D0929506

CONSTITUTIONAL LAW: PRINCIPLES AND POLICY
Cases and Materials

Seventh Edition

Jerome A. Barron
Harold H. Greene Professor of Law
The George Washington University Law School

C. Thomas Dienes
Lyle T. Alverson Professor of Law
The George Washington University Law School

Wayne McCormack
Professor of Law
University of Utah

Martin H. Redish
Louis and Harriet Ancel Professor of Law and Public Policy
Northwestern University

LexisNexis™

ISBN#: 0-8205-7033-8

Library of Congress Cataloging-in-Publication Data

Barron, Jerome A. et al.
Constitutional law : principles and policy / by Jerome A. Barron ... [et al.].
p. cm.
Includes index.
ISBN 0-8205-7033-8 (hardbound)
1. Constitutional law--United States--Cases. I. Barron, Jerome A.
KF4549.C655 2006
342.73--dc22 2006023808

This publication is designed to provide accurate and authoritative information in regard to the subject matter covered. It is sold with the understanding that the publisher is not engaged in rendering legal, accounting, or other professional services. If legal advice or other expert assistance is required, the services of a competent professional should be sought.

LexisNexis and the Knowledge Burst logo are trademarks of Reed Elsevier Properties Inc, used under license. Matthew Bender is a registered trademark of Matthew Bender Properties Inc.

Copyright © 2006 Matthew Bender & Company, Inc., a member of the LexisNexis Group.
All Rights Reserved.

No copyright is claimed in the text of statutes, regulations, and excerpts from court opinions quoted within this work. Permission to copy material exceeding fair use, 17 U.S.C. § 107, may be licensed for a fee of 10¢ per page per copy from the Copyright Clearance Center, 222 Rosewood Drive, Danvers, Mass. 01923, telephone (978) 750-8400.

Editorial Offices
744 Broad Street, Newark, NJ 07102 (973) 820-2000
201 Mission St., San Francisco, CA 94105-1831 (415) 908-3200
701 East Water Street, Charlottesville, VA 22902-7587 (434) 972-7600
www.lexis.com

(Pub.3018)

PREFACE

In this seventh edition of **Constitutional Law: Principles and Policy**, our effort has been to continue to make this book a teaching tool rather than an encyclopedia. Where a case is important, we have not stinted on according it the necessary space. We have learned over successive editions that teachers and students who use this book prefer fairly substantial edits of important cases rather than cases edited to the bone. Case editing in this new edition has been undertaken with this in mind, and also with the objective of fairly presenting conflicting constitutional philosophies. In keeping with this aim, case edits and summaries indicate not only the opinions of the Court in a given case, but also the positions taken by the Justices in their various concurrences and dissents.

As in the past, we continue to believe that the cases alone do not wholly describe the status of contemporary constitutional law. Therefore, in the notes that follow the cases, we have sought to acquaint the student with the essence of some of the recent significant constitutional commentary, past and present, as reflected both in books and in the law review literature. As in previous editions, we have included the text of the Constitution and a Table of the Justices. Finally, we have retained a commitment to our original purpose—to reflect fairly and fully the dynamism, controversy and excitement that characterize contemporary constitutional law.

We have tried to report the majority of the Supreme Court's constitutional decisions in the areas covered by this book since the last edition. But some of the cases that receive particular attention in this edition should be mentioned. In the Commerce Clause area, highlights of this new edition include *Gonzales v. Raich* (2005), the medical marijuana case, and its surprising reaffirmation of the affectation doctrine; and *Granholm v. Heald* (2005), the Dormant Commerce Clause wine case. In the area of Executive and Congressional relations, *Hamdi v. Rumsfeld* (2004), the enemy citizen combatant case, is given substantial space. *Hamdi* has significance not only for Executive and Congressional relations, but for what it has to say about the due process owed to citizen enemy combatants.

In the area of substantive due process, in the Texas criminal sodomy case *Lawrence v. Texas* (2003), the conflict over the meaning of liberty and the protection to be extended to individual autonomy is given extensive treatment. In the area of equal protection, *Grutter v. Bollinger* (2003) and *Gratz v. Bollinger* (2003) are front and center because of their implications not only for higher education, but for the future of affirmative action generally.

Unlike equal protection, the free expression area has been a fertile area for Supreme Court adjudication. Consequently, in this edition we have focused on such cases as *Virginia v. Black* (2003) and the emergence of true threats as an unprotected category of expression. We also report *Republican Party of Minnesota v. White* (2002) and *Watchtower Bible and Tract Society of New*

York, Inc. v. Village of Stratton (2002) to illustrate the Court's continuing use of and reliance on the content-based and content-neutral distinction.

In the area of freedom of religion, the battle between accommodationism and separationism has resulted in some landmark decisions. As a consequence, we have given substantial attention to the school voucher case, *Zelman v. Simmons-Harris* (2002). To illustrate how difficult it is to draw lines in this area, we have given extensive treatment to the Court's Ten Commandments cases, *McCreary County v. ACLU* (2005) and *Van Orden v. Perry* (2005), and their conflicting results.

In sum, this edition, like its predecessors, seeks to acquaint students with some of the formative and fundamental cases in American constitutional law and the principles that have flowed from them. At the same time, we have sought to keep instructors and students abreast of the continuing flow of constitutional adjudication and commentary.

Jerome A. Barron
C. Thomas Dienes
Wayne McCormack
Martin H. Redish

SUMMARY TABLE OF CONTENTS

TABLE OF CONTENTS

CONSTITUTION OF THE UNITED STATES

We the People of the United States, in Order to form a more perfect Union, establish Justice, insure domestic Tranquility, provide for the common defence, promote the general Welfare, and secure the Blessings of Liberty to ourselves and our Posterity, do ordain and establish this Constitution for the United States of America.

ARTICLE I

SECTION 1. All legislative Powers herein granted shall be vested in a Congress of the United States, which shall consist of a Senate and House of Representatives.

SECTION 2. [1]The House of Representatives shall be composed of Members chosen every second Year by the People of the several States, and the Electors in each State shall have the Qualifications requisite for Electors of the most numerous Branch of the State Legislature.

[2]No Person shall be a Representative who shall not have attained to the Age of twenty-five Years, and been seven Years a Citizen of the United States, and who shall not, when elected, be an Inhabitant of that State in which he shall be chosen.

[3]* [Representatives and direct Taxes shall be apportioned among the several States which may be included within this Union, according to their respective Numbers, which shall be determined by adding to the whole Number of free Persons, including those bound to Service for a Term of Years, and excluding Indians not taxed, three fifths of all other Persons.] The actual Enumeration shall be made within three Years after the first Meeting of the Congress of the United States, and within every subsequent Term of ten years, in such Manner as they shall by Law direct. The Number of Representatives shall not exceed one for every thirty Thousand, but each State shall have at Least one Representative; and until such enumeration shall be made, the State of New Hampshire shall be entitled to chuse three, Massachusetts eight, Rhode-Island and Providence Plantations one, Connecticut five, New-York six, New Jersey four, Pennsylvania eight, Delaware one, Maryland six, Virginia ten, North Carolina five, South Carolina five, and Georgia three.

[4]When vacancies happen in the Representation from any State, the Executive Authority thereof shall issue Writs of Election to fill such vacancies.

[5]The House of Representatives shall chuse their Speaker and other Officers; and shall have the sole Power of Impeachment.

---

* Note :The superior number preceding the paragraphs designates the number of the clause.

SECTION 3.* [1]The Senate of the United States shall be composed of two Senators from each State, [chosen by the Legislature] thereof, for six Years; and each Senator shall have one Vote.

[2]Immediately after they shall be assembled in Consequence of the first Election, they shall be divided as equally as may be into three Classes. The Seats of the Senators of the first Class shall be vacated at the Expiration of the Second Year, of the second Class at the Expiration of the fourth Year, and the third Class at the Expiration of the sixth Year, so that one-third may be chosen every second Year; [and if Vacancies happen by Resignation, or otherwise, during the Recess of the Legislature of any State, the Executive thereof may make temporary Appointments until the next Meeting of the Legislature, which shall then fill such Vacancies].**

[3]No Person shall be a Senator who shall not have attained to the Age of thirty Years, and been nine Years a Citizen of the United States, and who shall not, when elected, be an inhabitant of that State for which he shall be chosen.

[4]The Vice President of the United States shall be President of the Senate, but shall have no Vote, unless they be equally divided.

[5]The Senate shall chuse their other Officers, and also a President pro tempore, in the absence of the Vice President, or when he shall exercise the Office of President of the United States.

[6]The Senate shall have the sole Power to try all Impeachments. When sitting for that Purpose, they shall be on Oath or Affirmation. When the President of the United States is tried, the Chief Justice shall preside: And no Person shall be convicted without the Concurrence of two-thirds of the Members present.

[7]Judgment in Cases of Impeachment shall not extend further than to removal from Office, and disqualification to hold and enjoy any Office of honor, Trust, or Profit under the United States: but the Party convicted shall nevertheless be liable and subject to Indictment, Trial, Judgment, and Punishment, according to Law.

SECTION 4. [1]The Times, Places and Manner of holding Elections for Senators and Representatives, shall be prescribed in each State by the Legislature thereof; but the Congress may at any time by Law make or alter such Regulations, except as to the Places of chusing Senators.

[2]The Congress shall assemble at least once in every Year, and such Meeting shall [be on the first Monday in December,]unless they shall by Law appoint a different Day.***

* The part included in brackets was repealed by section 1 of amendment XVII.
** The part included in brackets was changed by clause 2 of amendment XVII.
*** The part included in brackets was changed by section 2 of amendment XX.

SECTION 5. [1]Each House shall be the Judge of the Elections, Returns, and Qualifications of its own Members, and a Majority of each shall constitute a Quorum to do Business; but a smaller Number may adjourn from day to day, and may be authorized to compel the Attendance of absent Members, in such Manner, and under such Penalties as each House may provide.

[2]Each House may determine the Rules of its Proceedings, punish its Members for disorderly Behavior, and, with the Concurrence of two thirds expel a Member.

[3]Each House shall keep a Journal of its Proceedings, and from time to time publish the same, excepting such Parts as may in their Judgment require Secrecy; and the Yeas and Nays of the Members of either House on any question shall, at the Desire of one fifth of those Present, be entered on the Journal.

[4]Neither House, during the Session of Congress, shall, without the Consent of the other, adjourn for more than three days, nor to any other Place than that in which the two Houses shall be sitting.

SECTION 6. [1]The Senators and Representatives shall receive a Compensation for their Services, to be ascertained by Law, and paid out of the Treasury of the United States. They shall in all Cases, except Treason, Felony and Breach of the Peace, be privileged from Arrest during their Attendance at the Session of their respective Houses, and in going to and returning from the same; and for any Speech or Debate in either House, they shall not be questioned in any other Place.

[2]No Senator or Representative shall, during the Time for which he was elected, be appointed to any civil Office under the Authority of the United States, which shall have been created, or the Emoluments whereof shall have been encreased during such time; and no Person holding any Office under the United States, shall be a Member of either House during his Continuance in Office.

SECTION 7. [1]All Bills for raising Revenue shall originate in the House of Representatives; but the Senate may propose or concur with Amendments as on other Bills.

[2]Every Bill which shall have passed the House of Representatives and the Senate, shall, before it become a Law, be presented to the President of the United States; if he approve he shall sign it, but if not he shall return it, with his Objections to that House in which it shall have originated, who shall enter the Objections at large on their Journal, and proceed to reconsider it. If after such Reconsideration two thirds of that House shall agree to pass the Bill, it shall be sent, together with the Objections, to the other House, by which it shall likewise be reconsidered, and if approved by two thirds of that House, it shall become a Law. But in all such Cases the Votes of both Houses shall be determined by Yeas and Nays, and the Names of the Persons voting for

and against the Bill shall be entered on the Journal of each House respectively. If any Bill shall not be returned by the President within ten Days (Sundays excepted) after it shall have been presented to him, the Same shall be a Law, in like Manner as if he had signed it, unless the Congress by their Adjournment prevent its Return, in which Case it shall not be a Law.

[3]Every Order, Resolution, or Vote to which the Concurrence of the Senate and House of Representatives may be necessary (except on a question of Adjournment) shall be presented to the President of the United States; and before the Same shall take Effect, shall be approved by him, or being disapproved by him, shall be repassed by two thirds of the Senate and House of Representatives, according to the Rules and Limitations prescribed in the Case of a Bill.

SECTION 8. 1The Congress shall have Power To lay and collect Taxes, Duties, Imposts and Excises, to pay the Debts and provide for the common Defence and general Welfare of the United States; but all Duties, Imposts and Excises shall be uniform throughout the United States;

[2]To borrow money on the credit of the United States;

[3]To regulate Commerce with foreign Nations, and among the several States, and with the Indian Tribes;

[4]To establish an uniform Rule of Naturalization, and uniform Laws on the subject of Bankruptcies throughout the United States;

[5]To coin Money, regulate the Value thereof, and of foreign Coin, and fix the Standard of Weights and Measures;

[6]To provide for the Punishment of counterfeiting the Securities and current Coin of the United States;

[7]To Establish Post Offices and post Roads;

[8]To promote the Progress of Science and useful Arts, by securing for limited Times to Authors and Inventors the exclusive Right to their respective Writings and Discoveries;

[9]To constitute Tribunals inferior to the supreme Court;

[10]To define and punish Piracies and Felonies committed on the high Seas, and Offenses against the Law of Nations;

[11]To declare War, grant Letters of Marque and Reprisal, and make Rules concerning Captures on Land and Water;

[12]To raise and support Armies, but no Appropriation of Money to that Use shall be for a longer Term than two Years;

[13]To provide and maintain a Navy;

[14]To make Rules for the Government and Regulation of the land and naval Forces;

[15]To provide for calling forth the Militia to execute the Laws of the Union, suppress insurrections and repel Invasions;

[16]To provide for organizing, arming, and disciplining the Militia, and for governing such Part of them as may be employed in the Service of the United States, reserving to the States respectively, the Appointment of the Officers, and the Authority of training the Militia according to the discipline prescribed by Congress;

[17]To exercise exclusive Legislation in all Cases whatsoever, over such District (not exceeding ten Miles square) as may, by Cession of particular States, and the acceptance of Congress, become the Seat of the Government of the United States, and to exercise like Authority over all Places purchased by the Consent of the Legislature of the State in which the Same shall be, for the Erection of Forts, Magazines, Arsenals, dock-Yards, and other needful Buildings; And

[18]To make all Laws which shall be necessary and proper for carrying into Execution the foregoing Powers, and all other Powers vested by this Constitution in the Government of the United States, or in any Department or Officer thereof.

SECTION 9. [1]The Migration or Importation of Such Persons as any of the States now existing shall think proper to admit, shall not be prohibited by the Congress prior to the Year one thousand eight hundred and eight, but a tax or duty may be imposed on such Importation, not exceeding ten dollars for each Person.

[2]The privilege of the Writ of Habeas Corpus shall not be suspended, unless when in Cases of Rebellion or Invasion the public Safety may require it.

[3]No Bill of Attainder or ex post facto Law shall be passed.

[4]* No capitation, or other direct, Tax shall be laid, unless in Proportion to the Census or Enumeration herein before directed to be taken.

[5]No Tax or Duty shall be laid on Articles exported from any State.

[6]No preference shall be given by any Regulation of Commerce or Revenue to the Ports of one State over those of another: nor shall Vessels bound to, or from, one State be obliged to enter, clear, or pay Duties in another.

---

* See also amendment XVI.

[7]No money shall be drawn from the Treasury, but in Consequence of Appropriations made by Law; and a regular Statement and Account of the Receipts and Expenditures of all public Money shall be published from time to time.

[8]No title of Nobility shall be granted by the United States: And no Person holding any Office of Profit or Trust under them, shall, without the Consent of the Congress, accept of any present, Emolument, Office, or Title, of any kind whatever, from any King, Prince, or foreign State.

SECTION 10. [1]No State shall enter into any Treaty, Alliance, or Confederation; grant Letters of Marque and Reprisal; coin Money; emit Bills of Credit; make any Thing but gold and silver Coin a Tender in Payment of Debts; pass any Bill of Attainder, ex post facto Law, or Law impairing the Obligation of Contracts, or grant any Title of Nobility.

[2]No State shall, without the Consent of the Congress, lay any Imposts or Duties on Imports or Exports, except what may be absolutely necessary for executing its inspection Laws; and the net Produce of all Duties and Imposts, laid by any State on Imports or Exports, shall be for the Use of the Treasury of the United States; and all such Laws shall be subject to the Revision and Control of the Congress.

[3]No State shall, without the Consent of Congress, lay any duty of Tonnage, keep Troops, or Ships of War in time of Peace, enter into any Agreement or Compact with another State, or with a foreign Power, or engage in War, unless actually invaded, or in such imminent Danger as will not admit of delay.

ARTICLE II

SECTION 1. [1]The executive Power shall be vested in a President of the United States of America. He shall hold his Office during the Term of four Years, and, together with the Vice-President, chosen for the same Term, be elected, as follows:

[2]Each State shall appoint, in such Manner as the Legislature thereof may direct, a Number of Electors, equal to the whole Number of Senators and Representatives to which the State may be entitled in the Congress: but no Senator or Representative, or Person holding an Office of Trust or Profit under the United States, shall be appointed an Elector.

[The Electors shall meet in their respective States, and vote by Ballot for two persons of whom one at least shall not be an Inhabitant of the same State with themselves. And they shall make a list of all the Persons voted for, and of the Number of Votes for each; which List they shall sign and certify, and transmit sealed to the Seat of the Government of the United States, directed to the President of the Senate. The President of the Senate shall, in the Presence of the Senate and House of Representatives, open all the Certificates, and the Votes shall then be counted. The Person having the greatest Number of Votes shall be the President, if such Number by a Majority of the whole Number of Electors appointed; and if there be more than one who have such Majority, and have an equal number of Votes, then the House of Representatives shall immediately chuse by Ballot one of them for President; and if no Person have a Majority, then from the five highest on the List the said House shall in like Manner chuse the President. But in chusing the President, the Votes shall be taken by States, the Representation from each State having one Vote; A quorum for this Purpose shall consist of a Member or Members from two-thirds of the States, and a Majority of all the States shall be necessary to a Choice. In every Case, after the Choice of the President the Person having the greatest Number of Votes of the Electors shall be the Vice President. But if there should remain two or more who have equal Votes, the Senate shall chuse from them by Ballot the Vice President.]*

[3]The Congress may determine the Time of chusing the Electors and the Day on which they shall give their Votes; which Day shall be the same throughout the United States.

[4]No person except a natural born Citizen, or a Citizen of the United States, at the time of the Adoption of this Constitution, shall be eligible to the Office of President; neither shall any Person be eligible to that Office who shall not have attained to the Age of thirty-five Years, and been fourteen Years a Resident within the United States.

[5]In case of the removal of the President from Office, or of his Death, Resignation or Inability to discharge the Powers and Duties of the said Office, the same shall devolve on the Vice President, and the Congress may by Law provide for the Case of Removal, Death, Resignation or Inability, both of the President, and Vice President, declaring what Officer shall then act as President, and such Officer shall act accordingly, until the Disability be removed, or a President shall be elected.

[6]The President shall, at stated Times, receive for his Services, a Compensation, which shall neither be encreased nor diminished during the Period for which he shall have been elected, and he shall not receive within that Period any other Emolument from the United States, or any of them.

[7]Before he enter on the Execution of His Office, he shall take the following Oath or Affirmation: "I do solemnly swear (or affirm) that I will faithfully execute the Office of President of the United States, and will to the best of my Ability, preserve, protect and defend the Constitution of the United States."

SECTION 2. [1]The President shall be Commander in Chief of the Army and Navy of the United States, and of the Militia of the several States, when called into the actual Service of the United States; he may require the Opinion, in writing, of the principal Officer in each of the executive Departments, upon any subject relating to the Duties of their respective Offices, and he shall have

* The part included in brackets has been superseded by section 3 of amendment XII.

Power to grant Reprieves and Pardons for Offences against the United States, except in Cases of Impeachment.

[2]He shall have Power, by and with the Advice and Consent of the Senate, to make Treaties, provided two-thirds of the Senators present concur; and he shall nominate, and by and with the Advice and Consent of the Senate, shall appoint Ambassadors, other public Ministers and Consuls, Judges of the supreme Court, and all other Officers of the United States, whose Appointments are not herein otherwise provided for, and which shall be established by Law; but the Congress may by Law vest the Appointment of such inferior Officers, as they think proper, in the President alone, in the Courts of Law, or in the Heads of Departments.

[3]The President shall have Power to fill up all Vacancies that may happen during the Recess of the Senate, by granting Commissions which shall expire at the End of their next Session.

SECTION 3. He shall from time to time give to the Congress Information of the State of the Union, and recommend to their Consideration such Measures as he shall judge necessary and expedient; he may, on extraordinary Occasions, convene both Houses, or either of them, and in Case of Disagreement between them, with Respect to the Time of Adjournment, he may adjourn them to such Time as he shall think proper; he shall receive Ambassadors and other public Ministers; he shall take Care that the Laws be faithfully executed, and shall Commission all the Officers of the United States.

SECTION 4. The President, Vice President and all civil Officers of the United States, shall be removed from Office on Impeachment for, and Conviction of, Treason, Bribery, or other high Crimes and Misdemeanors.

ARTICLE III

SECTION 1. The judicial Power of the United States, shall be vested in one supreme Court, and in such inferior Courts as the Congress may from time to time ordain and establish. The Judges, both of the supreme and inferior Courts, shall hold their Offices during good Behavior, and shall, at stated Times, receive for their Services a Compensation which shall not be diminished during their Continuance in Office.

SECTION 2. [1]The judicial Power shall extend to all Cases, in Law and Equity, arising under this Constitution, the Laws of the United States, and Treaties made, or which shall be made, under their Authority; to all Cases affecting Ambassadors, other public Ministers and Consuls; to all Cases of admiralty and maritime Jurisdiction; to Controversies to which the United States shall be a Party; to Controversies between two or more States; between a State and Citizens of another State;* between Citizens of different States; between Citizens of the same State claiming Lands under Grants of different States,

* This clause has been affected by amendment XI.

and between a State, or the Citizens thereof, and foreign States, Citizens or Subjects.

[2]In all Cases affecting Ambassadors, other public Ministers and Consuls, and those in which a State shall be Party, the supreme Court shall have original Jurisdiction. In all the other Cases before mentioned, the supreme Court shall have appellate Jurisidiction, both as to Law and Fact, with such Exceptions, and under such Regulations as the Congress shall make.

[3]The trial of all Crimes except in Cases of Impeachment shall be by Jury; and such Trial shall be held in the State where the said Crimes shall have been committed; but when not committed within any State, the Trial shall be at such Place or Places as the Congress may by Law have directed.

SECTION 3. [1]Treason against the United States shall consist only in levying War against them, or, in adhering to their Enemies, giving them Aid and Comfort. No Person shall be convicted of Treason unless on the Testimony of two Witnesses to the same overt Act, or on Confession in open Court.

[2]The Congress shall have power to declare the Punishment of Treason, but no Attainder of Treason shall work Corruption of Blood, or Forfeiture except during the Life of the Person attainted.

ARTICLE IV

SECTION 1. Full Faith and Credit shall be given in each State to the public Acts, Records, and judicial Proceedings of every other State. And the Congress may by general Laws prescribe the Manner in which such Acts, Records and Proceedings shall be proved, and the Effect thereof.

SECTION 2. [1]The Citizens of each State shall be entitled to all Privileges and Immunities of Citizens in the several States.

[2]A Person charged in any State with Treason, Felony, or other Crime, who shall flee from Justice, and be found in another State, shall on demand of the executive Authority of the State from which he fled, be delivered up, to be removed to the State having Jurisdiction of the Crime.

[3]** [No person held to Service or Labour in one State, under the Laws thereof, escaping into another, shall, in Consequence of any Law or Regulation therein, be discharged from such Service or Labour, but shall be delivered up on Claim of the Party to whom such Service or Labour may be due.]

SECTION 3. [1]New States may be admitted by the Congress into this Union; but no new State shall be formed or erected within the Jurisdiction of any other State; nor any State be formed by the Junction of two or more States, or parts of States, without the Consent of the Legislatures of the States concerned as well as of the Congress.

** This clause has been affected by amendment XIII.

2The Congress shall have Power to dispose of and make all needful Rules and Regulations respecting the Territory or other Property belonging to the United States; and nothing in this Constitution shall be so construed as to Prejudice any Claims of the United States, or of any particular State.

SECTION 4. The United States shall guarantee to every State in this Union a Republican Form of Government, and shall protect each of them against Invasion; and on Application of the Legislature, or of the Executive (when the Legislature cannot be convened) against domestic Violence.

ARTICLE V

The Congress, whenever two-thirds of both Houses shall deem it necessary, shall propose Amendments to this Constiution, or, on the Application of the Legislatures of two-thirds of the several States, shall call a Convention for proposing Amendments, which, in either Case, shall be valid to all Intents and Purposes, as part of this Constitution when ratified by the Legislatures of three-fourths of the several States, or by Conventions in three-fourths thereof, as the one or the other Mode of Ratification may be proposed by the Congress; Provided that no Amendment which may be made prior to the Year One thousand eight hundred and eight shall in any Manner affect the first and fourth Clauses in the Ninth Section of the first Article; and that no State, without its Consent, shall be deprived of its equal Sufferage in the Senate.

ARTICLE VI

1All Debts contracted and Engagements entered into, before the Adoption of this Constitution shall be as valid against the United States under this Constitution, as under the Confederation.

2This Constitution, and the Laws of the United States which shall be made in Pursuance thereof; and all Treaties made, or which shall be made, under the Authority of the United States, shall be the supreme Law of the Land; and the Judges in every State shall be bound thereby, any Thing in the Constitution or Laws of any State to the Contrary notwithstanding.

3The Senators and Representatives before mentioned, and the Members of the several State Legislatures, and all executive and judicial Officers, both of the United States and of the several States, shall be bound by Oath or Affirmation, to support this Constitution; but no religious Test shall ever be required as a Qualification to any Office or public Trust under the United States.

ARTICLE VII

The Ratification of the Conventions of nine States, shall be sufficient for the Establishment of this Constitution between the States so ratifying the Same.

AMENDMENT I

Congress shall make no law respecting an establishment of religion, or prohibiting the free exercise thereof; or abridging the freedom of speech, or of the press; or the right of the people peaceably to assemble and to petition the Government for a redress of grievances.

AMENDMENT II

A well regulated Militia, being necessary to the security of a free State, the right of the people to keep and bear Arms, shall not be infringed.

AMENDMENT III

No Soldier shall, in time of peace be quartered in any house, without the consent of the Owner, nor in time of war, but in a manner to be prescribed by law.

AMENDMENT IV

The right of the people to be secure in their persons, houses, papers, and effects, against unreasonable searches and seizures, shall not be violated, and no Warrants shall issue, but upon probable cause, supported by Oath or affirmation and particularly describing the Place to be searched, and the persons or things to be seized.

AMENDMENT V

No person shall be held to answer for a capital, or otherwise infamous crime, unless on a presentment or indictment of a Grand Jury, except in cases arising in the land or naval forces, or in the Militia, when in actual service in time of War or public danger; nor shall any person be subject for the same offence to be twice put in jeopardy of life or limb; nor shall be compelled in any criminal case to be a witness against himself, nor be deprived of life, liberty, or property, without due process of law; nor shall private property be taken for public use, without just compensation.

AMENDMENT VI

In all criminal prosecutions, the accused shall enjoy the right to a speedy and public trial, by an impartial jury of the State and district wherein the crime shall have been committed, which district shall have been previously ascertained by law, and to be informed of the nature and cause of the accusation: to be confronted with the witnesses against him; to have compulsory process for obtaining witnesses in his favor, and to have the Assistance of Counsel for his defence.

AMENDMENT VII

In suits at common law, where the value in controversy shall exceed twenty dollars, the right of trial by jury shall be preserved, and no fact tried by jury, shall be otherwise reexamined in any Court of the United States, than according to the rules of the common law.

AMENDMENT VIII

Excessive bail shall not be required, nor excessive fines imposed, nor cruel and unusual punishments inflicted.

AMENDMENT IX

The enumeration in the Constitution, of certain rights, shall not be construed to deny or disparage others retained by the people.

AMENDMENT X

The powers not delegated to the United States by the Constitution, nor prohibited by it to the States, are reserved to the States respectively, or to the people.
(Ratification of the first ten amendments was completed December 15, 1791.)

AMENDMENT XI

The Judicial power of the United States shall not be construed to extend to any suit in law or equity, commenced or prosecuted against one of the United States by Citizens of another State, or by Citizens or Subjects of any Foreign State.
(Declared ratified January 8, 1798.)

AMENDMENT XII

The electors shall meet in their respective states and vote by ballot for President and Vice-President, one of whom, at least, shall not be an inhabitant of the same state with themselves; they shall name in their ballots the person

voted for as President, and in distinct ballots the person voted for as Vice-President, and they shall make distinct lists of all persons voted for as President, and of all persons voted for as Vice-President, and of the number of votes for each, which lists they shall sign and certify, and transmit sealed to the seat of the government of the United States, directed to the President of the Senate; The President of the Senate shall, in presence of the Senate and House of Representatives, open all the certificates and the votes shall then be counted; The person having the greatest number of votes for President, shall be the President, if such number be a majority of the whole number of Electors appointed; and if no person have such majority, then from the persons having the highest numbers not exceeding three on the list of those voted for as President, the House of Representatives shall choose immediately, by ballot, the President. But in choosing the President, the votes shall be taken by states, the representation from each state having one vote; a quorum for this purpose shall consist of a member or members from two-thirds of the states, and a majority of all the states shall be necessary to a choice. [And if the House of Representatives shall not choose a President whenever the right of choice shall devolve upon them, before the fourth day of March next following, then the Vice-President shall act as President, as in the case of the death or other constitutional disability of the President.] * The person having the greatest number of votes as Vice-President, shall be the Vice-President, if such number be a majority of the whole number of Electors appointed, and if no person have a majority, then from the two highest numbers on the list, the Senate shall choose the Vice-President; a quorum for the purpose shall consist of two-thirds of the whole number of Senators, and a majority of the whole number shall be necessary to a choice. But no person constitutionally ineligible to the office of President shall be eligible to that of Vice-President of the United States.
(Declared ratified September 25, 1804.)

AMENDMENT XIII

SECTION 1. Neither slavery nor involuntary servitude, except as a punishment for crime whereof the party shall have been duly convicted, shall exist within the United States, or any place subject to their jurisdiction.

SECTION 2. Congress shall have power to enforce this article by appropriate legislation.
(Declared ratified December 18, 1865.)

AMENDMENT XIV

SECTION 1. All persons born or naturalized in the United States, and subject to the jurisdiction thereof, are citizens of the United States and of the State wherein they reside. No State shall make or enforce any law which shall abridge the privileges or immunities of citizens of the United States; nor shall

* The part included in the brackets has been superseded by section 3 of amendment XX.

any State deprive any person of life, liberty, or property, without due process of law; nor deny to any person within its jurisdiction the equal protection of the laws.

SECTION 2. Representatives shall be apportioned among the several States according to their respective numbers, counting the whole number of persons in each State, excluding Indians not taxed. But when the right to vote at any election for the choice of electors for President and Vice-President of the United States, Representatives in Congress, the Executive and Judicial officers of a State, or the members of the Legislature thereof, is denied to any of the male inhabitants of such State, being twenty-one years of age, and citizens of the United States, or in any way abridged, except for participation in rebellion, or other crime, the basis of representation therein shall be reduced in the proportion which the number of such male citizens shall bear to the whole number of male citizens twenty-one years of age in such State.

SECTION 3. No person shall be a Senator or Representative in Congress, or elector of President and Vice-President, or hold any office, civil or military, under the United States, or under any State, who, having previously taken an oath, as a member of Congress, or as an officer of the United States, or as a member of any State legislature, or as an executive or judicial officer of any State, to support the Constitution of the United States, shall have engaged in insurrection or rebellion against the same, or given aid or comfort to the enemies thereof. But Congress may by a vote of two-thirds of each House, remove such disability.

SECTION 4. The validity of the public debt of the United States, authorized by law, including debts incurred for payment of pensions and bounties for services in suppressing insurrection or rebellion, shall not be questioned. But neither the United States nor any State shall assume or pay any debt or obligation incurred in aid of insurrection or rebellion against the United States, or any claim for the loss or emancipation of any slave; but all such debts, obligations and claims shall be held illegal and void.

SECTION 5. The Congress shall have power to enforce, by appropriate legislation, the provisions of this article.
(Declared ratified July 28, 1868.)

AMENDMENT XV

SECTION 1. The right of citizens of the United States to vote shall not be denied or abridged by the United States or by any State on account of race, color, or previous condition of servitude

SECTION 2. The Congress shall have power to enforce this article by appropriate legislation.
(Declared ratified March 30, 1870.)

AMENDMENT XVI

The Congress shall have power to lay and collect taxes on incomes, from whatever source derived, without apportionment among the several States, and without regard to any census or enumeration.
(Declared ratified February 25, 1913.)

AMENDMENT XVII

The Senate of the United States shall be composed of two Senators from each State, elected by the people thereof, for six years; and each Senator shall have one vote. The electors in each State shall have the qualifications requisite for electors of the most numerous branch of the State legislatures.

When vacancies happen in the representation of any State in the Senate, the executive authority of such State shall issue writs of election to fill such vacancies: *Provided,* That the legislature of any State may empower the executive thereof to make temporary appointments until the people fill the vacancies by election as the legislature may direct.

This amendment shall not be so construed as to affect the election or term of any Senator chosen before it becomes valid as part of the Constitution.
(Declared ratified May 31, 1913.)

AMENDMENT XVIII

[SECTION 1. After one year from the ratification of this article the manufacture, sale, or transportation of intoxicating liquors within, the importation thereof into, or the exportation thereof from the United States and all territory subject to the jurisdiction thereof for beverage purposes is hereby prohibited.

[SECTION 2. The Congress and the several States shall have concurrent power to enforce this article by appropriate legislation.

[SECTION 3. This article shall be inoperative unless it shall have been ratified as an amendment to the Constitution by the legislatures of the several States, as provided in the Constitution, within seven years from the date of the submission hereof to the States by the Congress.] *

AMENDMENT XIX

The right of citizens of the United States to vote shall not be denied or abridged by the United States or by any State on account of sex.

Congress shall have power to enforce this article by appropriate legislation.
(Declared ratified August 26, 1920.)

* Amendment XVIII was repealed by section 1 of amendment XXI. (Declared ratified January 29, 1919.)

AMENDMENT XX

SECTION 1. The terms of the President and Vice-President shall end at noon on the 20th day of January, and the terms of Senators and Representatives at noon on the 3d day of January, of the years in which such terms would have ended if this article had not been ratified; and the terms of their successors shall then begin.

SECTION 2. The Congress shall assemble at least once in every year, and such meeting shall begin at noon on the 3d day of January, unless they shall by law appoint a different day.

SECTION 3. If, at the time for the beginning of the term of the President, the President elect shall have died, the Vice-President elect shall become President. If a President shall not have been chosen before the time fixed for the beginning of his term, or if the President elect shall have failed to qualify, then the Vice-President elect shall act as President until a President shall have qualified; and the Congress may by law provide for the case wherein neither a President elect nor a Vice-President elect shall have qualified, declaring who shall then act as President, or the manner in which one who is to act shall be selected, and such person shall act accordingly until a President or Vice-President shall have qualified.

SECTION 4. The Congress may by law provide for the case of the death of any of the persons from whom the House of Representatives may choose a President whenever the right of choice shall have devolved upon them and for the case of the death of any of the persons from whom the Senate may choose a Vice-President whenever the right of choice shall have devolved upon them.

SECTION 5. Sections 1 and 2 shall take effect on the 15th day of October following the ratification of this article.

SECTION 6. This article shall be inoperative unless it shall have been ratified as an amendment to the Constitution by the legislatures of three-fourths of the several States within seven years from the date of its submission. (Declared ratified February 6, 1933.)

AMENDMENT XXI

SECTION 1. The eighteenth article of amendment to the Constitution of the United States is hereby repealed.

SECTION 2. The transportation or importation into any State, Territory, or possession of the United States for delivery or use therein of intoxicating liquors, in violation of the laws thereof, is hereby prohibited.

SECTION 3. This article shall be inoperative unless it shall have been ratified as an amendment to the Constitution by conventions in the several States,

as provided in the Constitution, within seven years from the date of the submission hereof to the States by the Congress.
(Declared ratified December 5, 1933.)

AMENDMENT XXII

SECTION 1. No person shall be elected to the office of the President more than twice, and no person who has held the office of President, or acted as President, for more than two years of a term to which some other person was elected President shall be elected to the office of the President more than once. But this article shall not apply to any person holding the office of President when this Article was proposed by the Congress, and shall not prevent any person who may be holding the office of President, or acting as President, during the term within which this Article becomes operative from holding the office of President or acting as President during the remainder of such term.

SECTION 2. This article shall be inoperative unless it shall have been ratified as an amendment to the Constitution by the legislatures of three-fourths of the several States within seven years from the date of its submission to the States by the Congress.
(Declared ratified March 1, 1951.)

AMENDMENT XXIII

SECTION 1. The District constituting the seat of Government of the United States shall appoint in such manner as the Congress may direct:

A number of electors of President and Vice President equal to the whole number of Senators and Representatives in Congress to which the District would be entitled if it were a State, but in no event more than the least populous State; they shall be in addition to those appointed by the States, but they shall be considered, for the purposes of the election of President and Vice President, to be electors appointed by a State; and they shall meet in the District and perform such duties as provided by the twelfth article of amendment.

SECTION 2. The Congress shall have power to enforce this article by appropriate legislation.
(Declared ratified April 3, 1961.)

AMENDMENT XXIV

SECTION 1. The right of citizens of the United States to vote in any primary or other election for President or Vice President, for electors for President or Vice President, or for Senator or Representative in Congress, shall not be denied or abridged by the United States or any State by reason of failure to pay any poll tax or other tax.

SECTION 2. The Congress shall have power to enforce this article by appropriate legislation.
(Declared ratified February 4, 1962.)

AMENDMENT XXV

SECTION 1. In case of the removal of the President from office or of his death or resignation, the Vice President shall become President.

SECTION 2. Whenever there is a vacancy in the office of the Vice President, the President shall nominate a Vice President who shall take office upon confirmation by a majority vote of both Houses of Congress.

SECTION 3. Whenever the President transmits to the President pro tempore of the Senate and the Speaker of the House of Representatives his written declaration that he is unable to discharge the powers and duties of his office, and until he transmits to them a written declaration to the contrary, such powers and duties shall be discharged by the Vice President as Acting President.

SECTION 4. Whenever the Vice President and a majority of either the principal officers of the executive departments or of such other body as Congress may by law provide, transmit to the President pro tempore of the Senate and the Speaker of the House of Representatives their written declaration that the President is unable to discharge the powers and duties of his office, the Vice President shall immediately assume the powers and the duties of the office as Acting President.

Thereafter, when the President transmits to the President pro tempore of the Senate and the Speaker of the House of Representatives his written declaration that no inability exists, he shall resume the powers and duties of this office unless the Vice President and a majority of either the principal officers of the executive department or of such other body as Congress may by law provide, transmit within four days to the President pro tempore of the Senate and the Speaker of the House of Representatives their written declaration that the President is unable to discharge the powers and duties of his office. Thereupon Congress shall decide the issue, assembling within forty-eight hours for that purpose if not in session. If the Congress, within twenty-one days after receipt of the latter written declaration, or, if Congress is not in session, within twenty-one days after Congress is required to assemble, determines by two-thirds vote of both Houses that the President is unable to discharge the powers and duties of his office, the Vice President shall continue to discharge the same as Acting President; otherwise, the President shall resume the powers and duties of his office. (Declared ratified February 10, 1967.)

AMENDMENT XXVI

SECTION 1. The right of citizens of the United States, who are eighteen years of age or older, to vote shall not be denied or abridged by the United States or by any State on account of age.

SECTION 2. The Congress shall have power to enforce this article by appropriate legislation.
(Declared ratified July 1, 1971.)

AMENDMENT XXVII

No law varying the compensation for the services of the Senators and Representatives shall take effect, until an election of Representatives shall have intervened.
(Declared ratified May 7, 1992.)

Justices of the United States Supreme Court

Year	President	1 (Chief J.)	2	3	4	5	6	7	8	9
1789	Washington	John Jay	Rutledge, J.	Cushing	Wilson	Blair				
1790							Iredell			
1791			Johnson, T.							
1792										
1793			Paterson							
1794										
1795		Rutledge, J.								
1796		Ellsworth				Chase, Samuel				
1797	John Adams									
1798					Washington					
1799							Moore			
1800										
1801	Jefferson	Marshall, J. (Adams)								
1802										
1803										
1804							Johnson, W.			
1805										
1806			Livingston							
1807								Todd		
1808										
1809	Madison									
1810										

Year	President	1	2	3	4	5	6	7	8	9
1811				Story		Duvall				
1812										
1813										
1814										
1815										
1816										
1817	Monroe									
1818										
1819										
1820										
1821										
1822										
1823			Thompson							
1824										
1825	J. Q. Adams									
1826								Trimble		
1827										
1828										
1829	Jackson							McLean		
1830					Baldwin					
1831										
1832										
1833										
1834										

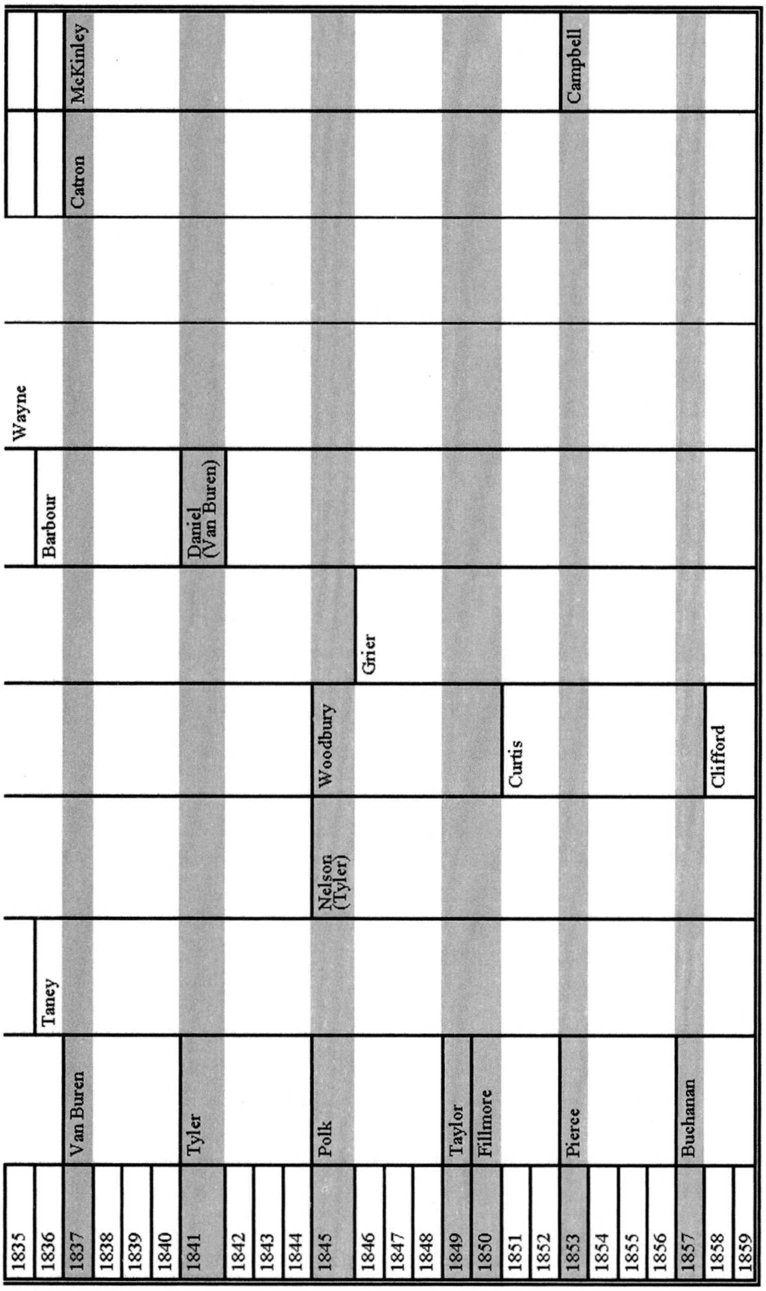
1835
1836
1837
1838
1839
1840
1841
1842
1843
1844
1845
1846
1847
1848
1849
1850
1851
1852
1853
1854
1855
1856
1857
1858
1859
Van Buren
Tyler
Polk
Taylor
Fillmore
Pierce
Buchanan
Taney
Nelson (Tyler)
Woodbury
Curtis
Clifford
Grier
Barbour
Daniel (Van Buren)
Wayne
Catron
McKinley
Campbell

Year	President	1 (Chief J.)	2	3	4	5	6	7	8	9
1860										
1861	Lincoln									
1862						Miller		Swayne	Field	Davis
1863									[10 seats	
1864		Chase, Salmon							until 1865]	
1865	A. Johnson									
1866										
1867										
1868										
1869	Grant									
1870					Strong		Bradley			
1871										
1872			Hunt							
1873										
1874		Waite								
1875										
1876										
1877	Hayes									Harlan (I)
1878										
1879										
1880					Woods					
1881	Garfield			Gray (Arthur)				Matthews (Garfield)		
1882			Blatchford							

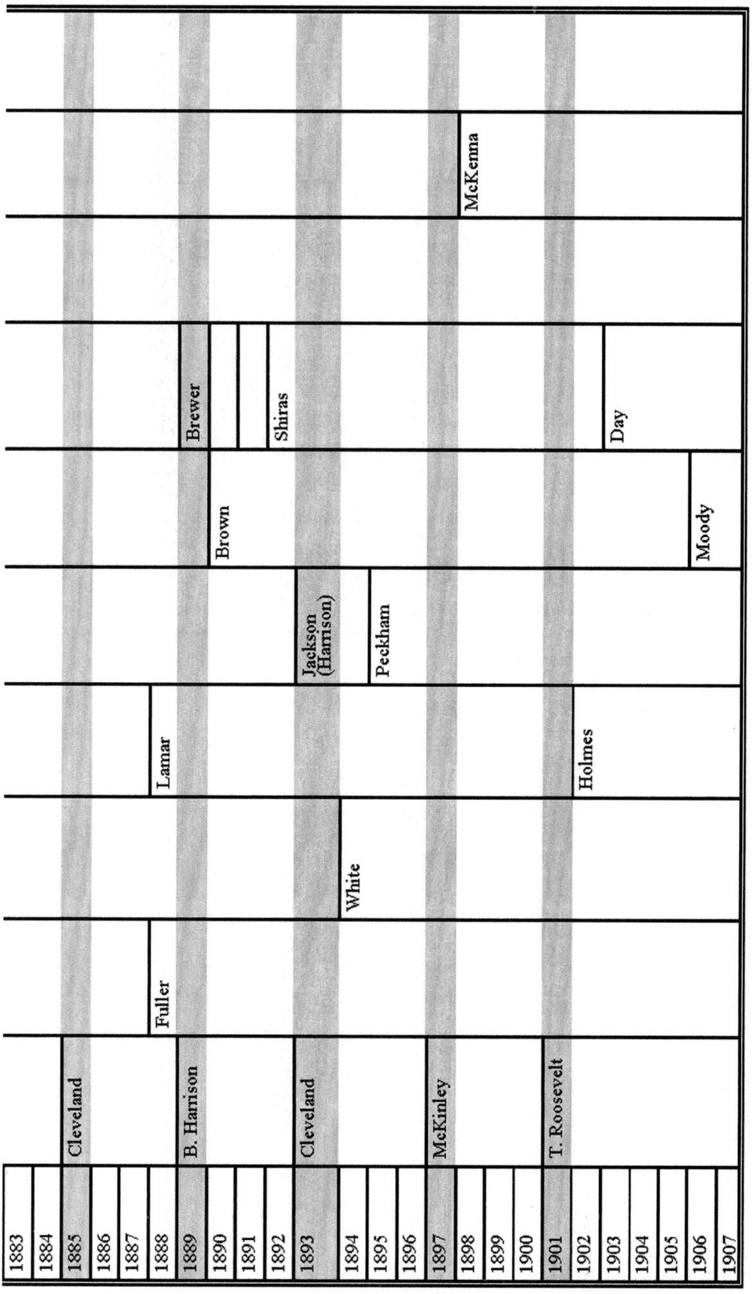
1883
1884
1885
1886
1887
1888
1889
1890
1891
1892
1893
1894
1895
1896
1897
1898
1899
1900
1901
1902
1903
1904
1905
1906
1907
Cleveland
B. Harrison
Cleveland
McKinley
T. Roosevelt
Fuller
White
Lamar
Holmes
Jackson (Harrison)
Peckham
Brown
Moody
Brewer
Shiras
Day
McKenna

Year	President	1 (Chief J.)	2	3	4	5	6	7	8	9
1908										
1909	Taft				Lurton					
1910		White	Van Devanter			Lamar		Hughes		
1911										
1912										Pitney
1913	Wilson									
1914					McReynolds					
1915										
1916						Brandeis		Clarke		
1917										
1918										
1919										
1920										
1921	Harding	Taft								
1922							Butler	Sutherland		
1923	Coolidge									Sanford (Harding)
1924										
1925									Stone	
1926										
1927										
1928										
1929	Hoover									
1930		Hughes								Roberts

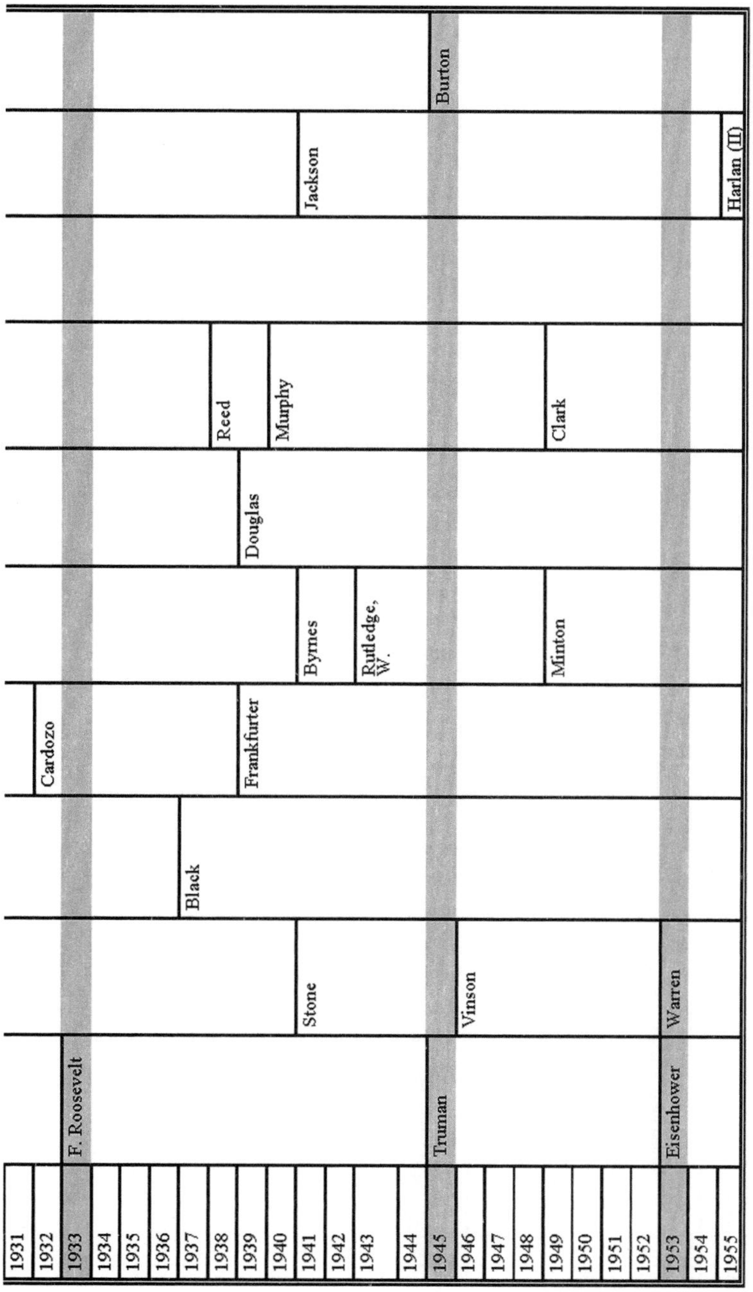
1931
1932
1933
1934
1935
1936
1937
1938
1939
1940
1941
1942
1943
1944
1945
1946
1947
1948
1949
1950
1951
1952
1953
1954
1955
F. Roosevelt
Truman
Eisenhower
Stone
Vinson
Warren
Black
Cardozo
Frankfurter
Byrnes
Rutledge, W.
Minton
Douglas
Reed
Murphy
Clark
Jackson
Harlan (II)
Burton

Year	President	1 (Chief J.)	2	3	4	5	6	7	8	9
1956					Brennan					
1957								Whittaker		
1958										Stewart
1959										
1060										
1961	Kennedy									
1962				Goldberg				White, B.		
1963	L.B. Johnson									
1964										
1965				Fortas						
1966										
1967							Marshall, T.			
1968										
1969	Nixon	Burger								
1970				Blackmun						
1971										
1972			Powell						Rehnquist	
1973										
1974	Ford									
1975						Stevens				
1976										
1977	Carter									
1978										
1979										

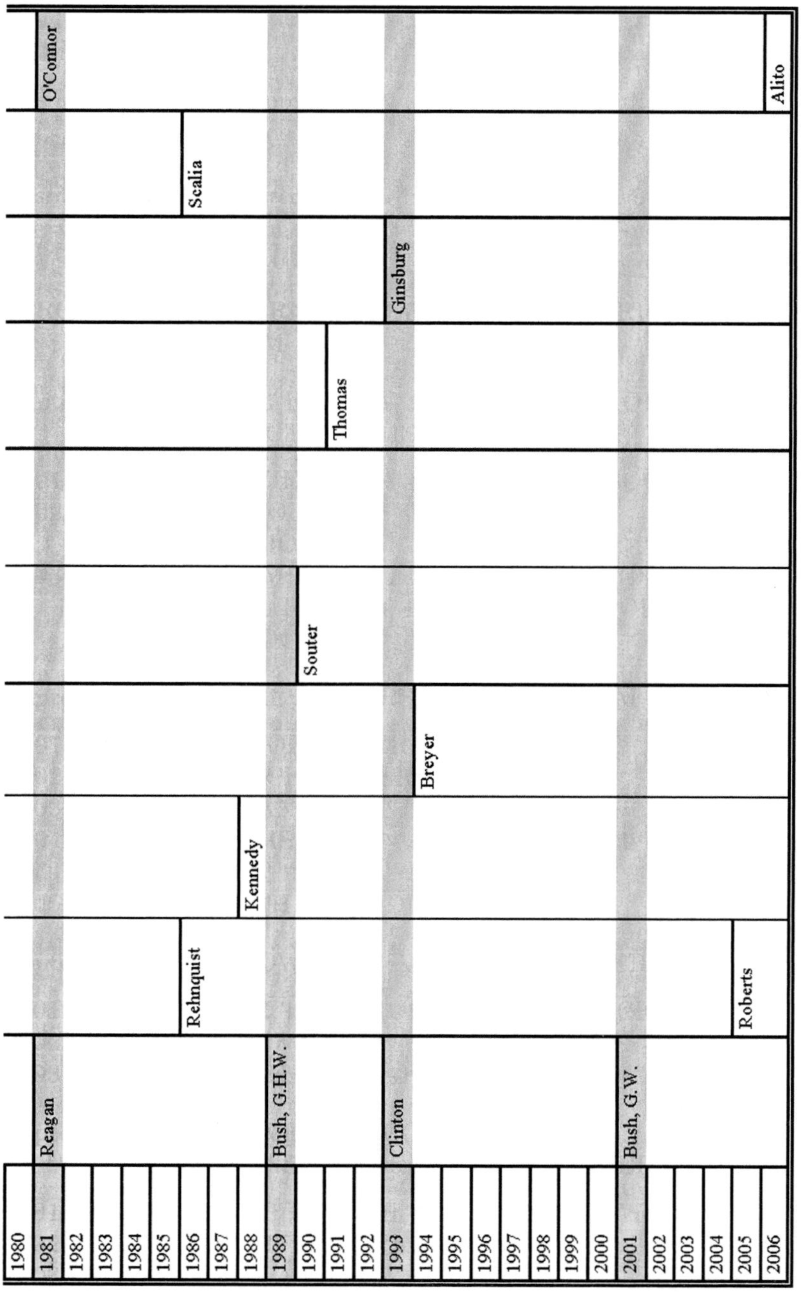
1980
1981
1982
1983
1984
1985
1986
1987
1988
1989
1990
1991
1992
1993
1994
1995
1996
1997
1998
1999
2000
2001
2002
2003
2004
2005
2006
Reagan
Bush, G.H.W.
Clinton
Bush, G.W.
Rehnquist
Roberts
Kennedy
Breyer
Souter
Thomas
Ginsburg
Scalia
O'Connor
Alito

INTRODUCTION: A BRIEF OVERVIEW OF AMERICAN CONSTITUTIONALISM

Rebellion and Independence

The English colonies in North America developed over a 150-year period prior to their break with the old country in 1776. Some of these colonies were organized as companies under royal charters from the crown, some were colonies under royal governors, and Georgia was a penal colony. The experience and structure of each differed slightly from the others, but all shared a common desire to end some of the abuses that they felt themselves to be suffering from the British crown. The delegates to the Continental Congress in 1776 were authorized to bargain with the crown in a concerted fashion to achieve various ill-defined goals, none of which included outright independence. When the Continental Congress declared independence on July 4, 1776, it came as a surprise to many citizens of the thirteen colonies.

One immediate consequence of the Declaration of Independence was the need to organize some entity through which to pursue the claim for independence itself. It would have been possible for each colony to press its claim for independence separately, as occurred with most of the Communist governments in Eastern Europe during the late 1980s. But the decision to pursue a collective solution was made at the time of the Declaration. Therefore, it was natural that there be a collective enterprise. The Continental Congress stayed in session through 1776 and 1777 to raise the Continental Army and pursue the War of Independence. The emerging concept of a collective federation was formalized in the Articles of Confederation adopted in 1777 and ratified in 1778.

The Articles of Confederation described the United States of America as a federation of independent states. There was a legislature but no judiciary nor executive. The model was something like the League of Nations following World War I (except that it had its own army) and something like the current United Nations (except that it had no executive). The Articles operated until replaced by the Constitution of the United States, drafted in 1787 and ratified in 1788. The chief defects of the Articles that led to the new Constitution were lack of central control over trade policies and lack of taxing power by the central government, although lack of a central court system or an executive were also impediments to the ability of the United States to function as a cohesive unit. A key question raised in 1787 and not yet fully resolved was the degree to which the states were independent units with its corollary of what amount of power that should be possessed by the central government.

State Constitutions and the Articles of Confederation

It might seem with the emergence of the new nation in 1776, and the perceived need for collective action mentioned above, that a unitary system such as existed in England would have been adopted. Instead, the new nation chose to govern itself as autonomous nation-states subject only to minimal collective action at the federal level. At least part of the reason for this choice must lie in practical necessity. The geographic dispersion of the American people and imperfect means of communication led naturally to the emergence of local traditions, interests, and values. Cultural heterogeneity among the colonies, tended further to promote separatism. Economic factors, such as differences in products and forms of economic activity, similarly reinforced localized interests. And finally the experience of the colonists with Great Britain had generated a fear of centralist tendencies and a desire to preserve local autonomy.

The foundations of our federalist structure, therefore, were already laid in November 1777, when the Continental Congress adopted the Articles of Confederation and recommended them to the states. The Articles were America's first real attempt to reconcile unity with diversity. But the colonial experience with Great Britain and the dominant belief that government was at best a necessary evil, something to be feared and circumscribed, necessarily determined the course of the new political union.

The Articles of Confederation reflected the colonial faith in state sovereignty as the only viable check on the abuse of centralized power when they pointedly declared: "Each state retains its sovereignty, freedom and independence, and every Power, Jurisdiction and Right, which is not by this confederation expressly delegated to the United States, in Congress assembled." The Articles were more in the nature of a treaty than a charter for unified government. Congress was denied the power to lay and collect taxes or duties or provide for a uniform currency. It had no regulatory power over interstate or foreign commerce and trade. Each state, regardless of its size was entitled to one vote; the vote of nine of the thirteen states was necessary to enact laws and a unanimous vote was required to amend the Articles. At a time when sectionalism was dominant, change was difficult to impossible.

Within the states, written constitutions established the new governments that took over from the British governors or chartered management companies. The concept of a written constitution thus was established at the state level before application to the national level. In these constitutions, tripartite organization of government was common. Most state constitutions provided for legislative, executive and judicial branches of government. There was frequently, however, no attempt to define the roles of the respective branches. Each had plenary authority within its sphere of operation, and it could be assumed that the scope of each was defined by its role.

Another common feature of the state constitutions was a listing of rights guaranteed to the individual. These listings borrowed heavily from the British traditions of Magna Carta and the Bill of Rights, and were influenced by the common-law glosses on those documents contained in Blackstone's COMMENTARIES ON THE LAWS OF ENGLAND.

Drafting and Ratification of the Constitution

The Confederation failed. It was increasingly clear that the central government had to be given sufficient powers to govern, at least in those matters for which the states individually were incompetent or perpetrating abuses. But fear of centralized power had not declined. Concern for individual liberty from accumulated power remained, and the jealous interest in preserving state sovereignty was widespread. It was this creative tension between efficiency in performing the tasks of government and restraint of centralized governmental power that dominated the debate over the constitutional allocation of powers between the nation and states.

The states sent delegates to a convention in the spring of 1787 with the mandate "to devise such further provisions as shall appear to them necessary to render the constitution of the federal government adequate to the exigencies of the Union." This was generally understood as suggesting the need to repair the two key deficiencies in the Articles, lack of taxing power and state autonomy in matters of trade and tariffs. Instead, the convention produced, on September 17, 1787, an entirely new document with three branches of federal government rather than one, a lengthy list of legislative and judicial powers, and authority to conduct all foreign affairs split between the legislative and executive branches. This document was placed before state conventions for ratification, thus triggering debates within each state between those supporting the new central government (known today as the Federalists) and those opposing creation of the new central government (known today as the Antifederalists). The necessary state ratifications were achieved by 1788 and the new government came into existence in 1789.

James Madison, Alexander Hamilton and John Jay authored a series of newspaper articles under the pseudonym of *Publius* to bolster the chances of ratification in New York. These articles eventually became known as the Federalist Papers and serve as a principal source of "legislative history" on several key principles in constitutional interpretation. In addition, Madison, a Virginian, made a fateful promise during the ratification debates in Virginia when the Antifederalist Patrick Henry founded his opposition to the new central government on the lack of any guarantees for individual liberty as against the new government. Madison promised that the new government would adopt a set of constitutional guarantees of individual liberty as soon as it was formed. Madison, as a member of the first House of Representatives, drafted a set of twelve proposals that were promulgated by Congress; ten of those were ratified in 1791 with the first eight known as the Bill of Rights.

Intellectual and Structural Traditions of the American Constitution

The British Background. Much of the British governmental structure inherited by the colonies was a reaction to or evolution from concepts of monarchy and the breakup of feudalism. England had, and still has, no single document that can be described as a written constitution. Britain, however, had a constitutional heritage expressed in several key documents executed by the crown or by Parliament. The structure of the U.S. Constitution drew heavily on the structure that had evolved in English practice. This is hardly surprising because that was the system with which colonists were most familiar. But it was also a system under which they had chafed and from which they would want to make some changes in crafting their new government.

The most important structural elements of British law, the common law authority of the courts and the legislative hegemony of Parliament, were not created by written document. The court system and the common law evolved from practices by which the crown had delegated authority to various officers to resolve disputes; this process began at least as early as the 13th Century and took roughly its current form during the eighteenth century. The dominance of Parliament stems from the Glorious Revolution of 1688 when the Stuart monarchs were replaced by William & Mary of Orange, who agreed to accept the promulgations of Parliament as binding law.

The central provisions of British law relating to rights of the person were Magna Carta (signed by King John, mythically Robin Hood's antagonist, in 1215), the Petition of Right Act (1628) and the Bill of Rights of 1689. It is critical to understand that even Magna Carta and the Bill of Rights are subject to amendment or repeal by Parliament on precisely the same basis as amendment or repeal of a provision of the tax code or any other statute. They are not, however, subject to amendment or repeal by the crown. The theory that the king was ceding certain rights in 1215 gave way by 1689 into the notion that certain rights pre-existed the monarch, whether by divine grant or natural law, and that neither a monarch nor any other government could eliminate those rights legitimately. In the "social compact" version of this theory, people create governments and give them certain powers, but the people are not capable of dealing away these central "inalienable" rights.

Many of the writings on which our constitutional history is based, such as John Locke's SECOND TREATISE ON CIVIL GOVERNMENT (1689) and Lord Coke's SECOND INSTITUTE, were reactions to the abuses of monarchical government. How their emphasis on natural law and individual rights, particularly rights of property, bear on apportioning power within a consciously tripartite and federalistic government remain intriguing questions. It is clear, however, that the Framers of the U.S. Constitution were acutely aware of some of these writings, most particularly of Montesquieu's articulation of the principles behind separating governmental powers among legislative, executive and judicial branches.

The Liberal and Republican Traditions. The Seventeenth and Eighteenth Centuries were times of intense political ferment, revolutions, and accompanying theorization in Europe and America. It would be helpful from our distant perspective if there had been two distinct competing theories, one of which had won, so that we would be able to guide ourselves by that message from the past. Unfortunately, the "competing" views were primarily addressed to the breakup of monarchy and feudalism; they shared many premises, were authored in a state of flux, and were addressed in many instances to conditions that no longer obtain. Nevertheless, in understanding where we are, it is helpful to understand where we came from. In that effort, modern scholars have isolated two competing strands of Euro-American political traditions, the "liberal" and the "republican" views, both of which attempted to articulate the premises for self-government, the values that government should pursue, and the mechanisms most likely to accomplish those goals. It is easy to trace the liberal tradition from writers who predated the Constitution into some of the premises of the new nation. It is less clear that the republican tradition tied directly into the opponents of the new constitution. The opponents made very specific arguments against the centralization of government and accretion of governmental power; whether these arguments stemmed directly from a separate intellectual tradition is an open question at this date. The summary below at least some background for your study.

The liberal tradition is most often associated with John Locke. Writing at the time of the Glorious Revolution in 1689, Locke sought to justify the notion of popular sovereignty, explaining why the people should govern themselves (or choose their rulers) rather than be ruled by a hereditary monarch. The tools for this purpose were available in the emerging notion of individual liberty fostered by the rise of the middle class and merchants in England, assisted by notions of natural law fostered by religious claims for freedom of the church from monarchical control. Locke emphasized individual autonomy and rights of the person as the basis for self-government. He was never clear about whether these were natural rights, existing in a state of nature prior to government, or whether these rights were created at the time of formation of government through the "social compact."

The difference between natural law and social compact theories would not have been critical to Locke nor to the Framers of the U.S. Constitution. Later in the nineteenth century a split that would affect our constitutional history developed between libertarians and utilitarians. John Stuart Mill, at least partially a utilitarian, published his essay *On Liberty* in 1859, claiming that individual liberties existed for their own sake, for the good of the individual, but also with some degree of value to others and to the structure of society. The overtly utilitarian Jeremy Bentham founded his conception of individual liberties on the premise that individual development was good for society so long as it fit into the overall objective of social organization, usually described as "the greatest good for the greatest number." The differences among these approaches and the natural law or social compact theories would become acute in late–twentieth–century America in the battle over individual liberties and civil rights as Republican presidents made judicial appointments in a conscious effort to overturn much of the work of the Warren Court. For present purposes, it is enough to realize that in 1787 the natural law and social compact theories had established a basis for believing that individual liberty was important and belonged equally to all people. This tenet was close to the heart of the liberal tradition. Utilitarianism and its potentially negative implications for individual liberties would come later.

With regard to political structure, as opposed to our modern concern for individual rights, the essential message of the liberal tradition was that liberty would be assured by popular sovereignty and was strongly equated with equality of people. Each of Jefferson's three ringing phrases in the Declaration of Independence was lifted directly from sources within this tradition:

> We hold these truths to be self-evident: That all men are created equal; that they are endowed by their Creator with certain inalienable rights; that among these are life, liberty, and the pursuit of happiness.

The Preamble to the Constitution reiterated the theme of popular sovereignty by proclaiming that the new government was created by "We the People." In the words of the Preamble, We the People "ordain and establish" government to pursue certain objectives and thus limit the powers of government to those which we choose. Two of the abiding concerns for constitutional interpretation thus become the extent to which We the People shall be involved in the day-to-day life of government and the extent to which We of a later day have the authority to reach differing interpretations of what We of an earlier day wrote.

The competing republican tradition can be traced principally to French origins in Montesquieu and Rousseau but also to British sources such as Edmund Burke. The republican tradition emphasizes communal well-being, full political participation by individuals, local control of public life in small communities, and thus a lessening of formal or central governmental power. Some of the opposition to the Constitution's ratification was rooted in this tradition. Patrick Henry, for example, opposed ratification both because it would create too large and centralized a government to permit local control of civic life and because it did not contain a specific guarantee of individual rights.

Republicanism's distrust of large government can play into competing strands of modern politics. One is the notion of "states' rights," which often includes a reaction against the "liberal" social agenda of the federal government. The other is a concern for individual rights and freedom. The problem for the republican tradition is that it presupposes a great deal of homogeneity within the community. The republican communitarian who would limit protection of individual rights to rely on communal civic values seems to assume that there will be no oppressed dissidents in the community; either everyone will share the same values or those values themselves will allow for an appropriate level of dissent. This vision runs head-on into the modern pluralistic society.

On the other hand, the problem for liberalism is that its emphasis on individuality presupposes equal opportunity for pursuit of happiness, a condition that may have had some legitimacy in the days of free and available land but that is increasingly less viable in an urbanized technological society. Most liberal writers emphasized that they were arguing for a condition of "formal" equality rather than for a guarantee of actual equality of results. The modern liberal (in the common sense of the term after the New Deal) has recognized this problem and sought to obtain governmental intervention to achieve actual equality of opportunity; this effort then threatens the individuality to which the liberal tradition aspired in the beginning.

The Contribution of Madison. James Madison was one of the principal draftsmen and a central apologist for the new Constitution in 1788. He began his famous discussion of federalism, FEDERALIST NO. 10, with the following proposition. "Among the numerous advantages promised by a well constructed Union, none deserves to be more accurately developed than its tendency to break and control the violence of faction." By faction Madison referred to "a number of citizens, whether amounting to a majority or minority of the whole, who are united and actuated by some common impulse of passion, or of interest, adverse to the rights of other citizens, or to the permanent and aggregate interests of the community." He argued that individual freedom would inevitably result, because of differences in either ability or opportunity, in an unequal distribution of wealth, which would in turn produce alliances based on self-interest. Through political arrangements, reasoned Madison, the dangers of faction might be controlled. Federation, he argued, made possible the governance by a common political authority of a large geographic area possessing multiple factions. The existence of such a pluralism of interests would guard against the accumulation of powers in a constant majority.

What Madison initially proposed as a rationale for separating power between federal and state governments could become a larger political theory promoting conscious creation of tension. The theory could be used to assert that a healthy tension is created in democratic processes by juxtaposing the three branches of government against each other (especially the courts against the legislature), the states against the federal government, rich against poor, merchants against consumers, employers against employees, and so on. If this approach were employed as a general presumption of interpretation for constitutional provisions, then competing views of a particular provision would be assessed according to the tendency of each to maintain a healthy state of tension between warring factions within society.

This "democratic republicanism" is essentially a blend of the liberal and republican traditions. It offers protection for individual liberty through the clash of self-interests represented in government through elected leadership. Madison also, however, became convinced of the need for explicit protection of individual rights against the community. His *Memoriam and Remonstrance*, which successfully persuaded the Virginia Assembly to prevent establishment of an official church and assure free exercise of religious preferences, predated the Constitution. He became the author of the Bill of Rights. Thus, Madison's own life and products reflected politically much of the tension that he advocated in political structures. It is a tension between reliance on virtual representation of self-interest as a check against governmental excesses and reliance on individual rights as a guarantee of liberty.

Stages of American Constitutional History

Some important historical figures and fundamental transitions in U.S. constitutional history may be familiar to you before you begin your study of the materials in this course. If not, here is an introduction to which you might want to refer back as you proceed through the course.

First, there are three Virginians who were important figures in the early years of the republic — Madison, Jefferson and John Marshall. The first person you will encounter in the cases is Marshall (Chief Justice 1801-1835). Marshall, unlike Jefferson and Madison, was a staunch Federalist. Jefferson wavered on the Federalist position, raising doubts about the new Constitution but not actively opposing it, serving in the first cabinet as Secretary of State under George Washington, and finally breaking away to run for President in 1800 on the Republican ticket against the Federalist incumbent John Adams. Madison was actively Federalist in obtaining ratification of the Constitution, then served as Jefferson's Secretary of State and was elected President in 1808 as a Republican. Marshall was a firm believer in the need for a strong central government. He served as Secretary of State in John Adams' administration and was appointed Chief Justice of the United States while still occupying the Secretary of State's office toward the end of Adams' term. The Supreme Court had not been a significant institution prior to Marshall's tenure. Several of his opinions established the basis for the power of the Supreme Court itself. Others formed the early underpinnings for manifestations of federal power over key matters such as regulation of commerce and foreign affairs.

The critical years leading to the Civil War were marked by disputes over the issue of slavery and the admission of new states to the Union. It was a new Republican party which became the leader in promoting abolition of slavery and a strong federal role in government to protect the interests of the industrialized North, challenged by a Democratic party oriented toward states' rights and the interests of the more agrarian South. Roger Taney (Chief Justice 1836-1864) was appointed to the Court by the Democratic President Andrew Jackson of Tennessee. It was Taney who authored the opinion in *Dred Scott v. Sanford*, reaction to which became a rallying cry for the abolitionists and was a factor in initiation of the Civil War. Taney also attempted unsuccessfully to block several wartime measures of President Abraham Lincoln, including suspension of the writ of habeas corpus.

The post-Civil War era saw attempts by the heavily Republican Congress to impose controls on the South, including Reconstruction and protection of civil rights for African-Americans. Doubts about the constitutionality of these efforts gave rise to the Thirteenth, Fourteenth, and Fifteenth Amendments, which are collectively known as the Post Civil War Amendments and serve as the cornerstone of judicial protection of civil rights against state governments. That cornerstone was not firmly fixed, however, until the middle of the twentieth century, almost 100 years after adoption of the amendments. One explanation for the delay is that the Compromise of 1876, which ended Reconstruction controls on the South, carried over into a judicial preference for state control of basic civil rights issues. Oddly enough, however, a Republican-dominated Supreme Court had announced that approach two years earlier in the *Slaughter-House Cases*.

The late nineteenth century saw the combination of industrialization and westward expansion of the nation. During this time, social reform movements attempted to regulate what were seen as some of the greater evils of the capitalist system. The reformers pursued minimum wage and maximum hour rules for employees along with collective bargaining rights on behalf of organized labor. Social reform legislation sought to eliminate abuses in the workplace, for example by prohibiting child labor or the employment of women in hazardous occupations. Meanwhile, some industries saw the advantage of regulation that would limit access to the market and limit competition. Setting of rates that could be charged by railroads and "public utilities" led to establishing limits on the size and weight of trucks, prices of many commodities, and similar maintenance of markets. Many of these efforts were met with the complaint that government regulation interfered with constitutionally protected rights of liberty and contract, a plea that was received sympathetically by a conservative Supreme Court during the early twentieth century.

The Great Depression brought an unmistakable demonstration of the existence and significance of an interlocked national economy along with strong political pressure from the New Deal government of Franklin D. Roosevelt. The Court reversed itself in 1937 to allow economic regulation of virtually any sort by either state or federal government. At the same time, the Court began to implement the provisions of the Bill of Rights against state governments through the rubric of the post-Civil War Amendments. The New Deal reformation was cemented when President Franklin D. Roosevelt appointed seven new justices to the Court during the four years from 1937 to 1941.

Following World War II and the Korean War, the stage was set for the Civil Rights Movement. At the Supreme Court, this revolution became known as the Warren Court Era after Earl Warren (Chief Justice 1953-1969). Warren was a Republican from California, appointed by Republican President Eisenhower, and was regarded as a tough law-and-order politician when appointed. His Court shaped new constitutional protection for individual rights and minority interests, particularly in matters affecting race and criminal procedure but also in matters such as free speech and legislative apportionment.

Republican presidential campaigns of the late 1960s and 1970s were run in large part against the Supreme Court as personified by Warren and Justice William O. Douglas. With the Republican hegemony of the Nixon, Reagan, and Bush presidencies, a number of conservative Justices changed the balance on the Court. But the trend was not all one-sided. President Clinton had two appointments to the Court, and some of the Republican appointees were not uniformly conservative reformers. The legacy of the Burger and Rehnquist Courts has yet to be fully understood.

The last quarter of the century saw a deeply fractured and divided Supreme Court struggling with issues of federal and state power without reaching a clear consensus on reform. There were isolated instances of retrenchment in some areas of criminal procedure and individual rights, such as religion and free speech. For the most part, the Court's agenda emphasized state powers and tended to restrict federal power, but it remains to be seen whether this "Revitalized Federalism" will have a lasting effect on the allocation of power between federal and state governments.

The Process and Significance of Appointing Supreme Court Justices

As the previous discussion implies, the appointment of Supreme Court Justices, indeed of all federal judges, is an important element of the American political scene. The formal steps in the process can be simply stated: when a vacancy occurs, whether by death or retirement (impeachment is also a distant possibility), the current President "nominates" a new member of the Court; the Senate then "confirms" or "rejects" the appointment. Within these formal steps, however, lie a host of engaging political and legal issues.

The role of the Senate is subject to a great deal of debate. The Constitution states that an appointment is made by the President "by and with the Advice and Consent of the Senate." This language implies that there could be an active give and take between President and Senate on who would be good judges for all the federal courts. In practice, however, the President has become virtually autonomous in the initial nomination step. There may well be active consultation between the President and leading members of his or her political party, but this is not a formal consultation with the Senate. The Senate then reviews the qualifications of the nominee through its Judiciary Committee and votes up or down on the nominee.

Because the Senate as a body plays only a reactive role rather than a more consultative role, the major debate has become whether it is appropriate for the Senate to consider the judicial philosophy of the candidate. On one extreme are those who say that the choice of judge is for the President subject only to the Senate's review of the nominee's character and a minimal level of competence for the job. On the other extreme are those who say that the Senate should have a consultative role and is free to reject a nominee just because a majority of the Senate do not agree with the nominee's philosophy or because they think there are better people out there for the job.

Your views on the merits of this debate may shift as you study the course of decisions in the Supreme Court.

Chapter 1

JUDICIAL REVIEW: INSTRUMENT OF AMERICAN CONSTITUTIONALISM

The origins, scope and legitimacy of judicial review in a democratic society are quite probably the most analyzed and debated issues of constitutional law and theory. Indeed, as subsequent chapters will demonstrate, in varying degrees these questions underlie virtually every issue of constitutional application. The intensity of the controversy is not surprising. However limited or defined, the concept of judicial review vests within a largely unrepresentative judiciary the all-but-irreversible power to invalidate the decisions of the majoritarian branches of government. On at least a superficial level, the concept appears at odds with the basic majoritarian premise of a democratic system. But the constitutional form of democracy we have chosen limits majority power both by substantive limitations in the grants of powers to each branch of government and by explicit prohibitions such as those in the Bill of Rights. Finding an acceptable balance between majoritarian government on the one hand and insulation of individual rights and fundamental constitutional principles from majoritarian encroachment on the other has not proven to be an easy task, despite its tremendous importance.

It is for these reasons that we begin the study of constitutional law with an examination of the theory of judicial review in a constitutional democracy. This initial chapter is divided into three sections. First, it will examine the history and theory behind the decisional sources of the American practice of judicial review: *Marbury v. Madison* and *Martin v. Hunter's Lessee*. Second, it will examine the different theories as to how the judicial review power may be exercised. Third, the chapter will consider a relatively narrow grouping of constitutional cases, generally categorized under the heading of "political question," in which the judiciary completely abstains from the exercise of its review function.

§ 1.01 JUDICIAL REVIEW IN A DEMOCRATIC SOCIETY

The Background of *Marbury v. Madison*

The Republicans won a solid victory in the election of 1800, but it was not clear who would be President. The electoral process at the time gave each elector two votes to cast for President. The person with the greatest number of votes would be President and the person with the second greatest would be Vice-President. All the Republican electors cast their two votes for Jefferson and Burr for President. The result was a tie for President between the running mates, throwing the election into the House of Representatives. Before the new Republican House was seated, the old Federalist Congress had to decide whether Jefferson or Burr should be President, triggering a debate which went on for several months and giving the Federalists the opportunity to do some lame-duck entrenchment of their position before leaving office.

John Marshall was President Adams' Secretary of State. On February 4, 1801, Marshall took office as Chief Justice of the United States while continuing to serve as Secretary of State. On February 13, the Federalist-dominated Congress enacted a Circuit Court Act creating several new judgeships. On February 17, the electoral tie was decided in favor of Jefferson and his inauguration was scheduled for March 4. On February 27, Congress enacted a bill creating 42 Justices of the Peace within the District of Columbia. The Senate completed confirmation of the Circuit Court Judges on March 2 and confirmation of the JPs on March 3. Adams signed the commissions of all the judges and JPs and gave them to Marshall for delivery to the recipients. Marshall's brother James was entrusted with the job of delivery but did not complete the job by midnight of the 3rd. James stated in an affidavit filed with the Court later that he had intended to deliver all the commissions but found that he "could not conveniently carry the whole" and that "several of them" were left in the Secretary of State's office.

Marbury was one of the JPs whose commission was undelivered. He sued James Madison, who was now Jefferson's Secretary of State, in the Supreme Court for a writ of mandamus ordering that the commission be delivered. His suit was not filed, however, until December of 1801. The Court held terms that began, by statute, in June and December each year. When the Court went out of session without reaching a decision on Marbury's petition, the Republican Congress could not resist the temptation of getting involved in the proceedings. The statute was changed in March 1802 to repeal the June and December terms and establish a single term beginning in February. Thus the Court could not reconvene to act on the case until February 1803.

Meanwhile, Congress attacked the Federalist-dominated judiciary in more direct ways. First, the Circuit Court Act was repealed. Second, a federal judge named Pickering was impeached and removed from office by the Senate; his offenses consisted essentially of alcoholism and a mild bit of insanity. He was obviously unfit for judicial office, but there was some question under the Constitution whether a judge could be removed from office in the absence of palpable "Treason, Bribery, or other High Crimes and Misdemeanors." After the Pickering trial, the House of Representatives impeached Justice Samuel Chase, an outspoken Federalist. The trial in the Senate resulted in nothing more than a vociferous attack on Chase's policies and opinions, with no showing of physical or moral unfitness. When Chase was acquitted, the threat of impeachment as a tool to reform the judiciary politically died. These events are chronicled well in CHARLES WARREN, THE SUPREME COURT IN UNITED STATES HISTORY (rev. ed. 1922) and ALBERT J. BEVERIDGE, THE LIFE OF JOHN MARSHALL (1919).

The stage for controversy was thus set when the Court reconvened in 1803 and turned to the *Marbury* case. *Marbury* was a power struggle between Federalists and Republicans, between Marshall and Jefferson, between the judiciary and the other branches of government.

MARBURY v. MADISON

5 U.S. (1 Cranch) 137, 2 L. Ed. 60 (1803)

Opinion of the Court [by CHIEF JUSTICE MARSHALL].

At the last term on the affidavits then read and filed with the clerk, a rule was granted in this case, requiring the secretary of state to show cause why a mandamus should not issue, directing him to deliver to William Marbury his commission as a justice of the peace for the county of Washington, in the District of Columbia.

No cause has been shown, and the present motion is for a mandamus. The peculiar delicacy of this case, the novelty of some of its circumstances, and the real difficulty attending the points which occur in it, require a complete exposition of the principles on which the opinion to be given by the court is founded.

In the order in which the court has viewed this subject, the following questions have been considered and decided.

1st. Has the applicant a right to the commission he demands?

2d. If he has a right, and that right has been violated, do the laws of his country afford him a remedy?

3d. If they do afford him a remedy, is it a mandamus issuing from this court?

The first object of inquiry is, 1st. Has the applicant a right to the commission he demands?

Mr. Marbury since his commission was signed by the President, and sealed by the Secretary of State, was appointed; and as the law creating the office, gave the officer a right to hold for five years, independent of the executive the appointment was not revocable, but vested in the officer legal rights, which are protected by the laws of his country. To withhold his commission, therefore, is an act deemed by the court not warranted by law, but violative of a vested legal right.

This brings us to the second inquiry; which is, 2d. If he has a right, and that right has been violated, do the laws of this country afford him a remedy?

The very essence of civil liberty certainly consists in the right of every individual to claim the protection of the laws, whenever he receives an injury. One of the first duties of government is to afford that protection. The government of the United States has been emphatically termed a government of laws, and not of men. It will certainly cease to deserve this high appellation, if the laws furnish no remedy for the violation of a vested legal right.

If this obloquy is to be cast on the jurisprudence of our country, it must arise from the peculiar character of the case. Is the act of delivering or withholding a commission to be considered as a mere political act, belonging to the executive department alone, for the performance of which entire confidence is placed by our constitution in the supreme executive; and for any misconduct respecting which, the injured individual has no remedy?

That there may be such cases is not to be questioned; but that every act of duty, to be performed in any of the great departments of government, constitutes such a case, is not to be admitted. It follows, then, that the question, whether the legality of an act of the head of a department be examinable in a court of justice or not, must always depend on the nature of that act.

By the constitution of the United States, the President is invested with certain important political powers, in the exercise of which he is to use his own discretion, and is accountable only to his country in his political character and to his own conscience. To aid him in the performance of these duties, he is authorized to appoint certain officers, who act by his authority, and in conformity with his orders.

In such cases, their acts are his acts; and whatever opinion may be entertained of the manner in which executive discretion may be used, still there exists, and can exist, no power to control that discretion. The subjects are political. They respect the nation, not individual rights, and being intrusted to the executive, the decision of the executive is exclusive. The application of this remark will be perceived by adverting to the act of congress for establishing the department of foreign affairs. This officer, as his duties were prescribed by that act, is to conform precisely to the will of the President. He is the mere organ by whom that will is communicated. The acts of such an officer, as an officer, can never be examinable by the courts.

But when the legislature proceeds to impose on that officer other duties; when he is directed peremptorily to perform certain acts; when the rights of individuals are dependent on the performance of those acts; he is so far the officer of the law; is amenable to the laws for his conduct; and cannot at his discretion sport away the vested right of others.

The conclusion from this reasoning is, that where the heads of departments are the political or confidential agents of the executive, merely to execute the will of the President, or rather to act in cases in which the executive possesses a constitutional or legal discretion, nothing can be more perfectly clear than that their acts are only politically examinable. But where a specific duty is assigned by law, and individual rights depend upon the performance of that duty, it seems equally clear that the individual who considers himself injured, has a right to resort to the laws of his country for a remedy.

It remains to be inquired whether, 3d. He is entitled to the remedy for which he applies. This depends on,

1st. The nature of the writ applied for; and, 2d. The power of this court.

This writ, if awarded, would be directed to an officer of government, and its mandate to him would be, to use the words of Blackstone, "to do a particular thing therein specified, which appertains to his office and duty, and which the court has previously determined, or at least supposes, to be consonant to right and justice." Or, in the words of Lord Mansfield, the applicant, in this case, has a right to execute an office of public concern, and is kept out by possession of that right. These circumstances certainly concur in this case.

Still, to render the mandamus a proper remedy, the officer to whom it is to be directed, must be one to whom, on legal principles, such writ may be directed; and the person applying for it must be without any other specific and legal remedy.

1st. With respect to the officer to whom it would be directed. The intimate political relation subsisting between the President of the United States and the heads of departments, necessarily renders any legal investigation of the acts of one of those high officers peculiarly irksome, as well as delicate; and excites some hesitation with respect to the propriety of entering into such investigation. Impressions are often received without much reflection or examination, and it is not wonderful that in such a case as this the assertion, by an individual, of his legal claims in a court of justice, to which claims it is the duty of that court to attend, should at first view be considered by some, as an attempt to intrude into the cabinet, and to intermeddle with the prerogatives of the executive.

It is scarcely necessary for the court to disclaim all pretensions to such jurisdiction. An extravagance, so absurd and excessive, could not have been entertained for a moment. The province of the court is, solely, to decide on the rights of individuals, not to inquire how the executive, or executive officers, perform duties in which they have a discretion. Questions in their nature political, or which are, by the constitution and laws, submitted to the executive, can never be made in this court.

But, if this be not such a question; if, so far from being an intrusion into the secrets of the cabinet, it respects a paper which, according to law, is upon record, and to a copy of which the law gives a right, on the payment of ten cents; if it be no intermeddling with a subject over which the executive can be considered as having exercised any control; what is there in the exalted station of the officer, which shall bar a citizen from asserting, in a court of justice, his legal rights, or shall forbid a court to listen to the claim, or to issue a mandamus directing the performance of a duty, not depending on executive discretion, but on particular acts of congress, and the general principles of law?

It is not by the office of the person to whom the writ is directed, but the nature of the thing to be done, that the propriety or impropriety of issuing a mandamus is to be determined. Where the head of a department acts in a case, in which executive discretion is to be exercised; in which he is the mere organ of executive will; it is again repeated, that any application to a court to control, in any respect, his conduct would be rejected without hesitation.

But where he is directed by law to do a certain act affecting the absolute rights of individuals, in the performance of which he is not placed under the particular direction of the President, and the performance of which the President cannot lawfully forbid, and therefore is never presumed to have forbidden; as for example, to record a commission, or a patent for land, which has received all the legal solemnities; or to give a copy of such record; in such cases, it is not perceived on what ground the courts of the country are further excused from the duty of giving judgment that right be done to an injured individual, than if the same services were to be performed by a person not the head of a department.

This, then, is a plain case for mandamus, either to deliver the commission, or a copy of it from the record; and it only remains to be inquired,

Whether it can issue from this court.

The act to establish the judicial courts of the United States authorizes the Supreme Court "to issue writs of mandamus in cases warranted by the principles and usages of law, to any courts appointed, or persons holding office, under the authority of the United States." The Secretary of State, being a person holding an office under the authority of the United States, is precisely within the letter of the description, and if this court is not authorized to issue a writ of mandamus to such an officer, it must be because the law is unconstitutional, and therefore absolutely incapable of conferring the authority, and assigning the duties which its words purport to confer and assign.

The constitution vests the whole judicial power of the United States in one Supreme Court, and such inferior courts as congress shall, from time to time, ordain and establish. This power is expressly extended to all cases arising under the laws of the United States; and, consequently, in some form, may be exercised over the present case; because the right claimed is given by a law of the United States.

In the distribution of this power it is declared that "the Supreme Court shall have original jurisdiction in all cases affecting ambassadors, other public ministers and consuls, and those in which a state shall be a party. In all other cases, the Supreme Court shall have appellate jurisdiction." It has been insisted, at the bar, that as the original grant of jurisdiction, to the Supreme and inferior courts, is general, and the clause, assigning original jurisdiction to the Supreme Court, contains no negative or restrictive words, the power remains to the legislature to assign original jurisdiction to that court in other cases than those specified in the article which has been recited; provided those cases belong to the judicial power of the United States.

If it had been intended to leave it in the discretion of the legislature to apportion the judicial power between the supreme and inferior courts according to the will of that body, it would certainly have been useless to have proceeded further than to have defined the judicial power, and the tribunals in which it should be vested. The subsequent part of the section is mere surplusage, is entirely without meaning, if such is to be the construction. If congress remains at liberty to give this court appellate jurisdiction, where the constitution has declared their jurisdiction shall be original; and original jurisdiction where the constitution has declared it shall be appellate; the distribution of jurisdiction, made in the constitution, is form without substance.

Affirmative words are often, in their operation, negative of other objects than those affirmed; and in this case, a negative or exclusive sense must be given to them, or they have no operation at all. It cannot be presumed that any clause in the constitution is intended to be without effect; and, therefore, such a construction is inadmissible, unless the words require it. The authority, therefore, given to the Supreme Court, by the act establishing the judicial courts of the United States, to issue writs of mandamus to public officers, appears not to be warranted by the constitution; and it becomes necessary to inquire whether a jurisdiction so conferred can be exercised.

The question, whether an act, repugnant to the constitution, can become the law of the land, is a question deeply interesting to the United States; but, happily, not of an intricacy proportioned to its interest. It seems only necessary to recognize certain principles, supposed to have been long and well established, to decide it.

That the people have an original right to establish, for their future government, such principles, as, in their opinion, shall most conduce to their own happiness is the basis on which the whole American fabric has been erected. The exercise of this original right is a very great exertion; nor can it, nor ought it, to be frequently repeated. The principles, therefore, so established, are deemed fundamental. And as the authority from which they proceed is supreme, and can seldom act, they are designed to be permanent.

This original and supreme will organizes the government, and assigns to different departments their respective powers. It may either stop here, or establish certain limits not to be transcended by those departments.

The government of the United States is of the latter description. The powers of the legislature are defined and limited; and that those limits may not be mistaken, or forgotten, the constitution is written. To what purpose are powers limited, and to what purpose is that limitation committed to writing, if these limits may, at any time, be passed by those intended to be restrained? The distinction between a government with limited and unlimited powers is abolished, if those limits do not confine the persons on whom they are imposed, and if acts prohibited and acts allowed, are of equal obligation. It is a proposition too plain to be contested, that the constitution controls any legislative act repugnant to it; or, that the legislature may alter the constitution by an ordinary act.

Between these alternatives there is no middle ground. The constitution is either a superior paramount law, unchangeable by ordinary means, or it is on a level with ordinary legislative acts, and, like other acts, is alterable when the legislature shall please to alter it.

If the former part of the alternative be true, then a legislative act contrary to the constitution is not law: if the latter part be true, then written constitutions are absurd attempts, on the part of the people, to limit a power in its own nature illimitable.

Certainly all those who have framed written constitutions contemplate them as forming the fundamental and paramount law of the nation, and, consequently, the theory of every such government must be, that an act of the legislature, repugnant to the constitution, is void.

This theory is essentially attached to a written constitution, and, is consequently, to be considered, by this court, as one of the fundamental principles of our society. It is not therefore to be lost sight of in the further consideration of this subject.

If an act of the legislature, repugnant to the constitution, is void, does it, notwithstanding its invalidity, bind the courts, and oblige them to give it effect? Or, in other words, though it be not law, does it constitute a rule as operative as if it was a law? This would be to overthrow in fact what was established in theory; and would seem, at first view, an absurdity too gross to be insisted on. It shall, however, receive a more attentive consideration.

It is emphatically the province and duty of the judicial department to say what the law is. Those who apply the rule to particular cases, must of necessity expound and interpret that rule. If two laws conflict with each other, the courts must decide on the operation of each. So if a law be in opposition to the constitution; if both the law and the constitution apply to a particular case, so that the court must either decide that case conformably to the law, disregarding the constitution; or conformably to the constitution, disregarding the law; the court must determine which of these conflicting rules governs the case. This is of the very essence of judicial duty.

If, then, the courts are to regard the constitution, and the constitution is superior to any ordinary act of the legislature, the constitution, and not such ordinary act, must govern the case to which they both apply.

Those, then, who controvert the principle that the constitution is to be considered, in court, as a paramount law, are reduced to the necessity of maintaining that courts must close their eyes on the constitution, and see only the law. This doctrine would subvert the very foundation of all written constitutions. It would declare that an act which, according to the principles and theory of our government, is entirely void, is yet, in practice, completely obligatory. It would declare that if the legislature shall do what is expressly forbidden, such act, notwithstanding the express prohibition, is in reality effectual. It would be giving to the legislature a practical and real omnipotence, with the same breath which professes to restrict their powers within narrow limits. It is prescribing limits, and declaring that those limits may be passed at pleasure.

That it thus reduces to nothing what we have deemed the greatest improvement on political institutions, a written constitution, would of itself be sufficient, in America, where written constitutions have been viewed with so much reverence, for rejecting the construction. But the peculiar expressions of the constitution of the United States furnish additional arguments in favor of its rejection.

The judicial power of the United States is extended to all cases arising under the constitution. Could it be the intention of those who gave this power, to say that in using it the constitution should not be looked into? That a case arising under the constitution should be decided without examining the instrument under which it arises? This is too extravagant to be maintained.

In some cases, then, the constitution must be looked into by the judges. And if they can open it at all, what part of it are they forbidden to read or to obey? [T]he framers of the constitution contemplated that instrument as a rule for the government of courts, as well as of the legislature. Why otherwise does it direct the judges to take an oath to support it? This oath certainly applies in an especial manner, to their conduct in their official character. How immoral to impose it on them, if they were to be used as the instruments, and the knowing instruments, for violating what they swear to support!

Why does a judge swear to discharge his duties agreeably to the constitution of the United States, if that constitution forms no rule for his government? If it is closed upon him, and cannot be inspected by him? If such be the real state of things, this is worse than solemn mockery. To prescribe, or to take this oath, becomes equally a crime.

It is also not entirely unworthy of observation, that in declaring what shall be the supreme law of the land, the constitution itself is first mentioned; and not the laws of the United States generally, but those only which shall be made in pursuance of the constitution, have that rank.

Thus, the particular phraseology of the constitution of the United States confirms and strengthens the principle, supposed to be essential to all written constitutions, that a law repugnant to the constitution is void; and that courts, as well as other departments, are bound by that instrument.

NOTES

1. *The political wisdom of Marshall.* The distinguished constitutional scholar Edward S. Corwin says that the Court in *Marbury v. Madison* wanted to make it clear that it thought that President Jefferson should have delivered the commissions to those who had been appointed to office under the previous administration. Yet, says Corwin, the Court feared "to invite a snub by actually asserting jurisdiction of the matter." The Court therefore "took the engaging position of declining to exercise power which the Constitution withheld from it, by making the occasion an opportunity to assert a far more transcendent power." Edward S. Corwin, The Doctrine of Judicial Review 9 (1914). The structure of the opinion in *Marbury* tends to corroborate Professor Corwin's thesis. The "lecture" Marshall gave Jefferson on the right of the justices to have their commissions, and the duty of the President to deliver them was really dicta because the Court held that it had no jurisdiction of the cause.

2. *The statutory issue.* Did Marshall read **Section 13 of the Judiciary Act of 1789** properly before deciding that it unconstitutionally conferred unauthorized original jurisdiction on the Supreme Court? The statute read as follows:

> That the Supreme Court shall have exclusive jurisdiction of all controversies of a civil nature, where a state is a party, except between a state and its citizens; and except also between a state and citizens of other states, or aliens, in which latter case it shall have original but not exclusive jurisdiction. And shall have exclusively all such jurisdiction of suits or proceedings against ambassadors or other public ministers, or their domestics, or domestic servants, as a court of law can have or exercise consistently with the law of nations; and original, but not exclusive jurisdiction of all suits brought by ambassadors or other public ministers, or in which a consul, or vice consul, shall be a party. And the trial of issues of fact in the Supreme Court in all actions at law against citizens of the United States shall be by jury. The Supreme Court shall also have appellate jurisdiction from the circuit courts and courts of the several states in the cases hereinafter specially provided for; and shall have power to issue writs of prohibition to the district courts, when proceeding as courts of admiralty and maritime jurisdiction, and writs of mandamus, in cases warranted by the principles and usages of law, to any courts appointed, or persons holding office, under the authority of the United States.

3. *Presidential discretion.* Marshall implicitly held that the President was subject to suit in the courts but gave no hint of how the Court would enforce a decree against a recalcitrant President. This issue arose anew in the famous controversy in 1973 and 1974 in which the special prosecutor and the Senate Select Committee on Presidential Campaign Activities (the Watergate Committee) sought the celebrated tapes from President Nixon. The President's lawyers relied on *Marbury* and a later opinion by Marshall written as Circuit Justice in the prosecution of Aaron Burr to argue that the President was immune from suit with regard to the exercise of his discretion.

Does Marshall's willingness to say that Jefferson should have delivered the commissions suggest that an appropriate court could have subjected the President to judicial process? In a per curiam opinion, *Nixon v. Sirica*, 487 F.2d 700, 712 (D.C. Cir. 1973), the court of appeals made the following response to the contention that executive discretion was judicially unreviewable:

> Finally, the President reminds us that the landmark decisions recognizing judicial power to mandamus Executive compliance with "ministerial" duties also acknowledged that the Executive Branch enjoys an unreviewable discretion in many areas of "political" or "executive" administration. While true, this is irrelevant to the issue of presidential immunity from judicial process. The discretionary-ministerial distinction concerns the nature of the act or omission under review, not the official title of the defendant. No case holds that an act is discretionary merely because the President is the actor. If the Constitution or the laws of evidence confer upon the President the absolute discretion to withhold material subpoenaed by a grand jury, then of course we would vacate, rather than approve with modification, the order entered below. However, this would be because the order touched upon matters within the President's sole discretion, not because the President is immune from process generally.

4. *The textual basis of judicial review.* There is no explicit reference in the text of the Constitution to the judiciary's power to exercise judicial review, but Marshall claims that the entire "phraseology . . . confirms and strengthens the principle." He points out three provisions that bear on the problem. Article III, § 2 extends "the judicial power" to "all cases, in law and equity, arising under this Constitution." The supremacy clause of Article VI states: "This Constitution and the laws of the United States which shall be made in pursuance thereof . . . shall be the supreme law of the land." And Article VI requires judges to take an oath to support the constitution. But almost all other public officials take the same oath, Article III apparently contemplates that some cases arising under the Constitution will go through the state courts, and "in pursuance of" surely contains some ambiguity. The issue is whether the Constitution gives the federal judiciary a special role in assessing the constitutionality of legislation, and the text provides no explicit answer.

5. *The structural basis of judicial review.* It is interesting that Marshall does not begin with the textual basis for the judicial review power but with an exegesis on the structure and nature of a written constitution. Compare Marshall's words with Hamilton's words in THE FEDERALIST NO. 78:

> The complete independence of the courts of justice is peculiarly essential in a limited Constitution. By a limited Constitution, I understand one which contains certain specified exceptions to the Legislative authority; such, for instance, as that it shall pass no bills of attainder, no ex post facto laws, and the like. Limitations of this kind can be preserved in practice no other way than through the medium of courts of justice; whose duty it must be to declare all acts contrary to the manifest tenor of the Constitution void. Without this, all the reservations of particular rights or privileges would amount to nothing.
>
> If it be said that the Legislative body are themselves the Constitutional judges of their own powers, and that the construction they put upon them is conclusive upon the other departments, it may be answered, that this cannot be the natural presumption, where it is not to be collected from any particular provisions in the Constitution. It is not otherwise to be supposed, that the Constitution could intend to enable the representatives of the people to substitute their will to that of their constituents. It is far more rational to suppose, that the courts were designed to be an intermediate body between the people and the Legislature, in order, among other things, to keep the latter within the limits assigned to their authority. The interpretation of the laws is the proper and peculiar province of the courts. A Constitution is, in fact, and must be regarded by the Judges as a fundamental law. It therefore belongs to them to ascertain its meaning as well as the meaning of any particular act proceeding from the Legislative body. If there should happen to be irreconcilable variance between the two, that which has the superior obligation and validity ought, of course, to be preferred; or, in other words the Constitution ought to be preferred to the statute, the intention of the people to the intention of their agents.

Professor Van Alstyne suggests that Marshall may have begged the critical question in *Marbury*. He argues that the real issue is "*who, according to the Constitution, is to make the determination as to whether any given law is in fact repugnant to the Constitution itself?*" William W. Van Alstyne, *A Critical Guide to Marbury v. Madison,* 1969 DUKE L.J. 1, 22.

It can be argued that in a constitutional democracy, the practice of judicial review by an unrepresentative and independent judiciary permissible is essential. The insularity, traditions, learning and decision-making advantages of the judiciary make it superior to the legislature in assessing constitutional arguments, thus legitimizing judicial review. MARTIN H. REDISH, THE FEDERAL COURTS IN THE POLITICAL ORDER (1991). On the hand, what weight should be given to the realization that judicial review is essentially an "undemocratic" force in American society? *See* ALEXANDER BICKEL, THE LEAST DANGEROUS BRANCH 23–33 (1962).

6. *The historical basis of judicial review.* While there still exists debate among respected scholars about the Framers' assumptions, the widely-held perception is that the judicial review power was intended. *See, e.g.,* EUGENE ROSTOW, THE SOVEREIGN PREROGATIVE: THE SUPREME COURT AND THE QUEST FOR LAW 150 (1962): "As far as the American Constitution is concerned, there can be little real doubt that the courts were intended from the beginning to have the power [of judicial review] they have exercised. The Federalist Papers are unequivocal; the Debates as clear as debates normally are." *See also* JULIUS GOEBEL, THE HISTORY OF THE SUPREME COURT OF THE UNITED STATES — ANTECEDENTS AND BEGINNINGS TO 1801 (1971).

7. *The British tradition.* In the British legal system, from which our jurisprudential heritage stems, the basic facts of life can be summed up in the single phrase of "parliamentary supremacy." It has been said that

> within the limits of physical possibility Parliament could make or unmake any law whatever. The courts can only interpret and may not question the validity of Acts of Parliament. No Parliament can bind its successor; otherwise the supremacy of succeeding Parliaments would be limited. The Bill of Rights [passed in 1688] could be cast overboard by the same process as a Prevention of Damage by Pests Act, namely by a repealing measure passed in ordinary form.

EMLYN C.S. WADE & GEORGE G. PHILLIPS, CONSTITUTIONAL LAW 46 (8th ed. 1970).

It is possible to find some contrary views in British jurisprudence. For example, Lord Coke felt quite differently back in the early 17th century:

> And it appears in our books, that in many cases, the common law will controul Acts of Parliament, and sometimes adjudge them to be utterly void: For when an Act of Parliament is against common right and reason, or repugnant, or impossible to be performed, the common law will controul it, and adjudge such Act to be void.

Dr. Bonham's Case, 8 Co. 113b, 118a (1608). Lord Coke's opinion was prior to the final struggles between Parliament and the Crown by which the legislative body finally achieved primacy in lawmaking.

What is left of the controlling authority of the common law is a presumption that Parliament does not change the common law without explicitly saying so. The presumption extends to many aspects of individual liberty such as criminal procedure rights, property, and access to the courts. Thus the common law as enforced and interpreted by the courts acts as a serious check on Parliament. Statutes will be interpreted to preserve common-law rights until Parliament musters the political will to enact a specific provision taking away a common-law right.

***A v. Home Secretary,* [2004] HL 56**. The House of Lords declared that emergency powers of executive detention granted in the Anti-Terrorism, Crime, and Security Act of 2001 were incompatible with obligations under the European Convention of Human Rights.

The House of Lords for the last couple of decades has performed its judicial function through an Appellate Committee of "Law Lords," who are appointed by the Queen and serve for a salary much like any other judge. There is no set procedure for how many Law Lords sit on a case or how they arrive at decisions. Formally, their decisions are still reported as recommendations to the full HL, but the "lay Lords" do not in fact vote on the final disposition. The Lords still cling to the principle of Parliamentary Supremacy so that there is no power to declare an Act invalid. Moreover, treaties such as the European Convention of Human Rights are not incorporated into domestic law. With the Human Rights Act of 1998, however, the HL was given the power to issue a "declaration of incompatibility" between an Act and the ECHR. The effect of the detention decision was basically advice to Parliament that a problem needs fixing. As the lead opinion stated:

> The Attorney General is fully entitled to insist on the proper limits of judicial authority, but he is wrong to stigmatise judicial decision-making as in some way undemocratic. . . . The effect is not, of course, to override the sovereign legislative authority of the Queen in Parliament, since if primary legislation is declared to be incompatible the validity of the legislation is unaffected and the remedy lies with the appropriate minister who is answerable to Parliament. The 1998 Act gives the courts a very specific, wholly democratic, mandate.

In June 2003, the Government proposed to abolish the judicial power of the House of Lords, to eliminate the office of Lord Chancellor (who sits as a Law Lord, is a member of Parliament, and is also an executive minister) and move the Appellate Committee to an independent role as the Supreme Court for the United Kingdom. This is taking place as a follow-up to "devolution" in which each of the states of the UK (Britain, Scotland, Wales, Northern Ireland) now has its own High Court. In various commentaries on the new proposal, it does not appear that anyone is seriously urging that the British adopt a concept of judicial review similar to that of the U.S. because Parliamentary Supremacy is still firmly fixed in that tradition. *See* ANDREW LASEUR, BUILDING THE UK'S NEW SUPREME COURT 7 (2004).

8. *Marbury and judicial supremacy.* *Marbury* does not necessarily stand for the proposition that the judiciary is "supreme" in constitutional interpretation. For example, there is nothing to prevent Congress from repealing a law that the Supreme Court has decided is constitutional, and there is nothing to prevent a President from vetoing a bill that the Supreme Court would likely uphold. Would it be fair to say that all three branches must find a law to be valid before it can be enforced? In *Cooper v. Aaron*, noted following the next case, the Court stated that *Marbury* stands for the proposition that "the federal judiciary is supreme in the exposition of the law of the Constitution." But *Cooper* involved state resistance to federal court orders, not the roles of co-ordinate branches of the federal government.

MARTIN v. HUNTER'S LESSEE
14 U.S. (1 Wheat.) 304, 4 L. Ed. 97 (1816)

[Lord Fairfax, a citizen of Virginia, willed his Virginia estates to his nephew, Denny Martin, a British subject. In 1789 after the American Revolution, Virginia confiscated lands owned by British subjects. Virginia granted a land patent over the Fairfax devise to David Hunter. Hunter brought an action of ejectment against Martin. The Virginia trial court held for Martin on the basis of the treaties of 1783 and 1794 between the United States and Great Britain, which protected British lands in the United States.

[The Virginia Court of Appeals, however, reversed and held for Hunter on the ground, inter alia, that Virginia's title to the land was perfected prior to the enactment of the treaties. In Fairfax's *Devisee v. Hunter's Lessee*, 11 U.S. (7 Cranch) 603 (1813), the Supreme Court reversed the Virginia Court of Appeals. The mandate of the Supreme Court directed the Virginia Court of Appeals to enter judgment for Martin. But that court refused to obey the Supreme Court's decree on the ground that § 25 of the Judiciary Act of 1789 which conferred appellate jurisdiction on the Supreme Court over the decisions of a state's highest tribunal was unconstitutional.

[The case was brought to the Supreme Court again. In a historic and fundamental decision, Mr. Justice Story, for the court, considered and rejected Virginia's challenge to the paramountcy of the Supreme Court of the United States.]

STORY, J., delivered the opinion of the court:

This is a writ of error from the Court of Appeals of Virginia, founded upon the refusal of that court to obey the mandate of this court, requiring the judgment rendered in this very cause, at February term, 1813, to be carried into due execution.

The third article of the constitution is that which must principally attract our attention. The language of the article throughout is manifestly designed to be mandatory upon the legislature. Its obligatory force is so imperative that Congress could not, without a violation of its duty, have refused to carry it into operation. The judicial power of the United States shall be vested (not may be vested) in one supreme court, and in such inferior courts as Congress may, from time to time, ordain and establish. Could Congress have lawfully refused to create a supreme court, or to vest in it the constitutional jurisdiction? The judicial power must, therefore, be vested in some court, by Congress; and to suppose that it was not an obligation binding on them, but might, at their pleasure, be omitted or declined, is to suppose that, under the sanction of the constitution they might defeat the constitution itself; a construction which would lead to such a result cannot be sound.

If, then, it is the duty of Congress to vest the judicial power of the United States, it is a duty to vest the whole judicial power. The language, if imperative as to one part, is imperative as to all. If it were otherwise, this anomaly would exist, that Congress might successively refuse to vest the jurisdiction in any one class of cases enumerated in the constitution, and thereby defeat the jurisdiction as to all; for the constitution has not singled out any class on which Congress are bound to act in preference to others.

The next consideration is as to the courts in which the judicial power shall be vested. It is manifest that a supreme court must be established; but whether it be equally obligatory to establish inferior courts is a question of some difficulty. If Congress may lawfully omit to establish inferior courts, it might follow that in some of the enumerated cases the judicial power could nowhere exist. It would seem, therefore, to follow that Congress are bound to create some inferior courts, in which to vest all that jurisdiction which, under the constitution, is exclusively vested in the United States, and of which the Supreme Court cannot take original cognizance. They might establish one or more inferior courts; they might parcel out the jurisdiction among such courts, from time to time, at their own pleasure. But the whole judicial power of the United States should be, at all times, vested either in an original or appellate form, in some courts created under its authority.

It being, then, established that the language of this clause is imperative, the next question is as to the cases to which it shall apply. The answer is found in the constitution itself. The judicial power shall extend to all the cases enumerated in the constitution. As the mode is not limited, it may extend to all such cases, in any form in which judicial power may be exercised. It may, therefore, extend to them in the shape of original or appellate jurisdiction, or both; for there is nothing in the nature of the cases which binds to the exercise of the one in preference to the other. But, even admitting that the language of the constitution is not mandatory, and that Congress may constitutionally omit to vest the judicial power in courts of the United States, it cannot be denied that when it is vested it may be exercised to the utmost constitutional extent.

This leads us to the consideration of the great question as to the nature and extent of the appellate jurisdiction of the United States. We have already seen that appellate jurisdiction is given by the constitution to the Supreme Court in all cases, where it has not original jurisdiction; subject, however, to such exceptions and regulations as Congress may prescribe. It is, therefore, capable of embracing every case enumerated in the constitution, which is not exclusively to be decided by way of original jurisdiction. But the exercise of appellate jurisdiction is far from being limited by the terms of the constitution to the Supreme Court. There can be no doubt that Congress may create a succession of inferior tribunals, in each of which it may vest appellate as well as original jurisdiction. The judicial power is delegated by the constitution in the most general terms, and may, therefore, be exercised by Congress under every variety of form, of appellate or original jurisdiction. And as there is nothing in the constitution which restrains or limits this power, it must, therefore, in all other cases, subsist in the utmost latitude of which, in its own nature, it is susceptible.

As, then, by the terms of the constitution, the appellate jurisdiction is not limited as to the Supreme Court, and as to this court it may be exercised in all other cases than those of which it has original cognizance, what is there to restrain its exercise over state tribunals in the enumerated cases? The appellate power is not limited by the terms of the third article to any particular courts. The words are, "the judicial power (which includes appellate power) shall extend to all cases," etc., and "in all other cases before mentioned the

Supreme Court shall have appellate jurisdiction." It is the case, then, and not the court, that gives the jurisdiction. If the judicial power extends to the case, it will be in vain to search in the letter of the constitution for any qualification as to the tribunal where it depends. It is incumbent, then, upon those who assert such a qualification to show its existence by necessary implication. If the text be clear and distinct, no restriction upon its plain and obvious import ought to be admitted, unless the inference be irresistible.

If the constitution meant to limit the appellate jurisdiction to cases pending in the courts of the United States, it would necessarily follow that the jurisdiction of these courts would, in all the cases enumerated in the constitution, be exclusive of state tribunals. How otherwise could the jurisdiction extend to all cases arising under the constitution, laws and treaties of the United States, or to all cases of admiralty and maritime jurisdiction? If some of these cases might be entertained by state tribunals, and no appellate jurisdiction as to them should exist, then the appellate power would not extend to all, but in some, cases. If state tribunals might exercise concurrent jurisdiction over all or some of the other classes of cases in the constitution without control, then the appellate jurisdiction of the United States might, as to such cases, have no real existence, contrary to the manifest intent of the constitution. Under such circumstances, to give effect to the judicial power, it must be construed to be exclusive; and this not only when the casus faederis should arise directly, but when it should arise, incidentally, in cases pending in state courts. This construction would abridge the jurisdiction of such courts far more than has been ever contemplated in any act of Congress.

On the other hand, if, as has been contended, a discretion be vested in Congress to establish, or not to establish, inferior courts at their own pleasure, and Congress should not establish such courts, the appellate jurisdiction of the Supreme Court would have nothing to act upon, unless it could act upon cases pending in the state courts. Under such circumstances it must be held that the appellate power would extend to state courts; for the constitution is peremptory that it shall extend to certain enumerated cases, which cases could exist in no other courts. Any other construction, upon this supposition, would involve this strange contradiction, that a discretionary power vested in Congress, and which they might rightfully omit to exercise, would defeat the absolute injunctions of the constitution in relation to the whole appellate power.

But it is plain that the framers of the constitution did contemplate that cases within the judicial cognizance of the United States not only might but would arise in the state courts, in the exercise of their ordinary jurisdiction. With this view the sixth article declares, that "this constitution, and the laws of the United States which shall be made in pursuance thereof, and all treaties made, or which shall be made, under the authority of the United States, shall be the supreme law of the land, and the judges in every state shall be bound thereby, anything in the constitution or laws of any state to the contrary notwithstanding." It is obvious that this obligation is imperative upon the state judges in their official, and not merely in their private, capacities. From the very nature of their judicial duties they would be called upon to pronounce the law applicable to the case in judgment. They were not to decide merely according to the laws or constitution of the state, but according to the constitution, laws and treaties of the United States — "the supreme law of the land."

It must, therefore, be conceded that the constitution not only contemplated, but meant to provide for cases within the scope of the judicial power of the United States, which might yet depend before state tribunals. It was foreseen that in the exercise of their ordinary jurisdiction, state courts would incidentally take cognizance of cases arising under the constitution, the laws and treaties of the United States. Yet to all these cases the judicial power, by the very terms of the constitution, is to extend. It cannot extend by original jurisdiction if that was already rightfully and exclusively attached in the state courts, which (as has been already shown) may occur; it must, therefore, extend by appellate jurisdiction, or not at all. It would seem to follow that the appellate power of the United States must, in such cases, extend to state tribunals; and if in such cases, there is no reason why it should not equally attach upon all others within the purview of the constitution.

It is a mistake that the constitution was not designed to operate upon states, in their corporate capacities. It is crowded with provisions which restrain or annul the sovereignty of the states in some of the highest branches of their prerogatives. The tenth section of the first article contains a long list of disabilities and prohibitions imposed upon the states. Surely, when such essential portions of state sovereignty are taken away, or prohibited to be exercised, it cannot be correctly asserted that the constitution does not act upon the states.

Nor can such a right be deemed to impair the independence of state judges. It is assuming the very ground in controversy to assert that they possess an absolute independence of the United States. In respect to the powers granted to the United States, they are not independent; they are expressly bound to obedience by the letter of the constitution; and if they should unintentionally transcend their authority, or misconstrue the constitution, there is no more reason for giving their judgments an absolute and irresistible force than for giving it to the acts of the other coordinate departments of state sovereignty.

It is further argued that no great public mischief can result from a construction which shall limit the appellate power of the United States to cases in their own courts; first, because state judges are bound by an oath to support the constitution of the United States, and must be presumed to be men of learning and integrity; and, secondly, because Congress must have an unquestionable right to remove all cases within the scope of the judicial power from the state courts to the courts of the United States, at any time before final judgment, though not after final judgment. As to the first reason — admitting that the judges of the state courts are, and always will be, of as much learning, integrity, and wisdom, as those of the courts of the United States (which we very cheerfully admit), it does not aid the argument. It is manifest that the constitution has proceeded upon a theory of its own, and given or withheld powers according to the judgment of the American people, by whom it was adopted. We can only construe its powers, and cannot inquire into the policy or principles which induced the grant of them. The constitution has presumed (whether rightly or wrongly we do not inquire) that state attachments, state prejudices, state jealousies, and state interests, might sometimes obstruct, or control, or be supposed to obstruct or control, the regular administration of justice.

This is not all. A motive of another kind, perfectly compatible with the most sincere respect for state tribunals, might induce the grant of appellate power over their decisions. That motive is the importance, and even necessity of uniformity of decisions throughout the whole United States, upon all subjects within the purview of the constitution. Judges of equal learning and integrity, in different states, might differently interpret a statute, or a treaty of the United States, or even the constitution itself. If there were no revising authority to control these jarring and discordant judgments, and harmonize them into uniformity, the laws, the treaties, and the constitution of the United States would be different in different states, and might, perhaps, never have precisely the same construction, obligation, or efficacy, in any two states.

On the whole, the court are of opinion that the appellate power of the United States does extend to cases pending in the state courts; and that the 25th section of the judiciary act, which authorizes the exercise of this jurisdiction in the specified cases, by a writ of error, is supported by the letter and spirit of the constitution. We find no clause in that instrument which limits this power; and we dare not interpose a limitation where the people have not been disposed to create one.

We have not thought it incumbent on us to give any opinion upon the question, whether this court have authority to issue a writ or mandamus to the Court of Appeals to enforce the former judgments, as we do not think it necessarily involved in the decision of this cause. It is the opinion of the whole court that the judgment of the Court of Appeals of Virginia, rendered on the mandate in this cause, be reversed, and the judgment of the District Court, held at Winchester, be, and the same is hereby affirmed.

[JUSTICE JOHNSON, concurring:]

It will be observed in this case, that the court disavows all intention to decide on the right to issue compulsory process to the state courts; thus leaving us, in my opinion, where the constitution and laws place us — supreme over persons and cases as far as our judicial powers extend, but not asserting any compulsory control over the state tribunals.

NOTES

1. *The state's position.* The Supreme Court of Appeals of Virginia had refused to obey the Supreme Court's mandate in *Martin v. Hunter's Lessee* and further declared that § 25 of the Judiciary Act of 1789 was unconstitutional. The opinion of the Virginia judges may be found in *Hunter v. Martin, Devisee of Fairfax*, 18 Va. (4 Munf.) 11 (1814). Each of four judges rendered separate opinions. Judge Cabell said:

> The constitution of the United States contemplates the independence of both governments and regards the residuary sovereignty of the states, as not less inviolable, than the delegated sovereignty of the United States. It must have been foreseen that controversies would

> sometimes arise as to the boundaries of the two jurisdictions. Yet the constitution has provided no umpire, has erected no tribunal by which they shall be settled.
>
> It has been contended that the constitution contemplated only the objects of appeal, and not the tribunals from which the appeal is to be taken; and intended to give to the Supreme Court of the United States appellate jurisdiction in all cases of federal cognizance. But this argument proves too much, and what is utterly inadmissible. It would give appellate jurisdiction, as well over the courts of England or France, as over the State courts; for, although I do not think the state courts are foreign courts in relation to the federal courts, yet I consider them not less independent than foreign courts.

The argument of Judge Cabell and the other judges who joined in the determination of the Virginia Supreme Court of Appeals to defy the decision of the Supreme Court in *Martin v. Hunter's Lessee* was based fundamentally on the so-called "compact" theory of the Constitution, i.e., the federal constitution was a compact among the states and the parties to that instrument were superior to the federal government which it created.

2. *The Supreme Court's position.* What were the arguments used by Justice Story to establish the constitutionality of § 25 of the Judiciary Act. Story hit three now familiar chords in constitutional litigation in his decision in *Martin v. Hunter's Lessee*: constitutional text, constitutional history, and political common sense. Certainly, the practical wisdom of the last of these was irrefutable. Justice Holmes stated a related thought in a later time: "I do not think the United States would come to an end if we lost our power to declare an Act of Congress void. I do think the Union would be imperiled if we could not make that declaration as to the laws of the several states." If Holmes is right, is *Martin* more important than *Marbury v. Madison*?

3. *Enforcement of decrees against the state.* Note that the Supreme Court in *Martin* did not face the question of whether it could order the Virginia Court of Appeals to enforce the Supreme Court's judgment. Instead the Court merely reinstated the judgment of the Virginia trial court, thus nicely avoiding the question of whether an asserted right to decide cases coming from the state supreme courts also carried with it the power to enforce those decisions. It certainly is a fair implication from Justice Johnson's concurring remarks in *Martin* that he thought the Supreme Court's appellate civil jurisdiction to render decisions in cases coming from the state supreme courts did not necessarily carry with it power to enforce those decisions.

The delicacy of how to treat defiance of the United States Supreme Court by the Virginia Court of Appeals in *Martin v. Hunter's Lessee* is, of course, indicated in the effort made by the court in its 1816 decision to avoid another confrontation with the Virginia Court of Appeals. The problem of securing compliance with decisions of the Supreme Court has been a recurring one in American constitutional law.

4. *The primacy of the judiciary.* The controversy concerning the power of the Supreme Court to bind state governments is not limited to defiance from the state courts. In *Cooper v. Aaron*, 358 U.S. 1 (1958), during the height of the crisis over the integration in the Little Rock public schools, the Supreme Court was faced with a contention that the governor and legislature of Arkansas were not bound by the Court's famous decision declaring state mandated school segregation unconstitutional. *Brown v. Board of Educ. (Brown I)*, 347 U.S. 483 (1954).

In *Cooper,* the Court held that state executives, legislators, and judges were alike bound to obey the decision of the Supreme Court. The Court relied on *Marbury* for the proposition that "the federal judiciary is supreme in the exposition of the law of the Constitution" and pointed out that "[e]very state legislator and executive, and judicial officer is solemnly committed by oath taken pursuant to Article VI, cl. 3, to support the Constitution." The Court then concluded by asserting that there was a constitutional duty on the part of the members of all the branches of state government to comply with its decisions:

> No state legislator or executive or judicial officer can war against the Constitution without violating his undertaking to support it. Chief Justice Marshall spoke for a unanimous Court in saying that: "If the legislatures of the several states may, at will, annul the judgments of the courts of the United States, and destroy the rights acquired under those judgments, the constitution itself becomes a solemn mockery." A Governor who asserts a power to nullify a federal court order is similarly restrained. If he had such power, said Chief Justice Hughes, in 1932, also for a unanimous Court, "it is manifest that the fiat of a state Governor, and not the Constitution of the United States, would be the supreme law of the land; that the restrictions of the Federal Constitution upon the exercise of state power would be but impotent phrases."

5. *Cohens v. Virginia*, 19 U.S. (6 Wheat.) 120 (1821). The issue of whether state courts could successfully defy and deny Supreme Court jurisdiction was raised again in this case. Congress had authorized the District of Columbia to conduct a lottery. Virginia, on the other hand, forbade lotteries. Virginia prosecuted and convicted two persons for selling District of Columbia lottery tickets in Virginia. The defendants appealed their convictions to the Supreme Court. *Martin v. Hunter's Lessee* may have settled the issue that the Supreme Court had appellate jurisdiction of civil cases coming from the state courts. But Cohens raised the issue of whether that settled the matter as far as the criminal jurisdiction of the state supreme courts was concerned. Virginia's argument was that the criminal cases were cases in which a state was a party. Article III of the Constitution gave the Supreme Court only original jurisdiction of cases when a state was a party, thus negating the possibility of appellate jurisdiction.

Marshall held in *Cohens* that state criminal cases like state civil cases came within the appellate jurisdiction of the Supreme Court:

> When we consider the situation of the government of the Union and of a state, in relation to each other; the nature of our constitution; the

> subordination of the state governments to that constitution; the great purpose for which jurisdiction over all cases arising under the constitution and laws of the United States, is confided to the judicial department; are we at liberty to insert in this general grant, an exception of those cases in which a state may be a party? Will the spirit of the constitution justify this attempt to control its words? We think it will not. We think a case arising under the constitution or laws of the United States, is cognizable in the Courts of the Union, whoever may be the parties to that case.

Although Marshall held that the Supreme Court had jurisdiction of the *Cohens* case, he held against the defendants who were appealing their Virginia convictions. Marshall held that Congress had not intended to authorize the sale of District of Columbia lottery tickets outside the District of Columbia. The decision in *Cohens* was received with hostility in Virginia. Nevertheless, because Virginia had won on the merits, there was no Supreme Court decision for Virginia to defy even if it had chosen to do so. Thus, Marshall employed once again in *Cohens* the strategy he had so shrewdly and so successfully used in *Marbury*. The individual case was decided in favor of the anti-Federalists but in the process of so deciding, a rationalization for the decision was asserted which entrenched and established the supremacy of federal judicial power.

§ 1.02 TECHNIQUES OF CONSTITUTIONAL INTERPRETATION

It is not enough just to know that courts in the American system have the power to declare acts of the legislature unconstitutional. The hard work comes in knowing when they should do so and why. The hard issues of constitutional law involve you in the debate over the proper role of the courts in interpreting the Constitution. The current section introduces some of the pervasive themes of interpretation that run throughout all of constitutional law. You may want to refer back to this section as you study some of the more controversial opinions in the later chapters of this book.

We all know intuitively that the Constitution is part of law and that we want law to be reasonably stable no matter who is applying it. A rule that depends on the whim of the judge is not law in the ordinary sense of the term. But some provisions of the Constitution are cast in terms that defy precision, such as "cruel and unusual punishment," "due process," and even "equal protection." One method for giving these terms content is to refer to the original intent of the drafters to see if they had a basic principle in mind that will solve the current problem. Another method is to refer to the structure of the governmental processes established by the Constitution to see if the structure suggests a solution to the problem. A third is to search for binding fundamental principles, either embedded in the Constitution itself or incorporated by reference to external sources, such as natural law.

What follows are brief excerpts from various authors struggling with this problem. In every instance, what the author, and what we as lawyers, are seeking is a method for giving content to the textual language at hand while controlling the discretion of the judges. What we want is enough stability to make the Constitution worthy of being considered part of the rule of law while still being faithful to the language and structure that brought us these open-ended phrases in the first place.

The first excerpt struggles with the question of whether the intent of the Framers should be considered important in interpreting constitutional language:

> Much use of language is characterized by vagueness, ambiguity or both; and knowing the intention with which language was used can often be useful in clarifying vagueness or resolving ambiguity. Words themselves, however, do bring a degree of "objective" meaning with them — a meaning independent of the intentions of any author employing them. It is only through such objective meaning that language expresses intentions. Once text and intent are seen as separable, the former comfortably assumes authoritativeness in a way that the latter cannot. Only the text is adopted.

Robert Bennett, *Objectivity in Constitutional Law*, 132 U. PA. L. REV. 445 (1984).

During the latter part of the 20th Century, a school of constitutional thought know as "original intent" was widely debated. Original intent became a centerpiece of the agenda of many conservatives disturbed at the progressive interpretations of the Warren Court era. One of its leading proponents, Judge and Professor Robert Bork, attempted to give a broader and more legitimate thrust to the use of intent:

> It is important to be plain at the outset what intentionalism means. It is not the notion that judges may apply a constitutional provision only to circumstances specifically contemplated by the framers. In so narrow a form the philosophy is useless. [A]ll an intentionalist requires is that the text, structure, and history of the Constitution provide him not with a conclusion but with a premise. That premise states a core value that the framers intended to protect.

Robert Bork, *The Constitution, Original Intent, and Economic Rights*, 23 SAN DIEGO L. REV. 823, 826 (1985).

Another attempt to place intent in a broader framework of common, or core, principles was made by Professor Perry:

> It is no doubt true that the ratifiers of at least some, perhaps many, constitutional provisions did not all share precisely the same understanding of the provisions. It is implausible to suppose, however, that there was no common, or core, understanding shared by (virtually) all of them. The task for the originalist judges — again, admittedly a difficult one — is to discover that common original understanding as best they can.

Michael Perry, *The Authority of Text, Tradition, and Reason: A Theory of Constitutional "Interpretation,"* 58 S. CAL. L. REV. 551, 600–01 (1985).

As the next excerpt demonstrates, a search for a theory of interpretation must take into account not only the relative clarity of particular phrases (compare "due process" with "35 years of age"), but also needs to explain why any particular approach is better than another in dealing with language that is not crystal clear. Some phrases in the Constitution might even have been chosen with an original intent of allowing changed interpretations to meet changing conditions and circumstances:

> [A theory that confines judges to the written Constitution] does seem to retain the substantial virtue of fitting better our ordinary notions of how law works: if your job is to enforce the Constitution then the Constitution is what you should be enforcing, not whatever may happen to strike you as a good idea at the time. Constitutional provisions exist on a spectrum ranging from the relatively specific to the extremely open-textured. [Some provisions seem] expected to govern a broader and more important range of problems. [Also,] we somehow sense that a line of growth was intended, that the language was not intended to be restricted to its 1791 meaning.

JOHN H. ELY, DEMOCRACY AND DISTRUST 12–13 (1980).

Moving beyond the text in some instances opens the door for some scholars who believe that the very structure of our federal system contemplates or even requires that judges be free to import values from sources other than the text alone:

> It seems to me that the courts do appropriately apply values not articulated in the constitutional text, and appropriately apply them in determining the constitutionality of legislation. In the important cases, references to and analysis of the constitutional text plays a minor role. The dominant norms of decision are those large conceptions of governmental structure and individual rights that are at best referred to, and whose content is scarcely at all specified, in the written constitution — dual federalism, vested rights, fair procedure, equality before the law.

Thomas Grey, *Do We Have an Unwritten Constitution?*, 27 STAN. L. REV. 703 (1975).

Importing values from other sources then forces a return to the question of why judicial review should even be allowed:

> [W]hy should judges regard constitutional texts as vesting them with the extraordinary authority to speak for the past against the present? In a nutshell: judges' regarding a written constitution as authoritative (so that they use it to overturn ordinary legislation) is justified by the likelihood that such judges would give greater protection of natural rights than would the legislature.

Michael S. Moore, *Justifying the Natural Law Theory of Constitutional Interpretation*, 69 FORD. L. REV. 2087, 2099 (2001).

Finally, one must ask the question whether any particular theory or general methodology of constitutional interpretation is either possible or desirable. Given the range of principles embodied in the document, and the range of problems coming before the courts, might it not be better to emphasize good legal reasoning with reference to external sources when they are helpful? Think back to Marshall's sources in *Marbury*, references to the structure of the federal government, a touch of history, and finally a quick look at textual provisions. Perhaps an approach that takes structure, history, and text all into account in persuasive degrees is the best guide to decision in any given situation. *See* Michael C. Dorf, *Create Your Own Constitutional Theory*, 87 CAL. L. REV. 593 (1999).

In recent years, a heated debate has erupted over the relevance of foreign practice and holdings in interpreting the U.S. Constitution. In *Atkins v. Virginia*, 536 U.S. 304 (2002), the Court held that imposition of the death penalty upon mentally retarded persons would violate the Cruel and Unusual Punishment Clause of the Eighth Amendment. Justice Stevens' opinion for the Court noted that virtually no other nation would allow execution of the mentally retarded. In *Lawrence v. Texas*, 539 U.S. 558 (2003), Justice Kennedy's majority opinion, striking down state laws criminalizing private homosexual conduct, relied on both foreign practice and an opinion of the European Court of Human Rights.

Dissenting in *Atkins*, Justice Scalia asserted that "the practices of the 'world community' " are "irrelevant" to American courts because their "notions of justice are (thankfully) not always those of our people. . . . We must never forget that it is a Constitution for the United States of America that we are expounding . . . . Where there is not first a settled consensus among our own people, the views of other nations, however enlightened the Justices of this Court may think them to be, cannot be imposed upon Americans through the Constitution."

In an unprecedented move, Justices Breyer and Scalia then engaged in a televised debate over the role of foreign holdings in U.S. constitutional interpretation. *See* Antonin Scalia & Stephen Breyer, *The Relevance of Foreign Law for American Constitutional Adjudication*, www.wcl.american.edu/secle/founders/2005/050113.cfm. Lower court judges have weighed in on the issue as well. Diarmuid F. O'Scannlain, *What Role Should Foreign Practice and Precedent Play in the Interpretation of Domestic Law*?, 80 NOTRE DAME L. REV. 1893 (2005) (Ninth Circuit Judge arguing that foreign holdings are relevant to some constitutional issues but not others); Patricia M. Wald, *The Use of International Law in the American Adjudicative Process*, 27 HARV. J.L. & PUB. POL'Y 431 (2004) (former D.C. Circuit Judge and Judge on the International Criminal Tribunal for Yugoslavia, arguing that U.S. judges should be more receptive to the holdings of judges around the world).

§ 1.03 JUDICIALLY IMPOSED LIMITS ON THE EXERCISE OF THE JUDICIAL REVIEW POWER: THE "POLITICAL QUESTION" DOCTRINE

To this point, the chapter has examined the sources, nature and rationale of the power of judicial review. In this section, we consider a doctrine which, while nominally accepting the principle of judicial review, posits that under certain circumstances the courts should decline to exercise that authority.

[A] THE APPORTIONMENT "THICKET"

Following the Depression and World War II, it became apparent to all political observers that massive population shifts had occurred from rural to urban areas. Despite these shifts in population, state legislatures had not been reapportioned (or redistricted) in many decades. The result was that some urban districts would have as many as 25 times as many voters as some rural districts. The claim was made that the vote of each urban dweller was only 1/25 as influential as that of the voter in a rural district. Cases challenging this situation on federal constitutional grounds began wending their way to the Supreme Court.

In the first of these cases, *Colegrove v. Green*, 328 U.S. 549 (1946), the Supreme Court had only seven sitting Justices, and they split 3-1-3. Justice Frankfurter, writing for the plurality of three who prevailed to dismiss the case, described the challenge as attempting to entice the Court into a "political thicket" because there were no standards by which to judge the validity of the state's apportionment scheme. After the Court dealt with a few other cases, including one in which a city had engaged in blatant racial gerrymandering, *Gomillion v. Lightfoot*, 364 U.S. 339 (1960), the stage was set for a full-scale challenge to a state legislative districting.

BAKER v. CARR
369 U.S. 186, 82 S. Ct. 691, 7 L. Ed. 2d 663 (1962)

JUSTICE BRENNAN delivered the opinion of the Court.

This civil action was brought under 42 U.S.C. §§ 1983 and 1988 to redress the alleged deprivation of federal constitutional rights. The complaint, alleging that by means of a 1901 statute of Tennessee apportioning the members of the General Assembly among the State's 95 counties, "these plaintiffs and others similarly situated, are denied the equal protection of the laws accorded them by the Fourteenth Amendment to the Constitution of the United States by virtue of the debasement of their votes," was dismissed by a three-judge court. The court held that it lacked jurisdiction of the subject matter and also that no claim was stated upon which relief could be granted. We hold that the dismissal was error, and remand the cause to the District Court for trial and further proceedings consistent with this opinion.

Tennessee's [state constitutional] standard for allocating legislative representation among her counties is the total number of qualified voters resident in the respective counties, subject only to minor qualifications. Decennial reapportionment in compliance with the constitutional scheme was effected by the General Assembly each decade from 1871 to 1901. In 1901 the General Assembly abandoned separate enumeration in favor of reliance upon the Federal Census and passed the Apportionment Act here in controversy. In the more than 60 years since that action, all proposals in both Houses of the General Assembly for reapportionment have failed to pass.

The relative standings of the counties in terms of qualified voters have changed significantly. It is primarily the continued application of the 1901 Apportionment Act to this shifted and enlarged voting population which gives rise to the present controversy.

[Appellants] seek a declaration that the 1901 statute is unconstitutional and an injunction restraining the appellees from acting to conduct any further elections under it. They also pray that unless and until the General Assembly enacts a valid reapportionment, the District Court should either decree a reapportionment by mathematical application of the Tennessee constitutional formulae to the most recent Federal Census figures, or direct the appellees to conduct legislative elections, primary and general, at large. They also pray for such other and further relief as may be appropriate.

Because we deal with this case on appeal from an order of dismissal granted on appellees' motions, precise identification of the issues presently confronting us demands clear exposition of the grounds upon which the District Court rested in dismissing the case. The dismissal order recited that the court sustained the appellees' grounds "(1) that the Court lacks jurisdiction of the subject matter, and (2) that the complaint fails to state a claim upon which relief can be granted."

In the setting of a case such as this, the recited grounds embrace two possible reasons for dismissal:

First: That the facts and injury alleged, the legal bases invoked as creating the rights and duties relied upon, and the relief sought, fail to come within that language of Article III of the Constitution and of the jurisdictional statutes which define those matters concerning which United States District Courts are empowered to act;

Second: That, although the matter is cognizable and facts are alleged which establish infringement of appellants' rights as a result of state legislative action departing from a federal constitutional standard, the court will not proceed because the matter is considered unsuited to judicial inquiry or adjustment.

We treat the first ground of dismissal as "lack of jurisdiction of the subject matter." The second we consider to result in a failure to state a justiciable cause of action.

In light of the District Court's treatment of the case, we hold today only (a) that the court possessed jurisdiction of the subject matter; (b) that a justiciable cause of action is stated upon which appellants would be entitled to appropriate relief; and (c) because appellees raise the issue before this Court, that the appellants have standing to challenge the Tennessee apportionment statutes. Beyond noting that we have no cause at this stage to doubt the

District Court will be able to fashion relief if violations of constitutional rights are found, it is improper now to consider what remedy would be most appropriate if appellants prevail at the trial.

Jurisdiction of the Subject Matter

The District Court was uncertain whether our cases withholding federal judicial relief rested upon a lack of federal jurisdiction or upon the inappropriateness of the subject matter for judicial consideration — what we have designated "nonjusticiability." The distinction between the two grounds is significant. In the instance of nonjusticiability, consideration of the cause is not wholly and immediately foreclosed; rather, the Court's inquiry necessarily proceeds to the point of deciding whether the duty asserted can be judicially identified and its reach judicially determined, and whether protection for the right asserted can be judicially molded. In the instance of lack of jurisdiction the cause either does not "arise under" the Federal Constitution, laws or treaties (or fall within one of the other enumerated categories of Art. III, § 2), or is not a "case or controversy" within the meaning of that section; or the cause is not one described by any jurisdictional statute. Our conclusion that this cause presents no nonjusticiable "political question" settles the only possible doubt that it is a case or controversy. Under the present heading of "Jurisdiction of the Subject Matter" we hold only that the matter set forth in the complaint does arise under the Constitution and is within 28 U.S.C. § 1343.

The appellees refer to *Colegrove v. Green*, [328 U.S. 549 (1946),] as authority that the District Court lacked jurisdiction of the subject matter. Appellees misconceive the holding of that case. The holding was precisely contrary to their reading of it. We hold that the District Court has jurisdiction of the subject matter of the federal constitutional claim asserted in the complaint.

Justiciability

In holding that the subject matter of this suit was not justiciable, the District Court relied on *Colegrove v. Green* and subsequent per curiam cases. We understand the District Court to have read the cited cases as compelling the conclusion that since the appellants sought to have a legislative apportionment held unconstitutional, their suit presented a "political question" and was therefore nonjusticiable. We hold that this challenge to an apportionment presents no nonjusticiable "political question." The cited cases do not hold the contrary.

Of course the mere fact that the suit seeks protection of a political right does not mean it presents a political question. Rather, it is argued that apportionment cases, whatever the actual wording of the complaint, can involve no federal constitutional right except one resting on the guaranty of a republican form of government, and that complaints based on that clause have been held to present political questions which are nonjusticiable.

We hold that the claim pleaded here neither rests upon nor implicates the Guaranty Clause and that its justiciability is therefore not foreclosed by our decisions of cases involving that clause.

[I]n the Guaranty Clause cases and in the other "political question" cases, it is the relationship between the judiciary and the coordinate branches of the Federal Government, and not the federal judiciary's relationship to the States, which gives rise to the "political question."

We have said that "in determining whether a question falls within [the political question] category, the appropriateness under our system of government of attributing finality to the action of the political departments and also the lack of satisfactory criteria for a judicial determination are dominant considerations." *Coleman v. Miller*, 307 U.S. 433, 454–455. The nonjusticiability of a political question is primarily a function of the separation of powers. Much confusion results from the capacity of the "political question" label to obscure the need for case-by-case inquiry. Deciding whether a matter has in any measure been committed by the Constitution to another branch of government, or whether the action of that branch exceeds whatever authority has been committed, is itself a delicate exercise in constitutional interpretation, and is a responsibility of this Court as ultimate interpreter of the Constitution. To demonstrate this requires no less than to analyze representative cases and to infer from them the analytical threads that make up the political question doctrine. We shall then show that none of those threads catches this case.

Foreign relations: There are sweeping statements to the effect that all questions touching foreign relations are political questions. Not only does resolution of such issues frequently turn on standards that defy judicial application, or involve the exercise of a discretion demonstrably committed to the executive or legislature; but many such questions uniquely demand single-voiced statement of the Government's views. Yet it is error to suppose that every case or controversy which touches foreign relations lies beyond judicial cognizance. For example, though a court will not ordinarily inquire whether a treaty has been terminated, since on that question "governmental action must be regarded as of controlling importance," if there has been no conclusive "governmental action" then a court can construe a treaty and may find it provides the answer.

Dates of duration of hostilities: Though it has been stated broadly that "the power which declared the necessity is the power to declare its cessation, and what the cessation requires," here too analysis reveals isolable reasons for the presence of political questions, underlying this Court's refusal to review the political department's determination of when or whether a war has ended. Dominant is the need for finality in the political determination, for emergency's nature demands "a prompt and unhesitating obedience."

Validity of enactments: In *Coleman v. Miller* this Court held that the questions of how long a proposed amendment to the Federal Constitution remained open to ratification, and what effect a prior rejection had on a subsequent ratification, were committed to congressional resolution and involved criteria of decision that necessarily escaped the judicial grasp. Similar considerations apply to the enacting process: "The respect due to coequal and independent departments," and the need for finality and certainty about the status of a statute contribute to judicial reluctance to inquire whether, as passed, it complied with all requisite formalities. But it is not true that courts will never delve into a legislature's records upon such a quest: If the enrolled statute lacks an effective date, a court will not hesitate to seek it in the legislative journals in order to preserve the enactment. The political question doctrine, a tool for maintenance of governmental order, will not be so applied as to promote only disorder.

It is apparent that several formulations which vary slightly according to the settings in which the questions arise may describe a political question, although each has one or more elements which identifies it as essentially a function of the separation of powers. Prominent on the surface of any case held to involve a political question is found a textually demonstrable constitutional commitment of the issue to a coordinate political department; or a lack of judicially discoverable and manageable standards for resolving it; or the impossibility of deciding without an initial policy determination of a kind clearly for nonjudicial discretion; or the impossibility of a court's undertaking independent resolution without expressing lack of the respect due coordinate branches of government; or an unusual need for unquestioning adherence to a political decision already made; or the potentiality of embarrassment from multifarious pronouncements by various departments on one question.

Unless one of these formulations is inextricable from the case at bar, there should be no dismissal for non-justiciability on the ground of a political question's presence. The doctrine of which we treat is one of "political questions," not one of "political cases." The courts cannot reject as "no law suit" a bona fide controversy as to whether some action denominated "political" exceeds constitutional authority. The cases we have reviewed show the necessity for discriminating inquiry into the precise facts and posture of the particular case, and the impossibility of resolution by any semantic cataloguing.

But it is argued that this case shares the characteristics of decisions that constitute a category not yet considered, cases concerning the Constitution's guaranty, in Art. IV, § 4, of a republican form of government. We shall discover that Guaranty Clause claims involve those elements which define a "political question," and for that reason and no other, they are nonjusticiable.

We come, finally, to the ultimate inquiry whether our precedents as to what constitutes a nonjusticiable "political question" bring the case before us under the umbrella of that doctrine. A natural beginning is to note whether any of the common characteristics which we have been able to identify and label descriptively are present. We find none: The question here is the consistency of state action with the Federal Constitution. We have no question decided, or to be decided, by a political branch of government coequal with this Court. Nor do we risk embarrassment of our government abroad, or grave disturbance at home if we take issue with Tennessee as to the constitutionality of her action here challenged. Nor need the appellants, in order to succeed in this action, ask the Court to enter upon policy determinations for which judicially manageable standards are lacking. Judicial standards under the Equal Protection Clause are well developed and familiar, and it has been open to courts since the enactment of the Fourteenth Amendment to determine, if on the particular facts they must, that a discrimination reflects no policy, but simply arbitrary and capricious action.

We conclude that the complaint's allegations of a denial of equal protection present a justiciable constitutional cause of action upon which appellants are entitled to a trial and a decision. The right asserted is within the reach of judicial protection under the Fourteenth Amendment.

JUSTICE CLARK, concurring.

Although I find the Tennessee apportionment statute offends the Equal Protection Clause, I would not consider intervention by this Court into so delicate a field if there were any other relief available to the people of Tennessee. But the majority of the people of Tennessee have no "practical opportunities for exerting their political weight at the polls" to correct the existing "invidious discrimination." Tennessee has no initiative and referendum. I have searched diligently for other "practical opportunities" present under the law. I find none other than through the federal courts. The majority of the voters have been caught up in a legislative strait jacket.

JUSTICE FRANKFURTER, whom JUSTICE HARLAN joins, dissenting.

The Court today reverses a uniform course of decision established by a dozen cases, including one by which the very claim now sustained was unanimously rejected only five years ago. The impressive body of rulings thus cast aside reflected the equally uniform course of our political history regarding the relationship between population and legislative representation — a wholly different matter from denial of the franchise to individuals because of race, color, religion or sex. Such a massive repudiation of the experience of our whole past in asserting destructively novel judicial power demands a detailed analysis of the role of this Court in our constitutional scheme. Disregard of inherent limits in the effective exercise of the Court's "judicial Power" not only presages the futility of judicial intervention in the essentially political conflict of forces by which the relation between population and representation has time out of mind been and now is determined. It may well impair the Court's position as the ultimate organ of "the supreme Law of the Land" in that vast range of legal problems, often strongly entangled in popular feeling, on which this Court must pronounce. The Court's authority — possessed of neither the purse nor the sword — ultimately rests on sustained public confidence in its moral sanction. Such feeling must be nourished by the Court's complete detachment, in fact and in appearance, from political entanglements and by abstention from injecting itself into the clash of political forces in political settlements.

For this Court to direct the District Court to enforce a claim to which the Court has over the years consistently found itself required to deny legal enforcement and at the same time to find it necessary to withhold any guidance to the lower court how to enforce this turnabout, new legal claim, manifests an odd — indeed an esoteric — conception of judicial propriety. To charge courts with the task of accommodating the incommensurable factors of policy that underlie these mathematical puzzles is to attribute, however flatteringly, omnicompetence to judges.

We were soothingly told at the bar of this Court that we need not worry about the kind of remedy a court could effectively fashion once the abstract constitutional right to have courts pass on a state-wide system of electoral districting is recognized as a matter of judicial rhetoric, because legislatures would heed the Court's admonition. This is not only an euphoric hope. It implies a sorry confession of judicial impotence in place of a frank acknowledgment that there is not under our Constitution a judicial remedy for every political mischief, for every undesirable exercise of legislative power. The Framers carefully and with deliberate forethought refused so to enthrone the judiciary. In this situation, as in others of like nature, appeal for relief does not belong here. Appeal must be to an informed, civically militant electorate. In a democratic society like ours, relief must come through an aroused popular conscience that sears the conscience of the people's representatives. In any event there is nothing judicially more unseemly nor more self-defeating than for this Court to make in terrorem pronouncements, to indulge in merely empty rhetoric, sounding a word of promise to the ear, sure to be disappointing to the hope.

The "political question" principle as applied in *Colegrove* has found wide application commensurate with its function as "one of the rules basic to the federal system and this Court's appropriate place within that structure." *Rescue Army v. Municipal Court.*

The *Colegrove* doctrine, in the form in which repeated decisions have settled it, was not an innovation. It represents long judicial thought and experience. From its earliest opinions this Court has consistently recognized a class of controversies which do not lend themselves to judicial standards and judicial remedies. To classify the various instances as "political questions" is rather a form of stating this conclusion than revealing of analysis.

The influence of these converging considerations — the caution not to undertake decision where standards meet for judicial judgment are lacking, the reluctance to interfere with matters of state government in the absence of an unquestionable and effectively enforceable mandate, the unwillingness to make courts arbiters of the broad issues of political organization historically committed to other institutions and for whose adjustment the judicial process is ill-adapted — has been decisive of the settled line of cases, reaching back more than a century, which holds that Art. IV, § 4, of the Constitution, guaranteeing to the States "a Republican Form of Government," is not enforceable through the courts.

The present case involves all of the elements that have made the Guarantee Clause cases non-justiciable. It is, in effect, a Guarantee Clause claim masquerading under a different label. But it cannot make the case more fit for judicial action that appellants invoke the Fourteenth Amendment rather than Art. IV, § 4, where, in fact, the gist of their complaint is the same — unless it can be found that the Fourteenth Amendment speaks with greater particularity to their situation. We have been admonished to avoid "the tyranny of labels."

Appellants appear as representatives of a class that is prejudiced as a class, in contradistinction to the polity in its entirety. However, the discrimination relied on is the deprivation of what appellants conceive to be their proportionate share of political influence. This, of course, is the practical effect of any allocation of power within the institutions of government. Hardly any distribution of political authority that could be assailed as rendering government nonrepublican would fail similarly to operate to the prejudice of some groups, and to the advantage of others, within the body politic.

What, then, is this question of legislative apportionment? Appellants invoke the right to vote and to have their votes counted. But they are permitted to vote and their votes are counted. They go to the polls, they cast their ballots, they send their representatives to the state councils. Their complaint is simply that the representatives are not sufficiently numerous or powerful — in short, that Tennessee has adopted a basis of representation with which they are dissatisfied. Talk of "debasement" or "dilution" is circular talk. One cannot speak of "debasement" or "dilution" of the value of a vote until there is first defined a standard of reference as to what a vote should be worth. What is actually asked of the Court in this case is to choose among competing bases of representation — ultimately, really, among competing theories of political philosophy — in order to establish an appropriate frame of government for the State of Tennessee and thereby for all of the States of the Union.

In such a matter, abstract analogies which ignore the facts of history deal in unrealities; they betray reason. This is not a case in which a State has, through a device however oblique and sophisticated, denied Negroes or Jews or redheaded persons a vote, or given them only a third or a sixth of a vote. That was *Gomillion v. Lightfoot*. What Tennessee illustrates is an old and still widespread method of representation — representation by local geographical division, only in part respective of population — in preference to others, others, forsooth, more appealing. Appellants contest this choice and seek to make this Court the arbiter of the disagreement. They would make the Equal Protection Clause the charter of adjudication, asserting that the equality which it guarantees comports, if not the assurance of equal weight to every voter's vote, at least the basic conception that representation ought to be proportionate to population, a standard by reference to which the reasonableness of apportionment plans may be judged.

To find such a political conception legally enforceable in the broad and unspecific guarantee of equal protection is to rewrite the Constitution. Certainly, "equal protection" is no more secure a foundation for judicial judgment of the permissibility of varying forms of representative government than is "Republican Form." Indeed since "equal protection of the laws" can only mean an equality of persons standing in the same relation to whatever governmental action is challenged, the determination whether treatment is equal presupposes a determination concerning the nature of the relationship. This, with respect to apportionment, means an inquiry into the theoretic base of representation in an acceptably republican state. For a court could not determine the equal-protection issue without in fact first determining the Republican-Form issue, simply because what is reasonable for equal protection purposes will depend upon what frame of government, basically, is allowed. To divorce "equal protection" from "Republican Form" is to talk about half a question.

The notion that representation proportioned to the geographic spread of population is so universally accepted as a necessary element of equality between man and man that it must be taken to be the standard of a political equality preserved by the Fourteenth Amendment — that it is, in appellants' words "the basic principle of representative government" — is, to put it bluntly, not true. However desirable and however desired by some among the great political thinkers and framers of our government, it has never been generally practiced, today or in the past. Unless judges, the judges of this Court, are to make their private views of political wisdom the measure of the Constitution — views which in all honesty cannot but give the appearance, if not reflect the reality, of involvement with the business of partisan politics so inescapably a part of apportionment controversies — the Fourteenth Amendment, "itself a historical product," provides no guide for judicial oversight of the representation problem.

Manifestly, the Equal Protection Clause supplies no clearer guide for judicial examination of apportionment methods than would the Guarantee Clause itself. Apportionment, by its character, is a subject of extraordinary complexity, involving — even after the fundamental theoretical issues concerning what is to be represented in a representative legislature have been fought out or compromised — considerations of geography, demography, electoral convenience, economic and social cohesions or divergencies among particular local groups, communications, the practical effects of political institutions like the lobby and the city machine, ancient traditions and ties of settled usage, respect for proven incumbents of long experience and senior status, mathematical mechanics, censuses compiling relevant data, and a host of others. Legislative responses throughout the country to the reapportionment demands of the 1960 Census have glaringly confirmed that these are not factors that lend themselves to evaluations of a nature that are the staple of judicial determinations or for which judges are equipped to adjudicate by legal training or experience or native wit. And this is the more so true because in every strand of this complicated, intricate web of values meet the contending forces of partisan politics. The practical significance of apportionment is that the next election results may differ because of it. Apportionment battles are overwhelmingly party or intra-party contests. It will add a virulent source of friction and tension in federal-state relations to embroil the federal judiciary in them.

Although the District Court had jurisdiction in the very restricted sense of power to determine whether it could adjudicate the claim, the case is of that class of political controversy which, by the nature of its subject, is unfit for federal judicial action. The judgment of the District Court, in dismissing the complaint for failure to state a claim on which relief can be granted, should therefore be affirmed.

[Dissenting opinion of Justice Harlan, joined by Justice Frankfurter, is omitted.]

NOTES

1. *The Brennan-Frankfurter debate*. Justice Brennan's opinion for the Court in *Baker v. Carr* identifies six indicia of a political question. The first two invoke the nature of the judicial function, while the last four refer in various ways to compelling needs for deference to the other branches of government. Justice Frankfurter, on the other hand, is primarily concerned with the loss of the Court's credibility if its mandates should be ignored by political bodies. We will deal with each of these problems in turn.

2. *Commitment to another branch*. The first indicator of a political question described by Justice Brennan is "a textually demonstrable constitutional commitment of the issue to a coordinate political department." Some observers use this facet of the doctrine to argue that there is really no such thing as a separate issue of justiciability at all. Professor Wechsler articulates what has come to be known as the "classical" form of the political question doctrine by asserting that this is the only acceptable use of the doctrine.

> [A]ll the doctrine can defensibly imply is that the courts are called upon to judge whether the Constitution has committed to another agency of government the autonomous determination of the issue raised, a finding that itself requires an interpretation that is *toto caelo* different from a broad discretion to abstain or intervene.

Herbert Wechsler, *Toward Neutral Principles of Constitutional Law*, 73 Harv. L. Rev. 1 (1959).

Luther v. Borden, 48 U.S. (7 How.) 1 (1849), is read by some observers to hold that cases arising under the "Guarantee Clause" [Art. IV, § 4: "The United States shall guarantee to every State in this Union a Republican Form of Government, and shall protect each of them against Invasion . . . ."] constitute nonjusticiable political questions. The case arose out of the Dorr rebellion of 1842 against the charter government of Rhode Island. The issue which the Court ultimately declined to resolve concerned which of the two competing governments constituted the proper government of the State of Rhode Island. The Court held that this was a matter for the "political branches" — President and Congress — to resolve in the first instance.

Professor Henkin argues that "the *Luther* decision gave [the political branches] no extra-ordinary deference," because the case can be read to mean that the phrase, "the United States shall guarantee" in Article IV "plausibly refers to the political branches, and it is not implausible to read it as excluding monitoring and enforcement by the courts." Louis Henkin, *Is There a "Political Question" Doctrine?*, 85 Yale L.J. 597, 609 (1976).

The role of the Court in deciding whether an issue is committed to another branch is also illustrated by *Powell v. McCormack*, 395 U.S. 486 (1969). Adam Clayton Powell was reelected to Congress while under heavy suspicion of wrongdoing in several ways. The House of Representatives refused to seat him on the grounds of improprieties committed as a Congressman. Although Article I, § 5, provides that "Each House shall be the Judge of the qualifications of its own Members," the Court rejected the argument that this constituted a textual commitment of "judicially unreviewable power to set qualifications for membership and to judge whether prospective members meet those qualifications." The "qualifications" of which each House is to be the sole judge are those listed in Article I, § 2 — age, citizenship, and residence. Although Powell could be removed for improprieties after being seated, that would require a two-thirds vote rather than a simple majority. Art. I, § 5, cl. 2.

3. *Is there law to apply? Standards for review*. The "lack of judicially discoverable and manageable standards for resolving" an issue is listed by

Justice Brennan as the second of the six indicia of a political question. The "standards" applying to the apportionment of legislatures were said by Justice Brennan to be familiar questions of discrimination. But questions left after *Baker* to be resolved in future litigation included some important questions, such as whether areas with greater natural resources or more dispersed populations were entitled to more votes per person than populated areas, whether historical boundaries (such as county lines) were entitled to weight in the apportionment process, and whether one house of a two-house legislature could reflect unequal population (like the U.S. Senate) for an anti-democratic checking function. Ultimately, the choice among any of the varied methods of drawing voting district lines arguably could be characterized as a nontraditional judicial function.

After several intermediate steps, the Court squarely faced its self-created dilemma in *Reynolds v. Sims*, 377 U.S. 533 (1964). The Court decided that "legislators represent people not trees," a conclusion that is not altogether obvious from the Constitution. The standard of review and relief finally adopted was that each person's vote in a state legislative election should count the same as every other person's vote, the one person-one vote principle. Over time, however, application of this principle has yielded to pressures of slight variations from district to district, reflection of historic local boundaries or difficulties of administration. The Court now seems willing to accept up to a 10% variance among district populations if there is a nondiscriminatory reason for the variance.

In *Davis v. Bandemer*, 478 U.S. 109 (1986), p. 916, the Supreme Court was faced with an equal protection challenge to legislative districting that was alleged to have discriminated against Democrats in favor of Republicans. Although the Court ultimately rejected the claim of discrimination, a plurality of four Justices would have held the issue to be justiciable under *Baker v. Carr*. Three Justices, led by Justice O'Connor, would have held that "partisan gerrymandering claims of major political parties raise a nonjusticiable political question that the judiciary should leave to the legislative branch as the Framers of the Constitution unquestionably intended." Justice O'Connor's opinion searched the history of the equal protection clause to demonstrate that it "does not supply judicially manageable standards for resolving purely political gerrymandering claims, and no group right to an equal share of political power was ever intended by the Framers of the Fourteenth Amendment." Does the O'Connor opinion sound more like a holding on the merits of the claim or a refusal to adjudicate? The controversy over the justiciability of political gerrymandering and the possibility of fashioning a fair standard for constitutional review continues. See the discussion of *Davis v. Bandemer* and its progeny in sec. 7.04 [C][2].

4. *Deference to other branches*. Justice Brennan's last four indicia all refer in one fashion or another to extreme cases for deference to another branch of government. The avoidance of "multifarious pronouncements by various departments on one question" probably refers mostly to foreign affairs. The others sound extremely amorphous and discretionary. They could be characterized as aspects of either a "prudential" or "functional" version of the political question doctrine. *See generally* Fritz Scharpf, *Judicial Review and* *the Political Question: A Functional Analysis*, 75 YALE L.J. 517 (1966). Professor Bickel, generally considered the leading advocate for these forms of the doctrine, described the elements in this manner:

> Such is the foundation of the political-question doctrine: the Court's sense of lack of capacity, compounded in unequal parts of (a) the strangeness of the issue and its intractability to principled resolution; (b) the sheer momentousness of it, which tends to unbalance judicial judgment; (c) the anxiety, not so much that the judicial judgment will be ignored, as that perhaps it should but will not be; (d) finally ("in a mature democracy"), the inner vulnerability, the self-doubt of an institution which is electorally irresponsible and has no earth to draw strength from.

ALEXANDER BICKEL, THE LEAST DANGEROUS BRANCH 184 (1962). Bickel defends his version of the doctrine by arguing: "[I]t is quite plain that some questions are held to be political pursuant to a decision on principle that there ought to be discretion free of principled rules." *Id.* What do you think this means? Do you agree with it? How would you characterize a holding that the rates of income tax, following adoption of the Sixteenth Amendment, are solely a matter for congressional determination and not subject to judicial review?

5. *Enforceability of judicial decrees.* Justice Frankfurter, dissenting in *Baker*, assumed that the Court's decree would fall on deaf ears and that the failure of the state legislatures to respond to the Court's mandates would be subversive of the Court. He argued that the Court's assertion of authority where the matter was better left to legislative remedies would undermine the Court's authority in areas where its responsibility was clear. He did not argue that the courts had no jurisdiction, but that they should stay out of this political hotbed for their own good.

As it happens, *Baker v. Carr* produced no massive resistance or disobedience. By and large, the process of reapportionment has been carried out to the satisfaction of the courts and political observers. Why? Perhaps the opinion is an example of what Eugene Rostow means by the democratic character of judicial review. EUGENE ROSTOW, THE SOVEREIGN PREROGATIVE: THE SUPREME COURT AND THE QUEST FOR LAW 167–68 (1962). The Court, Rostow wrote, is a teacher in a great national seminar. Sometimes the Court teaches badly. Sometimes the Court teaches well; and to teach well is occasionally to persuade.

A more serious challenge to the enforceability of the Court's mandate was presented in *United States v. Nixon*, p. 404. When the Special Watergate Prosecutor sought the Nixon White House tapes for use against indicted co-conspirators, the President claimed executive privilege protected the tapes from disclosure and did not promise to obey any court mandate that they be produced. In essence, the issue raised was whether the Court was, as Justice Brennan claimed in *Baker*, the "ultimate interpreter of the Constitution."

> For this nation, however, this issue presumably has been settled. Somehow or other, the courts have come into possession of the authority to resolve constitutional issues with finality. Although the intellectual

> operation entailed is like that used in the exercise of "judicial review," the function is altogether distinct. Exercise of the power of "constitutional review" places the courts in a relation with the other two branches totally different from that grounding "judicial review."

Frank Strong, *President, Congress, Judiciary: One Is More Equal Than the Others*, 60 A.B.A. J. 1052–53 (1974).

6. ***The role of the Supreme Court as a political institution.*** The following two excerpts present competing views of the political role of the Supreme Court.

> [T]he techniques and allied devices for staying the Court's hand, as is avowedly true at least of certiorari, cannot themselves be principled in the sense in which we have a right to expect adjudications on the merits to be principled. They mark the point at which the Court gives the electoral institutions their head and itself stays out of politics, and there is nothing paradoxical in finding that here is where the Court is most a political animal. But this is not to concede unchanneled, undirected, uncharted discretion. The antithesis of principle in an institution that represents decency and reason is not whim or even expediency, but prudence.

Alexander Bickel, The Least Dangerous Branch 127–33 (1962).

> Professor Bickel argues that "the Court is the place for principled judgment" or else "its insulation from the political process is inexplicable." It is my suggestion that the political process and the judiciary are not like Hindu castes forever barred from contact with each other in our system. Rather the judiciary is designed to have occasional political uses. The divorcement that Professor Bickel seeks would remove a forum for social change too useful and too important to justify limitation of the work of the Supreme Court to matters always susceptible to and always governed by principled judgment. The enormous resiliency, the constant possibilities for modest advance and subtle retreat, makes the court one of the most sensitive sources for social change in the United States.

Jerome Barron, *The Ambiguity of Judicial Review: A Response to Professor Bickel*, 1970 Duke L. J. 591.

[B] FOREIGN AFFAIRS AND POLITICAL QUESTIONS

In December 1978, President Carter announced that the United States would recognize the Peoples' Republic of China ("Communist China") as the sole government of China and would withdraw formal recognition from the Republic of China ("Taiwan"). At the same time, it was announced that the Mutual Defense Treaty between the United States and the Republic of China would be terminated. Many in the country and in the Congress reacted bitterly to these announcements on two grounds: (1) the moral ground that these actions constituted a shocking breach of faith, and (2) the constitutional ground that these actions could not be accomplished by the President unilaterally and were thus invalid.

Senator Barry Goldwater, joined by a number of other members of Congress from both the Senate and the House, filed suit in the federal district court in the District of Columbia. They sought declaratory and injunctive relief to prevent termination of the treaty by the President without senatorial or congressional consent. The complaint asserted that the President had no unilateral power under the Constitution to abrogate treaties. The district court dismissed the case, without prejudice, for lack of standing. Almost immediately after the district court order dismissed the suit, the Senate called up a resolution which specified fourteen different grounds that would authorize unilateral action by the President to terminate treaties. However, by a 59-35 vote, a substitute amendment authored by Senator Harry Byrd was presented to the Senate for its consideration. The Byrd Amendment would have required Senate approval as a prerequisite to termination of any mutual defense treaty between the United States and another country. No final action was ever taken on the resolution, principally because a dispute arose in the Senate on "whether the resolution would have retrospective or merely prospective effect."

After the Byrd Amendment was substituted, Senator Goldwater and the other plaintiffs filed a motion in the district court for amendment of the order of June 6, 1979, dismissing their complaint. The plaintiffs contended that the Senate action on the Byrd Amendment satisfied the court's criteria for creating a justiciable controversy. The district court granted the motion and ruled that the plaintiffs now had shown the requisite injury in fact, since their right to be consulted and their right to vote on treaty terminations had been denied. The district court also ruled that "the case did not present a nonjusticiable political question." Furthermore, the court reached the constitutional question and granted plaintiffs' cross motion for summary judgment, and an appeal to the United States Court of Appeals for the District of Columbia followed. The above statement of facts is based on the account in the per curiam decision of the court of appeals. *See Goldwater v. Carter*, 617 F.2d 697, 701 (D.C. Cir. 1979).

The court of appeals declared: "We find the President did not exceed his authority when he took action to withdraw from the ROC Treaty, by giving notice under Article X of the Treaty without consent of the Senate or other legislative concurrences." The court of appeals, in its per curiam opinion, insisted that it had not ignored the question of "justiciability." The court remarked, however, that there was only one issue in this case: "[W]hether the constitutional allocation of governmental power between two branches requires legislative consent to the termination" of the treaty.

GOLDWATER v. CARTER

444 U.S. 996, 100 S. Ct. 533, 62 L. Ed. 2d 428 (1979)

Order

Dec. 13, 1979. The petition for a writ of certiorari is granted. The judgment of the Court of Appeals is vacated and the case is remanded to the District Court with directions to dismiss the complaint.

JUSTICE MARSHALL concurs in the result.

JUSTICES WHITE and BLACKMUN join in the grant of the petition for a writ of certiorari but would set the case for argument and give it plenary consideration.

JUSTICE POWELL, concurring:

Although I agree with the result reached by the Court, I would dismiss the complaint as not ripe for judicial review. This Court has recognized that an issue should not be decided if it is not ripe for judicial review. Prudential considerations persuade me that a dispute between Congress and the President is not ready for judicial review unless and until each branch has taken action asserting its constitutional authority. Otherwise, we would encourage small groups or even individual Members of Congress to seek judicial resolution of issues before the normal political process has the opportunity to resolve the conflict.

In this case, a few Members of Congress claim that the President's action in terminating the treaty with Taiwan has deprived them of their constitutional role with respect to a change in the supreme law of the land. Congress has taken no official action. In the present posture of this case, we do not know whether there ever will be an actual confrontation between the Legislative and Executive Branches.

A simple hypothetical demonstrates the confusion that I find inherent in MR. JUSTICE REHNQUIST's concurring opinion. Assume that the President signed a mutual defense treaty with a foreign country and announced that it would go into effect despite its rejection by the Senate. Under MR. JUSTICE REHNQUIST's analysis that situation would present a political question even though Art. II, § 2, clearly would resolve the dispute. Although the answer to the hypothetical case seems self-evident because it demands textual rather than interstitial analysis, the nature of the legal issue presented is no different from the issue presented in the case before us. In both cases, the Court would interpret the Constitution to decide whether congressional approval is necessary to give a Presidential decision on the validity of a treaty the force of law. Such an inquiry demands no special competence or information beyond the reach of the judiciary.

Finally, the political-question doctrine rests in part on prudential concerns calling for mutual respect among the three branches of government. If this case were ripe for judicial review, none of these prudential considerations would be present. If the President and the Congress had reached irreconcilable positions, final disposition of the question presented by this case would eliminate, rather than create, multiple constitutional interpretations. The spectre of the Federal Government brought to a halt because of the mutual intransigence of the President and the Congress would require this Court to provide a resolution pursuant to our duty "to say what the law is."

Under the criteria enunciated in *Baker v. Carr*, we have the responsibility to decide whether both the Executive and Legislative Branches have constitutional roles to play in termination of a treaty. If the Congress, by appropriate formal action, had challenged the President's authority to terminate the treaty with Taiwan, the resulting uncertainty could have serious consequences for our country. In that situation, it would be the duty of this Court to resolve the issue.

JUSTICE REHNQUIST, with whom CHIEF JUSTICE BURGER, JUSTICE STEWART, and JUSTICE STEVENS join, concurring:

I am of the view that the basic question presented by the petitioners in this case is "political" and therefore nonjusticiable because it involves the authority of the President in the conduct of our country's foreign relations and the extent to which the Senate or the Congress is authorized to negate the action of the President.

Here, while the Constitution is express as to the manner in which the Senate shall participate in the ratification of a Treaty, it is silent as to that body's participation in the abrogation of a Treaty. In light of the absence of any constitutional provision governing the termination of a Treaty, and the fact that different termination procedures may be appropriate for different treaties, the instant case in my view "must surely be controlled by political standards."

Here we are asked to settle a dispute between coequal branches of our government, each of which has resources available to protect and assert its interests, resources not available to private litigants outside the judicial forum. Moreover, the effect of this action, as far as we can tell, is "entirely external to the United States, and [falls] within the category of foreign affairs." Finally, as already noted, the situation presented here is closely akin to that presented in *Coleman*, where the Constitution spoke only to the procedure for ratification of an amendment, not to its rejection.

Having decided that the question presented in this action is nonjusticiable, I believe that the appropriate disposition is for this Court to vacate the decision of the Court of Appeals and remand with instructions for the District Court to dismiss the complaint. This procedure derives support from our practice in disposing of moot actions in federal courts. The Court has required such decisions to be vacated in order to "prevent a judgment, unreviewable because of mootness, from spawning any legal consequences." It is even more imperative that this Court invoke this procedure to ensure that resolution of a "political question," which should not have been decided by a lower court, does not "spawn any legal consequences." An Art. III court's resolution of a question that is "political" in character can create far more disruption among the three coequal branches of government than the resolution of a question presented in a moot controversy. Since the political nature of the questions presented should have precluded the lower courts from considering or deciding the merits of the controversy, the prior proceedings in the federal courts must be vacated, and the complaint dismissed.

JUSTICE BRENNAN, dissenting:

I respectfully dissent from the order directing the District Court to dismiss this case, and would affirm the judgment of the Court of Appeals insofar as it rests upon the President's well-established authority to recognize, and withdraw recognition from, foreign governments.

In stating that this case presents a nonjusticiable "political question," the plurality, in my view, profoundly misapprehends the political question principle as it applies to matters of foreign relations. [T]he doctrine does not pertain when a court is faced with the antecedent question whether a particular branch has been constitutionally designated as the repository of political decisionmaking power. The issue of decisionmaking authority must be resolved as a matter of constitutional law, not political discretion; accordingly, it falls within the competence of the courts.

NOTES

1. ***Decision on the merits or avoidance?*** Professor Gaffney says the *Goldwater* case should not be viewed as a nonjusticiable political question, rejecting "the simplistic bifurcation of our national policy into hermetically sealed areas with domestic affairs susceptible of congressional participation, and foreign affairs the exclusive domain of the Executive." Edward Gaffney, *Goldwater v. Carter: The Constitutional Allocation of Power in Treaty Termination,* 6 YALE STUD. WORLD PUB. ORD. 115 (1979).

In a long and separate opinion in the court of appeals decision, in which he dissented in part and concurred in part, Judge MacKinnon observed: "We are not deciding a political question, but merely determining the procedure to be followed under the Constitution for the termination of a treaty." *Goldwater v. Carter*, 627 F.2d 697, 716 (1979). Does Justice Rehnquist's opinion in *Goldwater* constitute a refutation of this position? *Coleman v. Miller* involved a question of constitutional procedure, namely whether Congress was the final arbiter of the timeliness of state ratification resolutions. Application of the political question doctrine in *Coleman* could be viewed as a judicial resolution of the issue presented there.

Goldwater also may be seen as less a political question case than as another chapter in the steady accretion of executive power in the field of foreign relations. If the Court's invocation of the political question doctrine were in reality a subterfuge for a decision on the merits to defer to one of the elected branches, why would the Court bother to employ the political question rubric, rather than simply acknowledging what it was doing? What would be the costs of such honesty? What would be the benefits?

2. ***War powers and foreign affairs***. Is use of the political question doctrine in *Goldwater* analogous to its use to avoid judicial review of the constitutionality of the Vietnam War? *Compare Luftig v. McNamara*, 373 F.2d 664 (D.C. Cir. 1967) (validity of war is nonjusticiable) *with Orlando v. Laird*, 443 F.2d 1039 (2d Cir.), *cert. denied*, 404 U.S. 869 (1971) (justiciable but sufficiently authorized by Congress).

Dellums v. Bush, 752 F. Supp. 1141 (D.D.C. 1990), was a challenge by serveral Members of Congress to President Bush's proposed entry into Iraq without a congressional declaration or resolution. The district court held that it had "no hesitation in concluding that an offensive entry into Iraq by several hundred thousand United States servicemen . . . could be described as a 'war' within the meaning" of "the clause granting to the Congress, and to it alone, the authority to 'declare war.' " The district court, however, echoing Justice Powell's ripeness rationale, withheld relief while retaining jurisdiction of the case pending the questions of whether the President would actually order forces to combat and whether Congress would act in its full corporate capacity by resolution or otherwise. When Congress authorized U.S. military action against Iraq, the case was dismissed as moot.

[C] IMPEACHMENT — A POLITICAL QUESTION?

NIXON v. UNITED STATES
506 U.S. 224, 113 S. Ct. 732 (1993)

CHIEF JUSTICE REHNQUIST delivered the opinion of the Court.

Petitioner Walter L. Nixon, Jr., asks this court to decide whether Senate Rule XI, which allows a committee of Senators to hear evidence against an individual who has been impeached and to report that evidence to the full Senate, violates the Impeachment Trial Clause, Art. I, § 3, cl. 6. That Clause provides that the "Senate shall have the sole Power to try all Impeachments." But before we reach the merits of such a claim, we must decide whether it is "justiciable," that is, whether it is a claim that may be resolved by the courts. We conclude that it is not.

Nixon, a former Chief Judge of the United States District Court for the Southern District of Mississippi, was convicted by a jury of two counts of making false statements before a federal grand jury and sentenced to prison. Because Nixon refused to resign from his office as a United States District Judge, he continued to collect his judicial salary while serving out his prison sentence. On May 10, 1989, the House of Representatives adopted three articles of impeachment for high crimes and misdemeanors. The first two articles charged Nixon with giving false testimony before the grand jury and the third article charged him with bringing disrepute on the Federal Judiciary.

After the House presented the articles to the Senate, the Senate voted to invoke its own Impeachment Rule XI, under which the presiding officer appoints a committee of Senators to "receive evidence and take testimony." The Senate committee held four days of hearings, during which 10 witnesses, including Nixon, testified. Pursuant to Rule XI, the committee presented the full Senate with a complete transcript of the proceeding and a report stating the uncontested facts and summarizing the evidence on the contested facts. Nixon and the House impeachment managers submitted extensive final briefs to the full Senate and delivered arguments from the Senate floor during the three hours set aside for oral argument in front of that body. Nixon himself gave a personal appeal, and several Senators posed questions directly to both parties. The Senate voted by more than the constitutionally required two-thirds majority to convict Nixon on the first two articles. The presiding officer then entered judgment removing Nixon from his office as United States District Judge.

Nixon thereafter commenced the present suit, arguing that Senate Rule XI violates the constitutional grant of authority to the Senate to "try" all impeachments because it prohibits the whole Senate from taking part in the evidentiary hearings. *See* Art. I, § 3, cl. 6. Nixon sought a declaratory judgment that his impeachment conviction was void and that his judicial salary and privileges should be reinstated. The District Court held that his claim was nonjusticiable, and the Court of Appeals for the District of Columbia Circuit agreed.

A controversy is nonjusticiable — i.e., involves a political question — where there is "a textually demonstrable constitutional commitment of the issue to a coordinate political department; or a lack of judicially discoverable and manageable standards for resolving it . . . ." *Baker v. Carr*. But the courts must, in the first instance, interpret the text in question and determine whether and to what extent the issue is textually committed. *See ibid.; Powell v. McCormack*. As the decision makes clear, the concept of a textual commitment to a coordinate political department is not completely separate from the concept of a lack of judicially discoverable and manageable standards for resolving it; the lack of judicially manageable standards may strengthen the conclusion that there is a textually demonstrable commitment to a coordinate branch.

In this case, we must examine Art. I, § 3, cl. 6, to determine the scope of authority conferred upon the Senate by the Framers regarding impeachment. It provides:

> The Senate shall have the sole Power to try all Impeachments. When sitting for that Purpose, they shall be on Oath or Affirmation. When the President of the United States is tried, the Chief Justice shall preside: And no Person shall be convicted without the Concurrence of two thirds of the Members present.

The language and structure of this Clause are revealing. The first sentence is a grant of authority to the Senate, and the word "sole" indicates that this authority is reposed in the Senate and nowhere else. The next two sentences specify requirements to which the Senate proceedings shall conform: the Senate shall be on oath or affirmation, a two-thirds vote is required to convict, and when the President is tried the Chief Justice shall preside.

Petitioner argues that the word "try" in the first sentence imposes by implication an additional requirement on the Senate in that the proceedings must be in the nature of a judicial trial. From there petitioner goes on to argue that this limitation precludes the Senate from delegating to a select committee the task of hearing the testimony of witnesses, as was done pursuant to Senate Rule XI. " 'Try' means more than simply 'vote on' or 'review' or 'judge.' In 1787 and today, trying a case means hearing the evidence, not scanning a cold record." Petitioner concludes from this that courts may review whether or not the Senate "tried" him before convicting him.

There are several difficulties with this position which lead us ultimately to reject it. The word "try," both in 1787 and later, has considerably broader meanings than those to which petitioner would limit it. Based on the variety of definitions, we cannot say that the Framers used the word "try" as an implied limitation on the method by which the Senate might proceed in trying impeachments.

The conclusion that the use of the word "try" in the first sentence of the Impeachment Trial Clause lacks sufficient precision to afford any judicially manageable standard of review of the Senate's actions is fortified by the existence of the three very specific requirements that the Constitution does impose on the Senate when trying impeachments: the members must be under oath, a two-thirds vote is required to convict, and the Chief Justice presides when the President is tried. These limitations are quite precise, and their nature suggests that the Framers did not intend to impose additional limitations on the form of the Senate proceedings by the use of the word "try" in the first sentence.

Petitioner devotes only two pages in his brief to negating the significance of the word "sole" in the first sentence of Clause 6. As noted above, that sentence provides that "the Senate shall have the sole Power to try all Impeachments." We think that the word "sole" is of considerable significance. Indeed, the word "sole" appears only one other time in the Constitution — with respect to the House of Representatives' "sole Power of Impeachment." Art. I, § 2, cl. 5 (emphasis added). The common sense meaning of the word "sole" is that the Senate alone shall have authority to determine whether an individual should be acquitted or convicted.

The history and contemporary understanding of the impeachment provisions support our reading of the constitutional language. The parties do not offer evidence of a single word in the history of the Constitutional Convention or in contemporary commentary that even alludes to the possibility of judicial review in the context of the impeachment powers.

The Framers labored over the question of where the impeachment power should lie. Significantly, in at least two considered scenarios the power was placed with the Federal Judiciary. Indeed, Madison and the Committee of Detail proposed that the Supreme Court should have the power to determine impeachments. Despite these proposals, the Convention ultimately decided that the Senate would have "the sole Power to Try all Impeachments." According to Alexander Hamilton, the Senate was the "most fit depositary of this important trust" because its members are representatives of the people. The Supreme Court was not the proper body because the Framers "doubted whether the members of that tribunal would, at all times, be endowed with so eminent a portion of fortitude as would be called for in the execution of so difficult a task" or whether the Court "would possess the degree of credit and authority" to carry out its judgment if it conflicted with the accusation brought by the Legislature — the people's representative.

There are two additional reasons why the Judiciary, and the Supreme Court in particular, were not chosen to have any role in impeachments. First, the Framers recognized that most likely there would be two sets of proceedings for individuals who commit impeachable offenses — the impeachment trial and a separate criminal trial. In fact, the Constitution explicitly provides for two separate proceedings. *See* Art. I, § 3, cl. 7. The Framers deliberately separated the two forums to avoid raising the specter of bias and to ensure independent judgments. Certainly judicial review of the Senate's "trial" would introduce the same risk of bias as would participation in the trial itself.

Second, judicial review would be inconsistent with the Framers' insistence that our system be one of checks and balances. In our constitutional system, impeachment was designed to be the only check on the Judicial Branch by the Legislature. Nixon's argument would place final reviewing authority with respect to impeachments in the hands of the same body that the impeachment process is meant to regulate.

Nevertheless, Nixon argues that judicial review is necessary in order to place a check on the Legislature. Nixon fears that if the Senate is given unreviewable authority to interpret the Impeachment Trial Clause, there is a grave risk that the Senate will usurp judicial power. The Framers anticipated this objection and created two constitutional safeguards to keep the Senate in check. The first safeguard is that the whole of the impeachment power is divided between the two legislative bodies, with the House given the right to accuse and the Senate given the right to judge. This split of authority "avoids the inconvenience of making the same persons both accusers and judges; and guards against the danger of persecution from the prevalency of a factious spirit in either of those branches." The second safeguard is the two-thirds supermajority vote requirement. Hamilton explained that "as the concurrence of two-thirds of the senate will be requisite to a condemnation, the security to innocence, from this additional circumstance, will be as complete as itself can desire."

In addition to the textual commitment argument, we are persuaded that the lack of finality and the difficulty of fashioning relief counsel against justiciability. We agree with the Court of Appeals that opening the door of judicial review to the procedures used by the Senate in trying impeachments would "expose the political life of the country to months, or perhaps years, of chaos." This lack of finality would manifest itself most dramatically if the President were impeached. The legitimacy of any successor, and hence his effectiveness, would be impaired severely, not merely while the judicial process was running its course, but during any retrial that a differently constituted Senate might conduct if its first judgment of conviction were invalidated. Equally uncertain is the question of what relief a court may give other than simply setting aside the judgment of conviction. Could it order the reinstatement of a convicted federal judge, or order Congress to create an additional judgeship if the seat had been filled in the interim?

Petitioner finally contends that a holding of nonjusticiability cannot be reconciled with our opinion in *Powell v. McCormack*. Our conclusion in *Powell* was based on the fixed meaning of "qualifications" set forth in Art. I, § 2. The claim by the House that its power to "be the Judge of the Elections, Returns and Qualifications of its own Members" was a textual commitment of unreviewable authority was defeated by the existence of this separate provision specifying the only qualifications which might be imposed for House membership. The decision as to whether a member satisfied these qualifications was placed with the House, but the decision as to what these qualifications consisted of was not.

In the case before us, there is no separate provision of the Constitution which could be defeated by allowing the Senate final authority to determine the meaning of the word "try" in the Impeachment Trial Clause. We agree with Nixon that courts possess power to review either legislative or executive action that transgresses identifiable textual limits. But we conclude, after exercising that delicate responsibility, that the word "try" in the Impeachment Clause does not provide an identifiable textual limit on the authority which is committed to the Senate.

JUSTICE STEVENS, concurring.

For me, the debate about the strength of the inferences to be drawn from the use of the words "sole" and "try" is far less significant than the central fact that the Framers decided to assign the impeachment power to the Legislative Branch.

JUSTICE WHITE, with whom JUSTICE BLACKMUN joins, concurring in the judgment.

Petitioner contends that the method by which the Senate convicted him on two articles of impeachment violates Art. I, § 3, cl. 6 of the Constitution, which mandates that the Senate "try" impeachments. The Court is of the view that the Constitution forbids us even to consider his contention. I find no such prohibition and would therefore reach the merits of the claim. I concur in the judgment because the Senate fulfilled its constitutional obligation to "try" petitioner.

Even taking a wholly practical approach, I would prefer not to announce an unreviewable discretion in the Senate to ignore completely the constitutional direction to "try" impeachment cases. When asked at oral argument whether that direction would be satisfied if, after a House vote to impeach, the Senate, without any procedure whatsoever, unanimously found the accused guilty of being "a bad guy," counsel for the United States answered that the Government's theory "leads me to answer that question yes." Especially in light of this advice from the Solicitor General, I would not issue an invitation to the Senate to find an excuse, in the name of other pressing business, to be dismissive of its critical role in the impeachment process.

The majority finds a clear textual commitment in the Constitution's use of the word "sole" in the phrase "the Senate shall have the sole Power to try all impeachments." While the majority is right to interpret the term "sole" to indicate that the Senate ought to "function independently and without assistance or interference," it wrongly identifies the judiciary, rather than the House, as the source of potential interference with which the Framers were concerned when they employed the term "sole."

Even if the Impeachment Trial Clause is read without regard to its companion clause, the Court's willingness to abandon its obligation to review the constitutionality of legislative acts merely on the strength of the word "sole" is perplexing. Consider, by comparison, the treatment of Art. I, § 1, which grants "All legislative powers" to the House and Senate. As used in that context "all" is nearly synonymous with "sole" — both connote entire and exclusive authority. Yet the Court has never thought it would unduly interfere with the operation of the Legislative Branch to entertain difficult and important questions as to the extent of the legislative power. Quite the opposite, we have stated that the proper interpretation of the Clause falls within the province of the judiciary.

The historical evidence reveals above all else that the Framers were deeply concerned about placing in any branch the "awful discretion, which a court of impeachments must necessarily have." Viewed against this history, the discord between the majority's position and the basic principles of checks and balances underlying the Constitution's separation of powers is clear. In essence, the majority suggests that the Framers' conferred upon Congress a potential tool of legislative dominance yet at the same time rendered Congress' exercise of that power one of the very few areas of legislative authority immune from any judicial review. While the majority rejects petitioner's justiciability argument as espousing a view "inconsistent with the Framers' insistence that our system be one of checks and balances," it is the Court's finding of nonjusticiability that truly upsets the Framers' careful design. In a truly balanced system, impeachments tried by the Senate would serve as a means of controlling the largely unaccountable judiciary, even as judicial review would ensure that the Senate adhered to a minimal set of procedural standards in conducting impeachment trials.

The majority also contends that the term "try" does not present a judicially manageable standard. It is apparently on this basis that the majority distinguishes *Powell v. McCormack*. The majority finds this case different from *Powell* only on the grounds that, whereas the qualifications of Art. I, § 2 are readily susceptible to judicial interpretation, the term "try" does not provide an "identifiable textual limit on the authority which is committed to the Senate."

This argument comes in two variants. The first, which asserts that one simply cannot ascertain the sense of "try" which the Framers employed and hence cannot undertake judicial review, is clearly untenable. To begin with, one would intuitively expect that, in defining the power of a political body to conduct an inquiry into official wrongdoing, the Framers used "try" in its legal sense. That intuition is borne out by reflection on the alternatives. The third clause of Art. I, § 3 cannot seriously be read to mean that the Senate shall "attempt" or "experiment with" impeachments. It is equally implausible to say that the Senate is charged with "investigating" impeachments given that this description would substantially overlap with the House of Representatives' "sole" power to draw up articles of impeachment. Art. I, § 2, cl. 5.

The other variant of the majority position focuses not on which sense of "try" is employed in the Impeachment Trial Clause, but on whether the legal sense of that term creates a judicially manageable standard. The majority concludes that the term provides no "identifiable textual limit." Were the Senate, for example, to adopt the practice of automatically entering a judgment of conviction whenever articles of impeachment were delivered from the House, it is quite clear that the Senate will have failed to "try" impeachments. Indeed in this respect, "try" presents no greater, and perhaps fewer, interpretive difficulties than some other constitutional standards that have been found amenable to familiar techniques of judicial construction, including, for example, "Commerce . . . among the several States," and "due process of law."

The majority's conclusion that "try" is incapable of meaningful judicial construction is not without irony. One might think that if any class of concepts would fall within the definitional abilities of the judiciary, it would be that class having to do with procedural justice. Examination of the remaining question — whether proceedings in accordance with Senate Rule XI are compatible with the Impeachment Trial Clause — confirms this intuition.

In short, textual and historical evidence reveals that the Impeachment Trial Clause was not meant to bind the hands of the Senate beyond establishing a set of minimal procedures. Without identifying the exact contours of these procedures, it is sufficient to say that the Senate's use of a factfinding committee under Rule XI is entirely compatible with the Constitution's command that the Senate "try all impeachments." Petitioner's challenge to his conviction must therefore fail.

JUSTICE SOUTER, concurring in the judgment.

Whatever considerations feature most prominently in a particular case, the political question doctrine is "essentially a function of the separation of powers," existing to restrain courts "from inappropriate interference in the business of the other branches of Government." Not all interference is inappropriate or disrespectful, however, and application of the doctrine ultimately turns, as Learned Hand put it, on "how importunately the occasion demands an answer." L. HAND, THE BILL OF RIGHTS 15 (1958).

This occasion does not demand an answer. One can envision different and unusual circumstances that might justify a more searching review of impeachment proceedings. If the Senate were to act in a manner seriously threatening the integrity of its results, convicting, say, upon a coin-toss, or upon a summary determination that an officer of the United States was simply " 'a bad guy,' " (WHITE, J., concurring in judgment), judicial interference might well be appropriate. In such circumstances, the Senate's action might be so far beyond the scope of its constitutional authority, and the consequent impact on the Republic so great, as to merit a judicial response despite the prudential concerns that would ordinarily counsel silence. "The political question doctrine, a tool for maintenance of governmental order, will not be so applied as to promote only disorder."

NOTES

1. *Resuscitation of the political question doctrine.* Professor Gerhardt describes the potential impact of *Nixon* in the following terms:

> Few constitutional canons are criticized more often than the political question doctrine. *Nixon* breathed life back into the much-maligned political question doctrine [and] recognized that . . . Congress may make constitutional law — *i.e.*, make judgments about the scope and meaning of its constitutionally authorized impeachment functions — subject to change only if it later changes its mind or by a constitutional amendment.

Michael Gerhardt, *Rediscovering Nonjusticiability: Judicial Review of Impeachments After Nixon*, 1994 DUKE L.J. 231.

2. *Criticizing the resuscitation*. In the post-*Nixon* criticisms of the political question doctrine some see dangers beyond the classic separation of powers problems. Professor Brown criticizes the *Nixon* version of the doctrine because it could have implications for judicial refusal to decide questions of individual rights. Rebecca L. Brown, *When Political Questions Affect Individual Rights: The Other Nixon v. United States*, 1993 SUP. CT. REV. 125, 153.

3. *Bush v. Gore*, 531 U.S. 98 (2000). Consider the potential applicability of the political question doctrine to this highly publicized and controversial decision. The Court itself failed to invoke the doctrine but one Justice, in a dissenting opinion, advocated consideration of political question-like factors. The Florida Supreme Court had ordered manual recounts of ballots on which machines had failed to detect a vote for President in Florida's extremely close presidential election, in all counties where these so-called "undervotes" had not been subject to manual tabulation. The manual recounts were to begin at once. The United States Supreme Court granted an application for an emergency stay of the Florida court's mandate, and ultimately reversed in a per curiam opinion.

Noting that "the standards for accepting or rejecting contested ballots might vary not only from county to county but indeed within a single county from one recount to another," the Court concluded that "[t]his is not a process with sufficient guarantees of equal treatment." *See infra*, p. 925. Moreover, "the actual process by which the votes were to be counted under the Florida Supreme Court's decision raises further concerns. That order did not specify who would recount the ballots. The county canvassing boards were forced to pull together ad hoc teams comprised of judges from various Circuits who had no previous training in handling and interpreting ballots." Though as a purely theoretical matter, the Court could have remanded to the Florida Supreme Court to correct these constitutional defects, it chose instead simply to reverse. The Court reasoned that a remand would threaten the state's ability to reach a final electoral decision by December 18, the date prescribed by federal statute for insuring that the state's electoral votes would be counted. That would run counter to the Florida Supreme Court's prior interpretation of the state legislature's intent.

Justice Breyer, joined by Justices Stevens and Ginsburg, dissented. He initially argued, on the merits of the equal protection claim, that "the majority's reasoning would seem to invalidate any state provision for a manual recount of individual counties in a statewide election." As to the issue of remedy, he reasoned: "Whether there is time to conduct a recount prior to December 18 [six days after the date of the decision], when the electors are scheduled to meet, is a matter for the state courts to determine."

In a separate section of his opinion, joined also by Justice Souter, Justice Breyer invoked an analysis similar to that of the political question doctrine. "[N]o preeminent legal concern, or practical concern related to legal questions," he noted, "required this Court to hear this case, let alone to issue a stay that stopped Florida's recount process in its tracks."

He further argued that while "the selection of the President is of fundamental national importance," the importance "is political, not legal. And this Court should resist the temptation unnecessarily to resolve tangential disputes, where doing so threatens to determine the outcome of the election." Justice Breyer reasoned that "[t]he Constitution and federal statutes themselves make clear that restraint is appropriate. They set forth a road map of how to resolve disputes about electors, even after an election as close as this one. That road map foresees resolution of electoral disputes by *state* courts." In support, he noted that "the Twelfth Amendment commits to Congress the authority and responsibility to count electoral votes. A federal statute, the Electoral Count Act, enacted after the close 1876 Hayes-Tilden Presidential election, specifies that, after States have tried to resolve disputes (through 'judicial' or other means), Congress is the body primarily authorized to resolve remaining disputes." He found such a political process to be preferable to a judicial resolution: "The decision by both the Constitution's Framers and the 1886 Congress to minimize this Court's role in resolving presidential elections is as wise as it is clear. However awkward or difficult it may be for Congress to resolve difficult electoral disputes, Congress, being a political body, expresses the people's will far more accurately than does an unelected Court. And the people's will is what elections are about." Finally, he noted that "the Court is not acting to vindicate a fundamental constitutional principle," and that "in this highly politicalized matter, the appearance of a split decision runs the risk of undermining the public's confidence in the Court itself. Thus, the Court "risk[s] a self-inflicted wound — a wound that may harm not just the Court, but the nation," by deciding the case.

To what extent is Justice Breyer's argument similar to the political question doctrine? To what extent does it differ?

In what appears to be a response to Justice Breyer, the majority's per curiam opinion stated: "None are [sic] more conscious of the vital limits on judicial authority than are the members of this Court, and none stand [sic] more in admiration of the Constitution's design to leave the selection of the President to the people, through their legislatures, and to the political sphere. When contending parties invoke the process of the courts, however, it becomes our unsought responsibility to resolve the federal and constitutional issues the judicial system has been forced to confront." If one were to accept this reasoning, would there *ever* be a case in which the political question doctrine could be invoked? Is it a valid answer to the Court to suggest that a requirement of *judicial* process was fully satisfied by the adjudication of the matter in the Florida courts, and that the Supreme Court, pursuant to its certiorari jurisdiction, is *never* required "to resolve the federal and constitutional issues," merely because "contending parties invoke the process of the courts"? Consider also the following possible counter-response: Because the equal protection challenge was being made to the manual recount ordered by the Florida Supreme Court, absent review in the United States Supreme Court the petitioners would have had absolutely no judicial recourse for the alleged violation of constitutional rights.

Chapter 2
NATIONAL POWERS & FEDERALISM

This chapter introduces the basic dimensions of federalism through the scope of federal powers, along with a brief look at some structural limitations on the powers of state governments. The basic question for this chapter is whether the federal government is created by a collection of independent states (implying state dominance) or is instead a creature of all the people (implying that the states are subordinate units).

Federalism is not a uniquely American contribution to either constitutional or political theory. It is traceable at least to the Greek city-states and is in use in a number of other countries. *See* KENNETH C. WHEARE, FEDERAL GOVERNMENT (4th ed. 1963). Federalism has had a vital influence on the pattern of American constitutional development. As Professor Wechsler has written, "Federalism was the means and price of the formation of the Union. It was inevitable, therefore, that its basic concepts should determine much of our history." Herbert Wechsler, *The Political Safeguards of Federalism: The Role of the States in the Composition and Selection of the National Government,* 54 COLUM. L. REV. 543 (1954).

The Introduction set out some of the historical and intellectual background of the concept of federalism. There are political and social values in the system as well.

> The theoretical and pragmatic functions designed to be served by a federal system are not difficult to discern. The decentralization of political power makes perfect sense in a system premised on the fear of, and the desire to avoid, tyranny. As a result of its size, resources, and national perspective, the federal government is able to deal with certain problems that extend across the borders of the individual states. Yet because state governments can focus on the unique impact that a problem may have in a particular geographical or economic area, are closer to popular will, and can engage in social experimentation without the costs 'and risks incurred by conducting untested social programs at the national level, they provide a perspective that the federal government is unable to maintain.

MARTIN H. REDISH, THE CONSTITUTION AS POLITICAL STRUCTURE 25 (1995); *see also* DAVID L. SHAPIRO, FEDERALISM: A DIALOGUE 58–106 (1995).

There are drawbacks of a federal system. Scholars have pointed to three situations in which the exercise of independent state power could be problematic: (1) when "externalities" exist, i.e., when a particular state action (or inaction) give rises to considerably more intense problems in another state, resulting in a lack of incentive for the first state to avoid or cure those problems; (2) when states reduce commercial or environmental regulation as a means of attracting industry (the so-called "race to the bottom"); and (3) when individual states choose to depart from a broader national moral consensus (for example, in the area of civil rights or racial discrimination). *See generally* SHAPIRO at 34–57; Jacques LeBeouf, *The Economics of Federalism and the Proper Scope of the Federal Commerce Power*, 31 SAN DIEGO L. REV. 555 (1994).

The Framers had available to them several options in structuring the constitutional concept of federalism: They could have chosen (1) to provide the political branches of the federal government with unlimited discretion to promulgate laws deemed to be in the nation's best interests, while simultaneously insulating special enclaves of state power from federal encroachment, (2) to divide power between state and federal levels on the basis of predetermined consideration of the relative functional superiority of the two levels in handling various tasks, or (3) to provide the federal government with only specified powers, leaving the remaining powers to state authority.

As Article I, section 8 demonstrates, the Framers ultimately chose something along the lines of the third alternative. To make the structure more evident, the Tenth Amendment provides: "The powers not delegated to the United States by the Constitution nor prohibited by it to the States are reserved to the states respectively, or to the people." As you will see, there is a major debate over the question of whether this provision acts to create positive limits on federal power or whether it is instead a mere "tautology," stating the basic structure on which the entire rest of the Constitution rests.

What is the role of the Supreme Court in umpiring the federal system? In exercising the power of judicial review, should the courts give priority to checking abuses of the national power or should the courts give priority instead to maintaining national supremacy against intrusions by the individual states?

Professor Choper has argued that the Supreme Court should play no role in enforcing constitutional federalism:

> The federal judiciary should not decide constitutional questions respecting the ultimate power of the national government vis-à-vis the states; rather, the constitutional issue of whether federal action is beyond the authority of the central government and thus violates "states' rights" should be treated as nonjusticiable, final resolution being relegated to the political branches — i.e., Congress and the President.

JESSE CHOPER, JUDICIAL REVIEW AND THE NATIONAL POLITICAL PROCESS 175 (1980).

Choper has two reasons for advocating judicial abdication in federalism cases: (1) his desire "to ease the commendable and crucial task of judicial review in cases of individual liberties" and (2) his belief that the states need no countermajoritarian protection because their interests are already adequately represented in the political process. With regard to the first point, "it is neither intuitively nor empirically clear that the Court's so-called capital is transferable from one area of constitutional law to another." Martin Redish & Karen Drizin, *Constitutional Federalism and Judicial Review: The Role of Textual Analysis*, 62 N.Y.U. L. REV. 1, 36 (1987). The second point is the subject of intense debate in the Supreme Court opinions in *Garcia v. SAMTA*,

p. 120. *See* Larry Kramer, *Understanding Federalism*, 47 VAND. L. REV. 1485 (1994).

From today's perspective, the concept and role of federalism have undergone significant changes since 1789. As social problems grow more complex, as they cross state boundaries, and as demands for the rights of national citizenship become more intense, the demand for action by the national government grows. On the other hand, there has been a recent emphasis on returning power to the states and localities. The dilemma, however, is essentially the same as it was 184 years ago: "How do we make sure that the powers of government continue to be diffused while at the same time the chores of government are effectively performed?" Speech by Senator Edmund Muskie *quoted in* Leach, *Intergovernmental Cooperation and American Federalism*, in GOFFRIED DIETZE, ESSAYS ON THE AMERICAN CONSTITUTION 133 (1964).

Some additional insight to the development of U.S. federalism may be gained by comparing U.S. history to current events. European movements toward federalism and regional trade agreements reflect many of the same considerations.

§ 2.01 THE NATURE OF FEDERAL POWER

In *McCulloch v. Maryland,* the Supreme Court considered the constitutionality of congressional legislation creating the Second Bank of the United States. In 1791, amidst great controversy, Congress had incorporated the First Bank of the United States with power to issue bank notes, accept private deposits, discount promissory notes and carry on all the usual transactions of a local bank operated for the profit of shareholders. However, the controversy accompanying the creation of the bank was not to dissipate during the years of its operation.

> In the minds of much of the public the Bank of the United States was a ruthless and irresponsible institution, controlled by a small group of private bankers for personal profit. The Federal Government held a minor share of stock and held no actual control over the Bank's policies. While much of the antagonism was emotional, and while the bank perhaps received more blame for economic conditions than it deserved, a good deal of the disrepute was justified by poor management and selfish profit-seeking.

Harold Plous & Gordon Baker, *McCulloch v. Maryland: Right Principle, Wrong Case,* 9 STAN. L. REV. 710, 719 (1957). See 1 CHARLES WARREN, THE SUPREME COURT IN UNITED STATES HISTORY 499–540 (1922), for a historical treatment of the debate over the bank.

In 1811 the First Bank's charter had been allowed to expire. But on April 10, 1816, the Congress, again over bitter opposition, incorporated the Second Bank of the United States. It was over the constitutionality of this legislation that the battle in *McCulloch* was waged.

McCULLOCH v. MARYLAND
17 U.S. (4 Wheat.) 316, 4 L. Ed. 579 (1819)

[Pursuant to its charter, the Second Bank of the United States established a branch bank in Baltimore. On February 11, 1818, the General Assembly of Maryland enacted a statute imposing a tax on the face value of many of the notes issued by banks or their branches located in Maryland but not chartered by the state. Alternatively, the bank could make a payment of $15,000 annually.

[When the Baltimore branch of the Bank issued notes in contravention of the statute, an action of debt was brought on behalf of the state in the County Court of Baltimore County against McCulloch as cashier of the branch bank to recover the statutory penalty. The Maryland Court of Appeals affirmed judgment against McCulloch and the case came to the Supreme Court on a writ of error. Six counsel, including United States Attorney General William Wirt, Daniel Webster and William Pinckney for the bank and State Attorney General Luther Martin, Joseph Hopkinson, and Walter Jones for Maryland, argued the case for nine days. Justice Marshall, speaking for a unanimous Court including four Republicans, delivered his opinion only three days after argument.]

CHIEF JUSTICE MARSHALL delivered the opinion of the Court.

The first question made in the cause is, has Congress power to incorporate a bank? The power now contested was exercised by the first Congress elected under the present constitution. The bill for incorporating the Bank of the United States did not steal upon an unsuspecting legislature, and pass unobserved. Its principle was completely understood, and was opposed with equal zeal and ability. It would require no ordinary share of intrepidity to assert that a measure adopted under these circumstances was a bold and plain usurpation, to which the constitution gave no countenance.

These observations belong to the cause; but they are not made under the impression that, were the question entirely new, the law would be found irreconcilable with the constitution. In discussing this question, the counsel for the state of Maryland have deemed it of some importance, in the construction of the constitution, to consider that instrument not as emanating from the people, but as the act of sovereign and independent states. The powers of the general government, it has been said, are delegated by the states, who alone are truly sovereign; and must be exercised in subordination to the states, who alone possess supreme dominion.

It would be difficult to sustain this proposition. The convention which framed the constitution was indeed elected by the state legislatures. But the instrument, when it came from their hands, was a mere proposal, without obligation, or pretensions to it. It was reported to the then existing Congress of the United States, with a request that it might be submitted to a convention of delegates, chosen in each state by the people thereof, under the recommendation of its legislature, for their assent and ratification. This mode of proceeding was adopted; and by the convention, by Congress, and by the state legislatures, the instrument was submitted to the people. They acted upon it in the only manner in which they can act safely, effectively, and wisely, on such a subject, by assembling in convention. It is true, they assembled in their several states and where else should they have assembled? No political dreamer was ever wild enough to think of breaking down the lines which separate the states, and of compounding the American people into one common mass. Of consequence, when they act, they act in their states. But the measures they adopt do not, on that account, cease to be the measures of the people themselves, or become the measures of the state governments.

From these conventions the constitution derives its whole authority. The government proceeds directly from the people; is "ordained and established" in the name of the people; and is declared to be ordained, "in order to form a more perfect union, establish justice, insure domestic tranquility, and secure the blessings of liberty to themselves and to their posterity." The assent of the states, in their sovereign capacity, is implied in calling a convention, and thus submitting that instrument to the people. But the people were at perfect liberty to accept or reject it; and their act was final. It required not the affirmance, and could not be negatived, by the state governments. The constitution, when thus adopted, was of complete obligation, and bound the state sovereignties.

The government of the Union, then (whatever may be the influence of this fact on the case), is, emphatically, and truly, a government of the people. In form and in substance it emanates from them. Its powers are granted by them, and are to be exercised directly on them, and for their benefit.

This government is acknowledged by all to be one of enumerated powers. The principle, that it can exercise only the powers granted to it, is now universally admitted. But the question respecting the extent of the powers actually granted, is perpetually arising, and will probably continue to arise, as long as our system shall exist. The government of the United States though limited in its powers, is supreme; and its laws, when made in pursuance of the constitution, form the supreme law of the land, "anything in the constitution or laws of any state to the contrary notwithstanding."

Among the enumerated powers, we do not find that of establishing a bank or creating a corporation. But there is no phrase in the instrument which, like the articles of confederation, excludes incidental or implied powers; and which requires that everything granted shall be expressly and minutely described. Even the Tenth Amendment, which was framed for the purpose of quieting the excessive jealousies which had been excited, omits the word expressly, and declares only that the powers "not delegated to the United States, nor prohibited to the states, are reserved to the states or to the people"; thus leaving the question, whether the particular power which may become the subject of contest, has been delegated to the one government, or prohibited to the other, to depend on a fair construction of the whole instrument. The men who drew and adopted this amendment had experienced the embarrassments resulting from the insertion of this word in the articles of confederation, and probably omitted it to avoid those embarrassments. A constitution, to contain an accurate detail of all the subdivisions of which its great powers will admit, and of all the means by which they may be carried into execution, would partake of the prolixity of a legal code, and could scarcely be embraced by the human mind. It would probably never be understood by the public. Its nature, therefore, requires, that only its great outlines should be marked, its important objects designated, and the minor ingredients which compose those objects be deduced from the nature of the objects themselves. That this idea was entertained by the framers of the American constitution, is not only to be inferred from the nature of the instrument, but from the language. Why else were some of the limitations, found in the ninth section of the 1st article, introduced? It is also, in some degree, warranted by their having omitted to use any restrictive term which might prevent its receiving a fair and just interpretation. In considering this question, then, we must never forget, that it is a *constitution* we are expounding.

Although, among the enumerated powers of government, we do not find the word "bank" or "incorporation," we find the great powers to lay and collect taxes; to borrow money; to regulate commerce; to declare and conduct a war; and to raise and support armies and navies. The sword and the purse, all the external relations, and no inconsiderable portion of the industry of the nation, are entrusted to its government. It can never be pretended that these vast powers draw after them others of inferior importance, merely because they are inferior. Such an idea can never be advanced. But it may with great reason be contended, that a government, entrusted with such ample powers, on the due execution of which the happiness and prosperity of the nation so vitally depends, must also be entrusted with ample means for their execution. The power being given, it is the interest of the nation to facilitate its execution. It can never be their interest, and cannot be presumed to have been their intention, to clog and embarrass its execution by withholding the most appropriate means. If, indeed, such be the mandate of the constitution, we have only to obey; but that instrument does not profess to enumerate the means by which the powers it confers may be executed; nor does it prohibit the creation of a corporation, if the existence of such a being be essential to the beneficial exercise of those powers. It is, then, the subject of fair inquiry, how far such means may be employed.

The government which has a right to do an act, and has imposed on it the duty of performing that act, must, according to the dictates of reason, be allowed to select the means; and those who contend that it may not select any appropriate means, that one particular mode of effecting the object is excepted, take upon themselves the burden of establishing that exception.

But the constitution of the United States has not left the right of Congress to employ the necessary means, for the execution of the powers conferred on the government, to general reasoning. To its enumeration of powers is added that of making "all laws which shall be necessary and proper, for carrying into execution the foregoing powers, and all other powers vested by this constitution, in the government of the United States, or in any department [or officer] thereof."

The counsel for the state of Maryland have urged various arguments, to prove that this clause, though in terms a grant of power, is not so in effect; but is really restrictive of the general right, which might otherwise be implied, of selecting means for executing the enumerated powers.

[T]he argument on which most reliance is placed, is drawn from the peculiar language of this clause. Congress is not empowered by it to make all laws, which may have relation to the powers conferred on the government, but such only as may be "necessary and proper" for carrying them into execution. The word "necessary" is considered as controlling the whole sentence, and as limiting the right to pass laws for the execution of the granted powers, to such as are indispensable, and without which the power would be nugatory. That it excludes the choice of means, and leaves to Congress, in each case, that only which is most direct and simple.

Is it true, that this is the sense in which the word "necessary" is always used? Does it always import an absolute physical necessity, so strong that one thing, to which another may be termed necessary, cannot exist without that other? We think it does not. If reference be had to its use, in the common affairs of the world, or in approved authors, we find that it frequently imports no more than that one thing is convenient, or useful, or essential to another. To employ the means necessary to an end, is generally understood as employing any means calculated to produce the end, and not as being confined to those single means, without which the end would be entirely unattainable.

Let this be done in the case under consideration. The subject is the execution of those great powers on which the welfare of a nation essentially depends. It must have been the intention of those who gave these powers, to insure, as far as human prudence could insure, their beneficial execution. This could not be done by confiding the choice of means to such narrow limits as not to leave it in the power of Congress to adopt any which might be appropriate, and which were conducive to the end. This provision is made in a constitution intended to endure for ages to come, and consequently, to be adapted to the various crises of human affairs. To have prescribed the means by which government should, in all future time, execute its powers, would have been to change, entirely, the character of the instrument, and give it the properties of a legal code. It would have been an unwise attempt to provide, by immutable rules, for exigencies which, if foreseen at all, must have been seen dimly, and which can be best provided for as they occur. To have declared that the best means shall not be used, but those alone without which the power given would be nugatory, would have been to deprive the legislature of the capacity to avail itself of experience, to exercise its reason, and to accommodate its legislation to circumstances. If we apply this principle of construction to any of the powers of the government, we shall find it so pernicious in its operation that we shall be compelled to discard it.

In ascertaining the sense in which the word "necessary" is used in this clause of the constitution, we may derive some aid from that with which it is associated. Congress shall have power "to make all laws which shall be necessary and proper to carry into execution" the powers of the government. If the word "necessary" was used in that strict and rigorous sense for which the counsel for the state of Maryland contend, it would be an extraordinary departure from the usual course of the human mind, as exhibited in composition, to add a word, the only possible effect of which is to qualify that strict and rigorous meaning; to present to the mind the idea of some choice of means of legislation not straightened and compressed within the narrow limits for which gentlemen contend.

But the argument which most conclusively demonstrates the error of the construction contended for by the counsel for the state of Maryland, is founded on the intention of the convention, as manifested in the whole clause.

1st. The clause is placed among the powers of Congress, not among the limitations on those powers.

2d. Its terms purport to enlarge, not to diminish the powers vested in the government. It purports to be an additional power, not a restriction on those already granted. No reason has been, or can be assigned for thus concealing an intention to narrow the discretion of the national legislature under words which purport to enlarge it.

The result of the most careful and attentive consideration bestowed upon this clause is, that if it does not enlarge, it cannot be construed to restrain the powers of Congress, or to impair the right of the legislature to exercise its best judgment in the selection of measures to carry into execution the constitutional powers of the government. If no other motive for its insertion can be suggested, a sufficient one is found in the desire to remove all doubts respecting the right to legislate on that vast mass of incidental powers which must be involved in the constitution, if that instrument be not a splendid bauble.

We admit, as all must admit, that the powers of the government are limited, and that its limits are not to be transcended. But we think the sound construction of the constitution must allow to the national legislature that discretion, with respect to the means by which the powers it confers are to be carried into execution, which will enable that body to perform the high duties assigned to it, in the manner most beneficial to the people. Let the end be legitimate, let it be within the scope of the constitution, and all means which are appropriate, which are plainly adapted to that end, which are not prohibited, but consist with the letter and spirit of the constitution, are constitutional.

If a corporation may be employed indiscriminately with other means to carry into execution the powers of the government, no particular reason can be assigned for excluding the use of a bank, if required for its fiscal operations. To use one, must be within the discretion of Congress, if it be an appropriate mode of executing the powers of government. That it is a convenient, a useful, and essential instrument in the prosecution of its fiscal operations, is not now a subject of controversy.

But, were its necessity less apparent, none can deny its being an appropriate measure; and if it is, the degree of its necessity, as has been very justly observed, is to be discussed in another place. Should Congress, in the execution of its powers, adopt measures which are prohibited by the constitution; or should Congress, under the pretext of executing its powers, pass laws for the accomplishment of objects not entrusted to the government; it would become the painful duty of this tribunal, should a case requiring such a decision come before it, to say that such an act was not the law of the land. But where the law is not prohibited, and is really calculated to effect any of the objects entrusted to the government, to undertake here to inquire into the degree of its necessity, would be to pass the line which circumscribes the judicial department, and to tread on legislative ground. This court disclaims all pretensions to such a power.

It being the opinion of the court that the act incorporating the bank is constitutional, and that the power of establishing a branch in the state of Maryland might be properly exercised by the bank itself, we proceed to inquire: Whether the state of Maryland may, without violating the constitution, tax that branch?

That the power of taxation is one of vital importance; that it is retained by the states; that it is not abridged by the grant of a similar power to the government of the Union; that it is to be concurrently exercised by the two governments; are truths which have never been denied. But, such is the paramount character of the constitution that its capacity to withdraw any subject from the action of even this power, is admitted. The states are expressly forbidden to lay any duties on imports or exports, except what may be absolutely necessary for executing their inspection laws. If the obligation of this prohibition must be conceded — if it may restrain a state from the exercise of its taxing power on imports and exports — the same paramount character would seem to restrain, as it certainly may restrain, a state from such other exercise of this power as is in its nature incompatible with, and repugnant to, the constitutional laws of the Union. A law, absolutely repugnant to another, as entirely repeals that other as if express terms of repeal were used.

On this ground, the counsel for the bank place its claim to be exempted from the power of a state to tax its operations. There is no express provision for the case, but the claim has been sustained on a principle which so entirely pervades the constitution, is so intermixed with the materials which compose it, so interwoven with its web, so blended with its texture, as to be incapable of being separated from it, without rending it into shreds.

This great principle is, that the constitution and the laws made in pursuance thereof are supreme; that they control the constitution and laws of the respective states, and cannot be controlled by them. From this, which may be almost termed an axiom, other propositions are adduced as corollaries, on the truth or error of which, and on their application to this case, the cause has been supposed to depend. These are, 1st. That a power to create implies a power to preserve. 2d. That a power to destroy, if wielded by a different hand, is hostile to, and incompatible with, these powers to create and to preserve. 3d. That where this repugnance exists, that authority which is supreme must control, not yield to that over which it is supreme.

The power of Congress to create, and of course to continue, the bank, was the subject of the preceding part of this opinion; and is no longer to be considered as questionable. That the power of taxing [the bank] by the states may be exercised so as to destroy it, is too obvious to be denied. But taxation is said to be an absolute power, which acknowledges no other limits than those expressly prescribed in the constitution, and like sovereign powers of every other description, is trusted to the discretion of those who use it. But the very terms of this argument admit that the sovereignty of the state, in the article of taxation itself, is subordinate to, and may be controlled by the constitution of the United States. How far it has been controlled by that instrument must be a question of construction. In making this construction, no principle not declared can be admissible, which would defeat the legitimate operations of a supreme government. It is of the very essence of supremacy to remove all obstacles to its action within its own sphere, and so to modify every power vested in subordinate governments as to exempt its own operations from their own influence. This effect need not be stated in terms. It is so involved in the declaration of supremacy, so necessarily implied in it, that the expression of it could not make it more certain. We must, therefore, keep it in view while construing the constitution.

The argument on the part of the state of Maryland, is, not that the states may directly resist a law of Congress, but that they may exercise their acknowledged powers upon it, and that the constitution leaves them this right in the confidence that they will not abuse it. Before we proceed to examine this argument, and to subject it to the test of the constitution, we must be permitted to bestow a few considerations on the nature and extent of this original right of taxation, which is acknowledged to remain with the states. It is admitted that the power of taxing the people and their property is essential to the very existence of government, and may be legitimately exercised on the objects to which it is applicable, to the utmost extent to which the government may choose to carry it. The only security against the abuse of this power is found in the structure of the government itself. In imposing a tax the legislature acts upon its constituents. This is in general a sufficient security against erroneous and oppressive taxation.

The people of a state, therefore, give to their government a right of taxing themselves and their property, and as the exigencies of government cannot be limited, they prescribe no limits to the exercise of this right, resting confidently on the interest of the legislator, and on the influence of the constituent over their representative, to guard them against its abuse. But the means employed by the government of the Union have no such security, nor is the right of a state to tax them sustained by the same theory. Those means are not given by the people of a particular state, not given by the constituents of the legislature, which claim the right to tax them, but by the people of all the states. They are given by all, for the benefit of all — and upon theory, should be subjected to that government only which belongs to all.

All subjects over which the sovereign power of a state extends, are objects of taxation; but those over which it does not extend, are, upon the soundest principles, exempt from taxation. This proposition may almost be pronounced self-evident. The sovereignty of a state extends to everything which exists by its own authority, or is introduced by its permission; but does it extend to those means which are employed by Congress to carry into execution — powers conferred on that body by the people of the United States? We think it demonstrable that it does not. Those powers are not given by the people of a single state. They are given by the people of the United States, to a government whose laws, made in pursuance of the constitution, are declared to be supreme. Consequently, the people of a single state cannot confer a sovereignty which will extend over them.

That the power to tax involves the power to destroy; that the power to destroy may defeat and render useless the power to create; that there is a plain repugnance, in conferring on one government a power to control the constitutional measures of another, which other, with respect to those very measures, is declared to be supreme over that which exerts the control, are propositions not to be denied. But all inconsistencies are to be reconciled by the magic of the word CONFIDENCE. Taxation, it is said, does not necessarily and unavoidably destroy. To carry it to the excess of destruction would be an abuse, to presume which, would banish that confidence which is essential to all government.

But is this a case of confidence? Would the people of any one state trust those of another with a power to control the most insignificant operations of their state government? We know they would not. Why, then, should we suppose that the people of any one state should be willing to trust those of another with a power to control the operations of a government to which they have confided the most important and most valuable interests? In the legislature of the Union alone, are all represented. The legislature of the Union alone, therefore, can be trusted by the people with the power of controlling measures which concern all, in the confidence that it will not be abused. This, then, is not a case of confidence, and we must consider it as it really is.

If we apply the principle for which the state of Maryland contends, to the constitution generally, we shall find it capable of changing totally the character of that instrument. We shall find it capable of arresting all the measures of the government, and of prostrating it at the foot of the states. The American people have declared their constitution, and the laws made in pursuance thereof, to be supreme; but this principle would transfer the supremacy, in fact, to the states. If the controlling power of the states be established; if their supremacy as to taxation be acknowledged; what is to restrain their exercising this control in any shape they may please to give it? Their sovereignty is not confined to taxation. That is not the only mode in which it might be displayed. The question is, in truth, a question of supremacy; and if the right of the states to tax the means employed by the general government be conceded, the declaration that the constitution, and the laws made in pursuance thereof, shall be the supreme law of the land, is empty and unmeaning declamation.

It has also been insisted, that, as the power of taxation in the general and state governments is acknowledged to be concurrent, every argument which would sustain the right of the general government to tax banks chartered by the states, will equally sustain the right of the states to tax banks chartered by the general government. But the two cases are not on the same reason. The people of all the states have created the general government, and have conferred upon it the general power of taxation. The people of all the states, and the states themselves, are represented in Congress, and, by their representatives, exercise this power. When they tax the chartered institutions of the states, they tax their constituents; and these taxes must be uniform. But, when a state taxes the operations of the government of the United States, it acts upon institutions created, not by their own constituents, but by people over whom they claim no control. It acts upon the measures of a government created by others as well as themselves, for the benefit of others in common with themselves. The difference is that which always exists, and always must exist, between the action of the whole on a part, and the action of a part on the whole between the laws of a government declared to be supreme, and those of a government which, when in opposition to those laws, is not supreme.

But if the full application of this argument could be admitted, it might bring into question the right of Congress to tax the state banks, and could not prove the right of the states to tax the Bank of the United States. The court has bestowed on this subject its most deliberate consideration. The result is a conviction that the states have no power, by taxation or otherwise, to retard, impede, burden, or in any manner control the operations of the constitutional laws enacted by Congress to carry into execution the powers vested in the general government. This is, we think, the unavoidable consequence of that supremacy which the constitution has declared.

We are unanimously of opinion, that the law passed by the legislature of Maryland, imposing a tax on the Bank of the United States, is unconstitutional and void. This opinion does not deprive the states of any resources which they originally possessed. It does not extend to a tax paid by the real property of the bank, in common with other real property within the state, nor to a tax imposed on the interest which the citizens of Maryland may hold in this institution, in common with other property of the same description throughout the state. But this is a tax on the operations of the bank, and is, consequently, a tax on the operation of an instrument employed by the government of the Union to carry its powers into execution. Such a tax must be unconstitutional.

NOTES

1. *Nationalism versus localism.* The reaction to *McCulloch,* both pro and con, was immediate and intense. While much of the negative opinion was directed at the Court's legitimization of the national bank, most critics attacked Marshall's broad nationalist principles. Spencer Roane of Virginia, a strong antagonist of Marshall, writing in the newspapers under the pseudonyms of "Amphictyon" and "Hampden," claimed that Marshall's principles

> tend directly to consolidation of the States and to strip them of some of the most important attributes of their sovereignty. If the Congress of the United States should think proper to legislate to the full extent upon the principles now adjudicated by the Supreme Court, it is difficult to say how small be the remnant of powers left in the hands of the State authorities.

1 CHARLES WARREN, THE SUPREME COURT IN UNITED STATES HISTORY 517 (1922).

2. *Broad interpretation versus narrow interpretation.* In defining the delegated powers, should the courts adopt a broad or a narrow construction? The constitutional convention sent the following resolutions concerning the scope of national powers, which were originally proposed by Randolph, to its Committee of Detail:

> Resolved, that the national legislature ought, 1) to possess the legislative rights vested in Congress by the confederation, and 2) moreover, to legislate in all cases for the general interest of the Union, and 3)

> also in those to which the states are separately incompetent, or 4) in which the harmony of the United States may be interrupted by the exercise of individual legislation.

1 MAX FARRAND, THE RECORDS OF THE FEDERAL CONVENTION OF 1787, at 131 (1911). The convention consistently rejected attempts to more narrowly define the congressional power. It was the Committee of Detail that changed the language of this resolution into the language of Article 1, § 8, of the Constitution.

3. *The constitutional language.* Are the enumerated powers expressed in Article 1, § 8, limited to ends, or are means also specified? The power to raise armies is a *means* of effectuating the war power. Yet both are expressly provided for. Consider the argument in *McCulloch* of Luther Martin for Maryland: "If, then, the convention has specified some powers, which, being only means to accomplish the ends of government, might have been taken by implication; by what just rule of construction are other sovereign powers, equally vast and important, to be assumed by implication?"

What is the effect of the Tenth Amendment on this analysis? Marshall uses it to argue for implied powers. The corresponding provision in the Articles of Confederation was phrased in terms of "expressly delegated" powers and Congress rejected an attempt to insert "expressly" into the Tenth Amendment. I ANNALS OF CONG. 768.

4. *Implied powers, limited government, and federalism.* Is Marshall's theory of implied powers consistent with the principle of limited government? Of federalism? Spencer Roane of Virginia (alias Hampden) had argued that there is no difference between an "*unlimited* grant of power and a grant limited in its terms, but accompanied with *unlimited* means of carrying it into execution." 4 ALBERT J. BEVERIDGE, THE LIFE OF JOHN MARSHALL 316 (1919).

Does Marshall provide an adequate standard for limiting Congress' power, or is his theory, in fact, a general grant of legislative power? In *McCulloch,* he asserts that the Court must intervene when Congress "under the pretext of executing its powers" enacts laws designed to achieve objects not entrusted to the national government under the Constitution. It is not easy to imagine the Court's probing for Congress' true purpose or motive to determine whether Congress is acting "under the pretext" of executing its constitutional powers.

On the other hand, the need for a judicially enforced limit on Congress' power may be lessened by the political realities of our federalist system. "The actual extent of central intervention in the governance of our affairs is determined far less by the formal power distribution than by the sheer existence of the states and their political power to influence the action of the national authority." Wechsler, 54 COLUM. L. REV. at 544.

5. *The need for a "necessary and proper" clause.* Hamilton in THE FEDERALIST, NO. 33, contended that Congress would still have implied powers if there were no necessary and proper clause.

> [I]t may be affirmed with perfect confidence, that the constitutional operation of the intended government would be precisely the same, if [the clause] were entirely obliterated, as if [it] were repeated in every

> article. [It is] only declaratory of a truth, which would have resulted by necessary and unavoidable implication from the very act of constituting a Federal Government, and vesting it with certain specified powers. What is a power, but the ability or faculty of doing a thing? What is the ability to do a thing but the power of employing the *means* necessary to its execution? What is LEGISLATIVE power but a power of making laws? What are the *means* to execute a legislative power, but LAWS?

James Madison in THE FEDERALIST, NO. 44, states: "Had the Constitution been silent on this head, there can be no doubt that all the particular powers requisite as means of executing the general powers would have resulted to the government, by unavoidable implication." If Congress would have implied powers if there were no clause, shouldn't the inclusion of the "necessary and proper" language be read to limit the grant of power?

6. *Inherent domestic legislative powers.* It has been argued that Marshall's approach in *McCulloch* to Congress' power is excessively narrow; that Congress has general, inherent legislative power. In *Kansas v. Colorado*, 206 U.S. 46 (1907), the Court rejected a claim that Congress had power over reclamation of arid lands within a state. The opinion commented that "the proposition that there are legislative powers affecting the Nation as a whole which belong to, although not expressed in the grant of powers, is in direct conflict with the doctrine that this is a government of enumerated powers."

7. *Legislating pursuant to other constitutional provisions.* There are numerous express grants of congressional power outside Article I, § 8. *See, e.g.,* Article I, § 4, recognizing Congress' power to make or alter regulations for the election of senators and representatives; Article III, § 1, giving Congress power to establish inferior federal courts and to make "exception and regulations" regarding the appellate jurisdiction of the Supreme Court; Article IV, § 1, recognizing Congress' role in assuring full faith and credit. Similarly, amendments 13, 14, 15, 19, 23, 24, and 26 all include enabling clauses authorizing congressional legislation.

8. *Intergovernmental immunities.* Marshall claims that "the power to tax involves the power to destroy." Is Marshall's opinion limited to discriminatory state taxes or does it apply to all state taxes on federal instrumentalities? What constitutional provision did the Maryland tax violate? Charles Black has suggested that Marshall's reasoning is "essentially structural:" "It has to do in great part with what he conceives to be the warranted relational properties between the national government and the government of the states, with the structural corollaries of national supremacy — and, at one point, of the mode of formation of the Union." CHARLES BLACK, STRUCTURE AND RELATIONSHIP IN CONSTITUTIONAL LAW 15 (1969). Conversely, we need to ask whether there is a reciprocal state immunity from federal regulation. *See* § 2.02[c], *infra*.

9. *Legislating Pursuant to the Judicial Power.* In *Jinks v. Richland County*, 538 U.S. 456 (2003), the Court, per Justice Scalia, ruled 8-1 that Congress could extend state statutes of limitations so that state courts would be required to hear a claim that had originally been filed in federal court under that court's supplemental jurisdiction but that was dismissed by the federal court. 28 U.S.C. § 1367(d). Justice Scalia for the Court stated:

> [Section] 1367 (d) is necessary and proper for carrying into execution Congress's power "[t]o constitute Tribunals inferior to the Supreme Court," U.S. Const., Art. I, § 8, cl. 9, and to assure that those Tribunals may fairly and efficiently exercise "[t]he judicial Power of the United States," Art. III, § 1. As to "necessity": The federal courts can assuredly exist and function in the absence of § 1367 (d), but we long ago rejected the view that the Necessary and Proper Clause demands that an Act of Congress be "*absolutely* necessary" to the exercise of an enumerated power. *See McCulloch v. Maryland*. Rather, it suffices that § 1367 (d) is "conducive to the due administration of justice" in federal court, and is "plainly adapted" to that end.

10. Legislating Pursuant to the Treaty Power. In *Missouri v. Holland*, 252 U.S. 416 (1920), the Court upheld a federal statute protecting migratory birds. An earlier version of the statute had been struck down as beyond Congress' power under the Commerce Clause. The U.S. then entered into a treaty with Great Britain to protect endangered species migrating between the U.S. and Canada, and Congress re-enacted the statute. Justice Holmes found it not surprising that the treaty power could support legislation that would not be valid in the absence of an international agreement. "We do not mean to imply that there are no qualifications to the treaty-making power; but they must be ascertained in a different way. It is obvious that there may be matters of the sharpest exigency for the national well-being that an act of Congress could not deal with but that a treaty followed by such an act could."

In *Torres v. Mullin*, *cert. denied*, 124 S. Ct. 562 (2003), the Court refused to consider application of Article 36 of the Vienna Convention on Consular Relations. The treaty requires that a signatory nation (of which the U.S. is one) notify the consul of an arrested person's nation of his arrest and trial. The International Court of Justice held in the *LaGrand Case* (*F.R.G. v. U.S.*), 2001 ICJ No. 104, that U.S. courts may not foreclose convicted persons from raising this issue on appeal or even later in habeas corpus because there is no reason to suppose that either the accused or his counsel knew of the right at the time of trial. Mexico then sued the United States in the ICJ with respect to a number of Mexican nationals convicted in U.S. state courts without benefit of consular assistance, including several on death row. Torres is one of several on death row whose execution Mexico has sought to have stayed pending the ICJ ruling. His habeas corpus petition was denied by the Tenth Circuit and the Supreme Court denied certiorari in the case.

Justice Stevens provided an "opinion respecting the denial of certiorari" (he does not think it appropriate to "dissent" from a denial of certiorari, which in turn prompts some unusual pagination). He commented at 124 S. Ct. 919:

> Article VI, cl. 2, of our Constitution provides that the "Laws of the United States," expressly including "all Treaties made . . . under the Authority of the United States, shall be the supreme Law of the Land." The Court was unfaithful to that command when it held that Congress

> may not require county employees to check the background of prospective handgun purchasers, *Printz v. United States,* that Congress may not exercise its Article I powers to abrogate a State's common-law immunity from suit, *Seminole Tribe of Fla. v. Florida,* and that a State may not be required to provide its citizens with a remedy for its violation of their federal rights, *Alden v. Maine.* The Court is equally unfaithful to that command when it permits state courts to disregard the Nation's treaty obligations.

Justice Breyer, dissenting from the denial of certiorari at 124 S. Ct. 562, delved more thoroughly into the nature of treaty obligations. Although state and lower federal courts had held that this treaty was not "self-executing" and did not create "individual rights," the ICJ had disagreed. In Justice Breyer's view, if the ICJ is to be the authoritative interpreter of the treaty, then that interpretation would be binding on U.S. courts, both state and federal.

11. *U.S. Term Limits, Inc. v. Thornton*, 514 U.S. 779 (1995). The ongoing debate over what limits the Constitution places on the scope of federal power can be rephrased as a question of whether the federal government is a collection of people or a collection of state governments.

In the *Term Limits* case, the Court struck down "an amendment to the Arkansas State Constitution that prohibits the name of an otherwise-eligible candidate for Congress from appearing on the general election ballot if that candidate has already served three terms in the House of Representatives or two terms in the Senate. . . . Such a state-imposed restriction is contrary to the 'fundamental principle of our representative democracy,' embodied in the Constitution, that 'the people should choose whom they please to govern them.' *Powell v. McCormack,* 395 U.S. 486, 547 (1969). Allowing individual States to adopt their own qualifications for congressional service would be inconsistent with the Framers' vision of a uniform National Legislature representing the people of the United States. If the qualifications set forth in the text of the Constitution are to be changed, that text must be amended."

In dissent, Justice Thomas asserted:

> It is ironic that the Court bases today's decision on the right of the people to "choose whom they please to govern them." Under our Constitution, there is only one State whose people have the right to "choose whom they please" to represent Arkansas in Congress.
>
> Nothing in the Constitution deprives the people of each State of the power to prescribe eligibility requirements for the candidates who seek to represent them in Congress. The Constitution is simply silent on this question. And where the Constitution is silent, it raises no bar to action by the States or the people.

For the dissent, "[t]he ultimate source of the Constitution's authority is the consent of the people of each individual state, not the consent of the undifferentiated people of the nation as a whole."

Responding to the dissent, Justice Stevens for the majority argued that "the available historical and textual evidence, read in light of the basic principles of democracy underlying the Constitution . . . reveal the Framers' intent that neither Congress nor the States should possess the power to supplement the qualifications set forth in the text of the Constitution." Furthermore, the States could not have "reserved" this power because election of members of Congress was not a power that could have existed prior to ratification of the Constitution. It is a power that relates only to the federal government and must be decided by the federal government.

In a similar vein, Justice Kennedy concurred with the thought that "there exists a federal right of citizenship, a relationship between the people and their National Government, with which the States may not interfere."

Professor Sullivan says the core question in *Term Limits* was whether we are "one people insofar as we constitute the federal government, as the majority held, or rather, as the dissent would have it, irreducibly the peoples of the several states?"

> Sharply divided over whether constitutional text or history precluded state-imposed congressional term limits, the majority and dissenting opinions resorted ultimately to opposite structural default rules. According to the majority, the states have no powers respecting the federal government unless the Constitution expressly delegates them. It doesn't, so they don't. According to the dissent, the states may exercise all powers, even with respect to the federal government, that the Constitution does not expressly or by necessary implication withhold. It doesn't, so they do.

Kathleen Sullivan, *Dueling Sovereignties: Term Limits v. Thornton,* 109 Harv. L. Rev. 78, 79–80 (1995).

What does the Court mean when it asserts that "the basic principles of our democratic system" dictate that states lack power to add qualifications? On their face, do the Qualification Clauses embody these "basic principles"? If not, does the Court derive them from another constitutional provision? If no provision inculcates these principles, what renders a state's addition of qualifications unconstitutional? By way of examples, can a state disqualify convicted felons from voting in congressional elections or from serving in Congress? If so, how does this differ from term limits?

One unarguable effect of *Term Limits* is the end of state initiatives to impose term limits on members of Congress, leaving open the route of constitutional amendment. A more ephemeral effect is the degree to which it plays into the "states' rights" or "antifederalist" movement of the late twentieth century.

§ 2.02 THE COMMERCE POWER

[A] ESTABLISHING THE FOUNDATIONS (1790-1870)

"If there was any one object riding over every other in the adoption of the Constitution, it was to keep the commercial intercourse among the States free from all invidious and partial restraints." *Gibbons v. Ogden,* 22 U.S. (9 Wheat.) 1 (1824) (Johnson, J., concurring). In 1786, James Madison had written that "most of our political evils may be traced to our commercial ones." *See* 1 Charles Warren, The Supreme Court in United States History 568 (rev. ed. 1922). Problems of commerce were of central concern to the constitutional convention.

During the Confederation period, Congress had not been given the power to regulate commerce. While the national government had power to enter into treaties, the inability to ensure domestic compliance made the power meaningless. Foreign countries, especially Great Britain, faced with an impotent national government, freely imposed discriminatory trade restrictions on United States' goods and citizens. Interstate commerce fared no better. The states, in an effort to remedy the chaotic condition of their finances following the war, had begun to levy tariffs and imposts not only on foreign goods but on goods coming from or going to sister states. Such action naturally invited retaliation and trade wars were common. Again, the national government lacked power to act. As Madison stated in his "Preface to Debates in the Convention of 1787:"

> the want of authy. in Congs. to regulate Commerce had produced in foreign nations particularly G.B. a monopolizing policy injurious to the trade of the United States and destructive to their navigation. [The] same want of a general power over Commerce led to an exercise of this power separately, by the States, which not only proved abortive, but engendered rival, conflicting and angry regulation.

3 Max Farrand, Records of the Federal Convention of 1787.

Given this situation, it is not surprising that there was little debate at the constitutional convention on the question of giving Congress broad powers over commerce. As was stated by Alexander Hamilton in The Federalist, No. 11:

> The importance of the Union, in a commercial life, is one of those points, about which there is least room to entertain a difference of opinion, and which has in fact commanded the most general assent of men, who have any acquaintance with this subject.

Hamilton's words mildly foreshadowed the monumental struggles of the twentieth century over whether there exists a single "Union, in commercial life." The Commerce Clause, after an initial burst of interest, lay fallow for an entire century before the strains of an industrialized society created a new setting for concerted national action. But the foundations for expansion were set at the beginning by yet another Marshall opinion.

GIBBONS v. OGDEN

22 U.S. (9 Wheat.) 1, 6 L. Ed. 23 (1824)

[Livingston and Fulton had received from the New York legislature a monopoly for steamboat navigation within the jurisdictional waters of the state. Ogden was assigned the privilege of operating vessels between New York City and Elizabethtown, New Jersey. He subsequently sought to enjoin Gibbons, who operated under a federal license based on an act of Congress, from trading in the same waters. Gibbons appealed from an affirmance of a decree issuing the injunction.]

Chief Justice Marshall delivered the opinion of the Court.

The appellant contends that this decree is erroneous, because the laws which purport to give the exclusive privilege it sustains, are repugnant to the constitution and laws of the United States.

The words are: "Congress shall have power to regulate commerce with foreign nations, and among the several States, and with the Indian tribes."

The subject to be regulated is commerce; and our constitution being, as was aptly said at the bar, one of enumeration, and not of definition, to ascertain the extent of the power it becomes necessary to settle the meaning of the word. The counsel for the appellee would limit it to traffic, to buying and selling, or the interchange of commodities, and do not admit that it comprehends navigation. This would restrict a general term, applicable to many objects, to one of its significations. Commerce, undoubtedly, is traffic, but it is something more; it is intercourse. It describes the commercial intercourse between nations, and parts of nations, in all its branches, and is regulated by prescribing rules for carrying on that intercourse. The mind can scarcely conceive a system for regulating commerce between nations, which shall exclude all laws concerning navigation, which shall be silent on the admission of the vessels of the one nation into the ports of the other, and be confined to prescribing rules for the conduct of individuals, in the actual employment of buying and selling, or of barter.

If commerce does not include navigation, the government of the Union has no direct power over that subject, and can make no law prescribing what shall constitute American vessels, or requiring that they shall be navigated by American seamen. Yet this power has been exercised from the commencement of the government, has been exercised with the consent of all, and has been understood by all to be a commercial regulation. All America understands, and has uniformly understood, the word "commerce" to comprehend navigation. It was so understood, and must have been so understood, when the constitution was framed. The power over commerce, including navigation, was one of the primary objects for which the people of America adopted their government, and must have been contemplated in forming it. The convention must have used the word in that sense; because all have understood it in that sense, and the attempt to restrict it comes too late.

The word used in the constitution, then, comprehends, and has been always understood to comprehend, navigation within its meaning; and a power to regulate navigation is as expressly granted as if that term had been added to the word "commerce."

The subject to which the power is applied, is to commerce "among the several states." The word "among" means intermingled with. A thing which is among others, is intermingled with them. Commerce among the states cannot stop at the external boundary line of each state, but may be introduced into the interior.

It is not intended to say that these words comprehend that commerce which is completely internal, which is carried on between man and man in a state, or between different parts of the same state, and which does not extend to or affect other states. Such a power would be inconvenient, and is certainly unnecessary. Comprehensive as the word "among" is, it may very properly be restricted to that commerce which concerns more states than one. The phrase is not one which would probably have been selected to indicate the completely interior traffic of a state, because it is not an apt phrase for that purpose; and the enumeration of the particular classes of commerce to which the power was to be extended, would not have been made had the intention been to extend the power to every description. The enumeration presupposes something not enumerated; and that something, if we regard the language or the subject of the sentence, must be the exclusively internal commerce of a state. The genius and character of the whole government seem to be, that its action is to be applied to all the external concerns of the nation, and to those internal concerns which affect the states generally; but not to those which are completely within a particular state, which do not affect other states, and with which it is not necessary to interfere, for the purpose of executing some of the general powers of the government. The completely internal commerce of a state, then, may be considered as reserved for the state itself.

But, in regulating commerce with foreign nations, the power of Congress does not stop at the jurisdictional lines of the several states. It would be a very useless power if it could not pass those lines. The commerce of the United States with foreign nations, is that of the whole United States. Every district has a right to participate in it. The deep streams which penetrate our country in every direction, pass through the interior of almost every state in the Union, and furnish the means of exercising this right. If Congress has the power to regulate it, that power must be exercised whenever the subject exists. If it exists within the states, if a foreign voyage may commence or terminate at a port within a state, then the power of Congress may be exercised within a state.

We are now arrived at the inquiry, What is this power?

It is the power to regulate; that is, to prescribe the rule by which commerce is to be governed. This power, like all others vested in Congress, is complete in itself, may be exercised to its utmost extent, and acknowledges no limitations, other than are prescribed in the constitution. These are expressed in plain terms, and do not affect the questions which arise in this case, or which have been discussed at the bar. If, as has always been understood, the sovereignty of Congress, though limited to specified objects, is plenary as to those objects, the power over commerce with foreign nations, and among the several states, is vested in Congress as absolutely as it would be in a single government, having in its constitution the same restrictions on the exercise of the power as are found in the constitution of the United States. The wisdom and the discretion of Congress, their identity with the people, and the influence which their constituents possess at elections, are, in this, as in many other instances, as that, for example, of declaring war, the sole restraints on which they have relied, to secure them from its abuse. They are the restraints on which the people most often rely solely, in all representative governments.

The power of Congress, then, comprehends navigation within the limits of every state in the Union; so far as that navigation may be, in any manner, connected with "commerce with foreign nations, or among the several states, or with the Indian tribes." It may, of consequence, pass the jurisdictional line of New York, and act upon the very waters to which the prohibition now under consideration applies.

[Those sections of Chief Justice Marshall's opinion and Justice Johnson's concurrence dealing with the power of the states to regulate the subject matter of interstate commerce are set forth below, p. 220.]

NOTES

1. *Defining commerce.* Counsel for the appellee in *Gibbons v. Ogden* argued that commerce should be limited to "traffic, to buying and selling or to the exchange of commodities," and not "navigation." Marshall rejected this argument and gave a broad definition to the term commerce. Is such a broad definition of the term appropriate? After examining the debates at the Constitutional Convention, one commentator concludes:

> The inclusion of the subject-matter "navigation" within the "commerce" whose regulation was confided to Congress was thus conspicuously brought to the attention of all concerned at various stages in the formulation and adoption of the Constitution, was never objected to as an erroneous interpretation of the power, and in the upshot won wide acquiescence.

Albert Abel, *The Commerce Clause in the Constitutional Convention and in Contemporary Comment,* 25 MINN. L. REV. 432, 456 (1941).

2. *Intrastate activities.* Would Marshall's formulation of the commerce power permit Congress to regulate transactions even if there were no physical movement "between" states? Note that the Constitution does not use the words "interstate commerce." In 1787, it might have made little sense to ask whether Congress could regulate "local" activity if it "concerns more than one state." At that time, there were no electronic communications facilities, no stock or bond markets, and no history of what we know today as the effects felt in one state from a seemingly unrelated commercial transaction in another state.

In *The Daniel Ball,* 77 U.S. (10 Wall.) 557 (1871), the Court held that a vessel operating solely on the waters of Michigan's Grand River, exclusively within Michigan's borders, was nevertheless within the scope of Congress' regulatory powers because the ship "was employed in transporting goods destined for other states or goods brought from without the limits of Michigan and destined to places within that state." The Court concluded that the ship

> was employed as an instrument of [commerce among the States]; for whenever a commodity has begun to move as an article of trade from one State to another, commerce in that commodity between the States has commenced. The fact that several different and independent agencies are employed in transporting the commodity, some acting entirely in one State, and some acting through two or more States, does in no respect affect the character of the transaction. To the extent in which each agency acts in that transportation, it is subject to the regulation of Congress.

Despite Marshall's expansive language, the term "among" soon came to mean "between," and courts prior to the New Deal tended to require a showing of movement across state lines in order to constitute interstate commerce. As you read the materials below, consider the following:

> [I]f "among" the states had continued to be construed as covering all commercial transactions affecting more than one state and not merely as transactions "between" states, there would have been no need for the various "affectation" doctrines of recent years under which the commerce power has been expanded to reach intrastate activities.

Robert Stern, *The Scope of the Phrase Interstate Commerce,* 41 A.B.A.J. 823 (1955).

[B] FRAMING THE MODERN INTERSTATE COMMERCE POWER (1870-1976)

Little opportunity to apply Chief Justice Marshall's broad organic theory of commerce, or his expansive concept of national power, arose during most of the nineteenth century. Cases arising under the commerce clause essentially presented issues involving the power of the states to regulate the subject matter of interstate commerce. There was little perceived need or demand for positive federal legislation in the still-nascent national economy and hence no opportunity for judicial review of congressional action.

In the latter part of the nineteenth century, economic conditions changed. The Industrial Revolution produced working conditions that many people believed intolerable, reduced the dominance of the self-sustenance agrarian economy, and fostered inequality of bargaining power between worker and employer; these conditions prompted demands for reform of labor relations law. It was the era of the great trusts with interlocking components transcending state lines. Cross-continental railroads made state regulation of transportation hopelessly inadequate. Changing economic conditions produced an increasing demand for national intervention. Congressional action came initially through the Interstate Commerce Act of 1887 and the Sherman Anti-Trust Act of 1890. This legislation affected rate fixing practices, contracts, combinations and monopolistic activity which arguably occurred locally and was thus subject to state regulation. The question was whether Congress' power to regulate "commerce . . . among the States" provided sufficient constitutional nexus to make this legislation effective.

Apart from the problem of the economy, there arose pressing social, moral, health and safety concerns, such as child labor, gambling, obscenity, prostitution (known as the white slave traffic), lack of industrial safety, and unsafe and impure products. Again, the problems transcended state lines and the states individually either could not or would not act. Although there was a demand for social reform through federal legislation in the latter part of the nineteenth century, it was during the progressive era in the early twentieth century that the demand for federal intervention became especially intense. And again the national government responded through the enactment of social welfare legislation — the Pure Food and Drug Law of 1906, the Meat Inspection Acts of 1906 and 1907, the White Slave Traffic Act of 1910, and the Child Labor Act of 1916. But this legislation involved some of the most established preserves of state power. Could the Commerce Clause do the job?

[1] Searching for Federal Regulatory Power (1870-1932)

[a] Prohibiting commerce: a national police power?

The police power " '[a]ims directly to secure and promote the public welfare' by subjecting to restraint or compulsion the members of the community. It is the power by which the government abridges the freedom of action or the free use of property of the individual in order that the [public] welfare may not be jeopardized." Robert Cushman, *The National Police Power Under the Commerce Clause of the Constitution,* 3 MINN. L. REV. 289, 290 (1919). The Constitution does not grant Congress the power to enact legislation for the national morals, health, safety, and well-being; four resolutions seeking to confer such a power were rejected at the Constitutional Convention. Consequently, it is arguable that the police power protection is exclusively the responsibility of the states and that the federal government cannot legislate for social welfare objectives.

CHAMPION v. AMES [THE LOTTERY CASE]
188 U.S. 321, 23 S. Ct. 321, 47 L. Ed. 492 (1903)

[Appellant was arrested and indicted for violation of the Federal Lottery Act of 1895, prohibiting the importation, mailing, or interstate transit of lottery tickets. He appealed from an order of the circuit court dismissing a writ of habeas corpus, based on the alleged unconstitutionality of the federal statute. The importance and difficulty of the question presented is suggested by the fact that the case was argued three times before the Supreme Court, and the Court, in upholding the constitutionality of the Act, divided 5-4.]

JUSTICE HARLAN delivered the opinion of the Court.

We have said that the carrying from State to State of lottery tickets constitutes interstate commerce, and that the regulation of such commerce is within the power of Congress under the Constitution. Are we prepared to say that a provision which is, in effect, a *prohibition* of the carriage of such articles from State to State is not a fit or appropriate mode for the *regulation* of that particular kind of commerce? If lottery traffic, *carried on through interstate commerce*, is a matter of which Congress may take cognizance and over which its power may be exerted, can it be possible that it must tolerate the traffic, and simply regulate the manner in which it may be carried on? Or may not Congress, for the protection of the people of all the States, and under the power to regulate interstate commerce, devise such means, within the scope of the Constitution, and not prohibited by it, as will drive that traffic out of commerce among the States?

If a state, when considering legislation for the suppression of lotteries within its own limits, may properly take into view the evils that inhere in the raising of money, in that mode, why may not Congress, invested with the power to regulate commerce among the several states, provide that such commerce shall not be polluted by the carrying of lottery tickets from one state to another? In this connection it must not be forgotten that the power of Congress to regulate commerce among the states is plenary, is complete in itself, and is subject to no limitations except such as may be found in the Constitution. What provision in that instrument can be regarded as limiting the exercise of the power granted? What clause can be cited which, in any degree, countenances the suggestion that one may, of right, carry or cause to be carried from one state to another that which will harm the public morals? [S]urely it will not be said to be a part of anyone s liberty, as recognized by the supreme law of the land, that he shall be allowed to introduce into commerce among the states an element that will be confessedly injurious to the public morals.

If it be said that the act of 1895 is inconsistent with the Tenth Amendment, reserving to the states respectively, or to the people, the powers not delegated to the United States, the answer is that the power to regulate commerce among the states has been expressly delegated to Congress.

As a State may, for the purpose of guarding the morals of its own people, forbid all sales of lottery tickets within its limits, so Congress, for the purpose of guarding the people of the United States against the "widespread pestilence of lotteries" and to protect the commerce which concerns all the States, may prohibit the carrying of lottery tickets from one State to another. In legislating upon the subject of the traffic in lottery tickets, as carried on through interstate commerce, Congress only supplemented the action of those States — perhaps all of them — which, for the protection of the public morals, prohibit the drawing of lotteries, as well as the sale or circulation of lottery tickets, within their respective limits. It said, in effect, that it would not permit the declared policy of the States, which sought to protect their people against the mischiefs of the lottery business, to be overthrown or disregarded by the agency of interstate commerce. We should hesitate long before adjudging that an evil of such appalling character, carried on through interstate commerce, cannot be met and crushed by the only power competent to that end.

It is said, however, that if, in order to suppress lotteries carried on through interstate commerce, Congress may exclude lottery tickets from such commerce, that principle leads necessarily to the conclusion that Congress may arbitrarily exclude from commerce among the States any article, commodity or thing, of whatever kind or nature, or however useful or valuable, which it may choose, no matter with what motive, to declare shall not be carried from one State to another. It will be time enough to consider the constitutionality of such legislation when we must do so. The present case does not require the court to declare the full extent of the power that Congress may exercise in the regulation of commerce among the States. But, the possible abuse of a power is not an argument against its existence. There is probably no governmental power that may not be exerted to the injury of the public. If what is done by Congress is manifestly in excess of the powers granted to it, then upon the courts will rest the duty of adjudging that its action is neither legal nor binding upon the people. But if what Congress does is within the limits of its power, and is simply unwise or injurious, the remedy is that suggested by Chief Justice Marshall in *Gibbons v. Ogden,* when he said:

> The wisdom and the discretion of Congress, their identity with the people, and the influence which their constituents possess at elections, are, in this, as in many other instances, as that, for example, of declaring war, the sole restraints on which they have relied, to secure them from its abuse. They are the restraints on which the people must often rely solely, in all representative governments.

NOTE

The decision in the *Lottery Case* provided the doctrinal foundation for an outpouring of congressional social welfare legislation which was then legitimated by the Courts. This included legislation dealing with the white slave traffic (*Hoke v. United States,* 227 U.S. 308 (1913)); impure food and drugs (*Hipolite Egg Co. v. United States,* 220 U.S. 45 (1911)); *Weeks v. United States,* 245 U.S. 618 (1918)); shipment of prize fight films (*Weber v. Freed,* 239 U.S. 325 (1915)). But then came *Hammer v. Dagenhart.*

HAMMER v. DAGENHART

247 U.S. 251, 38 S. Ct. 529, 62 L. Ed. 1101 (1918)

Justice Day delivered the opinion of the Court.

A bill was filed in the United States district court for the western district of North Carolina by a father in his own behalf and as next friend of his two minor sons, one under the age of fourteen years and the other between the ages of fourteen and sixteen years, employees in a cotton mill at Charlotte, North Carolina, to enjoin the enforcement of the act of Congress intended to prevent interstate commerce in the products of child labor. The district court held the act unconstitutional and entered a decree enjoining its enforcement.

The attack upon the act rests upon three propositions: First. It is not a regulation of interstate and foreign commerce. Second. It contravenes the Tenth Amendment to the Constitution. Third. It conflicts with the Fifth Amendment to the Constitution. The controlling question for decision is: Is it within the authority of Congress in regulating commerce among the states to prohibit the transportation in interstate commerce of manufactured goods, the product of a factory in which, within thirty days prior to their removal therefrom, children under the age of fourteen have been employed or permitted to work, or children between the ages of fourteen and sixteen years have been employed or permitted to work more than eight hours in any day, or more than six days in any week, or after the hour of 7 o'clock P.M. or before the hour of 6 o'clock A.M.?

In *Gibbons v. Ogden,* CHIEF JUSTICE MARSHALL, speaking for this court, and defining the extent and nature of the commerce power, said: "It is the power to regulate — that is, to prescribe the rule by which commerce is to be governed." In other words, the power is one to control the means by which commerce is carried on, which is directly the contrary of the assumed right to forbid commerce from moving and thus destroy it as to particular commodities. But it is insisted that adjudged cases in this court establish the doctrine that the power to regulate given to Congress incidentally includes the authority to prohibit the movement of ordinary commodities, and therefore that the subject is not open for discussion. The cases demonstrate the contrary. They rest upon the character of the particular subjects dealt with and the fact that the scope of governmental authority, state or national, possessed over them, is such that the authority to prohibit is, as to them, but the exertion of the power to regulate.

[The Court summarized the holdings of the *Lottery Case* and its progeny noted above.] In each of these instances the use of interstate transportation was necessary to the accomplishment of harmful results. In other words, although the power over interstate transportation was to regulate, that could only be accomplished by prohibiting the use of the facilities of interstate commerce to effect the evil intended.

This element is wanting in the present case. The thing intended to be accomplished by this statute is the denial of the facilities of interstate commerce to those manufacturers in the states who employ children within the prohibited ages. The act in its effect does not regulate transportation among the states, but aims to standardize the ages at which children may be employed in mining and manufacturing within the states. The goods shipped are of themselves harmless. The act permits them to be freely shipped after thirty days from the time of their removal from the factory. When offered for shipment, and before transportation begins, the labor of their production is over, and the mere fact that they were intended for interstate commerce transportation does not make their production subject to Federal control under the commerce power.

Over interstate transportation, or its incidents, the regulatory power of Congress is ample, but the production of articles intended for interstate commerce is a matter of local regulation. If it were otherwise, all manufacture intended for interstate shipment would be brought under Federal control to the practical exclusion of the authority of the states — a result certainly not contemplated by the framers of the Constitution when they vested in Congress the authority to regulate commerce among the states. *Kidd v. Pearson,* 128 U.S. 1 (1888).

It is further contended that the authority of Congress may be exerted to control interstate commerce in the shipment of child-made goods because of the effect of the circulation of such goods in other states where the evil of this class of labor has been recognized by local legislation, and the right to thus employ child labor has been more rigorously restrained than in the state of production. In other words, that the unfair competition thus engendered may be controlled by closing the channels of interstate commerce to manufacturers in those states where the local laws do not meet what Congress deems to be the more just standard of other states.

There is no power vested in Congress to require the states to exercise their police power so as to prevent possible unfair competition. Many causes may co-operate to give one state, by reason of local laws or conditions, an economic advantage over others. The commerce clause was not intended to give to Congress a general authority to equalize such conditions. In some of the states laws have been passed fixing minimum wages for women; in others the local law regulates the hours of labor of women in various employments. Business done in such states may be at an economic disadvantage when compared with states which have no such regulations; surely, this fact does not give Congress the power to deny transportation in interstate commerce to those who carry on business where the hours of labor and the rate of compensation for women have not been fixed by a standard in the use in other states and approved by Congress.

The grant of power to Congress over the subject of interstate commerce was to enable it to regulate such commerce, and not to give it authority to control the states in their exercise of the police power over local trade and manufacture. The grant of authority over a purely Federal matter was not intended to destroy the local power always existing and carefully reserved to the states in the Tenth Amendment to the Constitution. Police regulations relating to the internal trade and affairs of the states have been uniformly recognized as within such control. The maintenance of the authority of the states over matters purely local is as essential to the preservation of our institutions as is the conservation of the supremacy of the Federal power in all matters entrusted to the nation by the Federal Constitution.

In interpreting the Constitution it must never be forgotten that the Nation is made up of States to which are entrusted the powers of local government. And to them and to the people the powers not expressly delegated to the National Government are reserved. To sustain this statute would not be, in our judgment, a recognition of the lawful exertion of congressional authority over interstate commerce, but would sanction an invasion by the Federal power of the control of a matter purely local in its character, and over which no authority has been delegated to Congress in conferring the power to regulate commerce among the states.

We have neither authority nor disposition to question the motives of Congress in enacting this legislation. The purposes intended must be attained consistently with constitutional limitations, and not by an invasion of the powers of the states. The far-reaching result of upholding the act cannot be more plainly indicated than by pointing out that if Congress can thus regulate matters entrusted to local authority by prohibition of the movement of commodities in interstate commerce, all freedom of commerce will be at an end, and the power of the states over local matters may be eliminated, and thus our system of government be practically destroyed.

JUSTICE HOLMES [joined by JUSTICE MCKENNA, JUSTICE BRANDEIS, and JUSTICE CLARKE], dissenting:

> The objection urged against the power is that the states have exclusive control over their methods of production and that Congress cannot meddle with them; and taking the proposition in the sense of direct intermeddling I agree to it and suppose that no one denies it. But if an act is within the powers specifically conferred upon Congress, it seems to me that it is not made any less constitutional because of the indirect effects that it may have, however obvious it may be that it will have those effects; and that we are not at liberty upon such grounds to hold it void.

The first step in my argument is to make plain what no one is likely to dispute — that the statute in question is within the power expressly given to Congress if considered only as to its immediate effects, and that if invalid it is so only upon some collateral ground. The statute confines itself to prohibiting the carriage of certain goods in interstate or foreign commerce. Congress is given power to regulate such commerce in unqualified terms. It would not be argued today that the power to regulate does not include the power to prohibit. Regulation means the prohibition of something, and when interstate commerce is the matter to be regulated I cannot doubt that the regulations may prohibit any part of such commerce that Congress sees fit to forbid.

The question, then, is narrowed to whether the exercise of its otherwise constitutional power by Congress can be pronounced unconstitutional because of its possible reaction upon the conduct of the states in a matter upon which I have admitted that they are free from direct control. I should have thought that that matter had been disposed of so fully as to leave no room for doubt. I should have thought that the most conspicuous decisions of this court had made it clear that the power to regulate commerce and other constitutional powers could not be cut down or qualified by the fact that it might interfere with the carrying out of the domestic policy of any State.

It does not matter whether the supposed evil precedes or follows the transportation. It is enough that, in the opinion of Congress, the transportation encourages the evil. I may add that in the cases on the so-called White Slave Act it was established that the means adopted by Congress as convenient to the exercise of its power might have the character of police regulations.

The notion that prohibition is any less prohibition when applied to things now thought evil I do not understand. But if there is any matter upon which civilized countries have agreed — far more unanimously than they have with regard to intoxicants and some other matters over which this country is now emotionally aroused — it is the evil of premature and excessive child labor. I should have thought that if we were to introduce our own moral conceptions where, in my opinion, they do not belong, this was preeminently a case for upholding the exercise of all its power by the United States.

But I had thought that the propriety of the exercise of a power admitted to exist in some cases was for the consideration of Congress alone, and that this court always had disavowed the right to intrude its judgment upon questions of policy or morals.

The act does not meddle with anything belonging to the states. They may regulate their internal affairs and their domestic commerce as they like. But when they seek to send their products across the state line they are no longer within their rights. If there were no Constitution and no Congress their power to cross the line would depend upon their neighbors. Under the Constitution such commerce belongs not to the states, but to Congress to regulate. It may carry out its views of public policy whatever indirect effect they may have upon the activities of the states. Instead of being encountered by a prohibitive tariff at her boundaries, the state encounters the public policy of the United States which it is for Congress to express. The public policy of the United States is shaped with a view to the benefit of the nation as a whole. If, as has been the case within the memory of men still living, a state should take a different view of the propriety of sustaining a lottery from that which generally prevails, I cannot believe that the fact would require a different decision from that reached in *Champion v. Ames*. Yet in that case it would be said with quite as much force as in this that Congress was attempting to intermeddle with the state's domestic affairs. The national welfare as understood by Congress may require a different attitude within its sphere from that of some self-seeking state. It seems to me entirely constitutional for Congress to enforce its understanding by all the means at its command.

NOTES

1. *Dual federalism.* *Hammer* is generally thought to have adopted a theory of "dual federalism." Professor Corwin asserted that this concept synthesizes four axioms:

> 1. The national government is one of enumerated powers only; 2. Also the purposes which it may constitutionally promote are few; 3. Within their respective spheres the two centers of government are "sovereign" and hence "equal"; 4. The relation of the two centers with each other is one of tension rather than collaboration.

Edward Corwin, *The Passing of Dual Federalism*, 36 VA. L. REV. 4 (1950).

In the words of another commentator, dual federalism envisions "two mutually exclusive, reciprocally limiting fields of power — that of the national government and of the States. The two authorities confront each other as equals at a precise constitutional line, defining their respective jurisdictions." Mason, *Federalism: The Role of the Court*, in VALERIE EARLE, FEDERALISM: INFINITE VARIETY IN THEORY AND PRACTICE 24–25 (1968). In what sense does the analysis adopted in *Hammer* represent adoption of the dual federalism theory?

Is the dual federalism model consistent with constitutional text? Consider the following textual argument against dual federalism:

> In Article I, Section 8, the Constitution enumerates most of Congress's powers. Yet Article I, Section 10 explicitly prohibits to the states

> specified powers granted to Congress under Section 8. If the Framers had assumed the existence of dual federalism, there arguably would have been no reason to include Section 10, because it would have been universally understood that the express grant of a particular power to the federal government would have automatically deprived the states of that power. [T]he fact that Section 10 expressly excludes only selected federal powers would seem to imply that to the contrary, the exercise of state authority in the areas of federal power *not* expressly prohibited was to be permitted (subject, of course, to the possibility of federal legislative preemption).

MARTIN H. REDISH, THE CONSTITUTION AS POLITICAL STRUCTURE 31 (1995).

2. *The Tenth Amendment.* Examine the language of the Tenth Amendment. Is it consistent with the analysis employed in *Hammer*? Note that Justice Day in *Hammer* sought to insert the word, "expressly" into the Tenth Amendment. The Constitutional Convention twice rejected proposals for such a revision. Compare the Court's defense of dual federalism in *Hammer* with the first Justice Harlan's treatment of the Tenth Amendment in the *Lottery Case.*

3. *A national police power.* Does the power to regulate commerce include some incidental power to prohibit the movement of goods?

> [A] modicum of reflection must suffice to show that any regulation whatsoever of commerce necessarily infers some measure of power to prohibit it, since it is the very nature of regulation to lay down terms on which the activity regulated will be permitted and for non-compliance with which it will not be permitted.

Edward Corwin, *Congress' Power to Prohibit Commerce: A Crucial Constitutional Issue,* 18 CORNELL L.Q. 477 (1933). Further, it would seem reasonable that Congress could enact police power-type legislation for the well-being of commercial activity itself, *e.g.*, safety statutes. Is there any judicially manageable standard for limiting the conditions that Congress may constitutionally impose as a price for engaging in interstate commerce?

The police power is usually defined to include protection of health, safety, welfare, and morals. In sustaining the Mann Act, prohibiting the transportation of women and girls across state lines for immoral purposes, the Court in *Hoke v. United States,* 227 U.S. 308 (1913), provided an especially broad statement of Congress' emerging police power:

> [S]urely if the facility of interstate transportation can be taken away from the demoralization of lotteries, the debasement of obscene literature, the contagion of diseased cattle or persons, the impurity of food and drugs, the like facility can be taken away from the systematic enticement to and the enslavement in prostitution and the debauchery of women, and more insistently of girls.
>
> The principle established by the cases is the simple one, when rid of confusing and distracting considerations, that Congress has power

> over transportation "among the several States," that the power is complete in itself, and that Congress, as an incident to it, may adopt not only means necessary but convenient to its exercise, and the means may have the quality of police regulations.

Justice Day in *Hammer* seeks to distinguish the prior "police power" cases on the basis of "the character of the particular subjects dealt with." Is the focus of the Court on the harmful character of the goods shipped or on a finding that "the use of interstate transportation was necessary to the accomplishment of harmful results?" Assuming the relevance of the character of the subject, who is to evaluate the harm, the Court or Congress?

4. *Effect and purpose.* The Court in *Hammer* concludes that the "effect" of the Child Labor Act is to regulate the age at which children may be employed in production, which occurs prior to transportation, and is "a matter of local regulation." But should an improper local "effect" obviate an otherwise constitutional regulation? Is that result consistent with the supremacy clause?

The attempt of the Court in *Hammer* to make the validity of congressional legislation turn on the character of the harm necessitates a probe of congressional purpose. Is this what was meant by Marshall in *McCulloch* that Congress cannot, "under the pretext of executing its powers," enact laws designed to achieve objectives not entrusted by the Constitution to the federal government?

5. *Regulating interstate competition.* Justice Day asserts that "[t]he commerce clause was not intended to give Congress a general authority to equalize economic conditions." The Court has repeatedly held that a state cannot enact legislation designed to give its producers a competitive advantage against out-of-state competition. *See* Chapter 3. "Why, then, should not Congress exercise the power which, after all, the Constitution confers upon *it* and not upon the Court, with the same objective in mind, and thereby equalize, if it can, conditions of competition among the states according to *its* view of sound social policy?" *See* Edward Corwin, *Congress' Power to Prohibit Commerce: A Crucial Constitutional Issue,* 18 CORNELL L.Q. 477, 496 (1933).

A primary motive in the adoption of the Commerce Clause was the elimination of economic rivalry which characterized the Confederation period. Under the Articles of Confederation, the states had the express right of prohibiting "the exportation or importation of any species of goods or commodities whatever." If the states surrendered this regulatory power, does it necessarily follow that Congress must have the power to prevent a vacuum of regulatory power? William Sutherland, *The Child Labor Cases and the Constitution,* 8 CORNELL L. REV. 338, 348 (1923).

6. *The Child Labor Tax Case.* Congress sought to circumvent the decision of *Hammer v. Dagenhart* by enacting a statute imposing a prohibitory tax upon manufacturers employing child labor. In *Bailey v. Drexel Furniture Co. (The Child Labor Tax Case),* 259 U.S. 20 (1922), Justice Taft for eight members of the Court, including three out of the four dissenters in *Hammer* (Holmes, Brandeis and McKenna), held the tax unconstitutional. Eventually, *Hammer v. Dagenhart* was overruled in *United States v. Darby,* p. 96.

[b] Streams of commerce

In *Stafford v. Wallace,* 258 U.S. 495 (1922), the Court upheld the constitutionality of the Packers and Stockyards Act of 1921 as applied to local dealers in Chicago stockyards. The Court spoke of a "stream" or "current" of commerce.

> The stockyards are not a place of rest or final destination. Thousands of head of livestock arrive daily by carload and trainload lots, and must be promptly sold and disposed of and moved out, to give place to the constantly flowing traffic that presses behind. The stockyards are but a throat through which the current flows, and the transactions which occur therein are only incident to this current from the West to the East, and from one state to another. Such transactions cannot be separated from the movement to which they contribute and necessarily take on its character.

It followed that the local activities were only a part of the interstate commerce that Congress could regulate. Citing to its earlier decision in *Swift v. United States,* 196 U.S. 375 (1905), the Court declared:

> The application of the commerce clause of the Constitution in the *Swift Case* was the result of the natural development of interstate commerce under modern conditions. It was the inevitable recognition of the great central fact that such streams of commerce from one part of the country to another, which are everflowing, are in their very essence the commerce among the states and with foreign nations, which historically it was one of the chief purposes of the Constitution to bring under national protection and control. This Court declined to defeat this purpose in respect of such a stream and take it out of complete national regulation by a nice and technical inquiry into the noninterstate character of some of its necessary incidents and facilities, when considered alone and without reference to their association with the movement of which they were an essential but subordinate part.

If Congress could reach activities at the throat, could it similarly regulate activity at the mouth, e.g., production? at the stomach, *e.g.*, sales to the consumer or use of the product?

[c] Direct and indirect effects

During the formative period of the early twentieth century, even if the Court were unwilling to characterize an activity as part of interstate commerce, congressional regulatory power might nevertheless be held to reach the activity if it directly affected commerce. Some local activities had such a "close and substantial" relation to interstate commerce that their regulation would be reasonable to foster and protect interstate commerce.

***Houston, E. & W. Tex. Ry. v. United States (The Shreveport Rate Cases),* 234 U.S. 342 (1914)**. The Court upheld federal controls over rates charged by a railroad for trips wholly within the state of Texas. The Interstate Commerce Commission had been created by Congress and charged with the authority to regulate freight charges of the railroads. The ICC found that rates between Tyler, Texas and Dallas were less than the rates between Tyler and Shreveport, Louisiana, which was closer than Dallas. The result, of course, would be that cotton and other East Texas products would be shipped to Dallas for processing rather than to Louisiana. The ICC ordered equalization of the freight charges. The Supreme Court upheld the rate order on the ground that congressional power over interstate commerce included "all matters having such a close and substantial relation to interstate traffic that the control is essential or appropriate to the security of the traffic, to the efficiency of the interstate service, and to the maintenance of conditions under which interstate commerce may be conducted upon fair terms and without molestation or hindrance."

Some of the most significant limitations on congressional power during these formative years resulted from the Supreme Court's holding that federal statutes could reach only "direct effects" on interstate commerce. The Sherman Antitrust Act of 1890 prohibited combinations or monopolies in restraint of trade which had an "effect" on interstate commerce.

***United States v. E.C. Knight & Co.*, 156 U.S. 1 (1895).** The Justice Department sought an injunction against the acquisition of other companies by the American Sugar Refining Co. which would give the company control of 98% of the sugar production in the country. The Court held that Congress could not regulate manufacturing, a local activity subject to the police powers of the states. "Commerce succeeds to manufacture, and is not part of it." *E.C. Knight* was followed in a number of cases dealing with mining and manufacturing, in which the Court held that those activities were not part of interstate commerce no matter how large and far-flung the company or industry involved.

Nor could Congress regulate manufacturing because of its relation to interstate commerce. Control over manufacturing "affects [commerce] only incidentally and indirectly." The challenged actions of the Sugar Trust "bore no direct relation to commerce between [among?] the States." Defining the commerce power to allow Congress to regulate local activities such as manufacturing would excessively intrude on state power. "Slight reflection will show that if the national power extends to all contracts and combinations in manufacture, agriculture, mining, and productive industries, whose ultimate result may affect external commerce, comparatively little of business operations and affairs would be left for state control."

[2] The New Deal Confrontation (1932-1937)

The stock market's crash of 1929 and the trauma of the Great Depression swept Franklin D. Roosevelt into office in 1932 with the promise of a New Deal for Americans. The programs of the New Deal were designed to ameliorate the impact of the depression by regulating prices of goods, regulating wages and hours of workers, providing jobs through public works programs, and strengthening federal controls on financial markets. The early challenges to the philosophy represented by the efforts, produced Supreme Court results that were not favorable to the administration.

***Carter v. Carter Coal Co.*, 298 U.S. 238 (1936).** The Court dealt with a challenge to the Bituminous Coal Conservation Act of 1935. Congress had attempted to regulate labor relations in the depressed coal industry by requiring collective bargaining and setting minimum wages and maximum hours. The wage and hour provisions were designed not so much to put more money into the pockets of individual workers as to force the creation of more jobs. The Court was not impressed by efforts to characterize coal mining as an industry affecting interstate commerce or as producing goods that would enter the stream of commerce. Justice Sutherland, for the Court, stated "Mining brings the subject of commerce into existence. Commerce disposes of it." Citing concern for the vitality of federalist principles, Justice Sutherland similarly limited Congress' power to reach local activity to that which "directly" affects commerce.

> Whether the effect of a given activity or condition is direct or indirect is not always easy to determine. The word "direct" implies that the activity or condition invoked or blamed shall operate proximately — not mediately, remotely, or collaterally — to produce the effect. It connotes the absence of an efficient intervening agency or condition. And the extent of the effect bears no logical relation to its character. The distinction between a direct and an indirect effect turns, not upon the magnitude of either the cause or the effect, but entirely upon the manner in which the effect has been brought about. If the production by one man of a single ton of coal intended for interstate sale and shipment, and actually so sold and shipped, affects interstate commerce indirectly, the effect does not become direct by multiplying the tonnage, or increasing the number of men employed, or adding to the expense or complexities of the business, or by all combined. It is quite true that rules of law are sometimes qualified by considerations of degree, as the government argues. But the matter of degree has no bearing upon the question here, since that question is not — What is the *extent* of the local activity or condition, or the *extent* of the effect produced upon interstate commerce? but: — What is the *relation* between the activity or condition and the effect?

All evils resulting from disruptive labor conditions were "local evils over which the federal government has no legislative control."

The "direct" effects test was also employed in *Schechter Poultry Corp. v. United States*, 295 U.S. 495 (1935). As part of the National Industrial Recovery Act, Congress authorized boards composed of industry representatives in local communities to set standards for wages and hours. Schechter was a poultry distributor in Brooklyn who received chickens from Pennsylvania, slaughtered and dressed them for delivery to retailers in the New York area. He required his employees to work longer hours than the maximum set by the local board and was prosecuted. The Court held that the chickens had left the stream of interstate commerce when they came to rest at Schechter's business in Brooklyn, and that the hours worked by his few employees had no direct effect on commerce.

Consider the critique by soon-to-be-Justice Jackson:

> [T]hese words [direct-indirect] are not in the Constitution. The majority in [*Carter*], asking [its] non-constitutional question, was able to answer it by simply observing that labor practices in mining must necessarily affect production first, and then interstate commerce. Since there was an intervening effect, the effect on commerce was indirect. And so a national government that has power, through the Federal Trade Commission, to prohibit the giving of prizes with penny candy shipped by the manufacturer from one state to another, was powerless to deal with the causes of critical stoppages in the gigantic bituminous coal industry.

Robert Jackson, The Struggle for Judicial Supremacy: A Study Of a Crisis in American Power Politics 162–63 (1941).

In 1937, President Roosevelt outlined his "court-packing plan," calling for the addition of a new seat on the Court for each Justice over the age of 70. This would have given the president six immediate appointments and a sympathetic majority of ten members of a Court of 15.

Whether for its own reasons or under the threat of court-packing, the Court recanted. In *NLRB v. Jones & Laughlin Steel Corp.*, 301 U.S. 1 (1937), Justice Roberts and Chief Justice Hughes joined the Court's liberal bloc to sustain broad national intervention in the economy. There is evidence available that the votes in this case were cast before the court-packing plan was announced. While the Court might have applied the stream of commerce doctrine to sustain application of the National Labor Relations Act to the vertically-integrated steel corporation, Chief Justice Hughes instead turned to the broader conception of Congress' commerce power:

> The fundamental principle is that the power to regulate commerce is the power to enact "all appropriate legislation" for "its protection and advancement." Although activities may be intrastate in character when separately considered, if they have such a close and substantial relation to interstate commerce that their control is essential or appropriate to protect that commerce from burdens and obstructions, Congress cannot be denied the power to exercise that control.

Noting the "serious effect upon interstate commerce" resulting from work stoppage in Jones & Laughlin's far-flung activities and the place of the steel industry in the national economy, the Court sustained Congress' power. The basis had been laid for the development of the modern affectation doctrine.

See Robert Stern, *The Commerce Clause and the National Economy, 1933-1946,* 59 Harv. L. Rev. 645, 883 (1946); AALS, Selected Essays 218 (1963), for an excellent discussion of the New Deal struggle.

[3] The Modern Commerce Power (1937-1976)

[a] Economic regulation

UNITED STATES v. DARBY

312 U.S. 100, 61 S. Ct. 451, 85 L. Ed. 609 (1941)

JUSTICE STONE delivered the opinion of the Court.

The two principal questions raised by the record in this case are, *first,* whether Congress has constitutional power to prohibit the shipment in interstate commerce of lumber manufactured by employees whose wages are less than a prescribed minimum or whose weekly hours of labor at that wage are greater than a prescribed maximum, and, *second,* whether it has power to prohibit the employment of workmen in the production of goods "for interstate commerce" at other than prescribed wages and hours.

The Fair Labor Standards Act set up a comprehensive legislative scheme for preventing the shipment in interstate commerce of certain products and commodities produced in the United States under labor conditions as respects wages and hours which fail to conform to standards set up by the Act.

The indictment charges that appellee is engaged, in the state of Georgia, in the business of acquiring raw materials, which he manufactures into finished lumber with the intent, when manufactured, to ship it in interstate commerce to customers outside the state, and that he does in fact so ship a large part of the lumber so produced.

The prohibition of shipment of the proscribed goods in interstate commerce.

While manufacture is not of itself interstate commerce the shipment of manufactured goods interstate is such commerce and the prohibition of such shipment by Congress is indubitably a regulation of the commerce. The power to regulate commerce is the power "to prescribe the rule by which commerce is to be governed." *Gibbons v. Ogden.* It extends not only to those regulations which aid, foster and protect the commerce, but embraces those which prohibit it. It is conceded that the power of Congress to prohibit transportation in interstate commerce includes noxious articles, stolen articles, kidnapped persons, and articles such as intoxicating liquor or convict made goods, traffic in which is forbidden or restricted by the laws of the state of destination.

The power of Congress over interstate commerce "is complete in itself, may be exercised to its utmost extent, and acknowledges no limitations, other than are prescribed in the Constitution." *Gibbons v. Ogden.* That power can neither be enlarged nor diminished by the exercise or non-exercise of state power. Congress, following its own conception of public policy concerning the restrictions which may appropriately be imposed on interstate commerce, is free to exclude from the commerce articles whose use in the states for which they are destined it may conceive to be injurious to the public health, morals or welfare, even though the state has not sought to regulate their use.

The motive and purpose of the present regulation are plainly to make effective the Congressional conception of public policy that interstate commerce should not be made the instrument of competition in the distribution of goods produced under substandard labor conditions, which competition is injurious to the commerce and to the states from and to which the commerce flows. The motive and purpose of a regulation of interstate commerce are matters for the legislative judgment upon the exercise of which the Constitution places no restriction and over which the courts are given no control. *McCray v. United States,* 195 U.S. 27; *Sonzinsky v. United States,* 300 U.S. 506, 513. Whatever their motive and purpose, regulations of commerce which do not infringe some constitutional prohibition are within the plenary power conferred on Congress by the Commerce Clause.

In the more than a century which has elapsed since the decision of *Gibbons v. Ogden,* these principles of constitutional interpretation have been so long and repeatedly recognized by this Court as applicable to the Commerce Clause, that there would be little occasion for repeating them now were it not for the decision of this Court twenty-two years ago in *Hammer v. Dagenhart.* In that case it was held by a bare majority of the Court over the powerful and now classic dissent of MR. JUSTICE HOLMES setting forth the fundamental issues involved, that Congress was without power to exclude the products of child labor from interstate commerce. The reasoning and conclusion of the Court's opinion there cannot be reconciled with the conclusion which we have reached, that the power of Congress under the Commerce Clause is plenary to exclude any article from interstate commerce subject only to the specific prohibitions of the Constitution.

Hammer v. Dagenhart has not been followed. The distinction on which the decision was rested that Congressional power to prohibit interstate commerce is limited to articles which in themselves have some harmful or deleterious property — a distinction which was novel when made and unsupported by any provision of the Constitution — has long since been abandoned. The thesis of the opinion that the motive of the prohibition or its effect to control in some measure the use or production within the states of the article thus excluded from the commerce can operate to deprive the regulation of its constitutional authority has long since ceased to have force. And finally we have declared, "The authority of the federal government over interstate commerce does not differ in extent or character from that retained by the states over intrastate commerce."

The conclusion is inescapable that *Hammer v. Dagenhart,* was a departure from the principles which have prevailed in the interpretation of the commerce clause both before and since the decision and that such vitality, as a precedent, as it then had has long since been exhausted. It should be and now is overruled.

Validity of the wage and hour requirements. Section 15(a) (2) and §§ 6 and 7 require employers to conform to the wage and hour provisions with respect to all employees engaged in the production of goods for interstate commerce. As appellee's employees are not alleged to be "engaged in interstate commerce" the validity of the prohibition turns on the question whether the employment, under other than the prescribed labor standards, of employees engaged in the production of goods for interstate commerce is so related to the commerce and so affects it as to be within the reach of the power of Congress to regulate it.

The obvious purpose of the Act was not only to prevent the interstate transportation of the proscribed product, but to stop the initial step toward transportation, production with the purpose of so transporting it. Congress was not unaware that most manufacturing businesses shipping their product in interstate commerce make it in their shops without reference to its ultimate destination and then, after manufacture, select some of it for shipment interstate and some intrastate according to the daily demands of their business; and that it would be practically impossible, without disrupting manufacturing businesses, to restrict the prohibited kind of production to the particular pieces of lumber, cloth, furniture or the like which later move in interstate rather than intrastate commerce.

The recognized need to drafting a workable statute and the well-known circumstances in which it was to be applied are persuasive of the conclusion, which the legislative history supports, that the "production for commerce" intended includes at least production of goods, which, at the time of production, the employer, according to the normal course of his business, all of the goods may not thereafter actually enter interstate commerce.

There remains the question whether such restriction on the production of goods for commerce is a permissible exercise of the commerce power. The power of Congress over interstate commerce is not confined to the regulation of commerce among the states. It extends to those activities intrastate which so affect interstate commerce or the exercise of the power of Congress over it as to make regulation of them appropriate means to the attainment of a legitimate end, the exercise of the granted power of Congress to regulate interstate commerce. *See McCulloch v. Maryland.*

The means adopted by § 15(a) (2) for the protection of interstate commerce by the suppression of the production of the condemned goods for interstate commerce is so related to the commerce and so affects it as to be within the reach of the commerce power. Congress, to attain its objective in the suppression of nationwide competition in interstate commerce by goods produced under substandard labor conditions, has made no distinction as to the volume or amount of shipments in the commerce or of production for commerce by any particular shipper or producer. It recognized that in present day industry, competition by a small part may affect the whole and that the total effect of the competition of many small producers may be great.

Our conclusion is unaffected by the Tenth Amendment. The amendment states but a truism that all is retained which has not been surrendered. There is nothing in the history of its adoption to suggest that it was more than declaratory of the relationship between the national and state governments as it had been established by the Constitution before the amendment or that its purpose was other than to allay fears that the new national government might seek to exercise powers not granted, and that the states might not be able to exercise fully their reserved powers.

NOTES

1. *Stone's opinion in Darby.* Alpheus T. Mason, Harlan Fiske Stone: Pillar of the Law (1956):

> [Justice Stone] had waited nearly five years for an opportunity to read out of constitutional jurisprudence that mainstay of laissez faire — "dual federalism" — the notion that the Tenth Amendment sets an independent limitation on the powers of Congress. "I have been thinking for sometime," he had written Charles A. Beard, "that the time might be opportune to say something in an opinion about the historic aspects of federal power. I think I shall improve the first opportunity to do something of the kind."

Id. at 553. Mason also noted that

> Hughes's dismay the year before retirement is reflected in his assignment of the opinion in *United States v. Darby,* to Justice Stone. [For Hughes] to uphold the Fair Labor Standards Act of 1938 would be to downgrade the Tenth Amendment to what it has never been for him — "a truism." Speaking for a unanimous court, Justice Stone ignored Hughes's refinements in the commerce cases decided since 1935, and went all the way back to John Marshall and *Gibbons v. Ogden.*

Id. at 145.

2. *Dual federalism.* After *Darby*, is there anything left of the doctrine of dual federalism or of Chief Justice Marshall's dictum in *McCulloch* that Congress could not, "under the pretext of executing its powers, pass laws for the accomplishment of objects not entrusted to the government?" Is there any limit on the conditions that Congress may impose for the privilege of using the channels of interstate commerce?

3. *Enterprise and "class of activities."* Under the FLSA, all employees involved in manufacturing goods for shipment in interstate commerce were covered, regardless of any particular employee's affect on commerce. This gave rise to the "enterprise" theory by which all aspects of an enterprise could be covered by federal regulation if the entity were engaged in interstate commerce. But should that be the case? In *Gonzales v. Raich*, p. 170, *infra*, the Court was faced with the argument that the federal Controlled Substances Act's ban on possession of marijuana could not constitutionally cover the personal possession of homegrown marijuana by a person who engaged in no interstate commerce and received a doctor's authorization for personal medical use. Should Congress be required to deal with specific "classes of activities" rather than a broad range of activities that in their total affect interstate commerce? In other words, can Congress expand the scope of its own authority by its definition of the class of activities that it chooses to consider to be part of its regulatory scheme?

WICKARD v. FILBURN

317 U.S. 111, 63 S. Ct. 82, 87 L. Ed. 122 (1942)

JUSTICE JACKSON delivered the opinion of the Court.

The appellee sought to enjoin enforcement against himself of the marketing penalty imposed by the amendment of May 26, 1941, to the Agricultural Adjustment Act of 1938, upon that part of his 1941 wheat crop which was available for marketing in excess of the marketing quota established for his farm. He also sought a declaratory judgment that the wheat marketing quota provisions of the Act as amended and applicable to him were unconstitutional because not sustainable under the Commerce Clause or consistent with the Due Process Clause of the Fifth Amendment.

The appellee for many years past has owned and operated a small farm in Montgomery County, Ohio, maintaining a herd of dairy cattle, selling milk, raising poultry, and selling poultry and eggs. It has been his practice to raise a small acreage of winter wheat, sown in the Fall and harvested in the following July; to sell a portion of the crop; to feed part to poultry and livestock on the farm, some of which is sold; to use some in making flour for home consumption; and to keep the rest for the following seeding. The intended disposition of the crop here involved has not been expressly stated.

In July of 1940, pursuant to the Agricultural Adjustment Act of 1938, as then amended, there were established for the appellee's 1941 crop a wheat acreage allotment of 11.1 acres and a normal yield of 20.1 bushels of wheat an acre. He was given notice of such allotment in July of 1940, before the Fall planting of his 1941 crop of wheat, and again in July of 1941, before it was harvested. He sowed, however, 23 acres, and harvested from his 11.9 acres of excess acreage 239 bushels, which under the terms of the Act as amended on May 26, 1941, constituted farm marketing excess, subject to a penalty of 49 cents a bushel, or $117.11 in all. The appellee has not paid the penalty and he has not postponed or avoided it by storing the excess under regulations of the Secretary of Agriculture, or by delivering it up to the Secretary. The Committee, therefore, refused him a marketing card, which was, under the terms of Regulations promulgated by the Secretary, necessary to protect a buyer from liability to the penalty and upon its protecting lien.

The general scheme of the Agricultural Adjustment Act of 1938 as related to wheat is to control the volume moving in interstate and foreign commerce in order to avoid surpluses and shortages and the consequent abnormally low or high wheat prices and obstructions to commerce. Within prescribed limits and by prescribed standards the Secretary of Agriculture is directed to ascertain and proclaim each year a national acreage allotment for the next crop of wheat, which is then apportioned to the states and their counties, and is eventually broken up into allotments for individual farms.

It is urged that, under the Commerce Clause of the Constitution, Article I, § 8, clause 3, Congress does not possess the power it has in this instance sought to exercise. The question would merit little consideration since our decision in *United States v. Darby,* sustaining the federal power to regulate production of goods for commerce, except for the fact that this Act extends federal regulation to production not intended in any part for commerce but wholly for consumption on the farm. The Act includes a definition of "market" and its derivatives, so that as related to wheat, in addition to its conventional meaning, it also means to dispose of "by feeding (in any form) to poultry or livestock which, or the products of which, are sold, bartered, or exchanged, or to be so disposed of." Hence, marketing quotas not only embrace all that may be sold without penalty but also what may be consumed on the premises.

Appellee says that this is a regulation of production and consumption of wheat. Such activities are, he urges, beyond the reach of Congressional power under the Commerce Clause, since they are local in character, and their effects upon interstate commerce are at most "indirect." In answer the Government argues that the statute regulates neither production nor consumption, but only marketing; and, in the alternative, that if the Act does go beyond the regulation of marketing it is sustainable as a "necessary and proper" implementation of the power of Congress over interstate commerce.

The Government's concern lest the Act be held to be a regulation of production or consumption, rather than of marketing, is attributable to a few dicta and decisions of this Court which might be understood to lay it down that activities such as "production," "manufacturing," and "mining" are strictly "local" and, except in special circumstances which are not present here, cannot be regulated under the commerce power because their effects upon interstate commerce are, as matter of law, only "indirect." Even today, when this power has been held to have great latitude, there is no decision of this Court that such activities may be regulated where no part of the product is intended for interstate commerce or intermingled with the subjects thereof.

But even if appellee's activity be local and though it may not be regarded as commerce, it may still, whatever its nature, be reached by Congress if it exerts a substantial economic effect on interstate commerce, and this irrespective of whether such effect is what might at some earlier time have been defined as "direct" or "indirect."

The effect of consumption of home-grown wheat on interstate commerce is due to the fact that it constitutes the most variable factor in the disappearance of the wheat crop. Consumption on the farm where grown appears to vary in an amount greater than 20 per cent of average production. The total amount of wheat consumed as food varies but relatively little, and use as seed is relatively constant.

The maintenance by government regulation of a price for wheat undoubtedly can be accomplished as effectively by sustaining or increasing the demand as by limiting the supply. The effect of the statute before us is to restrict the amount which may be produced for market and the extent as well to which one may forestall resort to the market by producing to meet his own needs. That appellees own contribution to the demand for wheat may be trivial by itself is not enough to remove him from the scope of federal regulation where, as here, his contribution, taken together with that of many others similarly situated, is far from trivial. *United States v. Darby.*

It is well established by decisions of this Court that the power to regulate commerce includes the power to regulate the prices at which commodities in that commerce are dealt in and practices affecting such prices. One of the primary purposes of the act in question was to increase the market price of wheat, and to that end to limit the volume thereof that could affect the market. It can hardly be denied that a factor of such volume and variability as home-consumed wheat would have a substantial influence on price and market conditions. This may arise because being in marketable condition such wheat overhangs the market and, if induced by rising prices, tends to flow into the market and check price increases. But if we assume that it is never marketed, it supplies a need of the man who grew it which would otherwise be reflected by purchasers in the open market. Home-grown wheat in this sense competes with wheat in commerce. The stimulation of commerce is a use of the regulatory function quite as definitely as prohibitions or restrictions thereon. This record leaves us in no doubt that Congress may properly have considered that wheat consumed on the farm where grown, if wholly outside the scheme of regulation, would have substantial effect in defeating and obstructing its purpose to stimulate trade therein at increased prices.

It is said, however, that this Act, forcing some farmers into the market to buy what they could provide for themselves, is an unfair promotion of the markets and prices of specializing wheat growers. It is of the essence of regulation that it lays a restraining hand on the self-interest of the regulated and that advantages from the regulation commonly fall to others. The conflicts of economic interest between the regulated and those who advantage by it are wisely left under our system to resolution by the Congress under its more flexible and responsible legislative process. Such conflicts rarely lend themselves to judicial determination. And with the wisdom, workability, or fairness, of the plan of regulation we have nothing to do.

The statute is also challenged as a deprivation of property without due process of law contrary to the Fifth Amendment, both because of its regulatory effect on the appellee and because of its alleged retroactive effect.

[The Court went on to hold that the application of the statute to the complainant did not violate the fifth amendment due process clause and reversed the district court.]

NOTES

1. ***A return to original intent?*** It has been urged that *Wickard* "completely swept away the old distinction between production and commerce; manufacturing, mining, and agriculture were now considered to be part of commerce and inseparable from it." PAUL BENSON, THE SUPREME COURT AND THE COMMERCE CLAUSE, 1937–1970, 101 (1970). Consider the following summation of the expansion of Congress commerce power: "This application of the clause to all business activities which concerns more state[s] than one, and not merely to direct trade and transportation between states, would seem to be precisely what was meant by Marshall's prophetic declaration." Robert Stern, *The Scope of the Phrase Interstate Commerce,* 41 A.B.A.J. 823, 871 (1955). Similarly, Justice Rutledge stated that "the 'affectation' approach was actually a revival of Marshall's 'necessary and proper' doctrine." *Mandeville Island Farms v. American Crystal Sugar Co.,* 334 U.S. 219, 232 n.11 (1948).

2. ***Changed circumstances.*** *Wickard* establishes that Congress may reach local activity if it exerts a "substantial economic effect" on interstate

commerce. How important is this limitation given our modern economy? The Court in *Wickard* appears willing to accept what in 1935 it had emphatically rejected, *i.e.*, that the interstate and intrastate aspects of the American economy are not distinct, separate and impenetrable and that the Tenth Amendment does not necessitate the drawing of a fixed line between the state and federal spheres of power. As Stern explains: "It may be true that the application of the principles now approved by the Supreme Court may leave only minor aspects of an economy free from the regulatory power of Congress. The reason for this, however, is not legal but economic." Robert Stern, *Problems of Yesteryear: Commerce and Due Process,* 4 VAND. L. REV. 446, 468 (1951).

3. ***Antitrust legislation.*** In construing federal legislation regulating commerce, the Court has refused to accept the argument that any activity perceptively connected with interstate commerce is itself in interstate commerce. In determining legislative intent, the Court has held that a statutory reference to interstate commerce by the Congress should not be considered as necessarily co-extensive with the full reach of commerce clause jurisdiction. Presumably, Congress would have to make it clear that co-extensiveness was its purpose, at least where a broad interpretation would trespass on areas traditionally assumed to be within the prerogative of state legislative jurisdiction.

On the other hand, in *McLain v. Real Estate Bd. of New Orleans,* 444 U.S. 232 (1980), the Court gave a broad reading to the jurisdictional provisions of the Sherman Act. The issue was whether the connection of real estate brokers with interstate commerce was sufficient to bring their commission-fixing arrangements within the ambit of the Sherman Act. The brokers succeeded in having the complaint dismissed in the district court by arguing that the brokerage business is wholly intrastate in nature and, hence, outside of the Sherman Act prohibition. The Supreme Court unanimously reversed. Chief Justice Burger, writing for the Court, stated that Sherman Act jurisdiction was present whenever the alleged illegal activities were part of the "stream of interstate commerce" or "substantially affect interstate commerce."

The Chief Justice cited the evidence presented to the trial court indicating that real estate financing and the insuring of titles to such property represents "appreciable commercial activity [occurring] in interstate commerce." To satisfy federal jurisdictional requirements, therefore, petitioners would have to show "that respondents' activities which allegedly have been infected by a price-fixing conspiracy 'as a matter of practical economics' have a not insubstantial effect on the interstate commerce involved."

[b] Protection of civil rights under the commerce clause

At common law, an innkeeper impliedly gave a general invitation to all members of the public to enter and use his premises without discrimination. But because slaves were considered property, they never received the benefit of these common-law rights. Following Emancipation, many states passed statutes abrogating the common-law rules and allowing operators of public accommodations to refuse service on any basis.

The Thirteenth, Fourteenth and Fifteenth Amendments were designed to remove at least some of these legal disabilities, and Congress sought through legislation to fashion a remedy to give these rights meaning. One such effort came in the Civil Rights Act of 1875 which provided:

> that all persons within the jurisdiction of the United States shall be entitled to full and equal enjoyment of the accommodations, advantages, facilities, and privileges of inns, public conveyances on land or water, theaters, or other places of public amusements; subject only to the conditions and limitations established by law, and applicable alike to citizens of every race and color, regardless of any previous condition of servitude.

The section was not limited to state action but could be applied even against private discrimination.

But as was to be the fate of much of the Civil War civil rights legislation, the courts undid the congressional handiwork. In the *Civil Rights Cases,* p. 1487, the Court declared the 1875 Act unconstitutional because the Fourteenth Amendment did not grant Congress power to legislate in the area of private discrimination. The Amendment, and thus the enforcement power of Congress, limited only official state discrimination rather than state-authorized private discrimination. It has been noted that the Court's "decision in the *Civil Rights Cases* was an important stimulus to the enactment of segregation statutes. It gave the assurance the South wanted that the federal government would not intervene to protect the civil rights of Negroes." John Hope Franklin, *History of Racial Segregation in the United States,* in 5 ANNALS OF CONG. 34 (1956).

Congress was not to legislate again in an effort to eliminate discrimination in public accommodations for eighty-seven years. In the interim, the Court struggled with the limitations imposed on direct judicial enforcement of the Civil War amendments by the state action requirement. But the increasing unwillingness of African-Americans in the South to accept segregation, increasing public awareness of the problems of segregated accommodations, the refusal of restaurants to serve African diplomats traveling between New York and Washington, and the death of President Kennedy, culminated in a demand for new federal intervention. In an attempt to revive the ideal of "freedom and equality for all," Congress passed the Civil Rights Act of 1964, but in doing so, it employed not only the Fourteenth Amendment guarantees but also the commerce clause.

CIVIL RIGHTS ACT OF 1964
Title II Injunctive Relief Against Discrimination in Places of Public Accommodation

> Sec. 201. (a) All persons shall be entitled to the full and equal enjoyment of the goods, services, facilities, privileges, advantages, and accommodations of any place of public accommodation, as defined in this section, without discrimination or segregation on the grounds of race, color, religion, or national origin.

(b) Each of the following establishments which serves the public is a place of public accommodation within the meaning of this title if its operations affect commerce, or if discrimination or segregation by it is supported by State action:

(1) any inn, hotel, motel, or other establishment which provides lodging to transient guests, other than an establishment located within a building which contains not more than five rooms for rent or hire and which is actually occupied by the proprietor of such establishment as his residence;

(2) any restaurant, cafeteria, lunchroom, lunch counter, soda fountain, or other facility principally engaged in selling food for consumption on the premises, including, but not limited to, any such facility located on the premises of any retail establishment; or any gasoline station; [if it serves or offers to serve interstate travelers or a substantial portion of the food which it serves, or gasoline or other products which it sells, has moved in commerce];

(3) any motion picture house, theater, concert hall, sports arena, stadium or other place of exhibition or entertainment; [if it customarily presents films, performances, athletic teams, exhibitions, or other sources of entertainment which move in commerce] . . . .

(e) The provisions of this title shall not apply to a private club or other establishment not in fact open to the public, except to the extent that the facilities of such establishment are made available to the customers or patrons of an establishment within the scope of subsection (b).

HEART OF ATLANTA MOTEL v. UNITED STATES

379 U.S. 241, 85 S. Ct. 348, 13 L. Ed. 2d 258 (1964)

JUSTICE CLARK delivered the opinion of the Court.

This is a declaratory judgment action attacking the constitutionality of Title II of the Civil Rights Act of 1964. A three-judge court sustained the validity of the Act and issued a permanent injunction restraining appellant from continuing to violate the Act. We affirm the judgment.

Appellant owns and operates the Heart of Atlanta Motel which has 216 rooms available to transient guests. The motel is located on Courtland Street, two blocks from downtown Peachtree Street. It is readily accessible to interstate highways 75 and 85 and state highways 23 and 41. Appellant solicits its patronage from outside the State of Georgia through various national advertising media, including magazines of national circulation; it maintains over 50 billboards and highway signs within the State, soliciting patronage for the motel; it accepts convention trade from outside Georgia and approximately 75% of its registered guests are from out of State. Prior to passage of the Act the motel had followed a practice of refusing to rent rooms to Negroes, and it alleged that it intended to continue to do so. In an effort to perpetuate that policy this suit was filed.

It is admitted that the operation of the motel brings it within the provisions of § 201(a) of the Act and that appellant refused to provide lodging for transient Negroes because of their race or color and that it intends to continue that policy unless restrained.

The sole question posed is, therefore, the constitutionality of the Civil Rights Act of 1964 as applied to these facts. The legislative history of the Act indicates that Congress based the Act on § 5 and the Equal Protection Clause of the Fourteenth Amendment as well as its power to regulate interstate commerce under Art. I, § 8, cl. 3, of the Constitution.

The Senate Commerce Committee made it quite clear that the fundamental object of Title II was to vindicate "the deprivation of personal dignity that surely accompanies denials of equal access to public establishments." At the same time, however, it noted that such an objective has been and could be readily achieved "by congressional action based on the commerce power of the Constitution." Our study of the legislative record, made in the light of prior cases, has brought us to the conclusion that Congress possessed ample power in this regard, and we have therefore not considered the other grounds relied upon. This is not to say that the remaining authority upon which it acted was not adequate, a question upon which we do not pass, but merely that since the commerce power is sufficient for our decision here we have considered it alone.

In light of our ground for decision, it might be well at the outset to discuss the *Civil Rights Cases,* which declared provisions of the Civil Rights Act of 1875 unconstitutional. We think that decision inapposite, and without precedential value in determining the constitutionality of the present Act. Unlike Title II of the present legislation, the 1875 Act broadly proscribed discrimination in "inns, public conveyances on land or water, theaters, and other places of public amusement," without limiting the categories of affected businesses to those impinging upon interstate commerce. In contrast, the applicability of Title II is carefully limited to enterprises having a direct and substantial relation to the interstate flow of goods and people, except where state action is involved. Further, the fact that certain kinds of businesses may not in 1875 have been sufficiently involved in interstate commerce to warrant bringing them within the ambit of the commerce power is not necessarily dispositive of the same question today. Our populace had not reached its present mobility, nor were facilities, goods and services circulating as readily in interstate commerce as they are today. Although the principles which we apply today are those first formulated by CHIEF JUSTICE MARSHALL in *Gibbons v. Ogden,* the conditions of transportation and commerce have changed dramatically, and we must apply those principles to the present state of commerce. The sheer increase in volume of interstate traffic alone would give discriminatory practices which inhibit travel a far larger impact upon the Nation's commerce than such practices had on the economy of another day. Finally, there is language in the *Civil Rights Cases* which indicates that the Court did not fully consider whether the 1875 Act could be sustained as an exercise of the commerce power.

While the [1964] Act as adopted carried no congressional findings the record of its passage through each house is replete with evidence of the burdens that discrimination by race or color places upon interstate commerce. This testimony included the fact that our people have become increasingly mobile with millions of people of all races traveling from State to State; that Negroes in particular have been the subject of discrimination in transient accommodations, having to travel great distances to secure the same; that often they have been unable to obtain accommodations and have had to call upon friends to put them up overnight; and that these conditions have become so acute as to require the listing of available lodging for Negroes in a special guidebook which was itself "dramatic testimony to the difficulties" Negroes encounter in travel. These exclusionary practices were found to be nationwide. This testimony indicated a qualitative as well as quantitative effect on interstate travel by Negroes. The former was the obvious impairment of the Negro traveler's pleasure and convenience that resulted when he continually was uncertain of finding lodging. As for the latter, there was evidence that this uncertainty stemming from racial discrimination had the effect of discouraging travel on the part of a substantial portion of the Negro community. We shall not burden this opinion with further details since the voluminous testimony presents overwhelming evidence that discrimination by hotels and motels impedes interstate travel.

The same interest in protecting interstate commerce which led Congress to deal with segregation in interstate carriers and the white-slave traffic has prompted it to extend the exercise of its power to gambling, to criminal enterprises, to deceptive practices in the sale of products, to fraudulent security transactions, to misbranding of drugs, to wages and hours, to members of labor unions, to crop control, to discrimination against shippers, to the protection of small business from injurious price cutting, to resale price maintenance, to professional football, and to racial discrimination by owners and managers of terminal restaurants.

That Congress was legislating against moral wrongs in many of these areas rendered its enactments no less valid. In framing Title II of this Act Congress was also dealing with what it considered a moral problem. But that fact does not detract from the overwhelming evidence of the disruptive effect that racial discrimination has had on commercial intercourse. It was this burden which empowered Congress to enact appropriate legislation, and, given this basis for the exercise of its power, Congress was not restricted by the fact that the particular obstruction to interstate commerce with which it was dealing was also deemed a moral and social wrong.

It is said that the operation of the motel here is of a purely local character. But, assuming this to be true, "[i]f it is interstate commerce that feels the pinch, it does not matter how local the operation which applies the squeeze." [T]he power of Congress to promote interstate commerce also includes the power to regulate the local incidents thereof, including local activities in both the States of origin and destination, which might have a substantial and harmful effect upon that commerce. One need only examine the evidence which we have discussed above to see that Congress may — as it has — prohibit racial discrimination by motels serving travelers, however local their operations may appear.

We, therefore, conclude that the action of the Congress in the adoption of the Act as applied here to a motel which concededly serves interstate travelers is within the power granted it by the Commerce Clause of the Constitution, as interpreted by this Court for 140 years. It may be argued that Congress could have pursued other methods to eliminate the obstructions it found in interstate commerce caused by racial discrimination. But this is a matter of policy that rests entirely with the Congress not within the courts. How obstructions in commerce may be removed — What means are to be employed — is within the sound and exclusive discretion of the Congress. It is subject only to one caveat — that the means chosen by it must be reasonably adapted to the end permitted by the Constitution. We cannot say that its choice here was not so adapted. The Constitution requires no more.

***Katzenbach v. McClung*, 379 U.S. 294 (1964).** A companion case to *Heart of Atlanta,* involved application of the 1964 Act to Ollie's Barbecue, which was off the beaten track in Birmingham, Alabama. A relatively small proportion of its customers were not local and only a portion of its food had been acquired through interstate commerce.

JUSTICE CLARK delivered the opinion of the Court.

Much is said about a restaurant business being local but "even if appellee's activity be local and though it may not be regarded as commerce, it may still, whatever its nature, be reached by Congress if it exerts a substantial economic effect on interstate commerce." *Wickard v. Filburn.* The appellees contend that Congress has arbitrarily created a conclusive presumption that all restaurants meeting the criteria set out in the Act "affect commerce." Stated another way, they object to the omission of a provision for a case-by-case determination — judicial or administrative — that racial discrimination in a particular restaurant affects commerce. But Congress' action in framing this Act was not unprecedented.

Here, [as in *United States v. Darby*], Congress has determined for itself that refusals of service to Negroes have imposed burdens both upon the interstate flow of food and upon the movement of products generally. Of course, the mere fact that Congress has said when particular activity shall be deemed to affect commerce does not preclude further examination by this Court. But where we find that the legislators, in light of the facts and testimony before them, have a rational basis for finding a chosen regulatory scheme necessary to the protection of commerce, our investigation is at an end. The only remaining question — one answered in the affirmative by the court below — is whether the particular restaurant either serves or offers to serve interstate travelers or serves food a substantial portion of which has moved in interstate commerce.

Confronted as we are with the facts laid before Congress, we must conclude that it had a rational basis for finding that racial discrimination in restaurants had a direct and adverse effect on the free flow of interstate commerce.

JUSTICE BLACK, concurring [in both cases].

I recognize that every remote, possible, speculative effect on commerce should not be accepted as an adequate constitutional ground to uproot and throw into the discard all our traditional distinctions between what is purely local, and therefore controlled by state laws, and what affects the national interest and is therefore subject to control by federal laws. I recognize too that some isolated and remote lunchroom which sells only to local people and buys almost all its supplies in the locality may possibly be beyond the reach of the power of Congress to regulate commerce, just as such an establishment is not covered by the present Act. But in deciding the constitutional power of Congress in cases like the two before us we do not consider the effect on interstate commerce of only one isolated, individual, local event, without regard to the fact that this single local event when added to many others of a similar nature may impose a burden on interstate commerce by reducing its volume or distorting its flow.

JUSTICE DOUGLAS, concurring [in both cases].

Though I join the Court's opinions, I am somewhat reluctant to rest solely on the Commerce Clause. My reluctance is not due to any conviction that Congress lacks power to regulate commerce in the interests of human rights. It is rather my belief that the right of people to be free of state action that discriminates against them because of race, like the "right of persons to move freely from State to State" "occupies a more protected position in our constitutional system than does the movement of cattle, fruit, steel and coal across state lines."

A decision based on the Fourteenth Amendment would have a more settling effect, making unnecessary litigation over whether a particular restaurant or inn is within the commerce definitions of the Act or whether a particular customer is an interstate traveler. Under my construction, the Act would apply to all customers in all the enumerated places of public accommodation. And that construction would put an end to all obstructionist strategies and finally close one door on a bitter chapter in American history.

JUSTICE GOLDBERG, concurring [in both cases].

In my concurring opinion in *Bell v. Maryland,* 378 U.S. 226, 317, I expressed my conviction that § 1 of the Fourteenth Amendment guarantees to all Americans the constitutional right "to be treated as equal members of the community with respect to public accommodations," and that "Congress [has] authority under § 5 of the Fourteenth Amendment, or under the Commerce Clause, Art. I, § 8, to implement the rights protected by § 1 of the Fourteenth Amendment. In the give-and-take of the legislative process, Congress can fashion a law drawing the guidelines necessary and appropriate to facilitate practical administration and to distinguish between genuinely public and private accommodations." The challenged Act is just such a law and, in my view, Congress clearly had authority under both § 5 of the Fourteenth Amendment and the Commerce Clause to enact the Civil Rights Act of 1964.

NOTES

1. *The choice of constitutional power.* While Congress wished to reverse the effect of the *Civil Rights Cases,* it was also concerned with the need to assure the constitutionality of the new legislation. The Court in the nineteenth century case had clearly provided an opening when it stated that its "remarks do not apply to those cases in which Congress was clothed with direct plenary power of legislation over the whole subject, accompanied with an expressed or implied denial of such powers to the States, as in the regulation of commerce."

Would there have been any advantages in relying on the Fourteenth Amendment rather than the Commerce Clause? As Justices Douglas and Goldberg indicate in their concurring opinions, the Fourteenth Amendment would seem to provide a more direct way of dealing with the problem of racial discrimination. Further, such a nexus would seem to provide broad federal power enabling Congress to legislate against discrimination in public accommodations, thereby eliminating the possible need to prove an interstate commerce nexus in the particular case. On the congressional use of the Fourteenth Amendment to reach *private* discrimination, see Chapter 10, § C.

2. *Scope of commerce.* If interstate commerce has begun, does Congress' police power extend to regulation of the goods even after they have reached their destination? Is the theory that Congress can regulate even local activity that has a social or moral effect on interstate commerce, *i.e.*, that interstate commerce should not be used to promote local discrimination?

3. *The "affectation" doctrine.* Is congressional power to enact Title II based on the premise that discrimination in public accommodations is an "economic burden" on interstate commerce? Note that the Act does not include specific findings of fact documenting such a burden. During the hearings, Assistant United States Attorney General Burke Marshall did state that:

> discrimination burdens Negro interstate travelers and thereby inhibits interstate travel. It artificially restricts the market available for interstate goods and services. It leads to the withholding of patronage by potential customers for such goods and services. It inhibits the holding of conventions and meetings in segregated cities. It interferes with businesses that wish to obtain the services of persons who do not choose to subject themselves to segregation and discrimination. And it restricts business enterprises in their choice of location for offices and plants, thus preventing the most effective allocation of national resources. Clearly, all of these are burdens on interstate commerce and they may therefore be dealt with by the Congress.

If discrimination were ended, would it matter that some whites might be deterred from traveling? From using food which has traveled through interstate commerce? Should such possible consequences be considered in determining the constitutionality of Title II?

4. *The character of the interstate connection.* Can Congress regulate racial discrimination in places of public accommodations because those places affect interstate commerce, or is it necessary that the government show that the racial discrimination itself affects interstate commerce? Burke Marshall stated:

> Let me dispel at the outset a possible misconception. We do not propose to regulate the businesses covered merely because they are engaged in some phase of interstate commerce. Discrimination by the establishments covered in the bill should be prohibited because it is that discrimination itself which adversely affects interstate commerce.

On another occasion during the hearing, he stated:

> Of course, there are limits on Congressional power under the Commerce Clause. It may be conceded that Congress does not hold the power to regulate all of a man's conduct solely because he has relationship with interstate commerce. What is required is that there be a relationship between interstate commerce and the evil to be regulated. Over the course of the years, various tests have been established for determining whether this relationship exists. The proposed legislation clearly meets these tests.

Hearings Before the Senate Committee on Commerce on S. 1732, 88th CONG., 1st Sess. (1963).

5. *A substantial effect.* The Court in *Katzenbach* has been criticized because in that case "where the connection with interstate commerce appears most tenuous, the Court dismissed the issue simply by referring to the analysis in *Heart of Atlanta.*" Is the substantial burden on interstate commerce produced by all those who satisfy the statutory standard, *i.e.*, serve a substantial amount of interstate commerce food? See Comment, 19 Sw. L.J. 329, 367 (1964), arguing that "[i]f the Court uses the *Wickard v. Filburn* yardstick, every hot dog stand in the country would be covered [since] the mustard obtained through interstate commerce and dispensed by the smallest hot dog stand would, if multiplied by all the hot dog stands in the country, surely affect commerce."

6. *Employment discrimination.* Title VII of the 1964 Civil Rights Act, as amended, declares it to be an "unlawful employment practice" for any employer having fifteen or more employees or labor organization engaged in an "industry affecting commerce" to discriminate on the basis of race, color, religion, sex, or national origin. "Industry affecting commerce" includes "any activity, business, or industry in commerce or in which a labor dispute would hinder or obstruct commerce or the free flow of commerce and includes any activity or industry 'affecting commerce' within the meaning of the Labor-Management Reporting and Disclosure Act of 1959."

In a Memorandum on Title VII's constitutionality, the Solicitor's Office of the Department of Labor argued:

> Since Congress in the exercise of its power over interstate commerce can make it unlawful to discriminate because of union membership and because of [union activity] under [the Fair Labor Standards Act and the National Labor Relations Act], it is clear that Congress also has power to prevent discrimination on the basis of race, color, religion or national origin.

The Memorandum also contended that it is established that the commerce power "extends to activities affecting commerce in any amount or volume not so minimal or sporadic as to fall within the doctrine of *de minimis non curat lex.*"

In *Fullilove v. Klutznick,* p. 725, the Court upheld a Minority Business Enterprise (MBE) provision of the Public Works Employment Act of 1977 requiring a ten percent set-aside of federal funds for local public works projects to be used to procure services or supplies from businesses owned and controlled by members of statutorily identified minority groups. In holding that the "objectives" of the program are within the powers of Congress, Chief Justice Burger stated:

> The legislative history of the MBE provision shows that there was a rational basis for Congress to conclude that the subcontracting practices of prime contractors could perpetuate the prevailing impaired access by minority businesses to public contracting opportunities, and that this inequity has an effect on interstate commerce. Thus Congress could take necessary and proper action to remedy the situation.

Such action was not dependent upon any showing that the prime contractors were responsible for a violation of antidiscrimination laws. Chief Justice Burger noted the use of Title VII of the Civil Rights Act of 1964 to prohibit practices "challenged as perpetuating the effects of [not unlawful] discrimination occurring prior to the effective date of the Act."

[C] STATE SOVEREIGNTY AND FEDERALISM

From the New Deal to 1976, the courts deferred to congressional use of its commerce power. Although constitutional concerns occasionally resulted in narrow statutory interpretation to check abuses, the constitutional grant of power provided a potent source of federal regulation. The results led one student of American federalism to observe that "[t]he radical transformation that has occurred in the structure of 'Our Federalism' in the nearly two centuries of our existence has emptied the concept of nearly all legal content and replaced it with a frank recognition of the legal hegemony of the national government." Henry Monaghan, *The Burger Court and Our Federalism,* 43 LAW & CONTEMP. PROBS. 39 (1980).

In the previous sections there were references to the use of the political process as an alternative to judicial review as a protective shield for federalist values. Chief Justice Marshall espoused this view from the outset in *Gibbons v. Ogden*: "The wisdom and the discretion of Congress, their identity with the people, and the influence which their constituents possess at elections, are the sole restraints on which they have relied, to secure them from its abuse." There is increasing sentiment, however, that these political checks have eroded in the post-New Deal era.

> [T]he new relationship of the states and state administrators to the federal government and the new politics of congressional representation have dramatically changed the workings of the process of federalism. It is now far less likely that the states interest in their continuing autonomy will consistently receive expression within the political branches of the federal government, or that the political process will yield dependable lines of accountability between the governed and the government.

Lewis Kaden, *Politics, Money, and State Sovereignty: The Judicial Role,* 79 Colum. L. Rev. 847, 868 (1979).

[1] Regulating State Activities: the Tenth Amendment

The Tenth Amendment provides: "The powers not delegated to the United States by the Constitution, nor prohibited by it to the States, are reserved to the States respectively, or to the people." In *Darby* the Court stated that the amendment is but a truism: the federal government cannot exercise powers not delegated to it. In rejecting dual federalism, *Darby* appeared to reject state power as a limitation on national power.

The Fair Labor Standards Act passed in 1938 and upheld in *Darby* exempted state government employment from its coverage. In 1966, Congress amended the statute to impose maximum hour and minimum wage controls on state hospitals and schools. The Supreme Court upheld the 1966 amendments in *Maryland v. Wirtz,* 392 U.S. 183 (1968), and characterized as "not tenable" the assertion that the federal commerce power "must yield to state sovereignty in the performance of governmental functions."

In *Fry v. United States,* 421 U.S. 542 (1975), the Court upheld application of the Economic Stabilization Act of 1970 to limit the wages and hours of state government employees. A prophetic footnote to the majority opinion by Justice Marshall, however, stated that the Tenth Amendment "expressly declares the constitutional policy that Congress may not exercise power in a fashion that impairs the States' integrity or their ability to function effectively in a federal system." In this case the "constitutional policy" was not violated. Justice Marshall stressed that the effectiveness of the Economic Stabilization Act would be drastically impaired if state employees were left uncovered. Further, the intrusion on state sovereignty by the federal legislation was viewed as limited because it lowered the amount that states could pay rather than increasing what they paid. But emphasizing these characteristics of the Stabilization Act indicated that the intergovernmental immunity doctrine might, in other contexts, limit the federal prerogative. Justice Rehnquist, dissenting, urged that *Maryland v. Wirtz* be reexamined. That development occurred just one year later.

NATIONAL LEAGUE OF CITIES v. USERY
426 U.S. 833, 96 S. Ct. 2465, 49 L. Ed. 2d 245 (1976)

Mr. Justice Rehnquist delivered the opinion for the Court.

The original Fair Labor Standards Act passed in 1938 specifically excluded the States and their political subdivisions from its coverage. In 1974, however, Congress enacted the most recent of a series of broadening amendments to the Act. By these amendments Congress has extended the minimum wage and maximum hour provisions to almost all public employees employed by the States and by their various political subdivisions. Appellants in these cases include individual cities and States, the National League of Cities, and the National Governors Conference; they brought an action in the District Court for the District of Columbia which challenged the validity of the 1974 amendments. They asserted in effect that when Congress sought to apply the Fair Labor Standards Act provisions virtually across the board to employees of state and municipal governments it "infringed a constitutional prohibition" running in favor of the States *as States.* [The lower court dismissed the complaints.]

This Court has never doubted that there are limits upon the power of Congress to override state sovereignty, even when exercising its otherwise plenary powers to tax or to regulate commerce which are conferred by Art. I of the Constitution. In *Fry*, the court recognized that an express declaration of this limitation is found in the Tenth Amendment:

> While the Tenth Amendment has been characterized as a "truism," stating merely that "all is retained which has not been surrendered," *United States v. Darby,* it is not without significance. The Amendment expressly declares the constitutional policy that Congress may not exercise power in a fashion that impairs the States' integrity or their ability to function effectively in a federal system.

It is one thing to recognize the authority of Congress to enact laws regulating individual businesses necessarily subject to the dual sovereignty of the government of the Nation and of the State in which they reside. It is quite another to uphold a similar exercise of congressional authority directed not to private citizens, but to the States as States. We have repeatedly recognized that there are attributes of sovereignty attaching to every state government which may not be impaired by Congress, not because Congress may lack an affirmative grant of legislative authority to reach the matter, but because the Constitution prohibits it from exercising the authority in that manner.

One undoubted attribute of state sovereignty is the States' power to determine the wages which shall be paid to those whom they employ in order to carry out their governmental functions, what hours those persons will work, and what compensation will be provided where these employees may be called upon to work overtime. The question we must resolve in this case, then, is whether these determinations are "functions essential to separate and independent existence," so that Congress may not abrogate the States' otherwise plenary authority to make them.

[As an example of the amendment's effects,] California [claimed that it could not pay overtime to cadets in training for highway patrol positions and] that it had thus been forced to reduce its academy training program from 2,080 hours to only 960 hours, a compromise undoubtedly of substantial importance to those whose safety and welfare may depend upon the preparedness of the California Highway Patrol.

Quite apart from the substantial costs imposed upon the States and their political subdivisions, the Act displaces state policies regarding the manner in which they will structure delivery of those governmental services which their citizens require. The Act, speaking directly to the States *qua* States, requires that they shall pay all but an extremely limited minority of their employees the minimum wage rates currently chosen by Congress. It may well be that as a matter of economic policy it would be desirable that States, just as private employers, comply with these minimum wage requirements. But it cannot be gainsaid that the federal requirement directly supplants the considered policy choices of the States' elected officials and administrators as to how they wish to structure pay scales in state employment. The only "discretion" left to them under the Act is either to attempt to increase their revenue to meet the additional financial burden imposed upon them by paying congressionally prescribed wages to their existing complement of employees, or to reduce that complement to a number which can be paid the federal minimum wage without increasing revenue.

This dilemma presented by the minimum wage restrictions may seem not immediately different from that faced by private employers, who have long been covered by the Act and who must find ways to increase their gross income if they are to pay higher wages while maintaining current earnings. The difference, however, is that a State is not merely a factor in the "shifting economic arrangements" of the private sector of the economy, but is itself a coordinate element in the system established by the framers for governing our federal union.

[B]oth the minimum wage and the maximum hour provisions will impermissibly interfere with the integral government functions of [States and their political subdivisions]. [E]ven if we accept appellee's assessments concerning the impact of the amendments, their application will nonetheless significantly alter or displace the States' abilities to structure employer-employee relationships in such areas as fire prevention, police protection, sanitation, public health, and parks and recreation. These activities are typical of those performed by state and local governments in discharging their dual functions of administering the public law and furnishing public services. Indeed, it is functions such as these which governments are created to provide, services such as these which the States have traditionally afforded their citizens. If Congress may withdraw from the States the authority to make those fundamental employment decisions upon which their systems for performance of these functions must rest, we think there would be little left of the States' "separate and independent existence."

Thus, even if appellants may have overestimated the effect which the Act will have upon their current levels and patterns of governmental activity, the dispositive factor is that Congress has attempted to exercise its Commerce Clause authority to prescribe minimum wages and maximum hours to be paid by the States in their capacities as sovereign governments. In so doing, Congress has sought to wield its power in a fashion that would impair the States' "ability to function effectively within a federal system." This exercise of congressional authority does not comport with the federal system of government embodied in the Constitution. We hold that insofar as the challenged amendments operate to directly displace the States' freedom to structure integral operations in areas of traditional governmental functions, they are not within the authority granted Congress by Art. I, § 8, cl. 3.[17]

[17] We express no view as to whether different results might obtain if Congress seeks to affect integral operations of state governments by exercising authority granted it under other sections of the Constitution such as the Spending Power, Art. I, § 8, cl. 1, or § 5 of the Fourteenth Amendment.

With respect to the Court's decision in *Wirtz,* [t]here are undoubtedly factual distinctions between the two situations, but in view of the conclusions expressed earlier in this opinion we do not believe the reasoning in *Wirtz* may any longer be regarded as authoritative.

[W]e have reaffirmed today that the States as States stand on a quite different footing than an individual or a corporation when challenging the exercise of Congress power to regulate commerce. Congress may not exercise that power so as to force directly upon the States its choices as to how essential decisions regarding the conduct of integral governmental functions are to be made. While there are obvious differences between the schools and hospitals involved in *Wirtz,* and the fire and police departments affected here, each provides an integral portion of those governmental services which the States and their political subdivisions have traditionally afforded their citizens. We are therefore persuaded that *Wirtz* must be overruled.

JUSTICE BLACKMUN, concurring.

I may misinterpret the Court's opinion, but it seems to me that it adopts a balancing approach, and does not outlaw federal power in areas such as environmental protection, where the federal interest is demonstrably greater and where state facility compliance with imposed federal standards would be essential. With this understanding on my part of the Court's opinion, I join it.

JUSTICE BRENNAN, with whom JUSTICE WHITE and JUSTICE MARSHALL join, dissenting:

[L]aws within the commerce power may not infringe individual liberties. But there is no restraint based on state sovereignty requiring or permitting judicial enforcement anywhere expressed in the Constitution.

My Brethren thus have today manufactured an abstraction without substance, founded neither in the words of the Constitution nor on precedent. An abstraction having such profoundly pernicious consequences is not made less so by characterizing the 1974 amendments as legislation directed against the "States *qua* States."

Certainly the paradigm of sovereign action — action *qua* State — is in the enactment and enforcement of state laws. Is it possible that my Brethren are signaling abandonment of the heretofore unchallenged principle that Congress "can, if it chooses, entirely displace the States to the full extent of the far-reaching Commerce Clause?" [T]he ouster of state laws obviously curtails or prohibits the States prerogatives to make policy choices respecting subjects clearly of greater significance to the "State *qua* State" than the minimum wage paid to state employees. The Supremacy Clause dictates this result under "the federal system of government embodied in the Constitution."

Judicial restraint in this area merely recognizes that the political branches of our Government are structured to protect the interests of the States, as well as the Nation as a whole, and that the States are fully able to protect their own interests in the premises. Congress is constituted of representatives in both Senate and House *elected from the States.* Decisions upon the extent of federal intervention under the Commerce Clause into the affairs of the

States are in that sense decisions of the States themselves. Judicial redistribution of powers granted the National Government by the terms of the Constitution violates the fundamental tenet of our federalism that the extent of federal intervention into the State's affairs in the exercise of delegated powers shall be determined by the States' exercise of political power through their representatives in Congress. *See* Wechsler, *The Political Safeguards of Federalism: The Role of the States in the Composition and Selection of the National Government,* 54 COLUM. L. REV. 543 (1954).

Are state and federal interests being silently balanced, as in the discussion of *Fry*? The best I can make of it is that the 1966 FLSA amendments are struck down and *Wirtz* is overruled on the basis of the conceptually unworkable essential function test; and that the test is unworkable is demonstrated by my Brethren's inability to articulate any meaningful distinctions among state-operated railroads, state-operated schools and hospitals, and state-operated police and fire departments.

We are left then with a catastrophic judicial body blow at Congress' power under the Commerce Clause. Even if Congress may nevertheless accomplish its objectives — for example by conditioning grants of federal funds upon compliance with federal minimum wage and overtime standards — there is an ominous portent of disruption of our constitutional structure implicit in today's mischievous decision. I dissent.

JUSTICE STEVENS, dissenting.

The Court holds that the Federal Government may not interfere with a sovereign state's inherent right to pay a substandard wage to the janitor at the state capitol. The principle on which the holding rests is difficult to perceive.

The Federal Government may, I believe, require the State to act impartially when it hires or fires the janitor, to withhold taxes from his pay check, to observe safety regulations when he is performing his job, to forbid him from burning too much soft coal in the capitol furnace, from dumping untreated refuse in an adjacent waterway, from overloading a state-owned garbage truck or from driving either the truck or the governor's limousine over 55 miles an hour. Even though these and many other activities of the capitol janitor are activities of the State *qua* State, I have no doubt that they are subject to federal regulation.

Since I am unable to identify a limitation on that federal power that would not also invalidate federal regulation of state activities that I consider unquestionably permissible, I am persuaded that this statute is valid. Accordingly, with respect and a great deal of sympathy for the views expressed by the Court, I dissent from its constitutional holding.

NOTES

1. *Constitutional sources.* What is the constitutional source of the limitation on federal power recognized in *National League of Cities*? The Court cites the footnote reference to the Tenth Amendment in *Fry* but never discusses the amendment's applicability. The Tenth Amendment reserves non-delegated power to the states "or to the people." How should one decide whether a power is reserved to state governments or to the people? And, if a power is reserved to the people, can they act through their representatives in Congress?

It is not uncommon to find structural limitations inherent in the Constitution. For example, the federal immunity from state taxation recognized in *McCulloch* may reflect the constitutional structure itself. And in *Texas v. White,* 74 U.S. (7 Wall.) 700, 725 (1869) (dealing with the legal effect of Southern secession during the Civil War), the Court stated: "The Constitution, in all its provisions, looks to an indestructible Union, composed of indestructible States." *National League of Cities* may be read as imposing state sovereignty as a structural limitation on federal commerce powers.

"State sovereignty has not been a viable legal concept since the ratification of the Federal Constitution. That fundamental document is basically inconsistent with the notion of states as separate sovereignties." Bernard Schwartz, *National League of Cities v. Usery — The Commerce Power and State Sovereignty Redivivus,* 46 FORDHAM L. REV. 1115, 1133 (1978).

2. *State sovereignty & equal footing.* In *Coyle v. Smith,* 221 U.S. 559 (1911), a federal statute requiring Oklahoma to retain a fixed state capital for a certain time as a condition of admission to the Union was held to violate the implicit requirement that new states be admitted on an "equal footing" with the original states. *National League* assumes further that federal action which would render all the states a mere form without meaningful substantive powers, should be set aside.

What entities share in sovereignty? Local governments and their agencies do not share in the states' Eleventh Amendment immunity from suit but apparently do share in the immunity recognized in *National League.* Thus, the limitation enforced in *National League* may be different from sovereign immunity. If a state chooses to have certain functions performed by a private corporation, does the corporation then share in the state's immunity? If a corporation performs functions traditionally and exclusively associated with government (e.g., fire or police services), does it share in sovereign immunity?

3. *Traditional functions.* In *National League,* Justice Rehnquist stresses "traditional governmental functions" in defining the occasions for immunity. How is the traditional character of the function to be determined? If the test were the length of time in which an activity had been carried on, then the test would disadvantage state innovations by excluding newly emerging state activities. Is the relevant distinction between "governmental" and "proprietary" functions performed by government? Justice Rehnquist states the critical test as whether the federal law impairs "functions essential to separate and independent existence" of the states and whether the law would "directly displace the States' freedom to structure integral operations in areas of traditional governmental functions." The word "integral" seems to call for a case-by-case determination of how important the particular state activity is.

4. From *National League* to *Garcia*

a. *Hodel v. Virginia Surface Mining Reclamation Ass'n,* 452 U.S. 264 (1981). The Court upheld various provisions of the Surface Mining Control and Reclamation Act of 1977, which enacted comprehensive regulation of strip coal mining. The Act was challenged as displacing state land use controls. Justice Marshall, for the Court, cited three requirements under *National League of Cities* in order for a claim based on the Tenth Amendment to succeed:

> First, there must be a showing that the challenged statute regulates the "States as States." Second, the federal regulation must address matters that are indisputably "attributes of state sovereignty." And third, it must be apparent that States' compliance with the federal law would directly impair their ability "to structure integral operations in areas of traditional functions."

b. *Federal Energy Regulatory Comm'n (FERC) v. Mississippi*, 456 U.S. 742 (1982). The Court reversed a lower court decision holding the Public Utility Regulatory Policies Act of 1978 (PURPA) unconstitutional on the basis of *National League of Cities.* Among other things, the Act required each state regulatory authority to implement rules requiring utilities to offer to sell and purchase electricity from qualifying cogeneration and small power production facilities.

PURPA was interpreted as simply requiring Mississippi authorities "to adjudicate disputes arising under the statute. Dispute resolution of this kind is the very type of activity customarily engaged in by the *Mississippi Public Service Commission*." Under *Testa v. Katt,* 330 U.S. 386 (1974), state courts must entertain federal claims unless there is a neutral reason for denying the particular class of claims, and PURPA simply required Mississippi to "open its doors to claimants." The Court considered it of no significance that the state commissions had administrative as well as judicial duties. "Any other conclusion would allow the States to disregard both the preeminent position held by federal law throughout the Nation, *cf. Martin v. Hunter's Lessee,* and the congressional determination that the federal rights granted by PURPA can appropriately be enforced through state adjudicatory machinery. Such an approach 'flies in the face of the fact that the States of the Union constitute a Nation' and 'disregards the purpose and effect of Article VI of the Constitution.' "

c. *Fitzpatrick v. Bitzer*, 427 U.S. 445 (1976). The Court held that Congress had the authority to include states as employers covered by Title VII of the Civil Rights Act of 1964. The "principle of state sovereignty," the Court stated, "is necessarily limited by the enforcement provisions of § 5 of the Fourteenth Amendment." In *City of Rome v. United States,* 446 U.S. 156 (1980), the Court rejected a challenge based on *National League of Cities* to the Voting Rights Act provisions regulating state and local voting requirements, stating:

> We agree with the court below that *Fitzpatrick* stands for the proposition that principles of federalism that might otherwise be an obstacle to congressional authority are necessarily overridden by the power to enforce the Civil War Amendments "by appropriate legislation." Those Amendments were specifically designed as an expansion of federal power and an intrusion on state sovereignty.

d. *EEOC v. Wyoming*, 460 U.S. 226 (1983). The Court rejected, 5-4, a Tenth Amendment challenge to an EEOC action against the state for violation of the Age Discrimination in Employment Act. Wyoming had a mandatory retirement rule at age 55 for game wardens; the ADEA prohibits mandatory retirement prior to age 70 unless age can be shown to be a "qualification reasonably necessary to the normal operation of the particular business."

The Act might have been authorized under the Fourteenth Amendment and thus upheld on the basis of *Fitzpatrick,* but the case was argued on the basis of the Commerce Clause. Justice Brennan, writing for the Court, stated, "We conclude that the degree of federal intrusion in this case is sufficiently less serious than it was in *National League of Cities* so as to make it unnecessary for us to override Congress's express choice to extend its regulatory authority to the States."

GARCIA v. SAN ANTONIO METROPOLITAN TRANSIT AUTHORITY

469 U.S. 528, 105 S. Ct. 1005, 83 L. Ed. 2d 1016 (1985)

[Passenger transportation for-hire within San Antonio originally was provided by a private company regulated and franchised by the city. In 1959, the city purchased the privately owned company, replacing it with a public authority, the San Antonio Mass Transit Authority (SAMTA). Federal government subsidies provided about 25% of the operating budget of SAMTA as well as about $35 million in capital grants. SAMTA officials had stated that federal subsidies were vital to its continued operation. In 1974, Congress repealed the overtime exemption for mass transportation employees under the Fair Labor Standards Act (FLSA). SAMTA complied with the FLSA's requirement until *National League of Cities.* But in 1979, the Wage and Hour Administration of the Department of Labor issued an opinion that SAMTA's operations were not immune from the application of the FLSA under *National League of Cities.*

[SAMTA filed this action against the Secretary of Labor in the United States District Court, seeking a declaratory judgment that *National League of Cities* precluded the application of the FLSA's overtime requirement to SAMTA's operations. On the same day, Garcia and several other SAMTA employees brought suit against SAMTA for overtime pay required under the FLSA.

[In 1981, the district court granted SAMTA's motion for summary judgment, ruling that the "local public mass transit systems constitute integral operations in areas of traditional government functions" under *National League of Cities.* In 1982, the Supreme Court in *Transportation Union v. Long Island R.R.,* 455 U.S. 678 (1982), ruled that the commuter rail service provided by Long Island Rail Road did not constitute a "traditional government function" and therefore did not enjoy immunity under *National League of Cities.*

[Thereafter, the Supreme Court vacated the district court judgment and remanded the case for further consideration in light of *Long Island.* On remand, the district court adhered to its original view and again entered judgment for SAMTA. The Secretary of Labor and Garcia took direct appeals from the district court to the United States Supreme Court.]

JUSTICE BLACKMUN delivered the opinion of the Court.

Although *National League of Cities* supplied some examples of "traditional governmental functions," it did not offer a general explanation of how a "traditional" function is to be distinguished from a "nontraditional" one. Since then, federal and state courts have struggled with the task, thus imposed, of identifying a traditional function for purposes of state immunity under the Commerce Clause.

In the present cases, a Federal District Court concluded that municipal ownership and operation of a mass-transit system is a traditional governmental function and thus, under *National League of Cities,* is exempt from the obligations imposed by the FLSA. Faced with the identical question, three Federal Courts of Appeals and one state appellate court have reached the opposite conclusion. Our examination of this "function" standard applied in these and other cases over the last eight years now persuades us that the attempt to draw the boundaries of state regulatory immunity in terms of "traditional governmental function" is not only unworkable but is inconsistent with established principles of federalism and, indeed, with those very federalism principles on which *National League of Cities* purported to rest. That case, accordingly, is overruled.

The District Court voiced a common concern: "Despite the abundance of adjectives, identifying which particular state functions are immune remains difficult." Just how troublesome the task has been is revealed by the results reached in other federal cases. Thus, courts have held that regulating ambulance services, licensing automobile drivers, operating a municipal airport, performing solid waste disposal, and operating a highway authority are functions *protected* under *National League of Cities.* At the same time, courts have held that issuance of industrial development bonds, regulation of intrastate natural gas sales, regulation of traffic on public roads, regulation of air transportation, operation of a telephone system, leasing and sale of natural gas, operation of a mental health facility, and provision of in-house domestic services for the aged and handicapped are *not* entitled to immunity. We find it difficult, if not impossible, to identify an organizing principle that places each of the cases in the first group on one side of a line and each of the cases in the second group on the other side. The constitutional distinction between licensing drivers and regulating traffic, for example, or between operating a highway authority and operating a mental health facility, is elusive at best.

A further cautionary note is sounded, [for example], by the Court's experience in the related field of state immunity from federal taxation. It was . . . uncertainty and instability that led the Court, in *New York v. United States,* 326 U.S. 572 (1946), unanimously to conclude that the distinction between "governmental" and "proprietary" functions was "untenable" and must be abandoned.

The distinction the Court discarded as unworkable in the field of tax immunity has proved no more fruitful in the field of regulatory immunity under the Commerce Clause. Neither do any of the alternative standards that might be employed to distinguish between protected and unprotected governmental functions appear manageable. We rejected the possibility of making immunity turn on a purely historical standard of "tradition" in *Long Island,* and properly so. The most obvious defect of a historical approach to state immunity is that it prevents a court from accommodating changes in the historical functions of States, changes that have resulted in a number of once-private functions like education being assumed by the States and their subdivisions.[9] At the same time, the only apparent virtue of a rigorous historical standard, namely, its promise of a reasonably objective measure for state immunity, is illusory. Reliance on history as an organizing principle results in linedrawing of the most arbitrary sort; the genesis of state governmental functions stretches over a historical continuum from before the Revolution to the present, and courts would have to decide by fiat precisely how longstanding a pattern of state involvement had to be for federal regulatory authority to be defeated.[10]

A nonhistorical standard for selecting immune governmental functions is likely to be just as unworkable as is a historical standard. The goal of identifying "uniquely" governmental functions, for example, has been rejected by the Court in the field of government tort liability in part because the notion of a "uniquely" governmental function is unmanageable. Another possibility would be to confine immunity to "necessary" governmental services, that is, services that would be provided inadequately or not at all unless the government provided them. The set of services that fits into this category, however, may well be negligible. The fact that an unregulated market produces less of some service than a State deems desirable does not mean that the State itself must provide the service; in most if not all cases, the State can "contract out" by hiring private firms to provide the service or simply by providing subsidies to existing suppliers. It also is open to question how well equipped courts are to make this kind of determination about the workings of economic markets.

We believe, however, that there is a more fundamental problem at work here, a problem that explains why the Court was never able to provide a basis for the governmental/proprietary distinction in the intergovernmental tax immunity cases and why an attempt to draw similar distinctions with respect to federal regulatory authority under *National League of Cities* is unlikely to succeed regardless of how the distinctions are phrased. The problem is that neither the governmental-proprietary distinction nor any other that purports to separate out important governmental functions can be faithful to the role of federalism in a democratic society. The essence of our federal system is that within the realm of authority left open to them under the Constitution, the States must be equally free to engage in any activity that their citizens choose

[9] Indeed, the "traditional" nature of a particular governmental function can be a matter of historical nearsightedness; today's self-evidently "traditional" function is often yesterday's suspect innovation.

[10] For much the same reasons, the existence *vel non* of a tradition of *federal* involvement in a particular area does not provide an adequate standard for state immunity. Most of the Federal Government's current regulatory activity originated less than 50 years ago with the New Deal, and a good portion of it has developed within the past two decades. The recent vintage of this regulatory activity does not diminish the strength of the federal interest in applying regulatory standards to state activities, nor does it affect the strength of the States' interest in being free from federal supervision.

for the common weal, no matter how unorthodox or unnecessary anyone else — including the judiciary — deems state involvement to be. Any rule of state immunity that looks to the "traditional," "integral," or "necessary" nature of governmental functions inevitably invites an unelected federal judiciary to make decisions about which state policies it favors and which ones it dislikes. "The science of government . . . is the science of experiment," and the States cannot serve as laboratories for social and economic experiment, if they must pay an added price when they meet the changing needs of their citizenry by taking up functions that an earlier day and a different society left in private hands.

We therefore now reject, as unsound in principle and unworkable in practice, a rule of state immunity from federal regulation that turns on a judicial appraisal of whether a particular governmental function is "integral" or "traditional." Any such rule leads to inconsistent results at the same time that it disserves principles of democratic self-governance, and it breeds inconsistency precisely because it is divorced from those principles. If there are to be limits on the Federal Government's power to interfere with state functions — as undoubtedly there are — we must look elsewhere to find them. We accordingly return to the underlying issue that confronted this Court in *National League of Cities* — the manner in which the Constitution insulates States from the reach of Congress' power under the Commerce Clause.

The States unquestionably do "retai[n] a significant measure of sovereign authority." They do so, however, only to the extent that the Constitution has not divested them of their original powers and transferred those powers to the Federal Government. As a result, to say that the Constitution assumes the continued role of the States is to say little about the nature of that role. With rare exceptions, like the guarantee, in Article IV, § 3, of state territorial integrity, the Constitution does not carve out express elements of state sovereignty that Congress may not employ its delegated powers to displace. The power of the Federal Government is a "power to be respected" as well, and the fact that the States remain sovereign as to all powers not vested in Congress or denied them by the Constitution offers no guidance about where the frontier between state and federal power lies. In short, we have no license to employ freestanding conceptions of state sovereignty when measuring congressional authority under the Commerce Clause.

When we look for the States' "residuary and inviolable sovereignty," THE FEDERALIST NO. 39 (J. Madison), in the shape of the constitutional scheme rather than in predetermined notions of sovereign power, a different measure of state sovereignty emerges. Apart from the limitation on federal authority inherent in the delegated nature of Congress' Article I powers, the principal means chosen by the Framers to ensure the role of the States in the federal system lies in the structure of the Federal Government itself. It is no novelty to observe that the composition of the Federal Government was designed in large part to protect the States from overreaching by Congress. The Framers thus gave the States a role in the selection both of the Executive and the Legislative Branches of the Federal Government. The States were vested with indirect influence over the House of Representatives and the Presidency by their control of electoral qualifications and their role in presidential elections.

U.S. Const., Art. I, § 2, and Art. II, § 1. They were given more direct influence in the Senate, where each State received equal representation and each Senator was to be selected by the legislature of his State. Art. I, § 3. The significance attached to the States' equal representation in the Senate is underscored by the prohibition of any constitutional amendment divesting a State of equal representation without the State's consent. Art. V.

In short, the Framers chose to rely on a federal system in which special restraints on federal power over the States inhered principally in the workings of the National Government itself, rather than in discrete limitations on the objects of federal authority. State sovereign interests, then, are more properly protected by procedural safeguards inherent in the structure of the federal system than by judicially created limitations on federal power.

The effectiveness of the federal political process in preserving the States' interests is apparent even today in the course of federal legislation. On the one hand, the States have been able to direct a substantial proportion of federal revenues into their own treasuries in the form of general and program-specific grants in aid. Moreover, at the same time that the States have exercised their influence to obtain federal support, they have been able to exempt themselves from a wide variety of obligations imposed by Congress under the Commerce Clause. The fact that some federal statutes such as the FLSA extend general obligations to the States cannot obscure the extent to which the political position of the States in the federal system has served to minimize the burdens that the States bear under the Commerce Clause.

We realize that changes in the structure of the Federal Government have taken place since 1789, not the least of which has been the substitution of popular election of Senators by the adoption of the Seventeenth Amendment in 1913, and that these changes may work to alter the influence of the States in the federal political process. Nonetheless, against this background, we are convinced that the fundamental limitation that the constitutional scheme imposes on the Commerce Clause to protect the "States as States" is one of process rather than one of result.

Insofar as the present cases are concerned, then, we need go no further than to state that we perceive nothing in the overtime and minimum-wage requirements of the FLSA, as applied to SAMTA, that is destructive of state sovereignty or violative of any constitutional provision. SAMTA faces nothing more than the same minimum-wage and overtime obligations that hundreds of thousands of other employers, public as well as private, have to meet.

In these cases, the status of public mass transit simply underscores the extent to which the structural protections of the Constitution insulate the States from federally imposed burdens. Congress has not simply placed a financial burden on the shoulders of States and localities that operate mass-transit systems, but has provided substantial countervailing financial assistance as well, assistance that may leave individual mass transit systems better off than they would have been had Congress never intervened at all in the area.

Of course, we continue to recognize that the States occupy a special and specific position in our constitutional system and that the scope of Congress' authority under the Commerce Clause must reflect that position. But the principal and basic limit on the federal commerce power is that inherent in all congressional action — the built-in restraints that our system provides through state participation in federal governmental action. The political process ensures that laws that unduly burden the States will not be promulgated. In the factual setting of these cases the internal safeguards of the political process have performed as intended.

These cases do not require us to identify or define what affirmative limits the constitutional structure might impose on federal action affecting the States under the Commerce Clause. *See Coyle v. Oklahoma.*

Though the separate concurrence providing the fifth vote in *National League of Cities* was "not untroubled by certain possible implications" of the decision, the Court in that case attempted to articulate affirmative limits on the Commerce Clause power in terms of core governmental functions and fundamental attributes of state sovereignty. But the model of democratic decision-making the Court there identified underestimated, in our view, the solicitude of the national political process for the continued vitality of the States. Attempts by other courts since then to draw guidance from this model have proved it both impracticable and doctrinally barren. In sum, in *National League of Cities* the Court tried to repair what did not need repair.

We do not lightly overrule recent precedent. We have not hesitated, however, when it has become apparent that a prior decision has departed from a proper understanding of congressional power under the Commerce Clause. *See United States v. Darby.* Due respect for the reach of congressional power within the federal system mandates that we do so now.

National League of Cities v. Usery is overruled.

JUSTICE POWELL, with whom THE CHIEF JUSTICE, JUSTICE REHNQUIST, and JUSTICE O'CONNOR join, dissenting.

A unique feature of the United States is the *federal* system of government guaranteed by the Constitution and implicit in the very name of our country. Despite some genuflecting in the Court's opinion to the concept of federalism, today's decision effectively reduces the Tenth Amendment to meaningless rhetoric when Congress acts pursuant to the Commerce Clause.

The Court finds that the test of State immunity approved in *National League of Cities* and its progeny is unworkable and unsound in principle. In finding the test to be unworkable, the Court begins by mischaracterizing *National League of Cities* and subsequent cases. In concluding that efforts to define state immunity are unsound in principle, the Court radically departs from long settled constitutional values and ignores the role of judicial review in our system of government.

Much of the Court's opinion is devoted to arguing that it is difficult to define *a priori* "traditional governmental functions." *National League of Cities* neither engaged in, nor required, such a task.[4] The Court discusses and

[4] In *National League of Cities,* we referred to the sphere of state sovereignty as including "traditional governmental functions," a realm which is, of course, difficult to define with precision. But the luxury of precise definitions is one rarely enjoyed in interpreting and applying the general provisions of our Constitution. Not surprisingly, therefore, the Court's attempt to demonstrate the impossibility of definition is unhelpful.

condemns as standards "traditional governmental function[s]," "purely historical" functions, " 'uniquely' governmental functions," and " 'necessary' governmental services." But nowhere does it mention that *National League of Cities* adopted a familiar type of balancing test for determining whether Commerce Clause enactments transgress constitutional limitations imposed by the federal nature of our system of government. Our subsequent decisions also adopted this approach of weighing the respective interests of the States and federal government.[5]

Today's opinion does not explain how the States' role in the electoral process guarantees that particular exercises of the Commerce Clause power will not infringe on residual State sovereignty. Members of Congress are elected from the various States, but once in office they are members of the federal government.[8] Although the States participate in the Electoral College, this is hardly a reason to view the President as a representative of the States' interest against federal encroachment. We noted recently the "hydraulic pressure inherent within each of the separate Branches to exceed the outer limits of its power." *Immigration and Naturalization Service v. Chadha.* The Court offers no reason to think that this pressure will not operate when Congress seeks to invoke its powers under the Commerce Clause, notwithstanding the electoral role of the States.[9]

---

[5] In undertaking such balancing, we have considered, on the one hand, the strength of the federal interest in the challenged legislation and the impact of exempting the States from its reach. Central to our inquiry into the federal interest is how closely the challenged action implicates the central concerns of the Commerce Clause, *viz.,* the promotion of a national economy and free trade among the states. Similarly, we have considered whether exempting States from federal regulation would undermine the goals of the federal program. On the other hand, we have also assessed the injury done to the States if forced to comply with federal Commerce Clause enactments.

[8] One can hardly imagine this Court saying that because Congress is composed of individuals, individual rights guaranteed by the Bill of Rights are amply protected by the political process. Yet, the position adopted today is indistinguishable in principle. The Tenth Amendment also is an essential part of the Bill of Rights.

[9] At one time in our history, the view that the structure of the federal government sufficed to protect the States might have had a somewhat more practical, although not a more logical, basis. Professor Wechsler, whose seminal article in 1954 proposed the view adopted by the Court today, predicated his argument on assumptions that simply do not accord with current reality. Professor Wechsler wrote: "National action has . . .always been regarded as exceptional in our polity, an intrusion to be justified by some necessity, the special rather than the ordinary case." Not only is the premise of this view clearly at odds with the proliferation of national legislation over the past 30 years, but "a variety of structural and political changes in this century have combined to make Congress particularly *insensitive* to state and local values." Advisory Comm'n on Intergovernmental Relations [ACIR], Regulatory Federalism: Policy, Process, Impact and Reform 50 (1984). The adoption of the Seventeenth Amendment (providing for direct election of senators), the weakening of political parties on the local level, and the rise of national media, among other things, have made Congress increasingly less representative of State and local interests, and more likely to be responsive to the demands of various national constituencies. As one observer explained, "As Senators and members of the House develop independent constituencies among groups such as farmers, businessmen, laborers, environmentalists, and the poor, each of which generally supports certain national initiatives, their tendency to identify with state interests and the positions of state officials is reduced." Kaden, Federalism in the Courts: Agenda for the 1980s, in ACIR.

See also Kaden, *Politics, Money, and State Sovereignty: The Judicial Role,* 79 COLUM. L. REV. 847 (1979) (changes in political practices and the breadth of national initiatives mean that the

The Court apparently thinks that the States' success at obtaining federal funds for various projects and exemptions from the obligations of some federal statutes is indicative of the "effectiveness of the federal political process in preserving the States interest." But such political success is not relevant to the question whether the political *processes* are the proper means of enforcing constitutional limitations. The States' role in our system of government is a matter of constitutional law, not of legislative grace.

More troubling than the logical infirmities in the Court's reasoning is the result of its holding, *i.e.,* that federal political officials, invoking the Commerce Clause, are the sole judges of the limits of their own power. This result is inconsistent with the fundamental principles of our constitutional system. *See, e.g.*, The Federalist No. 78 (Hamilton). At least since *Marbury v. Madison* it has been the settled province of the federal judiciary "to say what the law is" with respect to the constitutionality of acts of Congress. In rejecting the role of the judiciary in protecting the States from federal overreaching, the Court's opinion offers no explanation for ignoring the teaching of the most famous case in our history.

[T]he Court today propounds a view of federalism that pays only lip service to the role of the States. Although it says that the States "unquestionably do 'retai[n] a significant measure of sovereign authority,' " it fails to recognize the broad, yet specific areas of sovereignty that the Framers intended the States retain. Indeed, the Court barely acknowledges that the Tenth Amendment exists.[16] In *National League of Cities,* we identified the kinds of activities engaged in by state and local governments that affect the everyday lives of citizens. These are services that people are in a position to understand and evaluate, and in a democracy, have the right to oversee. We recognized that "it is functions such as these which governments are created to provide" and that the states and local governments are better able than the national government to perform them.

The Court maintains that the standard approved in *National League of Cities* "disserves principles of democratic self-government." In reaching this conclusion, the Court looks myopically only to persons elected to positions in the federal government. It disregards entirely the far more effective role of democratic self-government at the state and local levels. One must compare realistically the operation of the state and local governments with that of the federal government. My point is simply that members of the immense federal bureaucracy are not elected, know less about the services traditionally rendered by States and localities, and are inevitably less responsive to recipients of such services, than are state legislatures, city councils, boards of supervisors, and state and local commissions, boards, and agencies. It is

---

political branches "may no longer be as well suited as they once were to the task of safeguarding the role of the states in the federal system and protecting the fundamental value of federalism") and ACIR, Regulatory Federalism (detailing the "dramatic shift" in kind of federal regulation applicable to the States over the past two decades). Thus, even if one were to ignore the numerous problems with the Court's position in terms of constitutional theory, there would remain serious questions as to its factual premises.

[16] The Court's opinion mentions the Tenth Amendment only once, when it restates the question put to the parties for reargument in this case.

at these state and local levels — not in Washington as the Court so mistakenly thinks — that "democratic self-government" is best exemplified.

I return now to the balancing test approved in *National League of Cities* and accepted in *Hodel, Long Island R. Co.,* and *FERC v. Mississippi.* The financial impact on States and localities of displacing their control over wages, hours, overtime regulations, pensions, and labor relations with their employees could have serious, as well as unanticipated, effects on state and local planning, budgeting, and the levying of taxes.

The Court emphasizes that municipal operation of an intra-city mass transit system is relatively new in the life of our country. It nevertheless is a classic example of the type of service traditionally provided by local government. It is *local* by definition. It is this kind of state and local control and accountability that the Framers understood would insure the vitality and preservation of the federal system that the Constitution explicitly requires.

Although the Court's opinion purports to recognize that the States retain some sovereign power, it does not identify even a single aspect of state authority that would remain when the Commerce Clause is invoked to justify federal regulation. As I view the Court's decision today as rejecting the basic precepts of our federal system and limiting the constitutional role of judicial review, I dissent.

JUSTICE REHNQUIST, dissenting.

I join both JUSTICE POWELL's and JUSTICE O'CONNOR's thoughtful dissents. JUSTICE POWELL's reference to the "balancing test" approved in *National League of Cities* is not identical with the language in that case, which recognized that Congress could not act under its commerce power to infringe on certain fundamental aspects of state sovereignty that are essential to "the States' separate and independent existence." Nor is either test, or JUSTICE O'CONNOR's suggested approach, precisely congruent with JUSTICE BLACKMUN's views in 1976, when he spoke of a balancing approach which did not outlaw federal power in areas "where the federal interest is demonstrably greater." But under any one of these approaches the judgment in this case should be affirmed, and I do not think it incumbent on those of us in dissent to spell out further the fine points of a principle that will, I am confident, in time again command the support of a majority of this Court.

JUSTICE O'CONNOR, with whom JUSTICE POWELL and JUSTICE REHNQUIST join, dissenting.

The Framers perceived the interstate commerce power to be important but limited, and expected that it would be used primarily if not exclusively to remove interstate tariffs and to regulate maritime affairs and large-scale mercantile enterprise. In the decades since ratification of the Constitution, interstate economic activity has steadily expanded. This Court has been increasingly generous in its interpretation of the commerce power of Congress, primarily to assure that the National Government would be able to deal with national economic problems.

Incidental to this expansion of the commerce power, Congress has been given an ability it lacked prior to the emergence of an integrated national economy. Because virtually every *state* activity, like virtually every activity of a private individual, arguably "affects" interstate commerce, Congress can now supplant the States from the significant sphere of activities envisioned for them by the Framers. It is in this context that recent changes in the workings of Congress, such as the direct election of Senators and the expanded influence of national interest groups become relevant. These changes may well have lessened the weight Congress gives to the legitimate interests of States as States. As a result, there is now a real risk that Congress will gradually erase the diffusion of power between state and nation on which the Framers based their faith in the efficiency and vitality of our Republic.

Today, as federal legislation and coercive grant programs have expanded to embrace innumerable activities that were once viewed as local, the burden of persuasion has surely shifted, and the extraordinary has become ordinary. The political process has not protected against these encroachments on state activities, even though they directly impinge on a State's ability to make and enforce its laws. With the abandonment of *National League of Cities,* all that stands between the remaining essentials of state sovereignty and Congress is the latter's underdeveloped capacity for self-restraint.

The problems of federalism in an integrated national economy are capable of more responsible resolution than holding that the States as States retain no status apart from that which Congress chooses to let them retain. The proper resolution, I suggest, lies in weighing state autonomy as a factor in the balance when interpreting the means by which Congress can exercise its authority on the States as States. It is insufficient, in assessing the validity of congressional regulation of a State pursuant to the commerce power, to ask only whether the same regulation would be valid if enforced against a private party. That reasoning, embodied in the majority opinion, is inconsistent with the spirit of our Constitution. It remains relevant that a *State* is being regulated, as *National League of Cities* and every recent case have recognized. As far as the Constitution is concerned, a State should not be equated with any private litigant. Instead, the autonomy of a State is an essential component of federalism. If state autonomy is ignored in assessing the means by which Congress regulates matters affecting commerce, then federalism becomes irrelevant simply because the set of activities remaining beyond the reach of such a commerce power "may well be negligible."

It has been difficult for this Court to craft bright lines defining the scope of the state autonomy protected by *National League of Cities.* Such difficulty is to be expected whenever constitutional concerns as important as federalism and the effectiveness of the commerce power come into conflict. I would not shirk the duty acknowledged by *National League of Cities* and its progeny, and I share JUSTICE REHNQUIST's belief that this Court will in time again assume its constitutional responsibility.

NOTES

1. *State immunity from federal taxation.* In *McCulloch v. Maryland,* Chief Justice Marshall opined that there would be no constitutional infirmity in federal taxation of state activities because the states were adequately represented in the federal government. But for most of our history Congress has provided exemptions for various state activities from federal taxation. In *South Carolina v. Baker,* 485 U.S. 505 (1988), the Court, relying on *Garcia,* rejected a Tenth Amendment attack on section 310(b)(1) of the Tax Equity and Fiscal Responsibility Act of 1982, which removed the federal income tax exemption for interest earned on publicly offered long-term bonds issued by state and local governments unless those bonds are issued in registered form:

> *Garcia* holds that the limits [on Congress authority to regulate state activities] are structural, not substantive — i.e., that States must find their protection from congressional regulation through the national political process, not through judicially defined spheres of unregulable state activity. South Carolina contends that the political process failed here because Congress had no concrete evidence quantifying the tax evasion attributable to unregistered state bonds and relied instead on anecdotal evidence.
>
> Although *Garcia* left open the possibility that some extraordinary defects in the national political process might render congressional regulation of state activities invalid under the Tenth Amendment, the Court in *Garcia* had no occasion to identify or define the defects that might lead to such invalidation. Nor do we attempt any definitive articulation here. It suffices to observe that South Carolina has not even alleged that it was deprived of any right to participate in the national political process or that it was singled out in a way that left it politically isolated and powerless. [N]othing in *Garcia* or the Tenth Amendment authorizes courts to second-guess the substantive basis for congressional legislation.

Justices Stevens and Scalia and Chief Justice Rehnquist wrote separate concurrences, the Chief Justice noting that "[e]ven the more expansive conception of the Tenth Amendment espoused in *National League of Cities v. Usery* recognized that only congressional action that 'operate[s] to directly displace the States freedom to structure integral operations in areas of traditional governmental functions,' runs afoul of the authority granted Congress."

Justice O'Connor, dissenting, pointed out that "[l]ong-term debt obligations are an essential source of funding for state and local governments."

2. *Statutory construction.* Professor Field argues that the Court can achieve some of the objectives of the *Garcia* dissenters by tightly confining federal legislation without declaring it unconstitutional. She points out that constitutional doctrines are only one method of adjusting disputes between federal and state government and that

> far more often it is by interpreting a federal statute or framing a judicial doctrine by which the Court expands or contracts state authority. What the Court forgot in *National League* and remembered in *Garcia* is that, in most matters, the Constitution should be the last line of defense and not the first. In all but a limited class of cases, there are more flexible ways of adjusting conflicts while keeping the Court out of a direct confrontation with Congress.

Martha Field, *Garcia v. San Antonio Metropolitan Transit Authority: The Demise of a Misguided Doctrine,* 99 HARV. L. REV. 84, 118 (1985).

In ***Gregory v. Ashcroft*, 501 U.S. 452 (1991)**, the Court required that if Congress seeks to impose burdens on the states, it must do so by means of a clear statement. "This clear statement rule," said Justice O'Connor, speaking for the Court, "is nothing more than an acknowledgement that the States retain substantial sovereign powers under our constitutional scheme, powers with which Congress does not readily interfere." Is this rule a method of ascertaining legislative intent, or is it rather a method of assuring adherence to the federalism protections embodied in the political process?

3. *New York v. United States*, 505 U.S. 144 (1992). The Low-Level Radioactive Waste Policy Amendments Act of 1985 imposed upon states the obligation to provide for the disposal of low-level radioactive waste generated within their borders, provided monetary incentives for the development of disposal sites, and required a state to take title and possession of waste if it failed to provide for disposal of waste generated in that state by a specified date.

The Court upheld the monetary incentives but invalidated the "take title" provision. Justice O'Connor's opinion for the Court sought to distinguish the case from the line of cases culminating in *Garcia* because

> this is not a case in which Congress subjected a State to the same legislation applicable to private parties.
>
> Congress may not simply "commandee[r] the legislative process of the State by directly compelling them to enact and enforce a federal regulatory program."
>
> While Congress has substantial powers to govern the Nation directly, including areas of intimate concern to the States, the Constitution has never been understood to confer upon Congress the ability to require the States to govern according to Congress' instruction. Both the States and the United States existed before the Constitution. The people, through that instrument, established a more perfect union by substituting a national government, acting, with ample power, directly upon the citizens instead of the Confederate government, which acted with powers, greatly restricted, only upon the States. We have always understood that even where Congress has the authority under the Constitution to pass laws requiring or prohibiting certain acts, it lacks the power directly to compel the States to require or prohibit those acts.

Justice O'Connor pointed out that Congress can use two means to encourage states to regulate in a certain way: (1) attach conditions under its spending power and (2) give states a choice to regulate or be pre-empted by federal legislation where it has the power to regulate private activity under the commerce power. In either of these two situations, "the residents of the State retain the ultimate decision as to whether or not the state will comply."

> By contrast, where the Federal Government compels States to regulate, the accountability of both state and federal officials is diminished.

> [W]here the Federal Government directs the States to regulate, it may be state officials who will bear the brunt of public disapproval, while the federal officials who devised the regulatory program may remain insulated from the electoral ramifications of their decision.
>
> Whether one views the take title provision as lying outside Congress' enumerated powers, or as infringing upon state sovereignty reserved by the Tenth Amendment, the provision is inconsistent with the federal structure of our Government established by the Constitution.

Justice White, joined by Justices Blackmun and Stevens, dissented as to the invalidation of the "take title" provision. Justice Stevens' opinion pointed out that "the Federal Government directs state governments in many realms. The Government regulates state-operated railroads, state school systems, state prisons, state elections and a host of other state functions."

To what extent could Justice O'Connor's decision have been more properly grounded in the Guarantee Clause, Article IV, § 4? That provision directs the United States to "guarantee to every State in this Union a Republican Form of Government." Is there a sense in which the take-title provision actually undermines a state's republican form of government? Justice O'Connor concluded that because the Court had already found that the provision violates the Tenth Amendment, it need not examine it under the Guarantee Clause. She noted that the Clause "has been an infrequent basis for litigation throughout our history. In most of the cases in which the Court has been asked to apply the Clause, the Court has found the claims presented to be nonjusticiable under the 'political question' doctrine." *See generally* Deborah Merritt, *The Guarantee Clause and State Autonomy: Federalism for a Third Century*, 88 COLUM. L. REV. 1 (1988).

PRINTZ v. UNITED STATES

521 U.S. 898, 117 S. Ct. 2365, 138 L. Ed. 2d 914 (1997)

JUSTICE SCALIA delivered the opinion of the Court.

The question presented in these cases is whether certain interim provisions of the Brady Handgun Violence Prevention Act, commanding state and local law enforcement officers to conduct background checks on prospective handgun purchasers and to perform certain related tasks, violate the Constitution.

I

The Gun Control Act of 1968 (GCA) establishes a detailed federal scheme governing the distribution of firearms. In 1993, Congress amended the GCA by enacting the Brady Act. The Act requires the Attorney General to establish a national instant background check system by November 30, 1998, and immediately puts in place certain interim provisions until that system becomes operative. Under the interim provisions, a firearms dealer who proposes to transfer a handgun must first: (1) receive from the transferee a statement (the Brady Form), containing the name, address and date of birth of the proposed transferee along with a sworn statement that the transferee is not among any of the classes of prohibited purchasers; (2) verify the identity of the transferee by examining an identification document; and (3) provide the "chief law enforcement officer" (CLEO) of the transferee's residence with notice of the contents (and a copy) of the Brady Form. With some exceptions, the dealer must then wait five business days before consummating the sale, unless the CLEO earlier notifies the dealer that he has no reason to believe the transfer would be illegal.

The Brady Act creates two significant alternatives to the foregoing scheme. A dealer may sell a handgun immediately if the purchaser possesses a state handgun permit issued after a background check, or if state law provides for an instant background check. In States that have not rendered one of these alternatives applicable to all gun purchasers, CLEOs are required to perform certain duties. When a CLEO receives the required notice of a proposed transfer from the firearms dealer, the CLEO must "make a reasonable effort to ascertain within 5 business days whether receipt or possession would be in violation of the law, including research in whatever State and local record keeping systems are available and in a national system designated by the Attorney General." The Act does not require the CLEO to take any particular action if he determines that a pending transaction would be unlawful; he may notify the firearms dealer to that effect, but is not required to do so. If, however, the CLEO notifies a gun dealer that a prospective purchaser is ineligible to receive a handgun, he must, upon request, provide the would-be purchaser with a written statement of the reasons for that determination. Moreover, if the CLEO does not discover any basis for objecting to the sale, he must destroy any records in his possession relating to the transfer, including his copy of the Brady Form. Under a separate provision of the GCA, any person who "knowingly violates [the section of the GCA amended by the Brady Act] shall be fined under this title, imprisoned for no more than 1 year, or both."

Petitioners Jay Printz and Richard Mack, the CLEOs for Ravalli County, Montana, and Graham County, Arizona, respectively, filed separate actions challenging the constitutionality of the Brady Act's interim provisions. In each case, the District Court held that the provision requiring CLEOs to perform background checks was unconstitutional, but concluded that provision was severable from the remainder of the Act, effectively leaving a voluntary background-check system in place. A divided panel of the Court of Appeals for the Ninth Circuit reversed, finding none of the Brady Act's interim provisions to be unconstitutional.

II

From the description set forth above, it is apparent that the Brady Act purports to direct state law enforcement officers to participate, albeit only temporarily, in the administration of a federally enacted regulatory scheme. The petitioners here object to being pressed into federal service, and contend that congressional action compelling state officers to execute federal laws is unconstitutional. Because there is no constitutional text speaking to this precise question, the answer to the CLEOs' challenge must be sought in historical understanding and practice, in the structure of the Constitution, and in the jurisprudence of this Court. We treat those three sources, in that order, in this and the next two sections of this opinion.

Petitioners contend that compelled enlistment of state executive officers for the administration of federal programs is, until very recent years at least, unprecedented. The Government contends, to the contrary, that "the earliest Congresses enacted statutes that required the participation of state officials in the implementation of federal laws." The Government's contention demands our careful consideration, since early congressional enactments "provid[e] 'contemporaneous and weighty evidence' of the Constitution's meaning." Indeed, such "contemporaneous legislative exposition of the Constitution . . ., acquiesced in for a long term of years, fixes the construction to be given its provisions." Conversely if, as petitioners contend, earlier Congresses avoided use of this highly attractive power, we would have reason to believe that the power was thought not to exist.

The Government observes that statutes enacted by the first Congresses required state courts to record applications for citizenship, to transmit abstracts of citizenship applications and other naturalization records to the Secretary of State, and to register aliens seeking naturalization and issue certificates of registry. These early laws establish, at most, that the Constitution was originally understood to permit imposition of an obligation on state judges to enforce federal prescriptions, insofar as those prescriptions related to matters appropriate for the judicial power. That assumption was perhaps implicit in one of the provisions of the Constitution, and was explicit in another. In accord with the so-called Madisonian Compromise, Article III, § 1 established only a Supreme Court, and made the creation of lower federal courts optional with the Congress — even though it was obvious that the Supreme Court alone could not hear all federal cases throughout the United States. And the Supremacy Clause announced that "the Laws of the United States . . . shall be the supreme Law of the Land; and the Judges in every State shall be bound thereby." It is understandable why courts should have been viewed distinctively in this regard; unlike legislatures and executives, they applied the law of other sovereigns all the time.

[W]e do not think the early statutes imposing obligations on state courts imply a power of Congress to impress the state executive into its service. Indeed, it can be argued that the numerousness of these statutes, contrasted with the utter lack of statutes imposing obligations on the States' executive (notwithstanding the attractiveness of that course to Congress), suggests an assumed absence of such power.

In addition to early legislation, the Government also appeals to other sources we have usually regarded as indicative of the original understanding of the Constitution. It points to portions of THE FEDERALIST. But none of these statements necessarily implies — what is the critical point here — that Congress could impose these responsibilities without the consent of the States. They appear to rest on the natural assumption that the States would consent to allowing their officials to assist the Federal Government.

To complete the historical record, we must note that there is not only an absence of executive-commandeering statutes in the early Congresses, but there is an absence of them in our later history as well, at least until very recent years. The Government points to a number of federal statutes enacted within the past few decades that require the participation of state or local officials in implementing federal regulatory schemes. Some of these are connected to federal funding measures, and can perhaps be more accurately described as conditions upon the grant of federal funding than as mandates to the States; others, which require only the provision of information to the Federal Government, do not involve the precise issue before us here, which is the forced participation of the States' executive in the actual administration of a federal program. We of course do not address these or other currently operative enactments that are not before us; it will be time enough to do so if and when their validity is challenged in a proper case. For deciding the issue before us here, they are of little relevance. Even assuming they represent assertion of the very same congressional power challenged here, they are of such recent vintage that they are no more probative than the statute before us of a constitutional tradition that lends meaning to the text. Their persuasive force is far outweighed by almost two centuries of apparent congressional avoidance of the practice.

III

The constitutional practice we have examined above tends to negate the existence of the congressional power asserted here, but is not conclusive. We turn next to consideration of the structure of the Constitution, to see if we can discern among its "essential postulate[s]," *Principality of Monaco v. Mississippi*, a principle that controls the present cases.

It is incontestible that the Constitution established a system of "dual sovereignty." Although the States surrendered many of their powers to the new Federal Government, they retained "a residuary and inviolable sovereignty," THE FEDERALIST NO. 39 (J. Madison). This is reflected throughout the Constitution's text, including (to mention only a few examples) the prohibition on any involuntary reduction or combination of a State's territory, Art. IV, § 3; the Judicial Power Clause, Art. III, § 2, and the Privileges and Immunities Clause, Art. IV, § 2, which speak of the "Citizens" of the States; the amendment provision, Article V, which requires the votes of three-fourths of the States to amend the Constitution; and the Guarantee Clause, Art. IV, § 4, which "presupposes the continued existence of the states and . . . those means and instrumentalities which are the creation of their sovereign and reserved rights," *Helvering v. Gerhardt*. Residual state sovereignty was also implicit, of course, in the Constitution's conferral upon Congress of not all governmental powers, but only discrete, enumerated ones, Art. I, § 8, which implication was rendered express by the Tenth Amendment.

The Framers' experience under the Articles of Confederation had persuaded them that using the States as the instruments of federal governance was both ineffectual and provocative of federal-state conflict. *See* THE FEDERALIST NO. 15. Preservation of the States as independent political entities being the price of union, the Framers rejected the concept of a central government that would act upon and through the States, and instead designed a system in which the state and federal governments would exercise concurrent authority over the people — who were, in Hamilton's words, "the only proper objects of government," THE FEDERALIST NO. 15. We have set forth the historical record in more detail elsewhere, see *New York v. United States*, and need not repeat it here. It suffices to repeat the conclusion: "The Framers explicitly chose a Constitution that confers upon Congress the power to regulate individuals, not States." The great innovation of this design was that "our citizens would have two political capacities, one state and one federal, each protected from incursion by the other" — "a legal system unprecedented in form and design, establishing two orders of government, each with its own direct relationship, its own privity, its own set of mutual rights and obligations to the people who sustain it and are governed by it." *U.S. Term Limits, Inc. v. Thornton* (KENNEDY, J., concurring). The Constitution thus contemplates that a State's government will represent and remain accountable to its own citizens.

This separation of the two spheres is one of the Constitution's structural protections of liberty.

We have thus far discussed the effect that federal control of state officers would have upon the first element of the "double security" alluded to by Madison: the division of power between State and Federal Governments. It would also have an effect upon the second element: the separation and equilibration of powers between the three branches of the Federal Government itself. The Constitution does not leave to speculation who is to administer the laws enacted by Congress; the President, it says, "shall take Care that the Laws be faithfully executed," Art. II, § 3, personally and through officers whom he appoints (save for such inferior officers as Congress may authorize to be appointed by the "Courts of Law" or by "the Heads of Departments" who are themselves presidential appointees), Art. II, § 2. The Brady Act effectively transfers this responsibility to thousands of CLEOs in the 50 States, who are left to implement the program without meaningful Presidential control (if indeed meaningful Presidential control is possible without the power to appoint and remove). The insistence of the Framers upon unity in the Federal Executive — to insure both vigor and accountability — is well known. That unity would be shattered, and the power of the President would be subject to reduction, if Congress could act as effectively without the President as with him, by simply requiring state officers to execute its laws.

The dissent of course resorts to the last, best hope of those who defend *ultra vires* congressional action, the Necessary and Proper Clause. It reasons that the power to regulate the sale of handguns under the Commerce Clause, coupled with the power to "make all Laws which shall be necessary and proper for carrying into Execution the foregoing Powers," Art. I, § 8, conclusively establishes the Brady Act's constitutional validity, because the Tenth Amendment imposes no limitations on the exercise of delegated powers but merely prohibits the exercise of powers "not delegated to the United States." What destroys the dissent's Necessary and Proper Clause argument, however, is not the Tenth Amendment but the Necessary and Proper Clause itself.[17]

---

[17] When a "La[w] . . .for carrying into Execution" the Commerce Clause violates the principle of state sovereignty reflected in various constitutional provisions it is not a "La[w] . . .proper for carrying into Execution the Commerce Clause," and is thus, in the words of THE FEDERALIST, "merely [an] ac[t] of usurpation" which "deserve[s] to be treated as such." THE FEDERALIST NO. 33 (A. Hamilton).

The dissent perceives a simple answer in that portion of Article VI which requires that "all executive and judicial Officers, both of the United States and of the several States, shall be bound by Oath or Affirmation, to support this Constitution," arguing that by virtue of the Supremacy Clause this makes "not only the Constitution, but every law enacted by Congress as well," binding on state officers, including laws requiring state-officer enforcement. The Supremacy Clause, however, makes "Law of the Land" only "Laws of the United States which shall be made in Pursuance [of the Constitution]"; so the Supremacy Clause merely brings us back to the question discussed earlier, whether laws conscripting state officers violate state sovereignty and are thus not in accord with the Constitution.

IV

Finally, and most conclusively in the present litigation, we turn to the prior jurisprudence of this Court. In *Hodel v. Virginia Surface Mining & Reclamation Assn., Inc.* and *FERC v. Mississippi* we sustained statutes against constitutional challenge only after assuring ourselves that they did not require the States to enforce federal law.

When we were at last confronted squarely with a federal statute that unambiguously required the States to enact or administer a federal regulatory program, our decision should have come as no surprise. [I]n *New York v. United States* we concluded that Congress could constitutionally require the States to do neither. "The Federal Government," we held, "may not compel the States to enact or administer a federal regulatory program."

The Government contends that *New York* is distinguishable on the following ground: unlike the "take title" provisions invalidated there, the background-check provision of the Brady Act does not require state legislative or executive officials to make policy, but instead issues a final directive to state CLEOs. It is permissible, the Government asserts, for Congress to command state or local officials to assist in the implementation of federal law so long as "Congress itself devises a clear legislative solution that regulates private conduct" and requires state or local officers to provide only "limited, non-policy making help in enforcing that law."

The Government's distinction between "making" law and merely "enforcing" it, between "policy making" and mere "implementation," is an interesting one. It is perhaps not meant to be the same as, but it is surely reminiscent of, the line that separates proper congressional conferral of Executive power from unconstitutional delegation of legislative authority for federal separation-of-powers purposes. This Court has not been notably successful in describing the latter line; indeed, some think we have abandoned the effort to do so. We are doubtful that the new line the Government proposes would be any more distinct. How much is too much is not likely to be answered precisely; and an imprecise barrier against federal intrusion upon state authority is not likely to be an effective one.

Even assuming, moreover, that the Brady Act leaves no "policy making" discretion with the States, we fail to see how that improves rather than worsens the intrusion upon state sovereignty. It is an essential attribute of the States' retained sovereignty that they remain independent and autonomous within their proper sphere of authority. It is no more compatible with this independence and autonomy that their officers be "dragooned" into administering federal law, than it would be compatible with the independence and autonomy of the United States that its officers be impressed into service for the execution of state laws.

The Government purports to find support for its proffered distinction of *New York* in our decisions in *Testa v. Katt* and *FERC v. Mississippi.* We find neither case relevant. *Testa* stands for the proposition that state courts cannot refuse to apply federal law — a conclusion mandated by the terms of the Supremacy Clause ("the Judges in every State shall be bound [by federal law]"). As we have suggested earlier, that says nothing about whether state executive officers must administer federal law. As for *FERC*, it stated that "this Court never has sanctioned explicitly a federal command to the States to promulgate and enforce laws and regulations," and upheld the statutory provisions at issue precisely because they did not commandeer state government, but merely imposed preconditions to continued state regulation of an otherwise preempted field, and required state administrative agencies to apply federal law while acting in a judicial capacity, in accord with *Testa*.

The Government also maintains that requiring state officers to perform discrete, ministerial tasks specified by Congress does not violate the principle of *New York* because it does not diminish the accountability of state or federal officials. This argument fails even on its own terms. By forcing state governments to absorb the financial burden of implementing a federal regulatory program, Members of Congress can take credit for "solving" problems without having to ask their constituents to pay for the solutions with higher federal taxes. And even when the States are not forced to absorb the costs of implementing a federal program, they are still put in the position of taking the blame for its burdensomeness and for its defects. Under the present law, for example, it will be the CLEO and not some federal official who stands between the gun purchaser and immediate possession of his gun. And it will likely be the CLEO, not some federal official, who will be blamed for any error (even one in the designated federal database) that causes a purchaser to be mistakenly rejected.

Finally, the Government puts forward a cluster of arguments that can be grouped under the heading: "The Brady Act serves very important purposes, is most efficiently administered by CLEOs during the interim period, and places a minimal and only temporary burden upon state officers." There is considerable disagreement over the extent of the burden, but we need not pause over that detail. Assuming all the mentioned factors were true, they might be relevant if we were evaluating whether the incidental application to the States of a federal law of general applicability excessively interfered with the functioning of state governments. But where, as here, it is the whole object of the law to direct the functioning of the state executive, and hence to compromise the structural framework of dual sovereignty, such a "balancing" analysis is inappropriate. It is the very principle of separate state sovereignty that such a law offends, and no comparative assessment of the various interests can overcome that fundamental defect. We expressly rejected such an approach in *New York*.

We conclude categorically, as we concluded categorically in *New York:* "The Federal Government may not compel the States to enact or administer a federal regulatory program." The mandatory obligation imposed on CLEOs to perform background checks on prospective handgun purchasers plainly runs afoul of that rule.

V

We held in *New York* that Congress cannot compel the States to enact or enforce a federal regulatory program. Today we hold that Congress cannot circumvent that prohibition by conscripting the State's officers directly. The Federal Government may neither issue directives requiring the States to address particular problems, nor command the States' officers, or those of their political subdivisions, to administer or enforce a federal regulatory program. It matters not whether policy making is involved, and no case-by-case weighing of the burdens or benefits is necessary; such commands are fundamentally incompatible with our constitutional system of dual sovereignty.

JUSTICE O'CONNOR, concurring.

Our precedent and our Nation's historical practices support the Court's holding today. The Brady Act violates the Tenth Amendment to the extent it forces States and local law enforcement officers to perform background checks on prospective handgun owners and to accept Brady Forms from firearms dealers. Our holding, of course, does not spell the end of the objectives of the Brady Act. States and chief law enforcement officers may voluntarily continue to participate in the federal program. Congress is also free to amend the interim program to provide for its continuance on a contractual basis with the States if it wishes, as it does with a number of other federal programs. In addition, the Court appropriately refrains from deciding whether other purely ministerial reporting requirements are similarly invalid.

JUSTICE THOMAS, concurring.

Although I join the Court's opinion in full, I write separately to emphasize that the Tenth Amendment affirms the undeniable notion that under our Constitution, the Federal Government is one of enumerated, hence limited, powers. Accordingly, the Federal Government may act only where the Constitution authorizes it to do so. In my "revisionist" view, the Federal Government's authority under the Commerce Clause, which merely allocates to Congress the power "to regulate Commerce . . . among the several states," does not extend to the regulation of wholly intrastate, point-of-sale transactions. Absent the underlying authority to regulate the intrastate transfer of firearms, Congress surely lacks the corollary power to impress state law enforcement officers into administering and enforcing such regulations.

Even if we construe Congress' authority to regulate interstate commerce to encompass those intrastate transactions that "substantially affect" interstate commerce, I question whether Congress can regulate the particular transactions at issue here. The Constitution, in addition to delegating certain enumerated powers to Congress, places whole areas outside the reach of Congress' regulatory authority. The First Amendment, for example, is fittingly celebrated for preventing Congress from "prohibiting the free exercise" of religion or "abridging the freedom of speech." The Second Amendment similarly appears to contain an express limitation on the government's authority. That Amendment provides: "[a] well regulated Militia, being necessary to the security of a free State, the right of the people to keep and bear arms, shall not be infringed." This Court has not had recent occasion to consider the nature of the substantive right safeguarded by the Second Amendment. If, however, the Second Amendment is read to confer a personal right to "keep and bear arms," a colorable argument exists that the Federal Government's regulatory scheme, at least as it pertains to the purely intrastate sale or possession of firearms, runs afoul of that Amendment's protections. As the parties did not raise this argument, however, we need not consider it here. Perhaps, at some future date, this Court will have the opportunity to determine whether Justice Story was correct when he wrote that the right to bear arms "has justly been considered, as the palladium of the liberties of a republic." 3 J. STORY, *Commentaries*. In the meantime, I join the Court's opinion striking down the challenged provisions of the Brady Act as inconsistent with the Tenth Amendment.

JUSTICE STEVENS, with whom JUSTICE SOUTER, JUSTICE GINSBURG, and JUSTICE BREYER join, dissenting.

When Congress exercises the powers delegated to it by the Constitution, it may impose affirmative obligations on executive and judicial officers of state and local governments as well as ordinary citizens. This conclusion is firmly supported by the text of the Constitution, the early history of the Nation, decisions of this Court, and a correct understanding of the basic structure of the Federal Government.

These cases do not implicate the more difficult questions associated with congressional coercion of state legislatures addressed in *New York v. United States*. Nor need we consider the wisdom of relying on local officials rather than federal agents to carry out aspects of a federal program, or even the question whether such officials may be required to perform a federal function on a permanent basis. The question is whether Congress, acting on behalf of the people of the entire Nation, may require local law enforcement officers to perform certain duties during the interim needed for the development of a federal gun control program. It is remarkably similar to the question, heavily debated by the Framers of the Constitution, whether the Congress could require state agents to collect federal taxes. Or the question whether Congress could impress state judges into federal service to entertain and decide cases that they would prefer to ignore.

Indeed, since the ultimate issue is one of power, we must consider its implications in times of national emergency. Matters such as the enlistment of air raid wardens, the administration of a military draft, the mass inoculation of children to forestall an epidemic, or perhaps the threat of an international terrorist, may require a national response before federal personnel can be made available to respond. If the Constitution empowers Congress and the President to make an appropriate response, is there anything in the Tenth Amendment, "in historical understanding and practice, in the structure of the Constitution, [or] in the jurisprudence of this Court," that forbids the enlistment of state officers to make that response effective? More narrowly, what basis is there in any of those sources for concluding that it is the Members of this Court, rather than the elected representatives of the people, who should determine whether the Constitution contains the unwritten rule that the Court announces today?

Perhaps today's majority would suggest that no such emergency is presented by the facts of these cases. But such a suggestion is itself an expression of a policy judgment. And Congress' view of the matter is quite different from that implied by the Court today.

The Brady Act was passed in response to what Congress described as an "epidemic of gun violence." Whether or not the evaluation reflected in the enactment of the Brady Act is correct as to the extent of the danger and the efficacy of the legislation, the congressional decision surely warrants more respect than it is accorded in today's unprecedented decision.

I

The text of the Constitution provides a sufficient basis for a correct disposition of this case.

Article I, § 8, grants the Congress the power to regulate commerce among the States. Putting to one side the revisionist views expressed by JUSTICE THOMAS in his concurring opinion in *United States v. Lopez*, there can be no question that that provision adequately supports the regulation of commerce in handguns effected by the Brady Act. Moreover, the additional grant of authority in that section of the Constitution "[t]o make all Laws which shall be necessary and proper for carrying into Execution the foregoing Powers" is surely adequate to support the temporary enlistment of local police officers in the process of identifying persons who should not be entrusted with the possession of handguns. In short, the affirmative delegation of power in Article I provides ample authority for the congressional enactment.

Unlike the First Amendment, which prohibits the enactment of a category of laws that would otherwise be authorized by Article I, the Tenth Amendment imposes no restriction on the exercise of delegated powers. The Amendment confirms the principle that the powers of the Federal Government are limited to those affirmatively granted by the Constitution, but it does not purport to limit the scope or the effectiveness of the exercise of powers that are delegated to Congress. Thus, the Amendment provides no support for a rule that immunizes local officials from obligations that might be imposed on ordinary citizens. Indeed, it would be more reasonable to infer that federal law may impose greater duties on state officials than on private citizens because another provision of the Constitution requires that "all executive and judicial Officers, both of the United States and of the several States, shall be bound by Oath or Affirmation, to support this Constitution."

It is appropriate for state officials to make an oath or affirmation to support the Federal Constitution because, as explained in THE FEDERALIST, they "have an essential agency in giving effect to the federal Constitution." THE FEDERALIST NO. 44 (J. Madison). There can be no conflict between their duties to the State and those owed to the Federal Government because Article VI unambiguously provides that federal law "shall be the supreme Law of the Land," binding in every State. Thus, not only the Constitution, but every law enacted by Congress as well, establishes policy for the States just as firmly as do laws enacted by state legislatures.

There is not a clause, sentence, or paragraph in the entire text of the Constitution of the United States that supports the proposition that a local police officer can ignore a command contained in a statute enacted by Congress pursuant to an express delegation of power enumerated in Article I.

II

Under the Articles of Confederation the National Government had the power to issue commands to the several sovereign states, but it had no authority to govern individuals directly. Thus, it raised an army and financed its operations by issuing requisitions to the constituent members of the Confederacy, rather than by creating federal agencies to draft soldiers or to impose taxes. The basic change in the character of the government that the Framers conceived was designed to enhance the power of the national government, not to provide some new, unmentioned immunity for state officers. Because indirect control over individual citizens ("the only proper objects of government") was ineffective under the Articles of Confederation, Alexander Hamilton explained that "we must extend the authority of the Union to the persons of the citizens." THE FEDERALIST NO. 15.

Indeed, the historical materials strongly suggest that the Founders intended to enhance the capacity of the federal government by empowering it—as a part of the new authority to make demands directly on individual citizens—to act through local officials. Hamilton made clear that the new Constitution, "by extending the authority of the federal head to the individual citizens of the several States, will enable the government to employ the ordinary magistracy of each, in the execution of its laws." THE FEDERALIST NO. 27. Hamilton's meaning was unambiguous; the federal government was to have the power to demand that local officials implement national policy programs.

More specifically, during the debates concerning the ratification of the Constitution, it was assumed that state agents would act as tax collectors for the federal government. Opponents of the Constitution had repeatedly expressed fears that the new federal government's ability to impose taxes directly on the citizenry would result in an overbearing presence of federal tax collectors in the States. Federalists rejoined that this problem would not arise because, as Hamilton explained, "the United States . . . will make use of the State officers and State regulations for collecting" certain taxes. Similarly, Madison made clear that the new central government's power to raise taxes directly from the citizenry would "not be resorted to, except for supplemental purposes of revenue . . . and that the eventual collection, under the immediate authority of the Union, will generally be made by the officers . . . appointed by the several States." NO. 45.

The Court's response to this powerful historical evidence is weak. The majority suggests that "none of these statements necessarily implies . . . Congress could impose these responsibilities without the consent of the States." No fair reading of these materials can justify such an interpretation.

As Hamilton explained, the power of the government to act on "individual citizens" — including "employ[ing] the ordinary magistracy" of the States— was an answer to the problems faced by a central government that could act only directly "upon the States in their political or collective capacities." The Federalist, No. 27. The new Constitution would avoid this problem, resulting in "a regular and peaceable execution of the law of the Union."

This point is made especially clear in Hamilton's statement that "the legislatures, courts, and magistrates, of the respective members, will be incorporated into the operations of the national government as far as its just and constitutional authority extends; and will be rendered auxiliary to the enforcement of its laws." It is hard to imagine a more unequivocal statement that state judicial and executive branch officials may be required to implement federal law where the National Government acts within the scope of its affirmative powers.

The Court makes two unpersuasive attempts to discount the force of this statement. First, according to the majority, because Hamilton mentioned the Supremacy Clause without specifically referring to any "congressional directive," the statement does not mean what it plainly says. But the mere fact that the Supremacy Clause is the source of the obligation of state officials to implement congressional directives does not remotely suggest that they might be "incorporat[ed] into the operations of the national government" before their obligations have been defined by Congress. Federal law establishes policy for the States just as firmly as laws enacted by state legislatures, but that does not mean that state or federal officials must implement directives that have not been specified in any law. Second, the majority suggests that interpreting this passage to mean what it says would conflict with our decision in *New York v. United States*. But since the *New York* opinion did not mention Federalist No. 27, it does not affect either the relevance or the weight of the historical evidence provided by No. 27 insofar as it relates to state courts and magistrates.

Bereft of support in the history of the founding, the Court rests its conclusion on the claim that there is little evidence the National Government actually exercised such a power in the early years of the Republic. This reasoning is misguided in principle and in fact. While we have indicated that the express consideration and resolution of difficult constitutional issues by the First Congress in particular "provides 'contemporaneous and weighty evidence' of the Constitution's meaning since many of [its] Members . . . 'had taken part in framing that instrument,' " we have never suggested that the failure of the early Congresses to address the scope of federal power in a particular area or to exercise a particular authority was an argument against its existence. That position, if correct, would undermine most of our post-New Deal Commerce Clause jurisprudence.

More importantly, the fact that Congress did elect to rely on state judges and the clerks of state courts to perform a variety of executive functions, is surely evidence of a contemporary understanding that their status as state officials did not immunize them from federal service.

The Court assumes that the imposition of such essentially executive duties on state judges and their clerks sheds no light on the question whether executive officials might have an immunity from federal obligations. Even assuming that the enlistment of state judges in their judicial role for federal purposes is irrelevant to the question whether executive officials may be asked to perform the same function—a claim disputed below—the majority's analysis is badly mistaken.

We are far truer to the historical record by applying a functional approach in assessing the role played by these early state officials. The use of state judges and their clerks to perform executive functions was, in historical context, hardly unusual. And, of course, judges today continue to perform a variety of functions that may more properly be described as executive. The majority's insistence that this evidence of federal enlistment of state officials to serve executive functions is irrelevant simply because the assistance of "judges" was at issue rests on empty formalistic reasoning of the highest order.

III

[T]he presumption of validity that supports all congressional enactments has added force with respect to policy judgments concerning the impact of a federal statute upon the respective States. The majority points to nothing suggesting that the political safeguards of federalism identified in *Garcia* need be supplemented by a rule, grounded in neither constitutional history nor text, flatly prohibiting the National Government from enlisting state and local officials in the implementation of federal law.

Perversely, the majority's rule seems more likely to damage than to preserve the safeguards against tyranny provided by the existence of vital state governments. By limiting the ability of the Federal Government to enlist state officials in the implementation of its programs, the Court creates incentives for the National Government to aggrandize itself. In the name of States' rights, the majority would have the Federal Government create vast national bureaucracies to implement its policies. This is exactly the sort of thing that the early Federalists promised would not occur, in part as a result of the National Government's ability to rely on the magistracy of the states.

With colorful hyperbole, the Court suggests that the unity in the Executive Branch of the Federal Government "would be shattered, and the power of the President would be subject to reduction, if Congress could . . . require . . . state officers to execute its laws." Putting to one side the obvious tension between the majority's claim that impressing state police officers will unduly tip the balance of power in favor of the federal sovereign and this suggestion that it will emasculate the Presidency, the Court's reasoning contradicts *New York v. United States*.

That decision squarely approved of cooperative federalism programs, designed at the national level but implemented principally by state governments. *New York* disapproved of a particular method of putting such programs into place, not the existence of federal programs implemented locally. Indeed, nothing in the majority's holding calls into question the three mechanisms for constructing such programs that New York expressly approved. Congress may require the States to implement its programs as a condition of federal spending, [in order to avoid the threat of unilateral federal action in the area, or as a part of a program that affects States and private parties alike.] The majority's suggestion in response to this dissent that Congress' ability to create such programs is limited, is belied by the importance and sweep of the federal statutes that meet this description, some of which we described in *New York*.

Nor is there force to the assumption undergirding the Court's entire opinion that if this trivial burden on state sovereignty is permissible, the entire structure of federalism will soon collapse. These cases do not involve any mandate to state legislatures to enact new rules. When legislative action, or even administrative rule-making, is at issue, it may be appropriate for Congress either to pre-empt the State's lawmaking power and fashion the federal rule itself, or to respect the State's power to fashion its own rules. But this case, unlike any precedent in which the Court has held that Congress exceeded its powers, merely involves the imposition of modest duties on individual officers.

Far more important than the concerns that the Court musters in support of its new rule is the fact that the Framers entrusted Congress with the task of creating a working structure of intergovernmental relationships around the framework that the Constitution authorized. Neither explicitly nor implicitly did the Framers issue any command that forbids Congress from imposing federal duties on private citizens or on local officials. As a general matter, Congress has followed the sound policy of authorizing federal agencies and federal agents to administer federal programs. That general practice, however, does not negate the existence of power to rely on state officials in occasional situations in which such reliance is in the national interest.

IV

Finally, the Court advises us that the "prior jurisprudence of this Court" is the most conclusive support for its position. That "prior jurisprudence" is *New York v. United States*. Our statements [in *New York v. United States*], taken in context, clearly did not decide the question presented here, whether state executive officials — as opposed to state legislators — may in appropriate circumstances be enlisted to implement federal policy.

The majority relies upon dictum in *New York* to the effect that "[t]he Federal Government may not compel the States to enact or administer a federal regulatory program." But that language was wholly unnecessary to the decision of the case. It is, of course, beyond dispute that we are not bound by the dicta of our prior opinions. To the extent that it has any substance at all, *New York*'s administration language may have referred to the possibility that the State might have been able to take title to and devise an elaborate scheme for the management of the radioactive waste through purely executive policy making. But despite the majority's effort to suggest that similar activities are required by the Brady Act, it is hard to characterize the minimal requirement that CLEO's perform background checks as one involving the exercise of substantial policy making discretion on that essentially legislative scale.

In response to this dissent, the majority asserts that the difference between a federal command addressed to individuals and one addressed to the State itself "cannot be a constitutionally significant one." But there is abundant authority in our Eleventh Amendment jurisprudence recognizing a constitutional distinction between local government officials, such as the CLEO's who brought this action, and State entities that are entitled to sovereign immunity. To my knowledge, no one has previously thought that the distinction "disembowels" the Eleventh Amendment.

Importantly, the majority either misconstrues or ignores cases that are more directly on point. The burden on state officials that we approved in *FERC* was far more extensive than the minimal, temporary imposition posed by the Brady Act.

[I]n *Testa v. Katt*, the Court unanimously held that state courts of appropriate jurisdiction must occupy themselves adjudicating claims brought by private litigants under the federal Emergency Price Control Act of 1942, regardless of how otherwise crowded their dockets might be with state law matters. That is a much greater imposition on state sovereignty than the Court's characterization of the case as merely holding that "state courts cannot refuse to apply federal law." That characterization describes only the narrower duty to apply federal law in cases that the state courts have consented to entertain.

As *Testa* held, because the "Laws of the United States . . . [are] the supreme Law of the Land," state courts of appropriate jurisdiction must hear federal claims whenever a federal statute, such as the Emergency Price Control Act, requires them to do so. Hence, the Court's textual argument is quite misguided. The majority focuses on the Clause's specific attention to the point that "Judges in every State shall be bound." That language commands state judges to "apply federal law" in cases that they entertain, but it is not the source of their duty to accept jurisdiction of federal claims that they would prefer to ignore. Our opinion in *Testa* rested generally on the language of the Supremacy Clause, without any specific focus on the reference to judges.

Even if the Court were correct in its suggestion that it was the reference to judges in the Supremacy Clause, rather than the central message of the entire Clause, that dictated the result in *Testa*, the Court's implied *expressio unius* argument that the Framers therefore did not intend to permit the enlistment of other state officials is implausible. Throughout our history judges, state as well as federal, have merited as much respect as executive agents. The notion that the Framers would have had no reluctance to "press state judges into federal service" against their will but would have regarded the imposition of a similar—indeed, far lesser—burden on town constables as an intolerable affront to principles of state sovereignty, can only be considered perverse. If such a distinction had been contemplated by the learned and articulate men who fashioned the basic structure of our government, surely some of them would have said so.

The provision of the Brady Act that crosses the Court's newly defined constitutional threshold is more comparable to a statute requiring local police officers to report the identity of missing children to the Crime Control Center of the Department of Justice than to an offensive federal command to a sovereign state. If Congress believes that such a statute will benefit the people of the Nation, and serve the interests of cooperative federalism better than an enlarged federal bureaucracy, we should respect both its policy judgment and its appraisal of its constitutional power. Accordingly, I respectfully dissent.

JUSTICE SOUTER, dissenting.

I join JUSTICE STEVENS' dissenting opinion, but subject to the following qualifications. While I do not find anything dispositive in the paucity of early examples of federal employment of state officers for executive purposes, neither would I find myself in dissent with no more to go on than those few early instances in the administration of naturalization laws, for example, or such later instances as state support for federal emergency action. These illustrations of state action implementing congressional statutes are consistent with the Government's positions, but they do not speak to me with much force.

In deciding these cases, which I have found closer than I had anticipated, it is THE FEDERALIST that finally determines my position. I believe that the most straightforward reading of NO. 27 is authority for the Government's position here, and that this reading is both supported by NO. 44 and consistent with NOS. 36 and 45.

Hamilton in NO. 27 first notes that because the new Constitution would authorize the National Government to bind individuals directly through national law, it could "employ the ordinary magistracy of each [State] in the execution of its laws." Were he to stop here, he would not necessarily be speaking of anything beyond the possibility of cooperative arrangements by agreement. But he then addresses the combined effect of the proposed Supremacy Clause, U.S. Const., Art. VI, cl. 2, and state officers's oath requirement, U.S. Const., Art. VI, cl. 3, and he states that "the Legislatures, Courts and Magistrates of the respective members will be incorporated into the operations of the national government, as far as its just and constitutional authority extends; and will be rendered auxiliary to the enforcement of its laws." The natural reading of this language is not merely that the officers of the various branches of state governments may be employed in the performance of national functions; Hamilton says that the state governmental machinery "will be incorporated" into the Nation's operation, and because the "auxiliary" status of the state officials will occur because they are "bound by the sanctity of an oath," I take him to mean that their auxiliary functions will be the products of their obligations thus undertaken to support federal law, not of their own, or the States', unfettered choices.

Madison in NO. 44 supports this reading in his commentary on the oath requirement. He asks why state magistrates should have to swear to support the National Constitution, when national officials will not be required to oblige themselves to support the state counterparts. His answer is that national officials "will have no agency in carrying the State Constitutions into effect. The members and officers of the State Governments, on the contrary, will have an essential agency in giving effect to the Federal Constitution." He then describes the state legislative "agency" as action necessary for selecting the President, see U.S. Const., Art. II, § 1, and the choice of Senators, see U.S. Const., Art. I, § 3 (repealed by Amendment XVII). The Supremacy Clause itself, of course, expressly refers to the state judges' obligations under federal law, and other numbers of THE FEDERALIST give examples of state executive "agency" in the enforcement of national revenue laws.

Two such examples of anticipated state collection of federal revenue are instructive, each of which is put forward to counter fears of a proliferation of tax collectors. In NO. 45, Hamilton says that if a State is not given (or declines to exercise) an option to supply its citizens' share of a federal tax, the "eventual collection [of the federal tax] under the immediate authority of the Union, will generally be made by the officers, and according to the rules, appointed by the several States." And in NO. 36, he explains that the National Government would more readily "employ the State officers as much as possible, and to attach them to the Union by an accumulation of their emoluments," than by appointing separate federal revenue collectors.

In the light of all these passages, I cannot persuade myself that the statements from NO. 27 speak of anything less than the authority of the National Government, when exercising an otherwise legitimate power (the commerce power, say), to require state "auxiliaries" to take appropriate action. To be sure, it does not follow that any conceivable requirement may be imposed on any state official. I continue to agree, for example, that Congress may not require a state legislature to enact a regulatory scheme and that *New York v. United States* was rightly decided (even though I now believe its dicta went too far toward immunizing state administration as well as state enactment of such a scheme from congressional mandate); after all, the essence of legislative power, within the limits of legislative jurisdiction, is a discretion not subject to command. But insofar as national law would require nothing from a state officer inconsistent with the power proper to his branch of tripartite state government (say, by obligating a state judge to exercise law enforcement powers), I suppose that the reach of federal law as Hamilton described it would not be exceeded.

JUSTICE BREYER, with whom JUSTICE STEVENS joins, dissenting.

I would add to the reasons Justice Stevens sets forth the fact that the United States is not the only nation that seeks to reconcile the practical need for a central authority with the democratic virtues of more local control. At least some other countries, facing the same basic problem, have found that local control is better maintained through application of a principle that is the direct opposite of the principle the majority derives from the silence of our Constitution. The federal systems of Switzerland, Germany, and the European Union, for example, all provide that constituent states, not federal bureaucracies, will themselves implement many of the laws, rules, regulations, or decrees enacted by the central "federal" body.

Regardless, the Constitution itself is silent on the matter. Precedent supports the Government's position here. And the fact that there is not more precedent — that direct federal assignment of duties to state officers is not common — likely reflects, not a widely shared belief that any such assignment is incompatible with basic principles of federalism, but rather a widely shared practice of assigning such duties in other ways. Thus, there is neither need nor reason to find in the Constitution an absolute principle, the inflexibility of which poses a surprising and technical obstacle to the enactment of a law that Congress believed necessary to solve an important national problem.

NOTES

1. *Judicial activism and restraint*. Professor Hovenkamp, from a political economics perspective, criticizes the Court for taking an activist position with respect to review of "federal regulation thought to encroach on state prerogatives." With particular reference to *United States v. Lopez*, p. 153 *infra*, he comments that "activist Justices have struck down federal legislation on historically inaccurate constitutional grounds in an area, state-federal relations, where the political process has shown itself to be quite up to the task of allocating decisionmaking power." Herbert Hovenkamp, *Judicial Restraint and Constitutional Federalism*, 96 COLUM. L. REV. 2213 (1996).

By contrast, Professor Calabresi praises the Court's activism in this area and argues that there are good reasons why "the Justices should think federalism important." In particular he makes the familiar arguments that state autonomy encourages local accountability and encourages competitive experimentation, concluding that "there is a strong prima facie case for constitutionally mandated decentralization, which can be overcome when economies of scale, collective action problems, externalities, or civil rights issues are raised." STEVEN CALABRESI, 574 ANNALS OF THE AMER. ACAD. OF POL. & SOC. SCIENCE 24, 28 (March 2001).

2. *Protection of the States in the national political process*. Professor Choper, relied on by the majority in *Garcia*, recognizes that the political structures for safeguarding federalism may have changed but nevertheless asserts that both the theory and the practice of political structural control are still viable. For example, although members of the Senate and House are not elected by state governments, studies show that they tend to have "very long, resolute, and intimate ties to their districts." He points out that they tend to vote in the perceived interests of their local constituents even if this requires them to go against national party allegiances. JESSE CHOPER, JUDICIAL REVIEW AND THE NATIONAL POLITICAL PROCESS 178 (1980). He maintains that "[n]umerous structural aspects of the national political system serve to assure that states rights will not be trampled, and the lesson of practice is that they have not been."

Professor Choper relied on the earlier insights of Professor Wechsler, who had argued that "the states are the strategic yardsticks for the measurement of interest and opinion, the special centers of political activity, the separate geographical determinants of national as well as local politics." Herbert Wechsler, *The Political Safeguards of Federalism: The Role of the States in the Composition and Selection of the National Government*, 54 COLUM. L. REV. 543, 546 (1954).

How valid are these assumptions today? Consider the argument made by Professor Smith:

> [T]he *Garcia* majority's reliance on the political process as the guardian of state autonomy is perhaps unwarranted for several reasons. The expansion of the electorate, and the weakened effectiveness of state political parties has diluted states' influence over congressional composition. Likewise, increased interdependence between the states and the federal government has also contributed to a weakening in state

> control over the decisionmaking process that ultimately affects states' interests.

Stephen Smith, *State Autonomy After Garcia: Will the Political Process Protect States' Interests?*, 71 IOWA L. REV. 1527, 1550 (1986). *See also* William Van Alystyne, *Federalism, Congress, the States and the Tenth Amendment: Adrift in the Cellophane Sea*, 1987 DUKE L.J. 769.

Professor Kramer reviews the criticisms of the Wechsler position, finds that the structural bases of it have eroded with the loss of formal state roles in the federal system, but points out that political parties and their mechanisms yield similar protections for state governments in today's world. He concludes that the Wechsler conclusion is still sound although the reasons behind it have changed. Larry Kramer, *Putting the Politics Back Into the Political Safeguards of Federalism*, 100 COLUM. L. REV. 215 (2000).

Consider also the following critique of *Garcia*'s political process rationale:

> [E]ven if it is true that in most cases state interests will be adequately represented in Congress, that fact is beside the point as a matter of constitutional theory. All it implies is that relatively few serious constitutional challenges will be made on federalism grounds. Had the Framers been confident that the political process, standing alone, would provide sufficient protection to state interests, presumably they would have expressly vested in the federal government carte blanche authority to do what it deemed advisable. They clearly did not do so, and the states themselves, unwilling to rely solely on the enumeration structure of Article I, insisted on insertion of the even more explicit Tenth Amendment as a condition of ratification.

MARTIN H. REDISH, THE CONSTITUTION AS POLITICAL STRUCTURE 18–19 (1995).

3. *Reno v. Condon*, 528 U.S. 141 (2000). The Court upheld the federal Driver's Privacy Protection Act against a state federalism challenge. The Act prohibits both states and individuals from disclosing personally identifiable information from driver's license records without the person's consent except in specified contexts related to law enforcement needs. The effect is to eliminate a source of revenue for states that were selling mailing lists to private marketing firms. The Fourth Circuit held that this restriction violated the principles of *Printz* by commandeering state processes and officials. The Court, however, held that the Act did not require did not require the state affirmatively to legislate or enforce federal; instead, it prohibited action in the form of disclosure unless the state officials chose to obtain consent from the person affected. Nor did the regulation require state officials to assist in the regulation of conduct among private persons; rather, the federal statute regulated both public and private market suppliers of motor vehicle information.

4. *States and Federal Agencies.* In *Alaska Dep't of Envir. Conservation [ADEC] v. EPA*, 124 S. Ct. 983 (2004), the Court dealt with whether a federal agency could override a determination by a state agency. Under the federal

Clean Air Act, state agencies enforce federal requirements pursuant to an approved State Implementation Plan (SIP). In some areas of the country, stationary sources of emissions cannot construct new facilities or substantially modify existing facilities unless they employ best available control technology (BACT). Under the federal statutory scheme, the state agency makes a determination whether a proposed method of emission control constitutes BACT, but the EPA can issue orders to stop construction of any facility that it finds to be out of compliance with federal requirements.

In this case, a large zinc mining operation north of the Arctic Circle in Alaska sought to expand its operation by 40%. The method of emissions control that it preferred was approved by ADEC but EPA concluded that it was not the BACT for this application. EPA issued an order to halt construction, the State and company sought review in federal court, and the courts upheld the EPA's order.

Justice Ginsburg, for the majority of the Supreme Court, held that EPA's authority under the federal statute included the power to review state agency decisions and to set aside those that lack a "reasoned analysis." In response to the argument that EPA could thus effectively stop a construction project arbitrarily long after the project had begun, the Court responded: "EPA, we are confident, could not indulge in the inequitable conduct ADEC and the dissent hypothesize while the federal courts sit to review EPA's actions."

Justice Kennedy's dissent, joined by Chief Justice Rehnquist and Justices Scalia and Thomas, asserted that Congress could not have intended for a federal agency to exercise supervisory responsibility over a state government:

> The CAA is not the only statute that relies on a close and equal partnership between federal and state authorities to accomplish congressional objectives. Under the majority's reasoning, these other statutes, too, could be said to confer on federal agencies ultimate decisionmaking authority, relegating States to the role of mere provinces or political corporations, instead of coequal sovereigns entitled to the same dignity and respect.

[2] "Substantial Effects" on Commerce

In *United States v. Lopez* [p. 153 *infra*], the Supreme Court introduced new uncertainty into the scope of Congress' constitutional authority to regulate private activity pursuant to its commerce power. Because *Lopez* deals with a federal criminal statute passed pursuant to the commerce clause, it is necessary first to explore the pre-*Lopez* background of Congress' power to federalize crime.

As is demonstrated by the *Lottery Case,* the use of the commerce power to federalize criminal conduct typically dealt with through state criminal processes is not a modern phenomenon. But there has been an increasing incidence of the federalization of crime using this jurisdictional nexus since the 1930s. As control of criminal behavior has traditionally been considered a prerogative of the states in the exercise of their police power, what do these developments suggest concerning the health of federalism?

In modern society, local problems increasingly become national problems. Crime does not recognize artificial state boundaries but crime control has been a traditional prerogative of the states. State regulation has proven inadequate to the problems of organized crime, kidnapping, terrorism, etc., which frequently involve a number of jurisdictions. Crime generally adversely affects business conditions and arguably the level of interstate commerce. Again the questions arise: how can these problems be met consistent with the principles and values of federalism? To what extent does the Commerce Clause provide a jurisdictional nexus for national intervention federalizing criminal law? If the national government may act, is any local crime excluded from potential federal supervision? Are limits to be found through judicial review or political processes?

Until recently, most legislation federalizing crime has involved congressional regulation of interstate traffic. As the police power cases indicate, a plenary power to regulate commerce includes the power to prevent that commerce from being used for socially undesirable ends, and to impose protective conditions for the privilege of using the channels of interstate commerce.

***United States v. Sullivan*, 332 U.S. 689 (1948)**, involved the constitutionality of the Federal Food, Drug and Cosmetic Act of 1938, prohibiting "the doing of any act with respect to, a drug if such act is done while such article is held for sale after shipment in interstate commerce and results in such article being misbranded." It was alleged that properly labeled bottles of sulfathiazole tablets were shipped from Chicago, Illinois, to a consignee in Atlanta, Georgia. Respondent, a Georgia druggist, bought one of these properly labeled bottles in Atlanta and took it to his drug store in Columbus, Georgia, where he removed twelve tablets, placed them in pill boxes which were not properly marked, and resold them. He was indicted and convicted for violating the federal Act. The court of appeals reversed his conviction, interpreting the statutory language " 'while such article is held for sale after shipment in interstate commerce' as though Congress had said 'while such article is held for sale by a person who had himself received it by way of a shipment in interstate commerce.' " The Supreme Court reversed.

Justice Black, for the Court, concluded that:

> the language used by Congress broadly and unqualifiedly prohibits misbranding articles held for sale after shipment in interstate commerce, without regard to how long after the shipment the misbranding occurred, how many intrastate sales had intervened, or who had received the articles at the end of the interstate shipment.

As to the contention that the Act as construed was beyond Congress' constitutional power and invades powers reserved to the states, the Court upheld "the constitutional power of Congress under the commerce clause to regulate the branding of articles that have completed an interstate shipment and are being held for future sales in purely local or intrastate commerce." This power derived from the "full power to keep the channels of such commerce free from transportation of illicit or harmful articles, to make such as are injurious to the public health outlaws of such commerce, and to bar them from the facilities and privileges thereof." *McDermott v. Wisconsin,* 228 U.S. 115 (1913).

***Perez v. United States*, 402 U.S. 146 (1971)**, involved a conviction under the federal Consumer Credit Protection Act for engaging in "extortionate credit transactions." According to the majority, "Petitioner is one of the species commonly known as 'loan sharks' which Congress found are in large part under the control of 'organized crime.' 'Extortionate credit transactions' are defined as those characterized by the use or threat of the use of 'violence or other criminal means' in enforcement." The majority held that Congress had ample reason for belief that these transactions had an effect on interstate commerce.

> Where the *class of activities* is regulated and that *class* is within the reach of federal power, the courts have no power "to excise, as trivial, individual instances" of the class. Extortionate credit transactions, though purely intrastate, may in the judgment of Congress affect interstate commerce. In the setting of the present case there is a tie-in between local loan sharks and interstate crime. The findings by Congress are quite adequate on that ground. The essence of all these reports and hearings was summarized and embodied in formal congressional findings. They supplied Congress with the knowledge that the loan shark racket provides organized crime with its second most lucrative source of revenue, exacts millions from the pockets of people, coerces its victims into the commission of crimes against property, and causes the takeover by racketeers of legitimate businesses.

Justice Stewart, dissenting, observed that "under the statute before us a man can be convicted without any proof of interstate movement, of the use of the facilities of interstate commerce."

While the congressional prerogative to federalize local crime through the commerce power was obviously preceived to be broad, congressional legislation does not always use the full scope of the commerce jurisdiction. And, in some cases, the courts have interpreted the jurisdictional provisions of federal criminal laws in a way that avoids the question of the constitutional limits of the congressional power. *See United States v. Bass,* 404 U.S. 336 (1971) (narrowly interpreting federal firearms legislation to avoid commerce clause issues). *See also Scarborough v. United States,* 431 U.S. 563 (1976).

***United States v. Lopez*, 514 U.S. 549 (1995).** The Gun-Free School Zones Act of 1990 made it a federal crime "for any individual knowingly to possess a firearm at a place that the individual knows, or has reasonable cause to believe, is a school zone [within 1,000 feet of a private or public school]." The Supreme Court (Rehnquist, CJ) struck down this provision, commenting that the "Act neither regulates a commercial activity nor contains a requirement that the possession be connected in any way to interstate commerce." *Lopez* has been said to stand for the proposition that Congress must find either a "jurisdictional nexus" to interstate commerce or a "genuine economic effect" before it can regulate an activity.

After reviewing briefly the history of Commerce Clause adjudication, the Court noted that both Court and Congress in the modern era have thought it necessary to distinguish national from local concerns.

> [W]e have identified three broad categories of activity that Congress may regulate under its commerce power. First, Congress may regulate the use of the channels of interstate commerce. [citing *Darby* and *Heart of Atlanta*] Second, Congress is empowered to regulate and protect the instrumentalities of interstate commerce, or persons or things in interstate commerce, even though the threat may come only from intrastate activities. [citing transportation regulations] Finally, Congress' commerce authority includes the power to regulate those activities having a substantial relation to interstate commerce, *i.e.,* those activities that substantially affect interstate commerce.
>
> Within this final category, admittedly, our case law has not been clear whether an activity must "affect" or "substantially affect" interstate commerce in order to be within Congress' power to regulate it under the Commerce Clause. We conclude, consistent with the great weight of our case law, that the proper test requires an analysis of whether the regulated activity "substantially affects" interstate commerce.

One difficulty with the Act was that Congress had made no findings with regard to the impact on commerce from guns in schools. "We agree with the Government that Congress normally is not required to make formal findings as to the substantial burdens that an activity has on interstate commerce. But to the extent that congressional findings would enable us to evaluate the legislative judgment that the activity in question substantially affected interstate commerce, even though no such substantial effect was visible to the naked eye, they are lacking here."

The impacts on interstate commerce urged by the government were that the costs of violent crime would be spread throughout society through the mechanism of insurance. With specific reference to schools, the argument was that education would be diminished by the presence of guns in schools, and that a less educated populace "would have an adverse effect on the Nation's economic well-being."

> We pause to consider the implications of the Government's arguments. The Government admits, under its "costs of crime" reasoning, that Congress could regulate not only all violent crime, but all activities that might lead to violent crime, regardless of how tenuously they relate to interstate commerce. Similarly, under the Government's "national productivity" reasoning, Congress could regulate any activity that it found was related to the economic productivity of individual citizens: family law (including marriage, divorce, and child custody), for example. Under the theories that the Government presents in support of [the Act], it is difficult to perceive any limitation on federal power, even in areas such as criminal law enforcement or education where States historically have been sovereign. Thus, if we were to accept the Government's arguments, we are hard-pressed to posit any activity by an individual that Congress is without power to regulate.

Justices Kennedy and O'Connor concurred with "some pause" on the grounds that "unlike the earlier cases to come before the Court here neither the actors nor their conduct have a commercial character, and neither the purposes nor the design of the statute have an evident commercial nexus."

Justice Thomas concurred while objecting that the Court should not accept federal legislation on the basis of even "substantial effects" on interstate commerce. In his view the commerce power originally was, and now should be, limited to "selling, buying, and bartering, as well as transporting for these purposes." He would return to the reading of the commerce clause given in *E.C. Knight* and *Hammer*. "Agriculture and manufacturing involve the production of goods; commerce encompasses traffic in such articles."

Justices Souter and Breyer dissented on the grounds that Congress could rationally have found a connection between school violence, or threats of violence, and a variety of impacts to the national economy.

One commentator stated that "*Lopez* will not prove 'epochal,'" and that "there is less in *Lopez* than meets the eye." Louis Pollak, *Foreword*, 94 MICH. L. REV. 533, 550, 553 (1995). Another commentator argues that "as a practical matter, the main effect of *Lopez* is very likely to be nothing more than a renewed congressional interest in loading federal criminal statutes with findings and jurisdictional elements in order to demonstrate the close link between what Congress wishes to regulate and 'Commerce . . . among the several States.' *Lopez*, in short, may have little effect on the post-1937 norm of congressional omnicompetence." Jefferson Powell, *Enumerated Means and Unlimited Ends*, 94 MICH. L.REV. 651, 651–52 (1995).

On the other hand, Professor Calabresi noted that "[e]ven if *Lopez* produces no progeny and is soon overruled, the opinion has shattered forever the notion that, after fifty years of Commerce Clause precedent, we can never go back to the days of limited national power." Steven Calabresi, *"A Government of Limited and Enumerated Powers:" In Defense of United States v. Lopez,* 94 MICH. L. REV. 752 (1995). Professor Calabresi applauds this result, and dismisses concerns that have been expressed about the reassertion of constitutional limits on the scope of the commerce power:

> First, judicial enforcement of the Commerce Clause does not raise questions of interpretation or fact that are any more troubling than those that the Court regularly struggles with in the Bill of Rights and Fourteenth Amendment contexts. Second, the implications of public choice theory suggest that there is absolutely no reason to fear that a runaway Court ever will cripple the national government, disabling it from performing vital national functions. Third, the only valid fear that anyone ever should entertain about the Supreme Court's ability to enforce the Constitution in federalism cases is that the Court will do far too little, not that it will do too much.

Id. at 754–55.

UNITED STATES v. MORRISON

529 U.S. 598, 120 S. Ct. 1740, 146 L. Ed. 2d 658 (2000)

CHIEF JUSTICE REHNQUIST delivered the opinion of the Court.

In these cases we consider the constitutionality of 42 U.S.C. § 13981, which provides a federal civil remedy for the victims of gender-motivated violence. The United States Court of Appeals for the Fourth Circuit, sitting en banc, struck down § 13981 because it concluded that Congress lacked constitutional authority to enact the section's civil remedy. Believing that these cases are controlled by our decisions in *United States v. Lopez*, *United States v. Harris*, and the *In re Civil Rights Cases* (1883), we affirm.

I

Petitioner Christy Brzonkala enrolled at Virginia Polytechnic Institute (Virginia Tech) in the fall of 1994. In September of that year, Brzonkala met respondents Antonio Morrison and James Crawford, who were both students at Virginia Tech and members of its varsity football team. Brzonkala alleges that, within 30 minutes of meeting Morrison and Crawford, they assaulted and repeatedly raped her. After the attack, Morrison allegedly told Brzonkala, "You better not have any . . . diseases." In the months following the rape, Morrison also allegedly announced in the dormitory's dining room that he "like[d] to get girls drunk and . . . ." The omitted portions, quoted verbatim in the briefs on file with this Court, consist of boasting, debased remarks about what Morrison would do to women, vulgar remarks that cannot fail to shock and offend.

Brzonkala alleges that this attack caused her to become severely emotionally disturbed and depressed. She sought assistance from a university psychiatrist, who prescribed antidepressant medication. Shortly after the rape Brzonkala stopped attending classes and withdrew from the university.

In early 1995, Brzonkala filed a complaint against respondents under Virginia Tech's Sexual Assault Policy. During the school-conducted hearing on her complaint, Morrison admitted having sexual contact with her despite the fact that she had twice told him "no." After the hearing, Virginia Tech's Judicial Committee found insufficient evidence to punish Crawford, but found Morrison guilty of sexual assault and sentenced him to immediate suspension for two semesters.

Virginia Tech's dean of students upheld the judicial committee's sentence. However, in July 1995, Virginia Tech informed Brzonkala that Morrison intended to initiate a court challenge to his conviction under the Sexual Assault Policy. University officials told her that a second hearing would be necessary to remedy the school's error in prosecuting her complaint under that policy, which had not been widely circulated to students. The university therefore conducted a second hearing under its Abusive Conduct Policy, which was in force prior to the dissemination of the Sexual Assault Policy. Following this second hearing the Judicial Committee again found Morrison guilty and sentenced him to an identical 2-semester suspension. This time, however, the description of Morrison's offense was, without explanation, changed from "sexual assault" to "using abusive language."

Morrison appealed his second conviction through the university's administrative system. On August 21, 1995, Virginia Tech's senior vice president and provost set aside Morrison's punishment. She concluded that it was "excessive when compared with other cases where there has been a finding of violation of the Abusive Conduct Policy." Virginia Tech did not inform Brzonkala of this decision. After learning from a newspaper that Morrison would be returning to Virginia Tech for the fall 1995 semester, she dropped out of the university.

In December 1995, Brzonkala sued Morrison, Crawford, and Virginia Tech in the United States District Court for the Western District of Virginia. Her complaint alleged that Morrison's and Crawford's attack violated § 13981 and that Virginia Tech's handling of her complaint violated Title IX of the Education Amendments of 1972. Morrison and Crawford moved to dismiss this complaint on the grounds that it failed to state a claim and that § 13981's civil remedy is unconstitutional. The United States intervened to defend § 13981's constitutionality.

The District Court dismissed Brzonkala's Title IX claims against Virginia Tech for failure to state a claim upon which relief can be granted. It then held that Brzonkala's complaint stated a claim against Morrison and Crawford under § 13981, but dismissed the complaint because it concluded that Congress lacked authority to enact the section under either the Commerce Clause or § 5 of the Fourteenth Amendment.

A divided panel of the Court of Appeals reversed the District Court, reinstating Brzonkala's § 13981 claim and her Title IX hostile environment claim. The full Court of Appeals vacated the panel's opinion and reheard the case en banc. The en banc court then issued an opinion affirming the District Court's conclusion that Brzonkala stated a claim under § 13981 because her complaint alleged a crime of violence and the allegations of Morrison's crude and derogatory statements regarding his treatment of women sufficiently indicated that his crime was motivated by gender animus.[4] Nevertheless, the court by a divided vote affirmed the District Court's conclusion that Congress lacked constitutional authority to enact § 13981's civil remedy. Because the Court of Appeals invalidated a federal statute on constitutional grounds, we granted certiorari.

Every law enacted by Congress must be based on one or more of its powers enumerated in the Constitution. "The powers of the legislature are defined

---

[4] Section 13981 was part of the Violence Against Women Act of 1994, § 40302, 108 Stat. 1941-1942. It states that "[a]ll persons within the United States shall have the right to be free from crimes of violence motivated by gender." 42 U.S.C. § 13981(b). To enforce that right, subsection (c) declares:

> A person (including a person who acts under color of any statute, ordinance, regulation, custom, or usage of any State) who commits a crime of violence motivated by gender and thus deprives another of the right declared in subsection (b) of this section shall be liable to the party injured, in an action for the recovery of compensatory and punitive damages, injunctive and declaratory relief, and such other relief as a court may deem appropriate.

Section 13981 defines a "crim[e] of violence motivated by gender" as "a crime of violence committed because of gender or on the basis of gender, and due, at least in part, to an animus based on the victim's gender." § 13981(d)(1). It also provides that the term "crime of violence" includes any [felony, whether prosecuted as such or not].

and limited; and that those limits may not be mistaken or forgotten, the constitution is written." *Marbury v. Madison*. Congress explicitly identified the sources of federal authority on which it relied in enacting § 13981. It said that a "federal civil rights cause of action" is established "[p]ursuant to the affirmative power of Congress . . . under section 5 of the Fourteenth Amendment to the Constitution, as well as under section 8 of Article I of the Constitution." 42 U.S.C. § 13981(a). We address Congress' authority to enact this remedy under each of these constitutional provisions in turn.

II

As we discussed at length in *Lopez*, our interpretation of the Commerce Clause has changed as our Nation has developed. [I]t suffices to say that, in the years since *NLRB v. Jones & Laughlin Steel Corp.*, Congress has had considerably greater latitude in regulating conduct and transactions under the Commerce Clause than our previous case law permitted.

Lopez emphasized, however, that even under our modern, expansive interpretation of the Commerce Clause, Congress' regulatory authority is not without effective bounds.

> [E]ven [our] modern-era precedents which have expanded congressional power under the Commerce Clause confirm that this power is subject to outer limits. In Jones & Laughlin Steel, the Court warned that the scope of the interstate commerce power 'must be considered in the light of our dual system of government and may not be extended so as to embrace effects upon interstate commerce so indirect and remote that to embrace them, in view of our complex society, would effectually obliterate the distinction between what is national and what is local and create a completely centralized government.'

As we observed in *Lopez*, modern Commerce Clause jurisprudence has "identified three broad categories of activity that Congress may regulate under its commerce power." "First, Congress may regulate the use of the channels of interstate commerce." (citing *Heart of Atlanta Motel, Inc. v. United States*; *United States v. Darby*). "Second, Congress is empowered to regulate and protect the instrumentalities of interstate commerce, or persons or things in interstate commerce, even though the threat may come only from intrastate activities." (citing *Shreveport Rate Cases*; *Southern R. Co. v. United States*; *Perez*). "Finally, Congress' commerce authority includes the power to regulate those activities having a substantial relation to interstate commerce, . . . i.e., those activities that substantially affect interstate commerce." (citing *Jones & Laughlin Steel*).

Petitioners do not contend that these cases fall within either of the first two of these categories of Commerce Clause regulation. They seek to sustain § 13981 as a regulation of activity that substantially affects interstate commerce. Given § 13981's focus on gender-motivated violence wherever it occurs (rather than violence directed at the instrumentalities of interstate commerce, interstate markets, or things or persons in interstate commerce), we agree that this is the proper inquiry.

Since *Lopez* most recently canvassed and clarified our case law governing this third category of Commerce Clause regulation, it provides the proper framework for conducting the required analysis of § 13981.

Both petitioners and Justice Souter's dissent downplay the role that the economic nature of the regulated activity plays in our Commerce Clause analysis. But a fair reading of *Lopez* shows that the noneconomic, criminal nature of the conduct at issue was central to our decision in that case. ("Even *Wickard*, which is perhaps the most far reaching example of Commerce Clause authority over intrastate activity, involved economic activity in a way that the possession of a gun in a school zone does not"), ("Section 922(q) is not an essential part of a larger regulation of economic activity"), ("Admittedly, a determination whether an intrastate activity is commercial or noncommercial may in some cases result in legal uncertainty. But, so long as Congress' authority is limited to those powers enumerated in the Constitution, and so long as those enumerated powers are interpreted as having judicially enforceable outer limits, congressional legislation under the Commerce Clause always will engender 'legal uncertainty' "), ("The possession of a gun in a local school zone is in no sense an economic activity that might, through repetition elsewhere, substantially affect any sort of interstate commerce"). *Lopez's* review of Commerce Clause case law demonstrates that in those cases where we have sustained federal regulation of intrastate activity based upon the activity's substantial effects on interstate commerce, the activity in question has been some sort of economic endeavor.

The second consideration that we found important in analyzing § 922(q) was that the statute contained "no express jurisdictional element which might limit its reach to a discrete set of firearm possessions that additionally have an explicit connection with or effect on interstate commerce." Such a jurisdictional element may establish that the enactment is in pursuance of Congress' regulation of interstate commerce.

Third, we noted that neither § 922(q) "nor its legislative history contain[s] express congressional findings regarding the effects upon interstate commerce of gun possession in a school zone." While "Congress normally is not required to make formal findings as to the substantial burdens that an activity has on interstate commerce," the existence of such findings may "enable us to evaluate the legislative judgment that the activity in question substantially affect[s] interstate commerce, even though no such substantial effect [is] visible to the naked eye."

Finally, our decision in *Lopez* rested in part on the fact that the link between gun possession and a substantial effect on interstate commerce was attenuated. The United States argued that the possession of guns may lead to violent crime, and that violent crime "can be expected to affect the functioning of the national economy in two ways. First, the costs of violent crime are substantial, and, through the mechanism of insurance, those costs are spread throughout the population. Second, violent crime reduces the willingness of individuals to travel to areas within the country that are perceived to be unsafe." The Government also argued that the presence of guns at schools poses a threat to the educational process, which in turn threatens to produce a less efficient and productive workforce, which will negatively affect national productivity and thus interstate commerce.

We rejected these "costs of crime" and "national productivity" arguments because they would permit Congress to "regulate not only all violent crime, but all activities that might lead to violent crime, regardless of how tenuously they relate to interstate commerce." We noted that, under this but-for reasoning:

> Congress could regulate any activity that it found was related to the economic productivity of individual citizens: family law (including marriage, divorce, and child custody), for example. Under the[se] theories . . ., it is difficult to perceive any limitation on federal power, even in areas such as criminal law enforcement or education where States historically have been sovereign. Thus, if we were to accept the Government's arguments, we are hard pressed to posit any activity by an individual that Congress is without power to regulate.

With these principles underlying our Commerce Clause jurisprudence as reference points, the proper resolution of the present cases is clear. Gender-motivated crimes of violence are not, in any sense of the phrase, economic activity. While we need not adopt a categorical rule against aggregating the effects of any noneconomic activity in order to decide these cases, thus far in our Nation's history our cases have upheld Commerce Clause regulation of intrastate activity only where that activity is economic in nature.

Like the Gun-Free School Zones Act at issue in *Lopez*, § 13981 contains no jurisdictional element establishing that the federal cause of action is in pursuance of Congress' power to regulate interstate commerce. Although *Lopez* makes clear that such a jurisdictional element would lend support to the argument that § 13981 is sufficiently tied to interstate commerce, Congress elected to cast § 13981's remedy over a wider, and more purely intrastate, body of violent crime.

In contrast with the lack of congressional findings that we faced in *Lopez*, § 13981 is supported by numerous findings regarding the serious impact that gender-motivated violence has on victims and their families. But the existence of congressional findings is not sufficient, by itself, to sustain the constitutionality of Commerce Clause legislation. As we stated in *Lopez*, "[S]imply because Congress may conclude that a particular activity substantially affects interstate commerce does not necessarily make it so." Rather, "[w]hether particular operations affect interstate commerce sufficiently to come under the constitutional power of Congress to regulate them is ultimately a judicial rather than a legislative question, and can be settled finally only by this Court."

In these cases, Congress' findings are substantially weakened by the fact that they rely so heavily on a method of reasoning that we have already rejected as unworkable if we are to maintain the Constitution's enumeration of powers. Congress found that gender-motivated violence affects interstate commerce

> by deterring potential victims from traveling interstate, from engaging in employment in interstate business, and from transacting with business, and in places involved in interstate commerce; . . . by diminishing national productivity, increasing medical and other costs, and decreasing the supply of and the demand for interstate products.

Given these findings and petitioners' arguments, the concern that we expressed in *Lopez* that Congress might use the Commerce Clause to completely obliterate the Constitution's distinction between national and local authority seems well founded. The reasoning that petitioners advance seeks to follow the but-for causal chain from the initial occurrence of violent crime (the suppression of which has always been the prime object of the States' police power) to every attenuated effect upon interstate commerce. If accepted, petitioners' reasoning would allow Congress to regulate any crime as long as the nationwide, aggregated impact of that crime has substantial effects on employment, production, transit, or consumption. Indeed, if Congress may regulate gender-motivated violence, it would be able to regulate murder or any other type of violence since gender-motivated violence, as a subset of all violent crime, is certain to have lesser economic impacts than the larger class of which it is a part.

Petitioners' reasoning, moreover, will not limit Congress to regulating violence but may, as we suggested in *Lopez*, be applied equally as well to family law and other areas of traditional state regulation since the aggregate effect of marriage, divorce, and childrearing on the national economy is undoubtedly significant. Congress may have recognized this specter when it expressly precluded § 13981 from being used in the family law context. Under our written Constitution, however, the limitation of congressional authority is not solely a matter of legislative grace.[5]

We accordingly reject the argument that Congress may regulate noneconomic, violent criminal conduct based solely on that conduct's aggregate effect on interstate commerce. The Constitution requires a distinction between what is truly national and what is truly local. In recognizing this fact we preserve one of the few principles that has been consistent since the Clause was adopted. The regulation and punishment of intrastate violence that is not

[5] Justice Souter's dissent theory that *Gibbons v. Ogden, Garcia v. San Antonio Metropolitan Transit Authority*, and the Seventeenth Amendment provide the answer to these cases, is remarkable because it undermines this central principle of our constitutional system. As we have repeatedly noted, the Framers crafted the federal system of government so that the people's rights would be secured by the division of power. Departing from their parliamentary past, the Framers adopted a written Constitution that further divided authority at the federal level so that the Constitution's provisions would not be defined solely by the political branches nor the scope of legislative power limited only by public opinion and the legislature's self-restraint. It is thus a "permanent and indispensable feature of our constitutional system" that "the federal judiciary is supreme in the exposition of the law of the Constitution."

No doubt the political branches have a role in interpreting and applying the Constitution, but ever since *Marbury* this Court has remained the ultimate expositor of the constitutional text. As we emphasized in *United States v. Nixon*, "[I]n the performance of assigned constitutional duties each branch of the Government must initially interpret the Constitution, and the interpretation of its powers by any branch is due great respect from the others. . . . Many decisions of this Court, however, have unequivocally reaffirmed the holding of *Marbury* . . .that '[i]t is emphatically the province and duty of the judicial department to say what the law is.'"

Contrary to Justice Souter's suggestion, *Gibbons* did not exempt the commerce power from this cardinal rule of constitutional law. His assertion that, from *Gibbons* on, public opinion has been the only restraint on the congressional exercise of the commerce power is true only insofar as it contends that political accountability is and has been the only limit on Congress' exercise of the commerce power within that power's outer bounds. As the language surrounding that relied upon by Justice Souter makes clear, *Gibbons* did not remove from this Court the authority to define that boundary.

directed at the instrumentalities, channels, or goods involved in interstate commerce has always been the province of the States. Indeed, we can think of no better example of the police power, which the Founders denied the National Government and reposed in the States, than the suppression of violent crime and vindication of its victims.

III

Because we conclude that the Commerce Clause does not provide Congress with authority to enact § 13981, we address petitioners' alternative argument that the section's civil remedy should be upheld as an exercise of Congress' remedial power under § 5 of the Fourteenth Amendment. As noted above, Congress expressly invoked the Fourteenth Amendment as a source of authority to enact § 13981.

The principles governing an analysis of congressional legislation under § 5 are well settled. Section 5 states that Congress may " 'enforce,' by 'appropriate legislation' the constitutional guarantee that no State shall deprive any person of 'life, liberty or property, without due process of law,' nor deny any person 'equal protection of the laws.' " *City of Boerne v. Flores*. Section 5 is "a positive grant of legislative power," *Katzenbach v. Morgan*, that includes authority to "prohibit conduct which is not itself unconstitutional and [to] intrud[e] into 'legislative spheres of autonomy previously reserved to the States.' " *Flores* (quoting *Fitzpatrick v. Bitzer*). However, "[a]s broad as the congressional enforcement power is, it is not unlimited." *Oregon v. Mitchell*. In fact, as we discuss in detail below, several limitations inherent in § 5's text and constitutional context have been recognized since the Fourteenth Amendment was adopted.

Petitioners' § 5 argument is founded on an assertion that there is pervasive bias in various state justice systems against victims of gender-motivated violence. This assertion is supported by a voluminous congressional record. Specifically, Congress received evidence that many participants in state justice systems are perpetuating an array of erroneous stereotypes and assumptions. Congress concluded that these discriminatory stereotypes often result in insufficient investigation and prosecution of gender-motivated crime, inappropriate focus on the behavior and credibility of the victims of that crime, and unacceptably lenient punishments for those who are actually convicted of gender-motivated violence. Petitioners contend that this bias denies victims of gender-motivated violence the equal protection of the laws and that Congress therefore acted appropriately in enacting a private civil remedy against the perpetrators of gender-motivated violence to both remedy the States' bias and deter future instances of discrimination in the state courts.

Foremost among these limitations [on Congress' § 5 power] is the time-honored principle that the Fourteenth Amendment, by its very terms, prohibits only state action. "That Amendment erects no shield against merely private conduct, however discriminatory or wrongful." *Shelley v. Kraemer* [p. 1392].

Shortly after the Fourteenth Amendment was adopted, we decided two cases interpreting the Amendment's provisions, *United States v. Harris,* 106 U.S. 629 (1883), and the *Civil Rights Cases,* 109 U.S. 3 (1883). In *Harris*, the Court considered a challenge to § 2 of the Civil Rights Act of 1871. That section sought to punish "private persons" for "conspiring to deprive any one of the equal protection of the laws enacted by the State." We concluded that this law exceeded Congress' § 5 power because the law was "directed exclusively against the action of private persons, without reference to the laws of the State, or their administration by her officers."

We reached a similar conclusion in the *Civil Rights Cases*. In those consolidated cases, we held that the public accommodation provisions of the Civil Rights Act of 1875, which applied to purely private conduct, were beyond the scope of the § 5 enforcement power.

Petitioners argue that, unlike the situation in the *Civil Rights Cases*, here there has been gender-based disparate treatment by state authorities, whereas in those cases there was no indication of such state action. There is abundant evidence, however, to show that the Congresses that enacted the Civil Rights Acts of 1871 and 1875 had a purpose similar to that of Congress in enacting § 13981: There were state laws on the books bespeaking equality of treatment, but in the administration of these laws there was discrimination against newly freed slaves. The statement of Representative Garfield in the House and that of Senator Sumner in the Senate are representative:

"[T]he chief complaint is not that the laws of the State are unequal, but that even where the laws are just and equal on their face, yet, by a systematic maladministration of them, or a neglect or refusal to enforce their provisions, a portion of the people are denied equal protection under them." Cong. Globe, 42d Cong., 1st Sess., App. 153 (1871) (statement of Rep. Garfield).

"The Legislature of South Carolina has passed a law giving precisely the rights contained in your 'supplementary civil rights bill.' But such a law remains a dead letter on her statute-books, because the State courts, comprised largely of those whom the Senator wishes to obtain amnesty for, refuse to enforce it." Cong. Globe, 42d Cong., 2d Sess., 430 (1872) (statement of Sen. Sumner).

But even if that distinction were valid, we do not believe it would save § 13981's civil remedy. For the remedy is simply not "corrective in its character, adapted to counteract and redress the operation of such prohibited [s]tate laws or proceedings of [s]tate officers." *Civil Rights Cases*. Or, as we have phrased it in more recent cases, prophylactic legislation under § 5 must have a "congruence and proportionality between the injury to be prevented or remedied and the means adopted to that end." *Florida Prepaid Postsecondary Ed. Expense Bd. v. College Savings Bank*. Section 13981 is not aimed at proscribing discrimination by officials which the Fourteenth Amendment might not itself proscribe; it is directed not at any State or state actor, but at individuals who have committed criminal acts motivated by gender bias.

IV

Petitioner Brzonkala's complaint alleges that she was the victim of a brutal assault. But Congress' effort in § 13981 to provide a federal civil remedy can be sustained neither under the Commerce Clause nor under § 5 of the Fourteenth Amendment. If the allegations here are true, no civilized system of justice could fail to provide her a remedy for the conduct of respondent Morrison. But under our federal system that remedy must be provided by the Commonwealth of Virginia, and not by the United States. The judgment of the Court of Appeals is

Affirmed.

JUSTICE THOMAS, concurring.

The majority opinion correctly applies our decision in *United States v. Lopez* and I join it in full. I write separately only to express my view that the very notion of a "substantial effects" test under the Commerce Clause is inconsistent with the original understanding of Congress' powers and with this Court's early Commerce Clause cases. By continuing to apply this rootless and malleable standard, however circumscribed, the Court has encouraged the Federal Government to persist in its view that the Commerce Clause has virtually no limits. Until this Court replaces its existing Commerce Clause jurisprudence with a standard more consistent with the original understanding, we will continue to see Congress appropriating state police powers under the guise of regulating commerce.

JUSTICE SOUTER, with whom JUSTICES STEVENS, GINSBURG, and BREYER join, dissenting.

The Court says both that it leaves Commerce Clause precedent undisturbed and that the Civil Rights Remedy of the Violence Against Women Act of 1994, 42 U.S.C. § 13981, exceeds Congress's power under that Clause. I find the claims irreconcilable and respectfully dissent.[1]

I

Our cases, which remain at least nominally undisturbed, stand for the following propositions. Congress has the power to legislate with regard to activity that, in the aggregate, has a substantial effect on interstate commerce. The fact of such a substantial effect is not an issue for the courts in the first instance but for the Congress, whose institutional capacity for gathering evidence and taking testimony far exceeds ours. By passing legislation, Congress indicates its conclusion, whether explicitly or not, that facts support its exercise of the commerce power. The business of the courts is to review the congressional assessment, not for soundness but simply for the rationality of concluding that a jurisdictional basis exists in fact. Any explicit findings that Congress chooses to make, though not dispositive of the question of rationality, may advance judicial review by identifying factual authority on which Congress relied. Applying those propositions in these cases can lead to only one conclusion.

One obvious difference from *United States v. Lopez* is the mountain of data assembled by Congress, here showing the effects of violence against women on interstate commerce. Passage of the Act in 1994 was preceded by four years of hearings, which included testimony from physicians and law professors;

[1] Finding the law a valid exercise of Commerce Clause power, I have no occasion to reach the question whether it might also be sustained as an exercise of Congress's power to enforce the Fourteenth Amendment.

from survivors of rape and domestic violence; and from representatives of state law enforcement and private business. The record includes reports on gender bias from task forces in 21 States, and we have the benefit of specific factual findings in the eight separate Reports issued by Congress and its committees over the long course leading to enactment.

[In addition to data about the extent of rape, domestic violence, and sexual assault, Justice Souter's summary of the data pointed out impacts on commerce from women's refusal to attend after-dark entertainment, reduced productivity in the workplace, and the costs of treatment.]

Based on the data, Congress found that "crimes of violence motivated by gender have a substantial adverse effect on interstate commerce, by deterring potential victims from traveling interstate, from engaging in employment in interstate business, and from transacting with business, and in places involved, in interstate commerce . . . [,] by diminishing national productivity, increasing medical and other costs, and decreasing the supply of and the demand for interstate products . . . ."

Congress thereby explicitly stated the predicate for the exercise of its Commerce Clause power. Is its conclusion irrational in view of the data amassed? True, the methodology of particular studies may be challenged, and some of the figures arrived at may be disputed. But the sufficiency of the evidence before Congress to provide a rational basis for the finding cannot seriously be questioned.

While Congress did not, to my knowledge, calculate aggregate dollar values for the nationwide effects of racial discrimination in 1964, in 1994 it did rely on evidence of the harms caused by domestic violence and sexual assault, citing annual costs of $3 billion in 1990. Equally important, though, gender-based violence in the 1990s was shown to operate in a manner similar to racial discrimination in the 1960s in reducing the mobility of employees and their production and consumption of goods shipped in interstate commerce. Like racial discrimination, "[g]ender-based violence bars its most likely targets — women — from full partic[ipation] in the national economy."

If the analogy to the Civil Rights Act of 1964 is not plain enough, one can always look back a bit further. In *Wickard*, we upheld the application of the Agricultural Adjustment Act to the planting and consumption of homegrown wheat. The effect on interstate commerce in that case followed from the possibility that wheat grown at home for personal consumption could either be drawn into the market by rising prices, or relieve its grower of any need to purchase wheat in the market. The Commerce Clause predicate was simply the effect of the production of wheat for home consumption on supply and demand in interstate commerce. Supply and demand for goods in interstate commerce will also be affected by the deaths of 2,000 to 4,000 women annually at the hands of domestic abusers, and by the reduction in the work force by the 100,000 or more rape victims who lose their jobs each year or are forced to quit. Violence against women may be found to affect interstate commerce and affect it substantially.

II

The Act would have passed muster at any time between *Wickard* in 1942 and *Lopez* in 1995, a period in which the law enjoyed a stable understanding that congressional power under the Commerce Clause, complemented by the authority of the Necessary and Proper Clause, Art. I. § 8 cl. 18, extended to all activity that, when aggregated, has a substantial effect on interstate commerce. As already noted, this understanding was secure even against the turmoil at the passage of the Civil Rights Act of 1964, in the aftermath of which the Court not only reaffirmed the cumulative effects and rational basis features of the substantial effects test, but declined to limit the commerce power through a formal distinction between legislation focused on "commerce" and statutes addressing "moral and social wrong[s]." *Heart of Atlanta*.

The fact that the Act does not pass muster before the Court today is therefore proof, to a degree that *Lopez* was not, that the Court's nominal adherence to the substantial effects test is merely that. Although a new jurisprudence has not emerged with any distinctness, it is clear that some congressional conclusions about obviously substantial, cumulative effects on commerce are being assigned lesser values than the once-stable doctrine would assign them. These devaluations are accomplished not by any express repudiation of the substantial effects test or its application through the aggregation of individual conduct, but by supplanting rational basis scrutiny with a new criterion of review.

Thus the elusive heart of the majority's analysis in these cases is its statement that Congress's findings of fact are "weakened" by the presence of a disfavored "method of reasoning." This seems to suggest that the "substantial effects" analysis is not a factual enquiry, for Congress in the first instance with subsequent judicial review looking only to the rationality of the congressional conclusion, but one of a rather different sort, dependent upon a uniquely judicial competence.

CHIEF JUSTICE MARSHALL's seminal opinion in *Gibbons v. Ogden* construed the commerce power from the start with "a breadth never yet exceeded," *Wickard v. Filburn*. In particular, it is worth noting, the Court in *Wickard* did not regard its holding as exceeding the scope of CHIEF JUSTICE MARSHALL's view of interstate commerce; *Wickard* applied an aggregate effects test to ostensibly domestic, noncommercial farming consistently with CHIEF JUSTICE MARSHALL's indication that the commerce power may be understood by its exclusion of subjects, among others, "which do not affect other States." This plenary view of the power has either prevailed or been acknowledged by this Court at every stage of our jurisprudence. And it was this understanding, free of categorical qualifications, that prevailed in the period after 1937 through *Lopez*, as summed up by JUSTICE HARLAN: "Of course, the mere fact that Congress has said when particular activity shall be deemed to affect commerce does not preclude further examination by this Court. But where we find that the legislators . . . have a rational basis for finding a chosen regulatory scheme necessary to the protection of commerce, our investigation is at an end." *Maryland v. Wirtz*.

If we now ask why the formalistic economic/noneconomic distinction might matter today, after its rejection in *Wickard*, the answer is not that the majority fails to see causal connections in an integrated economic world. The answer is that in the minds of the majority there is a new animating theory that makes categorical formalism seem useful again. Just as the old formalism had value in the service of an economic conception, the new one is useful in serving a conception of federalism. It is the instrument by which assertions of national power are to be limited in favor of preserving a supposedly discernible, proper sphere of state autonomy to legislate or refrain from legislating as the individual States see fit. The legitimacy of the Court's current emphasis on the noncommercial nature of regulated activity, then, does not turn on any logic serving the text of the Commerce Clause or on the realism of the majority's view of the national economy. The essential issue is rather the strength of the majority's claim to have a constitutional warrant for its current conception of a federal relationship enforceable by this Court through limits on otherwise plenary commerce power. This conception is the subject of the majority's second categorical discount applied today to the facts bearing on the substantial effects test.

The Court finds it relevant that the statute addresses conduct traditionally subject to state prohibition under domestic criminal law, a fact said to have some heightened significance when the violent conduct in question is not itself aimed directly at interstate commerce or its instrumentalities. Again, history seems to be recycling, for the theory of traditional state concern as grounding a limiting principle has been rejected previously, and more than once. It was disapproved in *Darby*, and held insufficient standing alone to limit the commerce power in *Hodel*.

The objection to reviving traditional state spheres of action as a consideration in commerce analysis, however, not only rests on the portent of incoherence, but is compounded by a further defect just as fundamental. The defect, in essence, is the majority's rejection of the Founders' considered judgment that politics, not judicial review, should mediate between state and national interests as the strength and legislative jurisdiction of the National Government inevitably increased through the expected growth of the national economy. Whereas today's majority takes a leaf from the book of the old judicial economists in saying that the Court should somehow draw the line to keep the federal relationship in a proper balance, Madison, Wilson, and Marshall understood the Constitution very differently.

Although Madison had emphasized the conception of a National Government of discrete powers (a conception that a number of the ratifying conventions thought was too indeterminate to protect civil liberties), Madison himself must have sensed the potential scope of some of the powers granted (such as the authority to regulate commerce), for he took care in THE FEDERALIST NO. 46 to hedge his argument for limited power by explaining the importance of national politics in protecting the States' interests. The National Government "will partake sufficiently of the spirit [of the States], to be disinclined to invade the rights of the individual States, or the prerogatives of their governments." James Wilson likewise noted that "it was a favorite object in the Convention" to secure the sovereignty of the States, and that it had been achieved through the structure of the Federal Government. 2 ELLIOT'S DEBATES 438–439. The Framers of the Bill of Rights, in turn, may well have sensed that Madison and Wilson were right about politics as the determinant of the federal balance within the broad limits of a power like commerce, for they formulated the Tenth Amendment without any provision comparable to the specific guarantees proposed for individual liberties. In any case, this Court recognized the political component of federalism in the seminal *Gibbons* opinion. After declaring the plenary character of congressional power within the sphere of activity affecting commerce, THE CHIEF JUSTICE spoke for the Court in explaining that there was only one restraint on its valid exercise:

> The wisdom and the discretion of Congress, their identity with the people, and the influence which their constituents possess at elections, are, in this, as in many other instances, as that, for example, of declaring war, the sole restraints on which they have relied, to secure them from its abuse. They are the restraints on which the people must often rely solely, in all representative governments.

III

All of this convinces me that today's ebb of the commerce power rests on error, and at the same time leads me to doubt that the majority's view will prove to be enduring law. There is yet one more reason for doubt. Although we sense the presence of *Carter Coal*, *Schechter*, and *Usery* once again, the majority embraces them only at arm's-length. Where such decisions once stood for rules, today's opinion points to considerations by which substantial effects are discounted. Cases standing for the sufficiency of substantial effects are not overruled; cases overruled since 1937 are not quite revived. [T]he practice of ad hoc review cannot preserve the distinction between the judicial and the legislative, and this Court, in any event, lacks the institutional capacity to maintain such a regime for very long. This one will end when the majority realizes that the conception of the commerce power for which it entertains hopes would inevitably fail the test expressed in JUSTICE HOLMES's statement that "[t]he first call of a theory of law is that it should fit the facts." O. HOLMES, THE COMMON LAW 167 (Howe ed.1963). The facts that cannot be ignored today are the facts of integrated national commerce and a political relationship between States and Nation much affected by their respective treasuries and constitutional modifications adopted by the people. The federalism of some earlier time is no more adequate to account for those facts today than the theory of laissez-faire was able to govern the national economy 70 years ago.

NOTES

1. *Jones v. United States*, 529 U.S. 848 (2000). Jones used a Molotov cocktail to burn down his cousin's house and was convicted under the federal arson statute, which makes it a federal crime to "maliciously damag[e] or destro[y], . . . by means of fire or an explosive, any building . . . used in interstate or foreign commerce or in any activity affecting interstate or foreign commerce." The government argued that the house was involved in interstate commerce because it had been financed and insured by national companies and was supplied with utilities that operated in interstate commerce. Justice Ginsburg wrote the majority opinion, pointing out that this construction of the statute would make every building in the country, with the possible exception of a hermit's cabin, susceptible to coverage by the statute. This was not the likely intent of Congress and would raise severe constitutional issues under *Lopez*. The Court held that a private residence could not be construed to be "currently involved in interstate commerce."

2. *Solid Waste Agency of Northern Cook County v. United States Army Corps of Engineers*, 531 U.S. 159 (2001), presented another example of the use of statutory interpretation to avoid difficult Commerce Clause issues. The Court, per Chief Justice Rehnquist, held 5-4 that the Corps' interpretation of § 404(a) of the Clean Water Act, 33 U.S.C. § 1344(a), conferring federal authority over an abandoned sand and gravel pit that served as a habitat for migratory birds, exceeded the power granted to the Corps by Congress. Under the Clean Water Act, the Corps is authorized to issue permits for the discharge of dredged or fill material into navigable waters at waste disposal sites. In 1986, the Corps promulgated the "Migratory Bird Rule," the purpose of which was to broaden the Corps' jurisdiction to intrastate waters that serve as a habitat for migratory birds. The Corps denied a permit under this rule which defined "waters of the United States" to include "isolated wetlands and lakes, intermittent streams, prairie potholes, and other waters that aren't part of a tributary system to interstate waters or to navigable waters of the United States, the degradation or destruction of which could affect interstate commerce."

The Court found no clear statement from Congress that § 404(a) was intended to reach an abandoned sand and gravel pit containing nonnavigable waters and concluded that allowing the Corps to claim federal jurisdiction "would result in a significant impingement of the States' traditional and primary power over land and water use." The Chief Justice stated: "[W]here an otherwise acceptable construction of a statute would raise serious constitutional problems, the Court will construe the statute to avoid such problems unless such construction is plainly contrary to the intent of Congress." Justice Stevens, joined by Justices Souter, Ginsberg, and Breyer, dissenting, argued that "the term 'navigable waters' operates in the statute as a shorthand for 'waters over which federal authority may be properly asserted.' "

3. Judicial control of Congressional power. There are, of course, commentators who believe that *Lopez* and *Morrison* are wrongly decided and that the Court should have continued its lenient approach to Congress' power under the Commerce Clause. Professor Hovenkamp, for example, says that the "Court's activism is particularly unwelcome because the imbalance of power it seeks to 'correct' has historically proven to be self-correcting without the Court's intervention, and because the interest it seeks to protect — states' rights in the abstract — does not primarily implicate the individual liberty rights of under-represented persons." Herbert Hovenkamp, *Judicial Restraint and Constitutional Federalism*, 96 Colum. L. Rev. 2213 (1996). Similar views are expressed in Larry Kramer, *Putting the Politics Back Into the Political Safeguards of Federalism*, 100 Colum. L. Rev. 215 (2000).

4. The meaning of commerce. If *Lopez* and *Morrison* cement a changed approach to the breadth of Congress' interstate commerce power, it is important to describe that approach. Among the supporters of an interventionist role for the Court, the debate now turns to how far to extend the new restrictions. Justice Thomas, in *Lopez*, argued that "commerce" meant only buying, selling, and transporting goods for sale. Under this view, agriculture and manufacturing, the production of goods, precede commerce and would not be regulable by the federal government. The historical evidence for this view is summarized in Randy Barnett, *The Original Meaning of the Commerce Clause*, 68 U. CHI. L. REV. 101 (2001).

Professors Nelson and Poshaw dispute that claim, arguing that both the historical evidence and subsequent usage support a broader perspective of the word commerce. They believe that commerce includes both goods and services, along with the production of goods and the "bypoducts" of production, such as "environmental and safety effects." Grant Nelson & Robert Poshaw, *Rethinking the Commerce Clause: Applying First Principles to Uphold Federal Commercial Regulations but Preserve State Control Over Social Issues*, 85 IOWA L. REV. 1, 9 (1999). As the title of the article illustrates, even the broader perspective of "commerce" limits Congress' power to economic activity and leaves "social issues" such as family and general criminal law, to the states.

GONZALES v. RAICH
125 S. Ct. 2195 (2005)

JUSTICE STEVENS delivered the opinion of the Court.

California is one of at least nine States that authorize the use of marijuana for medicinal purposes. The question presented in this case is whether the power vested in Congress by Article I, § 8, of the Constitution "[t]o make all Laws which shall be necessary and proper for carrying into Execution" its authority to "regulate Commerce with foreign Nations, and among the several States" includes the power to prohibit the local cultivation and use of marijuana in compliance with California law.

I

In 1996, California voters passed Proposition 215, now codified as the Compassionate Use Act of 1996. The Act creates an exemption from criminal prosecution for physicians, as well as for patients and primary caregivers who possess or cultivate marijuana for medicinal purposes with the recommendation or approval of a physician. Respondents Angel Raich and Diane Monson are California residents who suffer from a variety of serious medical conditions and have sought to avail themselves of medical marijuana pursuant to the terms of the Compassionate Use Act. They are being treated by licensed, board-certified family practitioners, who have concluded, after prescribing a host of conventional medicines to treat respondents' conditions and to alleviate their associated symptoms, that marijuana is the only drug available that provides effective treatment. Both women have been using marijuana as a medication for several years pursuant to their doctors' recommendation, and both rely heavily on cannabis to function on a daily basis. Indeed, Raich's physician believes that forgoing cannabis treatments would certainly cause Raich excruciating pain and could very well prove fatal.

Respondent Monson cultivates her own marijuana, and ingests the drug in a variety of ways including smoking and using a vaporizer. Respondent Raich, by contrast, is unable to cultivate her own, and thus relies on two caregivers, litigating as "John Does," to provide her with locally grown marijuana at no charge. These caregivers also process the cannabis into hashish or keif, and Raich herself processes some of the marijuana into oils, balms, and foods for consumption.

On August 15, 2002, county deputy sheriffs and agents from the federal Drug Enforcement Administration (DEA) came to Monson's home. After a thorough investigation, the county officials concluded that her use of marijuana was entirely lawful as a matter of California law. Nevertheless, after a 3-hour standoff, the federal agents seized and destroyed all six of her cannabis plants.

Respondents thereafter brought this action against the Attorney General of the United States and the head of the DEA seeking injunctive and declaratory relief prohibiting the enforcement of the federal Controlled Substances Act (CSA), 21 U.S.C. § 801 *et seq.*, to the extent it prevents them from possessing, obtaining, or manufacturing cannabis for their personal medical use.

The District Court denied respondents' motion for a preliminary injunction. A divided panel of the Court of Appeals for the Ninth Circuit reversed and ordered the District Court to enter a preliminary injunction. The majority placed heavy reliance on our decisions in *United States v. Lopez* and *United States v. Morrison* to hold that this separate class of purely local activities was beyond the reach of federal power. In contrast, the dissenting judge concluded that the CSA, as applied to respondents, was clearly valid under *Lopez* and *Morrison*.

The case is made difficult by respondents' strong arguments that they will suffer irreparable harm because, despite a congressional finding to the contrary, marijuana does have valid therapeutic purposes. The question before us, however, is not whether it is wise to enforce the statute in these circumstances; rather, it is whether Congress' power to regulate interstate markets for medicinal substances encompasses the portions of those markets that are supplied with drugs produced and consumed locally. Well-settled law controls our answer. The CSA is a valid exercise of federal power, even as applied to the troubling facts of this case. We accordingly vacate the judgment of the Court of Appeals.

II

Marijuana itself was not significantly regulated by the Federal Government until 1937 when accounts of marijuana's addictive qualities and physiological effects, paired with dissatisfaction with enforcement efforts at state and local levels, prompted Congress to pass the Marihuana Tax Act (repealed 1970). Then in 1970, after declaration of the national "war on drugs," federal drug policy underwent a significant transformation. Prompted by a perceived need to consolidate the growing number of piecemeal drug laws and to enhance federal drug enforcement powers, Congress enacted the Comprehensive Drug Abuse Prevention and Control Act.

Title II of that Act, the CSA, repealed most of the earlier antidrug laws in favor of a comprehensive regime to combat the international and interstate traffic in illicit drugs. The main objectives of the CSA were to conquer drug abuse and to control the legitimate and illegitimate traffic in controlled substances.[2] Congress was particularly concerned with the need to prevent the diversion of drugs from legitimate to illicit channels.

To effectuate these goals, Congress devised a closed regulatory system making it unlawful to manufacture, distribute, dispense, or possess any controlled substance except in a manner authorized by the CSA. The CSA categorizes all controlled substances into five schedules. The drugs are grouped together based on their accepted medical uses, the potential for abuse, and their psychological and physical effects on the body.

In enacting the CSA, Congress classified marijuana as a Schedule I drug. This preliminary classification was based, in part, on the recommendation of the Assistant Secretary of HEW "that marihuana be retained within schedule I at least until the completion of certain studies now underway." Schedule I drugs are categorized as such because of their high potential for abuse, lack of any accepted medical use, and absence of any accepted safety for use in medically supervised treatment. These three factors, in varying gradations, are also used to categorize drugs in the other four schedules. For example, Schedule II substances also have a high potential for abuse which may lead to severe psychological or physical dependence, but unlike Schedule I drugs, they have a currently accepted medical use. By classifying marijuana as a Schedule I drug, as opposed to listing it on a lesser schedule, the manufacture,

---

[2] In particular, Congress made the following findings:

> (1) Many of the drugs included within this subchapter have a useful and legitimate medical purpose and are necessary to maintain the health and general welfare of the American people.
>
> (2) The illegal importation, manufacture, distribution, and possession and improper use of controlled substances have a substantial and detrimental effect on the health and general welfare of the American people.
>
> (3) A major portion of the traffic in controlled substances flows through interstate and foreign commerce. Incidents of the traffic which are not an integral part of the interstate or foreign flow, such as manufacture, local distribution, and possession, nonetheless have a substantial and direct effect upon interstate commerce because—
>
> > (A) after manufacture, many controlled substances are transported in interstate commerce,
> >
> > (B) controlled substances distributed locally usually have been transported in interstate commerce immediately before their distribution, and
> >
> > (C) controlled substances possessed commonly flow through interstate commerce immediately prior to such possession.
>
> (4) Local distribution and possession of controlled substances contribute to swelling the interstate traffic in such substances.
>
> (5) Controlled substances manufactured and distributed intrastate cannot be differentiated from controlled substances manufactured and distributed interstate. Thus, it is not feasible to distinguish, in terms of controls, between controlled substances manufactured and distributed interstate and controlled substances manufactured and distributed intrastate.
>
> (6) Federal control of the intrastate incidents of the traffic in controlled substances is essential to the effective control of the interstate incidents of such traffic.

21 U.S.C. §§ 801(1)–(6).

distribution, or possession of marijuana became a criminal offense, with the sole exception being use of the drug as part of a Food and Drug Administration pre-approved research study.

III

Respondents in this case do not dispute that passage of the CSA, as part of the Comprehensive Drug Abuse Prevention and Control Act, was well within Congress' commerce power. Nor do they contend that any provision or section of the CSA amounts to an unconstitutional exercise of congressional authority. Rather, respondents' challenge is actually quite limited; they argue that the CSA's categorical prohibition of the manufacture and possession of marijuana as applied to the intrastate manufacture and possession of marijuana for medical purposes pursuant to California law exceeds Congress' authority under the Commerce Clause.

Our case law firmly establishes Congress' power to regulate purely local activities that are part of an economic "class of activities" that have a substantial effect on interstate commerce. *See, e.g., Perez; Wickard v. Filburn.* As we stated in *Wickard*, "even if appellee's activity be local and though it may not be regarded as commerce, it may still, whatever its nature, be reached by Congress if it exerts a substantial economic effect on interstate commerce." We have never required Congress to legislate with scientific exactitude. When Congress decides that the " 'total incidence' " of a practice poses a threat to a national market, it may regulate the entire class. In this vein, we have reiterated that when " 'a general regulatory statute bears a substantial relation to commerce, the de minimis character of individual instances arising under that statute is of no consequence.' "

Our decision in *Wickard* is of particular relevance. In *Wickard*, we upheld the application of regulations promulgated under the Agricultural Adjustment Act of 1938, which were designed to control the volume of wheat moving in interstate and foreign commerce in order to avoid surpluses and consequent abnormally low prices. The regulations established an allotment of 11.1 acres for Filburn's 1941 wheat crop, but he sowed 23 acres, intending to use the excess by consuming it on his own farm. Filburn argued that even though we had sustained Congress' power to regulate the production of goods for commerce, that power did not authorize "federal regulation [of] production not intended in any part for commerce but wholly for consumption on the farm." JUSTICE JACKSON's opinion for a unanimous Court rejected this submission. He wrote:

> The effect of the statute before us is to restrict the amount which may be produced for market and the extent as well to which one may forestall resort to the market by producing to meet his own needs. That appellee's own contribution to the demand for wheat may be trivial by itself is not enough to remove him from the scope of federal regulation where, as here, his contribution, taken together with that of many others similarly situated, is far from trivial.

Wickard thus establishes that Congress can regulate purely intrastate activity that is not itself "commercial," in that it is not produced for sale, if it concludes that failure to regulate that class of activity would undercut the regulation of the interstate market in that commodity.

The similarities between this case and *Wickard* are striking. Like the farmer in *Wickard*, respondents are cultivating, for home consumption, a fungible commodity for which there is an established, albeit illegal, interstate market. Just as the Agricultural Adjustment Act was designed "to control the volume [of wheat] moving in interstate and foreign commerce in order to avoid surpluses" and consequently control the market price, a primary purpose of the CSA is to control the supply and demand of controlled substances in both lawful and unlawful drug markets. In *Wickard*, we had no difficulty concluding that Congress had a rational basis for believing that, when viewed in the aggregate, leaving home-consumed wheat outside the regulatory scheme would have a substantial influence on price and market conditions. Here too, Congress had a rational basis for concluding that leaving home-consumed marijuana outside federal control would similarly affect price and market conditions.

More concretely, one concern prompting inclusion of wheat grown for home consumption in the 1938 Act was that rising market prices could draw such wheat into the interstate market, resulting in lower market prices. The parallel concern making it appropriate to include marijuana grown for home consumption in the CSA is the likelihood that the high demand in the interstate market will draw such marijuana into that market. While the diversion of homegrown wheat tended to frustrate the federal interest in stabilizing prices by regulating the volume of commercial transactions in the interstate market, the diversion of homegrown marijuana tends to frustrate the federal interest in eliminating commercial transactions in the interstate market in their entirety. In both cases, the regulation is squarely within Congress' commerce power because production of the commodity meant for home consumption, be it wheat or marijuana, has a substantial effect on supply and demand in the national market for that commodity.

Nonetheless, respondents suggest that *Wickard* differs from this case in three respects: (1) the Agricultural Adjustment Act, unlike the CSA, exempted small farming operations; (2) *Wickard* involved a "quintessential economic activity" — a commercial farm — whereas respondents do not sell marijuana; and (3) the *Wickard* record made it clear that the aggregate production of wheat for use on farms had a significant impact on market prices. Those differences, though factually accurate, do not diminish the precedential force of this Court's reasoning.

The fact that Wickard's own impact on the market was "trivial by itself" was not a sufficient reason for removing him from the scope of federal regulation. That the Secretary of Agriculture elected to exempt even smaller farms from regulation does not speak to his power to regulate all those whose aggregated production was significant, nor did that fact play any role in the Court's analysis. Moreover, even though Wickard was indeed a commercial farmer, the activity he was engaged in — the cultivation of wheat for home consumption — was not treated by the Court as part of his commercial farming operation. And while it is true that the record in the *Wickard* case itself established the causal connection between the production for local use and the national market, we have before us findings by Congress to the same effect.

In assessing the scope of Congress' authority under the Commerce Clause, we stress that the task before us is a modest one. We need not determine whether respondents' activities, taken in the aggregate, substantially affect interstate commerce in fact, but only whether a "rational basis" exists for so concluding. Given the enforcement difficulties that attend distinguishing between marijuana cultivated locally and marijuana grown elsewhere, and concerns about diversion into illicit channels, we have no difficulty concluding that Congress had a rational basis for believing that failure to regulate the intrastate manufacture and possession of marijuana would leave a gaping hole in the CSA. That the regulation ensnares some purely intrastate activity is of no moment. As we have done many times before, we refuse to excise individual components of that larger scheme.

IV

To support their contrary submission, respondents rely heavily on two of our more recent Commerce Clause cases. In their myopic focus, they overlook the larger context of modern-era Commerce Clause jurisprudence preserved by those cases. Moreover, even in the narrow prism of respondents' creation, they read those cases far too broadly. Those two cases, of course, are *Lopez* and *Morrison*. As an initial matter, the statutory challenges at issue in those cases were markedly different from the challenge respondents pursue in the case at hand. Here, respondents ask us to excise individual applications of a concededly valid statutory scheme. In contrast, in both *Lopez* and *Morrison*, the parties asserted that a particular statute or provision fell outside Congress' commerce power in its entirety. This distinction is pivotal for we have often reiterated that "[w]here the class of activities is regulated and that class is within the reach of federal power, the courts have no power 'to excise, as trivial, individual instances' of the class." *Perez*.

At issue in *Lopez* was the validity of the Gun-Free School Zones Act of 1990, which was a brief, single-subject statute making it a crime for an individual to possess a gun in a school zone. The Act did not regulate any economic activity and did not contain any requirement that the possession of a gun have any connection to past interstate activity or a predictable impact on future commercial activity. The statutory scheme that the Government is defending in this litigation is at the opposite end of the regulatory spectrum. The CSA was a lengthy and detailed statute creating a comprehensive framework for regulating the production, distribution, and possession of five classes of "controlled substances." Marijuana was listed [in one of three subcategories of Schedule I]. That classification, unlike the discrete prohibition established by the Gun-Free School Zones Act of 1990, was merely one of many "essential part[s] of a larger regulation of economic activity, in which the regulatory scheme could be undercut unless the intrastate activity were regulated." *Lopez*.[3] Our opinion in *Lopez* casts no doubt on the validity of such a program.

Nor does this Court's holding in *Morrison*. The Violence Against Women Act of 1994 created a federal civil remedy for the victims of gender-motivated crimes of violence. The remedy was enforceable in both state and federal courts, and generally depended on proof of the violation of a state law. Despite congressional findings that such crimes had an adverse impact on interstate commerce, we held the statute unconstitutional because, like the statute in *Lopez*, it did not regulate economic activity. We concluded that "the noneconomic, criminal nature of the conduct at issue was central to our decision" in *Lopez*, and that our prior cases had identified a clear pattern of analysis: "Where economic activity substantially affects interstate commerce, legislation regulating that activity will be sustained." *Morrison*.

Unlike those at issue in *Lopez* and *Morrison*, the activities regulated by the CSA are quintessentially economic. The CSA is a statute that regulates the production, distribution, and consumption of commodities for which there is an established, and lucrative, interstate market. Prohibiting the intrastate possession or manufacture of an article of commerce is a rational (and commonly utilized) means of regulating commerce in that product. Because the CSA is a statute that directly regulates economic, commercial activity, our opinion in *Morrison* casts no doubt on its constitutionality.

The Court of Appeals was able to conclude otherwise only by isolating a "separate and distinct" class of activities that it held to be beyond the reach of federal power, defined as "the intrastate, noncommercial cultivation, possession and use of marijuana for personal medical purposes on the advice of a physician and in accordance with state law." The court characterized this class as "different in kind from drug trafficking." The differences between the members of a class so defined and the principal traffickers in Schedule I substances might be sufficient to justify a policy decision exempting the narrower class from the coverage of the CSA. The question, however, is whether Congress' contrary policy judgment, *i.e.*, its decision to include this narrower "class of activities" within the larger regulatory scheme, was constitutionally deficient. We have no difficulty concluding that Congress acted rationally in determining that none of the characteristics making up the purported class, whether viewed individually or in the aggregate, compelled an exemption from the CSA; rather, the subdivided class of activities defined by the Court of Appeals was an essential part of the larger regulatory scheme.

First, the fact that marijuana is used "for personal medical purposes on the advice of a physician" cannot itself serve as a distinguishing factor. The CSA designates marijuana as contraband for any purpose; in fact, by characterizing marijuana as a Schedule I drug, Congress expressly found that the drug has

[3] The principal dissent asserts that by "[s]eizing upon our language in *Lopez*," (opinion of O'Connor, J.), i.e., giving effect to our well-established case law, Congress will now have an incentive to legislate broadly. Even putting aside the political checks that would generally curb Congress' power to enact a broad and comprehensive scheme for the purpose of targeting purely local activity, there is no suggestion that the CSA constitutes the type of "evasive" legislation the dissent fears, nor could such an argument plausibly be made.

no acceptable medical uses. [E]ven if respondents are correct that marijuana does have accepted medical uses and thus should be redesignated as a lesser schedule drug,[4] the CSA would still impose controls beyond what is required by California law.

[I]f, as the principal dissent contends, the personal cultivation, possession, and use of marijuana for medicinal purposes is beyond the " 'outer limits' of Congress' Commerce Clause authority," it must also be true that such personal use of marijuana (or any other homegrown drug) for recreational purposes is also beyond those "outer limits," whether or not a State elects to authorize or even regulate such use. That is, the dissenters' rationale logically extends to place any federal regulation (including quality, prescription, or quantity controls) of any locally cultivated and possessed controlled substance for any purpose beyond the "outer limits" of Congress' Commerce Clause authority. One need not have a degree in economics to understand why a nationwide exemption for the vast quantity of marijuana (or other drugs) locally cultivated for personal use (which presumably would include use by friends, neighbors, and family members) may have a substantial impact on the interstate market for this extraordinarily popular substance. The congressional judgment that an exemption for such a significant segment of the total market would undermine the orderly enforcement of the entire regulatory scheme is entitled to a strong presumption of validity. Indeed, that judgment is not only rational, but "visible to the naked eye," *Lopez*, under any commonsense appraisal of the probable consequences of such an open-ended exemption.

Second, limiting the activity to marijuana possession and cultivation "in accordance with state law" cannot serve to place respondents' activities beyond congressional reach. The Supremacy Clause unambiguously provides that if there is any conflict between federal and state law, federal law shall prevail. It is beyond peradventure that federal power over commerce is "superior to that of the States to provide for the welfare or necessities of their inhabitants," however legitimate or dire those necessities may be. Just as state acquiescence to federal regulation cannot expand the bounds of the Commerce Clause, so too state action cannot circumscribe Congress' plenary commerce power.

Indeed, that the California exemptions will have a significant impact on both the supply and demand sides of the market for marijuana is not just "plausible" as the principal dissent concedes, it is readily apparent. The exemption for physicians provides them with an economic incentive to grant their patients permission to use the drug. In contrast to most prescriptions for legal drugs, which limit the dosage and duration of the usage, under California law the doctor's permission to recommend marijuana use is open-ended. The authority to grant permission whenever the doctor determines that a patient is afflicted with "any other illness for which marijuana provides relief," is broad enough to allow even the most scrupulous doctor to conclude that some recreational uses would be therapeutic. And our cases have taught

[4] We acknowledge that evidence proffered by respondents in this case regarding the effective medical uses for marijuana, if found credible after trial, would cast serious doubt on the accuracy of the findings that require marijuana to be listed in Schedule I. But the possibility that the drug may be reclassified in the future has no relevance to the question whether Congress now has the power to regulate its production and distribution. Respondents' submission, if accepted, would place all homegrown medical substances beyond the reach of Congress' regulatory jurisdiction.

us that there are some unscrupulous physicians who overprescribe when it is sufficiently profitable to do so.

So, from the "separate and distinct" class of activities identified by the Court of Appeals (and adopted by the dissenters), we are left with "the intrastate, noncommercial cultivation, possession and use of marijuana." Thus the case for the exemption comes down to the claim that a locally cultivated product that is used domestically rather than sold on the open market is not subject to federal regulation. Given the findings in the CSA and the undisputed magnitude of the commercial market for marijuana, our decisions in *Wickard v. Filburn* and the later cases endorsing its reasoning foreclose that claim.

JUSTICE SCALIA, concurring in the judgment.

I agree with the Court's holding that the Controlled Substances Act (CSA) may validly be applied to respondents' cultivation, distribution, and possession of marijuana for personal, medicinal use. I write separately because my understanding of the doctrinal foundation on which that holding rests is, if not inconsistent with that of the Court, at least more nuanced.

Since *Perez v. United States*, our cases have mechanically recited that the Commerce Clause permits congressional regulation of three categories: (1) the channels of interstate commerce; (2) the instrumentalities of interstate commerce, and persons or things in interstate commerce; and (3) activities that "substantially affect" interstate commerce. The first two categories are self-evident, since they are the ingredients of interstate commerce itself. *See Gibbons v. Ogden*. The third category, however, is different in kind, and its recitation without explanation is misleading and incomplete.

It is misleading because, unlike the channels, instrumentalities, and agents of interstate commerce, activities that substantially affect interstate commerce are not themselves part of interstate commerce, and thus the power to regulate them cannot come from the Commerce Clause alone. Rather, Congress's regulatory authority over intrastate activities that are not themselves part of interstate commerce (including activities that have a substantial effect on interstate commerce) derives from the Necessary and Proper Clause. And the category of "activities that substantially affect interstate commerce," *Lopez*, is incomplete because the authority to enact laws necessary and proper for the regulation of interstate commerce is not limited to laws governing intrastate activities that substantially affect interstate commerce. Where necessary to make a regulation of interstate commerce effective, Congress may regulate even those intrastate activities that do not themselves substantially affect interstate commerce.

Our cases show that the regulation of intrastate activities may be necessary to and proper for the regulation of interstate commerce in two general circumstances. Most directly, the commerce power permits Congress not only to devise rules for the governance of commerce between States but also to facilitate interstate commerce by eliminating potential obstructions, and to restrict it by eliminating potential stimulants. That is why the Court has repeatedly sustained congressional legislation on the ground that the regulated activities had a substantial effect on interstate commerce. [A]lthough Congress's authority to regulate intrastate activity that substantially affects interstate commerce is broad, it does not permit the Court to "pile inference upon inference," in order to establish that noneconomic activity has a substantial effect on interstate commerce.

As we implicitly acknowledged in *Lopez*, however, Congress's authority to enact laws necessary and proper for the regulation of interstate commerce is not limited to laws directed against economic activities that have a substantial effect on interstate commerce. Though the conduct in *Lopez* was not economic, the Court nevertheless recognized that it could be regulated as "an essential part of a larger regulation of economic activity, in which the regulatory scheme could be undercut unless the intrastate activity were regulated." This statement referred to those cases permitting the regulation of intrastate activities "which in a substantial way interfere with or obstruct the exercise of the granted power."

Although this power "to make . . . regulation effective" commonly overlaps with the authority to regulate economic activities that substantially affect interstate commerce,[5] and may in some cases have been confused with that authority, the two are distinct. The regulation of an intrastate activity may be essential to a comprehensive regulation of interstate commerce even though the intrastate activity does not itself "substantially affect" interstate commerce. Moreover, Congress may regulate even noneconomic local activity if that regulation is a necessary part of a more general regulation of interstate commerce. The relevant question is simply whether the means chosen are "reasonably adapted" to the attainment of a legitimate end under the commerce power. *Darby*.

Today's principal dissent objects that, by permitting Congress to regulate activities necessary to effective interstate regulation, the Court reduces *Lopez* and *Morrison* to "little more than a drafting guide." (opinion of O'Connor, J.). I think that criticism unjustified. Unlike the power to regulate activities that have a substantial effect on interstate commerce, the power to enact laws enabling effective regulation of interstate commerce can only be exercised in conjunction with congressional regulation of an interstate market, and it extends only to those measures necessary to make the interstate regulation effective. As *Lopez* itself states, and the Court affirms today, Congress may regulate noneconomic intrastate activities only where the failure to do so "could . . . undercut" its regulation of interstate commerce. This is not a power that threatens to obliterate the line between "what is truly national and what is truly local."

Finally, neither respondents nor the dissenters suggest any violation of state sovereignty of the sort that would render this regulation "inappropriate." *National League of Cities v. Usery*.

---

[5] *Wickard v. Filburn* presented such a case. Because the unregulated production of wheat for personal consumption diminished demand in the regulated wheat market, the Court said, it carried with it the potential to disrupt Congress's price regulation by driving down prices in the market. This potential disruption of Congress's interstate regulation, and not only the effect that personal consumption of wheat had on interstate commerce, justified Congress's regulation of that conduct.

* * *

JUSTICE O'CONNOR, with whom THE CHIEF JUSTICE and JUSTICE THOMAS join as to all but Part III, dissenting.

We enforce the "outer limits" of Congress' Commerce Clause authority not for their own sake, but to protect historic spheres of state sovereignty from excessive federal encroachment and thereby to maintain the distribution of power fundamental to our federalist system of government.

This case exemplifies the role of States as laboratories. The States' core police powers have always included authority to define criminal law and to protect the health, safety, and welfare of their citizens. Exercising those powers, California (by ballot initiative and then by legislative codification) has come to its own conclusion about the difficult and sensitive question of whether marijuana should be available to relieve severe pain and suffering. Today the Court sanctions an application of the federal Controlled Substances Act that extinguishes that experiment, without any proof that the personal cultivation, possession, and use of marijuana for medicinal purposes, if economic activity in the first place, has a substantial effect on interstate commerce and is therefore an appropriate subject of federal regulation. In so doing, the Court announces a rule that gives Congress a perverse incentive to legislate broadly pursuant to the Commerce Clause — nestling questionable assertions of its authority into comprehensive regulatory schemes — rather than with precision. That rule and the result it produces in this case are irreconcilable with our decisions in *Lopez* and *Morrison*.

Today's decision allows Congress to regulate intrastate activity without check, so long as there is some implication by legislative design that regulating intrastate activity is essential (and the Court appears to equate "essential" with "necessary") to the interstate regulatory scheme. Seizing upon our language in *Lopez* that the statute prohibiting gun possession in school zones was "not an essential part of a larger regulation of economic activity, in which the regulatory scheme could be undercut unless the intrastate activity were regulated," the Court appears to reason that the placement of local activity in a comprehensive scheme confirms that it is essential to that scheme. If the Court is right, then *Lopez* stands for nothing more than a drafting guide: Congress should have described the relevant crime as "transfer or possession of a firearm anywhere in the nation" — thus including commercial and noncommercial activity, and clearly encompassing some activity with assuredly substantial effect on interstate commerce. Had it done so, the majority hints, we would have sustained its authority to regulate possession of firearms in school zones. Furthermore, today's decision suggests we would readily sustain a congressional decision to attach the regulation of intrastate activity to a pre-existing comprehensive (or even not-so-comprehensive) scheme. If so, the Court invites increased federal regulation of local activity even if, as it suggests, Congress would not enact a new interstate scheme exclusively for the sake of reaching intrastate activity.

In contrast to the CSA's limitless assertion of power, Congress provided an exemption within the AAA for small producers. When Filburn planted the wheat at issue in *Wickard*, the statute exempted plantings less than 200 bushels (about six tons), and when he harvested his wheat it exempted plantings less than six acres. *Wickard*, then, did not extend Commerce Clause authority to something as modest as the home cook's herb garden. This is not to say that Congress may never regulate small quantities of commodities possessed or produced for personal use, or to deny that it sometimes needs to enact a zero tolerance regime for such commodities. It is merely to say that *Wickard* did not hold or imply that small-scale production of commodities is always economic, and automatically within Congress' reach.

Even assuming that economic activity is at issue in this case, the Government has made no showing in fact that the possession and use of homegrown marijuana for medical purposes, in California or elsewhere, has a substantial effect on interstate commerce. Similarly, the Government has not shown that regulating such activity is necessary to an interstate regulatory scheme. Whatever the specific theory of "substantial effects" at issue (*i.e.*, whether the activity substantially affects interstate commerce, whether its regulation is necessary to an interstate regulatory scheme, or both), a concern for dual sovereignty requires that Congress' excursion into the traditional domain of States be justified.

There is simply no evidence that homegrown medicinal marijuana users constitute, in the aggregate, a sizable enough class to have a discernable, let alone substantial, impact on the national illicit drug market — or otherwise to threaten the CSA regime. Explicit evidence is helpful when substantial effect is not "visible to the naked eye." And here, in part because common sense suggests that medical marijuana users may be limited in number and that California's Compassionate Use Act and similar state legislation may well isolate activities relating to medicinal marijuana from the illicit market, the effect of those activities on interstate drug traffic is not self-evidently substantial.

JUSTICE THOMAS, dissenting.

Respondents' local cultivation and consumption of marijuana is not "Commerce . . . among the several States." By holding that Congress may regulate activity that is neither interstate nor commerce under the Interstate Commerce Clause, the Court abandons any attempt to enforce the Constitution's limits on federal power. The majority supports this conclusion by invoking, without explanation, the Necessary and Proper Clause. Regulating respondents' conduct, however, is not "necessary and proper for carrying into Execution" Congress' restrictions on the interstate drug trade. Thus, neither the Commerce Clause nor the Necessary and Proper Clause grants Congress the power to regulate respondents' conduct.

As I explained at length in *United States v. Lopez*, the Commerce Clause empowers Congress to regulate the buying and selling of goods and services trafficked across state lines. The Clause's text, structure, and history all indicate that, at the time of the founding, the term " 'commerce' consisted of selling, buying, and bartering, as well as transporting for these purposes." Commerce, or trade, stood in contrast to productive activities like manufacturing and agriculture.

On this traditional understanding of "commerce," the Controlled Substances Act regulates a great deal of marijuana trafficking that is interstate and commercial in character. The CSA does not, however, criminalize only the interstate buying and selling of marijuana. Instead, it bans the entire market — intrastate or interstate, noncommercial or commercial — for marijuana. Respondents are correct that the CSA exceeds Congress' commerce power as applied to their conduct, which is purely intrastate and noncommercial.

More difficult, however, is whether the CSA is a valid exercise of Congress' power to enact laws that are "necessary and proper for carrying into Execution" its power to regulate interstate commerce. The Necessary and Proper Clause is not a warrant to Congress to enact any law that bears some conceivable connection to the exercise of an enumerated power. Nor is it, however, a command to Congress to enact only laws that are absolutely indispensable to the exercise of an enumerated power.

Congress has exercised its power over interstate commerce to criminalize trafficking in marijuana across state lines. The Government contends that banning Monson and Raich's intrastate drug activity is "necessary and proper for carrying into Execution" its regulation of interstate drug trafficking. However, in order to be "necessary," the intrastate ban must be more than "a reasonable means [of] effectuat[ing] the regulation of interstate commerce." It must be "plainly adapted" to regulating interstate marijuana trafficking — in other words, there must be an "obvious, simple, and direct relation" between the intrastate ban and the regulation of interstate commerce.

On its face, a ban on the intrastate cultivation, possession and distribution of marijuana may be plainly adapted to stopping the interstate flow of marijuana. Unregulated local growers and users could swell both the supply and the demand sides of the interstate marijuana market, making the market more difficult to regulate. But respondents do not challenge the CSA on its face. Instead, they challenge it as applied to their conduct. The question is thus whether the intrastate ban is "necessary and proper" as applied to medical marijuana users like respondents.

Respondents are not regulable simply because they belong to a large class (local growers and users of marijuana) that Congress might need to reach, if they also belong to a distinct and separable subclass (local growers and users of state-authorized, medical marijuana) that does not undermine the CSA's interstate ban.

But even assuming that States' controls allow some seepage of medical marijuana into the illicit drug market, there is a multibillion-dollar interstate market for marijuana. It is difficult to see how this vast market could be affected by diverted medical cannabis, let alone in a way that makes regulating intrastate medical marijuana obviously essential to controlling the interstate drug market.

Our federalist system, properly understood, allows California and a growing number of other States to decide for themselves how to safeguard the health and welfare of their citizens. I would affirm the judgment of the Court of Appeals. I respectfully dissent.

Notes and Questions

1. Justice O'Connor asserted that the Gun Free School Zone Act could become valid if Congress merely redrafted to ban possession or distribution of all guns throughout the U.S. except under a strict regulatory system that did not permit guns to be carried near schools. The majority answers in a footnote that there would be political barriers to such a move. Are the political barriers a constitutionally significant check on federal power?

2. Professor Pushaw says that *Raich* is not a case representing a major shift in Supreme Court doctrine because indeed neither *Lopez* nor *Morrison* represented a major development before it. "*Raich* illustrates the shortcomings of the *Lopez/Morrison* standards . . . Just as many scholars prematurely heralded *Lopez* as the beginning of a Commerce Clause revolution, others now may be too quick to characterize *Raich* as the end." Robert Pushaw, *The Medical Marijuana Case: A Commerce Clause Counter-Revolution?* 9 Lewis & Clark L. Rev. 879, 882, 884 (2005). Continuing his support for Justice Thomas' position that "commerce" is limited to buying and selling (see p. 170 *supra*), Professor Pushaw argues that position would be a more reliable standard than what can be gleaned from the current caselaw.

3. Assume that *Roe v. Wade* has been overruled. Could Congress then pass a law making it a federal crime to perform or obtain an abortion anywhere in the U.S.? If this were a problem itself, then Congress might forbid the use in providing abortions of any goods moving in interstate commerce. Since it would be very difficult to determine whether a particular piece of surgical equipment had moved in interstate commerce, Congress might then ban all abortions as part of the "class of activities" that affect interstate commerce. Would this be valid under *Darby* and *Gonzales*?

§ 2.03 THE TAXING AND SPENDING POWERS

Article I, § 8 of the Constitution begins with the statement that "the Congress shall have power to lay and collect taxes, duties, imposts and excises, to pay the debts and provide for the common defense and general welfare of the United States." Following this clause are 16 clauses setting out the so-called enumerated powers. Discerning a "plain meaning" of the taxing and spending language is itself no easy task. The most sensible reading might be that Congress may tax only for the purpose of paying debts and providing for the common defense and general welfare. If so, then the power to tax is apparently limited by the purposes for which the revenue may be spent. Another sensible reading is that the taxing and spending portions of the sentence operate independently, that taxing is not limited by the spending clause. Under that reading, there is still the question of whether taxes may be levied for regulatory purposes that are not listed in the enumerated powers.

The next question is whether there are any limitations on the power to spend. Defense spending seems easy enough to define; certainly recent decades have provided innumerable examples. But what debts may be paid and what constitutes the "general welfare?" There are three possible readings of this language. One is that only those debts incurred within the exercise of the enumerated powers are valid and only those purposes within the enumerated powers constitute the "general welfare." Second is that "general" welfare broadens the scope of spending beyond the enumerated powers so long as the spending is not for the "special" welfare of an identified person or group apart from the general operations of government. The third reading is that general welfare is a concept within the sole discretion of Congress not limited by either the enumerated powers or notions of special interests.

This section of the book deals with the scope of the taxing and spending powers together. For the purpose of context, you should be aware that the modern view of these powers has left taxing and spending virtually within the sole discretion of Congress. In 1989, total federal expenditures were about $1,200 billion ($1.2 trillion), of which $120 billion went to the states, approximately 20% of the total budgets of all the states. For fiscal year 2006, federal expenditures will be roughly $3,000 billion, of which about $423 billion will go to state and local governments. All the states together have a general fund revenue base of about $593 billion, so the federal portion of the states' budgets is now over 40%. The total revenue of all the states is only about 20% of what the federal government brings in. *See http://www.nasbo.org/Publications/fiscalsurvey/fsfall2005.pdf*. The allocation of power that goes with these dollars is obvious. The view has been expressed that

> the real transformation of "Our Federalism" has been worked in the modern federal role in taxation, borrowing and spending. The framers envisaged a "clear separation between state and federal governments, with each provided with the sources of public revenue necessary for support of the functions assigned to it." Once the Supreme Court recognized that congressional power to spend for the general welfare extends beyond the scope of the Article I, § 8 checklist, twentieth-century Congresses inevitably asserted the right to finance functions that traditionally the state had exclusively financed or regulated.

Henry Monaghan, *The Burger Court and "Our Federalism,"* 43 LAW & CONTEMP. PROBS. 39 (1980).

[A] AN ORIGINAL UNDERSTANDING OF THE CLAUSES?

The Court has consistently held that the general welfare clause in the Preamble is not a separate source of regulatory power for any branch of the national government. But why isn't the general welfare clause in Article I, § 8, when coupled with the necessary and proper clause, a separate source of federal regulatory power? Is the problem solely one of syntax?

> For one thing, it is a fact that in certain early printings of the Constitution the "common defense and general welfare" clause appears separately paragraphed, while in others it is set off from the "lay and collect" clause by a semi-colon and not, as modern usage would require, by the less awesome comma. To be sure, the semi-colon may have been due in the first instance to the splattering of a goose quill that needed trimming, for it is notorious that the fate of nations has often turned on just such minute points.

EDWARD S. CORWIN, THE TWILIGHT OF THE SUPREME COURT 153 (1934).

Does the problem lie in federal relationships? In a famous passage, Thomas Jefferson stated:

> [T]he laying of taxes is the power, and the general welfare the purpose for which the power is to be exercised. They [Congress] are not to lay taxes *ad libitum* for any purpose they please; but only to pay the debts or provide for the general welfare of the Union. In like manner, they are not to do anything they please, to provide for the general welfare, but only to lay taxes for that purpose. To consider the latter phrase, not as describing the purpose of the first, but as giving a distinct and independent power to do any act they please, which might be for the good of the Union, would render all the preceding and subsequent enumerations of power completely useless. It would reduce the whole instrument to a single phrase, that of instituting a Congress with power to do whatever would be for the good of the United States; and, as they would be the sole judges of the good or evil, it would also be a power to do whatever evil they please.

Writings of Thomas Jefferson 147–49 (Library ed. 1904).

Hamilton and Madison took very different positions regarding the purpose of the general welfare clause. The Supreme Court, at least in dictum, adopted the Hamiltonian position:

> Madison asserted it amounted to no more than a reference to the other powers enumerated in the subsequent clauses of the same section; that, as the United States is a government of limited and enumerated powers, the grant of power to tax and spend for the general national welfare must be confined to the enumerated legislative fields committed to the Congress. In this view the phrase is mere tautology, for taxation and appropriation are or may be necessary incidents of the exercise of any of the enumerated legislative powers. Hamilton, on the other hand, maintained the clause confers a power separate and distinct from those later enumerated, is not restricted in meaning by the grant of them, and Congress consequently has a substantive power to tax and to appropriate, limited only by the requirement that it shall be exercised to provide for the general welfare of the United States. Mr. Justice Story, in his *Commentaries,* espouses the Hamiltonian position. We shall not review the writings of public men and commentators or discuss the legislative practice. Study of all these leads us to conclude that the reading advocated by Mr. Justice Story is a correct one. While, therefore, the power to tax is not unlimited, its confines are set in the clause which confers it and not in those of § 8 which bestow and define the legislative powers of the Congress. It results that the power of Congress to authorize expenditure of public moneys for public purposes is not limited by the direct grants of legislative power found in the Constitution.

United States v. Butler, 297 U.S. 1, 65–66 (1936).

[B] THE EARLY CASES

The first case dealing specifically with the reach of federal taxing power was *Veazie Bank v. Fenno,* 75 U.S. (8 Wall.) 533 (1869), in which the Court upheld a federal tax on banknotes issued by state-chartered banks. The tax was upheld despite its apparent purpose and effect of imposing such a heavy burden on the notes as to drive them out of circulation. Because the power to coin money belonged to Congress, the tax could be upheld as a necessary and proper means of exercising a delegated power even if it were viewed as a penalty for regulatory purposes rather than a revenue-raising measure.

***United States v. Doremus*, 249 U.S. 86 (1919).** The Court dealt with the validity of the Harrison Act's imposition of a $1.00 licensing tax on sellers of narcotic drugs and requiring that all sales be noted on order forms, except those by a physician for medicinal purposes or by pharmacists upon prescription from a physician. While the revenue objectives of the legislation were minimal compared to its regulatory aspects, the Court sustained the legislation. The regulation was perceived as a method of assuring the collection of the tax.

> Congress, with full power over the subject, short of arbitrary and unreasonable action, which is not to be assumed, inserted these provisions in an act specifically providing for the raising of revenue. Considered of themselves, we think they tend to keep the traffic aboveboard and subject to inspection by those authorized to collect the revenue. They tend to diminish the opportunity of unauthorized persons to obtain the drugs and sell them clandestinely without paying the tax imposed by the federal law. Congress may have deemed it wise to prevent such possible dealings because of their effect upon the collection of the revenue.

Doremus seemed to imply that if Congress had a regulatory purpose rather than a revenue purpose, then the tax would be upheld only if the regulatory purpose were within its enumerated powers.

Judicial deference to the congressional judgment in this area seems to have reached its zenith in this early period in *McCray v. United States,* 195 U.S. 27 (1904), sustaining a federal tax of 10% per pound on colored oleomargarine and a tax on white oleomargarine of only ¼¢ per pound. The legislation, enacted under pressure from the dairy lobby, was quite clearly designed to drive colored oleomargarine off the market by making its price prohibitive. Nevertheless, the Court sustained the legislation as a valid taxing measure.

***Bailey v. Drexel Furniture Co.*, 259 U.S. 20 (1922).** The test of the *Doremus* position came after the Court invalidated Congress' attempt to regulate child labor under the commerce clause in *Hammer v. Dagenhart.* Congress then enacted a 10% excise tax on the net profits of certain businesses, such as mines and factories, employing child labor. The tax would be imposed on all profit for the year, regardless of the extent of the use of child labor, and could be escaped if the employer did not know that a child was under the age limit.

The Court struck down the child labor tax on the basis that it was not truly a tax and that its regulatory purposes were beyond the power of Congress.

> The difference between a tax and a penalty is sometimes difficult to define, and yet the consequences of the distinction in the required method of their collection often are important. Where the sovereign enacting the law has power to impose both tax and penalty, the difference between revenue production and mere regulation may be immaterial; but not so when one sovereign can impose a tax only, and the power of regulation rests in another. Taxes are occasionally imposed in the discretion of the legislature on proper subjects with the primary motive of obtaining revenue from them, and with the incidental motive of discouraging them by making their continuance onerous. They do not lose their character as taxes because of the incidental motive. But there comes a time in the extension of the penalizing features of the so-called tax when it loses its character as such and becomes a mere penalty, with the characteristics of regulation and punishment. Such is the case in the law before us. Although Congress does not invalidate the contract of employment, or expressly declare that the employment within the mentioned age is illegal, it does exhibit its intent practically to achieve the latter result by adopting the criteria of wrongdoing, and imposing its principal consequence on those who transgress its standard.

[C] TAXING AND SPENDING IN THE NEW DEAL ERA

The New Deal reversal on the Supreme Court was exemplified in the area of commerce power by *Carter Coal Co.* and *Jones & Laughlin Steel Co.* With regard to taxing and spending, the two corollary cases were *United States v. Butler* and *Steward Machine Co. v. Davis.*

***United States v. Butler*, 297 U.S. 1 (1936)**, dealt with the Agricultural Adjustment Act of 1933, which was designed to increase the price received by farmers for their products by controlling farm production. A tax could be imposed by the Secretary of Agriculture on the processors of selected commodities. The proceeds from this tax would be used by the Secretary to pay farmers to reduce their production for market. A processor of cotton brought suit to challenge the Act, and the Supreme Court initially held that the taxpayer had standing to challenge the Act because the tax was "an indispensable part in the plan of regulation." Justice Roberts for the Court then addressed the validity of the plan:

> We are not now required to ascertain the scope of the phrase "general welfare of the United States" or to determine whether an appropriation in aid of agriculture falls within it. Wholly apart from that question, another principle embedded in our Constitution prohibits the enforcement of the Agricultural Adjustment Act. The act invades the reserved rights of the states. It is a statutory plan to regulate and control agricultural production, a matter beyond the powers delegated to the federal government. The tax, the appropriation of the funds

raised, and the direction for their disbursement, are but parts of the plan. They are but means to an unconstitutional end.

If the taxing power may not be used as the instrument to enforce a regulation of matters of state concern with respect to which the Congress has no authority to interfere, may it, as in the present case, be employed to raise the money necessary to purchase a compliance which the Congress is powerless to command? The Government asserts that whatever might be said against the validity of the plan if compulsory, it is constitutionally sound because the end is accomplished by voluntary co-operation. There are two sufficient answers to the contention. The regulation is not in fact voluntary. The farmer, of course, may refuse to comply, but the price of such refusal is the loss of benefits. The amount offered is intended to be sufficient to exert pressure on him to agree to the proposed regulation. The power to confer or withhold unlimited benefits is the power to coerce or destroy. If the cotton grower elects not to accept the benefits, he will receive less for his crops; those who receive payments will be able to undersell him. The result may well be financial ruin.

But if the plan were one for purely voluntary co-operation it would stand no better so far as federal power is concerned. At best it is a scheme for purchasing with federal funds submission to federal regulation of a subject reserved to the states.

We are not here concerned with a conditional appropriation of money, nor with a provision that if certain conditions are not complied with the appropriation shall no longer be available. There is an obvious difference between a statute stating the conditions upon which moneys shall be expended and one effective only upon assumption of a contractual obligation to submit to a regulation which otherwise could not be enforced.

Justice Stone, joined by Justices Brandeis and Cardozo, filed a dissent mirroring their views on the power of Congress under the Commerce Clause.

***Steward Machine Co. v. Davis*, 301 U.S. 548 (1937)**, dealt with the validity of Title IX of the Social Security Act of 1935, which imposed a payroll tax on employers of eight or more persons, the proceeds of which went into the general revenue fund. If the taxpayer made contributions into a state unemployment fund certified by the federal government, however, he could receive a credit of up to ninety percent of the federal tax. Contributions to the state fund were to be made directly to the Secretary of the Treasury who then paid the state agency upon requisition. Title III of the Act provided for grants to the states from the general revenue fund to assist them in administering their unemployment compensation programs. Justice Cardozo's opinion for the Court first reviewed some of the data involving unemployment during the Depression and the billions of dollars that were already being spent for various forms of relief.

Who then is coerced through the operation of this statute? Not the taxpayer. He pays in fulfillment of the mandate of the local legislature.

> Not the state. Even now she does not offer a suggestion that in passing the unemployment law she was affected by duress. For all that appears she is satisfied with her choice, and would be sorely disappointed if it were now to be annulled. The difficulty with the petitioner's contention is that it confuses motive with coercion. "Every tax is in some measure regulatory. To some extent it interposes an economic impediment to the activity taxed as compared with others not taxed." *Sonzinsky v. United States.* In like manner every rebate from a tax when conditioned upon conduct is in some measure a temptation. But to hold that motive or temptation is equivalent to coercion is to plunge the law in endless difficulties. The outcome of such a doctrine is the acceptance of a philosophical determinism by which choice becomes impossible.
>
> In ruling as we do, we leave many questions open. We do not say that a tax is valid, when imposed by act of Congress, if it is laid upon the condition that a state may escape its operation through the adoption of a statute unrelated in subject matter to activities fairly within the scope of national policy and power. No such question is before us.

Note that both *Butler* and *Steward Machine* were actually challenges to taxes on the basis that the money was earmarked for allegedly unconstitutional spending programs. As a practical matter, most federal spending has been insulated from attack by an early Supreme Court holding that a taxpayer does not have standing to challenge a spending program directly. *Frothingham v. Mellon*, Chapter 11. The reasoning was that a general taxpayer's money is blended into the general treasury and is an insignificant part of each spending decision by the federal government. Only when a special tax is levied on certain activities for certain purposes, as in *Butler* and *Steward Machine,* could a challenge be made. Similarly, as in *Steward Machine,* a redistribution of wealth through grants to the states for specified purposes could not be challenged because the states could not complain of something in which they had the option to participate or not. The result has been to allow Congress to govern itself free of judicial review over the spending power through most of the twentieth century.

[D] THE POST-NEW DEAL ATTITUDE TOWARD TAXATION

United States v. Kahriger, 345 U.S. 22 (1953), raised two challenges to provisions of the Internal Revenue Act of 1951 which taxed persons engaged in the business of gambling (defined to target bookmakers) and required those persons to register with the IRS. A challenge to the registration provisions based on the fifth amendment privilege against self-incrimination was rejected by the Court but later accepted in large part in a subsequent case. *Marchetti v. United States,* 390 U.S. 39 (1968). The challenge addressed to Congress' power to enact the tax drew the following comment from the majority:

> Where federal legislation has rested on other congressional powers, such as the Necessary and Proper clause or the Commerce clause, this

> Court has generally sustained the statutes, despite their effect on matters ordinarily considered state concern. When federal power to regulate is found, its exercise is a matter for Congress. Where Congress has employed the taxing clause a greater variation in the decisions has resulted. The division in this Court has been more acute. Without any specific differentiation between the power to tax and other federal powers, the indirect results from the exercise of the power to tax have raised more doubts. It is hard to understand why the power to tax should raise more doubts because of indirect effects than other federal powers.

The *per curiam* opinion in *Buckley v. Valeo,* p. 1336, rejected a challenge to public financing of election campaigns based on the premise that such financing was contrary to the "general welfare." The Court provided an expansive view of the spending power. The general welfare clause, stated the Court, is not a limitation on congressional power. Rather, it is "a grant of power, the scope of which is quite expansive, particularly in view of the enlargement of power by the Necessary and Proper Clause." It was for Congress "to decide which expenditures will promote the general welfare." Any limitations "must be found elsewhere in the Constitution." Public financing of elections "as a means to reform the electoral process was clearly a choice within the granted power."

[E] CONDITIONAL GRANTS WITH REGULATORY EFFECTS

Is it now clear that Congress can, in the exercise of its spending power, condition disbursement upon compliance with stipulations normally within the realm of state power? Can a condition be totally unrelated to the subject of the grant? Are the conditions that may be imposed limited to those that are "necessary and proper" to effectuate the spending power? Consider Justice Cardozo's comment in *Steward Machine* that the Court was not saying "that a tax is valid if it is laid upon the condition that a State may escape its operation through the adoption of a statute unrelated in subject-matter to activities fairly within the scope of national policy and power." Does this limit the spending power?

In *Oklahoma v. United States Civil Serv. Comm'n,* 330 U.S. 127 (1947), the Court upheld a requirement that state employees comply with Hatch Act provisions regarding partisan political activities as a condition for receiving federal highway funds. The Court stated:

> While the United States is not concerned and has no power to regulate local political activities as such of state officials, it does have power to fix the terms upon which its money allotments to states shall be disbursed. The Tenth Amendment does not forbid the exercise of this power in the way that Congress has proceeded in this case.

It has been suggested that there has been not only a significant quantitative increase in the number of conditions that have been attached to federal grants in recent years but that there has also been a change in the character of the conditions being imposed.

> [A] closer look at some representative federal aid programs enacted under the authority to spend for the general welfare reveals that Congress has recently attached a much more elaborate range of conditions and penalties for noncompliance to its bounty to the state. Taken together, these measures, and others like them, have altered the shape of the federal system.

Lewis Kaden, *Politics, Money, and State Sovereignty: The Judicial Role,* 79 Colum. L. Rev. 847, 874 (1979). Some conditions are premised on independent justifications derived from the Constitution, such as anti-discrimination requirements. Others seek to control state policy by requiring state agencies to perform new functions or adopt a particular rule or standard of performance. Conditions may affect the structure and organization of state government by requiring creation of new administrative units. Penalties for violation of conditions may affect not only the particular program where the violation occurs but federal funding of other programs.

In recent years, increasing emphasis has been placed upon the concept of "Cooperative Federalism," contending that "the National Government and the States are mutually complementary parts of a *single* governmental mechanism all of whose powers are intended to realize the current purposes of government according to their applicability to the problem in hand." A primary method by which this doctrine has been implemented has been the "grants in aid" system whereby

> the National Government has held out inducements, primarily of a pecuniary kind, to the States to use their reserved power to support certain objectives of national policy in the field of expenditure. In other words, the greater financial strength of the National Government is joined to the wider coercive powers of the States. Thus since 1911, Congress has voted money to subsidize [projects] in return for which cooperating States have appropriated equal sums for the same purposes, and have brought their further powers to the support thereof along lines laid down by Congress.

Edward Corwin, *The Passing of Dual Federalism,* 36 Va. L. Rev. 1, 19, 20 (1950). The result has been increasing national involvement in traditionally local matters. In the area of education, health, housing, environmental control, land use, federal moneys and controls are of vital importance.

With the passing of *National League of Cities* and the expansive growth in federal regulatory power, it might be argued that the federal government may achieve its goals as easily through direct regulatory action as through conditional grants. But *New York v. United States* and *United States v. Lopez* suggest otherwise.

Rather than pursuing a remedy of cutting off funds to noncomplying states, plaintiffs usually choose to pursue the remedy of direct court enforcement of statutory "rights" by seeking injunctions to require compliance. Part of the explanation for converting the statute to a "regulatory" provision through the choice of remedy is that cutting off funds would actually work against the federal interests by removing both the incentive for compliance and the means of achieving compliance. If the defunding remedy is abandoned in favor of the regulatory remedy, there may be additional federalism concerns, as the notes following the next case illustrate.

SOUTH DAKOTA v. DOLE

483 U.S. 203, 107 S. Ct. 2793, 97 L. Ed. 2d 171 (1987)

CHIEF JUSTICE REHNQUIST delivered the opinion of the Court.

Petitioner South Dakota permits persons 19 years of age or older to purchase beer containing up to 3.2% alcohol. In 1984 Congress enacted 23 U.S.C. section 158 ("section 158"), which directs the Secretary of Transportation to withhold a percentage of federal highway funds otherwise allocable from States "in which the purchase or public possession of any alcoholic beverage by a person who is less than twenty-one years of age is lawful." The State sued in United States District Court seeking a declaratory judgment that section 158 violates the constitutional limitations on congressional exercise of the spending power and violates the Twenty-first Amendment to the United States Constitution. The District Court rejected the State's claims, and the Court of Appeals for the Eighth Circuit affirmed.

In this Court, the parties direct most of their efforts to defining the proper scope of the Twenty-first Amendment. South Dakota asserts that the setting of minimum drinking ages is clearly within the "core powers" reserved to the States under section 2 of the Amendment. Section 158, petitioner claims, usurps that core power. The Secretary in response asserts that the Twenty-first Amendment is simply not implicated by section 158; the plain language of section 2 confirms the States' broad power to impose restrictions on the sale and distribution of alcoholic beverages but does not confer on them any power to permit sales that Congress seeks to prohibit. That Amendment, under this reasoning, would not prevent Congress from affirmatively enacting a national minimum drinking age more restrictive than that provided by the various state laws; and it would follow a fortiori that the indirect inducement involved here is compatible with the Twenty-first Amendment.

Despite the extended treatment of the question by the parties, however, we need not decide in this case whether that Amendment would prohibit an attempt by Congress to legislate directly a national minimum drinking age. Here, Congress has acted indirectly under its spending power to encourage uniformity in the States drinking ages. As we explain below, we find this legislative effort within constitutional bounds even if Congress may not regulate drinking ages directly.

The Constitution empowers Congress to "lay and collect Taxes, Duties, Imposts, and Excises, to pay the Debts and provide for the common Defense and general Welfare of the United States." Incident to this power, Congress may attach conditions on the receipt of federal funds, and has repeatedly employed the power "to further broad policy objectives by conditioning receipt of federal moneys upon compliance by the recipient with federal statutory and administrative directives." *Fullilove v. Klutznick,* 448 U.S. 448, 474 (1980) (opinion of BURGER, C.J.). The breadth of this power was made clear in *United States v. Butler,* 297 U.S. 1, 66 (1936), where the Court, resolving a longstanding debate over the scope of the Spending Clause, determined that "the power of Congress to authorize expenditure of public moneys for public purposes is not limited by the direct grants of legislative power found in the Constitution." Thus, objectives not thought to be within Article I's enumerated legislative fields may nevertheless be attained through the use of the spending power and the conditional grant of federal funds.

The spending power is of course not unlimited, *Pennhurst State School and Hospital v. Halderman,* 451 U.S. 1, 17 (1981), but is instead subject to several general restrictions articulated in our cases. The first of these limitations is derived from the language of the Constitution itself: the exercise of the spending power must be in pursuit of "the general welfare." In considering whether a particular expenditure is intended to serve general public purposes, courts should defer substantially to the judgment of Congress. Second, we have required that if Congress desires to condition the States' receipt of federal funds, it "must do so unambiguously, enabling the States to exercise their choice knowingly, cognizant of the consequences of their participation." *Pennhurst State School v. Halderman.* Third, our cases have suggested (without significant elaboration) that conditions on federal grants might be illegitimate if they are unrelated "to the federal interest in particular national projects or programs." *Massachusetts v. United States,* 435 U.S. 444, 461 (1978) (plurality opinion). Finally, we have noted that other constitutional provisions may provide an independent bar to the conditional grant of federal funds.

South Dakota does not seriously claim that section 158 is inconsistent with any of the first three restrictions mentioned above. We can readily conclude that the provision is designed to serve the general welfare, especially in light of the fact that "the concept of welfare or the opposite is shaped by Congress." Congress found that the differing drinking ages in the States created particular incentives for young persons to combine their desire to drink with their ability to drive, and that this interstate problem required a national solution. The means it chose to address this dangerous situation were reasonably calculated to advance the general welfare. The conditions upon which States receive the funds, moreover, could not be more clearly stated by Congress. And the State itself, rather than challenging the germaneness of the condition to federal purposes, admits that it "has never contended that the congressional action was unrelated to a national concern in the absence of the Twenty-first Amendment." Indeed, the condition imposed by Congress is directly related to one of the main purposes for which highway funds are expended — safe interstate travel. This goal of the interstate highway system had been frustrated by varying drinking ages among the States. A presidential commission appointed to study alcohol-related accidents and fatalities on the Nation's highways concluded that the lack of uniformity in the States drinking ages created "an incentive to drink and drive" because "young persons commute to border States where the drinking age is lower." By enacting section 158, Congress conditioned the receipt of federal funds in a way reasonably calculated to address this particular impediment to a purpose for which the funds are expended.

The remaining question about the validity of section 158 — and the basic point of disagreement between the parties — is whether the Twenty-first Amendment constitutes an "independent constitutional bar" to the conditional grant of federal funds. Petitioner, relying on its view that the Twenty-first Amendment prohibits *direct* regulation of drinking ages by Congress, asserts that "Congress may not use the spending power to regulate that which it is prohibited from regulating directly under the Twenty-first Amendment." But our cases show that this "independent constitutional bar" limitation on the spending power is not of the kind petitioner suggests. *United States v. Butler,* for example, established that the constitutional limitations on Congress when exercising its spending power are less exacting than those on its authority to regulate directly.

We have also held that a perceived Tenth Amendment limitation on congressional regulation of state affairs did not concomitantly limit the range of conditions legitimately placed on federal grants. In *Oklahoma v. Civil Service Comm'n,* the Court considered the validity of the Hatch Act insofar as it was applied to political activities of state officials whose employment was financed in whole or in part with federal funds. The State contended that an order under this provision to withhold certain federal funds unless a state official was removed invaded its sovereignty in violation of the Tenth Amendment. Though finding that "the United States is not concerned with, and has no power to regulate, local political activities as such of state officials," the Court nevertheless held that the Federal Government "does have power to fix the terms upon which its money allotments to states shall be disbursed." The Court found no violation of the States sovereignty because the State could, and did, adopt "the 'simple expedient' of not yielding to what she urges is federal coercion. The offer of benefits to a state by the United States dependent upon cooperation by the state with federal plans, assumedly for the general welfare, is not unusual."

These cases establish that the "independent constitutional bar" limitation on the spending power is not, as petitioner suggests, a prohibition on the indirect achievement of objectives which Congress is not empowered to achieve directly. Instead, we think that the language in our earlier opinions stands for the unexceptionable proposition that the power may not be used to induce the States to engage in activities that would themselves be unconstitutional. Thus, for example, a grant of federal funds conditioned on invidiously discriminatory state action or the inaction of cruel and unusual punishment would be an illegitimate exercise of the Congress' broad spending power. But no such claim can be or is made here. Were South Dakota to succumb to the blandishments offered by Congress and raise its drinking age to 21, the State's action in so doing would not violate the constitutional rights of anyone.

Our decisions have recognized that in some circumstances the financial inducement offered by Congress might be so coercive as to pass the point at which "pressure turns into compulsion." *Steward Machine Co. v. Davis.* Here, however, Congress has directed only that a State desiring to establish a minimum drinking age lower than 21 lose a relatively small percentage of certain federal highway funds. Petitioner contends that the coercive nature of this program is evident from the degree of success it has achieved. We cannot conclude, however, that a conditional grant of federal money of this sort is unconstitutional simply by reason of its success in achieving the congressional objective.

When we consider, for a moment, that all South Dakota would lose if she adheres to her chosen course as to a suitable minimum drinking age is 5% of the funds otherwise obtainable under specified highway grant programs, the argument as to coercion is shown to be more rhetoric than fact. As we said a half century ago in *Steward Machine Co. v. Davis:*

> Every rebate from a tax when conditioned upon conduct is in some measure a temptation. But to hold that motive or temptation is equivalent to coercion is to plunge the law in[to] endless difficulties. The outcome of such a doctrine is the acceptance of a philosophical determinism by which choice becomes impossible. Till now the law has been guided by a robust common sense which assumes the freedom of the will as a working hypothesis in the solution of its problems.

Here Congress has offered relatively mild encouragement to the States to enact higher minimum drinking ages than they would otherwise choose. But the enactment of such laws remains the prerogative of the States not merely in theory but in fact. Even if Congress might lack the power to impose a national minimum drinking age directly, we conclude that encouragement to state action found in section 158 is a valid use of the spending power.

JUSTICE BRENNAN, dissenting.

I agree with Justice O'Connor that regulation of the minimum age of purchasers of liquor falls squarely within the ambit of those powers reserved to the States by the Twenty-first Amendment. Since States possess this constitutional power, Congress cannot condition a federal grant in a manner that abridges this right. The Amendment, itself, strikes the proper balance between federal and state authority. I therefore dissent.

JUSTICE O'CONNOR, dissenting.

My disagreement with the Court is relatively narrow on the Spending Power issue: it is a disagreement about the application of a principle rather than a disagreement on the principle itself. I agree with the Court that Congress may attach conditions on the receipt of federal funds to further "the federal interest in particular national projects or programs." I also subscribe to the established proposition that the reach of the Spending Power "is not limited by the direct grants of legislative power found in the Constitution."

But the Court's application of the requirement that the condition imposed be reasonably related to the purpose for which the funds are expended, is cursory and unconvincing. In my view, establishment of a minimum drinking age of 21 is not sufficiently related to interstate highway construction to justify so conditioning funds appropriated for that purpose.

When Congress appropriates money to build a highway, it is entitled to insist that the highway be a safe one. But it is not entitled to insist as a condition of the use of highway funds that the State impose or change regulations in other areas of the State's social and economic life because of an attenuated or tangential relationship to highway use or safety. Indeed, if the rule were otherwise, the Congress could effectively regulate almost any area of a State's social, political, or economic life on the theory that use of the interstate transportation system is somehow enhanced.

There is a clear place at which the Court can draw the line between permissible and impermissible conditions on federal grants. It is that while Congress has the power to *spend* for the general welfare, it has the power to *legislate* only for delegated purposes. The appropriate inquiry, then, is whether the spending requirement or prohibition is a condition on a grant or whether it is regulation. The difference turns on whether the requirement specifies in some way how the money should be spent, so that Congress' intent in making the grant will be effectuated. Congress has no power under the Spending Clause to impose requirements on a grant that go beyond specifying how the money should be spent. A requirement that is not such a specification is not a condition, but a regulation, which is valid only if it falls within one of Congress' delegated regulatory powers.

This approach harks back to *United States v. Butler,* the last case in which this Court struck down an Act of Congress as beyond the authority granted by the Spending Clause. There the Court wrote that "there is an obvious difference between a statute stating the conditions upon which moneys shall be expended and one effective only upon assumption of a contractual obligation to submit to a regulation which otherwise could not be enforced." The *Butler* Court saw the Agricultural Adjustment Act for what it was — an exercise of regulatory, not spending, power. The error in *Butler* was not the Court's conclusion that the Act was essentially regulatory, but rather its crabbed view of the extent of Congress regulatory power under the Commerce Clause. The Agricultural Adjustment Act was regulatory but it was regulation that today would likely be considered within Congress' Commerce Power.

While *Butler*'s authority is questionable insofar as it assumes that Congress has no regulatory power over farm production, its discussion of the Spending Power and its description of both the power's breadth and its limitations remains sound. The Court's decision in *Butler* also properly recognizes the gravity of the task of appropriately limiting the Spending Power. If the Spending Power is to be limited only by Congress notion of the general welfare, the reality, given the vast financial resources of the Federal Government, is that the Spending Clause gives "power to the Congress to tear down the barriers, to invade the states' jurisdiction, and to become a parliament of the whole people, subject to no restrictions save such as are self-imposed." This, of course, as *Butler* held, was not the Framers' plan and it is not the meaning of the Spending Clause.

[JUSTICE O'CONNOR concluded that the drinking age could not be regulated under the commerce clause because of the prohibitions of the Twenty-First Amendment.]

NOTES

1. *Civil rights.* Title VI of the 1964 Civil Rights Act, 42 U.S.C. § 2000d provides, "no person in the United States shall, on the ground of race, color, or national origin, be excluded from participation in, be denied the benefits of, or be subjected to discrimination under any program or activity receiving Federal assistance." In the event of a grantee's noncompliance with this mandate, the federal department or agency extending federal financial assistance may terminate or refuse to grant continuing assistance to the offending recipient. (§ 602.) By 1971, this sanction was available in over 400 loan and grant programs including aid to education, hospitals and other health facilities, and highway construction, providing the government with a viable alternative to judicial enforcement of the desegregation mandate.

There has been a natural reluctance to use the potent sanctions of Title VI because of its impact on recipients. The cutoff of benefits to welfare recipients or schools in poor districts would be drastic. It has been suggested, therefore, that the utility of this sanction may depend on the particular program involved. "In the areas of education and health, students and patients do not feel the immediate and full effect of a termination as the welfare recipients, for whom the weekly and monthly welfare grant is frequently the sole source of family income." In any case, the purpose of Title VI is not to withhold funds, but to induce recipients who rely on federal funds to desegregate. "An optimally effective Title VI would convince a recipient that: 1) the recipient needed the funds; 2) funds *would* be withheld; and 3) the recipient would rather comply than lose the funds. An actual cutoff would mean that Title VI had failed, since the particular administrative program would still be subject to discrimination." Comment, *Title VI of the Civil Rights Act of 1964 — Implementation and Impact,* 36 Geo. Wash. L. Rev. 824, 843 (1968).

As a result, private litigants have attempted to use Title VI and its corollaries (e.g., Title IX of the Education Amendments of 1972) to create private claims to relief. The relief would be a court order compelling or prohibiting certain actions "so long as the defendant receives federal funds." Although the Supreme Court has not passed directly on the issue, it has assumed that Title VI creates a private right of action for judicial enforcement. *Hills v. Gautreaux,* 425 U.S. 284 (1974); *Lau v. Nichols,* 414 U.S. 563 (1972). The Court has explicitly held that Title IX creates a private right of action. *Cannon v. University of Chicago,* 441 U.S. 677 (1979). By so construing the statutes, the Court has interpreted Congress as creating conditional "rights"; the citizen has a right to nondiscriminatory treatment enforceable by a court so long as the defendant receives federal funds. This is a regulatory use of the spending power that can itself alter the federal-state relation.

The Minority Business Enterprise Program, providing for a ten percent set-aside of federal public works grants, which was upheld in *Fullilove v. Klutznick,* p. 725, was primarily an exercise of Congress' spending power. Chief Justice Burger's plurality opinion reiterated that the spending power is an independent grant of power and that Congress may "further broad policy objectives by conditioning receipt of federal monies upon compliance by the recipient with federal statutory and administrative directives." This technique can be used "to induce governments and private parties to cooperate voluntarily with federal policy." The Court felt that it was unnecessary to "explore the outermost limitations on the objectives attainable through such an application of the Spending Power," since "[t]he reach of the Spending Power, within its sphere, is at least as broad as the regulatory powers of Congress." Since the objectives of the Act were within the scope of the commerce power and the Fourteenth Amendment, § 5, they were held to be within the scope of the spending power.

***Gonzaga University v. Doe,* 536 U.S. 273 (2002).** The Court held that the Family Educational Rights and Privacy Act (FERPA), which conditions grants to state agencies and educational institutions upon compliance with requirements regarding the privacy of student records, did not create individual, enforceable rights. The Court held that such funding provisions do not confer enforceable, individual rights unless Congress conveys in clear and unambiguous terms its intent to do so.

The Court, per Chief Justice Rehnquist, held that Congress' use of its spending authority in FERPA to condition grants on requirements regarding disclosure of student records did not create an individual, enforceable right. The Chief Justice stated that Congress must clearly intend to confer an individual, enforceable right, relying on the rule announced in *Pennhurst State School and Hospital v. Halderman*, 451 U.S. 1 (1981), where the Court held that the Developmentally Disabled Assistance and Bill of Rights Act did not create an individual right. There, the Court stated that "unless Congress 'speaks with a clear voice,' and manifests an 'unambiguous' intent to confer individual rights, federal funding provisions provide no basis for private enforcement by § 1983." By contrast, the Chief Justice contended, those cases where the Court did infer individual rights from spending legislation, such as *Wright v. Roanoake Redevelopment Corporation*, 479 U.S. 418 (1987), and *Wilder v. Virginia Hospital Association*, 496 U.S. 498 (1990), involved an unambiguous congressional intent to confer individual entitlements.

The Court next dismissed plaintiff's argument that this clear intent rule set too high a standard for § 1983 claims and that such a rule applies only where its claimed that the private right of action is implied directly from the statute. Justice Rehnquist declared:

> We now reject the notion that our cases permit anything short of an unambiguously conferred right to support a cause of action brought under § 1983. [I]t is rights, not the broader or vaguer "benefits" or "interests," that may be enforced under the authority of that section. [W]e further reject the notion that our implied right of action cases are separate and distinct from our § 1983 cases. [O]ur implied right of action cases should guide the determination of whether a statute confers rights enforceable under § 1983.

The Court concluded: "where the text and structure of a statute provide no indication that Congress intends to create new individual rights, there is no basis for a private suit, whether under § 1983 or under an implied right of action."

The Court went on to hold that FERPA fails to create enforceable rights because it lacks "rights-creating language," focuses on "aggregate" policy goals as opposed to individual needs, and provides an administrative remedy against offending institutions.

Justice Breyer, with whom Justice Souter joined concurring, argued that another factor indicating lack of congressional intent to create an individual right was the statute's "broad and unspecific" key language.

Justice Stevens, with whom Justice Ginsburg joined dissenting, argued that the FERPA creates an individual right for which § 1983 provided a remedy. According to Justice Stevens, the specific provision on which this case hinged clearly created a parental "right to withhold consent and prevent the unauthorized release of education record information by an educational institution." The provision at hand was "directed to the benefit of individual students and parents is binding on the states and is far from vague and amorphous."

2. *Relating conditions to regulatory power.* In light of *Dole,* how should the following questions be answered?

(1) Can grants to states be conditioned on acceptance by the state of conditions unrelated to the grant, such as compliance with standards on civil rights, air pollution, or treatment of persons with disabilities?

(2) Can grants be conditioned on state enforcement of matters as to which Congress claims no regulatory power, such as domestic relations law? Does it matter if the grant is general or specific in purpose?

(3) If conditional grants are not limited, does it matter whether the Court adheres to *Garcia* or reverts to limitations of the *National League* variety?

In *New York v. United States*, p. 131, *supra*, the Court rejected a Tenth Amendment challenge to the provisions of the federal statute providing monetary incentives. The Court characterized the provisions as "a conditional exercise of Congress' authority under the Spending Clause."

What effect, if any, should *Lopez* have on the conditional spending power? See Lynn Baker, *Conditional Federal Spending After* Lopez, 95 COLUM. L. REV. 1911, 1988 (1995), arguing "that the Court should now reinterpret the Spending Clause to work in concert, rather than in conflict, with its reading of the Commerce Clause." If the Court were to do so, what would Congress' resulting conditional spending power look like?

In *Sabri v. United States*, 124 S. Ct. 1941 (2004), a contractor was convicted of a federal crime for offering bribes to city officials when the city received millions of dollars in federal funding. The defendant argued that the prosecution should be required to show a connection between the bribe and some federal funding, but the Court disagreed.

> We can readily dispose of this position that, to qualify as a valid exercise of Article I power, the statute must require proof of connection with federal money as an element of the offense. We simply do not presume the unconstitutionality of federal criminal statutes lacking explicit provision of a jurisdictional hook, and there is no occasion even to consider the need for such a requirement where there is no reason to suspect that enforcement of a criminal statute would extend beyond a legitimate interest cognizable under Article I, § 8. Congress has authority under the Spending Clause to appropriate federal monies to promote the general welfare, and it has corresponding authority under the Necessary and Proper Clause, to see to it that taxpayer

dollars appropriated under that power are in fact spent for the general welfare, and not frittered away in graft or on projects undermined when funds are siphoned off or corrupt public officers are derelict about demanding value for dollars.

3. *Enforcement of spending power claims.* Congress frequently attempts to secure compliance by States with federal mandates by attaching conditions to federal grants. Several cases have raised the question of whether acceptance of a conditional grant is sufficient to waive the State's sovereign immunity. Thus far, the Supreme Court's response is that a claimed waiver will be effective only if the statutory language is "unequivocal."

Pennhurst State School & Hosp. v. Halderman, 451 U.S. 1 (1981) *(Pennhurst I),* arose when Congress provided funds for states to use in educating the handicapped and stated that states receiving federal funds were subjected to suit for failure to comply with the Act. Another section of the Act purported to declare a "Bill of Rights" for the handicapped, including a "right" to education in the "least restrictive environment." The Supreme Court held that in the absence of specific congressional statements, the requirements of the statutory "Bill of Rights" would not be enforced by lawsuit against the states.

In *Atascadero State Hosp. v. Scanlon,* 473 U.S. 234 (1983), the Court held that Congress had not been sufficiently explicit in the Rehabilitation Act of 1974 to subject the state hospital to suit for refusing to hire a handicapped applicant. Although a private employer would be subject to suit and although Congress could have subjected the state to suit under *Fitzpatrick*, the statute did not explicitly refer to states as potential defendants. Justice Brennan, joined by Justices Marshall, Blackmun, and Stevens, canvassed the history of sovereign immunity and found no support for the view in *Hans* that sovereign immunity was part of the policies implicit in the Eleventh Amendment.

In *Dellmuth v. Muth,* 491 U.S. 223 (1989), the Court held 5-4 that, in enacting the Education of the Handicapped Act (EHA), Congress had not evinced "an unmistakably clear intention to abrogate the States' constitutionally secured immunity from suit." The evidence, said Justice Kennedy for the Court, "must be both unequivocal and textual." Justice Brennan, again joined by Justices Marshall, Blackmun, and Stevens, dissenting, would have overruled *Hans* or, alternatively, would have found "that Congress in the EHA abrogated state immunity."

The same four justices dissented in *Papasan v. Allain,* 478 U.S. 265 (1986), in which the Court held that the Eleventh Amendment barred a suit seeking to reinstate the income from public school lands that had been sold by the state, allegedly in violation of trust responsibilities created by the grant of the lands from the federal government. The Court reasoned that the effect of the remedy would be the equivalent of a damage award for the value of the land. Justice Brennan argued, "It is highly unlikely that, having created a system in which federal law was to be supreme, the Framers of the Constitution or of the Eleventh Amendment nonetheless intended for that law to be unenforceable in the broad class of cases now barred by this Court's precedents. The Court's Eleventh Amendment jurisprudence is not supported by history or by sound legal reasoning. It is simply bad law."

§ 2.04 FEDERAL LEGISLATION IN AID OF CIVIL RIGHTS AND LIBERTIES

Much of the controversial aspects of federal legislative power revolves around the various forms of legislation in aid of civil rights, particularly attempts to deal with racial discrimination. Congress has used its commerce powers to remedy discrimination in public accommodations and used the spending power to cut off federal funds to grantees who discriminate. In the present section, we will place those measures into context with congressional power under one provision that speaks more directly to civil rights, the Fourteenth Amendment.

The initial thrust of congressional legislation in the second reconstruction was in the area of voting rights. But the results of the 1957, 1960, and 1964 [Title I] acts were generally disappointing. The legislation provided only weak remedies which were procedurally difficult to invoke. Government enforcement tended to be slow and limited. Reform proceeded on a case-by-case basis, with complainants forced to overcome litigation difficulties as well as local defiance. Even when a case was won, the local jurisdiction would often replace the condemned restrictive voting device with another that was equally restrictive.

The Voting Rights Cases

Congress tried a new tack with the Voting Rights Act of 1965, 42 U.S.C. § 1973, prohibiting the use of voter registration requirements to abridge the right to vote on account of race or color. In addition to providing for federal voting examiners (§ 1973(a)), the Act automatically suspends the use of voting tests to disqualify potential voters in states where the Attorney General finds that a test has been used, and less than fifty percent of the persons of voting age are registered to vote. Coverage can be removed if the District Court for the District of Columbia determines that no test has been used for five years to discriminate on account of race (§ 1973(b)). When a state subject to the Act attempts to add new voting qualifications, they must be approved by the Attorney General of the United States, or by a three-judge court of the District of Columbia (§ 1973(c)).

***South Carolina v. Katzenbach*, 383 U.S. 301 (1966).** In an original suit by six southern states subject to the Act, the Court upheld the constitutionality of these provisions. Authority for the legislation was found in the Fifteenth Amendment, § 2, which, the Court concluded, uses the same basic test "as in all cases concerning the express powers of Congress with relation to the reserve powers of the states: 'Let the end be legitimate, let it be within the scope of the Constitution, and all means which are appropriate, which are plainly adapted to that end, which are not prohibited, but consist with the letter and spirit of the Constitution, are constitutional.' *McCulloch v. Maryland*. . . . As against the reserved powers of the States, Congress may use any rational means to effectuate the constitutional prohibition of racial discrimination in voting."

> Congress had found that case-by-case litigation was inadequate to combat wide-spread and persistent discrimination in voting, because of the inordinate amount of time and energy required to overcome the obstructionist tactics invariably encountered in these lawsuits. After enduring nearly a century of systematic resistance to the Fifteenth Amendment, Congress might well decide to shift the advantage of time and inertia from the perpetrators of the evil to its victims.

The suspension of tests was a legitimate response to the problem because

> Congress knew that continuance of the tests and devices in use at the present time, no matter how fairly administered in the future, would freeze the effect of past discrimination in favor of unqualified white registrants. Congress permissibly rejected the alternative of requiring a complete re-registration of all voters, believing that this would be too harsh on many whites who had enjoyed the franchise for their entire adult lives.

***Katzenbach v. Morgan*, 384 U.S. 641 (1966).** In § 4(e) of the Voting Rights Act of 1965, Congress mandated that "no person who has successfully completed the sixth primary grade in a public school in, or a private school accredited by, the Commonwealth of Puerto Rico in which the language of instruction was other than English shall be denied the right to vote in any election because of his inability to read or write English." New York voters challenged the federal requirement on the ground that it diluted their votes in excess of Congress' power. The Supreme Court upheld the statute as a "proper exercise of the powers granted to Congress by § 5 of the Fourteenth Amendment."

> The Attorney General of the State of New York urges that § 4(e) cannot be sustained as appropriate legislation to enforce the Equal Protection Clause unless the judiciary decides — even with the guidance of a congressional judgment — that the application of the English literacy requirement prohibited by § 4(e) is forbidden by the Equal Protection Clause itself. We disagree. A construction of § 5 that would require a judicial determination that the enforcement of the state law precluded by Congress violated the Amendment, as a condition of sustaining the congressional enactment, would depreciate both congressional resourcefulness and congressional responsibility for implementing the Amendment.
>
> [O]ur decision in *Lassiter v. Northampton Election Bd.*, 360 U.S. 45 [(1954)], sustaining the North Carolina English literacy requirement as not in all circumstances prohibited by the first sections of the Fourteenth and Fifteenth Amendments, is inapposite. *Lassiter* did not present the question before us here: Without regard to whether the judiciary would find that the Equal Protection Clause itself nullifies New York's English literacy requirement as so applied, could Congress

prohibit the enforcement of the state law by legislating under § 5 of the Fourteenth Amendment?

The Court found at least two reasons that could justify federal intervention. One was that the statute "may be viewed as a measure to secure for the Puerto Rican community residing in New York nondiscriminatory treatment by government — both in the imposition of voting qualifications and the provision or administration of governmental services, such as public schools, public housing and law enforcement." Second was "the elimination of an invidious discrimination in establishing voter qualifications." Arguing that Congress "could have found" that Spanish-speaking citizens could be fully informed to exercise their votes, the Court stated that with its "specially informed legislative competence, it was Congress's prerogative to weigh these competing considerations."

Justice Harlan, joined by Justice Stewart, dissented. "When recognized state violations of federal constitutional standards have occurred, Congress is of course empowered by § 5 to take appropriate remedial measures to redress and prevent the wrongs. But it is a judicial question whether the condition with which Congress has thus sought to deal is in truth an infringement of the Constitution, something that is the necessary prerequisite to bringing the § 5 power into play at all." Justice Harlan emphasized that "to the extent that 'legislative facts' are relevant to a judicial determination, Congress is well equipped to investigate them, and such determinations are of course entitled to due respect." But in his view, Congress was not entitled to weigh "competing considerations" of what should be considered a violation of the Fourteenth Amendment.

***Oregon v. Mitchell*, 400 U.S. 112 (1970).** In the 1970 Voting Rights Act, Congress sought to lower the voting age from 21 to 18 in federal and state elections, to prohibit the use of literacy tests in state and national elections for five years, and to eliminate the use of state residency requirements in presidential and vice-presidential elections. The Court struck down (5-4) the provisions of the Act lowering the voting age to 18 in state elections, upheld (5-4) provisions lowering the voting age to 18 in federal elections, unanimously upheld the provisions of the Act proscribing literacy tests as a proper means of implementing the Fifteenth Amendment, and upheld (8-1) the residency provisions.

CITY OF BOERNE v. FLORES

521 U.S. 507, 117 S. Ct. 2157, 138 L. Ed. 2d 624 (1997)

JUSTICE KENNEDY delivered the opinion of the Court.

A decision by local zoning authorities to deny a church a building permit was challenged under the Religious Freedom Restoration Act of 1993 (RFRA). The case calls into question the authority of Congress to enact RFRA. We conclude the statute exceeds Congress' power.

I

Situated on a hill in the city of Boerne, Texas, some 28 miles northwest of San Antonio, is St. Peter Catholic Church. Built in 1923, the church's structure replicates the mission style of the region's earlier history. The church seats about 230 worshipers, a number too small for its growing parish. Some 40 to 60 parishioners cannot be accommodated at some Sunday masses. In order to meet the needs of the congregation the Archbishop of San Antonio gave permission to the parish to plan alterations to enlarge the building.

A few months later, the Boerne City Council passed an ordinance authorizing the city's Historic Landmark Commission to prepare a preservation plan with proposed historic landmarks and districts. Under the ordinance, the Commission must preapprove construction affecting historic landmarks or buildings in a historic district.

Soon afterwards, the Archbishop applied for a building permit so construction to enlarge the church could proceed. City authorities, relying on the ordinance and the designation of a historic district (which, they argued, included the church), denied the application. The Archbishop brought this suit challenging the permit denial in the United States District Court for the Western District of Texas.

The complaint contained various claims, but to this point the litigation has centered on RFRA and the question of its constitutionality. The archbishop relied upon RFRA as one basis for relief from the refusal to issue the permit. The district court concluded that by enacting RFRA Congress exceeded the scope of its enforcement power under § 5 of the Fourteenth Amendment. The court certified its order for interlocutory appeal and the Fifth Circuit reversed, finding RFRA to be constitutional. We reverse.

II

Congress enacted RFRA in direct response to the court's decision in *Employment Div., Dept. of Human Resources of Oregon v. Smith* [*infra* p. 1439]. There we considered a Free Exercise Clause claim brought by members of the Native American Church who were denied unemployment benefits when they lost their jobs because they had used peyote. Their practice was to ingest peyote for sacramental purposes, and they challenged an Oregon statute of general applicability which made use of the drug criminal. In evaluating the claim, we declined to apply the balancing test set forth in *Sherbert v. Verner* [text p. 1448], under which we would have asked whether Oregon's prohibition substantially burdened a religious practice and, if it did, whether the burden was justified by a compelling government interest.

The application of the *Sherbert* test, the *Smith* decision explained, would have produced an anomaly in the law, a constitutional right to ignore neutral laws of general applicability. The anomaly would have been accentuated, the court reasoned, by the difficulty of determining whether a particular practice was central to an individual's religion. The only instances where a neutral, generally applicable law had failed to pass constitutional muster, the *Smith* court noted, were cases in which other constitutional protections were at stake.

Four members of the court disagreed. They argued the law placed a substantial burden on the Native American Church members so that it could be upheld only if the law served a compelling state interest and was narrowly tailored to achieve that end. JUSTICE O'CONNOR concluded Oregon had satisfied the test, while JUSTICE BLACKMUN, joined by JUSTICE BRENNAN and JUSTICE MARSHALL, could see no compelling interest justifying the law's application to the members.

These points of constitutional interpretation were debated by members of Congress in hearings and floor debates. Many criticized the court's reasoning, and this disagreement resulted in the passage of RFRA. Congress announced:

"(1) [T]he framers of the Constitution, recognizing free exercise of religion as an unalienable right, secured its protection in the First Amendment to the Constitution;

"(2) laws 'neutral' toward religion may burden religious exercise as surely as laws intended to interfere with religious exercise;

"(3) governments should not substantially burden religious exercise without compelling justification;

"(4) in *Employment Division v. Smith* the Supreme Court virtually eliminated the requirement that the government justify burdens on religious exercise imposed by laws neutral toward religion; and

"(5) the compelling interest test as set forth in prior federal court rulings is a workable test for striking sensible balances between religious liberty and competing prior governmental interests."

The Act's stated purposes are:

> "(1) to restore the compelling interest test as set forth in *Sherbert v. Verner*, and to guarantee its application in all cases where free exercise of religion is substantially burdened; and
>
> "(2) to provide a claim or defense to persons whose religious exercise is substantially burdened by government."

RFRA prohibits "[g]overnment" from "substantially burden[ing]" a person's exercise of religion even if the burden results from a rule of general applicability unless the government can demonstrate the burden "(1) is in furtherance of a compelling governmental interest; and (2) is the least restrictive means of furthering that compelling governmental interest." The Act's mandate applies to any "branch, department, agency, instrumentality, and official (or other person acting under color of law) of the United States," as well as to any "state, or . . . subdivision of a state." § 2000bb-2(1). The Act's universal coverage is confirmed in § 2000bb-3(a), under which RFRA "applies to all federal and state law, and the implementation of that law, whether statutory or otherwise, and whether adopted before or after [RFRA's enactment]." in accordance with RFRA's usage of the term, we shall use "state law" to include local and municipal ordinances.

III

A

Congress relied on its Fourteenth Amendment enforcement power in enacting the most far reaching and substantial of RFRA's provisions, those which impose its requirements on the states. The parties disagree over whether RFRA is a proper exercise of Congress' § 5 power "to enforce" by "appropriate legislation" the constitutional guarantee that no state shall deprive any person of "life, liberty, or property, without due process of law" nor deny any person "equal protection of the laws."

In defense of the Act respondent contends that RFRA is permissible enforcement legislation. Congress, it is said, is only protecting by legislation one of the liberties guaranteed by the fourteenth amendment's due process clause, the free exercise of religion, beyond what is necessary under *smith*. It is said the Congressional decision to dispense with proof of deliberate or overt discrimination and instead concentrate on a law's effects accords with the settled understanding that § 5 includes the power to enact legislation designed to prevent as well as remedy constitutional violations. It is further contended that Congress' § 5 power is not limited to remedial or preventive legislation.

All must acknowledge that § 5 is "a positive grant of legislative power" to Congress, *Katzenbach v. Morgan,* legislation which deters or remedies constitutional violations can fall within the sweep of Congress' enforcement power even if in the process it prohibits conduct which is not itself unconstitutional and intrudes into "legislative spheres of autonomy previously reserved to the states." *Fitzpatrick v. Bitzer*. For example, the Court upheld a suspension of literacy tests and similar voting requirements under Congress' parallel power to enforce the provisions of the Fifteenth Amendment, as a measure to combat racial discrimination in voting, *South Carolina v. Katzenbach*, despite the facial constitutionality of the tests under *Lassiter v. Northampton County Bd. of Elections*. We have also concluded that other measures protecting voting rights are within Congress' power to enforce the Fourteenth and Fifteenth Amendments, despite the burdens those measures placed on the States.

Congress' power under § 5, however, extends only to "enforc[ing]" the provisions of the Fourteenth Amendment. The court has described this power as "remedial," *South Carolina v. Katzenbach*. The design of the amendment and the text of § 5 are inconsistent with the suggestion that Congress has the power to decree the substance of the fourteenth amendment's restrictions on the states. Legislation which alters the meaning of the free exercise clause cannot be said to be enforcing the clause. Congress does not enforce a constitutional right by changing what the right is. It has been given the power "to enforce," not the power to determine what constitutes a constitutional violation. Were it not so, what Congress would be enforcing would no longer be, in any meaningful sense, the "provisions of [the Fourteenth Amendment]."

While the line between measures that remedy or prevent unconstitutional actions and measures that make a substantive change in the governing law is not easy to discern, and Congress must have wide latitude in determining where it lies, the distinction exists and must be observed. There must be a congruence and proportionality between the injury to be prevented or remedied and the means adopted to that end. Lacking such a connection, legislation may become substantive in operation and effect. History and our case law support drawing the distinction, one apparent from the text of the Amendment.

The Fourteenth Amendment's history confirms the remedial, rather than substantive, nature of the enforcement clause. The Joint Committee on Reconstruction of the 39th Congress began drafting what would become the fourteenth amendment in January 1866. The objections to the Committee's first draft of the amendment, and the rejection of the draft, have a direct bearing on the central issue of defining Congress' enforcement power. In February, Republican Representative John Bingham of Ohio reported the following draft amendment to the House of Representatives on behalf of the Joint Committee:

> The Congress shall have power to make all laws which shall be necessary and proper to secure to the citizens of each state all privileges and immunities of citizens in the several states, and to all persons in the several states equal protection in the rights of life, liberty, and property.

The proposal encountered immediate opposition, which continued through three days of debate. Members of Congress from across the political spectrum criticized the amendment, and the criticisms had a common theme: the proposed amendment gave Congress too much legislative power at the expense of the existing constitutional structure. Democrats and conservative Republicans argued that the proposed amendment would give Congress a power to intrude into traditional areas of state responsibility, a power inconsistent with the federal design central to the Constitution.

As a result of these objections having been expressed from so many different quarters, the house voted to table the proposal until April. The Congressional action was seen as marking the defeat of the proposal. The amendment in its early form was not again considered. Instead, the Joint Committee began drafting a new article of amendment, which it reported to Congress on April 30, 1866.

Section 1 of the new draft Amendment imposed self-executing limits on the states. Section 5 prescribed that "[t]he Congress shall have power to enforce, by appropriate legislation, the provisions of this article." Under the revised Amendment, Congress' power was no longer plenary but remedial. Congress was granted the power to make the substantive constitutional prohibitions against the states effective. After revisions not relevant here, the new measure passed both houses and was ratified in July 1868 as the Fourteenth Amendment.

The design of the Fourteenth Amendment has proved significant also in maintaining the traditional separation of powers between Congress and the judiciary. The first eight amendments to the Constitution set forth self-executing prohibitions on governmental action, and this court has had primary authority to interpret those prohibitions. The Bingham draft, some thought, departed from that tradition by vesting in Congress primary power to interpret and elaborate on the meaning of the new amendment through legislation. As enacted, the Fourteenth Amendment confers substantive rights against the states which, like the provisions of the Bill of Rights, are self-executing. The power to interpret the Constitution in a case or controversy remains in the Judiciary.

The remedial and preventive nature of Congress' enforcement power, and the limitation inherent in the power, were confirmed in our earliest cases on the Fourteenth Amendment. Their treatment of Congress' § 5 power as corrective or preventive, not definitional, has not been questioned.

There is language in our opinion in *Katzenbach v. Morgan* which could be interpreted as acknowledging a power in Congress to enact legislation that expands the rights contained in § 1 of the Fourteenth Amendment. This is not a necessary interpretation, however, or even the best one. In *Morgan*, the court considered the constitutionality of § 4(e) of the Voting Rights Act of 1965, which provided that no person who had successfully completed the sixth primary grade in a public school in, or a private school accredited by, the Commonwealth of Puerto Rico in which the language of instruction was other than English could be denied the right to vote because of an inability to read or write English. New York's Constitution, on the other hand, required voters to be able to read and write English. The Court provided two related rationales for its conclusion that § 4(e) could "be viewed as a measure to secure for the Puerto Rican community residing in New York nondiscriminatory treatment by government." Under the first rationale, Congress could prohibit New York from denying the right to vote to large segments of its Puerto Rican community, in order to give Puerto Ricans "enhanced political power" that would be "helpful in gaining nondiscriminatory treatment in public services for the entire Puerto Rican community." Section 4(e) thus could be justified as a remedial measure to deal with "discrimination in governmental services." The second rationale, an alternative holding, did not address discrimination in the provision of public services but "discrimination in establishing voter qualifications." The Court perceived a factual basis on which Congress could have concluded that New York's literacy requirement "constituted an invidious discrimination in violation of the equal protection clause." Both rationales for upholding § 4(e) rested on unconstitutional discrimination by New York and Congress' reasonable attempt to combat it. As Justice Stewart explained in *Oregon v. Mitchell*, interpreting *Morgan* to give Congress the power to interpret the Constitution "would require an enormous extension of that decision's rationale."

If Congress could define its own powers by altering the Fourteenth Amendment's meaning, no longer would the Constitution be "superior paramount law, unchangeable by ordinary means." It would be "on a level with ordinary legislative acts, and, like other acts, . . . alterable when the legislature shall please to alter it." *Marbury v. Madison*. Under this approach, it is difficult to conceive of a principle that would limit Congressional power. Shifting legislative majorities could change the Constitution and effectively circumvent the difficult and detailed amendment process contained in Article V.

We now turn to consider whether RFRA can be considered enforcement legislation under § 5 of the Fourteenth Amendment.

B

Respondent contends that RFRA is a proper exercise of Congress' remedial or preventive power. The Act, it is said, is a reasonable means of protecting the free exercise of religion as defined by *Smith*. It prevents and remedies laws which are enacted with the unconstitutional object of targeting religious beliefs and practices. To avoid the difficulty of proving such violations, it is said, Congress can simply invalidate any law which imposes a substantial burden on a religious practice unless it is justified by a compelling interest and is the least restrictive means of accomplishing that interest. If Congress can prohibit laws with discriminatory effects in order to prevent racial discrimination in violation of the equal protection clause, then it can do the same, respondent argues, to promote religious liberty.

While preventive rules are sometimes appropriate remedial measures, there must be a congruence between the means used and the ends to be achieved. The appropriateness of remedial measures must be considered in light of the evil presented. Strong measures appropriate to address one harm may be an unwarranted response to another, lesser one.

A comparison between RFRA and the Voting Rights Act is instructive. In contrast to the record which confronted Congress and the judiciary in the voting rights cases, RFRA's legislative record lacks examples of modern instances of generally applicable laws passed because of religious bigotry. The history of persecution in this country detailed in the hearings mentions no episodes occurring in the past 40 years. As a general matter, it is for Congress to determine the method by which it will reach a decision.

Regardless of the state of the legislative record, RFRA cannot be considered remedial, preventive legislation, if those terms are to have any meaning. RFRA is so out of proportion to a supposed remedial or preventive object that it cannot be understood as responsive to, or designed to prevent, unconstitutional behavior. It appears, instead, to attempt a substantive change in Constitutional protections. Preventive measures prohibiting certain types of laws may be appropriate when there is reason to believe that many of the laws affected by the Congressional enactment have a significant likelihood of being unconstitutional.

The stringent test RFRA demands of state laws reflects a lack of proportionality or congruence between the means adopted and the legitimate end to be achieved. If an objector can show a substantial burden on his free exercise, the state must demonstrate a compelling governmental interest and show that the law is the least restrictive means of furthering its interest. Claims that a law substantially burdens someone's exercise of religion will often be difficult to contest. Requiring a state to demonstrate a compelling interest and show that it has adopted the least restrictive means of achieving that interest is the most demanding test known to constitutional law. Laws valid under *Smith* would fall under RFRA without regard to whether they had the object of stifling or punishing free exercise. We make these observations not to reargue the position of the majority in *Smith* but to illustrate the substantive alteration of its holding attempted by RFRA. Even assuming RFRA would be interpreted in effect to mandate some lesser test, say one equivalent to intermediate scrutiny, the statute nevertheless would require searching judicial scrutiny of state law with the attendant likelihood of invalidation. This is a considerable congressional intrusion into the states' traditional prerogatives and general authority to regulate for the health and welfare of their citizens.

The substantial costs RFRA exacts, both in practical terms of imposing a heavy litigation burden on the states and in terms of curtailing their traditional general regulatory power, far exceed any pattern or practice of unconstitutional conduct under the Free Exercise Clause as interpreted in *Smith*. Simply put, RFRA is not designed to identify and counteract state laws likely to be unconstitutional because of their treatment of religion. In most cases, the state laws to which RFRA applies are not ones which will have been motivated by religious bigotry. If a state law disproportionately burdened a particular class of religious observers, this circumstance might be evidence of an impermissible legislative motive. RFRA's substantial burden test, however, is not even a discriminatory effects or disparate impact test. It is a reality of the modern regulatory state that numerous state laws, such as the zoning regulations at issue here, impose a substantial burden on a large class of individuals. When the exercise of religion has been burdened in an incidental way by a law of general application, it does not follow that the persons affected have been burdened any more than other citizens, let alone burdened because of their religious beliefs.

When Congress acts within its sphere of power and responsibilities, it has not just the right but the duty to make its own informed judgment on the meaning and force of the Constitution. This has been clear from the early days of the republic. Were it otherwise, we would not afford Congress the presumption of validity its enactments now enjoy.

Our national experience teaches that the Constitution is preserved best when each part of the government respects both the Constitution and the proper actions and determinations of the other branches. When the court has interpreted the Constitution, it has acted within the province of the judicial branch, which embraces the duty to say what the law is. *Marbury v. Madison*. When the political branches of the government act against the background of a judicial interpretation of the Constitution already issued, it must be understood that in later cases and controversies the court will treat its precedents with the respect due them under settled principles, including stare decisis, and contrary expectations must be disappointed. RFRA was designed to control cases and controversies, such as the one before us; but as the provisions of the federal statute here invoked are beyond congressional authority, it is this Court's precedent, not RFRA, which must control.

It is for Congress in the first instance to "determin[e] whether and what legislation is needed to secure the guarantees of the Fourteenth Amendment," and its conclusions are entitled to much deference. *Katzenbach v. Morgan*. Congress' discretion is not unlimited, however, and the courts retain the power, as they have since *Marbury v. Madison*, to determine if Congress has exceeded its authority under the Constitution. Broad as the power of Congress is under the enforcement clause of the Fourteenth Amendment, RFRA contradicts vital principles necessary to maintain separation of powers and the federal balance. The judgment of the Court of Appeals sustaining the Act's constitutionality is reversed.

JUSTICE STEVENS, concurring.

In my opinion, RFRA is a "law respecting an establishment of religion" that violates the First Amendment to the Constitution.

If the historic landmark on the hill in Boerne happened to be a museum or an art gallery owned by an atheist, it would not be eligible for an exemption from the city ordinances that forbid an enlargement of the structure. Because the landmark is owned by the Catholic Church, it is claimed that RFRA gives its owner a federal statutory entitlement to an exemption from a generally applicable, neutral civil law. Whether the church would actually prevail under the statute or not, the statute has provided the church with a legal weapon that no atheist or agnostic can obtain. This governmental preference for religion, as opposed to irreligion, is forbidden by the First Amendment.

JUSTICE O'CONNOR, with whom JUSTICE BREYER joins except as to a portion of Part I, dissenting.

I dissent from the Court's disposition of this case. I agree with the Court that the issue before us is whether RFRA is a proper exercise of Congress' power to enforce § 5 of the Fourteenth Amendment. But as a yardstick for measuring the constitutionality of RFRA, the Court uses its holding in *Employment Div., Dept. Of Human Resources of Or. v. Smith*, the decision that prompted Congress to enact RFRA as a means of more rigorously enforcing the Free Exercise Clause. I remain of the view that *Smith* was wrongly decided, and I would use this case to reexamine the Court's holding there. Therefore, I would direct the parties to brief the question whether *Smith* represents the correct understanding of the Free Exercise Clause and set the case for reargument. If the Court were to correct the misinterpretation of the Free Exercise Clause set forth in *Smith*, it would simultaneously put our First Amendment jurisprudence back on course and allay the legitimate concerns of a majority in Congress who believed that *Smith* improperly restricted religious liberty. We would then be in a position to review RFRA in light of a proper interpretation of the Free Exercise Clause.

I agree with much of the reasoning set forth in Part III-A of the Court's opinion. Indeed, if I agreed with the court's standard in *Smith*, I would join the opinion. As the Court's careful and thorough historical analysis shows, Congress lacks the "power to decree the substance of the Fourteenth Amendment's restrictions on the states." Rather, its power under § 5 of the Fourteenth Amendment extends only to enforcing the amendment's provisions. In short, Congress lacks the ability independently to define or expand the scope of constitutional rights by statute. Accordingly, whether Congress has exceeded its § 5 powers turns on whether there is a "congruence and proportionality between the injury to be prevented or remedied and the means adopted to that end." This recognition does not, of course, in any way diminish Congress' obligation to draw its own conclusions regarding the Constitution's meaning. Congress, no less than this Court, is called upon to consider the requirements of the Constitution and to act in accordance with its dictates. But when it enacts legislation in furtherance of its delegated powers, Congress must make its judgments consistent with this Court's exposition of the Constitution and with the limits placed on its legislative authority by provisions such as the Fourteenth Amendment.

The Court's analysis of whether RFRA is a constitutional exercise of Congress' § 5 power, set forth in Part III-B of its opinion, is premised on the assumption that *Smith* correctly interprets the free exercise clause. This is an assumption that I do not accept. I continue to believe that *Smith* adopted an improper standard for deciding free exercise claims.

JUSTICE SOUTER, dissenting.

To decide whether the Fourteenth Amendment gives Congress sufficient power to enact the Religious Freedom Restoration Act, the Court measures the legislation against the free-exercise standard of *Employment Div., Dept. of Human Resources of Oregon v. Smith*. I have serious doubts about the precedential value of the *Smith* rule and its entitlement to adherence. These doubts are intensified today by the historical arguments going to the original understanding of the free exercise clause presented in JUSTICE O'CONNOR's opinion, which raises very substantial issues about the soundness of the *Smith* rule. But without briefing and argument on the merits of that rule, I am not now prepared to join JUSTICE O'CONNOR in rejecting it or the majority in assuming it to be correct. In order to provide full adversarial consideration, this case should be set down for reargument permitting plenary reexamination of the issue. Since the court declines to follow that course, our free-exercise law remains marked by an "intolerable tension," and the constitutionality of the Act of Congress to enforce the free-exercise right cannot now be soundly decided. I would therefore dismiss the writ of *certiorari* as improvidently granted, and I accordingly dissent from the Court's disposition of this case.

JUSTICE BREYER, dissenting.

I agree with JUSTICE O'CONNOR that the court should direct the parties to brief the question whether *Employment Div., Dept. of Human Resources of Oregon v. Smith*, was correctly decided, and set this case for reargument. I do not, however, find it necessary to consider the question whether, assuming *Smith* is correct, § 5 of the Fourteenth Amendment would authorize Congress to enact the legislation before us. Thus, while I agree with some of the views expressed in the first paragraph of Part I of JUSTICE O'CONNOR's dissent, I do not necessarily agree with all of them. I therefore join JUSTICE O'CONNOR's dissent, with the exception of the first paragraph of Part I.

NOTES

1. Congressional authority to interpret the Constitution. The Court makes a distinction between determining the meaning of the Constitution and finding the facts on which constitutional provisions might operate. In Professor McConnell's view, the Court did not need to work in such a stark dichotomy. "It is precisely in a close case that the independent judgment of Congress on a constitutional question should make a difference. When translating constitutional text into judicially enforceable doctrine, a responsible court necessarily takes into consideration not only the meaning of the constitutional provision at issue, but also the institutional implications of the doctrine for the allocation of power between the courts and the representative branches." Michael McConnell, *Institutions and Interpretation: A Critique of City of Boerne v. Flores*, 111 HARV. L. REV. 153, 155 (1997).

2. Implications for civil rights legislation. As amended in subsequent years, Title VII of the Civil Rights Act of 1964 provides remedies to employees without showing of intent to discriminate that would be required by direct constitutional analysis. Although Justice Kennedy goes to some lengths to avoid threatening congressional legislation dealing with discrimination, it would be extremely difficult to distinguish the Title VII definition of discrimination from the RFRA definition of free exercise, if Title VII were based on enforcement of equal protection. Rachel Toker, *Tying the Hands of Congress*, 33 HARV. C.R.-C.L. L. REV. 273, 305 (1997). To the extent that Congress bases its legislation on the commerce clause rather than section 5 of the Fourteenth Amendment, then this difficulty makes little difference.

The most likely effect of *City of Boerne*, therefore, is to reinforce Congress' practice of basing most of its civil rights legislation on the commerce clause. But does the retrenchment represented in *Lopez* and *Morrison* threaten the validity of federal legislation requiring the states to provide accommodations for the disabled or to prevent hostile work environments for women?

Might it be possible to revive the Violence Against Women Act as an enforcement of the civil rights of women? *See* Akhil Amar, *Foreword: The Document and the Doctrine*, 114 HARV. L. REV. 26 (2000).

§ 2.05 THE ELEVENTH AMENDMENT

In *Chisholm v. Georgia*, 2 U.S. (2 Dall.) 363 (1793), the Supreme Court held that the diversity jurisdiction of the federal courts under Article III permitted a citizen of one state to sue another state in federal court, rejecting an argument for sovereign immunity. The ratification of the Eleventh Amendment in 1798 undid the result in *Chisholm*. The Eleventh Amendment states: "The Judicial power of the United States shall not be construed to extend to any suit in law or equity, commenced or prosecuted against one of the United States by Citizens of another State, or by Citizens or Subjects of any Foreign State."

The language of the Eleventh Amendment appears to apply only to suits against a state by an out-of-stater, and the background from *Chisholm* would seem to imply that it referred only to diversity jurisdiction rather than suits based on federal law. Suppose suit is brought against a state by one of its own citizens with regard to a federal claim in a federal court, and the state has not consented to suit. Is the Eleventh Amendment a bar? Although the text of the amendment does not speak to this issue, the Supreme Court in *Hans v. Louisiana*, 134 U.S. 1 (1890), held that the Eleventh Amendment establishes sovereign immunity for states even from suits by their own citizens based on federal claims. The Eleventh Amendment immunity extends only to the state and its agencies, not to public subdivisions of the state, such as counties, municipalities, and their agencies.

Injunctive relief. The Court restricted the Eleventh Amendment in *Ex parte Young*, 209 U.S. 123 (1908). Justice Peckham reasoned in *Ex parte Young* that unconstitutional conduct by a state officer should not be considered state action on the ground that the state may not authorize unconstitutional action. Therefore, a suit in a federal court against a state officer acting unconstitutionally was not a suit against the state, and the Eleventh Amendment was not a bar. The constitutional contention in *Ex parte Young* was that the rates that railroads could charge had been set so low by the legislature as to constitute a confiscatory taking of the railroad's property. If the Minnesota law setting forth the objectionable rates constituted a deprivation of property without due process of law, then Young, the Attorney General, could be enjoined from enforcing it. The legal fiction of *Young* was necessary in the twentieth century to allow federal court implementation of federal constitutional protections against the states.

But in *Edelman v. Jordan*, 15 U.S. 651 (1974), the Court held that even in a suit directed against a public official, if relief involves a charge on the general revenues of the state and cannot be distinguished from an award of damages against the state, the Eleventh Amendment bars the award. The impediment to indirect suits against the states created by *Edelman* was modified in *Milliken v. Bradley (Milliken II)*, 433 U.S. 267 (1977), where the Court ruled that a federal court requirement that state defendants pay one-half the additional costs for remedial services under a school desegregation plan did not violate the Eleventh Amendment. The Court pointed out that *Edelman* had barred relief of an "accrued monetary liability" but had not barred the payment of state funds with respect to "compliance in the future with a substantive federal question determination":

> The decree to share the future costs of educational components in this case fits squarely within the prospective-compliance exception reaffirmed by *Edelman*. That exception, which had its genesis in *Ex parte Young*, permits federal courts to enjoin state officials to conform their conduct to requirements of federal law, notwithstanding a direct and substantial impact on the state treasury. The order challenged here does no more than that.

Civil rights actions. In *Fitzpatrick v. Bitzer*, 427 U.S. 445 (1976), the Court held that the Eleventh Amendment did not prevent Congress from authorizing the federal courts (in Title VII of the Civil Rights Act of 1964) to award back pay to state employees who had suffered state discrimination because of their sex. In this case, unlike *Edelman v. Jordan*, Congress had provided for suits against the state pursuant to legislative authority granted it under § 5 of the Fourteenth Amendment. The Eleventh Amendment bar to a back pay award against a state without its consent is thus limited by the power of Congress to authorize such awards pursuant to § 5 and *Fitzpatrick* was distinguishable from *Edelman* because of "the threshold fact of Congressional authorization."

Commerce power claims. After *Fitzpatrick*, a major question was whether Congress' ability to subject states to suit differed when it acted pursuant to its commerce or spending powers rather than its powers under the Fourteenth Amendment. *Edelman* did not ban all suits for "retroactive" relief against a state but held that Congress may authorize suit if the state is given clear notice that its conduct will be taken as a waiver of its sovereign immunity. Presumably, it should be easier to show a voluntary waiver of sovereign immunity in the case of a spending measure than in the case of a regulation under the commerce power. In the former, the state has a conscious choice to make, however coerced it may feel, about whether to take the federal funds subject to law suits if it does not obey all the mandates of the act. By contrast, it may come under the strictures of a commerce clause regulation without any official's consciously considering the question of suits against the state.

In *Pennsylvania v. Union Gas Co.*, 491 U.S. 1 (1989), a plurality of the Court ruled that Congress had authority to render a State liable for money damages in federal court when it legislated pursuant to its commerce power. Suit was brought by the United States against Union Gas to recover cleanup costs resulting from the escape of hazardous substances. Union Gas filed a third party complaint against Pennsylvania as a responsible party under the federal law. After having determined that Congress intended to hold the states liable under the federal law, the Court, per Justice Brennan, held 5-4 that Congress has authority under its Article I commerce powers to abrogate the states' Eleventh Amendment immunity. Justice Brennan's reasoning, however, drew only plurality support. The four dissenters described the plurality approach as "preserving *Hans* but permitting Congress to overrule it" through its Article I commerce powers and declared it "the worst of both worlds."

In *Seminole Tribe of Florida v. Florida*, 517 U.S. 44 (1996), a case dealing with Congress' power under the Indian Commerce Clause, a 5-4 Court overruled *Pennsylvania v. Union Gas*. The *Seminole Tribe* opinion by Chief Justice Rehnquist stated that "[i]n the five years since it was decided, *Union Gas* has proven to be a solitary departure from established law," that it had been a source of "confusion among the lower courts," and that it "essentially eviscerated our decision in *Hans*."

> In overruling *Union Gas* today, we reconfirm that the background principle of state sovereign immunity embodied in the Eleventh Amendment is not so ephemeral as to dissipate when the subject of the suit is an area . . . that is under the exclusive control of the Federal Government. Even when the Constitution vests in Congress complete lawmaking authority over a particular area, the Eleventh Amendment prevents congressional authorization of suits by private parties against unconsenting States.

The majority did, however, reiterate that Congress could subject the states to suit under its power to enforce the Fourteenth Amendment, as *Fitzpatrick* had held.

The dissenting justices believed that *Hans* need not be read as a constitutional holding but rather as an exercise in statutory interpretation. They disagreed with the majority's basic proposition that the Eleventh Amendment embodied a general policy of sovereign immunity. Justice Stevens noted that the decision "prevents Congress from providing a federal forum for a broad range of actions against States, from those sounding in copyright and patent law, to those concerning bankruptcy, environmental law, and the regulation of our vast national economy."

Spending power claims. As discussed in Chapter 3, Congress frequently attempts to secure compliance by States with federal mandates by attaching conditions to federal grants. Several cases have raised the question of whether acceptance of a conditional grant is sufficient to waive the State's sovereign immunity. Thus far, the Supreme Court's response is that a claimed waiver will be effective only if the statutory language is "unequivocal."

Pennhurst State School & Hosp. v. Halderman, 451 U.S. 1 (1981) *(Pennhurst I)*, arose when Congress provided funds for states to use in educating the handicapped and stated that states receiving federal funds were subjected to suit for failure to comply with the Act. Another section of the Act purported to declare a "Bill of Rights" for the handicapped, including a "right" to education in the "least restrictive environment." The Supreme Court held that in the absence of specific congressional statements, the requirements of the statutory "Bill of Rights" would not be enforced by lawsuit against the states.

In *Atascadero State Hosp. v. Scanlon*, 473 U.S. 234 (1983), the Court held that Congress had not been sufficiently explicit in the Rehabilitation Act of 1974 to subject the state hospital to suit for refusing to hire a handicapped applicant. Although a private employer would be subject to suit and although Congress could have subjected the state to suit under *Fitzpatrick*, the statute did not explicitly refer to states as potential defendants. Justice Brennan, joined by Justices Marshall, Blackmun, and Stevens, canvassed the history of sovereign immunity and found no support for the view in *Hans* that sovereign immunity was part of the policies implicit in the Eleventh Amendment.

In *Dellmuth v. Muth*, 491 U.S. 223 (1989), the Court held 5-4 that, in enacting the Education of the Handicapped Act (EHA), Congress had not evinced "an unmistakably clear intention to abrogate the States' constitutionally secured immunity from suit." The evidence, said Justice Kennedy for the Court, "must be both unequivocal and textual." Justice Brennan, again joined by Justices Marshall, Blackmun, and Stevens, dissenting, would have overruled *Hans* or, alternatively, would have found "that Congress in the EHA abrogated state immunity."

The Scope of Abrogation Under the Fourteenth Amendment. Following *Fitzpatrick* and *Seminole Tribe*, the most critical issues involving Eleventh Amendment immunity arise with Congress' exercise of authority under the Fourteenth Amendment. The authority from section 5 of the Fourteenth Amendment is often combined in the preambles or findings of legislation with findings that refer to the impact of an activity on interstate commerce. If Congress validly legislates under the Fourteenth Amendment, then it would seem that the Eleventh Amendment provides no immunity. But after *City of Boerne*, the validity of exercising Fourteenth Amendment power itself must be questioned.

In *Nevada Dep't of Human Resources v. Hibbs*, 538 U.S. 721 (2003), the Court upheld application of the Family and Medical Leave Act of 1993 to provide money damages against a state that did not comply with the family-care requirements of the Act. Although the Act was premised on alleviating discrimination against women in the workplace, it went beyond the strict commands of the Fourteenth Amendment by granting rights for men seeking time off from work to care for a dependent family member. *Boerne* had held that Congress could not redefine the meaning of constitutional provisions, and the Act's attempt to abrogate state immunity was challenged on the ground that Congress could not abrogate state immunity except to the extent of the right of nondiscrimination guaranteed by the Fourteenth Amendment itself. The Court, however, held that the power to "enforce" coupled with the "necessary and proper" clause gave Congress the power to adopt measures that were "congruent and proportional" to problems identified in enforcement of Fourteenth Amendment commands. An extensive review of evidence regarding discrimination against women in the workplace led to this conclusion:

> By creating an across-the-board, routine employment benefit for all eligible employees, Congress sought to ensure that family-care leave would no longer be stigmatized as an inordinate drain on the workplace caused by female employees, and that employers could not evade leave obligations simply by hiring men. By setting a minimum standard of family leave for *all* eligible employees, irrespective of gender, the FMLA attacks the formerly state-sanctioned stereotype that only women are responsible for family caregiving, thereby reducing employers' incentives to engage in discrimination by basing hiring and promotion decisions on stereotypes.

Chief Justice Rehnquist wrote the opinion for a 6-3 Court, but he then dissented in the following case.

The Americans with Disabilities Act (ADA) gave rise to two decisions of the Court. In the first, *Board of Trustees v. Garrett*, 531 U.S. 356 (2001), the Court held that the Eleventh Amendment prevented suits for money damages against States for violation of the nondiscrimination in employment provisions of the Act. In the second, *Tennessee v. Lane*, 124 S. Ct. 1978 (2004), the Court held that damages for interference with access to public programs and facilities was authorized under section 5 of the Fourteenth Amendment. The principal distinction between the two cases was that access to public programs and facilities would be required in some instances to assure that violations of due process did not occur, as for example in the instance of a litigant unable to obtain full access to the courthouse. In that kind of situation, the damages remedy would be "congruent and proportional" to the likelihood of a constitutional wrong. The majority went only so far as to hold that the ADA was valid "as it applies to the class of cases inplicating the fundamental right of access to the courts." Chief Justice Rehnquist, joined by Justices Kennedy and Thomas, complained that the "as-applied" approach would rewrite the statute and eliminate any incentive for Congress to be precise in its drafting. Justice Scalia in dissent objected that the "congruence and proportionality" test was designed for cases involving racial discrimination and should be so limited.

Chapter 3

STATE POWER IN AMERICAN FEDERALISM

Our focus in Chapter 2 was on the scope of national regulatory power in a federal system. The focus now turns to the other side of the equation, the regulatory powers of the states (and local governments acting as agents of the state). Again concern is with the scope of power, its sources and the limitations on the exercise of the power arising from the division of powers between the national and state governments. The federal Constitution does not purport to "grant" powers to the states, starting from the basic proposition that the states possess "plenary" authority as original sovereigns.

Some specific limitations on the regulatory power of the states are set forth in Article I, § 10. Further, some powers are clearly exclusive of state regulation, for example, the power to declare war or to legislate for the District of Columbia. But does a grant of power to the national government *necessarily* exclude the existence of a like power in the states?

The concept of mutually exclusive state and federal powers is referred to as the "dual federalism" model, defined as a governmental structure in which "each of the two sovereignties has its own exclusive area of authority and jurisdiction," DANIEL J. ELAZAR, THE AMERICAN PARTNERSHIP 22 (1962), or as one in which state and federal governments, "[w]ithin their respective spheres are 'sovereign' and hence equal." Edward Corwin, *The Passing of Dual Federalism,* 36 VA. L. REV. 1, 4 (1950). An alternative political theory, generally referred to as "cooperative federalism," posits that "[s]hared functions, without regard to neat allocations of responsibility, is the core of American governmental operation and of the theory of federalism as well. Intergovernmental collaboration rather than the priority of particular governmental levels is the working principle of the federal system." RICHARD H. LEACH, AMERICAN FEDERALISM 15 (1970). The choice of federalism theory may have significant influence upon the level of authority that the states may exercise over matters falling within Congress constitutionally ordained power.

The area in which this issue has arisen most clearly is the exercise of governmental power to regulate interstate commerce. Article I, § 8 of the Constitution delegates to Congress the authority to regulate commerce among the several states. The mere fact that the Constitution delegates a power to Congress, however, does not mean that Congress must exercise all of that power. If Congress has not acted, can the states, in the exercise of their police powers, regulate matters charged to the national government, or does the dormant grant of power itself limit the regulatory power of the states? Can the states exercise the granted power itself? What happens if Congress does legislate in regard to a particular subject? Does this necessarily preclude all state regulation? If the Supreme Court has held that certain state regulation is barred by a constitutional grant of power to the national government, can Congress, through legislation, authorize the states to act? Answers to these questions must flow from a constant redefinition of interfederal relationships. Once again, a question arises regarding the proper role of Congress and the courts in defining these relationships.

§ 3.01 STATE POWER TO REGULATE COMMERCE

[A] EFFECT OF THE GRANT OF POWER TO CONGRESS

GIBBONS v. OGDEN
22 U.S. (9 Wheat.) 1, 6 L. Ed. 23 (1824)

[The facts and initial part of the opinion relating to Congress' power to regulate commerce among the states are reprinted at p. 79. In the part of the opinion printed below, Chief Justice Marshall discusses the effect of the constitutional grant of commerce power to the national government and the effect of congressional regulation pursuant thereto on the regulatory power of the states.]

[I]t has been urged with great earnestness that, although the power of Congress to regulate commerce with foreign nations, and among the several states, be coextensive with the subject itself, and have no other limits than are prescribed in the Constitution, yet the states may severally exercise the same power within their respective jurisdictions. In support of this argument, it is said that they possessed it as an inseparable attribute of sovereignty before the formation of the Constitution, and still retain it, except so far as they have surrendered it by that instrument; that this principle results from the nature of the government, and is secured by the Tenth Amendment; that an affirmative grant of power is not exclusive, unless in its own nature it be such that the continued exercise of it by the former possessor is inconsistent with the grant, and that this is not of that description. The appellant, conceding these postulates, except the last, contends that full power to regulate a particular subject implies the whole power, and leaves no residuum; that a grant of the whole is incompatible with the existence of a right in another to any part of it.

The grant of the power to lay and collect taxes is, like the power to regulate commerce, made in general terms, and has never been understood to interfere with the exercise of the same power by the states; and hence has been drawn an argument which has been applied to the question under consideration. But the two grants are not, it is conceived, similar in their terms or their nature. Although many of the powers formerly exercised by the states are transferred to the government of the Union, yet the state governments remain, and constitute a most important part of our system. The power of taxation is indispensable to their existence, and is a power which, in its own nature, is capable of residing in, and being exercised by, different authorities at the same time. When, then, each government exercises the power of taxation, neither is exercising the power of the other. But when a state proceeds to regulate commerce with foreign nations, or among the several states, it is exercising the very power that is granted to Congress, and is doing the very thing which Congress is authorized to do. There is no analogy, then, between the power of taxation and the power of regulating commerce.

But the inspection laws are said to be regulations of commerce, and are certainly recognized in the Constitution as being passed in the exercise of a power remaining with the States.

That inspection laws may have a remote and considerable influence on commerce, will not be denied; but that a power to regulate commerce is the source from which the right to pass them is derived, cannot be admitted. The object of inspection laws is to improve the quality of articles produced by the labor of a country, to fit them for exportation, or it may be for domestic use. They act upon the subject before it becomes an article of foreign commerce, or of commerce among the states, and prepare it for that purpose. They form a portion of that immense mass of legislation which embraces everything within the territory of a state not surrendered to a general government; all which can be most advantageously exercised by the states themselves. Inspection laws, quarantine laws, health laws of every description, as well as laws for regulating the internal commerce of a state, and those which respect turnpike roads, ferries, etc., are component parts of this mass.

[I]f a state, in passing laws on subjects acknowledged to be within its control, and with a view to those subjects, shall adopt a measure of the same character with one which Congress may adopt, it does not derive its authority from the particular power which has been granted, but from some other which remains with the state, and may be executed by the same means. All experience shows that the same measures, or measures scarcely distinguishable from each other, may flow from distinct powers; but this does not prove that the powers themselves are identical. Although the means used in their execution may sometimes approach each other so nearly as to be confounded, there are other situations in which they are sufficiently distinct to establish their individuality.

In our complex system, presenting the rare and difficult scheme of one general government whose action extends over the whole, but which possesses only certain enumerated powers; and of numerous state governments, which retain and exercise all powers not delegated to the Union, contests respecting power must arise. Were it ever otherwise, the measures taken by the respective governments to execute their acknowledged powers would often be of the same description, and might sometimes interfere. This, however, does not prove that the one is exercising, or has a right to exercise the powers of the other.

It has been contended by the counsel for the appellant that, as the word to "regulate" implies in its nature full power over the thing to be regulated, it excludes, necessarily, the action of all others that would perform the same operation on the same thing. That regulation is designed for the entire result, applying to those parts which remain as they were, as well as to those which are altered. It produces a uniform whole, which is as much disturbed and deranged by changing what the regulating power designs to leave untouched, as that on which it has operated. There is great force in this argument, and the court is not satisfied that it has been refuted.

Since, however, in exercising the power of regulating their own purely internal affairs, whether of trading or police, the States may sometimes enact laws, the validity of which depends on their interfering with and being contrary to, an act of Congress passed in pursuance of the Constitution, the Court will enter upon an inquiry, whether the laws of New York, as expounded by the highest tribunal of that State, have, in their application to this case, come into collision with an Act of Congress, and deprive a citizen of a right to which that act entitles him. Should this collision exist, it will be immaterial whether those laws were passed in virtue of a concurrent power "to regulate commerce with foreign nations and among the several States," or in virtue of a power to regulate their domestic trade and police. In one case and the other, the acts of New York must yield to the law of Congress; and the decision sustaining the privilege they confer, against the right given by a law of the Union, must be erroneous.

[The Court construed the federal legislation to allow a licensee to engage in coastal trade. The New York Act granting a monopoly in navigation, therefore, was inconsistent with the rights granted under the federal act and, hence, unconstitutional. The decree below was reversed and the bill dismissed.]

[JUSTICE JOHNSON, concurring, contended that the Commerce Clause gave Congress exclusive power to regulate foreign and interstate commerce, thereby excluding any state regulatory power over such commerce.]

NOTES

1. ***Exclusive and shared powers***. In THE FEDERALIST NO. 32, Alexander Hamilton described the source of exclusive and shared powers, presaging the possibility of a concurrent state-federal power over the regulation of interstate commerce:

> [A]s the plan of the Convention aims only at a partial union or consolidation, the State governments would clearly retain all the rights of sovereignty which they before had, and which were not, by that act, *exclusively* delegated to the United States. This exclusive delegation, or rather this alienation of State sovereignty, would only exist in three cases: where the Constitution in express terms granted an exclusive authority to the Union; where it granted in one instance an authority to the Union, and in another prohibited the States from exercising the like authority; and where it granted an authority to the Union to which a similar authority in the States would be absolutely and totally *contradictory* and *repugnant.*

What the FEDERALIST PAPERS propagandized, in short, was that the Constitution created "at one and the same time both a consolidated and a federal government — a 'mixed' government." Howard Mann, *The Marshall Court: Nationalization of Private Rights and Personal Liberty from the Authority of the Commerce Clause,* 38 IND. L.J. 117, 193 (1963). Does the failure of the Framers to confront directly this issue suggest that the Commerce Clause was not intended, of its own force, to limit the states?

2. *Selective exclusiveness*. Daniel Webster, arguing for the appellant in *Gibbons,* relied strongly on the history of the formation of the Constitution, urging that the "very object intended, more than any other" was to divest the states of any power to regulate commerce in its "higher branches," which included the granting of monopolies in trade and navigation. Returning to Hamilton's approach in THE FEDERALIST NO. 32, Webster argued: "[S]o where the power, or any one subject, is given in general words, like the power to regulate commerce, the true method of construction would be, to consider of what parts the grant is composed, and which of those, from the nature of the thing, ought to be considered exclusive." While the meaning of the term "higher branches" is unclear, it is certain that Webster was not arguing for an absolutely exclusive commerce power, but rather for a doctrine of selective exclusiveness based on the particular regulation. Webster characterized the existing state regulations of transportation, trade, and traffic as "in their general character, rather regulations of police than of commerce, in the Constitutional understanding of that term." Thus, it followed that "quarantine laws, for example, may be considered as affecting commerce; yet they are, in their nature, health laws."

3. *Commerce and police powers*. Chief Justice Marshall argues that some state regulations, such as inspection laws, do not have their source in the power to regulate commerce among the states but in the police power. Does it matter if the police power or concurrent commerce power rationale is used? Professor (later Justice) Frankfurter observed:

> Because the "police power" is a response to the dynamic aspects of society, it has eluded attempts at definition. But precisely because it is such a response, it is one of the most fertile doctrinal sources for striking an accommodation between local interests and the demands of the commerce clause.

FELIX FRANKFURTER, THE COMMERCE CLAUSE UNDER MARSHALL, TANEY AND WAITE 27 (1937).

4. *Willson v. Black Bird Creek Marsh Co.*, 27 U.S. (2 Pet.) 245 (1829). The Court upheld a Delaware law authorizing a company to build a dam across a navigable creek flowing into the Delaware River. Justice Marshall, delivering the opinion of the Court, stressed the importance of such state regulation for flood control and health, urging that "[m]easures calculated to produce these objects, provided they do not come into collision with the powers of the general government, are undoubtedly within those which are reserved to the states." Because Congress had not passed any act of relevance, the challenge to the validity of the state legislation rested on its alleged repugnancy to the dormant power to regulate commerce among the several states. Marshall concluded: "We do not think that the act empowering the Black Bird Creek Marsh Company to place a dam across the Creeks, can under all the circumstances of the case, be considered as repugnant to the power to regulate commerce in its dormant state, or as being in conflict with any law passed on the subject."

Is Chief Justice Marshall retreating from his tentative approval of an exclusively federal commerce power? What does he mean by "under all the circumstances of the case"? Is it relevant that this stream was, according to counsel William Wirt, "one of those sluggish, reptile streams that do not run but creep, and which wherever it passes, spreads its venom, and destroys the health of all those who inhabit its marshes"?

[B] DEVELOPMENT OF THE DORMANT COMMERCE CLAUSE — THE *COOLEY* DOCTRINE

***Cooley v. Board of Wardens*, 53 U.S. (12 How.) 299 (1851).** Pennsylvania required vessels entering or leaving the port of Philadelphia to have a licensed pilot on board for navigating the Delaware River. Pilots could be licensed only by the Board of Wardens of Philadelphia Harbor. Cooley's violation of the statute resulted in a fine of $60 against him. On appeal to the Supreme Court, it was first argued that a federal statute explicitly authorized the states to regulate pilots in the harbors and ports of the United States. The Court, however, did not view the federal statute as significant because Congress could not delegate to the states a power over interstate commerce if that power had been removed from the states by operation of the Constitution. Therefore, the Court, in an opinion by Justice Curtis, moved to the basic question of whether the states had power over this aspect of commerce:

> [I]t would be in conformity with the contemporary exposition of the Constitution [when it was ratified] . . . to hold that the mere grant of such a power to Congress, did not imply a prohibition on the States to exercise the same power; that it is not the mere existence of such a power, but its exercise by Congress, which may be incompatible with the exercise of the same power by the States, and that the States may legislate in the absence of congressional regulations.
>
> The grant of commercial power to Congress does not contain any terms which expressly exclude the states from exercising an authority over its subject matter.
>
> The diversities of opinion, therefore, which have existed on this subject have arisen from the different views taken of the nature of this power. But when the nature of a power like this is spoken of, when it is said that the nature of the power requires that it should be exercised exclusively by Congress, it must be intended to refer to the subjects of that power, and to say they are of such a nature as to require exclusive legislation by Congress. Now, the power to regulate commerce, embraces a vast field, containing not only many, but exceedingly various subjects, quite unlike in their nature; some imperatively demanding a single uniform rule, operating equally on the commerce of the United States in every port; and some, like the subject now in question, as imperatively demanding that diversity, which alone can meet the local necessities of navigation.
>
> Either absolutely to affirm, or deny that the nature of [the commerce] power requires exclusive legislation by Congress, is to lose sight of the nature of the subjects of this power, and to assert concerning all of them, what is really applicable but to a part.

> Whatever subjects of this power are in their nature national, or admit only of one uniform system, or plan of regulation, may justly be said to be of such a nature as to require exclusive legislation by Congress. That this cannot be affirmed of laws for the regulation of pilots and pilotage is plain.

The Court then discussed the need for local supervision of harbor and river pilots, resulting from the vagaries of navigation in each locale. The federal statute deferring to the states on this subject became relevant as expressing the intent of Congress that pilotage was a subject allowing local control rather than requiring national uniformity.

Consider the analysis of *Cooley* contained in Martin Redish & Shane Nugent, *The Dormant Commerce Clause and the Constitutional Balance of Federalism,* 1987 DUKE L.J. 569, 577–79:

> [Justice Curtis'] approach simultaneously avoided confrontation with states rights advocates, yet reserved for the Court the ability to invalidate objectionable state legislation under a theory of *partial* exclusivity. Thus was born the "*Cooley* Rule of Selective Exclusiveness." Under the *Cooley* rule, only those state regulations affecting a specific category of interstate commerce — that which by its very nature requires exclusive federal regulation — are invalid by direct application of the commerce clause.

[C] SOURCES AND LEGITIMACY OF THE DORMANT COMMERCE CLAUSE

Cooley established that Article I's grant of power to Congress to regulate interstate commerce does not preclude all state regulation that affects such commerce. If Congress has acted pursuant to its commerce power, conflicting state legislation will of course fall because of the principle of federal supremacy. *Cooley* indicates, however, that under certain circumstances, state regulation of interstate commerce will fail, even in the absence of conflicting federal legislation. How to determine exactly what those circumstances are is a problem that pervades most of this chapter. An initial question, however, concerns the constitutional source and legitimacy for the invalidation of state legislation in the absence of conflicting federal legislation.

No provision of the Constitution explicitly prohibits states from burdening interstate commerce, although states are prohibited by Article I, § 10 from imposing tariffs and duties without control by Congress, and there is express protection of individuals against interstate discrimination in the privileges and immunities clause of Article IV, § 2. The constitutional basis for the invalidity of state legislation primarily stems from the negative implications of Article I's grant of the commerce power to Congress. The grant to Congress of the power to regulate interstate commerce is deemed to invalidate state legislation burdening interstate commerce. Traditionally, this constitutional dictate is referred to as the "dormant commerce clause," though that label has been criticized as misleading. *See* Julian Eule, *Laying the Dormant Commerce Clause to Rest,* 91 YALE L.J. 425 n.1 (1982).

As a matter of basic constitutional interpretation, does it make sense to infer a constitutional limitation on state authority from an affirmative grant of power to the federal government, even though the federal government has not exercised that power? Consider the following argument: When the Framers wished to impose direct limits on state authority, they did so explicitly in the body of the Constitution, as in the Privileges and Immunities Clause. Thus, if the Framers had intended to impose limitations on the states power to regulate interstate commerce beyond those imposed by Congress, they would have done so.

> [T]he dormant commerce clause is invalid because it reverses the political inertia established by the Constitution. Under the dormant commerce clause, the federal judiciary — the organ of the federal government most insulated from state influence and the organ traditionally feared most by the states — makes the initial legislative judgment whether state regulation of interstate commerce is reasonable. If the Court strikes down economic regulations, the states must somehow force Congress to reverse the decision of the Court through legislation — a process made difficult because of Congress's inherent political inertia. [H]istorical and textual analyses lead [to the conclusion] that this is clearly not the plan of the Constitution. State power to regulate interstate commerce was designed to be determined solely by the political judgment of Congress, where the states retain enough political power to *block* congressional action, since Congress's inertia is not against them.

Redish & Nugent, 1987 Duke L.J. at 573.

On the other hand, Professor Regan has argued that the dormant Commerce Clause is grounded in the Framers' intent in the drafting of the commerce power:

> There is much evidence that the main point of [the] grant [of power over interstate commerce] was not to empower Congress, but rather to disable the states from regulating commerce among themselves. Giving Congress the power to regulate internal commerce was one way of denying states that power, under the view that [the] granted regulatory powers were exclusive.

Donald Regan, *The Supreme Court and State Protectionism: Making Sense of the Dormant Commerce Clause,* 84 Mich. L. Rev. 1091, 1125 (1986).

In evaluating these conflicting arguments, it might be helpful to consider the reasons why the Supreme Court has recognized negative implications flowing from the dormant Commerce Clause. In other words, what economic, political, or social purposes does the dormant Commerce Clause serve? The following possibilities are the most frequently mentioned:

a. To preserve congressional authority over interstate commerce.

b. To preserve the principle of free trade, without governmental regulation or interference.

c. To avoid the "Balkanization" of the states — in other words, to preserve the Union by preventing the development of interstate friction that would derive from one state's imposition of burdens on commerce affecting other states.

d. To preserve the democratic process by preventing the legislature of one state from imposing special burdens on citizens of other states, who have no say in the makeup of that legislature.

Are any or all of these rationales valid? Are any or all of them of such great practical importance that the Supreme Court can properly assume that the Framers intended their protection, despite the absence of an explicit constitutional directive?

§ 3.02 THE MODERN FOCUS

Following *Cooley,* the Court struggled with the task of formulating standards to reconcile the national and local interests involved. The most important conceptual distinction the Court has drawn in developing these standards is the one between state regulations of interstate commerce that evenhandedly affect both in-state and out-of-state residents, and those that discriminate against out-of-staters. As will be seen in the next section, the latter type of regulation will be upheld relatively rarely. Regulations of the former variety, on the other hand, present more complex issues, involving a delicate balancing of competing interests. The first section below deals with discriminatory state regulations, and the section after that examines the legitimacy of evenhanded state regulation of interstate commerce.

[A] DISCRIMINATION: PURPOSE, MEANS, EFFECTS

In *South Carolina State Hwy. Dep't v. Barnwell Bros.,* p. 250, Justice Stone stated:

> The commerce clause, by its own force, prohibits discrimination against interstate commerce, whatever its form or method, and the decisions of this Court have recognized that there is scope for its like operation when state legislation nominally of local concern is in point of fact aimed at interstate commerce, or by its necessary operation is a means of gaining a local benefit by throwing the attendant burdens on those without the state. It was to end these practices that the commerce clause was adopted.

There has been general agreement in the Court that a state law that "discriminates" against interstate commerce usually is invalid. The rationale for such treatment is generally based on the historical purpose of the Commerce Clause to prevent interstate discrimination. But Justice Stone in *Barnwell* also suggested a justification based in political theory:

> Underlying the stated rule has been the thought, often expressed in judicial opinions, that when the regulation is of such a character that its burden falls principally upon those without the state, legislative

> action is not likely to be subjected to those political restraints which are normally exerted on legislation where it affects adversely some interests within the state.

Some commentators assert that the most persuasive, if any, justification for judicial enforcement of dormant commerce clause limits on the states is "the process-oriented protection of representational government." Julian Eule, *Laying the Dormant Commerce Clause to Rest*, 92 YALE L.J. 425, 443 (1982).

CITY OF PHILADELPHIA v. NEW JERSEY

437 U.S. 617, 98 S. Ct. 2531, 57 L. Ed. 2d 475 (1978)

[A New Jersey statute prohibited, with minor exceptions, the importation of solid or liquid waste from outside the state. The law was challenged by private operators of landfills in New Jersey and by cities in other states which had entered into contracts with the operators for waste disposal.

[Initially, the Court held that waste products, even if deemed valueless, constituted the movement of commerce within the meaning of the commerce clause. "All objects of interstate trade merit Commerce Clause protection; none is excluded by definition at the outset."]

MR. JUSTICE STEWART delivered the opinion of the Court.

The opinions of the Court through the years have reflected an alertness to the evils of "economic isolation" and protectionism, while at the same time recognizing that incidental burdens on interstate commerce may be unavoidable when a State legislates to safeguard the health and safety of its people. Thus, where simple economic protectionism is effected by state legislation, a virtually *per se* rule of invalidity has been erected. *See, e.g., Hood & Sons v. DuMond* [336 U.S. 525 (1949)]; *Baldwin v. G. A. F. Seelig* [p. 231]. The clearest example of such legislation is a law that overtly blocks the flow of interstate commerce at a State's borders. But where other legislative objectives are credibly advanced and there is no patent discrimination against interstate trade, the Court has adopted a much more flexible approach, the general contours of which were outlined in *Pike v. Bruce Church, Inc.* The crucial inquiry, must be directed to determining whether ch. 363 is basically a protectionist measure, or whether it can fairly be viewed as a law directed to legitimate local concerns, with effects upon interstate commerce that are only incidental.

The purpose of ch. 363 is set out in the statute itself as follows:

> The Legislature finds and determines that the volume of solid and liquid waste continues to rapidly increase, that the treatment and disposal of these wastes continues to pose an even greater threat to the quality of the environment of New Jersey, that the available and appropriate land fill sites within the State are being diminished, that the environment continues to be threatened by the treatment and disposal of waste which originated or was collected outside the State, and that the public health, safety and welfare require that the treatment and disposal within this State of all wastes generated outside of the State be prohibited.

The New Jersey Supreme Court accepted this statement of the state legislature's purpose. The state court additionally found that New Jersey's existing landfill sites will be exhausted within a few years; that to go on using these sites or to develop new ones will take a heavy environmental toll, both from pollution and from loss of scarce open lands; that new techniques to divert waste from landfills to other methods of disposal and resource recovery processes are under development, but that these changes will require time; and finally, that the extension of the lifespan of existing landfills, resulting from the exclusion of out-of-state waste, may be of crucial importance in preventing further virgin wetlands or other undeveloped lands from being devoted to landfill purposes. Based on these findings, the court concluded that ch. 363 was designed to protect not the State's economy, but its environment, and that its substantial benefits outweigh its "slight" burden on interstate commerce.

The appellants strenuously contend that ch. 363, "while outwardly cloaked 'in the currently fashionable garb of environmental protection,' is actually no more than a legislative effort to suppress competition and stabilize the cost of solid waste disposal for New Jersey residents." They cite passages of legislative history suggesting that the problem addressed by ch. 363 is primarily financial: Stemming the flow of out-of-state waste into certain landfill sites will extend their lives, thus delaying the day when New Jersey cities must transport their waste to more distant and expensive sites.

This dispute about ultimate legislative purpose need not be resolved, because its resolution would not be relevant to the constitutional issue to be decided in this case. Contrary to the evident assumption of the state court and the parties, the evil of protectionism can reside in legislative means as well as legislative ends. Thus, it does not matter whether the ultimate aim of ch. 363 is to reduce the waste disposal costs of New Jersey residents or to save remaining open lands from pollution, for we assume New Jersey has every right to protect its residents pocketbooks as well as their environment. And it may be assumed as well that New Jersey may pursue those ends by slowing the flow of *all* waste into the State's remaining landfills, even though interstate commerce may incidentally be affected. But whatever New Jersey's ultimate purpose, it may not be accomplished by discriminating against articles of commerce coming from outside the State unless there is some reason, apart from their origin, to treat them differently. Both on its face and in its plain effect, ch. 363 violates this principle of nondiscrimination.

The Court has consistently found parochial legislation of this kind to be constitutionally invalid, whether the ultimate aim of the legislation was to assure a steady supply of milk by erecting barriers to allegedly ruinous outside competition, *Baldwin v. G. A. F. Seelig,* or to create jobs by keeping industry within the State, *Foster Packing Co. v. Haydel*, or to preserve the State's financial resources from depletion by fencing out indigent immigrants, *Edwards v. California*. In each of these cases, a presumably legitimate goal was sought to be achieved by the illegitimate means of isolating the State from the national economy.

Also relevant here are the Court's decisions holding that a State may not accord its own inhabitants a preferred right of access over consumers in other

States to natural resources located within its borders. *Oklahoma v. Kansas Natural Gas Co.; Pennsylvania v. West Virginia.* These cases stand for the basic principle that a "State is without power to prevent privately owned articles of trade from being shipped and sold in interstate commerce on the ground that they are required to satisfy local demands or because they are needed by the people of the State." *Foster Packing Co. v. Haydel.* [6]

The New Jersey law at issue in this case falls squarely within the area that the Commerce Clause puts off-limits to state regulation. On its face, it imposes on out-of-state commercial interests the full burden of conserving the State's remaining landfill space. It is true that in our previous cases the scarce natural resource was itself the article of commerce, whereas here the scarce resource and the article of commerce are distinct. But that difference is without consequence. In both instances, the State has overtly moved to slow or freeze the flow of commerce for protectionist reasons. It does not matter that the State has shut the article of commerce inside the State in one case and outside the State in the other. What is crucial is the attempt by one State to isolate itself from a problem common to many by erecting a barrier against the movement of interstate trade.

It is true that certain quarantine laws have not been considered forbidden protectionist measures, even though they were directed against out-of-state commerce. But those quarantine laws banned the importation of articles such as diseased livestock that required destruction as soon as possible because their very movement risked contagion and other evils. Those laws thus did not discriminate against interstate commerce as such, but simply prevented traffic in noxious articles, whatever their origin.

The New Jersey statute is not such a quarantine law. There has been no claim here that the very movement of waste into or through New Jersey endangers health, or that waste must be disposed of as soon and as close to its point of generation as possible. The harms caused by waste are said to arise after its disposal in landfill sites, and at that point, as New Jersey concedes, there is no basis to distinguish out-of-state waste from domestic waste. If one is inherently harmful, so is the other. Yet New Jersey has banned the former while leaving its landfill sites open to the latter. The New Jersey law blocks the importation of waste in an obvious effort to saddle those outside the State with the entire burden of slowing the flow of refuse into New Jersey's remaining landfill sites. That legislative effort is clearly impermissible under the Commerce Clause of the Constitution.

Today, cities in Pennsylvania and New York find it expedient or necessary to send their waste into New Jersey for disposal, and New Jersey claims the right to close its borders to such traffic. Tomorrow, cities in New Jersey may find it expedient or necessary to send their waste into Pennsylvania or New York for disposal, and those States might then claim the right to close their borders. The Commerce Clause will protect New Jersey in the future, just as it protects her neighbors now, from efforts by one State to isolate itself in the stream of interstate commerce from a problem shared by all.

[6] We express no opinion about New Jersey's power, consistent with the Commerce Clause, to restrict to state residents access to state-owned resources, or New Jersey's power to spend state funds solely on behalf of state residents and businesses.

MR. JUSTICE REHNQUIST, with whom CHIEF JUSTICE BURGER joins, dissenting.

The question presented in this case is whether New Jersey must also continue to receive and dispose of solid waste from neighboring States, even though these will inexorably increase the health problems discussed above. The Court answers this question in the affirmative. New Jersey must either prohibit *all* landfill operations, leaving itself to cast about for a presently nonexistent solution to the serious problem of disposing of the waste generated within its own borders, or it must accept waste from every portion of the United States, thereby multiplying the health and safety problems which would result if it dealt only with such wastes generated within the State. Because past precedents establish that the Commerce Clause does not present appellees with such a Hobson's choice, I dissent.

The Court recognizes that States can prohibit the importation of items "which, on account of their existing condition, would bring in and spread disease, pestilence, and death, such as rags or other substances infected with the germs of yellow fever or the virus of smallpox, or cattle or meat or other provisions that are diseased or decayed or otherwise, from their condition and quality, unfit for human use or consumption." As the Court points out, "such quarantine laws have not been considered forbidden protectionist measures, *even though they were directed against out-of-state commerce.*"

Similarly, New Jersey should be free under our past precedents to prohibit the importation of solid waste because of the health and safety problems that such waste poses to its citizens. The fact that New Jersey continues to, and indeed must continue to, dispose of its own solid waste does not mean that New Jersey may not prohibit the importation of even more solid waste into the State. I simply see no way to distinguish solid waste, on the record of this case, from germ-infected rags, diseased meat, and other noxious items.

NOTES

1. *Economic protectionism*. Is *City of Philadelphia* a proper case for application of the dormant Commerce Clause concept? Note that the Court relies on *Baldwin v. G.A.F. Seelig, Inc.*, 294 U.S. 511 (1935), which held unconstitutional a New York statute that had established a system of minimum milk prices to be paid by dealers to producers and including a provision prohibiting sales of milk bought out-of-state at a price lower than the lawful price set for milk produced in-state. A New York City milk dealer who bought milk in Vermont at a below-minimum price and transported it to New York for sale brought suit in federal court challenging the law. In invalidating the law, Justice Cardozo, for the Court, reasoned:

> Such a power, if exerted, will set a barrier to traffic between one state and another as effective as if customs duties, equal to the price differential, had been laid upon the thing transported. Nice distinctions have been made at times between direct and indirect burdens. They are irrelevant when the avowed purpose of the obstruction, as well as its necessary tendency, is to suppress or mitigate the consequences of competition between the states. Such an obstruction is direct by the very terms of the hypothesis.

Justice Cardozo rejected the state's argument that "the economic motive is secondary and subordinate" to the goal of maintaining "a regular and adequate supply of pure and wholesome milk, the supply being put in jeopardy when the farmers of the state are unable to earn a living income."

> This would be to eat up the rule under the guise of an exception. Economic welfare is always related to health, for there can be no health if men are starving. Let such an exception be admitted, and all that a state will have to do in times of stress and strain is to say that its farmers and merchants and workmen must be protected against competition from without, lest they go upon the poor relief lists or perish altogether.

Explaining his view of the philosophy underlying the dormant Commerce Clause, Cardozo stated: "[The Constitution] was framed upon the theory that the peoples of the several states must sink or swim together, and that in the long run prosperity and salvation are in union and not division."

2. *Distinguishing between discrimination and protectionism*. To what extent are discrimination and protectionism identical? According to one commentator, courts usually blur the two concepts. *See* Catherine Gage O'Grady, *Targeting State Protectionism Instead of Interstate Discrimination Under the Dormant Commerce Clause,* 34 San Diego L. Rev. 571 (1997). Does *Baldwin* show that the two are not necessarily identical? Professor O'Grady argues that "economic protectionism and interstate discrimination are not synonyms and should not be treated as such." What is the difference? Which of the two is closer to the central concern underlying the dormant Commerce Clause? For the argument that "the primary concern in evaluating local regulations ought to be the long-recognized prohibition against resident economic protectionism," because "[t]he intentional, self-serving nature of a typical protectionist measure is likely to invoke anxiety in other states and invite hostile, retaliatory measures," *see* O'Grady, *supra*.

3. *Wildlife resources:* *Hughes v. Oklahoma*, 441 U.S. 322 (1979). The Supreme Court, per Justice Brennan, overruled a nineteenth-century precedent, *Geer v. Connecticut*, 161 U.S. 519 (1896), which had rejected a Commerce Clause challenge to a statute prohibiting the out-of-state transportation of game birds that had been killed within the state. *Geer* had reasoned that wildlife was owned in common by all the people of the state to the point that the state, as representative of its citizens, had virtually complete control over the resource: "The common ownership imports the right to keep the property if the sovereign so chooses, always within its jurisdiction for every purpose."

Geer was cited by the state of Oklahoma in support of its statute prohibiting the out-of-state transportation or shipment of minnows for sale which were seined or procured within the waters of the state. In reversing Hughes' conviction under the statute, the Supreme Court concluded that cases subsequent to *Geer* had undermined its premise that the common ownership thesis meant that no interstate commerce in wildlife was in fact involved. "We now conclude that challenges under the Commerce Clause to state regulations of wild animals should be considered according to the same general rule applied to state regulations of other natural resources, and therefore expressly overrule *Geer.*"

The Court concluded that the Oklahoma statute "on its face discriminates against interstate commerce." While this may often in itself be fatal, "[a]t a minimum such facial discrimination invokes the strictest scrutiny of any purported legitimate local purpose and of the absence of non-discriminatory alternatives."

Oklahoma claimed that the statute served the state's interest in maintaining the ecological balance in state waters by avoiding the removal of inordinate numbers of minnows. While the Court accepted this as a legitimate local purpose, the means selected were the most discriminatory alternative available. "Far from choosing the least discriminatory alternative, Oklahoma has chosen to 'conserve' its minnows in the way that most overtly discriminates against interstate commerce. The State places no limits on the number of minnows that can be taken by licensed minnow dealers; nor does it limit in any way how these minnows may be disposed of within the State. Yet it forbids the transportation of any commercially significant number of natural minnows out of the State for sale." The statute therefore was held to violate the Commerce Clause.

Justice Rehnquist, joined by Chief Justice Burger, dissented on the basis that the state has a substantial interest in preserving and regulating its natural resources for the benefit of its citizens.

4. *The quarantine precedents*. Justice Rehnquist, dissenting in *City of Philadelphia,* relied heavily on the precedent of the quarantine cases. In these cases, state regulations excluding commerce from other states were justified as necessary in order to avoid health and safety hazards to the public: "States have power to provide by law, suitable measures to prevent the introduction into the States of Articles of Trade, which on account of their existing condition, would bring in and spread disease, pestilence and death." *Baldwin v. Chicago & Nw. Ry.*, 125 U.S. 465, 489 (1888). As long as there is some inspection mechanism to assure that the incoming commerce is unsafe, the state is permitted to close its doors to the goods.

Justice Stewart sought to distinguish the quarantine cases. Consider the claim "[t]hat the Court's distinction is unconvincing since the purpose of the quarantine laws was to prevent the dangers that would arise after the item arrived in the state and was mingled with similar domestic items or was consumed by the people." *The Supreme Court, 1977 Term,* 92 Harv. L. Rev. 57, 62 n.39 (1978). Justice Rehnquist asserts that Stewart's distinction ignores the basic "fact of life" that New Jersey must put its garbage somewhere, while the transport of interstate waste through the state is just as potentially harmful as the introduction of diseased articles. It has been suggested that the Court's concern with the quarantine case precedent was the reason that a *per se* rule of invalidity was not adopted in *City of Philadelphia. Id.* Is a quarantine law discriminatory? Would it violate the Commerce Clause under the constitutional standards of *City of Philadelphia* and *Hughes*?

5. *Importing environmental problems*. In an unusual instance of the Court's upholding state discrimination against interstate commerce, *Maine* *v. Taylor*, 471 U.S. 131 (1986), rejected a challenge to a Maine criminal statute banning the importation of live baitfish from out of state. Justice Blackmun, for the Court, acknowledged that the Maine ban was discriminatory on its face and therefore called for the heightened scrutiny requirements of *Hughes v. Oklahoma*. "The statute must serve a legitimate local purpose and the purpose must be one that cannot be served as well by available non-discriminatory means."

Three prosecution experts had testified on the threat to Maine's fisheries posed by imported live baitfish. Their testimony indicated that Maine's wild fish would be at risk by parasites not common to domestic fisheries. Further, non-native species accidentally shipped with the baitfish could disturb the natural habitat of native fish and cause environmental disruption. In addition, they testified there was no satisfactory way to test shipments for parasites or for non-native species. Justice Blackmun concluded:

> The Commerce Clause significantly limits the ability of States and localities to regulate or otherwise burden the flow of interstate commerce, but it does not elevate free trade above all other values. As long as a State does not needlessly obstruct interstate trade or attempt to "place itself in a position of economic isolation," *Baldwin v. G.A.F. Seelig, Inc.*, it retains broad regulatory authority to protect the health and safety of its citizens and the integrity of its natural resources. The evidence in this case amply supports the District Court's findings that Maine's ban on the importation of live baitfish serves legitimate local purposes that could not adequately be served by available nondiscriminatory alternatives. This is not a case of arbitrary discrimination against interstate commerce; the record suggests that Maine has legitimate reasons, "apart from their origin, to treat (out-of-state baitfish) differently." *Philadelphia v. New Jersey*. The judgment of the Court of Appeals setting aside appellee's conviction is therefore reversed.

Dissenting in this "fishy case," Justice Stevens pointed out that Maine was the only state in the Union that banned out-of-state shipments of baitfish even though the type of fish banned thrives in Maine, "and, perhaps, not coincidentally, [is] the subject of a flourishing domestic industry." Justice Stevens found blatant discrimination requiring "rigorous justification," which did not exist. He would not give the benefit of the doubt to Maine regarding the uncertainty about possible ecological effects. "Ambiguity about dangers and alternatives should actually defeat rather than sustain the discriminatory measure. If Maine wishes to rely on its interest in ecological preservation, it must show that interest and the infeasibility of other alternatives with far greater specificity."

6. *Waste disposal restrictions*. In *Chemical Waste Management, Inc. v. Hunt*, 504 U.S. 334 (1992), the Supreme Court held invalid under the Commerce Clause an Alabama statute that imposed a special fee on out-of-state hazardous wastes disposed of inside the state. Relying on *Philadelphia v. New Jersey*, Justice White, speaking for the Court, stated: "No state may attempt to isolate itself from a problem common to the several States by raising barriers to the free flow of interstate trade." The Court noted that "[o]nce a state tax is found to discriminate against out-of-state commerce, it is typically struck down without further inquiry." The Court rejected the state's argument "that the additional fee imposed on out-of-state hazardous waste serves legitimate local purposes related to its citizens' health and safety." While acknowledging the possible legitimacy of the local interests, the Court noted that "only rhetoric, and not explanation, emerges as to why Alabama targets *only* interstate hazardous waste to meet these goals." It added that "[l]ess discriminatory alternatives are available to alleviate [the] concern" over the volume of waste entering the in-state facility.

In dissent, Chief Justice Rehnquist argued: "[T]he Court continues to err by its failure to recognize that waste — in this case admittedly *hazardous* waste — presents risks to the public health and environment that a State may legitimately wish to avoid, and that the State may pursue such an objective by means less Draconian than an outright ban."

Decided the same day was *Fort Gratiot Sanitary Landfill, Inc. v. Michigan Department of Natural Resources*, 504 U.S. 353 (1992). There the Court held unconstitutional the Waste Import Restrictions of Michigan's Solid Waste Management Act, which provided that solid waste generated in another county, state, or country cannot be accepted for disposal unless explicitly authorized in the receiving county's 20-year plan for providing for disposal of solid waste, as required by the Act. Justice Stevens, speaking for the Court, relied on *Philadelphia v. New Jersey* in holding the regulations to be unconstitutionally protectionist. The Court rejected the argument that the regulations were constitutional "because they treat waste from other Michigan counties no differently than waste from other States," reasoning that "a State (or one of its political subdivisions) may not avoid the strictures of the Commerce Clause by curtailing the movement of articles of commerce through subdivisions of the State, rather than through the State itself." Justice Stevens also rejected the argument that "the fact that the Michigan statute allows individual counties to accept solid waste from out of state qualif[ies] its discriminatory character." This fact, said the Court, "merely reduced the scope of the discrimination; for all categories of waste not excepted by the regulations, the discriminatory ban remained in place."

Chief Justice Rehnquist, joined by Justice Blackmun, dissented: "The legislation challenged today is simply one part of a broad package that includes a number of features. The Michigan legislation is thus quite unlike the simple outright ban that we confronted in *Philadelphia*." Arguing from principles of federalism, the Chief Justice reasoned that "[t]he Court today penalizes the State of Michigan for what to all appearances are its good-faith efforts, in turn encouraging each State to ignore the waste problem in the hope that another will pick up the slack."

In *C & A Carbone, Inc. v. Clarkstown*, 511 U.S. 383 (1994), the Court invalidated a Clarkstown, New York flow control ordinance which required that all solid waste be processed at a designated transfer station before leaving the municipality. Justice Kennedy, for the Court, described the processing function of the transfer station: "The station would receive bulk solid waste and separate recyclable from nonrecyclable items. Recyclable waste would be baled for shipment to a recycling facility; nonrecyclable waste to a suitable landfill or incinerator."

A local contractor constructed the facility and agreed to operate it for five years. At the end of the five-year period, the agreement called for the town to buy the facility for one dollar. During the period in which the facility was to be operated by the private contractor, the town guaranteed a minimum waste flow of 120,000 tons per year. The town authorized the contractor to charge the hauler a charge or tipping fee of $81 per ton. This fee "exceeded the disposal cost of unsorted solid waste on the private market." The town, therefore, concerned to assure the requisite flow of waste, promulgated a flow control ordinance which required "all nonhazardous solid waste within the town to be deposited at the [new] transfer station." The ordinance contained criminal sanctions for noncompliance.

C & A Carbone, who operated a recycling center in the town, challenged the flow control ordinance. At its recycling center Carbone received, sorted, and baled solid waste which it then shipped to other processing facilities. The Clarkstown flow control ordinance had a direct impact on the hauler since it required Carbone to bring the nonrecyclable residue from that waste to the town favored station. Carbone could not ship the nonrecyclable waste itself and was required to pay a tipping fee on trash that it had already sorted.

Despite the town's insistence that its ordinance was in effect only a quarantine since it only applied to waste within the town, the Court held that the flow control ordinance regulated interstate commerce:

> While the immediate effect of the ordinance is to direct local transport of solid waste to a designated site within the local jurisdiction, its economic effects are interstate in reach. The Carbone facility in Clarkstown receives and processes waste from places other than Clarkstown, including from out of state. By requiring Carbone to send the nonrecyclable portion of this waste to the [town favored] transfer station at an additional cost, the flow control ordinance drives up the cost for out-of-state interests to dispose of their solid waste. Furthermore, even as to waste originant in Clarkstown, the ordinance prevents everyone except the favored local operator from performing the initial processing step. The ordinance thus deprives out-of-state businesses of access to a local market.

Justice Souter, joined by the Chief Justice and Justice Blackmun, dissenting, contended that the Clarkstown ordinance does not extend a benefit to local private actors "but instead directly aids the government in satisfying a traditional governmental responsibility." The ordinance, therefore, did not discriminate against interstate commerce. Furthermore, there were "both analytical and practical differences" between this case and previous local processing cases:

> First, the terms of Clarkstown's ordinance favor a single processor, not the class of all such businesses located in Clarkstown. Second, the one proprietor so favored is essentially an agent of the municipal government, which (unlike Carbone or other private trash processors)

> must endure the removal of waste according to acceptable standards of public health. Any discrimination worked by [the ordinance] thus fails to produce the sort of entrepreneurial favoritism we have previously defined and condemned as protectionist.

As a matter of social and political theory, what are the relevant advantages and disadvantages of restricting state power to deal with waste management in favor of federal control? See Paul S. Weiland, Comment, *Federal and State Preemption of Environmental Law: A Critical Analysis,* 24 HARV. ENVTL. L. REV. 237, 239 (2000), listing as an advantage of federal control the fact that "centralization can overcome the problems associated with interjurisdictional negative externalities," which "exists when an agent does not bear all of the costs associated with her action. For example, if city A is located on a river upstream from city B and city A releases effluent into the river, this action may result in no adverse consequences for city A although it does have adverse consequences for city B. At least some of the costs associated with city A's action are externalized, that is, they are not borne by city A but are imposed on city B." Of what relevance was this concern to the decision in *City of Philadelphia*? The same commentator also notes, however, that "decentralization may be an appropriate response to the fact that environmental problems often tend to be place-specific." He further notes that both flexibility and innovation are more likely to occur in a decentralized regulatory system.

HUNT v. WASHINGTON STATE APPLE ADVERTISING COMMISSION

432 U.S. 333, 97 S. Ct. 2434, 53 L. Ed. 2d 383 (1977)

CHIEF JUSTICE BURGER delivered the opinion of the Court.

In 1973, North Carolina enacted a statute which required, *inter alia,* all closed containers of apples sold, offered for sale, or shipped into the State to bear "no grade other than the applicable U.S. grade or standard." In an action brought by the Washington State Apple Advertising Commission, a three-judge Federal District Court invalidated the statute insofar as it prohibited the display of Washington State apple grades on the ground that it unconstitutionally discriminated against interstate commerce.

Washington State is the Nation's largest producer of apples, its crops accounting for approximately 30% of all apples grown domestically and nearly half of all apples shipped in closed containers in interstate commerce. As might be expected, the production and sale of apples on this scale is a multimillion dollar enterprise which plays a significant role in Washington's economy. Because of the importance of the apple industry to the State, its legislature has undertaken to protect and enhance the reputation of Washington apples by establishing a stringent, mandatory inspection program, administered by the State's Department of Agriculture, which requires all apples shipped in interstate commerce to be tested under strict quality standards and graded accordingly. In all cases, the Washington State grades, which have gained substantial acceptance in the trade, are the equivalent of, or superior to, the comparable grades and standards adopted by the United States

Department of Agriculture (USDA). Compliance with the Washington inspection scheme costs the State's growers approximately $1 million each year.

In addition to its obvious consequence, prohibiting the display of Washington State apple grades on containers of apples shipped into North Carolina, the [statute] presented the Washington apple industry with a marketing problem of potentially nationwide significance. Washington apple growers annually ship in commerce approximately 40 million closed containers of apples, nearly 500,000 of which eventually find their way into North Carolina, stamped with the applicable Washington State variety and grade. [C]ompliance with North Carolina's unique regulation would have required Washington growers to obliterate the printed labels on containers shipped to North Carolina, thus giving their product a damaged appearance. Alternatively, they could have changed their marketing practices to accommodate the needs of the North Carolina market, *i.e.*, repack apples to be shipped to North Carolina in containers bearing only the USDA grade, and/or store the estimated portion of the harvest destined for that market in such special containers. As a last resort, they could discontinue the use of the preprinted containers entirely. None of these costly and less efficient options was very attractive to the industry. Moreover, in the event a number of other States followed North Carolina's lead, the resultant inability to display the Washington grades could force the Washington growers to abandon the State's expensive inspection and grading system which their customers had come to know and rely on over the 60-odd years of its existence.

Appellants do not really contest the District Court's determination that the challenged statute burdened the Washington apple industry by increasing its costs of doing business in the North Carolina market and causing it to lose accounts there. Rather, they maintain that any such burdens on the interstate sale of Washington apples were far outweighed by the local benefits flowing from what they contend was a valid exercise of North Carolina's inherent police powers designed to protect its citizenry from fraud and deception in the marketing of apples.

Prior to the statute's enactment, appellants point out, apples from 13 different States were shipped into North Carolina for sale. Seven of those States, including the State of Washington, had their own grading systems which, while differing in their standards, used similar descriptive labels (e.g., fancy, extra fancy, etc.). This multiplicity of inconsistent state grades, as the District Court itself found, posed dangers of deception and confusion not only in the North Carolina market, but in the Nation as a whole. The North Carolina statute, appellants claim, was enacted to eliminate this source of deception and confusion by replacing the numerous state grades with a single uniform standard. Moreover, it is contended that North Carolina sought to accomplish this goal of uniformity in an evenhanded manner as evidenced by the fact that its statute applies to all apples sold in closed containers in the State without regard to their point of origin. Nonetheless, appellants argue that the District Court gave "scant attention" to the obvious benefits flowing from the challenged legislation and to the long line of decisions from this Court holding that the States possess "broad powers" to protect local purchasers from fraud and deception in the marketing of foodstuffs. *E.g., Florida Lime & Avocado Growers, Inc. v. Paul*, 373 U.S. 132 (1963).

[H]owever, a finding that state legislation furthers matters of legitimate local concern, even in the health and consumer protection areas, does not end the inquiry. Such a view, we have noted, "would mean that the Commerce Clause of itself imposes no limitations on state action save for the rare instance where a state artlessly discloses an avowed purpose to discriminate against interstate goods." *Dean Milk Co. v. Madison.* Rather, when such state legislation comes into conflict with the Commerce Clause's overriding requirement of a national "common market," we are confronted with the task of effecting an accommodation of the competing national and local interests. *Pike v. Bruce Church, Inc.* We turn to that task.

[T]he challenged statute has the practical effect of not only burdening interstate sales of Washington apples, but also discriminating against them. This discrimination takes various forms. The first, and most obvious, is the statute's consequence of raising the costs of doing business in the North Carolina market for Washington apple growers and dealers, while leaving those of their North Carolina counterparts unaffected. [T]his disparate effect results from the fact that North Carolina apple producers, unlike their Washington competitors, were not forced to alter their marketing practices in order to comply with the statute. They were still free to market their wares under the USDA grade or none at all as they had done prior to the statute's enactment. Obviously, the increased costs imposed by the statute would tend to shield the local apple industry from the competition of Washington apple growers and dealers who are already at a competitive disadvantage because of their great distance from the North Carolina market.

Second, the statute has the effect of stripping away from the Washington apple industry the competitive and economic advantages it has earned for itself through its expensive inspection and grading system. The record demonstrates that the Washington apple-grading system has gained nationwide acceptance in the apple trade. Once again, the statute had no similar impact on the North Carolina apple industry and thus operated to its benefit.

Third, by prohibiting Washington growers and dealers from marketing apples under their State's grades, the statute has a leveling effect which insidiously operates to the advantage of local apple producers. [T]he Washington State grades are equal or superior to the USDA grades in all corresponding categories. Hence, with free market forces at work, Washington sellers would normally enjoy a distinct market advantage vis-a-vis local producers in those categories where the Washington grade is superior. However, because of the statute's operation, Washington apples which would otherwise qualify for and be sold under the superior Washington grades will now have to be marketed under their inferior USDA counterparts. Such "downgrading" offers the North Carolina apple industry the very sort of protection against competing out-of-state products that the Commerce Clause was designed to prohibit.

Despite the statute's facial neutrality, the Commission suggests that its discriminatory impact on interstate commerce was not an unintended byproduct and there are some indications in the record to that effect. However, we need not ascribe an economic protection motive to the North Carolina Legislature to resolve this case; we conclude that the challenged statute cannot stand insofar as it prohibits the display of Washington State grades even if enacted for the declared purpose of protecting consumers from deception and fraud in the marketplace.

When discrimination against commerce of the type we have found is demonstrated, the burden falls on the State to justify it both in terms of the local benefits flowing from the statute and the unavailability of nondiscriminatory alternatives adequate to preserve the local interests at stake. *Dean Milk Co. v. Madison.* North Carolina has failed to sustain that burden on both scores.

The several States unquestionably possess a substantial interest in protecting their citizens from confusion and deception in the marketing of foodstuffs, but the challenged statute does remarkably little to further that laudable goal at least with respect to Washington apples and grades. The statute, as already noted, permits the marketing of closed containers of apples under *no* grades at all. Such a result can hardly be thought to eliminate the problems of deception and confusion created by the multiplicity of differing state grades; indeed, it magnifies them by depriving purchasers of all information concerning the quality of the contents of closed apple containers. Moreover, although the statute is ostensibly a consumer protection measure, it directs its primary efforts, not at the consuming public at large, but at apple wholesalers and brokers who are the principal purchasers of closed containers of apples. And those individuals are presumably the most knowledgeable individuals in this area. Since the statute does nothing at all to purify the flow of information at the retail level, it does little to protect consumers against the problems it was designed to eliminate. Finally, we note that any potential for confusion and deception created by the Washington grades was not of the type that led to the statute's enactment. Since Washington grades are in all cases equal or superior to their USDA counterparts, they could only "deceive" or "confuse" a consumer to his benefit, hardly a harmful result.

In addition, it appears that nondiscriminatory alternatives to the outright ban of Washington State grades are readily available. For example, North Carolina could effectuate its goal by permitting out-of-state growers to utilize state grades only if they also marked their shipments with the applicable USDA label. In that case, the USDA grade would serve as a benchmark against which the consumer could evaluate the quality of the various state grades.

JUSTICE REHNQUIST took no part in the consideration or decision of the case.

NOTES

1. *Discrimination and protectionism*. Is *Hunt* properly deemed a case of economic discrimination? The North Carolina apple sellers were subject to the exact same limitations imposed on Washington apple sellers. Should the North Carolina law be invalidated simply because it denies out-of-state apple growers a competitive advantage? On the other hand, might these arguments be deemed overly naive? How do you think *Hunt* would have been decided had North Carolina had no apple crop of its own? In such a case, should the Court disregard its discriminatory-legislation analysis?

The Court in *Hunt* asserts that "we need not ascribe an economic protection motive to the North Carolina Legislature to resolve this case." When state legislation, nondiscriminatory on its face, is found to have a discriminatory impact, should it make a difference in drawing a constitutional calculus that the legislature had in fact intended to discriminate against out-of-state residents? Consider again the purposes served by the dormant commerce clause.

Legislative motivation was found irrelevant in *Hunt,* because even if that motivation were proper, the asserted justification was insufficient to allow such discriminatory impact. Assuming the asserted justification had, in fact, been found to be compelling, should the Court's decision be influenced by evidence that the legislature actually had intended to harm out-of-state competition? Is such a judicial inquiry into legislative motivation feasible? For an argument that such an inquiry is both feasible and necessary, see Regan, 84 Mich. L. Rev. at 1110-60.

2. *Less onerous alternatives*. The *Hunt* decision, like those involving overt discrimination, stresses the alternative means available to the state for achieving its permissible interests. The doctrine of "less onerous alternatives" has become a prime tool in striking down discriminatory legislation. Do you think such legislation either would or should be upheld if the Court fails to find a less onerous method of achieving the state's goal? What factors would influence your decision? On the other hand, should a state be required to exclude all possible alternatives? What if the alternative means would not be as effective in achieving the state's interest?

In *Dean Milk Co. v. Madison*, 340 U.S. 349 (1951), the Supreme Court, per Justice Clark, struck down a Madison, Wisconsin ordinance making it unlawful to sell milk as pasteurized unless it had been processed and bottled at an approved plant within a five-mile radius from the center of the city. The effect of this law was to exclude milk pasteurized at Dean Milk Company's plants in Illinois. While there were suggestions that the purpose of the ordinance was, in fact, to exclude higher grade milk from outside the Madison milkshed, the Court did not rely on a finding of discriminatory purpose. The state court had found that the law furthered health interests by promoting convenient, economical, and efficient plant inspection. But Justice Clark argued that to hold

> that the ordinance is valid simply because it professes to be a health measure would mean that the Commerce Clause of itself imposes no limitations on state action other than those laid down by the Due Process Clause, save for the rare instance when a state artlessly discloses an avowed purpose to discriminate against interstate goods.

Instead, Justice Clark looked to the character of this local health interest and the available means of protecting it. He began with the premise that

> this regulation, like the provision invalidated in *Baldwin v. G.A.F. Seelig, Inc.*, in *practical effect* excludes from distribution in Madison wholesome milk produced and pasteurized in Illinois. In thus erecting an economic barrier protecting a major local industry against competition from without the state, Madison plainly discriminates against

> interstate commerce. This it cannot do, even in the exercise of its unquestioned power to protect the health and safety of its people, if reasonable nondiscriminatory alternatives, adequate to conserve legitimate local interests are available [citing *Baldwin*].

The Court noted that this was true even though the ordinance also operated against Wisconsin milk outside the Madison milkshed.

In this instance, reasonable and adequate alternatives were available. Madison could use its own inspectors in Dean's plants and charge the costs of such inspections to the importing producers and processors. Or, they could employ the U.S. Public Health Services safety ratings and exclude milk not produced and pasteurized in conformity with their standards.

3. *Identifying discrimination*. In response to the 1973 oil shortage, the state of Maryland conducted a study which indicated that gasoline stations operated by producers or refiners received preferential treatment during the scarcity. This led to legislation which prohibited producers or refiners from operating retail service stations within Maryland, and required them to extend all "voluntary allowances" uniformly to all service stations that are supplied. In *Exxon Corp. v. Governor of Md.*, 437 U.S. 117 (1978), the Court, per Justice Stevens, upheld the statutory scheme against due process and commerce clause challenges.

Out-of-state oil producers claimed that the Maryland law was discriminatory. Since Maryland had no local producers or refiners, only interstate companies would bear the burden of divestiture of service stations. The law, they argued, had the practical effect of protecting in-state independent service station dealers from out-of-state competition by integrated petroleum companies. But the Court concluded that the Maryland Act was not discriminatory. The law "creates no barriers whatsoever against interstate independent dealers; it does not prohibit the flow of interstate goods, place added cost upon them or distinguish between in-state and out-of-state companies in the retail market." *Hunt* was specifically distinguished on the grounds that the challenged state statute in that case raised the cost of doing business for out-of-state dealers, and, in various other ways, favored the in-state dealer in the local market.

While the Court admitted that some out-of-state integrated petroleum companies would not enjoy the same privileged status in the Maryland market, it concluded that there was no competitive advantage given by the statute to in-state independent dealers against out-of-state dealers. "The fact that the burden of a state regulation falls on some interstate companies does not, by itself, establish a claim of discrimination against interstate commerce."

4. *West Lynn Creamery v. Healy*, 512 U.S. 186 (1994), invalidated a Massachusetts pricing order which imposed an assessment on all fluid milk sold by dealers to Massachusetts retailers, the proceeds of which were distributed to Massachusetts dairy farmers. Justice Stevens, for a majority of the Court, held that the order unconstitutionally discriminated against interstate commerce.

In the 1980s and early 1990s, Massachusetts dairy farmers started losing market share to lower cost producers in surrounding states. By 1992, about two-thirds of the milk sold in Massachusetts was produced out-of-state. A study conducted by the State showed that if the prices received by Massachusetts farmers for their milk were not increased, most of the remaining dairy farmers in the State would be forced out of business. Declaring a state of emergency, the Commissioner of the Massachusetts Department of Food and Agriculture issued an order which required every dealer in Massachusetts to pay an assessment into a fund established by the State. The proceeds of the fund were then distributed to Massachusetts dairy farmers.

West Lynn Creamery, Inc., a licensed Massachusetts milk dealer, challenged the order. Approximately 97% of the milk West Lynn purchases comes from outside Massachusetts. Le Comte Dairy, which purchases all its milk from West Lynn and then distributes the milk to retail outlets in Massachusetts also joined in the challenge. Initially, the challengers had complied with the pricing order, paying almost $200,000 into the fund. When they stopped making payments into the fund, the Commissioner began license revocation proceedings against them. The petitioners unsuccessfully asked the state courts to enjoin the enforcement of the order by the Commission on the ground that the order violated the dormant Commerce Clause.

Justice Stevens observed that, in prior decisions, the Court had invalidated state minimum price regulation which had the same effect as a tariff "neutralizing the advantage possessed by lower cost out-of-state producers." Under this precedent, the Massachusetts pricing order was clearly invalid:

> [The pricing order's] avowed purpose and its undisputed effect are to enable higher cost Massachusetts dairy farmers to compete with lower cost dairy farmers in other States. The "premium payments" are effectively a tax which makes milk produced out of State more expensive. Although the tax also applies to milk produced in Massachusetts, its effect on Massachusetts producers is entirely (indeed more than) offset by the subsidy provided exclusively to Massachusetts dairy farmers. Like an ordinary tariff, the tax is thus effectively imposed only on out-of-state products. The pricing order thus allows Massachusetts dairy farmers who produce at higher cost to sell at or below the price charged by lower cost out-of-state producers. [B]ecause the Federal Government [under the Agricultural Marketing Agreement Act] sets minimum prices, out-of-state producers may not even have the option of reducing prices in order to retain market share.

The State's principal argument was that since each part of its program — "a local subsidy and a non-discriminatory tax" — was valid, the combination of the two were equally valid: "In effect, [the State] argues, if the State may impose a valid tax on dealers, it is free to use the proceeds of the tax as it chooses; and if it may independently subsidize its farmers it is free to finance the subsidy by means of any legitimate tax."

Although Justice Stevens noted in a footnote that "[w]e have never squarely confronted the constitutionality of subsidies," he, nevertheless, observed that generally a "pure subsidy funded out of general revenue ordinarily imposes no burden on interstate commerce, but merely assists local business." But the funding source of the subsidy in this case came "principally from taxes on the sale of milk produced in other states."

Justice Scalia, joined by Justice Thomas, concurred in the result, but faulted the Court's reasoning: "[N]ot every state law which obstructs a national market violates the Commerce Clause." Scalia objected to what he called "a sweeping principle" in the Court's opinion that any state law which artificially aids in-state production when the same goods could be produced in other states at lower cost violates the Constitution. Justice Scalia declared that "a State subsidy would *clearly* be invalid" under the Court's approach since subsidies even if they are funded from general state revenues "are often admitted to have as their purpose — indeed, are nationally advertised as having as their purpose — making it more profitable to conduct business in-state than elsewhere, *i.e.*, distorting normal market incentives." Subsidies assist in-state business and "unquestionably neutralize advantages possessed by out-of-state enterprises." The Court's approach, Scalia asserted, would render many other state laws unconstitutional without regard to the *Pike* balancing test and greatly extend "the negative Commerce Clause beyond its current scope."

As an original matter, Justice Scalia had doubts about whether a negative Commerce Clause jurisprudence was justified at all. He conceded, however, that precedent had carried the day against him on this and engendered significant reliance interests:

> As a result, I will, on *stare decisis* grounds, enforce a self-executing "negative" Commerce Clause in two situations: (1) against a state law that facially discriminates against interstate commerce, and (2) against a state law that is indistinguishable from a type of law previously held unconstitutional by this Court.

Chief Justice Rehnquist, joined by Justice Blackmun, dissenting, saw the Massachusetts pricing order not only as a means of helping "struggling Massachusetts dairy farmers" but also to preserve a desired land use. Massachusetts in its pricing order had extended a subsidy to its dairy farmers such as had been approved in prior cases: "No decided case supports the Court's conclusion that the negative Commerce Clause prohibits the State from using money that it has lawfully obtained through a neutral tax on milk dealers and distributing it as a subsidy to dairy farmers."

In a parting shot, the Chief Justice accused the Court of confusing the dormant Commerce Clause with a mandate for laissez-faire economics:

> The wisdom of a messianic insistence on a grim sink-or-swim policy of laissez-faire economics would be debatable had Congress chosen to enact it; but Congress has done nothing of the kind. It is the Court which has imposed the policy under the dormant Commerce Clause, a policy which bodes ill for the values of federalism which have long animated our constitutional jurisprudence.

5. *Camps Newfound/Owatonna, Inc. v. Town of Harrison*, 520 U.S. 564 (1997). The Court held that an otherwise generally applicable Maine property tax violates the dormant Commerce Clause if its exemption for property owned by charitable institutions excludes organizations operated principally for the benefit of nonresidents.

Petitioner was a Maine nonprofit corporation that operated a summer camp for the benefit of children of the Christian Science faith. Because the majority of campers came from out-of-state, petitioner could not qualify under the statute for a complete exemption.

Justice Stevens, speaking for the Court, found that if the statute were aimed at profit-making activities, it would be unconstitutional: "It is not necessary to look beyond the text of this statute to determine that it discriminates against interstate commerce. The Maine law expressly distinguishes between entities that serve a principally interstate clientele and those that primarily serve an intrastate market, singling out camps that serve mostly in-staters for beneficial tax treatment, and penalizing those camps that do a principally interstate business. As a practical matter, the statute encourages affected entities to limit their out-of-state clientele, and penalizes the principally nonresident customers of businesses catering to a primarily interstate market." He added that "[t]o the extent that affected Maine organizations are not deterred by the statute from doing a principally interstate business, it is clear that discriminatory burdens on interstate commerce imposed by regulation or taxation may also violate the Commerce Clause." Because the town had made no effort to defend the statute under the stringent standards of the *per se* rule, the Court chose not to address that issue.

Though the Court acknowledged that it had never previously addressed the issue directly, it held that "the applicability of the dormant Commerce Clause to the nonprofit sector of the economy follows from our prior decisions." The Court reasoned that "[f]or purposes of Commerce Clause analysis, any categorical distinction between the activities of profit-making enterprises and not-for-profit entities is wholly illusory. Entities in both categories are major participants in interstate markets. And, although the summer camp involved in this case may have a relatively insignificant impact on the commerce of the entire Nation, the interstate commercial activities of nonprofit entities as a class are unquestionably significant."

The Court rejected the town's argument that the tax should be viewed as an indirect subsidy that caters principally to local needs: "Assuming, arguendo, that the Town is correct that a direct subsidy benefiting only those nonprofits serving principally Maine residents would be permissible, our cases do not sanction a tax exemption serving similar ends."

Justice Scalia, speaking on behalf of four justices, dissented:

> The Court's negative-commerce-clause jurisprudence has drifted far from its moorings. Originally designed to create a national market for commercial activity, it is today invoked to prevent a State from giving a tax break to charities that benefit the State's inhabitants. In my view, Maine's tax exemption, which excuses from taxation only that property used to relieve the State of its burden of caring for its residents, survives even our most demanding commerce-clause scrutiny.

6. *Pharmaceutical Research and Manufacturers of America v. Walsh,* 538 U.S. 644 (2003). The Court, per Justice Stevens, held that a rebate requirement included in the 2000 Maine Rx Program did not discriminate against interstate commerce in order to subsidize in-state retail sales and did not constitute impermissible extraterritorial regulation. A plurality of the Court held that the state program was not preempted by the mere existence of the federal Medicaid statute.

In 1990, in response to increasing Medicaid expenses, Congress passed federal legislation which required drug companies to enter into agreements with either the Secretary of Health and Human Services or individual states to provide rebates on the Medicaid sales of outpatient prescription drugs. Congress also allowed the states to "subject to authorization any covered outpatient drug" if certain limitations were followed.

In 2000, Maine enacted the "Maine Rx" program which is intended to permit individuals to buy drugs at discounts comparable to the rebate on Medicaid purchases. The State would "negotiate rebates with drug manufacturers to fund the reduced price for drugs offered to Maine Rx participants."

The Medicaid drug sales of those manufacturers that do not enter a rebate agreement are subject to a prior authorization procedure before qualifying for reimbursement. In an affidavit, one company executive noted that prior authorization [PA] "severely curtails access to the drug for covered patients and sharply reduces the drug's market share and sales, as the PA causes a shift of patients to competing drugs of other manufacturers that are not subject to a PA." An association of nonresident drug manufacturers claimed that the state program is pre-empted by the federal Medicaid statue because it "imposes a significant burden on Medicaid recipients by requiring prior authorization in certain circumstances without serving any valid Medicaid purpose." The Association argued the Maine program violates the Negative or Dormant Commerce Clause because it discriminates against interstate commerce in order to subsidize in-state retail sales and constitutes impermissible extraterritorial regulation. The district court granted the Association's motion for a preliminary injunction. In holding that the Maine program violated the Commerce Clause, the district court relied on *Healy v. Beer Institute* [p. 264], in holding that "Maine had no power to regulate the prices paid to drug manufacturers in transactions that occur out of the State." The First Circuit Court of Appeals reversed.

The Supreme Court affirmed. Justice Stevens first distinguished *Healy v. Beer Institute* and *Baldwin v. G.A.F. Seelig, Inc.*. In *Baldwin*, Justice Cardozo stated: "New York has no power to project its legislation into Vermont by regulating the price to be paid in that state for milk acquired there." The Association argued that the same reasoning applied to this case and what it described as "Maine's regulation of the terms of transactions that occur elsewhere." The Court rejected the Association's argument, since "unlike price control or price affirmation statutes, 'the Maine Act does not regulate the price of any out-of-state transaction, either by its express terms or by its inevitable effect. Maine does not insist that manufacturers sell their drugs to a wholesaler for a certain price. Similarly, Maine is not tying the price of its in-state products to out-of-state prices.' "

The Court also rejected the Association's discrimination claim. Justice Stevens distinguished *West Lynn Creamery, Inc. v. Healy*, where the Court held a Massachusetts milk pricing order invalid "because it had a discriminatory effect analogous to a protective tariff that taxed goods imported from neighboring states but does not tax similar products produced locally." The Association argued that Maine's Rx fund would also be created entirely from rebates paid by out-of-state drug companies and would also be used to subsidize sales by local pharmacies to local customers. The Court rejected the analogy by insisting that no disparate burden would be imposed on out of state companies. "A manufacturer could not avoid its rebate obligation by opening production facilities in Maine and would receive no benefit from the rebates even if it did so; the payments to the local pharmacists provide no special benefit to competitors of rebate-paying manufacturers."

Justice Scalia concurred in the judgment. He noted that "the Maine statute . . . is neither facially discriminatory against interstate commerce nor . . . similar to other state action that we have found invalid on negative-Commerce Clause grounds." Justice Scalia rejected the Association's negative Commerce Clause claim "because . . . the negative Commerce Clause, having no foundation in the text of the text of the Constitution and not lending itself to judicial application except in the invalidation of facially discriminatory action, should not be extended beyond such action and nondiscriminatory action of the precise sort hitherto invalidated." Justice Thomas concurred in the judgment, arguing that "the negative Commerce Clause has no basis in the text of the Constitution, makes little sense, and has proved virtually unworkable in application."

7. *Granholm v. Heald*, 544 U.S. 460 (2005). The Court held statutory schemes of both Michigan and New York for regulating the sale and importation of wine to be unconstitutionally discriminatory. Under Michigan's law, producers or distillers of alcoholic beverages, whether located in or out of state, generally were allowed to sell only to licensed in-state wholesalers, who, in turn, may sell only to in-state retailers. Licensed retailers sold to consumers at retail locations and, under certain circumstances, through home delivery. Though wine producers generally had to distribute their wine through wholesalers, there was an exception for Michigan's in-state wineries, who were eligible for licenses to ship directly to in-state consumers. Under the New York legislative scheme, as in Michigan, local wineries are allowed to make direct sales to consumers in New York on terms not available to out-of-state wineries. Noting that under the rule prohibiting state discrimination against interstate commerce "[r]ivalries among the States are kept to a minimum," the Court found both laws unconstitutional. The Court reasoned that under Michigan's law, "[t]he differential treatment requires all out-of-state wine, but not all in-state wine, to pass through an in-state wholesaler and retailer before reaching consumers." These two extra layers of overhead increase the cost of out-of-state wine to Michigan consumers. The cost differential, and in some cases the inability to secure a wholesaler for small shipments, can effectively bar small wineries from the Michigan market. While "[t]he New York regulatory scheme differs from Michigan's in that it does not ban direct shipments altogether," it was similarly discriminatory, because "[a]ll wine must be sold through a license fully accountable to New York, it just so happens that in order to become a licensee, a winery must have a physical presence in the State." This was discriminatory, because "[f]or most wineries, the expense of establishing a bricks-and-mortar distribution operation in one state, let alone all 50, is prohibitive. It comes as no surprise that not a single out-of-state winery has availed itself of New York's direct-shipping privilege."

The Court rejected the states' reliance on section 2 of the Twenty-First Amendment, which, as part of the repeal of Prohibition, provides: "The transportation or importation into any State, Territory, or possession of the United States for delivery or use therein of intoxicating liquors, in violation of the laws thereof, is hereby prohibited." The Court relied on its earlier holdings "that state regulation of alcohol is limited by the nondiscrimination principle of the Commerce Clause."

[B] UNDUE BURDENS: STRIKING THE BALANCE

Even if a state regulation serves a permissible state interest, and is not discriminatory in means or effect, the commerce clause inquiry does not end. An early effort suggesting a balancing approach to defining the limits on state power to regulate interstate commerce came in a dissenting opinion in *Di Santo v. Pennsylvania*, 273 U.S. 34 (1927), where the Court struck down a state statute requiring that all persons in the business of selling steamship tickets for transportation to or from foreign countries be licensed for a $50 fee. A license was granted only upon a showing of good character and fitness, and was revocable for misconduct. The Court did not consider the purpose of the Act, to prevent exploitation of poor immigrants, to be relevant. The statute fell because it was an unconstitutional "direct burden" on a well-recognized area of foreign commerce, "regardless of the purpose with which it was passed."

In a prophetic dissent, Justice Stone urged that the Court should balance federal and state interests and hold a state regulation valid if "a consideration of all the facts and circumstances, such as the nature of the regulation, its function, the character of the business involved and the actual effect on the flow of commerce, lead to the conclusion that the regulation concerns interests peculiarly local and does not infringe the national interest in maintaining the freedom of commerce across state lines." The *Di Santo* decision was overruled in *California v. Thompson*, 313 U.S. 109 (1941).

Justice Stone's *Di Santo* dissent found support in an influential article by Professor Noel Dowling, *Interstate Commerce and State Power,* 27 VA. L. REV. 1 (1940), proposing that "in the absence of affirmative consent, a Congressional negative will be presumed in the courts against state action which in its effect upon interstate commerce constitutes an unreasonable interference with national interests, the presumption being rebuttable at the pleasure of Congress." He argued that this was not only what the courts were doing in fact but would "involve an avowal that the Court is deliberately balancing national and local interests and making a choice as to which of the two should prevail."

Beginning in the 1970s, the Court decided to make a concerted effort to bring a degree of harmony and organization to the area. The dominant approach currently in use in cases of evenhanded state regulation is indicated in *Pike v. Bruce Church,* p. 252:

> Where the statute regulates evenhandedly to effectuate a legitimate local public interest, and its effects on interstate commerce are only incidental, it will be upheld unless the burden imposed on such commerce is clearly excessive in relation to the putative local benefits. If a legitimate local purpose is found, then the question becomes one of degree. And the extent of the burden that will be tolerated will of course depend on the nature of the local interest involved, and on whether it could be promoted as well with a lesser impact with interstate activities.

Pike requires the courts to determine if the benefit realized by the regulating state justifies the costs imposed by burdening the free flow of interstate commerce — *i.e.*, whether the law imposes an "undue burden" on interstate commerce. A number of troubling questions arise. Who has the burden of proof? Are some state interests ranked higher than others in the balance? The question of the proper role of the courts, Congress, and the states under the Commerce Clause once again arises. If a law is reasonably related to a permissible state interest and is not discriminatory in purpose, means or effect, it is arguable that this should terminate the judicial role. Under traditional due process analysis, it is considered inappropriate for the courts to go beyond the determination that a law reasonably serves a legitimate state interest. Judicial deference is accorded the legislative judgment. Is it proper for the courts to engage in the type of fact-finding and policy analysis needed for balancing? Should Congress, rather than the courts, check abusive state laws? Furthermore, is it proper for the courts actively to review nondiscriminatory state laws under the Commerce Clause at the same time they assume a posture of judicial deference to *federal* Commerce Clause regulation? Is there any basis for the different approach?

[1] Development of the Balancing Test

***Southern Pac. Co. v. Arizona ex rel. Sullivan,* 325 U.S. 761 (1945).** Chief Justice Stone, speaking for the Court, invalidated, under the dormant Commerce Clause, the Arizona Train Limit Law, which made it unlawful for any person or corporation to operate within the state a railroad train of more than fourteen passenger or seventy freight cars:

> There has been left to the states wide scope for the regulation of matters of local state concern, even though it in some measure affects commerce, provided it does not materially restrict the free flow of commerce across state lines, or interfere with it in matters with respect to which uniformity of regulation is of predominant national concern. Hence the matters for ultimate determination here are the nature and extent of the burden which the state regulation of interstate trains, adopted as a safety measure, imposes on interstate commerce, and whether the relative weights of the state and national interests involved are such as to make inapplicable the rule, generally

> observed, that the free flow of interstate commerce and its freedom from local restraints in matters requiring uniformity of regulation are interests safeguarded by the commerce clause from state interference.

Applying this standard, the Court found that "the Arizona Train Limit Law imposes a serious burden on the interstate commerce conducted by appellant. It materially impedes the movement of appellant's interstate trains through that state and interposes a substantial obstruction to the national policy proclaimed by Congress, to promote adequate, economical and efficient railway transportation service." In rejecting the asserted safety rationale for the law, the Court found that "such increased danger of accident and personal injury as may result from the greater length of trains is more than offset by the increase in the number of accidents resulting from the larger number of trains when train lengths are reduced," and therefore concluded that the law affords at most slight and dubious advantage, if any, over unregulated train lengths.

In holding the Arizona law unconstitutional, the Court distinguished *South Carolina State Hwy. Dep't v. Barnwell Bros.*, 303 U.S. 177 (1938), where the Court, per Justice Stone, had upheld a state statute prohibiting use on state highways of trucks whose width exceeded ninety inches or whose weight, including load, was over 20,000 pounds.

The district court in *Barnwell* had rejected due process claims but had concluded that the Commerce Clause imposed a more exacting standard of reasonableness than the Fourteenth Amendment. The Supreme Court, however, held that "[i]n the absence of [congressional] legislation the judicial function, under the Commerce Clause as well as the Fourteenth Amendment, stops with the inquiry whether the state legislature in adopting regulations such as the present has acted within its province, and whether the means chosen are reasonably adapted to the end sought."

The first inquiry was said to be answered by prior decisions "that a state may impose nondiscriminatory regulations with respect to the character of motor vehicles moving in interstate commerce as a safety measure and as a means of securing the economical use of its highways."

In assessing the second criterion, "[w]hen the action of a legislature is within the scope of its power, fairly debatable questions as to reasonableness, wisdom, and propriety are not for the determination of courts, but for the legislative body, on which rests the duty and responsibility of decision" (citing due process cases). The judicial function was solely "to ascertain upon the whole record whether it is possible to say that the legislative choice is without rational basis." Because the state legislative judgment had adequate support, the Fourteenth Amendment *and the Commerce Clause* were satisfied. Justice Stone specifically stated that "so long as the state action does not discriminate, the burden is one which the Constitution permits because it is an inseparable incident of the exercise of a legislative authority, which, under the Constitution, has been left to the states." A state regulation could be sustained "although it has burdened or impeded interstate commerce" and "materially interfere[s]" with interstate commerce.

In *Southern Pacific,* the Court noted that in the *Barnwell* decision "we were at pains to point out that there are few subjects of state regulation affecting interstate commerce which are so peculiarly of local concern as is the use of the state's highways. Unlike the railroads, local highways are built, owned and maintained by the state or its municipal subdivisions." In dissent, Justice Black argued that while "[i]t may be that offsetting dangers are possible in the operation of short trains, [t]he balancing of these probabilities is not in my judgment a matter for judicial determination, but one which calls for legislative consideration. Representatives elected by the people to make their laws, rather than judges appointed to interpret those laws, can best determine the policies which govern the people. That at least is the basic principle on which our democratic society rests." Is Justice Black's argument persuasive? Consider the response in Kenneth Karst, *Legislative Facts in Constitutional Litigation,* 1960 Sup. Ct. Rev. 75:

> The assumption seems to be that since ultimate questions of reasonableness are not "susceptible to solution" wholly on the basis [of] findings of fact, courts are somehow disqualified from deciding them. The assumption ignores centuries of judicial lawmaking when it denies the competency of courts to weigh competing social interests. The alternative to the educated judicial guess is relegation of the issue "to the category of political questions."

***Bibb v. Navajo Freight Lines,* 359 U.S. 520 (1959).** The Court held invalid "an Illinois statute requiring the use of a contour rear fender mudguard on trucks and trailers operated on the highways of that State." Although the Court ultimately invalidated the Illinois law, Justice Douglas, in his opinion for the Court, wrote that "safety measures carry a strong presumption of validity when challenged in court. If there are alternative ways of solving a problem, we do not sit to determine which of them is best suited to achieve a valid state objective. Policy decisions are for the state legislature, absent federal entry into the field."

Though at trial "Illinois introduced evidence seeking to establish that contour mudguards had a decided safety factor in that they prevented the throwing of debris into the faces of drivers of passing cars and into the windshields of a following vehicle," the district court concluded that it was "conclusively shown that the contour mud flap possesses no advantages over the conventional or straight mud flap previously required in Illinois and presently required in most of the states," and therefore held the law to be an undue burden on interstate commerce. In upholding the lower court's decision, Justice Douglas stated:

> Local regulations which would pass muster under the Due Process Clause might nonetheless fail to survive other challenges to constitutionality that bring the Supremacy Clause into play. Like any local law that conflicts with federal regulatory measures state regulations that seem afoul of the policy of free trade reflected in the Commerce Clause must also bow.
>
> This is one of those cases — few in number — where local safety measures that are nondiscriminatory place an unconstitutional burden on interstate commerce. A State which insists on a design out of

> line with the requirements of almost all the other States may sometimes place a great burden of delay and inconvenience on those interstate motor carriers entering or crossing its territory. Such a new safety device — out of line with the requirements of the other States — may be so compelling that the innovative State need not be the one to give way. But the present showing — balanced against the clear burden on commerce — is far too inconclusive to make this mudguard meet that test.

An important question to consider, in reading the next few cases, is the appropriateness of viewing nondiscriminatory state regulation of interstate *movement of goods* as being fungible with state regulation of interstate *transportation.* Is the state interest in imposing local regulations likely to be as great in both instances? Is the danger of interference with the free flow of commerce likely to be as great in both?

[2] Modernizing the Balancing Test

PIKE v. BRUCE CHURCH, INC.

397 U.S. 137, 90 S. Ct. 844, 25 L. Ed. 2d 174 (1970)

JUSTICE STEWART delivered the opinion of the Court.

The appellee [Bruce Church, Inc.] is a company engaged in extensive commercial farming operations in Arizona and California. The appellant is the official charged with enforcing the Arizona Fruit and Vegetable Standardization Act. A provision of the Act requires that, with certain exceptions, all cantaloupes grown in Arizona and offered for sale must be "packed in regular compact arrangement in closed standard containers approved by the supervisor." Invoking his authority under that provision, the appellant issued an order prohibiting the appellee company from transporting uncrated cantaloupes from its Parker, Arizona, ranch to nearby Blythe, California, for packing and processing. The company then brought this action in a federal court to enjoin the order as unconstitutional.

[T]he general rule that emerges can be phrased as follows: Where the statute regulates evenhandedly to effectuate a legitimate local public interest, and its effects on interstate commerce are only incidental, it will be upheld unless the burden imposed on such commerce is clearly excessive in relation to the putative local benefits. *Huron Cement Co. v. Detroit.* If a legitimate local purpose is found, then the question becomes one of degree. And the extent of the burden that will be tolerated will of course depend on the nature of the local interest involved, and on whether it could be promoted as well with a lesser impact on interstate activities. Occasionally the Court has candidly undertaken a balancing approach in resolving these issues, *Southern Pacific Co. v. Arizona,* but more frequently it has spoken in terms of "direct" and "indirect" effects and burdens.

At the core of the Arizona Fruit and Vegetable Standardization Act are the requirements that fruits and vegetables shipped from Arizona meet certain standards of wholesomeness and quality, and that they be packed in standard containers in such a way that the outer layer or exposed portion of the pack does not "materially misrepresent" the quality of the lot as a whole. The impetus for the Act was the fear that some growers were shipping inferior or deceptively packaged produce, with the result that the reputation of Arizona growers generally was being tarnished and their financial return concomitantly reduced. It was to prevent this that the Act was passed in 1929. The State has stipulated that its primary purpose is to promote and preserve the reputation of Arizona growers by prohibiting deceptive packaging.

We are not, then, dealing here with "state legislation in the field of safety where the propriety of local regulation has long been recognized," or with an Act designed to protect consumers in Arizona from contaminated or unfit goods. Its purpose and design are simply to protect and enhance the reputation of growers within the State. These are surely legitimate state interests. *Sligh v. Kirkwood*, 237 U.S. 52, 61. We have upheld a State's power to require that produce packaged in the State be packaged in a particular kind of receptacle, *Pacific States Box & Basket Co. v. White*, 296 U.S. 176. And we have recognized the legitimate interest of a State in maximizing the financial return to an industry within it. *Parker v. Brown*, 317 U.S. 341. Therefore, as applied to Arizona growers who package their produce in Arizona, we may assume the constitutional validity of the Act. We may further assume that Arizona has full constitutional power to forbid the misleading use of its name on produce that was grown or packed elsewhere. And, to the extent the Act forbids the shipment of contaminated or unfit produce, it clearly rests on sure footing.

But application of the Act through the appellant's order to the appellee company has a far different impact, and quite a different purpose. The cantaloupes grown by the company at Parker are of exceptionally high quality. The company does not pack them in Arizona and cannot do so without making a capital expenditure of approximately $200,000. The appellant's order would forbid the company to pack its cantaloupes outside Arizona, not for the purpose of keeping the reputation of its growers unsullied, but to enhance their reputation through the reflected good will of the company's superior produce. The appellant, in other words, is not complaining because the company is putting the good name of Arizona on an inferior or deceptively packaged product, but because it is not putting that name on a product that is superior and well packaged.

Although it is not easy to see why the other growers of Arizona are entitled to benefit at the company's expense from the fact that it produces superior crops, we may assume that the asserted state interest is a legitimate one. But the State's tenuous interest in having the company's cantaloupes identified as originating in Arizona cannot constitutionally justify the requirement that the company build and operate an unneeded $200,000 packing plant in the State. The nature of that burden is, constitutionally, more significant than its extent. For the Court has viewed with particular suspicion state statutes requiring business operations to be performed in the home State that could more efficiently be performed elsewhere. Even where the State is pursuing a clearly legitimate local interest, this particular burden on commerce has been declared to be virtually *per se* illegal.

While the order issued under the Arizona statute does not impose rigidity on an entire industry, it does impose a straitjacket on the appellee company with respect to the allocation of its interstate resources. Such an incidental consequence of a regulatory scheme could perhaps be tolerated if a more compelling state interest were involved. But here the State's interest is minimal at best certainly less substantial than a State's interest in securing employment for its people. If the Commerce Clause forbids a State to require work to be done within its jurisdiction to promote local employment, then surely it cannot permit a State to require a person to go into a local packing business solely for the sake of enhancing the reputation of other producers within its borders.

NOTES

1. ***Balancing the interests***. Reexamine the discussion of Justice Stone's dissent in *Di Santo* and Professor Dowling's article, p. 248. To what extent is the test developed in *Pike* similar to those suggested approaches? To what extent does the test developed in *Pike* amount to a simple balancing of competing interests? Is this properly a judicial function, or is it ultimately an issue for Congress? If it is, in fact, an issue for Congress, is it appropriate for the judiciary to make such a decision in the absence of a congressional determination?

2. ***Economic protectionism.*** Professor Regan argues that, despite the language in *Pike,* in the regulation of movement of goods, "the Court is concerned and should be concerned only with preventing purposeful protectionism." Donald Regan, *The Supreme Court and State Protectionism: Making Sense of the Dormant Commerce Clause,* 84 Mich. L. Rev. 1091, 1093 (1986). He argues that "neutral but burdensome" state regulations, those that are not protectionist in motivation, should be unaffected by the dormant Commerce Clause. Professor Regan asserts that Arizona's purpose in *Pike* falls within his definition of "protectionist" legislation, which includes those statutes that are "adopted for the purpose of improving the competitive position of local" (in-state) economic actors because they are local, and that are "analogous in form to the traditional instruments of protectionism — the tariff, the quota, or the outright embargo." *Id.* at 1094-95.

Do you agree that the Arizona legislation in *Pike* should be deemed "protectionist" merely because it is designed to promote Arizona's competitive position vis-a-vis other states by truthfully conveying the fact that the cantaloupes are from Arizona? Is not the whole point of a federal system to promote competition among the states? Might a more legitimate distinction, for purposes of the dormant Commerce Clause, be drawn between *pro*-competitive legislation, which aids a state's competitive position by promoting itself, and *anti*-competitive legislation, which improves a state's position by stifling out-of-state competition?

RAYMOND MOTOR TRANSPORTATION, INC. v. RICE
434 U.S. 429, 98 S. Ct. 787, 55 L. Ed. 2d 664 (1980)

Justice Powell delivered the opinion of the Court.

We consider on this appeal whether administrative regulations of the State of Wisconsin governing the length and configuration of trucks that may be operated within the State violate the Commerce Clause because they unconstitutionally burden or discriminate against interstate commerce. The three-judge District Court held that the regulations are not unconstitutional on either ground. Because we conclude that they unconstitutionally burden interstate commerce, we reverse.

Appellant Raymond Motor Transportation, Inc. (Raymond), a Minnesota corporation with its principal place of business in Minneapolis, is a common carrier of general commodities by motor vehicle. Operating pursuant to a certificate of public convenience and necessity granted by the Interstate Commerce Commission, Raymond provides service in eastern North Dakota, Minnesota, northern Illinois, and northwestern Indiana. Its primary interstate route is between Chicago and Minneapolis. It does not serve any points in Wisconsin. Appellant Consolidated Freightways Corporation of Delaware (Consolidated), a Delaware corporation with its principal place of business in Menlo Park, Cal., also is a common carrier of general commodities by motor vehicle.

Both Raymond and Consolidated use two different kinds of trucks. One consists of a three-axle power unit (tractor) which pulls a single two-axle trailer that is 40 feet long. The overall length of such a single-trailer unit (single) is 55 feet. This unit has been used on the Nation's highways for many years and is an industry standard. The other type truck consists of a two-axle tractor which pulls a single-axle trailer to which a single-axle dolly and a second single-axle trailer are attached. Each trailer is 27 feet long, and the overall length of such a double-trailer unit (double) is 65 feet.

The double, which has come into increasing use in recent years, is thought to have certain advantages over the single for general commodities shipping. Because of these advantages, Raymond would prefer to use doubles on its route between Chicago and Minneapolis. Consolidated would prefer to use doubles on its routes between Chicago, Detroit, and points east, and Minneapolis and points west, as well as on its routes commencing and ending in Milwaukee and Madison. The most direct route for all of this traffic is over Interstate Highways 90 and 94, both of which cross Wisconsin between Illinois and Minnesota. State law allows 65-foot doubles to be operated on interstate highways and access roads in Michigan, Illinois, Minnesota, and all of the States west from Minnesota to Washington through which Interstate Highways 90 and 94 run.

Wisconsin law, however, generally does not allow trucks longer than 55 feet to be operated on highways within that State. The key statutory provision is Wis. Stat. § 348.07 (1) (1975), which sets a limit of 55 feet on the overall length of a vehicle pulling one trailer. Any person operating a single-trailer unit of greater length must obtain a permit issued by the State Highway Commission. In addition, § 348.08(1) provides that no vehicle pulling more than one other vehicle shall be operated on a highway without a permit.

The Commission is authorized to issue various classes of annual permits for the operation of vehicles that do not conform to the above requirements. In particular, it may issue "trailer train" permits for the operation of combinations of more than two vehicles "consisting of truck tractors, trailers, semitrailers or wagons which do not exceed a total length of 100 feet," § 348.27(6).

The Commission may also "impose such reasonable conditions" and "adopt such reasonable rules" of operation with respect to vehicles operated under permit "as it deems necessary for the safety of travel and protection of the highways," § 348.25(3), including specification of the routes to be used by permittees.

The Commission has issued administrative regulations setting forth the conditions under which "trailer train" and other classes of permits will be issued. Although the Commission is empowered by § 348.27(6) to issue "trailer train" permits to operate double-trailer trucks up to 100 feet long, its regulations restrict such permits to "the operation of vehicles used for the transporting of municipal refuse or waste, or for the interstate or intra-state operations without load of vehicles in transit from manufacturer or dealer to purchaser or dealer, or for the purpose of repair." "Trailer train" permits also are issued "for the operation of a combination of three vehicles used for the transporting of milk from the point of production to the point of first processing."

The overture to this lawsuit began when Raymond and Consolidated each applied to the appropriate Wisconsin officials under § 348.27 (6) for annual permits to operate 65-foot doubles on Interstate Highways 90 and 94 between Illinois and Minnesota and, in Consolidated's case, on short stretches of four-lane divided highways between the interstate highways and freight terminals in Milwaukee and Madison. The permits were denied because appellants' proposed operations were not within the narrow scope of the administrative regulations that specify when "trailer train" permits will be issued. Appellants then filed suit in Federal District Court seeking declaratory and injunctive relief on the ground that the regulations barring the proposed operation of 65-foot doubles burden and discriminate against interstate commerce in violation of the Commerce Clause. The complaint alleged that the State's refusal to issue the requested permits disrupts and delays appellants' transportation of commodities in interstate commerce; that 65-foot doubles are as safe as, if not safer than, the 55-foot singles that are allowed to operate on Wisconsin highways without permits; and that the maze of statutory and administrative exceptions to the general prohibition against operating vehicles longer than 55 feet results in "over-length permits [being] routinely granted to classes of vehicles indistinguishable from those of the Plaintiffs in terms of size, safety, and divisibility of loads . . . ."

Appellants presented a great deal of evidence supporting their allegation that 65-foot doubles are as safe as, if not safer than, 55-foot singles when operated on limited-access, four-lane divided highways. The State, for reasons unexplained, made no effort to contradict this evidence of comparative safety with evidence of its own. The State produced no evidence, nor has it made any suggestion in this Court, that 65-foot doubles are less safe than 55-foot singles because of their extra trailer, as distinguished from their extra length.

Appellants also produced uncontradicted evidence showing that their operations are disrupted, their costs are raised, and their service is slowed by the challenged regulations. Finally, appellants' evidence demonstrated that Wisconsin routinely allows a great number and variety of vehicles over 55 feet long to be operated on the State's highways.

In the instant case, appellants do not dispute that a State has a legitimate interest in regulating motor vehicles using its roads in order to promote highway safety. Nor do they contend that federal regulation has pre-empted state regulation of truck length or configuration. They argue, however, that the burden imposed upon interstate commerce by the Wisconsin regulations challenged here is, in the language of *Pike v. Bruce Church, Inc.,* "clearly excessive in relation to the putative local benefits." Appellants contend that the regulations were shown by uncontradicted evidence to make no contribution to highway safety, while imposing a burden on interstate commerce that is substantial in terms of expense and delay. They analogize this case to *Bibb v. Navajo Freight Lines,* where the Court invalidated an Illinois law, defended on the ground that it promoted highway safety, that required trailers of trucks driven within Illinois to be equipped with contour mudguards.

The State replies that the general rule of *Pike* is not applicable to a State's regulation of motor vehicles in the promotion of safety. It contends that we should be guided, instead, by *South Carolina Highway Dept. v. Barnwell Bros., Inc.,* which upheld over Commerce Clause objections a state law that set stricter limitations on truck width and weight than did surrounding States laws. The State emphasizes that *Barnwell Bros.* applied a "rational relation" test rather than a "balancing" test, and argues that its regulations bear a rational relation to highway safety: Longer trucks take longer to pass or be passed than shorter trucks.

We acknowledge, as did the Court in *Bibb,* that there is language in *Barnwell Bros.* which, "read in isolation from . . . later decisions . . ., would suggest that no showing of burden on interstate commerce is sufficient to invalidate local safety regulations in absence of some element of discrimination against interstate commerce." But *Bibb* rejected such a suggestion by stating the test to be applied to state highway regulation in terms similar in principle to the subsequent formulation in *Pike v. Bruce Church, Inc.:*

> Unless we can conclude on the whole record that "the total effect of the law as a safety measure in reducing accidents and casualties is so slight or problematical as not to outweigh the national interest in keeping interstate commerce free from interferences which seriously impede it" . . . we must uphold the statute.

Thus, we cannot accept the State's contention that the inquiry under the Commerce Clause is ended without a weighing of the asserted safety purpose against the degree of interference with interstate commerce.

Nevertheless, it also is true that the Court has been most reluctant to invalidate under the Commerce Clause "state legislation in the field of safety where the propriety of local regulation has long been recognized." *Pike v. Bruce Church.* In no field has this deference to state regulation been greater than that of highway safety regulation.[2] Thus, those who would challenge state

[2] The Court's special deference to state highway regulations derives in part from the assumption that where such regulations do not discriminate on their face against interstate commerce, their burden usually falls on local economic interests as well as other States' economic interests, thus insuring that a State's own political processes will serve as a check against unduly burdensome regulations. *Compare South Carolina Highway Dept. v. Barnwell Bros. with Southern*

regulations said to promote highway safety must overcome a "strong presumption of [their] validity." *Bibb.*

Despite the strength of this presumption, we are persuaded by the record in this case that the challenged regulations unconstitutionally burden interstate commerce. The State's assertion that the challenged regulations contribute to highway safety is rebutted by appellants' evidence and undercut by the maze of exemptions from the general truck-length limit that the State itself allows.[3]

Moreover, appellants demonstrated, again without contradiction, that the regulations impose a substantial burden on the interstate movement of goods. The regulations substantially increase the cost of such movement, a fact which is not, as the District Court thought, entirely irrelevant. In addition, the regulations slow the movement of goods in interstate commerce by forcing appellants to haul doubles across the State separately, to haul doubles around the State altogether, or to incur the delays caused by using singles instead of doubles to pick up and deliver goods. *See Bibb.* Finally, the regulations prevent appellants from accepting interline transfers of 65-foot doubles for movement through Wisconsin from carriers that operate only in the 33 States where the doubles are legal. In our view, the burden imposed on interstate commerce by Wisconsin's regulations is no less than that imposed by the statute invalidated in *Bibb.*

One other consideration, although not decisive, lends force to our conclusion that the challenged regulations cannot stand. As we have noted, Wisconsin's regulatory scheme contains a great number of exceptions to the general rule that vehicles over 55 feet long cannot be operated on highways within the State. At least one of these exceptions discriminates on its face in favor of Wisconsin industries and against the industries of other States, and there are indications in the record that a number of the other exceptions, although neutral on their face, were enacted at the instance of, and primarily benefit, important Wisconsin industries. Viewed realistically, these exceptions may be the product of compromise between forces within the State that seek to retain the State's general truck-length limit, and industries within the State that complain that the general limit is unduly burdensome. Exemptions of this kind, however, weaken the presumption in favor of the validity of the general limit, because they undermine the assumption that the State's own political processes will act as a check on local regulations that unduly burden interstate commerce.

On this record, we are persuaded that the challenged regulations violate the Commerce Clause because they place a substantial burden on interstate commerce and they cannot be said to make more than the most speculative contribution to highway safety. Our holding is a narrow one, for we do not decide whether laws of other States restricting the operation of trucks over

---

Pacific Co. v. Arizona ex rel. Sullivan. It also derives from a recognition that the States shoulder primary responsibility for the construction, maintenance, and policing of their highways, and that highway conditions may vary widely from State to State. *See Bibb v. Navajo Freight Lines; Barnwell Bros.*

[3] The State's failure to present any evidence to rebut appellants' showing in itself sets this case apart from *Barnwell Bros.*, and even from *Bibb.*

55 feet long, or of double-trailer trucks, would be upheld if the evidence produced on the safety issue were not so overwhelmingly one-sided as in this case.[4]

The State of Wisconsin has failed to make even a colorable showing that its regulations contribute to highway safety. The judgment of the District Court is reversed, and the case is remanded for further proceedings consistent with this opinion.

JUSTICE STEVENS took no part in the consideration or decision of this case.

JUSTICE BLACKMUN, with whom THE CHIEF JUSTICE [BURGER], JUSTICE BRENNAN, and JUSTICE REHNQUIST join, concurring.

I join the opinion of the Court, but I add these comments to emphasize the narrow scope of today's decision.

First, the Court's reliance on *Pike v. Bruce Church, Inc.,* does not signal, for me, a new approach to review of state highway safety regulations under the Commerce Clause. Wisconsin argues that the Court previously has refused to balance safety considerations against burdens on interstate commerce. This contention misreads *Bibb v. Navajo Freight Lines,* which recognized the Court's responsibility to weigh the national interest in free-flowing commerce against "slight or problematical" safety interests.

Second, the reliance on *Pike* should not be read to equate the factual balance struck here with the balance established in *Pike* regarding the Arizona Fruit and Vegetable Standardization Act. Neither the *Pike* opinion nor today's decision suggests that a similar balance would be struck when a State legitimately asserts the existence of a safety justification for a regulation. In *Pike* itself the Court noted that it did not confront "state legislation in the field of safety where the propriety of local regulation has long been recognized." In other words, if safety justifications are not illusory, the Court will not second-guess legislative judgment about their importance in comparison with related burdens on interstate commerce. I therefore join the opinion of the Court because its ultimate balancing does not depart from this principle. Here, the Court does not engage in a balance of policies; it does not make a legislative choice. Instead, after searching the factual record developed by the parties, it concludes that the safety interests have not been shown to exist as a matter of law.

Nineteen years after *Bibb,* then, the Court has been presented with another of those cases — "few in number" — in which highway safety regulations uncon stitutionally burden interstate commerce. The contour-mudflaps law burdened the flow of commerce through Illinois in 1959 just as the length and configuration regulations burden the flow through Wisconsin today. It was shown that neither the mudflaps law nor the regulations contributed to highway safety. Giving the same legislative leeway to Wisconsin that the Court gave to Illinois, *Bibb v. Navajo Freight Lines* requires reversal of the judgment of the District Court.

---

[4] As one commentator has written, Commerce Clause adjudication must depend in large part "upon the thoroughness with which the lawyers perform their task in the conduct of constitutional litigation. Here, as in many other fields, constitutionality is conditioned upon the facts, and to the lawyers the courts are entitled to look for garnering and presenting the facts." Dowling, *Interstate Commerce and State Power,* 27 VA. L. REV. 1, 27-28 (1940).

NOTES

1. *The uses of precedent*. What, according to Justice Blackmun, should be the relevance of the *Pike* balancing analysis to cases involving highway safety regulations? Is this view different from that of the majority? *Should* the *Pike* balancing analysis apply to cases such as *Raymond*? Does the reformulation of the balancing test in *Pike* add anything to the analysis employed for transportation regulation in *Bibb* and *Southern Pacific,* which were both decided well before *Pike*?

2. *Kassel v. Consolidated Freightways Corp.*, 450 U.S. 662 (1981). Iowa by statute restricted "the length of vehicles that may use its highways. Unlike all other States in the West and Midwest, Iowa prohibits the use of 65-foot doubles."

Justice Powell for the Court stated:

> This case is *Raymond* revisited. Here as in *Raymond,* the State failed to present any persuasive evidence that 65-foot doubles are less safe than 55-foot singles. Moreover, Iowa's law is now out of step with the laws of all other midwestern and western states. Iowa thus substantially burdens the interstate flow of goods by truck. Iowa made a more serious effort to support the safety rationale of its law than did Wisconsin in *Raymond,* but its effort was no more persuasive.
>
> The Court normally does accord "special deference" to state highway safety regulations. This traditional deference "derives in part from the assumption that where such regulations do not discriminate on their face against interstate commerce, their burden usually falls on local economic interests as well as other States economic interests, thus insuring that a State's own political processes will serve as a check against unduly burdensome regulations." Less deference to the legislative judgment is due, however, where the local regulation bears disproportionately on out-of-state residents and businesses. Such a disproportionate burden is apparent here. Iowa's scheme, although generally banning large doubles from the State, nevertheless has several exemptions that secure to Iowans many of the benefits of large trucks while shunting to neighboring states many of the costs associated with their use.

Given the final quoted portion of Justice Powell's opinion, why do you suppose he did not simply apply the traditionally strong presumption against discriminatory legislation at the outset of his opinion?

Justice Brennan, joined by Justice Marshall, concurred in the *Kassel* judgment, based on their conclusion that the Governor had vetoed reform legislation for protectionist reasons, *i.e.*, it would benefit out-of-state trucking firms at the expense of Iowa citizens. Justice Brennan, however, did reject the Court's apparent acceptance of ad hoc balancing.

> I would emphasize that in the field of safety — and perhaps in the fields where the decisions of State lawmakers are deserving of a heightened degree of deference — the role of the courts is not to balance asserted burdens against intended benefits as it is in other fields.

> Compare *Raymond Motor Transportation Inc. v. Rice* (Blackmun, J., concurring) (safety regulation) with *Pike v. Bruce Church, Inc.,* (regulation intended "to protect and enhance the reputation of growers with the State"). In the field of safety, once the court has established that the intended safety benefit is not illusory, insubstantial, or nonexistent, it must defer to the State's lawmakers on the appropriate balance to be struck against other interests. I therefore disagree with my Brother Powell when he asserts that the degree of interference with interstate commerce may in the first instance be "weighed" against the State's safety interests.

Justice Rehnquist, dissenting for himself and two other Justices, contended that "[t]he result in this case suggests that the only state truck length limit that is valid is one which this Court has not been able to get its hands on." He asserted that, after ascertaining that a state regulation is a rational safety measure, the Court's only function is to assure that the regulation is not a pretext for discrimination. Only if the safety benefits were demonstratively trivial and the burden on interstate commerce great, should the Court determine that the safety concern is a pretext:

> Iowa adduced evidence supporting the relation between vehicle length and highway safety. The evidence indicated that longer vehicles take greater time to pass, thereby increasing the risks of accidents, particularly during the inclement weather not uncommon in Iowa. The 65-foot vehicle exposes a passing driver to visibility impairing splash and spray during bad weather for a longer period than do the shorter trucks permitted in Iowa. Longer trucks are more likely to clog intersections, and although there are no intersections on the Interstate Highways, the order below went beyond the highways themselves and the concerns about greater length at intersections would arise "at every trip origin, every trip destination, every intermediate stop for picking up trailers, reconfiguring loads, change of drivers, eating, refueling — every intermediate stop would generate this type of situation." The Chief of the Division of Patrol in the Iowa Department of Public Safety testified that longer vehicles pose greater problems at the scene of an accident. For example, trucks involved in accidents often must be unloaded at the scene, which would take longer the bigger the load.
>
> In rebuttal of Consolidated's evidence on the relative safety of 65-foot doubles to trucks permitted on Iowa's highways, Iowa introduced evidence that doubles are more likely than singles to jackknife or upset. The District Court concluded that this was so and that singles are more stable than doubles. Iowa also introduced evidence from Consolidated's own records showing that Consolidated's overall accident rate for doubles exceeded that of semis for three of the last four years, and that some of Consolidated's own drivers expressed a preference for the handling characteristics of singles over doubles.
>
> In sum, there was sufficient evidence presented at trial to support the legislative determination that length is related to safety, and

nothing in Consolidated's evidence undermines this conclusion. Under our Constitutional scheme there is only one legislative body which can pre-empt the rational policy determination of the Iowa Legislature and that is Congress. Forcing Iowa to yield to the policy choices of neighboring States perverts the primary purpose of the Commerce Clause, that of vesting power to regulate interstate commerce in Congress, where all the States are represented.

3. *CTS Corp. v. Dynamics Corp. of America*, 481 U.S. 69 (1987). The State of Indiana enacted legislation designed to make it more difficult for hostile takeovers of corporations with a substantial Indiana nexus. The Act applies only to "a corporation that has: (1) one hundred (100) or more shareholders; (2) its principal place of business, its principal office, or substantial assets within Indiana; and (3) either: (A) more than ten percent (10%) of its shareholders resident in Indiana; (B) more than ten percent (10%) of its shares owned by Indiana residents; or (C) ten thousand (10,000) shareholders resident in Indiana." Justice Powell for the Court described the operation of the statute as follows:

> The Act focuses on the acquisition of "control shares" in an issuing public corporation. Under the Act, an entity acquires "control shares" whenever it acquires shares that, but for the operation of the Act, would bring its voting power in the corporation to or above any of three thresholds: 20%, 33 1/3%, or 50%. An entity that acquires control shares does not necessarily acquire voting rights. Rather, it gains those rights only "to the extent granted by resolution approved by the shareholders of the issuing public corporation." [The Act] requires a majority vote of all disinterested shareholders holding each class of stock for passage of such a resolution. The practical effect of this requirement is to condition acquisition of control of a corporation on approval of a majority of the pre-existing disinterested shareholders.

Justice Powell first held that the statute was not discriminatory even though most tender offers would come from out of state, because the act operated the same regardless of the source of the offer. Second,

> This Court's recent Commerce Clause cases also have invalidated statutes that adversely may affect interstate commerce by subjecting activities to inconsistent regulations. The Indiana Act poses no such problem. So long as each State regulates voting rights only in the corporations it has created, each corporation will be subject to the law of only one State.

Finally, the statute was upheld by reference to state and national interests:

> Every State in this country has enacted laws regulating corporate governance. By prohibiting certain transactions, and regulating others, such laws necessarily affect certain aspects of interstate commerce. This necessarily is true with respect to corporations with shareholders in States other than the State of incorporation. Large

> corporations that are listed on national exchanges, or even regional exchanges, will have shareholders in many States and shares that are traded frequently. The markets that facilitate this national and international participation in ownership of corporations are essential for providing capital not only for new enterprises but also for established companies that need to expand their businesses. This beneficial free market system depends at its core upon the fact that a corporation — except in the rarest situations — is organized under, and governed by, the law of a single jurisdiction, traditionally the corporate law of the State of its incorporation.
>
> It thus is an accepted part of the business landscape in this country for States to create corporations, to prescribe their powers, and to define the rights that are acquired by purchasing their shares. A State has an interest in promoting stable relationships among parties involved in the corporations it charters, as well as in ensuring that investors in such corporations have an effective voice in corporate affairs.
>
> To the limited extent that the Act affects interstate commerce, this is justified by the State's interests in defining the attributes of shares in its corporations and in protecting shareholders. Congress has never questioned the need for state regulation of these matters. Nor do we think such regulation offends the Constitution. Accordingly, we reverse the judgment of the Court of Appeals.

Justice Scalia concurred on the basis that "having found that the Indiana Control Share Acquisitions Chapter neither 'discriminates against interstate commerce,' nor 'create[s] an impermissible risk of inconsistent regulation by different States,' I would conclude without further analysis that it is not invalid under the dormant Commerce Clause. While it has become standard practice at least since *Pike v. Bruce Church, Inc.* to consider, in addition to these factors, whether the burden on commerce imposed by a state statute 'is clearly excessive in relation to the putative local benefits,' such an inquiry is ill suited to the judicial function and should be undertaken rarely if at all."

Justice White, joined by Justices Blackmun and Stevens, dissented on the ground that "Indiana is directly regulating the purchase and sale of shares of stock in interstate commerce. . . . A state law which permits a majority of an Indiana corporation's stockholders to prevent individual investors, including out-of-state stockholders, from selling their stock to an out-of-state tender offeror and thereby frustrate any transfer of corporate control, is the archetype of the kind of state law that the Commerce Clause forbids."

Professor Regan notes "the absence of any reference to balancing in any of the opinions," and "take[s] some pleasure in observing that in none of the three opinions in *CTS* is there any favorable mention of *Pike*." Donald Regan, *Siamese Essays: (I) CTS Corp. v. Dynamics Corp. of America and Dormant Commerce Clause Doctrine; (II) Extraterritorial State Legislation,* 85 Mich. L. Rev. 1865, 1866–67 (1987). Do you agree with his assertion that "there is no statement in any of the three opinions of a balancing test of any kind"? Professor Regan explains the majority's discussion of the justifications for the

Indiana statute as relating to a potential constitutional challenge on grounds of "extraterritoriality," though he acknowledges that "none of the opinions in *CTS* talks about [that issue] explicitly." The term refers to the argument that the state has extended its legislative jurisdiction beyond the geographical scope permitted by due process. For a response to Regan's theory of extraterritoriality, see Mark Gergen, *Territoriality and the Perils of Formalism,* 86 MICH. L. REV. 1735 (1988), suggesting that Regan's extraterritoriality approach works poorly, if at all, as a check on the regulatory authority of states.

4. *The issue of extraterritoriality.* Consider the possible relevance to *CTS* of the Supreme Court's decision in *Healy v. Beer Institute*, 491 U.S. 324 (1989). The case involved a challenge to a Connecticut law that required beer companies to post prices monthly and affirm that those prices were not higher than they were in three contiguous states. In effect, the law limited the ability of out-of-state beer shippers to alter their prices outside of the state during the month in which they had affirmed prices in Connecticut. The Court noted that the "critical inquiry" under the dormant Commerce Clause was "whether the practical effect of the regulation is to control conduct beyond the boundaries of the State." On the basis of this inquiry, the Court held the statute unconstitutional, reasoning that it had the "extraterritorial effect of preventing brewers from undertaking competitive pricing in Massachusetts based on prevailing market conditions." The Court had previously struck down other state statutes on grounds of extraterritoriality. *See Brown-Forman Distillers Corp. v. New York State Liquor Authority*, 476 U.S. 573 (1986); *Edgar v. MITE Corp.*, 457 U.S. 624 (1982). In what way does extraterritorial legislation undermine the purposes sought to be fostered by the dormant Commerce Clause? How should a finding of extraterritoriality be made? Does it matter that the state, in affecting an out-of-stater's behavior in another state, is seeking to protect in-state interests. See, for example, *CTS.* To what extent is *Healy* different? Could the Connecticut statute invalidated in *Healy* have been found unconstitutional under more traditional protectionist grounds?

5. *The dormant Commerce Clause and the Internet.* How should the *Pike* test apply to a state's attempt to regulate the transmission of information or the conduct of transactions over the Internet? A number of scholars support "the emerging conventional wisdom among courts that the dormant Commerce Clause requires invalidation of state Internet communications regulations." Jack Goldsmith & Alan Sykes, *The Internet and the Dormant Commerce Clause,* 110 YALE L.J. 785 (2001). *See, e.g.*, Dan Burk, *Federalism in Cyberspace,* 28 CONN. L. REV. 1095, 1123–34 (1996); Glenn Harlan Reynolds, *Virtual Reality and "Virtual Welters": A Note on the Commerce Clause Implications of Regulating Cyberporn,* 82 VA. L. REV. 535, 537–42 (1996). Professors Goldsmith and Sykes, however, take issue with this view, arguing that it is "flawed in three respects: It rests on an impoverished understanding of the architecture of the Internet, it misreads dormant Commerce Clause jurisprudence, and it misunderstands the economics of state regulation of transborder transactions."

In what ways might state regulation of the Internet be thought to unduly burden the flow of interstate commerce? Consider the possibilities of inconsistent regulations by different states, the creation of economic externalities on those living in other states, and the problem of extraterritoriality. What justifications might a state make for regulation of, for example, Internet pornography? Of what relevance to this constitutional question, if any, is the *CTS* decision? The *Raymond* decision?

[C] STATE AS MARKET PARTICIPANT

REEVES, INC. v. STAKE

447 U.S. 429, 100 S. Ct. 2271, 65 L. Ed. 2d 244 (1980)

Justice Blackmun delivered the opinion of the Court.

The issue in this case is whether, consistent with the Commerce Clause, the State of South Dakota, in a time of shortage, may confine the sale of the cement it produces solely to its residents.

In 1919, South Dakota undertook plans to build a cement plant. The project, a product of the State's then prevailing Progressive political movement, was initiated in response to recent regional cement shortages that "interfered with and delayed both public and private enterprises," and that were "threatening the people of this state." Over the years, buyers in no less than nine nearby States purchased cement from the State's plant. Between 1970 and 1977, some 40% of the plant's output went outside the State. The plant's list of out-of-state cement buyers included petitioner Reeves, Inc., a ready-mix concrete distributor with facilities in Buffalo, Gillette, and Sheridan, Wyo. For 20 years the relationship between Reeves and the South Dakota cement plant was amicable, uninterrupted, and mutually profitable.

As the 1978 construction season approached, difficulties at the plant slowed production. Meanwhile, a booming construction industry spurred demand for cement both regionally and nationally. The plant found itself unable to meet all orders. Faced with the same type of "serious cement shortage" that inspired the plant's construction, the Commission "reaffirmed its policy of supplying all South Dakota customers first and to honor all contract commitments; with the remaining volume allocated on a first come, first served basis."

Reeves, which had no pre-existing long-term supply contract, was hit hard and quickly by this development. On June 30, 1978, the plant informed Reeves that it could not continue to fill Reeves' orders, and on July 5, it turned away a Reeves truck. Unable to find another supplier, Reeves was forced to cut production by 76% in mid-July. On July 19, Reeves brought this suit against the Commission, challenging the plant's policy of preferring South Dakota buyers, and seeking injunctive relief.

[*Hughes v. Alexandria Scrap Corp.*, 426 U.S. 79 (1976)] concerned a Maryland program designed to remove abandoned automobiles from the State's roadways and junkyards. To encourage recycling, a "bounty" was offered for every Maryland-titled junk car converted into scrap. Processors located both in and outside Maryland were eligible to collect these subsidies. The legislation, as initially enacted in 1969, required a processor seeking a bounty to present documentation evidencing ownership of the wrecked car. This requirement however, did not apply to "hulks," inoperable automobiles over eight years old. In 1974, the statute was amended to extend documentation requirements to hulks, which comprised a large majority of the junk cars being processed. Departing from prior practice, the new law imposed more exacting documentation requirements on out-of-state than in-state processors. By making it less remunerative for suppliers to transfer vehicles outside Maryland, the reform triggered a "precipitate decline in the number of bounty-eligible hulks supplied to appellee's [Virginia] plant from Maryland sources." Indeed, "[t]he practical effect was substantially the same as if Maryland had withdrawn altogether the availability of bounties on hulks delivered by unlicensed suppliers to licensed non-Maryland processors."

In the Court's view, *Alexandria Scrap* did not involve "the kind of action with which the Commerce Clause is concerned." Unlike prior cases voiding state laws inhibiting interstate trade, "Maryland has not sought to prohibit the flow of hulks, or to regulate the conditions under which it may occur. Instead, it has entered into the market itself to bid up their price," "as a purchaser, in effect, of a potential article of interstate commerce," and has restricted "its trade to its own citizens or businesses within the State."

Having characterized Maryland as a market participant, rather than as a market regulator, the Court found no reason to "believe the Commerce Clause was intended to require independent justification for [the State's] action." The Court couched its holding in unmistakably broad terms. "Nothing in the purposes animating the Commerce Clause prohibits a State, in the absence of congressional action, from participating in the market and exercising the right to favor its own citizens over others."

The basic distinction drawn in *Alexandria Scrap* between States as market participants and States as market regulators makes good sense and sound law. As that case explains, the Commerce Clause responds principally to state taxes and regulatory measures impeding free private trade in the national marketplace. There is no indication of a constitutional plan to limit the ability of the States themselves to operate freely in the free market. The precedents comport with this distinction.

Restraint in this area is also counseled by considerations of state sovereignty,[5] the role of each State "as guardian and trustee for its people," and "the long recognized right of trader or manufacturer, engaged in an entirely private business, freely to exercise his own independent discretion as to parties with whom he will deal." Moreover, state proprietary activities may be, and often are, burdened with the same restrictions imposed on private market participants. Evenhandedness suggests that, when acting as proprietors, States should similarly share existing freedoms from federal constraints, including the inherent limits of the Commerce Clause. Finally, as this case illustrates, the competing considerations in cases involving state proprietary action often

[5] Considerations of sovereignty independently dictate that marketplace actions involving "integral operations in areas of traditional governmental functions" — such as the employment of certain state workers — may not be subject even to congressional regulation pursuant to the commerce power. National League of Cities v. Usery, 426 U.S. 833, 852 (1976). It follows easily that the intrinsic limits of the Commerce Clause do not prohibit state marketplace conduct that falls within this sphere. Even where integral operations are not implicated, States may fairly claim some measure of a sovereign interest in retaining freedom to decide how, with whom, and for whose benefit to deal.

will be subtle, complex, politically charged, and difficult to assess under traditional Commerce Clause analysis. Given these factors, *Alexandria Scrap* wisely recognizes that, as a rule, the adjustment of interests in this context is a task better suited for Congress than this Court.

South Dakota, as a seller of cement, unquestionably fits the "market participant" label more comfortably than a State acting to subsidize local scrap processors. Thus, the general rule of *Alexandria Scrap* plainly applies here.

Undaunted by these considerations, petitioner advances four more arguments for reversal:

First, petitioner protests that South Dakota's preference for its residents responds solely to the "non-governmental objective" of protectionism. Therefore, petitioner argues, the policy is *per se* invalid.

We find the label "protectionism" of little help in this context. The State's refusal to sell to buyers other than South Dakotans is "protectionist" only in the sense that it limits benefits generated by a state program to those who fund the state treasury and whom the State was created to serve. Petitioner's argument apparently also would characterize as "protectionist" rules restricting to state residents the enjoyment of state educational institutions, energy generated by a state-run plant, police and fire protection, and agricultural improvement and business development programs. Such policies, while perhaps "protectionist" in a loose sense, reflect the essential and patently unobjectionable purpose of state government to serve the citizens of the State.[6]

Second, petitioner echoes the District Court's warning:

> If a state in this union were allowed to hoard its commodities or resources for the use of their own residents only, a drastic situation might evolve. For example, Pennsylvania or Wyoming might keep their coal, the northwest its timber, and the mining states their minerals. The result being that embargo may be retaliated by embargo and commerce would be halted at state lines.

This argument, although rooted in the core purpose of the Commerce Clause, does not fit the present facts. Cement is not a natural resource, like coal, timber, wild game, or minerals. It is the end-product of a complex process whereby a costly physical plant and human labor act on raw materials. South Dakota has not sought to limit access to the State's limestone or other materials used to make cement. Nor has it restricted the ability of private firms or sister States to set up plants within its borders. Moreover, petitioner has not suggested that South Dakota possesses unique access to the materials needed to produce cement.[7] Whatever limits might exist on a State's ability

[6] At bottom, the discrimination challenged in *Alexandria Scrap* was motivated by the same concern underlying South Dakota's resident preference policy — a desire to channel state benefits to the residents of the State supplying them. If some underlying "commendable as well as legitimate" purpose, is also required, it is certainly present here. In establishing the plant, South Dakota sought the most unstartling governmental goal: improvement of the quality of life in that State by generating a supply of a previously scarce product needed for "local" construction and governmental improvements.

[7] Nor has South Dakota cut off access to its own cement altogether, for the policy does not bar resale of South Dakota cement to out-of-state purchasers.

to invoke the *Alexandria Scrap* exemption to hoard resources which by happenstance are found there, those limits do not apply here.

Third, it is suggested that the South Dakota program is infirm because it places South Dakota suppliers of ready-mix concrete at a competitive advantage in the out-of-state market; Wyoming suppliers, such as petitioner, have little chance against South Dakota suppliers who can purchase cement from the State's plant and freely sell beyond South Dakota's borders. The force of this argument is seriously diminished, if not eliminated, by several considerations. The argument necessarily implies that the South Dakota scheme would be unobjectionable if sales in other States were totally barred. It therefore proves too much, for it would tolerate even a greater measure of protectionism and stifling of interstate commerce than the challenged system allows. Finally, the competitive plight of out-of-state ready-mix suppliers cannot be laid solely at the feet of South Dakota. It is attributable as well to their own States' not providing or attracting alternative sources of supply and to the suppliers' own failure to guard against shortages by executing long-term supply contracts with the South Dakota plant.

In its last argument, petitioner urges that, had South Dakota not acted, free market forces would have generated an appropriate level of supply at free market prices for all buyers in the region. Having replaced free market forces, South Dakota should be forced to replicate how the free market would have operated under prevailing conditions. This argument appears to us to be simplistic and speculative. The very reason South Dakota built its plant was because the free market had failed adequately to supply the region with cement.

JUSTICE POWELL, with whom JUSTICE BRENNAN, JUSTICE WHITE, and JUSTICE STEVENS join, dissenting.

The South Dakota Cement Commission has ordered that in times of shortage the state cement plant must turn away out-of-state customers until all orders from South Dakotans are filled. This policy represents precisely the kind of economic protectionism that the Commerce Clause was intended to prevent.[8]

The application of the Commerce Clause to this case should turn on the nature of the governmental activity involved. If a public enterprise undertakes an "integral operatio[n] in areas of traditional governmental functions," *National League of Cities v. Usery,* the Commerce Clause is not directly relevant. If, however, the State enters the private market and operates a commercial enterprise for the advantage of its private citizens, it may not evade the constitutional policy against economic balkanization.

This distinction derives from the power of governments to supply their own needs, and from the purpose of the Commerce Clause itself, which is designed to protect "the natural functioning of the interstate market." In procuring goods and services for the operation of government, a State may act without

[8] By "protectionism," I refer to state policies designed to protect private economic interests within the State from the forces of the interstate market. I would exclude from this term policies relating to traditional governmental functions, such as education, and subsidy programs like the one at issue in *Hughes v. Alexandria Scrap Corp.*

regard to the private marketplace and remove itself from the reach of the Commerce Clause. But when a State itself becomes a participant in the private market for other purposes, the Constitution forbids actions that would impede the flow of interstate commerce. These categories recognize no more than the "constitutional line between the State as Government and the State as trader."

The Court holds that South Dakota, like a private business, should not be governed by the Commerce Clause when it enters the private market. But precisely because South Dakota is a State, it cannot be presumed to behave like an enterprise engaged in an entirely private business. A State frequently will respond to market conditions on the basis of political rather than economic concerns. To use the Court's terms, a State may attempt to act as a "market regulator" rather than a "market participant." In that situation, it is a pretense to equate the State with a private economic actor. State action burdening interstate trade is no less state action because it is accomplished by a public agency authorized to participate in the private market.

The threshold issue is whether South Dakota has undertaken integral government operations in an area of traditional governmental functions, or whether it has participated in the marketplace as a private firm. If the latter characterization applies, we also must determine whether the State Commission's marketing policy burdens the flow of interstate trade. This analysis highlights the differences between the state action here and that before the Court in *Hughes v. Alexandria Scrap Corp.*

Unlike the market subsidies at issue in *Alexandria Scrap,* the marketing policy of the South Dakota Cement Commission has cut off interstate trade. The State can raise such a bar when it enters the market to supply its own needs. In order to ensure an adequate supply of cement for public uses, the State can withhold from interstate commerce the cement needed for public projects.

The State, however, has no parallel justification for favoring private, in-state customers over out-of-state customers. In response to political concerns that likely would be inconsequential to a private cement producer, South Dakota has shut off its cement sales to customers beyond its borders. That discrimination constitutes a direct barrier to trade of the type forbidden by the Commerce Clause, and involved in previous cases. The effect on interstate trade is the same as if the state legislature had imposed the policy on private cement producers. The Commerce Clause prohibits this severe restraint on commerce.

NOTES

1. *Rationale of participation*. What would the result have been in *Reeves* and *Hughes v. Alexandria Scrap Corp.* under conventional Commerce Clause analysis? In both cases the Court held that the Commerce Clause does not impose limitations on the state when it acts as a market participant rather than a market regulator. What is the rationale for this unique exclusion of an entire area of state activity from Commerce Clause constraints? The role of a state "as guardian and trustee for its people" is said to justify the "market participant" exception. Isn't this rationale equally applicable to *any* state regulation of commerce favoring its citizens, whether or not the state is a market participant? For example, reconsider the decision in *City of Philadelphia v. New Jersey*. Could not precisely the same argument have been made there to justify the state regulation?

Note also that the Court relied in part on the "state sovereignty" philosophy embodied in *National League of Cities*. What effect, if any, do you think the overruling of that decision in *Garcia,* should have on the "market participant" exception? Do the decisions in *New York v. U.S.* and *Lopez* alter that effect? In any event, is the sovereignty rationale logically inconsistent with the entire concept of the state as a market participant?

Finally, the Court relies on "the long recognized right of trader or manufacturer, engaged in an entirely private business, freely to exercise his own independent discretion as to parties with whom he will deal." Is this analogy persuasive? Is it realistic to compare a state, no matter what it is doing, to "an entirely private business"?

Reeves is criticized in Mark Gergen, *The Selfish State and the Market,* 66 TEX. L. REV. 1097, 1142–43 (1988):

> Ultimately preferences such as that in *Reeves* cannot be tolerated if we are to prevent state ownership of commercial enterprises from undermining our common market. States cannot be permitted to accomplish through ownership what they could not accomplish through regulation of commerce. Would we really permit a socialist government in Vermont to defeat free trade by collectivizing its retail establishments, factories, and farms?

2. *Participation and regulation*. *White v. Massachusetts Council of Constr. Employers*, 460 U.S. 204 (1983). How should the Court determine whether the state is acting as a market *participant* or as a market *regulator?* The mayor of Boston issued an executive order requiring that all construction projects funded in whole or in part by funds given or controlled by the city be performed by a work force consisting of at least half Boston residents. The state supreme court found the order barred by the negative implications of the dormant commerce clause, but the United States Supreme Court reversed: "*Alexandria Scrap* and *Reeves* stand for the proposition that when a state or local government enters the market as a participant it is not subject to the restraints of the Commerce Clause."

Justice Blackmun, joined by Justice White, concurred in part and dissented in part. He suggested that the "market participant" exception was inapplicable, because the executive order "goes much further" than *Reeves* or *Alexandria:*

> The city has not attempted merely to choose the "parties with whom [it] will deal." Instead, it has imposed as a condition of obtaining a public construction contract the requirement that *private firms* hire only Boston residents for 50% of specified jobs. Thus, the order directly restricts the ability of private employers to hire nonresidents, and thereby curtails nonresidents' access to jobs with private employers. I had thought it well established that, under the Commerce Clause, States and localities cannot impose restrictions granting their own

> residents either the exclusive right, or a priority, to private sector economic opportunities.

In a footnote in his opinion for the Court, Justice Rehnquist responded to Justice Blackmun:

> We agree with Justice Blackmun that there are some limits on a state or local government's ability to impose restrictions that reach beyond the immediate parties with which the government transacts business. We find it unnecessary in this case to define those limits with precision, except to say that we think the Commerce Clause does not require the city to stop at the boundary of formal privity of contract. In this case, the Mayor's executive order covers a discrete, identifiable class of economic activity in which the city is a major participant. Everyone affected by the order is, in a substantial if informal sense, "working for the city."

Serious questions may be raised about the consistency of the Court's treatment of employment requirements favoring in-state residents under the commerce clause with its treatment of similar situations under the privileges and immunities clause of Article IV, § 2. The issue will be reexamined in the notes following *Hicklin v. Orbeck.*

[D] INTERSTATE PRIVILEGES AND IMMUNITIES

HICKLIN v. ORBECK

437 U.S. 518, 98 S. Ct. 2482, 57 L. Ed. 2d 397 (1978)

Justice Brennan delivered the opinion of the Court.

In 1972, professedly for the purpose of reducing unemployment in the State, the Alaska Legislature passed an Act entitled "Local Hire Under State Leases." The key provision of "Alaska Hire," as the Act has come to be known, is the requirement that "all oil and gas leases, easements or right-of-way permits for oil or gas pipeline purposes, unitization agreements, or any renegotiation of any of the preceding to which the state is a party" contain a provision "requiring the employment of qualified Alaska residents" in preference to nonresidents. This employment preference is administered by providing persons meeting the statutory requirements for Alaskan residency with certificates of residence — "resident cards" — that can be presented to an employer covered by the Act as proof of residency. Appellants, individuals desirous of securing jobs covered by the Act but unable to qualify for the necessary resident cards, challenge Alaska Hire as violative of both the Privileges and Immunities Clause of Art. IV, § 2, and the Equal Protection Clause of the Fourteenth Amendment.

Appellants' principal challenge to Alaska Hire is made under the Privileges and Immunities Clause of Art. IV, § 2: "The Citizens of each State shall be entitled to all Privileges and Immunities of Citizens in the several States." That provision "establishes a norm of comity," *Austin v. New Hampshire*, 420

U.S. 656, 660 (1975), that is to prevail among the States with respect to their treatment of each other's residents. The purpose of the Clause, as described in *Paul v. Virginia*, 8 Wall. 168, 180 (1869), is

> to place the citizens of each State upon the same footing with citizens of other States, so far as the advantages resulting from citizenship in those States are concerned. It relieves them from the disabilities of alienage in other States; it inhibits discriminating legislation against them by other States; it gives them the right of free ingress into other States, and egress from them; it insures to them in other States the same freedom possessed by the citizens of those States in the acquisition and enjoyment of property and in the pursuit of happiness; and it secures to them in other States the equal protection of their laws. It has been justly said that no provision in the Constitution has tended so strongly to constitute the citizens of the United States one people as this.

Appellants' appeal to the protection of the Clause is strongly supported by this Court's decisions holding violative of the Clause state discrimination against nonresidents seeking to ply their trade, practice their occupation, or pursue a common calling within the State. For example, in *Ward v. Maryland*, 12 Wall. 418 (1871), a Maryland statute regulating the sale of most goods in the city of Baltimore fell to the privileges and immunities challenge of a New Jersey resident against whom the law discriminated. The statute discriminated against nonresidents of Maryland in several ways: It required nonresident merchants to obtain licenses in order to practice their trade without requiring the same of certain similarly situated Maryland merchants; it charged nonresidents a higher license fee than those Maryland residents who were required to secure licenses; and it prohibited both resident and nonresident merchants from using nonresident salesmen, other than their regular employees, to sell their goods in the city. In holding that the statute violated the Privileges and Immunities Clause, the Court observed that "the clause plainly and unmistakably secures and protects the right of a citizen of one State to pass into any other State of the Union for the purpose of engaging in lawful commerce, trade, or business without molestation." *Ward* thus recognized that a resident of one State is constitutionally entitled to travel to another State for purposes of employment free from discriminatory restrictions in favor of state residents imposed by the other State.

Again, *Toomer v. Witsell*, 334 U.S. 385 (1948), the leading modern exposition of the limitations the Clause places on a State's power to bias employment opportunities in favor of its own residents, invalidated a South Carolina statute that required nonresidents to pay a fee 100 times greater than that paid by residents for a license to shrimp commercially in the three-mile maritime belt off the coast of that State. The Court reasoned that although the Privileges and Immunities Clause "does not preclude disparity of treatment in the many situations where there are perfectly valid independent reasons for it," "[i]t does bar discrimination against citizens of other States where there is no substantial reason for the discrimination beyond the mere fact that they are citizens of other States." A "substantial reason for the discrimination" would not exist, the Court explained, "unless there is something to indicate that noncitizens constitute a peculiar source of the evil at which the [discriminatory] statute is aimed." Moreover, even where the presence or activity of nonresidents causes or exacerbates the problem the State seeks to remedy, there must be a "reasonable relationship between the danger represented by non-citizens, as a class, and the . . . discrimination practiced upon them." *Toomer*'s analytical framework was confirmed in *Mullaney v. Anderson*, 342 U.S. 415 (1952), where it was applied to invalidate a scheme used by the Territory of Alaska for the licensing of commercial fishermen in territorial waters; under that scheme residents paid a license fee of only $5 while nonresidents were charged $50.

Even assuming that a State may validly attempt to alleviate its unemployment problem by requiring private employers within the State to discriminate against nonresidents — an assumption made at least dubious by *Ward* — it is clear that under the *Toomer* analysis reaffirmed in *Mullaney,* Alaska Hire's discrimination against nonresidents cannot withstand scrutiny under the Privileges and Immunities Clause. For although the statute may not violate the Clause if the State shows "something to indicate that noncitizens constitute a peculiar source of the evil at which the statute is aimed," *Toomer v. Witsell,* and, beyond this, the State "has no burden to prove that its laws are not violative of the . . . Clause," *Baldwin v. Montana Fish and Game Comm'n,* (Brennan, J., dissenting), certainly no showing was made on this record that nonresidents were "a peculiar source of the evil Alaska Hire was enacted to remedy, namely, Alaska's uniquely high unemployment." What evidence the record does contain indicates that the major cause of Alaska's high unemployment was not the influx of nonresidents seeking employment, but rather the fact that a substantial number of Alaska's jobless residents — especially the unemployed Eskimo and Indian residents — were unable to secure employment either because of their lack of education and job training or because of their geographical remoteness from job opportunities; and that the employment of nonresidents threatened to deny jobs to Alaska residents only to the extent that jobs for which untrained residents were being prepared might be filled by nonresidents before the residents training was completed.

Moreover, even if the State's showing is accepted as sufficient to indicate that nonresidents were "a peculiar source of evil," *Toomer* and *Mullaney* compel the conclusion that Alaska Hire nevertheless fails to pass constitutional muster. For the discrimination the Act works against nonresidents does not bear a substantial relationship to the particular "evil" they are said to present. Alaska Hire simply grants all Alaskans, regardless of their employment status, education, or training, a flat employment preference for all jobs covered by the Act. A highly skilled and educated resident who has never been unemployed is entitled to precisely the same preferential treatment as the unskilled, habitually unemployed Arctic Eskimo enrolled in a job-training program. If Alaska is to attempt to ease its unemployment problem by forcing employers within the State to discriminate against nonresidents — again, a policy which may present serious constitutional questions — the means by which it does so must be more closely tailored to aid the unemployed the Act is intended to benefit. Even if a statute granting an employment preference to unemployed residents or to residents enrolled in job-training programs might be permissible, Alaska Hire's across-the-board grant of a job preference to all Alaskan residents clearly is not.

Relying on *McCready v. Virginia*, 94 U.S. 391 (1877), however, Alaska contends that because the oil and gas that are the subject of Alaska Hire are *owned* by the State, this ownership, of itself, is sufficient justification for the Act's discrimination against nonresidents, and takes the Act totally without the scope of the Privileges and Immunities Clause. We do not agree that the fact that a State owns a resource, of itself, completely removes a law concerning that resource from the prohibitions of the Clause. Although some courts, including the court below, have read *McCready* as creating an "exception" to the Privileges and Immunities Clause, we have just recently confirmed that "[i]n more recent years . . . the Court has recognized that the States' interest in regulating and controlling those things they claim to 'own' . . . is by no means absolute." *Baldwin v. Montana Fish and Game Comm'n.* Rather than placing a statute completely beyond the Clause, a State's ownership of the property with which the statute is concerned is a factor — although often the crucial factor — to be considered in evaluating whether the statute's discrimination against noncitizens violates the Clause. Dispositive though this factor may be in many cases in which a State discriminates against nonresidents, it is not dispositive here.

The reason is that Alaska has little or no proprietary interest in much of the activity swept within the ambit of Alaska Hire; and the connection of the State's oil and gas with much of the covered activity is sufficiently attenuated so that it cannot justifiably be the basis for requiring private employers to discriminate against nonresidents.

Although appellants raise no Commerce Clause challenge to the Act, the mutually reinforcing relationship between the Privileges and Immunities Clause of Art. IV, § 2, and the Commerce Clause — a relationship that stems from their common origin in the Fourth Article of the Articles of Confederation and their shared vision of federalism, see *Baldwin v. Montana Fish and Game Comm'n* — renders several Commerce Clause decisions appropriate support for our conclusion. [Prior cases] establish that the Commerce Clause circumscribes a State's ability to prefer its own citizens in the utilization of natural resources found within its borders, but destined for interstate commerce. Alaska's oil and gas here are bound for out-of-state consumption. Indeed, the construction of the Trans-Alaska Pipeline, on which project appellants' nonresidency has prevented them from working, was undertaken expressly to accomplish this end. Although the fact that a state-owned resource is destined for interstate commerce does not, of itself, disable the State from preferring its own citizens in the utilization of that resource, it does inform analysis under the Privileges and Immunities Clause as to the permissibility of the discrimination the State visits upon nonresidents based on its ownership of the resource. Here, the oil and gas upon which Alaska hinges its discrimination against nonresidents are of profound national importance. On the other hand, the breadth of the discrimination mandated by Alaska Hire goes far beyond the degree of resident bias Alaska's ownership of the oil and gas can justifiably support. The confluence of these realities points to but one conclusion: Alaska Hire cannot withstand constitutional scrutiny. As MR.

JUSTICE CARDOZO observed in *Baldwin v. G. A. F. Seelig, Inc.,* the Constitution "was framed upon the theory that the peoples of the several states must sink or swim together, and that in the long run prosperity and salvation are in union and not division."

NOTES

1. ***Privileges and immunities***. Article IV, § 2 has been narrowly construed only as a prohibition of discrimination against out-of-state citizens. *Toomer v. Witsell*, 334 U.S. 385, 396 (1948), defined the operative test for applying Article IV, § 2, in terms reminiscent of Commerce Clause balancing:

> Like many other constitutional provisions, the privileges and immunities clause is not an absolute. It does bar discrimination against citizens of other States where there is no substantial reason for the discrimination beyond the mere fact that they are citizens of other States. But it does not preclude disparity of treatment in the many situations where there are perfectly valid independent reasons for it. Thus the inquiry in each case must be concerned with whether such reasons do exist and whether the degree of discrimination bears a close relation to them. The inquiry must also, of course, be conducted with due regard for the principle that the States should have considerable leeway in analyzing local evils and in prescribing appropriate cures.

2. ***Discrimination and the dormant Commerce Clause***. The Supreme Court in *Hicklin* noted "the mutually reinforcing relationship" between Article IV, § 2 and the dormant commerce clause. Are the concepts redundant? As one distinction, the Privileges and Immunities Clause has been construed to exclude protection of corporations. *Blake v. McClung*, 172 U.S. 239 (1898).

3. ***United Building & Construction Trades Council v. City of Camden,* 465 U.S. 208 (1984)**. The Court remanded, under the Privileges and Immunities Clause, a municipal ordinance requiring that at least 40% of the employees of contractors and subcontractors working on city construction projects be Camden residents. Justice Rehnquist, speaking for the Court, initially rejected the state supreme court's conclusion that the clause was inapplicable to a municipal ordinance, which had the same effect on state residents living outside of the municipality as on out-of-staters:

> The fact that the ordinance in question is a municipal, rather than a state, law does not somehow place it outside the scope of the Privileges and Immunities Clause. First of all, one cannot easily distinguish municipal from state action in this case: the municipal ordinance would not have gone into effect without express approval by the State Treasurer. More fundamentally, a municipality is merely a political subdivision of the State from which its authority derives. It is as true of the Privileges and Immunities Clause as of the Equal Protection Clause that what "would be unconstitutional if done directly by the State can no more readily be accomplished by a city deriving its authority from the State. We have never read the clause so literally as to apply it only to distinctions based on state citizenship.

> A person who is not residing in a given State is *ipso facto* not residing in a city within that State. Thus, whether the exercise of a privilege is conditioned on state residency or on municipal residency he will just as surely be excluded."

Ultimately, the Court found that Camden's asserted justification required further factfinding by the lower court on the issue of whether nonresidents were a particular souce of unemployment problems in Camden. "Camden may, without fear of violating the Commerce Clause, pressure private employers engaged in public works projects funded in whole or in part by the city to hire city residents. But that same exercise of power to bias the employment decisions of private contractors and sub-contractors against out-of-state residents may be called to account under the Privileges and Immunities Clause."

The facts of *White* (p. 270) and *United Building* are, of course, strikingly similar, with the exception that *White* concerned a Commerce Clause challenge while *United Building* involved an attack under the privileges and immunities clause. Should the standards under the commerce clause and the privileges and immunities clause differ? Justice Rehnquist in *United Building* concluded that they do:

> The two Clauses have different aims and set different standards for state conduct. The Commerce Clause acts as an implied restraint upon state regulatory powers. Such powers must give way before the superior authority of Congress to legislate on (or leave unregulated) matters involving interstate commerce. When the state acts solely as a market participant, no conflict between state *regulation* and federal regulatory authority can arise. The Privileges and Immunities Clause, on the other hand, imposes a direct restraint on state action in the interests of interstate harmony. This concern with comity cuts across the market regulator-market participant distinction that is crucial under the Commerce Clause. It is discrimination against out-of-state residents on matters of fundamental concern which triggers the Clause, not regulation affecting interstate commerce. Thus, the fact that Camden is merely setting conditions on its expenditures for goods and services in the marketplace does not preclude the possibility that those conditions violate the Privileges and Immunities Clause.

Compare this analysis to *Hicklin* where the Court recognized "the mutually reinforcing relationship" between the two clauses, stemming "from their common origin and their shared vision of federalism." Reconsider the discussion of the possible rationales for the dormant Commerce Clause, discussed at the beginning of this chapter.

Is it true that the purpose of the negative implications theory of the dormant Commerce Clause is simply to assure that state power to regulate interstate commerce "give[s] way before the superior authority of Congress to legislate on (or leave unregulated) matters involving interstate commerce"? If it were, would we really need the concept in the first place? If Congress has, in fact, legislated, an ordinary preemption analysis will determine whether state legislation is permitted. The dormant Commerce Clause, by its very nature, operates only when Congress has *not* acted. In such an event, is it necessarily accurate to suggest that Congress has decided to "leave [the area] unregulated"? Would the dormant Commerce Clause not apply if it were determined simply that Congress had not even considered regulating the area? No inquiry into specific congressional intent in *not* regulating has ever been incorporated into a dormant Commerce Clause analysis.

Thus, if the dormant Commerce Clause applies, even when state regulation in no way interferes with any congressional plan to regulate or not regulate, the only purpose the concept could possibly serve would be a desire to preserve interstate comity. If one reaches this conclusion, is it legitimate to impose different standards under the Privileges and Immunities Clause and the dormant Commerce Clause?

4. *Importance of the interests involved.* There are occasions when the Court will not employ Article IV, § 2, against state laws which discriminate against nonresidents. A challenge to Montana's statutory elk-hunting license scheme based on the Privileges and Immunities Clause of Article IV, § 2, and Fourteenth Amendment equal protection was reviewed by the Court in *Baldwin v. Fish & Game Comm'n*, 436 U.S. 371 (1978). Under the 1976 Montana scheme, a Montana resident could purchase a license to hunt for elk for $9. A nonresident was required to purchase a combination license entitling him to hunt for a variety of designated game for $225. The resident could purchase a combination license granting all of the same hunting privileges for $30.

The Court, per Justice Blackmun, limited the Privileges and Immunities Clause as follows: "Only with respect to those 'privileges' and 'immunities' bearing upon the vitality of the Nation as a single entity must the State treat all citizens, resident and non-resident, equally." The Court concluded that hunting for elk in Montana "is not basic to the maintenance or well-being of the Union." The clause was read to prohibit only distinctions that "hinder the formation, the purpose or the development of a single union of States." Prior cases dealing with the important state interest in preserving and regulating the exploitation of its natural resources, including its wildlife, were emphasized. Further, out-of-state residents were not "deprived of a means of livelihood by the system or by access to any part of the State to which they may seek to travel." Simply, this did not involve a "fundamental" right under the Privileges and Immunities Clause.

Justice Brennan, joined by Justices White and Marshall, dissenting, challenged the Court's construction of Article IV, § 2. "I think the time has come to confirm explicitly that which has been implicit in our modern privileges and immunities decisions, namely that an inquiry into whether a given right is 'fundamental' has no place in our analysis of whether a State's discrimination against non-residents — who 'are not represented in the [discriminating] State's legislative halls,' violates the Clause. Rather, our primary concern is the State's justification for its discrimination."

The majority opinion also rejected an equal protection challenge because "[t]he legislative choice was an economic means not unreasonably related to the preservation of a finite resource and a substantial regulatory interest of the State."

5. *Attorney licensing and residence*. In *Supreme Court of New Hampshire v. Piper*, 470 U.S. 274 (1985), the Court held that the rules of the Supreme Court of New Hampshire limiting bar admission to state residents violated the Privileges and Immunities Clause of Art. IV, § 2. Justice Powell, for the Court, initially determined that the opportunity to practice law should be considered a national "fundamental right" under Art. IV, § 2. Justice Powell concluded that the practice of law does not involve "an exercise of state power justifying New Hampshire's residency requirement." While a state might restrict the right to hold elected office to residents, a lawyer is not " 'an officer' of the State in any political sense."

Having concluded that the state's residency rule deprived nonresidents of a protected privilege under Art. IV, § 2, the Court turned to the question of whether there was a substantial reason for the differential treatment and whether the discrimination practiced against nonresidents bore a substantial relationship to the state's objective. This included consideration of the availability of less restrictive means. The Court concluded: "The State neither advances a substantial reason for its discrimination against nonresident applicants to the bar, nor demonstrates that the discrimination practiced bears a close relationship to its proffered objectives."

Justice Rehnquist dissented, arguing that "there are significant state interests justifying this type of interstate discrimination." Just as a state may require that its lawmakers be residents without violating Art. IV, § 2, and may establish independently of the other states its own laws for governance of its citizens, so also New Hampshire should have a "right to decide that those people who in many ways will intimately deal with New Hampshire's self-governance should reside within that State." Justice Rehnquist distinguished legal practice from other occupations for Art. IV purposes because "law is one occupation that does not readily translate across state lines. Certain aspects of legal practice are distinctly and intentionally nonnational."

In *Supreme Court of Va. v. Friedman*, 487 U.S. 59 (1988), the Court, per Justice Kennedy, relying on *Piper,* struck down as violative of the Privileges and Immunities Clause a Virginia Supreme Court rule requiring out-of-state lawyers to become permanent residents of Virginia in order to be admitted to the state bar without examination. While acknowledging that "[t]he Clause does not preclude disparity in treatment where substantial reasons exist for the discrimination and the degree of discrimination bears a close relation to such reasons," the Court rejected the state's asserted justifications: "We acknowledge that a bar examination is one method of assuring that the admitted attorney has a stake in her professional license and concomitant interest in the integrity and standards of the bar. The question, however, is whether lawyers who are admitted in other States are less likely to respect the bar and further its interests solely because they are nonresidents. We cannot say this is the case."

Chief Justice Rehnquist, joined by Justice Scalia, dissented: "I continue to believe that the Privileges and Immunities Clause does not require States to ignore residency when admitting lawyers to practice in the way that they must ignore residency when licensing traders in foreign goods, or when licensing commercial shrimp fishermen."

Barnard v. Thorstenn, 489 U.S. 546 (1989), applying *Piper,* held that the bar admission residency requirements of the Virgin Islands, which are governed as a federal territory, violate the Privileges and Immunities Clause. Local court rules of the District Court of the Virgin Islands provided that applicants for bar admission must have resided in the Virgin Islands for at least one year and must state an intent to reside and practice law there following admission. The Court, per Justice Kennedy, held that none of the justifications offered for the rule was "sufficient to meet the Virgin Island's burden of demonstrating that the discrimination against nonresidents by Rule 56(6) is warranted by a substantial objective and bears a close or substantial relation to that objective."

Chief Justice Rehnquist, joined by Justices White and O'Connor, dissenting, urged that the case be remanded for trial to resolve genuine factual disputes about the uniqueness of legal practice in the Virgin Islands.

6. *Lunding v. New York Tax Appeals Tribunal,* 522 U.S. 287 (1998). The Court, per Justice O'Connor, held that a New York tax law, § 631(b)(6), violated the Privileges and Immunities Clause, Art. IV, § 2, since it prevented nonresidents from deducting alimony from their taxable income while allowing residents to deduct alimony expenses. Lunding, an attorney who resided in Connecticut but who worked in New York, filed suit challenging § 631(b)(6) as a violation of the Privileges and Immunities Clause claiming that he should be able to deduct 48% of his alimony expense because 48% of his income derived from activities conducted in New York. The New York Court of Appeals upheld the law reasoning that "substantial reasons for the disparity in tax treatment are apparent on the face of the statutory scheme."

The Supreme Court held 6-3 that the State had not shown substantial justification for the difference in treatment of nonresidents. One of the rights secured by Art. IV, § 2, is the right to carry on business in another state without being subjected to discriminatory taxation. While the Clause does not guarantee precise equality between residents and nonresidents, the constitutional rule is one of substantial equality of treatment.

New York argued that there is a distinction between business expenses related to the business income a nonresident earns in New York versus expenses "wholly linked to personal activities outside New York." New York claimed that because alimony was a personal expense the expense was more appropriately allocated to the state where the taxpayer resided. The Court rejected this argument because the statute prevented nonresidents from deducting any alimony expense, regardless of whether the alimony expense was related to New York. Thus, even if Lunding had been paying alimony to a New York resident (who would be taxed on the alimony as income), Lunding would be unable to deduct the expense from his New York income. Further, Justice O'Connor stressed "the inequities that could result when a nonresident with alimony obligations derives nearly all of her income from New York, a scenario that may be typical."

The Court concluded:

> Under the circumstances, we find that respondents have not presented a substantial justification for the categorical denial of alimony deductions to nonresidents. The State's failure to provide more than a cursory justification for § 631(b)(6) smacks of an effort to "penaliz[e] the citizens of other States by subjecting them to heavier taxation merely because they are such citizens," *Toomer*. We thus hold that § 631(b)(6) is an unwarranted denial to the citizens of other States of the privileges and immunities enjoyed by the citizens of New York.

Justice Ginsburg, joined by Chief Justice Rehnquist and Justice Kennedy, dissented, claiming that the majority developed a new "related-to-income" approach that would lead to allowing nonresidents to deduct any and every personal deduction allowed to residents— "[i]f that is the law of this case, long-settled provisions and decisions have been overturned, beyond the capacity of any legislature to repair." The dissent argued that the Court "previously held it sufficient . . .that 'the State has secured a reasonably fair distribution of burdens, and that no intentional discrimination has been made against nonresidents.' " The New York Court of Appeals had provided sufficient justification for section 631(b)(6) and the New York law was a fair adaptation, at the state level, of the current federal law.

7. *Hillside Dairy, Inc. v. Lyons*, 539 U.S. 59 (2003). The Supreme Court unanimously held that a claim under the Privileges and Immunities Clause of Art. IV, § 2 is not foreclosed because the challenged state regulations do not discriminate on their face on the basis of state citizenship or state residence. The Court also held that California's pricing and pooling system for determining the prices processors of fluid milk, pay to the producers of raw milk was not "legitimized" by § 144 of the Federal Agricultural Improvement and Reform Act against Commerce Clause challenge, on Congressional legitimization of state laws burdening interstate commerce.

Various corporate and individual out-of-state producers of milk filed suit in district court challenging a 1997 amendment to California's milk-pricing scheme, alleging that it violates the Commerce Clause and the Privileges and Immunities Clause of Art IV, § 2. The district court dismissed both claims without reaching the merits. The Court of Appeals for the Ninth Circuit held that a 1996 federal statute, § 144 of the Federal Agriculture Improvement and Reform Act ("§ 144"), immunized California's regulatory pricing and pooling regulations from Commerce Clause challenges. With respect to the Privileges and Immunities Clause claim, the Ninth Circuit held the corporations lacked standing, and that the individual's claim failed because the amendments did not "on their face, create classifications based on an individual's residency or citizenship."

The Court began by discussing the Commerce Clause issue. After discussing the history and precedent relating to § 144, Justice Stevens quoted the text of § 144:

> Nothing in this Act or any other provision of law shall be construed to preempt, prohibit or to otherwise limit the State of California,

> directly or indirectly, to establish or continue to affect any law, regulation, or requirement regarding (1) the percentage of milk solids or solids not fat in fluid milk products sold at retail or marketed in the State of California; or (2) the labeling of such fluid milk products with regard to milk solids or solids not fat.

The Court rejected California's argument that this language exempted its regulatory scheme from Commerce Clause challenges: "The text of the federal statute plainly covers California laws regulating the composition and labeling of fluid milk products, but does not mention laws regulating pricing." While Justice Stevens accepted the principle that Congress "has the power to authorize state regulations that burden or discriminate against interstate commerce," he stated that "we will not assume that it has done so unless such an intent is clearly expressed." While § 144 exempted any compositional and labeling laws imposed by California, it did not clearly express an intent to immunize pricing and pooling laws from Commerce Clause challenge. Justice Stevens said that "the mere fact that the composition and labeling laws relate to the sale of fluid milk is by no means sufficient to bring them within the scope of § 144." The Ninth Circuit erred in relying on § 144 to dismiss the challenge.

The Court then discussed the Privilege and Immunities claim. The Petitioners conceded the Ninth Circuit's conclusion that the corporate plaintiffs lacked standing to challenge the California laws under Art. II, § 2. Petitioners did challenge the Ninth Circuit holding that the claim of the individual challengers was barred "because the California laws 'do not, on their face, create classifications based on any individual's residency or citizenship.' " The Court held that "the absence of an express statement in the California laws and regulations identifying out-of-state citizenship as a basis for disparate treatment is not a sufficient basis for rejecting this claim." It did not decide whether Art. IV, § 2 prohibited "any classification with the practical effect of discriminating against [out-of-state] residents" nor did the Court reach the merits of the privileges and immunities claim. The judgment of the court of appeals was vacated and the cases were remanded.

Justice Thomas concurred in part and dissented in part. While he agreed that the Ninth Circuit was incorrect in their interpretation of the federal statute, he would affirm dismissal of the Commerce Clause claim because "[t]he negative Commerce Clause has no basis in the text of the Constitution, makes little sense, and has proved virtually unworkable in application." Therefore, Justice Thomas believes it "cannot serve as a basis for striking down a state statute."

§ 3.03 WHEN CONGRESS SPEAKS

The previous sections dealt with the negative implications of the dormant Commerce Clause when Congress has not spoken. In the present section, the focus shifts to consider the consequences when Congress speaks.

[A] LEGITIMIZING STATE BURDENS ON COMMERCE

In *Cooley v. Board of Wardens*, 53 U.S. (12 How.) 318 (1851), the Court stated:

> If the states were divested of the power to legislate on this subject by the grant of the commercial power to Congress, it is plain [that Congress] could not confer upon them power thus to legislate. If the Constitution excluded the states from making any laws regulating commerce, certainly Congress cannot regrant, or in any manner reconvey to the states that power.

Does this mean that the commerce power also limits the power of Congress? If Congress has plenary power over interstate commerce as *Gibbons* indicated, is there any limitation on its power to define the subjects of interstate commerce and the mode of their regulation? How could Justice Stone in *Southern Pac. Co. v. Arizona ex rel. Sullivan*, 325 U.S. 761 (1945), state that Congress has undoubted power to permit the states to regulate interstate commerce in a manner which would otherwise not be permissible?

In *Prudential Ins. Co. v. Benjamin*, 328 U.S. 408 (1946), the Court dealt with the validity of a 3% tax imposed on foreign, but not domestic, insurance companies by the state of South Carolina. A long line of decisions had held discriminatory taxes violative of the commerce clause. Further, two years earlier, in *United States v. Southeastern Underwriters Ass'n*, 322 U.S. 533 (1944), the Court had held that the insurance business was interstate commerce for purposes of the federal antitrust laws. Congress, however, had responded to the *Southeastern Underwriters* decision by passing the McCarran Act providing: "The business of insurance and every person engaged therein, shall be subject to the laws of the several states which relate to the regulation or taxation of such business."

Noting prior Court decisions validating congressional revisions of earlier Court holdings, Justice Rutledge for the Supreme Court stated:

> Whenever Congress' judgment has been uttered affirmatively to contradict the Court's previously expressed view that specific action taken by the states in Congress' silence was forbidden by the commerce clause, this body has accommodated its previous judgment to Congress' expressed approval.
>
> Some part of this readjustment may be explained in ways acceptable on any theory of the commerce clause, and the relations of Congress and the courts toward its functioning. Such explanations, however, hardly go to the root of the matter. For the fact remains that, in these instances, the sustaining of Congress' overriding action has involved something beyond correction of erroneous factual judgment in deference to Congress' presumably better-informed view of the facts, and also beyond giving due deference to its conception of the scope of its power, when it repudiates, just as when its silence is thought to support, the inference that it has forbidden state action.

> Congress intended to declare, and in effect declared, that uniformity of regulation, and of state taxation, are not required in reference to the business of insurance, by the national public interest, except in the specific respects otherwise specifically provided for. This necessarily was a determination by Congress that state taxes, which in its silence might be held invalid and discriminatory, do not place on interstate insurance business a burden which it is unable generally to bear or should not bear in the competition with local business.
>
> The power of Congress over commerce exercised entirely without reference to coordinated action of the states is not restricted, except as the Constitution expressly provides, by any limitation which forbids it to discriminate against interstate commerce in favor of local trade. Congress may keep the way open, confine it broadly or closely, or close it entirely, subject only to the restrictions upon its authority by other constitutional provisions and the requirement that it shall no invade the domains of action reserved exclusively for the states.
>
> This broad authority Congress may exercise alone, subject to those limitations, or in conjunction with coordinated action by the states, in which case limitations imposed by the preservation of their powers become inoperative and only those designed to forbid action altogether by any power or combination of powers in our governmental system remain effective. Here both Congress and South Carolina have acted, and in complete coordination, to sustain the tax. It is therefore reinforced by the exercise of all the power of government residing in our scheme.
>
> [Prudential's arguments] would reduce the joint exercise of power by Congress and the states to achieve common ends and the regulation of our society below the effective range of either power separately exerted, without basis in specific constitutional limitation or otherwise in the division itself. We know of no grounding, in either constitutional experience or spirit, for such a restriction. For great reasons of policy and history not now necessary to restate, these great powers were separated. They were not forbidden to cooperate or by doing so to achieve legislative consequences, particularly in the great fields of regulating commerce and taxation, which to some extent at least, neither could accomplish in isolated exception.

Prudential Insurance Co. v. Benjamin indicates that Congress can legitimate state action that would otherwise violate the Commerce Clause. *See Western & Southern Life Ins. Co. v. State Bd. of Equalization*, 451 U.S. 648 (1981) (California retaliatory tax against out-of-state insurance companies upheld on the basis of *Prudential Ins. Co. v. Benjamin*). If the negative implications on undue state interference with the free flow of commerce arose from presumed congressional intent, Congress could presumably remove the barrier. But if it is the Constitution, as interpreted by the Court, that prohibits the state action, how can Congress by ordinary legislation remove the prohibition? For the argument that "[t]he Court's willingness to allow Congress to overrule the Dormant Commerce Clause's limitations on state authority is fundamentally inconsistent with the Court's declared view that Congress may not authorize the states to violate the Constitution," and that "even worse, the Court has failed to provide a cogent explanation for this anomalous exception" to accepted precepts of judicial review, see Norman Williams, *Why Congress May Not "Overrule" the Dormant Commerce Clause*, 53 UCLA L. Rev. 153, 156 (2005).

[B] PREEMPTION BY FEDERAL STATUTE

In certain instances, the Constitution itself may preempt state power to act. *See, e.g.*, U.S. Const. Art. I, § 10, cl. 1. The cases in this chapter mostly have dealt with displacement by the Constitution of state power to regulate interstate commerce, subject to possible authorization by Congress through legislative action. Finally, Congress may choose to preempt state law in the course of establishing national rules even though absent such legislation states would have been permitted to act. It is to the latter subject that we now turn.

As *Gibbons v. Ogden* makes clear, a state law which conflicts with a valid federal law must give way under the Supremacy Clause of Article VI. Further, if Congress pursuant to its commerce powers expressly excludes state regulation, that is determinative since "the government of the Union, though limited in its powers, is supreme within its sphere of action." *McCulloch v. Maryland.* But what if the state law does not directly conflict with federal legislation and Congress does not expressly exclude the states from regulating? If the state law "stands as an obstacle to the accomplishment and execution of the full purposes and objectives of Congress," that in itself can result in its invalidation. *Jones v. Rath Packing Co.*, 430 U.S. 519, 526 (1977).

If some concurrent state regulation is permissible, what standard determines the permissible from the impermissible? The most important of the earlier preemption decisions are *Hines v. Davidowitz*, 312 U.S. 52 (1941), and *Pennsylvania v. Nelson*, 350 U.S. 497 (1956). In *Hines,* the Court invalidated Pennsylvania's Alien Registration Act because it was preempted by a comparable federal statute, noting that "[t]he basic subject of the state and federal laws is identical" and reasoning:

> There is not — and from the very nature of the problem there cannot be — any rigid formula or rule which can be used as a universal pattern to determine the meaning and purpose of every act of Congress. This Court, in considering the validity of state laws in the light of treaties or federal laws touching the same subject, has made use of the following expressions: conflicting; contrary to; occupying the field; repugnance; difference; irreconcilability; inconsistency; violation; curtailment; and interference. But none of these expressions provides an infallible constitutional yardstick. In the final analysis, there can be no one crystal clear distinctly marked formula. Our primary function is to determine whether, under the circumstances of this particular case, Pennsylvania's law stands as an obstacle to the accomplishment and execution of the full purposes and objectives of Congress.

In finding the state law preempted, the Court emphasized that "this legislation is in a field which affects international relations, the one aspect of our government that from the first has been most generally conceded imperatively to demand broad national authority," and that "this legislation deals with the rights, liberties, and personal freedoms of human beings, and is an entirely different category from state tax statutes or state pure food laws regulating the label on cans."

In *Nelson,* the Court held that a federal statute prohibiting the knowing advocacy of the overthrow of the Government of the United States by force and violence preempted the state sedition law, which proscribed the exact same conduct. The Court quoted *Rice v. Santa Fe Elevator Corp.*, 331 U.S. 218, 230 (1947), for the proposition that "[t]he scheme of federal regulation [is] so pervasive as to make reasonable the inference that Congress left no room for the States to supplement it."

For an interesting discussion of modern preemption theory, see David B. Spence & Paula Murphy, *The Law, Economics, and Politics of Federal Preemption Jurisprudence: A Quantitative Analysis,* 87 CALIF. L. REV. 1125 (1999). The authors note that "the question of whether a particular state or local environmental, health, and safety regulation should be preempted poses an ideological quandary for individual federal judges. For most judges, whether liberal or conservative, these cases pit one dimension of their ideology, their principles of federalism, against another, their policy preferences or attitudes toward the particular local regulation at issue. Generally speaking, conservatives and Republicans tend to favor less federal regulation and greater state power; conversely, liberals and Democrats tend to favor more federal regulation and less state power. However, most preemption cases involve a state or local regulation that is is more stringent than the corresponding federal regulation. For conservative judges, this means that upholding state power against a federal challenge will lead to more regulation, not less; ideologically liberal judges face exactly the opposite quandary." *Id.* at 1129.

To what extent should a judge's ideology or view of federalism appropriately affect her preemption determination? What question or questions should a judge be asking herself in making such a determination?

Chapter 4

EXECUTIVE AND CONGRESSIONAL RELATIONS: SEPARATION OF POWERS

James Madison in THE FEDERALIST, No. 47, wrote: "No political truth is certainly of greater intrinsic value, or is stamped with the authority of more enlightened patrons of liberty, than that accumulation of all powers, legislative, executive, and judiciary, in the same hands may justly be pronounced the very definition of tyranny." Building on the theoretical writings of Montesquieu and John Locke, and the practical experience of seventeenth-century England, the colonies and the Confederation (where executive and legislative powers were merged in the Congress), the Framers undertook to separate the legislative, executive, and judicial powers in the first three articles of the Constitution. But would this prevent tyranny? Left to itself, each branch might accumulate power with which to impose its will. Further, total separation, like total merger of powers, might well impair the effective performance of the government's business.

The answer was to reject an absolute separation of governmental functions. While the departments were formally separated and certain core functions were assigned to each of the separate institutions, the functions of the branches were also mingled and blended. There was created a "government of separated institutions sharing powers." RICHARD E. NEUSTADT, PRESIDENTIAL POWER 33 (1960). This was the system of checks and balances. As Madison explained: "The great security against a gradual concentration of the several powers in the same department consists in giving to those who administer each department the necessary constitutional means and personal motives to resist encroachment on the others. Ambition must be made to counteract ambition." THE FEDERALIST, No. 51. The President, for example, could veto legislation but the Congress could override the veto. The Executive could appoint officials and make treaties, but only with the concurrence of the Senate. The courts might invalidate laws passed by the Congress and signed by the President, but the Executive would appoint the judges with the Senate's approval.

As this discussion indicates, while the separation of powers principle serves to increase efficiency in government, this is not its only or even primary purpose. As Justice Brandeis said, dissenting in *Myers v. United States,* 272 U.S. 52, 293 (1926):

> The doctrine of the separation of powers was adopted by the Convention of 1787, not to promote efficiency, but to preclude the exercise of arbitrary power. The purpose was, not to avoid friction, but, by means of the inevitable friction incident to the distribution of the governmental powers among three departments, to save the people from autocracy.

The task of performing the essential functions of government while preserving this critical function of the separation of powers principle is the central focus of the present chapter.

Commentators have not been kind to recent Supreme Court separation of powers decisions. The Court is criticized for failing to provide any coherent doctrine and for vacillating between two approaches. There is the *formalist* model which sees the constitutional text as establishing bright lines separating the powers and responsibilities of the three branches. Formalist analysis tends to employ a literalist approach to interpreting constitutional language defining these separated powers. Martin Redish & Elizabeth Cisar, *"If Angels Were to Govern": The Need for Pragmatic Formalism in Separation of Powers Theory*, 41 DUKE L.J. 49, 465 (1991), present the formalist perspective:

> Each branch is limited to the exercise of the power given to it, which in turn, is exclusive of the power exercised by the other branches (with the limited exceptions explicitly provided in the text that allow one branch to check another). Under this structure, no case-by-case inquiry is made into the likelihood that tyranny will be threatened by a breach of branch separation, for the simple reason that there is no effective method of making that inquiry — at least until it is too late to avoid the danger.

The *functional* approach, in contrast, emphasizes the checks and balances principle more than strict separation. The functionalist tolerates a more fluid and flexible approach to the relations of the branches and perceives a greater open-ended, ambiguous quality to the constitutional language. For example, a self-proclaimed functionalist, Peter Strauss, *Formal and Functional Approaches to Separation of Powers Questions — A Foolish Inconsistency?*, 72 CORNELL L. REV. 488, 511–12 (1987), states:

> The Government we have built and now live with has attained a complexity and intermarriage of function that beggars the rationalistic tripartite schemes of the eighteenth century. Identifying a satisfactory principle for assessing the permissibility of distributions of governmental power, much less one that can be rooted in the "separation-of-powers" framework, may simply be too much to expect.

To what problems might a formalist approach give rise? Consider the argument made in Rebecca Brown, *Separated Powers and Ordered Liberty*, 139 U. PA. L. REV. 1513, 1524–25 (1991): "[Formalism] depends upon a belief that legislative, executive, and judicial powers are inherently distinguishable as well as separable from one another-a highly questionable premise. Moreover, formalism tends to produce excessively mechanical results." Professor Brown further argues that formalism "tends to straightjacket the government's ability to respond to new needs in creative ways, even if those ways pose no threat to whatever might be posited as the basic purposes of the constitutional structure." *Id.* at 1526.

On the other hand, consider the potential problems with a functionalist approach. Functionalism, it has been suggested, fails to provide "any comprehensible standard by which to judge particular incursions on the separation of powers." Moreover, functionalism undermines "the key structural assumption of separation-of-powers theory-that it will be impossible (at least until it is too late) to determine whether or not a particular breach of branch separation will seriously threaten the core political values of accountability, diversity and checking. Thus, functionalism, as the basis for the design of a doctrinal model of separation of powers, fails to fulfill the goals intended by the choice of a governmental system premised on separation of powers." MARTIN H. REDISH, THE CONSTITUTION AS POLITICAL STRUCTURE 125 (1995).

At times, the Court employs a formalist analysis and, on other occasions, a functional model. Is one approach preferable in all cases? Are there reasons to choose one model over another depending on the facts of the case? Consider the argument made in Bradford R. Clark, *Separation of Powers As a Safeguard of Federalism,* 79 TEX. L. REV. 1321, 1326 (2001), that "[m]any of the Court's most prominent decisions employing a formal approach involve enforcement of constitutionally prescribed lawmaking procedures designed to safeguard federalism. Formalism in this context operates to preserve state governance prerogatives by making federal law more difficult to adopt. Decisions taking a functional approach to separation of powers, by contrast, typically involve potential interference by one branch with the constitutional functions of another rather than attempts to evade federal lawmaking procedures." How legitimate is such a distinction? Does the fact that formalist protections are needed in the case of prescribed lawmaking procedures in order to protect federalism necessarily imply that such protections are *not* necessary to police one branch's incursions into the sphere of another? If the primary purpose of separation of powers protections was to prevent one or another branch from gaining tyrannical power, does it make sense to say that such protections are sufficiently important to justify formalist protection *only* when federalism concerns are also directly implicated? Why is it necessarily an either-or proposition?

One commentator has suggested that in reality there exists a "surprising, but robust, consensus" between formalists and functionalists. M. Elizabeth Magill, *The Real Separation in Separation of Powers Law,* 86 VA. L. REV. 1127, 1131 (2000). Professor Magill argues that "formalists and functionalists alike subscribe to a consensus about the objective of the system of separation of powers and also about the mechanisms by which that objective is to be achieved. First, courts and commentators agree on the following objective: The system of separation of powers is intended to prevent a single governmental institution from possessing and exercising too much power. Second, courts and commentators also basically, though not universally, agree on the mechanisms by which that objective is to be achieved. There are two components to those means. Commentators agree that governmental functions (legislative, executive, judicial) are to be dispersed among different governmental institutions. They also agree that, through the familiar features such as the President's limited veto, impeachment, and advice and consent, the institutions are given the means to protect the exercise of their own functions and check the exercise of functions by the others." *Id.* at 1147–49.

What are the concerns or values involved in the separation of powers cases? At times, the Court focuses on the need to assure that a branch will be able to perform certain "core" functions assigned to it by the Constitution. The emphasis is on avoiding diffusion of constitutional power and responsibility. At other times, the Court emphasizes preventing one branch from aggrandizing its own powers at the expense of the other branches. The focus is on avoiding concentration of governmental power. How do these concerns relate to the task of preserving individual liberties and to promoting government that is accountable to citizens, and yet is effective?

Throughout this book, consideration has been given to the role of the judiciary in relation to the other branches. In the present chapter, the focus will be on how the separation of powers principle has fared in the interplay between Congress and the executive branch. To what extent do these two branches exercise "exclusive" and "shared" powers? What principles guide the sharing of powers? Are the governing principles different in the domestic and foreign arenas?

Consider what should be the proper role of the judiciary in providing answers to the above questions, and in maintaining separation of powers generally. Professor Choper has argued:

> The federal judiciary should not decide constitutional questions concerning the respective powers of Congress and the President vis-a-vis one another; rather, the ultimate constitutional issues of whether executive action (or inaction) violates the prerogatives of Congress or whether legislative action (or inaction) transgresses the realm of the President should be held to be nonjusticiable, their final resolution to be remitted to the interplay of the national political process.

JESSE CHOPER, JUDICIAL REVIEW AND THE NATIONAL POLITICAL PROCESS 263 (1980). Choper grounds his theory on two premises: (1) that the political branches will themselves be able effectively to police separation-of-powers violations; and (2) that judicial resolution of separation-of-powers disputes will drain the judiciary's preciously limited institutional capital, which is needed more for the protection of individual rights, where those affected are likely to be unable to protect themselves. See *Id.* at 260–75.

Consider the following response to Choper's argument: "In structuring their unique governmental form, the Framers sought to avoid undue concentrations of power by resort two institutional devices designed to foster three political values: checking, diversification, and accountability. By simultaneously dividing power among the three branches and institutionalizing methods that allow each branch to check the two others, the Constitution reduces the likelihood that one faction or interest group that has managed to obtain control of one branch will be able to implement its political agenda in contravention of the wishes of the people. That the political structure adopted in the Constitution was designed simultaneously to preserve individual liberty and to avoid tyranny should come as no surprise to anyone reasonably well schooled in the theory of American government. But that fact makes all the more puzzling the modern tendency of both Court and commentators to treat these structural provisions with not-so-benign neglect. [A]ny purported dichotomy between constitutional structure and constitutional rights is a dangerous and false one. When political structure and constitutional rights are viewed as necessary but insufficient parts of a symbiotic, organic whole, one can easily see that in certain ways, the structural provisions are designed to reduce the possibility that individual liberties will, at some future point, be directly assaulted by government. In this manner, it was hoped, direct confrontation between government and liberty could be avoided." Redish, THE CONSTITUTION AS POLITICAL STRUCTURE at 4. See also Brown, 139 U. PA. L. REV., at 1514, arguing "that the structure of the government is a vital part of a constitutional organism whose final cause is the protection of individual rights."

If one were to begin interpretation of separation of powers with the premise that those structural protections were inserted for the purpose of preserving liberty, how, if at all, should that fact influence that interpretive process? Professor Brown has suggested that "when government action is challenged on separation-of-powers grounds, the Court should consider the potential effect of the arrangement on individual due-process interests." She contrasts her suggested doctrinal approach with an alternative approach that focuses on "the aim of preserving the government for its own sake," which she criticizes because "it does not look beyond any specific cases to a higher objective that the separation of powers may serve." *Id.* at 1514–16.

§ 4.01 PERSPECTIVES ON THE EXECUTIVE POWER

American history has been marked by the expansion of executive power, generally at the expense of Congress. Today the President is Head of State, Chief Legislator, Chief Administrator, Head of Foreign Relations, Commander in Chief, and Head of his Political Party, and a more recent nominee, Chief Prosecutor. But how has this occurred? Corwin notes that the colonists viewed "the executive magistracy" as "the natural enemy, the legislative assembly [as] the natural friend of liberty." EDWARD S. CORWIN, THE PRESIDENT: OFFICE AND POWERS, 1787–1957, at 4 (4th ed. 1957). Certainly, fear of the royal prerogative was well established during the colonial period; there was not even a separate executive office during the Confederation. Further, a review of the powers delegated in Articles I and II would suggest that the Congress, rather than the President, has the tools for achieving "leadership" in our balanced separation of powers system.

While the framers created a single independent President, who could be re-elected, the vague powers granted only suggest the potential of the institutionalized presidency. Cass Sunstein, *An Eighteenth Century President in a Twenty-First Century World*, 48 ARK. L. REV. 1 (1995):

> Insofar as it deals with presidential power, however, the American Constitution has proved to be a highly malleable document. With very few exceptions, the constitutional provisions relating to the president have not been changed at all since they were ratified in 1787. But in the late twentieth century, those provisions do not mean what they meant in 1787. The Constitution is a legal document, and it is enforced judicially; but its meaning was hardly fixed when it was ratified. In particular, the contemporary President has far broader powers than the original Constitution contemplated.

Franklin Delano Roosevelt's response to the economic crisis of the Great Depression and the emergency generated by World War II as well as the demands of international relations in modern times have done much to shape the modern American presidency. But there have been energetic presidents throughout our history who, responding to the needs of the times, or through personal disposition, have maximized the powers of the executive. Much of the present-day character of separation of powers, then, is a function of the perception and values of the men who have occupied the office.

Two polar views of their offices were presented by Teddy Roosevelt and William H. Taft. THEODORE ROOSEVELT, THE AUTOBIOGRAPHY OF THEODORE ROOSEVELT (W. Andrews ed. 1958): "The most important factor in getting the right spirit in my Administration, next to the insistence upon courage, honesty, and a genuine democracy of desire to serve the plain people, was my insistence upon the theory that the executive power was limited only by specific restrictions and prohibitions appearing in the Constitution or imposed by the Congress under its constitutional powers." W.H. TAFT, OUR CHIEF MAGISTRATE AND HIS POWERS (1916): "The true view of the Executive functions is, as I conceive it, that the President can exercise no power which cannot be fairly and reasonably traced to some specific grant of power or justly implied and included within such express grant as proper and necessary to its exercise. Such specific grant must be either in the federal Constitution or in an act of Congress passed in pursuance thereof. . . . My judgment is that the view of Mr. Roosevelt, ascribing an undefined residuum of power to the President is an unsafe doctrine and that it might lead under emergencies to results of an arbitrary character, doing irremediable injustice to private right."

NOTES

1. *Stewardship.* Judge Pine in the lower court decision in the *Steel Seizure* Case, p. 296, said that Roosevelt's stewardship theory does not "comport with our recognized theory of government." But consider the argument of John Locke:

> Where the legislative and executive power are in distinct hands, as they are in all moderated monarchies and well-framed governments, there the good of society requires that several things should be left to the discretion of him that has the executive power. For the legislature not being able to foresee and provide by law for all that may be useful to the community, the executor of the laws, having the power in his hands, but has, by the common law of nature, a right to make good of it for the good of society, in many cases where the municipal law has given no direction, till the legislative can be conveniently assembled to provide for it; nay, many things there are which the law can by no means provide for, and those must necessarily be left to the discretion of him that has the executive power in his hands, to be ordered by him as the public good and advantage shall require; nay, it is fit that the laws themselves should in some cases give way to the executive power, or rather to this fundamental law of nature and government — viz., that as much as may be all the members of the society are to be preserved.

John Locke, Two Treatises on Civil Government, Bk. II, ch. 14, §§ 159–66.

Is the stewardship theory premised on inherent presidential powers not dependent on constitutional grant? If such a power is recognized, a question would arise whether it would nevertheless be subject to constitutional limitation. Should it matter whether the subject matter is domestic or foreign?

2. *The vestiture clause.* Is Article II, § 1, vesting the "executive power" in the President, an independent grant of power or only a designation of the office? Does it vest all law-enforcing powers in the President? Consider the argument fashioned in Steven Calabresi & Saikrishna Prakash, *The President's Power to Execute the Law*, 104 Yale L.J. 541, 571 (1994):

> The Vesting Clauses of Article II and III contain nearly identical language in parallel grammatical formulations. Both omit the "herein granted" qualification that appears in the Vesting Clause of Article I, and both confer *general* grants of power (executive or judicial) on federal governmental entities that are then defined and limited by later provision of Article II and III.

Contrast this view with the position taken in Lawrence Lessig & Cass Sunstein, *The President and the Administration*, 94 Colum. L. Rev. 1, 47–48 (1994):

> [T]he framers intended the Vesting Clause to vest constitutionally little more than the enumerated executive powers. It says *who has the executive power*; not what that power is, just as the Vesting Clause of Article I says who has the legislative power (a Congress), while section 8 says what that power is, and the Vesting Clause of Article III says who has the judicial power (one Supreme Court at least) while section 2 specifies to what that power "extend[s]."

It has been argued by some commentators that the term "vested in the president" means that the powers were vested in one person, thereby indicating the outcome of the debate at the Constitutional Convention over whether there should be a plural or singular executive and was not intended to vest some unspecified powers in the President. On the other hand, in *Myers v. United States*, 272 U.S. 52 (1926), involving the President's power to remove government officials, Chief Justice Taft claimed that "[t]he vesting of the executive power in the President was essentially a grant of the power to execute the laws" not subject to qualification by statute, and that the specification was designed to lend emphasis "where emphasis was regarded as appropriate." Further, he noted that the First Congress in debating how the Secretary of the new Department of Foreign Relations might be removed, recognized that the President already had the power of removal, apparently through the "executive power" clause. But Justice Holmes, dissenting in *Myers*, asserted: "The duty of the President to see that the laws are executed is a duty that does not go beyond the laws or require him to achieve more than Congress sees fit to leave within his power."

3. *In re Neagle,* 135 U.S. 1 (1890). The Attorney General assigned Neagle, a United States marshal, to protect Supreme Court Justice Field, whose life had been threatened by one Terry. After Neagle had shot and killed Terry, he was arrested by state authorities and sought a writ of habeas corpus under federal statutes providing immunity from state prosecution for an act "in pursuance of a law of the United States." Although there was no definite statute authorizing Neagle's action, the Court issued the writ. While relying in part on statutes dealing with the powers of federal marshals, Justice Miller used broad language to characterize the executive power. Art. II, sec. 3, declaring that the President "shall take care that the laws be faithfully exectued," he reasoned, is not limited to the enforcement of acts of Congress or treaties according to their express terms, but instead includes "the rights, duties, and obligations growing out of the Constitution itself, our international relations, and all the protection implied by the nature of the government under the Constitution."

4. *In re Debs,* 158 U.S. 564 (1895). The Justice Department sought to enjoin Debs and other strikers from obstructing interstate commerce and the mails. Although there was no statutory basis for an injunction, the Court granted it, using language indicative of a broad executive power to act in the public interest:

> Every government, entrusted, by the very terms of its being, with powers and duties to be exercised and discharged for the general welfare, has a right to apply to its own courts for any proper assistance in the exercise of the one and the discharge of the other. [W]henever wrongs complained of are such as affect the public at large, and are in respect of matters which by the Constitution are entrusted to the care of the Nation, and concerning which the Nation owes the duty to all the citizens of securing to them their common rights, then the mere fact that the government has no pecuniary interest in the controversy is not sufficient to exclude it from the courts, or prevent it from taking measures therein to fully discharge those constitutional duties.

As Edward S. Corwin was later to note, "the Nation" here meant the President. "The significance of the Court's choice of terminology is that it was not basing its holding on the duty of the President 'to take care that the laws be faithfully executed,' but on a broader principle — national interest." Edward Corwin, *The Steel Seizure Case: A Judicial Brick Without Straw*, 53 COLUM. L. REV. 53, 54 (1953). Again, however, it should be noted that the Court did use statutes relating to the interstate commerce and postal powers in sustaining the injunction.

5. *United States v. Midwest Oil Co.,* 236 U.S. 459 (1915). This case represents one of the strongest precedents for broad executive power. Although a congressional statute indicated that public lands were to be open to public entry when "mineral deposits" were found, President Taft ordered withdrawal of land to prevent depletion of oil reserves. Although there was no direct statutory authorization for such action, the Court found adequate authority in the continued uncontested usage of the executive.

> Both officers, lawmakers and citizens naturally adjust themselves to any long-continued action of the Executive Department — on the

> presumption that unauthorized acts would not have been allowed to be so often repeated as to crystallize into a regular practice. That presumption is not reasoning in a circle but the basis of a wise and quieting rule that in determining the meaning of a statute or the existence of a power, weight shall be given to the usage itself — even when the validity of the practice is the subject of investigation.

The congressional enactments in this instance were "necessarily general," subject to emergencies and changed conditions justifying executive action. The important element was that Congress had not taken any action "which could, in any way, be construed as a denial of the right of the Executive to make temporary withdrawals of public land in the public interest."

Justice Day, dissenting, argued: "There is nothing in the Constitution suggesting or authorizing such augmentation of executive authority or justifying him in thus acting in aid of a power which the framers of the Constitution saw fit to vest exclusively in the legislative branch of the government." Does congressional acquiescence in executive action constitute congressional authorization of that action? Can it create a constitutional common law of executive power?

§ 4.02 ALLOCATING THE LAWMAKING POWER

The modern American President arguably makes as well as executes the law. Operating through the Executive Office, his role in framing legislation and influencing legislative outcomes, added to the veto and threat of veto, is a major factor in his domestic power position vis-a-vis the Congress. Through the issuance of executive orders and other policy directives, the executive further implements its legislative role. "Executive orders are presidential policy directives to the federal bureaucracy. Most executive orders implement legislative policies pursuant to specific grants of statutory authority to the President. Some important executive orders, however, implement what is essentially executive managerial policy pursuant to the President's independent authority under the Constitution and unspecified 'laws of the United States,' or to vague, general statutory grants of housekeeping or managerial authority." Peter Raven-Hansen, *Making Agencies Follow Orders: Judicial Review of Agency Violations of Executive Order 12,291*, 1983 Duke L.J. 285, 286.

Article I clearly establishes that "All legislative powers herein granted shall be vested in a Congress of the United States." The Article goes on to define the procedures for congressional lawmaking. While Chapter 2 of this text focused on the broad legislative power thus conferred, there are limitations, some of which flow from the doctrine of separation of powers. To what extent can Congress delegate its Article I responsibilities? What limitations exist on its powers to oversee the implementation of laws? With the growth of executive power and the advent of independent agencies, how can Congress maintain its role and its responsibilities in the separation of powers and checks and balances system?

[A] EXECUTIVE LAWMAKING

YOUNGSTOWN SHEET & TUBE CO. v. SAWYER [THE STEEL SEIZURE CASE]

343 U.S. 579, 72 S. Ct. 863, 96 L. Ed. 1153 (1952)

JUSTICE BLACK delivered the opinion of the Court.

We are asked to decide whether the President was acting within his constitutional power when he issued an order directing the Secretary of Commerce to take possession of and operate most of the Nation's steel mills. The mill owners argue that the President's order amounts to lawmaking, a legislative function which the Constitution has expressly confided to the Congress and not to the President. The Government's position is that the order was made on findings of the President that his action was necessary to avert a national catastrophe which would inevitably result from a stoppage of steel production, and that in meeting this grave emergency the President was acting within the aggregate of his constitutional powers as the Nation's Chief Executive and the Commander in Chief of the Armed Forces of the United States.

In the latter part of 1951, a dispute arose between the steel companies and their employees over terms and conditions that should be included in new collective bargaining agreements. Long-continued conferences failed to resolve the dispute. On December 18, 1951, the employees' representative, United Steelworkers of America, C.I.O., gave notice of an intention to strike when the existing bargaining agreements expired on December 31. The Federal Mediation and Conciliation Service then intervened in an effort to get labor and management to agree. This failing, the President on December 22, 1951, referred the dispute to the Federal Wage Stabilization Board to investigate and make recommendations for fair and equitable terms of settlement. The Board's report resulted in no settlement. On April 4, 1952, the Union gave notice of a nation-wide strike called to begin at 12:01 a.m. April 9. The indispensability of steel as a component of substantially all weapons and other war materials led the President to believe that the proposed work stoppage would immediately jeopardize our national defense and that governmental seizure of the steel mills was necessary in order to assure the continued availability of steel. Reciting these considerations for his action, the President, a few hours before the strike was to begin, issued Executive Order 10340. The order directed Secretary of Commerce to take possession of most of the steel mills and keep them running. The Secretary immediately issued his own possessory orders, calling upon the presidents of the various seized companies to serve as operating managers for the United States. They were directed to carry on their activities in accordance with regulations and directions of the Secretary. The next morning the President sent a message to Congress reporting his action. Twelve days later he sent a second message. Congress has taken no action.

Obeying the Secretary's orders under protest, the companies brought proceedings against him in the District Court. Their complaints charged that the seizure was not authorized by an act of Congress or by any constitutional provisions. The District Court was asked to declare the orders of the President and the Secretary invalid and to issue preliminary and permanent injunctions restraining their enforcement. Opposing the motion for preliminary injunction, the United States asserted that a strike disrupting steel production for even a brief period would so endanger the well-being and safety of the Nation that the President had "inherent power" to do what he had done — power "supported by the Constitution, by historical precedent, and by court decisions." The Government also contended that in any event no preliminary injunction should be issued because the companies had made no showing that their available legal remedies were inadequate or the their injuries from seizure would be irreparable. Holding against the Government on all points, the District Court on April 30 issued a preliminary injunction restraining the Secretary from "continuing the seizure and possession of the plants and from acting under the purported authority of Executive Order No., 10340." On the same day the Court of Appeals stayed the District Court's injunction. Deeming it best that the issues raised be promptly decided by this Court, we granted certiorari on May 3 and set the cause for argument on May 12.

The President's power, if any, to issue the order must stem either from an act of Congress or from the Constitution itself. There is no statute that expressly authorizes the President to take possession of property as he did here. Nor is there any act of Congress to which our attention has been directed from which such a power can fairly be implied. Indeed, we do not understand the Government to rely on statutory authorization for this seizure.

[T]he use of the seizure technique to solve labor disputes in order to prevent work stoppages was not only unauthorized by any congressional enactment; prior to this controversy, Congress had refused to adopt that method of settling labor disputes. When the Taft-Hartley Act was under consideration in 1947, Congress rejected an amendment which would have authorized such governmental seizures in cases of emergency. Instead, the plan sought to bring about settlements by use of the customary devices of mediation, conciliation, investigation by boards of inquiry, and public reports. In some instances temporary injunctions were authorized to provide cooling-off periods. All this failing, the unions were left free to strike after a secret vote by employees as to whether they wished to accept their employers' final settlement offer.

It is clear that if the President had authority to issue the order he did, it must be found in some provisions of the Constitution. And it is not claimed that express constitutional language grants this power to the President. The contention is that presidential power should be implied from the aggregate of his powers under the Constitution. Particular reliance is placed on provisions in Article II which say that "The executive Power shall be vested in a President"; that "he shall take Care that the Laws be faithfully executed"; and that he "shall be Commander in Chief of the Army and Navy of the United States."

The order cannot properly be sustained as an exercise of the President's military power as Commander in Chief of the Armed Forces. The Government attempts to do so by citing a number of cases upholding broad powers in military commanders engaged in day-to-day fighting in a theater of war. Such cases need not concern us here. Even though "theater of war" be an expanding concept, we cannot with faithfulness to our constitutional system hold that the Commander in Chief of the Armed Forces has the ultimate power as such to take possession of private property in order to keep labor disputes from stopping production. This is a job for the Nation's lawmakers, not for its military authorities.

Nor can the seizure order be sustained because of the several constitutional provisions that grant executive power to the President. In the framework of our Constitution, the President's power to see that the laws are faithfully executed refutes the idea that he is to be a lawmaker. The Constitution limits his functions in the lawmaking process to the recommending of laws he thinks wise and the vetoing of laws he thinks bad. And the Constitution is neither silent nor equivocal about who shall make laws which the President is to execute.

The President's order does not direct that a congressional policy be executed in a manner prescribed by Congress — it directs that a presidential policy be executed in a manner prescribed by the President. The power of Congress to adopt such public policies as those proclaimed by the order is beyond question. It can authorize the taking of private property for public use. It can make laws regulating the relationships between employers and employees, prescribing rules designed to settle labor disputes, and fixing wages and working conditions in certain fields of our economy. The Constitution did not subject this lawmaking power of Congress to presidential or military supervision or control.

It is said that other Presidents without congressional authority have taken possession of private business enterprises in order to settle labor disputes. But even if this be true, Congress has not thereby losts its exclusive contitutional authority to make laws necessary and proper to carry out the powers vested by the Constitution "in the Government of the United States, or any Department or Officer thereof." The Founders of this Nation entrusted the lawmaking power to the Congress alone in both good and bad times. It would do no good to recall the historical events, the fears of power and the hopes for freedom that lay behind their choice. Such a review would but confirm our holding that this seizure order cannot stand.

JUSTICE DOUGLAS, concurring.

The branch of government that has the power to pay compensation for a seizure is the only one able to authorize a seizure or make lawful one that the President has effected. That seems to me to be the necessary result of the condemnation provision in the Fifth Amendment. It squares with the theory of checks and balances expounded by MR. JUSTICE BLACK in the opinion of the Court in which I join.

JUSTICE FRANKFURTER, concurring.

We must put to one side consideration of what powers the President would have had if there had been no legislation whatever bearing on the authority asserted by the seizure, or if the seizure had been only for a short, explicitly temporary period, to be terminated automatically unless Congressional approval were given. These and other questions, like or unlike, are not now here. I would exceed my authority were I to say anything about them.

In adopting the provisions which it did, by the Labor Management Relations Act of 1947, for dealing with a "national emergency" arising out of a breakdown in peaceful industrial relations, Congress was very familiar with Governmental seizure as a protective measure. On a balance of considerations, Congress chose not to lodge this power in the President. It chose not to make available in advance a remedy to which both industry and labor were fiercely hostile.

The powers of the President are not as particularized as are those of Congress. But unenumerated powers do not mean undefined powers. The separation of powers built into our Constitution gives essential content to undefined provisions in the frame of our government.

To be sure, the content of the three authorities of government is not to be derived from an abstract analysis. The areas are partly interacting, not wholly disjointed. The Constitution is a framework for government. Therefore the way the framework has consistently operated fairly establishes that it has operated according to its true nature. Deeply embedded traditional ways of conducting government cannot supplant the Constitution or legislation, but they give meaning to the words of a text or supply them. It is an inadmissibly narrow conception of American constitutional law to confine it to the words of the Constitution and to disregard the gloss which life has written upon them. In short, a systematic, unbroken, executive practice, long pursued to the knowledge of the Congress and never before questioned, engaged in by Presidents who have also sworn to uphold the Constitution, making as it were such exercise of power part of the structure of our government, may be treated as a gloss on "executive Power" vested in the President by § 1 of Art. II.

[T]he list of executive assertions of the power of seizure in circumstances comparable to the present reduces to three in the six-month period from June to December of 1941. We need not split hairs in comparing those actions to the one before us, though much might be said by the way of differentiation. Without passing on their validity, as we are not called upon to do, it suffices to say that these three isolated instances do not add up, either in number, scope, duration or contemporaneous legal justification, to the kind of executive construction of the Constitution revealed in the *Midwest Oil* case. Nor do they come to us sanctioned by long-continued acquiescence of Congress giving decisive weight to a construction by the Executive of its powers.

Justice Jackson, concurring in the judgment and opinion of the Court.

The actual art of governing under our Constitution does not and cannot conform to judicial definitions of the power of any of its branches based on isolated clauses or even single Articles torn from context. While the Constitution diffuses power the better to secure liberty, it also contemplates that practice will integrate the dispersed powers into a workable government. It enjoins upon its branches separateness but interdependence, autonomy but reciprocity. Presidential powers are not fixed but fluctuate, depending upon their disjunction or conjunction with those of Congress. We may well begin by a somewhat oversimplified grouping of practical situations in which a President may doubt, or others may challenge, his powers, and by distinguishing roughly the legal consequences of this factor of relativity.

1. When the President acts pursuant to an express or implied authorization of Congress, his authority is at its maximum, for it includes all that he possesses in his own right plus all that Congress can delegate. In these circumstances, and in these only, may he be said (for what it may be worth) to personify the federal sovereignty. If this act is held unconstitutional under these circumstances, it usually means that the Federal Government as an undivided whole lacks power. A seizure executed by the President pursuant to an Act of Congress would be supported by the strongest of presumptions and the widest latitude of judicial interpretation, and the burden of persuasion would rest heavily upon any who might attack it.

2. When the President acts in absence of either a congressional grant or denial of authority, he can only rely upon his own independent powers, but there is a zone of twilight in which he and Congress may have concurrent authority, or in which its distribution is uncertain. Therefore, congressional inertia, indifference or quiescence may sometimes, at least as a practical matter, enable, if not invite, measures on independent presidential responsibility. In this area, any actual test of power is likely to depend on the imperatives of events and contemporary imponderables rather than on abstract theories of law.

3. When the President takes measures incompatible with the expressed or implied will of Congress, his power is at its lowest ebb, for then he can rely only upon his own constitutional powers minus any constitutional powers of Congress over the matter. Courts can sustain exclusive presidential control in such a case only by disabling the Congress from acting upon the subject. Presidential claim to a power at once so conclusive and preclusive must be scrutinized with caution, for what is at stake is the equilibrium established by our constitutional system.

Into which of these classifications does this executive seizure of the steel industry fit? It is eliminated from the first by admission, for it is conceded that no congressional authorization exists for this seizure. Can it then be defended under flexible tests available to the second category? It seems clearly eliminated from that class because Congress has not left seizure of private property an open field but has covered it by three statutory policies inconsistent with this seizure. None of these were invoked. This leaves the current seizure to be justified only by the severe tests under the third grouping, where it can be supported only by any remainder of executive power after subtraction of such powers as Congress may have over the subject. In short, we can sustain the President only by holding that seizure of such strike-bound industries is within his domain and beyond control by Congress. Thus, this Court's first review of such seizures occurs under circumstances which leave presidential power most vulnerable to attack and in the least favorable of possible constitutional postures.

I did not suppose, and I am not persuaded, that history leaves it open to question, at least in the courts, that the executive branch, like the Federal Government as a whole, possesses only delegated powers. The purpose of the Constitution was not only to grant power, but to keep it from getting out of hand. However, because the President does not enjoy unmentioned powers does not mean that the mentioned ones should be narrowed by a niggardly construction. Some clauses could be made almost unworkable, as well as immutable, by refusal to indulge some latitude of interpretation for changing times.

The Solicitor General seeks the power of seizure in three clauses of the Executive Article, the first reading, "The executive Power shall be vested in a President of the United States of America." I cannot accept the view that this clause is a grant in bulk of all conceivable executive power but regard it as an allocation to the presidential office of the generic powers thereafter stated.

The clause on which the Government next relies is that "The President shall be Commander in Chief of the Army and Navy of the United States." [The] argument tendered at our bar [is] that the President having, on his own responsibility, sent American troops abroad derives from that act "affirmative power" to seize the means of producing a supply of steel for them. I cannot foresee all that it might entail if the Court should endorse this argument. Nothing in our Constitution is plainer than that declaration of a war is entrusted only to Congress. Of course, a state of war may in fact exist without a formal declaration. But no doctrine that the Court could promulgate would seem to me more sinister and alarming than that a President whose conduct of foreign affairs is so largely uncontrolled, and often even is unknown, can vastly enlarge his mastery over the internal affairs of the country by his own commitment of the Nation's armed forces to some foreign venture.

The third clause in which the Solicitor General finds seizure powers is that "he shall take Care that the Laws be faithfully executed." That authority must be matched against words of the Fifth Amendment that "No person shall be deprived of life, liberty or property, without due process of law." One gives a governmental authority that reaches so far as there is law, the other gives a private right that authority shall go no farther. These signify about all there is of the principle that ours is a government of laws, not of men, and that we submit ourselves to rulers only if under rules.

The Solicitor General lastly grounds support of the seizure upon nebulous, inherent powers never expressly granted but said to have accrued to the office from the customs and claims of preceding administrations. The plea is for a resulting power to deal with a crisis or an emergency according to the necessities of the case, the unarticulated assumption being that necessity knows no law.

Loose and irresponsible use of adjectives colors all non-legal and much legal discussion of presidential powers. "Inherent" powers, "implied" powers, "incidental" powers, "plenary" powers, "war" powers and "emergency" powers are used, often interchangeably and without fixed or ascertainable meanings.

The vagueness and generality of the clauses that set forth presidential powers afford a plausible basis for pressures within and without an administration for presidential action beyond that supported by those whose responsibility it is to defend his actions in court. The claim of inherent and unrestricted presidential powers had long been a persuasive dialectical weapon in political controversy. While it is not surprising that counsel should grasp support from such unadjudicated claims of power, a judge cannot accept self-serving press statements of the attorney for one of the interested parties as authority in answering a constitutional question, even if the advocate was himself. But prudence has counseled that actual reliance on such nebulous claims stop short of provoking a judicial test.

The appeal, however, that we declare the existence of inherent powers *ex necessitate* to meet an emergency asks us to do what many think would be wise, although it is something the forefathers omitted. They knew what emergencies were, knew the pressures they engender for authoritative action, knew, too, how they afford a ready pretext for usurpation. We may also suspect that they suspected that emergency powers would tend to kindle emergencies. Aside from suspension of the privilege of the writ of habeas corpus in time of rebellion or invasion, when the public safety may require it, they made no express provision for exercise of extraordinary authority because of a crisis.

In the practical working of our Government we already have evolved a technique within the framework of the Constitution by which normal executive powers may be considerably expanded to meet an emergency. Congress may and has granted extraordinary authorities which lie dormant in normal times but may be called into play by the Executive in war or upon proclamation of a national emergency. Under this procedure we retain Government by law-special, temporary law, perhaps, but law nonetheless. The public may know the extent and limitations of the powers that can be asserted, and persons affected may be informed from the statute of their rights and duties.

In view of the ease, expedition and safety with which Congress can grant and has granted large emergency powers, certainly ample to embrace this crisis, I am quite unimpressed with the argument that we should affirm possession of them without statute. Such power either has no beginning or it has no end. If it exists, it need submit to no legal restraint. I am not alarmed that it would plunge us straightway into dictatorship, but it is at least a step in that wrong direction.

JUSTICE BURTON, concurring in both the opinion and judgment of the Court.

Does the President have inherent constitutional power to seize private property which makes congressional action in relation thereto unnecessary? We find no such power available to him under the present circumstances. The present situation is not comparable to that of an imminent invasion or threatened attack. We do not face the issue of what might be the President's constitutional power to meet such catastrophic situations. Nor is it claimed that the current seizure is in the nature of a military command addressed by the President, as Commander-in-Chief, to a mobilized nation waging, or imminently threatened with total war.

The controlling fact here is that Congress, within its constitutionally delegated power, has prescribed for the President specific procedures, exclusive of seizure, for his use in meeting the present type of emergency. Under these circumstances, the President's order of April 8 invaded the jurisdiction of Congress. It violated the essence of the principle of the separation of governmental powers.

JUSTICE CLARK, concurring in the judgment of the Court.

In my view the Constitution does grant to the President extensive authority in times of grave and imperative national emergency. In fact, to my thinking, such a grant may well be necessary to the very existence of the Constitution itself. In describing this authority I care not whether one calls it "residual," "inherent," "moral," "implied," "aggregate," "emergency," or otherwise.

I conclude that where Congress has laid down specific procedures to deal with the type of crisis confronting the President, he must follow those procedures in meeting the crisis; but that in the absence of such action by Congress, the President's independent power to act depends upon the gravity of the situation confronting the nation. I cannot sustain the seizure in question because here, Congress had prescribed methods to be followed by the President in meeting the emergency at hand.

Chief Justice Vinson, with whom Justices Reed and Minton join, dissenting.

In passing upon the question of Presidential powers in this case, we must first consider the context in which those powers were exercised.

Those who suggest that this is a case involving extraordinary powers should be mindful that these are extraordinary times. A world not yet recovered from the devastation of World War II has been forced to face the threat of another and more terrifying global conflict. In 1950, when the United Nations called upon member nations "to render every assistance" to repel aggression in Korea, the United States furnished its vigorous support. For almost two full years, our armed forces have been fighting in Korea, suffering casualties of over 108,000 men. Hostilities have not abated.

Congressional support of the action in Korea has been manifested by provisions for increased military manpower and equipment and for economic stabilization. The President has the duty to execute the foregoing legislative programs. Their successful execution depends upon continued production of steel and stabilized prices for steel.

One is not here called upon even to consider the possibility of executive seizure of a farm, a corner grocery store or even a single industrial plant. Such considerations arise only when one ignores the central fact of this case — that the Nation's entire basic steel production would have shut down completely if there had been no Government seizure. Even ignoring for the moment whatever confidential information the President may possess as "the Nation's organ for foreign affairs," the uncontroverted affidavits in this record amply support the finding that "a work stoppage would immediately jeopardize and imperil our national defense." Plaintiffs do not remotely suggest any basis for rejecting the President's finding that any stoppage of steel production would immediately place the Nation in peril. Accordingly, if the President has any power under the Constitution to meet a critical situation in the absence of express statutory authorization, there is no basis whatever for criticizing the exercise of such power in this case.

In passing upon the grave constitutional question presented in this case, we must never forget, as Chief Justice Marshall admonished, that the Constitution is "intended to endure for ages to come, and, consequently, to be adapted to the various crises of human affairs," and that "[i]ts means are adequate to its ends." Cases do arise presenting questions which could not have been foreseen by the Framers. In such cases, the Constitution has been treated as a living document adaptable to new situations. But we are not called upon today to expand the Constitution to meet a new situation. For, in this case, we need only look to history and time-honored principles of constitutional law.

A review of executive action demonstrates that our Presidents have on many occasions exhibited the leadership contemplated by the Framers when they made the President Commander in Chief, and imposed upon him the trust to take Case that the Laws be faithfully executed. With or without explicit statutory authorization, presidents have at such times dealt with national emergencies by acting promptly and resolutely to enforce legislative program until Congress could act. Congress and the courts have responded to such executive initiative with consistent approval.

Jefferson's initiative in the Louisiana Purchase, the Monroe Doctrine, and Jackson's removal of Government deposits from the Bank of the United States serve to demonstrate by deed what the Framers described by word when they vested the whole of the executive power in the President.

Without declaration of war, President Lincoln took energetic action with the outbreak of War Between the States. He summoned troops and paid them, out of the Treasury without appropriation therefor. He proclaimed a naval blockade of the Confederacy and seized ships violating that blockade. Congress, far from denying the validity of these acts, gave them express approval. The most striking action of President Lincoln was the Emancipation Proclamation, issued in aid of the successful prosecution of the War Between the States, but wholly without statutory authority. In an action finding a most apt precedent for this case, President Lincoln without statutory authority directed the seizure of rail and telegraph lines leading to Washington.

[The rest of Chief Justice Vinson's historical review of executive emergency action is omitted.]

This is but a cursory summary of executive leadership. But it amply demonstrates that Presidents have taken prompt action to enforce the laws and protect the country whether or not Congress happened to provide in advance for the particular method of execution. At the minimum, the executive actions reviewed herein sustain the action of the President in this case. And many of the cited examples of Presidential practice go far beyond the extent of power necessary to sustain the President's order to seize the steel mills. The fact that temporary executive seizures of industrial plants to meet an emergency have not been directly tested in this Court furnishes not the slightest suggestion that such action have been illegal. Rather, the fact that Congress and the courts have consistently recognized and given their support to such executive action indicates that such a power of seizure has been accepted through our history. History bears out the genius of the Founding Fathers, who created a Government subject to law but not left subject to inertia when vigor and initiative are required.

Focusing now on the situation confronting the President on the night of April 8, 1952, we cannot but conclude that the President was performing his duty under the Constitution to "take Care that the Laws be faithfully executed" — a duty described by President Benjamin Harrison as "the central idea of the office."

The President reported to Congress the morning after the seizure that he acted because a work stoppage in steel production would immediately imperil the safety of the Nation by preventing execution of the legislative programs for procurement of military equipment. And, while a shutdown could be averted by granting the price concessions requested by plaintiffs, granting such concessions would disrupt the price stabilization program also enacted by Congress. Rather than fail to execute either legislative program, the President acted to execute both.

Much of the argument in this case has been directed at straw men. We do not now have before us the case of a President acting solely on the basis of his own notions of the public welfare. Nor is there any question of unlimited executive power in this case. The President himself closed the door to any such claim when he sent his Message to Congress stating his purpose to abide by any action of Congress, whether approving or disapproving his seizure action. Here, the President immediately made sure that Congress was fully informed of the temporary action he had taken only to preserve the legislative programs from destruction until Congress could act.

The absence of a specific statute authorizing seizure of the steel mills as a mode of executing the laws — both the military procurement program and the anti-inflation program — has not until today been thought to prevent the President from executing the laws. Unlike an administrative commission confined to the enforcement of the statute under which it was created, or the head of a department when administering a particular statute, the President is a constitutional officer charged with taking care that a "mass of legislation" be executed. Flexibility as to mode of execution to meet critical situations is a matter of practical necessity. This practical construction of the "Take Care" clause, advocated by John Marshall, was adopted by this Court in *In re Neagle*, *In re Debs*, and other cases.

Whatever the extent of Presidential power on more tranquil occasions, and whatever the right of the President to execute legislative programs as he sees fit without reporting the mode of execution to Congress, the single Presidential purpose disclosed on this record is to faithfully execute the laws by acting in a an emergency to maintain the status quo, thereby preventing collapse of the legislative programs until Congress could act.

In *United States v. Midwest Oil Co.*, this Court approved executive action where, as here, the President acted to preserve an important matter until Congress could act — even though his action in that case was contrary to an express statute. In this case, there is no statute prohibiting the action taken by the President in a matter not merely important but threatening the very safety of the Nation. Executive inaction in such a situation, courting national disaster, is foreign to the concept of energy and initiative in the Executive as created by the Founding Fathers. The Constitution was itself "adopted in a period of grave emergency . . . . While emergency does not create power, emergency may furnish the occasion for the exercise of power." The Framers knew, as we should know in these times of peril, that there is real danger in Executive weakness. There is no cause to fear Executive tyranny so long as the laws of Congress are being faithfully executed. Certainly there is no basis for fear of dictatorship when the Executive acts, as he did in this case, only to save the situation until Congress could act.

The broad executive power granted by Article II to an officer on duty 365 days a year cannot, it is said, be invoked to avert disaster. Instead, the President must confine himself to sending a message to Congress recommending action. Under this messenger-boy concept of the Office, the President cannot even act to preserve legislative programs from destruction so that Congress will have something left to act upon. There is no judicial finding that the executive action was unwarranted because there was in fact no basis for the President's findings of the existence of an emergency for, under this view, the gravity of the emergency and the immediacy of the threatened disaster are considered irrelevant as a matter of law. The President informed Congress that even a temporary Government operation of plaintiff's properties was "thoroughly distasteful" to him, but was necessary to execute legislative programs essential to survival of the Nation. A sturdy judiciary should not be swayed by the unpleasantness or unpopularity of necessary executive action, but must independently determine for itself whether the President was acting, as required by the Constitution, to "take Care that the Laws be faithfully executed."

NOTES

1. ***Executive orders.*** It is difficult, if not impossible, to determine the frequency of executive lawmaking. While "executive orders" and "proclamations" are published in the Federal Register, there is no generally accepted definition of an "executive order," "executive proclamation," or of the myriad other executive regulatory documents. Yet it is clear that executive action is a vital source of government legal policy. Lincoln freed the slaves by proclamation; affirmative action in employment under government contracts is mandated, in large part, by Executive Order 11,246. Economic controls and the development of the government intelligence system have been largely handled through executive order. But what is the constitutional basis for this executive lawmaking? Does *Youngstown* mean that such executive action, when not taken pursuant to congressional statute, is unconstitutional? For the view that "[t]he increased use of executive orders and other presidential directives is a fundamental problem in modern-day America," see Tara Branum, *President or King? The Use and Abuse of Executive Orders in Modern-Day America*, 28 J. LEGIS. 1, 2 (2002).

2. ***Lawmaking powers.*** Before the Supreme Court in the *Steel Seizure* case, the Attorney General stated: "We, of course, do not contend that the President has 'unlimited and unrestrained' power. We contend only that in a situation of national emergency the President has authority *under the Constitution*, and subject to constitutional limitations, to take action of this type necessary to meet the emergency." (Emphasis added.)

What is the holding of *Youngstown*? Do a majority of justices agree with Justice Black that the executive has no domestic legislative-like powers unless granted by Congress? Assuming that a majority of justices recognize the existence of a constitutionally based, domestic executive legislative-like power, what is the constitutional source for such power? Note that there is no Necessary and Proper Clause in Article II. But consider the argument in THE FEDERALIST, Nos. 33 & 44, in regard to congressional powers, that the very grant of a power necessarily implies a grant of the means reasonably necessary to effectuate it.

There is also an argument that Congress is first among equals with respect to lawmaking, so that the executive and judicial branches have only those implied powers that are indispensable to their express powers. "[T]he absence of affirmative action by Congress may defeat an assertion of ancillary executive or judicial powers that cannot be defended as having been expressly provided in articles II and III or as necessarily implied by the nature of the expressed duties of those branches." William Van Alstyne, *The Role of Congress in Determining Incidental Powers of the President and of the Federal Courts: A Comment on the Horizontal Effect of the Sweeping Clause*, 40 LAW & CONTEMP. PROBS. 102, 118 (1976).

Congress had provided a method for handling serious national labor disputes in the Taft-Hartley Act. Further, in 1947 Congress had rejected a proposal authorizing presidential seizure. What is the relevance of these congressional actions for the constitutionality of the steel-seizure? Does *Youngstown* fall into Justice Jackson's second or third category?

3. *Aggregate residual power.* Perhaps the executive power to act might arise, not from any single grant of power, but from the aggregate of all the granted executive powers, expressed and implied.

> That the president does possess "residual" or "resultant" powers over and above, or in consequence of, its specifically granted powers to take temporary alleviative action in the presence of serious emergency is a proposition to which all but Justices Black and Douglas would probably have assented in the absence of the complicating issue that was created by the president's refusal to follow the procedures laid down in the Taft-Hartley Act.

Edward Corwin, *The Steel Seizure Case: A Judicial Brick Without Straw*, 53 COLUM. L. REV. 53, 65 (1953).

4. *Executive action in the absence of legislative action.* Corwin poses the question, "What is the lesson of the Steel Case?" He answers:

> Undoubtedly it tends to supplement presidential emergency power with a power to adopt temporary remedial legislation when Congress has been, in the judgment of the President, unduly remiss in taking cognizance of and acting on a given situation. In other words, the lesson of the case is that, just as nature abhors a vacuum, so does an age of emergency. Let Congress see to it, then, that no such vacuum occurs. The best escape from presidential autocracy in the age we inhabit is not, in short, judicial review, which can supply only a vacuum, but timely legislation.

EDWARD S. CORWIN, THE PRESIDENT: OFFICE AND POWERS 1787–1957, at 157 (4th ed. 1957).

Professor Henry Monaghan, in *The Protective Power of the Presidency*, 93 COLUM. L. REV. 1, 10 (1993), has looked back on the teaching of the *Steel Seizure* case:

> *Steel Seizure* represents the bedrock principle of the constitutional order: except perhaps when acting pursuant to some "specific" constitutional power, the President has no inherent power to invade private rights; the President not only cannot act *contra legem*, he or she must point to affirmative legislative authority when so acting.

But he does not reject "some narrow residuum of lawful authority to act in a genuine national emergency." Further, he argues for an implied executive protective power — "[T]he constitutional conception of a Chief Executive authorized to enforce the laws includes a general authority to protect and defend the personnel, property and instrumentalities of the United States from harm." *Id.* at 11.

Assuming the existence of some shared domestic lawmaking power, what rules should govern its exercise? Under what circumstances may the executive act in the absence of congressional authorization? Should the congressional or the executive judgment prevail if a conflict develops? Is the "twilight zone" approach of Justice Jackson to the sharing of powers operational or useful?

[B] CONGRESSIONAL LAWMAKING: LIMITATIONS AND RESPONSIBILITIES

[1] Delegation of Legislative Power

Much of the Executive's legislative role is a product of conscious legislative delegation of lawmaking power. Theoretically, power delegated to Congress cannot be redelegated to the Executive — *delegata potestas non potest delegari*. This doctrine "ensures to the extent consistent with orderly government administration that important choices of social policy are made by Congress, the branch of our government most responsive to the popular will." *Industrial Union Dep't v. American Petroleum Inst.*, 448 U.S. 607 (1980) (Rehnquist, J., concurring).

Why might delegation of legislative power to executive agencies be problematic, as a matter of American constitutional or political theory? Consider the following possibilities:

1. *Textual Problems*: According to Article I, the "legislative power" is vested in Congress. Hence were Congress to vest the legislative power in an agency located within the executive branch, this textual directive would be violated.

2. *Accountability Problems:* Where Congress delegates its lawmaking power to administrative agencies, fundamental policy making power is transferred from those representative of and accountable to the electorate to entities that are not directly accountable.

3. *Checking Problems:* Delegation of legislative power dangerously aggrandizes the power of the executive branch at the expense of the legislative branch, thereby undermining the delicate balance of authority among the branches, which was designed to avoid the onset of tyranny.

For a discussion of these issues, see MARTIN H. REDISH, THE CONSTITUTION AS POLITICAL STRUCTURE 135–61 (1995).

What are the arguments against a strong nondelegation doctrine? Consider the following possibilities:

1. *Voter Waiver*: To the extent members of Congress delegate legislative power but are nevertheless retained in office, the voters have chosen to accept such a practice. In the words of Professor Mashaw: "Assuming that our current representatives in the legislature vote for laws that contain vague delegations of authority, we are presumably holding them accountable for that at the polls. How is it that we are not being represented?" Jerry L. Mashaw, *Prodelegation: Why Administrators Should Make Political Decisions,* 1 J. L. ECON. & ORG. 81, 87 (1985).

2. *Comparative Accountability:* Because most important legislative judgments are made by powerful congressional subcommittees without the use of clear and open procedures, decision making by administrative agencies is actually preferable from the perspective of representationalism, because of their established and open processes. *See* Richard Stewart, *Beyond Delegation Doctrine*, 36 AM. U. L. REV. 323, 333 (1987).

3. *Comparative Representativeness:* Members of administrative agencies are appointed (usually for set terms) by the president, and the president is just as representative of the electorate as is Congress.

4. *The Impossibility of Fashioning Workable Standards:* No legislative directive can foresee every possible factual variation. Therefore in every case, those executing the law will necessarily exercise a certain degree of discretion. Thus, even if one were to assume that delegation of legislative power is constitutionally problematic, it is effectively impossible to fashion workable standards by which the courts could determine whether "too much" case-by-case discretion has, in fact, been delegated. For a response to this argument, see David Schoenbrod, *The Delegation Doctrine: Could the Court Give It Substance?,* 83 MICH. L. REV. 1223 (1985).

In *Mistretta v. United States*, 488 U.S. 361 (1989), the Court upheld sentencing guidelines for federal courts promulgated by the United States Sentencing Commission, an independent commission placed in the judicial branch under the Sentencing Reform Act of 1984. The Court, per Justice Blackmun, held that in establishing the Commission Congress neither delegated excessive legislative power nor violated separation of powers principles:

> Petitioner argues that in delegating the power to promulgate sentencing guidelines for every federal criminal offense to an independent Sentencing Commission, Congress has granted the Commission excessive legislative discretion in violation of the constitutionally based nondelegation doctrine. We do not agree.
>
> The nondelegation doctrine is rooted in the principle of separation of powers that underlies our tripartite system of government. We also

have recognized, however, that the separation-of-powers principle, and the nondelegation doctrine in particular, do not prevent Congress from obtaining the assistance of its coordinate Branches. In a passage now enshrined in our jurisprudence, Chief Justice Taft, writing for the Court, explained our approach to such cooperative ventures: "In determining what [Congress] may do in seeking assistance from another branch, the extent and character of that assistance must be fixed according to common sense and the inherent necessities of the government co-ordination." *J.W. Hampton Jr. & Co. v. United States,* 276 U.S. 394, 406 (1928). So long as Congress "shall lay down by legislative act an intelligible principle to which the person or body authorized to [exercise the delegated authority] is directed to conform, such legislative action is not a forbidden delegation of legislative power."

Applying this "intelligible principle" test to congressional delegations, our jurisprudence has been driven by a practical understanding that in our increasingly complex society, replete with ever changing and more technical problems, Congress simply cannot do its job absent an ability to delegate power under broad general directives.

After invalidating in 1935 two statutes as excessive delegations, we have upheld, again without deviation, Congress' ability to delegate power under broad standards. In light of our approval of these broad delegations, we harbor no doubt that Congress' delegation of authority to the Sentencing Commission is sufficiently specific and detailed to meet constitutional requirements. [A]lthough Congress granted the Commission substantial discretion in formulating guidelines, in actuality it legislated a full hierarchy of punishment — from near maximum imprisonment, to substantial imprison ment, to some imprisonment, to alternatives — and stipulated the most important offense and offender characteristics to place defendants within these categories.

The Act sets forth more than merely an "intelligible principle" or minimal standards. One court has aptly put it: "The statute outlines the policies which prompted establishment of the Commission, explains what the Commission should do and how it should do it, and sets out specific directives to govern particular situations." *United States v. Chambless,* 680 F. Supp. 793, 796 (E.D. La. 1988).

Developing proportionate penalties for hundreds of different crimes by a virtually limitless array of offenders is precisely the sort of intricate, labor-intensive task for which delegation to an expert body is especially appropriate. Although Congress has delegated significant discretion to the Commission to draw judgments from its analysis of existing sentencing practice and alternative sentencing models, "Congress is not confined to that method of executing its policy which involves the least possible delegation of discretion to administrative officers." *Yakus v. United States* [321 U.S. 414, 425–26 (1944)]. We have no doubt that in the hands of the Commission "the criteria which Congress has supplied are wholly adequate for carrying out the general policy and purpose" of the Act. *Sunshine Coal Co. v. Adkins,* 310 U.S. 381, 398 (1940).

In its most recent statement on the nondelegation doctrine, *Whitman v. American Trucking Associations*, 531 U.S. 457(2001), the Supreme Court upheld against constitutional attack section 109(b)(1) of the Clean Air Act, which instructs the Environmental Protection Agency (EPA) to set primary ambient air quality standards "the attainment and maintenance of which are requisite to protect the public health" with "an adequate margin of safety." Justice Scalia, speaking for the Court, concluded that "[t]he scope of discretion § 109(b)(1) allows is in fact well within the outer limits of our nondelegation precedents," since it satisfied the requisite "intelligible principle" standard, which had only been found to have been violated on two occasions, in the 1930s and '40s. The fact that the EPA was required to make judgments of degree, he found, is "not conclusive for delegation purposes." The EPA was therefore not exercising "legislative power," in violation of the directive of Article I of the Constitution.

In a separate concurring opinion, Justice Thomas indicated that while he agreed with the Court's conclusion that the "intelligible standards" principle was satisfied by the statute, "there are cases in which the principle is intelligible and yet the significance of the delegated decision is simply too great for the decision to be called anything other than 'legislative.' " However, since the parties had not raised that argument, he left for "a future day" more detailed consideration of that view. Justice Stevens, in a separate opinion, argued that "it would be both wiser and more faithful to what we have actually done in delegation cases to admit that agency rulemaking authority is 'legislative power.' "

Although in recent years the delegation doctrine has rarely been invoked by the Court, according to one scholar the doctrine still retains vitality. It is, Professor Lawson argues, "the Energizer Bunny of constitutional law: No matter how many times it gets broken, beaten, or buried, it just keeps on going and going." Gary Lawson, *Delegation and Original Meaning*, 88 VA. L. REV. 327, 330 (2002).

[2] The Legislative Veto

Broad congressional delegation of power has been a major factor in the expansion of the executive role. Increasingly, operative public policy is made in executive and independent agencies rather than in Congress. In an effort to restore balance, Congress has fashioned a variety of devices for controlling the exercise of delegated power. One attempt involves the so-called "legislative veto," by which Congress delegates power but reserves the ability to review proposed executive action to be taken pursuant to the statute. Some provisions require a congressional resolution of approval before the proposal can become effective, others provide for a one-House disapproval, and others provide for a joint resolution of disapproval. The constitutionality of many of these provisions, perhaps all, have been affected directly by the next case.

IMMIGRATION & NATURALIZATION SERVICE v. CHADHA

462 U.S. 919, 103 S. Ct. 2764, 77 L. Ed. 2d 317 (1983)

[The Court, per Chief Justice Burger, held 7-2 that the legislative veto provision in § 244(c)(2) of the Immigration and Naturalization Act ("Act") permitting a one-House veto over Executive Branch orders involving deportation of aliens is unconstitutional. Chadha was an East Indian living in the United States over one year after his nonimmigrant student visa had expired. He was ordered by the Immigration and Naturalization Service (INS) to show cause why he should not be deported. Chadha filed for a suspension of deportation under § 244(a)(1) of the Act, which permits the Attorney General to suspend deportation and grant an alien permanent residence in the United States, if he has resided in the country for over seven years, is of good moral character, and would suffer "extreme hardship" if deported. The immigration judge assigned to the case found that Chadha met these requirements and suspended his deportation. A report of the suspension was then submitted to Congress, as was called for by § 244(c)(1) of the Act. At that point, either House of Congress had the power under § 244(c)(2) of the Act to veto the Attorney General's order that Chadha not be deported. The section provides as follows:

> (2) In the case of an alien specified in paragraph (1) of subsection (a) of this subsection — if during the session of the Congress at which a case is reported or prior to the close of the session of the Congress next following the session at which a case is reported, either the Senate or the House of Representatives passes a resolution stating in substance that it does not favor the suspension of such deportation, the Attorney General shall thereupon deport such alien or authorize the alien's voluntary departure at his own expense under the order of deportation in the manner provided by law. If, within the time above specified, neither the Senate nor the House of Representatives shall pass such a resolution, the Attorney General shall cancel deportation proceedings.

During the final session in which Congress, pursuant to § 244(c)(2), could use its veto power, it did so. The House of Representatives, acting alone, passed a resolution vetoing the immigration judge's earlier decision to suspend Chadha's deportation. The resolution had not been submitted to the Senate nor presented to the President.

[The immigration judge then re-opened the deportation proceedings in order to implement the House order. Chadha moved to terminate the proceedings on the ground that § 244(c)(2) was unconstitutional. The immigration judge held he had no authority to rule on the constitutionality of § 244(c)(2). Chadha's appeal to the Board of Immigration Appeals produced the same result. The INS then joined Chadha in his appeal to the United States Court of Appeals. That court held that the House action under § 244(c)(2) violated the doctrine of separation of powers, and closed deportation proceedings against Chadha. The Supreme Court affirmed.

[The Court addressed several issues concerning the Court's authority to decide the principal issue raised. For example, the Court held that § 244(c)(2) was severable from the remainder of § 244: "Congress did not intend the validity of the Act as a whole, or of any part of the Act, to depend upon whether the veto clause of § 244(c)(2) was invalid." Most notably, § 406 of the Act expressly stated that if any particular provision of the Act were held invalid, the remainder of the Act would not be affected. As for the contention that the case presented a nonjusticiable political question, in that Chadha was challenging congressional authority to enact § 244(c)(2), the Court acknowledged that the controversy might be called "political." "But the presence of constitutional issues with significant political overtones does not automatically invoke the political question doctrine."]

CHIEF JUSTICE BURGER delivered the opinion of the Court.

We turn now to the question whether action of one House of Congress under § 244(c)(2) violates strictures of the Constitution. We begin, of course, with the presumption that the challenged statute is valid. Its wisdom is not the concern of the courts; if a challenged action does not violate the Constitution, it must be sustained. By the same token, the fact that a given law or procedure is efficient, convenient, and useful in facilitating functions of government, standing alone, will not save it if it is contrary to the Constitution. Convenience and efficiency are not the primary objectives — or the hallmarks — of democratic government and our inquiry is sharpened rather than blunted by the fact that Congressional veto provisions are appearing with increasing frequency in statutes which delegate authority to executive and independent agencies:

> Since 1932, when the first veto provision was enacted into law, 295 congressional veto-type procedures have been inserted in 196 different statutes as follows: from 1932 to 1939, five statutes were affected; from 1940–49, nineteen statutes; between 1950–59, thirty-four statutes; and from 1960–69, forty-nine. From the year 1970 through 1975, at least one hundred sixty-three such provisions were included in eighty-nine laws.

Justice White undertakes to make a case for the proposition that the one-House veto is a useful "political invention," and we need not challenge that assertion. We can even concede this utilitarian argument although the long range political wisdom of this "invention" is arguable. But policy arguments supporting even useful "political inventions" are subject to the demands of the Constitution which defines powers and, with respect to this subject, sets out just how those powers are to be exercised.

[W]e find that the purposes underlying the Presentment Clauses, Art. I, § 7, cls. 2, 3, and the bicameral requirement of Art. I, § 1 and § 7, cl. 2, guide our resolution of the important question presented in this case. The very structure of the articles delegating and separating powers under Arts. I, II, and III exemplify the concept of separation of powers and we now turn to Art. I.

The Presentment Clauses

The records of the Constitutional Convention reveal that the requirement that all legislation be presented to the President before becoming law was uniformly accepted by the Framers. Presentment to the President and the Presidential veto were considered so imperative that the draftsmen took special pains to assure that these requirements could not be circumvented. The decision to provide the President with a limited and qualified power to nullify proposed legislation by veto was based on the profound conviction of the Framers that the powers conferred on Congress were the powers to be most carefully circumscribed. It is beyond doubt that lawmaking was a power to be shared by both Houses and the President.

The President's role in the lawmaking process also reflects the Framers' careful efforts to check whatever propensity a particular Congress might have to enact oppressive, improvident, or ill-considered measures. The President's veto role in the legislative process was described later during public debate on ratification:

> The primary inducement to conferring the power in question upon the Executive is to enable him to defend himself; the secondary one is to increase the chances in favor of the community against the passing of bad laws through haste, inadvertence, or design. The Federalist No. 73 (A. Hamilton).

The Court also has observed that the Presentment Clauses serve the important purpose of assuring that a "national" perspective is grafted on the legislative process.

Bicameralism

The bicameral requirement of Art. I, §§ 1, 7 was of scarcely less concern to the Framers than was the Presidential veto and indeed the two concepts are interdependent. By providing that no law could take effect without the concurrence of the prescribed majority of the Members of both Houses, the Framers reemphasized their belief, already remarked upon in connection with the Presentment Clauses, that legislation should not be enacted unless it has been carefully and fully considered by the Nation's elected officials. Hamilton [pointed] up the need to divide and disperse power in order to protect liberty:

> In republican government, the legislative authority necessarily predominates. The remedy for this inconveniency is to divide the legislature into different branches; and to render them, by different modes of election and different principles of action, as little connected with each other as the nature of their common functions and their common dependence on the society will admit. THE FEDERALIST NO. 51.

However familiar, it is useful to recall that apart from their fear that special interests could be favored at the expense of public needs, the Framers were also concerned, although not of one mind, over the apprehensions of the smaller states. Those states feared a commonality of interest among the larger states would work to their disadvantage; representatives of the larger states, on the other hand, were skeptical of a legislature that could pass laws favoring a minority of the people. It need hardly be repeated here that the Great

Compromise, under which one House was viewed as representing the people and the other the states, allayed the fears of both the large and small states.

We see therefore that the Framers were acutely conscious that the bicameral requirement and the Presentment Clauses would serve essential constitutional functions. The President's participation in the legislative process was to protect the Executive Branch from Congress and to protect the whole people from improvident laws. The division of the Congress into two distinctive bodies assures that the legislative power would be exercised only after opportunity for full study and debate in separate settings. The President's unilateral veto power, in turn, was limited by the power of two thirds of both Houses of Congress to overrule a veto thereby precluding final arbitrary action of one person. It emerges clearly that the prescription for legislative action in Art. I, §§ 1, 7 represents the Framers' decision that the legislative power of the Federal government be exercised in accord with a single, finely wrought and exhaustively considered, procedure.

The Constitution sought to divide the delegated powers of the new federal government into three defined categories, legislative, executive and judicial, to assure, as nearly as possible, that each Branch of government would confine itself to its assigned responsibility. The hydraulic pressure inherent within each of the separate Branches to exceed the outer limits of its power, even to accomplish desirable objectives, must be resisted. Although not "hermetically" sealed from one another, *Buckley v. Valeo*, the powers delegated to the three Branches are functionally identifiable. When any Branch acts, it is presumptively exercising the power the Constitution has delegated to it. When the Executive acts, it presumptively acts in an executive or administrative capacity as defined in Art. II. And when, as here, one House of Congress purports to act, it is presumptively acting within its assigned sphere.

Beginning with this presumption, we must nevertheless establish that the challenged action under § 244(c)(2) is of the kind to which the procedural requirements of Art. I, § 7 apply. Not every action taken by either House is subject to the bicameralism and presentment requirements of Art. I. Whether actions taken by either House are, in law and fact, an exercise of legislative power depends not on their form but upon "whether they contain matter which is properly to be regarded as legislative in its character and effect." S. Rep. No. 1335, 54th Cong., 2d Sess., 8 (1897).

Examination of the action taken here by one House pursuant to § 244(c)(2) reveals that it was essentially legislative in purpose and effect. In purporting to exercise power defined in Art. I, § 8, cl. 4 to "establish an uniform Rule of Naturalization," the House took action that had the purpose and effect of altering the legal rights, duties and relations of persons, including the Attorney General, Executive Branch officials and Chadha, all outside the legislative branch. Section 244(c)(2) purports to authorize one House of Congress to require the Attorney General to deport an individual alien whose deportation otherwise would be cancelled under § 244. The one-House veto operated in this case to overrule the Attorney General and mandate Chadha's deportation; absent the House action, Chadha would remain in the United States. Congress has acted and its action has altered Chadha's status.

The legislative character of the one-House veto in this case is confirmed by the character of the Congressional action it supplants. Neither the House of Representatives nor the Senate contends that, absent the veto provision in § 244(c)(2), either of them, or both of them acting together, could effectively require the Attorney General to deport an alien once the Attorney General, in the exercise of legislatively delegated authority, had determined the alien should remain in the United States. Without the challenged provision in § 244(c)(2), this could have been achieved, if at all, only by legislation requiring deportation. Similarly, a veto by one House of Congress under § 244(c)(2) cannot be justified as an attempt at amending the standards set out in § 244(a)(1), or as a repeal of § 244 as applied to Chadha. Amendment and repeal of statutes, no less than enactment, must conform with Art. I.

The nature of the decision implemented by the one-House veto in this case further manifests its legislative character. After long experience with the clumsy, time consuming private bill procedure, Congress made a deliberate choice to delegate to the Executive Branch, and specifically to the Attorney General, the authority to allow deportable aliens to remain in this country in certain specified circumstances. It is not disputed that this choice to delegate authority is precisely the kind of decision that can be implemented only in accordance with the procedures set out in Art. I. Disagreement with the Attorney General's decision on Chadha's deportation — that is, Congress' decision to deport Chadha — no less than Congress' original choice to delegate to the Attorney General the authority to make that decision, involves determinations of policy that Congress can implement in only one way; bicameral passage followed by presentment to the President. Congress must abide by its delegation of authority until that delegation is legislatively altered or revoked.

Finally, we see that when the Framers intended to authorize either House of Congress to act alone and outside of its prescribed bicameral legislative role, they narrowly and precisely defined the procedure for such action. There are but four provisions in the Constitution, explicit and unambiguous, by which one House may act alone with the unreviewable force of law, not subject to the President's veto:

(a) The House of Representatives alone was given the power to initiate impeachments. Art. I, § 2, cl. 6;

(b) The Senate alone was given the power to conduct trials following impeachment on charges initiated by the House and to convict following trial. Art. I, § 3, cl. 5;

(c) The Senate alone was given final unreviewable power to approve or to disapprove presidential appointments. Art. II, § 2, cl. 2;

(d) The Senate alone was given unreviewable power to ratify treaties negotiated by the President. Art. II, § 2, cl. 2.

Clearly, when the Draftsmen sought to confer special powers on one House, independent of the other House, or of the President, they did so in explicit, unambiguous terms. These carefully defined exceptions from presentment and bicameralism underscore the difference between the legislative functions of Congress and other unilateral but important and binding one-House acts provided for in the Constitution. These exceptions are narrow, explicit, and separately justified; none of them authorize the action challenged here. On the contrary, they provide further support for the conclusion that Congressional authority is not to be implied and for the conclusion that the veto provided for in § 244(c)(2) is not authorized by the constitutional design of the powers of the Legislative Branch.

Since it is clear that the action by the House under § 244(c)(2) was not within any of the express constitutional exceptions authorizing one House to act alone, and equally clear that it was an exercise of legislative power, that action was subject to the standards prescribed in Article I. The bicameral requirement, the Presentment Clauses, the President's veto, and Congress' power to override a veto were intended to erect enduring checks on each Branch and to protect the people from the improvident exercise of power by mandating certain prescribed steps. To preserve those checks, and maintain the separation of powers, the carefully defined limits on the power of each Branch must not be eroded. To accomplish what has been attempted by one House of Congress in this case requires action in conformity with the express procedures of the Constitution's prescription for legislative action: passage by a majority of both Houses and presentment to the President.[22]

The veto authorized by § 244(c)(2) doubtless has been in many respects a convenient shortcut; the "sharing" with the Executive by Congress of its authority over aliens in this manner is, on its face, an appealing compromise. In purely practical terms, it is obviously easier for action to be taken by one House without submission to the President; but it is crystal clear from the records of the Convention, contemporaneous writings and debates, that the Framers ranked other values higher than efficiency.

The choices we discern as having been made in the Constitutional Convention impose burdens on governmental processes that often seem clumsy, inefficient, even unworkable, but those hard choices were consciously made by men who had lived under a form of government that permitted arbitrary governmental acts to go unchecked. With all the obvious flaws of delay, untidiness, and potential for abuse, we have not yet found a better way to

[22] Neither can we accept the suggestion that the one-House veto provision in § 244(c)(2) either removes or modifies the bicameralism and presentation requirements for the enactment of future legislation affecting aliens. The explicit prescription for legislative action contained in Art. I cannot be amended by legislation.

Justice White suggests that the Attorney General's action under § 244(c)(1) suspending deportation is equivalent to a proposal for legislation and that because Congressional approval is indicated "by failure to veto, the one-House veto satisfies the requirement of bicameral approval." However, as the Court of Appeals noted, that approach "would analogize the effect of the one house disapproval to the failure of one house to vote affirmatively on a private bill." Even if it were clear that Congress entertained such an arcane theory when it enacted § 244(c)(2), which Justice White does not suggest, this would amount to nothing less than an amending of Art. I. The legislative steps outlined in Art. I are not empty formalities; they were designed to assure that both Houses of Congress and the President participate in the exercise of lawmaking authority. This does not mean that legislation must always be preceded by debate; on the contrary, we have said that it is not necessary for a legislative body to "articulate its reasons for enacting a statute." United States Railroad Retirement Board v. Fritz, 449 U.S. 166, 179 (1980). But the steps required by Art. I, §§ 1, 7 make certain that there is an opportunity for deliberation and debate. To allow Congress to evade the strictures of the Constitution and in effect enact Executive proposals into law by mere silence cannot be squared with Art. I.

preserve freedom than by making the exercise of power subject to the carefully crafted restraints spelled out in the Constitution.

We hold that the Congressional veto provision in § 244(c)(2) is severable from the Act and that it is unconstitutional.

JUSTICE POWELL, concurring in the judgment.

The Court's decision, based on the Presentment Clauses, Art. I, § 7, cl. 2 and 3, apparently will invalidate every use of the legislative veto. The breadth of this holding gives one pause. Congress has included the veto in literally hundreds of statutes, dating back to the 1930s. Congress clearly views this procedure as essential to controlling the delegation of power to administrative agencies. One reasonably may disagree with Congress' assessment of the veto's utility, but the respect due its judgment as a coordinate branch of Government cautions that our holding should be no more extensive than necessary to decide this case. In my view, the case may be decided on a narrower ground. When Congress finds that a particular person does not satisfy the statutory criteria for permanent residence in this country it has assumed a judicial function in violation of the principle of separation of powers. Accordingly, I concur in the judgment.

The Constitution does not establish three branches with precisely defined boundaries. Rather, as Justice Jackson wrote, "[w]hile the Constitution diffuses power the better to secure liberty, it also contemplates that practice will integrate the dispersed powers into a workable government. It enjoins upon its branches separateness but interdependence, autonomy but reciprocity." *Youngstown Sheet & Tube Co. v. Sawyer* (concurring opinion). The Court thus has been mindful that the boundaries between each branch should be fixed "according to common sense and the inherent necessities of the governmental co-ordination." *J.W. Hampton, Jr. & Co. v. United States*, 276 U.S. 394, 406 (1928). But where one branch has impaired or sought to assume a power central to another branch, the Court has not hesitated to enforce the doctrine.

Functionally, the doctrine may be violated in two ways. One branch may interfere impermissibly with the other's performance of its constitutionally assigned function. *See Nixon v. Administrator of General Services*; *United States v. Nixon*. Alternatively, the doctrine may be violated when one branch assumes a function that more properly is entrusted to another. See *Youngstown Sheet & Tube Co. v. Sawyer*. This case presents the latter situation.

On its face, the House's action appears clearly adjudicatory. The House did not enact a general rule; rather it made its own determination that six specific persons did not comply with certain statutory criteria. It thus undertook the type of decision that traditionally has been left to other branches. Even if the House did not make a de novo determination, but simply reviewed the Immigration and Naturalization Service's findings, it still assumed a function ordinarily entrusted to the federal courts.

The impropriety of the House's assumption of this function is confirmed by the fact that its action raises the very danger the Framers sought to avoid — the exercise of unchecked power. In deciding whether Chadha deserves to be deported, Congress is not subject to any internal constraints that prevent it from arbitrarily depriving him of the right to remain in this country. Unlike the judiciary or an administrative agency, Congress is not bound by established substantive rules. Nor is it subject to the procedural safeguards, such as the right to counsel and a hearing before an impartial tribunal, that are present when a court or an agency adjudicates individual rights. The only effective constraint on Congress' power is political, but Congress is most accountable politically when it prescribes rules of general applicability. When it decides rights of specific persons, those rights are subject to "the tyranny of a shifting majority."

JUSTICE WHITE, dissenting.

Today the Court not only invalidates § 244(c)(2) of the Immigration and Nationality Act, but also sounds the death knell for nearly 200 other statutory provisions in which Congress has reserved a "legislative veto."

The prominence of the legislative veto mechanism in our contemporary political system and its importance to Congress can hardly be overstated. It has become a central means by which Congress secures the accountability of executive and independent agencies. Without the legislative veto, Congress is faced with a Hobson's choice: either to refrain from delegating the necessary authority, leaving itself with a hopeless task of writing laws with the requisite specificity to cover endless special circumstances across the entire policy landscape, or in the alternative, to abdicate its lawmaking function to the executive branch and independent agencies. To choose the former leaves major national problems unresolved; to opt for the latter risks unaccountable policymaking by those not elected to fill that role. Accordingly, over the past five decades, the legislative veto has been placed in nearly 200 statutes. The device is known in every field of governmental concern: reorganization, budgets, foreign affairs, war powers, and regulation of trade, safety, energy, the environment and the economy.

For all these reasons, the apparent sweep of the Court's decision today is regrettable. The Court's Article I analysis appears to invalidate all legislative vetoes irrespective of form or subject. Because the legislative veto is commonly found as a check upon rulemaking by administrative agencies and upon broad-based policy decisions of the Executive Branch, it is particularly unfortunate that the Court reaches its decision in a case involving the exercise of a veto over deportation decisions regarding particular individuals. Courts should always be wary of striking statutes as unconstitutional; to strike an entire class of statutes based on consideration of a somewhat atypical and more-readily indictable exemplar of the class is irresponsible.

If the legislative veto were as plainly unconstitutional as the Court strives to suggest, its broad ruling today would be more comprehensible. But, the constitutionality of the legislative veto is anything but clearcut. The issue divides scholars, courts, attorneys general, and the two other branches of the National Government. If the veto devices so flagrantly disregarded the requirements of Article I as the Court today suggests, I find it incomprehensible that Congress, whose members are bound by oath to uphold the Constitution, would have placed these mechanisms in nearly 200 separate laws over a period of 50 years.

We should not find the lack of a specific constitutional authorization for the legislative veto surprising, and I would not infer disapproval of the mechanism from its absence. From the summer of 1787 to the present the government of the United States has become an endeavor far beyond the contemplation of the Framers. Only within the last half century has the complexity and size of the Federal Government's responsibilities grown so greatly that the Congress must rely on the legislative veto as the most effective if not the only means to insure their role as the nation's lawmakers. But the wisdom of the Framers was to anticipate that the nation would grow and new problems of governance would require different solutions. Accordingly, our Federal Government was intentionally chartered with the flexibility to respond to contemporary needs without losing sight of fundamental democratic principles. In my view, neither Article I of the Constitution nor the doctrine of separation of powers is violated by this mechanism by which our elected representatives preserve their voice in the governance of the nation.

The power to exercise a legislative veto is not the power to write new law without bicameral approval or presidential consideration. The veto must be authorized by statute and may only negative what an Executive department or independent agency has proposed. On its face, the legislative veto no more allows one House of Congress to make law than does the presidential veto confer such power upon the President. Accordingly, the Court properly recognizes that it "must establish that the challenged action under § 244(c)(2) is of the kind to which the procedural requirements of Art. I, § 7 apply" and admits that "not every action taken by either House is subject to the bicameralism and presentation requirements of Art. I."

When the Convention did turn its attention to the scope of Congress' lawmaking power, the Framers were expansive. It is long-settled that Congress may "exercise its best judgment in the selection of measures, to carry into execution the constitutional powers of the government," and "avail itself of experience, to exercise its reason, and to accommodate its legislation to circumstances." *McCulloch v. Maryland.*

The Court heeded this counsel in approving the modern administrative state. The Court's holding today that all legislative-type action must be enacted through the lawmaking process ignores that legislative authority is routinely delegated to the Executive branch, to the independent regulatory agencies, and to private individuals and groups.

This Court's decisions sanctioning such delegations make clear that Article I does not require all action with the effect of legislation to be passed as a law. The wisdom and the constitutionality of these broad delegations are matters that still have not been put to rest. But for present purposes, these cases establish that by virtue of congressional delegation, legislative power can be exercised by independent agencies and Executive departments without the passage of new legislation. For some time, the sheer amount of law — the substantive rules that regulate private conduct and direct the operation of government — made by the agencies has far outnumbered the lawmaking engaged in by Congress through the traditional process. There is no question but that agency rulemaking is lawmaking in any functional or realistic sense of the term. These regulations bind courts and officers of the federal government, may pre-empt state law, and grant rights to and impose obligations on the public. In sum, they have the force of law.

If Congress may delegate lawmaking power to independent and executive agencies, it is most difficult to understand Article I as forbidding Congress from also reserving a check on legislative power for itself. Absent the veto, the agencies receiving delegations of legislative or quasi-legislative power may issue regulations having the force of law without bicameral approval and without the President's signature. It is thus not apparent why the reservation of a veto over the exercise of that legislative power must be subject to a more exacting test. In both cases, it is enough that the initial statutory authorizations comply with the Article I requirements.

Nor are there strict limits on the agents that may receive such delegations of legislative authority so that it might be said that the legislature can delegate authority to others but not to itself. While most authority to issue rules and regulations is given to the executive branch and the independent regulatory agencies, statutory delegations to private persons have also passed this Court's scrutiny. [T]he Court's decision today suggests that Congress may place a "veto" power over suspensions of deportation in private hands or in the hands of an independent agency, but is forbidden from reserving such authority for itself. Perhaps this odd result could be justified on other constitutional grounds, such as the separation of powers, but certainly it cannot be defended as consistent with the Court's view of the Article I presentment and bicameralism commands.

The Court also takes no account of perhaps the most relevant consideration: However resolutions of disapproval under § 244(c)(2) are formally characterized, in reality, a departure from the status quo occurs only upon the concurrence of opinion among the House, Senate, and President. Reservations of legislative authority to be exercised by Congress should be upheld if the exercise of such reserved authority is consistent with the distribution of and limits upon legislative power that Article I provides.

The central concern of the presentation and bicameralism requirements of Article I is that when a departure from the legal status quo is undertaken, it is done with the approval of the President and both Houses of Congress — or, in the event of a presidential veto, a two-thirds majority in both Houses. This interest is fully satisfied by the operation of § 244(c)(2). The President's approval is found in the Attorney General's action in recommending to Congress that the deportation order for a given alien be suspended. The House and the Senate indicate their approval of the Executive's action by not passing a resolution of disapproval within the statutory period. Thus, a change in the legal status quo — the deportability of the alien — is consummated only with the approval of each of the three relevant actors. The disagreement of any one of the three maintains the alien's pre-existing status: the Executive may choose not to recommend suspension; the House and Senate may each veto the recommendation. The effect on the rights and obligations of the affected individuals and upon the legislative system is precisely the same as if a private bill were introduced but failed to receive the necessary approval.

I do not suggest that all legislative vetoes are necessarily consistent with separation of powers principles. A legislative check on an inherently executive function, for example that of initiating prosecutions, poses an entirely different question. But the legislative veto device here — and in many other settings — is far from an instance of legislative tyranny over the Executive. It is a necessary check on the unavoidably expanding power of the agencies, both executive and independent, as they engage in exercising authority delegated by Congress.

[The Court's holding] reflects a profoundly different conception of the Constitution than that held by the Courts which sanctioned the modern administrative state. Today's decision strikes down in one fell swoop provisions in more laws enacted by Congress than the court has cumulatively invalidated in its history. I must dissent.

NOTES

1. *Breadth of the holding*. *Chadha* broadly repudiates legislative vetos on the basis of the structure of Article I rather than narrowly holding that the particular suspension of deportation violated separation of powers principles. Professor Strauss points out that there were many types of legislative vetos in various laws prior to *Chadha* and that the Court made no distinctions among them.

> Use of the veto as an instrument of the continuing political dialogue between President and Congress, on matters having high and legitimate political interest to both, and calling for flexibility for government generally, does not present the same problems as its use to control, in random and arbitrary fashion, those matters customarily regarded as the domain of administrative law.

Peter Strauss, *Was There a Baby in the Bathwater? A Comment on the Supreme Court's Legislative Veto Decision*, 1983 DUKE L.J. 789, 791–92. Does *Chadha* doom all use of the legislative veto?

2. *The formalist argument.* Chief Justice Burger's emphasis on structure and form in *Chadha* reflects the formalist approach. Describing the legislative veto as an "easy case," Professor Shane argues that in interpreting provisions in Articles I and II describing "conventionally understood structure and processes," a textualist approach is preferable in promoting control and accountability of government officials.

> When faced with a question to which the Constitution, plainly read, yields a plausible answer, I see no reason to believe that reading the text "creatively" will produce results more likely to foster good government. The functional arguments for and against legislative vetoes are numerous and have been made strongly, but I perceive no way in which a court could have confidence in one set of arguments or the other sufficient to overcome the answer all but dictated by the text when plainly read.

Peter Shane, *Conventionalism in Constitutional Interpretation and the Place of Administrative Agencies*, 36 AM. U. L. REV. 573, 596 (1987).

3. *The functionalist argument.* Other commentators criticize the "exceedingly literal and legalistic mode of analysis adopted in *Chadha*." Donald Elliott, *Why Our Separation of Powers Jurisprudence Is So Abysmal*, 57 Geo. Wash. L. Rev. 506, 514 (1989). Professor Elliott suggests that *Chadha* lacks an adequate analysis of the purpose behind the constitutional provisions and how they relate to the concerns of separation of powers doctrine. "Arguably, the legislative veto served to advance the true purposes of the principle of separation of powers that the Framers built into the Constitution by giving elected legislative officials an effective check over lawmaking by administrative bureaucrats." *Id.* at 516.

How would a functionalist decide the constitutionality of a one-House or two-House veto? "Under [a Madisonian view], the central issues would be the tendency of a challenged device to place a given branch beyond effective control by others, or to create an 'unnecessary and dangerous concentration of power in one branch,' or to interfere with a core function of another branch, to a degree unwarranted by 'overriding need' to accomplish some other objective." Strauss, 1983 Duke L.J. at 804.

Chadha can be perceived as a case in which Congress was enhancing its power at the expense of the executive branch. In such cases, judicial emphasis on the separate responsibilities of each of the branches may be appropriate.

> If the issue is whether a statute unreasonably expands or aggrandizes the powers of one branch, the separation theme is critical. If a statute concen trates within one branch functions that were formerly distributed among the branches, then the newly empowered branch can act without the restraint of the other branches. The separation of powers serves the same purpose as checks and balances — it prevents one branch from arbitrarily exercising too much power by ensuring that no single branch may act without the others.

Todd Peterson, *Prosecuting Executive Branch Officials for Contempt of Congress*, 66 N.Y.U.L. Rev. 563 (1991).

4. *Functionalist support for Chadha.* Is it possible to reach the result in *Chadha* without adopting the Court's formalist, textualist approach? Consider the argument that the legislative veto enhances the evils of factionalism by minimizing the difficulty of reaching consensus on a legislative policy choice. First, the veto excludes the President, who is more likely to represent a national constituency, from the consensus required to override an agency action. Further, it is easier to form a coalition of factional interests opposing an agency action, for any reason, than it would be to muster a consensus for a particular substitute policy choice. As a result, it is argued that the legislative veto operates to increase the extent of initial government regulation.

> The Framers expected that our constitutional structure, which makes it easier to block than to effect legislative change, would restrict the amount of legislation to which the people would be subject. The legislative veto, by circumventing the usual structure and creating an incentive for Congress to lower its decision costs by delegating power, tended to increase the size of government as a whole.

Harold Bruff, *Legislative Formality, Administrative Rationality*, 63 TEX. L. REV. 207, 220–22 (1984).

It has also been argued that legislative vetos provided "well-organized private groups an additional opportunity to fend off regulation. In this way, it undermined the central constitutional effort to diminish the power of well-organized private groups over governmental processes." Cass Sunstein, *Constitutionalism After the New Deal*, 101 HARV. L. REV. 421, 496 (1987). The one-house veto, for example, allows factions subject to particular agency action to avoid regulation by getting one of the houses to veto.

5. *Chadha and Representation.* One scholar argues that the real problem with the one-house veto was its harmful impact on representation: "It is no answer to say that, in *Chadha*, there was full representation because there was a vote by the entire House of Representatives. A one-house veto may cover the nation geographically but still presents risks of partial constitutional representation, because the Constitution demands the agreement of two different forms of constituency, one reflected in the Senate and the other in the House. Decisions by the House alone, and thus by population alone, will tend to reflect the majoritarian preferences of the larger population centers; by contrast, a decision by the Senate alone will tend to prefer the smaller states." V.F. Nourse, *Toward a New Constitutional Anatomy*, 56 STAN. L. REV 835, 861 (2004). Is Professor Nourse correct in asserting this is a *representation* concern? Isn't it far more appropriately categorized as a prophylactic means of preventing undue concentrations of power?

6. *Legislative acts.* A key factor in the Court's Article I analysis is its determination that the legislative veto is a "legislative act" requiring bicameralism and presentment. Yet the Court acknowledges that not every act of Congress is such a legislative act. How does the Court define "legislative act"? Article I, § 7, on presentment refers only to orders, resolutions, or votes requiring concurrence of the Senate and House.

> The question to be decided in Chadha was not whether the legislative veto is an exercise of Article I legislative power, but whether it is an exercise of Article I legislative power of the kind that requires presentment and bicameral action. The Court's presumption that the legislative veto is an exercise of Article I legislative power should only frame, rather than decide, the issue.

Donald Elliott, *INS v. Chadha: The Administrative Constitution, the Constitution, and the Legislative Veto*, 1983 SUP. CT. REV. 125, 134.

Does administrative rulemaking constitute a legislative act? Did the Attorney General affect rights in suspending Chadha's deportation; was the executive lawmaking? Professor Tribe notes that the Court's criteria for legislative act

> could apply with equal validity to nearly all exercises of delegated authority. Nearly all such actions alter legal rights, duties, and relations, thereby changing the legal status of persons outside the legislative branch in ways that, without the challenged delegation, could have been achieved, if at all, only by legislation. Both through

> rulemaking and through case-by-case dispositions, exercises of delegated authority change legal rights and privileges no less than do full-fledged laws.

Laurence Tribe, *The Legislative Veto Decision: A Law by Any Other Name?*, 21 HARV. J. ON LEGIS. 1, 9 (1984). Professor Strauss states: "Of course, the President and the agencies are lawmakers, in any conventional sense of the term, when they engage in rulemaking pursuant to constitutional or statutory authorization." Strauss, 1983 DUKE L.J. at 797. If it is true that administrative rule making is, in fact, law making, why would the *total* delegation of such law making power by Congress not violate the bicameralism and presentment requirements as much as does the *partial* delegation of legislative power to one house of Congress? What about the argument that in the case of congressional delegation of legislative power to administrative agencies, a constitutional safety net is provided by the availability of judicial review, which is unavailable in the case of a one-house veto? Of what value is judicial review as a means of assuring that agencies stayed within the bounds of their delegated authority, when Congress imposed no meaningful limits on that authority in the first place?

How were Chadha's rights altered by the veto? If his rights arise from the statute, doesn't the statutory right include the conditions prescribed in the statute, including the possibility of a legislative veto? Has Congress, as Justice White argues, simply "reserved" this authority by conditioning Chadha's statutory interest?

7. *The role of the courts.* Consider again Professor Choper's thesis that separation of powers issues should be treated as nonjusticiable, p. 290. Professor Nagel contends that *Chadha* reflects the Court's "affirmance of the centrality of judicial power." Robert Nagel, *The Legislative Veto, the Constitution, and the Courts*, 3 CONST. COMM. 71, 84 (1986):

> *Chadha* is justifiable, if at all, only on the ground that the judiciary, not the legislature, is the appropriate forum for deciding the practical questions that arise in the difficult, complicated effort to make the modern regulatory state democratically accountable. Its significance is that it confirms and accelerates the drive, which until *Chadha* could be discerned but not fully appreciated, toward the judicial monopolization of crucial questions of power definition and distribution.

[3] Budget Control

***Bowsher v. Synar*, 478 U.S. 714 (1986)**. In another example of the formalist approach in resolving separation of powers disputes, the Court held unconstitutional, 7-2, that portion of the Gramm-Rudman Act in which Congress assigned to the Comptroller General the authority to specify spending reductions binding on the President. Gramm-Rudman set a maximum deficit amount for each fiscal year between 1986 and 1991 (by which time the fiscal deficit would be reduced to zero). If the budget for any fiscal year exceeds the maximum amount, across-the-board cuts are required to reach the target deficit level. The procedures used for accomplishing these "automatic" reductions are spelled out in § 251 of the Act. Each year the Directors of the Office of Management and Budget (OMB) and the Congressional Budget Office (CBO) independently estimate the amount of the deficit for the upcoming year. If it exceeds the target level by more than a specified amount, the directors calculate the necessary reductions on a program-by-program basis. They then report their deficit estimates and reductions calculations to the Comptroller General (Comptroller). The Comptroller then reviews the recommendations and reports his conclusions to the President, who issues a "sequestration" order mandating the spending reductions specified by the Comptroller. Congress then has time to reduce spending to avoid the need for the sequestration order. If no reductions are made, the order becomes effective and the reductions are made.

The Court, per Chief Justice Burger, held that Congress had unconstitutionally encroached on the powers of the executive by vesting executive functions in the Comptroller who is subject to removal by Congress. "The Constitution," the Chief Justice argued, "does not contemplate an active role for Congress in the supervision of officers charged with the execution of the laws it enacts." Once the President appoints "executive officers" with the advice and consent of the Senate, "Congress cannot reserve for itself the power of removal of an officer charged with execution of the laws except by impeachment. To permit the execution of the laws to be vested in an officer answerable only to Congress would, in practical terms, reserve in Congress control over the execution of the laws." Congress has no authority to execute the laws and it cannot therefore "delegate to an officer under its control what it does not possess." To allow such a delegation, Chief Justice Burger argued, would effectively give Congress a veto power, by removing "or threatening to remove, an officer for executing the laws in any fashion found to be unsatisfactory by Congress." As in *Chadha*, such congressional control over the performance of executive functions is unconstitutional.

The Chief Justice then considered whether the Comptroller was under the control of Congress, concluding that he is. While the Comptroller is nominated by the President and confirmed by the Senate, "he is removable only at the initiative of Congress." This can be accomplished not only through impeachment proceedings but also by joint resolution at any time for (1) permanent disability; (2) inefficiency; (3) neglect of duty; (4) malfeasance; and (5) felony or conduct involving moral turpitude. The broad terms of the statutory grounds, Chief Justice Burger argued, would allow removal for any number of real or perceived "transgressions of the legislative will." The Chief Justice rejected Justice White's argument that the political realities demonstrate the independence, in fact, of the Comptroller from Congress. Congress, he found, has consistently viewed the Comptroller as an officer of the legislative branch. "Against this background, we see no escape from the conclusion that, because Congress has retained removal authority over the Comptroller, he may not be entrusted with executive power."

The Court then addressed the question whether the Comptroller was in fact given executive powers under Gramm-Rudman. Answering in the affirmative, the Chief Justice rejected the contention that the Comptroller's duties were ministerial and did not constitute "execution of the laws." Under Gramm-Rudman, the Comptroller prepares a report in which he specifies necessary budget reductions with "due regard" for the estimates and reductions submitted to him by the CBO and OMB, the President's fiscal and budgetary advisors. The Act allows the Comptroller to use his independent judgment and evaluation, requiring him to explain any differences he has with the OMB and CBO reports. Such interpretational powers, Chief Justice Burger argues, constitute an executive function. "The executive nature of the Comptroller's function under the Act is revealed in § 252(a)(3) which gives the Comptroller the ultimate authority to determine the budget cuts to be made. Indeed, the Comptroller commands the President himself to carry out, without the slightest variation, the directive of the Comptroller General as to the budget reductions." The Comptroller has the "ultimate authority" to determine budget cuts. The Chief Justice stressed that "[i]nterpreting a law enacted by Congress to implement the legislative mandate is the very essence of 'execution' of the law."

As the Court reasoned in *Chadha*, once Congress has enacted legislation, its participation ends. "By placing the responsibility for execution of [the Act] in the hands of an officer who is subject to removal only by itself, Congress has in effect retained control over the execution of the Act and has intruded into the executive function. The Constitution does not permit such an intrusion." The Court therefore affirmed the district court's judgment and invalidated the provision.

Justice White, in dissent, argued that the Act presents "no substantial threat to the basic scheme of separation of powers." Determining federal spending levels, Justice White contended, is a legislative function committed to Congress by Article I, § 9. The Act was designed to minimize the policy choices given to the Comptroller by creating "a precise and articulated set of criteria," while ensuring that congressional spending priorities remain unaltered. Justice White contended that "it is eminently reasonable and proper for Congress to vest the budget-cutting authority in an officer who is to the greatest degree possible nonpartisan and independent of the President and his political agenda and who therefore may be relied upon not to allow his calculations to be colored by political considerations. Such a delegation deprives the President of no authority that is rightfully his." While agreeing that Congress may not reserve an executive role for itself or its agents, Justice White did not agree that the power of Congress to remove the Comptroller by joint resolution constituted an impermissible execution of the law by Congress itself. Nor would he have found that the congressional removal power rendered the Comptroller an "agent" of Congress incapable of receiving executive power. The difficulty of removal makes congressional influence unlikely. In fact, Justice White contended, the Comptroller is one of the most independent officers in the entire federal establishment. None of the Comptrollers since 1921, he pointed out, has ever been threatened or removed.

Justice Blackmun filed a separate dissent arguing that the plaintiffs were not entitled to the relief requested (i.e., nullification of the automatic budget reduction provision). The proper remedy, he contended, would be to reject congressional removal of the Comptroller, if ever attempted, rather than nullifying the central provisions of Gramm-Rudman.

Under a "fallback" procedure in the Act, the report prepared by the Directors of OMB and CBO is now submitted to a specially created Temporary Joint

Committee on Deficit Reduction, which must report in five days to both houses of Congress a joint resolution setting forth the content of the report. Congress then votes on the resolution which, if passed and signed by the President, serves as the sequestration order.

[4] The Line Item Veto Act

In 1996, Congress passed and the President signed the Line Item Veto Act ("Act"), amending the Congressional Budget and Impoundment Control Act. Under the Act, the President was authorized to veto selected portions of spending and tax laws. The President could cancel dollar amounts of discretionary budget authority, any item of new direct spending, and certain tax benefits. This authority could be used when the President determined that such cancellation would reduce the federal budget deficit, not impair any essential government functions, and not harm the national interest. The President was required to notify Congress of such cancellation by a special message within five calendar days after enactment of the appropriation, authorization, revenue, or reconciliation law.

Presidential cancellation was to take effect when Congress receive the President's special message. If Congress disagreed, a majority of both Houses could pass a "disapproval bill" which, if signed by the President, nullified the cancellation. If the President vetoes the disapproval bill, Congress could override the veto by a two-thirds majority. The Act specified procedures for consideration by Congress of disapproval bills, including limitations on debate in both the House and Senate (e.g., limits on the use of the filibuster).

In *Clinton v. City of New York,* the Supreme Court faced the complex constitutional issues to which this statute gave rise.

In *Clinton v. City of New York,* 524 U.S. 417 (1998), the Supreme Court struck down the Line Item Veto Act ("Act"). Under the Act, the President was authorized to "veto" selected portions of spending and tax laws. The President could cancel dollar amounts of discretionary budget authority, any item of new direct spending, or certain tax benefits but only after a specific determination that cancellation would reduce the federal budget deficit, not impair any essential government functions, and not harm the national interest. The President was required to notify Congress of a cancellation by special message within five calendar days after enactment of the measure. If Congress disagreed, a majority of both Houses could pass a "disapproval bill" which, if signed by the President, nullified the cancellation. If the President vetoed the disapproval bill, Congress could override the veto by a two-thirds majority.

The majority opinion by Justice Stevens compared the resulting impact on legislation to amending existing legislation. Speaking of the two examples before the Court, he described them as "truncated versions of two bills that passed both Houses of Congress. They are not the product of the 'finely wrought' procedure that the Framers designed." Answering the argument that Congress can authorize the President to suspend the operation of certain laws under defined circumstances, he stated that in those situations, the President was "executing the policy that Congress had embodied in the statute. In contrast, whenever the President cancels an item of new direct spending or a limited tax benefit, he is rejecting the policy judgment made by Congress and relying on his own policy judgment."

In dissent, Justice Scalia argued that "there is not a dime's worth of difference between Congress' authorizing the President to cancel a spending item, and Congress' authorizing money to be spent on a particular item at the President's discretion." In a separate dissent, Justice Breyer argued that the requirements of Article I, § 7 were, in fact, complied with, since the Line Item Veto Act — which itself was enacted according to those procedural requirements — authorized the president's power of cancellation. He also argued that when the president cancelled the expenditures, he neither "repealed" nor "amended" the statute because his actions were in fact authorized by the statute. He was thus doing nothing more than following the law.

The functionalist argument for the majority position can be understood by a simplified example. If Congress adopted an appropriations bill with just three items in it, it is possible that none of the three would have carried a majority of Congress by itself. In other words, the entire package would pass or none of it would pass. But if the President then vetoed one of the three, it is quite possible that a majority (or at least more than one-third) of Congress would be very happy because two groups have their projects without having to pay for the third. In this scenario, the majority's characterization of the veto as an "amendment" of the legislation is quite sensible.

The dissents' functional argument is that Congress could have passed the measure with three contingent funding allocations and given the President discretion whether to spend any of the three. When the President decides to carry out two of the projects, he or she is carrying out the will of Congress.

If neither of these functional arguments carries the day, then are there formalistic reasons to choose one approach over the other?

NOTES

1. *Cancellation and impoundment.* Can the power of executive cancellation be distinguished, for constitutional purposes, from executive power to impound funds that have been authorized by Congress? If not, should that mean that cancellation should be deemed constitutional, or that impoundment should be deemed unconstitutional?

2. *Separation of powers.* Note that the Court concludes that because it hold that the Act's cancellation provisions violate Article I, § 7, "we find it unnecessary to consider the District Court's alternative holding that the Act 'impermissibly disrupts the balance of powers among the three branches of government.' " What is the difference between these lines of constitutional attack? Would it be inaccurate to suggest that the strict procedural requirements imposed in Article I, § 7 for the enactment of legislation were imposed for the very purpose of preventing the impermissible disruption of the balance of powers among the branches, since by their nature those procedures preclude lawmaking by branches other than Congress?

3. *Text.* According to one scholar, the Court in *Clinton* "moor[ed] its decision to a debatable interpretation of the constitutional text." Neal Devins,

Congressional Factfinding and the Scope of Judicial Review: A Preliminary Analysis, 50 DUKE L.J. 1190 (2001). Do you agree?

4. ***Delegation doctrine.*** To what extent is the decision in *Clinton* inconsistent with the Court's nondelegation jurisprudence (discussed text, pp. 308–311)? Does the nondelegation doctrine also implicate the lawmaking requirements of Article I, § 7? *See* Elena Kagan, *Presidential Administration*, 114 HARV. L. REV. 2245 (2001).

5. ***Statutory authorization.*** Note that in his dissent, Justice Breyer argues that the requirements of Article I, § 7 were, in fact, complied with, since the Line Item Veto Act — which itself was enacted according to those procedural requirements — authorized the president's power of cancellation. He also argues that when the president cancelled the expenditures, he neither "repealed" nor "amended" the statute because his actions were in fact authorized by the statute. He was thus doing nothing more than following the law. How persuasive is this response to the constitutional attack grounded in Article I, § 7? Consider the examples of valid congressional delegations of decision making power to the president, cited by Justice Breyer. To what extent are those examples distinguishable, for purposes of constitutionality, from the Line Item Veto Act?

[5] The Appointment and Removal Power

Article II, § 2, cl. 2, establishes the power to appoint officers of the United States in the President but provides that the Congress may vest the appointment of inferior officers in either the President alone, in the courts of law or in the heads of departments. In *Buckley v. Valeo*, 424 U.S. 1 (1976), the Court held that Congress had violated Article II by providing that a majority of the voting members of the Federal Election Commission were to be appointed by the President *pro tem* of the Senate and the Speaker of the House. Neither of these legislative officials was deemed to come within the terms "courts of law" or "heads of departments" as required by the appointments clause.

Even more troubling problems are presented by the removal power. What are the respective powers of Congress and the President in removing officials appointed under Article II? Most of the cases have involved the scope of the President's removal power. *Myers v. United States*, 272 U.S. 52 (1926), upholding presidential removal of a postmaster contrary to a tenure of office act, characterized "the power of removal [as] incident to the power of appointment." But in *Humphrey's Executor v. United States*, 295 U.S. 602 (1935), the Court rejected presidential removal of an FTC commissioner contrary to statute, since he was not a "purely executive officer" — the commissioner "occupies no place in the executive department and . . . exercises no part of the executive power vested by the Constitution in the President." When an officer exercises "quasi-legislative or quasi-judicial powers" or is an officer of the legislative or judicial departments, separation of powers rejects an "illimitable power of removal" in the President. The coercive power of removal was seen as threatening the independence of the commission, which, while "not wholly disconnected from the executive department," was created by Congress "as an agency of the legislative and judicial departments." *Wiener v. United States*, 357 U.S. 349 (1958), upholding a back pay claim by a commissioner of the War Claims Commission who had been removed, similarly recognized

> a sharp line of cleavage between officials who were part of the Executive establishment and were thus removable by virtue of the President's constitutional powers, and those who are members of a body "to exercise its judgment without the leave or hindrance of any other official or any department of the government," as to whom a power of removal exists only if Congress may fairly be said to have conferred it. This sharp differentiation derives from the difference in function between those who are part of the Executive establishment and those whose tasks require absolute freedom from Executive interference.

But increasingly, executive agencies perform quasi-legislative and quasi-judicial functions and the "independence" of the independent regulatory agencies from Congress and the President is questioned. Are the distinctions fashioned in *Humphrey's Executor* still meaningful? What is the status of the "fourth branch" of government? What are the implications of *Chadha* for exercising control over and promoting accountability of the administrative agencies?

The meaning of the Appointments Clause and the nature of the removal power came before the Court again in *Morrison v. Olson*, involving a challenge to the independent counsel provisions of the Ethics in Government Act. The Watergate scandals, resulting in the resignation of President Richard Nixon, had convinced the Congress that only an independent institution could be trusted to investigate and prosecute high ranking government officials. An official not appointed by the Executive or subject to executive removal at will and free of executive supervision of its prosecutorial operations, could provide an effective mechanism for promoting control and accountability. But *Chadha* and *Bowsher* suggest that the need and desirability of controlling the executive will not justify departures from the constitutional allocation of powers and responsibilities. If criminal investigation and prosecution is an "executive" function, can Congress divest or diminish the executive role in the appointment, removal and superintendence of the prosecutor consistent with separation of powers doctrine?

MORRISON v. OLSON

487 U.S. 654, 108 S. Ct. 2597, 101 L.Ed.2d 569 (1988)

Chief Justice Rehnquist delivered the opinion of the Court.

This case presents us with a challenge to the independent counsel provisions of the Ethics in Government Act of 1978, 28 U.S.C.A. sections 49, 591 *et seq.* We hold today that these provisions of the Act do not violate the Appointments Clause of the Constitution, Art. II, section 2, cl. 2, or the limitations of Article III, nor do they impermissibly interfere with the President's authority under Article II in violation of the constitutional principle of separation of powers.

Briefly stated, Title VI of the Ethics of Government Act allows for the appointment of an "independent counsel" to investigate and, if appropriate, prosecute certain high ranking government officials for violations of federal criminal laws. The Act requires the Attorney General, upon receipt of information that he determines is "sufficient to constitute grounds to investigate whether any person [covered by the Act] may have violated any Federal criminal law," to conduct a preliminary investigation of the matter. When the Attorney General has completed this investigation, or 90 days has elapsed, he is required to report to a special court [the Special Division] created by the Act "for the purpose of appointing independent counsels." If the Attorney General determines that "there are no reasonable grounds to believe that further investigation is warranted," then he must notify the Special Division of this result. In such a case, "the division of the court shall have no power to appoint an independent counsel." If, however, the Attorney General has determined that there are "reasonable grounds to believe that further investigation or prosecution is warranted," then he "shall apply to the division of the court for the appointment of an independent counsel." The Attorney General's application to the court "shall contain sufficient information to assist the [court] in selecting an independent counsel and in defining that independent counsel's prosecutorial jurisdiction." Upon receiving this application, the Special Division "shall appoint an appropriate independent counsel and shall define that independent counsel's prosecutorial jurisdiction."

With respect to all matters within the independent counsel's jurisdiction, the Act grants the counsel "full power and independent authority to exercise all investigative and prosecutorial functions and powers of the Department of Justice, the Attorney General, and any other officer or employee of the Department of Justice." The functions of the independent counsel include conducting grand jury proceedings and other investigations, participating in civil and criminal court proceedings and litigation, and appealing any decision in any case in which the counsel participates in an official capacity. Under section 594(a)(9), the counsel's powers include "initiating and conducting prosecutions in any court of competent jurisdiction, framing and signing indictments, filing informations, and handling all aspects of any case, in the name of the United States." The counsel may appoint employees, may request and obtain assistance from the Department of Justice, and may accept referral of matters from the Attorney General if the matter falls within the counsel's jurisdiction as defined by the Special Division. The Act also states that an independent counsel "shall, except where not possible, comply with the written or other established policies of the Department of Justice respecting enforcement of the criminal laws." In addition, whenever a matter has been referred to an independent counsel under the Act, the Attorney General and the Justice Department are required to suspend all investigations and proceedings regarding the matter. An independent counsel has "full authority to dismiss matters within [his] prosecutorial jurisdiction without conducting an investigation or at any subsequent time before prosecution, if to do so would be consistent" with Department of Justice policy.

Two statutory provisions govern the length of an independent counsel's tenure in office. The first defines the procedure for removing an independent counsel. Section 596(a)(1) provides: "An independent counsel appointed under this chapter may be removed from office, other than by impeachment and conviction, only by the personal action of the Attorney General and only for good cause, physical disability, mental incapacity, or any other condition that substantially impairs the performance of such independent counsel's duties."

If an independent counsel is removed pursuant to this section, the Attorney General is required to submit a report to both the Special Division and the Judiciary Committees of the Senate and the House "specifying the facts found and the ultimate grounds for such removal." Under the current version of the Act, an independent counsel can obtain judicial review of the Attorney General's action by filing a civil action in the United States District Court for the District of Columbia. Members of the Special Division "may not hear or determine any such civil action or any appeal of a decision in any such civil action." The reviewing court is authorized to grant reinstatement or "other appropriate relief."

The other provision governing the tenure of the independent counsel defines the procedures for "terminating" the counsel's office. Under section 596(b)(1), the office of an independent counsel terminates when he notifies the Attorney General that he has completed or substantially completed any investigations or prosecutions undertaken pursuant to the Act. In addition, the Special Division, acting either on its own or on the suggestion of the Attorney General, may terminate the office of an independent counsel at any time if it finds that "the investigation of all matters within the prosecutorial jurisdiction of such independent counsel . . . have been completed or so substantially completed that it would be appropriate for the Department of Justice to complete such investigations and prosecutions."

Finally, the Act provides for Congressional oversight of the activities of independent counsels. An independent counsel may from time to time send Congress statements or reports on his activities. The "appropriate committees of the Congress" are given oversight jurisdiction in regard to the official conduct of an independent counsel, and the counsel is required by the Act to cooperate with Congress in the exercise of this jurisdiction. The counsel is required to inform the House of Representatives of "substantial and credible information which [the counsel] receives . . . that may constitute grounds for an impeachment." In addition, the Act gives certain Congressional Committee Members the power to "request in writing that the Attorney General apply for the appointment of an independent counsel." The Attorney General is required to respond to this request within a specified time but is not required to accede to the request.

The proceedings in this case provide an example of how the Act works in practice. [In 1985, an investigation by the House Judiciary Committee led to a report which heavily criticized various Justice Department officials for their role in a dispute between the Administration and the House over the production of certain documents to House subcommittees. The report suggested that appellee Olson, then Assistant Attorney General for the Office of Legal Counsel, had given false testimony before a House subcommittee, and that other Justice Department officials had withheld certain documents from the Committee, thereby obstructing the Committee's investigation. This report was forwarded to the Attorney General, with a request for the appointment of an independent counsel to investigate the charges. The Attorney General applied to the Special Division for the appointment of an independent counsel to investigate appellee Olson. Appellant Morrison, independent counsel, caused a grand jury to issue and serve subpoenas *ad testificandum* and *duces tecum* upon the appellees. The appellees moved to quash the subpoenas, claiming that the independent counsel provisions of the Act were unconstitutional and the appellant had no authority to proceed. The district court denied the motions to quash, and a divided court of appeals reversed.]

The Appointments Clause of Article II reads as follows: "[The President] shall nominate, and by and with the Advice and Consent of the Senate, shall appoint Ambassadors, other public Ministers and Consuls, Judges of the Supreme Court, and all other Officers of the United States, whose Appointments are not herein otherwise provided for, and which shall be established by Law: but the Congress may by Law vest the Appointment of such inferior Officers, as they think proper, in the President alone, in the Courts of Law, or in the Heads of Departments." U.S. Const., Art. II, section 2, cl. 2.

The parties do not dispute that "[t]he Constitution for purposes of appointment . . . divides all its officers into two classes." *United States v. Germaine*, 99 U.S. 508, 509 (1879). As we stated in *Buckley v. Valeo*, "[p]rincipal officers are selected by the President with the advice and consent of the Senate. Inferior officers Congress may allow to be appointed by the President alone, by the heads of departments, or by the Judiciary." The initial question is, accordingly, whether appellant is an "inferior" or a "principal" officer. If she is the latter, as the Court of Appeals concluded, then the Act is in violation of the Appointments Clause.

The line between "inferior" and "principal" officers is one that is far from clear, and the Framers provided little guidance into where it should be drawn. We need not attempt here to decide exactly where the line falls between the two types of officers, because in our view appellant clearly falls on the "inferior officer" side of that line. Several factors lead to this conclusion.

First, appellant is subject to removal by a higher Executive Branch official. Although appellant may not be "subordinate" to the Attorney General [and the President] insofar as she possesses a degree of independent discretion to exercise the powers delegated to her under the Act, the fact that she can be removed by the Attorney General indicates that she is to some degree "inferior" in rank and authority.

Second, appellant is empowered by the Act to perform only certain, limited duties. An independent counsel's role is restricted primarily to investigation and, if appropriate, prosecution for certain federal crimes. Admittedly, the Act delegates to appellant "full power and independent authority to exercise all investigative and prosecutorial functions and powers of the Department of Justice," but this grant of authority does not include any authority to formulate policy for the Government or the Executive Branch, nor does it give appellant any administrative duties outside of those necessary to operate her office. The Act specifically provides that in policy matters appellant is to comply to the extent possible with the policies of the Department.

Third, appellant's office is limited in jurisdiction. Not only is the Act itself restricted in applicability to certain federal officials suspected of certain serious federal crimes, but an independent counsel can only act within the scope of the jurisdiction that has been granted by the Special Division pursuant to a request by the Attorney General.

Finally, appellant's office is limited in tenure. There is concededly no time limit on the appointment of a particular counsel. Nonetheless, the office of independent counsel is "temporary" in the sense that an independent counsel is appointed essentially to accomplish a single task, and when that task is over the office is terminated, either by the counsel herself or by action of the Special Division.

This conclusion is consistent with our few previous decisions that considered the question of whether a particular government official is a "principal" or an "inferior" officer. All of this is consistent with our reference in *United States v. Nixon* to the office of Watergate Special Prosecutor — whose authority was similar to that of appellant — as a "subordinate officer."

This does not, however, end our inquiry under the Appointments Clause. Appellees argue that even if appellant is an "inferior" officer, the Clause does not empower Congress to place the power to appoint such an officer outside the Executive Branch. They contend that the Clause does not contemplate congressional authorization of "interbranch appointments," in which an officer of one branch is appointed by officers of another branch. The relevant language of the Appointments Clause is worth repeating. It reads: ". . . but the Congress may by Law vest the Appointment of such inferior Officers, as they think proper, in the President alone, in the courts of Law, or in the Heads of Departments." On its face, the language of this "excepting clause" admits of no limitation on interbranch appointments. Indeed, the inclusion of "as they think proper" seems clearly to give Congress significant discretion to determine whether it is "proper" to vest the appointment of, for example, executive officials in the "courts of Law."

We do not mean to say that Congress' power to provide for interbranch appointments of "inferior officers" is unlimited. In addition to separation of powers concerns, which would arise if such provisions for appointment had the potential to impair the constitutional functions assigned to one of the branches, [Congress'] decision to vest the appointment power in the courts would be improper if there was some "incongruity" between the functions normally performed by the courts and the performance of their duty to appoint. In this case, however, we do not think it impermissible for Congress to vest the power to appoint independent counsels in a specially created federal court. We thus disagree with the Court of Appeals' conclusion that there is an inherent incongruity about a court having the power to appoint prosecutorial officers. We have recognized that courts may appoint private attorneys to act as prosecutor for judicial contempt judgments. Congress of course was concerned when it created the office of independent counsel with the conflicts of interest that could arise in situations when the Executive Branch is called upon to investigate its own high-ranking officers. If it were to remove the appointing authority from the Executive Branch, the most logical place to put it was in the Judicial Branch. In the light of the Act's provision making the judges of the Special Division ineligible to participate in any matters relating to an independent counsel they have appointed, we do not think that appointment of the independent counsels by the court runs afoul of the constitutional limitation on "incongruous" interbranch appointments.

Appellees next contend that the powers vested in the Special Division by the Act conflict with Article III of the Constitution. We have long recognized that by the express provision of Article III, the judicial power of the United States is limited to "Cases" and "Controversies." As a general rule, we have broadly stated that "executive or administrative duties of a nonjudicial nature may not be imposed on judges holding office under Art. III of the Constitution." The purpose of this limitation is to help ensure the independence of the Judicial Branch and to prevent the judiciary from encroaching into areas reserved for the other branches.

[The Court held that the powers vested in the Special Division by the Act do not conflict with Article III. Most of the vested powers are not solely "executive" functions but partake of more traditional judicial functions such as the court's grand jury role, issuance of search warrants and wiretap orders. While the role of the Special Division in terminating the independent counsel is more administrative, it "does not pose a sufficient threat of judicial intrusion into matters that are more properly within the Executive authority." Finally, the judges in the Special Division are sufficiently isolated to minimize any risk to judicial independence.]

We now turn to consider whether the Act is invalid under the constitutional principle of separation of powers. Two related issues must be addressed: The first is whether the provision of the Act restricting the Attorney General's power to remove the independent counsel to only those instances in which he can show "good cause," taken by itself, impermissibly interferes with the President's exercise of his constitutionally appointed functions. The second is whether, taken as a whole, the Act violates the separation of powers by reducing the President's ability to control the prosecutorial powers wielded by the independent counsel.

Unlike both *Bowsher* and *Myers*, this case does not involve an attempt by Congress itself to gain a role in the removal of executive officials other than its established powers of impeachment and conviction. The Act instead puts the removal power squarely in the hands of the Executive Branch; an independent counsel may be removed from office, "only by the personal action of the Attorney General, and only for good cause." There is no requirement of congressional approval of the Attorney General's removal decision, though the decision is subject to judicial review. In our view, the removal provisions of the Act make this case more analogous to *Humphrey's Executor v. United States*, and *Weiner v. United States*, than to *Myers* or *Bowsher*.

Appellees contend that *Humphrey's Executor* and *Wiener* are distinguishable from this case because they did not involve officials who performed a "core executive function." They argue that our decision in *Humphrey's Executor* rests on a distinction between "purely executive" officials and officials who exercise "quasi-legislative" and "quasi-judicial" powers. In their view, when a "purely executive" official is involved, the governing precedent is *Myers*, not *Humphrey's Executor*. And, under *Myers*, the President must have absolute discretion to discharge "purely" executive officials at will. We undoubtedly did rely on the terms "quasi-legislative" and "quasi-judicial" to distinguish the officials involved in *Humphrey's Executor* and *Wiener* from those in *Myers*, but our present considered view is that the determination of whether the Constitution allows Congress to impose a "good cause"-type restriction on the President's power to remove an official cannot be made to turn on whether or not that official is classified as "purely executive." The analysis contained in our removal cases is designed not to define rigid categories of those officials who may or may not be removed at will by the President, but to ensure that Congress does not interfere with the President's exercise of the "executive power" and his constitutionally appointed duty to "take care that the laws be faithfully executed" under Article II. We do not mean to suggest that an analysis of the functions served by the officials at issue is irrelevant. But the real question is whether the removal restrictions are of such a nature that they impede the President's ability to perform his constitu tional duty, and the functions of the officials in question must be analyzed in that light.

Considering for the moment the "good cause" removal provision in isolation from the other parts of the Act at issue in this case, we cannot say that the imposition of a "good cause" standard for removal by itself unduly trammels on executive authority. Although the counsel exercises no small amount of discretion and judgment in deciding how to carry out her duties under the Act, we simply do not see how the President's need to control the exercise of that discretion is so central to the functioning of the Executive Branch as to require as a matter of constitutional law that the counsel be terminable at will by the President.

Nor do we think that the "good cause" removal provision at issue here impermissibly burdens the President's power to control or supervise the independent counsel, as an executive official, in the execution of her duties under the Act. This is not a case in which the power to remove an executive official has been completely stripped from the President, thus providing no means for the President to ensure the "faithful execution" of the laws. Rather, because the independent counsel may be terminated for "good cause," the Executive, through the Attorney General, retains ample authority to assure that the counsel is competently performing her statutory responsibilities in a manner that comports with the provisions of the Act. Although we need not decide in this case exactly what is encompassed within the term "good cause" under the Act, the legislative history of the removal provision also makes clear that the Attorney General may remove an independent counsel for "misconduct." Here, as with the provision of the Act conferring the appointment authority of the independent counsel on the special court, the congressional determination to limit the removal power of the Attorney General was essential, in the view of Congress, to establish the necessary independence of the office. We do not think that this limitation as it presently stands sufficiently deprives the President of control over the independent counsel to interfere impermissibly with his constitutional obligation to ensure the faithful execution of the laws.

The final question to be addressed is whether the Act, taken as a whole, violates the principle of separation of powers by unduly interfering with the role of the Executive Branch. Time and again we have reaffirmed the importance in our constitutional scheme of the separation of governmental powers into the three coordinate branches. On the other hand, we have never held that the Constitution requires that the three Branches of Government "operate with absolute independence." *United States v. Nixon*.

We observe first that this case does not involve an attempt by Congress to increase its own powers at the expense of the Executive Branch. Unlike some of our previous cases, most recently *Bowsher v. Synar*, this case simply does not pose a "dange[r] of congressional usurpation of Executive Branch functions." Similarly, we do not think that the Act works any judicial usurpation of properly executive functions.

Finally, we do not think that the Act "impermissibly undermine[s]" the powers of the Executive Branch, or "disrupts the proper balance between the coordinate branches [by] prevent[ing] the Executive Branch from accomplishing its constitutionally assigned functions," *Nixon v. Administrator of General Services*. It is undeniable that the Act reduces the amount of control or supervision that the Attorney General and, through him, the President exercises over the investigation and prosecution of a certain class of alleged criminal activity. The Attorney General is not allowed to appoint the individual of his choice; he does not determine the counsel's jurisdiction; and his power to remove a counsel is limited. Nonetheless, the Act does give the Attorney General several means of supervising or controlling the prosecutorial powers that may be wielded by an independent counsel. Most importantly, the Attorney General retains the power to remove the counsel for "good cause," a power that we have already concluded provides the Executive with substantial ability to ensure that the laws are "faithfully executed" by an independent counsel. No independent counsel may be appointed without a specific request by the Attorney General, and the Attorney General's decision not to request appointment if he finds "no reasonable grounds to believe that further investigation is warranted" is committed to his unreviewable discretion. The Act thus gives the Executive a degree of control over the power to initiate an investigation by the independent counsel. Notwithstanding the fact that the counsel is to some degree "independent" and free from Executive supervision to a greater extent than other federal prosecutors, in our view these features of the Act give the Executive Branch sufficient control over the independent counsel to ensure that the President is able to perform his constitutionally assigned duties.

JUSTICE SCALIA, dissenting.

The framers of the Federal Constitution viewed the principle of separation of powers as the absolutely central guarantee of a just government. Madison wrote that "[n]o political truth is certainly of greater intrinsic value, or is stamped with the authority of more enlightened patrons of liberty." THE FEDERALIST NO. 47. Without a secure structure of separated powers, our Bill of Rights would be worthless, as are the bills of rights of many nations of the world that have adopted, or even improved upon, the mere words of ours.

Proposals to have multiple executives, or a council of advisors with separate authority, were rejected. Thus, while "[a]ll legislative Powers herein granted shall be vested in a Congress of the United States, which shall consist of a Senate *and* House of Representatives," (emphasis added), "[t]he executive Power shall be vested in *a President of the United States*" (emphasis added).

That is what this suit is about. Power. The allocation of power among Congress, the President and the courts in such fashion as to preserve the equilibrium the Constitution sought to establish — so that "a gradual concentration of the several powers in the same department," FEDERALIST NO. 51, (J. Madison), can effectively be resisted. Frequently an issue of this sort will come before the Court clad, so to speak, in sheep's clothing: the potential of the asserted principle to effect important change in the equilibrium of power is not immediately evident, and must be discerned by a careful and perceptive analysis. But this wolf comes as a wolf.

The context of this statute is acrid with the smell of threatened impeachment. Where, as here, a request for appointment of an independent counsel has come from the Judiciary Committee of either House of Congress, the Attorney General must, if he decides not to seek appointment, explain to that Committee why.

If to describe this case is not to decide it, the concept of a government of separate and coordinate powers no longer has meaning. The Court devotes most of its attention to such relatively technical details as the Appointments Clause and the removal power, addressing briefly and only at the end of its opinion the separation of powers. As my prologue suggests, I think that has it backwards. Our opinions are full of the recognition that it is the principle of separation of powers, and the inseparable corollary that each department's "defense must . . . be made commensurate to the danger of attack," FEDERALIST NO. 51 (J. Madison), which gives comprehensible content to the appointments clause, and determines the appropriate scope of the removal power.

Where a private citizen challenges action of the Government on grounds unrelated to separation of powers, harmonious functioning of the system demands that we ordinarily give some deference, or a presumption of validity, to the action of the political branches in what is agreed, between themselves at least, to be within their respective spheres. But where the issue pertain[s] to separation of powers, and the political branches are (as here) in disagreement, neither can be presumed correct. As one of the interested and coordinate parties to the underlying constitutional dispute, Congress, no more than the President, is entitled to the benefit of the doubt.

It seems to me that the decision of the Court of Appeals invalidating the present statute must be upheld on fundamental separation-of-powers principles if the following two questions are answered affirmatively: (1) Is the conduct of a criminal prosecution (and of an investigation to decide whether to prosecute) the exercise of purely executive power? (2) Does the statute deprive the President of the United States of exclusive control over the exercise of that power? Surprising to say, the Court appears to concede an affirmative answer to both questions, but seeks to avoid the inevitable conclusion that since the statute vests some purely executive power in a person who is not the President of the United States it is void.

[T]he independent [counsel] is vested with the "full power and independent authority to exercise all investigative and prosecutorial function and powers of the Department of Justice [and] the Attorney General." 28 U.S.C. § 594(a). Governmental investigation and prosecution of crimes is a quintessentially executive function.

As for the second question, whether the statute before us deprives the President of exclusive control over that quintessentially executive activity: The Court does not, and could not possibly, assert that it does not. That is indeed the whole object of the statute. Instead, the Court points out that the President, through his Attorney General, has at least some control. That concession is alone enough to invalidate the statute. It is not for us to determine, and we have never presumed to determine, how much of the purely executive powers of government must be within the full control of the President. The Constitution prescribes that they all are.

The utter incompatibility of the Court's approach with our constitutional traditions can be made more clear, perhaps, by applying it to the powers of the other two Branches. Is it conceivable that if Congress passed a statute depriving itself of less than full and entire control over some insignificant area of legislation, we would inquire whether the matter was "so central to the functioning of the Legislative Branch" as really to require complete control, or whether the statute gives Congress "sufficient control over the surrogate legislator to ensure that Congress is able to perform its constitutionally assigned duties"? Of course we would have none of that. Once we determined that a purely legislative power was at issue we would require it to be exercised, wholly and entirely, by Congress. Or to bring the point closer to home, consider a statute giving to non-Article III judges just a tiny bit of purely judicial power in a relatively insignificant field, with substantial control, though not total control, in the courts — perhaps "clear error" review, which would be a fair judicial equivalent of the Attorney General's "for cause" removal power here. Is there any doubt that we would not pause to inquire whether the matter was "so central to the functioning of the Judicial Branch" as really to require complete control, or whether we retained "sufficient control over the matters to be decided that we are able to perform our constitutionally assigned duties"? We would say that our "constitutionally assigned duties" include complete control over all exercises of the judicial power. We should say here that the President's constitutionally assigned duties include complete control over investigation and prosecution of violations of the law, and that the inexorable command of Article II is clear and definite: the executive power must be vested in the President of the United States.

Is it unthinkable that the President should have such exclusive power, even when alleged crimes by him or his close associates are at issue? No more so than that Congress should have the exclusive power of legislation, even when what is at issue is its own exemption from the burdens of certain laws. No more so than that this Court should have the exclusive power to pronounce the final decision on justiciable cases and controversies, even those pertaining to the constitutionality of a statute reducing the salaries of the Justices. A system of separate and coordinate powers necessarily involves an acceptance of exclusive power that can theoretically be abused. The checks against any Branch's abuse of its exclusive powers are twofold: First, retaliation by one of the other Branch's use of its exclusive powers: Congress, for example, can impeach the Executive who willfully fails to enforce the laws; the Executive can decline to prosecute under unconstitutional statutes; and the courts can dismiss malicious prosecutions: Second, and ultimately, there is the political check that the people will replace those in the political branches (the branches more "dangerous to the political rights of the Constitution," FEDERALIST NO. 78) who are guilty of abuse. Political pressures produced special prosecutors — for Teapot Dome and for Watergate, for example — long before this statute created the independent counsel.

The Court has, nonetheless, replaced the clear constitutional prescription that the executive power belongs to the President with a "balancing test." What are the standards to determine how the balance is to be struck, that is, how much removal of presidential power is too much? Many countries of the world get along with an Executive that is much weaker than ours — in fact, entirely dependent upon the continued support of the legislature. Once we depart from the text of the Constitution, just where short of that do we stop? The most amazing feature of the Court's opinion is that it does not even purport to give an answer. It simply announces, with no analysis, that the ability to control the decision whether to investigate and prosecute the President's closest advisors, and indeed the President himself, is not "so central to the functioning of the Executive Branch" as to be constitutionally required to be within the President's control. Apparently that is so because we say it is so.

Only someone who has worked in the field of law enforcement can fully appreciate the vast power and the immense discretion that are placed in the hands of a prosecutor with respect to the objects of his investigation. Under our system of government, the primary check against prosecutorial abuse is a political one. The prosecutors who exercise this awesome discretion are selected and can be removed by a President, whom the people have trusted enough to elect. Moreover, when crimes are not investigated and prosecuted fairly, nonselectively, with a reasonable sense of proportion, the President pays the cost in political damage to his administration. The President is directly dependent on the people, and since there is only one President, he is responsible. The people know whom to blame, whereas "one of the weightiest objections to a plurality in the executive . . . is that it tends to conceal faults and destroy responsibility." [FEDERALIST NO. 70.]

It is an additional advantage of the unitary Executive that it can achieve a more uniform application of the law. Perhaps that is not always achieved, but the mechanism to achieve it is there. The mini-Executive that is the independent counsel, however, operating in an area where so little is law and so much is discretion, is intentionally cut off from the unifying influence of the Justice Department, and from the perspective that multiple responsibilities provide. What would normally be regarded as a technical violation (there are no rules defining such things), may in her small world assume the proportions of an indictable offense. What would normally be regarded as an investigation that has reached the level of pursuing such picayune matters that it should be concluded, may to her be an investigation that ought to go on for another year. How frightening it must be to have your own independent counsel and staff appointed, with nothing else to do but to investigate you until investigation is no longer worthwhile — with whether it is worthwhile not depending upon what such judgments usually hinge on, competing responsibilities. And to have that counsel and staff decide, with no basis for comparison, whether what you have done is bad enough, willful enough, and provable enough, to warrant an indictment. How admirable the constitutional system that provides the means to avoid such a distortion. And how unfortunate the judicial decision that has permitted it.

[6] The Sentencing Commission

***Mistretta v. United States*, 488 U.S. 361 (1989)**. The Court employed a functionalist analysis in disposing of Mistretta's claim that the Sentencing Commission established by the 1984 Act was constituted in violation of the separation of powers. The 1984 Act established the Commission as "an independent commission in the judicial branch of the United States" to devise guidelines to be used for sentencing. The guidelines are binding on the courts, although judges may depart from the guidelines in cases where appropriate aggravating or mitigating circumstances exist.

The Commission is composed of seven voting members appointed by the President "by and with the consent of the Senate" for a term of six years, with no more than two full terms. At least three members must be federal judges who are selected from a list of six judges recommended to the President by the Judicial Conference of the United States. The Attorney General, or his designee, is an *ex officio* non-voting member, and no more than four members of the Commission may be members of the same political party. Members of the Commission are subject to removal by the President "only for neglect of duty or malfeasance in office or for other good cause shown."

Justice Blackmun noted that separation of powers is a "flexible" concept that does not require that the Branches be kept entirely separate and distinct.

> In adopting this flexible understanding of separation of powers, we simply have recognized Madison's teaching that the greatest security against tyranny — the accumulation of excessive authority in a single branch — lies not in a hermetic division between the Branches, but in a carefully crafted system of checked and balanced power within each Branch. Accordingly, as we have noted many times, the Framers "built into the tripartite Federal Government . . . a self-executing safeguard against the encroachment or aggrandizement of one branch at the expense of the other."

Either accretion to a single branch of power more appropriately diffused among the branches or undermining the authority and independence of one or another coordinate branch would violate the separation of powers doctrine. Acknowledging that the Commission was not a court and did not exercise judicial power, Justice Blackmun concluded that the vesting of nonadjudicatory activities in the judicial branch does not necessarily violate separation of powers. "Congress may delegate to the Judicial Branch nonadjudicatory functions that do not trench upon the prerogatives of another Branch and that are appropriate to the central mission of the Judiciary." Sentencing had been a shared function among the branches. "That Congress should vest such rulemaking in the Judicial Branch, far from being 'incongruous' or vesting within the Judiciary responsibilities that more appropriately belong to another Branch, simply acknowledges the role that the Judiciary has always played, and continues to play, in sentencing."

Nor did the political nature of the Commission's work threaten to undermine the integrity of the judicial branch or expand its powers beyond constitutional limits. First, the powers of the Commission are not significantly joined to the power of the judicial branch since the Commission does not exercise judicial power and is not controlled by nor accountable to the judicial branch. Further, the rulemaking power exercised by the Commission does not add to the aggregate of power previously exercised by the judicial branch in determining what sentence is appropriate for particular criminal conduct in particular circumstances.

Turning to Mistretta's claim that the composition of the Commission threatened the integrity of the judicial branch, the Court held that the inclusion of judicial officers on the Commission did not undermine judicial integrity. Unlike the Incompatibility Clause (Art. I, § 6), which applied to national legislators, the text of the Constitution includes no similar clause limiting the extrajudicial service of federal judges. Indeed Article III judges have historically participated in extrajudicial service. Service on the Sentencing Commission by federal judges is not in a judicial capacity but in an administrative role. "[T]he Constitution, at least as a *per se* matter, does not forbid judges from wearing two hats; it merely forbids them from wearing both hats at the same time." This does not mean that every type of extrajudicial service is appropriate under the Constitution. "The ultimate inquiry is whether a particular extrajudicial assignment undermines the integrity of the Judicial Branch."

> [P]articipation of Federal judges in the Sentencing Commission does not threaten, either in fact or in appearance, the impartiality of the Judicial Branch. We are drawn to this conclusion by one paramount consideration: that the Sentencing Commission is devoted exclusively to the development of rules to rationalize a process that has been and will continue to be performed by the Judicial Branch. [J]udicial participation on the Commission ensures that judicial experience and expertise will inform the promulgation of rules for the exercise of the Judicial Branch's own business — that of passing sentence on every criminal defendant. Since the Commission exercises no judicial power, the Act does not vest Article III powers in nonjudges nor does the mixed composition of the Commission involve a sharing of the judicial power.

Justice Scalia, dissenting, criticized the approach of the Court in recent separation of power decisions:

> Today's decision follows the regrettable tendency of our recent separation-of-powers jurisprudence, see *Morrison*, to treat the Constitution as though it were no more than a generalized prescription that the functions of the Branches should not be commingled too much — how much is too much is too be determined, case-by-case, by this Court. The Constitution is not that. Rather, as its name suggests, it is a prescribed structure, a framework, for the conduct of government. In designing that structure, the framers themselves considered how much commingling was, in the generality of things, acceptable, and

set forth their conclusions in the document. Consideration of the degree of commingling that a particular disposition produces may be appropriate at the margins, where the outline of the framework itself is not clear, but it seems to me far from a marginal question whether our constitutional structure allows for a body which is not the Congress, and yet exercises no governmental powers except the making of rules that have the effect of laws.

NOTES

1. ***A return to functionalism?*** A critical facet of *Morrison v. Olson* and *Mistretta* is the Court's abandonment of the rigid formalism used in *Chadha* and *Bowsher* in favor of a more functionalist approach. How would the independent counsel case be handled using formalism? Professor Shane argues that both text and history support the view that

> criminal prosecution [is not] an inherently or exclusively executive function. Prior references in judicial decisions to criminal prosecution as an executive function are dicta, explainable as a shorthand reference to the inappropriateness of subjecting prosecutorial discretion to excessive judicial supervision.

Peter Shane, *Independent Policy Making and Presidential Power: A Constitutional Analysis*, 57 GEO. WASH. L. REV. 596, 608 (1989).

But Justice Scalia, employing a formalistic analysis, dissented in *Morrison*. And the Court of Appeals, using a formalist analysis, had held the independent counsel provisions unconstitutional.

> An archformalist would not allow Congress to constrain the exercise of such a traditionally executive function as the conduct of criminal investigations and prosecutions. Nor would the archformalist accept the exercise of executive authority by one who has significant independence from the President. Finally, an archformalist would condemn the role of the Special Division.

Keith Werhan, *Towards an Eclectic Approach to Separation of Powers: Morrison v. Olson Examined,* 16 HASTINGS CONST. L.Q. 393, 414 (1989).

2. ***Textualism and originalism.*** In deciding the constitutionality of the independent counsel provisions, what effect should be given to textual provisions such as the Article II clause vesting executive power in the President? To the Article I clause establishing congressional power to enact laws "necessary and proper for carrying into Execution . . . all . . . Powers" vested in the national government. It has been argued that *Morrison* and *Mistretta* "do not test new institutional forms against the original design" and hence, are entitled to less deference than legitimating opinions paying closer attention to constitutional text, structure, and history." Stephen Carter, *Constitutional Improprieties: Reflection on Mistretta, Morrison, and Administrative Government*, 57 U. CHI. L. REV. 357, 358 (1990).

Should the *Morrison* Court have given greater consideration to the original understanding of the prosecutorial function? While there appears to have been a general acceptance by the parties in *Morrison* that prosecution is an essentially "executive" responsibility, the historical record is less clear. *See* Note, *Is Prosecution a Core Executive Function? Morrison v. Olson and the Framer's Intent,* 99 YALE L.J. 1069 (1990). If it is determined that criminal prosecution historically is not an exclusive executive function, what weight should be given to that finding in deciding the constitutionality of the independent counsel provisions?

It has been suggested that, even if prosecution is generally viewed as an executive function, a focus on the problem of political accountability and its limits justify the use of a more functional approach in the independent counsel context. Investigation of the possible misconduct of high level administrators "is fundamentally unlike ordinary administration, including most prosecution." Harold Bruff, *Independent Counsel and the Constitution*, 24 WILLAMETTE L. REV. 539, 548 (1988).

3. *A unitary executive?* Underlying the opinions in *Morrison* is a significant debate concerning the nature of the executive power established by the Framers. Steven Calabresi & Kevin Rhodes, *The Structural Constitution: Unitary Executive, Plural Judiciary*, 105 HARV. L. REV. 1153, 1165 (1995), define the position of the Unitarians:

> Unitary executive theorists read [the Vestiture] Clause, together with the Take Care Clause, as creating a hierarchical unified executive department under the direct control of the President. The practical consequence of this theory is dramatic: it renders unconstitutional independent agencies and counsels to the extent that they exercise discretionary executive power.

Similarly, two scholars stressing constitutional text argue: "The Executive Power Clause grants 'the executive Power' solely and exclusively to the President; it gives Congress no power whatever to create subordinate entities that may exercise 'the executive Power' until and unless the President delegates that power in some fashion." Steven Calabresi & Saikrishna Prakash, *The President's Power to Execute the Laws*, 104 YALE L.J. 541, 581 (1994).

Lawrence Lessig & Cass Sunstein, *The President and the Administration*, 94 COLUM. L. REV. 1 (1994), argue for a strong unitary executive based on changed circumstances and the need for executive officers making discretionary judgments about important domestic issues to be subject to presidential control. They emphasize the importance of accountability, coordination of the law and uniformity of regulation under the constitutional structure. But they deny that the principle of a unitary executive can be justified using original intent:

> Many think that under our constitutional system, the President must have the authority to control all government officials who implement the laws. [This] ignores strong evidence that the framers imagined not a clear executive hierarchy with the President at the summit, but a

large degree of congressional power to structure the administration as it thought proper.

4. *A distinction based on effects.* Is *Morrison v. Olson* a general repudiation of the formalist model in favor of functionalism or is there a way of explaining the different analysis used in these cases? Professor Peterson attempts to reconcile the formalism of *Chadha* and *Bowsher* with the functionalism of *Morrison* and *Mistretta* by arguing that "there is a significant difference between statutes that aggrandize a branch and statutes that restrict the power of a branch," and that "the courts may appropriately impose more formal restrictions on Congress's ability to enact statutes that breach lines of constitutional separation by increasing the powers of a particular branch." His view is that "statutory limitation of the power of a particular branch does not create as great a direct threat of the arbitrary and unchecked exercise of power," making a more functional approach desirable. Todd Peterson, *Prosecuting Executive Branch Officials for Contempt of Congress*, 66 N.Y.U. L. REV. 563 (1991). Professor Peterson notes that by creating the independent counsel, Congress did not increase the powers of a branch, "but rather further diffused power by placing limited prosecutorial power in an official independent from direct control of any of the three branches."

Michael Froomkin, *The Imperial Presidency's New Vestments*, 88 NW. U. L. REV. 1346, 1368–69 (1994), suggests that when congressional action involves an unenumerated executive power, the Court focuses on whether Congress "has impermissably aggrandized itself, not on whether the President's 'nebulous' executive power is being undermined." Abner Greene, *Checks and Balances in an Era of Presidential Lawmaking*, 61 U. CHI. L. REV. 123, 126 (1994), states: "The principle that synthesizes the case law is this: *Congress may give away legislative power and insulate such delegated power from total presidential control, but Congress may neither draw executive power to itself nor seek to legislate outside the Article I, Section 7 framework.*"

Is the distinction between an aggrandizement case and a case involving interference with the ability of another branch to perform its constitutional functions meaningful? Does the distinction justify different separation of powers analysis? Weren't the powers of the Special Division increased? After passage of the Act, didn't the ability of legislators to call for appointment of an independent counsel enhance the power of Congress vis a vis executive branch officials? It can be argued that the allocation of power between the branches is always relative — a loss of power by one branch is a relative gain of power to the others. Further, it can be argued that "[a]ggrandizement lies in the eyes of the beholder. It reflects (often unarticulated) value judgments about desirable allocation of power among the branches." Harold Bruff, 24 WILLAMETTE L. REV. at 547.

5. *The relevance of political practice.* Commentators who have examined historical political practice suggest that "each of the first thirty-two presidents — from George Washington up through Franklin D. Roosevelt --believed in a unitary executive," and that the independent counsel authorization in the Ethics in Government Act constituted an "experiment [ ] with unconstitutional limits on the president's removal power." They note that notwithstanding *Morrison*, "the Ethics in Government Act was allowed to lapse in June

1999 after both Democrats and Republicans grew to doubt its constitutionality and whether it represented good policy." Christopher Yoo, Steven Calabresi & Anthony Colangelo, *The Unitary Executive in the Modern Era, 1945-2004*, 90 Iowa L. Rev. 601, 606, 731 (2005).

6. *Inferior officers.* The Appointments Clause does not define the difference between a principal and an inferior officer. Neither the clause nor the historical record of the original intent deals with the problem of interbranch appointments. What effect, if any, should be given to these textual silences in separation of powers analysis? It can be argued that the absence of limiting language precludes the Court from imposing any limitation on Congress. Alternatively, the absence of text could be viewed as limiting Congress' ability to restrict executive appointment of executive branch officials. The Court of Appeals, in holding the method of appointment of independent counsel unconstitutional, observed that the ability of the President to enforce the laws is determined by the quality of executive officers selected — "it must be incongruous if an officer of one branch is authorized to appoint an officer of another branch who is assigned a duty central to the constitutional role of that other branch." *In re Sealed Case*, 838 F.2d 476, 494 (D.C. Cir. 1988).

7. *Executive management.* In prior cases, a congressional provision restricting removal of an official except for "good cause" was perceived as a meaningful, but proper, limit on executive power to remove quasi-legislative and quasi-judicial officers. But Congress could not limit presidential removal of purely executive officials. *Morrison* abandons this categorical regimen in favor of a more open-ended inquiry into whether the congressional restriction impedes the president's performance of his constitutional duties. Applying this standard, the Court concludes that the removal restriction does not "interfere with [the President's] constitutional obligation to ensure the faithful execution of the laws."

It has been argued that the *Morrison* Court places the President's supervisory responsibility over subordinate officials not under the Vestiture Clause, as might be expected, but under the Take Care Clause.

> But because the test of presidential control is whether the President is able to ensure that the counsel is performing "competently" and "in a manner that comports with the provisions of the Act," the Court must be conceiving the President's supervisory authority under the "take care" clause as purely ministerial in nature. Thus, the only constitutional "control" that the President is able to exercise free from congressional restraint is the control the Congress is least likely to restrain: taking care that all executive employees are doing what the Congress requires of them.

Stephen Carter, *The Independent Counsel Mess*, 102 Harv. L. Rev. 115 (1988). Carter claims that such a principle "wreaks havoc upon the system of checks and balances inherent in the separation of powers."

8. *The future.* What are the implications of *Morrison* and *Mistretta* for the constitutionality of administrative agencies combining executive, legislative and judicial functions? What are the implications of the decisions for future efforts by Congress to legislate executive accountability? Arguably, the decisions do not reflect a general deference to Congress in separation of powers disputes. (*Cf. Metroplitan Washington Airports Auth.*) And, as the notes above suggest, they do not necessarily presage an abandonment of focus on bright lines, constitutional text and original intent characterizing formalist analysis. But they do indicate that congressional limitations of executive power and the blending of judicial, legislative and executive functions in an official or agency may sometimes be upheld. They also indicate the continuing strength of functional analysis and balancing methodology on the Court.

§ 4.03 THE FOREIGN ARENA

The battles over legislative and executive prerogative have not been restricted to the domestic sphere. Nor were the principles fashioned in the preceding cases limited to domestic lawmaking. Nevertheless, as will become obvious, the principles governing the separation of powers in the domestic sphere, discussed above, are not fully applicable in the foreign arena.

> The foreign relations powers also reflect commitment to Separation and Checks-and-balances but what each branch can do alone, when the other is silent or even in the face of its opposition, is not determined by any "natural" division. As they have evolved, the foreign relations' powers appear not so much "separated" as fissured, along jagged lines indifferent to classical categories of governmental powers: some powers and functions belong to the President, some to Congress, some the President-and-Senate; some can be exercised by either the President or the Congress, some require the joint authority of both. Irregular, uncertain divisions render claims of usurpation more difficult to establish and the courts have not been available to adjudicate them.

Louis Henkin, Foreign Affairs and the Constitution 32 (1972). Are foreign affairs and war powers issues nonjusticiable? *See Goldwater v. Carter*, pp. 48–50.

[A] THE FOREIGN AFFAIRS POWER

[1] Presidential Authority

UNITED STATES v. CURTISS-WRIGHT EXPORT CORP.
299 U.S. 304, 57 S. Ct. 216, 81 L. Ed. 255 (1936)

[A Joint Resolution of Congress provided in Section 1: "[t]hat if the President finds that the prohibition of the sales of arms and munitions of war in the United States to those countries now engaged in armed conflict in the Chaco may contribute to the reestablishment of peace between those countries, and if he makes proclamation to that effect, it shall be unlawful to sell [any arms], except under such limitations and exceptions as the President prescribes." Section 2 provided penalties for violations.

[The appellees successfully challenged an indictment for conspiracy to sell arms in violation of the Resolution and a subsequent presidential proclamation. The district court held that the Resolution constituted an invalid delegation of legislative power. The case was heard by the Supreme Court on direct appeal.]

Justice Sutherland delivered the opinion of the Court.

Whether, if the Joint Resolution had related solely to internal affairs it would be open to the challenge that it constituted an unlawful delegation of legislative power to the Executive, we find it unnecessary to determine. The whole aim of the resolution is to affect a situation entirely external to the United States, and falling within the category of foreign affairs. The determination which we are called to make, therefore, is whether the Joint Resolution, as applied to that situation, is vulnerable to attack under the rule that forbids a delegation of the law-making power. In other words, assuming (but not deciding) that the challenged delegation, if it were confined to internal affairs, would be invalid, may it nevertheless be sustained on the ground that its exclusive aim is to afford a remedy for a hurtful condition within foreign territory?

It will contribute to the elucidation of the question if we first consider the differences between the powers of the Federal government in respect of foreign or external affairs and those in respect of domestic or internal affairs. That there are differences between them, and that these differences are fundamental, may not be doubted. The two classes of powers are different, both in respect of their origin and their nature. The broad statement that the Federal government can exercise no powers except those specifically enumerated in the Constitution, and such implied powers as are necessary and proper to carry into effect the enumerated powers, is categorically true only in respect to our internal affairs. In that field, the primary purpose of the Constitution was to carve from the general mass of legislative powers then possessed by the states such portions as it was thought desirable to vest in the Federal government, leaving those not included in the enumeration still in the states. That this doctrine applies only to powers which the states had, is self-evident. And since the states severally never possessed international powers, such powers could not have been carved from the mass of state powers but obviously were transmitted to the United States from some other source. During the colonial period, those powers were possessed exclusively by and were entirely under the control of the Crown.

As a result of the separation from Great Britain by the colonies, acting as a unit, the powers of external sovereignty passed from the Crown not to the colonies severally, but to the colonies in their collective and corporate capacity as the United States of America. The Union existed before the Constitution, which was ordained and established among other things to form "a more perfect Union." Prior to that event, it is clear that the Union, declared by the Articles of Confederation to be "perpetual," was the sole possessor of external sovereignty, and in the Union it remained without change save in so far as the Constitution in express terms qualified its exercise.

It results that the investment of the federal government with the powers of external sovereignty did not depend upon the affirmative grants of the

Constitution. The powers to declare and wage war, to conclude peace, to make treaties, to maintain diplomatic relations with other sovereignties, if they had never been mentioned in the Constitution, would have vested in the Federal government as necessary concomitants of nationality. Neither the Constitution nor the laws passed in pursuance of it have any force in foreign territory unless in respect of our own citizens and operations of the nation in such territory must be governed by treaties, international understandings and compacts, and the principles of international law. As a member of the family of nations, the right and power of the United States in that field are equal to the right and power of the other members of the international family. Otherwise, the United States is not completely sovereign. The power to acquire territory by discovery and occupation, the power to expel undesirable aliens, the power to make such international agreements as do not constitute treaties in the constitutional sense, none of which is expressly affirmed by the Constitution, nevertheless exist as inherently inseparable from the conception of nationality. This the Court recognized, and in each of the cases cited found the warrant for its conclusions not in the provisions of the Constitution, but in the law of nations.

Not only, as we have shown, is the Federal power over external affairs in origin and essential character different from that over internal affairs, but participation in the exercise of the power is significantly limited. In this vast external realm, with its important, complicated, delicate and manifold problems, the President alone has the power to speak or listen as a representative of the nation. He makes treaties with the advice and consent of the Senate; but he alone negotiates. Into the field of negotiation the Senate cannot intrude; and Congress itself is powerless to invade it.

It is important to bear in mind that we are here dealing not alone with an authority vested in the President by an exertion of legislative power, but with such an authority plus the very delicate, plenary and exclusive power of the President as the sole organ of the Federal government in the field of international relations — a power which does not require as a basis for its exercise an act of Congress, but which, of course, like every other governmental power, must be exercised in subordination to the applicable provisions of the Constitution. It is quite apparent that if, in the maintenance of our international relations, embarrassment — perhaps serious embarrassment — is to be avoided and success for our aims achieved, congressional legislation which is to be made effective through negotiation and inquiry within the international field must often accord to the President a degree of discretion and freedom from statutory restriction which would not be admissible were domestic affairs alone involved. Moreover, he, not Congress, has the better opportunity of knowing the conditions which prevail in foreign countries, and especially is this true in time of war. He has his confidential sources of information. He has his agents in the form of diplomatic, consular and other officials. Secrecy in respect of information gathered by them may be highly necessary, and the premature disclosure of it productive of harmful results. Indeed, so clearly is this true that the first President refused to accede to a request to lay before the House of Representatives the instructions, correspondence and documents relating to the negotiation of the Jay Treaty — a refusal the wisdom of which was recognized by the House itself and has never since been doubted.

In the light of the foregoing observations, it is evident that this court should not be in haste to apply a general rule which will have the effect of condemning legislation like that under review as constituting an unlawful delegation of legislative power. The principles which justify such legislation find overwhelming support in the unbroken legislative practice which has prevailed almost from the inception of the national government to the present day.

We deem it unnecessary to consider, seriatim, the several clauses which are said to evidence the unconstitutionality of the Joint Resolution as involving an unlawful delegation of legislative power. It is enough to summarize by saying that, both upon principle and in accordance with precedent, we conclude there is sufficient warrant for the broad discretion vested in the President to determine whether the enforcement of the statute will have a beneficial effect upon the reestablishment of peace in the affected countries; whether he shall make proclamation to bring the resolution into operation; whether and when the resolution shall cease to operate and to make proclamation accordingly; and to prescribe limitations and exceptions to which the enforcement of the resolution shall be subject.

[The Court went on to hold that the executive proclamation satisfied the Joint Resolution.] The judgment of the court below must be reversed and the cause remanded for further proceedings in accordance with the foregoing opinion.

[JUSTICE MCREYNOLDS dissented.]

NOTES

1. *Marshall's contribution.* Serving as a member of the House of Representa tives, John Marshall stated that the

> President is sole organ of the nation in its external relations, and is sole representative with foreign nations. Of consequence, the demand of a foreign nation can only be made on him. He possesses the whole Executive power. He holds and directs the force of the nation. Of consequence, any act to be performed by the force of the nation is to be performed through him.

10 ANNALS OF CONGRESS 596, 613–14 (1800).

2. *Presidents and monarchs.* Justice Sutherland in *Curtiss-Wright* argues for a broad executive prerogative in foreign affairs. Further, Locke, Blackstone and Montesquieu, who were all widely read by the Framers, characterize foreign relations as an "executive" power. But consider Alexander Bickel's critique that Sutherland's "grandiose conception, the almost regal conception of the President's independent role in foreign affairs never had any warrant in the constitution, is wrong in theory and unworkable in practice." *Hearings on S. 596 Before the Senate Comm. on Foreign Relations*, 92d Cong., 1st Sess. 26 (1971). Is the language in *Curtiss-Wright* on the executive power in foreign affairs dictum? Is Justice Sutherland's distinction between constitutional powers in the domestic and foreign affairs arenas workable? In that connection, it is debatable whether the *Steel Seizure* case or *Curtiss-Wright* itself is a domestic or foreign affairs case.

3. *Original Intent.* Historian Arthur Schlesinger argues that the Framers intended to establish "a partnership between Congress and the President in the conduct of foreign affairs with Congress as the senior partner." Arthur Schlesinger, *The Legislative — Executive Balance in International Affairs: The Intentions of the Framers*, THE WASH. Q., Winter 1989, at 102. On the other hand, it has been argued "that the Founding Fathers — in vesting 'the executive Power' in the President through article II, section 1 — intended to grant the President exclusive control over foreign affairs, subject to certain very important but limited exceptions spelled out in the text of the Constitution." Robert Turner, *The Constitution and the Iran-Contra Affair: Was Congress the Real Lawbreaker?*, 11 HOUSTON J. INT'L L. 83, 93 (1988). Professor Henkin offers the following on original intent:

> The framers, I am persuaded, had a reasonably clear idea of the powers they were conferring upon Congress: in general, they saw Congress as the principal "policymaking" (our term, not theirs) organ in foreign as in domestic affairs, and in their conception Congress was to dominate the political process. They had a much less clear view about the presidency. They allocated to the president particular functions, but these did not add up to a comprehensive, coherent conception of the office, or of the division of authority between Congress and president, in the mind of any of the framers, surely there was no consensus about it.

Louis Henkin, *Foreign Affairs and the Constitution*, 66 FOREIGN AFF. 284, 290 (1988).

Rostow argues that the quest for the original intention of the Founding Fathers should begin not with the language of the Constitution but with "the words in their full policy context." "The growth of our constitutional law of foreign relations, like the growth of every other branch of our law, was the result of solving policy problems through procedures which applied, and reconcile, the relevant goals of the Constitution." Eugene Rostow, *Responses*, 61 VA. L. REV. 797 (1975):

> In any event, it is bad jurisprudence to suppose that we should be bound in a straight jacket by original intention, even if we could discover it. Original intention is an important element in the evolution of constitutional law, but constitutional law, like every other branch of our legal system, is a process of living growth. Preoccupation with "original intention" leads to a kind of fundamentalism which to me is the antithesis of the wise law.

Id. at 798.

Examine the powers granted to Congress under Article I, § 8. To what extent do those powers concern the conduct of foreign affairs? Is it reasonable to believe that the very same framers who vested so many powers dealing with foreign affairs in the legislative branch proceeded on the implicit assumption that the president would exercise primary control over foreign affairs? For expression of the view that "Article II, Section 1, vesting the President with 'the executive Power,' incorporates the late eighteenth-century meaning typically ascribed to 'executive power,' " which "classified foreign affairs powers among the executive powers of government," see Saikrishna Prakash & Michael Ramsey, *Foreign Affairs and the Jeffersonian Executive: A Defense*, 89 MINN. L. REV. 1591 (2005). For an attack on this "residual theory" of foreign affairs power, see Curtis Bradley & Martin Flaherty, *Executive Power Essentialism and Foreign Affairs*, 102 MICH. L. REV. 545 (2004).

In any event, how relevant should original intent be in the absence of supporting constitutional text? How strong is the textual basis for the proposition that the president is to exercise the primary role in foreign affairs? How helpful is the so-called vestiture clause, at the beginning of Article II? Does it refer to foreign affairs? Is this argument circular, since it will ultimately turn on how one chooses to define "executive" power in the first place?

Even if one were to accept the original intent argument, is the decision in *Curtiss-Wright* legitimate? See Ramsey, 42 WM. & MARY L. REV. at 382, arguing that "the case against *Curtiss-Wright* need not turn upon the scope of presidential authority in foreign affairs. The truly radical part of *Curtiss-Wright* is not its emphasis on presidential power, but rather its claim that that power arose outside the Constitution." How effective is a written constitution as a restrictive document if the federal government, created by that document, is recognized to have powers derived from sources other than that constitution?

4. *Executive powers.* Does the constitutional support for a broad presidential control of foreign relations lie in the broad, uncertain Article II grant of the "executive power" to the President, in his duty to take care to see that the laws are faithfully executed or in his powers as Commander-in-Chief? The President has constitutional power to "receive Ambassadors and other public Ministers." Article II, § 3. This may be merely a ceremonial role or may confer substantive foreign affairs powers. Does it logically imply an exclusive power to recognize, or alternatively, to decline to recognize or withdraw recognition of foreign nations such as Cuba and China? Does it imply, as Thomas Jefferson wrote in 1790, that "[t]he transaction of business with foreign nations is executive altogether. It belongs, then to the head of that department, except as to such portion of it as are specially submitted to the Senate. Exceptions are to be construed strictly." 5 WRITINGS OF THOMAS JEFFERSON 161–62 (P. Ford ed. 1894). Corwin writes "there is no more securely established principle of constitutional practice than the exclusive right of the President to be the nation's intermediary in dealing with other nations." EDWARD S. CORWIN, THE PRESIDENT: OFFICE AND POWERS 1787–1957, at 184 (4th ed. 1957).

From these powers of reception, recognition and communication, does it then logically follow that the executive is responsible for the formulation of foreign policy? Henkin notes "it has sometimes been said that the President has power to conduct foreign relations but not to make foreign policy." But he concludes that "[i]n fact, a President could not conduct foreign relations without thereby making foreign policy. But if the division were feasible and meaningful it is contradicted by what Presidents have done and do daily beyond challenge." LOUIS HENKIN, FOREIGN AFFAIRS AND THE CONSTITUTION 47 (1972).

5. *Congressional powers.* On the other hand, Congress would appear to have the greater prerogative in foreign affairs if only bare constitutional grants of power were considered. In terms of major formal powers, Congress is authorized to regulate foreign commerce, to raise and maintain armies and navies and to declare war. Further, there is the extremely critical power of the purse which is often essential if foreign policy is to be effectuated. And then there are the implied foreign affairs powers, arising either from the inherent powers accompanying statehood or from the necessary and proper clause in relation to Article I or Article II express powers.

Apart from these formal powers, Congress also has broad informal controls available if disposed to use them, e.g., riders to legislation, Senate resolutions, the formal and informal actions of congressional committees. It has been suggested that the Framers "chose to grant Congress the dominant role in foreign affairs" and that this prerogative should be respected today. Gerhard Casper, *Responses*, 61 VA. L. REV. 777, 778 (1975).

6. *Shared powers.* The above suggests the potential for conflict or cooperation in the foreign arena. While some particular powers may be characterized as exclusive, the Constitution establishes a system of shared foreign affairs power.

> [T]he Constitution, considered only for its affirmative grants of powers capable of affecting the issue, is an invitation to struggle for the privilege of directing American Foreign Policy. In such a struggle the President has, it is true, certain great advantages but despite all this, actual practice under the Constitution has shown that, while the President is usually in a position to propose, the Senate and Congress are often in a technical position at least to dispose.

CORWIN at 171.

> A stranger reading the Constitution would get little inkling of such large Presidential authority. The structure of the federal government, the facts of national life, the realities and exigencies of international relations, the practices of diplomacy, have afforded Presidents unique temptations and unique opportunities to acquire unique powers.

HENKIN at 37.

What are the respective advantages and disadvantages of Congress and the Executive in dealing in foreign affairs? Can the presidential role be legitimized by the ongoing practices of our government from its beginnings?

7. *Delegation of power.* The primary issue in *Curtiss-Wright* involved the power of Congress to delegate power to the President to impose an arms embargo. It arose at the same time that the Court was limiting Congress' power to delegate lawmaking power in other arenas. Perhaps *Curtiss-Wright's* dichotomy between domestic and foreign affairs was an effort to distinguish those decisions. It is often suggested that the decision indicates that there is little limitation on delegation of foreign affairs powers. *But see Kent v. Dulles*, 357 U.S. 116 (1958), where the Court narrowly interpreted legislation involving passports, stating that if the "right to exit" is to be regulated it "must be pursuant to the law-making functions of the Congress and if that power is delegated, the standards must be adequate to pass scrutiny by the accepted tests."

In fact, congressional delegation of foreign affairs power has become a major factor in the growth of executive power. "Congress conceded and extended presidential primacy when it began to delegate to him huge grants of power with only general lines of guidance thus effectively leaving to the Executive the formulation of policy as well as large discretion in carrying it out." Louis Henkin, *"A More Effective System" for Foreign Relations: The Constitutional Framework*, 61 VA. L. REV. 751, 757 (1975). Henkin contends that "Congress allowed itself to become removed from the process of conducting foreign relations and foreign policy." When it was constitutionally required to act, "it often did not feel free to refuse to consummate policies which the President had developed for the United States, thus effectively confirming his authority to make them."

[2] Treaties and Executive Agreements

Article II, § 2, provides that the President shall have power, "by and with the Advice and Consent of the Senate, to make Treaties, provided two-thirds present concur." *Chadha* specifically recognized this as an area where one House may act alone. While it was originally intended that the Senate would actively advise the President as an executive counsel in the treaty making process (THE FEDERALIST, No. 64), this approach was altered almost immediately. The Senate's modern role is to review completed treaties. It may approve the treaty as written, approve it subject to conditions, reject and return it or simply withhold approval. Some treaties are not self-executing and require congressional implementing legislation. The President ratifies the treaty by signing the instrument of ratification. Termination of treaties remains an unresolved constitutional question.

In *Missouri v. Holland*, 252 U.S. 416 (1920), the Supreme Court held that the federal government, in entering into treaties, is not bound by the outer limits imposed on congressional authority in Article I. Justice Holmes, speaking for the Court, stated: "Acts of Congress are the pursuance of the Constitution, while treaties are declared to be so when made under the authority of the United States. . . . We do not mean to imply that there are no qualifications to the treaty-making power; but they must be ascertained in a different way. It is obvious that there may be matters of the sharpest exigency for the national well being that an act of Congress could not deal with but that a treaty followed by such an act could, and it is not lightly to be assumed that, in maters requiring national action, a 'power which must belong to and somewhere reside in every civilized government is not to be found.' " *Id.* at 433. Does this make sense? How relevant do you think it was that at the time of the decision — 1920 — the Court had, for the most part, construed congressional commerce power narrowly?

Treaties are not the only means by which the United States undertakes international obligations. As of January 1, 1983, the United States was a party to only 966 treaties, while 6571 executive agreements were in force. Cong.

Research Service (for the Senate Comm. on Foreign Relations), *Treaties and Other International Agreements: The Role of the United States Senate* (1984). The executive agreement, especially since the end of World War II, has increasingly replaced the formal treaty and consequently, the special prerogative of the Senate has been largely abrogated. Actually, only a small portion of executive agreements are made without some congressional involvement. There are three types of executive agreements: (1) congressional-executive agreements, either explicitly or implicitly authorized in advance by Congress or approved afterwards; (2) agreements pursuant to treaties; and (3) Presidential or sole executive agreements based on his independent constitutional authority. *Id.* at 6. It has been noted "that there are agreements which the President can make on his sole authority and others which he can make only with the consent of the Senate, but [no one] has told us which are which." HENKIN, FOREIGN AFFAIRS, AT 179. What is the constitutional authority for the use of such agreements? See *United States v. Belmont*, 301 U.S. 324 (1937) and *United States v. Pink*, 315 U.S. 203 (1942), recognizing the legal status of such compacts and their supremacy over inconsistent state law. Under the Case-Zablocki Act, all executive agreements must be reported to Congress within 60 days of their entry into force. Is such a limitation on presidential initiatives constitutional?

In 1993, after a hard fought political fight, the North American Free Trade Agreement (NAFTA) was approved by the Senate by a vote of 61-38. The House of Representatives had previously passed the accord by a vote of 234-200. Article II, § 2 of the Constitution provides that the President shall have the power, "by and with the Advice and Consent of the Senate, to make treaties, provided two-thirds present concur." Is NAFTA constitutional in the absence of approval by two-thirds of the Senate? And, what explains the involvement of the House in this process?

Noting that Article I, § 7, requires all revenue bills to originate in the House of Representatives, some commentators speculate that there is a danger in the treaty process if the House is left out of the process, as "[t]he resulting conflict between Senate and House may force the nation to breach treaty obligations the Senate and the President had only recently affirmed as binding." Bruce Ackerman & David Golove, *Is NAFTA Constitutional?*, 108 HARV. L. REV. 801, 923 (1995). Professors Ackerman and Golove point to numerous other constitutional examples allowing different legislative procedures for reaching the same end. "The text provides no fewer than four ways of passing a constitutional amendment. And . . . two ways of passing a statute — one with, and one without, the cooperation of the President. Similarly, Articles I and II set up alternative systems through which the nation can commit itself internationally — one with, and one without, the cooperation of the House." *Id.* at 920.

Professor Tribe notes that:

> whereas Article II specifies how treaties are to be made on behalf of the nation, and whereas Article I explains how states may enter into non-treaty agreements, the Constitution nowhere specifies a procedure by which the United States may enter non-treaty international agreements. Although this omission could in theory imply a genuine

> "hole" in constitutional "space," whereby *no* branch of the federal government is empowered to enter the United States into non-binding treaty agreements with foreign nations, such a conclusion would radically limit the power of the federal government over foreign affairs.

Laurence Tribe, *Taking Text and Structure Seriously: Reflections on Free-Form Method in Constitutional Interpretation,* 108 HARV. L. REV. 1223, 1268 (1995). Ultimately, Professor Tribe argues that if this power does exist in the federal government, "it seems clear that it is the President, not Congress, who has the authority to exercise the power on behalf of the nation." *Id.* at 1268–69. Professor Tribe concludes, "[o]ne gets the distinct impression from Professor Ackerman's heavy reliance on arguments from precedent and higher lawmaking that, but for the conclusion that he wishes to buttress, even he would see how shaky the status of the congressional-executive agreement is as a matter of constitutional text and structure." *Id.* at 1302.

An excellent example of the executive agreement as a vehicle for resolving major foreign affairs issues is provided by *Dames & Moore v. Regan.* As you read the case, consider the view that "[t]o understand the Supreme Court's decision in *Dames & Moore v. Regan,* one should perceive at the outset that it is basically a compromise between harsh international reality and abstract constitutional norms. Principle, as usual, gave way to realpolitik." Arthur S. Miller, *Dames and Moore v. Regan: A Political Decision by a Political Court,* 29 UCLA L. REV. 1104 (1982). Does emergency create power or make questions of constitutional power irrelevant?

DAMES & MOORE v. REGAN

453 U.S. 654, 101 S. Ct. 2972, 69 L. Ed. 2d 918 (1981)

[Diplomatic personnel in the American Embassy in Tehran, Iran, were seized as hostages on November 4, 1979. President Carter, acting pursuant to the International Emergency Economic Powers Act (IEEPA), declared a national emergency on November 14, 1979, and issued an executive order blocking the removal or transfer of all properties of the Iranian government. The Treasury Department promulgated regulations pursuant to the executive order, prohibiting attachments of Iranian property unless authorized by the Treasury Department. Subsequent regulations authorized certain judicial proceedings, including prejudgment attachments, against Iran, but did not allow entry of any judgment or decree. Dames & Moore brought suit in U.S. District Court on December 19, 1979, against the Government of Iran, the Atomic Energy Organization of Iran, and a number of Iranian banks for payments it claimed were owing. The district court issued prejudgment writs of attachment against the Iranian defendants' property and assets.

[On January 19, 1981, the United States and Iranian governments entered into an agreement for the release of the hostages. It provided for the establishment of an Iran-United States Claims Tribunal to provide final and binding arbitration of claims against either government. The United States was obligated to terminate all legal proceedings in United States courts against Iran and to nullify any attachments and judgments obtained in United States courts. The United States was also required to bring about the transfer of all Iranian assets held in United States banks. Executive Orders issued the same day revoked all licenses permitting the exercise of "any right, power or privilege" with regard to Iranian assets; "nullified" all non-Iranian interests acquired after November 19, 1981 in such assets, and required the transfer of assets to the Federal Reserve Bank in New York. These executive orders were ratified by President Reagan.

[Meanwhile, on January 27, 1981, the district court granted Dames & Moore's motion for summary judgment and awarded it the amount claimed plus interest, but on May 8, it stayed execution of the judgment. On April 28, Dames & Moore filed an action seeking to enjoin enforcement of the executive orders and treasury regulations implementing the Iran-U.S. agreement, alleging that the actions exceeded the Executive's statutory and constitutional powers. The district court dismissed the complaint. The Court granted certiorari and expedited review.]

JUSTICE REHNQUIST delivered the opinion of the Court.

[B]efore turning to the facts and law which we believe determine the result in this case, we stress that the expeditious treatment of the issues involved by all of the courts which have considered the President's actions makes us acutely aware of the necessity to rest decision on the narrowest possible ground capable of deciding the case. We attempt to lay down no general "guide-lines" covering other situations not involved here, and attempt to confine the opinion only to the very questions necessary to decision of the case.

The parties and the lower courts confronted with the instant questions have all agreed that much relevant analysis is contained in *Youngstown Sheet & Tube Co. v. Sawyer*. JUSTICE BLACK's opinion for the Court in that case, recognized that "[t]he President's power, if any, to issue the order must stem either from an act of Congress or from the Constitution itself." JUSTICE JACKSON's concurring opinion elaborated in a general way the consequences of different types of interaction between the two democratic branches in assessing presidential authority to act in any given case. JUSTICE JACKSON himself recognized that his three categories represented "a somewhat over-simplified grouping," and it is doubtless the case that executive action in any particular instance falls, not neatly in one of three pigeon-holes, but rather at some point along a spectrum running from explicit congressional authorization to explicit congressional prohibition. This is particularly true as respects cases such as the one before us, involving responses to international crises the nature of which Congress can hardly have been expected to anticipate in any detail.

In nullifying post-November 14, 1979, attachments and directing those persons holding blocked Iranian funds and securities to transfer them to the Federal Reserve Bank of New York for ultimate transfer to Iran, President Carter cited five sources of express or inherent power. The Government, however, has principally relied on § 203 of the IEEPA as authorization for these actions. [The Court holds that the nullification of attachments was authorized by the plain language of the IEEPA.] Because the President's action in nullifying the attachments and ordering the transfer of the assets was taken pursuant to specific congressional authorization, it is "supported by the strongest of presumptions and the widest latitude of judicial interpretation, and the burden of persuasion would rest heavily upon any who might attack it." *Youngstown* (JACKSON, J., concurring). Under the circumstances of this case, we cannot say that petitioner has sustained that heavy burden. A contrary ruling would mean that the Federal Government as a whole lacked the power exercised by the President, and that we are not prepared to say.

Although we have concluded that the IEEPA constitutes specific congressional authorization to the President to nullify the attachments and order the transfer of Iranian assets, there remains the question of the President's authority to suspend claims pending in American courts. Such claims have, of course, an existence apart from the attachments which accompanied them. In terminating these claims through Executive Order No. 12294, the President purported to act under authority of both the IEEPA and 22 U.S.C. § 1732, the so-called "Hostage Act."

We conclude that although the IEEPA authorized the nulification of the attachments, it cannot be read to authorize the suspension of the claims. The terms of the IEEPA do not authorize the President to suspend claims in American courts. This is the view of all the courts which have considered the question.

The Hostage Act, passed in 1868, provides:

> Whenever it is made known to the President that any citizen of the United States has been unjustly deprived of his liberty by or under the authority of any foreign government, it shall be the duty of the President forthwith to demand of that government the reasons of such imprisonment; and if it appears to be wrongful and in violation of the rights of American citizenship, the President shall forthwith demand the release of such citizen, and if the release so demanded is unreasonably delayed or refused, the President shall use such means, not amounting to acts of war, as he may think necesary and proper to obtain or effectuate the release; and all the facts and proceedings relative thereto shall as soon as practicable be communicated by the President to Congress.

We are reluctant to conclude that this provision constitutes specific authorization to the President to suspend claims in American courts. Although the broad language of the Hostage Act suggests it may cover this case, there are several difficuilties with such a view. The legislative history indicates that the Act was passed in response to a situation unlike the recent Iranian crisis. The legislative history is also somewhat ambiguous on the question whether Congress contemplated Presidential action such as that involved here or rather simply reprisals directed against the offending country and *its* citizens.

Concluding that neither the IEEPA nor the Hostage Act constitutes specific authorization of the President's action suspending claims, however, is not to say that these statutory provisions are entirely irrelevant to the question of the valildity of the President's action. We think both statutes highly relevant in the looser sense of indicating congressional acceptance of a broad scope for executive action in circumstances such as those presented in this case. [T]he

IEEPA delegates broad authority to the President to act in times of national emergency with respect to property of a foreign country. The Hostage Act similarly indicates congressional willingness that the President have broad discretion when responding to the hostile acts of foreign sovereigns.

Although we have declined to conclude that the IEEPA or the Hostage Act directly authorizes the Presient's suspension of claims for the reasons noted, we cannot ignore the general tenor of Congress' legislation in this area in trying to determine whether the President is acting alone or at least with the acceptance of Congress. As we have noted, Congress cannot anticipate and legislate with regard to every possible action the President may find it necessary to take or every possible situation in which he might act. Such failure of Congress specifically to delegate authority does not, "especially . . . in the areas of foreign policy and national security," imply "congressional disapproval" of action taken by the Executive. On the contrary, the enactment of legislation closely related to the question of the President's authority in a particular case which evinces legislative intent to accord the President broad discretion may be considered to "invite" "measures on independent presidential responsibility," *Youngstown* (JACKSON, J., concurring). At least this is so where there is no contrary indication of legislative intent and when, as here, there is a history of congressional acquiescence in conduct of the sort engaged in by the President. It is to that history which we now turn.

Not infrequently in affairs between nations, outstanding claims by nationals of one country against the government of another country are "sources of friction" between the two sovereigns. To resolve these difficulties, nations have often entered into agreements settling the claims of their respective nationals. Consistent with that principle, the United States has repeatedly exercised its sovereign authority to settle the claims of its nationals against foreign countries. Though those settlements have sometimes been made by treaty, there has also been a longstanding practice of settling such claims by executive agreement without the advice and consent of the Senate. Under such agreements, the President has agreed to renounce or extinguish claims of United States nationals against foreign governments in return for lump sum payments or the establishment of arbitration procedures. It is clear that the practice of settling claims continues today. Since 1952, the President has entered into at least 10 binding settlements with foreign nations, including an $80 million settlement with the People's Republic of China.

Crucial to our decision today is the conclusion that Congress has implicitly approved the practice of claim settlement by executive agreement. This is best demonstrated by Congress' enactment of the Internatiional Claims Settlement Act of 1949. The Act had two purposes: (1) to allocate to United States nationals funds received in the course of an executive claims settlement with Yugoslavia, and (2) to provide a procedure whereby funds resulting from future settlements could be distributed. To achieve these ends Congress created the International Claims Commission, now the Foreign Claims Settlement Commission, and gave it jurisdiction to make final and binding deceisions with respect to claims by United States nationals against settlement funds. By creating a procedure to implement future settlement agreements, Congress placed its stamp of approval on such agreements. Indeed, the legislative history of the Act observed that the United States was seeking settlements with countries other than Yugoslavia and that the bill contemplated settlements of a similar nature in the future.

Over the years Congress has frequently amended the International Claims Settlement Act to provide or particular problems arising out of settlement agreements, thus demonstrating Congress' continuing acceptance of the President's claim settlement authority. [T]he legislative history of the IEEPA further reveals that Congress has accepted the authority of the Executive to enter into settlement agreements. Though the IEEPA was enacted to provide for some limitation on the President's emergency powers, Congress stressed that "[n]othing in this act is intended . . . to interfere with the authority of the President to [block assets], or to impede the settlement of claims of U.S. citizens against foreign countries."

In addition to congressional acquiescence in the President's power to settle claims, prior cases of this Court have also recognized that the President does have some measure of power to enter into executive agreements without obtaining the advice and consent of the Senate. In *United States v. Pink*, 315 U.S. 203 (1942), for example, the Court upheld the validity of the Litvinov Assignment, which was part of an Executive Agreement whereby the Soviet Union assigned to the United States amounts owed to it by American nationals so that outstanding claims of other American nationals could be paid. The Court explained that the resolution of such claims was integrally connected with normalizing United States' relations with a foreign state.

In light of all of the foregoing — the inferences to be drawn from the character of the legislation Congress has enacted in the area and from the history of acquiescence in executive claims settlements — we conclude that the President was authorized to suspend pending claims pursuant to Executive Order No. 12294. As Justice Frankfurter pointed out in *Youngstown*, "a systematic, unbroken executive practice, long pursued to the knowledge of Congress and never before questioned may be treated as a gloss on 'Executive Power' vested in the President by § 1 of Art. II." Past practice does not, by itself, create power, but "long-continued practice, known to and acquiesced in by Congress, would raise a presumption that the [action] has been [taken] in pursuance of its consent. . . ." *United States v. Midwest Oil Co.* Such practice is present here and such a presumption is also appropriate. In light of the fact that Congress may be considered to have consented to the President's action in suspending claims, we cannot say that action exceeded the President's powers.

Just as importantly, Congress has not disapproved of the action taken here. Though Congress has held hearings on the Iranian Agreement itself, Congress has not enacted legislation, or even passed a resolution, indicating its displeasure with the Agreement. Quite the contrary, the relevant Senate Committee has stated that the establishment of the Tribunal is "of vital importance to the United States." We are thus clearly not confronted with a situation in which Congress has in some way resisted the exercise of presidential authority.

Finally, we re-emphasize the narrowness of our decision. We do not decide that the President possesses plenary power to settle claims, even as against foreign governmental entities. But where, as here, the settlement of claims has been determined to be a necessary incident to the resolution of a major foreign policy dispute between our country and another, and where, as here, we can conclude that Congress acquiesced in the President's action, we are not prepared to say that the President lacks the power to settle such claims.

[JUSTICE POWELL dissented in part on grounds that the nullification of attachment as a "taking" requiring "just compensation" should be left open for case by case resolution. The Court's treatment of this issue has been omitted.]

NOTES

1. *The power to settle private claims.* Professor Miller asks: "As a matter of abstract constitutional theory, where does Congress, or Congress and the President acting together, derive such a power [as was exercised in the Iranian Assets case]?" Miller, 29 UCLA L. REV. at 1111. Justice Rehnquist does not really address the source of the national power to act, but merely notes that the Court is unwilling to reject the existence of power. The long-standing practice of other nations in the international community may be relevant. Has the Sutherland thesis on sovereign foreign affairs power in *Curtiss-Wright* been accepted? Is the source of national power in the area of foreign affairs now irrelevant?

> Justice Rehnquist does not rely on Sutherland's theory regarding any inherent attributes of sovereignty, much less any doctrine which is not limited by the applicable provisions of the Constitution. Not only did the opinion refuse to enumerate principles that might authorize open-ended executive power relating to foreign affairs, it also refused to specify any limitations on that power other than the specific checks operating on all federal powers, such as the Bill of Rights.

John Nowak & Ronald Rotunda, *A Comment on the Creation and Resolution of a "Nonproblem":* Dames and Moore v. Regan, *The Foreign Affairs Power, and the Role of the Court*, 29 UCLA L. REV. 1129, 1155 (1982).

2. *Congressional acquiescence.* Had Congress consented to the President's action suspending claims in United States courts? Does congressional acquiescence constitute consent? Must Congress acquiesce in the general practice or in the specific case? Justice Rehniquist does not require a clear statement in the statutory authority even though individual rights were involved. Professor Koh asserts that "Justice Rehnquist construed a history of unchecked executive practice, the fact of IEEPA's existence, and the absence of express congressional disapproval of the president's action to demonstrate that Congress had *impliedly* authorized the act, thereby elevating the president's power from the twilight zone — Jackson's category two — to its height in Jackson's category one." KOH at 139. Professor Tribe similarly contrasts the effect of silence in *Dames & Moore* and *Youngstown*: "In *Dames & Moore v. Regan* . . . the Court treated Congress' silence as non-silence. Unlike those members of the *Steel Seizure* majority who viewed Congress' failure to enact *explicit* authorization of executive seizure as signalling its intent to forbid such actions, the Court in *Dames* found implicit congressional authorization of executive suspension of claims in three not-quite-applicable pieces of legislation plus, perhaps, the national mood of celebration." LAURENCE TRIBE, CONSTITUTIONAL CHOICES 39 (1985).

Would the President have constitiutional power to suspend the claims absent congressional acquiescence? What if Congress disagrees?

> Presidential exercise of power is always subject to ex post facto review by Congress to weigh both the genuineness of the urgency and the wisdom of the action. If Congress disagrees, it can repudiate the President formally. Congressional action in response to assertions of the presidential prerogative in these contexts should in turn trump the presidential power, and the process of constitutional lawmaking will continue.

Philip Trimble, *The President's Foreign Affairs Power,* in FOREIGN AFFAIRS AND THE CONSTITUTION 39, 46 (L. Henkin, et al., eds. 1990).

3. *American Insurance Association v. Garamendi,* 539 U.S. 396 (2003). The Court, per Justice Souter, in a 5-4 decision, held that a California State law, the Holocaust Victim Insurance Relief Act (HVIRA), requiring insurance companies doing business in the state to disclose "information about all policies sold in Europe between 1920 and 1945," by the company itself or any one "related" to it, was preempted by foreign affairs policy reflected in executive agreements mandating that all Holocaust claims go through the International Commission on Holocaust Era Insurance Claims.

At the conclusion of the Second World War, European insurance companies refused to honor the insurance policies of those who had died in the Holocaust on the grounds that death certificates or the proper policy paperwork were lacking. In order to aid the redevelopment of West Germany, the Allies agreed to delay all litigation against the German state or German corporations until "the final settlement of the problem of reparation." With the reunification of Germany in 1990, the German courts held that the moratorium could be lifted.

In response to the deluge of suits faced by German corporations and European insurance companies, Germany and the United States signed the German Foundation Agreement in July 2000, whereby Germany agreed to enact legislation establishing a Foundation funded with 10 billion deutsch marks to compensate all those "who suffered at the hands of German companies during the National Socialist era." In exchange, the U.S. government promised to advise federal courts handling such claims "that U.S. policy interests favor dismissal on any valid legal ground" and to use its best efforts to get state and local governments to respect the Foundation's exclusive mechanism.

In the Foundation Agreement, both countries agreed that the German Foundation would work with the International Commission on Holocaust Era Insurance Claims (ICHEIC), a voluntary organization founded by several European insurance companies, Israel and various Jewish and Holocaust survivor associations and the organization of American state insurance commissioners. ICHEIC has established procedures for handling demands against participating insurers. In the Foundation Agreement, Germany stipulated that insurance claims against German insurance companies would be processed according to ICHEIC procedures where applicable. The German Foundation has set aside monies to be used for working with ICHEIC and participating insurance companies have undertaken efforts for release of information on Holocaust victims with insurance claims. Justice Souter noted: "The German Foundation Pact has served as a model for similar agreements with Austria and France, and the United States Government continues to pursue comparable agreements with other countries."

Meanwhile, California passed the Holocaust Victims Insurance Relief Act (HVIRA), which specified that all insurance companies doing business in California must disclose all insurance policies issued by the company or any "related company" "to persons in Europe, which were in effect between 1920 and 1945," and list the persons' addresses, cities of origin, domiciles or the names of the beneficiaries. The law also mandated that any insurance company that failed to produce such a list would lose its California business license. U.S. Deputy Secretary of State Eizenstat wrote letters to the governor and insurance commissioner of California asking that the law not be enforced, as "actions by California, pursuant to this law, have already threatened to damage the cooperative spirit which the ICHEIC requires to resolve the important issue for Holocaust survivors." Concern was expressed that HVIRA could derail the German Foundation Agreement. After California tried to enforce the law, several insurance companies sought injunctive relief on the ground that HVIRA was unconstitutional. The district court issued a preliminary injunction. The Ninth Circuit reversed, but left the injunction in place pending consideration of a due process claim. On remand, the district court held that the law violated procedural due process, as the law "mandat[ed] license suspension for nonperformance of what may be impossible tasks without allowing for a meaningful hearing." The Ninth Circuit again reversed, holding that the tasks set out by the law were not impossible, and reiterating its prior holding that the state law violated "neither the Foreign Affairs nor the Foreign Commerce powers."

The Supreme Court reversed. Justice Souter, for the Court, stated:

> The principal argument for preemption made by petitioners and the United States as *amicus curiae* is that HVIRA interferes with foreign policy of the Executive Branch, as expressed principally in the executive agreements with Germany, Austria, and France. The major premises of the argument, at least, are beyond dispute. There is, of course, no question that at some point an exercise of state power that touches on foreign relations must yield to the National Government's policy, given the "concern for uniformity in this country's dealings with foreign nations" that animated the Constitution's allocation of foreign relations power to the National Government in the first place. *Banco Nacional de Cuba v. Sabbatino*, 376 U.S. 398, 427, n. 25 (1964).
>
> Nor is there any question generally that there is executive authority to decide what that policy should be. Although the source of the President's power to act in foreign affairs does not enjoy any textual detail, the historical gloss on the "executive Power" vested in Article

> II of the Constitution has recognized the President's "vast share of responsibility for the conduct of our foreign relations." *Youngstown Sheet & Tube Co. v. Sawyer*, (Frankfurter, J., concurring). While Congress holds express authority to regulate public and private dealings with other nations in its war and foreign commerce powers, in foreign affairs the President has a degree of independent authority to act. At a more specific level, our cases have recognized that the President has authority to make "executive agreements" with other countries, requiring no ratification by the Senate or approval by Congress, this power having been exercised since the early years of the Republic. *See Dames & Moore v. Regan.*
>
> The executive agreements at issue here do differ in one respect from those just mentioned insofar as they address claims associated with formerly belligerent states, but against corporations, not the foreign governments. But the distinction does not matter. Historically, wartime claims against even nominally private entities have become issues in international diplomacy, and three of the postwar settlements dealing with reparations implicating private parties were made by the Executive alone.
>
> Generally, then, valid executive agreements are fit to preempt state law, just as treaties are, and if the agreements here had expressly preempted laws like HVIRA, the issue would be straightforward. *See* [*United States v.*] *Belmont.* But petitioners and the United States as *amicus curiae* both have to acknowledge that the agreements include no preemption clause, and so leave their claim of preemption to rest on asserted interference with the foreign policy those agreements embody.

Since the executive agreements did not have explicit preemption clauses, Justice Souter next considered whether the State law interfered with the foreign policy those agreements embodied. He indicated that "the likelihood that state legislation will produce something more than incidental effect in conflict with express foreign policy of the National Government would require preemption of the state law." Further, "it would be reasonable to consider the strength of the state interest, judged by standards of traditional practice, when deciding how serious a conflict must be shown before declaring the state law preempted." He concluded: "Judged by these standards, we think petitioners and the Government have demonstrated a sufficiently clear conflict to require finding preemption here." First, "vindicating victims injured by acts or omissions of enemy corporations in wartime is thus within the traditional subject matter of foreign policy in which national, not state interests, are overriding, and which the National Government has addressed." In this case, "California seeks to use an iron fist where the President has chosen kid gloves." There is a "clear conflict" between the State law and federal executive policy. While this would have been sufficient "to require the state law to yield," Justice Souter also cited "the weakness of the State's interest. . . . in regulating disclosure of European Holocaust era insurance policies in the manner of HVIRA." Finally, the Court rejected California's argument that Congress had authorized state law of this sort. And "[g]iven the President's independent authority 'in the areas of foreign policy and national security, congressional silence is not to be equaled with congressional approval.' "

Justice Ginsburg, writing for herself and Justices Scalia, Thomas, and Stevens, dissented: "Although the federal approach differs from California's, no executive agreement or other formal expression of foreign policy disapproves state disclosure laws like the HVIRA." Since the agreement with the German government explicitly stated, that "[t]he United States does not suggest that its policy interests concerning the Foundation in themselves provide an independent legal basis for dismissal," Justice Ginsburg argued that the executive agreement was designed to not preempt any state initiatives. "No agreement so much as mentions the HVIRA's sole concern: public disclosure." Justice Ginsburg argued that there could be no preemption, as there was no official conflict. In response to the letters from Deputy Secretary of State Eizenstat to the contrary, Justice Ginsburg argued, " 'Executive Branch actions-press releases, letters, and *amicus* briefs' that 'express federal policy but lack the force of law' cannot render a state law unconstitutional under the Foreign Commerce Clause.' " Justice Ginsburg concluded: "As I see it, courts step out of their proper role when they rely on no legislative or even executive text, but only on inference and implication, to preempt state laws on foreign affairs grounds."

[B] THE WAR POWER

A reading of the Constitution on the war powers would, like foreign affairs powers generally, suggest a preponderance of influence in Congress. In addition to the principal power to declare war, Article I delegates powers to levy and collect taxes for the common defense, to define and punish piracies and felonies committed on the high seas and offenses against the law of nations, to grant letters of marque and reprisal, to make rules governing capture on land and water, to raise and support armies but limiting appropriations to two years, to provide and maintain a navy, to make rules regulating the land and naval forces, to provide for the organization, arming, discipline and calling forth of the militia, as well as the general power to make all laws necessary and proper for carrying into execution these powers and those granted elsewhere in the Constitution. In comparison, the Executive relies principally on the nebulous provision vesting the executive power in the President, the President's role as Commander-in-Chief, his duty to see that the laws are faithfully executed, his power to enter into treaties and the other powers relating to foreign relations.

Nevertheless, it has become increasingly obvious that this specification of powers is not indicative of the present operation of the separation of powers. While the Constitution envisions a sharing of the war powers, the reality is executive dominance. Today, "war" is seldom formally declared; deployment and use by the Executive of our armed forces in foreign lands is not unusual; Korea, Vietnam, Panama, Grenada, the Persian Gulf War, Haiti, and post-cold war collective actions such as Somalia and Bosnia, raise serious questions concerning Congress' continuing role in controlling the war power. ARTHUR SCHLESINGER, THE IMPERIAL PRESIDENCY (1973), cites decisions regarding war as the area in which "the imperial presidency received its decisive impetus." Whether this is a product of executive usurpation or congressional atrophy, the result is the same — presidential dominance of the war powers. What is the constitutional authority for the President's commitment of our armed forces absent a declaration of war? Do such presidential initiatives comport with the original understanding of executive-congressional relations? Can Congress constitutionally limit the President's commitment of armed forces absent a declaration of war? These and other problems were dramatically raised by the Persian Gulf Crisis.

[1] The Power to Engage in Military Action

1. *To "declare war."* At the Constitutional Convention, there was support for vesting the war power in the President, the Senate, the President and Senate together, and the Congress. The proposed draft vesting the power to "make" war in the legislature was deleted in favor of the congressional power to "declare" war. The debate suggests this was designed, not to enhance executive power, but to prevent "make" from being misconstrued as "conduct" war, which was an executive duty. Does this exclude Congress from making policy regarding the waging of war? The strategies relating to the use and movement of our Armed Forces? Does it limit the power of Congress to terminate a war?

Further, the change was designed to leave the Executive with "the power to repel sudden attacks" — that the "executive should be able to repel and not to commence war." 2 MAX FARRAND, THE RECORDS OF THE FEDERAL CONVENTION OF 1787, at 318–19 (rev. ed. 1966). Does "sudden attack" include all forms of self-defense? Does it include the threat of sudden attack as well as the reality? Does it include protection of the "Nation's security" in an "emergency" as the state department claims? *War Powers Legislation Hearings Before the Sen. Comm. on Foreign Relations*, 92d Cong., 1st Sess. 488 (1971).

2. *Commander-in-chief.* Alexander Hamilton, in THE FEDERALIST, No. 69:

> The president is to be commander-in-chief of the army and navy of the United States. In this respect, his authority would be nominally the same with that of the king of Great Britain, but in substance much inferior to it. It would amount to nothing more than the supreme command and direction of the military and naval forces, as first general and admiral of the confederacy while that of the British king extends to the declaring of war, and to the raising and regulating of fleets and armies, all which, by the Constitution under consideration, would appertain to the legislature.

Professor Henkin, commenting on the Hamilton perspective, notes that "generals and admirals even when they are 'first', do not determine the political purposes for which troops are to be used; they command them in the execution of policy made by others." He concludes that "[t]here is little evidence that the Framers intended more than to establish in the President civilian command of the forces for wars declared by Congress (or when the

United States was attacked)." LOUIS HENKIN, FOREIGN AFFAIRS AND THE CONSTITUTION 50–51 (1972).

Does the vesting of the "Executive power" in Article II, the President's foreign affairs power, or the concept of inherent power support the presidential claim for discretion in initiating hostilities without congressional authorization? Madison and James Wilson agreed that "executive powers do not include the rights of war and peace." 1 FARRAND at 70. As indicated in note 1, above, the framers considered and rejected vesting the power to declare war in the President because it was "too dangerous" to vest the war power in one person.

3. *Defining "war."* There is a question as to what constitutes the "war" that Congress may declare. The term may be used in an international law sense which would exclude a wide range of self-help measures short of juridical war. But if the President is empowered to employ the Armed Forces in all situations short of juridical war, Congress' power to declare "war" would be relatively meaningless. Should "war" be defined quantitatively, reflecting the level of intensity of the engagement? It has been suggested that "the meaning of 'war' in the context of the constitutional allocation of power to use force in foreign relations must be determined with reference to the purpose of the war-declaring clause: to safeguard the United States against unchecked executive decisions to commit the country to a trial of force." Note, 81 HARV. L. REV. 1771, 1774–75 (1968). Could Congress constitutionally limit the President's power to launch a first strike using nuclear weapons? *See* FIRST USE OF NUCLEAR WEAPONS: UNDER THE CONSTITUTION, WHO DECIDES? (P. Raven-Hansen ed. 1987).

4. *Practice.* Proponents of broad executive war powers argue principally from custom and usage. But again, there is substantial disagreement as to the proper interpretation of historical events. Nineteenth– and early twentieth–century experience with presidential use of our Armed Forces tended to be minor affairs which many would be unwilling to label "wars." They generally were premised on a self-defense theory or a neutrality theory of interposition — protection of American lives and property abroad while retaining a neutral posture between the conflicting parties.

In addition to the generally-accepted presidential power to repel attack without congressional authorization, there is also recognition of a power to rescue U.S. citizens. For example, in his Oct. 25, 1983, letter to the Speaker of the House on the Grenada operation, President Reagan cited, "the overriding importance of protecting the lives of the United States citizens in Grenada." Reprisal is another species of justification for presidential initiatives, closely related to a theory of self-defense. In explaining the air strikes against Libya on April 14, 1986, the President and the State Department cited various terrorist acts by Libya. It is sometimes argued that such acts of aggression against the United States and its nationals create a *de facto* war calling for action by the Commander in Chief. For an interesting and spirited exchange on the textual and historical issues surrounding the allocation of the warmaking power, see Michael Ramsey, *Textualism and War Powers*, 69 U. CHI. L. REV. 1543 (2002); John Yoo, *War and Constitutional Texts*, 69 U. CHI. L. REV. 1639 (2002); Michael Ramsey, *Text and History in the War Powers Debate: A Reply to Professor Yoo*, 69 U. CHI. L. REV. 1685 (2002).

5. *The Civil War.* The Civil War was an undeclared war. President Lincoln's April 1861 order declaring a blockade of Southern ports gave rise to one of the few Supreme Court statements on the war power. In the *Prize Cases*, 67 U.S. (2 Black) 635 (1865), the Court 5-4 upheld the blockade. Judge Grier, for the majority stated:

> By the Constitution, Congress alone has the power to declare a national or foreign war. It cannot declare war against a State, or any number of States, by virtue of any clause in the Constitution. The Constitution confers on the President the whole Executive power. He is bound to take care that the laws be faithfully executed. He is Commander-in-Chief of the Army and Navy of the United States. [He] has no power to initiate or declare a war either against a foreign nation or a domestic State. But by [Acts of Congress] he is authorized to call out the militia and use the military and naval forces of the United States in case of invasion by foreign nations, and to suppress insurrection against the government of a State or of the United States.
>
> If a war be made by invasion of a foreign nation, the President is not only authorized but bound to resist force by force. He does not initiate the war, but is bound to accept the challenge without waiting for any special legislative authority. And whether the hostile party be a foreign invader, or States organized in rebellion, it is none the less a war, although the declaration of it be 'unilateral.' [The] President was bound to meet [the Civil War] in the shape it presented itself, without waiting for Congress to baptize it with a name. If it were necessary to the technical existence of a war, that it should have a legislative sanction, we find it in almost every act passed at the extraordinary session of the Legislature of 1861, which was wholly employed in enacting laws to enable the Government to prosecute the war with vigor and efficiency.

Judge Nelson's dissent, stated:

> This great power over the business and property of the citizen is reserved to the legislative department by the express words of the Constitution. It cannot be delegated or surrendered to the Executive. Congress alone can determine whether war exists or should be declared, and until they have acted, no citizen of the State can be punished in his person or property, unless he had committed some offense against a law of Congress passed before the act was committed, which made it a crime and defined the punishment.

6. *Korea.* Any attempt at quantitative distinctions fails when consideration is given to the Korean "police action" taken without congressional authorization and with little congressional dissent. While consideration was given to having a *post hoc* resolution endorsing the action, the Executive believed this to be unnecessary. In 1951, Secretary of State Dean Acheson, testifying before Congress, explained:

> Not only has the President the authority to use the Armed Forces in carrying out the broad foreign policy of the United States and implementing treaties, but it is equally clear that this authority may not be interfered with by the Congress in the exercise of powers which it has under the Constitution.

Hearing Before the Sen. Comms. on Foreign Relations and Armed Services, 82d Cong., 1st Sess. 993 (1951). *See* Louis Fisher, *The Korean War: On What Legal Basis Did Truman Act?*, 89 AM. J. INT'L L. 21 (1995), who argues that President Truman's unilateral action was unconstitutional.

In sending troops to Korea, President Truman relied heavily on United Nations resolutions calling upon member states "to render every assistance" in repelling aggression against South Korea. In the Persian Gulf Crisis, would U.N. Resolution 678 have provided constitutional authority for presidential military action against Iraq? Would the President have authority to act pursuant to Resolution 678 even if Congress expressly denied authorization to act? Does the U.N. Charter envision a new order of U.N. authorized peace actions replacing the traditional method of warfare by member states? *See generally* Symposium, *Agora: The Gulf Crisis in International and Foreign Relations Law*, 85 AM. J. INT'L L. 63 (1991).

7. *Vietnam.* It was Vietnam that most dramatically presented the issue of the scope of presidential war powers and generated the debate leading to the War Powers Resolution. Professor Bickel stated:

> The decisions of 1965 may have differed only in degree from earlier stages in this process of growth [of executive war power]. But there comes a point when a difference of degree achieves the magnitude of a difference in kind. The decisions of 1965 amounted to an all but explicit transfer of the power to declare war from Congress, where the Constitution lodged it, to the President, on whom the framers refused to confer it.

Alexander Bickel, *The Constitution and the War*, 54 COMMENTARY 49, 50–51 (July 1972).

Leonard C. Meeker, Legal Adviser to the Department of State, provided the *Johnson Administration's Justification for the Vietnam War*, reprinted in 75 YALE L.J. 1085 (1966):

> There can be no question in present circumstances of the President's authority to commit United States forces to the defense of South Viet-Nam. The grant of authority to the President in Article II of the Constitution extends to the actions of the United States currently undertaken in Viet-Nam. In fact, however, it is unnecessary to determine whether this grant standing alone is sufficient to authorize actions taken in Viet-Nam. These actions rest not only on the exercise of Presidential powers under article II but on the SEATO treaty — a treaty advised and consented to by the Senate — and on actions of the Congress, particularly the joint resolution of August 10, 1964 [the Gulf of Tonkin Resolution].

Would similar arguments justify the offensive action against Iraq, absent the congressional declaration of Jan. 12, 1991? Note that the Tonkin Gulf Resolution, approved "all necessary measures . . . to prevent further aggression" and declared that "the United States is . . . prepared, as the President determines, to take all necessary steps, including the use of armed force . . . ."

Professor Ely, in his excellent two-part study of the Vietnam War concludes, "as the constitutional requirement of congressional authorization has historically been understood, Congress does indeed appear (years of denial and doubletalk notwithstanding) to have authorized each of [the] phases of the war." John Ely, *The American War in Indochina, Part I: The (Troubled) Constitutionality of the War They Told Us About,* 42 Stan. L. Rev. 877, 878 (1990). He adds:

> However, a Congress that lets the President call the shots on war and peace, and devotes itself instead to the construction of private political bomb shelters, is not what the framers of the Constitution had in mind in vesting the war power in the legislative process. If the point of the Constitution is to be served — that no one person is to have the authority to lead us into war — the "authorization" test must be reformulated, not so much to change its substantive standard as to clarify it, to prove a "bright line" test that will force Congress to take a clear stand one way or the other.

Does the War Powers Resolution, reprinted below, provide such a "bright line"?

[2] The War Powers Resolution

On November 7, 1973, Congress passed, over a presidential veto, the War Powers Resolution. Commenting on the proposal, a critic argued that it

> rests on heady new perspectives the Senate Foreign Relations Committee has discovered in the necessary and proper clause. Its doctrine would permit a plenipotentiary Congress to dominate the Presidency and the courts as well more completely than the House of Commons governs England; that is, it would permit Congress to amend the Constitution without the inconvenience of consulting the people.

The author warned that "[i]ts passage would be a constitutional disaster, depriving the government of the powers it needs most to safeguard the nation in a dangerous and unstable world." Eugene Rostow, *Great Cases Make Bad Law: The War Powers Act,* 50 Tex. L. Rev. 833, 835, 836 (1972). The executive has consistently echoed this critique, arguing that the Resolution is unconstitutional.

On the other hand, its proponents argued that

> the bill seeks to limit Presidential war-making in the absence of Congressional authorization, leaving the President free to defend the United States and its Armed Forces against sudden attack. The power to wage war, it may be categorically asserted, was vested by the

Constitution in Congress, not the President. If this be so, the bill merely seeks to restore the original design. It cannot be unconstitutional to go back to the Constitution.

Testimony of Raoul Berger, *War Powers Legislation, 1973, Hearings on S. 440 before the Sen. Comm. on Foreign Relations*, 93d Cong., 1st Sess. 5–6 (1973).

WAR POWERS RESOLUTION

50 U.S.C. §§ 1541–1548
(passed over President's veto November 7, 1973)
Purpose and Policy

SEC. 2. (a) It is the purpose of this joint resolution to fulfill the intent of the framers of the Constitution of the United States and insure that the collective judgment of both the Congress and the President will apply to the introduction of United States Armed Forces into hostilities, or into situations where imminent involvement in hostilities is clearly indicated by the circumstances, and to the continued use of such forces in hostilities or in such situations.

(b) Under article I, section 8, of the Constitution, it is specifically provided that the Congress shall have the power to make all laws necessary and proper for carrying into execution, not only its own powers but also all other powers vested by the Constitution in the Government of the United States, or in any department or officer thereof.

(c) The constitutional powers of the President as Commander-in-Chief to introduce United States Armed Forces into hostilities, or into situations where imminent involvement in hostilities is clearly indicated by the circumstances, are exercised only pursuant to (1) a declaration of war, (2) specific statutory authorization, or (3) a national emergency created by attack upon the United States, its territories or possessions, or its armed forces.

Consultation

SEC. 3. The President in every possible instance shall consult with Congress before introducing United States Armed Forces into hostilities or into situations where imminent involvement in hostilities is clearly indicated by the circumstances, and after every such introduction shall consult regularly with the Congress until United States Armed Forces are no longer engaged in hostilities or have been removed from such situations.

Reporting

SEC. 4. (a) In the absence of a declaration of war, in any case in which United States Armed Forces are introduced —

(1) into hostilities or into situations where imminent involvement in hostilities is clearly indicated by the circumstances;

(2) into the territory, airspace or waters of a foreign nation, while equipped for combat, except for deployments which relate solely to supply, replacement, repair, or training of such forces; or

(3) in numbers which substantially enlarge United States Armed Forces equipped for combat already located in a foreign nation;

the President shall submit within 48 hours to the Speaker of the House of Representatives and to the President pro tempore of the Senate a report, in writing, setting forth

(A) the circumstances necessitating the introduction of United States Armed Forces;

(B) the constitutional and legislative authority under which such introduction took place; and

(C) the estimated scope and duration of the hostilities or involvement.

(b) The President shall provide such other information as the Congress may request in the fulfillment of its constitutional responsibilities with respect to committing the Nation to war and to the use of United States Armed Forces abroad.

(c) Whenever United States Armed Forces are introduced into hostilities or into any situation described in subsection (a) of this section, the President shall, so long as such armed forces continue to be engaged in such hostilities or situation, report to the Congress periodically on the status of such hostilities or situation as well as on the scope and duration of such hostilities or situation, but in no event shall he report to the Congress less often than once every six months.

Congressional Action

Sec. 5. (b) Within sixty calendar days after a report is submitted or is required to be submitted pursuant to section 4(a)(1), whichever is earlier, the President shall terminate any use of United States Armed Forces with respect to which such report was submitted (or required to be submitted), unless the Congress (1) has declared war or has enacted a specific authorization for such use of United States Armed Forces, (2) has extended by law such sixty-day period, or (3) is physically unable to meet as a result of an armed attack upon the United States. Such sixty-day period shall be extended for not more than an additional thirty days if the President determines and certifies to the Congress in writing that unavoidable military necessity respecting the safety of United States Armed Forces requires the continued use of such armed forces in the course of bringing about a prompt removal of such forces.

(c) Notwithstanding subsection (b), at any time that United States Armed Forces are engaged in hostilities outside the territory of the United States, its possessions and territories without a declaration of war or specific statutory authorization, such forces shall be removed by the President if the Congress so directs by concurrent resolution.

Interpretation of Joint Resolution

Sec 8. (a) Authority to introduce United States Armed Forces into hostilities or into situations wherein involvement in hostilities is clearly indicated by the circumstances shall not be inferred -

(1) from any provision of law (whether or not in effect before the date of the enactment of this joint resolution), including any provision contained in any appropriation Act, unless such provision specifically authorizes the introduction of United States Armed Forces into hostilities or into such situation and states that it is intended to constitute specific statutory authorization within the meaning of this joint resolution; or

(2) from any treaty heretofore or hereafter ratified unless such treaty is implemented by legislation specifically authorizing the introduction of United States Armed Forces into hostilities or into such situation and stating that it is intended to constitute specific statutory authorization within the meaning of this joint [resolution].

(b) Nothing in this joint resolution -

(1) is intended to alter the constitutional authority of the Congress or of the President, or the provisions of existing treaties; or

(2) shall be construed as granting any authority to the President with respect to the introduction of United States Armed Forces into hostilities or into situation wherein involvement in hostilities is clearly indicated by the circumstances which authority he would not have had in the absence of this joint [resolution].

NOTES

1. *Constitutionality of the War Powers Resolution.* Much of the debate on the War Powers Resolution has been a matter of constitutional methodology. Proponents stress the intent of the Framers and opponents emphasize presidential usage and custom and the dynamic character of constitutional growth. Is the War Powers Resolution an unconstitutional infringement on presidential power? The position of the State Department was "that the description and allocation of war powers in the Constitution intentionally and wisely left the great questions of war and peace in specific cases to be resolved through fundamental political processes in which both the President and Congress participate." It contended that "the proposed legislation would alter this fundamental constitutional scheme. It would either expand or encroach on the underlying constitutional powers thought to be elaborated, a revision which in any event cannot be properly accomplished absent a constitutional amendment." *Statement of Charles N. Brower, Acting Legal Advisor, Dep't of State*, 1973 Hearings on S. 440, at 52.

Cyrus Vance, however, claims that such objections "mistake the nature and purpose of the statute."

> The purpose . . . is not to define or modify the constitutional powers of the President. Rather, the purpose was to establish a procedure through which Congress and the President can exercise their respective powers. [A] statute that establishes a procedural mechanism for such congressional expression is clearly a valid exercise of Congress's constitutional power to make all laws "necessary and proper" for the execution of powers constitutionally vested in the federal government.

Cyrus Vance, *Striking the Balance: Congress and the President Under the War Powers Resolution*, 133 U. Pa. L. Rev. 79, 85–86 (1984).

Professor Carter argues that "[t]he War Powers Resolution is not constitutional as an exercise of the war power. It is constitutional because it defines the war power." Such a definition coupled with a reasonable enforcement mechanism reflects a proper understanding of our checks and balances system.

> A proper understanding [of the system of checks and balances] leads ineluctably to the conclusion that, although the President might have broad authority to commit American forces in the absence of congressional action, Congress nevertheless holds the power to decide when the President's actions slide down the scale from use of troops in time

> of peace to use of troops in time of war. The War Powers Resolution is no more than a means to accomplish this legitimate end and, as a consequence, any constitutional challenge to its major provisions should fail.

Stephen Carter, *The Constitutionality of the War Powers Resolution*, 70 VA. L. REV. 101, 112 (1984).

In responding to the claim that past congressional acquiescence establishes executive war power, Professor Carter argues "that the President can exercise a purportedly inherent power if Congress has historically acquiesced and if Congress does not try to stop him." But he adds that "[i]f Congress does try to stop him, then by definition it is no longer acquiescing. In a fluid and dynamic system of checks and balances, this is the only conclusion that makes sense. It is surely not the case that all that is, is constitutional, so absent some constitutional equivalent of adverse possession, what Congress has given, Congress can also take back." *Id.* at 124. Can Congress always stop presidential military initiatives simply by cutting off funds? Would this be constitutional?

2. *The Chadha problem.* What is the status of § 5(b) & (c) of the War Powers Resolution after *Chadha*? In *Chadha*, Congress had delegated power to the executive, subject to congressional review. It can be argued that the Resolution is distinguishable, since "Congress never delegated the presidential authority curtailed by the joint resolution. Rather the authority is based on the President's executive power to act in emergencies while Congress considers appropriate legislation." Bennett Rushkoff, *In Defense of the War Powers Resolution*, 93 YALE L.J. 1330, 1349 (1984).

There also may be a difference between the attempt in § 5(b) to set a 60-day limit in the absence of congressional authorization and the assertion in § 5(c) that Congress can force a withdrawal at any time by passing a concurrent resolution. With regard to the latter, if *Chadha* were read to require presentment through a joint resolution, and if the President vetoed the resolution, then it would require a two-thirds majority to override the veto. This means that the President plus 34% of Congress could legally wage a war that 66% of Congress disapproved. It could be argued that this is appropriate because the war has already begun and it should take a super-majority to end it. On the other hand, it might be argued that *Chadha* does not apply to this situation because ending a war is not a "legislative act" within the meaning of that case; starting the war through declaration may be a legislative act, but continuing it requires the concurrence of both executive and legislature. When one branch withdraws its acquiescence, then the war should end.

3. *Efficacy of the War Powers Resolution.* Apart from the question of constitutionality of the War Powers Resolution, consider its efficacy in resolving the basic issues of the dispute over war powers. Numerous commentators have pointed out that after Vietnam, U.S. military actions around the globe have multiplied, that the resolution says nothing about "covert" operations not involving "armed forces," and that the President is free to operate for up to 60 days with no congressional involvement whatsoever.

4. Professor Ely attributed the inadequacies of the War Powers Resolution to the abdication of responsibility on the part of all three branches of government. "The War Powers Resolution hasn't worked, not because Congress's delineation of what should and should not count as authorization was inadequate, but rather because the President has not reported military actions to Congress as he is required to, and Congress has not had the backbone to call him on it, and the courts have abstained from getting involved even to the extent of 'remanding' the case to Congress." John Ely, *The American War in Indochina: The (Troubled) Constitutionality of the War They Told Us About,* 42 STAN. L. REV. 877, 878 (1990). Harold Koh, *War and Responsibility in the Dole-Gingrich Congress*, 50 U. MIAMI L. REV. 1, 9 (1995), also adopts a process-based view, stressing the need for "active institutional participation of all three branches . . . that promotes the creation and internalization of legal norms."

In JOHN H. ELY, WAR AND RESPONSIBILITY (1993), Professor Ely sought to provide a framework for what he described as a War Powers Resolution with teeth. He suggested allowing a maximum of 20 days for Congress to decide, rather than the current 90 days, and requiring that congressional authorization precede any military action unless there are compelling military reasons, in which case the President may request authorization from Congress contemporaneously with his order commencing military action. On the other hand, Professor Ely created a number of exceptions to his new resolution. The President would not be required to obtain advance authorization "where a clear threat to the national security has developed so rapidly as to preclude Congress's advance consideration of such authorization, or keeping the pendency of the United States to such a threat secret prior to its initiation is clearly essential to its military effectiveness." *Id.* at 133. It has been suggested that these exceptions may give away the whole store, making the "entire advance authorization provision hortatory." Jules Lobel, *"Little Wars" and the Constitution*, 50 U. MIAMI L. REV. 61, 75 (1995).

Ely conceded that "it is essentially impossible to write a statute that cannot be effectively defied by a President prepared to lie to cover his tracks," and that Congress may, in any event, still choose not to enforce the resolution, eradicating any benefit from a shortened period. In such cases, Professor Ely urged the judicial branch to intervene to require the political branches to fulfill their constitutional responsibility to decide on the use of military force, as this would offer an "educational process" capable of persuading Congress and the President to change the current pattern. Although "it is no business of [the judiciary] to decide what wars we fight," he reasoned that the judiciary's insulation from the political process "does situate them uniquely well to police malfunctions in that process." ELY at 54. Nevertheless, he admits that judicial enforcement of constitutional limitations in the war powers context or voluntary compliance is unlikely. ELY at 118, 126. According to Professor John Yoo, Presidents who have initiated hostilities have "generally consulted with, notified, and reported to Congress, consistent with the War Powers Resolution." John C. Yoo, *Applying the War Powers Resolution to the War on Terrorism*, 6 Green Bag 2d 175, 180 (2003). Professor Yoo acknowledges, however, that this has not always been the case. *Id.* at 180, n.35.

There is increasing support for simply repealing the War Powers Resolution. But others claim that it provides support for Congress in holding the President accountable, or at least forces a President contemplating the use of force to consider its limitations. Michael Glennon, *Too Far Apart: Repeal the War Powers Resolution*, 50 U. Miami L. Rev. 17, 31 (1995) concludes:

> Given the choice between no Resolution and one that doesn't work — one, indeed that confounds the congressional role rather than strengthens it; one that confuses public attention rather than focuses it; one that, with each use of force, deflects attention from underlying policy considerations as well as constitutional questions; one that gives the Congress no information about a crisis that it cannot get from the *New York Times*; and one that has rendered its law irrelevant — the better choice is no resolution.

An effort on June 7, 1995 to repeal the Resolution narrowly failed to pass the House by a vote of 217-201. Should the War Powers Resolution be strengthened? Should it be repealed?

In the case of President George W. Bush's invasion of Iraq in 2003, Congress enacted the Authorization for Use of Military Force (AUMF), Pub. L. 107-40, 115 Stat. 224 (2001). AUMF instructed the President to hunt down those who had perpetrated 9/11 or those who assisted or harbored the perpetrators, and to avoid the recurrence of this unprovoked attack. Section 2(a). According to one commentator, "[i]n light of the nature of the war to be fought, there was little, if any, serious concern that the President would overreach his constitutional authority." Douglas Kmiec, *Observing the Separation of Powers: The President's War Power Necessarily Remains "The Power to Wage War Successfully,"* 53 Drake L. Rev. 851, 855–56 (2005). The next sub-section deals with Supreme Court interpretation of this authorizing statute.

[3] The War Power in an Age of Terrorism

HAMDI v. RUMSFELD
524 U.S. 507 (2004)

O'Connor, J., announced the judgment of the Court and delivered an opinion, in which Rehnquist, C. J., and Kennedy and Breyer, JJ., joined. Souter, J., filed an opinion concurring in part, dissenting in part, and concurring in the judgment, in which Ginsburg, J., joined. Scalia, J., filed a dissenting opinion, in which Stevens, J., joined. Thomas, J., filed a dissenting opinion.

Justice O'Connor announced the judgment of the Court and delivered an opinion, in which The Chief Justice, Justice Kennedy, and Justice Breyer join.

At this difficult time in our Nation's history, we are called upon to consider the legality of the Government's detention of a United States citizen on United States soil as an "enemy combatant" and to address the process that is constitutionally owed to one who seeks to challenge his classification as such.

The United States Court of Appeals for the Fourth Circuit held that petitioner's detention was legally authorized and that he was entitled to no further opportunity to challenge his enemy-combatant label. We now vacate and remand. We hold that although Congress authorized the detention of combatants in the narrow circumstances alleged here, due process demands that a citizen held in the United States as an enemy combatant be given a meaningful opportunity to contest the factual basis for that detention before a neutral decisionmaker.

I

On September 11, 2001, the al Qaeda terrorist network used hijacked commercial airliners to attack prominent targets in the United States. Approximately 3,000 people were killed in those attacks. One week later, in response to these "acts of treacherous violence," Congress passed a resolution authorizing the President to "use all necessary and appropriate force against those nations, organizations, or persons he determines planned, authorized, committed, or aided the terrorist attacks" or "harbored such organizations or persons, in order to prevent any future acts of international terrorism against the United States by such nations, organizations or persons." Authorization for Use of Military Force ("the AUMF"). Soon thereafter, the President ordered United States Armed Forces to Afghanistan, with a mission to subdue al Qaeda and quell the Taliban regime that was known to support it.

This case arises out of the detention of a man whom the Government alleges took up arms with the Taliban during this conflict. His name is Yaser Esam Hamdi. Born an American citizen in Louisiana in 1980, Hamdi moved with his family to Saudi Arabia as a child. By 2001, the parties agree, he resided in Afghanistan. At some point that year, he was seized by members of the Northern Alliance, a coalition of military groups opposed to the Taliban government, and eventually was turned over to the United States military. The Government asserts that it initially detained and interrogated Hamdi in Afghanistan before transferring him to the United States Naval Base in Guantanamo Bay in January 2002. In April 2002, upon learning that Hamdi is an American citizen, authorities transferred him to a naval brig in Norfolk, Virginia, where he remained until a recent transfer to a brig in Charleston, South Carolina. The Government contends that Hamdi is an "enemy combatant," and that this status justifies holding him in the United States indefinitely — without formal charges or proceedings — unless and until it makes the determination that access to counsel or further process is warranted.

In June 2002, Hamdi's father, Esam Fouad Hamdi, filed the present petition for a writ of habeas corpus under 28 U.S.C. § 2241 in the Eastern District of Virginia, naming as petitioners his son and himself as next friend. The elder Hamdi alleges in the petition that he has had no contact with his son since the Government took custody of him in 2001, and that the Government has held his son "without access to legal counsel or notice of any charges pending against him." Although his habeas petition provides no details with regard to the factual circumstances surrounding his son's capture and detention, Hamdi's father has asserted in documents found elsewhere in the record that his son went to Afghanistan to do "relief work," and that he had been in that country less than two months before September 11, 2001, and could not have received military training. The 20-year-old was traveling on his own for the first time, his father says, and "because of his lack of experience, he was trapped in Afghanistan once that military campaign began."

[T]he Government filed a response and a motion to dismiss the petition. It attached to its response a declaration from one Michael Mobbs (hereinafter "Mobbs Declaration"), who identified himself as Special Advisor to the Under Secretary of Defense for Policy. Mobbs set forth what remains the sole evidentiary support that the Government has provided to the courts for Hamdi's detention. The declaration states that Hamdi "traveled to Afghanistan" in July or August 2001, and that he thereafter "affiliated with a Taliban military unit and received weapons training." It asserts that Hamdi "remained with his Taliban unit following the attacks of September 11" and that, during the time when Northern Alliance forces were "engaged in battle with the Taliban, . . . Hamdi's Taliban unit surrendered" to those forces, after which he "surrendered his Kalishnikov assault rifle" to them. The Mobbs Declaration also states that, because al Qaeda and the Taliban "were and are hostile forces engaged in armed conflict with the armed forces of the United States," "individuals associated with" those groups "were and continue to be enemy combatants." Mobbs states that Hamdi was labeled an enemy combatant "based upon his interviews and in light of his association with the Taliban." According to the declaration, a series of "U.S. military screening teams" determined that Hamdi met "the criteria for enemy combatants," and "a subsequent interview of Hamdi has confirmed that he surrendered and gave his firearm to Northern Alliance forces, which supports his classification as an enemy combatant."

The District Court found that the Mobbs Declaration fell "far short" of supporting Hamdi's detention. It criticized the generic and hearsay nature of the affidavit, calling it "little more than the government's 'say-so.' " It ordered the Government to turn over numerous materials for *in camera* review. The Fourth Circuit reversed, . . . [and] stressed that, because it was "undisputed that Hamdi was captured in a zone of active combat in a foreign theater of conflict," no factual inquiry or evidentiary hearing allowing Hamdi to be heard or to rebut the Government's assertions was necessary or proper. Concluding that the factual averments in the Mobbs Declaration, "if accurate," provided a sufficient basis upon which to conclude that the President had constitutionally detained Hamdi pursuant to the President's war powers, it ordered the habeas petition dismissed. Relying on *Ex parte Quirin,* 317 U.S. 1 (1942), the court emphasized that "one who takes up arms against the United States in a foreign theater of war, regardless of his citizenship, may properly be designated an enemy combatant and treated as such."

We now vacate the judgment below and remand.

II

The threshold question before us is whether the Executive has the authority to detain citizens who qualify as "enemy combatants." There is some debate as to the proper scope of this term, and the Government has never provided any court with the full criteria that it uses in classifying individuals as such. It has made clear, however, that, for purposes of this case, the "enemy combatant" that it is seeking to detain is an individual who, it alleges, was " 'part of or supporting forces hostile to the United States or coalition partners' " in Afghanistan and who " 'engaged in an armed conflict against the United States' " there. We therefore answer only the narrow question before us: whether the detention of citizens falling within that definition is authorized.

The Government maintains that no explicit congressional authorization is required, because the Executive possesses plenary authority to detain pursuant to Article II of the Constitution. We do not reach the question whether Article II provides such authority, however, because we agree with the Government's alternative position, that Congress has in fact authorized Hamdi's detention, through the AUMF.

Our analysis on that point, set forth below, substantially overlaps with our analysis of Hamdi's principal argument for the illegality of his detention. He posits that his detention is forbidden by 18 U.S.C. § 4001(a). Section 4001(a) states that "no citizen shall be imprisoned or otherwise detained by the United States except pursuant to an Act of Congress." Congress passed § 4001(a) in 1971 as part of a bill to repeal the Emergency Detention Act of 1950, which provided procedures for executive detention, during times of emergency, of individuals deemed likely to engage in espionage or sabotage. Congress was particularly concerned about the possibility that the Act could be used to reprise the Japanese internment camps of World War II. The Government again presses two alternative positions. First, it argues that § 4001(a), in light of its legislative history and its location in Title 18, applies only to "the control of civilian prisons and related detentions," not to military detentions. Second, it maintains that § 4001(a) is satisfied, because Hamdi is being detained "pursuant to an Act of Congress" — the AUMF. Again, because we conclude that the Government's second assertion is correct, we do not address the first. In other words, for the reasons that follow, we conclude that the AUMF is explicit congressional authorization for the detention of individuals in the narrow category we describe (assuming, without deciding, that such authorization is required), and that the AUMF satisfied § 4001(a)'s requirement that a detention be "pursuant to an Act of Congress" (assuming, without deciding, that § 4001(a) applies to military detentions).

The AUMF authorizes the President to use "all necessary and appropriate force" against "nations, organizations, or persons" associated with the September 11, 2001, terrorist attacks. There can be no doubt that individuals who fought against the United States in Afghanistan as part of the Taliban, an organization known to have supported the al Qaeda terrorist network responsible for those attacks, are individuals Congress sought to target in passing the AUMF. We conclude that detention of individuals falling into the limited category we are considering, for the duration of the particular conflict in which they were captured, is so fundamental and accepted an incident to war as to be an exercise of the "necessary and appropriate force" Congress has authorized the President to use.

The capture and detention of lawful combatants and the capture, detention, and trial of unlawful combatants, by "universal agreement and practice," are "important incidents of war." The purpose of detention is to prevent captured individuals from returning to the field of battle and taking up arms once again.

There is no bar to this Nation's holding one of its own citizens as an enemy combatant. In *Quirin*, one of the detainees, Haupt, alleged that he was a naturalized United States citizen. We held that "citizens who associate themselves with the military arm of the enemy government, and with its aid, guidance and direction enter this country bent on hostile acts, are enemy belligerents within the meaning of . . . the law of war." While Haupt was tried for violations of the law of war, nothing in *Quirin* suggests that his citizenship would have precluded his mere detention for the duration of the relevant hostilities. Nor can we see any reason for drawing such a line here. A citizen, no less than an alien, can be "part of or supporting forces hostile to the United States or coalition partners" and "engaged in an armed conflict against the United States"; such a citizen, if released, would pose the same threat of returning to the front during the ongoing conflict.

In light of these principles, it is of no moment that the AUMF does not use specific language of detention. Because detention to prevent a combatant's return to the battlefield is a fundamental incident of waging war, in permitting the use of "necessary and appropriate force," Congress has clearly and unmistakably authorized detention in the narrow circumstances considered here.

Hamdi objects, nevertheless, that Congress has not authorized the *indefinite* detention to which he is now subject. The Government responds that "the detention of enemy combatants during World War II was just as 'indefinite' while that war was being fought." We take Hamdi's objection to be not to the lack of certainty regarding the date on which the conflict will end, but to the substantial prospect of perpetual detention. We recognize that the national security underpinnings of the "war on terror," although crucially important, are broad and malleable. As the Government concedes, "given its unconventional nature, the current conflict is unlikely to end with a formal cease-fire agreement." The prospect Hamdi raises is therefore not far-fetched. If the Government does not consider this unconventional war won for two generations, and if it maintains during that time that Hamdi might, if released, rejoin forces fighting against the United States, then the position it has taken throughout the litigation of this case suggests that Hamdi's detention could last for the rest of his life.

It is a clearly established principle of the law of war that detention may last no longer than active hostilities. *See* Article 118 of the Geneva Convention (III) Relative to the Treatment of Prisoners of War ("Prisoners of war shall be released and repatriated without delay after the cessation of active hostilities").

Hamdi contends that the AUMF does not authorize indefinite or perpetual detention. Certainly, we agree that indefinite detention for the purpose of interrogation is not authorized. Further, we understand Congress' grant of authority for the use of "necessary and appropriate force" to include the authority to detain for the duration of the relevant conflict, and our understanding is based on longstanding law-of-war principles. If the practical circumstances of a given conflict are entirely unlike those of the conflicts that informed the development of the law of war, that understanding may unravel. But that is not the situation we face as of this date. Active combat operations against Taliban fighters apparently are ongoing in Afghanistan. The United States may detain, for the duration of these hostilities, individuals legitimately determined to be Taliban combatants who "engaged in an armed conflict against the United States." If the record establishes that United States troops are still involved in active combat in Afghanistan, those detentions are part of the exercise of "necessary and appropriate force," and therefore are authorized by the AUMF.

Ex parte Milligan, 4 Wall. 2, 125 (1866), does not undermine our holding about the Government's authority to seize enemy combatants, as we define that term today. In that case, the Court made repeated reference to the fact that its inquiry into whether the military tribunal had jurisdiction to try and punish Milligan turned in large part on the fact that Milligan was not a prisoner of war, but a resident of Indiana arrested while at home there. That fact was central to its conclusion. Had Milligan been captured while he was assisting Confederate soldiers by carrying a rifle against Union troops on a Confederate battlefield, the holding of the Court might well have been different. The Court's repeated explanations that Milligan was not a prisoner of war suggest that had these different circumstances been present he could have been detained under military authority for the duration of the conflict, whether or not he was a citizen.

Quirin was a unanimous opinion. It both postdates and clarifies *Milligan,* providing us with the most apposite precedent that we have on the question of whether citizens may be detained in such circumstances. Brushing aside such precedent — particularly when doing so gives rise to a host of new questions never dealt with by this Court — is unjustified and unwise.

III

Even in cases in which the detention of enemy combatants is legally authorized, there remains the question of what process is constitutionally due to a citizen who disputes his enemy-combatant status. Hamdi argues that he is owed a meaningful and timely hearing and that "extra-judicial detention [that] begins and ends with the submission of an affidavit based on third-hand hearsay" does not comport with the Fifth and Fourteenth Amendments. The Government counters that any more process than was provided below would be both unworkable and "constitutionally intolerable." Our resolution of this dispute requires a careful examination both of the writ of habeas corpus, which Hamdi now seeks to employ as a mechanism of judicial review, and of the Due Process Clause, which informs the procedural contours of that mechanism in this instance.

A

Though they reach radically different conclusions on the process that ought to attend the present proceeding, the parties begin on common ground. All agree that, absent suspension, the writ of habeas corpus remains available to every individual detained within the United States. All agree suspension of the writ has not occurred here. Thus, it is undisputed that Hamdi was properly before an Article III court to challenge his detention under 28 U.S.C. § 2241. Further, all agree that § 2241 and its companion provisions provide at least a skeletal outline of the procedures to be afforded a petitioner in federal habeas review. Most notably, § 2243 provides that "the person detained may, under oath, deny any of the facts set forth in the return or allege any other material facts," and § 2246 allows the taking of evidence in habeas proceedings by deposition, affidavit, or interrogatories.

The simple outline of § 2241 makes clear both that Congress envisioned that habeas petitioners would have some opportunity to present and rebut facts and that courts in cases like this retain some ability to vary the ways in which they do so as mandated by due process. The Government recognizes the basic procedural protections required by the habeas statute, but asks us to hold that, given both the flexibility of the habeas mechanism and the circumstances presented in this case, the presentation of the Mobbs Declaration to the habeas court completed the required factual development. It suggests two separate reasons for its position that no further process is due.

B

First, the Government urges the adoption of the Fourth Circuit's holding below — that because it is "undisputed" that Hamdi's seizure took place in a combat zone, the habeas determination can be made purely as a matter of law, with no further hearing or factfinding necessary. This argument is easily rejected. [T]he circumstances surrounding Hamdi's seizure cannot in any way be characterized as "undisputed," as "those circumstances are neither conceded in fact, nor susceptible to concession in law, because Hamdi has not been permitted to speak for himself or even through counsel as to those circumstances." Further, the "facts" that constitute the alleged concession are insufficient to support Hamdi's detention. Under the definition of enemy combatant that we accept today as falling within the scope of Congress' authorization, Hamdi would need to be "part of or supporting forces hostile to the United States or coalition partners" and "engaged in an armed conflict against the United States" to justify his detention in the United States for the duration of the relevant conflict. The habeas petition states only that "when seized by the United States Government, Mr. Hamdi resided in Afghanistan." An assertion that one *resided* in a country in which combat operations are taking place is not a concession that one was "*captured* in a zone of active combat operations in a foreign theater of war," and certainly is not a concession that one was "part of or supporting forces hostile to the United States or coalition partners" and "engaged in an armed conflict against the United States." Accordingly, we reject any argument that Hamdi has made concessions that eliminate any right to further process.

C

The Government's second argument requires closer consideration. This is the argument that further factual exploration is unwarranted and inappropriate in light of the extraordinary constitutional interests at stake. Under the

Government's most extreme rendition of this argument, "respect for separation of powers and the limited institutional capabilities of courts in matters of military decision-making in connection with an ongoing conflict" ought to eliminate entirely any individual process, restricting the courts to investigating only whether legal authorization exists for the broader detention scheme. At most, the Government argues, courts should review its determination that a citizen is an enemy combatant under a very deferential "some evidence" standard. Under this review, a court would assume the accuracy of the Government's articulated basis for Hamdi's detention, as set forth in the Mobbs Declaration, and assess only whether that articulated basis was a legitimate one.

In response, Hamdi emphasizes that this Court consistently has recognized that an individual challenging his detention may not be held at the will of the Executive without recourse to some proceeding before a neutral tribunal to determine whether the Executive's asserted justifications for that detention have basis in fact and warrant in law. He argues that the Fourth Circuit inappropriately "ceded power to the Executive during wartime to define the conduct for which a citizen may be detained, judge whether that citizen has engaged in the proscribed conduct, and imprison that citizen indefinitely," and that due process demands that he receive a hearing in which he may challenge the Mobbs Declaration and adduce his own counter evidence. The District Court, agreeing with Hamdi, apparently believed that the appropriate process would approach the process that accompanies a criminal trial. It therefore disapproved of the hearsay nature of the Mobbs Declaration and anticipated quite extensive discovery of various military affairs. Anything less, it concluded, would not be "meaningful judicial review."

Both of these positions highlight legitimate concerns. And both emphasize the tension that often exists between the autonomy that the Government asserts is necessary in order to pursue effectively a particular goal and the process that a citizen contends he is due before he is deprived of a constitutional right. The ordinary mechanism that we use for balancing such serious competing interests, and for determining the procedures that are necessary to ensure that a citizen is not "deprived of life, liberty, or property, without due process of law," is the test that we articulated in *Mathews v. Eldridge,* 424 U.S. 319 (1976). *Mathews* dictates that the process due in any given instance is determined by weighing "the private interest that will be affected by the official action" against the Government's asserted interest, "including the function involved" and the burdens the Government would face in providing greater process. The *Mathews* calculus then contemplates a judicious balancing of these concerns, through an analysis of "the risk of an erroneous deprivation" of the private interest if the process were reduced and the "probable value, if any, of additional or substitute safeguards." We take each of these steps in turn.

1

It is beyond question that substantial interests lie on both sides of the scale in this case. Hamdi's "private interest . . . affected by the official action," is the most elemental of liberty interests — the interest in being free from physical detention by one's own government. We have always been careful not to 'minimize the importance and fundamental nature' of the individual's right to liberty, and we will not do so today.

Nor is the weight on this side of the *Mathews* scale offset by the circumstances of war or the accusation of treasonous behavior, for "it is clear that commitment for *any* purpose constitutes a significant deprivation of liberty that requires due process protection," and at this stage in the *Mathews* calculus, we consider the interest of the *erroneously* detained individual. Indeed, as *amicus* briefs from media and relief organizations emphasize, the risk of erroneous deprivation of a citizen's liberty in the absence of sufficient process here is very real (noting ways in which "the nature of humanitarian relief work and journalism present a significant risk of mistaken military detentions"). Moreover, as critical as the Government's interest may be in detaining those who actually pose an immediate threat to the national security of the United States during ongoing international conflict, history and common sense teach us that an unchecked system of detention carries the potential to become a means for oppression and abuse of others who do not present that sort of threat. Because we live in a society in which "mere public intolerance or animosity cannot constitutionally justify the deprivation of a person's physical liberty," our starting point for the *Mathews v. Eldridge* analysis is unaltered by the allegations surrounding the particular detainee or the organizations with which he is alleged to have associated. We reaffirm today the fundamental nature of a citizen's right to be free from involuntary confinement by his own government without due process of law, and we weigh the opposing governmental interests against the curtailment of liberty that such confinement entails.

2

On the other side of the scale are the weighty and sensitive governmental interests in ensuring that those who have in fact fought with the enemy during a war do not return to battle against the United States. As discussed above, the law of war and the realities of combat may render such detentions both necessary and appropriate, and our due process analysis need not blink at those realities. Without doubt, our Constitution recognizes that core strategic matters of warmaking belong in the hands of those who are best positioned and most politically accountable for making them. *Youngstown Sheet & Tube Co. v. Sawyer* (acknowledging "broad powers in military commanders engaged in day-to-day fighting in a theater of war").

The Government also argues at some length that its interests in reducing the process available to alleged enemy combatants are heightened by the practical difficulties that would accompany a system of trial-like process. In its view, military officers who are engaged in the serious work of waging battle would be unnecessarily and dangerously distracted by litigation half a world away, and discovery into military operations would both intrude on the sensitive secrets of national defense and result in a futile search for evidence buried under the rubble of war. To the extent that these burdens are triggered by heightened procedures, they are properly taken into account in our due process analysis.

3

Striking the proper constitutional balance here is of great importance to the Nation during this period of ongoing combat. But it is equally vital that our calculus not give short shrift to the values that this country holds dear or to the privilege that is American citizenship. It is during our most challenging and uncertain moments that our Nation's commitment to due process is most severely tested; and it is in those times that we must preserve our commitment at home to the principles for which we fight abroad. *See United States v. Robel,* 389 U.S. 258, 264 (1967) ("It would indeed be ironic if, in the name of national defense, we would sanction the subversion of one of those liberties . . . which makes the defense of the Nation worthwhile").

With due recognition of these competing concerns, we believe that neither the process proposed by the Government nor the process apparently envisioned by the District Court below strikes the proper constitutional balance when a United States citizen is detained in the United States as an enemy combatant. That is, "the risk of erroneous deprivation" of a detainee's liberty interest is unacceptably high under the Government's proposed rule, while some of the "additional or substitute procedural safeguards" suggested by the District Court are unwarranted in light of their limited "probable value" and the burdens they may impose on the military in such cases.

We therefore hold that a citizen-detainee seeking to challenge his classification as an enemy combatant must receive notice of the factual basis for his classification, and a fair opportunity to rebut the Government's factual assertions before a neutral decisionmaker.

At the same time, the exigencies of the circumstances may demand that, aside from these core elements, enemy combatant proceedings may be tailored to alleviate their uncommon potential to burden the Executive at a time of ongoing military conflict. Hearsay, for example, may need to be accepted as the most reliable available evidence from the Government in such a proceeding. Likewise, the Constitution would not be offended by a presumption in favor of the Government's evidence, so long as that presumption remained a rebuttable one and fair opportunity for rebuttal were provided. Thus, once the Government puts forth credible evidence that the habeas petitioner meets the enemy-combatant criteria, the onus could shift to the petitioner to rebut that evidence with more persuasive evidence that he falls outside the criteria. A burden-shifting scheme of this sort would meet the goal of ensuring that the errant tourist, embedded journalist, or local aid worker has a chance to prove military error while giving due regard to the Executive once it has put forth meaningful support for its conclusion that the detainee is in fact an enemy combatant. In the words of *Mathews*, process of this sort would sufficiently address the "risk of erroneous deprivation" of a detainee's liberty interest while eliminating certain procedures that have questionable additional value in light of the burden on the *Government.*

We think it unlikely that this basic process will have the dire impact on the central functions of warmaking that the Government forecasts. The parties agree that initial captures on the battlefield need not receive the process we have discussed here; that process is due only when the determination is made to *continue* to hold those who have been seized. The Government has made clear in its briefing that documentation regarding battlefield detainees already is kept in the ordinary course of military affairs. Any factfinding imposition created by requiring a knowledgeable affiant to summarize these records to an independent tribunal is a minimal one. Likewise, arguments that military officers ought not have to wage war under the threat of litigation lose much of their steam when factual disputes at enemy-combatant hearings are limited to the alleged combatant's acts. This focus meddles little, if at all, in the strategy or conduct of war, inquiring only into the appropriateness of continuing to detain an individual claimed to have taken up arms against the United States. While we accord the greatest respect and consideration to the judgments of military authorities in matters relating to the actual prosecution of a war, and recognize that the scope of that discretion necessarily is wide, it does not infringe on the core role of the military for the courts to exercise their own time-honored and constitutionally mandated roles of reviewing and resolving claims like those presented here.

In sum, while the full protections that accompany challenges to detentions in other settings may prove unworkable and inappropriate in the enemy-combatant setting, the threats to military operations posed by a basic system of independent review are not so weighty as to trump a citizen's core rights to challenge meaningfully the Government's case and to be heard by an impartial adjudicator.

D

In so holding, we necessarily reject the Government's assertion that separation of powers principles mandate a heavily circumscribed role for the courts in such circumstances. Indeed, the position that the courts must forgo any examination of the individual case and focus exclusively on the legality of the broader detention scheme cannot be mandated by any reasonable view of separation of powers, as this approach serves only to *condense* power into a single branch of government. We have long since made clear that a state of war is not a blank check for the President when it comes to the rights of the Nation's citizens. *Youngstown Sheet & Tube.* Whatever power the United States Constitution envisions for the Executive in its exchanges with other nations or with enemy organizations in times of conflict, it most assuredly envisions a role for all three branches when individual liberties are at stake. Likewise, we have made clear that, unless Congress acts to suspend it, the Great Writ of habeas corpus allows the Judicial Branch to play a necessary role in maintaining this delicate balance of governance, serving as an important judicial check on the Executive's discretion in the realm of detentions. Thus, while we do not question that our due process assessment must pay keen attention to the particular burdens faced by the Executive in the context of military action, it would turn our system of checks and balances on its head to suggest that a citizen could not make his way to court with a challenge to the factual basis for his detention by his government, simply because the Executive opposes making available such a challenge. Absent suspension of the writ by Congress, a citizen detained as an enemy combatant is entitled to this process.

Because we conclude that due process demands some system for a citizen detainee to refute his classification, the proposed "some evidence" standard is inadequate. Any process in which the Executive's factual assertions go wholly unchallenged or are simply presumed correct without any opportunity for the alleged combatant to demonstrate otherwise falls constitutionally short. Aside from unspecified "screening" processes, and military interrogations in which the Government suggests Hamdi could have contested his classification, Hamdi has received no process. An interrogation by one's captor, however effective an intelligence-gathering tool, hardly constitutes a constitutionally adequate factfinding before a neutral decisionmaker. Plainly, the "process" Hamdi has received is not that to which he is entitled under the Due Process Clause.

There remains the possibility that the standards we have articulated could be met by an appropriately authorized and properly constituted military tribunal. Indeed, it is notable that military regulations already provide for such process in related instances, dictating that tribunals be made available to determine the status of enemy detainees who assert prisoner-of-war status under the Geneva Convention. In the absence of such process, however, a court that receives a petition for a writ of habeas corpus from an alleged enemy combatant must itself ensure that the minimum requirements of due process are achieved. Both courts below recognized as much, focusing their energies on the question of whether Hamdi was due an opportunity to rebut the Government's case against him. The Government, too, proceeded on this assumption, presenting its affidavit and then seeking that it be evaluated under a deferential standard of review based on burdens that it alleged would accompany any greater process.

JUSTICE SOUTER, with whom JUSTICE GINSBURG joins, concurring in part, dissenting in part, and concurring in the judgment.

It is undisputed that the Government has not charged [Hamdi] with espionage, treason, or any other crime under domestic law. It is likewise undisputed that for one year and nine months, on the basis of an Executive designation of Hamdi as an "enemy combatant," the Government denied him the right to send or receive any communication beyond the prison where he was held and, in particular, denied him access to counsel to represent him. The Government asserts a right to hold Hamdi under these conditions indefinitely, that is, until the Government determines that the United States is no longer threatened by the terrorism exemplified in the attacks of September 11, 2001.

In these proceedings on Hamdi's petition, he seeks to challenge the facts claimed by the Government as the basis for holding him as an enemy combatant. And in this Court he presses the distinct argument that the Government's claim, even if true, would not implicate any authority for holding him that would satisfy 18 U.S.C. § 4001(a), which bars imprisonment or detention of a citizen "except pursuant to an Act of Congress."

The Government responds that Hamdi's incommunicado imprisonment as an enemy combatant seized on the field of battle falls within the President's power as Commander in Chief under the laws and usages of war, and is in any event authorized by two statutes. Accordingly, the Government contends that Hamdi has no basis for any challenge by petition for habeas except to his own status as an enemy combatant; and even that challenge may go no further than to enquire whether "some evidence" supports Hamdi's designation; if there is "some evidence," Hamdi should remain locked up at the discretion of the Executive. At the argument of this case, in fact, the Government went further and suggested that as long as a prisoner could challenge his enemy combatant designation when responding to interrogation during incommunicado detention he was accorded sufficient process to support his designation as an enemy combatant. Since on either view judicial enquiry so limited would be virtually worthless as a way to contest detention, the Government's concession of jurisdiction to hear Hamdi's habeas claim is more theoretical than practical, leaving the assertion of Executive authority close to unconditional.

The plurality rejects any such limit on the exercise of habeas jurisdiction and so far I agree with its opinion. The plurality does, however, accept the Government's position that if Hamdi's designation as an enemy combatant is correct, his detention (at least as to some period) is authorized by an Act of Congress as required by § 4001(a), that is, by the Authorization for Use of Military Force. Here, I disagree and respectfully dissent. The Government has failed to demonstrate that the Force Resolution authorizes the detention complained of here even on the facts the Government claims. If the Government raises nothing further than the record now shows, the Non-Detention Act entitles Hamdi to be released.

The threshold issue is how broadly or narrowly to read the Non-Detention Act, the tone of which is severe: "No citizen shall be imprisoned or otherwise detained by the United States except pursuant to an Act of Congress." Should the severity of the Act be relieved when the Government's stated factual justification for incommunicado detention is a war on terrorism, so that the Government may be said to act "pursuant" to congressional terms that fall short of explicit authority to imprison individuals? With one possible though important qualification [relating to international law on treatment of prisoners, which is omitted here], the answer has to be no. For a number of reasons, the prohibition within § 4001(a) has to be read broadly to accord the statute a long reach and to impose a burden of justification on the Government.

First, the circumstances in which the Act was adopted point the way to this interpretation. The provision superseded a cold-war statute, the Emergency Detention Act of 1950, which had authorized the Attorney General, in time of emergency, to detain anyone reasonably thought likely to engage in espionage or sabotage. That statue was repealed in 1971 out of fear that it could authorize a repetition of the World War II internment of citizens of Japanese ancestry. Congress sought to preclude another episode like the one described in *Korematsu v. United States*.

When, therefore, Congress repealed the 1950 Act and adopted § 4001(a) for the purpose of avoiding another *Korematsu*, it intended to preclude reliance on vague congressional authority [such as had been relied upon in the Japanese internment] as authority for the detention or imprisonment at the discretion of the Executive. In requiring that any Executive detention be "pursuant to an Act of Congress," then, Congress necessarily meant to require a congressional enactment that clearly authorized detention or imprisonment.

Second, When Congress passed § 4001(a), it was acting in light of an interpretive regime that subjected enactments limiting liberty in wartime to the requirement of a clear statement and it presumably intended § 4001(a) to be read accordingly.

Finally, even if history had spared us the cautionary example of the internments in World War II, even if there had been no *Korematsu*, there would be a compelling reason to read § 4001(a) to demand manifest authority to detain before detention is authorized. The defining character of American constitutional government is its constant tension between security and liberty, serving both by partial helpings of each. In a government of separated powers, deciding finally on what is a reasonable degree of guaranteed liberty whether in peace or war (or some condition in between) is not well entrusted to the Executive Branch of Government, whose particular responsibility is to maintain security. For reasons of inescapable human nature, the branch of the Government asked to counter a serious threat is not the branch on which to rest the Nation's entire reliance in striking the balance between the will to win and the cost in liberty on the way to victory; the responsibility for security will naturally amplify the claim that security legitimately raises. A reasonable balance is more likely to be reached on the judgment of a different branch, just as Madison said in remarking that "the constant aim is to divide and arrange the several offices in such a manner as that each may be a check on the other — that the private interest of every individual may be a sentinel over the public rights." THE FEDERALIST NO. 51. Hence the need for an assessment by Congress before citizens are subject to lockup, and likewise the need for a clearly expressed congressional resolution of the competing claims.

Next, there is the Government's claim, accepted by the Court, that the terms of the Force Resolution are adequate to authorize detention of an enemy combatant under the circumstances described, a claim the Government fails to support sufficiently to satisfy § 4001(a) as read to require a clear statement of authority to detain. Since the Force Resolution was adopted one week after the attacks of September 11, 2001, it naturally speaks with some generality, but its focus is clear, and that is on the use of military power. It is fairly read to authorize the use of armies and weapons, whether against other armies or individual terrorists. But it never so much as uses the word detention, and there is no reason to think Congress might have perceived any need to augment Executive power to deal with dangerous citizens within the United States, given the well-stocked statutory arsenal of defined criminal offenses covering the gamut of actions that a citizen sympathetic to terrorists might commit.

Because I find Hamdi's detention forbidden by § 4001(a) and unauthorized by the Force Resolution, I would not reach any questions of what process he may be due in litigating disputed issues in a proceeding under the habeas statute or prior to the habeas enquiry itself. For me, it suffices that the Government has failed to justify holding him in the absence of a further Act of Congress, criminal charges, a showing that the detention conforms to the laws of war, or a demonstration that § 4001(a) is unconstitutional. I would therefore vacate the judgment of the Court of Appeals and remand for proceedings consistent with this view.

Since this disposition does not command a majority of the Court, however, the need to give practical effect to the conclusions of eight members of the Court rejecting the Government's position calls for me to join with the plurality in ordering remand on terms closest to those I would impose. Although I think litigation of Hamdi's status as an enemy combatant is unnecessary, the terms of the plurality's remand will allow Hamdi to offer evidence that he is not an enemy combatant, and he should at the least have the benefit of that opportunity.

It should go without saying that in joining with the plurality to produce a judgment, I do not adopt the plurality's resolution of constitutional issues that I would not reach. It is not that I could disagree with the plurality's determinations (given the plurality's view of the Force Resolution) that someone in Hamdi's position is entitled at a minimum to notice of the Government's claimed factual basis for holding him, and to a fair chance to rebut it before a neutral decision maker; nor, of course, could I disagree with the plurality's affirmation of Hamdi's right to counsel. On the other hand, I do not mean to imply agreement that the Government could claim an evidentiary presumption casting the burden of rebuttal on Hamdi, or that an opportunity to litigate before a military tribunal might obviate or truncate enquiry by a court on habeas.

Subject to these qualifications, I join with the plurality in a judgment of the Court vacating the Fourth Circuit's judgment and remanding the case.

JUSTICE SCALIA, with whom JUSTICE STEVENS joins, dissenting.

Petitioner, a presumed American citizen, has been imprisoned without charge or hearing in the Norfolk and Charleston Naval Brigs for more than two years, on the allegation that he is an enemy combatant who bore arms against his country for the Taliban. His father claims to the contrary, that he is an inexperienced aid worker caught in the wrong place at the wrong time. This case brings into conflict the competing demands of national security and our citizens' constitutional right to personal liberty. Although I share the Court's evident unease as it seeks to reconcile the two, I do not agree with its resolution.

Where the Government accuses a citizen of waging war against it, our constitutional tradition has been to prosecute him in federal court for treason or some other crime. Where the exigencies of war prevent that, the Constitution's Suspension Clause, allows Congress to relax the usual protections temporarily. Absent suspension, however, the Executive's assertion of military exigency has not been thought sufficient to permit detention without charge. No one contends that the congressional Authorization for Use of Military Force, on which the Government relies to justify its actions here, is an implementation of the Suspension Clause. Accordingly, I would reverse the decision below.

I

The very core of liberty secured by our Anglo-Saxon system of separated powers has been freedom from indefinite imprisonment at the will of the Executive. Blackstone stated this principle clearly:

> Of great importance to the public is the preservation of this personal liberty: for if once it were left in the power of any, the highest, magistrate to imprison arbitrarily whomever he or his officers thought proper . . . there would soon be an end of all other rights and immunities. . . . To bereave a man of life, or by violence to confiscate his estate, without accusation or trial, would be so gross and notorious an act of despotism, as must at once convey the alarm of tyranny throughout the whole kingdom. But confinement of the person, by secretly hurrying him to gaol, where his sufferings are unknown or forgotten; is a less public, a less striking, and therefore a more dangerous engine of arbitrary government. . . .
>
> To make imprisonment lawful, it must either be, by process from the courts of judicature, or by warrant from some legal officer, having authority to commit to prison; which warrant must be in writing, under the hand and seal of the magistrate, and express the causes of the commitment, in order to be examined into (if necessary) upon a *habeas corpus*. If there be no cause expressed, the gaoler is not bound to detain the prisoner.

1 W. BLACKSTONE, COMMENTARIES ON THE LAWS OF ENGLAND 132–133 (1765) (hereinafter Blackstone).

These words were well known to the Founders. Hamilton quoted from this very passage in THE FEDERALIST NO. 84. The two ideas central to Blackstone's understanding — due process as the right secured, and habeas corpus as the instrument by which due process could be insisted upon by a citizen illegally imprisoned — found expression in the Constitution's Due Process and Suspension Clauses.

The gist of the Due Process Clause, as understood at the founding and since, was to force the Government to follow those common-law procedures traditionally deemed necessary before depriving a person of life, liberty, or property. When a citizen was deprived of liberty because of alleged criminal conduct, those procedures typically required committal by a magistrate followed by indictment and trial. The Due Process Clause "in effect affirms the right of trial according to the process and proceedings of the common law."

To be sure, certain types of permissible *non*criminal detention — that is, those not dependent upon the contention that the citizen had committed a criminal act — did not require the protections of criminal procedure. However, these fell into a limited number of well-recognized exceptions — civil commitment of the mentally ill, for example, and temporary detention in quarantine of the infectious. It is unthinkable that the Executive could render otherwise criminal grounds for detention noncriminal merely by disclaiming an intent to prosecute, or by asserting that it was incapacitating dangerous offenders rather than punishing wrongdoing.

These due process rights have historically been vindicated by the writ of habeas corpus. In England before the founding, the writ developed into a tool for challenging executive confinement. It was not always effective. [As a result, the Habeas Corpus Act of 1679 added additional protections.]

The writ of habeas corpus was preserved in the Constitution — the only common-law writ to be explicitly mentioned. Hamilton lauded "the establishment of the writ of *habeas corpus*" in his Federalist defense as a means to protect against "the practice of arbitrary imprisonments . . . in all ages, [one of] the favourite and most formidable instruments of tyranny." THE FEDERALIST NO. 84. Indeed, availability of the writ under the new Constitution (along with the requirement of trial by jury in criminal cases) was his basis for arguing that additional, explicit procedural protections were unnecessary.

II

The allegations here, of course, are no ordinary accusations of criminal activity. Yaser Esam Hamdi has been imprisoned because the Government believes he participated in the waging of war against the United States. The relevant question, then, is whether there is a different, special procedure for imprisonment of a citizen accused of wrongdoing *by aiding the enemy in wartime*.

A

JUSTICE O'CONNOR, writing for a plurality of this Court, asserts that captured enemy combatants (other than those suspected of war crimes) have traditionally been detained until the cessation of hostilities and then released. That is probably an accurate description of wartime practice with respect to enemy *aliens*. The tradition with respect to American citizens, however, has been quite different. Citizens aiding the enemy have been treated as traitors subject to the criminal process.

The modern treason statute is 18 U.S.C. § 2381; it basically tracks the language of the constitutional provision. Other provisions of Title 18 criminalize various acts of warmaking and adherence to the enemy. The only citizen other than Hamdi known to be imprisoned in connection with military hostilities in Afghanistan against the United States *was* subjected to criminal process and convicted upon a guilty plea. *See United States v. Lindh,* 212 F. Supp. 2d 541 (ED Va. 2002).

B

There are times when military exigency renders resort to the traditional criminal process impracticable. English law accommodated such exigencies by allowing legislative suspension of the writ of habeas corpus for brief periods.

Our Federal Constitution contains a provision explicitly permitting suspension, but limiting the situations in which it may be invoked: "The privilege of the Writ of Habeas Corpus shall not be suspended, unless when in Cases of Rebellion or Invasion the public Safety may require it." Although this provision does not state that suspension must be effected by, or authorized by, a legislative act, it has been so understood, consistent with English practice and the Clause's placement in Article I.

The Suspension Clause was by design a safety valve, the Constitution's only "express provision for exercise of extraordinary authority because of a crisis," *Youngstown Sheet & Tube Co. v. Sawyer* (Jackson, J., concurring). Very early in the Nation's history, President Jefferson unsuccessfully sought a suspension of habeas corpus to deal with Aaron Burr's conspiracy to overthrow the Government. During the Civil War, Congress passed its first Act authorizing Executive suspension of the writ of habeas corpus, to the relief of those many who thought President Lincoln's unauthorized proclamations of suspension unconstitutional. Later Presidential proclamations of suspension relied upon the congressional authorization. During Reconstruction, Congress passed the Ku Klux Klan Act, which included a provision authorizing suspension of the writ, invoked by President Grant in quelling a rebellion in nine South Carolina counties.

III

Of course the extensive historical evidence of criminal convictions and habeas suspensions does not *necessarily* refute the Government's position in this case. When the writ is suspended, the Government is entirely free from judicial oversight. It does not claim such total liberation here, but argues that it need only produce what it calls "some evidence" to satisfy a habeas court that a detained individual is an enemy combatant. Even if suspension of the writ on the one hand, and committal for criminal charges on the other hand, have been the only *traditional* means of dealing with citizens who levied war against their own country, it is theoretically possible that the Constitution does not *require* a choice between these alternatives.

I believe, however, that substantial evidence does refute that possibility. First, the text of the 1679 Habeas Corpus Act makes clear that indefinite imprisonment on reasonable suspicion is not an available option of treatment for those accused of aiding the enemy, absent a suspension of the writ. In the United States, this Act was read as "enforcing the common law," and shaped the early understanding of the scope of the writ.

Writings from the founding generation also suggest that, without exception, the only constitutional alternatives are to charge the crime or suspend the writ. President Lincoln, when he purported to suspend habeas corpus without congressional authorization during the Civil War, apparently did not doubt that suspension was required if the prisoner was to be held without criminal trial. In his famous message to Congress on July 4, 1861, he argued only that he could suspend the writ, not that even without suspension, his imprisonment of citizens without criminal trial was permitted.

Further evidence comes from this Court's decision in *Ex parte Milligan*. There, the Court issued the writ to an American citizen who had been tried by military commission for offenses that included conspiring to overthrow the Government, seize munitions, and liberate prisoners of war. The Court rejected in no uncertain terms the Government's assertion that military jurisdiction was proper "under the laws and usages of war":

> It can serve no useful purpose to inquire what those laws and usages are, whence they originated, where found, and on whom they operate;

> they can never be applied to citizens in states which have upheld the authority of the government, and where the courts are open and their process unobstructed.

Milligan is not exactly this case, of course, since the petitioner was threatened with death, not merely imprisonment. But the reasoning and conclusion of *Milligan* logically cover the present case. The Government justifies imprisonment of Hamdi on principles of the law of war and admits that, absent the war, it would have no such authority. But if the law of war cannot be applied to citizens where courts are open, then Hamdi's imprisonment without criminal trial is no less unlawful than Milligan's trial by military tribunal.

IV

The Government argues that our more recent jurisprudence ratifies its indefinite imprisonment of a citizen within the territorial jurisdiction of federal courts. It places primary reliance upon *Ex parte Quirin,* a World War II case upholding the trial by military commission of eight German saboteurs, one of whom, Hans Haupt, was a U.S. citizen. The case was not this Court's finest hour. The Court upheld the commission and denied relief in a brief *per curiam* issued the day after oral argument concluded; a week later the Government carried out the commission's death sentence upon six saboteurs, including Haupt. The Court eventually explained its reasoning in a written opinion issued several months later.

Only three paragraphs of the Court's lengthy opinion dealt with the particular circumstances of Haupt's case. The Government argued that Haupt, like the other petitioners, could be tried by military commission under the laws of war. In agreeing with that contention, *Quirin* purported to interpret the language of *Milligan* quoted above (the law of war "can never be applied to citizens in states which have upheld the authority of the government, and where the courts are open and their process unobstructed") in the following manner:

> Elsewhere in its opinion . . . the Court was at pains to point out that Milligan, a citizen twenty years resident in Indiana, who had never been a resident of any of the states in rebellion, was not an enemy belligerent either entitled to the status of a prisoner of war or subject to the penalties imposed upon unlawful belligerents. We construe the Court's statement as to the inapplicability of the law of war to Milligan's case as having particular reference to the facts before it. From them the Court concluded that Milligan, not being a part of or associated with the armed forces of the enemy, was a non-belligerent, not subject to the law of war . . . .

[E]ven if *Quirin* gave a correct description of *Milligan*, or made an irrevocable revision of it, *Quirin* would still not justify denial of the writ here. In *Quirin* it was uncontested that the petitioners were members of enemy forces. They were "*admitted* enemy invaders," and it was "undisputed" that they had landed in the United States in service of German forces. The specific holding of the Court was only that, "upon the *conceded* facts," the petitioners were "plainly within [the] boundaries" of military jurisdiction. But where those jurisdictional facts are *not* conceded — where the petitioner insists that he is *not* a belligerent — *Quirin* left the pre-existing law in place: Absent suspension of the writ, a citizen held where the courts are open is entitled either to criminal trial or to a judicial decree requiring his release.

V

It follows from what I have said that Hamdi is entitled to a habeas decree requiring his release unless (1) criminal proceedings are promptly brought, or (2) Congress has suspended the writ of habeas corpus. A suspension of the writ could, of course, lay down conditions for continued detention, similar to those that today's opinion prescribes under the Due Process Clause. But there is a world of difference between the people's representatives' determining the need for that suspension (and prescribing the conditions for it), and this Court's doing so.

The plurality finds justification for Hamdi's imprisonment in the Authorization for Use of Military Force. [The AUMF] is not remotely a congressional suspension of the writ, and no one claims that it is. Contrary to the plurality's view, I do not think this statute even authorizes detention of a citizen with the clarity necessary to satisfy the interpretive canon that statutes should be construed so as to avoid grave constitutional concerns or with the clarity necessary to overcome the statutory prescription that "no citizen shall be imprisoned or otherwise detained by the United States except pursuant to an Act of Congress." 18 U.S.C. § 4001(a). But even if it did, I would not permit it to overcome Hamdi's entitlement to habeas corpus relief. The Suspension Clause of the Constitution, which carefully circumscribes the conditions under which the writ can be withheld, would be a sham if it could be evaded by congressional prescription of requirements *other than the common-law requirement of committal for criminal prosecution* that render the writ, though available, unavailing. If the Suspension Clause does not guarantee the citizen that he will either be tried or released, unless the conditions for suspending the writ exist and the grave action of suspending the writ has been taken; if it merely guarantees the citizen that he will not be detained unless Congress by ordinary legislation says he can be detained; it guarantees him very little indeed.

It should not be thought, however, that the plurality's evisceration of the Suspension Clause augments, principally, the power of Congress. As usual, the major effect of its constitutional improvisation is to increase the power of the Court. Having found a congressional authorization for detention of citizens where none clearly exists; and having discarded the categorical procedural protection of the Suspension Clause; the plurality then proceeds, under the guise of the Due Process Clause, to prescribe what procedural protections *it* thinks appropriate.

Having distorted the Suspension Clause, the plurality finishes up by transmogrifying the Great Writ — disposing of the present habeas petition by remanding for the District Court to "engage in a factfinding process that is both prudent and incremental." "In the absence of [the Executive's prior provision of procedures that satisfy due process], . . . a court that receives a petition for a writ of habeas corpus from an alleged enemy combatant must itself ensure that the minimum requirements of due process are achieved." This judicial remediation of executive default is unheard of. The role of habeas corpus is to determine the legality of executive detention, not to supply the omitted process necessary to make it legal. It is not the habeas court's function to make illegal detention legal by supplying a process that the Government could have provided, but chose not to. If Hamdi is being imprisoned in violation of the Constitution (because without due process of law), then his habeas petition should be granted; the Executive may then hand him over to the criminal authorities, whose detention for the purpose of prosecution will be lawful, or else must release him.

There is a certain harmony of approach in the plurality's making up for Congress's failure to invoke the Suspension Clause and its making up for the Executive's failure to apply what it says are needed procedures — an approach that reflects what might be called a Mr. Fix-it Mentality. The plurality seems to view it as its mission to Make Everything Come Out Right, rather than merely to decree the consequences, as far as individual rights are concerned, of the other two branches' actions and omissions. Has the Legislature failed to suspend the writ in the current dire emergency? Well, we will remedy that failure by prescribing the reasonable conditions that a suspension should have included. And has the Executive failed to live up to those reasonable conditions? Well, we will ourselves make that failure good, so that this dangerous fellow (if he is dangerous) need not be set free. The problem with this approach is not only that it steps out of the courts' modest and limited role in a democratic society; but that by repeatedly doing what it thinks the political branches ought to do it encourages their lassitude and saps the vitality of government by the people.

VI

Several limitations give my views in this matter a relatively narrow compass. They apply only to citizens, accused of being enemy combatants, who are detained within the territorial jurisdiction of a federal court. This is not likely to be a numerous group; currently we know of only two, Hamdi and Jose Padilla. Where the citizen is captured outside and held outside the United States, the constitutional requirements may be different. Moreover, even within the United States, the accused citizen-enemy combatant may lawfully be detained once prosecution is in progress or in contemplation. The Government has been notably successful in securing conviction, and hence long-term custody or execution, of those who have waged war against the state.

I frankly do not know whether these tools are sufficient to meet the Government's security needs, including the need to obtain intelligence through interrogation. It is far beyond my competence, or the Court's competence, to determine that. But it is not beyond Congress's. If the situation demands it, the Executive can ask Congress to authorize suspension of the writ — which can be made subject to whatever conditions Congress deems appropriate, including even the procedural novelties invented by the plurality today. To be sure, suspension is limited by the Constitution to cases of rebellion or invasion. But whether the attacks of September 11, 2001, constitute an "invasion," and whether those attacks still justify suspension several years later, are questions for Congress rather than this Court. If civil rights are to be curtailed during wartime, it must be done openly and democratically, as the Constitution requires, rather than by silent erosion through an opinion of this Court.

Many think it not only inevitable but entirely proper that liberty give way to security in times of national crisis — that, at the extremes of military exigency, *inter arma silent leges*. Whatever the general merits of the view that war silences law or modulates its voice, that view has no place in the interpretation and application of a Constitution designed precisely to confront war and, in a manner that accords with democratic principles, to accommodate it. Because the Court has proceeded to meet the current emergency in a manner the Constitution does not envision. I respectfully dissent.

JUSTICE THOMAS, dissenting.

The Executive Branch, acting pursuant to the powers vested in the President by the Constitution and with explicit congressional approval, has determined that Yaser Hamdi is an enemy combatant and should be detained. This detention falls squarely within the Federal Government's war powers, and we lack the expertise and capacity to second-guess that decision. As such, petitioners' habeas challenge should fail, and there is no reason to remand the case. The plurality reaches a contrary conclusion by failing adequately to consider basic principles of the constitutional structure as it relates to national security and foreign affairs and by using the balancing scheme of *Mathews v. Eldridge*. I do not think that the Federal Government's war powers can be balanced away by this Court. Arguably, Congress could provide for additional procedural protections, but until it does, we have no right to insist upon them. But even if I were to agree with the general approach the plurality takes, I could not accept the particulars. The plurality utterly fails to account for the Government's compelling interests and for our own institutional inability to weigh competing concerns correctly. I respectfully dissent.

I

"It is 'obvious and unarguable' that no governmental interest is more compelling than the security of the Nation." The national security, after all, is the primary responsibility and purpose of the Federal Government. But because the Founders understood that they could not foresee the myriad potential threats to national security that might later arise, they chose to create a Federal Government that necessarily possesses sufficient power to handle any threat to the security of the Nation.

The Founders intended that the President have primary responsibility — along with the necessary power — to protect the national security and to conduct the Nation's foreign relations. They did so principally because the structural advantages of a unitary Executive are essential in these domains. This is because "decision, activity, secrecy, and dispatch will generally characterise the proceedings of one man, in a much more eminent degree, than the proceedings of any greater number."

These structural advantages are most important in the national-security and foreign-affairs contexts. "Of all the cares or concerns of government, the direction of war most peculiarly demands those qualities which distinguish the exercise of power by a single hand." THE FEDERALIST No. 74 (A. Hamilton). Also for these reasons, John Marshall explained that "the President is the sole organ of the nation in its external relations, and its sole representative with foreign nations." To this end, the Constitution vests in the President "the executive Power," provides that he "shall be Commander in Chief of the" armed forces, and places in him the power to recognize foreign governments.

This Court has long recognized these features and has accordingly held that the President has *constitutional* authority to protect the national security and that this authority carries with it broad discretion.

Congress, to be sure, has a substantial and essential role in both foreign affairs and national security. But it is crucial to recognize that *judicial* interference in these domains destroys the purpose of vesting primary responsibility in a unitary Executive. Several points, made forcefully by Justice Jackson, are worth emphasizing. First, with respect to certain decisions relating to national security and foreign affairs, the courts simply lack the relevant information and expertise to second-guess determinations made by the President based on information properly withheld. Second, even if the courts could compel the Executive to produce the necessary information, such decisions are simply not amenable to judicial determination because "they are delicate, complex, and involve large elements of prophecy." Third, the Court has correctly recognized the primacy of the political branches in the foreign-affairs and national-security contexts.

For these institutional reasons and because "Congress cannot anticipate and legislate with regard to every possible action the President may find it necessary to take or every possible situation in which he might act," it should come as no surprise that "such failure of Congress . . . does not, 'especially . . . in the areas of foreign policy and national security,' imply 'congressional disapproval' of action taken by the Executive." *Dames & Moore v. Regan*. Rather, in these domains, the fact that Congress has provided the President with broad authorities does not imply — and the Judicial Branch should not infer — that Congress intended to deprive him of particular powers not specifically enumerated.

To be sure, the Court has at times held, in specific circumstances, that the military acted beyond its warmaking authority. But these cases are distinguishable in important ways. In *Ex parte Endo,* the Court held unlawful the detention of an admittedly law-abiding and loyal American of Japanese ancestry. It did so because the Government's asserted reason for the detention had nothing to do with the congressional and executive authorities upon which the Government relied. Those authorities permitted detention for the purpose of preventing espionage and sabotage and thus could not be pressed into service for detaining a loyal citizen. And in *Youngstown*, Justice Jackson emphasized that "Congress had not left seizure of private property an open field but had covered it by three statutory policies inconsistent with the seizure."

I acknowledge that the question whether Hamdi's executive detention is lawful is a question properly resolved by the Judicial Branch, though the question comes to the Court with the strongest presumptions in favor of the Government. The plurality agrees that Hamdi's detention is lawful if he is an enemy combatant. But the question whether Hamdi is actually an enemy combatant is "of a kind for which the Judiciary has neither aptitude, facilities nor responsibility and which has long been held to belong in the domain of political power not subject to judicial intrusion or inquiry." That is, although it is appropriate for the Court to determine the judicial question whether the President has the asserted authority, we lack the information and expertise to question whether Hamdi is actually an enemy combatant, a question the resolution of which is committed to other branches.

II

Although the President very well may have inherent authority to detain those arrayed against our troops, I agree with the plurality that we need not decide that question because Congress has authorized the President to do so. The Authorization for Use of Military Force (AUMF), authorizes the President to "use all necessary and appropriate force against those nations, organizations, or persons he determines planned, authorized, committed, or aided the terrorist attacks" of September 11, 2001.

The plurality, however, qualifies its recognition of the President's authority to detain enemy combatants in the war on terrorism in ways that are at odds with our precedent. Thus, the plurality relies primarily on Article 118 of the Geneva Convention (III) Relative to the Treatment of Prisoners of War, for the proposition that "it is a clearly established principle of the law of war that detention may last no longer than active hostilities." It then appears to limit the President's authority to detain by requiring that the record establish that United States troops are still involved in active combat in Afghanistan because, in that case, detention would be "part of the exercise of 'necessary and appropriate force.'" But I do not believe that we may diminish the Federal Government's war powers by reference to a treaty and certainly not to a treaty that does not apply. Further, we are bound by the political branches' determination that the United States is at war. And, in any case, the power to detain does not end with the cessation of formal hostilities.

Accordingly, the President's action here is "supported by the strongest of presumptions and the widest latitude of judicial interpretation." The question becomes whether the Federal Government (rather than the President acting alone) has power to detain Hamdi as an enemy combatant. More precisely, we must determine whether the Government may detain Hamdi given the procedures that were used.

III

I agree with the plurality that the Federal Government has power to detain those that the Executive Branch determines to be enemy combatants. But I do not think that the plurality has adequately explained the breadth of the President's authority to detain enemy combatants, an authority that includes making virtually conclusive factual findings. In my view, the structural considerations discussed above, as recognized in our precedent, demonstrate that we lack the capacity and responsibility to second-guess this determination.

In this context, due process requires nothing more than a good-faith executive determination. To be clear: The Court has held that an executive, acting pursuant to statutory and constitutional authority may, consistent with the Due Process Clause, unilaterally decide to detain an individual if the executive deems this necessary for the public safety *even if he is mistaken.* The Government's asserted authority to detain an individual that the President has determined to be an enemy combatant, at least while hostilities continue, comports with the Due Process Clause. As these cases also show, the Executive's decision that a detention is necessary to protect the public need not and should not be subjected to judicial second-guessing. Indeed, at least in the context of enemy-combatant determinations, this would defeat the unity, secrecy, and dispatch that the Founders believed to be so important to the warmaking function.

Justice Scalia relies heavily upon *Ex parte Milligan*. I admit that *Milligan* supports his position. But because the Executive Branch there, unlike here, did not follow a specific statutory mechanism provided by Congress, the Court did not need to reach the broader question of Congress' power, and its discussion on this point was arguably dicta. More importantly, the Court referred frequently and pervasively to the criminal nature of the proceedings instituted against Milligan. In fact, this feature serves to distinguish the state cases as well.

Although I do acknowledge that the reasoning of these cases might apply beyond criminal punishment, the punishment-nonpunishment distinction harmonizes all of the precedent. And, subsequent cases have at least implicitly distinguished *Milligan* in just this way. Because the Government does not detain Hamdi in order to punish him, as the plurality acknowledges, *Milligan* and the New York cases do not control.

NOTES

1. What does Justice Scalia, in dissent, mean when he asserts that "[i]t should not be thought . . . that the plurality's evisceration of the Suspension Clause augments, principally, the power of Congress. As usual the major effect of its constitutional improvisation is to increase the power of the Court"?

2. Examine the text of the Suspension Clause, Art. I, § 9, cl. 2. *Could* Congress have constitutionally invoked that provision in the *Hamdi* context?

3. According to Professor David Cole, writing prior to *Hamdi*, "[s]ince September 11 [2001], detention without trial has become, if not the norm, a huge exception. Thousands of people *not* involved in any terrorist activity have been locked up, many in secret, on pretextual charges or no charges at all, and effectively precluded from obtaining their release." David Cole, Enemy Aliens 46 (2003). Cole notes, however, that this has been achieved primarily with foreign nationals, while "[t]he few exceptions --Lindh, Padilla, and Hamdi

--have drawn highly disproportionate criticism, even though the charges and the evidence of Al Qaeda and Taliban ties appear to be stronger with respect to them than with respect to many of the foreign national detainees." *Id.* Should the two situations be treated differently, for constitutional purposes? *See also* David Cole, *The Priority of Morality: The Emergency Constitution's Blind Spot*, 113 YALE L. J. 1753, 1799 (2004) ("While the threat of future terrorism may well warrant rethinking constitutional structure, detaining innocent human beings to reassure a panicked public is not the sort of 'sweeping revision' the world, or the United States, should adopt."). Contrast Professor Cole's position with that taken in Bruce Ackerman, *The Emergency Constitution*, 113 YALE L. J. 1029, 1030 (2004): "To avoid a repeated cycle of repression, defenders of freedom must consider a more hard-headed doctrine — one that allows short-term emergency measures but draws the line against permanent restrictions. Above all else, we must prevent politicians from exploiting momentary panic to impose long-lasting limitations on liberty."

4. According to one commentator, "the due process regime the Court [in *Hamdi*] recommended provides only nominal protection for citizens seeking to challenge their detention." Nicholas Green, Note, *A "Blank Check": Judicial Review and the War Powers in Hamdi v. Rumsfeld*, 56 SO. CAR. L. REV. 581, 582 (2005). Rather, "[t]he Court's statements supporting judicial review act as a mask, hiding the broad authority that the Executive possesses and that the Court reinforced." *Id.* at 605. Do you agree?

5. Professors Bradley and Goldsmith have suggested that there are "two misconceptions relevant to interpreting the authority that Congress has granted in the AUMF. The first is that the powers being granted to the President are limited or truncated in some fashion because Congress has not declared war." The second is "that the powers granted to the President in the AUMF are limited or truncated in some fashion because an armed conflict with terrorists is not a 'real war.'" Curtis Bradley & Jack Goldsmith, *Congressional Authorization and the War on Terrorism*, 118 HARV. L. REV. 2047, 2056–57 (2005). They argue that "Presidents have exercised their full Commander-in-Chief powers in a number of military conflicts throughout U.S. history that involved many of the purportedly non-traditional elements present in the current conflict with terrorists." *Id.* at 2057.

In response, Professor Sunstein suggests that presidential power under the AUMF be determined by drawing an analogy to the deference given the executive branch in interpreting statutes under administrative law principles. Use of this approach leads him to conclude that "the President should have a great deal of discretion in interpreting ambiguities in the AUMF, subject to a constraint of reasonableness. The principal qualification is that if the President is infringing on constitutionally sensitive interests, the AUMF must be construed narrowly, whatever the President says." Cass Sunstein, *Administrative Law Goes to War*, 118 HARV. L. REV. 2663, 2664 (2005). Other contributions to the debate include Mark Tushnet, *Controlling Executive Power in the War on Terrorism*, 118 HARV. L. REV. 2673 (2005), and Curtis Bradley & Jack Goldsmith, *Rejoinder: The War on Terrorism: International Law, Clear Statement Requirements, and Constitutional Design*, 118 HARV. L. REV. 2683 (2005).

6. In *Rasul v. Bush*, 542 U.S. 466 (2004), the Court considered whether the U.S. District Courts have jurisdiction to adjudicate challenges to the detention of enemy foreign nationals who had been captured abroad and incarcerated at the United States Naval Base at Guantanamo Bay, Cuba, a territory over which, the Court noted, "the United States exercises plenary and exclusive jurisdiction but not 'ultimate sovereignty.' "A majority held that the District Court did, in fact, possess jurisdiction over the prisoners' habeas corpus actions, reversing both the District Court and Court of Appeals. The Court, in an opinion by Justice Stevens, held that the fact that the alien habeas petitioners who had been captured abroad were held in military custody did not bar district courts from exercising habeas jurisdiction. Justice Scalia, joined by two other justices dissented. "The consequences of this holding, as applied to aliens outside the country, is breathtaking," he argued, because "[o]ver the course of the last century, the United States has held millions of alien prisoners abroad. A great many of these prisoners would no doubt have complained about the circumstances of their capture and the terms of their confinement. The military is currently detaining over 600 prisoners at Guantanamo Bay alone; each detainee undoubtedly has complaints --real or contrived --about those terms and circumstances."

§ 4.04 PRIVILEGES AND IMMUNITIES IN THE SEPARATION OF POWERS

[A] EXECUTIVE PRIVILEGE

During the investigation of the break-in and cover-up of the Democratic National Committee headquarters at Watergate and other misconduct in the 1972 presidential election by the Senate Select Committee on Presidential Campaign Activities (the Watergate Committee), it was learned that President Nixon had recorded numerous presidential conversations on electronic tape. This touched off a new phase of the continuing controversy over the power of the Executive to withhold information from the coordinate branches of the government. Both the congressional committee and the Department of Justice's Special Prosecutor met executive opposition in their efforts to secure access to these tapes.

Dating back to its 1792 investigation of the disastrous St. Clair Expedition, Congress has sought, usually with success but sometimes with failure, information from the Executive. Since that time, the Executive has frequently claimed privilege to reject such demands. The modern assertion of a broad executive privilege against congressional demands is suggested by President Eisenhower's order to the Defense Department during the McCarthy-Army hearings in the 1950s:

> Because it is essential to efficient and effective administration that employees of the executive branch be in a position to be completely candid in advising with each other on official matters, and because it is not in the public interest that any of their conversations or communications be disclosed, you will instruct employees of your Department that in all of their appearances before the Subcommittee

of the Senate Committee on Government Operation, regarding the inquiry now before it, they are not to testify to any such conversations or communications or to produce any such document or reproductions. This principle must be maintained regardless of who would be benefitted by such disclosures.

I direct this action so as to maintain the proper separation of powers between the executive and legislative branches of the Government in accordance with my responsibilities and duties under the Constitution. This separation is vital to preclude the exercise of arbitrary power by any branch of the Government.

Similarly, litigation on behalf of or against the Government has spawned demands in the courts for information available only from the Executive.

Is the Executive subject to process issuing from the other branches? Does the Executive enjoy a constitutional privilege to withhold information? If there is a constitutional privilege, is it absolute or conditional? For example, can the courts review a claim of executive privilege consistent with separation of powers principles? Finally, how is the claim of executive privilege to be reconciled with the informational needs of the other branches?

UNITED STATES v. NIXON

418 U.S. 683, 94 S. Ct. 3090, 41 L. Ed. 2d 1039 (1974)

[On March 1, 1974, a federal grand jury in the District of Columbia indicted seven persons connected with the White House of conspiracy to defraud the United States and obstruct justice. While President Nixon was not indicted, he was named as an unindicted co-conspirator. The Watergate Special Prosecutor successfully moved for a subpoena duces tecum in the federal district court ordering the president to produce designated tapes, memoranda, and other papers relating to specified meetings between President Nixon and others. The President did release edited transcripts of some of the subpoenaed conversations but moved in court to quash the subpoena claiming "executive privilege."]

CHIEF JUSTICE BURGER delivered the opinion of the Court.

These cases present for review the denial of a motion, filed on behalf of the President of the United States, in the case of *United States v. Mitchell et al.* (D.C. Crim. No. 74-110), to quash a third-party subpoena duces tecum issued by the United States District Court for the District of Columbia, pursuant to Fed. Rule Crim. Proc. 17 (c). The subpoena directed the President to produce certain tape recordings and documents relating to his conversations with aides and advisers. The court rejected the President's claims of absolute executive privilege, of lack of jurisdiction, and of failure to satisfy the requirements of Rule 17(c). The President appealed to the Court of Appeals. We granted the United States' petition for certiorari before judgment, and also the President's responsive cross-petition for certiorari before judgment, because of the public importance of the issues presented and the need for their prompt resolution.

[The Court held that the district court's order was appealable since the President should not be required to disobey a court order to test its validity nor should a court be required to cite the President in order to invoke review.]

In the District Court, the President's counsel argued that the court lacked jurisdiction to issue the subpoena because the matter was an intra-branch dispute between a subordinate and superior officer of the Executive Branch and hence not subject to judicial resolution. That argument has been renewed in this Court with emphasis on the contention that the dispute does not present a "case" or "controversy" which can be adjudicated in the federal courts. The President's counsel argues that the federal courts should not intrude into areas committed to the other branches of Government. He views the present dispute as essentially a "jurisdictional" dispute within the Executive Branch which he analogizes to a dispute between two congressional committees. Since the Executive Branch has exclusive authority and absolute discretion to decide whether to prosecute a case, it is contended that a President's decision is final in determining what evidence is to be used in a given criminal case. Although his counsel concedes the President has delegated certain specific powers to the Special Prosecutor, he has not "waived nor delegated to the Special Prosecutor the President's duty to claim privilege as to all materials which fall within the President's inherent authority to refuse to disclose to any executive officer." The Special Prosecutor's demand for the items therefore presents, in the view of the President's counsel, a political question since it involves a "textually demonstrable" grant of power under Art. II.

The mere assertion of a claim of an "intra-branch dispute," without more, has never operated to defeat federal jurisdiction; justiciability does not depend on such a surface inquiry.

Our starting point is the nature of the proceeding for which the evidence is sought — here a pending criminal prosecution. It is a judicial proceeding in a federal court alleging violation of federal laws and is brought in the name of the United States as sovereign. Under the authority of Art. II, § 2, Congress has vested in the Attorney General the power to conduct the criminal litigation of the United States Government. It has also vested in him the power to appoint subordinate officers to assist him in the discharge of his duties. Acting pursuant to those statutes, the Attorney General has delegated the authority to represent the United States in these particular matters to a Special Prosecutor with unique authority and tenure. The regulation gives the Special Prosecutor explicit power to contest the invocation of executive privilege in the process of seeking evidence deemed relevant to the performance of these specially delegated duties.

So long as this regulation is extant it has the force of law. [I]t is theoretically possible for the Attorney General to amend or revoke the regulation defining the Special Prosecutor's authority. But he has not done so. So long as this regulation remains in force the Executive Branch is bound by it, and indeed the United States as the sovereign composed of the three branches is bound to respect and to enforce it. Moreover, the delegation of authority to the Special Prosecutor in this case is not an ordinary delegation by the Attorney General to a subordinate officer: with the authorization of the President, the Acting Attorney General provided in the regulation that the Special Prosecutor was not to be removed without the "consensus" of eight designated leaders of Congress.

The demands of and the resistance to the subpoena present an obvious controversy in the ordinary sense, but that alone is not sufficient to meet constitutional standards. In the constitutional sense, controversy means more than disagreement and conflict; rather it means the kind of controversy courts traditionally resolve. Here at issue is the production or nonproduction of specified evidence deemed by the Special Prosecutor to be relevant and admissible in a pending criminal case. It is sought by one official of the Government within the scope of his express authority; it is resisted by the Chief Executive on the ground of his duty to preserve the confidentiality of the communications of the President. Whatever the correct answer on the merits, these issues are "of a type which are traditionally justiciable." The independent Special Prosecutor with his asserted need for the subpoenaed material in the underlying criminal prosecution is opposed by the President with his steadfast assertion of privilege against disclosure of the material. This setting assures there is "that concrete adverseness which sharpens the presentation of issues upon which the court so largely depends for illumination of difficult constitutional questions." *Baker v. Carr*. Moreover, since the matter is one arising in the regular course of a federal criminal prosecution, it is within the traditional scope of Art. III power.

In light of the uniqueness of the setting in which the conflict arises, the fact that both parties are officers of the Executive Branch cannot be viewed as a barrier to justiciability. It would be inconsistent with the applicable law and regulation, and the unique facts of this case to conclude other than that the Special Prosecutor has standing to bring this action and that a justiciable controversy is presented for decision.

[The Court held that the prosecutor had made a sufficient showing, based on relevancy, admissibility and specificity to require production before trial. The denial of the President's motion to quash the subpoena was held to be consistent with Rule 17(c) of the Federal Rules of Criminal Procedure.]

Having determined that the requirements of Rule 17 (c) were satisfied, we turn to the claim that the subpoena should be quashed because it demands "confidential conversations between a President and his close advisors that it would be inconsistent with the public interest to produce." The first contention is a broad claim that the separation of powers doctrine precludes judicial review of a President's claim of privilege. The second contention is that if he does not prevail on the claim of absolute privilege, the court should hold as a matter of constitutional law that the privilege prevails over the subpoena duces tecum.

In the performance of assigned constitutional duties each branch of the Government must initially interpret the Constitution, and the interpretation of its powers by any branch is due great respect from the others. The President's counsel, as we have noted, reads the Constitution as providing an absolute privilege of confidentiality for all presidential communications. Many decisions of this Court, however, have unequivocally reaffirmed the holding of *Marbury v. Madison* that "it is emphatically the province and duty of the judicial department to say what the law is."

No holding of the Court has defined the scope of judicial power specifically relating to the enforcement of a subpoena for confidential presidential communications for use in a criminal prosecution, but other exercises of powers by the Executive Branch and the Legislative Branch have been found invalid as in conflict with the Constitution. Since this Court has consistently exercised the power to construe and delineate claims arising under express powers, it must follow that the Court has authority to interpret claims with respect to powers alleged to derive from enumerated powers.

Our system of government "requires that federal courts on occasion interpret the Constitution in a manner at variance with the construction given the document by another branch." *Powell v. McCormack*. Notwithstanding the deference each branch must accord the others, the "judicial power of the United States" vested in the federal courts by Art. III, § 1 of the Constitution can no more be shared with the Executive Branch than the Chief Executive, for example, can share with the Judiciary the veto power, or the Congress share with the Judiciary the power to override a presidential veto. Any other conclusion would be contrary to the basic concept of separation of powers and the checks and balances that flow from the scheme of a tripartite government. We therefore reaffirm that it is "emphatically the province and the duty" of this Court "to say what the law is" with respect to the claim of privilege presented in this case. *Marbury v. Madison*.

In support of his claim of absolute privilege, the President's counsel urges two grounds one of which is common to all governments and one of which is peculiar to our system of separation of powers. The first ground is the valid need for protection of communications between high government officials and those who advise and assist them in the performance of their manifold duties; the importance of this confidentiality is too plain to require further discussion. Human experience teaches that those who expect public dissemination of their remarks may well temper candor with a concern for appearances and for their own interests to the detriment of the decisionmaking process. Whatever the nature of the privilege of confidentiality of presidential communications in the exercise of Art. II powers the privilege can be said to derive from the supremacy of each branch within its own assigned area of constitutional duties. Certain powers and privileges flow from the nature of enumerated powers; the protection of the confidentiality of presidential communications has similar constitutional underpinnings.

The second ground asserted by the President's counsel in support of the claim of absolute privilege rests on the doctrine of separation of powers. Here it is argued that the independence of the Executive Branch within its own sphere, insulates a president from a judicial subpoena in an ongoing criminal prosecution, and thereby protects confidential presidential communications.

However, neither the doctrine of separation of powers, nor the need for confidentiality of high level communications, without more, can sustain an absolute, unqualified presidential privilege of immunity from judicial process under all circumstances. The President's need for complete candor and objectivity from advisers calls for great deference from the courts. However, when the privilege depends solely on the broad, undifferentiated claim of public interest in the confidentiality of such conversations, a confrontation with other values arises. Absent a claim of need to protect military, diplomatic or sensitive national security secrets, we find it difficult to accept the argument that even the very important interest in confidentiality of presidential communications is significantly diminished by production of such material for in camera inspection with all the protection that a district court will be obliged to provide.

The impediment that an absolute, unqualified privilege would place in the way of the primary constitutional duty of the judicial branch to do justice in criminal prosecutions would plainly conflict with the function of the courts under Art. III. In designing the structure of our Government and dividing and allocating the sovereign power among three coequal branches, the Framers of the Constitution sought to provide a comprehensive system, but the separate powers were not intended to operate with absolute independence. To read the Art. II powers of the President as providing an absolute privilege as against a subpoena essential to enforcement of criminal statutes on no more than a generalized claim of the public interest in confidentiality of nonmilitary and nondiplomatic discussions would upset the constitutional balance of "a workable government" and gravely impair the role of the courts under Art. III.

Since we conclude that the legitimate needs of the judicial process may outweigh presidential privilege, it is necessary to resolve those competing interests in a manner that preserves the essential functions of each branch. The expectation of a President to the confidentiality of his conversations and correspondence, like the claim of confidentiality of judicial deliberations, for example, has all the values to which we accord deference for the privacy of all citizens and added to those values the necessity for protection of the public interest in candid, objective, and even blunt or harsh opinions in presidential decisionmaking. A President and those who assist him must be free to explore alternatives in the process of shaping policies and making decisions and to do so in a way many would be unwilling to express except privately. These are the considerations justifying a presumptive privilege for presidential communications. The privilege is fundamental to the operation of government and inextricably rooted in the separation of powers under the Constitution. In *Nixon v. Sirica*, 487 F. 2d 700 (1973), the Court of Appeals held that such presidential communications are "presumptively privileged," and this position is accepted by both parties in the present litigation. We agree with Mr. Chief Justice Marshall's observation, therefore, that "in no case of this kind would a court be required to proceed against the President as against an ordinary individual." *United States v. Burr*, 25 Fed. Cas. 187, 191 (No. 14,694) (CCD Va. 1807).

But this presumptive privilege must be considered in light of our historic commitment to the rule of law. This is nowhere more profoundly manifest than in our view that "the twofold aim [of criminal justice] is that guilt shall not escape or innocence suffer." We have elected to employ an adversary system of criminal justice in which the parties contest all issues before a court of law. The need to develop all relevant facts in the adversary system is both fundamental and comprehensive. The ends of criminal justice would be defeated if judgments were to be founded on a partial or speculative presentation of the facts. The very integrity of the judicial system and public confidence in the system depend on full disclosure of all the facts, within the framework of the rules of evidence. To ensure that justice is done, it is imperative to the function of courts that compulsory process be available for the production of evidence needed either by the prosecution or by the defense. Only recently the Court restated the ancient proposition of law, albeit in the context of a grand jury inquiry rather than a trial, " 'that the public has a right to every man's evidence' except for those persons protected by a constitutional, common law, or statutory privilege." The privileges referred to by the Court are designed to protect weighty and legitimate competing interests.

In this case the President challenges a subpoena served on him as a third party requiring the production of materials for use in a criminal prosecution on the claim that he has a privilege against disclosure of confidential communications. He does not place his claim of privilege on the ground they are military or diplomatic secrets. As to these areas of Art. II duties the courts have traditionally shown the utmost deference to presidential responsibilities. No case of the Court, however, has extended this high degree of deference to a President's generalized interest in confidentiality. Nowhere in the Constitution, as we have noted earlier, is there any explicit reference to a privilege of confidentiality; yet to the extent this interest relates to the effective discharge of a President's powers, it is constitutionally based.

The right to the production of all evidence at a criminal trial similarly has constitutional dimensions. It is the manifest duty of the courts to vindicate those guarantees and to accomplish that it is essential that all relevant and admissible evidence be produced. In this case we must weigh the importance of the general privilege of confidentiality of presidential communications in performance of his responsibilities against the inroads of such a privilege on the fair administration of criminal justice.[19] The interest in preserving confidentiality is weighty indeed and entitled to great respect. However we cannot conclude that advisers will be moved to temper the candor of their remarks by the infrequent occasions of disclosure because of the possibility that such conversations will be called for in the context of a criminal prosecution.

On the other hand, the allowance of the privilege to withhold evidence that is demonstrably relevant in a criminal trial would cut deeply into the guarantee of due process of law and gravely impair the basic function of the courts. A President's acknowledged need for confidentiality in the communications of his office is general in nature, whereas the constitutional need for production of relevant evidence in a criminal proceeding is specific and central to the fair adjudication of a particular criminal case in the administration of justice. Without access to specific facts a criminal prosecution may be totally frustrated. The President's broad interest in confidentiality of communications will not be vitiated by disclosure of a limited number of conversations preliminarily shown to have some bearing on the pending criminal cases.

[19] We are not here concerned with the balance between the President's generalized interest in confidentiality and the need for relevant evidence in civil litigation, nor with that between the confidentiality interest and congressional demands for information, nor with the President's interest in preserving state secrets. We address only the conflict between the President's assertion of a generalized privilege of confidentiality against the constitutional need for relevant evidence to criminal trials

We conclude that when the ground for asserting privilege as to subpoenaed materials sought for use in a criminal trial is based only on the generalized interest in confidentiality, it cannot prevail over the fundamental demands of due process of law in the fair administration of criminal justice. The generalized assertion of privilege must yield to the demonstrated, specific need for evidence in a pending criminal trial. Here the District Court treated the material as presumptively privileged, proceeded to find that the Special Prosecutor had made a sufficient showing to rebut the presumption and ordered an in camera examination of the subpoenaed material. On the basis of our examination of the record we are unable to conclude that the District Court erred in ordering the inspection. Accordingly we affirm the order of the District Court that subpoenaed materials be transmitted to that court. We now turn to the important question of the District Court's responsibilities in conducting the in camera examination of presidential materials or communications delivered under the compulsion of the subpoena duces tecum.

Enforcement of the subpoena duces tecum was stayed pending this Court's resolution of the issues raised by the petitions for certiorari. Those issues now having been disposed of, the matter of implementation will rest with the District Court. "[T]he guard, furnished to [President] to protect him from being harassed by vexatious and unnecessary subpoenas, is to be looked for in the conduct of the [district] court after the subpoenas have issued; not in any circumstances which is to precede their being issued." *United States v. Burr*. Statements that meet the test of admissibility and relevance must be isolated; all other material must be excised. At this stage the District Court is not limited to representations of the Special Prosecutor as to the evidence sought by the subpoena; the material will be available to the District Court. It is elementary that in camera inspection of evidence is always a procedure calling for scrupulous protection against any release or publication of material not found by the court, at that stage, probably admissible in evidence and relevant to the issues of the trial for which it is sought. That being true of an ordinary situation, it is obvious that the District Court has a very heavy responsibility to see to it that presidential conversations, which are either not relevant or not admissible, are accorded that high degree of respect due the President of the United States. Mr. Chief Justice Marshall sitting as a trial judge in the *Burr* case was extraordinarily careful to point out that: "[I]n no case of this kind would a Court be required to proceed against the President as against an ordinary individual." Marshall's statement cannot be read to mean in any sense that a President is above the law, but relates to the singularly unique role under Art. II of a President's communications and activities, related to the performance of duties under that Article. Moreover, a President's communications and activities encompass a vastly wider range of sensitive material than would be true of any "ordinary individual." It is therefore necessary in the public interest to afford presidential confidentiality the greatest protection consistent with the fair administration of justice. The need for confidentiality even as to idle conversations with associates in which casual reference might be made concerning political leaders within the country or foreign statesmen is too obvious to call for further treatment. We have no doubt that the District Judge will at all times accord to presidential records that high degree of deference suggested in *United States v. Burr*, and will discharge his responsibility to see to it that until released to the Special Prosecutor no in camera material is revealed to anyone. This burden applies with even greater force to excised material; once the decision is made to excise, the material is restored to its privileged status and should be returned under seal to its lawful custodian.

Since this matter came before the Court during the pendency of a criminal prosecution, and on representations that time is of the essence, the mandate shall issue forthwith.

JUSTICE REHNQUIST took no part in the consideration or decision of these cases.

NOTES

1. *Cheney v. U.S. Dist. Court*, 542 U.S. 367 (2004). The Supreme Court held in *Cheney* that *Nixon*'s rejection of a broad claim of executive privilege did not apply in civil litigation in which the very purpose of the litigation was seeking disclosure of sensitive information. Shortly after entering office, President George W. Bush appointed a task force known as the National Energy Policy Development Group (NEPDG) to be chaired by Vice-President Cheney. Under federal law, a task force or advisory group that contains members from outside of government must disclose the membership and make public announcements of its meetings. The official members of the NEPDG were all government employees, but the Sierra Club and Judicial Watch filed suit alleging that a number of private sector executives were regularly consulted and became *de facto* members of the NEPDG. The lawsuit sought disclosure of membership and all deliberations of the group.

As part of plaintiffs' discovery request, the district court ordered the government officials, including the Vice-President, to disclose extensive information about meetings and documents related to the work of the NEPDG. The district court stated that any claims of executive privilege would be considered in relation to specific sensitive materials. The government officials sought a writ of mandamus from the court of appeals against this discovery order, which the court denied, and the government then appealed to the Supreme Court. Justice Kennedy's opinion for the Court emphasized that the executive officials were entitled to have their claim of executive privilege heard in general before discovery proceeded. He began by stating the basis of the court of appeals' denial of a broad claim of privilege:

If *Nixon* refused to recognize broad claims of confidentiality where the President had asserted executive privilege, the majority reasoned, *Nixon* must have rejected, *a fortiori*, petitioners' claim of discovery immunity where the privilege has not even been invoked. According to the majority, because the Executive Branch can invoke executive privilege to maintain the separation of powers, mandamus relief is premature.

This analysis, however, overlooks fundamental differences in the two cases. *Nixon* cannot bear the weight the Court of Appeals puts upon it. First, unlike this case, which concerns respondents' requests for information for use in a civil suit, *Nixon* involves the proper balance between the Executive's interest in the confidentiality of its communications and the "constitutional need for production of relevant evidence in a criminal proceeding." The Court's decision was explicit that it was "not . . . concerned with the balance between the President's generalized interest in confidentiality and the need for relevant evidence in civil litigation . . . . We address only the conflict between the President's assertion of a generalized privilege of confidentiality and the constitutional need for relevant evidence in criminal trials."

To be sure, *Nixon* held that the President cannot, through the assertion of a "broad [and] undifferentiated" need for confidentiality and the invocation of an "absolute, unqualified" executive privilege, withhold information in the face of subpoena orders. It did so, however, only after the party requesting the information — the special prosecutor — had satisfied his burden of showing the propriety of the requests. Here, as the Court of Appeals acknowledged, the discovery requests are anything but appropriate. They provide respondents all the disclosure to which they would be entitled in the event they prevail on the merits, and much more besides. In these circumstances, *Nixon* does not require the Executive Branch to bear the onus of critiquing the unacceptable discovery requests line by line.

2. *The Nixon precedent.* What relevance, if any, did President Nixon's alleged personal involvement in Watergate have on the Court's reasoning? Was it important that impeachment proceedings were underway? Is the unanimity of the result, without any concurrences, surprising? It is frequently argued that the Court failed to make a reasoned case for the propositions it announced. "[I]ts major pronouncements are essentially *ex cathedra*, its analysis of the major issues simplistic, and its doctrines supported far more by the fiat of the Justices' commissions than by the weight of either learning or reasoning." Paul Mishkin, *Great Cases and Soft Law: A Comment on* United States v. Nixon, 22 UCLA L. REV. 76 (1974). See also Akhil Amar, *Nixon's Shadow,* 83 MINN. L. REV. 1405 (1999), arguing that "the Tapes Case opinion reflected a troubling imperialism of its own-judicial imperialism-and featured remarkably sloppy reasoning."

It has been argued that the Court in *Nixon* relies too heavily on *Marbury v. Madison*, drawing from it "a misleadingly broad view of judicial competence, exclusivity and supremacy." Noting the role of Congress in impeachment controversies, Professor Gunther asserts "that the Court is not the ultimate arbiter of all constitutional questions and that the Court is not the only appropriate tribunal to resolve conflicts between the other branches." Gerald Gunther, *Judicial Hegemony and Legislative Autonomy: The Nixon Case and the Impeachment Process*, 22 UCLA L. REV. 30, 33, 37 (1974).

3. *The sources of executive privilege.* Professor Berger begins his work on executive privilege with this assertion:

> "Executive privilege" — the President's claim of constitutional authority to withhold information from Congress [or the judicial branch] — is a myth. Unlike most myths, the origins of which are lost in the mists of antiquity, "executive privilege" is a product of the nineteenth century, fashioned by a succession of presidents who created "precedents" to suit the occasion.

RAOUL BERGER, EXECUTIVE PRIVILEGE: A CONSTITUTIONAL MYTH 1 (1974).

The President's claim to resist disclosure has been based on history, recognition of an evidentiary privilege, and on the Constitution, in the separation of powers principle and as implied from express Article II powers.

a. The history of confrontation. Proponents of executive privilege place stress on the historical claims of presidents dating back to Washington to withhold information from Congress. According to one commentator, in modern times "President Eisenhower was particularly robust in his use of such claims. One factor in establishment of the Eisenhower doctrine of privilege was his commendable resistance to the army-McCarthy hearings." Jonathan Turley, *Paradise Lost: The Clinton Administration and the Erosion of Executive Privilege,* 60 MD. L. REV. 205, 238 (2001). Assuming that presidents have frequently claimed privilege against congressional intrusions successfully, how much weight should be given such precedent? Can custom and usage, uncontested in the courts, establish constitutional principles? Recall the language of United States v. Midwest Oil Co., 236 U.S. 459, 472–73 (1915):

> [G]overnment is a practical affair intended for practical men. Both officers, lawmakers, and citizens naturally adjust themselves to any long-continued action of the Executive Department — on the presumption that unauthorized acts would not have been allowed to be so often repeated as to crystallize into a regular practice. That presumption is not reasoning in a circle but the basis of a wise and quieting rule that in determining the meaning of a statute for the existence of a power, weight shall be given to the usage itself — even when the validity of the practice is the subject of investigation.

But it has been suggested that the use of acquiescence as implied authorization "is permissible only in the presence of certain key elements. Specifically, there must exist a custom comprised of acts of which the relevant nonacting branch is aware. There is simply no persuasive rationale for equating bare congressional silence with consent." Michael Glennon, *The Use of Custom in Resolving Separation of Powers Disputes*, 64 B.U.L. REV. 109, 148 (1984).

b. Evidentiary privilege. Executive claims for nondisclosure have also been based on common law and statute. *See, e.g., Environmental Protection Agency v. Mink*, 410 U.S. 73 (1973) (recognition of executive privilege for confidential information in the Freedom of Information Act). It has been claimed for military and state secrets, informers' identity, confidential reports and communications. There seems to be agreement that an evidentiary privilege is conditional and that the opposing interests in a particular case can be weighed by a court.

c. Separation of powers. Does the separation of powers principle support the claim for executive privilege in domestic matters against judicial demands for information? Against congressional demands? In Nixon v. Sirica, 487 F.2d 700 (D.C. Cir. 1973), the court upheld, with modifications, a district court order to the President to produce certain taped recordings for *in camera* inspection to determine if they were privileged. In resisting the subpoena the President stated, in part, that "[i]n doing so [he followed] the example of a long line of [his] predecessors as President of the United States who have consistently adhered to the position that the President is not subject to compulsory process from the courts." Arguing that "[t]he independence of the three Branches of our government is at the very heart of our Constitutional system," he contended that "[i]t would be wholly impermissible for the President to seek to compel some particular action by the courts" and it followed that "[i]t is equally impermissible for the courts to seek to compel some particular action from the President." He therefore concluded "that it would be inconsistent with the public interest and with the Constitutional position of the Presidency to make available recordings of meetings and telephone conversations in which I was a participant and I must respectfully decline to do so."

Does the separation of powers principle require an absolute independence of each of the branches from inquiry or supervision of the others? The ACLU amicus brief in *United States v. Nixon*, argued that "no branch is entirely 'master in its own house.' Each branch is subject to checks and balance from the others, and the separation of powers depends on interaction not isolation."

d. Implied powers. Do the Article II powers support executive privilege? The President's brief in the *Senate Select Committee* litigation [note 4 below], made this argument:

> The § 1 grant of "executive power" solely to the President is the most obvious and demonstrable source for the heretofore unchallenged right of the President to invoke executive privilege whenever the President deems it appropriate. Such an exercise of executive power is entirely consistent with the unbroken tradition of executive independence from legislative and judicial interference.

The brief then used Article II, § 2, empowering the President to require, in writing, the opinions of his principal officers in any subject.

> What the Senate Committee does not comprehend, although obvious to the Founding Fathers, is that the power to seek and receive advice would be a useless and empty power if the President could not keep his own counsel free from the review or scrutiny of the courts or the Congress. The very manner in which this inherent § 2 grant was made independent of Congressional interference bears witness to the intent of the Framers of the Constitution to preserve inviolate the confidentiality of the Executive Branch.

The President's counsel then considered Article II, § 3 which charges the President "from time to time [to] give to the Congress Information of the State of the Union."

> This vests in the President, not in the subpoena power of a Senate Committee, the power to determine when and what information he will provide to Congress. The same section imposes on the President the duty "to take care that the Laws be faithfully executed." As the President has clearly and forcefully maintained, the meetings and the conversations that the Senate Committee seeks to make public were

> participated in by the President pursuant to this Constitutional mandate. A performance of this executive duty cannot be brought under legal compulsion.

4. *Congressional demands.* *United States v. Nixon* deals only with special prosecutor demands for executive information to be used in a criminal trial. What is the status of executive claims of privilege against congressional demands for information?

> Executive privilege is at once the most refined form of government secrecy and the most direct executive challenge to Congress. Not only does executive privilege often interfere with the legislative work of Congress, but it has come to symbolize the troubled relations between Congress and the President and to identify their points of sharpest conflict.

Norman Dorsen & John Shattuck, *Executive Privilege, The Congress and the Courts*, 35 Ohio St. L.J. 1, 7 (1974).

In *Senate Select Comm. on Presidential Campaign Activities v. Nixon*, 498 F.2d 725 (D.C. Cir. 1974), the Watergate Committee had issued two subpoenas to the President: (1) for five specified tape recordings of conversations between President Nixon and John Dean; and, (2) for all records concerning the involvement of 25 named persons in any alleged criminal acts in connection with the 1972 presidential election. President Nixon claimed executive privilege, citing the need for confidentiality and the possible prejudicial effects on the Watergate criminal prosecution of public disclosure.

The district court quashed the second subpoena as too vague and conclusory to permit a meaningful response especially given the stringent requirements suggested by *Nixon v. Sirica* when a claim of executive privilege is made. The first subpoena was also quashed. While the district court rejected President Nixon's nonparticularized claim of a confidentiality privilege, its own independent weighing of the competing interests indicated that the public interest in the integrity of the criminal process took priority. The Committee appealed only from the second order. The court of appeals, *en banc*, per Chief Judge Bazelon, unanimously affirmed but on different grounds.

A presidential claim of a need for confidentiality, Chief Judge Bazelon said, is presumptively valid against compelled intrusion by an institution of government. The party seeking the information must make a strong showing of need — "a showing that the responsibilities of that institution cannot responsibly be fulfilled without access to records of the President's deliberations." Only then would the President be obliged to submit subpoenaed materials to the court, together with particularized claims, that would be weighed against the public interest served by disclosure. In this instance, the Watergate Committee had failed to make the requisite showing.

The *Select Committee* case suggests that the same principles outlined in *United States v. Nixon* would be applicable to congressional demands for executive information. On the other hand, Special Prosecutor Archibald Cox resisted an attempt by the Watergate Committee to join the Committee and grand jury cases, stating that

> the claim of Executive Privilege as against a legislative inquiry raises peculiar problems under the principle of separation of powers and the "political question" doctrine that are not involved when a Court is asked to rule on the producibility of evidence in a judicial proceeding, including a grand jury investigation. Moreover, the relevant interests which must be weighed when a claim of executive privilege is asserted against Congress are quite different than the interests involved in the grand jury proceeding.

Letter from Cox to Judge Sirica, in LEGAL DOCUMENTS RELATING TO THE SELECT COMM. ON PRESIDENTIAL CAMPAIGN ACTIVITIES, 93 Cong., 1st & 2d Sess. 649–50 (1974). Berger asserts that *Select Committee* is an unwarranted interference with congressional oversight powers because "what information Congress requires for the performance of investigatory functions was left in the discretion of Congress. To extend *United States v. Nixon* to make the courts the supervisor of Congress' exercise of that discretion is to engage in unauthorized 'blending' of powers." Raoul Berger, *Congressional Subpoenas to Executive Officials*, 75 COLUM. L. REV. 865, 875, 888 (1975).

5. *Executive documents and the public.* The Court wrote a postscript to *United States v. Nixon* in Nixon v. Administrator of General Services, 433 U.S. 425 (1977), upholding the constitutionality of the Presidential Recordings and Materials Preservation Act. The Act directed the General Services Administration (GSA) to take possession of Richard Nixon's White House papers and tape recordings, screen them and return to him those papers and materials which were personal and private. GSA is to preserve those papers having historical value and to make the materials available for use in judicial proceedings subject to "any rights, defenses or privileges which the Federal Government or any person may invoke." The Act also authorized the Administrator of GSA to issue regulations which would govern eventual public access to some of the materials pursuant to statutory guidelines. Upon resigning the presidency, Richard Nixon had executed a depository agreement with the Administrator of GSA providing for the storage of his White House papers and materials near his home in San Clemente. The agreement gave President Nixon far greater access and possessory rights to his presidential papers and tapes than did the Act which abrogated the depository agreement. President Nixon brought suit challenging the constitutionality of the Act.

The Court held, 7-2, per Justice Brennan, that the Act's disposition of presidential materials did not violate the principle of separation of powers. President Ford had signed the Act into law and President Carter, through the Solicitor General, had urged its validity. Therefore, the executive branch was a party to the Act's disposition of presidential materials. Moreover, the executive branch remained in full control of the custody and screening of the materials.

The Court, like the district court, rejected Nixon's separation of powers argument on the ground that it was based on an "archaic view of the separation of powers as requiring three airtight departments of government."

Instead, "the proper inquiry focuses on the extent to which (the Act) prevents the Executive Branch from accomplishing its constitutionally assigned functions." Since control of the materials was given to the executive branch there existed no likelihood that the Act would be unduly disruptive of executive functions. The Act was facially designed to ensure that the materials involved could only be released when release is not barred by privileges inherent in the executive branch.

Furthermore, the Court held that the Act did not violate the presidential privilege of confidentiality recognized in *United States v. Nixon*. The Court pointed out that the Act directed the Administrator of GSA to take into account "the need to protect any party's opportunity to assert any constitutionally-based right or privilege" and "the need (under the Act) to return purely private materials" to Nixon. The Court noted further: "[T]here never has been an expectation that the confidences of the Executive Office are absolute and unyielding" and in this instance, an "absolute barrier to all outside disclosure is not practically or constitutionally necessary."

Screening by archivists was deemed to constitute "a very limited intrusion by personnel in the Executive Branch sensitive to executive concern." Adequate justification had been shown "for this limited intrusion into executive confidentiality comparable to those held to justify the *in camera* inspection of the District Court sustained in *United States v. Nixon*." By virtue of the safeguards built into the Act, the Court held "that the claims of Presidential privilege must clearly yield to the important congressional purposes of preserving the materials and maintaining access to them for lawful government and historical purposes." Arguments based on the right of privacy and the Bill of Attainder Clause (Article I, § 9, cl. 3) were also rejected.

Chief Justice Burger dissented, calling the Court's holding "a grave repudiation of nearly 200 years of judicial precedent and historical practice." He labeled the Act in question "an exercise of executive — not legislative — power by the Legislative Branch." He also argued that the Act violated "the constitutionally based doctrine of Presidential privilege:" "A unanimous Court in *United States v. Nixon* could not have been clearer in holding that the privilege guaranteeing confidentiality of such communications derives from the Constitution, subject to compelled disclosure only in narrowly limited circumstances."

Justice Rehnquist dissented, saying that the result in the case "will daily stand as a veritable sword of Damocles over every succeeding president and his advisors." He rested his dissent exclusively on the view that the Act was a "clear violation of the constitutional principle of separation of powers." The Act would frustrate "candid and open discourse among the President, his advisors, foreign heads of State and Ambassadors, Members of Congress" and the others who deal with the President on a sensitive basis. As a result, "the effect of the Act and this Court's decision will undoubtedly restrain the necessary free flow of information to and from present and future Presidents."

[B] EXECUTIVE AND LEGISLATIVE IMMUNITY

[1] Presidential Immunity

In *Nixon v. Fitzgerald*, 457 U.S. 731 (1982), the Court, per Justice Powell, reversed a court of appeals decision and held that former President Nixon was entitled to absolute immunity from liability for civil damages predicated on his official acts. Because of the special nature of the office, the President has absolute immunity from damages liability for acts within the "outer perimeter" of his official responsibility.

The immunity issue arose after respondent Fitzgerald, a management analyst with the Air Force, was dismissed from his job in January 1970, during an alleged departmental reorganization and reduction in force in which his job was eliminated. One year earlier, Fitzgerald had testified before a congressional subcommittee about cost overruns and unexpected technical difficulties, much to the embarrassment of his supervisors in the Department of Defense. While the Civil Service Commission concluded that Fitzgerald's dismissal had offended applicable civil service regulations because it was motivated by "reasons purely personal" to respondent, it rejected his contention that his separation represented unlawful retaliation for his congressional testimony. Fitzgerald sued for damages, claiming his firing had been in retaliation for his testimony and naming Richard Nixon and various officials as defendants. The district court held that he had stated triable causes of action under two federal statutes and the First Amendment and that former President Nixon was not entitled to absolute presidential immunity. The court of appeals dismissed the appeal and the Supreme Court granted certiorari.

After disposing of claims challenging their jurisdiction over the controversy, the Court turned to a consideration of the merits. Prior decisions, Justice Powell noted, had "consistently recognized that government officials are entitled to some form of immunity from suits for civil damages." While a qualified immunity had been recognized for most state and federal officials, "some officials, notably judges and prosecutors, because of the special nature of their responsibilities require a full exemption from liability." The scope of the immunity of particular officials is to be determined by the Constitution, federal statutes, history, and public policy.

In the case of the President, immunity is "a functionally mandated incident of the President's unique office, rooted in the constitutional tradition of the separation of powers and supported by our history." The Court rejected Fitzgerald's claim that Nixon be limited to only qualified immunity, generally granted to governors and cabinet officers, since the "singular importance of the President's duties" and the adversarial character of the decisions involved demands a guarantee of absolute immunity from civil damages liability. The absence of such a guarantee "could distract a President from his public duties, to the detriment not only of the President and his office, but also the Nation that the President was designed to serve." Like the judge and the prosecutor, the President is a frequent national target for civil lawsuits.

Justice Powell also made clear the Court's reservations about exercising jurisdiction over the President, citing separation of powers concerns. "[A] court, before exercising jurisdiction, must balance the constitutional weight of the interest to be served against the dangers of intrusion on the authority and functions of the Executive Branch." In the case of a private suit for damages, the latter interest was seen as being the "weightier" of the two.

The Court rejected Fitzgerald's contention that Nixon's dismissal of a public employee would have been outside the "outer perimeter" of his official responsibility. "Because this mandate of office must include the authority to prescribe reorganizations and reductions in force, petitioner's alleged wrongful acts lay well within the outer perimeter of [the President's] authority."

Finally, the Court reassured the nation that there remains sufficient protection against presidential misconduct. Alternative remedies, such as impeachment, scrutiny by the press and by Congress, the need to maintain presidential influence and his place in history, and the President's own concerns in winning re-election, assured that the President would not be "above the law."

Justice White, joined by Justices Brennan, Marshall, and Blackmun dissenting, objected that the majority "makes no effort to distinguish categories of presidential conduct that should be absolutely immune from other categories of conduct that should not qualify for that level of immunity. Whatever the President does and however contrary to law he knows his conduct to be, he may, without fear of liability, injure federal employees or any other person within or without the government." White argued that, in other cases, absolute immunity attached only to the specific functions for which it is essential. The Court here abandoned this so-called "functional approach" for one that grants immunity to all Presidential acts, based on the "unique" nature of the office — this places "the President above the law. It is a reversion to the old notion that the King can do no wrong."

Although the majority attempted to support their decision with constitutional and separation of powers arguments, Justice White labeled the holding as simply a policy decision, "and in my view, very poor policy."

Absolute immunity has not historically been recognized as implicit in the Constitution. Justice White argued that no constitutional, textual or historical evidence exists to support a blanket immunity. The Court's "separation of powers" argument, he noted, is based on the extent to which private damages actions could prevent a President from "accomplishing [his] constitutionally assigned functions." But, "[w]hile absolute immunity might maximize executive efficiency and therefore be a worthwhile policy, lack of such immunity may not so disrupt the functioning of the presidency as to violate the separation of powers doctrine."

For the dissenters, immunity should turn on functional considerations: "The scope of immunity is determined by function, not office. Whatever may be true of the necessity of such a broad immunity in certain areas of executive responsibility, the only question that must be answered here is whether the dismissal of employees falls within a constitutionally assigned executive function, the performance of which would be substantially impaired by the possibility of a private action for damages. I believe it does not."

NOTES

1. ***Basis of the immunity.*** Could Congress establish a statutory cause of action against the President for civil damages? Is the immunity established in *Nixon v. Fitzgerald*, a constitutional rule or a prudential rule reflecting policy considerations. Stephen Carter, *The Political Aspects of Judicial Power: Some Notes on the Presidential Immunity Decision*, 131 U. PA. L. REV. 1341, 1401 (1983), argues that the case may reflect only a policy decision not to extend a judicially created remedy against the President.

> The message of *Nixon v. Fitzgerald* appears to be that the Supreme Court will not in the absence of extraordinary necessity act to save Congress from its own weakness, to punish a President that the legislature is unable to control. It is up to the political actors to save themselves. If they do not, then the federal courts, sitting on the sidelines, might finally be forced to enter the game. By the time they do, however, it may be too late. If it is, then the other players will have only themselves to blame.

2. ***Executive immunity generally.*** In a companion case to *Nixon v. Fitzgerald*, the Court in *Harlow v. Fitzgerald*, 457 U.S. 800 (1982), held that White House aides are not generally entitled to the same absolute immunity given the President with respect to civil damages liability. In the absence of a showing that public policy requires a grant of absolute immunity in a particular case, executive officials are only entitled to qualified immunity. "Government officials performing discretionary functions are shielded from liability for civil damages insofar as their conduct does not violate clearly established statutory or constitutional rights of which a reasonable person would have known."

3. ***Clinton v. Jones,* 520 U.S. 681 (1997)**. The Court here faced the question whether litigation of private actions for civil damages against an incumbent president on the basis of alleged wrongs committed prior to assuming office are to be deferred until he leaves office. A former state employee had sued President Clinton in federal district court, asserting federal and state claims arising out of allegedly improper sexual advances while he was governor of Arkansas. The President sought to dismiss the complaint without prejudice and the case stayed until he left office, arguing that "in all but the most exceptional cases the Constitution requires federal courts to defer such litigation until his term ends and that, in any event, respect for the office warrants such a stay." The Court, in an opinion by Justice Stevens, disagreed. It initially found that such a practice "cannot be sustained on the basis of precedent," because "none of [the previous] cases [involving sitting presidents] sheds any light on the constitutional issue before us." Moreover, policy considerations did not compel the result sought by the President: "The principal rationale for affording certain public servants immunity from suits for money damages arising out of their official acts is inapplicable to unofficial conduct. In cases involving prosecutors, legislators, and judges we have repeatedly explained that the immunity serves the public interest in enabling such officials to perform their designated functions effectively without fear that a particular decision may give rise to personal liability." Nor did the Court

find the historical evidence persuasive. It noted that "[n]one of [the] sources [to which the President points] shed much light on the question at hand," and in any event the evidence was, at the very least, conflicting as to the framers' understanding on the issue.

The President's "strongest argument," the Court stated, "is based on the text and structure of the Constitution." The President had argued "that he occupies a unique office with powers and responsibilities so vast and important that the public interest demands that he devote his undivided time and attention to his public duties." The President contended "that-as a byproduct of an otherwise traditional exercise of judicial power-burdens will be placed on the President that will hamper the performance of his official duties." He further asserted that "the doctrine of separation of powers places limits on the authority of the Federal Judiciary to interfere with the Executive Branch that would be transgressed by allowing [the] action to proceed."

In response, the Court indicated that there was little basis for concern about interference with the performance of the functions of the presidency: "[O]nly three sitting Presidents have been subjected to suit for their private actions. If the past is any indicator, it seems unlikely that a deluge of such litigation will ever engulf the Presidency. As for the case at hand, if properly managed by the District Court, it appears to us highly unlikely to occupy any substantial amount of petitioner's time." As to the broader separation-of-powers concern, the Court reasoned: "If the Judiciary may severely burden the Executive Branch by reviewing the legality of the President's official conduct, and if it may direct appropriate process to the President himself, it must follow that the federal courts have power to determine the legality of his unofficial conduct. The burden on the President's time and energy that is a mere byproduct of such review surely cannot be considered as onerous as the direct burden imposed by judicial review and the occasional invalidation of his official actions."

The Court concluded its discussion with a caveat: "Although we have rejected the argument that the potential burdens on the President violate separation-of-powers principles, those burdens are appropriate matters for the District Court to evaluate in its management of the case. The high respect that is owed to the office of the Chief Executive, though not justifying a categorical immunity, is a matter that should inform the conduct of the entire proceeding, including the timing and scope of discovery."

[2] The Speech and Debate Clause

Article I, § 6 provides that "for any Speech or Debate in either House, [members of Congress] shall not be questioned in any other place." This immunity extends to congressional aides when performing acts that would be immune if performed by the member of Congress. *Gravel v. United States*, 408 U.S. 606 (1972). But only "legislative acts" are protected, which Gravel defined to include matters which are "an integral part of the deliberative and communicating processes by which Members participate in Committee House proceedings with respect to the consideration and passage or rejection of proposed legislation or with respect to other matters which the Constitution places within the jurisdiction of either House." Applying this test, the Court held that Senator Gravel could not be prosecuted nor questioned for reading excerpts from the Pentagon Papers at a subcommittee meeting and for having the 47 volumes placed in the public record. Nor could the Senator or his aide be questioned concerning preparations for the meeting. On the other hand, Senator Gravel's arrangement with a private publisher to publish the papers was not a legislative act enjoining constitutional immunity. "Political acts" even though directed to informing and educating the public are not protected. Similarly, Senator Proxmire did not enjoy immunity from suit for allegedly defamatory statements in a press release made in presenting his Golden Fleece award — the acts were not "part of the deliberative process" or "essential to the deliberations in the Senate." *Hutchison v. Proxmire*, 443 U.S. 111 (1979).

United States v. Johnson, 383 U.S. 169 (1966), *United States v. Brewster*, 408 U.S. 501 (1972) and *United States v. Helstoski*, 442 U.S. 477 (1979), establish that references to past legislative acts of a Member cannot be introduced by the government in a criminal prosecution without undermining the values of Article I, § 6. On the other hand, "[p]romises by a Member to perform an act in the future are not legislative acts." *Helstoski*. Hence, evidence concerning bribery to vote or deliver a speech "at some future date" is admissible.

Chapter 5

LIMITATIONS ON GOVERNMENTAL POWER

We now turn from consideration of the allocation of governmental power to the limitations on governmental power. In an age of massive government, the task of securing individual rights and liberties becomes especially difficult. Further, fundamental constitutional rights often compete with each other and must be reconciled, *e.g.*, the demands of liberty and equality, the prohibition against discrimination and the right of free association, fair trial and freedom of the press. There is the problem of accommodating the principle of majoritarian democracy with sufficient protection for minority and individual rights. Questions arise whether constitutional guarantees impose only negative prohibitions or also affirmative duties on government and whether the provisions are addressed only to government officials or whether they apply also to private individuals and interest groups. And, in each instance, it is necessary to consider the proper role of the courts, legislature, and executive in resolving these problems.

Although we tend to think of constitutional rights and liberties in terms of the various constitutional amendments, there are, in fact a number of guarantees in the body of the original document. Article I, § 9, prohibits the suspension of the writ of habeas corpus except in cases of rebellion or invasion and Article I, §10, prohibits state laws that impair the obligation of contracts. Article I,§§ 9 and 10, prohibit either the state or federal government from passing bills of attainder or *ex post facto* laws. Article III,§ 2, guarantees trial by jury in criminal cases except in cases of impeachment. The requirements for a conviction of treason are specifically enumerated in Article III, § 3. Article VI, § 3, prohibits the use of religious tests as a qualification for public office. Article IV,§ 2, guarantees to citizens of each state privileges and immunities of the citizens in the several states.

Further, as was stressed earlier in the text, the separation and division of power, with provision for checks and balances, is itself a vital means of preventing the abuse of governmental power. By defining the powers of government, and denying those not granted, the government is theoretically limited in the demands it can make of the individual. Rights could be approached as the residue remaining to the individual after the powers of government have been defined. *See Entick v. Carrington,* 95 Eng. Rep. 807 (1765). Indeed, the Framers at the 1787 Convention placed such reliance on the principle of limited government achieved through enumerated powers that they defeated attempts to include a specification of individual rights. It was argued that there was no need for express guarantees since Congress had only such powers as had been delegated to it. In fact, it was argued that specification of rights might suggest the existence of federal powers that had not been delegated. The diversity of social and political interests in the new republic, the size of the polity, the mobility of its citizens, would all serve to secure liberty. On the other hand, state constitutions did specifically guarantee individual rights.

The state ratifying conventions produced a demand for inclusion of a specification of rights as the price of ratification. On June 8, 1789, James Madison presented a proposed set of amendments to the newly formed House of Representatives. From these came the first ten amendments, the Bill of Rights, which became part of the Constitution on December 15, 1791.

The concern of the present chapter is principally on the early search for limitations on federal and state governmental power imposed by the Due Process Clause of the Fifth Amendment and the guarantees in the first section of the Fourteenth Amendment.

§ 5.01 THE HISTORICAL PRELUDE

[A] NATURAL AND VESTED RIGHTS: UNWRITTEN LIMITATIONS ON GOVERNMENTAL POWER

The Declaration of Independence. When a question involving limitation on governmental power arises today, the initial reaction is to look for some potentially controlling constitutional provision. In the early days of the Republic, however, recourse was frequently made to the "unwritten law" ordained by "nature and nature's God." A general acceptance of this limitation on government in the seventeenth and eighteenth century is suggested in the Declaration of Independence.

The Declaration proceeds from the premise that it is a "self-evident truth" that "all men are created equal" and endowed with God-given, inalienable rights to life, liberty, and the pursuit of happiness. This is the philosophy of "natural rights." While influentially discussed in LOCKE'S SECOND TREATISE ON GOVERNMENT, its origins are traceable to ancient Greece and Rome. It is questionable that the designated rights were all viewed as equally inalienable, since some were partially surrendered as a consequence of living in civil society. Nevertheless, there was acceptance that there are limits on the claims that government can make on an individual that are not dependent on human laws and constitutions but belong naturally to all persons.

Judicial review and natural rights. If a government abuses its power, what is the remedy? The answer of the Declaration was revolution. A more temperate alternative is judicial invalidation. An early American example of judicial implementation of natural rights philosophy came in *Calder v. Bull*, 3 U.S. (3 Dall.) 386 (1798), involving the validity of a Connecticut law overturning a probate court decree and granting a new hearing to certain claimants under a will. The legislation was attacked as an *ex post facto* law prohibited by Article I, § 10. While the Court held that the constitutional provision applied only to penal, not civil legislation, Justice Samuel Chase commented on the limitations of governmental power arising from the social compact:

> I cannot subscribe to the omnipotence of a State Legislature, or that it is absolute and without control; although its authority should not

> be expressly restrained by the Constitution, or fundamental law, of the State. The purposes for which men enter into society will determine the nature and terms of the social compact; and as they are the foundation of the legislative power, they will decide what are proper objects of it. The nature, and ends of legislative power will limit the exercise of it. This fundamental principle flows from the very nature of our free Republican governments, that no man should be compelled to do what the laws do not require; nor to refrain from acts which the laws permit. There are acts which the Federal, or State, Legislature cannot do, without exceeding their authority. There are certain vital principles in our free republican governments, which will determine and overrule an apparent and flagrant abuse of legislative power; as to authorize manifest injustice by positive law; or to take away that security for personal liberty, or private property, for the protection whereof the government was established. An ACT of the Legislature (for I cannot call it a law), contrary to the great first principles of the social compact, cannot be considered a rightful exercise of legislative authority. The obligation of a law in governments established on express compact, and on republican principles, must be determined by the nature of the power, on which it is founded.

Justice Iredell, in a separate opinion, admitted that "some speculative jurists have held, that a legislative act against natural justice must, in itself, be void" but he rejected the power of a court, in the absence of any constitutional restraints, to declare the law void:

> The ideas of natural justice are regulated by no fixed standard: the ablest and the purest men have differed upon the subject; and all that the court could properly say, in such an event, would be, that the legislature (possessed of an equal right of opinion) had passed an act which, in the opinion of the judges, was inconsistent with the abstract principles of natural justice.

Which opinion do you think has the better argument? It has been suggested that

> [i]n the last analysis, the law of nature is nothing more or less than the popular conception of justice and right. Jefferson's use of it as a justification for revolution is less troublesome than its use by Chase as a basis for judicial review. A revolution will occur only when a group, powerful enough to overthrow the government, demands a change. But may the application of an unwritten law be left to a court with safety? To give [a court] such discretion is to give [it] a veto power over legislative enactments.

Lowell Howe, *The Meaning of "Due Process of Law" Prior to the Adoption of the Fourteenth Amendment*, 18 Cal. L. Rev. 583, 591 (1930). As you read the materials below, consider which opinion has emerged victorious, in form and in fact.

In any case, the natural rights philosophy was an integral part of judicial decisionmaking through much of the early nineteenth century. And, in the process, the courts fashioned what has been called "the basic doctrine of American constitutional law," the doctrine of vested rights.

The doctrine of vested rights. This doctrine, "setting out with the assumption that the property right is fundamental, treats any law impairing vested rights, whatever its intention, as a bill of pains and penalties, and so, void." Edward Corwin, *The Basic Doctrine of American Constitutional Law*, 12 MICH. L. REV. 243, 255 (1914). Property was a natural right protected by the social compact. To Locke, property was the most important of the natural rights because it was the one that generated civilization and assured to an individual the rewards of his or her labor and talents. "The idea that there was a sphere of private rights that lay absolutely beyond the authority of government, especially a republican government, was extraordinary, to say the least. There were virtually no precedents for such an idea in the Americans' colonial experience." Gordon S. Wood, *The Origins of Vested Rights in the Early Republic*, 85 VA. L. REV. 1421, 1439 (1999).

The shield erected around property rights from legislative attack is said by Corwin to have "represented the essential spirit and point of view of the founders of American Constitutional Law, who saw before them the same problem that had confronted the Convention of 1787, namely, the problem of harmonizing majority rule with minority rights, or more specifically, the republican institutions with the security of property, contracts, and commerce." Corwin, 12 MICH. L. REV. at 276.

In the light of its animus in favor of property, it is not surprising that critics of the doctrine of vested rights viewed it as a bulwark of aristocracy. The doctrine of vested rights was used by the courts principally as a bulwark of economic property interests against state legislative intrusion. But if the doctrine was to provide a secure base even for economic interests, it needed a constitutional nexus rather than the vagaries of natural rights jurisprudence.

***Fletcher v. Peck*, 10 U.S. (6 Cranch) 87 (1810)**, involved the Yazoo land-grant scandal. Many members of the Georgia legislature were bribed to grant 35 million acres of land to private companies at 1.5 cents per acre. A year later, a reform legislature attempted to rescind the grant, but much of the land had already been purchased by other investors. The question before the Court was whether either the "ex post facto" clause or the "impairment of the obligation of contract" clause protected the rights of bona fide purchasers. Chief Justice Marshall wrote the Court's opinion holding for the subsequent purchasers.

> If the legislature felt itself absolved from those rules of property which are common to all the citizens of the United States, and from those principles of equity which are acknowledged in all our courts, its act is to be supported by its power alone, and the same power may divest any other individual of his lands, if it shall be the will of the legislature so to exert it.
>
> It is the unanimous opinion of the court, that, in this case, the estate having passed into the hands of a purchaser for a valuable

> consideration, without notice, the state of Georgia was restrained, either by general principles which are common to all our free institutions, or by the particular provisions of the constitution of the United States, from passing a law whereby the estate of the plaintiff in the premises so purchased could be constitutionally and legally impaired and rendered null and void.

The Georgia rescinding statute was declared unconstitutional in *Fletcher* on three grounds. First, it was suggested that the grant in question was akin to a contract and, therefore, the "contract clause" was violated. Second, the Court states that "the rescinding act would have the effect of an ex post facto law." Finally, the Court found that the Georgia rescinding legislation had violated natural rights.

[B] DUE PROCESS AND SUBSTANTIVE RIGHTS

The Fifth Amendment guarantees that no person shall be deprived of life, liberty or property without due process of law. Could this provision provide a more secure constitutional nexus for the doctrine of natural rights?

Origins of the due process clause. The due process principle derives from the "law of the land" clause in Ch. 39 of Magna Carta, providing that "no freeman shall be taken, imprisoned, disseized, outlawed, or in any way destroyed, nor will we proceed against him or prosecute him, except by the lawful judgment of his peers, and by the law of the land." Later, Ch. 3 of 28 Edw. III (1355), guaranteed that "no man of what state or condition he be, shall be put out of his lands or tenements, nor taken, nor imprisoned, nor disinherited, nor put to death, without he be brought to answer by due process of law." This assurance was reaffirmed in the Petition of Right.

These guarantees in one form or the other found their way into most early state constitutions. While the law of the land and due process clauses came to be used interchangeably, American courts, unlike their English counterparts, treated the Due Process Clause as a restriction not only on the King or executive and the judiciary but also on the legislature. There is serious question, however, that either phrase was originally intended to provide a substantive, rather than a procedural, limitation on governmental power.

> To the lay mind the term "due process of law" suggests at once a form of trial, with the result that if it limits the legislature at all, it is only when that body is delineating the process whereby the legislative will is to be applied to specific cases; and a little research soon demonstrates that the lay mind is probably right so far as the history of the matter is concerned.

Edward S. Corwin, The Twilight of the Supreme Court: A History of Our Constitutional Theory 68–69 (1934).

State due process guarantees. While early state cases rejected attempts to read their "law of the land" or "due process" guarantees as a sanctuary for the doctrine of vested rights, the principle gradually found acceptance.

"Almost overnight the judiciary in America became not only the principal means by which popular legislatures were controlled and limited, but also the most effective instrument for sorting out individual disputes within a private sphere that the other institutions of government were forbidden to enter." Gordon S. Wood, *The Origins of Vested Rights in the Early Republic*, 85 VA L. REV. 1421, 1439 (1999).

Wynehamer v. People, 13 N.Y. (3 Kernan) 378 (1856), involved a New York penal statute forbidding the sale and storage of intoxicating liquors except for medicinal or sacramental purposes. The New York Court of Appeals held the act violative of the Due Process of Law Clause of the state constitution.

Judge Comstock for the Court, citing Blackstone for "the sanctity of private property, as against theories of public good," said that "there are some absolute private rights beyond [majority] reach, and among these the constitution places the right of property." Noting "the great danger in attempting to define the limits" of the natural rights philosophy which had previously been used to protect property, Judge Comstock preferred to ground a substantive restraint on legislative power in the due process guarantee. "The true interpretation of these constitutional phrases is, that where rights are acquired by the citizen under the existing law, there is no power in any branch of the government to take them away. Where rights of property are admitted to exist, the Legislature cannot say they shall exist no longer."

Judge Johnson, dissenting, branded the majority opinion as judicial usurpation, arguing that protection of citizens' rights from legislative abuse lay "in their reserved power of changing the representatives of the legislative sovereignty; and to that final and ultimate tribunal should all such errors and mistakes in legislation be referred for correction. . . . A government which does not possess the power to make all needful regulations with respect to internal trade and commerce, to impose such restrictions upon it as may be deemed necessary for the good of all, and even to prohibit and suppress entirely any particular traffic which is found to be injurious and demoralizing in its tendencies and consequences, is no government."

Fifth Amendment due process. At almost the same time as *Wynehamer*, the Supreme Court was giving Fifth Amendment due process a substantive content in dicta in the infamous *Dred Scott* decision, *Scott v. Sanford*, 60 U.S. (19 How.) 393 (1857). Although the case was decided on the ground that Dred Scott, being a "free Negro of African descent," was not entitled to sue in federal court as a "citizen" of the United States, the Court also considered the constitutionality of the Missouri Compromise. Congress had no power to prohibit slavery in specified areas, Chief Justice Taney stated, because the "powers over person and property are not only not granted to Congress, but are in express terms denied, and they are forbidden to exercise them."

The Bill of Rights as a limit on state legislative power. Neither of the above decisions, however, established the critical proposition that the Fifth Amendment due process guarantee was available to litigants challenging state legislation. In fact, the Court had earlier rejected the use of the Bill of Rights as a limitation on the use of state governmental power. In *Barron v. Baltimore*, 32 U.S. (7 Pet.) 243 (1833), the Court held that "the Fifth Amendment must be understood as restraining the power of the general government, not as applicable to the states." Chief Justice Marshall reasoned: "The constitution was ordained and established by the people of the United States for themselves, for their own government, and not for the government of the individual states. . . . [T]he limitations on power, if expressed in general terms, are naturally, and, we think, necessarily, applicable to the government created by the instrument."

In addition to this argument based on the nature of the federal Constitution, Marshall also argued that "had the framers of these amendments intended [the Bill of Rights] to be limitations on the powers of the state governments, they would have imitated the framers of the original constitution, and have expressed that intention." He noted specifically that Article I, §§ 9 and 10, particularly indicate whether they are to operate on the national or state government.

Finally, Marshall turned to the historical origin of the Bill of Rights.

> In almost every convention by which the constitution was adopted, amendments to guard against the abuse of power were recommended. These amendments demanded security against the apprehended encroachments of the general government — not against those of the local governments. In compliance with a sentiment thus generally expressed, to quiet fears thus extensively entertained, amendments were proposed by the required majority in Congress, and adopted by the states. These amendments contain no expression indicating an intention to apply them to the state governments. This court cannot so apply them.

Before the Civil War, then, those seeking protection for their vested economic property rights, and *a fortiori*, for their broader "property" interests in rights, from offensive state legislation, had to look either to state constitutions or to principles of natural justice. Federal constitutional protection was generally unavailable. The aftermath of the Civil War, however, was to provide new potential tools for limiting state regulatory power.

[C] THE RECONSTRUCTION AND CIVIL RIGHTS

The Civil War left some four million newly freed Blacks with little security in a hostile environment. State Black Codes, severely restricting the new freedmen's mobility, employment, and civil status, promised to replace the formal institution of slavery with a new form of subjugation. Between 1865 and 1875, three constitutional amendments and seven federal civil rights statutes were enacted providing both a shield and a sword for the protection of the individual. If these tools had been fully implemented many of the modern civil rights laws might never have been necessary. Eugene Gressman provides perspective on the potential impact of the Reconstruction:

> The changes made by this series of enactments and constitutional additions were of a most significant nature, altering substantially the balance between state and federal power. Civil rights were conceived of as inherent ingredients of national citizenship and as such were

> entitled to federal protection. And that protection was to be accorded in an affirmative fashion. [The] federal government was given effective weapons to combat and defend against all who would deprive inhabitants of the United States of their rights to be free of inequalities and distinction based on race, color and previous condition of servitude. These weapons were usable against both private individuals and those acting under color of state law.

Eugene Gressman, *The Unhappy History of Civil Rights Legislation*, 50 MICH. L. REV. 1323, 1336 (1952). But such was not to be the fate of the Reconstruction. Judicial invalidation, legislative repeal, and administrative nullification undermined the effectiveness of the legislative program.

The first constitutional assault of the Reconstruction period came with the ratification of the Thirteenth Amendment in December, 1865, abolishing slavery and involuntary servitude. Section 2 of the Amendment gave Congress power to enforce the prohibition by appropriate legislation. The need for such implementing legislation became immediately apparent as the southern Black Codes promised to undermine the new Amendment. Congress responded by enacting, over President Johnson's veto challenging the measure's constitutionality, the sweeping 1866 Civil Rights Act. Section 1 declared that all persons born in the United States are citizens thereof and that all such citizens, with a few designated exceptions,

> shall have the same right to make and enforce contracts, to sue, be parties, give evidence, to inherit, purchase, lease, sell, hold and convey real and personal property, and to full and equal benefits of all laws and proceedings for the security of personal and property, as is enjoyed by white citizens, and shall be subject to like punishment, pains, and penalties, and to none other, any law, statute, ordinance, regulation, or custom to the contrary notwithstanding.

Doubt concerning the adequacy of the Thirteenth Amendment to support this legislation, and the desire to assure against the repeal of its safeguards by a less demanding Congress, led to the adoption of the Fourteenth Amendment on July 9, 1868. Two years later, on March 30, 1870, the Fifteenth Amendment was ratified, guaranteeing the right to vote without regard to "race, color, or previous condition of servitude," applicable against both the state and the national government.

Using the enabling clauses of the three post-Civil War Amendments, Congress enacted a broad array of civil rights statutes protecting against discrimination in public accommodations, guaranteeing the right to vote, and protecting rights of contract, property, jury service, and the like. In the *Civil Rights Cases*, 109 U.S. 3 (1883), the Supreme Court declared unconstitutional the effort to outlaw private discrimination under the Fourteenth Amendment. Legislative and executive enthusiasm for enforcement of these provisions had already faded after the election of 1876. That left the question of whether the Supreme Court itself would vigorously interpret and enforce the three Amendments against state action. In *Plessy v. Ferguson*, 163 U.S. 537 (1896), the Court held that "separate but equal" facilities satisfied the "Equal Protection"

Clause of the Fourteenth Amendment. And in the *Slaughter-House Cases* below, the Court effectively emasculated the "Privileges or Immunities" Clause. It was not until later in the twentieth century that these three Amendments would become the source of significant constitutional protection for individual liberties.

§ 5.02 PRIVILEGES OR IMMUNITIES: THE CONCEPT THAT FAILED

The most significant of the three constitutional Amendments initiated by the Reconstruction Congress is the Fourteenth Amendment. Section 1 recognized citizenship based on birth or naturalization and extended protection against state denial of the privileges or immunities of United States citizens or of due process of law or equal protection of the laws to any person. But what did these guarantees mean and what was the purpose of the Amendment? What did it add to the guarantees of the Thirteenth Amendment? Was it intended to protect individual freedom against state interference — a constitutional nexus for the natural rights of man? Was it a protection for economic and commercial interests from intrusive state regulation — the doctrine of vested rights — constitutionalized? Did it make the guarantees of the Bill of Rights applicable to the states? What were the respective functions of the various guarantees of the section? The history of the Fourteenth Amendment remains clouded, uncertain and subject to varying interpretations. The present section will set forth some of the early directions that Fourteenth Amendment interpretation has traveled.

It might have been expected that the Court's initial venture into answering the above questions would involve the rights of newly freed slaves and other African-Americans. Instead, the first significant Fourteenth Amendment case arose out of a grant of a right to engage in the slaughtering of cattle.

SLAUGHTER-HOUSE CASES
83 U.S. (16 Wall.) 36, 21 L. Ed. 394 (1873)

[A Louisiana statute incorporated a company with a twenty-five-year monopoly to engage in the slaughtering business within a 1,154 square mile area in and around New Orleans. This suit was brought by butchers injured by the grant challenging its constitutionality.]

JUSTICE MILLER delivered the opinion of the Court:

It may, therefore, be considered as established, that the authority of the legislature of Louisiana to pass the present statute is ample, unless some restraint in the exercise of that power be found in the Constitution of that State or in the [thirteenth and fourteenth] amendments to the Constitution of the United States.

The plaintiffs in error, allege that the statute is a violation of the Constitution of the United States in these several particulars:

That it creates an involuntary servitude forbidden by the 13th article of amendment;

That it abridges the privileges and immunities of citizens of the United States;

That it denies to the plaintiffs the equal protection of the laws; and,

That it deprives them of their property without due process of law; contrary to the provisions of the 1st section of the 14th article of amendment.

This court is thus called upon for the first time to give construction to these articles.

[N]o one can fail to be impressed with the one pervading purpose found in them all, lying at the foundation of each, and without which none of them would have been even suggested; we mean the freedom of the slave race, the security and firm establishment of that freedom, and the protection of the newly made freeman and citizen from the oppressions of those who had formerly exercised unlimited dominion over him.

We do not say that no one else but the negro can share in this protection. Both the language and spirit of these articles are to have their fair and just weight in any question of construction. Undoubtedly, while negro slavery alone was in the mind of the Congress which proposed the 13th article, it forbids any other kind of slavery, now or hereafter. And so, if other rights are assailed by the states which properly and necessarily fall within the protection of these articles, that protection will apply though the party interested may not be of African descent. But what we do say, and what we wish to be understood, is, that in any fair and just construction of any section or phrase of these amendments, it is necessary to look to the purpose which we have said was the pervading spirit of them all, the evil which they were designed to remedy; and the process of continued addition to the Constitution until that purpose was supposed to be accomplished, as far as constitutional law can accomplish it.

The 1st section of the 14th article, to which our attention is more specially invited, opens with a definition of citizenship — not only citizenship of the United States, but citizenship of the states. No such definition was previously found in the Constitution, nor had any attempt been made to define it by act of Congress. It declares that persons may be citizens of the United States without regard to their citizenship of a particular state, and it overturns the *Dred Scott* decision by making all persons born within the United States and subject to its jurisdiction citizens of the United States. That its main purpose was to establish the citizenship of the negro can admit of no doubt.

The next observation is more important in view of the arguments of counsel in the present case. It is that the distinction between citizenship of the United States and citizenship of a state is clearly recognized and established. Not only may a man be a citizen of the United States without being a citizen of a state, but an important element is necessary to convert the former into the latter. He must reside within the state to make him a citizen of it, but it is only necessary that he should be born or naturalized in the United States to be a citizen of the Union.

It is quite clear, then, that there is a citizenship of the United States and a citizenship of a state, which are distinct from each other and which depend upon different characteristics or circumstances in the individual. We think this distinction and its explicit recognition in this Amendment of great weight in this argument, because the next paragraph of this same section, which is the one mainly relied on by the plaintiffs in error, speaks only of privileges and immunities of citizens of the United States, and does not speak of those of citizens of the several states. The argument, however, in favor of the plaintiffs, rests wholly on the assumption that the citizenship is the same and the privileges and immunities guaranteed by the clause are the same.

The language is, "No State shall make or enforce any law which shall abridge the privileges or immunities of citizens of the United States." It is a little remarkable, if this clause was intended as a protection to the citizen of a state against the legislative power of his own state, that the words "citizen of the state" should be left out when it is so carefully used, and used in contradistinction to "citizens of the United States" in the very sentence which precedes it. It is too clear for argument that the change in phraseology was adopted understandingly and with a purpose.

Of the privileges and immunities of the citizens of the United States, and of the privileges and immunities of the citizen of the state, and what they respectively are, we will presently consider; but we wish to state here that it is only the former which are placed by this clause under the protection of the Federal Constitution, and that the latter, whatever they may be, are not intended to have any additional protection by this paragraph of the amendment.

In the Constitution of the United States [Article IV, § 2, provides:] The citizens of each state shall be entitled to all the privileges and immunities of citizens of the several states. Fortunately we are not without judicial construction of this clause of the Constitution. The first and the leading case on the subject is that of *Corfield v. Coryell*, decided by MR. JUSTICE WASHINGTON in the circuit court for the district of Pennsylvania in 1823.

"The inquiry," he says, "is, what are the privileges and immunities of citizens of the several states? We feel no hesitation in confining these expressions to those privileges and immunities which are fundamental; which belong of right to the citizens of all free governments, and which have at all times been enjoyed by citizens of the several states which compose this Union, from the time of their becoming free, independent, and sovereign. What these fundamental principles are, it would be more tedious than difficult to enumerate." "They may all, however, be comprehended under the following general heads: protection by the government, with the right to acquire and possess property of every kind, and to pursue and obtain happiness and safety, subject, nevertheless, to such restraints as the government may prescribe for the general good of the whole."

The description, when taken to include others not named, but which are of the same general character, embraces nearly every civil right for the establishment and protection of which organized government is instituted. Throughout his opinion, they are spoken of as rights belonging to the individual as a citizen of a state. And they have always been held to be the class of rights which the state governments were created to establish and secure.

[Art. IV] did not create those rights, which it called privileges and immunities of citizens of the states. It threw around them in that clause no security for the citizen of the state in which they were claimed or exercised. Nor did it profess to control the power of the state governments over the rights of its own citizens. Its sole purpose was to declare to the several states, that whatever those rights, as you grant or establish them to your own citizens, or as you limit or qualify, or impose restrictions on their exercise, the same, neither more nor less, shall be the measure of the rights of citizens of other states within your jurisdiction.

It would be the vainest show of learning to attempt to prove by citations of authority, that up to the adoption of the recent Amendments, no claim or pretense was set up that those rights depended on the Federal government for their existence or protection, beyond the very few express limitations which the Federal Constitution imposed upon the states — such, for instance, as the prohibition against ex post facto laws, bills of attainder, and laws impairing the obligation of contracts. But with the exception of these and a few other restrictions, the entire domain of the privileges and immunities of citizens of the states, as above defined, lay within the constitutional and legislative power of the states, and without that of the Federal government. Was it the purpose of the Fourteenth Amendment, by the simple declaration that no state should make or enforce any law which shall abridge the privileges and immunities of citizens of the United States, to transfer the security and protection of all the civil rights which we have mentioned, from the states to the Federal government? And where it is declared that Congress shall have the power to enforce that article, was it intended to bring within the power of Congress the entire domain of civil rights heretofore belonging exclusively to the states?

All this and more must follow, if the proposition of the plaintiffs in error be sound. For not only are these rights subject to the control of Congress whenever in its discretion any of them are supposed to be abridged by state legislation, but that body may also pass laws in advance, limiting and restricting the exercise of legislative power by the states, in their most ordinary and usual functions, as in its judgment it may think proper on all such subjects. And still further, such a construction would constitute this court a perpetual censor upon all legislation of the states, on the civil rights of their own citizens, with authority to nullify such as it did not approve as consistent with those rights, as they existed at the time of the adoption of this Amendment. We are convinced that no such results were intended by the Congress which proposed these amendments, nor by the legislatures of the states, which ratified them.

Having shown that the privileges and immunities relied on in the argument are those which belong to citizens of the states as such, and that they are left to the state governments for security and protection, and not by this article placed under the special care of the Federal government, we may hold ourselves excused from defining the privileges and immunities of citizens of the United States which no state can abridge, until some case involving those privileges may make it necessary to do so. But lest it should be said that no such privileges and immunities are to be found if those we have been considering are excluded, we venture to suggest some which owe their existence to the Federal government, its national character, its Constitution, or its laws.

One of these is well described in the case of *Crandall v. Nevada*, 6 Wall. 36 (1868). It is said to be the right of the citizen of this great country, protected by implied guaranties of its Constitution, "to come to the seat of government to assert any claim he may have upon that government, to transact any business he may have with it, to seek its protection, to share its offices, to engage in administering its functions. He has the right of free access to its seaports, through which all operations of foreign commerce are conducted, to the sub-treasuries, land-offices, and courts of justice in the several states."

Another privilege of a citizen of the United States is to demand the care and protection of the Federal government over his life, liberty, and property when on the high seas or within the jurisdiction of a foreign government. The right to peaceably assemble and petition for redress of grievances, the privilege of the writ of habeas corpus, are rights of the citizen guaranteed by the Federal Constitution. The right to use the navigable waters of the United States, however they may penetrate the territory of the several states, and all rights secured to our citizens by treaties with foreign nations, are dependent upon citizenship of the United States, and not citizenship of a state. One of these privileges is conferred by the very article under consideration. It is that a citizen of the United States can, of his own volition, become a citizen of any state of the Union by a bona fide residence therein, with the same rights as other citizens of that state.

The argument has not been much pressed in these cases that the defendant's charter deprives the plaintiffs of their property without due process of law, or that it denies to them the equal protection of the law. We are not without judicial interpretation, both state and national, of the meaning of [the due process] clause. And it is sufficient to say that under no construction of that provision that we have ever seen, or any that we deem admissible, can the restraint imposed by the state of Louisiana upon the exercise of their trade by the butchers of New Orleans be held to be a deprivation of property within the meaning of that provision.

"Nor shall any state deny to any person within its jurisdiction the equal protection of the laws." In the light of the history of these amendments, and the pervading purpose of them, which we have already discussed, it is not difficult to give a meaning to this clause. The existence of laws in the states where the newly emancipated negroes resided, which discriminated with gross injustice and hardship against them as a class, was the evil to be remedied by this clause, and by it such laws are forbidden.

If, however, the states did not conform their laws to its requirements, then by the 5th section of the article of amendment Congress was authorized to enforce it by suitable legislation. We doubt very much whether any action of a state not directed by way of discrimination against the negroes as a class, or on account of their race, will ever be held to come within the purview of this provision. It is so clearly a provision for that race and that emergency, that a strong case would be necessary for its application to any other. But as it is a state that is to be dealt with, and not alone the validity of its laws, we may safely leave that matter until Congress shall have exercised its power, or some case of state oppression, by denial of equal justice in its courts, shall have claimed a decision at our hands. We find no such case in the one before us, and we do not deem it necessary to go over the argument again, as it may have relation to this particular clause of the Amendment.

JUSTICE FIELD, [joined by CHIEF JUSTICE CHASE and JUSTICES SWAYNE and BRADLEY,] dissenting:

The counsel of the plaintiffs in error contend that "wherever a law of a state, or a law of the United States, makes a discrimination between classes of persons, which deprive the one class of their freedom or their property, or which makes a caste of them to subserve the power, pride, avarice, vanity, or vengeance of others," there involuntary servitude exists within the meaning of the Thirteenth Amendment.

It is not necessary in my judgment, for the disposition of the present case in favor of the plaintiffs in error, to accept as entirely correct this conclusion of counsel. It, however, finds support in the act of Congress known as the civil rights act, which was framed and adopted upon a construction of the Thirteenth Amendment, giving to its language a similar breadth. Its 1st section declares that all persons born in the United States, and not subject to any foreign power, excluding Indians not taxed, are "citizens of the United States," and that "such citizens, of every race and color, without regard to any previous condition of slavery, or involuntary servitude, except as a punishment for crime, whereof the party shall have been duly convicted, shall have the same right in every state and territory in the United States to make and enforce contracts, to sue, be parties, and give evidence, to inherit, purchase, lease, sell, hold, and convey real and personal property, and to full and equal benefit of all laws and proceedings for the security of persons and property, as enjoyed by white citizens." This legislation was supported upon the theory that citizens of the United States as such were entitled to the rights and privileges enumerated, and that to deny to any such citizen equality in these rights and privileges with others was, to the extent of the denial, subjecting him to an involuntary servitude.

The provisions of the Fourteenth Amendment, which is properly a supplement to the thirteenth, cover, in my judgment, the case before us, and inhibit any legislation which confers special and exclusive privileges like these under consideration. The Amendment was adopted to obviate objections which had been raised and pressed with great force to the validity of the civil rights act, and to place the common rights of the American citizens under the protection of the National government.

A citizen of a state is now only a citizen of the United States residing in that state. The fundamental rights, privileges, and immunities which belong to him as a free man and as a free citizen, now belong to him as a citizen of the United States, and are not dependent upon his citizenship of any state. The Amendment does not attempt to confer any new privileges or immunities upon citizens or to enumerate or define those already existing. It assumes that there are such privileges and immunities which belong of right to citizens as such, and ordains that they shall not be abridged by state legislation. If this inhibition has no reference to privileges and immunities of this character, but only refers, as held by the majority of the court in their opinion, to such privileges and immunities as were before its adoption specially designated in the Constitution or necessarily implied as belonging to citizens of the United States, it was a vain and idle enactment, which accomplished nothing, and most unnecessarily excited Congress and the people on its passage. With privileges and immunities thus designated no state could ever have interfered by its laws, and no new constitutional provision was required to inhibit such interference. The supremacy of the Constitution and the laws of the United States always controlled any state legislation of that character. But if the Amendment refers to the natural and inalienable rights which belong to all citizens, the inhibition has a profound significance and consequence.

What, then, are the privileges and immunities which are secured against abridgement by state legislation? In the 1st section of the civil rights act Congress has given its interpretation to these terms, or at least has stated some of the rights, which, in its judgment, these terms include, the right "to make and enforce contracts, to sue, be parties and give evidence; to inherit, purchase, lease, sell, hold, and convey real personal property, and to full and equal benefit of all laws and proceedings for the security of person and property." That act, it is true, was passed before the Fourteenth Amendment, but the Amendment was adopted, to obviate objections to the act, or, speaking more accurately, I should say, to obviate objections to legislation of a similar character, extending the protection of the national government over the common right of all citizens of the United States. Accordingly, after its ratification Congress re-enacted the act under the belief that whatever doubts may have previously existed of its validity, they were removed by the Amendment.

The terms "privileges and immunities" are not new in the Amendment; they were in the Constitution before the Amendment was adopted. They are found in the 2d section of the 4th article. [The language from *Corfield v. Coryell, supra* is quoted.] The privileges and immunities designated are those which of right belong to the citizens of all free governments. Clearly among these must be placed the right to pursue a lawful employment in a lawful manner, without other restraint than such as equally affects all persons. What the clause in question did for the protection of the citizens of one state against hostile and discriminating legislation of other states, the Fourteenth Amendment does for the protection of every citizen of the United States against hostile and discriminating legislation, against him in favor of others whether they reside in the same or in different states. If, under the 4th article of the Constitution, equality of privileges and immunities is secured between citizens of different states, under the Fourteenth Amendment the same equality is secured between citizens of the United States.

Justice Bradley, dissenting:

Every citizen being primarily a citizen of the United States, and, secondarily, a citizen of the State where he resides, what, in general, are the privileges and immunities of a citizen of the United States? Is the right, liberty, or privilege of choosing any lawful employment one of them?

[I]n my judgment, the right of any citizen to follow whatever lawful employment he chooses to adopt (submitting himself to all lawful regulations) is one of his most valuable rights, and one which the legislature of a state cannot invade, whether restrained by its own Constitution or not. [Life, liberty, and property] are the fundamental rights which can only be taken away by due process of law, and which can only be interfered with, or the enjoyment of which can only be modified, by lawful regulations necessary or proper for the mutual good of all; and these rights, I contend, belong to the citizens of every free government. For the preservation, exercise and enjoyment of these rights the individual citizen, as a necessity, must be left free to adopt such calling, profession or trade as may seem to him most conducive to that end. Without this right he can not be a freeman. This right to choose one's calling is an essential part of that liberty which it is the object of the government to protect; and a calling, when chosen, is a man's property and right. Liberty and property are not protected where these rights are arbitrarily assailed.

[W]e are not bound to resort to implication, or to the constitutional history of England, to find an authoritative declaration of some of the most important privileges and immunities of citizens of the United States. It is in the Constitution itself. The Constitution, it is true, as it stood prior to the recent amendments, specifies, in terms, only a few of the personal privileges and immunities of citizens, but they are very comprehensive in their character. The States were merely prohibited from passing bills of attainder, ex post facto laws, laws impairing the obligation of contracts, and perhaps one or two more. But others of the greatest consequence were enumerated, although they were only secured, in express terms, from invasion by the Federal government; such as the right of habeas corpus, the right of trial by jury, of free exercise of religious worship, the right of free speech and a free press, the right peaceably to assemble for the discussion of public measures, the right to be secure against unreasonable searches and seizures, and above all, and including almost all the rest, the right of not being deprived of life, liberty, or property, without due process of law. These, and still others are specified in the original Constitution, or in the early amendments of it, as among the privileges and immunities of citizens of the United States, or, what is still stronger for the force of the argument, the rights of all persons, whether citizens or not.

But even if the Constitution were silent, the fundamental privileges and immunities of citizens, as such, would be no less real and no less inviolable than they now are. It was not necessary to say in words that the citizens of the United States should have and exercise all the privileges of citizens; the privilege of buying, selling, and enjoying property; the privilege of engaging in any lawful employment for a livelihood; the privilege of resorting to the laws for redress of injuries, and the like. Their very citizenship conferred these privileges, if they did not possess them before. And these privileges they would enjoy whether they were citizens of any State or not.

In my view, a law which prohibits a large class of citizens from adopting a lawful employment, or from following a lawful employment previously adopted, does deprive them of liberty as well as property, without due process of law. Their right of choice is a portion of their liberty; their occupation is their property. Such a law also deprives those citizens of the equal protection of the laws, contrary to the last clause of the section.

JUSTICE SWAYNE, dissenting:

> It is necessary to enable the government of the nation to secure to every one within its jurisdiction the rights and privileges enumerated, which, according to the plainest considerations of reason and justice and the fundamental principles of the social compact, all are entitled to enjoy. The construction adopted by the majority of my brethren defeats by a limitation not anticipated, the intent of those by whom the instrument was framed and of those by whom it was adopted.

NOTES

1. *An abolitionist perspective.* It has been suggested that "[t]he three much-discussed clauses of § 1 of the Fourteenth Amendment were the product of and perhaps took their meaning, application, and significance from a popular and primarily lay movement, which was moral, ethical, religious, revivalist rather than legal in character." JACOBUS TENBROEK, EQUAL UNDER LAW 116 (1965). The reference is to the abolitionist movement whose adherents constituted a major segment of the Joint Committee on Reconstruction of the 39th Congress that formulated the Fourteenth Amendment.

In the abolitionist perspective, the Fourteenth Amendment was "a meeting ground of constitutional and natural rights." Its guarantees "were required by justice. They were indispensable to liberty. They were what governments were instituted to protect and to protect equally by laws. They were the privileges and immunities of the United States. They were the natural and inherent rights of all men." TENBROEK at 128.

Under this interpretation, the Amendment intended to include the entire Bill of Rights and a great deal more, including

> the whole spectrum of rights embraced in such phrases as "natural rights," "fundamental rights," "the rights of man," "God-given rights" and so forth, and in such documents as the Declaration of Independence, the Preamble to the Constitution, and the Bill of Rights. In throwing together this miscellany of philosophical and historical antecedents, the interpreters of the amendments followed the example of the abolitionists of an earlier generation.

Henry Commager, *Historical Background of the Fourteenth Amendment*, in THE FOURTEENTH AMENDMENT: CENTENNIAL VOLUME 14, 24 (B. Schwartz ed. 1970).

It was the duty of Congress to protect these fundamental rights. "While section 1 of the Fourteenth Amendment was thus declaratory and confirmatory, section 5 corrected the one great constitutional defect, the one pressing want which years of systematic violation of men's natural rights demonstrated. It gave Congress power to protect those rights." TENBROEK at 233.

2. *National primacy.* A modern expression of the expansive view of the original intent of the Fourteenth Amendment's framers is provided by Robert Kaczorowski, *Revolutionary Constitutionalism in the Era of Civil War and Reconstruction*, 61 N.Y.U.L. REV. 863, 924 (1986):

> They believed that ultimate sovereignty over citizens was located in the national government, and that Congress and the federal courts possessed primary authority to protect citizens' fundamental rights. Because they believed that the thirteenth and fourteenth amendments directly secured the civil rights of United States citizens, [they] understood that these amendments conclusively established that the national government possessed both primary authority over civil rights and ultimate responsibility for safeguarding citizens' rights.

3. *Original intent.* John Bingham, the principal author of the Fourteenth Amendment, §1, specifically said that "the privileges and immunities of citizens of the United States, as contradistinguished from citizens of a state, are chiefly defined in the first eight amendments to the Constitution of the United States." Cong. Globe, 42d Cong., 1st Sess. app. 150 (1871). This and similar statements in Congress went unchallenged. After surveying the historical debate over the meaning of the Fourteenth Amendment, Professor Tribe concludes: "The [privileges or immunities] clause is best seen then, as incorporating the Bill of Rights against state governments without implying the exclusivity of that set of guarantees." I LAURENCE H. TRIBE, AMERICAN CONSTITUTIONAL LAW 1302 (3d ed. 2000). Professor Curtis similarly concludes that "in the thirty-five years or so before the 1868 ratification of the Fourteenth Amendment, common usage often referred to Bill of Rights liberties as 'privileges,' 'immunities,' or 'rights' of Americans or of citizens of the United States." Michael Kent Curtis, *Historical Linguistics, Inkblots,* and *Life After Death: The Privileges or Immunities of Citizens of the United States,* 78 N.C.L. REV. 1071, 1089 (2000).

Professor Tribe also argues: "*Corfield* can best be understood as an attempt to import the natural rights doctrine into the Constitution by way of the Privileges and Immunities Clause of Article IV" (*id.* at 1252) and that this *natural* rights approach provided the foundation for the *national* rights embodied in the Fourteenth Amendment. *Id.* at 1304–06. What role does Article IV play in the opinions of Justices Miller and Field? Does Justice Miller accurately quote the language of Art. IV?

4. *Federalism or revolution.* Why does the majority in *Slaughter-House* reject the abolitionist construction of the Fourteenth Amendment? Is Justice Miller's argument based on a counter-reading of history, on textual exegesis, or on competing value and policy choices? Justice Miller argues that the Framers could not have intended to restructure the American federal system in order to provide federal protection for civil rights. Compare Edward Corwin's assessment:

> The debates in Congress on the amendment leave one in little doubt of the intention of its framers to nationalize civil liberty in the United States, primarily for the benefit of the freedmen, to be sure, but incidentally for the benefit of all. This would be done, it was calculated, by converting State citizenship and its privileges and immunities into privileges and immunities of national citizenship. Then by section 5 of the amendment, which empowers Congress to enforce its other provisions by "appropriate legislation," that body would be made the

> ultimate authority in delimiting the entire sphere of private rights in relation to the powers of the States, leaving to the Supreme Court an intermediate role in this respect.

EDWARD S. CORWIN, LIBERTY AGAINST GOVERNMENT, at 118–19. Professor James W. Fox Jr., *Re-Readings and Misreadings: Slaughter-House, Privileges or Immunities, and Section Five Enforcement Powers*, 91 KY. L.J. 67 (2002), argues that, in the *Slaughter-House Cases*, "Miller wrongly relegated the fundamental privileges of citizenship, which were extensively discussed by the drafters of the Amendment and subsequent Congresses, to state privileges and immunities. In doing so, the Court greatly inhibited the ongoing congressional debate over specific definitions of the Clause in the context of Congressional enforcement powers under Section Five of the Amendment." Professor Fox argues that, contrary to modern Supreme Court interpretation, the original intent was that Congress had power under section five "to determine some of the content of the privileges and immunities of national citizenship." Consider the argument of Kevin Christopher Newsom, *Setting Incorporation Straight: A Reinterpretation of the Slaughter-House Cases*, 109 YALE L.J. 643, 648–49 (2000), "that Justice Miller's majority opinion in *Slaughter-House* did not foreclose the possibility of incorporating provisions of the Bill of Rights through the Privileges and Immunities Clause."

5. *Constitutionalizing civil rights.* By contrast, RAOUL BERGER, GOVERNMENT BY JUDICIARY (1977), argues that the three clauses of § 1 of the Amendment were all facets of the single concern to prohibit discrimination against freedmen in regard to a limited range of fundamental rights reflected in the 1866 Civil Rights Act. "Roughly speaking, the substantive rights were identified by the privileges and immunities clause; the equal protection clause was to bar legislative discrimination with respect to those rights; and the judicial machinery to secure them was to be supplied by nondiscriminatory due process of the several states." The substantive rights, Berger contends, included only (1) personal security; (2) freedom to move about; and (3) ownership and disposition of property. The incidental rights necessary for safeguarding these rights were enumerated in the 1866 Civil Rights Act which defined the outer limits of the Fourteenth Amendment privileges or immunities.

Critics of Berger's thesis claim that he has oversimplified the complexity of motivations that underlie the ambiguous provisions of the Fourteenth Amendment. Even if the Privileges or Immunities Clause was meant to constitutionalize the rights enumerated in the 1866 Civil Rights Act, this does not necessarily mean that the Amendment was so limited. Note that the Fourteenth Amendment does not enumerate specific rights as does the 1866 statute. "[I]f the rights of United States citizenship are the natural rights to life, liberty, and property, as repeatedly stated by the framers, then the rights specified in section one of the Civil Rights Act do not compromise the entire corpus of the rights of United States citizens." Kaczorowski, 61 N.Y.U. L. REV. at 924.

6. *Continuing uncertainty.* Chief Justice Earl Warren suggested in *Brown v. Board of Educ.* (*Brown I*), that the history of the Fourteenth Amendment is "[a]t best, inconclusive." Justice Brennan, concurring and dissenting in *Oregon v. Mitchell*, concluded that the "record left by the framers of the Fourteenth Amendment is thus too vague and imprecise," and the Amendment therefore remains "capable of being interpreted by future generations in accordance with the vision and needs of those generations." Thus, it has been urged that all a legal scholar or historian can hope to glean from the historical background of the Civil War Amendments is the "spirit" which gave them life and that a precise meaning of the words can never be determined. Commager, *Historical Background* at 14.

7. *Citizens and persons.* Whatever the historical purpose of the Privileges or Immunities Clause, it has been rendered virtually useless by judicial interpretation. There have been occasional attempted resurrections. *See, e.g.*, *Colgate v. Harvey*, 296 U.S. 404 (1935) (state statute held to abridge the privilege of a citizen to lend money, trade and make contracts), *overruled by Madden v. Kentucky*, 309 U.S. 83 (1940); *Hague v. C.I.O.*, 307 U.S. 496 (1939) (a minority of the Court argued that the right to peaceably assemble to discuss federal rights was a privilege of national citizenship while the majority used a due process rationale).

Is the failure of the Privileges or Immunities Clause as a source of the "fundamental" rights perhaps a fortunate, if accidental occurrence? Note that the Due Process and Equal Protection Clauses extend to "persons" rather than "citizens." The former, but not the latter, includes aliens and corporations. Further,

> [a] relationship between government and the governed that turns on citizenship can always be dissolved or denied. Citizenship is a legal construct, an abstraction, a theory. No matter what safeguards it may be equipped with, it is at best something that was given, and given to some and not to others, and it can be taken away. It has always been easier, it always will be easier, to think of someone as a non-citizen and to decide that he is a non-person which is the point of the *Dred Scott* case.

Alexander Bickel, *Citizenship in the American Constitution*, 15 ARIZ. L. REV. 369, 387 (1973).

8. *Resurrecting privileges or immunities*. One of the rights of national citizenship identified by Justice Miller was the right of a citizen of the United States to "become a citizen of any state of the Union by a bona fide residence therein with the same rights as other citizens of that state." In *Saenz v. Roe*, p. 888, the Court held that a state law limiting the welfare benefits that new arrivals could receive violated the right of interstate travel protected by the Privileges or Immunities Clause of the Fourteenth Amendment. Justice Stevens, for the Court, stated: "that newly arrived citizens 'have two political capacities, one state and one federal,' adds special force to their claim that they have the same rights as others who share their citizenship."

Does *Saenz* herald a new era of fundamental rights jurisprudence "predicated on the constitutional clause that ought to have been the basis for such a jurisprudence for more than a century"? Professor Lawrence Tribe believes it does not: "Observers of the Court who are inclined to see in the *Saenz* decision a harbinger of a fresh new jurisprudence of privileges and immunities may ultimately be proven right, and *Saenz* may indeed have been the first step on that clause's long road back to life from the *Slaughter-House Cases* — although I am inclined to doubt it . . . . *Saenz* revealed a Court far more comfortable protecting rights it can describe in architectural terms, especially in terms of federalism, than it is protecting rights that present themselves as spheres of personal autonomy or as dimensions of constitutionally mandated equality . . . ." Laurence H. Tribe, Saenz *Sans Prophecy: Does the Privileges or Immunities Revival Portend the Future—Or Reveal the Structure of the Present?* 113 HARV. L. REV. 110, 197–98 (1999).

§ 5.03 THE INCORPORATION DEBATE

The *Slaughter-House Cases* doomed the use of the Privileges or Immunities Clause as a constitutional source of fundamental rights limiting state action. Instead, it was to be the guarantee of liberty in the Fourteenth Amendment Due Process Clause that would serve as the vehicle whereby the states would be subjected to the fundamental rights and liberties of the federal Constitution. But what is the nature of the "liberty" protected by the Due Process Clause? Justice Bradley, dissenting in the *Slaughter-House Cases*, had suggested that the Fourteenth Amendment embodied all of the guarantees of the Bill of Rights and more. What rationale would support reading liberty to incorporate these enumerated guarantees? If not all of the Bill of Rights guarantees are to be incorporated, what is the standard for selecting those rights which are to be incorporated? Alternatively, if the meaning of liberty is not to be determined by the specifics of the first ten Amendments, but is to be interpreted independently of those rights, how is a court to determine if a claimed substantive interest or procedure is a part of due process liberty? The famous *Palko* case represents an early attempt to grapple with these problems.

Palko v. Connecticut, 302 U.S. 319 (1937), involved the validity under the Fourteenth Amendment of a Connecticut statute permitting criminal appeals by the state. Palko had been tried once, found guilty and sentenced to life imprisonment. Following appeal by the state, Palko was brought to trial again. Palko objected without success that he had been twice placed in jeopardy for the same offense. Nevertheless, he was convicted again and this time he was sentenced to death.

On appeal, Palko argued that if the federal government had twice tried him for the same offense the Double Jeopardy Clause of the Fifth Amendment would have invalidated the second trial and that the same result should be reached under the Fourteenth Amendment when state action is involved. Cardozo summarized and rejected Palko's argument: "We have said that in appellant's view the Fourteenth Amendment is to be taken as embodying the prohibitions of the Fifth. His thesis is even broader. Whatever could be a violation of the original Bill of Rights (amendments I to VIII) if done by the federal government is now equally unlawful by force of the fourteenth amendment if done by a state. There is no such general rule."

Cardozo conceded that some of the values protected in the Bill of Rights, *i.e.* freedom of expression, the free exercise of religion, the right of peaceable assembly, and the right of one accused of crime to the benefit of counsel, were also protected by the Fourteenth Amendment. But this was so, not "by force of the specific pledges of particular amendments" but because these values "have been found to be implicit in the concept of ordered liberty." In the Court's view, the double jeopardy complained of by Palko did not offend the "concept of ordered liberty." But the essential problem endured: Was it possible to provide judicial review in the field of individual liberties without having decision turn on the subjective reaction of the judicial mind to the wisdom of legislation? "Is there a 'rationalizing principle' that serves to give 'proper order' to these adjudications?" Sanford Kadish, *Methodology and Criteria on Due Process Adjudication: A Survey and Criticism*, 66 YALE L.J. 319, 320 (1957).

The inherent and insoluble ambiguity of judicial constitutional interpretation is reflected by the disappointment inherent in attempts at resolution of what are essentially problems of moral and ethical choice. In *Adamson v. California*, Justice Frankfurter and Justice Black each wrote separate opinions: Frankfurter wrote a concurrence, Black, a dissent. The issue between them was whether the California procedure which permits an adverse inference to be taken against an accused by his failure to take the stand violated the Due Process Clause of the Fourteenth Amendment. What matters for our purposes is not the different results that each of these men reached with regard to the issue at hand but rather what united them and what divided them. What united them was a common passion for objectivity, and a common quest for a doctrinal barometer by which to ascertain when the heavy hand of judicial review should be exerted against a state law. Both Black and Frankfurter agreed that the desired test should be one which would transcend the individual preference of judges.

ADAMSON v. CALIFORNIA

332 U.S. 46, 67 S. Ct. 1672, 91 L. Ed. 1903 (1947)

[Adamson was convicted in a California state court by a jury for murder in the first degree. Under the California procedure, which was atypical even at that time, if a defendant failed to explain or to deny evidence against him, that failure could be commented upon by the court and counsel and be considered by court and jury. The defendant Adamson failed to testify and the District Attorney commented on that failure. Adamson contended that his privilege against self-incrimination had thereby been infringed.

[The Court, per Justice Reed, easily disposed of Adamson's claim that the privilege against self-incrimination guaranteed by the Fifth Amendment was applicable to state action by reason of the Privileges or Immunities Clause of the Fourteenth Amendment. The force of precedent was clearly against such a claim. *Slaughter-House Cases.*

[Adamson had also claimed that his right to a fair trial, protected by the Due Process Clause of the Fourteenth Amendment, had been infringed. If he did take the stand, he would be subject to cross-examination about his prior criminal record for the purpose of impeaching his credibility. Disclosure of the prior criminal record might well prejudice his case in the instant proceeding. This, he contended, would violate due process liberty.

[The Court, however, rejected the claim. The Due Process Clause of the Fourteenth Amendment while guaranteeing fair trial did not "draw all the rights of the federal Bill of Rights under its protection." Further, there was nothing unfair in requiring a defendant to choose between leaving adverse evidence unanswered or responding, thereby subjecting himself to impeachment through disclosure of a prior criminal record. This was viewed as a dilemma facing any defendant. Therefore, "a state may control such a situation in accordance with its own ideas of the most efficient administration of criminal justice" without violating due process.

[Justice Frankfurter, although agreeing in the result, wrote a separate opinion in which he developed his position that the Due Process Clause of the Fourteenth Amendment should not be defined by mechanical reference to the Bill of Rights. In an influential concurrence which governed due process adjudication for nearly a decade and a half, Frankfurter detailed his position that the Due Process Clause of the Fourteenth Amendment had an independent potency and meaning apart from the Bill of Rights.]

Justice Frankfurter, concurring.

Only a technical rule of law would exclude from consideration that which is relevant, as a matter of fair reasoning, to the solution of a problem. Sensible and just-minded men, in important affairs of life, deem it significant that a man remains silent when confronted with serious and responsible evidence against himself which it is within his power to contradict. The notion that to allow jurors to do that which sensible and right-minded men do every day violates the "immutable principles of justice" as conceived by a civilized society is to trivialize the importance of "due process."

For historical reasons a limited immunity from the common duty to testify was written into the Federal Bill of Rights, and I am prepared to agree that, as part of that immunity, comment on the failure of an accused to take the witness stand is forbidden in federal prosecutions. It is so, of course, by explicit act of Congress. But to suggest that such a limitation can be drawn out of "due process" in its protection of ultimate decency in a civilized society is to suggest that the Due Process Clause fastened fetters of unreason upon the States.

Between the incorporation of the Fourteenth Amendment into the Constitution and the beginning of the present membership of the Court — a period of 70 years — the scope of that Amendment was passed upon by 43 judges. Of all these judges only one, who may respectfully be called an eccentric exception, even indicated the belief that the Fourteenth Amendment was a shorthand summary of the first eight Amendments theretofore limiting only the Federal Government, and that due process incorporated those eight Amendments as restrictions upon the powers of the States.

The short answer to the suggestion that the [due process clause] was a way of saying that every State must thereafter initiate prosecutions through indictment by a grand jury, must have a trial by a jury of twelve in criminal cases, and must have a trial by such a jury in common law suits where the amount in controversy exceeds twenty dollars, is that it is a strange way of saying it. It would be extraordinarily strange for a Constitution to convey such specific commands in such a roundabout and inexplicit way. Those reading the English language with the meaning which it ordinarily conveys, those conversant with the political and legal history of the concept of due process, those sensitive to the relations of the States to the central government as well as the relation of some of the provisions of the Bill of Rights to the process of justice, would hardly recognize the Fourteenth Amendment as a cover for the various explicit provisions of the first eight Amendments. Some of these are enduring reflections of experience with human nature, while some express the restricted views of Eighteenth-Century England regarding the best methods for the ascertainment of facts. The notion that the Fourteenth Amendment was a covert way of imposing upon the States all the rules which it seemed important to Eighteenth-Century statesmen to write into the Federal Amendments, was rejected by judges who were themselves witnesses of the process by which the Fourteenth Amendment became part of the Constitution.

Indeed, the suggestion that the Fourteenth Amendment incorporates the first eight Amendments as such is not unambiguously urged. Even the boldest innovator would shrink from suggesting to more than half the States that they may no longer initiate prosecutions without indictment by grand jury, or that thereafter all the States of the Union must furnish a jury of 12 for every case involving a claim above $20. There is suggested merely a selective incorporation of the first eight Amendments into the Fourteenth Amendment. Some are in and some are out, but we are left in the dark as to which are in and which are out. Nor are we given the calculus for determining which go in and which stay out. If the basis of selection is merely that those provisions of the first eight Amendments are incorporated which commend themselves to individual justices as indispensable to the dignity and happiness of a free man, we are thrown back to a merely subjective test. The protection against unreasonable search and seizure might have primacy for one judge, while trial by a jury of 12 for every claim above $20 might appear to another as an ultimate need in a free society. In the history of thought "natural law" has a much longer and much better founded meaning and justification than such subjective selection of the first eight Amendments for incorporation into the Fourteenth. If all that is meant is that due process contains within itself certain minimal standards which are "of the very essence of a scheme of ordered liberty," *Palko v. Connecticut*, putting upon this Court the duty of applying these standards from time to time, then we have merely arrived at the insight which our predecessors long ago expressed.

It may not be amiss to restate the pervasive function of the Fourteenth Amendment in exacting from the States observance of basic liberties. The Amendment neither comprehends the specific provisions by which the founders deemed it appropriate to restrict the federal government nor is it confined to them. The Due Process Clause of the Fourteenth Amendment has an independent potency, precisely as does the Due Process Clause of the Fifth Amendment in relation to the Federal Government. It ought not to require argument to reject the notion that due process of law meant one thing in the

Fifth Amendment and another in the Fourteenth. The Fifth Amendment specifically prohibits prosecution of an "infamous crime" except upon indictment; it forbids double jeopardy; it bars compelling a person to be a witness against himself in any criminal case; it precludes deprivation of "life, liberty, or property, without due process of law." Are Madison and his contemporaries in the framing of the Bill of Rights to be charged with writing into it a meaningless clause? To consider "due process of law" as merely a shorthand statement of other specific clauses in the same amendment is to attribute to the authors and proponents of this Amendment ignorance of, or indifference to, a historic conception which was one of the great instruments in the arsenal of constitutional freedom which the Bill of Rights was to protect and strengthen.

A construction which gives to due process no independent function but turns it into a summary of the specific provisions of the Bill of Rights would, as has been noted, tear up by the roots much of the fabric of law in the several States, and would deprive the States of opportunity for reforms in legal process designed for extending the area of freedom. It would assume that no other abuses would reveal themselves in the course of time than those which had become manifest in 1791. Such a view not only disregards the historic meaning of "due process." It leads inevitably to a warped construction of specific provisions of the Bill of Rights to bring within their scope conduct clearly condemned by due process but not easily fitting into the pigeon-holes of the specific provisions. It seems pretty late in the day to suggest that a phrase so laden with historic meaning should be given an improvised content consisting of some but not all of the provisions of the first eight Amendments, selected on an undefined basis, with improvisation of content for the provisions so selected.

And so, when, as in a case like the present, a conviction in a State court is here for review under a claim that a right protected by the Due Process Clause of the Fourteenth Amendment has been denied, the issue is not whether an infraction of one of the specific provisions of the first eight Amendments is disclosed by the record. The relevant question is whether the criminal proceedings which resulted in conviction deprived the accused of the due process of law to which the United States Constitution entitled him. Judicial review of that guaranty of the Fourteenth Amendment inescapably imposes upon this Court an exercise of judgment upon the whole course of the proceedings in order to ascertain whether they offend those canons of decency and fairness which express the notions of justice of English-speaking peoples even toward those charged with the most heinous offenses. These standards of justice are not authoritatively formulated anywhere as though they were prescriptions in a pharmacopoeia. But neither does the application of the Due Process Clause imply that judges are wholly at large. The judicial judgment in applying the Due Process Clause must move within the limits of accepted notions of justice and is not to be based upon the idiosyncrasies of a merely personal judgment. The fact that judges among themselves may differ whether in a particular case a trial offends accepted notions of justice is not disproof that general rather than idiosyncratic standards are applied. An important safeguard against such merely individual judgment is an alert deference to the judgment of the State court under review.

JUSTICE BLACK, dissenting:

This decision reasserts a constitutional theory spelled out in *Twining v. New Jersey*, that this Court is endowed by the Constitution with boundless power under "natural law" periodically to expand and contract constitutional standards to conform to the Court's conception of what at a particular time constitutes "civilized decency" and "fundamental principles of liberty and justice." Invoking this *Twining* rule, the Court concludes that although comment upon testimony in a federal court would violate the Fifth Amendment, identical comment in a state court does not violate today's fashion in civilized decency and fundamentals and is therefore not prohibited by the Federal Constitution as amended.

I would not reaffirm the *Twining* decision, I think that decision and the "natural law" theory of the Constitution upon which it relies, degrade the constitutional safeguards of the Bill of Rights and simultaneously appropriate for this Court a broad power which we are not authorized by the Constitution to exercise. My reasons for believing that the *Twining* decision should not be revitalized can best be understood by reference to the constitutional, judicial, and general history that preceded and followed the case.

In my judgment [the Amendment's] history conclusively demonstrates that the language of the first section of the Fourteenth Amendment, taken as a whole, was thought by those responsible for its submission to the people, and by those who opposed its submission, sufficiently explicit to guarantee that thereafter no state could deprive its citizens of the privileges and protections of the Bill of Rights. Whether this Court ever will, or whether it now should, in the light of past decisions, give full effect to what the Amendment was intended to accomplish is not necessarily essential to a decision here. However that may be, our prior decisions, including *Twining*, do not prevent our carrying out that purpose, at least to the extent of making applicable to the states, not a mere part, as the Court has, but the full protection of the Fifth Amendment's provision against compelling evidence from an accused to convict him of crime. And I further contend that the "natural law" formula which the Court uses to reach its conclusion in this case should be abandoned as an incongruous excrescence on our Constitution. I believe that formula to be itself a violation of our Constitution, in that it subtly conveys to courts, at the expense of legislatures, ultimate power over public policies in fields where no specific provision of the Constitution limits legislative power. And my belief seems to be in accord with the views expressed by this Court, at least for the first two decades after the Fourteenth Amendment was adopted.

I fear to see the consequences of the Court's practice of substituting its own concepts of decency and fundamental justice for the language of the Bill of Rights as its point of departure in interpreting and enforcing that Bill of Rights. If the choice must be between the selective process of the *Palko* decision applying some of the Bill of Rights to the States, or the *Twining* rule applying none of them, I would choose the *Palko* selective process. But rather than accept either of these choices, I would follow what I believe was the original purpose of the Fourteenth Amendment to extend to all the people of the nation the complete protection of the Bill of Rights. To hold that this Court can determine what, if any, provisions of the Bill of Rights will be enforced, and if so to what degree, is to frustrate the great design of a written Constitution.

Conceding the possibility that this Court is now wise enough to improve on the Bill of Rights by substituting natural law concepts for the Bill of Rights, I think the possibility is entirely too speculative to agree to take that course. I would therefore hold in this case that the full protection of the Fifth Amendment's proscription against compelled testimony must be afforded by California. This I would do because of reliance upon the original purpose of the Fourteenth Amendment.

It is an illusory apprehension that literal application of some or all of the provisions of the Bill of Rights to the States would unwisely increase the sum total of the powers of this Court to invalidate state legislation. The Federal Government has not been harmfully burdened by the requirement that enforcement of federal laws affecting civil liberty conform literally to the Bill of Rights. Who would advocate its repeal? It must be conceded, of course, that the natural-law-due-process formula, which the Court today reaffirms, has been interpreted to limit substantially this Court's power to prevent state violations of the individual civil liberties guaranteed by the Bill of Rights. But this formula also has been used in the past and can be used in the future, to license this Court, in considering regulatory legislation, to roam at large in the broad expanses of policy and morals and to trespass, all too freely, on the legislative domain of the States as well as the Federal Government.

Since *Marbury v. Madison* was decided, the practice has been firmly established for better or worse, that courts can strike down legislative enactments which violate the Constitution. This process, of course, involves interpretation, and since words can have many meanings, interpretation obviously may result in contraction or extension of the original purpose of a constitutional provision thereby affecting policy. But to pass upon the constitutionality of statutes by looking to the particular standards enumerated in the Bill of Rights and other parts of the Constitution is one thing; to invalidate statutes because of application of "natural law" deemed to be above and undefined by the Constitution is another. "In the one instance, courts proceeding within clearly marked constitutional boundaries seek to execute policies written into the Constitution; in the other they roam at will in the limitless area of their own beliefs as to reasonableness and actually select policies, a responsibility which the Constitution entrusts to the legislative representatives of the people." *Federal Power Commission v. Natural Gas Pipeline Co.*, 315 U.S. 575, 599, 601, n.4.

JUSTICE DOUGLAS joins in this opinion.

JUSTICE MURPHY, with whom JUSTICE RUTLEDGE concurs, dissenting:

While in substantial agreement with the views of MR. JUSTICE BLACK, I have one reservation and one addition to make. I agree that the specific guarantees of the Bill of Rights should be carried over intact into the first section of the Fourteenth Amendment. But I am not prepared to say that the latter is entirely and necessarily limited by the Bill of Rights. Occasions may arise where a proceeding falls so far short of conforming to fundamental standards of procedure as to warrant constitutional condemnation in terms of a lack of due process despite the absence of a specific provision in the Bill of Rights. That point, however, need not be pursued here inasmuch as the Fifth Amendment is explicit in its provision that no person shall be compelled in any criminal case to be a witness against himself. That provision, as MR. JUSTICE BLACK demonstrates, is a constituent part of the Fourteenth Amendment.

NOTES

1. *Original intent revisited.* Richard L. Aynes, *On Misreading John Bingham and the Fourteenth Amendment*, 103 YALE L.J. 57, 63–64 (1993), says that Justice Black "relied primarily on the views of John Bingham," the principal author of the Fourteenth Amendment, § 1. Justice Black reasoned that since Bingham believed that the privileges or immunities of U.S. citizens were "chiefly defined in the first eight amendments to the Constitution," Bingham must have meant that the Privileges or Immunities Clause of that Amendment would make the Bill of Rights enforceable against the states. Professor Aynes, who agrees with Justice Black, says Justice Frankfurter dismissed the statements of Bingham and relied on the *Slaughter-House Cases* repudiation of total incorporation. Compare the seminal article by Charles Fairman, *Does the Fourteenth Amendment Incorporate the Bill of Rights?,* 2 STAN. L. REV. 5 (1949), who reviewed the historical evidence, concluding that Justice Frankfurter's *Adamson* concurrence was correct.

2. *Fundamental values.* Justice Frankfurter thought any abiding judicial interpretation of the Due Process Clause of the Fourteenth Amendment had to meet two requirements. First, the judicial interpretation had to be a dynamic one, capable of changing with a maturing (or declining?) sense of decency. It would not and could not, he said, be imprisoned within the confines of a fixed formula. Second, the judicial interpretation had to be infused by an awareness that any judicial test which diminished state independence had to be used with reluctance. The test for invalidity was admittedly an awesome one: the procedure was to be invalidated when it offended the fundamental standards of decency. But what are these standards and how are they ascertained? Frankfurter answered that they were to be found in "accepted notions of justice of English-speaking peoples."

Justice Black in *Griswold v. Connecticut,* p. 493, commented that "the scientific miracles of this age have not yet produced a gadget which the Court can use to determine what traditions are rooted in the [collective] conscience of our people." The Court, he noted, lacked a Gallup poll. Is it possible to determine fundamental social values objectively?

It is probably a mistake to assume that Frankfurter's resolution of due process issues is necessitated by his methodology. Reference to civilized standards of decency, to "shocking the conscience" of the Court, are words deliberately chosen not to perform a task but to transmit a message. The message is that the task of deciding whether to invalidate state law must be exercised with restraint.

3. *The quest for certainty.* For Justice Black, this flexible approach to due process was unacceptable. Civilized standards of decency were too unconfined.

How could we have an objective constitutional interpretation given such an obscure guide? To Frankfurter this, of course, was a virtue because it demonstrated at the first level of disposition the "non-Euclidean" character of the problems presented to the court. To Black this imprecision was the undermining vice of the whole Frankfurter theory of due process, for in the end, Justice Black prophesied, what would be applied were the values of the judges themselves.

To Justice Black the history of the Fourteenth Amendment indicated the appropriate solution. The Fourteenth incorporated the first eight Amendments, nothing more or less. "[F]or Black, part of the appeal of incorporation lay in its mechanical quality — its apparent ability to reduce judicial discretion by establishing on exact identity between the broad language of the Fourteenth Amendment and the seemingly more specific rules of Amendments I-VIII." Akhil Amar, *The Bill of Rights and the Fourteenth Amendment,* 101 Yale L.J. 1193, 1227 (1992).

As a methodological approach, Justice Black's promised certainty in due process interpretation by resort to the cryptic and often uninterpreted phrases of the first eight Amendments seems certain to provide for the subjective value preferences of the judge, a result Justice Black abhors. What is the meaning of freedom of speech, establishment of religion, unreasonable search and seizure? What is a confession and when does the right to counsel attach? These questions cannot be answered by simple recourse to the language of the Bill of Rights. No matter how passionate Justice Black's pleas for literal constitutional interpretation, his impulses have been reformist and ethical; his search for the objective by resort to the "specifics" in the Bill of Rights was to prove illusory.

Is there an equally severe problem in that Justice Black's approach limits the definition of due process to the text of the Bill of Rights? *See* the Murphy-Rutledge dissent in *Adamson.*

4. *Selective incorporation.* While the Frankfurter "flexible" approach dominated due process decision-making for a decade and a half, it was to suffer a demise. But its replacement was not to be Justice Black's "total incorporation" methodology, but a process of "selective incorporation," a gradual process of inclusion and exclusion of those provisions of the Bill of Rights determined to be fundamental. It has been argued that: "Try as one might to avoid the phrase, 'ordered liberty' or something much like it remains as the principle of selection, to determine which specifics are 'incorporated,' and which are not. That judgment of selection is as likely to be 'subjective' as is the application of the traditional standard." Louis Henkin, *"Selective Incorporation" in the Fourteenth Amendment*, 73 Yale L.J. 74, 82 (1963). Henken asserts that "[s]elective incorporation finds no support in the language of the amendment, or in the history of its adoption." *Id* at 77–78.

While it is the selective process of incorporation, rather than Justice Black's total incorporation, that has triumphed, almost all of the substantive and procedural guarantees of the Bill of Rights have been incorporated in due process liberty. The notable exceptions are the Second and Third Amendments and the Fifth Amendment requirement of grand jury indictment in criminal trials, the Seventh Amendment right to jury trial in civil cases, and perhaps, the Eighth Amendment prohibition on excessive bail. Is there any reason why these rights should not be incorporated? When a right has been incorporated, the specific right, employing the same standards used in reviewing federal action, is generally used in reviewing state action.

5. *The continuing debate*. The debate over whether the Fourteenth Amendment was intended to incorporate the Bill of Rights continues. Professor Akhil Amar, *The Bill of Rights and the Fourteenth Amendment*, 101 YALE L.J. 1193, 1197 (1992), reviews the debate and offers a new model of incorporation:

> This synthesis, which I call "refined incorporation," begins with Black's insight that *all* of the privileges and immunities of citizens recognized in the Bill of Rights became applicable against states by dint of the Fourteenth Amendment. But not all of the provisions of the original Bill of Rights were indeed rights of citizens. Some instead were at least in part rights of states, and as such awkward to incorporate fully *against* states. The right question is whether the provision really guarantees a privilege or immunity of individual citizens rather than a right of states or the public at large. And when we ask this question, clause by clause, we must be attentive to the possibility, flagged by Frankfurter, that a particular principle in the Bill of Rights may change its shape in the process of absorption into the Fourteenth Amendment.

Professor Amar developed and applied "refined incorporation" in THE BILL OF RIGHTS: CREATION AND RECONSTRUCTION (1998).

§ 5.04 PROCEDURAL DUE PROCESS

The Due Process Clauses of the Fifth and Fourteenth Amendments provide that life, liberty and property shall not be taken from persons without due process of law. There is a commonsense meaning of due process — the guarantee of procedural fairness. Remedies for procedural due process violations mandate that the government change the processes used in dealing with persons but do not require any reform in the substantive rule itself. Given the penchant of lawyers for "fair procedure," this subject is a vital element defining the relations of government to the individual.

1. ***"Life, liberty, or property."*** Before government is obligated to accord any procedural fairness under the Fourteenth Amendment, the government must be depriving a person of "life, liberty, or property." A threat to one of these interests is a precondition for invoking the due process guarantees. But what is meant by life, liberty and property? Do these constitutional terms encompass all interests of value to the individual or are the relevant interests to be more narrowly confined? How is the meaning of life, liberty, and property to be ascertained and who is to do the defining?

In a series of law review articles in the mid-1960s, Professor Charles Reich had an unusual impact on the law, detailing the emergence of a "new property" in the form of government largesse. Prior to this time, government benefits were viewed by the courts as "privileges" that could be withdrawn at will rather than as "rights" to which people had claims of ownership. The rise in government awards of money, benefits, services, contracts, franchises and licenses meant that individuals were increasingly dependent on their relationship to government. Professor Reich urged that these benefits should be viewed as a type of property, protectable by due process. Charles Reich, *The New Property*, 73 YALE L.J. 733 (1964); Charles Reich, *Individual Rights and Social Welfare: The Emerging Legal Issues*, 74 YALE L.J. 1245 (1965); Charles Reich, *The Law of the Planned Society*, 75 YALE L.J. 1227 (1966).

***Goldberg v. Kelly*, 397 U.S. 254 (1970)**. The Supreme Court explicitly relied on and adopted the Reich view. In a case dealing with whether a state could terminate a person's welfare payments without a prior hearing, the Court said that the state did not even contest the question whether due process was required.

> Welfare benefits are a matter of statutory entitlement for persons qualified to receive them. Their termination involves state action that adjudicates important rights. The constitutional challenge cannot be answered by an argument that public assistance benefits are "a 'privilege' and not a 'right.'" Relevant constitutional restraints apply as much to the withdrawal of public assistance benefits as to disqualification for unemployment compensation; or to denial of a tax exemption; or to discharge from public employment.

The only significant question, therefore, was whether due proces required a pre-termination hearing, and the Court held that it did.

Following *Goldberg*, the Court was required to deal with complex questions of when the right arose. For example, the Court said that "discharge from public employment" required due process, but what was a "discharge" as opposed to a "refusal" to employ? In *Board of Regents v. Roth*, 408 U.S. 564 (1972) and *Perry v. Sindermann*, 408 U.S. 593 (1972), the Court dealt with claims of two college teachers who had been dismissed by their respective schools without hearings. Neither had achieved a formal status of "tenure." In *Roth*, the plaintiff had been denied renewal of his contract after the third year of teaching; the Court examined the rules of the College and found no "claim of entitlement" to renewal at that stage. In *Perry*, however, the plaintiff had been teaching in the state college system for some years and offered to show the "existence of rules and understandings, promulgated and fostered by state officials, that may justify his legitimate claim of entitlement to continued employment absent 'sufficient cause.'" The Court held that if he were successful in this showing, then he would have a legitimate property interest in continued employment.

> Proof of such a property interest would not, of course, entitle him to reinstatement. But such proof would obligate college officials to grant a hearing at his request, where he could be informed of the grounds for his nonretention and challenge their sufficiency.

Roth, on the other hand, could make no such showing. The Court emphasized: "Property interests, of course, are not created by the Constitution. Rather they are created and their dimensions are defined by existing rules or understandings that stem from an independent source such as state law — rules or understandings that secure certain benefits and that support claims of entitlement to those benefits."

Castle Rock v. Gonzales, 125 S. Ct. 2796 (2005). The Court in this case resolved the question whether police failure to enforce a restraining order against respondent's husband, leading to the murder of her children, deprived her of a property interest in the order without due process law. The Supreme Court held that it did not, because respondent lacked a protected property interest in the restraining order. Justice Scalia, writing for the Court, noted that "[o]ur cases recognize that a benefit is not a protected entitlement if government officials may grant or deny it in their discretion." While the lower court had found a property interest in the restraining order under state law, the Court indicated that it would not defer on the ultimate issue of "whether what Colorado law has given the respondent constitutes a property interest." The Court went further, refusing to defer to the lower court's finding of an entitlement. It made its own analysis of whether Colorado law gave respondent a right to enforcement of the restraining order.

The language of the Colorado statute appeared to be mandatory, e.g., "A police officer shall use every reasonable means to enforce a restraining order." But the Court concluded: "We do not believe that these provisions truly made enforcement of restraining orders *mandatory*. A well established tradition of police discretion has long coexisted with apparently mandatory arrest statues." Moreover, the Court held that "[e]ven if the statute could be said to have made enforcement of restraining orders 'mandatory' because of the domestic-violence context of the underlying statue, that would not necessarily mean that state law gave *respondent* an entitlement to *enforcement* of the mandate." Respondent's interest, the Court reasoned, "stems only from a State's *statutory* scheme—from a restraining order that was authorized by and tracked precisely the statute on which the Court of Appeals relied. She does not assert that she has any common-law or contractual entitlement to enforcement." The Colorado statute, the Court held, gave no unwavering right to enforcement. Finally, the Court held that "[e]ven if we were to think otherwise concerning the creation of an entitlement by Colorado, it is by no means clear than an individual entitlement to enforcement of a restraining order could constitute a 'property' interest for purposes of the Due Process Clause. Such a right would not, of course, resemble any traditional conception of property." While that fact alone did not automatically disqualify it from due process protection, such an entitlement would not have some ascertainable monetary value and arises incidentally, not out of some new species of governmental benefit.

Justice Stevens, on behalf of two members of the Court, dissented: "The majority's decision to plunge ahead with its own analysis of Colorado law imprudently departs from this Court's longstanding policy of paying 'deference [to] the views of a federal court as to the law of a State within its jurisdiction.' " Moroever, "[e]ven if the Court had good reason to doubt the Court of Appeals' determination of state law, it would . . . be a far wiser course to certify the question to the Colorado Supreme Court."

2. ***What process is due?*** Once the Court held, as it did in *Roth*, that constitutionally protected entitlements "are created and their dimensions are

defined by existing rules or understandings that stem from an independent source such as state law," certain commentators argued that a "paradox" resulted where the Court imposes procedural requirements not dictated by state legislative enactment:

> If the legislature has the greater authority to abolish a given right totally, it must, *a fortiori*, possess the lesser authority to modify some of the procedures that come into play when that right is terminated. Any legislative definition of a substantive property right must include procedural aspects and there can be no principled reason for allowing the legislature complete control over one aspect while not allowing them any control over the other.

Martin Redish & Lawrence Marshall, *Adjudicatory Independence and the Values of Procedural Due Process*, 95 YALE L.J. 455, 467 (1986).

The question naturally arose whether government could define the rules and understandings of employment so that no pre-termination hearing would be required. In other words, could the personnel regulations of a public employer provide for continued employment so long as the employee performed well but that employment could be terminated by the supervisor at any time? Would these "rules or understandings" constitute essentially employment at will?

In *Arnett v. Kennedy*, 416 U.S. 134 (1974), a plurality of three Justices led by Justice Rehnquist attempted to adopt the position that government could define the procedures as well as the content of employment. Justice Rehnquist wrote that the public employee must accept the "bitter with the sweet." And in *Bishop v. Wood*, 426 U.S. 341 (1976), Justice Rehnquist's position seemed to capture a majority of the Court. Petitioner's employment as a policeman had been terminated without affording him a hearing to determine the sufficiency of the cause for his discharge. He brought suit, contending that since a city ordinance classified him as a "permanent employee," he had a constitutional right to a pretermination hearing. The Supreme Court, in an opinion by Justice Stevens, rejected his argument:

> A property interest in employment can, of course, be created by ordinance, or by an implied contract. In either case, however, the sufficiency of the claim of entitlement must be decided by reference to state law. The North Carolina Supreme Court has held that an enforceable expectation of continued public employment in that State can exist only if the employer, by statute or contract, has actually granted some form of guarantee.
>
> On its face the ordinance on which petitioner relies may fairly be read as conferring such a guarantee. However, such a reading is not the only possible interpretation; the ordinance may also be construed as granting no right to continued employment but merely conditioning an employee's removal on compliance with certain specified procedures.

***Cleveland Bd. of Educ. v. Loudermill,* 470 U.S. 532 (1985).** A majority of the Court specifically rejected the "bitter with the sweet" approach.

> The point is straightforward: the Due Process Clause provides that certain substantive rights — life, liberty, and property — cannot be deprived except pursuant to constitutionally adequate procedures. The categories of substance and procedure are distinct. Were the rule otherwise, the Clause would be reduced to a mere tautology. "Property" cannot be defined by the procedures provided for its deprivation any more than can life or liberty. The right to due process "is conferred, not by legislative grace, but by constitutional guarantee. While the legislature may elect not to confer a property interest in [public] employment, it may not constitutionally authorize the deprivation of such an interest, once conferred, without appropriate procedural safeguards."

After *Loudermill*, it seems that a governmental entity may decide to have "employment at will" in which the employee has no claim of entitlement to continued employment, but if it grants any claim of entitlement, then the procedures for termination will be determined by federal constitutional law. Under these circumstances, why would a governmental employer provide anything but "at will" terms?

***Matthews v. Eldridge,* 424 U.S. 319 (1976).** Once it has been determined that due process attaches, what procedures are required? In *Goldberg*, p. 453, *supra*, the Court required a pre-termination hearing but allowed the hearing to be relatively informal, without cross-examination of witnesses or formal rules of evidence. In *Matthews v. Eldridge*, the Court distinguished *Goldberg* and held that due process does not require a hearing prior to the termination of social security disability benefits. While acknowledging that the disability benefits are a property interest protected by the due process clause, the Court determined that fairness did not require a hearing prior to termination of benefits. The following considerations were deemed relevant:

> First, the private interest that will be affected by the official action; second, the risk of an erroneous deprivation of such interest through the procedures used, and the probable value, if any, of additional or substitute procedural safeguards; and finally, the government's interest, including the function involved and the fiscal and administrative burden that the additional or substitute procedural requirement would entail.

The *Mathews v. Eldredge* factors, as they are now known, essentially call upon public administrators, and reviewing courts, to devise procedures that are as likely to avoid errors on important matters as seems reasonable in the particular administrative setting. The *Matthews* test was extended to judicial processes in suits between private parties in *Connecticut v. Doehr*, 501 U.S. 1 (1991).

See the Court's use of the *Matthews v. Eldridge* test in *Hamdi v. Rumsfeld*, p. 377, in determining what process is due to a citizen who has been detained in challenging his "enemy combatant" status. While a majority of the Court argued that the citizen-detainee is entitled to core procedures such as notice of the factual basis for the classification and a fair opportunity to rebut the government's factual claims before a neutral decisionmaker, only a plurality accepted Justice O'Connor's argument that "the exigencies of the circumstances may demand that, aside from these core elements, enemy combatant proceedings may be tailored to alleviate their uncommon potential to burden the Executive in such a time of ongoing military conflict."

3. **Institutional settings.** Finally, there is the problem that in many administrative settings, particularly those of governmental institutions, a great deal of discretion is vested in the administrator. In *University of Missouri v. Horowitz*, 435 U.S. 78 (1978), the Court dealt with a tricky problem presented by the dismissal of a medical student for repeated failures in the clinical portions of her education. The faculty warned her about her "personal hygiene" and deportment. When she continued to show up for rounds with dirty hands and the like, she was dismissed from school. The Court said that some judgments, such as the academic judgments involved in grading papers were not susceptible to review and a hearing before making them would make no sense. On the other hand, discipline for failure to follow a rule would require a hearing because there are specific facts to be determined and a decision on whether those facts fit an existing rule. In this close case, the Court held that the decision involved was an academic judgment requiring no hearing.

One of the most fertile grounds for due process litigation in institutional settings has been the prisons. *Goldberg v. Kelly* has had counterparts in decisions imposing a wide range of adjudicatory procedures on decisions to be made by state-run prisons. *Morrissey v. Brewer*, 408 U.S. 471 (1972) (parole revocation); *Gagnon v. Scarpelli*, 411 U.S. 778 (1973) (probation revocation). On the other hand, more limited procedural safeguards were accorded in *Wolff v. McDonnell*, 418 U.S. 539 (1974) (loss of good time credits). In *Meachum v. Fano*, 427 U.S. 215 (1976) (transfer to a prison with less favorable conditions), the Court held that there was no liberty interest sufficient to require due process protection. Further elaboration of the "entitlement" issue came in *Board of Pardons v. Allen*, 482 U.S. 369 (1987), in which the Court held that prisoners in Montana had a liberty interest in parole release. The statute governing parole board decisions mandated that "the board *shall* release on parole any person confined in the Montana state prison or the women's correction center when in its opinion there is reasonable probability that the prisoner can be released without detriment to the prisoner or to the community." And in *Washington v. Harper*, 494 U.S. 210 (1990), the Court, per Justice Kennedy, held that a Washington State Policy providing for involuntary administration of antipsychotic medication to mentally ill prisoners under defined procedures satisfied the requirements of the Due Process Clause.

Procedures whereby parents have their children voluntarily committed to state institutional mental health care came under judicial scrutiny in *Parham v. J.R.*, 442 U.S. 584 (1979). Children who had been committed pursuant to Georgia law sought a declaratory judgment that the state procedures violated due process because decision authority essentially rested with a medical professional. The Supreme Court, per Chief Justice Burger, reversed the district court, holding that the Georgia statutory procedures satisfied due process. The Court assumed that a child has a constitutionally protectible interest "not only in being free of unnecessary bodily restraints but also in not being labeled erroneously by some because of an improper decision by the state hospital superintendent." But in determining what procedures are required, the interest of the child must be considered with the interests of the parents in the child's welfare since they are "inextricably linked." Chief Justice Burger noted that parents generally act in the child's best interests and that no evidence of rampant abuse had been developed in the lower court.

Chapter 6

FORMS OF SUBSTANTIVE DUE PROCESS

INTRODUCTION

The *Slaughter-House Cases* could be described as a triumph of positivism over natural law. Judicial review would not result in invalidating a legislative enactment unless a specific, and narrowly interpreted, provision of the Constitution operated against the statute. The courts would not independently fashion individual rights. The dissenters, by contrast, did express a willingness to go beyond the literal confines of the Fourteenth Amendment to give content to its ambiguous phrases. It was not long before theories of natural law and vested rights began to creep into constitutional interpretation.

Beginning in the late nineteenth century, economic growth was beneficial for many people but left many victims in its wake. Reformers bent on protecting individuals and on protecting marketplaces from unfair or manipulative practices sought to impose government regulation on various business practices. Although most of the early initiatives were upheld under the prevailing views in *Slaughter-House*, the Supreme Court eventually invalidated much of the government protective regulation using a variety of constitutional rubrics. The most visible and consistent vehicle employed was "due process." The economic branch of substantive due process review died in the same judicial revolution of the 1930s that produced virtually unlimited congressional commerce power. Although interest in economic rights has resurfaced recently, both in academia and in the federal judiciary, the due process doctrine's articulation of those values remains quiescent for the moment.

In contrast to the fate of economic substantive due process, the Court has recognized a variety of fundamental personal rights, relating to general notions of "liberty" or "privacy." The most controversial and elaborate exposition of these personal rights began in the field of contraception and abortion. Constitutional protection has also been extended to marriage and family life, a right to refuse medical treatment, and some degree of sexual privacy.

Section 6.01 of this chapter traces the rise and fall of economic substantive due process and considers suggestions for more active judicial scrutiny of economic regulation, either using due process or some other constitutional rubric. Section 6.02 traces the development of fundamental personal rights doctrine and raises questions about the future directions of that form of substantive due process review.

The twin areas of economic and personal substantive due process are the easiest points in all of constitutional law in which to see the tension between demands for creative use of the judicial power to protect against governmental incursions and the competing desire for restraint by the judiciary in adhering to a written text. It will be important to appreciate that a person may believe quite differently about the role of the courts in the two areas because one person may have different views of the values that lie behind property and personal liberty for purposes of judicial protection. *See* Edwin Baker, *Property and its Relation to Constitutionally Protected Liberty*, 134 U. PA. L. REV. 741 (1986).

§ 6.01 ECONOMIC SUBSTANTIVE DUE PROCESS

[A] THE PATH TO *LOCHNER*

Munn v. Illinois, 113 U.S. 27 (1877), upheld a state statute limiting the rates charged by grain warehouses. The opinion was careful, however, to limit its discussion to the police power of the state to regulate private property that is "affected with a public interest." An owner would find that his property became "clothed with a public interest when used in a manner to make it of public consequence, and affect the community at large." The Court refused to inquire into the reasonableness of the rates since the setting of rates was a legislative prerogative. But the Court did add an interesting dictum: "Undoubtedly, in mere private contracts, relating to matters in which the public has no interest, what is reasonable must be ascertained judicially. But this is because the legislature has no control over such a contract."

Allgeyer v. Louisiana, 165 U.S. 578 (1897), invalidated a state statute making it illegal for any person to contract with an insurance company not licensed to do business in Louisiana. The Court recognized the power of the state to prohibit an insurance company from doing business within the state absent licensing, but held that prohibiting a person from making contact with an out-of-state company was a violation of the individual's right to contract protected by the Fourteenth Amendment's Due Process Clause.

> The liberty mentioned in that amendment means not only the right of the citizen to be free from the mere physical restraint of his person, as by incarceration, but the term is deemed to embrace the right of the citizen to be free in the enjoyment of all his faculties; to be free to use them in all lawful ways; to live and work where he will; to earn his livelihood by any lawful calling; to pursue any livelihood or avocation, and for that purpose to enter into all contracts which may be proper, necessary and essential to his carrying out to a successful conclusion the purposes above mentioned.

Nevertheless, in the years following *Slaughterhouse*, the constitutional protection of the liberty and property right to contract for employment, free of governmental interference, remained a minority position. For the time being, the police power of the state continued to receive judicial recognition. But the demands of the expanding industrialism for freedom from governmental restraint could not be denied. The social context was being revised.

> Due process was fashioned from the most respectable ideological stuff of the later nineteenth century. The ideas out of which it was shaped were in full accord with the dominant thought of the age. They were an aspect of common sense, a standard of economic orthodoxy, a test

of straight thinking and sound opinion. In the domain of thought their general attitude was on the present. In philosophy it was individualism; in government, laissez-faire; in economics, the natural law of supply and demand; in law, the freedom of contract. The system of thought had possessed every other discipline; it had in many a domain reshaped the law to its teachings.

Hamilton, *The Path of Due Process of Law*, 48 Ethics 269, 294–95 (1938).

LOCHNER v. NEW YORK

198 U.S. 45, 25 S. Ct. 539, 49 L. Ed. 937 (1905)

[Lochner was convicted of violating a New York statute prohibiting employers from employing workers in bakeries and confectionaries more than sixty hours per week or ten hours per day. His conviction was affirmed by the New York Court of Appeals.]

Justice Peckham delivered the opinion of the Court.

The statute necessarily interferes with the right of contract between the employer and employes, concerning the number of hours in which the latter may labor in the bakery of the employer. The general right to make a contract in relation to his business is part of the liberty of the individual protected by the Fourteenth Amendment of the federal Constitution. *Allgeyer v. Louisiana*. The right to purchase or to sell labor is part of the liberty protected by this amendment, unless there are circumstances which exclude the right. There are, however, certain powers, existing in the sovereignty of each state in the Union, somewhat vaguely termed police powers, the exact description and limitation of which have not been attempted by the courts. Those powers, broadly stated, and without, at present, any attempt at a more specific limitation, relate to the safety, health, morals and general welfare of the public. Both property and liberty are held on such reasonable conditions as may be imposed by the governing power of the state in the exercise of those powers, and with such conditions the Fourteenth Amendment was not designed to interfere.

It must, of course, be conceded that there is a limit to the valid exercise of the police power by the state. There is no dispute concerning this general proposition. In every case that comes before this Court, therefore, where legislation of this character is concerned, and where the protection of the federal Constitution is sought, the question necessarily arises: Is this a fair, reasonable, and appropriate exercise of the police power of the state, or is it an unreasonable, unnecessary, and arbitrary interference with the right of the individual to his personal liberty, or to enter into those contracts in relation to labor which may seem to him appropriate or necessary for the support of himself and his family? Of course the liberty of contract relating to labor includes both parties to it. The one has as much right to purchase as the other to sell labor.

This is not a question of substituting the judgment of the court for that of the legislature. If the act be within the power of the state it is valid, although the judgment of the court might be totally opposed to the enactment of such a law. But the question would still remain: Is it within the police power of the state? and that question must be answered by the Court.

Viewed in the light of purely labor law, with no reference whatever to the question of health, we think that a law like the one before us involves neither the safety, the morals, nor the welfare, of the public, and that the interest of the public is not in the slightest degree affected by such an act. The law must be upheld, if at all, as a law pertaining to the health of the individual engaged in the occupation of a baker. It does not affect any other portion of the public than those who are engaged in that occupation. Clean and wholesome bread does not depend upon whether the baker works but ten hours per day or only sixty hours a week. The limitation of the hours of labor does not come within the police power on that ground.

It is a question of which of two powers or rights shall prevail — the power of the state to legislate or the right of the individual to liberty of person and freedom of contract. The mere assertion that the subject relates, though but in a remote degree, to the public health, does not necessarily render the enactment valid. The act must have a more direct relation, as a means to an end, and the end itself must be appropriate and legitimate, before an act can be held to be valid which interferes with the general right of an individual to be free in his person and in his power to contract in relation to his own labor.

We think the limit of the police power has been reached and passed in this case. There is, in our judgment, no reasonable foundation for holding this to be necessary or appropriate as a health law to safeguard the public health, or the health of the individuals who are following the trade of a baker. If this statute be valid, and if, therefore, a proper case is made out in which to deny the right of an individual, sui juris, as employer or employe, to make contracts for the labor of the latter under the protection of the provisions of the federal Constitution, there would seem to be no length to which legislation of this nature might not go.

We think that there can be no fair doubt that the trade of a baker, in and of itself, is not an unhealthy one to that degree which would authorize the legislature to interfere with the right to labor, and with the right of free contract on the part of the individual, either as employer or employe. Some occupations are more healthy than others, but we think there are none which might not come under the power of the legislature to supervise and control the hours of working therein, if the mere fact that the occupation is not absolutely and perfectly healthy is to confer that right upon the legislative department of the government. It might be safely affirmed that almost all occupations more or less affect the health. There must be more than the mere fact of the possible existence of some small amount of unhealthiness to warrant legislative interference with liberty.

It is also urged, pursuing the same line of argument, that it is to the interest of the state that its population should be strong and robust, and therefore any legislation which may be said to tend to make people healthy must be valid as health laws, enacted under the police power. If this be a valid argument and a justification for this kind of legislation, it follows that the protection of the federal Constitution from undue interference with liberty of person and freedom of contract is visionary, wherever the law is sought to be justified as a valid exercise of the police power. Scarcely any law but might find shelter under such assumptions, and conduct, properly so called, as well as contract, would come under the restrictive sway of the legislature. We do not believe in the soundness of the views which uphold this law. On the contrary, we think that such a law as this, although passed in the assumed exercise of the police power, and as relating to the public health, or the health of the employes named, is not within that power, and is invalid. The act is not, within any fair meaning of the term, a health law, but is an illegal interference with the rights of individuals, both employers and employes, to make contracts regarding labor upon such terms as they may think best, or which they may agree upon with the other parties to such contracts. Statutes of the nature of that under review, limiting the hours in which grown and intelligent men may labor to earn their living, are mere meddlesome interferences with the rights of the individual, and they are not saved from condemnation by the claim that they are passed in the exercise of the police power and upon the subject of the health of the individual whose rights are interfered with, unless there be some fair ground, reasonable in and of itself, to say that there is material danger to the public health, or to the health of the employes, if the hours of labor are not curtailed.

This interference on the part of the legislatures of the several states with the ordinary trades and occupations of the people seems to be on the increase. It is impossible for us to shut our eyes to the fact that many of the laws of this character, while passed under what is claimed to be the police power for the purpose of protecting the public health or welfare, are, in reality, passed from other motives. It seems to us that the real object and purpose were simply to regulate the hours of labor between the master and his employes (all being men, sui juris), in a private business, not dangerous in any degree to morals, or in any real and substantial degree to the health of the employes. Under such circumstances the freedom of master and employe to contract with each other in relation to their employment, and in defining the same, cannot be prohibited or interfered with, without violating the federal Constitution.

JUSTICE HARLAN, with whom JUSTICES WHITE and DAY join, dissenting:

[Justice Harlan reviews the legislative evidence regarding the health dangers to bakers from excessive working hours.] I do not stop to consider whether any particular view of this economic question presents the sounder theory. What the precise facts are it may be difficult to say. It is enough for the determination of this case, and it is enough for this court to know, that the question is one about which there is room for debate and for an honest difference of opinion. There are many reasons of a weighty, substantial character, based upon the experience of mankind, in support of the theory that, all things considered, more than ten hours' steady work each day, from week to week, in a bakery or confectionery establishment, may endanger the health, and shorten the lives of the workmen, thereby diminishing their physical and mental capacity to serve the State, and to provide for those dependent upon them.

If such reasons exist that ought to be the end of this case, for the State is not amenable to the judiciary, in respect of its legislative enactments, unless such enactments are plainly, palpably, beyond all question, inconsistent with the Constitution of the United States.

JUSTICE HOLMES, dissenting.

This case is decided upon an economic theory which a large part of the country does not entertain. If it were a question whether I agreed with that theory, I should desire to study it further and long before making up my mind. But I do not conceive that to by my duty, because I strongly believe that my agreement or disagreement has nothing to do with the right of a majority to embody their opinions in law. It is settled by various decisions of this court that state constitutions and state laws may regulate life in many ways which we as legislators might think as injudicious, or if you like as tyrannical, as this, and which, equally with this, interfere with the liberty to contract. The Fourteenth Amendment does not enact Mr. Herbert Spencer's Social Statics. [A] constitution is not intended to embody a particular economic theory, whether of paternalism and the organic relation of the citizen to the state or of laissez faire. It is made for people of fundamentally differing views, and the accident of our finding certain opinions natural and familiar, or novel, and even shocking, ought not to conclude our judgment upon the question whether statutes embodying them conflict with the Constitution of the United States.

General propositions do not decide concrete cases. The decision will depend on a judgment or intuition more subtle than any articulate major premise. But I think that the proposition just stated, if it is accepted, will carry us far toward the end. Every opinion tends to become a law. I think that the word "liberty," in the Fourteenth Amendment, is perverted when it is held to prevent the natural outcome of a dominant opinion, unless it can be said that a rational and fair man necessarily would admit that the statute proposed would infringe fundamental principles as they have been understood by the traditions of our people and our law. It does not need research to show that no such sweeping condemnation can be passed upon the statute before us. A reasonable man might think it a proper measure on the score of health. Men whom I certainly could not pronounce unreasonable would uphold it as a first instalment of a general regulation of the hours of work. Whether in the latter aspect it would be open to the charge of inequality I think it unnecessary to discuss.

NOTES

1. *Liberty of contract.* *Lochner* completed the merger of the concepts of liberty and property in a due process-based "liberty of contract." *Lochner* proceeds on a doubtful assumption of equality of bargaining power between employer and employees, between two "persons" one of whom happens to be a corporation. ARTHUR S. MILLER, THE SUPREME COURT AND AMERICAN CAPITALISM 57–60 (1968), argues that "the Court considered the power of the individual worker to be equal to the power of the employer — even though that employer was a collectivity, a corporation, and a person in law only by application of a transparent legal fiction — an assumption that is difficult to explain except on grounds of willful blindness, or, perhaps, of a complete lack of knowledge of the facts of industrial life." Professor Miller asserts that the

Court "failed to see that freedom could be limited by centers of economic power — the corporation — as well as by government."

2. *The public interest.* The *Lochner* majority draws a sharp distinction between laws affecting private contract relations and laws bearing on the public well-being. Police powers extend only to the latter, *i.e.* matters of general public interest. Why isn't the public "in the slightest degree affected" by the hours a baker works? Professor, later Justice, Frankfurter noted that "[t]he underlying assumption was, of course, that industry presented only contract relations between individuals. That industry is part of society, the relation of business to the community, was naturally enough lost sight of in the days of pioneer development and free land." Felix Frankfurter, *Hours of Labor and Realism in Constitutional Law*, 29 HARV. L. REV. 353, 363 (1916).

3. *Means-end relationship.* The Holmes dissent in *Lochner* has received long-standing acclaim. How does he define the error of the majority? Is it an error in assessing the facts concerning the bakery business, or is it an error in legal reasoning? Does the error, for Justice Holmes, lie in the economic values of the majority, or in the judicial function in judging the validity of legislation under the Due Process Clause? Justice Harlan's dissent, unlike that of Holmes, undertakes to survey the evidence on the health consequences of working long hours in a bakery.

4. *The proper function of the court.* What should be the role of the courts in reviewing social and economic legislation?

> Even where the social undesirability of the law may be convincingly urged, invalidation of the law by a court debilitates popular democratic government. Most laws dealing with economic and social problems are matters of trial and error. [E]ven if a law is found wanting on trial, it is better that its defects should be demonstrated and removed than that the law should be aborted by judicial fiat. Such an assertion of judical power deflects responsibility from those on whom in a democratic society it ultimately rests — the people.

A.F.L. v. American Sash & Door Co., 335 U.S. 538, 553 (1949) (Frankfurter, J., concurring). Judge Hand similarly urged deference to the legislative judgment in socioeconomic questions since

> the whole matter is yet to such an extent experimental that no one can with justice apply to the concrete problems the yardstick of abstract economic theory. We do not know, and we cannot for a long time learn, what are the total results of such "meddlesome interference with the rights of the individual." [T]he legislature, with its paraphernalia of committee and commission, is the only public representative really fitted to experiment.

Learned Hand, *Due Process of Law and the Eight-Hour Day*, 21 HARV. L. REV. 495, 507–08 (1908).

5. *Economic explanations.* A modern commentator on *Lochner* suggests that its great significance

> lies in the fact that it was the focal point in a judicial move to fasten on the country by constitutional exegesis unsanctioned by the

> Constitution a pattern of economic organization believed by the Court to be essential to the fullest development of the nation's economy. Without appreciation of this dimension of *Lochner*, the lesson of this episode in constitutional history, however read, will be lost for evaluation of other instances where pressures build to induce the Court to discover in the Constitution what is not there but arguably ought to be in furtherance of fundamental postulates of political and social organization.

Frank Strong, *The Economic Philosophy of Lochner: Emergence, Embrasure and Emasculation*, 15 ARIZ. L. REV. 419 (1973).

Professor Hovenkamp urges that it would be simplistic to accuse the judges of the *Lochner* era as reading into the Constitution an economic theory that was not there. He reviews a variety of economic explanations for the *Lochner* era and finds each lacking. What the *Lochner* Court did, he asserts, was to act as judges always act, reading constitutional language against the backdrop of current understanding of the political economic system.

> Like judges of every era, they drew their wisdom — particularly the wisdom they applied to public law — from outside. To be sure, they operated under a set of rules of form that prevented them from citing this outside wisdom expressly, as judges frequently do today. They simply accepted as obvious, doctrine that had become part of the well-established, consensus models of other disciplines. In the case of substantive due process, the judges wrote into the Constitution a unique American perspective on classical economics.

Herbert Hovenkamp, *The Political Economy of Substantive Due Process*, 40 STAN. L. REV. 379, 393 (1988).

6. *Substantive due process and textual analysis.* It has been argued that

> the principle of textualism may well tell us that the doctrine of "substantive due process," whether in its economic or noneconomic form, is an impermissible interpretation. This is not because the concept gives the unrepresentative judiciary too much power, but because the concept of "substantive" process is an oxymoron. While the cryptic language of the due process clause may thus not reveal much, it *does* inescapably reveal that it is concerned with *process* which is something other than pure *substance*.

Martin Redish & Karen Drizin, *Constitutional Federalism and Judicial Review: The Role of Textual Analysis*, 62 N.Y.U.L. REV. 1, 22 (1987).

> There is some steely consistency to this hard-edged position [that "substantive due process" is an oxymoron], although on balance I believe that it is wrong. Process includes legislative process, and where the legislature acts in ways that are contrary to the general welfare, then it has not acted with due process. So stated the link between process and substantive outcomes becomes far closer.

Richard Epstein, *The Mistakes of 1937*, 11 Geo. Mason U.L. Rev. 5, 13 (1988).

7. Lochner as a method of review. Professor Sunstein claims that *Lochner* reflects a way of looking at the world that has not died out but simply been shifted to other arenas.

> For the *Lochner* Court, neutrality, understood in a peculiar way, was a constitutional requirement. Governmental intervention was constitutionally troublesome, whereas inaction was not; and both neutrality and inaction were defined as respect for the behavior of private actors pursuant to the common law, in light of the existing distribution of entitlements. Whether there was a departure from the requirement of neutrality, in short, depended on whether the government had altered the common law distribution of entitlements.

Cass Sunstein, *Lochner's Legacy*, 87 Colum. L. Rev. 873, 874 (1987).

[B] *LOCHNER* APPLIED

In the early twentieth century, the movement to reform evils generated by the factory system and industrial concentration, the Progressive Era, generated a mass of state and federal reform legislation. Unionization sought to provide greater equality of bargaining power between employees and employers. But *Lochner* characterized the judicial response.

> Courts continued to ignore newly arisen social needs. They applied complacently 18th century conceptions of the liberty of the individual and of the sacredness of private property. [T]he strain became dangerous; the constitutional limitations were invoked to stop the natural vent of legislation. In the course of relatively few years, hundreds of statutes which embodied attempts (often very crude) to adjust legal rights to the demands of social justice were nullified by the court, on the grounds that the statutes violated the constitutional guarantees of liberty or property.

Louis Brandeis, *The Living Law*, 10 Ill. L. Rev. 461, 464 (1916).

***Adair v. United States*, 208 U.S. 161 (1908)** struck down a federal law which made it a criminal offense for an interstate carrier to discharge an employee simply because of his membership in a labor union. The first Justice Harlan, who had dissented in *Lochner*, wrote the majority opinion premised on the "liberty of contract" guarantee of the Fifth Amendment.

> [I]t is not within the functions of government to compel any person in the course of his business and against his will to accept or retain the personal services of another, or to compel any person, against his will, to perform personal services for another. [T]he employer and the employee have equality of right, and any legislation that disturbs that equality is an arbitrary interference with the liberty of contract which no government can legally justify in a free land.

Justice Holmes in dissent argued that the law "simply prohibits the more powerful party to exact certain undertakings, or to threaten dismissal or unjustly discriminate on certain grounds against those already employed."

Seven years after *Adair*, the Court in *Coppage v. Kansas*, 236 U.S. 1 (1915), invalidated a similar state law. Justice Pitney, for the majority, recognized the inequality of bargaining position between employer and employee. "No doubt, wherever the right of private property exists, there must and will be inequalities of fortune; and thus it naturally happens that parties negotiating about a contract are not equally unhampered about circumstances." Nevertheless, as *Adair* had recognized, the constitutional guarantee of liberty of contract allowed the parties to determine the conditions of employment. "[T]he Fourteenth Amendment recognizes 'liberty' and 'property' as co-existent human rights, and debars the State from any unwarranted interference with either."

Justice Holmes in dissent urged the Court to overrule both *Adair* and *Lochner*, arguing that

> in present conditions a workman not unnaturally may believe that only by belonging to a union can he secure a contract that shall be fair to him. If that belief, whether right or wrong, may be held by a reasonable man, it seems to me that it may be enforced by law in order to establish the equality of position between the parties in which liberty of contract begins.

***Adkins v. Children's Hospital,* 261 U.S. 525 (1923)**, applied *Lochner* to invalidate a District of Columbia minimum wage law for women. Justice Sutherland, writing for the majority, while recognizing that there is "no such thing as absolute freedom of contract," stressed that "freedom of contract is, nevertheless, the general rule and restraint the exception."

Again, Justice Holmes dissented, challenging the expansion of the innocuous concept of liberty into a dogma of "liberty of contract":

> Contract is not specially mentioned in the text that we have to construe. It is merely an example of doing what you want to do, embodied in the word liberty. But pretty much all law consists in forbidding men to do some things that they want to do, and contract is no more exempt from law than other acts. This statute does not compel anybody to pay anything. It simply forbids employment at rates below those fixed as the minimum requirement of health and right living. In short, the law in its character and operation is like hundreds of so-called police laws that have been upheld.

It should not be assumed, however, that there were no deviations from the *Allgeyer-Lochner-Adair-Coppage* line of decision. ARTHUR S. MILLER, THE SUPREME COURT AND AMERICAN CAPITALISM 61–62 (1968), notes that "[t]he tendency in the United States towards equality, early noted by DeTocqueville, had by 1900 become sufficiently strong that the Court could not invalidate all efforts of legislatures to rectify imbalances in economic power. Its power was never complete. Some countervailing tendencies in judicial decisions may be seen in the early twentieth century." Nevertheless, "These cases, however, are aberrations; they reveal that the principle of substantive due process had begun slowly to erode about as soon as it had been created out of the whole cloth by the intellectual heirs of Mr. Justice Field."

***Muller v. Oregon,* 208 U.S. 412 (1908).** The Court unanimously upheld a state maximum hour law for women, reasoning that a "woman's physical structure and the performance of maternal functions place her at a disadvantage in the struggle for subsistence" and that "because healthy mothers are essential to vigorous offspring, the physical well-being of women becomes an object of public interest and care in order to preserve the strength and vigor of the race." The Court thus took "judicial cognizance" of considerations which made woman *sui generis*, so that "she is properly placed in a class by herself, and like legislation is not necessary for men and could not be sustained."

The decision in *Muller* was important both for its view of social legislation and as a portent for "women's protective legislation" that would be targeted as repressive by feminists of future generations. But it is now more famous for the manner in which its factual premises were established. Then Professor, and later Justice, Louis D. Brandeis submitted a brief containing a mass of socioeconomic data on the harm to women from excessive hours of employment.

> For the first time the arguments and briefs breathed the air of reality. [T]he support of legislation by an array of facts which established the reasonableness of the legislative action, however it may be with its wisdom — laid down a new technique for counsel charged with the responsibility of arguing such constitutional questions, and an obligation upon courts to insist upon such method of argument before deciding the issue, surely, at least, before deciding the issue adversely to the legislature.

Frankfurter, 29 Harv. L. Rev. at 364–65.

***Bunting v. Oregon,* 243 U.S. 426 (1917).** With then-Professor Felix Frankfurter submitting a two volume "Brandeis Brief," the Court sustained an Oregon law establishing a ten-hour day for male workers. No reference was made to *Lochner*, which was clearly contrary precedent. Simply, the statute was held to be a real health measure and therefore a proper exercise of the police power of the state. How do you explain *Muller* and *Bunting* in light of *Lochner*? And how do you explain *Adkins* in light of *Muller* and *Bunting*? Are minimum wage and maximum hour laws different in purpose or effect?

[C] THE COURT ABDICATES: THE FALL OF ECONOMIC SUBSTANTIVE DUE PROCESS

NEBBIA v. NEW YORK

291 U.S. 502, 54 S. Ct. 505, 78 L. Ed. 940 (1934)

[Nebbia was convicted for selling two quarts of milk below the minimum price set by a milk control board acting under a 1933 state law. The court of appeals affirmed.]

JUSTICE ROBERTS delivered the opinion of the Court.

Under our form of government the use of property and the making of contracts are normally matters of private and not of public concern. The general rule is that both shall be free of governmental interference. But neither property rights nor contract rights are absolute; for government cannot exist if the citizen may at will use his property to the detriment of his fellows, or exercise his freedom of contract to work them harm. Equally fundamental with the private right is that of the public to regulate it in the common interest.

The Fifth Amendment, in the field of federal activity, and the Fourteenth, as respects state action, do not prohibit governmental regulation for the public welfare. They merely condition the exertion of the admitted power, by securing that the end shall be accomplished by methods consistent with due process. And the guaranty of due process, as has often been held, demands only that the law shall not be unreasonable, arbitrary or capricious, and that the means selected shall have a real and substantial relation to the object sought to be attained. It results that a regulation valid for one sort of business, or in given circumstances, may be invalid for another sort, or for the same business under other circumstances, because the reasonableness of each regulation depends upon the relevant facts.

[The Court reviews the extensive legislative fact-finding on the dangers of price instability in the milk industry.] The milk industry in New York has been the subject of longstanding and drastic regulation in the public interest. In the light of the facts the order appears not to be unreasonable or arbitrary, or without relation to the purpose to prevent ruthless competition from destroying the wholesale price structure on which the farmer depends for his livelihood, and the community for an assured supply of milk.

But we are told that because the law essays to control prices it denies due process. Notwithstanding the admitted power to correct existing economic ills by appropriate regulation of business, even though an indirect result may be a restriction of the freedom of contract or a modification of charges for services or the price of commodities, the appellant urges that direct fixation of prices is a type of regulation absolutely forbidden. The argument runs that the public control of rates or prices is per se unreasonable and unconstitutional, save as applied to businesses affected with a public interest; that a business so affected is one in which property is devoted to an enterprise of a sort which the public itself might appropriately undertake, or one whose owner relies on a public grant or franchise for the right to conduct the business, or in which he is bound to serve all who apply; in short, such as is commonly called a public utility; or a business in its nature a monopoly. The milk industry, it is said, possesses none of these characteristics, and, therefore, not being affected with a public interest, its charges may not be controlled by the state.

It is clear that there is no closed class or category of businesses affected with a public interest, and the function of courts in the application of the Fifth and Fourteenth Amendments is to determine in each case whether circumstances vindicate the challenged regulation as a reasonable exertion of governmental authority or condemn it as arbitrary or discriminatory. The phrase "affected with a public interest" can, in the nature of things, mean no more than that an industry, for adequate reason, is subject to control for the public good. In several of the decisions of this Court wherein the expressions "affected with a public interest," and "clothed with a public use," have been brought forward as the criteria of the validity of price control, it has been admitted that they are not susceptible of definition and form an unsatisfactory test of the constitutionality of legislation directed at business practices or prices. These decisions must rest, finally, upon the basis that the requirements of due process were not met because the laws were found arbitrary in their operation and effect. But there can be no doubt that upon proper occasion and by appropriate measures the state may regulate a business in any of its aspects, including the prices to be charged for the products or commodities it sells.

So far as the requirement of due process is concerned, and in the absence of other constitutional restriction, a state is free to adopt whatever economic policy may reasonably be deemed to promote public welfare, and to enforce that policy by legislation adapted to its purpose. The courts are without authority either to declare such policy, or, when it is declared by the legislature, to override it. If the laws passed are seen to have a reasonable relation to a proper legislative purpose, and are neither arbitrary nor discriminatory, the requirements of due process are satisfied, and judicial determination to that effect renders a court functus officio. And it is equally clear that if the legislative policy be to curb unrestrained and harmful competition by measures which are not arbitrary or discriminatory it does not lie with the courts to determine that the rule is unwise. With the wisdom of the policy adopted, with the adequacy or practicability of the law enacted to forward it, the courts are both incompetent and unauthorized to deal. The course of decision in this Court exhibits a firm adherence to these principles.

If the law-making body within its sphere of government concludes that the conditions or practices in an industry make unrestricted competition an inadequate safeguard of the consumer's interests, produce waste harmful to the public, threaten ultimately to cut off the supply of a commodity needed by the public or portend the destruction of the industry itself, appropriate statutes passed in an honest effort to correct the threatened consequences may not be set aside because the regulation adopted fixes prices reasonably deemed by the legislature to be fair to those engaged in the industry and to the consuming public. And this is especially so where, as here, the economic maladjustment is one of price, which threatens harm to the producer at one end of the series and the consumer at the other. The Constitution does not secure to anyone liberty to conduct his business in such fashion as to inflict injury upon the public at large, or upon any substantial group of the people. Price control, like any other form of regulation, is unconstitutional only if arbitrary, discriminatory or demonstrably irrelevant to the policy the legislature is free to adopt, and hence an unnecessary and unwarranted interference with individual liberty.

Tested by these considerations we find no basis in the due process clause of the Fourteenth Amendment for condemning the provisions of the Agriculture and Markets Law here drawn into question.

[JUSTICE MCREYNOLDS, joined by JUSTICES VAN DEVANTER, SUTHERLAND and BUTLER, dissented.]

NOTES

1. ***The aftermath of Nebbia.*** *Nebbia* did not mark so abrupt a turning point as proponents of the New Deal would have liked. Between 1934 and 1937, the Court continued to invalidate a substantial part of President Roosevelt's program. Further, the *Lochner* line of cases had never been formally overruled. Nevertheless, the rationale of Justice Roberts in *Nebbia*, the changing composition of the Court and the demands of the New Deal assured the ultimate demise of *Lochner's* economics. Simply stated, its nineteenth century laissez-faire principles did not meet twentieth century needs. The majority's view that it was merely enforcing a natural condition of free bargaining based on common law norms became increasingly untenable. Principles of property and contract law protected by *Lochner* necessarily reflected economic policy choices. With *Nebbia*, the Court began a march that was to end, not with judicial review of the reasonableness of economic legislation characterized by restraint and deference to the legislative judgment, but with total judicial abdication.

Why did the Court make this shift in approach? Professor Hovenkamp points out that British and other European writers had been pursuing distributive and welfare economic theories long before those theories became popular in American thought. "When the dominant American economic ideology changed — not until the first three decades of the twentieth century — the legal ideology followed close behind." Hovenkamp, 40 STAN. L. REV. at 447.

2. ***The substantive change.*** A definitive change came in *West Coast Hotel Co. v. Parrish*, 300 U.S. 379 (1937), sustaining a state minimum wage law for women. The Court, per Chief Justice Hughes, overruled *Adkins* and accepted Justice Holmes' approach to the "liberty" guarantee.

> The Constitution does not speak of freedom of contract. It speaks of liberty and prohibits the deprivation of liberty without due process of law. In prohibiting that deprivation, the Constitution does not recognize an absolute and uncontrollable liberty. [T]he liberty safeguarded is liberty in a social organization which requires the protection of law against the evils which menace the health, safety, morals and welfare of the people. Liberty under the Constitution is thus necessarily subject to the restraints of due process, and regulation which is reasonable in relation to its subject and is adopted in the interests of the community is due process. This essential limitation of liberty in general governs freedom of contract in particular.

The Chief Justice asked: "What can be closer to the public interest than the health of women and their protection from unscrupulous and overreaching employers?" He stated that the protection of women is a legitimate purpose for state legislation and the requirement that a "minimum wage fairly fixed in order to meet the very necessities of existence" is a proper means to that end.

> The exploitation of a class of workers who are in an unequal position with respect to bargaining power and are thus relatively defenseless

> against the denial of a living wage is not only detrimental to their health and well being but casts a direct burden for their support upon the community. The community is not bound to provide what is in effect a subsidy for unconscionable employers. The community may direct its law-making power to correct the abuse which springs from our selfish disregard of the public interest.

It was now Justice Sutherland, joined by Justices Van Devanter, McReynolds and Butler who dissented, citing the principles of *Adkins*.

Any suspicion that *West Coast Hotel* might represent only judicial solicitude for the asserted needs of women was dispelled in 1941 in *United States v. Darby*, p. 96, upholding the minimum wage and maximum hour provisions of the Fair Labor Standards Act, declaring "it is no longer open to question that the fixing of a minimum wage is within the legislative power and that the bare fact of its exercise is not a denial of due process."

3. *The deferential approach.* In subsequent years, decisions distinguished and overruled almost all of the Court's earlier laissez-faire holdings on state and federal regulation in the economic sphere. In *Lincoln Federal Labor Union v. Northwestern Iron & Metal Co.*, 335 U.S. 525 (1949), the Court, per Justice Black, refused to follow *Adair* and *Coppage* and held constitutional a clause which forbade discrimination against nonunion employees. Justice Black declared:

> This court, beginning at least as early as 1934, when the *Nebbia* case was decided, has steadily rejected the due process philosophy enunciated in the *Adair-Coppage* line of cases. In doing so, it has consciously returned closer and closer to the earlier constitutional principle that states have power to legislate against what are found to be injurious practices in their internal commercial and business affairs, so long as their laws do not run afoul of some specific federal constitutional prohibition, or of some valid federal law. Under this constitutional doctrine, the due process clause is no longer to be so broadly construed that the Congress and state legislatures are put in a strait jacket when they attempt to suppress business and industrial conditions which they regard as offensive to the public welfare.

Ferguson v. Skrupa, 372 U.S. 726 (1963), holding constitutional a Kansas law making it unlawful for anyone to engage in the business of debt-adjusting, except as incident to the practice of law, spelled "the last rites for the economic philosophy of *Lochner*." Strong, 15 Ariz. L. Rev. at 454. In upholding the law, Justice Black declared:

> Under the system of government created by our Constitution, it is up to legislatures, not courts, to decide on the wisdom and utility of legislation. There was a time when the Due Process Clause was used by this Court to strike down laws which were thought unreasonable, that is, unwise or incompatible with some particular economic or social philosophy.

> The doctrine that prevailed in *Lochner, Coppage*, [and] *Adkins* has long since been discarded. We have returned to the original constitutional proposition that courts do not substitute their social and economic beliefs for the judgment of legislative bodies, who are elected to pass laws.
>
> In face of our abandonment of the use of the "vague contours" of the Due Process Clause to nullify laws which a majority of the Court believed to be economically unwise, [w]e conclude that the Kansas legislature was free to decide for itself that legislation was needed to deal with the business of debt adjusting. Unquestionably, there are arguments showing that the business of debt adjusting has social utility, but such arguments are properly addressed to the legislature, not to us. Whether the legislature takes for its textbook Adam Smith, Herbert Spencer, Lord Keynes, or some other is no concern of ours. The Kansas debt adjusting statute may be wise or unwise. But relief, if any be needed, lies not with us but with the body constituted to pass laws for the State of Kansas.

4. ***Resurrecting substantive due process?*** Professor Epstein has characterized the Court's ultimate rejection of economic substantive due process of the type fashioned in *Lochner* "as an intellectual mistake that ought to be undone if only we could find the way." He views the employer and employee as being the parties with an interest in the transaction and argues that interference with their choices is justified only when there is a risk that is "latent, which raises the prospect of employer misrepresentation or worker ignorance about those risks." Epstein, 11 GEO. MASON U.L. REV. at 15. But do wage and hour laws really have a focus on the current employer and employee? Are they not also useful for spreading jobs to people who are not currently employed?

[D] AN EVOLVING VIEW OF ECONOMIC LIBERTIES

Is it fair to allow government to wipe out one's occupation (as in *Ferguson*), to limit its utility (as in the many restrictions on optometrists), or to limit access to the occupation (as in apprenticeship and educational requirements)? Many people have objected to the self-serving use of the legislative process to insulate powerful lobbying groups from competition, such as physicians' successful arguments against optometrists and chiropractors. But the question is whether protection against abuse, if there is to be any, should be found in the constitution rather than through the legislative process itself. Notice that *Lochner* has never been overruled. Some commentators and judges would like to see it revived in some fashion.

The standard by which the Court currently purports to judge the validity of economic regulation was set forth in *United States v. Carolene Products Co.*, 304 U.S. 144 (1938):

> [T]he existence of facts supporting the legislative judgment is to be presumed, for regulatory legislation affecting ordinary commercial transactions is not to be pronounced unconstitutional unless in the light of the facts made known or generally assumed it is of such

> character as to preclude the assumption that it rests upon some rational basis within the knowledge and experience of the legislators.

The burden is on the challenging party to establish that the law has no rational relation to a permissible governmental purpose. Application of this standard has resulted in uniformly upholding economic legislation against due process challenges since the time of the New Deal.

In a famous footnote to the *Carolene Products* opinion, Justice Stone articulated a doctrine that was also to become a touchstone of developments in mid-twentieth-century American constitutionalism: "There may be narrower scope for operation of the presumption of constitutionality when legislation appears on its face to be within a specific prohibition of the Constitution, such as those of the first ten amendments." 304 U.S. at 152 n.4. Footnote 4 also left open the possibility of "more exacting judicial scrutiny" when legislation negatively impacted the political process itself or affected "discrete and insular minorities." Stone later amplified this position by referring to First Amendment rights of free speech and religion as occupying a "preferred position" over property rights or economic interests. *Jones v. Opelika*, 316 U.S. 584, 608 (1942). As will be seen below, when government imposes a significant burden on fundamental personal rights, the courts abandon the rationality standard in favor of a more demanding form of due process review.

On the other hand, in the context of procedural due process, it has been urged that "the dichotomy between personal liberties and property rights is a false one. Property does not have rights. People have rights. . . . In fact, a fundamental interdependence exists between the personal right to liberty and the personal right in property. Neither could have meaning without the other." *Lynch v. Household Fin. Corp.*, 405 U.S. 538, 552 (1972).

[1] A Burgeoning Counter-Revolution?

Judicial and critical attention to protecting property and economic interests has never been completely abandoned. There is at least one irony in the Supreme Court's differential treatment of speech and economic interests.

> Judges and professors are talkers both by profession and avocation. It is not surprising that they would view freedom of expression as primary to the free play of their personalities. But most men would probably feel that an economic right, such as freedom of occupation, was at least as vital to them as the right to speak their minds.

Robert McCloskey, *Economic Due Process and the Supreme Court: An Exhumation and Reburial*, 1962 Sup. Ct. Rev. 34, 46.

The "law and economics" movement, which has spawned a number of appointments to the federal bench from the ranks of law professors, has elaborated a model of "economic rights" which may have both natural law and utilitarian underpinnings. One of the most outspoken proponents of this model is Professor Epstein, who decries the judicial validation of government regulation from zoning to wage and hour laws. Richard Epstein, Takings:

PRIVATE PROPERTY AND THE POWER OF EMINENT DOMAIN (1985). In his view, "the greatest abuse known to the framers was the ceaseless imagination of legislative factions to devise new schemes for the costly and nonproductive transfer of wealth and power from one's opponents to one's friends." Richard Epstein, *Needed: Activist Judges for Economic Rights*, WALL ST. J., Nov. 14, 1985, at 32.

Other powerful voices have been added to this side of the debate. Judge Posner of the Seventh Circuit is a particularly vigorous advocate. Richard Posner, *The Constitution as an Economic Document*, 56 GEO. WASH. L. REV. 4 (1987). *See also* Christopher Wonnell, *Economic Due Process and the Preservation of Competition*, 11 HAST. CON. L.Q. 91 (1983). On the other side, "While this development has its attractive aspects, I conclude that the costs of reviving economic substantive due process still outweigh its benefits by a good margin." Michael Phillips, *Another Look at Economic Substantive Due Process*, 1987 WIS. L. REV. 265. The Court has recognized some economic rights in other settings. For example, rethink the cases on the dormant commerce clause and the Art. IV., § 2, privileges and immunities clause with this idea in mind. As another example, be alert to the economic substantive due process implications of the Court's decisions when you study the areas of commercial and corporate speech.

[2] Punitive Damages

In a series of cases that could be described as lying at the junction between procedural and substantive due process, the Court has set out guidelines for review of punitive damage awards by either state or federal courts. The Court has stated several times that the Due Process Clause prohibits "imposition of grossly excessive or arbitrary punishments on a tortfeasor." In *BMW of North America, Inc. v. Gore*, 517 U.S. 559 (1996), the Court considered "wrongdoing . . . by a national distributor of automobiles not to advise its dealers, and hence their customers, of predelivery damage to new cars when the cost of repair amounted to less than 3 percent of the car's suggested retail price." The purchaser of a "new" BMW discovered months later that the car had been repainted before he bought it. He recovered $4,000 in compensatory damages and a jury award of $4 million in punitive damages "based on a determination that the nondisclosure policy constituted 'gross, oppressive or malicious' fraud." When BMW argued that its practice of nondisclosure was lawful in at least 25 states, the Alabama courts reduced the punitive damage award to $2 million. As the Supreme Court later described its holding in *BMW*,

> We instructed courts reviewing punitive damages to consider three guideposts: 1) the degree of reprehensibility of the defendant's conduct; 2) the disparity between the actual or potential harm suffered by the plaintiff and the punitive damages award; and 3) the difference between the punitive damages awarded by the jury and the civil penalties authorized or imposed in comparable cases.

In *State Farm Mutual Auto. Ins. Co. v. Campbell*, 538 U.S. 408 (2003), the Court returned again to the constitutionality of punitive damage awards, holding 6-3, that a punitive damage award of $145 million, when compensatory damages were $1 million, was excessive and violated the Due Process Clause. The case involved a claim of bad faith in failing to settle a lawsuit within the limits of its insured's liability policy. Although State Farm eventually covered the entire damage award, the plaintiffs alleged harm from the stress and emotional distress of the situation. Over State Farm's objections, during both the liability and damages phases of the trial, the court allowed the admission of evidence of nationwide questionable practices by State Farm. This evidence covered twenty years of records and a variety of practices by State Farm beyond automobile insurance coverage. The jury awarded the Campbells $2.5 million in compensatory damages and $145 million in punitive damages, which was reduced to $1 million in compensatory damages and $25 million in punitive damages. On appeal, the Supreme Court of Utah reinstated the $145 million punitive damage award, reasoning that the wealth of State Farm and the reprehensibility of its actions warranted the large award.

With regard to the reprehensibility of the defendant's conduct, the U.S. Supreme Court stated:

> "The Utah Supreme Court's opinion makes explicit that State Farm was being condemned for its nationwide policies rather than for the conduct directed toward the Campbells . . . A State cannot punish a defendant for conduct that may have been lawful where it occurred . . . nor, as a general rule, does a State have legitimate concern in imposing punitive damages to punish a defendant for unlawful acts committed outside of the State's jurisdiction."

While not setting a "bright-line ratio" for punitive damages, Justice Kennedy stated: "Our jurisprudence and the principles it has now established demonstrate, however, that, in practice, few awards exceeding a single-digit ratio between punitive and compensatory damages, to a significant degree, will satisfy due process." Justice Ginsburg, dissenting, expressed her continuing opposition to "the Court's foray into punitive damages," territory traditionally within the State's domain." Justice Scalia, dissenting, argued that *Gore* was incorrectly decided and that the Due Process Clause contains no substantive protection against "excessive" or "unreasonable" punitive damages. In addition, he also argued that the "punitive damages jurisprudence which has sprung forth from *BMW v. Gore* is insusceptible of principled application." Justice Thomas, dissenting, also argued that the Constitution "does not constrain the size of punitive damages awards."

[3] The Takings Issue

The Fifth Amendment and Fourteenth Amendment contain the familiar protection of property against deprivation without due process. The Fifth Amendment also assures "nor shall private property be taken for public use without just compensation." The Takings Clause has generated substantial interest in recent decades as a possible limitation on state regulatory power.

Zoning was upheld as a general proposition in *Euclid v. Ambler Realty Co.*, 272 U.S. 365 (1926). Land-use regulations with more direct impact on activities such as mining were upheld in *Pennsylvania Coal Co. v. Mahon*, 260 U.S. 293 (1922). A few later cases found regulations to be violative of the takings clause in unusual situations. *Loretto v. Teleprompter Manhattan CATV*, 458 U.S. 419 (1982) (physical invasion of property through state law requiring landlords to permit cable companies to install cable facilities in apartment buildings effected a taking); *Kaiser Aetna v. United States*, 444 U.S. 164 (1979) (physical invasion after expensive development of site).

***Penn Central Trans. Co. v. New York*, 438 U.S. 104 (1978).** The City of New York established a commission to designate historical landmarks, preventing alteration of the exterior of a landmark without commission approval. Grand Central Station was so designated and the owner did not seek review of that decision. Subsequently, the owner contracted with a developer to seek erection of a multi-story building over the top of the station. When the commission rejected a petition to allow the construction, the owner challenged the landmark law as a taking. The Supreme Court responded that a restriction on use was not a per se taking. Unless the restriction prevented reasonable expectations of development, then the primary question in a "regulatory taking case is whether the restriction is "reasonably related to the promotion of the general welfare." The Court emphasized that the restrictions not only permitted beneficial use of the property but would allow some enhancements. Penn Central is mentioned frequently in subsequent cases as establishing a "balancing test" in which the public benefit is weighed against the burdens to the owner.

The Supreme Court accepted for review several cases in the 1980s in which it was alleged that a zoning or other land-use regulation constitutes a taking of private property without just compensation. Most of those cases were dismissed without reaching the merits because the plaintiff still had the opportunity to develop the land by seeking a zoning variance or similar relief. In a trilogy of cases in 1987, however, the Court served notice that the takings-compensation clause could have significant impact on land use regulations.

***First English Evangelical Lutheran Church of Glendale v. County of Los Angeles*, 482 U.S. 304 (1987).** The church owned a canyon piece of property on which it had conducted a camp for handicapped children. A flood in 1978 wiped out the camp facilities. As a result of the flood, the county enacted a moratorium on development in the canyons. The church then filed an action for damages. Under California law, the appropriate action to redress an excessive land-use regulation would be first to obtain a declaratory judgment or mandamus declaring the regulation to be a taking; if the local government agency then insisted on continuing the regulation in place, an inverse condemnation action could be brought to recover the fair market value of the property. The Supreme Court, through Chief Justice Rehnquist, held that the state could not refuse to award damages for the interim during which the validity of the regulation was being litigated. The Court remanded for further proceedings to determine whether the regulation constituted a taking. "We have no occasion to decide whether the ordinance at issue actually denied appellant all use of its property or whether the county might avoid the conclusion that a compensable taking had occurred by establishing that the denial of all use was insulated as a part of the State's authority to enact safety regulations. These questions, of course, remain open for decision on the remand we direct today." Justices Stevens, Blackmun, and O'Connor dissented.

***Nollan v. California Coastal Comm'n*, 483 U.S. 825 (1987).** The Court struck down a land-use regulation as a violation of the "taking without just compensation" rule. The Nollans bought a piece of beach-front property with an old bungalow on it. When they applied for a permit to tear down the old structure and erect a new home, the Coastal Commission said that they could have the permit only on condition that they grant a public easement across the beach for people to move back and forth between other, public beaches. The Supreme Court held that this condition was a taking of private property that did not substantially advance a legitimate state interest. Because the property was taken without compensation, the taking was invalid. Justices Brennan, Marshall, Blackmun, and Stevens dissented.

By contrast, in *Keystone Bituminous Coal Ass'n v. DeBenedictis*, 480 U.S. 470 (1987), the Supreme Court found that there was no taking of private property involved in a state law which required a mining company to leave in place fifty percent of the coal beneath public buildings, dwellings, or cemeteries. Justice Stevens, for the Court, held that there was a sufficient public purpose to justify the act on its face; finding a taking in any specific instance would require showing that the act resulted in substantial diminution of the value of a certain tract. Chief Justice Rehnquist dissented, joined by Justices Powell, O'Connor, and Scalia.

See John Humbach, *Economic Due Process and the Takings Clause*, 4 PACE ENV. L. REV. 311 (1987) ("it appears fair to conclude that traditional economic due process review was at least a part of what the Supreme Court was doing in the 1987 cases").

***Lucas v. South Carolina Coastal Council*, 505 U.S. 1003 (1992).** The Court held that a state regulation depriving a private property owner of all economically beneficial uses of land, except those that would be preventable under principles of state property and nuisance law, constituted a taking of private property. The plaintiff had purchased two oceanfront building lots in 1986 for almost a million dollars. In 1988 the state passed legislation restricting beachfront development; regulations adopted pursuant to the new statute precluded building on the two lots in question. In the findings of the trial court, the state action rendered the two lots "valueless." Justice Scalia, for a majority of the Supreme Court, said that the Court had previously

> described at least two discrete categories of regulatory action as compensable without case-specific inquiry into the public interest advanced in support of the restraint. The first encompasses regulations that compel the property owner to suffer a physical "invasion" of his property. . . . The second situation in which we have found categorical treatment appropriate is where regulation denies all economically beneficial or productive use of the land.

Nevertheless, Justice Scalia also recognized that the Court's cases had allowed the state to proscribe "noxious or harmful uses" of land under the nuisance doctrine. Moreover, regulations designed to confer mutual benefits to landowners had been upheld as part of the "background principles" under which owners take title to land. Putting all this together, the opinion summarized its holding as follows:

> Any limitation so severe [as to fall in the two categories] cannot be newly legislated or decreed (without compensation), but must inhere in the title itself, in the restrictions that background principles of the State's law of property and nuisance already place upon land ownership. A law or decree with such an effect must, in other words, do no more than duplicate the result that could have been achieved in the courts — by adjacent landowners (or other uniquely affected persons) under the State's law of private nuisance, or by the State under its complementary power to abate nuisances that affect the public generally, or otherwise.[16]

DOLAN v. CITY OF TIGARD

512 U.S. 374, 114 S. Ct. 2309, 124 L. Ed. 2d 304 (1994)

CHIEF JUSTICE REHNQUIST delivered the opinion of the Court.

Petitioner challenges the decision of the Oregon Supreme Court which held that the city of Tigard could condition the approval of her building permit on the dedication of a portion of her property for flood control and traffic improvements. We granted certiorari to resolve a question left open by our decision in *Nollan v. California Coastal Comm'n*, of what is the required degree of connection between the exactions imposed by the city and the projected impacts of the proposed development.

The State of Oregon enacted a comprehensive land use management program in 1973. Pursuant to the State's requirements, the city of Tigard developed a comprehensive plan and codified it in its Community Development Code (CDC). The CDC requires property owners in the area zoned Central Business District to comply with a 15% open space and landscaping requirement, which limits total site coverage, including all structures and paved parking, to 85% of the parcel. After the completion of a transportation study that identified congestion in the Central Business District as a particular problem, the city adopted a plan for a pedestrian/bicycle pathway intended to encourage alternatives to automobile transportation for short trips. The CDC requires that new development facilitate this plan by dedicating land for pedestrian pathways where provided for in the pedestrian/bicycle pathway plan.

The city also adopted a Master Drainage Plan (Drainage Plan). The Drainage Plan noted that flooding occurred in several areas along Fanno Creek, including areas near petitioner's property. The Drainage Plan also established that the increase in impervious surfaces associated with continued urbanization would exacerbate these flooding problems. To combat these risks, the Drainage Plan suggested a series of improvements to the Fanno Creek Basin,

[16] The principal "otherwise" that we have in mind is litigation absolving the State (or private parties) of liability for the destruction of "real and personal property, in cases of actual necessity, to prevent the spreading of a fire" or to forestall other grave threats to the lives and property of others.

including channel excavation in the area next to petitioner's property. Other recommendations included ensuring that the floodplain remains free of structures and that it be preserved as greenways to minimize flood damage to structures. The Drainage Plan concluded that the cost of these improvements should be shared based on both direct and indirect benefits, with property owners along the waterways paying more due to the direct benefit that they would receive.

Petitioner Florence Dolan owns a plumbing and electric supply store located on Main Street in the Central Business District of the city. The store covers approximately 9,700 square feet on the eastern side of a 1.67-acre parcel, which includes a gravel parking lot. Fanno Creek flows through the southwestern corner of the lot and along its western boundary. The year-round flow of the creek renders the area within the creek's 100-year floodplain virtually unusable for commercial development. The city's comprehensive plan includes the Fanno Creek floodplain as part of the city's greenway system.

Petitioner applied to the city for a permit to redevelop the site. Her proposed plans called for nearly doubling the size of the store to 17,600 square feet, and paving a 39-space parking lot. The City Planning Commission granted petitioner's permit application subject to conditions imposed by the city's CDC. [T]he Commission required that petitioner dedicate the portion of her property lying within the 100-year floodplain for improvement of a storm drainage system along Fanno Creek and that she dedicate an additional 15-foot strip of land adjacent to the floodplain as a pedestrian/bicycle pathway. The dedication required by that condition encompasses approximately 7,000 square feet, or roughly 10% of the property. In accordance with city practice, petitioner could rely on the dedicated property to meet the 15% open space and landscaping requirement mandated by the city's zoning scheme. The city would bear the cost of maintaining a landscaped buffer between the dedicated area and the new store.

The Commission made a series of findings concerning the relationship between the dedicated conditions and the projected impacts of petitioner's project. First, the Commission noted that "[i]t is reasonable to assume that customers and employees of the future uses of this site could utilize a pedestrian/ bicycle pathway adjacent to this development for their transportation and recreational needs." In addition, the Commission found that creation of a convenient, safe pedestrian/ bicycle pathway system as an alternative means of transportation "could offset some of the traffic demand on [nearby] streets and lessen the increase in traffic congestion."

The Commission went on to note that the required floodplain dedication would be reasonably related to petitioner's request to intensify the use of the site given the increase in the impervious surface. The Commission stated that the "anticipated increased storm water flow from the subject property to an already strained creek and drainage basin can only add to the public need to manage the stream channel and floodplain for drainage purposes." Based on this anticipated increased storm water flow, the Commission concluded that "the requirement of dedication of the floodplain area on the site is related to the applicant's plan to intensify development on the site." [The city's dedication requirements were upheld below.]

One of the principal purposes of the Takings Clause is "to bar Government from forcing some people alone to bear public burdens which, in all fairness and justice, should be borne by the public as a whole." Without question, had the city simply required petitioner to dedicate a strip of land along Fanno Creek for public use, rather than conditioning the grant of her permit to redevelop her property on such a dedication, a taking would have occurred. Such public access would deprive petitioner of the right to exclude others, "one of the most essential sticks in the bundle of rights that are commonly characterized as property."

In evaluating petitioner's claim, we must first determine whether the "essential nexus" exists between the "legitimate state interest" and the permit condition exacted by the city. *Nollan*. If we find that a nexus exists, we must then decide the required degree of connection between the exactions and the projected impact of the proposed development. We were not required to reach this question in *Nollan*, because we concluded that the connection did not meet even the loosest standard. Here, however, we must decide this question.

Undoubtedly, the prevention of flooding along Fanno Creek and the reduction of traffic congestion in the Central Business District qualify as the type of legitimate public purposes we have upheld. It seems equally obvious that a nexus exists between preventing flooding along Fanno Creek and limiting development within the creek's 100-year floodplain. Petitioner proposes to double the size of her retail store and to pave her now-gravel parking lot, thereby expanding the impervious surface on the property and increasing the amount of stormwater run-off into Fanno Creek. The same may be said for the city's attempt to reduce traffic congestion by providing for alternative means of transportation. In theory, a pedestrian/bicycle pathway provides a useful alternative means of transportation for workers and shoppers.

The second part of our analysis requires us to determine whether the degree of the exactions demanded by the city's permit conditions bear the required relationship to the projected impact of petitioner's proposed development. *Nollan*.

We think the "reasonable relationship" test adopted by a majority of the state courts is closer to the federal constitutional norm. But we do not adopt it as such, partly because the term "reasonable relationship" seems confusingly similar to the term "rational basis" which describes the minimal level of scrutiny under the Equal Protection Clause of the Fourteenth Amendment. We think a term such as "rough proportionality" best encapsulates what we hold to be the requirement of the Fifth Amendment. No precise mathematical calculation is required, but the city must make some sort of individualized determination that the required dedication is related both in nature and extent to the impact of the proposed development.

Justice Stevens' dissent relies upon a law review article for the proposition that the city's conditional demands for part of petitioner's property are "a species of business regulation that heretofore warranted a strong presumption of constitutional validity." But simply denominating a governmental measure as a "business regulation" does not immunize it from constitutional challenge on the grounds that it violates a provision of the Bill of Rights. We see no reason why the Takings Clause of the Fifth Amendment, as much a part of the Bill of Rights as the First Amendment or Fourth Amendment, should be relegated to the status of a poor relation. We turn now to analysis of whether the findings relied upon by the city here, first with respect to the floodplain easement, and second with respect to the pedestrian/bicycle path, satisfied these requirements.

It is axiomatic that increasing the amount of impervious surface will increase the quantity and rate of storm-water flow from petitioner's property. Therefore, keeping the floodplain open and free from development would likely confine the pressures on Fanno Creek created by petitioner's development. In fact, because petitioner's property lies within the Central Business District, the Community Development Code already required that petitioner leave 15% of it as open space and the undeveloped floodplain would have nearly satisfied that requirement. But the city demanded more — it not only wanted petitioner not to build in the floodplain, but it also wanted petitioner's property along Fanno Creek for its Greenway system. The city has never said why a public greenway, as opposed to a private one, was required in the interest of flood control.

The difference to petitioner, of course, is the loss of her ability to exclude others. It is difficult to see why recreational visitors trampling along petitioner's floodplain easement are sufficiently related to the city's legitimate interest in reducing flooding problems along Fanno Creek, and the city has not attempted to make any individualized determination to support this part of its request.

If petitioner's proposed development had somehow encroached on existing greenway space in the city, it would have been reasonable to require petitioner to provide some alternative greenway space for the public either on her property or elsewhere. But that is not the case here. We conclude that the findings upon which the city relies do not show the required reasonable relationship between the floodplain easement and the petitioner's proposed new building.

With respect to the pedestrian/bicycle pathway, we have no doubt that the city was correct in finding that the larger retail sales facility proposed by petitioner will increase traffic on the streets of the Central Business District. Dedications for streets, sidewalks, and other public ways are generally reasonable exactions to avoid excessive congestion from a proposed property use. But on the record before us, the city has not met its burden of demonstrating that the additional number of vehicle and bicycle trips generated by the petitioner's development reasonably relate to the city's requirement for a dedication of the pedestrian/bicycle pathway easement. No precise mathematical calculation is required, but the city must make some effort to quantify its findings in support of the dedication for the pedestrian/bicycle pathway beyond the conclusory statement that it could offset some of the traffic demand generated.

Cities have long engaged in the commendable task of land use planning, made necessary by increasing urbanization particularly in metropolitan areas such as Portland. The city's goals of reducing flooding hazards and traffic congestion, and providing for public greenways, are laudable, but there are outer limits to how this may be done.

JUSTICE STEVENS, with whom JUSTICE BLACKMUN and JUSTICE GINSBURG join, dissenting.

The Court recognizes as an initial matter that the city's conditions satisfy the "essential nexus" requirement announced in *Nollan v. California Coastal Comm'n*, because they serve the legitimate interests in minimizing floods and traffic congestions. The Court goes on, however, to erect a new constitutional hurdle in the path of these conditions. In addition to showing a rational nexus to a public purpose that would justify an outright denial of the permit, the city must also demonstrate "rough proportionality" between the harm caused by the new land use and the benefit obtained by the condition. The Court also decides for the first time that the city has the burden of establishing the constitutionality of its conditions by making an "individualized determination" that the condition in question satisfies the proportionality requirement.

Although limitation of the right to exclude others undoubtedly constitutes a significant infringement upon property ownership, restrictions on that right do not alone constitute a taking, and do not do so in any event unless they "unreasonably impair the value or use" of the property.

The Court's narrow focus on one strand in the property owner's bundle of rights is particularly misguided in a case involving the development of commercial property. As Professor Johnston has noted:

> The subdivider is a manufacturer, processor, and marketer of a product; land is but one of his raw materials. In subdivision control disputes, the developer is not defending hearth and home against the king's intrusion, but simply attempting to maximize his profits from the sale of a finished product. As applied to him, subdivision control exactions are actually business regulations. Johnston, *Constitutionality of Subdivision Control Exactions: The Quest for A Rationale*, 52 CORNELL L. Q. 871, 923 (1967).

The Court's assurances that its "rough proportionality" test leaves ample room for cities to pursue the "commendable task of land use planning," even twice avowing that "[n]o precise mathematical calculation is required," are wanting given the result that test compels here. Under the Court's approach, a city must not only "quantify its findings," and make "individualized determination[s]" with respect to the nature and the extent of the relationship between the conditions and the impact, but also demonstrate "proportionality." The correct inquiry should instead concentrate on whether the required nexus is present and venture beyond considerations of a condition's nature or germaneness only if the developer establishes that a concededly germane condition is so grossly disproportionate to the proposed development's adverse effects that it manifests motives other than land use regulation on the part of the city. The heightened requirement the Court imposes on cities is even more unjustified when all the tools needed to resolve the questions presented by this case can be garnered from our existing case law.

The Court has made a serious error by abandoning the traditional presumption of constitutionality and imposing a novel burden of proof on a city implementing an admittedly valid comprehensive land use plan. Even more consequential than its incorrect disposition of this case, however, is the Court's resurrection of a species of substantive due process analysis that it firmly rejected decades ago. The so-called "regulatory takings" doctrine has an obvious kinship with the line of substantive due process cases that *Lochner* exemplified. Besides having similar ancestry, both doctrines are potentially open-ended sources of judicial power to invalidate state economic regulations that Members of this Court view as unwise or unfair.

[JUSTICE SOUTER dissented principally on the ground that the landowner should bear the burden of proof on showing that the regulation was not related to a valid governmental objective.]

NOTES

1. *City of Monterey v. Del Monte Dunes at Monterey, Ltd.*, 526 U.S. 687 (1999). Del Monte Dunes, a land developer, was denied a city permit five times in attempts to develop its property. Each time the city imposed increasingly more rigorous requirements for approval. Del Monte finally sued the city, under 42 U.S.C. § 1983 claiming the city had effected an uncompensated regulatory taking. The jury was instructed that it should find for Del Monte if it found either that the developer had been deprived of all economically viable uses of its property, or if it found that the city's denial of the permit did not bear a reasonable relationship to the city's asserted legitimate public purpose. The jury found for Del Monte, and the Supreme Court affirmed.

The Court, per Justice Kennedy, first held that the reasonable proportionality standard established in *Dolan v. Tigard* was irrelevant to an inverse condemnation claim based upon the denial of a development permit. Because the jury verdict was based on a finding that the city's denial did not bear a reasonable relation to legitimate public interests, proportionality between the city's interests and its requirements on the developer were irrelevant.

Although the jury was instructed that the various purposes asserted by the city were legitimate public interests, they found that the denial of the permit was not reasonably related to those public purposes. That meant that the jury was not allowed to second-guess "the reasonableness, *per se,* of the customized ad hoc conditions imposed on the property's development." Justice Souter, joined by Justices O'Connor, Ginsburg, and Breyer, concurring in part and dissenting in part, agreed with the majority's judgement that the *Dolan* standard was inapplicable, but disagreed with the majority's judgement that Del Monte had a right to a jury trial. The ultimate issue in an inverse condemnation action (just compensation), Souter reasoned, is the same as that in a condemnation hearing for which there is no jury right, and therefore, there should be no right to a jury trial in an inverse condemnation action.

2. *Tahoe-Sierra Preservation Council, Inc. v. Tahoe Regional Planning Agency*, 535 U.S. 302 (2002). The Supreme Court held that a moratorium imposed during the process of formulating a comprehensive land use plan was not a *per se* taking requiring compensation under the Fifth Amendment. Justice Stevens writing for the Court declared: "In our view the answer to the abstract question whether a temporary moratorium effects a taking is neither "yes, always" nor "no, never"; the answer depends upon the particular circumstances of the case." An association of property owners and 400 individual property owners challenged facially the imposition of two moratoria on development of the area surrounding Lake Tahoe pending adoption of a comprehensive landuse plan by the Tahoe Regional Planning Agency (TRPA). The moratoria froze development on certain lands around Lake Tahoe for 32 months while the TRPA worked to adopt a regional plan that set standards for air and water quality, and conservation of soil and vegetation. The Supreme Court first declined to sever the 32-month period of the moratoria from the whole fee interest to determine if the property had been taken during that time. Instead, Justice Stevens held that in a regulatory takings claim, the proper focus is on the regulation's impact on the whole property interest: "An interest in real property is defined by the metes and bounds that describe its geographic dimensions and the term of years that describes the temporal aspect of the owner's interest. Both dimensions must be considered if the interest is to be considered in its entirety. Hence, a permanent deprivation of the owner's use of the entire area is a taking of the 'parcel as a whole,' whereas a temporary restriction that merely causes a diminution in value is not." Where the regulation does not effect a total taking of the whole parcel, *Penn Central* supplies the analytic framework. Justice Stevens concluded: "It may well be true that any moratorium that lasts for more than one year should be viewed with special skepticism. But given the fact that the District Court found that the 32 months required by TRPA to formulate the 1984 Regional Plan was not unreasonable, we could not possibly conclude that every delay of over one year is constitutionally unacceptable."

Chief Justice Rehnquist, with whom Justices Scalia and Thomas joined, dissenting, argued that the combined effect of the moratoria and injunction following the 1984 plan was a six-year restriction on all economically beneficial use of the property resulting in a taking. Such total deprivation of use, though it bears the label of "temporary," implicates the categorical rule announced in *Lucas*. Justice Thomas, with whom Justice Scalia joined dissenting, argued that any total deprivation of use of property is subject to *Lucas'* categorical rule even if the regulation is temporary and even if the property will recover its value when the prohibition is removed.

3. *Lawyer Trust Accounts.* In ***Phillips v. Washington Legal Foundation*, 524 U.S. 156 (1998),** the Supreme Court held 5-4 that interest income generated by escrow funds held in an Interest on Lawyers Trust Account (IOLTA) program is the "private property" of the owner of the principal. The Texas Supreme Court had issued an order that "an attorney who receives client funds that are 'nominal in amount or are reasonably anticipated to be held for a short period of time' must place such funds in a separate interest-bearing NOW account (an IOLTA account)." Interest from such accounts was to be paid to the Texas Equal Access to Justice Foundation, a nonprofit corporation that delivers legal services to low-income individuals. Indiana is the only state that does not have such a program. The IOLTA requirement was challenged as a violation of the Fifth Amendment which precludes taking property without just compensation. The district court granted summary judgment to Phillips, holding that there was no private property interest in the income generated by the money held in the IOLTA accounts. The Fifth Circuit reversed, holding that "any interest that accrues belongs to the owner of the principal." The Supreme Court affirmed. In remanding the case, the Court expressed no view on whether the funds had been "taken" by the State nor as to the amount of "just compensation" due if there was a taking.

Chief Justice Rehnquist, for the Court, said that state law was the basis for determining whether the interest income constituted private property. The principal in IOLTA accounts is clearly the private property of the client; only the status of the interest is in doubt. The well-established common law rule is that "interest follows principal." The Court rejected the argument that any value in the interest is government-created value. Rather, the value is created by the owner's principal. Chief Justice Rehnquist acknowledged: "[T]his would be a different case if the interest income generated by IOLTA accounts was transferred to the State as payment 'for services rendered' by the State. Our holding does not prohibit a State from imposing reasonable fees it incurs in generating and allocating interest income."

Justice Breyer, with Justices Stevens, Souter, and Ginsburg, dissented, contending that the "legal truism" that interest follows principal does not apply to this case. Texas did not take the owner's right to use his principal to generate a benefit for himself, but only the client's right to keep his principal from generating interest. Without IOLTA, it was not possible for the owner to generate interest on the principal. "Thus the question is whether 'interest,' *earned only as a result of IOLTA rules* and earned upon otherwise *barren* client principal 'follows principal.' Here, federal [banking] law ensured that, in the absence of IOLTA intervention, the client's principal would earn nothing." Since without the IOLTA program no interest could have been earned, the interest is not the private property of the owner of the principal.

***Brown v. Legal Foundation of Washington*, 538 U.S. 216 (2003).** The Court of Appeals for the Ninth Circuit, sitting en banc, held that the Washington State IOLTA program did not constitute a *per se* taking. Using the ad hoc approach of *Penn Central*, the appellate court held that the program did not constitute a taking and, that even if it were a taking, the just compensation would be zero.

The Supreme Court rejected the petitioners' claim that the deposit requirement of the IOLTA regulation constituted a taking, holding that the regulation required merely a transfer of principal and did not entail a confiscation of any interest. Justice Stevens for the majority stated that even if the deposit requirement were the first step in a regulatory taking, it would not constitute a taking by itself because it did not interfere with the petitioners' reasonable, investment backed expectations and did not result in a negative net-economic loss.

The Court also rejected the petitioners' second claim: that the IOLTA regulation requiring interest earned on IOLTA accounts to be transferred to the Legal Foundation of Washington constituted a taking, and that the taking required just compensation. Just compensation is measured by the property owner's loss, as opposed to the government's gain. A private party must be made whole and put in the same position they were in prior to the taking, but is not entitled to additional compensation. The Court reasoned that, absent the IOLTA program, the petitioners would not have earned any interest because their funds would never have been placed in interest bearing accounts due to the high transaction costs. Therefore, the amount they would have lost in having the money placed in an IOLTA account is zero.

Justice Scalia, joined by Chief Justice Rehnquist, Justice Kennedy, and Justice Thomas, dissented. Justice Scalia argued that the Court's holding contravened *Phillips* because once the Court determined that a taking had occurred, the just compensation awarded to the petitioners should be the fair market value of their interest that had "actually accrued" in the IOLTA account minus transaction costs, not what the value of their interest would have been had the State not taken their principal and deposited it in an IOLTA account.

4. *Eastern Enterprises v. Apfel,* 524 U.S. 498 (1998). The Court invalidated application of a federal multi-employer retirement plan that would have required payment into a pension fund of several million dollars by a company that had ceased to be engaged in coal mining decades earlier. The Court emphasized that the Constitution frowns on retroactive liability through several provisions, including the takings, *ex post facto*, and contracts clauses. The imposition of liability in this situation was particularly offensive in its interference with the company's "reasonable investment-backed expectations" because it had quit the coal mining business precisely because it was no longer profitable. As a final comment, the Court noted an argument that imposition of liability in this situation could be challenged as a violation of substantive due process. Although it declined to pass on the due process argument, the Court noted that its takings analysis "correlates" closely with due process.

LINGLE v. CHEVRON U.S.A., INC.
544 U.S. 528 (2005)

JUSTICE O'CONNOR delivered the opinion of the Court.

On occasion, a would-be doctrinal rule or test finds its way into our case law through simple repetition of a phrase however fortuitously coined. A quarter century ago, in *Agins v. City of Tiburon*, 447 U.S. 255, (1980), the Court declared that government regulation of private property "effects a taking if [such regulation] does not substantially advance legitimate state interests . . . ." Through reiteration in a half dozen or so decisions since *Agins*, this language has been ensconced in our Fifth Amendment takings jurisprudence. *See Monterey v. Del Monte Dunes at Monterey, Ltd.*, 526 U.S. 687, 704 (1999).

A Hawaii statute limits the rent that oil companies may charge to dealers who lease service stations owned by the companies. The lower courts held that the rent cap effected an uncompensated taking of private property because it did not substantially advance Hawaii's asserted interest in controlling retail gasoline prices.

> Our precedents stake out two categories of regulatory action that generally will be deemed per se takings for Fifth Amendment purposes. First, where government requires an owner to suffer a permanent physical invasion of her property however minor it must provide just compensation. *See Loretto v. Teleprompter*. A second categorical rule applies to regulations that completely deprive an owner of "all economically beneficial use" of her property. *Lucas*. We held in *Lucas*

that the government must pay just compensation for such "total regulatory takings," except to the extent that "background principles of nuisance and property law" independently restrict the owner's intended use of the property.

Outside these two relatively narrow categories (and the special context of land-use exactions discussed below), regulatory takings challenges are governed by the standards set forth in *Penn Central Transp. Co. v. New York City*, 438 U.S. 104 (1978).

The Court in *Penn Central* acknowledged that it had hitherto been "unable to develop any 'set formula'" for evaluating regulatory takings claims, but identified "several factors that have particular significance." Primary among those factors are "the economic impact of the regulation on the claimant and, particularly, the extent to which the regulation has interfered with distinct investment-backed expectations." In addition, the "character of the governmental action" for instance whether it amounts to a physical invasion or instead merely affects property interests through "some public program adjusting the benefits and burdens of economic life to promote the common good" may be relevant in discerning whether a taking has occurred. The *Penn Central* factors though each has given rise to vexing subsidiary questions have served as the principal guidelines for resolving regulatory takings claims that do not fall within the physical takings or *Lucas* rules.

There is no question that the "substantially advances" formula was derived from due process. Instead of addressing a challenged regulation's effect on private property, the "substantially advances" inquiry probes the regulation's underlying validity. But such an inquiry is logically prior to and distinct from the question whether a regulation effects a taking, for the Takings Clause presupposes that the government has acted in pursuit of a valid public purpose. The Clause expressly requires compensation where government takes private property "for public use." It does not bar government from interfering with property rights, but rather requires compensation "in the event of otherwise proper interference amounting to a taking." Conversely, if a government action is found to be impermissible for instance because it fails to meet the "public use" requirement or is so arbitrary as to violate due process that is the end of the inquiry. No amount of compensation can authorize such action.

Chevron's challenge to the Hawaii statute in this case illustrates the flaws in the "substantially advances" theory. To begin with, it is unclear how significantly Hawaii's rent cap actually burdens Chevron's property rights. The parties stipulated below that the cap would reduce Chevron's aggregate rental income on 11 of its 64 lessee-dealer stations by about $207,000 per year, but that Chevron nevertheless expects to receive a return on its investment in these stations that satisfies any constitutional standard. Moreover, Chevron asserted below, and the District Court found, that Chevron would recoup any reductions in its rental income by raising wholesale gasoline prices. In short, Chevron has not clearly argued — let alone established — that it has been singled out to bear any particularly severe regulatory burden. Rather, the gravamen of Chevron's claim is simply that Hawaii's rent cap will not actually serve the State's legitimate interest in protecting consumers against high gasoline prices. Whatever the merits of that claim, it does not sound under the Takings Clause. Chevron plainly does not seek compensation for a taking of its property for a legitimate public use, but rather an injunction against the enforcement of a regulation that it alleges to be fundamentally arbitrary and irrational.

It might be argued that this formula played a role in our decisions in *Nollan v. California Coastal Comm'n* and *Dolan v. City of Tigard*. But while the Court drew upon the language of *Agins* in these cases, it did not apply the "substantially advances" test that is the subject of today's decision. Both *Nollan* and *Dolan* involved Fifth Amendment takings challenges to adjudicative land-use exactions specifically, government demands that a landowner dedicate an easement allowing public access to her property as a condition of obtaining a development permit.

In each case, the Court began with the premise that, had the government simply appropriated the easement in question, this would have been a per se physical taking. The question was whether the government could, without paying the compensation that would otherwise be required upon effecting such a taking, demand the easement as a condition for granting a development permit the government was entitled to deny. The Court in *Nollan* answered in the affirmative, provided that the exaction would substantially advance the same government interest that would furnish a valid ground for denial of the permit. The Court further refined this requirement in *Dolan*, holding that an adjudicative exaction requiring dedication of private property must also be "'roughly proportional' . . . both in nature and extent to the impact of the proposed development."

Although *Nollan* and *Dolan* quoted *Agins*' language, the rule those decisions established is entirely distinct from the "substantially advances" test we address today. Whereas the "substantially advances" inquiry before us now is unconcerned with the degree or type of burden a regulation places upon property, *Nollan* and *Dolan* both involved dedications of property so onerous that, outside the exactions context, they would be deemed per se physical takings. In neither case did the Court question whether the exaction would substantially advance some legitimate state interest. Rather, the issue was whether the exactions substantially advanced the same interests that land-use authorities asserted would allow them to deny the permit altogether.

KENNEDY, J., concurring:

This separate writing is to note that today's decision does not foreclose the possibility that a regulation might be so arbitrary or irrational as to violate due process. The failure of a regulation to accomplish a stated or obvious objective would be relevant to that inquiry. Chevron voluntarily dismissed its due process claim without prejudice.

NOTE

***Kelo v. City of New London*, 125 S. Ct. 2655 (2005).** The Court held constitutional the exercise of eminent domain by New London, Connecticut, as part of a downtown development plan that was intended to add jobs and increase tax and other revenues. Petitioner challenged the exercise of this power on the grounds that the city's proposed use of the property for the development of an area of new private commercial establishments did not constitute a "public use," as required by the Takings Clause. Justice Stevens, writing for the Court, initially acknowledged the validity of "two polar propositions": first, "that the sovereign may not take the property of A for the sole purpose of transferring it to another private party B, even though A is paid just compensation," and second, "that a State may transfer property from one private party to another if future "use by the public" is the purpose of the taking."

The case turned, the Court reasoned, "on the question whether the City's development plan serves a 'public purpose,'" noting that it had always shown great deference on that issue. The Court rejected petitioner's proposed "new bright-line rule that economic development does not qualify as a public use," reasoning that "[p]romoting public economic development is a traditional and long accepted function of government." It further rejected the contention that allowing eminent domain to be used for economic development impermissibly blurs the boundary between private and public takings: "Quite simply, the government's pursuit of a public purpose will often benefit individual private parties." Finally, the Court rejected the argument that it should require a "reasonable certainty" that the expected public benefits will actually occur, finding it inconsistent with precedent.

Justice O'Connor, writing for four members of the Court, dissented: "To reason, as the Court does, that the incidental public benefits resulting from the subsequent ordinary use of private property render economic developments takings "for public use" is to wash out any distinction between private and public use of private property—and thereby effectively to delete the words "for public use" from the Takings Clause of the Fifth Amendment." Justice Thomas also dissented, arguing that "[i]f such 'economic development' takings are for a 'public use,' any taking is, and the Court has erased the Public Use Clause from our Constitution." In place of the majority's approach, he suggested that "the most natural reading of the Clause is that it allows the government to take property only if the government owns, or the public has a legal right to use, the property, as opposed to taking it for any public purpose of necessity whatsoever."

[4] The Contract Clause

Article I, § 10 of the Constitution provides: "No state shall pass any law impairing the obligation of Contracts." While the clause was originally intended to curb state legislative interference with existing debt obligations, during the early part of the nineteenth century it was transformed into an all-purpose tool limiting the state police power. The clause was interpreted to prohibit legislation that retroactively impaired substantive contractual obligations, both public and private. *Dartmouth College v. Woodward*, 17 U.S. (4 Wheat.) 518 (1819) (contract clause prohibited a statutory change in a public charter issued to Dartmouth College); *Sturges v. Crowinshield*, 17 U.S. (4 Wheat.) 122 (1819) (statute discharging obligations of debtors violates contract clause). But with the advent of due process, the Contract Clause was virtually abandoned. Thus, when economic due process itself suffered a demise in the 1930s, the Contract Clause similarly became a dead letter. *See Home Building & Loan Ass'n v. Blaisdell*, 290 U.S. 398 (1934) (state law extending mortgage redemption period following a foreclosure sale held not to violate the contract clause). For over thirty-five years the clause was to lie essentially dormant.

***Allied Structural Steel Co. v. Spannaus*, 438 U.S. 234 (1978)**. In 1963, Allied Structural Steel Company had adopted a pension plan assuring eligible employees of a fixed pension at age sixty-five as long as the company remained in business and elected to continue the pension plan in the existing form. The company, however, retained a virtually unrestricted right to amend or terminate the plan and distribute trust assets. In 1974 Minnesota enacted the Private Pension Act, whereby companies in Allied's position were subject to a "pension funding charge" if they terminated their pension plan or closed their offices in the state. The charge was assessed if the pension fund was not sufficient to provide full pensions to all employees who had worked ten years. Employers were required to purchase deferred annuities, payable to such employees at the normal retirement age, to satisfy the deficiency. When Allied began to close its Minnesota offices in 1974, it was notified that it owed a pension funding charge of approximately $185,000. Allied brought suit seeking injunctive and declaratory relief on grounds that the Act impaired its contractual obligations to its employees under its pension agreement.

The Supreme Court overturned the Minnesota statute. "If the Contract Clause is to retain any meaning at all, it must be understood to impose some limits upon the power of a State to abridge existing contractual relationships, even in the exercise of its otherwise legitimate police power." The Court heavily emphasized that the statute imposed a cost on the employer that the employer could not have anticipated, that it changed the vesting provisions of the plan to a 10-year full vesting, and that the change was a permanent change without an emergency justification resembling the economic shambles of the Depression under which *Blaisdell* was decided.

***United States Trust Co. v. New Jersey*, 431 U.S. 1 (1977)**. In the case of public contracts, a state may reserve the power to change its obligation either in the contract or the state constitution. Further, a state may not contract away its sovereign police power to legislate for the health, safety and well-being of its citizens. Fiscal powers, however, may be the subject of contract and when they are, the Contract Clause limits the state's ability to "impair" retroactively its undertakings.

In *United States Trust*, the Court held, per Justice Blackmun, that state statutes repealing a statutory covenant made by the two states limiting the ability of the Port Authority of New York and New Jersey to subsidize rail passenger transportation from revenues and reserves violates the Contract Clause. The repeal of the limitation eliminated an important security provision of bond holders and thus impaired the obligation of the state's contract. When a state impairs the obligation of its own contract, at least in fiscal matters, it must show that the impairment was both reasonable and necessary to serve important purposes claimed by the state.

In the two decades following *Allied* and *United States Trust*, no other state initiatives have been held to violate the Contract Clause.

§ 6.02 FUNDAMENTAL RIGHTS

In section 6.01, consideration was given to the rise and fall of substantive economic due process. But as economic due process rose and waned, the Fourteenth Amendment was being fashioned into a tool for the protection of procedural rights from state abuse through incorporation of some of the protections of the Bill of Rights (the procedural safeguards of the first eight amendments) into the amendment's Due Process Clause. In addition, the liberties protected by due process against state encroachment came to include the First Amendment guarantees of free speech, press and assembly, freedom of belief and association, free exercise of religion and freedom from state establishment of religion.

The process of selective incorporation described in the preceding paragraph was not terribly wrenching because the Court was employing protections explicitly mentioned in the Constitution, extending them to apply against the states. What has been more controversial is the development of unenumerated rights against state action. In the present section, the focus will be on the fashioning of rights relating to privacy, marriage and family that serve as a substantive restraint on the legislative power. One issue is whether this substantive review of the validity of government action differs from the substantive due process practiced in *Lochner* and condemned in *Nebbia* and its progeny. Is there any reason for substantive due process challenges to be treated differently in cases involving property rights and economic liberty (as in *Lochner*) than in cases involving other personal rights and liberties, such as privacy or free speech?

The Constitution does not expressly provide for a right of privacy — or, for that matter, for a right to vote, to marry, to bear children, to live as a family unit, or to travel. Can new rights be inferred from those that are enumerated or from structures and relationships within the constitutional framework? Can a judge properly look to principles and values outside of the Constitution?

If the Court does adopt a policy of active review on behalf of unexpressed rights, it will be charged with engaging in "Lochnerism" and natural law jurisprudence. To a certain extent, these issues were explored, primarily as a matter of constitutional theory, in Chapter 1. Here, we explore them as applied Supreme Court doctrine.

[A] CONTRACEPTION AND ABORTION

GRISWOLD v. CONNECTICUT
381 U.S. 479, 85 S. Ct. 1678, 14 L. Ed. 2d 510 (1965)

Justice Douglas delivered the opinion of the Court.

Appellant Griswold is Executive Director of the Planned Parenthood League of Connecticut. Appellant Buxton is a licensed physician and a professor at the Yale Medical School who served as Medical Director for the League at its Center in New Haven — a center open and operating from November 1 to November 10, 1961, when appellants were arrested. They gave information, instruction, and medical advice to married persons as to the means of preventing conception. They examined the wife and prescribed the best contraceptive device or material for her use. Fees were usually charged, although some couples were serviced free.

The statutes whose constitutionality is involved in this appeal are §§ 53-32 and 54-196 of the General Statutes of Connecticut (1958 rev.). The former provides:

> Any person who uses any drug, medicinal article or instrument for the purpose of preventing conception shall be fined not less than fifty dollars or imprisoned not less than sixty days nor more than one year or be both fined and imprisoned.

Section 54-196 provides:

> Any person who assists, abets, counsels, causes, hires or commands another to commit any offense may be prosecuted and punished as if he were the principal offender.

The appellants were found guilty as accessories and fined $100 each, against the claim that the accessory statute as so applied violated the Fourteenth Amendment. The Supreme Court of Errors affirmed that judgment.

[The Court initially held that the appellants had "standing to raise the constitutional rights of the married people with whom they had a professional relationship."]

Coming to the merits, we are met with a wide range of questions that implicate the Due Process Clause of the Fourteenth Amendment. Overtones of some arguments suggest that *Lochner v. New York* should be our guide. But we decline that invitation. We do not sit as a super-legislature to determine the wisdom, need, and propriety of laws that touch economic problems, business affairs, or social conditions. This law, however, operates directly on an intimate relation of husband and wife and their physician's role in one aspect of that relation.

The association of people is not mentioned in the Constitution nor in the Bill of Rights. The right to educate a child in a school of the parents' choice — whether public or private or parochial — is also not mentioned. Nor is the right to study any particular subject or any foreign language. Yet the First Amendment has been construed to include certain of those rights. By *Pierce v. Society of Sisters* [268 U.S. 510 (1925)], the right to educate one's children as one chooses is made applicable to the States by the force of the First and Fourteenth Amendments. By *Meyer v. Nebraska* [262 U.S. 390 (1923)], the same dignity is given the right to study the German language in a private school. In other words, the State may not, consistently with the spirit of the First Amendment, contract the spectrum of available knowledge. The right of freedom of speech and press includes not only the right to utter or to print, but the right to distribute, the right to receive, the right to read and freedom of inquiry, freedom of thought, and freedom to teach — indeed the freedom of the entire university community. Without those peripheral rights the specific rights would be less secure. And so we reaffirm the principle of the *Pierce* and the *Meyer* cases.

In other words, the First Amendment has a penumbra where privacy is protected from governmental intrusion. In like context, we have protected forms of "association" that are not political in the customary sense but pertain to the social, legal, and economic benefit of the members. *NAACP v. Button*, 371 U.S. 415, 430–431. The right of "association," like the right of belief, is more than the right to attend a meeting; it includes the right to express one's attitudes or philosophies by membership in a group or by affiliation with it or by other lawful means. Association in that context is a form of expression of opinion; and while it is not expressly included in the First Amendment its existence is necessary in making the express guarantees fully meaningful.

The foregoing cases suggest that specific guarantees in the Bill of Rights have penumbras, formed by emanations from those guarantees that help give them life and substance. Various guarantees create zones of privacy. The right of association contained in the penumbra of the First Amendment is one. The Third Amendment in its prohibition against the quartering of soldiers "in any house" in time of peace without the consent of the owner is another facet of that privacy. The Fourth Amendment explicitly affirms the "right of the people to be secure in their persons, houses, papers, and effects, against unreasonable searches and seizures." The Fifth Amendment in its Self-Incrimination Clause enables the citizen to create a zone of privacy which government may not force him to surrender to his detriment. The Ninth Amendment provides: "The enumeration in the Constitution, of certain rights, shall not be construed to deny or disparage others retained by the people." We have had many controversies over these penumbral rights of "privacy and repose." *See, e.g.*, *Breard v. Alexandria*, *Public Utilities Comm'n v. Pollak*, *Monroe v. Pape*, and *Skinner v. Oklahoma*. These cases bear witness that the right of privacy which presses for recognition here is a legitimate one.

The present case, then, concerns a relationship lying within the zone of privacy created by several fundamental constitutional guarantees. And it concerns a law which, in forbidding the use of contraceptives rather than regulating their manufacture or sale, seeks to achieve its goals by means having a maximum destructive impact upon that relationship. Such a law cannot stand in light of the familiar principle, so often applied by this Court, that a "governmental purpose to control or prevent activities constitutionally subject to state regulation may not be achieved by means which sweep unnecessarily broadly and thereby invade the area of protected freedoms." *NAACP v. Alabama*, 377 U.S. 288, 307. Would we allow the police to search the sacred precincts of marital bedrooms for telltale signs of the use of contraceptives? The very idea is repulsive to the notions of privacy surrounding the marriage relationship.

We deal with a right of privacy older than the Bill of Rights — older than our political parties, older than our school system. Marriage is a coming together for better or for worse, hopefully enduring, and intimate to the degree of being sacred. It is an association that promotes a way of life, not causes; a harmony in living, not political faiths; a bilateral loyalty, not commercial or social projects. Yet it is an association for as noble a purpose as any involved in our prior decisions.

Justice Goldberg, whom Chief Justice Warren and Justice Brennan join, concurring.

I agree with the Court that Connecticut's birth-control law unconstitutionally intrudes upon the right of marital privacy, and I join in its opinion and judgment. Although I have not accepted the view that "due process" as used in the Fourteenth Amendment incorporates all of the first eight amendments, I do agree that the concept of liberty protects those personal rights that are fundamental, and is not confined to the specific terms of the Bill of Rights. My conclusion that the concept of liberty is not so restricted and that it embraces the right of marital privacy though that right is not mentioned explicitly in the Constitution[17] is supported both by numerous decisions of this Court, referred to in the Court's opinion, and by the language and history of the Ninth Amendment. In reaching the conclusion that the right of marital privacy is protected, as being within the protected penumbra of specific guarantees of the Bill of Rights, the Court refers to the Ninth Amendment. I add these words to emphasize the relevance of that Amendment to the Court's holding.

This Court, in a series of decisions, has held that the Fourteenth Amendment absorbs and applies to the States those specifics of the first eight amendments which express fundamental personal rights. The language and history of the Ninth Amendment reveal that the Framers of the Constitution believed that there are additional fundamental rights, protected from governmental infringement, which exist alongside those fundamental rights specifically mentioned in the first eight constitutional amendments.

The Ninth Amendment is almost entirely the work of James Madison. It was introduced in Congress by him and passed the House and Senate with little or no debate and virtually no change in language. It was proffered to quiet expressed fears that a bill of specifically enumerated rights could not be sufficiently broad to cover all essential rights and that the specific mention of certain rights would be interpreted as a denial that others were protected.

While this Court has had little occasion to interpret the Ninth Amendment, "[i]t cannot be presumed that any clause in the constitution is intended to be without effect." The Ninth Amendment to the Constitution may be regarded by some as a recent discovery and may be forgotten by others, but since 1791 it has been a basic part of the Constitution which we are sworn to uphold. To hold that a right so basic and fundamental and so deep-rooted in our society as the right of privacy in marriage may be infringed because that right is not guaranteed in so many words by the first eight amendments to the Constitution is to ignore the Ninth Amendment and to give it no effect whatsoever. Moreover, a judicial construction that this fundamental right is not protected by the Constitution because it is not mentioned in explicit terms by one of the first eight amendments or elsewhere in the Constitution would violate the Ninth Amendment, which specifically states that "[t]he enumeration in the Constitution, of certain rights, shall not be *construed* to deny or disparage others retained by the people." (Emphasis added.)

A dissenting opinion suggests that my interpretation of the Ninth Amendment somehow "broaden[s] the powers of this Court." With all due respect, I believe that it misses the import of what I am saying. I do not take the

[17] This Court has never held that the Bill of Rights or the Fourteenth Amendment protects only those rights that the Constitution specifically mentions by name.

position of my Brother Black in his dissent in *Adamson v. California* that the entire Bill of Rights is incorporated in the Fourteenth Amendment, and I do not mean to imply that the Ninth Amendment is applied against the States by the Fourteenth. Nor do I mean to state that the Ninth Amendment constitutes an independent source of rights protected from infringement by either the States or the Federal Government. Rather, the Ninth Amendment shows a belief of the Constitution's authors that fundamental rights exist that are not expressly enumerated in the first eight amendments and an intent that the list of rights included there not be deemed exhaustive. As any student of this Court's opinions knows, this Court has held, often unanimously, that the Fifth and Fourteenth Amendments protect certain fundamental personal liberties from abridgment by the Federal Government or the States. The Ninth Amendment simply shows the intent of the Constitution's authors that other fundamental personal rights should not be denied such protection or disparaged in any other way simply because they are not specifically listed in the first eight constitutional amendments. I do not see how this broadens the authority of the Court; rather it serves to support what this Court has been doing in protecting fundamental rights.

Nor am I turning somersaults with history in arguing that the Ninth Amendment is relevant in a case dealing with a *State's* infringement of a fundamental right. While the Ninth Amendment — and indeed the entire Bill of Rights — originally concerned restrictions upon *federal* power, the subsequently enacted Fourteenth Amendment prohibits the States as well from abridging fundamental personal liberties. And, the Ninth Amendment, in indicating that not all such liberties are specifically mentioned in the first eight amendments, is surely relevant in showing the existence of other fundamental personal rights, now protected from state, as well as federal, infringement. In sum, the Ninth Amendment simply lends strong support to the view that the "liberty" protected by the Fifth and Fourteenth Amendments from infringement by the Federal Government or the States is not restricted to rights specifically mentioned in the first eight amendments.

In determining which rights are fundamental, judges are not left at large to decide cases in light of their personal and private notions. Rather, they must look to the "traditions and [collective] conscience of our people" to determine whether a principle is "so rooted [there] as to be ranked as fundamental." "Liberty" also "gains content from the emanations of specific [constitutional] guarantees" and "from experience with the requirements of a free society."

I agree fully with the Court that, applying these tests, the right of privacy is a fundamental personal right, emanating "from the totality of the constitutional scheme under which we live." Mr. Justice Brandeis, dissenting in *Olmstead v. United States*, 277 U.S. 438, 478, comprehensively summarized the principles underlying the Constitution's guarantees of privacy:

> The protection guaranteed by the [Fourth and Fifth] Amendments is much broader in scope. The makers of our Constitution undertook to secure conditions favorable to the pursuit of happiness. They recognized the significance of man's spiritual nature, of his feelings and of his intellect. They knew that only a part of the pain, pleasure and satisfactions of life are to be found in material things. They sought

> to protect Americans in their beliefs, their thoughts, their emotions and their sensations. They conferred, as against the Government, the right to be let alone — the most comprehensive of rights and the right most valued by civilized men.

The entire fabric of the Constitution and the purposes that clearly underlie its specific guarantees demonstrate that the rights to marital privacy and to marry and raise a family are of similar order and magnitude as the fundamental rights specifically protected.

The logic of the dissents would sanction federal or state legislation that seems to me even more plainly unconstitutional than the statute before us. Surely the Government, absent a showing of a compelling subordinating state interest, could not decree that all husbands and wives must be sterilized after two children have been born to them. Yet by their reasoning such an invasion of marital privacy would not be subject to constitutional challenge because, while it might be "silly," no provision of the Constitution specifically prevents the Government from curtailing the marital right to bear children and raise a family. While it may shock some of my Brethren that the Court today holds that the Constitution protects the right of marital privacy, in my view it is far more shocking to believe that the personal liberty guaranteed by the Constitution does not include protection against such totalitarian limitation of family size, which is at complete variance with our constitutional concepts. Yet, if upon a showing of a slender basis of rationality, a law outlawing voluntary birth control by married persons is valid, then, by the same reasoning, a law requiring compulsory birth control also would seem to be valid. In my view, however, both types of law would unjustifiably intrude upon rights of marital privacy which are constitutionally protected.

In a long series of cases this Court has held that where fundamental personal liberties are involved, they may not be abridged by the States simply on a showing that a regulatory statute has some rational relationship to the effectuation of a proper state purpose.

Although the Connecticut birth-control law obviously encroaches upon a fundamental personal liberty, the State does not show that the law serves any "subordinating [state] interest which is compelling" or that it is "necessary to the accomplishment of a permissible state policy." The State, at most, argues that there is some rational relation between this statute and what is admittedly a legitimate subject of state concern — the discouraging of extra-marital relations. It says that preventing the use of birth-control devices by married persons helps prevent the indulgence by some in such extra-marital relations. The rationality of this justification is dubious, particularly in light of the admitted widespread availability to all persons in the State of Connecticut, unmarried as well as married, of birth-control devices for the prevention of disease, as distinguished from the prevention of conception. But, in any event, it is clear that the state interest in safeguarding marital fidelity can be served by a more discriminately tailored statute, which does not, like the present one, sweep unnecessarily broadly, reaching far beyond the evil sought to be dealt with and intruding upon the privacy of all married couples. The State of Connecticut does have statutes, the constitutionality of which is beyond doubt, which prohibit adultery and fornication. These statutes demonstrate that means for achieving the same basic purpose of protecting marital fidelity are available to Connecticut without the need to "invade the area of protected freedoms."

Finally, it should be said of the Court's holding today that it in no way interferes with a State's proper regulation of sexual promiscuity or misconduct.

JUSTICE HARLAN, concurring in the judgment.

I fully agree with the judgment of reversal, but find myself unable to join the Court's opinion. The reason is that it seems to me to evince an approach to this case very much like that taken by my Brothers Black and Stewart in dissent, namely: the Due Process Clause of the Fourteenth Amendment does not touch this Connecticut statute unless the enactment is found to violate some right assured by the letter or penumbra of the Bill of Rights.

In my view, the proper constitutional inquiry in this case is whether this Connecticut statute infringes the Due Process Clause of the Fourteenth Amendment because the enactment violates basic values "implicit in the concept of ordered liberty," *Palko v. Connecticut*. For reasons stated at length in my dissenting opinion in *Poe v. Ullman*, I believe that it does. While the relevant inquiry may be aided by resort to one or more of the provisions of the Bill of Rights, it is not dependent on them or any of their radiations. The Due Process Clause of the Fourteenth Amendment stands, in my opinion, on its own bottom.

While I could not more heartily agree that judicial "self restraint" is an indispensable ingredient of sound constitutional adjudication, I do submit that the formula [Justice Black] suggested for achieving it is more hollow than real. "Specific" provisions of the Constitution, no less than "due process," lend themselves as readily to "personal" interpretations by judges whose constitutional outlook is simply to keep the Constitution in supposed "tune with the times." Judicial self-restraint will be achieved in this area, as in other constitutional areas, only by continual insistence upon respect for the teachings of history, solid recognition of the basic values that underlie our society, and wise appreciation of the great roles that the doctrines of federalism and separation of powers have played in establishing and preserving American freedoms. *See Adamson v. California* (Mr. Justice Frankfurter, concurring).

JUSTICE WHITE, concurring in the judgment.

In my view this Connecticut law as applied to married couples deprives them of "liberty" without due process of law, as that concept is used in the Fourteenth Amendment. I therefore concur in the judgment of the Court reversing these convictions under Connecticut's aiding and abetting statute. [Prior] decisions affirm that there is a "realm of family life which the state cannot enter" without substantial justification. *Prince v. Massachusetts*. Surely the right invoked in this case, to be free of regulation of the intimacies of the marriage relationship, "come[s] to this Court with a momentum for respect lacking when appeal is made to liberties which derive merely from shifting economic arrangements." *Kovacs v. Cooper* (opinion of Frankfurter, J.).

The Connecticut anti-contraceptive statute deals rather substantially with this relationship. For it forbids all married persons the right to use birth-control devices, regardless of whether their use is dictated by considerations of family planning, health, or indeed even of life itself. [T]he clear effect of these statutes, as enforced, is to deny disadvantaged citizens of Connecticut, those without either adequate knowledge or resources to obtain private counseling, access to medical assistance and up-to-date information in respect to proper methods of birth control. In my view, a statute with these effects bears a substantial burden of justification when attacked under the Fourteenth Amendment. [Citing equal protection and freedom of association cases.]

An examination of the justification offered, however, cannot be avoided by saying that the Connecticut anti-use statute invades a protected area of privacy and association or that it demeans the marriage relationship. The nature of the right invaded is pertinent, to be sure, for statutes regulating sensitive areas of liberty do, under the cases of this court require "strict scrutiny," *Skinner v. Oklahoma*, and "must be viewed in the light of less drastic means for achieving the same basic purpose." *Shelton v. Tucker*, 364 U.S. 479, 488. "Where there is a significant encroachment upon personal liberty, the State may prevail only upon showing a subordinating interest which is compelling." *Bates v. Little Rock*, 361 U.S. 516, 524. But such statutes, if reasonably necessary for the effectuation of a legitimate and substantial state interest, and not arbitrary or capricious in application, are not invalid under the Due Process Clause.

There is no serious contention that Connecticut thinks the use of artificial or external methods of contraception immoral or unwise in itself, or that the anti-use statute is founded upon any policy of promoting population expansion. Rather, the statute is said to serve the State's policy against all forms of promiscuous or illicit sexual relationships, be they premarital or extramarital, concededly a permissible and legitimate legislative goal.

Without taking issue with the premise that the fear of conception operates as a deterrent to such relationships in addition to the criminal proscriptions Connecticut has against such conduct, I wholly fail to see how the ban on the use of contraceptives by married couples in any way reinforces the State's ban on illicit sexual relationships. I find nothing in this record justifying the sweeping scope of this statute, with its telling effect on the freedoms of married persons, and therefore conclude that it deprives such persons of liberty without due process of law.

JUSTICE BLACK, with whom JUSTICE STEWART joins, dissenting.

The Court talks about a constitutional "right of privacy" as though there is some constitutional provision or provisions forbidding any law ever to be passed which might abridge the "privacy" of individuals. But there is not. There are, of course, guarantees in certain specific constitutional provisions which are designed in part to protect privacy at certain times and places with respect to certain activities. Such, for example, is the Fourth Amendment's guarantee against "unreasonable searches and seizures." But I think it belittles that Amendment to talk about it as though it protects nothing but "privacy." The average man would very likely not have his feelings soothed any more by having his property seized openly than by having it seized privately and by stealth. He simply wants his property left alone. And a person can be just as much, if not more, irritated, annoyed and injured by an unceremonious public arrest by a policeman as he is by a seizure in the privacy of his office or home.

One of the most effective ways of diluting or expanding a constitutionally guaranteed right is to substitute for the crucial word or words of a constitutional guarantee another word or words more or less flexible and more or less restricted in meaning. "Privacy" is a broad, abstract and ambiguous concept which can easily be shrunken in meaning but which can also, on the other hand, easily be interpreted as a constitutional ban against many things other than searches and seizures. I like my privacy as well as the next one, but I am nevertheless compelled to admit that government has a right to invade it unless prohibited by some specific constitutional provision. For these reasons I cannot agree with the Court's judgment and the reasons it gives for holding this Connecticut law unconstitutional.

Our Court certainly has no machinery with which to take a Gallup Poll. And the scientific miracles of this age have not yet produced a gadget which the Court can use to determine what traditions are rooted in the "[collective] conscience of our people." Moreover, one would certainly have to look far beyond the language of the Ninth Amendment to find that the Framers vested in this Court any such awesome veto powers over lawmaking, either by the States or by the Congress. Nor does anything in the history of the Amendment offer any support for such a shocking doctrine. That Amendment was passed, not to broaden the powers of this Court or any other department of "the General Government," but, as every student of history knows, to assure the people that the Constitution in all its provisions was intended to limit the Federal Government to the powers granted expressly or by necessary implication. This fact is perhaps responsible for the peculiar phenomenon that for a period of a century and a half no serious suggestion was ever made that the Ninth Amendment, enacted to protect state powers against federal invasion, could be used as a weapon of federal power to prevent state legislatures from passing laws they consider appropriate to govern local affairs. Use of any such broad, unbounded judicial authority would make of this Court's members a day-to-day constitutional convention.

Justice Stewart, whom Justice Black joins, dissenting.

I think this is an uncommonly silly law. As a practical matter, the law is obviously unenforceable, except in the oblique context of the present case. As a philosophical matter, I believe the use of contraceptives in the relationship of marriage should be left to personal and private choice, based upon each individual's moral, ethical, and religious beliefs. As a matter of social policy, I think professional counsel about methods of birth control should be available to all, so that each individual's choice can be meaningfully made. But we are not asked in this case to say whether we think this law is unwise, or even asinine. We are asked to hold that it violates the United States Constitution. And that I cannot do.

What provision of the Constitution, then, does make this state law invalid? The Court says it is the right of privacy "created by several fundamental constitutional guarantees." With all deference, I can find no such general right of privacy in the Bill of Rights, in any other part of the Constitution, or in any case ever before decided by this Court.

NOTES

1. *Textual approaches.* Professor Charles Black has noted that many persons viewed *Griswold* as creating "a methodological crisis in constitutional law" because

> nothing in the Constitution said in so many words that the state might not make contraception a crime. Somewhat more subtly put, and put in a manner more correspondent to past reality, many believed that no provision or set of provisions written in the Constitution could by any far-reaching process of "interpretation" be thought to refer to contraception.

Charles Black, *The Unfinished Business of the Warren Court*, 46 WASH. L. REV. 3, 32–33 (1970). Where does the Court find a right of privacy?

Justice Black, the consummate textualist, dissented in *Griswold* because he could find no right of privacy in the Constitution. But Justice Douglas, claiming to be interpreting the Bill of Rights guarantees, finds a right of privacy implied by various of the provisions. On other occasions, even Justice Black found such implied rights, e.g., a right of association inherent in the First Amendment guarantees, and a right of foreign travel. Further, Justice Black was willing to extend the equal protection mandate of *Brown v. Board of Education*, p. 687, to the federal government as part of Fifth Amendment due process liberty in *Bolling v. Sharpe*. Also note Justice Black's joining of the Fourth and Fifth Amendments to find a constitutional nexus for the exclusionary rule in *Mapp v. Ohio*, 367 U.S. 643 (1961). Is this legitimate constitutional interpretation? Could *Lochner's* right of contract be justified as an implication of Article I, § 10's Contract Clause?

2. *The Ninth Amendment.* While Justice Goldberg in his concurring opinion emphasizes the relevance of the Ninth Amendment, Justice Douglas' opinion makes only limited reference to it. Why shouldn't the Ninth Amendment serve as the primary textual grounding for the right of privacy? According to one commentator:

> Any provision that has survived [the amending] process must be presumed by interpreters of the Constitution to have some legitimate constitutional function, whether actual or only potential. Despite this long-respected presumption, the Supreme Court has generally interpreted the Ninth Amendment in a manner that denies it any role in the constitutional structure.

Randy Barnett, *Introduction: James Madison's Ninth Amendment*, in THE RIGHTS RETAINED BY THE PEOPLE 2 (R. Barnett ed. 1989).

Examine the language of the Ninth Amendment. What would be the implications for constitutional democratic theory if the Amendment were construed to authorize the judiciary to recognize unenumerated counter-majoritarian rights? *See* John H. Ely, Democracy and Distrust 34 (1980), suggesting that the Ninth Amendment "seems open-textured enough to support almost anything one might wish to argue, and that can get pretty scary." How does Justice Goldberg suggest limiting this danger? Is his suggestion a satisfactory answer? But if the Ninth Amendment is not read in this manner, how else can it reasonably be construed? Consider the following possible interpretation: The Ninth Amendment is nothing more than an anti-preemption provision. In other words, it makes clear that the enumeration of constitutionally protected rights is not intended to "occupy the field," and thereby preclude subsequent state-created supplementary rights that are not grounded in a specific textual provision. So construed, the Ninth Amendment would not authorize the judiciary to recognize new federally-protected constitutional rights. *See* Mark Goodman, The Ninth Amendment (1981). Is this a legitimate construction of the Ninth Amendment?

Assume that it could be established that the framers of the Ninth Amendment clearly contemplated the existence of rights above and beyond those enumerated in the Bill of Rights, on grounds of natural law — a philosophy well accepted at the time but one which in recent times has come into disfavor because of the widespread epistemological belief that no one can ascertain a higher law. Should we reject the framers' intent, because our moral and philosophical outlook is today so different from theirs?

According to one commentator, the Ninth Amendment has distinct advantages over substantive due process as a means of adjudicating privacy rights:

> First, Ninth Amendment adjudication would provide the textual foundation for the somewhat ephemeral (and consequently tenuous) constitutional right to personal autonomy. Second, Ninth Amendment adjudication would significantly alter the actual adjudication of personal autonomy claims. Properly conceived and applied, it would require a new focus on neglected but essential questions surrounding and infusing these disputes. These questions include: What is the appropriate limit on individual freedom in our society, and when does this freedom unduly infringe on the rights of others; what is the legitimate role that government can play in restricting the expression of freedom; and finally, what are the appropriate justifications for such restrictions?
>
> Substantive due process adjudication tends to ignore these questions and to obscure the conflict between individual freedom and legitimate government action. Instead, it focuses on positive descriptions of the historical treatment of such disputes exemplified by judges' decisions and legislatures' provisions.

Mark C. Niles, *Ninth Amendment Adjudication: An Alternative to Substantive Due Process Analysis of Personal Autonomy Rights*, 48 UCLA L. Rev. 85, 92 (2000).

If one rejects an interpretation of the Ninth Amendment that effectively vests in the judiciary the power to create new constitutional rights, how is the Ninth Amendment to be construed? Consider the following argument: The Ninth Amendment is nothing more than an "anti-preemption provision." In other words, it is merely designed to clarify that the Bill of Rights' enumeration of federally guaranteed rights is not intended to be an exhaustive list of legally recognized rights. As a result, Congress and state legislatures may supplement that list. For the view that the documentary history of the Ninth Amendment establishes that the Ninth and Tenth Amendments were intended to serve as twin guardians of federalism, see Kurt Lash, *The Lost Original Meaning of the Ninth Amendment*, 83 TEX. L. REV. 331 (2004). For the view that early courts and commentators interpreted the Ninth Amendment as a means of preserving the retained right of local self-government, see Kurt Lash, *The Lost Jusiprudence of the Ninth Amendment*, 83 TEX. L. REV. 597 (2005). On the general issue of Ninth Amendment interpretation, see Lawrence Claus, *Protecting Rights From Rights: Enumeration, Disparagement and the Ninth Amendment*, 79 NOTRE DAME L. REV. 585 (2004).

3. *Privacy and substantive due process.* Justice Douglas wrote many of the post-New Deal decisions repudiating *Lochner*. What is his justification, then, for the interventionist approach adopted in *Griswold*? In *Poe v. Ullman*, 367 U.S. 497 (1961), where the Court avoided the question decided in *Griswold* on justiciability grounds, Justice Douglas, dissenting, had said:

> The error of the old Court, as I see it, was not in entertaining inquiries concerning the constitutionality of social legislation but in applying the standards that it did. Social legislation dealing with business and economic matters touches no particularized prohibition of the Constitution, unless it be the provision of the Fifth Amendment that private property should not be taken for public use without just compensation. If it is free of the latter guarantee it has wide scope for application. Some go so far as to suggest that whatever the majority in the legislatures says goes, that there is no other standard of constitutionality. That reduces the legislative power to sheer voting strength and the judicial function to a matter of statistics.

One commentator has suggested that the problem with the breadth of Justice Douglas' interpretivism results from the fact that

> in extending the periphery, and in finding rights derived from the total scheme of the Bill of Rights, the Court [in *Griswold*] is applying essentially the same process as that used in the fundamental rights approach, but dignifying it with a different name and thereby creating the illusion of greater objectivity.

Paul Kauper, *Penumbras, Peripheries, Emanations, Things Fundamental and Forgotten: The Griswold Case*, 64 MICH. L. REV. 235, 253 (1965). Is there any real distinction between Douglas's interpretivism and the non-interpretivism of Justice Harlan?

It has been suggested that in his *Griswold* opinion, Justice Douglas

> wishes to avoid on the one hand the "natural law" principle which involves selecting rights includable in the due process clause of the

> 14th Amendment — a process that he and Justice Black had sought to avoid by demanding full incorporation of the Bill of Rights. At the same time, he wants to circumvent the limitations posed by Black's insistence that only those rights specified in the Bill of Rights or other provisions of the Constitution are protected. What results is a modified "natural law" yielding a body of rights whose content is suggested by specific constitutional provisions but whose scope and content are not restricted to, or by, the enumerated rights.

William Beaney, *The Griswold Case and the Expanding Right to Privacy*, 1966 WIS. L. REV. 979, 982. Does Justice Douglas succeed in avoiding natural law jurisprudence, or is his opinion an updated version of Justice Chase's opinion in *Calder v. Bull* p. 380? Professor Kauper stated: "Notwithstanding Justice Douglas' protestations, *Griswold* marked a significant revival of natural rights thinking, whatever the formal argument employed by the majority." Paul Kauper, *The Higher Law and the Rights of Man in a Revolutionary Society*, 18 U. MICH. L. QUAD. NOTES 9, 14 (Winter, 1974). Do you agree?

4. *Textual supplementation.* What are legitimate sources of reference for the interpretivist in determining the existence and scope of constitutional rights? A truly strict interpretivism would restrict the Court to reading the textual language. More commonly, the interpretivist seeks to ascertain the Framers' original intent or purpose by examining the historical record behind the framing of the constitutional provision in question. But can the interpretivist look to the development of a provision over time and still claim to be "interpreting" the Constitution? Paul Brest, *The Misconceived Quest for the Original Understanding*, 60 B.U.L. REV. 204 (1980), treats the constitutional text and original history as having "presumptive weight" but does not "treat them as authoritative or binding." Rather, "the presumption is defeasible over time in light of changing experiences and perceptions." He claims that "the practice of supplementing and derogating from the text and original understanding is itself part of our constitutional tradition." Is this interpretivism? Is it a legitimate approach?

5. *Open processes.* Can the interpretivist look to the constitutional structure and relationships to ascertain values and principles that can then be translated into implied constitutional rights? Professor Ely adopts such a form of modified interpretivism. He finds support in the Constitution for "representation-reinforcing" values which justify active judicial intervention in "ensuring broad participation in the processes and distributions of government." JOHN H. ELY, DEMOCRACY AND DISTRUST 87 (1980). For Ely, what distinguishes the United States Constitution is "a process of government, not a governing ideology." Aren't there a number of substantive values that can be derived from the Constitution, such as property and contractual liberty? Doesn't the Constitution reflect a commitment also to personal dignity and autonomy? Is there any special legitimacy in Ely's process-oriented approach?

For critiques of Professor Ely's approach, see Laurence Tribe, *The Puzzling Persistence of Process-Based Constitutional Theories*, 89 YALE L.J. 1063 (1980); Mark Tushnet, *Darkness on the Edge of Town: The Contributions of John Hart Ely to Constitutional Theory*, 89 YALE L.J. 1037 (1980). The more open-ended the "interpretivist" approach is to the sources of constitutional values and principles, the more subject the "interpretivist" is to charges of "Lochnerism," natural-law jurisprudence, and subjective decision-making. In short, the more "interpretivism" is modified, the more it begins to resemble "non-interpretivism."

Consider the following argument:

> A constitutional court composed of unelected, life-tenured judges, guided, in deciding issues at once emotional and politicized, only by a very old and in critical passages very vague constitution (yet one as difficult to amend as the U.S. Constitution is), is potentially an immensely powerful political organ—unless, despite the opportunities that are presented to the Justices, they manage somehow to behave like other judges. A court is supposed to be tethered to authoritative texts, such as constitutional and statutory provisions, and to previous judicial decisions; a legislature is not—it can roam free. But the Supreme Court, when it is deciding constitutional cases, is political in the sense of having and exercising discretionary power as capacious as a legislature's. It cannot abdicate that power, for there is nothing on which to draw to decide constitutional cases of any novelty other than discretionary judgment. To such cases the constitutional text and history, and the pronouncements in past opinions, do not speak clearly. Such cases occupy a broad open area where the conventional legal materials of decision run out and the Justices, deprived of those crutches, have to make a discretionary call.
>
> Richard Posner, *Foreword: A Political Court*, 119 HARV. L. REV. 31, 40 (2005).

Consider the relevance to a constitutional right of privacy of Professor Sunstein's theory of procedural "minimalism" in constitutional interpretation. Sunstein posits that, under this theory, "in the most difficult and controversial domains, the Court tends to choose relatively narrow and unambitious grounds." Instead of "accept[ing] a large-scale theory of constitutional interpretation; it proceeds by building cautiously on precedent, in the fashion of common law courts." Cass Sunstein, *Testing Minimalism: A Reply*, 104 MICH. L. REV. 123, 125 (2005). See also CASS SUNSTEIN, ONE CASE AT A TIME (1999). For a critique of Sunstein's approach, see Jonathan Molot, *Principled Minimalism: Restriking the Balance Between Judicial Minimalism and Neutral Principles*, 90 VA. L. REV. 1753 (2004).

6. *Supplemental values.* Professor Grey finds the distinguishing mark of non-interpretivism to be "its acceptance of the courts' additional role as the expounder of basic national ideals of individual liberty and fair treatment, even when the content of these ideals is not expressed as a matter of positive law in the written Constitution." Thomas Grey, *Do We Have an Unwritten Constitution?* 27 STAN. L. REV. 703, 706 (1975). The "characteristic contemporary metaphor" of modern judicial review, he claims, is "the living Constitution" with its provisions "suggesting restraints on government in the name of basic rights, yet sufficiently unspecific to permit the judiciary to elucidate the development and change in the content of those rights over time."

Professor Perry similarly has argued for non-interpretivism grounded on the principle of an "organic Constitution." Michael Perry, *Abortion, The Public Morals, and the Police Power: The Ethical Function of Substantive Due Process*, 23 UCLA L. Rev. 689 (1976).

Grey is not troubled by charges that he is a natural law jurisprude. Referring to the modern approach of fashioning rights, he states:

> The intellectual framework against which these rights have developed is different from the natural-rights tradition of the founding fathers — its rhetorical reference points are the Anglo-American tradition and basic American ideals, rather than human nature, the social contract, or the rights of man. But it is the modern offspring, in a direct and traceable line of legitimate descent, of the natural-rights tradition that is so deeply embedded in our constitutional origins.

Judge Bork, on the other hand, challenges reliance on nonconstitutional values in judicial review on the ground that

> the choice of "fundamental values" by the Court cannot be justified. Where constitutional materials do not clearly specify the value to be preferred, there is no principled way to prefer any claimed human value to any other. The judge must stick close to the text and the history, and their fair implications, and not construct new rights.

Robert Bork, *Neutral Principles and Some First Amendment Problems*, 47 Ind. L.J. 1, 8 (1971).

7. Tradition and values. Justice Harlan's *Griswold* concurrence is built on his classic statement of the fundamental rights approach dissenting in *Poe v. Ullman*:

> Due process has not been reduced to any formula; its content cannot be determined by reference to any code. The best that can be said is that through the course of this Court's decisions it has represented the balance which our Nation, built upon postulates of respect for the liberty of the individual, has struck between that liberty and the demands of organized society. The balance of which I speak is the balance struck by this country, having regard to what history teaches are the traditions from which it developed as well as the traditions from which it broke. That tradition is a living thing. A decision of this Court which radically departs from it could not long survive, while a decision which builds on what has survived is likely to be sound. No formula could serve as a substitute, in this area, for judgment and restraint.
>
> [I]nasmuch as this context is one not of words, but of history and purposes, the full scope of the liberty guaranteed by the Due Process Clause cannot be found in or limited by the precise terms of the specific guarantees elsewhere provided in the Constitution. This "liberty" is not a series of isolated points pricked out in terms of the taking of property; the freedom of speech, press, and religion; the right to keep

> and bear arms; the freedom from unreasonable searches and seizures; and so on. It is a rational continuum which, broadly speaking, includes a freedom from all substantial arbitrary impositions and purposeless restraints, and which also recognizes, what a reasonable and sensitive judgment must, that certain interests require particularly careful scrutiny of the state needs asserted to justify their abridgment.

8. *Scope of the right of privacy.* Prior to *Griswold*, privacy interests had found expression in search and seizure and self-incrimination cases. After *Griswold*, in *Stanley v. Georgia*, 394 U.S. 557 (1969), the Court struck down a conviction based on possession of obscene materials in one's own home, citing the First Amendment and the right to privacy. The privacy discussion emphasized the home as a critical locus of privacy, and the realm of beliefs and thoughts as essential parts of the "right to be let alone."

What relationship does the "privacy" protected in these cases bear to the right of privacy fashioned in *Griswold*? Is the right recognized in *Griswold* limited to marriage and familial privacy? Does it logically extend to all matters relating to sex? To the use of one's own body? To all matters relating to one's personality?

Justice White, concurring, claimed that "the State's policy against all forms of promiscuous or illicit sexual relationships" was "a permissible and legitimate legislative goal." Is this statement reconcilable with the logic of *Griswold*? Justice White authored the opinion of the Court in the subsequent case of *Bowers v. Hardwick*, p. 585, concerning homosexual conduct.

Justice Harlan similarly assumed the validity of laws proscribing adultery and other sexual conduct but emphasized that the contraceptive law raised the specter of the state's intrusion into the marital unit, even into the bedroom, thus triggering the right of privacy.

9. *Marital and familial privacy.* It has been suggested that "past decisions of the Court, notably the *Meyer* and *Pierce* cases, offered an immediate opening for finding that marital privacy, as a facet of the freedom of family life, was a fundamental right." Kauper, 64 MICH. L. REV. at 253. Does the privacy recognized in *Griswold* flow from the traditional values associated with marriage and family? Is it the right of married persons to use contraceptives that is being protected? This is certainly the perspective of *Griswold* offered by Professor Kauper:

> It required no judicial roving at large to reach the conclusion that the freedom of the marital relationship is a part of the bundle of rights associated with home, family, and marriage — rights supported by precedent, history, and common understanding. For a court to find that these rights are fundamental, whether because they are deeply written in the tradition and conscience of our people, are part of the concept of ordered liberty, are implicit in the notion of a free society, or emanate from the totality of the constitutional order, involves no immodest or startling exercise of judicial power.

Id. at 258. Similarly, it has been stated: "Whatever the constitutional right of privacy may mean in other contexts, the main object of constitutional protection in *Griswold* was the marital relationship." Kenneth Karst, *The Freedom of Intimate Association*, 89 YALE L.J. 624, 625 (1980).

10. *Eisenstadt v. Baird,* 405 U.S. 438 (1972). If *Griswold* were read to protect only the right of married couples to use contraceptives, the constitutionality of statutes limiting access to contraceptives, especially for unmarried persons, would remain in doubt. In *Eisenstadt*, the Court struck down a Massachusetts statute which, while allowing distribution of contraceptives to married persons by medical personnel, prohibited their distribution to unmarried persons. While the case was decided on equal protection grounds, the opinion indicated that the right of privacy recognized in *Griswold* could not be limited to married couples:

> [A]lthough "we need not and do not" decide the "important question" of whether such a prohibition "conflicts with fundamental human rights," whatever the rights of the individual to access to contraceptives may be, the rights must be the same for the married and the unmarried alike. If under *Griswold* the distribution of contraceptives to married persons cannot be prohibited, a ban on distribution to unmarried persons would be equally impermissible. It is true that in *Griswold* the right of privacy in question inhered in the marital relationship. Yet the marital couple is not an independent entity with a mind and heart of its own, but an association of two individuals, each with a separate intellectual and emotional makeup. If the right of privacy means anything, it is the right of the individual, married or single, to be free from unwarranted governmental intrusion into matters so fundamentally affecting a person as the decision whether to bear or beget a child.

Is this language from *Eisenstadt v. Baird* only a logical extension of *Griswold*? Consider the view that "*Eisenstadt* follows from *Griswold*, because the values of intimate association in the two cases are so closely parallel." Karst, 89 YALE L.J. at 624, 662. Does the right of privacy go beyond even marriage, family and sexual relationships to "intimate associations"?

11. *Carey v. Population Services Int'l,* 431 U.S. 678 (1977). The Court held unconstitutional provisions of the New York Education Law making it a crime (1) for any person to sell or distribute any contraceptive of any kind to a minor under the age of 16 years; (2) for anyone other than a licensed pharmacist to distribute contraceptives to persons over 16; and (3) for anyone, including licensed pharmacists, to advertise or display contraceptives. While Justice Brennan delivered the opinion of the Court, the Justices were sharply divided.

The Court did hold that "the constitutionally protected right of privacy extends to an individual's liberty to make choices regarding contraception." Justice Brennan stated that "[t]he decision whether to beget or bear a child is at the very heart of . . . constitutionally protected choices." While *Griswold* protected marital privacy, "in light of its progeny, the teaching of *Griswold* is that the Constitution protects individual decisions in matters of childbearing from unjustified intrusion by the State." The regulations limiting adult access to contraceptives to licensed pharmacists was not narrowly drawn to serve compelling State interests. The advertising limitations violated First Amendment freedom of expression.

Only Justices Stewart, Marshall, and Blackmun joined Justice Brennan in that portion of his opinion dealing with state law prohibitions on the distribution of contraceptives to those under sixteen years of age. While recognizing that "[m]inors, as well as adults, are protected by the Constitution and possess constitutional rights," Justice Brennan also noted that "the power of the state to control the conduct of children reaches beyond the scope of its authority over adults." It followed that "State restriction inhibiting privacy rights to minors are valid only if they serve any significant state interest that is not present in the case of an adult."

Chief Justice Burger dissented, as did Justice Rehnquist, who wrote:

> If those responsible for [the Civil War] amendments, by feats of valor or efforts of draftsmanship, could have lived to know that their efforts had enshrined in the Constitution the right of commercial vendors of contraceptives to peddle them to unmarried minors through such means as window displays and vending machines located in the men's room at truck stops, notwithstanding the considered judgment of the New York legislature to the contrary, it is not difficult to imagine their reaction.

What effect might the AIDS scare have on the reasoning of the dissenters in *Eisenstadt* and *Carey*?

12. *Property and liberty.* The members of the majority in *Griswold* rejected the judicial deference characteristic of economic due process, requiring a showing of more than mere rationality in order to sustain state legislation. Can the Supreme Court meaningfully distinguish substantive personal rights from substantive economic rights? Justice Frankfurter observed that

> there is truth behind the familiar contrast between rights of property and rights of man. But certainly in some of its aspects property is a function of personality, and conversely the free range of the human spirit becomes shriveled and constrained under economic dependence. Especially in a civilization like ours a sharp division between property rights and human rights largely falsifies reality.

FELIX FRANKFURTER, MR. JUSTICE HOLMES AND THE SUPREME COURT 74 (2d ed. 1961). Somewhat more colorfully, referring to professional licensing restrictions, Justice Douglas commented, "For many, it would be better to work in jail than to sit idle on the curb." *Barsky v. Bd. of Regents*, 347 U.S. 442, 472 (1953).

On the other hand, compare the following view:

> The different approach utilized by the courts in cases involving personal, individual liberties reflects in part the judicial sensitivity to the importance of the interests involved. It is highly questionable for a political system which purports to exalt human values to treat alleged violations of these interests in the same manner as challenges to the validity of ordinary economic controls. If we do purport to follow a hierachy of values, our legal policy must be fashioned in such a way as to reflect these differences. The elevation of human values over economic values in constitutional adjudication is a logical manifestation of this principle. To blandly throw basic human needs and aspirations into the same mix as business and industrial concerns goes far to vindicate the accusations of those critics of our system who claim we have distorted value priorities.

C. Thomas Dienes, Law, Politics and Birth Control 179 (1972). Can the differing standards of review be justified on the basis of differing judicial capabilities in the two situations?

> [T]he special scrutiny employed for laws affecting personal human liberties has reflected an assessment by the court of its competence vis-a-vis the legislature to decide complex social, economic, technical issues as opposed to those involving basic human freedoms guaranteed by the Constitution. Whereas legislatures usually have the capability for marshalling the intelligence necessary for effective policy formulation in the former area, the courts generally possess a greater insulation and the capacity for commitment to long-range principles vital to the preservation of personal guarantees. As has been noted: "Knowledge about civil and individual rights, unlike some economic data, is neither so technical nor so esoteric as to lie beyond the legitimate cognizance of the court." [Tussman & tenBroek, *The Equal Protection of the Laws*, 37 Cal. L. Rev. 341, 373 (1949).]

Dienes at 180. Is there something about the institutional roles of legislatures and courts that provides a different competence in these areas?

ROE v. WADE

410 U.S. 113, 93 S. Ct. 705, 35 L. Ed. 2d 147 (1973)

Justice Blackmun delivered the opinion of the Court.

This Texas federal appeal and its Georgia companion, *Doe v. Bolton*, present constitutional challenges to state criminal abortion legislation. The Texas statutes under attack here are typical of those that have been in effect in many States for approximately a century. Our task, of course, is to resolve the issue by constitutional measurement, free of emotion and of predilection. We seek earnestly to do this, and, because we do, we have inquired into, and in this opinion place some emphasis upon, medical and medical-legal history and what that history reveals about man's attitudes toward the abortion procedure over the centuries.

The Texas statutes make it a crime to "procure an abortion," as therein defined, or to attempt one, except with respect to "an abortion procured or attempted by medical advice for the purpose of saving the life of the mother." Jane Roe, a single woman sought a declaratory judgment that the Texas criminal abortion statutes were unconstitutional on their face, and an injunction restraining the defendant from enforcing the statutes. Roe alleged that she was unmarried and pregnant; that she wished to terminate her pregnancy by an abortion "performed by a competent, licensed physician, under safe, clinical conditions"; that she was unable to get a "legal" abortion in Texas because her life did not appear to be threatened by the continuation of her pregnancy; and that she could not afford to travel to another jurisdiction in order to secure a legal abortion under safe conditions.

[The district court held, on the merits, that the Texas statutes were unconstitutionally vague and constituted an overbroad infringement of the plaintiff's Ninth Amendment rights, but denied the injunction on abstention grounds. The disposition of the claims of the other litigants is omitted since the Supreme Court, on the basis of justiciability, standing and abstention, held that only Jane Roe was a proper litigant.]

[Justice Blackmun's extensive review of ancient attitudes towards abortion, the Hippocratic oath, the common law, the English statutory law and American law and the positions of medical and legal professional associations is omitted.]

Three reasons have been advanced to explain historically the enactment of criminal abortion laws in the nineteenth century and to justify their continued existence.

It has been argued occasionally that these laws were the product of a Victorian social concern to discourage illicit sexual conduct. Texas, however, does not advance this justification in the present case, and it appears that no court or commentator has taken the argument seriously.

A second reason is concerned with abortion as a medical procedure. When most criminal abortion laws were first enacted, the procedure was a hazardous one for the woman. Modern medical techniques have altered this situation. Appellants and various amici refer to medical data indicating that abortion in early pregnancy, this is, prior to the end of the first trimester, although not without its risk, is now relatively safe. Mortality rates for women undergoing early abortions, where the procedure is legal, appear to be as low as or lower than the rates for normal childbirth. Consequently, any interest of the State in protecting the woman from an inherently hazardous procedure, except when it would be equally dangerous for her to forgo it, has largely disappeared. Of course, important state interests in the area of health and medical standards do remain.

The third reason is the State's interest — some phrase it in terms of duty — in protecting prenatal life. Some of the argument for this justification rests on the theory that a new human life is present from the moment of conception. The State's interest and general obligation to protect life then extends, it is argued, to prenatal life. Only when the life of the pregnant mother herself is at stake, balanced against the life she carries within her, should the interest of the embryo or fetus not prevail. Logically, of course, a legitimate state interest in this area need not stand or fall on acceptance of the belief that life begins at conception or at some other point prior to live birth. In assessing the State's interest, recognition may be given to the less rigid claim that as long as at least potential life is involved, the State may assert interests beyond the protection of the pregnant woman alone.

The Constitution does not explicitly mention any right of privacy. In a line of decisions, the Court has recognized that a right of personal privacy, or a guarantee of certain areas or zones of privacy, does exist under the Constitution. This right of privacy, whether it be founded in the Fourteenth Amendment's concept of personal liberty and restrictions upon state action, as we feel it is, or, as the District Court determined, in the Ninth Amendment's reservation of rights to the people, is broad enough to encompass a woman's decision whether or not to terminate her pregnancy. The detriment that the State would impose upon the pregnant woman by denying this choice altogether is apparent. Specific and direct harm medically diagnosable even in early pregnancy may be involved. Maternity, or additional offspring, may force upon the woman a distressful life and future. Psychological harm may be imminent. Mental and physical health may be taxed by child care. There is also the distress, for all concerned, associated with the unwanted child, and there is the problem of bringing a child into a family already unable, psychologically and otherwise, to care for it. In other cases, as in this one, the additional difficulties and continuing stigma of unwed motherhood may be involved. All these are factors the woman and her responsible physician necessarily will consider in consultation.

On the basis of elements such as these, appellant and some amici argue that the woman's right is absolute and that she is entitled to terminate her pregnancy at whatever time, in whatever way, and for whatever reason she alone chooses. With this we do not agree. The Court's decisions recognizing a right of privacy also acknowledge that some state regulation in areas protected by that right is appropriate. As noted above, a State may properly assert important interests in safeguarding health, in maintaining medical standards, and in protecting potential life. At some point in pregnancy, these respective interests become sufficiently compelling to sustain regulation of the factors that govern the abortion decision. The privacy right involved, therefore, cannot be said to be absolute. In fact, it is not clear to us that the claim asserted by some amici that one has an unlimited right to do with one's body as one pleases bears a close relationship to the right of privacy previously articulated in the Court's decisions.

We, therefore, conclude that the right of personal privacy includes the abortion decision, but that this right is not unqualified and must be considered against important state interests in regulation. Where certain fundamental "rights" are involved, the Court has held that regulation limiting these rights may be justified only by a "compelling state interest," [citing equal protection and First Amendment cases], and that legislative enactments must be narrowly drawn to express only the legitimate state interests at stake.

The appellee and certain amici argue that the fetus is a "person" within the language and meaning of the Fourteenth Amendment. In support of this, they outline at length and in detail the well-known facts of fetal development. If this suggestion of personhood is established, the appellant's case, of course, collapses, for the fetus' right to life is then guaranteed specifically by the Amendment. On the other hand, the appellee conceded on the reargument that no case could be cited that holds that a fetus is a person within the meaning of the Fourteenth Amendment.

The Constitution does not define "person" in so many words. [The Court reviews all references to "person" in the Constitution.] But in nearly all these instances, the use of the word is such that it has application only postnatally. None indicates, with any assurance, that it has any possible prenatal application. All this, together with our observation, that throughout the major portion of the nineteenth century prevailing legal abortion practices were far freer than they are today, persuades us that the word "person," as used in the Fourteenth Amendment, does not include the unborn. This conclusion, however, does not of itself fully answer the contentions raised by Texas, and we pass on to other considerations.

The pregnant woman cannot be isolated in her privacy. She carries an embryo and, later, a fetus, if one accepts the medical definitions of the developing young in the human uterus. The situation therefore is inherently different from marital intimacy, or bedroom possession of obscene material, or marriage, or procreation, or education, with which *Eisenstadt*, *Griswold*, *Stanley*, *Loving*, *Skinner*, *Pierce*, and *Meyer* were respectively concerned.

Texas urges that, apart from the Fourteenth Amendment, life begins at conception and is present throughout pregnancy, and that, therefore, the State has a compelling interest in protecting that life from and after conception. We need not resolve the difficult question of when life begins. When those trained in the respective disciplines of medicine, philosophy, and theology are unable to arrive at any consensus, the judiciary, at this point in the development of man's knowledge, is not in a position to speculate as to the answer.

[W]e do not agree that, by adopting one theory of life, Texas may override the rights of the pregnant woman that are at stake. We repeat, however, that the State does have an important and legitimate interest in preserving and protecting the health of the pregnant woman, whether she be a resident of the State or a nonresident who seeks medical consultation and treatment there, and that it has still another important and legitimate interest in protecting the potentiality of human life. These interests are separate and distinct. Each grows in substantiality as the woman approaches term and, at a point during pregnancy, each becomes "compelling."

With respect to the State's important and legitimate interest in the health of the mother, the "compelling" point, in the light of present medical knowledge, is at approximately the end of the first trimester. This is so because of the now-established medical fact, that until the end of the first trimester mortality in abortion may be less than mortality in normal childbirth. It follows that, from and after this point, a State may regulate the abortion procedure to the extent that the regulation reasonably relates to the preservation and protection of maternal health. Examples of permissible state regulation in this area are requirements as to the qualifications of the person who is to perform the abortion; as to the licensure of that person; as to the facility in which the procedure is to be performed, that is, whether it must be a hospital or may be a clinic or some other place of less-than-hospital status; as to the licensing of the facility; and the like. This means, on the other hand, that, for the period of pregnancy prior to this "compelling" point, the attending physician, in consultation with his patient, is free to determine, without regulation by the State, that, in his medical judgment, the patient's pregnancy should be terminated. If that decision is reached, the judgment may be effectuated by an abortion free of interference by the State.

With respect to the State's important and legitimate interest in potential life, the "compelling" point is at viability. This is so because the fetus then presumably has the capability of meaningful life outside the mother's womb. State regulation protective of fetal life after viability thus has both logical and biological justifications. If the State is interested in protecting fetal life after viability, it may go so far as to proscribe abortion during that period, except when it is necessary to preserve the life or health of the mother.

Measured against these standards the Texas Penal Code, sweeps too broadly. The statute makes no distinction between abortions performed early in pregnancy and those performed later, and it limits to a single reason, "saving" the mother's life, the legal justification for the procedure. The statute, therefore, cannot survive the constitutional attack made upon it here.

This holding, we feel, is consistent with the relative weights of the respective interests involved, with the lessons and examples of medical and legal history, with the lenity of the common law, and with the demands of the profound problems of the present day. The decision leaves the State free to place increasing restrictions on abortion as the period of pregnancy lengthens, so long as those restrictions are tailored to the recognized state interests. The decision vindicates the right of the physician to administer medical treatment according to his professional judgment up to the points where important state interests provide compelling justifications for intervention. Up to those points, the abortion decision in all its aspects is inherently, and primarily, a medical decision, and basic responsibility for it must rest with the physician. If an individual practitioner abuses the privilege of exercising proper medical judgment, the usual remedies, judicial and intraprofessional, are available.

Justice Douglas, concurring [in *Doe v. Bolton* and *Roe v. Wade*].

While I join the opinion of the Court [except on the abstention issue], I add a few words. The Ninth Amendment obviously does not create federally enforceable rights. It merely says, "The enumeration in the Constitution, of certain rights, shall not be construed to deny or disparage others retained by the people." But a catalogue of these rights includes customary, traditional, and time-honored rights, amenities, privileges, and immunities that come within the sweep of "the Blessings of Liberty" mentioned in the preamble to the Constitution. Many of them, in my view, come within the meaning of the term "liberty" as used in the Fourteenth Amendment.

First is the autonomous control over the development and expression of one's intellect, interests, tastes, and personality. These are rights protected by the First Amendment and, in my view, they are absolute, permitting of no exceptions. The Free Exercise Clause of the First Amendment is one facet of this constitutional right. The right to remain silent as respects one's own beliefs, is protected by the First and the Fifth. The First Amendment grants the privacy of first-class mail. All of these aspects of the right of privacy are rights "retained by the people" in the meaning of the Ninth Amendment.

Second is freedom of choice in the basic decisions of one's life respecting marriage, divorce, procreation, contraception, and the education and upbringing of children. These rights, unlike those protected by the First Amendment, are subject to some control by the police power. These rights are "fundamental," and we have held that in order to support legislative action the statute must be narrowly and precisely drawn and that a "compelling state interest" must be shown in support of the limitation.[4]

Third is the freedom to care for one's health and person, freedom from bodily restraint or compulsion, freedom to walk, stroll, or loaf.

These rights, though fundamental, are likewise subject to regulation on a showing of "compelling state interest."

[A] woman is free to make the basic decision whether to bear an unwanted child. Elaborate argument is hardly necessary to demonstrate that childbirth may deprive a woman of her preferred lifestyle and force upon her a radically different and undesired future. For example, rejected applicants under the Georgia statute are required to endure the discomforts of pregnancy; to incur the pain, higher mortality rate, and aftereffects of childbirth; to abandon educational plans; to sustain loss of income; to forgo the satisfactions of careers; to tax further mental and physical health in providing child care; and, in some cases, to bear the lifelong stigma of unwed motherhood, a badge which may haunt, if not deter, later legitimate family relationships.

JUSTICE STEWART, concurring.

In 1963, this Court, in *Ferguson v. Skrupa* [p. 473], purported to sound the death knell for the doctrine of substantive due process. Barely two years later, in *Griswold v. Connecticut*, the Court held a Connecticut birth control law unconstitutional. In view of what had been so recently said in *Skrupa*, the Court's opinion in *Griswold* understandably did its best to avoid reliance on

[4] My Brother STEWART, writing in *Roe v. Wade*, says that our decision in *Griswold* reintroduced substantive due process that had been rejected in *Ferguson v. Skrupa*. *Skrupa* involved legislation governing a business enterprise; and the Court in that case, as had Mr. Justice Holmes on earlier occasions, rejected the idea that "liberty" within the meaning of the Due Process Clause of the Fourteenth Amendment was a vessel to be filled with one's personal choices of values, whether drawn from the laissez faire school, from the socialistic school, or from the technocrats. *Griswold* involved legislation touching on the marital relation and involving the conviction of a licensed physician for giving married people information concerning contraception. There is nothing specific in the Bill of Rights that covers that item. Nor is there anything in the Bill of Rights that in terms protects the right of association or the privacy in one's association. Yet we found those rights in the periphery of the First Amendment. Other peripheral rights are the right to educate one's children as one chooses, and the right to study the German language. These decisions, with all respect, have nothing to do with substantive due process. One may think they are not peripheral to other rights that are expressed in the Bill of Rights. But that is not enough to bring into play the protection of substantive due process.

There are, of course, those who have believed that the reach of due process in the Fourteenth Amendment included all of the Bill of Rights but went further. Such was the view of MR. JUSTICE MURPHY and MR. JUSTICE RUTLEDGE. *See Adamson v. California*. Perhaps they were right; but it is a bridge that neither I nor those who joined the Court's opinion in *Griswold* crossed.

the Due Process Clause of the Fourteenth Amendment as the ground for decision. Yet, the Connecticut law did not violate any provision of the Bill of Rights, nor any other specific provision of the Constitution. So it was clear to me then, and it is equally clear to me now, that the *Griswold* decision can be rationally understood only as a holding that the Connecticut statute substantively invaded the "liberty" that is protected by the Due Process Clause of the Fourteenth Amendment. As so understood, *Griswold* stands as one in a long line of pre-*Skrupa* cases decided under the doctrine of substantive due process, and I now accept it as such.

Several decisions of this Court make clear that freedom of personal choice in matters of marriage and family life is one of the liberties protected by the Due Process Clause of the Fourteenth Amendment. As recently as last Term, in *Eisenstadt v. Baird*, we recognized "the right of the individual, married or single, to be free from unwarranted governmental intrusion into matters so fundamentally affecting a person as the decision whether to bear or beget a child." That right necessarily includes the right of a woman to decide whether or not to terminate her pregnancy. "Certainly the interests of a woman in giving of her physical and emotional self during pregnancy and the interests that will be affected throughout her life by the birth and raising of a child are of a far greater degree of significance and personal intimacy than the right to send a child to private school protected in *Pierce v. Society of Sisters*, or the right to teach a foreign language protected in *Meyer v. Nebraska*." *Abele v. Markle*, 351 F. Supp. 224, 227 (Conn. 1972). Clearly, therefore, the Court today is correct in holding that the right asserted by Jane Roe is embraced within the personal liberty protected by the Due Process Clause of the Fourteenth Amendment.

It is evident that the Texas abortion statute infringes that right directly. Indeed, it is difficult to imagine a more complete abridgement of a constitutional freedom than that worked by the inflexible criminal statute now in force in Texas. The question then becomes whether the state interests advanced to justify this abridgement can survive the "particularly careful scrutiny" that the Fourteenth Amendment here requires. I think the Court today has thoroughly demonstrated that [the] state interests cannot constitutionally support the broad abridgment of personal liberty worked by the existing Texas law.

JUSTICE WHITE, with whom JUSTICE REHNQUIST joins, dissenting [in *Doe v. Bolton* and *Roe v. Wade*].

I find nothing in the language or history of the Constitution to support the Court's judgment. The Court simply fashions and announces a new constitutional right for pregnant mothers and, with scarcely any reason or authority for its action, invests that right with sufficient substance to override most existing state abortion statutes. The upshot is that the people and the legislatures of the 50 States are constitutionally disentitled to weigh the relative importance of the continued existence and development of the fetus, on the one hand, against a spectrum of possible impacts on the mother, on the other hand. As an exercise of raw judicial power, the Court perhaps has authority to do what it does today; but in my view its judgment is an improvident and extravagant exercise of the power of judicial review that the Constitution extends to this Court.

The Court apparently values the convenience of the pregnant mother more than the continued existence and development of the life or potential life that she carries. Whether or not I might agree with that marshalling of values, I can in no event join the Court's judgment because I find no constitutional warrant for imposing such an order of priorities on the people and legislatures of the States. In a sensitive area such as this, involving as it does issues over which reasonable men may easily and heatedly differ, I cannot accept the Court's exercise of its clear power of choice by interposing a constitutional barrier to state efforts to protect human life by investing mothers and doctors with the constitutionally protected right to exterminate it. This issue, for the most part, should be left with the people and to the political processes the people have devised to govern their affairs.

JUSTICE REHNQUIST, dissenting.

I have difficulty in concluding, as the Court does, that the right of "privacy" is involved in this case. Texas, by the statute here challenged, bars the performance of a medical abortion by a licensed physician on a plaintiff such as *Roe*. A transaction resulting in an operation such as this is not "private" in the ordinary usage of that word. Nor is the "privacy" that the Court finds here even a distant relative of the freedom from searches and seizures protected by the Fourth Amendment to the Constitution, which the Court has referred to as embodying a right to privacy.

If the Court means by the term "privacy" no more than that the claim of a person to be free from unwanted state regulation of consensual transactions may be a form of "liberty" protected by the Fourteenth Amendment, there is no doubt that similar claims have been upheld in our earlier decisions on the basis of that liberty. I agree with the statement of MR. JUSTICE STEWART in his concurring opinion that the "liberty," against deprivation of which without due process the Fourteenth Amendment protects, embraces more than the rights found in the Bill of Rights. But that liberty is not guaranteed absolutely against deprivation, only against deprivation without due process of law. The test traditionally applied in the area of social and economic legislation is whether or not a law such as that challenged has a rational relation to a valid state objective. The Due Process Clause of the Fourteenth Amendment undoubtedly does place a limit, albeit a broad one, on legislative power to enact laws such as this. If the Texas statute were to prohibit an abortion even where the mother's life is in jeopardy, I have little doubt that such a statute would lack a rational relation to a valid state objective. But the Court's sweeping invalidation of any restrictions on abortion during the first trimester is impossible to justify under that standard, and the conscious weighing of competing factors that the Court's opinion apparently substitutes for the established test is far more appropriate to a legislative judgment than to a judicial one.

While the Court's opinion quotes from the dissent of MR. JUSTICE HOLMES in *Lochner v. New York* the result it reaches is more closely attuned to the majority opinion of MR. JUSTICE PECKHAM in that case. As in *Lochner* and similar cases applying substantive due process standards to economic and social welfare legislation, the adoption of the compelling state interest standard will inevitably require this Court to examine the legislative policies and pass on the wisdom of these policies in the very process of deciding whether a particular state interest put forward may or may not be "compelling." The decision here to break pregnancy into three distinct terms and to outline the permissible restrictions the State may impose in each one, for example, partakes more of judicial legislation than it does of a determination of the intent of the drafters of the Fourteenth Amendment.

The fact that a majority of the States reflecting, after all, the majority sentiment in those States, have had restrictions on abortions for at least a century is a strong indication, it seems to me, that the asserted right to an abortion is not "so rooted in the traditions and conscience of our people as to be ranked as fundamental," *Snyder v. Massachusetts*, 291 U.S. 97 (1934). Even today, when society's views on abortion are changing, the very existence of the debate is evidence that the "right" to an abortion is not so universally accepted as the appellants would have us believe.

To reach its result, the Court necessarily has had to find within the scope of the Fourteenth Amendment a right that was completely unknown to the drafters of the Amendment. As early as 1821, the first state law dealing directly with abortion was enacted by the Connecticut Legislature. There apparently was no question concerning the validity of this provision or of any of the other state statutes when the Fourteenth Amendment was adopted. The only conclusion possible from this history is that the drafters did not intend to have the Fourteenth Amendment withdraw from the States the power to legislate with respect to this matter.

NOTES

1. *Doe v. Bolton,* 410 U.S. 179 (1973). In *Doe*, decided the same day as *Roe*, the Court upheld the Georgia abortion statutes, which were based on the ALI Modern Penal Code and similar to those adopted by about one fourth of the states. The Georgia version made abortion a crime except when

> performed by a physician duly licensed [and] based upon his best clinical judgment that an abortion is necessary because
>
> (1) A continuation of the pregnancy would endanger the life of the pregnant woman or would seriously and permanently injure her health; or,
>
> (2) The fetus would very likely be born with a grave, permanent, and irremediable mental or physical defect; or,
>
> (3) The pregnancy resulted from forcible or statutory rape.

Georgia also imposed a residency and various other procedural requirements.

The Court, per Justice Blackmun, held that the provision, as construed by the district court, was not unconstitutionally vague. The best clinical judgment of the physician, argued Justice Blackmun, is not restricted but "may be exercised in the light of all factors — physical, emotional, psychological, familial, and the woman's age — relevant to the well-being of the patient. All these factors may relate to health. This allows the attending physician the room he needs to make his best medical judgment. And it is room that operates for the benefit, not the disadvantage, of the pregnant woman."

The Court, however, reversed the district court's holding that three challenged procedural requirements were constitutional. First, a requirement that only hospitals accredited by the J.C.A.H. (Joint Commission on Accreditation of Hospitals) could perform abortions was found not "based on differences that are reasonably related to the purposes of the Act in which it is found," because non-abortion surgery at non-accredited hospitals was permitted if other state regulations were satisfied. The second and third provisions that the Court held unconstitutional were a requirement that an abortion be approved by a hospital staff committee and a requirement that the performing physician's judgment be confirmed by the examination of two other licensed physicians. The judgment of the woman's physician, licensed by the state and subject to disciplinary proceedings, Justice Blackmun concluded, was sufficient. No other medical or surgical procedure required such confirmation. "Required acquiescence by co-practitioners has no rational connection with a patient's needs and unduly infringes on the physician's right to practice."

The Court also concluded that its disposition of the procedural claims disposed of a challenge to the Georgia system as violative of equal protection on grounds that it discriminates against the poor.

2. *Privacy and abortion.* How would you describe the constitutional interest being protected in *Roe*? In what sense can the right protected in *Roe* be considered a form of "privacy"? Is it a right of privacy in the same sense as the right protected in *Griswold*? One commentator has suggested that the interests protected "are more obscured than illuminated by the Court's privacy language." Robert Bennett, *Abortion and Judicial Review: Of Burdens and Benefits, Hard Cases and Some Bad Law*, 75 Nw. U.L. Rev. 978, 991 (1981). Would a phrase such as the "right of self-determination" or even a "right of choice" have been a more felicitous choice, particularly in light of subsequent developments regarding rights to receive and refuse medical treatment?

Another approach to the abortion question is to link "bodily integrity" with a concept of "personhood" similar to that contained in other constitutional protections.

> [T]aking away women's ability to control their decision not to become mothers can be severely damaging to their very sense of self, for this denial of decisionmaking divides women from their wombs and uses their wombs for a purpose unrelated to women's own aspirations. Because bodily integrity is necessary for the formation of selfhood, it is essential that law recognize women's subjectivity in its construction of women's procreative lives.

Julia Hanigsberg, *Homologizing Pregnancy and Motherhood: A Consideration of Abortion*, 94 Mich. L. Rev. 371, 371–72 (1995).

3. *Criticisms of Roe.* *Roe* easily ranks as one of the most controversial of the Supreme Court's decisions, figuring prominently in presidential election campaigns and nominations to the Court over the last two decades. It would not be possible to detail all the objections to *Roe*, but the attempt here will be to capture the essence of the major strands of objections. The objections can be categorized in at least two ways, those objecting to the Court's methodology and those objecting to a perceived lack of sensitivity to the fetus.

a. Methodological objections

> What is frightening about *Roe* is that this super-protected right [of the woman to choose an abortion] is not inferable from the language of the Constitution, the framers' thinking respecting the specific problem in issue, any general value derivable from the provision they included, or the nation's governmental structure. Nor is it explainable in terms of the unusual political impotence of the group judicially protected vis-a-vis the interest that legislatively prevailed over it.

John Ely, *The Wages of Crying Wolf: A Comment on Roe v. Wade*, 82 YALE L.J. 920, 935–37 (1973).

Even Professor Tribe, a defender of the result in *Roe*, states: "One of the most curious things about *Roe* is that, behind its own verbal smokescreen, the substantive judgment on which it rests is nowhere to be found." Laurence Tribe, *Foreword: Toward a Model of Roles in the Due Process of Life and Law*, 87 HARV. L. REV. 1, 7 (1973).

Another type of methodological objection focuses on the Court's detailed prescription of the trimester framework and the permissible scope of state regulation within each trimester. The "rigid trimester framework" becomes the focus of dissenting opinions in post-*Roe* cases. It can be argued that a person might accept *Griswold*, yet still condemn *Roe* as "an aberration of judicial legislation." *See* William Van Alstyne, *Closing the Circle of Constitutional Review From Griswold v. Connecticut to Roe v. Wade: An Outline of a Decision Merely Overruling Roe*, 1989 DUKE L.J. 1677, 1684.

Professor Ely argues that *Roe* is a more dogmatic holding than *Lochner*. *Lochner* required a court to determine whether a particular regulation were reasonable whereas *Roe* sets out a "fundamental" right that can be invaded only for a "compelling" reason. Ely concludes,

> The problem with *Roe* is not so much that it bungles the question it sets itself but rather that it sets itself a question the Constitution has not made the court's business. The employment of a higher standard of judicial review, no matter how candid the recognition that it is indeed higher, loses some of its admirability when it is accompanied by neither a coherent account of why such a standard is appropriate nor any indication of why it has not been satisfied.

Ely, 82 YALE L.J. at 940–43.

b. "Fetal rights"

The most vociferous attacks on *Roe* have centered on the Court's conclusion that the state does not have a compelling interest in the fetus prior to viability. Bennett, 75 NW. U.L. REV. at 991, argues that

> the Court's reference to "potential life" does not fairly capture the seriousness of the interest pursued by "right-to-life" advocates; and

> it is their interest that the state has made its own. The life at stake, in the right-to-life view, is not "potential" but actual. The fetus is seen as equivalent in its humanness to infants and children and adults, since human life for them begins at conception. The interests the state pursues in criminal abortion laws are thus the same interests it pursues in murder laws: interests in asserting the sanctity of human life and in deterring attacks upon it.

Professor Noonan has also criticized the Court's emphasis on the fetus as a "potential life":

> This description was accurate if it meant there was existing life with a great deal of development yet to come, as one might say a 5-year-old is "potential life" meaning that he or she is only potentially what he or she will be at twenty-five. The Court's description was inaccurate if the Court meant to suggest that what was in the womb was pure potentiality, a zero that could not be protected by law.

John Noonan, *The Root and Branch of Roe v. Wade*, 63 NEB. L. REV. 668, 673 (1984).

Is it so clear that the Court ignored "the biological reality," as Professor Noonan suggests? Professor Noonan also suggests: "The Court seemed to be uncertain itself [on the characterization of a fetus as a life] and to take the position that if it were unsure, nobody else could be sure." Is this an accurate description of the Court's view? If so, is there anything wrong with the Court's adopting such a view?

Richard Epstein, *Substantive Due Process by Any Other Name: The Abortion Cases*, 1973 SUP. CT. REV. 159, 183:

> It remains true that for many purposes, the unborn — Mr. Justice Blackmun studiously avoids "person" — are regarded as persons, and it remains true as well that recent judicial trends have expanded, not limited their rights. Even if an unborn child is not treated as just another person, it is still necessary for Mr. Justice Blackmun to explain why the unborn child is not treated as a person in abortion cases, when it has been so regarded in other legal contexts.

There are two separate arguments regarding the status of the fetus. One is whether the fetus is a "person" under the due process guarantee; it is not at all clear what would be the significance of so categorizing. The second is that it would be permissible for the state to make the judgment call that the fetus is deserving of protection. The usual response of a court to a judgment based on unknowable or unprovable facts is to defer to the legislative judgment, but in this instance the legislative judgment has run up against a constitutionally based claim on the other side. The Court's opinion does not really address the second issue outside of the viability discussion; it seems to assume that only a claim of constitutional dimension on behalf of the fetus would warrant limitation on the constitutionally based right of the pregnant woman to control her own destiny. At the point of viability, according to the

Court, the state does have a compelling interest because at that point abortion begins to look more like homicide.

4. *Support for Roe.* Supporters of *Roe* have argued that it is only an "incremental development in constitutional doctrine" — "The couples' right to decide whether to have a family is the very same right as that established and protected in the cases dealing with contraception; considerations identical to those that justify protecting the broader class require careful scrutiny of regulations concerning abortion." This is based on the contention that privacy involves a sphere of interests:

> At the core of this sphere is the right of the individual to make for himself — except where a very good reason exists for placing the decision in society's hands — the fundamental decisions that shape family life: whom to marry; whether and when to have children; and with what values to rear those children.

Philip Heymann & Douglas Barzelay, *The Forest and the Trees: Roe v. Wade and Its Critics*, 53 B.U.L. Rev. 765, 772, 775, 777 n.61 (1973). Does *Roe* stand for the proposition that there is a constitutional right of a woman to control her own body? That there is a generic right of privacy in sexual matters?

A theoretical defense of *Roe* suggested by Philip Bobbitt, Constitutional Fate (1982), begins with the following ethical principle: "Government may not coerce intimate acts." *Id.* at 159. On the basis of this constitutional/ethical principle, he reasons that "[w]hatever else may be an intimate act, carrying a child within one's body and giving birth must be a profoundly intimate act." He acknowledges that arguably "a woman who voluntarily consents not merely to sexual intercourse but also to carrying a child for a period long enough so that she can both be presumed to be aware of her condition and to have had the time to reflect on it, has by her acquiescence waived any claim against the state's coercion. Because the mode in which the *Roe* argument I have given is ethical it cannot yield to waiver." Consider Martin Redish, *Judicial Review and Constitutional Ethics*, 82 Mich. L. Rev. 665, 676 (1984): "I fail to understand a logic that asserts that because a principle is ethical, it is not subject to waiver." Where does Bobbitt's ethical principle appear in the Constitution? "The barriers must be constitutional, it would seem, to account for our sense of absolute prohibition." Bobbitt also argues that government lacks authority to violate ethical principles, even those not expressly codified in a specific constitutional protection, because the Constitution should not be viewed as delegating to the government authority to violate such principles in the first place. Bobbitt, at 152, 155. Is this a legitimate means of avoiding the lack of a textual basis for the recognition of the right protected in *Roe*?

Professor Karst finds a reasoned basis for *Roe* in an evolving "freedom of intimate association" — "a close and familiar personal relationship with another that is in some significant way comparable to a marriage or family relationship." Kenneth Karst, *The Freedom of Intimate Association*, 89 Yale L.J. 624, 629 (1980). *Griswold* was based on the marital relationship but the decision to procreate reflects the same basic values as marriage. "The decision to have a child, whether within or outside marriage, strongly implicates the values of intimate association, particularly the values of caring and commitment, intimacy, and self-identification." Is this ethical theory stronger than Bobbitt's?

5. *An equal protection rationale.* If one were to reject reliance on a constitutional right of privacy as a basis for the abortion right, might it be persuasively argued that restricting a woman's ability to obtain an abortion violates equal protection, because the restriction discriminates against women? "Despite forceful and increasingly frequent arguments that the harm caused by restrictive abortion laws deny equal protection, at least as much as they impinge on personal privacy, the Court has steadfastly refused to consider abortion in this light." Erin Daly, *Reconsidering Abortion Law: Liberty, Equality, and the New Rhetoric of Planned Parenthood v. Casey,* 45 AM. U.L. REV. 77, 78 (1995). The reason for this failure, the same commentator claims, is that "the Court has failed to accord women the respect necessary to make equal protection claims appropriate."

6. *Minors — parental consent or notification.* In *Planned Parenthood v. Danforth*, p. 528, the Court held that a state could not require parental consent during the first trimester because that would give a third person a veto over the decision of a physician and his or her patient. In *City of Akron v. Akron Center for Reproductive Health, Inc.*, p. 528, the Court invalidated another parental notification and consent requirement. But in *Planned Parenthood v. Ashcroft*, p. 529, the Court upheld a parental consent requirement that had been interpreted to include a judicial substitute. The court of appeals had interpreted the Missouri statute to provide that a juvenile court in denying a petition for an abortion "for good cause" would be required "to find that the minor was not emancipated and was not mature enough to make her own decision and that an abortion was not in her best interests." The Supreme Court concluded that this interpretation of the statute was correct and that the statute, "as interpreted, avoids any constitutional infirmities."

In *Hodgson v. Minnesota*, 497 U.S. 417 (1990) and *Ohio v. Akron Center for Reproductive Health*, 497 U.S. 502 (1990), the Court reaffirmed the proposition that parental notification could be required before a minor's abortion provided that there is an alternative procedure for securing a judicial consent. The Minnesota statute required that both parents be notified and that one parent consent to the abortion. The statute went on to provide that if this combination were ruled unconstitutional, then the notification requirement would be effective unless the minor received a "court order permitting the abortion to proceed." A majority of the Supreme Court held the notification and consent requirement to be invalid. A different majority then held the notification with bypass procedure to be valid. Justice O'Connor, as the swing vote, explained her position on the bypass on the basis of precedent and the conclusion that "the interference with the internal operation of the family required by [the two-parent notification] simply does not exist where the minor can avoid notifying one or both parents by use of the bypass procedure."

Writing only for a plurality which included Chief Justice Rehnquist and Justices White and Scalia, Justice Kennedy concluded:

> A free and enlightened society may decide that each of its members should attain a clearer, more tolerant understanding of the profound

> philosophic choices confronted by a woman who is considering whether to seek an abortion. Her decision will embrace her own destiny and personal dignity, and the origins of the other human life that lie within the embryo. The State is entitled to assume that, for most of its people, the beginnings of that understanding will be within the family, society's most intimate association. It is both rational and fair for the State to conclude that, in most instances, the family will strive to give a lonely or even terrified minor advice that is both compassionate and mature. The statute in issue here is a rational way to further those ends. It would deny all dignity to the family to say that the State cannot take this reasonable step in regulating its health professions to ensure that, in most cases, a young woman will receive guidance and understanding from a parent.

7. From *Roe* to *Casey*: In the years following *Roe*, the abortion right endured a rollercoaster ride in a series of Supreme Court decisions culminating in the Court's decision in *Planned Parenthood of Southeastern Pennsylvania v. Casey* in 1992. What follows is a brief review of those decisions.

***a. Planned Parenthood of Central Missouri v. Danforth,* 428 U.S. 52 (1976).** The Court reconsidered the scope of *Roe*, holding:

(1) Viability need not be defined by a state in terms of a number of weeks but is a medical concept varying with each pregnancy.

(2) Requiring a woman's written consent to an abortion, even during the first trimester, is a permissible state regulation designed to assure full knowledge of the nature and consequences of the act.

(3) A state may not require consent of the spouse since the balance of interests favors the woman who physically bears the child and is most affected by the pregnancy.

(4) A state may not require parental consent during the first trimester since this gives third persons a veto over the decision of a physician and his/her patient.

(5) A state may require record keeping, even during the first trimester, so long as the record keeping is reasonably directed to the preservation of maternal health and properly respects the patient's confidentiality and privacy.

***b. City of Akron v. Akron Center for Reproductive Health, Inc.,* 462 U.S. 416 (1983).** The Court, in a 6-3 decision, reaffirmed *Roe* in striking down five provisions of a local ordinance regulating abortion. The invalidated provisions (1) required that all abortions performed after the first trimester of pregnancy be performed in a hospital; (2) set forth requirements for notification of and consent by parents before abortions may be performed on unmarried minors; (3) required that the attending physician make certain specific statements to the patient "to insure that the consent for an abortion is truly informed consent"; (4) required a 24-hour waiting period between the time the woman signs a consent form and the time the abortion is performed; and (5) required that fetal remains be "disposed of in a humane and sanitary manner."

In his opinion for the majority, Justice Powell stated:

> We reaffirm today that a State's interest in health regulation becomes compelling at approximately the end of the first trimester. The existence of a compelling state interest in health, however, is only the beginning of the inquiry. The State's regulation may be upheld only if it is reasonably designed to further that state interest. And the Court in *Roe* did not hold that it always is reasonable for a State to adopt an abortion regulation that applies to the entire second trimester. A State necessarily must have latitude in adopting regulations of general applicability in this sensitive area. But if it appears that during a substantial portion of the second trimester the State's regulation "depart[s] from accepted medical practice," the regulation may not be upheld simply because it may be reasonable for the remaining portion of the trimester. Rather, the State is obligated to make a reasonable effort to limit the effect of its regulations to the period in the trimester during which its health interest will be furthered.

Under this standard, the Court rejected all five of the ordinance's provisions, either because they unjustifiably placed "a significant obstacle in the path of women seeking an abortion," made unnecessarily blanket assumptions about the immaturity of minors, or constituted an undue attempt to persuade against abortion. Justice O'Connor, joined by Justices White and Rehnquist, dissented.

***c. Planned Parenthood Ass'n v. Ashcroft*, 462 U.S. 476 (1983)**. In this companion case to *City of Akron*, Justice Powell and Chief Justice Burger joined with the three dissenters from *Akron* (Justices O'Connor, White, and Rehnquist) to uphold several provisions of Missouri abortion statutes.

The Court upheld a provision of the Missouri law requiring the attendance of a second physician at the abortion of a viable fetus and requiring the second physician to "take all reasonable steps in keeping with good medical practice . . . to preserve the life and health of the viable unborn child; provided that it does not pose an increased risk to the life or health of the woman." Since many third-trimester abortions would be emergency operations, the state could reasonably assume that the first physician's attention and skills would be directed to preserving the woman's health and not protecting the life of the fetus.

> By giving immediate medical attention to a fetus that is delivered alive, the second physician will assure that the State's interests are protected more fully than the first physician alone would be able to do. And given the compelling interest that the State has in preserving life, we cannot say that the Missouri requirement of a second physician in those unusual circumstances where Missouri permits a third-trimester abortion is unconstitutional. Preserving the life of a viable fetus that is aborted may not often be possible, but the State legitimately may choose to provide safeguards for the comparatively few instances of live birth that occur. We believe that the second-physician requirement reasonably furthers the State's compelling interest in

> protecting the lives of viable fetuses and we reverse the judgment of the Court of Appeals holding that [provision] unconstitutional.

Another provision of the Missouri laws requiring that tissue removed in abortions be submitted to a pathologist for filing a report was also held constitutional. Justice Powell concluded: "On its face and in effect, [this requirement] is reasonably related to generally accepted medical standards and 'further[s] important health-related State concerns.' "

***d.Thornburgh v. American College of Obstetricians and Gynecologists,* 476 U.S. 747 (1986)**. The Court, following *Akron*, invalidated Pennsylvania statutes requiring the woman's informed consent after the delivering of specific information to her concerning, among other things, fetal characteristics at 2-week intervals. "A requirement that the woman give what is truly a voluntary and informed consent, as a general proposition, is, of course proper and is surely not unconstitutional," wrote Justice Blackmun, speaking for the majority. "But the State may not require the delivery of information designed 'to influence the woman's informed choice between abortion or childbirth.' " The Court also invalidated the statutory provisions requiring the filing of reports by the physician, which were then to be made available to the public. "The scope of the information required and its availability to the public belie any assertions by the Commonwealth that it is advancing any legitimate interest," said the Court. Finally, the Court invalidated provisions concerning the degree of care required for postviability abortions and the required presence of a second physician during an abortion when viability is possible.

Justice O'Connor, dissenting, elaborated on her theory of "undue burden" on the abortion choice in the following language:

> I remain of the views expressed in my dissent in *Akron*. The State has compelling interests in ensuring maternal health and in protecting potential human life, and these interests exist "throughout pregnancy." Under this Court's fundamental-rights jurisprudence, judicial scrutiny of state regulation of abortion should be limited to whether the state law bears a rational relationship to legitimate purposes such as the advancement of these compelling interests, with heightened scrutiny reserved for instances in which the State has imposed an "undue burden" on the abortion decision. An undue burden will generally be found "in situations involving absolute obstacles or severe limitations on the abortion decision," not wherever a state regulation "may 'inhibit' abortions to some degree." And if a state law does interfere with the abortion decision to an extent that is unduly burdensome, so that it becomes "necessary to apply an exacting standard of review," the possibility remains that the statute will withstand the stricter scrutiny.

***e. Webster v. Reproductive Health Services,* 492 U.S. 490 (1989)**. In *Webster*, the Court upheld a Missouri statute imposing significant restrictions on the abortion right. In so holding Chief Justice Rehnquist, in an opinion announcing the judgment of the Court but not speaking for a majority, rejected *Roe*'s trimester framework: "[T]he rigid *Roe* framework is hardly consistent with the notion of a Constitution cast in general terms, as ours is, and usually speaking in general principles, as ours does. The key elements of the *Roe* framework — trimesters and viability — are not found in the text of the Constitution or in any place else one would expect to find a constitutional principle." Justice Scalia wrote separately to accuse the plurality of "contriv-[ing] to avoid" overruling *Roe*. He would have overruled *Roe* "more explicitly." "The outcome of today's case will doubtless be heralded as a triumph of judicial statesmanship," he added. "It is not that, unless it is statesmanlike needlessly to prolong this Court's self-awarded sovereignty over a field where it has little proper business since the answers to most of the cruel questions posed are political and not judicial."

Justice Blackmun, concurring in part and dissenting in part, wrote: "Today, *Roe v. Wade* and the fundamental constitutional right of women to decide whether to terminate a pregnancy, survive but are not secure. Although the Court extricates itself from this case without making a single, even incremental change in the law of abortion, the plurality and Justice Scalia would overrule *Roe* (the first silently, the other explicitly) and would return to the States virtually unfettered authority to control the quintessentially intimate, personal, and life-directing decision whether to carry a fetus to term."

PLANNED PARENTHOOD OF SOUTHEASTERN PENNSYLVANIA v. CASEY

505 U.S. 833, 112 S. Ct. 2791, 120 L.Ed. 2d 674 (1992)

JUSTICE O'CONNOR, JUSTICE KENNEDY, and JUSTICE SOUTER announced the judgment of the Court and delivered the opinion of the Court with respect to Parts I, II, III, V-A, V-C, and VI, an opinion with respect to Part V-E, in which JUSTICE STEVENS joins, and an opinion with respect to Parts IV, V-B, and V-D.

I

Liberty finds no refuge in a jurisprudence of doubt. Yet 19 years after our holding that the Constitution protects a woman's right to terminate her pregnancy in its early stages, *Roe v. Wade*, that definition of liberty is still questioned. Joining the respondents as amicus curiae, the United States, as it has done in five other cases in the last decade, again asks us to overrule *Roe*.

At issue in these cases are five provisions of the Pennsylvania Abortion Control Act of 1982 as amended in 1988 and 1989. 18 PA. CONS. STAT. §§ 3203–3220 (1990). The Act requires that a woman seeking an abortion give her informed consent prior to the abortion procedure, and specifies that she be provided with certain information at least 24 hours before the abortion is performed. § 3205. For a minor to obtain an abortion, the Act requires the informed consent of one of her parents, but provides for a judicial bypass option if the minor does not wish to or cannot obtain a parent's consent. § 3206. Another provision of the Act requires that, unless certain exceptions apply, a married woman seeking an abortion must sign a statement indicating that she has notified her husband of her intended abortion. § 3209. The Act exempts compliance with these three requirements in the event of a "medical emergency," which is defined in § 3203 of the Act. In addition to the above provisions regulating the performance of abortions, the Act imposes certain reporting requirements on facilities that provide abortion services. §§ 3207(b), 3214(a), 3214(f).

Before any of these provisions took effect, the petitioners, who are five abortion clinics and one physician representing himself as well as a class of physicians who provide abortion services, brought this suit seeking declaratory and injunctive relief. Each provision was challenged as unconstitutional on its face. The District Court entered a preliminary injunction against the enforcement of the regulations, and, after a 3-day bench trial, held all the provisions at issue here unconstitutional, entering a permanent injunction against Pennsylvania's enforcement of them.

The Court of Appeals for the Third Circuit affirmed in part and reversed in part, upholding all of the regulations except for the husband-notification requirement.

The Court of Appeals found it necessary to follow an elaborate course of reasoning even to identify the first premise to use to determine whether the statute enacted by Pennsylvania meets constitutional standards. And at oral argument in this Court, the attorney for the parties challenging the statute took the position that none of the enactments can be upheld without overruling *Roe v. Wade*. We disagree with that analysis; but we acknowledge that our decisions after *Roe* cast doubt upon the meaning and reach of its holding. Further, the Chief Justice admits that he would overrule the central holding of *Roe* and adopt the rational relationship test as the sole criterion of constitutionality. State and federal courts as well as legislatures throughout the Union must have guidance as they seek to address this subject in conformance with the Constitution. Given these premises, we find it imperative to review once more the principles that define the rights of the woman and the legitimate authority of the State respecting the termination of pregnancies by abortion procedures.

After considering the fundamental constitutional questions resolved by *Roe*, principles of institutional integrity, and the rule of stare decisis, we are led to conclude this: the essential holding of *Roe v. Wade* should be retained and once again reaffirmed.

It must be stated at the outset and with clarity that *Roe*'s essential holding, the holding we reaffirm, has three parts. First is a recognition of the right of the woman to choose to have an abortion before viability and to obtain it without undue interference from the State. Before viability, the State's interests are not strong enough to support a prohibition of abortion or the imposition of a substantial obstacle to the woman's effective right to elect the procedure. Second is a confirmation of the State's power to restrict abortions after fetal viability, if the law contains exceptions for pregnancies which endanger a woman's life or health. And third is the principle that the State has legitimate interests from the outset of the pregnancy in protecting the health of the woman and the life of the fetus that may become a child. These principles do not contradict one another; and we adhere to each.

II

The most familiar of the substantive liberties protected by the Fourteenth Amendment are those recognized by the Bill of Rights. We have held that the Due Process Clause of the Fourteenth Amendment incorporates most of the Bill of Rights against the States. It is tempting, as a means of curbing the discretion of federal judges, to suppose that liberty encompasses no more than those rights already guaranteed to the individual against federal interference by the express provisions of the first eight amendments to the Constitution. But of course this Court has never accepted that view.

It is also tempting, for the same reason, to suppose that the Due Process Clause protects only those practices, defined at the most specific level, that were protected against government interference by other rules of law when the Fourteenth Amendment was ratified. *See Michael H. v. Gerald D.* (opinion of Scalia, J.). But such a view would be inconsistent with our law. It is a promise of the Constitution that there is a realm of personal liberty which the government may not enter. We have vindicated this principle before. Marriage is mentioned nowhere in the Bill of Rights and interracial marriage was illegal in most States in the nineteenth century, but the Court was no doubt correct in finding it to be an aspect of liberty protected against state interference by the substantive component of the Due Process Clause in *Loving v. Virginia.*

Neither the Bill of Rights nor the specific practices of States at the time of the adoption of the Fourteenth Amendment marks the outer limits of the substantive sphere of liberty which the Fourteenth Amendment protects. *See* U. S. CONST., Amend. 9. It is settled now, as it was when the Court heard arguments in *Roe v. Wade*, that the Constitution places limits on a State's right to interfere with a person's most basic decisions about family and parenthood.

The inescapable fact is that adjudication of substantive due process claims may call upon the Court in interpreting the Constitution to exercise that same capacity which by tradition courts always have exercised: reasoned judgment. Its boundaries are not susceptible of expression as a simple rule. That does not mean we are free to invalidate state policy choices with which we disagree; yet neither does it permit us to shrink from the duties of our office.

It is conventional constitutional doctrine that where reasonable people disagree the government can adopt one position or the other. That theorem, however, assumes a state of affairs in which the choice does not intrude upon a protected liberty.

Our law affords constitutional protection to personal decisions relating to marriage, procreation, contraception, family relationships, child rearing, and education. Our cases recognize "the right of the individual, married or single, to be free from unwarranted governmental intrusion into matters so fundamentally affecting a person as the decision whether to bear or beget a child." *Eisenstadt v. Baird*. Our precedents "have respected the private realm of family life which the state cannot enter." *Prince v. Massachusetts*. These matters, involving the most intimate and personal choices a person may make in a lifetime, choices central to personal dignity and autonomy, are central to the liberty protected by the Fourteenth Amendment. At the heart of liberty is the right to define one's own concept of existence, of meaning, of the universe, and of the mystery of human life. Beliefs about these matters could not define the attributes of personhood were they formed under compulsion of the State.

These considerations begin our analysis of the woman's interest in terminating her pregnancy but cannot end it, for this reason: though the abortion decision may originate within the zone of conscience and belief, it is more than a philosophic exercise. Abortion is a unique act. It is an act fraught with consequences for others: for the woman who must live with the implications of her decision; for the persons who perform and assist in the procedure; for the spouse, family, and society which must confront the knowledge that these procedures exist, procedures some deem nothing short of an act of violence against innocent human life; and, depending on one's beliefs, for the life or potential life that is aborted. Though abortion is conduct, it does not follow that the State is entitled to proscribe it in all instances. That is because the liberty of the woman is at stake in a sense unique to the human condition and so unique to the law. The mother who carries a child to full term is subject to anxieties, to physical constraints, to pain that only she must bear. That these sacrifices have from the beginning of the human race been endured by woman with a pride that ennobles her in the eyes of others and gives to the infant a bond of love cannot alone be grounds for the State to insist she make the sacrifice. Her suffering is too intimate and personal for the State to insist, without more, upon its own vision of the woman's role, however dominant that vision has been in the course of our history and our culture. The destiny of the woman must be shaped to a large extent on her own conception of her spiritual imperatives and her place in society.

It should be recognized, moreover, that in some critical respects the abortion decision is of the same character as the decision to use contraception, to which *Griswold v. Connecticut*, *Eisenstadt v. Baird*, and *Carey v. Population Services International*, afford constitutional protection. We have no doubt as to the correctness of those decisions. They support the reasoning in *Roe* relating to the woman's liberty because they involve personal decisions concerning not only the meaning of procreation but also human responsibility and respect for it.

It was this dimension of personal liberty that *Roe* sought to protect, and its holding invoked the reasoning and the tradition of the precedents we have discussed, granting protection to substantive liberties of the person. *Roe* was, of course, an extension of those cases and, as the decision itself indicated, the separate States could act in some degree to further their own legitimate interests in protecting pre-natal life. The extent to which the legislatures of the States might act to outweigh the interests of the woman in choosing to terminate her pregnancy was a subject of debate both in *Roe* itself and in decisions following it.

While we appreciate the weight of the arguments made on behalf of the State in the case before us, arguments which in their ultimate formulation conclude that *Roe* should be overruled, the reservations any of us may have in reaffirming the central holding of *Roe* are outweighed by the explication of individual liberty we have given combined with the force of stare decisis. We turn now to that doctrine.

III

A

Even when the decision to overrule a prior case is not, as in the rare instance, virtually foreordained, it is common wisdom that the rule of stare decisis is not an "inexorable command," and certainly it is not such in every constitutional case. Rather, when this Court reexamines a prior holding, its judgment is customarily informed by a series of prudential and pragmatic considerations designed to test the consistency of overruling a prior decision with the ideal of the rule of law, and to gauge the respective costs of reaffirming and overruling a prior case. Thus, for example, we may ask whether the rule has proved to be intolerable simply in defying practical workability, whether the rule is subject to a kind of reliance that would lend a special hardship to the consequences of overruling and add inequity to the cost of repudiation, whether related principles of law have so far developed as to have left the old rule no more than a remnant of abandoned doctrine, or whether facts have so changed or come to be seen so differently, as to have robbed the old rule of significant application or justification.

So in this case we may inquire whether *Roe*'s central rule has been found unworkable; whether the rule's limitation on state power could be removed without serious inequity to those who have relied upon it or significant damage to the stability of the society governed by the rule in question; whether the law's growth in the intervening years has left *Roe*'s central rule a doctrinal anachronism discounted by society; and whether *Roe*'s premises of fact have so far changed in the ensuing two decades as to render its central holding somehow irrelevant or unjustifiable in dealing with the issue it addressed.

Although *Roe* has engendered opposition, it has in no sense proven "unworkable," *see Garcia v. San Antonio Metropolitan Transit Authority*, representing as it does a simple limitation beyond which a state law is unenforceable. While *Roe* has, of course, required judicial assessment of state laws affecting the exercise of the choice guaranteed against government infringement, and although the need for such review will remain as a consequence of today's decision, the required determinations fall within judicial competence.

The inquiry into reliance counts the cost of a rule's repudiation as it would fall on those who have relied reasonably on the rule's continued application. Since the classic case for weighing reliance heavily in favor of following the earlier rule occurs in the commercial context, where advance planning of great precision is most obviously a necessity, it is no cause for surprise that some would find no reliance worthy of consideration in support of *Roe*.

One can readily imagine an argument stressing the dissimilarity of this case to one involving property or contract. Abortion is customarily chosen as an unplanned response to the consequence of unplanned activity or to the failure of conventional birth control, and except on the assumption that no intercourse would have occurred but for *Roe*'s holding, such behavior may appear to justify no reliance claim.

To eliminate the issue of reliance that easily, however, one would need to limit cognizable reliance to specific instances of sexual activity. But to do this would be simply to refuse to face the fact that for two decades of economic and social developments, people have organized intimate relationships and made choices that define their views of themselves and their places in society, in reliance on the availability of abortion in the event that contraception should fail. The ability of women to participate equally in the economic and social life of the Nation has been facilitated by their ability to control their reproductive lives. The Constitution serves human values, and while the effect of reliance on *Roe* cannot be exactly measured, neither can the certain cost of overruling *Roe* for people who have ordered their thinking and living around that case be dismissed.

No evolution of legal principle has left *Roe*'s doctrinal footings weaker than they were in 1973. No development of constitutional law since the case was decided has implicitly or explicitly left *Roe* behind as a mere survivor of obsolete constitutional thinking.

It will be recognized, of course, that *Roe* stands at an intersection of two lines of decisions, but in whichever doctrinal category one reads the case, the result for present purposes will be the same. [The line of cases on family and reproductive freedom and those on medical decisions both are consistent with *Roe*. And if *Roe* were *sui generis*, its only corollary would be a hypothetical state attempt to require an abortion.]

In any event, because *Roe*'s scope is confined by the fact of its concern with postconception potential life, a concern otherwise likely to be implicated only by some forms of contraception protected independently under *Griswold* and later cases, any error in *Roe* is unlikely to have serious ramifications in future cases.

We have seen how time has overtaken some of *Roe*'s factual assumptions: advances in maternal health care allow for abortions safe to the mother later in pregnancy than was true in 1973, and advances in neonatal care have advanced viability to a point somewhat earlier. But these facts go only to the scheme of time limits on the realization of competing interests, and the divergences from the factual premises of 1973 have no bearing on the validity of *Roe*'s central holding, that viability marks the earliest point at which the State's interest in fetal life is constitutionally adequate to justify a legislative ban on nontherapeutic abortions. The soundness or unsoundness of that constitutional judgment in no sense turns on whether viability occurs at approximately 28 weeks, as was usual at the time of *Roe*, at 23 to 24 weeks, as it sometimes does today, or at some moment even slightly earlier in pregnancy, as it may if fetal respiratory capacity can somehow be enhanced in the future. Whenever it may occur, the attainment of viability may continue to serve as the critical fact, just as it has done since *Roe* was decided; which is to say that no change in *Roe*'s factual underpinning has left its central holding obsolete, and none supports an argument for overruling it.

The sum of the precedential inquiry to this point shows *Roe*'s underpinnings unweakened in any way affecting its central holding. While it has engendered disapproval, it has not been unworkable. An entire generation has come of age free to assume *Roe*'s concept of liberty in defining the capacity of women to act in society, and to make reproductive decisions; no erosion of principle going to liberty or personal autonomy has left *Roe*'s central holding a doctrinal remnant; *Roe* portends no developments at odds with other precedent for the analysis of personal liberty; and no changes of fact have rendered viability more or less appropriate as the point at which the balance of interests tips. Within the bounds of normal stare decisis analysis, then, and subject to the considerations on which it customarily turns, the stronger argument is for affirming *Roe*'s central holding, with whatever degree of personal reluctance any of us may have, not for overruling it.

B

In a less significant case, stare decisis analysis could, and would, stop at the point we have reached. But the sustained and widespread debate *Roe* has provoked calls for some comparison between that case and others of comparable dimension that have responded to national controversies and taken on the impress of the controversies addressed. Only two such decisional lines from the past century present themselves for examination, and in each instance the result reached by the Court accorded with the principles we apply today.

The first example is that line of cases identified with *Lochner v. New York*, which imposed substantive limitations on legislation limiting economic autonomy in favor of health and welfare regulation, adopting, in JUSTICE HOLMES' view, the theory of laissez-faire. *West Coast Hotel Co. v. Parrish* signalled the demise of *Lochner*. In the meantime, the Depression had come and, with it, the lesson that seemed unmistakable to most people by 1937, that the interpretation of contractual freedom protected in [the *Lochner* line of cases] rested on fundamentally false factual assumptions about the capacity of a relatively unregulated market to satisfy minimal levels of human welfare.

The second comparison that twentieth century history invites is with the cases employing the separate-but-equal rule for applying the Fourteenth Amendment's equal protection guarantee. They began with *Plessy v. Ferguson*, holding that legislatively mandated racial segregation in public transportation works no denial of equal protection, rejecting the argument that racial separation enforced by the legal machinery of American society treats the black race as inferior. But this understanding of the facts and the rule it was stated to justify were repudiated in *Brown v. Board of Education*.

The Court in *Brown* addressed these facts of life by observing that whatever may have been the understanding in *Plessy*'s time of the power of segregation to stigmatize those who were segregated with a "badge of inferiority," it was clear by 1954 that legally sanctioned segregation had just such an effect, to the point that racially separate public educational facilities were deemed inherently unequal. Society's understanding of the facts upon which a constitutional ruling was sought in 1954 was thus fundamentally different from the basis claimed for the decision in 1896. While we think *Plessy* was wrong the day it was decided, we must also recognize that the *Plessy* Court's explanation for its decision was so clearly at odds with the facts apparent to the Court in 1954 that the decision to reexamine *Plessy* was on this ground alone not only justified but required.

West Coast Hotel and *Brown* each rested on facts, or an understanding of facts, changed from those which furnished the claimed justifications for the earlier constitutional resolutions. Each case was comprehensible as the Court's response to facts that the country could understand, or had come to understand already, but which the Court of an earlier day, as its own declarations disclosed, had not been able to perceive. As the decisions were thus comprehensible they were also defensible, not merely as the victories of one doctrinal school over another by dint of numbers (victories though they were), but as applications of constitutional principle to facts as they had not been seen by the Court before. In constitutional adjudication as elsewhere in life, changed circumstances may impose new obligations, and the thoughtful part of the Nation could accept each decision to overrule a prior case as a response to the Court's constitutional duty.

Because the case before us presents no such occasion it could be seen as no such response. Because neither the factual underpinnings of *Roe*'s central holding nor our understanding of it has changed (and because no other indication of weakened precedent has been shown) the Court could not pretend to be reexamining the prior law with any justification beyond a present doctrinal disposition to come out differently from the Court of 1973. To overrule prior law for no other reason than that would run counter to the view repeated in our cases, that a decision to overrule should rest on some special reason over and above the belief that a prior case was wrongly decided.

C

The examination of the conditions justifying *West Coast Hotel* and *Brown* is enough to suggest the terrible price that would have been paid if the Court had not overruled as it did. In the present case, however, as our analysis to this point makes clear, the terrible price would be paid for overruling. Our analysis would not be complete, however, without explaining why overruling *Roe*'s central holding would not only reach an unjustifiable result under principles of stare decisis, but would seriously weaken the Court's capacity to exercise the judicial power and to function as the Supreme Court of a Nation dedicated to the rule of law.

The root of American governmental power is revealed most clearly in the instance of the power conferred by the Constitution upon the Judiciary of the United States and specifically upon this Court. As Americans of each succeeding generation are rightly told, the Court cannot buy support for its decisions by spending money and, except to a minor degree, it cannot independently coerce obedience to its decrees. The Court's power lies, rather, in its legitimacy, a product of substance and perception that shows itself in the people's acceptance of the Judiciary as fit to determine what the Nation's law means and to declare what it demands. [T]he Court's legitimacy depends on making legally principled decisions under circumstances in which their principled character is sufficiently plausible to be accepted by the Nation.

The need for principled action to be perceived as such is implicated to some degree whenever this, or any other appellate court, overrules a prior case. This is not to say, of course, that this Court cannot give a perfectly satisfactory explanation in most cases. People understand that some of the Constitution's language is hard to fathom and that the Court's Justices are sometimes able to perceive significant facts or to understand principles of law that eluded their predecessors and that justify departures from existing decisions. However upsetting it may be to those most directly affected when one judicially derived rule replaces another, the country can accept some correction of error without necessarily questioning the legitimacy of the Court.

In two circumstances, however, the Court would almost certainly fail to receive the benefit of the doubt in overruling prior cases. There is, first, a point beyond which frequent overruling would overtax the country's belief in the Court's good faith. Despite the variety of reasons that may inform and justify a decision to overrule, we cannot forget that such a decision is usually perceived (and perceived correctly) as, at the least, a statement that a prior decision was wrong. There is a limit to the amount of error that can plausibly be imputed to prior courts. If that limit should be exceeded, disturbance of prior rulings would be taken as evidence that justifiable reexamination of principle had given way to drives for particular results in the short term. The legitimacy of the Court would fade with the frequency of its vacillation.

That first circumstance can be described as hypothetical; the second is to the point here and now. Where, in the performance of its judicial duties, the Court decides a case in such a way as to resolve the sort of intensely divisive controversy reflected in *Roe* and those rare, comparable cases, its decision has a dimension that the resolution of the normal case does not carry. It is the dimension present whenever the Court's interpretation of the Constitution calls the contending sides of a national controversy to end their national division by accepting a common mandate rooted in the Constitution.

The Court is not asked to do this very often, having thus addressed the Nation only twice in our lifetime, in the decisions of *Brown* and *Roe*. But when the Court does act in this way, its decision requires an equally rare precedential force to counter the inevitable efforts to overturn it and to thwart its implementation. Some of those efforts may be mere unprincipled emotional reactions; others may proceed from principles worthy of profound respect. But whatever the premises of opposition may be, only the most convincing justification under accepted standards of precedent could suffice to demonstrate that a later decision overruling the first was anything but a surrender to political pressure, and an unjustified repudiation of the principle on which the Court staked its authority in the first instance. So to overrule under fire in the absence of the most compelling reason to reexamine a watershed decision would subvert the Court's legitimacy beyond any serious question.

The Court's duty in the present case is clear. In 1973, it confronted the already-divisive issue of governmental power to limit personal choice to undergo abortion, for which it provided a new resolution based on the due process guaranteed by the Fourteenth Amendment. Whether or not a new social consensus is developing on that issue, its divisiveness is no less today than in 1973, and pressure to overrule the decision, like pressure to retain it, has grown only more intense. A decision to overrule *Roe*'s essential holding under the existing circumstances would address error, if error there was, at the cost of both profound and unnecessary damage to the Court's legitimacy, and to the Nation's commitment to the rule of law. It is therefore imperative to adhere to the essence of *Roe*'s original decision, and we do so today.

IV

From what we have said so far it follows that it is a constitutional liberty of the woman to have some freedom to terminate her pregnancy. We conclude that the basic decision in *Roe* was based on a constitutional analysis which we cannot now repudiate. The woman's liberty is not so unlimited, however, that from the outset the State cannot show its concern for the life of the unborn, and at a later point in fetal development the State's interest in life has sufficient force so that the right of the woman to terminate the pregnancy can be restricted.

That brings us, of course, to the point where much criticism has been directed at *Roe*, a criticism that always inheres when the Court draws a specific rule from what in the Constitution is but a general standard. We conclude, however, that the urgent claims of the woman to retain the ultimate control over her destiny and her body, claims implicit in the meaning of liberty, require us to perform that function. Liberty must not be extinguished for want of a line that is clear. And it falls to us to give some real substance to the woman's liberty to determine whether to carry her pregnancy to full term.

We conclude the line should be drawn at viability, so that before that time the woman has a right to choose to terminate her pregnancy. We adhere to this principle for two reasons. First, as we have said, is the doctrine of stare decisis.

The second reason is that the concept of viability, as we noted in *Roe*, is the time at which there is a realistic possibility of maintaining and nourishing a life outside the womb, so that the independent existence of the second life can in reason and all fairness be the object of state protection that now overrides the rights of the woman. Consistent with other constitutional norms, legislatures may draw lines which appear arbitrary without the necessity of offering a justification. But courts may not. We must justify the lines we draw. And there is no line other than viability which is more workable. To be sure, as we have said, there may be some medical developments that affect the precise point of viability, but this is an imprecision within tolerable limits given that the medical community and all those who must apply its discoveries will continue to explore the matter. The viability line also has, as a practical matter, an element of fairness. In some broad sense it might be said that a woman who fails to act before viability has consented to the State's intervention on behalf of the developing child.

The woman's right to terminate her pregnancy before viability is the most central principle of *Roe v. Wade*. It is a rule of law and a component of liberty we cannot renounce.

Yet it must be remembered that *Roe v. Wade* speaks with clarity in establishing not only the woman's liberty but also the State's "important and legitimate interest in potential life." That portion of the decision in *Roe* has been given too little acknowledgement and implementation by the Court in its subsequent cases. Those cases decided that any regulation touching upon the abortion decision must survive strict scrutiny, to be sustained only if drawn in narrow terms to further a compelling state interest. Not all of the cases decided under that formulation can be reconciled with the holding in *Roe* itself that the State has legitimate interests in the health of the woman and in protecting the potential life within her. In resolving this tension, we choose to rely upon *Roe*, as against the later cases.

Roe established a trimester framework to govern abortion regulations. Under this elaborate but rigid construct, almost no regulation at all is permitted during the first trimester of pregnancy; regulations designed to protect the woman's health, but not to further the State's interest in potential life, are permitted during the second trimester; and during the third trimester, when the fetus is viable, prohibitions are permitted provided the life or health of the mother is not at stake. Most of our cases since *Roe* have involved the application of rules derived from the trimester framework.

The trimester framework no doubt was erected to ensure that the woman's right to choose not become so subordinate to the State's interest in promoting fetal life that her choice exists in theory but not in fact. We do not agree, however, that the trimester approach is necessary to accomplish this objective. A framework of this rigidity was unnecessary and in its later interpretation sometimes contradicted the State's permissible exercise of its powers.

Though the woman has a right to choose to terminate or continue her pregnancy before viability, it does not at all follow that the State is prohibited from taking steps to ensure that this choice is thoughtful and informed. Even in the earliest stages of pregnancy, the State may enact rules and regulations designed to encourage her to know that there are philosophic and social arguments of great weight that can be brought to bear in favor of continuing the pregnancy to full term and that there are procedures and institutions to allow adoption of unwanted children as well as a certain degree of state assistance if the mother chooses to raise the child herself. It follows that States are free to enact laws to provide a reasonable framework for a woman to make a decision that has such profound and lasting meaning. This, too, we find consistent with *Roe*'s central premises, and indeed the inevitable consequence of our holding that the State has an interest in protecting the life of the unborn.

We reject the trimester framework, which we do not consider to be part of the essential holding of *Roe*. Measures aimed at ensuring that a woman's choice contemplates the consequences for the fetus do not necessarily interfere with the right recognized in *Roe*, although those measures have been found to be inconsistent with the rigid trimester framework announced in that case. A logical reading of the central holding in *Roe* itself, and a necessary reconciliation of the liberty of the woman and the interest of the State in promoting prenatal life, require, in our view, that we abandon the trimester framework as a rigid prohibition on all previability regulation aimed at the protection of fetal life. The trimester framework suffers from these basic flaws: in its formulation it misconceives the nature of the pregnant woman's interest; and in practice it undervalues the State's interest in potential life, as recognized in *Roe*.

Numerous forms of state regulation might have the incidental effect of increasing the cost or decreasing the availability of medical care, whether for abortion or any other medical procedure. The fact that a law which serves a valid purpose, one not designed to strike at the right itself, has the incidental effect of making it more difficult or more expensive to procure an abortion cannot be enough to invalidate it. Only where state regulation imposes an undue burden on a woman's ability to make this decision does the power of the State reach into the heart of the liberty protected by the Due Process Clause.

These considerations of the nature of the abortion right illustrate that it is an overstatement to describe it as a right to decide whether to have an abortion "without interference from the State." All abortion regulations interfere to some degree with a woman's ability to decide whether to terminate her pregnancy. It is, as a consequence, not surprising that despite the protestations contained in the original *Roe* opinion to the effect that the Court was not recognizing an absolute right, the Court's experience applying the trimester framework has led to the striking down of some abortion regulations which in no real sense deprived women of the ultimate decision. Not all governmental intrusion is of necessity unwarranted; and that brings us to the other basic flaw in the trimester framework: even in *Roe*'s terms, in practice it undervalues the State's interest in the potential life within the woman.

Roe v. Wade was express in its recognition of the State's "important and legitimate interest[s] in preserving and protecting the health of the pregnant woman [and] in protecting the potentiality of human life." The trimester framework, however, does not fulfill *Roe*'s own promise that the State has an interest in protecting fetal life or potential life. *Roe* began the contradiction by using the trimester framework to forbid any regulation of abortion designed to advance that interest before viability. Before viability, *Roe* and subsequent cases treat all governmental attempts to influence a woman's decision on behalf of the potential life within her as unwarranted. This treatment is, in our judgment, incompatible with the recognition that there is a substantial state interest in potential life throughout pregnancy.

The very notion that the State has a substantial interest in potential life leads to the conclusion that not all regulations must be deemed unwarranted. Not all burdens on the right to decide whether to terminate a pregnancy will be undue. In our view, the undue burden standard is the appropriate means of reconciling the State's interest with the woman's constitutionally protected liberty.

The concept of an undue burden has been utilized by the Court as well as individual members of the Court, including two of us, in ways that could be considered inconsistent. Because we set forth a standard of general application to which we intend to adhere, it is important to clarify what is meant by an undue burden.

A finding of an undue burden is a shorthand for the conclusion that a state regulation has the purpose or effect of placing a substantial obstacle in the path of a woman seeking an abortion of a nonviable fetus. A statute with this purpose is invalid because the means chosen by the State to further the interest in potential life must be calculated to inform the woman's free choice, not hinder it. And a statute which, while furthering the interest in potential life or some other valid state interest, has the effect of placing a substantial obstacle in the path of a woman's choice cannot be considered a permissible means of serving its legitimate ends. To the extent that the opinions of the Court or of individual Justices use the undue burden standard in a manner that is inconsistent with this analysis, we set out what in our view should be the controlling standard. In our considered judgment, an undue burden is an unconstitutional burden. Understood another way, we answer the question, left open in previous opinions discussing the undue burden formulation, whether a law designed to further the State's interest in fetal life which imposes an undue burden on the woman's decision before fetal viability could be constitutional. The answer is no.

Some guiding principles should emerge. What is at stake is the woman's right to make the ultimate decision, not a right to be insulated from all others in doing so. Regulations which do no more than create a structural mechanism by which the State, or the parent or guardian of a minor, may express profound respect for the life of the unborn are permitted, if they are not a substantial obstacle to the woman's exercise of the right to choose. Unless it has that effect on her right of choice, a state measure designed to persuade her to choose childbirth over abortion will be upheld if reasonably related to that goal. Regulations designed to foster the health of a woman seeking an abortion are valid if they do not constitute an undue burden.

Even when jurists reason from shared premises, some disagreement is inevitable. That is to be expected in the application of any legal standard which must accommodate life's complexity. We do not expect it to be otherwise with respect to the undue burden standard. We give this summary:

(a) To protect the central right recognized by *Roe v. Wade* while at the same time accommodating the State's profound interest in potential life, we will employ the undue burden analysis as explained in this opinion. An undue burden exists, and therefore a provision of law is invalid, if its purpose or effect is to place a substantial obstacle in the path of a woman seeking an abortion before the fetus attains viability.

(b) We reject the rigid trimester framework of *Roe v. Wade*. To promote the State's profound interest in potential life, throughout pregnancy the State may take measures to ensure that the woman's choice is informed, and measures designed to advance this interest will not be invalidated as long as their purpose is to persuade the woman to choose childbirth over abortion. These measures must not be an undue burden on the right.

(c) As with any medical procedure, the State may enact regulations to further the health or safety of a woman seeking an abortion. Unnecessary health regulations that have the purpose or effect of presenting a substantial obstacle to a woman seeking an abortion impose an undue burden on the right.

(d) Our adoption of the undue burden analysis does not disturb the central holding of *Roe v. Wade*, and we reaffirm that holding. Regardless of whether exceptions are made for particular circumstances, a State may not prohibit any woman from making the ultimate decision to terminate her pregnancy before viability.

(e) We also reaffirm *Roe*'s holding that "subsequent to viability, the State in promoting its interest in the potentiality of human life may, if it chooses, regulate, and even proscribe, abortion except where it is necessary, in appropriate medical judgment, for the preservation of the life or health of the mother."

These principles control our assessment of the Pennsylvania statute, and we now turn to the issue of the validity of its challenged provisions.

V

The Court of Appeals applied what it believed to be the undue burden standard and upheld each of the provisions except for the husband notification requirement. We agree generally with this conclusion, but refine the undue burden analysis in accordance with the principles articulated above. We now consider the separate statutory sections at issue.

A

Because it is central to the operation of various other requirements, we begin with the statute's definition of medical emergency. Under the statute, a medical emergency is "[t]hat condition which, on the basis of the physician's good faith clinical judgment, so complicates the medical condition of a pregnant woman as to necessitate the immediate abortion of her pregnancy to avert her death or for which a delay will create serious risk of substantial and irreversible impairment of a major bodily function."

Petitioners argue that the definition is too narrow, contending that it forecloses the possibility of an immediate abortion despite some significant health risks. If the contention were correct, we would be required to invalidate the restrictive operation of the provision, for the essential holding of *Roe* forbids a State from interfering with a woman's choice to undergo an abortion procedure if continuing her pregnancy would constitute a threat to her health.

The District Court found that there were three serious conditions which would not be covered by the statute: preeclampsia, inevitable abortion, and premature ruptured membrane. Yet, as the Court of Appeals observed, it is undisputed that under some circumstances each of these conditions could lead to an illness with substantial and irreversible consequences. While the definition could be interpreted in an unconstitutional manner, the Court of Appeals construed the phrase "serious risk" to include those circumstances. We conclude that, as construed by the Court of Appeals, the medical emergency definition imposes no undue burden on a woman's abortion right.

B

We next consider the informed consent requirement. Except in a medical emergency, the statute requires that at least 24 hours before performing an abortion a physician inform the woman of the nature of the procedure, the health risks of the abortion and of childbirth, and the "probable gestational age of the unborn child." The physician or a qualified nonphysician must inform the woman of the availability of printed materials published by the

State describing the fetus and providing information about medical assistance for childbirth, information about child support from the father, and a list of agencies which provide adoption and other services as alternatives to abortion. An abortion may not be performed unless the woman certifies in writing that she has been informed of the availability of these printed materials and has been provided them if she chooses to view them.

Our prior decisions establish that as with any medical procedure, the State may require a woman to give her written informed consent to an abortion. In this respect, the statute is unexceptional. Petitioners challenge the statute's definition of informed consent because it includes the provision of specific information by the doctor and the mandatory 24-hour waiting period. The conclusions reached by a majority of the Justices in the separate opinions filed today and the undue burden standard adopted in this opinion require us to overrule in part some of the Court's past decisions, decisions driven by the trimester framework's prohibition of all previability regulations designed to further the State's interest in fetal life.

To the extent *Akron I* and *Thornburgh* find a constitutional violation when the government requires, as it does here, the giving of truthful, nonmisleading information about the nature of the procedure, the attendant health risks and those of childbirth, and the "probable gestational age" of the fetus, those cases go too far, are inconsistent with *Roe*'s acknowledgment of an important interest in potential life, and are overruled. In attempting to ensure that a woman apprehend the full consequences of her decision, the State furthers the legitimate purpose of reducing the risk that a woman may elect an abortion, only to discover later, with devastating psychological consequences, that her decision was not fully informed. If the information the State requires to be made available to the woman is truthful and not misleading, the requirement may be permissible.

We also see no reason why the State may not require doctors to inform a woman seeking an abortion of the availability of materials relating to the consequences to the fetus, even when those consequences have no direct relation to her health. An example illustrates the point. We would think it constitutional for the State to require that in order for there to be informed consent to a kidney transplant operation the recipient must be supplied with information about risks to the donor as well as risks to himself or herself. We conclude that informed choice need not be defined in such narrow terms that all considerations of the effect on the fetus are made irrelevant. As we have made clear, we depart from the holdings of *Akron I* to the extent that we permit a State to further its legitimate goal of protecting the life of the unborn by enacting legislation aimed at ensuring a decision that is mature and informed, even when in so doing the State expresses a preference for childbirth over abortion. In short, requiring that the woman be informed of the availability of information relating to fetal development and the assistance available should she decide to carry the pregnancy to full term is a reasonable measure to insure an informed choice, one which might cause the woman to choose childbirth over abortion. This requirement cannot be considered a substantial obstacle to obtaining an abortion, and, it follows, there is no undue burden.

The Pennsylvania statute also requires us to reconsider the holding in *Akron I* that the State may not require that a physician, as opposed to a qualified assistant, provide information relevant to a woman's informed consent. Since there is no evidence on this record that requiring a doctor to give the information as provided by the statute would amount in practical terms to a substantial obstacle to a woman seeking an abortion, we conclude that it is not an undue burden. Our cases reflect the fact that the Constitution gives the States broad latitude to decide that particular functions may be performed only by licensed professionals, even if an objective assessment might suggest that those same tasks could be performed by others. Thus, we uphold the provision as a reasonable means to insure that the woman's consent is informed.

Our analysis of Pennsylvania's 24-hour waiting period between the provision of the information deemed necessary to informed consent and the performance of an abortion under the undue burden standard requires us to reconsider the premise behind the decision in *Akron I* invalidating a parallel requirement. The idea that important decisions will be more informed and deliberate if they follow some period of reflection does not strike us as unreasonable, particularly where the statute directs that important information become part of the background of the decision. The statute, as construed by the Court of Appeals, permits avoidance of the waiting period in the event of a medical emergency and the record evidence shows that in the vast majority of cases, a 24-hour delay does not create any appreciable health risk. In theory, at least, the waiting period is a reasonable measure to implement the State's interest in protecting the life of the unborn, a measure that does not amount to an undue burden.

Whether the mandatory 24-hour waiting period is nonetheless invalid because in practice it is a substantial obstacle to a woman's choice to terminate her pregnancy is a closer question. The findings of fact by the District Court indicate that because of the distances many women must travel to reach an abortion provider, the practical effect will often be a delay of much more than a day because the waiting period requires that a woman seeking an abortion make at least two visits to the doctor. The District Court also found that in many instances this will increase the exposure of women seeking abortions to "the harassment and hostility of anti-abortion protestors demonstrating outside a clinic." As a result, the District Court found that for those women who have the fewest financial resources, those who must travel long distances, and those who have difficulty explaining their whereabouts to husbands, employers, or others, the 24-hour waiting period will be "particularly burdensome."

These findings are troubling in some respects, but they do not demonstrate that the waiting period constitutes an undue burden. We do not doubt that, as the District Court held, the waiting period has the effect of "increasing the cost and risk of delay of abortions," but the District Court did not conclude that the increased costs and potential delays amount to substantial obstacles. [A]s we have stated, under the undue burden standard a State is permitted to enact persuasive measures which favor childbirth over abortion, even if those measures do not further a health interest.

We also disagree with the District Court's conclusion that the "particularly burdensome" effects of the waiting period on some women require its invalidation. A particular burden is not of necessity a substantial obstacle. Whether a burden falls on a particular group is a distinct inquiry from whether it is a substantial obstacle even as to the women in that group. Hence, on the record before us, and in the context of this facial challenge, we are not convinced that the 24-hour waiting period constitutes an undue burden.

We are left with the argument that the various aspects of the informed consent requirement are unconstitutional because they place barriers in the way of abortion on demand. Even the broadest reading of *Roe*, however, has not suggested that there is a constitutional right to abortion on demand. Rather, the right protected by *Roe* is a right to decide to terminate a pregnancy free of undue interference by the State. Because the informed consent requirement facilitates the wise exercise of that right it cannot be classified as an interference with the right *Roe* protects. The informed consent requirement is not an undue burden on that right.

C

Section 3209 of Pennsylvania's abortion law provides, except in cases of medical emergency, that no physician shall perform an abortion on a married woman without receiving a signed statement from the woman that she has notified her spouse that she is about to undergo an abortion. The woman has the option of providing an alternative signed statement certifying that her husband is not the man who impregnated her; that her husband could not be located; that the pregnancy is the result of spousal sexual assault which she has reported; or that the woman believes that notifying her husband will cause him or someone else to inflict bodily injury upon her. A physician who performs an abortion on a married woman without receiving the appropriate signed statement will have his or her license revoked, and is liable to the husband for damages.

The American Medical Association (AMA) has published a summary of the recent research in this field, which indicates that in an average 12-month period in this country, approximately two million women are the victims of severe assaults by their male partners. Physical violence is only the most visible form of abuse. Psychological abuse, particularly forced social and economic isolation of women, is also common. The vast majority of women notify their male partners of their decision to obtain an abortion. In many cases in which married women do not notify their husbands, the pregnancy is the result of an extramarital affair. Where the husband is the father, the primary reason women do not notify their husbands is that the husband and wife are experiencing marital difficulties, often accompanied by incidents of violence.

In well-functioning marriages, spouses discuss important intimate decisions such as whether to bear a child. But there are millions of women in this country who are the victims of regular physical and psychological abuse at the hands of their husbands. Should these women become pregnant, they may have very good reasons for not wishing to inform their husbands of their decision to obtain an abortion. Many may have justifiable fears of physical abuse, but may be no less fearful of the consequences of reporting prior abuse to the Commonwealth of Pennsylvania. Many may have a reasonable fear that notifying their husbands will provoke further instances of child abuse; these women are not exempt from § 3209's notification requirement. Many may fear devastating forms of psychological abuse from their husbands, including verbal harassment, threats of future violence, the destruction of possessions, physical confinement to the home, the withdrawal of financial support, or the disclosure of the abortion to family and friends. These methods of psychological abuse may act as even more of a deterrent to notification than the possibility of physical violence, but women who are the victims of the abuse are not exempt from § 3209's notification requirement. And many women who are pregnant as a result of sexual assaults by their husbands will be unable to avail themselves of the exception for spousal sexual assault, because the exception requires that the woman have notified law enforcement authorities within 90 days of the assault, and her husband will be notified of her report once an investigation begins. If anything in this field is certain, it is that victims of spousal sexual assault are extremely reluctant to report the abuse to the government; hence, a great many spousal rape victims will not be exempt from the notification requirement imposed by § 3209.

The spousal notification requirement is thus likely to prevent a significant number of women from obtaining an abortion. It does not merely make abortions a little more difficult or expensive to obtain; for many women, it will impose a substantial obstacle. We must not blind ourselves to the fact that the significant number of women who fear for their safety and the safety of their children are likely to be deterred from procuring an abortion as surely as if the Commonwealth had outlawed abortion in all cases.

This conclusion is in no way inconsistent with our decisions upholding parental notification or consent requirements. Those enactments, and our judgment that they are constitutional, are based on the quite reasonable assumption that minors will benefit from consultation with their parents and that children will often not realize that their parents have their best interests at heart. We cannot adopt a parallel assumption about adult women.

We recognize that a husband has a "deep and proper concern and interest . . . in his wife's pregnancy and in the growth and development of the fetus she is carrying." If this case concerned a State's ability to require the mother to notify the father before taking some action with respect to a living child raised by both, therefore, it would be reasonable to conclude as a general matter that the father's interest in the welfare of the child and the mother's interest are equal.

Before birth, however, the issue takes on a very different cast. After all, if the husband's interest in the fetus' safety is a sufficient predicate for state regulation, the State could reasonably conclude that pregnant wives should notify their husbands before drinking alcohol or smoking. A State may not give to a man the kind of dominion over his wife that parents exercise over their children.

Section 3209 embodies a view of marriage consonant with the common-law status of married women but repugnant to our present understanding of marriage and of the nature of the rights secured by the Constitution. Women do not lose their constitutionally protected liberty when they marry. The Constitution protects all individuals, male or female, married or unmarried, from the abuse of governmental power, even where that power is employed for the supposed benefit of a member of the individual's family.

D

We next consider the parental consent provision. Except in a medical emergency, an unemancipated young woman under 18 may not obtain an abortion unless she and one of her parents (or guardian) provides informed consent as defined above. If neither a parent nor a guardian provides consent, a court may authorize the performance of an abortion upon a determination that the young woman is mature and capable of giving informed consent and has in fact given her informed consent, or that an abortion would be in her best interests.

Our cases establish, and we reaffirm today, that a State may require a minor seeking an abortion to obtain the consent of a parent or guardian, provided that there is an adequate judicial bypass procedure. Under these precedents, in our view, the one-parent consent requirement and judicial bypass procedure are constitutional.

E

Under the recordkeeping and reporting requirements of the statute, every facility which performs abortions is required to file a report stating its name and address as well as the name and address of any related entity, such as a controlling or subsidiary organization. In the case of state-funded institutions, the information becomes public.

For each abortion performed, a report must be filed identifying: the physician (and the second physician where required); the facility; the referring physician or agency; the woman's age; the number of prior pregnancies and prior abortions she has had; gestational age; the type of abortion procedure; the date of the abortion; whether there were any pre-existing medical conditions which would complicate pregnancy; medical complications with the abortion; where applicable, the basis for the determination that the abortion was medically necessary; the weight of the aborted fetus; and whether the woman was married, and if so, whether notice was provided or the basis for the failure to give notice. Every abortion facility must also file quarterly reports showing the number of abortions performed broken down by trimester. In all events, the identity of each woman who has had an abortion remains confidential.

Subsection (12) of the reporting provision requires the reporting of, among other things, a married woman's "reason for failure to provide notice" to her husband. This provision in effect requires women, as a condition of obtaining an abortion, to provide the Commonwealth with the precise information we have already recognized that many women have pressing reasons not to reveal. Like the spousal notice requirement itself, this provision places an undue burden on a woman's choice, and must be invalidated for that reason.

VI

Our Constitution is a covenant running from the first generation of Americans to us and then to future generations. It is a coherent succession. Each generation must learn anew that the Constitution's written terms embody ideas and aspirations that must survive more ages than one. We accept our responsibility not to retreat from interpreting the full meaning of the covenant in light of all of our precedents. We invoke it once again to define the freedom guaranteed by the Constitution's own promise, the promise of liberty.

JUSTICE STEVENS, concurring in part and dissenting in part.

My disagreement with the joint opinion begins with its understanding of the trimester framework established in *Roe*. Contrary to the suggestion of the joint opinion, it is not a "contradiction" to recognize that the State may have a legitimate interest in potential human life and, at the same time, to conclude that that interest does not justify the regulation of abortion before viability (although other interests, such as maternal health, may). The fact that the State's interest is legitimate does not tell us when, if ever, that interest outweighs the pregnant woman's interest in personal liberty.

First, it is clear that, in order to be legitimate, the State's interest must be secular; consistent with the First Amendment the State may not promote a theological or sectarian interest.

Identifying the State's interests — which the States rarely articulate with any precision — makes clear that the interest in protecting potential life is not grounded in the Constitution. It is, instead, an indirect interest supported by both humanitarian and pragmatic concerns. Many of our citizens believe that any abortion reflects an unacceptable disrespect for potential human life and that the performance of more than a million abortions each year is intolerable; many find third-trimester abortions performed when the fetus is approaching personhood particularly offensive. The State has a legitimate interest in minimizing such offense. The State may also have a broader interest in expanding the population, believing society would benefit from the services of additional productive citizens — or that the potential human lives might include the occasional Mozart or Curie. These are the kinds of concerns that comprise the State's interest in potential human life.

In counterpoise is the woman's constitutional interest in liberty. One aspect of this liberty is a right to bodily integrity, a right to control one's person.

The woman's constitutional liberty interest also involves her freedom to decide matters of the highest privacy and the most personal nature. The authority to make such traumatic and yet empowering decisions is an element of basic human dignity. As the joint opinion so eloquently demonstrates, a woman's decision to terminate her pregnancy is nothing less than a matter of conscience.

Serious questions arise when a State attempts to "persuade the woman to choose childbirth over abortion." Decisional autonomy must limit the State's power to inject into a woman's most personal deliberations its own views of what is best. The State may promote its preferences by funding childbirth, by creating and maintaining alternatives to abortion, and by espousing the virtues of family; but it must respect the individual's freedom to make such judgments.

Under these principles, §§ 3205(a)(2)(i)–(iii) of the Pennsylvania statute are unconstitutional. Those sections require a physician or counselor to provide the woman with a range of materials clearly designed to persuade her to choose not to undergo the abortion. While the State is free, pursuant to § 3208 of the Pennsylvania law, to produce and disseminate such material, the State may not inject such information into the woman's deliberations just as she is weighing such an important choice.

Under this same analysis, §§ 3205(a)(1)(i) and (iii) of the Pennsylvania statute are constitutional. Those sections, which require the physician to inform a woman of the nature and risks of the abortion procedure and the medical risks of carrying to term, are neutral requirements comparable to those imposed in other medical procedures. Those sections indicate no effort by the State to influence the woman's choice in any way. If anything, such requirements enhance, rather than skew, the woman's decisionmaking.

The 24-hour waiting period required by §§ 3205(a)(1)–(2) of the Pennsylvania statute raises even more serious concerns. There is no evidence that the mandated delay benefits women or that it is necessary to enable the physician to convey any relevant information to the patient. The mandatory delay thus appears to rest on outmoded and unacceptable assumptions about the decisionmaking capacity of women.

The decision to terminate a pregnancy is profound and difficult. No person undertakes such a decision lightly — and States may not presume that a woman has failed to reflect adequately merely because her conclusion differs from the State's preference. A woman who has, in the privacy of her thoughts and conscience, weighed the options and made her decision cannot be forced to reconsider all, simply because the State believes she has come to the wrong conclusion.

Part of the constitutional liberty to choose is the equal dignity to which each of us is entitled. A woman who decides to terminate her pregnancy is entitled to the same respect as a woman who decides to carry the fetus to term. The mandatory waiting period denies women that equal respect.

The counseling provisions are similarly infirm. Whenever government commands private citizens to speak or to listen, careful review of the justification for that command is particularly appropriate. I conclude that the information requirements do not serve a useful purpose and thus constitute an unnecessary — and therefore undue — burden on the woman's constitutional liberty to decide to terminate her pregnancy.

Accordingly, while I disagree with Parts IV, V-B, and V-D of the joint opinion, I join the remainder of the Court's opinion.

JUSTICE BLACKMUN, concurring in part, concurring in the judgment in part, and dissenting in part.

I join parts I, II, III, V-A, V-C, and VI of the joint opinion of Justices O'Connor, Kennedy, and Souter.

I do not underestimate the significance of today's joint opinion. Yet I remain steadfast in my belief that the right to reproductive choice is entitled to the full protection afforded by this Court before *Webster*. And I fear for the darkness as four Justices anxiously await the single vote necessary to extinguish the light.

In brief, five Members of this Court today recognize that "the Constitution protects a woman's right to terminate her pregnancy in its early stages."

While I believe that the joint opinion errs in failing to invalidate the other regulations, I am pleased that the joint opinion has not ruled out the possibility that these regulations may be shown to impose an unconstitutional burden. The joint opinion makes clear that its specific holdings are based on the insufficiency of the record before it. I am confident that in the future evidence will be produced to show that "in a large fraction of the cases in which [these regulations are] relevant, [they] will operate as a substantial obstacle to a woman's choice to undergo an abortion."

Today, no less than yesterday, the Constitution and decisions of this Court require that a State's abortion restrictions be subjected to the strictest of judicial scrutiny. Our precedents and the joint opinion's principles require us to subject all non-*de minimis* abortion regulations to strict scrutiny. Under this standard, the Pennsylvania statute's provisions requiring content-based counseling, a 24-hour delay, informed parental consent, and reporting of abortion-related information must be invalidated.

State restrictions on abortion violate a woman's right of privacy in two ways. First, compelled continuation of a pregnancy infringes upon a woman's right to bodily integrity by imposing substantial physical intrusions and significant risks of physical harm.

Further, when the State restricts a woman's right to terminate her pregnancy, it deprives a woman of the right to make her own decision about reproduction and family planning — critical life choices that this Court long has deemed central to the right to privacy.

A State's restrictions on a woman's right to terminate her pregnancy also implicate constitutional guarantees of gender equality. State restrictions on abortion compel women to continue pregnancies they otherwise might terminate. By restricting the right to terminate pregnancies, the State conscripts women's bodies into its service, forcing women to continue their pregnancies, suffer the pains of childbirth, and in most instances, provide years of maternal care. The State does not compensate women for their services; instead, it assumes that they owe this duty as a matter of course. This assumption — that women can simply be forced to accept the "natural" status and incidents of motherhood — appears to rest upon a conception of women's role that has triggered the protection of the Equal Protection Clause.

Strict scrutiny of state limitations on reproductive choice still offers the most secure protection of the woman's right to make her own reproductive decisions, free from state coercion. No majority of this Court has ever agreed upon an alternative approach. The factual premises of the trimester framework have not been undermined, and the *Roe* framework is far more administrable, and far less manipulable, than the "undue burden" standard adopted by the joint opinion.

At long last, THE CHIEF JUSTICE admits it. Gone are the contentions that the issue need not be (or has not been) considered. There, on the first page, for all to see, is what was expected: "We believe that *Roe* was wrongly decided, and that it can and should be overruled consistently with our traditional approach to stare decisis in constitutional cases." If there is much reason to applaud the advances made by the joint opinion today, there is far more to fear from THE CHIEF JUSTICE's opinion.

THE CHIEF JUSTICE's criticism of *Roe* follows from his stunted conception of individual liberty. While recognizing that the Due Process Clause protects more than simple physical liberty, he then goes on to construe this Court's personal-liberty cases as establishing only a laundry list of particular rights, rather than a principled account of how these particular rights are grounded in a more general right of privacy. This constricted view is reinforced by THE CHIEF JUSTICE's exclusive reliance on tradition as a source of fundamental rights. In THE CHIEF JUSTICE's world, a woman considering whether to terminate a pregnancy is entitled to no more protection than adulterers, murderers, and so-called "sexual deviates." Given THE CHIEF JUSTICE's exclusive reliance on tradition, people using contraceptives seem the next likely candidate for his list of outcasts.

In one sense, the Court's approach is worlds apart from that of THE CHIEF JUSTICE and JUSTICE SCALIA. And yet, in another sense, the distance between the two approaches is short — the distance is but a single vote.

I am 83 years old. I cannot remain on this Court forever, and when I do step down, the confirmation process for my successor well may focus on the issue before us today. That, I regret, may be exactly where the choice between the two worlds will be made.

CHIEF JUSTICE REHNQUIST, with whom JUSTICES WHITE, SCALIA, and THOMAS join, concurring in the judgment in part and dissenting in part.

The joint opinion, following its newly-minted variation on stare decisis, retains the outer shell of *Roe v. Wade*, but beats a wholesale retreat from the substance of that case. We believe that *Roe* was wrongly decided, and that it can and should be overruled consistently with our traditional approach to stare decisis in constitutional cases. We would adopt the approach of the plurality in *Webster v. Reproductive Health Services,* and uphold the challenged provisions of the Pennsylvania statute in their entirety.

We agree with the Court of Appeals that our decision in *Roe* is not directly implicated by the Pennsylvania statute, which does not prohibit, but simply regulates, abortion. But, as the Court of Appeals found, the state of our post-*Roe* decisional law dealing with the regulation of abortion is confusing and uncertain, indicating that a reexamination of that line of cases is in order. Unfortunately for those who must apply this Court's decisions, the reexamination undertaken today leaves the Court no less divided than beforehand. Although they reject the trimester framework that formed the underpinning of *Roe*, JUSTICES O'CONNOR, KENNEDY, and SOUTER adopt a revised undue burden standard to analyze the challenged regulations. We conclude, however, that such an outcome is an unjustified constitutional compromise, one which leaves the Court in a position to closely scrutinize all types of abortion regulations despite the fact that it lacks the power to do so under the Constitution.

We have held that a liberty interest protected under the Due Process Clause of the Fourteenth Amendment will be deemed fundamental if it is "implicit in the concept of ordered liberty." *Palko v. Connecticut.*

In construing the phrase "liberty" incorporated in the Due Process Clause of the Fourteenth Amendment, we have recognized that its meaning extends beyond freedom from physical restraint. In *Pierce v. Society of Sisters*, we held that it included a parent's right to send a child to private school; in *Meyer v. Nebraska*, we held that it included a right to teach a foreign language in a parochial school. Building on these cases, we have held that the term "liberty" includes a right to marry, a right to procreate, and a right to use contraceptives. But a reading of these opinions makes clear that they do not endorse any all-encompassing "right of privacy."

In *Roe v. Wade*, the Court recognized a "guarantee of personal privacy" which "is broad enough to encompass a woman's decision whether or not to terminate her pregnancy." We are now of the view that, in terming this right fundamental, the Court in *Roe* read the earlier opinions upon which it based its decision much too broadly. Unlike marriage, procreation and contraception, abortion "involves the purposeful termination of potential life." *Harris v. McRae*. The abortion decision must therefore "be recognized as *sui generis*, different in kind from the others that the Court has protected under the rubric of personal or family privacy and autonomy." *Thornburgh v. American College of Obstetricians and Gynecologists*, (White, J., dissenting). One cannot ignore the fact that a woman is not isolated in her pregnancy, and that the decision to abort necessarily involves the destruction of a fetus.

Nor do the historical traditions of the American people support the view that the right to terminate one's pregnancy is "fundamental." The common law which we inherited from England made abortion after "quickening" an offense. At the time of the adoption of the Fourteenth Amendment, statutory prohibitions or restrictions on abortion were commonplace; in 1868, at least 28 of the then-37 States and 8 Territories had statutes banning or limiting abortion. By the turn of the century virtually every State had a law prohibiting or restricting abortion on its books. By the middle of the present century, a liberalization trend had set in. But 21 of the restrictive abortion laws in effect in 1868 were still in effect in 1973 when *Roe* was decided, and an overwhelming majority of the States prohibited abortion unless necessary to preserve the life or health of the mother. On this record, it can scarcely be said that any deeply rooted tradition of relatively unrestricted abortion in our history supported the classification of the right to abortion as "fundamental" under the Due Process Clause of the Fourteenth Amendment.

We think, therefore, both in view of this history and of our decided cases dealing with substantive liberty under the Due Process Clause, that the Court was mistaken in *Roe* when it classified a woman's decision to terminate her pregnancy as a "fundamental right" that could be abridged only in a manner which withstood "strict scrutiny."

The Court in *Roe* reached too far when it analogized the right to abort a fetus to the rights involved in *Pierce, Meyer, Loving*, and *Griswold*, and thereby deemed the right to abortion fundamental.

The joint opinion of JUSTICES O'CONNOR, KENNEDY, and SOUTER cannot bring itself to say that *Roe* was correct as an original matter, but the authors are of the view that "the immediate question is not the soundness of *Roe*'s resolution of the issue, but the precedential force that must be accorded to its holding." Instead of claiming that *Roe* was correct as a matter of original constitutional interpretation, the opinion therefore contains an elaborate discussion of stare decisis. This discussion of the principle of stare decisis appears to be almost entirely dicta, because the joint opinion does not apply that principle in dealing with *Roe*. *Roe* decided that a woman had a fundamental right to an abortion. The joint opinion rejects that view. *Roe* decided that abortion regulations were to be subjected to "strict scrutiny" and could be justified only in the light of "compelling state interests." The joint opinion rejects that view. *Roe* analyzed abortion regulation under a rigid trimester framework, a framework which has guided this Court's decisionmaking for 19 years. The joint opinion rejects that framework.

In our view, authentic principles of stare decisis do not require that any portion of the reasoning in *Roe* be kept intact. Erroneous decisions in such constitutional cases are uniquely durable, because correction through legislative action, save for constitutional amendment, is impossible. It is therefore our duty to reconsider constitutional interpretations that "depar[t] from a proper understanding" of the Constitution. *Garcia v. San Antonio Metropolitan Transit Authority*. Our constitutional watch does not cease merely because we have spoken before on an issue; when it becomes clear that a prior constitutional interpretation is unsound we are obliged to reexamine the question.

Nor does the joint opinion faithfully follow [its own analysis]. The opinion frankly concludes that *Roe* and its progeny were wrong in failing to recognize that the State's interests in maternal health and in the protection of unborn human life exist throughout pregnancy. But there is no indication that these components of *Roe* are any more incorrect at this juncture than they were at its inception.

The joint opinion thus turns to what can only be described as an unconventional — and unconvincing — notion of reliance, a view based on the surmise that the availability of abortion since *Roe* has led to "two decades of economic and social developments" that would be undercut if the error of *Roe* were recognized. The joint opinion's assertion of this fact is undeveloped and totally conclusory. In fact, one can not be sure to what economic and social developments the opinion is referring. Surely it is dubious to suggest that women have reached their "places in society" in reliance upon *Roe*, rather than as a result of their determination to obtain higher education and compete with men in the job market, and of society's increasing recognition of their ability to fill positions that were previously thought to be reserved only for men.

In the end, having failed to put forth any evidence to prove any true reliance, the joint opinion's argument is based solely on generalized assertions about the national psyche, on a belief that the people of this country have grown accustomed to the *Roe* decision over the last 19 years and have "ordered their thinking and living around" it. As an initial matter, one might inquire how the joint opinion can view the "central holding" of *Roe* as so deeply rooted in our constitutional culture, when it so casually uproots and disposes of that same decision's trimester framework. Furthermore, at various points in the past, the same could have been said about this Court's erroneous decisions that the Constitution allowed "separate but equal" treatment of minorities, or that "liberty" under the Due Process Clause protected "freedom of contract." The "separate but equal" doctrine lasted 58 years after *Plessy*, and *Lochner* protection of contractual freedom lasted 32 years. However, the simple fact that a generation or more had grown used to these major decisions did not prevent the Court from correcting its errors in those cases, nor should it prevent us from correctly interpreting the Constitution here.

Apparently realizing that conventional stare decisis principles do not support its position, the joint opinion advances a belief that retaining a portion of *Roe* is necessary to protect the "legitimacy" of this Court. Because the Court must take care to render decisions "grounded truly in principle," and not simply as political and social compromises, the joint opinion properly declares it to be this Court's duty to ignore the public criticism and protest that may arise as a result of a decision. Few would quarrel with this statement, although it may be doubted that Members of this Court, holding their tenure as they do during constitutional "good behavior," are at all likely to be intimidated by such public protests.

But the joint opinion goes on to state that when the Court "resolve[s] the sort of intensely divisive controversy reflected in *Roe* and those rare, comparable cases," its decision is exempt from reconsideration under established principles of stare decisis in constitutional cases. This is so, the joint opinion contends, because in those "intensely divisive" cases the Court has "call[ed] the contending sides of a national controversy to end their national division by accepting a common mandate rooted in the Constitution," and must therefore take special care not to be perceived as "surrender[ing] to political pressure" and continued opposition. This is a truly novel principle, one which is contrary to both the Court's historical practice and to the Court's traditional willingness to tolerate criticism of its opinions. Under this principle, when the Court has ruled on a divisive issue, it is apparently prevented from overruling that decision for the sole reason that it was incorrect, unless opposition to the original decision has died away.

Although many of the Court's decisions divide the populace to a large degree, we have not previously on that account shied away from applying normal rules of stare decisis when urged to reconsider earlier decisions. Over the past 21 years, for example, the Court has overruled in whole or in part 34 of its previous constitutional decisions.

The joint opinion picks out and discusses two prior Court rulings that it believes are of the "intensely divisive" variety, and concludes that they are of comparable dimension to *Roe*. It appears to us very odd indeed that the joint opinion chooses as benchmarks two cases in which the Court chose not to adhere to erroneous constitutional precedent, but instead enhanced its stature by acknowledging and correcting its error, apparently in violation of the joint opinion's "legitimacy" principle. One might also wonder how it is that the joint opinion puts these, and not others, in the "intensely divisive" category, and how it assumes that these are the only two lines of cases of comparable dimension to *Roe*. There is no reason to think that either *Plessy* or *Lochner* produced the sort of public protest when they were decided that *Roe* did. There were undoubtedly large segments of the bench and bar who agreed with the dissenting views in those cases, but surely that cannot be what the Court means when it uses the term "intensely divisive," or many other cases would have to be added to the list. In terms of public protest, however, *Roe*, so far as we know, was unique. But just as the Court should not respond to that sort of protest by retreating from the decision simply to allay the concerns of the protesters, it should likewise not respond by determining to adhere to the decision at all costs lest it seem to be retreating under fire. Public protests should not alter the normal application of stare decisis, lest perfectly lawful protest activity be penalized by the Court itself.

The joint opinion agrees that the Court's stature would have been seriously damaged if in *Brown* and *West Coast Hotel* it had dug in its heels and refused to apply normal principles of stare decisis to the earlier decisions. But the opinion contends that the Court was entitled to overrule *Plessy* and *Lochner* in those cases, despite the existence of opposition to the original decisions, only because both the Nation and the Court had learned new lessons in the interim. This is at best a feebly supported, post hoc rationalization for those decisions.

The joint opinion also agrees that the Court acted properly in rejecting the doctrine of "separate but equal" in *Brown*. In fact, the opinion lauds *Brown* in comparing it to *Roe*. This is strange, in that under the opinion's "legitimacy" principle the Court would seemingly have been forced to adhere to its erroneous decision in *Plessy* because of its "intensely divisive" character. To us, adherence to *Roe* today under the guise of "legitimacy" would seem to resemble more closely adherence to *Plessy* on the same ground. Fortunately, the Court did not choose that option in *Brown*, and instead frankly repudiated *Plessy*. The joint opinion concludes that such repudiation was justified only because of newly discovered evidence that segregation had the effect of treating one race as inferior to another. But it can hardly be argued that this was not urged upon those who decided *Plessy,* as JUSTICE HARLAN observed in his dissent that the law at issue "puts the brand of servitude and degradation upon a large class of our fellow-citizens, our equals before the law." It is clear that the same arguments made before the Court in *Brown* were made in *Plessy* as well. The Court in *Brown* simply recognized, as JUSTICE HARLAN had recognized beforehand, that the Fourteenth Amendment does not permit racial segregation. The rule of *Brown* is not tied to popular opinion about the evils of segregation; it is a judgment that the Equal Protection Clause does not permit racial segregation, no matter whether the public might come to believe that it is beneficial. On that ground it stands, and on that ground alone the Court was justified in properly concluding that the *Plessy* Court had erred.

There is also a suggestion in the joint opinion that the propriety of overruling a "divisive" decision depends in part on whether "most people" would now agree that it should be overruled. Either the demise of opposition or its progression to substantial popular agreement apparently is required to allow the Court to reconsider a divisive decision. How such agreement would be ascertained, short of a public opinion poll, the joint opinion does not say.

But surely even the suggestion is totally at war with the idea of "legitimacy" in whose name it is invoked. The Judicial Branch derives its legitimacy, not from following public opinion, but from deciding by its best lights whether legislative enactments of the popular branches of Government comport with the Constitution. The doctrine of stare decisis is an adjunct of this duty, and should be no more subject to the vagaries of public opinion than is the basic judicial task.

There are other reasons why the joint opinion's discussion of legitimacy is unconvincing as well. In assuming that the Court is perceived as "surrender-[ing] to political pressure" when it overrules a controversial decision, the joint opinion forgets that there are two sides to any controversy. The joint opinion asserts that, in order to protect its legitimacy, the Court must refrain from overruling a controversial decision lest it be viewed as favoring those who oppose the decision. But a decision to adhere to prior precedent is subject to the same criticism, for in such a case one can easily argue that the Court is responding to those who have demonstrated in favor of the original decision.

Roe is not this Court's only decision to generate conflict. Our decisions in some recent capital cases, and in *Bowers v. Hardwick*, have also engendered demonstrations in opposition. The joint opinion's message to such protesters appears to be that they must cease their activities in order to serve their cause, because their protests will only cement in place a decision which by normal standards of stare decisis should be reconsidered. Strong and often misguided criticism of a decision should not render the decision immune from reconsideration, lest a fetish for legitimacy penalize freedom of expression.

The end result of the joint opinion's paeans of praise for legitimacy is the enunciation of a brand new standard for evaluating state regulation of a woman's right to abortion — the "undue burden" standard. As indicated above, *Roe v. Wade* adopted a "fundamental right" standard under which state regulations could survive only if they met the requirement of "strict scrutiny." While we disagree with that standard, it at least had a recognized basis in constitutional law at the time *Roe* was decided. The same cannot be said for the "undue burden" standard, which is created largely out of whole cloth by the authors of the joint opinion. It is a standard which even today does not command the support of a majority of this Court. And it will not, we believe, result in the sort of "simple limitation," easily applied, which the joint opinion anticipates. In sum, it is a standard which is not built to last.

The sum of the joint opinion's labors in the name of stare decisis and "legitimacy" is this: *Roe v. Wade* stands as a sort of judicial Potemkin Village, which may be pointed out to passers by as a monument to the importance of adhering to precedent. But behind the facade, an entirely new method of analysis, without any roots in constitutional law, is imported to decide the constitutionality of state laws regulating abortion. Neither stare decisis nor "legitimacy" are truly served by such an effort.

We have stated above our belief that the Constitution does not subject state abortion regulations to heightened scrutiny. Accordingly, we think that the correct analysis is that set forth by the plurality opinion in *Webster*. A woman's interest in having an abortion is a form of liberty protected by the Due Process

Clause, but States may regulate abortion procedures in ways rationally related to a legitimate state interest.

The question before us is whether the spousal notification requirement rationally furthers any legitimate state interests. We conclude that it does. First, a husband's interests in procreation within marriage and in the potential life of his unborn child are certainly substantial ones. The State itself has legitimate interests both in protecting these interests of the father and in protecting the potential life of the fetus, and the spousal notification requirement is reasonably related to advancing those state interests. By providing that a husband will usually know of his spouse's intent to have an abortion, the provision makes it more likely that the husband will participate in deciding the fate of his unborn child, a possibility that might otherwise have been denied him. This participation might in some cases result in a decision to proceed with the pregnancy.

The State also has a legitimate interest in promoting "the integrity of the marital relationship." Petitioners argue that the notification requirement does not further any such interest; they assert that the majority of wives already notify their husbands of their abortion decisions, and the remainder have excellent reasons for keeping their decisions a secret. In the first case, they argue, the law is unnecessary, and in the second case it will only serve to foster marital discord and threats of harm. Thus, petitioners see the law as a totally irrational means of furthering whatever legitimate interest the State might have. But, in our view, it is unrealistic to assume that every husband-wife relationship is either (1) so perfect that this type of truthful and important communication will take place as a matter of course, or (2) so imperfect that, upon notice, the husband will react selfishly, violently, or contrary to the best interests of his wife. The spousal notice provision will admittedly be unnecessary in some circumstances, and possibly harmful in others, but "the existence of particular cases in which a feature of a statute performs no function (or is even counterproductive) ordinarily does not render the statute unconstitutional or even constitutionally suspect." *Thornburgh v. American College of Obstetricians and Gynecologists* (WHITE, J., dissenting). The Pennsylvania Legislature was in a position to weigh the likely benefits of the provision against its likely adverse effects, and presumably concluded, on balance, that the provision would be beneficial. Whether this was a wise decision or not, we cannot say that it was irrational. We therefore conclude that the spousal notice provision comports with the Constitution.

We would hold that each of the challenged provisions of the Pennsylvania statute is consistent with the Constitution. It bears emphasis that our conclusion in this regard does not carry with it any necessary approval of these regulations. Our task is, as always, to decide only whether the challenged provisions of a law comport with the United States Constitution. If, as we believe, these do, their wisdom as a matter of public policy is for the people of Pennsylvania to decide.

JUSTICE SCALIA, with whom THE CHIEF JUSTICE [REHNQUIST], JUSTICES WHITE and THOMAS join, concurring in the judgment in part and dissenting in part.

My views on this matter are unchanged from those I set forth in my separate opinions in *Webster v. Reproductive Health Services*, and *Ohio v. Akron Center for Reproductive Health (Akron II)* (Scalia, J., concurring). The States may, if they wish, permit abortion-on-demand, but the Constitution does not require them to do so. The permissibility of abortion, and the limitations upon it, are to be resolved like most important questions in our democracy: by citizens trying to persuade one another and then voting. As the Court acknowledges, "where reasonable people disagree the government can adopt one position or the other." The Court is correct in adding the qualification that this "assumes a state of affairs in which the choice does not intrude upon a protected liberty," but the crucial part of that qualification is the penultimate word. A State's choice between two positions on which reasonable people can disagree is constitutional even when (as is often the case) it intrudes upon a "liberty" in the absolute sense. Laws against bigamy, for example — which entire societies of reasonable people disagree with — intrude upon men and women's liberty to marry and live with one another. But bigamy happens not to be a liberty specially "protected" by the Constitution.

That is, quite simply, the issue in this case: not whether the power of a woman to abort her unborn child is a "liberty" in the absolute sense; or even whether it is a liberty of great importance to many women. Of course it is both. The issue is whether it is a liberty protected by the Constitution of the United States. I am sure it is not. I reach that conclusion not because of anything so exalted as my views concerning the "concept of existence, of meaning, of the universe, and of the mystery of human life." Rather, I reach it for the same reason I reach the conclusion that bigamy is not constitutionally protected — because of two simple facts: (1) the Constitution says absolutely nothing about it, and (2) the longstanding traditions of American society have permitted it to be legally proscribed.

The Court destroys the proposition, evidently meant to represent my position, that "liberty" includes "only those practices, defined at the most specific level, that were protected against government interference by other rules of law when the Fourteenth Amendment was ratified," (citing *Michael H. v. Gerald D.*, opinion of Scalia, J.). That is not, however, what *Michael H.* says; it merely observes that, in defining "liberty," we may not disregard a specific, "relevant tradition protecting, or denying protection to, the asserted right." But the Court does not wish to be fettered by any such limitations on its preferences. The Court's statement that it is "tempting" to acknowledge the authoritativeness of tradition in order to "cur[b] the discretion of federal judges," is of course rhetoric rather than reality; no government official is "tempted" to place restraints upon his own freedom of action, which is why Lord Acton did not say "Power tends to purify." The Court's temptation is in the quite opposite and more natural direction — towards systematically eliminating checks upon its own power; and it succumbs.

Beyond that brief summary of the essence of my position, I will not swell the United States Reports with repetition of what I have said before; and applying the rational basis test, I would uphold the Pennsylvania statute in its entirety. I must, however, respond to a few of the more outrageous arguments in today's opinion, which it is beyond human nature to leave unanswered. I shall discuss each of them under a quotation from the Court's opinion to which they pertain.

"The inescapable fact is that adjudication of substantive due process claims may call upon the Court in interpreting the Constitution to exercise that same capacity which by tradition courts always have exercised: reasoned judgment."

Assuming that the question before us is to be resolved at such a level of philosophical abstraction, in such isolation from the traditions of American society, as by simply applying "reasoned judgment," I do not see how that could possibly have produced the answer the Court arrived at in *Roe v. Wade*. Today's opinion describes the methodology of *Roe*, quite accurately, as weighing against the woman's interest the State's "important and legitimate interest in protecting the potentiality of human life." But "reasoned judgment" does not begin by begging the question, as *Roe* and subsequent cases unquestionably did by assuming that what the State is protecting is the mere "potentiality of human life." The whole argument of abortion opponents is that what the Court calls the fetus and what others call the unborn child is a human life. Thus, whatever answer *Roe* came up with after conducting its "balancing" is bound to be wrong, unless it is correct that the human fetus is in some critical sense merely potentially human. There is of course no way to determine that as a legal matter; it is in fact a value judgment. Some societies have considered newborn children not yet human, or the incompetent elderly no longer so.

The authors of the joint opinion, of course, do not squarely contend that *Roe v. Wade* was a correct application of "reasoned judgment"; merely that it must be followed, because of stare decisis. But in their exhaustive discussion of all the factors that go into the determination of when stare decisis should be observed and when disregarded, they never mention "how wrong was the decision on its face?" Surely, if "[t]he Court's power lies . . . in its legitimacy, a product of substance and perception," the "substance" part of the equation demands that plain error be acknowledged and eliminated. *Roe* was plainly wrong — even on the Court's methodology of "reasoned judgment," and even more so (of course) if the proper criteria of text and tradition are applied.

The emptiness of the "reasoned judgment" that produced *Roe* is displayed in plain view by the fact that, after more than 19 years of effort by some of the brightest (and most determined) legal minds in the country, after more than 10 cases upholding abortion rights in this Court, and after dozens upon dozens of amicus briefs submitted in this and other cases, the best the Court can do to explain how it is that the word "liberty" must be thought to include the right to destroy human fetuses is to rattle off a collection of adjectives that simply decorate a value judgment and conceal a political choice. The right to abort, we are told, inheres in "liberty" because it is among "a person's most basic decisions," it involves a "most intimate and personal choic[e]," it is "central to personal dignity and autonomy," it "originate[s] within the zone of conscience and belief," it is "too intimate and personal" for state interference, it reflects "intimate views" of a "deep, personal character," it involves "intimate relationships," and notions of "personal autonomy and bodily integrity," and it concerns a particularly "important decisio[n]." But it is obvious to anyone applying "reasoned judgment" that the same adjectives can be applied to many forms of conduct that this Court (including one of the Justices in today's majority, see *Bowers v. Hardwick*), has held are not entitled to constitutional protection — because, like abortion, they are forms of conduct that have long been criminalized in American society. Those adjectives might be applied, for example, to homosexual sodomy, polygamy, adult incest, and suicide, all of which are equally "intimate" and "deep[ly] personal" decisions involving "personal autonomy and bodily integrity," and all of which can constitutionally be proscribed because it is our unquestionable constitutional tradition that they are proscribable. It is not reasoned judgment that supports the Court's decision; only personal predilection.

"Liberty finds no refuge in a jurisprudence of doubt." One might have feared to encounter this august and sonorous phrase in an opinion defending the real *Roe v. Wade*, rather than the revised version fabricated today by the authors of the joint opinion. The shortcomings of *Roe* did not include lack of clarity: Virtually all regulation of abortion before the third trimester was invalid. But to come across this phrase in the joint opinion — which calls upon federal district judges to apply an "undue burden" standard as doubtful in application as it is unprincipled in origin — is really more than one should have to bear.

The joint opinion frankly concedes that the amorphous concept of "undue burden" has been inconsistently applied by the Members of this Court in the few brief years since that "test" was first explicitly propounded by JUSTICE O'CONNOR in her dissent in *Akron I*. Because the three Justices now wish to "set forth a standard of general application," the joint opinion announces that "it is important to clarify what is meant by an undue burden." I certainly agree with that, but I do not agree that the joint opinion succeeds in the announced endeavor. To the contrary, its efforts at clarification make clear only that the standard is inherently manipulable and will prove hopelessly unworkable in practice.

To the extent I can discern any meaningful content in the "undue burden" standard as applied in the joint opinion, it appears to be that a State may not regulate abortion in such a way as to reduce significantly its incidence. Thus, despite flowery rhetoric about the State's "substantial" and "profound" interest in "potential human life," and criticism of *Roe* for undervaluing that interest, the joint opinion permits the State to pursue that interest only so long as it is not too successful.

The Court's reliance upon stare decisis can best be described as contrived. It insists upon the necessity of adhering not to all of *Roe*, but only to what it calls the "central holding." It seems to me that stare decisis ought to be applied even to the doctrine of stare decisis, and I confess never to have heard of this new, keep-what-you-want-and-throw-away-the-rest version. The only principle the Court "adheres" to, it seems to me, is the principle that the Court must be seen as standing by *Roe*. That is not a principle of law (which is what I thought the Court was talking about), but a principle of Realpolitik — and a wrong one at that.

I cannot agree with, indeed I am appalled by, the Court's suggestion that the decision whether to stand by an erroneous constitutional decision must be strongly influenced — against overruling, no less — by the substantial and continuing public opposition the decision has generated. The Court's judgment that any other course would "subvert the Court's legitimacy" must be another consequence of reading the error-filled history book that described the deeply divided country brought together by *Roe*. In my history-book, the Court was covered with dishonor and deprived of legitimacy by *Dred Scott v. Sandford*, an erroneous (and widely opposed) opinion that it did not abandon, rather than by *West Coast Hotel Co. v. Parrish*, which produced the famous "switch in time" from the Court's erroneous (and widely opposed) constitutional opposition to the social measures of the New Deal. (Both *Dred Scott* and one line of the cases resisting the New Deal rested upon the concept of "substantive due process" that the Court praises and employs today. Indeed, *Dred Scott* was "very possibly the first application of substantive due process in the Supreme Court, the original precedent for *Lochner v. New York* and *Roe v. Wade*.")

[W]hether it would "subvert the Court's legitimacy" or not, the notion that we would decide a case differently from the way we otherwise would have in order to show that we can stand firm against public disapproval is frightening. It is a bad enough idea, even in the head of someone like me, who believes that the text of the Constitution, and our traditions, say what they say and there is no fiddling with them. But when it is in the mind of a Court that believes the Constitution has an evolving meaning, that the Ninth Amendment's reference to "othe[r]" rights is not a disclaimer, but a charter for action, and that the function of this Court is to "speak before all others for [the people's] constitutional ideals" unrestrained by meaningful text or tradition — then the notion that the Court must adhere to a decision for as long as the decision faces "great opposition" and the Court is "under fire" acquires a character of almost czarist arrogance. We are offended by these marchers who descend upon us, every year on the anniversary of *Roe*, to protest our saying that the Constitution requires what our society has never thought the Constitution requires. These people who refuse to be "tested by following" must be taught a lesson. We have no Cossacks, but at least we can stubbornly refuse to abandon an erroneous opinion that we might otherwise change — to show how little they intimidate us.

Of course, we have been subjected to what the Court calls "political pressure" by both sides of this issue. Maybe today's decision not to overrule *Roe* will be seen as buckling to pressure from that direction. Instead of engaging in the hopeless task of predicting public perception — a job not for lawyers but for political campaign managers — the Justices should do what is legally right by asking two questions: (1) Was *Roe* correctly decided? (2) Has *Roe* succeeded in producing a settled body of law? If the answer to both questions is no, *Roe* should undoubtedly be overruled.

NOTES

1. *Stenberg v. Carhart*, 530 U.S. 914 (2000). In an opinion by Justice Breyer, the Court invalidated a Nebraska statute prohibiting "partial-birth" abortions at any stage of pregnancy. "No partial birth abortion shall be performed in this state, unless such procedure is necessary to save the life of the mother whose life is endangered by a physical disorder, physical illness, or physical injury, including a life-endangering physical condition caused by or arising from the pregnancy itself." The statute defined "partial birth abortion" as: "an abortion procedure in which the person performing the abortion partially delivers vaginally a living unborn child before killing the unborn child and completing the delivery." It further defines "partially delivers vaginally a living unborn child before killing the unborn child" to mean "deliberately and intentionally delivering into the vagina a living unborn child, or a substantial portion thereof, for the purpose of performing a procedure that the person performing such procedure knows will kill the unborn child and does kill the unborn child." Penalties for violation of the statute included prison term up to 20 years and automatic revocation of a doctor's license to practice medicine in Nebraska. [Nebraska law already prohibited any post-viability abortion; no abortion, whether "partial-birth" or not, could occur if the fetus were capable of sustaining life outside the womb.]

Because the statute purported to prevent one form of abortion procedure, Justice Breyer began with an explanation of the different forms in current use. "Approximately 10% of all abortions are performed during the second trimester of pregnancy (12 to 24 weeks). In the early 1970s, inducing labor through the injection of saline into the uterus was the predominant method of second trimester abortion. Today, however, the medical profession has switched from medical induction of labor to surgical procedures for most second trimester abortions. The most commonly used procedure is called 'dilation and evacuation' (D&E). That procedure (together with a modified form of vacuum aspiration used in the early second trimester) accounts for about 95% of all abortions performed from 12 to 20 weeks of gestational age." After 15 weeks of gestation, or during weeks 16 to 20, the typical fetus will be too large for the D&E procedure to be performed safely for the mother. In many instances at this stage, the surgeon will employ a modified procedure in which the fetus is brought out of the uterus into the vagina intact. "Intact D&E proceeds in one of two ways, depending on the presentation of the fetus. If the fetus presents head first (a vertex presentation), the doctor collapses the skull; and the doctor then extracts the entire fetus through the cervix. If the fetus presents feet first (a breech presentation), the doctor pulls the fetal body through the cervix, collapses the skull, and extracts the fetus through the cervix. The breech extraction version of the intact D&E is also known commonly as 'dilation and extraction,' or D&X."

Although second trimester abortions may be regulated by the State for health and safety reasons, the Nebraska statute was found not to provide adequately for the mother's health. By banning "intact D&E" procedures, the state was actually forcing many women into more risky situations. "The State fails to demonstrate that banning D&X without a health exception may not create significant health risks for women, because the record shows that significant medical authority supports the proposition that in some circumstances, D&X would be the safest procedure."

The second problem with the statute was that it "unduly burdened" the abortion choice by broadly sweeping in many forms of D&E procedures. "Even if the statute's basic aim is to ban D&X, its language makes clear that it also covers a much broader category of procedures. The language does not track the medical differences between D&E and D&X — though it would have been a simple matter, for example, to provide an exception for the performance of D&E and other abortion procedures."

The Court concluded: "In sum, using this law some present prosecutors and future Attorneys General may choose to pursue physicians who use D & E procedures, the most commonly used method for performing previability second trimester abortions. All those who perform abortion procedures using that method must fear prosecution, conviction and imprisonment. The result is an undue burden upon a woman's right to make an abortion decision. We must consequently find the statute unconstitutional."

Chief Justice Rehnquist, Justice Thomas, and Justice Kennedy dissented on the grounds that *Casey* should be read as authorizing the states to regulate abortion practices for the purpose of promoting state interests related to the practice of medicine. As one of the three authors of the "joint opinion" in *Casey*, Justice Kennedy's position is perhaps of most significance: "It ill-serves the Court, its institutional position, and the constitutional sources it seeks to invoke to refuse to issue a forthright affirmation of Nebraska's right to declare that critical moral differences exist between the two procedures [D&E v. D&X]. The natural birth process has been appropriated; yet the Court refuses to hear the State's voice in defining its interests in its law. The Court's holding contradicts *Casey's* assurance that the State's constitutional position in the realm of promoting respect for life is more than marginal."

Justice Scalia dissented with his usual flair:

> I am optimistic enough to believe that, one day, *Stenberg v. Carhart* will be assigned its rightful place in the history of this Court's jurisprudence beside *Korematsu* and *Dred Scott*. The method of killing a human child — one cannot even accurately say an entirely unborn human child — proscribed by this statute is so horrible that the most clinical description of it evokes a shudder of revulsion. And the Court must know (as most state legislatures banning this procedure have concluded) that demanding a "health exception" — which requires the abortionist to assure himself that, in his expert medical judgment, this method is, in the case at hand, marginally safer than others (how can one prove the contrary beyond a reasonable doubt?) — is to give live-birth abortion free rein. The notion that the Constitution of the United States, designed, among other things, "to establish Justice, insure domestic Tranquility, . . . and secure the Blessings of Liberty to ourselves and our Posterity," prohibits the States from simply banning this visibly brutal means of eliminating our half-born posterity is quite simply absurd.

For a critical discussion of the decision, see Comment, *Slouching Toward Barbarism? The Quest to Limit Partial Birth Abortion After Stenberg v. Carhart*, 103 W. VA. L. REV. 219 (2000).

In 2003, Congress passed and the president signed the Partial-Birth Abortion Act, 18 U.S.C. § 1531, which provides:

> Any physician who, in or affecting interstate or foreign commerce, knowingly performs a partial birth abortion and thereby kills a human

> fetus shall be fined under this title or imprisoned not more than 2 years, or both. This subsection does not apply to a partial-birth abortion that is necessary to save the life of a mother whose life is endangered by a physical disorder, physical illness, or physical injury, including a life-endangering physical condition caused by or arising from the pregnancy itself.

Is this statute constitutional, under *Stenburg*? *See* Scott Hodges, Comment, *Constitutional Law: Beyond the Bounds of Roe: Does Stenberg v. Carhart Invalidate the Partial-Birth Abortion Ban Act of 2003?*, 57 OKLA. L. REV. 601 (2004).

2. *The future of abortion rights.* Justice Blackmun and some commentators worry that the joint opinion in *Casey* does not provide firm protection for the right of abortion choice. Professor Judges points out that the joint opinion offers a "ringing defense" of liberty and *stare decisis* that might have led to a "forceful reaffirmation of *Roe*."

> What follows in the joint opinion, however, is a substantial downsizing of *Roe*, the overruling of important post-*Roe* case law, and an invitation to legislatures to continue the cat-and-mouse game of testing *Roe*'s newly relaxed limits — all of which exacerbate the arbitrary allocation of abortion rights. The contrast is, to borrow a metaphor, "like a spectacularly successful football rally followed by a lost game."

Donald Judges, *Taking Care Seriously: Relational Feminism, Sexual Difference, and Abortion*, 73 N.C.L. REV. 1323, 1448 (1995).

[B] MARITAL AND FAMILIAL RIGHTS

While advocates of abortion reform have been able to find support for their position in *Griswold*, the dominant strain of that decision was on marital privacy — the use of contraceptives by the married couple. The majority opinions found support for due process liberty rights surrounding family life in *Meyer v. Nebraska* (state statute prohibiting instruction in certain foreign languages in private schools "materially interfere[s] with the power of parents to control the education of their own") and *Pierce v. Society of Sisters* (state law requiring parents to send children to public schools would "unreasonably interfere with the liberty of parents and guardians to direct the upbringing and education of children under their control"). In *Loving v. Virginia*, p. 657, holding that a state miscegenation law violated equal protection and due process, the Court referred to "the freedom to marry as one of the vital personal rights essential to the orderly pursuit of happiness by free men." Marriage was characterized as "one of the 'basic civil rights of man,' fundamental to our very existence and survival."

But the concept of marriage and family life is undergoing substantial change. How far will the constitutional protections accorded traditional relationships be extended to other forms of associations, such as cohabitation without marriage, or homosexual marriages? Is divorce also protected? What is a "family"? Does it include any group of individuals living together — for instance, communes, unmarried parents, a single parent with a child, or a homosexual parent with a child? Are laws restricting such groupings, or burdening intimate relationships, to be judged under strict scrutiny or traditional due process standards? Wilkinson and White have noted the usefulness of judicial review as a vehicle for adjusting legal principles to changing social conditions.

> [T]he effect of constitutional law in the domestic lifestyle area is potentially fourfold: to guarantee greater freedom of entry into and exit from formal family relationships, to encourage and validate role changes within the family or marriage partnership, to make available formal family status to unorthodox groups, and to confer legitimacy and recognition upon extrafamilial relationships.

Harvie Wilkinson & Edward White, *Constitutional Protection for Personal Lifestyles*, 62 CORNELL L. REV. 563, 567–68 (1977). But, they warn: "Deploying the Constitution to undermine conventional precepts of domestic morality is a step not lightly taken."

MOORE v. EAST CLEVELAND

431 U.S. 494, 97 S. Ct. 1932, 52 L. Ed. 2d 531 (1977)

JUSTICE POWELL announced the judgment of the Court, and delivered an opinion in which JUSTICES BRENNAN, MARSHALL, and BLACKMUN joined.

East Cleveland's housing ordinance, like many throughout the country, limits occupancy of a dwelling unit to members of a single family. But the ordinance contains an unusual and complicated definitional section that recognizes as a "family" only a few categories of related individuals. Because her family, living together in her home, fits none of those categories, appellant stands convicted of a criminal offense. The question in this case is whether the ordinance violates the Due Process Clause of the Fourteenth Amendment.

Appellant, Mrs. Inez Moore, lives in her East Cleveland home together with her son, Dale Moore, Sr., and her two grandsons, Dale, Jr., and John Moore, Jr. The two boys are first cousins rather than brothers; we are told that John came to live with his grandmother and with the elder and younger Dale Moore after his mother's death. In early 1973, Mrs. Moore received a notice of violation from the city, stating that John was an "illegal occupant" and directing her to comply with the ordinance. When she failed to remove him from her home, the city filed a criminal charge. Mrs. Moore moved to dismiss, claiming that the ordinance was constitutionally invalid on its face. Her motion was overruled, and upon conviction she was sentenced to five days in jail and a $25 fine. The Ohio Court of Appeals affirmed after giving full consideration to her constitutional claims, and the Ohio Supreme Court denied review.

When a city undertakes such intrusive regulation of the family, the usual judicial deference to the legislature is inappropriate. "This Court has long recognized that freedom of personal choice in matters of marriage and family life is one of the liberties protected by the Due Process Clause of the Fourteenth Amendment." *Cleveland Board of Education v. LaFleur*, 414 U.S.

632 (1974). Of course, the family is not beyond regulation. *See Prince v. Massachusetts*. But when the government intrudes on choices concerning family living arrangements, this Court must examine carefully the importance of the governmental interests advanced and the extent to which they are served by the challenged regulation. *See Poe v. Ullman* (HARLAN, J., dissenting). When thus examined, this ordinance cannot survive. The city seeks to justify it as a means of preventing overcrowding, minimizing traffic and parking congestion, and avoiding an undue financial burden on East Cleveland's school system. Although these are legitimate goals, the ordinance before us serves them marginally, at best.

The city would distinguish the cases based on *Meyer* [*v. Nebraska*] and *Pierce* [*v. Society of Sisters*]. It points out that none of them "gives grandmothers any fundamental rights with respect to grandsons," and suggests that any constitutional right to live together as a family extends only to the nuclear family — essentially a couple and their dependent children. But unless we close our eyes to the basic reasons why certain rights associated with the family have been accorded shelter under the Fourteenth Amendment's Due Process Clause, we cannot avoid applying the force and rationale of these precedents to the family choice involved in this case.

Substantive due process has at times been a treacherous field for this Court. There are risks when the judicial branch gives enhanced protection to certain substantive liberties without the guidance of the more specific provisions of the Bill of Rights. As the history of the *Lochner* era demonstrates, there is reason for concern lest the only limits to such judicial intervention become the predilections of those who happen at the time to be Members of this Court. That history counsels caution and restraint. But it does not counsel abandonment, nor does it require what the city urges here: cutting off any protection of family rights at the first convenient, if arbitrary boundary — the boundary of the nuclear family.

Appropriate limits on substantive due process come not from drawing arbitrary lines but rather from careful "respect for the teachings of history [and] solid recognition of the basic values that underlie our society." Our decisions establish that the Constitution protects the sanctity of the family precisely because the institution of the family is deeply rooted in this Nation's history and tradition.[12] It is through the family that we inculcate and pass down many of our most cherished values, moral and cultural.

Ours is by no means a tradition limited to respect for the bonds uniting the members of the nuclear family. The tradition of uncles, aunts, cousins, and especially grandparents sharing a household along with parents and children has roots equally venerable and equally deserving of constitutional recognition. Out of choice, necessity, or a sense of family responsibility, ithas

[12] Although he agrees that the Due Process Clause has substantive content, MR. JUSTICE WHITE in dissent expresses the fear that our recourse to history and tradition will "broaden enormously the horizons of the Clause." To the contrary, an approach grounded in history imposes limits on the judiciary that are more meaningful than any based on the abstract formula taken from *Palko v. Connecticut* and apparently suggested as an alternative. Indeed, the passage cited in MR. JUSTICE WHITE's dissent as "most accurately reflect[ing] the thrust of prior decisions" on substantive due process, expressly points to history and tradition as the source for "supplying content to this Constitutional concept." *Poe v. Ullman* (HARLAN, J., dissenting).

been common for close relatives to draw together and participate in the duties and the satisfactions of a common home. Decisions concerning child rearing, which [*Wisconsin v. Yoder*, p. 1432] *Meyer*, *Pierce* and other cases have recognized as entitled to constitutional protection, long have been shared with grandparents or other relatives who occupy the same household — indeed who may take on major responsibility for the rearing of the children.

JUSTICE STEVENS, concurring in the judgment.

There appears to be no precedent for an ordinance which excludes any of an owner's relatives from the group of persons who may occupy his residence on a permanent basis. Nor does there appear to be any justification for such a restriction on an owner's use of his property. The city has failed totally to explain the need for a rule which would allow a homeowner to have two grandchildren live with her if they are brothers, but not if they are cousins. Since this ordinance has not been shown to have any "substantial relation to the public health, safety, morals, or general welfare" of the city of East Cleveland, and since it cuts so deeply into a fundamental right normally associated with the ownership of residential property — that of an owner to decide who may reside on his or her property — it must fall under the limited standard of review of zoning decisions [employed by this Court]. Under that standard, East Cleveland's unprecedented ordinance constitutes a taking of property without due process and without just compensation.

CHIEF JUSTICE BURGER, dissenting.

It is unnecessary for me to reach the difficult constitutional issue this case presents. Appellant's deliberate refusal to use a plainly adequate administrative remedy provided by the city should foreclose her from pressing in this Court any constitutional objections to the city's zoning ordinance.

JUSTICE STEWART, with whom JUSTICE REHNQUIST joins, dissenting.

When the Court has found that the Fourteenth Amendment placed a substantive limitation on a State's power to regulate, it has been in those rare cases in which the personal interests at issue have been deemed "implicit in the concept of ordered liberty." *See Roe v. Wade*, quoting *Palko v. Connecticut*. The interest that the appellant may have in permanently sharing a single kitchen and a suite of contiguous rooms with some of her relatives simply does not rise to that level. To equate this interest with the fundamental decisions to marry and to bear and raise children is to extend the limited substantive contours of the Due Process Clause beyond recognition.

JUSTICE WHITE, dissenting.

That the Court has ample precedent for the creation of new constitutional rights should not lead it to repeat the process at will. The Judiciary, including this Court, is the most vulnerable and comes nearest to illegitimacy when it deals with judge-made constitutional law having little or no cognizable roots in the language or even the design of the Constitution. Realizing that the present construction of the Due Process Clause represents a major judicial gloss on its terms, as well as on the anticipation of the Framers, and that much of the underpinning for the broad, substantive application of the Clause disappeared in the conflict between the Executive and the Judiciary in the 1930s and 1940s, the Court should be extremely reluctant to breathe still further substantive content into the Due Process Clause so as to strike down legislation adopted by a State or city to promote its welfare. Whenever the Judiciary does so, it unavoidably pre-empts for itself another part of the governance of the country without express constitutional authority.

It seems to me that MR. JUSTICE DOUGLAS was closest to the mark in *Poe v. Ullman*, when he said that the trouble with the holdings of the "old Court" was not in its definition of liberty but in its definition of the protections guaranteed to that liberty — "not in entertaining inquiries concerning the constitutionality of social legislation but in applying the standards that it did."

The term "liberty" is not, therefore, to be given a crabbed construction. I have no more difficulty than MR. JUSTICE POWELL apparently does in concluding that appellant in this case properly asserts a liberty interest within the meaning of the Due Process Clause. The question is not one of liberty *vel non*. Rather, the issue is whether the precise interest involved — the interest in having more than one set of grandchildren live in her home — is entitled to such substantive protection under the Due Process Clause that this ordinance must be held invalid.

Under our cases, the Due Process Clause extends substantial protection to various phases of family life, but none requires that the claim made here be sustained. I cannot believe that the interest in residing with more than one set of grandchildren is one that calls for any kind of heightened protection under the Due Process Clause. To say that one has a personal right to live with all, rather than some, of one's grandchildren and that this right is implicit in ordered liberty is, as my Brother Stewart says, "to extend the limited substantive contours of the Due Process Clause beyond recognition." The present claim is hardly one of which it could be said that "neither liberty nor justice would exist if [it] were sacrificed." *Palko v. Connecticut*.

MR. JUSTICE POWELL would apparently construe the Due Process Clause to protect from all but quite important state regulatory interests any right or privilege that in his estimate is deeply rooted in the country's traditions. For me, this suggests a far too expansive charter for this Court and a far less meaningful and less confining guiding principle than MR. JUSTICE STEWART would use [*i.e.*, "implicit in the concept of ordered liberty"] for serious substantive due process review. What the deeply rooted traditions of the country are is arguable; which of them deserve the protection of the Due Process Clause is even more debatable. The suggested view would broaden enormously the horizons of the Clause; and, if the interest involved here is any measure of what the States would be forbidden to regulate, the courts would be substantively weighing and very likely invalidating a wide range of measures that Congress and state legislatures think appropriate to respond to a changing economic and social order.

Mrs. Moore's interest in having the offspring of more than one dependent son live with her qualifies as a liberty protected by the Due Process Clause; but, because of the nature of that particular interest, the demands of the Clause are satisfied once the Court is assured that the challenged proscription is the product of a duly enacted or promulgated statute, ordinance, or regulation and that it is not wholly lacking in purpose or utility. That under this ordinance any number of married children may reside with their mother and that this number might be as destructive of neighborhood values as one or more additional grandchildren is just another argument that children and grandchildren may not constitutionally be distinguished by a local zoning ordinance.

If there is power to maintain the character of a single-family neighborhood, as there surely is, some limit must be placed on the reach of the "family." Had it been our task to legislate, we might have approached the problem in a different manner than did the drafters of this ordinance; but I have no trouble in concluding that the normal goals of zoning regulation are present here and that the ordinance serves these goals by limiting, in identifiable circumstances, the number of people who can occupy a single household. The ordinance does not violate the Due Process Clause.

NOTES

1. *Substantive due process revisited.* *Moore* was the first case since 1937 in which the Court specifically invoked substantive due process to invalidate a law. No other right, such as privacy, was found in the Constitution or created from external sources. While the Court might also have employed equal protection analysis, Justice Powell relied on the arguably more sweeping substantive due process approach.

Professor Grano suggested that the decision in *Moore* demonstrates what is wrong with the "noninterpretivist" model of judicial review. He asserts that

> the prosecution of an elderly grandmother for coming to the aid of her family in a time of need shocks one's conscience . . . and should, in my view, outrage the moral sensibilities of others as well. Obviously, however, the city officials, prosecutor, and judge in *Moore*, who undoubtedly considered themselves decent, moral people, were not so outraged. I make this observation not to defend ethical relativism but only to question whether those of us on Mrs. Moore's side are justified in using constitutional adjudication to impose our morality on those who disagree.

Joseph Grano, *Judicial Review and a Written Constitution in a Democratic Society*, 28 WAYNE L. REV. 1, 11 (1981).

2. *The "family" precedents.* Is *Moore* simply a logical extension of *Meyer*, *Pierce* and *Griswold*? *Meyer* and *Pierce* both relied on the rights of the schools and teachers, as well as the parents, and religious considerations were present in *Pierce*. What is the Court's rationale for extending due process liberty to the non-nuclear family? It has been suggested that the Court in *Moore* "reached into a long history of cases dealing with a variety of issues and decided on a variety of constitutional bases, and it has found a persistent constitutional doctrine not specifically announced by any individual case." Tamila Jensen, *From Belle Terre to East Cleveland: Zoning, the Family, and the Right of Privacy*, 13 FAM. L.Q. 1, 15 (1979). How would you characterize the right recognized in *Moore*? Could it be viewed as a right to "family life"?

To what extent does *Moore* represent performance of the legitimate judicial function of discerning and enforcing the nation's underlying ethical values, such as enduring personal relationships? To what extent does *Moore* support recognition of a constitutional right to same-sex marriage?

3. *Village of Belle Terre v. Boraas,* 416 U.S. 1 (1974). The Court, in an opinion by Justice Douglas, upheld an ordinance that zoned for "single family dwellings," with "family" defined as one or more persons related by blood, adoption, or marriage, thus excluding groups of unrelated individuals. Justice Douglas characterized such an anti-commune zoning ordinance as social and economic legislation requiring judicial deference. Applying a rational basis test, the Court rejected the equal protection challenge. Justice Marshall in dissent argued that

> the choice of household companions — of whether a person's "intellectual and emotional needs" are best met by living with family, friends, professional associates, or others — involves deeply personal considerations as to the kind and quality of intimate relationships within the home. That decision surely falls within the ambit of the right to privacy protected by the Constitution.

Should *Belle Terre* have controlled the decision in *Moore*, as Justice Stewart, dissenting in *Moore*, argued? It has been suggested that "the court in *Moore* myopically saw the case as a dispute between 'a family' and 'the state' rather than as a dispute among citizens about the meaning of 'family.' " Robert Burt, *The Constitution of the Family*, 1979 SUP. CT. REV. 329. Professor Lupu comments that "the distinction that led to a 'fundamental liberty interest' in *Moore* alone lay in the method for pursuing that goal — Inez Moore chose one long sanctioned by legal institutions, while Bruce Boraas and his friends did not." Ira Lupu, *Untangling the Strands of the Fourteenth Amendment*, 77 MICH. L. REV. 981, 1052 (1979). If this is correct, the constitutional "protected family" is limited to what could be characterized as "traditional" associations. In light of Professor Tribe's analysis of the ethical value underlying *Moore*, how do you think he would view the asserted distinction between *Moore* and *Borass*?

4. *Troxel v. Granville,* 530 U.S. 57 (2000). A Washington State statute provided that any person may petition the court for visitation rights at any time and that the court may order visitation rights for any person when visitation may serve the best interest of the child. Grandparents had sought to use the statute to gain visitation rights to their granddaughters, even though the mother wanted less visitation than the grandparents sought. The Superior Court granted the grandparents' request, because it would be in the best interests of the children. The Washington Supreme Court held the statute facially unconstitutional. The Supreme Court affirmed 6-3 but there was no majority opinion.

In a plurality opinion, Justice O'Connor, joined by Chief Justice Rehnquist and Justices Ginsberg and Breyer, found that this "breathtakingly broad" statute, "as applied, exceeded the bounds of the Due Process Clause," by unduly interfering with the constitutionally protected right of a parent to raise his or her child. She found this conclusion to flow from prior precedent, which had "recognized the fundamental right of parents to make decisions concerning the care, custody, and control of their children."

Justice O'Connor refused, however, to definitively preclude state interference under all circumstances: "The problem here is not that the Washington Superior Court intervened, but that when it did so, it gave no special weight at all to [the mother's] determination of her daughters' best interests." In so doing, that court had "directly contravened the traditional presumption that a fit parent will act in the best interest of his or her child." The plurality further noted "that there is no allegation that [the mother] ever sought to cut off visitation entirely." Finally, Justice O'Connor pointed out that, "[s]ignificantly, many other States expressly provide by statute that courts may not award visitation unless a parent has denied (or unreasonably denied) visitation to the concerned third party." The plurality therefore concluded: "Considered together with the Superior Court's reasons for awarding visitation to the [grandparents], the combination of these factors demonstrates that the visitation order in this case was an unconstitutional infringement on [the mother's] fundamental right to make decisions concerning the care, custody, and control of her two daughters."

Justice Thomas, concurring in the judgment, agreed with the plurality that the Court's recognition "of a fundamental right of parents to direct the upbring of their children resolves this case" but would apply strict scrutiny "to infringements of fundamental rights" in affirming the judgment below. Justice Souter, concurring in the judgment, would have accepted the Washington Supreme Court's holding that the statute was facially overbroad and unconstitutional.

In dissent, Justice Scalia reasoned: "[W]hile I would think it entirely compatible with the commitment to representative democracy set forth in the founding documents to argue, in legislative chambers or in electoral campaigns, that the state has *no power* to interfere with parents' authority over the rearing of their children, I do not believe that the power which the Constitution confers upon me *as a judge* entitles me to deny legal effect to laws that (in my view) infringe upon what is (in my view) that unenumerated right."

According to one commentator, "the line the Court is attempting to walk between the preservation of parental rights and the recognition of nonparental claims is untenable." Emily Buss, *Adrift in the Middle: Parental Rights After* Troxel v. Granville, 2000 SUP. CT. REV. 279. "The central problem," Professor Buss argues, "is not that it affords parents too much protection, as some have argued, or that it affords parents too little protection, as others have argued, but that it tries to have it both ways." *Id.* at 279–80.

5. ***A pragmatic approach to family privacy.*** One scholar has argued that "there is an important and unfortunate disjunction between what the Court says about family privacy rights and how it actually goes about protecting those right in real cases." David Meyer, *The Paradox of Family Privacy*, 53 VAND. L. REV. 527, 529 (2000). Professor Meyer suggests that "[a]t one time or another, the Court has denominated each of the individual rights comprising family privacy as 'fundamental', suggesting that any significant governmental intrusions upon them should be subject to the narrowest possible limits. Yet the Court's actual behavior in specific cases has left a large wake of uncertainty and confusion." *Id.* at 528–29. The Court, he contends, has

taken a "meandering course" in which it has been "pragmatic, tacitly adjusting its scrutiny in light of the magnitude of the state's intrusion and the strength of the state's regulatory interests." *Id.* at 529.

6. *The right to marry.* While *Loving v. Virginia*, p. 661, recognized a right to marry as part of due process liberty, that case also was based on the equal protection guarantee's prohibition against invidious racial discrimination. An articulated, unequivocal "fundamental right to marry" was accepted in *Zablocki v. Redhail*, p. 902. There the Court held that a Wisconsin statute requiring persons obligated to pay child support payments to obtain court permission before they could marry, violated equal protection. The purported purpose of the statute was to prevent children from becoming public charges, but the effect of the statute was to severely burden certain persons, or even deny them the right to marry. Citing *Loving* and the family rights cases, the Court concluded that "it would make little sense to recognize a right of privacy with respect to other matters of family life and not with respect to entering the relationship that is the foundation of the family in our society." While Justice Marshall invalidated the statute under the rubric of equal protection, he relied on "the statute's broad infringement on the right to marry."

See Justice Stewart's concurring opinion in *Zablocki*, based on his conclusion that the statute is

> so alien to our traditions and so offensive to our shared notions of fairness [that it] offends the Due Process Clause of the Fourteenth Amendment. Today equal protection doctrine has become the Court's chief instrument for invalidating state laws. Yet, in a case like this one, the doctrine is no more than substantive due process by another name.

The Court considered the right to marry in the context of prisoners in *Turner v. Safley*, 482 U.S. 78 (1987), and held that prisoners had a right to marry under *Zablocki* that was violated by a prison regulation requiring permission of the warden, which would be given only under compelling circumstances. The regulation applied to prevent marriage between two prisoners in the absence of such "compelling" reasons as pregnancy. Prison officials attempted to justify it as an attempt to prevent jealousies within the prison population and on general security grounds. The Court, per Justice O'Connor, held that the regulation did not bear a "reasonable relation" to the proper security concerns of prison officials and therefore was invalid on its face. With regard to jealousies, the Court pointed out that those could exist with or without regard to formal marriage. With regard to general security concerns, the Court found that prison officials had over-reacted to a perceived problem. What are the implications of these decisions if any, for a right to same-sex marriage?

7. *Non-traditional relationships.* The above notes suggest that the parameters of "marriage" and "family" as protected constitutional values are still uncertain and evolving. What considerations should guide future decisions involving alternate lifestyles resembling the traditional associations? If private adult homosexuality is decriminalized, does that imply a right of homosexuals to marry? Consider the following perspective:

> There is, moreover, a difference between decriminalizing private, consensual conduct between homosexuals and affirmatively blessing such relationships through marriage. The former step signifies a removal of hostility and an expression of social tolerance that stops short of approval. The latter requires the state to give elevated and hallowed status to an alternative sexual lifestyle fundamentally at odds with the moral precepts of most Americans. Thus, even if private homosexual conduct were decriminalized as a matter of constitutional right, a freedom to marry would not follow.

Wilkinson & White, 62 CORNELL L. REV. at 572. Is cohabitation a constitutionally protected relationship?

MICHAEL H. & VICTORIA D. v. GERALD D.

491 U.S. 110, 109 S. Ct. 2333, 105 L. Ed. 2d 91 (1989)

JUSTICE SCALIA announced the judgment of the Court and delivered an opinion, in which THE CHIEF JUSTICE joins, and in all but note 6 of which JUSTICES O'CONNOR and KENNEDY join.

[Michael H. (described as "a neighbor") had "an adulterous affair" with Carole D. (described as "an international model") while she was married to Gerald D. (described as "a top executive in a French oil company"). Victoria D. was born to Carole and blood tests showed that there was a 98.07% probability that Michael was the father of Victoria. During Victoria's first three years, she resided always with her mother, who at times lived with Michael. On these occasions, Michael established a relationship with the child and held her out as his daughter. Carole finally reconciled with Gerald and she and Victoria have been living with him since 1984.

[Michael filed suit to establish his paternity and a right to visitation. Victoria, through her guardian ad litem, filed a cross-complaint asserting that she was entitled to maintain her filial relationship with both Michael and Gerald. Gerald intervened in the action and ultimately moved for summary judgment asserting that under § 621 of the California Evidence Code, which provides that a child born to a married woman living with her husband, who is neither impotent nor sterile, is presumed to be a child of the marriage. That presumption may only be rebutted by the husband or wife, and then only in limited circumstances. There were no triable issues of fact as to Victoria's paternity. The California Superior Court granted Gerald's motion for summary judgment, concluding that the evidence presented sufficed to demonstrate that Gerald and Carole were cohabitating at conception and birth and that Gerald was neither sterile nor impotent. The Court also denied visitation rights to Michael because it would impugn the integrity of the family unit.

[On appeal, Michael claimed that the Superior Court's application of § 621 violated his procedural and substantive due process rights. Victoria claimed that due process and equal protection rights were violated because only the father or mother but not the child could rebut the presumption. The California Court of Appeals affirmed the grant of summary judgment, upheld the statute and denied visitation rights. The California Supreme Court denied discretionary review. The United States Supreme Court affirmed the judgment.]

We address first the claims of Michael. At the outset, it is necessary to clarify what he sought and what he was denied. California law, like nature itself, makes no provision for dual fatherhood. Michael was seeking to be declared the father of Victoria. The immediate benefit he evidently sought to obtain from that status was visitation rights. But if Michael were successful in being declared the father, other rights would follow — most importantly, the right to be considered as the parent who should have custody. All parental rights, including visitation, were automatically denied by denying Michael status as the father.

Michael raises two related challenges to the constitutionality of § 621. First, he asserts that requirements of procedural due process prevent the State from terminating his liberty interest in his relationship with his child without affording him an opportunity to demonstrate his paternity in an evidentiary hearing. We believe this claim derives from a fundamental misconception of the nature of the California statute. While § 621 is phrased in terms of a presumption, that rule of evidence is the implementation of a substantive rule of law. California declares it to be, except in limited circumstances, irrelevant for paternity purposes whether a child conceived during and born into an existing marriage was begotten by someone other than the husband and had a prior relationship with him. Of course the conclusive presumption not only expresses the State's substantive policy but also furthers it, excluding inquiries into the child's paternity that would be destructive of family integrity and privacy.

This Court has struck down as illegitimate certain "irrebuttable presumptions." *See, e. g., Stanley v. Illinois*, 405 U.S. 645 (1972); *Vlandis v. Kline*, 412 U.S. 441 (1973); *Cleveland Board of Education v. LaFleur*, 414 U.S. 632 (1974). Those holdings did not, however, rest upon procedural due process. A conclusive presumption does, of course, foreclose the person against whom it is invoked from demonstrating, in a particularized proceeding, that applying the presumption to him will in fact not further the lawful governmental policy the presumption is designed to effectuate. But the same can be said of any legal rule that establishes general classifications, whether framed in terms of a presumption or not. [O]ur "irrebuttable presumption" cases must ultimately be analyzed as calling into question not the adequacy of procedures but — like our cases involving classifications framed in other terms [citing equal protection cases] — the adequacy of the "fit" between the classification and the policy that the classification serves. We therefore reject Michael's procedural due process challenge and proceed to his substantive claim.

Michael contends as a matter of substantive due process that because he has established a parental relationship with Victoria, protection of Gerald's and Carole's marital union is an insufficient state interest to support termination of that relationship. This argument is, of course, predicated on the assertion that Michael has a constitutionally protected liberty interest in his relationship with Victoria.

It is an established part of our constitutional jurisprudence that the term "liberty" in the Due Process Clause extends beyond freedom from physical restraint. *See, e.g., Pierce v. Society of Sisters; Meyer v. Nebraska*. In an attempt to limit and guide interpretation of the Clause, we have insisted not merely that the interest denominated as a "liberty" be "fundamental" (a concept that, in isolation, is hard to objectify), but also that it be an interest traditionally protected by our society.

This insistence that the asserted liberty interest be rooted in history and tradition is evident, as elsewhere, in our cases according constitutional protection to certain parental rights. Michael reads the landmark case of *Stanley v. Illinois* and [its progeny] as establishing that a liberty interest is created by biological fatherhood plus an established parental relationship — factors that exist in the present case as well. We think that distorts the rationale of those cases. As we view them, they rest not upon such isolated factors but upon the historic respect — indeed, sanctity would not be too strong a term — traditionally accorded to the relationships that develop within the unitary family.[3] In *Stanley*, for example, we forbade the destruction of such a family when, upon the death of the mother, the state had sought to remove children from the custody of a father who had lived with and supported them and their mother for 18 years.

Thus, the legal issue in the present case reduces to whether the relationship between persons in the situation of Michael and Victoria has been treated as a protected family unit under the historic practices of our society, or whether on any other basis it has been accorded special protection. We think it impossible to find that it has. In fact, quite to the contrary, our traditions have protected the marital family (Gerald, Carole, and the child they acknowledge to be theirs) against the sort of claim Michael asserts.

We have found nothing in the older sources, nor in the older cases, addressing specifically the power of the natural father to assert parental rights over a child born into a woman's existing marriage with another man. What Michael asserts here is a right to have himself declared the natural father and thereby to obtain parental prerogatives. What he must establish, therefore, is not that our society has traditionally allowed a natural father in his circumstances to establish paternity, but that it has traditionally accorded such a father parental rights, or at least has not traditionally denied them. What counts is whether the States in fact award substantive parental rights to the natural father of a child conceived within and born into an extant marital union that wishes to embrace the child. We are not aware of a single case, old or new, that has done so. This is not the stuff of which fundamental rights qualifying as liberty interests are made.[6]

---

[3] JUSTICE BRENNAN asserts that only "a pinched conception of 'the family'" would exclude Michael, Carole and Victoria from protection. We disagree. The family unit accorded traditional respect in our society, which we have referred to as the "unitary family," is typified, of course, by the marital family, but also includes the household of unmarried parents and their children. Perhaps the concept can be expanded even beyond this, but it will bear no resemblance to traditionally respected relationships — and will thus cease to have any constitutional significance — if it is stretched so far as to include the relationship established between a married woman, her lover and their child, during a three-month sojourn in St. Thomas, or during a subsequent 8-month period when, if he happened to be in Los Angeles, he stayed with her and the child.

[6] JUSTICE BRENNAN criticizes our methodology in using historical traditions specifically relating to the rights of an adulterous natural father, rather than inquiring more generally "whether parenthood is an interest that historically has received our attention and protection."

We do not understand why, having rejected our focus upon the societal tradition regarding the natural father's rights *vis-a-vis* a child whose mother is married to another man, JUSTICE

In *Lehr v. Robertson*, a case involving a natural father's attempt to block his child's adoption by the unwed mother's new husband, we observed that "[t]he significance of the biological connection is that it offers the natural father an opportunity that no other male possesses to develop a relationship with his offspring," and we assumed that the Constitution might require some protection of that opportunity. Where, however, the child is born into an extant marital family, the natural father's unique opportunity conflicts with the similarly unique opportunity of the husband of the marriage; and it is not unconstitutional for the State to give categorical preference to the latter. It is a question of legislative policy and not constitutional law whether California will allow the presumed parenthood of a couple desiring to retain a child conceived within and born into their marriage to be rebutted.

We do not accept JUSTICE BRENNAN's criticism that this result "squashes" the liberty that consists of "the freedom not to conform." It seems to us that reflects the erroneous view that there is only one side to this controversy — that one disposition can expand a "liberty" of sorts without contracting an equivalent "liberty" on the other side. Such a happy choice is rarely available. Here, to provide protection to an adulterous natural father is to deny protection to a marital father, and vice versa. If Michael has a "freedom not to conform" (whatever that means), Gerald must equivalently have a "freedom to conform." One of them will pay a price for asserting that "freedom" — Michael by being unable to act as father of the child he has adulterously begotten, or Gerald by being unable to preserve the integrity of the traditional

---

BRENNAN would choose to focus instead upon "parenthood." Why should the relevant category not be even more general — perhaps "family relationships"; or "personal relationships"; or even "emotional attachments in general"? Though the dissent has no basis for the level of generality it would select, we do: We refer to the most specific level at which a relevant tradition protecting, or denying protection to, the asserted right can be identified. If, for example, there were no societal tradition, either way, regarding the rights of the natural father of a child adulterously conceived, we would have to consult, and (if possible) reason from, the traditions regarding natural fathers in general. But there is such a more specific tradition, and it unqualifiedly denies protection to such a parent.

One would think that JUSTICE BRENNAN would appreciate the value of consulting the most specific tradition available, since he acknowledges that "[e]ven if we can agree . . . that 'family' and 'parenthood' are part of the good life, it is absurd to assume that we can agree on the contents of those terms and destructive to pretend that we do." Because such general traditions provide such imprecise guidance, they permit judges to dictate rather than discern the society's views. The need, if arbitrary decision-making is to be avoided, to adopt the most specific tradition as the point of reference — or at least to announce, as JUSTICE BRENNAN declines to do, some other criterion for selecting among the innumerable relevant traditions that could be consulted — is well enough exemplified by the fact that in the present case JUSTICE BRENNAN's opinion and JUSTICE O'CONNOR's opinion, which disapproves this footnote, both appeal to tradition, but on the basis of the tradition they select reach opposite results. Although assuredly having the virtue (if it be that) of leaving judges free to decide as they think best when the unanticipated occurs, a rule of law that binds neither by text nor by any particular, identifiable tradition, is no rule of law at all.

Finally, we may note that this analysis is not inconsistent with the result in cases such as *Griswold v. Connecticut*, or *Eisenstadt v. Baird*. None of those cases acknowledged a longstanding and still extant societal tradition withholding the very right pronounced to be the subject of a liberty interest and then rejected it. JUSTICE BRENNAN must do so here. In this case, the existence of such a tradition, continuing to the present day, refutes any possible contention that the alleged right is "so rooted in the traditions and conscience of our people as to be ranked as fundamental," *Snyder v. Massachusetts*, or "implicit in the concept of ordered liberty," *Palko v. Connecticut*.

family unit he and Victoria have established. Our disposition does not choose between these two "freedoms," but leaves that to the people of California. JUSTICE BRENNAN's approach chooses one of them as the constitutional imperative, on no apparent basis except that the unconventional is to be preferred.

We have never had occasion to decide whether a child has a liberty interest, symmetrical with that of her parent, in maintaining her filial relationship. We need not do so here because, even assuming that such a right exists, Victoria's claim must fail. Victoria's due process challenge is, if anything, weaker than Michael's. Her basic claim is not that California has erred in preventing her from establishing that Michael, not Gerald, should stand as her legal father. Rather, she claims a due process right to maintain filial relationships with both Michael and Gerald. This assertion merits little discussion, for, whatever the merits of the guardian ad litem's belief that such an arrangement can be of great psychological benefit to a child, the claim that a State must recognize multiple fatherhood has no support in the history or traditions of this country. Moreover, even if we were to construe Victoria's argument as forwarding the lesser proposition that, whatever her status *vis-a-vis* Gerald, she has a liberty interest in maintaining a filial relationship with her natural father, Michael, we find that, at best, her claim is the obverse of Michael's and fails for the same reasons.

Victoria claims in addition that her equal protection rights have been violated because, unlike her mother and presumed father, she had no opportunity to rebut the presumption of her legitimacy. We find this argument wholly without merit. When the husband or wife contests the legitimacy of their child, the stability of the marriage has already been shaken. In contrast, allowing a claim of illegitimacy to be pressed by the child — or, more accurately, by a court-appointed guardian ad litem — may well disrupt an otherwise peaceful union. Since it pursues a legitimate end by rational means, California's decision to treat Victoria differently from her parents is not a denial of equal protection.

JUSTICE O'CONNOR, with whom JUSTICE KENNEDY joins, concurring in part.

I concur in all but footnote 6 of JUSTICE SCALIA's opinion. This footnote sketches a mode of historical analysis to be used when identifying liberty interests protected by the Due Process Clause of the Fourteenth Amendment that may be somewhat inconsistent with our past decisions in this area. On occasion the Court has characterized relevant traditions protecting asserted rights at levels of generality that might not be "the most specific level" available. I would not foreclose the unanticipated by the prior imposition of a single mode of historical analysis.

JUSTICE STEVENS, concurring in the judgment.

As I understand this case, it raises two different questions about the validity of California's statutory scheme. First, is Cal. Evid. Code Ann. § 621 (West Supp. 1989) unconstitutional because it prevents Michael and Victoria from obtaining a judicial determination that he is her biological father — even if no legal rights would be affected by that determination? Second, does the California statute deny appellants a fair opportunity to prove that Victoria's best interests would be served by granting Michael visitation rights?

On the first issue I agree with JUSTICE SCALIA that the Federal Constitution imposes no obligation upon a State to "declare facts unless some legal consequence hinges upon the requested declaration."

On the second issue I do not agree with JUSTICE SCALIA's analysis. He seems to reject the possibility that a natural father might ever have a constitutionally protected interest in his relationship with a child whose mother was married to and cohabiting with another man at the time of the child's conception and birth. I think cases like *Stanley v. Illinois* and *Caban v. Mohammed* demonstrate that enduring "family" relationships may develop in unconventional settings. I therefore would not foreclose the possibility that a constitutionally protected relationship between a natural father and his child might exist in a case like this. Indeed, I am willing to assume for the purpose of deciding this case that Michael's relationship with Victoria is strong enough to give him a constitutional right to try to convince a trial judge that Victoria's best interest would be served by granting him visitation rights. I am satisfied, however, that the California statute, as applied in this case, gave him that opportunity.

Under the circumstances of the case before us, Michael was given a fair opportunity to show that he is Victoria's natural father, that he had developed a relationship with her, and that her interests would be served by granting him visitation rights. On the other hand, the record also shows that after its rather shaky start, the marriage between Carole and Gerald developed a stability that now provides Victoria with a loving and harmonious family home. In the circumstances of this case, I find nothing fundamentally unfair about the exercise of a judge's discretion that, in the end, allows the mother to decide whether her child's best interest would be served by allowing the natural father visitation privileges. Because I am convinced that the trial judge had the authority under state law both to hear Michael's plea for visitation rights and to grant him such rights if Victoria's best interests so warranted, I am satisfied that the California statutory scheme is consistent with the Due Process Clause of the Fourteenth Amendment.

JUSTICE BRENNAN, with whom JUSTICES MARSHALL and BLACKMUN join, dissenting.

In a case that has yielded so many opinions as has this one, it is fruitful to begin by emphasizing the common ground shared by a majority of this Court. Five Members of the Court refuse to foreclose "the possibility that a natural father might ever have a constitutionally protected interest in his relationship with a child whose mother was married to and cohabiting with another man at the time of the child's conception and birth." (STEVENS, J., concurring in judgment). Five Justices agree that the flaw inhering in a conclusive presumption that terminates a constitutionally protected interest without any hearing whatsoever is a procedural one. (WHITE, J., dissenting); (STEVENS, J., concurring in judgment). Four Members of the Court agree that Michael H. has a liberty interest in his relationship with Victoria (WHITE, J., dissenting), and one assumes for purposes of this case that he does (STEVENS, J., concurring in judgment).

In contrast, only two Members of the Court fully endorse JUSTICE SCALIA's view of the proper method of analyzing questions arising under the Due

Process Clause. (O'CONNOR, J., concurring in part). Nevertheless, because the plurality opinion's exclusively historical analysis portends a significant and unfortunate departure from our prior cases and from sound constitutional decision-making, I devote a substantial portion of my discussion to it.

Once we recognized that the "liberty" protected by the Due Process Clause of the Fourteenth Amendment encompasses more than freedom from bodily restraint, today's plurality opinion emphasizes, the concept was cut loose from one natural limitation on its meaning. This innovation paved the way, so the plurality hints, for judges to substitute their own preferences for those of elected officials. Dissatisfied with this supposedly unbridled and uncertain state of affairs, the plurality casts about for another limitation on the concept of liberty.

It finds this limitation in "tradition." Apparently oblivious to the fact that this concept can be as malleable and as elusive as "liberty" itself, the plurality pretends that tradition places a discernible border around the Constitution. The pretense is seductive; it would be comforting to believe that a search for "tradition" involves nothing more idiosyncratic or complicated than poring through dusty volumes on American history. Because reasonable people can disagree about the content of particular traditions, and because they can disagree even about which traditions are relevant to the definition of "liberty," the plurality has not found the objective boundary that it seeks.

Even if we could agree, moreover, on the content and significance of particular traditions, we still would be forced to identify the point at which a tradition becomes firm enough to be relevant to our definition of liberty and the moment at which it becomes too obsolete to be relevant any longer. The plurality supplies no objective means by which we might make these determinations. Indeed, as soon as the plurality sees signs that the tradition upon which it bases its decision (the laws denying putative fathers like Michael standing to assert paternity) is crumbling, it shifts ground and says that the case has nothing to do with that tradition, after all. "What is at issue here," the plurality asserts after canvassing the law on paternity suits, "is not entitlement to a state pronouncement that Victoria was begotten by Michael." But that is precisely what is at issue here, and the plurality's last-minute denial of this fact dramatically illustrates the subjectivity of its own analysis.

It is not that tradition has been irrelevant to our prior decisions. Throughout our decisionmaking in this important area runs the theme that certain interests and practices — freedom from physical restraint, marriage, child-bearing, childrearing, and others — form the core of our definition of "liberty." Our solicitude for these interests is partly the result of the fact that the Due Process Clause would seem an empty promise if it did not protect them, and partly the result of the historical and traditional importance of these interests in our society. In deciding cases arising under the Due Process Clause, therefore, we have considered whether the concrete limitation under consideration impermissibly impinges upon one of these more generalized interests.

Today's plurality, however, does not ask whether parenthood is an interest that historically has received our attention and protection; the answer to that question is too clear for dispute. Instead, the plurality asks whether the specific variety of parenthood under consideration — a natural father's relationship with a child whose mother is married to another man — has enjoyed such protection.

If we had looked to tradition with such specificity in past cases, many a decision would have reached a different result. Surely the use of contraceptives by unmarried couples, or even by married couples; the freedom from corporal punishment in schools; the freedom from an arbitrary transfer from a prison to a psychiatric institution; and even the right to raise one's natural but illegitimate children, were not "interest[s] traditionally protected by our society," at the time of their consideration by this Court. If we had asked, therefore, in *Eisenstadt, Griswold, Ingraham, Vitek,* or *Stanley* itself whether the specific interest under consideration had been traditionally protected, the answer would have been a resounding "no." That we did not ask this question in those cases highlights the novelty of the interpretive method that the plurality opinion employs today.

The plurality's interpretive method is more than novel; it is misguided. It ignores the good reasons for limiting the role of "tradition" in interpreting the Constitution's deliberately capacious language. In the plurality's constitutional universe, we may not take notice of the fact that the original reasons for the conclusive presumption of paternity are out of place in a world in which blood tests can prove virtually beyond a shadow of a doubt who sired a particular child and in which the fact of illegitimacy no longer plays the burdensome and stigmatizing role it once did. Nor, in the plurality's world, may we deny "tradition" its full scope by pointing out that the rationale for the conventional rule has changed over the years, as has the rationale for Cal. Evid. Code Ann. § 621; instead, our task is simply to identify a rule denying the asserted interest and not to ask whether the basis for that rule — which is the true reflection of the values undergirding it — has changed too often or too recently to call the rule embodying that rationale a "tradition." Moreover, by describing the decisive question as whether Michael and Victoria's interest is one that has been "traditionally protected by our society," rather than one that society traditionally has thought important (with or without protecting it), and by suggesting that our sole function is to "discern the society's views," the plurality acts as if the only purpose of the Due Process Clause is to confirm the importance of interests already protected by a majority of the States. Transforming the protection afforded by the Due Process Clause into a redundancy mocks those who, with care and purpose, wrote the Fourteenth Amendment.

In construing the Fourteenth Amendment to offer shelter only to those interests specifically protected by historical practice, moreover, the plurality ignores the kind of society in which our Constitution exists. We are not an assimilative, homogeneous society, but a facilitative, pluralistic one, in which we must be willing to abide someone else's unfamiliar or even repellant practice because the same tolerant impulse protects our own idiosyncracies. Even if we can agree, therefore, that "family" and "parenthood" are part of the good life, it is absurd to assume that we can agree on the content of those terms and destructive to pretend that we do. In a community such as ours, "liberty" must include the freedom not to conform. The plurality today squashes this freedom by requiring specific approval from history before protecting anything in the name of liberty.

The document that the plurality construes today is unfamiliar to me. It is not the living charter that I have taken to be our Constitution; it is instead a stagnant, archaic, hidebound document steeped in the prejudices and superstitions of a time long past. This Constitution does not recognize that times change, does not see that sometimes a practice or rule outlives its foundations. I cannot accept an interpretive method that does such violence to the charter that I am bound by oath to uphold.

The plurality's exclusive rather than inclusive definition of the "unitary family" is out of step with other decisions as well. This pinched conception of "the family," crucial as it is in rejecting Michael and Victoria's claim of a liberty interest, is jarring in light of our many cases preventing the States from denying important interests or statuses to those whose situations do not fit the government's narrow view of the family. From *Loving v. Virginia* to *Levy v. Louisiana*, and from *Gomez v. Perez,* to *Moore v. East Cleveland,* we have declined to respect a State's notion, as manifested in its allocation of privileges and burdens, of what the family should be. Today's rhapsody on the "unitary family" is out of tune with such decisions.

JUSTICE WHITE, with whom JUSTICE BRENNAN joins, dissenting.

California law, as the plurality describes it, tells us that, except in limited circumstances, California declares it to be "irrelevant for paternity purposes whether a child conceived during and born into a lawful marriage was begotten by someone other than the husband." This I do not accept, for the fact that Michael H. is the biological father of Victoria is to me highly relevant to whether he has rights, as a father or otherwise, with respect to the child. Because I believe that Michael H. has a liberty interest that cannot be denied without due process of the law, I must dissent.

Prior cases here have recognized the liberty interest of a father in his relationship with his child. In none of these cases did we indicate that the fathers' rights were dependent on the marital status of the mother or biological father. The basic principle enunciated in the Court's unwed father cases is that an unwed father who has demonstrated a sufficient commitment to his paternity by way of personal, financial, or custodial responsibilities has a protected liberty interest in a relationship with his child.

The interest in protecting a child from the social stigma of illegitimacy lacks any real connection to the facts of a case where a father is seeking to establish, rather than repudiate, paternity. The "stigma of illegitimacy" argument harks back to ancient common law when there were no blood tests to ascertain that the husband could not "by the laws of nature" be the child's father. I see no reason to debate the plurality's multilingual explorations into "spousal nonaccess" and ancient policy concerns behind bastardy laws.

The State's professed interest in the preservation of the existing marital unit is a more significant concern. To be sure, the intrusion of an outsider asserting that he is the father of a child whom the husband believes to be his own would be disruptive to say the least. On the facts of this case, however, Gerald was well aware of the liaison between Carole and Michael. The conclusive presumption of evidentiary rule § 621 virtually eliminates the putative father's chances of succeeding in his effort to establish paternity, but it by no means prevents him from asserting the claim. It may serve as a deterrent to such claims but does not eliminate the threat. Further, the argument that the conclusive presumption preserved the sanctity of the marital unit had more sway in a time when the husband was similarly prevented from challenging paternity.

NOTES

1. *Which tradition?* The critical difference in the approaches of Justice Scalia and Brennan lies in the breadth of their definitions of tradition to which a court can look for guidance in articulating the fundamental principles implicit in due process. Justice Scalia argues that the search should take place at "the most specific level at which a relevant tradition protecting, or denying protection for the asserted right can be identified."

> The selection of a level of generality necessarily involves value choices. Justice Scalia suggested that he had discovered a value-neutral method of selecting the appropriate level of generality. We conclude that Justice Scalia's proposal is inadequate. Far from providing judges with a value-neutral means for characterizing rights, it provides instead a method for disguising the importation of values.

Laurence Tribe & Michael Dorf, *Levels of Generality in the Definition of Rights,* 57 U. Chi. L. Rev. 1057, 1058–59 (1990).

Justice Brennan makes a similar criticism of footnote 6. Justice O'Connor does not want to "foreclose the unanticipated." The problem is whether those who differ with footnote 6 have articulated an acceptable method for controlling the discretion of the judges in formulating rights.

If one accepted Justice Scalia's concerns, would one also logically reject recognition of any form of constitutional protection based solely on considerations of tradition? As long as the tradition has not been formally embodied in constitutional text, why shouldn't society be able to alter it through normal majoritarian political processes?

2. *Individualism and family law.* According to one commentator, "*Michael H.* departs from individualism in family law, proclaiming that a third party intervening in a marriage via an extramarital affair with one of the marriage partners is afforded no guarantees whatsoever of what he or she may leave behind in that still intact family, even though sadly to the point of flesh and blood. In an era when marital infidelity is somewhat common, if not fashionable, this ought to be eye opening, dramatically rearranging the rights of individuals in subordination to the Original Design." Lynne Marie Kohm, *Marriage and the Intact Family: The Significance of Michael H. v. Gerald D.*, 22 Whittier L. Rev. 327, 375 (2000). Does this assessment overstate what was going on in *Michael H.*? If it is, in fact, accurate, what, if anything, does that say about the Court's view of its role in the development of unenumerated rights?

3. Note that while Justice Scalia is philosophically opposed to the judiciary's ascertainment of unenumerated constitutional rights, in *Michael H.,* He accepts at least a narrow form of such an approach. Is his opinion inconsistent with the view expressed in his opinion in *Casey*, p. 556? On the issue of Justice Scalia's constitutional philosophy, see Erwin Chemerinsky, *The Jurisprudence of Justice Scalia: A Critical Appraisal*, 22 U. HAW. L. REV. 385 (2000); J. Richard Broughton, *The Jurisprudence of Tradition and Justice Scalia's Unwritten Constitution*, 103 W. VA. L. REV. 19 (2000).

4. *The outer reaches of the historical approach*. Compare the two means of implementing substantive due process: Natural rights and historical tradition. Which is likely to be more expansive? For example, consider the issue of same sex marriage: Which of the two approaches is more likely to extend constitutional protection to this behavior? For the argument that "the U.S. Supreme Court's use of history in defining fundamental rights under substantive due process is sufficiently flexible to accommodate same-sex marriages within the fundamental right to marriage," see Veronica C. Abreu, Note, *The Malleable Use of History in Substantive Due Process Jurisprudence: How the "Deeply Rooted" Test Should Not Be a Barrier to Finding the Defense of Marriage Act Unconstitutional Under the Fifth Amendment's Due Process Clause*, 44 B.C.L. REV. 177, 179 (2002).

[C] HOMOSEXUALITY AND LIBERTY

***Bowers v. Hardwick*, 478 U.S. 186, 106 S. Ct. 2841, 92 L. Ed. 2d 140 (1986).** Respondent was charged with violating Georgia's statute criminalizing sodomy by committing the act with another male in the bedroom of respondent's home. After the District Attorney decided, tentatively, not to bring the case to the grand jury, respondent sued in federal district court, challenging the constitutionality of the statute, to the extent it criminalized consensual sodomy. The Court of Appeals, relying on cases such as *Griswold v. Connecticut*, held the statute unconstitutional. The Supreme Court, in an opinion by Justice White, reversed: "[W]e think it evident that none of the rights announced in those cases bears any resemblance to the claimed constitutional right of homosexuals to engage in acts of sodomy that is asserted in this case. No connection between family, marriage, or procreation on the one hand and homosexual activity on the other has been demonstrated." Justice White acknowledged that despite the language of the Due Process Clause of the Fifth and Fourteenth Amendments, which does not provide substantive protection, "the cases are legion in which those Clauses have been interpreted to have substantive content." However, "[s]triving to assure itself and the public that announcing rights not readily identifiable in the Constitution's text involves much more than the imposition of the Justices' own choice of values on the States and Federal Government, the Court has sought to identify the nature of the rights qualifying for heightened judicial protection." Included are "fundamental liberties that are 'implicit in the concept of ordered liberty,' such that 'neither liberty nor justice would exist if [they] were sacrificed' [citing *Palko v. Connecticut*]." Also included are those liberties that are "deeply rooted in the Nation's history." The Court found that "neither of these formulations would extend a fundamental right to homosexuals to engage in acts of consensual sodomy. Proscription against that conduct have ancient roots. Sodomy was a criminal offense at common law and was forbidden by the laws of the original thirteen states when they ratified the Bill of Rights, and "until

1961, all 50 states outlawed sodomy and today, 24 states and the District of Columbia continue to provide criminal penalties for sodomy performed in private and between consenting adults." Thus, "to claim that a right to engage in such conduct is 'deeply rooted in this Nation's history or tradition' or 'implicit in the concept of ordered liberty' is, at best, facetious." Because "[t]he Court is most vulnerable and comes nearest to illegitimacy when it deals with judge-made constitutional law having little or no cognizable roots in the language or design of the Constitution," the Court believed that there should be "great resistence to expand the substantive reach" of the Due Process Clauses.

Justice Blackmun, speaking for four Justices, dissented, arguing that the case was not about "a fundamental right to engage in homosexual sodomy," as the majority had asserted. Rather, it was about a fundamental "right to be let alone." The challenged statute "denies individuals the right to decide for themselves whether to engage in particular forms of private, consensual sexual activity." He added that "the Court's almost obsessive focus on homosexual activity is particularly hard to justify in light of the broad language Georgia has used. . . The sex or status of the persons who engage in the act is irrelevant as a matter of state law."

Justice Stevens also dissented: "Like the statute that is challenged in this case, the rationale of the Court's opinion applies equally to the prohibited conduct regardless of whether the parties who engage in it are married or unmarried, or are of the same of different sexes." He reasoned that "[i]f the Georgia statute cannot be enforced as it is written—if the conduct it seeks to prohibit is a protected form of liberty for the vast majority of Georgia's citizens—the State must assume the burden of justifying a selective application of its law." Both the homosexuals and the heterosexuals "have the same interest in deciding how he will live his own life, and, more narrowly, how he will conduct himself in his personal and voluntary associations with his companions. State intrusions into the private conduct of either is equally burdensome."

LAWRENCE v. TEXAS

539 U.S. 558, 123 S. Ct. 2472, 156 L.Ed.2d 508 (2003)

JUSTICE KENNEDY delivered the opinion of the Court.

Liberty protects the person from unwarranted government intrusions into a dwelling or other private places. In our tradition the State is not omnipresent in the home. And there are other spheres of our lives and existence, outside the home, where the State should not be a dominant presence. Freedom extends beyond spatial bounds. Liberty presumes an autonomy of self that includes freedom of thought, belief, expression, and certain intimate conduct. The instant case involves liberty of the person both in its spatial and more transcendent dimensions.

I

The question before the Court is the validity of a Texas statute making it a crime for two persons of the same sex to engage in certain intimate sexual conduct.

In Houston, Texas, officers of the Harris County Police Department were dispatched to a private residence in response to a reported weapons disturbance. They entered an apartment where one of the petitioners, John Geddes Lawrence, resided. The right of the police to enter does not seem to have been questioned. The officers observed Lawrence and another man, Tyron Garner, engaging in a sexual act. The two petitioners were arrested, held in custody over night, and charged and convicted before a Justice of the Peace.

The complaints described their crime as "deviate sexual intercourse, namely anal sex, with a member of the same sex (man)." The applicable state law is Tex. Penal Code Ann. § 21.06(a) (2003). It provides: "A person commits an offense if he engages in deviate sexual intercourse with another individual of the same sex." The statute defines "[d]eviate sexual intercourse" as follows:

> "(A) any contact between any part of the genitals of one person and the mouth or anus of another person; or
>
> "(B) the penetration of the genitals or the anus of an-other person with an object." § 21.01(1).

The petitioners exercised their right to a trial *de novo* in Harris County Criminal Court. They challenged the statute as a violation of the Equal Protection Clause of the Fourteenth Amendment and of a like provision of the Texas Constitution. Those contentions were rejected. The petitioners, having entered a plea of *nolo contendere*, were each fined $200 and assessed court costs of $141.25.

The Court of Appeals for the Texas Fourteenth District considered the petitioners' federal constitutional arguments under both the Equal Protection and Due Process Clauses of the Fourteenth Amendment. After hearing the case en banc the court, in a divided opinion, rejected the constitutional arguments and affirmed the convictions. The majority opinion indicates that the Court of Appeals considered our decision in *Bowers* v. *Hardwick* to be controlling on the federal due process aspect of the case. *Bowers* then being authoritative, this was proper.

We granted certiorari to consider three questions:

> "1. Whether Petitioners' criminal convictions under the Texas "Homosexual Conduct" law — which criminalizes sexual intimacy by same-sex couples, but not identical behavior by different-sex couples — violate the Fourteenth Amendment guarantee of equal protection of laws?
>
> "2. Whether Petitioners' criminal convictions for adult consensual sexual intimacy in the home violate their vital interests in liberty and privacy protected by the Due Process Clause of the Fourteenth Amendment?
>
> "3. Whether *Bowers v. Hardwick*, should be overruled?"

The petitioners were adults at the time of the alleged offense. Their conduct was in private and consensual.

II

We conclude the case should be resolved by determining whether the petitioners were free as adults to engage in the private conduct in the exercise of their liberty under the Due Process Clause of the Fourteenth Amendment to the Constitution. For this inquiry we deem it necessary to reconsider the Court's holding in *Bowers*.

There are broad statements of the substantive reach of liberty under the Due Process Clause in earlier cases, including *Pierce v. Society of Sisters,* and *Meyer v. Nebraska*; but the most pertinent beginning point is our decision in *Griswold v. Connecticut* After *Griswold* it was established that the right to make certain decisions regarding sexual conduct extends beyond the marital relationship. In *Eisenstadt v. Baird,* the Court invalidated a law prohibiting the distribution of contraceptives to unmarried persons. The case was decided under the Equal Protection Clause; but with respect to unmarried persons, the Court went on to state the fundamental proposition that the law impaired the exercise of their personal rights. The opinions in *Griswold* and *Eisenstadt* were part of the background for the decision in *Roe v. Wade*. *Roe* recognized the right of a woman to make certain fundamental decisions affecting her destiny and confirmed once more that the protection of liberty under the Due Process Clause has a substantive dimension of fundamental significance in defining the rights of the person.

In *Carey v. Population Services Int'l*, the Court confronted a New York law forbidding sale or distribution of contraceptive devices to persons under 16 years of age. Although there was no single opinion for the Court, the law was invalidated. Both *Eisenstadt* and *Carey*, as well as the holding and rationale in *Roe*, confirmed that the reasoning of *Griswold* could not be confined to the protection of rights of married adults. This was the state of the law with respect to some of the most relevant cases when the Court considered *Bowers v. Hardwick*.

The facts in *Bowers* had some similarities to the instant case. One difference between the two cases is that the Georgia statute prohibited the conduct whether or not the participants were of the same sex, while the Texas statute, as we have seen, applies only to participants of the same sex.

The Court began its substantive discussion in *Bowers* as follows: "The issue presented is whether the Federal Constitution confers a fundamental right upon homosexuals to engage in sodomy and hence invalidates the laws of the many States that still make such conduct illegal and have done so for a very long time." That statement, we now conclude, discloses the Court's own failure to appreciate the extent of the liberty at stake. To say that the issue in *Bowers* was simply the right to engage in certain sexual conduct demeans the claim the individual put forward, just as it would demean a married couple were it to be said marriage is simply about the right to have sexual intercourse. The laws involved in *Bowers* and here are, to be sure, statutes that purport to do no more than prohibit a particular sexual act. Their penalties and purposes, though, have more far-reaching consequences, touching upon the most private human conduct, sexual behavior, and in the most private of places, the home. The statutes do seek to control a personal relationship that, whether or not entitled to formal recognition in the law, is within the liberty of persons to choose without being punished as criminals.

This, as a general rule, should counsel against attempts by the State, or a court, to define the meaning of the relationship or to set its boundaries absent injury to a person or abuse of an institution the law protects. It suffices for us to acknowledge that adults may choose to enter upon this relationship in the confines of their homes and their own private lives and still retain their dignity as free persons. When sexuality finds overt expression in intimate conduct with another person, the conduct can be but one element in a personal bond that is more enduring. The liberty protected by the Constitution allows homosexual persons the right to make this choice.

Having misapprehended the claim of liberty there presented to it, and thus stating the claim to be whether there is a fundamental right to engage in consensual sodomy, the *Bowers* Court said: "Proscriptions against that conduct have ancient roots." In academic writings, and in many of the scholarly *amicus* briefs filed to assist the Court in this case, there are fundamental criticisms of the historical premises relied upon by the majority and concurring opinions in *Bowers*. We need not enter this debate in the attempt to reach a definitive historical judgment, but the following considerations counsel against adopting the definitive conclusions upon which *Bowers* placed such reliance.

At the outset it should be noted that there is no long-standing history in this country of laws directed at homosexual conduct as a distinct matter.

[E]arly American sodomy laws were not directed at homosexuals as such but instead sought to prohibit non-procreative sexual activity more generally. This does not suggest approval of homosexual conduct. It does tend to show that this particular form of conduct was not thought of as a separate category from like conduct between heterosexual persons. Laws prohibiting sodomy do not seem to have been enforced against consenting adults acting in private. Instead of targeting relations between consenting adults in private, nineteenth-century sodomy prosecutions typically involved relations between men and minor girls or minor boys, relations between adults involving force, relations between adults implicating disparity in status, or relations between men and animals.

[F]ar from possessing "ancient roots," *Bowers*, American laws targeting same-sex couples did not develop until the last third of the twentieth century. The reported decisions concerning the prosecution of consensual, homosexual sodomy between adults for the years 1880-1995 are not always clear in the details, but a significant number involved conduct in a public place. It was not until the 1970s that any State singled out same-sex relations for criminal prosecution, and only nine States have done so. Post-*Bowers* even some of these States did not adhere to the policy of suppressing homosexual conduct. Over the course of the last decades, States with samesex prohibitions have moved toward abolishing them.

In summary, the historical grounds relied upon in *Bowers* are more complex than the majority opinion and the concurring opinion by CHIEF JUSTICE BURGER indicate. Their historical premises are not without doubt and, at the very least, are overstated. It must be acknowledged, of course, that the Court in *Bowers* was making the broader point that for centuries there have been powerful voices to condemn homosexual conduct as immoral. These considerations do not answer the question before us, however. The issue is whether the majority may use the power of the State to enforce these views on the whole society through operation of the criminal law. [W]e think that our laws and traditions in the past half century are of most relevance here. These references show an emerging awareness that liberty gives substantial protection to adult persons in deciding how to conduct their private lives in matters pertaining to sex. This emerging recognition should have been apparent when *Bowers* was decided. In 1955 the American Law Institute promulgated the Model Penal Code and made clear that it did not recommend or provide for "criminal penalties for consensual sexual relations conducted in private." It justified its decision on three grounds: (1) The prohibitions undermined respect for the law by penalizing conduct many people engaged in; (2) the statutes regulated private conduct not harmful to others; and (3) the laws were arbitrarily enforced and thus invited the danger of blackmail.

In *Bowers* the Court referred to the fact that before 1961 all 50 States had outlawed sodomy, and that at the time of the Court's decision 24 States and the District of Columbia had sodomy laws. JUSTICE POWELL pointed out that these prohibitions often were being ignored, however. Georgia, for instance, had not sought to enforce its law for decades.

The sweeping references by CHIEF JUSTICE BURGER to the history of Western civilization and to Judeo-Christian moral and ethical standards did not take account of other authorities pointing in an opposite direction. A committee advising the British Parliament recommended in 1957 repeal of laws punishing homosexual conduct. Parliament enacted the substance of those recommendations 10 years later. Of even more importance, almost five years before *Bowers* was decided the European Court of Human Rights considered a case with parallels to *Bowers* and to today's case. An adult male resident in Northern Ireland alleged he was a practicing homosexual who desired to engage in consensual homosexual conduct. The laws of Northern Ireland forbade him that right. He alleged that he had been questioned, his home had been searched, and he feared criminal prosecution. The court held that the laws proscribing the conduct were invalid under the European Convention on Human Rights. *Dudgeonv. United Kingdom*, 45 Eur. Ct. H. R. (1981) ¶ 52. Authoritative in all countries that are members of the Council of Europe (21 nations then, 45 nations now), the decision is at odds with the premise in *Bowers* that the claim put forward was insubstantial in our Western civilization.

In our own constitutional system the deficiencies in *Bowers* became even more apparent in the years following its announcement. The 25 States with laws prohibiting the relevant conduct referenced in the *Bowers* decision are reduced now to 13, of which 4 enforce their laws only against homosexual conduct. In those States where sodomy is still proscribed, whether for samesex or heterosexual conduct, there is a pattern of nonenforcement with respect to consenting adults acting in private. The State of Texas admitted in 1994 that as of that date it had not prosecuted anyone under those circumstances.

Two principal cases decided after *Bowers* cast its holding into even more doubt. In *Planned Parenthood of Southeastern Pa. v. Casey*, the Court reaffirmed the substantive force of the liberty protected by the Due Process Clause. The *Casey* decision again confirmed that our laws and tradition afford constitutional protection to personal decisions relating to marriage, procreation, contraception, family relationships, child rearing, and education. In explaining the respect the Constitution demands for the autonomy of the person in making these choices, we stated as follows: "These matters, involving the most intimate and personal choices a person may make in a lifetime, choices central to personal dignity and autonomy, are central to the liberty protected by the Fourteenth Amendment. At the heart of liberty is the right to define one's own concept of existence, of meaning, of the universe, and of the mystery of human life. Beliefs about these matters could not define the attributes of personhood were they formed under compulsion of the State."

Persons in a homosexual relationship may seek autonomy for these purposes, just as heterosexual persons do. The decision in *Bowers* would deny them this right. The second post-*Bowers* case of principal relevance is *Romer v. Evans,* 517 U. S. 620 (1996). There the Court struck down classbased legislation directed at homosexuals as a violation of the Equal Protection Clause. *Romer* invalidated an amendment to Colorado's constitution which named as a solitary class persons who were homosexuals, lesbians, or bisexual either by "orientation, conduct, practices or relationships," *id.,* at 624, and deprived them of protection under state antidiscrimination laws. We concluded that the provision was "born of animosity toward the class of persons affected" and further that it had no rational relation to a legitimate governmental purpose. As an alternative argument in this case, counsel for the petitioners and some *amici* contend that *Romer* provides the basis for declaring the Texas statute invalid under the Equal Protection Clause. That is a tenable argument, but we conclude the instant case requires us to address whether *Bowers* itself has continuing validity. Were we to hold the statute invalid under the Equal Protection Clause some might question whether a prohibition would be valid if drawn differently, say, to prohibit the conduct both between same-sex and different-sex participants.

Equality of treatment and the due process right to demand respect for conduct protected by the substantive guarantee of liberty are linked in important respects, and a decision on the latter point advances both interests. If protected conduct is made criminal and the law which does so remains unexamined for its substantive validity, its stigma might remain even if it were not enforceable as drawn for equal protection reasons. When homosexual conduct is made criminal by the law of the State, that declaration in and of itself is an invitation to subject homosexual persons to discrimination both in the public and in the private spheres. The central holding of *Bowers* has been brought in question by this case, and it should be addressed. Its continuance as precedent demeans the lives of homosexual persons.

The stigma this criminal statute imposes, moreover, is not trivial. The offense, to be sure, is but a class C misdemeanor, a minor offense in the Texas legal system. Still, it remains a criminal offense with all that imports for the dignity of the persons charged. The petitioners will bear on their record the history of their criminal convictions. Just this Term we rejected various challenges to state laws requiring the registration of sex offenders. *Smith* v. *Doe*; *Connecticut Dept. of Public Safety v. Doe*. We are advised that if Texas convicted an adult for private, consensual homosexual conduct under the statute here in question the convicted person would come within the registration laws of a least four States were he or she to be subject to their jurisdiction. This underscores the consequential nature of the punishment and the statesponsored condemnation attendant to the criminal prohibition. Furthermore, the Texas criminal conviction carries with it the other collateral consequences always following a conviction, such as notations on job application forms, to mention but one example.

The foundations of *Bowers* have sustained serious erosion from our recent decisions in *Casey* and *Romer*. When our precedent has been thus weakened, criticism from other sources is of greater significance. In the United States criticism of *Bowers* has been substantial and continuing, disapproving of its reasoning in all respects, not just as to its historical assumptions. The courts of five different States have declined to follow it in interpreting provisions in their own state constitutions parallel to the Due Process Clause of the Fourteenth Amendment.

To the extent *Bowers* relied on values we share with a wider civilization, it should be noted that the reasoning and holding in *Bowers* have been rejected elsewhere. The European Court of Human Rights has followed not *Bowers* but its own decision in *Dudgeon v. United Kingdom*. Other nations, too, have taken action consistent with an affirmation of the protected right of homo-sexual adults to engage in intimate, consensual conduct. The right the petitioners seek in this case has been accepted as an integral part of human freedom in many other countries. There has been no showing that in this country the governmental interest in circumscribing personal choice is somehow more legitimate or urgent.

The doctrine of *stare decisis* is essential to the respect accorded to the judgments of the Court and to the stability of the law. It is not, however, an inexorable command. In *Casey* we noted that when a Court is asked to overrule a precedent recognizing a constitutional liberty interest, individual or societal reliance on the existence of that liberty cautions with particular strength against reversing course. The holding in *Bowers*, however, has not induced detrimental reliance comparable to some instances where recognized individual rights are involved. Indeed, there has been no individual or societal reliance on *Bowers* of the sort that could counsel against overturning its holding once there are compelling reasons to do so. *Bowers* itself causes uncertainty, for the precedents before and after its issuance contradict its central holding.

The rationale of *Bowers* does not withstand careful analysis. In his dissenting opinion in *Bowers* Justice Stevens came to these conclusions:

"Our prior cases make two propositions abundantly clear. First, the fact that the governing majority in a State has traditionally viewed a particular practice as immoral is not a sufficient reason for upholding a law prohibiting the practice; neither history nor tradition could save a law prohibiting miscegenation from constitutional attack. Second, individual decisions by married persons, concerning the intimacies of their physical relationship, even when not intended to produce offspring, are a form of 'liberty' protected by the Due Process Clause of the Fourteenth Amendment. Moreover, this protection extends to intimate choices by unmarried as well as married persons."

JUSTICE STEVENS' analysis, in our view, should have been controlling in *Bowers* and should control here. *Bowers* was not correct when it was decided, and it is not correct today. It ought not to remain binding precedent. *Bowers v. Hardwick* should be and now is overruled.

The present case does not involve minors. It does not involve persons who might be injured or coerced or who are situated in relationships where consent might not easily be refused. It does not involve public conduct or prostitution. It does not involve whether the government must give formal recognition to any relationship that homosexual persons seek to enter. The case does involve two adults who, with full and mutual consent from each other, engaged in sexual practices common to a homosexual lifestyle. The petitioners are entitled to respect for their private lives. The State cannot demean their existence or control their destiny by making their private sexual conduct a crime. Their right to liberty under the Due Process Clause gives them the full right to engage in their conduct without intervention of the government. The Texas statute furthers no legitimate state interest which can justify its intrusion into the personal and private life of the individual.

JUSTICE O'CONNOR, concurring in the judgment.

The Court today overrules *Bowers v. Hardwick*. I joined *Bowers*, and do not join the Court in overruling it. Nevertheless, I agree with the Court that Texas' statute banning same-sex sodomy is unconstitutional. Rather than relying on the substantive component of the Fourteenth Amendment's Due Process Clause, as the Court does, I base my conclusion on the Fourteenth Amendment's Equal Protection Clause.

The Equal Protection Clause of the Fourteenth Amendment "is essentially a direction that all persons similarly situated should be treated alike." *Cleburne v. Cleburne Living Center, Inc.* Under our rational basis standard of review, "legislation is presumed to be valid and will be sustained if the classification drawn by the statute is rationally related to a legitimate state interest." *Cleburne Living Center.*

Laws such as economic or tax legislation that are scrutinized under rational basis review normally pass constitutional muster, since "the Constitution presumes that even improvident decisions will eventually be rectified by the democratic processes." *Cleburne Living Center.* We have consistently held, however, that some objectives, such as "a bare . . . desire to harm a politically unpopular group," are not legitimate state interests. *Department of Agriculture* v. *Moreno,* [413 U.S. 528, 534 (1973)]. *See also Cleburne v. Cleburne Living Center*; *Romer v. Evans*. When a law exhibits such a desire to harm a politically unpopular group, we have applied a more searching form of rational basis review to strike down such laws under the Equal Protection Clause.

We have been most likely to apply rational basis review to hold a law unconstitutional under the Equal Protection Clause where, as here, the challenged legislation inhibits personal relationships [citing *Moreno*, *Eisenstadt v. Baird*, *Cleburne Living Center* and *Romer v. Evans*]. The dissent apparently agrees that if these cases have *stare decisis* effect, Texas' sodomy law would not pass scrutiny under the Equal Protection Clause, regardless of the type of rational basis review that we apply.

The statute at issue here makes sodomy a crime only if a person "engages in deviate sexual intercourse with another individual of the same sex." Sodomy between opposite-sex partners, however, is not a crime in Texas. That is, Texas treats the same conduct differently based solely on the participants. Those harmed by this law are people who have a same-sex sexual orientation and thus are more likely to engage in behavior prohibited by § 21.06. The Texas statute makes homosexuals unequal in the eyes of the law by making particular conduct — and only that conduct — subject to criminal sanction. It appears that prosecutions under Texas' sodomy law are rare. This case shows, however, that prosecutions under § 21.06 *do* occur. And while the penalty imposed on petitioners in this case was relatively minor, the consequences of conviction are not.

And the effect of Texas' sodomy law is not just limited to the threat of prosecution or consequence of conviction. Texas' sodomy law brands all homosexuals as criminals, thereby making it more difficult for homosexuals to be treated in the same manner as everyone else. Indeed, Texas itself has previously acknowledged the collateral effects of the law, stipulating in a prior challenge to this action that the law "legally sanctions discrimination against [homosexuals] in a variety of ways unrelated to the criminal law," including in the areas of "employment, family issues, and housing." Texas attempts to justify its law, and the effects of the law, by arguing that the statute satisfies rational basis review because it furthers the legitimate governmental interest of the promotion of morality. This case raises a different issue than *Bowers:* whether, under the Equal Protection Clause, moral disapproval is a legitimate state interest to justify by itself a statute that bans homosexual sodomy, but not heterosexual sodomy. It is not. Moral disapproval of this group, like a bare desire to harm the group, is an interest that is insufficient to satisfy rational basis review under the Equal Protection Clause. *See, e.g., Department of Agriculture v. Moreno*; *Romer* v. *Evans*. Indeed, we have never held that moral disapproval, without any other asserted state interest, is a sufficient rationale under the Equal Protection Clause to justify a law that discriminates among groups of persons.

Moral disapproval of a group cannot be a legitimate governmental interest under the Equal Protection Clause because legal classifications must not be "drawn for the purpose of disadvantaging the group burdened by the law." Texas' invocation of moral disapproval as a legitimate state interest proves nothing more than Texas' desire to criminalize homosexual sodomy. But the Equal Protection Clause prevents a State from creating "a classification of persons undertaken for its own sake." And because Texas so rarely enforces its sodomy law as applied to private, consensual acts, the law serves more as a statement of dislike and disapproval against homosexuals than as a tool to stop criminal behavior. The Texas sodomy law "raise[s] the inevitable inference that the disadvantage imposed is born of animosity toward the class of persons affected." Texas argues, however, that the sodomy law does not discriminate against homosexual persons. Instead, the State maintains that the law discriminates only against homosexual conduct. While it is true that the law applies only to conduct, the conduct targeted by this law is conduct that is closely correlated with being homosexual. Under such circumstances, Texas' sodomy law is targeted at more than conduct. It is instead directed toward gay persons as a class.

Indeed, Texas law confirms that the sodomy statute is directed toward homosexuals as a class. In Texas, calling a person a homosexual is slander *per se* because the word "homosexual" "impute[s] the commission of a crime." The State has admitted that because of the sodomy law, *being* homosexual carries the presumption of being a criminal. Texas' sodomy law therefore results in discrimination against homosexuals as a class in an array of areas outside the criminal law. In *Romer v. Evans,* we refused to sanction a law that singled out homosexuals "for disfavored legal status." The same is true here. The Equal Protection Clause " 'neither knows nor tolerates classes among citizens.' "

A State can of course assign certain consequences to a violation of its criminal law. But the State cannot single out one identifiable class of citizens for punishment that does not apply to everyone else, with moral disapproval as the only asserted state interest for the law. The Texas sodomy statute subjects homosexuals to "a lifelong penalty and stigma. A legislative classification that threatens the creation of an underclass . . . cannot be reconciled with" the Equal Protection Clause. *Plyler v. Doe* (POWELL, J., concurring).

Whether a sodomy law that is neutral both in effect and application, would violate the substantive component of the Due Process Clause is an issue that need not be decided today. I am confident, however, that so long as the Equal Protection Clause requires a sodomy law to apply equally to the private consensual conduct of homosexuals and heterosexuals alike, such a law would not long stand in our democratic society.

That this law as applied to private, consensual conduct is unconstitutional under the Equal Protection Clause does not mean that other laws distinguishing between heterosexuals and homosexuals would similarly fail under rational basis review. Texas cannot assert any legitimate state interest here, such as national security or preserving the traditional institution of marriage. Unlike the moral disapproval of same-sex relations — the asserted state interest in this case — other reasons exist to promote the institution of marriage beyond mere moral disapproval of an excluded group.

A law branding one class of persons as criminal solely based on the State's moral disapproval of that class and the conduct associated with that class runs contrary to the values of the Constitution and the Equal Protection Clause, under any standard of review.

JUSTICE SCALIA, with whom THE CHIEF JUSTICE and JUSTICE THOMAS join, dissenting.

"Liberty finds no refuge in a jurisprudence of doubt." *Planned Parenthood of Southeastern Pa. v. Casey*. That was the Court's sententious response, barely more than a decade ago, to those seeking to overrule *Roe v. Wade*. The Court's response today, to those who have engaged in a 17-year crusade to overrule

Bowers v. Hardwick, is very different. The need for stability and certainty presents no barrier.

Most of the rest of today's opinion has no relevance to its actual holding — that the Texas statute "furthers no legitimate state interest which can justify" its application to petitioners under rational-basis review. Though there is discussion of "fundamental proposition[s]," and "fundamental decisions," nowhere does the Court's opinion declare that homosexual sodomy is a "fundamental right" under the Due Process Clause; nor does it subject the Texas law to the standard of review that would be appropriate (strict scrutiny) if homosexual sodomy *were* a "fundamental right." Thus, while overruling the *outcome* of *Bowers*, the Court leaves strangely untouched its central legal conclusion: "[R]espondent would have us announce . . . a fundamental right to engage in homosexual sodomy. This we are quite unwilling to do." Instead the Court simply describes petitioners' conduct as "an exercise of their liberty" — which it undoubtedly is — and proceeds to apply an unheard-of form of rational-basis review that will have far-reaching implications beyond this case.

I

I begin with the Court's surprising readiness to reconsider a decision rendered a mere 17 years ago in *Bowers v. Hardwick*. I do not myself believe in rigid adherence to *stare decisis* in constitutional cases; but I do believe that we should be consistent rather than manipulative in invoking the doctrine. Today's opinions in support of reversal do not bother to distinguish — or indeed, even bother to mention — the paean to *stare decisis* coauthored by three Members of today's majority in *Planned Parenthood v. Casey*. There, when *stare decisis* meant preservation of judicially invented abortion rights, the widespread criticism of *Roe* was strong reason to *reaffirm* it. Today, however, the widespread opposition to *Bowers*, a decision resolving an issue as "intensely divisive" as the issue in *Roe*, is offered as a reason in favor of *overruling* it. Gone, too, is any "enquiry" (of the sort conducted in *Casey*) into whether the decision sought to be overruled has "proven 'unworkable.' "

Today's approach to *stare decisis* invites us to overrule an erroneously decided precedent (including an "intensely divisive" decision) *if:* (1) its foundations have been "eroded" by subsequent decisions; (2) it has been subject to "substantial and continuing" criticism; and (3) it has not induced "individual or societal reliance" that counsels against overturning. The problem is that *Roe* itself — which today's majority surely has no disposition to overrule — satisfies these conditions to at least the same degree as *Bowers*.

(1) A preliminary digressive observation with regard to the first factor: The Court's claim that *Planned Parenthood v. Casey*, "casts some doubt" upon the holding in *Bowers* (or any other case, for that matter) does not withstand analysis. As far as its holding is concerned, *Casey* provided a *less* expansive right to abortion than did *Roe*, *which was already on the books when Bowers was decided*. And if the Court is referring not to the holding of *Casey*, but to the dictum of its famed sweet-mystery-of-life passage. That "casts some doubt" upon either the totality of our jurisprudence or else (presumably the right answer) nothing at all.

I do not quarrel with the Court's claim that *Romer v. Evans*, "eroded" the "foundations" of *Bowers*' rational-basis holding. But *Roe* and *Casey* have been equally "eroded" by *Washington v. Glucksberg*, which held that *only* fundamental rights which are " 'deeply rooted in this Nation's history and tradition' " qualify for anything other than rational basis scrutiny under the doctrine of "substantive due process." *Roe* and *Casey*, of course, subjected the restriction of abortion to heightened scrutiny without even attempting to establish that the freedom to abort *was* rooted in this Nation's tradition.

(2) *Bowers*, the Court says, has been subject to "substantial and continuing [criticism], disapproving of its reasoning in all respects, not just as to its historical assumptions." Of course, *Roe* too (and by extension *Casey*) had been (and still is) subject to unrelenting criticism.

(3) That leaves, to distinguish the rock-solid, unamendable disposition of *Roe* from the readily overrulable *Bowers*, only the third factor. "[T]here has been," the Court says, "no individual or societal reliance on *Bowers* of the sort that could counsel against overturning its holding . . . ." It seems to me that the "societal reliance" on the principles confirmed in *Bowers* and discarded today has been overwhelming. Countless judicial decisions and legislative enactments have relied on the ancient proposition that a governing majority's belief that certain sexual behavior is "immoral and unacceptable" constitutes a rational basis for regulation. We ourselves relied extensively on *Bowers* when we concluded, in *Barnes v. Glen Theatre, Inc,* that Indiana's public indecency statute furthered "a substantial government interest in protecting order and morality." (plurality opinion) State laws against bigamy, same-sex marriage, adult incest, prostitution, masturbation, adultery, fornication, bestiality, and obscenity are likewise sustainable only in light of *Bowers*' validation of laws based on moral choices. Every single one of these laws is called into question by today's decision; the Court makes no effort to cabin the scope of its decision to exclude them from its holding. The impossibility of distinguishing homosexuality from other traditional "morals" offenses is precisely why *Bowers* rejected the rational-basis challenge.

What a massive disruption of the current social order, therefore, the overruling of *Bowers* entails. Not so the overruling of *Roe*, which would simply have restored the regime that existed for centuries before 1973, in which the permissibility of and restrictions upon abortion were determined legislatively State-by-State. To tell the truth, it does not surprise me, and should surprise no one, that the Court has chosen today to revise the standards of *stare decisis* set forth in *Casey*. It has thereby exposed *Casey*'s extraordinary deference to precedent for the result-oriented expedient that it is.

II

Having decided that it need not adhere to *stare decisis*, the Court still must establish that *Bowers* was wrongly decided and that the Texas statute, as applied to petitioners, is unconstitutional.

Texas Penal Code Ann. § 21.06(a) undoubtedly imposes constraints on liberty. So do laws prohibiting prostitution, recreational use of heroin, and, for that matter, working more than 60 hours per week in a bakery. But there is no right to "liberty" under the Due Process Clause, though today's opinion repeatedly makes that claim. The Fourteenth Amendment *expressly allows* States to deprive their citizens of "liberty," *so long as "due process of law" is provided.* Our opinions applying the doctrine known as "substantive due process" hold that the Due Process Clause prohibits States from infringing *fundamental* liberty interests, unless the infringement is narrowly tailored to serve a compelling state interest. *Washington v. Glucksberg* We have held repeatedly, in cases the Court today does not overrule, that *only* fundamental rights qualify for this so-called "heightened scrutiny" protection — that is, rights which are " 'deeply rooted in this Nation's history and tradition.' " All other liberty interests may be abridged or abrogated pursuant to a validly enacted state law if that law is rationally related to a legitimate state interest.

Bowers held, first, that criminal prohibitions of homosexual sodomy are not subject to heightened scrutiny because they do not implicate a "fundamental right" under the Due Process Clause. The Court today does not overrule this holding. Not once does it describe homosexual sodomy as a "fundamental right" or a "fundamental liberty interest," nor does it subject the Texas statute to strict scrutiny. Instead, having failed to establish that the right to homosexual sodomy is " 'deeply rooted in this Nation's history and tradition,' " the Court concludes that the application of Texas's statute to petitioners' conduct fails the rational-basis test, and overrules *Bowers*' holding to the contrary.

I shall address that rational-basis holding presently. First, however, I address some aspersions that the Court casts upon *Bowers'* conclusion that homosexual sodomy is not a "fundamental right" — even though, as I have said, the Court does not have the boldness to reverse that conclusion.

III

The Court's description of "the state of the law" at the time of *Bowers* only confirms that *Bowers* was right. The Court points to *Griswold v. Connecticut.* But that case *expressly disclaimed* any reliance on the doctrine of "substantive due process," and grounded the so-called "right to privacy" in penumbras of constitutional provisions *other than* the Due Process Clause. *Eisenstadt v. Baird,* likewise had nothing to do with "substantive due process"; it invalidated a Massachusetts law prohibiting the distribution of contraceptives to unmarried persons solely on the basis of the Equal Protection Clause. Of course *Eisenstadt* contains well known dictum relating to the "right to privacy," but this referred to the right recognized in *Griswold* — a right penumbral to the *specific* guarantees in the Bill of Rights, and not a "substantive due process" right. *Roe v. Wade* recognized that the right to abort an unborn child was a "fundamental right" protected by the Due Process Clause. We have since rejected *Roe*'s holding that regulations of abortion must be narrowly tailored to serve a compelling state interest, see *Planned Parenthood v. Casey*, and thus, by logical implication, *Roe*'s holding that the right to abort an unborn child is a "fundamental right."

After discussing the history of antisodomy laws, the Court proclaims that, "it should be noted that there is no longstanding history in this country of laws directed at homosexual conduct as a distinct matter." This observation in no way casts into doubt the "definitive [historical] conclusion," on which *Bowers* relied: that our Nation has a longstanding history of laws prohibiting *sodomy in general* — regardless of whether it was performed by same-sex or opposite-sex couples. It is (as *Bowers* recognized) entirely irrelevant whether the laws in our long national tradition criminalizing homosexual sodomy were "directed at homosexual conduct as a distinct matter." Whether homosexual sodomy was prohibited by a law targeted at same-sex sexual relations or by a more general law prohibiting both homosexual and heterosexual sodomy, the only relevant point is that it *was* criminalized — which suffices to establish that homosexual sodomy is not a right "deeply rooted in our Nation's history and tradition." The Court today agrees that homosexual sodomy was criminalized and thus does not dispute the facts on which *Bowers actually* relied.

Next the Court makes the claim, again unsupported by any citations, that "[l]aws prohibiting sodomy do not seem to have been enforced against consenting adults acting in private." The key qualifier here is "acting in private" — since the Court admits that sodomy laws *were* enforced against consenting adults. Surely that lack of evidence would not sustain the proposition that consensual sodomy on private premises with the doors closed and windows covered was regarded as a "fundamental right," even though all other consensual sodomy was criminalized. There are 203 prosecutions for consensual, adult homosexual sodomy reported in the West Reporting system and official state reporters from the years 1880-1995. There are also records of 20 sodomy prosecutions and 4 executions during the colonial period. *Bowers*' conclusion that homosexual sodomy is not a fundamental right "deeply rooted in this Nation's history and tradition" is utterly unassailable.

Realizing that fact, the Court instead says: "[W]e think that our laws and traditions in the past half century are of most relevance here. These references show *an emerging awareness* that liberty gives substantial protection to adult persons in deciding how to conduct their private lives *in matters pertaining to sex*." Apart from the fact that such an "emerging awareness" does not establish a "fundamental right," the statement is factually false. States continue to prosecute all sorts of crimes by adults "in matters pertaining to sex": prostitution, adult incest, adultery, obscenity, and child pornography. Sodomy laws, too, have been enforced "in the past half century," in which there have been 134 reported cases involving prosecutions for consensual, adult, homosexual sodomy. In relying, for evidence of an "emerging recognition," upon the American Law Institute's 1955 recommendation not to criminalize " 'consensual sexual relations conducted in private,' " the Court ignores the fact that this recommendation was "a point of resistance in most of the states that considered adopting the Model Penal Code."

In any event, an "emerging awareness" is by definition not "deeply rooted in this Nation's history and tradition[s]," as we have said "fundamental right" status requires. Constitutional entitlements do not spring into existence because some States choose to lessen or eliminate criminal sanctions on certain behavior. Much less do they spring into existence, as the Court seems to believe, because *foreign nations* decriminalize conduct. The *Bowers* majority opinion *never* relied on "values we share with a wider civilization," but rather rejected the claimed right to sodomy on the ground that such a right was not

" 'deeply rooted in *this Nation's* history and tradition,' " The Court's discussion of these foreign views (ignoring, of course, the many countries that have retained criminal prohibitions on sodomy) is therefore meaningless dicta. Dangerous dicta, however, since "this Court . . . should not impose foreign moods, fads, or fashions on Americans." *Foster v. Florida*, 537 U. S. 990, n. (2002) (THOMAS, J., concurring in denial of certiorari).

IV

I turn now to the ground on which the Court squarely rests its holding: the contention that there is no rational basis for the law here under attack. This proposition is so out of accord with our jurisprudence — indeed, with the jurisprudence of *any* society we know — that it requires little discussion. The Texas statute undeniably seeks to further the belief of its citizens that certain forms of sexual behavior are "immoral and unacceptable," *Bowers*, the same interest furthered by criminal laws against fornication, bigamy, adultery, adult incest, bestiality, and obscenity. *Bowers* held that this *was* a legitimate state interest. The Court today reaches the opposite conclusion. This effectively decrees the end of all morals legislation. If, as the Court asserts, the promotion of majoritarian sexual morality is not even a *legitimate* state interest, none of the above-mentioned laws can survive rational-basis review.

V

Finally, I turn to petitioners' equal-protection challenge, which no Member of the Court save JUSTICE O'CONNOR, embraces: On its face § 21.06(a) applies equally to all persons. Men and women, heterosexuals and homosexuals, are all subject to its prohibition of deviate sexual intercourse with someone of the same sex. To be sure, § 21.06 does distinguish between the sexes insofar as concerns the partner with whom the sexual acts are performed: men can violate the law only with other men, and women only with other women. But this cannot itself be a denial of equal protection, since it is precisely the same distinction regarding partner that is drawn in state laws prohibiting marriage with someone of the same sex while permitting marriage with someone of the opposite sex. The objection is made, however, that the antimiscegenation laws invalidated in *Loving v. Virginia*, similarly were applicable to whites and blacks alike, and only distinguished between the races insofar as the *partner* was concerned. In *Loving*, however, we correctly applied heightened scrutiny, rather than the usual rational-basis review, because the Virginia statute was "designed to maintain White Supremacy." A racially discriminatory purpose is always sufficient to subject a law to strict scrutiny, even a facially neutral law that makes no mention of race. No purpose to discriminate against men or women as a class can be gleaned from the Texas law, so rational-basis review applies. That review is readily satisfied here by the same rational basis that satisfied it in *Bowers* — society's belief that certain forms of sexual behavior are "immoral and unacceptable." This is the same justification that supports many other laws regulating sexual behavior that make a distinction based upon the identity of the partner — for example, laws against adultery, fornication, and adult incest, and laws refusing to recognize homosexual marriage.

JUSTICE O'CONNOR argues that the discrimination in this law which must be justified is not its discrimination with regard to the sex of the partner but its discrimination with regard to the sexual proclivity of the principal actor. Of course the same could be said of any law. A law against public nudity targets "the conduct that is closely correlated with being a nudist," and hence "is targeted at more than conduct"; it is "directed toward nudists as a class." But be that as it may. Even if the Texas law *does* deny equal protection to "homosexuals as a class," that denial *still* does not need to be justified by anything more than a rational basis, which our cases show is satisfied by the enforcement of traditional notions of sexual morality.

JUSTICE O'CONNOR simply decrees application of "a more searching form of rational basis review" to the Texas statute. The cases she cites do not recognize such a standard, and reach their conclusions only after finding, as required by conventional rational-basis analysis, that no conceivable legitimate state interest supports the classification at issue. *See Romer v. Evans*; *Cleburne v. Cleburne Living Center, Inc.*; *Department of Agriculture v. Moreno*. Nor does JUSTICE O'CONNOR explain precisely what her "more searching form" of rational-basis review consists of. It must at least mean, however, that laws exhibiting " 'a . . . desire to harm a politically unpopular group,' " are invalid *even though* there may be a conceivable rational basis to support them.

This reasoning leaves on pretty shaky grounds state laws limiting marriage to opposite-sex couples. JUSTICE O'CONNOR seeks to preserve them by the conclusory statement that "preserving the traditional institution of marriage" is a legitimate state interest. But "preserving the traditional institution of marriage" is just a kinder way of describing the State's *moral disapproval* of same-sex couples.

Today's opinion is the product of a Court, which is the product of a law-profession culture, that has largely signed on to the so-called homosexual agenda, by which I mean the agenda promoted by some homosexual activists directed at eliminating the moral opprobrium that has traditionally attached to homosexual conduct. One of the most revealing statements in today's opinion is the Court's grim warning that the criminalization of homosexual conduct is "an invitation to subject homosexual persons to discrimination both in the public and in the private spheres." It is clear from this that the Court has taken sides in the culture war, departing from its role of assuring, as neutral observer, that the democratic rules of engagement are observed. Many Americans do not want persons who openly engage in homosexual conduct as partners in their business, as scoutmasters for their children, as teachers in their children's schools, or as boarders in their home. They view this as protecting themselves and their families from a lifestyle that they believe to be immoral and destructive. The Court views it as "discrimination" which it is the function of our judgments to deter. So imbued is the Court with the law profession's anti-antihomosexual culture, that it is seemingly unaware that the attitudes of that culture are not obviously "mainstream;" that in most States what the Court calls "discrimination" against those who engage in homosexual acts is perfectly legal; that proposals to ban such "discrimination" under Title VII have repeatedly been rejected by Congress, that in some cases such "discrimination" is *mandated* by federal statute, see 10 U. S. C.

§ 654(b)(1) (mandating discharge from the armed forces of any service member who engages in or intends to engage in homosexual acts); and that in some cases such "discrimination" is a constitutional right, see *Boy Scouts of America v. Dale*.

Let me be clear that I have nothing against homosexuals, or any other group, promoting their agenda through normal democratic means. Social perceptions of sexual and other morality change over time, and every group has the right to persuade its fellow citizens that its view of such matters is the best. That homosexuals have achieved some success in that enterprise is attested to by the fact that Texas is one of the few remaining States that criminalize private, consensual homosexual acts. But persuading one's fellow citizens is one thing, and imposing one's views in absence of democratic majority will is something else. What Texas has chosen to do is well within the range of traditional democratic action, and its hand should not be stayed through the invention of a brand-new "constitutional right" by a Court that is impatient of democratic change.

One of the benefits of leaving regulation of this matter to the people rather than to the courts is that the people, unlike judges, need not carry things to their logical conclusion. The people may feel that their disapprobation of homosexual conduct is strong enough to disallow homosexual marriage, but not strong enough to criminalize private homosexual acts — and may legislate accordingly. The Court today pretends that it possesses a similar freedom of action, so that we need not fear judicial imposition of homosexual marriage, as has recently occurred in Canada (in a decision that the Canadian Government has chosen not to appeal). *See Halpern v. Toronto*, 2003 WL 34950 (Ontario Ct. App.). At the end of its opinion — after having laid waste the foundations of our rational-basis jurisprudence — the Court says that the present case "does not involve whether the government must give formal recognition to any relationship that homosexual persons seek to enter." Do not believe it. Today's opinion dismantles the structure of constitutional law that has permitted a distinction to be made between heterosexual and homosexual unions, insofar as formal recognition in marriage is concerned. This case "does not involve" the issue of homosexual marriage only if one entertains the belief that principle and logic have nothing to do with the decisions of this Court. Many will hope that, as the Court comfortingly assures us, this is so.

The matters appropriate for this Court's resolution are only three: Texas's prohibition of sodomy neither infringes a "fundamental right" (which the Court does not dispute), nor is unsupported by a rational relation to what the Constitution considers a legitimate state interest, nor denies the equal protection of the laws. I dissent.

JUSTICE THOMAS, dissenting.

I join JUSTICE SCALIA's dissenting opinion. I write separately to note that the law before the Court today "is . . . uncommonly silly." *Griswold v. Connecticut*. If I were a member of the Texas Legislature, I would vote to repeal it. Punishing someone for expressing his sexual preference through noncommercial consensual conduct with another adult does not appear to be a worthy way to expend valuable law enforcement resources. Notwithstanding this, I recognize that as a member of this Court I am not empowered to help petitioners and others similarly situated.

NOTES

1. ***Governmental action and judicial restraint.*** Arguments abound by which one could rationally oppose the economic substantive due process of *Lochner* yet support recognition of rights such as that asserted in *Lawrence*. Cass Sunstein, *Beyond the Republican Revival*, 97 YALE L.J. 1539, 1579 (1988), emphasizes the extent to which the *Lochner* Court posited the existence of a natural and prepolitical private sphere, one that served as a brake on legislation. [T]he problem with the *Lochner* Court was its reliance on common law and status quo baselines; the Court was unable to see the ways in which those baselines were implicated in, indeed a product of law. Pointing out that "traditional" disapprobation of homosexual practice is itself partly a creature of law, Sunstein argues that *Lochner's* invalidation of state legislation and *Bowers'* upholding of state legislation are virtually identical judicial decisions. If the Court in *Bowers* had in fact found a right of privacy to exist, would that right have been any less based in the concept of natural rights than the economic liberty interest recognized in *Lochner*?

A reasonable argument could be fashioned that *Lochner's* protection of economic and property interests actually has a firmer grounding in the history of the Constitution's creation than the right recognized in *Roe* or asserted in *Bowers*. If so, should that make a difference in terms of constitutional theory?

Might the decision in *Bowers* actually have been appropriately deemed less activist had it chosen to invalidate the Georgia statute on privacy grounds? Consider the view of one commentator that as written, *Bowers* appears to rest "on the collective distaste of the majority for the conduct under scrutiny." Thomas Stoddard, *Bowers v. Hardwick: Precedent by Personal Predilection*, 54 U. CHI. L. REV. 648, 649 (1986). *Cf.* Norman Vieira, *Hardwick and the Right of Privacy*, 55 U. CHI. L. REV. 1181 (1988): "One should ask whether the problem lies with the *Hardwick* decision or with the doctrine the Court was asked to apply."

2. ***Privacy, autonomy and political theory.*** Consider the implications of the revival among constitutional scholars of a focus on "civic republicanism" for the constitutional right asserted in *Lawrence*. Civic republican theory, in both its classical and modern manifestations, posits a "belief in the subordination of private interests to the public good." Cass Sunstein, *Beyond the Republican Revival*, 97 YALE L.J. 1539, 1541, 1550 (1988). It also carries the view "that there exists an objective public good apart from individual goods." Richard Fallon, *What Is Republicanism, and Is It Worth Reviving?*, 102 HARV. L. REV. 1695, 1698 (1989). *See also* Stephen Siegal, *The Marshall Court and Republicanism*, 67 TEX. L. REV. 903, 916 (1989): "A core tenet of republicanism was the belief that men most realized their humanity when they participated in public, communal life. Participation in public life involved the pursuit of the common good, an endeavor that required citizens to rise above and put aside self-interest." Under such a theory, should the privacy right asserted in *Lawrence* be valued?

Frank Michelman, *Law's Republic*, 97 YALE L.J. 1493, 1532–33 (1988) asserts that there is a republican argument to be made that the individual asserting a right to engage in homosexual behavior is being denied "due citizenship":

> It seems very likely that among the effects of a law like Georgia's on persons for whom homosexuality is an aspect of identity is denial or impairment of their citizenship, in the broad sense appropriate to modern republican constitutionalism: that of admission to full and effective participation in the various arenas of public life. It also denies citizenship by violating privacy.

If republicanism embraces protection of privacy, then what is the public good for which republicanism stands? If one accepts Michelman's logic, is there likely to be any practical difference between civic republican theory and a theory of liberal individualism? For discussion of the tensions between the right of privacy and civic republican theory, see Jed Rubenfeld, *The Right of Privacy*, 102 HARV. L. REV. 737, 761–70 (1989).

3. *The role of biological reproduction.* In *Bowers*, Justice White suggests that a key distinction between *Griswold* and *Roe* on the one hand and *Bowers* on the other is that the former dealt with biological reproduction while the latter does not. Is this a principled basis for distinction? See David Richards, *Constitutional Legitimacy and Constitutional Privacy*, 61 N.Y.U.L. REV. 800, 835 (1986), suggesting that "[c]ontrol of biological reproduction is artificially truncated as a principle of law; it does not correspond to any sensibly coherent theory that could be justified in the required way."

4. *Defining the issue.* Is Justice Blackmun right to view the issue as not whether an individual has the right to engage in homosexual conduct in private, but whether he has the right to be let alone? Should the outcome of the case change if one accepts Justice Blackmun's rephrasing of the issue? Should the dissent focus on the sweeping character of the Georgia sodomy statute which is not limited to homosexual conduct? Would *Roe v. Wade* have been more acceptable if the Court had simply held that the Texas statute was unconstitutionally overbroad?

If the Court had found homosexual conduct in private to be a fundamental liberty, might the Court then uphold legislation prohibiting such conduct when the state attempts to justify it as a health measure designed to stop the spread of AIDS, even though when the legislation was originally passed the AIDS problem was not considered?

5. *Impact of* Lawrence *on gay and lesbian rights.* Is *Lawrence* likely to have a significant political impact on the protection of gay and lesbian rights? Consider Christopher Leslie, *Lawrence v. Texas As the Perfect Storm*, 38 U.C. DAVIS L. REV. 509, 511–12 (2005): "Categorizing gay men and lesbians as criminals provided a plausible excuse for those who wanted to discriminate and punish homosexuals, regardless of any criminal laws. Once society determines that a person is a criminal, so the argument went, it is perfectly permissible to deny that person the rights and privileges that other law-abiding Americans take for granted. Labeled as criminals, gay and lesbian

Americans were subjected to discrimination from government officials at local, state, and federal levels, from private organizations and businesses, and from their fellow citizens." Did Justice Kennedy's opinion effectively undermine the basis for such discriminatory treatment? Consider Professor Leslie's contention that Justice O'Connor's approach "would not have ameliorated the true harms inflicted by sodomy laws." *Id.* at 542. If this is true, should the fact appropriately influence the Court's choice of constitutional rationale for its holding? On the general issue, see William Eskridge, *Lawrence's Jurisprudence of Tolerance: Judicial Review to Lower the Stakes of Identity Politics*, 88 MINN. L. REV. 1021 (2004).

6. ***Persuasiveness of equal protection alternative.*** How persuasive is Justice O'Connor's equal protection alternative? Professor Tribe has criticized it as a "constitutional 'halfway house' " that is "question-begging," because "if the Court had stopped short of holding that a ban on sodomy defined without regard to sex would be unconstitutional, then any state could freely prohibit or attach other negative consequences to the sexual intimacies to which homosexuals are distinctively drawn as long as it prohibited or similarly penalized the same acts when committed by opposite-sex couples." The state would then "be in a position to justify withholding employment, parenting, or other opportunities from those it labeled 'homosexual,' and permitting private individuals and other entities to do the same, on the now familiar rationale that gays and lesbians, unless sexually inactive, may be assumed to engage in conduct that the state is entitled to discourage and to denounce whereas no such assumption may be made about heterosexuals." Laurence Tribe, *Lawrence v. Texas: The "Fundamental Right" That Dare Not Speak Its Name,* 117 HARV. L. REV. 1893, 1911 (2004). Do you agree? Would a meaningful equal protection limit allow the state to do what Professor Tribe fears?

7. ***The Constitutional Implications of Lawrence.*** What, if anything, does the holding in *Lawrence*, imply about further applications of a constitutionally recognized personal right of autonomy? One scholar, for example, has argued that "proponents of same-sex marriage can use the Court's reasoning [in *Lawrence*] to support arguments that the state has substantive due process obligations to recognize such marriages." Carlos Ball, *The Positive in the Fundamental Right to Marry: Same-Sex Marriage in the Aftermath of Lawrence v. Texas*, 88 MINN. L. REV. 1184, 1186 (2004). Professor Ball reaches this conclusion, because "[t]here is an obligation arising from *Lawrence* for the state to respect the dignity of lesbians and gay men; that obligation will remain unfulfilled until (at least) the state gives full recognition to their committed relationships." *Id.* at 1219. Might reliance on Justice O'Connor's equal protection analysis provide a stronger constitutional foundation for the requirement that same-sex marriages be allowed than would a pure substantive due process analysis?

8. How central to the Court's analysis is its use of foreign law? Did use of foreign law hurt, more than help, the decision? One commentator suggests that "the foundation for the Court's opinion is its conception of natural justice. Because the Court is primarily concerned with maintaining the dignity and autonomy of free-willed individuals, such an idea is inconsistent with the notion of the Court announcing a relativistic communitarian standard." Darin

J. Hall, Note, *Not So Landmark After All? Lawrence v. Texas: Classical Liberalism and Due Process Jurisprudence*, 13 WM. & MARY BILL OF RTS. J. 617, 636 (2004).

[D] THE RIGHT TO "PERSONAL LIFESTYLE CHOICES"

In his classic work "On Liberty," John Stuart Mill provided a sweeping perspective on the proper limits of government intrusion on individual liberty:

> [T]he sole end for which mankind is warranted, individually or collectively, in interfering with the liberty of action of any of their number, is self-protection. [T]he only purpose for which power can be rightfully exercised over any member of a civilized community, against his will, is to prevent harm to others. His own good, either physical or moral, is not a sufficient warrant. He cannot rightfully be compelled to do or forbear because it will be better for him to do so, because it will make him happier, because, in the opinions of others, to do so would be wise, or even right. The only part of the conduct of anyone, for which he is amenable to society, is that which concerns others. In the part which merely concerns himself, his independence is, of right, absolute. Over himself, over his own body and mind, the individual is sovereign.

If one accepts Mill's analysis, how far does it reach? For example, Professors Wilkinson and White argue for recognition of a freedom in "personal lifestyle choices" — *i.e.* "an individual's decision to exercise control over the most personal aspects of his or her life." Wilkinson & White, 62 CORNELL L. REV. at 563, 564. What would be the effect of recognition of such a right on laws prohibiting marijuana use, public drunkenness, or "victimless crimes" generally? Do the cases discussed in this Chapter provide a doctrinal basis for the recognition of such a right? The Supreme Court apparently thinks not.

The Court rejected an effort to extend the privacy cases to police grooming regulations in *Kelley v. Johnson*, 425 U.S. 238 (1976). *Roe* and *Griswold* were distinguished, as involving "a substantial claim of infringement on the individual's freedom of choice with respect to certain basic matters as procreation, marriage, and family life." The present case involved a challenge to hair grooming regulations imposed upon police officers. While accepting, *arguendo*, that the citizenry at large may have a "liberty" interest in matters of personal appearance, Justice Rehnquist, for the Court, concluded that this was not determinative of the validity of such regulations for police officers. He rejected the premise "that the claim of a member of a uniformed civilian service based on the 'liberty' interest protected by the Fourteenth Amendment must necessarily be treated for constitutional purposes the same as a similar claim by a member of the general public." The Court held that the regulation did not violate any right guaranteed by the Fourteenth Amendment.

Justice Rehnquist reasoned that "[c]hoice of organization, dress, and equipment for law enforcement personnel is a decision entitled to the same sort of presumption of legislative validity as state choices designed to promote other claims within the cognizance of the state's police power. . . . The constitutional question to be decided is whether petitioner's determination that such regulations should be enacted is so irrational that it may be branded 'arbitrary,' and therefore a deprivation of respondent's 'liberty' interest in freedom to choose his own hair style." In this instance, the regulation was deemed a rational means of pursuing government's "overall need for discipline, *esprit de corps*, and uniformity" in its police force.

Justice Marshall, joined by Justice Brennan dissenting, argued that not only were the liberty interests of the Fourteenth Amendment implicated by this regulation of personal appearance but that no rational relationship existed between the challenged regulation and the identified state goals.

Putting aside for the moment the issue of the validity of the state's asserted justification for the regulation, what is the basis for the asserted liberty interest in personal appearance? Justice Marshall in his dissent argued that "the right in one's personal appearance is inextricably bound up with the historically recognized right of every individual to the possession and control of his own person; and, perhaps even more fundamentally, with 'the right to be let alone.' " Is this analysis persuasive? If so, is the right less important than "the individual's freedom of choice with respect to certain basic matters as procreation, marriage, and family life?" Might the interest in appearance be more closely analogized to the freedom of speech?

Assuming, as the Court did, the existence of a constitutionally protected interest in appearance, was the majority correct in concluding that the state interest in regulation outweighed it? Would the state interest be weaker, stronger or the same in regulating hair length of school students? Consider Wilkinson & White, 62 CORNELL L. REV. at 606: "Long hair on males is intrinsically no less healthy and no more distracting and disruptive of classroom work than long hair on females. Any difference is the result of custom alone; conformity to custom [seems] insufficient to justify the limitation on individual choice."

[E] HEALTH AND LIFE

[1] Rights to Treatment and Protection

The Court has thus far avoided broad statements on the issue of whether there is a constitutional right to treatment.

***O'Connor v. Donaldson*, 422 U.S. 563 (1975).** The Court, per Justice Stewart, unanimously held that involuntary confinement of a patient who was not dangerous to self or others without providing any treatment violates the due process guarantee. "A finding of 'mental illness' alone cannot justify a State's locking a person up against his will and keeping him indefinitely in simple custodial confinement." Justice Stewart noted there was "no reason now to decide whether mentally ill persons dangerous to themselves or to others have a right to treatment upon compulsory confinement by the State, or whether the State may compulsorily confine a nondangerous, mentally ill individual for the purpose of treatment."

In a concurring opinion, Chief Justice Burger was critical of the concept of a constitutional right to treatment.

> Given the present state of medical knowledge regarding abnormal human behavior and its treatment, few things would be more fraught with peril than to irrevocably condition a State's power to protect the mentally ill upon the providing of "such treatment as will give [them] a realistic opportunity to be cured." Nor can I accept the theory that a State may lawfully confine an individual thought to need treatment and justify that deprivation of liberty solely by providing some treatment. Our concepts of due process would not tolerate such a "trade-off."

***Youngberg v. Romeo*, 457 U.S. 307 (1982).** The Court was presented with the question whether a person who is involuntarily committed to a state institution for the mentally retarded has substantive rights under the due process guarantee to (1) safe conditions of confinement; (2) freedom from bodily restraint; and (3) training or "habilitation." Romeo, a profoundly retarded individual, had been injured on numerous occasions both because of his own violence and the violent reaction of other residents to him. Romeo's mother brought a § 1983 action on his behalf, claiming that officials at the institution failed to take appropriate preventive action and that they failed to provide him with "treatment or programs for his mental retardation."

Justice Powell, for the Court, found that precedent firmly established historic liberty interests in personal security and freedom from bodily restraint. These rights were "not extinguished by lawful confinement, even for penal purposes." Since denial of a person's right to personal security would constitute cruel and unusual punishment, "it must be unconstitutional to confine the involuntarily committed — who may not be punished at all — in unsafe conditions." Turning to the right of habilitation, Justice Powell acknowledged that this claim was "more troubling." Generally "the State is under no constitutional duty to provide substantive services for those within its borders." However, "when the State institutionalizes an individual who is thereafter wholly dependent on the State it is conceded that a duty to provide certain services and care does exist although even then a State necessarily has considerable discretion in determining the nature and scope of its responsibilities."

> If, as seems the case, respondent seeks only training related to safety and freedom from restraints, this case does not present the difficult question whether a mentally retarded person, involuntarily committed to a state institution, has some general constitutional right to training per se, even when no type or amount of training would lead to freedom. In the circumstances presented by this case, and on the basis of the record developed to date, we conclude that respondent's liberty interests require the State to provide minimally adequate or reasonable training to ensure safety and freedom from undue restraint. In view of the kinds of treatment sought by respondent and the evidence of record, we need go no further in the case.

DeShaney v. Winnebago Cty. Dept. of Social Services, **489 U.S. 189 (1989).** The Court rejected a claim that the State, by failing to protect a child from the physical abuse of his father, deprived the child of his "liberty" in violation of the due process guarantee.

Joshua DeShaney, a minor, had been placed in the custody of his father, Randy DeShaney, following his parents' divorce in 1980. Responding to reports that Joshua was being physically abused by his father, the Winnebago County Department of Social Services (DSS), in 1982, interviewed the father, who denied the accusations. The DSS did not pursue the matter any further at that time. When complaints to DSS persisted and evidence mounted that Joshua was indeed the victim of child abuse by his father, DSS took various steps to try to protect Joshua but did not remove him from his father's custody. Joshua was finally beaten so badly by his father in November, 1984, that he suffered permanent brain damage. Randy DeShaney was subsequently convicted of child abuse.

Joshua and his mother brought suit against Winnebago County and the DSS under 42 U.S.C. § 1983. The district court granted summary judgment for the government, which was affirmed by the Seventh Circuit Court of Appeals, and the Supreme Court.

Chief Justice Rehnquist, for the Court, held that the State is not constitutionally responsible for failing to affirmatively protect private citizens from harm which arises from other sources. "Our cases have recognized that the Due Process Clauses generally confer no affirmative right to governmental aid, even where such aid may be necessary to secure life, liberty, or property interests of which the government itself may not deprive the individual." The due process clause was intended "to protect the people from the State, not to ensure that the State protected them from each other." The Court concluded that "a State's failure to protect an individual against private violence simply does not constitute a violation of the Due Process Clause."

Justice Rehnquist rejected the argument by petitioners that there was a special relationship between the State and Joshua, because the State knew that Joshua faced a special danger of abuse from his father and had specifically undertaken to protect Joshua, which created a constitutional duty to protect him. Justice Rehnquist responded that the State had played no part in the creation of the danger of Joshua.

> It is true that in certain limited circumstances the Constitution imposes upon the State affirmative duties of care and protection with respect to particular individuals. In *Estelle v. Gamble,* 429 U.S. 97 (1976), we recognized that the Eighth Amendment's prohibition against cruel and unusual punishment, requires the State to provide adequate medical care to incarcerated prisoners. We reasoned that because the prisoner is unable "by reason of the deprivation of his liberty [to] care for himself," it is only "just" that the State be required to care for him. In *Youngberg v. Romeo* we extended this analysis beyond the Eighth Amendment setting, holding that the substantive component of the Fourteenth Amendment's Due Process Clause requires the State to provide involuntarily committed mental patients with such services

as are necessary to ensure their reasonable safety from themselves and others.

But these cases afford petitioners no help. Taken together, they stand only for the proposition that when the State takes a person into its custody and holds him there against his will, the Constitution imposes upon it a corresponding duty to assume some responsibility for his safety and general well-being. The rationale for this principle is simple enough: when the State by the affirmative exercise of its power so restrains an individual's liberty that it renders him unable to care for himself, and at the same time fails to provide for his basic human needs — *e.g.* food, clothing, shelter, medical care, and reasonable safety — it transgresses the substantive limits on state action set by the Eighth Amendment and the Due Process Clause. The affirmative duty to protect arises not from the State's knowledge of the individual's predicament or from its expression of intent to help him, but from the limitation which it has imposed on his freedom to act on his own behalf. In the substantive due process analysis, it is the State's affirmative act of restraining the individual's freedom to act on his own behalf — through incarceration, institutionalization, or other similar restraint of personal liberty — which is the "deprivation of liberty" triggering the protection of the Due Process Clause, not its failure to act to protect his liberty interests against harms inflicted by other means.

The *Estelle-Youngberg* analysis simply has no applicability to the present case. Petitioners concede that the harms Joshua suffered did not occur while he was in the State's custody, but while he was in the custody of his natural father, who was in no sense a state actor. While the State may have been aware of the dangers that Joshua faced in the free world, it played no part in their creation, nor did it do anything to render him any more vulnerable to them. That the State once took temporary custody of Joshua does not alter the analysis, for when it returned him to his father's custody, it placed him in no worse position than that which he would have been had it not acted at all; the State does not become the permanent guarantor of an individual's safety by having once offered him shelter. Under these circumstances, the State had no constitutional duty to protect Joshua.

Justice Brennan, joined by Justice Marshall and Justice Blackmun dissenting, argued that the government should be held responsible when it attempts to give aid to a private citizen but fails to follow through, particularly when that aid supplants private sources of aid. "I would recognize, as the Court apparently cannot, that the State's knowledge of [an] individual's predicament [and] its expressions of intent to help him can amount to a limitation of his freedom to act on his own behalf or to obtain help from others. Thus I would read *Youngberg* and *Estelle* to stand for the more generous proposition that, if a State cuts off private source of aid and then refuses aid itself, it cannot wash its hands of the harm." State inaction, as well as State action, reasoned the dissent, can implicate the due process guarantee. "My disagreement with the Court arises from its failure to see that inaction can be every bit as abusive of power as action, that oppression can result when a State undertakes a vital duty and then ignores it."

Justice Blackmun, dissenting separately, focused on the proper judicial reading of the open contours of the Fourteenth Amendment.

> Like the antebellum judges who denied relief to fugitive slaves, the Court today claims that its decision, however harsh, is compelled by existing legal doctrine. On the contrary, the question presented by the case is an open one, and our Fourteenth Amendment precedents may be read more broadly or narrowly depending on how one chooses to read them. Faced with the choice, I would adopt a "sympathetic" reading, one which comports with dictates of fundamental justice and recognizes that compassion need not be exiled from the province of judging.

***Sacramento v. Lewis,* 523 U.S. 833 (1998)**. The Supreme Court unanimously held that a police officer does not violate the Fourteenth Amendment's guarantee of substantive due process by causing death through indifference to human life in a high-speed automobile chase aimed at apprehending a suspected offender.

Sacramento County Sheriff's officers responded to a call to break up a fight. They saw a motorcycle approaching at high speed. Brian Willard, age 18, and Philip Lewis, age 16 and respondents' decedent, were riding the motorcycle. While it turned out that neither boy was involved in the fight for which the police were originally summoned, Officer Smith began a high-speed chase through a residential area reaching speeds upwards of 100 miles per hour and less than 100 feet between the motorcycle and Smith's car. The chase ended when the motorcycle tipped over on a sharp turn. Willard was not in the way of the car, but Smith's patrol car hit Lewis at 40 miles per hour, throwing him 70 feet and inflicting massive injuries; Lewis was pronounced dead at the scene. Lewis' parents sued Sacramento County, the Sacramento County Sheriff's Department, and Deputy Smith accusing them of depriving Lewis of his Fourteenth Amendment right to life. The Ninth Circuit reversed a district court dismissal holding the standard of fault to be applied to high-speed pursuits is "deliberate indifference to, or reckless disregard for, a person's right to life and personal security." The Supreme Court reversed and held that, "in such circumstances only a purpose to cause harm unrelated to the legitimate object of arrest will satisfy the element of arbitrary conduct shocking to the conscience, necessary for a due process violation."

Justice Souter, writing for the Court, began from the premise that Lewis and other respondents needed to overcome two principal objections to their claim. The first is that the subject is governed by a more definite provision of the Constitution to the exclusion of any possible application of substantive due process. The second is that the allegations are insufficient to state a substantive due process violation through executive abuse of power.

The first objection Lewis was able to overcome. Justice Souter noted the reluctance of the Court to expand the notion of substantive due process.

" 'Where a particular amendment provides an explicit textual source of constitutional protection against a particular sort of government behavior, that Amendment, not the more generalized notion of substantive due process, must be the guide for analyzing these claims.' " Sacramento argued that in chasing the motorcycle, Smith was attempting to make a seizure covered by the Fourth Amendment, and therefore the court should apply the reasonableness standard governing searches and seizures. The Court rejected the argument holding that substantive due process analysis is appropriate because Lewis' claim was not a search and seizure covered by the Fourth Amendment.

Second, Justice Souter addressed whether Lewis' allegations were sufficient to sustain a substantive due process claim. The core concept of due process is protection against arbitrary action. "[O]nly the most egregious official conduct can be said to be 'arbitrary in the constitutional sense.' " The measure of what violates the substantive component of the Due Process Clause is activity that "shocks the conscience" and offends the "decencies of civilized conduct." The Constitution does not guarantee a minimum standard of due care by government officials and impose a form of tort liability whenever someone with the authority of the government may negligently cause harm. It is in cases where there are deliberate decisions by government officials to deny a person life, liberty, or property that more likely will support a substantive due process claim by raising to the level of "conscience-shocking."

Certainly some official acts may be actionable under the Due Process Clause even if unintentional, provided the conduct is egregious enough, he reasoned. Rules of due process cannot be mechanically applied. "Deliberate indifference that shocks in one environment may not be so patently egregious in another, and our concern with preserving the constitutional proportions of substantive due process demands an exact analysis of circumstances before any abuse of power is considered as conscience-shocking." A much higher standard of fault than deliberate indifference must be demonstrated in a situation calling for fast action. "[H]igh-speed chases with no intent to harm suspects physically or to worsen their legal plight do not give rise to liability under the Fourteenth Amendment." Smith's action does not "shock the conscience." "Regardless of whether Smith's behavior offended the reasonableness held up by tort law or the balance struck in law enforcement's own codes of sound practice, it does not shock the conscience, and petitioners are not called upon to answer for it."

Justice Kennedy, with whom Justice O'Connor joins concurring, questioned whether a constitutional violation occurred in this case at all. The test of whether something "shocks the conscience" is laden with subjective assessments and therefore must be viewed with skepticism. "It suffices to conclude that neither our legal traditions nor the present needs of law enforcement justify finding a due process violation when unintended injuries occur after the police pursue a suspect who disobeys their lawful order to stop."

Justice Scalia, with whom Justice Thomas joins concurring, suggests a different test than "the Cellophane of subjectivity, the ol' 'shocks-the-conscience' test." Scalia suggests the Court ask whether the right Lewis asserts has traditionally been protected. Scalia found "no precedental support for a substantive-due-process right to be free from reckless police conduct during a car chase."

[2] The Right to Refuse Treatment

***Washington v. Harper*, 494 U.S. 210 (1990).** The Court considered the scope of the substantive due process protection enjoyed by an inmate subjected to involuntary treatment with antipsychotic drugs. A written state policy permitted involuntary treatment only if a psychiatrist determined that the inmate suffered from a "mental disorder" and was "gravely disabled" or posed a "likelihood of serious harm to himself, others or their property." This finding was subject to review by a medical committee. The respondent argued that the State could not override his choice to refuse the drugs unless he had been found to be incompetent, and then only if the factfinder exercising substituted judgment, determined that, if competent, the inmate would consent to the drug treatment. The Supreme Court disagreed.

Justice Kennedy began by affirming that in addition to the liberty interests created by the state policy, the respondent enjoyed a significant liberty interest under the due process clause in avoiding the unwanted administration of antipsychotic drugs. But he concluded that the State administrative scheme satisfied the due process mandate.

Applying the standard of reasonableness, Justice Kennedy first considered whether there existed "a 'valid, rational connection' between the prison regulation and the legitimate governmental interest put forward to justify it." There were few contexts, he reasoned, where the State had a greater interest in combatting the danger posed by a person to both himself and others than the prison environment. Where the root cause of the threat is the inmate's mental disability, the State's interest in security necessarily encompasses providing him with medical treatment.

The absence of "ready alternatives" to involuntary medication also provided evidence of the reasonableness of the state policy. Physical restraints or seclusion were not shown to be acceptable alternatives to antipsychotic drug treatment in terms of either medical effectiveness or their toll on institutional resources.

Justice Stevens, joined by Justice Brennan and Marshall, dissenting, began from the premise that a competent individual's right to refuse medication is a fundamental liberty deserving the highest order of protection. They accused the Court of virtually ignoring several physical and intellectual dimensions of that liberty.

> Every violation of a person's bodily integrity is an invasion of his or her liberty. The invasion is particularly intrusive if it creates a substantial risk of permanent injury and premature death. Moreover, any such action is degrading if it overrides a competent person's choice to reject a specific form of medical treatment. And when the purpose or effect of forced drugging is to alter the will and the mind of the subject, it constitutes a deprivation of liberty in the most literal and fundamental sense.

CRUZAN v. DIRECTOR, MISSOURI DEPARTMENT OF HEALTH

497 U.S. 261, 110 S. Ct. 2841, 111 L. Ed. 2d 224 (1990)

Chief Justice Rehnquist delivered the opinion of the Court.

Petitioner Nancy Beth Cruzan was rendered incompetent as a result of severe injuries sustained during an automobile accident. Co-petitioners Lester and Joyce Cruzan, Nancy's parents and co-guardians, sought a court order directing the withdrawal of their daughter's artificial feeding and hydration equipment after it became apparent that she had virtually no chance of recovering her cognitive faculties. The Supreme Court of Missouri held that because there was no clear and convincing evidence of Nancy's desire to have life-sustaining treatment withdrawn under such circumstances, her parents lacked authority to effectuate such a request. We granted certiorari, and now affirm.

On the night of January 11, 1983, Nancy Cruzan lost control of her car as she traveled down Elm Road in Jasper County, Missouri. The vehicle overturned, and Cruzan was discovered lying face down in a ditch without detectable respiratory or cardiac function. Paramedics were able to restore her breathing and heartbeat at the accident site, and she was transported to a hospital in an unconscious state. An attending neurosurgeon diagnosed her as having sustained probable cerebral contusions compounded by significant anoxia (lack of oxygen). The Missouri trial court in this case found that permanent brain damage generally results after 6 minutes in an anoxic state; it was estimated that Cruzan was deprived of oxygen from 12 to 14 minutes. She remained in a coma for approximately three weeks and then progressed to an unconscious state in which she was able to orally ingest some nutrition. In order to ease feeding and further the recovery, surgeons implanted a gastrostomy feeding and hydration tube in Cruzan with the consent of her then husband. Subsequent rehabilitative efforts proved unavailing. She now lies in a Missouri state hospital in what is commonly referred to as a persistent vegetative state: generally, a condition in which a person exhibits motor reflexes but evinces no indications of significant cognitive function. The State of Missouri is bearing the cost of her care.

After it had become apparent that Nancy Cruzan had virtually no chance of regaining her mental faculties her parents asked hospital employees to terminate the artificial nutrition and hydration procedures. All agree that such a removal would cause her death. The employees refused to honor the request without court approval. The parents then sought and received authorization from the state trial court for termination. The court found that a person in Nancy's condition had a fundamental right under the State and Federal Constitutions to refuse or direct the withdrawal of "death prolonging procedures." The court also found that Nancy's "expressed thoughts at age twenty-five in somewhat serious conversation with a housemate friend that if sick or injured she would not wish to continue her life unless she could live at least halfway normally suggests that given her present condition she would not wish to continue on with her nutrition and hydration."

The Supreme Court of Missouri reversed by a divided vote. The court recognized a right to refuse treatment embodied in the common-law doctrine of informed consent, but expressed skepticism about the application of that doctrine in the circumstances of this case. The court also declined to read a broad right of privacy into the State Constitution which would "support the right of a person to refuse medical treatment in every circumstance," and expressed doubt as to whether such a right existed under the United States Constitution. It then decided that the Missouri Living Will statute, embodied a state policy strongly favoring the preservation of life. The court found that Cruzan's statements to her roommate regarding her desire to live or die under certain conditions were "unreliable for the purpose of determining her intent," "and thus insufficient to support the co-guardians claim to exercise substituted judgment on Nancy's behalf." It rejected the argument that Cruzan's parents were entitled to order the termination of her medical treatment, concluding that "no person can assume that choice for an incompetent in the absence of the formalities required under Missouri's Living Will statutes or the clear and convincing, inherently reliable evidence absent here." The court also expressed its view that "[b]road policy questions bearing on life and death are more properly addressed by representative assemblies" than judicial bodies.

We granted certiorari to consider the question of whether Cruzan has a right under the United States Constitution which would require the hospital to withdraw life-sustaining treatment from her under these circumstances.

At common law, even the touching of one person by another without consent and without legal justification was a battery. This notion of bodily integrity has been embodied in the requirement that informed consent is generally required for medical treatment.

The logical corollary of the doctrine of informed consent is that the patient generally possesses the right not to consent, that is, to refuse treatment.

[M]ost courts have based a right to refuse treatment either solely on the common law right to informed consent or on both the common law right and a constitutional privacy right. [The Court's survey of state court decisions is omitted.]

As these cases demonstrate, the common-law doctrine of informed consent is viewed as generally encompassing the right of a competent individual to refuse medical treatment. Beyond that, these decisions demonstrate both similarity and diversity in their approach to decision of what all agree is a perplexing question with unusually strong moral and ethical overtones. State courts have available to them for decision a number of sources — state constitutions, statutes, and common law — which are not available to us. In this Court, the question is simply and starkly whether the United States Constitution prohibits Missouri from choosing the rule of decision which it did. This is the first case in which we have been squarely presented with the issue of whether the United States Constitution grants what is in common parlance referred to as a "right to die."

The principle that a competent person has a constitutionally protected liberty interest in refusing unwanted medical treatment may be inferred from our prior decisions. Just this Term, in the course of holding that a State's procedures for administering antipsychotic medication to prisoners were sufficient to satisfy due process concerns, we recognized that prisoners possess "a significant liberty interest in avoiding the unwanted administration of antipsychotic drugs under the Due Process Clause of the Fourteenth Amendment." *Washington v. Harper.*

But determining that a person has a "liberty interest" under the Due Process Clause does not end the inquiry;[3] "whether respondent's constitutional rights have been violated must be determined by balancing his liberty interests against the relevant state interests." *Youngberg v. Romeo.*

Petitioners insist that under the general holdings of our cases, the forced administration of life-sustaining medical treatment, and even of artificially-delivered food and water essential to life, would implicate a competent person's liberty interest. Although we think the logic of the cases discussed above would embrace such a liberty interest, the dramatic consequences involved in refusal of such treatment would inform the inquiry as to whether the deprivation of that interest is constitutionally permissible. But for purposes of this case, we assume that the United States Constitution would grant a competent person a constitutionally protected right to refuse lifesaving hydration and nutrition.

Petitioners go on to assert that an incompetent person should possess the same right in this respect as is possessed by a competent person. They rely primarily on our decisions in *Parham v. J.R.* and *Youngberg v. Romeo.* The difficulty with petitioners' claim is that in a sense it begs the question: an incompetent person is not able to make an informed and voluntary choice to exercise a hypothetical right to refuse treatment or any other right. Such a "right" must be exercised for her, if at all, by some sort of surrogate. Here, Missouri has in effect recognized that under certain circumstances a surrogate may act for the patient in electing to have hydration and nutrition withdrawn in such a way as to cause death, but it has established a procedural safeguard to assure that the action of the surrogate conforms as best it may to the wishes expressed by the patient while competent. Missouri requires that evidence of the incompetent's wishes as to the withdrawal of treatment be proved by clear and convincing evidence. The question, then, is whether the United States Constitution forbids the establishment of this procedural requirement by the State. We hold that it does not.

Whether or not Missouri's clear and convincing evidence requirement comports with the United States Constitution depends in part on what interests the State may properly seek to protect in this situation. Missouri relies on its interest in the protection and preservation of human life, and there can be no gainsaying this interest. As a general matter, the States — indeed, all civilized nations — demonstrate their commitment to life by treating homicide as serious crime. Moreover, the majority of States in this country have laws imposing criminal penalties on one who assists another to commit suicide. We do not think a State is required to remain neutral in the face of an informed and voluntary decision by a physically-able adult to starve to death.

[3] Although many state courts have held that a right to refuse treatment is encompassd by a generalized constitutional right of privacy, we have never so held. We believe this issue is more properly analyzed in terms of a Fourteenth Amendment liberty interest. *See Bowers v. Hardwick.*

But in the context presented here, a State has more particular interests at stake. The choice between life and death is a deeply personal decision of obvious and overwhelming finality. We believe Missouri may legitimately seek to safeguard the personal element of this choice through the imposition of heightened evidentiary requirements. It cannot be disputed that the Due Process Clause protects an interest in life as well as an interest in refusing life-sustaining medical treatment. Not all incompetent patients will have loved ones available to serve as surrogate decisionmakers. And even where family members are present, "[t]here will, of course, be some unfortunate situations in which family members will not act to protect a patient." A State is entitled to guard against potential abuses in such situations. Similarly, a State is entitled to consider that a judicial proceeding to make a determination regarding an incompetent's wishes may very well not be an adversarial one, with the added guarantee of accurate factfinding that the adversary process brings with it. Finally, we think a State may properly decline to make judgments about the "quality" of life that a particular individual may enjoy, and simply assert an unqualified interest in the preservation of human life to be weighed against the constitutionally protected interests of the individual.

In our view, Missouri has permissibly sought to advance these interests through the adoption of a "clear and convincing" standard of proof to govern such proceedings.

We think it self-evident that the interests at stake in the instant proceedings are more substantial, both on an individual and societal level, than those involved in a run-of-the-mine civil dispute. But not only does the standard of proof reflect the importance of a particular adjudication, it also serves as "a societal judgment about how the risk of error should be distributed between the litigants." The more stringent the burden of proof a party must bear, the more that party bears the risk of an erroneous decision. We believe that Missouri may permissibly place an increased risk of an erroneous decision on those seeking to terminate an incompetent individual's life-sustaining treatment. An erroneous decision to withdraw life-sustaining treatment is not susceptible of correction. One of the factors which [has] led the Court to require proof by clear and convincing evidence in a proceeding to terminate parental rights was that a decision in such a case was final and irrevocable. The same must surely be said of the decision to discontinue hydration and nutrition of a patient such as Nancy Cruzan, which all agree will result in her death.

It is also worth noting that most, if not all, States simply forbid oral testimony entirely in determining the wishes of parties in transactions which, while important, simply do not have the consequences that a decision to terminate a person's life does. Missouri's requirement of proof in this case may have frustrated the effectuation of the not-fully-expressed desires of Nancy Cruzan. But the Constitution does not require general rules to work faultlessly; no general rule can.

In sum, we conclude that a State may apply a clear and convincing evidence standard in proceedings where a guardian seeks to discontinue nutrition and hydration of a person diagnosed to be in a persistent vegetative state. We note that many courts which have adopted some sort of substituted judgment procedure in situations like this, whether they limit consideration of evidence to the prior expressed wishes of the incompetent individual, or whether they allow more general proof of what the individual's decision would have been, require a clear and convincing standard of proof for such evidence.

The Supreme Court of Missouri held that in this case the testimony adduced at trial did not amount to clear and convincing proof of the patient's desire to have hydration and nutrition withdrawn. In so doing, it reversed a decision of the Missouri trial court which had found that the evidence "suggest[ed]" Nancy Cruzan would not have desired to continue such measures, but which had not adopted the standard of "clear and convincing evidence" enunciated by the Supreme Court. The testimony adduced at trial consisted primarily of Nancy Cruzan's statements made to a housemate about a year before her accident that she would not want to live should she face life as a "vegetable," and other observations to the same effect. The observations did not deal in terms with withdrawal of medical treatment or of hydration and nutrition. We cannot say that the Supreme Court of Missouri committed constitutional error in reaching the conclusion that it did.

Petitioners alternatively contend that Missouri must accept the "substituted judgment" of close family members even in the absence of substantial proof that their views reflect the views of the patient.

No doubt is engendered by anything in this record but that Nancy Cruzan's mother and father are loving and caring parents. If the State were required by the United States Constitution to repose a right of "substituted judgment" with anyone, the Cruzans would surely qualify. But we do not think the Due Process Clause requires the State to repose judgment on these matters with anyone but the patient herself. Close family members may have a strong feeling — a feeling not at all ignoble or unworthy, but not entirely disinterested, either — that they do not wish to witness the continuation of the life of a loved one which they regard as hopeless, meaningless, and even degrading. But there is no automatic assurance that the view of close family members will necessarily be the same as the patient's would have been had she been confronted with the prospect of her situation while competent. All of the reasons previously discussed for allowing Missouri to require clear and convincing evidence of the patient's wishes lead us to conclude that the State may choose to defer only to those wishes, rather than confide the decision to close family members.

Justice O'Connor, concurring.

I agree that a protected liberty interest in refusing unwanted medical treatment may be inferred from our prior decisions and that the refusal of artificially delivered food and water is encompassed within that liberty interest. I write separately to clarify why I believe this to be so.

As the Court notes, the liberty interest in refusing medical treatment flows from decisions involving the State's invasions into the body. Because our notions of liberty are inextricably entwined with our idea of physical freedom and self-determination, the Court has often deemed state incursions into the body repugnant to the interests protected by the Due Process Clause. The State's imposition of medical treatment on an unwilling competent adult necessarily involves some form of restraint and intrusion. A seriously ill or dying patient whose wishes are not honored may feel a captive of the machinery required for life-sustaining measures or other medical interventions. Such forced treatment may burden that individual's liberty interests as much as any state coercion.

The State's artificial provision of nutrition and hydration implicates identical concerns. Artificial feeding cannot readily be distinguished from other forms of medical treatment. Whether or not the techniques used to pass food and water into the patient's alimentary tract are termed "medical treatment," it is clear they all involve some degree of intrusion and restraint. Requiring a competent adult to endure such procedures against her will burdens the patient's liberty, dignity, and freedom to determine the course of her own treatment. Accordingly, the liberty guaranteed by the Due Process Clause must protect, if it protects anything, an individual's deeply personal decision to reject medical treatment, including the artificial delivery of food and water.

I also write separately to emphasize that the Court does not today decide the issue whether a State must also give effect to the decisions of a surrogate decisionmaker. In my view, such a duty may well be constitutionally required to protect the patient's liberty interest in refusing medical treatment. Few individuals provide explicit oral or written instructions regarding their intent to refuse medical treatment should they become incompetent. States which decline to consider any evidence other than such instructions may frequently fail to honor a patient's intent. Such failures might be avoided if the State considered an equally probative source of evidence: the patient's appointment of a proxy to make health care decisions on her behalf. Delegating the authority to make medical decisions to a family member or friend is becoming a common method of planning for the future. These procedures for surrogate decisionmaking, which appear to be rapidly gaining in acceptance, may be a valuable additional safeguard of the patient's interest in directing his medical care. Moreover, as patients are likely to select a family member as a surrogate, giving effect to a proxy's decisions may also protect the "freedom of personal choice in matters of . . . family life." *Cleveland Board of Education v. LaFleur*, 414 U.S. 632 (1974).

Today's decision, holding only that the Constitution permits a State to require clear and convincing evidence of Nancy Cruzan's desire to have artificial hydration and nutrition withdrawn, does not preclude a future determination that the Constitution requires the States to implement the decisions of a patient's duly appointed surrogate. Nor does it prevent States from developing other approaches for protecting an incompetent individual's liberty interest in refusing medical treatment. As is evident from the Court's survey of state court decisions, no national consensus has yet emerged on the best solution for this difficult and sensitive problem. Today we decide only that one State's practice does not violate the Constitution; the more challenging task of crafting appropriate procedures for safeguarding incompetents' liberty interests is entrusted to the "laboratory" of the States in the first instance.

JUSTICE SCALIA, concurring.

While I agree with the Court's analysis today, and therefore join in its opinion, I would have preferred that we announce, clearly and promptly, that the federal courts have no business in this field; that American law has always accorded the State the power to prevent, by force if necessary, suicide — including suicide by refusing to take appropriate measures necessary to preserve one's life; that the point at which life becomes "worthless," and the point at which the means necessary to preserve it become "extraordinary" or "inappropriate," are neither set forth in the Constitution nor known to the nine Justices of this Court any better than they are known to nine people picked at random from the Kansas City telephone directory; and hence, that even when it is demonstrated by clear and convincing evidence that a patient no longer wishes certain measures to be taken to preserve her life, it is up to the citizens of Missouri to decide, through their elected representatives, whether that wish will be honored. It is quite impossible (because the Constitution says nothing about the matter) that those citizens will decide upon a line less lawful than the one we would choose; and it is unlikely (because we know no more about "life-and-death" than they do) that they will decide upon a line less reasonable.

The text of the Due Process Clause does not protect individuals against deprivations of liberty simpliciter. It protects them against deprivations of liberty "without due process of law." To determine that such a deprivation would not occur if Nancy Cruzan were forced to take nourishment against her will, it is unnecessary to reopen the historically recurrent debate over whether "due process" includes substantive restrictions. It is at least true that no "substantive due process" claim can be maintained unless the claimant demonstrates that the State has deprived him of a right historically and traditionally protected against State interference. *Michael H. v. Gerald D.* (plurality opinion); *Bowers v. Hardwick*. That cannot possibly be established here.

Petitioners rely on three distinctions to separate Nancy Cruzan's case from ordinary suicide: (1) that she is permanently incapacited and in pain; (2) that she would bring on her death not by any affirmative act but by merely declining treatment that provides nourishment; and (3) that preventing her from effectuating her presumed wish to die requires violation of her bodily integrity. None of these suffices. Suicide was not excused even when committed "to avoid those ills which [persons] had not the fortitude to endure."

The second asserted distinction — suggested by the recent cases canvassed by the Court concerning the right to refuse treatment — relies on the dichotomy between action and inaction. Suicide, it is said, consists of an affirmative act to end one's life; refusing treatment is not an affirmative act "causing" death, but merely a passive acceptance of the natural process of dying. Starving oneself to death is no different from putting a gun to one's temple as far as the common-law definition of suicide is concerned; the cause of death in both cases is the suicide's conscious decision to "pu[t] an end to his own existence."

The third asserted basis of distinction — that frustrating Nancy Cruzan's wish to die in the present case requires interference with her bodily integrity — is likewise inadequate, because such interference is impermissible only if one begs the question whether her refusal to undergo the treatment on her own is suicide. It has always been lawful not only for the State, but even for private citizens, to interfere with bodily integrity to prevent a felony. That general rule has of course been applied to suicide.

The dissents of Justices Brennan and Stevens make a plausible case for our intervention here only by embracing — the latter explicitly and the former by implication — a political principle that the States are free to adopt, but that is demonstrably not imposed by the Constitution. "The State," says Justice Brennan, "has no legitimate general interest in someone's life, completely abstracted from the interest of the person living that life, that could outweigh the person's choice *to avoid medical treatment*." The italicized phrase sounds moderate enough, and is all that is needed to cover the present case — but the proposition cannot *logically* be so limited. One who accepts it must also accept, I think, that the State has no such legitimate interest that could outweigh "the person's choice *to put an end to her life*." It seems to me, in other words, that Justice Brennan's position ultimately rests upon the proposition that it is none of the State's business if a person wants to commit suicide. Justice Stevens is explicit on the point: "Choices about death touch the core of liberty . . . . [N]ot much may be said with confidence about death unless it is said from faith, and that alone is reason enough to protect the freedom to conform choices about death to individual conscience." This is a view that some societies have held, and that our States are free to adopt if they wish. But it is not a view imposed by our constitutional traditions, in which the power of the State to prohibit suicide is unquestionable.

What I have said above is not meant to suggest that I would think it desirable, if we were sure that Nancy Cruzan wanted to die, to keep her alive by the means at issue here. I assert only that the Constitution has nothing to say about the subject. To raise up a constitutional right here we would have to create out of nothing (for it exists neither in text nor tradition) some constitutional principle whereby, although the State may insist that an individual come in out of the cold and eat food, it may not insist that he take medicine; and although it may pump his stomach empty of poison he has ingested, it may not fill his stomach with food he has failed to ingest. Are there, then, no reasonable and humane limits that ought not to be exceeded in requiring an individual to preserve his own life? There obviously are, but they are not set forth in the Due Process Clause. What assures us that those limits will not be exceeded is the same constitutional guarantee that is the source of most of our protection — what protects us, for example, from being assessed a tax of 100% of our income above the subsistence level, from being forbidden to drive cars, or from being required to send our children to school for 10 hours a day, none of which horribles is categorically prohibited by the Constitution. Our salvation is the Equal Protection Clause, which requires the democratic majority to accept for themselves and their loved ones what they impose on you and me. This Court need not, and has no authority to, inject itself into every field of human activity where irrationality and oppression may theoretically occur, and if it tries to do so it will destroy itself.

JUSTICE BRENNAN, with whom JUSTICE MARSHALL and JUSTICE BLACKMUN join, dissenting.

Because I believe that Nancy Cruzan has a fundamental right to be free of unwanted artificial nutrition and hydration, which right is not outweighed by any interests of the State, and because I find that the improperly biased procedural obstacles imposed by the Missouri Supreme Court impermissibly burden that right, I respectfully dissent. Nancy Cruzan is entitled to choose to die with dignity.

The starting point for our legal analysis must be whether a competent person has a constitutional right to avoid unwanted medical care. Earlier this Term, this Court held that the Due Process Clause of the Fourteenth Amendment confers a significant liberty interest in avoiding unwanted medical treatment. *Washington v. Harper*. Today, the Court concedes that our prior decisions "support the recognition of a general liberty interest in refusing medical treatment."

But if a competent person has a liberty interest to be free of unwanted medical treatment, as both the majority and Justice O'Connor concede, it must be fundamental. "We are dealing here with [a decision] which involves one of the basic civil rights of man." *Skinner v. Oklahoma ex rel. Williamson*. Whatever other liberties protected by the Due Process Clause are fundamental, "those liberties that are 'deeply rooted in this Nation's history and tradition'" are among them. *Bowers v. Hardwick*. The right to be free from medical attention without consent, to determine what shall be done with one's own body, is deeply rooted in this Nation's traditions, as the majority acknowledges. This right has long been "firmly entrenched in American tort law" and is securely grounded in the earliest common law. Thus, freedom from unwanted medical attention is unquestionably among those principles "so rooted in the traditions and conscience of our people as to be ranked as fundamental."

Although the right to be free of unwanted medical intervention, like other constitutionally protected interests, may not be absolute, no State interest could outweigh the rights of an individual in Nancy Cruzan's position. Whatever a State's possible interests in mandating life-support treatment under other circumstances, there is no good to be obtained here by Missouri's insistence that Nancy Cruzan remain on life-support systems if it is indeed her wish not to do so. Missouri does not claim, nor could it, that society as a whole will be benefited by Nancy's receiving medical treatment. No third party's situation will be improved and no harm to others will be averted.

The only state interest asserted here is a general interest in the preservation of life. But the State has no legitimate general interest in someone's life, completely abstracted from the interest of the person living that life, that could outweigh the person's choice to avoid medical treatment. "[T]he regulation of constitutionally protected decisions . . . must be predicated on legitimate state concerns other than disagreement with the choice the individual has made . . . . Otherwise, the interest in liberty protected by the Due Process Clause would be a nullity." *Hodgson v. Minnesota* (emphasis added). Thus, the State's general interest in life must accede to Nancy Cruzan's particularized and intense interest in self-determination in her choice of medical treatment. There is simply nothing legitimately within the State's purview to be gained by superseding her decision.

This is not to say that the State has no legitimate interests to assert here. As the majority recognizes, Missouri has a *parens patriae* interest in providing Nancy Cruzan, now incompetent, with as accurate as possible a determination of how she would exercise her rights under these circumstances. Second, if and when it is determined that Nancy Cruzan would want to continue treatment, the State may legitimately assert an interest in providing that treatment. But until Nancy's wishes have been determined, the only state interest that may be asserted is an interest in safe-guarding the accuracy of that determination.

Accuracy, therefore, must be our touchstone. Missouri may constitutionally impose only those procedural requirements that serve to enhance the accuracy of a determination of Nancy Cruzan's wishes or are at least consistent with an accurate determination. The Missouri "safeguard" that the Court upholds today does not meet that standard. The determination needed in this context is whether the incompetent person would choose to live in a persistent vegetative state on life-support or to avoid this medical treatment. Missouri's rule of decision imposes a markedly asymmetrical evidentiary burden. Only evidence of specific statements of treatment choice made by the patient when competent is admissible to support a finding that the patient, now in a persistent vegetative state, would wish to avoid further medical treatment. Moreover, this evidence must be clear and convincing. No proof is required to support a finding that the incompetent person would wish to continue treatment.

The majority claims that the allocation of the risk of error is justified because it is more important not to terminate life-support for someone who would wish it continued than to honor the wishes of someone who would not. An erroneous decision to terminate life-support is irrevocable, says the majority, while an erroneous decision not to terminate "results in a maintenance of the status quo." But, from the point of view of the patient, an erroneous decision in either direction is irrevocable. An erroneous decision to terminate artificial nutrition and hydration, to be sure, will lead to failure of that last remnant of physiological life, the brain stem, and result in complete brain death. An erroneous decision not to terminate life-support, however, robs a patient of the very qualities protected by the right to avoid unwanted medical treatment. His own degraded existence is perpetuated; his family's suffering is protracted; the memory he leaves behind becomes more and more distorted.

Even more than its heightened evidentiary standard, the Missouri court's categorical exclusion of relevant evidence dispenses with any semblence of accurate factfinding.

Too few people execute living wills or equivalently formal directives for such an evidentiary rule to ensure adequately that the wishes of incompetent persons will be honored. While it might be a wise social policy to encourage people to furnish such instructions, no general conclusion about a patient's choice can be drawn from the absence of formalities. The testimony of close friends and family members, on the other hand, may often be the best evidence available of what the patient's choice would be. It is they with whom the patient most likely will have discussed such questions and they who know the patient best.

I do not suggest that States must sit by helplessly if the choices of incompetent patients are in danger of being ignored. Even if the Court had ruled that Missouri's rule of decision is unconstitutional, as I believe it should have, States would nevertheless remain free to fashion procedural protections to safeguard the interests of incompetents under these circumstances. The Constitution provides merely a framework here: protections must be genuinely aimed at ensuring decisions commensurate with the will of the patient, and must be reliable as instruments to that end. Of the many States which have instituted such protections, Missouri is virtually the only one to have fashioned a rule that lessens the likelihood of accurate determinations. In contrast, nothing in the Constitution prevents States from reviewing the advisability of a family decision, by requiring a court proceeding or by appointing an impartial guardian ad litem.

JUSTICE STEVENS, dissenting.

Our Constitution is born of the proposition that all legitimate governments must secure the equal right of every person to "Life, Liberty, and the pursuit of Happiness." In the ordinary case we quite naturally assume that these three ends are compatible, mutually enhancing, and perhaps even coincident.

The Court would make an exception here. It permits the State's abstract, undifferentiated interest in the preservation of life to overwhelm the best interests of Nancy Beth Cruzan, interests which would, according to an undisputed finding, be served by allowing her guardians to exercise her constitutional right to discontinue medical treatment. Ironically, the Court reaches this conclusion despite endorsing three significant propositions which should save it from any such dilemma. First, a competent individual's decision to refuse life-sustaining medical procedures is an aspect of liberty protected by the Due Process Clause of the Fourteenth Amendment. Second, upon a proper evidentiary showing, a qualified guardian may make that decision on behalf of an incompetent ward. Third, in answering the important question presented by this tragic case, it is wise "not to attempt by any general statement, to cover every possible phase of the subject." Together, these considerations suggest that Nancy Cruzan's liberty to be free from medical treatment must be understood in light of the facts and circumstances particular to her.

I would so hold: in my view, the Constitution requires the State to care for Nancy Cruzan's life in a way that gives appropriate respect to her own best interests.

The portion of this Court's opinion that considers the merits of this case . . . fails to respect the best interests of the patient. It relies on what is tantamount to a waiver rationale: the dying patient's best interests are put to one side and the entire inquiry is focused on her prior expressions of intent. An innocent person's constitutional right to be free from unwanted medical treatment is thereby categorically limited to those patients who had the foresight to make an unambiguous statement of their wishes while competent. The Court's decision affords no protection to children, to young people who are victims of unexpected accidents or illnesses, or to the countless thousands of elderly persons who either fail to decide, or fail to explain, how they want to be treated if they should experience a similar fate. Because Nancy Beth Cruzan did not have the foresight to preserve her constitutional right in a living will, or some comparable "clear and convincing" alternative, her right is gone forever and her fate is in the hands of the state legislature instead of in those of her family, her independent neutral guardian ad litem, and an impartial judge — all of whom agree on the course of action that is in her best interests. The Court's willingness to find a waiver of this constitutional right reveals a distressing misunderstanding of the importance of individual liberty.

It seems to me that the Court errs insofar as it characterizes this case as involving "judgments about the 'quality' of life that a particular individual may enjoy." Nancy Cruzan is obviously "alive" in a physiological sense. But for patients like Nancy Cruzan, who have no consciousness and no chance of recovery, there is a serious question as to whether the mere persistence of their bodies is "life" as that word is commonly understood, or as it is used in both the Constitution and the Declaration of Independence. The State's unflagging determination to perpetuate Nancy Cruzan's physical existence is comprehensible only as an effort to define life's meaning, not as an attempt to preserve its sanctity.

If there is a shared thread among the various opinions on this subject, it may be that life is an activity which is at once the matrix for and an integration of a person's interests. In any event, absent some theological abstraction, the idea of life is not conceived separately from the idea of a living person. Yet, it is by precisely such a separation that Missouri asserts an interest in Nancy Cruzan's life in opposition to Nancy Cruzan's own interests. The resulting definition is uncommon indeed.

In short, there is no reasonable ground for believing that Nancy Beth Cruzan has any personal interest in the perpetuation of what the State has decided is her life. As I have already suggested, it would be possible to hypothesize such an interest on the basis of theological or philosophical conjecture. But even to posit such a basis for the State's action is to condemn it. It is not within the province of secular government to circumscribe the liberties of the people by regulations designed wholly for the purpose of establishing a sectarian definition of life.

My disagreement with the Court is thus unrelated to its endorsement of the clear and convincing standard of proof for cases of this kind. Indeed, I agree that the controlling facts must be established with unmistakable clarity. The critical question, however, is not how to prove the controlling facts but rather what proven facts should be controlling. In my view, the constitutional answer is clear: the best interests of the individual, especially when buttressed by the interests of all related third parties, must prevail over any general state policy that simply ignores those interests. Indeed, the only apparent secular basis for the State's interest in life is the policy's persuasive impact upon people other than Nancy and her family. The failure of Missouri's policy to heed the interests of a dying individual with respect to matters so private is ample evidence of the policy's illegitimacy.

Only because Missouri has arrogated to itself the power to define life, and only because the Court permits this usurpation, are Nancy Cruzan's life and liberty put into disquieting conflict. If Nancy Cruzan's life were defined by reference to her own interests, so that her life expired when her biological existence ceased serving any of her own interests, then her constitutionally protected interest in freedom from unwanted treatment would not come into conflict with her constitutionally protected interest in life. Conversely, if there were any evidence that Nancy Cruzan herself defined life to encompass every form of biological persistence by a human being, so that the continuation of treatment would serve Nancy's own liberty, then once again there would be no conflict between life and liberty. The opposition of life and liberty in this case are thus not the result of Nancy Cruzan's tragic accident, but are instead the artificial consequence of Missouri's effort, and this Court's willingness, to abstract Nancy Cruzan's life from Nancy Cruzan's person.

In this case, as is no doubt true in many others, the predicament confronted by the healthy members of the Cruzan family merely adds emphasis to the best interests finding made by the trial judge. Each of us has an interest in the kind of memories that will survive after death. To that end, individual decisions are often motivated by their impact on others. A member of the kind of family identified in the trial court's findings in this case would likely have not only a normal interest in minimizing the burden that her own illness imposes on others, but also an interest in having their memories of her filled predominantly with thoughts about her past vitality rather than her current condition. The meaning and completion of her life should be controlled by persons who have her best interests at heart — not by a state legislature concerned only with the "preservation of human life."

The Cruzan family's continuing concern provides a concrete reminder that Nancy Cruzan's interests did not disappear with her vitality or her consciousness. However commendable may be the State's interest in human life, it cannot pursue that interest by appropriating Nancy Cruzan's life as a symbol for its own purposes. Lives do not exist in abstraction from persons, and to pretend otherwise is not to honor but to desecrate the State's responsibility for protecting life. A State that seeks to demonstrate its commitment to life may do so by aiding those who are actively struggling for life and health. In this endeavor, unfortunately, no State can lack for opportunities: there can be no need to make an example of tragic cases like that of Nancy Cruzan.

NOTES

1. *The holding of Cruzan.* Does the Court's opinion stand for the proposition that there is no constitutional right of a physically incompetent individual to decline life-serving treatment? If not, how broad is the Court's holding? Is *Cruzan* appropriately viewed as a "right-to-die" case? *See* Yale Kamisar, *When Is There a Constitutional "Right to Die"? When Is There No Constitutional "Right to Live"?*, 25 Ga. L. Rev. 1203, 1214 (1991): "The Supreme Court is likely to make plain in a future case what I think is implicit in *Cruzan*: As a matter of constitutional law there is no distinction between a patient (such as Nancy Cruzan) whose condition has 'stabilized' or is not 'terminal' and a 'dying' or 'terminally ill' patient." Does *Cruzan* support such a suggestion?

2. *Assessing the interests involved.* Consider the following defense of the *Cruzan* decision:

> If [Nancy Cruzan] had no interest in further living, however, it does not necessarily follow that she also had an interest in dying. If allowing her to die cannot harm her because she no longer has

> interests in any meaningful sense, then she cannot be harmed by further maintenance, either. Nancy Cruzan simply had no further interests in being treated or not being treated.

John Robertson, *Cruzan and the Constitutional Status of Nontreatment Decisions for Incompetent Patients*, 25 GA. L. REV. 1139, 1158 (1991). Would it have made a difference if the plaintiffs in *Cruzan* had presented the claim as one on behalf of the parents to avoid watching their daughter, or her "shell," "suffer" the ignominy of persisting in a vegetative state? Does constitutional analysis depend more on the interest of the individual or the interest of the state? How relevant to the constitutional issue of the right to die is the fact that "many legal and bioethical commentators have decried [the *Cruzan*] decision"? John Robertson, *Assessing Quality of Life: A Response to Professor Kamisar*, 25 GA. L. REV. 1243 (1991).

WASHINGTON v. GLUCKSBERG

521 U.S. 702, 117 S. Ct. 2258, 138 L. Ed. 2d 772 (1997)

CHIEF JUSTICE REHNQUIST delivered the opinion of the Court.

The question presented in this case is whether Washington's prohibition against "caus[ing]" or "aid[ing]" a suicide offends the Fourteenth Amendment to the United States Constitution. We hold that it does not.

It has always been a crime to assist a suicide in the State of Washington. Today, Washington law provides: "A person is guilty of promoting a suicide attempt when he knowingly causes or aids another person to attempt suicide." "Promoting a suicide attempt" is a felony, punishable by up to five years' imprisonment and up to a $10,000 fine. §§ 9A.36.060(2) and 9A.20.021(1)(c). At the same time, Washington's Natural Death Act, enacted in 1979, states that the "withholding or withdrawal of life-sustaining treatment" at a patient's direction "shall not, for any purpose, constitute a suicide."

Petitioners in this case are the State of Washington and its Attorney General. Respondents Harold Glucksberg, M.D., Abigail Halperin, M.D., Thomas A. Preston, M.D., and Peter Shalit, M.D., are physicians who practice in Washington. These doctors occasionally treat terminally ill, suffering patients, and declare that they would assist these patients in ending their lives if not for Washington's assisted-suicide ban. In January 1994, respondents, along with three gravely ill, pseudonymous plaintiffs who have since died and Compassion in Dying, a nonprofit organization that counsels people considering physician-assisted suicide, sued in the United States District Court, seeking a declaration that Wash. Rev. Code § 9A.36.060(1) is, on its face, unconstitutional.

The plaintiffs asserted "the existence of a liberty interest protected by the Fourteenth Amendment which extends to a personal choice by a mentally competent, terminally ill adult to commit physician-assisted suicide." Relying primarily on *Planned Parenthood v. Casey* and *Cruzan v. Director, Missouri Dept. of Health*, the District Court agreed, and concluded that Washington's assisted-suicide ban is unconstitutional because it "places an undue burden on the exercise of [that] constitutionally protected liberty interest." The District Court also decided that the Washington statute violated the Equal Protection Clause's requirement that "all persons similarly situated . . . be treated alike."

A panel of the Court of Appeals for the Ninth Circuit reversed, emphasizing that "[i]n the two hundred and five years of our existence no constitutional right to aid in killing oneself has ever been asserted and upheld by a court of final jurisdiction." The Ninth Circuit reheard the case *en banc*, reversed the panel's decision, and affirmed the District Court. Like the District Court, the en banc Court of Appeals emphasized our *Casey* and *Cruzan* decisions. The court held that the State's assisted-suicide ban was unconstitutional "as applied to terminally ill competent adults who wish to hasten their deaths with medication prescribed by their physicians." The court did not reach the District Court's equal-protection holding. We granted *certiorari*, and now reverse.

We begin, as we do in all due-process cases, by examining our Nation's history, legal traditions, and practices. In almost every State — indeed, in almost every western democracy — it is a crime to assist a suicide. The States' assisted-suicide bans are not innovations. Rather, they are longstanding expressions of the States' commitment to the protection and preservation of all human life.

More specifically, for over 700 years, the Anglo-American common-law tradition has punished or otherwise disapproved of both suicide and assisting suicide.

Though deeply rooted, the States' assisted-suicide bans have in recent years been reexamined and, generally, reaffirmed. Because of advances in medicine and technology, Americans today are increasingly likely to die in institutions, from chronic illnesses. Public concern and democratic action are therefore sharply focused on how best to protect dignity and independence at the end of life, with the result that there have been many significant changes in state laws and in the attitudes these laws reflect. Many States, for example, now permit "living wills," surrogate health-care decisionmaking, and the withdrawal or refusal of life-sustaining medical treatment. At the same time, however, voters and legislators continue for the most part to reaffirm their States' prohibitions on assisting suicide.

The States are currently engaged in serious, thoughtful examinations of physician-assisted suicide and other similar issues. Attitudes toward suicide itself have changed, but our laws have consistently condemned, and continue to prohibit, assisting suicide. Despite changes in medical technology and notwithstanding an increased emphasis on the importance of end-of-life decisionmaking, we have not retreated from this prohibition. Against this backdrop of history, tradition, and practice, we now turn to respondents' constitutional claim.

The Due Process Clause guarantees more than fair process, and the "liberty" it protects includes more than the absence of physical restraint. The Clause also provides heightened protection against government interference with certain fundamental rights and liberty interests. In a long line of cases, we have held that, in addition to the specific freedoms protected by the Bill of Rights, the "liberty" specially protected by the Due Process Clause includes the rights to marry; to have children; to direct the education and upbringing of one's children; to marital privacy; to use contraception; to bodily integrity, and to abortion. We have also assumed, and strongly suggested, that the Due Process Clause protects the traditional right to refuse unwanted lifesaving medical treatment. *Cruzan.*

But we "ha[ve] always been reluctant to expand the concept of substantive due process because guideposts for responsible decisionmaking in this unchartered area are scarce and open-ended." *Collins* [*v. Harker Heights*]. By extending constitutional protection to an asserted right or liberty interest, we, to a great extent, place the matter outside the arena of public debate and legislative action. We must therefore "exercise the utmost care whenever we are asked to break new ground in this field," *ibid*, lest the liberty protected by the Due Process Clause be subtly transformed into the policy preferences of the members of this Court.

Our established method of substantive-due-process analysis has two primary features: First, we have regularly observed that the Due Process Clause specially protects those fundamental rights and liberties which are, objectively, "deeply rooted in this Nation's history and tradition" [*Moore v. City of East Cleveland*], and "implicit in the concept of ordered liberty," such that "neither liberty nor justice would exist if they were sacrificed," *Palko v. Connecticut.* Second, we have required in substantive-due-process cases a "careful description" of the asserted fundamental liberty interest. *Collins*, *Cruzan.* Our Nation's history, legal traditions, and practices thus provide the crucial "guideposts for responsible decisionmaking," that direct and restrain our exposition of the Due Process Clause.

JUSTICE SOUTER, relying on JUSTICE HARLAN's dissenting opinion in *Poe v. Ullman* [p. 507], would largely abandon this restrained methodology, and instead ask "whether [Washington's] statute sets up one of those 'arbitrary impositions' or 'purposeless restraints' at odds with the Due Process Clause of the Fourteenth Amendment." In our view, however, the development of this Court's substantive-due-process jurisprudence, has been a process whereby the outlines of the "liberty" specially protected by the Fourteenth Amendment — never fully clarified, to be sure, and perhaps not capable of being fully clarified — have at least been carefully refined by concrete examples involving fundamental rights found to be deeply rooted in our legal tradition. This approach tends to rein in the subjective elements that are necessarily present in due-process judicial review. In addition, by establishing a threshold requirement — that a challenged state action implicate a fundamental right — before requiring more than a reasonable relation to a legitimate state interest to justify the action, it avoids the need for complex balancing of competing interests in every case.

Turning to the claim at issue here, respondents assert a "liberty to choose how to die" and a right to "control of one's final days," and describe the asserted liberty as "the right to choose a humane, dignified death," and "the liberty to shape death." As noted above, we have a tradition of carefully formulating the interest at stake in substantive-due-process cases. For example, although *Cruzan* is often described as a "right to die" case we were, in fact, more precise: we assumed that the Constitution granted competent persons a "constitutionally protected right to refuse lifesaving hydration and nutrition." The Washington statute at issue in this case prohibits "aid[ing] another person to attempt suicide," and, thus, the question before us is whether the "liberty" specially protected by the Due Process Clause includes a right to commit suicide which itself includes a right to assistance in doing so.

We now inquire whether this asserted right has any place in our Nation's traditions. Here we are confronted with a consistent and almost universal tradition that has long rejected the asserted right, and continues explicitly to reject it today, even for terminally ill, mentally competent adults. To hold for respondents, we would have to reverse centuries of legal doctrine and practice, and strike down the considered policy choice of almost every State.

Respondents contend, however, that the liberty interest they assert is consistent with this Court's substantive-due-process line of cases, if not with this Nation's history and practice. Pointing to *Casey* and *Cruzan*, respondents read our jurisprudence in this area as reflecting a general tradition of "self-sovereignty," and as teaching that the "liberty" protected by the Due Process Clause includes "basic and intimate exercises of personal autonomy." According to respondents, our liberty jurisprudence, and the broad, individualistic principles it reflects, protects the "liberty of competent, terminally ill adults to make end-of-life decisions free of undue government interference." The question presented in this case, however, is whether the protections of the Due Process Clause include a right to commit suicide with another's assistance. With this "careful description" of respondents' claim in mind, we turn to *Casey* and *Cruzan*.

Respondents contend that in *Cruzan* we "acknowledged that competent, dying persons have the right to direct the removal of life-sustaining medical treatment and thus hasten death," and that "the constitutional principle behind recognizing the patient's liberty to direct the withdrawal of artificial life support applies at least as strongly to the choice to hasten impending death by consuming lethal medication." The right assumed in *Cruzan*, however, was not simply deduced from abstract concepts of personal autonomy. Given the common-law rule that forced medication was a battery, and the long legal tradition protecting the decision to refuse unwanted medical treatment, our assumption was entirely consistent with this Nation's history and constitutional traditions. The decision to commit suicide with the assistance of another may be just as personal and profound as the decision to refuse unwanted medical treatment, but it has never enjoyed similar legal protection. Indeed, the two acts are widely and reasonably regarded as quite distinct. In *Cruzan* itself, we recognized that most States outlawed assisted suicide — and even more do today — and we certainly gave no intimation that the right to refuse unwanted medical treatment could be somehow transmuted into a right to assistance in committing suicide.

Respondents also rely on *Casey*. [R]espondents emphasize the statement in *Casey* that: "At the heart of liberty is the right to define one's own concept of existence, of meaning, of the universe, and of the mystery of human life. Beliefs about these matters could not define the attributes of personhood were they formed under compulsion of the State."

By choosing this language, the Court's opinion in *Casey* described, in a general way and in light of our prior cases, those personal activities and decisions that this Court has identified as so deeply rooted in our history and traditions, or so fundamental to our concept of constitutionally ordered liberty, that they are protected by the Fourteenth Amendment. The opinion moved from the recognition that liberty necessarily includes freedom of conscience and belief about ultimate considerations to the observation that "though the abortion decision may originate within the zone of conscience and belief, it is more than a philosophic exercise." That many of the rights and liberties protected by the Due Process Clause sound in personal autonomy does not warrant the sweeping conclusion that any and all important, intimate, and personal decisions are so protected, and *Casey* did not suggest otherwise.

The history of the law's treatment of assisted suicide in this country has been and continues to be one of the rejection of nearly all efforts to permit it. That being the case, our decisions lead us to conclude that the asserted "right" to assistance in committing suicide is not a fundamental liberty interest protected by the Due Process Clause. The Constitution also requires, however, that Washington's assisted-suicide ban be rationally related to legitimate government interests. This requirement is unquestionably met here. Washington's assisted-suicide ban implicates a number of state interests.

First, Washington has an "unqualified interest in the preservation of human life." The State's prohibition on assisted suicide, like all homicide laws, both reflects and advances its commitment to this interest. This interest is symbolic and aspirational as well as practical. Respondents admit that "[t]he State has a real interest in preserving the lives of those who can still contribute to society and enjoy life." The Court of Appeals also recognized Washington's interest in protecting life, but held that the "weight" of this interest depends on the "medical condition and the wishes of the person whose life is at stake." Washington, however, has rejected this sliding-scale approach and, through its assisted-suicide ban, insists that all persons' lives, from beginning to end, regardless of physical or mental condition, are under the full protection of the law. As we have previously affirmed, the States "may properly decline to make judgments about the 'quality' of life that a particular individual may enjoy," *Cruzan*. This remains true, as *Cruzan* makes clear, even for those who are near death.

Those who attempt suicide — terminally ill or not — often suffer from depression or other mental disorders. Research indicates, however, that many people who request physician-assisted suicide withdraw that request if their depression and pain are treated. Thus, legal physician-assisted suicide could make it more difficult for the State to protect depressed or mentally ill persons, or those who are suffering from untreated pain, from suicidal impulses.

The State also has an interest in protecting the integrity and ethics of the medical profession. And physician-assisted suicide could, it is argued, undermine that the trust that is essential to the doctor-patient relationship by blurring the time-honored line between healing and harming.

Next, the State has an interest in protecting vulnerable groups — including the poor, the elderly, and disabled persons — from abuse, neglect, and mistakes. We have recognized the real risk of subtle coercion and undue influence in end-of-life situations. *Cruzan*. If physician-assisted suicide were permitted, many might resort to it to spare their families the substantial financial burden of end-of-life health-care costs. The State's interest here goes beyond protecting the vulnerable from coercion; it extends to protecting disabled and terminally ill people from prejudice, negative and inaccurate stereotypes, and "societal indifference." The State's assisted-suicide ban reflects and reinforces its policy that the lives of terminally ill, disabled, and elderly people must be no less valued than the lives of the young and healthy, and that a seriously disabled person's suicidal impulses should be interpreted and treated the same way as anyone else's.

Finally, the State may fear that permitting assisted suicide will start it down the path to voluntary and perhaps even involuntary euthanasia. The Court of Appeals struck down Washington's assisted-suicide ban only "as applied to competent, terminally ill adults who wish to hasten their deaths by obtaining medication prescribed by their doctors." Washington insists, however, that the impact of the court's decision will not and cannot be so limited. If suicide is protected as a matter of constitutional right, it is argued, "every man and woman in the United States must enjoy it." Thus, it turns out that what is couched as a limited right to "physician-assisted suicide" is likely, in effect, a much broader license, which could prove extremely difficult to police and contain. Washington's ban on assisting suicide prevents such erosion. This concern is further supported by evidence about the practice of euthanasia in the Netherlands. The Dutch government's own study suggests that, despite the existence of various reporting procedures, euthanasia in the Netherlands has not been limited to the competent, terminally ill adults who are enduring physical suffering, and that regulation of the practice may not have prevented abuses in cases involving vulnerable persons, including severely disabled neonates and elderly persons suffering from dementia.

We need not weigh exactingly the relative strengths of these various interests. They are unquestionably important and legitimate, and Washington's ban on assisted suicide is at least reasonably related to their promotion and protection. We therefore hold that Wash. Rev. Codes § 9A.36.060(1) does not violate the Fourteenth Amendment, either on its face or "as applied to competent, terminally ill adults who wish to hasten their deaths by obtaining medication prescribed by their doctors."

Throughout the Nation, Americans are engaged in an earnest and profound debate about the morality, legality, and practicality of physician-assisted suicide. Our holding permits this debate to continue, as it should in a democratic society. The decision of the *en banc* Court of Appeals is reversed, and the case is remanded for further proceedings consistent with this opinion.

JUSTICE SOUTER, concurring in the judgment.

My understanding of unenumerated rights in the wake of [JUSTICE HARLAN's dissent in *Poe v. Ullman*] and subsequent cases avoids the absolutist failing of many older cases without embracing the opposite pole of equating reasonableness with past practice described at a very specific level. That understanding begins with a concept of "ordered liberty," *Poe* (HARLAN, J.);

comprising a continuum of rights to be free from "arbitrary impositions and purposeless restraints," *Poe* (HARLAN, J.).

After the *Poe* dissent, as before it, this enforceable concept of liberty would bar statutory impositions even at relatively trivial levels when governmental restraints are undeniably irrational as unsupported by any imaginable rationale. Such instances are suitably rare. The claims of arbitrariness that mark almost all instances of unenumerated substantive rights are those resting on "certain interests requir[ing] particularly careful scrutiny of the state needs asserted to justify their abridgment." In the face of an interest this powerful a State may not rest on threshold rationality or a presumption of constitutionality, but may prevail only on the ground of an interest sufficiently compelling to place within the realm of the reasonable a refusal to recognize the individual right asserted.

This approach calls for a court to assess the relative "weights" or dignities of the contending interests, and to this extent the judicial method is familiar to the common law. Common law method is subject, however, to two important constraints in the hands of a court engaged in substantive due process review. First, such a court is bound to confine the values that it recognizes to those truly deserving constitutional stature, either to those expressed in constitutional text, or those exemplified by "the traditions from which [the Nation] developed," or revealed by contrast with "the traditions from which it broke." *Poe* (HARLAN, J., dissenting).

The second constraint, again, simply reflects the fact that constitutional review, not judicial lawmaking, is a court's business here. It is only when the legislation's justifying principle, critically valued, is so far from being commensurate with the individual interest as to be arbitrarily or pointlessly applied that the statute must give way. Only if this standard points against the statute can the individual claimant be said to have a constitutional right.

Although the *Poe* dissent disclaims the possibility of any general formula for due process analysis (beyond the basic analytic structure just described), JUSTICE HARLAN of course assumed that adjudication under the Due Process Clauses is like any other in stance of judgment dependent on common-law method, being more or less persuasive according to the usual canons of critical discourse. When identifying and assessing the competing interests of liberty and authority, for example, the breadth of expression that a litigant or a judge selects in stating the competing principles will have much to do with the outcome and may be dispositive. As in any process of rational argumentation, we recognize that when a generally accepted principle is challenged, the broader the attack the less likely it is to succeed. The principle's defenders will, indeed, often try to characterize any challenge as just such a broadside, perhaps by couching the defense as if a broadside attack had occurred.

Just as results in substantive due process cases are tied to the selections of statements of the competing interests, the acceptability of the results is a function of the good reasons for the selections made. It is here that the value of common-law method becomes apparent, for the usual thinking of the common law is suspicious of the all-or-nothing analysis that tends to produce legal petrification instead of an evolving boundary between the domains of old principles. Common-law method tends to pay respect instead to detail, seeking to understand old principles afresh by new examples and new counter-examples. The "tradition is a living thing," *Poe* (HARLAN, J., dissenting), albeit one that moves by moderate steps carefully taken. "The decision of an apparently novel claim must depend on grounds which follow closely on well-accepted principles and criteria. The new decision must take its place in relation to what went before and further [cut] a channel for what is to come." Exact analysis and characterization of any due process claim is critical to the method and to the result.

It is in the abortion cases that the most telling recognitions of the importance of bodily integrity and the concomitant tradition of medical assistance have occurred. The analogies between the abortion cases and this one are several. Even though the State has a legitimate interest in discouraging abortion, the Court recognized a woman's right to a physician's counsel and care. Like the decision to commit suicide, the decision to abort potential life can be made irresponsibly and under the influence of others, and yet the Court has held in the abortion cases that physicians are fit assistants. Without physician assistance in abortion, the woman's right would have too often amounted to nothing more than a right to self-mutilation, and without a physician to assist in the suicide of the dying, the patient's right will often be confined to crude methods of causing death, most shocking and painful to the decedent's survivors.

The argument supporting respondents' position progresses through three steps of increasing forcefulness. First, it emphasizes the decriminalization of suicide. Reliance on this fact is sanctioned under the standard that looks not only to the tradition retained, but to society's occasional choices to reject traditions of the legal past. While the common law prohibited both suicide and aiding a suicide, with the prohibition on aiding largely justified by the primary prohibition on self-inflicted death itself, the State's rejection of the traditional treatment of the one leaves the criminality of the other open to questioning that previously would not have been appropriate. The second step in the argument is to emphasize that the State's own act of decriminalization gives a freedom of choice much like the individual's option in recognized instances of bodily autonomy. One of these, abortion, is a legal right to choose in spite of the interest a State may legitimately invoke in discouraging the practice, just as suicide is not subject to choice, despite a state interest in discouraging it. The third step is to emphasize that respondents claim the right to assistance not on the basis of some broad principle that would be subject to exceptions if the continuing interest of the State's in discouraging suicide were to be recognized at all. Respondents base their claim on the traditional right to medical care and counsel, subject to the limiting conditions of informed, responsible choice when death is imminent, conditions that support a strong analogy to rights of care in other situations in which medical counsel and assistance have been available as a matter of course. There can be no stronger claim to a physician's assistance than at the time when death is imminent, a moral judgement implied by the State's own recognition of the legitimacy of medical procedures necessarily hastening the moment of impending death.

It is my judgment, the importance of the individual interest here, as within that class of "certain interests" demanding careful scrutiny of the State's contrary claim cannot be gainsaid. Whether that interest might in some circumstances, or at some time, be seen as "fundamental" to the degree entitled to prevail is not, however, a conclusion that I need draw here, for I am satisfied that the State's interests are sufficiently serious to defeat the present claim that its law is arbitrary or purposeless.

The State has put forward several interests to justify the Washington law as applied to physicians treating terminally ill patients, even those competent to make responsible choices: protecting life generally, discouraging suicide even if knowing and voluntary, and protecting terminally ill patients from involuntary suicide and euthanasia, both voluntary and nonvoluntary.

It is not necessary to discuss the exact strengths of the first two claims of justification in the present circumstances, for the third is dispositive for me. That third justification is different from the first two, for it addresses specific features of respondents' claim, and it opposes that claim not with a moral judgment contrary to respondents', but with a recognized state interest in the protection of non-responsible individuals and those who do not stand in relation either to death or to their physicians as do the patients whom respondents describe. The State claims interests in protecting patients from mistakenly and involuntarily deciding to end their lives, and in guarding against both voluntary and involuntary euthanasia. Leaving aside any difficulties in coming to a clear concept of imminent death, mistaken decisions may result from inadequate palliative care or a terminal prognosis that turns out to be error; coercion and abuse may stem from the large medical bills that family members cannot bear or unreimbursed hospitals decline to shoulder. Voluntary and involuntary euthanasia may result once doctors are authorized to prescribe lethal medication in the first instance, for they might find it pointless to distinguish between patients who administer their own fatal drugs and those who wish not to, and their compassion for those who suffer may obscure the distinction between those who ask for death and those who may be unable to request it. The argument is that a progression would occur, obscuring the line between the ill and the dying, and between the responsible and the unduly influenced, until ultimately doctors and perhaps others would abuse a limited freedom to aid suicides by yielding to the impulse to end another's suffering under conditions going beyond the narrow limits the respondents propose. The State thus argues, essentially, that respondents' claim is not as narrow as it sounds, simply because no recognition of the interest they assert could be limited to vindicating those interests and affecting no others. The State says that the claim, in practical effect, would entail consequences that the State could, without doubt, legitimately act to prevent.

The mere assertion that the terminally sick might be pressured into suicide decisions by close friends and family members would not alone be very telling. Of course that is possible, not only because the costs of care might be more than family members could bear but simply because they might naturally wish to see an end of suffering for someone they love. But one of the points of restricting any right of assistance to physicians, would be to condition the right on an exercise of judgment by someone qualified to assess the patient's responsible capacity and detect the influence of those outside the medical relationship.

The State, however, goes further, to argue that dependence on the vigilance of physicians will not be enough. First, the lines proposed here (particularly the requirement of a knowing and voluntary decision by the patient) would be more difficult to draw than the lines that have limited other recently recognized due process rights. Second, this difficulty could become the greater by combining with another fact within the realm of plausibility, that physicians simply would not be assiduous to preserve the line. They have compassion, and those who would be willing to assist in suicide at all might be the most susceptible to the wishes of a patient, whether the patient were technically quite responsible or not. Physicians, and their hospitals, have their own financial incentives, too, in this new age of managed care. Whether acting from compassion or under some other influence, a physician who would provide a drug for a patient to administer might well go the further step of administering the drug himself; so, the barrier between assisted suicide and euthanasia could become porous, and the line between voluntary and involuntary euthanasia as well. The case for the slippery slope is fairly made out here, not because recognizing one due process right would leave a court with no principled basis to avoid recognizing another, but because there is a plausible case that the right claimed would not be readily containable by reference to facts about the mind that are matters of difficult judgment, or by gatekeepers who are subject to temptation, noble or not.

Respondents propose an answer to all this, the answer of state regulation with teeth. Legislation proposed in several States, for example, would authorize physician-assisted suicide but require two qualified physicians to confirm the patient's diagnosis, prognosis, and competence; and would mandate that the patient make repeated requests witnessed by at least two others over a specified time span; and would impose reporting requirements and criminal penalties for various acts of coercion.

But at least at this moment there are reasons for caution in predicting the effectiveness of the teeth proposed. Respondents' proposals, as it turns out, sound much like the guidelines now in place in the Netherlands, the only place where experience with physician-assisted suicide and euthanasia has yielded empirical evidence about how such regulations might affect actual practice. Dutch physicians must engage in consultation before proceeding, and must decide whether the patient's decision is voluntary, well considered, and stable, whether the request to die is enduring and made more than once, and whether the patient's future will involve unacceptable suffering. There is, however, a substantial dispute today about what the Dutch experience shows. Some commentators marshall evidence that the Dutch guidelines have in practice failed to protect patients from involuntary euthanasia and have been violated with impunity. The day may come when we can say with some assurance which side is right, but for now it is the substantiality of the factual disagreement, and the alternatives for resolving it, that matter. They are, for me, dispositive of the due process claim at this time.

[W]e therefore have a clear question about which institution, a legislature or a court, is relatively more competent to deal with an emerging issue as to which facts currently unknown could be dispositive. The answer has to be, for the reasons already stated, that the legislative process is to be preferred.

While I do not decide for all time that respondents' claim should not be recognized, I acknowledge the legislative institutional competence as the better one to deal with that claim at this time.

JUSTICE O'CONNOR, concurring.*

Death will be different for each of us. For many, the last days will be spent in physical pain and perhaps the despair that accompanies physical deterioration and a loss of control of basic bodily and mental functions. Some will seek medication to alleviate that pain and other symptoms.

The Court frames the issue in this case as whether the Due Process Clause of the Constitution protects a "right to commit suicide which itself includes a right to assistance in doing so," and concludes that our Nation's history, legal traditions, and practices do not support the existence of such a right. I join the Court's opinions because I agree that there is no generalized right to "commit suicide." But respondents urge us to address the narrower question whether a mentally competent person who is experiencing great suffering has a constitutionally cognizable interest in controlling the circumstances of his or her imminent death. I see no need to reach that question in the context of the facial challenges to the New York and Washington laws at issue here. The parties and *amici* agree that in these States a patient who is suffering from a terminal illness and who is experiencing great pain has no legal barriers to obtaining medication, from qualified physicians, to alleviate that suffering, even to the point of causing unconsciousness and hastening death. In this light, even assuming that we would recognize such an interest, I agree that the State's interests in protecting those who are not truly competent or facing imminent death, or those whose decisions to hasten death would not truly be voluntary, are sufficiently weighty to justify a prohibition against physician-assisted suicide.

In sum, there is no need to address the question whether suffering patients have a constitutionally cognizable interest in obtaining relief from the suffering that they may experience in the last days of their lives. There is no dispute that dying patients in Washington and New York can obtain palliative care, even when doing so would hasten their deaths. The difficulty in defining terminal illness and the risk that a dying patient's request for assistance in ending his or her life might not be truly voluntary justifies the prohibitions on assisted suicide we uphold here.

JUSTICE STEVENS, concurring in the judgments.**

Today, the Court decides that Washington's statute prohibiting assisted suicide is not invalid "on its face," that is to say, in all or most cases in which it might be applied. That holding, however, does not foreclose the possibility that some applications of the statute might well be invalid.

As originally filed, this case presented a challenge to the Washington statute on its face and as it applied to three terminally ill, mentally competent patients and to four physicians who treat terminally ill patients. After the District Court issued its opinion holding that the statute placed an undue

---

* [*Ed. Note:*Justice O'Connor's concurring opinion applies to *Vacco v. Quill.*]

** [*Ed. Note:* Justice Stevens' concurring opinion applies to *Vacco v. Quill.*]

burden on the right to commit physician-assisted suicide, the three patients died. Although the Court of Appeals considered the constitutionality of the statute "as applied to the prescription of life-ending medication for use by terminally ill, competent adult patients who wish to hasten their deaths," the court did not have before it any individual plaintiff seeking to hasten her death or any doctor who was threatened with prosecution for assisting in the suicide of a particular patient; its analysis and eventual holding that the statute was unconstitutional was not limited to a particular set of plaintiffs before it.

History and tradition provide ample support for refusing to recognize an open-ended constitutional right to commit suicide. Much more than the State's paternalistic interest in protecting the individual from the irrevocable consequences of an ill-advised decision motivated by temporary concerns is at stake. There is truth in John Donne's observation that "No man is an island." The State has an interest in preserving and fostering the benefits that every human being may provide to the community — a community that thrives on the exchange of ideas, expressions of affection, shared memories and humorous incidents as well as on the material contributions that its members create and support. The value to others of a person's life is far too precious to allow the individual to claim a constitutional entitlement to complete autonomy in making a decision to end that life. Thus, I fully agree with the Court that the "liberty" protected by the Due Process Clause does not include a categorical "right to commit suicide which itself includes a right to assistance in doing so."

But just as our conclusion that capital punishment is not always unconstitutional did not preclude later decisions holding that it is sometimes impermissibly cruel, so is it equally clear that a decision upholding a general statutory prohibition of assisted suicide does not mean that every possible application of the statute would be valid. A State, like Washington, that has authorized the death penalty and thereby has concluded that the sanctity of human life does not require that it always be preserved, must acknowledge that there are situations in which an interest in hastening death is legitimate. Indeed, not only is that interest sometimes legitimate, I am also convinced that there are times when it is entitled to constitutional protection.

In *Cruzan* the Court assumed that the interest in liberty protected by the Fourteenth Amendment encompassed the right of a terminally ill patient to direct the withdrawal of life-sustaining treatment. As the Court correctly observes today, that assumption "was not simply deduced from abstract concepts of personal autonomy." Instead, it was supported by the common-law tradition protecting the individual's general right to refuse unwanted medical treatment. [B]ut I insist that the source of Nancy Cruzan's right to refuse treatment was not just a common-law rule. Rather, this right is an aspect of a far broader and more basic concept of freedom that is even older than the common law. This freedom embraces, not merely a person's right to refuse a particular kind of unwanted treatment, but also her interest in dignity, and in determining the character of the memories that will survive long after her death. In recognizing that the State's interests did not outweigh Nancy Cruzan's liberty interest in refusing medical treatment, *Cruzan* rested not simply on the common-law right to refuse medical treatment, but — at least implicitly — on the even more fundamental right to make this "deeply personal decision" (O'CONNOR, J., concurring).

Thus, the common-law right to protection from battery, which included the right to refuse medical treatment in most circumstances, did not mark "the outer limits of the substantive sphere of liberty" that supported the Cruzan family's decision to hasten Nancy's death. *Planned Parenthood of Southeastern Pa. v. Casey* [p. 474]. Those limits have never been precisely defined. They are generally identified by the importance and character of the decision confronted by the individual. Avoiding intolerable pain and the indignity of living one's final days incapacitated and in agony is certainly "[a]t the heart of [the] liberty . . . to define one's own concept of existence, of meaning, of the universe, and of the mystery of human life." *Casey*.

While I agree with the Court that *Cruzan* does not decide the issue presented by these cases, *Cruzan* did give recognition, not just to vague, unbridled notions of autonomy, but to the more specific interest in making decisions about how to confront an imminent death. Although there is no absolute right to physician-assisted suicide, *Cruzan* makes it clear that some individuals who no longer have the option of deciding whether to live or to die because they are already on the threshold of death have a constitutionally protected interest that may outweigh the State's interest in preserving life at all costs. The liberty interest at stake in a case like this differs from, and is stronger than, both the common-law right to refuse medical treatment and the unbridled interest in deciding whether to live or die. It is an interest in deciding how, rather than whether, a critical threshold shall be crossed.

The state interests supporting a general rule banning the practice of physician-assisted suicide do not have the same force in all cases. First and foremost of these interests is the "unqualified interest in the preservation of human life," which is equated with "the sanctity of life." That interest not only justifies — it commands — maximum protection of every individual's interest in remaining alive, which in turn commands the same protection for decisions about whether to commence or to terminate life-support systems or to administer pain medication that may hasten death. Properly viewed, however, this interest is not a collective interest that should always outweigh the interests of a person who because of pain, incapacity, or sedation finds her life intolerable, but rather, an aspect of individual freedom.

Many terminally ill people find their lives meaningful even if filled with pain or dependence on others. Some find value in living through suffering; some have an abiding desire to witness particular events in their families' lives; many believe it a sin to hasten death. Individuals of different religious faiths make different judgments and choices about whether to live on under such circumstances. There are those who will want to continue aggressive treatment; those who would prefer terminal sedation; and those who will seek withdrawal from life-support systems and death by gradual starvation and dehydration. Although as a general matter the State's interest in the contributions each person may make to society outweighs the person's interest in ending her life, this interest does not have the same force for a terminally ill patient faced not with the choice of whether to live, only of how to die. Allowing the individual, rather than the State, to make judgments "about the 'quality' of life that a particular individual may enjoy" does not mean that the lives of terminally-ill, disabled people have less value than the lives of those who are healthy. Rather, it gives proper recognition to the individual's interest in choosing a final chapter that accords with her life story, rather than one that demeans her values and poisons memories of her.

Similarly, the State's legitimate interests in preventing suicide, protecting the vulnerable from coercion and abuse, and preventing euthanasia are less significant in this context. I agree that the State has a compelling interest in preventing persons from committing suicide because of depression, or coercion by third parties. But the State's legitimate interest in preventing abuse does not apply to an individual who is not victimized by abuse, who is not suffering from depression, and who makes a rational and voluntary decision to seek assistance in dying. Although, diagnosing depression and other mental illness is not always easy, mental health workers and other professionals expert in working with dying patients can help patients cope with depression and pain, and help patients assess their options.

Relatedly, the State and *amici* express the concern that patients whose physical pain is inadequately treated will be more likely to request assisted suicide. Encouraging the development and ensuring the availability of adequate pain treatment is of utmost importance; palliative care, however, cannot alleviate all pain and suffering. An individual adequately informed of the care alternatives thus might make a rational choice for assisted suicide. For such an individual, the State's interest in preventing potential abuse and mistake is only minimally implicated.

The final major interest asserted by the State is its interest in preserving the traditional integrity of the medical profession. The fear is that a rule permitting physicians to assist in suicide is inconsistent with the perception that they serve their patients solely as healers. But for some patients, it would be a physician's refusal to dispense medication to ease their suffering and make their death tolerable and dignified that would be inconsistent with the healing role. For doctors who have long-standing relationships with their patients, who have given their patients advice on alternative treatments, who are attentive to their patient's individualized needs, and who are knowledgeable about pain symptom management and palliative care options, heeding a patient's desire to assist in her suicide would not serve to harm the physician-patient relationship. Furthermore, because physicians are already involved in making decisions that hasten the death of terminally ill patients — through termination of life support, withholding of medical treatment, and terminal sedation — there is in fact significant tension between the traditional view of the physician's role and the actual practice in a growing number of cases.

Although, as the Court concludes today, these potential harms are sufficient to support the State's general public policy against assisted suicide, they will not always outweigh the individual liberty interest of a particular patient. Unlike the Court of Appeals, I would not say as a categorical matter that these state interests are invalid as to the entire class of terminally ill, mentally competent patients. I do not, however, foreclose the possibility that an individual plaintiff seeking to hasten her death, or a doctor whose assistance was sought, could prevail in a more particularized challenge. Future cases will determine whether such a challenge may succeed.

There remains room for vigorous debate about the outcome of particular cases that are not necessarily resolved by the opinions announced today. How such cases may be decided will depend on their specific facts. In my judgment, however, it is clear that the so-called "unqualified interest in the preservation of human life," *Cruzan; Glucksberg,* is not itself sufficient to outweigh the interest in liberty that may justify the only possible means of preserving a dying patient's dignity and alleviating her intolerable suffering.

JUSTICE GINSBURG, concurring in the judgments.*

I concur in the Court's judgments in these cases substantially for the reasons stated by Justice O'Connor in her concurring opinion.

JUSTICE BREYER, concurring in the judgments.**

I believe that JUSTICE O'CONNOR's views, which I share, have greater legal significance than the Court's opinion suggests. I join her separate opinion, except insofar as it joins the majority.

I agree with the Court that the critical question in both of the cases before us is whether "the 'liberty' specially protected by the Due Process Clause includes a right" of the sort that the respondents assert. *Washington v. Glucksberg*. I do not agree, however, with the Court's formulation of that claimed "liberty" interest. The Court describes it as a "right to commit suicide with another's assistance." But I would not reject the respondents' claim without considering a different formulation, for which our legal tradition may provide greater support. That formulation would use words roughly like a "right to die with dignity." But irrespective of the exact words used, at its core would lie personal control over the manner of death, professional medical assistance, and the avoidance of unnecessary and severe physical suffering — combined.

As JUSTICE SOUTER points out, JUSTICE HARLAN's dissenting opinion in *Poe v. Ullman* offers some support for such a claim. In that opinion, JUSTICE HARLAN referred to the "liberty" that the Fourteenth Amendment protects as including "a freedom from all substantial arbitrary impositions and purposeless restraints" and also as recognizing that "certain interests require particularly careful scrutiny of the state needs asserted to justify their abridgment." The "certain interests" to which JUSTICE HARLAN referred may well be similar (perhaps identical) to the rights, liberties, or interests that the Court today, as in the past, regards as "fundamental."

JUSTICE HARLAN concluded that marital privacy was such a "special interest." He found in the Constitution a right of "privacy of the home" — with the home, the bedroom, and "intimate details of the marital relation" at its heart — by examining the protection that the law had earlier provided for related, but not identical, interests described by such words as "privacy," "home," and "family." The respondents here essentially ask us to do the same. They argue that one can find a "right to die with dignity" by examining the

* [*Ed. Note:* Justice Ginsburg's concurring opinion applies to *Vacco v. Quill.*]

** [*Ed. Note:* Justice Breyer's concurring opinion applies to *Vacco v. Quill.*]

protection the law has provided for related, but not identical, interests relating to personal dignity, medical treatment, and freedom from state-inflicted pain.

I do not believe, however, that this Court need or now should decide whether or a not such a right is "fundamental." That is because, in my view, the avoidance of severe physical pain (connected with death) would have to comprise an essential part of any successful claim and because, as JUSTICE O'CONNOR points out, the laws before us do not force a dying person to undergo that kind of pain. Rather, the laws of New York and of Washington do not prohibit doctors from providing patients with drugs sufficient to control pain despite the risk that those drugs themselves will kill. And under these circumstances the laws of New York and Washington would overcome any remaining significant interests and would be justified, regardless.

Were the legal circumstances different — for example, were state law to prevent the provision of palliative care, including the administration of drugs as needed to avoid pain at the end of life — then the law's impact upon serious and otherwise unavoidable physical pain (accompanying death) would be more directly at issue. And as JUSTICE O'CONNOR suggests, the Court might have to revisit its conclusions in these cases.

VACCO v. QUILL

521 U.S. 793, 117 S. Ct. 2293, 138 L. Ed. 2d 834 (1997)

CHIEF JUSTICE REHNQUIST delivered the opinion of the Court.

In New York, as in most States, it is a crime to aid another to commit or attempt suicide, but patients may refuse even lifesaving medical treatment. The question presented by this case is whether New York's prohibition on assisting suicide therefore violates the Equal Protection Clause of the Fourteenth Amendment. We hold that it does not.

Petitioners are various New York public officials. Respondents are physicians who practice in New York. They assert that although it would be "consistent with the standards of [their] medical practice[s]" to prescribe lethal medication for "mentally competent, terminally ill patients" who are suffering great pain and desire a doctor's help in taking their own lives, they are deterred from doing so by New York's ban on assisting suicide. Respondents, and three gravely ill patients who have since died, sued the State's Attorney General in the United States District Court. They urged that because New York permits a competent person to refuse life-sustaining medical treatment, and because the refusal of such treatment is "essentially the same thing" as physician-assisted suicide, New York's assisted-suicide ban violates the Equal Protection Clause.

The District Court disagreed: "[I]t is hardly unreasonable or irrational for the State to recognize a difference between allowing nature to take its course, even in the most severe situations, and intentionally using an artificial death -producing device."

The Court of Appeals for the Second Circuit reversed. The court determined that, despite the assisted-suicide ban's apparent general applicability, "New York law does not treat equally all competent persons who are in the final stages of fatal illness and wish to hasten their deaths," because "those in the final stages of terminal illness who are on life-support systems are allowed to hasten their deaths by directing the removal of such systems; but those who are similarly situated, except for the previous attachment of life-sustaining equipment, are not allowed to hasten death by self-administering prescribed drugs." In the court's view, "[t]he ending of life by [the withdrawal of life-support systems] is nothing more nor less than assisted suicide." The Court of Appeals then examined whether this supposed unequal treatment was rationally related to any legitimate state interests, and concluded that "to the extent that [New York's statutes] prohibit a physician from prescribing medications to be self-administered by a mentally competent, terminally-ill person in the final stages of his terminal illness, they are not rationally related to any legitimate state interest." We granted certiorari, and now reverse.

The Equal Protection Clause commands that no State shall "deny to any person within its jurisdiction the equal protection of the laws." This provision creates no substantive rights. Instead, it embodies a general rule that States must treat like cases alike but may treat unlike cases accordingly. If a legislative classification or distinction "neither burdens a fundamental right nor targets a suspect class, we will uphold [it] so long as it bears a rational relation to some legitimate end." *Romer v. Evans* [p. 792].

New York's statutes outlawing assisting suicide affect and address matters of profound significance to all New Yorkers alike. They neither infringe fundamental rights nor involve suspect classifications. These laws are therefore entitled to a "strong presumption of validity."

On their faces, neither New York's ban on assisting suicide nor its statutes permitting patients to refuse medical treatment treat anyone differently than anyone else or draw any distinctions between persons. Everyone, regardless of physical condition, is entitled, if competent, to refuse unwanted lifesaving medical treatment; no one is permitted to assist a suicide. Generally speaking, laws that apply evenhandedly to all "unquestionably comply" with the Equal Protection Clause.

The Court of Appeals, however, concluded that some terminally ill people — those who are on life-support systems — are treated differently than those who are not, in that the former may "hasten death" by ending treatment, but the latter may not "hasten death" through physician-assisted suicide. This conclusion depends on the submission that ending or refusing lifesaving medical treatment "is nothing more nor less than assisted suicide." Unlike the Court of Appeals, we think the distinction between assisting suicide and withdrawing life-sustaining treatment, a distinction widely recognized and endorsed in the medical profession and in our legal traditions, is both important and logical; it is certainly rational.

The distinction comports with fundamental legal principles of causation and intent. First, when a patient refuses life-sustaining medical treatment, he dies from an underlying fatal disease or pathology; but if a patient ingests lethal medication prescribed by a physician, he is killed by that medication.

Furthermore, a physician who withdraws, or honors a patient's refusal to begin, life-sustaining medical treatment purposefully intends, or may so intend, only to respect his patient's wishes and "to cease doing useless and futile or degrading things to the patient when [the patient] no longer stands to benefit from them." Assisted Suicide in the United States, Hearing before the Subcommittee on the Constitution of the House Committee on the Judiciary (1996) (testimony of Dr. Leon R. Kass). The same is true when a doctor provides aggressive palliative care; in some cases, painkilling drugs may hasten a patient's death, but the physician's purpose and intent is, or may be, only to ease his patient's pain. A doctor who assists a suicide, however, "must, necessarily and indubitably, intend primarily that the patient be made dead." Similarly, a patient who commits suicide with a doctor's aid necessarily has the specific intent to end his or her own life, while a patient who refuses or discontinues treatment might not.

The law has long used actors' intent or purpose to distinguish between two acts that may have the same result. Put differently, the law distinguishes actions taken "because of" a given end from actions taken "in spite of" their unintended but foreseen consequences.

Given these general principles, it is not surprising that many courts, including New York courts, have carefully distinguished refusing life-sustaining treatment from suicide. Similarly, the overwhelming majority of state legislatures have drawn a clear line between assisting suicide and withdrawing or permitting the refusal of unwanted lifesaving medical treatment by prohibiting the former and permitting the latter. Thus, even as the States move to protect and promote patients' dignity at the end of life, they remain opposed to physician-assisted suicide.

New York is a case in point. The State enacted its current assisted-suicide statutes in 1965. Since then, New York has acted several times to protect patients' common-law right to refuse treatment. In so doing, however, the State has neither endorsed a general right to "hasten death" nor approved physician-assisted suicide.

This Court has also recognized, at least implicitly, the distinction between letting a patient die and making that patient die. In *Cruzan v. Director, Mo. Dept. of Health*, we concluded that "[t]he principle that a competent person has a constitutionally protected liberty interest in refusing unwanted medical treatment may be inferred from our prior decisions," and we assumed the existence of such a right for purposes of that case. But our assumption of a right to refuse treatment was grounded not, as the Court of Appeals supposed, on the proposition that patients have a general and abstract "right to hasten death," but on well established, traditional rights to bodily integrity and freedom from unwanted touching. In fact, we observed that "the majority of States in this country have laws imposing criminal penalties on one who assists another to commit suicide." Cruzan therefore provides no support for the notion that refusing life-sustaining medical treatment is "nothing more nor less than suicide."

For all these reasons, we disagree with respondents' claim that the distinction between refusing lifesaving medical treatment and assisted suicide is "arbitrary" and "irrational." Granted, in some cases, the line between the two may not be clear, but certainty is not required, even were it possible. Logic and contemporary practice support New York's judgment that the two acts are different, and New York may therefore, consistent with the Constitution, treat them differently. By permitting everyone to refuse unwanted medical treatment while prohibiting anyone from assisting a suicide, New York law follows a longstanding and rational distinction.

New York's reasons for recognizing and acting on this distinction — including prohibiting intentional killing and preserving life; preventing suicide; maintaining physicians' role as their patients' healers; protecting vulnerable people from indifference, prejudice, and psychological and financial pressure to end their lives; and avoiding a possible slide towards euthanasia — are discussed in greater detail in our opinion in Glucksberg. These valid and important public interests easily satisfy the constitutional requirement that a legislative classification bear a rational relation to some legitimate end.*

NOTES

1. Contrast the constitutional rights sought to be asserted in *Vacco* and *Glucksberg* with those asserted in *Roe* and *Cruzan*. Are the assertions of constitutional right distinguishable? How viable is the Court's asserted distinction between a constitutional right to refuse treatment and a constitutional right to assisted suicide?

2. Do you agree with the suggestion that "the decisions in *Vacco* and *Glucksberg* have left enough room for experimentation to suggest that the Court may allow physician-assisted suicides"? Note, *Physician-Assisted Suicide: Does the "End" Justify the Means?* 40 Ariz. L. Rev. 1471, 1492 (1998).

3. One commentator has recently argued that under the dictates of substantive due process, "strict scrutiny is required for laws that prevent patients from using medical marijuana as a last resort for the treatment of pain or nausea," and that "a law completely banning the use of marijuana will, as applied to some patients, infringe upon an array of fundamental rights. . ." Note, *Last Resorts and Fundamental Rights: The Substantive Due Process Implications of Prohibitions on Medical Marijuana*, 118 Harv. L. Rev. 1985, 1985 (2005). Reliance is placed on "basic liberties," such as "the rights to live, to die with dignity, to avoid pain, and to make autonomous choices—in consultation with a doctor—about medical treatment." *Id.* Do the preceding cases support this position? For another argument for the extension of substantive due process to new activities, see Note, *Assessing the Viability of a Substantive Due Process Right to In Vitro Fertilization*, 118 Harv. L. Rev. 2792 (2005).

Postscript

Section 6.02 of this chapter has focused on the use of due process liberty as a conduit for recognition of various rights relating to personal autonomy including sexual privacy, marriage and family, personal lifestyle and a right to treatment, and the problems of defining and protecting those rights. Other chapters will focus on additional rights expressly or impliedly drawn from the

* [*Ed. Note:* Justice Souter wrote a separate concurring opinion in *Vacco v. Quill*.]

Constitution or created from external sources. Again, due process liberty will generally be the vehicle for imposing these restrictions on government. In Chapter 7, dealing with equal protection, there will be occasion to consider "fundamental rights" such as interstate migration or travel, marriage, voting, and access to justice. We will also have occasion in that chapter to consider instances in which the Court has rejected rights, such as welfare and education. In Chapters 8 and 9, the focus will be on the broad substantive guarantees of the First Amendment, encompassing express rights such as speech, press, assembly, and religion, and implied rights such as association and belief. It is due process "liberty" that serves to impose these substantive rights, and a correspondingly more exacting standard of judicial review than rationality, on the states.

Chapter 7

THE MEANING OF EQUAL PROTECTION

The Fourteenth Amendment provides, in part, "No State . . . shall deny to any person the equal protection of the laws." A comparable guarantee, applicable against the federal government, has been read into the Fifth Amendment Due Process Clause. Prior to the 1950s, in the absence of race discrimination, the Court interpreted the equal protection guarantee as imposing only a minimal restraint on the government's ability to use classifications in awarding benefits or imposing burdens. Due process, not equal protection, was the tool of substantive judicial review. Indeed, review of government action under the Clause was so restrained that Justice Holmes once referred to equal protection as "the last resort of constitutional arguments." *Buck v. Bell,* 274 U.S. 200, 208 (1927).

It has been argued that equality is a term so devoid of meaning — "an empty vessel with no moral content of its own" — that it should be banished from moral and legal discourse as an analytic term. Peter Westen, *The Empty Idea of Equality*, 95 HARV. L. REV. 537, 542, 547 (1982). Claims to equal treatment, Westen argues, are, in fact, claims to some substantive right; use of the rubrics of equality are unnecessary and confusing. He asks: would the phrase "Equal justice under law" mean less if it read: "Justice Under Law"? The argument has been repeated and developed. *See* Christopher J. Peters, *Equality Revisited*, 110 HARV. L. REV. 1210 (1997). As you read the material below, consider the opposing view that there are core values to the Equal Protection Clause, including principles of equality of respect and the equal dignity of persons. *See, e.g.*, Kenneth Karst, *Why Equality Matters*, 17 GA. L. REV. 255 (1983). Similarly, Kenneth W. Simons, *The Logic of Egalitarian Norms*, 80 B.U. L. REV. 694, 697 (2000), says: "the norm of equality, with its distinctive logic and force, has powerfully shaped the analysis of a range of social issues . . . Our discourse would be greatly impoverished, and moral argument would be greatly and unnecessarily complicated, if we abjured the concept of a right to equal treatment."

Whatever the abstract value of equality, during the Warren Court years the equal protection guarantee became a prime resort for overturning legislation. As Professor Bickel stated, "a broadly conceived egalitarianism was the main theme in the music to which the Warren Court marched." ALEXANDER BICKEL, THE SUPREME COURT AND THE IDEA OF PROGRESS 103 (1970). A two-tier system of review gradually emerged. In most social and economic cases, the Court applies the traditional standard reflecting deference to the government's substantive policy judgment. If there is any rational relation between the legal classification and a permissible government objective, equal protection is satisfied. The burden is on the challenging party to prove the lack of a reasonable basis. If there are findings of fact that would sustain the legislation, it will be assumed that the government has made these factual findings. When this standard is applied, judicial deference is the order of the day.

In other cases, however, the Court applies "strict scrutiny," closely examining the governmental classification. Under strict scrutiny, the government has the burden of justifying its different treatment of groups or "classes" of persons by showing that the classification is necessary to achieve a compelling government interest. There are two occasions for such an activist standard of judicial review — when the government employs a "suspect classification," disadvantaging a protected class, or when the government's classification scheme significantly burdens the exercise of a "fundamental right," including some rights derived from the Equal Protection Clause itself. Just as traditional review usually results in a rejection of the equal protection challenge, strict scrutiny review almost always produces a holding that equal protection is violated. It is "strict in theory and fatal in fact." Gerald Gunther, *Foreword: In Search of Evolving Doctrine on a Changing Court: A Model for a Newer Equal Protection*, 86 HARV. L. REV. 1 (1972).

With the passing of the Warren Court and the transition from the Burger to the Rehnquist Court, the standard of review has become more uncertain. Strict scrutiny is still retained for suspect classifications and fundamental rights, but these apparently have become closed categories, at least as a formal matter. While the Court has reined in the occasions for strict scrutiny, however, it has departed from the two-tier approach in two ways. First, the Court has added a new tier of "intermediate" equal protection review. Usually this standard requires that the government establish that the classification is substantially related to the achievement of an important governmental objective. In the gender discrimination context, the Court has described this burden as "demanding," requiring the government demonstrate an "exceedingly persuasive justification." *United States v. Virginia*, text, p. 820. Second, in some cases, even while using the language of traditional rationality review, the Court has abandoned judicial deference, applied a more exacting scrutiny and held that the law violates the Equal Protection Clause. This is sometimes referred to as "rationality review with teeth" or rationality review "with bite."

The standards of review employed by the Court in equal protection cases are hardly self-defining. Difficult questions abound. How is the reasonableness of a classification to be determined? What is the rationale, if any, for different standards of equal protection review? When is a classification suspect? When does a classification "significantly burden" a "fundamental right" and how does this form of equal protection review relate to substantive due process analysis? These are some of the puzzles that perplex the student of the modern law of equal protection.

§ 7.01 FASHIONING THE CONCEPTS: TRADITIONAL EQUAL PROTECTION

RAILWAY EXPRESS AGENCY v. NEW YORK
336 U.S. 106, 69 S. Ct. 463, 93 L. Ed. 533 (1949)

JUSTICE DOUGLAS delivered the opinion of the Court.

Section 124 of the Traffic Regulations of the City of New York promulgated by the Police Commissioner provides:

No person shall operate, or cause to be operated, in or upon any street an advertising vehicle; provided that nothing herein contained shall prevent the putting of business notices upon business delivery vehicles, so long as such vehicles are engaged in the usual business or regular work of the owner and not used merely or mainly for advertising.

Appellant is engaged in a nation-wide express business. It operates about 1,900 trucks in New York City and sells the space on the exterior sides of these trucks for advertising. That advertising is for the most part unconnected with its own business. It was convicted in the magistrate's court and fined. The Court of Appeals affirmed.

The [lower court] concluded that advertising on vehicles using the streets of New York City constitutes a distraction to vehicle drivers and to pedestrians alike and therefore affects the safety of the public in the use of the streets. We do not sit to weigh evidence on the due process issue in order to determine whether the regulation is sound or appropriate; nor is it our function to pass judgment on its wisdom.

The question of equal protection of the laws is pressed more strenuously on us. It is pointed out that the regulation draws the line between advertisements of products sold by the owner of the truck and general advertisements. It is argued that unequal treatment on the basis of such a distinction is not justified by the aim and purpose of the regulation. It is said, for example, that one of appellant's trucks carrying the advertisement of a commercial house would not cause any greater distraction of pedestrians and vehicle drivers than if the commercial house carried the same advertisement on its own truck. Yet the regulation allows the latter to do what the former is forbidden from doing. It is therefore contended that the classification which the regulation makes has no relation to the traffic problem since a violation turns not on what kind of advertisements are carried on trucks but on whose trucks they are carried.

That, however, is a superficial way of analyzing the problem, even if we assume that it is premised on the correct construction of the regulation. The local authorities may well have concluded that those who advertise their own wares on their trucks do not present the same traffic problem in view of the nature or extent of the advertising which they use. It would take a degree of omniscience which we lack to say that such is not the case. If that judgment is correct, the advertising displays that are exempt have less incidence on traffic than those of appellants.

We cannot say that that judgment is not an allowable one. Yet if it is, the classification has relation to the purpose for which it is made and does not contain the kind of discrimination against which the Equal Protection Clause affords protection. It is by such practical considerations based on experience rather than by theoretical inconsistencies that the question of equal protection is to be answered. And the fact that New York City sees fit to eliminate from traffic this kind of distraction but does not touch what may be even greater ones in a different category, such as the vivid displays on Times Square, is immaterial. It is no requirement of equal protection that all evils of the same genus be eradicated or none at all.

JUSTICE JACKSON, concurring.

My philosophy as to the relative readiness with which we should resort to these two clauses [due process and equal protection] is almost diametrically opposed to the philosophy which prevails on this Court. While claims of denial of equal protection are frequently asserted, they are rarely sustained. But the Court frequently uses the due process clause to strike down measures taken by municipalities to deal with activities in their streets and public places which the local authorities consider to create hazards, annoyances or discomforts to their inhabitants. And I have frequently dissented when I thought local power was improperly denied.

The burden should rest heavily upon one who would persuade us to use the due process clause to strike down a substantive law or ordinance. Even its provident use against municipal regulations frequently disables all government — state, municipal and federal — from dealing with the conduct in question because the requirement of due process is also applicable to State and Federal Governments. Invalidation of a statute or an ordinance on due process grounds leaves ungoverned and ungovernable conduct which many people find objectionable.

Invocation of the equal protection clause, on the other hand, does not disable any governmental body from dealing with the subject at hand. It merely means that the prohibition or regulation must have a broader impact. I regard it as salutary doctrine that cities, states and the Federal Government must exercise their powers so as not to discriminate between their inhabitants except upon some reasonable differentiation fairly related to the object of regulation. This equality is not merely abstract justice. The framers of the Constitution knew, and we should not forget today, that there is no more effective practical guaranty against arbitrary and unreasonable government than to require that the principles of law which officials would impose upon a minority must be imposed generally. Conversely, nothing opens the door to arbitrary action so effectively as to allow those officials to pick and choose only a few to whom they will apply legislation and thus to escape the political retribution that might be visited upon them if larger numbers were affected. Courts can take no better measure to assure that laws will be just than to require that laws be equal in operation.

That the difference between carrying on any business for hire and engaging in the same activity on one's own is a sufficient one to sustain some types of regulations of the one that is not applied to the other, is almost elementary. But it is usual to find such regulations applied to the very incidents wherein the two classes present different problems, such as in charges, liability and quality of service.

The difference, however, is invoked here to sustain a discrimination in a problem in which the two classes present identical dangers. The courts of New York have declared that the sole nature and purpose of the regulation before us is to reduce traffic hazards. There is not even a pretense here that the traffic hazard created by the advertising which is forbidden is in any manner or degree more hazardous than that which is permitted. It is urged with considerable force that this local regulation does not comply with the equal protection clause because it applies unequally upon classes whose differentiation is in no way relevant to the objects of the regulation.

As a matter of principle and in view of my attitude toward the equal protection clause, I do not think differences of treatment under law should be approved on classification because of differences unrelated to the legislative purpose. The equal protection clause ceases to assure either equality or protection if it is avoided by any conceivable difference that can be pointed out between those bound and those left free.

But it is not difficult to see that, in a day of extravagant advertising more or less subsidized by tax deduction, the rental of truck space could become an obnoxious enterprise. While I do not think highly of this type of regulation, that is not my business, and in view of the control I would concede to cities to protect citizens in quiet and orderly use for their proper purposes of the highways and public places, I think the judgment below must be affirmed.

NOTES

Rationality and Deference

1. *Rational basis review.* The Court has stated that a "classification must be reasonable, not arbitrary, and must rest upon some ground of difference having a fair and substantial relation to the object of the legislation, so that all persons similarly circumstanced shall be treated alike." *Royster Guano Co. v. Virginia*, 253 U.S. 412, 415 (1920). What was the nature of the classification in issue in *Railway Express*? Are "all persons similarly circumstanced treated alike"? The determination of whether persons are "similarly situated" implies the existence of some standard of comparison. How did the Court determine the validity of the classification under the Equal Protection Clause?

Railway Express is an example of traditional equal protection review used for most social and economic classifications. The "fair and substantial relation" language used in *Royster Guano*, which is frequently quoted in modern equal protection cases using traditional review standards, would suggest a significant degree of judicial scrutiny of classifications. But this is not the case. In fact, the courts usually defer and ask only if the classification is rationally related to a legitimate government interest.

2. *Probing legislative purposes.* If the courts are to inquire into the rationality of the relationship of a classification to a permissible government purpose, it is necessary to determine whether the law has a permissible purpose. Identifying "the purpose" of a group lawmaker can be difficult. What was the purpose of the law in *Railway Express* according to the majority? According to Justice Jackson? Consider the following formulation of the purpose: "[T]o promote public safety slightly by reducing the number of distractions on the sides of moving vehicles to the extent this is feasible without jeopardizing the economic well-being of those merchants who advertise on their own trucks." Note, 82 YALE L.J. 123, 144 (1972). Do you agree with the view that "[i]t is always possible to define the legislative purpose of a statute in such a way that the statutory classification is rationally related to it."? *Id.* at 128.

3. *Means-end relationship.* Like due process, traditional equal protection requires that there be a rational relationship between the means selected and a permissible government purpose. In evaluating the reasonableness of a classification under this standard, the courts frequently examine the means-end relationship in terms of the "under-inclusiveness" or "over-inclusiveness" of the classification. "Under-inclusion occurs when a state benefits or burdens persons in a manner that furthers a legitimate public purpose but does not confer this same benefit or place this same burden on others who are similarly situated." Persons who should be covered under the law are excluded or exempted. "An over-inclusive classification includes not only those who are similarly situated with respect to the purpose but others who are not so situated as well." A classic example of over-inclusiveness was the internment of Japanese-Americans during the second World War because of the alleged danger of sabotage by some Japanese-Americans. Oddly, from our later perspective, this example of over-inclusiveness was upheld rather than struck down by the Court. Note, *Developments in the Law — Equal Protection*, 82 HARV. L. REV. 1065, 1084–87 (1969). *See* Joseph Tussman & Jacobus tenBroek, *The Equal Protection of the Laws*, 37 CAL. L. REV. 341 (1949).

Is the law in *Railway Express* under-inclusive or over-inclusive? Is it relevant that the ban in *Railway Express* does not extend to "vivid displays on Time Square" which present even greater safety hazards? Preventing government from proceeding one step at a time, given limited public resources, might severely impede needed action and prevent experimentation. But blanket acceptance of a step by step approach invites an arbitrary selection process.

4. *The practice of deference.* The judicial deference reflected in traditional equal protection review is the controlling standard for most social and economic classifications. In the absence of some reason for invoking a more active standard of review, the courts are to defer to the legislative judgment, requiring only that the classification is not arbitrary and irrational. Between 1930 and 1985, only one case involving economic regulation was held unconstitutional under the Equal Protection Clause.

In *Morey v. Doud*, 354 U.S. 457 (1957), the Court, 6-3, struck down the Illinois Community Currency Exchanges Act, a statute regulating currency exchanges selling money orders, but excepting those issuing money orders of the United States Post Office, American Express Co., Postal Telegraph Co., and Western Union Telegraph Co. Only the exception for American Express was challenged on appeal. The state argued that the purpose of the Act's provisions was to protect the public when dealing with currency exchanges and that since American Express was an enterprise of unquestioned solvency and high financial standing, the legislative exception was reasonable. The Court, however, determined that the Act's provisions "make it clear that the statute was intended to afford the public continuing protection. The discrimination in favor of the American Express Company does not conform to this purpose."

In *New Orleans v. Dukes*, 427 U.S. 297 (1976), *Morey v. Doud* was overruled. *Dukes* involved a New Orleans ordinance prohibiting vendors selling from pushcarts in the French Quarter of New Orleans. The prohibition was designed to preserve the historic charm of the quarter and to maintain its attraction for tourists. However, it contained a "grandfather clause" which exempted street vendors who had been operating on French Quarter streets for eight years or more. Only two vendors, who had been street vending in the French Quarter for twenty years, qualified for the exemption. The ordinance was challenged by a pushcart vendor who had been in business in the French Quarter for only two years at the time the prohibition went into effect. The Supreme Court in a per curiam opinion ruled against the plaintiff pushcart vendor and declared the ordinance to be constitutional:

> When local economic regulation is challenged solely as violating the Equal Protection Clause, this Court consistently defers to legislative determinations as to the desirability of particular statutory discrimination. States are accorded wide latitude in the regulation of their local economies under their police powers, and rational distinctions may be made with substantially less than mathematical exactitude. Legislatures may implement their program step by step in such economic areas, adopting regulations that only partially ameliorate a perceived evil and deferring complete elimination of the evil to future regulations. In short, the judiciary may not sit as a superlegislature to judge the wisdom or desirability of legislative policy determinations made in areas that neither affect fundamental rights nor proceed along suspect lines; in the local economic sphere, it is only the invidious discrimination, the wholly arbitrary act, which cannot stand consistently with the Fourteenth Amendment.
>
> It is suggested that the "grandfather provision," allowing the continued operation of some vendors was a totally arbitrary and irrational method of achieving the city's purpose. But rather than proceeding by the immediate and absolute abolition of all pushcart food vendors, the city could rationally choose initially to eliminate vendors of more recent vintage. This gradual approach to the problem is not constitutionally impermissible. The city could reasonably decide that newer businesses were less likely to have built up substantial reliance interests in continued operation in the Vieux Carre and that the two vendors which qualified under the "grandfather clause" had themselves become part of the distinctive character and charm that distinguishes the Vieux Carre. We cannot say that these judgments so lack rationality that they constitute a constitutionally impermissible denial of equal protection.

Alternative Approaches to Rationality Review

Even as a statement of a minimum threshold of constitutionality, the rationality standard seldom is applied rigorously. It is more often a statement of a conclusion that the law is constitutional than a standard of actual evaluation. As a result, there have been recurring suggestions that the Court put some actual teeth into rationality review of social and economic classifications. As we will see later, the current Supreme Court has applied heightened scrutiny in special situations involving "disfavored" groups, but the focus here is on social and economic legislation and rationality review.

5. *Legislative coherence.* Professor Gunther, in a seminal article, argues that the Court should be "less willing to supply justifying rationales by exercising its imagination." He would have the Court consider only the state's proffered purpose. "If the Court were to require an articulation of purpose from an authoritative state source rather than hypothesizing one on its own, there would at least be indirect pressure on the legislature to state its own reasons for selecting particular means and classifications [and thus] improve the quality of the political process [by] encouraging a fuller airing in the political arena of the grounds for legislative action." Gunther's means-oriented standard of review would also have the Justices gauge the reasonableness of questionable means on the basis of materials that are offered to the Court, rather than "resorting to rationalizations created by perfunctory judicial hypothesizing." Gerald Gunther, *In Search of Evolving Doctrine on a Changing Court: A Model for Newer Equal Protection,* 86 HARV. L. REV. 1, 21 (1972).

6. *A public interest approach.* One view is that the demand for rationality under the Due Process and Equal Protection Clauses is designed to assure that lawmaking serves the public interest rather than the interests of particular factions or groups. Professor Sunstein notes that a variety of constitutional clauses, including Equal Protection, are designed to prevent "naked preferences" — "the distribution of resources or opportunities to one group rather than another solely on the ground that those favored have exercised raw political power to obtain what they want." Cass Sunstein, *Naked Preferences and the Constitution*, 84 COLUM. L. REV. 1689 (1984).

In economic regulation cases, can the political process be relied on to produce choices that are designed to serve the public interest? Sunstein argues that the attacks on current equal protection analysis, "suggest that a more vigorous equal protection doctrine would protect a wide range of other groups from disabilities created by the political process. In addition, it would raise the level of means-ends scrutiny, thus responding to the suggestion that rationality review is too deferential in practice." *Id.* at 1716.

7. *A pluralist approach.* A different view is that any demand for meaningful judicial review involves an unrealistic instrumental model of the legislative process where laws are carefully fashioned to achieve identifiable public welfare objectives. A realistic approach to the legislative process accepts the interplay of competing interest groups. "Many public policies are better explained as the outcome of a pure power struggle — clothed in a rhetoric of public interest that is a mere figleaf — among narrow interest or pressure groups. The ability of such groups to obtain legislation derives from their money, votes, cohesiveness, ability to make credible threats of violence or other disorder if their demands are not met, and other factors all totally unrelated to the abstract merit of the policy at issue." Richard Posner, *The DeFunis Case and the Constitutionality of Preferential Treatment of Racial Minorities*, 1974 SUP. CT. REV. 1, 27. Judge Posner argues that instead of asking for rational pursuit of the public interest, "[t]he real 'justification' for most legislation is simply that it is the product of the constitutionally created political process of our society."

The Judicial Response

8. *United States Railroad Retirement Bd. v. Fritz*, 449 U.S. 166 (1980). The Court upheld a section of the Railroad Retirement Act of 1974, which denied dual "windfall" retirement benefits to some railroad workers but not others. Justice Rehnquist, for the Court, reasoned that Congress could properly conclude that workers who retired while still employed in the railroad industry had a greater equitable claim to dual benefits than those workers who were no longer in the railroad industry when they became eligible for dual benefits. Justice Rehnquist said it is "constitutionally sufficient" if there are "plausible reasons" for the legislative action. It is "constitutionally irrelevant" whether these reasons in fact formed the basis for the legislative decision, "because this Court has never insisted that a legislative body articulate its reasons for enacting a statute."

Justice Brennan, joined by Justice Marshall, dissenting, rejected what he considered to be the Court's "tautological approach to statutory purpose" that "virtually immunizes social and economic classifications from judicial review."

> [B]y presuming purpose from result, the Court reduces analysis to tautology. It may always be said that Congress intended to do what it in fact did. If that were the extent of our analysis, we would find every statute, no matter how arbitrary or irrational, perfectly tailored to achieve its purpose. But equal protection scrutiny under the rational-basis test requires the courts first to deduce the independent objectives of the statute, usually from statements of purpose and other evidence in the statute and legislative history, and second to analyze whether the challenged classification rationally furthers achievement of those objectives. The Court's tautological approach will not suffice.
>
> The standard we have applied is properly deferential to the Legislative Branch: where Congress has articulated a legitimate governmental objective, and the challenged classification rationally furthers that objective, we must sustain the provision. In other cases, however, the courts must probe more deeply. Where Congress has expressly stated the purpose of a piece of legislation, but where the challenged classification is either irrelevant to or counter to that purpose, we must view any *post hoc* justifications proffered by Government attorneys with skepticism. A challenged classification may be sustained only if it is rationally related to achievement of an *actual* legitimate governmental purpose.

Justice Stevens, concurring in the judgment, accepted Justice Brennan's argument that the Court's approach was tautological and that equal protection guarantee requires something more than a "conceivable" or "plausible" explanation for unequal treatment. But he did not agree that a classification must further the "actual purpose" of the legislature. "Actual purpose is sometimes unknown. Moreover, undue emphasis on actual motivation may result in identically worded statutes being held valid in one State and invalid in a neighboring State. I therefore believe that we must discover a correlation between the classification and either the actual purpose of the statute or a legitimate purpose that we may reasonably presume to have motivated an impartial legislature."

9. *FCC v. Beach Communications, Inc.*, 508 U.S. 307 (1993). The Court, per Justice Thomas, unanimously upheld a provision of the Cable Communications Policy Act of 1984. The provision made Satellite Master Antenna Television (SMATV) facilities that serviced separately owned and managed buildings subject to regulation but exempted SMATV facilities "that service one or more buildings under common ownership or management." The Court affirmed the appropriateness of the deferential standard of review for equal protection challenges to economic regulation:

> Whether embodied in the Fourteenth Amendment or inferred from the Fifth, equal protection is not a license for courts to judge the wisdom, fairness, or logic of legislative choices. In areas of social and economic policy, a statutory classification that neither proceeds along suspect lines nor infringes fundamental constitutional rights must be upheld against equal protection challenge if there is any reasonably conceivable state of facts that could provide a rational basis for the classification. Where there are "plausible reasons" for Congress' action, "our inquiry is at an end." *United States Railroad Retirement Board v. Fritz.* This standard of review is a paradigm of judicial restraint. On rational-basis review, a classification comes to us bearing a strong presumption of validity, and those attacking the rationality of the classification have the burden "to negate every conceivable basis which might support it." Moreover, because we never require a legislature to articulate its reasons for enacting a statute, it is entirely irrelevant for constitutional purposes whether the conceived reason for the challenged distinction actually motivated the legislature. Thus, the absence of "legislative facts" explaining the distinction "on the record," has no significance in rational-basis analysis.

Justice Thomas indicated that the deferential standard of review is particularly apt where legislative line-drawing is involved since line-drawing is a legislative and not a judicial responsibility. "Such scope-of-coverage provisions are unavoidable components of most economic or social legislation. In establishing the franchise, Congress had to draw the line somewhere; it had to choose which facilities to franchise. This necessity renders the precise coordinates of the resulting legislative judgement virtually unreviewable, since the legislature must be allowed leeway to approach a perceived problem incrementally."

The Court concluded that the common ownership distinction was a rational one. Justice Thomas acknowledged that the assumptions that might be used to support the challenged distinction might be erroneous but he concluded: "[T]he very fact that they are 'arguable' is sufficient, on rational-basis review, to 'immunize' the Congressional choice from constitutional challenge."

Justice Stevens, concurred in the judgment, but expressed concern that the Court's approach "sweeps too broadly, for it is difficult to imagine a legislative classification that could *not* be supported by a 'reasonably conceivable set of facts.' Judicial review under the 'conceivable set of facts' test is tantamount to no review at all." Justice Stevens argued that "something more" is required by the equal protection guarantee. "In my view, when the actual rationale for legislative classification is unclear, we should inquire whether the classification is rationally related to 'a legitimate purpose that we may *reasonably presume* to have motivated an impartial legislature.' "

10. *Fitzgerald v. Racing Ass'n of Central Iowa*, 539 U.S. 103 (2003). A unanimous Court, applying the rational basis test, held that imposition of a different tax rate on slot machines at racetracks and riverboats does not violate the Equal Protection Clause.

In 1994, Iowa enacted a law imposing a graduated tax on racetrack slot machines adjusted revenues. The top rate started at 10% but was configured to automatically rise to 36% over time. Since the law did not address the tax rate on adjusted revenues applying to riverboat slot machines, the current maximum rate of 20% remained on riverboat slot machines. A number of racetracks brought suit in state court contending that the 20%/36% tax differential violated equal protection. While the state district court upheld the statute, the Iowa Supreme Court reversed, concluding that, since "the differential tax completely defeats the alleged purpose of the statute, namely, 'to help the racetracks recover from economic distress,' that there could 'be no rational reason for this differential tax.' "

The Court, per Justice Breyer, determined that the rational basis standard applies since the Iowa "law distinguishes for tax purposes among revenues obtained within the State of Iowa by two enterprises, each of which does business in the State." Applying the deferential test, Justice Breyer observed that the Iowa law "might predominantly serve one general objective, say, helping the racetracks, while containing subsidiary provisions that seek to achieve other desirable (perhaps even contrary) ends as well, thereby producing a law that balanced objectives, but still serves the general objectives when seen as a whole." The Iowa Supreme Court could not deny "that the 1994 legislation, seen as a whole, can rationally be understood to do what that court says it seeks to do, namely, advance the racetrack's economic interests. Its grant to the racetracks of authority to operate slot machines should help the racetracks economically to some degree — even if its simultaneous imposition of a tax on slot machine adjusted revenues means that the law provides less help than respondents might like. At least a rational legislator might so believe." Legislators, not courts, were given broad constitutional authority "within the bounds of rationality" to decide who gets help under the tax laws and how much help they get. Judicial review "is 'at an end' once the court identifies a plausible basis on which the legislature may have relied."

Justice Breyer concluded that "[o]nce one realizes that not every provision in a law must share a single objective, one has no difficulty finding the necessary rational support for the 20 percent/36 percent differential here at issue." While that difference might be harmful to the racetracks, it is helpful to the riverboats who also were facing financial distress. "These two characterizations are but opposite sides of the same coin. Each reflects a rational way for a legislator to view the matter." And there could have been a variety of other rational considerations supporting the different tax rates. Justice Breyer summarized the Court's conclusion that there was " 'a plausible policy reason for the classification,' that the legislature 'rationally may have considered true' the related justifying 'legislative facts,' and that the 'relationship of the classification to its goal is not so attenuated as to render the distinction arbitrary or irrational.' "

11. *Rationality with bite?* The Supreme Court continues to adhere to the highly deferential rationality test discussed above. There have been some cases, however, purporting to use a rationality test, where the Court uses rationality language but engages in a more demanding scrutiny and holds government action unconstitutional on equal protection grounds. Robert C. Farrell, *Successful Rational Bases Claims in the Supreme Court From the 1971 Term Through* Romer v. Evans, 32 IND. L. REV. 357 (1999), identifies 10 such cases of "heightened rationality" out of 110 using rationality review over the last 25 years but says "[t]he Court never explains why it has selected a particular case for heightened rationality." Further, "[t]he Court's analysis differs from case to case. None of the cases has had a significant precedential impact on subsequent cases. For the most part, once the case has been decided, the Court ignores it." And, after reviewing the cases, he concludes: "[the] search for an underlying principle that would explain the results in the heightened rationality cases appears to be unsuccessful. Rather, it appears that the Court, without explanation, decided in a particular case to use heightened rationality and thus the claim succeeded . . . The Court continues to write opinions as if they matter, but the Court's jurisprudence of heightened rationality is difficult to understand."

Later in the Chapter, in a section on "Rational Basis 'With Teeth,' " two cases often cited as examples of rationality with bite are reported. In *City of Cleburne v. Cleburne Living Center*, p. 852, the Court held that the denial of a special use permit for the operation of a group home for the mentally retarded, while other similarly situated operations were allowed to operate, violated equal protection. In *Romer v. Evans*, p. 862, the Court held that a state constitutional amendment discriminating against homosexuals violated equal protection. In both cases, the Court claimed to be using rationality review. In *Lawrence v. Texas*, p. 583, Justice O'Connor, concurring, used a "more searching form of rational basis review" in holding that a Texas statute banning same-sex sodomy violates the Equal Protection Clause. As you read these cases, and others included in the section, consider whether you can identify any explanation for the Court's use of more active scrutiny in applying rational basis equal protection. Should the courts ever engage in such active review in socio-economic regulation cases?

§ 7.02 SUSPECT CLASSIFICATIONS — RACE

[A] DISCRIMINATION THROUGH LAW AND ITS ADMINISTRATION

LOVING v. VIRGINIA
388 U.S. 1, 87 S. Ct. 1817, 18 L. Ed. 2d 1010 (1967)

Chief Justice Warren delivered the opinion of the Court.

This case presents a constitutional question never addressed by this Court: whether a statutory scheme adopted by the State of Virginia to prevent marriages between persons solely on the basis of racial classifications violates the Equal Protection and Due Process Clauses of the Fourteenth Amendment. For reasons which seem to us to reflect the central meaning of those constitutional commands, we conclude that these statutes cannot stand consistently with the Fourteenth Amendment.

In June 1958, two residents of Virginia, Mildred Jeter, a Negro woman, and Richard Loving, a white man, were married in the District of Columbia pursuant to its laws. Shortly after their marriage, the Lovings returned to Virginia and established their marital abode in Caroline County. [They were subsequently convicted of violating Virginia's ban on interracial marriages. The State Supreme Court of Appeals upheld the law and affirmed the convictions.]

In upholding the constitutionality of these provisions in the decision below, the Supreme Court of Appeals of Virginia referred to its 1955 decision in *Naim v. Naim*, 197 Va. 80, 87 S.E.2d 749 that the State's legitimate purposes were "to preserve the racial integrity of its citizens," and to prevent "the corruption of blood," "a mongrel breed of citizens," and "the obliteration of racial pride," obviously an endorsement of the doctrine of White Supremacy. The court also reasoned that marriage has traditionally been subject to state regulation without federal intervention, and, consequently, the regulation of marriage should be left to exclusive state control by the Tenth Amendment.

In cases involving distinctions not drawn according to race, the Court has merely asked whether there is any rational foundation for the discriminations, and has deferred to the wisdom of the state legislatures. In the case at bar, however, we deal with statutes containing racial classifications, and the fact of equal application does not immunize the statute from the very heavy burden of justification which the Fourteenth Amendment has traditionally required of state statutes drawn according to race.

The State argues that statements in the Thirty-ninth Congress about the time of the passage of the Fourteenth Amendment indicate that the Framers did not intend the Amendment to make unconstitutional state miscegenation laws. [W]e have said in connection with a related problem, that although these historical sources "cast some light" they are not sufficient to resolve the problem; "[a]t best, they are inconclusive. The most avid proponents of the post-War Amendments undoubtedly intended them to remove all legal distinctions among 'all persons born or naturalized in the United States.' Their opponents, just as certainly, were antagonistic to both the letter and the spirit of the Amendments and wished them to have the most limited effect." *Brown v. Board of Education*. The clear and central purpose of the Fourteenth Amendment was to eliminate all official state sources of invidious racial discrimination in the States. *Slaughter-House Cases*; *Strauder v. West Virginia*.

There can be no question but that Virginia's miscegenation statutes rest solely upon distinctions drawn according to race. The statutes proscribe generally accepted conduct if engaged in by members of different races. Over the years, this Court has consistently repudiated "[d]istinctions between citizens solely because of their ancestry" as being "odious to a free people whose institutions are founded upon the doctrine of equality." *Hirabayashi v. United States*, 320 U.S. 81, 100 (1943). At the very least, the Equal Protection Clause demands that racial classifications, especially suspect in criminal statutes, be subjected to the "most rigid scrutiny," *Korematsu v. United States*, 323 U.S. 214, 216 (1944), and, if they are ever to be upheld, they must be shown to be necessary to the accomplishment of some permissible state objective, independent of the racial discrimination which it was the object of the Fourteenth Amendment to eliminate. Indeed, two members of this Court have already stated that they "cannot conceive of a valid legislative purpose which makes the color of a person's skin the test of whether his conduct is a criminal offense." *McLaughlin v. Florida* (STEWART, J., joined by Douglas, J., concurring).

There is patently no legitimate overriding purpose independent of invidious racial discrimination which justifies this classification. The fact that Virginia prohibits only interracial marriages involving white persons demonstrates that the racial classifications must stand on their own justification, as measures designed to maintain White Supremacy. We have consistently denied the constitutionality of measures which restrict the rights of citizens on account of race. There can be no doubt that restricting the freedom to marry solely because of racial classifications violates the central meaning of the Equal Protection Clause.

These statutes also deprive the Lovings of liberty without due process of law in violation of the Due Process Clause of the Fourteenth Amendment. The freedom to marry has long been recognized as one of the vital personal rights essential to the orderly pursuit of happiness by free men.

Marriage is one of the "basic civil rights of man," fundamental to our very existence and survival. *Skinner v. State of Oklahoma*. To deny this fundamental freedom on so unsupportable a basis as the racial classifications embodied in these statutes, classifications so directly subversive of the principle of equality at the heart of the Fourteenth Amendment, is surely to deprive all the State's citizens of liberty without due process of law. The Fourteenth Amendment requires that the freedom of choice to marry not be restricted by invidious racial discriminations. Under our Constitution, the freedom to marry or not marry a person of another race resides with the individual and cannot be infringed by the State.

NOTES

The Antidiscrimination Principle

1. ***The principle involved.*** *Loving* rejects application of the traditional rationality test for laws that "rest solely upon distinctions drawn according to race." Professor Brest defines the "antidiscrimination principle" as "the general principle disfavoring classifications and other decisions and practices that depend on the race (or ethnic origin) of the parties affected." Paul Brest, *Foreword: In Defense of the Antidiscrimination Principle*, 90 HARV. L. REV. 1 (1976). Jack Balkin & Reva Siegel, *The American Civil Rights Tradition: Anticlassification or Antisubordination*, 58 U. MIAMI L. REV. 9 (2003), define the "anticlassification" or "antidicriminiation principle" as holding "that the government may not classify people either overtly or surreptitiously on the basis of a forbidden category: for example, their race."

2. ***Strauder v. West Virginia,* 100 U.S. 303 (1880).** The murder conviction of a black defendant when African-Americans were excluded by state law from jury service was overturned as violative of the equal protection guarantee. The Court asserted that the Fourteenth Amendment established that "the law in the States shall be the same for the Black as for the White; that all persons, whether colored or white, shall stand equal before the laws of the States, and in regard to the colored race, for whose protection the amendment was primarily designed, that no discrimination shall be made against them by law because of their color."

The Amendment was said to imply "a positive immunity, or right, most valuable to the colored race — the right to exemption from unfriendly legislation against them distinctively as colored — exemption from legal discrimination, implying inferiority in civil society, lessening the security of their enjoyment of the rights which others enjoy, and discriminations which are steps toward reducing them to the conditions of a subject race."

In *Strauder,* blacks were denied a government benefit available to whites. But in *Loving,* neither blacks nor whites could marry a person of the other race. In a portion of the opinion not reprinted above, the Court's answer to the state's argument that the statute had "equal application" to both races was that the statute nevertheless was an invidious racial classification.

3. ***Palmore v. Sidoti,* 466 U.S. 429 (1984).** The Court held, per Chief Justice Burger, that a state court's consideration of private racial biases and the injury they might inflict on the child as a basis for removing an infant child from the custody of its natural mother violated the Equal Protection Clause. Linda Palmore and Anthony Sidoti, both whites, were divorced in May 1980, and the mother was awarded custody of their three-year old daughter. In September 1981, the father sought custody of the child by filing a petition to modify the previous judgment due to changed conditions. The charge was that the child's mother was cohabiting with a black man whom she later married. A Florida state court found that there was no question as to either parent's devotion to the child or the care they would provide for her. The state court, however, concluded that the best interests of the child would be served by awarding custody to the father. "This Court feels that despite the strides

that have been made in bettering relations between the races in this country, it is inevitable that Melanie will, if allowed to remain in her present situation and attains school age and thus more vulnerable to peer pressures, suffer from the social stigmatization that is sure to come."

The United States Supreme Court reversed:

> A core purpose of the Fourteenth Amendment was to do away with all governmentally-imposed discrimination based on race. Classifying persons according to their race is more likely to reflect racial prejudice than legitimate public concerns; the race, not the person, dictates the category. Such classifications are subject to the most exacting scrutiny; to pass constitutional muster, they must be justified by a compelling governmental interest and must be "necessary . . . to the accomplishment" of its legitimate purpose, *McLaughlin v. Florida*.
>
> The goal of granting custody based on the best interests of the child is indisputably a substantial governmental interest for purposes of the Equal Protection Clause. It would ignore reality to suggest that racial and ethnic prejudices do not exist or that all manifestations of those prejudices have been eliminated. There is a risk that a child living with a step-parent of a different race may be subject to a variety of pressures and stresses not present if the child were living with parents of the same racial or ethnic origin.
>
> The question, however, is whether the reality of private biases and the possible injury they might inflict are permissible considerations for removal of an infant child from the custody of its natural mother. We have little difficulty concluding that they are not. The Constitution cannot control such prejudices but neither can it tolerate them. Private biases may be outside the reach of the law, but the law cannot, directly or indirectly, give them effect. The effects of racial prejudice, however real, cannot justify a racial classification removing an infant child from the custody of its natural mother found to be an appropriate person to have such custody.

Can race be considered in adoption proceedings? Lower courts have allowed race to be "a factor in determining where to place a child, but the use of race as the sole reason to make or change an adoption placement is not constitutional." Rita L. Simon & Howard Altstein, *The Relevance of Race in Adoption Law and Social Practice*, 11 NOTRE DAME J.L. ETHICS & PUB. POL'Y 171, 178 (1997). Explaining this result, the authors state: "In sum, an inherently suspect, indeed presumptively invalid, racial classification in the adoption statute is, in a constitutional sense, necessary to advance a compelling governmental interest: the best interest of the child. It thus survives strict scrutiny — a result that is unusual, as racial classifications go, but not precluded." See R. Richard Banks, *The Color of Desire: Fulfilling Adoptive Parents' Racial Preference Through Discriminatory State Action*, 107 YALE L.J. 875, 964 (1998), who argues for "strict nonaccommodation" to private racial preferences in order to "alter race politics through counteracting the social processes and racial understandings that perpetuate both racial conflict and racial inequality."

4. *Justification.* If race classifications are so onerous, should they be *per se* impermissible rather than suspect? Should "invidious racial discrimination" be *per se* impermissible? In *Korematsu v. United States*, 321 U.S. 214 (1944), the Court upheld a wartime conviction for violation of a military order excluding Americans of Japanese ancestry from certain designated military areas on the west coast. Justice Black, for the majority, began with the premise that "all legal restrictions which curtail the civil rights of a single racial group are immediately suspect. That is not to say that all such restrictions are unconstitutional. It is to say that courts must subject them to the most rigid scrutiny. Pressing public necessity may sometimes justify the existence of such restrictions; racial antagonism never can."

In this instance, wartime necessity and the alleged inability to separate the loyal from the disloyal were used to justify a conclusion that "exclusion of the whole group [was] a military imperative." *See Hirabayashi v. United States*, 320 U.S. 81 (1943) (wartime curfew order upheld). For a critical perspective, see Symposium, *The Long Shadow of Korematsu*, 40 B.C.L. Rev. 1 (1998). Note that classifications based on national origin and ethnicity are treated in the same manner as race classifications. Should they be?

The Rationale of Suspectness

5. *The role of history.* The debate over the historical purpose of the Fourteenth Amendment is discussed in Chapter 5. *Strauder*, *Loving* and *Palmore* all emphasize the historical purpose of the Fourteenth Amendment to eliminate state-supported invidious racial discrimination. In *Loving*, Virginia argued that it was not the intent of the framers of the Fourteenth Amendment to upset the miscegenation laws which were common at the time. Similarly, Professor Bickel acknowledged that "the obvious conclusion to which the evidence easily leads is that section 1 of the Fourteenth Amendment, like section 1 of the Civil Rights Act of 1866, carried out the relatively narrow objective of the Moderates, and hence, as originally understood, was meant to apply neither to jury service, nor suffrage, nor antimiscegenation statutes, nor segregation." Alexander Bickel, *The Original Understanding and the Segregation Decision*, 69 Harv. L. Rev. 1 (1955). Assuming the Framers did not intend to eliminate miscegenation laws, what effect should this have on a present day court judging their constitutionality?

Bickel went on to speculate that the historical meaning of the Amendment may be more subtle. "But may it not be that the Moderates and the Radicals reached a compromise permitting them to go to the country with language which they could, where necessary, defend against damaging alarms raised by the opposition, but which at the same time was sufficiently elastic to permit reasonable future advances?" Under this interpretation, the "future effect" of the Amendment "was left to future determination." If the "original understanding" is not controlling, what standards or principles should guide the judicial elaboration of the equal protection guarantee?

6. *The role of social science.* In oral argument in *Loving*, Justice Harlan asked: "Assuming that the argument is rejected that as a matter of history the Fourteenth Amendment was supposed to leave state restraints on interracial marriage intact, what then would be the constitutional status of Virginia's statute under contemporary Fourteenth Amendment principles?"

The Assistant Attorney General for Virginia, in responding to Justice Harlan's question, pointed to a copious volume on the lectern: ALBERT I. GORDON, INTERMARRIAGE — INTERFAITH, INTERRACIAL, INTERETHNIC. The data collected in the book indicated that children of mixed marriages suffered greater difficulties, psychological or otherwise, than children of more homogeneous unions. In other words, Virginia was saying that social science techniques indicated the psychological undesirability of interracial marriage. Note the similar argument in *Palmore*.

The Supreme Court of Appeals for Virginia, however, rejected reliance on such arguments: "A decision by this Court reversing [precedents] upon considerations of such text writers would be judicial legislation in the raw sense of that term. Such arguments are properly addressable to the legislature, which enacted the law in the first place, and not to this Court, whose prescribed role in the separated powers of government is to adjudicate, and not to legislate." *Loving v. Commonwealth*, 206 Va. 924, 147 S.E.2d 78 (1966). In *Loving* and *Palmore*, it was argued that the law was being used as a proxy for the legitimate state objective of protecting children. Yet the law failed. Why?

7. *Equal worth and respect.* In *Palmore*, the Court suggests that racial classifications should be subject to heightened scrutiny because of the possibility of "prejudice." Judge Linde asks, "What is it that 'suspect classifications' are suspected of?" He answers: "The suspicion, in that phrase, is suspicion of prejudice — not simply prejudgment based on ignorance and mistaken notions of fact, but invidious prejudgment, grounded in notions of superiority and inferiority, in beliefs about relative worth, attitudes that deny the premise of human equality and that will not be readily sacrificed to mere facts." Hans Linde, *Due Process of Lawmaking*, 55 NEB. L. REV. 197, 201–02 (1976).

Professor Karst similarly argues that the "substantive core" of the equal protection guarantee is in the "principle of equal citizenship." This principle requires that government "treat each individual as a person, one who is worthy of respect, one who 'belongs.' Accordingly, the principle guards against degradation or the imposition of stigma." Kenneth Karst, *Foreword: Equal Citizenship Under the Fourteenth Amendment*, 91 HARV. L. REV. 1, 6 (1977).

Ronald Dworkin offers the following "postulate of political morality":

> Government must treat those whom it governs with concern, that is, as human beings who are capable of suffering and frustration, and with respect, that is, as human beings who are capable of forming and acting on intelligent conceptions of how their lives should be lived. Government must not only treat people with concern and respect, but with equal concern and respect. It must not distribute goods or opportunities unequally on the ground that some citizens are entitled to more because they are worthy of more concern.

RONALD M. DWORKIN, TAKING RIGHTS SERIOUSLY 272–73 (1977).

Professor Deborah Hellman, *The Expressive Dimension of Equal Protection*, 85 MINN. L. REV. 1, 15 (2000), applies this principle to *Loving*: "The statute expressed that whites are superior and that the purity of the white race and no other is of supreme importance to the state. The principle of equal concern forbids the state from adopting or endorsing this view."

8. *Discrete and insular minorities.* Could the special treatment afforded racial classifications be functionally justified given the special needs for judicial protection of "discrete and insular minorities" who are denied effective representation through ordinary political processes? In *United States v. Carolene Products Co.*, 303 U.S. 144, 152–53 n.4 (1938), Justice Stone provided one of the most important footnotes in constitutional law. In it he suggested, *inter alia*, that statutes "directed at" racial minorities might be subjected to a "more exacting judicial scrutiny" under the Fourteenth Amendment. He asked, "whether prejudice against discrete and insular minorities may be a special condition, which tends seriously to curtail the operation of those political processes ordinarily to be relied upon to protect minorities, and which may call for a correspondingly more searching judicial inquiry."

Professor Ely has employed the *Carolene Products* footnote as a predicate for justifying judicial intervention under the Equal Protection Clause to assure that the political processes whereby values are identified and accommodated are not unduly constricted because of prejudice. However, the mere fact that a group loses in the political marketplace does not mean the representative system of government is malfunctioning. We should treat as suspicious those classifications "that disadvantage groups we know to be the object of widespread vilification, groups we know others (specifically those who control the legislative process) might wish to injure." JOHN H. ELY, DEMOCRACY AND DISTRUST 153 (1980). If racial minorities actively participate in the political process, would the basis for heightened review of racial classifications be eliminated?

Professor Fiss argued for invoking equal protection against government action which "aggravates the subordinate position of a specially disadvantaged group." In reference to racial classifications against blacks, he stated: "[B]lacks should be viewed as having three characteristics that are relevant in the formulation of equal protection theory: (a) they are a social group; (b) the group has been in a position of perpetual subordination; and (c) the political power of the group is severely circumscribed. Blacks are a specially disadvantaged group, and I would view the Equal Protection Clause as a protection for such groups." Owen Fiss, *Groups and the Equal Protection Clause*, 5 J. PHIL. & PUB. AFF. 107, 154–55 (1976). *See Issues in Legal Scholarship, The Origins and Fate of Antisubordination Theory: A Symposium on Owen Fiss's "Groups and the Equal Protection Clause."* www.bepress.com "Antisubordination theorists contend that guarantees of equal citizenship cannot be realized under conditions of pervasive social stratification and argue that law should reform institutions and practices that enforce the secondary social status of historically oppressed groups." Jack M. Balkin & Reva B. Siegel, *The American Civil Rights Tradition: Anticlassification or Antisubordination?*, 58 U. MIAMI L. REV. 9 (2003).

Discriminatory Administration or Enforcement

9. *Yick Wo v. Hopkins,* 118 U.S. 356 (1886). If an administrator establishes a policy that facially segregates racially, it is clear that the strict scrutiny standard should be applicable. But frequently, discrimination is not embodied in an overt discriminatory rule. *Yick Wo v. Hopkins*, dealt with a San Francisco ordinance that required a permit to operate a laundry unless the laundry was located in a brick or stone building. Yick Wo, a Chinese alien who had operated a laundry in the same building for twenty-two years, was convicted for doing business without a permit and was imprisoned for nonpayment of the $10 fine. The Supreme Court of California denied his petition for a writ of habeas corpus. The record established that of the 320 laundries in San Francisco, 240 were owned by Chinese aliens and 310 were constructed of wood as was Yick Wo's. While 200 Chinese who had applied for laundry licenses had been denied, all applications by non-Chinese had been granted.

In reversing the conviction, Justice Matthews, for the United States Supreme Court, found it unnecessary to determine if the statute was invalid in that it vested excessive opportunity for discrimination in the administrator.

> [T]he facts shown establish an administration directed so exclusively against a particular class of persons as to warrant and require the conclusion, that, whatever may have been the intent of the ordinances as adopted, they are applied by the public authorities charged with their administration, and thus representing the State itself, with a mind so unequal and oppressive as to amount to a practical denial by the State of the equal protection of the laws which is secured to the petitioners, as to all other persons, by the broad and benign provisions of [the Fourteenth Amendment]. Though the law itself be fair on its face and impartial in appearance, yet, if it is applied and administered by public authorities with an evil eye and unequal hand, so as practically to make unjust and illegal discriminations between persons in similar circumstances, material to their rights, the denial of equal justice is still within the prohibition of the Constitution.

Citing the grossly disparate statistics on permit applications and approvals, the Court concluded: "The fact of this discrimination is admitted. No reason for it is shown, and the conclusion cannot be resisted, that no reason for it exists except hostility to the race and nationality to which the petitioners belong and which in the eye of the law is not justified. The discrimination is, therefore, illegal and the public administration which enforces it is a denial of the equal protection of the laws."

In *Yick Wo*, the ordinance was facially neutral regarding race or national origin. There was no formal legal rule or policy establishing a racial classification. What was the basis for holding that the Equal Protection Clause was violated? How did the Court determine that there was discrimination? Is the Court holding that the statistical disparity between Chinese and non-Chinese license applicants establishes an equal protection violation?

[B] DISCRIMINATORY PURPOSE AND IMPACT

WASHINGTON v. DAVIS

426 U.S. 229, 96 S. Ct. 2040, 48 L. Ed. 2d 597 (1976)

JUSTICE WHITE delivered the opinion of the Court.

This case involves the validity of a qualifying test administered to applicants for positions as police officers in the District of Columbia Metropolitan Police Department. The test was sustained by the District Court but invalidated by the Court of Appeals. We are in agreement with the District Court and hence reverse the judgment of the Court of Appeals.

According to the findings and conclusions of the District Court, to be accepted by the Department and to enter an intensive 17-week training program, the police recruit was required to satisfy certain physical and character standards, to be a high school graduate or its equivalent, and to receive a grade of at least 40 out of 80 on "Test 21," which is "an examination that is used generally throughout the federal service," which "was developed by the Civil Service Commission, not the Police Department," and which was "designed to test verbal ability, vocabulary, reading and comprehension."

The validity of Test 21 was the sole issue before the court on the motions for summary judgment. The District Court noted that there was no claim of "an intentional discrimination or purposeful discriminatory acts" but only a claim that Test 21 bore no relationship to job performance and "has a highly discriminatory impact in screening out black candidates." Respondents' evidence, the District Court said, warranted three conclusions: "(a) The number of black police officers, while substantial, is not proportionate to the population mix of the city. (b) A higher percentage of blacks fail the Test than whites. (c) The Test has not been validated to establish its reliability for measuring subsequent job performance." This showing was deemed sufficient to shift the burden of proof to the defendants in the action, petitioners here; but the court nevertheless concluded that on the undisputed facts respondents were not entitled to relief. The District Court relied on several factors. Since August 1969, 44% of new police force recruits had been black; that figure also represented the proportion of blacks on the total force and was roughly equivalent to 20-to 29-year-old blacks in the 50-mile radius in which the recruiting efforts of the Police Department had been concentrated. It was undisputed that the Department had systematically and affirmatively sought to enroll black officers, many of whom passed the test but failed to report for duty. The District Court rejected the assertion that Test 21 was culturally slanted to favor whites and was "satisfied that the undisputable facts prove the test to be reasonably and directly related to the requirements of the police recruit training program and that it is neither so designed nor operates [sic] to discriminate against otherwise qualified blacks."

The tendered constitutional issue [on appeal] was whether the use of Test 21 invidiously discriminated against Negroes and hence denied them due process of law contrary to the commands of the Fifth Amendment. The Court of Appeals, addressing that issue, announced that it would be guided by *Griggs v. Duke Power Co.*, 401 U. S. 424 (1971), a case involving the interpretation and application of Title VII of the Civil Rights Acts of 1964, and held that the statutory standards elucidated in that case were to govern the due process question tendered in this one. The court went on to declare that lack of discriminatory intent in designing and administering Test 21 was irrelevant; the critical fact was rather that a far greater proportion of blacks — four times as many — failed the test than did whites. This disproportionate impact, standing alone and without regard to whether it indicated a discriminatory purpose, was held sufficient to establish a constitutional violation, absent proof by petitioners that the test was an adequate measure of job performance in addition to being an indicator of probable success in the training program, a burden which the court ruled petitioners had failed to discharge.

As the Court of Appeals understood Title VII, employees or applicants proceeding under it need not concern themselves with the employer's possibly discriminatory purpose but instead may focus solely on the racially differential impact of the challenged hiring or promotion practices. This is not the constitutional rule. We have never held that the constitutional standard for adjudicating claims of invidious racial discrimination is identical to the standards applicable under Title VII, and we decline to do so today.

The central purpose of the Equal Protection Clause is the prevention of official conduct discriminating on the basis of race. But our cases have not embraced the proposition that a law or other official act, without regard to whether it reflects a racially discriminatory purpose, is unconstitutional solely because it has a racially disproportionate impact.

Almost 100 years ago, *Strauder v. West Virginia*, established that the exclusion of Negroes from grand and petit juries in criminal proceedings violated the Equal Protection Clause, but the fact that a particular jury or a series of juries does not statistically reflect the racial composition of the community does not in itself make out an invidious discrimination forbidden by the Clause. "A purpose to discriminate must be present which may be proven by systematic exclusion of eligible jurymen of the proscribed race or by unequal application of the law to such an extent as to show intentional discrimination."

The school desegregation cases have also adhered to the basic equal protection principle that the invidious quality of a law claimed to be racially discriminatory must ultimately be traced to a racially discriminatory purpose. That there are both predominantly black and predominantly white schools in a community is not alone violative of the Equal Protection Clause. The essential element of de jure segregation is "a current condition of segregation resulting from intentional state action." *Keyes v. School Dist. No. 1* [p. 633]. "The differentiating factor between de jure segregation and so-called de facto segregation is purpose or intent to segregate." *Id.* The Court has also recently rejected allegations of racial discrimination based solely on the statistically disproportionate racial impact of various provisions of the Social Security Act because "[t]he acceptance of appellants' constitutional theory would render suspect each difference in treatment among the grant classes, however lacking in racial motivation and however otherwise rational the treatment might be." *Jefferson v. Hackney*, 406 U. S. 535, 548 (1972).

This is not to say that the necessary discriminatory racial purpose must be express or appear on the face of the statute, or that a law's disproportionate impact is irrelevant in cases involving Constitution-based claims of racial discrimination. A statute, otherwise neutral on its face, must not be applied so as invidiously to discriminate on the basis of race. *Yick Wo v. Hopkins*. It is also clear from the cases dealing with racial discrimination in the selection of juries that the systematic exclusion of Negroes is itself such an "unequal application of the law . . . as to show intentional discrimination." With a prima facie case made out, "the burden of proof shifts to the State to rebut the presumption of unconstitutional action by showing that permissible racially neutral selection criteria and procedures have produced the monochromatic result."

Necessarily, an invidious discriminatory purpose may often by inferred from the totality of the relevant facts, including the fact, if it is true, that the law bears more heavily on one race than another. It is also not infrequently true that the discriminatory impact — in the jury cases for example, the total or seriously disproportionate exclusion of Negroes from jury venires — may for all practical purposes demonstrate unconstitutionality because in various circumstances the discrimination is very difficult to explain on nonracial grounds. Nevertheless, we have not held that a law, neutral on its face and serving ends otherwise within the power of government to pursue, is invalid under the Equal Protection Clause simply because it may affect a greater proportion of one race than of another. Disproportionate impact is not irrelevant, but it is not the sole touchstone of an invidious racial discrimination forbidden by the Constitution. Standing alone, it does not trigger the rule that racial classifications are to be subjected to the strictest scrutiny and are justifiable only by the weightiest of considerations.

[V]arious Courts of Appeals have held in several contexts, including public employment, that the substantially disproportionate racial impact of a statute or official practice standing alone and without regard to discriminatory purpose, suffices to prove racial discrimination violating the Equal Protection Clause absent some justification going substantially beyond what would be necessary to validate most other legislative classifications. The cases impressively demonstrate that there is another side to the issue; but, with all due respect, to the extent that those cases rested on or expressed the view that proof of discriminatory racial purpose is unnecessary in making out an equal protection violation, we are in disagreement. Test 21, which is administered generally to prospective Government employees, concededly seeks to ascertain whether those who take it have acquired a particular level of verbal skill; and it is untenable that the Constitution prevents the Government from seeking modestly to upgrade the communicative abilities of its employees rather than to be satisfied with some lower level of competence, particularly where the job requires special ability to communicate orally and in writing.

Nor on the facts of the case before us would the disproportionate impact of Test 21 warrant the conclusion that it is a purposeful device to discriminate against Negroes. [T]he test is neutral on its face and rationally may be said to serve a purpose the Government is constitutionally empowered to pursue. Even agreeing with the District Court that the differential racial effect of Test

21 called for further inquiry, we think the District Court correctly held that the affirmative efforts of the Metropolitan Police Department to recruit black officers, the changing racial composition of the recruit classes and of the force in general, and the relationship of the test to the training program negated any inference that the Department discriminated on the basis of race or that "a police officer qualifies on the color of his skin rather than ability."

Under Title VII, Congress provided that when hiring and promotion practices disqualifying substantially disproportionate numbers of blacks are challenged, discriminatory purpose need not be proved, and that it is an insufficient response to demonstrate some rational basis for the challenged practices. It is necessary, in addition, that they be "validated" in terms of job performance in any one of several ways, perhaps by ascertaining the minimum skill, ability, or potential necessary for the position at issue and determining whether the qualifying tests are appropriate for the selection of qualified applicants for the job in question. However this process proceeds, it involves a more probing judicial review of, and less deference to, the seemingly reasonable acts of administrators and executives than is appropriate under the Constitution where special racial impact, without discriminatory purpose, is claimed. We are not disposed to adopt this more rigorous standard for the purposes of applying the Fifth and the Fourteenth Amendments in cases such as this.

A rule that a statute designed to serve neutral ends is nevertheless invalid, absent compelling justification, if in practice it benefits or burdens one race more than another would be far reaching and would raise serious questions about, and perhaps invalidate, a whole range of tax, welfare, public service, regulatory, and licensing statutes that may be more burdensome to the poor and to the average black than to the more affluent white.

Given that rule, such consequences would perhaps be likely to follow. However, in our view, extension of the rule beyond those areas where it is already applicable by reason of statute, such as in the field of public employment, should await legislative prescription.

[The Court went on to hold that no statutory violation had been established. JUSTICE STEWART concurred on the Court's constitutional holding.]

[JUSTICES BRENNAN and MARSHALL dissented on the statutory disposition and did not reach the constitutional issues.]

JUSTICE STEVENS, concurring [and joining the Court's opinion].

The requirement of purposeful discrimination is a common thread running through the cases [by the Court]. Frequently the most probative evidence of intent will be objective evidence of what actually happened rather than evidence describing the subjective state of mind of the actor. For normally the actor is presumed to have intended the natural consequences of his deeds. This is particularly true in the case of governmental action which is frequently the product of compromise, of collective decisionmaking, and of mixed motivation. It is unrealistic, on the one hand, to require the victim of alleged discrimination to uncover the actual subjective intent of the decisionmaker or, conversely, to invalidate otherwise legitimate action simply because an improper motive affected the deliberation of a participant in the decisional process. A law conscripting clerics should not be invalidated because an atheist voted for it.

My point in making this observation is to suggest that the line between discriminatory purpose and discriminatory impact is not nearly as bright, and perhaps not quite as critical, as the reader of the Court's opinion might assume. I agree, of course, that a constitutional issue does not arise every time some disproportionate impact is shown. On the other hand, when the disproportion is as dramatic as in *Gomillion v. Lightfoot*, or *Yick Wo v. Hopkins*, it really does not matter whether the standard is phrased in terms of purpose or effect. Therefore, although I accept the statement of the general rule in the Court's opinion, I am not yet prepared to indicate how that standard should be applied in the many cases which have formulated the governing standard in different language.

NOTES

1. *Purpose and effect.* In *Gomillion v. Lightfoot*, 364 U.S. 339 (1960), the Court held an Alabama law that changed the city boundaries of Tuskegee from a square "to an uncouth twenty-eight-sided figure" unconstitutional under the Fifteenth Amendment. It was alleged that the law removed all but four or five of the 400 black voters, but no whites. Justice Frankfurter, for the Court, held that if this allegation were established, "the conclusion would be irresistible, tantamount for all practicable purposes to a mathematical demonstration, that the legislation is solely concerned with segregating white and colored voters." As Justice Frankfurter put it, "Acts generally lawful may become unlawful when done to accomplish an unlawful end."

Gomillion establishes that the antidiscrimination principle of *Loving* is not limited to facial or explicit invidious racial classifications. As David Strauss, *Discriminatory Intent and the Taming of Brown*, 56 U. Chi. L. Rev. 935, 948 (1989), put it: "If explicit racial classifications are unlawful, it makes little sense to allow a government that is subtle enough to use an ostensibly neutral surrogate for race to get away with maintaining the Jim Crow regime." But is it enough that a law has a discriminatory racially disproportionate impact?

In *Washington v. Davis*, the Court correctly states that in no prior case had the Supreme Court held that disproportionate impact would itself trigger strict scrutiny. But it might have added that the Court had not held that discriminatory racial purpose was constitutionally required; nor had it been clearly established that legislative purpose could even be probed. In fact, the ambiguity of the Court's pre-*Davis* handling of the purpose-effect issue invited lower court confusion. Should discriminatory purpose be a constitutional requirement?

2. *The meaning of purpose.* What does the Court in *Washington v. Davis* mean by purpose? In *Personnel Administrator v. Feeney*, text, p. 798, the Court upheld a Massachusetts law giving veterans a lifetime preference for state civil service positions. Since 98% of Massachusetts veterans were males, the law overwhelmingly favored males for public employment. The challenger argued that "a person intends the natural and probable consequence of his voluntary actions." But the Court responded: " 'Discriminatory purpose,' however, implies more than intent as volition or intent as awareness of consequences. It implies that the decisionmaker, in this case a state legislature, selected or reaffirmed a particular course of action at least in part 'because of,' not merely 'in spite of,' its adverse effects upon an identifiable group." But the Court found nothing in the record that demonstrated "that this preference for veterans was originally devised or subsequently re-enacted because it would accomplish the collateral goal of keeping women in a stereotypic and predefined place in [public employment]." There was a nondiscriminatory explanation for the disparate impact — a desire to benefit veterans, male and female alike. Professor Strauss says: "the discriminatory intent standard requires that race play no role in government decisions." He refers to this as the "reversing the groups test" and says it poses this question: "suppose the adverse effects of the challenged government decision fell on whites instead of blacks . . . Would the decision be different? If the answer is yes, then the decision was made with discriminatory intent." 56 U. CHI. L. REV. at 956.

3. *Unconscious racism.* Charles Lawrence, *The Id, the Ego, and Equal Protection: Reckoning with Unconscious Racism*, 39 STAN. L. REV. 317, 322 (1987), argues that much of the behavior that produces racial discrimination is a result of unconscious racism. "Traditional notions of intent do not reflect the fact that decisions about racial matters are influenced in large part by factors that can be characterized as neither intentional — in the sense that certain outcomes are self-consciously sought — nor unintentional — in the sense that the outcomes are random, fortuitous, and uninfluenced by the decisionmaker's beliefs, desires, and wishes." He claims that we are not aware of the extent to which our beliefs about race are affected by our cultural heritage and how those beliefs in turn affect our actions. "[W]here the goal is the eradication of invidious racial discrimination, the law must recognize racism's primary source." *Id.* at 323. He urges use of strict scrutiny when government actions are unconsciously influenced by race.

In *Trojan Horses of Race*, 118 HARV. L. REV. 1489, 1494 (2005), Professor Jerry Kang similarly argues that social cognition research "demonstrates that most of us have implicit biases in the form of negative beliefs (stereotypes) and attitudes (prejudice) against racial minorities. These implicit biases, however, are not well reflected in explicit self-reported measures. This diassociation arises not solely because we try to sound more politically correct. Even when we are honest, we simply lack introspective insight. Finally, and most importantly, these implicit biases have real-world consequences—not only in the extraordinary case of shooting a gun, but also in the more mundane, everyday realm of social interactions." Does acceptance of "unconscious racism" justify the use of strict scrutiny when government actions cause disparate racial consequences?

4. *Problems with requiring purpose.* Deborah Hillman, *The Expressive Dimension of Equal Protection*, 85 MINN. L. REV. 1, 3 (2000), summarizes some of the concerns with requiring intent: "Briefly, the intent doctrine has been criticized as incoherent because determining the intent of a group like a legislative body is both philosophically as well as practically problematic. Second, even at the individual level, it is often difficult to know or assess the precise reasons for an individual's action. Unconscious or subtle motives may guide us without our recognition of their influence. Third, moral responsibility for actions extends beyond those actions one specifically intends. Surely the failure to take the interests of a group into account—indifference rather than animus—is to deny those affected the law's equal protection. Fourth and finally, while intent is relevant to assessing the moral culpability of legislative actors, courts ought to interpret the Equal Protection Clause to police how people are treated by their government. We ought to be interested in the permissibility of laws, not in the purity of legislative motives." Barbara Flagg, *"Was Blind but Now I See:" White Race Consciousness and the Requirement of Discriminatory Intent*, 91 MICH. L. REV. 953, 966 (1993), says that the problems associated with probing for intent include issues of ascertainability, futility, and disutility. "The difficulty of ascertaining legislative motive was apparent. Futility referred to the ability of the legislature to rehabilitate an invalidated law simply by reenacting it with a recitation of 'permissible' purposes. Disutility represented the concern that declaring legislative acts unconstitutional on the basis of motive alone might result in the invalidation of laws that were otherwise beneficial in their operation."

In Title VII employment cases, where Congress has provided that the prima facie case of discrimination can be based on disparate treatment or disparate impact, "there has long been a dispute over whether disparate impact doctrine is an evidentiary dragnet designed to discover hidden instances of intentional discrimination or a more aggressive attempt to dismantle racial hierarchies regardless of whether anything like intentional discrimination is present." Richard A. Primus, *Equal Protection and Disparate Impact: Round Three*, 117 HARV. L. REV. 493, 518 (2003). Professor Primus suggests that under the evidentiary approach, "disparate impact is a prophylactic measure that is necessary because deliberate discrimination can be difficult to prove." *Id.* at 520. Use of disparate impact "irrespective of an employer's state of mind," reflects a desire to eliminate the vestiges of past illegal racial discrimination in employment. *Id.* at 523–524. It is claimed that this was why the Court in *Griggs* accepted disparate impact even though Title VII at that time did not expressly provide for it. Is the disparate impact doctrine in Title VII cases justified as a remedy for "subconscious discrimination?" *See id.* at 532–535. Does the use of disparate impact to establish a Title VII violation raise qual protection problems? Is it a form of affirmative action? *Id.* at 536–552.

5. *Explanations for requiring purpose.* Given the harm that can be occasioned by disparate racial impact, why has the Court made discriminatory purpose a necessary condition for more searching judicial inquiry? One possible answer is that government has no constitutional duty to remedy a harm it has not caused. Assuming that the racially segregated condition is not the product of intentional government conduct, it is argued, the Equal Protection Clause imposes no obligation on government to remedy the condition or to take account of it in decisionmaking. The remedy for such harms under our constitutional system lies in the political process, and the Constitution does not guarantee any individual or group a favorable outcome in the legislative process. It is only when that process is not open to the disadvantaged class, i.e., it is malfunctioning, that the courts should intervene.

Professor Mary Frug, *Securing Job Equality for Women: Labor Market Hostility to Working Mothers*, 59 B.U. L. REV. 55, 82 (1979), cites two principal problems involved in using an impact test to trigger a more demanding judicial scrutiny. "First, a rule that disparate racial impact alone could render governmental action suspect would fundamentally change the prevailing theory of racial equality, which has principally functioned to prohibit the use of race as a governmental decisionmaking factor. The second major argument supporting *Davis* is the nearly insurmountable institutional burdens that would be placed on both the legislature and the judiciary if governmental actions with disparate racial impact triggered the exacting justification racially specific governmental action requires." If the Court were to hold that demonstrating disparate racial impact is sufficient to trigger close judicial scrutiny, would this necessitate race-conscious action programs to cure the disparities?

VILLAGE OF ARLINGTON HEIGHTS v. METROPOLITAN HOUSING DEVELOPMENT CORP.

429 U.S. 252, 97 S. Ct. 555, 50 L. Ed. 2d 450 (1977)

[Metropolitan Housing Development Corp. (MHDC) was seeking to develop a racially integrated, low-income, multiple-family housing project in the Village of Arlington Heights. While MHDC had leased land, hired an architect, and initiated development, successful completion depended on having the zoning changed from a single-family classification. When the village denied the zoning change, MHDC brought suit alleging racial discrimination in violation of the Fourteenth Amendment and a violation of the Fair Housing Act of 1968. The district court entered judgment for the village but the court of appeals reversed, concluding that the "ultimate effect" of the official action was racially discriminatory and therefore violated the equal protection guarantee.]

JUSTICE POWELL delivered the opinion of the Court.

Our decision last Term in *Washington v. Davis* made it clear that official action will not be held unconstitutional solely because it results in a racially disproportionate impact. Proof of racially discriminatory intent or purpose is required to show a violation of the Equal Protection Clause.

Davis does not require a plaintiff to prove that the challenged action rested solely on racially discriminatory purposes. Rarely can it be said that a legislature or administrative body operating under a broad mandate made a decision motivated solely by a single concern, or even that a particular purpose was the "dominant" or "primary" one. In fact, it is because legislators and administrators are properly concerned with balancing numerous competing considerations that courts refrain from reviewing the merits of their decisions, absent a showing of arbitrariness or irrationality. But racial discrimination is not just another competing consideration. When there is a proof that a discriminatory purpose has been a motivating factor in the decision, this judicial deference is no longer justified.

Determining whether invidious discriminatory purpose was a motivating factor demands a sensitive inquiry into such circumstantial and direct evidence of intent as may be available. The impact of the official action — whether it "bears more heavily on one race than another," — may provide an important starting point. Sometimes a clear pattern, unexplainable on grounds other than race, emerges from the effect of the state action even when the governing legislation appears neutral on its face. *Yick Wo v. Hopkins*. The evidentiary inquiry is then relatively easy. But such cases are rare. Absent a pattern as stark as that in *Gomillion* or *Yick Wo*, impact alone is not determinative, and the Court must look to other evidence.

The historical background of the decision is one evidentiary source, particularly if it reveals a series of official actions taken for invidious purposes. The specific sequence of events leading up [to] the challenged decision also may shed some light on the decisionmaker's purposes. For example, if the property involved here always had been zoned R-5 but suddenly was changed to R-3 when the town learned of MHDC's plans to erect integrated housing, we would have a far different case. Departures from the normal procedural sequence also might afford evidence that improper purposes are playing a role. Substantive departures too may be relevant, particularly if the factors usually considered important by the decisionmaker strongly favor a decision contrary to the one reached. The legislative or administrative history may be highly relevant, especially where there are contemporary statements by members of the decisionmaking body, minutes of its meetings, or reports. In some extraordinary instances the members might be called to the stand at trial to testify concerning the purpose of the official action, although even then such testimony frequently will be barred by privilege.

The foregoing summary identifies, without purporting to be exhaustive, subjects of proper inquiry in determining whether racially discriminatory intent existed. With these in mind, we now address the case before us. [T]he impact of the Village's decision does arguably bear more heavily on racial minorities. Minorities comprise 18% of the Chicago area population, and 40% of the income groups said to be eligible for Lincoln Green. But there is little about the sequence of events leading up to the decision that would spark suspicion. The area around the Viatorian property has been zoned R-3 since 1959, the year when Arlington Heights first adopted a zoning map. Single-family homes surround the 80-acre site, and the Village is undeniably committed to single-family homes as its dominant residential land use. The rezoning request progressed according to the usual procedures. The Plan Commission even scheduled two additional hearings, at least in part to accommodate MHDC and permit it to supplement its presentation with answers to questions generated at the first hearing.

The statements by the Plan Commission and Village Board members, as reflected in the official minutes, focused almost exclusively on the zoning aspects of the MHDC petition, and the zoning factors on which they relied are not novel criteria in the Village's rezoning decisions. There is no reason to doubt that there has been reliance by some neighboring property owners on the maintenance of single-family zoning in the vicinity. The Village originally adopted its buffer policy long before MHDC entered the picture and has applied the policy too consistently for us to infer discriminatory purpose from its application in this case. Finally, MHDC called one member of the Village Board to the stand at trial. Nothing in her testimony supports an inference of invidious purpose.

In sum, the evidence does not warrant overturning the concurrent findings of both courts below. Respondents simply failed to carry their burden of proving that discriminatory purpose was a motivating factor in the Village's decision.[21] This conclusion ends the constitutional inquiry. The Court of Appeals' further finding that the Village's decision carried a discriminatory "ultimate effect" is without independent constitutional significance.

Respondents' complaint also alleged that the refusal to rezone violated the Fair Housing Act. They continue to urge here that a zoning decision made by a public body may, and that petitioners' action did, violate [the Act]. The Court of Appeals, however, proceeding in a somewhat unorthodox fashion, did not decide the statutory question. We remand the case for further consideration of respondents' statutory claims.

[Justice Stevens took no part in the decision. Justice Marshall, joined by Justice Brennan, concurred in part and dissented in part while Justice White dissented, all urging a remand to the lower courts for further evidentiary proceedings.]

NOTES

1. ***Proving purpose.*** *Washington v. Davis* provides guidance on how discriminatory purpose is to be proved, including the possibility of inferences from statistical impact and from "the totality of the relevant facts." *Arlington Heights* affords a more complete guide to the relevant evidentiary sources. But *Arlington Heights* also demonstrates the difficulty of the challenger's burden of proof. A number of commentators have characterized *Arlington Heights* as a primer to government officials on how to build an appropriate record to prevent a finding of discriminatory intent.

Michael Selmi, *Proving Intentional Discrimination: The Reality of Supreme Court Rhetoric*, 86 Geo. L.J. 279, 290 (1997), notes that the element of intent is inferred from the language of facially discriminatory practice and policies, but adds that "[m]ore commonly, statutes and policies challenged as discriminatory are facially neutral, and the court must infer intent from the fact of differential treatment. This inference is generally based on the accumulated evidence, which is almost always circumstantial in character." Professor Selmi develops the argument that "despite its rhetoric regarding the importance of ferreting out subtle discrimination, the Court has only seen discrimination, absent a facial classification, in the most obvious situations — situations that could not be explained on any basis other than race. Whenever the Court found room to accept a nondiscriminatory explanation for a disputed act, it did so." *Id.* at 284.

---

[21] Proof that the decision by the Village was motivated in part by a racially discriminatory purpose would not necessarily have required invalidation of the challenged decision. Such proof would, however, have shifted to the Village the burden of establishing that the same decision would have resulted even had the impermissible purpose not been considered. If this were established, the complaining party in a case of this kind no longer fairly could attribute the injury complained of to improper consideration of a discriminatory purpose. In such circumstances, there would be no justification for judicial interference with the challenged decision. But in this case respondents failed to make the required threshold showing.

2. *Causation.* Professor Selmi notes that while intent can be established through proof of animus or motive, "neither animus or motive is *required* to prove intent." Instead, "the key question is whether race made a difference in the decisionmaking process, a question that targets causation, rather than subjective mental states." 86 Geo. L.J. at 288–289.

Even if the plaintiff establishes that the law is explainable in part by a racially discriminatory purpose, *Arlington Heights* indicates that the government need not show a compelling justification if it can demonstrate that "the same decision would have resulted even had the impermissible purpose not been considered."

> The effect of *Arlington Heights* therefore is to restructure the burden of proof in racial discrimination cases so that the justifications ordinarily brought forward in defense as compelling, become the basis to refute the prima facie case of racial discrimination in the first instance. This re-ordered sequence of proof as articulated in *Arlington Heights*, promises more judicial success for the municipality relying on allegedly compelling justifications for its differential code enforcement program.

Daniel Mandelker, *Differential Enforcement of Housing Codes — The Constitutional Dimension*, 55 U. Det. J. Urb. L. 517, 606 (1978).

It can be argued that if a law disadvantages a racial minority and racial discrimination is a motivating force for the law, this should be sufficient to trigger strict scrutiny. The fact that, in retrospect, the state would have taken the same action apart from the discriminatory purpose does not serve to purge the harmful racial effects of the law nor the racial motivation behind it. *See* Larry Alexander, *Introduction: Motivation and Constitutionality*, 15 San Diego L. Rev. 925, 945 (1978), who argues "that treating blacks in certain ways violates the equal protection clause and thus invites judicial, not just political, remedy, even if it satisfies completely some non-racial principle."

3. *Historical intent.* In *Hunter v. Underwood*, 471 U.S. 222 (1985), a unanimous Court, per Justice Rehnquist, held that § 182 of the Alabama Constitution, which provides for disenfranchisement of misdemeanants convicted of committing crimes involving "moral turpitude," violates equal protection. Appellees, a black and a white person, were disenfranchised because they each had been convicted of presenting a worthless check. They sought declaratory and injunctive relief against application of § 182 to misdemeanants. The district court found that disenfranchisement of African-Americans was a major purpose at the convention which adopted the Alabama Constitution, but that it had not been shown that § 182 was itself based upon this racism. Further, the court reasoned that the invalid purpose would not render § 182 invalid since the section served a permissible motive, "governing exercise of the franchise by those convicted of crimes." The Court of Appeals for the Eleventh Circuit held that the district court's findings were clearly erroneous and reversed. It found that (1) "discriminatory intent was a motivating factor" for § 182; (2) a competing permissible intent did not exist; and (3) that "§ 182 would not have been enacted in absence of the racially discriminatory motivation [and] as applied to misdemeanants violated the Fourteenth Amendment."

The Supreme Court affirmed. Justice Rehnquist noted that § 182 on its face is racially neutral, applying equally to anyone convicted of one of the designated crimes, but the Court of Appeals had found that this facially neutral provision had an indisputably discriminatory impact. Given such a finding supported by the record, the court of appeals was correct in examining the purpose or intent behind § 182. The proceedings of the convention, several historical studies, and the expert testimony of two historians "demonstrated conclusively that § 182 was enacted with the intent of disenfranchising blacks." The fact that the convention may also have been motivated by the additional purpose of discriminating against poor whites (even assuming this qualified as a permissible purpose) "would not render nugatory the purpose to discriminate against all blacks, and it is beyond peradventure that the latter was a 'but for' motivation for the enactment of § 182." Therefore, the Court concluded that the "original enactment [of § 182] was motivated by a desire to discriminate against blacks on account of race and the section continues to this day to have that effect. As such, it violates equal protection under *Arlington Heights*."

4. *Jury discrimination.* In *Batson v. Kentucky*, 476 U.S. 79 (1986), the Court held that equal protection is violated when a prosecutor uses his peremptory challenges to exclude certain jurors solely on the basis of their race. Justice Powell relied heavily on the principles of *Strauder v. West Virginia* establishing that "the State denies a black defendant equal protection of the laws when it puts him on trial before a jury from which members of his race have been purposely excluded." While a defendant has no right to a jury composed in whole or in part of persons of his own race, "he does have the right to be tried by a jury whose members are selected pursuant to nondiscriminatory criteria. The Equal Protection Clause guarantees the defendant that the State will not exclude members of his race from the jury venire on account of race, or on the false assumption that members of his race are not qualified to serve as jurors." Discriminatory jury selection harms not only the defendant but the entire community since it "undermine[s] public confidence in the fairness of our system of justice" and stimulates race prejudice which impedes securing equal justice for black citizens.

Once the prima facie case is made, the burden shifts to the state to justify the exclusion on some "neutral ground," although this need not rise to the level justifying exercise of a challenge for cause. "[T]he prosecutor must articulate a neutral explanation related to the particular case to be tried. The trial court then will have the duty to determine if the defendant has established purposeful discrimination."

In *Purkett v. Elem*, 514 U.S. 755 (1995), the Court reversed an Eighth Circuit decision holding that a prosecutor's decision to strike two black veniremen based on their "long hair," "goatees," and "suspicious" looks was racially discriminatory. The per curiam opinion held that *Batson* "does not demand an explanation that is persuasive, or even plausible." In dissent, Justice Stevens, joined by Justice Beyer, complained that "the Court replaces the *Batson* standard with the surprising announcement that any neutral explanation, no matter how 'implausible or fantastic,' even if it's 'silly or superstitious' is sufficient to rebut a prima facie case of discrimination." Stevens added, "It is not too much to ask that a prosecutor's explanation for his strikes be race neutral, reasonably specific, *and* trial related."

Robin Charlow, *Tolerating Deception and Discrimination after Batson*, 50 STAN. L. REV. 9, 36 (1997), says that *Elem* established "that, at least in the *Batson* context, it is indeed the subjective motivation of the actor that is crucial to the doctrine of discriminatory intent." Leonard C. Cavise, *The Batson Doctrine: The Supreme Court's Utter Failure to Meet the Challenge of Discrimination in Jury Selection*, 1999 WIS. L. REV. 501, notes that while "many feared peremptory challenges would become an endangered species" following the *Batson* decision, "those fears have been laid to rest by a Supreme Court anxious to render its own decision as meaningless, ineffective, and unthreatening as possible. Only the most overtly discriminatory or impolitic lawyer can be caught in *Batson's* toothless bite and, even then, the wound will be only superficial."

5. *Voting Discrimination.* In *Mobile v. Bolden*, 446 U.S. 55 (1980), the Court rejected an equal protection challenge to an at-large election system in Mobile, Alabama. A plurality concluded that the plaintiffs had failed to prove that the system was "conceived or operated as [a] purposeful device to further racial discrimination," even though the lower courts had held that an invidious discriminatory purpose could be inferred from the totality of the facts. The plurality examined each of the elements of proof of discriminatory purpose independently and found it inadequate.

In *Rogers v. Lodge*, 458 U.S. 613 (1982), the Court appeared to retreat from the stringent evidentiary standards for proving purpose that it had erected in *Mobile*. The case involved a challenge to the at-large electoral system maintained since 1911 by Burke County, Georgia. While a slight majority of the population in the county in 1980 was Black and while Blacks in 1978 constituted thirty-eight percent of the registered voters, no Black had ever been elected to the five-person Board of Commissioners. The district court, writing before *Mobile* was decided, held that while the at-large system of election was "racially neutral when adopted, [it] is being maintained for invidious purposes." The court of appeals, affirming, concluded that the district court had correctly anticipated *Mobile's* requirement that appellees were required to prove that the at-large voting system was maintained for a discriminatory purpose and that the lower court's conclusion that the state's burden had not been met was "virtually mandated by the overwhelming proof."

Justice White, who had dissented in *Mobile*, now wrote for a majority in affirming the lower court judgment. While reaffirming the *Mobile* principle that a prerequisite to a finding of unconstitutional vote dilution is a finding of a discriminatory intent, the Supreme Court looked to the "totality of circumstances" and deferred to the district court factfinding which appeared to rely on the same type of considerations that had been rejected in *Mobile* (e.g., the failure of any Black candidates to be elected; the impact of past discrimination on the ability of Blacks to participate effectively in the political process; the insensitivity and unresponsiveness of elected officials in Burke County to the needs of the Black community; past discrimination in education and in the legal system; and the socio-economic status of Burke County

Blacks). The lower court had also relied on other factors which enhanced the tendency of multi-member districts to minimize the voting strength of racial minorities, such as the requirement of a majority for election, the sheer geographic size of the county, the requirement that candidates run for specific seats, and the absence of any residency requirement. Justice White concluded that "none of the District Court's findings underlying its ultimate finding of intentional discrimination appears to us to be clearly erroneous."

6. *The death penalty.* In *McCleskey v. Kemp*, 481 U.S. 279 (1987), Justice Powell for the Court rejected a challenge to application of the death penalty in Georgia murder cases. Statistical evidence (the Baldus study) showed "defendants charged with killing white persons received the death penalty in 11% of the cases, but defendants charged with killing blacks received the death penalty in only 1% of the cases. The raw numbers also indicate a reverse racial disparity according to the race of the defendant: 4% of the black defendants received the death penalty, as opposed to 7% of the white defendants." When the death penalty cases were grouped by combination of race of defendant and race of victim, the following data emerged: "the death penalty was assessed in 22% of the cases involving black defendants and white victims; 8% of the cases involving white defendants and white victims; 1% of the cases involving black defendants and black victims; and 3% of the cases involving white defendants and black victims. Similarly, prosecutors sought the death penalty in 70% of the cases involving black defendants and white victims; 32% of the cases involving white defendants and white victims; 15% of the cases involving black defendants and black victims; and 19% of the cases involving white defendants and black victims."

McCleskey was a black defendant convicted of murdering a police officer in the course of an armed robbery. He was sentenced to death and challenged the sentence on both equal protection and cruel and unusual punishment grounds. With regard to the equal protection claim, the opinion by Justice Powell reiterated the "purposeful discrimination" test and stated that

> to prevail under the Equal Protection Clause, McCleskey must prove that the decisionmakers in his case acted with discriminatory purpose. He offers no evidence specific to his own case that would support an inference that racial considerations played a part in his sentence. Instead, he relies solely on the Baldus study. McCleskey argues that the Baldus study compels an inference that his sentence rests on purposeful discrimination. McCleskey's claim that these statistics are sufficient proof of discrimination, without regard to the facts of a particular case, would extend to all capital cases in Georgia, at least where the victim was white and the defendant is black.
>
> [E]ach particular decision to impose the death penalty is made by a petit jury selected from a properly constituted venire. Each jury is unique in its composition, and the Constitution requires that its decision rest on consideration of innumerable factors that vary according to the characteristics of the individual defendant and the facts of the particular capital offense. Thus, the application of an inference drawn from the general statistics to a specific decision in a trial and sentencing simply is not comparable to the application of an inference

> drawn from general statistics to a specific venire-selection or Title VII case. In those cases, the statistics relate to fewer entities, and fewer variables are relevant to the challenged decisions.
>
> Finally, McCleskey's statistical proffer must be viewed in the context of his challenge. McCleskey challenges decisions at the heart of the State's criminal justice system. Implementation of [criminal] laws necessarily requires discretionary judgments. Because discretion is essential to the criminal justice process, we would demand exceptionally clear proof before we would infer that the discretion has been abused. The unique nature of the decisions at issue in this case also counsel against adopting such an inference from the disparities indicated by the Baldus study. Accordingly, we hold that the Baldus study is clearly insufficient to support an inference that any of the decisionmakers in McCleskey's case acted with discriminatory purpose.

Justices Brennan, Marshall, Blackmun, and Stevens dissented. After reviewing the history of conscious racial discrimination in the Georgia criminal justice system and observing that history could have produced even unconscious race bias in jurors, Justice Brennan pointed out that the jury has complete discretion in choosing life or death, and need not articulate its basis for selecting life imprisonment. The Georgia sentencing system therefore provides considerable opportunity for racial considerations, however subtle and unconscious, to influence charging and sentencing decisions. History and its continuing legacy thus buttress the probative force of McCleskey's statistics. Formal dual criminal laws may no longer be in effect, and intentional discrimination may no longer be prominent. Nonetheless, subtle, less consciously held racial attitudes continue to be of concern, and the Georgia system gives such attitudes considerable room to operate.

Professor Kennedy asserts that the *McCleskey* majority was "trapped by visions of old conquests — the battles against de jure segregation and overt, intentional discrimination." He says that this view "ignores the chameleon-like ability of prejudice to adapt unobtrusively to new surroundings and, further, to hide itself even from those firmly within its grip." Randall Kennedy, *McCleskey v. Kemp: Race, Capital Punishment and the Supreme Court*, 101 Harv. L. Rev. 1388, 1419 (1988). Note, *Constitutional Risks to Equal Protection in the Criminal Justice System*, 114 Harv. L. Rev. 2098 (2001), argues that the *McCleskey* Court's emphasis on "particularized harm" causes courts to ignore "more subtle, systematic risks" of government action. Often a criminal defendant cannot prove "that racial discrimination more likely than not tainted his particular conviction." Sometimes, all statistical analysis will reveal is that disparities remain even after all plausible non-racial factors have been accounted for. "The risk of particularized harm is of special concern in equal protection cases today as social mores have largely driven racial discrimination underground, making discrimination far more likely to occur surreptitiously." The author concludes that the same problem of establishing racial discrimination through statutes applies in sentencing, prosecution and policing. *Id.* at 2106.

7. *Selective prosecution.* In *United States v. Armstrong*, 517 U.S. 456 (1996), the defendant in a federal prosecution for possession of crack cocaine alleged that the U.S. Attorney's Office routinely prosecuted only black defendants for this offense and sought discovery from the government's files regarding the race of persons accused but not prosecuted. In an opinion by Chief Justice Rehnquist, the Supreme Court upheld the trial court's refusal to provide discovery absent an initial showing by "some credible evidence" of a failure to prosecute persons of different race than the defendant's. In order to prove a selective-prosecution claim, the claimant must demonstrate that the prosecutorial policy had a discriminatory effect and was motivated by a discriminatory purpose. To establish a discriminatory effect in a race case, the claimant must show that similarly situated individuals of a different race were not prosecuted. "We think the required threshold — a credible showing of different treatment of similarly situated persons — adequately balances the Government's interest in vigorous prosecution and the defendant's interest in avoiding selective prosecution."

Richard H. McAndrews, *Race and Selective Prosecution: Discovering the Pitfalls of Armstrong*, 73 Chi-Kent L. Rev. 605 (1998), is critical of the discovery rules imposed in *Armstrong*. "Criminal defendants in this country almost never win claims that prosecutors acted with racially discriminatory purpose in bringing a charge. No wonder, given that prosecutors control almost all the information relevant to determining their motive. Commentators have noted the dilemma: the defendant 'cannot obtain discovery unless she first makes a threshold showing . . . of selective prosecution . . . Yet making a sufficient preliminary showing of discriminatory intent may be impossible without some discovery.' "

8. *Context and intent.* Does the intent requirement operate the same way regardless of the fact context? Consider the claim that the intent requirement operates "differently in different contexts in order to 'balance' individual and societal interests consistently with the ideology of traditional liberalism. Where (as in housing and employment) this ideology either relegates decisionmaking to markets or allows the state much leeway in allocating goods, intent makes judicial supervision of decisionmaking difficult. On the other hand, where liberal ideology insists on particular types of nonmarket allocation (as in voting, jury selection, and sometimes education), intent makes judicial intervention more likely." Daniel Ortiz, *The Myth of Intent in Equal Protection*, 41 Stan. L. Rev. 1105, 1107 (1989). For example, Professor Ortiz argues that "the intent test in the jury selection cases differs from the intent test in housing and employment cases in two important respects: it places both a light burden on the individual and a heavier burden on the state." *Id.* at 1122.

[C] DISCRIMINATION IN EDUCATION: AN AFFIRMATIVE DUTY TO EQUALIZE?

[1] Establishing the Foundations: *Plessy* and *Brown*

By the late nineteenth century, southern blacks were being subjected to a new form of slavery in the form of Jim Crow segregation. Michael Klarman,

From Jim Crow to Civil Rights: The Supreme Court and the Struggle for Racial Equality 59–60 (2004), says that "[m]ost Jim Crow laws merely described white supremacy; they did not produce it. Entrenched social mores, reinforced by economic power and the threat and reality of physical violence, were primarily responsible for bolstering the South's racial hierarchy." Nevertheless, denied political equality by restrictive voting laws, Negroes were now relegated to social inferiority by state law. "In bulk and detail as well as in effectiveness of enforcement, the segregation codes were comparable with the black codes of the old regime, though the laxity that mitigated the harshness of the black codes was replaced by a rigidity that was more typical of the segregation code. That code lent the sanction of law to a racial ostracism that extended to churches and schools, to housing and jobs, to eating and drinking." C. Vann Woodward, The Strange Career of Jim Crow 7 (2d ed. 1966). But in *Strauder v. West Virginia*, p. 659, the Supreme Court had said that the Fourteenth Amendment conferred "the right to exemption from unfriendly legislation against [Negroes] distinctively as colored."

***Plessy v. Ferguson*, 163 U.S. 537 (1896)**. The Court considered these apparently inconsistent legal commands in the context of a statute requiring "equal but separate" railway accommodations for whites and blacks, concluding:

> The object of the [Fourteenth] Amendment was undoubtedly to enforce the absolute equality of the two races before the law, but, in the nature of things, it could not have been intended to abolish distinctions based upon color, or to enforce social, as distinguished from political equality, or a commingling of the two races upon terms unsatisfactory to either. Laws permitting, and even requiring, their separation, in places where they are liable to be brought into contact, do not necessarily imply the inferiority of either race to the other, and have been generally, if not universally, recognized as within the competency of the state legislatures in the exercise of their police power.
>
> [T]he case reduces itself to the question whether the statute of Louisiana is a reasonable regulation, and with respect to this there must necessarily be a large discretion on the part of the legislature. In determining the question of reasonableness it is at liberty to act with reference to the established usages, customs, and traditions of the people, and with a view to the promotion of their comfort, and the preservation of the public peace and good order. Gauged by this standard, we cannot say that a law which authorizes or even requires the separation of the two races in public conveyances is unreasonable or more obnoxious to the Fourteenth Amendment than the acts of Congress requiring separate schools for colored children in the District of Columbia, the constitutionality of which does not seem to have been questioned, or the corresponding acts of state legislatures.
>
> We consider the underlying fallacy of the plaintiff's argument to consist in the assumption that the enforced separation of the two races stamps the colored race with a badge of inferiority. If this be so, it is not by reason of anything found in the act, but solely because the

> colored race chooses to put that construction upon it. The argument also assumes that social prejudices may be overcome by legislation, and that equal rights cannot be secured to the negro except by an enforced commingling of the two races. We cannot accept this proposition. If the two races are to meet upon terms of social equality, it must be the result of natural affinities, a mutual appreciation of each other's merits, and a voluntary consent of individuals.

In dissent, Justice Harlan argued:

> In respect of civil rights, common to all citizens, the Constitution of the United States does not, I think, permit any public authority to know the race of those entitled to be protected in the enjoyment of such rights. Every true man has pride of race, and under appropriate circumstances, when the rights of others, his equals before the law, are not to be affected, it is his privilege to express such pride and to take such action based upon it as to him seems proper. But I deny that any legislative body or judicial tribunal may have regard to the race of citizens when the civil rights of those citizens are involved. Indeed such legislation as that here in question is inconsistent, not only with that equality of rights which pertains to citizenship, national and state, but with the personal liberty enjoyed by every one within the United States.
>
> [I]n view of the Constitution, in the eye of the law, there is in this country no superior, dominant, ruling class of citizens. There is no caste here. Our Constitution is color-blind, and neither knows nor tolerates classes among citizens. In respect of civil rights, all citizens are equal before the law. The destinies of the two races in this country are indissolubly linked together, and the interests of both require that the common government of all shall not permit the seeds of race hate to be planted under the sanction of law. What can more certainly arouse race hate, what more certainly create and perpetuate a feeling of distrust between these races, than state enactments which in fact proceed on the ground that colored citizens are so inferior and degraded that they cannot be allowed to sit in public coaches occupied by white citizens? That, as all will admit, is the real meaning of such legislation as was enacted in Louisiana.

There is little discussion in *Plessy* regarding the "equal" facet of separate but equal., Michael J. Klarman, *The Plessy Era*, 1998 SUP. CT. REV. 303, 378, notes that in the early twentieth century, "segregation in practice, whether in public education or railroad travel, rarely afforded blacks anything approaching equality." In *Missouri ex rel. Gaines v. Canada*, 305 U.S. 337 (1938), the Court held unconstitutional a Missouri plan whereby the state provided a law school for Whites and financed legal education for Negroes in other states. Chief Justice Hughes reasoned that Missouri must give equal protection of the laws in its own jurisdiction.

> By the operation of the laws of Missouri a privilege has been created for white law students which is denied to Negroes by reason of their

race. The white resident is afforded legal education within the State; the Negro resident having the same qualifications is refused it there and must go outside the State to obtain it. That is a denial of the equality of legal right to the enjoyment of the privilege which the State has set up, and the provision for the payment of tuition fees in another State does not remove the discrimination.

In 1950, the Court decided two cases that went far in undermining state imposed educational segregation, regardless of the equality and tangible facilities. *McLaurin v. Oklahoma Regents for Higher Education*, 339 U.S. 637 (1950), held that black graduate students who were consigned to certain desks in the classroom and special areas of the library and cafeteria were not being afforded their "present and personal right" to equal protection of the laws. Such restrictions "handicapped" McLaurin "in his pursuit of effective graduate education" since they "impair and inhibit his ability to study, to engage in discussions and exchange views with other students, and, in general, to learn his profession."

In *Sweatt v. Painter*, 339 U.S. 629 (1950), again avoiding the "broader issues," the Court found inequality even though the state maintained separate law schools for blacks and whites within the state. Numerous inequalities in tangible resources were noted, including many difficult to measure, such as the reputation of the faculty, the experience of the administrators, the influence of alumni, and community standing. And the Court went on to more intangible features, noting the difference between the segregated schools in opportunity for "the interplay of ideas and the exchange of views with which the law is concerned."

By the early 1950s, the NAACP had to decide whether to continue pursuing equality of schools or to challenge the very premise of "separate" schools. World War II had produced significant changes in American race relations. The stage was set for *Brown v. Board of Education*.

BROWN v. BOARD OF EDUCATION [BROWN I]
347 U.S. 483, 74 S. Ct. 686, 98 L. Ed. 873 (1954)

Chief Justice Warren delivered the opinion of the Court.

These cases come to us from the States of Kansas, South Carolina, Virginia and Delaware. In each of the cases, minors of the Negro race, through their legal representatives, seek the aid of the courts in obtaining admission to the public schools of their community on a nonsegregated basis. In each instance, they have been denied admission to schools attended by white children under laws requiring or permitting segregation according to race.

The plaintiffs contend that segregated public schools are not "equal" and cannot be made "equal," and that hence they are deprived of the equal protection of the laws. Because of the obvious importance of the question presented, the Court took jurisdiction. Argument was heard in the 1952 Term, and reargument was heard this Term on certain questions propounded by the Court. Reargument was largely devoted to the circumstances surrounding the adoption of the Fourteenth Amendment in 1868. This discussion and our own investigation convince us that, although these sources cast some light, it is not enough to resolve the problem with which we are faced. At best, they are inconclusive. The most avid proponents of the post-War Amendments undoubtedly intended them to remove all legal distinctions among "all persons born or naturalized in the United States." Their opponents, just as certainly, were antagonistic to both the letter and the spirit of the Amendments and wished them to have the most limited effect. What others in Congress and state legislatures had in mind cannot be determined with any degree of certainty.

In the first cases in this Court construing the Fourteenth Amendment, decided shortly after its adoption, the Court interpreted it as proscribing all state-imposed discriminations against the Negro race. The doctrine of "separate but equal" did not make its appearance in this Court until 1896 in the case of *Plessy v. Ferguson*, involving not education but transportation. American courts have since labored with the doctrine for over half a century.

Our decision cannot turn on merely a comparison of tangible factors in the Negro and white schools involved in each of the cases. We must look instead to the effect of segregation itself on public education. In approaching this problem, we cannot turn the clock back to 1868 when the Amendment was adopted, or even to 1896 when *Plessy v. Ferguson* was written. We must consider public education in the light of its full development and its present place in American life throughout the Nation. Only in this way can it be determined if segregation in public schools deprives these plaintiffs of the equal protection of the laws.

Today, education is perhaps the most important function of state and local governments. Compulsory school attendance laws and the great expenditures for education both demonstrate our recognition of the importance of education to our democratic society. It is required in the performance of our most basic public responsibilities, even service in the armed forces. It is the very foundation of good citizenship. Today it is a principal instrument in awakening the child to cultural values, in preparing him for later professional training, and in helping him to adjust normally to his environment. In these days, it is doubtful that any child may reasonably be expected to succeed in life if he is denied the opportunity of an education. Such an opportunity, where the state has undertaken to provide it, is a right which must be made available to all on equal terms.

We come then to the question presented: Does segregation of children in public schools solely on the basis of race, even though the physical facilities and other "tangible" factors may be equal, deprive the children of the minority group of equal educational opportunities? We believe that it does.

In *Sweatt v. Painter*, in finding that a segregated law school for Negroes could not provide them equal educational opportunities, this Court relied in large part on "those qualities which are incapable of objective measurement but which make for greatness in a law school." Such considerations apply with added force to children in grade and high schools. To separate them from others of similar age and qualifications solely because of their race generates a feeling of inferiority as to their status in the community that may affect their hearts and minds in a way unlikely ever to be undone. The effect of this separation on their educational opportunities was well stated by a finding in the Kansas case by a court which nevertheless felt compelled to rule against the Negro plaintiffs:

> Segregation of white and colored children in public schools has a detrimental effect upon the colored children. The impact is greater when it has the sanction of the law; for the policy of separating the races is usually interpreted as denoting the inferiority of the Negro group. A sense of inferiority affects the motivation of a child to learn. Segregation with the sanction of law, therefore, has a tendency to retard the educational and mental development of Negro children and to deprive them of some of the benefits they would receive in a racially integrated school system.

Whatever may have been the extent of psychological knowledge at the time of *Plessy v. Ferguson*, this finding is amply supported by modern authority.[11] Any language in *Plessy v. Ferguson* contrary to this finding is rejected.

We conclude that in the field of public education the doctrine of "separate but equal" has no place. Separate educational facilities are inherently unequal. Therefore, we hold that the plaintiffs and others similarly situated for whom the actions have been brought are, by reason of the segregation complained of, deprived of the equal protection of the laws guaranteed by the Fourteenth Amendment. This disposition makes unnecessary any discussion whether such segregation also violates the Due Process Clause of the Fourteenth Amendment.

Because these are class actions, because of the wide applicability of this decision, and because of the great variety of local conditions, the formulation of decrees in these cases presents problems of considerable complexity. On reargument, the consideration of appropriate relief was necessarily subordinated to the primary question — the constitutionality of segregation in public education. We have now announced that such segregation is a denial of the equal protection of the laws. In order that we may have the full assistance of the parties in formulating decrees, the cases will be restored to the docket, and the parties are requested to present further argument.

NOTES

1. *The holding of* Brown. While *Brown I* is clearly a landmark decision, there is substantial disagreement as to what the Court held and the basis for its holding. Reva B. Siegel, *Equality Talk: Antisubordination and Anticlassification Values in Constitutional Struggles over* Brown, 117 HARV. L. REV. 1470, 1478–79 (2004), comments that "[w]hen Brown was first handed down,

[11] K.B. CLARK, EFFECT OF PREJUDICE AND DISCRIMINATION ON PERSONALITY DEVELOPMENT (MIDCENTURY WHITE HOUSE CONFERENCE ON CHILDREN AND YOUTH, 1950); WITMER & KOTINSKY, PERSONALITY IN THE MAKING (1952), c. VI; Deutscher and Chein, *The Psychological Effects of Enforced Segregation: A Survey of Social Science Opinion*, 26 J.PSYCHOL. 259 (1948); Chein, *What are the Psychological Effects of Segregation Under Conditions of Equal Facilities?*, 3 INT. J. OPINION AND ATTITUDE RES. 229 (1949); BRAMELD, EDUCATIONAL COSTS, IN DISCRIMINATION AND NATIONAL WELFARE (McIver, ed., 1949), 44–48; FRAZIER, THE NEGRO IN THE UNITED STATES (1949), 674–681. *And see generally* MYRDAL, AN AMERICAN DILEMMA (1944).

contemporaries understood that the Court had taken the momentous step of declaring that segregation in public education was unconstitutional, yet it was not clear exactly how the Fourteenth Amendment would alter the organization of schools or how it would affect the many other institutions in the United States in which race played a shaping role. [I]ts ultimate logic and practical application still remained unclear." Remember that *Loving v. Virginia*, p. 657, invalidating miscegenation laws, had not yet been decided. Professor Jack Balkin, *What* Brown *Teaches Us About Its Constitutional Theory*, 90 VA. L. REV. 1537, 1567 (2004), suggests that the meaning of *Brown* has shifted over time: "The *Brown* we have today has been formalized and domesticated, limited in its remedial scope, and made palatable for mass consumption."

As you consider the various alternatives, consider the political position of the Court at the time:

> The Court knew, of course, that its judgment would have an unparalleled impact on the daily lives of a very substantial portion of the population and that the response to many of those affected would be in varying degrees hostile. It was necessary, therefore, if ever it had been, to exert to the utmost the prestige, the oracular authority of the institution. To this end, it was desirable that the Court speak unanimously, with one voice from the deep. And the less said, the less chance of internal disagreement. By the same token, it was wise to present as small a target as possible to marksmen on the outside.

Alexander Bickel, *The Original Understanding and the Segregation Decision*, 69 HARV. L. REV. 1, 2 (1955).

2. *Original intent.* The Court in *Brown* found the history of the Fourteenth Amendment inconclusive regarding the status of racial segregation in education. It has been argued that because separate schools were common at the time that the Fourteenth Amendment was drafted, it could not have been intended to upset the system of segregated schools. ROBERT H. BORK, THE TEMPTING OF AMERICA 75–76 (1990), says that "[t]he inescapable fact is that those who ratified the amendment did not think it outlawed segregated education or segregation in any aspect of life."

Alexander Bickel has suggested that the Fourteenth Amendment implemented "the relatively narrow objectives of the moderates," and therefore was not intended to apply to segregated education, but that the language of the Amendment was left sufficiently flexible to accommodate future growth. As Bickel put it: "[W]e are dealing with a constitutional amendment, not a statute." In a proposed redraft of the *Brown* opinion, Professor Pollak agrees that the history of the Fourteenth Amendment does not disclose any intent on the part of the framers to end educational segregation but asserts that this is not dispositive: "For one thing, it is familiar constitutional history that this court has progressively brought within the ambit of the Fourteenth Amendment many issues and many litigants probably not contemplated by those who framed and ratified the amendment. Moreover—and of more immediate moment—we read the history of the Amendment as contemplating an essentially dynamic development by Congress and this Court of the liberties outlined in such generalized terms in the Amendment." Louis Pollak, *Racial*

Discrimination and Judicial Integrity: A Reply to Professor Wechsler, 108 U. Pa. L. Rev. 1 (1959).

Michael W. McConnell, *Originalism and the Desegregation Decisions* 81 Va. L. Rev. 947, 952 (1995), says: "In the fractured discipline of constitutional law, there is something very close to a consensus that *Brown* was inconsistent with the original understanding of the Fourteenth Amendment, except perhaps at an extremely high and indeterminate level of abstraction." But after an extensive reexamination of the historical evidence, McConnell concludes "that school segregation was understood during Reconstruction to violate the principle of equality of the Fourteenth Amendment." *Id.* at 1140. Michael J. Klarman, *Brown, Originalism, and Constitutional Theory: A Response to Professor McConnell*, 81 Va. L. Rev. 1881, 1883 (1995), argues that "[McConnell] fails to show either that *Brown* is correct on originalist grounds, or even, as he more modestly suggests, that *Brown* is 'within the legitimate range of interpretations' of the Fourteenth Amendment." Professor Klarman also claims that McConnell's efforts demonstrate the difficulties of originalist constitutional theory. For Professor McConnell's defense, see *The Originalist Justification for Brown: A Reply to Professor Klarman*, 81 Va. L. Rev. 1937 (1995). Is it important that *Brown* be justified in terms of original intent?

3. *The educational context.* Robert Carter, who argued *Brown* for the NAACP to the Supreme Court states: "We were looking to *Brown* to establish, through constitutional doctrine, equal educational opportunity for black children in real life." Robert Carter, *Reexamining Brown Twenty-five Years Later: Looking Backward Into the Future*, 14 Harv. C.R. — C.L.L. Rev. 615 (1979). Chief Justice Warren's statement that "separate educational facilities are inherently unequal," his comments on the effects of segregation on the child and his citation in footnote 11 of social science authorities have received extensive commentary. At the trial, social scientists were used by the NAACP as expert witnesses. The Virginia and South Carolina courts rejected such evidence while the Delaware and Kansas courts accepted it. The NAACP brief to the Supreme Court contained an extensive social science appendix signed by thirty-five distinguished social scientists, concluding that "enforced segregation is psychologically detrimental to the members of the segregated group." In oral argument, the social science findings were described by Robert Carter as "the heart of our case."

What role did the social science evidence of harm to Black children play in the decision in *Brown*? Would the decision have been the same even if no empirical evidence of psychological and educational harm had been provided? The social psychologist who played a leading role in *Brown* contends: "The role of social science in the *Brown* decision was crucial, in the Court's opinion, in supplying persuasive evidence that segregation itself means inequality." Kenneth Clark, *The Social Scientists, The Brown Decision and Contemporary Confusion*, in Argument: The Oral Argument Before the Supreme Court in Brown v. Board of Education of Topeka 1952–55 (L. Friedman ed. 1969). Professor Siegel, 117 Harv. L. Rev., at 1481, notes that, "as contemporaries realized, the language of classification was conspicuously absent in *Brown*, which emphasized that racially segregated schools harmed children by causing in them powerful feelings of 'inferiority as to their status in the community.' The decision did not condemn racial classification as such; rather, it addressed the harmful consequences of separating children in a specific institutional context."

4. *An antidiscrimination focus.* Immediately after *Brown I*, the Court issued a series of per curiam decisions holding state imposed segregation in various public facilities unconstitutional on the basis of *Brown I. See, e.g., Mayor of Baltimore v. Dawson,* 350 U.S. 877 (1955) (beaches); *Holmes v. Atlanta*, 350 U.S. 879 (1955) (municipal golf courses); *Gayle v. Browder*, 352 U.S. 903 (1956) (buses); *New Orleans City Park Improvement Ass'n v. Detiege*, 358 U.S. 54 (1958) (parks). It is difficult to understand how these varying factual contexts could be summarily handled if *Brown* is based on the special place of education in our society and the harm of state imposed segregation on the child. Commenting on these decisions, Professor Paul Kauper, *The Supreme Court and the Rule of Law*, 50 MICH. L. REV. 531, 549 (1961), stated: "It will be remembered that the famous school desegregation decision rested squarely and peculiarly on the finding that segregation in public schools resulted in harmful, discriminatory effects on Negro children. Yet in view of a series of later per curiam decisions, it must now be inferred that the school desegregation decision really was grounded on a broader principle, namely, that all segregation legislation is invalid since it rests on an impermissible basis of classification." In *Missouri v. Jenkins*, 515 U.S. 70 (1995), Justice Thomas, concurring, stated that "*Brown I* itself did not need to rely upon any psychological or social-science research in order to announce the simple, yet fundamental truth that the government cannot discriminate among its citizens on the basis of race."

Does *Brown* hold that state imposed racial segregation, regardless of the context, is violative of equal protection? Is *Plessy* overruled? Is the Court adopting the dissent of Justice Harlan in *Plessy* and returning to *Strauder*? Is the Court saying that racial classifications are per se impermissible?

In *Bolling v. Sharpe*, 347 U.S. 497 (1954), a companion case to *Brown*, the Court held that the educational segregation laws of the District of Columbia violated the Due Process Clause of the Fifth Amendment — "discrimination may be so unjustifiable as to be violative of due process." Chief Justice Warren, for a unanimous Court, began with the premise that "[c]lassifications based solely upon race must be scrutinized with particular care since they are contrary to our traditions and hence constitutionally suspect. Liberty under law extends to the full range of conduct which the individual is free to pursue, and it cannot be restricted except for a proper governmental objective." Applying this standard, the Chief Justice concluded: "Segregation in public education is not reasonably related to any proper governmental objective and thus it imposes on Negro children of the District of Columbia a burden that constitutes an arbitrary deprivation of their liberty in violation of the Due Process Clause." Why did Chief Justice Warren in *Brown* not use the "suspect classifications" approach employed in *Bolling*?

5. *A matter of ethics.* "If desegregation decisions are to be stable, consistent, and manageable, courts have little choice but to rely on ethical principles. The cases can be explained only by reference to such principles." Mark Yudof, *Equal Educational Opportunity and the Courts*, 51 TEX. L. REV. 411, 446

(1973). Is *Brown* ultimately a question of ethics, a subjective judgment of how our society should be run? How would you frame the principle underlying *Brown*?

In *Toward Neutral Principles of Constitutional Law*, 73 HARV. L. REV. 1 (1959), Herbert Wechsler argued that state-imposed segregation involved "the denial by the state of freedom to associate, a denial that impinges in the same way on any groups or races that may be involved." Critics of *Brown* claimed that "integration forces an association upon those for whom it is unpleasant or repugnant." Is the *Brown* Court simply choosing which claim of harm should prevail? Is there any "neutral principle" that supports *Brown*?

For Professor Black, any suggestion that racial segregation could be consistent with equality was laughable. "Segregation is historically and contemporaneously associated in a functioning complex with practices which are indisputably and grossly discriminatory of the Negro race, as such, by state law." Charles Black, *The Lawfulness of the Segregation Decisions*, 69 YALE L.J. 421 (1980). Jeb Rubenfeld, *Affirmative Action*, 107 YALE L.J. 427, 469 (1997), argues that their could be no state justification for the *de jure* racial segregation in *Brown*. "In 1950s America, the untouchability imputed to blacks by separate-but-equal was visible on the face of the law. Once the Court became willing to recognize the true purpose of separate-but-equal, no means-end scrutiny applied, for the very purpose of equal protection review — in all three varieties — is nothing other than to assist in determining a law's true purpose. Hence, the true question in *Brown*, as in *Plessy*, was solely whether a state could constitutionally enforce a law the purpose of which was to legalize black untouchability."

[2] Making *Brown* Work: Judicial and Administrative Implementation

BROWN v. BOARD OF EDUCATION [BROWN II]
349 U.S. 294, 75 S. Ct. 753, 99 L. Ed. 1083 (1955)

CHIEF JUSTICE WARREN delivered the opinion of the Court.

These cases were decided on May 17, 1954. The opinions of that date, declaring the fundamental principle that racial discrimination in public education is unconstitutional, are incorporated herein by reference. All provisions of federal, state, or local law requiring or permitting such discrimination must yield to this principle. There remains for consideration the manner in which relief is to be accorded.

Full implementation of these constitutional principles may require solution of varied local school problems. School authorities have the primary responsibility for elucidating, assessing, and solving these problems; courts will have to consider whether the action of school authorities constitutes good faith implementation of the governing constitutional principles. Because of their proximity to local conditions and the possible need for further hearings, the courts which originally heard these cases can best perform this judicial appraisal. Accordingly, we believe it appropriate to remand the cases to those courts.

In fashioning and effectuating the decrees, the courts will be guided by equitable principles. Traditionally, equity has been characterized by a practical flexibility in shaping its remedies and by a facility for adjusting and reconciling public and private needs. These cases call for the exercise of these traditional attributes of equity power. At stake is the personal interest of the plaintiffs in admission to public schools as soon as practicable on a nondiscriminatory basis. To effectuate this interest may call for elimination of a variety of obstacles in making the transition to school systems operated in accordance with the constitutional principles set forth in our May 17, 1954, decision. Courts of equity may properly take into account the public interest in the elimination of such obstacles in a systematic and effective manner. But it should go without saying that the vitality of these constitutional principles cannot be allowed to yield simply because of disagreement with them.

While giving weight to these public and private considerations, the courts will require that the defendants make a prompt and reasonable start toward full compliance with our May 17, 1954, ruling. Once such a start has been made, the courts may find that additional time is necessary to carry out the ruling in an effective manner. The burden rests upon the defendants to establish that such time is necessary in the public interest and is consistent with good faith compliance at the earliest practicable date. To that end, the courts may consider problems related to administration, arising from the physical condition of the school plant, the school transportation system, personnel, revision of school districts and attendance areas into compact units to achieve a system of determining admission to the public schools on a nonracial basis, and revision of local laws and regulations which may be necessary in solving the foregoing problems. They will also consider the adequacy of any plans the defendants may propose to meet these problems and to effectuate a transition to a racially nondiscriminatory school system. During this period of transition, the courts will retain jurisdiction of these cases.

The judgments below, except that in the Delaware case, are accordingly reversed and the cases are remanded to the District Courts to take such proceedings and enter such orders and decrees consistent with this opinion as are necessary and proper to admit to public schools on a racially nondiscriminatory basis with all deliberate speed the parties to these cases. The judgment in the Delaware case — ordering the immediate admission of the plaintiffs to schools previously attended only by white children — is affirmed on the basis of the principles stated in our May 17, 1954, opinion, but the case is remanded to the Supreme Court of Delaware for such further proceedings as that Court may deem necessary in light of this opinion.

NOTES

1. *Personal rights and public remedies.* In *McLaurin* and earlier segregation cases, the right to equal protection had been treated as a "personal and present right." The unusual character of the *Brown II* decree is noted by Professor Bickel, who points out that a normal judicial decree tells specific parties to do specific things. "The equivalent in these cases would have been a decree ordering the named children, and perhaps, since these were class actions, all children in the five school districts effected, who were similarly situated, to be admitted forthwith to the white schools of their choice. The question is, why should the Court not have issued such a decree? Indeed, one might have asked whether the Court could do other than issue such a decree?" ALEXANDER BICKEL, THE LEAST DANGEROUS BRANCH: THE SUPREME COURT AT THE BAR OF POLITICS 247 (1962).

Consider the later explanation of Chief Justice Warren in an interview:

> In these days you'll find a lot of people who are saying that they should have said, "These people must be allowed to go to this school." Well, if they had, it was the opinion, my opinion and most of us, that it would have solved nothing. We would have one or two Negroes go to a white school, but that would be all there was to it. So we treated it as a class action, so that everyone in the same situation as they were would be treated in the same manner judicially.

Earl Warren, 1891–1974, THE WASHINGTON POST, July 14, 1974 at C3.

2. *Personal and group rights.* Is the right recognized in *Brown* a personal right or a right of blacks as a class? William Bradford Reynolds, *Individualism v. Group Rights: The Legacy of Brown*, 93 YALE L.J. 995 (1984), commenting on *Brown*, stated that "both Court and counsel recognized that the civil right at issue — the right to race-neutral assignment — belonged to each individual student and therefore could not be reconciled with the group-oriented notion that the Constitution requires integration through race-conscious student assignments."

Burke Marshall, *A Comment on the Nondiscrimination Principle in a "Nation of Minorities"*, 93 YALE L.J. 1006 (1984) emphasizes the group character of the rights and duties involved in segregation. He points out that the costs of segregation are borne by various groups in society and the benefits of desegregation vary by the group to which one happens to belong: "The state did not merely disregard a constitutional command protecting individuals against racial discrimination when it discriminated against Ms. Brown; it violated the equal protection clause by running a segregated (or dual) school system that was a primary, but by no means a unique, component of a state-imposed caste system. . . . Once this is recognized explicitly, it is plain that how the state must act has nothing to do with Ms. Brown personally, as an individual."

Consider the language of the court in *United States v. Jefferson County Bd. of Educ.*, 372 F.2d 836, 868 (5th Cir. 1966):

> The gradual transition the Supreme Court authorized was to allow the states time to solve the administration problems inherent in that changeover. No delay would have been necessary if the right at issue in *Brown* had been only the right of individual Negro plaintiffs to admission to a white school. Moreover, the delay of one year in deciding *Brown II* and the gradual remedy *Brown II* fashioned can be justified only on the ground that the "personal and present" right of the individual plaintiffs must yield to the overriding right of Negroes as a class to a completely integrated public education.

3. *"With all deliberate speed."* Since the Court had the equitable power to fashion a suitable remedy appropriate to the case, why did it adopt the "all deliberate speed" formula? Whereas *Brown I* was met with fervid hostility in the South, *Brown II* was well received and even cheered in southern state legislatures. Wasn't delay an open invitation to resistance and evasion? But Bickel asserted, "The system would have worked no differently, no matter what was the form of the Supreme Court's decree." Alexander Bickel, *The Decade of School Desegregation: Progress and Prospects*, 64 COLUM. L. REV. 193, 201 (1964).

Chief Justice Warren, in the interview referred to above, explained the use of the phrase "with all deliberate speed": "[I]t was suggested that that would be a way to proceed in the case because we realize that under our federal system there were so many blocks preventing an immediate solution of the thing in reality, that the best we could look for would be a progression of action, and to keep it going, in a proper manner, we adopted that phrase, 'all deliberate speed.' "

It has been suggested "that the Justices were primarily concerned about white opposition, not administrative adjustments. Fully aware that they were commanding a sweeping transformation of long-standing and entrenched practices and customs, the Justices wished to project a flexibility that would reduce intransigence and promote flexibility among whites. In addition, the Court sought to protect itself as an institution by avoiding orders that would be successfully defied." Paul Gewirtz, *Remedies and Resistance*, 92 YALE L.J. 585, 611–12 (1983). Are these legitimate considerations for a court in framing remedies for constitutional wrongs?

4. *Public actions.* The special character of *Brown* was to persist in the prolonged effort to realize its promise. School desegregation cases, comparable to litigation involving prisons, mental hospitals, etc., are "public actions," differing markedly from the ordinary lawsuit involving simply the particular plaintiff and defendant. The objective of the public action is not "to resolve disputes between individuals, but rather to give meaning to our public values." Owen Fiss, *Foreword: The Forms of Justice*, 93 HARV. L. REV. 1 (1979). *Brown II* can be viewed as introducing a new "genre of constitutional litigation" involving judicially-managed structural reform of public bureaucratic institutions. *Brown II* did not provide much guidance for lower courts on how they were to achieve the reformation. "[I]t was but a recognition of the magnitude of the task and an attempt to buy time." It was the lower federal courts that, in the ensuing years, "discovered what the task required and adjusted procedural forms to meet the felt necessities." *Id.* at 1.

[3] Defining the Desegregation Mandate: An Affirmative Duty To Integrate?

Professor Michael J. Klarman claims that *Brown* had little *direct* effect on school segregation. But he argues that the decision had significant *indirect* effects by stimulating "massive resistence," often violent, in the South and a consequent Northern backlash producing political support for congressional action. FROM JIM CROW TO CIVIL

> RIGHTS: THE SUPREME COURT AND THE STRUGGLE FOR RACIAL EQUALITY Ch. 7 (2004). Resistance to *Brown* took many forms that endangered the vindication of rights: violence; flight from public schools; boycotts; hostility and incitements; foot-dragging by officials legally obliged to desegregate; and new acts of official segregation. It was the relentless refusal of citizens and public officials to accept the meaning of *Brown* — their persistent failure to accept change and to act in good faith to implement the law — that required the courts to intrude with such coercion, with such detail, with such stubborn patience and courage, and with strategic and managerial preoccupations that strained the boundaries of the traditional judicial function.

Paul Gewirtz, *Remedies and Resistance*, 92 YALE L.J. 585, 588 (1983). Yet a decade after *Brown*, only 1.17 percent of black children in the South attended school with white children. It was not until passage of the 1964 Civil Rights Act that there were significant inroads on school segregation in the South.

The desegregation of Little Rock High School met with official resistance by Governor Orval Faubus until President Eisenhower dispatched federal troops to protect black school children entering the school. In *Cooper v. Aaron*, 358 U.S. 1 (1958), each member of the Supreme Court signed an opinion stating that rights of school children were "not to be sacrificed or yielded to the violence and disorder which have followed upon the actions of the Governor and Legislature."

Southern school districts often adopted "freedom of choice" plans which allowed a pupil to choose his or her own public school. New Kent County, Virginia, which had been *de jure* segregated prior to *Brown*, adopted such a plan in 1965. Nevertheless, by 1968 no white children were in the Negro school and eighty-five percent of the black children in the system were still in the all-Negro school. In *Green v. County School Board*, 391 U.S. 430 (1968), the Court held the plan unconstitutional.

Justice Brennan, for the Court, framed the question as "whether, under all the circumstances here, respondent School Board's adoption of a 'freedom-of-choice' plan which allows a pupil to choose his own public school constitutes adequate compliance with the Board's responsibilities to achieve a system of determining admission to the public schools on a non-racial basis." He contended that, under *Brown II*, school boards "then operating state-compelled dual systems were nevertheless clearly charged with the affirmative duty to take whatever steps might be necessary to convert to a unitary system in which racial discrimination would be eliminated root and branch."

In the summer of 1969, the federal government, in an unusual position, requested a delay in implementing desegregation orders in thirty Mississippi school districts. The Fifth Circuit granted the request, but the Supreme Court in *Alexander v. Holmes County Board of Education*, 396 U.S. 19 (1969), reversed per curiam, stating: "Continued operation of segregated schools under a standard of allowing 'all deliberate speed' for desegregation is no longer constitutionally permissible. Under explicit holdings of this Court the obligation of every school district is to terminate dual school systems at once and to operate now and hereafter only unitary schools."

SWANN v. CHARLOTTE-MECKLENBURG BOARD OF EDUCATION

402 U.S. 1, 91 S. Ct. 1267, 28 L. Ed. 2d 554 (1971)

[These cases arose from attempts to desegregate the school district of metropolitan Charlotte, North Carolina, which had a racial composition of approximately 71 percent White and 29 percent Negro. After finding several Board plans unacceptable, the district court appointed its own expert. It subsequently approved a modified Board plan for secondary schools, but accepted its expert's plan involving zoning, pairing and grouping, and the consequent busing of pupils resulting in student bodies of between 9 and 38 percent Negro throughout the elementary school system. The court of appeals affirmed as to the secondary schools, but held that the elementary school plan would place an unreasonable burden on the Board and the system's pupils. On remand, the district court identified three acceptable alternative plans and ordered its expert's plan to remain in effect if the Board failed to accept one of the three. The Board "acquiesced" in the expert's plan.]

CHIEF JUSTICE BURGER delivered the opinion of the Court.

This case and those argued with it arose in states having a long history of maintaining two sets of schools in a single school system deliberately operated to carry out a governmental policy to separate pupils in schools solely on the basis of race. That was what *Brown v. Board of Education* was all about. These cases present us with the problem of defining in more precise terms than heretofore the scope of the duty of school authorities and district courts in implementing *Brown I* and the mandate to eliminate dual systems and establish unitary systems at once.

The problems encountered by the district courts and courts of appeals make plain that we should now try to amplify guidelines, however incomplete and imperfect, for the assistance of school authorities and courts. The failure of local authorities to meet their constitutional obligations aggravated the massive problem of converting from the state-enforced discrimination of racially separate school systems. This process has been rendered more difficult by changes since 1954 in the structure and patterns of communities, the growth of student population, movement of families, and other changes, some of which had marked impact on school planning, sometimes neutralizing or negating remedial action before it was fully implemented. Rural areas accustomed for half a century to the consolidated school systems implemented by bus transportation could make adjustments more readily than metropolitan areas with dense and shifting population, numerous schools, congested and complex traffic patterns.

The objective today remains to eliminate from the public schools all vestiges of state-imposed segregation. Segregation was the evil struck down by *Brown I* as contrary to the equal protection guarantees of the Constitution. That was the violation sought to be corrected by the remedial measures of *Brown II*. That was the basis for the holding in *Green* that school authorities are "clearly charged with the affirmative duty to take whatever steps might be necessary to convert to a unitary system in which racial discrimination would be eliminated root and branch."

If school authorities fail in their affirmative obligations under these holdings, judicial authority may be invoked. Once a right and a violation have been shown, the scope of a district court's equitable powers to remedy past wrongs is broad, for breadth and flexibility are inherent in equitable remedies. The task is to correct, by a balancing of the individual and collective interests, the condition that offends the Constitution.

In seeking to define even in broad and general terms how far this remedial power extends it is important to remember that judicial powers may be exercised only on the basis of a constitutional violation. Remedial judicial authority does not put judges automatically in the shoes of school authorities whose powers are plenary. Judicial authority enters only when local authority defaults.

[The Court's discussion of desegregation of faculty, staff, transportation, extra-curricular activities and facilities is omitted. The Court stated, "Independent of student assignment, where it is possible to identify a 'white school' or a 'Negro school' simply by reference to the racial composition of teachers and staff, the quality of school buildings and equipment, or the organization of sports activities, a prima facie case of violation of substantive constitutional rights under the Equal Protection Clause is shown."]

The central issue in this case is that of student assignment, and there are essentially four problem areas:

(1) Racial Balances or Racial Quotas

We do not reach in this case the question whether a showing that school segregation is a consequence of other types of state action, without any discriminatory action by the school authorities, is a constitutional violation requiring remedial action by the school desegregation decree. This case does not present that question and we therefore do not decide it.

Our objective in dealing with the issues presented by these cases is to see that school authorities exclude no pupil of a racial minority from any school, directly or indirectly, on account of race; it does not and cannot embrace all the problems of racial prejudice, even when those problems contribute to disproportionate racial concentrations in some schools.

In this case it is urged that the District Court has imposed a racial balance requirement of 71%-29% on individual schools. [The district court opinion] contains intimations that the "norm" is a fixed mathematical racial balance reflecting the pupil constituency of the system. If we were to read the holding of the District Court to require, as a matter of substantive constitutional right, any particular degree of racial balance or mixing, that approach would be disapproved and we would be obliged to reverse. The constitutional command to desegregate schools does not mean that every school in every community must always reflect the racial composition of the school system as a whole.

[But, in this case] the use made of mathematical ratios was no more than a starting point in the process of shaping a remedy, rather than an inflexible requirement. As we said in *Green*, a school authority's remedial plan or a district court's remedial decree is to be judged by its effectiveness. Awareness of the racial composition of the whole school system is likely to be a useful starting point in shaping a remedy to correct past constitutional violations. In sum, the very limited use made of mathematical ratios was within the equitable remedial discretion of the District Court.

(2) One-Race Schools

The record in this case reveals the familiar phenomenon that in metropolitan areas minority groups are often found concentrated in one part of the city. In some circumstances certain schools may remain all or largely of one race until new schools can be provided or neighborhood patterns change. Schools all or predominately of one race in a district of mixed population will require close scrutiny to determine that school assignments are not part of state-enforced segregation.

In light of the above, it should be clear that the existence of some small number of one-race, or virtually one-race, schools within a district is not in and of itself the mark of a system which still practices segregation by law. The court should scrutinize such schools, and the burden upon the school authorities will be to satisfy the court that their racial composition is not the result of present or past discriminatory action on their part.

An optional majority-to-minority transfer provision has long been recognized as a useful part of every desegregation plan. Provision for optional transfer of those in the majority racial group of a particular school to other schools where they will be in the minority is an indispensable remedy for those students willing to transfer to other schools in order to lessen the impact on them of the state-imposed stigma of segregation. In order to be effective, such a transfer arrangement must grant the transferring student free transportation and space must be made available in the school to which he desires to move.

(3) Remedial Altering of Attendance Zones

Absent a constitutional violation there would be no basis for judicially ordering assignment of students on a racial basis. All things being equal, with no history of discrimination, it might well be desirable to assign pupils to schools nearest their homes. But all things are not equal in a system that has been deliberately constructed and maintained to enforce racial segregation. The remedy for such segregation may be administratively awkward, inconvenient and even bizarre in some situations and may impose burdens on some; but all awkwardness and inconvenience cannot be avoided in the interim period when remedial adjustments are being made to eliminate the dual school systems.

In this area, we must of necessity rely to a large extent, as this Court has for more than 16 years, on the informed judgment of the district courts in the first instance and on courts of appeals. We hold that the pairing and grouping of non-contiguous school zones is a permissible tool and such action is to be considered in light of the objectives sought.

(4) Transportation of Students

No rigid guidelines as to student transportation can be given for application to the infinite variety of problems presented in thousands of situations. Bus transportation has been an integral part of the public education system for years, and was perhaps the single most important factor in the transition from the one-room schoolhouse to the consolidated school. Eighteen million of the nation's public school children, approximately 39% were transported to their schools by bus in 1969–1970 in all parts of the country. The importance of bus transportation as a normal and accepted tool of educational policy is readily discernible in this and the companion case.

An objection to transportation of students may have validity when the time or distance of travel is so great as to risk either the health of the children or significantly impinge on the educational process. On the facts of this case, we are unable to conclude that the order of the District Court is not reasonable, feasible and workable. However, in seeking to define the scope of remedial power or the limits on remedial power of courts in an area as sensitive as we deal with here, words are poor instruments to convey the sense of basic fairness inherent in equity. Substance, not semantics, must govern, and we have sought to suggest the nature of limitations without frustrating the appropriate scope of equity.

At some point, these school authorities and others like them should have achieved full compliance with this Court's decision in *Brown I*. The systems will then be "unitary" in the sense required by our decisions in *Green* and *Alexander*. It does not follow that the communities served by such systems will remain demographically stable, for in a growing, mobile society, few will do so. Neither school authorities nor district courts are constitutionally required to make year-by-year adjustments of the racial composition of student bodies once the affirmative duty to desegregate has been accomplished and racial discrimination through official action is eliminated from the system. This does not mean that federal courts are without power to deal with future problems; but in the absence of a showing that either the school authorities or some other agency of the State has deliberately attempted to fix or alter demographic patterns to affect the racial composition of the schools, further intervention by a district court should not be necessary.

For the reasons herein set forth, the judgment of the Court of Appeals is affirmed as to those parts in which it affirmed the judgment of the District Court.

NOTES

1. *Significance of Swann*. Professor Fiss suggests that *Swann* took four additional steps beyond previous segregation cases: (1) "[E]ven if geographic proximity, not race, were the basis for [school attendance] zones and thus for assignments, the Board's duty to convert to a 'unitary non-racial school system' would not be satisfied." What is the rationale for preventing school districts from using a neutral assignment policy? (2) The recognition of an evidentiary presumption that past discrimination is causally related to present segregation. "The school board will also have to show that its past discriminatory conduct — involving racial designation of schools, site selection, and determination of school size — is not a link in the causal chain producing the segregation. This will be very difficult to do, and the difficulty of overcoming a presumption will tend to accentuate the fact that gives rise to it, namely, the segregated patterns, and this will be reflected in the board's assignment policies." (3) The Court said that a district must do everything possible to eliminate these patterns of segregation. Integration is not merely a value to be considered; in the hierarchy of values "integration assumes a role of paramount importance." (4) *Swann* "validates the use of race in student assignments when the goal is integration rather than segregation." Owen Fiss, *The Charlotte-Mecklenburg Case — Its Significance for Northern School Desegregation*, 38 U. Chi. L. Rev. 697, 699–703 (1971). Is it now clear that the Equal Protection Clause does not command a colorblind Constitution at least when color consciousness is ordered to remedy past discrimination?

2. *The mandate of Swann.* In *Swann*, Chief Justice Burger said that "the greatest possible degree of actual desegregation" must be the goal. What does this mean? If there is a plan that would yield a student racial mixture more closely mirroring the racial composition of the community must it be used? Must a *de jure* school system achieve a greater degree of racial mixture than would have been obtained if it had never intentionally segregated? Is there now a right to an "integrated education?"

In *Davis v. Board of School Comm'rs*, 402 U.S. 33 (1971). a companion case to *Swann*, the Court dealt with a desegregation plan from Mobile, Alabama. The plan used unified geographic zones and provided for no busing, which left some all-black schools. Chief Justice Burger stated that " 'neighborhood school zoning,' whether based strictly on home-to-school distance or on 'unified geographic zones,' is not the only constitutionally permissible remedy; nor is it *per se* adequate to meet the remedial responsibilities of local boards. Having once found a violation, the district judge or school authorities should make every effort to achieve the greatest possible degree of actual desegregation, taking into account the practicalities of the situation. A district court may and should consider the use of all available techniques. The measure of any desegregation plan is its effectiveness."

Since the district courts had failed to consider the use of busing and alternative zoning, the case was remanded.

3. *An obligation to integrate?* The possibility that *Swann* might demand the use of all reasonable means available to achieve the best racial mix is also suggested by *Wright v. Council of Emporia*, 407 U.S. 451 (1972). The Court, per Justice Stewart, rejected an attempt of the town of Emporia to withdraw from the county school system, which had been ordered to desegregate, holding "that a new school district may not be created where its effect would be to impede the process of dismantling a dual system." But note that the Court adopted this effects test only for a school system under an affirmative duty to desegregate.

Chief Justice Burger, joined by Justices Blackmun, Powell and Rehnquist, dissenting in *Wright* (the first dissents registered in educational desegregation cases), criticized

> the gravely mistaken view that a plan providing more consistent racial ratios is somehow more unitary than one which tolerates a lack of racial balance. Since the goal is to dismantle dual school systems rather than to reproduce in each classroom a microcosmic reflection of the racial proportions of a given geographical area, there is no basis for saying that a plan providing a uniform racial balance is more effective or constitutionally preferred. School authorities may wish to pursue that goal as a matter of policy, but we have made it plain that it is not constitutionally mandated.

Consider the consequences of a judicial finding that the school district has *de jure* segregated and is under an affirmative duty to desegregate. "Once the court finds liability, in other words, *de facto* segregation becomes the operative constitutional standard until the district achieves unitariness. For this period of time, adverse impact, not motivation, controls." Daniel Ortiz, *The Myth of Intent in Equal Protection*, 41 Stan. L. Rev. 1105, 1133 (1989).

[4] Desegregation and Achieving Unitary Status

The consequences of a judicial determination that a school district has achieved a unitary status are significant. For example, the federal court steps out and the school board regains its autonomous authority. In addition, new allegations of segregation would require the initiation of an entirely new lawsuit in which no reliance could be placed on segregative conduct occurring prior to the order of unitary status. The school is not necessarily legally responsible for resegregation. When does a formerly *de jure* segregated school system achieve unitary status?

***Board of Educ. v. Dowell*, 498 U.S. 237 (1991).** The Oklahoma City schools operated for five years under a 1972 decree requiring desegregation following a finding of *de jure* segregation. In 1977, the Board obtained an order "terminating the case" on the basis that the schools had achieved unitary status. In 1984, the Board promulgated a new plan alleviating substantial amounts of busing of black school children, with the predicted effect that a number of schools would return to primarily single-race status. The district court refused to reopen the case, ruling that its 1977 order was final.

The Supreme Court held that the 1977 order did not foreclose review of the Board's actions because of ambiguity about the effect of finding that a school district had achieved unitary status. But the Court held the 1984 plan could be valid, and the 1972 injunction dissolved, if the Board could show (1) that it "has complied in good faith with the desegregation decree since it was entered" and (2) that "the vestiges of past discrimination had been eliminated to the extent practicable."

The court stressed the "temporary" nature of federal court supervision and the importance of local control of education: "Dissolving a desegregation decree after the local authorities have operated in compliance with it for a reasonable period of time properly recognized that 'necessary concern for the important values of local control of public school systems dictates that a federal court's regulatory control of such systems not extend beyond the time required to remedy the effects of past intentional discrimination.' "

Justice Marshall, joined by justices Blackmun and Stevens, dissenting, argued that a "desegregation decree cannot be lifted so long as conditions likely to inflict the stigmatic injury condemned in *Brown I* persist and there remain feasible methods of eliminating such conditions."

***Freeman v. Pitts,* 503 U.S. 467 (1992).** The Supreme Court held that in the course of supervising a desegregation plan, a district court has the authority to relinquish supervision and control of a school district in incremental stages, prior to achieving full compliance in every area of school operations: "We have said that the [district] court's end purpose must be to remedy the violation and in addition to restore state and local authorities to the control of a school system that is operating in compliance with the Constitution. Partial relinquishment of judicial control, where justified by the facts of the case, can be an important and significant step in fulfilling the district court's duty to return the operations and control of schools to local authorities."

***Missouri v. Jenkins,* 515 U.S. 70 (1995)** (*Jenkins III*). In a case dealing with the Kansas City School District, which had been proceeding in federal court since 1977, the Supreme Court held (5-4) that a federal court could not order salary increases and remedial education programs on the ground that "student achievement levels were still at or below the national norms at many grade levels."

The majority opinion by Chief Justice Rehnquist emphasized that "the nature and scope of the remedy are to be determined by the violation, [which] means that federal-court decrees must directly address and relate to the constitutional violation itself." The test for constitutional violations in school desegregation cases is "whether the [constitutional violator] has complied in good faith with the desegregation decree since it was entered, and whether the vestiges of past discrimination have been eliminated to the extent practicable." The Court found that the challenged portion of the federal court's remedy "results in so many imponderables and is so far removed from the task of eliminating the racial identifiability of the schools [in Kansas City] that we believe it is beyond the admittedly broad discretion of the District Court." Justice Rehnquist observed that racial disparities in achievement levels are not necessarily attributable to past racial discrimination — "[N]umerous external factors beyond the control of [the defendants] affect minority student achievement."

Justice Souter, joined by Justices Stevens, Ginsburg, and Breyer, dissented on the ground that the parties had not had sufficient notice to address the nature of the underlying violation as a premise for the ordered remedy.

Wendy Parker, *The Future of School Desegregation*, 94 Nw. U.L. Rev. 1157, 1177 (2000), provides a perspective on these three Supreme Court cases from the 1990s. "The Court identifies one value that, from the perspective of plaintiffs, limits the effectiveness of judicial remedies: local control. Specifically, the Court instructs in *Dowell*, *Freeman*, and *Jenkins III* that the value of local control must be recognized in crafting a remedy and judging its effectiveness. In a related vein, the Court's perception of how a school district would look absent a defendant's violations further narrows the remedial process. The Court accepts racial segregation as a natural consequence of purely private behavior. In *Dowell*, for example, the Court found no fault in the possibility of immediate resegregation of the Oklahoma City elementary schools. Similarly, in *Freeman*, the Court accepted the presence of segregation even in a school district operating under court order. Finally, in *Jenkins III*, the Court presumed that private forces caused disparities in the achievement scores of African-American and white schoolchildren, and it accepted the disparities as a fact of American life. This acceptance of racial segregation and racial disparities calls into question the purpose of school desegregation remedies and their potential for actual integration."

Many commentators see the recent Supreme Court decisions limiting remedies and approving termination orders for school districts achieving unitary status as the prelude to a general rollback in *Brown* and its progeny. And yet the limited and ambiguous nature of those holdings and the fragmented character of the Court, make predictions questionable: "If equal opportunity means the end of racial isolation and the achievement of equal funding or outputs, the court long ago gave a negative answer . . . . If equal opportunity means freedom from present intentional racial discrimination in the public schools, its future is secure. If it also means freedom for the lingering effects of past discrimination, its future hangs in the balance." Brian Landsberg, *Equal Educational Opportunity: The Rehnquist Court Revisits Green and Swann*, 42 Emory L.J. 821, 860–61 (1993). Professor Parker conducted two empirical studies covering court-ordered desegregation of 192 school districts, concluding that "the vast majority of school desegregation litigation continues, with no hint of impending termination." 94 Nw. U.L. Rev. at 1159. She finds that the real problem is "disregard and neglect" and argues for more effective judicial involvement in implementing remedies. *Id.* at 1121.

[5] The Court Looks North: the De Jure — De Facto Distinction

While the desegregation of southern schools has met with at least some limited success, school segregation in the North has only intensified. Today, education in the North is as, if not more, racially segregated than in the South.

But if education in the North is as segregated as in the South, its causes have been more difficult to isolate. While many jurisdictions had statutes requiring dual school systems, most had been eliminated before *Brown*. In many northern areas racial segregation in education can be traced to intentionally discriminatory school board policies involving gerrymandered school attendance zones, transfer policies, and school construction and closing policies. But in other instances, educational segregation appears to be a product primarily of increasing residential racial segregation. These differing forms of educational segregation may even exist in different schools in the same school district.

***Keyes v. School Dist. No. 1*, 413 U.S. 189 (1973).** This was a challenge to the racial and ethnic makeup of the Denver, Colorado school system. Denver had never maintained a statutory dual school system comparable to those invalidated in *Brown I* and its progeny. Nevertheless, the district court in *Keyes* held that by practices such as manipulating student attendance zones and using mobile classrooms, the Denver school board had maintained for almost a decade, "an unconstitutional policy of deliberate racial segregation" in schools in the Park Hill area of the city. Almost forty percent of Denver's black student population had been directly affected by these practices. But the court also held that this finding "did not, in itself, impose on the school board any affirmative duty to eliminate segregation throughout the school district, including the heavily segregated core city schools." The plaintiffs apparently conceded the need to prove that the segregated schooling was brought about or maintained by intentional state action.

The Supreme Court, per Justice Brennan, rejected the school board's claim that it was necessary for plaintiffs to establish de jure segregation as to each school in a school system.

> [W]here plaintiffs prove that the school authorities have carried out a systematic program of segregation affecting a substantial portion of the students, schools, teachers, and facilities within the school system, it is only common sense to conclude that there exists a predicate for a finding of the existence of a dual school system. [R]acially inspired school board actions have an impact beyond the particular schools that are the subject of those actions.

Justice Brennan reasoned that "there is a high probability that where school authorities have effectuated an intentionally segregative policy in a meaningful portion of the school system, similar impermissible considerations have motivated their actions in other areas of the system."

The Court then considered how the school board could rebut the prima facie case. "In discharging [its] burden, it is not enough, of course, that the school authorities rely upon some allegedly logical, racially neutral explanation for their actions. Their burden is to adduce proof sufficient to support a finding that segregative intent was not among the factors that motivated their actions."

Justice Powell concurred in part and dissented in part, arguing that the Court should abandon any requirement that a plaintiff establish intentional state segregation in order to establish a constitutional violation.

> I would not perpetuate the *de jure/de facto* distinction nor would I leave to petitioners the initial tortuous effort of identifying "segregative acts" and deducing "segregatory intent." I would hold, quite simply, that where segregated public schools exist within a school district to a substantial degree, there is a prima facie case that the duly constituted public authorities (I will usually refer to them collectively as the "school board") are sufficiently responsible to impose upon them a nationally applicable burden to demonstrate they nevertheless are operating a genuinely integrated school system.
>
> The principal reason for abandonment of the *de jure/de facto* distinction is that, in view of the evolution of the holding in *Brown I* into the affirmative duty doctrine, the distinction no longer can be justified on a principled basis.

Justice Rehnquist dissented:

> [I]n a school district the size of Denver's, it is quite conceivable that the School Board might have engaged in the racial gerrymandering of the attendance boundary between two particular schools in order to keep one largely Negro and Hispano, and the other largely Anglo, as the District Court found to have been the fact in this case. Such action would have deprived affected minority students who were the victims of such gerrymandering of their constitutional right to equal protection of the law. But if the school board had been evenhanded in its drawing of the attendance lines for other schools in the district, minority students required to attend other schools within the district would have suffered no such deprivation. It certainly would not reflect normal English usage to describe the entire district as "segregated" on such a state of facts, and it would be a quite unprecedented application of principles of equitable relief to determine that if the gerrymandering of one attendance zone were proven, particular racial mixtures could be required by a federal district court for every school in the district.

***Columbus Bd. of Educ. v. Penick,* 443 U.S. 449 (1979).** The Court, per Justice White, affirmed a district court finding that present school segregation in Columbus was a product of school board conduct "animated by an unconstitutional segregative purpose" having a current segregative impact justifying a system-wide remedy. Although Columbus had not maintained formally segregated schools since 1888, the district court found that in 1954, when *Brown I* was decided, the School Board was deliberately maintaining an enclave of racially segregated schools in a substantial part of the school system. Citing *Keyes*, this finding provided the basis for the district court's conclusion that the "Columbus Public Schools were officially segregated in 1954." Because the Columbus system was *de jure* segregated in 1954, it was under a "duty to dismantle its dual system." But the lower courts found that the Columbus Board "had failed to discharge this duty" and "knowingly continues its failure to eliminate the consequences of its past segregative policies" to the present time. Further, "in the intervening years there has been a series of Board actions and practices that could not 'reasonably be explained without reference to racial concerns,' and which 'intentionally aggravated, rather than alleviated,' racial separation in the schools."

The Court held that, on the basis of these findings, the lower court could reasonably conclude that "at the time of trial there was systemwide segregation in the Columbus schools that was the result of recent and remote intentionally segregative actions of the Columbus Board." And it was justified in finding that these "purposefully segregative practices with current systemwide impact," required a systemwide remedy.

***Dayton Bd. of Educ. v. Brinkman,* 443 U.S. 526 (1979)** (*Dayton II*). The district court had dismissed the complaint, finding the plaintiffs "had failed to prove that acts of intentional segregation over 20 years old had any current incremental segregative effects." But the Court of Appeals reversed and the Supreme Court, 5-4, agreed. Justice White accepted the appellate court's conclusion that at the time of *Brown I*, the Dayton Board "was purposefully operating segregated schools in a substantial part of the district." Under *Keyes*, this justified an inference that segregation throughout the system was intentional, absent rebutting evidence which had not been provided by the Board.

> Part of the affirmative duty imposed by our cases, as we decided in *Wright v. Council of City of Emporia* is the obligation not to take any action that would impede the process of disestablishing the dual system and its effects. The Dayton Board, however, had engaged in many post-*Brown* actions that had the effect of increasing or perpetuating segregation. The District Court ignored this compounding of the original constitutional breach on the ground that there was no direct evidence of continued discriminatory purpose. But the measure of the post-*Brown* conduct of a school board under an unsatisfied duty to liquidate a dual system is the effectiveness, not the purpose, of the actions in decreasing or increasing the segregation caused by the dual system.

"[I]f intentional segregation sufficient to trigger the *Keyes* shift in burden of proof ever occurred in a particular school district, local authorities are responsible for desegregating the entire district unless, after 1955, the school board's policies had the effect of undoing the results of the intentional segregation." Peter Shane, *School Desegregation Remedies and the Fair Governance of Schools*, 132 U. PA. L. REV. 1041, 1072 (1984).

[6] Interdistrict Desegregation

Prior to the decision in ***Milliken v. Bradley*, 418 U.S. 717 (1974)**, the attorney for the plaintiff had predicted that the decision would be the *Brown* of the North. BBC-TV Documentary, "Deep South . . . Deep North." In fact, the decision may be more analogous to *Plessy v. Ferguson*. For the first time, a majority of the Supreme Court rejected the desegregation claims of black children. As a result, the effective desegregation of northern-style segregated metropolitan schools has been made far more difficult.

Metropolitan Detroit resembles many big cities. Whites have increasingly left the central city for the suburbs leaving a predominantly black city surrounded by predominantly white enclaves. Any attempt to eliminate substantial racial imbalance in even a *de jure* segregated city is doomed to failure unless the surrounding jurisdictions can be joined in fashioning a remedy. But how far can the courts go in ignoring jurisdictional boundaries? Is the state or the local district the proper defendant?

After allowing limited intervention by outlying school districts, the district court concluded that there was state action; found that the Detroit-only desegregation plans would only make Detroit more identifiably Black and increase white flight, and hence "would not accomplish desegregation within the corporate geographical limits of the city"; concluded that school district lines "are simply matters of political convenience and may not be used to deny Constitutional rights"; defined a desegregation area of Detroit and fifty-three suburban school districts; appointed a panel to fashion "an effective desegregation plan" based on fifteen clusters, each containing part of the Detroit system and two or more suburban districts, designed to "achieve the greatest degree of actual desegregation to the end that, upon implementation, no school, grade or classroom [would be] substantially disproportionate to the overall racial composition"; and ordered the Detroit Board of Education to purchase or lease at least 295 school buses under an interim plan for 1972–1973. The court of appeals, *en banc*, affirmed. The appellate court said: "If we hold that school district boundaries are absolute barriers to a Detroit school desegregation plan, we would be opening a way to nullify *Brown v. Board of Education.*"

The Supreme Court, Chief Justice Burger writing for the Court, narrowly defined the occasions for interdistrict remedies.

> The controlling principle consistently expounded in our holdings is that the scope of the remedy is determined by the nature and extent of the constitutional violation. Before the boundaries of separate and autonomous school districts may be set aside by consolidating the separate units for remedial purposes or by imposing a cross-district remedy, it must first be shown that there has been a constitutional violation within one district that produces a significant segregative effect in another district. Specifically it must be shown that racially discriminatory acts of the state or local school districts, or of a single school district have been a substantial cause of inter-district segregation.
>
> To approve the remedy ordered by the court would impose on the outlying districts, not shown to have committed any constitutional violation, a wholly impermissible remedy based on a standard not hinted at in *Brown I* and *II* or any holding of this Court. The constitutional right of the Negro respondents residing in Detroit is to attend a unitary school system in that district. Unless petitioners drew the district lines in a discriminatory fashion, or arranged for White students residing in the Detroit district to attend schools in Oakland and Macomb Counties, they were under no constitutional duty to make provisions for Negro students to do so. The view of the dissenters can be supported only by drastic expansion of the constitutional right itself, an expansion without any support in either constitutional principle or precedent.

Justice Marshall, joined by Justices White, Douglas, and Brennan, cited a number of factors supporting the lower court decision that the state of Michigan itself had a constitutional duty to remedy Detroit's segregation.

> The actions of the State itself directly contributed to Detroit's segregation. Under the Fourteenth Amendment, the State is ultimately responsible for the actions of its local agencies. And finally, given the structure of Michigan's educational system, Detroit's segregation cannot be viewed as the problem of an independent and separate entity. Michigan operates a single statewide system of education, a substantial part of which was shown to be segregated in this case.

Professor Wilkinson contends that the *Milliken* Court "falsely limited the search for suburban complicity." He argues, "What had to be explained in Detroit was the overconcentration of blacks in the ghetto and that of whites in the suburbs." Noting the lower court's findings on government complicity in metropolitan residential (and hence educational) segregation, Wilkinson frames the question: "To what extent had racially motivated zoning laws, location of public housing projects, racially restrictive covenants on FHA and VA mortgages created the white character of Detroit's suburban neighborhoods and the black character of core city neighborhoods." Wilkinson says that "victimization could not be understood or genuine restoration attempted without looking at housing." But he concludes that the *Milliken* Court was able "to finesse the issue since the Court of Appeals had not considered segregated housing patterns." J. HARVIE WILKINSON, FROM BROWN TO BAKKE 222–23 (1979). Would the Detroit school board be legally responsible for de jure actions of housing authorities?

[7] Questioning Desegregation

A 2003 report by the Harvard Civil Rights Project reported "[A] substantial group of American schools are virtually all non-white. These school educate one-sixth of the nation's black students and one-fourth of black students in the Northeast and Midwest. One-ninth of Latino students attend schools where 99–100% of the student body is composed of minority students." ERIKA FRANKENBERG ET AL., THE CIVIL RIGHTS PROJECT AT HARVARD UNIV., A MULTICULTRUAL SOCIETY WITH SEGREGATED SCHOOLS: ARE WE LOSING THE DREAM? 5 (2003). Professor Molly S. McUsic, *The Future of Brown v. Board of Education: Economic Integration of the Public Schools*, 117 HARV. L. REV. 1334 (2004), argues that "Even as *Brown* principles stand beyond mainstream debate and praise for *Brown* borders on homage, legal scholars will be obliged to note that as a legal decision, the influence of *Brown* is thirty years past its peak, and the changes it prompted are everywhere being reversed."

The setback to desegregation has disillusioned many who sought to realize the broader promise of *Brown*. Increasing opposition to desegregation, particularly in big cities, and the resulting problem of white flight presents a further challenge to desegregation goals. Discontent in black communities with some desegregation remedies such as busing of black children into white schools raises further questions about the value of integration. For those who define the promise of *Brown* in terms of "equal educational opportunity," there is increasing uncertainty whether desegregation is educationally beneficial for black children. For a defense of the gains realized through desegregation of education, see James Liebman, *Implementing Brown in the Nineties*, 76 VA. L. REV. 349, 356–360 (1990) ("the reigning legal view today is that reforms like desegregation are anathema today precisely because they can and do constitutionally redistribute [educational resources] on the basis of race").

Alex Johnson, *Bid Whist, Tonk and United States v. Fordice: Why Integrationism Fails African-Americans Again*, 81 CAL. L. REV. 1401, 1427 (1993), observes that "something odd happened as *de jure* segregation disappeared and *de facto* segregation took its place. Ironically, a significant portion of the African-American community came to view the liberal notion of integration as undesirable. . . . [T]he Court's assimilationist brand of integration came to be perceived as a badge of inferiority by African-Americans, thus bringing it full circle to *Plessy*." Johnson argues that "integration can only be achieved by respecting this unique culture through the maintenance and operation of *separate* institutions that allow African-Americans to join together in 'collective associations which have . . . educational and social dimensions.'" *Id.* at 1403.

A number of black leaders have called for a reexamination of goals and strategies. In his chronicles on the civil rights movement, Professor Derrick Bell observes, "Symbolically, the sacrificed black children in the Chronicle represent literally thousands like themselves who are the casualties of desegregation, their schooling irreparably damaged even though they themselves did not dramatically disappear. It certainly calls into question the real beneficiaries in the thousands of school-desegregation cases that the former Legal Defense Fund director, Jack Greenberg, aptly called the 'trench warfare' of the civil rights movement." Derrick A. Bell, And We Are Not Saved 107 (1987). While acknowledging the numerous civil rights laws and precedents that are available, he argues that "the protection they provide is diluted by lax enforcement, by the establishment of difficult-to-meet standards of proof, and, worst of all, by the increasing irrelevance of antidiscrimination laws to race-related disadvantages, now as likely to be the result as much of social class as of color." *Id.* at 5. For Bell, a preferable approach to desegregation as the desired end "is to focus on obtaining real educational effectiveness which may entail the improvement of presently segregated schools as well as the creation or preservation of model black schools." Derrick Bell, *Brown v. Board of Education and the Interest Convergence Dilemma*, 93 Harv. L. Rev. 518, 530, 532 (1980). In a later book, Silent Covenants: Brown v. Board of Education and the Unfulfilled Hopes For Racial Reform (2004), Bell is critical of *Brown* and argues that it would have been better had the Court retained *Plessy* but rigorously enforced the demand for equality in "separate but equal."

[D] BENIGN QUOTAS, PREFERENTIAL TREATMENT, AND AFFIRMATIVE ACTION

[1] Education

As the cases in the previous section indicate, the courts today frequently require the use of race in fashioning remedies for *de jure* segregation. On the other hand, Justice Harlan in *Plessy v. Ferguson*, said that the Constitution is "color-blind." Can the government voluntarily choose to give preference to racial minorities in distributing benefits? Can race be used in an effort to achieve and stabilize desegregation? Is the proper focus of equal protection analysis on individual wrongdoers and individual victims or on group harms? These are some of the problems of affirmative action — a subject which has seriously divided former allies of the desegregation movement. The focus is not on whether the shackles of racism should be removed, but whether the competitors bearing the heritage of racism must now be given assistance in the name of equal opportunity.

Some of the questions generated by affirmative action might have been answered when Marco De Funis, a disappointed white applicant to the University of Washington Law School, brought suit challenging the school's minority admissions program. But in *De Funis v. Odegaard*, 416 U.S. 312 (1974), the Court held that the case had become moot. Only Justice Douglas addressed the merits of the affirmative action question. His dissenting opinion appeared to treat race conscious affirmative action programs as almost *per se* unconstitutional. "The consideration of race as a measure of an applicant's qualification normally introduces a capricious and irrelevant factor working on invidious discrimination." Whatever the person's race, he argued, an applicant has a constitutional right to have his application considered on its individual merits in a racially neutral way." Justice Douglas concluded: "So far as race is concerned, any state-sponsored preference to one race over another in [a] competition [is] invidious and violative of the Equal Protection Clause."

The Court was provided with another opportunity to address the constitutionality of state-sponsored voluntary affirmative action programs in *Regents of University of California v. Bakke*. Michael Selmi, *The Life of Bakke: An Affirmative Action Retrospective*, 87 GEO. L.J. 981, 982 (1999), claims that "[a] careful look at the arguments made and analyzed in *Bakke* demonstrates that nary a new argument has been advanced in the last twenty years." Consider the following view: "A coherent doctrinal underpinning is what the *Bakke* decision most conspicuously lacks, although it does provide a how-to-do-it handbook for the admission of minority applicants to professional schools." Karst & Horowitz, *The Bakke Opinion and Equal Protection Doctrine*, 14 HARV. C.R.—C.L. L. REV. 7 (1979).

REGENTS OF THE UNIVERSITY OF CALIFORNIA v. BAKKE

438 U.S. 265, 98 S. Ct. 2733, 57 L. Ed. 2d 750 (1978)

JUSTICE POWELL announced the judgment of the Court.

This case presents a challenge to the special admissions program of the petitioner, the Medical School of the University of California at Davis, which is designed to assure the admission of a specified number of students from certain minority groups.

For the reason stated in the following opinion, I believe that so much of the judgment of the California court as holds petitioner's special admissions program unlawful and directs that respondent be admitted to the Medical School must be affirmed. For the reasons expressed in a separate opinion, my Brothers THE CHIEF JUSTICE [BURGER], MR. JUSTICE STEWART, MR. JUSTICE REHNQUIST, and MR. JUSTICE STEVENS concur in this judgment. I also conclude for the reasons stated in the following opinion that the portion of the court's judgment enjoining petitioner from according any consideration to race in its admissions process must be reversed. For reasons expressed in separate opinions, my Brothers MR. JUSTICE BRENNAN, MR. JUSTICE WHITE, MR. JUSTICE MARSHALL, and MR. JUSTICE BLACKMUN concur in this judgment.

I

The special admissions program operated with a separate committee, a majority of whom were members of minority groups. On a 1974 form [applicants were asked] whether they wished to be considered as members of a "minority group," which the medical school apparently viewed as "Blacks," "Chicanos," "Asians," and "American Indians." If these questions were answered affirmatively, the application was forwarded to the special admissions committee. No formal definition of "disadvantage" was ever produced, but the chairman of the special committee screened each application to see whether it reflected economic or educational deprivation. The special committee continued to recommend special applicants until a number prescribed by faculty vote were admitted. [I]n 1973 and 1974, when the class size [was] 100, the prescribed number of special admissions [was] 16.

From 1971 through 1974, the special program resulted in the admission of 21 black students, 30 Mexican-Americans, and 12 Asians, for a total of 63 minority students. Over the same period, the regular admissions program produced one black, six Mexican-Americans, and 37 Asians, for a total of 44 minority students. Although disadvantaged whites applied to the special program in large numbers, none received an offer of admission through that process. Indeed, in 1974, at least, the special committee explicitly considered only "disadvantaged" special applicants who were members of one of the designated minority groups.

Allan Bakke is a white male who applied to the Davis Medical School in both 1973 and 1974. Bakke's application was rejected. In both years, applicants were admitted under the special program with grade point averages, MCAT scores, and benchmark scores significantly lower than Bakke's.

II

[Justice Powell initially dealt with the question of whether Bakke had a right of action under Title VI of the Civil Rights Act of 1964.] The language of § 601, like that of the Equal Protection Clause, is majestic in its sweep:

> No person in the United States shall, on the ground of race, color, or national origin, be excluded from participation in, be denied the benefits of, or be subjected to discrimination under any program or activity receiving Federal financial assistance.

Examination of the voluminous legislative history of Title VI reveals a congressional intent to halt federal funding of entities that violate a prohibition of racial discrimination similar to that of the Constitution. In view of the clear legislative intent, Title VI must be held to proscribe only those racial classifications that would violate the Equal Protection Clause or the Fifth Amendment.

III

[A]. En route to [a] crucial battle over the scope of judicial review, the parties fight a sharp preliminary action over the proper characterization of the special admissions program. Petitioner prefers to view it as establishing a "goal" of minority representation in the medical school. Respondent, echoing the courts below, labels it a racial quota.

This semantic distinction is beside the point: the special admissions program is undeniably a classification based on race and ethnic background. To the extent that there existed a pool of at least minimally qualified minority applicants to fill the 16 special admissions seats, white applicants could compete only for 84 seats in the entering class, rather than the 100 open to minority applicants. Whether this limitation is described as a quota or a goal, it is a line drawn on the basis of race and ethnic status. The guarantee of equal protection cannot mean one thing when applied to one individual and something else when applied to a person of another color. If both are not accorded the same protection, then it is not equal.

Nevertheless, petitioner argues that the court below erred in applying strict scrutiny to the special admission programs because white males, such as respondent, are not a "discrete and insular minority" requiring extraordinary protection from the majoritarian political process. *Carolene Products Co.*, at 152–153, n. 4. This rationale, however, has never been invoked in our decisions as a prerequisite to subjecting racial or ethnic distinctions to strict scrutiny. Nor has this Court held that discreetness and insularity constitute necessary preconditions to a holding that a particular classification is invidious. These characteristics may be relevant in deciding whether or not to add new types of classifications to the list of "suspect" categories or whether a particular classification survives close examination. Racial and ethnic classifications, however, are subject to stringent examination without regard to these additional characteristics. Racial and ethnic distinctions of any sort are inherently suspect and thus call for the most exacting judicial examination.

[B]. Petitioner urges us to adopt for the first time a more restrictive view of the Equal Protection Clause and hold that discrimination against members of the white "majority" cannot be suspect if its purpose can be characterized as "benign."[34] The clock of our liberties, however, cannot be turned back to 1868. It is far too late to argue that the guarantee of equal protection to all persons permits the recognition of special wards entitled to a degree of protection greater than that accorded others.

Once the artificial line of a "two-class theory" of the Fourteenth Amendment is put aside, the difficulties entailed in varying the level of judicial review according to a perceived "preferred" status of a particular racial or ethnic minority are intractable. The concepts of "majority" and "minority" necessarily reflect temporary arrangements and political judgments. [T]he white "majority" itself is composed of various minority groups, most of which can lay claim to a history of prior discrimination at the hands of the state and private individuals. There is no principled basis for deciding which groups would merit

[34] In the view of MR. JUSTICE BRENNAN, MR. JUSTICE WHITE, MR. JUSTICE MARSHALL, and MR. JUSTICE BLACKMUN, the pliable notion of "stigma" is the crucial element in analyzing racial classifications. The Equal Protection Clause is not framed in terms of "stigma." Certainly the word has no clearly defined constitutional meaning. It reflects a subjective judgment that is standardless. All state-imposed classifications that rearrange burdens and benefits on the basis of race are likely to be viewed with deep resentment by the individuals burdened.

"heightened judicial solicitude" and which would not. Courts would be asked to evaluate the extent of the prejudice and consequent harm suffered by various minority groups. The kind of variable sociological and political analysis necessary to produce such rankings simply does not lie within the judicial competence — even if they otherwise were politically feasible and socially desirable.

Moreover, there are serious problems of justice connected with the idea of preference itself. First, it may not always be clear that a so-called preference is in fact benign. Courts may be asked to validate burdens imposed upon individual members of particular groups in order to advance the group's general interest. Nothing in the Constitution supports the notion that individuals may be asked to suffer otherwise impermissible burdens in order to enhance the societal standing of their ethnic groups. Second, preferential programs may only reinforce common stereotypes holding that certain groups are unable to achieve success without special protection based on a factor having no relationship to individual worth. Third, there is a measure of inequity in forcing innocent persons in respondent's position to bear the burdens of redressing grievances not of their making. Disparate constitutional tolerance of such classifications well may serve to exacerbate racial and ethnic antagonisms rather than alleviate them.

If it is the individual who is entitled to judicial protection against classifications based upon his racial or ethnic background because such distinctions impinge upon personal rights, rather then the individual only because of his membership in a particular group, then constitutional standards may be applied consistently. When [political judgments] touch upon an individual's race or ethnic background, he is entitled to a judicial determination that the burden he is asked to bear on that basis is precisely tailored to serve a compelling governmental interest. The Constitution guarantees that right to every person regardless of his background.

IV

We have held that in "order to justify the use of a suspect classification, a State must show that its purpose or interest is both constitutionally permissible and substantial, and that its use of the classification is 'necessary to the accomplishment' of its purpose or the safeguarding of its interest." The special admissions program purports to serve the purposes of: (i) "reducing the historic deficit of traditionally disfavored minorities in medical schools and the medical profession"; (ii) countering the effects of societal discrimination; (iii) increasing the number of physicians who will practice in communities currently underserved; and (iv) obtaining the educational benefits that flow from an ethnically diverse student body. It is necessary to decide which, if any, of these purposes is substantial enough to support the use of a suspect classification.

[A]. If petitioner's purpose is to assure within its student body some specified percentage of a particular group merely because of its race or ethnic origin, such a preferential purpose must be rejected not as insubstantial but as facially invalid. Preferring members of any one group for no reason other than race or ethnic origin is discrimination for its own sake. This the Constitution forbids. *Loving*.

[B]. The State certainly has a legitimate and substantial interest in ameliorating, or eliminating where feasible, the disabling effects of identified discrimination. [But we] have never approved a classification that aids persons perceived as members of relatively victimized groups at the expense of other innocent individuals in the absence of judicial, legislative, or administrative findings of constitutional or statutory violations. After such findings have been made, the governmental interest in preferring members of the injured groups at the expense of others is substantial, since the legal rights of the victims must be vindicated. In such a case, the extent of the injury and the consequent remedy will have been judicially, legislatively, or administratively defined. Also, the remedial action usually remains subject to continuing oversight to assure that it will work the least harm possible to other innocent persons competing for the benefit. Without such findings of constitutional or statutory violations, it cannot be said that the government has any greater interest in helping one individual than in refraining from harming another. Thus, the government has no compelling justification for inflicting such harm.

Petitioner does not purport to have made, and is in no position to make, such findings. Its broad mission is education, not the formulation of any legislative policy or the adjudication of particular claims of illegality. For reasons similar to those stated in Part III of this opinion, isolated segments of our vast governmental structures are not competent to make those decisions, at least in the absence of legislative mandates and legislatively determined criteria. Before relying upon these sorts of findings in establishing a racial classification, a governmental body must have the authority and capability to establish, in the record, that the classification is responsive to identified discrimination. Lacking this capability, petitioner has not carried its burden of justification on this issue.

Hence, the purpose of helping certain groups whom the faculty of the Davis Medical School perceived as victims of "societal discrimination" does not justify a classification that imposes disadvantages upon persons like respondent, who bear no responsibility for whatever harm the beneficiaries of the special admissions program are thought to have suffered. To hold otherwise would be to convert a remedy heretofore reserved for violations of legal rights into a privilege that all institutions throughout the Nation could grant at their pleasure to whatever groups are perceived as victims of societal discrimination. That is a step we have never approved.

[C]. Petitioner simply has not carried its burden of demonstrating that it must prefer members of particular ethnic groups over all other individuals in order to promote better health care delivery to deprived citizens. Indeed, petitioner has not shown that its preferential classification is likely to have any significant effect on the problem.

[D]. The fourth goal asserted by petitioner is the attainment of a diverse student body. This clearly is a constitutionally permissible goal for an institution of higher education. Academic freedom, though not a specifically enumerated constitutional right, long has been viewed as a special concern of the First Amendment. The freedom of a university to make its own judgments as to education includes the selection of its student body. Thus, in arguing that its universities must be accorded the right to select those students who will contribute the most to the "robust exchange of ideas," petitioner invokes a countervailing constitutional interest, that of the First Amendment. In this light, petitioner must be viewed as seeking to achieve a goal that is of paramount importance in the fulfillment of its mission. An otherwise qualified medical student with a particular background — whether it be ethnic, geographic, culturally advantaged or disadvantaged — may bring to a professional school of medicine experiences, outlooks and ideas that enrich the training of its student body and better equip its graduates to render with understanding their vital service to humanity.

Ethnic diversity, however, is only one element in a range of factors a university properly may consider in attaining the goal of a heterogeneous student body. Although a university must have wide discretion in making the sensitive judgments as to who should be admitted, constitutional limitations protecting individual rights may not be disregarded. Respondent urges — and the courts below have held — that petitioner's dual admissions program is a racial classification that impermissibly infringes his rights under the Fourteenth Amendment. As the interest of diversity is compelling in the context of a university's admissions program, the question remains whether the program's racial classification is necessary to promote this interest.

V

It may be assumed that the reservation of a specified number of seats in each class for individuals from the preferred ethnic groups would contribute to the attainment of considerable ethnic diversity in the student body. But petitioner's argument that this is the only effective means of serving the interest of diversity is seriously flawed. In a most fundamental sense the argument misconceives the nature of the state interest that would justify consideration of race or ethnic background. It is not an interest in simple ethnic diversity, in which a specified percentage of the student body is in effect guaranteed to be members of selected ethnic groups, with the remaining percentage an undifferentiated aggregation of students. The diversity that furthers a compelling state interest encompasses a far broader array of qualifications and characteristics of which racial or ethnic origin is but a single though important element. Petitioner's special admissions program, focused solely on ethnic diversity, would hinder rather than further attainment of genuine diversity.

Nor would the state interest in genuine diversity be served by expanding petitioner's two-track system into a multitrack program with a prescribed number of seats set aside for each identifiable category of applicants. The experience of other university admissions programs, which take race into account in achieving the educational diversity valued by the First Amendment, demonstrates that the assignment of a fixed number of places to a minority group is not a necessary means toward that end. An illuminating example is found in the Harvard College program.

In such an admissions program, race or ethnic background may be deemed a "plus" in a particular applicant's file, yet it does not insulate the individual from comparison with all other candidates for the available seats. The file of a particular black applicant may be examined for his potential contribution to diversity without the factor of race being decisive when compared, for example, with that of an applicant identified as an Italian-American if the latter is thought to exhibit qualities more likely to promote beneficial educational pluralism. Such qualities could include exceptional personal talents, unique work or service experience, leadership potential, maturity, demonstrated compassion, a history of overcoming disadvantage, ability to communicate with the poor, or other qualifications deemed important. In short, an admissions program operated in this way is flexible enough to consider all pertinent elements of diversity in light of the particular qualifications of each applicant, and to place them on the same footing for consideration, although not necessarily according them the same weight. Indeed, the weight attributed to a particular quality may vary from year to year depending upon the "mix" both of the student body and the applicants for the incoming class.

This kind of program treats each applicant as an individual in the admissions process. The applicant who loses out on the last available seat to another candidate receiving a "plus" on the basis of ethnic background will not have been foreclosed from all consideration for that seat simply because he was not the right color or had the wrong surname. It would mean only that his combined qualifications, which may have included similar nonobjective factors, did not outweigh those of the other applicant. His qualifications would have been weighed fairly and competitively, and he would have no basis to complain of unequal treatment under the Fourteenth Amendment.

It has been suggested that an admissions program which considers race only as one factor is simply a subtle and more sophisticated — but no less effective — means of according racial preference than the Davis program. A facial intent to discriminate, however, is evident in petitioner's preference program and not denied in this case. No such facial infirmity exists in an admissions program where race or ethnic background is simply one element — to be weighed fairly against other elements — in the selection process. In short, good faith would be presumed in the absence of a showing to the contrary in the manner permitted by our cases.

In summary, it is evident that the Davis special admission program involves the use of an explicit racial classification never before countenanced by this Court. It tells applicants who are not Negro, Asian, or "Chicano" that they are totally excluded from a specific percentage of the seats in an entering class. No matter how strong their qualifications, quantitative and extracurricular, including their own potential for contribution to educational diversity, they are never afforded the chance to compete with applicants from the preferred groups for the special admission seats. At the same time, the preferred applicants have the opportunity to compete for every seat in the class.

The fatal flaw in petitioner's preferential program is its disregard of individual rights as guaranteed by the Fourteenth Amendment. Such rights are not absolute. But when a State's distribution of benefits or imposition of burdens hinges on the color of a person's skin or ancestry, that individual is entitled to a demonstration that the challenged classification is necessary to promote a substantial state interest. Petitioner has failed to carry this burden.

For this reason, that portion of the California court's judgment holding petitioner's special admissions program invalid under the Fourteenth Amendment must be affirmed.

In enjoining petitioner from ever considering the race of any applicant, however, the courts below failed to recognize that the State has a substantial interest that legitimately may be served by a properly devised admissions program involving the competitive consideration of race and ethnic origin. For this reason, so much of the California court's judgment as enjoins petitioner from any consideration of the race of any applicant must be reversed.

VI

With respect to respondent's entitlement to an injunction directing his admission to the Medical School, petitioner has conceded that it could not carry its burden of proving that, but for the existence of its unlawful special admissions program, respondent still would not have been admitted. Hence, respondent is entitled to the injunction, and that portion of the judgment must be affirmed.

JUSTICE STEVENS, with whom CHIEF JUSTICE BURGER, and JUSTICES STEWART and REHNQUIST join, concurring in the judgment in part and dissenting in part.

[T]he meaning of the Title VI ban on exclusion is crystal clear: Race cannot be the basis of excluding anyone from participation in a federally funded program. [N]othing in the legislative history justifies the conclusion that the broad language of § 601 should not be given its natural meaning. We are dealing with a distinct statutory prohibition, enacted at a particular time with particular concerns in mind; neither its language nor any prior interpretation suggests that its place in the Civil Rights Act, won after long debate, is simply that of a constitutional appendage. In unmistakable terms the Act prohibits the exclusion of individuals from federally funded programs because of their race. As succinctly phrased during the Senate debate, under Title VI it is not "permissible to say 'yes' to one person, but to say 'no' to another person, only because of the color of his skin."

The University's special admissions program violated Title VI of the Civil Rights Act of 1964 by excluding Bakke from the medical school because of his race. It is therefore our duty to affirm the judgment ordering Bakke admitted to the University. Accordingly, I concur in the Court's judgment insofar as it affirms the judgment of the Supreme Court of California. To the extent that it purports to do anything else, I respectfully dissent.

JUSTICES BRENNAN, WHITE, MARSHALL, and BLACKMUN, concurring in the judgment in part and dissenting.

The Court today, in reversing in part the judgment of the Supreme Court of California, affirms the constitutional power of Federal and State Government to act affirmatively to achieve equal opportunity for all. [T]he central meaning of today's opinions [is]: Government may take race into account when it acts not to demean or insult any racial group, but to remedy disadvantages cast on minorities by past racial prejudice, at least when appropriate findings have been made by judicial, legislative, or administrative bodies with competence to act in this area.

The assertion of human equality is closely associated with the proposition that differences in color or creed, birth or status, are neither significant nor relevant to the way in which persons should be treated. Nonetheless, the position that such factors must be "[c]onstitutionally an irrelevance," summed up by the shorthand phrase "[o]ur Constitution is color-blind," *Plessy v. Ferguson* (HARLAN, J., dissenting), has never been adopted by this Court as the proper meaning of the Equal Protection Clause. Indeed, we have expressly rejected this proposition on a number of occasions. Our cases have always implied that an "overriding statutory purpose," could be found that would justify racial classifications. We conclude, therefore, that racial classifications are not per se invalid under the Fourteenth Amendment. Accordingly, we turn to the problem of articulating what our role should be in reviewing state action that expressly classifies by race.

[W]hites [do not] as a class have any of the "traditional indicia of suspectness: the class is not saddled with such disabilities, or subjected to such a history or purposeful unequal treatment, or relegated to such a position of political powerlessness as to command extraordinary protection from the majoritarian political process." Moreover, if the University's representations are credited, this is not a case where racial classifications are "irrelevant and therefore prohibited." Nor has anyone suggested that the University's purposes contravene the cardinal principle that racial classifications that stigmatize — because they are drawn on the presumption that one race is inferior to another or because they put the weight of government behind racial hatred and separatism — are invalid without more.

On the other hand, the fact that this case does not fit neatly into our prior analytic framework for race cases does not mean that it should be analyzed by applying the very loose rational-basis standard of review that is the very least that is always applied in equal protection cases. Instead, a number of considerations — developed in gender discrimination cases but which carry even more force when applied to racial classifications — lead us to conclude that racial classifications designed to further remedial purposes "must serve important governmental objectives and must be substantially related to achievement of those objectives." *Califano v. Webster*, quoting *Craig v. Boren*.

[B]ecause of the significant risk that racial classifications established for ostensibly benign purposes can be misused, causing effects not unlike those created by invidious classifications, it is inappropriate to inquire only whether there is any conceivable basis that might sustain such a classification. Instead, to justify such a classification an important and articulated purpose for its use must be shown. In addition, any statute must be stricken that stigmatizes any group or that singles out those least well represented in the political process to bear the brunt of a benign program. Thus our review under the Fourteenth Amendment should be strict — not " 'strict' in theory and fatal in fact," because it is stigma that causes fatality — but strict and searching nonetheless.

Davis' articulated purpose of remedying the effects of past societal discrimination is, under our cases, sufficiently important to justify the use of race-conscious admissions programs where there is a sound basis for concluding that minority underrepresentation is substantial and chronic, and that the handicap of past discrimination is impeding access of minorities to the medical school. [Prior cases adopting race-consciousness] cannot be distinguished simply by the presence of judicial findings of discrimination, for race-conscious remedies have been approved where such findings have not been made. Indeed, the requirement of a judicial determination of a constitutional or statutory violation as a predicate for race-conscious remedial actions would be self-defeating. Such a requirement would severely undermine efforts to achieve voluntary compliance with the requirements of law.

We therefore conclude that Davis' goal of admitting minority students disadvantaged by the effects of past discrimination is sufficiently important to justify use of race-conscious admissions criteria.

The second prong of our test — whether the Davis program stigmatizes any discrete group or individual and whether race is reasonably used in light of the program's objectives — is clearly satisfied by the Davis program.

It is not even claimed that Davis' program in any way operates to stigmatize or single out any discrete and insular, or even any identifiable, nonminority group. Nor will harm comparable to that imposed upon racial minorities by exclusion or separation on grounds of race be the likely result of the program. Nor was Bakke in any sense stamped as inferior by the Medical School's rejection of him. Indeed, it is conceded by all that he satisfied those criteria regarded by the School as generally relevant to academic performance better than most of the minority members who were admitted. Moreover, there is absolutely no basis for concluding that Bakke's rejection as a result of Davis' use of racial preference will affect him throughout his life in the same way as the segregation of the Negro school children in *Brown I* would have affected them. Unlike discrimination against racial minorities, the use of racial preferences for remedial purposes does not inflict a pervasive injury upon individual whites in the sense that wherever they go or whatever they do there is a significant likelihood that they will be treated as second-class citizens because of their color.

In addition, there is simply no evidence that the Davis program discriminates intentionally or unintentionally against any minority group which it purports to benefit. The program does not establish a quota in the invidious sense of a ceiling on the number of minority applicants to be admitted. Nor can the program reasonably be regarded as stigmatizing the program's beneficiaries or their race as inferior. The Davis program does not simply advance less qualified applicants; rather, it compensates applicants, whom it is uncontested are fully qualified to study medicine, for educational disadvantage which it was reasonable to conclude was a product of state-fostered discrimination.

We disagree with the lower courts' conclusion that the Davis program's use of race was unreasonable in light of its objectives. First, as petitioner argues, there are no practical means by which it could achieve its ends in the foreseeable future without the use of race-conscious measures. With respect to any factor (such as poverty or family educational background) that may be used as a substitute for race as an indicator of past discrimination, whites greatly outnumber racial minorities simply because whites make up a far larger percentage of the total population and therefore far outnumber minorities in absolute terms at every socio-economic level. Moreover, while race is positively correlated with differences in GPA and MCAT scores, economic disadvantage is not. Thus, it appears that economically disadvantaged whites do not score less well than economically advantaged whites, while economically advantaged blacks score less well than do disadvantaged whites. These statistics graphically illustrate that the University's purpose to integrate its classes by compensating for past discrimination could not be achieved by a general preference for the economically disadvantaged or the children of parents of limited education unless such groups were to make up the entire class.

Second, the Davis admissions program does not simply equate minority status with disadvantage. Rather, Davis considers on an individual basis each applicant's personal history to determine whether he or she has likely been disadvantaged by racial discrimination.

Finally, Davis' special admissions program cannot be said to violate the Constitution simply because it has set aside a predetermined number of places for qualified minority applicants rather than using minority status as a positive factor to be considered in evaluating the applications of disadvantaged minority applicants. For purposes of constitutional adjudication, there is no difference between the two approaches. In any admissions program which accords special consideration to disadvantaged racial minorities, a determination of the degree of preference to be given is unavoidable, and any given preference that results in the exclusion of a white candidate is no more or less constitutionally acceptable than a program such as that at Davis.

The "Harvard" program, as those employing it readily concede, openly and successfully employs a racial criterion for the purpose of ensuring that some of the scarce places in institutions of higher education are allocated to disadvantaged minority students. That the Harvard approach does not also make public the extent of the preference and the precise workings of the system while the Davis program employs a specific, openly stated number, does not condemn the latter plan for purposes of Fourteenth Amendment adjudication. It may be that the Harvard plan is more acceptable to the public than is the Davis "quota." If it is, any State, including California, is free to adopt it in preference to less acceptable alternative, just as it is generally free, as far as the Constitution is concerned, to abjure granting any racial preferences in its admissions program. But there is no basis for preferring a particular preference program simply because in achieving the same goals that the Davis Medical School is pursuing, it proceeds in a manner that is not immediately apparent to the public.

JUSTICE MARSHALL.

While I applaud the judgment of the Court that a university may consider race in its admissions process, it is more than a little ironic that, after several hundred years of class-based discrimination against Negroes, the Court is unwilling to hold that a class-based remedy for that discrimination is permissible. In declining to so hold, today's judgment ignores the fact that for several hundred years Negroes have been discriminated against, not as individuals, but rather solely because of the color of their skins. It is unnecessary in twentieth-century America to have individual Negroes demonstrate that they have been victims of racial discrimination; the racism of our society has been so pervasive that none, regardless of wealth or position, has managed to escape its impact. The experience of Negroes in America has been different in kind, not just in degree, from that of other ethnic groups. It is not merely the history of slavery alone but also that a whole people were marked as inferior by the law. And that mark has endured. The dream of America as the great melting pot has not been realized for the Negro; because of his skin color he never even made it into the pot.

These differences in the experience of the Negro make it difficult for me to accept that Negroes cannot be afforded greater protection under the Fourteenth Amendment where it is necessary to remedy the effects of past discrimination. In the Civil Rights Cases, the Court wrote that the Negro emerging from slavery must cease "to be the special favorite of the laws." We cannot in light of the history of the last century yield to that view. It is because of a legacy of unequal treatment that we now must permit the institutions of this society to give consideration to race in making decisions about who will hold the positions of influence, affluence and prestige in America. For far too long, the doors to those positions have been shut to Negroes. If we are ever to become a fully integrated society, one in which the color of a person's skin will not determine the opportunities available to him or her, we must be willing to take steps to open those doors. I do not believe that anyone can truly look into America's past and still find that a remedy for the effects of that past is impermissible.

JUSTICE BLACKMUN.

I suspect that it would be impossible to a arrange an affirmative action program in a racially neutral way and have it successful. To ask that this be so is to demand the impossible. In order to get beyond racism, we must first take account of race. There is no other way. And in order to treat some persons equally, we must treat them differently. We cannot — we dare not — let the Equal Protection Clause perpetrate racial supremacy.

NOTES

1. ***A per se rule?*** *Bakke* did indicate that, given the proper factual predicate, five Justices were willing to hold that the state may use race as a factor in its decisionmaking. Voluntary affirmative action programs not instituted as a remedy for proven de jure racial segregation were not *per se* impermissible under the equal protection guarantee.

Should government be allowed to justify its actions when persons are thereby disadvantaged because of their race? Professor Van Alstyne warns that the standards of review permitting justification of race-conscious remedies are "a sieve that encourages renewed race-based laws, racial discrimination, racial competition, racial spoils systems, and more judicial sport. It is *Plessy v. Ferguson* all over again, in new and modest dress." William Van Alstyne, *Rites of Passage: Race, the Supreme Court and the Constitution*, 46 U. CHI. L. REV. 775–97 (1979). The benign use of race to overcome racism, he argues, has historically been a failure and is ultimately defeating. "Rather, one gets beyond racism by getting beyond it now: by a complete, resolute, and credible commitment never to tolerate in one's own life — or in the life or practices of one's government — the differential treatment of other human beings by race." Is ample protection against renewed racism provided through the use of more stringent standards of judicial review? ALEXANDER BICKEL, THE MORALITY OF CONSENT 132–33 (1975) championed a color-blindness principle: "The lesson of the great decisions of the Supreme Court and the lesson of contemporary history have been the same for at least a generation: discrimination on the basis of race is illegal, immoral, unconstitutional, inherently wrong, and destructive of democratic society. Now this is to be unlearned and we are told that this is not a matter of fundamental principle but only a matter of whose ox is gored."

2. *Heightened scrutiny.* No justice in *Bakke* advocated use of the mere rationality standard. But if Justice Brennan is correct that the usual reasons for a more searching judicial inquiry are not present when the discrimination is against whites, why shouldn't rationality be the standard of review? Professor Ely in a pre-*Bakke* evaluation of affirmative action, argued that "special scrutiny is not appropriate when White people have decided to favor Black people at the expense of White people. A White majority is unlikely to disadvantage itself for reasons of racial prejudice; nor is it likely to be tempted either to underestimate the needs and deserts of Whites relative to those of others, or to overestimate the costs of devising an alternative classification that would extend to certain Whites the advantages generally extended to Blacks." John Ely, *The Constitutionality of Reverse Racial Discrimination*, 41 U. CHI. L. REV. 723 (1974).

3. *Strict scrutiny or intermediate review.* Why does Justice Powell invoke strict scrutiny? His emphasis is on an individual right to fair, *i.e.*, equal, treatment by government — no person should be significantly burdened by government because of his or her race. Professor Tribe states that Powell seems "to express an aversion not simply to classifications based on race but to mass process as such." His *Bakke* opinion recognizes "an individual's right to be treated by the government as a unique and not a fungible being — a right that would retain vitality even in contexts that do not involve classifications based on race." Laurence Tribe, *Perspectives on Bakke: Equal Protection, Procedural Fairness or Structural Justice?*, 92 HARV. L. REV. 864, 867 (1979).

Does a concern for individualized justice justify use of strict scrutiny under equal protection even for "benign" classifications? Does it focus on the costs to whites rather than on the need for relief of racial minorities? Consider the following: "The harm to those excluded from affirmative action is real. In standard affirmative action plans, the principal harm takes the form of opportunity costs inflicted on those denied positions because of their race. These costs are high, they are demoralizing, and they deserve to be taken very seriously by all who must decide whether to support or oppose affirmative action as a matter of policy. But they do not differ in a constitutional sense from the harms inflicted on the better-off by programs that offer special opportunities to the poor, on the able-bodied by laws that require special accommodations for the preferences to veterans. All these programs are instances of affirmative action. It is impossible that the only kind of affirmative action made unconstitutional under the Civil War Amendments is the kind that would offer assistance to blacks." Jeb Rubenfeld, *Affirmative Action*, 107 YALE L.J. 427, 464 (2000). What is the nature of the burden on Bakke from the Davis program?

4. *Individual and group rights.* *Brown II* suggested the problem of whether equal protection protects individual or group interests. In the affirmative action cases, the issue of the role of group rights under our Constitution takes center stage.

Professor Brest finds the group orientation inconsistent not only with our underlying political theory of liberalism, "focusing on the rights of individuals, including rights of distributive justice," but also with the traditional antidiscrimination principle and notions of individual autonomy "which attributes no moral significance to membership in racial groups." Paul Brest, *Foreword: In Defense of the Antidiscrimination Principle*, 90 HARV. L. REV. 1, 48–52 (1976).

Professor Marshall argues, "The equal protection clause is not primarily concerned with the protection of individuals against invidious discrimination. On the contrary, it cannot sensibly be interpreted in any other way than — as argued principally by Owen Fiss — in terms of its protection of groups, and of individuals only by reason of their membership in groups." Burke Marshall, *A Comment on the Nondiscrimination Principle in a "Nation of Minorities,"* 93 YALE L.J. 1006, 1007 (1984).

> I think that we would have no debate over whether or not a policy of nondiscrimination or colorblindness is an ideal for an ideal society. The problem is that ours is not an ideal society. Ours is a society that is still permeated by racial discrimination and even more so by the traces of racial oppression that was permitted legally as well as socially and economically up until a little less than thirty years ago. [D]iscrimination is not . . . against individuals. It is discrimination against a people. And the remedy, therefore, has to correct and cure and compensate for the discrimination against the people and not just the discrimination against the identifiable persons.

Id. at 1006.

5. *Remedying societal discrimination and integration.* The Court has approved use of race conscious plans to remedy proven government *de jure* segregation in the education and employment contexts. While the Board of Regents did not admit to past racial or ethnic discrimination, the Board claimed that the Davis plan was designed to remedy past societal discrimination. Why did Justice Powell conclude that this did not satisfy the demands of strict scrutiny?

Consider the argument of Professor Robert Post, *Fashioning the Legal Constitution: Culture, Courts, and Law*, 117 HARV. L. REV. 4, 63 (2003): "Although Powell's exposition of the compelling educational interest of diversity had been intellectually elegant and precise, it had displayed little or no relationship to the actual reasons why affirmative action had become prominent in American higher education. These reasons were based almost entirely on the felt need to remedy deep social dislocations associated with race." Why does the Brennan group accept remediation as a sufficient interest justifying race-conscious admissions? Professor Elizabeth Anderson says: "From a compensatory point of view, patterns of segregation are objectionable as effects of massive, continuing, and illegal private housing and employment discrimination, historic state policies supporting segregation of neighborhoods and schools, officially race-neutral policies that have dramatic racial effects (e.g., white flight)." *Integration, Affirmative Action, and Strict Scrutiny*, 77 N.Y.U.L. REV. 1195, 1200–01 (2002).

In evaluating the government interest in compensating for past societal discrimination, what weight should be given to the fact that the beneficiaries of the affirmative action program have generally not been personally discriminated against by the government institution? Does it matter that the white persons who are burdened by the use of affirmative action have not personally engaged in racial discrimination? Again, the issue of whether equal protection embodies group or individual interests is vital in answering these questions.

Consider the different theories of compensation and reparations noted in *Bakke*. In an amicus brief filed on behalf of the Anti-Defamation League of B'nai B'rith, Professors Bickel and Kurland argued: "Generalized historical assertions about conditions somewhere in the United States some time in the past is not the premise of the remedial cases decided by this Court, nor should it be. If such a predicate were allowed to replace careful, specific findings of discrimination as the necessary condition for maintaining racial discrimination, such racial preferences would be constitutionally sanctioned in a wide range of circumstances that would denigrate if not destroy the concept of racial equality specified in the Equal Protection Clause."

Alternatively, should it be possible to justify a race-conscious admissions program as a means of promoting a forward-looking policy of integration, not dependent on past wrongdoing? "The integrative view focuses more on the causal impact of segregation on two core ideals: equality of opportunity and democracy. Segregation is objectionable as a continuing cause of multiple, systematic, mutually reinforcing race-based inequalities, operating independently of and in conjunction with discrimination, in both the economic and political spheres." Anderson, 77 N.Y.U.L. REV. at 1201–02. Professor Anderson explains the goal of integration: "Consider, in this light, one of the forward-looking claims made on behalf of race-conscious admissions: that racial diversity in the student body helps break down racial stereotypes. Our interest in doing so is a matter of justice, of ending societal discrimination. But it is not about compensating for past wrongs. It is about constructing a better future. Members of underrepresented racial groups are admitted under integrative affirmative action programs, not as victims of discrimination, but as agents of integration, contributing to the education of their fellow students." *Id.* at 1223–24.

6. *Diversity.* Why is "student diversity" a compelling interest for Justice Powell? Consider the argument that "diversity put the justification for racial preferences squarely on improving the educational experience of all students, rather than on helping a favored few. If, as educators insisted and Powell believed, racial, ethnic, and other kinds of diversity in the classroom enhanced the education of all students, then the search for minority representation could be seen as sound educational policy, not racial favoritism." John Jeffries, Bakke *Revisited*, 2003 Sup. Ct. Rev. 1, 9. Justice Powell's emphasis on diversity has been lauded as a practical means of restructuring student body composition. "Invocation of diversity was Powell's master stroke. It was also his healing gesture. Diversity was the most acceptable public rationale for affirmative action, because it has been historically clearly related to a university's function. It was the most traditional justification, because the most analogous to geographic preference." J. Harvie Wilkinson, From Brown to Bakke 303 (1979).

Some commentators, however, have questioned the use of diversity as a justification for racial preference. "I doubt that race or ethnicity is such an indicator [of diversity]. I think that differences in economic status, for example, are much more important indicators of different experiences and perceptions. But, of course, there are economically advantaged and economically disadvantaged persons in every racial and ethnic group. Thus, racial preferences in admissions to higher education are justified if important differences are associated with race or not." Lino Graglia, *Racially Discriminatory Admission to Public Institutions of Higher Education*, 9 Sw. U.L. Rev. 583, 588 (1977).

Charles R. Lawrence III, *Two Views of the River: A Criteria of the Liberal Defense of Affirmative Action*, 101 Colum. L. Rev. 928, 931 (2001), who strongly supports affirmative action, worries that liberal supporters of diversity may avoid questioning the way that traditional admissions criteria "continues to perpetuate race and class privilege" pushing other more radical substantive defenses to the background, including "the need to remedy past discrimination, address present discriminatory practices, and [reexamine] traditional notions of merit and the role of universities in the reproduction of elites."

7. *Narrow tailoring: race plus.* Is the failing of the Davis plan in its use of a two-track admissions procedure? Can a university consider the numbers or percentage of minority admissions in order to assure a racial and ethnic blend? Are quotas, goals, or percentages permissible? Professor Laurence H. Tribe, *Perspectives on Bakke: Equal Protection, Procedural Fairness or Structural Justice?* 92 Harv. L. Rev. 864, 866 (1979), asks: "If it is not 'discriminatory' in some invidious or otherwise forbidden sense to prefer minorities on a case-by-case basis, why is it 'discriminatory' to do so more mechanically and in gross?" Consider the view that "under the Powell opinion the relevant criteria in determining the permissibility of a race-conscious admissions program are the number of traits that are given special weight and the degree to which those traits are considered in a competitive fashion. The opinion does not make clear, however, just how these criteria relate to each other and exactly how they are to be measured." Vincent Blasi, *Bakke as Precedent: Does Mr. Justice Powell Have a Theory?*, 67 Cal. L. Rev. 2, 33 (1979).

Justice Powell's use of the Harvard Plan does provide some guidance for admission directors in devising acceptable affirmative action programs. Some commentators contend that it is unlikely that the Harvard Plan would produce any different admission results than a more blatant race conscious plan. In short, it is only a facade, a cover, for covert racial preferences. Professor Tushnet bluntly points out that "the Harvard program was a more genteel way of accomplishing the same results as the plan in *Bakke*, and on the margins a plus factor has precisely the same effect as that plan; Powell's position was 'pure sophistry.'" Mark Tushnet, *Justice Lewis F. Powell and the Jurisprudence of Centrism*, 93 MICH. L. REV. 1854, 1875 (1995).

John C. Jeffries, Bakke *Revisited*, 2003 SUP. CT. REV. 1, 2 says that while Justice Powell dismisses the distinction between goals and quotas as "besides the point," his opinion "came to rest on precisely that ground." He argues that "the difference between the affirmative action plans that Powell found unconstitutional and those that he was prepared to uphold was not substantive, or even formalistic, but essentially aesthetic. Considered purely as a matter of craft—of consistency with precedent, coherency as doctrine, and clarity of result—Powell's *Bakke* opinion must be judged a failure." But Jeffries suggests that there are advantages to Justice Powell's approach: "If the advantages accorded racial and ethnic minorities are not explicitly stated, they need not be explicitly undone. If adjustments are not announced and contested, a steady progression of divisive debates can perhaps be avoided. The burying of racial preferences in 'plus' factors for certain individuals obscures and softens the sense of injury that even the most dedicated proponents of affirmative action must acknowledge will be felt by those who are disadvantaged for reasons they cannot control. [S]chools will be better, happier, and more productive places if the lines separating the students who inhabit them are not harshly drawn." *Id.* at 20.

8. *Powell's objective.* Professor John Jefferies, Powell's clerk and biographer, explains his motivation: "Powell saw little prospect that the compensatory rationale would place any meaningful limit on the duration of such preferences. Powell thought of affirmative action as a transition, a short-term departure from the ideal of color-blindness justified only by pressing necessity. Allowing minority set-asides to continue until all effects of past societal discrimination had been eliminated might mean they would last forever. Powell therefore crafted an approach designed both to permit affirmative action and to constrain it." 2003 SUP. CT. REV. at 9.

Post-Bakke

Justice Powell's opinion in *Bakke* received widespread praise from commentators who termed it a "Solomonic judgment," an act of "judicial statesmanship" providing something for everybody and quelling threatened divisiveness. For example, Professor Tribe suggests that the *Bakke* decision may have been ideal as a matter of politics or judicial statecraft. "The headlines could cry 'Bakke Wins Admission,' while the lawyers and admissions officers would quietly read the subtitles: 'Affirmative action upheld.'" Tribe, 92 HARV. L. REV. at 864–65.

Justice Powell's decision allowed affirmative action in education to survive. And for the next quarter century, it was Powell's pragmatic resolution that would be viewed, practically and legally, as the law of the land. Justice Powell's analysis could be said to provide the narrowest grounds for the holding concurred in by a majority of concurring justices. *Marks v. United States*, 430 U.S. 188 (1977). But there were those who argued that Justice Powell in *Bakke* wrote only for himself and that his diversity rationale was not binding precedent.

In an extremely closely watched case, *Hopwood v. Texas*, 78 F.3d 932 (5th Cir.), the racial preferences of the admissions program at the University of Texas School of Law were declared invalid by the Fifth Circuit. The Fifth Circuit determined that Justice Powell's opinion in *Bakke* did not accurately reflect current Supreme Court doctrine and declared that "the use of ethnic diversity simply to achieve racial heterogeneity, even as part of the consideration of a number of factors, is unconstitutional." The Supreme Court denied certiorari.

As we began the new century, David Cole, *Call It Integration*, LEGAL TIMES, March 19, 2001, at 64, said, "Affirmative action in higher education has never been more established — and more vulnerable — than it is today." While race-conscious programs existed throughout higher education, lawsuits were filed in Georgia, Michigan, Washington and Texas, producing conflicting results on whether "diversity" is a compelling interest in higher education. The Supreme Court returned to affirmative action in the educational context in *Grutter v. Bollinger*, p. 736, and *Gratz v. Bollinger*, p. 756. As you read the following cases on employment and licensing in the intervening years, consider the view that "[t]he *Hopwood* majority's conclusion that the Powell opinion has been undermined by subsequent precedent reads more into that precedent than is warranted. *Hopwood* relies on dicta from cases involving employment and contracting, which may be distinguishable from the educational admissions context." Lackland H. Bloom, Jr. Hopwood, Bakke *and the Future of the Diversity Justification*, 29 TEXAS TECH. L. REV. 1, 64 (1998).

[2] Employment and Licensing — From *Bakke* to *Adarand*

***Fullilove v. Klutznik*, 448 U.S. 448 (1980).** The Court upheld a "set aside" provision in the Public Works Act of 1977, requiring state and local governments receiving federal public works grants, to allocate at least 10% of the funds for purchasing services from minority business enterprises (MBE). MBEs were defined as businesses controlled by designated minorities, *i.e.*, Negroes, Spanish-speaking, Orientals, Indians, Eskimos and Aleuts. Both the district court and court of appeals rejected the equal protection challenge and the Supreme Court affirmed.

Chief Justice Burger, announcing the decision of the Court, in an opinion joined only by Justices White and Powell, did not adopt either of the tests articulated in *Bakke* because the MBE program would be upheld under "close examination" using either standard.

Citing the school desegregation cases, Chief Justice Burger rejected the claim "that in the remedial context the Congress must act in a wholly 'colorblind' fashion."

> Here we deal, as we noted earlier, not with the limited remedial powers of a federal court, for example, but with the broad remedial powers of Congress. It is fundamental that in no organ of government, state or federal, does there repose a more comprehensive remedial power than in the Congress, expressly charged by the Constitution with competence and authority to enforce equal protection guarantees. Congress not only may induce voluntary action to assure compliance with existing federal statutory or constitutional antidiscrimination provisions, but also, where Congress has authority to declare certain conduct unlawful, it may, as here, authorize and induce state action to avoid such conduct.

The Chief Justice was more concerned with the contention that the MBE program impermissibly deprived innocent nonminority businesses of government contracting opportunities. He concluded that this was "an incidental consequence of the program, not part of its objective."

Justice Powell wrote a separate concurrence, stressing the difference between the Regents in *Bakke*, who "were not competent to make, and had not made, findings sufficient to uphold the use of the race-conscious remedy they adopted" and Congress.

Justice Marshall, joined by Justices Brennan and Blackmun, concurred using their *Bakke* intermediate review standard.

> As the Court demonstrates, it is indisputable that Congress' articulated purpose for enacting the set-aside provision was to remedy the present effects of past racial discrimination. Congress had a sound basis for concluding that minority-owned construction enterprises, though capable, qualified, and ready and willing to work, have received a disproportionately small amount of public contracting business because of the continuing effects of past discrimination. In these circumstances, remedying these present effects of past racial discrimination is a sufficiently important governmental interest to justify the use of racial classifications.

Justice Stewart, joined by Justice Rehnquist, dissenting, adopted a virtually *per se* rule to race-conscious affirmative action, exempting only remedial programs for proven past race discrimination.

> Under our Constitution, the government may never act to the detriment of a person solely because of that person's race. The color of a persons's skin and the country of his origin are immutable facts that bear no relation to ability, disadvantage, moral culpability, or any other characteristics of constitutionally permissible interest to government. In short, racial discrimination is by definition invidious discrimination. The rule cannot be any different when the persons injured by a racially biased law are not members of a racial minority.

Justice Steven's dissent was not as sweeping. He was not "convinced that the [Equal Protection] Clause contains an absolute prohibition against any statutory classification based on race." But he took issue with Congress' procedures in passing the MBE measure. Specifically, Justice Stevens faulted Congress for failing to detail how it arrived at the 10% set-aside figure or its definition of minority groups. He concluded that the provision could not "be characterized as a narrowly tailored racial classification."

***Wygant v. Jackson Board of Education*, 476 U.S. 267 (1986).** A badly fragmented Court held unconstitutional a provision in a collective bargaining agreement giving preferential treatment to some employees because of their race or national origin. Between 1969 and 1971, the number of minority teachers in the Jackson, Michigan public schools increased as a result of "affirmative steps" taken by the Board to settle a civil rights complaint. But, in 1971 many of the newly hired teachers had to be laid off. To quell rising racial unrest, the Board and teachers union entered into a new agreement in 1972, providing a seniority system for layoffs, "except that at no time will there be a greater percentage of minority personnel laid off than the current percentage of minority personnel employed at the time of the layoff." When white workers having greater seniority than retained minority workers were laid off, the white employees challenged the racial preference. The district court upheld the racial preference as an attempt to remedy societal discrimination by providing "role models" for minority school children. The Court of Appeals affirmed.

Justice Powell, announcing the judgment of the Court in an opinion joined only by Chief Justice Burger, Justice Rehnquist and, in part, Justice O'Connor, adopted strict scrutiny and held that the interest in providing minority role models to overcome societal discrimination was not compelling.

> This Court never has held that societal discrimination alone is sufficient to justify a racial classification. Rather, the Court has insisted upon some showing of prior discrimination by the governmental unit involved before allowing limited use of racial classifications in order to remedy such discrimination. Societal discrimination, without more, is too amorphous a basis for imposing a racially classified remedy. The role model theory announced by the District Court and the resultant holding typify this indefiniteness. No one doubts that there has been serious racial discrimination in this country. But as the basis for imposing discriminatory *legal* remedies that work against innocent people, societal discrimination is insufficient and over expansive. In the absence of particularized findings, the court could uphold remedies that are ageless in their reach into the past, and timeless in their ability to affect the future.

Justice Powell also stressed the burden imposed by the racial preference on innocent white workers, but Justice O'Connor did not join this portion of the plurality opinion:

> While hiring goals impose a diffuse burden, often foreclosing only one of several opportunities, layoffs impose the entire burden of achieving racial equality on particular individuals, often resulting in serious disruption of their lives. That burden is too intrusive. Other, less

intrusive means of accomplishing similar purposes — such as the adoption of hiring goals — are available.

Justice O'Connor, concurring, asserted that remedying past discrimination could be a compelling objective but concluded that the policy here was not tied to prior conduct. "[B]ecause the layoff provision here acts to maintain levels of minority hiring that have no relation to remedying employment discrimination, it cannot be adjudged 'narrowly tailored' to effectuate its asserted remedial purpose."

Justice White, concurring, focused on the harm caused by the race-conscious layoff provision. "Whatever the legitimacy of hiring goals or quotas may be, the discharge of white teachers to make room for blacks, none of whom has been shown to be a victim of any racial discrimination, is quite a different matter. I cannot believe that in order to integrate a work force, it would be permissible to discharge whites and hire blacks until the latter comprised a suitable percentage of the work force."

Justice Marshall, joined by Justices Brennan and Blackmun, dissenting, stressed the efforts of the union and Board to "solve serious educational problems in the public schools."

Justice Stevens, dissenting, did not believe it was necessary to find past racial discrimination in order to justify a program designed to further the "legitimate interest in employing more black teachers in the future."

> [In] our present society, race is not always irrelevant to sound governmental decisionmaking. In the context of public education, it is quite obvious that a school board may reasonably conclude that an integrated faculty will be able to provide benefits to the student body that could not be provided by an all white, or nearly all white, faculty. It is one thing for a white child to be taught by white teachers that color, like beauty, is only "skin deep"; it is far more convincing to experience that truth on a day to day basis during the routine, ongoing learning process.

***City of Richmond v. J.A. Croson Co.*, 488 U.S. 469 (1989).** For the first time, a majority of the Court applied strict scrutiny in reviewing an affirmative action program. The program at issue was the city's "Minority Business Utilization Plan," a plan essentially identical to that upheld in *Fullilove*, requiring prime contractors awarded city construction contracts to subcontract at least 30% of the dollar amount of each contract to one or more "Minority Business Enterprises" (MBEs). Any MBE in the nation could qualify.

The Court 6-3 held the plan unconstitutional. Justice O'Connor, writing for a plurality, explained that *Fullilove* was not controlling. While Congress could address the effects of society-wide discrimination in the construction industry, that did not mean that the states are free to use race-conscious remedies since "[s]ection 1 of the Fourteenth Amendment is an explicit constraint on *state* power," (emphasis added) including state remedial power.

Strict scrutiny applied to this local program:

> The Richmond Plan denies certain citizens the opportunity to compete for a fixed percentage of public contracts based solely upon their race. To whatever racial group these citizens belong, their "personal rights" to be treated with equal dignity and respect are implicated by a rigid rule erecting race as the sole criterion in an aspect of public decisionmaking. Absent searching judicial inquiry into the justification for such race-based measures, there is simply no way of determining what classifications are "benign" or "remedial" and what classifications are in fact motivated by illegitimate notions of racial inferiority or simple racial politics. Indeed, the purpose of strict scrutiny is to "smoke out" illegitimate uses of race by assuring that the legislative body is pursing a goal important enough to warrant use of a highly suspect tool. The test also ensures that the means chosen "fit" this compelling goal so closely that there is little or no possibility that the motive for the classification was illegitimate racial prejudice or stereotype. We thus reaffirm the view expressed by the plurality in *Wygant* that the standard of review under the equal protection clause is not dependent on the race of those burdened or benefitted by a particular classification.

Justice O'Connor, writing now for the Court, concluded that the city failed to demonstrate a compelling remedial interest. The assertion that there had been past discrimination in the entire construction industry "provides no guidance for a legislative body to determine the precise scope of the injury it seeks to remedy. It 'has no logical stopping point.' " Further, "none of the evidence presented by the city points to any identified discrimination in the Richmond construction industry." There was nothing indicating a *prima facie* case of a specific, identified constitutional or statutory violation by anyone in the Richmond construction industry requiring remediation.

The city had adopted the remedial plan after a public hearing at which there was no direct evidence presented that the city had discriminated on the basis of race in granting contracts, or that its prime contractors had discriminated against minority subcontractors. In addition to "highly conclusionary statements" by city officials that the plan was remedial, the city relied on evidence such as statistics showing that a.67% of the city's prime construction contracts had been awarded to minority businesses in recent years even though the population was 50% black; evidence that a variety of local contractor associations had virtually no MBE members; and congressional findings on discrimination in the construction industry used in *Fullilove*.

While the district court had accepted this evidence, the Supreme Court did not. Examining each of the lower court findings of discrimination *seriatim*, Justice O'Connor rejected the statistical evidence since there was no corresponding information on the number of minority MBEs in the city or the extent of MBEs participating in subcontracting. Further, she rejected the evidence on associational membership.

> For low minority membership in these associations to be relevant, the city would have to link it to the number of local MBEs eligible for membership. If the statistical disparity between eligible MBEs and

> MBE membership were great enough, an inference of discriminatory exclusion could arise. In such a case, the city would have a compelling interest in preventing its tax dollars from assisting these organizations in maintaining a racially segregated construction market.

But the city had not provided the necessary probative evidence. Concerning the congressional findings relied on by the city, Justice O'Connor noted that while Congress in *Fullilove* was acting pursuant to 5 of the Fourteenth Amendment, state and local governments must make findings identifying discrimination "with some specificity before they may use race-conscious relief." Justice O'Connor, for the Court, also indicated serious doubt that the Richmond plan was narrowly tailored. She was especially critical of the 30% quota, which "cannot be said to be narrowly tailored to any goals except perhaps outright racial balancing."

Justice Stevens, concurring in part and concurring in the judgment, first stated that he disagreed "with the premise that seems to underlie" the decision, "that a governmental decision that rests on a racial classification is never permissible except as a remedy for a past wrong." However, Justice Stevens emphasized that the city had failed to make a sufficient showing that "the public interest in the efficient performance of its construction contracts will be served by granting a preference to minority-business enterprises." He also noted that the plan was an attempt by a "legislative body, rather than a court, to fashion a remedy for a past wrong."

Justice Scalia concurred in the judgment:

> I do not agree that, despite the Fourteenth Amendment, state and local governments may in some circumstances discriminate on the basis of race in order (in a broad sense) 'to ameliorate the effects of past discrimination.' At least where state or local action is at issue, only a social emergency rising to the level of imminent danger to life and limb—for example, a prison race riot, requiring temporary segregation of inmates—can justify an exception to the principle embodied in the Fourteenth Amendment that "[o]ur Constitution is color-blind and neither nor tolerates classes among citizens," *Plessy v. Ferguson* (Harlan, J., dissenting). In my view there is only one circumstance in which the States may act by race to "undo the effects of past discrimination": where that is necessary to eliminate their own maintenance of a system of unlawful racial classification.

Justice Kennedy, concurring in part and concurring in the judgement, acknowledged the force of Justice Scalia's opinion emphasizing the moral imperative of racial neutrality. Nevertheless, he concluded that a decision invalidating all racial preferences that are not "necessary remedies to victims of unlawful discrimination" would be "a significant break with our precedents that require a case-by-case test."

Justice Marshall, joined by Justices Brennan and Blackmun, dissenting, would hold that counteracting "the continuing impact of government acceptance or use of private institutions or structures once wrought by discrimination" is an important government interest, and that the city's plan is substantially related to this interest.

> When government channels all its contracting funds to a white-dominated community of established contractors whose racial homogeneity is the product of private discrimination, it does more than place its imprimatur on the practices which forged and which continue to define that community. It also provides a measurable boost to those economic entities that have thrived within it, while denying important economic benefits to those entities which, but for prior discrimination, might well be better qualified to receive valuable government contracts.

***Metro Broadcasting, Inc. v. FCC*, 497 U.S. 547 (1990).** Justice Brennan, for a majority of the Court, upheld two policies of the Federal Communications Commission: "(1) a program awarding an enhancement for minority ownership in comparative proceedings for new licenses, and (2) the minority 'distress sale' program, which permits a limited category of existing radio and television broadcast stations to be transferred only to minority-controlled firms."

> It is of overriding significance in these cases that the FCC's minority ownership programs have been specifically approved — indeed, mandated — by Congress. In *Fullilove v. Klutznick*, [we] explained that deference was appropriate in light of Congress' institutional competence as the national legislature, as well as Congress' powers under the Commerce Clause, the Spending Clause, and the Civil War Amendments.
>
> A majority of the Court in *Fullilove* did not apply strict scrutiny to the race-based classification at issue. We hold that benign race-conscious measures mandated by Congress — even if those measures are not "remedial" in the sense of being designed to compensate victims of past governmental or societal discrimination — are constitutionally permissible to the extent that they serve important governmental objectives within the power of Congress and are substantially related to achievement of those objectives.
>
> Our decision last Term in *Richmond v. J.A. Croson Co.*, concerning a minority set-aside program adopted by a municipality, does not prescribe the level of scrutiny to be applied to a benign racial classification employed by Congress. In fact, much of the language and reasoning in *Croson* reaffirmed the lesson of *Fullilove* that race-conscious classifications adopted by Congress to address racial and ethnic discrimination are subject to a different standard than such classifications prescribed by state and local governments.

The Court found that a "governmental objective of broadcast diversity" was served by increasing levels of minority ownership of radio stations.

> The judgment that there is a link between expanded minority ownership and broadcast diversity does not rest on impermissible stereotyping. Although all station owners are guided to some extent by

market demand in their programming decisions, Congress and the Commission have determined that there may be important differences between the broadcasting practices of minority owners and those of their nonminority counterparts. This judgment — and the conclusion that there is a nexus between minority ownership and broadcasting diversity — is corroborated by a host of empirical evidence. Evidence suggests that an owner's minority status influences the selection of topic for news coverage and the presentation of editorial viewpoint, especially on matters of particular concern to minorities. In addition, studies show that a minority owner is more likely to employ minorities in managerial and other important roles where they can have an impact on station policies.

Finally, we do not believe that the minority ownership policies at issue impose impermissible burdens on nonminorities. [A] congressionally mandated benign race-conscious program that is substantially related to the achievement of an important governmental interest is consistent with equal protection principles so long as it does not impose undue burdens on nonminorities. *Cf. Fullilove.*

Justice Stevens concurred:

[T]he Court demonstrates that this case falls within the extremely narrow category of governmental decisions for which racial or ethnic heritage may provide a rational basis for differential treatment. The public interest in broadcast diversity — like the interest in an integrated police force, diversity in the composition of a public school faculty or diversity in the student body of a professional school — is in my view unquestionably legitimate.

Justice O'Connor, joined by Chief Justice Rehnquist and Justices Scalia and Kennedy dissenting, asserted that "the Constitution requires that the Court apply a strict standard of scrutiny to evaluate racial classifications such as those contained in the challenged FCC policies. *See Richmond v. J.A. Croson Co.* The Constitution's guarantee of equal protection binds the Federal Government as it does the States, and no lower level of scrutiny applies to the Federal Government's use of race classifications." Justice O'Connor argued that *Fullilove* stood for the proposition that congressional determinations could satisfy strict scrutiny under the proper circumstances.

The Court asserts that *Fullilove* supports its novel application of intermediate scrutiny to "benign" racial conscious measures adopted by Congress. Three reasons defeat this claim. First, *Fullilove* concerned an exercise of Congress' powers under § 5 of the Fourteenth Amendment. Second, *Fullilove* applies at most only to congressional measures that seek to remedy identified past discrimination. Finally, even if *Fullilove* applied outside a remedial exercise of Congress' § 5 power, it would not support today's adoption of the intermediate standard of review proffered by Justice Marshall but rejected in *Fullilove*.

With regard to the interest in program diversity, the dissenters insisted that minority ownership was not substantially connected to this interest unless one engaged in impermissible racial stereotyping.

> The FCC has used race as a proxy for whatever views it believes to be underrepresented in the broadcasting spectrum. This reflexive or unthinking use of a suspect classification is the hallmark of an unconstitutional policy. . . . The FCC has failed to implement a case-by-case determination [of program viewpoint], and that failure is particularly unjustified when individualized hearings already occur, as in the comparative licensing program.

Justice Kennedy, joined by Justice Scalia, dissenting, characterized the majority opinion as a return to "*Plessy*'s deferential approach to racial classifications. I cannot agree with the Court that the Constitution permits the Government to discriminate among its citizens on the basis of race in order to serve interests so trivial as 'broadcast diversity.' "

***Adarand Constructors, Inc. v. Pena,* 515 U.S. 200 (1995).** The United States Department of Transportation awarded a prime contract with terms that gave the prime contractor a bonus if it hired subcontractors certified as small businesses controlled by "socially and economically disadvantaged individuals." Federal law provided that the prime contractor could presume certain minorities were "socially and economically disadvantaged individuals." Adarand sued claiming that the presumption discriminated on the basis of race in violation of the Fifth Amendment.

The Court held the program must be subjected to strict scrutiny review and remanded the case. Justice O'Connor, writing for the majority (except insofar as it might be inconsistent with Justice Scalia's concurrence), surveyed the precedent, noting that the cases as explained in *Croson* demonstrated three "general propositions" for racial classifications under the Fourteenth and Fifth Amendments: skepticism, consistency, and congruence. *Skepticism* mandates that racial preferences are subject to "a most searching examination." *Consistency* requires that the same standard of review is employed no matter which racial groups are burdened or benefitted by a particular classification.' " Finally, *congruence* dictates that the analysis for such classifications is the same under both the Fifth and Fourteenth Amendments. "Taken together, these three propositions lead to the conclusion that any person, of whatever race, has the right to demand that any governmental actor subject to the Constitution justify any racial classification subjecting that person to unequal treatment under the strictest judicial scrutiny."

Metro Broadcasting, Justice O'Connor said, departed from prior precedent because "it turned its back on *Croson's* explanation of why strict scrutiny of all governmental racial classifications is essential," and rejected the principle of congruence by subjecting federal governmental action, and in doing so also underminded the other two propositions.

> The three propositions underminded by *Metro Broadcasting* all derive from the basic principle that the fifth and Fourteenth Amendments to the Constitution protect persons, not groups. It follows from that

> principle that all governmental action based on race—a group classification long recognized as "in most circumstances irrelevant and therefore prohibited"—should be subjected to detailed judicial inquiry to ensure that the personal right to equal protection of the laws has not been infringed. Accordingly, we hold today that all racial classifications imposed by whatever federal, state, or local governmental actor, must be analyzed by a reviewing court under strict scrutiny. To the extent that *Metro Broadcasting* is inconsistent with that holding, it is overruled.

But Justice O'Connor stressed that the principle of consistency does not mean that review is "strict in theory, but fatal on fact." Consistency says nothing about the ultimate validity of the law under review. "The unhappy persistence of both the practice and the lingering effects of racial discrimination against minority groups in this country is an unfortunate reality, and the government is not disqualified from acting in response to it."

While Justice O'Connor recognized that members of the Court had taken different views on the scope of Congressional authority under 5 of the Fourteenth Amendment to deal with racial discrimination, she denied that the principle of congruence violated "any principle of appropriate respect for a co-equal Branch of the Government." Strict scrutiny remained "the best way to ensure that courts will consistently give racial classification that kind of detailed examination, both as to ends and as to means."

Justice Scalia, concurring in part and concurring in the judgment, stated that "government can never have a 'compelling interest' in discriminating on the basis of race in order to 'make up' for past racial discrimination in the opposite direction." "[U]nder our Constitution there can be no such thing as a creditor or a debtor race." Although Justice Scalia thought it was "unlikely, if not impossible, that the challenged program would survive under this understanding of strict scrutiny," he was "content to leave that to be decided on remand."

Justice Thomas concurred in part and concurred in the judgment: "I believe that there is a 'moral [and] constitutional equivalence,' between laws designed to subjugate a race and those that distribute benefits on the basis of race in order to foster some current notion of equality. Government cannot make us equal; it can only recognize, respect, and protect us as equal before the law. [T]here can be no doubt that racial paternalism and its unintended consequences can be as poisonous and pernicious as any other form of discrimination."

Justice Stevens, joined by Justice Ginsburg, in dissent, criticized the majority for being "preoccupied with abstract standards." Requiring consistency, according to Justice Stevens, "would disregard the difference between a 'No Trespassing' sign and a welcome mat." He explained that "[a]s a matter of constitutional and democratic principle, a decision by representatives of the majority to discriminate against the members of a minority race is fundamentally different from those same representatives' decision to impose incidental costs on the majority of their constituents in order to provide a benefit to a disadvantaged minority." Consistency would "produce the anomalous result" that affirmative action programs designed to remedy discrimination against racial minorities would be subject to higher scrutiny than programs designed to remedy discrimination against women. Justice Stevens faulted the majority's focus on congruence for "ignor[ing] important practical and legal differences between federal and state or local decisionmakers."

Justice Souter, joined by Justices Ginsburg and Breyer, dissenting, thought the decision to apply strict scrutiny in these circumstances would not necessarily alter the outcome of cases, such as *Fulliove*. "Surely the transition from the *Fullilove* plurality view (in which Justice Powell joined) to today's strict scrutiny (which will presumably be applied as Justice Powell employed it) does not signal a change in the standard by which the burden of a remedial racial preference is to be judged as reasonable or not at any given time."

Justice Ginsburg, joined by Justice Breyer, dissenting, would have upheld the challenged program, but in an effort at damage control, chose to view the Court's decision "as one that allows our precedent to evolve, still to be informed by and responsive to changing conditions."

> The divisions in this difficult case should not obscure the Court's recognition of the persistence of racial inequality and a majority's acknowledgement of Congress' authority to act affirmatively, not only to end discrimination, but also to counteract discrimination's lingering effects.

The Court's opinion had rejected the notion that strict scrutiny is fatal in fact. Rather, it demands review that is searching to ferret out malign discrimination, masquerading as benign. "Bias both conscious and unconscious, reflecting traditional and unexamined habits of thought, keeps up barriers that must come down if equal opportunity and nondiscrimination are ever genuinely to become this country's law and practice."

Commenting on skepticism and consistency, David Strauss, Affirmative Action and the Public Interest, 1995 SUP. CT. REV. 1, 11, states: "[W]hile the nominal standards [for benign and invidious racial programs] are the same, the actual standards are not. The actual standard for measures that discriminate against minorities is absolute invalidity, subject to an exception for truly extraordinary circumstances. The standard for affirmative action is not so restrictive." What is the position of the *Adarand* Court on skepticism and consistency?

Focusing on congruence, might the operation of strict standard differ in federal and state cases? A Justice Department Memorandum from Assistant Attorney General Walter Dellinger to General Counsels, June 28, 1995, states:

> [I]n particular, the Court [in *Adarand*] expressly left open the question of what deference the judiciary should give to determinations by Congress that affirmative action is necessary to remedy discrimination against racial and ethnic minority groups. Unlike state and local governments, Congress may be able to rely on national findings of discrimination to justify remedial racial and ethnic classifications; it may not have to base such measures on evidence of discrimination in every geographical locale or sector of the economy that is affected. On

the other hand, as with state and local governments under *Croson,* Congress may not predicate race-based remedial measures on generalized, historical societal discrimination.

[3] Education Revisited

GRUTTER v. BOLLINGER

539 U.S. 306, 123 S. Ct. 2325, 156 L. Ed. 2d 304 (2003)

JUSTICE O'CONNOR delivered the opinion of the Court.

This case requires us to decide whether the use of race as a factor in student admissions by the University of Michigan Law School (Law School) is unlawful.

I

The Law School ranks among the Nation's top law schools. It receives more than 3,500 applications each year for a class of around 350 students. Seeking to "admit a group of students who individually and collectively are among the most capable," the Law School looks for individuals with "substantial promise for success in law school" and "a strong likelihood of succeeding in the practice of law and contributing in diverse ways to the well-being of others." More broadly, the Law School seeks "a mix of students with varying backgrounds and experiences who will respect and learn from each other." In 1992, the dean of the Law School charged a faculty committee with crafting a written admissions policy to implement these goals. In particular, the Law School sought to ensure that its efforts to achieve student body diversity complied with this Court's most recent ruling on the use of race in university admissions. *See Regents of Univ. of Cal. v. Bakke*. Upon the unanimous adoption of the committee's report by the Law School faculty, it became the Law School's official admissions policy.

The hallmark of that policy is its focus on academic ability coupled with a flexible assessment of applicants' talents, experiences, and potential "to contribute to the learning of those around them." The policy requires admissions officials to evaluate each applicant based on all the information available in the file, including a personal statement, letters of recommendation, and an essay describing the ways in which the applicant will contribute to the life and diversity of the Law School. In reviewing an applicant's file, admissions officials must consider the applicant's undergraduate grade point average (GPA) and Law School Admissions Test (LSAT) score because they are important (if imperfect) predictors of academic success in law school. The policy stresses that "no applicant should be admitted unless we expect that applicant to do well enough to graduate with no serious academic problems."

The policy makes clear, however, that even the highest possible score does not guarantee admission to the Law School. Nor does a low score automatically disqualify an applicant. Rather, the policy requires admissions officials to look beyond grades and test scores to other criteria that are important to the Law School's educational objectives. So-called " 'soft' variables" such as "the enthusiasm of recommenders, the quality of the undergraduate institution, the quality of the applicant's essay, and the areas and difficulty of undergraduate course selection" are all brought to bear in assessing an "applicant's likely contributions to the intellectual and social life of the institution."

The policy aspires to "achieve that diversity which has the potential to enrich everyone's education and thus make a law school class stronger then the sum of its parts." The policy does not restrict the types of diversity contributions eligible for "substantial weight" in the admissions process, but instead recognizes "many possible bases for diversity admissions." The policy does, however, reaffirm the Law School's long-standing commitment to "one particular type of diversity." that is, "racial and ethnic diversity with special reference to the inclusion of students which have been historically discriminated against, like African-Americans, Hispanics and Native Americans, who without this commitment might not be represented in our student body in meaningful numbers." By enrolling a " 'critical mass' of [underrepresented] minority students," the Law School seeks to "ensur[e] their ability to make unique contributions to the character of the Law School."

The policy does not define diversity "solely in terms of racial and ethnic status." Nor is the policy "insensitive to the competition among all students for admission to the [L]aw [S]chool." Rather, the policy seeks to guide admissions officers in "producing classes both diverse and academically outstanding, classes made up of students who promise to continue the tradition of outstanding contribution by Michigan Graduates to the legal profession."

Petitioner Barbara Grutter is a white Michigan resident who applied to the Law School in 1996 with a 3.8 grade point average and 161 LSAT score. The Law School initially placed petitioner on a waiting list, but subsequently rejected her application. In December 1997, petitioner filed suit in the United States District Court. Petitioner alleged that respondents discriminated against her on the basis of race in violation of the Fourteenth Amendment; Title VI of the Civil Rights Act of 1964; and 42 U.S.C. § 1981. Petitioner further alleged that her application was rejected because the Law School uses race as a "predominant" factor, giving applicants who belong to certain minority groups "a significantly greater chance of admission than students with similar credentials from disfavored racial groups." Petitioner also alleged that respondents "had no compelling interest to justify their use of race in the admissions process." Petitioner requested compensatory and punitive damages, an order requiring the Law School from continuing to discriminate on the basis of race. Petitioner clearly has standing to bring this lawsuit.

The District Court granted petitioner's motion for class certification and bifurcation of the trial into liability and damages phases. The class was defined as " 'all persons who (A) applied for and were not granted admission to the University of Michigan Law School for the academic years since (and including) 1995 until the time that judgment is entered herein; and (B) were members of those racial or ethnic groups, including Caucasian, that Defendants treated less favorably in considering their applications for admission to the Law School.' "

During the 15-day bench trial, the parties introduced extensive evidence concerning the Law School's use of race in the admissions process. [The Court's discussion of the evidence is omitted.] In the end, the District Court concluded that the Law School's use of race as a factor in admissions decisions was unlawful. Applying strict scrutiny, the District Court determined that the Law School's asserted interest in assembling a diverse student body was not compelling because "the attainment of a racially diverse class . . . was not recognized as such by *Bakke* and is not a remedy for past discrimination." The District Court went on to hold that even if diversity were compelling, the Law School had not narrowly tailored its use of race to further that interest. The District Court granted petitioner's request for declaratory relief and enjoined the Law School from using race as a factor in its admissions decisions. The Court of Appeals entered a stay of the injunction pending appeal.

Sitting en banc, the Court of Appeals reversed the District Court's judgment and vacated the injunction. The Court of Appeals first held that JUSTICE POWELL's opinion in *Bakke* was binding precedent establishing diversity as a compelling state interest. According to the Court of Appeals, JUSTICE POWELL's opinion with respect to diversity comprised the controlling rationale for the judgment of this Court under the analysis set forth in *Marks v. United States,* 430 U.S. 188 (1977). The Court of Appeals also held that the Law School's use of race was narrowly tailored because race was merely a "potential 'plus' factor" and because the Law School's program was "virtually identical" to the Harvard admissions program described approvingly by JUSTICE POWELL and appended to his *Bakke* opinion. Four dissenting judges would have held the Law School's use of race unconstitutional.

We granted certiorari to resolve the disagreement among the Courts of Appeals on a question of national importance: Whether diversity is a compelling interest that can justify the narrowly tailored use of race in selecting applicants for admission to public universities. Compare *Hopwood* v. *Texas,* 78 F. 3d 932 (CA5 1996) (*Hopwood I*) (holding that diversity is not a compelling state interest), with *Smith v. University of Wash. Law School*, 233 F. 3d 1188 (CA9 2000) (holding that it is).

II

We last addressed the use of race in public higher education over 25 years ago. Since this Court's splintered decision in *Bakke*, JUSTICE POWELL's opinion announcing the judgment of the Court has served as the touchstone for constitutional analysis of race-conscious admissions policies. Public and private universities across the Nation have modeled their own admissions programs on JUSTICE POWELL's views on permissible race-conscious policies.

[The Court's extended discussion of JUSTICE POWELL's opinion in *Bakke* is omitted.]

In the wake of our fractured decision in *Bakke*, courts have struggled to discern whether JUSTICE POWELL's diversity rationale, set forth in part of the opinion joined by no other Justice, is nonetheless binding precedent under *Marks*. In that case, we explained that "[w]hen a fragmented Court decided a case and no single rationale explaining the result enjoys the assent of five

Justices, the holding of the Court may be viewed as that position taken by those Members who concurred in the judgments on the narrowest grounds." As the divergent opinions of the lower courts demonstrate, however, "[t]his test is more easily stated than applied to the various opinions supporting the result in [*Bakke*]." We do not find it necessary to decide whether Justice Powell's opinion is binding under *Marks*. More important, for the reasons set out below, today we endorse Justice Powell's view that student body diversity is a compelling state interest that can justify the use of race in university admissions.

We have held that all racial classifications imposed by government "must be analyzed by a reviewing court under strict scrutiny." This means that such classifications are constitutional only if they are narrowly tailored to further compelling governmental interests. Strict scrutiny is not "strict in theory, but fatal in fact." *Adarand Constructors, Inc. v. Pena*. Although all governmental uses of race are subject to strict scrutiny, not all are invalidated by it. When race-based action is necessary to further a compelling governmental interest, such action does not violate the constitutional guarantee of equal protection so long as the narrow-tailoring requirement is also satisfied.

Context matters when reviewing race-based governmental action under the Equal Protection Clause. In *Adarand Constructors, Inc. v. Pena*, we made clear that strict scrutiny must take " 'relevant differences' into account." Indeed, as we explained, that is its "fundamental purpose." Not every decision influenced by race is equally objectionable and strict scrutiny is designed to provide a framework for carefully examining the importance and the sincerity of the reasons advanced by the governmental decisionmaker for the use of race in that particular context.

III

A.

With these principles in mind, we turn to the question whether the Law School's use of race is justified by a compelling state interest. Before this Court, as they have throughout this litigation, respondents assert only one justification for their use of race in the admissions process: obtaining "the educational benefits that flow from a diverse student body." In other words, the Law School asks us to recognize, in the context of higher education, a compelling state interest in student body diversity.

We first wish to dispel the notion that the Law School's argument has been foreclosed, either expressly or implicitly, by our affirmative-action cases decided since *Bakke*. It is true that some language in those opinions might be read to suggest that remedying past discrimination is the only permissible justification for race-based governmental action. *See, e.g.*, *Richmond v. J. A. Croson Co.*, (plurality opinion) (stating that unless classifications based on race are "strictly reserved for remedial settings, they may in fact promote notions of racial inferiority and lead to a politics of racial hostility"). But we have never held that the only governmental use of race that can survive strict scrutiny is remedying past discrimination. Nor, since *Bakke*, have we directly addressed the use of race in the context of public higher education. Today, we hold that the Law School has a compelling interest in attaining a diverse student body.

The Law School's educational judgment that such diversity is essential to its educational mission is one to which we defer. The Law School's assessment that diversity will, in fact, yield educational benefits is substantiated by respondents and their *amici*. Our scrutiny of the interest asserted by the Law School is no less strict for taking into account complex educational judgments in an area that lies primarily within the expertise of the university. Our holding today is in keeping with our tradition of giving a degree of deference to a university's academic decisions, within constitutionally prescribed limits.

We have long recognized that, given the important purpose of public education and the expansive freedoms of speech and thought associated with the university environment, universities occupy a special niche in our constitutional tradition. In announcing the principle of student body diversity as a compelling state interest, JUSTICE POWELL invoked our cases recognizing a constitutional dimension, grounded in the First Amendment, of educational autonomy: "The freedom of a university to make its own judgments as to education includes the selection of its student body." *Bakke*. From this premise, JUSTICE POWELL reasoned that by claiming "the right to select those students who will contribute the most to the 'robust exchange of ideas,' "a university "seek[s] to achieve a goal that is of paramount importance in the fulfillment of its mission." Our conclusion that the Law School has a compelling interest in a diverse student body is informed by our view that attaining a diverse student body is at the heart of the Law School's proper institutional mission, and that "good faith" on the part of a university is "presumed" absent "a showing to the contrary."

As part of its goal of "assembling a class that is both exceptionally academically qualified and broadly diverse," the Law School seeks to "enroll a 'critical mass' of minority students." The Law School's interest is not simply "to assure within its student body some specified percentage of a particular group merely because of its race or ethnic origin." That would amount to outright racial balancing, which is patently unconstitutional. Rather, the Law School's concept of critical mass is defined by reference to the educational benefits that diversity is designed to produce.

These benefits are substantial. As the District Court emphasized, the Law School's admissions policy promotes "cross-racial understanding," helps to break down racial stereotypes, and "enables [students] to better understand persons of different races." These benefits are "important and laudable," because "classroom discussion is livelier, more spirited, and simply more enlightening and interesting" when the students have "the greatest possible variety of backgrounds." The Law School's claim of a compelling interest is further bolstered by its *amici*, who point to the educational benefits that flow from student body diversity. In addition to the expert studies and reports entered into evidence at trial, numerous studies show that student body diversity promotes learning outcomes, and "better prepares them as professionals." These benefits are not theoretical but real, as major American businesses have made clear that the skills needed in today's increasingly global marketplace can only be developed through exposure to widely diverse people, cultures, ideas, and viewpoints. What is more, high-ranking retired officers and civilian leaders of the United States military assert that, "[b]ased on [their] decades of experience," a "highly qualified, racially diverse officer corps. . .is essential to the military's ability to fulfill its principle mission to provide national security." The primary sources for the Nation's officer corps are the service academies and the Reserve Officers Training Corps (ROTC), the latter compromising students already admitted to participating colleges and *both* highly qualified *and* racially diverse unless the service academies and the ROTC used limited race-conscious recruiting and admissions policies."

We have repeatedly acknowledged the overriding importance of preparing students for work and citizenship, describing education as pivotal to "sustaining our political and cultural heritage" with a fundamental role in maintaining the fabric of society. *Plyler v. Doe* [text, p. 945]. This Court has long recognized that "education. . .is the very foundation of good citizenship." *Brown v. Board of Education*. For this reason, the diffusion of knowledge and opportunity through public institutions of higher education must be accessible to all individuals regardless of race or ethnicity. Effective participation by members of all racial and ethnic groups in the civic life of our Nation is essential if the dream of one Nation, indivisible, is to be realized.

Moreover, universities, and in particular, law schools, represent the training ground for a large number of our Nation's leaders. Individuals with law degrees occupy roughly half the sate governorships, more than half the seats in the United States Senate, and more than a third of the seats in the United States hours of Representatives. The pattern is even more striking when it comes to highly selective law schools. In order to cultivate a set of leaders with legitimacy in the eyes of the citizenry, it is necessary that the path to leadership be visibly open to talented and qualified individuals of ever race and ethnicity. All members of our heterogeneous society must have confidence in the openness and integrity of the educational institutions that provide this training.

The Law School does not premise its need for critical mass on "any belief that minority students always (or even consistently) express some characteristic minority viewpoint on any issue." To the contrary, diminishing the force of such stereotypes is both a crucial part of the Law School's mission, and one that it cannot accomplish with only token numbers of minority students. Just as growing up in a particular region or having particular professional experiences in likely to affect an individual's views, so too is one's own, unique experience of being a racial minority in a society, like our own, in which race unfortunately still matters. The Law School has determined, based on its experience and expertise, that a "critical mass" of underrpresented minorities is necessary to further its compelling interest in securing the educational benefits of a diverse student body. Even in the limited circumstance when drawing racial distinctions is permissible to further compelling state interest, government is still "constrained in how it may pursue that end: [T]he means chosen to accomplish the [government's] asserted purpose must be specifically and narrowly framed to accomplish that purpose." *Shaw v. Hunt* [text, p. 774]. The purpose of the narrow tailoring requirement is to ensure that "the means chosen 'fit'. . .th[e] compelling goal so closely that there is little or no possibility that the motive for the classification was illegitimate racial prejudice or stereotype." *Richmond v. J. A. Croson Co.* (plurality opinion)

Since *Bakke,* we have had no occasion to define the contours of the narrow-tailoring inquiry with respect to race-conscious university admission programs. That inquiry must be calibrated to fit the distinct issues raised by the use of race to achieve student body diversity in public higher education. Contrary to JUSTICE KENNEDY's assertion, we do not "abandon[] strict scrutiny." Rather, as we have already explained, we adhere to *Adarand*'s teaching that the very purpose of strict scrutiny is to take such "relevant differences into account."

We find that the Law School's admissions program bears the hallmarks of a narrowly tailored plan. As JUSTICE POWELL made clear in *Bakke*, truly individualized consideration demands that race be used in a flexible, nonmechanical way. It follows from this mandate that universities cannot establish quotas for members of certain racial groups or put members of those groups on separate admissions tracks. Nor can universities insulate applicants who belong to certain racial or ethnic groups from the competition for admission. Universities can, however, consider race or ethnicity more flexibly as a "plus" factor in the context of individualized consideration of each and every applicant.

We are satisfied that the Law School's admissions program, like the Harvard plan described by JUSTICE POWELL, does not operate as a quota. Properly understood, a "quota" is a program in which a certain fixed number or proportion of opportunities are "reserved exclusively for certain minority groups." *Richmond v. J. A. Croson Co.* In contrast, "A permissible goal. . .require[s] only a good-faith effort. . .to come within a range demarcated by the goal itself," *Sheet Metal Workers v. EEOC* [478 U.S. 421, 495 (1986)], and permits consideration of race as a "plus" factor in any given case while still ensuring that each candidate "compete[s] with all other qualified applicants," *Johnson v. Transportation Agency, Santa Clara Cty.*, 480 U.S. 616, 638 (1987).

The Law School's goal of attaining a critical mass of underrepresented minority students does not transform its program into a quota. As the Harvard plan described by JUSTICE POWELL recognized, there is of course "some relationship between numbers and achieving the benefits to be derived from a diverse student body, and between numbers and providing a reasonable environment for those students admitted." Nor, as JUSTICE KENNEDY posits, does the Law School's consultation of the "daily reports," which keep track of the racial and ethnic composition of the class (as well as of residency and gender), "suggest[] there was no further attempt at individual review save for race itself" during the final stages of the admissions process. To the contrary, the Law School's admissions officers testified without contradiction that they never gave race any more or less weight based on the information contained in these reports. Moreover, as JUSTICE KENNEDY concedes, between 1993 and 2000, the number of African-American, Latino, and Native-American students in each class at the Law School varied from 13.5 to 20.1 percent, a range inconsistent with a quota.

The Chief Justice believes that the Law School's policy conceals an attempt to achieve racial balancing, and cites admissions data to contend that the Law School discriminates among different groups within the critical mass. But, as The Chief Justice concedes, the number of underrepresented minority students who ultimately enroll in the Law School differs substantially from their representation in the applicant pool and varies considerably for each group from year to year.

That a race-conscious admissions program does not operate as a quota does not, by itself, satisfy the requirement of individualized consideration. When using race as a "plus" factor in university admissions, a university's admissions program must remain flexible enough to ensure that each applicant is evaluated as an individual and not in a way that makes an applicant's race or ethnicity the defining feature of his or her application. The importance of this individualized consideration in the context of a race conscious admissions program is paramount.

Here, the Law School engages in a highly individualized, holistic review of each applicant's file, giving serious consideration to all the ways an applicant might contribute to a diverse educational environment. The Law School affords this individualized consideration to applicants of all races. There is no policy, either *de jure* or *de facto*, of automatic acceptance or rejection based on any single "soft" variable. Unlike the program at issue in *Gratz v. Bollinger*, the Law School awards no mechanical, predetermined diversity "bonuses" based on race or ethnicity. We also find that, like the Harvard plan Justice Powell referenced in *Bakke*, the Law School's race-conscious admissions program adequately ensures that all factors that may contribute to student body diversity are meaningfully considered alongside race in admissions decisions. With respect to the use of race itself, all underrepresented minority students admitted by the Law School have been deemed qualified. By virtue of our Nation's struggle with racial inequality, such students are both likely to have experiences of particular importance to the Law School's mission, and less likely to be admitted in meaningful numbers on criteria that ignore those experiences.

The Law School does not, however, limit in any way the broad range of qualities and experiences that may be considered valuable contributions to student body diversity. All applicants have the opportunity to highlight their own potential diversity contributions through the submission of a personal statement, letters of recommendation, and an essay describing the ways in which the applicant will contribute to the life and diversity of the Law School.

What is more, the Law School actually gives substantial weight to diversity factors besides race. The Law School frequently accepts nonminority applicants with grades and test scores lower than underrepresented minority applicants (and other nonminority applicants) who are rejected. This shows that the Law School seriously weighs many other diversity factors besides race that can make a real and dispositive difference for nonminority applicants as well. By this flexible approach, the Law School sufficiently takes into account, practice as well as theory, a wide variety of characteristics besides race and ethnicity that contribute to a diverse student body.

Petitioner and the United States argue that the Law School's plan is not narrowly tailored because race-neutral means exist to obtain the educational benefits of student body diversity that the Law School seeks. We disagree. Narrow tailoring does not require exhaustion of every conceivable race-neutral alternative. Nor does it require a university to choose between maintaining a reputation for excellence or fulfilling a commitment to provide educational opportunities to members of all racial groups. Narrow tailoring does, however, require serious, good faith consideration of workable race-neutral alternatives that will achieve the diversity the university seeks.

We agree with the Court of Appeals that the Law School sufficiently considered workable race-neutral alternatives. The District Court took the Law School to task for failing to consider race-neutral alternatives such as "using a lottery system" or "decreasing the emphasis for all applicants on undergraduate GPA and LSAT scores." But these alternatives would require a dramatic sacrifice of diversity, the academic quality of all admitted students, or both.

We acknowledge that "there are serious problems of justice connected with the idea of preference itself." *Bakke*. Narrow tailoring, therefore, requires that a race-conscious admissions program not unduly harm members of any racial group. We agree that, in the context of its individualized inquiry into the possibly diversity contributions of all applicants, the Law School's race-conscious admission program does not unduly harm nonminority applicants.

We are mindful, however, that "[a] core purpose of the Fourteenth Amendment was to do away with all governmentally imposed discrimination based on race." *Palmore v. Sidoti*. Accordingly, race-conscious admissions policies must be limited in time. This requirement reflects that racial classifications, however compelling their goals, are potentially so dangerous that they may be employed no more broadly than the interest demands. Enshrining a permanent justification for racial preferences would offend this fundamental equal protection principle. We see no reason to exempt race-conscious admissions programs from the requirement that all governmental use of race must have a logical end point. The Law School, too, concedes that all "race-conscious programs must have reasonable durational limits."

In the context of higher education, the durational requirement can be met by sunset provisions in race-conscious admissions policies and periodic reviews to determine whether racial preferences are still necessary to achieve student body diversity. Universities in California, Florida, and Washington State, where racial preferences in admissions are prohibited by state law, are currently engaged in experimenting with a wide variety of alternative approaches. Universities in other States can and should draw on the most promising aspects of these race-neutral alternatives as they develop.

The requirement that all race-conscious admissions programs have a termination point "assure[s] all citizens that the deviation from the norm of equal treatment of all racial and ethnic groups is a temporary matter, a measure taken in the service of the goal of equality itself." *Richmond v. J. A. Croson Co.* (plurality opinion). We take the Law School at its word that it would "like nothing better than to find a race-neutral admissions formula" and will terminate its race-conscious admissions program as soon as practicable. It has been 25 years since JUSTICE POWELL first approved the use of race to further an interest in student body diversity in the context of public higher education. Since that time, the number of minority applicants with high grades and test scores has indeed increased. We expect that 25 years from now, the use of racial preferences will no longer be necessary to further the interest approved today.

IV

In summary, the Equal Protection Clause does not prohibit the Law School's narrowly tailored use of race in admissions decisions to further a compelling interest in obtaining the educational benefits that flow from a diverse student body. Consequently, petitioner's statutory claims based on Title VI and 42 U. S. C. § 1981 also fail. Judgment of the Court of Appeals for the Sixth Circuit, accordingly, is affirmed.

Justice Ginsburg, with whom Justice Breyer joins, concurring.

The Court [observes] that race-conscious programs "must have a logical end point." The Court further observes that "[i]t has been 25 years since Justice Powell first approved the use of race to further an interest in student body diversity in the context of public higher education." For at least part of that time, however, the law could not fairly be described as "settled," and in some regions of the Nation, overtly race-conscious admissions policies have been proscribed. Moreover, it was only 25 years before *Bakke* that this Court declared public school segregation unconstitutional, a declaration that, after prolonged resistance, yielded an end to a law-enforced racial caste system, itself the legacy of centuries of slavery. *See Brown v. Board of Education.* It is well documented that conscious and unconscious race bias, even rank discrimination based on race, remain alive in our land, impeding realization of our highest values and ideals. As to public education, data for the years 2000–2001 show that 71.6% of African-American children and 76.3% of Hispanic children attended a school in which minorities made up a majority of the student body. And schools in predominantly minority communities lag far behind others measured by the educational resources available to them.

However strong the public's desire for improved education systems may be, it remains the current reality that many minority students encounter markedly inadequate and unequal educational opportunities. From today's vantage point, one may hope, but not firmly forecast, that over the next generations' span, progress toward nondiscrimination and genuinely equal opportunity will make it safe to sunset affirmative action.

Justice Scalia, with whom Justice Thomas joins, concurring in part and dissenting in part.

The "educational benefit" that the University of Michigan seeks to achieve by racial discrimination consists, according to the Court, of "crossracial understanding." and "better prepar[ation of] students for an increasingly diverse workforce and society," "all of which is necessary not only for work, but also for good 'citizenship.' " This is not, of course, an "educational benefit" on which students will be graded on their Law School transcript (Works and

Plays Well with Others: B) or tested by the bar examiners (Q: Describe in 500 words or less your cross-racial understanding). For it is a lesson of life rather than law— essentially the same lesson taught to (or rather learned by, for it cannot be "taught" in the usual sense) people three feet shorter and twenty years younger than the full-grown adults at the University of Michigan Law School, in institutions ranging from Boy Scout troops to public-school kindergartens. If properly considered an "educational benefit" at all, it is surely not one that is either uniquely relevant to law school or uniquely "teachable" in the formal educational setting. *And therefore*: If it is appropriate for the University of Michigan Law School to use racial discrimination for the purpose of putting together a "critical mass" that will convey generic lessons in socialization and good citizenship, surely it is no less appropriate — indeed, *particularly* appropriate — for the civil service system of the State of Michigan to do so. The nonminority individuals who are deprived of a legal education, a civil service job, or any job at all by reason of their skin color will surely understand.

Unlike a clear constitutional holding that racial preferences in state educational institutions are impermissible, or even a clear anticonstitutional holding that racial preferences in state educational institutions are OK, today's *Grutter-Gratz* split double header seems perversely designed to prolong the controversy and the litigation. Some future lawsuits will presumably focus on whether the discriminatory scheme in question contains enough evaluation of the applicant "as an individual," and sufficiently avoids "separate admissions tracks" to fall under *Grutter* rather than *Gratz*. Some will focus on whether a university has gone beyond the bounds of a " 'good faith effort' " and has so zealously pursued its "critical mass" as to make it an unconstitutional *de facto* quota system, rather than merely " 'a permissible goal.' " Other lawsuits may focus on whether, in the particular setting at issue, any educational benefits flow from racial diversity. Still other suits may challenge the bona fides of the institution's expressed commitment to the educational benefits of diversity that immunize the discriminatory scheme in *Grutter*. And still other suits may claim that the institution's racial preferences have gone below or above the mystical *Grutter*-approved "critical mass." Finally, litigation can be expected on behalf of minority groups intentionally short changed in the institution's composition of its generic minority "critical mass." I do not look forward to any of these cases. The Constitution proscribes government discrimination on the basis of race, and state-provided education is no exception.

JUSTICE THOMAS, with whom JUSTICE SCALIA joins as to Parts I–VII, concurring in part and dissenting in part.

I believe blacks can achieve in every avenue of American life without the meddling of university administrators. Because I wish to see all students succeed whatever their color, I share, in some respect, the sympathies of those who sponsor the type of discrimination advanced by the University of Michigan Law School (Law School). The Constitution does not, however, tolerate institutional devotion to the status quo in admissions policies when such devotion ripens into racial discrimination. Nor does the Constitution countenance the unprecedented deference the Court gives to the Law School, an approach inconsistent with the very concept of "strict scrutiny."

No one would argue that a university could set up a lower general admission standard and then impose heightened requirements only on black applicants. Similarly, a university may not maintain a high admission standard and grant exemptions to favored races. The Law School, of its own choosing, and for its own purposes, maintains an exclusionary admissions system that it knows produces racially disproportionate results. Racial discrimination is not a permissible solution to the self-inflicted wounds of this elitist admissions policy.

The majority upholds the Law School's racial discrimination not by interpreting the people's Constitution, but by responding to a faddish slogan of the cognoscenti. Nevertheless, I concur in part in the Court's opinion. First, I agree with the Court insofar as its decision, which approves of only one racial classification, confirms that further use of race in admissions remains unlawful. Second, I agree with the Court's holding that racial discrimination in higher education admissions will be illegal in 25 years. I respectfully dissent from the remainder of the Court's opinion and the judgment, however, because I believe that the Law School's current use of race violates the Equal Protection Clause and that the Constitution means the same thing today as it will in 300 months.

I

The majority agrees that the Law School's racial discrimination should be subjected to strict scrutiny. Where the Court has accepted only national security [*Korematsu*], and rejected even the best interests of a child [*Palmore v. Sidotti*], as a justification for racial discrimination, I conclude that only those measures the State must take to provide a bulwark against anarchy, or to prevent violence, will constitute a "pressing public necessity." The Constitution abhors classifications based on race, not only because those classifications can harm favored races or are based on illegitimate motives, but also because every time the government places citizens on racial registers and makes race relevant to the provision of burdens or benefits, it demeans us all.

II

Unlike the majority, I seek to define with precision the interest being asserted by the Law School before determining whether that interest is so compelling as to justify racial discrimination. The Law School maintains that it wishes to obtain "educational benefits that flow from student body diversity." The Law School's argument, as facile as it is, can only be understood in one way: Classroom aesthetics yields educational benefits, racially discriminatory admissions policies are required to achieve the right racial mix, and therefore the policies are required to achieve the educational benefits. It is the *educational benefits* that are the end, or allegedly compelling state interest, not "diversity."

One must also consider the Law School's refusal to entertain changes to its current admissions system that might produce the same educational benefits. The Law School adamantly disclaims any race-neutral alternative that would reduce "academic selectivity," which would in turn "require the Law School to become a very different institution, and to sacrifice a core part of its educational mission." In other words, the Law School seeks to improve marginally the education it offers without sacrificing too much of its exclusivity and elite status.

The proffered interest that the majority vindicates today, then, is not simply "diversity." Instead the Court upholds the use of racial discrimination as a tool to advance the Law School's interest in offering a marginally superior education while maintaining an elite institution. Unless each constituent part of this state interest is of pressing public necessity, the Law School's use of race is unconstitutional. I find each of them to fall far short of this standard.

III

A close reading of the Court's opinion reveals that all of its legal work is done through one conclusory statement: The Law School has a "compelling interest in securing the educational benefits of a diverse student body." No serious effort is made to explain how these benefits fit with the state interests the Court has recognized (or rejected) as compelling, or to place any theoretical constraints on an enterprising court's desire to discover still more justifications for racial discrimination. In the absence of any explanation, one might expect the Court to fall back on the judicial policy of *stare decisis*. But the Court eschews even this weak defense of its holding, shunning an analysis of the extent to which JUSTICE POWELL's opinion in *Regents of Univ. Of Cal. v. Bakke*, is binding, in favor of an unfounded wholesale adoption of it.

JUSTICE POWELL's opinion in *Bakke* and the Court's decision today to rest on the fundamentally flawed proposition that racial discrimination can be contextualized so that a goal, such as classroom aesthetics, can be compelling in one context but not in another. This "we know it when we see it" approach to evaluating state interests is not capable of judicial application. Under the proper standard, there is no pressing public necessity in maintaining a public law school at all and, it follows, certainly not an elite law school. Likewise, marginal improvements in legal education do not qualify as a compelling state interest.

This Court has limited the scope of equal protection review to interests and activities that occur within that State's jurisdiction. The Equal Protection Clause does not permit States to justify racial discrimination on the basis of what the rest of the Nation "may do or fail to do." The only interests that can satisfy the Equal Protection Clause's demands are those found within a State's jurisdiction. The only cognizable state interests vindicated by operating a public law school are, therefore, the education of that State's citizens and the training of that State's lawyers. [T]he Law School trains few Michigan residents and overwhelmingly serves students, who, as lawyers, leave the State of Michigan. By contrast, Michigan's other public law school, Wayne State University Law School, sends 88% of its graduates on to serve the people of Michigan. It does not take a social scientist to conclude it is precisely the Law School's status as an elite institution that causes it to be a way-station for the rest of the country's lawyers, rather than a training ground for those who will remain in Michigan. The Law School's decision to be an elite institution does little to advance the welfare of the people of Michigan or any cognizable interest of the State of Michigan. Again, the fact that few Sates choose to maintain elite law schools raises a strong inference that there is nothing compelling about the elite status.

IV

The interest in remaining elite and exclusive that the majority thinks so obviously critical requires the use of admissions "standards" than, in turn, create the Law School's "need" to discriminate on the basis of race. The majority errs, however, because race-neutral alternatives must only be "workable," and do "about as well" *in vindicating the compelling state interest.* The Court never explicitly holds that the Law School's desire to retain the status quo in "academic selectivity" is itself a compelling state interest, and, as I have demonstrated, it is not. Therefore, the Law School should be forced to choose between its classroom aesthetic and its exclusionary admissions system—it cannot have it both ways.

With the adoption of different admissions methods, such as accepting all students who meet minimum qualifications, the Law School could achieve its vision of the racially aesthetic student body without the use of racial discrimination. The Law School concedes this, but the Court holds, implicitly and under the guise of narrow tailoring, that the Law School has a compelling state interest in doing what it wants to do. I cannot agree.

The Court bases its unprecedented deference to the Law School—a deference antithetical to strict scrutiny—on an idea of "educational autonomy" grounded in the First Amendment. In my view, there is no basis for a right of public universities to do what would otherwise violate the Equal Protection Clause. In my view, "[i]t is the business" of this Court to explain itself when it cites provisions of the Constitution to invent new doctrines— including the idea that the First Amendment authorizes a public university to do what would otherwise violate the Equal Protection Clause. The majority fails in its summary effort to prove this point.

The Court's deference to the Law School's conclusion that its racial experimentation leads to educational benefits will, if adhered to, have serious collateral consequences. The Court relies heavily on social science evidence to justify its deference. The Court never acknowledges, however, the growing evidence that racial (and other sorts of) heterogeneity actually impairs learning among black students.

Moreover one would think, in light of the Court's decision in *United States v. Virginia* [text, p. 820] that before being given license to use racial discrimination, the Law School would be required to radically reshape its admissions process, even to the point of sacrificing some elements of its character. In *Virginia*, where the standard of review dictated that greater flexibility be granted to VMI's educational policies than the Law School deserves here, this

Court gave no deference. Apparently where the status quo being defended is that of the elite establishment—here the Law School—rather than a less fashionable Southern military institution, the Court will defer without serious inquiry and without regard to the applicable legal standard.

Virginia is also notable for the fact that the Court relied on the "experience" of formerly single-sex institutions, such as the service academies, to conclude that admission of women to VMI would be "manageable." Today, however, the majority ignores the "experience" of those institutions that have been forced to abandon explicit racial discrimination in admissions. The sky has not fallen at Boalt Hall at the University of California, Berkeley, for example. Prior to Proposition 209's adoption of Cal. Const., Art. 1, § 31(a), which bars the State from "grant[ing] preferential treatment . . .on the basis of race . . . in the operation of . . . public education," Boalt Hall enrolled 20 blacks and 28 Hispanics in its first-year class for 1996. In 2002, without deploying express racial discrimination in admissions, Boalt's entering class enrolled 14 blacks and 36 Hispanics.

V

Putting aside the absence of any legal support for the majority's reflexive deference, there is much to be said for the view that the use of tests and other measures to "predict" academic performance is a poor substitute for a system that gives every applicant a chance to prove he can succeed in the study of law. The rallying cry that in the absence of racial discrimination in admissions there would be a true meritocracy ignores the fact that the entire process is poisoned by numerous exceptions to "merit." For example, in the national debate on racial discrimination in higher education admissions, much has been made of the fact that elite institutions utilize a so-called "legacy" preference to give the children of alumni an advantage in admissions. This, and other, exceptions to a "true" meritocracy give the lie to protestations that merit admissions are in fact the order of the day at the Nation's universities. The Equal Protection Clause does not, however, prohibit the use of unseemly legacy preferences or many other kinds of arbitrary admissions procedures.

[N]o modern law school can claim ignorance of the poor performance of blacks, relatively speaking, on the Law School Admissions Test (LSAT). Nevertheless, law schools continue to use the test and then attempt to "correct" for black underperformance by using racial discrimination in admissions so as to obtain their aesthetic student body. The Law School's continued adherence to measures it knows produce racially skewed results is not entitled to deference by this Court. Having decided to use the LSAT, the Law School must accept the constitutional burdens that come with this decision. The Court will not even deign to make the Law School try other methods, however, preferring instead to grant a 25-year license to violate the Constitution.

VI

The absence of any articulated legal principle supporting the majority's principal holding suggests another rationale. I believe what lies beneath the Court's decision today are the benighted notions that one can tell when racial discrimination benefits (rather than hurts) minority groups, and that racial discrimination is necessary to remedy general societal ills. This Court's precedents supposedly settled both issues, but clearly the majority still cannot commit to the principle that racial classifications are *per se* harmful and that almost no amount of benefit in the eye of the beholder can justify such classifications. [N]owhere in any of the filings in this Court is any evidence that the purported "beneficiaries" of this racial discrimination prove themselves by performing at (or even near) the same level as those students who receive no preferences.

The silence in this case is deafening to those of us who view higher education's purpose as imparting knowledge and skills to students, rather than a communal, rubber stamp, credentialing process. The Law School is not looking for those students who, despite a lower LSAT score or undergraduate grade point average, will succeed in the study of law. The Law School seeks only a facade — it is sufficient that the class looks right, even if it does not perform right.

The Law School tantalizes unprepared students with the promise of a University of Michigan degree and all the opportunities that it offers. These overmatched students take the bait, only to find that they cannot succeed in the cauldron of competition. And this mismatch crisis is not restricted to elite institutions. While these students may graduate with law degrees, there is no evidence that they have received a qualitatively better legal education (or become better lawyers) than if they had gone to a less "elite" law school for which they were better prepared. And the aestheticists will never address the real problems facing "underrepresented minorities," instead continuing their social experiments on other people's children.

It is uncontested that each year, the Law School admits a handful of blacks who would be admitted in the absence of racial discrimination. Who can differentiate between those who belong and those who do not? The majority of blacks are admitted to the Law School because of discrimination, and because of this policy all are tarred as undeserving. This problem of stigma does not depend on determinacy as to whether those stigmatized are actually the "beneficiaries" of racial discrimination. When blacks take positions in the highest places of government, industry, or academia, it is an open question today whether their skin color played a part in their advancement.

Finally, the Court's disturbing reference to the importance of the country's law schools as training grounds meant to cultivate "a set of leaders with legitimacy in the eyes of the citizenry," through the use of racial discrimination deserves discussion. As noted earlier, the Court has soundly rejected the remedying of societal discrimination as a justification for governmental use of race. For those who believe that every racial disproportionality in our society is caused by some kind of racial discrimination, there can be no distinction between remedying societal discrimination and erasing racial disproportionalities in the country's leadership caste.

VII

As the foregoing makes clear, I believe the Court's opinion to be, in most respects, erroneous, I do, however, find two points on which I agree. First,

I not that the issue of unconstitutional racial discrimination among the groups the Law School prefers is not presented in this case, because petitioner has never argued that the Law School engages in such a practice, and the Law School maintains that it does not. I join the Court's opinion insofar as it confirms that this type of racial discrimination remains unlawful.

The Court also holds that racial discrimination in admissions should be given another 25 years before it is deemed no longer narrowly tailored to the Law School's fabricated compelling state interest. While I agree that in 25 years the practices of the Law School will be illegal, they are, for the reasons I have given, illegal now. The majority does not and cannot rest its time limitation on any evidence that the gap in credentials between black and white students is shrinking or will be gone in that timeframe. Nor is the Court's holding that racial discrimination will be unconstitional in 25 years made contingent on the gap closing in that time.

CHIEF JUSTICE REHNQUIST, with whom JUSTICE SCALIA, JUSTICE KENNEDY, and JUSTICE THOMAS join, dissenting.

I do not believe, that the University of Michigan Law School's (Law School) means are narrowly tailored to the interest it asserts. The Law School claims it must take the steps it does to achieve a "critical mass" of underrepresented minority students. But its actual program bears no relation to this asserted goal. Stripped of its "critical mass" veil, the Law School's program is revealed as a naked effort to achieve racial balancing. Before the Court's decision today, we consistently applied the same strict scrutiny analysis regardless of the government's purported reason for using race and regardless of the setting in which race was being used. Although the Court recites the language of our strict scrutiny analysis, its application of that review is unprecedented in its deference.

In practice, the Law School's program bears little or no relation to its asserted goal of achieving "critical mass." Respondents explain that the Law School seeks to accumulate a "critical mass" of *each* underrpresented minority group. But the record demonstrates that the Law School's admissions practices with respect to these groups differ dramatically and cannot be defended under any consistent use of the term "critical mass." From 1995–2000, the Law School admitted between 1,130 and 1,310 students. Of those, between 13 and 19 were Native American, between 91 and 108 were African-Americans, and between 47 and 56 were Hispanic. If the Law School is admitting between 91 and 108 African-Americans in order to achieve "critical mass," thereby preventing African-American students from feeling "isolated or like spokespersons fro their race," one would think that a number of the same order of magnitude would be necessary to accomplish the same purpose for Hispanics and Native Americans. Similarily, even if all of the Native American applicants admitted in a given year matriculate, which the record demonstrates is not at all the case, how can this possibly constitute a "critical mass" of Native Americans in a class of over 350 students? But respondents offer no race-specific reasons for such disparities. Instead, they simply emphasize the importance of achieving "critical mass," without any explanation of why that concept is applied differently among the three underrepresented minority groups. These different numbers, moreover, come only as a result of substantially different treatment among the three underrepresented minority groups.

These statistics have a significant bearing on petitioner's case. Respondents have never offered any race-specific arguments explaining why significantly more individuals from one underrepresented minority group are needed in order to achieve "critical mass" or further student body diversity. But the Law School's disparate admissions practices with respect to these minority groups demonstrate that its alleged goal of "critical mass" is simply a sham. Surely strict scrutiny cannot permit these sort of disparities without at least some explanation. Only when the "critical mass" label is discarded does a likely explanation for these numbers emerge. [T[he correlation between the percentage of the Law School's pool of applicants who are members of the three minority groups and the percentage of the admitted applicants who are members of these same groups is far too precise to be dismissed as merely the result of the school paying "some attention to [the] numbers." As the tables below show, from 1995 through 2000 the percentage of admitted applicants who were members of these minority groups closely tracked the percentage of individuals in the school's applicant pool who were from the same groups. [The statistical tables are omitted.]

The tight correlation between the percentage of applicants and admittees of a given race, must result from careful race based planning by the Law School. It suggests a formula for admission based on the aspirational assumption that all applicants are equally qualified academically, and therefore that the proportion of each group admitted should be the same as the proportion of that group in the applicant pool.

I do not believe that the Constitution gives the Law School such free rein in the use of race. The Law School has offered no explanation for its actual admissions practices and, unexplained, we are bound to conclude that the Law School has managed its admissions program, not to achieve a "critical mass," but to extend offers of admission to members of selected minority groups in proportion to their statistical representation in the applicant pool. But this is precisely the type of racial balancing that the Court itself calls "patently unconstitutional."

Finally, I believe that the Law School's program fails strict scrutiny because it is devoid of any reasonably precise time limit on the Law School's use of race in admissions. The Court suggests a possible 25-year limitation on the Law School's current program. Respondents, on the other hand, remain more ambiguous, explaining that "the Law School of course recognizes that race-conscious programs must have reasonable durational limits, and the Sixth Circuit properly found such a limit in the Law School's resolve to cease considering race when genuine race-neutral alternatives become available." These discussions of a time limit are the vaguest of assurances. In truth, they permit the Law School's use of racial preferences on a seemingly permanent basis. Thus, an important component of strict scrutiny — that a program be limited in time — is casually subverted.

JUSTICE KENNEDY, dissenting.

The separate opinion by JUSTICE POWELL in *Regents of Univ. of Cal. v. Bakke* is based on the principle that a university admission program may take account of race as one, nonpredominant factor in a system designed to consider each applicant as an individual, provided the program can meet the test of strict scrutiny by the judiciary. This is a unitary formulation. If strict scrutiny is abandoned or manipulated to distort its real and accepted meaning, the Court lacks authority to approve the use of race even in this modest, limited way. The opinion by JUSTICE POWELL in my view states the correct rule for resolving this case. The Court, however, does not apply strict scrutiny. By trying to say otherwise, it undermines both the test and its own controlling precedents.

JUSTICE POWELL's approval of the use of race in university admissions reflected a tradition, grounded in the First Amendment, of acknowledging a university's conception of its educational mission. Our precedents provide a basis for the Court's acceptance of a university's considered judgment that racial diversity among students can further its educational task, when supported by empirical evidence.

It is unfortunate, however, that the Court takes the first part of JUSTICE POWELL's rule but abandons the second. Having approved the use of race as a factor in the admissions process, the majority proceeds to nullify the essential safeguard JUSTICE POWELL insisted upon as the precondition of the approval. The safeguard was rigorous judicial review, with strict scrutiny as the controlling standard. The Court confuses deference to a university's definition of its educational objective with deference to the implementation of this goal. In the context of university admissions the objective of racial diversity can be accepted based on empirical data known to us, but deference is not to be given with respect to the methods by which it is pursued.

The Court, in a review that is nothing short of perfunctory, accepts the University of Michigan Law School's assurances that its admissions process meets with constitutional requirements. The majority fails to confront the reality of how the Law School's admissions policy is implemented. The dissenting opinion by THE CHIEF JUSTICE, which I join in full, demonstrates beyond question why the concept of critical mass is a delusion used by the Law School to mask its attempt to make race an automatic factor in most instances and to achieve numerical goals indistinguishable from quotas. It remains to point out how critical mass becomes inconsistent with individual consideration in some more specific aspects of the admissions process.

About 80 to 85 percent of the places in the entering class are given to applicants in the upper range of Law School Admissions Test scores and grades. An applicant with these credentials likely will be admitted without consideration of race or ethnicity. With respect to the remaining 15 to 20 percent of the seats, race is likely outcome determinative for many members of minority groups. That is where the competition becomes tight and where any given applicant's chance of admission is far smaller if he or she lacks minority status. At this point the numerical concept of critical mass has the real potential to compromise individual review.

The Law School has not demonstrated how individual consideration is, or can be, preserved at this stage of the application process given the instruction to attain what it calls critical mass. In fact the evidence shows otherwise. There was little deviation among admitted minority students during the years from 1995 to 1998. The percentage of enrolled minorities fluctuated only by 0.3%, from 13.5% to 13.8%. The number of minority students to whom offers were extended varied by just a slightly greater magnitude of 2.2%, from the high of 15.6% in 1995 to the low of 13.4% in 1998.

The District Court relied on this uncontested fact to draw an inference that the Law School's pursuit of critical mass mutated into the equivalent of a quota. Admittedly, there were greater fluctuations among enrolled minorities in the preceding years, 1987–1994, by as much as 5 or 6%. The percentage of minority offers, however, at no point fell below 12%, historically defined by the Law School as the bottom of its critical mass range. The greater variance during the earlier years, in any event, does not dispel suspicion that the school engaged in racial balancing.

The Law School has the burden of proving, in conformance with the standard of strict scrutiny, that it did not utilize race in an unconstitutional way. At the very least, the constancy of admitted minority students and the close correlation between the racial breakdown of admitted minorities and the composition of the applicant pool require the Law School either to produce a convincing explanation or to show it has taken adequate steps to ensure individual assessment. The Law School does neither.

The obvious tension between the pursuit of critical mass and the requirement of individual review increased by the end of the admissions season. Most of the decisions where race may decide the outcome are made during this period. The admissions officers consulted the daily reports which indicated the composition of the incoming class along racial lines. The consultation of daily reports during the last stages in the admissions process suggests there was no further attempt at individual review save for race itself. The admissions officers could use the reports to recalibrate the plus factor given to race depending on how close they were to achieving the Law School's goal of critical mass. The bonus factor of race would then become divorced from individual review; it would be premised instead on the numerical objective set by the Law School. The Law School made no effort to guard against this danger. It provided no guidelines to its admissions personnel on how to reconcile individual assessment with the directive to admit a critical mass of minority students. The admissions program could have been structured to eliminate at least some of the risk that the promise of individual evaluation was not being kept.

It is difficult to assess the Court's pronouncement that race-conscious admissions programs will be unnecessary 25 years from now. If it is intended to mitigate the damage the Court does to the concept of strict scrutiny, neither petitioners nor other rejected law school applicants will find solace in knowing the basic protection put in place by Justice Powell will be suspended for a full quarter of a century. Deference is antithetical to strict scrutiny, not consistent with it.

As to the interpretation that the opinion contains its own self-destruct mechanism, the majority's abandonment of strict scrutiny undermines this objective. Were the courts to apply a searching standard to race-based admissions schemes, that would force educational institutions to seriously explore race-neutral alternatives. The Court, by contrast, is willing to be satisfied by the

Law School's profession of its own good faith. Other programs do exist which will be more effective in bringing about the harmony and mutual respect among all citizens that our constitutional tradition has always sought. They, and not the program under review here, should be the model, even if the Court defaults by not demanding it. It is regrettable the Court's important holding allowing racial minorities to have their special circumstances considered in order to improve their educational opportunities is accompanied by a suspension of the strict scrutiny which was the predicate of allowing race to be considered in the first place. For these reasons, though I reiterate my approval of giving appropriate consideration to race in this one context, I must dissent in the present case.

GRATZ v. BOLLINGER

539 U.S. 244, 123 S. Ct. 2411, 156 L. Ed. 2d 257 (2003)

CHIEF JUSTICE REHNQUIST delivered the opinion of the Court.

We granted certiorari in this case to decide whether "the University of Michigan's use of racial preferences in undergraduate admissions violate[s] the Equal Protection Clause of the Fourteenth Amendment, Title VI of the Civil Rights Act of 1964 or 42 U. S. C. § 1981." Because we find that the manner in which the University considers the race of applicants in its undergraduate admissions guidelines violates these constitutional and statutory provisions, we reverse that proportion of the District Court's decision upholding the guidelines.

Petitioners Jennifer Gratz and Patrick Hamacher both applied for admission to the University of Michigan's (University College of Literature, Science, and the Arts (LSA) as residents of the State of Michigan. Both petitioners are Caucasian. Gratz, who applied for admission for the fall of 1995 was notified in January of that year that a final decision regarding her admission had been delayed until April. This delay was based upon the University's determination that, although Gratz was "well qualified," she was "less competitive than the students who ha[d] been admitted on first review." Gratz was notified in April that the LSA was unable to offer her admission. She enrolled in the University of Michigan at Dearborn, from which she graduated in the spring of 1999.

Hamacher applied for admission to the LSA for the fall of 1997. A final decision as to his application was also postponed because, though his "academic credentials [were] in the qualified range, they [were] not at the level needed for first review admission." Hamacher's application was subsequently denied in April 1997, and he enrolled at Michigan State University.

In October 1997, Gratz and Hamacher filed a lawsuit in the United States District Court for the Eastern District of Michigan against the University of Michigan, the LSA, James Duderstadt, and Lee Bollinger. Petitioners' complaint was a class-action suit alleging "violations and threatened violations of the rights of the plaintiffs and the class they represent to equal protection of the laws under the Fourteenth Amendment . . ., and for racial discrimination in violation of 42 U. S. C. §§ 1981, 1983, and 2000d *et seq.*" Petitioners sought, *inter alia*, compensatory and punitive damages for past violations, declaratory relief finding that respondents violated petitioners' "rights to nondiscriminatory treatment," an injunction prohibiting respondents from "continuing to discriminate on the basis of race in violation of the Fourteenth Amendment," and an order requiring the LSA to offer Hamacher admission as a transfer student.

The District Court granted petitioners' motion for class certification. The certified class consisted of "those individuals who applied for and were not granted admission to the College of Literature, Science and the Arts of the University of Michigan for all academic years from 1995 forward and who are members of those racial or ethnic groups, including Caucasian, that defendants treated less favorably on the basis of race in considering their application for admission." And Hamacher, whose claim the District Court found to challenge a " 'practice of racial discrimination pervasively applied on a classwide basis,' " was designated as the class representative.

The University has changed its admissions guidelines a number of times during the period relevant to this litigation, and we summarize the most significant of these changes briefly. The University's Office of Undergraduate Admissions (OUA) oversees the LSA admissions process. In order to promote consistency in the review of the large number of applications received, the OUA uses written guidelines for each academic year. Admissions counselors make admissions decisions in accordance with these guidelines.

OUA considers a number of factors in making admissions decisions, including high school grades, standardized test scores, high school quality, curriculum strength, geography, alumni relationships, and leadership. OUA also considers race. During all periods relevant to this litigation, the University has considered African-Americans, Hispanics, and Native Americans to be "underrepresented minorities," and it is undisputed that the University admits "virtually every qualified . . . applicant" from these groups.

[The Court's discussion of the admissions process prior to 1989 which is not at issue on appeal is omitted.]

Beginning with the 1998 academic year, the OUA dispensed with [prior admissions procedures] in favor of a "selection index," on which an applicant could score a maximum of 150 points. This index was divided linearly into ranges generally calling for admissions dispositions as follows: 100–150 (admit); 95–99 (admit or postpone); 90–94 (postpone or admit); 75–89 (delay or postpone); 74 and below (delay or reject).

Each application received points based on high school grade point average, standardized test scores, academic quality of an applicant's high school, strength or weakness of high school curriculum, in-state residency, alumni relationship, personal essay, and personal achievement or leadership. Of particular significance here, under a "miscellaneous" category, an applicant was entitled to 20 points based upon his or her membership in an underrepresented racial or ethnic minority group. The University explained that the " 'development of the selection index for admissions in 1998 changed only the mechanics, not the substance of how race and ethnicity were considered in admissions.' "

During 1999 and 2000, the OUA used the selection index, under which every applicant from an underrepresented racial or ethnic minority group was awarded 20 points. Starting in 1999, however, the University established an Admissions Review Committee (ARC), to provide an additional level of consideration for some applications. Under the new system, counselors may, in their discretion, "flag" an application for the ARC to review after determining that the applicant (1) is academically prepared to succeed at the University, (2) has achieved a minimum selection index score, and (3) possesses a quality or characteristic important to the University's composition of its freshman class, such as high class rank, unique life experiences, challenges, circumstances, interests or talents, socioeconomic disadvantage, and underrepresented race, ethnicity, or geography. After reviewing "flagged" applications, the ARC determines whether to admit, defer, or deny each applicant.

The District Court began its analysis by reviewing this Court's decision in *Bakke*. Although the court acknowledged that no decision from this Court since *Bakke* has explicitly accepted the diversity rationale discussed by JUSTICE POWELL, it also concluded that this Court had not, in the years since *Bakke*, rule out such a justification for the use of race. The District Court concluded that respondents and their *amici curiae* had presented "solid evidence" that a racially and ethnically diverse student body produces significant educational benefits such that achieving such a student body constitutes a compelling government interest.

The court next considered whether the LSA's admissions guidelines were narrowly tailored to achieve that interest. Again relying on JUSTICE POWELL's opinion in *Bakke*, the District Court determined that the admission program the LSA began using in 1999 is a narrowly tailored means of achieving the University's interest in the educational benefits that flow from a racially and ethnically diverse student body. The court emphasized that the LSA's current program does not utilize rigid quotas or seek to admit a predetermined number of minority students. The award of 20 points for membership in an underrepresented minority group, in the District Court's view, was not the functional equivalent of a quota because minority candidates were not insulated from review by virtue of those points. Likewise, the court rejected the assertion that the LSA's program operates like the two-track system JUSTICE POWELL found objectionable in *Bakke* on the grounds that LSA applicants are not cometing for different groups of seats. The court also dismissed petitioners' assertion that the LSA's current system is nothing more than a means by which to achieve racial balancing. The court explained that the LSA does not seek to achieve a certain proportion of minority students, let alone a proportion that represents the community.

The District Court found the admissions guidelines the LSA used from 1995 through 1998 to be more problematic. In the court's view, the University's prior practice of "protecting" or "reserving" seats for underrepresented minority applicants effectively kept nonprotected applicants from competing for those slots. This system, the court concluded, operated as the functional equivalent of a quota and rand afoul of JUSTICE POWELL's opinion in *Bakke*. Based on these findings, the court granted petitioners' motion for summary judgment with respect to the LSA's admission programs in existence from 1995 through 1998, and respondents' motion with respect to the LSA's admission programs for 1999 and 2000. Accordingly, the District Court denied petitioners' request for injunctive relief. The District Court issued an order consistent with its rulings and certified two questions for interlocutory appeal to the Sixth Circuit pursuant. Both parties appealed aspects of the District Court's rulings, and the Court of Appeals heard the case en banc on the same day as *Grutter v. Bollinger*. The Sixth Circuit later issued an opinion in *Gutter*, upholding the admissions program used by the University of Michigan Law School, and the petitioner in that case sought a writ of certiorari from this Court. Petitioners asked this Court to grant certiorari in this case as well, despite the fact that the Court of Appeals had not yet rendered a judgment, so that this Court could address the constitutionality of the consideration of race in university admissions in a wider range of circumstances. We did so.

II

We consider first whether petitioners have standing to seek declaratory and injunctive relief, and, finding that they do, we next consider the merits of their claims.

A

Although no party has raised the issue, JUSTICE STEVENS argues that petitioners lack Article III standing to seek injunctive relief with respect to the University's use of race in undergraduate admissions. He first contends that because Hamacher did not "actually appl[y] for admission as a transfer student [,] [h]is claim of future injury is at best 'conjectural or hypothetical' rather than 'real and immediate.' " But whether Hamacher "actually applied" for admission as a transfer student is not determinative of his ability to seek injunctive relief in this case. If Hamacher had submitted a transfer application and had been rejected, he would still need to allege an intent to apply again in order to seek prospective relief. If JUSTICE STEVENS means that because Hamacher did not apply to transfer, directly conflicts with the finding of fact entered by the District Court that Hamacher "intends to transfer to the University of Michigan when defendants cease the use of race as an admission preference." It is well established that intent may be relevant to standing in an Equal Protection challenge.

In bringing his equal protection challenge against the University's use of race in undergraduate admissions, Hamacher alleged that the University had denied him the opportunity to compete for admission on an equal basis. When Hamacher applied to the University as a freshman applicant, he was denied admission even though an underrepresented minority applicant with his qualifications would have been admitted. After being denied admission, Hamacher demonstrated that he was "able and ready" to apply as a transfer student should the University cease to use race in undergraduate admissions. He therefore has standing to seek prospective relief with respect to the University's continued use of race in undergraduate admissions.

JUSTICE STEVENS raises a second argument as to standing. He contends that the University's use of race in undergraduate transfer admissions differs from its use of race in undergraduate freshman admissions, and that therefore Hamacher lacks standing to represent absent class members challenging the latter. As an initial matter, there is a question whether the relevance of this variation, if any, is a matter of Article III standing at all or whether it goes to the propriety of class certification pursuant to Federal Rule of Civil Procedure 23(a). The parties have not briefed the question of standing versus adequacy, however, and we need not resolve the question today: Regardless of whether the requirement is deemed one of adequacy or standing, it is clearly satisfied in this case.

In sum, the same set of concerns is implicated by the University's use of race in evaluating all undergraduate admissions applications under the guidelines. We therefore agree with the District Court's carefully considered decision to certify this class-action challenge to the University's consideration of race in undergraduate admissions. Indeed, class action treatment was particularly important in this case because "the claims of the individual students run the risk of becoming moot" and the "[t]he class action vehicle . . . provides a mechanism for ensuring that a justiciable claim is before the Court." Thus, we think it clear that Hamacher's personal stake, in view of both his past injury and the potential injury he faced at the time of certification, demonstrates that he may maintain this class-action challenge to the University's use of race in undergraduate admissions.

B

Petitioners argue, first and foremost, that the University's use of race in undergraduate admissions violates the Fourteenth Amendment. Specifically, they contend that this Court has only sanctioned the use of racial classifications to remedy identified discrimination, a justification on which respondents have never relied. Petitioners further argue that "diversity as a basis for employing racial references is simply too open-ended, ill-defined, and indefinite to constitute a compelling interest capable of supporting narrowly-tailored means." But for the reasons set forth today in *Grutter v. Bollinger*, the Court has rejected these arguments of petitioners. Petitioners alternatively argue that even if the University's interest in diversity can constitute a compelling state interest, the District Court erroneously concluded that the University's use of race in its current freshman admissions policy is narrowly tailored to achieve such an interest.

Petitioners argue that the guidelines the University began using in 1999 do not "remotely resemble the kind of consideration of race and ethnicity that JUSTICE POWELL endorsed in *Bakke*." Respondents reply that the University's current admissions program is narrowly tailored and avoids the problems of the Medical School of the University of California at Davis program "hews closely" to both the admissions program described by JUSTICE POWELL as well as the Harvard College admissions program that he endorsed. Specifically, respondents contend that the LSA's policy provides the individualized consideration that "JUSTICE POWELL considered a hallmark of a constitutionally appropriate admissions program." For the reasons set out below, we do not agree. We find that the University's policy, which automatically distributes 20 points, or one-fifth of the points needed to guarantee admission, to every single "underrepresented minority" applicant solely because of race, is not narrowly tailored to achieve the interest in educational diversity that respondents claim justifies their program. JUSTICE POWELL's opinion in *Bakke* emphasized the importance of considering each particular applicant as an individual, assessing all of the qualities that individual possesses, and in turn, evaluating that individual's ability to contribute to the unique setting of higher education. The admissions program JUSTICE POWELL described, however, did not contemplate that any single characteristic automatically ensured a specific and identifiable contribution to a university's diversity. Instead, under the approach JUSTICE POWELL described, each characteristic of a particular applicant was to be considered in assessing the applicant's entire application.

The current LSA policy does not provide such individualized consideration. The LSA's policy automatically distributes 20 points to every single applicant from an "underrepresented minority" group, as defined by the University. The only consideration that accompanies this distribution of points is a factual review of an application to determine whether in individual is a member of one of these minority groups. Moreover, unlike JUSTICE POWELL's example, where the race of a "particular black applicant" could be considered without being decisive, the LSA's automatic distribution of 20 points has the effect of making "the factor of race . . . decisive" for virtually every minimally qualified underrepresented minority applicant.

Even if student C's "extraordinary artistic talent" rivaled that of Monet or Picasso, the applicant would receive, at most, five points under the LSA's system. At the same time, every single underrepresented minority applicant, including students A and B, would automatically receive 20 points for submitting and application. Clearly, the LSA's system does not offer applicants the individualized selection process described in Harvard's example. Instead of considering how the differing backgrounds, experiences, and characteristics of students A, B, and C might benefit the University, admissions counselors reviewing LSA applications would simply award both A and B 20 points because their applications indicate that they are African-American, and student C would receive up to 5 points for his "extraordinary talent."

Respondents emphasize the fact that the LSA has created the possibility of an applicant's file being flagged for individualized consideration by the ARC. We think that the flagging program only emphasizes the flaws of the University's system as a whole when compared to that described by JUSTICE POWELL. Again, students A, B, and C illustrate the point. First, student A would never be flagged. This is because as the University has conceded, the effect of automatically awarding 20 points is that virtually every qualified applicant "with promise of superior academic performance," would certainly fit this description. Thus, the result of the automatic distribution of 20 points is that the University would never consider student A's individual background, experiences, and characteristics to assess his individual "potential contribution to diversity." Instead, every applicant like student A would simply be admitted.

It is possible that students B and C would be flagged and considered as individuals. This assumes that student B was not already admitted because of the automatic 20-point distribution, and that student C could muster at least 70 additional points. But the fact that the "review committee can look at the applications individually and ignore the points," once an application is flagged, is of little comfort under our strict scrutiny analysis. The record does not reveal precisely how many applications are flagged for this individualized consideration, but it is undisputed that such consideration is the exception and not the rule in the operation of the LSA's admissions program. Additionally, this individualized review is only provided *after* admissions counselors automatically distribute the University's version of a "plus" that makes race a decisive factor for virtually every minimally qualified underrepresented minority applicant.

Respondents contend that "[t]he volume of applications and the presentation of applicant information make it impractical for [LSA] to use the . . .admissions system" upheld by the Court today in *Grutter*. But the fact that the implementation of a program capable of providing individualized consideration might present administrative challenges does not render constitutional an otherwise problematic system. Nothing in JUSTICE POWELL's opinion in *Bakke* signaled that a university may employ whatever means it desires to achieve the state's goal of diversity without regard to the limits imposed by our strict scrutiny analysis.

We conclude, therefore, that because the University's use of race in its current freshman admissions policy is not narrowly tailored to achieve respondents' asserted compelling interest in diversity, the admissions policy violates the Equal Protection Clause of the Fourteenth Amendment. We further find that the admissions policy also violates Title VI and 42 U. S. C. § 1981. Accordingly, we reverse that portion of the District Court's decision granting respondents summary judgment with respect to liability and remand the case for proceedings consistent with this opinion.

JUSTICE O'CONNOR, concurring.

Unlike the law school admission policy the Court upholds today in *Grutter v. Bollinger*, the procedures employed by the University of Michigan's (University) Office of Undergraduate Admissions do not provide for a meaningful individualized review of applicants. The law school considers the various diversity qualifications of each applicant, including race, on a case-by-case basis. By contrast, the Office of Undergraduate Admissions relies on the selection index to assign *every* underrepresented minority applicant the same, *automatic* 20-point bonus without consideration of the particular background, experiences, or qualities of each individual applicant. And this mechanized selection index score, by and large, automatically determines the admissions decision for each applicant. The selection index thus precludes admission counselors from conducting the type of individualized consideration the Court's opinion in Grutter requires: consideration of each applicant's individualized qualifications, including the contribution each individual's race or ethnic identity will make to the diversity of the student body, taking into account diversity within and among all racial and ethnic groups.

Although the Office of Undergraduate Admission does assign 20 points to some "soft" variables other than race, the points available for other diversity contributions, such as leadership and service, personal achievement, and geographic diversity, are capped at much lower levels. Even the most outstanding national high school leader could never receive more than five points for his or her accomplishments — a mere quarter of the points automatically assigned to an underrepresented minority solely based on the facto of his or her race. Of course, as JUSTICE POWELL made clear in *Bakke*, a university need not "necessarily accor[d]" all diversity factors "the same weight," and the "weight attributed to a particular quality may vary from year to year depending on the 'mix' both of the student body and the applicants for the in-coming class." But the selection index by setting up automatic, predetermined point allocations for the soft variables, ensures that the diversity contributions of applicants cannot be individually assessed. This policy stands in sharp contrast to the law school's admissions plan, which enables admissions officers to make nuanced judgments with respect to the contribution each applicant is likely to make to the diversity of the incoming class. *See Grutter v. Bollinger*.

The only potential source of individualized consideration appears to be the Admissions Review Committee. The evidence in the record, however, reveals very little about how the review committee actually functions. And what evidence there is indicates that the committee is a kind of afterthought, rather than an integral component of a system of individualized review. Given these circumstances, the addition of the Admissions Review Committee to the admissions process cannot offset the apparent absence of individualized consideration from the Office of Undergraduate Admissions' general practices.

For these reasons, the record before us does not support the conclusion that the University of Michigan's admissions program for its College of Literature, Science, and the Arts — to the extent that it considers race — provides the necessary individualized consideration. The University, of course, remains free to modify its system so that it does so. But the current system, as I understand it, is a nonindividualized, mechanical one. As a result, I join the Court's opinion reversing the decision of the District Court.

JUSTICE THOMAS, concurring.

I join the Court's opinion because I believe it correctly applies our precedents, including today's decision in *Grutter v. Bollinger*. For similar reasons to those given in my separate opinion in that case, however, I would hold that a State's use of racial discrimination in higher education admissions is categorically prohibited by the Equal Protection Clause.

JUSTICE BREYER, concurring in the judgment.

I concur in the judgment of the Court though I do not join its opinion. I join JUSTICE O'CONNOR's opinion except insofar as it joins that of the Court. I join Part I of JUSTICE GINSBURG's dissenting opinion, but I do not dissent from the Court's reversal of the District Court's decision. I agree with JUSTICE GINSBURG that, in implementing the Constitution's equality instruction, government decisionmakers may properly distinguish between policies of inclusion and exclusion, for the former are more likely to prove consistent with the basic constitutional obligation that the law respect each individual equally.

JUSTICE STEVENS, with whom JUSTICE SOUTER joins, dissenting.

Petitioners seek forward-looking relief enjoining the University of Michigan from continuing to use its current race-conscious freshman admissions policy. Yet, unlike the plaintiff in *Grutter v. Bollinger*, the petitioners in this case had already enrolled at other schools before they filed their class-action complaint in this case. Neither petitioner was in the process of reapplying to Michigan through the freshman admissions process at the time this suit was field, and neither has done so since. There is a total absence of evidence that either petitioner would receive any benefit from the prospective relief sought by their lawyer. While some unidentified members of the class may very well have standing to seek prospective relief, it is clear that neither petitioner does. Our precedents therefore require dismissal of the action. Michigan submitted that Hamacher suffered " 'no threat of imminent future injury' " given that he had already enrolled at another undergraduate institution. The District Court rejected Michigan's contention, concluding that Hamacher had standing to seek injunctive relief because the complaint alleged that he intended to apply to Michigan as a transfer student. The District court, accordingly, certified Hamacher as the sole class representative and limited the claims of the class to injunctive and declaratory relief.

When petitioners sought certiorari from this Court, Michigan did not cross-petition for review of the District Court's judgment concerning the admissions policies that Michigan had in place when Gratz and Hamacher applied for admission in 1994 and 1996 respectively. Accordingly, we have before us only that portion of the District Court's judgment that upheld Michigan's new freshman admissions policy.

Both Hamacher and Gratz, of course, have standing to seek damages as compensation for the alleged wrongful denial of their respective applications under Michigan's old freshman admissions system. However, like the plaintiff in *Los Angeles v. Lyons*, 461 U.S. 95 (1983), who had standing to recover damages caused by chokeholds administered by the police in the past but had no standing to seek injunctive relief preventing future chokeholds, petitioners' past injuries do not give them standing to obtain injunctive relief to protect third parties from similar harms. To seek forward-looking, injunctive relief, petitioners must show that they face an imminent threat of future injury. This they cannot do given that when this suit was filed, neither faced an impending threat of future injury based on Michigan's new freshman admissions policy. Petitioner's attempt to base Hamacher's standing in this suit on a hypothetical transfer application fails for several reasons. First, there is no evidence that Hamacher ever actually applied for admission as a transfer student at Michigan. His claim of future injury is at best "conjectural or hypothetical" rather than "real and immediate." Second, as petitioners' counsel conceded at oral argument, the transfer policy is not before this Court and was not addressed by the District Court. Third, the differences between the freshman and the transfer admissions policies make it extremely unlikely, at best, that an injunction requiring respondents to modify the freshman admissions program would have any impact on Michigan's transfer policy. This is especially true in light of petitioners' unequivocal disavowal of any request for equitable relief that would totally preclude the use of race in the processing of all admissions applications.

Because Michigan's transfer policy was not challenged by petitioners and is not before this Court, we do not know whether Michigan would defend its transfer policy on diversity grounds, or whether it might try to justify its transfer policy on other grounds, such as a remedial interest. Because the transfer policy has never been the subject of this suit, we simply do not know (1) whether Michigan would defend its transfer policy on "diversity" grounds or some other grounds, or (2) how the absence of a point system in the transfer policy might impact a narrow tailoring analysis of that policy. To have standing, it is elementary that the petitioners' own interests must be implicated. Because neither petitioner has a personal stake in this suit for prospective relief, neither has standing.

It is true that the petitioners' complaint was filed as a class action and that Hamacher had been certified as the representative of a class, some of whose members may well have standing to challenge the LSA freshman admissions program that is presently in effect. But the fact that a suit may be a class action. . .adds nothing to the question of standing, for even named plaintiffs who represent a class must allege and show that they personally have been injured, not that injury has been suffered by other, unidentified members of the class to which they belong and which they purport to represent. *Simon v. Eastern Ky. Welfare Rights Organization.* While unidentified members of the class he represents may well have standing to challenge Michigan's current freshman admission policy, Hamacher cannot base his standing to sue on injuries suffered by other members of the class.

As this case comes to us, our precedents leave us no alternative but to dismiss the writ for lack of jurisdiction. Neither petitioner has a personal stake in the outcome of the case, and neither has standing to seek prospective relief on behalf of unidentified class members who may or may not have standing to litigate on behalf of themselves. Accordingly, I respectfully dissent.

JUSTICE SOUTER, with whom JUSTICE GINSBURG joins as to Part II, dissenting.

I

The Court's finding of Article III standing rests on two propositions: first, that both the University of Michigan's undergraduate college's transfer policy and its freshman admissions policy seek to achieve student body diversity through the "use of race," and second, that Hamacher has standing to challenge the transfer policy on the grounds that diversity can never be a "compelling state interest" justifying the use of race in any admissions decision, freshman or transfer. The Court concludes that, because Hamacher's argument, if successful, would seal the fate of both policies, his standing to challenge the transfer policy also allows him to attack the freshman admissions policy. I agree with JUSTICE STEVENS's critique that the Court thus ignores the basic principle of Article III standing that a plaintiff cannot challenge a government program that does not apply to him.

But even on the Court's indulgent standing theory, the decision should not go beyond a recognition that diversity can serve as a compelling state interest justifying race-conscious decisions in education. Since, as the Court says, "petitioners did not raise a narrow tailoring challenge to the transfer policy," our decision in *Grutter* is fatal to Hamacher's sole attack upon the transfer policy, which is the only policy before this Court that he claims aggrieved him. Hamacher's challenge to that policy having failed, his standing is presumably spent. The further question whether the freshman admissions plan is narrowly tailored to achieving student body diversity remains legally irrelevant to Hamacher and should await a plaintiff who is actually hurt by it.

II

The cases now contain two pointers toward the line between the valid and the unconstitutional in race-conscious admissions schemes. *Grutter* reaffirms the permissibility of individualized consideration of race to achieve a diversity of students, at least where race is not assigned a preordained value in all cases. On the other hand, JUSTICE POWELL's opinion in *[Bakke]*, rules out a racial quota or set-aside, in which race is the sole fact of eligibility for certain places in a class. Although the freshman admissions system here is subject to argument on the merits, I think it is closer to what *Grutter* approves than to what *Bakke* condemns, and should not be held unconstitutional on the current record.

The record does not describe a system with a quota like the one struck down in *Bakke*, which "insulate[d]" all nonminority candidates from competition from certain seats. The *Bakke* plan "focused *solely* on ethnic diversity" and effectively told nonminority applicants that "[n]o matter how strong their qualifications, quantitative and extracurricular, including their own potential for contribution to educational diversity, they are never afforded the chance to compete with applicants from the preferred groups for the [set-aside] special admissions seats."

The plan here, in contrast, lets all applicants compete for all places and values an applicant's offering for any place not only on grounds of race, but on grades, test scores, strength of high school, quality of course of study, residence, alumni relationships, leadership, personal character, socioeconomic disadvantage, athletic ability, and quality of a personal essay. A nonminority applicant who scores highly in these other categories can readily garner a selection index exceeding that of a minority applicant who gets the 20-point bonus.

Subject to one qualification to be taken up below, this scheme of considering, through the selection index system, all of the characteristics that the college thinks relevant to student diversity for every one of the student places to be filled fits JUSTICE POWELL's description of a constitutionally acceptable program: one that considers "all pertinent elements of diversity in light of the particular qualifications of each applicant" and places each element "on the same footing for consideration, although not necessarily according them the same weight.

The one qualification to this description of the admissions process is that membership in an underrepresented minority is given a weight of 20 points on the 150-point scale. On the face of things, however, this assignment of specific points does not set race apart from all other weighted considerations. Nonminority students may receive 20 points for athletic ability, socioeconomic disadvantage, attendance at a socioeconomically disadvantaged or predominantly minority high school, or at the Provost's discretion; they may also receive 10 points for being residents of Michigan, 6 for residence in an underrepresented Michigan county, 5 for leadership and service, and so on.

The Court nonetheless finds fault with a scheme that "automatically" distributes 20 points to minority applicants. The objection goes to the use of points to quantify and compare characteristics, or to the number of points awarded due to race, but on either reading the objection is mistaken.

The very nature of a college's permissible practice of awarding value to racial diversity means that race must be considered in a way that increases some applicants' chances for admission. Since college admission is not left entirely to inarticulate intuition, it is hard to see what is inappropriate in assigning some stated value to a relevant characteristic, whether it be reasoning ability, writing style, running speed, or minority race. JUSTICE POWELL's plus factors necessarily are assigned some values. The college simply does by a numbered scale what the law school accomplishes in its "holistic review," *Grutter*; the distinction does not imply that applicants to the undergraduate college are denied individualized consideration or a fair chance to compete on the basis of all the various merits their applications may disclose.

Nor is it possible to say that the 20 points convert race into a decisive factor comparable to reserving minority places as in *Bakke*. The present record obviously shows that nonminority applicants may achieve higher selection point totals than minority applicants owing to characteristics other than race, and the fact that the university admits "virtually every qualified underrepresented minority applicant," may reflect nothing more than the likelihood that very few qualified minority applicants apply, as well as the possibility that self-selection results in a strong minority applicant pool. It suffices for me, as it did for the District Court, that there are no *Bakke*-like set-asides and that consideration of an applicant's whole spectrum of ability is no more ruled out by giving 20 points for race than by giving the same points for athletic ability or socioeconomic disadvantage.

Any argument that the "tailoring" amounts to a set-aside, then, boils down to the claim that a plus factor of 20 points makes some observers suspicious, where a factor of 10 points might not. But suspicion does not carry petitioners' ultimate burden of persuasion in this constitutional challenge, and it surely does not warrant condemning the college's admissions scheme on this record. Because the District Court (correctly, in my view) did not believe that the specific point assignment was constitutionally troubling, it made only limited and general findings on other characteristics of the university's admissions practice, such as the conduct of individualized review by the Admissions Review Committee. As the Court indicates, we know very little about the actual role of the review committee. The point system cannot operate as a *de facto* set-aside if the greater admissions process, including review by the committee, results in individualized review sufficient to meet the Court's standards. Since the record is quiet, if not silent, on the case-by-case work of the committee, the Court would be on more defensible ground by vacating and remanding for evidence about the committee's specific determinations.

Without knowing more about how the Admissions Review Committee actually functions, it seems especially unfair to treat the candor of the admissions plan as an Achilles' heel. Drawing on admissions systems used at public universities in California, Florida, and Texas, the United States contends that Michigan could get student diversity in satisfaction of its compelling interest by guaranteeing admission to a fixed percentage of the top students from each high school in Michigan. The "percentage plans" are just as race conscious as the point scheme (and fairly so), but they get their racially diverse results without saying directly what they are doing or why they are doing it. In contrast, Michigan states its purpose directly and, if this were a doubtful case for me, I would be tempted to give Michigan an extra point of its own for its frankness. Equal protection cannot become an exercise in which the winners are the ones who hide the ball.

III

If this plan were challenged by a plaintiff with proper standing under Article III, I would affirm the judgment of the District Court granting summary judgment to the college. As it is, I would vacate the judgment for lack of jurisdiction, and I respectfully dissent.

JUSTICE GINSBURG, with whom JUSTICE SOUTER joins, dissenting.*

I

Educational institutions, the Court acknowledges, are not barred from any and all consideration of race when making admissions decisions. *See Grutter v. Bollinger*. But the Court once again maintains that the same standard of review controls judicial inspection of all official race classifications. This insistence on "consistency," *Adarand*, would be fitting were our Nation free of the vestiges of rank discrimination long reinforced by law. But we are not far distant from an overtly discriminatory past, and the effects of centuries of law-sanctioned inequality remain painfully evident in our communities and schools.

In the wake "of a system of racial caste only recently ended," large disparities endure. Unemployment, poverty, and access to health care vary disproportionately by race. Neighborhoods and schools remain racially divided. African-American and Hispanic children are all too often educated in poverty-stricken and underperforming institutions. Adult African-Americans and Hispanics generally earn less than whites with equivalent levels of education. Equally credentialed job applicants receive different receptions depending on their race. Irrational prejudice is still encountered in real estate markets and consumer transactions.

The Constitution instructs all who act for the government that they may not "deny to any person . . . the equal protection of the laws." In implementing this equality instruction, as I see it, government decisionmakers may properly distinguish between policies of exclusion and inclusion. Actions designed to

* JUSTICE BREYER joins Part I of this opinion.

burden groups long denied full citizenship stature are not sensibly ranked with measures taken to hasten the day when entrenched discrimination and its after effects have been extirpated.

Our jurisprudence ranks race a "suspect" category, "not because [race] is inevitably an impermissible classification, but because it is one which usually, to our national shame, has been drawn for the purpose of maintaining racial inequality." But where race is considered "for the purpose of achieving equality," no automatic proscription is in order.

The mere assertion of a laudable governmental purpose, of course, should not immunize a race-conscious measure from careful judicial inspection. Close review is needed "to ferret out classifications in reality malign, but masquerading as benign," *Adarand*, and to "ensure that preferences are not so large as to trammel unduly upon the opportunities of others or interfere too harshly with legitimate expectations of persons in once preferred groups."

II

Examining in this light the admissions policy employed by the University of Michigan's College of Literature, Science, and the Arts (College), and for the reasons well stated by JUSTICE SOUTER, I see no constitutional infirmity. Like other top-ranking institutions, the College has many more applicants for admission than it can accommodate in an entering class. Every applicant admitted under the current plan, petitioners do not here dispute, is qualified to attend the College. The racial and ethnic groups to which the College accords special consideration (African-Americans, Hispanics, and Native-Americans) historically have been relegated to inferior status by law and social practice; their members continue to experience class-based discrimination to this day. There is no suggestion that the College adopted its current policy in order to limit or decrease enrollment by any particular racial or ethnic group, and no seats are reserved on the basis of race. Nor has there been any demonstration that the College's program unduly constricts admissions opportunities for students who do not receive special consideration based on race.

The stain of generations of racial oppression is still visible in our society, and the determination to hasten its removal remains vital. One can reasonably anticipate, therefore, that colleges and universities will seek to maintain their minority enrollment—and the networks and opportunities thereby opened to minority graduates—whether or not they can do so in full candor through adoption of affirmative action plans of the kind here at issue. Without recourse to such plans, institutions of higher education may resort to camouflage. If honesty is the best policy, surely Michigan's accurately described, fully disclosed College affirmative action program is preferable to achieving similar numbers through winks, nods, and disguises.

NOTES

1. ***Student diversity.*** The Court in *Grutter* holds that Michigan has a compelling interest in attaining a diverse student body. What makes this

interest compelling? Robert C. Post, *Foreword: Fashioning the Legal Constitution: Culture, Courts, and Law*, 117 HARV. L. REV. 4 (2005) argues: "Although *Grutter* casts itself as merely endorsing Justice Powell's opinion in *Bakke*, *Grutter's* analysis of diversity actually differs quite dramatically from Powell's. In contrast to Powell's opinion in *Bakke*, *Grutter* does not offer an account of the intrinsic value of the educational process. It instead conceives of education as instrumental for the achievement of extrinsic social goods like professionalism, citizenship, or leadership. It follows from this way of conceptualizing the problem that the Law School can have a compelling interest in using diversity to facilitate the attainment of these social goods *only* if there is an independently compelling interest in the actual attainment of these goods. *Grutter's* justifications for diversity thus potentially reach far more widely than do Powell's." Professor Post claims that unlike Powell's emphasis on educational benefits in *Bakke*, in *Grutter* diversity functions as " 'a code word for representation in enjoyment of social goods by major ethnic groups who have some claim to past mistreatment.' " *Id.* at 64. Has the Court now implicitly accepted "remedying societal discrimination" as a compelling interest? Has the Court adopted forward looking integration as a compelling interest? Consider the following: "So, the most important function of affirmative action recognized in *Grutter* is forward-looking: to make possible the effective functioning of lending American institutions that have been historically segregated (or stratified) by integrating them at all levels." Kenneth Karst, *The Revival of Forward-Looking Affirmative Action*, 104 COLUM. L. REV. 68, 71.

> *Grutter* transforms the diversity rationale in the course of adopting it, expanding the concept of diversity so that it explicitly embraces antisubordination values. Yet the Court masks the antisubordination rationale for its decision and imposes practical requirements on the admissions process designed to limit its institutional expression. At every turn, *Grutter* deploys anticlassification discourse to limit and to disguise the expression of antisubordination values. The case demonstrates the Court's deep desire to shield interpretation of the Equal Protection Clause from concerns about groups, social structure, caste, and subordination. In other words, *Grutter* fervently warns against interpreting the Equal Protection Clause in terms of the very values the decision in fact vindicates. Protestations to the contrary notwithstanding, *Grutter* embodies an antisubordination understanding of the clause.

Reva B. Siegel, *Equality Talk: Antisubordination and Anticlassification Values in Constitutional Struggles over Brown*, 117 HARV. L. REV. 1470, 1539–40 (2004).

2. *Elite institutions.* Are Justices Thomas and Scalia correct that the Court is elevating maintenance of an elite law school to a compelling interest? Must a law school be forced to sacrifice the educational benefits of a more qualified student body in order to obtain the educational benefits of diversity, and vice-versa? Consider the following: "If it were indeed true that racial diversity could somehow be achieved without reference to race, there would be no need to choose between racial diversity and admissions selectivity. Yet under current conditions, color-blindness would force exactly that choice. Thomas and Scalia recognized and confronted that dilemma. They were understandably reluctant to advocate resegregation, so instead they attacked academic selectivity. The full measure of their disdain for 'elite' institutions became evident in their scorn for those who run them. For Thomas and Scalia, law school administrators are mere 'aestheticists,' unconcerned with students' 'knowledge and skills,' seeking only the 'facade' of a class that 'looks right, even if it does not perform right.' " John C. Jefferies, Jr., Bakke *Revisited*, 55 SUP. CT. REV. 1, 17 (2003).

3. *Narrow tailoring.* Professor Post lists four requirements that the Court uses in *Grutter-Gratz* in determining if a diversity plan is narrowly tailored: "A race-based affirmative action program (1) must 'not unduly harm members of any racial group'; (2) can be implemented only if there has been a 'serious, good faith consideration of workable race-neutral alternatives that will achieve the diversity the university seeks'; (3) 'must be limited in time'; and (4) must afford each applicant 'truly individualized consideration.' " 117 HARV. L. REV. at 67. The requirement of individualized consideration is the most important. But Professor Post contends "that the Court never makes clear whether the Michigan undergraduate program fails the individualized consideration because it quantifies the contribution of race to diversity by 'a specific and identifiable' measure or instead because the program employs a measure that is 'decisive.' " *Id.* at 70–71. Do you agree that, after *Gratz*, "[r]acial inequalities can be addressed but only where the relevance of racial differences is masked"? *Id.* at 75. If the Court defers to the University in defining its academic mission, why can't the University define "critical mass" in terms of "specific," "identifiable," even "decisive" numbers?

4. *Affirmative action in 25 years.* Do you agree with Justice Thomas that the Court held that affirmative action in public higher education will be unconstitutional in 25 years? Or is the 25-year statement merely aspirational? Even if Justice Thomas is correct that there is a 25-year sunset provision for affirmative action, is such an outcome consistent with the Court's holding that diversity is a compelling interest? Wouldn't a time limit be consistent only if the compelling interest in such a program were remedial? *See* Post, 117 HARV. L. REV. at 67 n.306 ("[T]he justification of diversity, unlike remedy, has no built-in time horizon; if diversity is necessary for the quality of education, it is necessary at any and all times.").

5. *Benign classifications, strict scrutiny, and deference.* In *Bakke*, four Justices argued that intermediate scrutiny is the proper standard to review benign racial classifications. In *Gratz*, Justice Ginsburg (joined by Justice Souter) also argued for a standard lower than strict scrutiny: "Actions designed to burden groups long denied full citizenship stature are not sensibly ranked with measures taken to hasten the day when entrenched discrimination and its effects have been extirpated."

While the Court in *Grutter* accepted strict scrutiny as the appropriate standard of review, the dissenting Justices and commentators noted that the Court's deferential application of the standard seemed contrary to the idea of strict scrutiny. *See, e.g.,* Wendy Parker, *Connecting the Dots: Grutter, School*

Desegregation, and Federalism, 45 WM. & MARY L. REV. 1691, 1693 (2004) ("[I]n holding that diversity could be a compelling governmental interest, the majority took the school officials at their word when the school officials said they needed racial diversity for educational reasons and, in holding that the program was narrowly tailored, the majority gave the defendants the benefit of the doubt in the operation of the racial preferences."); *Grutter*, 539 U.S. at 380 (Rehnquist, C.J., dissenting) ("Although the Court recites the language of our strict scrutiny analysis, its application of that review is unprecedented in its deference.").

Do you think the Court correctly applied strict scrutiny in *Grutter*? Or has the Court moved closer to the position of the dissenters in *Bakke* by applying a strict scrutiny in a manner that resembles a less strict standard of review? Consider the following:

> One interpretation of this deference, however, is that it revives the distinction between benign and odious uses of race in the application of strict scrutiny—a distinction more explicitly drawn in Justice Ginsburg's dissenting opinion in *Gratz*. Under this interpretation, the use of race is benign when educational decisionmakers exercise their judgment to serve the larger integrative and democratic values of society. The educational judgment of university officials merits deference because their holistic assessment of candidates assures all applicants that their potential contributions will be thoughtfully considered, and avoids ignoble social purposes, such as arbitrary racial balancing, and the consequences of an ill-designed social program that perpetuates stereotypes. Explicit considerations of race are broadly legitimating when they apply on an individual basis, encompass an expansive group of beneficiaries (including whites), undergo reevaluation from time to time, and galvanize more systematic interventions to make race-neutral alternatives available.

Lani Guinier, *Admissions Rituals as Political Acts: Guardians at the Gates of Our Democratic Ideas*, 117 HARV. L. REV. 113, 180–181 (2003).

6. *Social pressures.* The former president of the University of Michigan, Lee C. Bollinger, says a decision was made "to discuss this issue in all its dimensions fully and frankly in public as well as in the courtroom." Lee C. Bollinger, *A Comment on* Grutter *and* Gratz v. Bollinger, 103 COLUM. L. REV. 1589, 1592 (2003). This included an effort to emphasize what was at stake in the litigation by actively involving individuals and groups in the litigation. *Id.* at 1594–95. The result was dramatic. There were 102 amicus briefs filed in the cases, 83 supporting the University. One hundred twenty-four House members and 13 Senators joined briefs supporting the University (no members of Congress joined the challengers). Twenty-three states and the Virgin Islands joined one of three briefs arguing for the University; only Florida supported petitioner. Ninety-one colleges and universities and the major educational associations supported the University with none opposing affirmative action. Big business, labor, civil rights groups and a coalition of former high-ranking officers and civilians leaders of the military filed amicus briefs supporting the University. While the Bush administration argued that the

Michigan plan constituted an unconstitutional quota, the President announced that he strongly supports racial diversity in higher education. The Justice Department brief was limited to attacking the University plan, but did not challenge racial diversity as a compelling interest. Neil Devins, *Explaining* Grutter v. Bollinger, 152 U. PA. L. REV. 347, 367 (2003) summarizes this public involvement: "Social and political forces beating against the Court in the *Grutter* and *Gratz* cases include the amicus filings by both interest groups and lawmakers, the Bush administration's decision to embrace racial diversity as an important and legitimate governmental end, the continuing salience of race discrimination in judicial confirmation politics, the ouster of Senate majority leader Trent Lott for making racially insensitive comments, and the awareness of the difficulties of implementing a Court ruling or severely limiting race-conscious admissions." What effect do you think these social and political forces had on the Court? What effect should they have?

[E] RACE-CONSCIOUS REDISTRICTING

The 1990 census required many states to redistrict because of population shifts during the preceding decade. The U.S. Department of Justice and a variety of interest groups, some racially constituted or oriented, succeeded in having a number of districts drawn with a majority in each district of racial groups that otherwise constituted a minority in the state (so-called majority-minority districts). The Justice Department's encouraging of "majority-minority" districting by the states has been said by some political analysts to have been a significant factor in the surprising showing of the Republican Party in elections for the House of Representatives in 1994. By blocking together voters with a strong Democratic leaning, the theory goes, redistricting can leave open several other districts for capture by Republicans.

The Justice Department acted under the Voting Rights Act of 1965, which prohibits the use of any electoral practice or procedure which "results in a denial or abridgement" of the right to vote on the bases of race or color. Section 2 guarantees that racial minorities shall have the same opportunity as other members of the electorate "to participate in the political process and to elect members of their choice." As a result of 1982 Amendments, a violation of § 2 can be proven by discriminatory effects alone but § 2 rejects a right to proportional representation. Section 5 of the Act requires that political jurisdictions covered under the Act (because of a history of low minority voting participation and the historic use of certain voting tests and devices) must secure preclearance of changes in voting laws or procedures from the Attorney General of the United States or the United States District Court for the District of Columbia.

In an article frequently cited by the Supreme Court in the following cases, Professors Richard H. Pildes and Richard G. Niemi, *Expressive Harms, "Bizarre Districts," and Voting Rights: Evaluating Election-District Appearances After* Shaw v. Reno, 92 MICH. L. REV. 483 (1993), note the fertile ground for legal controversy: "Voting-rights controversies today arise from two alternative conceptions of representative government colliding like tectonic plates. On one side is the long-standing Anglo-American commitment to organizing political representation around geography. On the other side is the increasing power of the Voting Rights of 1965 (VRA), which organizes political representation around the concept of interest."

***Shaw v. Reno*, 509 U.S. 630 (1993).** The Supreme Court held that a state congressional districting scheme would be invalid as "racial gerrymandering" if the shape of the district were "unexplainable on grounds other than race." North Carolina had created two "bizarre" districts, each of which contained a majority of black voters. One ran along the I-95 corridor almost the whole width of the state and the other was a "hook" shape in the eastern part of the state. Justice O'Connor for the majority wrote that "segregation of voters" was an entirely separate constitutional violation from vote dilution and that "reapportionment is one area in which appearances do matter." The Court concluded that a plaintiff "may state a claim by alleging that the legislation, though race-neutral on its face, rationally cannot be understood as anything other than an effort to separate voters into different districts on the basis of race, and that the separation lacks sufficient justification." Justices White, Blackmun, Stevens, and Souter dissented.

***Miller v. Johnson*, 515 U.S. 900 (1995).** In the Supreme Court's first vindication of a *Shaw* claim, the Court invalidated Georgia's 1990 redistricting plan. The state legislature twice was denied preclearance under § 5 of the Voting Rights Act for previous redistricting plans, and enacted a plan that created three majority-minority districts. The plan significantly increased the number of counties that were split between districts and included one majority-minority district that stretched from Atlanta to Savannah, picking up the black populations of each city while including smaller tracts of rural areas between. The Court held that to succeed in a *Shaw* claim, a plaintiff must show that race was the legislature's predominant factor" for drawing districts by proving that the legislature "subordinated traditional race-neutral distracting principles to racial considerations." Although the shape of the district may be relevant to this inquiry, an unusual shape is not required to succeed in defeating a redistricting plan. The Court held that race was the predominant intent of the Georgia legislature in drawing its plan, and Georgia could not overcome the application of strict scrutiny.

Justice O'Connor concurred, noting that she viewed the majority's standard as "demanding," but that the "vast majority" of congressional districts would be upheld under the majority's standard even though race may have been considered in the redistricting. Justice Ginsburg, joined by Justices Stevens, Breyer, and Souter, dissented, arguing that the districts in question were not oddly shaped and that the legislature adhered to traditional districting principles. The dissent also distinguished race-conscious redistricting purposes, states "assemble people in groups" instead of "assign[ing] voters to districts based on merit or achievement."

***Shaw v. Hunt*, 517 U.S. 899 (1996).** On remand in the original *Shaw v. Reno* case, the district court had held the two North Carolina districts to be justified as attempts by the state to comply with the Voting Rights Act. On appeal, the Supreme Court first held that only the two appellants who live in District 12 had standing to challenge their district. The remaining appellants, who did not reside in either of the challenged districts, lacked standing. Although accepting that the districting plan reflected urban-rural considerations, political party considerations, and protection of incumbents, the Court concluded: "Race was the criterion that, in the State's view, could not be compromised; respecting communities of interest and protecting Democratic incumbents came into play only after the race-based decision had been made." Because race was the "predominant" consideration, subordinating race-neutral districting policies, strict scrutiny applied.

The Court then held that District 12 was not justified by any compelling state interest in eradicating the effects of past discrimination because the district court had found that past discrimination did not actually precipitate the use of race in the redistricting plan. The state also argued that District 12 was created in an effort to satisfy both §§ 2 & 5 of the Voting Rights Act. The plan could not be justified as a necessary remedy for compliance with § 5 because that section itself is "ameliorative" and not racially discriminatory. Assuming that avoiding minority vote dilution under § 2 liability, the minority group must be shown to be "geographically compact," and the Court did not see that District 12 contained a "geographically compact" population of any race.

***Bush v. Vera*, 517 U.S. 952 (1996).** Justice O'Connor, for a plurality joined by Chief Justice Rehnquist and Justice Kennedy, held that three majority-minority Texas congressional districts were unconstitutional under *Shaw I and Miller*. While Justice O'Connor noted that strict scrutiny did not "apply merely because redistricting is performed with consciousness of race" and did not "apply to all cases of intentional creation of majority-minority districts," this was a "mixed motive case," and after a detailed review, Justice O'Connor concluded that race predominated over traditional districting criteria such as incumbency protection, and therefore strict scrutiny was triggered.

The state asserted three compelling interests to overcome strict scrutiny. First, the state claimed that drawing majority-minority districts was required by § 2 of the Voting Rights Act ("VRA"). Justice O'Connor, while assuming without deciding that compliance with § 2 was a compelling interest concluded that the plan was not narrowly tailored because the districts did not comply with a requirement that districts be "compact" as a precondition for § 2 claims. Second, the state argued that it had a compelling interest in remedying past discrimination. Justice O'Connor rejected this interest because it was essentially the same as the first—VRA § 2 dealt with vote dilution which was the only type of past discrimination sought to be remedied by the state. Finally, Justice O'Connor rejected the state's claim that VRA § 5 constituted a compelling interest because § 5 required only "that the minority's opportunity to elect representatives of its choice not be diminished," and drawing additional majority-minority districts was not required to avoid "retrogressoin."

Justice O'Connor, the author of the plurality opinion, took the unusual step of writing a separate concurring opinion to add that, in her judgment, compliance with VRA § 2 was indeed a compelling state interest and § 2 was fully consistent with *Shaw I*. Justice Thomas, with Justice Scalia, concurred in the judgment, but would hold that "[s]trict scrutiny applies to all governmental classifications based on race." Justice Kennedy also concurred separately.

Justice Stevens, with Justices Ginsburg and Breyer dissenting, argued that race was not the predominant legislative motive, and pointed out that a legislature's use of racial data in districting where race highly correlates with political affiliation "is neither irrational, nor invidious," and thus not "unjustified." Justice Stevens also argued that the Court's jurisprudence in this area "threatens to create harms more significant than any suffered by the individual plaintiffs challenging these districts." Justice Sourter, joined by Justices Ginsburg and Breyer dissenting, criticized the Court for its "failure to devise a concept of *Shaw* harm that distinguishes those who are injured from those who are not" and for "its inability to provide any manageable standard to distinguish forbidden districting conduct from the application of traditional state districting principles and the plans that they produce."

***Abrams v. Johnson*, 521 U.S. 74 (1997).** The Court upheld the electoral district lines for Georgia's congressional delegation that had been devised on remand from *Miller*. The district court had originally deferred to the Georgia Legislature to draw a new plan, but the legislature was unable to reach agreement. The court then drew up its own plan, containing only one majority black district. On review, the Supreme Court found that the revised plan violated neither the terms of the Voting Rights Act of 1965 nor the Constitution's one person, one vote requirement. The majority reasoned that while ordinarily congressional districts are to be designed to achieve population equality "as nearly as practicable," slight deviations may be allowed under certain circumstances. The district court had justified such deviations on the state's "strong historical preference" for not splitting counties outside the Atlanta area. The district court also focused on the need to maintain core districts and communities of interest. After noting the legislature's inability to develop a plan, the Supreme Court stated that "[t]he District Court was left to embark on a delicate task with limited legislative guidance. The court was most careful to take into account traditional state districting factors, and it remained sensitive to the constitutional requirement of equal protection of the laws."

Justice Breyer, in dissent and speaking on behalf of four justices, concluded that the district court should have maintained two, rather than only one, "majority-minority" districts. The decision, he stated, "departs dramatically from the Georgia Legislature's preference for two such district plans."

***Hunt v. Cromartie*, 526 U.S. 541 (1999).** The Supreme Court, for the third time in six years, reviewed a claim that the North Carolina legislature had racially gerrymandered the Twelfth Congressional District. In response to *Shaw II*, North Carolina in 1997 enacted a new districting plan. The new District 12, was shorter but retained a "snakelike" shape. Blacks now accounted for 47% of the district's total population; 43% of the voting age population and, 46% of registered voters. Voters filed suit against state officials alleging that the new District 12 was again a product of unconstitutional racial gerrymandering. Both parties moved for summary judgment. The district court 2-1 granted plaintiff's summary judgement motion and enjoined elections under the plan. It held that "the uncontroverted material facts" showed that the districting was "facially race-driven" and therefore violated equal protection. The Supreme Court reversed.

The Supreme Court held that, although the State did not contest the plaintiff's circumstantial evidence supporting an inference of a racial motivation, a genuine dispute of material fact existed as to the legislature's motivation for drawing the district lines, making summary judgment inappropriate. Justice Thomas, for the Court, stated that "[t]he legislature's motivation is itself a factual question." The State had argued that the reconfiguration was based on political, and not racial, motives and supported its argument with affidavits from legislators who stated that the district lines were drawn in order to "preserve the existing partisan balance in the State's congressional delegation . . . ." The State had also introduced the affidavit of an expert who analyzed election result data for precincts in District 2 and those surrounding it, including all 234 boundary segments of District 12. He found a correlation between party preference and race composition which supported both the political and racial motivation arguments. The expert further analyzed "divergent boundary segments," which are those areas where the concentration of blacks was higher inside the District while Democrats were greater outside and vice versa. He concluded that because the legislature had included the precincts with a higher concentration of Democrats more often than the black precincts, the data supported the political motivation theory more than the racial theory.

In deciding a motion for summary judgement, a court must examine the evidence in the light most favorable to the non-moving party when deciding whether a genuine dispute of material fact exists. The Supreme Court held that the District Court was required to accept the State's political motivation explanation as true and should have decided that a genuine dispute existed as to the legislature's motivation. The Supreme Court has held that political gerrymandering is constitutional "even if it so happens that the most loyal Democrats happen to be black Democrats and even if the State were conscious of that fact." The evidence was susceptible to two different interpretations and it was up to the trier of fact, not the trial court, to decide between them.

***Easley v. Cromartie*, 532 U.S. 234 (2001).** After remand of *Hunt*, the three-judge district court, following a three-day trial, again held (over a dissent) that the legislature had unconstitutionally drawn District 12's new 1997 boundaries because race was the predominant factor behind those boundaries. The district court relied on three factors: the district's shape, its splitting of towns and counties, and its high African-American voting population. The Supreme Court, in a 5-4 decision, reversed, finding that this factual finding was clearly erroneous. Justice Breyer, writing for the majority, held: "Given the undisputed evidence that racial identification is highly correlated with political affiliation in North Carolina, these facts [relied upon by the district court] in and of themselves cannot, as a matter of law, support the District Court's judgement." He concluded that "[t]he evidence taken together, however, does not show that racial considerations predominated in the drawing of District 12's boundaries. That is because race in this case correlates closely with political behavior. The basic question is whether the legislature drew District 12's because of race rather than political behavior (coupled with traditional, non-racial districting considerations)." He found that the "demanding" burden of proof on one challenging a district's boundaries on racial grounds could not be deemed to have been satisfied.

In dissent, Justice Thomas, joined by Justices Scalia and Kennedy and the Chief Justice, found that "[i]n light of the direct evidence of racial motive and the inferences that may be drawn from the circumstantial evidence, I am satisfied that the District Court's finding was permissible, even if not compelled by the record."

Redistricting cases and equal protection. Like *Baker v. Carr, Shaw I* established a cause of action under the Equal Protection Clause. In racial districting cases alleging vote dilution, the plaintiffs typically allege that they have been harmed through the diminution of their voting strength. But *Shaw* is a race case in a voting context, not a voting case. "*Shaw* turns out not really to be a case about the right to vote, at least not the right the Court had identified in its earlier decisions. Rather, *Shaw* forms an integral piece of an ongoing struggle between the Supreme court and the political branches over how to address the enduring problems of race in America." Pamela Karlan, *All Over the Map: The Supreme Court's Voting Trilogy,* 1993 SUP. CT. REV. 254, 246. See Pamela S. Karlan and Daryl J. Levinson, *Why Voting Is Different*, 84 CALIF. L. REV. 1201, 1202 (1996), arguing "that the Court's attempt to integrate voting rights law into its more general approach to affirmative action is both misguided and incoherent."

Melissa L. Saunders, *Reconsidering* Shaw: *The* Miranda *of Race-Conscious Districting*, 109 YALE L.J. 1603, 1605 (2000), suggests that "[t]he *Shaw* doctrine, is not only inconsistent with the Court's traditional equal protection jurisprudence, but is also incomprehensible." She claims that "[t]he difficulty with *Shaw* and its progeny, from the standpoint of traditional equal protection jurisprudence, is that these cases permit courts to declare laws unconstitutional under the Equal Protection Clause in the absence of evidence that the laws subject any identifiable class of persons to special disadvantage." *Id.* at 1610. Professors Saunders argues that the cases reflect a "prophylactic" rule "that overprotects individual constitutional rights in some cases in order to ensure adequate protection of those rights across a range of cases." *Id.* at 1606. *See also* Melissa L. Saunders, *Equal Protection, Class Legislation, and Colorblindness*, 96 MICH. L. REV. 245, 326 (1997) ("For all its moral attractiveness though, the notion that the Equal Protection Clause gives every person a substantive right not to be dealt with by the state on the basis of race remains flatly inconsistent with the original understanding." She argues that a racially discriminatory effect is needed for presumptive unconstitutionality).

Identifying harm. Piles & Niemi, 92 MICH. L. REV. at 506–07, referred to the constitutional injury in *Shaw I* as "expressive harm."

> An expressive harm is one that results from the ideas or attitudes expressed through a governmental action, rather than from the more tangible or material consequences the action brings about. Public policies can violate the Constitution not only because they bring about concrete costs, but because the very meaning they convey demonstrates inappropriate respect for relevant public values. On this unusual conception of constitutional harm, when a governmental action expresses disrespect for such values, it can violate the Constitution.

The authors note that "the harm is not concrete to particular individuals, singled out for distinct burdens" but rather is general or social. See Samuel

Issacharoff & Thomas C. Goldstein, *Identifying the Harm in Racial Gerrymandering Claims*, 1 MICH. J. RACE & L. 47 (1996), who discuss the various theories of constitutional harm used in the racial districting cases, especially Justice O'Connor's concern with the "extreme" use of race in districting.

The lack of individualized injury presented difficult standing problems for the plaintiffs, on which Justice Stevens has focused. Indeed, it could be argued that the harm identified by the Court principally falls on either the minority voters who are pejoratively lumped together or on voters outside the district who otherwise would be included. But the plaintiffs with standing in all these cases have been white voters included in the challenged district. How are they harmed?

Race-consciousness plus. In *Bush v. Vera*, the Court makes it clear that simple race-conscious districting is not sufficient to trigger strict scrutiny. Why isn't the purpose to classify on a racial basis sufficient to trigger the heightened standard? It has been suggested that if *Shaw* were "a run-of-the mill equal protection case," strict scrutiny "would apply not just to 'bizarre' districts, but 'all the way down.' If a plaintiff could successfully show that a compact district had been drawn for racial purposes . . . the usual equal protection rules would apply [i.e., strict scrutiny]." Alexander Aleinikoff & Samuel Issacharoff, *Race and Redistricting: Drawing Constitutional Lines After* Shaw v. Reno, 92 MICH. L. REV. 588, 606–07 (1993). But the authors warn that "[r]edistricting is an area in which classifications of all kinds — most notably partisan, socioeconomic, racial, and ethnic are the lifeblood of the process." *Id.* at 607. "Even assuming the validity of long-term aspirations toward a constitutional norm of color blindness, the fact remains that this society can no longer tolerate an absence of minority representation in its elite institutions, be they professional academies or legislative halls. Accordingly, [only] excessive or unalterable race-based decisionmaking will be deemed to inflict dignitary harm on affected individuals and to threaten systemic legitimacy because of its inherent divisiveness." *Id.* at 650.

In *Miller*, the Court focuses on whether race is the *predominant* motivation for the districting, subordinating traditional race-neutral districting principles. What are "traditional" districting principles? Is race, ethnicity or national origin a traditional districting principle? A legitimate proxy for traditional principles? What role does "bizarreness" play? It has been argued that "*Miller*'s 'predominant factor' test is, if anything, more indeterminant than *Shaw*'s 'bizarreness' standard." Pamela Karlan, *Still Hazy After All These Years: Voting Rights in the Post-Shaw Era,* 26 CUMB. L. REV. 287, 288 (1995).

In traditional equal protection law, a plaintiff does not have to prove race was a "predominant motivation" for strict scrutiny to apply. Why is racial districting different? "One would have to be not only colorblind, but deaf and dumb as well, not to recognize that questions of racial justice and issues with a racial valence form a significant part of the current legislative agenda. [I]f courts were to apply strict scrutiny to every districting decision in which [race was a predominant factor] they would have to scrutinize not only a few majority-black congressional districts, but many majority-white districts as well, since 'substantial' numbers of voters are moved into or out of those districts on the basis of race. That courts are unwilling to engage in that kind of wholesale scrutiny rests on assumptions every bit as 'offensive and demeaning' as those the Supreme Court beholds in others. The Court lacked a majority for the proposition that all majority-black districts are constitutionally suspect." *Id.* at 303–05. But see Richard Pildes, *Principled Limitations on Racial and Partisan Redistricting*, 106 YALE L.J. 2505, 2506 (1997) (arguing that "[w]hatever the merits of motive-based approaches in mediating group conflicts in other constitutional contexts, in the redistricting arena [the predominant factor] approach will not be capable of sustaining constitutional doctrine in a coherent, administerable, or useful form.").

Applying strict scrutiny. Absent identifiable past discrimination to be remedied, the focus of justifying excessive race conscious districting centers on § 2 and § 5 of the 1965 Voting Rights Act. It has been suggested that, "[n]either *Miller* nor *Shaw*, however, really explicates the role of the Act beyond making two obvious points: a state cannot rely on an unconstitutional or erroneous interpretation of the Act and preclearance cannot foreclose a constitutional challenge." Karlan, 26 CUMB. L. REV. at 307. Given the whipsawing between political interests and the Justice Department on the one side and the "activist federal judiciary" on the other, Professor Karlan concludes: "There is now no realistic way for a jurisdiction to avoid costly and divisive litigation." Peter J. Rubin, *Reconnecting Doctrine and Purpose: A Comprehensive Approach to Strict Scrutiny After* Adarand *and* Shaw, 149 U. PA. L. REV. 1, 54 (2000), says: "The states thus find themselves in a box. They appear, under federal antidiscrimination law, to be both required to use and prohibited from using race as they draw their electoral district lines. When confronted with this reality, the Court has not engaged in the analytical rethinking that would be required to make the law more coherent." Does *Hunt v. Cromartie* (*Cromartie II*) reflect such a rethinking?

Impact of racial redistricting cases. Professor Pamela Karlan, *Easing the Spring: Strict Scrutiny and Affirmative Action After the Redistricting Cases*, 43 WM. & MARY L. REV. 1569, 1593–94 (2002), argues that in the racial redistricting cases, "the Court has been forced to confront the consequences that expansive resort to strict scrutiny might produce, and it has blinked. First, the Court has significantly tightened the trigger for strict scrutiny: under *Adarand*, all racial classifications must be analyzed under strict scrutiny, but under *Shaw* and its progeny, only when race predominates and subordinates race-neutral considerations does it prompt heightened scrutiny. Second, it has recognized that compliance with federal law can constitute a compelling state interest for taking race into account even when the federal law goes beyond what the Constitution itself requires. It has permitted states to take race into account to prevent their election from having a disparate impact on minority voters. In short, the Court has been unwilling to use strict scrutiny to dismantle the crown jewel of the Second Reconstruction. Faced with the prospect of a wholesale ouster of minority representatives from federal and state legislative bodies, the Court has created a more forbearant version of strict scrutiny. The question is whether that version has legs beyond redistricting."

Following the 2000 round of redistricting, the increased litigation predicted by many commentators failed to materialize. Why? Professor Richard Pildes,

Foreword: The Constitutionalization of Democratic Politics, 118 HARV. L. REV. 28, 67–69 (2004), argues that the "vague constitutional constraints" of *Shaw* and its progeny became "self-enforcing" because they were "internalized" by state legislators responsible for redistricting. "States continued to draw safe minority districts; *Shaw* had almost no effect on the number of African Americans elected to Congress. At the same time, states did not create the exceptionally contorted districts that had sometimes been used in the 1990s to enhance minority representation. And rather than a deluge of *Shaw* litigation, there has been almost no such litigation at all. Instead, state legislators and other actors internalized the vague legal constraints of *Shaw* in ways that generated a stable equilibrium. Though the law itself could not generate that stability ex ante by establishing necessary and sufficient criteria for the application of *Shaw*, political practice nonetheless became stable. In the 2000 round of redistricting, legislators and their counsels recognized the obligation to comply with the VRA, but they also internalized a sense of constraint from *Shaw*; the prevailing view was that minority districts were required when they could be created in a manner consistent with the design of other districts, but that exceptionally contorted minority districts were neither required nor constitutional."

§ 7.03 NOT-SO-SUSPECT CLASSIFICATIONS

Even if it were accepted that the Fourteenth Amendment was historically directed against racial classifications burdening African-Americans, that does not determine the status of other classifications such as alienage, gender, illegitimacy, age, and wealth. The language of the Amendment is not limited to racial classifications, and as Bickel noted: "[T]he fact that the proposed constitutional amendment was couched in more general terms could not have escaped those who voted for it." Alexander Bickel, *The Original Understanding of the Segregation Decision*, 69 HARV. L. REV. 1, 60 (1955). But this does not necessarily mean that other classifying traits should be treated as "suspect" and subjected to the same degree of judicial scrutiny as accorded classifications based on race or ethnicity.

Why are racial classifications treated as suspect? When this question was asked earlier, two strands of thought in addition to history were suggested, *i.e.*, avoidance of irrational prejudice and the desire to protect "discrete and insular minorities." Are there other considerations? Race is immutable, rarely relevant to the governmental decision in question, a basis for historic malign treatment and generally a visible characteristic. Are other classifications suspect if they possess or lack some of these attributes? For example, immutability could encompass factors such as sex, age, illegitimacy, physical capacity, and intelligence. Gender classifications can be a facade masking irrelevant stereotypes, but gender classifications may be based on relevant physical differences.

As we consider the standards for determining suspectness, consideration must also be given to defining the standard of review. There is nothing that commands adherence to a rigid two-tiered system. It has been suggested that the Court's unwillingness to recognize new suspect classifications is attributable to the consequences of strict scrutiny. "First, this standard of review has been 'strict' in theory and fatal in fact. Moreover, there is no historical tie between the fourteenth amendment and nonracial characteristics which would justify the Court's de facto prohibition of such classifications. Finally, and most importantly, laws which contain such classifications may be entirely reasonable and appropriate legislative decisions." John Nowak, *Realigning the Standards of Review Under the Equal Protection Guarantee — Prohibited, Neutral and Permissive Classifications*, 62 GEO. L.J. 1071 (1974). Alternative standards could be fashioned by employing fixed formulas or a sliding scale reflecting the particular characteristics of the law in question.

[A] ALIENAGE: THE "SOMETIMES SUSPECT" CLASSIFICATION

Increasing controversy over immigration policy, concern over aliens after 9/11, and the public benefits available to aliens, documented and undocumented, give added importance to the legal treatment of alienage classifications. California's Proposition 187, for example, would deny a variety of benefits, including education, to aliens. *See Plyler v. Doe,* p. 945 and notes following. Federal legislation similarly restricts welfare benefits for aliens. Indeed, legislation has been introduced in Congress that even proposes a constitutional amendment altering the Fourteenth Amendment to eliminate birthright citizenship for children of undocumented aliens. Such measures not only seek to deter immigration but reflect the perception of aliens as outsiders. "[I]n the view of its adherents, the exclusion of aliens from access to various rights and benefits properly preserves the benefits of membership for those deemed to belong within the moral boundaries of the national community." Linda Bosniak, *Membership, Equality and the Difference That Alienage Makes*, 69 N.Y.U.L. REV. 1047, 1053 (1994). Bosniak recognizes that alienage has to do with governmental power and sovereignty, which are virtually unconstrained. "Yet alienage as a legal category also lies in the world of social relationships among territorially present persons. In this world, government power to impose disabilities on people based on their status is substantially constrained. Formal commitments to norms of equal treatment and the elimination of caste-like status have importantly shaped American public law, particularly during the past several decades. From this perspective, aliens appear to be at once indistinguishable from citizens and precisely the sort of social group that requires the law's protection." *Id.* at 1056. See Linda Bosniak, *Universal Citizenship and the Problem of Alienage*, 94 NW. U.L. REV. 963, 967–68 (2000), arguing that the modern approach to citizenship focuses on the "notion that citizenship entails universality." This "universal ideal," Professor Bosniak says, "requires not only citizenship for all but also recognized [fundamental] rights for citizens." *Id.* at 968. Nevertheless, she acknowledges that "the universal ideal is far from realized in fact for many of the political community's residents, even in formal terms." *Id.* at 975.

An alien is a "person" protected by the due process and equal protection clauses. But what standard of review should be used? If original intent were the sole guide, it is likely that alienage classification would not qualify for strict scrutiny. "The framers clearly believed that aliens were entitled to some rights; at the same time, however, they carefully noted and preserved the distinction between aliens and citizens. Thus, their theory of equality cannot have encompassed a general belief that the concept of citizenship should be viewed as irrelevant to state action." Earl Maltz, *The Constitution and Nonracial Discrimination: Alienage, Sex, and the Framers' Ideal of Equality*, 7 CONST. COMM. 251, 264 (1990).

Is there any justification for treating alienage as a suspect classification? Can alienage classifications be analogized to race? Reflect on Alexander Bickel's thought provoking comment: "I find it gratifying that we live under a Constitution to which the concept of citizenship matters very little, that prescribes decencies and wise modalities of government quite without regard to the concept of citizenship." ALEXANDER BICKEL, THE MORALITY OF CONSENT 53–54 (1975).

Professor Ely has argued that the "discrete and insular minorities" rationale calls for heightened scrutiny. "Aliens cannot vote in any state, which means that any representation they will receive will be exclusively 'virtual.' That fact should at the very least require an unusually strong showing of a favorable environment for empathy, something that is lacking here. Moreover, our legislatures are composed almost entirely of citizens who have always been such." JOHN H. ELY, DEMOCRACY AND DISTRUST 161–62 (1980).

***Graham v. Richardson*, 403 U.S. 365 (1971).** The Court, per Justice Blackmun, struck down a state fifteen-year residency requirement for aliens as a pre-condition for eligibility for welfare benefits. Justice Blackmun declared "that classifications based on alienage, like those based on nationality or race, are inherently suspect and subject to close judicial scrutiny. Aliens as a class are a prime example of a single 'discrete and insular' minority for whom such heightened judicial solicitude is appropriate." Justice Blackmun went on to conclude "that a State's desire to preserve limited welfare benefits for its own citizens (the special interest doctrine) is inadequate to justify restricting benefits to citizens and long time resident aliens." *See Sugarman v. Dougall*, 413 U.S. 634 (1973) (striking down a New York citizenship requirement for all competitive civil service positions as "neither narrowly confined nor precise in its application"); *In re Griffiths*, 413 U.S. 717 (1973) (invalidating a Connecticut rule restricting admission to the bar to citizens of the United States as unnecessary to the accomplishment of valid state purposes).

Justice Rehnquist wrote a dissent for both *Sugarman* and *Griffiths* attacking the use of the more stringent standard of review. He argued that

> there is no language used in the Amendment, or any historical evidence as to the intent of the Framers, which would suggest in the slightest degree that it was intended to render alienage a "suspect" classification, that it was designed in any way to protect "discrete and insular minorities" other than racial minorities, or that it would in any way justify the result reached by the Court in these two cases.

He noted the frequent references in the Constitution differentiating between aliens and citizens, including the provisions in section 1 of the Fourteenth Amendment.

BERNAL v. FAINTER

467 U.S. 216, 104 S. Ct. 2312, 81 L. Ed. 2d 175 (1984)

JUSTICE MARSHALL delivered the opinion of the Court.

The question posed by this case is whether a statute of the State of Texas violates the Equal Protection Clause of the Fourteenth Amendment of the United States Constitution by denying aliens the opportunity to become notaries public. The Court of Appeals for the Fifth Circuit held that the statute does not offend the Equal Protection Clause. We granted certiorari and now reverse.

Petitioner, a native of Mexico, is a resident alien who has lived in the United States since 1961. He works as a paralegal for Texas Rural Legal Aid, Inc., helping migrant farm workers on employment and civil rights matters. In order to administer oaths to these workers and to notarize their statements for use in civil litigation, petitioner applied in 1978 to become a notary public. Under Texas law, notaries public authenticate written instruments, administer oaths, and take out-of-court depositions. The Texas Secretary of State denied petitioner's application because he failed to satisfy the statutory requirement that a notary public be a citizen of the United States. TEX. CIV. STAT. ANN., Art. 5949(2).

As a general matter, a State law that discriminates on the basis of alienage can be sustained only if it can withstand strict judicial scrutiny. In order to withstand strict scrutiny, the law must advance a compelling State interest by the least restrictive means available.

We have, however, developed a narrow exception to the rule that discrimination based on alienage triggers strict scrutiny. This exception has been labeled the "political function" exception and applies to laws that exclude aliens from positions intimately related to the process of democratic self-government. The contours of the "political function" exception are outlined by our prior decisions. [I]n *Cabell v. Chavez-Salido*, 454 U.S. 432 (1982), we held that a State may bar aliens from positions as probation officers because they, like police and teachers, routinely exercise discretionary power, involving a basic governmental function, that places them in a position of direct authority over other individuals.

The rationale behind the political function exception is that within broad boundaries a State may establish its own form of government and limit the right to govern those who are full-fledged members of the political community. Some public positions are so closely bound up with the formulation and implementation of self-government that the State is permitted to exclude from those positions persons outside the political community, hence persons who have not become part of the process of democratic self-determination.

To determine whether a restriction based on alienage fits within the narrow political function exception, we devised in *Cabell* a two-part test.

> First, the specificity of the classification will be examined: a classification that is substantially overinclusive or underinclusive tends to undercut the governmental claim that the classification serves legitimate political ends. Second, even if the classification is sufficiently

tailored, it may be applied in the particular case only to "persons holding state elective or important nonelective executive, legislative, and judicial positions," those officers who "participate directly in the formulation, execution, or review of broad public policy" and hence "perform functions that go right to the heart of representative government."

We now turn to Article 5949(2) to determine whether it satisfies the *Cabell* test. The statute provides that "[t]o be eligible for appointment as a Notary Public, a person shall be a resident citizen of the United States and of this state." Unlike the statute invalidated in *Sugarman*, Article 5949(2) does not indiscriminately sweep within its ambit a wide range of offices and occupations but specifies only one particular post with respect to which the State asserts a right to exclude aliens. Clearly, then, the statute is not overinclusive; it applies narrowly to only one category of persons: those wishing to obtain appointments as notaries. Less clear is whether Article 5942(2) is fatally underinclusive. Texas does not require court reporters to be United States citizens even though they perform some of the same services as notaries. Nor does Texas require that its Secretary of State be a citizen, even though he holds the highest appointive position in the State and performs many important functions, including supervision of the licensing of all notaries public. We need not decide this issue, however, because of our decision with respect to the second prong of the *Cabell* test.

In support of the proposition that notaries public fall within that category of officials who perform functions that "go to the heart of representative government," the State emphasizes that notaries are designated as public officers by the Texas Constitution.

We recognize the critical need for a notary's duties to be carried out correctly and with integrity. But a notary's duties, important as they are, hardly implicate responsibilities that go to the heart of representative government. Rather, these duties are essentially clerical and ministerial. In contrast to state troopers, *Foley v. Connelie*, notaries do not routinely exercise the State's monopoly of legitimate coercive force. Nor do notaries routinely exercise the wide discretion typically enjoyed by public school teachers when they present materials that educate youth respecting the information and values necessary for the maintenance of a democratic political system. *See Ambach v. Norwick*. To be sure, considerable damage could result from the negligent or dishonest performance of a notary's duties. But the same could be said for the duties performed by cashiers, building inspectors, the janitors who clean up the offices of public officials, and numerous other categories of personnel upon whom we depend for careful, honest service. What distinguishes such personnel from those to which the political function exception is properly applied is that the latter are either invested with policy-making responsibility or broad discretion in the execution of public policy that requires the routine exercise of authority over individuals. Neither of these characteristics pertain to the functions performed by Texas notaries. We conclude, then, that the "political function" exception is inapplicable to Article 5949(2) and that the statute is therefore subject to strict judicial scrutiny.

To satisfy strict scrutiny, the State must show that Article 5949(2) furthers a compelling State interest by the least restrictive means practically available. Respondent maintains that Article 5949(2) serves its "legitimate concern that notaries be reasonably familiar with state law and institutions" and "that notaries may be called upon years later to testify to acts they have performed." However both of these asserted justifications utterly fail to meet the stringent requirements of strict scrutiny. There is nothing in the record that indicates that resident aliens, as a class, are so incapable of familiarizing themselves with Texas law as to justify the State's absolute and class-wide exclusion. Similarly inadequate is the State's purported interest in insuring the later availability of notaries' testimony. This justification fails because the State fails to advance a factual showing that the unavailability of notaries' testimony presents a real, as opposed to a merely speculative, problem to the State. Without a factual underpinning, the State's asserted interest lacks the weight we have required of interests properly denominated as compelling.

JUSTICE REHNQUIST, dissenting.

I dissent for the reasons stated in my dissenting opinion in *Sugarman v. Dougall*.

NOTES

1. ***Political function.*** The "political function" principle represents an exception from the general use of strict scrutiny review of state laws based on alienage. One observer has pointed out that the political function approach makes it difficult to challenge alienage classifications: "[T]he *Foley-Ambach* approach places the primary burden on the alien to show that the position in question does not affect the political community, rather than placing the primary burden on the state, as it had been, to justify a classification based on alienage. It presents the Court and litigants with the complex problem of defining the political community. In addition, it diminishes the protected status of aliens." Marilyn Walter, *The Alien's Right to Work and the Political Community's Right to Govern*, 25 WAYNE L. REV. 1181, 1198 (1979).

Professor Alex Aleinikoff, *Citizens, Aliens, Membership and the Constitution*, 7 CONST. COMM. 9, 23 (1990), argues that "both immigration practice and the daily lives of resident aliens suggest that true 'membership' in the life of the nation begins at the point of admission for permanent residence." Michael Scaperlanda, *Partial Membership: Aliens and the Constitutional Community*, 81 IOWA L. REV. 707 (1996), distinguishes a "membership" paradigm where a governmental entity is involved in defining its community from a "personhood" paradigm emphasizing the rights of the noncitizen. He argues "that membership provides the baseline norm governing all aspects of our alienage jurisprudence, with the personhood tradition subordinated to a secondary status." *Id.* at 716.

2. ***Federal alienage classifications.*** Strict scrutiny has not been used for federal alienage classifications. The powers vested in the national government to regulate naturalization and foreign affairs provides broad discretion over the admission of aliens, the substantive basis for their deportation and their treatment while in this country. See Victor C. Romero, *The Congruence*

Principle Applied: Rethinking Equal Protection Review of Federal Alienage Classifications After Adarand Constructors, Inc. v. Pena, 76 Or. L. Rev. 425, 429 (1997), arguing "that the principle of congruence [used in *Adarand*] should be applied to alienage classifications so that federal alienage classifications are scrutinized in the same manner as state alienage classifications."

Mathews v. Diaz, 426 U.S. 67 (1976), presented the question of whether Congress may condition an alien's eligibility for participation in a federal medical insurance program on continuous residence in the United States for a five-year period and admission for "a permanent residence." The Supreme Court, per Justice Stevens, held both conditions constitutional, declaring that the real question in this case was "whether the statutory discrimination within the class of aliens — allowing benefits to some aliens but not to others — is permissible." In resolving this question, Justice Stevens stated: "The reasons that preclude judicial review of political questions also dictate a narrow standard of review of decisions made by the Congress or the President in the area of immigration and naturalization." In the present case, those who qualified for medical benefits under the congressional test could "reasonably be presumed to have a greater affinity to the United States than those who do not. In short citizens and those who are most like citizens qualify. Those who are less like citizens do not." Both conditions were "unquestionably reasonable."

3. *A preemption alternative.* A number of commentators have suggested that a preferable method of dealing with state laws burdening aliens is preemption analysis. The pervasive federal power over immigration and foreign affairs permits the federal government to preclude excessive state regulation. In *Toll v. Moreno*, 458 U.S. 1 (1982), the Court held, in an opinion by Justice Brennan, that the University of Maryland's policy barring domiciled nonimmigrant aliens and their dependents with "G-4" visas from acquiring in-state status for purposes of admissions and fees violated the supremacy clause. The University granted preferential tuition treatment to citizens and immigrants domiciled in the state, but denied the benefits to nonimmigrants holding G-4 visas, issued to officers of international organizations and members of their immediate families, even though they were domiciled in the state.

Professor Aleinikoff questions the approach in *Diaz*, arguing that "the courts have wrongly assumed that every federal regulation based on alienage is necessarily sustainable as an exercise of the immigration power." Alex Aleinikoff, *Federal Regulation of Aliens and the Constitution*, 83 Am. J. Int'l L. 862, 869 (1989). He argues that courts "ought to examine the justifications offered on behalf of federal regulations based on alienage to see if they meet traditional constitutional standards of permissibility."

[B] GENDER CLASSIFICATIONS: "ALL [PERSONS] ARE CREATED EQUAL"

Concern with gender classifications was clearly not an animating force in the enactment of the equal protection guarantee. Indeed, given the pervasive discrimination against women at the time, it could be questioned whether the framers even envisioned women as beneficiaries of the Fourteenth Amendment. Ruth Ginsburg, *Sexual Equality Under the Fourteenth and Equal Rights Amendments*, 1979 WASH. U.L.Q. 161, states: "[T]he framers of the fourteenth amendment did not contemplate sex equality. Boldly dynamic interpretation, departing radically from the original understanding, is required to tie to the fourteenth amendment's equal protection clause a command that government treat men and women as individuals equal in rights, responsibilities, and opportunities."

Nineteenth-century evidence includes *Bradwell v. Illinois*, 83 U.S. 130, 141 (1872), upholding the exclusion of women from law practice, in which Justice Bradley stated: "Man is, or should be, woman's protector and defender. The natural and proper timidity and delicacy which belongs to the female sex evidently unfits it for many of the occupations of civil life. The paramount destiny and mission of woman are to fulfill the noble and benign offices of wife and mother. This is the law of the Creator. And the rules of civil society must be adapted to the general constitution of things, and cannot be based upon exceptional cases."

Nevertheless, from the outset, the Court has read "persons" to include women. And, in recent years, the Court has even employed a more searching standard of review to gender classification.

[1] Identifying Standards — The Formative Period

Prior to the 1970s, the Court generally upheld gender classifications using traditional review. But in *Reed v. Reed*, 404 U.S. 71 (1971), the Court, per Chief Justice Burger, unanimously struck down an Idaho law giving males a preference over females as administrators of estates. The appellant's brief had argued "that designation of sex as a suspect classification is overdue, is the only wholly satisfactory standard for dealing with the claim in this case, and should be the starting point for assessing that claim. Nonetheless, it should be apparent that the reasonable relation test also must yield a conclusion in favor of the appellant."

Chief Justice Burger framed the question as: "Whether the difference in the sex of competing applicants for letters of administration bears a rational relationship to a state objective that is sought to be advanced." Relying entirely on traditional equal protection cases as precedent, the Court nevertheless found that the statute violated equal protection. While the state interest in reducing the work load of probate courts was deemed "not without some legitimacy," the state's manner of advancing that interest did not satisfy equal protection standards:

> To give a mandatory preference to members of either sex over members of the other, merely to accomplish the elimination of hearings on the merits, is to make the very kind of arbitrary legislative choice forbidden by the Equal Protection Clause of the Fourteenth Amendment; and whatever may be said as to the positive values of avoiding intra-family controversy, the choice in this context may not lawfully be mandated solely on the basis of sex.

Persons within the various classes of relationship to the intestate were similarly situated. "By providing dissimilar treatment for men and women who are thus similarly situated, the challenged section violates the Equal Protection Clause."

While *Reed* uses the terminology of traditional equal protection, Professor Gunther suggests that this may be misleading. "Clear priority classifications are plainly relevant to the State's interest in reducing administrative disputes. Only by importing some special suspicion of sex-related means from the new equal protection area can the result be made entirely persuasive. Yet application of new equal protection criteria is precisely what *Reed v. Reed* purported to avoid." Gerald Gunther, *Foreword: In Search of Evolving Doctrine on a Changing Court: A Model for a Newer Equal Protection*, 86 Harv. L. Rev. 1, 34 (1972).

On March 22, 1972, forty-nine years after it was first introduced, the Senate completed congressional approval of an equal rights amendment.

> Section 1. Equality of rights under the law shall not be denied or abridged by the United States or by any State on account of sex.
>
> Section 2. The Congress shall have the power to enforce, by appropriate legislation, the provisions of this article.
>
> Section 3. The Amendment shall take effect two years after the date of ratification.

"The fundamental legal principle underlying the Equal Rights Amendment is that the law must deal with particular attributes of individuals, not with a classification based on the broad and impermissible attribute of sex." Brown, Emerson, Falk & Freedman, *The Equal Rights Amendment: A Constitutional Basis for Equal Rights for Women*, 80 Yale L.J. 871, 893 (1971). Proponents of the measure argued that it would make sex classifications per se impermissible with two exceptions, *i.e.* personal privacy and physical characteristics unique to one sex.

March 22, 1979, was the original time limit provided for ratification, but proponents obtained from Congress a three-year extension with which to gain the remaining number of states for ratification. The extension period ended in June 1982, still lacking the requisite number of states.

FRONTIERO v. RICHARDSON

411 U.S. 677, 93 S. Ct. 1764, 36 L. Ed. 2d 583 (1973)

Justice Brennan announced the judgment of the Court in an opinion in which Justice Douglas, Justice White, and Justice Marshall join.

The question before us concerns the right of a female member of the uniformed services to claim her spouse as a "dependent" for the purposes of obtaining increased quarters allowances and medical and dental benefits on an equal footing with male members. Under these statutes, a serviceman may claim his wife as a "dependent" without regard to whether she is in fact dependent upon him for any part of her support. A servicewoman, on the other hand, may not claim her husband as a "dependent" under these programs unless he is in fact dependent upon her for over one-half of his support. At the outset, appellants contend that classifications based upon sex, like classifications based upon race, alienage, and national origin, are inherently suspect and must therefore be subjected to close judicial scrutiny. We agree and, indeed, find at least implicit support for such an approach in our unanimous decision only last Term in *Reed v. Reed.*

[T]he Court [in *Reed*] held the statutory preference for male applicants unconstitutional. In reaching this result, the Court implicitly rejected appellee's apparently rational explanation of the statutory scheme, and concluded that, by ignoring the individual qualifications of particular applicants, the challenged statute provided "dissimilar treatment for men and women who are similarly situated." This departure from "traditional" rational basis analysis with respect to sex-based classifications is clearly justified.

There can be no doubt that our Nation has had a long and unfortunate history of sex discrimination. Traditionally, such discrimination was rationalized by an attitude of "romantic paternalism" which, in practical effect, put women not on a pedestal, but in a cage. As a result of notions such as these, our statute books gradually became laden with gross, stereotypical distinctions between the sexes and, indeed, throughout much of the nineteenth century the position of women in our society was, in many respects, comparable to that of blacks under the pre-Civil War slave codes. Neither slaves nor women could hold office, serve on juries, or bring suit in their own names, and married women traditionally were denied the legal capacity to hold or convey property or to serve as legal guardians of their own children. And although blacks were guaranteed the right to vote in 1870, women were denied even that right — which is itself "preservative of other basic civil and political rights" — until adoption of the Nineteenth Amendment half a century later. It is true, of course, that the position of women in America has improved markedly in recent decades. Nevertheless, it can hardly be doubted that, in part because of the high visibility of the sex characteristic, women still face pervasive, although at times more subtle, discrimination in our educational institutions, on the job market and, perhaps most conspicuously, in the political arena.

Moreover, since sex, like race and national origin, is an immutable characteristic determined solely by the accident of birth, the imposition of special disabilities upon the members of a particular sex because of their sex would seem to violate "the basic concept of our system that legal burdens should bear some relationship to individual responsibility." And what differentiates sex from such nonsuspect statuses as intelligence or physical disability, and aligns it with the recognized suspect criteria, is that the sex characteristic frequently bears no relation to ability to perform or contribute to society. As a result, statutory distinctions between the sexes often have the effect of invidiously relegating the entire class of females to inferior legal status without regard to the actual capabilities of its individual members.

[In passing the ERA], Congress has itself concluded that classifications based upon sex are inherently invidious, and this conclusion of a coequal branch of Government is not without significance to the question presently under consideration. With these considerations in mind, we can only conclude that classifications based upon sex, like classifications based upon race, alienage, or national origin, are inherently suspect, and must therefore be subjected to strict judicial scrutiny. Applying the analysis mandated by that stricter standard of review, it is clear that the statutory scheme now before us is constitutionally invalid.

[T]he Government concedes that the differential treatment accorded men and women under these statutes serves no purpose other than mere "administrative convenience." In essence, the Government maintains that, as an empirical matter, wives in our society frequently are dependent upon their husbands, while husbands rarely are dependent upon their wives. Thus, the Government argues that Congress might reasonably have concluded that it would be both cheaper and easier simply conclusively to presume that wives of male members are financially dependent upon their husbands, while burdening female members with the task of establishing dependency in fact.[22]

The Government offers no concrete evidence, however, tending to support its view that such differential treatment in fact saves the Government any money. In order to satisfy the demands of strict judicial scrutiny, the Government must demonstrate, for example, that it is actually cheaper to grant increased benefits with respect to all male members, than it is to determine which male members are in fact entitled to such benefits and to grant increased benefits only to those members whose wives actually meet the dependency requirement. Here, however, there is substantial evidence that, if put to the test, many of the wives of male members would fail to qualify for benefits. And in light of the fact that the dependency determination with respect to the husbands of female members is presently made solely on the basis of affidavits rather than through the more costly hearing process, the Government's explanation of the statutory scheme is, to say the least, questionable.

In any case, our prior decisions make clear that, although efficacious administration of governmental programs is not without some importance, "The Constitution recognizes higher values than speed and efficiency." *Stanley v. Illinois*, 405 U.S. 645, 656 (1972). And when we enter the realm of "strict judicial scrutiny," there can be no doubt that "administrative convenience" is not a shibboleth, the mere recitation of which dictates constitutionality. On the contrary, any statutory scheme which draws a sharp line between the sexes, solely for the purpose of achieving administrative convenience, necessarily commands "dissimilar treatment for men and women who are similarly situated," and therefore involves the "very kind of arbitrary legislative choice forbidden by the [Constitution]." *Reed v. Reed*.

JUSTICE POWELL, with whom THE CHIEF JUSTICE [BURGER] and JUSTICE BLACKMUN join, concurring in the judgment.

I agree that the challenged statutes constitute an unconstitutional discrimination against service women in violation of the Due Process Clause of the Fifth Amendment, but I cannot join the opinion of MR. JUSTICE BRENNAN. It is unnecessary for the Court in this case to characterize sex as a suspect

[22] It should be noted that these statutes are not in any sense designed to rectify the effects of past discrimination against women.

classification, with all of the far-reaching implications of such a holding. *Reed v. Reed*, which abundantly supports our decision today, did not add sex to the narrowly limited group of classifications which are inherently suspect. In my view, we can and should decide this case on the authority of *Reed* and reserve for the future any expansion of its rationale.

There is another, and I find compelling, reason for deferring a general categorizing of sex classifications as invoking the strictest test of judicial scrutiny. The Equal Rights Amendment, which if adopted will resolve the substance of this precise question, has been approved by the Congress and submitted for ratification by the States. If this Amendment is duly adopted, it will represent the will of the people accomplished in the manner prescribed by the Constitution. By acting prematurely and unnecessarily, as I view it, the Court has assumed a decisional responsibility at the very time when state legislatures, functioning within the traditional democratic process, are debating the proposed Amendment. It seems to me that this reaching out to preempt by judicial action a major political decision which is currently in process of resolution does not reflect appropriate respect for duly prescribed legislative processes.

JUSTICE STEWART concurs in the judgment, agreeing that the statutes before us work an invidious discrimination in violation of the Constitution. *Reed v. Reed*.

JUSTICE REHNQUIST dissents for the reasons stated by Judge Rives in his opinion for the District Court.

CRAIG v. BOREN

429 U.S. 190, 97 S. Ct. 451, 50 L. Ed. 2d 397 (1976)

JUSTICE BRENNAN delivered the opinion of the Court.

The interaction of two sections of an Oklahoma statute, §§ 241 and 245, prohibits the sale of "nonintoxicating" 3.2% beer to males under the age of 21 and to females under the age of 18. The question to be decided is whether such a gender-based differential constitutes a denial to males 18-20 years of age of the Equal Protection of the Laws in violation of the Fourteenth Amendment.

To withstand constitutional challenge, previous cases establish that classifications by gender must serve important governmental objectives and must be substantially related to achievement of those objectives. In light of the weak congruence between gender and the characteristic or trait that gender purport[s] to represent, it [is] necessary that the legislatures choose either to realign their substantive laws in a gender-neutral fashion, or to adopt procedures for identifying those instances where the sex-centered generalization actually [comports] with fact.

In this case, "*Reed* we feel is controlling." We turn then to the question whether, under *Reed*, the difference between males and females with respect to the purchase of 3.2% beer warrants the differential in age drawn by the Oklahoma statute. We conclude that it does not.

We accept for purposes of discussion the District Court's identification of the objective underlying §§ 241 and 245 as the enhancement of traffic safety.

Clearly, the protection of public health and safety represents an important function of state and local governments. However, appellees' statistics in our view cannot support the conclusion that the gender-based distinction closely serves to achieve that objective and therefore the distinction cannot under *Reed* withstand equal protection challenge.

The appellees introduced a variety of statistical surveys. First, an analysis of arrest statistics for 1973 demonstrated that 18-20-year-old male arrests for "driving under the influence" and "drunkenness" substantially exceeded female arrests for that same age period. Similarly, youths aged 17–21 were found to be overrepresented among those killed or injured in traffic accidents, with males again numerically exceeding females in this regard. Third, a random roadside survey in Oklahoma City revealed that young males were more inclined to drive and drink beer than were their female counterparts. Fourth, Federal Bureau of Investigation nationwide statistics exhibited a notable increase in arrests for "driving under the influence." Finally, statistical evidence gathered in other jurisdictions, particularly Minnesota and Michigan, was offered to corroborate Oklahoma's experience by indicating the pervasiveness of youthful participation in motor vehicle accidents following the imbibing of alcohol.

Even were this statistical evidence accepted as accurate, it nevertheless offers only a weak answer to the equal protection question presented here. The most focused and relevant of the statistical surveys, arrests of 18-20-year-olds for alcohol-related driving offenses, exemplifies the ultimate unpersuasiveness of this evidentiary record. Viewed in terms of the correlation between sex and the actual activity that Oklahoma seeks to regulate — driving while under the influence of alcohol — the statistics broadly establish that .18% of females and 2% of males in that age group were arrested for that offense. While such a disparity is not trivial in a statistical sense, it hardly can form the basis for employment of a gender line as a classifying device. Certainly if maleness is to serve as a proxy for drinking and driving, a correlation of 2% must be considered an unduly tenuous "fit." Indeed, prior cases have consistently rejected the use of sex as a decisionmaking factor even though the statutes in question certainly rested on far more predictive empirical relationships than this.

There is no reason to belabor this line of analysis. It is unrealistic to expect either members of the judiciary or state officials to be well versed in the rigors of experimental or statistical technique. But this merely illustrates that proving broad sociological propositions by statistics is a dubious business, and one that inevitably is in tension with the normative philosophy that underlies the Equal Protection Clause. Suffice to say that the showing offered by the appellees does not satisfy us that sex represents a legitimate, accurate proxy for the regulation of drinking and driving. In fact, when it is further recognized that Oklahoma's statute prohibits only the selling of 3.2% beer to young males and not their drinking the beverage once acquired (even after purchase by their 18–20-year-old female companions), the relationship between gender and traffic safety becomes far too tenuous to satisfy Reed's requirement that the gender-based difference be substantially related to achievement of the statutory objective. We hold, therefore, that under *Reed*, Oklahoma's 3.2% beer statute invidiously discriminates against males 18-20 years of age.

[The Court's discussion of the effect of the Twenty-First Amendment is omitted.]

JUSTICE POWELL, concurring.

I join the opinion of the Court as I am in general agreement with it. I do have reservations as to some of the discussion concerning the appropriate standard for equal protection analysis and the relevance of the statistical evidence. Accordingly, I add this concurring statement.

With respect to the equal protection standard, I agree that *Reed v. Reed* is the most relevant precedent. But I find it unnecessary, in deciding this case, to read that decision as broadly as some of the Court's language may imply. *Reed* and subsequent cases involving gender-based classifications make clear that the Court subjects such classifications to a more critical examination than is normally applied when "fundamental" constitutional rights and "suspect classes" are not present.

It seems to me that the statistics offered by appellees and relied upon by the District Court do tend generally to support the view that young men drive more, possibly are inclined to drink more, and — for various reasons — are involved in more accidents than young women. Even so, I am not persuaded that these facts and the inferences fairly drawn from them justify this classification based on a three-year age differential between the sexes, and especially one that is so easily circumvented as to be virtually meaningless. Putting it differently, this gender-based classification does not bear a fair and substantial relation to the object of the legislation.

JUSTICE STEVENS, concurring.

There is only one Equal Protection Clause. It requires every State to govern impartially. It does not direct the courts to apply one standard of review in some cases and a different standard in other cases. Whatever criticism may be leveled at a judicial opinion implying that there are at least three such standards applies with the same force to a double standard. I am inclined to believe that what has become known as the two-tiered analysis of equal protection claims does not describe a completely logical method of deciding cases, but rather is a method the Court has employed to explain decisions that actually apply a single standard in a reasonably consistent fashion. The classification is not totally irrational.

[The] legislation imposes a restraint on one hundred percent of the males in the class allegedly because about 2% of them have probably violated one or more laws relating to the consumption of alcoholic beverages. It is unlikely that this law will have a significant deterrent effect either on that 2% or on the law-abiding 98%. But even assuming some such slight benefit, it does not seem to me that an insult to all of the young men of the State can be justified by visiting the sins of the 2% on the 98%.

JUSTICE STEWART, concurring in the judgment.

The disparity created by these Oklahoma statutes amounts to total irrationality. For the statistics upon which the State now relies, whatever their other shortcomings, wholly fail to prove or even suggest that 3.2% beer is somehow more deleterious when it comes into the hands of a male aged 18–20 than of a female of like age. The disparate statutory treatment of the sexes here, without even a colorably valid justification or explanation, thus amounts to invidious discrimination. *See Reed v. Reed.*

JUSTICE REHNQUIST, dissenting.

The Court's disposition of this case is objectionable on two grounds. First is its conclusion that men challenging a gender-based statute which treats them less favorably than women may invoke a more stringent standard of judicial review than pertains to most other types of classifications. Second is the Court's enunciation of this standard, without citation to any source, as being that "classifications by gender must serve important governmental objectives and must be substantially related to achievement of those objectives." The only redeeming feature of the Court's opinion, to my mind, is that it apparently signals a retreat by those who joined the plurality opinion in *Frontiero v. Richardson* from their view that sex is a "suspect" classification for purposes of equal protection analysis. I think the Oklahoma statute challenged here need pass only the "rational basis" equal protection analysis, and I believe that it is constitutional under that analysis.

Most obviously unavailable to support any kind of special scrutiny in this case, is a history or pattern of past discrimination, such as was relied on by the plurality in *Frontiero* to support its invocation of strict scrutiny. There is no suggestion in the Court's opinion that males in this age group are in any way peculiarly disadvantaged, subject to systematic discriminatory treatment, or otherwise in need of special solicitude from the courts. [B]efore today, no decision of this Court has applied an elevated level of scrutiny to invalidate a statutory discrimination harmful to males, except where the statute impaired an important personal interest protected by the Constitution. There being no such interest here, and there being no plausible argument that this is a discrimination against females, the Court's reliance on our previous sex-discrimination cases is ill-founded. It treats gender classification as a talisman which — without regard to the rights involved or the persons affected — calls into effect a heavier burden of judicial review.

The Court's conclusion that a law which treats males less favorably than females "must serve important governmental objectives and must be substantially related to achievement of those objectives" apparently comes out of thin air. The Equal Protection Clause contains no such language, and none of our previous cases adopt that standard. I would think we have had enough difficulty with the two standards of review which our cases have recognized — the norm of "rational basis," and the "compelling state interest" required where a "suspect classification" is involved — so as to counsel weightily against the insertion of still another "standard" between those two. How is this Court to divine what objectives are important? How is it to determine whether a particular law is "substantially" related to the achievement of such objective, rather than related in some other way to its achievement? Both of the phrases used are so diaphanous and elastic as to invite subjective judicial preferences or prejudices relating to particular types of legislation, masquerading as judgments whether such legislation is directed at "important" objectives or, whether the relationship to those objectives is "substantial" enough.

I would have thought that if this Court were to leave anything to decision by the popularly elected branches of the Government, where no constitutional claim other than that of equal protection is invoked, it would be the decision as to what governmental objectives to be achieved by law are "important," and which are not. As for the second part of the Court's new test, the Judicial Branch is probably in no worse position than the Legislative or Executive Branches to determine if there is any rational relationship between a classification and the purpose which it might be thought to serve. But the introduction of the adverb "substantially" requires courts to make subjective judgments as to operational effects, for which neither their expertise nor their access to data fits them. And even if we manage to avoid both confusion and the mirroring of our own preferences in the development of this new doctrine, the thousands of judges in other courts who must interpret the Equal Protection Clause may not be so fortunate.

The rationality of a statutory classification for equal protection purposes does not depend upon the statistical "fit" between the class and the trait sought to be singled out. It turns on whether there may be a sufficiently higher incidence of the trait within the included class than in the excluded class to justify different treatment. Therefore the present equal protection challenge to this gender-based discrimination poses only the question whether the incidence of drunk driving among young men is sufficiently greater than among young women to justify differential treatment. Notwithstanding the Court's critique of the statistical evidence, that evidence suggests clear differences between the drinking and driving habits of young men and women. Those differences are grounds enough for the State reasonably to conclude that young males pose by far the greater drunk-driving hazard, both in terms of sheer numbers and in terms of hazard on a per-driver basis. The gender-based difference in treatment in this case is therefore not irrational.

[CHIEF JUSTICE BURGER also dissented separately, although he was "in general agreement with JUSTICE REHNQUIST's dissent."]

NOTES

1. ***Is strict scrutiny appropriate?*** Are gender classifications sufficiently analogous to race classifications to merit heightened review? In *Bakke*, Justice Brennan accepted such an analogy noting that like race, "gender-based classifications too often [have] been inexcusably utilized to stereotype and stigmatize politically powerless segments of society." On the other hand, Justice Powell in *Bakke*, noting that the Court had not drawn the analogy, asserted that "the perception of racial classifications as inherently odious stems from a lengthy and tragic history that gender-based classifications do not share." In *Frontiero*, the Solicitor General acknowledged that "sex, like race or national origin, is a visible and immutable biological characteristic that bears no necessary relation to ability." Brief for Appellees, *Frontiero v. Richardson*. Sex is a congenital and generally immutable characteristic. Further, gender classifications are based on status rather than behavior and personal responsibility, and thus raise problems of "individualized justice." Is this reasoning sufficient to justify use of strict or heightened scrutiny?

2. *Relevant factor or stereotype?* Does a gender-based classification imply inferiority; does it impose a stigma? The Solicitor General in *Frontiero* argued that "legislation affecting women [unlike] that affecting racial or ethnic minorities [is not] commonly perceived as implying a stigma of inferiority or a badge of opprobrium which suggests that the affected class lacks equal dignity." There are many laws recognizing sex differences which do not imply inferior status, *e.g.*, separate public washrooms, requirements that women wear bathing suit tops on public beaches. But many laws are based on "archaic stereotypes" about women's roles.

Professor Wasserstrom has argued, "It is even clearer in the case of sex than in the case of race that one's sexual identity is a centrally important, crucially relevant category within our culture." He thinks that sexual identity is more important than one's race because "there are substantially different role expectations and role assignments to persons in accordance with their sexual physiology, and the position of the two sexes in the culture are distinct." Richard Wasserstrom, *Racism, Sexism, and Preferential Treatment: An Approach to the Topics*, 24 UCLA L. Rev. 581, 587 (1977).

Professor Tribe asserts that each of the sex-based classifications invalidated by the Supreme Court involved a governmental reliance on an existing stereotype to justify the convenience of using that norm as a basis for decision. "The Supreme Court's thoughtful response to this argument has recognized the argument's essence as self-fulfilling prophecy: The 'accuracy' of government's assumption is derived in some significant degree from the chill on sex-role experimentation and change generated by the classifications themselves." Laurence H. Tribe, American Constitutional Law 1565 (2d ed. 1988).

3. *Political access.* Does the "discrete and insular minorities" theory apply to gender classifications? Professor Ely says not, at least for classifications enacted after women were enfranchised in 1920. "The degree of contact between men and women could hardly be greater, and neither, of course, are women 'in the closet' as homosexuals historically have been. Finally, lest you think I missed it, women have about half the votes, apparently more. . . . [I]f women don't protect themselves from sex discrimination in the future, it won't be because they can't. It will rather be because for one reason or another — substantive disagreement or more likely the assignment of a low priority to the issue — they don't choose to." John H. Ely, Democracy and Distrust 164, 169 (1980). Does the lack of significant female representation in legislatures or the power centers of business refute the Ely position?

Lillian BeVier, *Thoughts From a "Real" Woman,* 18 Harv. J.L. & Pub. Pol'y 457, 458 (1995), citing women's right to vote, rejects special constitutional protection, arguing: "At this point in time, issues of concern to women have such special salience that it is quite implausible to claim that women need special constitutional protection because politicians routinely ignore them." Akhil Amar, *Women and the Constitution,* 18 Harv. J.L. & Pub. Pol'y 465, 475 (1995), responds: "When women become half of those who vote in legislatures, I'll probably join Professor BeVier."

4. *Operation of the tests.* How does intermediate review compare with strict scrutiny and traditional rationality review? Is it a balancing test? "[T]he middle tier has no predictable application. Whether or not a given classification furthers an 'important governmental interest,' or is 'substantially related' to this interest, are subjective determinations, and a conservative majority is as likely to conclude one way as a liberal majority is to conclude the other." E.A. Hull, *Sex Discrimination and the Equal Protection Clause: An Analysis of Kahn v. Shevin and Orr v. Orr*, 30 SYRACUSE L. REV. 639, 671 (1979).

An empirical study of the different forms of review in gender cases concluded that, in contrast to the relatively predictable outcomes under strict scrutiny and rational basis, "when courts apply the intermediate standard, litigants alleging sex discrimination are nearly as likely to win as they are to lose." Lee Epstein et al., *Constitutional Sex Discrimination*, 1 TENN. J.L. & POL'Y 11, 67 (2004). The authors also not that, "litigants challenging sex-based classifications are more than twice as likely to prevail now than they were prior to *Craig*." *Id.* at 53.

PERSONNEL ADMINISTRATOR v. FEENEY
442 U.S. 256, 99 S. Ct. 2282, 60 L. Ed. 2d 870 (1979)

JUSTICE STEWART delivered the opinion of the Court.

This case presents a challenge to the constitutionality of the Massachusetts Veterans Preference Statute, Mass. Gen. Laws, ch. 31, § 23, on the ground that it discriminates against women in violation of the Equal Protection Clause of the Fourteenth Amendment. Under ch. 31, § 23, all veterans who qualify for state civil service positions must be considered for appointment ahead of any qualifying nonveterans. The preference operates overwhelmingly to the advantage of males.

When this litigation was commenced, over 98% of the veterans in Massachusetts were male; only 1.8% were female. And over one-quarter of the Massachusetts population were veterans. During the decade between 1963 and 1973 when the appellee was actively participating in the State's merit selection system, 47,005 new permanent appointments were made in the classified official service. Forty-three percent of those hired were women, and 57% were men. Of the women appointed, 1.8% were veterans, while 54% of the men had veteran status. A large unspecified percentage of the female appointees were serving in lower paying positions for which males traditionally had not applied. On each of 50 sample eligible lists that are part of the record in this case, one or more women who would have been certified as eligible for appointment on the basis of test results were displaced by veterans whose test scores were lower.

At the outset of this litigation the State conceded that for "many of the permanent positions for which males and females have competed" the veterans' preference has "resulted in a substantially greater proportion of female eligibles than male eligibles" not being certified for consideration. The impact of the veterans' preference law upon the public employment opportunities of women has thus been severe. This impact lies at the heart of the appellee's federal constitutional claim. The sole question for decision on this appeal is whether Massachusetts, in granting an absolute lifetime preference to veterans, has discriminated against women in violation of the Equal Protection Clause of the Fourteenth Amendment.

Although public employment is not a constitutional right and the States have wide discretion in framing employee qualifications, precedents dictate that any state law overtly or covertly designed to prefer males over females in public employment would require an exceedingly persuasive justification to withstand a constitutional challenge under the Equal Protection Clause of the Fourteenth Amendment. When a statute gender-neutral on its face is challenged on the ground that its effects upon women are disproportionably adverse, a two-fold inquiry is thus appropriate. The first question is whether the statutory classification is indeed neutral in the sense that it is not gender based. If the classification itself, covert or overt, is not based upon gender, the second question is whether the adverse effect reflects invidious gender-based discrimination. *See Village of Arlington Heights*. In this second inquiry, impact provides an "important starting point," but purposeful discrimination is "the condition that offends the Constitution."

The question whether ch. 31, § 23 establishes a classification that is overtly or covertly based upon gender must first be considered. The appellee has conceded that ch. 31, § 23 is neutral on its face. She has also acknowledged that state hiring preferences for veterans are not per se invalid, for she has limited her challenge to the absolute lifetime preference that Massachusetts provides to veterans. The District Court made two central findings that are relevant here: first, that ch. 31, § 23 serves legitimate and worthy purposes; second, that the absolute preference was not established for the purpose of discriminating against women. The appellee has thus acknowledged and the District Court has thus found that the distinction between veterans and nonveterans drawn by ch. 31, § 23 is not a pretext for gender discrimination. The appellee's concession and the District Court's finding are clearly correct.

If the impact of this statute could not be plausibly explained on a neutral ground, impact itself would signal that the real classification made by the law was in fact not neutral. *See Washington v. Davis*; *Village of Arlington Heights*. But there can be but one answer to the question whether this veteran preference excludes significant numbers of women from preferred state jobs because they are women or because they are nonveterans. Apart from the fact that the definition of "veterans" in the statute has always been neutral as to gender and that Massachusetts has consistently defined veteran status in a way that has been inclusive of women who have served in the military, this is not a law that can plausibly be explained only as a gender-based classification. Indeed, it is not a law that can rationally be explained on that ground. Veteran status is not uniquely male. Although few women benefit from the preference, the nonveteran class is not substantially all-female. To the contrary, significant numbers of nonveterans are men, and all nonveterans — male as well as female — are placed at a disadvantage. Too many men are affected by ch. 31, § 23 to permit the inference that the statute is but a pretext for preferring men over women.

Moreover, as the District Court implicitly found, the purpose of the statute provides the surest explanation for its impact. Just as there are cases in which impact alone can unmask an invidious classification, *cf. Yick Wo v. Hopkins*, there are others, in which — notwithstanding impact — the legitimate noninvidious purposes of a law cannot be missed. This is one. The distinction made by ch. 31, § 23, is, as it seems to be, quite simply between veterans and nonveterans, not between men and women.

The dispositive question, then, is whether the appellee has shown that a gender-based discriminatory purpose has, at least in some measure, shaped the Massachusetts veterans' preference legislation. As did the District Court, she points to two basic factors which in her view distinguish ch. 31, § 23 from the neutral rules at issue in the *Washington v. Davis* and *Arlington Heights* cases. The first is the nature of the preference, which is said to be demonstrably gender-biased in the sense that it favors a status reserved under federal military policy primarily to men. The second concerns the impact of the absolute lifetime preference upon the employment opportunities of women, an impact claimed to be too inevitable to have been unintended. The appellee contends that these factors, coupled with the fact that the preference itself has little if any relevance to actual job performance, more than suffice to prove the discriminatory intent required to establish a constitutional violation.

To the extent that the status of veteran is one that few women have been enabled to achieve, every hiring preference for veterans, however modest or extreme, is inherently gender-based. If Massachusetts by offering such a preference can be said intentionally to have incorporated into its state employment policies the historical gender-based federal military personnel practices, the degree of the preference would or should make no constitutional difference. Invidious discrimination does not become less so because the discrimination accomplished is of a lesser magnitude. Discriminatory intent is simply not amenable to calibration. It either is a factor that has influenced the legislative choice or it is not. The District Court's conclusion that the absolute veterans' preference was not originally enacted or subsequently reaffirmed for the purpose of giving an advantage to males as such necessarily compels the conclusion that the State intended nothing more than to prefer "veterans." Given this finding, simple logic suggests that an intent to exclude women from significant public jobs was not at work in this law. To reason that it was, by describing the preference as "inherently non-neutral" or "gender-based," is merely to restate the fact of impact, not to answer the question of intent.

The appellee's ultimate argument rests upon the presumption, common to the criminal and civil law, that a person intends the natural and foreseeable consequences of his voluntary actions. The decision to grant a preference to veterans was of course "intentional." So, necessarily, did an adverse impact upon nonveterans follow from that decision. And it cannot seriously be argued that the legislature of Massachusetts could have been unaware that most veterans are men. It would thus be disingenuous to say that the adverse consequences of this legislation for women were unintended, in the sense that they were not volitional or in the sense that they were not foreseeable.

"Discriminatory purpose," however, implies more than intent as volition or intent as awareness of consequences. It implies that the decisionmaker, in this case a state legislature, selected or reaffirmed a particular course of action at least in part "because of," not merely "in spite of," its adverse effects upon an identifiable group.[25] Yet nothing in the record demonstrates that this preference for veterans was originally devised or subsequently re-enacted because it would accomplish the collateral goal of keeping women in a stereotypic and predefined place in the Massachusetts Civil Service.

To the contrary, the statutory history shows that the benefit of the preference was consistently offered to "any person" who was a veteran. That benefit has been extended to women under a very broad statutory definition of the term veteran. The preference formula itself, which is the focal point of this challenge, was first adopted — so it appears from this record — out of a perceived need to help a small group of older Civil War veterans. It has since been reaffirmed and extended only to cover new veterans. When the totality of legislative actions establishing and extending the Massachusetts veterans' preference are considered, the law remains what it purports to be: a preference for veterans of either sex over nonveterans of either sex, not for men over women.

Justice Stevens, with whom Justice White joins, concurring.

While I concur in the Court's opinion, I confess that I am not at all sure that there is any difference between the two questions posed. If a classification is not overtly based on gender, I am inclined to believe the question whether it is covertly gender-based is the same as the question whether its adverse effects reflect invidious gender-based discrimination. However the question is phrased, for me the answer is largely provided by the fact that the number of males disadvantaged by Massachusetts' Veterans Preference (1,867,000) is sufficiently large — and sufficiently close to the number of disadvantaged females (2,954,000) — to refute the claim that the rule was intended to benefit males as a class over females as a class.

Justice Marshall, with whom Justice Brennan joins, dissenting.

Although acknowledging that in some circumstances, discriminatory intent may be inferred from the inevitable or foreseeable impact of a statute, the Court concludes that no such intent has been established here. I cannot agree. In my judgment, Massachusetts' choice of an absolute veterans' preference system evinces purposeful gender-based discrimination. And because the statutory scheme bears no substantial relationship to a legitimate governmental objective, it cannot withstand scrutiny under the Equal Protection Clause.

That a legislature seeks to advantage one group does not, as a matter of logic or of common sense, exclude the possibility that it also intends to disadvantage another. Individuals in general and lawmakers in particular frequently act for a variety of reasons. Thus, the critical constitutional inquiry is not whether an illicit consideration was the primary or but-for cause of a

[25] This is not to say that the inevitability or foreseeability of consequences of a neutral rule has no bearing upon the existence of discriminatory intent. Certainly, when the adverse consequences of a law upon an identifiable group are as inevitable as the gender-based consequences of ch. 31, § 23, a strong inference that the adverse effects were desired can reasonably be drawn. But in this inquiry — made as it is under the Constitution — an inference is a working tool, not a synonym for proof. When as here, the impact is essentially an unavoidable consequence of a legislative policy that has in itself always been deemed to be legitimate, and when, as here, the statutory history and all of the available evidence affirmatively demonstrate the opposite, the inference simply fails to ripen into proof.

decision, but rather whether it had an appreciable role in shaping a given legislative enactment.

Although neutral in form, the statute is anything but neutral in application. It inescapably reserves a major sector of public employment to "an already established class which, as a matter of historical fact, is 98% male." Where the foreseeable impact of a facially neutral policy is so disproportionate, the burden should rest on the State to establish that sex-based considerations played no part in the choice of the particular legislative scheme.

Clearly, that burden was not sustained here. The legislative history of the statute reflects the Commonwealth's patent appreciation of the impact the preference system would have on women, and an equally evident desire to mitigate that impact only with respect to certain traditionally female occupations. Until 1971, the statute and implementing civil service regulations exempted from operation of the preference any job requisitions "especially calling for women." In practice, this exemption, coupled with the absolute preference for veterans, has created a gender-based civil service hierarchy, with women occupying low grade clerical and secretarial jobs and men holding more responsible and remunerative positions. Thus, for over 70 years, the Commonwealth has maintained, as an integral part of its veterans' preference system, an exemption relegating female civil service applicants to occupations traditionally filled by women. Such a statutory scheme both reflects and perpetuates precisely the kind of archaic assumptions about women's roles which we have previously held invalid.

To survive challenge under the Equal Protection Clause, statutes reflecting gender-based discrimination must be substantially related to the achievement of important governmental objectives. Appellants here advance three interests in support of the absolute preference system: (1) assisting veterans in their readjustment to civilian life; (2) encouraging military enlistment; and (3) rewarding those who have served their country. Although each of those goals is unquestionably legitimate, the "mere recitation of a benign compensatory purpose" cannot of itself insulate legislative classifications from constitutional scrutiny. And in this case, the Commonwealth has failed to establish a sufficient relationship between its objectives and the means chosen to effectuate them.

[The dissent's analysis of the state interests is omitted.]

NOTES

1. *Identifying gender-based discrimination.* Do all laws that disadvantage women more than men (or vice versa) constitute gender discrimination? Judge Diane Wood, *Sex Discrimination in Life and Law*, 1999 U. CHI. LEGAL F. 1, notes that "[w]hatever lack of clarity there is in the terms 'sex' when we think about proscriptions against sex discrimination, it is nothing in comparison to the confusion that abounds with respect to the notion of 'discrimination' in this area. Is 'discrimination' just the flip side of equality or does an anti-discrimination principle evoke something different from the norm of equal treatment?" She observes that "courts have not traditionally used the term 'sex' to encompass issues relating to sexual orientation, [y]et it is easy to see how the two ideas are at least closely related, if not overlapping or coincident." Is the ban on same-sex marriage a form of gender discrimination? Is the regulation or prohibition of abortion a form of gender discrimination?

Mary Becker, *The Sixties Shift to Formal Equality and the Courts: An Argument for Pragmatism and Politics*, 40 Wm. & Mary L. Rev. 209, 210 (1998), says that by the end of the 1960's the primary focus of gender discrimination was on formal equality — "the idea that men and women are similarly situated, and therefore, should have the same rights and opportunities." But she argues that times have changed. "At best formal equality can only get women who look like men the rights men enjoy. It cannot generate new rules that accommodate women's styles and lifestyles as well as mens." *Id.* at 259. Professor Becker concludes that in today's world, "formal equality is a barrier to the flexibility and experimentation needed to combat the new, sex neutral ways in which law supports patriarchy." *Id.* at 272. Does this analysis suggest a different approach to identifying prohibited gender discrimination?

2. *Geduldig v. Aiello*, 417 U.S. 484 (1974). The Court upheld a California disability insurance program which exempted from coverage any work loss resulting from normal pregnancy using the rational basis test. Justice Stewart, for the Court, found no discrimination with respect to the persons or groups eligible for participation:

> There is no evidence in the record that the selection of the risk insured by the program worked to discriminate against any definable group or class in terms of the aggregate risk protection derived by that group or class from the program. There is no risk from which men are protected and women are not. Likewise, there is no risk from which women are protected and men are not.

In a footnote, gender discrimination cases were distinguished since the insurance program:

> does not exclude anyone from benefit eligibility because of gender but merely removes one physical condition — pregnancy — from the list of compensable disabilities. While it is true that only women can become pregnant, it does not follow that every legislative classification concerning pregnancy is a sex-based classification like those considered in Reed and Frontiero. Normal pregnancy is an objectively identifiable physical condition with unique characteristics. Absent a showing that distinctions involving pregnancy are mere pretexts designed to effect an invidious discrimination against the members of one sex or the other, lawmakers are constitutionally free to include or exclude pregnancy from the coverage of legislation such as this on any reasonable basis, just as with respect to any other physical condition.

The two classes were not men and women but "pregnant women and non-pregnant persons," the latter class including both males and females.

Justice Brennan, joined by Justices Douglas and Marshall, dissenting, argued that

> by singling out for less favorable treatment a gender-linked disability peculiar to women, the State has created a double standard for disability compensation. In effect, one set of rules is applied to females and another to males. Such dissimilar treatment of men and women, on the basis of physical characteristics inextricably linked to one sex, inevitably constitutes sex discrimination.

See *General Elec. Co. v. Gilbert*, 429 U.S. 125 (1976), applying the *Geduldig v. Aiello* approach to Title VII. This approach to pregnancy classification in employment was subsequently reversed by a congressional amendment of Title VII. 92 Stat. 2076 (1978).

3. *Abortion clinic access.* *Bray v. Alexandria Women's Health Clinic*, 506 U.S. 263 (1993), rejected an effort to use federal civil rights law, 42 U.S.C. § 1985(3), which provides a federal cause of action for conspiracies to deprive a person or class of persons of constitutional rights, against Operation Rescue's efforts to block access to abortion clinics. Justice Scalia, for the majority, held that the abortion clinic had shown no "racial, or perhaps otherwise class-based, individious discriminatory animus behind the conspirator's action." Justice Scalia reasoned that the term class "connotes something more than a group of individuals who share a desire to engage in conduct that the § 1985(3) defendant disfavors." Here, Operation Rescue's demonstrations had a harmful effect on women seeking abortions but did not discriminate against women in general. Justice Scalia rejected the proposition "that since voluntary abortion is an activity engaged in only by women, to disfavor it is *ipso facto* to discriminate invidiously against women as a class." It should be noted that the Court was interpreting only statutory requirements and not directly addressing the Constitution's equal protection guarantee. Congress then adopted the Freedom of Access to Clinic Entrances Act of 1994, 18 U.S.C. § 248.

4. *Requiring intent.* As in the race cases, *Feeney* requires a plaintiff to prove intent to discriminate on the basis of gender and rejects knowledge or foreseeability as the measure of intent. Reva Siegel, *Why Equal Protection No Longer Protects: The Evolving Forms of Status-Enforcing State Action*, 49 STAN. L. REV. 1111, 1134 (1997), says that "in rejecting forms of conscious intent it termed 'volition' or 'awareness of consequences,' the Court deemed tort standards of foreseeability an inadequate basis for holding state actors accountable for their actions under the Equal Protection Clause. Instead, in *Feeney*, the Court asked plaintiffs to prove that legislators adopting a policy that would foreseeably injure women or minorities had acted with the express purpose of injuring women or minorities — in short, a legislative state of mind akin to malice." She argues that "the form of discriminatory purpose the Court asked plaintiffs to prove in *Feeney* . . . is one that the sociological and psychological studies of racial bias suggest plaintiffs will rarely be able to prove." *Id.* at 1137.

5. *Intent in Feeney.* Given the extreme disparate impact of Massachusetts' lifetime gender preference for veterans, why does plaintiff fail in *Feeney*? Consider the following from Eric Schnapper, *Two Categories of Discriminatory Intent*, 17 HARV. C.R.-C.L. L. REV. 31, 44 (1982): "The *Feeney* opinion persuasively demonstrates that harming women was not the goal of the veterans' preference. But the adverse impact on women was the social cost of achieving the goal of helping veterans. Unconsidered was why the legislature was willing to accept that cost or why the state had chosen this extreme form of preference to reward veterans for their service to the nation rather than any of the wide variety of less discriminatory means available."

[2] "Real Gender Differences"

Equal protection requires that those who are similarly situated should be treated alike. But there *are* differences between men and women. For example, only women can become pregnant or have an abortion. To what extent are decision makers constitutionally allowed to use such differences in fashioning laws? Are such classifications "suspect" and subject to heightened scrutiny? *Must* decisionmakers consider such differences in fashioning policy in order to assure equality? Equal protection may not be afforded if persons that are different are treated alike. Is the objective to minimize the impact of sexual differences in an effort to achieve a gender neutral society? Or, should the focus be on recognizing the unique characteristics and needs of each gender?

Professor Martha Minow, *Foreword: Justice Engendered*, 101 Harv. L. Rev. 10, 12–13 (1987), poses three versions of the "dilemma of difference." First is the dilemma that difference may be recreated by noticing it or destroyed by ignoring it. The second version is the "riddle of neutrality" — that government may "freeze in place" sexual disparities by refusing to recognize differences but may reinforce stereotypes by recognizing differences. Third is the dilemma posed by having to choose between granting decision-makers broad discretion and imposing fixed rules. "Formal rules constrain public or private discretion, but their very specificity may make differences significant."

MICHAEL M. v. SUPERIOR COURT

450 U.S. 464, 101 S. Ct. 1200, 67 L. Ed. 2d 437 (1981)

Justice Rehnquist announced the judgment of the Court and delivered an opinion in which The Chief Justice [Burger], and Justices Stewart and Powell joined.

The question presented in this case is whether California's "statutory rape" law, § 261.5 of the California Penal Code, violates the Equal Protection Clause of the Fourteenth Amendment. Section 261.5 defines unlawful sexual intercourse as "an act of sexual intercourse accomplished with a female not the wife of the perpetrator, where the female is under the age of 18 years." The statute thus makes men alone criminally liable for the act of sexual intercourse.

In July 1978, a complaint was filed in the Municipal Court of Sonoma County, Cal., alleging that petitioner, then a 17 1/2 year old male, had had unlawful sexual intercourse with a female under the age of 18, in violation of § 261.5. Prior to trial, petitioner sought to set aside the information on both state and federal constitutional grounds, asserting that § 261.5 unlawfully discriminated on the basis of gender. The trial court and the California Court of Appeal denied petitioner's request for relief and petitioner sought review in the Supreme Court of California [which upheld the statute].

As is evident from our opinions, the Court has had some difficulty in agreeing upon the proper approach and analysis in cases involving challenges to gender-based classifications. [W]e have not held that gender-based classifications are "inherently suspect" and thus we do not apply so-called "strict scrutiny" to those classifications. Our cases have held, however, that the traditional minimum rationality test takes on a somewhat "sharper focus" when gender-based classifications are challenged. In *Reed v. Reed*, for example, the Court stated that a gender-based classification will be upheld if it bears a "fair and substantial relationship" to legitimate state ends, while in *Craig v. Boren*, the Court restated the test to require the classification to bear a "substantial relationship" to "important governmental objectives."

Underlying these decisions is the principle that a legislature may not "make overbroad generalizations based on sex which are entirely unrelated to any differences between men and women or which demean the ability or social status of the affected class." But because the Equal Protection Clause does not "demand that a statute necessarily apply equally to all persons" or require "things which are different in fact to be treated in law as though they were the same," this Court has consistently upheld statutes where the gender classification is not invidious, but rather realistically reflects the fact that the sexes are not similarly situated in certain circumstances. As the Court has stated, a legislature may "provide for the special problems of women."

Applying those principles to this case, the fact that the California Legislature criminalized the act of illicit sexual intercourse with a minor female is a sure indication of its intent or purpose to discourage that conduct. Precisely why the legislature desired that result is of course somewhat less clear. This Court has long recognized that "inquiries into congressional motives or purposes are a hazardous matter," and the search for the "actual" or "primary" purpose of a statute is likely to be elusive. Here, for example, the individual legislators may have voted for the statute for a variety of reasons. Some legislators may have been concerned about preventing teenage pregnancies, others about protecting young females from physical injury or from the loss of "chastity," and still others about promoting various religious and moral attitudes towards premarital sex.

The justification for the statute offered by the State, and accepted by the Supreme Court of California, is that the legislature sought to prevent illegitimate teenage pregnancies. That finding, of course, is entitled to great deference. And although our cases establish that the State's asserted reason for the enactment of a statute may be rejected, "if it could not have been a goal of the legislation," this is not such a case. We are satisfied not only that the prevention of illegitimate pregnancy is at least one of the "purposes" of the statute, but that the State has a strong interest in preventing such pregnancy. At the risk of stating the obvious, teenage pregnancies, which have increased dramatically over the last two decades, have significant social, medical and economic consequences for both the mother and her child, and the State. Of particular concern to the State is that approximately half of all teenage pregnancies end in abortion. And of those children who are born, their illegitimacy makes them likely candidates to become wards of the State.

We need not be medical doctors to discern that young men and young women are not similarly situated with respect to the problems and the risks of sexual intercourse. Only women may become pregnant and they suffer disproportionately the profound physical, emotional and psychological consequences of sexual activity. The statute at issue here protects women from sexual intercourse at an age when those consequences are particularly severe.[7]

The question thus boils down to whether a State may attack the problem of sexual intercourse and teenage pregnancy directly by prohibiting a male from having sexual intercourse with a minor female.[8] We hold that such a statute is sufficiently related to the State's objectives to pass constitutional muster. Because virtually all of the significant harmful and inescapably identifiable consequences of teenage pregnancy fall on the young female, a legislature acts well within its authority when it elects to punish only the participant who, by nature, suffers few of the consequences of his conduct. It is hardly unreasonable for a legislature acting to protect minor females to exclude them from punishment. Moreover, the risk of pregnancy itself constitutes a substantial deterrence to young females. No similar natural sanctions deter males. A criminal sanction imposed solely on males thus serves to roughly "equalize" the deterrents on the sexes.

We are unable to accept petitioner's contention that the statute is impermissibly underinclusive and must, in order to pass judicial scrutiny, be broadened so as to hold the female as criminally liable as the male. It is argued that this statute is not necessary to deter teenage pregnancy because a gender-neutral statute, where both male and female would be subject to prosecution, would serve that goal equally well. The relevant inquiry, however, is not whether the statute is drawn as precisely as it might have been, but whether the line chosen by the California Legislature is within constitutional limitations. In any event, we cannot say that a gender-neutral statute would be as effective as the statute California has chosen to enact. The State persuasively contends that a gender-neutral statute would frustrate its interest in effective enforcement. Its view is that a female is surely less likely to report violations of the statute if she herself would be subject to criminal prosecution. In an area already fraught with prosecutorial difficulties, we decline to hold that the Equal Protection Clause requires a legislature to enact a statute so broad that it may well be incapable of enforcement.

In upholding the California statute we also recognize that this is not a case where a statute is being challenged on the grounds that it "invidiously

---

[7] Although petitioner concedes that the State has a "compelling" interest in preventing teenage pregnancy, he contends that the "true" purpose of § 261.5 is to protect the virtue and chastity of young women. As such, the statute is unjustifiable because it rests on archaic stereotypes. What we have said above is enough to dispose of that contention. The question for us — and the only question under the Federal Constitution — is whether the legislation violates the Equal Protection Clause of the Fourteenth Amendment, not whether its supporters may have endorsed it for reasons no longer generally accepted. Even if the preservation of female chastity were one of the motives of the statute, and even if that motive be impermissible, petitioner's argument must fail because "it is a familiar practice of constitutional law that this court will not strike down an otherwise constitutional statute on the basis of an alleged illicit legislative motive." *United States v. O'Brien*.

[8] We do not understand petitioner to question a state's authority to make sexual intercourse among teenagers a criminal act, at least on a gender-neutral basis. The Court has long recognized that a State has even broader authority to protect the physical, mental, and moral well-being of its youth, than of its adults.

discriminates" against females. To the contrary, the statute places a burden on males which is not shared by females. But we find nothing to suggest that men, because of past discrimination or peculiar disadvantages, are in need of the special solicitude of the courts. Nor is this a case where the gender classification is made "solely for administrative convenience," or rests on "the baggage of sexual stereotypes." As we have held, the statute instead reasonably reflects the fact that the consequences of sexual intercourse and pregnancy fall more heavily on the female than on the male.

JUSTICE STEWART, concurring.

The Constitution is violated when government, state or federal, invidiously classifies similarly situated people on the basis of the immutable characteristics with which they were born. Thus, detrimental racial classifications by government always violate the Constitution, for the simple reason that, so far as the Constitution is concerned, people of different races are always similarly situated. *See Fullilove v. Klutznick* (dissenting opinion). By contrast, while detrimental gender classifications by government often violate the Constitution, they do not always do so, for the reason that there are differences between males and females that the Constitution necessarily recognizes. In this case we deal with the most basic of these differences: females can become pregnant as the result of sexual intercourse; males cannot.

[W]e have recognized that in certain narrow circumstances men and women are not similarly situated, and in these circumstances a gender classification based on clear differences between the sexes is not invidious, and a legislative classification realistically based upon those differences is not unconstitutional. Applying these principles to the classification enacted by the California Legislature, it is readily apparent that § 261.5 does not violate the Equal Protection Clause. Young women and men are not similarly situated with respect to the problems and risk associated with intercourse and pregnancy, and the statute is realistically related to the legitimate state purpose of reducing those problems and risks.

JUSTICE BLACKMUN, concurring in the judgment.

I cannot vote to strike down the California statutory rape law, for I think it is a sufficiently reasoned and constitutional effort to control the problem at its inception. For me, there is an important difference between this state action and a State's adamant and rigid refusal to face, or even to recognize, the "significant consequences" — to the woman — of a forced or unwanted conception. I am persuaded that, although a minor has substantial privacy rights in intimate affairs connected with procreation, California's efforts to prevent teenage pregnancy are to be viewed differently [from] efforts to inhibit a woman from dealing with pregnancy once it has become an inevitability.

JUSTICE BRENNAN, with whom JUSTICES WHITE and MARSHALL join, dissenting.

It is disturbing to find the Court so splintered on a case that presents such a straighforward issue: whether the admittedly gender-based classification in Cal. Penal Code § 261.5 bears a sufficient relationship to the State's asserted goal of preventing teenage pregnancies to survive the "mid-level" constitutional scrutiny mandated by *Craig v. Boren*.

[E]ven assuming that prevention of teenage pregnancy is an important governmental objective and that it is in fact an objective of § 261.5, California still has the burden of proving that there are fewer teenage pregnancies under its gender-based statutory rape law than there would be if the law were gender-neutral. To meet this burden, the State must show that because its statutory rape law punishes only males, and not females, it more effectively deters minor females from having sexual intercourse.

However, a State's bare assertion that its gender-based statutory classification substantially furthers an important governmental interest is not enough to meet its burden of proof under *Craig v. Boren*. Rather, the State must produce evidence that will persuade the Court that its assertion is true. The State has not produced such evidence in this case. Moreover, there are at least two serious flaws in the State's assertion that law enforcement problems created by a gender-neutral statutory rape law would make such a statute less effective than a gender-based statute in deterring sexual activity.

First, the experience of other jurisdictions, and California itself, belies the plurality's conclusion that a gender-neutral statutory rape law "may well be incapable of enforcement." There are now at least 37 States that have enacted gender-neutral statutory rape laws. California has introduced no evidence that those states have been handicapped by the enforcement problems the plurality finds so persuasive. In addition, the California Legislature in recent years has revised other sections of the Penal Code to make them gender-neutral. Again, the State has introduced no evidence to explain why a gender-neutral statutory rape law would be any more difficult to enforce than those statutes.

The second flaw in the State's assertion is that even assuming that a gender-neutral statute would be more difficult to enforce, the State has still not shown that those enforcement problems would make such a statute less effective than a gender-based statute in deterring minor females from engaging in sexual intercourse. Common sense, however, suggests that a gender-neutral statutory rape law is potentially a greater deterrent of sexual activity than a gender-based law, for the simple reason that a gender-neutral law subjects both men and women to criminal sanctions and thus arguably has a deterrent effect on twice as many potential violators. Even if fewer persons were prosecuted under the gender-neutral law, as the State suggests, it would still be true that twice as many persons would be subject to arrest. The State's failure to prove that a gender-neutral law would be a less effective deterrent than a gender-based law, like the State's failure to prove that a gender-neutral law would be difficult to enforce, should have led this Court to invalidate § 261.5.

Until very recently, no California court or commentator had suggested that the purpose of California's statutory rape law was to protect young women from the risk of pregnancy. Indeed, the historical development of § 261.5 demonstrates that the law was initially enacted on the premise that young women, in contrast to young men, were to be deemed legally incapable of consenting to an act of sexual intercourse. Because their chastity was considered particularly precious, those young women were felt to be uniquely in need of the State's protection. In contrast, young men were assumed to be capable of making such decisions for themselves; the law therefore did not offer them any special protection.

It is perhaps because the gender classification in California's statutory rape law was initially designed to further these outmoded sexual stereotypes, rather than to reduce the incidence of teenage pregnancies, that the State has been unable to demonstrate a substantial relationship between the classification and its newly asserted goal. But whatever the reason, the State has not shown that Cal. Penal Code § 261.5 is any more effective than a gender-neutral law would be in deterring minor females from engaging in sexual intercourse. It has therefore not met its burden of proving that the statutory classification is substantially related to the achievement of its asserted goal.

JUSTICE STEVENS, dissenting.

[I]f, as in this case, there is an apparent connection between the discrimination and the fact that only women can become pregnant, it may be appropriate to presume that the classification is lawful. This presumption, however, may be overcome by a demonstration that the apparent justification for the discrimination is illusory or wholly inadequate. Thus, instead of applying a "mid-level" form of scrutiny in all sex discrimination cases, perhaps the burden is heavier in some than in others. Nevertheless, as I have previously suggested, the ultimate standard in these, as in all other equal protection cases, is essentially the same. Professor Cox recently noted that however the level of scrutiny is described, in the final analysis, "the Court is always deciding whether in its judgment the harm done to the disadvantaged class by the legislative classification is disproportionate to the public purposes the measure is likely to achieve." Cox, *Book Review*, 94 HARV L. REV. 700, 706 (1981).

[T]he plurality is quite correct in making the assumption that the joint act that this law seeks to prohibit creates a greater risk of harm for the female than for the male. But the plurality surely cannot believe that the risk of pregnancy confronted by the female — any more than the risk of venereal disease confronted by males as well as females — has provided an effective deterrent to voluntary female participation in the risk-creating conduct. Yet the plurality's decision seems to rest on the assumption that the California Legislature acted on the basis of that rather fanciful notion.

In my judgment, the fact that a class of persons is especially vulnerable to a risk that a statute is designed to avoid is a reason for making the statute applicable to that class. The argument that a special need for protection provides a rational explanation for an exemption is one I simply do not comprehend. In this case, the fact that a female confronts a greater risk of harm than a male is a reason for applying the prohibition to her — not a reason for granting her a license to use her own judgment on whether or not to assume the risk. Surely, if we examine the problem from the point of view of society's interest in preventing the risk-creating conduct from occurring at all, it is irrational to exempt 50% of the potential violators.

In my opinion, the only acceptable justification for a general rule requiring disparate treatment of the two participants in a joint act must be a legislative judgment that one is more guilty than the other. The risk-creating conduct that this statute is designed to prevent requires the participation of two persons — one male and one female. The question raised by this statute is whether the State, consistently with the Federal Constitution, may always punish the male and never the female when they are equally responsible or when the female is the more responsible of the two.

It would seem to me that an impartial lawmaker could give only one answer to that question. The fact that the California Legislature has decided to apply its prohibition only to the male may reflect a legislative judgment that in the typical case the male is actually the more guilty party. Any such judgment must, in turn, assume that the decision to engage in the risk-creating conduct is always — or at least typically — a male decision. If that assumption is valid, the statutory classification should also be valid. But what is the support for the assumption? It is not contained in the record of this case or in any legislative history or scholarly study that has been called to our attention. I think it is supported to some extent by traditional attitudes toward male-female relationships. But the possibility that such an habitual attitude may reflect nothing more than an irrational prejudice makes it an insufficient justification for discriminatory treatment that is otherwise blatantly unfair. For, as I read this statute, it requires that one, and only one, of two equally guilty wrongdoers be stigmatized by a criminal conviction.

Finally, even if my logic is faulty and there actually is some speculative basis for treating equally guilty males and females differently, I still believe that any such speculative justification would be outweighed by the paramount interest in even-handed enforcement of the law. A rule that authorizes punishment of only one of two equally guilty wrongdoers violates the essence of the constitutional requirement that the sovereign must govern impartially.

***Rostker v. Goldberg*, 453 U.S. 57 (1981).** The Court, per Justice Rehnquist, held that Congress' decision to authorize the draft registration only of men does not violate the Fifth Amendment Due Process Clause. The Military Selective Service Act (the MSSA), empowers the President to require males, but not females, between the ages of 18 and 26, to register for possible conscription. In 1980, President Carter decided to reactivate draft registration, which had been discontinued in 1975. In his request to Congress for funding, the President recommended the MSSA be amended to permit the registration and conscription of women. While Congress allocated funds for reactivating the registration, it declined to amend the MSSA and allocated only such funds as were required for registering males. By proclamation on July 2, 1980, the President ordered registration of males to begin on July 21, 1980.

In rejecting the Fifth Amendment challenge, Justice Rehnquist began from the premise that the deference normally due decisions of Congress is increased when Congress is acting under its authority over national defense and military affairs: "[P]erhaps in no other area has the Court accorded Congress greater deference. Not only is the scope of Congress' constitutional power in this area broad, but the lack of competence on the part of the courts is marked. [T]he tests and limitations to be applied may differ because of the military context." But the Court did not expressly adopt the rationality test argued by the government.

> We do not think that the substantive guarantee of due process or certainty in the law will be advanced by any further "refinement" in the applicable tests as suggested by the Government. Announced

> degrees of "deference" to legislative judgments, just as levels of "scrutiny" which this Court announces that it applies to particular classifications made by a legislative body, may all too readily become facile abstractions used to justify a result. In this case the courts are called upon to decide whether Congress, acting under an explicit constitutional grant of authority, has by that action transgressed an explicit guarantee of individual rights which limits the authority so conferred. Simply labeling the legislative decision "military" on the one hand or "gender-based" on the other does not automatically guide a court to the correct constitutional result.

It could not be denied, Justice Rehnquist reasoned, that the government's interest in raising and supporting armies is an "important governmental interest," under the *Craig* test. The congressional decision to register only males resulted from an assessment that any future draft would be characterized by a need for combat troops and, since women as a group are not eligible for combat, Congress exempted them from registration. "The reason women are exempted from registration is not because military needs can be met by drafting men. This is not a case of Congress arbitrarily choosing to burden one of two similarly situated groups. [M]en and women, because of the combat restrictions on women, are simply not similarly situated for purposes of a draft or registration for a draft."

Justice White, joined by Justice Brennan, dissenting, rejected the position that Congress had concluded that all non-combat positions should be filled with combat ready personnel. Nor had Congress determined that all women who could serve in wartime without adversely affecting combat readiness could be filled by volunteers. Instead, the record indicated that 80,000 persons would have to be conscripted to fill positions not requiring combat-ready men. Justice White did indicate a willingness to remand for fact-finding "on this crucial issue."

Justice Marshall, joined by Justice Brennan, dissenting, was critical of the Court for placing "its imprimatur on one of the most potent remaining public expressions of 'ancient canards about the proper role of women.'"

> In my judgment, there simply is no basis for concluding in this case that excluding women from registration is substantially related to the achievement of a concededly important governmental interest in maintaining an effective defense.
>
> In this case, the Government makes no claim that preparing for a draft of combat troops cannot be accomplished just as effectively by registering both men and women but drafting only men if only men turn out to be needed. Nor can the Government argue that this alternative entails the additional cost and administrative inconvenience of registering women. This Court has repeatedly stated that the administrative convenience of employing a gender classification is not an adequate constitutional justification under the *Craig v. Boren* test.

***Caban v. Mohammed,* 441 U.S. 380 (1979).** The Court held unconstitutional, 5-4, a state law permitting the mother, but not the father, of an illegitimate child to block the child's adoption by withholding consent. Justice Powell, for the Court, invoked the *Craig v. Boren* intermediate standard of review, finding the law "another example of 'overbroad generalizations' in gender-based classifications." The Court rejected the state's claim that the classification could be justified by the closer relation of a mother to her child, concluding that "maternal and paternal roles are not invariably different in importance." Even if this assumption were generally accurate for newborn infants, "this generalization concerning parent-child relations would become less acceptable as a basis for legislative distinctions as the age of the child increased." Indeed, the present case challenged the assumption. The father had lived with the mother and two children (age four and six) in a natural family relationship for several years and had participated in the care and support of the children. There was no reason to believe that the mother had a closer relationship to the children. Justice Powell concluded: "we reject, therefore, the claim that the broad, gender-based distinction of [the statute] is required by any universal difference between maternal and paternal relations at every phase of a child's development."

Justice Stewart, dissenting, argued that men and women were "not in fact similarly situated in the area covered by the law in question," and hence, equal protection was not violated.

> With respect to a large group of adoptions — those of newborn children and infants — unwed mothers and unwed fathers are simply not similarly situated. Our law has given the unwed mother the custody of her illegitimate children precisely because it is she who bears the child and because the vast majority of unwed fathers have been unknown, unavailable, or simply uninterested. This custodial preference has carried with it a correlative power in the mother to place her child for adoption or not to do so.

Justice Stevens dissenting, joined by Chief Justice Burger and Justice Rehnquist, found sufficient justification for the law in the state interest in facilitating adoption. "[A]s a matter of equal protection analysis, it is perfectly obvious that at the time and immediately after a child is born out of wedlock differences between men and women justify some differential treatment of the mother and father in the adoption process." Since the law was justified in the most common cases, *i.e.* involving newborns and infants in the mothers' custody, "we should presume that the law is entirely valid and require the challenger to demonstrate that its unjust applications are sufficiently numerous and serious to render it invalid." The lower courts had found the number of fathers similarly situated to the father in the present case was small and that the disadvantage to such a class "insignificant by comparison to the benefits of the rule as it now stands."

***Parham v. Hughes,* 441 U.S. 347 (1979).** The Court held, 5-4, that neither the Due Process nor the Equal Protection Clause of the Fourteenth Amendment is violated by a state statute which denies the father of an illegitimate child who has not legitimated the child the right to sue for the child's wrongful death. The plurality opinion of Justice Stewart, joined by Chief Justice Burger and Justices Rehnquist and Stevens, concluded that the sex discrimination cases were inapposite since mothers and fathers of illegitimate children are not similarly situated in regard to the statute. Under state law, only the father of the illegitimate could take voluntary unilateral action to make the illegitimate child legitimate. The statute was held to be rationally related to resolving the difficult problem of proving paternity for illegitimate children and the related danger of spurious claims against intestate estates. It is not irrational to solve the problem of establishing paternity by limiting recovery for wrongful death only to those fathers of illegitimate children who have established paternity by legitimating their children. It is constitutionally irrelevant that the state might have chosen alternative means of establishing paternity.

Justice Powell concurred in the judgment but applied the intermediate standard of review applicable to gender-based classifications. He concluded that the state statute was substantially related to the state's objective of avoiding difficult problems in proving paternity.

Justice White, joined by Justices Brennan, Marshall, and Blackmun, dissented. Initially, they took issue with the Court's use of the rational basis test for what they deemed to be a gender-based discrimination.

> There is a startling circularity in [the plurality's] argument. The issue before the Court is whether Georgia may require unmarried fathers, but not unmarried mothers, to have pursued the statutory legitimization procedure in order to bring suit for the wrongful death of their children. Seemingly, it is irrelevant that as a matter of state law mothers may not legitimate their children, for they are not required to do so in order to maintain a wrongful death action. That only fathers may resort to the legitimization process cannot dissolve the sex discrimination in requiring them to. Under the plurality's bootstrap rationale, a State could require that women, but not men, pass a course in order to receive a taxi license, simply by limiting admission to the course to women.

Applying an intermediate standard of review, the dissent concluded that the Equal Protection Clause was not satisfied. The classification was not adequately related to the state's interest in avoiding problems of proving paternity. "The legitimization requirement is not only a rule concerning the competency of evidence but an absolute prerequisite to recovery for the wrongful death of a child, barring many who are capable of proving their parenthood, solely because they are fathers."

Nguyen v. INS (2001), text, p. 838. The Court held 5-4 that a federal statute requiring that children born outside of the United States and out of wedlock to fathers who are U.S. citizens be legitimized or obtain found proof of paternity by age 18 in order to obtain citizenship but imposing no similar requirement for mothers, does not violate equal protection.

NOTES

1. ***A dual standard?*** Is there a different standard of review used in *Michael M.* and *Rostker* from that used in *Craig v. Boren*? It has been suggested that these cases reflect two different approaches to the nature and significance of sex classifications. The approach reflected in *Craig v. Boren* creates a presumption of invalidity for all intentional sex classifications. The Court applies intermediate review, examining whether the actual purpose is important. The classification must be a "highly accurate proxy" for the characteristic said to distinguish men and women and any sex-neutral alternative must be shown to be less effective. A second approach, reflected in *Michael M.* and *Rostker*, focuses on whether women and men are "different in fact" in the context of the law at issue. If so, sex is not a neutral factor and the classification is not as suspect.

Ann Freedman, *Sex Equality, Sex Differences, and the Supreme Court,* 92 YALE L.J. 913, 931 (1983), is critical of Justices Rehnquist and Stewart's view of "real" differences: " 'Real' differences are defined broadly to include definitional differences, legally created differences, and differences that result from past discrimination against women. In cases involving 'real' differences, review of the relationship between the classification and the goal is deferential. This approach is also associated with a high degree of tolerance for facially sex-neutral rules that have a disparate impact on one sex." Should a law reflecting "real differences" still be treated as suspect to smoke out invidious gender discrimination or to determine if the real differences justify different legal treatment?

Suppose the statutory rape law is treated as a law for the protection of women — what legal consequences should follow? Consider the following: "By refusing to grant women autonomy and by protecting them in ways that men are not protected, the state treats women's bodies — and therefore women themselves as objects. Men are treated differently. Their bodies are considered part of them, subject to their free control." Frances Olsen, *Statutory Rape: A Feminist Critique of Rights Analysis*, 63 TEX. L. REV. 387, 406 (1984).

2. ***The nature of differences.*** A key question is how do you determine if sex differences are real; how do you determine if men and women are "similarly situated"? Some external standard must be used to define whether the classes are like or unlike. Are "real sex differences" simply a matter of demonstrating an aggregate statistical difference between men and women? Should the approach be limited to biological and physiological differences or does it include psychological and value differences? Cultural and legislatively created differences? And, even if there are real gender differences, how do we determine if the differences should be legally relevant? "We think we know what is real, what differences are real, and what really matters, even though sometimes we realize that our perceptions and desires are influenced by others." Minow, 101 HARV. L. REV. at 73.

In *Michael M.*, the difference is said to be biological. But it has been argued that *Michael M.* is based on assumptions concerning male responsibility in childbearing, the role of women *vis-a-vis* males in raising the children, and male aggressiveness and female passivity in sexual relationships. "When the

Court acts on the assumption that these stereotypes are natural, biological and unalterable, it reinforces and perpetuates the stereotypes." Sylvia Law, *Rethinking Sex and the Constitution*, 132 U. PA. L. REV. 955, 999–1000 (1984).

Catharine MacKinnon, *Reflections of Sex Equality Under Law*, 100 YALE L.J. 1281, 1304–05 (1991), takes issue with the Court's failure to identify accurately the relevant difference:

> Women and men are not similarly situated with regard to sexual assault in the sense that they are not equally subject to it or equally subjected to it. Underage girls form a credible disadvantaged group for equal protection purposes when the social facts of sexual assault are faced, facts which prominently feature one-sided sexual aggression by older males. It seems that in order to imagine equality, one must first be blind to inequality and to see inequality blinds one to seeing that equality is possible.

Consider the relevance of the Court's treatment of pregnancy classifications on the issue of reproductive freedom. "Because pregnancy is unique to women and there is no male analogue to women's childbearing ability, the Court has found that men and women are not 'similarly situated.' Thus, reproductive-based classifications need only meet the most minimal standard of review, leaving women's reproductive freedom virtually unprotected under the Equal Protection Clause." Stephanie Ridder & Lisa Woll, *Transforming the Grounds: Autonomy and Reproductive Freedom*, 2 YALE J.L. & FEMINISM 75, 80 (1989).

MacKinnon, 100 YALE L.J. at 1319, argues: "Because the social organization of reproduction is a major bulwark of women's social inequality, any constitutional interpretation of a sex equality principle must prohibit laws, state policies, or official practices and acts that deprive women of reproductive control or punish women for their reproductive role or capacity."

The "real sex difference" in *Rostker* is grounded on legislation disabling women from serving in combat. Consider the following: "The majority's acceptance, [in *Rostker*], of legally created differences as a basis for other sex-based laws seems inconsistent with any serious commitment to eliminating sex discrimination. If legislatures can create 'real' sex differences at will by passing sex-based laws, the equal protection clause can easily be circumvented." Freedman, 92 YALE L.J. at 939.

3. *Feminist constitutional jurisprudence.* There are differing approaches among feminists on how to approach sex classifications, especially those reflecting sex differences. Some writers tend to stress the antidiscrimination principle, formal equality and the need for sex-neutral laws, *i.e.* an assimilation or "sameness" perspective. Acceptance of sexual inequalities is criticized as a demand for special treatment rather than pursuit of the goal of equal treatment. "[W]e can't have it both ways, [and] we need to think carefully about which way we want to have it." Wendy Williams, *The Equality Crisis: Some Reflections on Culture, Courts and Feminism*, 8 WOMEN'S RTS. L. REP. 175, 196 (1982).

Other commentators accept that there are "differences" between men and women that may properly be reflected in different legal treatment. For example, much femininist jurisprudence focuses on "the tension between women's primary concern with intimacy or connection and men's primary focus on separation or autonomy." Suzanna Sherry, *Civic Virtue and the Feminine Voice in Constitutional Adjudication*, 72 VA. L. REV. 543, 580 (1986). *See* Robin West, *Jurisprudence and Gender*, 55 U. CHI. L. REV. 1 (1988), who similarly explores sexual and cultural differences and their legal relevance. *See generally* CAROL GILLIGAN, IN A DIFFERENT VOICE (1982), which significantly influenced the stress in feminist jurisprudence on women's greater capacity for connection with others.

CATHARINE A. MACKINNON, FEMINISM UNMODIFIED (1987), concludes that both the difference and the assimilation approaches are defective because they are premised on defining man as the norm against which woman is measured.

> Under the sameness standard, women are measured according to our correspondence with man, our equality judged by our proximity to his measure. Under the difference standard, we are measured according to our lack of correspondence with him, our womanhood judged by our distance from his measure. Gender neutrality is thus simply the male standard, and the special protection rule is simply the female standard, but do not be deceived: masculinity, or maleness, is the referent for both.

Id. at 34. She proposes focusing, not on whether men and women are "similarly situated" or different, but on "expos[ing] that which women have had little choice but to be confined to, in order to change it." *Id.* at 40. Professor MacKinnon's emphasis is on male dominance and oppression of women. The goal is to use law as an instrument to effectuate women's liberation.

Kathryn Abrams, *The Constitution of Women*, 48 ALA. L. REV. 861, 874 (1997), after surveying each of the above theories, offers the following perspective: "The goal should not be to find yet another theory that describes gender discrimination by reference to some single pattern, but rather to generate a multi-faceted theory which clarifies that discrimination against women differs in different contexts and which affects distinct subgroups of women in varying ways. The goal is not to formulate a new image of women that better captures their essence, but to propagate images of women that are plural and acknowledge the ambiguities in their experience."

[3] The Modern Standards

***Mississippi University for Women v. Hogan,* 458 U.S. 718 (1982).** Mississippi operated a number of coeducational professional nursing programs at various state-supported colleges and one nursing program limited to women at MUW. The male plaintiff wanted to enroll in the MUW program near his home and to receive credit for nursing work that he could continue if enrolled at this particular school. Justice O'Connor for the Supreme Court held that the intermediate standard of review established in *Craig v. Boren* required the state to show an "exceedingly persuasive justification" for a sex-based classification.

Mississippi's "primary justification for maintaining the single-sex admissions policy of MUW is that it compensates for discrimination against women and, therefore, constitutes affirmative action." Justice O'Connor's response to this argument was that women had not been discriminated against in the field of nursing. "Rather than compensate for discriminatory barriers faced by women, MUW's policy of excluding males from admission to the School of Nursing tends to perpetuate the stereotypical view of nursing as an exclusively woman's job."

Justice Powell, joined by Justice Rehnquist, dissented:

> The Court's opinion bows deeply to conformity. Left without honor — indeed, held unconstitutional — is an element of diversity that has characterized much of American education. The Court in effect holds today that no State now may provide even a single institution of higher learning open only to women students.

Chief Justice Burger and Justice Blackmun in separate dissents reiterated these themes of diversity and the threats of this case to all single-sex educational institutions.

***J.E.B. v. Alabama,* 511 U.S. 127 (1994).** The Court in *Batson v. Kentucky* had held race-based use of peremptory jury challenges to be unconstitutional. In *J.E.B.*, the Court, in an opinion by Justice Blackmun, held that the gender-based exercise of peremptory challenges by the prosecutor in a paternity and child support action was unconstitutional. The facts recited by Justice Blackmun were relatively simple:

> On behalf of T.B., the mother of a minor child, Alabama filed a complaint for paternity and child support against petitioner J.E.B. The trial court assembled a panel of 36 potential jurors, 12 males and 24 females. After the court excused three jurors for cause, only 10 of the remaining 33 jurors were male. The State then used 9 of its 10 peremptory strikes to remove male jurors; petitioner used all but one of his strikes to remove female jurors. As a result, all the selected jurors were female.

Justice Blackmun pointed out that gender-based discrimination in the exercise of peremptory challenges "is a relatively recent phenomenon" for the simple reason that women were not even allowed to serve on juries in most states until this century. He adopted the "exceedingly persuasive justification" standard from *MUW v. Hogan* as the guiding principle for assessing intentional discrimination on the basis of sex.

> Far from proffering an exceptionally persuasive justification for its gender-based peremptory challenges, respondent maintains that its decision to strike virtually all the males from the jury in this case "may reasonably have been based upon the perception, supported by history, that men otherwise totally qualified to serve upon a jury might be more sympathetic and receptive to the arguments of a man alleged in a paternity action to be the father of an out-of-wedlock child, while women equally qualified to serve upon a jury might be more sympathetic and receptive to the arguments of the complaining witness who bore the child."

> We shall not accept as a defense to gender-based peremptory challenges "the very stereotype the law condemns." Respondent's rationale, not unlike those regularly expressed for gender-based strikes, is reminiscent of the arguments advanced to justify the total exclusion of women from juries. Respondent offers virtually no support for the conclusion that gender alone is an accurate predictor of juror's attitudes; yet it urges this Court to condone the same stereotypes that justified the wholesale exclusion of women from juries and the ballot box.[11] Respondent seems to assume that gross generalizations that would be deemed impermissible if made on the basis of race are somehow permissible when made on the basis of gender.

Justice O'Connor, concurring, expressed her concern that "today's important blow against gender discrimination is not costless" she acknowledged "that like race, gender matters. A plethora of studies make clear that in rape cases, for example, female jurors are somewhat more likely to vote to convict than male jurors . . . [O]ne need not be a sexist to share the intuition that in certain cases a person's gender and resulting life experience will be relevant to his or her view of the case." Justice O'Connor expressed her "belief that today's holding should be limited to the *government's* use of gender-based peremptory strikes."

Chief Justice Rehnquist, dissented on the basis that

> there are sufficient differences between race and gender discrimination such that the principle of *Batson* should not be extended to peremptory challenges to potential jurors based on sex. Under the Equal Protection Clause, these differences mean that the balance should tilt in favor of peremptory challenges when sex, not race, is the issue. Unlike the Court, I think the State has shown that jury strikes on the basis of gender "substantially further" the State's legitimate interest in achieving a fair and impartial trial through the venerable practice of peremptory challenges. The two sexes differ, both biologically and, to a diminishing extent, in experience. It is not merely "stereotyping" to say that these differences may produce a difference in outlook which is brought to the jury room.

Justice Scalia, joined by Chief Justice Rehnquist and Justice Thomas, dissented in more caustic terms:

> Today's opinion is an inspiring demonstration of how thoroughly up-to-date and right-thinking we Justices are in matters pertaining to the sexes (or as the Court would have it, the genders), and how sternly

[11] Even if a measure of truth can be found in some of the gender stereotypes used to justify gender-based peremptory challenges, that fact alone cannot support discrimination on the basis of gender in jury selection. We have made abundantly clear in past cases that gender classifications that rest on impermissible stereotypes violate the Equal Protection Clause, even when some statistical support can be conjured up for the generalization. The generalization advanced by Alabama in support of its asserted right to discriminate on the basis of gender is, at the least, overbroad, and serves only to perpetuate the same "outmoded notions of the relative capabilities of men and women," that we have invalidated in other contexts.

we disapprove the male chauvinist attitudes of our predecessors. The price to be paid for this display — a modest price, surely — is that most of the opinion is quite irrelevant to the case at hand.

The core of the Court's reasoning is that peremptory challenges on the basis of any group characteristic subject to heightened scrutiny are inconsistent with the guarantee of the Equal Protection Clause. That conclusion can be reached only by focusing unrealistically upon individual exercises of the peremptory challenge, and ignoring the totality of the practice. Since all groups are subject to the peremptory challenge (and will be made the object of it, depending upon the nature of the particular case) it is hard to see how any group is denied equal protection. That explains why peremptory challenges coexisted with the Equal Protection Clause for 120 years. This case is a perfect example of how the system as a whole is even-handed. While the only claim before the Court is petitioner's complaint that the prosecutor struck male jurors, for every man struck by the government petitioner's own lawyer struck a woman. To say that men were singled out for discriminatory treatment in this process is preposterous. The situation would be different if both sides systematically struck individuals of one group, so that the strikes evinced group-based animus and served as a proxy for segregated venire lists. The pattern here, however, displays not a systemic sex-based animus but each side's desire to get a jury favorably disposed to its case. That is why the Court's characterization of respondent's argument as "reminiscent of the arguments advanced to justify the total exclusion of women from juries," is patently false. Women were categorically excluded from juries because of doubt that they were competent; women are stricken from juries by peremptory challenge because of doubt that they are well disposed to the striking party's case. There is discrimination and dishonor in the former, and not in the latter.

Kathryn Abrams, *The Constitution of Women*, 48 ALA L. REV. 861, 878 (1997), suggests Justice Blackmun's opinion would have been more satisfactory had he "noted that some experientially-based, gender-specific differences exist, but [he] concluded that acknowledging them through peremptory challenges carried too great a risk of rehabilitating stereotypes."

UNITED STATES v. VIRGINIA

518 U.S. 515, 116 S. Ct. 2264, 135 L. Ed. 2d 735 (1996)

JUSTICE GINSBURG delivered the opinion of the Court.

Virginia's public institutions of higher learning include an incomparable military college, Virginia Military Institute (VMI). The United States maintains that the Constitution's equal protection guarantee precludes Virginia from reserving exclusively to men the unique educational opportunities VMI affords. We agree.

Founded in 1839, VMI is today the sole single-sex school among Virginia's 15 public institutions of higher learning. VMI's distinctive mission is to produce "citizen-soldiers," men prepared for leadership in civilian life and in military service. VMI pursues this mission through pervasive training of a kind not available anywhere else in Virginia. Assigning prime place to character development, VMI uses an "adversative method" modeled on English public schools and once characteristic of military instruction. VMI constantly endeavors to instill physical and mental discipline in its cadets and impart to them a strong moral code. The school's graduates leave VMI with heightened comprehension of their capacity to deal with duress and stress, and a large sense of accomplishment for completing the hazardous course.

Neither the goal of producing citizen-soldiers nor VMI's implementing methodology is inherently unsuitable to women. And the school's impressive record in producing leaders has made admission desirable to some women. Nevertheless, Virginia has elected to preserve exclusively for men the advantages and opportunities a VMI education affords.

VMI produces its "citizen-soldiers" through "an adversative, or doubting, model of education" which features "[p]hysical rigor, mental stress, absolute equality of treatment, absence of privacy, minute regulation of behavior, and indoctrination in desirable values."

VMI cadets live in spartan barracks where surveillance is constant and privacy nonexistent; they wear uniforms, eat together in the mess hall, and regularly participate in drills. Entering students are incessantly exposed to the rat line, "an extreme form of the adversative model," comparable in intensity to Marine Corps boot camp. Tormenting and punishing, the rat line bonds new cadets to their fellow sufferers and, when they have completed the 7-month experience, to their former tormentors.

VMI's "adversative model" is further characterized by a hierarchical "class system" of privileges and responsibilities, a "dyke system" for assigning a senior class mentor to each entering class "rat," and a stringently enforced "honor code," which prescribes that a cadet "does not lie, cheat, steal nor tolerate those who do."

In 1990, prompted by a complaint filed with the Attorney General by a female high-school student seeking admission to VMI, the United States sued the Commonwealth of Virginia and VMI, alleging that VMI's exclusively male admission policy violated the Equal Protection Clause of the Fourteenth Amendment.

The District Court ruled in favor of VMI, however, and rejected the equal protection challenge pressed by the United States. The District Court reasoned that education in "a single-gender environment, be it male or female," yields substantial benefits. VMI's school for men brought diversity to an otherwise coeducational Virginia system, and that diversity was "enhanced by VMI's unique method of instruction." If single-gender education for males ranks as an important governmental objective, it becomes obvious, the District Court concluded, that the only means of achieving the objective "is to exclude women from the all-male institution — VMI."

The Court of Appeals for the Fourth Circuit disagreed and vacated the District Court's judgment. The appellate court held: "The Commonwealth of Virginia has not . . . advanced any state policy by which it can justify its determination, under an announced policy of diversity, to afford VMI's unique type of program to men and not to women." Remanding the case, the appeals court assigned to Virginia, in the first instance, responsibility for selecting a remedial course. The court suggested these options for the State: Admit women to VMI; establish parallel institutions or programs; or abandon state support, leaving VMI free to pursue its policies as a private institution.

In response to the Fourth Circuit's ruling, Virginia proposed a parallel program for women: Virginia Women's Institute for Leadership (VWIL). The 4-year, state-sponsored undergraduate program would be located at Mary Baldwin College, a private liberal arts school for women, and would be open, initially, to about 25 to 30 students. Although VWIL would share VMI's mission — to produce "citizen-soldiers" — the VWIL program would differ, as does Mary Baldwin College, from VMI in academic offerings, methods of education, and financial resources.

Virginia returned to the District Court seeking approval of its proposed remedial plan, and the court decided the plan met the requirements of the Equal Protection Clause.

A divided Court of Appeals affirmed the District Court's judgment. This time, the appellate court determined to give "greater scrutiny to the selection of means than to the [State's] proffered objective." "[P]roviding the option of a single-gender college education may be considered a legitimate and important aspect of a public system of higher education," the appeals court observed; that objective, the court added, is "not pernicious." Moreover, the court continued, the adversative method vital to a VMI education "has never been tolerated in a sexually heterogeneous environment." The method itself "was not designed to exclude women," the court noted, but women could not be accommodated in the VMI program, the court believed, for female participation in VMI's adversative training "would destroy . . . any sense of decency that still permeates the relationship between the sexes."

Having determined, deferentially, the legitimacy of Virginia's purpose, the court considered the question of means. Exclusion of "men at Mary Baldwin College and women at VMI," the court said, was essential to Virginia's purpose, for without such exclusion, the State could not "accomplish [its] objective of providing single-gender education."

The court recognized that, as it analyzed the case, means merged into end, and the merger risked "bypass[ing] any equal protection scrutiny." The court therefore added another inquiry, a decisive test it called "substantive comparability." The key question, the court said, was whether men at VMI and women at VWIL would obtain "substantively comparable benefits at their institution or through other means offered by the [S]tate." Although the appeals court recognized that the VWIL degree "lacks the historical benefit and prestige" of a VMI degree, it nevertheless found the educational opportunities at the two schools "sufficiently comparable."

The cross-petitions in this case present two ultimate issues. First, does Virginia's exclusion of women from the educational opportunities provided by VMI — extraordinary opportunities for military training and civilian leadership development — deny to women "capable of all of the individual activities required of VMI cadets," the equal protection of the laws guaranteed by the Fourteenth Amendment? Second, if VMI's "unique" situation — as Virginia's sole single-sex public institution of higher education — offends the Constitution's equal protection principle, what is the remedial requirement?

We note, once again, the core instruction of this Court's pathmarking decisions in *J.E.B. v. Alabama* and *Mississippi Univ. for Women*: Parties who seek to defend gender-based government action must demonstrate an "exceedingly persuasive justification" for that action.

To summarize the Court's current directions for cases of official classification based on gender: Focusing on the differential treatment or denial of opportunity for which relief is sought, the reviewing court must determine whether the proffered justification is "exceedingly persuasive." The burden of justification is demanding and it rests entirely on the State. The State must show "at least that the [challenged] classification serves 'important governmental objectives and that the discriminatory means employed' are 'substantially related to the achievement of those objectives.' " The justification must be genuine, not hypothesized or invented post hoc in response to litigation. And it must not rely on overbroad generalizations about the different talents, capacities, or preferences of males and females.

The heightened review standard our precedent establishes does not make sex a proscribed classification. Supposed "inherent differences" are no longer accepted as a ground for race or national origin classifications. Physical differences between men and women, however, are enduring: "[T]he two sexes are not fungible; a community made up exclusively of one [sex] is different from a community composed of both."

"Inherent differences" between men and women, we have come to appreciate, remain cause for celebration, but not for denigration of the members of either sex or for artificial constraints on an individual's opportunity. Sex classifications may be used to compensate women "for particular economic disabilities [they have] suffered," *Califano v. Webster*, to "promot[e] equal employment opportunity," *see California Federal Sav. & Loan Assn. v. Guerra*, 479 U.S. 272, 289 (1987), to advance full development of the talent and capacities of our Nation's people.[7] But such classifications may not be used, as they once were, to create or perpetuate the legal, social, and economic inferiority of women.

Measuring the record in this case against the review standard just described, we conclude that Virginia has shown no "exceedingly persuasive justification" for excluding all women from the citizen-soldier training afforded

[7] Several amici have urged that diversity in educational opportunities is an altogether appropriate governmental pursuit and that single-sex schools can contribute importantly to such diversity. Indeed, it is the mission of some single-sex schools "to dissipate, rather than perpetuate, traditional gender classifications." *See* Brief for Twenty-Six Private Women's Colleges as Amici Curiae 5. We do not question the State's prerogative evenhandedly to support diverse educational opportunities. We address specifically and only an educational opportunity recognized by the District Court and the Court of Appeals as "unique," an opportunity available only at Virginia's premier military institute, the State's sole single-sex public university or college. *Cf. Mississippi Univ. for Women v. Hogan* ("Mississippi maintains no other single-sex public university or college. Thus, we are not faced with the question of whether States can provide 'separate but equal' undergraduate institutions for males and females.").

by VMI. We therefore affirm the Fourth Circuit's initial judgment, which held that Virginia had violated the Fourteenth Amendment's Equal Protection Clause. Because the remedy proffered by Virginia — the Mary Baldwin VWIL program — does not cure the constitutional violation, i.e., it does not provide equal opportunity, we reverse the Fourth Circuit's final judgment in this case.

The Fourth Circuit initially held that Virginia had advanced no state policy by which it could justify, under equal protection principles, its determination "to afford VMI's unique type of program to men and not to women." Virginia challenges that "liability" ruling and asserts two justifications in defense of VMI's exclusion of women. First, the Commonwealth contends, "single-sex education provides important educational benefits," and the option of single-sex education contributes to "diversity in educational approaches." Second, the Commonwealth argues, "the unique VMI method of character development and leadership training," the school's adversative approach, would have to be modified were VMI to admit women. We consider these two justifications in turn.

Single-sex education affords pedagogical benefits to at least some students, Virginia emphasizes, and that reality is uncontested in this litigation. Similarly, it is not disputed that diversity among public educational institutions can serve the public good. But Virginia has not shown that VMI was established, or has been maintained, with a view to diversifying, by its categorical exclusion of women, educational opportunities within the State. In cases of this genre, our precedent instructs that "benign" justifications proffered in defense of categorical exclusions will not be accepted automatically; a tenable justification must describe actual state purposes, not rationalizations for actions in fact differently grounded.

Neither recent nor distant history bears out Virginia's alleged pursuit of diversity through single-sex educational options. Virginia describes the current absence of public single-sex higher education for women as "an historical anomaly." But the historical record indicates action more deliberate than anomalous: First, protection of women against higher education; next, schools for women far from equal in resources and stature to schools for men; finally, conversion of the separate schools to coeducation.

In sum, we find no persuasive evidence in this record that VMI's male-only admission policy "is in furtherance of a state policy of 'diversity.' " No such policy, the Fourth Circuit observed, can be discerned from the movement of all other public colleges and universities in Virginia away from single-sex education. A purpose genuinely to advance an array of educational options, as the Court of Appeals recognized, is not served by VMI's historic and constant plan — a plan to "affor[d] a unique educational benefit only to males." However "liberally" this plan serves the State's sons, it makes no provision whatever for her daughters. That is not equal protection.

Virginia next argues that VMI's adversative method of training provides educational benefits that cannot be made available, unmodified, to women. Alterations to accommodate women would necessarily be "radical," so "drastic," Virginia asserts, as to transform, indeed "destroy," VMI's program. Neither sex would be favored by the transformation, Virginia maintains: Men would be deprived of the unique opportunity currently available to them;

women would not gain that opportunity because their participation would "eliminat[e] the very aspects of [the] program that distinguish [VMI] from . . . other institutions of higher education in Virginia."

The District Court forecast from expert witness testimony, and the Court of Appeals accepted, that coeducation would materially affect "at least these three aspects of VMI's program — physical training, the absence of privacy, and the adversative approach." And it is uncontested that women's admission would require accommodations, primarily in arranging housing assignments and physical training programs for female cadets. It is also undisputed, however, that "the VMI methodology could be used to educate women." In sum, as the Court of Appeals stated, "neither the goal of producing citizen soldiers," VMI's raison d'etre, "nor VMI's implementing methodology is inherently unsuitable to women."

It may be assumed, for purposes of this decision, that most women would not choose VMI's adversative method. As Fourth Circuit Judge Motz observed, however, in her dissent from the Court of Appeals' denial of rehearing en banc, it is also probable that "many men would not want to be educated in such an environment." (On that point, even our dissenting colleague might agree.) Education, to be sure, is not a "one size fits all" business. The issue, however, is not whether "women — or men — should be forced to attend VMI"; rather, the question is whether the State can constitutionally deny to women who have the will and capacity, the training and attendant opportunities that VMI uniquely affords.

The notion that admission of women would downgrade VMI's stature, destroy the adversative system and, with it, even the school, is a judgment hardly proved, a prediction hardly different from other "self-fulfilling prophec-[ies]," once routinely used to deny rights or opportunities. When women first sought admission to the bar and access to legal education, concerns of the same order were expressed. Medical faculties similarly resisted men and women as partners in the study of medicine. More recently, women seeking careers in policing encountered resistance based on fears that their presence would "undermine male solidarity;" deprive male partners of adequate assistance; and lead to sexual misconduct. Field studies did not confirm these fears.

Women's successful entry into the federal military academies, and their participation in the Nation's military forces, indicate that Virginia's fears for the future of VMI may not be solidly grounded. The State's justification for excluding all women from "citizen-soldier" training for which some are qualified, in any event, cannot rank as "exceedingly persuasive," as we have explained and applied that standard.

Virginia and VMI trained their argument on "means" rather than "end," and thus misperceived our precedent. Single-sex education at VMI serves an "important governmental objective," they maintained, and exclusion of women is not only "substantially related," it is essential to that objective. By this notably circular argument, the "straightforward" test *Mississippi Univ. for Women* described, was bent and bowed.

The State's misunderstanding and, in turn, the District Court's, is apparent from VMI's mission: to produce "citizen-soldiers," individuals "imbued with love of learning, confident in the functions and attitudes of leadership, possessing a high sense of public service, advocates of the American democracy and free enterprise system, and ready . . . to defend their country in time of national peril." Surely that goal is great enough to accommodate women, who today count as citizens in our American democracy equal in stature to men. Just as surely, the State's great goal is not substantially advanced by women's categorical exclusion, in total disregard of their individual merit, from the State's premier "citizen-soldier" corps. Virginia, in sum, "has fallen far short of establishing the 'exceedingly persuasive justification' " that must be the solid base for any gender-defined classification.

In the second phase of the litigation, Virginia presented its remedial plan — maintain VMI as a male-only college and create VWIL as a separate program for women. Inspecting the VMI and VWIL educational programs to determine whether they "afford[ed] to both genders benefits comparable in substance, [if] not in form and detail," the Court of Appeals concluded that Virginia had arranged for men and women opportunities "sufficiently comparable" to survive equal protection evaluation. The United States challenges this "remedial" ruling as pervasively misguided.

A remedial decree, this Court has said, must closely fit the constitutional violation; it must be shaped to place persons unconstitutionally denied an opportunity or advantage in "the position they would have occupied in the absence of [discrimination]." *See Milliken v. Bradley*. The constitutional violation in this case is the categorical exclusion of women from an extraordinary educational opportunity afforded men. A proper remedy for an unconstitutional exclusion, we have explained, aims to "eliminate [so far as possible] the discriminatory effects of the past" and to "bar like discrimination in the future."

Virginia chose not to eliminate, but to leave untouched, VMI's exclusionary policy. For women only, however, Virginia proposed a separate program, different in kind from VMI and unequal in tangible and intangible facilities.

VWIL affords women no opportunity to experience the rigorous military training for which VMI is famed. Instead, the VWIL program "deemphasize[s]" military education, and uses a "cooperative method" of education "which reinforces self-esteem."

VWIL students receive their "leadership training" in seminars, externships, and speaker series, episodes and encounters lacking the "[p]hysical rigor, mental stress, . . . minute regulation of behavior, and indoctrination in desirable values" made hallmarks of VMI's citizen-soldier training. Kept away from the pressures, hazards, and psychological bonding characteristic of VMI's adversative training, VWIL students will not know the "feeling of tremendous accomplishment" commonly experienced by VMI's successful cadets.

Virginia maintains that these methodological differences are "justified pedagogically," based on "important differences between men and women in learning and developmental needs," "psychological and sociological differences" Virginia describes as "real" and "not stereotypes." The Task Force charged with developing the leadership program for women, drawn from the staff and faculty at Mary Baldwin College, "determined that a military model and, especially VMI's adversative method, would be wholly inappropriate for educating and training most women."

As earlier stated, generalizations about "the way women are," estimates of what is appropriate for most women, no longer justify denying opportunity to women whose talent and capacity place them outside the average description. Notably, Virginia never asserted that VMI's method of education suits most men.

In contrast to the generalizations about women on which Virginia rests, we note again these dispositive realities: VMI's "implementing methodology" is not "inherently unsuitable to women"; "some women . . . do well under [the] adversative model"; "some women, at least, would want to attend [VMI] if they had the opportunity"; "some women are capable of all of the individual activities required of VMI cadets," and "can meet the physical standards [VMI] now impose[s] on men."[19] It is on behalf of these women that the United States has instituted this suit, and it is for them that a remedy must be crafted, a remedy that will end their exclusion from a state-supplied educational opportunity for which they are fit, a decree that will "bar like discrimination in the future."

In myriad respects other than military training, VWIL does not qualify as VMI's equal. VWIL's student body, faculty, course offerings, and facilities hardly match VMI's. Nor can the VWIL graduate anticipate the benefits associated with VMI's 157-year history, the school's prestige, and its influential alumni network. Virginia, in sum, while maintaining VMI for men only, has failed to provide any "comparable single-gender women's institution." Instead, the Commonwealth has created a VWIL program fairly appraised as a "pale shadow" of VMI in terms of the range of curricular choices and faculty stature, funding, prestige, alumni support and influence.

When Virginia tendered its VWIL plan, the Fourth Circuit did not inquire whether the proposed remedy, approved by the District Court, placed women denied the VMI advantage in "the position they would have occupied in the absence of [discrimination]." Instead, the Court of Appeals considered whether the State could provide, with fidelity to the equal protection principle, separate and unequal educational programs for men and women.

The Fourth Circuit plainly erred in exposing Virginia's VWIL plan to a deferential analysis, for "all gender-based classifications today" warrant "heightened scrutiny." Valuable as VWIL may prove for students who seek the program offered, Virginia's remedy affords no cure at all for the opportunities and advantages withheld from women who want a VMI education and can make the grade. In sum, Virginia's remedy does not match the constitutional violation; the State has shown no "exceedingly persuasive justification" for withholding from women qualified for the experience premier training of the kind VMI affords.

---

[19] Admitting women to VMI would undoubtedly require alterations necessary to afford members of each sex privacy from the other sex in living arrangements, and to adjust aspects of the physical training programs. *See* Brief for Petitioner 27–29; *cf.* note following 10 U.S.C. § 4342 (academic and other standards for women admitted to the Military, Naval, and Air Force Academies "shall be the same as those required for male individuals, except for those minimum essential adjustments in such standards required because of physiological differences between male and female individuals"). Experience shows such adjustments are manageable.

A prime part of the history of our Constitution, historian Richard Morris recounted, is the story of the extension of constitutional rights and protections to people once ignored or excluded. VMI's story continued as our comprehension of "We the People" expanded. There is no reason to believe that the admission of women capable of all the activities required of VMI cadets would destroy the Institute rather than enhance its capacity to serve the "more perfect Union."

JUSTICE THOMAS took no part in the consideration or decision of this case.

CHIEF JUSTICE REHNQUIST, concurring in judgment.

The Court holds first that Virginia violates the Equal Protection Clause by maintaining the Virginia Military Institute's (VMI's) all-male admissions policy, and second that establishing the Virginia Women's Institute for Leadership (VWIL) program does not remedy that violation. While I agree with these conclusions, I disagree with the Court's analysis and so I write separately.

Two decades ago in *Craig v. Boren*, we announced that "[t]o withstand constitutional challenge, . . . classifications by gender must serve important governmental objectives and must be substantially related to achievement of those objectives." We have adhered to that standard of scrutiny ever since. While the majority adheres to this test today, it also says that the State must demonstrate an "exceedingly persuasive justification" to support a gender-based classification. It is unfortunate that the Court thereby introduces an element of uncertainty respecting the appropriate test.

Before this Court, Virginia has sought to justify VMI's single-sex admissions policy primarily on the basis that diversity in education is desirable, and that while most of the public institutions of higher learning in the State are coeducational, there should also be room for single-sex institutions. I agree with the Court that there is scant evidence in the record that this was the real reason that Virginia decided to maintain VMI as men only. But, unlike the majority, I would consider only evidence that postdates our decision in *Hogan*, and would draw no negative inferences from the State's actions before that time. I think that after *Hogan*, the State was entitled to reconsider its policy with respect to VMI, and to not have earlier justifications, or lack thereof, held against it.

Even if diversity in educational opportunity were the State's actual objective, the State's position would still be problematic. The difficulty with its position is that the diversity benefitted only one sex; there was single-sex public education available for men at VMI, but no corresponding single-sex public education available for women. When *Hogan* placed Virginia on notice that VMI's admissions policy possibly was unconstitutional, VMI could have dealt with the problem by admitting women; but its governing body felt strongly that the admission of women would have seriously harmed the institution's educational approach. Was there something else the State could have done to avoid an equal protection violation? Since the State did nothing, we do not have to definitively answer that question.

Had Virginia made a genuine effort to devote comparable public resources to a facility for women, and followed through on such a plan, it might well have avoided an equal protection violation. I do not believe the State was faced with the stark choice of either admitting women to VMI, on the one hand, or abandoning VMI and starting from scratch for both men and women, on the other.

[I]t is not the "exclusion of women" that violates the Equal Protection Clause, but the maintenance of an all-men school without providing any — much less a comparable — institution for women. Accordingly, the remedy should not necessarily require either the admission of women to VMI, or the creation of a VMI clone for women. An adequate remedy in my opinion might be a demonstration by Virginia that its interest in educating men in a single-sex environment is matched by its interest in educating women in a single-sex institution.

In the end, the women's institution Virginia proposes, VWIL, fails as a remedy, because it is distinctly inferior to the existing men's institution and will continue to be for the foreseeable future. VWIL simply is not, in any sense, the institution that VMI is. In particular, VWIL is a program appended to a private college, not a self-standing institution; and VWIL is substantially underfunded as compared to VMI. I therefore ultimately agree with the Court that Virginia has not provided an adequate remedy.

JUSTICE SCALIA, dissenting.

Today the Court . . . rejects (contrary to our established practice) the factual findings of two courts below, sweeps aside the precedents of this Court, and ignores the history of our people. As to facts: it explicitly rejects the finding that there exist "gender-based developmental differences" supporting Virginia's restriction of the "adversative" method to only a men's institution, and the finding that the all-male composition of the Virginia Military Institute (VMI) is essential to that institution's character. As to precedent: it drastically revises our established standards for reviewing sex-based classifications. And as to history: it counts for nothing the long tradition, enduring down to the present, of men's military colleges supported by both States and the Federal Government.

Much of the Court's opinion* is devoted to deprecating the closed-mindedness of our forebears with regard to women's education, and even with regard to the treatment of women in areas that have nothing to do with education. Closed-minded they were — as every age is, including our own, with regard to matters it cannot guess, because it simply does not consider them debatable. The virtue of a democratic system with a First Amendment is that it readily enables the people, over time, to be persuaded that what they took for granted is not so, and to change their laws accordingly. That system is destroyed if the smug assurances of each age are removed from the democratic process and written into the Constitution. So to counterbalance the Court's criticism of our ancestors, let me say a word in their praise: they left us free to change. The same cannot be said of this most illiberal Court, which has embarked on a course of inscribing one after another of the current preferences of the society (and in some cases only the counter-majoritarian preferences of the society's law-trained elite) into our Basic Law. Today it

* [Most of the majority's historical references are edited out of this version. — Ed.]

enshrines the notion that no substantial educational value is to be served by an all-men's military academy — so that the decision by the people of Virginia to maintain such an institution denies equal protection to women who cannot attend that institution but can attend others. Since it is entirely clear that the Constitution of the United States — the old one — takes no sides in this educational debate, I dissent.

I have no problem with a system of abstract tests such as rational-basis, intermediate, and strict scrutiny (though I think we can do better than applying strict scrutiny and intermediate scrutiny whenever we feel like it). Such formulas are essential to evaluating whether the new restrictions that a changing society constantly imposes upon private conduct comport with that "equal protection" our society has always accorded in the past. But in my view the function of this Court is to preserve our society's values regarding (among other things) equal protection, not to revise them; to prevent backsliding from the degree of restriction the Constitution imposed upon democratic government, not to prescribe, on our own authority, progressively higher degrees. For that reason it is my view that, whatever abstract tests we may choose to devise, they cannot supersede — and indeed ought to be crafted so as to reflect — those constant and unbroken national traditions that embody the people's understanding of ambiguous constitutional texts. More specifically, it is my view that "when a practice not expressly prohibited by the text of the Bill of Rights bears the endorsement of a long tradition of open, widespread, and unchallenged use that dates back to the beginning of the Republic, we have no proper basis for striking it down." *Rutan v. Republican Party* (SCALIA, J., dissenting). The same applies, *mutatis mutandis*, to a practice asserted to be in violation of the post-Civil War Fourteenth Amendment.

[T]he tradition of having government-funded military schools for men is as well rooted in the traditions of this country as the tradition of sending only men into military combat. The people may decide to change the one tradition, like the other, through democratic processes; but the assertion that either tradition has been unconstitutional through the centuries is not law, but politics-smuggled-into-law.

And the same applies, more broadly, to single-sex education in general, which, as I shall discuss, is threatened by today's decision with the cut-off of all state and federal support. Government-run non military educational institutions for the two sexes have until very recently also been part of our national tradition. "[It is] [c]oeducation, historically, [that] is a novel educational theory. From grade school through high school, college, and graduate and professional training, much of the Nation's population during much of our history has been educated in sexually segregated classrooms." *Mississippi Univ. for Women v. Hogan* (POWELL, J., dissenting). These traditions may of course be changed by the democratic decisions of the people, as they largely have been.

Today, however, change is forced upon Virginia, and reversion to single-sex education is prohibited nationwide, not by democratic processes but by order of this Court. Even while bemoaning the sorry, bygone days of "fixed notions" concerning women's education, the Court favors current notions so fixedly that it is willing to write them into the Constitution of the United States by application of custom-built "tests." This is not the interpretation of a Constitution, but the creation of one.

Only the amorphous "exceedingly persuasive justification" phrase, and not the standard elaboration of intermediate scrutiny, can be made to yield this conclusion that VMI's single-sex composition is unconstitutional because there exist several women (or, one would have to conclude under the Court's reasoning, a single woman) willing and able to undertake VMI's program. Intermediate scrutiny has never required a least-restrictive-means analysis, but only a "substantial relation" between the classification and the state interests that it serves. The reasoning in our other intermediate-scrutiny cases has similarly required only a substantial relation between end and means, not a perfect fit. In *Rostker v. Goldberg*, we held that selective-service registration could constitutionally exclude women, because even "assuming that a small number of women could be drafted for noncombat roles, Congress simply did not consider it worth the added burdens of including women in draft and registration plans." There is simply no support in our cases for the notion that a sex-based classification is invalid unless it relates to characteristics that hold true in every instance.

It is hard to consider women a "discrete and insular minorit[y]" unable to employ the "political processes ordinarily to be relied upon," when they constitute a majority of the electorate. And the suggestion that they are incapable of exerting that political power smacks of the same paternalism that the Court so roundly condemns. Moreover, a long list of legislation proves the proposition false [citing various civil rights laws].

The question to be answered, I repeat, is whether the exclusion of women from VMI is "substantially related to an important governmental objective."

It is beyond question that Virginia has an important state interest in providing effective college education for its citizens. That single-sex instruction is an approach substantially related to that interest should be evident enough from the long and continuing history in this country of men's and women's colleges. But beyond that, as the Court of Appeals here stated: "That single-gender education at the college level is beneficial to both sexes is a fact established in this case."

But besides its single-sex constitution, VMI is different from other colleges in another way. It employs a "distinctive educational method," sometimes referred to as the "adversative, or doubting, model of education." No one contends that this method is appropriate for all individuals; education is not a "one size fits all" business. Just as a State may wish to support junior colleges, vocational institutes, or a law school that emphasizes case practice instead of classroom study, so too a State's decision to maintain within its system one school that provides the adversative method is "substantially related" to its goal of good education. Moreover, it was uncontested that "if the state were to establish a women's VMI-type [i.e., adversative] program, the program would attract an insufficient number of participants to make the program work"; and it was found by the District Court that if Virginia were to include women in VMI, the school "would eventually find it necessary to drop the adversative system altogether." Thus, Virginia's options were an adversative method that excludes women or no adversative method at all.

Virginia did not make this determination regarding the make-up of its public college system on the unrealistic assumption that no other colleges exist. Substantial evidence in the District Court demonstrated that the Commonwealth has long proceeded on the principle that "[h]igher education resources should be viewed as a whole — public and private" — because such an approach enhances diversity and because "it is academic and economic waste to permit unwarranted duplication." It is thus significant that, whereas there are "four all-female private [colleges] in Virginia," there is only "one private all-male college," which "indicates that the private sector is providing for th[e] [former] form of education to a much greater extent that it provides for all-male education." In these circumstances, Virginia's election to fund one public all-male institution and one on the adversative model — and to concentrate its resources in a single entity that serves both these interests in diversity — is substantially related to the State's important educational interests.

The Court today has no adequate response to this clear demonstration of the conclusion produced by application of intermediate scrutiny. Rather, it relies on a series of contentions that are irrelevant or erroneous as a matter of law, foreclosed by the record in this case, or both.

1. I have already pointed out the Court's most fundamental error, which is its reasoning that VMI's all-male composition is unconstitutional because "some women are capable of all of the individual activities required of VMI cadets," and would prefer military training on the adversative model. This unacknowledged adoption of what amounts to (at least) strict scrutiny is without antecedent in our sex-discrimination cases and by itself discredits the Court's decision.

2. The Court suggests that Virginia's claimed purpose in maintaining VMI as an all-male institution — its asserted interest in promoting diversity of educational options — is not "genuin[e]," but is a pretext for discriminating against women. But whether it is part of the evidence to prove that diversity was the Commonwealth's objective is quite separate from whether it is part of the evidence to prove that anti-feminism was not.

3. In addition to disparaging Virginia's claim that VMI's single-sex status serves a state interest in diversity, the Court finds fault with Virginia's failure to offer education based on the adversative training method to women. It dismisses the District Court's " 'findings' on 'gender-based developmental differences' " on the ground that "[t]hese 'findings' restate the opinions of Virginia's expert witnesses, opinions about typically male or typically female 'tendencies.' " How remarkable to criticize the District Court on the ground that its findings rest on the evidence (i.e., the testimony of Virginia's witnesses)! That is what findings are supposed to do. It is indefensible to tell the Commonwealth that "[t]he burden of justification is demanding and it rests entirely on [you]," and then to ignore the District Court's findings because they rest on the evidence put forward by the Commonwealth — particularly when, as the District Court said, "[t]he evidence in the case . . . is virtually uncontradicted.

Ultimately, in fact, the Court does not deny the evidence supporting these findings. It instead makes evident that the parties to this case could have saved themselves a great deal of time, trouble, and expense by omitting a trial. The Court simply dispenses with the evidence submitted at trial — it never says that a single finding of the District Court is clearly erroneous — in favor of the Justices' own view of the world.

4. The Court contends that Virginia, and the District Court, erred, and "misperceived our precedent," by "train[ing] their argument on 'means' rather than 'end.' " The Court focuses on "VMI's mission," which is to produce individuals "imbued with love of learning, confident in the functions and attitudes of leadership, possessing a high sense of public service, advocates of the American democracy and free enterprise system, and ready . . . to defend their country in time of national peril." "Surely," the Court says, "that goal is great enough to accommodate women."

The Court's analysis at least has the benefit of producing foreseeable results. Applied generally, it means that whenever a State's ultimate objective is "great enough to accommodate women" (as it always will be), then the State will be held to have violated the Equal Protection Clause if it restricts to men even one means by which it pursues that objective — no matter how few women are interested in pursuing the objective by that means, no matter how much the single-sex program will have to be changed if both sexes are admitted, and no matter how beneficial that program has theretofore been to its participants.

5. The Court argues that VMI would not have to change very much if it were to admit women. The principal response to that argument is that it is irrelevant: If VMI's single-sex status is substantially related to the government's important educational objectives, as I have demonstrated above and as the Court refuses to discuss, that concludes the inquiry. There should be no debate in the federal judiciary over "how much" VMI would be required to change if it admitted women and whether that would constitute "too much" change.[5]

6. Finally, the absence of a precise "all-women's analogue" to VMI is irrelevant. Although there is no precise female-only analogue to VMI, Virginia has created during this litigation the Virginia Women's Institute for Leadership (VWIL), a state-funded all-women's program run by Mary Baldwin College. I have thus far said nothing about VWIL because it is, under our established test, irrelevant, so long as VMI's all-male character is "substantially related" to an important state goal. But VWIL now exists, and the Court's treatment of it shows how far-reaching today's decision is.

VWIL was carefully designed by professional educators who have long experience in educating young women. The program rejects the proposition that there is a "difference in the respective spheres and destinies of man and woman," and is designed to "provide an all-female program that will achieve substantially similar outcomes [to VMI's] in an all-female environment." After holding a trial where voluminous evidence was submitted and making detailed

[5] The Court's do-it-yourself approach to factfinding is exemplified by its invocation of the experience of the federal military academies to prove that not much change would occur. In fact, the District Court noted that "the West Point experience" supported the theory that a coeducational VMI would have to "adopt a [different] system," for West Point found it necessary upon becoming coeducational to "move away" from its adversative system.

findings of fact, the District Court concluded that "there is a legitimate pedagogical basis for the different means employed [by VMI and VWIL] to achieve the substantially similar ends." The Court of Appeals undertook a detailed review of the record and affirmed. But it is Mary Baldwin College, which runs VWIL, that has made the point most succinctly:

> It would have been possible to develop the VWIL program to more closely resemble VMI, with adversative techniques associated with the rat line and barracks-like living quarters. Simply replicating an existing program would have required far less thought, research, and educational expertise. But such a facile approach would have produced a paper program with no real prospect of successful implementation.

Brief for Mary Baldwin College as Amicus Curiae 5. It is worth noting that none of the United States' own experts in the remedial phase of this case was willing to testify that VMI's adversative method was an appropriate methodology for educating women. This Court, however, does not care.

As is frequently true, the Court's decision today will have consequences that extend far beyond the parties to the case. What I take to be the Court's unease with these consequences, and its resulting unwillingness to acknowledge them, cannot alter the reality.

[T]he rationale of today's decision is sweeping: for sex-based classifications, a redefinition of intermediate scrutiny that makes it indistinguishable from strict scrutiny. Indeed, the Court indicates that if any program restricted to one sex is "uniqu[e]," it must be opened to members of the opposite sex "who have the will and capacity" to participate in it. [8] I suggest that the single-sex program that will not be capable of being characterized as "unique" is not only unique but nonexistent.

In any event, regardless of whether the Court's rationale leaves some small amount of room for lawyers to argue, it ensures that single-sex public education is functionally dead. The costs of litigating the constitutionality of a single-sex education program, and the risks of ultimately losing that litigation, are simply too high to be embraced by public officials. No state official in his right mind will buy such a high-cost, high-risk lawsuit by commencing a single-sex program. The enemies of single-sex education have won; by persuading only seven Justices (five would have been enough) that their view of the world is enshrined in the Constitution, they have effectively imposed that view on all 50 States.

This is especially regrettable because, as the District Court here determined, educational experts in recent years have increasingly come to "support [the] view that substantial educational benefits flow from a single-gender environment, be it male or female, that cannot be replicated in a coeducational setting." "The evidence in th[is] case," for example, "is virtually uncontradicted" to that effect. Until quite recently, some public officials have attempted

[8] In this regard, I note that the Court — which I concede is under no obligation to do so — provides no example of a program that would pass muster under its reasoning today: not even, for example, a football or wrestling program. On the Court's theory, any woman ready, willing, and physically able to participate in such a program would, as a constitutional matter, be entitled to do so.

to institute new single-sex programs, at least as experiments. In 1991, for example, the Detroit Board of Education announced a program to establish three boys-only schools for inner-city youth; it was met with a lawsuit, a preliminary injunction was swiftly entered by a District Court that purported to rely on *Hogan*, and the Detroit Board of Education voted to abandon the litigation and thus abandon the plan. Today's opinion assures that no such experiment will be tried again.

There are few extant single-sex public educational programs. The potential of today's decision for widespread disruption of existing institutions lies in its application to private single-sex education. Government support is immensely important to private educational institutions. Mary Baldwin College — which designed and runs VWIL — notes that private institutions of higher education in the 1990–1991 school year derived approximately 19 percent of their budgets from federal, state, and local government funds, not including financial aid to students. Charitable status under the tax laws is also highly significant for private educational institutions, and it is certainly not beyond the Court that rendered today's decision to hold that a donation to a single-sex college should be deemed contrary to public policy and therefore not deductible if the college discriminates on the basis of sex.

The issue will be not whether government assistance turns private colleges into state actors, but whether the government itself would be violating the Constitution by providing state support to single-sex colleges. When the Government was pressed at oral argument concerning the implications of these cases for private single-sex education if government-provided single-sex education is unconstitutional, it stated that the implications will not be so disastrous, since States can provide funding to racially segregated private schools, "depend[ing] on the circumstances." I cannot imagine what those "circumstances" might be.

The only hope for state-assisted single-sex private schools is that the Court will not apply in the future the principles of law it has applied today. That is a substantial hope, I am happy and ashamed to say. After all, did not the Court today abandon the principles of law it has applied in our earlier sex-classification cases? And does not the Court positively invite private colleges to rely upon our ad-hocery by assuring them this case is "unique"?

NOTES

1. *The standard of review.* In *VMI,* the United States argued that the Court should adopt strict scrutiny for sex-based classifications. *See* Deborah Brake, *Sex as a Suspect Class: An Argument for Applying Strict Scrutiny to Gender Discrimination,* 6 CONST. L.J. 953 (1996) ("By adopting strict scrutiny for gender discrimination, the Supreme Court could resolve . . . anomalies and avoid future confusion and misapplication of intermediate scrutiny in lower courts."). The Court declined the invitation. But Justice Ginsburg's opinion does provide an unusually careful explication of the intermediate standard of review. There had been criticism prior to *VMI* that the intermediate test was often applied with less than full vigor. Speaking after *VMI*, Judith Lichtman of the Women's Legal Defense Fund said "[t]here was a murkiness, a lack of clarity, within the federal system on [the standard]. By clarifying it and putting it into the historical context of Supreme Court law, [Justice Ginsburg] has made it the very strong standard we believed it to be." *High Court Goes for "Skeptical" Scrutiny on Gender,* NAT'L L.J., July 8, 1996, at A12.

Justice Scalia claims Justice Ginsburg "drastically revises" the established standards for review of sex-based classification. He cites the Court's use of "the amorphous 'exceedingly persuasive justification' phrase" rather than "the standard elaboration of intermediate scrutiny." But that phrase was used in prior cases as indicative of intermediate review. Justice O'Connor in *MUW,* like Justice Ginsburg in *VMI,* looked to the actual purpose of the challenged law. Justice Scalia suggests that Justice Ginsburg is using "a least restrictive means analysis." Is he correct?

2. *Ends and means.* What is the objective of the VMI program? Educational diversity? Producing citizen-soldiers? Single-sex education? Educating students? The court of appeals in the remedial proceeding (*VMI II*) asked if the all-male admission policy was substantially related to achieving the benefits of a single sex education. The court acknowledged that, under this analysis "means merged into end, and the merger risked bypassing any educational scrutiny." Therefore, it added a test of "substantive comparability." Jon Soderberg, *The "Constitutional" Assault on the Virginia Military Institute,* 53 WASH. & LEE L. REV. 429, 457 (1996), refers to the *VMI II* approach as "a modified intermediate scrutiny that . . . attempts to impart some flexibility to the intermediate scrutiny equal protection analysis." The dissenting judge in *VMI II* argued that all of the identified interests were "rationalizations compelled by the emergencies of the litigation rather than an actual overriding purpose of the proposed separate-but-equal arrangement." What does Justice Ginsburg identify as the state's objective for intermediate review? Justice Scalia?

3. *Separate but equal.* Are the means to be defined in terms of VMI's all-male admissions policy or the state's separate-but-equal program? If the state had established that the VWIL and VMI programs were substantially comparable, would intermediate review be satisfied? Compare the following:

> [If] military training or education is constructed so that it is a problem for women "to fit," then the answer is to reconstruct the military and military service so that both men and women "fit." Only women and men together, with whatever rearrangements that fact requires, can define what military service is. Side-by-side arrangements will only enshrine the male model — the status quo — as *the* model and consign the female experience to be judged as inferior.

Mary Cheh, *An Essay on VMI and Military Service: Yes, We Do Have To Be Equal Together,* 50 WASH. & LEE L. REV. 49, 55–56 (1993).

> A new VMI-type experience for women would be separate and unequal, not in the sense that an all-female education *is inferior* to an all-male education, but simply because "new" is not *identical* to "old." [A] flexible, or "pro-choice," version of intermediate scrutiny would allow

> women to choose superior leadership training or opt for the traditional coeducational experience.

Soderberg, 53 WASH. & LEE L. REV. at 458–59. What is Justice Ginsburg's position on separate-but-equal? Justice Scalia? Why does Chief Justice Rehnquist concur?

Consider the role of "sameness" versus the "difference" feminist debate in this legal controversy. "Throughout the VMI litigation, Virginia . . . did what feminist theorists have long criticized in [the legal system] — they assumed the correctness of a masculine male standard and asked only whether women could fit it, not whether it was an appropriate standard for persons of either sex." Mary Ann Case, *Two Cheers for Cheerleading: The Noisy Integration of VMI and the Quiet Success of Virginia Women in Leadership*, 1999 U. CHI. LEGAL F. 347. Professor Case says "[t]his unquestioning acceptance of a masculine standard, at least for men if not also for women, and the failure to consider the possibility of a feminine standard applied sex-neutrally is one of the central problems of gender discrimination." She notes an argument used in oral argument in VMI. Suppose women were barred from legal practice for 150 years and a tough adversative method developed in practice and in law schools. And then women were admitted to practice but offered only a legal education with a less aggressive methodology. Would equal protection be satisfied?

4. *The future of single sex education.* The constitutionality of the all-male program at the Citadel, and its "parallel sister school" at South Carolina Institute of Leadership for Women (SCIL) was also challenged. Would that program necessarily be unconstitutional after *VMI*? If Virginia and South Carolina left in place the all-women's programs at VWIL and SCIL, while "integrating" the formerly all-men's schools, would those programs be unconstitutional? Anita Blair, *The Equal Protection Clause and Single-Sex Public Education: United States v. Virginia and Virginia Military Institute*, 6 CONST. L.J. 999, 1000 (1996), argues that "[a] ruling requiring VMI to admit women would seriously jeopardize other single-sex schools, both public and private. If public single-sex programs are held to violate fundamental United States law, even private schools must admit both men and women or else forego tax-exempt status and, more importantly, tax deductions for their donors."

In response, it has been argued that, in addition to ignoring the distinction between public and private schools, "[the parity] argument obscures the distinction between 'invidious' discrimination and 'benign' discrimination, whose purpose is to equalize the playing field. [T]he argument obscures the distinction between single-sex education for women, which in some instances has demonstrable pedagogical value, and single sex education for men, which, thus far, has been shown to have at best a null effect and even, perhaps, serious disadvantages." Sara Mandelbaum, *"As VMI Goes . . .": The Domino Effect and Other Stubborn Myths*, 6 CONST. L.J. 979, 980–81 (1996).

Professor Jill Hasday, *The Principle and Practice of Women's "Full Citizenship": A Case of Sex-Segregated Public Education*, 101 MICH. L. REV. 755, 758 (2002), argues that if the Court's goal in *VMI* is to give women "full citizenship stature" and to prevent the perpetuation of the "legal, social, and economic inferiority of women," the Court "would be wise to focus much more constitutional scrutiny on coeducational public schools directly, examining them also as possible sources of women's inequality," rather than sex-segregated education. She claims that, the "historical record reveals that differences of form like that between sex-segregated and coeducational public education can actually prove relatively unimportant in terms of their substantive impact on women's status." *Id.* at 759.

Compare Amy H. Nemko, *Single-Sex Public Education After VMI: The Case for Women's School's*, 21 HARV. WOMEN'S L.J. 19, 22 (1998) ("While in many cases classifications on the basis of sex are synonymous with sex discrimination, in other cases, sex classifications permit equal protection to be achieved within a framework that recognizes difference.") with Christopher H. Pyle, *Women's Colleges: Is Segregation by Sex Still Justifiable After* United States v. Virginia?, 77 B.U.L. REV. 209, 271 (1997) ("[t]here seems no way that private women's colleges can escape the logic of equal protection and individual rights advanced in *United States v. Virginia*. Like racially segregated schools, they may duck, bob, and weave, but eventually the Court's — and society's — rejection of the sweeping generalizations upon which they were founded and with which they are now defended must catch up to them. The message seems clear: Invalid stereotypes, no less than invidious discrimination, will be fatal to government funding of colleges which exclude applicants on the basis of sex").

Would high school programs providing separate science and math classes for females violate equal protection? A separate school for African-American males with a program and faculty designed for their special needs? Professor Gary J. Simson, *Separate But Equal and Single-Sex Schools*, 90 CORNELL L. REV. 443, 451 (2005); asks: "With regard to coordinate single-sex schools [i.e. male and female] should the suspicion of discrimination shift [the] burden to the state to disprove stigma and other types of disadvantages to girls? If no such disadvantage is found to exist, coordinate public single-sex schools easily pass constitutional muster. Although the state is obviously taking sex into account in establishing such schools, it is not treating anyone any better or worse on the basis of sex. No sex classification exists, and therefore the higher level of scrutiny triggered by sex classifications does not come into play. If, however, disadvantage to girls is found to exist, the state is clearly classifying on the basis of sex, and middle-tier scrutiny applies. Whatever the precise ingredients of middle-tier scrutiny, it is dubious that the system of coordinate single-sex schools in question could survive such review. Coordinate single-sex schools do not seem to promise substantial academic and developmental benefits that could not be achieved in coed environment. On the other hand, the coordinate schools carry with them by virtue of their single-sex character a significant disadvantage to girls not generated by coed schools." *Id.* at 453.

5. *Nguyen v. INS*, 533 U.S. 53 (2001). A federal statute requires that children born outside of the United States and out of wedlock to fathers who are U.S. citizens be legitimized or obtain formal proof of paternity by age 18 in order to obtain citizenship. It does not require any similar action by mothers who are United States citizens. In *Miller v. Albright*, 523 U.S. 420 (1998), a fragmented Supreme Court rejected a challenge to the statute without deciding the constitutional issue.

In its subsequent decision in *Nguyen v. INS*, a majority of the Court held that the federal statute making it more difficult for a child born abroad and out of wedlock to one parent who was a United States citizen does not violate the equal protection guarantee of the fifth amendment.

The petitioner had been born out of wedlock in Vietnam to a United States citizen father and a Vietnamese citizen mother, who became a lawful permanent resident of the United States at age 6. At the age of 22, the petitioner pleaded guilty in a Texas state court to two counts of sexual assault on a child. Later the Immigration and Naturalization Service (INS) initiated deportation proceedings against him. His father obtained an order of parentage from a state court while petitioner's appeal was pending before the Board of Immigration Appeals, but the Board dismissed the appeal because petitioner had not complied with the statute's requirements for one born out of wedlock and abroad to a citizen father and noncitizen mother.

Justice Kennedy, in the opinion for the Court upholding the statute, applied intermediate scrutiny. Since this standard was satisfied in that "[t]he fit between the means and the important end is 'exceedingly persuasive,' " the Court did not decide whether a lesser degree of scrutiny applies because the statute implicated Congress' immigration and naturalization power. Nor did it decide whether a court could grant citizenship as relief on terms other than those specified by Congress. Justices Scalia and Thomas, concurring, would hold that it could not.

The Court held that the gender-based discrimination against unmarried fathers was justified: "Congress' decision to impose requirements on unmarried fathers that differ from those on unmarried mothers is based on the significant difference between their respective relationships to the potential citizen at the time of birth." Two important governmental interests were served by the distinction.

First is "the importance of assuring that a biological parent-child relationship exists." The Court reasoned that "[i]n the case of the father, the uncontestable fact is that he need not be present at the birth. If he is present, furthermore, that circumstance is not incontrovertible proof of fatherhood. Fathers and mothers are not similarly situated with regard to the proof of biological parenthood." Congress need not elect a particular method of establishing paternity e.g., clear and convincing evidence from DNA testing, nor a gender-neutral approach. "The issue is not the use of gender specific terms instead of neutral terms.Just as neutral terms can mask discrimination that is unlawful, gender specific terms can mask a permissible distinction. The equal protection question is whether the distinction is lawful."

Second is "the determination to ensure that the child and the citizen parent have some demonstrated opportunity or potential to develop not just a relationship that is recognized, as a formal matter, by the law, but one that consists of the real, everyday ties that provide a connection between child and citizen parent and, in turn, the United States." In the case of a citizen mother, "the very event of birth" provides the opportunity for a meaningful relationship, one that does not automatically exist as to the father's relationship. Thus, Congress could properly seek to "ensur[e] some opportunity for a tie between citizen father and foreign born child which is a reasonable substitute for the opportunity manifest between mother and child at the time of birth."

Justice Kennedy concluded:

> To fail to acknowledge even our most basic biological difference — such as the fact that a mother must be present at birth but the father need not be — risks making the guarantee of equal protection superficial, and so disserving it. Mechanistic classification of all our differences as stereotypes would operate to obscure those misconceptions and prejudices that are real. The distinction embodied in the statutory scheme here at issue is not marked by misconception and prejudice, nor does it show disrespect for either class. The difference between men and women in relation to the birth process is a real one, and the principle of equal protection does not forbid Congress to address the problem at hand in a manner specific to each gender.

Justice O'Connor, joined by three other members of the Court, dissented, noting that "[w]hile the Court invokes heightened scrutiny, the manner in which it explains and applies this standard is a stranger to our precedents." She argued that the party defending the statute must show "exceedingly persuasive justification," that the courts must inquire "into the actual purposes of the discrimination" and that "overbroad sex-based generalizations are impermissible even when they enjoy empirical support." She questioned the verifiability rationale used by the majority: "While it is doubtless true that a mother's blood relation to a child is uniquely 'verifiable from the birth itself, the majority has not shown that a mother's birth relation is uniquely verifiable *by the INS*, much less that any greater verifiability warrants a sex-based, rather than a sex-neutral statute." She stressed that sex-neutral alternatives, such as a requirement that both mothers and fathers prove parenthood within 30 days, were available: "In our prior cases, the existence of comparable or superior sex-neutral alternatives has been a powerful reason to reject a sex-based classification."

[4] Compensatory Action in Gender Cases

In a number of the above cases, the government sought to justify its disparate treatment of men and women as a "benign" classification designed to remedy past discrimination against women or to protect women as a class from harms entailed by their social position. As in *MUW v. Hogan*, the Court often pierces the veil and characterizes the law as premised on archaic stereotypes about women's proper place in society. But what if a law is actually remedial in character, designed to compensate and redress past wrongs? What treatment should be accorded laws discriminating against males for the purpose of aiding females?

a. Reconsider Justice Powell's and Justice Brennan's discussion of affirmative action in gender cases in *Bakke*. There are significant differences in result and approach in affirmative action in race cases and gender cases. Consider the reported remarks of Justice Stewart: "[T]he female of the species has the best of both worlds. She can attack laws that unreasonably discriminate against her while preserving those that favor her." HARV. L. SCH. REC., March 23, 1973, p. 15, *quoted in* Ruth Ginsburg, *Some Thoughts on Benign Classification in the Context of Sex*, 10 CONN. L. REV. 813, 818 n.32 (1978).

b. Two companion Social Security Act cases suggest the problems posed when the government claims a compensatory justification for gender classifications.

***Califano v. Goldfarb*, 430 U.S. 199 (1977).** The Court held unconstitutional a Social Security Act provision providing survivors benefits to a widow regardless of dependency, but providing such benefits to a widower only if he proved he had been receiving at least half of his support from his deceased wife. Justice Brennan, in a plurality opinion, concluded that under the Act, "female insurers received less protection for their spouses solely because of their sex."

Justice Rehnquist, joined by Chief Justice Burger and Justices Stewart and Blackmun, dissented on the ground that providing benefits to widows while not to similarly situated widowers "is a differing treatment which 'rest[s] upon some ground of difference having a fair and substantial relation to the object of the legislation.' "

***Califano v. Webster*, 430 U.S. 313 (1977).** A 1972 amendment to the Social Security Act introduced a formula for computing benefits which permitted women to exclude more lower earning wage years than a similarly situated male. In a per curiam opinion, the Court upheld the classification as a benign measure designed "to compensate women for past economic discrimination." The Court, utilizing an intermediate standard of review, accepted that "[r]eduction of the disparity in economic condition between men and women caused by the long history of discrimination against women has been recognized as an important government objective."

Four Justices concurred on the basis of Justice Rehnquist's dissent in *Goldfarb*.

Consider the following assessment of *Webster* and *Goldfarb* by now-Justice Ginsburg: "Two points are highlighted in the opinions. (1) Where, as in *Webster*, legislation directly addresses past discrimination and serves to ameliorate it, disparate treatment of the sexes, at least as an interim measure, is constitutional. (2) Where, as in widower *Goldfarb*'s case, differential treatment is rooted in traditional role-typing and is not deliberately and specifically aimed at redressing past injustice, differential treatment based on sex is unconstitutional." Ruth Ginsburg, *Sex Equality and the Constitution*, 52 TUL. L. REV. 451, 471 (1978). *See* Heather Nelson, *"Fatal In Fact"?: An Examination of the Viability of Affirmative Action for Women in a Post-Adarand Era*, 21 WOMEN'S RTS. L. REP. 151, 157 (2000) ("In short, the 'compensatory' cases discussed above demonstrate that the Court has been willing to consider an argument it has rejected as a justification for race-based affirmative action programs: that the social and economic history of women as a group has left them with particular social and economic needs and that these needs can be addressed through remedial legislative schemes.").

c. *Wengler v. Druggists Mutual Insurance Co.*, 446 U.S. 142 (1980). The Court, in an opinion by Justice White, held invalid a workers' compensation scheme "under which a widower is not entitled to death benefits unless he either is mentally or physically incapacitated from wage earning or proves actual dependence on his wife's earnings. In contrast, a widow qualifies for death benefits without having to prove actual dependence on her husband's earnings." The Court viewed the law as discriminating against both women workers and male survivors. Justice Rehnquist dissented.

d. *Orr v. Orr*, 440 U.S. 268 (1979). The Court, per Justice Brennan, held unconstitutional Alabama alimony statutes authorizing courts to award alimony to a wife but not to a husband. Using intermediate review, Justice Brennan rejected the state argument that the law was justified as a means of providing help to needy spouses, using sex as a proxy for need. While assisting needy spouses was "a legitimate and important governmental objective," the law was not "substantially related" to achieving the objective. "Under the statute, individualized hearings at which the parties' relative financial circumstances are considered already occur. There is no reason, therefore, to use sex as a proxy for need. Needy males could be helped along with needy females with little if any additional burden on the State."

e. *Benign classification or paternalism?* Legislation which appears to be benign, in fact may serve to preserve traditional stereotyping of women. It is often difficult to determine when a law is benign and compensatory rather than merely paternalistic. States enacted laws which instituted special maximum hour laws and provided rest periods and rest facilities for women workers because they were deemed weaker than their male counterparts. Now-Justice Ginsburg points out "the historical tendency of lawmakers and jurists to regard virtually all gender-based classifications as designed for women's benefit or protection." She notes that "[o]ccupations from bartending to lawyering were once closed to women, ostensibly to spare them from exposure to noxious atmosphere. Chivalrous, benign impulses were said to motivate regulations governing the hours and conditions of women's work, but not of men's." Ruth Ginsburg, *Some Thoughts on Benign Classifications in the Context of Sex*, 10 CONN. L. REV. 813, 814–15 (1978).

The Court was willing to go behind the government's stated benign purpose in *Wengler*. Justice Ginsburg notes that "the [Social Security cases] declare post hoc rationalization unacceptable to sustain law in fact rooted in a 'romantically paternalistic' view of women as men's subordinates." Ruth Ginsburg, *Sexual Equality Under the Fourteenth and Equal Rights Amendments*, 1979 WASH. U. L. REV. 161, 169. A number of commentators have suggested that Justice Brennan's opinions in post-*Frontiero* gender cases such as *Orr v. Orr* often seem to use a strict scrutiny approach to the means-end analysis even while employing the language of intermediate review.

[C] ILLEGITIMACY CLASSIFICATIONS

The illegitimate child at common law was "filius nullius," the child of no one. He or she had no right to support or inheritance from the putative father and bore the stigma of bastard. Statutes in most states have today erased many of these legal disabilities. Yet, the vestiges of unequal treatment of illegitimates remain. Further, the rate of illegitimate birth has soared in modern times, especially as traditional attitudes towards marriage and family have changed. What approach should the Court adopt towards review of illegitimacy classifications?

***Levy v. Louisiana*, 391 U.S. 68 (1968).** The Court, per Justice Douglas, held unconstitutional Louisiana's Wrongful Death Act which prevented an illegitimate child from recovering for the death of his mother. While branding the law irrational, Justice Douglas clearly engaged in more searching review.

> [W]e have been extremely sensitive when it comes to basic civil rights (*Skinner v. Oklahoma*; *Harper v. Virginia State Board of Elections*) and have not hesitated to strike down an invidious classification even though it had history and tradition on its side. The rights asserted here involve the intimate, familial relationship between a child and his own mother. Legitimacy or illegitimacy of birth has no relation to the nature of the wrong allegedly inflicted on the mother. These children, though illegitimate, were dependent on her; she cared for them and nurtured them; they were indeed hers in the biological and the spiritual sense; in her death they suffered wrong in the sense that any dependent would.

***Labine v. Vincent*, 401 U.S. 532 (1971).** A Louisiana law barred illegitimate children from sharing equally with legitimate children in the estates of their fathers who died intestate, even though the children were acknowledged. Such "natural children" could inherit by will, or succeed to the estate of their father "to the exclusion only of the State." Unacknowledged children could not claim by intestate succession and had only a limited ability to be beneficiaries under a will. A legitimated or adopted child was treated as any legitimate child. The Court, per Justice Black, upheld the law. The dissenters in *Levy* were joined by the new arrivals, Chief Justice Warren Burger and Justice Blackmun.

Levy was limited to cases "where the State had created an insurmountable barrier to [the] illegitimate child." In the present case, Justice Black observed, the father could have executed a will, could have legitimated the child by marrying her mother, or by an acknowledgment of paternity he could have stated his desire to legitimate. While the Justices might not agree with the policy choices of the state legislature, Justice Black stated, this was not a basis for invalidation of the law.

> [T]he power to make rules to establish, protect, and strengthen family life as well as to regulate the disposition of property left in Louisiana by a man dying there is committed by the Constitution of the United States and the people of Louisiana to the legislature of that State. Absent a specific constitutional guarantee, it is for that legislature, not the life-tenured judges of this Court to select from among possible laws.

In a cryptic footnote, Justice Black added: "Even if we were to apply the 'rational basis' test to the Louisiana intestate succession statute, that statute clearly has a rational basis in view of Louisiana's interest in promoting family life and of directing the disposition of property left within the State." What standard was the Court applying?

Justice Brennan, in dissent, charged that "for reasons not articulated, the Court refuses to consider in this case whether there is any reason at all, or any basis whatever, for the difference in treatment that Louisiana accords to publicly acknowledged illegitimates and to legitimate children."

***Weber v. Aetna Casualty & Surety Co.*, 406 U.S. 164 (1972).** *Labine* was distinguished and *Levy* was deemed controlling, in holding unconstitutional a Louisiana workman's compensation law barring unacknowledged illegitimate children from collecting death benefits. Justice Powell, for the Court, concluded that *Labine* was premised on the traditional deference accorded state regulation of the disposition of property at death. While Justice Powell endorsed the enhanced judicial scrutiny employed in *Levy*, he was less than clear on the nature of the review standard or its rationale:

> Having determined that *Levy* is the applicable precedent we briefly reaffirm here the reasoning which produced that result. The tests to determine the validity of state statutes under the Equal Protection Clause have been variously expressed, but this Court requires, at a minimum, that a statutory classification bear some rational relationship to a legitimate state purpose. Though the latitude given state economic and social regulation is necessarily broad, when state statutory classifications approach sensitive and fundamental personal rights, this Court exercises a stricter scrutiny, *Brown v. Board of Education*, *Harper v. Virginia State Board of Elections*. The essential inquiry is, however, inevitably a dual one: What legitimate state interest does the classification promote? What fundamental personal rights might the classification endanger?

While Justice Powell stressed that "fundamental personal rights" were implicated, he also emphasized the character of illegitimacy as a classifying trait. Visiting the state's condemnation of illicit relationships on the illegitimate child, he asserted, is "illogical and unjust." Further, "imposing disabilities on the illegitimate child is contrary to the basic concept of our system that legal burdens should bear some relationship to individual responsibility or wrongdoing." The Court went on to hold that the exclusion of illegitimates had "no significant relationship" to the legitimate objectives sought to be served by the worker's compensation law.

***Mathews v. Lucas*, 427 U.S. 495 (1976).** The Court, per Justice Blackmun, upheld provisions of the Social Security Act imposing a more stringent burden of proving dependency for death benefits on some classes of illegitimate children. While recognizing some similarities between illegitimacy and racial and national origin classifications, the Court stressed the differences:

> It is true, of course, that the legal status of illegitimacy, however defined, is, like race or national origin, a characteristic determined by causes not within the control of the illegitimate individual, and it bears no relation to the individual's ability to participate in and contribute to society. But where the law is arbitrary in such a way, we have had no difficulty in finding the discrimination impermissible on less demanding standards than those advocated here. And such

> irrationality in some classifications does not in itself demonstrate that other, possibly rational, distinctions made in part on the basis of legitimacy are inherently untenable. Moreover, while the law has long placed the illegitimate child in an inferior position relative to the legitimate in certain circumstances, particularly in regard to obligations of support or other aspects of family law, perhaps in part because the roots of the discrimination rest in the conduct of the parents rather than the child, and perhaps in part because illegitimacy does not carry an obvious badge, as race or sex do, this discrimination against illegitimates has never approached the severity or pervasiveness of the historic legal and political discrimination against women and Negroes.

Citing *Labine*, Justice Blackmun concluded "that the Act's discrimination between individuals on the basis of their legitimacy does not 'command extraordinary protection from the majoritarian political process,' which our most exacting scrutiny would entail."

Instead of strict scrutiny, the Court required the challengers to prove the "insubstantiality" of the relation of the classification to the likelihood of dependency. While *Weber* standards were cited as controlling and the review was described as "not toothless," the Court gave broad leeway to the congressional judgment. The materiality of the relation of the classification to dependency need not be "scientifically substantiated." Nor, "in this realm of less than strictest scrutiny," was Congress prevented from considering the relative amounts spent for welfare benefits and for administration. The judicial function was limited, according to Justice Blackmun, to determining

> whether Congress' assumptions are so inconsistent or insubstantial as not to be reasonably supportive of its conclusions that individualized factual inquiry in order to isolate each nondependent child in a given class of cases is unwarranted as an administrative exercise. In the end, the precise accuracy of Congress' calculations is not a matter of specialized judicial competence; and we have no basis to question their detail beyond the evident consistency and substantiality.

In *Mathews v. Lucas*, the plaintiff failed to show that the classifications were not "reasonably related to the likelihood of dependency at death." Presumptions of dependency, reasoned the Court, serve "administrative convenience" by reducing the burden and expense of case-by-case determination. The presumption need only "approximate rather than precisely mirror" the results of individualized decisions.

Justice Stevens, joined by Justices Brennan and Marshall dissented:

> The opinion tells us very little, about the "applicable level of scrutiny." It is not "our most exacting scrutiny"; on the other hand, if the classification derives "possibly rational" support from another source, it is not "inherently untenable" simply because it rests in part on illegitimacy. I believe an admittedly illogical and unjust result should not be accepted without both a better explanation and also something more than a "possibly rational" basis.

LALLI v. LALLI

439 U.S. 259, 99 S. Ct. 518, 58 L. Ed. 2d 503 (1978)

[In *Trimble v. Gordon*, 430 U.S. 762 (1977), the Supreme Court, per Justice Powell, had held unconstitutional an Illinois statute providing that an illegitimate child could recover from the father only if (1) the child had been acknowledged by the father, and, (2) the child had been legitimated by the intermarriage of the parents. Applying an intermediate standard of review, the Court had rejected the state's argument that the requirements were justified in order to encourage legitimate family relationships and to maintain an accurate and efficient method of estate administration.

[CHIEF JUSTICE BURGER and JUSTICES STEWART and BLACKMUN dissented in *Trimble*, finding the case "constitutionally indistinguishable" from *Labine v. Vincent*. JUSTICE REHNQUIST, in a lengthy separate dissent criticized severely the Court's departure from the rational basis test in non-race cases. He concluded that the Illinois law alleviated some of the difficulties of proof in intestate succession of illegimates from their fathers. Since the law was "not mindless and patently irrational," it was constitutional.

[In *Lalli*, the Court considered the implications of *Trimble* (and *Labine*) on a New York law (§ 4-1.2) providing that illegitimate children can inherit by intestate succession from their father only if a court of competent jurisdiction has, during the lifetime of the father, made an order of filiation declaring paternity. Legitimate children are not subject to any such requirement. Robert Lalli failed to secure such an order of filiation during his putative father's lifetime but sought to tender evidence establishing paternity in support of his and his sister's claim to be included as distributees of the estate. The lower court, relying on the statute, rejected the tender of proof and the New York Court of Appeals affirmed.]

JUSTICE POWELL announced the judgment of the Court in an opinion, in which THE CHIEF JUSTICE [BURGER] and JUSTICE STEWART join.

We begin our analysis with *Trimble* [where we] concluded that the Illinois statute discriminated against illegitimate children in a manner prohibited by the Equal Protection Clause. Although, as decided in *Mathews v. Lucas* and reaffirmed in *Trimble* classifications based on illegitimacy are not subject to "strict scrutiny," they nevertheless are invalid under the Fourteenth Amendment if they are not substantially related to permissible state interests. Upon examination, we found that the Illinois law failed that test.

Two state interests were proposed which the statute was said to foster: the encouragement of legitimate family relationships and the maintenance of an accurate and efficient method of disposing of an intestate decedent's property. Granting that the State was appropriately concerned with the integrity of the family unit, we viewed the statute as bearing "only the most attenuated relationship to the asserted goal." We again rejected the argument that "persons will shun illicit relations because the offspring may not one day reap the benefits" that would accrue to them were they legitimate. *Weber*. The statute therefore was not defensible as an incentive to enter legitimate family relationships.

Illinois' interest in safeguarding the orderly disposition of property at death was more relevant to the statutory classification. We recognized that devising "an appropriate legal framework" in the furtherance of that interest "is a matter particularly within the competence of the individual States." An important aspect of that framework is a response to the often difficult problem of proving the paternity of illegitimate children and the related danger of spurious claims against intestate estates. These difficulties, we said, "might justify a more demanding standard for illegitimate children claiming under their fathers' estates than that required either for illegitimate children claiming under their mothers' estates or for legitimate children generally."

The Illinois statute, however, was constitutionally flawed because, by insisting upon not only an acknowledgment by the father, but also the marriage of the parents, it excluded "at least some significant categories of illegitimate children of intestate men [whose] inheritance rights can be recognized without jeopardizing the orderly settlement of estates or the dependability of titles to property passing under intestacy laws. We concluded that the Equal Protection Clause required that a statute placing exceptional burdens on illegitimate children in the furtherance of proper state objectives must be more "carefully tuned to alternative considerations," than was true of the broad disqualification in the Illinois law.

The New York statute, enacted in 1965, was intended to soften the rigors of previous law which permitted illegitimate children to inherit only from their mothers. By lifting the absolute bar to paternal inheritance, § 4-1.2 tended to achieve its desired effect. As in *Trimble*, however, the question before us is whether the remaining statutory obstacles to inheritance by illegitimate children can be squared with the Equal Protection Clause. At the outset we observe that § 4-1.2 is different in important respects from the statutory provision overturned in *Trimble*. Under § 4-1.2, the marital status of the parents is irrelevant. The single requirement at issue here is an evidentiary one — that the paternity of the father be declared in a judicial proceeding sometime before his death. The child need not have been legitimated in order to inherit from his father. Had the appellant in *Trimble* been governed by § 4-1.2, she would have been a distributee of her father's estate.

A related difference between the two provisions pertains to the state interests said to be served by them. The Illinois law was defended, in part, as a means of encouraging legitimate family relationships. No such justification has been offered in support of § 4-1.2. The Court of Appeals disclaimed that the purpose of the statute, "even in small part, was to discourage illegitimacy, to mold human conduct or to set societal norms." The absence in § 4-1.2 of any requirement that the parents intermarry or otherwise legitimate a child born out of wedlock and our review of the legislative history of the statute confirm this view. Our inquiry, therefore, is focused narrowly. We are asked to decide whether the discrete procedural demands that § 4-1.2 places on illegitimate children bear an evident and substantial relation to the particular state interests this statute is designed to serve.

The primary state goal underlying the challenged aspects of § 4-1.2 is to provide for the just and orderly disposition of property at death. We long have recognized that this is an area with which the States have an interest of considerable magnitude. This interest is directly implicated in paternal inheritance by illegitimate children because of the peculiar problems of proof that are involved. Establishing maternity is seldom difficult. Proof of paternity, by contrast, frequently is difficult when the father is not part of a formal family unit.

Although the overarching purpose of [§ 4-1.2] was "to alleviate the plight of the illegitimate child," the Bennett Commission [which proposed the law] considered it necessary to impose the strictures of § 4-1.2 in order to mitigate serious difficulties in the administration of the estates of both testate and intestate decedents.

> [T]he illegitimate must be served with process. How does one cite and serve an illegitimate of whose existence neither family nor personal representative may be aware? And of greatest concern, how [sic] achieve finality of decree in any estate when there always exists the possibility however remote of a secret illegitimate lurking in the buried past of a parent or an ancestor of a class of beneficiaries?

Even where an individual claiming to be the illegitimate child of a deceased man makes himself known, the difficulties facing an estate are likely to persist. Because of the particular problems of proof, spurious claims may be difficult to expose.

As the State's interests are substantial, we now consider the means adopted by New York to further these interests. The administration of an estate will be facilitated, and the possibility of delay and uncertainty minimized, where the entitlement of an illegitimate child to notice and participation is a matter of judicial record before the administration commences. Fraudulent assertions of paternity will be much less likely to succeed, or even to arise, where the proof is put before a court of law at a time when the putative father is available to respond, rather than first brought to light when the distribution of the assets of an estate is in the offing. We do not question that there will be some illegitimate children who would be able to establish their relationship to their deceased fathers without serious disruption of the administration of estates and that, as applied to such individuals, § 4-1.2 appears to operate unfairly. But few statutory classifications are entirely free from the criticism that they sometimes produce inequitable results. Our inquiry under the Equal Protection Clause does not focus on the abstract "fairness" of a state law, but on whether the statute's relation to the state interests it is intended to promote is so tenuous that it lacks the rationality contemplated by the Fourteenth Amendment.

Inheritance is barred only where there has been a failure to secure evidence of paternity during the father's lifetime in the manner prescribed by the State. This is not a requirement that inevitably disqualifies an unnecessarily large number of children born out of wedlock. As the history of § 4-1.2 clearly illustrates, the New York Legislature desired to "grant to illegitimates in so far as practicable rights of inheritance on a par with those enjoyed by legitimate children," while protecting the important state interests we have described. Section 4-1.2 represents a carefully considered legislative judgment as to how this balance best could be achieved.

Even if, as Mr. Justice Brennan believes, § 4-1.2 could have been written somewhat more equitably, it is not the function of a court "to hypothesize independently on the desirability or feasibility of any possible alternative[s]" to the statutory scheme formulated by New York. *Mathews v. Lucas*. "These matters of practical judgment and empirical calculation are for [the State]. In the end, the precise accuracy of [the State's] calculations is not a matter of specialized judicial competence; and we have no basis to question their detail beyond the evident consistency and substantiality."

We conclude that the requirement imposed by § 4-1.2 on illegitimate children who would inherit from their fathers is substantially related to the important state interests the statute is intended to promote. We therefore find no violation of the Equal Protection Clause.

[Justice Rehnquist concurs in the judgment of affirmance "for the reasons stated in his dissent in *Trimble v. Gordon.*"]

Justice Stewart, concurring.

It seems to me that Mr. Justice Powell's opinion convincingly demonstrates the significant differences between the New York law at issue here and the Illinois law at issue in *Trimble v. Gordon*. Therefore, I cannot agree with the view expressed in the concurring opinion that *Trimble v. Gordon* is now "a derelict," or with the implication that in deciding the two cases the way it has this Court has failed to give authoritative guidance to the courts and legislatures of the several States.

Justice Blackmun, concurring in the judgment.

It seems to me that the Court today gratifyingly reverts to the principles set forth in *Labine v. Vincent*. What Mr. Justice Black said for the Court in *Labine* applies with equal force to the present case and, as four of us thought, to the Illinois situation with which *Trimble* was concerned. I would overrule *Trimble*, but the Court refrains from doing so on the theory that the result in *Trimble* is justified because of the peculiarities of the Illinois Probate Act there under consideration. This, of course, is an explanation, but, for me, it is an unconvincing one. I therefore must regard *Trimble* as a derelict, explainable only because of the overtones of its appealing facts and offering little precedent for constitutional analysis of State intestate succession laws. If *Trimble* is not a derelict, the corresponding statutes of other States will be of questionable validity until this Court passes on them, one by one, as being on the *Trimble* side of the line, or the *Vincent-Lalli* side.

Justice Brennan, with whom Justices White, Marshall, and Stevens join, dissenting.

Trimble v. Gordon declares that the state interest in the accurate and efficient determination of paternity can be adequately served by requiring the illegitimate child to offer into evidence a "formal acknowledgment of paternity." The New York statute is inconsistent with this command. Under the New York scheme, an illegitimate child may inherit intestate only if there has been a judicial finding of paternity during the lifetime of the father. The present case illustrates the injustice of the departure from *Trimble* worked by today's decision sustaining the New York rule. All interested parties concede that Robert Lalli is the son of Mario Lalli. Mario Lalli supported Robert during his son's youth. Mario Lalli formally acknowledged Robert Lalli as his son. Yet, for want of a judicial order of filiation entered during Mario's lifetime, Robert Lalli is denied his intestate share of his father's estate.

There is no reason to suppose that the injustice of the present case is aberrant. Indeed it is difficult to imagine an instance in which an illegitimate child acknowledged and voluntarily supported by his father, would ever inherit intestate under the New York scheme. Social welfare agencies, busy as they are with errant fathers, are unlikely to bring paternity proceedings against fathers who support their children. Similarly, children who are acknowledged and supported by their father are unlikely to bring paternity proceedings against him. Finally, fathers who do not even bother to make out wills (and thus die intestate) are unlikely to take the time to bring formal filiation proceedings. Thus, as a practical matter, by requiring judicial filiation orders entered during the lifetime of the father, the New York statute makes it virtually impossible for acknowledged and freely supported illegitimate children to inherit intestate.

Two interests are said to justify this discrimination against illegitimates. First, it is argued, reliance upon mere formal public acknowledgments of paternity would open the door to fraudulent claims of paternity. I cannot accept this argument. I adhere to the view that when "a father has formally acknowledged his child there is no possible difficulty of proof, and no opportunity for fraud or error. This purported interest [in avoiding fraud] can offer no justification for distinguishing between a formally acknowledged illegitimate child and a legitimate one." *Labine v. Vincent* (BRENNAN, J., dissenting).

But even if my confidence in the accuracy of formal public acknowledgments of paternity were unfounded, New York has available less drastic means of screening out fraudulent claims of paternity. In addition to requiring formal acknowledgments of paternity, New York might require illegitimates to prove paternity by an elevated standard of proof, e.g., clear and convincing evidence, or even beyond a reasonable doubt. Certainly here, where there is no factual dispute as to the relationship between Robert and Mario Lalli, there is no justification for denying Robert Lalli his intestate share.

Second, it is argued, the New York statute protects estates from belated claims by unknown illegitimates. I find this justification even more tenuous than the first. Publication notice and a short limitations period in which claims against the estate could be filed could serve the asserted state interest as well, if not better, than the present scheme. In any event, the fear that unknown illegitimates might assert belated claims hardly justifies cutting off the rights of known illegitimates such as Robert Lalli.

I see no reason to retreat from our decision in *Trimble v. Gordon*. The New York statute on review here, like the Illinois statute in *Trimble*, excludes "forms of proof which do not compromise the State['s] interests." The statute thus discriminates against illegitimates through means not substantially related to the legitimate interests that the statute purports to promote. I would invalidate the statute.

NOTES

1. *Suspect classifications.* Should status classifications based on illegitimacy be treated as suspect? Two commentators argue that illegitimacy shares with race several attributes: it is an immutable characteristic beyond a person's control that carries a history of discriminatory treatment and deters political clout. "Indeed the stigma of 'bastardy' in American society is so strong that illegitimates may be even more disabled than nonwhites from forming a political force to affect changes on a social or legislative level." John Gray & David Rudovsky, *The Court Acknowledges the Illegitimate: Levy v. Louisiana and Glona v. American Guarantee & Liability Insurance Co.*, 118 U. Pa. L. Rev. 1, 6–7 (1969).

The extent to which a more searching standard of review is employed in illegitimacy cases could turn on the probability that the law was motivated by prejudice, by notions about superiority and inferiority. When statutes involve the need to compensate minors for loss of financial support of parents, children are similarly situated regardless of legitimacy. "In such a situation, absent some other apparent explanation, one would normally presume that the denial of benefits was the result of prejudice." Closer judicial scrutiny, therefore, is justified. Other challenged laws involve "extrinsic ethical judgments regarding circumstances under which members of society should have enforceable claims against third parties" — in such cases, prejudice is less likely and a more searching review is not indicated. Earl Maltz, *Illegitimacy and Equal Protection*, 1980 Ariz. St. L.J. 831.

2. *Gender and illegitimacy.* While *Lalli* suggests the adoption of an intermediate standard of review using the terminology of *Craig v. Boren*, there is real doubt whether the review in illegitimacy cases is as searching as that in gender cases. *Mathews v. Lucas* indicates that the challenger has the burden of proof in illegitimacy cases. In *Lalli v. Lalli*, Justice Powell suggested that the "less onerous alternatives" requirement did not apply in illegitimacy cases. Is this true in gender cases? Can it be argued that illegitimacy classes are "functionally suspect" as has been said of gender classifications?

Are sex classifications more invidious than illegitimacy classifications? Illegitimates generally have not been barred from schools or jobs or other social roles because of their status. It has been argued that different treatment is justified on grounds that "antibastard legislation is not pervasive, but has been limited to treating the illegitimate less well than his legitimate sibling only in regard to parental obligations and third-party or governmental obligations predicated upon an injury to or incapacitation or death of a parent." Arnold Loewy, *A Different and More Viable Theory of Equal Protection*, 57 N.C. L. Rev. 3, 22 (1978).

3. *Implications of Lalli.* Some commentators see the decision as signalling a judicial retreat. *Lalli* is described by one as troubling because many statutory benefits depend on inheritance rights. "The second more troubling aspect of *Lalli* is that it appears to signal a retreat by the Court from its earlier position of broadly condemning this form of discrimination." Christina Kellett, *The Burger Decade: More Than Toothless Scrutiny for Laws Affecting Illegitimates*, 57 U. Det. J. Urb. L. 791, 808 (1980).

[D] RATIONAL BASIS "WITH TEETH"

[1] Mental Retardation, Age, Poverty

CITY OF CLEBURNE v. CLEBURNE LIVING CENTER, INC.
473 U.S. 432, 105 S. Ct. 3249, 87 L. Ed. 2d 313 (1985)

[In 1980, Jan Hannah purchased a building in Cleburne, Texas, with the intention of leasing it to the Cleburne Living Center (CLC) for the operation of a group home for the mentally retarded. The city informed CLC that under the zoning regulations applicable to the site a special use permit would be required for the operation of the group home. After holding a public hearing, the city council voted to deny the special use permit. CLC filed suit in federal district court alleging that the zoning ordinance violated the equal protection rights of the prospective residents of the home. The district court held the ordinance constitutional. The court of appeals reversed holding that mental retardation was a quasi-suspect classification, and that, using the intermediate level of scrutiny, the ordinance "violated the Equal Protection Clause because it did not substantially further an important governmental interest."]

JUSTICE WHITE delivered the opinion of the Court.

We hold that a lesser standard of scrutiny is appropriate, but conclude that under that standard the ordinance is invalid as applied in this case. The general rule is that legislation is presumed to be valid and will be sustained if the classification drawn by the statute is rationally related to a legitimate state interest. When social or economic legislation is at issue, the Equal Protection Clause allows the states wide latitude, and the Constitution presumes that even improvident decisions will eventually be rectified by the democratic processes.

The general rule gives way, however, when a statute classifies by race, alienage or national origin. These factors are so seldom relevant to the achievement of any legitimate state interest that laws grounded in such considerations are deemed to reflect prejudice and antipathy — a view that those in the burdened class are not as worthy or deserving as others. For these reasons and because such discrimination is unlikely to be soon rectified by legislative means, these laws are subjected to strict scrutiny and will be sustained only if they are suitably tailored to serve a compelling state interest. Legislative classifications based on gender also call for a heightened standard of review. That factor generally provides no sensible ground for differential treatment. Official discriminations resting on [illegitimacy] are also subject to somewhat heightened review.

We have declined, however, to extend heightened review to differential treatment based on age:

> "While the treatment of the aged in this Nation has not been wholly free of discrimination, such persons, unlike, say, those who have been discriminated against on the basis of race or national origin, have not experienced a "history of purposeful unequal treatment' or been subjected to unique disabilities on the basis of stereotyped

characteristics not truly indicative of their abilities." *Massachusetts Board of Retirement v. Murgia*, 427 U.S. 307, 313 (1976).

The lesson of *Murgia* [upholding a law imposing compulsory retirement at age 50 for police officers] is that where individuals in the group affected by a law have distinguishing characteristics relevant to interests the state has the authority to implement, the courts have been very reluctant, as they should be in our federal system and with our respect for the separation of powers, to closely scrutinize legislative choices as to whether, how and to what extent those interests should be pursued. In such cases, the Equal Protection Clause requires only a rational means to serve a legitimate end.

Against this background, we conclude for several reasons that the Court of Appeals erred in holding mental retardation a quasi-suspect classification calling for a more exacting standard of judicial review than is normally accorded economic and social legislation. First, it is undeniable, and it is not argued otherwise here, that those who are mentally retarded have a reduced ability to cope with and function in the everyday world. Nor are they all cut from the same pattern: as the testimony in this record indicates, they range from those whose disability is not immediately evident to those who must be constantly cared for.[9] They are thus different, immutably so, in relevant respects, and the states' interest in dealing with and providing for them is plainly a legitimate one. How this large and diversified group is to be treated under the law is a difficult and often a technical matter, very much a task for legislators guided by qualified professionals and not by the perhaps ill-informed opinions of the judiciary. Heightened scrutiny inevitably involves substantive judgments about legislative decisions, and we doubt that the predicate for such judicial oversight is present where the classification deals with mental retardation.

Second, the distinctive legislative response, both national and state, to the plight of those who are mentally retarded demonstrates not only that they have unique problems, but also that the lawmakers have been addressing their difficulties in a manner that belies a continuing antipathy or prejudice and a corresponding need for more intrusive oversight by the judiciary.

Third, the legislative response, which could hardly have occurred and survived without public support, negates any claim that the mentally retarded are politically powerless in the sense that they have no ability to attract the

[9] Mentally retarded individuals fall into four distinct categories. The vast majority — approximately 89% — are classified as "mildly" retarded, meaning that their IQ is between 50 and 70. Approximately 6% are "moderately" retarded, with IQs between 35 and 50. The remaining two categories are "severe" (IQs of 20 to 35) and "profound" (IQs below 20). These last two categories together account for about 5% of the mentally retarded population.

Mental retardation is not defined by reference to intelligence or IQ alone, however. The American Association on Mental Deficiency (AAMD) has defined mental retardation as "significantly subaverage general intellectual functioning existing concurrently with deficits in adaptive behavior and manifested during the developmental period." "Deficits in adaptive behavior" are limitations on general ability to meet the standards of maturation, learning, personal independence, and social responsibility expected for an individual's age level and cultural group. Mental retardation is caused by a variety of factors, some genetic, some environmental, and some unknown.

attention of the lawmakers. Any minority can be said to be powerless to assert direct control over the legislature, but if that were a criterion for higher level scrutiny by the courts, much economic and social legislation would now be suspect.

Fourth, if the large and amorphous class of the mentally retarded were deemed quasi-suspect for the reasons given by the Court of Appeals, it would be difficult to find a principled way to distinguish a variety of other groups who have perhaps immutable disabilities setting them off from others, who cannot themselves mandate the desired legislative responses, and who can claim some degree of prejudice from at least part of the public at large. One need mention in this respect only the aging, the disabled, the mentally ill, and the infirm. We are reluctant to set out on that course, and we decline to do so.

Doubtless, there have been and there will continue to be instances of discrimination against the retarded that are in fact invidious, and that are properly subject to judicial correction under constitutional norms. But the appropriate method of reaching such instances is not to create a new quasi-suspect classification and subject all governmental action based on that classification to more searching evaluation. Rather, we should look to the likelihood that governmental action premised on a particular classification is valid as a general matter, not merely to the specifics of the case before us. Because mental retardation is a characteristic that the government may legitimately take into account in a wide range of decisions, and because both state and federal governments have recently committed themselves to assisting the retarded, we will not presume that any given legislative action, even one that disadvantages retarded individuals, is rooted in considerations that the Constitution will not tolerate.

Our refusal to recognize the retarded as a quasi-suspect class does not leave them entirely unprotected from invidious discrimination. To withstand equal protection review, legislation that distinguishes between the mentally retarded and others must be rationally related to a legitimate governmental purpose. This standard, we believe, affords government the latitude necessary both to pursue policies designed to assist the retarded in realizing their full potential, and to freely and efficiently engage in activities that burden the retarded in what is essentially an incidental manner. The State may not rely on a classification whose relationship to an asserted goal is so attenuated as to render the distinction arbitrary or irrational. *See Zobel v. Williams*; *United States Department of Agriculture v. Moreno*. Furthermore, some objectives — such as "a bare . . . desire to harm a politically unpopular group," *Moreno* — are not legitimate state interests. Beyond that, the mentally retarded, like others, have and retain their substantive constitutional rights in addition to the right to be treated equally by the law.

We turn to the issue of the validity of the zoning ordinance insofar as it requires a special use permit for homes for the mentally retarded. We inquire first whether requiring a special use permit for the Featherston home in the circumstances here deprives respondents of the equal protection of the laws. If it does, there will be no occasion to decide whether the special use permit provision is facially invalid where the mentally retarded are involved, or to put it another way, whether the city may never insist on a special use permit for a home for the mentally retarded in an R-3 zone. This is the preferred course of adjudication since it enables courts to avoid making unnecessarily broad constitutional judgments.

The constitutional issue is clearly posed. The City does not require a special use permit in an R-3 zone for apartment houses, multiple dwellings, boarding and lodging houses, fraternity or sorority houses, dormitories, apartment hotels, hospitals, sanitariums, nursing homes for convalescents or the aged (other than for the insane or feeble-minded or alcoholics or drug addicts), private clubs or fraternal orders, and other specified uses. It does, however, insist on a special permit for the Featherston home, and it does so, as the District Court found, because it would be a facility for the mentally retarded. May the city require the permit for this facility when other care and multiple dwelling facilities are freely permitted?

It is true, as already pointed out, that the mentally retarded as a group are indeed different from others not sharing their misfortune, and in this respect they may be different from those who would occupy other facilities that would be permitted in an R-3 zone without a special permit. But this difference is largely irrelevant unless the Featherston home and those who would occupy it would threaten legitimate interests of the city in a way that other permitted uses such as boarding houses and hospitals would not. Because in our view the record does not reveal any rational basis for believing that the Featherston home would pose any special threat to the city's legitimate interests, we affirm the judgment below insofar as it holds the ordinance invalid as applied in this case.

It is true that they suffer disability not shared by others; but why this difference warrants a density regulation that others need not observe is not at all apparent. At least this record does not clarify how, in this connection, the characteristics of the intended occupants of the Featherston home rationally justify denying to those occupants what would be permitted to groups occupying the same site for different purposes. Those who would live in the Featherston home are the type of individuals who, with supporting staff, satisfy federal and state standards for group housing in the community; and there is no dispute that the home would meet the federal square-footage-per-resident requirement for facilities of this type. In the words of the Court of Appeals, "The City never justifies its apparent view that other people can live under such 'crowded' conditions when mentally retarded persons cannot."

In the courts below the city also urged that the ordinance is aimed at avoiding concentration of population and at lessening congestion of the streets. These concerns obviously fail to explain why apartment houses, fraternity and sorority houses, hospitals and the like, may freely locate in the area without a permit. So, too, the expressed worry about fire hazards, the serenity of the neighborhood, and the avoidance of danger to other residents fail rationally to justify singling out a home such as 201 Featherston for the special use permit, yet imposing no such restrictions on the many other uses freely permitted in the neighborhood.

The short of it is that requiring the permit in this case appears to us to rest on an irrational prejudice against the mentally retarded, including those who would occupy the Featherston facility and who would live under the closely supervised and highly regulated conditions expressly provided for by state and federal law.

The judgment of the Court of Appeals is affirmed insofar as it invalidates the zoning ordinance as applied to the Featherston home. The judgment is otherwise vacated.

JUSTICE STEVENS, with whom THE CHIEF JUSTICE [REHNQUIST] joins, concurring.

[O]ur cases reflect a continuum of judgmental responses to differing classifications which have been explained in opinions by terms ranging from "strict scrutiny" at one extreme to "rational basis" at the other. I have never been persuaded that these so called "standards" adequately explain the decisional process. Cases involving classifications based on alienage, illegal residency, illegitimacy, gender, age, or — as in this case — mental retardation, do not fit well into sharply defined classifications.

In every equal protection case, we have to ask certain basic questions. What class is harmed by the legislation, and has it been subjected to a "tradition of disfavor" by our laws? What is the public purpose that is being served by the law? What is the characteristic of the disadvantaged class that justifies the disparate treatment? In most cases the answer to these questions will tell us whether the statute has a "rational basis." The answers will result in the virtually automatic invalidation of racial classifications and in the validation of most economic classifications, but they will provide differing results in cases involving classifications based on alienage, gender, or illegitimacy. But that is not because we apply an "intermediate standard of review" in these cases; rather it is because the characteristics of these groups are sometimes relevant and sometimes irrelevant to a valid public purpose, or, more specifically, to the purpose that the challenged laws purportedly intended to serve.

Every law that places the mentally retarded in a special class is not presumptively irrational. The differences between mentally retarded persons and those with greater mental capacity are obviously relevant to certain legislative decisions. An impartial lawmaker — indeed, even a member of a class of persons defined as mentally retarded — could rationally vote in favor of a law providing funds for special education and special treatment for the mentally retarded. A mentally retarded person could also recognize that he is a member of a class that might need special supervision in some situations, both to protect himself and to protect others. Restrictions on his right to drive cars or to operate hazardous equipment might well seem rational even though they deprived him of employment opportunities and the kind of freedom of travel enjoyed by other citizens.

Even so, the Court of Appeals correctly observed that through ignorance and prejudice the mentally retarded "have been subjected to a history of unfair and often grotesque mistreatment." The record convinces me that this permit was required because of the irrational fears of neighboring property owners, rather than for the protection of the mentally retarded persons who would reside in respondent's home. Accordingly, I join the opinion of the Court.

JUSTICE MARSHALL, with whom JUSTICES BRENNAN and BLACKMUN join, concurring in the judgment in part and dissenting in part.

The Court holds the ordinance invalid on rational basis grounds and disclaims that anything special, in the form of heightened scrutiny, is taking place. Yet Cleburne's ordinance surely would be valid under the traditional rational basis test applicable to economic and commercial regulation. In my view, it is important to articulate, as the Court does not, the facts and principles that justify subjecting this zoning ordinance to the searching review — the heightened scrutiny — that actually leads to its invalidation. Moreover, in invalidating Cleburne's exclusion of the "feebleminded" only as applied to respondents, rather than on its face, the Court radically departs from our equal protection precedents. Because I dissent from this novel and truncated remedy, and because I cannot accept the Court's disclaimer that no "more exacting standard" than ordinary rational basis review is being applied, I write separately.

However labelled, the rational basis test invoked today is most assuredly not the rational basis test. The Court, for example, concludes that legitimate concerns for fire hazards or the serenity of the neighborhood do not justify singling out respondents to bear the burdens of these concerns, for analogous permitted uses appear to pose similar threats. Yet under the traditional and most minimal version of the rational basis test, "reform may take one step at a time, addressing itself to the phase of the problem which seems most acute to the legislative mind." *Williamson v. Lee Optical Co.* The "record" is said not to support the ordinance's classifications, but under the traditional standard we do not sift through the record to determine whether policy decisions are squarely supported by a firm factual foundation. Finally, the Court further finds it "difficult to believe" that the retarded present different or special hazards than other groups. In normal circumstances, the burden is not on the legislature to convince the Court that the lines it has drawn are sensible; legislation is presumptively constitutional, and a State "is not required to resort to close distinctions or to maintain a precise, scientific uniformity with reference" to its goals.

I have long believed the level of scrutiny employed in an equal protection case should vary with "the constitutional and societal importance of the interest adversely affected and the recognized invidiousness of the basis upon which the particular classification is drawn." *San Antonio Independent School District v. Rodriguez* (Marshall, J. dissenting). When a zoning ordinance works to exclude the retarded from all residential districts in a community, these two considerations require that the ordinance be convincingly justified as substantially furthering legitimate and important purposes.

In light of the importance of the interest at stake and the history of discrimination the retarded have suffered, the Equal Protection Clause requires us to do more than review the distinctions drawn by *Cleburne*'s zoning ordinance as if they appeared in a taxing statute or in economic or commercial legislation. The searching scrutiny I would give to restrictions on the ability of the retarded to establish community group homes leads me to conclude that *Cleburne*'s vague generalizations for classifying the "feeble minded" with drug addicts, alcoholics, and the insane, and excluding them where the elderly, the ill, the boarder, and the transient are allowed, are not substantial or important enough to overcome the suspicion that the ordinance rests on impermissible assumptions or outmoded and perhaps invidious stereotypes.

NOTES

1. *Real differences.* Martha Minow, *When Difference Has Its Home: Group Homes for the Mentally Retarded, Equal Protection and Legal Treatment of Difference*, 22 HARV. C.R. — C.L.L. REV. 111, 122 (1987), argues that the *Cleburne* majority "treats mental deficiency as a real and immutable difference, and the majority's mental universe is inhabited by various groups, some with immutable differences that set them apart from the rest of society and thus warrant different legal treatment." Instead of this "abnormal persons" approach, she urges a "social relations" analysis which challenges the assumed differences between legally-defined groups. "Such suspicion stems not only from an awareness of historical errors in the attribution of difference, but also from a view that attribution itself hides the power of these who classify as well as those defined as different." *Id.* at 129. Do the Stevens or Marshall opinions in *Cleburne* reflect this perspective? Does it make all classification suspect?

2. *The limits of suspectness.* While mental retardation and age classifications do not share all of the characteristics that make race suspect, neither do alienage, gender, and illegitimacy. And yet the latter classifications do receive a more searching judicial scrutiny, at least in some cases. Why are mental retardation and age not subject to heightened scrutiny? In the case of the aged, perhaps the answer lies in the fact that we are all potentially among the aged and hence are not as likely to discriminate against that class. Perhaps it is the lack of a discrete class of "aged" that can readily be identified. But are such considerations applicable to the mentally retarded or mentally ill? Perhaps the distinguishing factor is that the political process itself may provide adequate protection against legislation hostile to the aged or the mentally retarded. Today, discrimination based on illness and physical or mental handicaps is generally handled by statute.

3. *Rationality with bite.* On the other hand, is *Cleburne* really an application of the deferential rationality standard? Or is the Court simply using the language of rationality while employing a more searching mode of judicial scrutiny? See p. 656, n. 11, on "rationality with bite." Cass Sunstein, *Foreword: Leaving Things Undecided*, 110 HARV. L. REV. 4, 61 (1996), says that in *Cleburne* (and *Romer*) "the Court was concerned that a politically unpopular group was facing discrimination as a result of irrational hatred and fear." He argues that the cases "reflect the possible use of rationality review as a kind of magical trump card, or perhaps joker, hidden in the pack and used on special occasions. In these cases, rationality review, traditionally little more than a rubber stamp, is used to invalidate badly motivated laws without refining a new kind of scrutiny. In this way too, they are minimalist; they have no progeny." *See* Ashutosh Bhagwat, *Purpose Scrutiny in Constitutional Analysis*, 85 CALIF. L. REV. 297, 312 (1997) ("In [*Cleburne* and *Romer*], the Court applied its lowest standard of scrutiny, the rational basis test, but nonetheless struck down the regulations because it perceived that the actual ends — as distinct from the proffered ends — motivating the legislation were illegitimate."); Robert C. Farrell, *Successful Rational Basis Claims in the Supreme Court from the 1971 Term Through* Romer v. Evans, 32 IND. L. REV. 357, 398 (1999) ("the [*Cleburne*] Court used several non-deferential techniques. Specifically, the Court's analysis moved back and forth between rejecting purposes as impermissible, and rejecting as inadequate or nonexistent the connection between the differing treatment of the mentally retarded and an alleged, permissible purpose.").

Is Congress better equipped to determine the need for protection of particular groups against discrimination? Using *Cleburne* as an example, Professor William D. Araiza, *The Section 5 Power and the Rational Basis Standard of Equal Protection*, 79 TUL. L. REV. 519, 564 (2005), argues that "[the] characteristics of rational basis review make it less of an effective guard against unthinking or animus-based action, and more an arbitrary lightning bolt that, when effective at all, completely wipes out one action but leaves similarly problematic conduct untouched. Congress, with the flexibility inherent in legislation, can craft a result that is once broader, in the sense of applying to a general species of potentially problematic government action, and more naunced, in the sense of imposing rules that fall between complete approval and outright prohibition."

4. *Heller v. Doe,* 509 U.S. 312 (1993). The Court, per Justice Kennedy, upheld, 5-4, a Kentucky statutory scheme for the involuntary commitment of mentally retarded or mentally ill individuals against an equal protection and procedural due process challenge. The state statutes provided for the commitment of those who constituted a danger to themselves or others, who could reasonably benefit from the available treatment, and for whom the least restrictive alternative is placement in the relevant facility.

The Kentucky statutory scheme for involuntary commitment distinguished between the mentally retarded and the mentally ill in two respects. First, the burden of proof in proceedings for the involuntary commitment of the mentally retarded is clear and convincing evidence. The standard in proceedings for the involuntary commitment of the mentally ill is beyond a reasonable doubt. Second, guardians and members of the immediate family of a mentally retarded person who is the subject of a proceeding to involuntarily commit were permitted to participate in the proceeding as if they were full parties. Not so for the guardians and immediate family members of a mentally ill person who is the subject of an involuntary commitment proceeding.

The Court accepted the state's argument that a lower standard of proof in commitments for mental retardation was justified since that condition was easier to diagnose than is the case with mental illness: "In assigning the burden of proof, Kentucky was determining the 'risk of error' faced by the subject of the proceedings. If diagnosis is more difficult in cases of mental illness than in instances of mental retardation, a higher burden of proof for the former tends to equalize the risks of an erroneous determination that the subject of a commitment proceeding has the condition in question." In addition, as a generality, treatment of the mentally retarded is far less invasive than the treatment given the mentally ill. The latter are subjected to medical and psychiatric treatment rather than, as is the case with the mentally retarded, "education and training."

A rational basis existed as well for the state's decision to allow immediate family members and guardians to participate in involuntary commitment proceedings for the mentally retarded but not for the mentally ill. Such persons may have intimate and valuable knowledge of the mentally retarded person's capacities and experiences. But mental illness may often arise only after the person involved is an adult and the immediate family members may furnish neither care nor support. In addition, privacy considerations in the case of adults who formerly were of sound mental health may call for limiting the number of persons involved in the involuntary commitment proceeding of a mentally ill person.

Justice Souter, joined by Justices Blackmun, O'Connor and Stevens dissented, concluding that the differing standards of proof for involuntary commitment are not supported by any rational justification. "We do not lower burdens of proof merely because it is easy to prove the proposition at issue, nor do we raise them merely because it is difficult. We do not presume that a curtailment of liberty of those who are disabled is, because of their disability, less severe than the same loss to those who are ill."

Professor Farrell, 32 IND. L. REV. at 400, argues that the claim of discrimination in *Heller* was "quite similar" to the claim of discrimination in *Cleburne*. But the *Heller* Court "cited *Cleburne* only once and purported to find in *Cleburne* the same [deferential] rational basis standard it was using in *Heller*." But he argues that the Court was wrong: "The rational basis review in *Heller* bears very little similarity to the rational basis review in *Cleburne*."

5. *Village of Willowbrook v. Olech*, 528 U.S. 562 (2000). Olech, a homeowner, sued when the Village of Willowbrook attempted to impose a 33-foot easement in order to hookup her property to the municipal water supply while other property owners had been required to grant only a 15-foot easement. The Court held that Olech could constitute a class of one since "the number of individuals in a class is immaterial for equal protection analysis."

While Olech had alleged the Village's action were motivated by ill-will, the Court held that allegations that the Village's actions were "irrational and wholly arbitrary" and that the Village had finally "relented" by allowing the hookup for a 15-foot easement, "quite apart from the Village's subjective motivation, are sufficient to state a claim under traditional equal protection analysis."

6. *Discrimination against the poor.* The question of the proper standard of review to be applied to classifications between the rich and the poor runs through a number of the cases in the section on fundamental rights equal protection. One of the themes of the Warren Court's egalitarianism was the suggestion that a wealth classification should itself be sufficient to trigger a more searching judicial scrutiny. But it has been noted that "there is no evidence that the framers [of the Fourteenth Amendment] were concerned with the distribution of income." Ralph Winter, *Poverty, Economic Equality, and the Equal Protection Clause*, 1972 SUP. CT. REV. 41, 98. Winter argues that discrimination based on wealth was common during the nineteenth century and there is no legislative history supporting the view that the Fourteenth Amendment was intended to protect the poor as a class. How critical is this factor? Winter argues that the poor are not even an identifiable class because "there is no transcendent income line below which is poverty. The fact is that any person who has less material income than someone else will feel deprived. [T]he poverty problem is a relative inequality problem rather than some sort of absolute affliction." *Id.*

The capacity to pay for goods and services is a characteristic feature of our society. What would be the consequence of using a stricter standard of review for wealth classification? Does it matter if the wealth classification is de jure or de facto? Owen Fiss, *The Forms of Justice*, 93 Harv. L. Rev. 1, 7 (1979), notes that "poverty was not identified by footnote four [of the *Carolene Products* decision] as a category of legislative failure, and for good reason. The absence of wealth is so pervasive a handicap, it is experienced by so many groups in society, even the majority itself, that to recognize it as a category of legislative failure would stand the theory of the *Carolene Products* footnote on its head — it would undermine the premise of majoritarianism itself."

Stephen Loffredo, *Poverty, Democracy and Constitutional Law*, 141 U. Pa. L. Rev. 1277, 1285 (1993), argues that the political powerlessness of the poor requires some form of enhanced judicial protection. "[T]he Court's laissez-faire jurisprudence poses a dangerous dilemma: the political process provides little security for even the most basic interests of the poor, while the absence of a judicial check on the process has encouraged political discourse and decision making to degenerate into a virtual free-fire zone with respect to the lives of poor people. The lack of serious judicial review, and the resulting legislative failure to engage in reasoned deliberation, has produced a politics marked by scapegoating, stereotyping, and stigmatization."

In *James v. Valtierra*, 402 U.S. 137 (1971), the Court reversed a lower court's determination that an article of the California Constitution requiring referendum approval for any low-rent public housing project denied equal protection. The Court, per Justice Black, noted that California frequently used the referendum "to give citizens a voice on questions of public policy," and argued that "[p]rovisions for referendums demonstrate devotion to democracy, not to bias, discrimination, prejudice." Requiring a mandatory referendum for public housing while other referendums resulted from citizen initiative was not deemed a critical distinction. While those seeking public housing might face roadblocks not faced by other groups, "a law making procedure that 'disadvantages' a particular group does not always deny equal protection."

Justice Marshall, joined by Justices Blackmun and Brennan in dissent, argued that because the article explicitly applied only to low-income housing, and not to other publicly assisted housing developments, it was discriminatory on its face. He characterized the article as "an explicit classification on the basis of poverty — a suspect classification which demands exacting judicial scrutiny." For the dissent, "singling out the poor to bear a burden not placed on any other class of citizens tramples the values that the Fourteenth Amendment was designed to protect."

Harris v. McRae, p. 929, and *San Antonio Sch. Dist. v. Rodriguez*, p. 936, similarly rejected heightened scrutiny for wealth classifications.

[2] Sexual Orientation

ROMER v. EVANS

517 U.S. 620, 116 S. Ct. 1620, 134 L. Ed. 2d 855 (1996)

JUSTICE KENNEDY delivered the opinion of the Court.

One century ago, the first JUSTICE HARLAN admonished this Court that the Constitution "neither knows nor tolerates classes among citizens." *Plessy v. Ferguson* (dissenting opinion). Unheeded then, those words now are understood to state a commitment to the law's neutrality where the rights of persons are at stake. The Equal Protection Clause enforces this principle and today requires us to hold invalid a provision of Colorado's Constitution.

I

The enactment challenged in this case is an amendment to the Constitution of the State of Colorado, adopted in a 1992 statewide referendum. The parties and the state courts refer to it as "Amendment 2," its designation when submitted to the voters. The impetus for the amendment and the contentious campaign that preceded its adoption came in large part from ordinances that had been passed in various Colorado municipalities. For example, the cities of Aspen and Boulder and the City and County of Denver each had enacted ordinances which banned discrimination in many transactions and activities, including housing, employment, education, public accommodations, and health and welfare services. What gave rise to the statewide controversy was the protection the ordinances afforded to persons discriminated against by reason of their sexual orientation. *See* BOULDER REV. CODE § 12-1-1 (defining "sexual orientation" as "the choice of sexual partners, i.e., bisexual, homosexual or heterosexual"); DENVER REV. MUNICIPAL CODE, Art. IV § 28-92 (defining "sexual orientation" as "[t]he status of an individual as to his or her heterosexuality, homosexuality or bisexuality"). Amendment 2 repeals these ordinances to the extent they prohibit discrimination on the basis of "homosexual, lesbian or bisexual orientation, conduct, practices or relationships." COLO. CONST., Art. II, § 30b.

Yet Amendment 2, in explicit terms, does more than repeal or rescind these provisions. It prohibits all legislative, executive or judicial action at any level of state or local government designed to protect the named class, a class we shall refer to as homosexual persons or gays and lesbians. The amendment reads:

> *No Protected Status Based on Homosexual, Lesbian, or Bisexual Orientation.* Neither the State of Colorado, through any of its branches or departments, nor any of its agencies, political subdivisions, municipalities or school districts, shall enact, adopt or enforce any statute, regulation, ordinance or policy whereby homosexual, lesbian or bisexual orientation, conduct, practices or relationships shall constitute or otherwise be the basis of or entitle any person or class of persons to have or claim any minority status, quota preferences, protected status or claim of discrimination. This Section of the Constitution shall be in all respects self-executing.

Soon after Amendment 2 was adopted, this litigation to declare its invalidity and enjoin its enforcement was commenced in the District Court for the City and County of Denver. Among the plaintiffs (respondents here) were homosexual persons, some of them government employees. They alleged that enforcement of Amendment 2 would subject them to immediate and substantial risk of discrimination on the basis of their sexual orientation. Other plaintiffs (also respondents here) included the three municipalities whose ordinances we have cited and certain other governmental entities which had acted earlier to protect homosexuals from discrimination but would be prevented by Amendment 2 from continuing to do so. Although Governor Romer had been on record opposing the adoption of Amendment 2, he was named in his official capacity as a defendant, together with the Colorado Attorney General and the State of Colorado.

The trial court granted a preliminary injunction to stay enforcement of Amendment 2, and an appeal was taken to the Supreme Court of Colorado. Sustaining the interim injunction and remanding the case for further proceedings, the State Supreme Court held that Amendment 2 was subject to strict scrutiny under the Fourteenth Amendment because it infringed the fundamental right of gays and lesbians to participate in the political process. *Evans v. Romer*, 854 P.2d 1270 (Colo. 1993) (*Evans I*). To reach this conclusion, the state court relied on our voting rights cases and on our precedents involving discriminatory restructuring of governmental decisionmaking. On remand, the State advanced various arguments in an effort to show that Amendment 2 was narrowly tailored to serve compelling interests, but the trial court found none sufficient. It enjoined enforcement of Amendment 2, and the Supreme Court of Colorado, in a second opinion, affirmed the ruling. *Evans v. Romer*, 882 P. 2d 1335 (Colo.1994) (*Evans II*). We granted certiorari and now affirm the judgment, but on a rationale different from that adopted by the State Supreme Court.

II

The State's principal argument in defense of Amendment 2 is that it puts gays and lesbians in the same position as all other persons. So, the State says, the measure does no more than deny homosexuals special rights. This reading of the amendment's language is implausible. We rely not upon our own interpretation of the amendment but upon the authoritative construction of Colorado's Supreme Court. The state court, deeming it unnecessary to determine the full extent of the amendment's reach, found it invalid even on a modest reading of its implications. The critical discussion of the amendment, set out in *Evans I*, is as follows:

> The immediate objective of Amendment 2 is, at a minimum, to repeal existing statutes, regulations, ordinances, and policies of state and local entities that barred discrimination based on sexual orientation.*

* [Aspen, Boulder, and Denver all prohibited discrimination in employment, housing and public accommodations on the basis of sexual orientation; a State Executive Order prohibited employment discrimination on the basis of sexual orientation; the Colorado Insurance Code prohibited

> The "ultimate effect" of Amendment 2 is to prohibit any governmental entity from adopting similar, or more protective statutes, regulations, ordinances, or policies in the future unless the state constitution is first amended to permit such measures.

Sweeping and comprehensive is the change in legal status effected by this law. So much is evident from the ordinances that the Colorado Supreme Court declared would be void by operation of Amendment 2. Homosexuals, by state decree, are put in a solitary class with respect to transactions and relations in both the private and governmental spheres. The amendment withdraws from homosexuals, but no others, specific legal protection from the injuries caused by discrimination, and it forbids reinstatement of these laws and policies.

The change that Amendment 2 works in the legal status of gays and lesbians in the private sphere is far-reaching, both on its own terms and when considered in light of the structure and operation of modern anti-discrimination laws. That structure is well illustrated by contemporary statutes and ordinances prohibiting discrimination by providers of public accommodations. "At common law, innkeepers, smiths, and others who 'made profession of a public employment,' were prohibited from refusing, without good reason, to serve a customer." The duty was a general one and did not specify protection for particular groups. The common law rules, however, proved insufficient in many cases.

[Modern] statutes and ordinances depart from the common law by enumerating the groups or persons within their ambit of protection. Enumeration is the essential device used to make the duty not to discriminate concrete and to provide guidance for those who must comply. In following this approach, Colorado's state and local governments have not limited anti-discrimination laws to groups that have so far been given the protection of heightened equal protection scrutiny under our cases. Rather, they set forth an extensive catalogue of traits which cannot be the basis for discrimination, including age, military status, marital status, pregnancy, parenthood, custody of a minor child, political affiliation, physical or mental disability of an individual or of his or her associates — and, in recent times, sexual orientation.

Amendment 2 bars homosexuals from securing protection against the injuries that these public-accommodations laws address. That in itself is a severe consequence, but there is more. Amendment 2, in addition, nullifies specific legal protections for this targeted class in all transactions in housing, sale of real estate, insurance, health and welfare services, private education, and employment.

Not confined to the private sphere, Amendment 2 also operates to repeal and forbid all laws or policies providing specific protection for gays or lesbians from discrimination by every level of Colorado government. The State Supreme Court cited two examples of protections in the governmental sphere

health insurance providers from determining insurability and premiums based on sexual orientation; and various state colleges prohibited discrimination based on sexual orientation. — Ed.]

that are now rescinded and may not be reintroduced. The first is [an] Executive Order which forbids employment discrimination against "all state employees, classified and exempt on the basis of sexual orientation." Also repealed, and now forbidden, are "various provisions prohibiting discrimination based on sexual orientation at state colleges." The repeal of these measures and the prohibition against their future reenactment demonstrates that Amendment 2 has the same force and effect in Colorado's governmental sector as it does elsewhere and that it applies to policies as well as ordinary legislation.

Amendment 2's reach may not be limited to specific laws passed for the benefit of gays and lesbians. It is a fair, if not necessary, inference from the broad language of the amendment that it deprives gays and lesbians even of the protection of general laws and policies that prohibit arbitrary discrimination in governmental and private settings. At some point in the systematic administration of these laws, an official must determine whether homosexuality is an arbitrary and thus forbidden basis for decision. Yet a decision to that effect would itself amount to a policy prohibiting discrimination on the basis of homosexuality, and so would appear to be no more valid under Amendment 2 than the specific prohibitions against discrimination the state court held invalid.

If this consequence follows from Amendment 2, as its broad language suggests, it would compound the constitutional difficulties the law creates. The state court did not decide whether the amendment has this effect, however, and neither need we. In the course of rejecting the argument that Amendment 2 is intended to conserve resources to fight discrimination against suspect classes, the Colorado Supreme Court made the limited observation that the amendment is not intended to affect many anti-discrimination laws protecting non-suspect classes, *Romer II*. In our view that does not resolve the issue. In any event, even if, as we doubt, homosexuals could find some safe harbor in laws of general application, we cannot accept the view that Amendment 2's prohibition on specific legal protections does no more than deprive homosexuals of special rights. To the contrary, the amendment imposes a special disability upon those persons alone. Homosexuals are forbidden the safeguards that others enjoy or may seek without constraint. They can obtain specific protection against discrimination only by enlisting the citizenry of Colorado to amend the state constitution or perhaps, on the State's view, by trying to pass helpful laws of general applicability. This is so no matter how local or discrete the harm, no matter how public and widespread the injury. We find nothing special in the protections Amendment 2 withholds. These are protections taken for granted by most people either because they already have them or do not need them; these are protections against exclusion from an almost limitless number of transactions and endeavors that constitute ordinary civic life in a free society.

III

The Fourteenth Amendment's promise that no person shall be denied the equal protection of the laws must co-exist with the practical necessity that most legislation classifies for one purpose or another, with resulting disadvantage to various groups or persons. We have attempted to reconcile the principle with the reality by stating that, if a law neither burdens a fundamental right nor targets a suspect class, we will uphold the legislative classification so long as it bears a rational relation to some legitimate end.

Amendment 2 fails, indeed defies, even this conventional inquiry. First, the amendment has the peculiar property of imposing a broad and undifferentiated disability on a single named group, an exceptional and, as we shall explain, invalid form of legislation. Second, its sheer breadth is so discontinuous with the reasons offered for it that the amendment seems inexplicable by anything but animus toward the class that it affects; it lacks a rational relationship to legitimate state interests.

Taking the first point, even in the ordinary equal protection case calling for the most deferential of standards, we insist on knowing the relation between the classification adopted and the object to be attained. The search for the link between classification and objective gives substance to the Equal Protection Clause; it provides guidance and discipline for the legislature, which is entitled to know what sorts of laws it can pass; and it marks the limits of our own authority. In the ordinary case, a law will be sustained if it can be said to advance a legitimate government interest, even if the law seems unwise or works to the disadvantage of a particular group, or if the rationale for it seems tenuous. The laws challenged in [cases such as *Duke* & *Railway Express*] were narrow enough in scope and grounded in a sufficient factual context for us to ascertain that there existed some relation between the classification and the purpose it served. By requiring that the classification bear a rational relationship to an independent and legitimate legislative end, we ensure that classifications are not drawn for the purpose of disadvantaging the group burdened by the law.

Amendment 2 confounds this normal process of judicial review. It is at once too narrow and too broad. It identifies persons by a single trait and then denies them protection across the board. The resulting disqualification of a class of persons from the right to seek specific protection from the law is unprecedented in our jurisprudence. The absence of precedent for Amendment 2 is itself instructive; "[d]iscriminations of an unusual character especially suggest careful consideration to determine whether they are obnoxious to the constitutional provision."

It is not within our constitutional tradition to enact laws of this sort. Central both to the idea of the rule of law and to our own Constitution's guarantee of equal protection is the principle that government and each of its parts remain open on impartial terms to all who seek its assistance. "Equal protection of the laws is not achieved through indiscriminate imposition of inequalities." Respect for this principle explains why laws singling out a certain class of citizens for disfavored legal status or general hardships are rare. A law declaring that in general it shall be more difficult for one group of citizens than for all others to seek aid from the government is itself a denial of equal protection of the laws in the most literal sense. "The guaranty of 'equal protection of the laws is a pledge of the protection of equal laws.' "

A second and related point is that laws of the kind now before us raise the inevitable inference that the disadvantage imposed is born of animosity toward the class of persons affected. "[I]f the constitutional conception of 'equal protection of the laws' means anything, it must at the very least mean that a bare . . . desire to harm a politically unpopular group cannot constitute a legitimate governmental interest." Even laws enacted for broad and ambitious purposes often can be explained by reference to legitimate public policies which justify the incidental disadvantages they impose on certain persons. Amendment 2, however, in making a general announcement that gays and lesbians shall not have any particular protections from the law, inflicts on them immediate, continuing, and real injuries that outrun and belie any legitimate justifications that may be claimed for it. We conclude that, in addition to the far-reaching deficiencies of Amendment 2 that we have noted, the principles it offends, in another sense, are conventional and venerable; a law must bear a rational relationship to a legitimate governmental purpose, and Amendment 2 does not.

The primary rationale the State offers for Amendment 2 is respect for other citizens' freedom of association, and in particular the liberties of landlords or employers who have personal or religious objections to homosexuality. Colorado also cites its interest in conserving resources to fight discrimination against other groups. The breadth of the Amendment is so far removed from these particular justifications that we find it impossible to credit them. We cannot say that Amendment 2 is directed to any identifiable legitimate purpose or discrete objective. It is a status-based enactment divorced from any factual context from which we could discern a relationship to legitimate state interests; it is a classification of persons undertaken for its own sake, something the Equal Protection Clause does not permit. "[C]lass legislation . . . [is] obnoxious to the prohibitions of the Fourteenth Amendment. . . ." *Civil Rights Cases.*

We must conclude that Amendment 2 classifies homosexuals not to further a proper legislative end but to make them unequal to everyone else. This Colorado cannot do. A State cannot so deem a class of persons a stranger to its laws. Amendment 2 violates the Equal Protection Clause, and the judgment of the Supreme Court of Colorado is affirmed.

Justice Scalia, with whom The Chief Justice and Justice Thomas join, dissenting.

The Court has mistaken a Kulturkampf for a fit of spite. The constitutional amendment before us here is not the manifestation of a "bare . . . desire to harm" homosexuals, but is rather a modest attempt by seemingly tolerant Coloradans to preserve traditional sexual mores against the efforts of a politically powerful minority to revise those mores through use of the laws. That objective, and the means chosen to achieve it, are not only unimpeachable under any constitutional doctrine hitherto pronounced (hence the opinion's heavy reliance upon principles of righteousness rather than judicial holdings); they have been specifically approved by the Congress of the United States and by this Court.

In holding that homosexuality cannot be singled out for disfavorable treatment, the Court contradicts a decision, unchallenged here, pronounced only 10 years ago, *see Bowers v. Hardwick*, and places the prestige of this institution behind the proposition that opposition to homosexuality is as reprehensible as racial or religious bias. Whether it is or not is precisely the cultural debate that gave rise to the Colorado constitutional amendment (and to the preferential laws against which the amendment was directed). Since the Constitution of the United States says nothing about this subject, it is left to be resolved by normal democratic means, including the democratic adoption of provisions in state constitutions. This Court has no business imposing upon all Americans the resolution favored by the elite class from which the Members of this institution are selected, pronouncing that "animosity" toward homosexuality, is evil. I vigorously dissent.

I

Let me first discuss Part II of the Court's opinion, [which rejects] the State's arguments that Amendment 2 "puts gays and lesbians in the same position as all other persons," and "does no more than deny homosexuals special rights."

In reaching this conclusion, the Court considers it unnecessary to decide the validity of the State's argument that Amendment 2 does not deprive homosexuals of the "protection [afforded by] general laws and policies that prohibit arbitrary discrimination in governmental and private settings." I agree that we need not resolve that dispute, because the Supreme Court of Colorado has resolved it for us. In *Evans I*, the Colorado court stated: "[I]t is significant to note that Colorado law currently proscribes discrimination against persons who are not suspect classes, including discrimination based on age, marital or family status, veterans' status, and for any legal, off-duty conduct such as smoking tobacco. Of course Amendment 2 is not intended to have any effect on this legislation, but seeks only to prevent the adoption of anti-discrimination laws intended to protect gays, lesbians, and bisexuals." The clear import of the Colorado court's conclusion that [the state statute regarding "off-duty conduct"] is not affected is that "general laws and policies that prohibit arbitrary discrimination" would continue to prohibit discrimination on the basis of homosexual conduct as well. This analysis, which is fully in accord with (indeed, follows inescapably from) the text of the constitutional provision, lays to rest such horribles, raised in the course of oral argument, as the prospect that assaults upon homosexuals could not be prosecuted. The amendment prohibits special treatment of homosexuals, and nothing more.

Despite all of its hand-wringing about the potential effect of Amendment 2 on general antidiscrimination laws, the Court's opinion ultimately does not dispute all this, but assumes it to be true. The only denial of equal treatment it contends homosexuals have suffered is this: They may not obtain preferential treatment without amending the state constitution. That is to say, the principle underlying the Court's opinion is that one who is accorded equal treatment under the laws, but cannot as readily as others obtain preferential treatment under the laws, has been denied equal protection of the laws. If merely stating this alleged "equal protection" violation does not suffice to refute it, our constitutional jurisprudence has achieved terminal silliness.

The central thesis of the Court's reasoning is that any group is denied equal protection when, to obtain advantage (or, presumably, to avoid disadvantage), it must have recourse to a more general and hence more difficult level of political decisionmaking than others. The world has never heard of such a principle, which is why the Court's opinion is so long on emotive utterance and so short on relevant legal citation. And it seems to me most unlikely that any multilevel democracy can function under such a principle. For whenever a disadvantage is imposed, or conferral of a benefit is prohibited, at one of the higher levels of democratic decisionmaking (i.e., by the state legislature rather than local government, or by the people at large in the state constitution rather than the legislature), the affected group has (under this theory) been denied equal protection. To take the simplest of examples, consider a state law prohibiting the award of municipal contracts to relatives of mayors or city councilmen. Once such a law is passed, the group composed of such relatives must, in order to get the benefit of city contracts, persuade the state legislature — unlike all other citizens, who need only persuade the municipality. It is ridiculous to consider this a denial of equal protection, which is why the Court's theory is unheard-of.

The Court's entire novel theory rests upon the proposition that there is something special — something that cannot be justified by normal "rational basis" analysis — in making a disadvantaged group (or a nonpreferred group) resort to a higher decisionmaking level. That proposition finds no support in law or logic.

II

I turn next to whether there was a legitimate rational basis for the substance of the constitutional amendment — for the prohibition of special protection for homosexuals.[1] It is unsurprising that the Court avoids discussion of this question, since the answer is so obviously yes. The case most relevant to the issue before us today is not even mentioned in the Court's opinion: In *Bowers v. Hardwick*, we held that the Constitution does not prohibit what virtually all States had done from the founding of the Republic until very recent years — making homosexual conduct a crime. That holding is unassailable, except by those who think that the Constitution changes to suit current fashions. But in any event it is a given in the present case: Respondents' briefs did not urge overruling *Bowers*, and at oral argument respondents' counsel expressly disavowed any intent to seek such overruling. If it is constitutionally permissible for a State to make homosexual conduct criminal, surely it is constitutionally permissible for a State to enact other laws merely disfavoring homosexual conduct. ("After all, there can hardly be more palpable discrimination against a class than making the conduct that defines the class criminal." *Padula v. Webster*, 822 F. 2d 97, 103 (1987).) And

[1] The Court evidently agrees that "rational basis" — the normal test for compliance with the Equal Protection Clause — is the governing standard. The trial court rejected respondents' argument that homosexuals constitute a "suspect" or "quasi-suspect" class, and respondents elected not to appeal that ruling to the Supreme Court of Colorado. And the Court implicitly rejects the Supreme Court of Colorado's holding that Amendment 2 infringes upon a "fundamental right" of "independently identifiable class[es]" to "participate equally in the political process."

a fortiori it is constitutionally permissible for a State to adopt a provision not even disfavoring homosexual conduct, but merely prohibiting all levels of state government from bestowing special protections upon homosexual conduct. Respondents (who, unlike the Court, cannot afford the luxury of ignoring inconvenient precedent) counter *Bowers* with the argument that a greater-includes-the-lesser rationale cannot justify Amendment 2's application to individuals who do not engage in homosexual acts, but are merely of homosexual "orientation." Some courts of appeals have concluded that, with respect to laws of this sort at least, that is a distinction without a difference. The Supreme Court of Colorado itself appears to be of this view. ("Amendment 2 targets this class of persons based on four characteristics: sexual orientation; conduct; practices; and relationships. Each characteristic provides a potentially different way of identifying that class of persons who are gay, lesbian, or bisexual. These four characteristics are not truly severable from one another because each provides nothing more than a different way of identifying the same class of persons.")

But assuming that, in Amendment 2, a person of homosexual "orientation" is someone who does not engage in homosexual conduct but merely has a tendency or desire to do so, *Bowers* still suffices to establish a rational basis for the provision. If it is rational to criminalize the conduct, surely it is rational to deny special favor and protection to those with a self-avowed tendency or desire to engage in the conduct. Indeed, where criminal sanctions are not involved, homosexual "orientation" is an acceptable stand-in for homosexual conduct. A State "does not violate the Equal Protection Clause merely because the classifications made by its laws are imperfect." Just as a policy barring the hiring of methadone users as transit employees does not violate equal protection simply because some methadone users pose no threat to passenger safety, and just as a mandatory retirement age of 50 for police officers does not violate equal protection even though it prematurely ends the careers of many policemen over 50 who still have the capacity to do the job, Amendment 2 is not constitutionally invalid simply because it could have been drawn more precisely so as to withdraw special antidiscrimination protections only from those of homosexual "orientation" who actually engage in homosexual conduct. As Justice Kennedy wrote, when he was on the Court of Appeals, in a case involving discharge of homosexuals from the Navy: "Nearly any statute which classifies people may be irrational as applied in particular cases. Discharge of the particular plaintiffs before us would be rational, under minimal scrutiny, not because their particular cases present the dangers which justify Navy policy, but instead because the general policy of discharging all homosexuals is rational."

III

The foregoing suffices to establish what the Court's failure to cite any case remotely on point would lead one to suspect: No principle set forth in the Constitution, nor even any imagined by this Court in the past 200 years, prohibits what Colorado has done here. But the case for Colorado is much stronger than that. What it has done is not only unprohibited, but eminently reasonable, with close, congressionally approved precedent in earlier constitutional practice.

First, as to its eminent reasonableness. The Court's opinion contains grim, disapproving hints that Coloradans have been guilty of "animus" or "animosity" toward homosexuality, as though that has been established as Unamerican. Of course it is our moral heritage that one should not hate any human being or class of human beings. But I had thought that one could consider certain conduct reprehensible — murder, for example, or polygamy, or cruelty to animals — and could exhibit even "animus" toward such conduct. Surely that is the only sort of "animus" at issue here: moral disapproval of homosexual conduct, the same sort of moral disapproval that produced the centuries-old criminal laws that we held constitutional in *Bowers*. The Colorado amendment does not, to speak entirely precisely, prohibit giving favored status to people who are homosexuals; they can be favored for many reasons — for example, because they are senior citizens or members of racial minorities. But it prohibits giving them favored status because of their homosexual conduct — that is, it prohibits favored status for homosexuality.

But though Coloradans are, as I say, entitled to be hostile toward homosexual conduct, the fact is that the degree of hostility reflected by Amendment 2 is the smallest conceivable. The Court's portrayal of Coloradans as a society fallen victim to pointless, hate-filled "gay-bashing" is so false as to be comical. Colorado not only is one of the 25 States that have repealed their antisodomy laws, but was among the first to do so [in 1971]. But the society that eliminates criminal punishment for homosexual acts does not necessarily abandon the view that homosexuality is morally wrong and socially harmful; often, abolition simply reflects the view that enforcement of such criminal laws involves unseemly intrusion into the intimate lives of citizens.

There is a problem, however, which arises when criminal sanction of homosexuality is eliminated but moral and social disapprobation of homosexuality is meant to be retained. The Court cannot be unaware of that problem; it is evident in many cities of the country, and occasionally bubbles to the surface of the news, in heated political disputes over such matters as the introduction into local schools of books teaching that homosexuality is an optional and fully acceptable "alternate life style." The problem (a problem, that is, for those who wish to retain social disapprobation of homosexuality) is that, because those who engage in homosexual conduct tend to reside in disproportionate numbers in certain communities, have high disposable income, and of course care about homosexual-rights issues much more ardently than the public at large, they possess political power much greater than their numbers, both locally and statewide. Quite understandably, they devote this political power to achieving not merely a grudging social toleration, but full social acceptance, of homosexuality.

I do not mean to be critical of these legislative successes; homosexuals are as entitled to use the legal system for reinforcement of their moral sentiments as are the rest of society. But they are subject to being countered by lawful, democratic countermeasures as well.

That is where Amendment 2 came in. It sought to counter both the geographic concentration and the disproportionate political power of homosexuals by (1) resolving the controversy at the statewide level, and (2) making the election a single-issue contest for both sides. It put directly, to all the citizens of the State, the question: Should homosexuality be given special protection? They answered no. The Court today asserts that this most democratic of procedures is unconstitutional. Lacking any cases to establish that facially absurd proposition, it simply asserts that it must be unconstitutional, because it has never happened before.

[T]here is a [close] analogy, one that involves precisely the effort by the majority of citizens to preserve its view of sexual morality statewide, against the efforts of a geographically concentrated and politically powerful minority to undermine it. The constitutions of the States of Arizona, Idaho, New Mexico, Oklahoma, and Utah to this day contain provisions stating that polygamy is "forever prohibited." Polygamists, and those who have a polygamous "orientation," have been "singled out" by these provisions for much more severe treatment than merely denial of favored status; and that treatment can only be changed by achieving amendment of the state constitutions. The Court's disposition today suggests that these provisions are unconstitutional, and that polygamy must be permitted in these States on a state-legislated, or perhaps even local-option, basis — unless, of course, polygamists for some reason have fewer constitutional rights than homosexuals.

The United States Congress, by the way, required the inclusion of these antipolygamy provisions in the constitutions of Arizona, New Mexico, Oklahoma, and Utah, as a condition of their admission to statehood. (For Arizona, New Mexico, and Utah, moreover, the Enabling Acts required that the antipolygamy provisions be "irrevocable without the consent of the United States and the people of said State" — so that not only were "each of [the] parts" of these States not "open on impartial terms" to polygamists, but even the States as a whole were not; polygamists would have to persuade the whole country to their way of thinking.) Thus, this "singling out" of the sexual practices of a single group for statewide, democratic vote — so utterly alien to our constitutional system, the Court would have us believe — has not only happened, but has received the explicit approval of the United States Congress.

Has the Court concluded that the perceived social harm of polygamy is a "legitimate concern of government," and the perceived social harm of homosexuality is not?

IV

I strongly suspect that the answer to the last question is yes, which leads me to the last point I wish to make: The Court today, announcing that Amendment 2 "defies . . . conventional [constitutional] inquiry," and "confounds [the] normal process of judicial review," employs a constitutional theory heretofore unknown to frustrate Colorado's reasonable effort to preserve traditional American moral values. The Court's stern disapproval of "animosity" towards homosexuality might be compared with what an earlier Court (including the revered JUSTICES HARLAN and BRADLEY) said in *Murphy v. Ramsey*, 114 U.S. 15 (1885), rejecting a constitutional challenge to a United States statute that denied the franchise in federal territories to those who engaged in polygamous cohabitation: "[C]ertainly no legislation can be supposed more wholesome and necessary in the founding of a free, self-governing commonwealth, fit to take rank as one of the co-ordinate States of the Union, than that which seeks to establish it on the basis of the idea of the family, as consisting in and springing from the union for life of one man and one woman in the holy estate of matrimony; the sure foundation of all that is stable and noble in our civilization; the best guaranty of that reverent morality which is the source of all beneficent progress in social and political improvement." I would not myself indulge in such official praise for heterosexual monogamy, because I think it no business of the courts (as opposed to the political branches) to take sides in this culture war.

When the Court takes sides in the culture wars, it tends to be with the knights rather than the villeins — and more specifically with the Templars, reflecting the views and values of the lawyer class from which the Court's Members are drawn. How that class feels about homosexuality will be evident to anyone who wishes to interview job applicants at virtually any of the Nation's law schools. The interviewer may refuse to offer a job because the applicant is a Republican; because he is an adulterer; because he went to the wrong prep school or belongs to the wrong country club; because he eats snails; because he is a womanizer; because she wears real-animal fur; or even because he hates the Chicago Cubs. But if the interviewer should wish not to be an associate or partner of an applicant because he disapproves of the applicant's homosexuality, then he will have violated the pledge which the Association of American Law Schools requires all its member-schools to exact from job interviewers: "assurance of the employer's willingness" to hire homosexuals. Bylaws of the Association of American Law Schools, Inc. § 6-4(b). This law-school view of what "prejudices" must be stamped out may be contrasted with the more plebeian attitudes that apparently still prevail in the United States Congress, which has been unresponsive to repeated attempts to extend to homosexuals the protections of federal civil rights laws, and which took pains to exclude them specifically from the Americans With Disabilities Act of 1990.

Today's opinion has no foundation in American constitutional law, and barely pretends to. The people of Colorado have adopted an entirely reasonable provision which does not even disfavor homosexuals in any substantive sense, but merely denies them preferential treatment. Amendment 2 is designed to prevent piecemeal deterioration of the sexual morality favored by a majority of Coloradans, and is not only an appropriate means to that legitimate end, but a means that Americans have employed before. Striking it down is an act, not of judicial judgment, but of political will. I dissent.

NOTES

1. *The Court's rationale.* The immediate reaction to *Romer*, even by many who favored its result, was that it "conspicuously failed to articulate a principled justification. [Justice Kennedy's] opinion was rooted neither in original meaning nor in precedent, and provided little guidance for future controversies." Taylor, *Is Judicial Restraint Dead?*, Legal Times (July 29, 1996), S27.

The Court declined to adopt the rationale of the Colorado Supreme Court that Amendment 2 violated equal protection by infringing the fundamental right of gays and lesbians to participate in the political process. The claim that discrimination based on sexual orientation is a suspect classification requiring heightened judicial scrutiny was not argued to the Court.

Professor Kathleen Sullivan, *Decisions Expand Equal Protection Rights*, NATIONAL L.J. (July 19), 1996, C7, suggests that Justice Kennedy's opinion is an amalgam of two alternative theories argued to the Court. First, she cites an amicus brief by a group of constitutional law scholars as arguing for a literal reading of the Equal Protection Clause. "[A] state may not forbid arbitrary and irrational discrimination except when committed against homosexuals." A second theory argued that Amendment 2 was so over-and under-inclusive in serving any legitimate ends "that it must be understood as based ultimately on naked animosity towards gay people alone."

2. *A per se rule?* Why is Amendment 2 "an exceptional and . . . invalid form of legislation?" *Leading Cases*, 110 HARV. L. REV. 135, 163 (1996) says: "The [*Romer*] Court founded its decision on a rule that legislation making it more burdensome for a single group of citizens to seek the government's protection is a per se denial of equal protection of the laws." Cass Sunstein, *Foreword: Leaving Things Undecided*, 110 HARV. L. REV. 4, 63 (1996), argues that "[i]f *Romer* is to be defended, it must be because the grounds for Amendment 2 are, in a deliberative democracy, properly ruled off-limits, because the Amendment reflects a judgment that certain citizens should be treated as social outcasts." Daniel Farber and Susanna Sherry, *The Pariah Principle* 13 CONST. COMM. 257, 258 (1996), suggest that *Romer* reflects the principle "that the government may not designate any societal group as untouchable, regardless of whether the group in question is generally like left-handers (or, under current doctrine, homosexuals)." Akhil Amar, *Attainder and Amendment 2:* Romer's *Rightness*, 95 MICH. L. REV. 203, 203–204 (1996), carries this theme further, suggesting that "the sociology and principles underlying the Attainder Clause powerfully illuminate the facts of *Romer*, the opinions in *Romer*, and the spirit of the Equal Protection Clause itself." Joseph Jackson, *Persons of Equal Worth:* Romer v. Evans *and the Policies of Equal Protection*, 45 UCLA L. REV. 453 (1997), argues *Romer* "illuminated the core of equal protection: government must respect the principle that all persons have equal intrinsic worth. Obviously, this principle bars laws rooted in hostility toward a particular group. Even when animosity is lacking, however, the principle bars laws that seek to entrench a social hierarchy — to keep a group 'in its place.' "

Justice Scalia denies that Amendment 2 denies homosexuals the protection of general laws and policies. He argues that the Court is holding that equal protection is violated by forcing disadvantaged groups to have recourse to general and more difficult levels of decisionmaking. Is he correct? *Leading Cases*, 110 HARV. L. REV. at 161–62, responds that "the per se rule does not implicate the imposition of just any disadvantage on any random group; it implicates, for a singled-out class, the denial of the rights to seek the *protections of the laws*." Is it a violation of equal protection to impose a "unique disability" on a class?

3. *Rationality or animus.* Colorado argued that Amendment 2 rationally furthered legitimate state policies. Why does the argument fail? Is the

Amendment's over-or under-inclusiveness fatal under rationality review? Professor Sunstein argues that, like *Cleburne* "the proffered justifications were so weakly connected with the measures at issue" that they appeared to be imposed on the basis of animus against homosexuals. 110 HARV. L. REV. at 61–63. Barbara J. Flagg, *'Animus' and Moral Disapproval: A Comment on* Romer v. Evans, 82 MINN. L. REV. 833, 834 (1998), says that "the majority characterized the ultimate driving force behind Amendment 2 as constitutionally impermissible animus, rather than moral disapproval, and so held that it failed rational basis review." What is the difference? Justice Scalia argues that the only animus at issue is moral disapproval of homosexual conduct similar to that expressed in *Bowers v. Hardwick*. Sunstein, 110 HARV. L. REV. at 62, responds that *Romer* means that "it is no longer legitimate to discriminate against homosexuals as a class simply because the state wants to discourage homosexuality or homosexual behavior. The state must justify discrimination on some other, public regarding ground."

4. *The role of Bowers v. Hardwick.* Much of the criticism of Justice Kennedy's opinion in *Romer* has been directed at the Court's failure even to discuss *Bowers v. Hardwick*. Cass Sunstein, *Sexual Orientation and the Constitution: A Note on the Relationship Between Due Process and Equal Protection*, 55 U. CHI. L. REV. 1161, 1174 (1988), argues that *Bowers* is not dispositive. While due process emphasizes values that are traditionally protected, the Equal Protection Clause "does not safeguard tradition; it protects against traditions, however long-standing and deeply rooted." *See also* Cass Sunstein, *Homosexuality and the Constitution*, 70 IND. L.J. 1 (1994): "To say the least, [discrimination based on sexual orientation] is not squarely covered by *Bowers*." Can a meaningful distinction be made between regulating conduct and status? *Bowers v. Hardwick* was overruled in *Lawrence v. Texas*, p. 587.

5. *Lawrence v. Texas (O'Connor, J., concurring).* To what extent does *Romer* provide support for Justice O'Connor's concurring opinion in *Lawrence v. Texas* arguing that the Texas homosexual sodomy law should be held unconstitutional on the basis of the Equal Protection Clause. Citing *City of Cleburne* and *Romer*, Justice O'Connor said: "When a law exhibits such a desire to harm a politically unpopular group, we have applied a more searching form of rational basis of review to strike down such laws under the Equal Protection Clause. We have been most likely to apply rational basis review to hold a law unconstitutional under Equal Protection Clause where, as here, the challenged law inhibits personal relationships."

Responding to the argument that the law discriminates only against homosexual conduct, not homosexual persons, she stated: "While it is true that the law applies only to conduct, the conduct targeted by this law is conduct that is closely correlated with being a homosexual. Under such circumstances, Texas' sodomy law is targeted at more than conduct. It is instead directed towards gay persons as a class." Citing *Romer*, she continued, "we refused to sanction a law that singled out homosexuals 'for disfavored legal status.' The same is true here. The Equal Protection Clause, 'neither knows nor tolerates classes among citizens.' "

As for the state's use of morality as a justification, she again returned to *Romer* stating: "Moral disapproval of this group, like a bare desire to harm the group, is an interest that is insufficient to satisfy rational basis review under the Equal Protection Clause. Indeed, we have never held that moral disapproval, without any other asserted state interest, is a sufficient rationale under the Equal Protection Clause to justify a law that discriminates among groups of persons." Such discrimination violates the Equal Protection Clause "under any standard of review."

Justice Scalia, dissenting, claimed Justice O'Connor "simply decrees application of a more searching form of rational basis review," arguing that none of the precedent recognized such a standard. Rather, the precedent rested on the Court's conclusion "that no conceivable legitimate state interest supports the classification at issue." In *Lawrence*, the Texas statute was justified by "society's belief that certain forms of sexual behaviors are 'immoral and unacceptable.' "

6. *Same-sex marriage.* In *Baehr v. Lewin*, 852 P.2d 44 (Haw. 1993), the Hawaii Supreme Court held that a law restricting marriage to opposite-sex couples came within the state constitutional prohibition against sexual discrimination. The case was remanded, with an order to analyze the restriction under "strict scrutiny." Andrew Koppelman, *Why Discrimination Against Lesbians and Gay Men Is Sex Discrimination*, 69 N.Y.U.L. REV. 197, 203 (1994) sets out the argument this way: "Laws against gays rest upon a normative stereotype: the bald conviction that certain behavior — for example, sex with women — is appropriate for members of one sex, but not for members of the other sex. Since intermediate scrutiny of gender-based discrimination is appropriate, and laws that discriminate against gays cannot withstand intermediate scrutiny, our legal argument is concluded. A court applying received doctrine should invalidate any statute that singles out gays for unequal treatment." Koppleman suggests that "In the same way that the prohibition of miscegenation [in *Loving v. Virginia*] preserved the polarities to race on which white supremacy rested, the prohibition of homosexuality preserves the polarities of gender on which rests the subordination of women." *Id.* at 202.

But Richard F. Duncan, *From* Loving *to* Romer *Homosexual Marriage and Moral Discernment*, 12 BYU J. PUB. L. 239, 247 (1998), argues: "Marriage is a dual gender relationship in the sense that a lawful marriage requires participation by both man and woman. Marriage laws apply the same equal standard to each gender — neither men nor women may marry a person of the same gender. Neither the benefits nor the burden of these laws are distributed unequally to men or women as a class. Therefore, these laws do not discriminate on the basis of gender." Duncan rejects the *Loving* analogy: "[I]n the end, the 'case for same-sex marriage' fails because it lacks the quality that animated the Supreme Court's opinion in *Loving* — a well-developed sense of moral discernment . . . Because race is irrelevant to what makes a relationship a marriage, it was immoral and unconstitutional for Virginia to forbid interracial marriages. However, unlike Virginia's racist restriction on marriage, the dual-gender requirement is based upon the inherent sexual complementarity of husband and wife." *Id.* at 251. Professor Duncan has also argued that "[i]f *Romer* governs the constitutionality of laws defining marriage as a relationship of one man and one woman, these laws will certainly be upheld because they are sufficiently narrow and focused to enable the Court to ascertain their eminent reasonableness." Duncan, 6 WM. & MARY BILL OF RTS. J. at 156.

Cass Sunstein, *What Did Lawrence Hold? Of Autonomy, Desuetude, Sexuality, And Marriage*, 2003 SUP. CT. REV. 27 (2003) says that "at first glance, *Lawrence* has nothing at all do to with same-sex marriage." However, "if *Lawrence* is put together with *Loving* it would seem plausible to say that the government would have to produce a compelling justification for refusing to recognize such marriages, and compelling justifications are not easy to find. If we emphasize an equality rationale, the subtext of *Lawrence*, then bans on same-sex marriages are in serious constitutional trouble."

Professor Sunstein says that Justice O'Connor was "aware of the potentially broad implications" of *Lawrence*, and "with her eye firmly on the military and family law, she said that 'Texas cannot assert any legitimate state interest here, such as national security or preserving the traditional institution of marriage.' " Explaining that bans on same-sex marriage could be upheld after her conclusion that moral disapproval is not a sufficient basis for discriminating among groups of persons, Justice O'Connor stated that "other reasons exist to promote the institution of marriage beyond moral disapproval of an excluded group." *See also* Nan D. Hunter, *Symposium: Gay Rights After* Lawrence: *Living with* Lawrence, 88 MINN. L. REV. 1103 (2004) ("Justice O'Connor believes that 'preserving the traditional institution of marriage' is a legitimate state of interest and presumably would satisfy the rational-basis test that would be used to decide a gay marriage case.").

In *Lawrence v. Texas: The "Fundamental Right" That Dare Not Speak Its Name*, 117 HARV. L. REV. 1893 (2004), Professor Tribe "argue[s] that the underlying theory and most important passages of *Lawrence* suggest ready (though not immediate) applicability of the holding to same-sex marriage." The principal basis against the argument the *Lawrence* will lead to same sex marriages "appears to be the *Lawrence* Court's observation that the case before it did 'not involve whether the government must give formal recognition to any relationship that homosexual persons seek to enter.' And involved no 'injury to a person or abuse of an institution the law protects.' " Addressing the argument of harm to the institution of marriage by same-sex couples, Professor Tribe states that "[i]t would seem implausible for this Court to accept [harms to the institution of marriage] since its one and only reference to what would demean those who are married the right to have sexual intercourse.' The obvious implication of this blunt statement is that marriage is not (only) about sex, but also about intimacy, companionship, and love-phenomena that have a public no less than a private face. Just as the *Loving* Court came to realize that racial boundaries cannot define such a relationship, so this Court ought to come to a similar conclusion with respect to sexual orientation."

See *Goodridge v. Department of Public Health*, 798 N.E.2d 941 (Mass. 2003), holding that the state ban on same-sex marriage violated the Massachusetts state constitution. The court concluded "that the marriage ban does not meet the rational basis test for either due process or equal protection."

7. ***The limits of suspectness.*** Should sexual orientation be treated as a suspect or quasi-suspect classification? *Developments in the Law — Sexual Orientation and the Law*, 102 HARV. L. REV. 1508, 1525–34 (1989), sets forth the case for heightened scrutiny of discrimination based on sexual orientation. The authors point to a history of discrimination, a perceived lack of political clout, and the lack of "relationship to ability to perform or contribute." They add: "Moreover, even if the scientific research has suggested that sexual orientation is largely immutable: once an individual's sexual orientation is established early in life, it is difficult, if not impossible for her to alter it." Eskridge, 74 IND. L.J. at 1100–1101, similarly argues that "[t]he Supreme Court has found sex and other classifications questionable, because they frequently bear no relation to ability to perform or contribute to society, are typically motivated by stereotypical rather than fact-based thinking, and pervasively affect classes of citizens traditionally subjected to legal disabilities. Gay legal history suggests a prima facie case for sexual orientation classifications to fit this mold. But lower courts have almost universally rejected heightened scrutiny for sexual orientation classification."

§ 7.04 FUNDAMENTAL RIGHTS AND INTERESTS

The last section demonstrates that a more searching standard of judicial review under the Equal Protection Clause can be triggered because of the basis on which the government allocates benefits or imposes burdens. But the Court has also invoked a heightened standard of review because of the nature of the interests affected by the classification. A fee charged for a driver's license might easily pass constitutional muster, while a fee charged as a precondition for voting might produce a more exacting judicial scrutiny and ultimately fail. Voting is apparently a more "fundamental" interest than being permitted to drive.

But what makes an interest "fundamental?" Must the interest be a constitutional right like freedom of speech or privacy? Is it enough that the classification involves an interest of great importance to the individual to justify close judicial scrutiny under the Equal Protection Clause? Total political and social equality as a constitutional obligation of government, requiring government to equalize the availability of all important goods of our society, is probably unrealistic. It is therefore necessary to consider the character of the inequalities that will be judicially tolerated and the character of the inequalities to be constitutionally condemned.

One of the earliest efforts to use a more searching standard of equal protection review based on the nature of the interest at stake came in *Skinner v. Oklahoma ex rel. Williamson*, 316 U.S. 535 (1942), where the Court struck down a state law providing for sexual sterilization of persons convicted more than twice of felonies involving moral turpitude. While Justice Stone, concurring, urged the use of due process to invalidate the Act, Justice Douglas, for the majority, held the law violative of equal protection. Among the inequalities in the Act, Justice Douglas emphasized that while larceny was a basis for sterilization, embezzlement was not, even though "the nature of the two crimes is intrinsically the same and they are punishable in the same manner." While purporting to "give Oklahoma that large deference which [previous equal protection cases] require," Justice Douglas emphasized that the Court was "dealing here with legislation which involves one of the basic civil rights of man. Marriage and procreation are fundamental to the very existence and survival of the race"; the classification "touches a sensitive and important area of human rights." In such cases, "strict scrutiny of the classification which a State makes is essential." Was Justice Douglas recognizing a constitutional "right to marry" or "right to procreate"? Are only classifications producing inequalities in the enjoyment of "fundamental constitutional rights" demanding of "strict scrutiny," or do the demands of equal protection cut even deeper?

During the Warren Court years, the Court began to fashion substantive values and interests directly from the Equal Protection Clause — a new "substantive equal protection" began to emerge. While "fundamental interests" such as voting or access to criminal justice strictly might not be constitutional rights protected by the due process guarantee like freedom of speech, the right of interstate migration or the rights relating to marriage, family and privacy, laws discriminating among classes in their ability to enjoy such interests would be subjected to a stricter scrutiny. Especially when the ability of individuals to enjoy these "fundamental interests" was determined by their wealth, a more searching review was called for. Indeed, the Court employed the most demanding form of review, strict scrutiny, which required the government to justify its classification by showing it was necessary to promote a compelling government objective. But if certain interests were to be singled out, labelled "fundamental," and the classifications subjected to strict scrutiny, how was "fundamental" to be determined? What interests would qualify — welfare, education, housing, or medical care? Would the Equal Protection Clause become a vehicle for the fashioning of an "egalitarian revolution," requiring government to remedy inequalities in realizing the goods and values of the society?

During the era of the Burger and Rehnquist Courts, enthusiasm for the "fundamental interests" branch of the new equal protection has waned. While the Warren Court precedents have not been overruled, new substantive rights have not been derived from the Equal Protection Clause.

What does the fundamental rights and interests branch of equal protection add to the constitutional protection available to the individual? To the extent that the classification burdens an interest that is independently safeguarded by the Due Process Clause, is the protection afforded by the Equal Protection Clause redundant? Should heightened judicial scrutiny be used for classifications burdening "fundamental interests" that are not otherwise protected by the Constitution?

[A] THE RIGHT OF INTERSTATE MIGRATION

SHAPIRO v. THOMPSON

394 U.S. 618, 89 S. Ct. 1322, 22 L. Ed. 2d 600 (1969)

JUSTICE BRENNAN delivered the opinion of the Court.

These three appeals were restored to the calendar for reargument. Each is an appeal from a decision of a three-judge District Court holding unconstitutional a State or District of Columbia statutory provision which denies welfare assistance to residents of the State or District who have not resided within their jurisdictions for at least one year immediately preceding their applications for such assistance. We affirm the judgments of the District Courts in the three cases.

There is no dispute that the effect of the waiting-period requirement in each case is to create two classes of needy resident families indistinguishable from each other except that one is composed of residents who have resided a year or more, and the second of residents who have resided less than a year, in the jurisdiction. On the basis of this sole difference the first class is granted and the second class is denied welfare aid upon which may depend the ability of the families to obtain the very means to subsist — food, shelter, and other necessities of life. The interests which appellants assert are promoted by the classification either may not constitutionally be promoted by government or are not compelling governmental interests.

Primarily, appellants justify the waiting-period requirement as a protective device to preserve the fiscal integrity of state public assistance programs. It is asserted that people who require welfare assistance during their first year of residence in a State are likely to become continuing burdens on state welfare programs. Therefore, the argument runs, if such people can be deterred from entering the jurisdiction by denying them welfare benefits during the first year, state programs to assist long-time residents will not be impaired by a substantial influx of indigent newcomers.

We do not doubt that the one-year waiting period device is well suited to discourage the influx of poor families in need of assistance. An indigent who desires to migrate, resettle, find a new job, start a new life will doubtless hesitate if he knows that he must risk making the move without the possibility of falling back on state welfare assistance during his first year of residence, when his need may be most acute. But the purpose of inhibiting migration by needy persons into the State is constitutionally impermissible.

This Court long ago recognized that the nature of our Federal Union and our constitutional concepts of personal liberty unite to require that all citizens be free to travel throughout the length and breadth of our land uninhibited by statutes, rules, or regulations which unreasonably burden or restrict this movement. We have no occasion to ascribe the source of this right to travel interstate to a particular constitutional provision.

Alternatively, appellants argue that even if it is impermissible for a State to attempt to deter the entry of all indigents, the challenged classification may be justified as a permissible state attempt to discourage those indigents who would enter the State solely to obtain larger benefits. We observe first that none of the statutes before us is tailored to serve that objective. Rather, the class of barred newcomers is all-inclusive, lumping the great majority who come to the State for other purposes with those who come for the sole purpose of collecting higher benefits.

More fundamentally, a State may no more try to fence out those indigents who seek higher welfare benefits than it may try to fence out indigents generally. Implicit in any such distinction is the notion that indigents who enter a State with the hope of securing higher welfare benefits are somehow less deserving than indigents who do not take this consideration into account. But we do not perceive why a mother who is seeking to make a new life for herself and her children should be regarded as less deserving because she considers, among other factors, the level of a State's public assistance. Surely such a mother is no less deserving than a mother who moves into a particular State in order to take advantage of its better educational facilities.

Appellants argue further that the challenged classification may be sustained as an attempt to distinguish between new and old residents on the basis of the contribution they have made to the community through the payment of taxes. We have difficulty seeing how long-term residents who qualify for welfare are making a greater present contribution to the State in taxes than indigent residents who have recently arrived. Appellants' reasoning would logically permit the State to bar new residents from schools, parks, and libraries or deprive them of police and fire protection. Indeed it would permit the State to apportion all benefits and services according to the past tax contributions of its citizens. The Equal Protection Clause prohibits such an apportionment of state services.

We recognize that a State has a valid interest in preserving the fiscal integrity of its programs. It may legitimately attempt to limit its expenditures, whether for public assistance, public education, or any other program. But a State may not accomplish such a purpose by invidious distinctions between classes of its citizens. It could not, for example, reduce expenditures for education by barring indigent children from its schools. Similarly, in the cases before us, appellants must do more than show that denying welfare benefits to new residents saves money. The saving of welfare costs cannot justify an otherwise invidious classification.

Appellants next advance as justification certain administrative and related governmental objectives allegedly served by the waiting-period requirement. They argue that the requirement (1) facilitates the planning of the welfare budget; (2) provides an objective test of residency; (3) minimizes the opportunity for recipients fraudulently to receive payments from more than one jurisdiction; and (4) encourages early entry of new residents into the labor force. [The Court rejects each of these justifications.]

We conclude that appellants in these cases do not use and have no need to use the one-year requirement for the governmental purposes suggested. Thus, even under traditional equal protection tests a classification of welfare applicants according to whether they have lived in the State for one year would seem irrational and unconstitutional. But, of course, the traditional criteria do not apply in these cases. Since the classification here touches on the fundamental right of interstate movement, its constitutionality must be judged by the stricter standard of whether it promotes a compelling state interest. Under this standard, the waiting period requirement clearly violates the Equal Protection Clause.[21]

[21] We imply no view of the validity of waiting-period or residence requirements determining eligibility to vote, eligibility for tuition-free education, to obtain a license to practice a profession, to hunt or fish, and so forth. Such requirements may promote compelling state interests on the one hand, or, on the other, may not be penalties upon the exercise of the constitutional right of interstate travel.

[The Court held that the Social Security Act had not approved use of waiting periods.]

The waiting-period requirement in the District of Columbia Code violates the Due Process Clause of the Fifth Amendment.

JUSTICE STEWART, concurring.

The Court today does not "pick out particular human activities, characterize them as 'fundamental,' and give them added protection." To the contrary, the Court simply recognizes, as it must, an established constitutional right, and gives to that right no less protection than the Constitution itself demands.

CHIEF JUSTICE WARREN, with whom JUSTICE BLACK joins, dissenting.

Congress has imposed a residence requirement in the District of Columbia and authorized the States to impose similar requirements. The issue before us must therefore be framed in terms of whether Congress may create minimal residence requirements, not whether the States, acting alone, may do so. *See Prudential Insurance Co. v. Benjamin.*

Residence requirements do not create a flat prohibition, for potential welfare recipients may move from State to State and establish residence wherever they please. Nor is any claim made by appellees that residence requirements compel them to choose between the right to travel and another constitutional right. Any burden inheres solely in the fact that a potential welfare recipient might take into consideration the loss of welfare benefits for a limited period of time if he changes his residence. Not only is this burden of uncertain degree, but appellees themselves assert there is evidence that few welfare recipients have in fact been deterred by residence requirements.

The insubstantiality of the restriction imposed by residence requirements must then be evaluated in light of the possible congressional reasons for such requirements. Our cases require only that Congress have a rational basis for finding that a chosen regulatory scheme is necessary to the furtherance of interstate commerce. *See, e.g., Katzenbach v. McClung.* Certainly, a congressional finding that residence requirements allowed each State to concentrate its resources upon new and increased programs of rehabilitation ultimately resulting in an enhanced flow of commerce as the economic condition of welfare recipients progressively improved is rational and would justify imposition of residence requirements under the Commerce Clause. Since the congressional decision is rational and the restriction on travel insubstantial, I conclude that residence requirements can be imposed by Congress as an exercise of its power to control interstate commerce consistent with the constitutionally guaranteed right to travel.

JUSTICE HARLAN, dissenting.

The "compelling interest" doctrine, which today is articulated more explicitly than ever before, constitutes an increasingly significant exception to the long-established rule that a statute does not deny equal protection if it is rationally related to a legitimate governmental objective. The "compelling interest" doctrine has two branches. The branch which requires that classifications based upon "suspect" criteria be supported by a compelling interest apparently had its genesis in cases involving racial classifications, which have been regarded as inherently "suspect." Today the list apparently has been further enlarged to include classifications based upon recent interstate movement, and perhaps those based upon the exercise of any constitutional right. I think that this branch of the "compelling interest" doctrine is sound when applied to racial classifications, for historically the Equal Protection Clause was largely a product of the desire to eradicate legal distinctions founded upon race.

The second branch of the "compelling interest" principle is more troublesome. For it has been held that a statutory classification is subject to the "compelling interest" test if the result of the classification may be to affect a "fundamental right," regardless of the basis of the classification.

I think this branch of the "compelling interest" doctrine particularly unfortunate and unnecessary. It is unfortunate because it creates an exception which threatens to swallow the standard equal protection rule. Virtually every state statute affects important rights. This Court has repeatedly held, for example, that the traditional equal protection standard is applicable to statutory classifications affecting such fundamental matters as the right to pursue a particular occupation, the right to receive greater or smaller wages or to work more or less hours, and the right to inherit property. Rights such as these are in principle indistinguishable from those involved here, and to extend the "compelling interest" rule to all cases in which such rights are affected would go far toward making this Court a "super-legislature." This branch of the doctrine is also unnecessary. When the right affected is one assured by the federal Constitution, any infringement can be dealt with under the Due Process Clause. But when a statute affects only matters not mentioned in the federal Constitution and is not arbitrary or irrational, I must reiterate that I know of nothing which entitles this Court to pick out particular human activities, characterize them as "fundamental," and give them added protection under an unusually stringent equal protection test.

I conclude with the following observations. Today's decision, it seems to me, reflects to an unusual degree the current notion that this Court possesses a peculiar wisdom all its own whose capacity to lead this Nation out of its present troubles is contained only by the limits of judicial ingenuity in contriving new constitutional principles to meet each problem as it arises. For anyone who, like myself, believes that it is an essential function of this Court to maintain the constitutional divisions between state and federal authority and among the three branches of the Federal Government, today's decision is a step in the wrong direction. This resurgence of the expansive view of "equal protection" carries the seeds of more judicial interference with the state and federal legislative process. I consider it particularly unfortunate that this judicial roadblock to the powers of Congress in this field should occur at the very threshold of the current discussions regarding the "federalizing" of these aspects of welfare relief.

NOTES

1. ***The right to interstate migration.*** While the right to travel was specifically recognized in the Articles of Confederation, it is not mentioned

in the Constitution. Nevertheless, there is substantial precedent recognizing its existence. But, as in *Shapiro*, the Court has not specified its source. In *United States v. Guest*, 383 U.S. 745 (1966), the Court stated: "The Constitutional right to travel from one State to another occupies a position fundamental to the concept of our Federal Union. It is a right that has been firmly established and repeatedly recognized. [T]he right finds no explicit mention in the Constitution. The reason, it has been suggested, is that a right so elementary was conceived from the beginning to be a necessary concomitant of the stronger Union the Constitution created. In any event, freedom to travel throughout the United States has long been recognized as a basic right under the Constitution."

2. *The relevance of equality.* Why doesn't the Court strike these laws on right to travel grounds alone without invoking the Equal Protection Clause? Professor Barrett notes that in *Shapiro* the Court never discussed the extent of the burden on the freedom to travel, or related the travel right to the state interests involved. Edward Barrett, *Judicial Supervision of Legislative Classifications — A More Modest Role for Equal Protection?* 1976 B.Y.U.L. Rev. 89, 116. He suggests that this omission indicates that it was unnecessary to use equal protection analysis because "the statutes could easily have been held invalid because they discriminated against the exercise of a constitutionally protected interest, and such discrimination could not be justified since the recent residents, as such, did not present any unique evil."

3. *Penalty analysis.* The Court considered the applicability of *Shapiro* to a one-year durational residency requirement as a condition to an indigent's receiving non-emergency hospital or medical care at public expense in *Memorial Hospital v. Maricopa County*, 415 U.S. 250 (1973). Justice Marshall, for the majority, found *Shapiro* to be controlling and held that the state failed to demonstrate a compelling state interest for burdening the right to interstate travel.

In explaining the scope of *Shapiro*, Justice Marshall noted that the right of travel was involved there only in the limited sense of a right to migrate "with an intent to settle and abide." Not all residency requirements were invalidated even though "a bona fide residence requirement would burden the right to travel, if travel meant merely movement." The Court in *Shapiro* had not even declared durational residency requirements per se unconstitutional but held that they may not deter or "penalize" the constitutional right to travel. "Whatever the ultimate parameters of the *Shapiro* penalty analysis, it is at least clear that medical care is as much a 'basic necessity of life' to an indigent as welfare assistance. And, government privileges or benefits necessary to basic sustenance have often been viewed as being of greater constitutional significance than less essential forms of governmental entitlements."

4. *Sosna v. Iowa*, 419 U.S. 393 (1975). The Court, 6-3, per Justice Rehnquist, sustained the constitutionality of a one-year residency requirement for divorce in Iowa, characterizing the requirement as "a part of Iowa's comprehensive statutory regulation of domestic relations, an area that has long been regarded as a virtually exclusive province of the states." *Shapiro* and *Maricopa County* were distinguished as cases in which the durational residency requirements "were justified on the basis of budgetary or record-keeping considerations which were held insufficient to outweigh the constitutional claims of the individuals," whereas Iowa's "interest in requiring that those who seek a divorce from its courts be genuinely attached to the state, as well as a desire to insulate divorce decrees from the likelihood of collateral attack, require a different resolution of the constitutional issue." Nor was appellant "irretrievably foreclosed from obtaining some part of what she sought," as was the case with the welfare recipients in *Shapiro*, or the indigent patient in *Maricopa County*; her access to the courts was merely delayed.

Justice Marshall noted in his dissent that the Court did not examine "whether the right to obtain a divorce is of sufficient importance that its denial to recent immigrants constitutes a penalty on interstate travel." Justice Marshall characterized the majority's approach as an "ad hoc balancing test, under which the State's putative interest in ensuring that its divorce petitioners establish some roots in Iowa is said to justify the one-year residency requirement."

5. *Durational residency and voting.* A requirement that a person be a resident of the state for a year and of the county for three months before being allowed to vote was held violative of equal protection in *Dunn v. Blumstein*, 405 U.S. 330 (1972). Justice Marshall, for the Court, used the strict scrutiny standard of review because, "[b]y denying some citizens the right to vote, such laws deprive them of 'a fundamental political right,' preservative of all rights" and because such a durational residency requirement, "directly impinges on the exercise of a second fundamental personal right, the right to travel."

The Court considered the state interests in assuring the "purity of the ballot box" and having "knowledgeable voters." While admitting that "the prevention of fraud is a legitimate and compelling government goal," the Court found it impossible to view the durational residency requirement as necessary to achieve that state interest. "Fixing a constitutionally acceptable period is surely a matter of degree. It is sufficient to note here that 30 days appears to be an ample period of time for the State to complete whatever administrative tasks are necessary to prevent fraud — and a year, or three months, too much."

Similarly, the use of a conclusive presumption to assure knowledgeable voters was, "much too crude," and the relationship between the state interest in an informed electorate and durational residency requirements was "too attenuated." Justice Marshall explained: "The classifications created by durational residence requirements obviously permit any long time resident to vote regardless of his knowledge of the issues — and obviously many long time residents do not have any. On the other hand, the classifications bar from the franchise many other, admittedly new, residents who have become at least minimally, and often fully, informed about the issues."

Chief Justice Burger, dissenting, argued that "some lines must be drawn. To challenge such lines by the 'compelling state interest' standard is to condemn them all. So far as I am aware, no state law has ever satisfied this seemingly insurmountable standard, and I doubt one ever will, for it demands nothing less than perfection."

But one year later, in *Marston v. Lewis*, 410 U.S. 679 (1973), the Court, per curiam, upheld Arizona's 50-day durational voting residency requirement and 50-day voter registration cutoff requirement. Noting the frequency of mistakes by volunteer registrars and the close timing of primaries and general elections, the Court found, "a recent and amply justifiable [state] judgment that 50 days rather than 30 is necessary to promote the State's important interest in accurate voter lists. The Constitution is not so rigid that that determination and others like it may not stand." Justice Marshall dissented, arguing that *Dunn* indicated that a 30-day residency requirement "provided the State with 'an ample period of time to complete whatever administrative tasks are necessary to prevent fraud' in the process of voter registration." He accepted that district court's conclusion that the state had failed to meet its "heavy burden" of justification "in light of reasonably available and less restrictive alternatives." *See Starns v. Malkerson*, 401 U.S. 935 (1971), in which the Court summarily affirmed the lower court decision upholding Minnesota's one-year durational residency requirement for receiving in-state tuition benefits.

6. *Residency and durational residency.* In *McCarthy v. Philadelphia Civil Service Comm'n*, 424 U.S. 645 (1976), the Court, *per curiam* and without argument, upheld as "not irrational" a municipal regulation requiring employees of the city of Philadelphia to be residents of the city. While acknowledging that prior cases had invalidated durational residency requirements, the Court indicated that it had never "questioned the validity of a condition placed upon municipal employment that a person be a resident at the time of his application." Because the Philadelphia regulation involved a requirement of bona fide continuing residency, rather than one of prior durational residency, the travel cases did not support appellant's claim.

7. *Zobel v. Williams*, 457 U.S. 55 (1982). An Alaskan statutory scheme by which the state distributes income derived from its natural resources to its adult citizens in varying amounts, depending on the length of each citizen's residence, was held to violate the equal protection rights of newer state citizens. In 1976, Alaska adopted a constitutional amendment establishing a Permanent Fund into which the state must deposit at least 25% of its mineral income each year. In 1980, the legislature enacted a dividend distribution program, under which each citizen 18 years of age or older would receive one dividend unit for each year of residency subsequent to 1959, the first year of statehood. A one-year resident would receive one unit, or $50, while a resident of Alaska since it became a state would receive 21 units, or $1050.

Residents of Alaska since 1978 brought suit in 1980 challenging the dividend distribution plan as violative of their right to equal protection, their right to migrate to Alaska, to establish residency there and to enjoy full rights of Alaska citizenship on the same terms as all other citizens of the state. The Alaska Supreme Court sustained the constitutionality of the statute.

Chief Justice Burger, for the Court, began from the premise that the Alaska statute was neither a residency nor a durational residency requirement. Instead, the dividend law created "fixed, permanent distinctions between an ever increasing number of perpetual classes of concededly bona fide residents, based on how long they have been in the state." The statutory scheme could not pass even the minimal rationality test.

The first two objectives advanced by the state, i.e., creating a financial incentive for individuals to establish and maintain an Alaska residence and to encourage prudent management of the Permanent Fund, were held not to be rationally related to the classification between newer residents and those in Alaska since 1959 — the state interest was "not in any way served by granting greater dividends to persons for their residency during the 21 years prior to the enactment." The third objective — to reward citizens for past contributions — was not a legitimate state purpose. "If the States can make the amount of a cash dividend depend on length of residence, what would preclude varying university tuition on a sliding scale based on years of residence — or even limiting access to finite public facilities, eligibility for student loans, for civil service jobs, or for government contracts by length of residence? Alaska's reasoning could open the door to state apportionment of other rights, benefits and services according to length of residency. It would permit the states to divide citizens into expanding numbers of permanent classes. Such a result would be clearly impermissible."

Justice Brennan, joined by Justices Marshall, Blackmun and Powell, concurred on the basis of the "right to travel" and also because of "the idea of constitutionally protected equality." "[T]he past-contribution rationale is so far-reaching in its potential application, and the relationship between residence and contribution to the State so vague and insupportable, that it amounts to little more than a restatement of the criterion for discrimination that it purports to justify."

Justice O'Connor, concurring, employed the Privileges and Immunities Clause of Article IV, § 2. Alaska, in her view, had failed to prove that new residents were a peculiar source of any evil or that the discrimination bore a substantial relationship to the amount that people might have contributed to the state.

Justice Rehnquist, dissenting, argued that the state interest in recognizing past contributions satisfied rationality review: "[T]he illegitimacy of a State's recognizing the past contributions of its citizens has been established by the Court only in certain cases considering an infringement of the right to travel, and the majority itself rightly declines to apply the strict scrutiny analysis of those right-to-travel cases. The distribution scheme at issue in this case impedes no person's right to travel to and settle in Alaska; if anything, the prospect of receiving annual cash dividends would encourage immigration to Alaska."

8. *Attorney General of N.Y. v. Soto-Lopez,* 476 U.S. 898 (1986). The Court held that a preference in civil service employment opportunities offered by the state of New York solely to resident veterans who lived in the state at the time they entered military service violated the constitutional rights of resident veterans who lived outside the state when they entered military service. Justice Brennan, joined by Justices Marshall, Blackmun, and Powell, concluded that the preference violated the appellees' "constitutionally protected rights to migrate and to equal protection of the law." The plurality concluded that "the state has not met its heavy burden of proving that it has selected a means of pursuing a compelling state interest which does not impinge unnecessarily on constitutionally protected interests." Once veterans establish a bona fide residence in a state, they may not be discriminated against solely based on the date of their arrival. As long as New York offers resident veterans a civil service employment preference, they are constitutionally required to do so without regard to residence at the time of entry into the service.

Chief Justice Burger, joined by Justice White, while concurring in the judgment, would have decided the case on the authority of *Zobel* using equal protection rational basis analysis. New York's scheme, he concluded, could not survive rational basis scrutiny purely as a matter of equal protection law. He did not, therefore, address the heightened equal protection scrutiny or right to travel analysis used by Justice Brennan.

Justice O'Connor, joined by Justice Rehnquist and Justice Stevens, dissenting, took issue with the Court's "free-floating right to migrate," its equal protection analysis, and its failure "to make clear how much of its analysis is necessary or sufficient to find a violation of the 'right to migrate' independently of an Equal Protection Clause violation." Justice O'Connor contended that the right had not been penalized nor significantly burdened by New York. There was no direct restriction on the freedom to move to New York or to establish residency. Nor did the program penalize the right to travel by denying newcomers fundamental rights or essential services until they have satisfied a durational residency requirement. Further, the preference scheme did not force newcomers to accept an inferior status to all other residents of New York; they have the same status as nonveteran New Yorkers. She concluded that "heightened scrutiny under the 'right to migrate' or the Equal Protection Clause is inappropriate."

SAENZ v. ROE

526 U.S. 489, 119 S. Ct. 1518, 143 L. Ed. 2d 689 (1999)

JUSTICE STEVENS delivered the opinion of the Court.

In 1992, California enacted a statute limiting the maximum welfare benefits available to newly arrived residents. The scheme limits the amount payable to a family that has resided in the State for less than 12 months to the amount payable by the State of the family's prior residence. The questions presented by this case are whether the 1992 statute was constitutional when it was enacted and, if not, whether an amendment to the Social Security Act enacted by Congress in 1996 affects that determination.

The word "travel" is not found in the text of the Constitution. Yet the "constitutional right to travel from one State to another" is firmly embedded in our jurisprudence, *United States v. Guest.* In this case California argues that, unlike the legislation reviewed in *Shapiro*, it does not penalize the right to travel because new arrivals are not ineligible for benefits during their first year of residence. California submits that, instead of being subjected to the strictest scrutiny, the statute should be upheld if it is supported by a rational basis and that the State's legitimate interest in saving over $10 million a year satisfies that test. [The United States] has participated as amicus curiae in this Court. It has advanced the novel argument that the [federal statute] allows the States to adopt a "specialized choice-of-law-type provision" that "should be subject to an intermediate level of constitutional review," merely requiring that durational residency requirements be "substantially related to an important governmental objective." The debate about the appropriate standard of review, together with the potential relevance of the federal statute, persuades us that it will be useful to focus on the source of the constitutional right on which respondents rely.

The "right to travel" discussed in our cases embraces at least three different components. It protects the right of a citizen of one State to enter and to leave another State, the right to be treated as a welcome visitor rather than an unfriendly alien when temporarily present in the second State, and, for those travelers who elect to become permanent residents, the right to be treated like other citizens of that State.

It was the right to go from one place to another, including the right to cross state borders while en route, that was vindicated in *Edwards v. California* which invalidated a state law that impeded the free interstate passage of the indigent. We reaffirmed that right in *United States v. Guest,* which afforded protection to the "right to travel freely to and from the State of Georgia and to use highway facilities and other instrumentalities of interstate commerce within the State of Georgia." Given that [the California law] imposed no obstacle to respondents' entry into California, we think the State is correct when it argues that the statute does not directly impair the exercise of the right to free interstate movement. For the purposes of this case, therefore, we need not identify the source of that particular right in the text of the Constitution. The right of "free ingress and egress to and from" neighboring States, which was expressly mentioned in the text of the Articles of Confederation, may simply have been "conceived from the beginning to be a necessary concomitant of the stronger Union the Constitution created."

The second component of the right to travel is, however, expressly protected by the text of the Constitution. The first sentence of Article IV, § 2, provides: "The Citizens of each State shall be entitled to all Privileges and Immunities of Citizens in the several States." Thus, by virtue of a person's state citizenship, a citizen of one State who travels in other States, intending to return home at the end of his journey, is entitled to enjoy the "Privileges and Immunities of Citizens in the several States" that he visits. There may be a substantial reason for requiring the nonresident to pay more than the resident for a hunting license, or to enroll in the state university, but our cases have not identified any acceptable reason for qualifying the protection afforded by the Clause for "the citizen of State A who ventures into State B to settle there and establish a home." *Zobel* (O'CONNOR, J., concurring in judgment). Permissible justifications for discrimination between residents and nonresidents are simply inapplicable to a nonresident's exercise of the right to move into another State and become a resident of that State.

What is at issue in this case, then, is this third aspect of the right to travel—the right of the newly arrived citizen to the same privileges and immunities enjoyed by other citizens of the same State. That right is protected not only by the new arrival's status as a state citizen, but also by her status as a citizen of the United States. That additional source of protection is plainly identified in the opening words of the Fourteenth Amendment:

> All persons born or naturalized in the United States, and subject to the jurisdiction thereof, are citizens of the United States and of the State wherein they reside. No State shall make or enforce any law which shall abridge the privileges or immunities of citizens of the United States.

Despite fundamentally differing views concerning the coverage of the Privileges or Immunities Clause of the Fourteenth Amendment, most notably expressed in the majority and dissenting opinions in the SlaughterHouse Cases, it has always been common ground that this Clause protects the third component of the right to travel. Writing for the majority in the Slaughter-House Cases, JUSTICE MILLER explained that one of the privileges conferred by this Clause "is that a citizen of the United States can, of his own volition, become a citizen of any State of the Union by a bona fide residence therein, with the same rights as other citizens of that State."

That newly arrived citizens "have two political capacities, one state and one federal," adds special force to their claim that they have the same rights as others who share their citizenship. Neither mere rationality nor some intermediate standard of review should be used to judge the constitutionality of a state rule that discriminates against some of its citizens because they have been domiciled in the State for less than a year. The appropriate standard may be more categorical than that articulated in *Shapiro*, but it is surely no less strict.

Because this case involves discrimination against citizens who have completed their interstate travel, the State's argument that its welfare scheme affects the right to travel only "incidentally" is beside the point. Were we concerned solely with actual deterrence to migration, we might be persuaded that a partial withholding of benefits constitutes a lesser incursion on the right to travel than an outright denial of all benefits. But since the right to travel embraces the citizen's right to be treated equally in her new State of residence, the discriminatory classification is itself a penalty.

It is undisputed that respondents and the members of the class that they represent are citizens of California and that their need for welfare benefits is unrelated to the length of time that they have resided in California. We thus have no occasion to consider what weight might be given to a citizen's length of residence if the bona fides of her claim to state citizenship were questioned. Moreover, because whatever benefits they receive will be consumed while they remain in California, there is no danger that recognition of their claim will encourage citizens of other States to establish residency for just long enough to acquire some readily portable benefit, such as a divorce or a college education, that will be enjoyed after they return to their original domicile.

The classifications challenged in this case—and there are many—are defined entirely by (a) the period of residency in California and (b) the location of the prior residences of the disfavored class members. The favored class of beneficiaries includes all eligible California citizens who have resided there for at least one year, plus those new arrivals who last resided in another country or in a State that provides benefits at least as generous as California's.

Thus, within the broad category of citizens who resided in California for less than a year, there are many who are treated like lifetime residents. And within the broad sub-category of new arrivals who are treated less favorably, there are many smaller classes whose benefit levels are determined by the law of the States from whence they came. California must therefore explain not only why it is sound fiscal policy to discriminate against those who have been citizens for less than a year, but also why it is permissible to apply such a variety of rules within that class.

These classifications may not be justified by a purpose to deter welfare applicants from migrating to California for three reasons. First, although it is reasonable to assume that some persons may be motivated to move for the purpose of obtaining higher benefits, the empirical evidence reviewed by the District Judge, which takes into account the high cost of living in California, indicates that the number of such persons is quite small—surely not large enough to justify a burden on those who had no such motive. Second, California has represented to the Court that the legislation was not enacted for any such reason. Third, even if it were, as we squarely held in *Shapiro v. Thompson,* such a purpose would be unequivocally impermissible.

Disavowing any desire to fence out the indigent, California has instead advanced an entirely fiscal justification for its multitiered scheme. [It] will save the State approximately $10.9 million a year. The question is not whether such saving is a legitimate purpose but whether the State may accomplish that end by the discriminatory means it has chosen. An evenhanded, across-the-board reduction of about 72 cents per month for every beneficiary would produce the same result. But our negative answer to the question does not rest on the weakness of the State's purported fiscal justification. It rests on the fact that the Citizenship Clause of the Fourteenth Amendment expressly equates citizenship with residence: "That Clause does not provide for, and does not allow for, degrees of citizenship based on length of residence." *Zobel.* It is equally clear that the Clause does not tolerate a hierarchy of 45 subclasses of similarly situated citizens based on the location of their prior residence. Thus [California law] is doubly vulnerable: Neither the duration of respondents' California residence, nor the identity of their prior States of residence, has any relevance to their need for benefits. In short, the State's legitimate interest in saving money provides no justification for its decision to discriminate among equally eligible citizens.

The question that remains is whether congressional approval of durational residency requirements in the 1996 amendment to the Social Security Act somehow resuscitates the constitutionality of [the California law]. That question is readily answered, for we have consistently held that Congress may not authorize the States to violate the Fourteenth Amendment. Moreover, the protection afforded to the citizen by the Citizenship Clause of that Amendment is a limitation on the powers of the National Government as well as the States.

Citizens of the United States, whether rich or poor, have the right to choose to be citizens "of the State wherein they reside." U.S. Const., Amndt. 14, § 1. The States, however, do not have any right to select their citizens. The Fourteenth Amendment, like the Constitution itself, was, as Justice Cardozo put it, "framed upon the theory that the peoples of the several states must sink or swim together, and that in the long run prosperity and salvation are in union and not division." *Baldwin v. G.A.F. Seelig, Inc.*

CHIEF JUSTICE REHNQUIST, with whom JUSTICE THOMAS joins, dissenting.

The Court today breathes new life into the previously dormant Privileges or Immunities Clause of the Fourteenth Amendment—a Clause relied upon by this Court in only one other decision, *Colgate v. Harvey*, 296 U.S. 404 (1935), overruled five years later by *Madden v. Kentucky*, 309 U.S. 83 (1940). It uses this Clause to strike down what I believe is a reasonable measure falling under the head of a "good-faith residency requirement." Because I do not think any provision of the Constitution—and surely not a provision relied upon for only the second time since its enactment 130 years ago—requires this result, I dissent.

Much of the Court's opinion is unremarkable and sound. The right to travel clearly embraces the right to go from one place to another, and prohibits States from impeding the free interstate passage of citizens. The traditional conception of the right to travel is simply not an issue in this case.

I also have no difficulty with aligning the right to travel with the protections afforded by the Privileges and Immunities Clause of Article IV, § 2, to nonresidents who enter other States "intending to return home at the end of [their] journey." Like the traditional right-to-travel guarantees discussed above, however, this Clause has no application here, because respondents expressed a desire to stay in California and become citizens of that State. Respondents therefore plainly fall outside the protections of Article IV, § 2.

Finally, I agree with the proposition that a "citizen of the United States can, of his own volition, become a citizen of any State of the Union by a bona fide residence therein, with the same rights as other citizens of that State." *Slaughter-House Cases.*

But I cannot see how the right to become a citizen of another State is a necessary "component" of the right to travel, or why the Court tries to marry these separate and distinct rights. A person is no longer "traveling" in any sense of the word when he finishes his journey to a State which he plans to make his home. Indeed, under the Court's logic, the protections of the Privileges or Immunities Clause recognized in this case come into play only when an individual stops traveling with the intent to remain and become a citizen of a new State. The right to travel and the right to become a citizen are distinct, their relationship is not reciprocal, and one is not a "component" of the other. Indeed, the same dicta from the Slaughter-House Cases quoted by the Court actually treats the right to become a citizen and the right to travel as separate and distinct rights under the Privileges or Immunities Clause of the Fourteenth Amendment. At most, restrictions on an individual's right to become a citizen indirectly affect his calculus in deciding whether to exercise his right to travel in the first place, but such an attenuated and uncertain relationship is no ground for folding one right into the other.

No doubt the Court has, in the past 30 years, essentially conflated the right to travel with the right to equal state citizenship in striking down durational residence requirements similar to the one challenged here. *See, e.g., Shapiro v. Thompson; Dunn v. Blumstein; Maricopa County.* The Court today tries to clear much of the underbrush created by these prior right-to-travel cases, abandoning its effort to define what residence requirements deprive individuals of "important rights and benefits" or "penalize" the right to travel. Under its new analytical framework, a State, outside certain ill-defined circumstances, cannot classify its citizens by the length of their residence in the State without offending the Privileges or Immunities Clause of the Fourteenth Amendment. The Court thus departs from *Shapiro* and its progeny, and, while paying lipservice to the right to travel, the Court does little to explain how the right to travel is involved at all. Instead, as the Court's analysis clearly demonstrates, this case is only about respondents' right to immediately enjoy all the privileges of being a California citizen in relation to that State's ability to test the goodfaith assertion of this right. The Court has thus come full circle by effectively disavowing the analysis of *Shapiro*, segregating the right to travel and the rights secured by Article IV from the right to become a citizen under the Privileges or Immunities Clause, and then testing the residence requirement here against this latter right. For all its misplaced efforts to fold the right to become a citizen into the right to travel, the Court has essentially returned to its original understanding of the right to travel.

In unearthing from its tomb the right to become a state citizen and to be treated equally in the new State of residence, however, the Court ignores a State's need to assure that only persons who establish a bona fide residence receive the benefits provided to current residents of the State. The Court has consistently recognized that while new citizens must have the same opportunity to enjoy the privileges of being a citizen of a State, the States retain the ability to use bona fide residence requirements to ferret out those who intend to take the privileges and run. As this Court explained in *Martinez v. Bynum* "A bona fide residence requirement, appropriately defined and uniformly applied, furthers the substantial state interest in assuring that services provided for its residents are enjoyed only by residents. The *Martinez* Court explained that "residence" requires "both physical presence and an intention to remain," and approved a Texas law that restricted eligibility for tuition-free education to families who met this minimum definition of residence.

While the physical presence element of a bona fide residence is easy to police, the subjective intent element is not. It is simply unworkable and futile to require States to inquire into each new resident's subjective intent to remain. Hence, States employ objective criteria such as durational residence requirements to test a new resident's resolve to remain before these new citizens can enjoy certain in-state benefits. Recognizing the practical appeal of such criteria, this Court has repeatedly sanctioned the State's use of durational residence requirements before new residents receive in-state tuition rates at state universities. The Court has done the same in upholding a 1-year residence requirement for eligibility to obtain a divorce in state courts, see *Sosna v. Iowa* and in upholding political party registration restrictions that amounted to a durational residency requirement for voting in primary elections, see *Rosario v. Rocketidler*, 410 U.S. 752, 760–762, (1973). If States can require individuals to reside in-state for a year before exercising the right to educational benefits, the right to terminate a marriage, or the right to vote in primary elections that all other state citizens enjoy, then States may surely do the same for welfare benefits.

The Court today recognizes that States retain the ability to determine the bona fides of an individual's claim to residence, but then tries to avoid the issue. It asserts that because respondents' need for welfare benefits is unrelated to the length of time they have resided in California, it has "no occasion to consider what weight might be given to a citizen's length of residence if the bona fides of her claim to state citizenship were questioned." But I do not understand how the absence of a link between need and length of residency bears on the State's ability to objectively test respondents' resolve to stay in California.

The Court tries to distinguish education and divorce benefits by contending that the welfare payment here will be consumed in California, while a college education or a divorce produces benefits that are "portable" and can be enjoyed after individuals return to their original domicile. But this "you can't take it with you" distinction is more apparent than real, and offers little guidance to lower courts who must apply this rationale in the future. Welfare payments are a form of insurance, giving impoverished individuals and their families the means to meet the demands of daily life while they receive the necessary training, education, and time to look for a job. The cash itself will no doubt be spent in California, but the benefits from receiving this income and having the opportunity to become employed or employable will stick with the welfare recipient if they stay in California or go back to their true domicile.

I therefore believe that the durational residence requirement challenged here is a permissible exercise of the State's power to "assur[e] that services provided for its residents are enjoyed only by residents."

Finally, Congress' express approval of durational residence requirements for welfare recipients like the one established by California only goes to show the reasonableness of [the California law]. The National Legislature, where people from Mississippi as well as California are represented, has recognized the need to protect state resources in a time of experimentation and welfare reform. As States like California revamp their total welfare packages, they should have the authority and flexibility to ensure that their new programs are not exploited. Congress has decided that it makes good welfare policy to give the States this power. California has reasonably exercised it through an objective, narrowly tailored residence requirement. I see nothing in the Constitution that should prevent the enforcement of that requirement.

JUSTICE THOMAS, with whom THE CHIEF JUSTICE joins, dissenting.

In my view, the majority attributes a meaning to the Privileges or Immunities Clause that likely was unintended when the Fourteenth Amendment was enacted and ratified. Unlike the majority, I would look to history to ascertain the original meaning of the Clause. [A]t the time the Fourteenth Amendment was adopted, people understood that "privileges or immunities of citizens" were fundamental rights, rather than every public benefit established by positive law. Accordingly, the majority's conclusion— that a State violates the Privileges or Immunities Clause when it "discriminates" against citizens who have been domiciled in the State for less than a year in the distribution of welfare benefit appears contrary to the original understanding and is dubious at best.

The *Slaughter-House Cases* sapped the Clause of any meaning. Although the majority appears to breathe new life into the Clause today, it fails to address its historical underpinnings or its place in our constitutional jurisprudence. Because I believe that the demise of the Privileges or Immunities Clause has contributed in no small part to the current disarray of our Fourteenth Amendment jurisprudence, I would be open to reevaluating its meaning in an appropriate case. Before invoking the Clause, however, we should endeavor to understand what the framers of the Fourteenth Amendment thought that it meant. We should also consider whether the Clause should displace, rather than augment, portions of our equal protection and substantive due process jurisprudence. The majority's failure to consider these important questions raises the specter that the Privileges or Immunities Clause will become yet another convenient tool for inventing new rights, limited solely by the "predilections of those who happen at the time to be Members of this Court."

NOTES

1. *A structural right?* Laurence H. Tribe, Saenz *Sans Prophecy: Does the Privileges or Immunities Revival Portend the Future — Or Reveal the Structure of the Present*, 113 HARV. L. REV. 110, 112 (1999), suggests that freedom of interstate movement and migration may be the paradigmatic case of rights which "partake simultaneously of personal self-government and of the system of definitions and relationships that describe the form of state and federal self-government that the original Constitution as modified by the Fourteenth Amendment brought about." Professor Tribe says that "[t]he component of the right of travel confirmed in *Saenz* involved the elaboration of a structural principle of equal citizenship more than the protection of an individual right of interstate movement, or indeed of any individual right deriving from either the Privileges and Immunities Clause of Article IV or the Privileges or Immunities Clause of the Fourteenth Amendment neither of which speaks in terms of travel, interstate mobility, or anything of the sort." *Id.* at 154. He doubts that *Saenz* is "a harbinger of a fresh new jurisprudence of privileges and immunities." Professor Tribe concludes: "Rather than a glimpse into a future written in terms of privileges or immunities, the *Saenz* decision seems to me to have offered a window into the present and the recent past. *Saenz* revealed a Court far more comfortable protecting rights that it can describe in architectural terms, especially in terms of federalism, than it is protecting rights that present themselves as spheres of personal autonomy or as dimensions of constitutionality mandated equality — even by modes of analysis that are in essence structural." *Id.* at 198.

2. *Congressional legislation.* Congress had authorized states to adopt rules like that of California. There was concern that states, fearful of becoming welfare magnets, would engage in a race to the bottom. *Saenz* holds that the protections afforded by the Citizenship Clause also limits the powers of the national government. Jide Nzelibe, *Free Movement: A Federalist Reinterpretation,* 49 AM. U.L. REV. 433, 435 (1999), says that "although the discussion of interstate travel and migration always has been mired in the language of personal rights and discrimination, [the right to travel] is . . . grounded purely in our federalist structure and is not traceable to the spirit of specific provisions in the Bill of Rights." The author argues that "when viewed as a limitation on interstate conflict, it is illogical to construe the free movement principle also as a limitation on the powers of the national government." *Id.* at 465.

3. *Bona fide residence.* Would the California law be unconstitutional under *Shapiro* and its progeny? Does it "penalize" the exercise of the travel right? Does *Saenz* prohibit discrimination against newly arrived residents in all public benefits programs? Roderick M. Hills, Jr., *Poverty, Residency and Federalism: States' Duty of Impartiality Towards Newcomers*, 1999 SUP. CT. REV. 277, 298, says that "neither the *Saenz* Court nor the precedents that it attempts to reconcile provide an adequate account of what it means to be a bona fide resident of a state. The precedents suggest that the definition of state residence will vary with the particular program to which a new resident seeks access — suffrage is easier to get than reduced tuition at a state university — but the precedents do not explain why or how." He claims that the *Saenz* Court adopted a nondiscrimination theory — "once a new resident demonstrates that he or she is a bona fide resident, then states are categorically barred from drawing distinctions that burden that new resident based on length of residence." *Id.* at 282. Professor Hills argue that the *Saenz* Court provided no convincing argument for this theory and "the Court did not resolve the confusion in the precedents about the meaning of bona fide residency." *Id.* at 283.

Professor Hills seeks to develop a functional theory of bona fide residency. "I suggest that the definition of bona fide residence should be rooted in a balance between two rival considerations. On the one hand, states cannot undermine our common national citizenship by trying to transform themselves into tightly cohesive or socially homogenous communities—what I call 'affective communities.' Therefore, the Court should be especially suspicious of state laws that treat newcomers as unwelcome strangers out of cultural or social hostility toward those newcomers. On the other hand, states have a legitimate interest in limiting eligibility for their redistributive programs to those residents whose migration into the state was motivated by a purpose other than becoming eligible for the redistributive program. Otherwise, the newcomers who migrate to a state to take advantage of a redistributive subsidy—persons whom I shall call 'subsidy-motivated migrants'— might undermine the state's incentives to maintain the redistributive programs that attracted the migrants to the state in the first place." *Id.* at 299. While *Saenz* was correct to reject discrimination against indigent newcomers in welfare benefits given the danger of "cultural animosity," Hills says, the Court should have limited its categorical nondiscrimination rule to the context. *Id.* at 335. Can durational residency requirements ever be used to measure bona fide residence? What is the effect of *Saenz* on *Shapiro* and its fundamental rights equal protection progeny?

4. *Same-sex marriage.* Vermont has adopted a "civil union" statute recognizing a quasi-marital relationship between same-sex couples. However, several states have adopted Defense of Marriage Acts (DOMAs) or similar provisions refusing to recognize the marriage or union of a same-sex couple celebrated in another state. Mark Strasser, *The Privileges of National Citizenship: On* Saenz, *Same-Sex Couples, and the Right to Travel*, 52 Rutgers L. Rev. 553 (2000), argues that "states that prohibit the recognition of same-sex marriages performed in another domiciliary violate privilege and immunities guarantees by discriminating against nonresidents who are forced to choose between remaining in a state where the marriage was performed or surrendering their marriage in order to migrate to a new state. Thus, if interpreted broadly, the Defense of Marriage Act (DOMA) and the so-called 'mini-Domas' passed by individual states violate a right of national citizenship and effectively undermine the concept of national sovereignty." Professor Strasser explains: "If the privileges of national citizenship do not include something as fundamental as the right to have one's marriage (valid in the domicile at the time of celebration) recognized in each state through which one might travel or to which one might migrate, then it is not clear what interests could possibly meet the relevant standard. Certainly, those state-imposed prices of admission which have already been held to trigger the relevant protections would be viewed by many as much less dear than the cost involved in having one's valid marriage no longer recognized, the wishes both members of the couple notwithstanding." *Id.* at 587. He concludes: "The Court must declare DOMA and the mini DOMAs violations of privileges and immunities guarantees. Any other holding would contribute to this country's becoming a mere league of separate sovereign states rather than a single great community consisting of all the states united." *Id.* at 588.

[B] RIGHTS RELATING TO MARRIAGE AND FAMILY

ZABLOCKI v. REDHAIL

434 U.S. 374, 98 S. Ct. 673, 54 L. Ed. 2d 8 (1978)

[Wisconsin statute § 245.10 required that court approval be obtained before the marriage of any parent under an obligation to support minor children not in that parent's custody. Court approval could not be granted unless the applicant submitted proof of compliance with the support obligation and demonstrated that the children covered by the support order were not, and were not likely to become, public charges. Persons acquiring marriage licenses in violation of the statute were subject to criminal penalties.

[As a result of a paternity action that had been brought against him while still in high school, Redhail had been under a court-ordered support obligation since May 1972. From May 1972 until August 1974, Redhail was unemployed and indigent, and was unable to make support payments. In September 1974, wishing to marry a woman who was expecting his child, Redhail applied for and was denied a marriage license. His support obligations were in arrears in excess of $3,700, and his illegitimate child had been a public charge since her birth, receiving AFDC benefits. The parties stipulated that the child would have remained a public charge even if Redhail's support payments had been current.

[Redhail brought a class action challenging the statute as violative of equal protection and due process. The three-judge district court held the statute unconstitutional under the Equal Protection Clause.]

JUSTICE MARSHALL delivered the opinion of the Court.

In evaluating § 245.10 under the Equal Protection Clause, "we must first determine what burden of justification the classification created thereby must meet, by looking to the nature of the classification and the individual interests affected." Since our past decisions make clear that the right to marry is of fundamental importance, and since the classification at issue here significantly interferes with the exercise of that right, we believe that "critical examination" of the state interests advanced in support of the classification is required. The leading decision of this Court on the right to marry is *Loving v. Virginia*.

It is not surprising that the decision to marry has been placed on the same level of importance as decisions relating to procreation, childbirth, child-rearing, and family relationships. As the facts of this case illustrate, it would make little sense to recognize a right of privacy with respect to other matters of family life and not with respect to the decision to enter the relationship that is the foundation of the family in our society. [I]f appellee's right to procreate means anything at all, it must imply some right to enter the only relationship in which the State of Wisconsin allows sexual relations legally to take place.

By reaffirming the fundamental character of the right to marry, we do not mean to suggest that every state regulation which relates in any way to the incidents of or prerequisites for marriage must be subjected to rigorous scrutiny. To the contrary, reasonable regulations that do not significantly interfere with decisions to enter into the marital relationship may legitimately be imposed. [*See Califano v. Jobst*, p. 902.] The statutory classification at issue here, however, clearly does interfere directly and substantially with the right to marry.

Under the challenged statute, no Wisconsin resident in the affected class may marry in Wisconsin or elsewhere without a court order, and marriages contracted in violation of the statute are both void and punishable as criminal offenses. Some of those in the affected class, like appellee, will never be able to obtain the necessary court order, because they either lack the financial means to meet their support obligations or cannot prove that their children will not become public charges. These persons are absolutely prevented from getting married. Many others, able in theory to satisfy the statute's requirements, will be sufficiently burdened by having to do so that they will in effect be coerced into foregoing their right to marry. And even those who can be persuaded to meet the statute's requirements suffer a serious intrusion into their freedom of choice in an area in which we have held such freedom to be fundamental.[12]

[12] The directness and substantiality of the interference with the freedom to marry distinguish the instant case from *Califano v. Jobst*. As the opinion for the Court [in *Jobst*] expressly noted, the rule terminating benefits upon marriage was not "an attempt to interfere with the individual's freedom to make a decision as important as marriage." The Social Security provisions placed no direct legal obstacle in the path of persons desiring to get married, and — notwithstanding our

When a statutory classification significantly interferes with the exercise of a fundamental right, it cannot be upheld unless it is supported by sufficiently important state interests and is closely tailored to effectuate only those interests. At argument, appellant's counsel suggested that, since permission to marry cannot be granted unless the applicant shows that he has satisfied his court-determined support obligations to the prior children and that those children will not become public charges, the statute provides incentive for the applicant to make support payments to his children. This "collection device" rationale cannot justify the statute's broad infringement on the right to marry.

First, with respect to individuals who are unable to meet the statutory requirements, the statute merely prevents the applicant from getting married, without delivering any money at all into the hands of the applicant's prior children. More importantly, regardless of the applicant's ability or willingness to meet the statutory requirements, the State already has numerous other means for exacting compliance with support obligations, means that are at least as effective as the instant statute's and yet do not impinge upon the right to marry.

There is also some suggestion that § 245.10 protects the ability of marriage applicants to meet support obligations to prior children by preventing the applicants from incurring new support obligations. But the challenged provisions of § 245.10 are grossly underinclusive with respect to this purpose, since they do not limit in any way new financial commitments by the applicant other than those arising out of the contemplated marriage. The statutory classification is substantially overinclusive as well: given the possibility that the new spouse will actually better the applicant's financial situation, by contributing income from a job or otherwise, the statute in many cases may prevent affected individuals from improving their ability to satisfy their prior support obligations. And, although it is true that the applicant will incur support obligations to any children born during the contemplated marriage, preventing the marriage may only result in the children being born out of wedlock, as in fact occurred in appellee's case. Since the support obligation is the same whether the child is born in or out of wedlock, the net result of preventing the marriage is simply more illegitimate children.

CHIEF JUSTICE BURGER, concurring.

Unlike the intentional and substantial interference with the right to marry effected by the Wisconsin statute at issue here, the Social Security Act provisions challenged in *Jobst* did not constitute an "attempt to interfere with the individual's freedom to make a decision as important as marriage," and, at most, had an indirect impact on that decision. It is with this understanding that I join the Court's opinion today.

JUSTICE STEWART, concurring in the judgment.

Brother Rehnquist's imaginative recasting of the case — there was no evidence that the laws significantly discouraged, let alone made "practically impossible," any marriages. Indeed, the provisions had not deterred the individual who challenged the statute from getting married, even though he and his wife were both disabled. *See Califano v. Jobst* (because of availability of other federal benefits, total payments to the Jobsts after marriage were only $20 per month less than they would have been had Mr. Jobst's child benefits not been terminated).

Like almost any law, the Wisconsin statute now before us affects some people and does not affect others. But to say that it thereby creates "classifications" in the equal protection sense strikes me as little short of fantasy. The problem in this case is not one of discriminatory classifications, but of unwarranted encroachment upon a constitutionally protected freedom. I think that the Wisconsin statute is unconstitutional because it exceeds the bounds of permissible state regulation of marriage, and invades the sphere of liberty protected by the Due Process Clause of the Fourteenth Amendment.

I do not agree with the Court that there is a "right to marry" in the constitutional sense. That right, or more accurately, that privilege, is under our federal system peculiarly one to be defined and limited by state law. A State may not only "significantly interfere with decisions to enter into the marriage relationship," but may in many circumstances absolutely prohibit it. But, just as surely, in regulating the intimate human relationship of marriage, there is a limit beyond which a State may not constitutionally go.

The Constitution does not specifically mention freedom to marry, but it is settled that the "liberty" protected by the Due Process Clause of the Fourteenth Amendment embraces more than those freedoms expressly enumerated in the Bill of Rights. And the decisions of this Court have made clear that freedom of personal choice in matters of marriage and family life is one of the liberties so protected.

It is evident that the Wisconsin law now before us directly abridges that freedom. The question is whether the state interests that support the abridgement can overcome the substantive protections of the Constitution. [T]he State's legitimate concern with the financial soundness of prospective marriages must stop short of telling people they may not marry because they are too poor or because they might persist in their financial irresponsibility. The invasion of constitutionally protected liberty and the chance of erroneous prediction are simply too great. A legislative judgment so alien to our traditions and so offensive to our shared notions of fairness offends the Due Process Clause of the Fourteenth Amendment.

Today equal protection doctrine has become the Court's chief instrument for invalidating state laws. Yet, in a case like this one, the doctrine is no more than substantive due process by another name. Although the Court purports to examine the bases for legislative classifications and to compare the treatment of legislatively defined groups, it actually erects substantive limitations on what States may do. Thus, the effect of the Court's decision in this case is not to require Wisconsin to draw its legislative classifications with greater precision or to afford similar treatment to similarly situated persons. Rather, the message of the Court's opinion is that Wisconsin may not use its control over marriage to achieve the objectives of the state statute. Such restrictions on basic governmental power are at the heart of substantive due process.

The Court is understandably reluctant to rely on substantive due process. But to embrace the essence of that doctrine under the guise of equal protection serves no purpose but obfuscation. "[C]ouched in slogans and ringing phrases," the Court's equal protection doctrine shifts the focus of the judicial inquiry away from its proper concerns, which include "the nature of the individual interest affected, the extent to which it is affected, the rationality of the connection between legislative means and purpose, the existence of alternative means for effectuating the purpose, and the degree of confidence we may have that the statute reflects the legislative concern for the purpose that would legitimately support the means chosen."

JUSTICE POWELL, concurring in the judgment.

I write separately because the majority's rationale sweeps too broadly in an area which traditionally has been subject to pervasive state regulation. The Court apparently would subject all state regulation which "directly and substantially" interferes with the decision to marry in a traditional family setting to "critical examination" or "compelling state interest" analysis. Presumably, "reasonable regulations that do not significantly interfere with decisions to enter into the marital relationship may legitimately be imposed." The Court does not present, however, any principled means for distinguishing between the two types of regulations. Since state regulation in this area typically takes the form of a prerequisite or barrier to marriage or divorce, the degree of "direct" interference with the decision to marry or to divorce is unlikely to provide either guidance for state legislatures or a basis for judicial oversight.

State power over domestic relations is not without constitutional limits. The Due Process Clause requires a showing of justification "when the government intrudes on choices concerning family living arrangements" in a manner which is contrary to deeply rooted traditions. Furthermore, under the Equal Protection Clause the means chosen by the State in this case must bear "a fair and substantial relation" to the object of the legislation. [*Reed v. Reed*; *Craig v. Boren*.]

The Wisconsin measure in this case does not pass muster under either due process or equal protection standards. Appellant identifies three objectives which are supposedly furthered by the statute in question: (i) a counseling function; (ii) an incentive to satisfy outstanding support obligations; and (iii) a deterrent against incurring further obligations. The opinion of the Court amply demonstrates that the asserted objective[s do not justify] this statute.

JUSTICE STEVENS, concurring in the judgment.

Because of the tension between some of the language in MR. JUSTICE MARSHALL's opinion and the Court's unanimous holding in *Califano v. Jobst*, a further exposition of the reasons why the Wisconsin statute offends the Equal Protection Clause of the Fourteenth Amendment is necessary.

When a State allocates benefits or burdens, it may have valid reasons for treating married and unmarried persons differently. A classification based on marital status is fundamentally different from a classification which determines who may lawfully enter into the marriage relationship. The individual's interest in making the marriage decision independently is sufficiently important to merit special constitutional protection. It is not, however, an interest which is constitutionally immune from even-handed regulation. Thus, laws prohibiting marriage to a child, a close relative, or a person afflicted with venereal disease, are unchallenged even though they "interfere directly and substantially with the right to marry." This Wisconsin statute has a different character.

Under this statute, a person's economic status may determine his eligibility to enter into a lawful marriage. A noncustodial parent whose children are "public charges" may not marry even if he has met his court-ordered obligations. Thus, within the class of parents who have fulfilled their court-ordered obligations, the rich may marry and the poor may not. This type of statutory discrimination is, I believe, totally unprecedented, as well as inconsistent with our tradition of administering justice equally to the rich and to the poor.

The statute appears to reflect a legislative judgment that persons who have demonstrated an inability to support their offspring should not be permitted to marry and thereafter to bring additional children into the world. Even putting to one side the growing number of childless marriages and the burgeoning number of children born out of wedlock, that sort of reasoning cannot justify this deliberate discrimination against the poor.

In sum, the public charge provision is either futile or perverse insofar as it applies to childless couples, couples who will have illegitimate children if they are forbidden to marry, couples whose economic status will be improved by marriage, and couples who are so poor that the marriage will have no impact on the welfare status of their children in any event. Even assuming that the right to marry may sometimes be denied on economic grounds, this clumsy and deliberate legislative discrimination between the rich and the poor is irrational in so many ways that it cannot withstand scrutiny under the Equal Protection Clause of the Fourteenth Amendment.

JUSTICE REHNQUIST, dissenting.

I would view this legislative judgment in the light of the traditional presumption of validity. I think that under the Equal Protection Clause the statute need pass only the "rational basis test," and that under the Due Process Clause it need only be shown that it bears a rational relation to a constitutionally permissible objective. The statute so viewed is a permissible exercise of the State's power to regulate family life and to assure the support of minor children, despite its possible imprecision in the extreme cases envisioned in the concurring opinions.

NOTES

1. *Califano v. Jobst,* 434 U.S. 47 (1977). The Court upheld provisions of the Social Security Act creating an exception to a general rule that benefits for a disabled child of a wage earner terminated on the child's marriage. The exception, which provided that benefits would not be terminated if the child married a person also entitled to benefits under the Act, was challenged as violative of equal protection by a disabled child whose benefits were terminated on his marriage to another disabled person who was not entitled to benefits under the Act.

Justice Stevens, for a unanimous Court, concluded that the general rule of termination of benefits upon marriage was valid, "[s]ince it was rational for Congress to assume that marital status is a relevant test of probable dependency." The exception also withstood challenge under the equal protection principles in Fifth Amendment Due Process even though "the limited exception may have an impact on a secondary beneficiary's desire to marry, and may make some suitors less welcome than others." The Court concluded that "Congress could reasonably take one firm step toward the goal of eliminating the hardship caused by the general marriage rule without accomplishing its entire objective in the same piece of legislation."

2. *A right to marry?* Justice Marshall, citing inter alia, *Loving v. Virginia*, *Griswold v. Connecticut*, and *Skinner v. Oklahoma*, suggests that "past decisions make clear that the right to marry is of fundamental importance." What is the source of the right to marry? Do prior decisions clearly establish the fundamental nature of the right?

3. *Penalty analysis.* If the right to marry is fundamental, why wasn't the statute in *Jobst* subjected to a "critical examination"? It has been urged: "The key to a clear application of the *Redhail* test lies in the identification of what constitutes a significant interference with the right to marry." *Developments in the Law — The Constitution and the Family*, 93 Harv. L. Rev. 1156, 1251 (1980). Did the statute in *Zablocki* represent a more significant burden on the right to marry than that in *Jobst*? The Court's footnote distinction of *Jobst* appears to rest primarily on the "availability of other federal benefits" that made the impact of the "marriage penalty" relatively minimal. How would we know if, for example, the "marriage penalty" in federal income tax law became too great?

Although focusing on First Amendment and privacy rights, Professor Michael Dorf, *Incidental Burdens on Fundamental Rights*, 109 Harv. L. Rev. 1175, 1232–33 (1996), has attempted to generalize the judicial concern with whether an incidental burden on a fundamental right is sufficiently "substantial" to merit heightened scrutiny. He argues that "the substantiality requirement is a sensible response to competing concerns: on the one hand, the best understanding of constitutional text, history, structure, and purpose suggests that incidental burdens matter; on the other hand, for government to function effectively, most incidental burdens must be deemed inoffensive. The substantiality requirement mediates this conflict." Does "penalty analysis" reflect this concern with the severity of the burden on the right? Professor Dorf notes that the language of *Zablocki* "closely parallels the undue burden standard of *Casey*." *Id.* At 1220.

4. *Equal protection or due process?* What is the classification in *Zablocki*? Against whom does the law discriminate? Professor Lupu observes, "[T]he majority opinion, resting wholly on the equal protection clause, seems almost completely unconcerned with the question of 'classification' or 'discrimination.' The de facto wealth classification generated by the Wisconsin scheme — the very poor were blocked from marriage regardless of their satisfaction of support obligations — received only the scantiest attention." Ira Lupu, *Untangling the Strands of the Fourteenth Amendment*, 77 Mich. L. Rev. 981, 1025 (1979).

Several commentators have questioned the Court's use of equal protection to strike down regulations burdening fundamental rights because "the concern in these cases is not with the classifying factor, but rather with the importance of the state interest asserted and the closeness of the relationship with the classification and that interest. Initially, one wonders why it is necessary to utilize equal protection at all when the interest is independently protected by the Constitution." Barrett, *Judicial Supervision of Legislative Classifications — A More Modest Role for Equal Protection?* 1976 B.Y.U. L. REV. 89. Professor Tribe, Saenz *Sans Prophecy: Does the Privileges Immunities Revivial Portend the Future — Or Reveal the Structure of the Present?*, 113 HARV. L. REV. 110, 122 (1999), says that "rights inferred from the essentially individualistic and private dimensions of self-government — rights of personal autonomy and self-determination that are abridged not by unequal distribution or uneven access but instead by government usurpation or denial — are not fundamental for the distinctly distribution-oriented purposes of heightened review under the Equal Protection Clause, where challenged government action cannot be said to invade the personal sphere those rights define or to leave any group completely without access to those rights."

Given the due process roots of the right to marry and the use of substantive due process as a ground of decision in prior cases, why was the decision in *Zablocki* grounded on the Equal Protection Clause? Is there any difference in the functions served by the equal protection and due process guarantees? Does review of governmental action burdening the exercise of fundamental rights differ depending on whether due process or equal protection analysis is employed? Equal protection analysis has tended to use a rigid tiered approach, whereas due process more frequently has reflected a flexible approach, such as ad hoc balancing.

When a statute or regulation is determined to impinge unconstitutionally upon exercise of a fundamental right, does the state's future ability to regulate in that area differ depending on whether an equal protection or a due process analysis has been employed? Justice Stewart argues that the effect of the majority's decision in *Zablocki* is not to require the state to "draw its legislative classifications with greater precision," but to tell the state that it cannot "use its control over marriage to achieve the objectives of the state statute."

That invalidating a statute on equal protection rather than on due process grounds may produce anomalous results can be demonstrated by asking what remedy should be ordered following the opinion in *Skinner v. Oklahoma*, p. 878. Could the state decide that all convicted felons be sterilized to remove the equal protection difficulty? Despite the Court's recognition that it was dealing with fundamental rights, the statute was not invalidated because it infringed those rights, but because it did so unequally. The logical implication of invalidating the statutory scheme on equal protection grounds might be that a statute providing for sterilization of those convicted of both larceny and embezzlement would withstand judicial scrutiny. But this result would involve an even greater invasion of a fundamental right.

But Professor Cass Sunstein, *The Right to Marry*, 26 CARDOZO L. REV. 2081 (2005), argues that "the right to marry should be taken as part of the 'fundamental rights' branch of equal protection not as part of substantive due process." *Id.* at 2083. Reliance on substantive due process, he argues, has been based on the intuitive connection between sexuality and reproduction (protected by substantive due process) and marriage is not easily analyzed in the same terms. *Id.* at 2097. Like the right to vote, "the right to marry is a right of equal access to a publicly-administered institution. If a state abolished the official institution of marriage, it would be acting constitutionally, so long as it did not also abolish private marriage ceremonies. The state is under no obligation to confer either the expressive or the material benefits of marriage. [The right to marry] is a right of access, by those who enjoy it, to the expressive and material benefits that official marriage provides." *Id.* at 2118. He stresses that "so long as the institution of marriage exists, the relevant right entitles people, not to any particular set of expressive benefits, but to exactly that panoply of benefits that the relevant state offers." *Id.* at 2084. Applying his approach to same-sex marriage, he says: "I contend that, in principle, bans on same-sex marriage do run into real problems under the Equal Protection Clause, but that federal courts should be extremely reluctant to invalidate such bans for prudential reasons involving their limited role in the constitutional order. The issue of same-sex marriage is best handled through democratic arenas and at the state level (most plausibly including decisions of state courts)." *Id.* at 2085.

[C] EQUAL ACCESS TO THE FRANCHISE

[1] Denial of the Franchise

HARPER v. VIRGINIA STATE BOARD OF ELECTIONS
383 U.S. 663, 86 S. Ct. 1079, 16 L. Ed. 2d 169 (1966)

Justice Douglas delivered the opinion of the Court.

These are suits by Virginia residents to have declared unconstitutional Virginia's poll tax [$1.50 annual tax]. The three-judge District Court dismissed the complaint.

While the right to vote in federal elections is conferred by Art. I, § 2, of the Constitution, the right to vote is nowhere expressly mentioned. It is argued that the right to vote in state elections is implicit, particularly by reason of the First Amendment and that it may not constitutionally be conditioned upon the payment of a tax or fee. We do not stop to canvass the relation between voting and political expression. For it is enough to say that once the franchise is granted to the electorate, lines may not be drawn which are inconsistent with the Equal Protection Clause of the Fourteenth Amendment.

We conclude that a State violates the Equal Protection Clause of the Fourteenth Amendment whenever it makes the affluence of the voter or payment of any fee an electoral standard. Voter qualifications have no relation to wealth nor to paying or not paying this or any other tax. Our cases demonstrate that the Equal Protection Clause of the Fourteenth Amendment restrains the States from fixing voter qualifications which invidiously discriminate.

Long ago in *Yick Wo v. Hopkins*, the Court referred to "the political franchise of voting" as a "fundamental political right, because preservative of all rights." Recently in *Reynolds v. Sims*, 377 U.S. 533 (1964), we said, "Undoubtedly, the right of suffrage is a fundamental matter in a free and democratic society. Especially since the right to exercise the franchise in a free and unimpaired manner is preservative of other basic civil and political rights, any alleged infringement of the right of citizens to vote must be carefully and meticulously scrutinized." We say the same whether the citizen, otherwise qualified to vote, has $1.50 in his pocket or nothing at all, pays the fee or fails to pay it. The principle that denies the State the right to dilute a citizen's vote on account of his economic status or other such factors by analogy bars a system which excludes those unable to pay a fee to vote or who fail to pay.

It is argued that a State may exact fees from citizens for many different kinds of licenses; that if it can demand from all an equal fee for a driver's license, it can demand from all an equal poll tax for voting. But we must remember that the interest of the State, when it comes to voting, is limited to the power to fix qualifications. Wealth, like race, creed, or color, is not germane to one's ability to participate intelligently in the electoral process. Lines drawn on the basis of wealth or property, like those of race are traditionally disfavored. *See Griffin v. Illinois*; *Douglas v. California*. To introduce wealth or payment of a fee as a measure of a voter's qualifications is to introduce a capricious or irrelevant factor. The degree of the discrimination is irrelevant. In this context — that is, as a condition of obtaining a ballot — the requirement of fee paying causes an "invidious" discrimination (*Skinner v. Oklahoma*), that runs afoul of the Equal Protection Clause.

We agree, of course, with MR. JUSTICE HOLMES that the Due Process Clause of the Fourteenth Amendment "does not enact Mr. Herbert Spencer's Social Statics" (*Lochner v. New York*). Likewise, the Equal Protection Clause is not shackled to the political theory of a particular era. In determining what lines are unconstitutionally discriminatory, we have never been confined to historic notions of equality, any more than we have restricted due process to a fixed catalogue of what was at a given time deemed to be the limits of fundamental rights. Notions of what constitutes equal treatment for purposes of the Equal Protection Clause do change. (*Brown v. Board of Educ.*)

In a recent searching re-examination of the Equal Protection Clause, we held, as already noted, that "the opportunity for equal participation by all voters in the election of state legislators" is required. *Reynolds v. Sims*. We decline to qualify that principle by sustaining this poll tax. Our conclusion, like that in *Reynolds v. Sims*, is founded not on what we think governmental policy should be, but on what the Equal Protection Clause requires.

We have long been mindful that where fundamental rights and liberties are asserted under the Equal Protection Clause, classifications which might invade or restrain them must be closely scrutinized and carefully confined. *See, e.g., Skinner v. Oklahoma*. Those principles apply here. For to repeat, wealth or fee paying has, in our view, no relation to voting qualifications; the right to vote is too precious, too fundamental to be so burdened or conditioned.

JUSTICE BLACK, dissenting.

State poll tax legislation can "reasonably," "rationally" and without an "invidious" or evil purpose to injure anyone be found to rest on a number of state policies including (1) the State's desire to collect its revenue, and (2) its belief that voters who pay a poll tax will be interested in furthering the State's welfare when they vote. Certainly it is rational to believe that people may be more likely to pay taxes if payment is a prerequisite to voting. And if history can be a factor in determining the "rationality" of discrimination in a state law, then whatever may be our personal opinion, history is on the side of "rationality" of the State's poll tax policy. Property qualifications existed in the Colonies and were continued by many States after the Constitution was adopted.

The Court denies that it is using the "natural-law due-process formula." I find no statement in the Court's opinion, however, which advances even a plausible argument as to why the alleged discriminations which might possibly be effected by Virginia's poll tax law are "irrational," "unreasonable," "arbitrary," or "invidious" or have no relevance to a legitimate policy which the State wishes to adopt. I can only conclude that the primary, controlling, predominate, if not the exclusive reason for declaring the Virginia law unconstitutional is the Court's deep-seated hostility and antagonism, which I share, to making payment of a tax a prerequisite to voting.

JUSTICE HARLAN, whom JUSTICE STEWART joins, dissenting.

The Equal Protection Clause prevents States from arbitrarily treating people differently under their laws. The test evolved by this Court for determining whether an asserted justifying classification exists is whether such a classification can be deemed to be founded on some rational and otherwise constitutionally permissible state policy. This standard reduces to a minimum the likelihood that the federal judiciary will judge state policies in terms of the individual notions and predilections of its own members, and until recently it has been followed in all kinds of "equal protection" cases.

Reynolds v. Sims, among its other breaks with the past, also marked a departure from these traditional and wise principles. Unless its "one man, one vote" thesis of state legislative apportionment is to be attributed to the unsupportable proposition that "Equal Protection" simply means indiscriminate equality, it seems inescapable that what *Reynolds* really reflected was but this Court's own views of how modern American representative government should be run. For it can hardly be thought that no other method of apportionment may be considered rational.

In substance the Court's analysis of the equal protection issue goes no further than to say that the electoral franchise is "precious" and "fundamental," and to conclude that "[t]o introduce wealth or payment of a fee as a measure of a voter's qualifications is to introduce a capricious or irrelevant factor." These are of course captivating phrases, but they are wholly inadequate to satisfy the standard governing adjudication of the equal protection issue: Is there a rational basis for Virginia's poll tax as a voting qualification? I think the answer to that question is undoubtedly "yes."

Property and poll-tax qualifications, very simply, are not in accord with current egalitarian notions of how a modern democracy should be organized. It is of course entirely fitting that legislatures should modify the law to reflect such changes in popular attitudes. However, it is all wrong, in my view, for the Court to adopt the political doctrines popularly accepted at a particular moment of our history and to declare all others to be irrational and invidious, barring them from the range of choice by reasonably minded people acting through the political process. It was not too long ago that MR. JUSTICE HOLMES felt impelled to remind the Court that the Due Process Clause of the Fourteenth Amendment does not enact the laissez-faire theory of society. *Lochner*. The times have changed, and perhaps it is appropriate to observe that neither does the Equal Protection Clause of that Amendment rigidly impose upon America an ideology of unrestrained egalitarianism.

KRAMER v. UNION FREE SCHOOL DISTRICT
395 U.S. 621, 89 S. Ct. 1886, 23 L. Ed. 2d 583 (1969)

CHIEF JUSTICE WARREN delivered the opinion of the Court.

In this case we are called on to determine whether § 2012 of the New York Education Law is constitutional. The legislation provides that in certain New York school districts residents who are otherwise eligible to vote in state and federal elections may vote in the school district election only if they (1) own (or lease) taxable real property within the district, or (2) are parents (or have custody of) children enrolled in the local public schools. Appellant, a bachelor who neither owns nor leases taxable real property, filed suit in federal court claiming that § 2012 denied him equal protection. With one judge dissenting, a three-judge District Court dismissed appellant's complaint. Finding that § 2012 does violate the Equal Protection Clause of the Fourteenth Amendment, we reverse.

[I]n this case, we must give the statute a close and exacting examination. This careful examination is necessary because statutes distributing the franchise constitute the foundation of our representative society. Any unjustified discrimination in determining who may participate in political affairs or in the selection of public officials undermines the legitimacy of representative government. Statutes granting the franchise to residents on a selective basis always pose the danger of denying some citizens any effective voice in the governmental affairs which substantially affect their lives. Therefore, if a challenged state statute grants the right to vote to some bona fide residents of requisite age and citizenship and denies the franchise to others, the Court must determine whether the exclusions are necessary to promote a compelling state interest.

The presumption of constitutionality and the approval given "rational" classifications in other types of enactments are based on an assumption that the institutions of state government are structured so as to represent fairly all the people. However, when the challenge to the statute is in effect a challenge of this basic assumption, the assumption can no longer serve as the basis for presuming constitutionality. And, the assumption is no less under attack because the legislature which decides who may participate at the various levels of political choice is fairly elected.

Nor is the need for close judicial examination affected because the district meetings and the school board do not have "general" legislative powers. Our exacting examination is not necessitated by the subject of the election; rather, it is required because some resident citizens are permitted to participate and some are not.

We turn therefore to question whether the exclusion is necessary to promote a compelling state interest. First appellees argue that the State has a legitimate interest in limiting the franchise in school district elections to "members of the community of interest" — those "primarily interested in such elections." Second, appellees urge that the State may reasonably and permissibly conclude that "property taxpayers" (including lessees of taxable property who share the tax burden through rent payments) and parents of the children enrolled in the district's schools are those "primarily interested" in school affairs.

We need express no opinion as to whether the State in some circumstances might limit the exercise of the franchise to those "primarily interested" or "primarily affected." Of course, we therefore do not reach the issue of whether these particular elections are of the type in which the franchise may be so limited. For, assuming arguendo that New York legitimately might limit the franchise in these school district elections to those "primarily interested in school affairs," close scrutiny of the § 2012 classifications demonstrates that they do not accomplish this purpose with sufficient precision to justify denying appellant the franchise.

Whether classifications allegedly limiting the franchise to those resident citizens "primarily interested" deny those excluded equal protection of the law depends, inter alia, on whether all those excluded are in fact substantially less interested or affected than those the statute includes. In other words, the classifications must be tailored so that the exclusion of appellant and members of his class is necessary to achieve the articulated state goal. Section 2012 does not meet the exacting standard of precision we require of statutes which selectively distribute the franchise. The classifications in § 2012 permit inclusion of many persons who have, at best, a remote and indirect interest, in school affairs and on the other hand, exclude others who have a distinct and direct interest in the school meeting decisions. Nor do appellees offer any justification for the exclusion of seemingly interested and informed residents.

JUSTICE STEWART, with whom JUSTICES BLACK and HARLAN join, dissenting.

Clearly a State may reasonably assume that its residents have a greater stake in the outcome of elections held within its boundaries than do other persons. Likewise, it is entirely rational for a state legislature to suppose that residents, being generally better informed regarding state affairs than are nonresidents, will be more likely than nonresidents to vote responsibly. And the same may be said of legislative assumptions regarding the electoral competence of adults and literate persons on the one hand, and of minors and illiterates on the other. So long as the classification is rationally related to a permissible legislative end, therefore — as are residence, literacy, and age requirements imposed with respect to voting — there is no denial of equal protection.

[T]he asserted justification for applying such a [strict] standard cannot withstand analysis. The voting qualifications at issue have been promulgated, not by Union Free School District No. 15, but by the New York State Legislature, and the appellant is of course fully able to participate in the election of representatives in that body. There is simply no claim whatever here that the state government is not "structured so as to represent fairly all the people," including the appellant.

Nor is there any other justification for imposing the Court's "exacting" equal protection test. This case does not involve racial classifications, which in light of the genesis of the Fourteenth Amendment have traditionally been viewed as inherently "suspect." And this statute is not one that impinges upon a constitutionally protected right, and that consequently can be justified only by a "compelling" state interest. For "the Constitution of the United States does not confer the right of suffrage upon any one." *Minor v. Happersett*. In any event, it seems to me that under any equal protection standard, short of a doctrinaire insistence that universal suffrage is somehow mandated by the Constitution, the appellant's claim must be rejected.

NOTES

1. *Voting as a fundamental right.* Is voting a protected constitutional right like freedom of speech or the right of privacy? If so, what is its source? In *Wesberry v. Sanders*, 376 U.S. 1, 17 (1964), Justice Black said: "Other rights, even the most basic, are illusory if the right to vote is undermined." Consider also the language of the Court in *Reynolds v. Sims* that "the right to exercise the franchise in a free and unimpaired manner is preservative of other basic civil and political rights."

But note that *Kramer* acknowledged that important public offices can be filled by appointment rather than election. And *Harper* indicates only that "once the franchise is granted to the electorate, lines may not be drawn which are inconsistent with the Equal Protection Clause of the Fourteenth Amendment." This language indicates that there is no constitutional mandate that a state must extend the vote in the first instance. Further, Article I, § 2, and Article II, § 1, recognize broad state discretion in conducting elections. And *Kramer* suggests that age, residency, and citizenship limitations on the franchise need only be rational. Laurence H. Tribe, Saenz *Sans Prophecy: Does the Privileges or Immunities Revival Portend the Future — Or Reveal the Structure of the Present?*, 113 HARV. L. REV. 110, 121–122 (1999), says voting "might be denied altogether with respect to a particular state or local office or referendum question without triggering any constitutional concern. All that matters with voting — unlike other constitutional rights as religious worship, free speech, peaceable assembly, or travel — is that access to the right, if granted at all, must be granted equally." Professor Tribe contrasts personal rights based on notions of autonomy and self determination from rights such as voting. "Rights derived from norms of equal distribution inherent in the Constitution's structure should of course be recognized as fundamental for purposes of equal protection analysis and given effect through strict scrutiny. This is so particularly when those rights, like equality of the franchise, are constitutive of self-government in its collective, public dimension." *Id.* at 122.

2. *Equal access to the franchise.* In *United States v. Carolene Products Co.*, 304 U.S. 144, 152 n.4 (1938), Justice Stone, after noting that there may be a narrower scope for the presumption of constitutionality when "specific constitutional rights" are implicated, added that it was "unnecessary to consider now whether legislation which restricts those political processes which can ordinarily be expected to bring about repeal of undesirable legislation, is to be subjected to more exacting judicial scrutiny under the general prohibitions of the Fourteenth Amendment than are most other types of legislation."

Relying on *Carolene Products*, Professor Ely urges more active equal protection review of voting classifications in order to maintain "open political processes." He states that "unblocking stoppages in the democratic process is what judicial review ought preeminently to be about, and denial of the vote seems the quintessential stoppage." John H. Ely, Democracy and Distrust 17 (1980). Does this justify use of strict scrutiny? Ely summarizes the voting cases as involving rights "(1) that are essential to the democratic process and (2) whose dimensions cannot safely be left to our elected representatives, who have an obvious vested interest in the status quo."

3. *Salyer Land Co. v. Tulare Lake Basin Water Storage Dist.*, 410 U.S. 719 (1973). The Court, per Justice Rehnquist, applied the rationality test and upheld a law permitting only landowners to vote in water storage district general elections and apportioning votes in those elections according to the assessed valuation of land. The Court concluded that the water storage district "by reason of its special limited purpose and of the disproportionate effect of its activities on landowners as a group" was an exception to the *Kramer* requirements. Is this "penalty" analysis? Is *Kramer* inapplicable because the burden on the franchise is not as severe?

4. *Ball v. James*, 451 U.S. 355 (1981). The Court invoked the *Salyer* exception in upholding a scheme for electing directors of a large water reclamation district in Arizona (the Salt River District). The district limited voting eligibility to landowners and apportioned voting power according to the amount of land a voter owned. Justice Stewart, for the Court, following the lead of *Salyer*, looked to the nature of the services provided in determining whether the one-man, one-vote principle of *Reynolds v. Sims* applied. He asked "whether the purpose of the district is sufficiently specialized and narrow and whether its activities bear on landowners so disproportionately as to distinguish the district from those public entities whose more general governmental functions demand application of the *Reynolds* principle."

Justice Stewart acknowledged that the services provided by the *Salt River District* in the present case were "more diverse and affect far more people than those of the Tulare Lake Basin District" in *Salyer*. Nevertheless, he concluded: "The constitutionally relevant fact is that all water delivered by Salt River District, like the water delivered by the Tulare Lake Basin District, is distributed according to land ownership, and the District does not and cannot control the use to which the landowners who are entitled to the water choose to put it."

[2] Dilution of the Franchise

The voting cases discussed thus far involved a denial of the franchise to particular classes. But the Court in *Kramer* noted that the equality mandate also applies to a dilution of the vote. Professor Heather K. Gerken, *Understanding the Right to an Undiluted Vote*, 114 Harv. L. Rev. 1663, 1681 (2001), identifies three differences of dilution claims from conventional claims based on the individual right to vote: "First, although the harm of dilution can be understood as an individual injury, fairness is measured in group terms. Second, the right of an individual to an undiluted vote rises and falls with the treatment of the group. Third, the right is unindividuated among members of the group; no group member is more or less injured than any other group member." Professor Gerken says that "[t]aken together, [these principles] provide what amounts to a diagnostic test for identifying aggregate harms and serve as a basis for creating a broader conceptual framework to understand these harms. She concludes that "if we are going to recognize an aggregate harm like dilution, we must take account of its group-like qualities." *Id.* at 1742.

***Reynolds v. Sims,* 377 U.S. 533 (1964).** In mandating one-person, one-vote apportionment for both houses of a state legislature, the Court spoke of the right of each voter to "an equally effective voice in the election of members of his state legislature." A vote can be so diluted in effectiveness that it is little more than a symbolic act. The *Reynolds* Court continued:

> Legislators represent people, not trees or acres. Legislators are elected by voters, not farms or cities or economic interests. As long as ours is a representative form of government, and our legislatures are those instruments of government elected directly by and directly representative of the people, the right to elect legislators in a free and unimpaired fashion is a bedrock of our political system. It could hardly be gainsaid that a constitutional claim had been asserted by an allegation that certain otherwise qualified voters had been entirely prohibited from voting for members of their state legislature. And, if a State should provide that the votes of citizens in one part of the State should be given two times, or five times, or 10 times the weight of votes of citizens in another part of the State, it could hardly be contended that the right to vote of those residing in the disfavored areas had not been effectively diluted.
>
> Logically, in a society ostensibly grounded on representative government, it would seem reasonable that a majority of the people of a State could elect a majority of the State's legislators. To conclude differently, and to sanction minority control of state legislative bodies, would appear to deny majority rights in a way that far surpasses any possible denial of minority rights that might otherwise be thought to result. Since legislatures are responsible for enacting laws by which all citizens are to be governed, they should be bodies which are collectively responsive to the popular will. And the concept of equal protection has been traditionally viewed as requiring the uniform treatment of persons standing in the same relation to the governmental action questioned or challenged. With respect to the allocation of legislative representation, all voters, as citizens of a State, stand in the same relation regardless of where they live.
>
> We are told that the matter of apportioning representation in a state legislature is a complex and many-faceted one. We are advised that

> States can rationally consider factors other than population in apportioning legislative representation. We are admonished not to restrict the power of the States to impose differing views as to political philosophy on their citizens. We are cautioned about the dangers of entering into political thickets and mathematical quagmires. Our answer is this: a denial of constitutionally protected rights demands judicial protection; our oath and our office require no less of us. To the extent that a citizen's right to vote is debased, he is that much less a citizen. The fact than an individual lives here or there is not a legitimate reason for overweighting or diluting the efficacy of his vote. The complexions of societies and civilizations change, often with amazing rapidity. A nation once primarily rural in character becomes predominantly urban. Representation schemes once fair and equitable become archaic and outdated. But the basic principle of representative government remains, and must remain, unchanged — the weight of a citizen's vote cannot be made to depend on where he lives.
>
> We hold that, as a basic constitutional standard, the Equal Protection Clause requires that the seats in both houses of a bicameral state legislature must be apportioned on a population basis. Simply stated, an individual's right to vote for state legislators is unconstitutionally impaired when its weight is in a substantial fashion diluted when compared with votes of citizens living in other parts of the State.

Wesberry v. Sanders, 376 U.S. (1964), used Article I, § 2, of the Constitution to fashion the same principle for congressional districting. But the courts have implemented the guiding principle differently. In *Mahan v. Howell*, 410 U.S. 315 (1973), the Court permitted a 16.4 percent variation from numerical equality in a state apportionment scheme in order to maintain historic political boundaries. And in *White v. Regester*, 412 U.S. 755 (1973), a 9.9 percent variation was permitted without even requiring justification. In *Gaffney v. Cummings*, 412 U.S. 735 (1973), the Court stated: "It is now time to recognize that minor deviations from mathematical equality among state legislative districts are insufficient to make out a prima facie case so as to require justification by the State." The Court has been more stringent in applying one-person, one-vote principles to congressional districting. In fact, the Courts have required that states "come as nearly as practicable to population equality" in congressional districting. In rejecting a .7% maximum percentage deviation between districts in *Karcher v. Daggett*, 462 U.S. 725 (1983), the Court noted that the state must show "with some specificity that a particular objective required the specific deviation in its plan."

Samuel Issacharoff, *Judging Politics: The Elusive Quest for Judicial Review of Political Fairness*, 71 Tex. L. Rev. 1643, 1648 (1993) observes that the Supreme Court emphasis on "numerical standards of apportionment" following *Baker v. Carr* served three purposes: it was quantifiable and based on "unassailable empirical data," it was readily manageable by the courts, and it should avoid gerrymandering. "The optimism of the 1960s allowed the Court the easy transition from the chosen constitutional path — the equipopulation principle — to the ultimate constitutional objective — political fairness."

Professor Issacharoff notes that the equipopulation principle met its greatest success in the context of "equal individual access to the political process. . . . The most difficult problem in the apportionment context arose as individuals claimed rights to effective use of the franchise based on group identities." *Id.* at 1652.

The Constitution cannot guarantee an effective vote in the sense of a guarantee that your candidate will win, or that you have a right to be in a district with like-minded voters. What, then, is the scope of the equal protection guarantee against the dilution of the franchise?

***Mobile v. Bolden,* 446 U.S. 55 (1980).** The Court rejected an equal protection challenge to Mobile's at-large election system. While the case dealt principally with whether the system impermissibly discriminated on the basis of race, Justice Marshall, in dissent, argued that Mobile's electoral system, even apart from its racial bias, violated equal protection, because it impinged on the "fundamental right to equal electoral participation."

> We decided a series of vote-dilution cases under the Fourteenth Amendment that were designed to protect electoral minorities from precisely the combination of electoral laws and historical and social factors found in the present cases. *Reynolds v. Sims* and its progeny focused solely on the discriminatory effects of malapportionment. The equal protection problem attacked by the "one person, one vote" principle is, then, one of vote dilution: under *Reynolds*, each citizen must have an "equally effective voice" in the election of representatives. In the present cases, the alleged vote dilution, though caused by the combined effects of the electoral structure and social and historical factors rather than by unequal population distribution, is analytically the same concept: the unjustified abridgment of a fundamental right.

Justice Stewart, in a plurality opinion, contended that Justice Marshall was advocating a system of proportional representation.

> The theory of this dissenting opinion appears to be that every "political group," or at least every such group that is in the minority, has a federal constitutional right to elect candidates in proportion to its numbers. Moreover, a political group's "right" to have its candidates elected is said to be a "fundamental interest," the infringement of which may be established without proof that a State has acted with the purpose of impairing anybody's access to the political process. This dissenting opinion finds the "right" infringed in the present case because no Negro has been elected to the Mobile City Commission.
>
> Whatever appeal the dissenting opinion's view may have as a matter of political theory, it is not the law. The Equal Protection Clause of the Fourteenth Amendment does not require proportional representation as an imperative of political organization. The entitlement that the dissenting opinion assumes to exist simply is not to be found in the Constitution of the United States. It is of course true that a law that impinges upon a fundamental right explicitly or implicitly secured by the Constitution is presumptively unconstitutional. But plainly

> "[i]t is not the province of this court to create substantive constitutional rights in the name of guaranteeing equal protection of the laws." [The] right to equal participation in the electoral process does not protect any "political group," however defined, from electoral defeat.

Justice Marshall responded:

> The plurality's response is that my approach amounts to nothing less than a constitutional requirement of proportional representation for groups. That assertion amounts to nothing more than a red herring: I explicitly reject the notion that the Constitution contains any such requirement. The constitutional protection against vote dilution found in our prior cases does not extend to those situations in which a group has merely failed to elect representatives in proportion to its share of the population. To prove unconstitutional vote dilution, the group is also required to carry the far more onerous burden of demonstrating that it has been effectively fenced out of the political process. Typical of the plurality's mischaracterization of my position is its assertion that I would provide protection against vote dilution for "every 'political group,' or at least every such group that is in the minority." The vote-dilution doctrine can logically apply only to groups whose electoral discreetness and insularity allow dominant political factions to ignore them. In short, the distinction between a requirement of proportional representation and the discriminatory-effect test I espouse is by no means a difficult one, and it is hard for me to understand why the plurality insists on ignoring it.
>
> A requirement of proportional representation would indeed transform this Court into a "super-legislature," and would create the risk that some groups would receive an undeserved windfall of political influence. In contrast, the protection against vote dilution recognized by our prior cases serves as a minimally intrusive guarantee of political survival for a discrete political minority that is effectively locked out of governmental decisionmaking processes. So understood, the doctrine hardly "create[s] substantive constitutional rights in the name of guaranteeing equal protection of the laws." Rather, the doctrine is a simple reflection of the basic principle that the Equal Protection Clause protects "[t]he right of a citizen to equal representation and to have his vote weighted equally with those of all other citizens." *Reynolds v. Sims.*

Does one-person-one-vote achieve "fair and effective representation?" Does the Constitution guarantee equality of the franchise or equality of representation? Is it an individual right or a group right at issue? Justice Stevens, concurring in the judgment in *Mobile*, stated: "[T]here is a fundamental distinction between state action that inhibits an individual's right to vote and state action that affects the political strength of various groups that compete for leadership in a democratically governed community. That distinction divides so-called vote dilution practices into two different categories 'governed by entirely different constitutional considerations.' "

***Davis v. Bandemer*, 478 U.S. 109 (1986).** After the 1980 round of redistricting, Indiana Democrats filed suit claiming that the new reapportionment plan constituted an unconstitutional political gerrymander. The Supreme Court held that such claims were justiciable, but no majority could agree on the proper standard under the Equal Protection Clause. Justice White, writing for a plurality that included Justices Brennan, Marshall, and Blackmun, would have held that to prove unconstitutional political gerrymandering, plaintiffs "were required to prove both intentional discrimination against an identifiable political group and actual discriminatory effect on that group." While rejecting proportional representation, the plurality said that plaintiffs would have to show that "the electoral system is arranged in a manner that will consistently degrade a voter's or a group of voters' influence on the political process as a whole." Under this standard, the plurality concluded that the plaintiffs had not met their burden.

Justice Powell with Justice Stevens, concurring in part and dissenting in part, agreed that the claim was justiciable, but disagreed on the standard to be used for adjudicating such claims. They favored a "sensitive and searching inquiry" which considered "the shapes of voting districts and adherence to established political subdivision boundaries, the nature of the legislative procedures by which the apportionment law was adopted and legislative history reflecting contemporaneous legislative goals[,] as well as evidence concerning population disparities and statistics tending to show vote dilution." Justices Powell and Stevens would have upheld the district court's finding of an unconstitutional gerrymander.

Justice O'Connor, with Chief Justice Burger and Justice Rehnquist, concurred in the judgment, but would have held that claims of political gerrymandering are nonjusticiable because of "the intractable difficulties in deriving a judicially manageable standard from the Equal Protection Clause." Justice O'Connor distinguished political gerrymanders from racial ones, noting that "while membership in a racial group is an immutable characteristic, voters can — and often do — move from one party to the other or support candidates from both parties." She also voiced concern that judicial interference in these situations "is likely to move in the direction of proportional representation for political parties." Finally, Justice O'Connor noted that an internal check existed against an "overambitious gerrymander" — by trying to increase seats for a political party, voters who reliably vote for that party must be moved out of districts controlled by the party, thus increasing the chance that the other party wins that seat.

***Vieth v. Jubelirer*, 541 U.S. 267 (2004).** In this challenge to a Pennsylvania congressional districting plan, it was alleged that the Republican majority in the state legislature had created districts that would disfavor Democratic Party candidates for Congress. The "complaint alleged that the districts created were 'meandering and irregular,' and 'ignored all traditional redistricting criteria, including the preservation of local government boundaries, solely for the sake of partisan advantage.' " The district court approved a revised plan. The Supreme Court affirmed.

Justice Scalia, writing for a plurality that included Chief Justice Rehnquist and Justices O'Connor and Thomas, would have overruled *Bandemer* and held that claims of political gerrymandering are nonjusticiable. Justice Scalia rejected the tests proposed by the plurality and dissent in *Bandemer*, the appellants, and each of the three dissenting opinions in *Vieth*, and concluded that after "[e]ighteen years of judicial effort with virtually nothing to show for it not judicially discernible and manageable standards for adjudicating political gerrymandering claims have emerged."

Justice Kennedy concurred in the judgment, concluding that this claim must be dismissed and agreeing that no equal protection test against which to measure political gerrymandering claims has emerged. But he would not "foreclose all possibility of judicial relief if some limited and precise rationale were found to correct an established violation of the Constitution in some redistricting cases." Citing *Baker v. Carr* as an example where equal protection claims were held justiciable absent specific standards, Justice Kennedy thought it important "to err on the side of caution" because "[a] determination by the Court to deny all hopes of intervention could erode confidence in the courts as much as would a premature decision to intervene."

Justice Stevens, Justice Souter (joined by Justice Ginsburg), and Justice Breyer each dissented separately, offering a different equal protection standard for political gerrymandering claims. Justice Stevens would draw from standards formulated in the racial gerrymandering cases and "ask whether the legislature allowed partisan considerations to dominate and control the lines drawn, forsaking all neutral principles." Justice Souter would require a plaintiff to satisfy a five-part test in order to make out a prima facie case, including a showing that "the district of [plaintiff's] residence paid little or no heed to those traditional districting principles whose disregard can be shown straightforwardly" and that "the defendants acted intentionally to manipulate the shape of the district in order to" remove or displace members of the plaintiff's political group. Finally, Justice Breyer concluded that "courts should be able to identify the presence of one important gerrymandering evil, the unjustified entrenching in power of a political party that the voters have rejected," and that courts "should be able to separate the unjustified abuse of partisan boundary-drawing considerations to achieve that end from their more ordinary and justified use."

NOTES

1. *Individual or group rights.* While one-person-one-vote is frequently justified in terms of individual voting rights, it is argued that "the claims that gerrymandering violates individual voting rights cannot withstand analysis." Daniel Lowenstein & Jonathan Steinberg, *The Quest for Legislative Districting in the Public Interest: Elusive or Illusory?*, 33 U.C.L.A. L. Rev. 1, 136 (1985). Martin Shapiro, *Gerrymandering, Unfairness, and the Supreme Court*, 33 UCLA L. Rev. 227, 232 (1985) says: "The one-person-one-vote standard rests on nineteenth century liberal political theory which used individuals as the basic unit of politics. From the perspective of twentieth century liberal theories, which use groups as the basic units of politics, the notion that a one-person-one-vote standard will assure fair representation is nonsense."

Does judicial acceptance of traditional community interests as a basis for deviating from one-person-one-vote in state apportionment cases implicitly accept minority representation? Group rights? Do racial gerrymander cases such as *Gomillion v. Lightfoot*, 364 U.S. 339 (1960), accept group rights? Lani Guinier, *Groups, Representation, and Race-Conscious Districting: A Case of the Emperor's Clothes*, 71 TEX. L. REV. 1589, 1682 (1993), argues that gerrymandering simply indicates the group nature of districting. "The concept of representation necessarily applies to groups: groups of voters elect representatives; individuals do not. Because representation is primarily about political influence, not political service, bottom-up representation becomes the essential link to a genuine voice in the process of self-government. Districting is a form of group-interest representation, albeit an imperfectly realized one." Similarly, Professor Richard Pildes, *The Supreme Court, 2003 Term, Foreword: The Constitutionalization of Democratic Politics*, 118 HARV. L. REV. 28, 58 (2004), notes: " 'Representational rights,' as Justice Kennedy called the claims at stake [in *Vieth*], are not individual ones. Structural judgments about the proper processes of redistricting or about the fair distribution of seats among groups, given the distribution of votes cast, are unavoidable."

Professor Heather Gerken, *Lost in the Political Thicket*, 153 U. PA. L. REV. 503, 522 (2004), suggests an approach that focuses on "discrete structural harms" in analyzing vote dilution and related claims: "Discrete structural harms, then, seem to represent a midway point between a purely individualist framework and a purely structural approach. For instance, injuries like vote dilution where identification of an individual harm requires reference to the relative treatment of a group — inflict a sufficiently concrete harm upon members of a group to impose some limits on judicial intervention. But the *measure* of the harm nonetheless requires a structural judgment by the court."

2. *Proportional representation.* "Those who argue that some forms of partisanship in districting are unconstitutional, and should be justiciable, rarely explicitly propose proportional representation as the standard against which challenged schemes can be measured for constitutionality and often take great pains to insist otherwise. But their opponents often contend that they have no alternative." Mitchell N. Berman, *Managing Gerrymandering*, 83 TEX. L. REV. 781, 820–21 (2005). It has been argued that, in implementing the Voting Rights Acts, § 5, proportional representation of racial groups often appears to be an accepted norm. *See* Alan Howard & Bruce Howard, *The Dilemma of the Voting Rights Act — Recognizing the Emerging Political Equality Norm*, 83 COLUM. L. REV. 1615 (1983).

The specter of "proportional representation" haunts the opinions in the dilution cases. Why? It may be that proportional representation "would create a political structure that would make the maintenance of other central constitutional values more difficult." Sanford Levinson, *Gerrymandering and the Brooding Omnipresence of Proportional Representation: Why Won't It Go Away?*, 33 U.C.L.A. L. REV. 257, 271 (1985). Does the problem lie in proportional representation or in judicial adoption of proportional representation as a Fourteenth Amendment command?

3. *Standards for political gerrymandering.* Between *Bandemer* and *Veith*, different Justices have suggested five different standards under which to review claims of political gerrymandering. Justice Scalia cites this as evidence that no such standards exist: "the mere fact that these four dissenters come up with three different standards — all of them different from the two proposed in *Bandemer* and the one proposed here by appellants — goes a long way to establishing that there is no constitutionally discernible standard." Justice Breyer responds that "dissenters might instead believe that the more thorough, specific reasoning that accompanies separate statements will stimulate further discussion. And that discussion could lead to change in the law." Justice Kennedy notes that "by the timeline of the law 18 years is rather a short period" and that "the rapid evolution of technologies in the apportionment field suggests yet unexplored possibilities."

Does the problem of formulating objective neutral criteria for decision justify judicial avoidance or a deferential standard of judicial review? Perhaps *Bandemer* and *Vieth* can be compared to *Baker v. Carr*, establishing justiciability and inviting litigation that will fashion standards of judicial review. *See Vieth*, 541 U.S. at 310 (Kennedy, J., concurring in the judgment) ("Our willingness to enter the political thicket of the apportionment process with respect to one-person, one-vote claims makes it particularly difficult to justify a categorical refusal to entertain claims against this other type of gerrymandering.").

4. *Bipartisan gerrymanders.* A related problem to political gerrymandering is that of bipartisan gerrymandering. A bipartisan gerrymander is one in which legislators create "safe" districts for incumbents of both parties. As Professor Richard Pildes, 118 Harv. L. Rev. at 60–61, puts it: "When neither party controls the legislative process, incumbents of both parties sometimes agree on a bipartisan, or 'sweetheart,' gerrymander. These agreements reflect a convenant not to compete between the incumbents of the two parties. [C]ourts should be aware of the emerging prevalence of bipartisan gerrymandering as they address the need for constitutional checks on self-entrenching practices and the form that such oversight should take."

Are there equal protection concerns associated with bipartisan gerrymanders? Are these concerns greater or lesser than those associated with partisan gerrymanders? Consider the following: "In the partisan gerrymandering context, the claimed victims of discrimination have ample recourse to political redress, even if not immediate satisfaction within the jurisdiction in question. But beyond the question of political redress, the magnitude of the risk of discriminatory partisan gerrymandering is overwhelmed by the fact of nondiscriminatory bipartisan gerrymandering that renders elections in the United States immune to voter preferences." Samuel Issacharoff & Pamela S. Karlan, *Where to Draw the Line?: Judicial Review of Political Gerrymanders*, 153 U. Pa. L. Rev. 541, 571 (2004).

5. *Racial gerrymandering.* The Court has reviewed racial gerrymandering that resulted in majority-minority voting districts. What are the differences between race and political affiliation — immutability of the characteristic? Relevance to the political process? Are there other distinctions that you find persuasive?

Professor Guinier, 71 Tex. L. Rev. at 1591–92, claims that "critics of race-conscious districting have misdirected their fire"; that they fail to realize that representation is itself a group process. "Perhaps unwittingly, they also reveal a bias toward the representation of a particular racial group rather than their discomfort with group representation itself. In a society as deeply cleaved by issues of racial identity as ours, there is no one race. In the presence of such racial differences, a system of representation that fails to provide group representation loses legitimacy."

In *(E)Racing Democracy: The Voting Rights Cases*, 108 HRV. L. REV. at 132, Professor Guinier argues that courts should adopt race-conscious group representation "as a universal remedial principle of democratic accountability and legitimacy. Finally, in choosing remedies to guarantee representation opportunities for politically cohesive racial groups, courts should select remedies that also have the potential to empower other politically cohesive groups. This is especially true when successful voting rights challenges by racial minority groups expose more systematic problems with current political arrangements."

6. *Access to the ballot.* The value of the franchise can also be diluted by laws restricting access by independent candidates and minority parties to the ballot. Such restrictions place "burdens on two different, although overlapping, kinds of rights — the right of individuals to associate for the advancement of political beliefs and the right of qualified voters, regardless of their political persuasion, to cast their votes effectively." *Williams v. Rhodes*, 393 U.S. 23 (1968). *Williams* involved an Ohio law permitting parties receiving 10% of the vote in the gubernatorial election to quality automatically for the following presidential election but requiring other parties to satisfy structural requirements and submit substantial proof of community support (e.g., filing petitions, signed by 15% of qualified electors voting in the prior gubernatorial election, nine months before the election).

The Ohio law, the Court observed, made it "virtually impossible for a new political party to be placed on the state ballot." Only a compelling state interest could justify such a restriction. But the Ohio law was not drawn merely to promote the two party system; it gave a "complete monopoly" to the Republicans and Democrats. Less restrictive ballot access requirements were available.

The Court has accepted that some restrictions on ballot access are permissible if they reasonably serve the state's important interests "in protecting the integrity of their political process from frivolous or fraudulent candidacies, in ensuring that their election process are efficient, in avoiding voter confusion caused by an overcrowded ballot, and in avoiding the expense and burden of run-off elections." *Clements v. Fashing*, 457 U.S. 957 (1982), upholding a state law barring an office holder from running for a different office.

The use of filing fees for ballot access, with no alternative means of access, seldom satisfies strict scrutiny. *See, e.g., Lubin v. Panish*, 415 U.S. 709 (1979) (filing fee of 1% of salary for office sought held unconstitutional). But the disposition of laws requiring signed petitions demonstrating community support is less certain. If the law "affords minority political parties a real and substantially equal opportunity for ballot qualification," they will be upheld. For example, in *American Party of Texas v. White*, 415 U.S. 767 (1974), the Court upheld a ballot access requirement that parties which had not demonstrated significant voter support in the previous elections provide petitions signed by 1% of voters and limiting the pool of signatories to those who had not participated in another party's primary or nominating process. Similarly, in *Storer v. Brown*, 415 U.S. 724 (1974), a one year disaffiliation provision for candidates was upheld as furthering the state's compelling interest in the stability of its political system. But, if the ballot access provisions are virtually exclusionary of independents and minority parties, the requirements will be held invalid under *Williams*.

7. *Bush v. Gore,* 531 U.S. 98 (2000), text, p. 58. In a per curiam opinion joined by five justices, the Court held that Florida recount procedures "do not satisfy the minimum requirements for non-arbitrary treatment of voters necessary to secure the fundamental right [to vote] and violated the equal protection guarantee." Since a recount complying with equal protection could not be completed in the time remaining, the Court reversed the judgement of the Florida Supreme Court ordering the recount.

The Court began by setting forth the basis for holding that equal protection extended to the counting and recounting of votes.

> When the state legislature vests the right to vote for President in its people, the right to vote as the legislature has prescribed is fundamental; and one source of its fundamental nature lies in the equal weight accorded to each vote and the equal dignity owed to each voter. The right to vote is protected in more than the initial allocation of the franchise. Equal protection applies as well to the manner of its exercise. Having once granted the right to vote on equal terms, the State may not, by later arbitrary and disparate treatment, value one person's vote over that of another. *See, e.g., Harper v. Virginia Bd. of Elections*; *Reynolds v. Sims*.

The Florida recount procedures did not meet the standard. While the Florida Supreme Courts command that the recount was designed to determine the "intent of the voters" was acceptable, "[t]he problem inheres in the absence of specific standards to ensure its equal application. The formulation of uniform rules to determine intent based on these recurring circumstances is practicable and, we conclude necessary."

The Court notes that "[t]he standards for accepting or rejecting contested ballots might vary not only from county to county but indeed within a single county from one recount team to another." The recount was not limited to undervotes but extended to ballots which contain more than one vote, or overvotes. The order was not specific on who would count the ballots. The Court summarized:

> The recount process, in its features here described, is inconsistent with the minimum procedures necessary to protect the fundamental right of each voter in the special instance of a statewide recount under the authority of a single state judicial officer. Our consideration is limited to the present circumstances, for the problem of equal protection in election processes generally presents many complexities.
>
> The question before the Court is not whether local entities, in the exercise of their expertise, may develop different systems for implementing elections. Instead, we are presented with a situation where

a state court with the power to assure uniformity has ordered a statewide recount with minimal procedural safeguards. When a court orders a statewide remedy, there must be at least some assurance that the rudimentary requirements of equal treatment and fundamental fairness are satisfied.

Seven Justices of the Court agree that there are constitutional problems with the recount ordered by the Florida Supreme Court that demand a remedy. *See* (SOUTER, J., dissenting); (BREYER, J., dissenting). The only disagreement is to a remedy. None are more conscious of the vital limits on judicial authority than are the members of this Court, and none stand more in admiration of the Constitution's design to leave the selection of the President to the people, through their legislatures, and to the political sphere. When contending parties invoke the process of the courts, however, it becomes our unsought responsibility to resolve the federal and constitutional issues the judicial system has been forced to confront.

Justice Stevens, joined by Justices Ginsburg and Breyer, dissented.

[P]etitioners [are not] correct in asserting that the failure of the Florida Supreme Court to specify in detail the precise manner in which the "intent of the voter" is to be determined rises to the level of a constitutional violation. We found such a violation when individual votes within same State were weighted unequally, *see, e.g.*, *Reynolds v. Sims*, but we have never before called into question the substantive standard by which a State determines that a vote has been legally cast. And there is no reason to think that the guidance provided to the factfinders, specially the various canvassing boards, by the "intent of the voter" standard is any less sufficient — or will lead to results any less uniform — than, for example, the "beyond a reasonable doubt" standard employed everyday by ordinary citizens in courtrooms across this country.

Admittedly, the use of differing substandards for determining voter intent in different counties employing similar voting systems may raise serious concerns. Those concerns are alleviated — if not eliminated — by the fact that a single impartial magistrate will ultimately adjudicate all objections arising from the recount process. Of course, as a general matter, "the interpretation of constitutional principles must not be too literal. We must remember that the machinery of government would not work if it were government would not work if it were not allowed a little play in its joints." If it were otherwise, Florida's decision to leave to each county the determination of what balloting system to employ — despite enormous difference in accuracy — might run afoul of equal protection. So, too, might the similar decisions of the vast majority of state legislatures to delegate to local authorities certain decisions with respect to voting systems and ballot design.

Justice Souter, joined by Justice Breyer, also dissented.

> Petitioners have raised an equal protection claim (or, alternatively, a due process claim) in the charge that unjustifiably disparate standards are applied in different electoral jurisdictions to otherwise identical facts. It is true that the Equal Protection Clause does not forbid the use of a variety of voting mechanisms within a jurisdiction, even though different mechanisms will have different levels of effectiveness in recording voters' intentions; local variety can be justified by concerns about cost, the potential value of innovation, and so on. But evidence in the record here suggests that a different order of disparity obtains under rules for determining a voter's intent that have been applied (and could continue to be applied) to identical types of ballots used in identical brands of machines and exhibiting identical physical characteristics (such as "hanging" or "dimpled" chads) I can conceive of no legitimate state interest served by these differing treatments of the expressions of voters' fundamental rights. The differences appear wholly arbitrary.

For discussion of *Bush v. Gore* from both sides of the political spectrum, see Symposium: *Bush v. Gore*, 68 U. CHI. L. REV. 613–791 (2001). For a critical analysis, see Jack M. Balkin, Bush v. Gore *and the Boundary Between Law and Politics*, 110 YALE L.J. 1407 (2001). *See also* Richard Posner, *Florida 2000: A Legal and Statistical Analysis of the Election Deadlock and the Ensuing Litigation*, 2000 SUP. CT. REV. 1.

[D] EQUAL ACCESS TO THE COURTS

In *Griffin v. Illinois*, 351 U.S. 12 (1956), the Court held that both equal protection and due process were violated by a state law denying free transcripts to indigent convicted criminal defendants, where the transcript was necessary to "adequate and effective" appellate review. Justice Black, in a plurality opinion, concluded that while a state need not provide appellate review, if it does so, then it cannot "do so in a way that discriminates against some convicted defendants on account of their poverty." In a frequently quoted passage, Justice Black stated, "There can be no equal justice where the kind of trial a man gets depends on the amount of money he has."

This concept of equal access to criminal justice is also found in *Douglas v. California*, 372 U.S. 353 (1963), recognizing the right of an indigent convict to counsel when the first appeal is granted as a matter of right. Justice Douglas for the Court stated

> Absolute equality is not required; lines can be and are drawn and we often sustain them. But where the merits of the one and only appeal an indigent has as of right are decided without benefit of counsel, we think an unconstitutional line has been drawn between rich and poor.

Justice Harlan dissented in both *Griffin* and *Douglas*. Although agreeing that equal protection prevents a state "from discriminating between 'rich' and 'poor' as such, this principle does not mean that it prevents the State from adopting a law of general applicability that may affect the poor more harshly than it does the rich."

> Laws such as these do not deny equal protection to the less fortunate for one essential reason: the Equal Protection Clause does not impose on the States "an affirmative duty to lift the handicaps flowing from differences in economic circumstances." To so construe it would be to read into the Constitution a philosophy of leveling that would be foreign to many of our basic concepts of the proper relations between government and society. The State may have a moral obligation to eliminate the evils of poverty, but it is not required by the Equal Protection Clause to give to some whatever others can afford.

Griffin-Douglas fashioned an uncertain right of equal access to criminal justice grounded, at least in part, in the Equal Protection Clause. The Court did not rely on any independent fundamental right such as travel or marriage. Nor did the Court label wealth a suspect or quasi-suspect classification. But the nature of the defendant's interest and the nature of the classifying trait were patently important. In *Maher v. Roe*, p. 930, the Court emphasized that *Griffin-Douglas* were grounded in the criminal justice system, a governmental monopoly in which participation is compelled.

The governmental monopoly over a required process was also at stake in *Boddie v. Connecticut*, 401 U.S. 371 (1971). The Court, Justice Harlan now writing the majority opinion, held unconstitutional state requirements for payment of court fees and costs for service of process (approximately sixty dollars average costs) in order to bring an action for divorce. The Court did not invoke equal protection, but instead relied on the due process guarantee:

> Our conclusion is that, given the basic position of the marriage relationship in this society's hierarchy of values and the concomitant state monopolization of the means for legally dissolving this relationship, due process does prohibit the State from denying, solely because of inability to pay, access to its courts to individuals who seek judicial dissolution of their marriages.

But in *United States v. Kras*, 409 U.S. 434 (1973), the Court (5-4), per Justice Blackmun, held that a provision of the Bankruptcy Act imposing a fifty dollar fee did not violate due process or equal protection protected by the Fifth Amendment. *Boddie* was distinguished. First the petitioner's "alleged interest in the elimination of his debt burden, and in obtaining his desired new start in life, although important, does not rise to the same constitutional level. If Kras is not discharged in bankruptcy, his position will not be materially altered in any constitutional sense. Gaining or not gaining a discharge will effect no change with respect to basic necessities." It followed that "no fundamental interest is gained or lost depending on the availability of a discharge of bankruptcy." Further, "the government's control over the establishment, enforcement, or dissolution of debts [is not] nearly so exclusive as Connecticut's control over the marriage relationship in *Boddie*." Justice Blackmun argued, "However unrealistic the remedy may be in a particular situation, a debtor, in theory, and often in actuality, may adjust his debts by negotiated agreement with his creditors. Government's role with respect to the private commercial relationship is qualitatively and quantitatively different than its role in the establishment, enforcement, and dissolution of marriage."

In *M.L.B. v. S.L.J.*, 519 U.S. 102 (1996), the Court held that a state may not revoke a mother's right to appeal from the termination of her parental rights because of her inability to comply with statutes requiring her to pay record preparation fees in advance. In so holding, the Court emphasized that "[c]hoices about marriage, family life, and the upbringing of children are among associational rights this Court has ranked of basic importance in our society," citing *Boddie*. Thus, a case "involving the State's authority to sever permanently a parent-child bond demands the close consideration the Court has long required when a family association so undeniably important is at stake." The Court's decision reflected both equal protection and due process principles: "The equal protection concern relates to the legitimacy of fencing out would-be appellants based solely on their inability to pay core costs. The due process concern homes in on the essential fairness of the state-ordered proceeding anterior to adverse state action."

The fact that a criminal case was not involved did not affect the Court's holding. Unlike most civil cases, reasoned the Court, the stakes — forced dissolution of parental rights — are more substantial than the mere loss of money.

[E] LIMITING FUNDAMENTAL RIGHTS AND INTERESTS

The Warren Court clearly broke new ground in equal protection doctrine. There was an increasing expectation that the Equal Protection Clause might be used to impose on states an affirmative constitutional duty to equalize access to important government benefits such as housing, medical care, and education. But the egalitarian revolution was only in a nascent stage when the personnel of the Court began to change. As many of the previous cases indicate, with the Burger and Rehnquist Courts the use of the Equal Protection Clause as a vehicle for promoting equality of public access to goods and benefits has waned. There has not been a direct reversal of precedent; instead, fine distinctions have been drawn and opportunities to extend the governing principles have been rejected.

The judicial value structure that had provided the impetus for the new directions based on social meliorism during the Warren Court years was now in the minority on the Court. Fundamental rights and interests have not been expanded to encompass welfare interests or a right to a minimum standard of living. Government need not fund medically necessary abortions for welfare recipients even if maternity benefits are provided. The government has no constitutional duty to provide decent housing (*see Lindsey v. Normet*, 405 U.S. 56 (1972)) or to equalize educational resources.

In the present section, the focus will be on this change of direction and the reasons given for limiting fundamental rights and interests. In examining the cases, consider whether a more searching standard of review might have been applied and how the opinion and decisions would have been framed, and what value choices would be made. What do the decisions suggest for the future of equal protection?

[1] Equality Through Welfare

In the late 1960s, Professor Michelman wrote a seminal article suggesting that government was under an affirmative constitutional duty to provide "minimum protection" for the basic welfare needs of an individual — food, shelter, health care, education — which he labeled "just wants." Frank Michelman, *On Protecting the Poor Through the Fourteenth Amendment*, 83 HARV. L. REV. 7 (1969). *See* Michelman, *Welfare Rights in a Constitutional Democracy*, 1979 WASH. U.L. REV. 659. While Michelman's thesis received strong support, it also was bitterly attacked. "[S]uch a use of judicial power is absolutely wrong. In terms of a sensible division of functions between the Court and the elected branches, it resembles more a call for partial rule by junta (of between five and nine men) than for an acceptable interpretation of the structure of the Constitution." Ralph Winter, *Poverty, Economic Equality, and the Equal Protection Clause*, 1972 SUP. CT. REV. 41, 43. For a historical study of the constitutional welfare rights movement and the theory and judgments underlying it, see William E. Forbath, *Constitutional Welfare Rights: A History, Critique and Reconstruction*, 69 FORDHAM L. REV. 1827 (2001) ("Dusk seems to have come for constitutional welfare rights, an intellectual and practical project of many revered lawyers, judges, and scholars during the 1960s and 1970s." *Id.* at 1822); Frank I. Michelman, *Democracy-Based Resistence to a Constitutional Right of Social Citizenship: A Comment on Forbath*, 69 FORDHAM L. REV. 1893 (2001).

***Dandridge v. Williams*, 397 U.S. 471 (1970).** The Court upheld a Maryland "family maximum grant" law placing a dollar ceiling on AFDC benefits available to a welfare family. The standard of need increased with each additional child but the increments became proportionately smaller until the maximum was reached. The appellees argued that the law discriminated against larger families in violation of the equal protection guarantee.

Justice Stewart, writing for the Court, characterized the law as falling "[i]n the area of economics and social welfare" and applied the rational basis test.

> To be sure, the cases enunciating this fundamental standard under the Equal Protection Clause, have in the main involved state regulation of business or industry. The administration of public welfare assistance, by contrast, involves the most basic economic needs of impoverished human beings. We recognize the dramatically real factual difference between the cited cases and this one, but we can find no basis for applying a different constitutional standard. [I]t is a standard that is true to the principle that the Fourteenth Amendment gives the federal courts no power to impose upon the States their views of wise economic or social policy.
>
> By combining a limit on the recipient's grant with permission to retain money earned, without reduction in the amount of the grant,

> Maryland provides an incentive to seek gainful employment. And by keying the maximum family AFDC grants to the minimum wage a steadily employed head of a household receives, the State maintains some semblance of an equitable balance between families on welfare and those supported by an employed breadwinner.
>
> We do not decide today that the Maryland regulation is wise, that it best fulfills the relevant social and economic objectives that Maryland might ideally espouse, or that a more just and humane system could not be devised. Conflicting claims of morality and intelligence are raised by opponents and proponents of almost every measure, certainly including the one before us. But the intractable economic, social, and even philosophical problems presented by public welfare assistance programs are not the business of this Court.

Justice Marshall, in dissent, criticized "the Court's emasculation of the Equal Protection Clause as a constitutional principle applicable to the area of social welfare administration" and asserted that "the Court's decision today is wholly without precedent." LAURENCE H. TRIBE, AMERICAN CONSTITUTIONAL LAW 1663 (2d ed. 1988), suggests that *Dandridge* represents an end to the expansion of equal protection as a device for protecting the poor in areas where the basic necessities of life hang in the balance. "[T]he *Dandridge* reluctance to intervene in welfare legislation represents a deep current in Burger Court concerns; the talismanic characteristic of 'state regulations in the social and economic field' lies poised and ready to spring any time the Court decides not to intervene, and poses a constant threat to challenges of inequalities and arbitrariness in public assistance laws."

Other than Justice Stewart's references in *Dandridge* to "overreaching" and the First Amendment, there was only minimal reference to fundamental interests by the majority. Thomas Dienes, *To Feed the Hungry: Judicial Retrenchment in Welfare Adjudication*, 58 CAL. L. REV. 555 (1970), noted some of the roads not taken: "[T]he *Williams* Court might have considered the impact of the maximum grant on such interests as the right to privacy in the marital relationship (where a viable marriage exists), the freedom to choose family size, and the interest in maintaining a harmonious marital union. Similarly, the effect of the provision to induce the dissolution of the parent-child relationship as the price of adequate funds for subsistence and to place further strains on familial stability in the family already struggling to maintain itself against the disruptive effects of poverty also deserves judicial cognizance."

Apart from whether there are constitutional rights burdened by the maximum grant, the interests at stake are different in character from the interests in the business and economic regulation and tax cases. Is the Court's approach in *Dandridge* consistent with its treatment of welfare in *Shapiro v. Thompson*, criticizing the effect of the classification involved as denying "food, shelter, and the other necessities of life" or in *Goldberg v. Kelly*, stressing the importance of the welfare interest? Consider Justice Marshall's argument in dissent in *Dandridge*:

This case, involving the literally vital interests of a powerless minority — poor families without breadwinners — is far removed from the area of business regulation, as the Court concedes. Why then is the standard used in those cases imposed here? We are told no more than that this case falls in "the area of economics and social welfare," with the implication that from there the answer is obvious. In my view, equal protection analysis of this case is not appreciably advanced by the a priori definition of a "right," fundamental or otherwise. Rather, concentration must be placed upon the character of the classification in question, the relative importance to individuals in the class discriminated against of the governmental benefits that they do not receive, and the asserted state interests in support of the classification.

***United States Department of Agriculture v. Moreno,* 413 U.S. 528 (1973).** The Court, per Justice Brennan, struck down § 3(e) of the Food Stamp Act which, with certain exceptions, excludes from participation in the program any household containing an individual who is unrelated to any other member of the household as violative of equal protection. The classification was said to be "clearly irrelevant to the declared purpose of the Act to safeguard the health and well-being of the Nation's population and raise levels of nutrition among low-income households." Nor did it "rationally further some [other] legitimate governmental interest."

Justice Douglas applied a strict scrutiny standard to the provision since he found that it curtailed the right to associate "to combat the common foe of hunger." Justice Rehnquist, joined by the Chief Justice, dissenting, argued that "the limitation which Congress enacted could, in the judgment of reasonable men, conceivably deny food stamps to members of households which have been formed solely for the purpose of taking advantage of the Food Stamp program. [T]his was a permissible congressional decision quite consistent with the underlying policy of the Act."

[2] Welfare and Abortion Funding

A major battleground of the war between pro-life and abortion forces has been the question of government funding of abortions for welfare recipients. Unlike the constitutions of many third world countries, the American Constitution is generally not read to impose affirmative duties on government to promote individual rights and interests. Instead, it is perceived as a series of prohibitions on government actions interfering with personal interests. Is denial of abortion funding to a welfare recipient simply a refusal to provide a benefit, or is it an impermissible interference with the right of the woman to choose an abortion? Can government, consistent with the equal protection guarantee, provide maternal benefits at the same time it denies abortion funding? Can government provide medically necessary services to welfare recipients but refuse to provide medically-necessary abortions? What standard of review is the Court to apply in determining the validity of such laws? These are some of the questions posed by the abortion funding cases.

HARRIS v. McRAE

448 U.S. 297, 100 S. Ct. 2671, 65 L. Ed. 2d 784 (1980)

JUSTICE STEWART delivered the opinion of the Court.

This case presents statutory and constitutional questions concerning the public funding of abortions under Title XIX of the Social Security Act, commonly known as the "Medicaid" Act, and recent annual appropriations acts containing the so-called "Hyde Amendment." The statutory question is whether Title XIX requires a State that participates in the Medicaid program to fund the cost of medically necessary abortions for which federal reimbursement is unavailable under the Hyde Amendment. The constitutional question, which arises only if Title XIX imposes no such requirement, is whether the Hyde Amendment, by denying public funding for certain medically necessary abortions, contravenes the liberty or equal protection guarantees of the Due Process Clause of the Fifth Amendment, or either of the Religion Clauses of the First Amendment.

The Medicaid program was created in 1965 for the purpose of providing federal financial assistance to States that choose to reimburse certain costs of medical treatment for needy persons. Although participation in the Medicaid program is entirely optional, once a State elects to participate, it must comply with the requirements of Title XIX.

Since September 1976, Congress has prohibited — either by an amendment to the annual appropriations bill for the Department of Health, Education, and Welfare or by a joint resolution — the use of any federal funds to reimburse the cost of abortions under the Medicaid program except under certain specified circumstances. This funding restriction is commonly known as the "Hyde Amendment," after its original congressional sponsor, Representative Hyde. The current version of the Hyde Amendment, applicable for fiscal year 1980, provides:

> [N]one of the funds provided by this joint resolution shall be used to perform abortions except where the life of the mother would be endangered if the fetus were carried to term; or except for such medical procedures necessary for the victims of rape or incest when such rape or incest has been reported promptly to a law enforcement agency or public health service.

[On the statutory question, the Court held that Title XIX does not require a participating State to pay for those medically necessary abortions for which federal reimbursement is unavailable under the Hyde Amendment. The Court then turned to the constitutional issues.]

It is well settled that, quite apart from the guarantee of equal protection, if a law "impinges upon a fundamental right explicitly or implicitly secured by the Constitution [it] is presumptively unconstitutional." *Mobile v. Bolden* (plurality opinion). Accordingly, before turning to the equal protection issue in this case, we examine whether the Hyde Amendment violates any substantive rights secured by the Constitution. We address first the appellees' argument that the Hyde Amendment, by restricting the availability for certain medically necessary abortions under Medicaid, impinges on the "liberty" protected by the Due Process Clause as recognized in *Roe v. Wade* and its progeny.

In *Maher v. Roe*, 432 U.S. 464 (1977), the Court was presented with the question whether the scope of personal constitutional freedom recognized in *Roe v. Wade* included an entitlement to Medicaid payments for abortions that are not medically necessary. At issue in *Maher* was a Connecticut welfare regulation under which Medicaid recipients received payments for medical services incident to childbirth, but not for medical services incident to nontherapeutic abortions. The District Court held that the regulation violated the Equal Protection Clause of the Fourteenth Amendment because the unequal subsidization of childbirth and abortion impinged on the "fundamental right to abortion" recognized in *Wade* and its progeny.

It was the view of this Court that "the District Court misconceived the nature and scope of the fundamental right recognized in *Roe*." The doctrine of *Roe v. Wade*, the Court held in *Maher*, "protects the woman from unduly burdensome interference with her freedom to decide whether to terminate her pregnancy," such as the severe criminal sanctions at issue in *Roe v. Wade*, or the absolute requirement of spousal consent for an abortion challenged in *Planned Parenthood of Central Missouri v. Danforth*. But the constitutional freedom recognized in *Wade* and its progeny, the *Maher* Court explained, did not prevent Connecticut from making "a value judgment favoring childbirth over abortion, and . . . implement[ing] that judgment by the allocation of public funds." As the Court elaborated:

> The Connecticut regulation before us is different in kind from the laws invalidated in our previous abortions decisions. The Connecticut regulation places no obstacles — absolute or otherwise — in the pregnant woman's path to an abortion. An indigent woman who desires an abortion suffers no disadvantage as a consequence of Connecticut's decision to fund childbirth; she continues as before to be dependent on private sources for the service she desires. The State may have made childbirth a more attractive alternative, thereby influencing the woman's decision, but it has imposed no restriction on access to abortions that was not already there. The indigency that may make it difficult — and in some cases, perhaps, impossible — for some women to have abortions is neither created nor in any way affected by the Connecticut regulation.

The Court in *Maher* noted that its description of the doctrine recognized in *Wade* and its progeny signaled "no retreat" from those decisions. In explaining why the constitutional principle recognized in *Wade* and later cases — protecting a woman's freedom of choice — did not translate into a constitutional obligation of Connecticut to subsidize abortions, the Court cited the "basic difference between direct state interference with a protected activity and state encouragement of an alternative activity consonant with legislative policy. Constitutional concerns are greatest when the State attempts to impose its will by force of law; the State's power to encourage actions deemed to be in the public interest is necessarily far broader." Thus, even though the

Connecticut regulation favored childbirth over abortion by means of subsidization of one and not the other, the Court in *Maher* concluded that the regulation did not impinge on the constitutional freedom recognized in *Wade* because it imposed no governmental restriction on access to abortions.

The Hyde Amendment, like the Connecticut welfare regulation at issue in *Maher*, places no governmental obstacle in the path of a woman who chooses to terminate her pregnancy, but rather, by means of unequal subsidization of abortion and other medical services, encourages alternative activity deemed in the public interest. The present case does differ factually from *Maher* insofar as that case involved a failure to fund nontherapeutic abortions, whereas the Hyde Amendment withholds funding of certain medically necessary abortions. Accordingly, the appellees argue that because the Hyde Amendment affects a significant interest not present or asserted in *Maher* — the interest of a woman in protecting her health during pregnancy — and because that interest lies at the core of the personal constitutional freedom recognized in *Wade*, the present case is constitutionally different from *Maher*. It is the appellees' view that to the extent that the Hyde Amendment withholds funding for certain medically necessary abortions, it clearly impinges on the constitutional principle recognized in *Wade*.

It is evident that a woman's interest in protecting her health was an important theme in *Wade*. In concluding that the freedom of a woman to decide whether to terminate her pregnancy falls within the personal liberty protected by the Due Process Clause, the Court in *Wade* emphasized the fact that the woman's decision carries with it significant personal health implications — both physical and psychological. In fact, [b]ecause even the compelling interest of the State in protecting potential life after fetal viability was held to be insufficient to outweigh a woman's decision to protect her life or health, it could be argued that the freedom of a woman to decide whether to terminate her pregnancy for health reasons does in fact lie at the core of the constitutional liberty identified in *Wade*.

But, regardless of whether the freedom of a woman to choose to terminate her pregnancy for health reasons lies at the core or the periphery of the due process liberty recognized in *Wade*, it simply does not follow that a woman's freedom of choice carries with it a constitutional entitlement to the financial resources to avail herself of the full range of protected choices. The reason why was explained in *Maher*: although government may not place obstacles in the path of a woman's exercise of her freedom of choice, it need not remove those not of its own creation. Indigency falls in the latter category. The financial constraints that restrict an indigent woman's ability to enjoy the full range of constitutionally protected freedom of choice are the product not of governmental restrictions on access to abortions, but rather of her indigency. Although Congress has opted to subsidize medically necessary services generally, but not certain medically necessary abortions, the fact remains that the Hyde Amendment leaves an indigent woman with at least the same range of choice in deciding whether to obtain a medically necessary abortion as she would have had if Congress had chosen to subsidize no health care costs at all. We are thus not persuaded that the Hyde Amendment impinges on the constitutionally protected freedom of choice recognized in *Wade*.[19]

Although the liberty protected by the Due Process Clause affords protection against unwarranted government interference with freedom of choice in the context of certain personal decisions, it does not confer an entitlement to such funds as may be necessary to realize all the advantages of that freedom. To hold otherwise would mark a drastic change in our understanding of the Constitution. To translate the limitation on governmental power implicit in the Due Process Clause into an affirmative funding obligation would require Congress to subsidize the medically necessary abortion of an indigent woman even if Congress had not enacted a Medicaid program to subsidize other medically necessary services. Nothing in the Due Process Clause supports such an extraordinary result. Whether freedom of choice that is constitutionally protected warrants federal subsidization is a question for Congress to answer, not a matter of constitutional entitlement. Accordingly, we conclude that the Hyde Amendment does not impinge on the due process liberty recognized in *Wade*.

It remains to be determined whether the Hyde Amendment violates the equal protection component of the Fifth Amendment. This challenge is premised on the fact that, although federal reimbursement is available under Medicaid for medically necessary services generally, the Hyde Amendment does not permit federal reimbursement of all medically necessary abortions. The District Court held, and the appellees argue here, that this selective subsidization violates the constitutional guarantee of equal protection. The guarantee of equal protection under the Fifth Amendment is not a source of substantive rights or liberties,[25] but rather a right to be free from invidious discrimination in statutory classifications and other governmental activity. It is well-settled that where a statutory classification does not itself impinge on a right or liberty protected by the Constitution, the validity of classification must be sustained unless "the classification rests on grounds wholly irrelevant to the achievement of [any legitimate governmental] objective."

[19] The appellees argued that the Hyde Amendment is unconstitutional because it "penalizes" the exercise of a woman's choice to terminate a pregnancy by abortion. This argument falls short of the mark. In *Maher*, the Court found only a "semantic difference" between the argument that Connecticut's refusal to subsidize nontherapeutic abortions "unduly interfere[d]" with the exercise of the constitutional liberty recognized in *Wade* and the argument that it "penalized" the exercise of that liberty. And, regardless of how the claim was characterized, the *Maher* Court rejected the argument that Connecticut's refusal to subsidize protected conduct, without more, impinged on the constitutional freedom of choice. This reasoning is equally applicable in the present case. A substantial constitutional question would arise if Congress had attempted to withhold all Medicaid benefits from an otherwise eligible candidate simply because that candidate had exercised her constitutionally protected freedom to terminate her pregnancy by abortion. But the Hyde Amendment does not provide for such a broad disqualification from receipt of public benefits. Rather, the Hyde Amendment, like the Connecticut welfare provision at issue in *Maher*, represents simply a refusal to subsidize certain protected conduct. A refusal to fund protected activity, without more, cannot be equated with the imposition of a "penalty" on that activity.

[25] An exception to this statement is to be found in *Reynolds v. Sims*, and its progeny. Although the Constitution of the United States does not confer the right to vote in state elections, *Reynolds* held that if a State adopts an electoral system, the Equal Protection Clause of the Fourteenth Amendment confers upon a qualified voter a substantive right to participate in the electoral process equally with other qualified voters.

For the reasons stated above, we have already concluded that the Hyde Amendment violates no constitutionally protected substantive rights. We now conclude as well that it is not predicated on a constitutionally suspect classification. In reaching this conclusion, we again draw guidance from the Court's decision in *Maher v. Roe*. As to whether the Connecticut welfare regulation providing funds for childbirth but not for nontherapeutic abortions discriminated against a suspect class, the Court in *Maher* observed:

> An indigent woman desiring an abortion does not come within the limited category of disadvantaged classes so recognized by our cases. Nor does the fact that the impact of the regulation falls upon those who cannot pay lead to a different conclusion. In a sense, every denial of welfare to an indigent creates a wealth classification as compared to nonindigents who are able to pay for the desired goods or services. But this Court has never held that financial need alone identifies a suspect class for purposes of equal protection analysis.

Thus, the Court in *Maher* found no basis for concluding that the Connecticut regulation was predicated on a suspect classification.

It is our view that the present case is indistinguishable from *Maher* in this respect. Here, as in *Maher*, the principal impact of the Hyde Amendment falls on the indigent. But that fact does not itself render the funding restriction constitutionally invalid, for this Court has held repeatedly that poverty, standing alone, is not a suspect classification. *See, e.g., James v. Valtierra*. That *Maher* involved the refusal to fund nontherapeutic abortions, whereas the present case involves the refusal to fund medically necessary abortions, has no bearing on the factors that render a classification "suspect" within the meaning of the constitutional guarantee of equal protection.

The remaining question then is whether the Hyde Amendment is rationally related to a legitimate governmental objective. It is the Government's position that the Hyde Amendment bears a rational relationship to its legitimate interest in protecting the potential life of the fetus. We agree. [T]he Hyde Amendment, by encouraging childbirth except in the most urgent circumstances, is rationally related to the legitimate governmental objective of protecting potential life. By subsidizing the medical expenses of indigent women who carry their pregnancies to term while not subsidizing the comparable expenses of women who undergo abortions (except those whose lives are threatened), Congress has established incentives that make childbirth a more attractive alternative than abortion for persons eligible for Medicaid. These incentives bear a direct relationship to the legitimate congressional interest in protecting potential life. Nor is it irrational that Congress has authorized federal reimbursement for medically necessary services generally, but not for certain medically necessary abortions. Abortion is inherently different from other medical procedures, because no other procedure involves the purposeful termination of a potential life.

After conducting an extensive evidentiary hearing into issues surrounding the public funding of abortions, the District Court concluded that "[t]he interests of the federal government in the fetus and in preserving it are not sufficient, weighed in the balance with the woman's threatened health, to justify withdrawing medical assistance unless the woman consents to carry the fetus to term." In making an independent appraisal of the competing interests involved here, the District Court went beyond the judicial function. Such decisions are entrusted under the Constitution to Congress, not the courts. It is the role of the courts only to ensure that congressional decisions comport with the Constitution.

Where, as here, the Congress has neither invaded a substantive constitutional right or freedom, nor enacted legislation that purposefully operates to the detriment of a suspect class, the only requirement of equal protection is that congressional action be rationally related to legitimate governmental interest. The Hyde Amendment satisfies that standard. It is not the mission of this Court or any other to decide whether the balance of competing interests reflected in the Hyde Amendment is wise social policy.

JUSTICE BRENNAN, with whom JUSTICES MARSHALL and BLACKMUN join, dissenting.

Roe and its progeny established that the pregnant woman has a right to be free from state interference with her choice to have an abortion — a right which, at least prior to the end of the first trimester, absolutely prohibits any governmental regulation of that highly personal decision. The proposition for which these cases stand thus is not that the State is under an affirmative obligation to ensure access to abortions for all who may desire them; it is that the State must refrain from wielding its enormous power and influence in a manner that might burden the pregnant woman's freedom to choose whether to have an abortion. The Hyde Amendment's denial of public funds for medically necessary abortions plainly intrudes upon this constitutionally protected decision, for both by design and in effect it serves to coerce indigent pregnant women to bear children that they would otherwise elect not to have.

The fundamental flaw in the Court's due process analysis, then, is its failure to acknowledge that the discriminatory distribution of the benefits of governmental largesse can discourage the exercise of fundamental liberties just as effectively as can an outright denial of those rights through criminal and regulatory sanctions. Implicit in the Court's reasoning is the notion that as long as the government is not obligated to provide its citizens with certain benefits or privileges, it may condition the grant of such benefits on the recipient's relinquishment of his constitutional rights.

JUSTICE STEVENS, dissenting.

This case involves a special exclusion of women who, by definition, are confronted with a choice between two serious harms: serious health damage to themselves on the one hand and abortion on the other. The competing interests are the interest in maternal health and the interest in protecting potential human life. It is now part of our law that the pregnant woman's decision as to which of these conflicting interests shall prevail is entitled to constitutional protection.

If a woman has a constitutional right to place a higher value on a avoiding either serious harm to her own health or perhaps an abnormal childbirth than on protecting potential life, the exercise of that right cannot provide the basis for the denial of a benefit to which she would otherwise be entitled. The Court's sterile equal protection analysis evades this critical though simple point.

NOTES

1. *A right to abortion funding.* The claim of those seeking abortion funding is usually not premised on a claim of a due process right to public support for abortion. As indicated above, American constitutional law has not generally recognized an affirmative duty of government to correct the inequities in society. There are, however, occasions when the Court has imposed an affirmative duty on the government to provide free services to indigents or an affirmative constitutional duty to remedy private discrimination. *See, e.g., Boddie v. Connecticut* (state cannot deny access to divorce courts solely because of a person's inability to pay consistent with due process); *White Primary Cases*, p. 1496 (state cannot disclaim responsibility for racial discrimination in election primaries conducted by private groups).

This duty, however, has generally been imposed only where the state possesses a monopoly over an important commodity or service or the activity is "traditionally and exclusively" a state function. Does the state have a practical monopoly on abortion services for the indigent?

2. *Penalizing rights.* In the abortion funding cases, the Court rejects the claim that the challenged laws impose an impermissible burden or penalty on the exercise of a fundamental right. Professor Simson, disagreeing with the *Maher* Court's conclusions, describes the abortion right as based on "an interest in deciding free from state interference whether or not to seek an abortion in the first place." It was this right, Professor Simson argues, that the *Maher* case undermined. "[B]y offering to pay indigent women's childbirth expenses but not the cost of their having abortions, Connecticut substantially interferes with needy women's decisions as to whether or not to have an abortion. Under Connecticut's discriminatory funding scheme, money becomes a factor that weighs heavily against abortions." Gary Simson, *Abortion, Poverty and the Equal Protection of the Laws*, 13 Ga. L. Rev. 505, 508–09 (1979). Does *Harris* avoid fundamental rights expansion "by a rule requiring direct, substantial, and absolute obstruction of the opportunity to exercise the right?" James Kushner, *Substantive Equal Protection: The Rehnquist Court and the Fourth Tier of Judicial Review*, 53 Mo. L. Rev. 423, 434 (1988). How does this argument fare when applied to *Harris v. McRae*? Note that the Hyde Amendment would not permit therapeutic, medically necessary abortions. Could a state constitutionally fund abortions while refusing to pay maternity benefits?

3. *Unconstitutional conditions.* It is a basic constitutional principle that government cannot condition the receipt of a public benefit on surrender of constitutional rights. Kathleen Sullivan, *Unconstitutional Conditions*, 102 Harv. L. Rev. 1415 (1989), explains that "the doctrine of unconstitutional conditions holds that government may not grant a benefit on the condition that the beneficiary surrender a constitutional right, even if the government may withhold that benefit altogether. It reflects the triumph of the view that government may not do indirectly what it may not do directly over the view that the greater power to deny a benefit includes the lesser power to impose a condition on its receipt."

Can this principle be applied to the refusal of government to fund abortions while it funds childbirth? Has government "bought up" the abortion rights of the poor by offering to pay the cost of childbirth? *See Rust v. Sullivan*, p. 1142, upholding regulations limiting the ability of recipients of federal funding from engaging in abortion referral, advocacy and counseling activities. Professor Sullivan offers this possible explanation for the failure of the unconstitutional condition doctrine in the abortion funding cases: "Not only has [the Court] found coercion sometimes empirically wanting, but it has also found coercion conceptually impossible when government has merely declined to subsidize a right. This penalty/nonsubsidy distinction has increasingly determined the outcomes of unconstitutional conditions challenges. 'Penalties' coerce; 'nonsubsidies' do not." Sullivan, 102 HARV. L. REV. at 1439.

4. *State purposes.* Professor Perry contends that floor debates on the Hyde Amendment relied explicitly on the view that abortion is "morally objectionable" and that *Roe v. Wade* made that view "illicit." Michael Perry, *Why the Supreme Court Was Plainly Wrong in the Hyde Amendment Case: A Brief Comment on Harris v. McRae*, 32 STAN. L. REV. 1113 (1980). Thus, "the central question in *McRae* ought to have been whether the Hyde Amendment is predicated on the illicit view. [T]he crucial question, which the Court completely overlooked, is whether the 'value judgment favoring childbirth' embodied in governmental 'encouragement of an alternative activity' is predicated on the view that abortion is per se — and not because of its effect on other government interests — morally objectionable." Peter Westen, *Correspondence*, 33 STAN. L. REV. 1187 (1981), responds that "[n]o one can deny that Professor Perry's conclusion follows from his premises. As with most syllogisms, however, the real issue is the validity of the major premise — that *Roe* necessarily prohibited the state from taking any action premised on moral objections to abortion."

[3] Economic Inequalities and a Right to Education

Education was identified by Michelman as one of his "just wants" affected by economic inequality. Denial of equal educational opportunity may arise not only from racial discrimination but also from fiscal disparities between educational districts. The problem arises from traditional reliance on the property tax for the bulk of the local share of educational revenues. Since the taxable property wealth of districts varies greatly, so do the resources available per child. Resources available for education reflect in part the property wealth of the district. But the question is whether this presents a constitutional problem.

SAN ANTONIO INDEPENDENT SCHOOL DIST. v. RODRIGUEZ

411 U.S. 1, 93 S. Ct. 1278, 36 L. Ed. 2d 16 (1973)

JUSTICE POWELL delivered the opinion of the Court.

This suit attacking the Texas system of financing public education was initiated by Mexican-American parents [as] a class action on behalf of school children throughout the State who are members of minority groups or who are poor and reside in school districts having a low property tax base. The District Court held that the Texas system discriminates on the basis of wealth in the manner in which education is provided for its people. Finding that wealth is a "suspect" classification and that education is a "fundamental" interest, the District Court held that the Texas system could be sustained only if the State could show that it was premised upon some compelling state interest. On this issue the court concluded that "[n]ot only are defendants unable to demonstrate compelling state interests they fail even to establish a reasonable basis for these classifications."

The wealth discrimination discovered by the District Court in this case, and by several other courts that have recently struck down school financing laws in other States, is quite unlike any of the forms of wealth discrimination heretofore reviewed by this Court. The Texas system of school finance might be regarded as discriminating (1) against "poor" persons whose incomes fall below some identifiable level of poverty or who might be characterized as functionally "indigent," or (2) against those who are relatively poorer than others, or (3) against all those who, irrespective of their personal incomes, happen to reside in relatively poorer school districts. The individuals, or groups of individuals, who constituted the class discriminated against in our prior cases shared two distinguishing characteristics: because of their impecunity they were completely unable to pay for some desired benefit, and as a consequence, they sustained an absolute deprivation of a meaningful opportunity to enjoy that benefit.

Only appellees' first possible basis for describing the class disadvantaged by the Texas school-financing system — discrimination against a class of definably "poor" persons — might arguably meet the criteria established in these prior cases. Even a cursory examination, however, demonstrates that neither of the two distinguishing characteristics of wealth classifications can be found here.

First, in support of their charge that the system discriminates against the "poor," appellees have made no effort to demonstrate that it operates to the peculiar disadvantage of any class fairly definable as indigent, or as composed of persons whose incomes are beneath any designated poverty level. Indeed, there is reason to believe that the poorest families are not necessarily clustered in the poorest property districts.

Second, neither appellees nor the District Court addressed the fact that, unlike each of the foregoing cases, lack of personal resources has not occasioned an absolute deprivation of the desired benefit. The argument here is not that the children in districts having relatively low assessable property values are receiving no public education; rather, it is that they are receiving a poorer quality education than that available to children in districts having more assessable wealth. Apart from the unsettled and disputed question whether the quality of education may be determined by the amount of money expended for it, a sufficient answer to appellees' argument is that, at least where wealth is involved, the Equal Protection Clause does not require absolute equality or precisely equal advantages.

For these two reasons — the absence of any evidence that the financing system discriminates against any definable category of "poor" people or that it results in the absolute deprivation of education — the disadvantaged class is not susceptible of identification in traditional terms.

However described, it is clear that appellees' suit asks this Court to extend its most exacting scrutiny to review a system that allegedly discriminates against a large, diverse, and amorphous class, unified only by the common factor of residence in districts that happen to have less taxable wealth than other districts. The system of alleged discrimination and the class it defines have none of the traditional indicia of suspectness: the class is not saddled with such disabilities, or subjected to such a history of purposeful unequal treatment, or relegated to such a position of political powerlessness as to command extraordinary protection from the majoritarian political process.

We thus conclude that the Texas system does not operate to the peculiar disadvantage of any suspect class. But in recognition of the fact that this Court has never heretofore held that wealth discrimination alone provides an adequate basis for invoking strict scrutiny, appellees have not relied solely on this contention. They also assert that the State's system impermissibly interferes with the exercise of a "fundamental" right and that accordingly the prior decisions of this Court require the application of the strict standard of judicial review. It is this question — whether education is a fundamental right, in the sense that it is among the rights and liberties protected by the Constitution — which has so consumed the attention of courts and commentators in recent years.

The importance of a service performed by the State does not determine whether it must be regarded as fundamental for purposes of examination under the Equal Protection Clause. The lesson of [prior] cases in addressing the question now before the Court is plain. It is not the province of this Court to create substantive constitutional rights in the name of guaranteeing equal protection of the laws. Thus, the key to discovering whether education is "fundamental" is not to be found in comparisons of the relative societal significance of education as opposed to subsistence or housing. Nor is it to be found by weighing whether education is as important as the right to travel. Rather, the answer lies in assessing whether there is a right to education explicitly or implicitly guaranteed by the Constitution. *Eisenstadt v. Baird*; *Dunn v. Blumstein*; *Skinner v. Oklahoma*.

Education, of course, is not among the rights afforded explicit protection under our Federal Constitution. Nor do we find any basis for saying it is implicitly so protected. It is appellees' contention, however, that education is distinguishable from other services and benefits provided by the State because it bears a peculiarly close relationship to other rights and liberties accorded protection under the Constitution. Specifically, they insist that education is itself a fundamental personal right because it is essential to the effective exercise of First Amendment freedoms and to intelligent utilization of the right to vote. In asserting a nexus between speech and education, appellees urge the right to speak is meaningless unless the speaker is capable of articulating his thoughts intelligently and persuasively. Likewise, they argue that the corollary right to receive information becomes little more than a hollow privilege when the recipient has not been taught to read, assimilate, and utilize available knowledge.

We need not dispute any of these propositions. Yet we have never presumed to possess either the ability or the authority to guarantee to the citizenry the most effective speech or the most informed electoral choice. That these may be desirable goals of a system of freedom of expression and of a representative form of government is not to be doubted. But they are not values to be implemented by judicial intrusion into otherwise legitimate state activities.

Even if it were conceded that some identifiable quantum of education is a constitutionally protected prerequisite to the meaningful exercise of either right, we have no indication that the present levels of educational expenditure in Texas provide an education that falls short. [T]hat argument provides no basis for finding an interference with fundamental rights where only relative differences in spending levels are involved and where no charge fairly could be made that the system fails to provide each child with an opportunity to acquire the basic minimal skills necessary for the enjoyment of the rights of speech and of full participation in the political process.

Furthermore, the logical limitations on appellees' nexus theory are difficult to perceive. How, for instance, is education to be distinguished from the significant personal interests in the basics of decent food and shelter? Empirical examination might well buttress an assumption that the ill-fed, ill-clothed, and ill-housed are among the most ineffective participants in the political process and that they derive the least enjoyment from the benefits of the First Amendment. If so appellees' thesis would cast serious doubt on the authority of *Dandridge v. Williams*.

In one further respect we find this a particularly inappropriate case in which to subject state action to strict judicial scrutiny. Each of our prior cases involved legislation which "deprived," "infringed," or "interfered" with the free exercise of some such fundamental personal right or liberty. A critical distinction between those cases and the one now before us lies in what Texas is endeavoring to do with respect to education. Every step leading to the establishment of the system Texas utilizes today — including the decisions permitting localities to tax and expend locally, and creating and continuously expanding the state aid — was implemented in an effort to extend public education and to improve its quality. Of course, every reform that benefits some more than others may be criticized for what it fails to accomplish. But we think it plain that, in substance, the thrust of the Texas system is affirmative and reformatory and, therefore, should be scrutinized under judicial principles sensitive to the nature of the State's efforts and to the rights reserved to the States under the Constitution.

We need not rest our decision, however, solely on the inappropriateness of the strict-scrutiny test. A century of Supreme Court adjudication under the Equal Protection Clause affirmatively supports the application of the traditional standard of review, which requires only that the State's system be shown to bear some rational relationship to legitimate state purposes. This case represents a direct attack on the way in which Texas has chosen to raise and disburse state and local tax revenues. In so doing, appellees would have the Court intrude in an area in which it has traditionally deferred to state legislatures.

In addition to matters of fiscal policy, this case also involves the most persistent and difficult questions of educational policy, another area in which this Court's lack of specialized knowledge and experience counsels against premature interference with the informed judgments made at the state and local levels. Education, perhaps even more than welfare assistance, presents a myriad of "intractable economic, social, and even philosophical problems." *Dandridge v. Williams.*

In sum, to the extent that the Texas system of school finance results in unequal expenditures between children who happen to reside in different districts, we cannot say that such disparities are the product of a system that is so irrational as to be invidiously discriminatory. One also must remember that the system here challenged is not peculiar to Texas or to any other State. In its essential characteristics the Texas plan for financing public education reflects what many educators for a half century have thought was an enlightened approach to a problem for which there is no perfect solution. We are unwilling to assume for ourselves a level of wisdom superior to that of legislators, scholars, and educational authorities in 50 States, especially where the alternatives proposed are only recently conceived and nowhere yet tested.

These practical considerations, of course, play no role in the adjudication of the constitutional issues presented here. But they serve to highlight the wisdom of the traditional limitations on this Court's function.

JUSTICE WHITE, with whom JUSTICES DOUGLAS and BRENNAN join, dissenting.

If the State aims at maximizing local initiative and local choice, by permitting school districts to resort to the real property tax if they choose to do so, it utterly fails in achieving its purpose in districts with property tax bases so low that there is little if any opportunity for interested parents, rich or poor, to augment school district revenues. Requiring the State to establish only that unequal treatment is in furtherance of a permissible goal, without also requiring the State to show that the means chosen to effectuate that goal are rationally related to its achievement, makes equal protection analysis no more than an empty gesture.

JUSTICE MARSHALL, with whom JUSTICE DOUGLAS concurs, dissenting.

To begin, I must once more voice my disagreement with the Court's rigidified approach to equal protection analysis. The Court apparently seeks to establish today that equal protection cases fall into one of two neat categories which dictate the appropriate standard of review — strict scrutiny or mere rationality. But this Court's decisions in the field of equal protection defy such easy categorization. A principled reading of what this Court has done reveals that it has applied a spectrum of standards in reviewing discrimination allegedly violative of the Equal Protection Clause. This spectrum clearly comprehends variations in the degree of care with which the Court will scrutinize particular classifications, depending, I believe, on the constitutional and societal importance of the interest adversely affected and the recognized invidiousness of the basis upon which the particular classification is drawn. I find in fact that many of the Court's recent decisions embody the very sort of reasoned approach to equal protection analysis for which I previously argued. *Dandridge v. Williams* (dissenting opinion).

I therefore cannot accept the majority's labored efforts to demonstrate that fundamental interests, which call for strict scrutiny of the challenged classification, encompass only established rights which we are somehow bound to recognize from the text of the Constitution itself. To be sure, some interests which the Court has deemed to be fundamental for purposes of equal protection analysis are themselves constitutionally protected rights. [*Shapiro v. Thompson*.] But it will not do to suggest that the "answer" to whether an interest is fundamental for purposes of equal protection analysis is always determined by whether that interest "is a right explicitly or implicitly guaranteed by the Constitution."

I would like to know where the Constitution guarantees the right to procreate, *Skinner v. Oklahoma*, or the right to vote in state elections, *e.g.*, *Reynolds v. Sims*, or the right to an appeal from a criminal conviction, *e.g.*, *Griffin v. Illinois*. These are instances in which, due to the importance of the interests at stake, the Court has displayed a strong concern with the existence of discriminatory state treatment. But the Court has never said or indicated that these are interests which independently enjoy full-blown constitutional protection.

The majority is, of course, correct when it suggests that the process of determining which interests are fundamental is a difficult one. But I do not think the problem is insurmountable. And I certainly do not accept the view that the process need necessarily degenerate into an unprincipled, subjective "picking-and-choosing" between various interests or that it must involve this Court in creating "substantive constitutional rights in the name of guaranteeing equal protection of the laws." Although not all fundamental interests are constitutionally guaranteed, the determination of which interests are fundamental should be firmly rooted in the text of the Constitution. The task in every case should be to determine the extent to which constitutionally guaranteed rights are dependent on interests not mentioned in the Constitution. As the nexus between the specific constitutional guarantee and the nonconstitutional interest draws closer, the nonconstitutional interest becomes more fundamental and the degree of judicial scrutiny applied when the interest is infringed on a discriminatory basis must be adjusted accordingly. Thus, it cannot be denied that interests such as procreation, the exercise of the state franchise, and access to criminal appellate processes are not fully guaranteed to the citizen by our Constitution. But these interests have nonetheless been afforded special judicial consideration in the face of discrimination because they are, to some extent, interrelated with constitutional guarantees.

[T]he Court concludes that public education is not constitutionally guaranteed. It is true that this Court has never deemed the provision of free public education to be required by the Constitution. Nevertheless, the fundamental importance of education is amply indicated by the prior decisions of this Court, by the unique status accorded public education by our society, and by the close relationship between education and some of our most basic constitutional values. It is this very sort of intimate relationship between a particular personal interest and specific constitutional guarantees that has heretofore caused the Court to attach special significance, for purposes of equal protection analysis, to individual interests such as procreation and the exercise of state franchise.

The factors just considered, including the relationship between education and the social and political interests enshrined within the Constitution, compel us to recognize the fundamentality of education and to scrutinize with appropriate care the basis for state discrimination affecting equality of educational opportunity in Texas' school districts — a conclusion which is only strengthened when we consider the character of the classification in this case.

This is not to say that the form of wealth classification in this case does not differ significantly from those recognized in the previous decisions of this Court. Our prior cases have dealt essentially with discrimination on the basis of personal wealth. Here, by contrast, the children of the disadvantaged Texas school districts are being discriminated against not necessarily because of their personal wealth or the wealth of their families, but because of the taxable property wealth of the residents of the district in which they happen to live. The appropriate question, then, is whether the same degree of judicial solicitude and scrutiny that has previously been afforded wealth classifications is warranted here. [W]e have generally gauged the invidiousness of wealth classifications with an awareness of the importance of the interests being affected and the relevance of personal wealth to those interests. *See Harper v. Virginia Bd. of Elections.*

[I]nsofar as group wealth discrimination involves wealth over which the disadvantaged individual has no significant control, it represents in fact a more serious basis of discrimination than does personal wealth. For such discrimination is no reflection of the individual's characteristics or his abilities. And thus — particularly in the context of a disadvantaged class composed of children — we have previously treated discrimination on a basis which the individual cannot control as constitutionally disfavored.

The disability of the disadvantaged class in this case extends as well into the political processes upon which we ordinarily rely as adequate for the protection and promotion of all interests. Here legislative reallocation of the State's property wealth must be sought in the face of inevitable opposition from significantly advantaged districts that have a strong vested interest in the preservation of the status quo. Nor can we ignore the extent to which, in contrast to our prior decisions, the State is responsible for the wealth discrimination in this instance. [T]his case, in contrast to the Court's previous wealth discrimination decisions, can only be seen as "unusual in the extent to which governmental action is the cause of the wealth classifications." In the final analysis, then, the invidious characteristics of the group wealth classification present in this case merely serve to emphasize the need for careful judicial scrutiny of the State's justifications for the resulting interdistrict discrimination in the educational opportunity afforded to the schoolchildren of Texas.

The nature of our inquiry into the justifications for state discrimination is essentially the same in all equal protection cases: We must consider the substantiality of the state interests sought to be served, and we must scrutinize the reasonableness of the means by which the State has sought to advance its interests. At the outset, I do not question that local control of public education, as an abstract matter, constitutes a very substantial state interest. But I need not now decide how I might ultimately strike the balance were we confronted with the situation where the State's sincere concern for local control inevitably produced educational inequality. For on this record, it is apparent that the State's purported concern with local control is offered primarily as an excuse rather than as a justification for interdistrict inequality.

In fact, the Texas scheme produces precisely the opposite result. Local school districts cannot choose to have the best education in the State by imposing the highest tax rate. Instead, the quality of the educational opportunity offered by any particular district is largely determined by the amount of taxable property located in a district — a factor over which local voters can exercise no control. At the same time, appellees have pointed out a variety of alternative financing schemes which may serve the State's purported interest in local control as well as, if not better than, the present scheme without the current impairment of the educational opportunity of vast numbers of Texas schoolchildren.

NOTES

1. *Fundamental rights.* *Rodriguez* establishes that the importance of the interest is, in itself, insufficient to trigger strict scrutiny under the new equal protection. In *Serrano v. Priest*, 96 Cal. Rptr. 601, 487 P.2d 1241 (1971), the state court, in addition to holding district wealth to be suspect, also held that education was fundamental. "[F]irst, education is a major determinant of an individual's chances for economic and social success in our competitive society; second, education is a unique influence on a child's development as a citizen and his participation in political and community life. [E]ducation is the lifeline of both the individual and society."

Compare Edward B. Foley, Rodriguez *Revisited: Constitutional Theory and School Finance*, 32 Ga. L. Rev. 475, 479 (1998), who argues that "as long as all children receive a certain minimum level of educational opportunity, the fact that some children receive better opportunities does not necessarily violate the principle of intrinsic equality. This is true even if the educational inequalities are caused by inequalities in the taxable wealth of the local communities in which these children reside. Thus, the result in *Rodriguez* is not inconsistent with interpreting the Equal Protection Clause to conform to the dictates of intrinsic equality." But he claims that "[t]he principle of intrinsic equality does require a minimum level of educational opportunity. [T]he Constitution guarantees all children of normal intelligence the opportunity to receive an education that prepares them for the rights and responsibilities of adult citizenship in a democratic society. Indeed, the *Rodriguez* Court explicitly recognized this possibility."

2. *The demise of fundamental rights equal protection.* Michael J. Klarman, *An Interpretative History of Modern Equal Protection*, 90 Mich. L. Rev. 213, 288 (1991) says, "Not only did Rodriguez reject the notion implicit in Brown, that education was a fundamental right, but also the Court declares its unwillingness to identify for equal protection purposes fundamental rights that were not explicitly embraced in, or implicitly derivable from, the constitutional text." Professor Klarman concludes: "Rodriguez seemed, in short, to compel the conclusion that future fundamental rights strand expansion was out of the question." Laurence Tribe, Saenz *Sans Prophecy: Does the Privileges* *or Immunities Revival Portend the Future — or Reveal the Past*, 113 Harv. L. Rev. 110, 125 (1999), says "the *Rodriguez* Court more or less buried the equal protection jurisprudence of which *Shapiro* had been a part, indicating that the era of judicially generated fundamental rights had drawn to a close."

3. *Village of Belle Terre v. Boraas*, 416 U.S. 1 (1974). A zoning ordinance limiting occupancy of one-family dwelling places to traditional families, or groups of not more than two unrelated persons, was upheld in, against claims that it violated the rights to travel, privacy, association, and equal protection. Justice Douglas, for the majority, characterized the law as involving "social and economic legislation" and applied the traditional rational basis test. He saw the measure as a form of aesthetic zoning. "A quiet place where yards are wide, people few, and motor vehicles restricted are legitimate guidelines in a land use project addressed to family needs. The police power is ample to lay out zones where family values, youth values, and the blessings of quiet seclusion and clean air make the area a sanctuary for people."

The limitation of families to two unrelated persons was dismissed by noting that "every line drawn by a legislature leaves some out that might well have been included. That exercise of discretion, however, is a legislative not a judicial function."

Justice Marshall, dissenting, argued that the limitation on unrelated households to two persons, while placing no limitations on households of related individuals, "burdens the students' rights of association and privacy guaranteed by the First and Fourteenth Amendments." Applying "strict equal protection scrutiny," he reasoned that "Belle Terre imposes upon those who deviate from the community norm in their choice of living companions significantly greater restrictions than are applied to residential groups who are related by blood or marriage, and comprise the established order within the community. The town has, in effect, acted to fence out those individuals whose choice of lifestyle differs from that of its current residents." While admitting the community's interest in aesthetic zoning, Justice Marshall found the means chosen both over-and under-inclusive and contended that they could be "as effectively achieved by means of an ordinance that did not discriminate on the basis of constitutionally protected choices of lifestyle."

4. *Marshall v. United States*, 414 U.S. 417 (1974). The Court (6-3), per Chief Justice Burger, upheld a provision of the Narcotics Rehabilitation Act of 1966 disqualifying individuals with two prior felony convictions from taking advantage of the rehabilitative benefits of the Act. Following the logic of the court of appeals that "there is no 'fundamental right' to rehabilitation from narcotic addiction at public expense," the Court applied a rational basis standard of review. Congress could rationally conclude that an addict with a multiple-felony record is less likely to benefit from rehabilitative treatment, might present an impediment to the treatment of others, and could be a greater threat to society upon release.

5. *State constitutional law.* All of the arguments made in *Rodrigez* have been replayed in litigation brought under state constitutions but occasionally with different results. In addition to equal protection, state constitutions also generally contain an education clause, usually requiring that state legislatures provide "a thorough and efficient system" of public schools. Enrich,

Leaving Equality Behind: New Directions in School Finance Reform, 48 VAND. L. REV. 101, 108–9 (1995), notes that in addition to arguments for equality of funding or quality of education, these cases also raise another line of argument:

> [T]he claimed right is a substantive right to a particular category of governmental services — public schooling. This reorientation opens the way to a crucial shift of focus, away from educational equality and toward educational adequacy. Adequacy arguments, instead of asking comparative questions about the differences in the resources or opportunities available to children in different districts, look directly at the quality of the educational services delivered to children in disadvantaged districts and ask evaluative questions about whether those services are sufficient to satisfy the state's constitutional obligations.

Professor Enrich indicates that these adequacy arguments avoid some problems of equality arguments, such as the difficulty of defining the "precise content" of equality for educational funding and that "equality — whatever its precise meaning and whatever its centrality among our shared societal and legal norms — can suddenly loom too large, threatening to demand too much and to overwhelm other important concerns." Douglas S. Reed, *Twenty-Five Years After* Rodriguez: *School Finance Litigation and the Impact of the New Judicial Federalism,* 32 LAW & SOC'Y REV. 175, 176 (1998), notes that these claims have been pursued to state supreme courts in 36 states, winning 20 of the decisions. He concludes "that within the realm of school finance reform, state supreme courts have had a significant and durable impact on the distribution of educational resource." *Id.* at 214. *See generally* Macchiarola & Diaz, *Disorder in the Courts: The Aftermath of* San Antonio Independent School District v. Rodriguez *in the State Courts,* 30 VAL. U.L. REV. 551 (1996).

PLYLER v. DOE

457 U.S. 202, 102 S. Ct. 2382, 72 L. Ed. 2d 786 (1982)

JUSTICE BRENNAN delivered the opinion of the Court.

The question presented by these cases is whether, consistent with the Equal Protection Clause of the Fourteenth Amendment, Texas may deny to undocumented school-age children the free public education that it provides to children who are citizens of the United States or legally admitted aliens. In May 1975, the Texas legislature revised its education laws to withhold from local school districts any state funds for the education of children who were not "legally admitted" into the United States. The 1975 revision also authorized local school districts to deny enrollment in their public schools to children not "legally admitted" to the country. These cases involve constitutional challenges to those provisions.

Appellants argue at the outset that undocumented aliens, because of their immigration status, are not "persons within the jurisdiction" of the State of Texas, and that they therefore have no right to the equal protection of Texas law. We reject this argument. Whatever his status under the immigration laws, an alien is surely a "person" in any ordinary sense of that term. Aliens, even aliens whose presence in this country is unlawful, have long been recognized as "persons" guaranteed due process of law by the Fifth and Fourteenth Amendments. Indeed, we have clearly held that the Fifth Amendment protects aliens whose presence in this country is unlawful from invidious discrimination by the Federal Government.

[W]e have treated as presumptively invidious those classifications that disadvantage a "suspect class," or that impinge upon the exercise of a "fundamental right." With respect to such classifications, it is appropriate to enforce the mandate of equal protection by requiring the State to demonstrate that its classification has been precisely tailored to serve a compelling governmental interest. In addition, we have recognized that certain forms of legislative classification, while not facially invidious, nonetheless give rise to recurring constitutional difficulties; in these limited circumstances we have sought the assurance that the classification reflects a reasoned judgment consistent with the ideal of equal protection by inquiring whether it may fairly be viewed as furthering a substantial interest of the State. We turn to a consideration of the standard appropriate for the evaluation of § 21.031.

Sheer incapability or lax enforcement of the laws barring entry into this country, coupled with the failure to establish an effective bar to the employment of undocumented aliens, has resulted in the creation of a substantial "shadow population" of illegal migrants — numbering in the millions — within our borders. This situation raises the specter of a permanent caste of undocumented resident aliens, encouraged by some to remain here as a source of cheap labor, but nevertheless denied the benefits that our society makes available to citizens and lawful residents. The existence of such an underclass presents most difficult problems for a Nation that prides itself on adherence to principles of equality under law.[19]

The children who are plaintiffs in these cases are special members of this underclass. Persuasive arguments support the view that a State may withhold its beneficence from those whose very presence within the United States is the product of their own unlawful conduct. These arguments do not apply with the same force to classifications imposing disabilities on the minor children of such illegal entrants. At the least, those who elect to enter our territory by stealth and in violation of our law should be prepared to bear the consequences, including, but not limited to, deportation. But the children of those illegal entrants are not comparably situated. Their "parents have the ability to conform their conduct to societal norms," and presumably the ability

[19] We reject the claim that "illegal aliens" are a "suspect class." No case in which we have attempted to define a suspect class has addressed the status of persons unlawfully in our country. Unlike most of the classifications that we have recognized as suspect, entry into this class, by virtue of entry into this country, is the product of voluntary action. Indeed, entry into the class is itself a crime. In addition, it could hardly be suggested that undocumented status is a "constitutional irrelevancy." With respect to the actions of the federal government, alienage classifications may be intimately related to the conduct of foreign policy, to the federal prerogative to control access to the United States, and to the plenary federal power to determine who has sufficiently manifested his allegiance to become a citizen of the Nation. No State may independently exercise a like power. But if the Federal Government has by uniform rule prescribed what it believes to be appropriate standards for the treatment of an alien subclass, the States may, of course, follow the federal direction.

to remove themselves from the State's jurisdiction; but the children who are plaintiffs in these cases "can affect neither their parents' conduct nor their own status." Even if the State found it expedient to control the conduct of adults by acting against their children, legislation directing the onus of a parent's misconduct against his children does not comport with fundamental conceptions of justice.

Of course, undocumented status is not irrelevant to any proper legislative goal. Nor is undocumented status an absolutely immutable characteristic since it is the product of conscious, indeed unlawful, action. But § 21.031 is directed against children, and imposes its discriminatory burden on the basis of a legal characteristic over which children can have little control. It is thus difficult to conceive of a rational justification for penalizing these children for their presence within the United States. Yet that appears to be precisely the effect of § 21.031.

Public education is not a "right" granted to individuals by the Constitution. *San Antonio School District*. But neither is it merely some governmental "benefit" indistinguishable from other forms of social welfare legislation. Both the importance of education in maintaining our basic institutions, and the lasting impact of its deprivation on the life of the child, mark the distinction. We have recognized "the public school as a most vital civic institution for the preservation of a democratic system of government," and as the primary vehicle for transmitting "the values on which our society rests." In addition, education provides the basic tools by which individuals might lead economically productive lives to the benefit of us all. In sum, education has a fundamental role in maintaining the fabric of our society. We cannot ignore the significant social costs borne by our Nation when select groups are denied the means to absorb the values and skills upon which our social order rests.

In addition to the pivotal role of education in sustaining our political and cultural heritage, denial of education to some isolated group of children poses an affront to one of the goals of the Equal Protection Clause: the abolition of governmental barriers presenting unreasonable obstacles to advancement on the basis of individual merit. Paradoxically, by depriving the children of any disfavored group of an education, we foreclose the means by which that group might raise the level of esteem in which it is held by the majority. But more directly, "education prepares individuals to be self-reliant and self-sufficient participants in society." Illiteracy is an enduring disability. The inability to read and write will handicap the individual deprived of a basic education each and every day of his life. The inestimable toll of that deprivation on the social, economic, intellectual and psychological well-being of the individual, and the obstacle it poses to individual achievement, makes it most difficult to reconcile the cost or the principle of a status-based denial of basic education with the framework of equality embodied in the Equal Protection Clause. What we said 28 years ago in *Brown v. Board of Education* still holds true: "Today, education is perhaps the most important function of state and local governments."

These well-settled principles allow us to determine the proper level of deference to be afforded § 21.031. Undocumented aliens cannot be treated as a suspect class because their presence in this country in violation of federal law is not a "constitutional irrelevancy." Nor is education a fundamental right; a State need not justify by compelling necessity every variation in the manner in which education is provided to its population. *See San Antonio School Dist. v. Rodriguez*. But more is involved in this case than the abstract question whether § 21.031 discriminates against a suspect class, or whether education is a fundamental right. Section 21.031 imposes a lifetime hardship on a discrete class of children not accountable for their disabling status. The stigma of illiteracy will mark them for the rest of their lives. By denying these children a basic education, we deny them the ability to live within the structure of our civic institutions, and foreclose any realistic possibility that they will contribute in even the smallest way to the progress of our Nation. In determining the rationality of § 21.031, we may appropriately take into account its costs to the Nation and to the innocent children who are its victims. In light of these countervailing costs, the discrimination contained in § 21.031 can hardly be considered rational unless it furthers some substantial goal of the State.

Appellants argue that the classification at issue furthers an interest in the "preservation of the state's limited resources for the education of its lawful residents." Of course, a concern for the preservation of resources standing alone can hardly justify the classification used in allocating those resources. The State must do not more than justify its classification with a concise expression of an intention to discriminate. Apart from the asserted state prerogative to act against undocumented children solely on the basis of their undocumented status — an asserted prerogative that carries only minimal force in the circumstances of this case — we discern three colorable state interests that might support § 21.031.

First, appellants appear to suggest that the State may seek to protect the State from an influx of illegal immigrants. While a State might have an interest in mitigating the potentially harsh economic effects of sudden shifts in population, § 21.031 hardly offers an effective method of dealing with an urgent demographic or economic problem. There is no evidence in the record suggesting that illegal entrants impose any significant burden on the State's economy.

Second, while it is apparent that a state may "not reduce expenditures for education by barring [some arbitrarily chosen class of] children from its schools," appellants suggest that undocumented children are appropriately singled out for exclusion because of the special burdens they impose on the State's ability to provide high quality public education. But the record in no way supports the claim that exclusion of undocumented children is likely to improve the overall quality of education in the State. As the District Court noted, the State failed to offer any "credible supporting evidence that a proportionately small diminution of the funds spent on each child [which might result from devoting some State funds to the education of the excluded group] will have a grave impact on the quality of education." In terms of educational cost and need undocumented children are "basically indistinguishable" from legally resident alien children.

Finally, appellants suggest that undocumented children are appropriately singled out because their unlawful presence within the United States renders them less likely than other children to remain within the boundaries of the

State, and to put their education to productive social or political use within the State. Even assuming that such an interest is legitimate, it is an interest that is most difficult to quantify. The State has no assurance that any child, citizen or not, will employ the education provided by the State within the confines of the State's borders. In any event, the record is clear that many of the undocumented children disabled by this classification will remain in this country indefinitely, and that some will become lawful residents or citizens of the United States. It is difficult to understand precisely what the State hopes to achieve by promoting the creation and perpetuation of a subclass of illiterates within our boundaries, surely adding to the problems and costs of unemployment, welfare, and crime. It is thus clear that whatever savings might be achieved by denying these children an education, they are wholly insubstantial in light of the costs involved to these children, the State, and the Nation.

If the State is to deny a discrete group of innocent children the free public education that it offers to other children residing within its borders, that denial must be justified by a showing that it furthers some substantial state interest. No such showing was made here.

JUSTICE MARSHALL, concurring.

While I join the Court opinion, I do so without in any way retreating from my opinion in *San Antonio School District v. Rodriguez*. I continue to believe that an individual's interest in education is fundamental. Furthermore, I believe that the facts of these cases demonstrate the wisdom of rejecting a rigidified approach to equal protection analysis, and of employing an approach that allows for varying levels of scrutiny depending upon "the constitutional and societal importance of the interest adversely affected and the recognized invidiousness of the basis upon which the particular classification is drawn." It continues to be my view that a class-based denial of public education is utterly incompatible with the Equal Protection Clause of the Fourteenth Amendment.

JUSTICE BLACKMUN, concurring.

I believe the Court's experience has demonstrated that the *Rodriguez* formulation does not settle every issue of "fundamental rights" arising under the Equal Protection Clause. Only a pendant would insist that there are no meaningful distinctions among the multitude of social and political interests regulated by the States, and *Rodriguez* does not stand for quite so absolute a proposition. To the contrary, *Rodriguez* implicitly acknowledged that certain interests, though not constitutionally guaranteed, must be accorded a special place in equal protection analysis.

It is arguable, of course, that the Court never should have applied fundamental rights doctrine. JUSTICE HARLAN, for one, maintained that strict equal protection scrutiny was appropriate only when racial or analogous classifications were at issue. But it is too late to debate that point, and I believe that accepting the principle of the voting cases — the idea that state classifications bearing on certain interests pose the risk of allocating rights in a fashion inherently contrary to any notion of "equality" — dictates the outcome here.

In my view, when the State provides an education to some and denies it to others, it immediately and inevitably creates class distinctions of a type fundamentally inconsistent with [the] purposes of the Equal Protection Clause. Children denied an education are placed at a permanent and insurmountable competitive disadvantage, for an uneducated child is denied even the opportunity to achieve. And when those children are members of an identifiable group, that group — through the State's action — will have been converted into a discrete underclass. Other benefits provided by the State, such as housing and public assistance, are of course important; to an individual in immediate need, they may be more desirable than the right to be educated. But classifications involving the complete denial of education are in a sense unique, for they strike at the heart of equal protection values by involving the State in the creation of permanent class distinctions. In a sense, then, denial of an education is the analogue of denial of the right to vote: the former relegates the individual to second-class social status; the latter places him at a permanent political disadvantage.

JUSTICE POWELL, concurring.

I join the opinion of the Court, and write separately to emphasize the unique character of the case before us. The classification in question severely disadvantages children who are the victims of a combination of circumstances. Access from Mexico into this country, across our 2,000–mile border, is readily available and virtually uncontrollable. Illegal aliens are attracted by our employment opportunities, and perhaps by other benefits as well. This is a problem of serious national proportions, as the Attorney General recently has recognized. Perhaps because of the intractability of the problem, Congress — vested by the Constitution with the responsibility of protecting our borders and legislating with respect to aliens — has not provided effective leadership in dealing with this problem. It therefore is certain that illegal aliens will continue to enter the United States and, as the record makes clear, an unknown percentage of them will remain here. I agree with the Court that their children should not be left on the streets uneducated.

Although the analogy is not perfect, our holding today does find support in decisions of this Court with respect to the status of illegitimates. In this case, the State of Texas effectively denies to the school age children of illegal aliens the opportunity to attend the free public schools that the State makes available to all residents. They are excluded only because of a status resulting from the violation by parents or guardians of our immigration laws and the fact that they remain in our country unlawfully. The respondent children are innocent in this respect. They can "affect neither their parents' conduct nor their own status."

Our review in a case such as this is properly heightened. The classification at issue deprives a group of children of the opportunity for education afforded all other children simply because they have been assigned a legal status due to a violation of law by their parents. These children thus have been singled out for a lifelong penalty and stigma. A legislative classification that threatens the creation of an underclass of future citizens and residents cannot be reconciled with one of the fundamental purposes of the Fourteenth Amendment. In these unique circumstances, the Court properly may require that the State's interests be substantial and that the means bear a "fair and substantial relation" to these interests.[3]

In my view, the State's denial of education to these children bears no substantial relation to any substantial state interest. Both of the district courts found that an uncertain but significant percentage of illegal alien children will remain in Texas as residents and many eventually will become citizens. The discussion by the Court of the State's purported interests demonstrates that they are poorly served by the educational exclusion. Indeed, the interests relied upon by the State would seem to be insubstantial in view of the consequences to the State itself of wholly uneducated persons living indefinitely within its borders. By contrast, access to the public schools is made available to the children of lawful residents without regard to the temporary nature of their residency in the particular Texas school district.

CHIEF JUSTICE BURGER, with whom JUSTICES WHITE, REHNQUIST, and O'CONNOR join, dissenting.

The Court acknowledges that, except in those cases when state classifications disadvantage a "suspect class" or impinge upon a "fundamental right," the Equal Protection Clause permits a State "substantial latitude" in distinguishing between different groups of persons. Moreover, the Court expressly — and correctly — rejects any suggestion that illegal aliens are a suspect class, or that education is a fundamental right. Yet by patching together bits and pieces of what might be termed quasi-suspect-class and quasi-fundamental-rights analysis, the Court spins out a theory custom-tailored to the facts of these cases. In the end, we are told little more than that the level of scrutiny employed to strike down the Texas law applies only when illegal alien children are deprived of a public education. If ever a court was guilty of an unabashedly result-oriented approach, this case is a prime example.

The Court first suggests that these illegal alien children, although not a suspect class, are entitled to special solicitude under the Equal Protection Clause because they lack "control" over or "responsibility" for their unlawful entry into this country. Similarly, the Court appears to take the position that § 21.031 is presumptively "irrational" because it has the effect of imposing "penalties" on "innocent" children. However, the Equal Protection Clause does not preclude legislators from classifying among persons on the basis of factors and characteristics over which individuals may be said to lack "control." Indeed, in some circumstances persons generally, and children in particular, may have little control over or responsibility for such things as their ill-health, need for public assistance, or place of residence. Yet a state legislature is not barred from considering, for example, relevant differences between the mentally-healthy and the mentally-ill, or between the residents of different

[3] THE CHIEF JUSTICE argues in his dissenting opinion that this heightened standard of review is inconsistent with the Court's decision in *San Antonio School District v. Rodriguez*. But in *Rodriguez* no group of children was singled out by the State and then penalized because of their parent's status. Rather, funding for education varied across the State because of the tradition of local control. Nor, in that case, was any group of children totally deprived of all education as in this case. If the resident children of illegal aliens were denied welfare assistance, made available by government to all other children who qualify, this also — in my opinion — would be an impermissible penalizing of children because of their parents' status.

counties, simply because these may be factors unrelated to individual choice or to any "wrongdoing."

The Court's analogy to cases involving discrimination against illegitimate children is grossly misleading. The State has not thrust any disabilities upon appellees due to their "status of birth." Rather, appellees' status is predicated upon the circumstances of their concededly illegal presence in this country, and is a direct result of Congress' obviously valid exercise of its "broad constitutional powers" in the field of immigration and naturalization.

The second strand of the Court's analysis rests on the premise that, although public education is not a constitutionally-guaranteed right, "neither is it merely some governmental 'benefit' indistinguishable from other forms of social welfare legislation." Whatever meaning or relevance this opaque observation might have in some other context, it simply has no bearing on the issues at hand. Indeed, it is never made clear what the Court's opinion means on this score.

The importance of education is beyond dispute. Yet we have held repeatedly that the importance of a governmental service does not elevate it to the status of a "fundamental right" for purposes of equal protection analysis. *San Antonio School District v. Rodriguez*; *Lindsey v. Normet*. In *San Antonio School District*, Justice Powell, speaking for the Court, expressly rejected the proposition that state laws dealing with public education are subject to special scrutiny under the Equal Protection Clause. Moreover, the Court points to no meaningful way to distinguish between education and other governmental benefits in this context. Is the Court suggesting that education is more "fundamental" than food, shelter, or medical care?

Once it is conceded — as the Court does — that illegal aliens are not a suspect class, and that education is not a fundamental right, our inquiry should focus on and be limited to whether the legislative classification at issue bears a rational relationship to a legitimate state purpose.

Without laboring what will undoubtedly seem obvious to many, it simply is not "irrational" for a State to conclude that it does not have the same responsibility to provide benefits for persons whose very presence in the State and this country is illegal as it does to provide for persons lawfully present. By definition, illegal aliens have no right whatever to be here, and the State may reasonably, and constitutionally, elect not to provide them with governmental services at the expense of those who are lawfully in the State.

***Martinez v. Bynum,* 461 U.S. 321 (1983).** The Court upheld § 21.031 of the Texas Education Code which denies tuition-free education to a minor living apart from his or her "parent, guardian, or other person having lawful control of him under an order of a court," if the child's presence in the school district is "for the primary purpose of attending the public free schools." Roberto Morales, a United States citizen by birth whose parents reside in Mexico, lived with his sister, Martinez, for the primary purpose of attending school in the McAllen, Texas school district. Martinez and four other custodians of school age children sought a declaratory judgment that § 21.031 was unconstitutional on its face as a denial of equal protection and the right of interstate travel. The district court granted judgment for the defendant state education officials and the court of appeals affirmed.

Justice Powell, speaking for the Supreme Court, held that the statute was a bona fide residence requirement and that it met constitutional standards. No suspect classification was implicated by the Texas scheme and education, he declared, has been held not to constitute a fundamental right. Justice Powell explained the Court's view on the validity of the residency requirements:

> A bona fide residence requirement, appropriately defined and uniformly applied, furthers the substantial state interest in assuring that services provided for its residents are enjoyed only by residents. Such a requirement with respect to attendance in public free schools does not violate the Equal Protection Clause of the Fourteenth Amendment. It does not burden or penalize the constitutional right of interstate travel, for any person is free to move to a State and to establish residence there. A bona fide residence requirement simply requires that the person does establish residence before demanding the services that are restricted to residents.

The Court also stressed the importance of local control of education and the substantial adverse effect on planning and operations if schools were to be prevented from imposing residency requirements.

The only question, then, was whether § 21.031 is a residence requirement. Traditionally, said Justice Powell, residency requires both "physical presence and an intention to remain" in the jurisdiction. Section 21.031 was deemed more generous than this traditional two-part minimum standard.

> It compels a school district to permit a child such as Morales to attend school without paying tuition if he has a bona fide intention to remain in the school district indefinitely, for he then would have a reason for being there other than his desire to attend school: his intention to make his home in the district. . . . In short, § 21.031 grants the benefits of residency to everyone who satisfies the traditional residence definition and to some who legitimately could be classified as nonresidents. Since there is no indication that this extension of the traditional definition has any impermissible basis, we certainly cannot say that § 21.031(b) violates the Constitution. The Constitution permits a state to restrict eligibility for tuition-free education to its bona fide residents. [The Texas law] is a bona fide residence requirement that satisfies constitutional standards.

***Kadrmas v. Dickinson Pub. Schools*, 487 U.S. 450 (1988).** The Court, per Justice O'Connor, rejected an equal protection challenge to a North Dakota statute authorizing school districts which chose not to "reorganize" into larger districts to charge a fee for schoolbus service, not to exceed the district's estimated cost for providing the service. The Court initially rejected applicability of either the "strict scrutiny" standard or the somewhat less exacting "heightened" scrutiny employed in *Plyler*:

> [Heightened scrutiny] has generally been applied only in cases that involved discriminatory classification based on sex or illegitimacy.

> *Plyler* did not fit this pattern. We have not extended this holding beyond the "unique circumstances" that provoked its "unique confluence of theories and rationales." Nor do we think that the case before is today is governed by the holding in *Plyler*. Unlike the children in that case, [the appellant school child] has not been penalized by the government for illegal conduct by her parents. On the contrary, [she] was denied access to the school bus only because her parents would not agree to pay the same user fee charged to all other families that took advantage of the service. The case before us does not resemble *Plyler*, and we decline to extend the rationale of the decision to cover this case.

Justice Marshall, joined by Justice Brennan, dissented:

> Today, the Court continues the retreat form the promise of equal educational opportunity by holding that a school district's refusal to allow an indigent child who lives 16 miles from the nearest school to use a schoolbus service without paying a fee does not violate the Equal Protection Clause. Because I do no believe that this Court should sanction discrimination against the poor with respect to "perhaps the most important function of state and local government," *Brown v. Board of Educ.*, I dissent.

Justice Stevens, joined by Justice Blackmun, also dissented, because of the state's disparate treatment between "reorganized" and "nonreorganized" school districts: Though the state had an interest in encouraging district reorganization, "after the voters in a school district have had a fair opportunity to decide whether or not to reorganize, there is no longer any justification at all for allowing the nonreorganized districts to place an obstacle in the paths of poor children seeking an education in some parts of the State that has not been removed in other parts of the State."

NOTES

1. *Critiques of Plyler.* Michael Perry, *Equal Protection, Judicial Activism and the Intellectual Agenda of Constitutional Theory: Reflections on and Beyond* Plyler v. Doe, 44 U. PITT. L. REV. 329, 339–40 (1983), argues that there is no basis for increasing judicial activism in *Plyler*: "Introducing a standard less deferential than the traditional one out of solicitude for the principle of equal protection makes no sense, because the Texas statute simply does not implicate, much less offend the principle of equal protection."

But Thomas Gerety, *Children in the Labyrinth: The Complexities of Plyler v. Doe*, 44 U. PITT. L. REV. 379, 395, 397–98 (1983), argues that the sliding scale approach is adequate to justify the result in *Plyler*: "Only an attentiveness to the burden of the classification brings us to the intuitive result: the burden of the classification is grievous because it deprives certain people of the rudiments of literacy; it is grievous, besides, because it falls on children, and not just on any children or on any alien children but on alien children without papers — the one group of children whose parents will be least able to complain or to devise alternatives."

2. *The standard of review?* Does *Plyler* represent a rejection of a rigid tiered approach to fundamental rights and interests review? Is it an acceptance of Justice Marshall's sliding scale analysis or the case by case approach urged by Justice Stevens? Dennis Hutchinson, *More Substantive Equal Protection? A Note on* Plyler v. Doe, 1982 Sup. Ct. Rev. 167, 192–193, offers the following evaluation of *Plyler*'s precedential value: "The demise of strict scrutiny for racial classifications, occasioned by the cases involving affirmative action, the explosive growth of the middle tier of scrutiny since *Craig v. Boren*; and the ten-year-old plea for real 'bite' in the 'mere rationality' standard have had the combined effect of turning the interpretation of the Equal Protection Clause into an exercise of balancing competing interests whose weights are a function of prior case law only to a limited degree." Following *Romer v. Evans*, is there additional support for this proposition?

3. *Proposition 187.* In November 1994, the California voters passed Proposition 187. The effect of the measure was to add a provision to the California Constitution prohibiting the use of state funds for provision of various services to illegal aliens. Among the services included were education (both K-12 and higher education), health care, welfare, and a variety of social services. The lower court enjoined Proposition 187 and the decision was not appealed. Does *Plyler* dictate the result on all aspects of this measure, extending beyond education and children? "Brennan never explained how the denial of schooling to a child differs from the denial of other governmental benefits to an undocumented parent, upon whose income and well-being the child's welfare ultimately depends." Peter Schuck, *The Message of Proposition 187*, 26 Pac. L.J. 989, 992 (1995).

Professor Linda Bosniak, *Membership, Equality, and the Difference that Alienage Makes,* 69 N.Y.U.L. Rev. 1047, 1120–22 (1994), notes that *Plyler* has limited value as precedent for alienage discrimination beyond its context of denial of education to children:

> Although Justice Brennan showed enormous compassion for the alien children who are direct targets of the state's challenged law, his solicitude did not extend nearly so far when it came to the children's parents. Had the case involved denial of state benefits to undocumented adults (whose undocumented status, it is assumed, would be the result of their own, voluntary action), and had the case not specifically involved educational rights (which the Court treats as fundamentally important in this case), the outcome might well have differed.

But Professor Bosniak notes that Justice Brennan in *Plyler* also pictured adult undocumented aliens as victims of government's ambivalent policies toward their illegal entry and continued presence. Professor Gerald Newman, *Aliens as Outlaws: Government Services, Proposition 187 and the Structure of Equal Protection Doctrine,* 42 UCLA L. Rev. 1425, 1449–50 (1995) argues:

> For "illegal" alien adults, judicial enforcement of the minimal level of government services consistent with equal protection is justified by

the evident inadequacy of the political process to ensure that level. As with other categories of aliens, their unrepresented status and the lack of sympathy due to their foreignness render them vulnerable to hostile discrimination. The additional factor of the state's frustration at the federal government's inability or unwillingness to achieve total enforcement of the immigration statutes exposes them to mistreatment that falls below the level that every human being can rightfully expect for a government that exercises power over her.

Chapter 8

FREEDOM OF EXPRESSION

The First Amendment explicitly protects freedom of speech and press only from being abridged by federal legislation. In *Gitlow v. New York,* 268 U.S. 652 (1925), the Court said that "we may and do assume that freedom of speech and of the press — which are protected by the First Amendment from abridgment by Congress — are among the fundamental personal rights and 'liberties' protected by the due process clause of the Fourteenth Amendment from impairment by the States."

Historically, however, there are some categories of expression that have not received any level of protection. Those most frequently mentioned are fraud, defamation, and obscenity. Disclosure of official secrets is also assumed to be "abridgable" without First Amendment protection. These categories seem to reflect types of expression that would cause harms that are appropriately preventable by society. To use a familiar example, falsely shouting "Fire" in a crowded theater is universally deemed to be unprotected by the First Amendment. But is it speech? or is it something else?

One way of approaching freedom of expression, therefore, is to attempt to place various forms of expression into categories of protected or unprotected expression. Most twentieth-century free speech analysis was preoccupied with the quest for definable categories, asking how much harm is required before government is allowed to intervene — i.e., how close is a statement to being like "Fire" in a crowded theater? Obviously, the content of the speech is critical to this inquiry. The opposite side of that coin, and one leading possibly to a different doctrinal approach, is to ask what interest government has in suppressing a particular form of expression. In recent years, the Supreme Court has tended (primarily under Justice Scalia's prodding) in the latter direction, probing governmental objectives rather than the nature of particular speech. In this approach, government neutrality toward content or viewpoint becomes an important goal.

Section 8.01 explores the basics of free speech doctrine by examining arguable interests of government in regulating, either because of the content of the speech or the circumstances in which it is presented; this section will present the question of whether a categorical approach is desirable. Section 8.02 looks at two categories of expression that have been particularly difficult to describe, commercial speech and obscenity. Section 8.03 turns to issues of particular interest to the media, including the category of defamation. Section 8.04 then deals with a distinct set of freedoms implied from the First Amendment and called the right of association.

§ 8.01 FREE SPEECH DOCTRINE

[A] REGULATING ADVOCACY: THE CLEAR AND PRESENT DANGER DOCTRINE

The earliest and most enduring of the judicial efforts to formulate a standard for content-based control of speech arose in the context of national security — the clear and present danger doctrine. This doctrine presents a need for analysis of the values reflected in the functional approaches to First Amendment theory. Three explanations for freedom of speech have dominated discussion — the marketplace model, the citizen participant model, and the individual liberty model — although variations and other approaches are regularly introduced.

[1] The Origins of the Clear and Present Danger Doctrine: Functions of Freedom of Expression

Supreme Court consideration of the specific protection afforded by the First Amendment against governmental legislation or action restrictive of freedom of expression did not really begin until after World War I. The introduction of conscription in the United States in World War I plus the resulting American alliance with Czarist Russia provoked a reaction from communist and radical groups in the United States. The activities of these groups, insofar as they defied the Espionage Act of 1917, provoked the beginning of modern First Amendment law in the Supreme Court. The Espionage Act prohibited obstruction of recruiting or the encouragement of insubordination in the armed services. Radical discontent with conscription precipitated a confrontation between government and socialist dissidents which required the Supreme Court to elaborate on the scope of First Amendment protection.

***Schenck v. United States*, 249 U.S. 47 (1919).** Schenck, General Secretary of the Socialist Party, along with other defendants, mailed leaflets to draft-age men stating that the draft was in violation of the Thirteenth Amendment's prohibition of slavery. The leaflets were deemed by the government to encourage obstruction of the draft; Schenck and his associates were indicted and convicted for conspiring to violate the Espionage Act. On appeal to the Supreme Court, the defendants claimed that the government's use of defendants' speech to establish a violation of the Espionage Act was unconstitutional, but the Court affirmed the convictions. The Court gave judicial approval to this federal burden on expression. Yet *Schenck* is considered one of the seminal cases in First Amendment law. The opinion, written by Justice Oliver Wendell Holmes, permanently impacted First Amendment doctrine..

In *Schenck*, Holmes described the clear and present danger doctrine in the following manner:

> We admit that in many places and in ordinary times the defendants in saying all that was said in the circular would have been within their constitutional rights. But the character of every act depends upon the circumstances in which it is done. The most stringent protection of free speech would not protect a man in falsely shouting fire in a

theatre and causing a panic. It does not even protect a man from an injunction against uttering words that may have all the effect of force. The question in every case is whether the words used are used in such circumstances and are of such a nature as to create a clear and present danger that they will bring about the substantive evils that Congress has a right to prevent. It is a question of proximity and degree. When a nation is at war many things that might be said in time of peace are such a hindrance to its effort that their utterance will not be endured so long as men fight and that no Court should regard them as protected by any constitutional right. It seems to be admitted that if an actual obstruction of the recruiting service were proved, liability for words that produced that effect might be enforced.

ABRAMS v. UNITED STATES

250 U.S. 616, 40 S. Ct. 17, 63 L. Ed. 1173 (1919)

[In the same year in which *Schenck* was decided, the Court produced another influential decision in the free speech area. Once again the influential opinion was authored by Holmes, but this time he was in dissent. The words of his dissent, particularly the passage that sets forth the famous marketplace of ideas theory of freedom of expression, are still quoted long after the majority opinion by Justice Clarke has been forgotten.

[Abrams, along with others, published pamphlets attacking the special American expeditionary force sent to challenge the new Communist revolutionary government of Russia. They were convicted under 1918 amendments to the Espionage Act, *inter alia*, for publishing language "intended to incite, provoke or encourage resistance" to the war effort and of conspiring "to urge, incite and advocate" curtailment of production of war materials. The Supreme Court, citing *Schenck*, held that the publication and distribution of the pamphlet during the war was not protected by the First Amendment. Finding the evidence sufficient to sustain the jury verdict, the Court affirmed the convictions.]

Justice Holmes, jointed by Justice Brandeis, dissenting.

I do not doubt for a moment that by the same reasoning that would justify punishing persuasion to murder, the United States constitutionally may punish speech that produces or is intended to produce a clear and imminent danger that it will bring about forthwith certain substantive evils that the United States constitutionally may seek to prevent. The power undoubtedly is greater in time of war than in time of peace because war opens dangers that do not exist at other times.

But as against dangers peculiar to war, as against others, the principle of the right to free speech is always the same. It is only the present danger of immediate evil or an intent to bring it about that warrants Congress in setting a limit to the expression of opinion where private rights are not concerned. Now nobody can suppose that the surreptitious publishing of a silly leaflet by an unknown man, without more, would present any immediate danger that its opinions would hinder the success of the government arms or have any appreciable tendency to do so. Publishing those opinions for the very purpose of obstructing, however, might indicate a greater danger and at any rate would have the quality of an attempt. [But] I do not see how anyone can find the intent required by the statute in any of the defendants' words.

In this case sentences of twenty years imprisonment have been imposed for the publishing of two leaflets that I believe the defendants had as much right to publish as the Government has to publish the Constitution of the United States now vainly invoked by them.

Persecution for the expression of opinions seems to me perfectly logical. If you have no doubt of your premises or your power and want a certain result with all your heart you naturally express your wishes in law and sweep away all opposition. To allow opposition by speech seems to indicate that you think the speech impotent, as when a man says that he has squared the circle, or that you do not care wholeheartedly for the result, or that you doubt either your power or your premises. But when men have realized that time has upset many fighting faiths, they may come to believe even more than they believe the very foundations of their own conduct that the ultimate good desired is better reached by free trade in ideas — that the best test of truth is the power of the thought to get itself accepted in the competition of the market, and that truth is the only ground upon which their wishes safely can be carried out. That at any rate is the theory of our Constitution. It is an experiment, as all life is an experiment. Every year if not every day we have to wager our salvation upon some prophecy based upon imperfect knowledge. While that experiment is part of our system I think that we should be eternally vigilant against attempts to check the expression of opinions that we loathe and believe to be fraught with death, unless they so imminently threaten immediate interference with the lawful and pressing purposes of the law that an immediate check is required to save the country. I wholly disagree with the argument of the Government that the First Amendment left the common law as to seditious libel in force. History seems to me against the notion. I had conceived that the United States through many years had shown its repentance for the Sedition Act of 1798, by repaying fines that it imposed. Only the emergency that makes it immediately dangerous to leave the correction of evil counsels to time warrants making any exception to the sweeping command, "Congress shall make no law abridging the freedom of speech." Of course, I am speaking only of expressions of opinion and exhortations, which were all that were uttered here, but I regret that I cannot put into more impressive words my belief that in their conviction upon this indictment the defendants were deprived of their rights under the Constitution of the United States.

NOTES

The Marketplace Model

1. *Reliance on competition.* In a sense, the marketplace of ideas theory, advocated in Justice Holmes's dissent in *Abrams*, represents the application of Social Darwinism to ideas, just as earlier Social Darwinism had been applied to economic theory. Holmes' marketplace of ideas theory was not, of course, a new proposition. The theory rose out of deep currents in British political thought. English poet and political thinker, John Milton, writing in the seventeenth century, advocated the same *laissez-faire* clash of ideas extolled by Holmes in *Abrams*:

> And though all the winds of doctrine were let loose to play upon the earth, so Truth be in the field, we do injuriously by licensing and prohibiting to misdoubt her strength. Let her and Falsehood grapple; who ever knew truth put to the worse in a free and open encounter?

John Milton, Areopagitica (1644).

The English political economist John Stuart Mill expressed similar ideas in the nineteenth century. Compare Holmes' marketplace analogy in *Abrams* with the following passage from Mill:

> But the peculiar evil of silencing the expression of an opinion is, that it is robbing the human race; posterity as well as the existing generation; those who dissent from the opinion, still more than those who hold it. If the opinion is right, they are deprived of the opportunity of exchanging error for truth; if wrong, they lose, what is almost as great a benefit, the clearer perception and livelier impression of truth, produced by its collision with error.

John S. Mill, On Liberty (1859).

2. *Criticisms of the marketplace model.* The marketplace of ideas theory has been subject to strenuous attack. For example, consider the following critique:

> In one sense, the theory appears to suffer from an internal contradiction: the theory's goal is the attainment of truth, yet it posits that we can never really know the truth, so we must keep looking. But, if we can never attain the truth, why bother to continue the fruitless search? More importantly, any theory positing that the value of free speech is the search for truth creates a great danger that someone will decide that he finally has attained knowledge of the truth. At that point, that individual (or society) may feel fully justified, as a matter of both morality and logic in shutting off expression of any views that are contrary to this "truth."

Martin Redish, *The Value of Free Speech*, 130 U. Pa. L. Rev. 591, 617 (1982).

Are some kinds of truth, however, different from others? Suppose an individual wishes to advertise the opinion that cigarette smoking does not cause cancer, although the surgeon general has reached the opposite conclusion? Can "false" advertising or fraudulent statements be punished consistently with the marketplace theory? Can the government constitutionally punish the following statements because of their supposed falsity: (a) "We invaded Iraq for oil, not for freedom"; (b) "the government lied to us about weapons of mass destruction"; "Nike employs slave labor in foreign countries to manufacture its shoes."

Consider also the view that "the classic model is flawed because it requires that people be able to use their rational capacities to eliminate distortion caused by the form and frequency of message presentation and to find the core of relevant information or argument. This assumption cannot be accepted. Emotional or 'irrational' appeals have great impact." Edwin Baker, *Scope of the First Amendment Freedom of Speech*, 25 UCLA L. REV. 964, 976 (1978).

3. *The problem of monopoly.* The philosopher of the radical left, Herbert Marcuse, launched the following attack against the marketplace of ideas theory: "Different opinions and 'philosophies' can no longer compete peacefully for adherence and persuasion on rational grounds. The 'marketplace of ideas' is organized and delimited by those who determine the national and individual interest." Herbert Marcuse, *Repressive Tolerance* in R. WOLFF, B. MOORE & H. MARCUSE, A CRITIQUE OF PURE TOLERANCE 110 (1965).

Marcuse believes that the free discussion of ideas is an illusion, that the marketplace of ideas is so distorted by economic reality that the dissenting idea or viewpoint really does not have a fair chance: "Under the rule of monopolistic media — themselves the mere instruments of economic and political power — a mentality is created from which right and wrong, true and false are predefined whenever they effect the vital interests of the society." What is a tolerance which is not repressive? Marcuse distinguishes "liberating tolerance" from "repressive tolerance": "Liberating tolerance, then, would mean intolerance against movements from the right, and tolerance of movements from the left." *Id.*

4. *Market failure and modern communications.* Professor Barron argued almost four decades ago that the marketplace of ideas was unrealistic: "Our constitutional theory is in the grip of a romantic conception of free expression, a belief that the 'marketplace of ideas' is freely accessible. But if ever there were a self-operating marketplace of ideas, it has long ceased to exist." Jerome Barron, *Access to the Press A New First Amendment Right*, 80 HARV. L. REV. 1641, 1648 (1967):

> The "marketplace of ideas" has rested on the assumption that protecting the right of expression is equivalent to providing for it. But changes in the communications industry have destroyed the equilibrium in that marketplace. Yet the Holmesian theory is not abandoned even though the advent of radio and television has made even more evident that philosophy's unreality. A realistic view of the first amendment requires recognition that a right of expression is somewhat thin if it can be exercised only at the sufferance of the managers of mass communications.

If the marketplace is not functioning, does government have a constitutional obligation to make it work? Consider the suggestion that "even the venerable metaphor of the marketplace of ideas may have continuing force if the marketplace is thought of not so much as a site where prices are determined and purchases made but rather as a place where people gather to browse, to taste, and to commingle aimlessly." Vincent Blasi, *The Checking Value in First Amendment Theory*, 1977 AM. B. FOUND. RES. J. 521, 551.

The advent of a wide-open electronic forum known as the Internet or the World Wide Web may come close to Professor Blasi's vision. Does it also restore the romantic vision of the market, whose loss Professor Barron had recorded?

The Citizen Participant Model

5. *Original intent and sedition.* Holmes remarked in *Abrams* that he disagreed with the argument made by the government in that case that the "First Amendment left the common law as to seditious libel in force." This is a reference to the enactment in 1798, seven years after the ratification of the Constitution, of the Alien and Sedition Acts. The Sedition Act of 1798 prohibited the publication of "false, scandalous, or malicious" criticism of the government, Congress, or the President designed to bring established governmental authority into "contempt, or disrepute." The Act was never tested in the Supreme Court. In 1801, President Jefferson, an antagonist of the Federalist-inspired legislation designed to strike at his Democrat-Republican Party's sympathy for revolutionary France, allowed the legislation to lapse.

For some, the failure to re-enact the Act, and the eventual repayment by the government of the fines imposed under the Act, justified Holmes' conclusion that the weight of history was against the notion that the First Amendment and the Sedition Act could coexist. ZECHARIAH CHAFEE, FREE SPEECH IN THE UNITED STATES (1941). For others, the passage of the Act so soon after the enactment of the first amendment illustrates that the Framers and their contemporaries had not understood the First Amendment as placing an absolute restraint on governmental restrictions on political expression. LEONARD W. LEVY, LEGACY OF SUPPRESSION: FREEDOM OF SPEECH AND PRESS IN EARLY AMERICAN HISTORY (1960); Walter Berns, *Freedom of the Press and the Alien and Sedition Laws: A Reappraisal*, 1970 SUP. CT. REV. 109.

6. *The scope of self-governance.* Justice Brandeis in his concurring opinion in *Whitney v. California*, p. 975, asserted that "political discussion is a political duty." Later, Professor Meiklejohn grounded the First Amendment on the principle of self-government and consent to authority — "The principle of freedom of speech springs from the necessities of self-government." ALEXANDER MEIKLEJOHN, FREE SPEECH: AND ITS RELATION TO SELF-GOVERNMENT 26 (1948):

> Just as far as, at any point, the citizens who are to decide an issue are denied acquaintance with information or doubt or disbelief or criticism which is relevant to that issue, just so far the result must be ill-considered, ill-balanced planning for the general good. It is that mutilation of the thinking process of the community against which the First Amendment to the Constitution is directed.

From these premises Meiklejohn argued for absolute protection of "public" speech. But this utilitarian view does not guarantee any individual protection of his or her speech — it is only required "that everything worth saying shall be said." Indeed, Meiklejohn specifically criticized Holmes' excessive individualism.

7. *Political speech.* An extension of Meiklejohn's argument, providing First Amendment protection only to political speech, was made in Robert Bork,

Neutral Principles and Some First Amendment Problems, 47 IND. L.J. 1 (1971). Judge Bork argued that the benefits of non-political speech are "indistinguishable from the functions or benefits of all other human activity." He reasoned that "[a]n individual may develop his faculties from trading on the stock market, following his profession as a river-port pilot, working as a barmaid, engaging in sexual activity, playing tennis, rigging prices or in any of thousands of endeavors." It is only the "discovery and spread of political truth that distinguishes speech from any other form of human activity," and is therefore the only principled basis upon which to provide greater protection to speech than to other activities.

In response to Judge Bork, it has been argued that

> there are numerous non-communicative, nonspeech activities that may be thought to aid in the attainment of political truth. For example, working as a farmer could help one understand the problems and benefits of farm price supports; working as a doctor could do the same with respect to socialized medicine; living in a large urban area and taking public transportation might convince one of the need for greater federal aid to cities and mass transit. Thus, nonspeech activities could aid attainment of knowledge of political truth as much as does any political discourse. Bork's logic therefore must be rejected, because it inescapably results in the content of speech protected by the first amendment being a null set; there is no category of expression that furthers a value or values unique to speech.

MARTIN REDISH, FREEDOM OF EXPRESSION: A CRITICAL ANALYSIS 17–18 (1984).

Another answer to the Bork-Meikeljohn argument would be based on whether there are other kinds of private or nonpolitical speech that serve the political process. For example, do art or music often carry a political message? Should protection of art or music turn on whether they carry such a message?

The Individual Liberty Model

8. *Basis of the liberty model.* The citizen-participant and market models both emphasize utilitarian values of freedom of expression. But as Brandeis observed in *Whitney v. California*, speech may also have an intrinsic value — liberty is valued "both as an end and as a means." John Stuart Mill in ON LIBERTY stressed,

> Human nature is not a machine to be built after a model, and set to do exactly the work prescribed for it, but a tree, which requires to grow and develop itself on all sides, according to the tendency of the inward forces which make it a living thing.

This emphasis on liberty to develop one's faculties to promote individual autonomy and to further self-determination has been called "the most coherent theory of the First Amendment."

> The liberty model holds that the free speech clause protects not a marketplace but rather an arena of individual liberty from certain

> types of governmental restrictions. Speech is protected not as a means to a collective good but because of the value of speech conduct to the individual. The liberty theory justifies protection because of the way the protected conduct fosters individual self-realization and self-determination without improperly interfering with the legitimate claims of others.

Edwin Baker, *Scope of the First Amendment Freedom of Speech*, 25 UCLA L. REV. 964, 966 (1978).

9. *The demands of autonomy.* Consider Professor Scanlon's view that freedom of expression is essential to the rational autonomous person who requires a wide range of information — "An autonomous person cannot accept without independent consideration the judgment [of] others as to what he should believe or what he should do." Thomas Scanlon, *A Theory of Freedom of Expression*, 1 PHIL. & PUB. AFF. 204 (1972). *See also* David Strauss, *Persuasion, Autonomy, and Freedom of Expression*, 91 COLUM. L. REV. 334 (1991), describing the "persuasion principle" in this way: "Except, perhaps, in extraordinary circumstances, the government may not restrict speech because it fears, however justifiably, that the speech will persuade those who hear it to do something of which the government disapproves." Can these theories co-exist with the clear-and-present-danger test?

Does all communication further self-development? Other behavior which arguably furthers human experience and growth is regulated and even prohibited by government, and the constitutional demands of liberty require only that the law be reasonable. Does regulation of freedom of speech deserve any different treatment? Professor Schauer asserts that "if there is no principle of free speech independent of a more general liberty, then free speech is more a platitude than a principle"? FREDERICK F. SCHAUER, FREE SPEECH: A PHILOSOPHICAL ENQUIRY 6 (1982).

Evaluating the "Clear and Present Danger" Test

10. *Criticisms.* The clear-and-present-danger test has been subjected to severe criticism over the years. In the words of Professor Strong, "there are few who would grieve at [the test's] total demise." Frank Strong, *Fifty Years of "Clear and Present Danger": From Schenck to Brandenburg — and Beyond*, 1969 SUP. CT. REV. 41. Some of the important criticisms were described by Professor Paul Freund:

> The truth is that the clear-and-present-danger test is an oversimplified judgment unless it takes account also of a number of other factors: the relative seriousness of the danger in comparison with the value of the occasion for speech or political activity; the availability of more moderate controls than those which the state has imposed; and perhaps the specific intent with which the speech or activity is launched. No matter how rapidly we utter the phrase, "clear and present danger," or how closely we hyphenate the words, they are not a substitute for the weighing of values.

PAUL FREUND, ON UNDERSTANDING THE SUPREME COURT 27–28 (1949).

Professor Emerson attacked the test because "it assumes that once expression immediately threatens the attainment of some valid social objective, the expression can be prohibited." There is a fallacy in this logic, he suggests, because "[t]o permit the state to cut off expression as soon as it comes close to being effective is essentially to allow only abstract or innocuous expression. In short, a legal formula found solely in terms of effectiveness of the expression in influencing action is incompatible with the existence of free expression." THOMAS EMERSON, TOWARD A GENERAL THEORY OF THE FIRST AMENDMENT 51–52 (1966). *See also* David Dow & R. Scott Shieldes, *Rethinking the Clear and Present Danger Test*, 73 IND. L.J. 1217, 1218 (1998), suggesting that the clear and present danger test "cannot coexist with those modern notions of individual responsibility that underlie our laws and our form of government itself."

John Ely also severely criticizes the clear and present danger analysis. One of his objections is that the test determines the level of constitutional protection on the basis of the danger of the expression: "balancing tests inevitably become intertwined with the ideological predispositions of those doing the balancing — or if not that, at least with the relative confidence or paranoia of the age in which they are doing it." John Ely, *Flag Desecration: A Case Study in the Roles of Categorization and Balancing in First Amendment Analysis*, 88 HARV. L. REV. 1482, 1501 (1975). He argues that "[s]o long as the constitutional test is geared to the threat posed by the specific communication in issue, courts will tend to be swept along by the same sorts of fears that moved the legislators and the prosecutorial authorities, and the First Amendment is likely to end up a very theoretical barrier." JOHN H. ELY, DEMOCRACY AND DISTRUST 107 (1980).

11. *The Masses test.* If the courts do not focus on the danger of unlawful advocacy in deciding whether to protect it, upon what else can they focus? The words themselves? The speaker's intent? Would another approach produce a more speech-protective result? Consider the opinion of Judge Learned Hand, when he was a district judge, in *Masses Publishing Co. v. Patten,* 244 F. 535 (S.D.N.Y.), *rev'd*, 246 F. 24 (2d Cir. 1917). The New York Postmaster had advised the plaintiff, publisher of a revoluntionary periodical, that his publication would not be sent through the mail, pursuant to the Espionage Act, because it tended to hamper the United States in its war effort. The publisher sought a preliminary injunction against the journal's exclusion, which Judge Hand granted.

"One may not counsel or advise others to violate the law as it stands," Hand wrote. "While, of course, this may be accomplished as well by indirection as expressly," he stated, "[i]f one stops short of urging to resist the law, it seems to me one should not be held to have attempted to cause its violation." He construed the Act to be limited to the direct advocacy of resistance to the recruiting and enlistment service, which the journal in question had not done.

While Hand's decision was reversed on appeal, his theory has withstood the test of time and has received plaudits from modern commentators as a viable, protectionist alternative to the clear and present danger test. *See, e.g.*, Kent Greenawalt, *Speech and Crime*, 1980 AM. B. FOUND. RES. J. 645, 702; Gerald

Gunther, *Learned Hand and the Origins of Modern First Amendment Doctrine: Some Fragments of History*, 27 STAN. L. REV. 719, 729 (1975). The emphasis of the *Masses* test is on permitting speech unless the words are a direct incitement. *See* Vincent Blasi, *Learned Hand and the Self-Government Theory of the First Amendment*, 61 U. COLO. L. REV. 1, 3 (1990) ("even in *Abrams*, Holmes's focus was on the predicted consequence of the speech, not its content"). Was Marc Antony engaged in incitement when he delivered his famed funeral oration? In *Gitlow v. New York*, the next major case, Holmes pointed out that punishing incitement might allow government intervention before any real threat existed.

12. *An absolutist alternative.* What other alternative modes of First Amendment interpretation are conceivable? Consider the so-called "absolutist" position advocated by Justice Black:

> The beginning of the First Amendment is that "Congress shall make no law." I understand that it is rather old-fashioned and shows a slight naivete to say that "no law" means no law. It is one of the most amazing things about the ingeniousness of the times that strong arguments are made, which almost convince me, that it is very foolish of me to think "no law" means no law. But what it says is "Congress shall make no law." My view is, without deviation, without exception, without any ifs, buts, or whereases, that freedom of speech means that you shall not do something to people either for the views they have or the views they express or the words they speak or write.

Edmond Cahn, *Justice Black and First Amendment "Absolutes": A Public Interview*, 37 N.Y.U.L. REV. 549, 553–54, 559 (1962). Professor Meiklejohn similarly attacked the clear and present danger doctrine because it was designed to permit what he believed the First Amendment forbade, i.e., governmental restriction of public speech. ALEXANDER MEIKLEJOHN, FREE SPEECH AND ITS RELATION TO SELF-GOVERNMENT 29 (1948).

Justice Black attempted to make the touchstone of First Amendment protection depend on whether "speech" or "action" was being regulated. In his view, "speech" has absolute protection. "Action," on the other hand, is subject to reasonable regulation. *See generally* Hugo Black, *The Bill of Rights*, 35 N.Y.U. L. REV. 865 (1960). How would an absolutist respond to Justice Holmes' example regarding falsely crying fire in a crowded theater?

In the late 1940s, when Congress was considering legislation restricting expression in response to the communist scare, the debate on whether the First Amendment permitted any such legislation resumed. In a review of Meiklejohn's book, Professor Chafee defended the utility of the clear and present danger doctrine as a basis for resolving such problems and criticized Meiklejohn's absolutist approach.

> No matter how terrible and immediate the dangers may be, he keeps saying, the First Amendment will not let Congress or anybody else in the Government try to deal with Communists who have not yet committed unlawful acts. It is hopeless to use reasoning like this in order to win votes against [anti-Communist legislation]. Such a view may be courageous, but it won't work.

Zechariah Chafee, *Book Review*, 62 HARV. L. REV. 891, 894 (1949). For Chafee, Meiklejohn's and Justice Black's pleas for absolute First Amendment protection, although perhaps admirable as a theoretical ideal, were bound to founder on the harsh shores of political reality. Chafee wrote: "The true alternative to Holmes' view of the First Amendment was not at all the perfect immunity for public discussion which Mr. Meiklejohn desires. It was no immunity at all in the face of legislation."

It is worth noting that Professor Meiklejohn's view of absolute First Amendment protection was less encompassing than might appear. In Meiklejohn's view, the language to emphasize in the First Amendment is "freedom of speech." Abridgement of speech per se is not prohibited. Meiklejohn concludes that it is "public" speech which is absolutely protected. "Private" speech, speech not concerning public affairs or political criticism, is deemed to be a lower species of expression.

Is an "absolute" construction of the First Amendment dictated by the amendment's language? Is it viable? Consider the following argument:

> An absolute construction [of the First Amendment] is (1) not required by the language of the amendment, (2) not dictated by the intent of the framers, and (3) impossible in practice. As to the issue of language, the phrase "freedom of speech" is not necessarily the same as "speech," and is certainly not self-defining. As to the intent of the framers, what little evidence there is suggests that, to the extent they thought about it at all, they intended an extremely narrow construction of the first amendment, and certainly not an absolute construction. Finally, I simply refuse to believe that anything in first amendment language or policy requires us to protect the statement of a mob leader, outside a poorly defended prison, urging his torch-carrying compatriots to lynch a prisoner inside. Once it is acknowledged that the free speech interest must give way in such a situation to a competing social interest, acceptance of at least some form of balancing process is established. The question is simply where to draw the line.

Martin Redish, *The Value of Free Speech*, 130 U. PA. L. REV. 591, 623–24 (1982).

Might an "absolutist" legitimately authorize punishment of the mob leader for urging a lynching outside a poorly-defended prison? Professor Emerson believed that

> a fundamental distinction must be drawn between conduct which consists of "expression" and conduct which consists of "action." "Expression" must be freely allowed and encouraged. "Action" can be controlled, subject to other constitutional requirements, but not by controlling expression.

THOMAS I. EMERSON, THE SYSTEM OF FREEDOM OF EXPRESSION 17–19 (1970). How would Emerson's suggested distinction apply to the urging of a mob leader to storm a poorly-defended jail? Is the speech-action dichotomy preferable to the clear-and-present danger test?

13. ***Absolutism and values.*** Laurent Frantz, *Is the First Amendment Law? — A Reply To Professor Mendelson*, 51 Cal. L. Rev. 729, 750–53 (1963), argues that the word "absolute" is no more definite than many words. "Much of what is frequently derided as a demand for 'absolute' seems to me nothing more than a demand that the Court should ask first, 'Is this the type of governmental action that the first amendment forbids?' "

[2] Developing the Doctrine: The Formative Years

GITLOW v. NEW YORK
268 U.S. 652, 45 S. Ct. 625, 69 L. Ed. 1138 (1925)

[Gitlow, a member of the left wing of the Socialist Party, was indicted and convicted under New York's criminal anarchy statute for publishing a radical "manifesto." The New York Criminal Anarchy statute forbade the publication of material advocating or "teaching the duty, necessity, or propriety of overthrowing or overturning organized government by force or violence." Gitlow's Manifesto had criticized the approach of the moderate socialists in seeking to obtain political power through democratic processes. Gitlow, instead, advocated mass strikes by the proletariat. On review, the Supreme Court affirmed Gitlow's conviction.]

Justice Sanford delivered the opinion of the Court.

For present purposes we may and do assume that freedom of speech and of the press — which are protected by the First Amendment from abridgment by Congress — are among the fundamental personal rights and "liberties" protected by the due process clause of the Fourteenth Amendment from impairment by the States.

By enacting the present statute the State has determined, through its legislative body, that utterances advocating the overthrow of organized government by force, violence and unlawful means, are so inimical to the general welfare and involve such danger of substantive evil that they may be penalized in the exercise of its police power. That determination must be given great weight. Every presumption is to be indulged in favor of the validity of the statute. [P]olice "statutes may only be declared unconstitutional where they are arbitrary or unreasonable attempts to exercise authority vested in the State in the public interest." That utterances inciting to the overthrow of organized government by unlawful means, present a sufficient danger of substantive evil to bring their punishment within the range of legislative discretion, is clear. Such utterances, by their very nature, involve danger to the public peace and to the security of the State. They threaten breaches of the peace and ultimate revolution. And the immediate danger is none the less real and substantial, because the effect of a given utterance cannot be accurately foreseen. The State cannot reasonably be required to measure the danger from every such utterance in the nice balance of a jeweler's scale. A single revolutionary spark may kindle a fire that, smouldering for a time, may burst into a sweeping and destructive conflagration. It cannot be said that the State is acting arbitrarily or unreasonably when in the exercise of its judgment as to the measures necessary to protect the public peace and safety, it seeks to extinguish the spark without waiting until it has enkindled the flame or blazed into the conflagration. It cannot reasonably be required to defer the adoption of measures for its own peace and safety until the revolutionary utterances lead to actual disturbances of the public peace or imminent and immediate danger of its own destruction; but it may, in the exercise of its judgment, suppress the threatened danger in its incipiency.

This being so it may be applied to every utterance — not too trivial to be beneath the notice of the law — which is of such a character and used with such intent and purpose as to bring it within the prohibition of the statute. In other words, when the legislative body has determined generally, in the constitutional exercise of its discretion, that utterances of a certain kind involve such danger of substantive evil that they may be punished, the question whether any specific utterance coming within the prohibited class is likely, in and of itself, to bring about the substantive evil, is not open to consideration. It is sufficient that the statute itself be constitutional and that the use of the language comes within its prohibition.

It is clear that the question in such cases is entirely different from that involved in those cases where the statute merely prohibits certain acts involving the danger of substantive evil, without any reference to language itself, and it is sought to apply its provisions to language used by the defendant for the purpose of bringing about the prohibited results. There, if it be contended that the statute cannot be applied to the language used by the defendant because of its protection by the freedom of speech or press, it must necessarily be found, as an original question, without any previous determination by the legislative body, whether the specific language used involved such likelihood of bringing about the substantive evil as to deprive it of the constitutional protection. In such case it has been held that the general provisions of the statute may be constitutionally applied to the specific utterance of the defendant if its natural tendency and probable effect was to bring about the substantive evil which the legislative body might prevent. And the general statement in the *Schenck* Case, that the "question in every case is whether the words used are used in such circumstances and are of such a nature as to create a clear and present danger that they will bring about the substantive evils," — upon which great reliance is placed in the defendant's argument — was manifestly intended, as shown by the context, to apply only in cases of this class, and has no application to those like the present, where the legislative body itself has previously determined the danger of substantive evil arising from utterances of a specified character.

And finding, for the reasons stated, that the statute is not in itself unconstitutional, and that it has not been applied in the present case in derogation of any constitutional right, the judgment of the Court of Appeals is affirmed.

MR. JUSTICE HOLMES [joined by JUSTICE BRANDEIS], dissenting.

MR. JUSTICE BRANDEIS and I are of opinion that this judgment should be reversed. If what I think the correct test is applied, it is manifest that there was no present danger of an attempt to overthrow the government by force on the part of the admittedly small minority who shared the defendant's views. It is said that this manifesto was more than a theory, that it was an incitement. Every idea is an incitement. It offers itself for belief and if believed it is acted on unless some other belief outweighs it or some failure of energy stifles the movement at its birth. The only difference between the expression of an opinion and an incitement in the narrower sense is the speaker's enthusiasm for the result. Eloquence may set fire to reason. But whatever may be thought of the redundant discourse before us it had no chance of starting a present conflagration. If in the long run the beliefs expressed in proletarian dictatorship are destined to be accepted by the dominant forces of the community, the only meaning of free speech is that they should be given their chance and have their way.

If the publication of this document had been laid as an attempt to induce an uprising against government at once and not at some indefinite time in the future it would have presented a different question. The object would have been one with which the law might deal, subject to the doubt whether there was any danger that the publication could produce any result, or in other words, whether it was not futile and too remote from possible consequences. But the indictment alleges the publication and nothing more.

WHITNEY v. CALIFORNIA

274 U.S. 357, 47 S. Ct. 641, 71 L. Ed. 1095 (1927)

[*Whitney v. California* is an example of still another First Amendment case in which the enduring principles are not from the opinion of the Court but the separate opinion of a Justice who did not join the Court's opinion.

[Anita Whitney attended a Communist Party Convention in California where she was elected an alternate member of the Party's state executive committee. She was indicted and convicted under the California Criminal Syndicalism Act. Criminal Syndicalism was defined under the law "as any doctrine, advocating [or] teaching unlawful methods of terrorism as a means of accomplishing a change in industrial ownership or control, or effecting any political change." Whitney argued that although it turned out that the majority of delegates attending the convention favored violence as a means of securing political change, she did not favor violence and in fact had worked for positions that would prevent the Communist Labor Party of California from being used for such purposes.

[The Court, per Justice Sanford, rejected her defense on the ground that she was raising issues of fact which had been found against her by the lower court and which the Supreme Court, as an appellate court, could not re-open for consideration. The Court affirmed her conviction, declaring that acting in concert was a greater threat to the public order than the expressions or acts of individuals acting separately.]

JUSTICE BRANDEIS [joined by JUSTICE HOLMES], concurring.

Miss Whitney was convicted of the felony of assisting in organizing, in the year 1919, the Communist Labor Party of California, of being a member of it, and of assembling with it. These acts are held to constitute a crime, because the party was formed to teach criminal syndicalism. The statute which made these acts a crime restricted the right of free speech and of assembly theretofore existing. The claim is that the statute, as applied, denied to Miss Whitney the liberty guaranteed by the Fourteenth Amendment.

The felony which the statute created is a crime very unlike the old felony of conspiracy or the old misdemeanor of unlawful assembly. The mere act of assisting in forming a society for teaching syndicalism, of becoming a member of it, or assembling with others for that purpose is given the dynamic quality of crime. There is guilt although the society may not contemplate immediate promulgation of the doctrine. Thus the accused is to be punished, not for attempt, incitement or conspiracy, but for a step in preparation, which, if it threatens the public order at all, does so only remotely. The novelty in the prohibition introduced is that the statute aims, not at the practice of criminal syndicalism, nor even directly at the preaching of it, but at association with those who propose to preach it.

Despite arguments to the contrary which had seemed to me persuasive, it is settled that the due process clause of the Fourteenth Amendment applies to matters of substantive law as well as to matters of procedure. Thus all fundamental rights comprised within the term liberty are protected by the federal Constitution from invasion by the states. The right of free speech, the right to teach and the right of assembly are, of course, fundamental rights. These may not be denied or abridged. But, although the rights of free speech and assembly are fundamental, they are not in their nature absolute. Their exercise is subject to restriction, if the particular restriction proposed is required in order to protect the state from destruction or from serious injury, political, economic or moral. That the necessity which is essential to a valid restriction does not exist unless speech would produce, or is intended to produce, a clear and imminent danger of some substantive evil which the state constitutionally may seek to prevent has been settled.

It is said to be the function of the Legislature to determine whether at a particular time and under the particular circumstances the formation of, or assembly with, a society organized to advocate criminal syndicalism constitutes a clear and present danger of substantive evil; and that by enacting the law here in question the Legislature of California determined that question in the affirmative. *Compare Gitlow v. New York.* The Legislature must obviously decide, in the first instance, whether a danger exists which calls for a particular protective measure. But where a statute is valid only in case certain conditions exist, the enactment of the statute cannot alone establish the facts which are essential to its validity. Prohibitory legislation has repeatedly been held invalid, because unnecessary, where the denial of liberty involved was that of engaging in a particular business. The powers of the courts to strike down an offending law are no less when the interests involved are not property rights, but the fundamental personal rights of free speech and assembly.

This Court has not yet fixed the standard by which to determine when a danger shall be deemed clear; how remote the danger may be and yet be deemed present; and what degree of evil shall be deemed sufficiently substantial to justify resort to abridgment of free speech and assembly as the means of protection. To reach sound conclusions on these matters, we must bear in mind why a state is, ordinarily, denied the power to prohibit dissemination of social, economic and political doctrine which a vast majority of its citizens believes to be false and fraught with evil consequence.

Those who won our independence believed that the final end of the state was to make men free to develop their faculties, and that in its government the deliberative forces should prevail over the arbitrary. They valued liberty both as an end and as a means. They believed liberty to be the secret of happiness and courage to be the secret of liberty. They believed that freedom to think as you will and to speak as you think are means indispensable to the discovery and spread of political truth; that without free speech and assembly discussion would be futile; that with them, discussion affords ordinarily adequate protection against the dissemination of noxious doctrine; that the greatest menace to freedom is an inert people; that public discussion is a political duty; and that this should be a fundamental principle of the American government. They recognized the risks to which all human institutions are subject. But they knew that order cannot be secured merely through fear of punishment for its infraction; that it is hazardous to discourage thought, hope and imagination; that fear breeds repression; that repression breeds hate; that hate menaces stable government; that the path of safety lies in the opportunity to discuss freely supposed grievances and proposed remedies; and that the fitting remedy for evil counsels is good ones. Believing in the power of reason as applied through public discussion, they eschewed silence coerced by law — the argument of force in its worst form. Recognizing the occasional tyrannies of governing majorities, they amended the Constitution so that free speech and assembly should be guaranteed.

Fear of serious injury cannot alone justify suppression of free speech and assembly. Men feared witches and burnt women. It is the function of speech to free men from the bondage of irrational fears. To justify suppression of free speech there must be reasonable ground to fear that serious evil will result if free speech is practiced. There must be reasonable ground to believe that the danger apprehended is imminent. There must be reasonable ground to believe that the evil to be prevented is a serious one. Every denunciation of existing law tends in some measure to increase the probability that there will be violation of it. Condonation of a breach enhances the probability. Expressions of approval add to the probability. Propagation of the criminal state of mind by teaching syndicalism increases it. Advocacy of law-breaking heightens it still further. But even advocacy of violence, however reprehensible morally, is not a justification for denying free speech where the advocacy falls short of incitement and there is nothing to indicate that the advocacy would be immediately acted on. The wide difference between advocacy and incitement, between preparation and attempt, between assembling and conspiracy, must be borne in mind. In order to support a finding of clear and present danger it must be shown either that immediate serious violence was to be expected or was advocated, or that the past conduct furnished reason to believe that such advocacy was then contemplated.

Those who won our independence by revolution were not cowards. They did not fear political change. They did not exalt order at the cost of liberty. To courageous, self-reliant men, with confidence in the power of free and fearless reasoning applied through the processes of proper government, no danger flowing from speech can be deemed clear and present, unless the incidence of the evil apprehended is so imminent that it may befall before there is opportunity for full discussion. If there be time to expose through discussion the falsehood and fallacies, to avert the evil by the processes of education, the remedy to be applied is more speech, not enforced silence. Only an emergency can justify repression. Such must be the rule if authority is to be reconciled with freedom. Such, in my opinion, is the command of the Constitution. It is therefore always open to Americans to challenge a law abridging free speech and assembly by showing that there was no emergency justifying it.

Moreover, even imminent danger cannot justify resort to prohibition of these functions essential to effective democracy, unless the evil apprehended is relatively serious. The fact that speech is likely to result in some violence or in destruction of property is not enough to justify its suppression. There must be the probability of serious injury to the State. Among free men, the deterrents ordinarily to be applied to prevent crime are education and punishment for violations of the law, not abridgment of the rights of free speech and assembly.

Whenever the fundamental rights of free speech and assembly are alleged to have been invaded, it must remain open to a defendant to present the issue whether there actually did exist at the time a clear danger, whether the danger, if any, was imminent, and whether the evil apprehended was one so substantial as to justify the stringent restriction interposed by the Legislature. The legislative declaration, like the fact that the statute was passed and was sustained by the highest court of the State, creates merely a rebuttable presumption that these conditions have been satisfied.

Whether in 1919, when Miss Whitney did the things complained of, there was in California such clear and present danger of serious evil, might have been made the important issue in the case. She might have required that the issue be determined either by the court or the jury. She claimed below that the statute as applied to her violated the federal Constitution; but she did not claim that it was void because there was no clear and present danger of serious evil, nor did she request that the existence of these conditions of a valid measure thus restricting the rights of free speech and assembly be passed upon by the court or a jury. On the other hand, there was evidence on which the court or jury might have found that such danger existed. I am unable to assent to the suggestion in the opinion of the court that assembling with a political party, formed to advocate the desirability of a proletarian revolution by mass action at some date necessarily far in the future, is not a right within the protection of the Fourteenth Amendment. In the present case, however, there was other testimony which tended to establish the existence of a conspiracy, on the part of members of the International Workers of the World, to commit present serious crimes, and likewise to show that such a conspiracy would be furthered by the activity of the society of which Miss Whitney was a member. Under these circumstances the judgment of the State court cannot be disturbed.

NOTES

1. *The judicial review problem.* Justice Brandeis in *Whitney* argued that the majority's test is equivalent to no judicial review at all. He stated that "the enactment of the statute cannot alone establish the facts which are essential to its validity." Why is this? At least in part the answer might lie in the different nature of the legislative and judicial functions. The legislature is legislating for the future, unable to determine the particular circumstances under which speech may take place. But, as Brandeis said, "the question whether, at the time and under the circumstances, the conditions existed which are essential to validity under the Federal Constitution" is a question that the legislature cannot answer.

2. *Deference to the legislature.* Criticism of the Holmes-Brandeis view in *Gitlow* and *Whitney* is found in Robert Bork, *Neutral Principles and Some First Amendment Problems,* 47 IND. L.J. 1 (1971). Judge Bork argues that the current state of the law "should have been built on Justice Sanford's majority opinions in *Gitlow* and *Whitney*" and lodges the following criticism of the Holmes-Brandeis position:

> Justice Holmes' dissent in *Gitlow* and Justice Brandeis' concurrence in *Whitney* insisted that the Court must also find that, as Brandeis put it, the speech would produce, or is intended to produce, a clear and imminent danger of some substantive evil which the state constitutionally may seek to prevent. Neither of them explained why the danger must be "clear and imminent" before a particular instance of speech could be punished.

Id. at 32. Judge Bork defends Justice Sanford's opinions for the Court: "The legislatures had struck at speech not aimed at the discovery and spread of political truth but aimed rather at destroying the premises of our political system and the means by which we define political truth. There is no value that judges can independently give such speech in opposition to a legislative determination."

Brandeis believed that the courts should decide the imminence of danger. The quarrel over the branch of government appropriate to define the reach of First Amendment protection shifts the battle to the larger and perennial battleground over the wisdom of an extended concept of judicial review. On the one hand, the argument is that if a Bill of Rights does not ever serve to curb a legislative majority against legislative wishes, what purpose does a Bill of Rights serve? The argument is the familiar one that the very purpose of constitutionalism is occasionally to set aside legislation desired by the majority. On the other hand, the argument is that in a democratic society judicial invalidation of a legislative determination that certain speech is inimical "to the premises of our political system" is neither neutral nor democratically arrived at. Perhaps a skeptic like Holmes, or a libertarian like Brandeis, would suggest that the only assumption that the first amendment makes is that there are no inviolable "premises" in "our political system."

[3] The Doctrine Tested: Failure in Crisis

DENNIS v. UNITED STATES
341 U.S. 494, 71 S. Ct. 857, 95 L. Ed. 1137 (1951)

CHIEF JUSTICE VINSON announced the judgment of the Court and an opinion in which JUSTICE REED, JUSTICE BURTON and JUSTICE MINTON join.

Petitioners were indicted in July, 1948, for violation of the conspiracy provisions of the Smith Act during the period of April, 1945, to July, 1948. A verdict of guilty as to all the petitioners was returned by the jury on October 14, 1949. The Court of Appeals affirmed the convictions. 183 F.2d 201. We granted certiorari, limited to the following two questions: (1) Whether either § 2 or § 3 of the Smith Act, inherently or as construed and applied in the instant case, violates the First Amendment and other provisions of the Bill of Rights; (2) whether either § 2 or § 3 of the Act, inherently or as construed and applied in the instant case, violates the First and Fifth Amendments because of indefiniteness.

Sections 2 and 3 of the Smith Act provide as follows:

> Sec. 2. (a) It shall be unlawful for any person —
>
> (1) to knowingly or willfully advocate, abet, advise, or teach the duty, necessity, desirability, or propriety of overthrowing or destroying any government in the United States by force or violence, or by the assassination of any officer of any such government;
>
> (3) to organize or help to organize any society, group, or assembly of persons who teach, advocate, or encourage the overthrow or destruction of any government in the United States by force or violence; or to be or become a member of, or affiliate with, any such society, group, or assembly of persons, knowing the purposes thereof.
>
> Sec. 3. It shall be unlawful for any person to attempt to commit, or to conspire to commit, any of the acts prohibited by the provisions of this title.

The indictment charged the petitioners with wilfully and knowingly conspiring (1) to organize as the Communist Party of the United States of America a society, group and assembly of persons who teach and advocate the overthrow and destruction of the Government of the United States by force and violence, and (2) knowingly and wilfully to advocate and teach the duty and necessity of overthrowing and destroying the Government of the United States by force and violence. The indictment further alleged that § 2 of the Smith Act proscribes these acts and that any conspiracy to take such action is a violation of § 3 of the Act.

Our limited grant of the writ of certiorari has removed from our consideration any question as to the sufficiency of the evidence to support the jury's determination that petitioners are guilty of the offense charged. Whether on this record petitioners did in fact advocate the overthrow of the Government by force and violence is not before us, and we must base any discussion of this point upon the conclusions stated in the opinion of the Court of Appeals, which treated the issue in great detail. That court held that the record amply supports the necessary finding of the jury that petitioners, the leaders of the Communist Party in this country, intended to initiate a violent revolution whenever the propitious occasion appeared.

The obvious purpose of the statute is to protect existing Government, not from change by peaceable, lawful and constitutional means, but from change by violence, revolution and terrorism. That it is within the power of the Congress to protect the Government of the United States from armed rebellion is a proposition which requires little discussion. Whatever theoretical merit there may be to the argument that there is a "right" to rebellion against dictatorial governments is without force where the existing structure of the government provides for peaceful and orderly change. We reject any principle of governmental helplessness in the face of preparation for revolution, which principle, carried to its logical conclusion, must lead to anarchy. No one could conceive that it is not within the power of Congress to prohibit acts intended to overthrow the Government by force and violence. The question with which we are concerned here is not whether Congress has such power, but whether the means which it has employed conflict with the First and Fifth Amendments to the Constitution.

One of the bases for the contention that the means which Congress has employed are invalid takes the form of an attack on the face of the statute on the grounds that by its terms it prohibits academic discussion of the merits of Marxism-Leninism, that it stifles ideas and is contrary to all concepts of a free speech and a free press.

The very language of the Smith Act negates the interpretation which petitioners would have us impose on that Act. It is directed at advocacy, not discussion. Thus, the trial judge properly charged the jury that they could not convict if they found that petitioners did "no more than pursue peaceful studies and discussions or teaching and advocacy in the realm of ideas." He further charged that it was not unlawful "to conduct in an American college and university a course explaining the philosophical theories set forth in the books which have been placed in evidence." Such a charge is in strict accord with the statutory language, and illustrates the meaning to be placed on those words. Congress did not intend to eradicate the free discussion of political theories, to destroy the traditional rights of Americans to discuss and evaluate ideas without fear of governmental sanction. Rather Congress was concerned with the very kind of activity in which the evidence showed these petitioners engaged.

But although the statute is not directed at the hypothetical cases which petitioners have conjured, its application in this case has resulted in convictions for the teaching and advocacy of the overthrow of the Government by force and violence, which, even though coupled with the intent to accomplish that overthrow, contains an element of speech. For this reason, we must pay special heed to the demands of the First Amendment marking out the boundaries of speech. The rule we deduce from [prior] cases is that where an offense is specified by a statute in nonspeech or nonpress terms, a conviction relying upon speech or press as evidence of violation may be sustained only when the speech or publication created a "clear and present danger" of attempting or accomplishing the prohibited crime, *e.g.*, interference with enlistment. The dissents, we repeat, in emphasizing the value of speech, were addressed to the argument of the sufficiency of the evidence.

Although no case subsequent to *Whitney* and *Gitlow* has expressly overruled the majority opinions in those cases, there is little doubt that subsequent opinions have inclined toward the Holmes-Brandeis rationale. [But] neither Justice Holmes nor Justice Brandeis ever envisioned that a shorthand phrase should be crystallized into a rigid rule to be applied inflexibly without regard to the circumstances of each case. Speech is not an absolute, above and beyond control by the legislature when its judgment, subject to review here, is that certain kinds of speech are so undesirable as to warrant criminal sanction. Nothing is more certain in modern society than the principle that there are no absolutes, that a name, a phrase, a standard has meaning only when associated with the considerations which gave birth to the nomenclature. To those who would paralyze our Government in the face of impending threat by encasing it in a semantic straitjacket we must reply that all concepts are relative.

In this case we are squarely presented with the application of the "clear and present danger" test, and must decide what that phrase imports. Overthrow of the Government by force and violence is certainly a substantial enough interest for the Government to limit speech. Indeed, this is the ultimate value of any society, for if a society cannot protect its very structure from armed internal attack, it must follow that no subordinate value can be protected. If, then, this interest may be protected, the literal problem which is presented is what has been meant by the use of the phrase "clear and present danger" of the utterances bringing about the evil within the power of Congress to punish.

Obviously, the words cannot mean that before the Government may act, it must wait until the putsch is about to be executed, the plans have been laid and the signal awaited. If Government is aware that a group aiming at its overthrow is attempting to indoctrinate its members and to commit them to a course whereby they will strike when the leaders feel the circumstances permit, action by the Government is required. Certainly an attempt to overthrow the Government by force, even though doomed from the outset because of inadequate numbers or power of the revolutionists, is a sufficient evil for Congress to prevent. The damage which such attempts create both physically and politically to a nation makes it impossible to measure the validity in terms of the probability of success, or the immediacy of a successful attempt. In the instant case the trial judge charged the jury that they could not convict unless they found that petitioners intended to overthrow the Government "as speedily as circumstances would permit." This does not mean, and could not properly mean, that they would not strike until there was certainty of success. What was meant was that the revolutionists would strike when they thought the time was ripe. We must therefore reject the contention that success or probability of success is the criterion.

The situation with which JUSTICES HOLMES and BRANDEIS were concerned in *Gitlow* was a comparatively isolated event, bearing little relation in their minds to any substantial threat to the safety of the community. They were not confronted with any situation comparable to the instant one — the development of an apparatus designed and dedicated to the overthrow of the Government, in the context of world crisis after crisis.

Chief Judge Learned Hand, writing for the majority below, interpreted the phrase as follows: "In each case [courts] must ask whether the gravity of the 'evil,' discounted by its improbability, justifies such invasion of free speech as is necessary to avoid the danger." We adopt this statement of the rule. As articulated by Chief Judge Hand, it is as succinct and inclusive as any other we might devise at this time. It takes into consideration those factors which we deem relevant, and relates their significance. More we cannot expect from words.

Likewise, we are in accord with the court below, which affirmed the trial court's finding that the requisite danger existed. The mere fact that from the period 1945 to 1948 petitioners' activities did not result in an attempt to overthrow the Government by force and violence is of course no answer to the fact that there was a group that was ready to make the attempt. The formation by petitioners of such a highly organized conspiracy, with rigidly disciplined members subject to call when the leaders, these petitioners, felt that the time had come for action, coupled with the inflammable nature of world conditions, similar uprisings in other countries, and the touch-and-go nature of our relations with countries with whom petitioners were in the very least ideologically attuned, convince us that their convictions were justified on this score. And this analysis disposes of the contention that a conspiracy to advocate, as distinguished from the advocacy itself, cannot be constitutionally restrained, because it comprises only the preparation. It is the existence of the conspiracy which creates the danger. If the ingredients of the reaction are present, we cannot bind the Government to wait until the catalyst is added.

We hold that §§ 2(a)(1), 2(a)(3) and 3 of the Smith Act, do not inherently, or as construed or applied in the instant case, violate the First Amendment and other provisions of the Bill of Rights, or the First and Fifth Amendments because of indefiniteness. Petitioners intended to overthrow the Government of the United States as speedily as the circumstances would permit. Their conspiracy to organize the Communist Party, and to teach and advocate the overthrow of the Government of the United States by force and violence, created a "clear and present danger" of an attempt to overthrow the Government by force and violence. They were properly and constitutionally convicted for violation of the Smith Act. The judgments of conviction are affirmed.

Justice Clark took no part in the consideration or decision of this case.

Justice Frankfurter, concurring in affirmance of the judgment.

Absolute rules would inevitably lead to absolute exceptions, and such exceptions would eventually corrode the rules. The demands of free speech in a democratic society as well as the interest in national security are better served by candid and informed weighing of the competing interests, within the confines of the judicial process, than by announcing dogmas too inflexible for the non-Euclidian problems to be solved.

But how are competing interests to be assessed? Since they are not subject to quantitative ascertainment, the issue necessarily resolves itself into asking, who is to make the adjustment? — who is to balance the relevant factors and ascertain which interest is in the circumstances to prevail? Full responsibility for the choice cannot be given to the courts. Courts are not representative bodies. They are not designed to be a good reflex of a democratic society. Their judgment is best informed, and therefore most dependable, within narrow limits. Their essential quality is detachment, founded on independence. History teaches that the independence of the judiciary is jeopardized when courts become embroiled in the passions of the day and assume primary responsibility in choosing between competing political, economic and social pressures.

Primary responsibility for adjusting the interests which compete in the situation before us of necessity belongs to the Congress. The nature of the power to be exercised by this Court has been delineated in decisions not charged with the emotional appeal of situations such as that now before us. We are to set aside the judgment of those whose duty it is to legislate only if there is no reasonable basis for it. We are to determine whether a statute is sufficiently definite to meet the constitutional requirements of due process, and whether it respects the safeguards against undue concentration of authority secured by separation of power.

JUSTICE JACKSON, concurring.

The "clear and present danger" test was an innovation by JUSTICE HOLMES in the *Schenck* case, reiterated and refined by him and MR. JUSTICE BRANDEIS in later cases, all arising before the era of World War II revealed the subtlety and efficacy of modernized revolutionary techniques used by totalitarian parties. In those cases, they were faced with convictions under so-called criminal syndicalism statutes aimed at anarchists but which, loosely construed, had been applied to punish socialism, pacifism, and left-wing ideologies, the charges often resting on far-fetched inferences which, if true, would establish only technical or trivial violations. They proposed "clear and present danger" as a test for the sufficiency of evidence in particular cases.

I would save it, unmodified, for application as a "rule of reason" in the kind of case for which it was devised. When the issue is criminality of a hot-headed speech on a street corner, or circulation of a few incendiary pamphlets, or parading by some zealots behind a red flag, or refusal of a handful of school children to salute our flag, it is not beyond the capacity of the judicial process to gather, comprehend, and weigh the necessary materials for decision whether it is a clear, and present danger of substantive evil or a harmless letting off of steam. It is not a prophecy, for the danger in such cases has matured by the time of trial or it was never present. The test applies and has meaning where a conviction is sought to be based on a speech or writing which does not directly or explicitly advocate a crime but to which such tendency is sought to be attributed by construction or by implication from external circumstances. The formula in such cases favors freedoms that are vital to our society, and, even if sometimes applied too generously, the consequences cannot be grave. But its recent expansion has extended, in particular to Communists, unprecedented immunities. Unless we are to hold our Government captive in a judge-made verbal trap, we must approach the problem of a well-organized, nation-wide conspiracy, as realistically as our predecessors faced the trivialities that were being prosecuted until they were checked with a rule of reason.

If we must decide that this Act and its application are constitutional only if we are convinced that petitioner's conduct creates a "clear and present danger" of violent overthrow, we must appraise imponderables, including international and national phenomena which baffle the best informed foreign offices and our most experienced politicians. We would have to foresee and predict the effectiveness of Communist propaganda, opportunities for infiltration, whether, and when, a time will come that they consider propitious for action, and whether and how fast our existing government will deteriorate. No doctrine can be sound whose application requires us to make a prophecy of that sort in the guise of a legal decision. The judicial process is not adequate to a trial of such far-flung issues. The answers given would reflect our own political predilections and nothing more.

The authors of the clear and present danger test never applied it to a case like this, nor would I. What really is under review here is a conviction of conspiracy. The Constitution does not make conspiracy a civil right. The basic rationale of the law of conspiracy is that a conspiracy may be an evil in itself, independently of any other evil it seeks to accomplish. Having held that a conspiracy alone is a crime and its consummation is another, it would be weird legal reasoning to hold that Congress could punish the one only if there was "clear and present danger" of the second.

JUSTICE BLACK, dissenting.

[L]et us assume, contrary to all constitutional ideas of fair criminal procedure, that petitioners although not indicted for the crime of actual advocacy, may be punished for it. Even on this radical assumption, the other opinions in this case show that the only way to affirm these convictions is to repudiate directly or indirectly the established "clear and present danger" rule. This the Court does in a way which greatly restricts the protections afforded by the First Amendment. The opinions for affirmance indicate that the chief reason for jettisoning the rule is the expressed fear that advocacy of Communist doctrine endangers the safety of the Republic. Undoubtedly, a governmental policy of unfettered communication of ideas does entail dangers. To the Founders of this Nation, however, the benefits derived from free expression were worth the risk. They embodied this philosophy in the First Amendment's command that "Congress shall make no law abridging the freedom of speech, or of the press." I have always believed that the First Amendment is the keystone of our Government, that the freedoms it guarantees provide the best insurance against destruction of all freedom. At least as to speech in the realm of public matters, I believe that the "clear and present danger" test does not "mark the furthermost constitutional boundaries of protected expression" but does "no more than recognize a minimum compulsion of the Bill of Rights." *Bridges v. California,* 314 U.S. 252, 263.

Public opinion being what it now is, few will protest the conviction of these Communist petitioners. There is hope, however, that in calmer times, when present pressures, passions and fears subside, this or some later Court will restore the First Amendment liberties to the high preferred place where they belong in a free society.

JUSTICE DOUGLAS, dissenting.

If this were a case where those who claimed protection under the First Amendment were teaching the techniques of sabotage, the assassination of the President, the filching of documents from public files, the planting of bombs, the art of street warfare, and the like, I would have no doubts. The freedom to speak is not absolute; the teaching of methods of terror and other seditious conduct should be beyond the pale along with obscenity and immorality. This case was argued as if those were the facts. But the fact is that no such evidence was introduced at the trial. So far as the present record is concerned, what petitioners did was to organize people to teach and themselves teach the Marxist-Leninist doctrine.

The vice of treating speech as the equivalent of overt acts of a treasonable or seditious character is emphasized by a concurring opinion, which by invoking the law of conspiracy makes speech do service for deeds which are dangerous to society. The doctrine of conspiracy has served divers and oppressive purposes and in its broad reach can be made to do great evil. But never until today has anyone seriously thought that the ancient law of conspiracy could constitutionally be used to turn speech into seditious conduct. Yet that is precisely what is suggested. I repeat that we deal here with speech alone, not with speech plus acts of sabotage or unlawful conduct. Not a single seditious act is charged in the indictment. To make a lawful speech unlawful because two men conceive it is to raise the law of conspiracy to appalling proportions. That course is to make a radical break with the past and to violate one of the cardinal principles of our constitutional scheme.

There comes a time when even speech loses its constitutional immunity. Speech innocuous one year may at another time fan such destructive flames that it must be halted in the interests of the safety of the Republic. That is the meaning of the clear and present danger test. When conditions are so critical that there will be no time to avoid the evil that the speech threatens, it is time to call a halt. Otherwise, free speech which is the strength of the Nation will be the cause of its destruction. Yet free speech is the rule, not the exception. The restraint to be constitutional must be based on more than fear, on more than passionate opposition against the speech, on more than a revolted dislike for its contents. There must be some immediate injury to society that is likely if speech is allowed.

NOTES

1. ***The gravity-probability formulation.*** Chief Justice Vinson said he agreed with the test used by Judge Learned Hand in the court of appeals, which was "whether the gravity of the 'evil,' discounted by its improbability, justifies such invasion of free speech as is necessary to avoid the danger." Under the gravity of the evil formulation, if the evil is sufficiently great, speech may be punished even though its probability is minimal. But what is the evil with which the Smith Act is concerned? Is it overthrow of the government or revolution or attempts to overthrow the government or even the conspiracy itself? Each of these dangers involves different probabilities and different degrees of seriousness.

Vinson was certain that the clear and present danger test, properly understood, did not mean that government is prohibited from acting "until the putsch is about to be executed." He denied that "success or probability of success" was appropriate in applying the clear and present danger test. Operating from these premises Vinson was driven to set aside the factor of time in applying the clear and present danger test.

Professor Strong describes the *Dennis* outcome as follows:

> In the hour of its greatest test, against the tough opponent of national security at mid-twentieth century, the rule of clear and present danger lost its bid for general acceptance as a requirement that for state or federal restriction of speech to be valid it must be shown that a legitimate objective of government is imminently and substantially imperiled.

Frank Strong, *Fifty Years of "Clear and Present Danger": From Schenck to Bran denburg — And Beyond*, 1969 SUP. CT. REV. 41, 52.

2. *The evidence presented at the trial.* Note that the Court refused to review the sufficiency of the evidence at trial. Should it have? Consider the following summary of the government's case at trial:

> The government's legal strategy enabled it to avoid the need to present evidence concerning the specific activities of the individual defendants. Instead, the government reasoned that because the defendants had indisputably organized the Communist Party of the United States, following its predecessor's brief dissolution during World War II, to obtain a conviction it needed to establish only that the Communist Party proceeded on the assumption that the change in America's governmental institutions necessary to bring about a truly socialist system must come through resort to violence. The most interesting aspect of the government's case was what it did *not* seek to establish. The government made no effort to prove that this attempted overthrow was in any sense imminent, or even in the concrete planning stages. It failed to introduce any evidence to show that anyone in the party had made even the slightest effort to prepare for any such attempt. Moreover, the government made no effort to demonstrate that any of the individual defendants themselves had at any time directly advocated the violent overthrow of the government.
>
> The government sought to demonstrate that the CPUSA had conspired to organize and teach the advocacy of overthrow by introducing into evidence various books, pamphlets, and articles. The most recent work introduced into evidence by the government was first published in 1928.
>
> When the government rested, its entire case was grounded on dated philosophical treatises and isolated testimony that individual communists had preached the necessity of violent overthrow of the government in order to achieve a socialist revolution. It was clear that the prosecution had failed to put on the powerful case that most had expected.

MARTIN H. REDISH, THE LOGIC OF PERSECUTION: FREE EXPRESSION AND THE MCCARTHY ERA 83–85 (2005).

3. In the 1990s, previously classified documents (the "Venona" documents) — decoded cable messages sent by Soviet intelligence agents back to Moscow — were released, revealing that members of the Communist Party of the United States of America had been heavily involved in espionage (i.e., the clandestine transfer of secret or classified information to a foreign power) or the facilitation of espionage on behalf of the Soviet Union during the 1940s. *See* Redish, *supra* at 2–8. Should this fact in any way affect the relevance of the First Amendment for the *Dennis* prosecution? *See id.* at 72–80. To what extent does the organization for purposes of advocacy that the Communists were alleged to have engaged in in *Dennis* differ from the espionage in which the Venona documents demonstrate they engaged? Can the former be properly described as "speech" while the latter be described as uprotected "conduct" even though espionage necessarily involves some form of communication? Consider Eugene Volokh, *Speech As Conduct: Generally Applicable Laws, Illegal Courses of Conduct, "Situation-Altering Utterances," and the Uncharted Zones*, 90 CORNELL L. REV. 1277, 1284 (2005), arguing that "[s]peech and conduct — or more precisely the speech and nonspeech elements of some behavior — should indeed be distinguished, and the nonspeech elements may be much more heavily regulated." Professor Volokh concludes that "[e]xpression can generally be regulated to prevent harms that flow from its noncommunicative elements, but not harms that flow from what the expression expresses." How would Professor Volokh's analysis deal with espionage?

4. *Clear and present danger, balancing, and the First Amendment.* In *Dennis*, Professor Strong argues, the Court's watering-down of the "clear and present danger" test made it roughly equivalent to the highly deferential "balancing-of-interests" test which Justice Frankfurter had been advocating all along. If the Holmes-Brandeis "clear and present danger" test was roughly analogous to Justice Black's "preferred freedom" doctrine, we can see how far the First Amendment theory strayed in *Dennis*. Was *Dennis* an aberration produced by the excesses of the "Red Scare" or did it merely dramatize inherent weaknesses of the clear and present danger test?

Justice Black in *Konigsberg v. State Bar,* 366 U.S. 36 (1961), also noted "the sudden transformation of the 'clear and present danger test' in *Dennis v. United States*" whereby the test "was diluted and weakened by being recast in terms of [a] 'balancing' formula." He expressed doubt "that Justices Holmes and Brandeis would even have recognized their test." What is the effect of *Dennis* on the Holmes-Brandeis formulation? Did Chief Justice Vinson employ a balancing test even while using the language of clear and present danger? Justice Black, in dissent in *Dennis*, criticized any test which sustained laws "suppressing freedom of speech and press on the basis of Congress' or our own notions of mere 'reasonableness.' "

5. *Deference to Congress.* Justice Frankfurter's attack on the clear and present danger doctrine in *Dennis* argues for a balancing approach for cases where the values of freedom of expression and national security are in conflict. But Frankfurter intends the balancing to be done by the Congress, rather than by the Court. What difference does it make? It is Congress which has passed the law which is under attack as violative of the First Amendment. If the congressional determination is to be upheld on the theory that the congressional balancing decision should be respected, there is no place for judicial review. Unless it can be said that Congress engaged in no balancing process whatever, the congressional determination controls. In his opinion in *Dennis*, Frankfurter extolls his approach as implementing the popular or democratic will and as causing no lasting damage to civil liberties:

> But it is relevant to remind that in sustaining the power of Congress in a case like this nothing irrevocable is done. The democratic process at all events is not impaired or restricted. Power and responsibility remain with the people and immediately with their representatives. All the Court says is that Congress was not forbidden by the Court to pass this enactment and that a prosecution under it may be brought against a conspiracy such as the one before us.

Are majoritarianism and constitutionalism necessarily synonymous? The purpose behind constitutional limitations such as the Bill of Rights, after all, is to protect certain values from destruction by a legislative majority. In this sense, a basic American constitutional goal is limitation of majority will. Therefore, it is somewhat anomalous if majority preference, as expressed in a statute, is given too heavy a weight in evaluating whether such a statute violates a constitutional limitation such as the First Amendment.

6. *Yates v. United States,* 354 U.S. 298 (1957). The favorable result in *Dennis* encouraged the government to continue its program of criminal prosecution of Communists under the Smith Act. The target broadened to reach not just the Party leaders but the small-fry in the Party leadership as well. Attempts by persons convicted as a result of these prosecutions to win Supreme Court review failed in the years immediately following *Dennis*. Finally, the Court granted certiorari in the case of *Yates v. United States*.

Although *Yates* was professedly a case involving judicial construction of the Smith Act rather than a case involving direct interpretation of the First Amendment, the Court in *Yates* clearly narrowed the scope of *Dennis*. A key passage in *Yates* is found in this excerpt from Justice Harlan's opinion for the Court:

> We are thus faced with the question whether the Smith Act prohibits advocacy and teaching of forcible overthrow as an abstract principle, divorced from any effort to instigate action to that end, so long as such advocacy or teaching is engaged in with evil intent. We hold that it does not. The distinction between advocacy of abstract doctrine and advocacy directed at promoting unlawful action is one that has been consistently recognized in the opinions of this Court.

A troubling question was whether the distinction between "advocacy of abstract doctrine" and "advocacy directed at promoting unlawful action" had been recognized in *Dennis*. Justice Harlan in *Yates* preferred to read *Dennis* as if the distinction had been honored there:

> The Government's reliance on this Court's decision in *Dennis* is misplaced. It is true that at one point in the late Chief Justice's opinion

> it is stated that the Smith Act "is directed at advocacy, not discussion." [B]ut it is clear that the reference was to advocacy of action, not ideas, for in the very next sentence the opinion emphasizes that the jury was properly instructed that there could be no conviction for "advocacy in the realm of ideas." The two concurring opinions in that case likewise emphasized the distinction with which we are concerned.

Justice Harlan in *Yates* stated the *Dennis* holding anew:

> The essence of the *Dennis* holding was that indoctrination of a group in preparation for future violent action, as well as exhortation to immediate action, by advocacy found to be directed to "action for the accomplishment" of forcible overthrow, to violence "as a rule or principle of action," and employing "language of incitement," is not constitutionally protected when the group is of sufficient size and cohesiveness, is sufficiently oriented towards action, and other circumstances are such as reasonable to justify apprehension that action will occur.

Justice Clark, dissenting, believed that *Dennis* and *Yates* were inconsistent. The charge to the jury of the trial judge in *Yates* was in his view correct. Clark did not agree that *Dennis* required, as Harlan put it in *Yates*, that the jury be told that the Smith Act "does not denounce advocacy in the sense of preaching abstractly the forcible overthrow of the government." Justice Clark made the following caustic comments about the Harlan statement in *Yates* on the "essence of *Dennis*":

> I have read this statement over and over but do not seem to grasp its meaning for I see no resemblance between it and what the respected Chief Justice wrote in *Dennis*, nor do I find any such theory in the concurring opinions. As I see it, the trial judge charged in essence all that was required under *Dennis* opinions, whether one takes the view of the Chief Justice or of those concurring in the judgment.

The key development in *Yates* was that it precluded the idea that advocacy of abstract doctrine could be punishable consistent with the First Amendment. Advocacy of action, as defined by Harlan in *Yates*, alone was punishable. In this view, *Yates* was considered a welcome advance by libertarians over *Dennis*. But there was no mention in *Yates* that the danger be imminent; danger in the future might be sufficient. Commenting on the effect of *Yates* on *Dennis*, Judge Linde states:

> Since the action advocated might lie in the undefined future, [*Yates*' emphasis was on] the content of the proscribed advocacy, not the immediacy of any danger it might create. Furthermore, reaffirmance in *Yates* of the *Dennis* instruction concerning "overthrow as speedily as circumstances would permit" referred to the required subjective intent of the advocate, not to the objective dangers of his advocacy.

Hans Linde, *"Clear and Present Danger" Reexamined: Dissonance in the Brandenburg Concerto*, 22 Stan. L. Rev. 1163, 1166 (1970).

[4] The Modern Doctrine: Speech and Context

BRANDENBURG v. OHIO

395 U.S. 444, 89 S. Ct. 1827, 23 L. Ed. 2d 430 (1969)

Per Curiam.

The appellant, a leader of a Ku Klux Klan group, was convicted under the Ohio Criminal Syndicalism statute for "advocat[ing] the duty, necessity, or propriety of crime, sabotage, violence, or unlawful methods of terrorism as a means of accomplishing industrial or political reform" and for "voluntarily assembl[ing] with any society, group, or assemblage of persons formed to teach or advocate the doctrines of criminal syndicalism." Ohio Rev. Code Ann. § 2923.13.[1]

The Ohio Criminal Syndicalism Statute was enacted in 1919. From 1917 to 1920, identical or quite similar laws were adopted by 20 States and two territories. In 1927, this Court sustained the constitutionality of California's Criminal Syndicalism Act, the text of which is quite similar to that of the laws of Ohio. *Whitney v. California*. The Court upheld the statute on the ground that, without more, "advocating" violent means to effect political and economic change involves such danger to the security of the State that the State may outlaw it. But *Whitney* has been throughly discredited by later decisions. *See Dennis v. United States*. These later decisions have fashioned the principle that the constitutional guarantees of free speech and free press do not permit a State to forbid or proscribe advocacy of the use of force or of law violation except where such advocacy is directed to inciting or producing imminent lawless action and is likely to incite or produce such actions.[2] A statute which fails to draw this distinction impermissibly intrudes upon the freedoms guaranteed by the First and Fourteenth Amendments. It sweeps within its condemnation speech which our Constitution has immunized from governmental control.

Measured by this test, Ohio's Criminal Syndicalism Act cannot be sustained. The Act punishes persons who "advocate or teach the duty, necessity, or propriety" of violence "as a means of accomplishing industrial or political reform"; or who publish or circulate or display any book or paper containing such advocacy; or who "justify" the commission of violent acts "with intent to

---

[1] [At a Ku Klux Klan Rally, appellant had made the following statement: "We're not a revengent organization, but if our President, our Congress, our Supreme Court, continues to suppress the white, Caucasian race, it's possible that there might have to be some revengence taken." — Eds.]

[2] It was on the theory that the Smith Act embodied such a principle and that it had been applied only in conformity with it that this Court sustained the Act's constitutionality. That this was the basis for Dennis was emphasized in Yates in which the Court overturned convictions for advocacy of the forcible overthrow of the Government under the Smith Act, because the trial judge's instructions had allowed conviction for mere advocacy, unrelated to its tendency to produce forcible action.

exemplify, spread or advocate the propriety of the doctrines of criminal syndicalism"; or who "voluntarily assemble" with a group formed "to teach or advocate the doctrines of criminal syndicalism." Neither the indictment nor the trial judge's instructions to the jury in any way refined the statute's bald definition of the crime in terms of mere advocacy not distinguished from incitement to imminent lawless action.

Accordingly, we are here confronted with a statute which, by its own words and as applied, purports to punish mere advocacy and to forbid, on pain of criminal punishment, assembly with others merely to advocate the described type of action. Such a statute falls within the condemnation of the First and Fourteenth Amendments. The contrary teaching of *Whitney v. California* cannot be supported, and that decision is therefore overruled.

JUSTICE BLACK, concurring.

I agree with the views expressed by MR. JUSTICE DOUGLAS in his concurring opinion in this case that the "clear and present danger" doctrine should have no place in the interpretation of the First Amendment. I join the Court's opinion, which, as I understand it, simply cites *Dennis v. United States*, but does not indicate any agreement on the Court's part with the "clear and present danger" doctrine on which *Dennis* purported to rely.

JUSTICE DOUGLAS, concurring.

While I join the opinion of the Court, I desire to enter a caveat. Though I doubt if the "clear and present danger" test is congenial to the First Amendment in time of a declared war, I am certain it is not reconcilable with the First Amendment in days of peace. I see no place in the regime of the First Amendment for any "clear and present danger" test, whether strict and tight as some would make it, or free-wheeling as the Court in *Dennis* rephrased it.

When one reads the opinions closely and sees when and how the "clear and present danger" test has been applied, great misgivings are aroused. First, the threats were often loud but always puny and made serious only by judges so wedded to the status quo that critical analysis made them nervous. Second, the test was so twisted and perverted in *Dennis* as to make the trial of those teachers of Marxism an all-out political trial which was part and parcel of the cold war that has eroded substantial parts of the First Amendment.

Action is often a method of expression and within the protection of the First Amendment. Suppose one tears up his own copy of the Constitution in eloquent protest to a decision of this Court. May he be indicted? Suppose one rips his own Bible to shreds to celebrate his departure from one "faith" and his embrace of atheism. May he be indicted? The line between what is permissible and not subject to control and what may be made impermissible and subject to regulation is the line between ideas and overt acts.

The example usually given by those who would punish speech is the case of one who falsely shouts fire in a crowded theatre. This is, however, a classic case where speech is brigaded with action. They are indeed inseparable and a prosecution can be launched for the overt acts actually caused. Apart from rare instances of that kind, speech is, I think, immune from prosecution. Certainly there is no constitutional line between advocacy of abstract ideas as in Yates and advocacy of political action as in *Scales*. The quality of advocacy turns on the depth of the conviction; and government has no power to invade that sanctuary of belief and conscience.

NOTES

1. *The* Brandenburg *opinion.*Is it troubling that the Supreme Court issued its *Brandenburg* decision as an anonymous per curiam opinion? Further, in purporting to summarize and clarify fifty years' worth of free speech doctrine, why did *Brandenburg* spend only one brief paragraph on this issue? The per curiam opinion summarized past decisions by saying that legislative proscription of advocacy is not constitutional except when such advocacy (1) is directed to inciting or producing imminent lawless action, and (2) is likely to incite or produce such action. Professor Gunther has said of *Brandenburg*:

> [I]n *Brandenburg v. Ohio*, the Warren Court built on *Yates* and *Scales* to produce its clearest and most protective standard under the first amendment. And *Brandenburg* continues to be adhered to by the Burger Court. [It] combines the most protective ingredients of the *Masses* incitement emphasis with the most useful elements of the clear and present danger heritage.

Gunther, 27 STAN. L. REV. at 754.

Professor BeVier finds in *Brandenburg* "[a] rule successfully mating principle with pragmatic and institutional concerns." The test affords the Supreme Court an opportunity to review the judgment of lower courts through review of "constitutional fact." "Through a rule based on both content and context, the Court retains the potential of each approach to correct juries' inclinations to punish unpopular speakers in addition to dangerously inciteful ones without succumbing to the limitations of either rule." Lillian BeVier, *The First Amendment and Political Speech: An Inquiry into the Substance and Limit of Principle*, 30 STAN. L. REV. 299, 342 (1978).

In spite of such praise, Professor Emerson criticizes even the revised danger test for allowing early governmental intervention, for being ad hoc and vague, and for failing to take into account other options for societal protection. Thomas Emerson, *First Amendment Doctrine and the Burger Court*, 68 CAL. L. REV. 422, 437 (1980).

2. *A revised clear and present danger test?* Why does the *Brandenburg* Court fail to mention the clear and present danger doctrine by name or refer to the Holmes-Brandeis legacy? Might the test be viewed as a rejection of clear-and-present-danger's use of a weighted balancing test, in favor of a definitional speech-acts test? Consider Jed Rubenfeld, *The First Amendment's Purpose,* 53 STAN. L. REV. 767, 829 (2001) ("*Brandenburg* clearly implies that the probability that speech may bring about an unlawful act is not a sufficient constitutional basis for criminalizing it, unless the speech is so closely, immediately, and intentionally engaged with a particular unlawful act that the speech is itself part and parcel of that act, or an attempt (in the criminal law sense of the word) to bring it about.").

Alternatively, could the reason that the Court did not invoke the clear-and-present-danger precedents be that it actually intended to provide *less* protection to inciting speech than the Holmes-Brandeis formulation intended to provide? Might the Court have meant, simply, to reiterate the less speech-protective dichotomy-recognized in *Dennis* and elaborated upon in *Yates*-between purely abstract advocacy, which is protected, and advocacy of concrete criminal conduct at some undetermined future time, which is unprotected? Is that the reason that the Court cited both *Dennis* and *Yates* in footnote 2? See Laura Donohue, *Terrorist Speech and the Future of Free Expression*, 27 CARDOZO L. REV. 233, 248 (2005): "Relying on *Brandenberg* as a guarantee that speech necessary to the liberal democratic discourse is protected. . . may be somewhat naive." Professor Donohue asserts that the opinion "stopped short of ruling on the fate of *Schenck*, *Dennis*, or *Yates*." *Id.* at 249. Is she correct? On the relevance of footnote 2, see MARTIN REDISH, THE LOGIC OF PERSECUTION: FREE EXPRESSION AND THE MCCARTHY ERA 104 (2005): "This footnote would seem to suggest that, despite its strong words in the text of its opinion, in reality all the Court intended to do in *Brandenberg* was apply the distinction. . . between protected 'abstract' advocacy on the one hand and unprotected advocacy of concrete future conduct at some undetermined point, on the other." But if that were, in fact, the Court's intent, would it have made sense for the Court to use the language of imminence in the body of its test — language which had long been associated with the Holmes-Brandeis version of clear and present danger?

3. *Criminal instruction.* To what extent should the standard developed in *Brandenburg* be applied to cases in which the speech sought to be regulated instructed another in how to commit a crime? Consider the application of *Brandenburg* by the Fourth Circuit Court in *Rice v. Paladin Enterprises, Inc.*, 128 F.3d 233 (4th Cir. 1997), *cert. denied*, 523 U.S. 1074 (1998). Defendant was the publisher of *Hit Man: A Technical Manual for Independent Contractors.* As the name implies, the book provided a how-to-do-it description for hit men-people hired to murder another individual or individuals. Relying on the book as a guide, an individual who had been hired as a hit man murdered a woman, her eight-year-old quadriplegic son, and the son's nurse.

In criminal trials, the murderer had been sentenced to death and the man who had hired him sentenced to prison. The relatives and representatives of the decedents brought a civil suit against Paladin, alleging that its book had aided and abetted the murderer in the commission of his crimes. Paladin stipulated, for purposes of argument, that in marketing *Hit Man*, it "intended to attract and assist criminals and would-be criminals who desire information and instructions on how to commit crimes," and that it "intended and had knowledge" that the book actually "would be used, upon receipt, by criminals and would-be criminals to plan and execute the crime of murder for hire." It further stipulated that its publication of the manual had actually assisted the murderer in the preparation of the murders in question.

Paladin relied on *Brandenburg* to establish that its publication of the manual was protected by the First Amendment, since even with its concessions about use of the book, temporal imminence between publication of the book and commission of the crime was lacking. The court rejected the argument: "[W]hile even speech advocating lawlessness has long enjoyed protections under the First Amendment, it is equally well established that speech which, in its effect, is tantamount to legitimately proscribable nonexpressive conduct may itself be legitimately proscribed, punished, or regulated incidentally to the constitutional enforcement of generally applicable statutes." 128 F.3d at 243. The court further reasoned that "the First Amendment is generally inapplicable to charges of aiding and abetting" violations of law. The court then noted that "a jury could reasonably find that Paladin aided and abetted the murders at issue through the quintessential speech act of providing step-by-step instructions for murder (replete with photographs, diagrams, and narration) so comprehensive and detailed that it is as if the instructor were literally present with the would-be murderer not only in the preparation and planning, but in the actual commission of, and follow-up to, the murder." *Id.* at 249.

At the same time, perhaps puzzlingly, the court noted that "[a]id and assistance in the form of this kind of speech bears no resemblance to the 'theoretical advocacy' [or] 'the mere abstract teaching [of] the moral propriety or even moral necessity for a resort to force and violence,'" quoting *Brandenburg*. Instead, the court found, the manual amounted to the "advocacy and teaching of concrete action," quoting *Yates*. It was thus unclear whether the court was relying on the speech-act concept, on which it appeared to be relying initially, or instead on the precept that only abstract advocacy of unlawful conduct is protected. What practical difference might it make in future cases if the court is taken as having relied on one rather than the other? How legitimate a response to a First Amendment argument is the contention that the conduct amounts to aiding and abetting, in violation of state statute? Doesn't the First Amendment take precedence over a conflicting statute?

How important should the inability of the reader or listener to obtain the information absent communication by the speaker be in undertaking a First Amendment analysis in cases of criminal instruction? For example, the *Hit Man* manual gave the following advice: "[In order to dispose of a corpse,] you can simply cut off the head after burying the body. Take the head to some deserted location, place a stick of dynamite in the mouth, and blow the telltale dentition to smithereens! After this, authorities can't use the victim's dental records to identify his remains." Is this something a hit man could not have learned without reliance on the manual? If the hit man had seen it done this way in a movie, and then followed the same course of action in committing murder, could the movie producer be held liable, consistent with the First Amendment? What implications would such a conclusion have for the First Amendment? Is the movie hypothetical distinguishable from the Hit Man manual situation? The court noted that the hit man "faithfully followed the book's instructions in making a home-made silencer, using a rental car with stolen out-of-state tags, murdering the victims in their own home, using an AR-7 rifle to shoot the victims in the eyes from point blank range, and concealing his involvement in the murders." Should the level of constitutional protection turn at all on the hit man's ability either to intuit such behavior on his own or to discover it through other means? How relevant is the fact in reality that the book was not written by a hit man at all, but in fact had been secretly written by an elderly lady who had absolutely no experience as a hit man?

Consider the extent of First Amendment protection that should be given to the speech in each of the following situations:

a. Information on the Internet explaining how to build a bomb.

b. A communication providing an enemy of our nation with secret troop movements.

c. A speech attacking the tax system as theft, and explaining how to evade taxes illegally.

To a certain extent, at least, the court relied on more than merely the conveyance of concrete information. It further noted that "*Hit Man* does not merely detail how to commit murder and murder for hire; through powerful prose in the second person and imperative voice, it encourages its readers in their specific acts of murder. It reassures those contemplating the crime that they may proceed with their plans without fear of either personal failure or punishment." 128 F.3d at 252. Does the court's reliance on this factor support or undermine its conclusion that the manual is not protected by the First Amendment?

4. *Applying Brandenburg.* In *Hess v. Indiana*, 414 U.S. 105 (1973), the Court reversed a conviction under a state disorderly conduct statute on the basis of *Brandenburg*. The defendant, an anti-war demonstrator, had been convicted for using words such as "we'll take the fucking street later." In its per curiam opinion, the Court characterized such speech as amounting "to nothing more than advocacy of illegal action at some indefinite future time. This is not sufficient to permit the State to punish Hess' speech." The Court invoked the *Brandenburg* test:

> Since the uncontroverted evidence showed that Hess' statement was not directed to any person or any group of persons, it cannot be said that he was advocating, in the normal sense, any action. And since there was no evidence or rational inference from the import of the language, that his words were intended to produce, and likely to produce, imminent disorder, those words could not be punished by the State on the ground that they had "a tendency to lead to violence."

5. *Coercive Speech.* Should speech that is directly coercive — for example, threats or blackmail — receive any First Amendment protection? If not, how feasible is it to distinguish coercive speech from advocacy of unlawful conduct? Consider *NAACP v. Claiborne Hardware Co.*, 458 U.S. 586 (1982). There on two occasions the field secretary of the NAACP in Mississippi had warned that any African Americans who broke the boycott of white merchants would have their necks broken. The Court unanimously held that the statements did not constitute unprotected threats, noting that merely because "expressions were intended to exercise a coercive impact on respondent does not remove them from the reach of the First Amendment." Do you agree with this conclusion? One commentator has suggested that the test for protection should be whether "the speaker explicitly or implicitly suggests that he or his co-conspirators will be the ones to carry out the threat." Jennifer Rothman, *Freedom of Speech* *and True Threats*, 25 HARV. L. J. & PUB. POL. 283, 289 (2001). Why should the presence of this factor make a difference?

[B] THE STRUCTURE OF SPEECH REGULATION

[1] Content-Based and Content-Neutral Regulation

In the last section, the focus was on government regulation of speech advocating illegal conduct. Government sought to regulate the advocacy — the speech — because of some harm which was said to flow from the speaker's message, e.g. violent overthrow of government, violence, destruction of property or other illegal conduct. The clear and present danger doctrine assumes that some speech is protected by the First Amendment and some is not. That speech which presents the requisite degree of danger is proscribable; the rest is not. One approach is to treat such unprotected speech as a "category" of speech which is not entitled to full or to any First Amendment protection. Thus, the Court has fashioned certain categories of speech where general First Amendment principles do not apply, e.g., incitement, fighting words, true threats, obscenity, child pornography.

An approach of increasing importance in First Amendment law focuses on the nature of the government regulation. The Court has distinguished between content-based and content-neutral regulations. When government undertakes to regulate speech because of its content or message — because of what is said — the law is especially burdened under the First Amendment. "[A]bove all else, the First Amendment means that government has no power to restrict expression because of its message, its ideas, its subject matter, or its content." *Police Department v. Mosely,* 408 U.S. 92, 95 (1972). While this is an overstatement, it does reflect the important principle that when government uses content-based regulation, the government must establish that the speech falls into a category of unprotected or low value speech, or, the regulation is presumptively unconstitutional. In the area of content-based regulation, the courts also distinguish between subject matter regulations on the one hand and viewpoint regulation on the other. The idea of this distinction is that regulations discriminating on the basis of viewpoint are even more suspect than those discriminating on the basis of subject matter. But both forms of regulation are treated as content-based.

On the other hand, when government regulates for reasons unrelated to the speaker's message, even though freedom of expression is incidentally burdened, First Amendment review is less demanding. Content-neutral time, place or manner regulations, for example, are often reviewed under an intermediate form of balancing analysis, e.g, the law must be narrowly tailored to serve a significant or substantial government interest and leave open ample alternative channels of communication. It is sufficient if the law directly and effectively furthers the end. Government need not use less restrictive means. In some cases, the Court uses the influential standard from *United States v. O'Brien*, 391 U.S. 367, 374 (1968) (text, p. 1072): "A government regulation is sufficiently justified . . . if it furthers an important or substantial government interest; if the government interest is unrelated to the suppression of free expression; and if the incidental restriction of alleged First

Amendment freedoms is no greater than is essential to the furtherance of that interest." The Court has treated these two formulations as essentially the same standard.

Michael C. Dorf, *Incidental Burdens on Fundamental Rights*, 109 HARV. L. REV. 1175, 1180 (1996), notes that "[a]t least formally, the Supreme Court requires intermediate scrutiny of [content-neutral] laws that impose an incidental burden on free speech, although in practice, the standard applied often appear to be quite deferential." But he argues that there are exceptions: "Although not entirely self-consciously, the Court has closely scrutinized incidental burdens that it deems *substantial*." See Geoffrey R. Stone, *Content-Neutral Restrictions*, 54 U. CHI. L. REV. 46, 114 (1987), who similarly notes the deferential approach used for most content-neutral regulation but says that heightened scrutiny is used "whenever an incidental restriction either has a highly disproportionate impact on free expression or directly penalizes expressive activity. And the latter exception is applied quite liberally whenever the challenged restriction significantly limits the opportunities for free expression."

What is the rationale for these distinctions? How is content-based regulation distinguished from content-neutral regulation? Is the distinction appropriate and useful? How are these structural principles implemented in different fact contexts? These are the difficult questions running through the cases that follow.

***Turner Broadcasting System, Inc. v. FCC*, 512 U.S. 622 (1994)** (*Turner I*), text, p. 1308. Federal law requires that cable television systems devote a portion of their channels to the transmission of local broadcast television stations. The Court 5-4, per Justice Kennedy, held that the must-carry rules are content-neutral regulations. First, the rules "on their face, impose burdens and confer benefits without reference to the content of the speech." While the rules interfered with editorial discretion, "the extent of the interference does not depend on the cable operators' programming." Nor was Congress' purpose in enacting the rules content-based. Congress' overriding objective in enacting the must-carry rules "was not to favor programming of a particular subject matter, viewpoint, or format, but rather to preserve free access to free television programming for the 40 percent of Americans without cable." It followed that "the must-carry provisions do not pose such inherent dangers to free expression, or present such potential for censorship or manipulation, as to justify application of the most exacting level of First Amendment scrutiny." The regulation should be reviewed under "the intermediate level of scrutiny applicable to content-neutral restrictions that impose an incidental burden on speech." The case was remanded. *See Turner II*, text, p. 1312. The dissent argued that the must-carry rules were content-based regulations since "[t]he interest in ensuring access to a multiplicity of diverse and antagonistic sources of information, no matter how praiseworthy, is directly tied to the content of what the speakers will likely say."

The Court in *Turner I* provided a useful discussion of the structural principles underlying the content-based, content-neutral distinction.

> At the heart of the First Amendment lies the principle that each person should decide for him or herself the ideas and beliefs deserving

of expression, consideration, and adherence. Our political system and cultural life rest upon this ideal. Government action that stifles speech on account of its message, or that requires the utterance of a particular message favored by the Government seeks not to advance a legitimate regulatory goal, but to suppress unpopular ideas or information or manipulate the public debate through coercion rather than persuasion. These restrictions "rais[e] the specter that the Government may effectively drive certain ideas or viewpoints from the marketplace." *Simon & Schuster, Inc. v. Members of the New York State Crime Victims Bd.* [text, p. 996].

For these reasons, the First Amendment, subject only to narrow and well-understood exceptions does not countenance governmental control over the content of messages expressed by private individuals. Our precedents thus apply the most exacting scrutiny to regulations that suppress, disadvantage, to regulations that suppress, disadvantage, or impose differential burdens upon speech because of its content. Laws that compel speakers to utter or distribute speech bearing a particular message are subject to the same rigorous scrutiny. In contrast, regulations that are unrelated to the content of speech are subject to an intermediate level of scrutiny, because in most cases they pose a less substantial risk of excising certain ideas or viewpoints from the public dialogue.

Deciding whether a particular regulation is content-based or content-neutral is not always a simple task. We have said that the "principal inquiry in determining content-neutrality . . .is whether the government has adopted a regulation of speech because of [agreement or] disagreement with the message it conveys." *Ward v. Rock Against Racism*. The purpose, or justification, of a regulation will often be evident on its face. But while a content-based purpose may be sufficient in certain circumstances to show that a regulation is content-based, it is not necessary to such a showing in all cases (" 'illicit legislative intent is not the sine qua non of a violation of the First Amendment' "). Nor will the mere assertion of a content-neutral purpose be enough to save a law which, on its face, discriminates based on content.

Compare *Turner I* and *II* with *Reno v. ACLU*, text, p. 1234, invalidating statutory provisions regulating indecency on the Internet and *United States v. Playboy Entertainment Corp.*, text, p. 1247, invalidating statutory provisions regulating sexually explicit cable channels, both of which hold the regulations to be content-based and use strict scrutiny review.

***Police Department of the City of Chicago v. Mosley*, 408 U.S. 92 (1972).** In a suit brought by a person who had been picketing a Chicago high school because of alleged racial discrimination, the Supreme Court declared the following city ordinance unconstitutional on its face. The ordinance prohibited picketing "within 150 feet of any primary or secondary school building while the school is in session and one-half hour before the school is in session and one-half hour after the school session has been concluded, *provided* that this subsection does not prohibit the peaceful picketing of any school involved in a labor dispute."

The majority opinion authored by Justice Marshall combined equal protection analysis with public forum concepts, and seemed to announce principles applicable to all free speech cases. Consider Kenneth Karst, *Equality as a Central Principle in the First Amendment*, 43 U. CHI. L. REV. 20, 21 (1975): "The principle of equality, when understood to mean equal liberty, is not just a peripheral support for the freedom of expression, but rather part of the 'central meaning of the First Amendment.' "

> Because Chicago treats some picketing differently from others, we analyze this ordinance in terms of the Equal Protection Clause of the Fourteenth Amendment. Of course, the equal protection claim in this case is closely intertwined with First Amendment interests; the Chicago ordinance affects picketing, which is expressive conduct; moreover, it does so by classifications formulated in terms of the subject of the picketing. As in all equal protection cases, however, the crucial question is whether there is an appropriate governmental interest suitably furthered by the differential treatment.
>
> Necessarily, then, under the Equal Protection Clause, not to mention the First Amendment itself, government may not grant the use of a forum to people whose views it finds acceptable, but deny use to those wishing to express less favored or more controversial views. And it may not select which issues are worth discussing or debating in public facilities. Once a forum is opened up to assembly or speaking by some groups, government may not prohibit others from assembling or speaking on the basis of what they intend to say. Selective exclusions from a public forum may not be based on content alone, and may not be justified by reference to content alone. [T]o permit the continued building of our politics and culture, and to assure self-fulfillment for each individual, our people are guaranteed the right to express any thought, free from government censorship. The essence of this forbidden censorship is content "control."

Chicago attempted to persuade the Court that labor picketing would be less disruptive of school affairs than other kinds of picketing, but the Court was unwilling to accept the factual premises of the argument. " 'Peaceful' nonlabor picketing [is] obviously no more disruptive than 'peaceful' labor picketing. But Chicago's ordinance permits the latter and prohibits the former."

Chief Justice Burger concurred with the "reservation that some of the language used in the discussion of the First Amendment could, if read out of context, be misleading. Numerous holdings of this Court attest to the fact that the First Amendment does not literally mean that we 'are guaranteed the right to express any thought, free from government censorship.' "

***Simon & Schuster, Inc. v. Members of the New York State Crime Victims Board*, 502 U.S. 105 (1991).** The Court invalidated New York's so-called "Son of Sam" law, which required an entity contracting with an accused or convicted person for a depiction of the crime to turn over any income under that contract to an escrow fund for the victim. The Court found the Son of Sam law to be a "content-based statute," because "[i]t singles out income derived from expressive activity for a burden the State places on no other income, and it is directed only at works with a specified content." The Court warned that "[i]n the context of financial regulation, the Government's ability to impose content-based burdens on speech raises the specter that the Government may effectively drive certain ideas or viewpoints from the marketplace. The First Amendment presumptively places this sort of discrimination beyond the power of the Government." Because the law "establishes a financial disincentive to create or publish works with a particular content," it could be upheld only if it served a compelling interest and were narrowly drawn to serve that interest. The state could not "offer any justification for a distinction between this expressive activity and other activity in connection with its interest in transferring the fruits of crime from criminals to their victims." The Court concluded that "the State has a compelling interest in compensating victims from the fruits of crime, but little if any interest in limiting such compensation to the proceeds of the wrongdoer's speech about the crime." The law was not narrowly-tailored to the state's "undisputed compelling interest in ensuring that criminals do not profit from their crimes." The law was "significantly overinclusive" reaching such works as the AUTOBIOGRAPHY OF MALCOLM X, Thoreau's CIVIL DISOBEDIENCE and even the CONFESSIONS OF SAINT AUGUSTINE.

Justice Kennedy, concurring, rejected use of a strict scrutiny for such a content-based regulation in favor of a *per se* rule, subject to categorical exceptions. "Here a law is directed to speech alone where the speech in question is not obscene, not defamatory, not words tantamount to an act otherwise criminal, not an impairment of some other constitutional right, not an incitement to lawless action, and not calculated or likely to bring about imminent harm the state has the substantive power to prevent. No further inquiry is necessary to reject the state's argument that the statute should be upheld." While he acknowledged that other categories of unprotected expression might emerge, he argued that the "use of these traditional legal categories is preferable to the sort of ad hoc balancing that the Court henceforth must perform in every case if the analysis here used becomes our standard test." Is strict scrutiny a balancing test? For an argument that it isn't, see Eugene Volokh, *Freedom of Speech, Permissible Tailoring and Transcending Strict Scrutiny*, 144 U. PA. L. REV. 2417, 2438–39 (1996). *Compare* Stephen Gottlieb, *Compelling Governmental Interests and Constitutional Discourse*, 55 ALB. L. REV. 549, 551 (1992) ("Strict scrutiny is a form of balancing with a rigorous burden of proof placed on the government.").

***Renton v. Playtime Theatres, Inc.*, 475 U.S. 41 (1986),** text, p. 1220. The Court upheld a city ordinance prohibiting adult motion picture theatres from locating within 1000 feet of any residential zone, church, park, or school. The challenged regulation restricted speech by reference to the type of movie theatre involved, treating "theatres that specialize in adult films differently from other kinds of theatres" for zoning purposes. The Court, per Justice Rehnquist, noted that, while the regulation applied only to a particular category of speech, it was justified on grounds unrelated to that speech. Rather, the ordinance was designed to deal with the "secondary effects of such theatres in the surrounding community," such as crime and effects on property values. The ordinance was a valid content-neutral time, place and manner regulation which was "designed to serve a substantial government interest and [which] allows for reasonable alternative avenues of communication." The city had not used its zoning power "as a pretext for suppressing expression" but had made some areas available for adult theaters while "preserving the quality of life in the community at large." Do you agree that the ordinance's purpose in *Renton* removes it from the category of "content-based" restrictions?

In *City of Los Angeles v. Alameda Books, Inc.*, 535 U.S. 425 (2002), text, p. 1221, the Court sought "to clarify the standard for determining whether [an] ordinance serves a substantial government interest under *Renton*." While the Court reversed a lower court decision invalidating, at the summary judgement stage, a Los Angeles ordinance prohibiting the establishment of more than one adult entertainment business in the same building, there was no majority opinion.

Justice O'Connor, joined by Chief Justice Rehnquist and Justices Scalia and Thomas, concluded that the law was a content-neutral time, place and manner regulation subject to intermediate review under *Renton*. "[O]ur cases require only that municipalities rely upon evidence that is 'reasonably believed to be relevant' to the secondary effects that they seek to address." In the present case, "it is rational for the city to infer that reducing the concentration of adult operations in a neighborhood, whether within separate establishments or in one establishment, will reduce crime rates."

Justice Kennedy concurred in the judgment since the city should not have been foreclosed from making the requisite showing under *Renton* by a grant of summary judgment. Justice Kennedy wrote separately for two reasons. First, the designation of adult entertainment zoning as "content-neutral" announced in *Renton* was a legal fiction. Justice Kennedy argued: "if the statute describes the speech by content then it is content-based. And the ordinance in *Renton* treated theaters that specialized in adult films differently from other kinds of theaters. These ordinances are content-based and we should call them so." Justice Kennedy continued: "Nevertheless, the central holding of *Renton* is sound: A zoning restriction that is designed to decrease secondary effects and not speech should be subject to intermediate rather than strict scrutiny. Generally, the government has no power to restrict speech based on content but there are exceptions to the rule. And zoning regulations do not automatically raise the specter of impermissible content discriminations, even if they are content-based, because they have a prima facie legitimate purpose: to limit the negative externalities of land use. The zoning context provides a built-in legitimate rationale, which rebuts the usual presumption that content-based restrictions are unconstitutional. For this reason, we apply intermediate rather than strict scrutiny."

Second, Justice Kennedy addressed the application of the *Renton* standard. He contended that "a city must advance some basis to show that its regulation has the purpose and effect of suppressing secondary effects, while leaving the quantity and accessibility of speech substantially intact." The plurality had addressed the secondary effects prong by arguing that the city could say that the concentration of businesses under one roof would attract the same number of patrons as the concentration of separate establishments. However, the plurality's approach might expand *Renton* since it failed to consider whether, in addressing these secondary effects, the regulation would also reduce speech. Los Angeles must show the ordinance would not burden the speech at issue, that it will "cause two businesses to split rather than to close, that the quantity of speech will be substantially undiminished, and that the total secondary effects will be significantly reduced."

Justice Souter, joined by Justice Stevens and Ginsburg, dissenting, agreed that "intermediate scrutiny" applied. But he noted: "[t]he variants of middle-tier tests cover a grab bag of restrictive statutes, with a corresponding variety of justifications." Zoning of business based on their sales of expressive adult materials does involve a risk of content-based restriction. "Thus, the Court has recognized that this kind of regulation, though often called content-neutral, occupies a kind of limbo between full-blown, content-based restrictions and regulations that apply without any reference to the substance of what is said."

Justice Souter contended that there was a simple safeguard against possible viewpoint discrimination. "If combating secondary effects of property devaluation and crime is truly the reason for the regulation, it is possible to show by empirical evidence that the effects exist, that they are caused by the expressive activity subject to the zoning can be expected either to ameliorate them or to enhance the capacity of the government to combat them (say, by concentrating them in one area), without suppressing the expressive activity itself."

In a portion of the dissent also joined by Justice Breyer, Justice Souter contended that the city failed to justify the ordinance under intermediate scrutiny. "[T]he government's freedom of experimentation cannot displace its burden under the intermediate scrutiny standard to show that the restriction on speech is no greater than essential to realizing an important objective, in this case policing crime. Since we cannot make even a best guess that the city's breakup policy will have any effect on crime or law enforcement, we are a very far crime from any assurance against covert content-based regulation."

***Boos v. Barry*, 485 U.S. 312 (1988).** A District of Columbia ordinance prohibited the display of any sign within 500 feet of a foreign embassy if that sign tends to bring that foreign government into "public odium" or "public disrepute." The argument was made that the ordinance was not content-based, "because the government is not itself selecting between viewpoints; the permissible message on a picket sign is determined solely by the policies of a foreign government." While the Court agreed that the ordinance was not "viewpoint-based" (since the ordinance "determines which viewpoint is acceptable in a neutral fashion by looking to the policies of foreign governments"), the law was nevertheless properly characterized as "content-based," because "the government has determined that an entire category of speech — signs or displays critical of foreign governments — is not to be permitted."

The government had relied on *Renton*, arguing "that here too the real concern is a secondary effect, namely, our international law obligation to shield diplomats from speech that offends their dignity." The Court rejected reliance on *Renton*, however, because "[r]egulations that focus on the direct impact of speech on its audience present a different situation. Listeners' reaction to speech are not the type of 'secondary effects' we referred to in *Renton*." Could the government have recast its argument in order to bring the ordinance within the "secondary effects" rationale? For example, might the government have successfully contended that the ordinance was designed merely to avoid undermining U.S. relations with foreign governments that might result from the prohibited demonstrations?

***Hill v. Colorado*, 530 U.S. 703 (2000).** A Colorado statute enacted to protect abortion clinics from harassment made it unlawful for any person within 100 feet of a health care facility's entrance to "knowingly approach" within 8 feet of another person, without that person's consent, in order to pass "a leaflet or handbill to, displa[y] a sign to, or engag[e] in oral protest, education or counseling with [that] person."

The majority, in upholding the statue against a facial attack, reasoned that regulation was a content-neutral time-place-manner regulation. First, the statute was "not a 'regulation of speech' " but rather was a "regulation of the places where some speech may occur." Second, the Court held that the law "was not adopted 'because of disagreement with the message [the protest] conveys.' " Instead, the " 'restrictions apply equally to all demonstrators, regardless of viewpoint, and the statutory language makes no reference to the content of the speech.' " Third, "the State's interests in protecting access and privacy, and providing the police with clear guidelines, are unrelated to the content of the demonstrators' speech. As we have repeatedly explained, government regulation of expressive activity is 'content neutral' if it is justified without reference to the content of regulated speech." The Court found that the statute regulated solely on the basis of categories of speech — namely, location of protest, education and counseling.

Justice Scalia, dissenting, disagreed, finding the regulation to be unambiguously content-based. " 'The vice of content-based legislation — what renders it deserving of the high standard of strict scrutiny — is not that it is always used for invidious, thought-control purposes, but that it lends itself to use for those purposes.' A restriction that operates only on speech that communicates a message of protest, education, or counseling presents exactly this risk." Who has the better of the argument?

REPUBLICAN PARTY OF MINNESOTA v. WHITE
536 U.S. 765, 122 S. Ct. 2528, 153 L. Ed. 2d 694 (2002)

JUSTICE SCALIA delivered the opinion of the Court.

The question presented in this case is whether the First Amendment permits the Minnesota Supreme Court to prohibit candidates for judicial election in that State from announcing their views on disputed legal and political issues.

Since Minnesota's admission to the Union in 1858, the State's Constitution has provided for the selection of all state judges by popular election. Since 1912, those elections have been nonpartisan. Since 1974, they have been subject to a legal restriction which states that a "candidate for a judicial office, including an incumbent judge," shall not "announce his or her views on disputed legal or political issues." This prohibition is known as the "announce clause." Incumbent judges who violate it are subject to discipline, including removal, censure, civil penalties, and suspension without pay. Lawyers who run for judicial office also must comply with the announce clause. Those who violate it are subject to, *inter alia*, disbarment, suspension, and probation.

[T]he announce clause prohibits a judicial candidate from stating his views on any specific nonfanciful legal question within the province of the court for which he is running, except in the context of discussing past decisions—and in the latter context as well, if he expresses the view that he is not bound by *stare decisis*. [T]he clause both prohibits speech on the basis of its content and burdens a category of speech that is "at the core of our First Amendment freedoms"—speech about the qualifications of candidates for public office. The Court of Appeals concluded that the proper test to be applied to determine the constitutionality of such a restriction is what our cases have called strict scrutiny; the parties do not dispute that this is correct. Under the strict-scrutiny test, respondents have the burden to prove that the announce clause is (1) narrowly tailored, to serve (2) a compelling state interest. In order for respondents to show that the announce clause is narrowly tailored, they must demonstrate that it does not "unnecessarily circumscrib[e] protected expression." *Brown v. Hartlage,* 456 U.S. 45, 54 (1982).

The Court of Appeals concluded that respondents had established two interests as sufficiently compelling to justify the announce clause: preserving the impartiality of the state judiciary and preserving the appearance of the impartiality of the state judiciary. Respondents reassert these two interests before us, arguing that the first is compelling because it protects the due process rights of litigants, and that the second is compelling because it preserves public confidence in the judiciary. Respondents are rather vague, however, about what they mean by "impartiality." Clarity on this point is essential before we can decide whether impartiality is indeed a compelling state interest, and, if so, whether the announce clause is narrowly tailored to achieve it.

One meaning of "impartiality" in the judicial context—and of course its root meaning—is the lack of bias for or against either *party* to the proceeding. Impartiality in this sense assures equal application of the law. That is, it guarantees a party that the judge who hears his case will apply the law to him in the same way he applies it to any other party. This is the traditional sense in which the term is used.

We think it plain that the announce clause is not narrowly tailored to serve impartiality (or the appearance of impartiality) in this sense. Indeed, the clause is barely tailored to serve that interest *at all*, inasmuch as it does not restrict speech for or against particular *parties*, but rather speech for or against particular *issues*. To be sure, when a case arises that turns on a legal issue on which the judge (as a candidate) had taken a particular stand, the party taking the opposite stand is likely to lose. But not because of any bias against that party, or favoritism toward the other party. *Any* party taking that position is just as likely to lose. The judge is applying the law (as he sees it) evenhandedly.

It is perhaps possible to use the term "impartiality" in the judicial context (though this is certainly not a common usage) to mean lack of preconception in favor of or against a particular *legal view*. This sort of impartiality would be concerned, not with guaranteeing litigants equal application of the law, but rather with guaranteeing them an equal chance to persuade the court on the legal points in their case. Impartiality in this sense may well be an interest served by the announce clause, but it is not a *compelling* state interest, as strict scrutiny requires. A judge's lack of predisposition regarding the relevant legal issues in a case has never been thought a necessary component of equal justice, and with good reason. For one thing, it is virtually impossible to find a judge who does not have preconceptions about the law. Indeed, even if it were possible to select judges who did not have preconceived views on legal issues, it would hardly be desirable to do so. "Proof that a Justice's mind at the time he joined the Court was a complete *tabula rasa* in the area of constitutional adjudication would be evidence of lack of qualification, not lack of bias." The Minnesota Constitution positively forbids the selection to courts of general jurisdiction of judges who are impartial in the sense of having no views on the law. And since avoiding judicial preconceptions on legal issues is neither possible nor desirable, pretending otherwise by attempting to preserve the "appearance" of that type of impartiality can hardly be a compelling state interest either.

A third possible meaning of "impartiality" (again not a common one) might be described as openmindedness. This quality in a judge demands, not that he have no preconceptions on legal issues, but that he be willing to consider views that oppose his preconceptions, and remain open to persuasion, when the issues arise in a pending case. This sort of impartiality seeks to guarantee each litigant, not an *equal* chance to win the legal points in the case, but at least *some* chance of doing so. It may well be that impartiality in this sense, and the appearance of it, are desirable in the judiciary, but we need not pursue that inquiry, since we do not believe the Minnesota Supreme Court adopted the announce clause for that purpose. Respondents argue that the announce clause serves the interest in openmindedness, or at least in the appearance of openmindedness, because it relieves a judge from pressure to rule a certain way in order to maintain consistency with statements the judge has previously made. The problem is, however, that statements in election campaigns are such an infinitesimal portion of the public commitments to legal positions that judges (or judges-to-be) undertake, that this object of the prohibition is implausible. Before they arrive on the bench (whether by election or otherwise) judges have often committed themselves on legal issues that they must later rule upon.

The short of the matter is this: In Minnesota, a candidate for judicial office may not say "I think it is constitutional for the legislature to prohibit same-sex marriages." He may say the very same thing, however, up until the very day before he declares himself a candidate, and may say it repeatedly (until litigation is pending) after he is elected. As a means of pursuing the objective of open-mindedness that respondents now articulate, the announce clause is so woefully underinclusive as to render belief in that purpose a challenge to the credulous.

Moreover, the notion that the special context of electioneering justifies an *abridgment* of the right to speak out on disputed issues sets our First Amendment jurisprudence on its head. "[D]ebate on the qualifications of candidates" is "at the core of our electoral process and of the First Amendment freedoms," not at the edges. We have never allowed the government to prohibit candidates from communicating relevant information to voters during an election.

JUSTICE GINSBURG would do so—and much of her dissent confirms rather than refutes our conclusion that the purpose behind the announce clause is not openmindedness in the judiciary, but the undermining of judicial elections. JUSTICE GINSBURG greatly exaggerates the difference between judicial and legislative elections. Not only do state-court judges possess the power to "make" common law, but they have the immense power to shape the States' constitutions as well. Which is precisely why the election of state judges became popular. There is an obvious tension between the article of Minnesota's popularly approved Constitution which provides that judges shall be elected, and the Minnesota Supreme Court's announce clause which places most subjects of interest to the voters off limits. (The candidate-speech restrictions of all the other States that have them are also the product of judicial fiat.) The disparity is perhaps unsurprising, since the ABA, which originated the announce clause, has long been an opponent of judicial elections. That opposition may be well taken (it certainly had the support of the Founders of the Federal Government), but the First Amendment does not permit it to achieve its goal by leaving the principle of elections in place while preventing candidates from discussing what the elections are about. The Minnesota Supreme Court's canon of judicial conduct prohibiting candidates for judicial election from announcing their views on disputed legal and political issues violates the First Amendment. Accordingly, we reverse the grant of summary judgment to respondents and remand the case for proceedings consistent with this opinion.

JUSTICE O'CONNOR, concurring.

I join the opinion of the Court but write separately to express my concerns about judicial elections generally. Respondents claim that "[t]he Announce Clause is necessary . . . to protect the State's compelling governmental interes[t] in an actual and perceived . . . impartial judiciary." I am concerned that, even aside from what judicial candidates may say while campaigning, the very practice of electing judges undermines this interest. We of course want judges to be impartial, in the sense of being free from any personal stake in the outcome of the cases to which they are assigned. But if judges are subject to regular elections they are likely to feel that they have at least some personal stake in the outcome of every publicized case. Elected judges cannot help being aware that if the public is not satisfied with the outcome of a particular case, it could hurt their reelection prospects. Even if judges were able to suppress their awareness of the potential electoral consequences of their decisions and refrain from acting on it, the public's confidence in the judiciary could be undermined simply by the possibility that judges would be unable to do so.

Moreover, contested elections generally entail campaigning. And campaigning for a judicial post today can require substantial funds. Unless the pool of judicial candidates is limited to those wealthy enough to independently fund their campaigns, a limitation unrelated to judicial skill, the cost of campaigning requires judicial candidates to engage in fundraising. Yet relying on campaign donations may leave judges feeling indebted to certain parties or interest groups. Even if judges were able to refrain from favoring donors, the mere possibility that judges' decisions may be motivated by the desire to repay campaign contributors is likely to undermine the public's confidence in the judiciary. Despite these significant problems, 39 States currently employ some form of judicial elections for their appellate courts, general jurisdiction trial courts, or both.

JUSTICE KENNEDY, concurring.

I agree with the Court that Minnesota's prohibition on judicial candidates announcing their legal views is an unconstitutional abridgment of the freedom of speech. There is authority for the Court to apply strict scrutiny analysis to resolve some First Amendment cases, see, *e.g., Simon & Schuster, Inc. v. Members of N. Y. State Crime Victims Bd.* and the Court explains in clear and forceful terms why the Minnesota regulatory scheme fails that test. So I join its opinion.

I adhere to my view, however, that content-based speech restrictions that do not fall within any traditional exception should be invalidated without inquiry into narrow tailoring or compelling government interests. The speech at issue here does not come within any of the exceptions to the First Amendment recognized by the Court. The political speech of candidates is at the heart of the First Amendment, and direct restrictions on the content of candidate speech are simply beyond the power of government to impose.

Minnesota may choose to have an elected judiciary. It may strive to define those characteristics that exemplify judicial excellence. It may enshrine its definitions in a code of judicial conduct. It may adopt recusal standards more rigorous than due process requires, and censure judges who violate these standards. What Minnesota may not do, however, is censor what the people hear as they undertake to decide for themselves which candidate is most likely to be an exemplary judicial officer. Deciding the relevance of candidate speech is the right of the voters, not the State. *See Brown v. Hartlage,* 456 U. S. 45, 60 (1982). The law in question here contradicts the principle that unabridged speech is the foundation of political freedom. By abridging speech based on its content, Minnesota impeaches its own system of free and open elections.

JUSTICE STEVENS, with whom JUSTICE SOUTER, JUSTICE GINSBURG, and JUSTICE BREYER join, dissenting.

By obscuring the fundamental distinction between campaigns for the judiciary and the political branches, and by failing to recognize the difference between statements made in articles or opinions and those made on the campaign trail, the Court defies any sensible notion of the judicial office and the importance of impartiality in that context. The Court's disposition rests on two seriously flawed premises—an inaccurate appraisal of the importance of judicial independence and impartiality, and an assumption that judicial candidates should have the same freedom to express themselves on matters of current public importance" as do all other elected officials. Elected judges, no less than appointed judges, occupy an office of trust that is fundamentally different from that occupied by policymaking officials.

There is a critical difference between the work of the judge and the work of other public officials. In a democracy, issues of policy are properly decided by majority vote; it is the business of legislators and executives to be popular. But in litigation, issues of law or fact should not be determined by popular vote; it is the business of judges to be indifferent to unpopularity. [W]e do know that a judicial candidate, who announces his views in the context of a campaign, is effectively telling the electorate: "Vote for me because I believe X, and I will judge cases accordingly." Once elected, he may feel free to disregard his campaign statements, but that does not change the fact that the judge announced his position on an issue likely to come before him *as a reason to vote for him.* Minnesota has a compelling interest in sanctioning such statements.

A candidate for judicial office who goes beyond the expression of "general observation about the law in order to obtain favorable consideration" of his candidacy, demonstrates either a lack of impartiality or a lack of understanding of the importance of maintaining public confidence in the impartiality of the judiciary.

Even when "impartiality" is defined in its narrowest sense to embrace only "the lack of bias for or against either *party* to the proceeding," the announce clause serves that interest. Expressions that stress a candidate's unbroken record of affirming convictions for rape, for example, imply a bias in favor of a particular litigant (the prosecutor) and against a class of litigants (defendants in rape cases). Contrary to the Court's reasoning in its first attempt to define impartiality, an interpretation of the announce clause that prohibits such statements serves the State's interest in maintaining both the appearance of this form of impartiality and its actuality.

The Court boldly asserts that respondents have failed to carry their burden of demonstrating "that campaign statements are uniquely destructive of openmindedness." But the very purpose of most statements prohibited by the announce clause is to convey the message that the candidate's mind is not open on a particular issue. The Court seems to have forgotten its prior evaluation of the importance of maintaining public confidence in the "disinterestedness" of the judiciary. *Mistretta v. United States,* 488 U. S. 361, 407 (1989). Conversely, the judicial reputation for impartiality and openmindedness is compromised by electioneering that emphasizes the candidate's personal predilections rather than his qualifications for judicial office. The disposition of this case on the flawed premise that the criteria for the election to judicial office should mirror the rules applicable to political elections is profoundly misguided. I therefore respectfully dissent.

JUSTICE GINSBURG, with whom JUSTICE STEVENS, JUSTICE SOUTER, and JUSTICE BREYER join, dissenting.

The speech restriction must fail, in the Court's view, because an electoral process is at stake; if Minnesota opts to elect its judges, the Court asserts, the State may not rein in what candidates may say. I do not agree with this unilocular, "an election is an election," approach. Instead, I would differentiate elections for political offices, in which the First Amendment holds full sway, from elections designed to select those whose office it is to administer justice without respect to persons. Minnesota's choice to elect its judges, I am persuaded, does not preclude the State from installing an election process geared to the judicial office.

Judges are not political actors. They do not sit as representatives of particular persons, communities, or parties; they serve no faction or constituency. Even when they develop common law or give concrete meaning to constitutional text, judges act only in the context of individual cases, the outcome of which cannot depend on the will of the public. Thus, the rationale underlying unconstrained speech in elections for political office—that representative government depends on the public's ability to choose agents who will act at its behest—does not carry over to campaigns for the bench. As to persons aiming to occupy the seat of judgment, the Court's unrelenting reliance on decisions involving contests for legislative and executive posts is manifestly out of place. In view of the magisterial role judges must fill in a system of justice, a role that removes them from the partisan fray, States may limit judicial campaign speech by measures impermissible in elections for political office.

All parties to this case agree that, whatever the validity of the Announce Clause, the State may constitutionally prohibit judicial candidates from pledging or promising certain results. When a judicial candidate promises to rule a certain way on an issue that may later reach the courts, the potential for due process violations is grave and manifest. If successful in her bid for office, the judicial candidate will become a judge, and in that capacity she will be under pressure to resist the pleas of litigants who advance positions contrary to her pledges on the campaign trail. If the judge fails to honor her campaign promises, she will not only face abandonment by supporters of her professed views, she will also "ris[k] being assailed as a dissembler," willing to say one thing to win an election and to do the opposite once in office. By removing this source of "possible temptation" for a judge to rule on the basis of self-interest, the pledges or promises prohibition furthers the State's "compellin[g] interest in maintaining a judiciary fully capable of performing" its appointed task.

In addition to protecting litigants' due process rights, the parties in this case further agree, the pledges or promises clause advances another compelling state interest: preserving the public's confidence in the integrity and impartiality of its judiciary. Prohibiting a judicial candidate from pledging or promising certain results if elected directly promotes the State's interest in preserving public faith in the bench. When a candidate makes such a promise during a campaign, the public will no doubt perceive that she is doing so in the hope of garnering votes. And the public will in turn likely conclude that when the candidate decides an issue in accord with that promise, she does so at least in part to discharge her undertaking to the voters in the previous election and to prevent voter abandonment in the next. The perception of that unseemly *quid pro quo*—a judicial candidate's promises on issues in return for the electorate's votes at the polls— inevitably diminishes the public's faith in the ability of judges to administer the law without regard to personal or political self-interest. Uncoupled from the Announce Clause, the ban on pledges or promises is easily circumvented. By prefacing a campaign commitment with the caveat, "although I cannot promise anything," or by simply avoiding the language of promises or pledges altogether, a candidate could declare with impunity how she would decide specific issues. Semantic sanitizing of the candidate's commitment would not, however, diminish its pernicious effects on actual and perceived judicial impartiality.

By targeting statements that do not technically constitute pledges or promises but nevertheless "publicly mak[e] known how [the candidate] would decide" legal issues, the Announce Clause prevents this end run around the letter and spirit of its companion provision. No less than the pledges or promises clause itself, the Announce Clause is an indispensable part of Minnesota's effort to maintain the health of its judiciary, and is therefore constitutional for the same reasons.

For more than three-quarters of a century, States like Minnesota have endeavored, through experiment tested by experience, to balance the constitutional interests in judicial integrity and free expression within the unique setting of an elected judiciary. The Announce Clause, borne of this long effort, "comes to this Court bearing a weighty title of respect." I would uphold it as an essential component in Minnesota's accommodation of the complex and competing concerns in this sensitive area. Accordingly, I would affirm the judgment of the Court of Appeals for the Eighth Circuit.

WATCHTOWER BIBLE AND TRACT SOCIETY OF NEW YORK, INC. v. VILLAGE OF STRATTON

536 U.S. 150, 122 S. Ct. 2080, 153 L. Ed. 2d 205 (2002)

JUSTICE STEVENS delivered the opinion of the Court.

Petitioners contend that a village ordinance making it a misdemeanor to engage in door-to-door advocacy without first registering with the mayor and receiving a permit violates the First Amendment. Through this facial challenge, we consider the door-to-door canvassing regulation not only as it applies to religious proselytizing, but also to anonymous political speech and the distribution of handbills.

We granted certiorari to decide the following question: "Does a municipal ordinance that requires one to obtain a permit prior to engaging in the door-to-door advocacy of a political cause and to display upon demand the permit, which contains one's name, violate the First Amendment protection accorded to anonymous pamphleteering or discourse?"

For over fifty years, the Court has invalidated restrictions on door-to-door convassing and pamphleteering. From these decisions, several themes emerge that guide our consideration of the ordinance at issue here.

First, the cases emphasize the value of the speech involved. For example, in *Murdock v. Pennsylvania* [319 U.S. 105, 109 (1943)], the Court noted that "hand distribution of religious tracts is an age-old form of missionary evangelism—as old as the history of printing presses." In addition, the cases discuss extensively the historical importance of door-to-door canvassing and pamphleteering as vehicles for the dissemination of ideas. In *Schneider v. State (Town of Irvington*) [308 U.S. 147 (1939)], the petitioner was a Jehovah's Witness who had been convicted of canvassing without a permit based on evidence that she had gone from house to house offering to leave books or booklets. Writing for the Court, Justice Roberts stated that "pamphlets have proved most effective instruments in the dissemination of opinion. And perhaps the most effective way of bringing them to the notice of individuals is their distribution at the homes of the people."

Despite the emphasis on the important role that door-to-door canvassing and pamphleteering has played in our constitutional tradition of free and open discussion, these early cases also recognized the interests a town may have in some form of regulation, particularly when the solicitation of money is involved. In *Cantwell v. Connecticut*, [310 U.S. 296 (1943)], the Court held that an ordinance requiring Jehovah's Witnesses to obtain a license before soliciting door to door was invalid because the issuance of the license depended on the exercise of discretion by a city official. Our opinion recognized that "a State may protect its citizens from fraudulent solicitation by requiring a stranger in the community, before permitting him publicly to solicit funds for any purpose, to establish his identity and his authority to act for the cause which he purports to represent." Similarly, in *Martin v. City of Struthers*, [319 U.S. 141 (1943)],the Court recognized crime prevention as a legitimate interest served by these ordinances and noted that "burglars frequently pose as canvassers, either in order that they may have a pretense to discover whether a house is empty and hence ripe for burglary, or for the purpose of spying out the premises in order that they may return later." Despite recognition of these interests as legitimate, our precedent is clear that there must be a balance between these interests and the effect of the regulations on First Amendment rights. We "must 'be astute to examine the effect of the challenged legislation' and must 'weigh the circumstances and . . . appraise the substantiality of the reasons advanced in support of the regulation.' " Finally, the cases demonstrate that efforts of the Jehovah's Witnesses to resist speech regulation have not been a struggle for their rights alone. In *Martin*, after cataloging the many groups that rely extensively upon this method of communication, the Court summarized that "[d]oor to door distribution of circulars is essential to the poorly financed causes of little people."

Although these World War II-era cases provide guidance for our consideration of the question presented, they do not answer one preliminary issue that the parties adamantly dispute. That is, what standard of review ought we use in assessing the constitutionality of this ordinance. We find it unnecessary, however, to resolve that dispute because the breadth of speech affected by the ordinance and the nature of the regulation make it clear that the Court of Appeals erred in upholding it.

The Village argues that three interests are served by its ordinance: the prevention of fraud, the prevention of crime, and the protection of residents' privacy. We have no difficulty concluding, in light of our precedent, that these are important interests that the Village may seek to safeguard through some form of regulation of solicitation activity. We must also look, however, to the amount of speech covered the ordinance and whether there is an appropriate balance between the affected speech and the governmental interests that the ordinance purports to serve. The text of the Village's ordinance prohibits "canvassers" from going on private property for the purpose of explaining or promoting any "cause," unless they receive a permit and the residents visited have not opted for a "no solicitation" sign. Had this provision been construed to apply only to commercial activities and the solicitation of funds, arguably the ordinance would have been tailored to the Village's interest in protecting the privacy of its residents and preventing fraud. Yet, even though the Village has explained that the ordinance was adopted to serve those interests, it has never contended that it should be so narrowly interpreted.

The mere fact that the ordinance covers so much speech raises constitutional concerns. It is offensive—not only to the values protected by the First Amendment, but to the notion of a free society—that in the context of everyday public discourse a citizen must first inform the government of her desire to speak to her neighbors and then obtain a permit to do so. Even if the issuance of permits by the mayor's office is a ministerial task that is performed promptly and at no cost to the applicant, a law requiring a permit to engage in such speech constitutes a dramatic departure from our national heritage and constitutional tradition. Three obvious examples illustrate the pernicious effect of such a permit requirement. First, as our cases involving distribution of unsigned handbills demonstrate, there are a significant number of persons who support causes anonymously. "The decision to favor anonymity may be motivated by fear of economic or official retaliation, by concern about social ostracism, or merely by a desire to preserve as much of one's privacy as possible." *McIntyre v. Ohio Elections Comm'n* [514 U.S. 334 (1995)]. The requirement that a canvasser must be identified in a permit application filed in the mayor's office and available for public inspection necessarily results in a surrender of that anonymity.

Second, requiring a permit as a prior condition on the exercise of the right to speak imposes an objective burden on some speech of citizens holding religious or patriotic views. As our World War II-era cases dramatically demonstrate, there are a significant number of persons whose religious scruples will prevent them from applying for such a license. There are no doubt other patriotic citizens, who have such firm convictions about their constitutional right to engage in uninhibited debate in the context of door-to-door advocacy, that they would prefer silence to speech licensed by a petty official.

[T]hird, there is a significant amount of spontaneous speech that is effectively banned by the ordinance. A person who made a decision on a holiday or a weekend to take an active part in a political campaign could not begin to pass out handbills until after he or she obtained the required permit. Even a spontaneous decision to go across the street and urge a neighbor to vote against the mayor could not lawfully be implemented without first obtaining the mayor's permission.

The breadth and unprecedented nature of this regulation does not alone render the ordinance invalid. Also central to our conclusion that the ordinance does not pass First Amendment scrutiny is that it is not tailored to the Village's stated interests. Even if the interest in preventing fraud could adequately support the ordinance insofar as it applies to commercial transactions and the solicitation of funds, that interest provides no support for its application to petitioners, to political campaigns, or to enlisting support for unpopular causes. The Village, however, argues that the ordinance is nonetheless valid because it serves the two additional interests of protecting the privacy of the resident and the prevention of crime. With respect to the former, it seems clear that § 107 of the ordinance, which provides for the posting of "No Solicitation" signs and which is not challenged in this case, coupled with the resident's unquestioned right of refuse to engage in conversation with unwelcome visitors, provides ample protection for the unwilling listener. The annoyance caused by an uninvited knock on the front door is the same whether or not the visitor is armed with a permit.

With respect to the latter, it seems unlikely that the absence of a permit would preclude criminals from knocking on doors and engaging in conversations not covered by the ordinance. Moreover, the Village did not assert an interest in crime prevention below, and there is an absence of any evidence of a special crime problem related to door-to-door solicitation in the record before us.

The judgment of the Court of Appeals is reversed, and the case is remanded for further proceedings consistent with this opinion.

JUSTICE BREYER, with whom JUSTICE SOUTER and JUSTICE GINSBURG join, concurring.

While joining the Court's opinion, I write separately to note that the dissent's "crime prevention" justification for this ordinance is not a strong one. For one thing, there is no indication that the legislative body that passed the ordinance considered this justification. Stratton did not rely on the rationale in the courts below, and its general references to "deter[ring] crime" in its brief to this Court cannot fairly be construed to include any other than the fraud it discusses specifically. In the intermediate scrutiny context, the Court ordinarily does not supply reasons the legislative body has not given. I can only conclude that if the village of Stratton thought preventing burglaries and violent crimes was an important justification for this ordinance, it would have said so.

Because Stratton did not rely on the crime prevention justification, because Stratton has not now "present[ed] more than anecdote and supposition," and because the relationship between the interest and the ordinance is doubtful, I am unwilling to assume that these conjectured benefits outweigh the cost of abridging the speech covered by the ordinance.

JUSTICE SCALIA, with whom JUSTICE THOMAS joins, concurring in the judgment.

I concur in the judgment, for many but not all of the reasons set forth in the opinion for the Court. If a licensing requirement is otherwise lawful, it is in my view not invalidated by the fact that some people will choose, for religious reasons, to forgo speech rather than observe it. That would convert an invalid free-exercise claim, into a valid free-speech claim—and a more destructive one at that. Whereas the free-exercise claim, if acknowledged, would merely exempt Jehovah's Witnesses from the licensing requirement, the free-speech claim exempts *everybody*, thanks to Jehovah's Witnesses. As for the Court's fairy-tale category of "patriotic citizens," who would rather be silenced than licensed in a manner that the Constitution (but for their "patriotic" objection) would permit: If our free-speech jurisprudence is to be determined by the predicted behavior of such crackpots, we are in a sorry state indeed.

Chief Justice Rehnquist, dissenting.

The town had little reason to suspect that the negligible burden of having to obtain a permit runs afoul of the First Amendment. For over 60 years, we have categorically stated that a permit requirement for door-to-door canvassers, which gives no discretion to the issuing authority, is constitutional. The Court today, however, abruptly changes course and invalidates the ordinance.

Just as troubling as the Court's ignoring over 60 years of precedent is the difficulty of discerning from the Court's opinion what exactly it is about the Stratton ordinance that renders it unconstitutional. It is not clear what test the Court is applying, or under which part of that indeterminate test the ordinance fails. We are instead told that the "breadth of speech affected" and "the nature of the regulation" render the permit requirement unconstitutional. Under a straightforward application of the applicable First Amendment framework, however, the ordinance easily passes muster.

There is no support in our case law for applying anything more stringent than intermediate scrutiny to the ordinance. The ordinance is content-neutral and does not bar anyone from going door-to-door in *Stratton*. It merely regulates the manner in which one must canvass: A canvasser must first obtain a permit. [T]his test applies to content-neutral time, place, or manner restrictions on speech in public forums. The next question is whether the ordinance serves the important interests of protecting privacy and preventing fraud and crime. With respect to the interest in protecting privacy, the Court concludes that "[t]he annoyance caused by an uninvited knock on the front door is the same whether or not the visitor is armed with a permit." True, but that misses the key point: the permit requirement results in fewer uninvited knocks. Those who have complied with the permit requirement are less likely to visit residences with no trespassing signs, as it is much easier for the authorities to track them down.

The Court also fails to grasp how the permit requirement serves *Stratton*'s interest in preventing crime. We have approved of permit requirements for those engaging in protected First Amendment activity because of a common-sense recognition that their existence both deters and helps detect wrongdoing.

Of course, the *Stratton* ordinance does not guarantee that no canvasser will ever commit a burglary or violent crime. The Court seems to think this dooms the ordinance, erecting an insurmountable hurdle that a law must provide a fool-proof method of preventing crime. In order to survive intermediate scrutiny, however, a law need not solve the crime problem, it need only further the interest in preventing crime. Some deterrence of serious criminal activity is more than enough to survive intermediate scrutiny.

The final requirement of intermediate scrutiny is that a regulation leave open ample alternatives for expression. Undoubtedly, ample alternatives exist here. Most obviously, canvassers are free to go door-to-door after filling out the permit application. And those without permits may communicate on public sidewalks, on street corners, through the mail, or through the telephone.

Intermediate scrutiny analysis thus confirms what our cases have long said: A discretionless permit requirement for canvassers does not violate the First Amendment. Today, the Court elevates its concern with what is, at most, a negligible burden on door-to-door communication above this established proposition.

NOTES

1. *Identifying content-based regulation.* Susan H. Williams, *Content Discrimination and the First Amendment*, 139 U. PA. L. REV. 615, 620–21 (1991), argues "that content discrimination is not one concept but many. There are several different types of content discrimination. The government's purpose [to discriminate] is one type of discrimination, but it is only one. Content discrimination may occur in the impact of the regulation on the marketplace of ideas available to listeners, as when a regulation bans a certain format that is systematically associated with particular speakers or points of view, thereby reducing the availability of that point of view in the marketplace. Content discrimination may also occur in the impact of the regulation on the speaker's chosen message, as when a regulation removes certain symbols or symbolic activities from the range of expression available to speakers."

2. *Content-based as applied.* In *Speech as Conduct: Generally Applicable Laws, Illegal Courses of Conduct, "Situation-Altering Utterances," and the Unchartered Zones*, 90 CORNELL L. REV. 1277, 1286–87 (2005), Professor Eugene Volokh discusses laws that can be considered " 'content-based as applied,' because of the content of the speech triggers its application." He uses the example of a person who, by publishing a book describing how a crime can be easily executed, breaks a law prohibiting the aiding and abetting of a crime. "The law doesn't merely have the effect of restricting some speech more then other speech — most content-neutral laws do that. Rather, the law applies to speech precisely because of the harms that supposedly flow from the content of the speech: Publishing and distributing the book violates the aiding and abetting law because of what the book says." *Id.* He argues that such laws should be presumptively unconstitutional just like facially content-based laws. "[T]he premise of modern First Amendment law is that the government generally may not (with a few narrow exceptions) punish speech because of a fear, even a justified fear, that people will make the wrong decisions based on that speech: '[T]he people in our democracy are entrusted with the responsibility for judging and evaluating the relative merits of conflicting arguments. [I]f there by any danger that the people cannot evaluate the information and arguments advanced by [speakers], it is a danger contemplated by the Framers of the First Amendment.' Thus, punishing speech because its content persuades, informs, or offends especially conflicts with the free speech guarantee, more so than punishing speech for reasons unrelated to its potential persuasive, informative, or offensive effect." *Id.* at 1304.

3. *Evaluating the content distinction.* Does it make sense to distinguish between content-based and content-neutral regulations for purposes of judicial review? *See also* pp. 1071–1090 on expressive conduct. Consider the following attack on the distinction: "That governmental regulation impedes all forms of speech rather than only selected viewpoints or subjects, does not alter the fact that the regulation impairs the free flow of expression. Whatever rationale one adopts for the constitutional protection of speech, the goals behind that rationale are undermined by *any* limitation on expression, content-based or not. [E]ven if content-neutral restrictions equally affected all competing points of view, such restrictions may undermine the functioning of the marketplace [of ideas] by keeping the public equally ignorant of *all* positions on issues, rather than merely one viewpoint." Martin Redish, *The Content Distinction in First Amendment Analysis*, 34 Stan. L. Rev. 113, 128, 130 (1981).

What are the arguments supporting the distinction? Consider Geoffrey Stone, *Restrictions of Speech Because of its Content: The Peculiar Case of Subject Matter Restrictions*, 46 U. Chi. L. Rev. 81 (1978), arguing that content-based regulations deserve special disdain, because they violate the principle that denies the government power to restrict speech because it disapproves the message conveyed. In *Content Regulation and the First Amendment*, 25 Wm. & Mary L. Rev. 189 (1983), Stone argues: "Any law that substantially prevents the communication of a particular idea, viewpoint, or item of information violates the First Amendment except, perhaps, in the most extraordinary of circumstances. This is so, not because such a law restricts 'a lot' of speech, but because by effectively excising a specific message from public debate, it mutilates 'the thinking process of the community' and is thus incompatible with the central precepts of the First Amendment." "

Professor Volokh argues that there is also a practical reason for distinguishing between content-based and content-neutral regulations: "Allowing content-based restrictions (whether facially content-based or content-based as applied) is likely to burden speech more than allowing content-neutral restrictions." Volokh, 90 Cornell L. Rev. at 1305.

[2] The Doctrine of Prior Restraint: Forms of Control — the Structure of the Doctrine

Many have argued that the freedom of speech comprehended in the original understanding of the First Amendment was limited to prohibition of prior restraints, i.e., imposition of limitations or prohibition of speech before it is disseminated. Prior restraints are to be contrasted with "subsequent punishment" — the imposition of penalties for speech that has already been disseminated. Imposition of a prior restraint can be accomplished, for example, by insisting on the speaker's obtaining a license or permit prior to speaking, by court injunction, or by any other method that prohibits a specific message as opposed to prohibiting a category of messages.

While the modern Court has clearly rejected the narrow reading that would limit the free speech guarantee to prior restraints, the historical record arguably calls for closer judicial attention when government seeks to employ prior restraints. The modern Court has said: "Any prior restraint on expression comes to this Court with a 'heavy presumption' against its constitutional validity." *Organization for a Better Austin v. Keefe,* 402 U.S. 415, 419 (1971). But the judicial disfavor accorded prior restraint has not been based solely on history. The functional values served by the First Amendment also are used to justify a stringent standard of review. Speech restrained prior to publication is not exposed to the marketplace. The citizen is denied exposure to the message. The individual cannot learn from speech which is never spoken.

Professor Emerson provides a valuable summary of the rationale for the prior restraint doctrine:

> A system of prior restraint is in many ways more inhibiting than a system of subsequent punishment; it is likely to bring under government scrutiny a far wider range of expressions; it shuts off communication before it takes place; suppression by a stroke of the pen is more likely to be applied than suppression through a criminal process; the procedures do not require attention to the safeguards of the criminal process; the system allows less opportunity for public appraisal and criticism; the dynamics of the system drive toward excesses, as the history of all censorship shows.

THOMAS EMERSON, THE SYSTEM OF FREEDOM OF EXPRESSION 506 (1970); *see generally* Thomas Emerson, *The Doctrine of Prior Restraint*, 20 LAW & CONTEMP. PROBS. 648 (1955).

What regulations should be characterized as "prior restraints?" And what are the appropriate judicial standards to be used? The *Keefe* quotation above suggests that prior restraints are not absolutely prohibited, but we then need to distinguish the permissible from the impermissible prior restraint.

NEAR v. MINNESOTA

283 U.S. 697, 51 S. Ct. 625, 75 L. Ed. 2d 1357 (1931)

MR. CHIEF JUSTICE HUGHES delivered the opinion of the Court.

[A Minnesota statute passed in 1925 declared that a person who "engaged in the business of regularly or customarily producing, publishing or circulating . . . a malicious, scandalous and defamatory newspaper, magazine or other periodical is guilty of a nuisance" and may be enjoined from further committing or maintaining the nuisance. *The Saturday Press* attacked the mayor, chief of police and other law enforcement officials in Minneapolis, asserting that "a Jewish gangster" was in control of gambling, bootlegging and racketeering in Minneapolis. According to the Supreme Court, "There is no question but that the articles made serious accusations against the public officers named and others in connection with the prevalence of crimes and the failure to expose and punish them." The County Attorney sought and obtained an injunction against further publication of The Saturday Press or "any publication whatsoever which is a malicious, scandalous or defamatory newspaper."]

If we cut through mere details of procedure, the operation and effect of the statute in substance is that public authorities may bring the owner or publisher of a newspaper or periodical before a judge upon a charge of conducting a business of publishing scandalous and defamatory matter — in particular that the matter consists of charges against public officers of official dereliction — and unless the owner or publisher is able and disposed to bring competent evidence to satisfy the judge that the charges are true and are published with good motives and for justifiable ends, his newspaper or periodical is suppressed and further publication is made punishable as a contempt. This is of the essence of censorship.

The question is whether a statute authorizing such proceedings in restraint of publication is consistent with the conception of the liberty of the press as historically conceived and guaranteed. In determining the extent of the constitutional protection, it has been generally, if not universally, considered that it is the chief purpose of the guaranty to prevent previous restraints upon publication. The struggle in England, directed against the legislative power of the licenser, resulted in renunciation of the censorship of the press. The liberty deemed to be established was thus described by Blackstone: "The liberty of the press is indeed essential to the nature of a free state; but this consists in laying no previous restraints upon publications, and not in freedom from censure for criminal matter when published. Every freeman has an undoubted right to lay what sentiments he pleases before the public; to forbid this, is to destroy the freedom of the press; but if he publishes what is improper, mischievous or illegal, he must take the consequence of his own temerity." The distinction was early pointed out between the extent of the freedom with respect to censorship under our constitutional system and that enjoyed in England.

The criticism upon Blackstone's statement has not been because immunity from previous restraint upon publication has not been regarded as deserving of special emphasis, but chiefly because that immunity cannot be deemed to exhaust the conception of the liberty guaranteed by State and Federal Constitutions. We have no occasion to inquire as to the permissible scope of subsequent punishment. For whatever wrong the appellant has committed or may commit, by his publications, the state appropriately affords both public and private redress by its libel laws. As has been noted, the statute in question does not deal with punishments; it provides for no punishment, except in case of contempt for violation of the court's order, but for suppression and injunction — that is, for restraint upon publication.

The objection has also been made that the principle as to immunity from previous restraint is stated too broadly, if every such restraint is deemed to be prohibited. That is undoubtedly true; the protection even as to previous restraint is not absolutely unlimited. But the limitation has been recognized only in exceptional cases. No one would question but that a government might prevent actual obstruction to its recruiting service or the publication of the sailing dates of transports or the number and location of troops. On similar grounds, the primary requirements of decency may be enforced against obscene publications. The security of the community life may be protected against incitements to acts of violence and the overthrow by force of orderly government. These limitations are not applicable here. Nor are we now concerned with questions as to the extent of authority to prevent publications in order to protect private rights according to the principles governing the exercise of the jurisdiction of courts of equity.

The fact that for approximately one hundred and fifty years there has been almost an entire absence of attempts to impose previous restraints upon publications relating to the malfeasance of public officers is significant of the deep-seated conviction that such restraints would violate constitutional right. Public officers, whose character and conduct remain open to debate and free discussion in the press, find their remedies for false accusations in actions under libel laws not in proceedings to restrain the publication of newspapers and periodicals. The general principle that the constitutional guaranty of the liberty of the press gives immunity from previous restraints has been approved in many decisions under state constitutions.

The importance of this immunity has not lessened. While reckless assaults upon public men, and efforts to bring obloquy upon those who are endeavoring faithfully to discharge official duties, exert a baleful influence and deserve the severest condemnation in public opinion, it cannot be said that this abuse is greater, and it is believed to be less, than that which characterized the period in which our institutions took shape. Meanwhile, the administration of government has become more complex, the opportunities for malfeasance and corruption have multiplied, crime has grown to most serious proportions, and the danger of its protection by unfaithful officials and of the impairment of the fundamental security of life and property by criminal alliances and official neglect, emphasizes the primary need of a vigilant and courageous press, especially in great cities. The fact that the liberty of the press may be abused by miscreant purveyors of scandal does not make any the less necessary the immunity of the press from previous restraint in dealing with official misconduct. Subsequent punishment for such abuses as may exist is the appropriate remedy, consistent with constitutional privilege.

The statute in question cannot be justified by reason of the fact that the publisher is permitted to show, before injunction issues, that the matter published is true and is published with good motives and for justifiable ends. If such a statute, authorizing suppression and injunction on such a basis, is constitutionally valid, it would be equally permissible for the Legislature to provide that at any time the publisher of any newspaper could be brought before a court, or even an administrative officer (as the constitutional protection may not be regarded as resting on mere procedural details), and required to produce proof of the truth of his publication, or of what he intended to publish and of his motives, or stand enjoined. If this can be done, the Legislature may provide machinery for determining in the complete exercise of its discretion what are justifiable ends and restrain publication accordingly. And it would be but a step to a complete system of censorship. The recognition of authority to impose previous restraint upon publication in order to protect the community against the circulation of charges of misconduct, and especially of official misconduct, necessarily would carry with it the admission of the authority of the censor against which the constitutional barrier was erected. The preliminary freedom, by virtue of the very reason for its existence, does not depend, as this court has said, on proof of truth.

For these reasons we hold the statute, so far as it authorized the proceedings in this action, to be an infringement of the liberty of the press guaranteed by the Fourteenth Amendment. We should add that this decision rests upon the operation and effect of the statute, without regard to the question of the truth of the charges contained in the particular periodical. The fact that the public officers named in this case, and those associated with the charges of official dereliction, may be deemed to be impeccable, cannot affect the conclusion that the statute imposes an unconstitutional restraint upon publication.

JUSTICE BUTLER, joined by JUSTICES VAN DEVANTER, MCREYNOLDS, and SUTHERLAND, dissenting.

The Minnesota statute does not operate as a previous restraint on publication within the proper meaning of that phrase. It does not authorize administrative control in advance such as was formerly exercised by the licensers and censors, but prescribes a remedy to be enforced by a suit in equity. In this case there was previous publication made in the course of the business of regularly producing malicious, scandalous, and defamatory periodicals. The business and publications unquestionably constitute an abuse of the right of free press. The statute denounces the things done as a nuisance on the ground, as stated by the state Supreme Court, that they threaten morals, peace, and good order. There is no question of the power of the state to denounce such transgressions. The restraint authorized is only in respect of continuing to do what has been duly adjudged to constitute a nuisance. There is nothing in the statute purporting to prohibit publications that have not been adjudged to constitute a nuisance. It is fanciful to suggest similarity between the granting or enforcement of the decree authorized by this statute to prevent *further* publication of malicious, scandalous, and defamatory articles and the *previous restraint* upon the press by licensers as referred to by Blackstone and described in the history of the times to which he alludes.

It is well known, as found by the state Supreme Court, that existing libel laws are inadequate effectively to suppress evils resulting from the kind of business and publications that are shown in this case. The doctrine that measures such as the one before us are invalid because they operate as previous restraints to infringe freedom of press exposes the peace and good order of every community and the business and private affairs of every individual to the constant and protracted false and malicious assaults of any insolvent publisher who may have purpose and sufficient capacity to contrive and put into effect a scheme or program for oppression, blackmail or extortion.

NOTES

1. *Rationale for the doctrine.* Thomas Emerson, *The Doctrine of Prior Restraint*, 20 LAW & CONTEMP. PROBS. 648, 648 (1955):

> [T]he doctrine deals with limitations of form rather than substance. The issue is not whether the government may impose a particular restriction of substance in an area of public expression, such as forbidding obscenity in newspapers, but whether it may do so by a particular method, such as advance screening of newspaper copy. In other words, restrictions which could be validly imposed when enforced by subsequent punishment are, nevertheless, forbidden if attempted by prior restraint.

Are prior restraints really more invasive of First Amendment interests than are subsequent punishment systems? Take *Near* as an example. Would First

Amendment interests have been less undermined if, instead of employing an injunction system, the state had imposed criminal penalties for publications of the type outlawed? Professor Emerson argues that one advantage of the prior restraint doctrine is that "[i]t does not require the same degree of judicial balancing that the courts have held to be necessary in [most First Amendment contexts]. Hence, it does not involve the same necessity for the court to pit its judgment on controversial matters of economics, politics, or social theory against that of the legislature." *Id.* at 648. On the general issue of the validity of a special presumption against prior restraints, compare Vincent Blasi, *Toward a Theory of Prior Restraint: The Central Linkage*, 66 MINN. L. REV. 11 (1983), with Martin Redish, *The Proper Role of the Prior Restraint Doctrine in First Amendment Theory*, 70 VA. L. REV. 53 (1984).

2. *The Near exceptions.* Under *Near*, the norm is intended to be freedom from prior restraint. Valid prior restraints are intended to be the exception, and the Court lists national security, obscenity, and incitements to violence as exceptions. "Unfortunately, Chief Justice Hughes never explains what makes his three exceptions exceptional, nor does he indicate whether these exceptions are meant to be exclusive categories or whether additions can be made to them in the future, as the need arises." JEROME BARRON & C. THOMAS DIENES, HANDBOOK OF FREE SPEECH AND FREE PRESS 35 (1979).

3. *Identifying prior restraints.* Justice Butler argues that the regulation challenged in *Near* was not a prior restraint at all because an injunction could be obtained only after a judicial determination and could be directed only against repeat publications of similar nature. Licenses, censorship, and injunctions, for instance, operate to burden expression before the communication takes place and are therefore recognized modes of prior restraint, whether the restraint is imposed by the court or an administrative official.

The difficulty is that the Supreme Court has sometimes applied the term "prior restraint" so liberally as to deprive it of a hard meaning. Thus, the Court has used that phrase in striking down a gross receipts tax on newspapers, *Grosjean v. American Press,* 297 U.S. 233 (1936), as well as in a case invalidating controls on mailing privileges, *Lamont v. Postmaster General,* 381 U.S. 301 (1965). *Compare Pittsburgh Press Co. v. Pittsburgh Comm'n on Human Relations,* 413 U.S. 376 (1973), upholding a municipal human relations ordinance forbidding newspapers from carrying sex-designated want ads. The commission's orders were not deemed prior restraints because the availability of a judicial review procedure assured that restrictions on protected expression would be curtailed: "The special vice of a prior restraint is that communication will be suppressed, either directly or by inducing excessive caution in the speaker, before an adequate [judicial] determination that it is unprotected by the First Amendment." It should not be thought, therefore, that just because a law prevents a communication from occurring that the control automatically becomes a prior restraint. Disorderly conduct, breach of the peace, obscenity laws, etc., even when "narrowly drawn" to conform to Supreme Court requirements, inhibit free expression and tend to produce self-censorship. There is obviously an ambiguous borderland where controls exist which can be classified either as examples of subsequent punishment or as prior restraints. For the party seeking to invalidate the control, however, characterizing a regulation as a prior restraint may induce a court to demand a heavy burden of justification which is required to sustain a prior restraint.

4. *Judicial restraints.* Should a distinction be drawn between administrative restraints and judicial restraints? Does one form present a greater threat to First Amendment rights? Are First Amendment interests better served if a court, rather than an administrator, decides that a restraint on speech is necessary? *See* John Jeffries, *Rethinking Prior Restraint*, 92 Yale L.J. 409 (1983); Redish, 70 Va. L. Rev. at 53. *See also* Mark Lemley & Eugene Volokh, *Freedom of Speech and Injunctions in Intellectual Property Cases*, 48 Duke L.J. 147, 210–211 (1998), arguing that the prior restraint doctrine should not prohibit "permanent injunctions of unprotected speech, entered after a full consideration of the merits whether at trial or on summary judgment." To the same effect, see Ariel Bendor, *Prior Restraint, Incommensurability and the Constitutionalism of Means*, 68 Ford. L. Rev. 289, 346–47 (1999). To a certain extent, the Supreme Court has recognized that administrative restraints are more harmful. However, in a number of cases, the Court has imposed its heavy negative presumption on judicial injunctions, without distinguishing such restraints from the administrative variety. *See, e.g.*, *Nebraska Press Ass'n v. Stuart,* 427 U.S. 539 (1976), where the Court reversed a "gag" order, issued by a state trial judge, which, as modified by the Nebraska Supreme Court, restrained the news media from publishing or broadcasting accounts of confessions or admissions made by an accused except those made to members of the press. The Court, in an opinion by Chief Justice Burger, noted that First Amendment guarantees "afford special protection against orders that prohibit the publication or broadcast of particular information or commentary — orders that impose a 'previous' or 'prior' restraint on speech." The opinion concluded: "We cannot say on this record that alternatives to a prior restraint on petitioners would not have sufficiently mitigated the adverse effects of pretrial publicity so as to make prior restraint unnecessary." Thus, the Court imposed its heavy presumption against prior restraints, even though the restraint had been judicially imposed.

In examining *Nebraska Press*, reconsider the question whether prior restraints actually are more harmful than subsequent punishment schemes, as the prior restraint doctrine presumes. Would or should the result have been different if the case had arisen as a criminal prosecution of a member of the press for violating a state statute that prohibited dissemination of an accused's admissions? In other words, was the constitutional defect in *Nebraska Press* the method of regulation of expression or was it the substance of the interference with expression?

NEW YORK TIMES CO. v. UNITED STATES

403 U.S. 713, 91 S. Ct. 2140, 29 L. Ed. 2d 822 (1971)

[A former Pentagon employee, Dr. Daniel Ellsberg, had a change of heart about the merit of American involvement in the Vietnam war. Ellsberg turned over a secret classified government report which formed a record of American involvement in war in Vietnam. In June 1971, the New York Times decided to publish these papers, which became known as the Pentagon Papers.

[The United States government sought a temporary restraining order prohibiting the publication of the papers. A hearing was held on June 18 in the District Court for the Southern District of New York. On June 19, the district court granted a 10-day restraining order but refused a permanent injunction. On June 22, argument was held in the United States Court of Appeals for the Second Circuit, which reversed the trial court on June 23 and held that the Times should be restrained from publishing pending a government showing that prohibition of the papers placed the national security in jeopardy. Meanwhile, the United States Court of Appeals for the District of Columbia refused to grant the government's request to restrain publication of the papers by the WASHINGTON POST. The two cases were reviewed simultaneously in the Supreme Court, with argument on June 26, resulting in the following decision on June 30. The total elapsed time from filing in the district court to decision in the Supreme Court was less than two weeks.]

PER CURIAM.

We granted certiorari in these cases in which the United States seeks to enjoin THE NEW YORK TIMES and the WASHINGTON POST from publishing the contents of a classified study entitled "History of U.S. Decision-Making Process on Viet Nam Policy."

"Any system of prior restraints of expression comes to this Court bearing a heavy presumption against its constitutional validity." *Bantam Books, Inc. v. Sullivan*. The Government "thus carries a heavy burden of showing justification for the imposition of such a restraint." *Organization for a Better Austin v. Keefe*. The District Court for the Southern District of New York in the *New York Times* case, and the District Court for the District of Columbia and the Court of Appeals for the District of Columbia Circuit in the *Washington Post* case held that the Government had not met that burden. We agree.

The judgment of the Court of Appeals for the District of Columbia Circuit is therefore affirmed. The order of the Court of Appeals for the Second Circuit is reversed.

[Following this short per curiam opinion, each of the Justices of the Supreme Court filed an opinion. Those opinions are summarized below.]

JUSTICE BLACK: The government's position in the principal case, said Justice Black, constituted a "bold and dangerously far reaching contention that the courts should take it upon themselves to 'make' a law abridging freedom of the press in the name of equity, presidential power and national security." He rejected the theory that "inherent Presidential power" could justify a prior restraint. Justice Black made it clear that even if an injunction had been authorized by statute, he would have found such a statute invalid. He said with dismay that "some of my Brethren are apparently willing to hold that the publication of news may sometimes be enjoined. Such a holding would make a shambles of the First Amendment." But this is, rather astringently expressed to be sure, the essence of the doctrine of *Near v. Minnesota*. "Restraint would be recognized only in exceptional cases." But Chief Justice Hughes had observed in *Near*: "No one would question but that a government might prevent actual obstruction of its recruiting service or the publication of the sailing dates of transports or the number and location of troops." The government in the *Pentagon Papers Case* relied on national security as a justification for enjoining publication. Justice Black rejected the justification saying that the word "security" was too broad and vague a term to utilize as an exception to first amendment protection.

JUSTICE DOUGLAS: Justice Douglas asserted that "the First Amendment leaves no room for governmental restraint on the press," although he did emphasize that no existing federal legislation authorized a press restraint or publication. It may be argued that Douglas' emphasis on the lack of statutory authorization for the injunctive relief sought by the government suggests that for Douglas the situation might have been altered if there had been a statute explicitly covering the case.

JUSTICE BRENNAN: Justice Brennan concluded that "the First Amendment stands as an absolute bar to the imposition of judicial restraints in circumstances of the kind presented by these cases." But he did recognize that there is a "single extremely narrow class of cases in which the First Amendment's bar on prior judicial restraint may be overridden." Brennan says the case law indicates this occurs when the nation "is at war." But even if the "present world situation" were equivalent, "only governmental allegation and proof that publication must inevitably, directly and immediately cause the occurrence of an event kindred to imperiling the safety of a transport already at sea can support the issuance of an interim restraining order." Notice that Justice Brennan would provide a freedom from prior restraint which is almost, but not quite, absolute. Recall the emphasis by Chief Justice Hughes in *Near* that exceptions to the doctrine of freedom from prior restraint were exceptional.

JUSTICE STEWART: Justice Stewart thought the other branches of the national government could not and should not unduly transgress on the discretion and privacy the President believed necessary for the conduct of international affairs and negotiations: "The responsibility must be where the power is. If the Constitution gives the Executive a large degree of unshared power in the conduct of foreign affairs and the maintenance of our national defense, then under the Constitution the Executive must have the largely unshared duty to determine and preserve the degree of internal security necessary to exercise that power successfully." Justice Stewart's view leaves the constitutionality of official secrets classifications very far from judicial scrutiny. Does this view of executive prerogative, or inherent presidential power, permit a classification system that constitutes an invalid prior restraint?

Despite Justice Stewart's sympathy for the need for some confidentiality on the part of the Executive in the conduct of international affairs, he joined the majority opinion in holding that the publication of the *Pentagon Papers* could not be enjoined. His reasons for reaching this result follow:

> This is not to say that Congress and the courts have no role to play. Undoubtedly Congress has the power to enact specific and appropriate criminal laws to protect government property and preserve government secrets. Congress has passed such laws, and several of them are of very colorable relevance to the apparent circumstances of these cases. And if a criminal prosecution is instituted, it will be the responsibility of the courts to decide the applicability of the criminal law under which the charge is brought. Moreover, if Congress should

> pass a specific law authorizing civil proceedings in this field, the courts would likewise have the duty to decide the constitutionality of such a law as well as its applicability to the facts proved.
>
> But in the cases before us we are asked neither to construe specific regulations nor to apply specific laws. We are asked, instead, to perform a function that the Constitution gave to the Executive, not the Judiciary. We are asked, quite simply, to prevent the publication by two newspapers of material that the Executive Branch insists should not, in the national interest, be published. I am convinced that the Executive is correct with respect to some of the documents involved. But I cannot say that disclosure of any of them will surely result in direct, immediate, and irreparable damage to our Nation or its people. That being so, there can under the First Amendment be but one judicial resolution of the issues before us. I join the judgments of the Court.

Justice Stewart did not make the absence of legislation the dispositive factor as an absolute matter. He suggested that the Court could enjoin publication if publication threatened "irreparable damage" to the nation.

JUSTICE WHITE: Justice White announced his disagreement with the view that "in no circumstances would the First Amendment permit an injunction about publishing information about government plans or operations." But he rejected the government's position that there exists inherent presidential power which authorizes injunction of a publication by the press if the publication presented a "grave and irreparable" threat to the public interest. He based his conclusion in the present case on two factors: The absence of a statute permitting a prior restraint, and the failure of the government to show the kind of necessity required to justify a prior restraint in the absence of legislation.

Justice White did suggest that if the publishers violated existing federal legislation by publishing the Pentagon Papers (and he implied that they might), the publishers might, consistently with the First Amendment, be punished subsequently to publication:

> What is more, terminating the ban on publication of the relatively few sensitive documents the Government now seeks to suppress does not mean that the law either requires or invites newspapers or others to publish them or that they will be immune from criminal action if they do. Prior restraints require an unusually heavy justification under the First Amendment; but failure by the government to justify prior restraints does not measure its constitutional entitlement to a conviction for criminal publication. That the government chose to proceed by injunction does not mean that it could not successfully proceed in another way.

JUSTICE MARSHALL: For Justice Marshall the issue was not, as the government contended, whether the First Amendment barred a court from prohibiting a newspaper from publishing material whose publication jeopardized the national security. The issue he said was more fundamental: "whether this Court or the Congress has the power to make law."

Marshall emphasized that the separation of powers doctrine prevented judicial issuance of an injunction in these circumstances: "It would, however, be utterly inconsistent with the concept of separation of power for this Court to use its power of contempt to prevent behavior that Congress has specifically declined to prohibit." For Marshall it was crucial was that "Congress had specifically rejected legislation that would have clearly given the President the power he seeks here and made the current activity of the newspapers unlawful."

Justice Marshall did not indicate whether, if Congress had given the President the authority to seek an injunction against the press where warranted by national security, such a statute would have been consistent with the First Amendment.

CHIEF JUSTICE BURGER, dissenting: In the early part of the Chief Justice's opinion he made clear that for him the First Amendment was not an absolute: "Only those who view the First Amendment as an absolute in all circumstances — a view I respect, but reject — can find such a case as this to be simple or easy." He complained that the cases had proceeded in such haste through the courts that no judge who had passed on the case knew all the facts of the case. As a result, he said, "only those judges to whom the First Amendment is absolute and permits of no restraint in any circumstances or for any reason, are really in a position to act."

Burger argued that the TIMES had "unauthorized possession of the documents for three to four months, during which it has had its expert analysts studying them, presumably digesting them and preparing the material for publication." In these circumstances, the Chief Justice asked: "Would it have been unreasonable, since the newspaper could anticipate the government's objections to release of secret material, to give the government an opportunity to review the entire collection and determine whether agreement could be reached on publication?"

On the question of the TIMES' refusal to allow the government to examine the Pentagon Papers in its possession, on the ground of protecting its sources, he made the following caustic observation:

> Interestingly the TIMES explained its refusal to allow the government to examine its own purloined documents by saying in substance this might compromise their sources and informants! The TIMES thus asserts a right to guard the secrecy of its sources while denying that the Government of the United States has that power.

Perhaps the most interesting aspect of Chief Justice Burger's opinion was his apparent belief that the President possessed inherent power to classify documents and shield them from public scrutiny. He apparently did not believe that either the doctrine of separation of powers or the strictures of the First Amendment served to destroy justification for an injunction issued on the basis of inherent presidential power. A major theme of the dissent was a protest against the TIMES' position that it was the absolute trustee of the public's right to know.

JUSTICE BLACKMUN, dissenting: Justice Blackmun began his dissent with a protest that the government and the courts had been given far less time to arrive at accommodation between the public's right to know and the national security than had THE NEW YORK TIMES.

Blackmun concluded his dissent with an admonition that if harm resulted to the nation from publication of the *Papers* in controversy the fault would lie with the press:

> [I]f, with the Court's action today, these newspapers proceed to publish the critical documents and there results therefrom "the death of soldiers, the destruction of alliances, the greatly increased difficulty of negotiation with our enemies, the inability of our diplomats to negotiate," to which list I might add the factors of prolongation of the war and of further delay in the freeing of United States prisoners, then the Nation's people will know where the responsibility for these sad consequences rests.

JUSTICE HARLAN, dissenting: Justice Harlan expressed the view that the haste with which the Supreme Court had considered the *Pentagon Papers Case* had obscured the resolution of fundamental constitutional questions presented by the case:

> 1. Whether the Attorney General is authorized to bring these suits in the name of the United States. This question involves as well the construction and validity of a singularly opaque statute — the Espionage Act, 18 U.S.C. § 793(e).
>
> 2. Whether the First Amendment permits the federal courts to enjoin publication of stories which would present a serious threat to national security. *See Near v. Minnesota.*
>
> 3. Whether the threat to publish highly secret documents is of itself a sufficient implication of national security to justify an injunction on the theory that regardless of the contents of the documents harm enough results simply from the demonstration of such a breach of secrecy.
>
> 4. Whether the unauthorized disclosure of any of these particular documents would seriously impair the national security.
>
> 5. What weight should be given to the opinion of high officers in the Executive Branch of the government with respect to questions 3 and 4.
>
> 6. Whether the newspapers are entitled to retain and use the documents notwithstanding the seemingly uncontested facts that the documents, or the originals of which they are duplicates, were purloined from the government's possession and that the newspapers received them with knowledge that they had been feloniously acquired.

7. Whether the threatened harm to the national security or the government's possessory interest in the documents justifies the issuance of an injunction against publication in light of —

a. The strong First Amendment policy against prior restraints on publication;

b. The doctrine against enjoining conduct in violation of criminal statutes; and

c. The extent to which the materials at issue have apparently already been otherwise disseminated.

In Justice Harlan's view, the power "to evaluate the 'pernicious' influence of premature disclosure" was lodged to some extent in the inherent power of the Executive. Unlike Chief Justice Burger, however, Justice Harlan clearly assigned a role to the judiciary in reviewing an initial executive determination against disclosure. The courts must determine that the subject matter lies within the foreign relations power and that the determination of the irreparable harm to national security be made by the head of the executive department concerned.

Justice Harlan's suggested judicial procedure for weighing whether an executive determination to prohibit disclosure of documents is constitutionally permissible does not appear to require that the government turn over the documents to the court. If that is true, how does the judiciary satisfy itself that the subject matter of the documents lies within the proper compass of the President's foreign relations power?

NOTES

1. ***Prior restraint and publication.*** Was the prior restraint doctrine really applicable in the *Pentagon Papers* decision? In the *Pentagon Papers Case*, unlike *Near*, the suppression had been imposed by a court that had access to the specific papers in controversy. Unlike the situation in *Near*, the courts in the *Pentagon Papers Case* were not being asked to enjoin future publications whose contents were unknown, and the order restraining publication in the *Pentagon Papers Case* was temporary in character. Moreover, unlike the *Near* situation, the *Pentagon Papers Case* involved the area of foreign relations and national security where competing constitutional claims, such as the constitutional status of executive prerogative, were present.

Is the reference to prior restraint, then, little more than a symbolic matter? Is it a way of saying that restraining orders against the press by courts are presumptively impermissible in our society?

2. ***The Progressive case.*** A potential opportunity for clarification of *Pentagon Papers* arose in *United States v. Progressive, Inc.*, 467 F. Supp. 990 (W.D. Wis.), *appeal dismissed*, 610 F.2d 819 (7th Cir. 1979), involving the government's effort to secure an injunction against The Progressive's publication of an article providing technical information on the making of a hydrogen bomb. The government argued that the synthesis of information in the publication would threaten national security, even though all the information

in the article was allegedly obtained from public sources. In granting a temporary injunction, the district court noted that the Atomic Energy Act authorizes injunctions to prevent disclosure of defined restricted data. More importantly, the judge was concerned that although a mistake in ruling against the magazine would curtail the defendant's rights "in a drastic and substantial fashion," a mistake in ruling against the government risked thermonuclear annihilation.

> Because of this "disparity of risk," because the government has met its heavy burden of showing justification for the imposition of a prior restraint, [and] because the Court is unconvinced that suppression of the objected-to technical portions of the [article] would not in any plausible fashion impede the defendants in their laudable crusade to stimulate public knowledge of nuclear armament and bring about enlightened debate on national policy questions, the Court finds that the objected-to portions of the article fall within the narrow area recognized by the Court in *Near v. Minnesota* in which a prior restraint on publication is appropriate.

The Court concluded: "In view of the showing of harm made by the United States, a preliminary injunction would be warranted even in the absence of statutory authorization [the Atomic Energy Act of 1954] because of the existence of the likelihood of direct, immediate and irreparable injury to our nation and its people [*Pentagon Papers*] (Justice Stewart)." The Supreme Court denied a mandamus petition seeking to expedite review. When other newspapers began to publish comparable materials to that in the Progressive article, the government abandoned its effort to secure the restraining order.

Professor Cheh has suggested that the trial court in the *Progressive* case, although purportedly accepting *Pentagon Papers* as controlling,

> succumbed to the danger that the *New York Times* test was designed to prevent. Instead of requiring that the government meet its heavy burden of proof with clear and convincing evidence, the court weighed the interests on both sides. It balanced the gravity of the risk, posited to be death from nuclear annihilation, against the importance to the public of knowing the specific details of the hydrogen bomb manufacture. With the issues thus presented, the result was a foregone conclusion.

Mary Cheh, *The Progressive Case and the Atomic Energy Act: Waking to the Dangers of Government Information Controls*, 48 GEO. WASH. L. REV. 163, 200 (1980); *see also* L.A. Powe, *The H-Bomb Injunction*, 61 U. COLO. L. REV. 55, 76 (1990): "Judges, after all, are not editors; they are accustomed to deciding post hoc, and the posture of national security prior restraint forces guesses about the unknown future. If the consequences are as grave as those in *United States v. The Progressive, Inc.*, what do we expect?"

3. *Government employee disclosures.* *Snepp v. United States,* 444 U.S. 507 (1980) (per curiam), illustrates another method by which the government has sought to prevent publication of materials deemed detrimental to national security. In 1968, Frank Snepp entered into an agreement with the Central Intelligence Agency (CIA) whereby, as a condition of employment, he agreed to submit any information or material concerning the CIA for clearance prior to its publication, during or after his term of employment. After leaving the service, Snepp, without securing clearance, published DECENT INTERVAL, concerning CIA activities in Vietnam, which admittedly contained no classified information. The district court, determining that Snepp had breached his "position of trust" by violating the agreement, issued an injunction requiring clearance of future publication and imposing a constructive trust on all profits from the book for the benefit of the government. The court of appeals affirmed, but modified the decree to eliminate the constructive trust.

The Supreme Court summarily affirmed the district court, rejecting even the court of appeals' modification of the district court decree. Denying the constructive trust "would deprive the Government of this equitable and effective means of protecting intelligence that may contribute to national security." The Court disposed of any First Amendment problem in a footnote:

> We agree with the Court of Appeals that Snepp's agreement is an "entirely appropriate" exercise of the C.I.A. director's statutory mandate to "protec[t] intelligence sources and methods from unauthorized disclosure." Moreover, this Court's cases make clear that — even in the absence of an express agreement — the C.I.A could have acted to protect substantial government interests by imposing reasonable restrictions on employee activities that in other contexts might be protected by the First Amendment. The Government has a compelling interest in protecting both the secrecy of information important to our national security and the appearance of confidentiality so essential to the effective operation of our foreign intelligence service. The agreement that Snepp signed is a reasonable means for protecting this vital interest.

Justice Stevens, joined by Justices Brennan and Marshall, dissenting, rejected the constructive trust as an inappropriate remedy "because the profits are [not] the direct result of the breach." Justice Stevens rejected any suggestion that an agency would have authority to censor employee publications of unclassified information on the basis that the publication could be "detrimental to vital interests" or otherwise be deemed "harmful." Rather, the valid interest of government would allow it to control only the disclosure of classified information.

Professor Cox contends that pre-publication agreements subject employees' "right to criticize the government to an excessively severe and time-consuming prior restraint. [In *Snepp*,] C.I.A. censorship appears to have gone beyond matters relevant to security. The pressure to trim in order to satisfy the censor is ever present. It is not enough that *Snepp's* entirely voluntary undertaking should operate as a waiver of his constitutional rights." Archibald Cox, *Freedom of Expression in the Burger Court*, 94 HARV. L. REV. 1, 9 (1980).

WALKER v. BIRMINGHAM

388 U.S. 307, 87 S. Ct. 1824, 18 L. Ed. 2d 1210 (1967)

[Eight African-American ministers, including the late Martin Luther King, led civil rights marches in Birmingham during Easter week, 1963, in defiance of an *ex parte* restraining order banning all marches, parades, sit-ins or other demonstrations in violation of the Birmingham parade ordinance. The petitioners were held in contempt for violating the ex parte order. The state courts held that petitioners could not violate the injunction and later challenge its validity.]

JUSTICE STEWART delivered the opinion of the Court.

We are asked to say that the Constitution compelled Alabama to allow the petitioners to violate this injunction, to organize and engage in these mass street parades and demonstrations, without any previous effort on their part to have the injunction dissolved or modified, or any attempt to secure a parade permit in accordance with its terms. [W]e cannot accept the petitioners' contentions in the circumstances of this case. Without question the state court that issued the injunction had, as a court of equity, jurisdiction over the petitioners and over the subject matter of the controversy. And this is not a case where the injunction was transparently invalid or had only a frivolous pretense to validity. We have consistently recognized the strong interest of state and local governments in regulating the use of their streets and other public places.

The generality of the language contained in the Birmingham parade ordinance upon which the injunction was based would unquestionably raise substantial constitutional issues concerning some of its provisions. The petitioners, however, did not even attempt to apply to the Alabama courts for an authoritative construction of the ordinance. Had they done so, those courts might have given the licensing authority granted in the ordinance a narrow and precise scope.

The breadth and vagueness of the injunction itself would also unquestionably be subject to substantial constitutional question. But the way to raise that question was to apply to the Alabama courts to have the injunction modified or dissolved. The injunction in all events clearly prohibited mass parading without a permit, and the evidence shows that the petitioners fully understood that prohibition when they violated it.

This case would arise in quite a different constitutional posture if the petitioners, before disobeying the injunction, had challenged it in the Alabama courts, and had been met with delay or frustration of their constitutional claims. But there is no showing that such would have been the fate of a timely motion to modify or dissolve the injunction. There was an interim of two days between the issuance of the injunction and the Good Friday march. The petitioners give absolutely no explanation of why they did not make some application to the state court during that period. The injunction had issued *ex parte*; if the court had been presented with the petitioners' contentions, it might well have dissolved or at least modified its order in some respects. If it had not done so, Alabama procedure would have provided for an expedited process of appellate review. It cannot be presumed that the Alabama courts would have ignored the petitioners' constitutional claims. Indeed, these contentions were accepted in another case by an Alabama appellate court that struck down on direct review the conviction under this very ordinance of one of these same petitioners.

[P]recedents clearly put the petitioners on notice that they could not bypass orderly judicial review of the injunction before disobeying it. Any claim that they were entrapped or misled is wholly unfounded, a conclusion confirmed by evidence in the record showing that when the petitioners deliberately violated the injunction they expected to go to jail.

The rule of law that Alabama followed in this case reflects a belief that in the fair administration of justice no man can be judge in his own case, however exalted his station, however righteous his motives, and irrespective of his race, color, politics, or religion. This Court cannot hold that the petitioners were constitutionally free to ignore all the procedures of the law and carry their battle to the streets. One may sympathize with the petitioners' impatient commitment to their cause. But respect for judicial process is a small price to pay for the civilizing hand of law which alone can give abiding meaning to constitutional freedom.

Chief Justice Warren, with whom Justices Brennan and Fortas join, dissenting.

It has never been thought that violation of a statute indicated such a disrespect for the legislature that the violator always must be punished even if the statute was unconstitutional. On the contrary, some cases have required that persons seeking to challenge the constitutionality of a statute first violate it to establish their standing to sue. Indeed, it shows no disrespect for law to violate a statute on the ground that it is unconstitutional and then to submit one's case to the courts with the willingness to accept the penalty if the statute is held to be valid.

This injunction was such potent magic that it transformed the command of an unconstitutional statute into an impregnable barrier, challengeable only in what likely would have been protracted legal proceedings and entirely superior in the meantime even to the United States Constitution.

Justice Brennan, with whom Chief Justice Warren and Justices Douglas and Fortas join, dissenting.

Under cover of exhortation that the Negro exercise "respect for judicial process," the Court empties the Supremacy Clause of its primacy by elevating a state rule of judicial administration above the right of free expression guaranteed by the Federal Constitution. And the Court does so by letting loose a devastatingly destructive weapon for suppression of cherished freedoms heretofore believed indispensable to maintenance of our free society. I cannot believe that this distortion in the hierarchy of values upon which our society has been and must be ordered can have any significance beyond its function as a vehicle to affirm these contempt convictions.

The vitality of First Amendment protections has been deemed to rest in large measure upon the ability of the individual to take his chances and express himself in the face of such restraints, armed with the ability to challenge those restraints if the State seeks to penalize that expression. The most striking examples of the right to speak first and challenge later, and of peculiar moment for the present case, are the cases concerning the ability of an individual to challenge a permit or licensing statute giving broad discretion to an individual or group, such as the Birmingham permit ordinance, despite the fact that he did not attempt to obtain a permit or license.

Yet by some inscrutable legerdemain these constitutionally secured rights to challenge prior restraints invalid on their face are lost if the State takes the precaution to have some judge append his signature to an *ex parte* order which recites the words of the invalid statute. The State neatly insulates its legislation from challenge by mere incorporation of the identical stifling, overbroad, and vague restraints on exercise of the First Amendment freedoms into an even more vague and pervasive injunction obtained invisibly and upon a stage darkened lest it be open to scrutiny by those affected. The *ex parte* order of the judicial officer exercising broad equitable powers is glorified above the presumably carefully considered, even if hopelessly invalid, mandates of the legislative branch. I would expect this tribunal, charged as it is with the ultimate responsibility to safeguard our constitutional freedoms, to regard the *ex parte* injunctive tool to be far more dangerous than statutes to First Amendment freedoms. One would expect this Court particularly to remember the stern lesson history taught courts, in the context of the labor injunction, that the *ex parte* injunction represents the most devastating of restraints on constitutionally protected activities. Today, however, the weapon is given complete invulnerability in the one context in which the danger from broad prior restraints has been thought to be the most acute. Were it not for the *ex parte* injunction, petitioners could have paraded first and challenged the permit ordinance later. But because of the *ex parte* stamp of a judicial officer on a copy of the invalid ordinance they are barred not only from challenging the permit ordinance, but also the potentially more stifling yet unconsidered restraints embodied in the injunction itself.

The Court today lets loose a devastatingly destructive weapon for infringement of freedoms jealously safeguarded not so much for the benefit of any given group of any given persuasion as for the benefit of all of us. We cannot permit fears of "riots" and "civil disobedience" generated by slogans like "Black Power" to divert our attention from what is here at stake — not violence or the right of the State to control its streets and sidewalks, but the insulation from attack of ex parte orders and legislation upon which they are based even when patently impermissible prior restraints on the exercise of First Amendment rights, thus arming the state courts with the power to punish as a "contempt" what they otherwise could not punish at all.

NOTES

1. *Shuttlesworth v. Birmingham*, 394 U.S. 147 (1969). The Court, per Justice Stewart, overturned the conviction of Reverend Shuttlesworth, who led fifty-two people in a protest march without a permit as required by a Birmingham licensing ordinance. He had been informed that no license would be issued under the ordinance, which required that licenses be issued unless the City Commission concluded that "the public welfare, peace, safety, health, decency, good order, morals or convenience require that it be refused."

Although the ordinance as subsequently construed by the Alabama Supreme Court "would pass Constitutional muster," Justice Stewart reasoned it was impossible to know its limited construction at the time of the protest, and the conviction, therefore, could not stand. Justice Stewart also held that Shuttlesworth's failure to test the licensing statute was not determinative: "[O]ur decisions have made clear that a person faced with such an unconstitutional licensing law may ignore it, and engage with impunity in the exercise of the right of free expression for which the law purports to require a license." Does it make sense to treat *Shuttlesworth* differently from *Walker*?

2. *Ex parte orders and injunctions.* Note that in *Walker* the prior restraint came in the form of an *ex parte* restraining order, which means that it was issued before the defendant had an opportunity to be heard. In the post-*Walker* decision in *Carroll v. President & Comm'rs,* 393 U.S. 175 (1968), the Court held an *ex parte* restraining order of a proposed rally unconstitutional "because of a basic infirmity in the procedure by which it was obtained," and concluded that "there is no place within the area of basic freedoms guaranteed by the First Amendment for such orders where no showing is made that it is impossible to serve or to notify the opposing parties and to give them an opportunity to participate." Does this decision effectively overrule *Walker*, or are the two cases distinguishable?

3. *Jurisdiction and contempt orders.* *Walker* deals with applicability of what is often called the "collateral bar" rule, which "provides that, with relatively rare but complex exceptions, an individual who has knowingly violated an injunction cannot defend against a contempt citation on the ground that the injunction was invalid." Martin Redish, *The Proper Role of the Prior Restraint Doctrine in First Amendment Theory*, 70 VA. L. REV. 53, 93 (1984).

Though the origins of the doctrine are earlier, the leading case applying it is *United States v. United Mine Workers,* 330 U.S. 258 (1947). There the Court upheld imposition of stiff fines on a union and its president for willful violation of a judicial order restraining them from striking. The Court rejected the union's argument that the district court lacked jurisdiction to issue the restraining order, and held "that an order issued by a court with jurisdiction over the subject matter and person must be obeyed by the parties until it is reversed by orderly and proper proceedings. This is true without regard even for the constitutionality of the Act under which the order is issued."

In cases preceding *United Mine Workers*, the Supreme Court had recognized an exception to the collateral bar rule when the defendant in the contempt proceeding successfully challenged the issuing court's jurisdiction. In *United Mine Workers*, the Court narrowed the exception to cases in which the issuing court's claim to jurisdiction was frivolous. Note the *Walker* Court's summary disposition of the "frivolousness" exception.

4. *Collateral bar and prior restraints.* The principles of standing and ripeness are reversed in cases dealing with violation of a criminal statute rather than injunctions. Although one who challenges the statute in advance of violating it is usually said not to present a "ripe" or "live" controversy [see Chapter 11], one who intentionally violates a criminal statute may nevertheless defend on the ground that the act under which he is prosecuted is unconstitutional.

It has been suggested that if the collateral bar rule were abolished, there would be no reason to treat prior restraints with any greater disdain than subsequent punishment systems. Stephen Barnett, *The Puzzle of Prior Restraint*, 29 STAN. L. REV. 539 (1977). Do you agree that if an individual subjected to a prior restraint of expression were allowed to defend in a contempt proceeding on the ground that the restraint was unconstitutional, prior restraints and subsequent punishment for violation of criminal statutes would be fungible for First Amendment purposes? Consider how the dissenters in *Walker* attempted to avoid the difficulty of the collateral bar rule in that case. Do you find any of the methods to be persuasive?

[3] The First Amendment Overbreadth Doctrine

"The overbreadth doctrine postulates that the government may not achieve its concededly valid purpose by means that sweep unnecessarily broadly, reaching constitutionally protected as well as unprotected activity." MARTIN H. REDISH, FREEDOM OF EXPRESSION: A CRITICAL ANALYSIS 216–20 (1984). The result, when this doctrine is applied, is that a person who could be convicted under a narrowly drawn statute is acquitted because others whose expression is protected would be covered by the overly broad statute.

What purpose or purposes are served by the overbreadth doctrine? Consider the argument of Professor Chen that the overbreadth doctrine can "serve as a useful tool to test the legitimacy of lawmakers' motives; the closer the fit between the government's chosen means and its valid objectives, the more likely it is that lawmakers truly sought to fulfill those objectives." Alan Chen, *Statutory Speech Bubbles, First Amendment Overbreadth, and Improper Legislative Purpose*, 38 HARV. C.R. — C.L. L. REV. 31 (2003). Why should we care what the legislature's motive was for enacting a restriction on expression? If it is assumed that a "bad" (i.e., viewpoint suppressive) legislative motivation renders a law unconstitutional, does it logically follow that a "good" motivation (i.e., unrelated to the goal of viewpoint suppression) necessarily render the law constitutional?

Overbreadth and standing. It is traditionally assumed that the most distinctive consequence of the overbreadth doctrine is its departure from generally accepted standing principles, which posit that one may not invoke the constitutional rights of another. *See, e.g., United States v. Raines,* 362 U.S. 17 (1960). Following its decision in *Thornhill v. Alabama,* 310 U.S. 88 (1940), the Supreme Court has allowed an individual whose conduct might well be prohibited by a properly and narrowly drawn statute to object to an existing statute on the basis of First Amendment overbreadth, or, in other words, because the existing law conceivably could be applied to another whose conduct would be protected by the First Amendment.

One commentator has argued that the overbreadth doctrine represents no departure from traditional standing principles because "[u]nder 'conventional' standing principles, a litigant has always had the right to be judged in accordance with a constitutionally valid rule of law." Henry Monaghan, *Overbreadth*, 1981 SUP. CT. REV. 1, 3. The Supreme Court, however, continues to view First Amendment overbreadth as "strong medicine," and a substantial departure from traditional standing rules, as emphasized in *Broadrick v. Oklahoma*, below. Should an individual whose conduct can be prohibited be allowed to challenge a law on the grounds that, because of overbreadth, it could conceivably be applied unconstitutionally to another? What are the competing considerations?

Another commentator has made the following suggestion:

> In general, Supreme Court holdings of overbreadth that are rendered in reviewing state court enforcement actions should confer immunity on all conduct occurring after the judgment is entered and before a constitutionally adequate narrowing construction is obtained. In injunctive and declaratory judgment actions in the lower federal courts, a different rule should obtain. Non-parties . . . should not be able to claim immunity as a necessary consequence of the federal judgment.

Richard Fallon, *Making Sense of Overbreadth*, 100 YALE L.J. 853, 908 (1991).

Overbreadth and vagueness contrasted. A law will often be challenged for vagueness, as well as on overbreadth grounds. It is occasionally suggested that the overbreadth analysis is largely a manifestation of the same concerns behind the void-for-vagueness doctrine as that doctrine applies in the First Amendment context. It is undoubtedly true that there exists a substantial overlap between the two doctrines. The Court will often establish a law's vagueness by citing possible examples of an unconstitutionally broad application of the statute's language. Moreover, both vices lead to the danger of selective enforcement: a vague law because no one knows how far it reaches, and an overbroad law because its sweep is so far-reaching that prosecutors may select for punishment among those who fall within the law's reach. Finally, it is true that both types of laws can lead to a chill on the exercise of First Amendment rights.

It is important, however, not to overstate either the conceptual overlap of the two doctrines or the Supreme Court's fungible use of them. One of the most significant vices of a vague statute is that the individual is not given fair warning that his or her conduct will run afoul of the statutory ban. Yet a law may be considered overbroad, even though it all too clearly describes exactly what conduct it is prohibiting. A law will be invalidated for overbreadth even when the statute's reach is clearly defined, if that reach goes too far. The concern about fair warning, so important in the vagueness analysis, is not relevant to this inquiry. The greatest practical danger of a failure to recognize that the vagueness-overbreadth overlap is not complete is that a reviewing court may incorrectly accept a law when it concludes that the statutory terms are clear, or alternatively when there is no overbreadth despite ambiguity or vagueness in the statute.

***Broadrick v. Oklahoma*, 413 U.S. 601 (1973).** A First Amendment challenge was made to section 818 of Oklahoma's Merit System of Personnel Administration Act, which restricted the political activities of the state's classified civil servants. Paragraph seven of the section provided that "[n]o employee in the civil service [shall] in any manner be concerned in soliciting or receiving any assessment [or] contribution for any political organization, candidacy or other political purpose." The paragraph also prohibited employees from "tak[ing] part in the management or affairs of any political party or in any political campaign, except to exercise his right as a citizen privately to express his opinion and cast his vote." The Court, in an opinion by Justice White, rejected both vagueness and overbreadth challenges to the Act:

> [W]e have little doubt that § 818 [is] not so vague that "men of common intelligence must necessarily guess at its meaning." Whatever other problems there are with § 818, it is all but frivolous to suggest that the section fails to give adequate warning of what activities it proscribes or fails to set out "explicit standards" for those who must apply it. Moreover, even if the outermost boundaries of § 818 may be imprecise, any such uncertainty has little relevance here, where appellants' conduct falls squarely within the "hard core" of the statute's proscriptions.
>
> Appellants assert that § 818 has been construed as applying to such allegedly protected political expression as the wearing of political buttons or the displaying of bumper stickers. But appellants did not engage in any such activity. They are charged with actively engaging in partisan political activities — including the solicitation of money — among their coworkers for the benefit of their superiors.
>
> Embedded in the traditional rules governing constitutional adjudication is the principle that a person to whom a statute may constitutionally be applied will not be heard to challenge that statute on the ground that it may conceivably be applied unconstitutionally to others. In the past, the Court has recognized some limited exceptions to these principles, but only because of the most "weighty countervailing policies." [One] exception has been carved out in the area of the First Amendment.
>
> The consequence of our departure from traditional rules of standing in the First Amendment area is that any enforcement of a statute thus placed at issue is totally forbidden until and unless a limiting construction or partial invalidation so narrows it as to remove the seeming threat of deterrence to constitutionally protected expression. Application of the overbreadth doctrine in this manner is, manifestly, strong medicine. It has been employed by the Court sparingly and only as a last resort. [T]he plain import of our cases is, at the very least, that facial overbreadth adjudication is an exception to our traditional rules of practice and that its function, a limited one at the outset, attenuates as the otherwise unprotected behavior that it forbids the State to sanction moves from "pure speech" toward conduct and that conduct — even if expressive — falls within the scope of otherwise valid criminal laws that reflect legitimate state interests in maintaining comprehensive controls over harmful, constitutionally unprotected conduct. Although such laws, if too broadly worded, may deter protected speech to some unknown extent, there comes a point where that effect — at best a prediction — cannot, with confidence, justify invalidating a statute on its face and so prohibiting a State from enforcing the statute against conduct that is admittedly within its

> power to proscribe. To put the matter another way, particularly where conduct and not merely speech is involved, we believe that the overbreadth of a statute must not only be real, but substantial as well, judged in relation to the statute's plainly legitimate sweep. It is our view that § 818 is not substantially overbroad and that whatever overbreadth may exist should be cured through case-by-case analysis of the fact situations to which its sanctions, assertedly, may not be applied.

Four Justices dissented in *Broadrick*. Justice Brennan, dissenting, reasoned:

> [T]he Court makes no effort to define what it means by "substantial overbreadth." We have never held that a statute should be held invalid on its face merely because it is possible to conceive of a single impermissible application, and in that sense a requirement of substantial overbreadth is already implicit in the doctrine. Whether the Court means to require some different or greater showing of substantiality is left obscure by today's opinion, in large part because the Court makes no effort to explain why the overbreadth of the Oklahoma Act, while real, is somehow not quite substantial.
>
> More fundamentally, the Court offers no rationale to explain its conclusion that, for purposes of overbreadth analysis, deterrence of conduct should be viewed differently from deterrence of speech, even where both are equally protected by the First Amendment. Indeed, in the case before us it is hard to know whether the protected activity falling within the Act should be considered speech or conduct.

Overbreadth and the public forum. Justice White provided the foundation for *Broadrick* in his earlier dissent in *Coates v. City of Cincinnati,* 402 U.S. 611, 617 (1971). The case involved a challenge to an ordinance making it a crime for "three or more persons to assemble . . . on any of the sidewalks . . . and there conduct themselves in a manner annoying to persons passing byY." The majority found the ordinance unconstitutionally vague and overbroad. Justice White argued:

> Even accepting the overbreadth doctrine with respect to statutes clearly reaching speech, the Cincinnati ordinance does not purport to bar or regulate speech as such. It prohibits persons from assembling and "conduct[ing]" themselves in a manner annoying to other persons. Even if the assembled defendants in this case were demonstrating and picketing, we have long recognized that picketing is not solely a communicative endeavor and has aspects which the State is entitled to regulate even though there is incidental impact on speech.

Do you understand either the rationale or scope of Justice White's dichotomy between pure words and so-called "expressive conduct"? Consider the type of expressive conduct involved in *Broadrick*. Is the political activity involved there less worthy of First Amendment protection because it does not consist of spoken words?

The *Broadrick* limitation was not mentioned in *Lewis v. City of New Orleans,* 415 U.S. 130 (1974), where the Court struck down an ordinance that made it a crime "to curse or revile or to use obscene or opprobrious language toward or with reference to any member of the city police while in the actual performance of his duty." According to one commentator, the decision indicated "very strongly that *Broadrick* was to have little, if any, effect on overbreadth review of statutes directly aimed at regulating speech." *Note*, 49 N.Y.U. L. REV. 532, 544 (1974).

In *Los Angeles City Council v. Taxpayers for Vincent,* 466 U.S. 789 (1984), the Court upheld against an overbreadth attack a municipal ordinance prohibiting the posting of signs on public property. In so doing, the Court examined the scope of the "substantiality" requirement: "The concept of 'substantial overbreadth' is not readily reduced to an exact definition. It is clear, however, that the mere fact that one can conceive of some impermissible applications of a statute is not sufficient to render it susceptible to an overbreadth challenge. In short, there must be a realistic chance that the statute itself will significantly compromise recognized First Amendment protections of parties not before the Court for it to be facially challenged on overbreadth grounds."

In *Board of Airport Commissioners v. Jews for Jesus,* 482 U.S. 569 (1987), the Court found to be unconstitutionally overbroad a resolution of the Los Angeles Board of Airport Commissioners which provided that "the Central Terminal Area at Los Angeles International Airport [LAX] is not open for First Amendment activities by an individual and/or entity." Justice O'Connor, speaking for the Court, noted that "the resolution at issue in this case reaches the universe of expressive activity, and, by prohibiting all protected expression, purports to create a virtual 'First Amendment Free Zone' at LAX. The resolution does not merely regulate expressive activity in the Central Terminal Area that might create problems such as congestion or the disruption of the activities of those who use LAX." She reasoned that the Resolution must therefore prohibit "even talking and reading, or the wearing of campaign buttons or symbolic clothing. Under such a sweeping ban, virtually every individual who enters LAX may be found to violate the resolution by engaging in some 'First Amendment activity.' We think it obvious that such a ban cannot be justified even if LAX were a nonpublic forum because no conceivable governmental interest would justify such an absolute prohibition of speech." The Court rejected the argument that the Resolution should be construed to apply only to expressive activity unrelated to airport purposes: "The line between airport-related speech and non-airport-related speech is, at best, murky."

Overbreadth and charitable solicitations. The *Broadrick* limitation received only brief reference in *Village of Schaumburg v. Citizens for a Better Environment,* 444 U.S. 620 (1980), involving an overbreadth challenge to an ordinance prohibiting door-to-door or on-street solicitation of contributions by charitable organizations that do not use at least 75% of their receipts for "charitable purposes." The opinion, written by Justice White (author of *Broadrick*), emphasized that the First Amendment has long been thought to protect on-street and door-to-door solicitation and that "[o]ur cases long have protected speech even though it is in the form of a solicitation to pay or contribute money."

In *Secretary of State of Maryland v. Joseph H. Munson Co.,* 467 U.S. 947 (1984), the Supreme Court expanded its holding in *Village of Schaumburg.* The issue in *Munson* was "whether a Maryland statute with a like percentage limitation, but with provisions that render it more 'flexible' than the *Schaumburg* ordinance, can withstand constitutional attack." The Maryland law authorized a waiver of the 25% limitation whenever it would effectively prevent the charitable organization from raising contributions.

The Court's opinion, written by Justice Blackmun, concluded that the added flexibility was insufficient to save the statute from an overbreadth attack. It concluded also that the "substantial" overbreadth requirement of *Broadrick* and *Ferber* did not present a problem to a finding of unconstitutionality. Justice Rehnquist, joined by Justices Powell and O'Connor and the Chief Justice, dissented, contending that "[t]he Court is simply mistaken when it claims that there is no 'core of easily identifiable and constitutionally proscribable conduct that the statute prohibits' " and that "donor confidence is enhanced by such a regulation, and the intended objects of the public's bounty are benefited." He contended that "the Court simply ignores or sleights some crucial differences between this statute and the ordinance at issue in *Schaumburg.*"

Overbreadth and the child pornography problem. In sharp contrast to *Schaumburg's* failure to employ *Broadrick* is a decision that significantly expands the reach of *Broadrick's* limitations on the use of overbreadth analysis. In *New York v. Ferber,* 458 U.S. 747 (1982), the Court reversed the New York Court of Appeals' invalidation, on overbreadth grounds, of a state statute that prohibited the knowing promotion of a sexual performance by a child under the age of sixteen by distributing material that depicts such a performance. The New York court had found the law to be overbroad, because it would have forbidden the distribution of material with serious literary, scientific, or educational value. The state court had rejected applicability of the *Broadrick* exception, since it believed that "pure speech" was involved.

The Supreme Court stated that "[t]his case convinces us that the rationale of *Broadrick* is sound and should be applied in the present context involving the harmful employment of children to make sexually explicit materials for distribution," even though more traditional forms of expression were the subject of regulation. The Court held that the special "substantiality" requirement of *Broadrick* was applicable because

> the extent of deterrence of protected speech can be expected to decrease with the declining reach of the regulation. This observation appears equally applicable to the publication of books and films as it is to activities, such as picketing or participation in election campaigns, which have previously been categorized as involving conduct plus speech. We see no appreciable difference between the position of a publisher or bookseller in doubt as to the reach of New York's child pornography law and the situation faced by the Oklahoma state employees with respect to that state's restriction on partisan political activity. Indeed, it could reasonably be argued that the bookseller,

> with an economic incentive to sell materials that may fall within the statute's scope, may be less likely to be deterred than the employee who wishes to engage in political campaign activity.

The message of *Ferber* appears to be that all overbreadth challenges should be tested by the special "substantiality" requirement, which was devised originally in *Broadrick* only for regulation of expressive conduct.

Osborne v. Ohio, 495 U.S. 103 (1990), also rejected an overbreadth challenge to a child pornography statute after the state supreme court limited application of the statute to materials that involved either a "lewd exhibition of or a graphic focus on the genitals" of a minor "neither the child nor ward of the person charged."

Massachusetts v. Oakes, 491 U.S. 576 (1989), involved a conviction for possession of seductive photos of the defendant's teenage step-daughter. The conviction was reversed by the state supreme court on overbreadth grounds. The U.S. Supreme Court tben vacated for mootness because the statute was amended in the meantime to narrow its scope, and the case was remanded to determine whether the defendant's activities fell within the prior statute.

***City of Chicago v. Morales,* 527 U.S. 41 (1999)**. In 1992, the Chicago City Council passed the Gang Congregation Ordinance in response to the public loitering of gang members to intimidate neighborhoods and establish control over identifiable areas: "Whenever a police officer observes a person whom he reasonably believes to be a criminal street gang member loitering in a public place with one or more persons, he shall order all such persons to disperse and remove themselves from the area." "Loiter" was defined to mean "to remain in one place with no apparent purpose." Any person who disobeyed the order to disperse was subject to arrest and penalties of $500, six months imprisonment, and 120 hours of community service.

The Chicago Police Department issued General Order 92-4 establishing guidelines to limit the discretion of police officers, including detailed criteria for defining street gangs, designated areas of enforcement (which were not made public), and designated officers authorized to make arrests under the ordinance. In three years of enforcement, the police issued over 89,000 orders to disperse and arrested over 42,000 people for violating the ordinance.

The Illinois Supreme Court invalidated the ordinance, holding "that the gang loitering ordinance violates due process of law in that it is impermissibly vague on its face and an arbitrary restriction on personal liberties." The Supreme Court affirmed: "We are mindful that 'the preservation of liberty depends in part on the maintenance of social order.' However, in this instance the city has enacted an ordinance that affords too much discretion to the police and too little notice to citizens who wish to use the public streets."

Justice Stevens, for the Court, concluded that the ordinance also failed to establish minimum guidelines to limit the discretion of police officers. "It matters not whether the reason that a gang member and his father, for example, might loiter near Wrigley Field is to rob an unsuspecting fan or just to get a glimpse of Sammy Sosa leaving the ballpark; in either event, if their purpose is not apparent to a nearby officer, she may indeed, she shall order them to disperse." Furthermore, the police department's general order of internal guidelines was an insufficient limitation on police discretion because it did not provide any notice to the public.

The Illinois Supreme Court interpreted the definition of "loiter" to provide "absolute discretion to police officers to determine what activities constitute loitering." Justice Stevens noted that the Supreme Court has "no authority to construe the language of a state statute more narrowly than the construction given by that State's highest court." [*Smiley v. Kansas,* 196 U.S. 447 (1905).] Nevertheless, Justice Stevens analyzed the city's arguments challenging the Illinois Supreme Court's interpretation and found them to be unpersuasive.

The city argued the ordinance limited officer discretion in three ways: it allowed arrest only of someone with no apparent purpose and not moving along; it allowed arrest only if a person disobeyed a dispersal order; and it required the officer to reasonably believe that one of the loiterers is a member of a criminal street gang. Justice Stevens reasoned the first two arguments did not even address the question of police discretion to issue an order to disperse. The third argument did place a limitation on police, however "[t]hat limitation would no doubt be sufficient if the ordinance only applied to loitering that had an apparently harmful purpose or effect, or possibly if it only applied to loitering by persons reasonably believed to be criminal gang members. But this ordinance, for reasons that are not explained in the findings of the city council, requires no harmful purpose and applies to non-gang members as well as suspected gang members." In fact, Stevens noted that the ordinance was "ironically" inapplicable when loiterers had an apparent purpose, even if this purpose was criminal.

Writing for a plurality (Justices Souter and Ginsburg joined), Justice Stevens observed that laws could be attacked on their face under two doctrines-the overbreadth doctrine and the vagueness doctrine. The overbreadth doctrine, Justice Stevens noted, is inappropriate because "the law does not have a sufficiently substantial impact on conduct protected by the First Amendment." The law did not prohibit speech; did not apply to assemblies "designed to demonstrate a group's support of, or opposition to, a particular point of view," nor did the law "prohibit any form of conduct that is apparently intended to convey a message." But, Justice Stevens continued, "the freedom to loiter for innocent purposes is part of the liberty' protected by the Due Process Clause of the Fourteenth Amendment. [I]ndeed, it is apparent that an individual's decision to remain in a public place of his choice is as much a part of his liberty as the freedom of movement inside frontiers that is a part of our heritage' or the right to move to whatsoever place one's own inclination may direct' identified in Blackstone's COMMENTARIES."

Nonetheless, Justice Stevens found there was no need to evaluate the ordinance under the due process overbreadth doctrine. Rather, he reasoned, "it is clear that the vagueness of this enactment makes a facial challenge appropriate. This is not an ordinance that simply regulates business behavior and contains a scienter requirement.' It is a criminal law that contains no mens rea requirement, and infringes on constitutionally protected rights. When vagueness permeates the text of such a law, it is subject to facial attack."

Justice Stevens, speaking for the plurality, rejected Justice Scalia's argument that a successful facial challenge must "establish that no set of circumstances exists under which the Act would be valid" [*United States v. Salerno,* 481 U.S. 739 (1987)], arguing that "the *Salerno* formulation [h]as never been the decisive factor in any decision of this Court, including *Salerno* itself."

Justice Stevens' plurality opinion also argued: "Vagueness may invalidate a criminal law for either of two independent reasons. First, it may fail to provide the kind of notice that will enable ordinary people to understand what conduct it prohibits; second, it may authorize and even encourage arbitrary and discriminatory enforcement." Justice Stevens observed: "The Illinois Supreme Court recognized that the term 'loiter' may have a common and accepted meaning, but the definition of that term in this ordinance to remain in one place with no apparent purpose does not. It is difficult to imagine how any citizen of the city of Chicago standing in a public place with a group of people would know if he or she had any apparent purpose. If she were talking to another person, would she have an apparent purpose? If she were frequently checking her watch and looking expectantly down the street, would she have an apparent purpose? [T]he vagueness that dooms this ordinance is not the product of uncertainty about the normal meaning of 'loitering,' but rather about what loitering is covered by the ordinance and what is not." Stevens suggested that the ordinance would be valid if loitering were "combined with some other overt act or evidence of criminal intent."

The city's argument that loiterers were not subject to arrest until after they had disobeyed a police officer's order to disperse, and that this order served as actual notice was unpersuasive for two reasons. First, such an order comes too late "to enable the ordinary citizen to conform his or her conduct to the law. [B]ecause an officer may issue an order only after prohibited conduct has already occurred, it cannot provide the kind of advance notice that will protect the putative loiterer from being ordered to disperse." Furthermore, Stevens reasoned that "[i]f the loitering is in fact harmless and innocent, the dispersal order itself is an unjustified impairment of liberty. [S]uch an order cannot retroactively give adequate warning of the boundary between the permissible and the impermissible applications of the law."

Second, the vague phrasing of the dispersal order compounded the inadequacy of the notice required because it did not specify how far and how long the loiterers must disperse. "Lack of clarity in the description of the loiterer's duty to obey a dispersal order might not render the ordinance unconstitutionally vague if the definition of the forbidden conduct were clear, but it does buttress our conclusion that the entire ordinance fails to give the ordinary citizen adequate notice of what is forbidden and what is permitted."

Justice O'Connor, joined by Justice Breyer, concurring in the judgment and concurring in part, agreed that the law was unconstitutionally vague, but wished to "characterize more clearly the narrow scope of today's holding." Justice O'Connor observed that several reasonable alternatives remained open to Chicago to combat the threat of gang violence, including laws that prohibit loitering with a "harmful purpose," loitering laws that target only gang members, and laws that include limits on the area and manner of enforcement. Justice O'Connor believed the Illinois Supreme Court had erred in considering the intent of the drafters in determining whether the ordinance was vague, but agreed that the Illinois Supreme Court's construction was binding on the Supreme Court.

Justice Kennedy, concurring in part, reasoned that because the ordinance reached such a broad range of innocent conduct, it was not saved by the requirement that a loiterer disobey a police order before being subject to arrest. Adequacy of notice was still lacking: "A citizen, while engaging in a wide array of innocent conduct, is not likely to know when he may be subject to a dispersal order based on the officer's own knowledge of the identity or affiliations of other persons with whom the citizen is congregating; nor may the citizen be able to assess what an officer might conceive to be the citizen's lack of an apparent purpose."

Justice Breyer, concurring in part, agreed that the overbreadth doctrine was inapplicable, and argued that the ordinance created a "major, not a minor, limitation upon the free state of nature" because police discretion was limited by only two restrictions: by the officer's reasonable belief that one of the loiterers is a gang member; and by the officer's determination that a person is remaining in a public place with "no apparent purpose." The first limitation "leaves many individuals, gang members and nongang members alike, subject to its strictures" and the second limitation is "not a limitation at all." "The ordinance is unconstitutional, not because a policeman applied this discretion wisely or poorly in a particular case, but rather because the policeman enjoys too much discretion in every case. And if every application of the ordinance represents an exercise of unlimited discretion, than the ordinance is invalid in all its applications. [T]he city of Chicago may no more apply this law to the defendants, no matter how they behaved, than it could apply an (imaginary) statute that said, 'It is a crime to do wrong,' even to the worst of murderers. [B]ut I believe this ordinance is unconstitutional, not because it provides insufficient notice, but because it does not provide sufficient minimal standards to guide law enforcement officers."

Justice Scalia, dissenting, criticized the majority on the grounds that "the majority today invalidates this perfectly reasonable measure by ignoring our rules governing facial challenges, by elevating loitering to a constitutionally guaranteed right, and by discerning vagueness where, according to the usual standards, none exists."

Justice Scalia rejected successful facial challenges, except in free-speech cases subject to the doctrine of overbreadth, must show a law is "unenforceable in all its applications" and stated that "it is highly questionable whether federal courts have any business making such a declaration." He argued: "When our normal criteria for facial challenges are applied, it is clear that the Justices in the majority have transposed the burden of proof. Instead of requiring the respondents, who are challenging the Ordinance, to show that it is invalid in all its applications, they have required the petitioner to show it is valid in all it applications. [B]ut the ultimate demonstration of the inappropriateness of the Court's holding of facial invalidity is the fact that it is doubtful whether some of these respondents could even sustain an as-applied challenge on the basis of the majority's own criteria."

Justice Scalia rejected the existence of any "Fundamental Freedom to Loiter" on the basis of the "vast historical tradition of criminalizing the activity" detailed in Justice Thomas' dissent.

Justice Scalia asserted that the plurality's contention that the ordinance is a criminal law with no mens rea requirement is incorrect, because the only act made punishable by the ordinance is failure to obey an officer's order to disperse, not loitering itself. Further, he argues that the ordinance is not vague because what the order actually subjects to criminal penalty is failure to obey an order to disperse. Such an order gives a person actual notice and is not vague. He refuses to be bound by the Illinois Supreme Court's interpretation of "apparent purpose" because he asserts it is a legal conclusion, not a construction of the language of the ordinance. Furthermore, the ordinance "vests no more discretion in the police than innumerable other measures authorizing police orders to preserve the public peace and safety."

Finally, Justice Scalia argued that the alternative measures noted by Justice O'Connor have not been effective, and furthermore, "in our democratic system, how much harmless conduct to proscribe is not a judgement to be made by the courts. So long as constitutionally guaranteed rights are not affected, and so long as the proscription has a rational basis, all sorts of perfectly harmless activity by millions of perfectly innocent people can be forbidden."

Justice Thomas, joined by Chief Justice Rehnquist and Justice Scalia, dissenting, disagreed with the Court that the ordinance was vague because "any fool would know that a particular category of conduct would be within [its] reach." Police have a well-established duty and power to preserve the public peace, including the power to disperse groups threatening it, under which police must inevitably exercise discretion. Laws prohibiting vagrancy and loitering have a long history in this country, extending back to colonial times. Justice Thomas contended therefore, that "the asserted freedom to loiter for innocent purposes' is in no way deeply rooted in this Nation's history and tradition." Justice Thomas concludes: "Today the Court focuses extensively on the rights of gang members and their companions. It can safely do so the people who will have to live with the consequences of today's opinion do not live in our neighborhoods. [B]y focusing exclusively on the imagined rights of [criminals] the Court today has denied our most vulnerable citizens the very thing that Justice Stevens elevates above all else the freedom of movement.' And that is a shame."

[C] FIGHTING WORDS, TRUE THREATS, AND OFFENSIVE SPEECH

***Chaplinsky v. New Hampshire,* 315 U.S. 568 (1942).** Chaplinsky was a Jehovah's Witness who distributed pamphlets on the streets of Rochester, New Hampshire. Some residents complained to the city marshal that Chaplinsky was denouncing all religion as a "racket." Although the marshal did tell the irate citizens that Chaplinsky was engaged in lawful activity, he also warned Chaplinsky that the crowd was restless. Chaplinsky made this statement to the marshal outside city hall: "You are a God-damned racketeer and a damned fascist and the whole government of Rochester are Fascists or agents of Fascists." He was prosecuted under a New Hampshire statute which forbade "addressing any offensive, derisive or annoying word to any other person who is lawfully in any street or other public place, nor call him by any offensive or derisive name."

The state supreme court put a gloss on the statute. Only those words were forbidden which had a "direct tendency to cause acts of violence by the persons to whom, individually, the remark is addressed." This gave birth to "fighting words" as a First Amendment doctrine. The Supreme Court endorsed the New Hampshire Supreme Court's statement of the doctrine:

> The word "offensive" is not to be defined in terms of what a particular addressee thinks. The test is what men of common intelligence would understand to be words likely to cause an average addressee to fight. The English language has a number of words and expressions which by general consent are "fighting words" when said without a disarming smile. Such words, as ordinary men know, are likely to cause a fight. The statute, as construed, does no more than prohibit the face-to-face words plainly likely to cause a breach of the peace by the speaker — including "classical fighting words," words in current use less "classical" but equally likely to cause violence, and other disorderly words, including profanity, obscenity and threats.

The Supreme Court observed: "Argument is unnecessary to demonstrate that the appellations 'damned racketeer' and 'damned Fascist' are epithets likely to provoke the average person to retaliation, and thereby cause a breach of the peace."

The Supreme Court in *Chaplinsky* set forth a principle which, although later substantially modified, has had enduring significance:

> There are certain well-defined and narrowly limited classes of speech, the prevention and punishment of which have never been thought to raise any Constitutional problem. These include the lewd and obscene, the profane, the libelous, and the insulting or "fighting" words — those which by their very utterance inflict injury or tend to incite an immediate breach of the peace. It has been well observed that such utterances are of such slight social value as a step to truth that any benefit that may be derived from them is clearly out-weighed by the social interest in order and morality.

COHEN v. CALIFORNIA

403 U.S. 15, 91 S. Ct. 1780, 29 L. Ed. 2d 284 (1971)

Mr. Justice Harlan delivered the opinion of the Court.

This case may seem at first blush too inconsequential to find its way into our books, but the issue it presents is of no small constitutional significance. [Cohen] was convicted of violating that part of California Penal Code § 415 which prohibits "maliciously and willfully disturb[ing] the peace or quiet of any neighborhood or person by offensive conduct." He was given 30 days' imprisonment. The facts upon which his conviction rests are as follows:

> On April 26, 1968, the defendant was observed in the Los Angeles County Courthouse in the corridor outside of division 20 of the municipal court wearing a jacket bearing the words "Fuck the Draft" which were plainly visible. There were women and children present in the corridor. The defendant was arrested. The defendant testified that he wore the jacket knowing that the words were on the jacket as a means of informing the public of the depth of his feelings against the Vietnam War and the draft.
>
> The defendant did not engage in, nor threaten to engage in, nor did anyone as the result of his conduct in fact commit or threaten to commit any act of violence. The defendant did not make any loud or unusual noise, nor was there any evidence that he uttered any sound prior to his arrest.

In affirming[,] the Court of Appeal held that "offensive conduct" means "behavior which has a tendency to provoke others to acts of violence or to in turn disturb the peace," and that the State had proved this element because, on the facts of this case, "[i]t was certainly reasonably foreseeable that such conduct might cause others to rise up to commit a violent act against the person of the defendant or attempt to forcibly remove his jacket." The California Supreme Court declined review by a divided vote. We now reverse.

In order to lay hands on the precise issue which this case involves, it is useful first to canvass various matters which this record does not present.

The conviction quite clearly rests upon the asserted offensiveness of the words Cohen used to convey his message to the public. The only "conduct" which the State sought to punish is the fact of communication. Thus, we deal here with a conviction resting solely upon "speech," not upon any separately identifiable conduct which allegedly was intended by Cohen to be perceived by others as expressive of particular views but which, on its face, does not necessarily convey any message and hence arguably could be regulated without effectively repressing Cohen's ability to express himself. *Cf. United States v. O'Brien* [p. 1072]. Further, the State certainly lacks power to punish Cohen for the underlying content of the message the inscription conveyed. At least so long as there is no showing of an intent to incite disobedience to or disruption of the draft, Cohen could not, consistently with the First and Fourteenth Amendments, be punished for asserting the evident position on the inutility or immorality of the draft his jacket reflected. *Yates v. United States.*

Appellant's conviction, then, rests squarely upon his exercise of the "freedom of speech" protected from arbitrary governmental interference by the Constitution and can be justified, if at all, only as a valid regulation of the manner in which he exercised that freedom, not as a permissible prohibition on the substantive message it conveys. This does not end the inquiry, of course, for the First and Fourteenth Amendments have never been thought to give absolute protection to every individual to speak whenever or wherever he pleases, or to use any form of address in any circumstances that he chooses. In this vein, too, however, we think it important to note that several issues typically associated with such problems are not presented here.

In the first place, Cohen was tried under a statute applicable throughout the entire State. Any attempt to support this conviction on the ground that the statute seeks to preserve an appropriately decorous atmosphere in the courthouse where Cohen was arrested must fail in the absence of any language in the statute that would have put appellant on notice that certain kinds of otherwise permissible speech or conduct would nevertheless, under California law, not be tolerated in certain places.

In the second place, as it comes to us, this case cannot be said to fall within those relatively few categories of instances where prior decisions have established the power of government to deal more comprehensively with certain forms of individual expression simply upon a showing that such a form was employed. This is not, for example, an obscenity case. Whatever else may be necessary to give rise to the States' broader power to prohibit obscene expression, such expression must be, in some significant way, erotic. It cannot plausibly be maintained that this vulgar allusion to the Selective Service System would conjure up such psychic stimulation in anyone likely to be confronted with Cohen's crudely defaced jacket.

This Court has also held that States are free to ban the simple use, without a demonstration of additional justifying circumstances, of so-called "fighting words," those personally abusive epithets which, when addressed to the ordinary citizen, are, as a matter of common knowledge, inherently likely to provoke violent reaction. *Chaplinsky v. New Hampshire*. While the four-letter word displayed by Cohen in relation to the draft is not uncommonly employed in a personally provocative fashion, in this instance it was clearly not "directed to the person of the hearer." *Cantwell v. Connecticut,* 310 U.S. 296, 309 (1940). No individual actually or likely to be present could reasonably have regarded the words on appellant's jacket as a direct personal insult. Nor do we have here an instance of the exercise of the State's police power to prevent a speaker from intentionally provoking a given group to hostile reaction. *Cf. Feiner v. New York* [p. 1047]; *Terminiello v. Chicago,* 337 U.S. 1 (1949). There is, as noted above, no showing that anyone who saw Cohen was in fact violently aroused or that appellant intended such a result.

Finally, in arguments before this Court much has been made of the claim that Cohen's distasteful mode of expression was thrust upon unwilling or unsuspecting viewers, and that the State might therefore legitimately act as it did in order to protect the sensitive from otherwise unavoidable exposure to appellant's crude form of protest. Of course, the mere presumed presence of unwitting listeners or viewers does not serve automatically to justify curtailing all speech capable of giving offense. While this Court has recognized that government may properly act in many situations to prohibit intrusion into the privacy of the home of unwelcome views and ideas which cannot be totally banned from the public dialogue, we have at the same time consistently stressed that "we are often 'captives' outside the sanctuary of the home and subject to objectionable speech." The ability of government, consonant with the Constitution, to shut off discourse solely to protect others from hearing it is, in other words, dependent upon a showing that substantial privacy interests are being invaded in an essentially intolerable manner. Any broader view of this authority would effectively empower a majority to silence dissidents simply as a matter of personal predilections.

Given the subtlety and complexity of the factors involved, if Cohen's "speech" was otherwise entitled to constitutional protection, we do not think the fact that some unwilling "listeners" in a public building may have been briefly exposed to it can serve to justify this breach of the peace conviction where, as here, there was no evidence that persons powerless to avoid appellant's conduct did in fact object to it, and where that portion of the statute upon which Cohen's conviction rests evinces no concern, either on its face or as construed by the California courts, with the special plight of the captive auditor, but, instead, indiscriminately sweeps within its prohibitions all "offensive conduct" that disturbs "any neighborhood or person."

Against this background, the issue flushed by this case stands out in bold relief. It is whether California can excise, as "offensive conduct," one particular scurrilous epithet from the public discourse, either upon the theory of the court below that its use is inherently likely to cause violent reaction or upon a more general assertion that the States, acting as guardians of public morality, may properly remove this offensive word from the public vocabulary.

The rationale of the California court is plainly untenable. At most it reflects an "undifferentiated fear or apprehension of disturbance [which] is not enough to overcome the right to freedom of expression." *Tinker v. Des Moines Indep. Community School Dist.* [p. 1136]. We have been shown no evidence that substantial numbers of citizens are standing ready to strike out physically at whoever may assault their sensibilities with execrations like that uttered by Cohen. There may be some persons about with such lawless and violent proclivities, but that is an insufficient base upon which to erect, consistently with constitutional values, a governmental power to force persons who wish to ventilate their dissident views into avoiding particular forms of expression. The argument amounts to little more than the self-defeating proposition that to avoid physical censorship of one who has not sought to provoke such a response by a hypothetical coterie of the violent and lawless, the States may more appropriately effectuate that censorship themselves.

Admittedly, it is not so obvious that the First and Fourteenth Amendments must be taken to disable the States from punishing public utterance of this unseemly expletive in order to maintain what they regard as a suitable level of discourse within the body politic. We think, however, that examination and reflection will reveal the shortcomings of a contrary viewpoint.

The constitutional right of free expression is powerful medicine in a society as diverse and populous as ours. It is designed and intended to remove governmental restraints from the arena of public discussion, putting the decision as to what views shall be voiced largely into the hands of each of us, in the hope that use of such freedom will ultimately produce a more capable citizenry and more perfect polity and in the belief that no other approach would comport with the premise of individual dignity and choice upon which our political system rests.

To many, the immediate consequence of this freedom may often appear to be only verbal tumult, discord, and even offensive utterance. These are, however, within established limits, in truth necessary side effects of the broader enduring values which the process of open debate permits us to achieve. That the air may at times seem filled with verbal cacophony is, in this sense not a sign of weakness but of strength. We cannot lose sight of the fact that, in what otherwise might seem a trifling and annoying instance of individual distasteful abuse of a privilege, these fundamental societal values are truly implicated.

Against this perception of the constitutional policies involved, we discern certain more particularized considerations that peculiarly call for reversal of this conviction. First, the principle contended for by the State seems inherently boundless. How is one to distinguish this from any other offensive word? Surely the State has no right to cleanse public debate to the point where it is grammatically palatable to the most squeamish among us. Yet no readily ascertainable general principle exists for stopping short of that result were we to affirm the judgment below. For, while the particular four-letter word being litigated here is perhaps more distasteful than most others of its genre, it is nevertheless often true that one man's vulgarity is another's lyric. Indeed, we think it is largely because governmental officials cannot make principled distinctions in this area that the Constitution leaves matters of taste and style so largely to the individual.

Additionally, we cannot overlook the fact, because it is well illustrated by the episode involved here, that much linguistic expression serves a dual communicative function: it conveys not only ideas capable of relatively precise, detached explication, but otherwise inexpressible emotions as well. In fact, words are often chosen as much for their emotive as their cognitive force. We cannot sanction the view that the Constitution, while solicitous of the cognitive content of individual speech, has little or no regard for that emotive function which, practically speaking, may often be the more important element of the overall message sought to be communicated.

Finally, and in the same vein, we cannot indulge the facile assumption that one can forbid particular words without also running a substantial risk of suppressing ideas in the process. Indeed, governments might soon seize upon the censorship of particular words as a convenient guise for banning the expression of unpopular views. We have been able, as noted above, to discern little social benefit that might result from running the risk of opening the door to such grave results.

It is, in sum, our judgment that, absent a more particularized and compelling reason for its actions, the State may not, consistently with the First and Fourteenth Amendments, make the simple public display here involved of this single four-letter expletive a criminal offense. Because that is the only arguably sustainable rationale for the conviction here at issue, the judgment below must be reversed.

Justice Blackmun, with whom Chief Justice Burger and Justice Black join [dissenting].

Cohen's absurd and immature antic, in my view, was mainly conduct and little speech. Further, the case appears to me to be well within the sphere of *Chaplinsky v. New Hampshire*, where MR. JUSTICE MURPHY, a known champion of First Amendment freedoms, wrote for a unanimous bench. As a consequence, this Court's agonizing over First Amendment values seems misplaced and unnecessary.

NOTES

1. *The hostile audience problem — Feiner v. New York,* 340 U.S. 315 (1951). A speaker was interrupted by a policeman who demanded that he stop because his remarks in derogation of the President, the mayor of Syracuse, and the American Legion, which incurred both approval and hostility from his audience, appeared to be about to cause a fight. When the speaker refused to stop, he was arrested for disturbing the peace. The Supreme Court upheld Feiner's conviction against a contention that the arrest violated free speech.

Feiner is often thought to exemplify the "hostile audience" problem: If a speaker angers a crowd to the point that either the physical security of the speaker is endangered or a public disorder is likely, who should the police arrest? The speaker or the crowd? Is it relevant that the speaker is not inciting to violence? If the audience outnumbers the police, do logistical considerations become constitutional law? If the crowd is many and menacing, and the police are few, are the police constitutionally justified in carrying away the speaker? Compare the various responses of the Justices to these questions in the excerpts which follow.

Chief Justice Vinson, speaking for the Court, affirmed Feiner's conviction:

Petitioner was thus neither arrested nor convicted for the making or the content of his speech. Rather, it was the reaction which it actually engendered. We are well aware that the ordinary murmurings and objections of a hostile audience cannot be allowed to silence a speaker, and are also mindful of the possible danger of giving overzealous police officials complete discretion to break up otherwise lawful public meetings. But we are not faced here with such a situation. It is one thing to say that the police cannot be used as an instrument for the suppression of unpopular views, and another to say that, when as here the speaker passes the bounds of argument or persuasion and undertakes incitement to riot, they are powerless to prevent a breach of the peace.

Justice Black vigorously dissented in *Feiner*:

As to the existence of a dangerous situation on the streetcorner, it seems far-fetched to suggest that the "facts" show any imminent threat of riot or uncontrollable disorder. Moreover, assuming that the "facts" did indicate a critical situation, I reject the implication of the Court's opinion that the police had no obligation to protect petitioner's constitutional right to talk. The police of course have power to prevent breaches of the peace. But if, in the name of preserving order, they ever can interfere with a lawful public speaker, they first must make all reasonable efforts to protect him. Here the police duty was to protect petitioner's right to talk, even to the extent of arresting the man who threatened to interfere. Instead, they shirked that duty and acted only to suppress the right to speak.

Here the petitioner was "asked" then "told" then "commanded" to stop speaking, but a man making a lawful address is certainly not required to be silent merely because an officer directs it. Petitioner was entitled to know why he should cease doing a lawful act. Not once was he told. I understand that people in authoritarian countries must obey arbitrary orders. I had hoped there was no such duty in the United States.

Is *Feiner* consistent with the emphasis in *New York Times Co. v. Sullivan*, p. 1256, on the "profound national commitment to the principle that debate on public issues shall be uninhibited, robust, and wide-open, and that it may well include vehement, caustic, and sometimes unpleasantly sharp attacks on government and public officials?"

2. *The Skokie cases.* Is a Nazi march and display of the swastika in a largely Jewish town protected expression? In the late 1970s, the American Nazi Party loudly proclaimed its intent to parade through a predominantly Jewish suburb of Chicago. Skokie numbered among its citizens many survivors of Nazi concentration camps. The village government enacted ordinances designed to prevent the Nazi parades. In *Collin v. Smith,* 578 F.2d 1197, 1206 (7th Cir. 1978), these ordinances were declared to be unconstitutional:

> It would be grossly insensitive to deny, as we do not, that the proposed demonstration would seriously disturb, emotionally and mentally, at least some, and probably many of the Village's residents. The problem with engrafting an exception on the First Amendment for such situations is that they are indistinguishable in principle from speech that "invite(s) dispute[,] induces a condition of unrest, creates dissatisfaction with conditions as they are, or even stirs people to anger." *Terminiello v. Chicago,* 337 U.S. 1, 4 (1949). Yet these are among the "high purposes" of the First Amendment.

The village of Skokie then sued to enjoin the Nazis from displaying the swastika on the grounds that it was likely to foment a breach of the peace and constitute a nuisance. A state lower court issued the injunction. But the Illinois Supreme Court reversed. *Village of Skokie v. National Socialist Party,* 373 N.E.2d 21 (Ill. 1978):

> Plaintiff urges, and the appellate court has held, that the exhibition of the Nazi symbol, the swastika, addresses to ordinary citizens a message which is tantamount to fighting words. Plaintiff further asks this court to extend *Chaplinsky*, which upheld a statute punishing the use of such words, and hold that the fighting words doctrine permits a prior restraint on defendants' symbolic speech. In our judgment we are precluded from doing so.
>
> The display of the swastika, as offensive to the principles of a free nation as the memories it recalls may be, is symbolic political speech intended to convey to the public the beliefs of those who display it. It does not, in our opinion, fall within the definition of "fighting words," and that doctrine cannot be used here to overcome the heavy presumption against the constitutional validity of a prior restraint.

> Nor can we find that the swastika, while not representing fighting words, is nevertheless so offensive and peace threatening to the public that its display can be enjoined. We do not doubt that the sight of this symbol is abhorrent to the Jewish citizens of Skokie, and that the survivors of the Nazi persecutions, tormented by their recollections, may have strong feelings regarding its display. Yet it is entirely clear that this factor does not justify enjoining defendants' speech.
>
> In summary, as we read the controlling Supreme Court opinions, use of the swastika is a symbolic form of free speech entitled to first amendment protections. Its display on uniforms or banners by those engaged in peaceful demonstrations cannot be totally precluded solely because that display may provoke a violent reaction by those who view it. Particularly is this true where, as here, there has been advance notice by the demonstrators of their plans so that they have become, as the complaint alleges, "common knowledge" and those to whom sight of the swastika banner or uniforms would be offensive are forewarned and need not view them. A speaker who gives prior notice of his message has not compelled a confrontation with those who voluntarily listen.

The Illinois court also addressed what is usually known as the "hostile audience" problem, relying on the opinion from *Collin*:

> [T]he Court of Appeals for the Seventh Circuit, in reversing the denial of defendant Collin's application for a permit to speak in Chicago's Marquette Park, noted that courts have consistently refused to ban speech because of the possibility of unlawful conduct by those opposed to the speaker's philosophy. Starting with *Terminiello v. City of Chicago* and continuing to *Gregory v. City of Chicago*, 394 U.S. 111 (1969), it has become patent that a hostile audience is not a basis for restraining otherwise legal First Amendment activity. [I]f the actual behavior is not sufficient to sustain a conviction under a statute, then certainly the anticipation of such events cannot sustain the burden necessary to justify a prior restraint.

3. *The rationale of the "fighting words" doctrine.* Justice Harlan's opinion in *Cohen* begins from the premise that government can regulate the words, the speech content, or the message being communicated, only if it satisfies *Yates'* incitement test. Why not use *Brandenburg*? Harlan rejects the state's efforts to label Cohen's actions as conduct and use less stringent standards of review.

Justice Harlan states that the "prevention and punishment of [insulting or fighting words] have never been thought to raise any Constitutional problem." But the common law provided no remedy for insults and indeed did not allow insults to serve as a justification for assault by the insulted person. It is certainly questionable whether society generally should want to promote the view that insults can prompt the ordinary reasonable person to throw the first punch or reach for a concealed weapon. Does Justice Harlan's rationale depend on the listener's being considered a reasonable person?

4. *The relation between the clear-and-present danger doctrine and the fighting words doctrine.* As formulated in *Chaplinsky*, the fighting words doctrine does seem to differ from the clear and present danger doctrine. The danger doctrine arguably focuses on the occasions when the government's interests justify suppression of advocacy because of the potential danger created by positive response of listeners under the existing conditions. The fighting words doctrine, on the other hand, could be said to exclude a particular mode of speech — "verbal assaults in face-to-face encounters" — from First Amendment protection. Further, the reactions of the actual addressees was the focal point of the danger test, but not of the fighting words test which looked to the probable reactions of reasonable persons. But the Court's subsequent attention to the reactions of the particular addressee suggests that the fighting words doctrine is rapidly becoming only a form of the clear and present danger doctrine. Must breach of the peace and disorderly conduct statutes now be drawn to reflect the modern clear and present danger doctrine? *See* Thomas Shea, *"Don't Bother to Smile When You Call Me That" — Fighting Words and the First Amendment*, 63 KY. L.J. 1 (1975).

Cohen, in rejecting the State's ability to regulate offensive language employs "a balancing test, restrained by two factors: A strong concern for sharpness of focus in regulatory schemes, and a rebuttable presumption against recognizing new justifications for content regulation." Daniel Farber, *Content Regulation and the First Amendment: A Revisionist View*, 68 GEO. L.J. 727, 741 (1980). *Compare* John Ely, *Flag Desecration: A Case Study in the Roles of Categorization and Balancing in First Amendment Analysis*, 88 HARV. L. REV. 1482, 1493 (1975), finding "little trace of balancing" in *Cohen*.

Professor Gard has argued that the fighting words doctrine should be abandoned because such language deserves First Amendment protection:

> The doctrine, which operates, at best, to penalize individuals for failing to show others the respect society deems proper and, at worst, to penalize individuals for vehement criticism of government officials, is simply not constitutionally justifiable. Whatever the desirability of maintaining a polite society, the first amendment prohibits the government from seeking its preservation by means of censoring expression entitled to constitutional protection.

Stephen Gard, *Fighting Words as Free Speech*, 58 WASH. U.L.Q. 531, 536 (1980). *See also* MARTIN H. REDISH, FREEDOM OF EXPRESSION: A CRITICAL ANALYSIS 55–56 (1984):

> The theoretical fallacy in the *Chaplinsky* doctrine is the assumption that the value of free speech is a means to attain truth. Once one recognizes that the primary value of free speech is a means of fostering individual development and aiding the making of life-affecting decisions, the inappropriateness of distinguishing between the value of different types of speech becomes clear.
>
> Why not view *Chaplinsky's* comments as a personal catharsis, as a means to vent his frustration at a system he deemed to be oppressive? Is it not a mark of individuality to be able to attack a society viewed as oppressing the individual?

5. *Offensive language.* *Cohen* addresses particularly the question of whether the state can proscribe offensive language. *Chaplinsky* asserted that profane words lack social value and included insulting words along with "fighting words" as words that "by their very utterance inflict injuries." In *Rosenfeld v. New Jersey,* 408 U.S. 901, 905 (1972), Justice Powell, in dissent, defined offensive expression to include "the willful use of scurrilous language calculated to offend the sensibilities of an unwilling audience." Justice Powell argued that "[t]he shock and sense of affront, and sometimes the injury to mind and spirit, can be as great from words as from physical attack." What is Justice Harlan's response to the Powell argument? *Cohen* was deemed controlling in *Rosenfeld*, which vacated and remanded a conviction under a statute prohibiting "loud and offensive or profane or indecent language" for the use of the term "mother fucking" four times in a speech before the school board. *See Brown v. Oklahoma,* 408 U.S. 914 (1972), vacating and remanding a conviction for use of the words "mother fucking" to the police pursuant to a statute prohibiting "obscene or lascivious language."

Compare Justice Powell's opinion for the Court in *Erznoznik v. City of Jacksonville,* 422 U.S. 205, 210 (1975), striking down an ordinance prohibiting drive-ins from showing films containing nudity when the screen was visible from the public street. "Much that we encounter offends esthetic, if not our political and moral, sensibilities. Nevertheless, the Constitution does not permit the government to decide which types of otherwise protected speech are sufficiently offensive to require protection for the unwilling listener or viewer." But, in a footnote, Justice Powell distinguished this principle from the "deliberate verbal assault."

6. *Verbal assaults.* Professor Bickel rejected Justice Harlan's views in *Cohen*:

> There is such a thing as verbal violence, a kind of cursing, assaultive speech that amounts to almost physical aggression, bullying that is no less punishing because it is simulated. This sort of speech constitutes an assault. More, and equally important, it may create a climate, an environment in which conduct and actions that were not possible before become possible.

ALEXANDER BICKEL, THE MORALITY OF CONSENT 72 (1975). By way of contrast, Professor Farber, like Justice Harlan, argues:

> Use of offensive language reveals the existence of something offensive and ugly, whether in the situation described by the speaker or in the speaker's mind itself. In either event, the language reveals an important though unpleasant truth about the world. Suppressing this language violates a cardinal principle of a free society, that truths are better confronted than repressed. As long as we live in an ugly world, ugly speech must have its forum. We cannot expect to have, nor should we require, true civility in discourse until we achieve civility in society.

Daniel Farber, *Civilizing Public Discourse: An Essay on Professor Bickel, Justice Harlan, and the Enduring Significance of Cohen v. California*, 1980 DUKE L.J. 283.

7. *Regulation of hate speech: Theoretical issues.* One of the most controversial issues in modern free speech analysis is the level of protection to be afforded to so-called "hate speech" — speech that espouses hatred for or attacks on racial, religious or ethnic groups. Professor Matsuda contends that racist insults carry harms in themselves. "From the victim's perspective, all of these implements inflict wounds, wounds that are neither random nor isolated." She also implies, however, that the words should be controlled before they lead to physical impacts. "Violence is a necessary and inevitable part of the structure of racism. It is the final solution, as fascists know, barely held at bay while the tactical weapons of segregation, disparagement, and hate propaganda do their work." Mari Matsuda, *Public Response to Racist Speech: Considering the Victim's Story,* 87 MICH. L. REV. 2320, 2332–33, 2335 (1989). *See also* Richard Delgado, *Words That Wound: A Tort Action for Racial Insults, Epithets and Name-Calling,* 17 HARV. C.R.-C.L.L. REV. 133 (1982).

How should judges, especially those not trained in psychology, evaluate the question of whether words inflict harms? What are the costs, if any, of regulating hate speech? How do the different theoretical rationales for free speech protection interact with such regulation?

Consider the possible relevance to the issue of hate speech regulation of the debate over the concept of low value speech.

> If taken to an extreme, the generally salutary antipathy to 'censorship' would protect those who defraud consumers; who conspire, threaten, and bribe; who disclose to unfriendly countries plans to develop military technology; who use children to produce pornography; who disclose the names of rape victims; and who spread knowing falsehoods about private citizens. And if judges are unwilling to distinguish between high-and low-value speech, government will be unable to control these forms of expression without simultaneously lowering the burden of justification and thus endangering other speech that belongs at the center of constitutional concern.

Cass Sunstein, *Low Value Speech Revisited,* 83 NW. U.L. REV. 555, 561 (1989).

The statement, "Subjugate women!," appearing on a political pamphlet, may convey exactly the same meaning to its audience as a pornographic picture of a woman in bondage. If that is the case, then there seems to be a good argument for regarding the pamphlet as having the same value as speech. If the pamphlet is high value speech, then so too it would appear is the pornographic picture. Conversely, if the latter is low — or no — value speech, then so is the pamphlet.

Larry Alexander, *Low Value Speech,* 83 NW. U.L. REV. 547, 547–48 (1989). See p. 1253 on female pornography.

***R.A.V. v. City of St. Paul,* 505 U.S. 377 (1992).** Petitioner allegedly burned a cross on the yard of a black family. He was charged with violating the St. Paul Bias-Motivated Crime Ordinance, which criminalized "place[ing] on public or private property a symbol, object, appellation, characterization or graffiti, including, but not limited to, a burning cross or Nazi swastika, which one knows or has reasonable grounds to know arouses anger, alarm or resentment in others on the basis of race, color, creed, religion or gender." The Minnesota Supreme Court construed the ordinance to prohibit only those expressions that would constitute "fighting words" under *Chaplinsky v. New Hampshire*. Assuming arguendo that all of the expression reached by the ordinance is proscribeable under the "fighting words" doctrine, the Supreme Court unanimously held that the ordinance was facially unconstitutional, but divided on the reasoning.

Justice Scalia, writing for the majority, held that the ordinance is facially unconstitutional in that it prohibits otherwise permitted speech solely on the basis of the subjects the speech addresses. Initially, Justice Scalia rejected the notion that the government may regulate, in any manner, speech that falls within one of the *Chaplinsky* categories:

> "We have sometimes said that these categories of expression are not within the area of constitutionally protected speech," or that the "protection of the First Amendment does not extend" to them. Such statements must be taken in context, however, and are no more literally true than is the occasionally repeated shorthand characterizing obscenity "as not being speech at all." What they mean is that these areas of speech can, consistently with the First Amendment, be regulated because of their constitutionally proscribable content (obscenity, defamation, etc.)—-not that they are categories of speech entirely invisible to the Constitution, so that they may be made the vehicles for content discrimination unrelated to their distinctively proscribable content. Thus, the government may proscribe libel; but it may not make the further content discrimination of proscribing only libel critical of the government."

But Justice Scalia noted that "[e]ven the prohibition against content discrimination that we assert the First Amendment requires is not absolute." The presumptive invalidity of content discrimination is subject to exceptions where there is no danger of driving certain ideas or viewpoints from the market.

> First, when the basis for the content discrimination consists of entirely of the very reason the entire class of speech at issue is proscribable, no significant danger of idea or viewpoint discrimination exists. Such a reason, having been adjudged neutral enough to support exclusion of the entire class of speech from First Amendment protection, is also neutral enough to form the basis of distinction within the class. To illustrate: A State might choose to prohibit only that obscenity which is the most patently offensive in its prurience — i.e., that which involves the most lascivious displays of sexual activity. But it may not prohibit, for example, only that obscenity which includes offensive political messages. Similarly, the federal government can criminalize only those threats of violence directed against the president, since the reasons why threats are outside First Amendment have special force when applied to the President.

> Second, [a]nother valid basis for according differential treatment to even a content-defined subclass of proscribable speech is that the subclass happens to be associated with particular "secondary effects" of speech, so that the regulation is justified without reference to the content of the speech. *Renton v. Playtime Theatres, Inc.* An example of a regulation falling under this exception would be a law prohibiting only those obscene live performances that involved minors. Similarly, Title VII's prohibition of sex discrimination in the workplace would allow regulation of sexually derogatory fighting words.
>
> Finally, an exception for content-based regulations in a category of proscribeable speech may exist so long as "the nature of the content discrimination is such that there is no realistic possibility that official suppression of ideas is afoot.

Justice Scalia then applied this framework to the St. Paul ordinance: "[T]he ordinance applies only to 'fighting words' that insult, or provoke violence 'on the basis of race, color, creed, religion or gender.' Displays containing abusive invective, no matter how vicious or severe, are permissible unless they are addressed to one of the specified disfavored topics. Those who wish to use 'fighting words' in connection with other ideas to express hostility, for example, on the basis of political affiliation, union membership, or homosexuality are not covered." He concluded: "The First Amendment does not permit St. Paul to impose special prohibitions on those speakers who express views on disfavored subjects."

Nor did the content-based discrimination reflected in the St. Paul ordinance come within any of the specific exceptions to the First Amendment prohibition, nor within a more general exception for content discrimination that does not threaten censorship of ideas. It did not fall within the first exception, since "the reason why fighting words are categorically excluded from the protection of the First Amendment is not that their content communicates any particular idea, but that their content embodies a particularly intolerable (and socially unnecessary) mode of expressing whatever idea the speaker wishes to convey. St. Paul has not singled out an especially offensive mode of expression — it has not, for example, selected for prohibition only those fighting words that communicate ideas in a threatening (as opposed to a merely obnoxious) manner. Rather, it has proscribed fighting words of whatever manner that communicate messages of racial, gender, or religious intolerance. Selectivity of this sort creates the possibility that the city is seeking to handicap the expression of particular ideas."

Justice Scalia rejected St. Paul's argument that the ordinance survived strict scrutiny because "the ordinance helps to ensure the basic human rights of members of groups that have historically been subjected to discrimination." While noting that this interest was compelling, the content discrimination was not "reasonably necessary" to achieve this interest. The existence of content-neutral alternatives — banning all fighting words — was determinative. Justice Scalia concluded that "The only interest distinctively served by the content limitation is that of displaying the city council's special hostility towards the particular biases thus singled out. That is precisely what the First Amendment forbids."

Justice White, joined by Justices Blackmun and O'Connor, and in part by Justice Stevens, concurred in the judgment. He first criticized the majority's assertion that there are restrictions on the ability of government to regulate within the *Chaplinsky* categories: "[T]he Court announces that earlier Courts did not mean their repeated statements that certain categories of expression are not within the area of constitutionally protected speech.' To the contrary, those statements meant precisely what they said: The categorical approach is a firmly entrenched part of our First Amendment jurisprudence. It is inconsistent to hold that the government may proscribe an entire category of speech because the content of that speech is evil, but that the government may not treat a subset of that category differently without violating the First Amendment; the content of the subset is by definition worthless and undeserving of constitutional protection."

Justice White also faulted the majority for adopting, what he referred to as, an "underbreadth" doctrine:

> "The overbreadth doctrine has the redeeming virtue of attempting to avoid the chilling of protected expression, but the Court's new 'underbreadth' creation serves no desirable function. Instead, it permits, indeed invites, the continuation of expressive conduct that in this case is evil and worthless in First Amendment terms, until the city of St. Paul cures the underbreadth by adding to its ordinance a catch-all phrase such as 'and all other fighting words that may constitutionally be subject to this ordinance.' Any contribution of this holding to First Amendment jurisprudence is surely a negative one, since it necessarily signals that expressions of violence, such as the message of intimidation and racial hatred conveyed by burning a cross on someone lawn, are of sufficient value to outweigh the social interest in order and morality that has traditionally placed such fighting words outside the First Amendment."

Justice White also accused the Court of "discarding our firmly established strict scrutiny analysis." "Under the majority's view, a narrowly drawn content-based ordinance could never pass constitutional muster if the object of that legislation could be accomplished by banning a wider category of speech."

Justice White noted that the majority's concern about content-based regulations within *Chaplinsky* categories of unprotected speech is unnecessary because "the Equal Protection Clause requires that the regulation of unprotected speech be rationally related to a legitimate government interest. Thus, [a] defamation statute that drew distinctions on the basis of political affiliation or 'an ordinance prohibiting only those legally obscene works that contain criticism of the city government,' would unquestionably fail rational basis review."

Justice White preferred to decide the case under the more traditional overbreadth doctrine. The state supreme court had interpreted the ordinance to permit the city to "[p]rohibit expression that 'by its very utterance' causes 'anger, alarm or resentment.' " But, according to Justice White, "such generalized reactions are not sufficient to strip expression of its constitutional protection."

Justice Blackmun, concurring in the judgment, posited that "[t]he majority opinion signals one of two possibilities: it will serve as precedent for future cases, or it will not." In the former case, "by deciding that a State cannot regulate speech that causes great harm unless it also regulates speech that does not (setting law and logic on their heads), the Court seems to abandon the categorical approach, and inevitably to relax the level of scrutiny applicable to content-based laws. As Justice White points out, this weakens the traditional protections of speech. If all expressive activity must be accorded the same protection, that protection will be scant."

In the second case, the decision "will be regarded as an aberration — a case where the Court manipulated doctrine to strike down an ordinance whose premise it opposed, namely, that racial threats and verbal assaults are of greater harm than other fighting words." He expressed concern "that the Court has been distracted from its proper mission by the temptation to decide the issue over politically correct speech and cultural diversity, neither of which is presented here. If this is the meaning of today opinion, it is perhaps even more regrettable." Justice Blackmun agreed with Justice White that the ordinance "reaches beyond fighting words to speech protected by the First Amendment."

Justice Stevens, joined in part by Justices White and Blackmun, concurred in the judgment, but wrote "separately to suggest how the allure of absolute principles has skewed the analysis of both the majority and Justice White's opinion." Justice Stevens criticized the majority for its holding that content-based regulations are presumptively invalid: "Drawing on broadly worded dicta, the Court establishes a near-absolute ban on content-based regulations of expression and holds that the First Amendment prohibits the regulation of fighting words by subject matter. Thus, while the Court rejects the 'all-or-nothing-at-all' nature of the categorical approach, it promptly embraces an absolutism of its own: within a particular proscribable category of expression, the Court holds, a government must either proscribe all speech or no speech at all." Justice Stevens criticized the Court's rejection of content-based regulation.

> [O]ur decisions demonstrate that content-based distinctions, far from being presumptively invalid, are an inevitable and indispensable aspect of a coherent understanding of the First Amendment. This is true at every level of First Amendment law. In broadest terms, our entire First Amendment jurisprudence creates a regime based on the content of speech. The scope of the First Amendment is determined by the content of expressive activity. Likewise, whether speech falls within one part of the categories of "unprotected" or "proscribable" expression is determined, in part, by its content. Even within categories of protected expression, the First Amendment status of speech is fixed by its content.

Justice Stevens criticized Justice White's opinion because of his "reservations about the 'categorical approach' to the First Amendment." Justice

Stevens argued that the categorical approach "sacrifices subtlety for clarity." "fits poorly with the complex reality of expression," "inevitably give[s] rise only to fuzzy boundaries," and is "unworkable," "ultimately futile," and "destined to fail."

***Wisconsin v. Mitchell*, 508 U.S. 476 (1993).** The Court upheld a Wisconsin statute which enhanced criminal penalties when the victim is selected because of race. When a group of black men and boys attacked and beat a white boy severely, the two-year sentence of one of the perpetrators was enhanced to seven years because the perpetrator had selected the victim because of the victim's race. The Wisconsin Supreme Court struck down the law on the ground that it violated the First Amendment because it was overbroad and punished what the legislature deemed to be "offensive thought."

Unlike *R.A.V.*, the Wisconsin statute went beyond punishing expression and punished the underlying conduct: "[A] physical assault is not by any stretch of the imagination expressive conduct protected by the First Amendment." The defendant contended that since the rationale for enhancing the criminal penalty was his discriminatory motive in selecting the victim, the Wisconsin law punished thoughts and beliefs in violation of the First Amendment. The Court rejected this contention. While a person may not be punished because of his abstract beliefs, *Dawson v. Delaware,* 503 U.S. 159 (1992) (use of evidence that the defendant was a member of a white supremacist prison gang in a capital-sentencing hearing, when the evidence has no relevance to the issues in the hearing, violates the First Amendment), motive is frequently an important factor in determining penalties for criminal conduct.

In addition, motive played the same role under the Wisconsin penalty enhancement law as it does under antidiscrimination laws. Such laws are aimed at unprotected conduct, not activity protected by the First Amendment. This same reasoning was used by the Chief Justice to distinguish *R.A.V.*:

> [W]hereas the ordinance struck down in *R.A.V.* was explicitly directed at expression (*i.e.*, "speech" or "messages"), the statute in this case is aimed at conduct unprotected by the First Amendment.

Chief Justice Rehnquist stressed the rationale for the Wisconsin penalty enhancement law:

> [T]he Wisconsin statute singles out for enhancement bias-inspired conduct because this conduct is thought to inflict greater individual and societal harm. For example, according to the State, and its *amici*, bias-motivated crimes are more likely to provoke retaliatory crimes, inflict distinct emotional harms on their victims, and incite community unrest. The State's desire to redress these perceived harms provides an adequate explanation for its penalty-enhance ment provision over and above mere disagreement with offenders' beliefs and biases.

There was no First Amendment barrier against the "evidentiary use of speech" in order to prove motive or intent or the elements of a crime. Similarly, in *Price Waterhouse v. Hopkins,* 490 U.S. 228 (1989), the Court had allowed the evidentiary use of speech by the defendant in a Title VII discrimination claim.

Contrast the following competing views on the issue involved in *Mitchell*:

> If we conclude that constitutional protection of freedom of thought should be accepted, the fact that sentencing enhancement laws do not directly impede or penalize communicative activity cannot automatically insulate them from constitutional attack. Because such laws are adopted for the very purpose of penalizing thought processes and political motivations found to be offensive by those in power, they constitute classic abridgements of the constitutionally protected freedom of thought.

Martin Redish, *Freedom of Thought as Freedom of Expression: Hate Crime Sentencing Enhancement and First Amendment Theory*, 1992 Criminal Justice Ethics 29, 37.

> Assume, for instance, that a judge has two murderers before her for sentencing — one who killed his rich aunt in order to inherit her fortune and another who killed his aunt in order to save her further suffering from a painfully debilitative disease. Giving the greedy nephew a more severe sentence than the compassionate nephew may raise interesting questions about the theory of punishment but it does not raise free speech concerns. The greedy nephew is being punished not for holding certain abstract beliefs, but for *acting* on those beliefs in a way that makes his conduct more reprehensible, more dangerous, or perhaps more in need of deterrence than the compassionately motivated nephew.

James Weinstein, *Hate Crime and Punishment: A Comment on* Wisconsin v. Mitchell, 73 Ore. L.Rev. 345, 349–50 (1994).

Consider the following hypothetical statute: "A person convicted of a crime will have his or her sentence doubled if it is found that the crime was motivated out of a belief in the pro-life cause." Would such a statute be held constitutional? If not, to which situation is the statute in *Mitchell* more analogous, this hypothetical or the one described by Professor Weinstein?

VIRGINIA v. BLACK

538 U.S. 343 123 S. Ct. 1536, 155 L. Ed. 2d 535 (2003)

Justice O'Connor announced the judgment of the Court and delivered the opinion of the Court with respect to Parts I, II, and III, and an opinion with respect to Parts IV and V, in which The Chief Justice, Justice Stevens, and Justice Breyer join. In this case we consider whether the Commonwealth of Virginia's statute banning cross burning with "an intent to intimidate a person or group of persons" violates the First Amendment. We conclude that while a State, consistent with the First Amendment, may ban cross burning carried out with the intent to intimidate, the provision in the Virginia statute treating any cross burning as prima facie evidence of intent to intimidate renders the statute unconstitutional in its current form.

I

Respondents Barry Black, Richard Elliott, and Jonathan O'Mara were convicted separately of violating Virginia's cross-burning statute, § 18.2-423. That statute provides: "It shall be unlawful for any person or persons, with the intent of intimidating any person or group of persons, to burn, or cause to be burned, a cross on the property of another, a highway or other public place. Any person who shall violate any provision of this section shall be guilty of a Class 6 felony.

"Any such burning of a cross shall be prima facie evidence of an intent to intimidate a person or group of persons."

On August 22, 1998, Barry Black led a Ku Klux Klan rally in Carroll County, Virginia. Twenty-five to thirty people attended this gathering, which occurred on private property with the permission of the owner, who was in attendance. The property was located on an open field in Cana, Virginia.

When the sheriff of Carroll County learned that a Klan rally was occurring in his county, he went to observe it from the side of the road. During the approximately one hour that the sheriff was present, about 40 to 50 cars passed the site, a "few" of which stopped to ask the sheriff what was happening on the property. Eight to ten houses were located in the vicinity of the rally. Rebecca Sechrist, who was related to the owner of the property where the rally took place, "sat and watched to see what [was] going on" from the lawn of her in-laws' house. She looked on as the Klan prepared for the gathering and subsequently conducted the rally itself. During the rally, Sechrist heard Klan members speak about "what they were" and "what they believed in." The speakers "talked real bad about the blacks and the Mexicans." One speaker told the assembled gathering that "he would love to take a. 30/.30 and just randomly shoot the blacks." The speakers also talked about "President Clinton and Hillary Clinton," and about how their tax money "goes to . . . the black people." Sechrist testified that this language made her "very . . . scared."

At the conclusion of the rally, the crowd circled around a 25-to 30-foot cross. The cross was between 300 and 350 yards away from the road. According to the sheriff, the cross "then all of a sudden . . . went up in a flame." As the cross burned, the Klan played Amazing Grace over the loudspeakers. Sechrist stated that the cross burning made her feel "awful" and "terrible." The sheriff then went down the driveway, entered the rally, and asked "who was responsible for burning the cross." Black responded, "I guess I am because I'm the head of the rally."

Black was charged with burning a cross with the intent of intimidating a person or group of persons, in violation of § 18.2-423. At his trial, the jury was instructed that "intent to intimidate means the motivation to intentionally put a person or a group of persons in fear of bodily harm. Such fear must arise from the willful conduct of the accused rather than from some mere temperamental timidity of the victim." The trial court also instructed the jury that "the burning of a cross by itself is sufficient evidence from which you may infer the required intent." When Black objected to this last instruction on First Amendment grounds, the prosecutor responded that the instruction was "taken straight out of the [Virginia] Model Instructions." The jury found Black guilty, and fined him $2,500. The Court of Appeals of Virginia affirmed Black's conviction.

On May 2, 1998, respondents Richard Elliott and Jonathan O'Mara, as well as a third individual, attempted to burn a cross on the yard of James Jubilee. Jubilee, an African-American, was Elliott's next-door neighbor in Virginia Beach, Virginia. Four months prior to the incident, Jubilee and his family had moved from California to Virginia Beach. Before the cross burning, Jubilee spoke to Elliott's mother to inquire about shots being fired from behind the Elliott home. Elliott's mother explained to Jubilee that her son shot firearms as a hobby, and that he used the backyard as a firing range.

On the night of May 2, respondents drove a truck onto Jubilee's property, planted a cross, and set it on fire. Their apparent motive was to "get back" at Jubilee for complaining about the shooting in the backyard. Respondents were not affiliated with the Klan. The next morning, as Jubilee was pulling his car out of the driveway, he noticed the partially burned cross approximately 20 feet from his house. After seeing the cross, Jubilee was "very nervous" because he "didn't know what would be the next phase," and because "a cross burned in your yard . . . tells you that it's just the first round."

Elliott and O'Mara were charged with attempted cross burning and conspiracy to commit cross burning. O'Mara pleaded guilty to both counts, reserving the right to challenge the constitutionality of the cross-burning statute. The judge sentenced O'Mara to 90 days in jail and fined him $2,500. The judge also suspended 45 days of the sentence and $1,000 of the fine.

At Elliott's trial, the judge originally ruled that the jury would be instructed "that the burning of a cross by itself is sufficient evidence from which you may infer the required intent." At trial, however, the court instructed the jury that the Commonwealth must prove that "the defendant intended to commit cross burning," that "the defendant did a direct act toward the commission of the cross burning," and that "the defendant had the intent of intimidating any person or group of persons." The court did not instruct the jury on the meaning of the word "intimidate," nor on the prima facie evidence provision of § 18.2-423. The jury found Elliott guilty of attempted cross burning and acquitted him of conspiracy to commit cross burning. It sentenced Elliott to 90 days in jail and a $2,500 fine. The Court of Appeals of Virginia affirmed the convictions of both Elliott and O'Mara. Each respondent appealed to the Supreme Court of Virginia, arguing that § 18.2-423 is facially unconstitutional. The Supreme Court of Virginia consolidated all three cases, and held that the statute is unconstitutional on its face. It held that the Virginia cross-burning statute "is analytically indistinguishable from the ordinance found unconstitutional in *R.A.V.*, [text, p. 1053]. The Virginia statute, the court held, discriminates on the basis of content since it "selectively chooses only cross burning because of its distinctive message." The court also held that the prima facie evidence provision renders the statute overbroad because "the enhanced probability of prosecution under the statute chills the expression of protected speech." Three justices dissented, concluding that the Virginia cross-burning statute passes constitutional muster because it proscribes only conduct that constitutes a true threat.

Burning a cross in the United States is inextricably intertwined with the history of the Klu Klux Klan. Cross burnings have been used to communicate both threats of violence and messages of shared ideology. Often, the Klan used cross burnings as a tool of intimidation and a threat of impending violence. Throughout the history of the Klan, cross burnings have also remained potent symbols of shared group identity and ideology. The burning cross became a symbol of the Klan itself and a central feature of Klan gatherings.

To this day, regardless of whether the message is a political one or whether the message is also meant to intimidate, the burning of a cross is a "symbol of hate." *Capitol Square Review and Advisory Bd. v. Pinette*, [515 U.S. 753 (1995)] (THOMAS, J., concurring). And while cross burning sometimes carries no intimidating message, at other times the intimidating message is the *only* message conveyed. For example, when a cross burning is directed at a particular person not affiliated with the Klan, the burning cross often serves as a message of intimidation, designed to inspire in the victim a fear of bodily harm. Moreover, the history of violence associated with the Klan shows that the possibility of injury or death is not just hypothetical. The person who burns a cross directed at a particular person often is making a serious threat, meant to coerce the victim to comply with the Klan's wishes unless the victim is willing to risk the wrath of the Klan. Indeed, as the cases of respondents Elliott and O'Mara indicate, individuals without Klan affiliation who wish to threaten or menace another person sometimes use cross burning because of this association between a burning cross and violence.

In sum, while a burning cross does not inevitably convey a message of intimidation, often the cross burner intends that the recipients of the message fear for their lives. And when a cross burning is used to intimidate, few if any messages are more powerful.

III

The protections afforded by the First Amendment are not absolute, and we have long recognized that the government may regulate certain categories of expression consistent with the Constitution. *Chaplinsky v. New Hampshire.* Thus, for example, a State may punish those words "which by their very utterance inflict injury or tend to incite an immediate breach of the peace." *Chaplinsky v. New Hampshire.* Furthermore, "the constitutional guarantees of free speech and free press do not permit a State to forbid or proscribe advocacy of the use of force or of law violation except where such advocacy is directed to inciting or producing imminent lawless action and is likely to incite or produce such action." *Brandenburg v. Ohio*. And the First Amendment also permits a State to ban a "true threat." *Watts v. United States*, 394 U.S. 705, 708 (1969) (per curiam); *R.A.V. v. City of St. Paul; Madsen v. Women's Health Center, Inc*, [text, p. 1125]; *Schenck v. Pro-Choice Network of Western N.Y.*, [text, p. 1132].

"True threats" encompass those statements where the speaker means to communicate a serious expression of an intent to commit an act of unlawful violence to a particular individual or group of individuals. *See Watts v. United States* [394 U.S. 705 (1969)] ("political hyberbole" is not a true threat). The speaker need not actually intend to carry out the threat. Rather, a prohibition on true threats "protects individuals from the fear of violence" and "from the disruption that fear engenders," in addition to protecting people "from the possibility that the threatened violence will occur." [*R.A.V.*] Intimidation in the constitutionally proscribable sense of the word is a type of true threat, where a speaker directs a threat to a person or group of persons with the intent of placing the victim in fear of bodily harm or death. Respondents do not contest that some cross burnings fit within this meaning of intimidating speech, and rightly so. [T]he history of cross burning in this country shows that cross burning is often intimidating, intended to create a pervasive fear in victims that they are a target of violence. We did not hold in *R.A.V.* that the First Amendment prohibits *all* forms of content-based discrimination within a proscribable area of speech. Rather, we specifically stated that some types of content discrimination did not violate the First Amendment. [T]he First Amendment permits content discrimination "based on the very reasons why the particular class of speech at issue . . . is proscribable."

Similarly, Virginia's statute does not run afoul of the First Amendment insofar as it bans cross burning with intent to intimidate. Unlike the statute at issue in *R.A.V.*, the Virginia statute does not single out for opprobrium only that speech directed toward "one of the specified disfavored topics." It does not matter whether an individual burns a cross with intent to intimidate because of the victim's race, gender, or religion, or because of the victim's "political affiliation, union membership, or homosexuality." Moreover, as a factual matter it is not true that cross burners direct their intimidating conduct solely to racial or religious minorities. Indeed, in the case of Elliott and O'Mara, it is at least unclear whether the respondents burned a cross due to racial animus.

The First Amendment permits Virginia to outlaw cross burnings done with the intent to intimidate because burning a cross is a particularly virulent form of intimidation. Instead of prohibiting all intimidating messages, Virginia may choose to regulate this subset of intimidating messages in light of cross burning's long and pernicious history as a signal of impending violence. Thus, just as a State may regulate only that obscenity which is the most obscene due to its prurient content, so too may a State choose to prohibit only those forms of intimidation that are most likely to inspire fear of bodily harm. A ban on cross burning carried out with the intent to intimidate is fully consistent with our holding in *R.A.V.* and is proscribable under the First Amendment.

IV

The Supreme Court of Virginia ruled in the alternative that Virginia's cross-burning statute was unconstitutionally overbroad due to its provision stating that "any such burning of a cross shall be prima facie evidence of an intent to intimidate a person or group of persons." The court below did not reach whether this provision is severable from the rest of the crossburning statute under Virginia law. In this Court, as in the Supreme Court of Virginia, respondents do not argue that the prima facie evidence provision is unconstitutional as applied to any one of them. Rather, they contend that the provision is unconstitutional on its face.

The Supreme Court of Virginia has not ruled on the meaning of the prima facie evidence provision. It has, however, stated that "the act of burning a cross alone, with no evidence of intent to intimidate, will nonetheless suffice for arrest and prosecution and will insulate the Commonwealth from a motion to strike the evidence at the end of its case-in-chief." The jury in the case of Richard Elliott did not receive any instruction on the prima facie evidence provision, and the provision was not an issue in the case of Jonathan O'Mara because he pleaded guilty. The court in Barry Black's case, however, instructed the jury that the provision means: "The burning of a cross, by itself, is sufficient evidence from which you may infer the required intent." This jury instruction is the same as the Model Jury Instruction in the Commonwealth of Virginia.

The prima facie evidence provision, as interpreted by the jury instruction, renders the statute unconstitutional. Because this jury instruction is the Model Jury Instruction, and because the Supreme Court of Virginia had the opportunity to expressly disavow the jury instruction, the jury instruction's construction of the prima facie provision "is a ruling on a question of state law that is as binding on us as though the precise words had been written into" the statute. As construed by the jury instruction, the prima facie provision strips away the very reason why a State may ban cross burning with the intent to intimidate. The prima facie evidence provision permits a jury to convict in every cross-burning case in which defendants exercise their constitutional right not to put on a defense. And even where a defendant like Black presents a defense, the prima facie evidence provision makes it more likely that the jury will find an intent to intimidate regardless of the particular facts of the case. The provision permits the Commonwealth to arrest, prosecute, and convict a person based solely on the fact of cross burning itself.

It is apparent that the provision as so interpreted " 'would create an unacceptable risk of the suppression of ideas.' " *Secretary of State of Md. v. Joseph H. Munson Co.* The act of burning a cross may mean that a person is engaging in constitutionally proscribable intimidation. But that same act may mean only that the person is engaged in core political speech. The prima facie evidence provision in this statute blurs the line between these two meanings of a burning cross. As interpreted by the jury instruction, the provision chills constitutionally protected political speech because of the possibility that a State will prosecute—and potentially convict—somebody engaging only in lawful political speech at the core of what the First Amendment is designed to protect.

As the history of cross burning indicates, a burning cross is not always intended to intimidate. Rather, sometimes the cross burning is a statement of ideology, a symbol of group solidarity. It is a ritual used at Klan gatherings, and it is used to represent the Klan itself. Indeed, occasionally a person who burns a cross does not intend to express either a statement of ideology or intimidation. Cross burnings have appeared in movies such as Mississippi Burning, and in plays such as the stage adaptation of Sir Walter Scott's THE LADY OF THE LAKE.

The prima facie provision makes no effort to distinguish among these different types of cross burnings. It does not distinguish between a cross burning done with the purpose of creating anger or resentment and a cross burning done with the purpose of threatening or intimidating a victim. It does not distinguish between a cross burning at a public rally or a cross burning on a neighbor's lawn. It does not treat the cross burning directed at an individual differently from the cross burning directed at a group of like-minded believers. It allows a jury to treat a cross burning on the property of another with the owner's acquiescence in the same manner as a cross burning on the property of another without the owner's permission. To this extent I agree with Justice Souter that the prima facie evidence provision can "skew jury deliberations toward conviction in cases where the evidence of intent to intimidate is relatively weak and arguably consistent with a solely ideological reason for burning."

It may be true that a cross burning, even at a political rally, arouses a sense of anger or hatred among the vast majority of citizens who see a burning cross. But this sense of anger or hatred is not sufficient to ban all cross burnings. The prima facie evidence provision in this case ignores all of the contextual factors that are necessary to decide whether a particular cross burning is intended to intimidate. The First Amendment does not permit such a shortcut.

For these reasons, the prima facie evidence provision, as interpreted through the jury instruction and as applied in Barry Black's case, is unconstitutional on its face. We recognize that the Supreme Court of Virginia has not authoritatively interpreted the meaning of the prima facie evidence provision. Unlike Justice Scalia, we refuse to speculate on whether *any* interpretation of the prima facie evidence provision would satisfy the First Amendment. Rather, all we hold is that because of the interpretation of the prima facie evidence provision given by the jury instruction, the provision makes the statute facially invalid at this point. We also recognize the theoretical possibility that the court, on remand, could interpret the provision in a manner different from that so far set forth in order to avoid the constitutional objections we have described. We leave open that possibility.

We also leave open the possibility that the provision is severable, and if so, whether Elliott and O'Mara could be retried under § 18.2-423.

V

With respect to Barry Black, we agree with the Supreme Court of Virginia that his conviction cannot stand, and we affirm the judgment of the Supreme Court of Virginia. With respect to Elliott and O'Mara, we vacate the judgment of the Supreme Court of Virginia, and remand the case for further proceedings.

Justice Stevens, concurring.

Cross burning with "an intent to intimidate," unquestionably qualifies as the kind of threat that is unprotected by the First Amendment. For the reasons stated in the separate opinions that Justice White and I wrote in *R.A.V. v. St. Paul* that simple proposition provides a sufficient basis for upholding the basic prohibition in the Virginia statute even though it does not cover other types of threatening expressive conduct. With this observation, I join JUSTICE O'CONNOR's opinion.

JUSTICE SCALIA, with whom JUSTICE THOMAS joins as to Parts I and II, concurring in part, concurring in the judgment in part, and dissenting in part.

I agree with the Court that, under our decision in *R.A.V. v. St. Paul*, a State may, without infringing the First Amendment, prohibit cross burning carried out with the intent to intimidate. Accordingly, I join Parts I-III of the Court's opinion. I also agree that we should vacate and remand the judgment of the Virginia Supreme Court so that that Court can have an opportunity authoritatively to construe the prima-facie-evidence provision. I write separately, however, to describe what I believe to be the correct interpretation of § 18.2-423, and to explain why I believe there is no justification for the plurality's apparent decision to invalidate that provision on its face.

I

The established meaning in Virginia of the term "prima facie evidence" appears to be perfectly orthodox: It is evidence that suffices, on its own, to establish a particular fact. But it is hornbook law that this is true only to the extent that the evidence goes unrebutted. Put otherwise, where the Commonwealth has demonstrated through its case in chief that the defendant burned a cross in public view, this is sufficient, at least until the defendant has come forward with rebuttal evidence, to create a jury issue with respect to the intent element of the offense.

II

The question presented, then, is whether, given this understanding of the term "prima facie evidence," the cross-burning statute is constitutional. Some individuals who engage in protected speech may, because of the prima-facie-evidence provision, be subject to conviction. Such convictions, assuming they are unconstitutional, could be challenged on a case-by-case basis. The plurality, however, with little in the way of explanation, leaps to the conclusion that the *possibility* of such convictions justifies facial invalidation of the statute.

In deeming § 18.2-423 facially invalid, the plurality presumably means to rely on some species of overbreadth doctrine. But it must be a rare species indeed. We have noted that "in a facial challenge to the overbreadth and vagueness of a law, a court's first task is to determine whether the enactment reaches a substantial amount of constitutionally protected conduct." *Hoffman Estates v. Flipside, Hoffman Estates, Inc.*, 455 U.S. 489, 494 (1982). If one looks only to the core provision of § 18.2-423—"it shall be unlawful for any person or persons, with the intent of intimidating any person or group of persons, to burn, or cause to be burned, a cross . . ."—it appears *not* to capture any protected conduct; that language is limited in its reach to conduct which a State is, under the Court's holding, allowed to prohibit. In order to identify *any* protected conduct that is affected by Virginia's cross-burning law, the plurality is compelled to focus not on the statute's core prohibition, but on the prima-facie-evidence provision, and hence on *the process* through which the prohibited conduct may be found by a jury.

The plurality is thus left with a strikingly attenuated argument to support the claim that Virginia's cross-burning statute is facially invalid. The class of persons that the plurality contemplates could impermissibly be convicted under § 18.2-423 includes only those individuals who (1) burn a cross in public view, (2) do not intend to intimidate, (3) are nonetheless charged and prosecuted, and (4) refuse to present a defense. Conceding (quite generously, in my view) that this class of persons exists, it cannot possibly give rise to a viable facial challenge, not even with the aid of our First Amendment overbreadth doctrine. The notion that the set of cases identified by the plurality in which convictions might improperly be obtained is sufficiently large to render the statute *substantially* overbroad is fanciful.

III

As the analysis in Part I, demonstrates, I believe the prima-facie-evidence provision in Virginia's cross-burning statute is constitutionally unproblematic. Nevertheless, because the Virginia Supreme Court has not yet offered an authoritative construction of § 18.2-423, I concur in the Court's decision to vacate and remand the judgment with respect to respondents Elliott and O'Mara. I also agree that respondent Black's conviction cannot stand. Still, I cannot go along with the Court's decision to affirm the judgment with respect to Black. In that judgment, the Virginia Supreme Court, having erroneously concluded that § 18.2-423 is overbroad, not only vacated Black's conviction, but dismissed the indictment against him as well. Because I believe the constitutional defect in Black's conviction is rooted in a jury instruction and not in the statute itself, I would not dismiss the indictment and would permit the Commonwealth to retry Black if it wishes to do so.

JUSTICE SOUTER, with whom JUSTICE KENNEDY and JUSTICE GINSBURG join, concurring in the judgment in part and dissenting in part.

I agree with the majority that the Virginia statute makes a content-based distinction within the category of punishable intimidating or threatening expression, the very type of distinction we considered in *R.A.V. v. St. Paul*. I disagree that any exception should save Virginia's law from unconstitutionality under the holding in *R.A.V.* or any acceptable variation of it. [T]he specific prohibition of cross burning with intent to intimidate selects a symbol with particular content from the field of all proscribable expression meant to intimidate. To be sure, that content often includes an essentially intimidating message, that the cross burner will harm the victim, most probably in a physical way, given the historical identification of burning crosses with arson, beating, and lynching. But even when the symbolic act is meant to terrify, a burning cross may carry a further, ideological message of white Protestant supremacy. The ideological message not only accompanies many threatening uses of the symbol, but is also expressed when a burning cross is not used to threaten but merely to symbolize the supremacist ideology and the solidarity of those who espouse it.

The issue is whether the statutory prohibition restricted to this symbol falls within one of the exceptions to *R.A.V.*'s general condemnation of limited content-based proscription within a broader category of expression proscribable generally. I do not think that the Virginia statute qualifies for this virulence exception as *R.A.V.* explained it. The statute fits poorly with the illustrative examples given in *R. A. V.*, none of which involves communication generally associated with a particular message, and in fact, the majority's discussion of a special virulence exception here moves that exception toward a more flexible conception than the version in *R.A.V.* I will reserve judgment on that doctrinal development, for even on a pragmatic conception of *R.A.V.* and its exceptions the Virginia statute could not pass muster, the most obvious hurdle being the statute's prima facie evidence provision. That provision is essential to understanding why the statute's tendency to suppress a message disqualifies it from any rescue by exception from *R.A.V.*'s general rule.

R.A.V. defines the special virulence exception to the rule barring content-based subclasses of categorically proscribable expression this way: prohibition by subcategory is nonetheless constitutional if it is made "entirely" on the "basis" of "the very reason" that "the entire class of speech at issue is proscribable" at all. The Court explained that when the subcategory is confined to the most obviously proscribable instances, "no significant danger of idea or viewpoint discrimination exists," and the explanation was rounded out with some illustrative examples. None of them, however, resembles the case before us.

I read *R.A.V.*'s examples of the particular virulence exception as covering prohibitions that are not clearly associated with a particular viewpoint, and that are consequently different from the Virginia statute. On that understanding of things, I necessarily read the majority opinion as treating *R.A.V.*'s virulence exception in a more flexible, pragmatic manner than the original illustrations would suggest. Actually, another way of looking at today's decision would see it as a slight modification of *R.A.V.*'s third exception, which allows content-based discrimination within a proscribable category when its "nature" is such "that there is no realistic possibility that official suppression of ideas is afoot." The majority's approach could be taken as recognizing an exception to *R.A.V.* when circumstances show that the statute's ostensibly valid reason for punishing particularly serious proscribable expression probably is not a ruse for message suppression, even though the statute may have a greater (but not exclusive) impact on adherents of one ideology than on others.

My concern here, in any event, is not with the merit of a pragmatic doctrinal move. For whether or not the Court should conceive of exceptions to *R.A.V.*'s general rule in a more practical way, no content-based statute should survive even under a pragmatic recasting of *R.A.V.* without a high probability that no "official suppression of ideas is afoot." I believe the prima facie evidence provision stands in the way of any finding of such a high probability here.

As I see the likely significance of the evidence provision, its primary effect is to skew jury deliberations toward conviction in cases where the evidence of intent to intimidate is relatively weak and arguably consistent with a solely ideological reason for burning. What is significant is not that the provision permits a factfinder's conclusion that the defendant acted with proscribable and punishable intent without any further indication, because some such indication will almost always be presented. What is significant is that the provision will encourage a factfinder to err on the side of a finding of intent to intimidate when the evidence of circumstances fails to point with any clarity either to the criminal intent or to the permissible one. The effect of such a distortion is difficult to remedy, since any guilty verdict will survive sufficiency review unless the defendant can show that, "viewing the evidence in the light most favorable to the prosecution, [no] rational trier of fact could have found the essential elements of the crime beyond a reasonable doubt." The provision will thus tend to draw nonthreatening ideological expression within the ambit of the prohibition of intimidating expression, as JUSTICE O'CONNOR notes.

To the extent the prima facie evidence provision skews prosecutions, then, it skews the statute toward suppressing ideas. Thus, the appropriate way to consider the statute's prima facie evidence term, in my view, is not as if it were an overbroad statutory definition amenable to severance or a narrowing construction. The question here is not the permissible scope of an arguably overbroad statute, but the claim of a clearly content-based statute to an exception from the general prohibition of content-based proscriptions, an exception that is not warranted if the statute's terms show that suppression of ideas may be afoot.

It is difficult to conceive of an intimidation case that could be easier to prove than one with cross burning, assuming any circumstances suggesting intimidation are present. The provision, apparently so unnecessary to legitimate prosecution of intimidation, is therefore quite enough to raise the question whether Virginia's content-based statute seeks more than mere protection against a virulent form of intimidation. It consequently bars any conclusion that an exception to the general rule of *R.A.V.* is warranted on the ground "that there is no realistic [or little realistic] possibility that official suppression of ideas is afoot." Since no *R.A.V.* exception can save the statute as content based, it can only survive if narrowly tailored to serve a compelling state interest, a stringent test the statute cannot pass; a content-neutral statute banning intimidation would achieve the same object without singling out particular content.

I conclude that the statute under which all three of the respondents were prosecuted violates the First Amendment, since the statute's content-based distinction was invalid at the time of the charged activities, regardless of whether the prima facie evidence provision was given any effect in any respondent's individual case. In my view, severance of the prima facie evidence provision now could not eliminate the unconstitutionality of the whole statute at the time of the respondents' conduct. I would therefore affirm the judgment of the Supreme Court of Virginia vacating the respondents' convictions and dismissing the indictments. Accordingly, I concur in the Court's judgment as to respondent Black and dissent as to respondents Elliott and O'Mara.

JUSTICE THOMAS, dissenting.

Although I agree with the majority's conclusion that it is constitutionally permissible to "ban . . . cross burning carried out with intent to intimidate," I believe that the majority errs in imputing an expressive component to the activity in question. In my view, whatever expressive value cross burning has, the legislature simply wrote it out by banning only intimidating conduct undertaken by a particular means. A conclusion that the statute prohibiting cross burning with intent to intimidate sweeps beyond a prohibition on certain conduct into the zone of expression overlooks not only the words of the statute but also reality. To me, the majority's brief history of the Ku Klux Klan only reinforces this common understanding of the Klan as a terrorist organization, which, in its endeavor to intimidate, or even eliminate those its dislikes, uses the most brutal of methods. It strains credulity to suggest that a state legislature that adopted a litany of segregationist laws self-contradictorily intended to squelch the segregationist message. Even for segregationists, violent and terroristic conduct, the Siamese twin of cross burning, was intolerable. The ban on cross burning with intent to intimidate demonstrates that even segregationists understood the difference between intimidating and terroristic conduct and racist expression. It is simply beyond belief that, in passing the statute now under review, the Virginia legislature was concerned with anything but penalizing conduct it must have viewed as particularly vicious. Accordingly, this statute prohibits only conduct, not expression. And, just as one cannot burn down someone's house to make a political point and then seek refuge in the First Amendment, those who hate cannot terrorize and intimidate to make their point. In light of my conclusion that the statute here addresses only conduct, there is no need to analyze it under any of our First Amendment tests.

Even assuming that the statute implicates the First Amendment, in my view, the fact that the statute permits a jury to draw an inference of intent to intimidate from the cross burning itself presents no constitutional problems. Therein lies my primary disagreement with the plurality. "The threshold inquiry is ascertaining the constitutional analysis applicable to [a jury instruction involving a presumption] is to determine the nature of the presumption it describes." We have categorized the presumptions as either permissive inferences or mandatory presumptions. To the extent we do have a construction of this statute by the Virginia Supreme Court, we know that both the majority and the dissent agreed that the presumption was "a statutorily supplied *inference.*" The plurality, however, is troubled by the presumption because this is a First Amendment case. First, it is, at the very least, unclear that the inference comes into play during arrest and initiation of a prosecution, that is, prior to the instructions stage of an actual trial. Second, as I explained above, the inference is rebuttable and, as the jury instructions given in this case demonstrate, Virginia law still requires the jury to find the existence of each element, including intent to intimidate, beyond a reasonable doubt. Moreover, even in the First Amendment context, the Court has upheld such regulations where conduct that initially appears culpable, ultimately results in dismissed charges.

NOTES

1. *Applying R.A.V.* In *R.A.V.*, Justice White argued that the Court's opinion "necessarily signals that expressions of violence, such as the message of intimidation and racial hatred conveyed by burning a cross on someone's lawn, are of sufficient value to outweigh the social interest in order and morality that has traditionally placed such fighting words outside the First Amendment." The Virginia Supreme Court, in holding the cross burning cross law facially unconstitutional in *Black,* argued that the Virginia law "is analytically indistinguishable from the ordinance found unconstitutional in *R.A.V.*" How does the Court in *Black* reconcile its decision with *R.A.V.*? Does Justice Scalia's first exception in *R.A.V.* apply? Isn't there a danger of viewpoint discrimination in *Black*? Is cross burning always ideological, even when threatening, as Justice Souter, dissenting, suggests?

Consider the following: "If Virginia can permissibly regulate cross burning because Virginia is regulating 'a particularly virulent form of intimidation,' one could argue that St. Paul should have been able to single out fighting words uttered on the basis of race, gender, and religion because such fighting words are likely to cause anger and incite immediate violence. Notably, the Constitution is not neutral with respect to discrimination on the basis of racial, gender, and religious identity; it demonstrates a clear commitment to racial, gender and religious equity. If cross-burning itself is a particularly virulent type of intimidation, then burning a cross on the basis of the victim's race must certainly be an even more virulent type of intimidation. If one were to apply *Black's* reasoning to *R.A.V.*, not only should the Court have upheld St. Paul's ordinance, but the ordinance presented a more compelling case for affirmance than the statute in *Black*." Guy-Uriel E. Charles, *Colored Speech: Cross Burnings, Epistemics, and the Triumph of the Crits?*, 93 Geo. L.J. 575, 604–05 (2005).

2. *Identifying true threats.* In defining intimidation as a true threat, the Court includes any threat to a person or group of persons intended to place the victim in fear of bodily harm or death. Professor Gey contends that this broad and ambiguous definition threatens the speech-protective standard dictated in *Brandenburg v. Ohio* and potentially strips significant meaning from the First Amendment. "The only manifestation of fear that should be relevant to the application of 'true threats' analysis is the personalized and immediate fear of a person who is singled out and told in no uncertain terms that he or she is specifically targeted for attack. If a generalized, diffuse fear can be used as a justification for sanctioning speech, then all aggressively antagonistic dissent will be subject to suppression." Steven G. Gey, *A Few Questions About Cross Burning, Intimidation, and Free Speech,* 80 Notre Dame L. Rev. 1287, 1349 (2005). What is the relation of the true threat doctrine in *Black* to *Brandenburg* and to the fighting words doctrine of *Chaplinsky*?

3. *First Amendment intent.* The Court holds that the prima facie evidence clause of the Virginia law renders it facially unconstitutional because it permits a jury to convict in cross-burning cases even where the defendant does not have an intent to intimidate. Is Justice O'Connor using the overbreadth doctrine? Professor Schauer raises the question whether a potential defendant should be required to possess intent if the harm the legislature seeks to protect against is the fear resulting from such a threat, and not the threat itself. "[I]t may be right that the speaker can be prosecuted because he is as responsible for the ordinary meaning of his words as he is for the ordinary consequences of pulling the trigger on a gun ('I didn't know it was going to go off' is unlikely to be a good defense, even if guns sometimes misfire)." Frederick Schauer, *Intentions, Conventions, and the First Amendment: The Case of Cross-Brurning*, 2003 Sup. Ct. Rev. 197, 220 (2003). *See also* Jeannie Bell, *O Say,*

Can You See: Free Expression by the Light of Fiery Crosses, 39 Harv. C.R.-C.L. L. Rev. 335, 370 (2004) ("The legacy of cross-burning makes the impact of their behavior reasonably foreseeable. [S]imilar harm results from burning the cross regardless of whether they intend to intimidate."). Professor Bell endorses a victim-centered approach to dealing with cross-burnings which would allow for prosecution in all cases in which a defendant burned a cross with a directly targeted victim. *Id.* at 375. "Burned crosses are not intended as symbolic instruments of racists views, but rather as instruments designed to terrorize." *Id.* at 338. Does the First Amendment require a specific intent for crimes punishing speech?

[D] EXPRESSIVE CONDUCT

Conduct can be used as a means of communicating ideas — the medium can be the message. In *West Virginia State Board of Education v. Barnette,* 319 U.S. 624 (1943), Justice Jackson recognized for the Court that symbolic action could sometimes be the most effective form of expressing an idea: "There is no doubt that the [compulsory] flag salute is a form of utterance. Symbolism is a primitive but effective way of communicating ideas. The use of an emblem or flag to symbolize some system, idea, institution, or personality is a short cut from mind to mind." In *Stromberg v. California,* 283 U.S. 359 (1931), the Supreme Court struck down on First Amendment grounds a state statute that prohibited "the display of a red flag as a symbol of opposition by peaceful and legal means to organized government."

What standards should be applied to conduct that communicates? An anarchist who shoots the president to express opposition to government cannot, of course, claim First Amendment protection. Should "symbolic" speech be extended the same first amendment protection accorded "pure speech?" Can government proscribe the idea being communicated under the guise of a content-neutral regulation of conduct? Should the courts probe the purpose or motive underlying the control? Should we seek to determine if the speech or action element predominates and extend first amendment protection only to the former? The *O'Brien* case provided some judicial answers, however nebulous and debatable, to these questions.

UNITED STATES v. O'BRIEN

391 U.S. 367, 88 S. Ct. 1673, 20 L. Ed. 2d 672 (1968)

Chief Justice Warren delivered the opinion of the Court.

On the morning of March 31, 1966, David Paul O'Brien and three companions burned their Selective Service registration certificates on the steps of the South Boston Courthouse. A sizeable crowd, including several agents of the Federal Bureau of Investigation, witnessed the event. Immediately after the burning, members of the crowd began attacking O'Brien and his companions. An FBI agent ushered O'Brien to safety inside the courthouse. After he was advised of his right to counsel and to silence, O'Brien stated to FBI agents that he had burned his registration certificate because of his beliefs, knowing that he was violating federal law. He produced the charred remains of the certificate, which, with his consent, were photographed.

For this act, O'Brien was indicted, tried, convicted, and sentenced in the United States District Court for the District of Massachusetts. He did not contest the fact that he had burned the certificate. He stated in argument to the jury that he burned the certificate publicly to influence others to adopt his antiwar beliefs, as he put it, "so that other people would reevaluate their positions with Selective Service, with the armed forces, and reevaluate their place in the culture of today, to hopefully consider my position."

By [a] 1965 Amendment, Congress added to § 12(b)(3) of the 1948 [Universal Military Training and Service] Act the provision here at issue, subjecting to criminal liability not only one who "forges, alters, or in any manner changes" but also one who "knowingly destroys, [or] knowingly mutilates" a certificate. We note at the outset that the 1965 Amendment plainly does not abridge free speech on its face, and we do not understand O'Brien to argue otherwise. Amended § 12(b)(3) on its face deals with conduct having no connection with speech. It prohibits the knowing destruction of certificates issued by the Selective Service System, and there is nothing necessarily expressive about such conduct. The Amendment does not distinguish between public and private destruction, and it does not punish only destruction engaged in for the purpose of expressing views.

O'Brien nonetheless argues that the 1965 Amendment is unconstitutional in its application to him, and is unconstitutional as enacted because what he calls the "purpose" of Congress was "to suppress freedom of speech." We consider these arguments separately.

O'Brien first argues that the 1965 Amendment is unconstitutional as applied to him because his act of burning his registration certificate was protected "symbolic speech" within the First Amendment. His argument is that the freedom of expression which the First Amendment guarantees includes all modes of "communication of ideas by conduct," and that his conduct is within this definition because he did it [as a] "demonstration against the war and against the draft."

We cannot accept the view that an apparently limitless variety of conduct can be labelled "speech" whenever the person engaging in the conduct intends thereby to express an idea. However, even on the assumption that the alleged communicative element in O'Brien's conduct is sufficient to bring into play the First Amendment, it does not necessarily follow that the destruction of a registration certificate is constitutionally protected activity. This Court has held that when "speech" and "nonspeech" elements are combined in the same course of conduct, a sufficiently important governmental interest in regulating the nonspeech element can justify incidental limitations on First Amendment freedoms. To characterize the quality of the governmental interest which must appear, the Court has employed a variety of descriptive terms: compelling; substantial; subordinating; paramount; cogent; strong. Whatever imprecision inheres in these terms, we think it clear that a governmental regulation is sufficiently justified if it is within the constitutional power of the government; if it furthers an important or substantial governmental interest; if the governmental interest is unrelated to the suppression of free expression; and if the incidental restriction on alleged First Amendment freedom is no greater than is essential to the furtherance of that interest. We find that the 1965

Amendment to § 462(b)(3) of the Universal Military Training and Service Act meets all of these requirements, and consequently that O'Brien can be constitutionally convicted for violating it.

1. The registration certificate serves as proof that the individual described thereon has registered for the draft. The classification certificate shows the eligibility classification of a named but undescribed individual.

2. The information supplied on the certificates facilitates communication between registrants and local boards, simplifying the system and benefiting all concerned.

3. The smooth functioning of the system requires that local boards be continually aware of the status and whereabouts of registrants, and the destruction of certificates deprives the system of a potentially useful notice device.

4. The regulatory scheme involving Selective Service certificates includes clearly valid prohibitions against the alteration, forgery or similar deceptive misuse of certificates.

The many functions performed by Selective Service certificates establish beyond doubt that Congress has a legitimate and substantial interest in preventing their wanton and unrestrained destruction and assuring their continuing availability by punishing people who knowingly and wilfully destroy or mutilate them.

We think it apparent that the continuing availability to each registrant of his Selective Service certificates substantially furthers the smooth and proper functioning of the system that Congress has established to raise armies. We think it also apparent that the Nation has a vital interest in having a system for raising armies that functions with maximum efficiency and is capable of easily and quickly responding to continually changing circumstances. For these reasons, the Government has a substantial interest in assuring the continuing availability of issued Selective Service certificates.

It is equally clear that the 1965 Amendment specifically protects this substantial governmental interest. We perceive no alternative means that would more precisely and narrowly assure the continuing availability of issued Selective Service certificates than a law which prohibits their wilful mutilation or destruction. The 1965 Amendment prohibits such conduct and does nothing more. In other words, both the governmental interest and the operation of the 1965 Amendment are limited to the non-communicative aspect of O'Brien's conduct. The governmental interest and the scope of the 1965 Amendment are limited to preventing a harm to the smooth and efficient functioning of the Selective Service System. When O'Brien deliberately rendered unavailable his registration certificate, he wilfully frustrated this governmental interest. For this noncommunicative impact of his conduct, and for nothing else, he was convicted.

The case at bar is therefore unlike one where the alleged governmental interest in regulating conduct arises in some measure because the communication allegedly integral to the conduct is itself thought to be harmful.

In conclusion, we find that because of the Government's substantial interest in assuring the continuing availability of issued Selective Service certificates, because amended § 462(b) is an appropriately narrow means of protecting this interest and condemns only the independent noncommunicative impact of conduct within its reach, and because the noncommunicative impact of O'Brien's act of burning his registration certificate frustrated the Government's interest, a sufficient governmental interest has been shown to justify O'Brien's conviction.

O'Brien finally argues that the 1965 Amendment is unconstitutional as enacted because what he calls the "purpose" of Congress was "to suppress freedom of speech." We reject this argument because under settled principles the purpose of Congress, as O'Brien uses that term, is not a basis for declaring this legislation unconstitutional.

It is a familiar principle of constitutional law that this Court will not strike down an otherwise constitutional statute on the basis of an alleged illicit legislative motive. Inquiries into congressional motives or purposes are a hazardous matter. When the issue is simply the interpretation of legislation, the Court will look to statements by legislators for guidance as to the purpose of the legislature, because the benefit to sound decision-making in this circumstance is thought sufficient to risk the possibility of misreading Congress' purpose. It is entirely a different matter when we are asked to void a statute that is, under well-settled criteria, constitutional on its face, on the basis of what fewer than a handful of Congressmen said about it. What motivates one legislator to make a speech about a statute is not necessarily what motivates scores of others to enact it, and the stakes are sufficiently high for us to eschew guesswork. We decline to void essentially on the ground that it is unwise legislation which Congress had the undoubted power to enact and which could be reenacted in its exact form if the same or another legislator make a "wiser" speech about it.

JUSTICE HARLAN, concurring.

I wish to make explicit my understanding that [the majority opinion] does not foreclose consideration of First Amendment claims in those rare instances when an "incidental" restriction upon expression, imposed by a regulation which furthers an "important or substantial" governmental interest and satisfies the Court's other criteria, in practice has the effect of entirely preventing a "speaker" from reaching a significant audience with whom he could not otherwise lawfully communicate. This is not such a case, since O'Brien manifestly could have conveyed his message in many ways other than by burning his draft card.

JUSTICE MARSHALL took no part in the consideration or decision of these cases.

[JUSTICE DOUGLAS dissented on the ground that the basic but undecided constitutional issue in the case was whether conscription was unconstitutional in the absence of a declaration of war.]

NOTES

1. *Speech or conduct?* O'Brien's lawyers attempted to attack the application of the law to their client by arguing that his action was symbolic speech protected under the First Amendment. In responding to this argument, the *O'Brien* Court began from the premise that it would be unacceptable to label an "apparently limitless variety of conduct" as speech merely because "the person engaging in the conduct intends thereby to express an idea."

THOMAS EMERSON, THE SYSTEM OF FREEDOM OF EXPRESSION (1970), had earlier suggested approaching symbolic speech cases by determining whether the speech or conduct element "is predominant in the conduct under consideration." This approach would be based on "a commonsense reaction, made in light of the functions and operations of a system of freedom of expression." In Emerson's view, *O'Brien* was wrongly decided because the action was speech rather than conduct, and thus entitled to full First Amendment protection. On the other hand, if the protester had subsequently been punished for nonpossession of a draft card, Emerson reasoned, that punishment would be based on conduct, not speech, and hence would not be judged by First Amendment standards.

Justice Douglas made much the same speech-action distinction in *Brandenburg* when he said that speech "brigaded" with conduct should not be protected under the First Amendment, and Justice Black regularly applied this speech-action dichotomy. Does the test provide a viable way of disposing of symbolic speech cases?

Compare *O'Brien* to *Tinker v. Des Moines School District,* 393 U.S. 503 (1969). There the Court invalidated a school's ban on students' wearing armbands as a protest against the Vietnam War. The Court noted that the regulated activity "involves direct, primary First Amendment rights akin to 'pure speech.'" Is *Tinker* distinguishable from *O'Brien*?

Commenting on the speech-action dichotomy, Professor Ely argued that "burning a draft card to express opposition to the draft is an undifferentiated whole, 100% action and 100% expression. It involves no conduct that is not at the same time communication, and no communication that does not result from conduct. Attempts to determine which element 'predominates' will therefore inevitably degenerate into question-begging judgments about whether the activity should be protected." John Ely, *Flag Desecration: A Case Study in the Roles of Categorization and Balancing in First Amendment Anaylsis*, 88 HARV. L. REV. 1482, 1495 (1975). Similarly Professor Henkin argued that a "constitutional distinction between speech and conduct is specious. Speech is conduct, and actions speak." Louis Henkin, *On Drawing Lines*, 82 HARV. L. REV. 63, 79 (1968). Professor Henkin suggested that "the meaningful constitutional distinction is not between speech and conduct but between conduct that speaks, communicates, and other kinds of conduct." For Professor Emerson's response to critics of the speech-action approach, see Thomas Emerson, *First Amendment Doctrine and the Burger Court*, 68 CAL. L. REV. 422, 477–81 (1980).

Note also Professor Volokh's argument that while speech and conduct should be distinguished, typical "it's not speech, it's conduct" doctrines would force courts to focus on the wrong questions and reach the wrong results. Professor Volokh states that courts should instead focus on a distinction more like that of *O'Brien*: "Expression can generally be regulated to prevent harms that flow from its noncommunicative (elements noise, traffic obstruction, and the like), but not harms that flow from what the expression expresses. Neither generally applicable laws nor specially targeted laws should be allowed to restrict speech because of what the speech says, unless the speech falls within one of the exceptions to protection (e.g., threats or false statements of fact) or unless the restriction passes strict scrutiny." Eugene Volokh, *Speech as Conduct: Generally Applicable Laws, Illegal Course of Conduct, "Situation-Altering Utterances," and the Uncharted Zones*, 90 CORNELL L. REV. 1277, 1284 (2005).

2. *Content-Neutrality.* Suppose the 1965 Amendment had made criminal the destruction or mutilation of a draft card as a means of "expressing opposition to the Vietnam War." Same analysis and result? Notice that O'Brien's lawyers tried to attack the 1965 Amendment itself as invalid by showing that the congressional motivation was to suppress communication. Why wasn't the legislative intent behind the 1965 Amendment more seriously considered by the Court? In spite of its protestations, the Court in *O'Brien* did consider the legislative history and indicated that O'Brien had not proved bad congressional motive. Note that the Court in equal protection — suspect classification cases requires that discriminatory purpose be established.

Professor Tribe argues that a law is content-based "if on its face [it] is targeted at ideas or information that government seeks to suppress, or if a governmental action neutral on its face was motivated by (*i.e.*, would not have occurred but for) an intent to single out constitutionally protected speech for control or penalty." LAURENCE TRIBE, AMERICAN CONSTITUTIONAL LAW 794 (2d ed. 1988). Professor Ely suggests that the determination of whether a law is content control turns on "whether the harm that the state is seeking to avert is one that grows out of the fact that the defendant is communicating, and more particularly out of the way people can be expected to react to his message, or rather would arise even if the defendant's conduct had no communicative significance whatever." Ely, 88 HARV. L. REV. at 1497.

3. *O'Brien's balancing test.* If the speech-action dichotomy is not accepted, it becomes necessary to determine whether the burden on freedom of expression values produced by applying the 1965 Amendment to O'Brien's conduct is constitutionally excessive. Assuming that the amendment is content-neutral and that government has the power to act, *O'Brien* asks whether the law "furthers an important or substantial governmental interest" and whether "the incidental restriction on alleged First Amendment freedoms is no greater than is essential to the furtherance of that interest." Is this just another balancing test? Is it appropriate for all freedom of expression cases — a speech test for all seasons? "[F]or most expressive conduct, the purpose of expression is protected but the method of expression is regulable." *Note, Making Sense of Hybrid Speech: A New Model for Commercial Speech and Expressive Conduct*, 118 HARV. L. REV. 2836, 2840 (2005). Intermediate scrutiny is said to be the resulting compromise, "allowing government to retain significant power to regulate in these areas but acknowledging that the First Amendment still provides some protection." *Id.* at 2841.

Apart from the value of the *O'Brien* test as stated, what do you think of the Court's application of the test to the facts? Consider Professor Ely's assessment that the Court, in fact, attached "trivial functional significance" to the "critical word 'substantial.'" Ely, 88 HARV. L. REV. at 1483–86. It has been claimed that "[a]lthough the *O'Brien* test remains good law, the Court has never used it to invalidate laws that incidentally burden expressive conduct. In fact, the Court has created a waivable presumption that such laws do not violate the First Amendment." 118 HARV. L. REV. at 2852. Is the problem that many laws have an incidental effect on the First Amendment? Consider the critique by Michael C. Dorf, *Incidental Burdens and Fundamental Rights*, 109 HARV. L. REV. 1175, 1204 (1996): "In some sense, the *O'Brien* test is the worst of all possible worlds. A large category of content-neutral laws is susceptible to an *O'Brien* challenge. Litigation over regulations in this category imposes substantial costs on society but yields few tangible benefits. Because most of the challenged laws will survive, most of the cases actually litigated will not benefit free speech. Nor does the prospect of *O'Brien* scrutiny deter potentially speech-chilling laws, because legislators enacting content-neutral laws will not ordinarily contemplate free speech issues: by definition, such laws are aimed at problems that do not arise from the communicative impact of speech. Thus, if *O'Brien* scrutiny is to remain toothless, it hardly seems worth retaining as a discrete First Amendment test."

TEXAS v. JOHNSON

491 U.S. 397, 109 S. Ct. 2533, 105 L. Ed. 2d 342 (1989)

JUSTICE BRENNAN delivered the opinion of the Court.

After publicly burning an American flag as a means of political protest, Gregory Lee Johnson was convicted of desecrating a flag in violation of Texas law. This case presents the question whether his conviction is consistent with the First Amendment. We hold that it is not.

While the Republican National Convention was taking place in Dallas in 1984, respondent Johnson participated in a political demonstration dubbed the "Republican War Chest Tour." [T]he purpose of this event was to protest the policies of the Reagan administration and of certain Dallas-based corporations. The demonstrators marched through the Dallas streets, chanting political slogans and stopping at several corporate locations to stage "die-ins" intended to dramatize the consequences of nuclear war. He did, however, accept an American flag handed to him by a fellow protestor who had taken it from a flag pole outside one of the targeted buildings. The demonstration ended in front of Dallas City Hall, where Johnson unfurled the American flag, doused it with kerosene, and set it on fire. While the flag burned, the protestors chanted, "America, the red, white, and blue, we spit on you." After the demonstrators dispersed, a witness to the flag-burning collected the flag's remains and buried them in his backyard.

Of the approximately 100 demonstrators, Johnson alone was charged with a crime. The only criminal offense with which he was charged was the desecration of a venerated object in violation of Tex. Penal Code Ann. § 42.09 (a)(3) (1989).[1] After a trial, he was convicted, sentenced to one year in prison,

[1] Tex. Penal Code Ann. Section 42.09 (1989) [provided]: "Section 42.09. Desecration of Venerated Object. (a) A person commits an offense if he intentionally or knowingly desecrates: (1) a public monument; (2) a place of worship or burial; or (3) a state or national flag. (b) For purposes of this section 'desecrate' means deface, damage, or otherwise physically mistreat in a way that the actor knows will seriously offend one or more persons likely to observe or discover his action."

and fined $2,000. The Court of Appeals for the Fifth District of Texas at Dallas affirmed Johnson's conviction but the Texas Court of Criminal Appeals reversed, holding that the State could not, consistent with the First Amendment, punish Johnson for burning the flag in these circumstances.

We granted certiorari, and now affirm.

Johnson was convicted of flag desecration for burning the flag rather than for uttering insulting words. This fact somewhat complicates our consideration of his conviction under the First Amendment. We must first determine whether Johnson's burning of the flag constituted expressive conduct, permitting him to invoke the First Amendment in challenging his conviction. *See, e.g., Spence v. Washington*. If his conduct was expressive, we next decide whether the State's regulation is related to the suppression of free expression. *See, e.g., United States v. O'Brien*; *Spence*. If the State's regulation is not related to expression, then the less stringent standard we announced in *United States v. O'Brien* for regulations of noncommunicative conduct controls. If it is, then we are outside of *O'Brien's* test, and we must ask whether this interest justifies Johnson's conviction under a more demanding standard. A third possibility is that the State's asserted interest is simply not implicated on these facts, and in that event the interest drops out of the picture.

In deciding whether particular conduct possess sufficient communicative elements to bring the First Amendment into play, we have asked whether "[a]n intent to convey a particularized message was present, and [whether] the likelihood was great that the message would be understood by those who viewed it." [In] *Spence v. Washington,* 418 U.S. 405 (1974), for example, we emphasized that Spence's taping of a piece sign to his flag was "roughly simultaneous with and concededly triggered by the Cambodian incursion and the Kent State tragedy." The State of Washington had conceded, in fact, that Spence's conduct was a form of communication, and we stated that "the State's concession is inevitable on this record." Texas conceded that Johnson's conduct was expressive conduct. Johnson burned an American flag as part — indeed, as the culmination — of a political demonstration that coincided with the convening of the Republican Party and its renomination of Ronald Reagan for President. The expressive, overtly political nature of this conduct was both intentional and overwhelmingly apparent.

The Government generally has a freer hand in restricting expressive conduct than it has in restricting the written or spoken word. It may not, however, proscribe particular conduct because it has expressive elements. It is, in short, not simply the verbal or nonverbal nature of the expression, but the governmental interest at stake, that helps to determine whether a restriction on that expression is valid.

[W]e have limited the applicability of *O'Brien*'s relatively lenient standard to those cases in which "the governmental interest is unrelated to the suppression of free expression." In stating, moreover, that *O'Brien's* test "in the last analysis is little, if any, different from the standard applied to time, place, or manner restrictions," we have highlighted the requirement that the governmental interest in question be unconnected to expression in order to come under *O'Brien's* less demanding rule.

In order to decide whether *O'Brien's* test applies here, therefore, we must decide whether Texas has asserted an interest in support of Johnson's conviction that is unrelated to the suppression of expression. If we find that an interest asserted by the State is simply not implicated on the facts before us, we need not ask whether *O'Brien's* test applies. The State offers two separate interests to justify this conviction: preventing breaches of the peace, and preserving the flag as a symbol of nationhood and national unity. We hold that the first interest is not implicated on this record and that the second is related to the suppression of expression.

Texas claims that its interest in preventing breaches of the peace justifies Johnson's conviction for flag desecration. However, no disturbance of the peace actually occurred or threatened to occur because of Johnson's burning of the flag. The State's position, therefore, amounts to a claim that an audience that takes serious offense at particular expression is necessarily likely to disturb the peace and that the expression may be prohibited on this basis. Our precedents do not countenance such a presumption. On the contrary, they recognize that a principal "function of free speech under our system of government is to invite dispute." Thus, we have not permitted the Government to assume that every expression of a provocative idea will incite a riot. To accept Texas' arguments that it need only demonstrate "the potential for a breach of the peace," and that every flag-burning necessarily possesses that potential, would be to eviscerate our holding in *Brandenburg*. This we decline to do.

Nor does Johnson's expressive conduct fall within that small class of "fighting words" that are "likely to provoke the average person to retaliation, and thereby cause a breach of the peace." *Chaplinsky v. New Hampshire*. No reasonable onlooker would have regarded Johnson's generalized expression of dissatisfaction with the policies of the Federal Government as a direct personal insult or an invitation to exchange fisticuffs.

We thus conclude that the State's interest in maintaining order is not implicated on these facts. The State need not worry that our holding will disable it from preserving the peace. We do not suggest that the First Amendment forbids a State to prevent "imminent lawless action."

The State also asserts an interest in preserving the flag as a symbol of nationhood and national unity. These concerns blossom only when a person's treatment of the flag communicates some message, and thus are related "to the suppression of free expression" within the meaning of *O'Brien*. We are thus outside of *O'Brien's* test altogether.

It remains to consider whether the State's interest in preserving the flag as a symbol of nationhood and national unity justifies Johnson's conviction. Johnson was not, prosecuted for the expression of just any idea; he was prosecuted for his expression of dissatisfaction with the policies of this country, expression situated at the core of our First Amendment values. Johnson was prosecuted because he knew that his politically charged expression would cause "serious offense." If he had burned the flag as a means of disposing of it because it was dirty or torn, he would not have been convicted of flag desecration under this Texas law: federal law designates burning as the preferred means of disposing of a flag "when it is in such condition that it is no longer a fitting emblem for display," and Texas has no quarrel with this means of disposal. The Texas law is thus not aimed at protecting the physical integrity of the flag in all circumstances, but is designed instead to protect it only against impairments that would cause serious offense to others.

Whether Johnson's treatment of the flag violated Texas law thus depended on the likely communicative impact of his expressive conduct. Our decision in *Boos v. Barry* tells us that this restriction on Johnson's expression is content-based. According to the principles announced in *Boos*, Johnson's political expression was restricted because of the content of the message he conveyed. We must therefore subject the State's asserted interest in preserving the special symbolic character of the flag to "the most exacting scrutiny."

Texas argues that its interest in preserving the flag as a symbol of nationhood and national unity survives this close analysis. According to Texas, if one physically treats the flag in a way that would tend to cast doubt on either the idea that nationhood and national unity are the flag's referents or that national unity actually exists, the message conveyed thereby is a harmful one and therefore may be prohibited.

If there is a bedrock principle underlying the First Amendment, it is that the Government may not prohibit the expression of an idea simply because society finds the idea itself offensive or disagreeable. We have not recognized an exception to this principle even where our flag has been involved. In *Street v. New York,* 394 U.S. 576 (1969), we held that a State may not criminally punish a person for uttering words critical of the flag. Nor may the Government, we have held, compel conduct that would evince respect for the flag.

In short, nothing in our precedents suggests that a State may foster its own view of the flag by prohibiting expressive conduct relating to it. To bring its argument outside our precedents, Texas attempts to convince us that even if its interest in preserving the flag's symbolic role does not allow it to prohibit words or some expressive conduct critical of the flag, it does permit it to forbid the outright destruction of the flag. The State's argument cannot depend here on the distinction between written or spoken words and nonverbal conduct. That distinction, we have shown, is of no moment where the nonverbal conduct is expressive, as it is here, and where the regulation of that conduct is related to expression, as it is here.

Texas' focus on the precise nature of Johnson's expression, moreover, misses the point of our prior decisions: their enduring lesson, that the Government may not prohibit expression simply because it disagrees with its message, is not dependent on the particular mode in which one chooses to express an idea. If we were to hold that a State may forbid flag-burning wherever it is likely to endanger the flag's symbolic role, but allow it wherever burning a flag promotes that role — as where, for example, a person ceremoniously burns a dirty flag — we would be saying that when it comes to impairing the flag's physical integrity, the flag itself may be used as a symbol — as a substitute for the written or spoken word or a "short cut from mind to mind" — only in one direction. We would be permitting a State to "prescribe what shall be orthodox" by saying that one may burn the flag to convey one's attitude toward it and its referents only if one does not endanger the flag's representation of nationhood and national unity.

To conclude that the Government may permit designated symbols to be used to communicate only a limited set of messages would be to enter territory having no discernible or defensible boundaries. Could the Government, on this theory, prohibit the burning of state flags? Of copies of the Presidential seal? Of the Constitution? In evaluating these choices under the First Amendment, how would we decide which symbols were sufficiently special to warrant this unique status? To do so, we would be forced to consult our own political preferences, and impose them on the citizenry, in the very way that the First Amendment forbids us to do. There is, moreover, no indication — either in the text of the Constitution or in our cases interpreting it — that a separate juridical category exists for the American flag alone. It is not the State's ends, but its means, to which we object. It cannot be gainsaid that there is a special place reserved for the flag in this Nation. To say that the Government has an interest in encouraging proper treatment of the flag, however, is not to say that it may criminally punish a person for burning a flag as a means of political protest.

We are fortified in today's conclusion by our conviction that forbidding criminal punishment for conduct such as Johnson's will not endanger the special role played by our flag or the feelings it inspires. We are tempted to say, in fact, that the flag's deservedly cherished place in our community will be strengthened, not weakened, by our holding today. Our decision is a reaffirmation of the principles of freedom and inclusiveness that the flag best reflects, and of the conviction that our toleration of criticism such as Johnson's is a sign and source of our strength. It is the Nation's resilience, not its rigidity, that Texas sees reflected in the flag — and it is that resilience that we reassert today.

The way to preserve the flag's special role is not to punish those who feel differently about these matters. It is to persuade them that they are wrong. And, precisely because it is our flag that is involved, one's response to the flag-burner may exploit the uniquely persuasive power of the flag itself. We can imagine no more appropriate response to burning a flag than waving one's own, no better way to counter a flag-burner's message than by saluting the flag that burns, no surer means of preserving the dignity even of the flag that burned than by — as one witness here did — according its remains a respectful burial. We do not consecrate the flag by punishing its desecration, for in doing so we dilute the freedom that this cherished emblem represents.

Johnson was convicted for engaging in expressive conduct. The State's interest in preventing breaches of the peace does not support his conviction because Johnson's conduct did not threaten to disturb the peace. Nor does the State's interest in preserving the flag as a symbol of nationhood and national unity justify his criminal conviction for engaging in political expression. The judgment of the Texas Court of Criminal Appeals is therefore affirmed.

JUSTICE KENNEDY, concurring.

It is poignant but fundamental that the flag protects those who hold it in contempt. For all the record shows, this respondent was not a philosopher and perhaps did not even possess the ability to comprehend how repellant his statements must be to the Republic itself. But whether or not he could appreciate the enormity of the offense he gave, the fact remains that his acts were speech, in both the technical and the fundamental meaning of the Constitution. So I agree with the Court that he must go free.

CHIEF JUSTICE REHNQUIST, with whom JUSTICE WHITE and JUSTICE O'CONNOR join, dissenting.

The American flag, throughout more than 200 years of our history, has come to be the visible symbol embodying our Nation. It does not represent the views of any particular political party, and it does not represent any particular political philosophy. The flag is not simply another "idea" or "point of view" competing for recognition in the marketplace of ideas. Millions and millions of Americans regard it with an almost mystical reverence regardless of what sort of social, political, or philosophical beliefs they may have. I cannot agree that the First Amendment invalidates the Act of Congress, and the laws of 48 of the 50 States, which make criminal the public burning of the flag.

Here it may equally well be said that the public burning of the American flag by Johnson was no essential part of any exposition of ideas, and at the same time it had a tendency to incite a breach of the peace. Johnson was free to make any verbal denunciation of the flag that he wished; indeed, he was free to burn the flag in private. But his act, like Chaplinsky's provocative words, conveyed nothing that could not have been conveyed and was not conveyed just as forcefully in a dozen different ways. As with "fighting words," so with flag burning, for purposes of the First Amendment: It is "no essential part of any exposition of ideas, and [is] of such slight social value as a step to truth that any benefit that may be derived from [it] is clearly outweighed" by the public interest in avoiding a probable breach of the peace.

The result of the Texas statute is obviously to deny one in Johnson's frame of mind one of many means of "symbolic speech." Far from being a case of "one picture being worth a thousand words," flag burning is the equivalent of an inarticulate grunt or roar that, it seems fair to say, is most likely to be indulged in not to express any particular idea, but to antagonize others. Surely one of the high purposes of a democratic society is to legislate against conduct that is regarded as evil and profoundly offensive to the majority of people — whether it be murder, embezzlement, pollution, or flag burning.

The Court decides that the American flag is just another symbol, about which not only must opinions pro and con be tolerated, but for which the most minimal public respect may not be enjoined. The government may conscript men into the Armed Forces where they must fight and perhaps die for the flag, but the government may not prohibit the public burning of the banner under which they fight. I would uphold the Texas statute as applied in this case.

JUSTICE STEVENS, dissenting.

Even if flag burning could be considered just another species of symbolic speech under the logical application of the rules that the Court has developed in its interpretation of the First Amendment in other contexts, this case has an intangible dimension that makes those rules inapplicable. The value of the flag as a symbol cannot be measured. Even so, I have no doubt that the interest in preserving that value for the future is both significant and legitimate.

The content of respondent's message has no relevance whatsoever to the case. The case has nothing to do with "disagreeable ideas." It involves disagreeable conduct that, in my opinion, diminishes the value of an important national asset. The Court is therefore quite wrong in blandly asserting that respondent "was prosecuted for his expression of dissatisfaction with the policies of this country, expression situated at the core of our First Amendment values." Respondent was prosecuted because of the method he chose to express his dissatisfaction with those policies.

The ideas of liberty and equality have been an irresistible force. If those ideas are worth fighting for — and our history demonstrates that they are — it cannot be true that the flag that uniquely symbolizes their power is not itself worthy of protection from unnecessary desecration.

NOTES

1. *United States v. Eichman*, 496 U.S. 310 (1990). The Flag Protection Act of 1989, 18 U.S.C. § 700, enacted by Congress after the decision in *Johnson*, provided that "[w]hoever knowingly mutilates, defaces, physically defiles, burns, maintains on the floor or ground, or tramples upon any flag of the United States" is subject to criminal penalties. Justice Brennan, speaking for the Court, held the Act unconstitutional.

> The Government contends that the Flag Protection Act is constitutional because, unlike the statute addressed in *Johnson*, the Act does not target expressive conduct on the basis of the content of its message. The Government asserts an interest in "protect[ing] the physical integrity of the flag under all circumstances" in order to safeguard the flag's identity "as the unique and unalloyed symbol of the Nation." The Act proscribes conduct that damages or mistreats a flag, without regard to the actor's motive, his intended message, or the likely effects of his conduct on onlookers. By contrast, the Texas statute expressly prohibited only those acts of physical flag desecration "that the actor knows will seriously offend" onlookers, and the former federal statute prohibited only those acts of desecration that "cas[t] contempt upon" the flag.

Despite these suggested distinctions, Justice Brennan concluded that

> the Government's asserted interest is "related to the suppression of free expression," and concerned with the content of such expression. The Government's interest in protecting the "physical integrity" of a privately owned flag rests upon a perceived need to preserve the flag's status as a symbol of our Nation and certain national ideals. . . . Although Congress cast the Flag Protection Act in somewhat broader terms than the Texas statute at issue in *Johnson*, the Act still suffers from the same fundamental flaw: it suppresses expression out of concern for its likely communicative impact.

The Court "decline[d] the Government's invitation to reassess [the] conclusion [in *Johnson*] in light of Congress' recent recognition of a purported 'national consensus' favoring a prohibition on flag-burning." Justice Stevens, joined by Justices White, O'Connor, and Chief Justice Rehnquist, dissented.

2. *Street v. New York,* 394 U.S. 576 (1969). The Court earlier had invalidated a conviction for flag desecration because the defendant had been charged with both burning a flag and verbally casting contempt upon it. In his dissent in *Street*, Justice Fortas argued:

> If a state statute provided that it is a misdemeanor to burn one's shirt or trousers or shoes on the public thoroughfare, it could hardly be asserted that the citizen's constitutional right is violated. If the arsonist asserted that he was burning his shirt or trousers or shoes as a protest against the Government's fiscal policies, for example, it is hardly possible that his claim to First Amendment shelter would prevail against the State's claim of a right to avert danger to the public and to avoid obstruction of traffic as a result of the fire.

How persuasive is this argument as a rationale for flag desecration regulation, in light of the fact that flag desecration ordinances do not prohibit the burning of any flag, only the American flag?

3. *The Spence test.* *Texas v. Johnson* cites the *Spence* test which is often used to determine if conduct implicates the First Amendment. Robert Post, *Recuperating First Amendment Doctrine*, 47 Stan L. Rev. 1249, 1252 (1995), argues that "any action can at any time be communicative in a manner that satisfies the *Spence* test." He offers the example of a racist who commits a violent crime to communicate a message of racial prejudice and hate. All of the elements of *Spence*, he says, are satisfied but "[i]n such a case we do not say that the state's interest in prohibiting violence outweighs the defendant's interest in communication as such, but rather that the First Amendment does not come into the case at all." Professor Post argues: "First Amendment analysis is relevant only when the values served by the First Amendment are implicated. These values do not attach to abstract acts of communication as such but rather to the social contexts that envelop and give constitutional significance to acts of communication . . .The *Spence* test fails because it ignores social context; it does not state a significant condition for bringing the First Amendment into play because social contexts can sometimes render individual act of communication into events without First Amendment value." *Id.* at 1255. Post goes on to argue that *Spence* also fails to consider "why the state seeks to impose regulations." *Id.* Is this where the *O'Brien* inquiry — whether "the governmental interest is unrelated to the suppression of free expression" — comes into play?

4. *The values involved.* Professor Ely has argued that "the state may assert an interest — which justifies control over even privately burned flags — similar to that asserted in the case of the interrupting audience. The state's interest in both of these cases might be characterized as an interest in preventing the jamming of signals, an interest not in preventing the defendant from expressing himself but rather in keeping him from interfering with the expression of others." John Ely, *Flag Desecration: A Case Study in the Roles of Categorization and Balancing in First Amendment Analysis*, 88 Harv. L. Rev. 1482, 1504 (1975).

Could one refuse to protect public sensibilities through flag desecration laws, yet nevertheless uphold regulation of hate speech to protect the sensibilities of the targeted groups? *See* Frank Michelman, *Saving Old Glory: On Constitutional Iconography*, 42 STAN. L. REV. 1337, 1362 (1990), arguing that although "some speech acts are so antithetical to any serious profession of aspiration toward American political community, and so destructive of movement toward it, that a Constitution depicting that aspiration cannot shelter such acts against the community's prohibition, and at the same time retain the force of apparent moral seriousness." But, he concludes that "flag burning is a poor candidate for typifying speech acts of that kind." This is because "flag burning is not a repudiation of the nation's ideals or of aspiration towards political community. Rather, the flag burner charges the nation with betraying the ideals as the flag burner understands them." He argues that regulation of hate speech, on the other hand, "is calculated to aid and reinforce denial of basic human respect, and hence full citizenship."

This distinction is criticized in Martin Redish & Gary Lippman, *Freedom of Expression and the Civic Republican Revival in Constitutional Theory: The Ominous Implications*, 79 CAL. L. REV. 267, 311 (1991): "When the dust settles, all Professor Michelman has done is solipsistically transform the unprotected category of speech from what the *majority* finds offensive or undermining of community to include solely what *he* finds meets these criteria."

Nude Dancing

***Barnes v. Glen Theatre, Inc.*, 501 U.S. 560 (1991).** Two places of adult live entertainment, Kitty Kat Lounge and Glen Theatre, and individual go-go dancers, wishing to provide totally nude dancing, brought suit to enjoin enforcement of the Indiana public indecency statute. The indecency law, which made it a misdemeanor to appear "in a state of nudity," had been interpreted to apply to establishments serving liquor and presenting go-go dancing and to require use of G-strings and pasties. A fragmented Supreme Court 5-4 rejected the First Amendment challenge.

Chief Justice Rehnquist, joined by Justices O'Connor and Kennedy, began by acknowledging that there was support for the lower court's conclusion "that nude dancing of the kind to be performed here is expressive conduct within the outer perimeters of the First Amendment, though we view it as only marginally so." He then turned to the proper level of protection to be afforded the expressive conduct. "Applying the four-part *O'Brien*, we find that Indiana's public indecency statute is justified despite its incidental limitations on some expressive activity. [T]he public indecency statute is clearly within the constitutional power of the State and furthers substantial governmental interests. [T]he statute's purpose of protecting societal order and morality is clear from its text and history. Public indecency statutes of this sort are of ancient origin, and presently exist in at least 47 States. Public indecency, including nudity, was a criminal offense at common law. Public indecency statutes such as the one before us reflect moral disapproval of people appearing in the nude among strangers in public places."

Chief Justice Rehnquist then argued that the interest in order and morality was unrelated to the suppression of free expression. [W]e do not think that when Indiana applies its statute to the nude dancing in these nightclubs it is proscribing nudity because of the erotic message conveyed by the dancers. Presumably numerous other erotic performances are presented at these establishments and similar clubs without any interference from the state, so long as the performers wear a scant amount of clothing. Likewise, the requirement that the dancers don pasties and a G-string does not deprive the dance of whatever erotic message it conveys; it simply makes the message slightly less graphic. The perceived evil that Indiana seeks to address is not erotic dancing, but public nudity. The appearance of people of all shapes, sizes and ages in the nude at a beach, for example, would convey little if any erotic message, yet the state still seeks to prevent it. Public nudity is the evil the state seeks to prevent, whether or not it is combined with expressive activity." Even though nude dancing has a communicative element "it was not the dancing that was prohibited, but simply its being done in the nude."

The Chief Justice concluded with the final part of the *O'Brien* test. "The statutory prohibition is not a means to some greater end, but an end in itself. It is without cavil that the public indecency statute is 'narrowly tailored'; Indiana's requirement that the dancers wear at least pasties and a G-string is modest, and the bare minimum necessary to achieve the state's purpose."

Justice Scalia concurred only in the judgment. "I agree that the judgment of the Court of Appeals must be reversed. In my view, however, the challenged regulation must be upheld, not because it survives some lower level of First-Amendment scrutiny, but because, as a general law regulating conduct and not specifically directed at expression, it is not subject to First-Amendment scrutiny at all."

Justice Scalia argued that the indecency law was not targeted at indecent, offensive speech. "The purpose of Indiana's nudity law would be violated, I think, if 60,000 fully consenting adults crowded into the Hoosierdome to display their genitals to one another, even if there were not an offended innocent in the crowd. Our society prohibits, and all human societies have prohibited, certain activities not because they harm others but because they are considered, in the traditional phrase, '*contra bonos mores*,' *i.e.*, immoral. Since the Indiana regulation is a general law not specifically targeted at expressive conduct, its application to such conduct does not in my view implicate the First Amendment."

Justice Scalia argued that "virtually every law restricts conduct, and virtually any prohibited conduct can be performed for an expressive purpose — if only expressive of the fact that the actor disagrees with the prohibition. It cannot reasonably be demanded, therefore, that every restriction of expression incidentally produced by a general law regulating conduct pass normal First-Amendment scrutiny, or even — as some of our cases have suggested, *see e.g.*, *United States v. O'Brien* — that it be justified by an 'important or substantial' government interest. Nor do our holdings require such justification: we have never invalidated the application of a general law simply because the conduct that it reached was being engaged in for expressive purposes and the government could not demonstrate a sufficiently important state interest. All our holdings (though admittedly not some of our discussion) support the conclusion that 'the only First Amendment analysis applicable to laws that do not directly or indirectly impede speech is the threshold inquiry of whether the purpose of the law is to suppress communication. If not, that is the end of the matter so far as First Amendment guarantees are concerned; if so, the court then proceeds to determine whether there is substantial justification for the proscription.' Such a regime ensures that the government does not act to suppress communication, without requiring that all conduct-restricting regulation (which means in effect all regulation) survive an enhanced level of scrutiny."

Justice Scalia noted that the Court had adopted such a regime in the context of the Free Exercise Clause. "In *Employment Division, Oregon Dept. of Human Resources v. Smith*, [text, p. 1458], we held that general laws not specifically targeted at religious practices did not require heightened First Amendment scrutiny even though they diminished some people's ability to practice their religion. Relatively few can plausibly assert that their illegal conduct is being engaged in for religious reasons; but almost anyone can violate almost any law as a means of expression."

Justice Souter, concurring in the judgment, agreed that the *O'Brien* test applied, but concluded that it was satisfied. But he relied "not on the possible sufficiency of society's moral views to justify the limitations at issue, but on the State's substantial interest in combating the secondary effects of adult entertainment establishments of the sort typified by respondents' establishments. I think that we may legitimately consider petitioners' assertion that the statute is applied to nude dancing because such dancing 'encourages prostitution, increases sexual assaults, and attracts other criminal activity.' To say that pernicious secondary effects are associated with nude dancing establishments is not necessarily to say that such effects result from the persuasive effect of the expression inherent in nude dancing. It is to say, rather, only that the effects are correlated with the existence of establishments offering such dancing, without deciding what the precise causes of the correlation actually are. Because the State's interest in banning nude dancing results from a simple correlation of such dancing with other evils, rather than from a relationship between the other evils and the expressive component of the dancing, the interest is unrelated to the suppression of free expression."

Justice White, joined by Justices Marshall, Blackmun and Stevens, dissenting, argued that prior cases such as *O'Brien* and *Bowers v. Hardwick*, involved "truly general proscriptions on individual conduct," whereas "Indiana does not suggest that its statute applies to, or could be applied, to nudity wherever it occurs, including the home." The State did not apply the indecency law to nudity in performance such as plays, ballets or operas." The Indiana law was not a general prohibition.

"Legislators do not just randomly select certain conduct for proscription; they have reasons for doing so and those reasons illuminate the purpose of the law that is passed. Indeed, a law may have multiple purposes. The purpose of forbidding people from appearing nude in parks, beaches, hot dog stands, and like public places is to protect others from offense. But that could not possibly be the purpose of preventing nude dancing in theaters and barrooms since the viewers are exclusively consenting adults who pay money to see these dances. The purpose of the proscription in these contexts is to protect the viewers from what the State believes is the harmful message that nude dancing communicates. Since the State permits the dancers to perform if they wear pasties and G-strings but forbids nude dancing, it is precisely because of the distinctive, expressive content of the nude dancing performances at issue in this case that the State seeks to apply the statutory prohibition. It is only because nude dancing performances may generate emotions and feelings of eroticism and sensuality among the spectators that the State seeks to regulate such expressive activity, apparently on the assumption that creating or emphasizing such thoughts and ideas in the minds of the spectators may lead to increased prostitution and the degradation of women. But generating thoughts, ideas, and emotions is the essence of communication. The nudity element of nude dancing performances cannot be neatly pigeonholed as mere 'conduct' independent of any expressive component of the dance. That fact dictates the level of First Amendment protection to be accorded the performances at issue here. Content based restrictions 'will be upheld only if narrowly drawn to accomplish a compelling governmental interest.' "

Applying the more demanding standard of review, the dissent concluded: "[E]ven if there were compelling interests, the Indiana statute is not narrowly drawn. If the State is genuinely concerned with prostitution and associated evils, it can adopt restrictions that do not interfere with the expressiveness of nonobscene nude dancing performances. For instance, the State could perhaps require that, while performing, nude performers remain at all times a certain minimum distance from spectators, that nude entertainment be limited to certain hours, or even that establishments providing such entertainment be dispersed throughout the city. Likewise, the State clearly has the authority to criminalize prostitution and obscene behavior. Banning an entire category of expressive activity, however, generally does not satisfy the narrow tailoring requirement of strict First Amendment scrutiny."

***Erie v. Pap's A.M.*, 529 U.S. 277 (2000).** The Court again upheld a public nudity statute 5-4 and once again there was no Court opinion. The public nudity law of Erie, Pennsylvania, has an indecency law prohibiting appearing in a state of nudity, and requiring the use of a G-string and pasties in nude dancing establishment's such as Kandyland, owned by Pap's A.M., which challenged the law. The Pennsylvania Supreme Court, finding that *Barnes* had provided no clear precedent, adopted Justice White's dissenting opinion and held that the law was content-based and unconstitutional under strict scrutiny review.

Justice O'Connor, joined by Chief Justice Rehnquist and Justices Kennedy and Breyer, accepted that "nude dancing of the type at issue here is expressive conduct, although we think that it falls only within the outer ambit of the First Amendment's protection." But the plurality concluded that the law was content-neutral to be reviewed under the *O'Brien* standard. On its face, the law was a general prohibition — "[I]t does not target nudity that contains an erotic message; rather, it bans all public nudity, regardless of whether that nudity is accompanied by expressive activity." "[E]ven if Erie's public nudity ban has some minimal effect on the erotic message by muting that portion of the expression that occurs when the last stitch is dropped, the dancers at Kandyland and other such establishments are free to perform wearing pasties and G-strings. Any effect on the overall expression is *de minimis*. If States are to be able to regulate secondary effects, then *de minimis* intrusions on expression such as those at issue here cannot be sufficient to render the ordinance content-based."

The plurality then applied the *O'Brien* test, concluding the Erie ordinance was justified. "The asserted interests of regulating conduct through a public nudity ban and of combating the harmful secondary effects associated with nude dancing are undeniably important. Because the nude dancing at Kandyland is of the same character as the adult entertainment at issue in *Renton* [and] *Young v. American Mini Theatres Inc.*, it was reasonable for Erie to conclude that such nude dancing was likely to produce the same secondary effects. And Erie could reasonably rely on the evidentiary foundation set forth in *Renton* and *American Mini Theatres* to the effect that secondary effects are caused by the presence of even one adult entertainment establishment in a given neighborhood. The ordinance also satisfies *O'Brien's* third factor, that the government interest is unrelated to the suppression of free expression. The fourth and final *O'Brien* factor — that the restriction is no greater that is essential to the furtherance of the government interest — is satisfied as well. The ordinance regulates conduct, and any incidental impact on the expressive element of nude dancing is *de minimis*. The requirement that dancers wear pasties and G-strings is a minimal restriction in furtherance of the asserted government interests, and the restriction leaves ample capacity to convey the dancer's erotic message."

Justice Scalia, joined by Justice Thomas, concurred in the judgement, on the basis of his opinion in *Barnes* that the law "is not subject to First Amendment scrutiny at all" since the law was generally applicable, not targeted against expressive conduct. "Moreover, even were I to conclude that the city of Erie had specifically singled out the activity of nude dancing, I still would not find that this regulation violated the First Amendment unless I could be persuaded (as on this record I cannot) that it was the communicative character of nude dancing that prompted the ban. The traditional power of government to foster good morals (*bonos mores*), and the acceptability of the traditional judgement (if Erie wishes to endorse it) that nude public dancing itself is immoral, have not been repealed by the First Amendment."

Justice Souter concurred in part and dissented in part. "Erie's stated interest in combating the secondary effects associated with nude dancing establishments is an interest unrelated to the suppression of expression under *United States v. O'Brien*, and the city's regulation is thus properly considered under the *O'Brien* standards. I do not believe, however, that the current record allows us to say that the city has made a sufficient evidentiary showing to sustain its regulation, and I would therefore vacate the decision of the Pennsylvania Supreme Court and remand the case for further proceedings." Justice Souter acknowledged that he had erred in not demanding such an evidentiary showing in *Barnes*. In any case, "[t]he record before us now does not permit the conclusion that Erie's ordinance is reasonably designed to mitigate real harms."

Justice Stevens, joined by Justice Ginsburg, dissenting, argued: "Far more important than the question whether nude dancing is entitled to the protection of the First Amendment are the dramatic changes in legal doctrine that the Court endorses today. Until now, the 'secondary effects' of commercial enterprises featuring indecent entertainment have justified only the regulation of their location. For the first time, the Court has now held that such effects may justify the total suppression of protected speech. Indeed, the plurality opinion concludes that admittedly trivial advancements of a State's interests may provide the basis for censorship."

[E] REGULATING THE PUBLIC FORUM

One issue that plays an important role in analysis of the right of freedom of speech in the public forum concerns the nature of the governmental regulation. Think about the following two examples. First, a legislature prohibits demonstrations critical of the government within 100 yards of the capitol. Second, a municipality prohibits any demonstration (defined as a gathering of three or more persons) within 100 yards of a hospital. In the former, the government is regulating the content of the communication — it is a content-based control. In the latter, the government is regulating only on the basis of the time, place, and manner in which the communication occurs. The law is content-neutral. Should the standards of review differ in these two cases? "The most puzzling aspect of the distinction between content-based and content-neutral restrictions is that either restriction reduces the sum total of information or opinion disseminated. That governmental regulation impedes all forms of speech, rather than only selected viewpoints or subjects, does not alter the fact that the regulation impairs the free flow of expression." Martin Redish, *The Content Distinction in First Amendment Analysis*, 34 STAN. L. REV. 113, 128 (1981).

Courts will generally uphold content-neutral, narrowly drawn, reasonable regulation of the time, place, and manner of expression. But the question naturally arises, what is "reasonable"? Generally, the answer to this involves some form of balancing test. The courts weigh the severity of the burden imposed by the restraint on freedom of expression against the government interest in maintaining the regulation. The time, place, and manner cases often highlight the important concept of the public forum.

Public fora are places recognized by the courts as being appropriate sites for public debate and protest. Courts today accept that streets and public parks and the grounds surrounding legislative assemblies can be used for speech activities. But can protest be excluded from places with special government purposes, such as military bases, libraries, schools, prisons, government office buildings, and courts? Can picketing and soliciting of a residence be prevented in the name of privacy? What about public areas that, while not truly sensitive or restricted, have not traditionally been utilized for expressive purposes?

Even when the forum is amenable to protest activities, the character of the communication may still have some effect on the constitutionality of the government regulation. The soap-box orator is different from protests involving hundreds of singing, chanting, marching protestors carrying picket signs, but how does government deal with the difference?

[1] Defining the Public Forum

INTERNATIONAL SOCIETY FOR KRISHNA CONSCIOUSNESS, INC. v. LEE*
505 U.S. 672, 112 S.Ct. 2701, 120 L.Ed.2d 541 (1992)

CHIEF JUSTICE REHNQUIST delivered the opinion of the Court.

Petitioner International Society for Krishna Consciousness, Inc. (ISKCON) is a not-for-profit religious corporation whose members perform a ritual known as sankirtan. The ritual consists of "going into public places, disseminating religious literature and soliciting funds to support the religion." The primary purpose of this ritual is raising funds for the movement.

Respondent Walter Lee, now deceased, was the police superintendent of the Port Authority of New York and New Jersey and was charged with enforcing the regulation at issue. The Port Authority owns and operates three major airports in the greater New York City area: John F. Kennedy International Airport (Kennedy), La Guardia Airport (La Guardia), and Newark International Airport (Newark). The three airports collectively form one of the world's busiest metropolitan airport complexes. They serve approximately 8% of this country's domestic airline market and more than 50% of the trans-Atlantic market. By decade's end they are expected to serve at least 110 million passengers annually.

The airports are funded by user fees and operated to make a regulated profit. Most space at the three airports is leased to commercial airlines, which bear primary responsibility for the leasehold. The Port Authority retains control over unleased portions, including La Guardia's Central Terminal Building, portions of Kennedy's International Arrivals Building, and Newark's North Terminal Building. The terminals are generally accessible to the general public and contain various commercial establishments such as restaurants, snack stands, bars, newsstands, and stores of various types. Virtually all who visit the terminals do so for purposes related to air travel. These visitors principally include passengers, those meeting or seeing off passengers, flight crews, and terminal employees.

The Port Authority has adopted a regulation forbidding within the terminals the repetitive solicitation of money or distribution of literature. The regulation states:

> The following conduct is prohibited within the interior areas of buildings or structures at an air terminal if conducted by a person to or with passers-by in a continuous or repetitive manner:

* [*ISKCON v. Lee* deals with a ban on soliciation of funds in the airport. A companion case, *Lee v. ISKCON*, p. 1103, deals with a ban on distribution of printed materials. The Court in the first case upholds the ban on solicitation, then a different majority strikes down the ban on distribution. — Ed.]

(a) The sale or distribution of any merchandise, including but not limited to jewelry, food stuffs, candles, flowers, badges and clothing.

(b) The sale or distribution of flyers, brochures, pamphlets, books or any other printed or written material.

(c) Solicitation and receipt of funds.

The regulation governs only the terminals; the Port Authority permits solicitation and distribution on the sidewalks outside the terminal buildings. The regulation effectively prohibits petitioner from performing sankirtan in the terminals. The Court of Appeals concluded that, presented with the issue, this Court would find that the ban on solicitation was reasonable, but the ban on distribution was not. Petitioner sought certiorari respecting the Court of Appeals' decision that the terminals are not public fora and upholding the solicitation ban. Respondent cross-petitioned respecting the court's holding striking down the distribution ban. We granted both petitions, to resolve whether airport terminals are public fora, a question on which the Circuits have split and on which we once before granted certiorari but ultimately failed to reach. *Board of Airport Comm'rs v. Jews for Jesus, Inc.*

It is uncontested that the solicitation at issue in this case is a form of speech protected under the First Amendment. But it is also well settled that the government need not permit all forms of speech on property that it owns and controls. Where the government is acting as a proprietor, managing its internal operations, rather than acting as lawmaker with the power to regulate or license, its action will not be subjected to the heightened review to which its actions as a lawmaker may be subject. Thus, we have upheld a ban on political advertisements in city-operated transit vehicles, even though the city permitted other types of advertising on those vehicles. Similarly, we have permitted a school district to limit access to an internal mail system used to communicate with teachers employed by the district. *Perry Education Assn. v. Perry Local Educators' Ass'n.*

These cases reflect, either implicitly or explicitly, a "forum-based" approach for assessing restrictions that the government seeks to place on the use of its property. *Cornelius v. NAACP Legal Defense and Educational Fund, Inc.* Under this approach, regulation of speech on government property that has traditionally been available for public expression is subject to the highest scrutiny. Such regulations survive only if they are narrowly drawn to achieve a compelling state interest. The second category of public property is the designated public forum, whether of a limited or unlimited character — property that the state has opened for expressive activity by part or all of the public. Regulation of such property is subject to the same limitations as that governing a traditional public forum. Finally, there is all remaining public property. Limitations on expressive activity conducted on this last category of property must survive only a much more limited review. The challenged regulation need only be reasonable, as long as the regulation is not an effort to suppress the speaker's activity due to disagreement with the speaker's view.

The parties do not disagree that this is the proper framework. Rather, they disagree whether the airport terminals are public fora or nonpublic fora. They also disagree whether the regulation survives the "reasonableness" review governing nonpublic fora, should that prove the appropriate category. Like the Court of Appeals, we conclude that the terminals are nonpublic fora and that the regulation reasonably limits solicitation.

Our recent cases provide additional guidance on the characteristics of a public forum. In *Cornelius* we noted that a traditional public forum is property that has as "a principal purpose the free exchange of ideas." [A] public forum [is not] created "whenever members of the public are permitted freely to visit a place owned or operated by the Government." The decision to create a public forum must instead be made "by intentionally opening a nontraditional forum for public discourse." *Cornelius*. Finally, we have recognized that the location of property also has bearing because separation from acknowledged public areas may serve to indicate that the separated property is a special enclave, subject to greater restriction.

[P]recedents foreclose the conclusion that airport terminals are public fora. Reflecting the general growth of the air travel industry, airport terminals have only recently achieved their contemporary size and character. Moreover, even within the rather short history of air transport, it is only "[i]n recent years [that] it has become a common practice for various religious and non-profit organizations to use commercial airports as a forum for the distribution of literature, the solicitation of funds, the proselytizing of new members, and other similar activities." Thus, the tradition of airport activity does not demonstrate that airports have historically been made available for speech activity. Nor can we say that these particular terminals, or airport terminals generally, have been intentionally opened by their operators to such activity; the frequent and continuing litigation evidencing the operators' objections belies any such claim. In short, there can be no argument that society's time-tested judgment, expressed through acquiescence in a continuing practice, has resolved the issue in petitioner's favor.

Petitioner attempts to circumvent the history and practice governing airport activity by pointing our attention to the variety of speech activity that it claims historically occurred at various "transportation nodes" such as rail stations, bus stations, wharves, and Ellis Island. Even if we were inclined to accept petitioner's historical account describing speech activity at these locations, an account respondent contests, we think that such evidence is of little import for two reasons. First, much of the evidence is irrelevant to public fora analysis, because sites such as bus and rail terminals traditionally have had private ownership. The development of privately owned parks that ban speech activity would not change the public fora status of publicly held parks. But the reverse is also true. The practices of privately held transportation centers do not bear on the government's regulatory authority over a publicly owned airport.

Second, the relevant unit for our inquiry is an airport, not "transportation nodes" generally. When new methods of transportation develop, new methods for accommodating that transportation are also likely to be needed. And with each new step, it therefore will be a new inquiry whether the transportation necessities are compatible with various kinds of expressive activity. To make a category of "transportation nodes," therefore, would unjustifiably elide what may prove to be critical differences of which we should rightfully take account. The "security magnet," for example, is an airport commonplace that lacks a counterpart in bus terminals and train stations. And public access to air terminals is also not infrequently restricted. To blithely equate airports with other transportation centers, therefore, would be a mistake.

The differences among such facilities are unsurprising since as noted, airports are commercial establishments funded by users fees and designed to make a regulated profit, and where nearly all who visit do so for some travel related purpose. As commercial enterprises, airports must provide services attractive to the marketplace. In light of this, it cannot fairly be said that an airport terminal has as a principal purpose "promoting the free exchange of ideas." *Cornelius*. To the contrary, the record demonstrates that Port Authority management considers the purpose of the terminals to be the facilitation of passenger air travel, not the promotion of expression. Even if we look beyond the intent of the Port Authority to the manner in which the terminals have been operated, the terminals have never been dedicated (except under the threat of court order) to expression in the form sought to be exercised here: i.e., the solicitation of contributions and the distribution of literature.

The terminals here are far from atypical. Although many airports have expanded their function beyond merely contributing to efficient air travel, few have included among their purposes the designation of a forum for solicitation and distribution activities. Thus, we think that neither by tradition nor purpose can the terminals be described as satisfying the standards we have previously set out for identifying a public forum. The restrictions here challenged, therefore, need only satisfy a requirement of reasonableness. We have no doubt that under this standard the prohibition on solicitation passes muster.

We have on many prior occasions noted the disruptive effect that solicitation may have on business. Passengers who wish to avoid the solicitor may have to alter their path, slowing both themselves and those around them. The result is that the normal flow of traffic is impeded. This is especially so in an airport, where "air travelers, who are often weighted down by cumbersome baggage may be hurrying to catch a plane or to arrange ground transportation." Delays may be particularly costly in this setting, as a flight missed by only a few minutes can result in hours worth of subsequent inconvenience.

In addition, face-to-face solicitation presents risks of duress that are an appropriate target of regulation. The skillful, and unprincipled, solicitor can target the most vulnerable, including those accompanying children or those suffering physical impairment and who cannot easily avoid the solicitation. The unsavory solicitor can also commit fraud through concealment of his affiliation or through deliberate efforts to shortchange those who agree to purchase. Compounding this problem is the fact that, in an airport, the targets of such activity frequently are on tight schedules. This in turn makes such visitors unlikely to stop and formally complain to airport authorities. As a result, the airport faces considerable difficulty in achieving its legitimate interest in monitoring solicitation activity to assure that travelers are not interfered with unduly.

The Port Authority has concluded that its interest in monitoring the activities can best be accomplished by limiting solicitation and distribution to the sidewalk areas outside the terminals. This sidewalk area is frequented by an overwhelming percentage of airport users. Thus the resulting access of those who would solicit the general public is quite complete. In turn we think it would be odd to conclude that the Port Authority's terminal regulation is unreasonable despite the Port Authority having otherwise assured access to an area universally traveled.

The inconveniences to passengers and the burdens on Port Authority officials flowing from solicitation activity may seem small, but viewed against the fact that "pedestrian congestion is one of the greatest problems facing the three terminals," the Port Authority could reasonably worry that even such incremental effects would prove quite disruptive. As a result, we conclude that the solicitation ban is reasonable.

JUSTICE O'CONNOR [concurring in *Lee v. International Society of Krishna Consciousness, Inc.,* and concurring in the judgment in *International Society of Krishna Consciousness Inc. v. Lee*].

In the decision below, the Court of Appeals upheld a ban on solicitation of funds within the airport terminals operated by the Port Authority of New York and New Jersey, but struck down a ban on the repetitive distribution of printed or written material within the terminals. I would affirm both parts of that judgment.

I agree that publicly owned airports are not public fora. Unlike public streets and parks, both of which our First Amendment jurisprudence has identified as "traditional public fora," airports do not count among their purposes the "free exchange of ideas," they have not "by long tradition or by government fiat been devoted to assembly and debate"; nor have they "time out of mind, been used for purposes of communicating thoughts between citizens, and discussing public questions." Although most airports do not ordinarily restrict public access, "[p]ublicly-owned or –operated property does not become a 'public forum' simply because members of the public are permitted to come and go at will. "[W]hen government property is not dedicated to open communication the government may — without further justification — restrict use to those who participate in the forum's official business." *Perry*. There is little doubt that airports are among those publicly owned facilities that could be closed to all except those who have legitimate business there. Public access to airports is thus not "inherent in the open nature of the locations," as it is for most streets and parks, but is rather a "matter of grace by government officials." *United States v. Kokinda*, (BRENNAN, J., dissenting). I also agree with the Court that the Port Authority has not expressly opened its airports to the types of expression at issue here, and therefore has not created a "limited" or "designated" public forum relevant to this case.

For these reasons, the Port Authority's restrictions on solicitation and leafletting within the airport terminals do not qualify for the strict scrutiny that applies to restriction of speech in public fora. That airports are not public fora, however, does not mean that the government can restrict speech in whatever way it likes. "The Government, even when acting in its proprietary capacity, does not enjoy absolute freedom from First Amendment constraints." *Kokinda*.

We have said that a restriction on speech in a nonpublic forum is "reasonable" when it is "consistent with the [government's] legitimate interest in preserv[ing] the property for the use to which it is lawfully dedicated." *Perry*. Ordinarily, this inquiry is relatively straightforward, because we have almost always been confronted with cases where the fora at issue were discrete, single-purpose facilities. The Port Authority urges that this case is no different and contends that it, too, has dedicated its airports to a single purpose — facilitating air travel — and that the speech it seeks to prohibit is not consistent with that purpose. But the wide range of activities promoted by the Port Authority is no more directly related to facilitating air travel than are the types of activities in which ISKCON wishes to engage. In my view, the Port Authority is operating a shopping mall as well as an airport. The reasonableness inquiry, therefore, is not whether the restrictions on speech are "consistent with . . .preserving the property" for air travel, but whether they are reasonably related to maintaining the multipurpose environment that the Port Authority has deliberately created.

Applying that standard, I agree with the Court that the ban on solicitation is reasonable. Face-to-face solicitation is incompatible with the airport's functioning in a way that the other, permitted activities are not.

In my view, however, the regulation banning leafletting cannot be upheld as reasonable on this record. I therefore concur in the judgment striking down that prohibition. While the difficulties posed by solicitation in a nonpublic forum are sufficiently obvious that its regulation may "ring of common-sense," the same is not necessarily true of leafletting. To the contrary, we have expressly noted that leafletting does not entail the same kinds of problems presented by face-to-face solicitation. With the possible exception of avoiding litter, it is difficult to point to any problems intrinsic to the act of leafletting that would make it naturally incompatible with a large, multipurpose forum such as those at issue here.

Of course, it is still open for the Port Authority to promulgate regulations of the time, place, and manner of leafletting which are "content-neutral, narrowly tailored to serve a significant government interest, and leave open ample alternative channels of communication." For example, during the many years that this litigation has been in progress, the Port Authority has not banned sankirtan completely from JFK International Airport, but has restricted it to a relatively uncongested part of the airport terminals, the same part that houses the airport chapel. In my view, that regulation meets the standards we have applied to time, place, and manner restrictions of protected expression.

JUSTICE KENNEDY, with whom JUSTICE BLACKMUN, JUSTICE STEVENS, and JUSTICE SOUTER join as to Part I, concurring in the judgment.

While I concur in the judgment affirming in this case, my analysis differs in substantial respects from that of the Court. In my view the airport corridors and shopping areas outside of the passenger security zones, areas operated by the Port Authority, are public forums, and speech in those places is entitled to protection against all government regulation inconsistent with public forum principles. The Port Authority's blanket prohibition on the distribution or sale of literature cannot meet those stringent standards, and I agree it is invalid under the First and Fourteenth Amendments. The Port Authority's rule disallowing in-person solicitation of money for immediate payment, however, is in my view a narrow and valid regulation of the time, place, and manner of protected speech in this forum, or else is a valid regulation of the nonspeech element of expressive conduct. I would sustain the Port Authority's ban on solicitation and receipt of funds.

I

Under [the] categorical view the application of public-forum analysis to airport terminals seems easy. Airports are of course public spaces of recent vintage, and so there can be no time-honored tradition associated with airports of permitting free speech. And because governments have often attempted to restrict speech within airports, it follows a fortiori under the Court's analysis that they cannot be so-called "designated" forums. So, the Court concludes, airports must be nonpublic forums, subject to minimal First Amendment protection.

This analysis is flawed at its very beginning. It leaves the government with almost unlimited authority to restrict speech on its property by doing nothing more than articulating a non-speech-related purpose for the area, and it leaves almost no scope for the development of new public forums absent the rare approval of the government. The Court's error lies in its conclusion that the public-forum status of public property depends on the government's defined purpose for the property, or on an explicit decision by the government to dedicate the property to expressive activity. In my view, the inquiry must be an objective one, based on the actual, physical characteristics and uses of the property.

The First Amendment is a limitation on government, not a grant of power. Its design is to prevent the government from controlling speech. Yet under the Court's view the authority of the government to control speech on its property is paramount, for in almost all cases the critical step in the Court's analysis is a classification of the property that turns on the government's own definition or decision, unconstrained by an independent duty to respect the speech its citizens can voice there. The Court acknowledges as much, by reintroducing today into our First Amendment law a strict doctrinal line between the proprietary and regulatory functions of government which I thought had been abandoned long ago.

The Court's approach is contrary to the underlying purposes of the public forum doctrine. Public places are of necessity the locus for discussion of public issues, as well as protest against arbitrary government action. At the heart of our jurisprudence lies the principle that in a free nation citizens must have the right to gather and speak with other persons in public places. The recognition that certain government-owned property is a public forum provides open notice to citizens that their freedoms may be exercised there without fear of a censorial government, adding tangible reinforcement to the idea that we are a free people.

The Court's analysis rests on an inaccurate view of history. The notion that traditional public forums are property which have public discourse as their principal purpose is a most doubtful fiction. The types of property that we have recognized as the quintessential public forums are streets, parks, and sidewalks. It would seem apparent that the principal purpose of streets and sidewalks, like airports, is to facilitate transportation, not public discourse, and we have recognized as much. Similarly, the purpose for the creation of public parks may be as much for beauty and open space as for discourse. Thus under the Court's analysis, even the quintessential public forums would appear to lack the necessary elements of what the Court defines as a public forum.

The Court's answer to these objections appears to be a recourse to history as justifying its recognition of streets, parks, and sidewalks, but apparently no other types of government property, as traditional public forums. The Court ignores the fact that the purpose of the public forum doctrine is to give effect to the broad command of the First Amendment to protect speech from governmental interference.

One of the places left in our mobile society that is suitable for discourse is a metropolitan airport. It is of particular importance to recognize that such spaces are public forums because in these days an airport is one of the few government-owned spaces where many persons have extensive contact with other members of the public.

I agree with the Court that government property of a type which by history and tradition has been available for speech activity must continue to be recognized as a public forum. In my view, however, constitutional protection is not confined to these properties alone. Under the proper circumstances I would accord public forum status to other forms of property, regardless of its ancient or contemporary origins and whether or not it fits within a narrow historic tradition. If the objective, physical characteristics of the property at issue and the actual public access and uses which have been permitted by the government indicate that expressive activity would be appropriate and compatible with those uses, the property is a public forum. The most important considerations in this analysis are whether the property shares physical similarities with more traditional public forums, whether the government has permitted or acquiesced in broad public access to the property, and whether expressive activity would tend to interfere in a significant way with the uses to which the government has as a factual matter dedicated the property. In conducting the last inquiry, courts must consider the consistency of those uses with expressive activities in general, rather than the specific sort of speech at issue in the case before it; otherwise the analysis would be one not of classification but rather of case-by-case balancing, and would provide little guidance to the State regarding its discretion to regulate speech. Courts must also consider the availability of reasonable time, place, and manner restrictions in undertaking this compatibility analysis. The possibility of some theoretical inconsistency between expressive activities and the property's uses should not bar a finding of a public forum, if those inconsistencies can be avoided through simple and permitted regulations.

The second category of the Court's jurisprudence, the so-called designated forum, provides little, if any, additional protection for speech. Where government property does not satisfy the criteria of a public forum, the government retains the power to dedicate the property for speech, whether for all expressive activity or for limited purposes only. I do not quarrel with the fact that speech must often be restricted on property of this kind to retain the purpose for which it has been designated. And I recognize that when property has been designated for a particular expressive use, the government may choose to eliminate that designation. But this increases the need to protect speech in other places, where discourse may occur free of such restrictions. In some sense the government always retains authority to close a public forum, by selling the property, changing its physical character, or changing its principal use. Otherwise the State would be prohibited from closing a park, or eliminating a street or sidewalk, which no one has understood the public forum doctrine to require. The difference is that when property is a protected public forum the State may not by fiat assert broad control over speech or expressive activities; it must alter the objective physical character or uses of the property, and bear the attendant costs, to change the property's forum status.

Under this analysis, it is evident that the public spaces of the Port Authority's airports are public forums. An airport corridor is of course not a street, but that is not the proper inquiry. The question is one of physical similarities, sufficient to suggest that the airport corridor should be a public forum for the same reasons that streets and sidewalks have been treated as public forums by the people who use them.

Plaintiffs do not seek access to the secured areas of the airports, nor do I suggest that these areas would be public forums. And while most people who come to the Port Authority's airports do so for a reason related to air travel, either because they are passengers or because they are picking up or dropping off passengers, this does not distinguish an airport from streets or sidewalks, which most people use for travel.

[P]erhaps most important, it is apparent from the record, and from the recent history of airports, that when adequate time, place, and manner regulations are in place, expressive activity is quite compatible with the uses of major airports.

We have long recognized that the right to distribute flyers and literature lies at the heart of the liberties guaranteed by the Speech and Press Clauses of the First Amendment. The Port Authority's rule, which prohibits almost all such activity, is among the most restrictive possible of those liberties. The regulation is in fact so broad and restrictive of speech, JUSTICE O'CONNOR finds it void even under the standards applicable to government regulations in nonpublic forums. I have no difficulty deciding the regulation cannot survive the far more stringent rules applicable to regulations in public forums.

II

It is my view, however, that the Port Authority's ban on the "solicitation and receipt of funds" within its airport terminals should be upheld under the standards applicable to speech regulations in public forums. The regulation may be upheld as either a reasonable time, place, and manner restriction, or as a regulation directed at the nonspeech element of expressive conduct. The two standards have considerable overlap in a case like this one.

I am in full agreement with the statement of the Court that solicitation is a form of protected speech. If the Port Authority's solicitation regulation prohibited all speech which requested the contribution of funds, I would conclude that it was a direct, content-based restriction of speech in clear violation of the First Amendment. The Authority's regulation does not prohibit all solicitation, however; it prohibits the "solicitation and receipt of funds." I do not understand this regulation to prohibit all speech that solicits funds. It reaches only personal solicitations for immediate payment of money. Otherwise, the "receipt of funds" phrase would be written out of the provision. The regulation does not cover, for example, the distribution of preaddressed envelopes along with a plea to contribute money to the distributor or his organization. As I understand the restriction it is directed only at the physical exchange of money, which is an element of conduct interwoven with otherwise expressive solicitation. In other words, the regulation permits expression that solicits funds, but limits the manner of that expression to forms other than the immediate receipt of money.

It is apparent that the justification for the solicitation ban is unrelated to the content of speech or the identity of the speaker. There can also be no doubt that the prevention of fraud and duress is a significant government interest. The government cannot, of course, prohibit speech for the sole reason that it is concerned the speech may be fraudulent. But the Port Authority's regulation does not do this. It recognizes that the risk of fraud and duress is intensified by particular conduct, the immediate exchange of money; and it addresses only that conduct.

Much of what I have said about the solicitation of funds may seem to apply to the sale of literature, but the differences between the two activities are of sufficient significance to require they be distinguished for constitutional purposes. The Port Authority's flat ban on the distribution or sale of printed material must, in my view, fall in its entirety. The application of our time, place, and manner test to the ban on sales leads to a result quite different from the solicitation ban. For one, the government interest in regulating the sales of literature is not as powerful as in the case of solicitation. The danger of a fraud arising from such sales is much more limited than from pure solicitation, because in the case of a sale the nature of the exchange tends to be clearer to both parties. Also, the Port Authority's sale regulation is not as narrowly drawn as the solicitation rule, since it does not specify the receipt of money as a critical element of a violation. And perhaps most important, the flat ban on sales of literature leaves open fewer alternative channels of communication than the Port Authority's more limited prohibition on the solicitation and receipt of funds. Given the practicalities and ad hoc nature of much expressive activity in the public forum, sales of literature must be completed in one transaction to be workable. Attempting to collect money at another time or place is a far less plausible option in the context of a sale than when soliciting donations, because the literature sought to be sold will under normal circumstances be distributed within the forum. Thus the Port Authority's regulation allows no practical means for advocates and organizations to sell literature within the public forums which are its airports.

Against all of this must be balanced the great need, recognized by our precedents, to give the sale of literature full First Amendment protection. We have long recognized that to prohibit distribution of literature for the mere reason that it is sold would leave organizations seeking to spread their message without funds to operate. The effect of a rule of law distinguishing between sales and distribution would be to close the marketplace of ideas to less affluent organizations and speakers, leaving speech as the preserve of those who are able to fund themselves. One of the primary purposes of the public forum is to provide persons who lack access to more sophisticated media the opportunity to speak. A prohibition on sales forecloses that opportunity for the very persons who need it most. And while the same arguments might be made regarding solicitation of funds, the answer is that the Port Authority has not prohibited all solicitation, but only a narrow class of conduct associated with a particular manner of solicitation.

For these reasons I agree that the Court of Appeals should be affirmed in full in finding the Port Authority's ban on the distribution or sale of literature unconstitutional, but upholding the prohibition on solicitation and immediate receipt of funds.

JUSTICE SOUTER, with whom JUSTICE BLACKMUN and JUSTICE STEVENS join, concurring in the judgment in *Lee v. International Society of Krishna Consciousness, Inc.*] and dissenting in *International Society for Krishna Consciousness, Inc. v. Lee*].

I

I join in Part I of JUSTICE KENNEDY's opinion and the judgment of affirmance in [*Lee v. Interrnational Society of Krishna Consciousness, Inc.*]. I agree with JUSTICE KENNEDY's view of the rule that should determine what is a public forum and with his conclusion that the public areas of the airports at issue here qualify as such.

Public forum analysis is stultified not only by treating its archetypes as closed categories, but by treating its candidates so categorically as to defeat their identification with the archetypes. We need not say that all "transportation nodes" or all airports are public forums in order to find that certain metropolitan airports are. Thus, the enquiry may and must relate to the particular property at issue and not necessarily to the "precise classification of the property." It is true that property of some types will invariably be public forums. But to find one example of a certain property type (e.g., airports, post offices, etc.) that is not a public forum is not to rule out all properties of that sort. One can imagine a public airport of a size or design or need for extraordinary security that would render expressive activity incompatible with its normal use. But that would be no reason to conclude that one of the more usual variety of metropolitan airports is not a public forum.

I also agree with JUSTICE KENNEDY's statement of the public forum principle: we should classify as a public forum any piece of public property that is "suitable for discourse" in its physical character, where expressive activity is "compatible" with the use to which it has actually been put. Applying this test, I have no difficulty concluding that the unleased public areas at airports like the metropolitan New York airports at issue in this case are public forums.

II

From the Court's conclusion, however, sustaining the total ban on solicitation of money for immediate payment, I respectfully dissent.

Even if I assume arguendo that the ban on the petitioners' activity at issue here is both content-neutral and merely a restriction on the manner of communication, the regulation must be struck down for its failure to satisfy the requirements of narrow tailoring to further a significant state interest, and availability of "ample alternative channels for communication."

As JUSTICE KENNEDY's opinion indicates, the respondent comes closest to justifying the restriction as one furthering the government's interest in preventing coercion and fraud. The claim to be preventing coercion is weak to start with. While a solicitor can be insistent, a pedestrian on the street or airport concourse can simply walk away or walk on. Since there is here no evidence of any type of coercive conduct, over and above the merely importunate character of the open and public solicitation, that might justify a ban, the regulation cannot be sustained to avoid coercion.

As for fraud, our cases do not provide government with plenary authority to ban solicitation just because it could be fraudulent. The evidence of fraudulent conduct here is virtually nonexistent.

Even assuming a governmental interest adequate to justify some regulation, the present ban would fall when subjected to the requirement of narrow tailoring.

Finally, I do not think the Port Authority's solicitation ban leaves open the "ample" channels of communication required of a valid content-neutral time, place and manner restriction. A distribution of preaddressed envelopes is unlikely to be much of an alternative. The practical reality of the regulation, which this Court can never ignore, is that it shuts off a uniquely powerful avenue of communication for organizations like the International Society for Krishna Consciousness, and may, in effect, completely prohibit unpopular and poorly funded groups from receiving funds in response to protected solicitation.

LEE v. INTERNATIONAL SOCIETY FOR KRISHNA CONSCIOUSNESS, INC.

505 U.S. 830, 112 S. Ct. 2709, 120 L. Ed. 2d 669 (1992)

For the reasons expressed in the opinions of JUSTICES O'CONNOR, KENNEDY, and SOUTER in *International Society for Krishna Consciousness, Inc. v. Lee*, the judgment of the Court of Appeals holding that the ban on distribution of literature in the Port Authority airport terminals is invalid under the First Amendment is

Affirmed.

CHIEF JUSTICE REHNQUIST, with whom JUSTICES WHITE, SCALIA, and THOMAS join, dissenting.

Leafletting presents risks of congestion similar to those posed by solicitation. It presents, in addition, some risks unique to leafletting. And of course, as with solicitation, these risks must be evaluated against a backdrop of the substantial congestion problem facing the Port Authority and with an eye to the cumulative impact that will result if all groups are permitted terminal access. Viewed in this light, I conclude that the distribution ban, no less than the solicitation ban, is reasonable. I therefore dissent from the Court's holding striking the distribution ban.

Suffice it to say that the risks and burdens posed by leafletting are quite similar to those posed by solicitation. The weary, harried, or hurried traveler may have no less desire and need to avoid the delays generated by having literature foisted upon him than he does to avoid delays from a financial solicitation. And while a busy passenger perhaps may succeed in fending off a leafletter with minimal disruption to himself by agreeing simply to take the proffered material, this does not completely ameliorate the dangers of congestion flowing from such leafletting. Others may choose not simply to accept the material but also to stop and engage the leafletter in debate, obstructing those who follow. Moreover, those who accept material may often simply drop it on the floor once out of the leafletter's range, creating an eyesore, a safety hazard, and additional clean-up work for airport staff.

In addition, a differential ban that permits leafletting but prohibits solicitation, while giving the impression of permitting the Port Authority at least half of what it seeks, may in fact prove for the Port Authority to be a much more Pyrrhic victory. Under the regime that is today sustained, the Port Authority is obliged to permit leafletting. But monitoring leafletting activity in order to ensure that it is only leafletting that occurs, and not also soliciting, may prove little less burdensome than the monitoring that would be required if solicitation were permitted. At a minimum, therefore, I think it remains open whether at some future date the Port Authority may be able to reimpose a complete ban, having developed evidence that enforcement of a differential ban is overly burdensome. Until now it has had no reason or means to do this, since it is only today that such a requirement has been announced.

NOTES

1. *Defining the forum.* One of the earliest Court acknowledgments of the public forum concept came in *Hague v. Congress for Industrial Organization*, 307 U.S. 496 (1939), where the Court extended constitutional protection to protest on the public streets:

> Wherever the title of streets and parks may rest, they have immemorially been held in trust for the use of the public and, time out of mind, have been used for purposes of assembly, communicating thoughts between citizens, and discussing public questions. Such use of the streets and public places has, from ancient times, been a part of the privileges, immunities, rights, and liberties of citizens.

This often-quoted language was used by the Court to extend the concept of the public forum to public streets. Do you see how the very same language might be relied upon to limit the scope of the concept?

For a time, it appeared that the concept of the public forum would constantly expand to accommodate First Amendment expression. In *Edwards v. South Carolina,* 372 U.S. 229 (1963), the forum was extended to statehouse grounds and in *Brown v. Louisiana,* 383 U.S. 131 (1966), the Court recognized that even a public library could be a public forum, if the protest were not inconsistent with the facility's primary purpose as a library. Similarly, school property can be part of the public forum, again subject to reasonable time, place, and manner constraints. *Grayned v. City of Rockford,* 408 U.S. 104 (1972); *Tinker v. City of Des Moines Indep. School Dist.*, p. 1052.

Relatively early on, however, it became clear that the scope of the public forum is not unlimited. In *Adderley v. Florida,* 385 U.S. 39 (1965), the Court held that jailhouse grounds were not a "public forum," and therefore demonstrators protesting the arrest of their schoolmates could constitutionally be convicted under state trespass laws. Justice Black, writing for the Court, noted that jails are "built for security purposes" and, unlike the state capitol grounds in *Edwards*, are not generally open to the public.

Military bases have been excluded from the public forum category. In *Greer v. Spock,* 428 U.S. 828 (1976), the Court upheld military post requirements that approval of the base commander be obtained prior to political activity on the base. Justice Stewart, for the Court, rejected the proposition that "whenever members of the public are permitted to visit a place owned or operated by the Government, then that place becomes a 'public forum' for purposes of the First Amendment." The Court has also rejected the contention that the advertising space of a municipally owned rapid transit system is part of the public forum. *Lehman v. City of Shaker Heights,* 418 U.S. 298 (1974).

2. *Critiquing the modern doctrine.* In critiquing modern public forum doctrine, two distinct questions may be asked: (a) does it make sense to distinguish between public and private fora for First Amendment purposes in the first place? (b) If so, does the distinction actually drawn by the Court make sense? As to the former question, is it necessary to begin First Amendment analysis with an a priori categorization? Why shouldn't courts examine each case on its own terms, considering whether government is justified in restricting expression? Why should government be given so much more leeway in so-called "private" fora? As to the second question, does the distinction adopted by the Court in *Krishna Consciousness* make sense? Is the label, "private" forum, a misnomer for the category of cases to which the Court applies it? After *Krishna Consciousness*, has the government effectively been given the power to insulate itself from meaningful constitutional review? Is there any other way the Court could have drawn the dichotomy?

A number of scholars have been highly critical of the Court's development of its public forum doctrine. For example, Professor Steven Gey argues "that the existing public forum doctrine is inadequate in three major respects: First, because it limits the key reference point of the traditional public forum to antiquated public spaces that have a decreasing impact on the everyday communicative lives of modern citizens. Second, because the Supreme Court has created a mutated middle category of 'limited' public forums that are defined tautologically in terms of the government's intent as to whether speech may take place in the forum. And third, with [one] exception, the Court has been reluctant to extend the application of the public forum beyond the context of physical forums-which limits the doctrine's usefulness in an era when an increasing proportion of public debate occurs electronically between conversants who are separated geographically by great distances." Steven Gey, *Reopening the Public Forum-From Sidewalks to Cyberspace,* 58 OHIO ST. L.J. 1535, 1634 (1998).

According to Professor Calvin Massey, "[t]he public forum problem has never been resolved adequately because the Court has attempted to straddle two incompatible theories of free speech. The affirmative theory — the notion that governments are obliged to promote public discourse — tugs in the direction of ever-expanding public access to public property. The negative theory — the idea that governments are obliged to remain neutral in public discourse — pulls in the direction of equal access rather than expanding access. The doctrinal edifice that bridges this chasm relies on determining the forum status of public property-public forum or not? — to ascertain the standard of review. This came about because early in the development of public forum doctrine the Court conceived of the public forum problem in terms of property." He concludes that "[b]ecause the Court has severely constricted the public forum concept, affirmative theory today is merely a vestigal element in public forum doctrine." Calvin Massey, *Public Fora, Neutral Governments, and the Prism of Property*, 50 HASTINGS L.J. 309, 352 (1999).

3. *United States v. Kokinda,* 497 U.S. 720 (1990). The Court upheld a United States Postal Service regulation that prohibited "[s]oliciting alms and contributions" on postal premises. The Court found unpersuasive defendants' argument that "although the sidewalk is on postal service property, because it is not distinguishable from the municipal sidewalk across the parking lot from the post office's entrance, it must be a traditional public forum." Justice O'Connor, speaking for the plurality, responded: "The Postal Service has not expressly dedicated its sidewalks to any expressive activity. Indeed, postal property is expressly dedicated to only one means of communication: the posting of public notices on designated bulletin boards. No postal service regulation opens postal sidewalks to any First Amendment activity." Justice Kennedy concurred in the judgment. He acknowledged that "there remains a powerful argument that, because of the wide range of activities that the Government permits to take place on this postal sidewalk, it is more than a nonpublic forum." He concluded, however, that the regulation should be upheld because it is "narrow in its purpose, design, and effect, does not discriminate on the basis of content or viewpoint, is narrowly drawn to serve an important governmental interest, and permits respondents to engage in a broad range of activity to express their views, including the solicitation of financial support."

Justice Brennan, joined all or in part by three justices, dissented: "It is only common sense that a public sidewalk adjacent to a public building to which citizens are freely admitted is a natural location for speech to occur."

4. *"Private" shopping centers.* *Amalgamated Food Employees Local 590 v. Logan Valley Plaza, Inc.*, 391 U.S. 308 (1968), suggested that the public forum concept might be extended even to privately owned shopping centers which were "the functional equivalent" of municipal business districts. But

Lloyd Corp. v. Tanner, 407 U.S. 551 (1972), refused to extend the public forum concept to protest activity unrelated to the activities of the shopping center, at least within a privately enclosed center. "There is no open-ended invitation to the public, for any and all purposes, however incompatible with the interests of both the stores and the shoppers whom they serve." And, in *Hudgens v. NLRB,* 424 U.S. 507 (1976), *Logan Valley* was overruled. The Court reasoned that *Tanner's* distinction between related and unrelated protests was content-oriented and therefore impermissible. Because the private character of the shopping center would allow the owners to exclude unrelated communication, it must also permit exclusion of related expression. As Justice Black had written earlier in *Marsh v. Alabama*, p. 1476, only "when property has taken on all the attributes of a town" does it become dedicated to the public use.

5. *Residential picketing.* In *Frisby v. Schultz,* 487 U.S. 474 (1988), the Court, per Justice O'Connor, upheld a city ordinance that, as construed, completely banned any picketing focused on and taking place in front of a particular residence. "Our prior holdings make clear that a public street does not lose its status as a traditional public forum simply because it runs through a residential neighborhood." But the Court found that the ordinance served "a significant government interest," namely "the protection of residential privacy." "The devastating effect of targeted picketing on the quiet enjoyment of the home is beyond doubt." Moreover, the ordinance was directed only at targetted picketing and did not prevent "more general dissemination of a message." The Court ultimately concluded that "[b]ecause the picketing prohibited by the ordinance is speech directed primarily at those who are presumptively unwilling to receive it, the State has a substantial and justifiable interest in banning it."

Justice Brennan, joined by Justice Marshall, dissented: "[S]ubstantial regulation is permitted to neutralize the intrusive or unduly coercive aspects of picketing around the home. But to say that picketing may be substantially regulated is not to say that it may be prohibited in its entirety." Justice Stevens dissented on overbreadth grounds.

ARKANSAS EDUCATIONAL TELEVISION COMMISSION v. FORBES

523 U.S. 666, 118 S. Ct. 1633, 140 L. Ed.2d 875 (1998)

JUSTICE KENNEDY delivered the opinion of the Court.

A state-owned public television broadcaster sponsored a candidate debate from which it excluded an independent candidate with little popular support. The issue before us is whether, by reason of its state ownership, the station had a constitutional obligation to allow every candidate access to the debate. We conclude that, unlike most other public television programs, the candidate debate was subject to constitutional constraints applicable to nonpublic fora under our forum precedents. Even so, the broadcaster's decision to exclude the candidate was a reasonable, viewpoint-neutral exercise of journalistic discretion.

Petitioner, the Arkansas Educational Television Commission (AETC), is an Arkansas state agency owning and operating a network of five noncommercial television stations (Arkansas Educational Television Network or AETN). The eight members of AETC are appointed by the Governor for eight-year terms and are removable only for good cause. To insulate its programming decisions from political pressure, AETC employs an Executive Director and professional staff who exercise broad editorial discretion in planning the network's programming. AETC has also adopted the Statement of Principles of Editorial Integrity in Public Broadcasting, which counsel adherence to "generally accepted broadcasting industry standards, so that the programming service is free from pressure from political or financial supporters."

In the spring of 1992, AETC staff began planning a series of debates between candidates for federal office in the November 1992 elections. AETC decided to televise a total of five debates, scheduling one for the Senate election and one for each of the four congressional elections in Arkansas. AETC staff developed a debate format allowing about 53 minutes during each one-hour debate for questions to and answers by the candidates. Given the time constraint, the staff and Simmons "decided to limit participation in the debates to the major party candidates or any other candidate who had strong popular support."

On June 17, 1992, AETC invited the Republican and Democratic candidates for Arkansas' Third Congressional District to participate in the AETC debate for that seat. Two months later, after obtaining the 2,000 signatures required by Arkansas law, respondent Ralph Forbes was certified as an independent candidate qualified to appear on the ballot for the seat. Forbes was a perennial candidate who had sought, without success, a number of elected offices in Arkansas. On August 24, 1992, he wrote to AETC requesting permission to participate in the debate for his district, scheduled for October 22, 1992. On September 4, AETC Executive Director Susan Howarth denied Forbes' request, explaining that AETC had "made a bona fide journalistic judgement that our viewers would be best served by limiting the debate" to the candidates already invited.

On October 19, 1992, Forbes filed suit against AETC, seeking injunctive and declaratory relief as well as damages. Forbes claimed he was entitled to participate in the debate under both the First Amendment and 47 U.S.C. § 315, which affords political candidates a limited right of access to television air time. Forbes has long since abandoned his statutory claims, and so the issue is whether his exclusion from the debate was consistent with the First Amendment. The Court of Appeals held it was not, applying our public forum precedents. Appearing as amicus curiae in support of petitioners, the Solicitor General argues that our forum precedents should be of little relevance in the context of television broadcasting. At the outset, then, it is instructive to ask whether public forum principles apply to the case at all.

Having first arisen in the context of streets and parks, the public forum doctrine should not be extended in a mechanical way to the very different context of public television broadcasting. In the case of streets and parks, the open access and viewpoint neutrality commanded by the doctrine is "compatible with the intended purpose of the property." *Perry Ed. Assn. v. Perry Local Educators' Assn.* So too was the requirement of viewpoint neutrality compatible with the university's funding of student publications in *Rosenberger v.*

Rector and Visitors of Univ. of Va. In the case of television broadcasting, however, broad rights of access for outside speakers would be antithetical, as a general rule, to the discretion that stations and their editorial staff must exercise to fulfill their journalistic purpose and statutory obligations.

Congress has rejected the argument that "broadcast facilities should be open on a nonselective basis to all persons wishing to talk about public issues." *Columbia Broadcasting System, Inc. v. Democratic National Committee.* Instead, television broadcasters enjoy the "widest journalistic freedom" consistent with their public responsibilities.

As a general rule, the nature of editorial discretion counsels against subjecting broadcasters to claims of viewpoint discrimination. Programming decisions would be particularly vulnerable to claims of this type because even principled exclusions rooted in sound journalistic judgment can often be characterized as viewpoint-based. To comply with their obligation to air programming that serves the public interest, broadcasters must often choose among speakers expressing different viewpoints. "That editors newspaper or broadcast can and do abuse this power is beyond doubt," *Columbia Broadcasting System, Inc.* but "[c]alculated risks of abuse are taken in order to preserve higher values." *Id.* Much like a university selecting a commencement speaker, a public institution selecting speakers for a lecture series, or a public school prescribing its curriculum, a broadcaster by its nature will facilitate the expression of some viewpoints instead of others. Were the judiciary to require, and so to define and approve, pre-established criteria for access, it would risk implicating the courts in judgments that should be left to the exercise of journalistic discretion.

When a public broadcaster exercises editorial discretion in the selection and presentation of its programming, it engages in speech activity. Although programming decisions often involve the compilation of the speech of third parties, the decisions nonetheless constitute communicative acts. Claims of access under our public forum precedents could obstruct the legitimate purposes of television broadcasters. Were the doctrine given sweeping application in this context, courts "would be required to oversee far more of the day-to-day operations of broadcasters' conduct, deciding such questions as whether a particular individual or group has had sufficient opportunity to present its viewpoint and whether a particular viewpoint has already been sufficiently aired." *Columbia Broadcasting System.* "The result would be a further erosion of the journalistic discretion of broadcasters," transferring "control over the treatment of public issues from the licensees who are accountable for broadcast performance to private individuals" who bring suit under our forum precedents. In effect, we would "exchange public trustee broadcasting, with all its limitations, for a system of self-appointed editorial commentators."

In the absence of any congressional command to "[r]egimen[t] broadcasters" in this manner, we are disinclined to do so through doctrines of our own design. This is not to say the First Amendment would bar the legislative imposition of neutral rules for access to public broadcasting. Instead, we say that, in most cases, the First Amendment of its own force does not compel public broadcasters to allow third parties access to their programming.

Although public broadcasting as a general matter does not lend itself to scrutiny under the forum doctrine, candidate debates present the narrow exception to the rule. For two reasons, a candidate debate like the one at issue here is different from other programming. First, unlike AETC's other broadcasts, the debate was by design a forum for political speech by the candidates. Consistent with the long tradition of candidate debates, the implicit representation of the broadcaster was that the views expressed were those of the candidates, not its own. The very purpose of the debate was to allow the candidates to express their views with minimal intrusion by the broadcaster. In this respect the debate differed even from a political talk show, whose host can express partisan views and then limit the discussion to those ideas.

Second, in our tradition, candidate debates are of exceptional significance in the electoral process. Deliberation on the positions and qualifications of candidates is integral to our system of government, and electoral speech may have its most profound and widespread impact when it is disseminated through televised debates.

As we later discuss, in many cases it is not feasible for the broadcaster to allow unlimited access to a candidate debate. Yet the requirement of neutrality remains; a broadcaster cannot grant or deny access to a candidate debate on the basis of whether it agrees with a candidate's views. Viewpoint discrimination in this context would present not a "[c]alculated ris[k]," *Columbia Broadcasting System*, but an inevitability of skewing the electoral dialogue.

The special characteristics of candidate debates support the conclusion that the AETC debate was a forum of some type. The question of what type must be answered by reference to our public forum precedents, to which we now turn.

Forbes argues, and the Court of Appeals held, that the debate was a public forum to which he had a First Amendment right of access. Under our precedents, however, the debate was a nonpublic forum, from which AETC could exclude Forbes in the reasonable, viewpoint-neutral exercise of its journalistic discretion.

For our purposes, it will suffice to employ the categories of speech fora already established and discussed in our cases. "[T]he Court [has] identified three types of fora: the traditional public forum, the public forum created by government designation, and the nonpublic forum." *Cornelius v. NAACP Legal Defense Ed. Fund, Inc.* Traditional public fora are defined by the objective characteristics of the property, such as whether, "by long tradition or by government fiat," the property has been "devoted to assembly and debate." *Perry Ed. Assn.* The government can exclude a speaker from a traditional public forum "only when the exclusion is necessary to serve a compelling state interest and the exclusion is narrowly drawn to achieve that interest." *Cornelius*.

Designated public fora, in contrast, are created by purposeful governmental action. "The government does not create a [designated] public forum by inaction or by permitting limited discourse, but only by intentionally opening a nontraditional public forum for public discourse." [*Cornelius*] Hence "the Court has looked to the policy and practice of the government to ascertain whether it intended to designate a place not traditionally open to assembly and debate as a public forum." *Cornelius*. If the government excludes a speaker who falls within the class to which a designated public forum is made generally available, its action is subject to strict scrutiny.

Other government properties are either nonpublic fora or not fora at all. The government can restrict access to a nonpublic forum "as long as the restrictions are reasonable and [are] not an effort to suppress expression merely because public officials oppose the speaker's view." *Cornelius*.

In summary, traditional public fora are open for expressive activity regardless of the government's intent. The objective characteristics of these properties require the government to accommodate private speakers. The government is free to open additional properties for expressive use by the general public or by a particular class of speakers, thereby creating designated public fora. Where the property is not a traditional public forum and the government has not chosen to create a designated public forum, the property is either a nonpublic forum or not a forum at all.

The parties agree the AETC debate was not a traditional public forum. The Court has rejected the view that traditional public forum status extends beyond its historic confines, see *ISKCON* and even had a more expansive conception of traditional public fora been adopted, the almost unfettered access of a traditional public forum would be incompatible with the programming dictates a television broadcaster must follow. The issue, then, is whether the debate was a designated public forum or a nonpublic forum.

Under our precedents, the AETC debate was not a designated public forum. To create a forum of this type, the government must intend to make the property "generally available," *Widmar v. Vincent*, to a class of speakers. In *Widmar*, for example, a state university created a public forum for registered student groups by implementing a policy that expressly made its meeting facilities "generally open" to such groups. A designated public forum is not created when the government allows selective access for individual speakers rather than general access for a class of speakers. In *Perry*, for example, the Court held a school district's internal mail system was not a designated public forum even though selected speakers were able to gain access to it.

And in *Cornelius* itself, the Court held the Combined Federal Campaign (CFC) charity drive was not a designated public forum because "[t]he Government's consistent policy ha[d] been to limit participation in the CFC to appropriate' [i.e., charitable rather than political] voluntary agencies and to require agencies seeking admission to obtain permission from federal and local Campaign officials.

These cases illustrate the distinction between "general access," which indicates the property is a designated public forum, and "selective access," which indicates the property is a nonpublic forum. On one hand, the government creates a designated public forum when it makes its property generally available to a certain class of speakers, as the university made its facilities generally available to student groups in *Widmar*. On the other hand, the government does not create a designated public forum when it does no more than reserve eligibility for access to the forum to a particular class of speakers, whose members must then, as individuals, "obtain permission," to use it. For instance, the Federal Government did not create a designated public forum in *Cornelius* when it reserved eligibility for participation in the CFC drive to charitable agencies, and then made individual, non-ministerial judgments as to which of the eligible agencies would participate.

The *Cornelius* distinction between general and selective access furthers First Amendment interests. By recognizing the distinction, we encourage the government to open its property to some expressive activity in cases where, if faced with an all-or-nothing choice, it might not open the property at all. That this distinction turns on governmental intent does not render it unprotective of speech. Rather, it reflects the reality that, with the exception of traditional public fora, the government retains the choice of whether to designate its property as a forum for specified classes of speakers.

Here, the debate did not have an open-microphone format. Contrary to the assertion of the Court of Appeals, AETC did not make its debate generally available to candidates for Arkansas' Third Congressional District seat. Instead, just as the Federal Government in *Cornelius* reserved eligibility for participation in the CFC program to certain classes of voluntary agencies, AETC reserved eligibility for participation in the debate to candidates for the Third Congressional District seat (as opposed to some other seat). At that point, just as the Government in *Cornelius* made agency-by-agency determinations as to which of the eligible agencies would participate in the CFC, AETC made candidate-by-candidate determinations as to which of the eligible candidates would participate in the debate. "Such selective access, unsupported by evidence of a purposeful designation for public use, does not create a public forum." *Cornelius*. Thus the debate was a nonpublic forum.

In addition to being a misapplication of our precedents, the Court of Appeals' holding would result in less speech, not more. In ruling that the debate was a public forum open to all ballot-qualified candidates, the Court of Appeals would place a severe burden upon public broadcasters who air candidates' views. Were it faced with the prospect of cacophony, on the one hand, and First Amendment liability, on the other, a public television broadcaster might choose not to air candidates' views at all. A broadcaster might decide "the safe course is to avoid controversy, and by so doing diminish the free flow of information and ideas." *Turner Broadcasting System, Inc.*

The debate's status as a nonpublic forum, however, did not give AETC unfettered power to exclude any candidate it wished. As JUSTICE O'CONNOR has observed, nonpublic forum status "does not mean that the government can restrict speech in whatever way it likes." *ISKCON*. To be consistent with the First Amendment, the exclusion of a speaker from a nonpublic forum must not be based on the speaker's viewpoint and must otherwise be reasonable in light of the purpose of the property. *Cornelius*.

In this case, the jury found Forbes' exclusion was not based on "objections or opposition to his views." The record provides ample support for this finding, demonstrating as well that AETC's decision to exclude him was reasonable. AETC Executive Director Susan Howarth testified Forbes' views had "absolutely" no role in the decision to exclude him from the debate. She further testified Forbes was excluded because (1) "the Arkansas voters did not consider him a serious candidate"; (2) "the news organizations also did not consider him a serious candidate"; (3) "the Associated Press and a national election result reporting service did not plan to run his name in results on election night"; (4) Forbes "apparently had little, if any, financial support, failing to report campaign finances to the Secretary of State's office or to the Federal Election Commission"; and (5) "there [was] no 'Forbes for Congress' campaign headquarters other than his house." Forbes himself described his campaign organization as "bedlam" and the media coverage of his campaign as "zilch." It is, in short, beyond dispute that Forbes was excluded not because of his viewpoint but because he had generated no appreciable public interest.

There is no substance to Forbes' suggestion that he was excluded because his views were unpopular or out of the mainstream. His own objective lack of support, not his platform, was the criterion. Indeed, the very premise of Forbes' contention is mistaken. A candidate with unconventional views might well enjoy broad support by virtue of a compelling personality or an exemplary campaign organization. By the same token, a candidate with a traditional platform might enjoy little support due to an inept campaign or any number of other reasons.

Nor did AETC exclude Forbes in an attempted manipulation of the political process. The evidence provided powerful support for the jury's express finding that AETC's exclusion of Forbes was not the result of "political pressure from anyone inside or outside [AETC]." There is no serious argument that AETC did not act in good faith in this case. AETC excluded Forbes because the voters lacked interest in his candidacy, not because AETC itself did.

The broadcaster's decision to exclude Forbes was a reasonable, viewpoint-neutral exercise of journalistic discretion consistent with the First Amendment. The judgment of the Court of Appeals is REVERSED.

Justice Stevens, with whom Justice Souter, and Justice Ginsburg, join, dissenting.

The Court has decided that a state-owned television network has no "constitutional obligation to allow every candidate access to" political debates that it sponsors. I do not challenge that decision. The judgment of the Court of Appeals should nevertheless be affirmed. The official action that led to the exclusion of respondent Forbes from a debate with the two major-party candidates for election to one of Arkansas' four seats in Congress does not adhere to well-settled constitutional principles. The ad hoc decision of the staff of the Arkansas Educational Television Commission (AETC) raises precisely the concerns addressed by "the many decisions of this Court over the last 30 years, holding that a law subjecting the exercise of First Amendment freedoms to the prior restraint of a license, without narrow, objective, and definite standards to guide the licensing authority, is unconstitutional." *Shuttlesworth v. Birmingham*.

In its discussion of the facts, the Court barely mentions the standardless character of the decision to exclude Forbes from the debate. In its discussion of the law, the Court understates the constitutional importance of the distinction between state ownership and private ownership of broadcast facilities. I shall therefore first add a few words about the record in this case and the history of regulation of the broadcast media, before explaining why I believe the judgment should be affirmed.

Two months before Forbes was officially certified as an independent candidate qualified to appear on the ballot under Arkansas law, the AETC staff had already concluded that he "should not be invited" to participate in the televised debates because he was "not a serious candidate as determined by the voters of Arkansas." He had, however, been a serious contender for the Republican nomination for Lieutenant Governor in 1986 and again in 1990. Although he was defeated in a run-off election, in the three-way primary race conducted in 1990—just two years before the AETC staff decision—he had received 46.88% of the statewide vote and had carried 15 of the 16 counties within the Third Congressional District by absolute majorities. Nevertheless, the staff concluded that Forbes did not have "strong popular support."

Given the fact that the Republican winner in the Third Congressional District race in 1992 received only 50.22% of the vote and the Democrat received 47.20%, it would have been necessary for Forbes, who had made a strong showing in recent Republican primaries, to divert only a handful of votes from the Republican candidate to cause his defeat. Thus, even though the AETC staff may have correctly concluded that Forbes was "not a serious candidate," their decision to exclude him from the debate may have determined the outcome of the election in the Third District.

If a comparable decision were made today by a privately owned network, it would be subject to scrutiny under the Federal Election Campaign Act unless the network used "pre-established objective criteria to determine which candidates may participate in [the] debate." No such criteria governed AETC's refusal to permit Forbes to participate in the debate. Indeed, whether that refusal was based on a judgment about "newsworthiness"—as AETC has argued in this Court—or a judgment about "political viability"—as it argued in the Court of Appeals—the facts in the record presumably would have provided an adequate basis either for a decision to include Forbes in the Third District debate or a decision to exclude him, and might even have required a cancellation of two of the other debates.

AETC is a state agency whose actions "are fairly attributable to the State and subject to the Fourteenth Amendment, unlike the actions of privately owned broadcast licensees." The AETC staff members therefore "were not ordinary journalists: they were employees of government." The Court implicitly acknowledges these facts by subjecting the decision to exclude Forbes to constitutional analysis. Yet the Court seriously underestimates the importance of the difference between private and public ownership of broadcast facilities, despite the fact that Congress and this Court have repeatedly recognized that difference.

In *Columbia Broadcasting System, Inc. v. Democratic National Committee*, the Court held that a licensee is neither a common carrier, nor a public forum that must accommodate "the right of every individual to speak, write, or publish," *id.* Speaking for a plurality, CHIEF JUSTICE BURGER expressed the opinion that the First Amendment imposes no constraint on the private network's journalistic freedom.

The case before us today involves only the right of a state-owned network to regulate speech that plays a central role in democratic government. Because AETC is owned by the State, deference to its interest in making ad hoc decisions about the political content of its programs necessarily increases the risk of government censorship and propaganda in a way that protection of privately owned broadcasters does not.

The Court recognizes that the debates sponsored by AETC were "by design a forum for political speech by the candidates." The Court also acknowledges the central importance of candidate debates in the electoral process. Thus, there is no need to review our cases expounding on the public forum doctrine to conclude that the First Amendment will not tolerate a state agency's arbitrary exclusion from a debate forum based, for example, on an expectation that the speaker might be critical of the Governor, or might hold unpopular views about abortion or the death penalty. Indeed, the Court so holds today.

It seems equally clear, however, that the First Amendment will not tolerate arbitrary definitions of the scope of the forum. We have recognized that "[o]nce it has opened a limited forum, the State must respect the lawful boundaries it has itself set." *Rosenberger v. Rector* and *Visitors of Univ. of Va.* It follows, of course, that a State's failure to set any meaningful boundaries at all cannot insulate the State's action from First Amendment challenge. The dispositive issue in this case, then, is not whether AETC created a designated public forum or a nonpublic forum, as the Court concludes, but whether AETC defined the contours of the debate forum with sufficient specificity to justify the exclusion of a ballot-qualified candidate.

AETC asks that we reject Forbes' constitutional claim on the basis of entirely subjective, ad hoc judgments about the dimensions of its forum. The First Amendment demands more, however, when a state government effectively wields the power to eliminate a political candidate from all consideration by the voters. All stations must act as editors, and when state-owned stations participate in the broadcasting arena, their editorial decisions may impact the constitutional interests of individual speakers. A state-owned broadcaster need not plan, sponsor, and conduct political debates, however. When it chooses to do so, the First Amendment imposes important limitations on its control over access to the debate forum.

AETC's control was comparable to that of a local government official authorized to issue permits to use public facilities for expressive activities. In cases concerning access to a traditional public forum, we have found an analogy between the power to issue permits and the censorial power to impose a prior restraint on speech. Thus, in our review of an ordinance requiring a permit to participate in a parade on city streets, we explained that the ordinance, as written, "fell squarely within the ambit of the many decisions of this Court over the last 30 years, holding that a law subjecting the exercise of First Amendment freedoms to the prior restraint of a license, without narrow, objective, and definite standards to guide the licensing authority, is unconstitutional." *Shuttlesworth.*

The televised debate forum at issue in this case may not squarely fit within our public forum analysis, but its importance cannot be denied. Given the special character of political speech, particularly during campaigns for elected office, the debate forum implicates constitutional concerns of the highest order, as the majority acknowledges. Indeed, the planning and management of political debates by state-owned broadcasters raise serious constitutional concerns that are seldom replicated when state-owned television networks engage in other types of programming. Surely the Constitution demands at least as much from the Government when it takes action that necessarily impacts democratic elections as when local officials issue parade permits.

The reasons that support the need for narrow, objective, and definite standards to guide licensing decisions apply directly to the wholly subjective access decisions made by the staff of AETC. The importance of avoiding arbitrary or viewpoint-based exclusions from political debates militates strongly in favor of requiring the controlling state agency to use (and adhere to) pre-established, objective criteria to determine who among qualified candidates may participate. When the demand for speaking facilities exceeds supply, the State must "ration or allocate the scarce resources on some acceptable neutral principle." *Rosenberger*. A constitutional duty to use objective standards i.e., "neutral principles"—for determining whether and when to adjust a debate format would impose only a modest requirement that would fall far short of a duty to grant every multiple-party request. Such standards would also have the benefit of providing the public with some assurance that state-owned broadcasters cannot select debate participants on arbitrary grounds.

Like the Court, I do not endorse the view of the Court of Appeals that all candidates who qualify for a position on the ballot are necessarily entitled to access to any state-sponsored debate. I am convinced, however, that the constitutional imperatives that motivated our decisions in cases like *Shuttlesworth* command that access to political debates planned and managed by state-owned entities be governed by pre-established, objective criteria. Requiring government employees to set out objective criteria by which they choose which candidates will benefit from the significant media exposure that results from state-sponsored political debates would alleviate some of the risk inherent in allowing government agencies—rather than private entities—to stage candidate debates.

NOTES

1. Consider the majority's use of the argument that the exercise of a broadcaster's editorial discretion constitutes a communicative act, and therefore should not be interfered with by the imposition of First Amendment-dictated access. To what extent should this reasoning be deemed relevant to a state-owned broadcasting entity? How important is the fact that despite its holding, the Court acknowledged the possibility of legislatively imposed access rules?

2. To what extent would it be proper to deem the Internet a public forum? What are the competing arguments? *See generally* Dawn Nunziato, *The Death of the Public Forum in Cyberspace*, 20 BERKELEY TECH. L. J. 1115 (2005); Note, *Linking Public Websites to the Public Forum*, 87 VA. L. REV. 1007 (2001); Note, *Sidewalks in Cyberspace: Making Space for Public Forums in the Electronic Environment*, 12 HARV. J. L. & TECH. 149 (1998).

[2] Time, Place, and Manner Regulation

***Grayned v. City of Rockford*, 408 U.S. 104 (1972).** In upholding a narrowly drawn statute restricting protest activity around a schoolhouse during class hours, the Court provided a classic summary of the permissible scope of time, place, and manner controls:

> [G]overnment has no power to restrict [speech] activity because of its message [but] reasonable "time, place and manner" regulations may be necessary to further significant governmental interests, and are permitted. For example, two parades cannot march on the same street simultaneously and government may allow only one. A demonstration or parade on a large street during rush hour might put an intolerable burden on the essential flow of traffic, and for that reason could be prohibited. If overamplified loud speakers assault the citizenry, government may turn them down.
>
> The nature of the place, "the pattern of its normal activities, dictates the kinds of regulations of time, place and manner that are reasonable." Although a silent vigil may not unduly interfere with a public library, making a speech in the reading room almost certainly would. That same speech should be perfectly appropriate in a park. The crucial question is whether the manner of expression is basically compatible with the normal activity of a particular place at a particular time. Our cases make clear that in assessing the reasonableness of regulation, we must weigh heavily the fact that communication is involved; the regulation must be narrowly tailored to further the State's legitimate interest. "Access to [public places] for the purpose of exercising [First Amendment rights] cannot constitutionally be denied broadly." Free expression must not, in the guise of regulation, be abridged or denied.

***Clark v. Community for Creative Non-Violence*, 468 U.S. 288 (1984).** The Supreme Court considered the issue "whether a National Park Service regulation prohibiting camping in certain parks violates the First Amendment when applied to prohibit demonstrators from sleeping in Lafayette Park and the Mall [in Washington, D.C.] in connection with a demonstration intended to call attention to the plight of the homeless." A majority held the prohibition to constitute a valid time-place-manner regulation, even assuming, arguendo, that the demonstrator's activities could be considered protected speech:

> The requirement that the regulation be content neutral is clearly satisfied. Neither was the regulation faulted, nor could it be, on the ground that without overnight sleeping the plight of the homeless could not be communicated in other ways. The regulation otherwise left the demonstration intact, with its symbolic city, signs and the presence of those who were willing to take their turns in a day-and-night vigil.
>
> It is also apparent to us that the regulation narrowly focuses on the Government's substantial interest in maintaining the parks in the heart of our capital in an attractive and intact condition, readily

> available to the millions of people who wish to see and enjoy them by their presence. To permit camping — using those areas as living accommodations — would be totally inimical to these purposes.

Justice Marshall, joined by Justice Brennan, dissented:

> According to the majority, the significant government interest advanced by denying respondents' request to engage in sleep-speech is the interest in "maintaining the parks in the heart of our capital in an attractive and intact condition." That interest is indeed significant. However, neither the Government nor the majority adequately explains how prohibiting respondents' planned activity will substantially further that interest. The majority fails to offer any evidence indicating that the absence of an absolute ban on sleeping would present administrative problems to the Park Service that are substantially more difficult than it ordinarily confronts. A mere apprehension of difficulties should not be enough to overcome the right to free expression.
>
> [T]he Court has dramatically lowered its scrutiny of governmental regulation once it has determined that such regulations are content-neutral. The minimal scrutiny prong of this two-tiered approach has led to an unfortunate diminution of First Amendment protection. By narrowly limiting its concern to whether a given regulation creates a content-based distinction, the Court has seemingly overlooked the fact that content-neutral restrictions are also capable of unnecessarily restricting protected expressive activity. The Court, however, has transformed the ban against content-distinctions from a floor that offers all persons at least equal liberty under the First Amendment into a ceiling that restricts persons to the protection of First Amendment equality — but nothing more.

***Heffron v. International Society for Krishna Consciousness,* 452 U.S. 640 (1981).** Pursuant to state law, the Minnesota Agricultural Society conducted an annual state fair. The fair authorities issued a rule requiring that all persons or groups seeking to sell, exhibit or distribute materials at the fair do so from fixed locations on the fairgrounds. Although the rules did not bar walking around on the fairgrounds, all sales, distributions and fund solicitations had to be conducted from a booth rented from the fair authorities on a first-come, first-served basis. ISKCON sued, alleging that the rule violated the first amendment by suppressing the Society's religious practice of Sankirtan, a ritual requiring members to go into public places to distribute material and solicit donations for the Krishna religion. The Supreme Court, in an opinion by Justice White, upheld the rule:

> It is common ground that the First Amendment does not guarantee the right to communicate one's views at all times and places or in any manner that may be desired. As the Minnesota Supreme Court recognized, the activities of [ISKCON] are subject to reasonable time, place and manner restrictions. We have often approved restrictions

> of that kind provided that they are justified without reference to the content of the regulated speech, that they serve a significant governmental interest, and that in doing so they leave open ample alternative channels for communication of the information.

The Court found that the rule was not content-based, and served the significant governmental interest in "the need to maintain the orderly movement of the crowd given the large number of exhibitors and persons attending the Fair." The Court rejected the argument that this threat could be avoided by less restrictive means, "such as penalizing disorder or disruption, limiting the number of solicitors, or putting more narrowly drawn restrictions on the location and movement" of the Society's representatives.

Justice Brennan, joined by two other justices, concurred in part and dissented in part: "By prohibiting distribution of literature outside the booths, the fair officials sharply limit the number of fairgoers to whom the proselytizers and candidates can communicate their messages."

***Ward v. Rock Against Racism,* 491 U.S. 781 (1989).** Justice Kennedy, speaking for the Court, held valid, against a First Amendment challenge, a New York City regulation which required performers at the Naumburg Acoustic Bandshell in Central Park to use the city's sound amplification equipment and a sound technician provided by the city.

Rock Against Racism (ROCK), a sponsor of yearly rock concerts at the Bandshell for which it furnished its own sound equipment and technicians, challenged this regulation, and the Second Circuit invalidated it. Although agreeing that content-neutral time, place and manner regulations are permissible, the Second Circuit said they must constitute the least intrusive means of accomplishing a legitimate purpose of the regulation. The Second Circuit mentioned the availability of a number of less restrictive alternatives such as directing ROCK's technicians to keep the volume below specified levels. The Supreme Court reversed.

Was the New York City regulation content neutral? ROCK argued that it was not because the city was seeking "to assert artistic control over performers at the Bandshell by enforcing a bureaucratically determined, value-laden conception of good sound." The Court rejected this contention and pointed to the finding of the district court that the "city requires its sound technician to defer to the wishes of sponsors concerning sound mix."

The Court also rejected the Second Circuit's position that New York City was required to choose the least intrusive means to handle the noise problem in Central Park:

> Lest any confusion on the point remain, we reaffirm today that a regulation of the time, place, or manner of protected speech must be narrowly tailored to serve the government's legitimate content-neutral interests but that it need not be the least-restrictive or least-intrusive means of doing so. It is undeniable that the city's substantial interest in limiting sound volume is served in a direct and effective way by the requirement that the city's sound technician control the mixing board during the performance. The alternative methods hypothesized

by the Court of Appeals reflect nothing more than a disagreement with the city over how much control of volume is appropriate or how the level of control is to be achieved.

Justice Marshall, joined by Justices Brennan and Stevens, dissented:

> Until today, a key safeguard of free speech has been the government's obligation to adopt the least intrusive restriction necessary to achieve its goals. By abandoning the requirement that time, place, and manner regulations must be narrowly tailored, the majority replaces constitutional scrutiny with mandatory deference.
>
> By holding that the guidelines are valid time, place, and manner restrictions, notwithstanding the availability of less intrusive but effective means of controlling volume, the majority deprives the narrow tailoring requirement of all meaning.

Content-Based Time, Place, Manner Regulations. The regulations discussed to this point have been content-neutral. In *Burson v. Freeman,* 504 U.S. 191 (1992), the Court considered the constitutionality of a content-based time-place-manner regulation. The case involved a challenge to Tennessee statutes prohibiting the solicitation of votes and the display of campaign materials within 100 feet of the entrance to a polling place on election day. Justice Blackmun, speaking for four Justices, held that while the statutes must be subjected to exacting scrutiny, "[t]he interests advanced by Tennessee obviously are compelling ones." He concluded that

> an examination of the history of election regulation in this country reveals a persistent battle against two evils: voter intimidation and election fraud. [A]ll 50 states settled on the same solution: a secret ballot secured in part by a restricted zone around the voting compartments. We find that this wide-spread and time-tested consensus demonstrates that some restricted zone is necessary in order to serve the State's compelling interest in preventing voter intimidation and election fraud.

Justice Stevens, joined by Justices O'Connor and Souter, dissented:

> The speech and conduct prohibited in the campaign-free zone is classic political expression. Therefore, I fully agree with the plurality that Tennessee must show that its "regulation is necessary to serve a compelling state interest and that it is narrowly drawn to achieve that end." I do not agree, however, that Tennessee has made anything approaching such a showing.

Pointing to the extremely broad scope of the campaign-free zone in certain states, Justice Stevens concluded that "[t]he fact that campaigning-free zones cover such a large area in some States unmistakably identifies censorship of election-day campaigning as an animating force behind these restrictions."

Justice Scalia, concurring in the judgment, found that no public forum was involved, because "the streets and sidewalks around polling places have traditionally *not* been devoted to assembly and debate."

[3] Licensing and the Public Forum

LOVELL v. CITY OF GRIFFIN
303 U.S. 444, 58 S. Ct. 666, 82 L. Ed. 949 (1938)

CHIEF JUSTICE HUGHES delivered the opinion of the Court.

Appellant, Alma Lovell, was convicted in the Recorder's Court of the City of Griffin, Georgia, of the violation of a city ordinance and was sentenced to imprisonment for fifty days in default of the payment of a fine of fifty dollars. The Superior Court of the county refused sanction of a petition for review; the Court of Appeals affirmed the judgment of the Superior Court; and the Supreme Court of the State denied an application for certiorari. The case comes here on appeal. The ordinance in question is as follows:

> Section 1. That the practice of distributing, either by hand or otherwise, circulars, handbooks, advertising, or literature of any kind, whether said articles are being delivered free, or whether same are being sold, within the limits of the City of Griffin, without first obtaining written permission from the City Manager of the City of Griffin, such practice shall be deemed a nuisance, and punishable as an offense against the City of Griffin.

The violation, which is not denied, consisted of the distribution without the required permission of a pamphlet and magazine in the nature of religious tracts, setting forth the gospel of the "Kingdom of Jehovah." Appellant did not apply for a permit. The Court of Appeals sustained the constitutional validity of the ordinance.

The ordinance is comprehensive with respect to the method of distribution. It covers every sort of circulation "either by hand or otherwise." There is thus no restriction in its application with respect to time or place. It is not limited to ways which might be regarded as inconsistent with the maintenance of public order or as involving disorderly conduct, the molestation of the inhabitants, or the misuse or littering of the streets. The ordinance prohibits the distribution of literature of any kind at any time, at any place, and in any manner without a permit from the City Manager.

We think that the ordinance is invalid on its face. Whatever the motive which induced its adoption, its character is such that it strikes at the very foundation of the freedom of the press by subjecting it to license and censorship. While this freedom from previous restraint upon publication cannot be regarded as exhausting the guaranty of liberty, the prevention of that restraint was a leading purpose in the adoption of the constitutional provision. Legislation of the type of the ordinance in question would restore the system of license and censorship in its baldest form.

The liberty of the press is not confined to newspapers and periodicals. It necessarily embraces pamphlets and leaflets. These indeed have been historic weapons in the defense of liberty, as the pamphlets of Thomas Paine and others in our own history abundantly attest. The press in its historic connotation comprehends every sort of publication which affords a vehicle of information and opinion. The ordinance cannot be saved because it relates to distribution and not to publication. "Liberty of circulating is as essential to that freedom as liberty of publishing; indeed, without the circulation, the publication would be of little value." *Ex parte Jackson*, 96 U.S. 727, 733 (1877).

As the ordinance is void on its face, it was not necessary for appellant to seek a permit under it. She was entitled to contest its validity in answer to the charge against her.

NOTES

1. *Administrative discretion.* *Lovell* was followed in a series of subsequent Supreme Court decisions. For example, in *Kunz v. New York,* 340 U.S. 290 (1951), the Court reversed the conviction of a controversial Baptist minister whose permit for street-preaching was revoked because of his having ridiculed and denounced other religious beliefs. He continued to hold street meetings despite the loss of the permit, and was convicted of violating the permit ordinance. The Court's opinion, by Chief Justice Vinson, noted that the ordinance "gives an administrative official discretionary power to control in advance the right of citizens to speak on religious matters [on the streets]. As such, the ordinance is clearly invalid as a prior restraint. New York cannot vest restraining control over the right to speak on religious subjects in an administrative official where there are no appropriate standards to guide his action." *See also Cantwell v. Connecticut,* 310 U.S. 296 (1940); *Thornhill v. Alabama,* 310 U.S. 88 (1940); *Niemotko v. Maryland,* 340 U.S. 268 (1951).

2. *The duty to comply or challenge.* In *Poulos v. New Hampshire,* 345 U.S. 395 (1953), a Jehovah's Witness was refused a license to use a public park for religious services, even though he had complied with all procedural requirements for obtaining the license. He nevertheless held the service, and was arrested and convicted of violating a city ordinance prohibiting the holding of any parade or exhibition without first obtaining a license from the city council. Unlike *Lovell*, the appellant (a) had requested a license and had been denied it, and (b) did not challenge the ordinance as overbroad on its face but rather as unconstitutional as applied to him. The Supreme Court affirmed his conviction. The Court emphasized that, under the state supreme court's construction, the ordinance required "uniform, non-discriminatory and consistent administration of the granting of licenses for public meetings on public streets." Even though both the state supreme court and the United States Supreme Court agreed that the refusal to grant appellant a license was unconstitutional, they both affirmed appellant's conviction for holding a service without a license.

The opinion of Justice Reed noted appellant's argument "that if he can be punished for violation of the valid ordinance because he exercised his right of free speech, after the wrongful refusal of the license, the protection of the Constitution is illusory." However, the opinion concluded that "to allow applicants to proceed without the required permits to run businesses, erect structures, purchase firearms, transport or store explosives or inflammatory products, hold public meetings without prior safety arrangements or take other unauthorized action is apt to cause breaches of the peace or create public dangers. Delay is unfortunate, but the expense and annoyance of litigation is a price citizens must pay for life in an orderly society where the rights of the First Amendment have a real and abiding meaning." Does Justice Reed persuade you? Is *Poulos* distinguishable from *Lovell* and the cases following it?

3. *Parade permits.* Note that, in contrast to some of the cases dealing with the licensing of leaflet distribution, none of the Court's decisions totally prohibits the use of a licensing requirement for public parades or demonstrations. In the well-known case of *Cox v. New Hampshire,* 312 U.S. 569 (1941), decided after *Lovell*, the Court held that "regulation of the use of the streets for parades and processions is a traditional exercise of control by local government" and therefore upheld a New Hampshire statute requiring a license for the holding of a parade or procession on a public street. The Supreme Court cited the state supreme court's conclusion that "[t]he obvious advantage of requiring application for a permit was giving the public authorities notice in advance so as to afford opportunity for proper policing." *Lovell* was distinguishable, said Chief Justice Hughes, speaking for the Court, because there "the ordinance prohibited the distribution of literature of any kind at any time, at any place, and in any manner without a permit from the city manager, thus striking at the very foundation of the freedom of the press by subjecting it to license and censorship."

Do you agree that this distinction saves the New Hampshire statute challenged in *Cox*? Is the state's interest in licensing "organized" demonstrations more compelling than its interest in regulating "unorganized" expressive activity on the public streets? Does the state have a sufficiently strong interest in licensing demonstrations to justify the use of prior restraint inherent in a licensing system? Assuming no unreasonable or discriminatory denial of licenses, how, if at all, does such a licensing requirement invade free speech interests?

Professor Baker is highly critical of *Cox* on the ground that the only offense of the Jehovah's Witnesses was their desire to express themselves:

> During a single hour on the evening of July 8, 1939, approximately 26,000 people passed by an intersection in Manchester, New Hampshire. Included among those 26,000 were about eighty-eight people divided into four or five small groups. The people in each group walked single file and carried small staffs and signs. It appears that the only legally relevant difference between the conduct of these eighty-eight and the thousands of other people was that these Jehovah's Witnesses walked in small, organized groups or "moving assemblies" and that they walked in order to be expressive rather than to engage in shopping, business, travel or other similar pursuits.

Edwin Baker, *Unreasoned Reasonableness: Mandatory Parade Permits and Time, Place and Manner Regulations*, 78 Nw. U.L. Rev. 937, 992–93 (1983). A counter-argument is made by Professor Blasi:

> From the standpoint of efficiency, it makes sense for a city to regulate the content of a demonstration before the event. The damage done by libelous, privacy-invading, or violence-inciting speech is often irreparable; preventing the speech from ever working its harm is better both for the putative victims and the speakers, who are faced only with permit denials and injunctions rather than criminal convictions.

Vincent Blasi, *Prior Restraints on Demonstrations*, 68 MICH. L. REV. 1481, 1504-05 (1970).

4. *Forsyth County v. The Nationalist Movement,* 505 U.S. 123 (1992). The Court held invalid on its face an ordinance requiring applicants for a permit to conduct a parade or assembly on public property to pay in advance a fee of up to $1,000 and authorizing the county administrator to determine the amount of the fee by assessing the amount required to meet the expenses of providing security for the event. Justice Blackmun, speaking for five Justices, initially noted that the ordinance amounted to a prior restraint. While conceding that "the Court has recognized that government, in order to regulate competing uses of public forums, may impose a permit requirement on those wishing to hold a march, parade, or rally," he also noted that such a scheme "may not delegate overly broad licensing discretion to a government official. Further, any permit scheme controlling the time, place, and manner of speech must not be based on the content of the message, must be narrowly tailored to serve a significant governmental interest, and must leave open ample alternatives for communication."

On the basis of this analysis, the Court found the ordinance unconstitutional:

> The ordinance contains more than the possibility of censorship through uncontrolled discretion. As construed by the county, the ordinance often requires that the fee be based on the content of the speech. The fee assessed will depend on the administrator's measure of the amount of hostility likely to be created by the speech based on its content. Those wishing to express views unpopular with bottle-throwers, for example, may have to pay more for their permit.

The Court rejected the argument "that the $1,000 cap on the fee ensures that the ordinance will not result in content-based discrimination. Neither the $1,000 cap on the fee charged, nor even some lower nominal cap, could save the ordinance because in this context, the level of the fee is irrelevant. A tax based on the content of speech does not become more constitutional because it is a small tax."

Chief Justice Rehnquist, joined by three other justices, dissented on the ground that "there are no lower court factual findings on the scope or administration of the ordinance."

5. *Prohibition of leaflet distribution.* *Lovell* involved a requirement of permission from a city official before leaflets could be distributed. On occasion, municipalities have attempted other means of regulating leaflet distribution.

One of those methods was a simple total prohibition of their distribution on city streets.

In *Schneider v. State,* 308 U.S. 147 (1939), the Supreme Court held unconstitutional four city ordinances prohibiting the public distribution of leaflets. Justice Roberts, author of the famous "public forum" dictum in *Hague v. CIO*, wrote for the Court:

> Although a municipality may enact regulations in the interest of the public safety, health, welfare or convenience, these may not abridge the individual liberties secured by the Constitution to those who wish to speak, write, print or circulate information or opinions.

The Court rejected the asserted justification that the ordinances were designed to avoid littering: "This constitutional protection does not deprive a city of all power to prevent street littering. Amongst these is the punishment of those who actually throw papers on the streets." How successful a method of preventing littering is "the punishment of those who actually throw papers on the streets" likely to be? Should it matter?

6. *City of Lakewood v. Plain Dealer Publishing Co.,* 486 U.S. 750 (1988). The Court, in an opinion by Justice Brennan, upheld a facial challenge to an ordinance licensing the placement of newsracks because "the face of the ordinance itself contains no explicit limits on the Mayor's discretion." The ordinance authorized denial of an application for a permit on "such other terms and conditions deemed necessary and reasonable by the Mayor."

> The City asks us to presume that the Mayor will deny a permit application only for reasons related to the health, safety, or welfare of Lakewood citizens, and that additional terms and conditions will be imposed only for similar reasons. This presumes the Mayor will act in good faith and adhere to standards absent from the statute's face. But this is the very presumption that the doctrine forbidding unbridled discretion disallows.

Justice White, joined by Justices Stevens and O'Connor, dissented on the grounds that a facial attack was inappropriate: "Our normal approach has been to determine whether a law is unconstitutional as applied in the particular case before the Court. This rule is also the usual approach we follow when reviewing laws that require licenses or permits to engage in business or other activities." The majority believed that a facial examination was appropriate, because the individual was required to apply for licenses annually, and because the licensing system was "directed narrowly and specifically at expression or conduct commonly associated with expression: the circulation of newspapers."

[4] Injunctions and the Public Forum

MADSEN v. WOMEN'S HEALTH CENTER
512 U.S. 753, 114 S.Ct. 2516, 129 L. Ed. 2d 593 (1994)

CHIEF JUSTICE REHNQUIST delivered the opinion of the Court.

Petitioners challenge the constitutionality of an injunction entered by a Florida state court which prohibits antiabortion protestors from demonstrating in certain places and in various ways outside of a health clinic that performs abortions. We hold that the establishment of a 36-foot buffer zone on a public street from which demonstrators are excluded passes muster under the First Amendment, but that several other provisions of the injunction do not.

Respondents operate abortion clinics throughout central Florida. Petitioners and other groups and individuals are engaged in activities near the site of one such clinic in Melbourne, Florida. They picketed and demonstrated where the public street gives access to the clinic. In September 1992, a Florida state court permanently enjoined petitioners from blocking or interfering with public access to the clinic, and from physically abusing persons entering or leaving the clinic. Six months later, respondents sought to broaden the injunction, complaining that access to the clinic was still impeded by petitioners' activities and that such activities had also discouraged some potential patients from entering the clinic, and had deleterious physical effects on others. The trial court thereupon issued a broader injunction, which is challenged here.

The court found that, despite the initial injunction, protesters continued to impede access to the clinic by congregating on the paved portion of the street — Dixie Way — leading up to the clinic, and by marching in front of the clinic's driveways. It found that as vehicles heading toward the clinic slowed to allow the protesters to move out of the way, "sidewalk counselors" would approach and attempt to give the vehicle's occupants antiabortion literature. The number of people congregating varied from a handful to 400, and the noise varied from singing and chanting to the use of loudspeakers and bullhorns.

The protests, the court found, took their toll on the clinic's patients. A clinic doctor testified that, as a result of having to run such a gauntlet to enter the clinic, the patients "manifested a higher level of anxiety and hypertension causing those patients to need a higher level of sedation to undergo the surgical procedures, thereby increasing the risk associated with such procedures." The noise produced by the protestors could be heard within the clinic, causing stress in the patients both during surgical procedures and while recuperating in the recovery rooms. And those patients who turned away because of the crowd to return at a later date, the doctor testified, increased their health risks by reason of the delay. Doctors and clinic workers, in turn, were not immune even in their homes.

This and similar testimony led the state court to conclude that its original injunction had proved insufficient "to protect the health, safety and rights of women in Brevard and Seminole County, Florida, and surrounding counties seeking access to [medical and counseling] services." The state court therefore amended its prior order, enjoining a broader array of activities.

[The amended injunction prohibits demonstrators from entering the premises of the Clinic; from obstructing or interfering with access to any building or parking lot of the Clinic; from demonstrating within 36 feet of the Clinic; from using noise or images observable to or within earshot of the patients inside the Clinic during surgical procedures and recovery periods; from physically approaching any person seeking the services of the Clinic in an area within 300 feet of the Clinic, unless such person indicates a desire to communicate; from demonstrating or using sound amplification equipment within 300 feet of the residence of any of the staff or obstructing the entrances, exits or driveways of the residences of any of the staff; from physically abusing, intimidating, harassing, or assaulting persons at the Clinic or at any of the homes of staff of the Clinic; from harassing, intimidating or threatening any person who assists in providing services at the respondents' Clinic. The injunction also prohibits persons from encouraging other persons to commit any of the prohibited acts.]

The Florida Supreme Court upheld the constitutionality of the trial court's amended injunction. Shortly before the Florida Supreme Court's opinion was announced, the United States Court of Appeals for the Eleventh Circuit heard a separate challenge to the same injunction. The Court of Appeals struck down the injunction.

We begin by addressing petitioners' contention that the state court's order, because it is an injunction that restricts only the speech of antiabortion protesters, is necessarily content or viewpoint based. Accordingly, they argue, we should examine the entire injunction under the strictest standard of scrutiny. We disagree. To accept petitioners' claim would be to classify virtually every injunction as content– or viewpoint-based.

The fact that the injunction in the present case did not prohibit activities of those demonstrating in favor of abortion is justly attributable to the lack of any similar demonstrations by those in favor of abortion, and of any consequent request that their demonstrations be regulated by injunction. There is no suggestion in this record that Florida law would not equally restrain similar conduct directed at a target having nothing to do with abortion; none of the restrictions imposed by the court were directed at the contents of petitioner's message.

Our principal inquiry in determining content neutrality is whether the government has adopted a regulation of speech "without reference to the content of the regulated speech." We thus look to the government's purpose as the threshold consideration. Here, the state court imposed restrictions on petitioners incidental to their antiabortion message because they repeatedly violated the court's original order. That petitioners all share the same viewpoint regarding abortion does not in itself demonstrate that some invidious content-or viewpoint-based purpose motivated the issuance of the order. It suggests only that those in the group whose conduct violated the court's order happen to share the same opinion regarding abortions being performed at the clinic. In short, the fact that the injunction covered people with a particular viewpoint does not itself render the injunction content or viewpoint based.[2] Accordingly, the injunction issued in this case does not demand the level of heightened scrutiny set forth in *Perry Education Ass'n*. And we proceed to discuss the standard which does govern.

If this were a content-neutral, generally applicable statute, instead of an injunctive order, its constitutionality would be assessed under the standard set forth in *Ward v. Rock Against Racism*, and similar cases. Given that the forum around the clinic is a traditional public forum, we would determine whether the time, place, and manner regulations were "narrowly tailored to serve a significant governmental interest."

There are obvious differences, however, between an injunction and a generally applicable ordinance. Ordinances represent a legislative choice regarding the promotion of particular societal interests. Injunctions, by contrast, are remedies imposed for violations (or threatened violations) of a legislative or judicial decree. Injunctions also carry greater risks of censorship and discriminatory application than do general ordinances. Injunctions, of course, have some advantages over generally applicable statutes in that they can be tailored by a trial judge to afford more precise relief than a statute where a violation of the law has already occurred.

We believe that these differences require a somewhat more stringent application of general First Amendment principles in this context. In past cases evaluating injunctions restricting speech, we have relied upon such general principles while also seeking to ensure that the injunction was no broader than necessary to achieve its desired goals. Our close attention to the fit between the objectives of an injunction and the restrictions it imposes on speech is consistent with the general rule, quite apart from First Amendment considerations, "that injunctive relief should be no more burdensome to the defendants than necessary to provide complete relief to the plaintiffs." Accordingly, when evaluating a content-neutral injunction, we think that our standard time, place, and manner analysis is not sufficiently rigorous. We must ask instead whether the challenged provisions of the injunction burden no more speech than necessary to serve a significant government interest.

JUSTICE SCALIA contends that precedent compels the application of strict scrutiny in this case. JUSTICE SCALIA fails to cite a single case, and we are aware of none, in which we have applied this standard to a content-neutral injunction. He cites a number of cases in which we have struck down, with little or no elaboration, prior restraints on free expression. As we have explained, however, we do not believe that this injunction constitutes a prior restraint, and we therefore believe that the "heavy presumption" against its constitutionality does not obtain here.

We begin with the 36-foot buffer zone. We have noted a distinction between the type of focused picketing banned from the buffer zone and the type of

[2] Not all injunctions which may incidentally affect expression are "prior restraints" in the sense that that term was used in *New York Times Co.* Here petitioners are not prevented from expressing their message in any one of several different ways; they are simply prohibited from expressing it within the 36-foot buffer zone. Moreover, the injunction was issued not because of the content of petitioners' expression, as was the case in *New York Times Co.*, but because of their prior unlawful conduct.

generally disseminated communication that cannot be completely banned in public places, such as handbilling and solicitation. Here the picketing is directed primarily at patients and staff of the clinic.

The need for a complete buffer zone near the clinic entrances and driveway may be debatable, but some deference must be given to the state court's familiarity with the facts and the background of the dispute between the parties even under our heightened review. Moreover, one of petitioners' witnesses during the evidentiary hearing before the state court conceded that the buffer zone was narrow enough to place petitioners at a distance of no greater than 10 to 12 feet from cars approaching and leaving the clinic. Protesters standing across the narrow street from the clinic can still be seen and heard from the clinic parking lots. We also bear in mind the fact that the state court originally issued a much narrower injunction, providing no buffer zone, and that this order did not succeed in protecting access to the clinic. The failure of the first order to accomplish its purpose may be taken into consideration in evaluating the constitutionality of the broader order. On balance, we hold that the 36-foot buffer zone around the clinic entrances and driveway burdens no more speech than necessary to accomplish the governmental interest at stake.

We hold that the limited noise restrictions imposed by the state court order burden no more speech than necessary to ensure the health and well-being of the patients at the clinic. The First Amendment does not demand that patients at a medical facility undertake Herculean efforts to escape the cacophony of political protests. "If overamplified loudspeakers assault the citizenry, government may turn them down." That is what the state court did here, and we hold that its action was proper.

The same, however, cannot be said for the "images observable" provision of the state court's order. This broad prohibition on all "images observable" burdens more speech than necessary to achieve the purpose of limiting threats to clinic patients or their families. Similarly, if the blanket ban on "images observable" was intended to reduce the level of anxiety and hypertension suffered by the patients inside the clinic, it would still fail. The only plausible reason a patient would be bothered by "images observable" inside the clinic would be if the patient found the expression contained in such images disagreeable. But it is much easier for the clinic to pull its curtains than for a patient to stop up her ears, and no more is required to avoid seeing placards through the windows of the clinic. This provision of the injunction violates the First Amendment.

The state court ordered that petitioners refrain from physically approaching any person seeking services of the clinic "unless such person indicates a desire to communicate" in an area within 300 feet of the clinic. The state court was attempting to prevent clinic patients and staff from being "stalked" or "shadowed" by the petitioners as they approached the clinic.

But it is difficult, indeed, to justify a prohibition on all uninvited approaches of persons seeking the services of the clinic, regardless of how peaceful the contact may be, without burdening more speech than necessary to prevent intimidation and to ensure access to the clinic. Absent evidence that the protesters' speech is independently proscribable (i.e., "fighting words" or threats), or is so infused with violence as to be indistinguishable from a threat of physical harm, this provision cannot stand. "As a general matter, we have indicated that in public debate our own citizens must tolerate insulting, and even outrageous, speech in order to provide adequate breathing space to the freedoms protected by the First Amendment." *Boos v. Barry*. The "consent" requirement alone invalidates this provision; it burdens more speech than is necessary to prevent intimidation and to ensure access to the clinic.

The final substantive regulation challenged by petitioners relates to a prohibition against picketing, demonstrating, or using sound amplification equipment within 300 feet of the residences of clinic staff. The prohibition also covers impeding access to streets that provide the sole access to streets on which those residences are located. The same analysis applies to the use of sound amplification equipment here as that discussed above: the government may simply demand that petitioners turn down the volume if the protests overwhelm the neighborhood.

As for the picketing, our prior decision upholding a law banning targeted residential picketing remarked on the unique nature of the home, as "the last citadel of the tired, the weary, and the sick." *Frisby*. But the 300-foot zone around the residences in this case is much larger than the zone provided for in the ordinance which we approved in *Frisby*. [T]he 300-foot zone would ban "general marching through residential neighborhoods, or even walking a route in front of an entire block of houses." *Ibid.* The record before us does not contain sufficient justification for this broad a ban on picketing; it appears that a limitation on the time, duration of picketing, and number of pickets outside a smaller zone could have accomplished the desired result.

In sum, we uphold the noise restrictions and the 36-foot buffer zone around the clinic entrances and driveway because they burden no more speech than necessary to eliminate the unlawful conduct targeted by the state court's injunction. We strike down as unconstitutional the 36-foot buffer zone as applied to the private property to the north and west of the clinic, the "images observable" provision, the 300-foot no-approach zone around the clinic, and the 300-foot buffer zone around the residences, because these provisions sweep more broadly than necessary to accomplish the permissible goals of the injunction.

JUSTICE STEVENS, concurring in part and dissenting in part.

I agree with the Court that a different standard governs First Amendment challenges to generally applicable legislation than the standard that measures such challenges to judicial remedies for proven wrongdoing. Unlike the Court, however, I believe that injunctive relief should be judged by a more lenient standard than legislation. As the Court notes, legislation is imposed on an entire community, regardless of individual culpability. By contrast, injunctions apply solely to an individual or a limited group of individuals who, by engaging in illegal conduct, have been judicially deprived of some liberty — the normal consequence of illegal activity. Given this distinction, a statute prohibiting demonstrations within 36 feet of an abortion clinic would probably violate the First Amendment, but an injunction directed at a limited group of persons who have engaged in unlawful conduct in a similar zone might well be constitutional.

I conclude that, under the circumstances of this case, the prohibition against "physically approaching" in the 300-foot zone around the clinic withstands petitioners' First Amendment challenge. [JUSTICE STEVENS concluded that the other provisions of the injunction were not properly before the Court.]

JUSTICE SCALIA, with whom JUSTICE KENNEDY and JUSTICE THOMAS join, concurring in the judgment in part and dissenting in part.

The judgment in today's case has an appearance of moderation and Solomonic wisdom, upholding as it does some portions of the injunction while disallowing others. That appearance is deceptive. The entire injunction in this case departs so far from the established course of our jurisprudence that in any other context it would have been regarded as a candidate for summary reversal. But the context here is abortion. Today the ad hoc nullification machine claims its latest, greatest, and most surprising victim: the First Amendment.

Because I believe that the judicial creation of a 36-foot zone in which only a particular group, which had broken no law, cannot exercise its rights of speech, assembly, and association, and the judicial enactment of a noise prohibition, applicable to that group and that group alone, are profoundly at odds with our First Amendment precedents and traditions, I dissent.

The Court creates, brand-new for this abortion-related case, an additional standard that is (supposedly) "somewhat more stringent," than intermediate scrutiny, yet not as "rigorous," as strict scrutiny. The Court does not give this new standard a name, but perhaps we could call it intermediate-intermediate scrutiny. [A] restriction upon speech imposed by injunction (whether nominally content based or nominally content neutral) is at least as deserving of strict scrutiny as a statutory, content-based restriction.

That is so for several reasons: The danger of content-based statutory restrictions upon speech is that they may be designed and used precisely to suppress the ideas in question rather than to achieve any other proper governmental aim. But that same danger exists with injunctions. Although a speech-restricting injunction may not attack content as content, it lends itself just as readily to the targeted suppression of particular ideas. The proceedings before us here illustrate well enough what I mean. The injunction was sought against a single-issue advocacy group by persons and organizations with a business or social interest in suppressing that group's point of view.

The second reason speech-restricting injunctions are at least as deserving of strict scrutiny is obvious enough: they are the product of individual judges rather than of legislatures — and often of judges who have been chagrined by prior disobedience of their orders. The right to free speech should not lightly be placed within the control of a single man or woman. And the third reason is that the injunction is a much more powerful weapon than a statute, and so should be subjected to greater safeguards. Normally, when injunctions are enforced through contempt proceedings, only the defense of factual innocence is available. The collateral bar rule of *Walker v. Birmingham* eliminates the defense that the injunction itself was unconstitutional. Thus, persons subject to a speech-restricting injunction who have not the money or not the time to lodge an immediate appeal face a Hobson's choice: they must remain silent, since if they speak their First Amendment rights are no defense in subsequent contempt proceedings. This is good reason to require the strictest standard for issuance of such orders.

Finally, I turn to the Court's application of the second part of its test: whether the provisions of the injunction "burden no more speech than necessary" to serve the significant interest protected.

This test seems to me amply and obviously satisfied with regard to the noise restriction that the Court approves. With regard to the 36-foot speech-free zone, however, it seems to me just as obvious that the test which the Court sets for itself has not been met.

Assuming a "significant state interest" of the sort cognizable for injunction purposes (i.e., one protected by a law that has been or is threatened to be violated) in both (1) keeping pedestrians off the paved portion of Dixie Way, and (2) enabling cars to cross the public sidewalk at the clinic's driveways without having to slow down or come to even a "momentary" stop, there are surely a number of ways to protect those interests short of banishing the entire protest demonstration from the 36-foot zone. For starters, the Court could have (for the first time) ordered the demonstrators to stay out of the street (the original injunction did not remotely require that). It could have limited the number of demonstrators permitted on the clinic side of Dixie Way. And it could have forbidden the pickets to walk on the driveways.

But I need not engage in such precise analysis, since the Court itself admits that the requirement is not to be taken seriously. "The need for a complete buffer zone," it says, "may be debatable, but some deference must be given to the state court's familiarity with the facts and the background of the dispute between the parties even under our heightened review." In application, in other words, the "burden no more speech than is necessary" test has become an "arguably burden no more speech than is necessary" test. This renders the Court's intermediate-intermediate scrutiny not only no more stringent than plain old intermediate scrutiny, but considerably less stringent.

What we have decided seems to be, and will be reported by the media as, an abortion case. But it will go down in the lawbooks, it will be cited, as a free-speech injunction case — and the damage its novel principles produce will be considerable. The proposition that injunctions against speech are subject to a standard indistinguishable from (unless perhaps more lenient in its application than) the "intermediate scrutiny" standard we have used for "time, place, and manner" legislative restrictions; the notion that injunctions against speech need not be closely tied to any violation of law, but may simply implement sound social policy; and the practice of accepting trial-court conclusions permitting injunctions without considering whether those conclusions are supported by any findings of fact — these latest by-products of our abortion jurisprudence ought to give all friends of liberty great concern.

NOTES

1. *Content neutrality.* Was the injunction in *Madsen* content-based? Would its prohibitions have been more content-based had they come in the form of a statute? The Freedom of Access to Clinic Entrances Act of 1994, 18 U.S.C. § 248, authorizes federal injunctive relief against anyone who "by force or threat of force or by physical obstruction, intentionally injures, intimidates or interferes with or attempts to injure, intimidate or interfere with any person because that person is or has been, . . . obtaining or providing reproductive health services." Should this statute be found unconstitutional as a content-based regulation?

2. *Intermediate scrutiny.* The Court suggests that "a somewhat more stringent" standard of review is employed for review of injunctions than of statutes. Why should this be so? Compare the discussion of prior restraints and the collateral bar rule, p. 1039.

3. *Appellate review of injunctions.* For the most part, the Court in *Madsen* employs a narrow, fact-specific approach in reaching its decision. Are there any drawbacks to such an approach? But Justice Scalia takes the Court to task for giving deference to the trial court on the need for a buffer zone. What difference does it really make whether the Court engages in its own factual determinations or accepts the facts of the trial court? What are the future dangers to free speech to which Justice Scalia alludes?

4. *Schenck v. Pro-Choice Network of Western New York,* 519 U.S. 357 (1997). The Court in this decision elaborated upon *Madsen*. Abortion doctors and clinics sought to enjoin defendant individuals and organizations from blockading the clinics or engaging in other illegal conduct. The clinics had been subjected to numerous large-scale blockades in which protestors marched, stood, knelt, sat, or lay in clinic parking lot driveways and doorways, blocking or hindering cars from entering the lots and patients and clinic employees from entering the clinic. In addition, smaller protesting groups had sought to stop or disrupt clinic operations by, among other things, surrounding, crowding, jostling, grabbing, pushing, shoving, yelling and spitting at women entering the clinics. Local police were apparently unable to respond effectively to the protestors. On the sidewalks outside the clinics, protestors called "sidewalk counselors" used similar methods to dissuade women headed toward the clinics from having abortions.

The federal district court issued a temporary restraining order and subsequently a preliminary injunction, banning demonstrations within fifteen feet of doorways, parking lot entrances, and driveways of clinics ("fixed buffer zones"), or within fifteen feet of any person or vehicle seeking access to or leaving the clinics ("floating buffer zones"). The injunction also allowed two sidewalk counselors inside the buffer zones, but required them to "cease and desist" their efforts if asked by the counselor to do so.

Chief Justice Rehnquist, speaking for the Court, initially concluded that "[g]iven the factual similarity between this case and *Madsen*, we conclude that the governmental interests underlying the injunction in *Madsen* ensuring public safety and order, promoting the free flow of traffic on streets and sidewalks, protecting property rights, and protecting a woman's freedom to seek pregnancy-related services also underlie the injunction here, and in combination are certainly significant enough to justify an appropriately tailored injunction to secure unimpeded physical access to the clinics."

Nevertheless, the Court struck down the floating buffer zones, "because they burden more speech than is necessary to serve the relevant governmental interests. The floating buffer zones prevent defendants—except for the sidewalk counselors, while they are tolerated by the targeted individual—from communicating a message from a normal conversational distance or handing leaflets to people entering or leaving the clinics who are walking on the public sidewalks." The Court held "that because this broad prohibition on speech 'floats,' it cannot be sustained on the record." In certain instances, the Court noted, the floating buffer zone might result in pushing the demonstrator off the sidewalk and into the street. The Court found that the zones' "lack of certainty leads to a substantial risk that much more speech will be burdened than the injunction by its terms prohibits. That is, attempts to stand 15 feet from someone entering or leaving a clinic and to communicate a message—certainly protected on the face of the injunction—will be hazardous if one wishes to remain in compliance with the injunction." The Court suggested that "there may well be ways to both effect separation and yet provide certainty," but failed to elaborate.

The Court, however, upheld the injunction's imposition of fixed buffer zones around the doorways, driveways, and driveway entrances: "These buffer zones are necessary to ensure that people and vehicles trying to enter or exit the clinic property or clinic parking lots can do so. As in *Madsen*, the record shows that protestors purposely or effectively blocked or hindered people from entering and exiting the clinic doorways, from driving cars to and away from clinic entrances, and from dividing in or out of clinic parking lots. Based on this conduct the District Court was entitled to conclude that the only way to ensure access was to move back the demonstrators away from the doorways and parking lot entrances."

The Court rejected the challenge to the "cease and desist" provision limiting the exception for sidewalk counselors: "We doubt that the District Court's reason for including that provision—to protect the right of the people approaching and entering the facilities to be left alone—accurately reflects our First Amendment jurisprudence in this area. *Madsen* sustained an injunction designed to secure physical access to the clinic, but not on the basis of any generalized right to be let alone." However, the Court added that "the entire exception for sidewalk counselors was an effort to enhance petitioners' speech rights, and the 'cease and desist' limitation must be assessed in that light."

Justice Scalia, concurring in part and dissenting in part, criticized the majority's review of the district court's injunction: "Instead of evaluating the injunction before us on the basis of the reasons for which it was issued, the Court today postulates other reasons that might have justified it and pronounces those never-determined reasons adequate. This is contrary to the settled practice governing appellate review of injunctions." He noted that "[t]he Court candidly concedes that the nonexistent right to be left alone' underlay the District Court's imposition of the cease-and-desist provision. It appears not to grasp, however, the decisive import of this concession." He found that by basing its conclusion on the constitutionality of the injunction "on the basis of what the issuing court might reasonably have found as to necessity, rather than on the basis of what it in fact found," the majority was making "a destructive inroad upon First Amendment law."

5. *Hill v. Colorado,* 530 U.S. 703 (2000). As a follow-up to injunctions attempting to protect abortion clinics from harassment, some states passed statutes for the same purpose. In an opinion by Justice Stevens, the Court upheld a statute of this type against a facial challenge. "Colo. Rev. Stat. § 18-9-122(3) makes it unlawful" for any person within 100 feet of a health care facility's entrance "to 'knowingly approach' within 8 feet of another person, without that person's consent," in order to pass " 'a leaflet or handbill to, displa[y] a sign to, or engag[e] in oral protest, education, or counseling with [that] person.'&thi;

To the majority, the case involved a simple balancing of the rights of speakers with the interests of unwilling listeners. Challengers attempted to portray the statute as creating a "floating zone" of privacy around the unwilling listener, thus forcing the speaker to move to avoid that zone. The Court, however, pointed out that this was not the case. "Although the statute prohibits speakers from approaching unwilling listeners, it does not require a standing speaker to move away from anyone passing by. Nor does it place any restriction on the content of any message that anyone may wish to communicate to anyone else, either inside or outside the regulated areas." As a content-neutral time, place, and manner protection of the privacy of persons entering medical facilities, the statute passed facial muster. The majority also rejected arguments of vagueness, overbreadth, and prior restraint. On the latter point, the statute does not address any particular person or message but sets out a standard of conduct for all.

Justice Scalia, joined by Justice Thomas, dissented:

> The Court today concludes that a regulation requiring speakers on the public thoroughfares bordering medical facilities to speak from a distance of eight feet is "not a regulation of speech," but "a regulation of the places where some speech may occur," and that a regulation directed to only certain categories of speech (protest, education, and counseling) is not "content-based." For these reasons, it says, the regulation is immune from the exacting scrutiny we apply to content-based suppression of speech in the public forum. The Court then determines that the regulation survives the less rigorous scrutiny afforded content-neutral time, place, and manner restrictions because it is narrowly tailored to serve a government interest protection of citizens' "right to be let alone" that has explicitly been disclaimed by the State, probably for the reason that, as a basis for suppressing peaceful private expression, it is patently incompatible with the guarantees of the First Amendment. None of these remarkable conclusions should come as a surprise. What is before us, after all, is a speech regulation directed against the opponents of abortion, and it therefore enjoys the benefit of the "ad hoc nullification machine" that the Court has set in motion to push aside whatever doctrines of constitutional law stand in the way of that highly favored practice. *Madsen v. Women's Health Center, Inc.*, 512 U. S. 753, 785 (1994) (Scalia, J., concurring in judgment in part and dissenting in part). Having deprived abortion opponents of the political right to persuade the electorate that abortion should be restricted by law, the Court today

> continues and expands its assault upon their individual right to persuade women contemplating abortion that what they are doing is wrong. Because, like the rest of our abortion jurisprudence, today's decision is in stark contradiction of the constitutional principles we apply in all other contexts, I dissent.

Justice Kennedy also dissented: "For the first time, the Court approves a law which bars a private citizen from passing a message, in a peaceful manner and on a profound moral issue, to a fellow citizen on a public sidewalk."

[F] SPEECH IN RESTRICTED ENVIRONMENTS

The principles relating to freedom of expression developed thus far are subject to an important caveat. The Court has fashioned exceptions for "special contexts" or "restricted environments," where the ordinary speech-protective rules are either not applied or are applied in a materially different and often greatly diminished fashion. When government controls speech in these restricted environments — speech in the public schools, speech by military personnel, speech in prisons, speech of government employees — it is not imposing generally applicable regulations on civil society. It curtails the speech of only a sector of the public having a special relationship to the government. On the other hand, the speech of millions of people is involved in these special contexts and a significant amount of speech may never be heard in the marketplace of ideas.

Similarly, there are occasions when government does not so much regulate the marketplace of ideas as participate in the marketplace. Government may itself speak or it may subsidize the speech of others. It is not surprising that when it acts in this arguably nonregulatory fashion, government will claim the prerogative of deciding on what it will say or not say, what views it will select to support or not support. But government intervention in the marketplace, into political dialogue, can markedly skew the debate. Given the reliance on government subsidies, there is the concern that government can influence or determine the speech of grant recipients and ultimately of what ideas we receive and don't receive.

[1] Student Speech

Application of free speech protection to speech in the academic forum presents a serious dilemma: On the one hand, schools are places where those in authority must be in a position to assure an environment free from unwanted distractions, so the goals of education may be achieved. On the other hand, students in an academic environment are presumably being trained to assume roles as functioning citizens in society, so it might be unwise to ignore one of the primary means by which individuals develop, both intellectually and socially. See the argument fashioned in Thomas Dienes & Annemargaret Connolly, *When Students Speak: Judicial Review in the Academic Marketplace*, 7 YALE L. & POL'Y REV. 343, 351 (1989): "[T]o shelter children from the marketplace by exposing them only to government-approved ideas may frustrate, if not destroy, a child's ability to develop as a rational decision-maker."

The Supreme Court initially appeared quite protective of the free speech right in the academic environment. In *West Virginia State Board of Education v. Barnette,* 319 U.S. 624 (1943), the Court held that school children could not be required to participate in a salute to the flag. In *Tinker v. Des Moines School District,* 393 U.S. 503 (1969), the Court held that students had a first amendment right to wear black arm bands in school as a protest against the Vietnam War. In so holding, Justice Fortas, speaking for the Court, stated:

> First Amendment rights, applied in light of the special characteristics of the school environment, are available to teachers and students. It can hardly be argued that either students or teachers shed their constitutional rights to freedom of speech or expression at the schoolhouse gate. In order for the State in the person of school officials to justify prohibition of a particular expression of opinion, it must be able to show that its action was caused by something more than a mere desire to avoid the discomfort and unpleasantness that always accompany an unpopular viewpoint. [A student] may express his opinions, . . . if he does so without "materially and substantially interfer[ing] with the requirements of appropriate discipline in the operation of the school" and without colliding with the rights of others.

The exact reach of the decision is unclear, however, because the Court also deemed relevant the fact that "the school authorities did not purport to prohibit the wearing of all symbols of political or controversial significance." Thus, there may well have been an underlying fear on the part of the Court that what was actually involved was viewpoint regulation.

In *Board of Education v. Pico,* 457 U.S. 853 (1982), the Court, in a plurality decision, found that local school boards may not remove books from school libraries simply because they dislike the ideas contained in those books.

The Court's view appeared to become more restrictive of free speech rights in the academic forum in *Bethel School District No. 43 v. Fraser,* 478 U.S. 675 (1986). There the Court, in an opinion by Chief Justice Burger, held that the First Amendment does not prevent a school district from disciplining a high school student for giving a lewd speech at a high school assembly. *Tinker* was distinguished, because of "[t]he marked distinction between the political 'message' of the armbands in *Tinker* and the sexual content of respondent's speech in this case." While conceding the existence of *Cohen v. California,* the Court reasoned that "[i]t does not follow, however, that simply because the use of an offensive form of expression may not be prohibited to adults making what the speaker considers a political point, that same latitude must be permitted to children in a public school."

HAZELWOOD SCHOOL DISTRICT v. KUHLMEIER
484 U.S. 260, 108 S. CT. 562, 98 L. ED. 2D 592 (1988)

JUSTICE WHITE delivered the opinion of the Court.

This case concerns the extent to which educators may exercise editorial control over the contents of a high school newspaper produced as part of the school's journalism curriculum. Petitioners are the Hazelwood School District in St. Louis County, Missouri; various school officials; Robert Eugene Reynolds, the principal of Hazelwood East High School, and Howard Emerson, a teacher in the school district. Respondents are three former Hazelwood East students who were staff members of SPECTRUM, the school newspaper. They contend that school officials violated their First Amendment rights by deleting two pages of articles from the May 13, 1983, issue of SPECTRUM.

Spectrum was written and edited by the Journalism II class at Hazelwood East. The Board of Education allocated funds from its annual budget for printing, [supplies, textbooks, and a portion of the journalism teacher's salary — supplemented by some proceeds from sales of the newspaper]. The Journalism II course was taught by Robert Stergos for most of the 1982-1983 academic year. Stergos left Hazelwood East to take a job in private industry on April 29, 1983, when the May 13 edition of SPECTRUM was nearing completion, and petitioner Emerson took his place as newspaper adviser for the remaining weeks of the term.

The practice at Hazelwood East during the spring 1983 semester was for the journalism teacher to submit page proofs of each SPECTRUM issue to Principal Reynolds for his review prior to publication. On May 10, Emerson delivered the proofs of the May 13 edition to Reynolds, who objected to two of the articles scheduled to appear in that edition. One of the stories described three Hazelwood East students' experiences with pregnancy; the other discussed the impact of divorce on students at the school. Reynolds was concerned that, although the pregnancy story used false names "to keep the identity of these girls a secret," the pregnant students still might be identifiable from the text. He also believed that the article's references to sexual activity and birth control were inappropriate for some of the younger students at the school. In addition, Reynolds was concerned that a student identified by name in the divorce story had complained that her father "wasn't spending enough time with my mom, my sister and I" prior to the divorce, "was always out of town on business or out late playing cards with the guys," and "always argued about everything" with her mother. Reynolds believed that the student's parents should have been given an opportunity to respond to these remarks or to consent to their publication. He was unaware that Emerson had deleted the student's name from the final version of the article.

Reynolds believed that there was no time to make the necessary changes in the stories before the scheduled press run and that the newspaper would not appear before the end of the school year if printing were delayed to any significant extent. He concluded that his only options under the circumstances were to publish a four-page newspaper instead of the planned six-page newspaper, eliminating the two pages on which the offending stories appeared, or to publish no newspaper at all. Accordingly, he directed Emerson to withhold from publication the two pages containing the stories on pregnancy and divorce.[1] He informed his superiors of the decision, and they concurred.

[1] The two pages deleted from the newspaper also contained articles on teenage marriage, runaways, and juvenile delinquents, as well as a general article on teenage pregnancy. Reynolds testified that he had no objection to these articles and that they were deleted only because they appeared on the same pages as the two objectionable articles.

We deal first with the question whether SPECTRUM may appropriately be characterized as a forum for public expression. The public schools do not possess all of the attributes of streets, parks, and other traditional public forums that "time out of mind, have been used for purposes of assembly, communicating thoughts between citizens, and discussing public questions." Hence, school facilities may be deemed to be public forums only if school authorities have "by policy or by practice" opened those facilities "for indiscriminate use by the general public," or by some segment of the public, such as student organizations. If the facilities have instead been reserved for other intended purposes, "communicative or otherwise," then no public forum has been created, and school officials may impose reasonable restrictions on the speech of students, teachers, and other members of the school community.

In sum, the evidence relied upon by the Court of Appeals fails to demonstrate the "clear intent to create a public forum" that existed in cases in which we found public forums to have been created. School officials did not evince either "by policy or by practice" any intent to open the pages of SPECTRUM to "indiscriminate use" by its student reporters and editors, or by the student body generally. Instead, they "reserve[d] the forum for its intended purpos[e]," as a supervised learning experience for journalism students. Accordingly, school officials were entitled to regulate the contents of SPECTRUM in any reasonable manner. It is this standard, rather than our decision in *Tinker*, that governs this case.

The question whether the First Amendment requires a school to tolerate particular student speech — the question that we addressed in *Tinker* — is different from the question whether the First Amendment requires a school affirmatively to promote particular student speech. [A] school may in its capacity as publisher of a school newspaper or producer of a school play "disassociate itself," *Fraser*, not only from speech that would "substantially interfere with [its] work . . .or impinge upon the rights of other students," *Tinker*, but also from speech that is, for example, ungrammatical, poorly written, inadequately researched, biased or prejudiced, vulgar or profane, or unsuitable for immature audiences. A school must be able to set high standards for the student speech that is disseminated under its auspices — standards that may be higher than those demanded by some newspaper publishers or theatrical producers in the "real" world — and may refuse to disseminate student speech that does not meet those standards. Otherwise, the schools would be unduly constrained from fulfilling their role as "a principal instrument in awakening the child to cultural values, in preparing him for later professional training, and in helping him to adjust normally to his environment." *Brown v. Board of Education*.

Accordingly, we conclude that the standard articulated in *Tinker* for determining when a school may punish student expression need not also be the standard for determining when a school may refuse to lend its name and resources to the dissemination of student expression. Instead, we hold that educators do not offend the First Amendment by exercising editorial control over the style and content of student speech in school-sponsored expressive activities so long as their actions are reasonably related to legitimate pedagogical concerns.

In sum, we cannot reject as unreasonable Principal Reynolds' conclusion that neither the pregnancy article nor the divorce article was suitable for publication in SPECTRUM. Accordingly, no violation of First Amendment rights occurred.

JUSTICE BRENNAN, with whom JUSTICE MARSHALL and JUSTICE BLACKMUN join, dissenting.

The mere fact of school sponsorship does not, as the Court suggests, license such thought control in the high school, whether through school suppression of disfavored viewpoints or through official assessment of topic sensitivity. The former would constitute unabashed and unconstitutional viewpoint discrimination as well as an impermissible infringement of the students' "right to receive information and ideas." Just as a school board may not purge its state-funded library of all books that "offen[d] [its] social, political and moral tastes," school officials may not, out of like motivation, discriminatorily excise objectionable ideas from a student publication. The State's prerogative to dissolve the student newspaper entirely (or to limit its subject matter) no more entitles it to dictate which viewpoints students may express on its pages, than the State's prerogative to close down the schoolhouse entitles it to prohibit the nondisruptive expression of antiwar sentiment within its gates.

NOTES

1. Tinker *today.* Erwin Chemerinsky, *Students Do Leave Their First Amendment Rights at the Schoolhouse Gates: What's Left of Tinker?*, 48 DRAKE L. REV. 527, 542 (2000), argues that "[I]t is appropriate to see *Bethel* and *Hazelwood*, in their specific holdings and their general approach, as being limited to public schools' ability to regulate speech in official programs and courses. Therefore, even in light of *Bethel* and *Hazelwood*, there remains First Amendment protection of student speech in non-curricular areas where there is no evidence of disruption of school activities." But he adds that while the holding of *Tinker* may persist, "the *Tinker* majority's approach to student speech is no longer followed. The Court has made it clear that it views schools as authoritarian institutions and it therefore will defer to school officials in student speech cases." *Id.* at 541.

2. *Speech in the military.* In what ways do the competing interests differ when the "restricted environment" is the military, rather than the schools? Which situation provides a stronger basis for restricting free speech rights? Consider C. Thomas Dienes, *When the First Amendment is Not Preferred: The Military and Other "Special Contexts,"* 56 U. CINN. L. REV. 779, 816–17 (1988): "[F]irst Amendment autonomy concerns are important to the military society. The ability to make choices and the need for educated, well-developed persons is regarded by the military itself as critical in the modern army. And the capacity for effective decision-making is said to be a necessary ingredient for being a good officer. Stagnation born by excessive conformity would seem an especially serious concern in the military bureaucracy. From either an intrinsic or an instrumentalist perspective, it is difficult to believe that the interests of the military society are served by inhibiting the development of those skills and capacities required for full participation in any society."

Compare the counter-argument made in *Chappell v. Wallace,* 462 U.S. 296, 300 (1983): "[I]n the civilian life of a democracy many command few; in the military, however, this is reversed, for military necessity makes demands on its personnel 'without counterpart in civilian life.' " Should a distinction be drawn between the level of protection given to the right of members of the military to speak on the one hand and to the right of others to communicate to the military? Should the issue of free speech protection for the military necessarily be viewed as an all-or-nothing choice?

3. ***Free speech and government employment.*** To what extent are the free speech issues in student speech and military speech cases analogous to the free speech implications that arise from the penalization of a government employee for engaging in expression?

***Pickering v. Board of Education,* 391 U.S. 563 (1963).** The Court overturned the Board's dismissal of a teacher for publishing in a newspaper a letter criticizing the Board's allocation of school funds between educational and athletic programs and the methods used to inform the school district's taxpayers of the real reasons why additional tax revenues were being sought. The letter contained information which was false. "The theory that public employment which may be denied altogether may be subjected to any conditions, regardless of how unreasonable, has been uniformly rejected [quoting *Keyishian v. Board of Regents,* 385 U.S. 589, 605–06 (1967)]. At the same time, it cannot be gainsaid that the State has interests as an employer in regulating the speech of its employees that differ significantly from those it possesses in connection with regulation of the speech of the citizenry in general." In striking a balance in this case, the Court found that the teacher could not be dismissed absent a showing of knowledge of falsity or reckless disregard of truth or falsity.

***Connick v. Myers,* 461 U.S. 138 (1983).** The Court restricted the balancing test in *Pickering* to "speech on a matter of public concern." On the other hand, "[w]hen employee expression cannot be fairly considered as relating to any matter of political, social, or other concern to the community, government officials should enjoy wide latitude in managing their offices, without intrusive oversight by the judiciary in the name of the [First Amendment]." Justice White, for the Court, explained that the Court was not saying that private employee speech was a category of low-value speech.

> We hold only that when a public employee speaks not as a citizen upon matters of public concern, but instead as an employee upon matters only of personal interest, absent the most unusual circumstances, a federal court is not the appropriate forum in which to review the wisdom of a personnel decision taken by a public agency allegedly in reaction to the employee's behavior. Our responsibility is to ensure that citizens are not deprived of fundamental rights by virtue of working for the government; this does not require a grant of immunity for employee grievances not afforded by the First Amendment to those who do not work for the state.

Justice White said that "[whether an employee's speech addressed a matter of public concern must be determined by the content, form, and context of a given statement, as revealed by the whole record."

***Rankin v. McPherson,* 483 U.S. 378 (1987).** The Court held that a clerical employee in a county constable's office could not constitutionally be discharged for remarking, after hearing of an attempt on the life of the President, "if they go for him again, I hope they get him." After concluding that the speech in question involved "a matter of public concern," the Court applied the *Pickering* analysis, requiring the state to justify the discharge. "While McPherson's statement was made at the workplace," the Court reasoned, "there is no evidence that it interfered with the efficient functioning of the office." The Court added that "[n]or was there any danger that McPherson had discredited the office by making her statement in public."

***Waters v. Churchill,* 511 U.S. 661 (1994).** Justice O'Connor focused on why a government is given a freer hand in controlling employee speech that in regulating the speech of the general public. "The key to First Amendment analysis of government employment decisions, is this: the government's interest in achieving its goals as effectively and efficiently as possible is elevated from a relatively subordinate interest when it acts as sovereign to a significant one when it acts as employer. The government cannot restrict the speech of the public at large just in the name of efficiency. But where the government is employing someone for the very purpose of effectively achieving its goals, such restrictions may well be appropriate."

***City of San Diego v. Roe,* 543 U.S. 77 (2004).** The Court held, *per curiam*, that the First Amendment did not protect a police officer who was terminated for selling videotapes of himself engaging in sexually explicit acts. The First Amendment was not violated even though the expression was not an internal workplace grievance, took place while he was off-duty and away from the workplace and was unrelated to his employment. The police officer's expression did not fall within the principle of *United States v. Treasury Employees*, 513 U.S. 454, 465 (1995): "when government employees speak or write on their own time on topics unrelated to their employment, the speech can have First Amendment protection, absent some governmental justification 'far stronger than mere speculation' in regulating it." In the present case, the police department "demonstrated legitimate and substantial interests of its own that were compromised by his speech." The officer used his uniform, referred to his law enforcement duties, and engaged in a "parody," bringing "the mission of the employer and the professionalism of its officers into serious disrepute." Nor was the officer's expression protected under *Pickering/Connick* since the speech here did not involve a matter of public concern. The officer's activities "did nothing to inform the public about any aspect of the SDPD's functioning or operation." Instead "Roe's expression was widely broadcast, linked to his offcial status as a police officer, and designed to exploit his employer's image."

[2] Publicly Funded Speech

Professor Robert Post, *Subsidized Speech,* 106 YALE L.J. 151 (1996), argues that "[s]ubsidized speech challenges two fundamental assumptions of ordinary First Amendment doctrine. It renders uncertain the status of speakers, forcing us to determine whether speakers should be characterized as independent participants in the formation of public opinion or instead as instrumentalities of the government. And it renders uncertain the status of government action forcing us to determine whether subsidies should be characterized as government regulations imposed on persons or instead as a form of government participation in the marketplace of ideas."

***Rust v. Sullivan*, 500 U.S. 173 (1991).** The Court 5-4 rejected a facial challenge to Department of Health and Human Services (HHS) regulations limiting the ability of Title X fund recipients to engage in abortion related activities. Title X, providing for federal family planning project grants to public and nonprofit private agencies, provides that: "none of the funds appropriate under this subchapter shall be used in programs where abortion is a method of family planning." While this provision had been interpreted only to prohibit the performance of abortions, in 1988 the Secretary promulgated new regulations attaching three principal conditions to Title X grants. First, the regulations provided that a "Title X project may not provide counseling concerning the use of abortion as a method of family planning or provide referral for abortion as a method of family planning." The project is prohibited from referring a pregnant woman to an abortion provider, even upon specific request. One permissible response to such an inquiry is that "the project does not consider abortion an appropriate method of family planning and therefore does not counsel or refer for abortion." Second, the new regulations broadly prohibited Title X projects from engaging in activities that "encourage, promote or advocate abortion as a method of family planning." Third, the regulations required that Title X projects to be structured so that they are "physically and financially separate" from prohibited abortion activities. To be deemed physically and financially separate, "a Title X project must have an objective integrity and independence from prohibited activities. Mere bookkeeping separation of Title X funds from other monies is not sufficient."

Chief Justice Rehnquist, for the Court, held that the agency's interpretation of the statute was a "permissible construction" given its language and legislative history. He then turned to the petitioner's argument that the regulations violated the First Amendment by impermissibly discriminating on the basis of viewpoint since they required that recipients provide information that promotes childbirth while prohibiting all discussion about abortion as a lawful option. The Court rejected the argument.

> There is no question but that the statutory prohibition is constitutional. The Government can, without violating the Constitution, selectively fund a program to encourage certain activities it believes to be in the public interest, without at the same time funding an alternate program which seeks to deal with the problem in another way. In so doing, the Government has not discriminated on the basis of viewpoint; it has merely chosen to fund one activity to the exclusion of the other. The challenged regulations implement the statutory prohibition by prohibiting counseling, referral, and the provision of information regarding abortion as a method of family planning. They are designed to ensure that the limits of the federal program are observed.
>
> To hold that the Government unconstitutionally discriminates on the basis of viewpoint when it chooses to fund a program dedicated

> to advance certain permissible goals, because the program in advancing those goals necessarily discourages alternate goals, would render numerous government programs constitutionally suspect. When Congress established a National Endowment for Democracy to encourage other countries to adopt democratic principles, it was not constitutionally required to fund a program to encourage competing lines of political philosophy such as Communism and Fascism. Petitioners' assertions ultimately boil down to the position that if the government chooses to subsidize one protected right, it must subsidize analogous counterpart rights. But the Court has soundly rejected that proposition. Within far broader limits than petitioners are willing to concede, when the government appropriates public funds to establish a program it is entitled to define the limits of that program.

Chief Justice Rehnquist similarly rejected the petitioner's "unconstitutional conditions" argument that the regulations violated the First Amendment since they conditioned the receipt of Title X finding on surrender of the right to engage in abortion advocacy and counseling.

> [H]ere the government is not denying a benefit to anyone, but is instead simply insisting that public funds be spent for the purposes for which they were authorized. The Secretary's regulations do not force the Title X grantee to give up abortion-related speech; they merely require that the grantee keep such activities separate and distinct from Title X activities. Title X expressly distinguishes between a Title X grantee and a Title X project. The regulations govern the scope of the Title X project's activities, and leave the grantee unfettered in its other activities. The Title X grantee can continue to perform abortions, provide abortion-related services, and engage in abortion advocacy; it simply is required to conduct those activities through programs that are separate and independent from the project that receives Title X funds. In contrast, our "unconstitutional conditions" cases involve situations in which the government has placed a condition on the recipient of the subsidy rather than on a particular program or service, thus effectively prohibiting the recipient from engaging in the protected conduct outside the scope of the federally funded program.
>
> By requiring that the Title X grantee engage in abortion-related activity separately from activity receiving federal funding, Congress has not denied it the right to engage in abortion-related activities. Congress has merely refused to fund such activities out of the public fisc, and the Secretary has simply required a certain degree of separation from the Title X project in order to ensure the integrity of the federally funded program.

But the Court did suggest a caveat:

> This is not to suggest that funding by the Government, even when coupled with the freedom of the fund recipients to speak outside the

> scope of the Government-funded project, is invariably sufficient to justify government control over the content of expression. For example, this Court has recognized that the existence of a Government "subsidy," in the form of Government-owned property, does not justify the restriction of speech in areas that have "been traditionally open to the public for expressive activity," or have been "expressly dedicated to speech activity." Similarly, we have recognized that the university is a traditional sphere of free expression so fundamental to the functioning of our society that the Government's ability to control speech within that sphere by means of conditions attached to the expenditure of Government funds is restricted by the vagueness and overbreadth doctrines of the First Amendment.

Justice Blackmun, joined by Justices Marshall and Stevens, dissented from the Courts disposition of the constitution claims. "Until today, the Court never has upheld viewpoint-based suppression of speech simply because that suppression was a condition upon the acceptance of public funds. Whatever may be the Government's power to condition the receipt of its largess upon the relinquishment of constitutional rights, it surely does not extend to a condition that suppresses the recipient's cherished freedom of speech based solely upon the content or viewpoint of that speech. By refusing to fund those family-planning projects that advocate abortion because they advocate abortion, the Government plainly has targeted a particular viewpoint."

Justice Blackmun also argued:

> By manipulating the content of the doctor/patient dialogue, the Regulations upheld today force each of the petitioners "to be an instrument for fostering public adherence to an ideological point of view [he or she] finds unacceptable." The Court concludes that the challenged Regulations do not violate the First Amendment rights of Title X staff members because any limitation of the employees' freedom of expression is simply a consequence of their decision to accept employment at a federally funded project. But it has never been sufficient to justify an otherwise unconstitutional condition upon public employment that the employee may escape the condition by relinquishing his or her job. It is beyond question "that a government may not require an individual to relinquish rights guaranteed him by the First Amendment as a condition of public employment."
>
> Under the majority's reasoning, the First Amendment could be read to tolerate any governmental restriction upon an employee's speech so long as that restriction is limited to the funded workplace. This is a dangerous proposition, and one the Court has rightly rejected in the past.

***Rosenberger v. Rector and Visitors of University of Virginia*, 515 U.S. 819 (1995).** The Court held unconstitutional a University of Virginia policy excluding religious organizations from its subsidy program for student publications. The subsidy program was held to be a limited public forum and the University was engaged in impermissible viewpoint discrimination. When the

University argued that this case "involves the provision of funds rather than access to public facilities," the Court, per Justice Kennedy, responded.

> When the University determines the content of the education it provides, it is the University speaking, and we have permitted the government to regulate the content of what is or is not expressed when it is the speaker or when it enlists private entities to convey its own message. In the same vein, in *Rust v. Sullivan*, the government did not create a program to encourage private speech but instead used private speakers to transmit specific information pertaining to its own program. We recognized that when the government appropriates public funds to promote a particular policy of its own it is entitled to say what it wished. When the government disburses public funds to private entities to convey a governmental message, it may take legitimate and appropriate steps to ensure that its message is neither garbled nor distorted by the grantee.
>
> It does not follow, however, that viewpoint-based restrictions are proper when the University does not itself speak or subsidizes transmittal of a message it favors but instead expends funds to encourage a diversity of views from private speakers. A holding that the University may not discriminate based on the viewpoint of private persons whose speech it facilities does not restrict the University's own speech, which is controlled by different principles.
>
> The distinction between the University's own favored message and the private speech of students is evident in the case before us. The University declares that the student groups eligible for support are not the University's agents, are not subject to its control, and are not its responsibility. Having offered to pay the third-party contractors on behalf of private speakers who convey their own messages, the University may not silence the expression of selected viewpoints.

Professor Robert Post, *Subsidized Speech*, 106 YALE L.J. at 155, suggests that the Court's point in *Rosenberger* "is that when the state itself speaks, it may adopt a determinate content and viewpoint even 'when it enlists private entities to convey its own message.' But when the state attempts to restrict the independent contributions of citizens to public discourse, even if those contributions are subsidized, First Amendment rules prohibiting content and viewpoint discrimination will apply. The reasoning of *Rosenberger* thus rests on two premises First, speech may be subsidized and yet remain within public discourse; the mere fact of subsidization is not sufficient to justify classifying speech as within or outside public discourse. Second, substantive First Amendment analysis will depend on whether the citizen who speaks is characterized as a public functionary or as an independent participant in public discourse." He argues that "the Court's use of the viewpoint/content distinction, when applied within managerial domains, actually expresses the difference between those restraints on speech that are instrumentally necessary to the attainment of legitimate managerial purpose, and those that are not." *Id.* at 167. Thus, he argues that the inclusion of religious views in *Rosenberger* was based on the conclusion that the discrimination "is irrelevant to any legitimate educational purpose served by the university's grant program." *Id.* In *Rust*, did the Court decide that the government was restricting speech in a "managerial domain" in order to accomplish legitimate managerial ends? Professor Post concludes that "the viewpoint discrimination [in *Rust*] cannot be justified by reference to managerial authority." *Id.* at 174.

NATIONAL ENDOWMENT FOR THE ARTS v. FINLEY
524 U.S. 569, 118 S. CT. 2168, 141 L. ED.2D 500 (1998)

JUSTICE O'CONNOR delivered the opinion of the Court.

The National Foundation on the Arts and Humanities Act, as amended in 1990, requires the Chairperson of the National Endowment for the Arts (NEA) to ensure that "artistic excellence and artistic merit are the criteria by which [grant] applications are judged, taking into consideration general standards of decency and respect for the diverse beliefs and values of the American public." 20 U.S.C. § 954(d)(1). In this case, we review the Court of Appeals' determination that § 954(d)(1), on its face, impermissibly discriminates on the basis of viewpoint and is void for vagueness under the First and Fifth Amendments. We conclude that § 954(d)(1) is facially valid, as it neither inherently interferes with First Amendment rights nor violates constitutional vagueness principles.

Applications for NEA funding are initially reviewed by advisory panels composed of experts in the relevant field of the arts. Under the 1990 Amendments to the enabling statute, those panels must reflect "diverse artistic and cultural points of view" and include "wide geographic, ethnic, and minority representation," as well as "lay individuals who are knowledgeable about the arts." The panels report to the 26-member National Council on the Arts (Council), which, in turn, advises the NEA Chairperson. The Chairperson has the ultimate authority to award grants but may not approve an application as to which the Council has made a negative recommendation.

Since 1965, the NEA has distributed over three billion dollars in grants to individuals and organizations, funding that has served as a catalyst for increased state, corporate, and foundation support for the arts. Congress has recently restricted the availability of federal funding for individual artists, confining grants primarily to qualifying organizations and state arts agencies, and constraining sub-granting. Throughout the NEA's history, only a handful of the agency's roughly 100,000 awards have generated formal complaints about misapplied funds or abuse of the public's trust. Two provocative works, however, prompted public controversy in 1989 and led to congressional revaluation of the NEA's funding priorities and efforts to increase oversight of its grant-making procedures. The Institute of Contemporary Art at the University of Pennsylvania had used $30,000 of a visual arts grant it received from the NEA to fund a 1989 retrospective of photographer Robert Mapplethorpe's work. The exhibit, entitled The Perfect Moment, included homoerotic photographs that several Members of Congress condemned as pornographic. Members also denounced artist Andres Serrano's work Piss Christ, a photograph of a crucifix immersed in urine. Serrano had been awarded a $15,000 grant from the Southeast Center for Contemporary Art, an organization that received NEA support.

When considering the NEA's appropriations for fiscal year 1990, Congress reacted to the controversy surrounding the Mapplethorpe and Serrano photographs by eliminating $45,000 from the agency's budget, the precise amount contributed to the two exhibits by NEA grant recipients. Ultimately, Congress adopted [§ 954(d)(1)], which directs the Chairperson, in establishing procedures to judge the artistic merit of grant applications, to "take into consideration general standards of decency and respect for the diverse beliefs and values of the American public."

The four individual respondents in this case, Karen Finley, John Fleck, Holly Hughes, and Tim Miller, are performance artists who applied for NEA grants before § 954(d)(1) was enacted. An advisory panel recommended approval of respondents' projects, both initially and after receiving Frohnmayer's request to reconsider three of the applications. A majority of the Council subsequently recommended disapproval, and in June 1990, the NEA informed respondents that they had been denied funding. Respondents filed suit, alleging that the NEA had violated their First Amendment rights.

Respondents raise a facial constitutional challenge to § 954(d)(1), and consequently they confront "a heavy burden" in advancing their claim. Facial invalidation "is, manifestly, strong medicine" that "has been employed by the Court sparingly and only as a last resort." *Broadrick v. Oklahoma* [text, p. 1033] (noting that "facial challenges to legislation are generally disfavored"). To prevail, respondents must demonstrate a substantial risk that application of the provision will lead to the suppression of speech. Respondents argue that the provision is a paradigmatic example of viewpoint discrimination because it rejects any artistic speech that either fails to respect mainstream values or offends standards of decency. The premise of respondents' claim is that § 954(d)(1) constrains the agency's ability to fund certain categories of artistic expression. The NEA, however, reads the provision as merely hortatory, and contends that it stops well short of an absolute restriction. We do not decide whether the NEA's view—that the formulation of diverse advisory panels is sufficient to comply with Congress' command—is in fact a reasonable reading of the statute. It is clear, however, that the text of § 954(d)(1) imposes no categorical requirement.

That § 954(d)(1) admonishes the NEA merely to take "decency and respect" into consideration, and that the legislation was aimed at reforming procedures rather than precluding speech, undercut respondents' argument that the provision inevitably will be utilized as a tool for invidious viewpoint discrimination. In cases where we have struck down legislation as facially unconstitutional, the dangers were both more evident and more substantial. [T]he "decency and respect" criteria do not silence speakers by expressly "threatening censorship of ideas." Thus, we do not perceive a realistic danger that § 954(d)(1) will compromise First Amendment values.

The NEA's enabling statute contemplates a number of indisputably constitutional applications for both the "decency" prong of § 954(d)(1) and its reference to "respect for the diverse beliefs and values of the American public." Educational programs are central to the NEA's mission. And it is well established that "decency" is a permissible factor where "educational suitability" motivates its consideration. We recognize, of course, that reference to permissible applications would not alone be sufficient to sustain the statute against respondents' First Amendment challenge. But neither are we persuaded that, in other applications, the language of § 954(d)(1) itself will give rise to the suppression of protected expression. Any content-based considerations that may be taken into account in the grant-making process are a consequence of the nature of arts funding. The NEA has limited resources and it must deny the majority of the grant applications that it receives, including many that propose "artistically excellent" projects. As the dissent below noted, it would be "impossible to have a highly selective grant program without denying money to a large amount of constitutionally protected expression." The "very assumption" of the NEA is that grants will be awarded according to the "artistic worth of competing applications," and absolute neutrality is simply "inconceivable."

Respondent's reliance on our decision in *Rosenberger v. Rector and Visitors* of *Univ.* of *Va.,* is therefore misplaced. Although the scarcity of NEA funding does not distinguish this case from *Rosenberger,* the competitive process according to which the grants are allocated does. In the context of arts funding, in contrast to many other subsidies, the Government does not indiscriminately "encourage a diversity of views from private speakers," The NEA's mandate is to make aesthetic judgments, and the inherently content-based "excellence" threshold for NEA support sets it apart from the subsidy at issue in *Rosenberger*—which was available to all student organizations that were "related to the educational purpose of the University," and from comparably objective decisions on allocating public benefits, such as access to a school auditorium or a municipal theater, or the second class mailing privileges available to "all newspapers and other periodical publications."

Respondents do not allege discrimination in any particular funding decision. (In fact, after filing suit to challenge § 954(d)(1), two of the individual respondents received NEA grants.) Thus, we have no occasion here to address an as-applied challenge in a situation where the denial of a grant may be shown to be the product of invidious viewpoint discrimination. If the NEA were to leverage its power to award subsidies on the basis of subjective criteria into a penalty on disfavored viewpoints, then we would confront a different case.

Finally, although the First Amendment certainly has application in the subsidy context, we note that the Government may allocate competitive funding according to criteria that would be impermissible were direct regulation of speech or a criminal penalty at stake. So long as legislation does not infringe on other constitutionally protected rights, Congress has wide latitude to set spending priorities. Congress may "selectively fund a program to encourage certain activities it believes to be in the public interest, without at the same time funding an alternative program which seeks to deal with the problem in another way." In doing so, "the Government has not discriminated on the basis of viewpoint; it has merely chosen to fund one activity to the exclusion of the other."

The lower courts also erred in invalidating § 954(d)(1) as unconstitutionally vague. Under the First and Fifth Amendments, speakers are protected from arbitrary and discriminatory enforcement of vague standards. The terms of the provision are undeniably opaque, and if they appeared in a criminal statute or regulatory scheme, they could raise substantial vagueness concerns. It is unlikely, however, that speakers will be compelled to steer too far clear of any "forbidden area" in the context of grants of this nature. We recognize, as a practical matter, that artists may conform their speech to what they believe to be the decision-making criteria in order to acquire funding. But when the Government is acting as patron rather than as sovereign, the consequences of imprecision are not constitutionally severe.

In the context of selective subsidies, it is not always feasible for Congress to legislate with clarity. Indeed, if this statute is unconstitutionally vague, then so too are all government programs awarding scholarships and grants on the basis of subjective criteria such as "excellence." Section 954(d)(1) merely adds some imprecise considerations to an already subjective selection process. It does not, on its face, impermissibly infringe on First or Fifth Amendment rights.

JUSTICE SCALIA, with whom JUSTICE THOMAS joins, concurring in the judgment.

"The operation was a success, but the patient died." What such a procedure is to medicine, the Court's opinion in this case is to law. It sustains the constitutionality of 20 U.S.C. § 954(d)(1) by gutting it. The most avid congressional opponents of the provision could not have asked for more. I write separately because, unlike the Court, I think that § 954(d)(1) must be evaluated as written, rather than as distorted by the agency it was meant to control. By its terms, it establishes content-and viewpoint-based criteria upon which grant applications are to be evaluated. And that is perfectly constitutional.

[I]t is entirely, 100% clear that decency and respect are to be taken into account in evaluating applications. This is so apparent that I am at a loss to understand what the Court has in mind (other than the gutting of the statute) when it speculates that the statute is merely "advisory." To the extent a particular applicant exhibits disrespect for the diverse beliefs and values of the American public or fails to comport with general standards of decency, the likelihood that he will receive a grant diminishes. In other words, the presence of the "take into consideration" clause "cannot be regarded as mere surplusage; it means something." And the "something" is that the decision-maker, all else being equal, will favor applications that display decency and respect, and disfavor applications that do not. This unquestionably constitutes viewpoint discrimination. That conclusion is not altered by the fact that the statute does not "compel" the denial of funding,

It is evident in the legislative history that § 954(d)(1) was prompted by, and directed at, the public funding of such offensive productions as Serrano's "Piss Christ," the portrayal of a crucifix immersed in urine, and Mapplethorpe's show of lurid homoerotic photographs. Thus, even if one strays beyond the plain text it is perfectly clear that the statute was meant to disfavor-that is, to discriminate against-such productions. Not to ban their funding absolutely, to be sure (though as I shall discuss, that also would not have been unconstitutional); but to make their funding more difficult.

More fundamentally, of course, all this legislative history has no valid claim upon our attention at all. The law at issue in this case is to be found in the text of § 954(d)(1), which passed both Houses and was signed by the President. And that law unquestionably disfavors-discriminates againstindecency and disrespect for the diverse beliefs and values of the American people. I turn, then, to whether such viewpoint discrimination violates the Constitution.

With the enactment of § 954(d)(1), Congress did not *abridge* the speech of those who disdain the beliefs and values of the American public, nor did it abridge indecent speech. Those who wish to create indecent and disrespectful art are as unconstrained now as they were before the enactment of this statute. *Avant-garde* artistes such as respondents remain entirely free to *epater les bourgeois;* they are merely deprived of the additional satisfaction of having the bourgeoisie taxed to pay for it. It is preposterous to equate the denial of taxpayer subsidy with measures "aimed at the suppression of dangerous ideas." *Regan v. Taxation without Representation* of *Wash.* One might contend, I suppose, that a threat of rejection by the only available source of free money would constitute coercion and hence "abridgment" within the meaning of the First Amendment. But even if one accepts the contention, it would have no application here. The NEA is far from the sole source of funding for art—even indecent, disrespectful, or just plain bad art. Accordingly, the Government may earmark NEA funds for projects it deems to be in the public interest without thereby abridging speech.

The nub of the difference between me and the Court is that I regard the distinction between "abridging" speech and funding it as a fundamental divide, on this side of which the First Amendment is inapplicable. The Court, by contrast, seems to believe that the First Amendment, despite its words, has some ineffable effect upon funding, imposing constraints of an indeterminate nature which it announces (without troubling to enunciate any particular test) are not violated by the statute here-or, more accurately, are not violated by the quite different, emasculated statute that it imagines. The government, I think, may allocate both competitive and noncompetitive funding ad libitum, insofar as the First Amendment is concerned.

Finally, what is true of the First Amendment is also true of the constitutional rule against vague legislation: it has no application to funding. Insofar as it bears upon First Amendment concerns, the vagueness doctrine addresses the problems that arise from government regulation of expressive conduct, not government grant programs. In the former context, vagueness produces an abridgment of lawful speech; in the latter it produces, at worst, a waste of money.

Justice Souter, dissenting.

The decency and respect proviso mandates viewpoint-based decisions in the disbursement of government subsidies, and the Government has wholly failed to explain why the statute should be afforded an exemption from the fundamental rule of the First Amendment that viewpoint discrimination in the exercise of public authority over expressive activity is unconstitutional. The Court's conclusions that the proviso is not viewpoint based, that it is not a regulation, and that the NEA may permissibly engage in viewpoint-based discrimination, are all patently mistaken. Nor may the question raised be answered in the Government's favor on the assumption that some constitutional applications of the statute are enough to satisfy the demand of facial constitutionality, leaving claims of the proviso's obvious invalidity to be dealt with later in response to challenges of specific applications of the discriminatory standards. This assumption is irreconcilable with our long standing and sensible doctrine of facial overbreadth, applicable to claims brought under the First Amendment's speech clause. I respectfully dissent.

"If there is a bedrock principle underlying the First Amendment, it is that the government may not prohibit the expression of an idea simply because society finds the idea itself offensive or disagreeable." *Texas v. Johnson.*

When called upon to vindicate this ideal, we characteristically begin by asking "whether the government has adopted a regulation of speech because of disagreement with the message it conveys. The government's purpose is the controlling consideration." *Ward v. Rock Against Racism.* The answer in this case is damning. One need do nothing more than read the text of the statute to conclude that Congress's purpose in imposing the decency and respect criteria was to prevent the funding of art that conveys an offensive message; the decency and respect provision on its face is quintessentially viewpoint based, and quotations from the Congressional Record merely confirm the obvious legislative purpose.

[A] statute disfavoring speech that fails to respect America's "diverse beliefs and values" is the very model of viewpoint discrimination; it penalizes any view disrespectful to any belief or value espoused by someone in the American populace. Boiled down to its practical essence, the limitation obviously means that art that disrespects the ideology, opinions, or convictions of a significant segment of the American public is to be disfavored, whereas art that reinforces those values is not. After all, the whole point of the proviso was to make sure that works like Serrano's ostensibly blasphemous portrayal of Jesus would not be funded, while a reverent treatment, conventionally respectful of Christian sensibilities, would not run afoul of the law. Nothing could be more viewpoint-based than that.

A second basic strand in the Court's treatment of today's question, and the heart of JUSTICE SCALIA's, in effect assumes that whether or not the statute mandates viewpoint discrimination, there is no constitutional issue here because government art subsidies fall within a zone of activity free from First Amendment restraints. The Government calls attention to the roles of government-as-speaker and government-as-buyer, in which the government is of course entitled to engage in viewpoint discrimination.

The Government freely admits, however, that it neither speaks through the expression subsidized by the NEA, nor buys anything for itself with its NEA grants. [T]he Government acts as a patron, financially underwriting the production of art by private artists and impresarios for independent consumption. Accordingly, the Government would have us liberate government-as-patron from First Amendment strictures not by placing it squarely within the categories of government-as-buyer or government-as-speaker, but by recognizing a new category by analogy to those accepted ones. The analogy is, however, a very poor fit, and this patronage falls embarrassingly on the wrong side of the line between government-as-buyer or -speaker and government-as-regulator-of-private-speech.

Rosenberger controls here. The NEA, like the student activities fund in *Rosenberger, is* a subsidy scheme created to encourage expression of a diversity of views from private speakers. Given this congressional choice to sustain freedom of expression, *Rosenberger* teaches that the First Amendment forbids decisions based on viewpoint popularity. So long as Congress chooses to subsidize expressive endeavors at large, it has no business requiring the NEA to turn down funding applications of artists and exhibitors who devote their "freedom of thought, imagination, and inquiry" to defying our tastes, our beliefs, or our values. It may not use the NEA's purse to "suppress . . .dangerous ideas." *Regan v. Taxation with Representation* of *Wash.*

Since the decency and respect proviso of § 954(d)(1) is substantially overbroad and carries with it a significant power to chill artistic production and display, it should be struck down on its face. The Court does not strike down the proviso, however. Instead, it preserves the irony of a statutory mandate to deny recognition to virtually any expression capable of causing offense in any quarter as the most recent manifestation of a scheme enacted to "create and sustain . . . a climate encouraging freedom of thought, imagination, and inquiry." § 951(7).

NOTES

1. Contrast *Rosenberger* with the subsequent decision in *Legal Services Corporation v. Velasquez,* 531 U.S. 533 (2001). The Legal Services Corporation Act authorizes the Legal Services Corporation (LSC) to distribute funds appropriated by Congress to local grantee organizations that provided free legal assistance to indigent clients in, among other things, welfare benefit claims. Since 1996, however, Congress had prohibited the funding of any organization that represented clients in an effort to amend or otherwise challenge existing welfare law. Grantees were not allowed to continue representation in a welfare matter where at any point such an issue became apparent. The Supreme Court held, 5-4, that such limitations violate the First Amendment.

Justice Kennedy, writing for the majority, sought to distinguish *Rust* on the grounds that the expression there "amounted to government speech." He noted that "[n]either the latitude for government speech nor its rationale applies to subsidies for private speech in every instance, however." Subsidization of litigation through the LSC program, he concluded, "was designed to facilitate private speech, not to promote a governmental message. The lawyer utilizing LSC funds, he reasoned, "is not the government's speaker," because "Congress funded LSC grantees to provide attorneys to represent the interests of indigent clients," not to convey a particular government message. Of particular importance to his analysis was the fact that the funding of private litigation is not normally used as a means of government speech: "[T]he government seeks to use an existing medium of expression and to control it in a class of cases, in ways which distort its usual functioning. Where the government uses or attempts to regulate a particular medium, we have been informed by its accepted usage in determining whether a particular restriction on speech is necessary for the program's purposes and limitations."

Not entirely clear was the relevance of separation-of-powers considerations to the Court's First Amendment analysis. In finding the law unconstitutional, the Court pointed to the proclamation of judicial power contained in *Marbury v. Madison* and noted that "[a]n informed, independent judiciary presumes an informed, independent bar." The statutory limitation on funding was of concern, because as a result "cases would be presented by LSC attorneys who could not advise the courts of serious questions of statutory validity." Thus, "[b]y seeking to prohibit the analysis of certain legal issues and to truncate presentation to the courts, the enactment under review prohibits speech and expression upon which courts must depend for the proper exercise of the judicial power. Congress cannot wrest the law from the Constitution which is its source." Seemingly synthesizing First Amendment and separation-of-powers considerations, the Court found that "[a] scheme so inconsistent with accepted separation-of-powers principles is an insufficient basis to sustain or uphold the restriction on speech."

Justice Scalia, dissenting, argued that "discrimination on the basis of viewpoint," a prerequisite to a finding of a subsidy's unconstitutionality, was not present. Was this conclusion accurate? In commenting on the Court's asserted distinction of *Rust* as a case involving government speech, he stated: "This is so unpersuasive it hardly needs response. If the private doctors' confidential advice to their patients at issue in *Rust* constituted 'government speech,' it is hard to imagine what subsidized speech would *not* be government speech." He concluded his First Amendment analysis by making a point "that is embarrassingly simple: The LSC subsidy neither prevents anyone from speaking nor coerces anyone to change speech, and is indistinguishable in all relevant respects from the subsidy upheld in *Rust v. Sullivan.*"

Neither the majority nor dissent focused its analysis on the possible relevance of *Finley*. Does that decision have any relevance to the First Amendment analysis?

2. *The search for coherent doctrine.* Steven J. Heyman, *State-Supported Speech*, 1999 WIS. L. REV. 1119, 1130, provides the following perspective on the above line of cases: "*Finley* clearly reveals the incoherence and disarray of the Court's subsidized-speech jurisprudence. To be sure, some elements of doctrine appear relatively settled. When the government itself seeks to convey a message, either directly or through private surrogates, it will be allowed to control what is said. There is also general agreement that when the government funds expression, it has wide authority over aspects of content (such as subject matter) that the Justices regard as relatively neutral. On the other hand, viewpoint discrimination is impermissible in programs that indiscriminately support a diversity of private expression (at least if the Court concludes that a public forum has been created). Finally, the 'unconstitutional conditions' doctrine applies when government seeks to impose limits on speech beyond the scope of a public program. Yet, however clear the issue may be at the periphery, it remains deeply obscure at the core."

Professor Heyman argues that the cases reflect two contradictory positions. One view, reflected in the positions of Chief Justice Rehnquist and Justice Scalia, is that "the First Amendment imposes few if any constraints on the government's power over speech it supports." The other view, which Heyman says is championed by Justices Blackmun and Souter, "holds that funding decisions should be subject to the same strict standards that apply to the regulation of speech."

Professor Heyman argues that both views wrongly ask whether denials of support constitute censorship. He argues that the problem is one "of distributive justice in the modern liberal state." Thus, "funding should be distributed in a way that is consonant with both the community's purposes in establishing a program and with constitutional principles of respect for persons." *Id.* at 1198.

Compare Abner S. Greene, *Government of the Good*, 53 VAND. L. REV. 1, 68–69 (2000), who argues: "Government both may and should promote contested conceptions of the good, through direct speech acts and through funding private. Speech with conditions attached." He argues that government speech or subsidization is invalid only if it monopolizes a speech market, or "coerces" rather than "persuades" citizen choice or if it masks the fact that it is government imposing the conditions, i.e., "ventriloquism."

3. *Unconstitutional conditions.* What role should the unconstitutional conditions doctrine play in these subsidy cases? Consider as the paradigm case of that doctrine the following situation: An individual may have no constitutional right to receive welfare, but the government may nevertheless not condition receipt of welfare on an agreement not to criticize the President of the United States. Are the regulations challenged in the above cases appropriately viewed in this manner? Consider also the following case: Congress hires Company A to print the Congressional Record. Instead of printing what members of Congress have said on the floor of Congress, however, Company A prints in the Record its opposition to restrictions on abortion rights. Therefore, Congress cancels its contract with Company A. We may assume that this would not be deemed a case of "unconstitutional conditions." How is it to be distinguished from the welfare hypothetical? To which hypothetical are the situations in *Rust, Rosenberger, and Finley* more analogous? *See* Martin Redish & Daryl Kessler, *Governmental Subsidies and Free Expression*, 80 MINN. L. REV. 543 (1996).

Frederick Schauer, *Principles, Institutions, and the First Amendment*, 112 HARV. L. REV. 84, 103–104 (1998), says "Nothing within unconstitutional conditions doctrine provides the resources for permitting content-based conditions of producing good art, or contemporary art, or original art, while striking down a condition that only art supporting the President would be subsidized. For such a distinction we must look elsewhere, and we thus see why the cases that a generation ago would have attracted unconstitutional conditions language are now commonly focused on the distinction between different forms of content regulation. That the principle of unconstitutional conditions is not so much as mentioned in any of the different opinions in *Finley* is less an oversight than an epitaph."

4. *Explaining* Finley. Randall P. Bezanson, *The Government Speech Forum:* Forbes *and* Finley *and Government Speech Selection Judgments*, 83 IOWA L. REV. 053, 994 (1998), argues that *Finley* is best understood as a government speech case. "The government was interested in controlling some speech by private artists in order to express its own views, not in acting as a regulator of the artists' speech. The expressive message resided, in *Finley*, in the program of support over the entire range of subsidized work, not in the particular work of art. The government's program occupied but a small place in a large and diverse, otherwise dominantly private, market of philanthropy, patronage, and commerce in art."

Frederick Schauer, 112 HARV. L. REV. at 94, criticizes the "implausible doctrinal structure" used in *Finley*. "Most implausible of all . . . is the view, superficially determinative of the result in *Finley*, that the decency standard is permissible because it is only a factor and not a categorical rule." He argues that, "if a legislature directed an airport commission to take into consideration a group's patriotism or Republicanism as a factor in deciding whether to allow it to solicit funds, it is unlikely that the factor/rule distinction would save the viewpoint discrimination." *Id.* at 95. Professor Schauer instead finds an explanation for *Finley* in the link between the viewpoint discriminatory process used and the largely non-governmental social institution of the arts. "In light of other relatively contemporary cases, the Court's most explicitly stressed features of a factor/rule distinction and a subsidy/prohibition distinction do not, even when take together, appear to explain the result. But if the nature of art, the culture of art, and the practice of arts funding are in important ways special or distinct and if the nominally governmental structure of NEA decisionmaking connects with this culture and its institutions, then the nature of art may have done the [critical] work in *Finley*."

UNITED STATES v. AMERICAN LIBRARY ASSOCIATION, INC.

539 U.S. 194 123 S. Ct. 2297, 156 L. Ed. 2d 221 (2003)

CHIEF JUSTICE REHNQUIST announced the judgment of the Court and delivered an opinion, in which JUSTICE O'CONNOR, JUSTICE SCALIA, and JUSTICE THOMAS joined.

To address the problems associated with the availability of Internet pornography in public libraries, Congress enacted the Children's Internet Protection Act (CIPA). Under CIPA, a public library may not receive federal assistance to provide Internet access unless it installs software to block images that constitute obscenity or child pornography, and to prevent minors from obtaining access to material that is harmful to them. The District Court held these provisions facially invalid on the ground that they induce public libraries to violate patrons' First Amendment rights. We now reverse.

To help public libraries provide their patrons with Internet access, Congress offers two forms of federal assistance. First, the E-rate program established by the Telecommunications Act of 1996 entitles qualifying libraries to buy Internet access at a discount. Second, pursuant to the Library Services and Technology Act, the Institute of Museum and Library Services makes grants to state library administrative agencies to "electronically lin[k] libraries with educational, social, or information services," "assis[t] libraries in accessing information through electronic networks," and "pa[y] costs for libraries to acquire or share computer systems and telecommunications technologies." These programs have succeeded greatly in bringing Internet access to public libraries.

By connecting to the Internet, public libraries provide patrons with a vast amount of valuable information. But there is also an enormous amount of pornography on the Internet, much of which is easily obtained. The accessibility of this material has created serious problems for libraries, which have found that patrons of all ages, including minors, regularly search for online pornography. Some patrons also expose others to pornographic images by leaving them displayed on Internet terminals or printed at library printers.

Upon discovering these problems, Congress became concerned that the E-rate and LSTA programs were facilitating access to illegal and harmful pornography." But Congress also learned that filtering software that blocks access to pornographic Web sites could provide a reasonably effective way to prevent such uses of library resources. By 2000, before Congress enacted CIPA, almost 17% of public libraries used such software on at least some of their Internet terminals, and 7% had filters on all of them. A library can set such software to block categories of material, such as "Pornography" or "Violence." When a patron tries to view a site that falls within such a category, a screen appears indicating that the site is blocked. But a filter set to block pornography may sometimes block other sites that present neither obscene nor pornographic material, but that nevertheless trigger the filter. To minimize this problem, a library can set its software to prevent the blocking of material that falls into categories like "Education," "History," and "Medical." A library may also add or delete specific sites from a blocking category, and anyone can ask companies that furnish filtering software to unblock particular sites.

Responding to this information, Congress enacted CIPA. It provides that a library may not receive E-rate or LSTA assistance unless it has "a policy of Internet safety for minors that includes the operation of a technology protection measure . . . that protects against access" by all persons to "visual depictions" that constitute "obscen[ity]" or "child pornography," and that protects against access by minors to "visual depictions" that are "harmful to minors." The statute defines a "[t]echnology protection measure" as "a specific technology that blocks or filters Internet access to material covered by" CIPA. CIPA also permits the library to "disable" the filter "to enable access for bona fide research or other lawful purposes."

Under the E-rate program, disabling is permitted "during use by an adult." Under the LSTA program, disabling is permitted during use by any person.

Appellees are a group of libraries, library associations, library patrons, and Web site publishers. They sued the United States and the Government agencies and officials responsible for administering the E-rate and LSTA programs in District Court, challenging the constitutionality of CIPA's filtering provisions.

After a trial, the District Court ruled that CIPA was facially unconstitutional and enjoined the relevant agencies and officials from withholding federal assistance for failure to comply with CIPA. The District Court held that Congress had exceeded its authority under the Spending Clause, because, in the court's view, "any public library that complies with CIPA's conditions will necessarily violate the First Amendment." Based on both of these grounds, the court held that the filtering software contemplated by CIPA was a content-based restriction on access to a public forum, and was therefore subject to strict scrutiny. Applying this standard, the District Court held that, although the Government has a compelling interest "in preventing the dissemination of obscenity, child pornography, or, in the case of minors, material harmful to minors," the use of software filters is not narrowly tailored to further those interests. We now reverse.

Congress has wide latitude to attach conditions to the receipt of federal assistance in order to further its policy objectives. *South Dakota v. Dole*]. But Congress may not "induce" the recipient "to engage in activities that would themselves be unconstitutional." We have held in two analogous contexts that the government has broad discretion to make content-based judgments in deciding what private speech to make available to the public. The principles underlying [*Arkansas Ed. Television Communication v. Forbes*] and [*National Endowment for Arts v. Finley*] also apply to a public library's exercise of judgment in selecting the material it provides to its patrons. Just as forum analysis and heightened judici scrutiny are incompatible with the role of public television stations and the role of the NEA, they are also incompatible with the discretion that public libraries must have to fulfill their traditional missions. Public library staffs necessarily consider content in making collection decisions and enjoy broad discretion in making them.

The public forum principles on which the District Court relied are out of place in the context of this case. Internet access in public libraries is neither a "traditional" nor a "designated" public forum. First, this resource—which did not exist until quite recently—has not "immemorially been held in trust for the use of the public and, time out of mind, . . . been used for purposes of assembly, communication of thoughts between citizens, and discussing public questions."

Nor does Internet access in a public library satisfy our definition of a "designated public forum." To create such a forum, the government must make an affirmative choice to open up its property for use as a public forum.

The situation here is very different. A public library does not acquire Internet terminals in order to create a public forum for Web publishers to express themselves, any more than it collects books in order to provide a public forum for the authors of books to speak. It provides Internet access, not to "encourage a diversity of views from private speakers," but for the same reasons it offers other library resources: to facilitate research, learning, and recreational pursuits by furnishing materials of requisite and appropriate quality.

The District Court disagreed because, whereas a library reviews and affirmatively chooses to acquire every book in its collection, it does not review every Web site that it makes available. Based on this distinction, the court reasoned that a public library enjoys less discretion in deciding which Internet materials to make available than in making book selections. We do not find this distinction constitutionally relevant.

A library's failure to make quality-based judgments about all the material it furnishes from the Web does not somehow taint the judgments it does make.

A library's need to exercise judgment in making collection decisions depends on its traditional role in identifying suitable and worthwhile material; it is no less entitled to play that role when it collects material from the Internet than when it collects material from any other source.

Like the District Court, the dissents fault the tendency of filtering software to "overblock"—that is, to erroneously block access to constitutionally protected speech that falls outside the categories that software users intend to block. Assuming that such erroneous blocking presents constitutional difficulties, any such concerns are dispelled by the ease with which patrons may have the filtering software disabled. When a patron encounters a blocked site, they need only ask a librarian to unblock it or (at least in the case of adults) disable the filter. As the District Court found, libraries have the capacity to permanently unblock any erroneously blocked site and the Solicitor General stated at oral argument that a "library may . . . eliminate the filtering with respect to specific sites . . . at the request of a patron."

The District Court viewed unblocking and disabling as inadequate because some patrons may be too embarrassed to request them. But the Constitution does not guarantee the right to acquire information at a public library without any risk of embarrassment.

Appellees urge us to affirm the District Court's judgment on the alternative ground that CIPA imposes an unconstitutional condition on the receipt of federal assistance. Under this doctrine, "the government 'may not deny a benefit to a person on a basis that infringes his constitutionally protected . . . freedom of speech' even if he has no entitlement to that benefit."

Appellees argue that CIPA imposes an unconstitutional condition on libraries that receive E-rate and LSTA subsidies by requiring them, as a condition on their receipt of federal funds, to surrender their First Amendment right to provide the public with access to constitutionally protected speech. The Government counters that this claim fails because Government entities do not have First Amendment rights.

We need not decide this question because, even assuming that appellees may assert an "unconstitutional conditions" claim, this claim would fail on the merits. Within broad limits, "when the Government appropriates public funds to establish a program it is entitled to define the limits of that program." *Rust v. Sullivan*. The same is true here. The E-rate and LSTA programs were intended to help public libraries fulfill their traditional role of obtaining material of requisite and appropriate quality for educational and informational purposes. Congress may certainly insist that these "public funds be spent for the purposes for which they were authorized." Especially because public libraries have traditionally excluded pornographic material from their other collections, Congress could reasonably impose a parallel limitation on its Internet assistance programs. As the use of filtering software helps to carry out these programs, it is a permissible condition under *Rust*.

Justice Stevens asserts the premise that "[a] federal statute penalizing a library for failing to install filtering software on every one of its Internet-accessible computers would unquestionably violate [the First] Amendment." But—assuming again that public libraries have First Amendment rights—CIPA does not "penalize" libraries that choose not to install such software, or deny them the right to provide their patrons with unfiltered Internet access. Rather, CIPA simply reflects Congress' decision not to subsidize their doing so. To the extent that libraries wish to offer unfiltered access, they are free to do so without federal assistance. Appellees mistakenly contend, in reliance on *Legal Services Corporation v. Velazquez*, that CIPA's filtering conditions "[d]istor[t] the [u]sual [f]unctioning of [p]ublic [l]ibraries." In *Velazquez*, the Court concluded that a Government program of furnishing legal aid to the indigent differed from the program in *Rust* "[i]n th[e] vital respect" that the role of lawyers who represent clients in welfare disputes is to advocate *against* the Government, and there was thus an assumption that counsel would be free of state control. The Court concluded that the restriction on advocacy in such welfare disputes would distort the usual functioning of the legal profession and the federal and state courts before which the lawyers appeared. Public libraries, by contrast, have no comparable role that pits them against the Government, and there is no comparable assumption that they must be free of any conditions that their benefactors might attach to the use of donated funds or other assistance.

Because public libraries' use of Internet filtering software does not violate their patrons' First Amendment rights, CIPA does not induce libraries to violate the Constitution, and is a valid exercise of Congress' spending power. Nor does CIPA impose an unconstitutional condition on public libraries.

JUSTICE KENNEDY, concurring in the judgment.

If, on the request of an adult user, a librarian will unblock filtered material or disable the Internet software filter without significant delay, there is little to this case. The Government represents this is indeed the fact. If some libraries do not have the capacity to unblock specific Web sites or to disable the filter or if it is shown that an adult user's election to view constitutionally protected Internet material is burdened in some other substantial way, that would be the subject for an as-applied challenge, not the facial challenge made in this case.

JUSTICE BREYER, concurring in the judgment.

In ascertaining whether the statutory provisions are constitutional, I would apply a form of heightened scrutiny, examining the statutory requirements in question with special care. The Act directly restricts the public's receipt of information. And it does so through limitations imposed by outside bodies (here Congress) upon two critically important sources of information—the Internet as accessed via public libraries. For that reason, we should not examine the statute's constitutionality as if it raised no special First Amendment concern—as if, like tax or economic regulation, the First Amendment demanded only a "rational basis" for imposing a restriction. Nor should we accept the Government's suggestion that a presumption in favor of the statute's constitutionality applies.

At the same time, in my view, the First Amendment does not here demand application of the most limiting constitutional approach—that of "strict scrutiny." The statutory restriction in question is, in essence, a kind of "selection" restriction (a kind of editing). It affects the kinds and amount of materials that the library can present to its patrons. And libraries often properly engage in the selection of materials, either as a matter of necessity (*i.e.*, due to the scarcity of resources) or by design (i.e., in accordance with collection development policies). "[S]trict scrutiny" implies too limiting and rigid a test for me to believe that the First Amendment requires it in this context.

In such cases the Court has asked whether the harm to speech-related interests is disproportionate in light of both the justifications and the potential alternatives. It has considered the legitimacy of the statute's objective, the extent to which the statute will tend to achieve that objective, whether there are other, less restrictive ways of achieving that objective, and ultimately whether the statute works speech-related harm that, in relation to that objective, is out of proportion. This approach does not substitute a form of "balancing" for less flexible, though more speech protective, forms of "strict scrutiny." Rather, it *supplements* the latter with an approach that is more flexible but nonetheless provides the legislature with less than ordinary leeway in light of the fact that constitutionally protected expression is at issue.

The Act's restrictions satisfy these constitutional demands. The Act seeks to restrict access to obscenity, child pornography, and, in respect to access by minors, material that is comparably harmful. These objectives are "legitimate," and indeed often "compelling." Due to present technological limitations, however, the software filters both "overblock," screening out some perfectly legitimate material, and "underblock," allowing some obscene material to escape detection by the filter. But no one has presented any clearly superior or better fitting alternatives. At the same time, the Act contains an important exception that limits the speech-related harm that "overblocking" might cause. As the plurality points out, the Act allows libraries to permit any adult patron access to an "overblocked" Web site; the adult patron need only ask a librarian to unblock the specific Web site or, alternatively, ask the librarian, "Please disable the entire filter."

The Act does impose upon the patron the burden of making this request. But it is difficult to see how that burden (or any delay associated with compliance) could prove more onerous than traditional library practices associated with segregating library materials in, say, closed stacks, or with interlibrary lending practices that require patrons to make requests that are not anonymous and to wait while the librarian obtains the desired materials from elsewhere. Perhaps local library rules or practices could further restrict the ability of patrons to obtain "overblocked" Internet material. But we are not now considering any such local practices. We here consider only a facial challenge to the Act itself. Given the comparatively small burden that the Act imposes upon the library patron seeking legitimate Internet materials, I cannot say that any speech-related harm that the Act may cause is disproportionate when considered in relation to the Act's legitimate objectives. I therefore agree with the plurality that the statute does not violate the First Amendment, and I concur in the judgment.

JUSTICE STEVENS, dissenting.

I agree with the plurality that it is neither inappropriate nor unconstitutional for a local library to experiment with filtering software as a means of curtailing children's access to Internet Web sites displaying sexually explicit images. I also agree with the plurality that the 7% of public libraries that decided to use such software on *all* of their Internet terminals in 2000 did not act unlawfully. Whether it is constitutional for the Congress of the United States to impose that requirement on the other 93%, however, raises a vastly different question. Rather than allowing local decisionmakers to tailor their responses to local problems, the Children's Internet Protection Act (CIPA) operates as a blunt nationwide restraint on adult access to "an enormous amount of valuable information" that individual librarians cannot possibly review. Most of that information is constitutionally protected speech. In my view, this restraint is unconstitutional.

The unchallenged findings of fact made by the District Court reveal fundamental defects in the filtering software that is now available or that will be available in the foreseeable future. Given the quantity and ever-changing character of Web sites offering free sexually explicit material, it is inevitable that a substantial amount of such material will never be blocked. Because of this "underblocking," the statute will provide parents with a false sense of security without really solving the problem that motivated its enactment. Conversely, the software's reliance on words to identify undesirable sites necessarily results in the blocking of thousands of pages that "contain content that is completely innocuous for both adults and minors, and that no rational person could conclude matches the filtering companies' category definitions, such as 'pornography' or 'sex.' " In my judgment, a statutory blunderbuss that mandates this vast amount of "overblocking" abridges the freedom of speech protected by the First Amendment.

The effect of the overblocking is the functional equivalent of a host of individual decisions excluding hundreds of thousands of individual constitutionally protected messages from Internet terminals located in public libraries throughout the Nation. Neither the interest in suppressing unlawful speech nor the interest in protecting children from access to harmful materials justifies this overly broad restriction on adult access to protected speech. "The Government may not suppress lawful speech as the means to suppress unlawful speech." *Ashcroft v. Free Speech Coalition.*

Until a blocked site or group of sites is unblocked, a patron is unlikely to know what is being hidden and therefore whether there is any point in asking for the filter to be removed. It is as though the statute required a significant part of every library's reading materials to be kept in unmarked, locked rooms or cabinets, which could be opened only in response to specific requests. Some curious readers would in time obtain access to the hidden materials, but many would not. Inevitably, the interest of the authors of those works in reaching the widest possible audience would be abridged. Moreover, because the procedures that different libraries are likely to adopt to respond to unblocking requests will no doubt vary, it is impossible to measure the aggregate effect of the statute on patrons' access to blocked sites. Unless we assume that the statute is a mere symbolic gesture, we must conclude that it will create a significant prior restraint on adult access to protected speech.

The plurality incorrectly argues that the statute does not impose "an unconstitutional condition on public libraries." On the contrary, it impermissibly conditions the receipt of Government funding on the restriction of significant First Amendment rights. As the plurality recognizes, we have always assumed that libraries have discretion when making decisions regarding what to include in, and exclude from, their collections. Given our Nation's deep commitment "to safeguarding academic freedom" and to the "robust exchange of ideas," a library's exercise of judgment with respect to its collection is entitled to First Amendment protection.

A federal statute penalizing a library for failing to install filtering software on every one of its Internet-accessible computers would unquestionably violate that Amendment. I think it equally clear that the First Amendment protects libraries from being denied funds for refusing to comply with an identical rule. An abridgment of speech by means of a threatened denial of benefits can be just as pernicious as an abridgment by means of a threatened penalty. Our cases holding that government employment may not be conditioned on the surrender of rights protected by the First Amendment illustrate the point. The issue in this case does not involve governmental attempts to control the speech or views of its employees. It involves the use of its treasury to impose controls on an important medium of expression. The question, then, is whether requiring the filtering software on all Internet-accessible computers distorts that medium. As I have discussed above, the over-and underblocking of the software does just that.

[U]nder this statute, if a library attempts to provide Internet service for even *one* computer through an E-rate discount, that library must put filtering software on *all* of its computers with Internet access, not just the one computer with E-rate discount. This Court should not permit federal funds to be used to enforce this kind of broad restriction of First Amendment rights, particularly when such a restriction is unnecessary to accomplish Congress' stated goal. The abridgment of speech is equally obnoxious whether a rule like this one is enforced by a threat of penalties or by a threat to withhold a benefit. I would affirm the judgment of the District Court.

Justice Souter, with whom Justice Ginsburg joins, dissenting.

[T]he unblocking provisions simply cannot be construed, even for constitutional avoidance purposes, to say that a library must unblock upon adult request, no conditions imposed and no questions asked. First, the statute says only that a library "may" unblock, not that it must. In addition, it allows unblocking only for a "bona fide research or other lawful purposes," and if the "lawful purposes" criterion means anything that would not subsume and render the "bona fide research" criterion superfluous, it must impose some limit on eligibility for unblocking. There is therefore necessarily some restriction, which is surely made more onerous by the uncertainty of its terms and the generosity of its discretion to library staffs in deciding who gets complete Internet access and who does not. We therefore have to take the statute on the understanding that adults will be denied access to a substantial amount of nonobscene material harmful to children but lawful for adult examination, and a substantial quantity of text and pictures harmful to no one.

We likewise have to examine the statute on the understanding that the restrictions on adult Internet access have no justification in the object of protecting children. Children could be restricted to blocked terminals, leaving other unblocked terminals in areas restricted to adults and screened from casual glances. And of course the statute could simply have provided for unblocking at adult request, with no questions asked. The statute could, in other words, have protected children without blocking access for adults or subjecting adults to anything more than minimal inconvenience, just the way (the record shows) many librarians had been dealing with obscenity and indecency before imposition of the federal conditions. Instead, the Government's funding conditions engage in overkill to a degree illustrated by their refusal to trust even a library's staff with an unblocked terminal, one to which the adult public itself has no access.

The question for me, then, is whether a local library could itself constitutionally impose these restrictions on the content otherwise available to an adult patron through an Internet connection, at a library terminal provided for public use. The answer is no. A library that chose to block an adult's Internet access to material harmful to children (and whatever else the undiscriminating filter might interrupt) would be imposing a content-based restriction on communication of material in the library's control that an adult could otherwise lawfully see. This would simply be censorship. True, the censorship would not necessarily extend to every adult, for an intending Internet user might convince a librarian that he was a true researcher or had a "lawful purpose" to obtain everything the library's terminal could provide. But as to those who did not qualify for discretionary unblocking, the censorship would be complete and, like all censorship by an agency of the Government, presumptively invalid owing to strict scrutiny in implementing the Free Speech Clause of the First Amendment.

The Court's plurality does not treat blocking affecting adults as censorship, but chooses to describe a library's act in filtering content as simply an instance of the kind of selection from available material that every library (save, perhaps, the Library of Congress) must perform. But this position does not hold up.

Public libraries are indeed selective in what they acquire to place in their stacks, as they must be. There is only so much money and so much shelf space, and the necessity to choose some material and reject the rest justifies the effort to be selective with an eye to demand, quality, and the object of maintaining the library as a place of civilized enquiry by widely different sorts of people. Selectivity is thus necessary and complex, and these two characteristics explain why review of a library's selection decisions must be limited: the decisions are made all the time, and only in extreme cases could one expect particular choices to reveal impermissible reasons (reasons even the plurality would consider to be illegitimate), like excluding books because their authors are Democrats or their critiques of organized Christianity are unsympathetic. Review for rational basis is probably the most that any court could conduct, owing to the myriad particular selections that might be attacked by someone, and the difficulty of untangling the play of factors behind a particular decision.

At every significant point, however, the Internet blocking here defies comparison to the process of acquisition. The proper analogy therefore is not to passing up a book that might have been bought; it is either to buying a book and then keeping it from adults lacking an acceptable "purpose," or to buying an encyclopedia and then cutting out pages with anything thought to be unsuitable for all adults.

The plurality claims to find support for its conclusions in the "traditional missio[n]" of the public library. The plurality thus argues, in effect, that the traditional responsibility of public libraries has called for denying adult access to certain books, or bowdlerizing the content of what the libraries let adults see. But, in fact, the plurality's conception of a public library's mission has been rejected by the libraries themselves. And no library that chose to block adult access in the way mandated by the Act could claim that the history of public library practice in this country furnished an implicit gloss on First Amendment standards, allowing for blocking out anything unsuitable for adults. Institutional history of public libraries in America discloses an evolution toward a general rule, now firmly rooted, that any adult entitled to use the library has access to any of its holdings.

Thus, there is no preacquisition scarcity rationale to save library Internet blocking from treatment as censorship, and no support for it in the historical development of library practice. To these two reasons to treat blocking differently from a decision declining to buy a book, a third must be added. Quite simply, we can smell a rat when a library blocks material already in its control, just as we do when a library removes books from its shelves for reasons having nothing to do with wear and tear, obsolescence, or lack of demand. Content-based blocking and removal tell us something that mere absence from the shelves does not.

Removal of books or selective blocking by controversial subject matter is not a function of limited resources and less likely than a selection decision to reflect an assessment of esthetic or scholarly merit. There is no good reason, then, to treat blocking of adult enquiry as any thing different from the censorship it presumptively is. For this reason, I would hold in accordance with conventional strict scrutiny that a library's practice of blocking would violate an adult patron's First and Fourteenth Amendment right to be free of Internet censorship, when unjustified (as here) or by any legitimate interest in screening children for harmful material. On that ground, the Act's blocking requirement in its current breadth calls for unconstitutional action by a library recipient, and is itself unconstitutional.

NOTES

1. *Spending limits and unconstitutional conditions.* The district court decided that, apart from CIPA, any public library installing filters would violate the First Amendment by restricting patron access to a public forum. Why does the plurality reject the district court's analysis? Is a library's decision to install filters just a "collection decision" analogous to book acquisitions? The plurality argues that discretionary content-based decisions are involved in both cases requiring judicial deference. Perhaps the proper analogy is to book removal and "censorship," as Justice Souter claims. How does Justice Stevens come out on the question of whether, absent CIPA, a public library can install filters consistent with the First Amendment? The plurality rejects the argument of the American Library Association that CIPA imposes an unconstitutional condition on public libraries, using *Rust*. How is *Velazquez* distinguished? All four members of the plurality dissented in *Velazquez*.

Justice Stevens characterizes CIPA as "penalizing" libraries for failing to install filters — do you agree?

2. *Distortion or enhancement.* Professor Lillian R. Bevier, United States v. American Library Association: *Wither First Amendment Doctrine,* 55 SUP. CT. REV. 16 (2003), argues that *American Library Association* "was an easy case, that the decision was correct as an application of existing doctrine, and that the doctrine it applied is defensible and coherent." She characterizes Justice Rehnquist's plurality opinion as an example of "the Distortion Model of the First Amendment" — in the absence of government deliberately manipulating the content or outcome of the political debate, or censoring or selectively denying speech opportunities to disfavored views, the courts defer to the political branches. She argues that the separate opinions in *American Library Association* reflect "the Enhancement Model" which "charges the Court with responsibility to maximize the quantity of speech to which citizens have access." But, she argues that enhancement runs counter to current First Amendment doctrine which focuses on negative rights — "It is a doctrine not of entitlement but of protection from government."

Justice Rehnquist rejected the claim of library patrons and web site operators that Congress had exceeded First Amendment limits on the spending power by denying their claim of a right of access to the Internet as a public forum. Professor Bevier comments: "The conclusion that public libraries could constitutionally install Internet filters that incidentally overblock sexually explicit protected material, at least if they made it easy for patrons to have the filters disabled, determined the legitimacy of CIPA as an exercise of congressional spending power." She continues — by concluding that CIPA did not impose a penalty on libraries but "merely reflected Congress' permissible decision not to subsidize such a choice [not to install filtering devices]," the plurality disposed of the unconstitutional conditions challenge.

3. *A federalism approach?* Professor Desai argues that the Supreme Court in *American Library Association* would have done better to focus on the "underlying principles of constitutional federalism" rather than the First Amendment. Concentrating on federalism "would have given the Court the opportunity to invalidate an overbroad regulation such as CIPA and yet would have permitted a wide variety of regulatory approaches to vexing problems such as sexually explicit speech on library Internet terminals." Anuj C. Desai, *Filters and Federalism: Public Library Internet Access, Local Control, and the Federal Spending Power*, 7 U. PA. J. CONST. L. 3, 4 (2004). Professor Desai endorses Justice Stevens' dissent, which would have found the federal statute unconstitutional but still permitted local libraries the choice of whether to filter Internet content. *Id.* at 45. Instead, he says, that the Court's judgment forces federal funding recipients to filter their Internet access regardless of whether they have had issues with access to sexually explicit materials on the Internet: "By constitutionalizing the question in terms of the First Amendment, [the] 'independent constitutional bar' rule [on federal spending] left the Court with an all-or-nothing solution. In contrast, if the Court had viewed the constitutional question through the lens of federalism and had invalidated it on that ground, a variety of approaches — some including filters, some not — would have remained available." *Id.* at 60–62. See also Professor

Mark Rosen's critique of the plurality's "One-Size-Fits-All" approach: "[A] local library's decision to install an Internet filter implicates the Constitution differently than the federal government's requirement that local libraries install such filters. Whereas a federal act 'operates as a blunt nationwide restraint,' an individual library's decision is a decision by the locality that can be tailored to fit local circumstances." Mark D. Rosen, *The Surprisingly Strong Case for Tailoring Constitutional Principles*, 153 U. Pa. L. Rev. 1513, 1539–41 (2005).

4. ***Implications?*** Professor Dawn C. Nunziato, *The Death of the Public Forum in Cyberspace*, 20 Berkeley Tech. L. J. 1115, 1161 (2005), claims that the *American Library Association* decision establishes a "dangerous speech-restrictive precedent" by holding that no public forum existed even in "this rare instance of public ownership and control over Internet speech forums." *Id.* at 1157. "Courts should reject such a simplistic analysis of public forums, which forecloses by its very terms the recognition of an Internet forum as a public forum for First Amendment purposes. Instead, courts should undertake a functional analysis to determine whether such places are currently widely used for purposes of 'communication of thoughts between citizens, and discussing public questions' and serve the same speech-facilitating purposes served in real space by public sidewalks and parks." *Id.* at 1162. Does a library which provides Internet access create a public forum? Consider the following: "The *American Library Association* decision resolved the immediate question of CIPA's facial validity, but it is not clear how any future as-applied challenges may fare or whether the case will be influential beyond its specific context. An important reason for this uncertainty, which also explains the splintered opinions and the ambiguous direction of the Court, is that the case was a poor fit under the established First Amendment doctrines of the public forum and unconstitutional conditions. The more precise problem this case presents is the need to determine which kind of First Amendment rules apply to public institutions that are created for the purpose of spreading information and engaging in expressive activities. In this regard, *American Library Association* may be considered a missed opportunity to clarify an ambiguous area of constitutional law." Robert Corn-Revere, United States v. American Library Association: *A Missed Opportunity for the Supreme Court to Clarify Application of First Amendment Law to Publicly Funded Experience Institution*, 2003 Cato Sup. Ct. Rev. 104, 120.

§ 8.02 CALIBRATING FIRST AMENDMENT PROTECTION

The principle that there are categories of expression which do not merit First Amendment protection, or at least not full First Amendment protection, has had enduring vitality. In the past, it was possible to say that the categories of defamation, obscenity, fighting words, and official secrets were entitled to no First Amendment protection. We saw in the *Pentagon Papers Cases* that the national security interest resulted only in a content-based balancing approach to publication of official secrets, rather than a categorical exclusion from First Amendment protection. We have also considered the "category" of "fighting words," noting particularly Justice Scalia's insistence in *R.A.V.* that the Court would no longer follow a categorical approach to any areas of "unprotected" speech. Apparently, that category has been abandoned in favor of considering the impacts of offensive or hate speech. Even Justice Stevens in *R.A.V.* expressed serious "reservations about the categorical approach."

In this section, two categories of speech — commercial and pornographic — with limited or no constitutional protection will be considered. A third category, defamation, is considered in Section 8.03 with other issues related to publication and the media.

Commercial speech, originally cast out of the First Amendment, has been brought back into the fold; but that does not mean that it is accorded full First Amendment protection. As will be seen, commercial speech appears to occupy some intermediate place, enjoying neither the full protection of political speech nor the absence of First Amendment protection accorded obscenity.

Roth v. United States read obscenity out of the First Amendment as totally lacking redeeming social value. As amended by *Miller v. California*, there it remains today. Since *Roth*, obscenity law has revolved around the definitional question of whether the material is obscene, and the determination of what is obscene is no easy matter. Further, in cases involving "indecent" publications, several holdings have suggested that government may be able to consider the content of the expression in framing appropriate regulations, such as zoning or broadcast rules. There is even one area in which non-obscene, indecent, speech is excluded from First Amendment protection, i.e., child pornography. And an argument receiving substantial attention in recent years is that female pornography should be treated as not speech and placed outside the scope of the First Amendment.

[A] COMMERCIAL SPEECH: THE "IN-BETWEEN" CATEGORY

[1] Commercial Advertising

In *Valentine v. Chrestensen,* 316 U.S. 52 (1942), the Supreme Court unanimously held that commercial speech was outside the ambit of the First Amendment and therefore subject to regulation by government. The question in *Chrestensen* was whether a municipal anti-litter ordinance could be enforced against the exhibitor of a submarine who criticized the police commissioner on the back of his advertising handbill. The Supreme Court seemed to assume that commercial speech would not be protected by the First Amendment but stressed that Chrestensen had printed his noncommercial message solely to evade the ordinance. The Court's evaluation of Chrestensen's subjective intent, in other words, deprived him of First Amendment protection, and his First Amendment claim was seen as a mere ploy to escape a municipal ordinance. *Valentine v. Chrestensen* had sown the seeds of a constitutional doctrine of significance: the theory that the First Amendment does not protect "purely" commercial speech.

Valentine v. Chrestensen was decided against the background of the judicial aversion of that time to substantive due process. Two commentators offer the following speculation: "Had Chrestensen had the foresight not to sue, and had no other commercial speech cases arrived at the Court until the 1960s or the 1970s — when the days of economic substantive due process had receded into the more distant past and First Amendment protections had matured and become more absolute — things might have come out otherwise." Alex Kozinski & Stuart Banner, *The Anti-History and Pre-History of Commercial Speech*, 71 TEX. L. REV. 747, 774–75 (1993). Is it likely that if *Valentine* had been decided on First Amendment grounds instead of under substantive due process, the distinction between commercial speech and non-commercial speech would not have emerged?

In *Virginia State Board of Pharmacy v. Virginia Citizens Consumer Council, Inc.*, 425 U.S. 748 (1976), the Court radically transformed the view expressed in *Chrestensen* that commercial speech was unprotected speech. *Virginia Pharmacy* held unconstitutional a Virginia statute which prohibited pharmacists from advertising the price of prescription drugs. Justice Blackmun said:

> Our question is whether speech which does "no more than propose a commercial transaction," *Pittsburgh Press Co. v. Pittsburgh Commission on Human Relations*, is so removed from any "exposition of ideas," *Chaplinsky v. New Hampshire*, and from "truth, science, morality, and arts in general, in its diffusion of liberal sentiments on the administration of Government," *Roth v. United States*, that it lacks all protection. Our answer is that it is not.
>
> Advertising, however tasteless and excessive it sometimes may seem, is nonetheless dissemination of information as to who is producing and selling what product, for what reason, and at what price. So long as we preserve a predominantly free enterprise economy, the allocation of our resources in large measure will be made through numerous private economic decisions. It is a matter of public interest that those decisions, in the aggregate, be intelligent and well informed. To this end, the free flow of commercial information is indispensable. And if it is indispensable to the proper allocation of resources in a free enterprise system, it is also indispensable to the formation of intelligent opinions as to how that system ought to be regulated or altered. Therefore, even if the First Amendment were thought to be primarily an instrument to enlighten public decisionmaking in a democracy, we could not say that the free flow of information does not serve that goal.

While holding that commercial speech, like other varieties of speech, was protected, Justice Blackmun also observed in a much quoted and cited footnote that commercial speech was nevertheless different from other kinds of speech and, therefore, perhaps still somewhat more subject to regulation:

> In concluding that commercial speech enjoys First Amendment protection, we have not held that it is wholly undifferentiable from other forms. There are commonsense differences between speech that does "no more than propose a commercial transaction," and other varieties. Even if the differences do not justify the conclusion that commercial speech is valueless, and thus subject to complete suppression by the State, they nonetheless suggest that a different degree of

> protection is necessary to insure that the flow of truthful and legitimate commercial information is unimpaired. The truth of commercial speech, for example, may be more easily verifiable by its disseminator than, let us say, news reporting or political commentary, in that ordinarily the advertiser seeks to disseminate information about a specific product or service that he himself provides and presumably knows more about than anyone else. Also, commercial speech may be more durable than other kinds. Since advertising is the *sine qua non* of commercial profits, there is little likelihood of its being chilled by proper regulation and foregone entirely.
>
> Attributes such as these, the greater objectivity and hardiness of commercial speech, may make it less necessary to tolerate inaccurate statements for fear of silencing the speaker. They may also make it appropriate to require that a commercial message appear in such a form, or include such additional information, warnings and disclaimers, as are necessary to prevent its being deceptive.

Is *Virginia Board* "inexplicable under traditional First Amendment principles?" Thomas Jackson & John Jeffries, *Commercial Speech: Economic Due Process and the First Amendment*, 65 VA. L. REV. 1 (1979). The authors argue that the First Amendment protects only a limited range of values, concluding that "[m]easured in terms of traditional first amendment principles commercial speech is remarkable for its insignificance. It neither contributes to self-government nor nurtures the realization of the individual personality." *Id.* Thomas Emerson, *First Amendment Doctrine and the Burger Court*, 68 CAL. L. REV. 422 (1980) and Edwin Baker, *Commercial Speech: A Problem in the Theory of Freedom*, 62 IOWA L. REV. 1 (1976), similarly conclude that commercial speech does not fall within the realm of First Amendment speech. For competing views, see Martin Redish, *The First Amendment in the Marketplace: Commercial Speech and the Value of Free Expression*, 39 GEO. WASH. L. REV. 429, 443–44 (1971); Martin Redish, *The Value of Free Speech*, 130 U. PA. L. REV. 591, 633 (1982).

In an implicit argument for regulation Ronald Collins & David Skover, *Commerce and Communication*, 71 TEX. L. REV. 697, 720–22 (1993) subject advertising to the following critique: "Advertising pressure does more than influence content; it sometimes dictates it. Even non-libelous political dissent, when critical of advertisers, is subject to outright suppression. Commercial speech represents commercial power." In rebuttal, consider Rodney Smolla, *Information, Imagery, and the First Amendment: A Case for Expansive Protection of Commercial Speech*, 71 TEX. L. REV. 777, 782–83 (1993):

> The very "excesses" of modern advertising that might at first make it seem a likely candidate for heavy legal regulation are actually the attributes that most qualify such speech for the heightened constitutional protection we routinely grant other categories of speech. The refusal of current First Amendment jurisprudence to accept a schism between the rational and the irrational elements of speech (or, to use slightly different terms, between the intellectual and emotional content of speech) is sound. Commercial speech should be no exception.

In *Friedman v. Rogers,* 440 U.S. 1 (1977), a Texas statute providing that optometry could not be practiced under a trade name was upheld. Unlike information about the price which was involved in *Virginia Pharmacy*, the communication of trade names, Justice Powell declared for the Court, was a form of speech that had no intrinsic meaning. Compare this holding with due process challenges (both substantive and procedural) to similar restrictions on corporate practice of pharmacy and optometry. *Gibson v. Berryhill,* 411 U.S. 564 (1973); *North Dakota St. Bd. of Pharmacy v. Snyder's Drug Stores,* 414 U.S. 156 (1973).

***Bolger v. Youngs Drug Products Corp.,* 463 U.S. 60 (1983).** The Supreme Court, per Justice Marshall, held that 39 U.S.C. § 3001(e)(2), prohibiting the mailing of unsolicited advertisements for contraceptives, violated the First Amendment as applied to a mailing by Youngs Drug Products, a producer of contraceptives. When Youngs proposed a public mailing of unsolicited advertisements, including informational pamphlets promoting its products but also discussing venereal disease and family planning, the postal service notified the manufacturer that the proposed mailings would violate federal law.

Although Youngs contended that the proposed mailings constituted "fully protected" speech, the Court found that most of its mailings fell "within the core notion of commercial speech — speech which does no more than propose a commercial transaction." But the informational pamphlets were not merely proposals to deal.

> We have made clear that advertising which "links a product to a current public debate" is not thereby entitled to the constitutional protection afforded noncommercial speech. A company has the full panoply of protections available to its direct comments on public issues, so there is no reason for providing similar constitutional protection when such statements are made in the context of commercial transactions. Advertisers should not be permitted to immunize false or misleading product information from government regulation simply by including references to public issues.

After determining that the mailings constituted commercial speech, the Court nevertheless held that the mailings were protected speech. While recognizing the state's authority to deal effectively with false, deceptive or misleading sales techniques and commercial speech related to illegal activities, Justice Marshall noted that the government had never claimed that Youngs' mailings fell into any of these categories. "To the contrary, advertising for contraceptives not only implicates substantial individual and societal interests in the free flow of commercial information, but also relates to activity that is protected from unwarranted state interference."

***Cincinnati v. Discovery Network, Inc.,* 507 U.S. 410 (1993).** The Court, per Justice Stevens, invalidated a ban on commercial newsracks. The city of Cincinnati had imposed a ban on newsracks which distributed commercial publications but no ban on newspaper newsracks. Cincinnati justified its ban on commercial newsracks because of its interests in safety and esthetics on its sidewalks. The Court was not persuaded:

> It was the city's burden to establish a "reasonable fit" between its legitimate interests in safety and esthetics and its choice of a limited and selective prohibition of newsracks as the means chosen to serve those interests.

The "reasonable fit" was lacking here. Although the ban on commercial newsracks would remove 62 commercial newsracks from the streets of the city, 1500-2000 newspaper racks would still be on the streets. In such circumstances, the safety and esthetic benefit to be obtained from a ban just on commercial newsracks was marginal indeed.

In dissent, Chief Justice Rehnquist, joined by Justices White and Thomas, attacked the majority for failing to give sufficient leeway to regulatory concerns. "That there may be other — less restrictive — means by which Cincinnati could have gone about addressing its safety and esthetic concerns, then, does not render its prohibitions against [commercial] newsracks unconstitutional." In Chief Justice Rehnquist's view, the fact of the matter was that Cincinnati had just burdened *less* speech than necessary to accomplish all its objectives.

Does *Cincinnati* represent a refusal by the Court to be a prisoner of the categorical approach?

Defining commercial speech. One of the criticisms of according a new First Amendment status to commercial speech is that the new status of commercial speech might end up eroding core areas of protected speech. If commercial speech is to be accorded a lesser degree of First Amendment protection, it is vital to establish a workable definition of the term.

In *Virginia Pharmacy*, commercial speech is defined as "proposing a commercial transaction." In *Central Hudson*, below, commercial speech is defined as "expression related solely to the economic interests of the speaker and its audience." It has been pointed out, however, that in *Bolger*, the Court "returns to the 'proposing a commercial transaction' notion. It again seems to equate commercial speech and commercial advertising." Steven Shiffrin, *The First Amendment and Economic Regulation: Away From A General Theory of the First Amendment*, 78 Nw. U.L. Rev. 1212, 1222 (1983).

Motivations of speakers and regulators. Regulation of health claims made on behalf of commercial products can raise fundamental questions about the integrity of the commercial speech doctrine. Texas brought a proceeding against the Quaker Oats Company on the ground that it has "embarked upon a campaign of deception" with the objective of enticing Texans concerned about their cholesterol levels and heart disease to consume the company's oatmeal and oat bran products "as a substitute for medical treatment." The State of Texas alleged that Quaker's motivation in this campaign stemmed from the "base purpose of selling as much of Quaker's products as possible." Is the Quaker Oats ad protected by the commercial speech doctrine?

A First Amendment stepchild? Why should there be so much controversy about whether First Amendment protection should be accorded to commercial speech? The following explanation has been offered:

> The commercial speech doctrine is the stepchild of first amendment jurisprudence: Liberals don't much like commercial speech because it's commercial; conservatives mistrust it because it's speech. Yet, in a free market economy, the ability to give and receive information about commercial matters may be as important, sometimes more important, than expression of a political, artistic, or religious nature.

Alex Kozinski and Stuart Banner, *Who's Afraid of Commercial Speech?*, 76 Va. L. Rev. 627, 652 (1990).

[2] Advertising by Regulated Utilities

CENTRAL HUDSON GAS & ELEC. CORP. v. PUBLIC SERVICE COMM'N

447 U.S. 557, 100 S. Ct. 2343, 65 L. Ed. 2d 341 (1980)

Justice Powell delivered the opinion of the Court.

This case presents the question whether a regulation of the Public Service Commission of the State of New York violates the First and Fourteenth Amendments because it completely bans promotional advertising by an electrical utility.

In December 1973, the Commission, appellee here, ordered electric utilities in New York State to cease all advertising that "promot[es] the use of electricity." The order was based on the Commission's finding that "the interconnected utility system in New York State does not have sufficient fuel stocks or sources of supply to continue furnishing all customer demands for the 1973-1974 winter." Three years later, when the fuel shortage had eased, the Commission requested comments from the public on its proposal to continue the ban on promotional advertising. Central Hudson Gas & Electric Corporation, the appellant in this case, opposed the ban on First Amendment grounds. After reviewing the public comments, the Commission extended the prohibition in a Policy Statement issued on February 25, 1977. The Policy Statement divided advertising expenses "into two broad categories: promotional — advertising intended to stimulate the purchase of utility services — and institutional and informational, a broad category inclusive of all advertising not clearly intended to promote sales." The Commission declared all promotional advertising contrary to the national policy of conserving energy. It acknowledged that the ban is not a perfect vehicle for conserving energy. Still, the Commission adopted the restriction because it was deemed likely to "result in some dampening of unnecessary growth" in energy consumption.

The Commission's order explicitly permitted "informational" advertising designed to encourage "*shifts* of consumption" from peak demand times to periods of low electricity demand. (Emphasis in original.) Informational advertising would not seek to increase aggregate consumption, but would invite a leveling of demand throughout any given 24-hour period. The agency offered to review "specific proposals by the companies for specifically described [advertising] programs that meet these criteria." Appellant challenged the order in state court, arguing that the Commission had restrained commercial speech in violation of the First and Fourteenth Amendments. The Commission's order was upheld by the trial court and at the intermediate appellate level. The New York Court of Appeals affirmed.

The Commission's order restricts only commercial speech, that is, expression related solely to the economic interests of the speaker and its audience. In applying the First Amendment to this area, we have rejected the "highly paternalistic" view that government has complete power to suppress or regulate commercial speech. Even when advertising communicates only an incomplete version of the relevant facts, the First Amendment presumes that some accurate information is better than no information at all.

Nevertheless, our decisions have recognized "the 'common-sense' distinction between speech proposing a commercial transaction, which occurs in an area traditionally subject to government regulation, and other varieties of speech." The Constitution therefore accords a lesser protection to commercial speech than to other constitutionally guaranteed expression. The protection available for particular commercial expression turns on the nature both of the expression and of the governmental interests served by its regulation.

The First Amendment's concern for commercial speech is based on the informational function of advertising. Consequently, there can be no constitutional objection to the suppression of commercial messages that do not accurately inform the public about lawful activity. The government may ban forms of communications more likely to deceive the public than to inform it.

If the communication is neither misleading nor related to unlawful activity, the government's power is more circumscribed. The State must assert a substantial interest to be achieved by restrictions on commercial speech. Moreover, the regulatory technique must be in proportion to that interest. The limitation on expression must be designed carefully to achieve the State's goal. Compliance with this requirement may be measured by two criteria. First, the restriction must directly advance the state interest involved; the regulation may not be sustained if it provides only ineffective or remote support for the government's purpose. Second, if the governmental interest could be served as well by a more limited restriction on commercial speech, the excessive restrictions cannot survive.

Under the first criterion, the Court has declined to uphold regulations that only indirectly advance the state interest involved. The second criterion recognizes that the First Amendment mandates that speech restrictions be "narrowly drawn." The regulatory technique may extend only as far as the interest it serves. The State cannot regulate speech that poses no danger to the asserted state interest, nor can it completely suppress information when narrower restrictions on expression would serve its interest as well.

In commercial speech cases, then, a four-part analysis has developed. At the outset, we must determine whether the expression is protected by the First Amendment. For commercial speech to come within that provision, it at least must concern lawful activity and not be misleading. Next, we ask whether the asserted governmental interest is substantial. If both inquiries yield positive answers, we must determine whether the regulation directly advances the governmental interest asserted, and whether it is not more extensive than is necessary to serve that interest.

[T]he critical inquiry in this case [is] whether the Commission's complete suppression of speech ordinarily protected by the First Amendment is no more extensive than necessary to further the State's interest in energy conservation. The Commission's order reaches all promotional advertising, regardless of the impact of the touted service on overall energy use. But the energy conservation rationale, as important as it is, cannot justify suppressing information about electric devices or services that would cause no net increase in total energy use. In addition, no showing has been made that a more limited restriction on the content of promotional advertising would not serve adequately the State's interests.

The Commission also has not demonstrated that its interest in conservation cannot be protected adequately by more limited regulation of appellant's commercial expression. To further its policy of conservation, the Commission could attempt to restrict the format and content of Central Hudson's advertising. It might, for example, require that the advertisements include information about the relative efficiency and expense of the offered service, both under current conditions and for the foreseeable future. In the absence of a showing that more limited speech regulations would be ineffective, we cannot approve the complete suppression of Central Hudson's advertising.

Justice Blackmun, with whom Justice Brennan joins, concurring.

It appears that the Court would permit the State to ban all direct advertising of air conditioning, assuming that a more limited restriction on such advertising would not effectively deter the public from cooling its homes. In my view, our cases do not support this type of suppression. If a governmental unit believes that use or over-use of air conditioning is a serious problem, it must attack that problem directly, by prohibiting air conditioning or regulating thermostat levels. Just as the Commonwealth of Virginia may promote professionalism of pharmacists directly, so too New York may not promote energy conservation "by keeping the public in ignorance." *Virginia Pharmacy Board*.

Justice Rehnquist, dissenting.

The Court's analysis in my view is wrong in several respects. Initially, I disagree with the Court's conclusion that the speech of a state-created monopoly, which is the subject of a comprehensive regulatory scheme, is entitled to protection under the First Amendment. I also think that the Court errs here in failing to recognize that the state law is most accurately viewed as an economic regulation and that the speech involved (if it falls within the scope of the First Amendment at all) occupies a significantly more subordinate position in the hierarchy of First Amendment values than the Court gives it today. Finally, the Court in reaching its decision improperly substitutes its own judgment for that of the State in deciding how a proper ban on promotional advertising should be drafted. With regard to this latter point, the Court adopts as its final part of a four-part test a "no more extensive than necessary" analysis that will unduly impair a state legislature's ability to adopt legislation reasonably designed to promote interests that have always been rightly thought to be of great importance to the State. I think New York's ban on such advertising falls within the scope of permissible state regulation of an economic activity by an entity that could not exist in corporate form, say nothing of enjoy monopoly status, were it not for the laws of New York.

This Court has previously recognized that although commercial speech may be entitled to First Amendment protection, that protection is not as extensive as that accorded to the advocacy of ideas. The test adopted by the Court elevates the protection accorded commercial speech that falls within the scope of the First Amendment to a level that is virtually indistinguishable from that of noncommercial speech. I think the Court in so doing has effectively accomplished the "devitalization" of the First Amendment that it counseled against in *Ohralik*. I think it has also by labeling economic regulation of business conduct as a restraint on "free speech" gone far to resurrect the discredited doctrine of cases such as *Lochner*. New York's order here is in my view more akin to an economic regulation to which virtually complete deference should be accorded by this Court.

NOTES

1. ***Extent of protection for commercial speech.*** Notice that Justice Powell, for the Court in *Central Hudson*, suggests that even an "incomplete version of the relevant facts" in commercial advertising merits First Amendment protection. Is that view inconsistent with the Court's decision in *Friedman* upholding a Texas law barring the use of trade names?

2. ***Comparison to political speech.*** The Court has never accepted the proposition that political speech can be suppressed merely because it is deceptive or misleading. Error does not deprive "pure" speech of constitutional protection. *See New York Times v. Sullivan*, p. 1156. But apparently this principle does not extend to commercial speech. What is the rationale for allowing government to proscribe commercial speech that is misleading?

Jackson and Jeffries argue that applying the First Amendment to commercial concerns is "diverting" a civil liberty to the interests of business:

> Nothing could be more hostile to the traditional understanding of the freedom of speech than governmental evaluations of the deceptiveness of political statements. Yet nothing could be more palpably wrong-headed than the extension of this approach to protect deceptive or misleading solicitations of commercial transactions.

Jackson & Jeffries, 65 VA. L. REV. at 1.

Most of the commentators supporting limitation on full First Amendment expression cite the lack of any value of commercial speech in protecting self-expression and individual development. But many commercial statements include artistic and ideological statements. "Advocacy advertising" is hardly rare. Even more important, the values of the marketplace of ideas and political participation in a democracy provided the foundations in Virginia Board for extending First Amendment protection to commercial speech. "Since commercial messages necessarily contain social and political implications, they possess the same potential as other forms of speech to challenge those in political power and constitute a portion of the political dialogue on policy issues." The Supreme Court, 1979 Term, 94 HARV. L. REV. 159, 166 (1980).

For the view that commercial speech and commercialism in our culture has ravaged the marketplace of ideas, consider the following:

> In sum, today's mass advertising often has less to do with products than lifestyles, less to do with facts than image, and less to do with reason than romance. It is more a total cultural system than an exclusively informational one; it is "a social discourse whose unifying theme is the meaning of consumption." This system refactors the marketplace-of-ideas equation: The ideas component is de-emphasized in favor of the marketplace component.

Ronald L.K. Collins & David M. Skover, The Death of Discourse 81 (1996).

Do the differences between commercial speech and political speech in terms of a capability for verification and durability justify a different standard of review? Justice Blackmun concurring in *Central Hudson* would argue that prior decisions used these distinctions only to justify the inapplicability of the overbreadth doctrine to commercial speech and to justify greater tolerance for time, place, and manner regulation of commercial expression. Is it desirable to use different standards of review for government controls based on speech content?

Is it an exaggeration for Justice Rehnquist to say that the Court's new "test" for protecting commercial speech elevates commercial speech to a First Amendment status "that is virtually indistinguishable from that of noncommercial speech"? After all, one important difference between clearly protected political speech and less clearly protected commercial speech is still very much alive as a result of Justice Powell's four-part test in Central Hudson: protection will be accorded to commercial speech only if it is not misleading.

[3] Professional Advertising and Solicitation

Lawyer advertising, originally an aspect of commercial speech doctrine, has spawned such a rich case law that it has now "developed its own distinct area of common law." Kozinski and Banner, 76 Va. L. Rev. at 630. These commentators observe, "At present, the law of attorney advertising has grown to such an extent that it has been able to seal itself off from its roots in first amendment theory." Thus, despite the relative youth of the commercial speech doctrine "judges often decide these [lawyer advertising] cases with reference only to prior law."

***Bates v. State Bar*, 433 U.S. 350 (1977).** The Court held unconstitutional a state bar association prohibition, enforced by the state supreme court, on all advertising by lawyers. Two members of the Arizona State Bar had opened a legal clinic designed to provide legal services to persons of moderate income who were not eligible for government legal aid. In order to keep costs down, the lawyers accepted only routine matters, such as uncontested divorces and uncontested adoptions. After operating the clinic for two years, they determined that advertising was necessary to obtain the high volume of business required to make their low cost legal services feasible. Accordingly, they placed an advertisement in a daily newspaper in Phoenix where they announced they were offering "legal services at very reasonable fees." The ad then listed the types of services provided and the fees charged. The two lawyers were disciplined under the bar association rule barring attorney advertising. The attorneys challenged the rule on the authority of Virginia Pharmacy, but the Arizona Supreme Court upheld the bar committee's determination under the advertising prohibition.

The Supreme Court, per Justice Blackmun, ruled that commercial speech, which would aid in providing informed and reliable decisionmaking, merit some First Amendment protection which was impaired by the disciplinary rule. "Like the Virginia statutes [involved in Virginia Pharmacy], the disciplinary rule serves to inhibit the free flow of commercial information and to keep the public in ignorance."

In considering the justifications offered for the advertising prohibition, Justice Blackmun initially emphasized the narrowness of the issue presented. Questions concerning advertising of the quality of legal services and of restrictions on in-person solicitation of clients were not in controversy. The heart of the dispute in the present case was "whether lawyers may constitutionally advertise the prices at which certain routine services will be performed."

The Court went on to reject a variety of justifications offered by the state bar and then stated:

> In the usual case involving a restraint on speech, a showing that the challenged rule served unconstitutionally to suppress speech would end our analysis. In the First Amendment context, the Court has permitted attack on overly broad statutes without requiring that the person making the attack demonstrate that in fact his specific conduct was protected. Having shown that the disciplinary rule interferes with protected speech, appellants ordinarily could expect to benefit regardless of the nature of their acts.

In the commercial speech context, however, the Court chose not to apply the overbreadth doctrine. Justice Blackmun noted that the overbreadth doctrine was "strong medicine," the justification for which applies "weakly, if at all, in the ordinary commercial context" since there are "'commonsense differences' between commercial speech and other varieties."

It was necessary therefore to consider whether the appellants' advertisement was constitutionally protected. In holding that "advertising by attorneys may not be subjected to a blanket suppression," Justice Blackmun emphasized that the Court was not holding "that advertising by attorneys may not be regulated in any way." He then suggested some limitations on advertising that were not expressly foreclosed by the decision. "Advertising that is false, deceptive, or misleading of course is subject to restraint. Since the advertiser knows his product and has a commercial interest in its dissemination, we have little worry that regulation to assure truthfulness will discourage protected speech." Further, the Court was not addressing the question of advertising the quality of services. He noted that such advertisements "are not susceptible to measurement or verification; accordingly, such claims may be so likely to be misleading as to warrant restriction."

Justice Blackmun also noted that rejection of a blanket prohibition on price advertising did not foreclose the use of "reasonable restrictions on the time, place, and manner of advertising." Nor did the ruling prevent the suppression of advertising concerning transactions that are themselves illegal. Finally, "the special problems of advertising on the electronic broadcast media will warrant special consideration."

The Court ended where it had begun — by stressing the narrow character of its holding.

> The constitutional issue in this case is only whether the State may prevent publication in a newspaper of appellants' truthful advertisement concerning the availability and terms of routine legal services. We rule simply that the flow of such information may not be restrained, and we therefore hold the present application of the disciplinary rule against appellants to be violative of the First Amendment.

***Ohralik v. Ohio State Bar Ass'n*, 436 U.S. 447 (1978).** The Court, per Justice Powell, resolved an issue expressly left open in *Bates v. State Bar*, holding that the Bar, acting with state authorization, "constitutionally may discipline a lawyer for soliciting clients in person, for pecuniary gain, under circumstances likely to pose dangers that the State has a right to prevent." *Compare In re Primus*, 436 U.S. 412 (1978), where the Court held that a state may not punish

> a member of its Bar [an ACLU attorney] who, seeking to further political and ideological goals through associational activity, including litigation, advises a layperson of her legal rights and discloses in a subsequent letter that free legal assistance is available from a nonprofit organization with which the lawyer and her associates are affiliated.

Are the differences in results between *Ohralik* and *In re Primus* a continuing illustration of the fact that commercial speech still occupies an inferior position vis-a-vis political speech?

Justice Powell in Ohralik described the diminished standard of protection for commercial speech as an effort to maintain full protection for full First Amendment speech.

> To require a parity of constitutional protection for commercial and non-commercial speech alike could invite dilution, simply by a leveling process, of the force of the First Amendment's guarantee with respect to the latter kind of speech. Rather than subject the First Amendment to such a devitalization, we instead have afforded commercial speech a limited measure of protection, commensurate with its subordinate position in the scale of First Amendment values, while allowing modes of regulation that might be impermissible in the realm of non-commercial expression.

***Edenfield v. Fane*, 507 U.S. 761 (1993).** A state ban on in-person solicitation by CPA's was struck down as violative of the First Amendment. Justice

Kennedy for the Court held that the state failed to show that its rule advanced state interests in a direct and material manner. Ohralik was distinguished on the ground that CPA in-person solicitation, unlike more persuasive lawyer in-person solicitation, is "not inherently conducive to overreaching and other forms of misconduct." CPA's are not trained in the art of persuasion. There was, therefore, slight risk that innocent persons would be misled. All the CPA sought to do was to "communicate nondeceptive information proposing a lawful commercial transaction."

***Zauderer v. Office of Disciplinary Counsel of the Supreme Court of Ohio*, 471 U.S. 626 (1985).** The Court upheld application of state disciplinary rules to an attorney who had failed to disclose in his ads that, if a lawsuit did not succeed, the client might be liable for the costs of the litigation. Philip Zauderer, an Ohio lawyer, had run a newspaper advertisement indicating his wish to represent women who had suffered injuries from the effects of using the Dalkon Shield Intrauterine Device. A special feature of the ad was that it contained a drawing of the device. Justice White for the Court said:

> Appellant contends that assessing the validity of the Ohio Supreme Court's decision to discipline him for his failure to include in the Dalkon Shield advertisement the information that clients might be liable for significant litigation costs even if their lawsuits were unsuccessful entails precisely the same inquiry as determining the validity of the restrictions on advertising content discussed above. Appellant, however, overlooks material differences between disclosure requirements and outright prohibitions on speech. In requiring attorneys who advertise their willingness to represent clients on a contingent-fee basis to state that the client may have to bear certain expenses even if he loses, Ohio has not attempted to prevent attorneys from conveying information to the public; it has only required them to provide somewhat more information than they might otherwise be inclined to present. We have, to be sure, held that in some instances, compulsion to speak may be as violative of the First Amendment as prohibitions on speech. *See, e.g., Wooley v. Maynard*; *Miami Herald Publishing Co. v. Tornillo.*
>
> But the interests at stake in this case are not of the same order as those discussed in *Wooley* [and] *Tornillo*. Ohio has not attempted to "prescribe what shall be orthodox in politics, nationalism, religion, or other matters of opinion or force citizens to confess by word or act their faith therein." *Barnette*. The State has attempted only to prescribe what shall be orthodox in commercial advertising, and its prescription has taken the form of a requirement that appellant include in his advertising purely factual and uncontroversial information about the terms under which his services will be available. Because the extension of First Amendment protection to commercial speech is justified principally by the value to consumers of the information such speech provides, appellant's constitutionally protected interest in not providing any particular factual information in his advertising is minimal.

The Court in *Zauderer* used the review standard employed in *Ohralik* — the Court "asked only if the (disclosure) requirements were narrowly related to the state interest in preventing deception of consumers." Why didn't the Court adopt the *Central Hudson* test "for evaluating this minimal burden on speech from disclosure laws?" Are some burdens on commercial speech so minimal as to be subject only to a rationality standard? Which ones? Why?

Ohralik and *Zauderer* are cases where government regulation of the activities of professionals has been challenged on the ground that the regulation of these activities is protected expression under the First Amendment. In *Ohralik* disciplinary rules prohibiting personal solicitation by lawyers were upheld, while in *Zauderer* disciplinary rules prohibiting printed advertising containing advice and information on specific legal issues were struck down. *Zauderer* suggests that when print solicitation rather than in-person solicitation is involved, a higher standard of review is applied.

***Florida Bar v. Went For It Inc.*, 515 U.S. 618 (1995).** The Supreme Court upheld (5-4) a Florida Bar Rule that prohibited "personal injury lawyers from sending targeted direct-mail solicitations to victims and their relatives for 30 days following an accident or disaster." The opinion by Justice O'Connor for the majority accepted the state's assertion that the harm to be avoided was the "outrage and irritation with the state-licensed legal profession that the practice of direct solicitation only days after accidents has engendered." Therefore, the state could restrict even mail solicitation as well as face-to-face solicitation in an effort to enhance public confidence in the profession and protect the sensitivities of accident victims and their families.

Justice Kennedy was joined in dissent by Justices Stevens, Souter, and Ginsburg. "With all respect for the Court, in my view its solicitude for the privacy of victims and its concern for our profession are misplaced and self-defeating. [W]hen an accident results in death or injury, it is often urgent at once to investigate the occurrence, identify witnesses, and preserve evidence."

***Peel v. Illinois Attorney Registration and Disciplinary Commission*, 496 U.S. 91 (1990).** The Court held that a state could not, consistent with the First Amendment, categorically prohibit a lawyer from advertising his certification as a trial specialist. Lawyer Gary Peel had been certified as a trial specialist by the National Board of Trial Advocacy. The Illinois Attorney Registration and Disciplinary Commission filed a complaint against Peel alleging that by holding himself out as a "specialist" Peel had violated a provision of the Illinois Code of Professional Responsibility. The Illinois Supreme Court censured Peel; the United States Supreme Court reversed.

A plurality of the Court, Justice Stevens joined by Justices Brennan, Blackmun, and Kennedy, said the issue was whether the letterhead "was misleading, and, even if it was not, whether the potentially misleading character of such a statement creates an interest sufficiently substantial to justify a categorical ban on their use." Justice Stevens declared that Peel's letterhead was not misleading because the claim of certification was verifiable and because of the "complete absence of deception in the case." The Illinois court had erred by confusing "the distinction between statements of opinion or quality and statements of objective facts that may support an inference of quality."

Justice O'Connor, joined by Chief Justice Rehnquist and Justice Scalia, dissented and observed that the result reached in the case illustrated the difficulties presented by "rote application of the commercial speech doctrine" to state regulation of professional standards for lawyers. She argued that prior cases did not mandate the invalidation of the state regulation at issue. Furthermore she protested the Court's "micromanagement of the State's inherent authority to police the ethical standards of the profession within its borders."

***Ibanez v. Florida Department of Business and Professional Regulation, Board of Accountancy*, 512 U.S. 136 (1994).** The Supreme Court held that the Florida Board had wrongly reprimanded attorney Silvia Ibanez for her use of the words "Certified Public Accountant" (CPA) and "Certified Financial Planner" (CFP) in the yellow pages listing for attorneys and on her law office stationery. Justice Ginsburg, writing for the Court, began from the premise that the use by Ibanez of the CPA and CFP designations was commercial speech and that "only false, deceptive or misleading commercial speech may be banned." Under *Central Hudson*, commercial speech that is not false, deceptive, or misleading may be regulated "but only if the State shows that the restriction directly and materially advances a substantial state interest in a manner no more extensive than necessary to serve that interest." Regulation will not be permitted if it only furnishes "remote support" to the purpose served by the regulation. *Edenfield v. Fane*. Justice Ginsburg concluded: "Measured against these standards the order reprimanding Ibanez cannot stand."

[4] Advertising of "Prohibitable" Transactions

***Posadas de Puerto Rico Associates v. Tourism Co. of Puerto Rico*, 478 U.S. 328 (1986).** Puerto Rico has legalized certain forms of gambling in specific places to encourage tourism. Advertising of these licensed gambling parlors to the Puerto Rican public was prohibited but "restricted advertising" outside of Puerto Rico was permitted. Under the Games of Chance Act, the Tourism Company of Puerto Rico was authorized to issue regulations which stated in pertinent part:

> No concessionaire, nor his agent or employee is authorized to advertise the gambling parlors to the public in Puerto Rico. The advertising of our games of chance is hereby authorized through newspapers, magazines, radio, television and other publicity media outside Puerto Rico subject to the prior editing and approval by the Tourism Development Company of the advertisement to be submitted in draft to the company.

Posadas brought a declaratory judgment against the Tourism Company in the Superior Court of Puerto Rico on the ground that the Game of Chance Act and its implementing regulations violated protected commercial speech. The Puerto Rico court reasoned that the legislature was concerned with advertising directed to the residents of Puerto Rico. In light of this, the court issued a narrowing interpretation of the statute as follows:

> We hereby allow, within the jurisdiction of Puerto Rico, advertising by the casinos addressed to tourists, provided they do not invite the residents of Puerto Rico to visit the casino, even though said announcements may incidentally reach the hands of a resident. We hereby authorize advertising in the mass communication media of the country, where the trade name of the hotel is used even though it may contain a reference to the casino provided that the word casino is never used alone nor specified. Since a clausus enumeration of this regulation is unforeseeable, any other situation or incident relating to the legal restriction must be measured in light of the public policy of promoting tourism. If the object of the advertisement is the tourist, it passes legal scrutiny.

Justice Rehnquist for the Court first observed, "Because this case involves the restriction of pure commercial speech which does 'no more than propose a commercial transaction,' our First Amendment analysis is guided by the general principles identified in *Central Hudson*." With respect to the first two prongs of the test, the majority found that gambling posed substantial problems in Puerto Rico and that casino gambling could rationally be distinguished from other forms of gambling such as card games and cockfighting.

With respect to whether the prohibition was more broad than necessary to accomplish the purpose, the Court announced a standard of deference to legislative judgment. "We think it is up to the legislature to decide whether" other means of achieving its goals would be "as effective."

Finally came the surprising and significant part of the *Posadas* opinion:

> Appellant also makes the related argument that, having chosen to legalize casino gambling for residents of Puerto Rico, the First Amendment prohibits the legislature from using restrictions on advertising to accomplish its goal of reducing demand for such gambling. We disagree. In our view, appellant has the argument backwards. As we noted in the preceding paragraph, it is precisely because the government could have enacted a wholesale prohibition of the underlying conduct that it is permissible for the government to take the less intrusive step of allowing the conduct, but reducing the demand through restrictions on advertising. It would surely be a Pyrrhic victory for casino owners such as appellant to gain recognition of a First Amendment right to advertise their casinos to the residents of Puerto Rico, only to thereby force the legislature into banning casino gambling by residents altogether. It would just as surely be a strange constitutional doctrine which would concede to the legislature the authority to totally ban a product or activity, but deny to the legislature the authority to forbid the stimulation of demand for the product or activity through advertising on behalf of those who would profit from such increased demand. Legislative regulation of products or activities deemed harmful, such as cigarettes, alcoholic beverages, and prostitution, has varied from outright prohibition on the one hand, to legalization of the product or activity with restrictions on stimulation of its demand

> on the other hand. To rule out the latter, intermediate kind of response would require more than we find in the First Amendment.

Justice Brennan, joined by Justices Marshall and Blackmun, dissented.

> I see no reason why commercial speech should be afforded less protection than other types of speech where, as here, the government seeks to suppress commercial speech in order to deprive consumers of accurate information concerning lawful activity. However, no differences between commercial and other kinds of speech justify protecting commercial speech less extensively where, as here, the government seeks to manipulate private behavior by depriving citizens of truthful information concerning lawful activities. Accordingly, I believe that where the government seeks to suppress the dissemination of nonmisleading commercial speech relating to legal activities, for fear that recipients will act on the information provided, such regulation should be subject to strict judicial scrutiny.

Justice Stevens also dissented, noting various discriminatory aspects of the revised regulations as narrowed by the Puerto Rico courts.

The standard for commercial speech. *Virginia Pharmacy* and *Bates* suggested that legislative prohibitions on entire categories of commercial speech were going to be impermissible. Yet, in *Posadas*, a ban on the category of speech, i.e., a ban by the Puerto Rican Government on advertisements that encourage Puerto Ricans to patronize casinos in Puerto Rico, was upheld. To reach this result, Chief Justice Rehnquist uses the *Central Hudson* test which presumably is a more demanding test than the rationality standard. Yet, as used, does it function very differently than the rationality standard?

Is the only solution to the evisceration of the protection intended to be afforded by the *Central Hudson* test, the adoption of a strict scrutiny standard for commercial speech? Is this what Justice Brennan is advocating? The problem, of course, with the adoption of a strict scrutiny standard in the commercial speech area is that it might protect too much. Could one still have securities laws?

Greater includes the lesser? In *Posadas*, Chief Justice Rehnquist stated his now well-known and controversial greater-includes-the-lesser argument. Consider the argument that because Rehnquist at least formally adhered to the *Central Hudson* test, it is hard to believe that the Court intended to adopt the greater-includes-the lesser argument. Moreover, he believes this argument is analytically flawed:

> The fatal flaw in Justice Rehnquist's reasoning is that he actually has reversed the "greater" and the "lesser." His logic effectively reduces the greater first amendment protection of expression to the considerably lesser Fifth Amendment protection afforded commercial conduct.

Martin Redish, *Product Health Claims and the First Amendment: Scientific Expression and the Twilight Zone of Commercial Speech*, 43 VAND. L. REV. 1433, 1441–42 (1990).

It is further argued that the greater-includes-the-lesser argument is inconsistent with a line of First Amendment doctrine proclaimed in *Schenck v. United States,* 249 U.S. 47 (1919), providing "at least some degree of first amendment protection" to advocacy of unlawful conduct. If the logic of Rehnquist's argument is accepted, "presumably Congress could ban *all* such advocacy, because by hypothesis Congress could ban — indeed, already has banned — the conduct advocated by such expression."

***Rubin v. Coors Brewing Co.,* 514 U.S. 476 (1995).** Evidence that *Central Hudson* is not as deferential as its critics contend is found in this case. In an opinion by Justice Thomas, a unanimous Court invalidated a portion of 27 U.S.C. § 205(e)(2), which prohibited beer labels from displaying alcohol content. The statute was passed shortly after adoption of the Twenty-First Amendment and the repeal of Prohibition. The statute allows display of alcoholic content on bottles of distilled spirits and wine, but "statements of, or statements likely to be considered as statements of, alcoholic content of malt beverages are prohibited unless required by State law."

Justice Thomas applied *Central Hudson* this way:

> We conclude that § 205(e)(2) cannot directly and materially advance its asserted interest because of the overall irrationality of the Government's regulatory scheme. While the laws governing labeling prohibit the disclosure of alcohol content unless required by state law, federal regulations apply a contrary policy to beer advertising. Like § 205(e)(2), these restrictions prohibit statements of alcohol content in advertising, but, unlike § 205(e)(2), they apply only in States that affirmatively prohibit such advertisements. As only 18 States at best prohibit disclosure of content in advertisements, brewers remain free to disclose alcohol content in advertisements, but not on labels, in much of the country. The failure to prohibit the disclosure of alcohol content in advertising, which would seem to constitute a more influential weapon in any strength war than labels, makes no rational sense if the government's true aim is to suppress strength wars.
>
> Other provisions of the FAAA and its regulations similarly undermine § 205(e)(2)'s efforts to prevent strength wars. While § 205(e)(2) bans the disclosure of alcohol content on beer labels, it allows the exact opposite in the case of wines and spirits. Thus, distilled spirits may contain statements of alcohol content, and such disclosures are required for wines with more than 14 percent alcohol. If combatting strength wars were the goal, we would assume that Congress would regulate disclosure of alcohol content for the strongest beverages as well as for the weakest ones. Further, the Government permits brewers to signal high alcohol content through use of the term "malt liquor."
>
> To be sure, the government's interest in combatting strength wars remains a valid goal. But the irrationality of this unique and puzzling regulatory framework ensures that the labelling ban will fail to achieve that end. There is little chance that § 205(e)(2) can directly and materially advance its aim, while other provisions of the same act directly undercut its efforts.

Justice Stevens concurred with the comment that "Congress may not seek to accomplish [its] purpose through a policy of consumer ignorance."

44 LIQUORMART v. RHODE ISLAND

517 U.S. 484, 116 S. Ct. 1495, 134 L.Ed. 2d 34 (1996)

[A liquor retailer challenged a Rhode Island statutory bar against advertisements of retail liquor prices except at the place of sale. Rhode Island defended its statute on the ground that the Twenty-First Amendment gives the states the authority to regulate alcoholic beverages within their borders. Rejecting this contention, a full majority of the Court held that "the Twenty-First Amendment does not qualify the constitutional prohibition against laws abridging the freedom of speech embodied in the First Amendment." With regard to the First Amendment aspects of the case, however, the Court was badly fractionated.]

JUSTICE STEVENS, joined by JUSTICES KENNEDY and GINSBURG with respect to Part IV; joined by JUSTICES KENNEDY, SOUTER, and GINSBURG with respect to Part V; joined by JUSTICES KENNEDY, THOMAS and GINSBURG with respect to Part VI.

IV

As our review of the case law reveals, Rhode Island errs in concluding that all commercial speech regulations are subject to a similar form of constitutional review simply because they target a similar category of expression. The mere fact that messages propose commercial transactions does not in and of itself dictate the constitutional analysis that should apply to decisions to suppress them.

When a State regulates commercial messages to protect consumers from misleading, deceptive, or aggressive sales practices, or requires the disclosure of beneficial consumer information, the purpose of its regulation is consistent with the reasons for according constitutional protection to commercial speech and therefore justifies less than strict review. However, when a State entirely prohibits the dissemination of truthful, nonmisleading commercial messages for reasons unrelated to the preservation of a fair bargaining process, there is far less reason to depart from the rigorous review that the First Amendment generally demands.

Sound reasons justify reviewing the latter type of commercial speech regulation more carefully. Most obviously, complete speech bans, unlike content-neutral restrictions on the time, place, or manner of expression, are particularly dangerous because they all but foreclose alternative means of disseminating certain information.

Precisely because bans against truthful, nonmisleading commercial speech rarely seek to protect consumers from either deception or overreaching, they usually rest solely on the offensive assumption that the public will respond "irrationally" to the truth. The First Amendment directs us to be especially skeptical of regulations that seek to keep people in the dark for what the government perceives to be their own good. That teaching applies equally to state attempts to deprive consumers of accurate information about their chosen products.

V

In this case, there is no question that Rhode Island's price advertising ban constitutes a blanket prohibition against truthful, nonmisleading speech about a lawful product. There is also no question that the ban serves an end unrelated to consumer protection. Accordingly, we must review the price advertising ban with "special care," *Central Hudson*, mindful that speech prohibitions of this type rarely survive constitutional review.

The State argues that the price advertising prohibition should nevertheless be upheld because it directly advances the State's substantial interest in promoting temperance, and because it is no more extensive than necessary.

Although the record suggests that the price advertising ban may have some impact on the purchasing patterns of temperate drinkers of modest means, the State has presented no evidence to suggest that its speech prohibition will significantly reduce market-wide consumption. Moreover, the evidence suggests that the abusive drinker will probably not be deterred by a marginal price increase, and that the true alcoholic may simply reduce his purchases of other necessities.

As is evident, any conclusion that elimination of the ban would significantly increase alcohol consumption would require us to engage in the sort of "speculation or conjecture" that is an unacceptable means of demonstrating that a restriction on commercial speech directly advances the State's asserted interest.

The State also cannot satisfy the requirement that its restriction on speech be no more extensive than necessary. It is perfectly obvious that alternative forms of regulation that would not involve any restriction on speech would be more likely to achieve the State's goal of promoting temperance. As the State's own expert conceded, higher prices can be maintained either by direct regulation or by increased taxation. Per capita purchases could be limited as is the case with prescription drugs. Even educational campaigns focused on the problems of excessive, or even moderate, drinking might prove to be more effective.

As a result, even under the less than strict standard that generally applies in commercial speech cases, the State has failed to establish a "reasonable fit" between its abridgment of speech and its temperance goal. It necessarily follows that the price advertising ban cannot survive the more stringent constitutional review that *Central Hudson* itself concluded was appropriate for the complete suppression of truthful, nonmisleading commercial speech.

VI

The State responds by arguing that it merely exercised appropriate "legislative judgment" in determining that a price advertising ban would best promote temperance. Relying on the *Central Hudson* analysis set forth in *Posadas*, Rhode Island first argues that, because expert opinions as to the effectiveness of the price advertising ban "go both ways," the Court of Appeals correctly concluded that the ban constituted a "reasonable choice" by the legislature. The State next contends that precedent requires us to give particular deference to that legislative choice because the State could, if it chose, ban the sale of alcoholic beverages outright. Finally, the State argues that deference is appropriate because alcoholic beverages are so-called "vice" products.

The State's first argument fails to justify the speech prohibition at issue.

The reasoning in *Posadas* does support the State's argument, but, on reflection, we are now persuaded that *Posadas* erroneously performed the First Amendment analysis. The casino advertising ban was designed to keep truthful, nonmisleading speech from members of the public for fear that they would be more likely to gamble if they received it. As a result, the advertising ban served to shield the State's antigambling policy from the public scrutiny that more direct, nonspeech regulation would draw.

Given our longstanding hostility to commercial speech regulation of this type, *Posadas* clearly erred in concluding that it was "up to the legislature" to choose suppression over a less speech-restrictive policy. The *Posadas* majority's conclusion on that point cannot be reconciled with the unbroken line of prior cases striking down similarly broad regulations on truthful, nonmisleading advertising when non-speech-related alternatives were available.

We also cannot accept the State's second contention, which is premised entirely on the "greater-includes-the-lesser" reasoning endorsed toward the end of the majority's opinion in *Posadas*. Further consideration persuades us that the "greater-includes-the-lesser" argument should be rejected for the important reason that it is inconsistent with both logic and well-settled doctrine.

Although we do not dispute the proposition that greater powers include lesser ones, we fail to see how that syllogism requires the conclusion that the State's power to regulate commercial *activity* is "greater" than its power to ban truthful, nonmisleading commercial *speech*. Contrary to the assumption made in *Posadas*, we think it quite clear that banning speech may sometimes prove far more intrusive than banning conduct. [A] local ordinance banning bicycle lessons may curtail freedom far more than one that prohibits bicycle riding within city limits. In short, we reject the assumption that words are necessarily less vital to freedom than actions, or that logic somehow proves that the power to prohibit an activity is necessarily "greater" than the power to suppress speech about it.

As a matter of First Amendment doctrine, the *Posadas* syllogism is even less defensible. The text of the First Amendment makes clear that the Constitution presumes that attempts to regulate speech are more dangerous than attempts to regulate conduct. That presumption accords with the essential role that the free flow of information plays in a democratic society. As a result, the First Amendment directs that government may not suppress speech as easily as it may suppress conduct, and that speech restrictions cannot be treated as simply another means that the government may use to achieve its ends.

These basic First Amendment principles clearly apply to commercial speech; indeed, the *Posadas* majority impliedly conceded as much by applying the

Central Hudson test. Thus, it is no answer that commercial speech concerns products and services that the government may freely regulate. Our decisions from *Virginia Pharmacy Bd.* on have made plain that a State's regulation of the sale of goods differs in kind from a State's regulation of accurate information about those goods. Thus, just as it is perfectly clear that Rhode Island could not ban all obscene liquor ads except those that advocated temperance, we think it equally clear that its power to ban the sale of liquor entirely does not include a power to censor all advertisements that contain accurate and nonmisleading information about the price of the product.

Finally, we find unpersuasive the State's contention that the price advertising ban should be upheld because it targets commercial speech that pertains to a "vice" activity. [T]he scope of any "vice" exception to the protection afforded by the First Amendment would be difficult, if not impossible, to define. [A] vice label that is unaccompanied by a corresponding prohibition against the commercial behavior at issue fails to provide a principled justification for the regulation of commercial speech about that activity.

JUSTICE SCALIA, concurring in part and concurring in the judgment.

I share Justice Thomas's discomfort with the *Central Hudson* test, which seems to me to have nothing more than policy intuition to support it. I also share Justice Stevens' aversion towards paternalistic governmental policies that prevent men and women from hearing facts that might not be good for them. On the other hand, it would also be paternalism for us to prevent the people of the States from enacting laws that we consider paternalistic, unless we have good reason to believe that the Constitution itself forbids them.

Since I do not believe we have before us the wherewithal to declare *Central Hudson* wrong—or at least the wherewithal to say what ought to replace it—I must resolve this case in accord with our existing jurisprudence. I am not disposed to develop new law, or reinforce old, on this issue, and accordingly I merely concur in the judgment of the Court. I believe, however, that Justice Stevens' treatment of the application of the Twenty-First Amendment to this case is correct, and accordingly join [those] Parts of Justice Stevens' opinion.

JUSTICE THOMAS, concurring in Parts I, II, VI, and VII, and concurring in the judgment.

In cases such as this, in which the government's asserted interest is to keep legal users of a product or service ignorant in order to manipulate their choices in the marketplace, the balancing test adopted in *Central Hudson* should not be applied, in my view. Rather, such an "interest" is per se illegitimate and can no more justify regulation of "commercial" speech than it can justify regulation of "noncommercial" speech.

Both JUSTICE STEVENS and JUSTICE O'CONNOR appear to adopt a stricter, more categorical interpretation of the fourth prong of *Central Hudson* than that suggested in some of our other opinions, one that could, as a practical matter, go a long way toward the position I take. [Their] opinions would appear to commit the courts to striking down restrictions on speech whenever a direct regulation (i.e., a regulation involving no restriction on speech regarding lawful activity at all) would be an equally effective method of dampening demand by legal users. But it would seem that directly banning a product (or rationing it, taxing it, controlling its price, or otherwise restricting its sale in specific ways) would virtually always be at least as effective in discouraging consumption as merely restricting advertising regarding the product would be, and thus virtually all restrictions with such a purpose would fail the fourth prong of the *Central Hudson* test. I welcome this outcome; but, rather than "applying" the fourth prong of Central Hudson to reach the inevitable result that all or most such advertising restrictions must be struck down, I would adhere to the doctrine adopted in *Virginia Pharmacy Bd.* and in JUSTICE BLACKMUN's *Central Hudson* concurrence, that all attempts to dissuade legal choices by citizens by keeping them ignorant are impermissible.

In my view, the *Central Hudson* test asks the courts to weigh the incommensurable — the value of knowledge versus the value of ignorance — and to apply contradictory premises — that informed adults are the best judges of their own interests, and that they are not. Rather than continuing to apply a test that makes no sense to me where the asserted state interest is of the type involved here, I would return to the reasoning and holding of *Virginia Pharmacy Bd.* Under that decision, these restrictions fail.

JUSTICE O'CONNOR, with whom CHIEF JUSTICE REHNQUIST, JUSTICE SOUTER, and JUSTICE BREYER join, concurring in the judgment.

I agree with the Court that Rhode Island's price-advertising ban is invalid. I would resolve this case more narrowly, however, by applying our established *Central Hudson* test to determine whether this commercial-speech regulation survives First Amendment scrutiny. Rhode Island's regulation fails the final prong [of *Central Hudson*]; that is, its ban is more extensive than necessary to serve the State's interest.

[I]n order for a speech restriction to pass muster under the final prong, there must be a fit between the legislature's goal and method, "a fit that is not necessarily perfect, but reasonable; that represents not necessarily the best single disposition but one whose scope is in proportion to the interest served." *Bd. of Trustees of St. Univ. of New York v. Fox.*

If the target is simply higher prices generally to discourage consumption, the regulation imposes too great, and unnecessary, a prohibition on speech in order to achieve it. The State has other methods at its disposal — methods that would more directly accomplish this stated goal without intruding on sellers' ability to provide truthful, nonmisleading information to customers. A tax, for example, would have a far more certain and direct effect on prices, without any restriction on speech. The principal opinion suggests further alternatives.

It is true that *Posadas* accepted as reasonable, without further inquiry, Puerto Rico's assertions that the regulations furthered the government's interest and were no more extensive than necessary to serve that interest. Since *Posadas*, however, this Court has examined more searchingly the State's professed goal, and the speech restriction put into place to further it, before accepting a State's claim that the speech restriction satisfies First Amendment scrutiny. The closer look that we have required since *Posadas* comports better with the purpose of the analysis set out in *Central Hudson*, by requiring the State to show that the speech restriction directly advances its interest and is narrowly tailored. Under such a closer look, Rhode Island's price-advertising ban clearly fails to pass muster.

Because Rhode Island's regulation fails even the less stringent standard set out in *Central Hudson*, nothing here requires adoption of a new analysis for the evaluation of commercial speech regulation. The principal opinion acknowledges that "even under the less than strict standard that generally applies in commercial speech cases, the State has failed to establish a reasonable fit between its abridgement of speech and its temperance goal." Because we need go no further, I would not here undertake the question whether the test we have employed since *Central Hudson* should be displaced.

NOTES

1. *New Approaches.* Justice Stevens' opinion in *Liquormart* applied *Central Hudson* but without enthusiasm. This is hardly surprising since in the *Coors* case Justice Stevens, concurring, made clear his disenchantment with *Central Hudson*. Would Stevens prefer to return to *Virginia Pharmacy*?

Justice O'Connor criticized Justice Stevens for not applying the "established *Central Hudson*" test in *Liquormart*. Justice Stevens said that blanket prohibitions against truthful nonmisleading advertising must be examined with "special care" under *Central Hudson*. Is this "special care" requirement a new hurdle imposed on advertising regulation unjustified by *Central Hudson*?

44 Liquormart is outspoken in its hostility to *Posadas*. Stevens would discard *Posadas* altogether and O'Connor declined to follow it. But Justice O'Connor did not call for its overruling. Why not?

Professor Robert Post offers the following critical assessment of the commercial speech doctrine: Commercial speech received protection because of its informational function. However, public discourse is protected to assure citizen participation in a democratic society. The information-protection rationale of commercial speech explains why commercial speech can be subject to restrictions that would not be tolerated in the case of public discourse; prior restraint, over breadth and compelled disclosure are all, in some circumstances, permissible restraints *vis-a-vis* commercial speech. But the *Central Hudson* test is inadequate to accomplish the informational function of commercial speech. Professor Post makes a forecast on the future of the commercial speech doctrine: "My best guess, therefore, is that the commercial speech doctrine will either continue to unfold the implications of its Meiklejohnian foundations by developing the doctrinal tools necessary to assess the impact of state regulation on the actual circulation of commercial information, or it will abandon these foundations as the Justices seek to merge commercial speech with public discourse." Robert Post, *The Constitutional Status of Commercial Speech*, 48 UCLA L. Rev. 1, 55 (2000).

Compare Professor Post's theoretical approach to commercial speech doctrine to the following far more pragmatic analysis. Professor Suzanna Sherry argues that "concrete, atheoretical concerns" play a substantial role in the Supreme Court's commercial speech cases. This pragmatic approach, she asserts, is demonstrated by the Court's reliance on empirical data in some commercial speech cases. Thus, *Lorillard* relied on empirical studies to justify its conclusion that "limiting exposure to tobacco advertising directly advanced the state's interest in reducing underage use of cigars and smokeless tobacco products, thus satisfying the third prong of the Central Hudson test." Similarly, she observes: "In *44 Liquormart*, the Court credited the district court findings of fact based on empirical studies of liquor consumption patterns, rejecting the appellate court's finding of 'inherent merit' in the state's argument that competitive price advertising would lower prices and thus increase alcohol sales." Suzanna Sherry, *Hard Cases Make Good Judges*, 99 Nw. U. L. Rev. 3, 12–13 (2004).

2. *Tobacco advertising.* The Food and Drug Administration is considering proposals which limit "tobacco promotions and advertising aimed at young people." The Clinton administration distinguished its proposal from the Rhode Island ban on liquor price advertising on the grounds that its proposal is not as comprehensive, it is a health measure, and aimed only at young people. Washington Post, p. A4, May 14, 1996. Would a ban on tobacco advertising aimed at young people be valid? Would content neutrality be a problem?

3. *Advertising and the media.* Some writers have argued that advertisers play the role of censor in contemporary American society:

> Advertisers, not governments, are the primary censors of media content in the United States. Or perhaps it should be said that advertisers are second after the media themselves, the "gate-keepers," which engage in self-censorship for both good and bad reasons.

C. Edwin Baker, Advertising and a Democratic Press 99 (1994). Given his misgivings about advertising, Professor Baker believes the current commercial speech doctrine tends to favor regulation of commercial speech: "Although possibly commercial speech should never have been protected at all, under current doctrine any good policy justification for a tax or regulation should defeat an advertiser's First Amendment claims." *Id.* at 130. Do *Coors* and *44 Liquormart* suggest that this assessment of the Court's commercial speech doctrine should be revised?

GREATER NEW ORLEANS BROADCASTING ASSOCIATION, INC. v. UNITED STATES

527 U.S. 173, 119 S. Ct. 1923, 144 L.Ed. 2d 161 (1999)

[A federal statute, 18 U.S.C. Sec. 1304, banned the advertising of casino gambling on radio and television. The law applied even to jurisdictions such as Louisiana where casino gambling was legal. Some broadcasters in the greater New Orleans area instituted a First Amendment challenge law. The Supreme Court, per Justice Stevens, held unanimously that the application of 18 U.S.C. Sec. 1304 to casino gambling broadcast ads in Louisiana violated the First Amendment.]

Justice Stevens delivered the opinion of the Court.

In this case, there is no need to break new ground. *Central Hudson*, as applied in our more recent commercial speech cases, provides an adequate basis for decision. All parties to this case agree that the messages petitioners wish to broadcast constitute commercial speech, and that these broadcasts would satisfy the first part of the *Central Hudson* test: Their content is not misleading and concerns lawful activities, i.e., private casino gambling in Louisiana and Mississippi.

The second part of the *Central Hudson* test asks whether the asserted governmental interest served by the speech restriction is substantial. The Solicitor General identifies two such interests: (1) reducing the social costs associated with "gambling" or "casino gambling," and (2) assisting States that "restrict gambling" or "prohibit casino gambling" within their own borders. Underlying Congress' statutory scheme, the Solicitor General contends, is the judgment that gambling contributes to corruption and organized crime; underwrites bribery, narcotics trafficking, and other illegal conduct; imposes a regressive tax on the poor; and "offers a false but sometimes irresistible hope of financial advancement."

We can accept the characterization of these two interests as "substantial," but that conclusion is by no means self-evident. No one seriously doubts that the Federal Government may assert a legitimate and substantial interest in alleviating the societal ills recited above, or in assisting like-minded States to do the same. But in the judgment of both the Congress and many state legislatures, the social costs that support the suppression of gambling are offset, and sometimes outweighed, by countervailing policy considerations, primarily in the form of economic benefits. That Congress has generally exempted state-run lotteries and casinos from federal gambling legislation reflects a decision to defer to, and even promote, differing gambling policies in different States. Whatever its character in 1934 when § 1304 was adopted, the federal policy of discouraging gambling in general, and casino gambling in particular, is now decidedly equivocal.

The third part of the *Central Hudson* test asks whether the speech restriction directly and materially advances the asserted governmental interest. Consequently, "the regulation may not be sustained if it provides only ineffective or remote support for the government's purpose." *Central Hudson*. We have observed that "this requirement is critical; otherwise, 'a State could with ease restrict commercial speech in the service of other objectives that could not themselves justify a burden on commercial expression.'" *Rubin v. Coors Brewing Co.* [text, p. 1192.]

The fourth part of the test complements the direct-advancement inquiry of the third, asking whether the speech restriction is not more extensive than necessary to serve the interests that support it. As applied to petitioners' case, § 1304 cannot satisfy these standards. With regard to the first asserted interest — alleviating the social costs of casino gambling by limiting demand — the Government contends that its broadcasting restrictions directly advance that interest because "promotional" broadcast advertising concerning casino gambling increases demand for such gambling, which in turn increases the amount of casino gambling that produces those social costs. Additionally, the Government believes that compulsive gamblers are especially susceptible to the pervasiveness and potency of broadcast advertising. Assuming the accuracy of this causal chain, it does not necessarily follow that the Government's speech ban has directly and materially furthered the asserted interest.

While it is no doubt fair to assume that more advertising would have some impact on overall demand for gambling, it is also reasonable to assume that much of that advertising would merely channel gamblers to one casino rather than another. More important, any measure of the effectiveness of the Government's attempt to minimize the social costs of gambling cannot ignore Congress' simultaneous encouragement of tribal casino gambling, which may well be growing at a rate exceeding any increase in gambling or compulsive gambling that private casino advertising could produce.

The second interest asserted by the Government — the derivative goal of "assisting" States with policies that disfavor private casinos — adds little to its case. We cannot see how this broadcast restraint, ambivalent as it is, might directly and adequately further any state interest in dampening consumer demand for casino gambling if it cannot achieve the same goal with respect to the similar federal interest.

Furthermore, even assuming that the state policies on which the Federal Government seeks to embellish are more coherent and pressing than their federal counterpart, § 1304 sacrifices an intolerable amount of truthful speech about lawful conduct when compared to all of the policies at stake and the social ills that one could reasonably hope such a ban to eliminate.

Accordingly, respondents cannot overcome the presumption that the speaker and the audience, not the Government, should be left to assess the value of accurate and nonmisleading information about lawful conduct. Had the Federal Government adopted a more coherent policy, or accommodated the rights of speakers in States that have legalized the underlying conduct, this might be a different case. But under current federal law, as applied to petitioners and the messages that they wish to convey, the broadcast prohibition in 18 U.S.C. § 1304 and 47 CFR § 73.1211 (1998) violates the First Amendment. The judgment of the Court of Appeals is therefore REVERSED.

CHIEF JUSTICE REHNQUIST, concurring.

Title 18 U.S.C. § 1304 regulates broadcast advertising of lotteries and casino gambling. I agree with the Court that "the operation of § 1304 and its attendant regulatory regime is so pierced by exemptions and inconsistencies," that it violates the First Amendment.

JUSTICE THOMAS, concurring in the judgment.

I continue to adhere to my view that "in cases such as this, in which the government's asserted interest is to keep legal users of a product or service ignorant in order to manipulate their choices in the marketplace," the *Central Hudson* test should not be applied because "such an 'interest' is per se illegitimate and can no more justify regulation of 'commercial speech' than it can justify regulation of 'noncommercial' speech." *44 Liquormart, Inc. v. Rhode Island* (concurring in part and concurring in the judgment). Accordingly, I concur only in the judgment.

NOTES

1. *Significance of Greater New Orleans.* Two commentators note that in Greater New Orleans the Court once again declared that *Central Hudson* remained a part of constitutional jurisprudence despite doubts about its continuing utility both within the Court and the academy. Furthermore, *Greater New Orleans* clearly sounded the death knell for any lingering validity the "greater-includes-the-lesser" rationale of Posadas might still have had: "In other words, government power to ban a product or activity does not alone reduce First Amendment protection for truthful, non-deceptive commercial speech about that product or activity. Instead the government must regulate in a more direct manner that is less intrusive upon the First Amendment rights commercial speakers and the public." Michael Hoefges and Milgros Rivera-Sanchez, *"Vice" Advertising Under the Supreme Court's Commercial Speech Doctrine: The Shifting Central Hudson Analysis*, 22 HASTINGS COMM & ENT. L.J. 345, 386 (2000).

Professor Rodney Smolla summarizes the flow of commercial speech cases since *Virginia Pharmacy*: "The arc of the cases is unmistakable: in decision after decision the Supreme Court has advanced protection for advertising, repeatedly striking down regulation grounded in paternalistic motivations or speculative judgments by government regulators." Smolla, *Free the Fortune 500! The Debate Over Corporate Speech and the First Amendment*, 54 CASE W. RES. L. REV. 1277, 1292 (2004). He suggests that the case law signifies that abandonment of *Central Hudson* is imminent: "The opinions of several Justices in *44 Liquormart* seemed to signal the possibility that the Court was willing to expand even more the already substantial First Amendment protection granted to commercial speech." This "possibility was raised again in *Greater New Orleans Broadcasting*" where the Court was invited to repudiate *Central Hudson* but declined to do so. He concludes: "[W]hile the Court continues to apply *Central Hudson*, it does so against the backdrop of growing momentum for doctrinal change that would provide even greater [First Amendment] protection for advertising." *Id.* at 1297–1298.

2. *First Amendment status of "Vice" Advertising.* With respect to "vice" advertising and the commercial speech doctrine, generally, consider the following: "Virtually every nation in the world is free to adopt as, as one element of its strategy for combating tobacco use, regulations designed to restrict demand-inducing advertising. A construction of the First Amendment that permits restrictions only on deceptive advertising and advertising for illegal projects — as proposed by Justice Thomas and perhaps Justice Stevens — would, in effect, remove this as a regulatory option in the United States. The government would be forced into one of two polar positions: either making tobacco use illegal and thereby permitting restrictions of nondeceptive tobacco advertising, or continuing to allow adults to use tobacco products legally and thereby permitting unrestricted promotion of tobacco products. From a policy perspective, this regulatory straight jacket makes little sense. If cigarettes were introduced today, knowing what we know about them as a product, there is little doubt that they would be banned. And any advertising for them would thus also be banned, and this would be constitutional under the Thomas/Stevens commercial speech theory." Thomas Merrill, *The Constitution and the Cathedral: Prohibiting, Purchasing, Possibly Condemning Tobacco Advertising*, 93 NW. U. L. REV. 1143, 1203 (1999).

Why does Professor Merrill says that if tobacco were a banned substance, tobacco advertising could also be banned? Is it because, under *Central Hudson*, the advertising of an illegal product merits no First Amendment protection?

3. *Tobacco Advertising and Free Speech: Lorillard Tobacco Co. v. Reilly*, 533 U.S. 525 (2001): In *Lorillard*, the Court applied its commercial speech analysis developed in *44 Liquormart* and *Greater New Orleans* to the issue of tobacco advertising regulation. The Attorney General of Massachusetts promulgated comprehensive regulations governing the advertising and sale of cigarettes, smokeless tobacco, and cigars. The purpose of the regulations was, according to the Attorney General, "to eliminate deception and unfairness in the way cigarettes and smokeless tobacco products are marketed, sold and distributed in Massachusetts in order to address the incidence of cigarette smoking and smokeless tobacco use by children under legal age and in order to prevent access to such products by underage consumers." Specifically, the regulations prohibited outdoor tobacco advertising (including advertising seen from within a retail establishment) in any location that is within a 1,000-foot radius of any public playground, playground area in a public park, elementary school or secondary school. In addition, they prohibited point-of-sale advertising any portion of which is placed lower than five feet from the floor of any retail establishment located within that 1,000–foot radius.

The tobacco companies challenged the regulations on both preemption and First Amendment grounds. The Court held, per Justice O'Connor, that the regulations of cigarette advertising were preempted by federal statute and that it therefore did not need to consider the First Amendment challenge. Because the relevant federal statute applied solely to cigarettes, however, the Court did deal with the First Amendment challenge to the regulations of advertising for smokeless tobacco and cigars. The tobacco companies urged the Court to "reject the *Central Hudson* analysis and apply strict scrutiny." As in *Greater New Orleans*, the Court saw "no need to break new ground. *Central Hudson*, as applied in our more recent commercial speech cases, provides an adequate basis for decision."

Because the Attorney General conceded, for purposes of the case, that the speech being regulated advertised a lawful product in a truthful manner, the only elements of the four-part *Central Hudson* test relevant to the case were the final two: "the relationship between the harm that underlies the State's interest and the means identified by the State to advance that interest" and the requirement of "a reasonable fit between the means and ends of the regulatory scheme." The Court found that the 1,000-foot radius regulations satisfied the third element of *Central Hudson*, rejecting the cigar and smokeless tobacco manufacturers' assertion that "the Attorney General cannot prove that advertising has a causal link to tobacco use such that limiting advertising will materially alleviate any problem of underage use of their products." The Court "disagree[d] with petitioners' claim that there is no evidence that preventing targeted campaigns and limiting youth exposure to advertising will decrease underage use of smokeless tobacco and cigars." The Court noted that it had previously "acknowledged the theory that product advertising stimulates demand for products, while suppressed advertising may have the opposite effect."

The Court nevertheless held the 1,000-foot radius prohibition unconstitutional: "Whatever the strength of the Attorney General's evidence to justify the outdoor advertising regulations, however, we conclude that the regulations do not satisfy the fourth step of the *Central Hudson* analysis." In reaching the conclusion that the regulations went further than necessary, the Court noted that "the Attorney General did not seem to consider the impact of the 1,000-foot restriction on commercial speech in major metropolitan areas. The Attorney General apparently selected the 1,000-foot distance based on the FDA's decision to impose an identical 1,000-foot restriction when it attempted to regulate cigarette and smokeless tobacco advertising. But the FDA's 1,000-foot regulation was not an adequate basis for the Attorney General to tailor the Massachusetts regulations. The degree to which speech is suppressed — or alternative avenues for speech remain available — under a particular regulatory scheme tends to be case-specific." Therefore "[t]he uniformly broad sweep of the geographical limitations demonstrates a lack of tailoring." Moreover, "the range of communications restricted seems unduly broad." The Court conceded that "[t]he State's interest in preventing underage tobacco use is substantial and even compelling, but it is no less true that the sale and use of tobacco products by adults is a legal activity. We must consider that tobacco retailers and manufacturers have an interest in conveying truthful information about their products to adults, and adults have a corresponding interest in receiving truthful information about tobacco products. As the State protects children from tobacco advertisements, tobacco manufacturers and retailers and their adult consumers still have a protected interest in communication." It further noted that "a retailer in Massachusetts may have no means of communicating to passersby on the street that it sells tobacco products because alternative forms of advertisement, like newspapers, do not allow that retailer to propose an instant transaction in the way that onsite advertising does."

Finally, the Court found that the point-of-sale advertising regulations "fail both the third and fourth steps of the *Central Hudson* analysis," because the 5-foot rule does not advance the goal of curbing youth demand for tobacco products: "Not all children are less than 5 feet tall, and those who are certainly have the ability to look up and take in their surroundings."

Justice Kennedy, joined by Justice Scalia, concurred in part and in the judgment: "The obvious overbreadth of the outdoor advertising restrictions suffices to invalidate them under the fourth part of the test in *Central Hudson*. As a result, in my view, there is no need to consider whether the restrictions satisfy the third part of the test, a proposition about which there is considerable doubt. Neither are we required to consider whether *Central Hudson* should be retained in the face of the substantial objections that can be made to it. My continuing concerns that the test gives insufficient protection to truthful, nonmisleading commercial speech require me to refrain from expressing agreement with the Court's application of the third part of *Central Hudson*."

Justice Thomas also filed a separate concurring opinion: "I share the Court's view that the regulations fail even the intermediate scrutiny of *Central Hudson*. At the same time, I continue to believe that when the government seeks to restrict truthful speech in order to suppress the ideas it conveys, strict scrutiny is appropriate, whether or not the speech in question may be characterized as 'commercial.' " As to the specific argument that the regulations were justified by the need to protect children, Justice Thomas wrote: "The theory that public debate should be limited in order to protect impressionable children has a long historical pedigree: Socrates was condemned for being 'a doer of evil, inasmuch as he corrupts the youth.' But the theory has met with a less enthusiastic reception in this Court than it did in the Athenian assembly." He noted that "[o]utside of the broadcasting context, we have adhered to the view that 'the governmental interest in protecting children from harmful materials' does not 'justify an unnecessarily broad suppression of speech addressed to adults.' "

He also rejected the argument that, because of its health risks to children and its addictive nature, tobacco presented a unique case for justifying advertising regulation: "Respondents say that tobacco companies are covertly targeting children in their advertising. Fast food companies do so openly." Moreover, "even though fast food is not addictive in the same way tobacco is, children's exposure to fast food advertising can have deleterious consequences that are difficult to reverse." The same is true, he argued, for underage drinking. Thus, accepting the argument in the tobacco context could not be confined to that situation: "Calls for limits on expression always are made when the specter of some threatened harm is looming. The identity of the harm may vary. People will be inspired by totalitarian dogmas and subvert the Republic. They will be inflamed by racial demagoguery and embrace hatred and bigotry. Or they will be enticed by cigarette advertisements and choose to smoke, risking disease. It is therefore no answer for the State to say that the makers of cigarettes are doing harm: perhaps they are. But in that respect they are no different from the purveyors of other harmful products, or the advocates of harmful ideas. When the State seeks to silence them, they are all entitled to the protection of the First Amendment."

Justice Breyer, joined by Justice Souter, concurred in part and dissented in part: "While the ultimate question before us is one of law, the answer to that question turns on complicated factual questions relating to the practical effects of the regulations. As the record does not reveal the answer to these disputed questions of fact, the court should have denied summary judgment to both parties and allowed the parties to present further evidence."

THOMPSON v. WESTERN STATES MEDICAL CENTER
535 U.S. 357, 122 S. Ct. 1497, 152 L. Ed. 2d 563 (2002)

JUSTICE O'CONNOR delivered the opinion of the Court.

Section 503A of the Food and Drug Administration Modernization Act of 1997 (FDAMA or Act), exempts "compounded drugs" from the Food and Drug Administration's standard drug approval requirements as long as the providers of those drugs abide by several restrictions, including that they refrain from advertising or promoting particular compounded drugs. Respondents, a group of licensed pharmacies that specialize in compounding drugs, sought to enjoin enforcement of the subsections of the Act dealing with advertising and solicitation, arguing that those provisions violate the First Amendment's free speech guarantee.

Drug compounding is a process by which a pharmacist or doctor combines, mixes, or alters ingredients to create a medication tailored to the needs of an individual patient. Compounding is typically used to prepare medications that are not commercially available, such as medication for a patient who is allergic to an ingredient in a mass-produced product.

We granted certiorari, to consider whether the FDAMA's prohibitions on soliciting prescriptions for, and advertising, compounded drugs violate the First Amendment. The parties agree that the advertising and soliciting prohibited by the FDAMA constitute commercial speech. Neither party has challenged the appropriateness of applying the *Central Hudson* framework to the speech-related provisions at issue here. Although several Members of the Court have expressed doubts about the *Central Hudson* analysis and whether it should apply in particular cases, there is no need in this case to break new ground.

Preserving the effectiveness and integrity of the FDCA's new drug approval process is clearly an important governmental interest, and the Government has every reason to want as many drugs as possible to be subject to that approval process. The Government also has an important interest, however, in permitting the continuation of the practice of compounding so that patients with particular needs may obtain medications suited to those needs. And it would not make sense to require compounded drugs created to meet the unique needs of individual patients to undergo the testing required for the new drug approval process.

Assuming it is true that drugs cannot be marketed on a large scale without advertising, the FDAMA's prohibition on advertising compounded drugs might indeed "directly advanc[e]" the Government's interests. *Central Hudson.* Even assuming that it does, however, the Government has failed to demonstrate that the speech restrictions are "not more extensive than is necessary to serve [those] interest[s]." In previous cases addressing this final prong of the *Central Hudson* test, we have made clear that if the Government could achieve its interests in a manner that does not restrict speech, or that restricts less speech, the Government must do so.

Several non-speech-related means of drawing a line between compounding and large-scale manufacturing might be possible here. First, it seems that the Government could use the very factors the FDA relied on to distinguish compounding from manufacturing in its 1992 Compliance Policy Guide. For example, the Government could ban the use of "commercial scale manufacturing or testing equipment for compounding drug products." It could prohibit pharmacists from compounding more drugs in anticipation of receiving prescriptions than in response to prescriptions already received. It could prohibit pharmacists from "[o]ffering compounded drugs at wholesale to other state licensed persons or commercial entities for resale." Alternately, it could limit the amount of compounded drugs, either by volume or by numbers of prescriptions, that a given pharmacist or pharmacy sells out of State. Another possibility not suggested by the Compliance Policy Guide would be capping the amount of any particular compounded drug, either by drug volume, number of prescriptions, gross revenue, or profit that a pharmacist or pharmacy may make or sell in a given period of time. It might even be sufficient to rely solely on the non-speech-related provisions of the FDAMA, such as the requirement that compounding only be conducted in response to a prescription or a history of receiving a prescription, and the limitation on the percentage of a pharmacy's total sales that out-of-state sales of compounded drugs may represent. The Government has not offered any reason why these possibilities, alone or in combination, would be insufficient to prevent compounding from occurring on such a scale as to undermine the new drug approval process.

Even if the Government had argued that the FDAMA's speech-related restrictions were motivated by a fear that advertising compounded drugs would put people who do not need such drugs at risk by causing them to convince their doctors to prescribe the drugs anyway, that fear would fail to justify the restrictions. Aside from the fact that this concern rests on the questionable assumption that doctors would prescribe unnecessary medications (an assumption the dissent is willing to make based on one magazine article and one survey, neither of which was relied upon by the Government), this concern amounts to a fear that people would make bad decisions if given truthful information about compounded drugs. We have previously rejected the notion that the Government has an interest in preventing the dissemination of truthful commercial information in order to prevent members of the public from making bad decisions with the information.

Accordingly, we affirm the Court of Appeals' judgment that the speech-related provisions of FDAMA § 503A are unconstitutional.

JUSTICE THOMAS, concurring.

I concur because I agree with the Court's application of the test set forth in *Central Hudson.* I continue, however, to adhere to my view that cases such as this should not be analyzed under the *Central Hudson* test. *44 Liquormart, Inc. v. Rhode Island* (opinion concurring in part and concurring in judgment).

JUSTICE BREYER, with whom THE CHIEF JUSTICE, JUSTICE STEVENS, and JUSTICE GINSBURG join, dissenting.

I do not deny that the statute restricts the circulation of some truthful information. It prevents a pharmacist from including in an advertisement the information that "this pharmacy will compound Drug X." Nonetheless, this Court has not previously held that commercial advertising restrictions automatically violate the First Amendment. Rather, the Court has applied a more flexible test. It has examined the restriction's proportionality, the relation between restriction and objective, the fit between ends and means. In doing so, the Court has asked whether the regulation of commercial speech "directly advances" a "substantial" governmental objective and whether it is "more extensive than is necessary" to achieve those ends. It has done so because it has concluded that, from a constitutional perspective, commercial speech does not warrant application of the Court's strictest speech-protective tests. And it has reached this conclusion in part because restrictions on commercial speech do not often repress individual self-expression; they rarely interfere with the functioning of democratic political processes; and they often reflect a democratically determined governmental decision to regulate a commercial venture in order to protect, for example, the consumer, the public health, individual safety, or the environment.

The Court, in my view, gives insufficient weight to the Government's regulatory rationale, and too readily assumes the existence of practical alternatives. It thereby applies the commercial speech doctrine too strictly. In my view, the Constitution demands a more lenient application, an application that reflects the need for distinctions among contexts, forms of regulation, and forms of speech, and which, in particular, clearly distinguishes between "commercial speech" and other forms of speech demanding stricter constitutional protection. Otherwise, an overly rigid "commercial speech" doctrine will transform what ought to be a legislative or regulatory decision about the best way to protect the health and safety of the American public into a constitutional decision prohibiting the legislature from enacting necessary protections. As history in respect to the Due Process Clause shows, any such transformation would involve a tragic constitutional misunderstanding.

Consider the following assessment of *Greater New Orleans*, *Thompson* and *Lorillard*: "Starting in 1999 — [n]ineteen years after *Central Hudson* — the four part test had become comfortable enough, and had produced enough precedent, that all the Justices except Justice Thomas agreed that there was no need to rethink it. Were the test more rigid, this agreement might signal a hardening or a move toward formalism; but with the flexible intermediate scrutiny — which does sometimes produce disagreements over results — it instead suggests a Court that is willing to stop fighting about terminology and instead look hard at what is actually at stake in each case." Suzanna Sherry, *Hard Cases Make Good Judges*, 99 Nw. U. L. Rev. 3 (2004). Do you agree that all Justices except Thomas do not wish to rethink *Central Hudson*? Did the majority in *Thompson* take a "hard look" at what was really at stake in the case or does the case indicate a "move toward formalism?"

[B] OBSCENE AND INDECENT SPEECH

Lewdness, offensiveness, and profanity have not been excluded from First Amendment protection. But in the 1957 decision, *Roth v. United States*, obscenity was cast out. And, arguably, in a 1978 decision, *FCC v. Pacifica Foundation*, p. 1224, indecency was also cast out — at least in the special context of the electronic media where the presence of children cannot be controlled. By 1973, when the Court in *Miller v. California* framed the modern standards relating to obscenity, some thirty obscenity decisions had been rendered, none of which won the support of a majority of the Justices. As you read the cases below, ask yourself if there is a category of expression that should be denied First Amendment protection. What is the rationale for excluding the obscene from the judicial review normally accorded to content-based restrictions? Is it possible to fashion narrower standards that specifically address particular state concerns such as the protection of children, pandering, or community deterioration? If "obscenity" or "pornography" is to be suppressed, what standards and definitions can be used that are not excessively vague and overbroad?

Some Justices have suggested that sexually explicit, "indecent" speech, even if not obscene, can be subjected to a regimen of regulation that would not be acceptable for political speech. Subject matter regulation of the circumstances under which such expression occurs would be permissible as long as the government maintains ideological neutrality and the regulation is not excessively burdensome, judged by a balancing standard. Is such an exception to the usual strict scrutiny accorded to content-based restrictions desirable? Does it perhaps provide a predicate for restoring obscene speech to First Amendment status, while recognizing the concerns of communities over sexually explicit materials? Is such a standard of "indecency" more workable than the standards fashioned for obscenity?

Should the *Pacifica* rationale for indecency regulation on broadcasting be extended to other electronic media? *Pacifica* has been much criticized, but it has also shown surprising durability. In a 1996 decision, *Denver Area Educational Television Consortium*, the plurality opinion approved extending the *Pacifica* rationale, at least in part, to cable television, but four years later in *United States v. Playboy Entertainment Group*, text, p. 1247, the Court did not apply *Pacifica* and applied the strict scrutiny standard to a cable indecency regulation.

Recently, a new category — "kiddie porn" or child pornography — has been added to the domain of unprotected expression. Has this domain any fixed frontiers? Should it be extended to female pornography? *See* ANDREA DWORKIN, PORNOGRAPHY: MEN POSSESSING WOMEN (1981). Should civil regulation of indecent and obscene publication draw a different judicial response than criminal prosecution? These are the questions that perplex courts as they consider the problems posed by sexually explicit materials.

[1] Beginnings of the Two-Level Approach

ROTH v. UNITED STATES

354 U.S. 476, 77 S. Ct. 1304, 1 L. Ed. 2d 1498 (1957)

JUSTICE BRENNAN delivered the opinion of the Court.

The dispositive question is whether obscenity is utterance within the area of protected speech and press. Although this is the first time the question has been squarely presented to this Court, either under the First Amendment or under the Fourteenth Amendment, expressions found in numerous opinions indicate that this Court has always assumed that obscenity is not protected by the freedoms of speech and press.

In light of this history, it is apparent that the unconditional phrasing of the First Amendment was not intended to protect every utterance. This phrasing did not prevent this Court from concluding that libelous utterances are not within the area of constitutionally protected speech. *Beauharnais v. People of State of Illinois,* 343 U.S. 250, 266. At the time of the adoption of the First Amendment, obscenity law was not as fully developed as libel law, but there is sufficiently contemporaneous evidence to show that obscenity, too, was outside the protection intended for speech and press.

The protection given speech and press was fashioned to assure unfettered interchange of ideas for the bringing about of political and social changes desired by the people. All ideas having even the slightest redeeming social importance — unorthodox ideas, controversial ideas, even ideas hateful to the prevailing climate of opinion — have the full protection of the guaranties, unless excludable because they encroach upon the limited area of more important interests. But implicit in the history of the First Amendment is the rejection of obscenity as utterly without redeeming social importance. This rejection for that reason is mirrored in the universal judgment that obscenity should be restrained, reflected in the international agreement of over 50 nations, in the obscenity laws of all of the 48 States, and in the 20 obscenity laws enacted by the Congress from 1842 to 1956. We hold that obscenity is not within the area of constitutionally protected speech or press.

It is strenuously urged that these obscenity statutes offend the constitutional guaranties because they punish incitation to impure sexual thoughts, not shown to be related to any overt antisocial conduct which is or may be incited in the persons stimulated to such thoughts. It is insisted that the constitutional guaranties are violated because convictions may be had without proof either that obscene material will perceptibly create a clear and present danger of antisocial conduct, or will probably induce its recipients to such conduct. But, in light of our holding that obscenity is not protected speech, the complete answer to this argument is in the holding of this Court in *Beauharnais v. Illinois*.

However, sex and obscenity are not synonymous. Obscene material is material which deals with sex in a manner appealing to prurient interest. The portrayal of sex, *e.g.*, in art, literature and scientific works, is not itself sufficient reason to deny material the constitutional protection of freedom of speech and press. Sex, a great and mysterious motive force in human life, has indisputably been a subject of absorbing interest to mankind through the ages; it is one of the vital problems of human interest and public concern.

The early leading standard of obscenity allowed material to be judged merely by the effect of an isolated excerpt upon particularly susceptible persons. *Regina v. Hicklin*, [1868] L.R. 3 Q.B. 360. Some American courts adopted this standard but later decisions have rejected it and substituted this test: whether to the average person, applying contemporary community standards, the dominant theme of the material taken as a whole appeals to prurient interest. The *Hicklin* test, judging obscenity by the effect of isolated passages upon the most susceptible persons, might well encompass material legitimately treating with sex, and so it must be rejected as unconstitutionally restrictive of the freedoms of speech and press. On the other hand, the substituted standard provides safeguards adequate to withstand the charge of constitutional infirmity.

Both trial courts below sufficiently followed the proper standard. Both courts used the proper definition of obscenity.

It is argued that the statutes do not provide reasonably ascertainable standards of guilt and therefore violate the constitutional requirements of due process. The federal obscenity statute makes punishable the mailing of material that is "obscene, lewd, lascivious, or filthy or other publication of an indecent character." The California statute makes punishable, *inter alia*, the keeping for sale or advertising material that is "obscene or indecent." The thrust of the argument is that these words are not sufficiently precise because they do not mean the same thing to all people, all the time, everywhere. Many decisions have recognized that these terms of obscenity statutes are not precise. This Court, however, has consistently held that lack of precision is not itself offensive to the requirements of due process.

In summary, then, we hold that these statutes, applied according to the proper standard for judging obscenity, do not offend constitutional safeguards against convictions based upon protected material, or fail to give men in acting adequate notice of what is prohibited.

CHIEF JUSTICE WARREN, concurring in the result.

The line dividing the salacious or pornographic from literature or science is not straight and unwavering. Present laws depend largely upon the effect that the materials may have upon those who receive them. It is manifest that the same object may have a different impact, varying according to the part of the community it reached. But there is more to these cases. It is not the book that is on trial; it is a person. The conduct of the defendant is the central issue, not the obscenity of a book or picture. The nature of the materials is, of course, relevant as an attribute of the defendant's conduct, but the materials are thus placed in context from which they draw color and character. A wholly different result might be reached in a different setting.

The defendants in both these cases were engaged in the business of purveying textual or graphic matter openly advertised to appeal to the erotic interest of their customers. They were plainly engaged in the commercial exploitation of the morbid and shameful craving for materials with prurient effect. I believe that the State and Federal Governments can constitutionally punish such conduct.

JUSTICE HARLAN, concurring in the result in No. 61, and dissenting in No. 582.

I concur in *Alberts v. California*.

Nothing in the Constitution requires California to accept as truth the most advanced and sophisticated psychiatric opinion. It seems to me clear that it is not irrational, in our present state of knowledge, to consider that pornography can induce a type of sexual conduct which a State may deem obnoxious to the moral fabric of society. In fact the very division of opinion on the subject counsels us to respect the choice made by the State.

I dissent in *Roth v. United States*.

We are faced here with the question whether the federal obscenity statute, as construed and applied in this case, violates the First Amendment to the Constitution. To me, this question is of quite a different order than one where we are dealing with state legislation under the Fourteenth Amendment. I do not think it follows that state and federal powers in this area are the same, and that just because the State may suppress a particular utterance, it is automatically permissible for the Federal Government to do the same.

[T]he interests which obscenity statutes purportedly protect are primarily entrusted to the care, not of the Federal Government, but of the States. Congress has no substantive power over sexual morality. Such powers as the Federal Government has in this field are but incidental to its other powers, here the postal power, and are not of the same nature as those possessed by the States, which bear direct responsibility for the protection of the local moral fabric.

JUSTICE DOUGLAS, with whom JUSTICE BLACK concurs, dissenting.

The test of obscenity the Court endorses today gives the censor free range over a vast domain. To allow the State to step in and punish mere speech or publication that the judge or the jury thinks has an undesirable impact on thoughts but that is not shown to be a part of unlawful action is drastically to curtail the First Amendment. If we were certain that impurity of sexual thoughts impelled to action, we would be on less dangerous ground in punishing the distributors of this sex literature. But it is by no means clear that obscene literature, as so defined, is a significant factor in influencing substantial deviations from the community standards.

NOTES

1. *Utility and danger.* Commenting on the "two-level speech theory" emerging from *Roth*, Professor Kalven stressed the important role played by the evaluation of the content of the publication in the theory.

> The first question is whether it belongs to a category that has any social utility. If it does not, it may be banned. If it does, there is a further question of measuring the clarity and proximity and gravity of any danger from it. It is thus apparent that the issue of social utility of a communication has become as crucial a part of our theory as the issue of danger.

Harry Kalven, *The Metaphysics of the Law of Obscenity*, 1960 SUP. CT. REV. 1.

2. *The English test.* Obscenity under *Roth* is material which is (1) without redeeming social importance, and which (2) to the average person, applying contemporary community standards, appeals to the prurient interest in its dominant theme taken as a whole.

Why did the Supreme Court refuse to adopt the English test for obscenity, the *Hicklin* test, which made the standard for obscenity the effect of an isolated passage among the most susceptible persons? Is it because the English do not operate under a written constitutional command such as the First Amendment? The American test obviously gives more latitude to freedom of expression. The definition of obscenity will clearly be narrower if the arbiter of what is obscene is the average rather than the susceptible person. Notice the *Roth* test rejects *Hicklin* in another way. The dominant theme of the material must appeal to the prurient interest. An isolated passage, unlike the case under *Hicklin*, would be insufficient to support a judgment that particular printed material is obscene.

3. *Vagueness.* Is the *Roth* test for obscenity unacceptably vague? Is it true that the Supreme Court would not tolerate, let alone propound, such vague rules of constitutionality in any context but the obscenity cases? Consider the following statement by Justice Stewart in his concurring opinion in *Jacobellis v. Ohio*, 378 U.S. 184, 197 (1964):

> I have reached the conclusion that under the First and Fourteenth Amendments criminal laws in this area [of obscenity] are constitutionally limited to hard-core pornography. I shall not attempt today further to define the kinds of material I understand to be embraced within that shorthand description, and perhaps I could never succeed in intelligibly doing so. But I know it when I see it.

Consider also the following defense of Justice Stewart's statement:

> Justice Stewart did not think he was applying a personal, idiosyncratic notion of "hard-core pornography." [Instead,] "hard-core pornography" was a category of pornography that virtually *all* people would view as beyond the pale, that virtually all would think suppressible. This requirement of near consensus was self-consciously a speech-protective standard of wide tolerance allowing only the most minimal censorship, and it actually gives more guidance than the vague, multifactor test that the court's majority has used.

Paul Gewirtz, *On "I Know It When I See It"*, 105 YALE L.J. 1023, 1037 (1996).

Prof. Gewirtz concedes that this definition will not be accepted by feminist critics who will respond: "What you claim is reality is not what I claim is reality." But Gewirtz counters that at least Stewart's statement stands "as an acknowledgement of the subjectivity that exists in judging." In that case, how useful is the Stewart statement?

GINZBURG v. UNITED STATES
383 U.S. 463, 86 S. Ct. 942, 16 L. Ed. 2d 31 (1966)

JUSTICE BRENNAN delivered the opinion of the Court.

In the cases in which this Court has decided obscenity questions since *Roth*, it has regarded the materials as sufficient in themselves for the determination of the question. In the present case, however, the prosecution charged the offense in the context of the circumstances of production, sale, and publicity and assumed that, standing alone, the publications themselves might not be obscene. We agree that the question of obscenity may include consideration of the setting in which the publications were presented as an aid to determining the question of obscenity, and assume without deciding that the prosecution could not have succeeded otherwise. [W]e view the publications against a background of commercial exploitation of erotica solely for the sake of their prurient appeal.

The record in that regard amply supports the decision of the trial judge that the mailing of all three publications offended the statute.

The three publications were EROS, a hard-cover magazine of expensive format; LIAISON, a bi-weekly newsletter; and THE HOUSEWIFE'S HANDBOOK ON SELECTIVE PROMISCUITY (hereinafter the HANDBOOK), a short book.

Besides testimony as to the merit of the material, there was abundant evidence to show that each of the accused publications was originated or sold as stock in trade of the sordid business of pandering — "the business of purveying textual or graphic matter openly advertised to appeal to the erotic interest of their customers." EROS early sought mailing privileges from the postmasters of Intercourse and Blue Ball, Pennsylvania. The trial court found the obvious, that these hamlets were chosen only for the value their names would have in furthering petitioners' efforts to sell their publications on the basis of salacious appeal; the facilities of the post offices were inadequate to handle the anticipated volume of mail, and the privileges were denied. Mailing privileges were then obtained from the postmaster of Middlesex, New Jersey. EROS and Liaison thereafter mailed several million circulars soliciting subscriptions from that post office; over 5,500 copies of the HANDBOOK were mailed.

The "leer of the sensualist" also permeates the advertising for the three publications. The circulars sent for EROS and Liaison stressed the sexual candor of the respective publications, and openly boasted that the publishers would take full advantage of what they regarded an unrestricted license allowed by law in the expression of sex and sexual matters.

This evidence, in our view, was relevant in determining the ultimate question of obscenity and, in the context of this record, serves to resolve all ambiguity and doubt. The deliberate representation of petitioners' publications as erotically arousing, for example, stimulated the reader to accept them as prurient; he looks for titillation, not for saving intellectual content. Similarly, such representation would tend to force public confrontation with the potentially offensive aspects of the work; the brazenness of such an appeal heightens the offensiveness of the publications to those who are offended by such material. And the circumstances of presentation and dissemination of material are equally relevant to determining whether social importance claimed for material in the courtroom was, in the circumstances, pretense or reality — whether it was the basis upon which it was traded in the market place or a spurious claim for litigation purposes. Where the purveyor's sole emphasis is on the sexually provocative aspects of his publications, that fact may be decisive in the determination of obscenity. Certainly in a prosecution which, as here, does not necessarily imply suppression of the materials involved, the fact they originate or are used as a subject of pandering is relevant to the application of the *Roth* test.

We perceive no threat to First Amendment guarantees in thus holding that in close cases evidence of pandering may be probative with respect to the nature of the material in question and thus satisfy the *Roth* test.

[The dissenting opinions of JUSTICES BLACK, DOUGLAS, HARLAN and STEWART are omitted.]

NOTES

1. *The methodology of Ginzburg.* The dissenting Justices in *Ginzburg* were troubled by its new direction in the law of obscenity. Justice Stewart called Ginzburg's conviction a denial of due process of law. Justice Harlan termed the majority's treatment of the federal obscenity statute "an astonishing piece of judicial improvisation." Does the advent of the "pandering" concept mean that the sender of constitutionally protected materials can be convicted of criminal offense because of the subjective reactions of judge and jury? The Court seemed truly offended by Ginzburg's attempt to secure mailing privileges from Intercourse, Pennsylvania and Middlesex, New Jersey. Was the Court so personally offended by Ginzburg's cheeky attitude that it fashioned a new rule to uphold his conviction? Justice Black, true to his absolutist, "plain meaning" view of the First Amendment, vigorously criticized the subjectivity of the majority approach. Under the *Ginzburg* formulation, Black said, "the law becomes certain for the first and last time."

2. *Special protection for minors.* In *Ginsberg v. New York,* 390 U.S. 629 (1968), the Supreme Court upheld the constitutionality of a state law prohibiting distribution to minors of materials deemed to be obscene as to minors — whether or not the materials were constitutionally protected (i.e., not obscene) as to adults. The Court expressly embraced the notion of "variable obscenity" propounded by Lockhart and McClure. By distinguishing the target audience and its particular susceptibilities, the New York legislature in *Ginsberg* successfully walked the tightrope between overbroad obscenity regulation and no regulation at all. In *Ginsberg*, the Court held that a properly drafted anti-obscenity statute addressed to distribution to minors would pass muster. What is crucial for the Court in *Ginsberg*? The intent of the distributor? The way the material is treated by the intended audience?

However, the Court did not explicitly face several crucial questions in *Ginsberg*: Were the materials at issue in the case actually obscene? Was the New York statute validated merely because the state's power to regulate the conduct of children is greater than its power over adults?

3. *A right to possess.* In *Stanley v. Georgia,* 394 U.S. 557 (1969), the Court limited the domain of the newly created and unprotected category of obscene expression by holding that the constitutional value of privacy limited the reach of the state. In the course of a search of a home in Georgia for evidence of illegal bookmaking activities, the police found obscene films. The accused was therefore arrested and charged with possession of obscene matter. *Stanley* held that the mere possession of obscene matter which an individual reads or watches in his own home could not constitutionally be made a crime. Justice Marshall declared for the Court:

> Whatever may be the justifications for other statutes regulating obscenity, we do not think they reach into the privacy of one's own home. If the First Amendment means anything, it means that a State has no business telling a man, sitting alone in his own house, what books he may read or what films he may watch. Our whole constitutional heritage rebels at the thought of giving government the power to control men's minds.

If obscenity is "utterly without redeeming social importance" and therefore merits no constitutional protection whatsoever, why can't the state proscribe private possession of obscene materials? Is the Court's answer to this question that the difference between *Roth* and *Stanley* is fully understandable because a competing constitutional value was at stake in *Stanley* which was not present in *Roth*, *i.e.* a First Amendment-based right of privacy. Some commentators viewed *Stanley* as a silent departure from the fundamental holding of *Roth* that obscenity is not constitutionally-protected speech.

[2] The Burger Court, Federalism and Obscenity

MILLER v. CALIFORNIA
413 U.S. 15, 93 S. Ct. 2607, 37 L. Ed. 2d 419 (1973)

Chief Justice Burger delivered the opinion of the Court.

This case involves the application of a state's criminal obscenity statute to a situation in which sexually explicit materials have been thrust by aggressive sales action upon unwilling recipients who had in no way indicated any desire to receive such materials. This Court has recognized that the States have a legitimate interest in prohibiting dissemination or exhibition of obscene material when the mode of dissemination carries with it a significant danger of offending the sensibilities of unwilling recipients or of exposure to juveniles. It is in this context that we are called on to define the standards which must be used to identify obscene material that a State may regulate without infringing the First Amendment as applicable to the States through the Fourteenth Amendment.

While *Roth* presumed "obscenity" to be "utterly without redeeming social value," Memoirs required that to prove obscenity it must be affirmatively established that the material is "utterly without redeeming social value." Thus, even as they repeated the words of *Roth*, the *Memoirs* plurality produced a drastically altered test that called on the prosecution to prove a negative, i.e., that the material was "utterly without redeeming social value" — a burden virtually impossible to discharge under our criminal standards of proof. Such considerations caused Justice Harlan to wonder if the "utterly without redeeming social value" test had any meaning at all.

Apart from the initial formulation in the *Roth* case, no majority of the Court has at any given time been able to agree on a standard to determine what constitutes obscene, pornographic material subject to regulation under the States' police power. We have seen "a variety of views among the members of the Court unmatched in any other course of constitutional adjudication." This is not remarkable, for in the area of freedom of speech and press the courts must always remain sensitive to any infringement on genuinely serious literary, artistic, political, or scientific expression. This is an area in which there are few eternal verities. The case we now review was tried on the theory that the California Penal Code § 311 approximately incorporates the three-stage *Memoirs* test. But now the *Memoirs* test has been abandoned as unworkable by its author[4] and no member of the Court today supports the *Memoirs* foundation.

This much has been categorically settled by the Court, that obscene material is unprotected by the First Amendment. "The First and Fourteenth Amendments have never been treated as absolutes." We acknowledge, however, the inherent dangers of undertaking to regulate any form of expression. State

[4] *See* the dissenting opinion of Justice Brennan in *Paris Adult Theatre I v. Slaton* [p.1219].

statutes designed to regulate obscene materials must be carefully limited. As a result, we now confine the permissible scope of such regulation to works which depict or describe sexual conduct. That conduct must be specifically defined by the applicable state law, as written or authoritatively construed. A state offense must also be limited to works which, taken as a whole, appeal to the prurient interest in sex, which portray sexual conduct in a patently offensive way, and which, taken as a whole, do not have serious literary, artistic, political, or scientific value.

The basic guidelines for the trier of fact must be: (a) whether "the average person, applying contemporary community standards" would find that the work, taken as a whole, appeals to the prurient interest, (b) whether the work depicts or describes, in a patently offensive way, sexual conduct specifically defined by the applicable state law, and (c) whether the work, taken as a whole, lacks serious literary, artistic, political, or scientific value. We do not adopt as a constitutional standard the "utterly without redeeming social value" test of *Memoirs v. Massachusetts*; that concept has never commanded the adherence of more than three Justices at one time. If a state law that regulates obscene material is thus limited, as written or construed, the First Amendment values applicable to the States through the Fourteenth Amendment are adequately protected by the ultimate power of appellate courts to conduct an independent review of constitutional claims when necessary.

We emphasize that it is not our function to propose regulatory schemes for the States. That must await their concrete legislative efforts. It is possible, however, to give a few plain examples of what a state statute could define for regulation under the second part (b) of the standard announced in this opinion:

(a) Patently offensive representations or descriptions of ultimate sexual acts, normal or perverted, actual or simulated.

(b) Patently offensive representation or descriptions of masturbation, excretory functions and lewd exhibition of the genitals.

Sex and nudity may not be exploited without limit by films or pictures exhibited or sold in places of public accommodation any more than live sex and nudity can be exhibited or sold without limit in such public places. At a minimum, prurient, patently offensive depiction or description of sexual conduct must have serious literary, artistic, political, or scientific value to merit First Amendment protection. For example, medical books for the education of physicians and related personnel necessarily use graphic illustrations and descriptions of human anatomy. In resolving the inevitably sensitive questions of fact and law, we must continue to rely on the jury system, accompanied by the safeguards that judges, rules of evidence, presumption of innocence and other protective features provide, as we do with rape, murder and a host of other offenses against society and its individual members.

Under the holdings announced today, no one will be subject to a prosecution for the sale or exposure of obscene materials unless these materials depict or describe patently offensive "hard-core" sexual conduct specifically defined by the regulating state law as written or construed. We are satisfied that these specific prerequisites will provide fair notice to a dealer in such materials that his public and commercial activities may bring prosecution.

It is certainly true that the absence, since *Roth*, of a single majority view of this Court as to proper standards for testing obscenity has placed a strain on both state and federal courts. But today, for the first time since *Roth* was decided in 1957, a majority of this Court has agreed on concrete guidelines to isolate "hard core" pornography from expression protected by the First Amendment. Now we may abandon the casual practice of *Redrup v. New York*, 386 U.S. 767 (1967) and attempt to provide positive guidance to the federal and state courts alike.

This may not be an easy road, free from difficulty. But no amount of "fatigue" should lead us to adopt a convenient "institutional" rationale—an absolutist, "anything goes"-view of the First Amendment—because it will lighten our burdens. "Such an abnegation of judicial supervision in this field would be inconsistent with our duty to uphold the constitutional guarantees." Nor should we remedy "tension between state and federal courts" by arbitrarily depriving the States of a power reserved to them under the Constitution, a power which they have enjoyed and exercised continuously from before the adoption of the First Amendment to this day. "Our duty admits of no 'substitute for facing up to the tough individual problems of constitutional judgment involved in every obscenity case.' "

Under a national Constitution, fundamental First Amendment limitations on the powers of the States do not vary from community to community, but this does not mean that there are, or should or can be, fixed, uniform national standards of precisely what appeals to the "prurient interest" or is "patently offensive." These are essentially questions of fact, and our nation is simply too big and too diverse for this Court to reasonably expect that such standards could be articulated for all 50 States in a single formulation, even assuming the prerequisite consensus exists. When triers of fact are asked to decide whether "the average person, applying contemporary community standards" would consider certain materials "prurient," it would be unrealistic to require that the answer be based on some abstract formulation. The adversary system, with lay jurors as the usual ultimate fact-finders in criminal prosecutions, has historically permitted triers-of-fact to draw on the standards of their community, guided always by limiting instructions on the law. To require a State to structure obscenity proceedings around evidence of a national "community standard" would be an exercise in futility.

We conclude that neither the State's alleged failure to offer evidence of "national standards," nor the trial court's charge that the jury consider state community standards, were constitutional errors.[5] Nothing in the First Amendment requires that a jury must consider hypothetical and unascertainable "national standards" when attempting to determine whether certain materials are obscene as a matter of fact.

It is neither realistic nor constitutionally sound to read the First Amendment as requiring that the people of Maine or Mississippi accept public depiction of conduct found tolerable in Las Vegas, or New York City. People

[5] [Community standards were ascertained by reference to the testimony of a police officer with many years of specialization in obscenity offenses. He had conducted an extensive statewide survey — the Chief Justice said nothing more specific about the survey — and had given expert evidence on 26 occasions in the year prior to the *Miller* trial.]

in different States vary in their tastes and attitudes, and this diversity is not to be strangled by the absolutism of imposed uniformity. We hold the requirement that the jury evaluate the materials with reference to "contemporary standards of the State of California" serves this protective purpose and is constitutionally adequate.

In sum we (a) reaffirm the *Roth* holding that obscene material is not protected by the First Amendment, (b) hold that such material can be regulated by the States, subject to the specific safeguards enunciated above, without a showing that the material is "utterly without redeeming social value," and (c) hold that obscenity is to be determined by applying "contemporary community standards," not "national standards."

PARIS ADULT THEATRE I v. SLATON

413 U.S. 49, 93 S. Ct. 2628, 37 L. Ed. 2d 446 (1973)

[On the same day as *Miller*, the Court, per Chief Justice Burger, affirmed, 5-4, a Georgia Supreme Court holding that two "adult" movies were constitutionally unprotected. The decision was notable because it held that courts were not obliged to require "expert" affirmative evidence that the materials were obscene. Further, the Court held that the state could validly regulate use of obscene material in local commerce and in places of public accommodation even if those using such materials voluntarily sought them out.]

CHIEF JUSTICE BURGER delivered the opinion of the Court.

[W]e hold that there are legitimate state interests at stake in stemming the tide of commercialized obscenity, even assuming it is feasible to enforce effective safeguards against exposure to juveniles and to passersby. These include the interest of the public in the quality of life and the total community environment, the tone of commerce in the great city centers, and, possibly, the public safety itself.

The idea of a "privacy" right and a place of public accommodation are, in this context, mutually exclusive. Conduct or depictions of conduct that the state police power can prohibit on a public street does not become automatically protected by the Constitution merely because the conduct is moved to a bar or a "live" theatre stage, any more than a "live" performance of a man and woman locked in a sexual embrace at high noon in Times Square is protected by the Constitution because they simultaneously engage in a valid political dialogue. [W]e reject the claim that the State of Georgia is here attempting to control the minds or thoughts of those who patronize theatres. Preventing unlimited display or distribution of obscene material, which by definition lacks any serious literary, artistic, political or scientific value as communication, is distinct from a control of reason and the intellect. Where communication of ideas, protected by the First Amendment, is not involved, nor the particular privacy of the home protected by *Stanley*, nor any of the other "areas or zones" of constitutionally protected privacy, the mere fact that, as a consequence, some human "utterances" or "thoughts" may be incidentally affected does not bar the State from acting to protect legitimate state interests.

JUSTICE BRENNAN, dissenting.

I am convinced that the approach initiated 15 years ago in *Roth v. United States*, and culminating in the Court's decision today, cannot bring stability to this area of the law without jeopardizing fundamental First Amendment values, and I have concluded that the time has come to make a significant departure from that approach.

Our experience since *Roth* requires us not only to abandon the effort to pick out obscene materials on a case-by-case basis, but also to reconsider a fundamental postulate of *Roth*: that there exists a definable class of sexually oriented expression that may be totally suppressed by the Federal and State Governments. Assuming that such a class of expression does in fact exist, I am forced to conclude that the concept of "obscenity" cannot be defined with sufficient specificity and clarity to provide fair notice to persons who create and distribute sexually oriented materials, to prevent substantial erosion of protected speech as a by-product of the attempt to suppress unprotected speech, and to avoid very costly institutional harms.

In short, while I cannot say that the interests of the State — apart from the question of juveniles and unconsenting adults — are trivial or nonexistent, I am compelled to conclude that these interests cannot justify the substantial damage to constitutional rights and to this Nation's judicial machinery that inevitably results from state efforts to bar the distribution even of unprotected material to consenting adults. I would hold, therefore, that at least in the absence of distribution to juveniles or obtrusive exposure to unconsenting adults, the First and Fourteenth Amendments prohibit the state and federal governments from attempting wholly to suppress sexually oriented materials on the basis of their allegedly "obscene" contents. Nothing in this approach precludes those governments from taking action to serve what may be strong and legitimate interests through regulation of the manner of distribution of sexually-oriented material.

NOTES

1. *The revised test.* What are the major changes in obscenity law resulting from *Miller*? Certainly one of the most obvious revisions is the Court's reformulation of the *Roth* definition of obscenity. The scope of the definition of obscenity is expanded in *Miller* by substituting for an inquiry of "utterly without redeeming social importance" an inquiry which asks whether the "work, taken as a whole, lacks serious literary, artistic, political or scientific value."

By removing the protection provided by the "utterly without redeeming social importance" test, does the Court make it easier for the state to cast an obscenity net beyond the limits of "hard-core" pornography? This is an important issue because it has been urged that one of the functions of that part of the *Roth* definition of obscenity which required that the material in question be "utterly without redeeming social importance" was designed to constitutionally proscribe "hard-core" pornography and nothing else. It is interesting to note that Chief Justice Burger apparently believed that the *Miller* definition of obscenity will reach only "hard-core" pornography. Ironically, under the *Roth* test the perimeters of "hard-core" pornography were perhaps more secure than under *Miller*. After all, is it not far easier to say that a book lacks "serious value" than it is to say that it is "utterly without redeeming social importance"?

The Court's efforts in *Miller* and subsequent cases to define obscenity have received the following searing critique, among others:

> In defining obscenity, the Court has advanced an incoherent formula that requires the application of "community standards" without any specification of what constitutes a "community"; the identification of national "reasonable" judgments about artistic and literary taste, a subject on which reason may be of little guidance, and on which the nation is likely to have no consensus; the differentiation of healthy from "shameful or morbid" sexual interests; and the determination that speech is "patently offensive," a judgment which in nonsexual circumstances is a reason for protecting nor criminalizing speech.

David Cole, *Playing by Pornography's Rules: The Regulation of Sexual Expression,* 143 U. PA. L. REV. 111, 112 (1994). In what respects does *Miller* bring *greater* clarity to the definition of obscenity than *Roth*?

2. *The vagueness and overbreadth problems.*

Miller sought to achieve greater specificity and avoid charges of vagueness by providing definite instructions on what type of materials were obscene. Was the Court successful? In *Ward v. Illinois,* 431 U.S. 767 (1977), the Court held, per Justice White, that the *Miller* requirement of specificity in defining obscenity standards was satisfied by a state statute, phrased in general terms, which adopted the patently offensive formulation of *Miller* since this adoption impliedly incorporated *Miller* examples of patently offensive sexual representations. This reading was supported by subsequent state court decisions using the *Miller* examples in defining the kinds of materials proscribed. These prior decisions also established that the defendant had adequate notice of the types of materials that were covered under the state obscenity laws. Sadomasochistic materials are among the types of patently offensive sexual representations that a state may constitutionally reach under its obscenity laws.

3. *Post-Miller pandering.* In *Splawn v. California,* 431 U.S. 595 (1977), the Supreme Court affirmed the continuing vitality of *Ginzburg* holding, *inter alia*, 5-4, per Justice Rehnquist, that a state court could validly instruct a jury to consider "motives of commercial exploitation on the part of persons in the chain of distribution of the material other than himself." The Court made clear that the trial court could permissibly instruct the jury pursuant to the "commercial exploitation" test of *Ginzburg* even though the jury might otherwise have found that the film was protected under the standards introduced in *Miller v. California*.

Justice Stevens, joined by Justices Brennan, Stewart and Marshall, dissented.

> Truthful statements which are neither misleading nor offensive are protected by the First Amendment even though made for a commercial purpose. *Virginia Pharmacy Board v. Virginia Consumer Council.*

4. *Community standards.* Certainly, one of the most celebrated and publicized aspects of *Miller* is the rejection of the idea formerly endorsed in *Jacobellis v. Ohio,* 378 U.S. 184 (1964), that what offends contemporary community standards is to be judged by a national standard. The Court denied that "there are, or should or can be, fixed, uniform national standards of precisely what appeals to the 'prurient interest' or is 'patently offensive.' "

Who should determine what appeals to the "prurient interest of a community"? According to Chief Justice Burger, speaking for the Court in *Miller*, the jury should make this determination. If these determinations should be left to the jury, then is it not possible that "Deep Throat" may be held to appeal to the prurient interest of Xenia, Ohio but not to the prurient interest of Shaker Heights, Ohio? If this is true, is it also true as Chief Justice Burger says in *Miller* that "fundamental First Amendment limitations on the powers of the States do not vary from community to community"?

5. *Federal standards.* How is the *Miller* standard to be applied in a federal obscenity prosecution? The Court answered that question as follows in *Hamling v. United States,* 418 U.S. 87 (1974):

> Since this case was tried in the Southern District of California, and presumably jurors from throughout that judicial district were available to serve on the panel which tried petitioners, it would be the standards of that "community" upon which the jurors would draw. But this is not to say that a District Court would not be at liberty to admit evidence of standards existing in some place outside of this particular district, if it felt such evidence would assist the jury in the resolution of the issues which they were to decide.

See Smith v. United States, 431 U.S. 291 (1977) (holding, 5-4, that, in federal prosecutions, the meaning of contemporary community standards with respect to what constitutes appeal to the prurient interest and patent offensiveness under the test of *Miller v. California* is to be determined by jurors in light of their understanding of local contemporary community standards).

6. *Jenkins v. Georgia,* 418 U.S. 153 (1974). *Miller v. California* was greeted with considerable criticism in the press and the arts and with a new, if sporadic, wave of censorious obscenity prosecutions in some localities throughout the country. Did *Miller* really mean that the new definition of "unprotected speech" had been indefinably broadened? Was the definition of obscenity now to be at the totally unstandardized mercy of the local jury? In *Jenkins*, the manager of a movie theatre in Albany, Georgia, had been convicted under the Georgia state obscenity statute for showing the film "Carnal Knowledge." The jury had convicted prior to the announcement of *Miller* and the Georgia Supreme Court affirmed after the announcement of *Miller*.

Jenkins, the "Carnal Knowledge" case, was important for what it said on the role of the jury. Even though questions of appeal to the "prurient interest" or of patent offensiveness are "essentially questions of fact," it would be a serious misreading of *Miller* to conclude that juries have unbridled discretion in determining what is "patently offensive." The Court reminded the state that in *Miller* it had said that in first amendment cases it still retained its power to conduct an "independent review of constitutional claims when necessary." The Court pointed out that there were substantive constitutional limitations on what a jury could hold to be obscene. In the Court's view, the jury was limited to a narrow area by *Miller*: "materials [which] depict or describe patently offensive 'hard core' sexual conduct."

7. *Serious value.* The third prong of the *Miller* test for defining obscenity requires that a work, taken as a whole, must lack *serious* literary, artistic, political or scientific values. In *Pope v. Illinois,* 481 U.S. 497 (1987), the Court held, per Justice White, that this prong of the *Miller* test should be determined by an objective rather than a local community standard:

> The proper inquiry is not whether an ordinary member of any given community would find serious, literary, artistic, political or scientific value in allegedly obscene material, but whether a reasonable person would find such value in the material, taken as a whole.

Justice Stevens dissented and argued that the communicative material at issue (magazines sold at an adult bookstore) merited First Amendment protection "if *some reasonable person* could consider it as having serious, literary, artistic, political or scientific value." Otherwise, a juror asked to apply a "reasonable person" standard "might well believe that the majority of the population who found no value in such a book are more reasonable than the minority who do find value."

8. *Arcara v. Cloud Books, Inc.,* 478 U.S. 697 (1986). This case presented the question whether the First Amendment prevents the enforcement of a statute authorizing the closure of premises used for prostitution and lewdness if the premises are also used as an adult bookstore. The New York Court of Appeals had held that the statute in question could not be constitutionally applied to close a bookstore since that would violate the *O'Brien* test, which requires that a statute incidentally restricting speech be no broader than is necessary to achieve its purposes. The Supreme Court, per Chief Justice Burger, upheld application of the statute:

> [W]e have not traditionally subjected every criminal and civil sanction imposed through legal process to "least restrictive means" scrutiny simply because each particular remedy will have some effect on the First Amendment activities of those subject to sanction. Rather, we have subjected such restrictions to scrutiny only where it was conducted with a significant expressive element that drew the legal remedy in the first place, as in *O'Brien*, or where a statute based on a nonexpressive activity has the inevitable effect of singling out those engaged in expressive activity, as in *Minneapolis Star*. This case involves neither situation, and we conclude the First Amendment is not implicated by the enforcement of a public health regulation of general application against the physical premises in which respondents happen to sell books.

The key point of the Court was that the *O'Brien* test has no "relevance to a statute directed at imposing sanctions on nonexpressive activity."

Justice Blackmun, joined by Justices Brennan and Marshall, dissenting, declared that [u]ntil today "it had never been suggested that government could suppress speech 'without justification' as long as it did so through generally applicable regulations that have 'nothing to do with any expressive conduct.' "

9. *Procedural safeguards.* In *Freedman v. Maryland,* 380 U.S. 51 (1965), the Court imposed procedural requirements on censorship boards:

(1) The board has the burden of showing that a film is unprotected expression.

(2) Only a judicial proceeding will suffice to impose a valid final restraint on a film's exhibition.

(3) The state, either by statute, or by "authoritative judicial construction," must afford the exhibitor a procedure under which he is either issued a license or the censorship board is required to go to court to restrain the showing of the film in controversy.

The Court in *Freedman* made it very clear that this decision by a movie censorship board to license or to enjoin must occur within a brief and specified period of time. Why this emphasis on time? Why this preference for judicial rather than administrative determinations of obscenity? Is it for the same reason the issue of obscenity is an issue of law for the judge rather than of fact for the jury? *Cf. Jacobellis v. Ohio,* 378 U.S. 184 (1964). In a jurisdiction where judges are elected rather than appointed as are members of censorship boards, is it clear that the judges will have the "necessary sensitivity to freedom of expression"? *See generally* Henry Monaghan, *First Amendment "Due Process,"* 83 Harv. L. Rev. 518 (1970).

[3] Indecent Speech: Content Control Outside Obscenity

YOUNG v. AMERICAN MINI THEATRES, INC.

427 U.S. 50, 96 S. Ct. 2440, 49 L. Ed. 2d 310 (1976)

[The Court, per Justice Stevens, upheld two 1972 Detroit zoning ordinances providing that an adult theater may not (unless a waiver was granted) be located within 1,000 feet of any two other "regulated uses" or within 500 feet of a residential area. In addition to adult theaters, the term "regulated uses" covered establishments such as adult bookstores, cabarets, bars, taxi dance halls and hotels. A theater was deemed to be an "adult" theater if it was used to present "material distinguished or characterized by an emphasis on matter depicting 'Specified Sexual Activities' or 'Specified Anatomical Areas.' "

[First, the Court upheld the ordinances against a double flanked attack on the ground of vagueness. The first flank of that attack was based on the theory that the motion picture operators received inadequate notice from the ordinance. The Court rejected this contention, holding that if there was any element of vagueness in the ordinances, it had not affected the operators of the two motion picture theaters who brought the suit. Justice Stevens reasoned as follows: "[E]ven if there may be some uncertainty about the effect of the ordinances on other litigants, they are unquestionably applicable to these respondents. The record indicates that both theaters proposed to offer adult fare on a regular basis. Neither respondent has alleged any basis for claiming or anticipating any waiver of the restriction as applied to its theater."

[The second flank of the vagueness attack was predicated on the argument of the operators that they were unable to determine how much sexually explicit material may be portrayed before the material will be deemed "characterized by an emphasis" on such matters. The Court said such doubts, if necessary, could be resolved by a "narrowing construction" in the state courts.

[The Court also ruled that licensing or zoning ordinances are not invalid prior restraints under the First Amendment.]

JUSTICE STEVENS delivered the opinion of the Court.

Petitioners acknowledge that the ordinances prohibit theaters which are not licensed as "adult motion picture theaters" from exhibiting films which are protected by the First Amendment. Respondents argue that the ordinances are therefore invalid as prior restraints on free speech. The ordinances are not challenged on the ground that they impose a limit on the total number of adult theaters which may operate in the city of Detroit. There is no claim that distributors or exhibitors of adult films are denied access to the market or, conversely, that the viewing public is unable to satisfy its appetite for sexually explicit fare. Viewed as an entity, the market for this commodity is essentially unrestrained.

It is true, however, that adult films may only be exhibited commercially in licensed theaters. But that is also true of all motion pictures. The city's general zoning laws require all motion picture theaters to satisfy certain locational as well as other requirements; we have no doubt that the municipality may control the location of theaters as well as the location of other commercial establishments, either by confining them to certain specified commercial zones or by requiring that they be dispersed throughout the city. The mere fact that the commercial exploitation of material protected by the First Amendment is subject to zoning and other licensing requirements is not a sufficient reason for invalidating these ordinances.

Putting to one side for the moment the fact that adult motion picture theaters must satisfy a locational restriction not applicable to other theaters, we are also persuaded that the 1,000-foot restriction does not, in itself, create an impermissible restraint on protected communication. The city's interest in planning and regulating the use of property for commercial purposes is clearly adequate to support that kind of restriction applicable to all theaters within the city limits. In short, apart from the fact that the ordinances treat adult theaters differently from other theaters and the fact that the classification is predicated on the content of material shown in the respective theaters, the regulation of the place where such films may be exhibited does not offend the First Amendment.

The question whether speech is, or is not, protected by the First Amendment often depends on the content of the speech. Even within the area of protected speech, a difference in content may require a different governmental response.

In *New York Times Co. v. Sullivan*, we recognized that the First Amendment places limitations on the States' power to enforce their libel laws. The essence of that rule is the need for absolute neutrality by the Government, its regulation of communication may not be affected by sympathy or hostility for the point of view being expressed by the communicator. Thus, although the content of a story must be examined to decide whether it involves a public figure or a public issue, the Court's application of the relevant rule may not depend on its favorable or unfavorable appraisal of that figure or that issue.

We have recently held that the First Amendment affords some protection to commercial speech. We have also made it clear, however, that the content of a particular advertisement may determine the extent of its protection. More directly in point are opinions dealing with the question whether the First Amendment prohibits the state and federal governments from wholly suppressing sexually oriented materials on the basis of their "obscene character." In *Ginsberg v. New York*, the Court upheld a conviction for selling to a minor magazines which were concededly not "obscene" if shown to adults. Indeed, the Members of the Court who would accord the greatest protection to such materials have repeatedly indicated that the State could prohibit the distribution or exhibition of such materials to juveniles and consenting adults. Surely the First Amendment does not foreclose such a prohibition; yet it is equally clear that any such prohibition must rest squarely on an appraisal of the content of material otherwise within a constitutionally protected area.

Such a line may be drawn on the basis of content without violating the Government's paramount obligation of neutrality in its regulation of protected communication. For the regulation of the places where sexually explicit films may be exhibited is unaffected by whatever social, political, or philosophical message the film may be intended to communicate; whether the motion picture ridicules or characterizes one point of view or another, the effect of the ordinances is exactly the same.

Moreover, even though we recognize that the First Amendment will not tolerate the total suppression of erotic materials that have some arguably artistic value, it is manifest that society's interest in protecting this type of expression is of a wholly different, and lesser, magnitude than the interest in untrammeled political debate that inspired Voltaire's immortal comment. Whether political oratory or philosophical discussion moves us to applaud or to despise what is said, every schoolchild can understand why our duty to defend the right to speak remains the same. But few of us would march our sons and daughters off to war to preserve the citizen's right to see "Specified Sexual Activities" exhibited in the theaters of our choice. Even though the First Amendment protects communication in this area from total suppression, we hold that the State may legitimately use the content of these materials as the basis for placing them in a different classification from other motion pictures.

The remaining question is whether the line drawn by these ordinances is justified by the city's interest in preserving the character of its neighborhoods. The record discloses a factual basis for the Common Council's conclusion that this kind of restriction will have the desired effect.[34] It is not our function to appraise the wisdom of its decision to require adult theaters to be separated rather than concentrated in the same areas. In either event, the city's interest in attempting to preserve the quality of urban life is one that must be accorded high respect. Moreover, the city must be allowed a reasonable opportunity to experiment with solutions to admittedly serious problems.

Since what is ultimately at stake is nothing more than a limitation on the place where adult films may be exhibited,[35] even though the determination of whether a particular film fits that characterization turns on the nature of its content, we conclude that the city's interest in the present and future character of its neighborhoods adequately supports its classification of motion pictures. We hold that the zoning ordinances requiring that adult motion picture theaters not be located within 1,000 feet of two other regulated uses does not violate the Equal Protection Clause of the Fourteenth Amendment.

JUSTICE STEWART, with whom JUSTICES BRENNAN, MARSHALL, and BLACKMUN join, dissenting.

What this case does involve is the constitutional permissibility of selective interference with protected speech whose content is thought to produce distasteful effects. It is elementary that a prime function of the First Amendment is to guard against just such interference. By refusing to invalidate Detroit's ordinance the Court rides roughshod over cardinal principles of First Amendment law, which require that time, place and manner regulations that affect protected expression be content-neutral except in the limited context of a captive or juvenile audience. In place of these principles the Court invokes a concept wholly alien to the First Amendment. Since "few of us would march our sons and daughters off to war to preserve the citizen's right to see 'Specified Sexual Activities' exhibited in the theaters of our choice," the Court implies that these films are not entitled to the full protection of the Constitution.

The fact that the "offensive" speech here may not address "important" topics — "ideas of social and political significance," in the Court's terminology — does not mean that it is less worthy of constitutional protection. Moreover, in the absence of a judicial determination of obscenity, it is by no means clear that the speech is not "important" even on the Court's terms.

---

[34] The Common Council's determination was that a concentration of "adult" movie theaters causes the area to deteriorate and become a focus of crime effects which are not attributable to theaters showing other types of films. It is this secondary effect which this zoning ordinance attempts to avoid, not the dissemination of "offensive" speech. In contrast, in *Erznoznik*, the justifications offered by the city rested primarily on the city's interest in protecting its citizens from exposure to unwanted, "offensive" speech. The only secondary effect relied on to support that ordinance was the impact on traffic — an effect which might be caused by a distracting open-air movie even if it did not exhibit nudity.

[35] The situation would be quite different if the ordinance had the effect of suppressing, or greatly restricting access to, lawful speech. Here, however, the District Court specifically found that "[t]he Ordinances do not affect the operation of existing establishments but only the location of new ones. There are myriad locations in the City of Detroit which must be over 1,000 feet from existing regulated establishments. This burden on First Amendment rights is slight."

NOTES

1. *Content regulation.* Can a meaningful distinction be made, as Justice Stevens suggests, between a content-based law which is ideological, thus based on the viewpoint of the speech in question, and regulations which consider content but maintain neutrality towards the idea being expressed? Professor Farber suggests that such a distinction is critical to a proper understanding of *Mini Theatres*: "The classification at issue in *Mini Theatres* was not suspect as one based directly on viewpoint. In this respect, the classification is like a subject-matter classification." Daniel Farber, *Content Regulation and the First Amendment: A Revisionist View*, 68 GEO. L. REV. 727 (1980). Nevertheless, he warns that "such classifications are not entirely free from suspicion. Like gender classifications they may be based on invidious purposes. For these reasons, something more than minimal scrutiny given to classifications in economic regulatory schemes is necessary."

2. *City of Renton v. Playtime Theatres, Inc.*, 475 U.S. 41 (1986). The Court, per Justice Rehnquist, held that a city zoning ordinance which prohibited adult motion picture theatres from locating within 1,000 feet of any residential zone, single or multiple family dwelling, church, park, or school was constitutional. The ordinance was held to be a valid form of time, place,and manner regulation. Relying on *Young v. American Mini Theatres*, the regulations were deemed to be content neutral:

> [T]he Renton ordinance is aimed not at the content of the films shown at "adult motion picture theatres," but rather at the secondary effects of such theaters on the surrounding community. The District Court found that the City Council's "pre-dominant concerns" were with the secondary effects of adult theaters, and not with the content of adult films themselves. The appropriate inquiry in this case, then, [using the standards applicable to "content-neutral" time, place and manner regulations] is whether the Renton ordinance is designed to serve a substantial governmental interest and allows for reasonable alternative avenues of communication.

Renton was not required, as the court of appeals had ruled, to undertake specific studies related to Renton, but could rely on the studies of other cities such as Seattle that adult movie theatres would have unwanted effects on the quality of life in Renton. Although Renton's method of regulating adult movie theatres differed from the methods used by other cities, it was not the Court's function to require either concentration of adult theatres or their dispersion. The Renton ordinance constituted a "valid" governmental response to the admittedly serious problems created by adult theatres:

> Renton has not used "the power to zone as a pretext for suppressing expression" (*American Mini Theatres*) (Powell, J. concurring), but rather has sought to make some areas available for adult theatres and their patrons, while at the same time preserving the quality of life in the community at large by preventing those theatres from locating in other areas. This, after all, is the essence of zoning.

Justice Brennan, in a dissent joined by Justice Marshall, said that the ordinance was not content-neutral and discriminated on its face against adult movie theatres. The record, said Justice Brennan, did not support the Court's assertion that the "ordinance was designed to further Renton's substantial interest in preserv[ing] the quality of urban life."

The significance of *Renton* is that no proof of independent harm to the city is required to justify either concentration or dispersion of adult theatres. This contrasts markedly with *Schad* where independent harm to the city was shown. Doesn't the rationale of *Renton* show that the difference between using a time, place, manner analysis or a strict scrutiny standard is critical?

CITY OF LOS ANGELES v. ALAMEDA BOOKS, INC.

535 U.S. 425 122 S. Ct. 1728, 152 L.Ed.2d 670 (2002)

[A Los Angeles ordinance prohibiting the operation of more than one adult entertainment business in the same building was upheld on the basis of the *Renton* secondary effects doctrine. The city sought to satisfy the substantial governmental interest prong of the secondary effects doctrine by relying on a 1977 study which concluded that adult businesses "are associated with higher rates of prostitution, robbery, assaults and thefts" in the surrounding neighborhoods. The Court of Appeals ruled that the city could not rely on the 1977 study which was conducted "some years" before the enactment of the present version of the ordinance. The Supreme Court reversed.]

JUSTICE O'CONNOR announced the judgment of the Court and delivered an opinion, in which THE CHIEF JUSTICE, JUSTICE SCALIA, and JUSTICE THOMAS join.

The Court of Appeals misunderstood the implications of the 1977 study. While the study reveals that areas with high concentrations of adult establishments are associated with high crime rates, areas with high concentrations of adult establishments are also areas with high concentrations of adult operations, albeit each in separate establishments. It was therefore consistent with the findings of the 1977 study, and thus reasonable, for Los Angeles to suppose that a concentration of adult establishments is correlated with high crime rates because a concentration of operations in one locale draws, for example, a greater concentration of adult consumers to the neighborhood, and a high density of such consumers either attracts or generates criminal activity. The assumption behind this theory is that having a number of adult operations in one single adult establishment draws the same dense foot traffic as having a number of distinct adult establishments in close proximity, much as minimalls and department stores similarly attract the crowds of consumers. Under this view, it is rational for the city to infer that reducing the concentration of adult operations in a neighborhood, whether within separate establishments or in one large establishment, will reduce crime rates.

In *Renton v. Playtime Theatres, Inc.*, we specifically refused to set such a high bar for municipalities that want to address merely the secondary effects of protected speech. We held that a municipality may rely on any evidence that is "reasonably believed to be relevant" for demonstrating a connection between speech and a substantial, independent government interest. This is not to say that a municipality can get away with shoddy data or reasoning. The municipality's evidence must fairly support the municipality's rationale for its ordinance. If plaintiffs fail to cast direct doubt on this rationale, either by demonstrating that the municipality's evidence does not support its rationale or by furnishing evidence that disputes the municipality's factual findings, the municipality meets the standard set forth in *Renton.* If plaintiffs succeed in casting doubt on a municipality's rationale in either manner, the burden shifts back to the municipality to supplement the record with evidence renewing support for a theory that justifies its ordinance. This case is at a very early stage in this process. It arrives on a summary judgment motion by respondents defended only by complaints that the 1977 study fails to prove that the city's justification for its ordinance is necessarily correct. Therefore, we conclude that the city, at this stage of the litigation, has complied with the evidentiary requirement in *Renton.*

Unlike the city of Renton, the city of Los Angeles conducted its own study of adult businesses. We have concluded that the Los Angeles study provides evidence to support the city's theory that a concentration of adult operations in one locale attracts crime, and can be reasonably relied upon to demonstrate that Los Angeles Municipal Code § 12.70(C) (1983) is designed to promote the city's interest in reducing crime. Therefore, the city need not present foreign studies to overcome the summary judgment against it.

Justice Souter, with whom Justice Stevens and Justice Ginsburg join, and with whom Justice Breyer joins in part, dissenting.

From a policy of dispersing adult establishments, the city has thus moved to a policy of dividing them in two. The justification claimed for this application of the new policy remains, however, the 1977 survey, as supplemented by the authority of one decided case on regulating adult arcades in another State. The case authority is not on point, and the 1977 survey provides no support for the breakup policy. Its evidentiary insufficiency bears emphasis and is the principal reason that I respectfully dissent from the Court's judgment today.

[T]he Court has recognized that this kind of regulation, though called content neutral, occupies a kind of limbo between full-blown, content-based restrictions and regulations that apply without any reference to the substance of what is said. It would in fact make sense to give this kind of zoning regulation a First Amendment label of its own, and if we called it content correlated, we would not only describe it for what it is, but keep alert to a risk of content-based regulation that it poses. The risk lies in the fact that when a law applies selectively only to speech of particular content, the more precisely the content is identified, the greater is the opportunity for government censorship. Adult speech refers not merely to sexually explicit content, but to speech reflecting a favorable view of being explicit about sex and a favorable view of the practices it depicts; a restriction on adult content is thus also a restriction turning on a particular viewpoint, of which the government may disapprove.

This risk of viewpoint discrimination is subject to a relatively simple safeguard, however. If combating secondary effects of property devaluation and crime is truly the reason for the regulation, it is possible to show by empirical evidence that the effects exist, that they are caused by the expressive activity subject to the zoning, and that the zoning can be expected either to ameliorate them or to enhance the capacity of the government to combat them (say, by concentrating them in one area), without suppressing the expressive activity itself. This capacity of zoning regulation to address the practical problems without eliminating the speech is, after all, the only possible excuse for speaking of secondary-effects zoning as akin to time, place, or manner regulations.

The plurality overlooks a key distinction between the zoning regulations at issue in Renton and Young, and this new Los Angeles breakup requirement. In those two cases, the municipalities' substantial interest for purposes of intermediate scrutiny was an interest in choosing between two strategies to deal with crime or property value, each strategy tied to the businesses' location, which had been shown to have a causal connection with the secondary effects: the municipality could either concentrate businesses for a concentrated regulatory strategy, or disperse them in order to spread out its regulatory efforts.

If we take the city's breakup policy at its face, enforcing it will mean that in every case two establishments will operate instead of the traditional one. Since the city presumably does not wish merely to multiply adult establishments, it makes sense to ask what offsetting gain the city may obtain from its new breakup policy. The answer may lie in the fact that two establishments in place of one will entail two business overheads in place of one: two monthly rents, two electricity bills, two payrolls. Every month business will be more expensive than it used to be, perhaps even twice as much. That sounds like a good strategy for driving out expressive adult businesses. It sounds, in other words, like a policy of content-based regulation.

[4] Indecency Regulation on Broadcasting

FEDERAL COMMUNICATIONS COMM'N v. PACIFICA FOUNDATION

438 U.S. 726, 98 S. Ct. 3026, 58 L. Ed. 2d 198 (1978)

JUSTICE STEVENS delivered the opinion of the Court (Parts I, II, III, and IV-C) and an opinion in which THE CHIEF JUSTICE and JUSTICE REHNQUIST join in part.

This case requires that we decide whether the Federal Communications Commission has any power to regulate a radio broadcast that is indecent but not obscene.

A satiric humorist named George Carlin recorded a 12-minute monologue entitled "Filthy Words" before a live audience in a California theater. He began by referring to his thoughts about "the words you couldn't say on the public, ah, airwaves, um, the ones you definitely wouldn't say, ever." He proceeded to list those words and repeat them over and over again in a variety of colloquialisms. The transcript of the recording, which is appended to this opinion, indicates frequent laughter from the audience.

At about 2 o'clock in the afternoon on Tuesday, October 30, 1973, a New York radio station owned by respondent, Pacifica Foundation, broadcast the "Filthy Words" monologue. A few weeks later a man, who stated that he had heard the broadcast while driving with his young son, wrote a letter complaining to the Commission.

In its Memorandum Opinion the Commission stated that it intended to "clarify the standards which will be utilized in considering" the growing number of complaints about indecent speech on the airwaves. Advancing several reasons for treating broadcast speech differently from other forms of expression, the Commission found a power to regulate indecent broadcasting in two statutes: 18 U.S.C. § 1464, which forbids the use of "any obscene, indecent, or profane language by means of radio communications," and 47 U.S.C. § 303(g), which requires the Commission to "encourage the larger and more effective use of radio in the public interest."

[T]he Commission concluded that certain words depicted sexual and excretory activities in a patently offensive manner, noted that they "were broadcast at a time when children were undoubtedly in the audience (*i.e.*, in the early afternoon)," and that the prerecorded language, with these offensive words "repeated over and over," was "deliberately broadcast." In summary, the Commission stated: "We therefore hold that the language as broadcast was indecent and prohibited by 18 U.S.C. 1464."

[The Court sustained the FCC decision.]

Pacifica makes two constitutional attacks on the Commission's order. First, it argues that the Commission's construction of the statutory language broadly encompasses so much constitutionally protected speech that reversal is required even if Pacifica's broadcast of the "Filthy Words" monologue is not itself protected by the First Amendment. Second, Pacifica argues that inasmuch as the recording is not obscene, the Constitution forbids any abridgment of the right to broadcast it on the radio.

The first argument fails because our review is limited to the question whether the Commission has the authority to proscribe this particular broadcast. As the Commission itself emphasized, its order was "issued in a specific factual context." That approach is appropriate for courts as well as the Commission when regulation of indecency is at stake, for indecency is largely a function of context — it cannot be adequately judged in the abstract.

When the issue is narrowed to the facts of this case, the question is whether the First Amendment denies government any power to restrict the public broadcast of indecent language in any circumstances. For if the government has any such power, this was an appropriate occasion for its exercise.

The words of the Carlin monologue are unquestionably "speech" within the meaning of the First Amendment. It is equally clear that the Commission's objections to the broadcast were based in part on its content. The order must therefore fall if, as Pacifica argues, the First Amendment prohibits all governmental regulation that depends on the content of speech. Our past cases demonstrate, however, that no such absolute rule is mandated by the Constitution.

Although these words ordinarily lack literary, political, or scientific value, they are not entirely outside the protection of the First Amendment. Some uses of even the most offensive words are unquestionably protected. Indeed, we may assume, arguendo, that this monologue would be protected in other contexts. Nonetheless, the constitutional protection accorded to a communication containing such patently offensive sexual and excretory language need not be the same in every context. It is a characteristic of speech such as this that both its capacity to offend and its "social value," to use MR. JUSTICE MURPHY's term, vary with the circumstances. Words that are commonplace in one setting are shocking in another. To paraphrase MR. JUSTICE HARLAN, one occasion's lyric is another's vulgarity. *Cf. Cohen v. California.*

In this case it is undisputed that the content of Pacifica's broadcast was "vulgar," "offensive," and "shocking." Because content of that character is not entitled to absolute constitutional protection under all circumstances, we must consider its context in order to determine whether the Commission's action was constitutionally permissible.

We have long recognized that each medium of expression presents special First Amendment problems. *Joseph Burstyn, Inc. v. Wilson.* And of all forms of communication, it is broadcasting that has received the most limited First Amendment protection. Thus, although other speakers cannot be licensed except under laws that carefully define and narrow official discretion, a broadcaster may be deprived of his license and his forum if the Commission decides that such an action would serve "the public interest, convenience, and necessity." Similarly, although the First Amendment protects newspaper publishers from being required to print the replies of those whom they criticize, *Miami Herald Publishing Co. v. Tornillo*, it affords no such protection to broadcasters; on the contrary, they must give free time to the victims of their criticism. *Red Lion Broadcasting Co., Inc. v. FCC.*

The reasons for these distinctions are complex, but two have relevance to the present case. First, the broadcast media have established a uniquely pervasive presence in the lives of all Americans. Patently offensive, indecent material presented over the airwaves confronts the citizen, not only in public, but also in the privacy of the home, where the individual's right to be let alone plainly outweighs the First Amendment rights of an intruder. *Rowan v. Post Office Department.* Because the broadcast audience is constantly tuning in and out, prior warnings cannot completely protect the listener or viewer from unexpected program content. To say that one may avoid further offense by turning off the radio when he hears indecent language is like saying that the remedy for an assault is to run away after the first blow. One may hang up on an indecent phone call, but that option does not give the caller a constitutional immunity or avoid a harm that has already taken place.

Second, broadcasting is uniquely accessible to children, even those too young to read. Although Cohen's written message might have been incomprehensible to a first grader, Pacifica's broadcast could have enlarged a child's vocabulary in an instant. Other forms of offensive expression may be withheld from the young without restricting the expression at its source. Bookstores and motion picture theaters, for example, may be prohibited from making indecent material available to children. The ease with which children may obtain access to broadcast material, coupled with the concerns recognized in [*Ginsberg v. New York*], amply justify special treatment of indecent broadcasting.

It is appropriate, in conclusion, to emphasize the narrowness of our holding. This case does not involve a two-way radio conversation between a cab driver and a dispatcher, or a telecast of an Elizabethan comedy. We have not decided that an occasional expletive in either setting would justify any sanction or, indeed, that this broadcast would justify a criminal prosecution. The Commission's decision rested entirely on a nuisance rationale under which context is all-important. The concept requires consideration of a host of variables. The time of day was emphasized by the Commission. The content of the program in which the language is used will also affect the composition of the audience, and differences between radio, television, and perhaps closed-circuit transmissions, may also be relevant. As Mr. Justice Sutherland wrote, a "nuisance may be merely a right thing in the wrong place — like a pig in the parlor instead of the barnyard." We simply hold that when the Commission finds that a pig has entered the parlor, the exercise of its regulatory power does not depend on proof that the pig is obscene.

Justice Powell, with whom Justice Blackmun joins, concurring.

In my view, the result in this case does not turn on whether Carlin's monologue, viewed as a whole, or the words that comprise it, have more or less "value" than a candidate's campaign speech. This is a judgment for each person to make, not one for the judges to impose upon him. The result turns instead on the unique characteristics of the broadcast media, combined with society's right to protect its children from speech generally agreed to be inappropriate for their years, and with the interest of unwilling adults in not being assaulted by such offensive speech in their homes.

Justice Brennan, with whom Justice Marshall joins, dissenting.

For the second time in two years, *see Young v. American Mini Theatres*, the Court refuses to embrace the notion, completely antithetical to basic First Amendment values, that the degree of protection the First Amendment affords protected speech varies with the social value ascribed to that speech by five Members of this Court. Moreover, as do all parties, all Members of the Court agree that the Carlin monologue aired by Station WBAI does not fall within one of the categories of speech, such as "fighting words," or obscenity, that is totally without First Amendment protection. Yet despite the Court's refusal to create a sliding scale of First Amendment protection calibrated to this Court's perception of the worth of a communication's content, and despite our unanimous agreement that the Carlin monologue is protected speech, a majority of the Court nevertheless finds that, on the facts of this case, the FCC is not constitutionally barred from imposing sanctions on Pacifica for its airing of the Carlin monologue. This majority apparently believes that the FCC's disapproval of Pacifica's afternoon broadcast of Carlin's "Dirty Words" recording is a permissible time, place, and manner regulation.

Whatever the minimal discomfort suffered by a listener who inadvertently tunes into a program he finds offensive during the brief interval before he can simply extend his arm and switch stations or flick the "off" button, it is surely worth the candle to preserve the broadcaster's right to send, and the right of those interested to receive, a message entitled to full First Amendment protection.

The Court's balance, of necessity, fails to accord proper weight to the interests of listeners who wish to hear broadcasts the FCC deems offensive. It permits majoritarian tastes completely to preclude a protected message from entering the homes of a receptive, unoffended minority. No decision of this Court supports such a result.

Because the Carlin monologue is obviously not an erotic appeal to the prurient interests of children, the Court, for the first time, allows the government to prevent minors from gaining access to materials that are not obscene, and are therefore protected, as to them.

In concluding that the presence of children in the listening audience provides an adequate basis for the FCC to impose sanctions for Pacifica's broadcast of the Carlin monologue, the opinions of my Brother Powell, and my Brother STEVENS, both stress the time-honored right of a parent to raise his child as he sees fit — a right this Court has consistently been vigilant to protect. *See Wisconsin v. Yoder*; *Pierce v. Society of Sisters*. Yet this principle supports a result directly contrary to that reached by the Court. *Yoder* and *Pierce* hold that parents, not the government, have the right to make certain decisions regarding the upbringing of their children.

For my own part, even accepting that this case is limited to its facts, I would place the responsibility and the right to weed worthless and offensive communications from the public airways where it belongs and where, until today, it resided: in a public free to choose those communications worthy of its attention from a marketplace unsullied by the censor's hand.

JUSTICE STEWART, joined by JUSTICES BRENNAN, WHITE, and MARSHALL, also dissented.]

NOTES

1. *The broadcast media.* Is *Pacifica*, then, another anomaly in First Amendment law? Justice Stevens offers an explanation: "And of all forms of communication, it is broadcasting that has received the most limited First Amendment protection." But why have the electronic media been accorded less First Amendment protection than the print media? Is part of the answer, at least in the context of the *Pacifica* decision, to be found in the fact that the state has greater latitude to regulate broadcasting in the interest of its children? Justice Stevens emphasizes two factors: broadcasting is (1) a "uniquely pervasive presence" and (2) "uniquely accessible to children." To these factors must be added the peculiarly repetitive quality of the "indecent expression" in *Pacifica* plus the time the material was broadcast. Is *Pacifica* then a case with unusual facts which involve basically just a time-place-manner regulation? Is the trouble with this explanation that the content of the expression appears to be basic to the decision?

2. *"Dial-a-porn."* In *Sable Communication of California, Inc. v. FCC,* 492 U.S. 115 (1989), a federal statute totally banning "dial-a-porn," i.e., sexually-oriented messages which were indecent but not obscene, was held unconstitutional. Justice White, speaking for the Court in *Sable*, distinguished *Pacifica* which did not involve a total ban on broadcasting indecent material but instead sought to channel such material to times of day when children would not be exposed to it. *Pacifica* had relied on the unique pervasive and intrusive quality of broadcasting as well as its unique accessibility to children. "Dial-a-porn" was different than broadcasting:

> [T]he [dial-in] medium requires the listener to take affirmative steps to receive the communication. There is no "captive audience" problem here; callers will generally not be unwilling listeners. The context of dial-in-services, where a caller seeks and is willing to pay for the communication is manifestly different from a situation in which a listener does not want the received message.

The Court rejected the government's argument that nothing less than a total ban would prevent children from obtaining access to "dial-a-porn" messages. Technological means were available to prevent such access. Indeed, the FCC had determined "that its credit card, access code, and scrambling rules were a satisfactory solution to the problem of keeping indecent dial-a-porn messages out of the reach of minors." In view of the technology available, the statute imposing a total ban was "not a narrowly tailored effort to serve the compelling interest of preventing minors from being exposed to indecent telephone messages."

3. *Cable Television and Indecency Regulation.*

***Denver Area Educational Telecommunications Consortium, Inc. v. FCC*, 518 U.S. 727 (1996).** The Supreme Court considered First Amendment challenges to three provisions of the Cable Television Consumer Protection and Competition Act of 1992 as implemented by FCC regulations. Sec. 10(a) permits a cable operator to refuse to carry leased access programming that "depicts sexual or excretory activities or organs in a patently offensive way as measured by contemporary community standards." Sec. 10(b) seeks to limit the access of children to indecent programming and requires the FCC to promulgate rules requiring cable operators transmitting indecent material on leased access channels to segregate such programming on a separate channel which is blocked unless the subscriber requests otherwise. Sec. 10(c) mandates that the FCC issue regulations that authorize cable operators to deny the used of public, educational and governmental channels (public access channels) for programming "which contains obscene material, sexually explicit conduct, or material soliciting or promoting unlawful conduct."

A badly fractionated Court upheld § 10(a) by a 7-2 vote, struck down § 10(c) by a 5-4 vote, and struck down § 10(b) by a 6-3 vote. As a result of the decision, indecency on public access channels receives more favored treatment than indecency on leased access channels. The requirement that indecent material be segregated on a separate channel was, however, struck down. The discussion in *Denver Consortium* of the First Amendment issues relating to access channels is set forth at p. 1302. The aspects of the case that deal with the regulation of indecency on cable are set forth here.

Justice Breyer, joined by Justices Stevens, O'Connor and Souter, concluded that § 10(a) was valid for several reasons. First, *Sable*, *Ginsberg* and *Ferber* all support the compelling governmental interest in protecting "children from exposure to patently offensive sex-related material." Second, § 10(a) is a very specialized provision. "[B]ut for a previous act of Congress" there would have been "no path of access of an operator's control." Third, the problem Congress addressed in *Pacifica* is remarkably similar to the problem addressed by Congress here:

> All [the *Pacifica* factors] are present here. Cable television broadcasting, including access channel broadcasting, is as "accessible to children" as over-the-air broadcasting. Cable television systems, including access channels, "have established a uniquely pervasive presence in the lives of all Americans." *Pacifica.* There is nothing to stop "adults who feel the need" from finding similar programming elsewhere, say, on tape or in theatres.

Fourth, Justice Breyer pointed out that Sec. 10(a) is permissive, i.e., it did not *require* the cable operator to ban indecent material on leased access channels but simply permitted the operator to do so: "[A]lthough [§ 10(a)] does create a risk that a program will not appear, that risk is not the same as the certainty that accompanies a governmental ban." Justice Breyer rejected the contention that the material as defined in the provisions and as amplified by the FCC was too vague. FCC regulations had added as a guideline language similar to the definition of obscenity set forth in *Miller v. California*:

> The language, while vague, attempts to identify the category of materials that Justice Stewart thought could be described only in terms of "I know it when I see it." *Jacobellis v. Ohio.* Sec.10(a) and the FCC regulations, with *Miller*'s qualifiers, [appear] to refer to material that would be offensive enough to fall within that category but for the fact that the material also has "serious literary, artistic, political or scientific value" or nonprurient purposes. This history suggests that the statute's language aims at the kind of programming to which its sponsors referred — pictures of oral sex, bestiality and rape. [W]e conclude that the statute is not impermissibly vague.

With respect to § 10(b), Justice Breyer delivered the opinion of the Court:

> [Section 10(b)] and its implementing regulations require cable operators to place "patently offensive" leased channel programming on a separate channel; to block that channel; to unblock that channel within 30 days of a subscriber's request for reblocking. Also, leased access channel programmers must notify cable operators of an intended "patently offensive" broadcast up to 30 days before its scheduled broadcast date. These requirements have obvious restrictive effects. The several up-to-30-day delays, along with a single channel segregation, means that a subscriber cannot decide to watch a single program without considerable advance planning. Moreover, the "written notice" requirement will further restrict viewing by subscribers who fear for their reputations. Further, the added costs and burdens that these requirements impose upon a cable system operator may

> encourage that operator to ban programming that the operator would otherwise permit to run, even if only late at night.

Justice Breyer concluded that this restriction was not " 'narrowly tailored' to meet its legitimate objective." For example, § 551 of the 1996 Telecommunications Act provides that in the future television sets will have to be manufactured "with a so-called 'V-chip' — a device that will be able automatically to identify and block sexually explicit or violent programs." Justice Breyer said of these measures:

> [T]hey are significantly less restrictive than the provision here at issue. They do not force the viewer to receive all "patently offensive" programming or none; they will not lead the viewer automatically to judge the few by the reputation of the many; and they will not automatically place the occasional viewer's name on a special list.

Justice Breyer, joined by Justices Stevens and Souter, concluded that § 10(c) authorizing cable operators to ban obscene and indecent material on public access channels was unconstitutional. Justice Breyer declared that the government had failed to show that there was a sufficient problem regarding "patently offensive" broadcasts to children to warrant the restriction set forth in § 10(c):

> [Section 10(c)] would not significantly restore editorial rights of cable operators, but would greatly increase the risk that certain categories of programming (say, borderline offensive programs) will not appear. [Further,] we conclude that the Government cannot show Sec. 10(c) is necessary to protect children or that it is appropriately tailored to secure that end.

Justice Souter, concurring, agreed with the plurality that cable indecency, should be governed by *Pacifica* for the present:

> [T]oday's plurality opinion observes rightly that the characteristics of broadcast radio that rendered indecency particularly threatening in *Pacifica*, that is, its intrusion into the house and accessibility to children are also present in the case of cable television. It would seem, then, that the appropriate category for cable indecency should be as contextually detailed as the *Pacifica* example.
>
> Rather than definitively settling the issue now, Justice Breyer wisely reasons by analogy rather than by rule, concluding that the speech and the restriction at issue in this case may usefully be measured against the ones at issue in *Pacifica*. [U]ntil a category of indecency can be defined both with reference to the new technology and with a prospect of durability, the job of courts will be just what Justice Breyer does today: recognizing established First Amendment interests through a close analysis that constrains the Congress, without wholly incapacitating it in all matters of the significance apparent here.

Justice Kennedy, joined by Justice Ginsburg, dissenting in part and concurring in part, would hold § 10(a) as well as §§ 10(b) and (c) unconstitutional:

> [The government] argues the nature of the speech in question — indecent broadcast (or cablecast) — is subject to the lower standard of review it contends was applied in *Pacifica*. *Pacifica* did not purport, however, to apply a special standard for indecent broadcasting. Emphasizing the narrowness of its holding, *Pacifica* conducted a context-specific analysis of the FCC's restriction on indecent programming during daytime hours. It relied on the general rule that "broadcasting has received the most limited First Amendment protection." We already have rejected the application of this standard of review to infringements on the liberties of cable operators, even though they control an important communications medium. *Turner Broadcasting*. There is even less cause for a lower standard here.

Justice Kennedy said that the appropriate standard for both §§ 10(a) and 10(c) was strict scrutiny. Under that standard, these provisions failed since they were not "narrowly tailored to serve a compelling interest":

> First, to the extent some operators may allow indecent programming, children in localities those operators serve will be left unprotected. Second, to the extent cable operators prohibit indecent programming on access channels, not only children but adults will be deprived of it. Secs. 10(a) and (c) present a classic case of discrimination based on its content.

Justice Thomas, joined by Chief Justice Rehnquist and Justice Scalia, concurring in the judgment in part and dissenting in part, agreed that § 10(a) did not violate the First Amendment but thought that §§ 10(b) and (c) did not violate the First Amendment either:

> [Section] 10(b) does nothing more than adjust the nature of government-imposed leased access requirements in order to emulate the market forces that keep indecent programming primarily on premium channels (without permitting the operator to charge susbcribers for that programming).
>
> Unlike Secs. 10(a) and (c), Sec. 10(b) clearly implicates petitioners' free speech rights. Though Sec. 10(b) by no means bans indecent speech, it clearly places content-based restrictions on the transmission of private speech by requiring cable operators to block and segregate indecent programming that the operator has agreed to carry. Consequently, Sec. 10(b) must be subjected to strict scrutiny and can be upheld only if it furthers a compelling governmental interest by the least restrictive means available. The parties agree that Congress has a "compelling interest in protecting the physical and psychological well-being of minors" and that its interest "extends to shielding minors from the influence of [indecent speech] that is not obscene by adult standards." *See Ginsberg v. New York*. Because Sec. 10(b) is narrowly

> tailored to achieve that well-established compelling interest, I would uphold it. I therefore dissent from the Court's decision to the contrary.

Consider the following assessment of *Denver Area*: "One of the difficulties *Denver Area* presents is that the examination proceeds from very different focal points by various Justices. Justice Breyer and Justice Souter analyzed the issue by determining which standard is appropriate to govern a new medium like cable. Justice Kennedy, on the other hand, looked beyond the medium. His question related to which standard of review is appropriate for the regulation of indecent speech. Kennedy's corollary to this question focused on the *Pacifica* standard as a narrow holding bred in broadcasting which should not be extended to newer electronic media. Justice Breyer's balancing approach serves as a tentative standard for the beginning of a new electronic media age. The balancing is candid, contextual, and media deferential, and it yielded, rather than thwarted [speech] protective results in *Denver Area*." Jerome A. Barron, *The Electronic Media and the Flight from First Amendment Doctrine: Justice Breyer's New Balancing Approach*, 31 U. of Mich. J. of L. Ref. 817, 865–866 (1998).

***United States v. Playboy Entertainment Gp.*, 529 U.S. 803 (2000).** A cable television programmer sought a declaratory judgment that Sec. 505 of the Telecommunications Act of 1996, the "signal bleed" provision, requiring cable operators either to scramble sexually explicit channels or limit programming on such channels to certain hours, was unconstitutional. The Supreme Court, Justice Kennedy, held that the provision constituted a content-based restriction subject to strict scrutiny. Because the government failed to show that this mechanism was the least restrictive means of achieving its goal of preventing children from hearing or seeing images resulting from "signal bleed," it violated the First Amendment's free speech clause. "Signal bleed" refers to inadequate blocking or scrambling of signals so that a discernible image may appear on the scrambled channel from time to time. Because the technology of scrambling does not prevent signal bleed in most cases, local cable operators elected to broadcast sexually explicit programming to only during the permitted hours, effectively limiting programmers' access to television sets at much of prime time viewing hours. A less restrictive statutory alternative, Sec. 504 of the Act, promoting viewer blocking on an individual basis, was found by the Court to be available and to be effective to serve the government's interest in protecting children from unwanted exposure to sexually explicit material.

Justice Breyer, joined by Chief Justice Rehnquist, and Justices O'Connor and Scalia, dissented on the ground that Sec. 504's viewer opt-out procedure was not a less restrictive alternative: "[D]uring the 14 months the Government was enjoined from enforcing Sec. 505 'fewer than 0.5% of cable subscribers requested full blocking' under Sec. 504." Justice Breyer insisted First Amendment standards permit Congress to enact legislation that "increases the costs associated with certain speech where doing so serves a compelling interest that cannot be served through the adoption of a less restrictive, similarly effective alternative." Where the protection of children is at issue, the First Amendment poses a barrier that properly is high, but not insurmountable.

Although he joined the Breyer dissent, Justice Scalia filed a separate dissent saying that the case could be resolved on the ground that the law at issue was regulating "the business of obscenity." Relying on *Ginzburg v. U.S.* test, p. 1205, he contended that the challenged law, Sec. 505, like the activity sanctioned in *Ginzburg,* did not merit First Amendment protection: "We have recognized that commercial entities which engage in 'the sordid business of pandering' by 'deliberately emphasiz[ing] the sexually provocative aspects of [their nonobscene products], in order to catch the salaciously disposed,' engage in constitutionally unprotected behavior."

Justice Kennedy in *Playboy Entertainment Group* said that a distinction between cable television and broadcast television was the point on which the case turned: "Cable systems have the capacity to block unwanted channels on a household-by-household basis. The option to block reduces the likelihood, so concerning to the Court in *Pacifica*, that traditional First Amendment scrutiny would deprive the Government of all authority to address this sort of problem." The Court in *Playboy Entertainment* applied strict scrutiny to indecent speech. Arguably, this could be interpreted to mean that *Pacifica* has been eclipsed, if not reversed, by *Playboy Entertainment.* But Justice Kennedy emphasized that broadcast television, unlike cable television, cannot be blocked. What is the standard of review for regulation of indecency on cable television after *Playboy Entertainment Group*? Have the rulings on this issue in *Denver Area* been superseded?

[5] Indecency Recalculation on the Internet

RENO v. AMERICAN CIVIL LIBERTIES UNION
521 U.S. 844, 117 S. Ct. 2329, 138 L.Ed. 2d. 874 (1997)

JUSTICE STEVENS delivered the opinion of the Court.

At issue is the constitutionality of two statutory provisions enacted to protect minors from "indecent" and "patently offensive" communications on the Internet. Notwithstanding the legitimacy and importance of the congressional goal of protecting children from harmful materials, we agree with the three-judge District Court that the statute abridges "the freedom of speech" protected by the First Amendment.

Sexually explicit material on the Internet includes text, pictures, and chat and "extends from the modestly titillating to the hardest-core." These files are created, named, and posted in the same manner as material that is not sexually explicit, and may be accessed either deliberately or unintentionally during the course of an imprecise search. "Once a provider posts its content on the Internet, it cannot prevent that content from entering any community."

Though such material is widely available, users seldom encounter such content accidentally. "A document's title or a description of the document will usually appear before the document itself and in many cases the user will receive detailed information about a site's content before he or she need take the step to access the document. Almost all sexually explicit images are preceded by warnings as to the content." For that reason, the "odds are slim" that a user would enter a sexually explicit site by accident.

The Telecommunications Act of 1996 was an unusually important legislative enactment. [I]ts primary purpose was to reduce regulation and encourage "the rapid deployment of new telecommunications technologies." Title V — known as the "Communications Decency Act of 1996" (CDA) — contains provisions that were either added in executive committee after the hearings were concluded or as amendments offered during floor debate on the legislation. An amendment offered in the Senate was the source of the two statutory provisions challenged in this case. They are informally described as the "indecent transmission" provision and the "patently offensive display" provision.

The first, 47 U.S.C.A. § 223(a), prohibits the knowing transmission of obscene or indecent messages to any recipient under 18 years of age. It provides in pertinent part:

> "(a) Whoever —
>
> "(1) in interstate or foreign communications —
>
> "(B) by means of a telecommunications device knowingly —
>
> "(i) makes, creates, or solicits, and
>
> "(ii) initiates the transmission of,
>
> "any comment, request, suggestion, proposal, image, or other communication which is obscene or indecent, knowing that the recipient of the communication is under 18 years of age, regardless of whether the maker of such communication placed the call or initiated the communication;
>
> "(2) knowingly permits any telecommunications facility under his control to be used for any activity prohibited by paragraph (1) with the intent that it be used for such activity,
>
> "shall be fined under Title 18, or imprisoned not more than two years, or both."

The second provision, § 223(d), prohibits the knowing sending or displaying of patently offensive messages in a manner that is available to a person under 18 years of age. It provides:

> "(d) Whoever —
>
> "(1) in interstate or foreign communications knowingly —
>
> "(A) uses an interactive computer service to send to a specific person or persons under 18 years of age, or
>
> "(B) uses any interactive computer service to display in a manner available to a person under 18 years of age,
>
> "any comment, request, suggestion, proposal, image, or other communication that, in context, depicts or describes, in terms patently offensive as measured by contemporary community standards, sexual or excretory activities or organs, regardless of whether the user of such service placed the call or initiated the communication; or

> "(2) knowingly permits any telecommunications facility under such person's control to be used for an activity prohibited by paragraph (1) with the intent that it be used for such activity,
>
> "shall be fined under Title 18, or imprisoned not more than two years, or both."

The breadth of these prohibitions is qualified by two affirmative defenses. *See* § 223(e)(5). One covers those who take "good faith, reasonable, effective, and appropriate actions" to restrict access by minors to the prohibited communications. § 223(e)(5)(A). The other covers those who restrict access to covered material by requiring certain designated forms of age proof, such as a verified credit card or an adult identification number or code. § 223(e)(5)(B).

On February 8, 1996, immediately after the President signed the statute, 20 plaintiffs filed suit against the Attorney General of the United States and the Department of Justice challenging the constitutionality of §§ 223(a)(1) and 223(d). The two cases were consolidated, and a three-judge District Court was convened pursuant to § 561 of the Act. After an evidentiary hearing, that court entered a preliminary injunction against enforcement of both of the challenged provisions.

The judgment of the District Court enjoins the Government from enforcing the prohibitions in § 223(a)(1)(B) insofar as they relate to "indecent" communications, but expressly preserves the Government's right to investigate and prosecute the obscenity or child pornography activities prohibited therein. The injunction against enforcement of §§ 223(d)(1) and (2) is unqualified because those provisions contain no separate reference to obscenity or child pornography.

In arguing for reversal, the Government contends that the CDA is plainly constitutional under three of our prior decisions: (1) *Ginsberg v. New York* [text, p. 1207]; (2) *FCC v. Pacifica Foundation* [text, p. 1224]; and (3) *Renton v. Playtime Theatres, Inc.* [text, p. 1220] A close look at these cases, however, raises — rather than relieves — doubts concerning the constitutionality of the CDA.

In four important respects, the statute upheld in *Ginsberg* was narrower than the CDA. First, we noted in *Ginsberg* that "the prohibition against sales to minors does not bar parents who so desire from purchasing the magazines for their children." Under the CDA, by contrast, neither the parents' consent — nor even their participation — in the communication would avoid the application of the statute. Second, the New York statute applied only to commercial transactions, whereas the CDA contains no such limitation. Third, the New York statute cabined its definition of material that is harmful to minors with the requirement that it be "utterly without redeeming social importance for minors." The CDA fails to provide us with any definition of the term "indecent" as used in § 223(a)(1) and, importantly, omits any requirement that the "patently offensive" material covered by § 223(d) lack serious literary, artistic, political, or scientific value. Fourth, the New York statute defined a minor as a person under the age of 17, whereas the CDA, in applying to all those under 18 years, includes an additional year of those nearest majority.

[T]here are significant differences between the order upheld in *Pacifica* and the CDA. First, the order in *Pacifica*, issued by an agency that had been regulating radio stations for decades, targeted a specific broadcast that represented a rather dramatic departure from traditional program content in order to designate when — rather than whether — it would be permissible to air such a program in that particular medium. The CDA's broad categorical prohibitions are not limited to particular times and are not dependent on any evaluation by an agency familiar with the unique characteristics of the Internet. Second, unlike the CDA, the Commission's declaratory order was not punitive; we expressly refused to decide whether the indecent broadcast "would justify a criminal prosecution." Finally, the Commission's order applied to a medium which as a matter of history had "received the most limited First Amendment protection," in large part because warnings could not adequately protect the listener from unexpected program content. The Internet, however, has no comparable history.

In *Renton*, we upheld a zoning ordinance that kept adult movie theaters out of residential neighborhoods. The ordinance was aimed, not at the content of the films shown in the theaters, but rather at the "secondary effects" — such as crime and deteriorating property values — that these theaters fostered. According to the Government, the CDA is constitutional because it constitutes a sort of "cyberzoning" on the Internet. But the CDA applies broadly to the entire universe of cyberspace. And the purpose of the CDA is to protect children from the primary effects of "indecent" and "patently offensive" speech, rather than any "secondary" effect of such speech.

Neither before nor after the enactment of the CDA have the vast democratic fora of the Internet been subject to the type of government supervision and regulation that has attended the broadcast industry. Moreover, the Internet is not as "invasive" as radio or television. The District Court specifically found that "[c]ommunications over the Internet do not 'invade' an individual's home or appear on one's computer screen unbidden. Users seldom encounter content 'by accident.' It also found that "[a]lmost all sexually explicit images are preceded by warnings as to the content," and cited testimony that " 'odds are slim' that a user would come across a sexually explicit sight by accident."

Finally, unlike the conditions that prevailed when Congress first authorized regulation of the broadcast spectrum, the Internet can hardly be considered a "scarce" expressive commodity. It provides relatively unlimited, low-cost capacity for communication of all kinds. This dynamic, multifaceted category of communication includes not only traditional print and news services, but also audio, video, and still images, as well as interactive, real-time dialogue. Through the use of chat rooms, any person with a phone line can become a town crier with a voice that resonates farther than it could from any soapbox. Through the use of Web pages, mail exploders, and newsgroups, the same individual can become a pamphleteer. [O]ur cases provide no basis for qualifying the level of First Amendment scrutiny that should be applied to this medium.

The Government argues that the statute is no more vague than the obscenity standard this Court established in *Miller v. California* [text p. 1216]. But that is not so. Because the CDA's "patently offensive" standard (and, we assume *arguendo*, its synonymous "indecent" standard) is one part of the three-prong *Miller* test, the Government reasons, it cannot be unconstitutionally vague. The Government's assertion is incorrect as a matter of fact. The second prong of the *Miller* test — the purportedly analogous standard — contains a critical requirement that is omitted from the CDA: That the proscribed material be "specifically defined by the applicable state law." This requirement reduces the vagueness inherent in the open-ended term "patently offensive" as used in the CDA. Moreover, the *Miller* definition is limited to "sexual conduct," whereas the CDA extends also to include (1) "excretory activities" as well as (2) "organs" of both a sexual and excretory nature.

The Government's reasoning is also flawed. Just because a definition including three limitations is not vague, it does not follow that one of those limitations, standing by itself, is not vague. Each of *Miller's* additional two prongs — (1) that, taken as a whole, the material appeal to the "prurient" interest, and (2) that it "lac[k] serious literary, artistic, political, or scientific value" — critically limits the uncertain sweep of the obscenity definition.

In contrast to *Miller* and our other previous cases, the CDA thus presents a greater threat of censoring speech that, in fact, falls outside the statute's scope. Given the vague contours of the coverage of the statute, it unquestionably silences some speakers whose messages would be entitled to constitutional protection. That danger provides further reason for insisting that the statute not be overly broad. The CDA's burden on protected speech cannot be justified if it could be avoided by a more carefully drafted statute.

We are persuaded that the CDA lacks the precision that the First Amendment requires when a statute regulates the content of speech. In order to deny minors access to potentially harmful speech, the CDA effectively suppresses a large amount of speech that adults have a constitutional right to receive and to address to one another. That burden on adult speech is unacceptable if less restrictive alternatives would be at least as effective in achieving the legitimate purpose that the statute was enacted to serve. In evaluating the free speech rights of adults, we have made it perfectly clear that "[s]exual expression which is indecent but not obscene is protected by the First Amendment." It is true that we have repeatedly recognized the governmental interest in protecting children from harmful materials. *See Ginsberg*; *Pacifica*. But that interest does not justify an unnecessarily broad suppression of speech addressed to adults.

The breadth of the CDA's coverage is wholly unprecedented. Unlike the regulations upheld in *Ginsberg* and *Pacifica*, the scope of the CDA is not limited to commercial speech or commercial entities. Its open-ended prohibitions embrace all nonprofit entities and individuals posting indecent messages or displaying them on their own computers in the presence of minors. The general, undefined terms "indecent" and "patently offensive" cover large amounts of nonpornographic material with serious educational or other value. Moreover, the "community standards" criterion as applied to the Internet means that any communication available to a nation-wide audience will be judged by the standards of the community most likely to be offended by the message. The regulated subject matter may extend to discussions about prison rape or safe sexual practices, artistic images that include nude subjects, and arguably the card catalogue of the Carnegie Library.

For the purposes of our decision, we need neither accept nor reject the Government's submission that the First Amendment does not forbid blanket prohibition on all "indecent" and "patently offensive" messages communicated to a 17–year–old — no matter how much value the message may contain and regardless of parental approval. It is at least clear that the strength of the Government's interest in protecting minors is not equally strong throughout the coverage of this broad statute. Under the CDA, a parent allowing her 17–year–old to use the family computer to obtain information on the Internet that she, in her parental judgment, deems appropriate could face a lengthy prison term. Similarly, a parent who sent his 17–year–old college freshman information on birth control via e-mail could be incarcerated even though neither he, his child, nor anyone in their home community, found the material "indecent" or "patently offensive," if the college town's community thought otherwise.

The breadth of this content-based restriction of speech imposes an especially heavy burden on the Government to explain why a less restrictive provision would not be as effective as the CDA. It has not done so. The arguments in this Court have referred to possible alternatives such as requiring that indecent material be "tagged" in a way that facilitates parental control of material coming into their homes, making exceptions for messages with artistic or educational value, providing some tolerance for parental choice, and regulating some portions of the Internet — such as commercial web sites — differently than others, such as chat rooms. Particularly in the light of the absence of any detailed findings by the Congress, or even hearings addressing the special problems of the CDA, we are persuaded that the CDA is not narrowly tailored if that requirement has any meaning at all.

The record demonstrates that the growth of the Internet has been and continues to be phenomenal. As a matter of constitutional tradition, in the absence of evidence to the contrary, we presume that governmental regulation of the content of speech is more likely to interfere with the free exchange of ideas than to encourage it. The interest in encouraging freedom of expression in a democratic society outweighs any theoretical but unproven benefit of censorship.

JUSTICE O'CONNOR, with whom THE CHIEF JUSTICE joins, concurring in the judgment in part and dissenting in part.

I write separately to explain why I view the Communications Decency Act of 1996 as little more than an attempt by Congress to create "adult zones" on the Internet. Our precedent indicates that the creation of such zones can be constitutionally sound. Despite the soundness of its purpose, however, portions of the CDA are unconstitutional because they stray from the blueprint our prior cases have developed for constructing a "zoning law" that passes constitutional muster.

Although the prospects for the eventual zoning of the Internet appear promising, I agree with the Court that we must evaluate the constitutionality of the CDA as it applies to the Internet as it exists today. Given the present state of cyberspace, I agree with the Court that the "display" provision cannot pass muster. Until gateway technology is available throughout cyberspace, and it is not in 1997, a speaker cannot be reasonably assured that the speech he displays will reach only adults because it is impossible to confine speech to an "adult zone." Thus, the only way for a speaker to avoid liability under the CDA is to refrain completely from using indecent speech. But this forced silence impinges on the First Amendment right of adults to make and obtain this speech and, for all intents and purposes, "reduce[s] the adult population [on the Internet] to reading only what is fit for children." As a result, the "display" provision cannot withstand scrutiny.

The "indecency transmission" and "specific person" provisions present a closer issue, for they are not unconstitutional in all of their applications. As discussed above, the "indecency transmission" provision makes it a crime to transmit knowingly an indecent message to a person the sender knows is under 18 years of age. The "specific person" provision proscribes the same conduct, although it does not as explicitly require the sender to know that the intended recipient of his indecent message is a minor. § 223(d)(1)(A). Appellant urges the Court to construe the provision to impose such a knowledge requirement, and I would do so.

So construed, both provisions are constitutional as applied to a conversation involving only an adult and one or more minors — e.g., when an adult speaker sends an e-mail knowing the addressee is a minor, or when an adult and minor converse by themselves or with other minors in a chat room. In this context, these provisions are no different from the law we sustained in *Ginsberg*. Restricting what the adult may say to the minors in no way restricts the adult's ability to communicate with other adults. He is not prevented from speaking indecently to other adults in a chat room (because there are no other adults participating in the conversation) and he remains free to send indecent e-mails to other adults. The relevant universe contains only one adult, and the adult in that universe has the power to refrain from using indecent speech and consequently to keep all such speech within the room in an "adult" zone.

The analogy to *Ginsberg* breaks down, however, when more than one adult is a party to the conversation. If a minor enters a chat room otherwise occupied by adults, the CDA effectively requires the adults in the room to stop using indecent speech. The CDA is therefore akin to a law that makes it a crime for a bookstore owner to sell pornographic magazines to anyone once a minor enters his store. Even assuming such a law might be constitutional in the physical world as a reasonable alternative to excluding minors completely from the store, the absence of any means of excluding minors from chat rooms in cyberspace restricts the rights of adults to engage in indecent speech in those rooms.

The Court neither "accept[s] nor reject[s]" the argument that the CDA is facially overbroad because it substantially interferes with the First Amendment rights of minors. I would reject it. *Ginsberg* established that minors may constitutionally be denied access to material that is obscene as to minors.

Our cases require a proof of "real" and "substantial" overbreadth, *Broadrick v. Oklahoma* [text, p. 1033], and appellees have not carried their burden in this case. In my view, the universe of speech constitutionally protected as to minors but banned by the CDA — i.e., the universe of material that is "patently offensive," but which nonetheless has some redeeming value for minors or does not appeal to their prurient interest — is a very small one. Appellees cite no examples of speech falling within this universe and do not attempt to explain why that universe is substantial "in relation to the statute's plainly legitimate sweep." That the CDA might deny minors the right to obtain material that has some "value" is largely beside the point. While discussions about prison rape or nude art may have some redeeming education value for adults, they do not necessarily have any such value for minors, and under *Ginsberg*, minors only have a First Amendment right to obtain patently offensive material that has "redeeming social importance for minors." Accordingly, in my view, the CDA does not burden a substantial amount of minors' constitutionally protected speech.

NOTE

Professor Krotozynski contends that *Reno v. ACLU* signifies that "at least for the moment" childproofing the Internet is not possible since the Supreme Court is not willing to sustain restrictions on content available to adults to make such childproofing possible. At the same time he observes: "[T]here are ways of eradicating child pornography from the Internet — government control over websites and government blocking of unlicensed websites would effectively end the Internet trade in kiddie porn." But he believes the Supreme Court would be unlikely to sustain such regulation and Congress is unlikely to enact it. The result, he concludes, is that "child pornography will be a social cost imposed on our society in exchange for the wonders of instant information from virtually any location in the country with a telephone." Ronald J. Krotoszynski, Jr., *Childproofing the Internet*, 41 Brandeis L. J. 447, 462 (2003). After reading the Internet regulation cases which follow, consider whether you agree with his assessment.

ASHCROFT v. AMERICAN CIVIL LIBERTIES UNION
535 U.S. 564, 122 S. Ct. 1700, 152 L. Ed.2d 771 (2002)

Justice Thomas announced the judgment of the Court and delivered the opinion of the Court with respect to Parts I, II, and IV.

This case presents the narrow question whether the Child Online Protection Act's (COPA or Act) use of "community standards" to identify "material that is harmful to minors" violates the First Amendment. We hold that this aspect of COPA does not render the statute facially unconstitutional.

I

Apparently responding to our objections to the breadth of the CDA's coverage, Congress limited the scope of COPA's coverage in at least three ways. First, while the CDA applied to communications over the Internet as a whole, including, for example, e-mail messages, COPA applies only to material displayed on the World Wide Web. Second, unlike the CDA, COPA covers only communications made "for commercial purposes." And third, while the CDA prohibited "indecent" and "patently offensive" communications, COPA restricts only the narrower category of "material that is harmful to minors."

In their complaint, respondents alleged that, although they believed that the material on their Web sites was valuable for adults, they feared that they would be prosecuted under COPA because some of that material "could be construed as 'harmful to minors' in some communities. Respondents' facial challenge claimed, inter alia, that COPA violated adults' rights under the First and Fifth Amendments because it (1) "created an effective ban on constitutionally protected speech by and to adults"; (2) "[was] not the least restrictive means of accomplishing any compelling governmental purpose"; and (3) "[was] substantially overbroad."

The District Court granted respondents' motion for a preliminary injunction, barring the Government from enforcing the Act until the merits of respondents' claims could be adjudicated. The United States Court of Appeals for the Third Circuit affirmed.

II

Miller adopted the use of "community standards" from *Roth*, which repudiated an earlier approach for assessing objectionable material. The Court preserved the use of community standards in formulating the *Miller* test, explaining that they furnish a valuable First Amendment safeguard: "The primary concern . . . is to be certain that . . . [material] will be judged by its impact on an average person, rather than a particularly susceptible or sensitive person—or indeed a totally insensitive one." *Miller.*

III

The Court of Appeals, however, concluded that this Court's prior community standards jurisprudence "has no applicability to the Internet and the Web" because "Web publishers are currently without the ability to control the geographic scope of the recipients of their communications." We therefore must decide whether this technological limitation renders COPA's reliance on community standards constitutionally infirm. In addressing this question, the parties first dispute the nature of the community standards that jurors will be instructed to apply when assessing, in prosecutions under COPA, whether works appeal to the prurient interest of minors and are patently offensive with respect to minors. Respondents contend that jurors will evaluate material using "local community standards," while petitioner maintains that jurors will not consider the community standards of any particular geographic area, but rather will be "instructed to consider the standards of the adult community as a whole, without geographic specification." In the context of this case, which involves a facial challenge to a statute that has never been enforced, we do not think it prudent to engage in speculation as to whether certain hypothetical jury instructions would or would not be consistent with COPA, and deciding this case does not require us to do so. It is sufficient to note that community standards need not be defined by reference to a precise geographic area. Absent geographic specification, a juror applying community standards will inevitably draw upon personal "knowledge of the community or vicinage from which he comes." Because juries would apply different standards across the country, and Web publishers currently lack the ability to limit access to their sites on a geographic basis, the Court of Appeals feared that COPA's "community standards" component would effectively force all speakers on the Web to abide by the "most puritan" community's standards. And such a requirement, the Court of Appeals concluded, "imposes an overreaching burden and restriction on constitutionally protected speech."

In evaluating the constitutionality of the CDA, this Court expressed a similar concern over that statute's use of community standards to identify patently offensive material on the Internet. We noted that "the 'community standards' criterion as applied to the Internet means that any communication available to a nationwide audience will be judged by the standards of the community most likely to be offended by the message." *Reno.* The Court of Appeals below relied heavily on this observation, stating that it was "not persuaded that the Supreme Court's concern with respect to the 'community standards' criterion has been sufficiently remedied by Congress in COPA."

The CDA's use of community standards to identify patently offensive material, however, was particularly problematic in light of that statute's unprecedented breadth and vagueness. The statute covered communications depicting or describing "sexual or excretory activities or organs" that were "patently offensive as measured by contemporary community standards"— a standard somewhat similar to the second prong of *Miller's* threeprong test. But the CDA did not include any limiting terms resembling *Miller's* additional two prongs. It neither contained any requirement that restricted material appeal to the prurient interest nor excluded from the scope of its coverage works with serious literary, artistic, political, or scientific value. The tremendous breadth of the CDA magnified the impact caused by differences in community standards across the country, restricting Web publishers from openly displaying a significant amount of material that would have constituted protected speech in some communities across the country but run afoul of community standards in others.

COPA, by contrast, does not appear to suffer from the same flaw because it applies to significantly less material than did the CDA and defines the harmful-to-minors material restricted by the statute in a manner parallel to the *Miller* definition of obscenity.

If a publisher chooses to send its material into a particular community, this Court's jurisprudence teaches that it is the publisher's responsibility to abide by that community's standards. The publisher's burden does not change simply because it decides to distribute its material to every community in the Nation. Nor does it change because the publisher may wish to speak only to those in a "community where avant garde culture is the norm," (Kennedy, J., concurring in judgment), but nonetheless utilizes a medium that transmits its speech from coast to coast. If a publisher wishes for its material to be judged only by the standards of particular communities, then it need only take the simple step of utilizing a medium that enables it to target the release of its material into those communities. Respondents argue that COPA is "unconstitutionally overbroad" because it will require Web publishers to shield some material behind age verification screens that could be displayed openly in many communities across the Nation if Web speakers were able to limit access to their sites on a geographic basis. "To prevail in a facial challenge," however, "it is not enough for a plaintiff to show 'some' overbreadth." *Reno.* (O'CONNOR, J., concurring in judgment in part and dissenting in part). Rather, "the overbreadth of a statute must not only be real, but substantial as well." *Broadrick v. Oklahoma* [text, p. 1041]. At this stage of the litigation, respondents have failed to satisfy this burden, at least solely as a result of COPA's reliance on community standards. Because Congress has narrowed the range of content restricted by COPA in a manner analogous to *Miller*'s definition of obscenity, we conclude, consistent with our holdings, that any variance caused by the statute's reliance on community standards is not substantial enough to violate the First Amendment.

IV

The scope of our decision today is quite limited. We hold only that COPA's reliance on community standards to identify "material that is harmful to minors" does not *by itself* render the statute substantially overbroad for purposes of the First Amendment. We do not express any view as to whether COPA suffers from substantial overbreadth for other reasons, whether the statute is unconstitutionally vague, or whether the District Court correctly concluded that the statute likely will not survive strict scrutiny analysis once adjudication of the case is completed below. While respondents urge us to resolve these questions at this time, prudence dictates allowing the Court of Appeals to first examine these difficult issues. Petitioner does not ask us to vacate the preliminary injunction entered by the District Court, and in any event, we could not do so without addressing matters yet to be considered by the Court of Appeals. As a result, the Government remains enjoined from enforcing COPA absent further action by the Court of Appeals or the District Court. For the foregoing reasons, we vacate the judgment of the Court of Appeals and remand the case for further proceedings.

JUSTICE O'CONNOR, concurring in part and concurring in the judgment.

The plurality's opinion argues that, even under local community standards, the variation between the most and least restrictive communities is not so great with respect to the narrow category of speech covered by COPA as to, alone, render the statute substantially overbroad. But respondents' failure to prove substantial overbreadth on a facial challenge in this case still leaves open the possibility that the use of local community standards will cause problems for regulation of obscenity on the Internet, for adults as well as children, in future cases.

I agree with JUSTICE KENNEDY that, given Internet speakers' inability to control the geographic location of their audience, expecting them to bear the burden of controlling the recipients of their speech, as we did in *Hamling* and *Sable*, may be entirely too much to ask, and would potentially suppress an inordinate amount of expression.

For these reasons, adoption of a national standard is necessary in my view for any reasonable regulation of Internet obscenity.

Our precedents do not forbid adoption of a national standard. Although jurors asked to evaluate the obscenity of speech based on a national standard will inevitably base their assessments to some extent on their experience of their local communities, I agree with Justice Breyer that the lesser degree of variation that would result is inherent in the jury system and does not necessarily pose a First Amendment problem. In my view, a national standard is not only constitutionally permissible, but also reasonable.

While I would prefer that the Court resolve the issue before it by explicitly adopting a national standard for defining obscenity on the Internet, given respondents' failure to demonstrate substantial overbreadth due solely to the variation between local communities, I join Parts I, II, III-B, and IV of Justice Thomas' opinion and the judgment.

Justice Stevens, dissenting.

In its original form, the community standard provided a shield for communications that are offensive only to the least tolerant members of society. In the context of the Internet, however, community standards become a sword, rather than a shield. If a prurient appeal is offensive in a puritan village, it may be a crime to post it on the World Wide Web. COPA not only restricts speech that is made available to the general public, it also covers a medium in which speech cannot be segregated to avoid communities where it is likely to be considered harmful to minors. The Internet presents a unique forum for communication because information, once posted, is accessible everywhere on the network at once. The speaker cannot control access based on the location of the listener, nor can it choose the pathways through which its speech is transmitted. By approving the use of community standards in this context, Justice Thomas endorses a construction of COPA that has "the intolerable consequence of denying some sections of the country access to material, there deemed acceptable, which in others might be considered offensive to prevailing community standards of decency."

If the material were forwarded through the mails, as in *Hamling*, or over the telephone, as in Sable, the sender could avoid destinations with the most restrictive standards. Given the undisputed fact that a provider who posts material on the Internet cannot prevent it from entering any geographic community, (opinion of Thomas, J.), a law that criminalizes a particular communication in just a handful of destinations effectively prohibits transmission of that message to all of the 176.5 million Americans that have access to the Internet. In light of this fundamental difference in technologies, the rules applicable to the mass mailing of an obscene montage or to obscene dial-a-porn should not be used to judge the legality of messages on the World Wide Web.

NOTES

1. ***National Contemporary Community Standards.*** Professor Etzioni, like Justice O'Connor, argues for the adoption of national contemporary community standards but with some "leeway" for the addition of local standards: "Aside from upholding national standards in the protection of minors, communities should be given some leeway, in grey areas, to add some standards of their own. The term 'grey areas,' to be defined by Congress and the courts, is used to indicate that communities would not be free to ignore the First Amendment, but only to add some measures or provide further definitions, for instance [as to] what they consider harmful. Those who argue that the Internet makes it impossible to impose local standards should take heart from the fact that it is technically possible." Amitai Etzioni, *Do Children Have the Same First Amendment Rights as Adults?* 79 CHI-KENT L. REV. 3, 22-23 (2004). Would this proposal for adding local community standards in "grey areas" to national community standards violate the First Amendment?

2. *Ashcroft v. ACLU*, 542 U.S. 656 (2004). The litigation over the Child Online Protection Act (COPA) returned to the Court after the remand ordered in 2002. The Court of Appeals on remand "concluded that the statute was not narrowly tailored to serve a compelling Government interest, was overbroad, and was not the least restrictive means available for the Government to serve the interest of preventing minors from using the Internet to gain access to materials that are harmful to them." The Supreme Court, in an opinion by Justice Kennedy, affirmed the preliminary injunction against enforcement only on the ground that less restrictive alternatives existed:

> The primary alternative considered by the District Court was blocking and filtering software. Blocking and filtering software is an alternative that is less restrictive than COPA, and, in addition, likely more effective as a means of restricting children's access to materials harmful to them. The District Court, in granting the preliminary injunction, did so primarily because the plaintiffs had proposed that filters are a less restrictive alternative to COPA and the Government had not shown it would be likely to disprove the plaintiffs' contention at trial.
>
> Filters are less restrictive than COPA. They impose selective restrictions on speech at the receiving end, not universal restrictions at the source. Under a filtering regime, adults without children may gain access to speech they have a right to see without having to identify themselves or provide their credit card information. Even adults with children may obtain access to the same speech on the same terms simply by turning off the filter on their home computers. Above all, promoting the use of filters does not condemn as criminal any category of speech, and so the potential chilling effect is eliminated, or at least much diminished. All of these things are true, moreover, regardless of how broadly or narrowly the definitions in COPA are construed.
>
> Filters also may well be more effective than COPA. First, a filter can prevent minors from seeing all pornography, not just pornography posted to the Web from America. The District Court noted in its factfindings that one witness estimated that 40% of harmful-to-minors content comes from overseas. COPA does not prevent minors from having access to those foreign harmful materials. That alone makes it possible that filtering software might be more effective in serving Congress' goals. Effectiveness is likely to diminish even further if COPA is upheld, because the providers of the materials that would be covered by the statute simply can move their operations overseas. It is not an answer to say that COPA reaches some amount of materials that are harmful to minors; the question is whether it would reach more of them than less restrictive alternatives. In addition, the

> District Court found that verification systems may be subject to evasion and circumvention, for example by minors who have their own credit cards. Finally, filters also may be more effective because they can be applied to all forms of Internet communication, including e-mail, not just communications available via the World Wide Web.

Justice Scalia dissented on the ground that the First Amendment did not require strict scrutiny of this statute. "Nothing in the First Amendment entitles the type of material covered by COPA to that exacting standard of review. We have recognized that commercial entities which engage in the sordid business of pandering by deliberately emphasizing the sexually provocative aspects of [their nonobscene products], in order to catch the salaciously disposed, engage in constitutionally unprotected behavior."

Justice Breyer, joined by Chief Justice Rehnquist and Justice O'Connor, dissented on the grounds that the statute's objectives could not in fact be carried out by less restrictive means. Justice Breyer first emphasized that COPA actually limits only a small category of expression. "The only significant difference between the present statute and Miller's definition consists of the addition of the words 'with respect to minors,' and 'for minors.' But the addition of these words to a definition that would otherwise cover only obscenity expands the statute's scope only slightly. That is because the material in question (while potentially harmful to young children) must, first, appeal to the 'prurient interest' of, i.e., seek a sexual response from, some group of adolescents or postadolescents (since young children normally do not so respond). And material that appeals to the 'prurient interests' of some group of adolescents or postadolescents will almost inevitably appeal to the 'prurient interests' of some group of adults as well."

Justice Breyer then analyzed the compelling interest of the Government in preventing exposure of minors to harmful material in relation to the proposed alternatives:

> Conceptually speaking, the presence of filtering software is not an alternative legislative approach to the problem of protecting children from exposure to commercial pornography. Rather, it is part of the status quo, *i.e.*, the backdrop against which Congress enacted the present statute. It is always true, by definition, that the status quo is less restrictive than a new regulatory law. It is always less restrictive to do nothing than to do something. But "doing nothing" does not address the problem Congress sought to address—namely that, despite the availability of filtering software, children were still being exposed to harmful material on the Internet.
>
> First, the Government might "act to encourage" the use of blocking and filtering software. The problem is that any argument that rests upon this alternative proves too much. If one imagines enough government resources devoted to the problem and perhaps additional scientific advances, then, of course, the use of software might become as effective and less restrictive. Obviously, the Government could give all parents, schools, and Internet cafes free computers with filtering programs already installed, hire federal employees to train parents

and teachers on their use, and devote millions of dollars to the development of better software. The result might be an alternative that is extremely effective. But the Constitution does not, because it cannot, require the Government to disprove the existence of magic solutions, *i.e.*, solutions that, put in general terms, will solve any problem less restrictively but with equal effectiveness.

3. *Aftermath of Ashcroft v. ACLU II.* First Amendment Internet lawyer Paul Smith believes that the aftermath of this second COPA ruling will show that regulating the Internet is likely to be "much more ineffective." Since a "web site can be posted anywhere in the world," Smith thinks "efforts to extend American law to foreign based websites are bound, ultimately, to lead to problems when other countries attempt to apply to American Web speakers limitations that would never be tolerated under the First Amendment." Smith concludes that laws enacted by government will be defeated by technology "which will have the final say." Paul Smith, *The First Amendment in the Internet Age*, in Joseph Rusomanno, ed., DEFENDING THE FIRST AMENDMENT, COMMENTARY ON FIRST AMENDMENT ISSUES AND CASES (2005). In this view, if parents wish to deny access to sexually explicit websites to their children, they will have to do so without effective help from government. Does this argument strengthen or weaken First Amendment defenses to future Internet regulation in this area?

4. *First Amendment Standards of Review and The Internet.* When confronted in *Reno v. ACLU* and *Denver Area* with federal legislation dealing with indecency, the Court used differing standards of review. In *Denver Area*, the plurality opinion for the Court used a balancing approach while *Reno* used the strict scrutiny standard of review. Why the difference? Two commentators suggest an explanation. *Denver Area* was a situation where different classes of speakers were in conflict with each other. Cable programmers, cable system operators, and the viewing audience all presented conflicting First Amendment claims. "*Reno v. ACLU* involved speech-repressive legislation with respect to which the affected classes of speakers — Internet Service Providers, civil liberties groups, media organizations — were on the same side against the government." JEROME A. BARRON & C. THOMAS DIENES, FIRST AMENDMENT LAW IN A NUTSHELL 132 (3d. ed. 2004).

[6] Child Pornography: Unprotected Expression?

***New York v. Ferber*, 458 U.S. 747 (1982).** The Court unanimously upheld a New York criminal statute prohibiting persons from knowingly promoting sexual performances by children under the age of sixteen by distributing material which depicts such performances. Ferber's conviction for distributing films devoted almost exclusively to depicting young boys masturbating had been overturned by the New York Court of Appeals on grounds that the state statute violated the First Amendment since it was not limited to obscenity as defined in *Miller v. California*.

In reversing, the Supreme Court, per Justice White, concluded that "the states are entitled to greater leeway in the regulation of pornographic depictions of children." The Court offered a variety of reasons for not applying the *Miller* standards. First: "It is evident beyond the need for elaboration that a state's interest 'in safeguarding the physical and psychological well-being of a minor' is 'compelling.' " Second: "The distribution of photographs and films depicting sexual activities by juveniles is intrinsically related to the sexual abuse of children." Third: "The advertising and selling of child pornography provides an economic motive for and is thus an integral part of the production of such materials, an activity illegal throughout the nation." Fourth: "The value of permitting live performances and photographic reproductions of children engaged in lewd sexual conduct is exceedingly modest, if not de minimis." Fifth: "Recognizing and classifying child pornography as a category of material outside the protection of the First Amendment is not incompatible with our earlier decisions."

More specifically, the Court adjusted the *Miller* standards as follows: "a trier of fact need not find that the material appeals to the prurient interest of the average person; it is not required that sexual conduct portrayed be done so in a patently offensive manner; and the material at issue need not be considered as a whole. We note that the distribution or descriptions or other depictions of sexual conduct, not otherwise obscene, which do not involve live performance or photographic or other visual reproduction of live performances, retains first amendment protection. As with obscenity laws, criminal responsibility may not be imposed without some element of scienter on the part of the defendant." Since the New York law was found to comport with these standards, there was nothing unconstitutionally underinclusive about its singling out this particular category of material as not entitled to First Amendment protection.

Nor was the New York statute unconstitutionally overbroad because it prohibited the distribution of materials with serious literary, scientific, or educational value or material which did not threaten the harm sought to be combatted by the state. The Court considered this

> the paradigmatic case of a state statute whose legitimate reach dwarfs its arguably impermissible applications. How often, if ever, it may be necessary to employ children to engage in conduct clearly within the reach of the [New York statute] in order to produce educational, medical, or artistic works cannot be known with certainty. Yet we seriously doubt that these arguably impermissible applications of the statute amount to more than a tiny fraction of the materials within the statute's reach. Nor will we assume that the New York courts will widen the possibly invalid reach of the statute by giving an expansive construction to [its] proscriptions.

The Court therefore invoked the principle of *Broadrick v. Oklahoma,* 413 U.S. 601 (1973), that a law was "not substantially overbroad and whatever overbreadth exists should be cured through case-by-case analysis of the fact situations to which its sanctions, assertedly, may not be applied." As applied to Ferber and to others distributing similar material, the statute did not violate the First Amendment.

Justice O'Connor concurred in order to note that "the compelling interests identified in today's opinion, suggest that the Constitution might in fact permit New York to ban knowing distribution of works depicting minors engaged in explicit sexual conduct, regardless of the social value of the depictions." The Court did not hold, said Justice O'Connor, that New York must except from the statute material with serious literary, scientific, or educational value. Justice Brennan, joined by Justice Marshall, concurring, directly rejected Justice O'Connor's view. Application of the statute "to depictions of children that in themselves do have serious literary, artistic, scientific, or medical value, would violate the First Amendment." Such depictions would, by definition, have social value and the state interest in suppressing such materials "is likely to be far less compelling."

Justice Stevens, concurring in the judgment, concluded that this "generally marginal speech does not warrant the extraordinary protection afforded by the overbreadth doctrine. Because I have no difficulty with the statute's application in this case, I concur in the Court's judgment." Justice Blackmun concurred in the result.

***Osborne v. Ohio*, 495 U.S. 103 (1990).** The Court, per Justice White, upheld a conviction under an Ohio criminal statute that prohibited a person from possessing or viewing "any material or performance that shows a minor who is not the person's child or ward in a state of nudity" unless either it is "presented for a bona fide, artistic, medical, scientific, educational, religious, governmental, judicial or other proper purpose, by or to a . . . person having a proper interest in the material or performance," or "the person knows that the parents, guardian, or custodian has consented in writing." After police, acting pursuant to a valid search, found four photographs of a nude male adolescent posed in sexually explicit positions, Osborne was convicted and sentenced to six months in jail under the Ohio statute. The Ohio state courts upheld the conviction.

Justice White reasoned that *Stanley v. Georgia* did not compel a ruling that the statute was unconstitutional "because the interests underlying child pornography prohibitions far exceed the interests" which motivated the Georgia law. *Stanley* held legislation unconstitutional which was premised on the "desirability of controlling a person's private thoughts." But here the interest at stake was no "paternalistic interest" in regulating an individual's thoughts. The Ohio statute was concerned with protecting the "victims of child pornography" and destroying the "market for the exploitative use of children."

Relying on *Ferber*, the Court declared that a "State's interest in 'safeguarding the physical and psychological well-being of a minor' is 'compelling.' " Justice White said it was reasonable for Ohio to assume that the production of child pornography would be decreased if those who possessed and viewed the product were penalized "thereby decreasing demand." Rejecting the contention that there were other measures available besides punishing possession to diminish the market for child pornography, Justice White stated:

> Given the importance of the state's interest in protecting the victims of child pornography, we cannot fault Ohio for attempting to stamp out this vice at all levels in the distribution chain. According to the State, since the time of our decision in *Ferber*, much of the child pornography has been driven underground; as a result, it is now

> difficult, if not impossible, to solve the child pornography problem by only attacking production and distribution.

Other state interests served by the statute, the Court declared were that the ban on possession encouraged the possessors of child pornography to destroy it. This was desirable since the continued existence of the child victim's abuse haunted them for years thereafter. In addition, destruction of child pornography materials prevented its use by pedophiles "to seduce other children into sexual activity."

Osborne contended "that the statute as written is substantially overbroad." However, the Ohio Supreme Court had given a narrowing construction to the statute and limited its application to prohibit "the possession or viewing of material or performance of a minor who is in a state of nudity, where such nudity constitutes a lewd exhibition or involves a graphic focus on the genitals, and where the person depicted is neither the child or ward of the person charged." By so limiting the statute's scope, the Ohio Supreme Court "avoided penalizing persons for viewing or possessing innocuous photographs of naked children."

Justice Brennan, joined by Justices Marshall and Stevens, dissented on the ground that the statute was plainly overbroad since "simple nudity, without more" was defined to constitute child pornography." Moreover, "Ohio's 'graphic focus' test is impermissibly capacious." The "graphic focus" phrase was "a stranger to obscenity regulation" and suffered from the same vagueness infirmities as the "lewd exhibition" phrase.

ASHCROFT v. THE FREE SPEECH COALITION

535 U.S. 234 122 S. Ct. 1389, 152 L.Ed.2d 403 (2002)

[The Court invalidated the Child Pornography Prevention Act (CPPA) which proscribed virtual child pornography on the ground that it trespassed on freedom of speech. The CPPA extended the federal prohibition on child pornography to sexually explicit images that were designed to suggest the actors were children or at least minors even though that was not the case. These images were created by the use of "adults who looked like minors or by using computer imaging." New technology had made it "possible to create realistic images of children who do not exist."]

Justice Kennedy delivered the opinion of the Court.

Under Miller, the First Amendment requires that redeeming value be judged by considering the work as a whole. Where the scene is part of the narrative, the work itself does not for this reason become obscene, even though the scene in isolation might be offensive. For this reason, and the others we have noted, the CPPA cannot be read to prohibit obscenity, because it lacks the required link between its prohibitions and the affront to community standards prohibited by the definition of obscenity.

The Government seeks to address this deficiency by arguing that speech prohibited by the CPPA is virtually indistinguishable from child pornography, which may be banned without regard to whether it depicts works of value.

In contrast to the speech in *Ferber*, speech that itself is the record of sexual abuse, the CPPA prohibits speech that records no crime and creates no victims by its production. Virtual child pornography is not "intrinsically related" to the sexual abuse of children, as were the materials in *Ferber*. While the Government asserts that the images can lead to actual instances of child abuse, the causal link is contingent and indirect. The harm does not necessarily follow from the speech, but depends upon some unquantified potential for subsequent criminal acts.

The Government says these indirect harms are sufficient because, as *Ferber* acknowledged, child pornography rarely can be valuable speech. This argument, however, suffers from two flaws. First, *Ferber*'s judgment about child pornography was based upon how it was made, not on what it communicated. The case reaffirmed that where the speech is neither obscene nor the product of sexual abuse, it does not fall outside the protection of the First Amendment. The second flaw in the Government's position is that *Ferber* did not hold that child pornography is by definition without value. On the contrary, the Court recognized some works in this category might have significant value, but relied on virtual images—the very images prohibited by the CPPA—as an alternative and permissible means of expression: *Ferber*, then, not only referred to the distinction between actual and virtual child pornography, it relied on it as a reason supporting its holding. *Ferber* provides no support for a statute that eliminates the distinction and makes the alternative mode criminal as well.

The CPPA, for reasons we have explored, is inconsistent with *Miller* and finds no support in *Ferber*. The Government seeks to justify its prohibitions in other ways. It argues that the CPPA is necessary because pedophiles may use virtual child pornography to seduce children. The precedents establish, however, that speech within the rights of adults to hear may not be silenced completely in an attempt to shield children from it. Here, the Government wants to keep speech from children not to protect them from its content but to protect them from those who would commit other crimes. The objective is to prohibit illegal conduct, but this restriction goes well beyond that interest by restricting the speech available to lawabiding adults.

The Government submits further that virtual child pornography whets the appetites of pedophiles and encourages them to engage in illegal conduct. This rationale cannot sustain the provision in question. The mere tendency of speech to encourage unlawful acts is not a sufficient reason for banning it.

Finally, the Government says that the possibility of producing images by using computer imaging makes it very difficult for it to prosecute those who produce pornography by using real children. Experts, we are told, may have difficulty in saying whether the pictures were made by using real children or by using computer imaging. The necessary solution, the argument runs, is to prohibit both kinds of images. The argument, in essence, is that protected speech may be banned as a means to ban unprotected speech. This analysis turns the First Amendment upside down. The Government may not suppress lawful speech as the means to suppress unlawful speech. Protected speech does not become unprotected merely because it resembles the latter. The Constitution requires the reverse. The overbreadth doctrine prohibits the

Government from banning unprotected speech if a substantial amount of protected speech is prohibited or chilled in the process.

CHIEF JUSTICE REHNQUIST, with whom JUSTICE SCALIA joins in part, dissenting.

I agree with Part II of JUSTICE O'CONNOR's opinion concurring in the judgment in part and dissenting in part. Congress has a compelling interest in ensuring the ability to enforce prohibitions of actual child pornography, and we should defer to its findings that rapidly advancing technology soon will make it all but impossible to do so.

In sum, while potentially impermissible applications of the CPPA may exist, I doubt that they would be "substantial . . . in relation to the statute's plainly legitimate sweep." *Broadrick*. The aim of ensuring the enforceability of our Nation's child pornography laws is a compelling one. The CPPA is targeted to this aim by extending the definition of child pornography to reach computer-generated images that are virtually indistinguishable from real children engaged in sexually explicit conduct. The statute need not be read to do any more than precisely this, which is not offensive to the First Amendment.

NOTE

Professor Krotoszynski offers the following defense and appraisal of the *Free Speech Coalition* case: "[T]he Supreme Court rightly decided *Free Speech Coalition*. The contrary view would sweep up a great deal of serious art and literature. If the Free Speech Clause protects art and literature, this result cannot be correct especially when *Ferber's* central rationale — avoiding direct harm to children in the production of erotica — is utterly absent. Notwithstanding the furor over *Free Speech Coalition*, the case does not meaningfully address the most problematic aspects of attempting to excise child pornography from the community. The case only establishes the definition of child pornography, limiting it to materials featuring real children." Ronald J. Krotoszynski, Jr., *Childproofing the Internet*, 41 BRANDEIS L.J. 447, 459–461 (2003).

[7] Female Pornography: Unprotected Expression?

Osborne allowed suppression of material on the bases that creation of the material could harm a participant and that improper use of the material could seduce other participants. Can sexually pornographic materials be suppressed on the basis that they are psychologically harmful to women or that they contribute to a pattern of subordination of women?

The view that pornography is an aspect of the systemic subordination of women is found in Kathleen Bean, *A Radical Feminist View of Pornography*, 1 J. CONTEMP. LEGAL ISSUES 19, 22 (1987):

> Pornography [is not] speech about sex or morality or sexual domination or sexual submissiveness. Pornography is a part of a systematic male-dominated hierarchy subordinating women. Pornography is not personal speech, but a political act of discrimination, violating the civil

> rights of women. Pornography is the act, the pain, the harm; it does not "speak" that women are subordinate. It is woman-subordinate.

In *American Booksellers Ass'n Inc. v. Hudnut,* 771 F.2d 323 (7th Cir. 1985), an Indianapolis ordinance prohibiting pornography, defined as "the graphic, sexually explicit subordination of women, whether in pictures or words," was declared violative of free speech. Judge Easterbrook declared: "The state may not ordain preferred viewpoints in this way. The Constitution forbids the state to declare one perspective right and silence opponents." Judge Easterbrook rejected the argument that female pornography was " 'low value' speech" and, therefore, "enough like obscenity" to permit Indianapolis to prohibit it. Indianapolis relied on *Pacifica* and *Mini Theatres*. Judge Easterbrook said that those cases did not "select among viewpoints." Moreover, the very reasons that Indianapolis sought to prohibit pornography suggested that pornography was not low value speech. Indianapolis sought to prohibit pornography because of its adverse impact upon the way women are perceived and treated in society. In his view, such speech, "influences social relations and politics on a grand scale," and thus "controls attitudes at home and in the legislature." The Supreme Court affirmed without opinion. *Hudnut v. American Booksellers Ass'n Inc.,* 475 U.S. 1001 (1986).

Andrea Dworkin and Professor Catharine MacKinnon proposed an ordinance for the city of Minneapolis which would treat pornography as a civil rights violation. The statute contemplated civil remedies rather than criminal penalties. Writing in defense of the proposed statute, Professor Mackinnon observed that much less evidence of harm than can be found to exist in the case of pornography has been deemed sufficient to validate legislation designed to remedy other harms involving speech interests. "Under *Miller*, obscenity was allowed to be made criminal in the name of the 'danger of offending the sensibilities of unwilling recipients, or exposure to juveniles.' " Catharine MacKinnon, *Pornography, Civil Rights and Speech*, 20 Harv. C.R. — C.L.L. Rev. 1, 61 (1985). Professor MacKinnon contends that pornography perpetuates the subordination of women and, therefore, blocks the achievement of equality between the sexes: "Pornography strips and devastates women of credibility, from our accounts of sexual assault to our everyday reality of sexual subordination."

In *Regina v. Butler,* 89 D.L.R. 4th 449 (Can. 1992), the Supreme Court of Canada proved to be a receptive forum for MacKinnon's idea that the harmful, degrading and subordinating effects of pornographic expression on women can justify its regulation. *Butler* reversed the dismissal by a lower court of criminal pornography charges. Professor Zimmerman questions the harmful effects rationale: "Harm? Well, the court agreed that there was no convincing empirical proof that 'dehumanizing' pornography causes actual harm — but it concluded nonetheless that the legislature was entitled to rely on the large body of opinion that violent or dehumanizing depictions are injurious to women." Diane Zimmerman, *Am I Caught in a Time Warp, Or What? Reflections on Pornography and Purity*, 38 N.Y.L. Sch. L. Rev. 335, 342 (1993). Furthermore, she is troubled by the portrait of women which is presented by the antipornography literature: "Women are presented as trapped in an identity that has been determined for us by what all-powerful men imagine us to be. Therefore, the argument runs, women need active protection by government from this male-dominated, hierarchical imaging if we are to stand a chance of redefining ourselves or gaining control of the circumstances of our lives." She concludes that "if history is any guide, adopting the role of victim, of person-in-need-of-protection — for any purpose — is a game we should be chary of playing."

Professor Sunstein argues, on the other hand, that there is a category of expression which he defines as pornography which can be regulated consistent with the First Amendment. Pornography is defined as follows: "[R]egulable pornography must (a) be sexually explicit, (b) depict women as enjoying or deserving some form of physical abuse, and (c) have the purpose and effect of producing sexual arousal." Cass Sunstein, *Pornography and the First Amendment*, 1986 Duke L.J. 589, 592. This definition is described as drawing on "feminist approaches to the problems of pornography" and as a departure from "current law, which is directed at 'obscenity'." How does Sunstein's definition of pornography differ from the *Miller* definition of obscenity?

Sunstein also argues that although as a general proposition "inquiries into general powerlessness should not be used to defend restrictions on expression," the case of pornography is different: "The pornography industry has such power to condition men and women that it has the effect of silencing the antipornography cause in particular and women in general." *Id.* at 623–24. In this view, pornography inhibits speech by silencing those, particularly women, who would engage in speech to counter pornography.

Professor Chevigny has rebutted Sunstein's argument about the special nature of pornography: "Pornography's message is powerful precisely because it does not argue but represents what it has to say in a way that arouses some of the audience. The same is true of all persuasion." Paul Chevigny, *Pornography and Cognition: A Reply to Cass Sunstein*, 1989 Duke L.J. 420, 430. Propaganda for pornography is dangerous for the same reasons that propaganda for racism is dangerous. But Chevigny argues that censorship is no more an appropriate way to deal with pornography than it would be an appropriate response to racism: "If expression is dangerous enough to be a candidate for suppression, then it is important enough to warrant a persuasive response."

Do the political right and the political left have different views on pornography? In a review of two books dealing at least in part with pornography — Richard A. Posner, Sex and Reason (1992) and Edward De Grazia, Girls Lean Back Everywhere: The Law of Obscenity and the Assault on Genius (1992) — Professor MacKinnon observes that the left and the right share a common bond on the subject of pornography:

> In their policy positions and ways of writing, then, Posner and de Grazia exemplify the two complementary strategies through which pornography has historically been protected. The conservative strategy is to cover it up. The liberal strategy is to parade it. If it is covered up, the harm will not be seen; if it is made public enough, the harm will not be seen, either. Both strategies allow the harm to be done

while protecting pornography from the perception that it harms anyone.

Catherine MacKinnon, *Pornography Left and Right*, 30 Harv. C.R. – C.L.L. Rev. 143, 161 (1995).

Both authors, she concludes, believe that pornography should be protected when it has value. The debate then is between harm and value. In such a debate she believes there is no contest: "There is something monstrous in balancing 'value' against *harm*, things against people, this on which left and right speak as one. [W]hen injury to women and children can be balanced against the 'value' of pornography, women and children do not have human status."

§ 8.03 FREEDOM OF THE PRESS: PROBLEMS OF PUBLICATION, NEWSGATHERING, AND ACCESS

In 1975, in a now famous lecture at Yale Law School, Justice Stewart contended that the press should be accorded special status under the Press Clause of the First Amendment because of the unique role performed by the press in our society. In Stewart's view, the Framers intended by the Press Clause to "create a fourth institution outside the government as an additional check to the three official branches." In his Yale Law School lecture, Justice Stewart noted that the only institution accorded specific protection by the language of the constitutional text is the press: "[T]he Free Press Clause extends protection to an institution." Potter Stewart, *Or of the Press*, 26 Hastings L.J. 631 (1975). For Justice Stewart, the references in the text of the First Amendment to freedom of the press and freedom of speech are not interchangeable or redundant terms, but rather they are freighted with special meaning. He based the constitutional privilege fashioned in *New York Times v. Sullivan* on the Press Clause.

New York Times v. Sullivan posed the question of whether the First Amendment permitted a law of libel; under long-standing assumptions, libel previously had been treated as a category outside the protection of the First Amendment. The Court modified this assumption in holding that the law of "libel can claim no talismanic immunity from constitutional limitations. It must be measured by standards that satisfy the First Amendment." The result was to constitutionalize the common law tort of libel.

There are implications in the defamation cases for torts such as the right of privacy and infliction of emotional distress, which also affect the public debate. Then there are First Amendment issues involved in the gathering of news, such as whether reporters have a privilege against being required to disclose their sources to criminal investigators. Finally, there are significant First Amendment issues involved in the customary regulatory controls on modern media, including the Internet.

[A] DEFAMATION AND PRIVACY: THE RIGHT TO PUBLISH

[1] The *New York Times v. Sullivan* Doctrine and its Progeny

Although the Court in *New York Times v. Sullivan* did not hold that the law of libel was unconstitutional, it did say that the central meaning of the First Amendment was to encourage robust and vigorous criticism of government. If the press had to live in fear of severe libel judgments, the Court believed that criticism of government would be stilled or lessened. To avoid this, the Court held that when elected public officials are involved, libel judgments will be permissible only when the libel has been published with actual malice. The result of the decision was to give the press an incentive to engage in criticism of elected public officials. The Court did not concern itself with whether elected public officials would have an opportunity to respond to criticism. Is it reasonable to assume that the public official always has access to the press to voice his or her side of a dispute?

NEW YORK TIMES CO. v. SULLIVAN

376 U.S. 254, 84 S. Ct. 710, 11 L. Ed. 2d 686 (1964)

Justice Brennan delivered the opinion of the Court.

We are required for the first time in this case to determine the extent to which the constitutional protections for speech and press limit a State's power to award damages in a libel action brought by a public official against critics of his official conduct.

Respondent L. B. Sullivan is one of the three elected Commissioners of the City of Montgomery, Alabama. He testified that he was "Commissioner of Public Affairs and the duties are supervision of the Police Department, Fire Department, Department of Cemetery and Department of Scales." A jury in the Circuit Court of Montgomery County awarded him damages of $500,000, the full amount claimed, against all the petitioners, and the Supreme Court of Alabama affirmed.

Respondent's complaint alleged that he had been libeled by statements in a full-page advertisement that was carried in the New York Times on March 29, 1960. Of the 10 paragraphs of text in the advertisement, the third and a portion of the sixth were the basis of respondent's claim of libel. They read as follows:

Third paragraph:

> In Montgomery, Alabama, after students sang "My Country, 'Tis of Thee" on the State Capitol steps, their leaders were expelled from school, and truckloads of police armed with shotguns and tear-gas ringed the Alabama State College Campus. When the entire student body protested to state authorities by refusing to re-register, their dining hall was padlocked in an attempt to starve them into submission.

Sixth paragraph:

> Again and again the Southern violators have answered Dr. King's peaceful protests with intimidation and violence. They have bombed his home almost killing his wife and child. They have assaulted his person. They have arrested him seven times — for "speeding," "loitering" and similar "offenses." And now they have charged him with "perjury" — a felony under which they would imprison him for ten years.

Although neither of these statements mentions respondent by name, [r]espondent and six other Montgomery residents testified that they read some or all of the statements as referring to him in his capacity as Commissioner. It is uncontroverted that some of the statements contained in the two paragraphs were not accurate descriptions of events which occurred in Montgomery.

In affirming the judgment [against THE NEW YORK TIMES], the Supreme Court of Alabama sustained the trial judge's rulings and instructions in all respects. It rejected petitioners' constitutional contentions with the brief statements that "The First Amendment of the U.S. Constitution does not protect libelous publications" and "The Fourteenth Amendment is directed against State action and not private action." We reverse the judgment. We hold that the rule of law applied by the Alabama courts is constitutionally deficient for failure to provide the safeguards for freedom of speech and of the press that are required by the First and Fourteenth Amendments in a libel action brought by a public official against critics of his official conduct. We further hold that under the proper safeguards the evidence presented in this case is constitutionally insufficient to support the judgment for respondent.

Respondent relies heavily, as did the Alabama courts, on statements of this Court to the effect that the Constitution does not protect libelous publications. Those statements do not foreclose our inquiry here. None of the cases sustained the use of libel laws to impose sanctions upon expression critical of the official conduct of public officials. [W]e consider this case against the background of a profound national commitment to the principle that debate on public issues should be uninhibited, robust, and wide-open, and that it may well include vehement, caustic, and sometimes unpleasantly sharp attacks on government and public officials. The present advertisement, as an expression of grievance and protest on one of the major public issues of our time, would seem clearly to qualify for the constitutional protection. The question is whether it forfeits that protection by the falsity of some of its factual statements and by its alleged defamation of respondent.

Authoritative interpretations of the First Amendment guarantees have consistently refused to recognize an exception for any test of truth, whether administered by judges, juries, or administrative officials — and especially not one that puts the burden of proving truth on the speaker. That erroneous statement is inevitable in free debate, and that it must be protected if the freedoms of expression are to have the "breathing space" that they "need to survive," [has been previously recognized].

Injury to official reputation affords no more warrant for repressing speech that would otherwise be free than does factual error. Where judicial officers are involved, this Court has held that concern for the dignity and reputation of the courts does not justify the punishment as criminal contempt of criticism of the judge or his decision. *Bridges v. California,* 314 U.S. 252. This is true even though the utterance contains "half truths" and "misinformation." Such repression can be justified, if at all, only by a clear and present danger of the obstruction of justice. If judges are to be treated as "men of fortitude, able to thrive in a hardy climate," surely the same must be true of other government officials, such as elected city commissioners. Criticism of their official conduct does not lose its constitutional protection merely because it is effective criticism and hence diminishes their official reputations.

If neither factual error nor defamatory content suffices to remove the constitutional shield from criticism of official conduct, the combination of the two elements is no less inadequate. This is the lesson to be drawn from the great controversy over the Sedition Act of 1798, which first crystallized a national awareness of the central meaning of the First Amendment. Although the Sedition Act was never tested in this Court, the attack upon its validity has carried the day in the court of history.

What a State may not constitutionally bring about by means of a criminal statute is likewise beyond the reach of its civil law of libel. The fear of damage awards under a rule such as that invoked by the Alabama courts here may be markedly more inhibiting than the fear of prosecution under a criminal statute. The judgment awarded in this case — without the need for any proof of actual pecuniary loss — was one thousand times greater than the maximum fine provided by the Alabama criminal statute, and one hundred times greater than that provided by the Sedition Act. And since there is no double-jeopardy limitation applicable to civil lawsuits, this is not the only judgment that may be awarded against petitioners for the same publication.[18] Whether or not a newspaper can survive a succession of such judgments, the pall of fear and timidity imposed upon those who would give voice to public criticism is an atmosphere in which the First Amendment freedoms cannot survive.

A rule compelling the critic of official conduct to guarantee the truth of all his factual assertions — and to do so on pain of libel judgments virtually unlimited in amount — leads to a comparable "self-censorship." Allowance of the defense of truth, with the burden of proving it on the defendant, does not mean that only false speech will be deterred. Even courts accepting this defense as an adequate safeguard have recognized the difficulties of adducing legal proofs that the alleged libel was true in all its factual particulars. Under such a rule, would-be critics of official conduct may be deterred from voicing their criticism, even though it is believed to be true and even though it is in fact true, because of doubt whether it can be proved in court or fear of the expense of having to do so. They tend to make only statements which "steer far wider of the unlawful zone." The rule thus dampens the vigor and limits

[18] The Times states that four other libel suits based on the advertisement have been filed against it by others who have served as Montgomery City Commissioners and by the Governor of Alabama; that another $500,000 verdict has been awarded in the only one of these cases that has yet gone to trial; and that the damages sought in the other three total $2,000,000.

the variety of public debate. It is inconsistent with the First and Fourteenth Amendments.

The constitutional guarantees require, we think, a federal rule that prohibits a public official from recovering damages for a defamatory falsehood relating to his official conduct unless he proves that the statement was made with "actual malice" — this is, with knowledge that it was false or with reckless disregard of whether it was false or not.

Such a privilege for criticism of official conduct is appropriately analogous to the protection accorded a public official when he is sued for libel by a private citizen. In *Barr v. Matteo,* 360 U.S. 564, 575, this Court held the utterance of a federal official to be absolutely privileged if made "within the outer perimeter" of his duties. The States accord the same immunity to statements of their highest officers, although some differentiate their lesser officials and qualify the privilege they enjoy. But all hold that all officials are protected unless actual malice can be proved. The reason for the official privilege is said to be that the threat of damage suits would otherwise "inhibit the fearless, vigorous, and effective administration of policies of government" and "dampen the ardor of all but the most resolute, or the most irresponsible, in the unflinching discharge of their duties." Analogous considerations support the privilege for the citizen-critic of government. It is as much his duty to criticize as it is the official's duty to administer. *See Whitney v. California* (concurring opinion of MR. JUSTICE BRANDEIS). As Madison said, "the censorial power is in the people over the Government, and not in the Government over the people." It would give public servants an unjustified preference over the public they serve, if critics of official conduct did not have a fair equivalent of the immunity granted to the officials themselves.

We conclude that such a privilege is required by the First and Fourteenth Amendments. We hold today that the Constitution delimits a State's power to award damages for libel in actions brought by public officials against critics of their official conduct. Since this is such an action, the rule requiring proof of actual malice is applicable. While Alabama law apparently requires proof of actual malice for an award of punitive damages, where general damages are concerned malice is "presumed." Such a presumption is inconsistent with the federal rule. Since the trial judge did not instruct the jury to differentiate between general and punitive damages, it may be that the verdict was wholly an award of one or the other. But it is impossible to know, in view of the general verdict returned. Because of this uncertainty, the judgment must be reversed and the case remanded.

Since respondent may seek a new trial, we deem that considerations of effective judicial administration require us to review the evidence in the present record to determine whether it could constitutionally support a judgment for respondent. This Court's duty is not limited to the elaboration of constitutional principles; we must also in proper cases review the evidence to make certain that those principles have been constitutionally applied. This is such a case, particularly since the question is one of alleged trespass across "the line between speech unconditionally guaranteed and speech which may legitimately be regulated." In cases where that line must be drawn, the rule is that we "examine for ourselves the statements in issue and the circumstances under which they were made to see whether they are of a character which the principles of the First Amendment, as adopted by the Due Process Clause of the Fourteenth Amendment, protect." We must "make an independent examination of the whole record," so as to assure ourselves that the judgment does not constitute a forbidden intrusion on the field of free expression.

Applying these standards, we consider that the proof presented to show actual malice lacks the convincing clarity which the constitutional standard demands, and hence that it would not constitutionally sustain the judgment for respondent under the proper rule of law. The case of the individual petitioners requires little discussion. Even assuming that they could constitutionally be found to have authorized the use of their names on the advertisement, there was no evidence whatever that they were aware of any erroneous statements or were in any way reckless in that regard. The judgment against them is thus without constitutional support. As to the TIMES, we similarly conclude that the facts do not support a finding of actual malice. [The Court's review of the evidence is omitted.]

We also think the evidence was constitutionally defective in another respect: it was incapable of supporting the jury's finding that the allegedly libelous statements were made "of and concerning" respondent. [The Alabama court's ruling would result in] transmuting criticism of government, however impersonal it may seem on its face, into personal criticism, and hence potential libel, of the officials of whom the government is composed. Raising as it does the possibility that a good-faith critic of government will be penalized for his criticism, the proposition relied on by the Alabama courts strikes at the very center of the constitutionally protected area of free expression. We hold that such a proposition may not constitutionally be utilized to establish that an otherwise impersonal attack on governmental operations was a libel of an official responsible for those operations. Since it was relied on exclusively here, and there was no other evidence to connect the statements with respondent, the evidence was constitutionally insufficient to support a finding that the statements referred to respondent.

The judgment of the Supreme Court of Alabama is reversed and the case is remanded to that court for further proceedings not inconsistent with this opinion.

JUSTICE BLACK, with whom JUSTICE DOUGLAS joins, concurring.

I base my vote to reverse on the belief that the First and Fourteenth Amendments not merely "delimit" a State's power to award damages to "a public official against critics of his official conduct" but completely prohibit a State from exercising such a power. The Court goes on to hold that a State can subject such critics to damages if "actual malice" can be proved against them. "Malice," even as defined by the Court, is an elusive, abstract concept, hard to prove and hard to disprove. The requirement that malice be proved provides at best an evanescent protection for the right critically to discuss public affairs and certainly does not measure up to the sturdy safeguard embodied in the First Amendment. Unlike the Court, therefore, I vote to reverse exclusively on the ground that the TIMES and the individual defendants had an absolute, unconditional constitutional right to publish in the TIMES advertisement their criticisms of the Montgomery agencies and officials.

The half-million-dollar verdict does give dramatic proof, however, that state libel laws threaten the very existence of an American press virile enough to publish unpopular views on public affairs and bold enough to criticize the conduct of public officials.

[JUSTICE GOLDBERG, concurring, also argued that the Constitution affords "an absolute, unconditional privilege to criticize official conduct despite the harm that may flow from excesses and abuses."]

NOTES

1. *Scope of the privilege to publish.* In *New York Times v. Sullivan*, Justice Brennan cites the profound national commitment to "uninhibited, robust, and wide-open" debate on public issues. If support for unfettered discussion is so unequivocal, why isn't the First Amendment privilege absolute? Is Justice Brennan balancing the competing interests? Is Justice Brennan saying that defamatory publication made with actual malice is not "freedom of speech" within the meaning of the First Amendment? If Justice Brennan is giving absolute protection to First Amendment speech, but defining protected speech to exclude defamation with actual malice, what is the basis for the exclusion? In *Garrison v. Louisiana,* 379 U.S. 64 (1964), the Court stated: "[T]he use of the known lie is at once at odds with the premises of democratic government and with the orderly manner in which economic social, or political change is to be effected. Calculated falsehood[,] the knowingly false statement and the false statement made with reckless disregard of the truth, do not enjoy constitutional protection."

2. *Criticism of government.* Professor Kalven, in an article published shortly after the *New York Times* decision was announced, predicted that the case might well mark a shift in the Supreme Court's approach to the issue of free speech. Harry Kalven, *The New York Times Case: A Note on "The Central Meaning of the First Amendment,"* 1964 SUP. CT. REV. 191. Kalven believed that the Court took the opportunity in *New York Times* to restate that "central meaning" — a quote from Justice Brennan's opinion — in terms of the old criminal offense of seditious libel. The Court, in *New York Times* according to Professor Kalven, formulated a "crucial syllogism":

> The central meaning of the [First] Amendment is that seditious libel cannot be made the subject of governmental sanction. The Alabama [libel law] is closely akin to making seditious libel an offense. The Alabama rule therefore violated the meaning of the Amendment.

What is the "governmental sanction" being discussed here? Alabama did not convict the *Times* of the criminal offense of seditious libel, i.e., criticizing the public officials of Montgomery, Alabama.

Professor Kalven thought that, by stressing the primary right of citizens to freely criticize their government, the Court had carved out an area of expression which is "off-limits" to governmental interference or sanction except under the most crucial emergency circumstances. Any attempt by the government, direct or indirect, to impinge on this "off-limits" area would then be presumed to violate the First Amendment. Such a formulation is, to say the least, at odds with the balancing tests by which the Supreme Court has often viewed free speech issues in the past. Doesn't the determination of what is "actual malice" under *New York Times* still constitute a "balancing of interests" test? Is the Court engaged in "definitional balancing"?

3. *The civil rights context.* As Justice Brennan pointed out in *New York Times*, the facts of the case concerned "one of the major public issues of our time" — the civil rights struggle. Professor Kalven suggested that the Court was "compelled by the political realities of the case to decide it in favor of THE NEW YORK TIMES." He suggested that the *New York Times* rule itself and the explanation of free speech doctrine accompanying it was developed by the Court in order to justify the politically ordained result. If "political realities" can be the impetus to a "new meaning" for the First Amendment, might this not operate, in a given political context, to restrict civil liberties as well as to expand them? Could it be that, in the *New York Times* case, political realities coincided with, rather than dictated, the result? If the Court had been concerned with nothing more than political realities, why didn't it reverse for insufficient evidence, and avoid the First Amendment issue entirely?

4. *Right of access and debate.* If encouragement of "uninhibited, robust and wide-open" debate on public issues is the operating premise of the Court's opinion in *New York Times*, why didn't the Court take steps to assure debate? Should the Court have imposed some obligation on the press to assure that the debate which it considered so important actually transpired? If the press is to be more free from libel suits than ever before in the interest of promoting searing social criticism, shouldn't individuals or groups attacked in the press have some right of reply in the same forum? In such circumstances, does the First Amendment require a right of reply? In Jerome Barron, *Access to the Press — A New First Amendment Right*, 80 HARV. L. REV. 1641 (1967), the view is expressed that it was precisely in terms of assuring debate in the press, the *raison d'etre* of the *New York Times v. Sullivan decision*, that the case was a failure.

5. *Refining the privilege.* The *New York Times* case soon spawned a considerable progeny. *See Garrison v. Louisiana,* 379 U.S. 64 (1964) (*Times* rule applies to criminal libel); *Rosenblatt v. Baer,* 383 U.S. 75 (1966) (*Times* applies to nonelected public officials); *Curtis Publishing Co. v. Butts* and *Associated Press v. Walker,* 388 U.S. 130 (1967) (majority of justices indicate that *Times* standards apply to public figures); *St. Amant v. Thompson,* 390 U.S. 727 (1968) ("reckless disregard" defined subjectively as "serious doubts as to the truth of [the] publication"); *Monitor Patriot Co. v. Roy,* 401 U.S. 265 (1971) (a charge of criminal conduct is relevant to an official's or candidate's fitness for office for purposes of applying the *Times* rule).

6. *False light privacy.* In *Time, Inc. v. Hill,* 385 U.S. 374 (1967), the Supreme Court made it clear that the First Amendment interest in vigorous and robust public discussion was going to affect the law of privacy as well as the law of libel. In the *Hill* case, a suit based on New York's right of privacy statute was brought against Life magazine by a family whose experience as hostages of three escaped convicts was falsely exploited by LIFE magazine. The Hills won a verdict for $50,000 compensatory damages and $25,000 punitive damages which was later cut on retrial to $25,000 compensatory damages and no punitive damages.

The Supreme Court reversed, holding that the *New York Times* doctrine should be applied to the New York privacy statute to redress false reports of matters of public interest. The Court held that the plaintiff must prove that defendant had published the report with reckless disregard of the truth or falsity of what was said. Since the proof would conceivably be interpreted as supporting a jury finding of negligent misstatement by the magazine or of reckless disregard of truth, the Supreme Court ordered a new trial. Are the members of the *Hill* family public figures? If they were, they were such only after Life had publicized them. Does this mean that any private person is a public figure if he brings a suit for invasion of his right of privacy? After all, a privacy plaintiff will only be written about if he is newsworthy. Moreover, if newsworthiness is the touchstone of the qualified privilege conferred by the *New York Times* doctrine in privacy cases, doesn't this give even a wider berth to the press than did the "public figure" standard?

Because the New York courts made newsworthiness the key to the privilege, the Supreme Court was brought face to face with interest in an issue has more First Amendment significance than the particular status of the plaintiff. The *Hill* case was not analogous to the problem of seditious libel which was such an impetus to the formulation of the *New York Times* rule. Certainly, on its face, the *Hill* facts were far removed from criticism of government officials. Can you discern a thread connecting *Hill* to the seditious libel issue? Is the underlying principle or strategy of *Hill* reminiscent of *New York Times*?

7. *Private person — public issue.* With *Rosenbloom v. Metromedia,* 403 U.S. 29 (1971), the *New York Times* rule came full circle. Discarding the public official-public figure standard, a plurality of the Court argued that in the interest of wide-open and robust debate of public issues, the actual malice rule must apply even to private citizens caught up in events of public or general interest. But, there were five separate opinions filed in *Rosenbloom*, and they were strikingly different. The Court's plurality opinion, consisting of Justices Brennan, Burger, and Blackmun, extended the *New York Times* rule to private citizens thrust into the public eye by involvement in news events. The actual malice standard was applied to public issues involving private figures. But it was only a plurality opinion. Does the rationale of *New York Times v. Sullivan* support such an extension?

[2] Halting the Advance of the *Times* Doctrine

GERTZ v. ROBERT WELCH, INC.

418 U.S. 323, 94 S. Ct. 2997, 35 L. Ed. 2d 585 (1974)

JUSTICE POWELL delivered the opinion of the Court.

In 1968 a Chicago policeman named Nuccio shot and killed a youth named Nelson. The state authorities prosecuted Nuccio for the homicide and ultimately obtained a conviction for murder in the second degree. The Nelson family retained petitioner Elmer Gertz, a reputable attorney, to represent them in civil litigation against Nuccio.

Respondent publishes AMERICAN OPINION, a monthly outlet for the views of the John Birch Society. Early in the 1960s the magazine began to warn of a nationwide conspiracy to discredit local law enforcement agencies and create in their stead a national police force capable of supporting a communist dictatorship. As part of the continuing effort to alert the public to this assumed danger, the managing editor of American Opinion commissioned an article on the murder trial of officer Nuccio. For this purpose he engaged a regular contributor to the magazine. In March of 1969 respondent published the resulting article under the title "FRAME-UP: Richard Nuccio And The War On Police." The article purports to demonstrate that the testimony against Nuccio at his criminal trial was false and that his prosecution was part of the communist campaign against the police.

In his capacity as counsel for the Nelson family in the civil litigation, petitioner attended the coroner's inquest into the boy's death and initiated actions for damages, but he neither discussed officer Nuccio with the press nor played any part in the criminal proceeding. Notwithstanding petitioner's remote connection with the prosecution of Nuccio, respondent's magazine portrayed him as an architect of the "frame-up." According to the article, the police file on petitioner took "a big, Irish cop to lift." The article stated that petitioner had been an official of the "Marxist League for Industrial Democracy, originally known as the Intercollegiate Socialist Society, which has advocated the violent seizure of our government." It labelled Gertz a "Leninist" and a "Communist-fronter." It also stated that Gertz had been an officer of the National Lawyers Guild, described as a communist organization that "probably did more than any other outfit to plan the Communist attack on the Chicago police during the 1968 Democratic convention."

These statements contained serious inaccuracies. The managing editor of American Opinion made no effort to verify or substantiate the charges against petitioner. Petitioner filed a diversity action for libel in the United States District Court for the Northern District of Illinois. He claimed that the falsehoods published by respondent injured his reputation as a lawyer and a citizen. [Following a jury verdict, the district court entered judgment for respondent Robert Welch, Inc.] Petitioner appealed to contest the applicability of the *New York Times* standard to this case. The Court of Appeals affirmed. For the reasons stated below, we reverse.

The principal issue in this case is whether a newspaper or broadcaster that publishes defamatory falsehoods about an individual who is neither a public official nor a public figure may claim a constitutional privilege against liability for the injury inflicted by those statements.

We begin with the common ground. Under the First Amendment there is no such thing as a false idea. However pernicious an opinion may seem, we depend for its correction not on the conscience of judges and juries but on the competition of other ideas. But there is no constitutional value in false statements of fact. Neither the intentional lie nor the careless error materially advances society's interest in "uninhibited, robust, and wide-open" debate on public issues. *New York Times Co. v. Sullivan.* They belong to that category of utterances which "are no essential part of any exposition of ideas, and are of such slight social value as a step to truth that any benefit that may be derived from them is clearly outweighed by the social interest in order and morality." *Chaplinsky v. New Hampshire.*

Although the erroneous statement of fact is not worthy of constitutional protection, it is nevertheless inevitable in free debate. Our decisions recognize that a rule of strict liability that compels a publisher or broadcaster to guarantee the accuracy of his factual assertions may lead to intolerable self-censorship. Allowing the media to avoid liability only by proving the truth of all injurious statements does not accord adequate protection to First Amendment liberties.

The need to avoid self-censorship by the news media is, however, not the only societal value at issue. The *New York Times* standard defines the level of constitutional protection appropriate to the context of defamation of a public person. Those who, by reason of the notoriety of their achievements or the vigor and success with which they seek the public's attention, are properly classed as public figures and those who hold governmental office may recover for injury to reputation only on clear and convincing proof that the defamatory falsehood was made with knowledge of its falsity or with reckless disregard for the truth. This standard administers an extremely powerful antidote to the inducement to media self-censorship of the common law rule of strict liability for libel and slander. And it exacts a correspondingly high price from the victims of defamatory falsehood. Plainly many deserving plaintiffs, including some intentionally subjected to injury, will be unable to surmount the barrier of the *New York Times* test. For the reasons stated below, we conclude that the state interest in compensating injury to the reputation of private individuals requires that a different rule should obtain with respect to them.

The first remedy of any victim of defamation is self-help — using available opportunities to contradict the lie or correct the error and thereby to minimize its adverse impact on reputation. Public officials and public figures usually enjoy significantly greater access to the channels of effective communication and hence have a more realistic opportunity to counteract false statements than private individuals normally enjoy.[9] Private individuals are therefore more vulnerable to injury, and the state interest in protecting them is correspondingly greater.

More important than the likelihood that private individuals will lack effective opportunities for rebuttal, there is a compelling normative consideration underlying the distinction between public and private defamation plaintiffs. An individual who decides to seek governmental office must accept certain necessary consequences of that involvement in public affairs. He runs the risk of closer public scrutiny than might otherwise be the case. And society's interest in the officers of government is not strictly limited to the formal discharge of official duties. As the Court pointed out in *Garrison v. Louisiana,* 379 U.S. 64, 77 (1964), the public's interest extends to "anything that might touch on an official's fitness for office."

Hypothetically, it may be possible for someone to become a public figure through no purposeful action of his own, but the instances of truly involuntary

[9] Of course, an opportunity for rebuttal seldom suffices to undo harm of defamatory falsehood. Indeed, the law of defamation is rooted in our experience that the truth rarely catches up with a lie. But the fact that the self-help remedy of rebuttal, standing alone, is inadequate to its task does not mean that it is irrelevant to our inquiry.

public figures must be exceedingly rare. For the most part those who attain this status have assumed roles of especial prominence in the affairs of society. Some occupy positions of such persuasive power and influence that they are deemed public figures for all purposes. More commonly, those classed as public figures have thrust themselves to the forefront of particular public controversies in order to influence the resolution of the issues involved. In either event, they invite attention and comment.

Even if the foregoing generalities do not obtain in every instance, the communications media are entitled to act on the assumption that public officials and public figures have voluntarily exposed themselves to increased risk of injury from defamatory falsehoods concerning them. No such assumption is justified with respect to a private individual. He has not accepted public office nor assumed an "influential role in ordering society." *Curtis Publishing Co. v. Butts* (opinion of WARREN, C. J.). He has relinquished no part of his interest in the protection of his own good name, and consequently he has a more compelling call on the courts for redress of injury inflicted by defamatory falsehood. Thus, private individuals are not only more vulnerable to injury than public officials and public figures; they are also more deserving of recovery.

For these reasons we conclude that the States should retain substantial latitude in their efforts to enforce a legal remedy for defamatory falsehood injurious to the reputation of a private individual. The extension of the *New York Times* test proposed by the *Rosenbloom* plurality would abridge this legitimate state interest to a degree that we find unacceptable. And it would occasion the additional difficulty of forcing state and federal judges to decide on an ad hoc basis which publications address issues of "general or public interest" and which do not — to determine, in the words of MR. JUSTICE MARSHALL, "what information is relevant to self-government." *Rosenbloom v. Metromedia, Inc.* We doubt the wisdom of committing this task to the conscience of judges. Nor does the Constitution require us to draw so thin a line between the drastic alternatives of the *New York Times* privilege and the common law of strict liability for defamatory error. The "public or general interest" test for determining the applicability of the *New York Times* standard to private defamation actions inadequately serves both of the competing values at stake. On the one hand, a private individual whose reputation is injured by defamatory falsehood that does concern an issue of public or general interest has no recourse unless he can meet the rigorous requirements of *New York Times*. This is true despite the factors that distinguish the state interest in compensating private individuals from the analogous interest involved in the context of public persons. On the other hand, a publisher or broadcaster of a defamatory error which a court deems unrelated to an issue of public or general interest may be held liable in damages even if it took every reasonable precaution to ensure the accuracy of its assertions. And liability may far exceed compensation for any actual injury to the plaintiff, for the jury may be permitted to presume damages without proof of loss and even to award punitive damages.

We hold that, so long as they do not impose liability without fault, the States may define for themselves the appropriate standard of liability for a publisher or broadcaster of defamatory falsehood injurious to a private individual. This approach provides a more equitable boundary between the competing concerns involved here. It recognizes the strength of the legitimate state interest in compensating private individuals for wrongful injury to reputation, yet shields the press and broadcast media from the rigors of strict liability for defamation. At least this conclusion obtains where, as here, the substance of the defamatory statement "makes substantial danger to reputation apparent."

[Further] we hold that the States may not permit recovery of presumed or punitive damages, at least when liability is not based on a showing of knowledge of falsity or reckless disregard for the truth. The largely uncontrolled discretion of juries to award damages where there is no loss unnecessarily compounds the potential of any system of liability for defamatory falsehood to inhibit the vigorous exercise of First Amendment freedoms. Additionally, the doctrine of presumed damages invites juries to punish unpopular opinion rather than to compensate individuals for injury sustained by the publication of a false fact. More to the point, the States have no substantial interest in securing for plaintiffs such as this petitioner gratuitous awards of money damages far in excess of any actual injury.

It is necessary to restrict defamation plaintiffs who do not prove knowledge of falsity or reckless disregard for the truth to compensation for actual injury. We need not define "actual injury," as trial courts have wide experience in framing appropriate jury instructions in tort action. Suffice it to say that actual injury is not limited to out-of-pocket loss. Indeed, the more customary types of actual harm inflicted by defamatory falsehood include impairment of reputation and standing in the community, personal humiliation, and mental anguish and suffering. Of course, juries must be limited by appropriate instructions, and all awards must be supported by competent evidence concerning the injury, although there need be no evidence which assigns an actual dollar value to the injury.

We also find no justification for allowing awards of punitive damages against publishers and broadcasters held liable under state-defined standards of liability for defamation. Like the doctrine of presumed damages, jury discretion to award punitive damages unnecessarily exacerbates the danger of media self-censorship, but, unlike the former rule, punitive damages are wholly irrelevant to the state interest that justifies a negligence standard for private defamation actions. They are not compensation for injury. Instead, they are private fines levied by civil juries to punish reprehensible conduct and to deter its future occurrence. In short, the private defamation plaintiff who establishes liability under a less demanding standard than that stated by *New York Times* may recover only such damages as are sufficient to compensate him for actual injury.

Notwithstanding our refusal to extend the *New York Times* privilege to defamation of private individuals, respondent contends that we should affirm the judgment below on the ground that petitioner is either a public official or a public figure. There is little basis for the former assertion. Respondent's characterization of petitioner as a public figure raises a different question. That designation may rest on either of two alternative bases. In some instances an individual may achieve such pervasive fame or notoriety that he becomes a public figure for all purposes and in all contexts. More commonly, an individual voluntarily injects himself or is drawn into a particular public controversy and thereby becomes a public figure for a limited range of issues. In either case such persons assume special prominence in the resolution of public questions.

Petitioner has long been active in community and professional affairs. He has served as an officer of local civil groups and of various professional organizations, and he has published several books and articles on legal subjects. Although petitioner was consequently well-known in some circles, he had achieved no general fame or notoriety in the community. None of the prospective jurors called at the trial had ever heard of petitioner prior to this litigation, and respondent offered no proof that this response was atypical of the local population. We would not lightly assume that a citizen's participation in community and professional affairs rendered him a public figure for all purposes. Absent clear evidence of general fame or notoriety in the community, and pervasive involvement in the affairs of society, an individual should not be deemed a public personality for all aspects of his life. It is preferable to reduce the public figure question to a more meaningful context by looking to the nature and extent of an individual's participation in the particular controversy giving rise to the defamation.

In this context it is plain that petitioner was not a public figure. He played a minimal role at the coroner's inquest, and his participation related solely to his representation of a private client. He took no part in the criminal prosecution of officer Nuccio. Moreover, he never discussed either the criminal or civil litigation with the press and was never quoted as having done so. He plainly did not thrust himself into the vortex of this public issue, nor did he engage the public's attention in an attempt to influence its outcome. We are persuaded that the trial court did not err in refusing to characterize petitioner as a public figure for the purpose of this litigation.

We therefore conclude that the *New York Times* standard is inapplicable to this case and that the trial court erred in entering judgment for respondent. Because they jury was allowed to impose liability without fault and was permitted to presume damages without proof of injury, a new trial is necessary. We reverse and remand for further proceedings in accord with this opinion.

Justice Blackmun, concurring.

The Court was sadly fractionated in *Rosenbloom*. A result of that kind inevitably leads to uncertainty. I feel that it is of profound importance for the Court to come to rest in the defamation area and to have a clearly defined majority position that eliminates the unsureness engendered by *Rosenbloom's* diversity. If my vote were not needed to create a majority, I would adhere to my prior view. A definitive ruling, however, is paramount.

Justice Brennan, dissenting.

Matters of public or general interest do not "suddenly become less so merely because a private individual is involved or because in some sense the individual did not 'voluntarily' choose to become involved." *See Times, Inc. v. Hill.* I reject the argument that my *Rosenbloom* view improperly commits to judges the task of determining what is and what is not an issue of "general or public interest."[3] I noted in *Rosenbloom* that performance of this task would not always be easy. But surely the courts, the ultimate arbiters of all disputes concerning clashes of constitutional values, would only be performing one of their traditional functions in undertaking this duty. The public interest is necessarily broad; any residual self-censorship that may result from the uncertain contours of the "general or public interest" concept should be of far less concern to publishers and broadcasters than that occasioned by state laws imposing liability for negligent falsehood.

JUSTICE WHITE, dissenting.

[T]he Court, in a few printed pages, has federalized major aspects of libel law by declaring unconstitutional in important respects the prevailing defamation law in all or most of the 50 States. Under the new rule the plaintiff can lose, not because the statement is true, but because it was not negligently made.

So too, the requirement of proving special injury to reputation before general damages may be awarded will clearly eliminate the prevailing rule, worked out over a very long period of time, that, in the case of defamations not actionable per se, the recovery of general damages for injury to reputation may also be had if some form of material or pecuniary loss is proved. Finally, an inflexible federal standard is imposed for the award of punitive damages. No longer will it be enough to prove ill will and an attempt to injure.

These are radical changes in the law and severe invasions of the prerogatives of the States. They should at least be shown to be required by the First Amendment or necessitated by our present circumstances. Neither has been demonstrated. I fail to see how the quality or quantity of public debate will be promoted by further emasculation of state libel laws for the benefit of the news media. If anything, this trend may provoke a new and radical imbalance in the communications process. *Cf.* Barron, *Access to the Press — A New First Amendment Right*, 80 HARV. L. REV. 1641, 1657 (1967). It is not at all inconceivable that virtually unrestrained defamatory remarks about private citizens will discourage them from speaking out and concerning themselves with social problems. This would turn the First Amendment on its head.

This case ultimately comes down to the importance the Court attaches to society's "pervasive and strong interest in preventing and redressing attacks upon reputation." *Rosenblatt v. Baer*. From all that I have seen, the Court has miscalculated and denigrates that interest at a time when escalating assaults on individuality and person dignity counsel otherwise. At the very least, the issue is highly debatable, and the Court has not carried its heavy burden of proof to justify tampering with state libel laws.

[3] Parenthetically, my Brother WHITE argues that the Court's view and mine will prevent a plaintiff — unable to demonstrate some degree of fault — from vindicating his reputation by securing a judgment that the publication was false. This argument overlooks the possible enactment of statutes, not requiring proof of fault, which provide for an action or retraction or for publication of a court's determination of falsity if the plaintiff is able to demonstrate that false statements have been published concerning his activities. Although it may be that question could be raised concerning the constitutionality of such statutes, certainly nothing I have said today (and, as I read the Court's opinion, nothing said there) should be read to imply that a private plaintiff unable to prove fault, must inevitably be denied the opportunity to secure a judgment upon the truth or falsity of statements published about him. *Cf. Rosenbloom v. Metromedia, Inc.*

[The dissenting opinions of Chief Justice Burger and Justice Douglas are omitted.]

NOTES

1. *The significance of Gertz.* In *Gertz*, the Court rejected the extension of the *New York Times* doctrine to publications concerning matters of "general or public interest." A fundamental reason for this rejection was that the Court was persuaded that the opportunity for self-help rebuttal was far less available to private figures than is the case with public figures. The Court's assessment of the opportunity for reply on the part of the libel plaintiff thus appears to be crucial to whether the *New York Times* rule may be invoked by the libel defendant. *Gertz* was decided on the same day as *Miami Herald Publ'g Co. v. Tornillo*, p. 1302. *Tornillo* rejected right of reply legislation as a means of making an accommodation between the *New York Times v. Sullivan* doctrine and its broad protection for media criticism and the ability of those criticized to respond. Taking the two cases together, do you agree with the Court's implicit assumption that damages rather than reply as a remedy for defamation is less inhibitory of freedom of the press?

Unwilling to uphold a mandatory right of reply and yet fearful that self-help rebuttal would be inadequate for private figures, the Court retreated from the continuous inflation of *New York Times v. Sullivan*. The *Rosenbloom* plurality was set aside: the status of the plaintiff rather than the content of the publication was to be the touchstone for application of the *New York Times* doctrine.

The focal point of inquiry of the public law of libel after *Gertz* has not been whether the publication in question involves a "public issue" but rather whether the libel plaintiff is a public or a private figure. In the latter event, the *New York Times* standard was not available to the libel defendant. What standards would apply in such a case?

How does the state's interest in protecting reputation in private defamation cases involving private plaintiffs differ from those cases involving public plaintiffs? What is the "compelling normative consideration" that, in part, moves the Court to perceive an altered balance of interests? Is the Court's distinction between public and private plaintiffs more judicially manageable than the *Rosenbloom* public interest standard? Suppose you were arguing to a state court that is trying to choose a standard of liability for private plaintiff defamation after *Gertz* — how would you argue?

2. *The Brennan approach.* Justice Brennan authored the plurality opinion in *Rosenbloom* with its sympathetic reference to right of reply legislation as a way both to extend the *New York Times v. Sullivan* doctrine to a still larger area of defamation law and yet to assure some opportunity to individuals to counter adverse criticism in the media. Brennan said nothing in *Tornillo* to explain his surprising willingness to invalidate right of reply legislation. But in his dissent in *Gertz v. Welch*, Brennan did cite, apparently with some continuing approval, the text and footnote from his plurality opinion for the Court in *Rosenbloom*, which favored right of reply legislation.

3. *Dun & Bradstreet, Inc. v. Greenmoss Builders, Inc.*, 472 U.S. 749 (1985). The rule of *Gertz* prohibiting recovery of presumed or punitive damages absent proof of actual malice was held not to apply when the defamatory statements do not involve an issue of public concern. Dun & Bradstreet, a credit reporting agency, sent a report to five subscribers indicating that Greenmoss Builders, Inc., a construction contractor, had filed for bankruptcy. The report was false and Greenmoss sought compensatory and punitive damages. A jury trial resulted in an award of $50,000 in presumed damages and $200,000 in punitive damages, even though actual malice had not been established. The trial court granted a new trial. The Vermont Supreme Court reversed holding "that as a matter of federal constitution law the media protections outlined in *Gertz* are inapplicable to nonmedia defamation actions."

The Supreme Court reversed but on different grounds. In a plurality opinion, Justice Powell, was joined by Justices Rehnquist and O'Connor.

> We have never considered whether the *Gertz* balance obtains when the defamatory statements involve no issue of public concern. To make this determination, we must employ the approach approved in *Gertz* and balance the State's interest in compensating private individuals for injury to their reputation against the First Amendment interest in protecting this type of expression. This state interest is identical to the one weighed in *Gertz*. There we found that it was "strong and legitimate." A State should not lightly be required to abandon it.
>
> The First Amendment interest, on the other hand, is less important than the one weighed in *Gertz*. We have long recognized that not all speech is of equal First Amendment importance. It is speech on " 'matters of public concern' " that is "at the heart of the First Amendment's protection." In contrast, speech on matters of purely private concern is of less First Amendment concern. As a number of state courts, including the court below, have recognized, the role of the Constitution in regulating state libel law is far more limited when the concerns that activated *New York Times* and *Gertz* are absent.
>
> In light of the reduced constitutional value of speech involving no matters of public concern, we hold that the state interest adequately supports awards of presumed and punitive damages — even absent a showing of "actual malice."

Focusing on the private economic interests involved and the fact that the report was sent to only five subscribers, the Court held that the publication was not public speech.

Justice Brennan, joined by Justices Marshall, Blackmun, and Stevens, dissenting, rejected the majority's conclusion that the speech in issue did not involve a matter of public concern. "The credit reporting of Dun & Bradstreet falls within any reasonable definition of 'public concern' consistent with our precedents. Justice Powell's reliance on the fact that Dun & Bradstreet publishes credit reports 'for profit' is wholly unwarranted. Time and again we have made clear that speech loses none of its constitutional protection 'even though it is carried in a form that is "sold" for profit.' *Virginia Pharmacy Board*. More importantly, an announcement of the bankruptcy of a local company is information of potentially great concern to residents of the community where the company is located."

4. *Philadelphia Newspapers, Inc. v. Hepps*, 475 U.S. 767 (1986). *Gertz* was not the end of the Court's willingness to obliterate rules of state law on the basis of the First Amendment. Hepps sued the PHILADELPHIA INQUIRER for publishing that he and others had links to organized crime and had used those links to influence the state government process. In *Hepps*, the Court ruled 5-4 that plaintiffs suing newspapers for libel in matters of public concern must prove that the statements complained of are false. The Pennsylvania law had been that the defendant had the burden of proving the truth of the statement complained of. Justice O'Connor, joined by Brennan, Marshall, Blackmun, and Powell, declared: "We recognize that requiring the plaintiff to show falsity will insulate from liability some speech that is false, but unprovably so. To provide 'breathing space,' for true speech on matters of public concern, the Court has been willing to insulate even demonstrably false speech from liability, and has imposed additional requirements of fault upon the plaintiff in a suit for defamation. We therefore do not break new ground here in insulating speech that is not even demonstrably false."

5. *Opinion and fact*. For a while an end run around the *Times* rule was accomplished by reliance on the opinion defense. This defense was based on a *dictum* in *Gertz*:

> Under the First Amendment there is no such thing as a false idea. However, pernicious an opinion may seem, we depend for its correction not on the conscience of judges and juries but on the competition of other ideas. But there is no constitutional value in false statements of fact.

From this statement courts began constructing an absolute First Amendment based privilege for statements of opinion on matters of public concern. By 1990, over two-thirds of the state and almost all of the federal circuit courts of appeal had recognized a First Amendment opinion privilege. False statements of fact could be actionable defamation but false opinion could not. The crucial question then became whether a defamatory statement should be categorized as "opinion" or "fact." This issue itself was a matter of law for the court. Doubtless, it was not without significance that if a court could conclude that the defamatory statement before it was "opinion," the case was over.

In *Milkovich v. Lorain Journal Co.,* 497 U.S. 1 (1990), the Supreme Court, per Chief Justice Rehnquist, rejected a First Amendment-based opinion privilege in defamation cases. Chief Justice Rehnquist denied that the *Gertz dictum* "was intended to create a wholesale defamation exemption for anything that might be labeled 'opinion.'" Expressions of opinion, the Court observed, often imply assertions of objective fact:

> If a speaker says, "In my opinion John Jones is a liar," he implies a knowledge of facts which lead to the conclusion that John Jones told an untruth. Even if the speaker states the facts upon which he bases

> his opinion, if those facts are either incorrect or incomplete, or if his assessment of them is erroneous, the statement may still imply a false assertion of fact. Simply couching such statements in terms of opinion does not dispel these implications; and the statement, "In my opinion, John Jones is a liar," can cause as much damage to reputation as the statement, "Jones is a liar."

Chief Justice Rehnquist rejected creating an "artificial dichotomy between 'opinion' and fact." Rehnquist said that the key to understanding when a statement of opinion was actionable defamation and when it was not is found in the *Hepps* case:

> *Hepps* stands for the proposition that a statement on matters of public concern must be provable as false before there can be liability under state defamation law, at least in situations, like the present, where a media defendant is involved. Thus, unlike the statement, "In my opinion Mayor Jones is a liar," the statement, "In my opinion Mayor Jones shows his abysmal ignorance by accepting the teachings of Marx and Lenin," would not be actionable. *Hepps* ensures that a statement of opinion relating to matters of public concern which does not contain a provable false factual connotation will receive full constitutional protection.

Milkovich focuses on implied false and defamatory meaning. If a statement cannot be proven to be false, there can be no liability. In the case of satire or parody, there is no liability because such statements cannot reasonably be considered to be defamatory statements of fact. Since *Milkovich* emphasizes false statements of fact, in theory pivotal decision making is given to the jury which determines questions of fact. Since juries are often less sympathetic to the media, will the consequence of *Milkovich* be to undermine the *Times* doctrine? On the other hand, it can be argued that *Milkovich* strengthens the *Times* doctrine since it blocks the opinion defense which was becoming a way of avoiding the doctrine.

Consider the suggestion that *Milkovich* "constitutionalized" the determination of whether a challenged publication had a defamatory meaning: "[T]he Court's threshold requirement of a false, defamatory meaning in *Milkovich* appears to be less an isolated response to the dilemma posed by a specific case and more a significant explication of the substantive, constitutional barriers envisioned by *New York Times* in public figure libel cases." Thomas Dienes & Lee Levine, *Implied Libel, Defamatory Meaning and State of Mind: The Promise of* New York Times v. Sullivan, 778 IOWA L. REV. 237, 280 (1993). In short, a court must consider the First Amendment in determining whether a publication is capable of bearing a defamatory meaning — whether it reasonably can be said to be defamatory statement of fact — and whether it is verifiable.

Given its complexity and cost, is libel law worth saving? Professor David Anderson contends that although it is possible to conceive of a world without libel law "it would be a less civil world, a less just world for victims of defamation, a world less anchored to truth and reason." David Anderson, *Is*

Libel Law Worth Reforming? 140 U. PA. L. REV. 487, 551 (1991). Professor Anderson believes the libel law should be reformed and that the Supreme Court should reform it: "The system of libel law the Court has created so permeates the field that other agencies of reform are effectively disabled." If the Supreme Court were to reform libel law, with the aim of achieving "new accommodations of speech and reputational interests as a matter of constitutional law," *id.* at 553–54, what changes should the Court make in the public law of libel as it now exists? Consider the claim of Professor David A. Logan, *Libel Law in the Trenches: Reflections on Current Data on Libel Litigation*, 87 VA. L. REV. 503, 508 (2001): "[T]he *New York Times/Gertz* regime has eviscerated the law of libel to the point that it now poses little serious threat to the First Amendment rights of the media, and the image of the contemporary media, cowed by the threat of libel claims, is unsupported by the available evidence. More generally, the data are testament that a First Amendment culture has taken deep root in both the federal and state judiciaries and support the view that the Court's libel decisions rank among the great civil liberties victories of the last half-century." *Compare* BRUCE W. SANFORD, DON'T SHOOT THE MESSINGER: HOW OUR GROWING HATRED OF THE MEDIA THREATENS FREE SPEECH FOR ALL OF US 9 (1999) (arguing that the growing gulf between the public and the media suggests that "[a] golden age that for fifty years saw the creation and expansion of a First Amendment right of the public to receive information has concluded.").

[3] The Emotional Distress Tort

Time, Inc. v. Hill involved a plaintiff's attempt to use the privacy tort to avoid the strictures of the *Times* doctrine. A more recent attempt which might have led to similar consequences involved the tort of intentional infliction of emotional distress. Since the elements of the emotional distress tort, are quite different from defamation, is application of an actual malice test still required by the First Amendment? In the context of the emotional distress tort is the actual malice test even relevant? Can the state interests served by the emotional distress tort be reconciled with the First Amendment?

HUSTLER MAGAZINE v. FALWELL

485 U.S. 46, 108 S. Ct. 876, 99 L. Ed. 2d 41 (1988)

CHIEF JUSTICE REHNQUIST delivered the opinion of the Court.

Petitioner HUSTLER MAGAZINE, Inc., is a magazine of nationwide circulation. Respondent Jerry Falwell, a nationally known minister who has been active as a commentator on politics and public affairs, sued petitioner and its publisher, petitioner Larry Flynt, to recover damages for invasion of privacy, libel, and intentional infliction of emotional distress. The District Court directed a verdict against respondent on the privacy claim, and submitted the other two claims to a jury. The jury found for petitioners on the defamation claim, but found for respondent on the claim for intentional infliction of emotional distress and awarded damage. We now consider whether this award is consistent with the First and Fourteenth Amendments of the United States Constitution.

The inside front cover of the November 1983 issue of HUSTLER MAGAZINE featured a "parody" of an advertisement for Campari Liqueur that contained the name and picture of respondent and was entitled "Jerry Falwell talks about his first time." This parody was modeled after actual Campari ads that included interviews with various celebrities about their "first times." Although it was apparent by the end of each interview that this meant the first time they sampled Campari, the ads clearly played on the sexual double entendre of the general subject of "first times." Copying the form and layout of these Campari ads, HUSTLER's editors chose respondent as the featured celebrity and drafted an alleged "interview" with him in which he states that his "first time" was during a drunken incestuous rendezvous with his mother in an outhouse. The HUSTLER parody portrays respondent and his mother as drunk and immoral, and suggests that respondent is a hypocrite who preaches only when he is drunk. In small print at the bottom of the page, the ad contains the disclaimer, "ad parody — not to be taken seriously." The magazine's table of contents also lists the ad as "Fiction; Ad and Personality Parody."

Soon after the November issue of HUSTLER became available to the public, respondent brought this diversity action in the United States District Court for the Western District of Virginia against HUSTLER MAGAZINE, Inc., Larry C. Flynt, and Flynt Distributing Co. Respondent stated in his complaint that publication of the ad parody in HUSTLER entitled him to recover damages for libel, invasion of privacy, and intentional infliction of emotional distress. The case proceeded to trial. At the close of the evidence, the District Court granted a directed verdict for petitioners on the invasion of privacy claim. The jury then found against respondent on the libel claim, specifically finding that the ad parody could not "reasonably be understood as describing actual facts about [respondent] or actual events in which [he] participated." The jury ruled for him on the intentional infliction of emotional distress claim, however, and stated that he should be awarded $100,000 in compensatory damages, as well as $50,000 each in punitive damages from petitioners. Petitioners' motion for judgment notwithstanding the verdict was denied. On appeal, the United States Court of Appeals for the Fourth Circuit affirmed the judgment against petitioners.

This case presents us with a novel question involving First Amendment limitations upon a State's authority to protect its citizens from the intentional infliction of emotional distress. We must decide whether a public figure may recover damages for emotional harm caused by the publication of an ad parody offensive to him, and doubtless gross and repugnant in the eyes of most. Respondent would have us find that a State's interest in protecting public figures from emotional distress is sufficient to deny First Amendment protection to speech that is patently offensive and is intended to inflict emotional injury, even when that speech could not reasonably have been interpreted as stating actual facts about the public figure involved. This we decline to do.

In respondent's view, and in the view of the Court of Appeals, so long as the utterance was intended to inflict emotional distress, was outrageous, and did in fact inflict serious emotional distress, it is of no constitutional import whether the statement was a fact or an opinion, or whether it was true or false. It is the intent to cause injury that is the gravamen of the tort, and the State's interest in preventing emotional harm simply outweighs whatever interest a speaker may have in speech of this type. Generally speaking the law does not regard the intent to inflict emotional distress as one which should receive much solicitude, and it is quite understandable that most if not all jurisdictions have chosen to make it civilly culpable where the conduct in question is sufficiently "outrageous." But in the world of debate about public affairs, many things done with motives that are less than admirable are protected by the First Amendment. Thus while such a bad motive may be deemed controlling for purposes of tort liability in other areas of the law, we think the First Amendment prohibits such a result in the area of public debate about public figures.

Respondent contends, however, that the caricature in question here was so "outrageous" as to distinguish it from more political cartoons. There is no doubt that the caricature of respondent and his mother published in HUSTLER is at best a distant cousin of the political cartoons, and a rather poor relation at that. If it were possible by laying down a principled standard to separate the one from the other, public discourse would probably suffer little or no harm. But we doubt that there is any such standard, and we are quite sure that the pejorative description "outrageous" does not supply one. "Outrageousness" in the area of political and social discourse has an inherent subjectiveness about it which would allow a jury to impose liability on the basis of the jurors' taste or views, or perhaps on the basis of their dislike of a particular expression.

We conclude that public figures and public officials may not recover for the tort of intentional infliction of emotional distress by reason of publications such as the one here at issue without showing in addition that the publication contains a false statement of fact which was made with "actual malice," *i.e.*, with knowledge that the statement was false or with reckless disregard as to whether or not it was true. This is not merely a "blind application" of the *New York Times* standard, it reflects our considered judgment that such a standard is necessary to give adequate "breathing space" to the freedoms protected by the First Amendment. The judgment of the Court of Appeals is accordingly reversed.

JUSTICE WHITE, concurring in the judgment.

As I see it, the decision in *New York Times v. Sullivan* has little to do with this case, for here the jury found that the ad contained no assertion of fact. But I agree with the Court that the judgment below, which penalized the publication of the parody, cannot be squared with the First Amendment.

NOTE

Professor Post argues that "the *Falwell* opinion prohibits the tort of intentional infliction of emotional distress from enforcing, in the absence of a knowingly false assertion of fact, precisely those norms which define civility and hence which would restrain speech likely to be experienced as coercive and violative of identity." Robert Post, *The Constitutional Concept of Public Discourse: Outrageous Opinion, Democratic Deliberation, and Hustler Magazine v. Falwell*, 103 HARV. L. REV. 601, 624 (1990).

Falwell rejected the distinction which the emotional distress tort makes between "outrageous opinion and non-outrageous opinion" as unprincipled due to its inherently subjective character and its variability from individual to individual. Post says, however, that the concept of outrageousness speaks to community values rather than personal values or preferences. He claims that "what is driving the *Falwell* opinion is not that the distinction between outrageous and non-outrageous speech is subjective or arbitrary, but rather that it is constitutionally inappropriate as a standard for the legal regulation of public discourse." *Id.* at 625–26. Professor Post offers as an alternative view that "the boundaries of public discourse cannot be fixed in a neutral fashion. From the perspective of the logic of democratic self-governance, any restriction of the domain of public discourse must necessarily constitute a forcible truncation of possible lines of democratic development. We can and do have firm convictions about the core of the domain, but its periphery will remain both ideological and vague, subject to an endless negotiation between democracy and community life." *Id.* at 683–84. Is Post suggesting that there is a false absolutism, a masking of basic conflicts, in the rationale of *Falwell*? In terms of the day to day life of free expression, are the outcomes of cases likely to differ depending on whether Post's analysis is used? Is Post's analysis consistent with *Cohen v. California*?

[4] Privacy and the First Amendment — Publishing Names of Rape Victims

Earlier in connection with *Time, Inc. v. Hill*, we discussed false light privacy and its relationship to *New York Times v. Sullivan*. We observed the close relationship between the First Amendment interest in newsworthiness and the state's desire to protect personal privacy. Another area involving the same First Amendment clash is so-called "true privacy" — the aspect of the privacy tort which is known as public disclosure of embarrassing private facts. The cases which follow involve the publication of intimate facts which would be offensive to a reasonable person. In each case the privacy claim was subordinated to the First Amendment interest in the publication of truthful information about matters of public record and public concern. Is the theory of these cases that truthful information which is a matter of public record is *a fortiori* a matter of public interest and therefore protected by the First Amendment?

Consider whether truthful publication of embarrassing facts which were *not* matters of public record would be protected by the First Amendment. Should the answer turn on the degree of public interest in the private facts? For example, should publication in sexual assault cases turn on sociological estimates of the value of disclosure versus secrecy in combatting the crime? [Feminist authors disagree on this question.] Finally, can the privacy tort survive the first amendment theory of these cases?

Susan M. Giles suggests that, in the future, the Court may hold that "public figures could never recover for publication of true private facts (concluding that states' lesser interest in providing a remedy for those who have assumed the risk of such publicity is outweighed by the interest of the public in true information about such public persons)." In the case of a private citizen, where the matter is of public concern "the Court could continue to hold that, upon proof that the information is of public concern and that it was lawfully acquired, there can be no liability for publication in the absence of a governmental interest of the 'highest order.' " A situation involving private citizens and private facts would have the strongest case for recovery: the "Court may well conclude that there is a low First Amendment interest in facts of no public concern (even though true), a high state interest in giving a remedy to a private person, and thus recovery should be allowed, perhaps with some limitation on damages." *Public Plaintiffs and Private Facts: Should the "Public Figure" Doctrine Be Transplanted into Privacy Law?*, 83 NEB L. REV. 1204 (2005).

***Cox Broadcasting Corp. v. Cohn,* 420 U.S. 469 (1975).** The Court established the right of the press to report facts disclosed in a court trial and in court records open to the public. In news broadcasts of a rape trial, an Atlanta television station reported the name of a rape victim who died as a result of the incident. Georgia law made it a crime to publish the name of a rape victim. The name of the victim, a minor, was obtained by a television news reporter from a clerk of the court who gave the news reporter a copy of the indictment. On the basis of the statute, the girl's father brought an action for invasion of his privacy. The state supreme court held that a cause of action for damages for invasion of privacy was legally cognizable in these circumstances. The broadcaster contended that recognition of such a cause of action violated the First and Fourteenth Amendments.

In a decision carefully limited to the facts the Supreme Court, per Justice White, reversed:

> At the very least, the First and Fourteenth Amendments will not allow exposing the press to liability for truthfully publishing information released to the public in official court records. If there are privacy interests to be protected in judicial proceedings, the States must respond by means which avoid public documentation or other exposure of private information. Their political institutions must weigh the interests in privacy with the interests of the public to know and of the press to publish. Once true information is disclosed in public court documents open to public inspection, the press cannot be sanctioned for publishing it.

The Court refused to rule on the contention of the media that accurate publication of information cannot constitutionally be punished by either civil or criminal actions for invasion of privacy. The Court also said: "We mean to imply nothing about any constitutional questions which might arise from a state policy not allowing access by the public and press to various kinds of official records, such as records of juvenile-court proceedings."

***Florida Star v. B.J.F.,* 491 U.S. 524 (1989),** the Court held, per Justice Marshall, that the imposition of civil damages on a newspaper for publishing the name of a rape victim which it had obtained from a publicly released police report violated the First Amendment. This result was reached despite the fact that Florida had a statute which forbade publication of the name of the victim of a sexual offense.

The FLORIDA STAR, a weekly newspaper, published a story about a robbery and a sexual assault perpetrated on B.J.F. from a police report on B.J.F. identifying her by her full name. The report was placed in the Sheriff's Department press room. A FLORIDA STAR reporter-trainee prepared a story based on the report. In printing B.J.F.'s full name, the STAR violated its own internal policy of not publishing the names of rape victims. B.J.F. brought suit against the STAR on the theory that the newspaper had been negligent *per se* in violating the Florida statute forbidding the publication of the names of victims of sexual offenses. A jury award to B.J.F. of both compensatory and punitive damages was upheld in the Florida courts but the Supreme Court reversed.

An important factor in the case was the manner by which the FLORIDA STAR obtained the "identifying information in question." The state had much narrower means at its disposal to prevent the publication of this information than "the extreme step of punishing truthful speech." B.J.F.'s identity would never have been disclosed "were it not for the erroneous, if inadvertent, inclusion by the department of her full name in an incident report made available in a press room open to the public." Since the government had failed to police itself in disseminating information, imposition of damages against the press could not be viewed as "a narrowly tailored means of safeguarding anonymity."

> Our holding today is limited. We do not hold that truthful publication is automatically constitutionally protected, or that there is no zone of personal privacy within which the State may protect the individual from intrusion by the press, or even that a State may never punish publication of the name of the victim of a sexual offense. We hold only that where a newspaper publishes truthful information which it has lawfully obtained, punishment may lawfully be imposed, if at all, only when narrowly tailored to a state interest of the highest order, and that no such interest is satisfactorily served by imposing liability . . .under the facts of this case.

Justice White, joined by Chief Justice Rehnquist and Justice O'Connor, dissented:

> If the First Amendment prohibits wholly private persons (such as B.J.F.) from recovering for the publication of the fact that she was raped, I doubt that there remain any "private facts" which persons may assume will not be published in the newspapers, or broadcast on television.
>
> More recently, in *Cox Broadcasting*, we acknowledged the possibility that the First Amendment may prevent a state from ever subjecting the publication of truthful but private information to civil liability. Today we hit the bottom of the slippery slope. I would find a place to draw the line higher on the hillside: a spot high enough to protect B.J.F.'s desire for privacy and peace-of-mind in the wake of a horrible personal tragedy. There is no public interest in publishing the names, addresses, and phone numbers of persons who are the victims of crime

> — and no public interest in immunizing the press from liability in rare cases where a State's efforts to protect a victim's privacy have failed.

Professor Edelman asks a fundamental question about *Florida Star*: What is "the constitutional difference between false and defamatory speech — for which the plaintiff can recover — and the equally injurious truthful speech that invades the plaintiff's privacy?" Peter Edelman, *Free Press v. Privacy: Haunted by the Ghost of Justice Black*, 68 Tex. L. Rev. 1195, 1198 (1990). The action based on the latter type of injurious speech is virtually wiped out with the "near extinction of an individual's right to prevent disclosure of private facts." *Id.* Prof. Edelman takes particular aim at the great weight the Court gives the fact that the material published by the newspaper was lawfully obtained: "[In most situations], the lawfulness of acquisition is an inept measure of the competing interests of speech and privacy in the private-fact disclosure context. A far superior standard is available through consideration of such significant issues as the plaintiff's status and the newsworthiness of the disclosed fact." *Id.* at 1206. Edelman says that the task presented in *Florida Star* was to balance an individual's interest in privacy against the interest in free expression of truth information. He protests, however, that rather than candidly undertaking this task the Court strikes a "balance implicitly, choosing the absolutist position without saying so." *Id.* at 1214–15.

***Bartnicki v. Vopper*, 532 U.S. 514 (2001).** The case presented the issue of "what degree of protection, if any, the First Amendment provides to speech that discloses the contents of an illegally intercepted communication." Individuals whose cellular telephone conversation had been intercepted and taped by an unknown third party sued media defendants who broadcast the tape and the individual who had given the tape to the media, pursuant to federal and state wiretapping laws, which prohibit not only the actual interception and taping but also the act of intentionally disclosing to any other person the contents of such an intercepted communication. The conversation was between a union's chief negotiator and president discussing a proposed teachers strike at a local high school in the course of collective-bargaining negotiations which were both contentious and the recipient of a good deal of media attention. In the course of the conversation, the union president raised the possibility of violence in order to stop the board of education's intransigence. Finding that the issue presented "a conflict of the highest order," the Court held "that the disclosures made by respondents in this suit are protected by the First Amendment."

Justice Stevens, writing for the majority, conceded that the federal law, as well as its state analog, "is in fact a content-neutral law of general applicability," because "[t]he statute does not distinguish based on the content of the intercepted conversations, nor is it justified by reference to the content of those conversations." He nevertheless concluded that, as applied to the conversation in question, the law violated the First Amendment. The Court rejected the so-called "dry up the market" theory, which justifies restrictions on secondary behavior because they will have the effect to deterring the primary illegal action. The argument, as applied to this context, was that prohibiting disclosure would deter the act of intercepting the conversation. The Court responded that "there is no empirical evidence to support the assumption that the prohibition against disclosures reduces the number of illegal interceptions." It reasoned that "[t]he justification for any such novel burden on expression must be 'far stronger than mere speculation about serious harms.' "

The Court also rejected the second asserted justification, which it conceded was "considerably stronger." The argument was that "the fear of public disclosure of private conversations might well have a chilling effect on private speech." In rejecting this argument, however, the Court emphasized that "[w]e need not decide whether that interest is strong enough to justify the application of [the federal wiretapping statute] to disclosures of trade secrets or domestic gossip or other information of purely private concern (reserving the question whether truthful publication of private matters unrelated to public affairs can be constitutionally proscribed)." This was due to the fact that "[t]he enforcement of that provision in this case, however, implicates the core purposes of the First Amendment because it imposes sanctions on the publication of truthful information of public concern." In this case, the "naked prohibition against disclosure is fairly characterized as a regulation of pure speech." Relying on *Time, Inc. v. Hill* and *New York Times Co. v. Sullivan*, the Court noted that "[o]ne of the costs associated with participation in public affairs is an attendant loss of privacy."

Justice Breyer, joined by Justice O'Connor, concurred in what he saw to be the Court's "narrow" holding, "limited to the special circumstances present here: (1) the radio broadcasters acted lawfully (up to the time of final public disclosure); and (2) the information publicized involved a matter of unusual public concern, namely a threat of potential physical harm to others." Justice Breyer noted that "[t]he statutory restrictions before us directly enhance private speech," but that "as applied in these circumstances, [they] do not reasonably reconcile the competing constitutional objectives. Rather, they disproportionately interfere with media freedom." He reasoned that because the intercepted conversation "rais[ed] a significant concern for the safety of others it followed that "the speakers had little or no legitimate interest in maintaining the privacy of the particular conversation." He noted, however, his view that "the Constitution permits legislatures to respond flexibly to the challenges future technology may pose to the individual's interest in basic personal privacy."

The Chief Justice, joined by Justices Scalia and Thomas, dissented. He referred to the Court's "matter of public concern" standard as "an amorphous concept that the Court does not even attempt to define." He reasoned that "the Court's decision diminishes, rather than enhances, the purposes of the First Amendment: chilling the speech of the millions of Americans who rely upon electronic technology to communicate each day."

Professor Rodney A. Smolla, *Information as Contraband: The First Amendment and Liability for Trafficking in Speech*, 96 NW. U.L. REV. 1099 (2002), states that the Court's decision in *Bartnicki* is in great need of deciphering. "[T]he confusing alignment of the Justices makes the precise holding of the case far from clear, and what at first blush seemed a setback for the protection of privacy may on further review prove a backhanded victory." Although Justice Stevens's majority opinion was nominally joined by five other Justices, "two of the Justices of the majority — Breyer and O'Connor — concurred in an opinion written by Justice Breyer that appeared to dramatically trim the reach and rationale of the majority opinion." What would have been the result in *Bartnicki* if the broadcasters had known the identity of the party intercepting the communication?

Professor David Kohler argues that the holding in *Bartnicki v. Vopper* is a large step away from the ideals of *New York Times Co. v. Sullivan*. "Whereas in *Sullivan* speech as a value to be protected virtually above all others, in *Bartnicki* it is a commodity to be weighted in relative terms with other important interests." Professor Kohler expresses discomfort with the concurring opinion in *Bartnicki*, which he says states that "not only must speech be of public concern to trump the kinds of privacy interests implicated by *Bartnicki*, it must also be of unusual public concern — in this case a perceived threat of violence — and must be about someone whose interest in privacy is particularly low — in this case a public figure. Because the vote of these two justices was necessary for the majority, it would appear that the concurrence might, in fact, have some teeth." *Forty Years After* New York Times v. Sullivan: *The Good, the Bad, and the Ugly*, 83 OR. L. REV. 1203 (2004).

Eugene Volokh, *Freedom of Speech and Information Privacy: The Troubling Implications of a Right to Stop People from Speaking About You*, 52 STAN. L. REV. 1049, 1122 (2000), argues that "despite their intuitive appeal, restrictions on speech that reveals personal information are constitutional under current doctrine only if they are imposed by contract, express or implied." He concludes that "expanding the doctrine to create a new exception may give supporters of information privacy speech restrictions much more than they bargained for. All the proposals for such expansion — whether based on an intellectual property theory, a commercial speech theory, a private concern speech theory, or a compelling government interest theory — would, if accepted, become strong precedent for other speech restrictions, including ones that have already been proposed." Does *Bartnicki v. Vopper* support Professor Volokh's conclusions? Writing on *Bartnicki v. Vopper* and similar cases prior to the Court's decision, Professor Volokh said: "Speech by people who have never promised to remain quiet about something may not be suppressed simply because someone else wrongfully revealed the information (at least absent some overwhelming national security concerns), even if the leaker breached a contract or even broke the law; a contrary rule would dramatically undermine newspapers' ability to report. Intercepting confidential communications is properly outlawed, but a newspaper need not stay silent about such communications if they come into newspaper's hands."

Compare Daniel J. Solove, *The Virtues of Knowing Less: Justifying Privacy Protections Against Disclosure*, 53 DUKE L.J. 967, 997 (2003), who criticizes Volokh for losing sight of the ends of the First Amendment by focusing too heavily on the means. "Privacy regulations that promote speech should not simply be viewed in terms of their speech-restrictive elements; they should be understood holistically, in terms of their overall purpose in the protection of free speech." Professor Solove argues that "information must be considered in context, which means that the relationships in which the information is transferred and the ways in which it is used become the central focus of inquiry." *Id.* at 1065.

[B] MEDIA ACCESS TO INFORMATION

Should the right of the press to acquire information be as fully protected as its right to disseminate information? Justice Stevens in a dissent has commented: "But it has always been apparent that the freedom to obtain information that the government has a legitimate interest in not disclosing is far narrower than the freedom to disseminate information, which is 'virtually obsolete' in most contexts." *Press Enterprise Co. v. Superior Ct. (Press Enterprise II),* 478 U.S. 1 (1986).

Justice Stewart asserted that the Press Clause of the First Amendment was a "structural provision of the Constitution extending protection to the press as an institution" and possessed a potency independent of the speech clause. This position has not been accepted by the Court, nor has it led to an acceptance of the view that the press right to acquire information should be superior to that of other members of the public. The Court's desire to reject the principle that the media has rights beyond those of the general public has often produced opinions which seem to undercut the First Amendment rights of the public. Yet the First Amendment status of the right of the press and the public to acquire information has gathered new strength.

Madison said that "a popular government, without popular information, or the means of acquiring it, is but a prologue to a force or a tragedy, or perhaps both." But as the Court noted *in Cox Broadcasting Corp. v. Cohn,* 420 U.S. 469, 490–91 (1975), "in a society in which each individual has but limited time and resources with which to observe at first hand the operations of his government, he relies necessarily upon the press to bring to him in convenient form the facts of those operations." *See* OWEN FISS, THE IRONY OF FREE SPEECH 50 (1996): "In exercising [its] sovereign prerogative, citizens depend upon a number of institutions to inform them about the positions of various contenders for office and to report and evaluate the ongoing policies and practices of government. In modern society the organized press, including television, is perhaps the principal institution that performs this function, and in order to discharge these democratic responsibilities the press needs a certain measure of autonomy from the state."

C. THOMAS DIENES, LEE LEVINE & ROBERT LIND, NEWSGATHERING AND THE LAW § 1.05 (3rd ed. 2005), note that "[I]f the press is to perform its informing and checking functions, it must be free to publish and to obtain information affecting matters of public concern. The constitutional freedom of the press to publish is well established. The freedom of the press to gather the news, free of excessive governmental interference, and its ability to obtain access to governmental institutions and to information in the hands of government are, however, less certain." Ever since *Branzburg v. Hayes*, acknowledged that "newsgathering is not without its First Amendment protections" and that "without some protection for seeking out the news, freedom of the press could be eviscerated," new protection has been accorded to newsgathering.

Assuming some right of the press to gather news, the question is the breadth of that right. Can the journalist resist the inquiries of grand juries and of the courts in criminal and civil proceedings? Does the press have the right of access to government institutions such as prisons, mental hospitals, and government documents? Can courts be closed to protect the interests of the parties? Are the First Amendment rights of the press any different than the rights of the public generally? If there is a right to gather news, what correlative duties does the right impose on government? Should the First Amendment encompass affirmative rights as well as negative prohibitions? The rationale for recognition of a right of the press to acquire information rests on the premise that the press, in implementing the public's right to receive information, serves a surrogate for the public.

One scholar has argued against constitutionalizing a public right to know: "The Constitution yields no normative standards by which the claim of access to governmental information can be evaluated and the question of whether citizens' demands for information ought to be honored is not merely quite unsuitable for judicial resolution, but also seems plainly to have been committed to the branches of government entrusted with making and administering the laws." Lillian BeVier, *An Informed Public, and Informing Press: The Search for a Constitutional Principle*, 68 CAL. L. REV. 482 (1980).

Despite reservations such as these, a First Amendment right of press access to the criminal process, even though it flows from recognition of a general public right of access, has now been recognized. The right to attend trials announced in *Richmond Newspapers, Inc. v. Virginia,* 448 U.S. 555 (1980), by Chief Justice Burger was declared a guaranteed First Amendment right of the public including the press. From these beginnings, a broad right of access to the criminal process has emerged. "Today, this right of access has spread to criminal and civil proceedings generally and lower courts continue to explore the boundaries of the access right, as well as the contours of constitutional protection for the newsgathering process generally." DIENES, LEVINE & LIND, at § 1.05.

Nevertheless, the War Against Terror has posed new challenges for maintaining public access to government proceedings and records. "The war against terrorism and the armed conflicts in Afghanistan and Iraq have made the press's task of informing the public increasingly difficult. The Reporters Committee for Freedom of the Press has observed that, '[i]n the days immediately following September 11, the U.S. Government embarked on an unprecedented path of secrecy. The atmosphere of terror induced public officials to abandon the country's culture of openness and opt for secrecy as a way of ensuring safety and security.' [REPORTERS COMM. FOR FREEDOM OF THE PRESS, HOMEFRONT CONFIDENTIAL: HOW THE WAR ON TERRORISM AFFECTS ACCESS TO INFORMATION AND THE PUBLIC'S RIGHT TO KNOW (6th ed. Sept. 2005)]. Professor David Cole asserts that, by January 2004, more than 5,000 foreign nationals had been subjected to detention as the government pursued its antiterrorism efforts. Many were detained without charges; more than 600 detainees charged with immigration violations were tried in secret. [David Cole, *The Priority of Morality: The Emergency Constitution's Blind Spot*, 113 YALE L.J. 1753 (2004)]." DIENES, LEVINE & LIND, at § 1.06.

Thus far, we have spoken of a right on the part of the press and the public to have access to governmental institutions. What of the right of the public to have access to the media? Does the First Amendment guarantee a free press or a fair press? What should be the center of First Amendment concern, diversity of expression or editorial autonomy? There is growing concentration of ownership of the media. In an era of large newspaper chains and great media combines, is it realistic to expect that there can be diversity of expression without diversity of ownership? What is the role, if any, of the first amendment in resolving questions of access to the media?

One of the authors of this text has contended: "The changing nature of the communications process has made it imperative that the law show concern for the public interest in effective utilization of media for the expression of diverse points of view. Confrontation of ideas, a topic of eloquent affection in contemporary decisions, demands some recognition of a right to be heard as a constitutional principle." Jerome Barron, *Access to the Press—A New First Amendment Right,* 80 HARV. L. REV. 1641 (1967).

A right of access implies a right of participation in the channels of communication. Is such a right a constitutional right? If not, can government legislate such a right consistent with the First Amendment? Should there be different access rules for the broadcast media and the print media? Currently, we have two First Amendment models for dealing with these media; one for the print media and one for the broadcast media. New technology breeds yet new media which may not be totally responsive to either of these models. Is a cable system more like a broadcasting station or a newspaper? Since cable has a multiplicity of channels the scarcity rationale arguably ought not to apply. And what First Amendment standards should apply to the Internet, where access is generally available and any user can claim to be a reporter. *See* David A. Anderson, *Freedom of Press*, 80 TEXAS L. REV. 429, 528 (2002) ("It is impossible or at least impractical to extend press perequisites equally to all information providers, and it is difficult to distinguish the press from the rest because the press is 'disappearing inside the larger world of communications.' ").

[1] Journalist's Privilege: *Branzburg* and Beyond

***Branzburg v. Hayes*, 408 U.S. 665 (1972).** If a reporter in pursuit of a story uncovers information which the law enforcement arm of the state cannot easily acquire, may the state secure access to this information by the issuance of a subpoena to the reporter to testify or to turn over materials gathered by the reporter? Assuming that enforcement of the subpoena could restrain journalists by making it impossible for them to assure confidentiality to their sources, does the First Amendment prohibit restraints on the information-gathering process? In 1972, three cases came before the Supreme Court for review of the question of whether the First Amendment provided a privilege to newsmen to refuse to testify in circumstances where the press is unwillingly being made an arm of government. "The issue in these cases is whether requiring newsmen to appear and testify before state or federal grand juries abridges the freedom of speech and press guaranteed by the First Amendment. We hold that it does not."

Justice White summarized the first amendment claims as follows:

> [T]o gather news it is often necessary to agree either not to identify [sources] or to publish only part of the facts revealed, or both. [I]f the reporter is nevertheless forced to reveal these confidences to a grand

> jury, the source so identified and other confidential sources of other reporters will be measurably deterred from furnishing publishable information, all to the detriment of the free flow of information protected by the First Amendment. The heart of the claim is that the burden on news gathering from compelling reporters to disclose confidential information outweighs any public interest in obtaining this information.

While acknowledging that "newsgathering is not without its First Amendment protections," the Court stressed that "the First Amendment does not guarantee the press a constitutional right of special access to information not available to the public generally." Justice White cited the numerous laws of general applicability that the press is required to obey along with the general public, such as the antitrust laws, labor laws, and defamation laws. "The use of confidential sources by the press is not forbidden or restricted; reporters remain free to seek news from any source by means within the law. The sole issue before us is the obligation of reporters to respond to grand jury subpoenas as other citizens do and to answer questions relevant to an investigation into the commission of crime."

As for the incidental burden on the free flow of information, Justice White expressed skepticism. The estimates on the inhibition from forced disclosure were labelled "widely divergent and to a great extent speculative." Against this speculative burden on the press' capacity to gather information and on the free flow of information, the Court placed the public interest in the special role of the grand jury in law enforcement. "Fair and effective law enforcement aimed at providing security for the person and property of the individual is a fundamental function of government, and a grand jury plays an important, constitutionally mandated role in this process." The Court stressed that the public has a right to every man's evidence and concluded:

> On the record now before us, we perceive no basis for a holding that the public interest in law enforcement and insuring effective grand jury proceedings is insufficient to override the consequential, but uncertain, burden on news gathering which is said to result from insisting that reporters, like other citizens, respond to relevant questions put to them in the course of a valid grand jury investigation or criminal trial. Until now the only testimonial privilege for unofficial witnesses that is rooted in the Federal Constitution is the Fifth Amendment privilege against compelling self-incrimination. We are asked to create another by interpreting the First Amendment to grant newsmen testimonial privilege that other citizens do not enjoy. This we decline to do.

Justice White took a very stern view with regard to crimes that the journalist has witnessed as distinguished from sources that he does not wish to identify, stating: "Insofar as any reporter in these cases undertook not to reveal or testify about the crime he witnessed, his claim of privilege under the First Amendment presents no substantial question. The crimes of news sources are no less reprehensible and threatening to the public interest when witnessed by a reporter than when they are not."

Justice Powell in a separate concurrence stated that "state and federal authorities are not free to 'annex' the news media as 'an investigative arm of government.' " If a newsman is asked questions in a grand jury proceeding which are not asked in good faith, the journalist may secure the protection of the court "on a motion to quash and an appropriate protective order may be entered. The asserted claim to privilege should be judged on its facts by the striking of a proper balance between the freedom of the press and the obligation of all citizens to give relevant testimony with respect to criminal conduct. The balance of the vital constitutional and societal interests on a case-by-case basis accords with the tried and traditional way of adjudicating such questions. In short, the courts will be available to newsmen under circumstances where legitimate First Amendment interests require protection."

Justice Douglas, dissenting, argued that the First Amendment conferred an absolute privilege on the reporter to refuse to divulge news sources. Douglas criticized the qualified privilege view and THE NEW YORK TIMES for supporting that view: "THE NEW YORK TIMES, whose reporting functions are at issue here, takes the amazing position that First Amendment rights are to be balanced against other needs of convenience of government."

Justice Stewart, joined by Justices Brennan and Marshall in dissent, began from a very different premise than that adopted by the Court. The reporter's constitutional right to a confidential relationship with his source stems from the broad societal interest in a full and free flow of information to the public. "News must not be unnecessarily cut off at its source, for without freedom to acquire information the right to publish would be impermissibly compromised." Nor did the dissent concur with the majority's assessment of the burden imposed by forced disclosure. Confidentiality between the reporter and his or her source was deemed essential to newsgathering. The right to a confidential relationship between a reporter and his source was said to follow from three factual predicates: "(1) newsmen require informants to gather news; (2) confidentiality is essential to the creation and maintenance of a news-gathering relationship with informants; and (3) the existence of an unbridled subpoena power will deter sources from divulging information or deter reporters from gathering and publishing information." The dissenters criticized the Court's demand for verification: "[W]e have never before demanded that First Amendment rights rest on elaborate empirical studies demonstrating beyond any conceivable doubt that deterrent effects exist."

Justice Stewart described the procedure by which a qualified privilege could be administered:

> I would hold that the government must (1) show that there is probable cause to believe that the newsman has information which is clearly relevant to a specific probable violation of law; (2) demonstrate that the information sought cannot be obtained by alternative means less destructive of First Amendment rights; (3) demonstrate a compelling and overriding interest in the information. This is not to say that a grand jury could not issue its subpoena until such a

showing were made, and it is not to say that a newsman would in any way be privileged to ignore any subpoena that was issued. Obviously, before the government's burden to make such a showing were triggered, the reporter would have to move to quash the subpoena, asserting the basis on which he considered the particular relationship a confidential one.

NOTES

1. *The effect of Branzburg.* Justice Powell's pivotal concurring opinion provided the crucial fifth vote in *Branzburg*. Though the outlines of Powell's protective order procedure are unclear, his opinion does suggest that the *Branzburg* doctrine of no First Amendment-based judicially created journalist's privilege is not as absolute a bar as it might appear.

Justice Powell suggested a balancing of interests. The Stewart threefold inquiry, although set forth in a dissent, has had significant influence. In the post-*Branzburg* era, most states and federal circuits have recognized a First Amendment based journalist's privilege in contexts other than grand jury subpoenas.. On its facts, *Branzburg* represented a defeat for a First Amendment based journalist's privilege, yet the actual impact of the decision has been to give life in the lower courts to a First Amendment-based privilege, particularly on the civil side. The Stewart dissent in *Branzburg* has provided an analytical basis for these developments.

2. *Other confidential relationships.* The Court has not been willing to reconsider the rejection of a First Amendment-based journalist's privilege in *Branzburg*. In *University of Pennsylvania v. EEOC,* 493 U.S. 411 (1990), a unanimous Supreme Court, per Justice Blackmun, held *inter alia*, that a university's failure in a Title VII case before the Equal Employment Opportunity Commission (EEOC) to disclose relevant "confidential peer review information," acquired during tenure review, was not protected under the First Amendment: "We were unwilling [in *Branzburg*] as we are today, to embark the judiciary on a long and difficult journey to an uncertain destination."

3. *Cohen v. Cowles Media Co.,* 501 U.S. 663 (1991). This case presented a reverse twist on the journalist privilege problem. Cohen, who was in the advertising business and was a political operative for the Republican Party, offered some reporters some hitherto unknown information about the arrest record of the Democratic candidate for Lieutenant-Governor. The offer was made upon the condition that the reporters would keep his identity secret.

Although the reporters made such a promise to Cohen, their editors refused to honor the promise. The editors considered the identity of the source more newsworthy than the relatively minor arrests which Cohen had disclosed. Upon publication of his identity Cohen was fired from his advertising agency. Cohen sued the newspapers who had breached their promise to him. Justice White spoke for a sharply divided Court:

> The question before us is whether the First Amendment prohibits a plaintiff from recovering damages, under state promissory estoppel law, for a newspaper's breach of a promise of confidentiality given to the plaintiff in exchange for information. We hold that it does not.

The media defendants had argued that *Florida Star* had established that the state may not constitutionally punish publication of lawfully acquired information. Justice White disagreed:

> This case, however, is not controlled by this line of cases but rather by the equally well-established line of decisions holding that generally applicable laws do not offend the First Amendment simply because their enforcement against the press has incidental effects on its ability to gather and report the news. [T]he truthful information sought to be published must have been lawfully acquired. The press may not with impunity break and enter an office or dwelling to gather news. Neither does the First Amendment relieve a newspaper reporter of the obligation shared by all citizens to respond to a grand jury subpoena and answer questions relevant to a criminal investigation, even though the reporter might be required to reveal a confidential source. *Branzburg v. Hayes.*

Justice Souter, joined by Justices Marshall, Blackmun and O'Connor, dissented. The state interest in enforcing "a newspaper's promise of confidentiality" was "insufficient to outweigh the interest in unfettered publication of the information revealed in this case." But for the Court, "[t]he parties themselves determine the scope of their legal obligations, and any restrictions which may be placed on the publication of truthful information are self-imposed."

Is there a First Amendment interest at stake in *Cohen* besides the right of the press to publish truthful information? "There are First Amendment interests in protecting both confidentiality and publication. *Cohen* represents a collision between these two First Amendment interests. None of the opinions [in *Cohen*] acknowledged that the First Amendment interests in securing an unclogged information flow may be hampered by refusing to enforce promises to sources to keep their identities confidential." Jerome Barron, *Cohen v. Cowles Media and Its Significance for First Amendment Law and Journalism*, 3 Wm.& Mary Bill of Rts. L.J. 419, 463 (1994). The First Amendment protects "freedom of the press" but who is the press? Was the press in *Cohen* the reporters who wished to honor the promise they had made to Dan Cohen, or was it the editors who did not wish to do so? *Id.* at 454.

Is the First Amendment status of newsgathering affected by the conduct of the newsgatherers? Consider the following: "Although there was nothing unlawful about the newsgathering activity at issue, the [*Cohen*] majority was not ready to give its imprimatur to the newspaper's conduct. [T]he *Cohen* majority [hints that it] saw the matter of newsgathering conduct as potentially relevant to resolving a close case, even where that conduct could surely not be called 'unlawful' in any conventional sense." Robert O'Neil, *Tainted Sources, First Amendment Rights and Journalistic Wrongs*, 4 Wm. & Mary Bill of Rts. L. J. 1005, 1012 (1996). *Cohen* raises the issue of First Amendment concerns over contractual liability resulting from the newsgathering process. Most of the cases, however, have involved "newsgathering torts." *See* Dienes, Levine & Lind, at chs. 13-15.

4. ***Wilson v. Layne*, 526 U.S. 603 (1999).** During the execution of an arrest warrant, Deputy United States Marshals and Montgomery County, Maryland police officers invited a newspaper reporter and a photographer from the WASHINGTON POST to accompany them, on a "media ride along." The media personnel entered the home of Charles and Geraldine Wilson to observe and photograph the execution of the warrant, but they did not participate in the execution of the warrant nor did they assist the law enforcement officers in any way.

The Wilsons sued the federal law enforcement officers in their personal capacities for damages. Suit was brought against the federal officials under *Bivens v. Six Unknown Federal Narcotics Agents,* 403 U.S. 388 (1871), and suit was brought against local law enforcement personnel under 42 U.S.C. § 1983. The Wilsons contended that by bringing members of the media into their home to observe and record the execution of an arrest warrant the law enforcement officials had violated their Fourth Amendment rights. Speaking for the Court, Chief Justice Rehnquist agreed: "We hold that such a 'media ride along' does violate the Fourth Amendment, but that because the state of the law was not clearly established at the time the search in this case took place, the officers are entitled to the defense of qualified immunity. While the Court recognized that the press has an important role in informing the public about the criminal justice systems, "[t]he Fourth Amendment also protects a very important right and in the present case it is in terms of that right that the media ride-alongs must be judged."

Good police public relations cannot justify a media ride-along intrusion into a private home. Even the need for accurate reporting about the police "bears no direct relation to the constitutional justification for the police intrusion into a home in order to execute a felony arrest warrant." The Court ruled that it was a violation of the Fourth Amendment for police officers to bring the media or other third parties into a home during the execution of a warrant when their presence "was not in aid of the execution of the warrant." What if the search involves a business rather than a home?

[2] Press Access to Government Institutions

RICHMOND NEWSPAPERS, INC. v. VIRGINIA
448 U.S. 555, 100 S. Ct. 2814, 65 L. Ed. 2d 973 (1980)

CHIEF JUSTICE BURGER announced the judgment of the Court and delivered an opinion in which JUSTICES WHITE and STEVENS joined.

The narrow question presented in this case is whether the right of the public and press to attend criminal trials is guaranteed under the United States Constitution.

In March 1976, one Stevenson was indicted for the murder of a hotel manager who had been found stabbed to death on December 2, 1975. Tried promptly in July 1976, Stevenson was convicted of second-degree murder in the Circuit Court of Hanover County, Va. The Virginia Supreme Court reversed the conviction in October 1977, holding that a bloodstained shirt purportedly belonging to Stevenson had been improperly admitted into evidence. [Two more trials followed.] Stevenson was tried in the same court for a fourth time beginning on September 11, 1978. Present in the courtroom when the case was called were appellants Wheeler and McCarthy, reporters for appellant Richmond Newspapers, Inc. Before the trial began, counsel for the defendant moved that it be closed to the public.

The trial judge, who had presided over two of the three previous trials, asked if the prosecution had any objection to clearing the courtroom. The prosecutor stated he had no objection and would leave it to the discretion of the court. Presumably referring to Virginia Code § 19.2-266, the trial judge then announced: "[T]he statute gives me that power specifically and the defendant has made the motion." He then ordered "that the Courtroom be kept clear of all parties except the witnesses when they testify."[2] The record does not show that any objections to the closure order were made by anyone present at the time, including appellants Wheeler and McCarthy. Later that same day, however, appellants sought a hearing on a motion to vacate the closure order. The trial judge granted the request and scheduled a hearing to follow the close of the day's proceedings. When the hearing began, the court ruled that the hearing was to be treated as part of the trial; accordingly, he again ordered the reporters to leave the courtroom, and they complied.

At the closed hearing, counsel for appellants observed that no evidentiary findings had been made by the court prior to the entry of its closure order and pointed out that the court had failed to consider any other, less drastic measures within its power to ensure a fair trial. Counsel for appellants argued that constitutional considerations mandated that before ordering closure, the court should first decide that the rights of the defendant could be protected in no other way.

Counsel for defendant Stevenson pointed out that this was the fourth time he was standing trial. He also referred to "difficulty with information between jurors," and stated that he "didn't want information to leak out," be published by the media, perhaps inaccurately, and then be seen by the jurors. Defense counsel argued that these things, plus the fact that "this is a small community," made this a proper case for closure. The court denied the motion to vacate and ordered the trial to continue the following morning "with the press and public excluded."

[T]he Virginia Supreme Court, finding no reversible error, denied the petition for appeal.

We begin consideration of this case by noting that the precise issue presented here has not previously been before this Court for decision. In *Gannett Co. v. DePasquale,* 443 U.S. 368 (1979), the Court was not required to decide whether a right of access to trials, as distinguished from hearing on pre trial motions, was constitutionally guaranteed. The Court held that the Sixth Amendment's guarantee to the accused of a public trial gave neither

[2] Virginia Code § 19.2-266 provides in part:

> In the trial of all criminal cases, whether the same be felony or misdemeanor cases, the court may, in its discretion, exclude from the trial any persons whose presence would impair the conduct of a fair trial, provided that the right of the accused to a public trial shall not be violated.

the public nor the press an enforceable right of access to a pretrial suppression hearing. But here for the first time the Court is asked to decide whether a criminal trial itself may be closed to the public upon the unopposed request of a defendant, without any demonstration that closure is required to protect the defendant's superior right to a fair trial, or that some other overriding consideration requires closure.

[The Court's historical summary is omitted.]

In earlier times, both in England and America, attendance at court was a common mode of "passing the time." With the press, cinema, and electronic media now supplying the representations or reality of the real life drama once available only in the courtroom, attendance at court is no longer a widespread pastime. Instead of acquiring information about trials by firsthand observation or by word of mouth from those who attended, people now acquire it chiefly through the print and electronic media. In a sense, this validates the media claim of functioning as surrogates for the public. While media representatives enjoy the same right of access as the public, they often are provided special seating and priority of entry so that they may report what people in attendance have seen and heard. This "contribute[s] to public understanding of the rule of law and to comprehension of the functioning of the entire criminal justice system." *Nebraska Press Assn. v. Stuart* (BRENNAN, J., concurring).

From this unbroken, uncontradicted history, supported by reasons as valid today as in centuries past, we are bound to conclude that a presumption of openness inheres in the very nature of a criminal trial under our system of justice. This conclusion is hardly novel; without a direct holding on the issue, the Court has voiced its recognition of it in a variety of contexts over the years. Despite the history of criminal trials being presumptively open since long before the Constitution, the State presses its contention that neither the Constitution nor the Bill of Rights contains any provision which by its terms guarantees to the public the right to attend criminal trials. Standing alone, this is correct, but there remains the question whether, absent an explicit provision, the Constitution affords protection against exclusion of the public from criminal trials.

The Bill of Rights was enacted against the backdrop of the long history of trials being presumptively open. Public access to trials was then regarded as an important aspect of the process itself. In guaranteeing freedoms such as those of speech and press, the First Amendment can be read as protecting the right of everyone to attend trials so as to give meaning to those explicit guarantees. Free speech carries with it some freedom to listen. What this means in the context of trials is that the First Amendment guarantees of speech and press, standing alone, prohibit government from summarily closing courtroom doors which had long been open to the public at the time that amendment was adopted.

It is not crucial whether we describe this right to attend criminal trials to hear, see, and communicate observations concerning them as a "right of access," *cf. Gannett* (POWELL, J., concurring); *Saxbe v. Washington Post Co.*; *Pell v. Procunier*, or a "right to gather information," for we have recognized that "without some protection for seeking out the news, freedom of the press could be eviscerated." *Branzburg v. Hayes*. The explicit, guaranteed rights to speak and to publish concerning what takes place at a trial would lose much meaning if access to observe the trial could, as it was here, be foreclosed arbitrarily.

We hold that the right to attend criminal trials is implicit in the guarantees of the First Amendment; without the freedom to attend such trials, which people have exercised for centuries, important aspects of freedom of speech and "of the press could be eviscerated." *Branzburg*.

Having concluded there was a guaranteed right of the public under the First and Fourteenth Amendments to attend the trial of Stevenson's case, we return to the closure order challenged by appellants. The Court in *Gannett* made clear that although the Sixth Amendment guarantees the accused a right to a public trial, it does not give a right to a private trial. Despite the fact that this was the fourth trial of the accused, the trial judge made no findings to support closure; no inquiry was made as to whether alternative solutions would have met the need to ensure fairness; there was no recognition of any right under the Constitution for the public or press to attend the trial. In contrast to the pretrial proceeding dealt with in *Gannett*, there exist in the context of the trial itself various tested alternatives to satisfy the constitutional demands of fairness. *See, e.g.*, *Nebraska Press Association v. Stuart*; *Sheppard v. Maxwell*. There was no suggestion that any problems with witnesses could not have been dealt with by their exclusion from the courtroom or their sequestration during the trial. Nor is there anything to indicate that sequestration of the jurors would not have guarded against their being subjected to any improper information. All of the alternatives admittedly present difficulties for trial courts, but none of the factors relied on here was beyond the realm of the manageable. Absent an overriding interest articulated in findings, the trial of a criminal case must be open to the public.[18]

JUSTICE REHNQUIST, dissenting.

For the reasons stated in my separate concurrence in *Gannett Co., Inc. v. DePasquale*, I do not believe that either the First or Sixth Amendments, as made applicable to the States by the Fourteenth, require that a State's reasons for denying public access to a trial, where both the prosecuting attorney and the defendant have consented to an order of closure approved by the judge, are subject to any additional constitutional review at our hands. The issue here is not whether the "right" to freedom of the press conferred by the First Amendment to the Constitution overrides the defendant's "right" to a fair trial conferred by other amendments to the Constitution; it is instead whether any provision in the Constitution may fairly be read to prohibit what the trial judge in the Virginia state court system did in this case. Being unable to find any such prohibition in the First, Sixth, Ninth, or any other Amendments to the United States Constitution, or in the Constitution itself, I dissent.

---

[18] We have no occasion here to define the circumstances in which all or parts of a criminal trial may be closed to the public, but our holding today does not mean that the First Amendment rights of the public and representatives of the press are absolute. Just as a government may impose reasonable time, place, and manner restrictions upon the use of its streets in the interest of such objectives as the free flow of traffic, *see, e.g.*, *Cox v. New Hampshire*, so may a trial judge, in the interest of the fair administration of justice, impose reasonable limitations on access to a trial.

NOTES

1. *Press-Enterprise Co. v. Superior Court [Press-Enterprise II],* 478 U.S. 1 (1986). The Court held, per Chief Justice Burger, that a qualified First Amendment right of access to criminal proceedings applied to preliminary hearings as conducted in California. Robert Diaz, a nurse, was charged with murdering 12 patients by administering massive doses of the heart drug lidocaine. A preliminary hearing was held at which Dianz moved to exclude the public from the proceedings. A California statute, Cal. Penal Code § 868, required such proceedings to be open unless exclusion of the public is deemed necessary "to protect the defendant's right to a fair and impartial trial." The magistrate granted the motion on the ground that closure was necessary in view of the national publicity. A 41-day preliminary hearing was held during which time the state presented medical and scientific evidence. Press-Enterprise Co. asked that the transcript of the proceedings be released at the close of the preliminary hearing. The request was refused and the record was sealed. The California Supreme Court held that there was no First Amendment right of access to preliminary hearings. The California court "reasoned that the right of access to criminal proceedings recognized in *Press-Enterprise Co. v. Superior Court,* 464 U.S. 501 (1984) (*Press-Enterprise I*) [selection of jurors] extended only to actual criminal trials."

The United States Supreme Court reversed and held that the California Supreme Court failed to consider the First Amendment right of access to criminal proceedings. Chief Justice Burger declared:

> The considerations that led the Court to apply the First Amendment right of access to criminal trials in *Richmond Newspapers* and *Globe* and the selection of jurors in *Press-Enterprise I* lead us to conclude that the right of access applies to preliminary hearings as conducted in California. Since a qualified First Amendment right of access attaches to preliminary hearings in California, the proceedings cannot be closed unless specific, on the record findings are made demonstrating that "closure is essential to preserve higher values and is narrowly tailored to serve that interest." *Press-Enterprise I. See also Globe Newspaper*. If the interest asserted is the right of the accused to a fair trial, the preliminary hearing shall be closed only if specific findings are made demonstrating that first, there is a substantial probability that the defendant's right to a fair trial will be prejudiced by publicity that closure would prevent and, second, reasonable alternatives to closure cannot adequately protect the defendant's free trial rights.

Justice Stevens, joined by Justice Rehnquist, dissented in part: "[T]he Court reverses — without comment or explanation or any attempt at reconciliation — the holding in *Gannett* that a 'reasonable probability of prejudice' is enough to overcome the First Amendment right of access to a preliminary proceeding."

2. *The test for openness.* As the cases discussed in this section illustrate, it has been difficult for the Court to identify those parts of the process which should be open and those which should not. If the criminal trial is to be open, is that true as well for the preliminary hearing? What about the *voir dire*?

Indeed, what about the jury room itself? "The fashioning of a First Amendment-based right to public access to judicial proceedings has generally involved application of a two-part inquiry designed to determine if the press and public enjoy a presumptive right to be present. First, there is the historical inquiry: 'whether the place and process have historically been open to the press and general public.' Second, there is the functional inquiry: 'whether public access plays a significant positive role in the functioning of the particular process in question.' This judicial emphasis on tradition and function mirrors the methodology traditionally employed in constitutional due process analysis." Should the absence of a tradition of openness be dispositive that no public right of access exists? In the functional part of the test, should the focus be on the value of access to the functioning of the proceeding in question or on "the public interest in information concerning public affairs." DIENES, LEVINE & LIND, at § 2.02.

[C] ACCESS TO THE MEDIA

[1] A Right of Access to the Electronic Media?

RED LION BROADCASTING CO. v. FCC

395 U.S. 367, 89 S. Ct. 1794, 23 L. Ed. 2d 371 (1969)

JUSTICE WHITE delivered the opinion of the Court.

The Federal Communications Commission has for many years imposed on radio and television broadcasters the requirement that discussion of public issues be presented on broadcast stations, and that each side of those issues must be given fair coverage. This is known as the fairness doctrine, which originated very early in the history of broadcasting and has maintained its present outlines for some time. It is an obligation whose content has been defined in a long series of FCC rulings in particular cases, and which is distinct from the statutory requirement of § 315 of the Communications Act that equal time be allotted all qualified candidates for public office.

The broadcasters challenge the fairness doctrine and its specific manifestations in the personal attack and political editorial rules on conventional First Amendment grounds, alleging that the rules abridge their freedom of speech and press. Their contention is that the First Amendment protects their desire to use their allotted frequencies continuously to broadcast whatever they choose, and to exclude whomever they choose from ever using that frequency. No man may be prevented from saying or publishing what he thinks, or from refusing in his speech or other utterances to give equal weight to the views of his opponents. This right, they say, applies equally to broadcasters.

It would be strange if the First Amendment, aimed at protecting and furthering communications, prevented the Government from making radio communication possible by requiring licenses to broadcast and by limiting the number of licenses so as not to overcrowd the spectrum. No one has a First Amendment right to a license or to monopolize a radio frequency; to deny a station license because "the public interest" requires it "is not a denial of free speech." *National Broadcasting Co. v. United States,* 319 U.S. 190, 227 (1943).

There is nothing in the First Amendment which prevents the Government from requiring a licensee to share his frequency with others and to conduct himself as a proxy or fiduciary with obligations to present those views and voices which are representative of his community and which would otherwise, by necessity, be barred from the airwaves.

This is not to say that the First Amendment is irrelevant to public broadcasting. On the contrary, it has a major role to play as the Congress itself recognized in § 326, which forbids FCC interference with "the right of free speech by means of radio communication." Because of the scarcity of radio frequencies, the Government is permitted to put restraints on licensees in favor of others whose views should be expressed on this unique medium. But the people as a whole retain their interest in free speech by radio and their collective right to have the medium function consistently with the ends and purposes of the First Amendment. It is the right of the viewers and listeners, not the right of the broadcasters, which is paramount. It is the purpose of the First Amendment to preserve an uninhibited marketplace of ideas in which truth will ultimately prevail, rather than to countenance monopolization of that market, whether it be by the Government itself or a private licensee. It is the right of the public to receive suitable access to social, political, esthetics, moral, and other ideas and experiences which is crucial here. That right may not constitutionally be abridged either by Congress or by the FCC.

Nor can we say that it is inconsistent with the First Amendment goal of producing an informed public capable of conducting its own affairs to require a broadcaster to permit answers to personal attacks occurring in the course of discussing controversial issues, or to require that the political opponents of those endorsed by the station be given a chance to communicate with the public. Otherwise, station owners and a few networks would have unfettered power to make time available only to the highest bidders, to communicate only their own views on public issues, people and candidates, and to permit on the air only those with whom they agreed. There is no sanctuary in the First Amendment for unlimited private censorship operating in a medium not open to all. "Freedom of the press from governmental interference under the First Amendment does not sanction repression of that freedom by private interests."

[I]f present licensees should suddenly prove timorous, the Commission is not powerless to insist that they give adequate and fair attention to public issues. It does not violate the First Amendment to treat licensees given the privilege of using scarce radio frequencies as proxies for the entire community, obligated to give suitable time and attention to matters of great public concern. To condition the granting or renewal of licenses on a willingness to present representative community views on controversial issues is consistent with the ends and purposes of those constitutional provisions forbidding the abridgment of freedom of speech and freedom of the press. Congress need not stand idly by and permit those with licenses to ignore the problems which beset the people or to exclude from the airways anything but their own views of fundamental questions.

NOTES

1. ***Separate First Amendment Model for Broadcasting?*** The *Red Lion* case is often contrasted with *Miami Herald Publishing Co. v. Tornillo, infra*, p. 1302, to signify that there are different First Amendment models for different media. The *Red Lion* case is said to signify deference to government regulation of the broadcast media and the *Tornillo* case is said to signify that heightened review is the appropriate approach to First Amendment challenges to government regulation of the print media.

For a powerful assault on the idea of a separate First Amendment model for broadcasting, consider the following critique: "Perhaps the most persuasive explanation for the Broadcast Model's persistence has its roots in public choice theory. A growing body of scholarship has argued that the current structure of broadcast regulation is the product of rent seeking. Unlike other users of spectrum based technologies, broadcasters receive their licenses for free. In addition, [t]he FCC has adopted policies that have restricted entry in a manner that has enhanced the values of those licenses still further. By creating such rents, Congress was able to protect politicians against any adverse impact that television might have over elections. The tremendous benefits that broadcasters receive from this arrangement led them not to challenge the imposition of such regulations in most cases. Broadcasters are all too aware that the elimination of such public interest obligations would destroy any justification for continuing to receive benefits." Christopher S. Yoo, *The Rise and Demise of the Technology-Specific Approach to the First Amendment*, 91 GEO. L.J. 245 (2003). Doesn't the *Red Lion* case itself indicate that broadcasters *do* challenge government regulation and are not necessarily willing participants in the "bargain" that Professor Yoo describes?

Should we have First Amendment parity — one First Amendment standard for all media? Or should we have a separate standard for each new medium of communication? For further discussion of this issue, see the *Denver Area case, infra*.

2. ***Fate of the Fairness Doctrine.*** On August 4, 1987, the FCC abolished the fairness doctrine. The decision was upheld by the United States Court of Appeals for the District of Columbia. *Syracuse Peace Council v. FCC,* 867 F.2d 654 (D.C. Cir. 1989). However, the decision was not based on First Amendment grounds but on the ground that "the FCC's decision that the Fairness Doctrine no longer served the public interest was neither arbitrary, capricious nor an abuse of discretion."

COLUMBIA BROADCASTING SYSTEM v. DEMOCRATIC NATIONAL COMMITTEE

412 U.S. 94, 93 S. Ct. 2080, 36 L. Ed. 2d 772 (1973)

[The Democratic National Committee and the Business Executives Move for Vietnam Peace sought unsuccessfully to buy time from broadcasters for the exposition of social and political issues. The DNC asked the FCC to issue a declaratory ruling that "under the First Amendment, a broadcaster may not, as a general policy, refuse to sell time to responsible entities such as the DNC, for the solicitation of funds and for comment on public issues." The FCC refused to issue such a ruling. The court of appeals reversed, held that a "broadcaster's fixed policy of refusing editorial advertisements violates the First Amendment," and remanded to the FCC "to develop procedures and guidelines for administering a First Amendment right of access."

The Supreme Court, per CHIEF JUSTICE BURGER, reversed the court of appeals and held that a broadcaster who meets the fairness doctrine obligation has no duty under either the First Amendment or the Federal Communications Act to accept editorial advertisements.]

CHIEF JUSTICE BURGER delivered the opinion of the Court.

The Commission was justified in concluding that the public interest in providing access to the marketplace of "ideas and experiences" would scarcely be served by a system so heavily weighted in favor of the financially affluent, or those with access to wealth. Even under a first-come-first-served system, proposed by the dissenting Commissioner in these cases, the views of the affluent could well prevail over those of others, since they would have it within their power to purchase time more frequently. Moreover, there is the substantial danger, as the Court of Appeals acknowledged, that the time allotted for editorial advertising could be monopolized by those of one political persuasion. Nor can we accept the Court of Appeals' view that every potential speaker is "the best judge" of what the listening public ought to hear or indeed the best judge of the merits of his or her views. All journalistic tradition and experience is to the contrary. For better or worse, editing is what editors are for; and editing is selection and choice of material. That editors — newspaper or broadcast — can and do abuse this power is beyond doubt, but that is not reason to deny the discretion Congress provided. Calculated risks of abuse are taken in order to preserve higher values. It was reasonable for Congress to conclude that the public interest in being informed requires periodic accountability on the part of those who are entrusted with the use of broadcast frequencies, scarce as they are. In the delicate balancing historically followed in the regulation of broadcasting Congress and the Commission could appropriately conclude that the allocation of journalistic priorities should be concentrated in the licensee rather than diffused among many. This policy gives the public some assurance that the broadcaster will be answerable if he fails to meet their legitimate needs. No such accountability attaches to the private individual, whose only qualifications for using the broadcast facility may be abundant funds and a point of view. To agree that debate on public issues should be "robust and wide-open" does not mean that we should exchange "public trustee" broadcasting, with all its limitations, for a system of self-appointed editorial commentators. By minimizing the difficult problems involved in implementing such a right or access, the Court of Appeals failed to come to grips with another problem of critical importance to broadcast regulation and the First Amendment — the risk of an enlargement of government control over the content of broadcast discussion of public issues. Under the Fairness Doctrine the Commission's responsibility is to judge whether a licensee's overall performance indicates a sustained good faith effort to meet the public interest in being fully and fairly informed. The Commission's responsibilities under a right-of-access system would tend to draw it into a continuing case-by-case determination of who should be heard and when.

[JUSTICE BRENNAN, joined by JUSTICE MARSHALL, dissented.]

NOTES

1. *Private and public censorship.* Justice Brennan in dissent in *CBS* thought the massive governmental regulation of broadcasting so intertwined the activities of "private broadcasters" with government as to suffuse broadcasters with the First Amendment obligations we demand of government.

To the emphasis on journalistic discretion, which the Court said would be threatened by requiring acceptance of editorial advertising, Justice Brennan replied that journalistic discretion, if it is unaccompanied by no access obligations, may perpetuate as much censorship as it is supposed to thwart. In fact, Brennan pointed out that the briefs to the Court demonstrate that private censorship by the networks is a continuing reality:

> The briefs of the broadcaster-petitioners in this case illustrate the type of "journalistic discretion" licensees now exercise in this regard. Thus ABC suggests that it would refuse to air those views which it considers "scandalous" or "crackpot," while CBS would exclude those issues as "insignificant" or "trivial." Similarly, NBC would bar speech that strays "beyond the bounds of normally accepted taste" and WTOP would protect the public from subjects that are "slight, parochial or inappropriate."

Does the application of an eighteenth century conception of freedom of the press to network programming policies make sense?

Isn't the result in *CBS v. DNC* inconsistent with the idea that public or political speech is the core area of First Amendment protection? Does *CBS v. DNC* suggest that public or political speech has no specific First Amendment claim to network time? A blanket restriction on the sale of such time was held to be permissible under the First Amendment. Are the First Amendment implications of the result in *CBS v. DNC* completely answered by saying that the networks are private not public and, therefore, not subject to First Amendment requirements?

2. *CBS v. DNC — A Case of Competing First Amendment Rights?* One of the editors of this casebook has made the following analysis of *CBS v. DNC*:

"[T]he networks particularly attacked the position of the access claimants that they had a First Amendment right of access to the electronic media. The networks argued the First Amendment supported them, not the access claimants. The right of access, the networks contended, was completely at odds with the exercise of editorial judgement, which was certainly protected by the First Amendment. It did not occur to the network lawyers that both the access claimants and the networks might each have a claim to First Amendment protection. The significance and the difficulty of the access issue lies in the fact that it presents a case of competing First Amendment rights." Jerome A. Barron, *Creating A New First Amendment Right, Miami Herald Publishing Co., and the Story of Access to the Media*, in Joseph Russomano (ed.) DEFENDING THE FIRST: COMMENTARY ON FIRST AMENDMENT ISSUES AND CASES 1–22 (2005).

3. *Columbia Broadcasting System v. FCC,* 453 U.S. 367 (1981). The Court per Chief Justice Burger considered the First Amendment validity of § 312(a)(7) of the Communications Act, which provides that the FCC may revoke any license or construction permit for "willful or repeated failure to allow reasonable access" or "purchase of reasonable amounts of time by a legally qualified federal political candidate." The Carter administration had sought time for a 30-minute program between 8:00 p.m. and 10:30 p.m. in the early part of December, 1979, from the three major television networks. The networks declined to make the requested time available. Accordingly, the Carter/Mondale Presidential Committee filed a complaint under § 312(a)(7) with the FCC. The FCC ruled that the networks had violated the statute and the court of appeals affirmed. The Supreme Court affirmed the court of appeals and held that § 312(a)(7) did more than codify a generalized public interest standard and required broadcasters "to respond to the individualized situation of a particular candidate."

> Petitioners are correct that the Court has never approved a general right of access to the media. *See, e.g., Miami Herald Publishing Co. v. Tornillo*; *CBS, Inc. v. Democratic National Committee.* Nor do we do so today. Section 312 (a)(7) creates a limited right to "reasonable" access that pertains only to legally qualified federal candidates and may be invoked by them only for the purpose of advancing their candidacies once a campaign has commenced. The Commission has stated that, in enforcing the statute, it will "provide leeway to broadcasters and not merely attempt de novo to determine the reasonableness of their judgments." If broadcasters have considered the relevant factors in good faith, the Commission will uphold their decisions.

The Court distinguishes a general right of access to the media, which it says it has never approved, from a limited statutory right of "reasonable" access, which it does approve. What are the distinguishing factors? The First Amendment interest of candidates and voters would be relevant in a general right of access context, as well as a limited right. Is the point that the specific right of access does less violence to the First Amendment rights of broadcasters?

4. *Ownership and control.* In the case of the electronic media, the Court has not been as hostile to the development of governmentally enforced procedures to assure a marketplace of ideas as it has in the print media. Thus, in *FCC v. National Citizens Comm. for Broadcasting,* 436 U.S. 775 (1978), the Supreme Court ruled, per Justice Marshall, that a prospective FCC ban on common ownership of newspapers and broadcast stations in the same community did not violate the First Amendment. There is no unabridgeable first amendment right to broadcast, because the inherent limitations of the broadcast spectrum require allocation and regulation of stations:

> [E]fforts to " 'enhanc[e] the volume and quality of coverage' of public issues" through regulation of broadcasting may be permissible where similar efforts to regulate the print media would not be. *Red Lion Broadcasting Co. v. FCC*; compare *Miami Herald Publishing Co. v. Tornillo.* Here the regulations are not content-related; moreover, their purpose and effect is to promote free speech, not to restrict it.

The ban was said to foster diversity of expression and encourage, rather than restrict, free speech. The FCC decision to limit the rule to prospective operation was not irrational.

5. *FCC v. League of Women Voters*, 4678 U.S. 364 (1984). The Supreme Court, per Justice Brennan, struck down a provision of the Public Broadcasting Act of 1967 barring noncommercial educational broadcasting stations receiving grants from the Corporation for Public Broadcasting from editorializing. The statute's sweeping ban was deemed to far exceed what was necessary "to protect against the risk of governmental interference or to prevent the public from assuming that editorials by public broadcasting stations represent the official view of government." The ban constituted a content control. But because broadcasting "operates under restraints not imposed upon other media," the Court applied an intermediate standard of review rather than strict scrutiny: "[W]e hold only that the specific interests sought to be advanced by the [statutory] ban on editorializing are either not sufficiently substantial or are not served in a sufficiently limited manner to justify the substantial abridgment of important journalistic freedoms which the First Amendment jealously protects."

Justice Stevens, dissenting, declared that the interest "in maintaining government neutrality in the free market of ideas" outweighed the "impact on expression" flowing from the statutory ban. Justice Rehnquist, joined by the Chief Justice and Justice White, dissented: "[B]ecause Congress' decision to enact [the statutory ban] is a rational exercise of its spending powers and is strictly neutral, I would hold that nothing in the First Amendment makes it unconstitutional."

Does *League of Women Voters* change the standard of review for content controls in broadcasting ?

[2] A Right of Access to the Print Media?

MIAMI HERALD PUBLISHING CO. v. TORNILLO
418 U.S. 241, 94 S. Ct. 2831, 39 L. Ed. 2d 1 (1974)

Chief Justice Burger delivered the opinion of the Court.

The issue in this case is whether a state statute granting a political candidate a right to equal space to reply to criticism and attacks on his record by a newspaper, violates the guarantees of a free press.

In the fall of 1972, appellee, Executive Director of the Classroom Teachers Association, apparently a teachers' collective-bargaining agent, was a candidate for the Florida House of Representatives. On September 20, 1972, and again on September 29, 1972, appellant printed editorials critical of appellee's candidacy. In response to these editorials appellee demanded that appellant print verbatim his replies, defending the role of the Classroom Teachers Association and the organization's accomplishments for the citizens of Dade County. Appellant declined to print the appellee's replies, and appellee brought suit in Circuit Court, Dade County, seeking declaratory and injunctive relief and actual and punitive damages in excess of $5,000. The action was premised on Florida Statute § 104.38, a "right of reply" statute which provides that if a candidate for nomination or election is assailed regarding his personal character or official record by any newspaper, the candidate has the right to demand that the newspaper print, free of cost to the candidate, any reply the candidate may make to the newspaper's charges. The reply must appear in as conspicuous a place and in the same kind of type as the charges which prompted the reply, provided it does not take up more space than the charges. Failure to comply with the statute constitutes a first-degree misdemeanor.

Appellant contends the statute is void on its face because it purports to regulate the content of a newspaper in violation of the First Amendment. Alternatively it is urged that the statute is void for vagueness since no editor could know exactly what words would call the statute into operation. It is also contended that the statute fails to distinguish between critical comment which is and is not defamatory.

The appellee and supporting advocates of an enforceable right of access to the press vigorously argue that Government has an obligation to ensure that a wide variety of views reach the public. The contentions of access proponents will be set out in some detail. It is urged that at the time the First Amendment to the Constitution was enacted in 1791 as part of our Bill of Rights the press was broadly representative of the people it was serving. While many of the newspapers were intensely partisan and narrow in their views, the press collectively presented a broad range of opinions to readers. Entry into publishing was inexpensive; pamphlets and books provided meaningful alternatives to the organized press for the expression of unpopular ideas and often treated events and expressed views not covered by conventional newspapers. A true marketplace of ideas existed in which there was relatively easy access to the channels of communication.

Access advocates submit that although newspapers of the present are superficially similar to those of 1791 the press of today is in reality very different from that known in the early years of our national existence. In the past half century a communications revolution has seen the introduction of radio and television into our lives, the promise of a global community through the use of communications satellites, and the spectre of a "wired" nation by means of an expanding cable television network with two-way capabilities. The printed press, it is said, has not escaped the effects of this revolution. Newspapers have become big business and there are far fewer of them to serve a larger literate population. Chains of newspapers, national newspapers, national wire and news services, and one-newspaper towns, are the dominant features of a press that has become noncompetitive and enormously powerful and influential in its capacity to manipulate popular opinion and change the course of events. Major metropolitan newspapers have collaborated to establish news services national in scope. Such national news organizations provide syndicated "interpretative reporting" as well as syndicated features and commentary, all of which can serve as part of the new school of "advocacy journalism."

The elimination of competing newspapers in most of our large cities, and the concentration of control of media that results from the only newspaper being owned by the same interests which own a television station and a radio station, are important components of this trend toward concentration of control of outlets to inform the public.

The result of these vast changes has been to place in a few hands the power to inform the American people and shape public opinion. Much of the editorial opinion and commentary that is printed is that of syndicated columnists distributed nationwide and, as a result, we are told, on national and world issues there tends to be a homogeneity of editorial opinion, commentary, and interpretative analysis. The abuses of bias and manipulative reportage are, likewise, said to be the result of the vast accumulations of unreviewable power in the modern media empires. In effect, it is claimed, the public has lost any ability to respond or to contribute in a meaningful way to the debate on issues. The monopoly of the means of communication allows for little or no critical analysis of the media except in professional journals of very limited readership.

[I]t is reasoned that the only effective way to insure fairness and accuracy and to provide for some accountability is for government to take affirmative action. The First Amendment interest of the public in being informed is said to be in peril because the "marketplace of ideas" is today a monopoly controlled by the owners of the market.

Proponents of enforced access to the press take comfort from language in several of this Court's decisions which suggests that the First Amendment acts as a sword as well as a shield, that it imposes obligations on the owners of the press in addition to protecting the press from government regulation. In *New York Times Co. v. Sullivan*, the Court spoke of "a profound national commitment to the principle that debate on public issues should be uninhibited, robust, and wide-open." It is argued that the "uninhibited, robust" debate is not "wide-open" but open only to a monopoly in control of the press. Appellee cites the plurality opinion in *Rosenbloom v. Metromedia, Inc.*, which he suggests seemed to invite experimentation by the States in right to access regulation of the press.[18]

However much validity may be found in these arguments, at each point the implementation of a remedy such as an enforceable right of access necessarily calls for some mechanism, either governmental or consensual. If it is governmental coercion, this at once brings about a confrontation with the express provisions of the First Amendment and the judicial gloss on that amendment developed over the years. [T]he Court has expressed sensitivity as to whether a restriction or requirement constituted the compulsion exerted by government on a newspaper to print that which it would not otherwise print. The clear implication has been that any such a compulsion to publish that which " 'reason' tells them should not be published" is unconstitutional. A responsible press is an undoubtedly desirable goal, but press responsibility is not mandated by the Constitution and like many other virtues it cannot be legislated.

Appellee's argument that the Florida statute does not amount to a restriction of appellant's right to speak because "the statute in question here has

[18] "If the States fear that private citizens will not be able to respond adequately to publicity involving them, the solution lies in the direction of ensuring their ability to respond, rather than in stifling public discussion of matters of public concern. Barron, *Access to the Press — A New First Amendment Right*, 80 HARV. L. REV. 1641, 1666–1678."

not prevented the Miami Herald from saying anything it wished" begs the core question. Compelling editors or publishers to publish that which " 'reason' tells them should not be published" is what is at issue in this case. The Florida statute operates as a command in the same sense as a statute or regulation forbidding appellant from publishing specified matter. Governmental restraint on publishing need not fall into familiar or traditional patterns to be subject to constitutional limitations on governmental powers. The Florida statute exacts a penalty on the basis of the content of a newspaper. The first phase of the penalty resulting from the compelled printing of a reply is exacted in terms of the cost in printing and composing time and materials and in taking up space that could be devoted to other material the newspapers may have preferred to print. It is correct, as appellee contends, that a newspaper is not subject to the finite technological limitations of time that confront a broadcaster but it is not correct to say that, as an economic reality, a newspaper can proceed to infinite expansion of its column space to accommodate the replies that a government agency determines or a statute commands the readers should have available.

Faced with the penalties that would accrue to any newspaper that published news or commentary arguably within the reach of the right of access statute, editors might well conclude that the safe course is to avoid controversy and that, under the operation of the Florida statute, political and electoral coverage would be blunted or reduced. Government enforced right of access inescapably "dampens the vigor and limits the variety of public debate," *New York Times Co. v. Sullivan*.

Even if a newspaper would face no additional costs to comply with a compulsory access law and would not be forced to forego publication of news or opinion by the inclusion of a reply, the Florida statute fails to clear the barriers of the First Amendment because of its intrusion into the function of editors. A newspaper is more than a passive receptacle or conduit for news, comment, and advertising. The choice of material to go into a newspaper, and the decisions made as to limitations on the size of the paper, and content, and treatment of public issues and public officials — whether fair or unfair — constitutes the exercise of editorial control and judgment. It has yet to be demonstrated how governmental regulation of this crucial process can be exercised consistent with First Amendment guarantees of a free press as they have evolved to this time. Accordingly, the judgment of the Supreme Court of Florida is reversed.

JUSTICE BRENNAN, with whom JUSTICE REHNQUIST joins, concurring.

I join the Court's opinion which, as I understand it, addresses only "right of reply" statutes and implies no view upon the constitutionality of "retraction" statutes affording plaintiffs able to prove defamatory falsehoods a statutory action to require publication of a retraction.

NOTES

1. ***Autonomy and diversity.*** One scholar has provided the following assessment of the *Tornillo* case:

> The Court's failure to accord any weight to the interest in diversity of expression, presumably protected by Florida statute, indicates the inadequacy of efforts to cast the first amendment solely in instrumental terms. The Court sees a core of principle in the first amendment from which it will not exact instrumental justification. If this view of *Miami Herald* is warranted, the decision represents a judicial preference for the principle of publisher autonomy over the competing policies of diversity of expression.

BENNO C. SCHMIDT, FREEDOM OF THE PRESS VS. PUBLIC ACCESS 237–38 (1976).

Schmidt's view is that *Tornillo* expresses an absolute preference for autonomy over the competing value of diversity of expression.

2. *Market dominance.* One of the editors of this casebook, Professor Barron, made the following argument in his brief to the Supreme Court in the *Tornillo* case on the inability of Pat Tornillo to obtain access to respond to the Miami Herald's editorial attacks on him:

> Absent the Florida right of reply statute, Tornillo would be effectively muzzled in Dade County, Florida. The facts of this case illustrate the loneliness of someone in a position like Tornillo's. When Tornillo sought to enforce his right to reply remedy in court, the Attorney General of the state of Florida announced his intention not to defend the statute. On appeal to the Supreme Court of Florida, the local ACLU chapter allied itself with the Herald. In this court, the amici on behalf of the Herald are almost impossible to count. Newspaper and broadcaster trade associations, newspaper chains, and other mass media ownership groups have all joined to protest Tornillo's attempt to enforce the Florida right of reply statute.

Professor Powe has responded to these concerns about market domination and unfairness in the press as follows:

> Beyond the chilling effect and the necessary infringement of autonomy, the idea of enforced fairness requires placing an amazing amount of faith in government decision-making to implement fairness.

Lucas Powe, *Tornillo*, 1987 S. CT. REV. 345, 363–64.

3. *A "reasonable" right of access to the print media?* Immediately after the *Tornillo* decision, it was argued that the case had not entirely foreclosed the question of mandatory access to the print media. *The Supreme Court, 1973 Term*, 88 HARV. L. REV. 41, 179–80 (1973). The reasoning was that, under *Tornillo*, compulsory access was only presumptively invalid rather than invalid per se. Possible consequences of this distinction were described as follows: "An interpretation of *Miami Herald* which makes compulsory access only presumptively unconstitutional could permit retraction statutes to be upheld if the important state interest in promoting the vindication of personal reputation was deemed sufficiently compelling."

Note that in *CBS v. FCC*, the Court upheld the reasonable access for federal political candidates provision of the Federal Communications Act on the ground that *Tornillo* intended to invalidate a general right of access statute but did not intend to invalidate specific rights of access legislation.

After *CBS v. DNC*, was the result in *Tornillo* inevitable? The *Miami Herald* in its brief and oral argument so contended. Appellee *Tornillo*, however, distinguished CBS and other pre-*Tornillo* access cases in its brief as follows:

> In the CBS case, at least as the FCC and the Supreme Court viewed the issues, nothing in the federal statutes or in FCC decision or regulations justified the recognition of a limited right of access to public television time. In other words, the access to editorial advertising claim was grounded on the First Amendment itself, there was no statute providing access rights.

Tornillo was distinguishable because in *Tornillo*, unlike CBS, there was a statutory basis for the access claim. Why wasn't *Red Lion* the relevant precedent for the disposition of the *Tornillo* case?

4. *The print and broadcast First Amendment models.* One commentator underscores the distinction between the two First Amendment models or approaches as reflected by the *Red Lion* and *Tornillo* decisions: "If the rights of the communication entity's owners were intended to trump all other claims to First Amendment protection for all media, *Tornillo* would have been the ideal occasion to make that statement. The *Tornillo* Court instead directed itself to the print media alone and did not so much as cite *Red Lion*, the most obvious contrary electronic media precedent then extant." Jerome A. Barron, *The Electronic Media and the Flight From First Amendment Doctrine: Justice Breyer's New Balancing Approach*, 31 U. Mich. J.L. Ref. 817, 870 (1998).

Professor Marvin Ammori agrees that there are two First Amendment traditions — a paper tradition and an electronic communications tradition. But he argues that the print or paper tradition is over-emphasized by law school casebooks while the electronic communications tradition "is ignored and harshly criticized." Ammori, *Another Worthy Tradition: How the Free Speech Curriculum Ignores Electronic Media and Distorts Free Speech Doctrine*, 70 Mo. L. Rev. 59, 60–61 (2005). Ammori says the objectives of these two traditions are in conflict. The "core doctrine" of the paper tradition "protects street corner speakers and pamphleteers." This print or paper focused tradition is animated by "an unwavering distrust of government." Paper tradition advocates "lament that its doctrine does not extend to electronic media, which receive what they call 'less' speech freedom. They have long attacked *Red Lion's* reasoning." *Id.* at 64–65. Ammori concludes: "The communications tradition conflicts with five central tenets of paper tradition. As law students learn, paper tradition posits: (1) equating structural regulation and content regulation; (2) a marked public/private distinction, with an indifference to supposedly private speech power; (3) a nearly fatal presumption against content-based speech regulations; (4) a consistent preference for clear rules over standards or balancing; and (5) little distinction between entities' and individuals' speech." *Id.* at 69. The focus of the communications tradition is on speech in the electronic media and on whether individuals actually have power to communicate: "Its primary aim is speech diversity not government distrust. Unlike paper tradition, it permits government constitutional leeway to adopt structural regulations." Such regulations usually favor public debate and seek to "advance social values like viewpoints diversity and localism." *Id.* at 64–65.

[3] Access in the Cable Context

[H]ow should the First Amendment implications of cable regulation be evaluated? Professor Daniel Brenner suggests that "the key to cable's first amendment regime lies in distinguishing, as reasonably as possible, among the expressive and nonexpressive activities of operators." Daniel Brenner, *Cable Television and the Freedom of Expression*, 1988 DUKE L.J. 329, 331. Such a "regime should provide the First Amendment protection when content-related expressive activities are involved and pull back that protection when such activities are not."

Assuming that the expressive activities of cable can be identified, what First Amendment model should be used to evaluate those activities. The *Tornillo* or newspaper model? The *Red Lion* or broadcast model? Some other model such as the *O'Brien* test?

TURNER BROADCASTING SYSTEM, INC. v. FCC
512 U.S. 622, 114 S. Ct. 2445, 129 L.Ed. 2d 497 (1994)

JUSTICE KENNEDY announced the judgment of the Court and delivered the opinion of the Court, except as to Part III-B.

Sections 4 and 5 of the Cable Television Consumer Protection and Competition Act of 1992 require cable television systems to devote a portion of their channels to the transmission of local broadcast television stations. This case presents the question whether these provisions abridge the freedom of speech or of the press, in violation of the First Amendment.

On October 5, 1992, Congress overrode a Presidential veto to enact the Cable Television Consumer Protection and Competition Act of 1992. At issue in this case is the constitutionality of the so-called must-carry provisions, which require cable operators to carry the signals of a specified number of local broadcast television stations.

There can be no disagreement on an initial premise: Cable programmers and cable operators engage in and transmit speech, and they are entitled to the protection of the speech and press provisions of the First Amendment. By requiring cable systems to set aside a portion of their channels for local broadcasters, the must-carry rules regulate cable speech in two respects: The rules reduce the number of channels over which cable operators exercise unfettered control, and they render it more difficult for cable programmers to compete for carriage on the limited channels remaining. Nevertheless, because not every interference with speech triggers the same degree of scrutiny under the First Amendment, we must decide at the outset the level of scrutiny applicable to the must-carry provisions.

We address first the Government's contention that regulation of cable television should be analyzed under the same First Amendment standard that applies to regulation of broadcast television. It is true that our cases have permitted more intrusive regulation of broadcast speakers than of speakers in other media. But the rationale for applying a less rigorous standard of First Amendment scrutiny to broadcast regulation, whatever its validity in the cases elaborating it, does not apply in the context of cable regulation.

[T]he inherent physical limitation on the number of speakers who may use the broadcast medium has been thought to require some adjustment in traditional First Amendment analysis to permit the Government to place limited content restraints, and impose certain affirmative obligations, on broadcast licensees. *Red Lion*.

Although courts and commentators have criticized the scarcity rationale since its inception, we have declined to question its continuing validity as support for our broadcast jurisprudence, and see no reason to do so here. The broadcast cases are inapposite in the present context because cable television does not suffer from the inherent limitations that characterize the broadcast medium. Indeed, given the rapid advances in fiber optics and digital compression technology, soon there may be no practical limitation on the number of speakers who may use the cable medium. Nor is there any danger of physical interference between two cable speakers attempting to share the same channel. In light of these fundamental technological differences between broadcast and cable transmission, application of the more relaxed standard of scrutiny adopted in *Red Lion* and the other broadcast cases is inapt when determining the First Amendment validity of cable regulation. Because the must-carry provisions impose special obligations upon cable operators and special burdens upon cable programmers, some measure of heightened First Amendment scrutiny is demanded.

Insofar as they pertain to the carriage of full power broadcasters, the must-carry rules, on their face, impose burdens and confer benefits without reference to the content of speech.

It is true that the must-carry provisions distinguish between speakers in the television programming market. But they do so based only upon the manner in which speakers transmit their messages to viewers, and not upon the messages they carry: Broadcasters, which transmit over the airwaves, are favored, while cable programmers, which do not, are disfavored. Cable operators, too, are burdened by the carriage obligations, but only because they control access to the cable conduit. So long as they are not a subtle means of exercising a content preference, speaker distinctions of this nature are not presumed invalid under the First Amendment.

By preventing cable operators from refusing carriage to broadcast television stations, the must-carry rules ensure that broadcast television stations will retain a large enough potential audience to earn necessary advertising revenue — or, in the case of noncommercial broadcasters, sufficient viewer contributions, to maintain their continued operation. In so doing, the provisions are designed to guarantee the survival of a medium that has become a vital part of the Nation's communication system, and to ensure that every individual with a television set can obtain access to free television programming.

Tornillo and *Pacific Gas & Electric* do not control this case. [U]nlike the access rules struck down in those cases, the must-carry rules are content-neutral in application. They are not activated by any particular message spoken by cable operators and thus exact no content-based penalty.

[T]he asserted analogy to *Tornillo* ignores an important technological difference between newspapers and cable television. [W]hen a newspaper asserts exclusive control over its own news copy, it does not thereby prevent other newspapers from being distributed to willing recipients in the same locale. The same is not true of cable. When an individual subscribes to cable, the physical connection between the television set and the cable network gives the cable operator bottleneck, or gatekeeper, control over most (if not all) of the television programming that is channeled into the subscriber's home. A cable operator, unlike speakers in other media, can thus silence the voice of competing speakers with a mere flick of the switch.

In sum, the must-carry provisions do not pose such inherent dangers to free expression, or present such potential for censorship or manipulation, as to justify application of the most exacting level of First Amendment scrutiny. We agree with the District Court that the appropriate standard by which to evaluate the constitutionality of must-carry is the intermediate level of scrutiny applicable to content-neutral restrictions that impose an incidental burden on speech.

To satisfy this standard, a regulation need not be the least speech-restrictive means of advancing the Government's interests. Narrow tailoring in this context requires, that the means chosen do not "burden substantially more speech than is necessary to further the government's legitimate interests."

Congress declared that the must-carry provisions serve three interrelated interests: (1) preserving the benefits of free, over-the-air local broadcast television, (2) promoting the widespread dissemination of information from a multiplicity of sources, and (3) promoting fair competition in the market for television programming. None of these interests is related to the "suppression of free expression," *O'Brien*, or to the content of any speakers' messages. And viewed in the abstract, we have no difficulty concluding that each of them is an important governmental interest.

III B

In defending the factual necessity for must-carry, the Government relies in principal part on Congress' legislative finding that, absent mandatory carriage rules, the continued viability of local broadcast television would be "seriously jeopardized."

We agree that courts must accord substantial deference to the predictive judgments of Congress. That Congress' predictive judgments are entitled to substantial deference does not mean, however, that they are insulated from meaningful judicial review altogether.

In sum, because there are genuine issues of material fact still to be resolved on this record, we hold that the District Court erred in granting summary judgment in favor of the Government. [W]e think it necessary to permit the parties to develop a more thorough factual record, and to allow the District Court to resolve any factual disputes remaining, before passing upon the constitutional validity of the challenged provisions.

JUSTICE STEVENS, concurring in part and concurring in the judgment.

The must-carry provisions are amply "justified by special characteristics of the cable medium," namely, "the bottleneck monopoly power exercised by cable operators and the dangers this power poses to the viability of broadcast television." Cable operators' control of essential facilities provides a basis for intrusive regulation that would be inappropriate and perhaps impermissible for other communicative media.

It is thus my view that we should affirm the judgment of the District Court. Were I to vote to affirm, however, no disposition of this appeal would command the support of a majority of the Court. Accordingly, because I am in substantial agreement with Justice Kennedy's analysis of the case, I concur in the judgment vacating and remanding for further proceedings.

JUSTICE O'CONNOR, with whom JUSTICES SCALIA and GINSBURG join, and with whom JUSTICE THOMAS joins [in part], concurring in part and dissenting in part.

Preferences for diversity of viewpoints, for localism, for educational programming, and for news and public affairs all make reference to content. They may not reflect hostility to particular points of view, or a desire to suppress certain subjects because they are controversial or offensive. They may be quite benignly motivated. But benign motivation, we have consistently held, is not enough to avoid the need for strict scrutiny of content-based justifications. The First Amendment does more than just bar government from intentionally suppressing speech of which it disapproves. It also generally prohibits the government from excepting certain kinds of speech from regulation because it thinks the speech is especially valuable.

This is why the Court is mistaken in concluding that the interest in diversity — in "access to a multiplicity" of "diverse and antagonistic sources" — is content neutral. The interest in ensuring access to a multiplicity of diverse and antagonistic sources of information, no matter how praiseworthy, is directly tied to the content of what the speakers will likely say.

Accordingly, I would reverse the judgment below.

NOTES

1. *Turner redivivus.* On remand, a three judge federal court held 2-1, that, using the *O'Brien* standard, there was substantial evidence justifying the congressional judgment that must-carry was necessary "to protect the economic health of the broadcast industry and that the burden to the cable industry would not be substantial." *Turner Broadcasting v. FCC,* 910 F. Supp. 734 (D.C. Cir. 1995).

2. *Turner critiqued.* A critical view of *Turner* is taken in Ashutosh Bhagwat, *Of Markets and Media: The First Amendment, the New Mass Media, and the Political Components of Culture*, 74 N.C. L. REV. 141, 200 (1995):

> [T]he Supreme Court decided *Turner* incorrectly. [T]he must-carry rules are designed systematically to favor speech of a particular content. [They] favor speech that is "local" in origin and give disproportionate coverage to local issues and points of view. [This] is sufficient

> to condemn the must carry rules as vehicles for an impermissible political preference on the part of Congress. [T]he rules interfere directly with market choices by coercing the carriage, and therefore the consumption of particular speech.

In a more sympathetic interpretation of *Turner*, Professor Baker asks for a distinction between the First Amendment treatment of legal regulation of individuals and media entities: "[L]aw has little role in structuring individuals. In contrast, Congressional conceptions of the public good ought to inform the inevitable choices in the manner of structuring legally created entities, and, often, [these conceptions] will include content-oriented judgments." Edwin Baker, *Turner Broadcasting: Content-Based Regulation of Persons and Presses*, 1994 SUP. CT. REV. 57, 62.

Whose description is more useful for First Amendment issues arising from emerging communications technology?

3. *Access in different media.* Professor Sunstein says that *Turner* "adopted ingredients of an entirely new model of the First Amendment." Cass Sunstein, *The First Amendment in Cyberspace*, 104 YALE L. J. 1757, 1765 (1995). *Turner* emphasized "ensuring general public (viewer access) to free programming." Further, *Turner* legitimized "governmental efforts to control the information superhighway so as to ensure viewer and listener access." *Id.* at 1774.

Sunstein concedes that applying *Turner* to other technologies may be difficult since these technologies may lack cable's bottleneck control problem. *Id.* at 1780. For example, he says, that the Internet raises "no bottleneck control problem." Do you agree? Was there a bottleneck problem in *Tornillo*?

4. *Turner Broadcasting System, Inc. v. FCC,* 520 U.S. 180 (1997) [*Turner II*]. The Court answered the question it had remanded for further consideration in *Turner I*: Whether the "must-carry" provisions advance important non-speech related governmental interests and do not burden substantially more speech than necessary to further those interests. After 18 months of additional factfinding, the district court concluded that substantial evidence supported Congress's judgment that the must-carry provisions further important governmental interests in assisting in preserving the existence of local on-air broadcast stations by assuring their carriage on cable systems.

In a 5-4 decision, the Supreme Court affirmed. Justice Kennedy, writing for the majority, reasoned:

> The harm Congress feared was that stations dropped or denied carriage would be at a "serious risk of financial difficulty," and would "deteriorate to a substantial degree or fail altogether." Congress had before it substantial evidence to support its conclusion. Congress was advised the viability of a broadcast station depends to a material extent on its ability to secure cable carriage.
>
> Must-carry ensures that a number of local broadcasters retain cable carriage, with the concomitant audience access and advertising revenues needed to support a multiplicity of stations.

The Court further found that "the burden imposed by must-carry is congruent to the benefits it affords," and that it "is narrowly tailored to preserve a multiplicity of broadcast stations for the 40 percent of American households without cable."

Justice Kennedy spoke for only four justices, however, when he justified must-carry on Congress's legitimate antitrust concern over undue concentrations of power within the cable industry.

Justice Breyer, declining to concur in this portion of the Court's opinion, reasoned:

> Whether or not the statute does or does not sensibly compensate for some significant market defect, it undoubtedly seeks to provide over-the-air viewers who *lack* cable with a rich mix of over-the-air programming by guaranteeing the over-the air stations that provide such programming with the extra dollars that an additional cable audience will generate. I do not deny that the compulsory carriage that creates the "guarantee" extracts a serious First Amendment price. It interferes with the protected interests of the cable operators to choose their own programming; it prevents displaced cable program providers from obtaining an audience; and it will sometimes prevent some cable viewers from watching what, in its absence, would have been their preferred set of programs. This "price" amounts to a "suppression of speech." But there are important First Amendment interests on the other side as well. Indeed *Turner [I]* rested in part upon the proposition that "assuring that the public has access to a multiplicity of information sources is a governmental purpose of the highest order, for it promotes values central to the First Amendment." With important First Amendment interests on both sides of the equation, the key question becomes one of proper fit. That question, in my view, requires a reviewing court to determine both whether there are significantly less restrictive ways to achieve Congress' over-the-air programing objectives, and also to decide whether the statute, in its effort to achieve those objectives, strikes a reasonable balance between potentially speech-restricting and speech-enhancing consequences. Finally, I believe that Congress could reasonably conclude that the statute will help the typical over-the-air viewer (by maintaining an expanded range of choice) more than it hurt the typical cable subscriber (by restricting cable slots otherwise available for preferred programming.

Justice O'Connor, writing for four justices, dissented, because she "remain[ed] convinced that the statute is not a measured response to congressional concerns about monopoly power."

5. *Denver Area Educational Telecommunications Consortium, Inc. v. FCC*, 518 U.S. 727 (1996). The validity of three provisions of the 1992 Cable Act, regulating indecency on leased and public access cable channels, were considered by the Supreme Court. Section 10(a) of the Act authorized the cable operator to permit or prohibit indecent programming on leased access channels. Section 10(c) of the Act permitted cable operators to permit or prohibit indecent programming on public access channels. Section 10(b), applying to leased access channels, required cable operators to segregate and block patently offensive programming on a single channel. The Court held that § 10(a) was constitutional but that §§ 10(b) and 10(c) violated the First Amendment. The portions of the opinions in *Denver Consortium* dealing with the regulation of indecent programming on cable are set forth on p. 1236. The portions of these opinions in *Denver Consortium* dealing with First Amendment issues relating to the regulation of access channels are set forth here.

Justice Breyer, joined by Justices Stevens, O'Connor and Souter, found that section 10(a) did not violate the First Amendment:

> [Petitioners] say, cable system operators have more power to "censor" program viewing than do broadcasters, for individual communities typically have only one cable system, linking broadcasters and other program providers with each community's many subscribers. Moreover, concern about system operators' exercise of this considerable power originally led government — local and federal — to insist that operators provide leased and public access channels free of operator editorial control. Under these circumstances, petitioners conclude, Congress' "permissive" law, in actuality, will "abridge" their free speech.
>
> [T]he First Amendment embodies an overarching commitment to protect speech from Government regulation through close judicial scrutiny, thereby enforcing the Constitution's constraints, but without imposing judicial formulae so rigid that they become a straightjacket that disables Government from responding to serious problems.
>
> Justices Kennedy and Thomas would have us further declare which [First Amendment approach] we are applying here. But no definitive choice among competing analogies (broadcast, common carrier, bookstore) allows us to declare a rigid single standard, good for now and for all future media and purposes. [A]ware as we are of the changes taking place in the law, the technology, and the industrial structure, related to communications, *see* Telecommunications Act of 1996, we believe it unwise and unnecessary definitively to pick one analogy or one specific set of words now.
>
> Rather than decide these issues, we can decide this case more narrowly, by closely scrutinizing Sec.10(a) to assure that it properly addresses an extremely important problem, without imposing, in light of the relevant interests, an unnecessarily great restriction on speech.

Justice Breyer said that although § 10(c), barring indecent material on public access channels, was similar to § 10(a), barring indecent material on leased access channels, there were important differences. Cable operators dedicate channels for public access purposes "as part of the consideration they give municipalities that award them cable franchises." Thus, cable operators never had editorial control over public access channels. Second, public access cable systems are subject to locally accountable entities which makes it "unlikely that many children will in fact be exposed to programming considered patently offensive in that community."

Justice Souter, concurring, shared the "Court's unwillingness to announce a definitive categorical analysis in this case"; he doubted the Court's capacity to develop a "definitive level-of-scrutiny" for cable:

> [W]e can hardly settle rules for review of regulation on the assumption that cable will remain a separable and useful category of First Amendment scrutiny. And as broadcast, cable, and the cyber-technology of the Internet and the World Wide Web approach the day of using a common receiver, we can hardly assume that standards for judging the regulation of one of them will not have immense, but now unknown and unknowable, effects on the others. Accordingly, in charting a course that will permit reasonable regulation in light of the values of competition, we have to accept the likelihood that the media of communication will become less categorical and more protean. [A] proper choice among existing doctrinal categories is not obvious.

Justice Kennedy, joined by Justice Ginsburg, concurred in part and dissented in part.

> The plurality opinion, insofar as it upholds Sec. 10(a) of of the 1992 Cable Act, is adrift. The opinion treats concepts such as public forum, broadcaster, and common carrier as mere labels rather than as categories with settled legal significance; it applies no standard, and by this omission loses sight of existing First Amendment doctrine. When confronted with a threat to free speech in the context of an emerging technology, we ought to have the discipline to analyze the case by existing elaborations of constant First Amendment principles. Rather than undertake this task, however, the plurality just declares that, all things considered, Sec. 10(a) seems fine.

Although Justice Kennedy agreed that §§ 10(b) & (c) were invalid, he thought that past precedents required the Court to hold § 10(a) invalid as well:

> Secs. 10(a) and (c) are unusual. They do not require direct action against speech, but do authorize a cable operator to deny the use of its property to certain forms of speech. As a general matter, a private person may exclude certain speakers from his or her property without violating the First Amendment, and if Secs. 10(a) and (c) were no more than affirmations of this principle they might be unremarkable. Access channels, however, are property of the cable operator dedicated or otherwise reserved for programming of other speakers or the government. A public access channel is a public forum, and laws requiring leased access channels create common carrier obligations. When the government identifies certain speech on the basis of its content as vulnerable to exclusion from a common carrier or public forum, strict scrutiny applies. However compelling Congress' interest in shielding children from indecent programming, the provisions in this case are not drawn with enough care to withstand scrutiny under our precedents.
>
> While it protests against standards, the plurality does seem to favor one formulation of the question in this case: namely, whether the Act

"properly addresses an extremely important problem, without imposing, in light of the relevant interests, an unnecessarily great restriction on speech." This description of the question accomplishes little, save to clutter our First Amendment case law by adding an untested rule with an uncertain relationship to the others we use to evaluate laws restricting speech. The novelty and complexity of this case is a reason to look for help from other areas of our First Amendment jurisprudence, not a license to wander into uncharted areas of the law with no compass other than our own opinions about good policy.

Justice Thomas, joined by Chief Justice Rehnquist and Justice Scalia, concurred in the judgment in part and dissented in part.

I agree with the plurality's conclusion that Sec. 10(a) is constitutionally permissible, but I disagree with its conclusion that Secs. 10(b) and (c) violate the First Amendment. For many years, we have failed to articulate how and to what extent the First Amendment protects cable operators, programmers and viewers from state and federal regulation. I think it is time we did so, and I cannot go along with the plurality's assiduous attempts to avoid addressing that issue openly. The text of the First Amendment makes no distinction between print, broadcast, and cable media, but we have done so.

Our First Amendment distinctions between media, dubious from their infancy, placed cable in a doctrinal wasteland in which regulators and cable operators alike could not be sure whether cable was entitled to the substantial First Amendment protections afforded the print media or was subject to the more onerous obligations shouldered by the broadcast media.

By recognizing the general primacy of the cable operator's editorial rights over the rights of programmers and viewers, *Turner* raises serious questions about the merits of petitioners' claims. None of the petitioners in these cases are cable operators; they are all cable viewers or access programmers or their representative organizations. It is not intuitively obvious that the First Amendment protects the interests petitioners assert, and neither petitioners nor the plurality have adequately explained the source or justification of those asserted rights.

In the process of deciding not to decide on a governing standard, Justice Breyer purports to discover in our cases an expansive, general principle permitting government to "directly regulate speech to address extraordinary problems, where its regulations are appropriately tailored to resolve those problems without imposing an unnecessarily great restriction on speech." This heretofore unknown standard is facially subjective and openly invites balancing of asserted speech interests to a degree not ordinarily permitted. It is true that the standard I endorse lacks the "flexibility" inherent in the plurality's balancing approach, but that relative rigidity is required by our precedents and is not of my own making.

Further, Justice Thomas contended that "leased and public access were a type of forced speech." Accordingly, *Turner* required that the "federal access requirements" should have been subjected to "some form of heightened scrutiny." The access requirements restrict the free speech rights of cable operators and expand the speech opportunities of access programmers. But the point was that access programmers "have no underlying constitutional rights to speak through the cable medium."

> Sec. 10(a) and (c) do not burden a programmer's right to seek access for its indecent programming on an operator's system. Rather, they merely restore part of the editorial discretion an operator would have absent government regulation without burdening the programmer's underlying speech rights.

Consider the following appraisal of *Denver Area*: "[U]nder Justice Breyer's balancing analysis, a regulation will prevail when a governmental access for expression interest outweighs the government interest in suppression of expression. A regulation will fail, on the other hand, when no access interest is involved, and the government interest is clearly suppression of speech alone. Access rights must be weighed against the free speech rights of the cable operator. For Justice Thomas, no First Amendment rights conflicted in *Denver Area* because the only rights asserted that merit First Amendment status were those of the cable operator." Jerome A. Barron, *The Electronic Media and the Flight from First Amendment Doctrine: Justice Breyer's New Balancing Approach*, 31 U. MICH. J.L. REF. 817, 853, 868 (1998). In this analysis, Breyer and Thomas were deemed polar opposites in *Denver Area*: "Under Justice Breyer's perspective, existing First Amendment doctrine was insufficiently pluralistic and inadequately sensitive to the unique issues raised by newly emerging electronic media. Justice Thomas, on the other hand, asserted that First Amendment law in the United States is too pluralistic, too sensitive to specific media, and insufficiently respectful of First Amendment principles." *Id.* at 872. Justice Breyer for the plurality in *Denver Area* resists selecting a new First Amendment standard for cable indecency regulation. The First Amendment standard that Justice Breyer uses to evaluate the access provisions under review in *Denver Area* appears to be simply a new verbal formulation for old-fashioned balancing. *Turner I*, however, declared that strict scrutiny was the appropriate standard for content-based cable regulation. Does *Denver Area*, therefore, conflict with *Turner I* ? See the discussion of *Pacifica* in *Denver Area* set forth in the indecency section, p. 1201.

From a First Amendment perspective, what is the downside of failing to develop a first amendment standard for cable or, indeed, for any new emerging electronic technology? Justice Thomas defined First Amendment rights in his opinion in *Denver* as completely co-extensive with property rights. Is that consistent with the Supreme Court's broadcast First Amendment cases?

Justice Thomas basically equates First Amendment rights with property rights: the entity that owns the medium has First Amendment rights to the exclusion of others. One commentator has subjected this view to the following critique: "[T]he programming decisions of commercial television broadcasters should not qualify as 'editorial discretion' protected by the First Amendment to the extent that they involve entrepreneurially motivated decisions to manufacture and to sell market-driven content. What appears to be speech is, fundamentally and essentially, property — property that has been molded in the way that any entrepreneur shapes his product. It is a product shaped by market incentives. It is a product governed by the behavioral pressures of consumer sovereignty. Choices to create and to sell this product should be understood as property interests protected under the Fifth Amendment, rather than as speech protected by the First Amendment." David Chang, *Selling the Market-Driven Message: Commercial Television, Consumer Sovereignly, and the First Amendment*, 85 MINN. L. REV. 451, 581–583 (2000).

§ 8.04 FREEDOM OF ASSOCIATION

[A] THE NATURE OF THE RIGHT

There is no specific mention of a right of association in the Constitution. Nevertheless, in *NAACP v. Alabama,* 357 U.S. 449 (1958), the Court stated: "[I]t is beyond debate that freedom to engage in association for the advancement of beliefs and ideas is an inseparable aspect of the 'liberty' assured by the Due Process Clause of the Fourteenth Amendment, which embraces freedom of speech." For the Court, it was obvious that "[e]ffective advocacy of both public and private points of view, particularly controversial ones, is undeniably enhanced by group association as this Court has more than once recognized by remarking upon the close nexus between the freedoms of speech and assembly."

Nor is there a specific reference to a freedom of belief in the Constitution. But in rejecting the state's ability to require a flag salute by school children, the Court in *West Virginia State Board of Education v. Barnette,* 319 U.S. 624 (1943), stated: "If there is any fixed star in our constitutional horizon, it is that no official, high or petty, can prescribe what shall be orthodox in politics, nationalism, religion, or other matters of opinion." While not expressly provided for, then, there is no doubt today that the rights of association and belief are implied in the various guarantees of the First Amendment and due process liberty.

The rights of association and belief arise in a variety of contexts. They are most clearly implicated when government seeks to proscribe membership directly in a particular political group or association, *e.g.*, by imposing criminal sanctions on membership in the Communist Party of the United States. But, other more indirect methods for achieving governmental interests are available that also implicate implied First Amendment rights. For example, legislative investigations into associational activities arguably chill the exercise of the rights of association and belief.

> The mere summoning of a witness and compelling him to testify, against his will, about his beliefs, expressions or associations is a measure of governmental interference. When those forced revelations concern matters that are unorthodox, unpopular, or even hateful to the general public, the reaction in the life of the witness may be disastrous.

Watkins v. United States, 354 U.S. 178 (1957).

Government has also sought to register political organizations and to force disclosure of membership lists and other information from groups engaged in activity deemed detrimental to the public welfare. Such compelled disclosure can chill the exercise of First Amendment rights.

More recently, the rights of association and belief have been implicated in controls on the electoral process. With an increasingly vital role played by big money and big interests in the election process, government has sought to force disclosure and impose limitations on campaign contributions and expenditures. But arguably, such regulations limit freedom of expression, at least if money talks, and limit political association and belief, in any case. To what extent may a state or Congress regulate the structure and activities of the political parties that play such a vital role in determining who will govern?

Finally, if there is a freedom to associate and believe, is there also a freedom not to associate and believe? Can government undertake to force workers to contribute to union activities, or individuals to express beliefs to which they may not adhere? To what extent may government force associations to accept unwanted members in pursuit of equal rights? These are some of the questions explored in this section.

[1] The Communist Party Cases

In June 1961, the Supreme Court decided three cases, *Communist Party of the United States v. Subversive Activities Control Board,* 367 U.S. 1 (1961); *Scales v. United States,* 367 U.S. 203 (1961); and *Noto v. United States,* 367 U.S. 290 (1961), which upheld national security laws and took a narrow view of the First Amendment guarantee of freedom of association. The three cases involved federal legislation directed at the American Communist Party and its members, *i.e.*, the Smith Act of 1940, as amended, and the Subversive Activities Control Act of 1950. 18 U.S.C. § 2385; 50 U.S.C. § 781. *Compare United States v. Robel,* 389 U.S. 258 (1967), invalidating a loyalty-security program as an overbroad intrusion on the right of association.

The Communist Party Cases arose out of legislation enacted by Congress at the height of popular feeling against Communism. The cases wound their way through years of litigation, and finally reached the Supreme Court for adjudication in 1961, after the most intense anti-Communist feeling had diminished. Nevertheless, the Court exercised extreme deference to the legislative findings made in 1950. In the *SACB* case, for example, the legislative findings supporting the requirement that the Communist Party of the United States register and disclose its membership lists and other information were deemed not "unfounded and irrational imaginings." The "magnitude of the public interests" outweighed the minimal burden on associational values, especially since the law only prescribed conditions for organizing, and did not proscribe the organizing itself.

The *Scales* decision is indicative of the Court's deference but also established important propositions for the future. *Scales* concerned a constitutional challenge to a provision of the federal statute which had been the focal point of the *Dennis-Yates* cases, the Smith Act. This law included a membership clause which made it a felony for any person to be a member of an organization which advocated the forceful overthrow of the government, knowing the purposes of the organization. The Court, per Justice Harlan, virtually rewrote the membership clause, reading into it an element of specific intent on the defendant's part to incite illegal action as required in *Yates*. Scales was found to have such specific intent, but in *Noto* the Court held that such evidence was lacking.

Justice Black, in dissent, argued that if the Court as here, refused to analyze legislative "findings," then Congress, not the court, would become the arbiter of First Amendment freedoms, a result Justice Black rejected. Justice Douglas also dissented.

At least, the *Scales-Noto* decisions indicate that membership in an organization cannot be punished without a showing that the defendant actively affiliated with the organization, knowing of its illegal objectives, with the specific intent to further those objectives. Moreover, the organizational objectives that can be proscribed are limited to those that satisfy the requirements of the clear and present danger doctrine. As Justice Harlan in *Scales* recognized, "a blanket prohibition of association with a group having both legal and illegal aims would indeed [present] a real danger that legitimate political expression or association would be impaired."

[2] Legislative Investigations

Watkins was prosecuted under 2 U.S.C. § 192 for contempt of Congress for refusing to answer questions "pertinent to the questions under inquiry." Although willing to testify on other matters, Watkins refused to say whether or not certain persons he knew were or had been members of the Communist Party. He refused to plead the Fifth Amendment, but said he would not answer questions about persons who had long since severed their associations with the Communist movement. On review of his contempt conviction, the Supreme Court, per Chief Justice Warren, reversed. *Watkins v. United States,* 354 U.S. 178 (1957).

From the point of view of first Amendment rights, the crucial aspect of the Court's opinion in *Watkins* was the holding that the questions propounded to a witness by a legislative investigating committee must meet a high standard of pertinency. The pertinency requirement in the statute was held to demand the same precision and clarity which the due process clause of the Fifth Amendment required in any criminal offense.

The *Watkins* approach was somewhat obscured in *Barenblatt v. United States,* 360 U.S. 109 (1959). In *Barenblatt* the Court, per Justice Harlan, reviewed petitioner's contempt conviction for refusing to answer certain questions of a subcommittee of the House Un-American Activities Committee. Justice Harlan recognized that "the First Amendment in some circumstances protects an individual from being compelled to disclose his associational relationships." Nevertheless,

> the protections of the First Amendment, unlike a proper claim of the privilege against self-incrimination under the Fifth Amendment, do not afford a witness the right to resist inquiry in all circumstances.

> Where First Amendment rights are asserted to bar governmental interrogation resolution of the issue always involves a balancing by the courts of the competing private and public interests at stake in the particular circumstances shown.

Purporting to balance the interests, Harlan stressed Congress' "wide power to legislate in the field of Communist activity in this Country, and to conduct appropriate investigations in aid thereof" which "[i]n the last analysis rests on the right of self-preservation, 'the ultimate value of any society.' *Dennis v. United States*."

Justice Black, joined by Chief Justice Warren and Justice Douglas, dissenting, did not agree "that laws directly abridging First Amendment freedoms can be justified by a congressional or judicial balancing process." Even assuming interests were to be balanced, Justice Black argued that the majority ignored its own test.

> In the first place, it completely leaves out the real interest in Barenblatt's silence, the interest of the people as a whole in being able to join organizations, advocate causes and make political "mistakes" without later being subjected to governmental penalties for having dared to think for themselves. It is this right, the right to error politically, which keeps us strong as a Nation.

Although in *Barenblatt* congressional power to investigate was upheld, the investigative powers of state legislatures were curtailed in *Gibson v. Florida Legislative Investigation Comm.*, 372 U.S. 539 (1963), involving an investigation of the NAACP, and establishing a compelling state interest test:

> The strong associational interest in maintaining the privacy of membership lists of groups engaged in the constitutionally protected free trade in ideas and beliefs may not be substantially infringed upon such a slender showing as here made by the respondent. While, of course, all legitimate organizations are the beneficiaries of these protections, they are all the more essential here, where the challenged privacy is that of persons espousing beliefs already unpopular with their neighbors and the deterrent and "chilling" effect on the free exercise of constitutionally enshrined rights of free speech, expression, and association are consequently the more immediate and substantial.

Does *Gibson* limit *Barenblatt*, or are the decisions distinguishable? For a modern analysis of the First Amendment implications of legislative investigations into Communist activities in the 1950s, see Martin Redish & Christopher McFadden, *HUAC, the Hollywood Ten, and the First Amendment Right of Non-Association*, 85 Minn. L. Rev. 1669 (2001).

[3] The NAACP Cases

NAACP support for civil rights efforts in Alabama incurred the wrath of state officials. In 1956, state Attorney General John Patterson demanded in a subpoena that the NAACP disclose the names of its Alabama members. In *NAACP v. Alabama ex rel. Patterson,* 357 U.S. 449 (1958), the Court unanimously held, per Justice Harlan, that disclosure would violate the First Amendment guarantee of freedom of association, applicable to the states through the due process clause of the Fourteenth Amendment. Justice Harlan's opinion, however, applied a mere balancing-of-interests approach which future cases followed.

One clue to a difference between *NAACP* and *SACB* is found in the *NAACP* opinion itself. An earlier Supreme Court decision, *Bryant v. Zimmerman,* 278 U.S. 63 (1928), had upheld a New York law requiring registration of Ku Klux Klan members. Naturally, the state of Alabama relied upon *Bryant* in its own case before the Court. But Justice Harlan distinguished *Bryant* on the ground that the Ku Klux Klan was an organization dedicated to unlawful acts and violence. Could it be argued that groups espousing dissident beliefs may be regarded by legislatures and courts as prone to unlawful acts, and therefore vulnerable to forced disclosure of membership? Isn't this precisely the constitutional danger the Court sought to avoid in *NAACP v. Alabama*? The NAACP was not a respectable organization in the minds of state officials of Alabama, but it was viewed more positively by the members of the Court. Is this a proper basis on which to protect one organization but not another?

In *NAACP v. Claiborne Hardware Co.,* 458 U.S. 886 (1982), the Court, per Justice Stevens, ruled that participants in a civil rights boycott could not be held liable for damages absent a showing that violent activity caused the resultant harm. The case arose in 1966 when the local chapter of the NAACP launched a boycott of all white merchants in Claiborne County, Mississippi, seeking to force civic and business leaders to comply with a list of demands for equality and racial justice. While the boycott consisted largely of speeches and other nonviolent activity, some threats and acts of violence did occur. In 1969, plaintiff white merchants filed suit for injunctive relief and damages against the NAACP, among others. The lower court found defendants jointly and severally liable for all of the merchants' lost earnings during a seven-year period, amounting to over $1,000,000, and issued a permanent injunction. The Mississippi Supreme Court upheld the result on the basis of malicious interference with the plaintiff's business, although it did remand for a recomputation of damages.

In reversing, the Supreme Court, per Justice Stevens, held that petitioner's nonviolent activities were entitled to First Amendment protection. The Court recognized the importance and effectiveness of group association — "The right to associate does not lose all constitutional protection merely because some members of the group may have participated in conduct or advocated doctrine that itself is not protected." Moreover, most of the boycott's activities fell within the realm of speech, assembly, association, and petition, all protected activity under the First Amendment. "While states have broad power to regulate economic activity, we do not find a comparable right to prohibit peaceful political activity such as that found in the boycott in this case. . . . For liability to be imposed by reason of association alone, it is necessary to establish that the group itself possessed unlawful goals and that the individual held a specific intent to further those illegal aims."

[4] Economic Regulation and Association

***Lyng v. International Union, UAW*, 485 U.S. 360 (1988).** The Court held that section 109 of the Omnibus Budget Reconciliation Act of 1981, providing that no household may become eligible to participate in the food stamp program while any of its members is on strike or receive an increase in the allotment of food stamps it is already receiving because the striking member's income is decreased, did not infringe a striker's right to associate with his family or the associational rights of strikers and their unions. Justice White, writing for the majority, stated:

> [I]t is "exceedingly unlikely" that § 109 will "prevent any group of persons from dining together." Even if isolated instances can be found in which a striking individual may have left the other members of the household in order to increase their allotment of food stamps, "in the overwhelming majority of cases [the statute] probably has no effect at all." The statute certainly does not "order" any individuals not to dine together; nor does it in any other way " 'directly and substantially' interfere with family living arrangements."

The Court also reasoned that the statute "does not 'order' appellees not to associate together for the purpose of conducting a strike, or for any other purpose, and it does not 'prevent' them from associating together or burden their ability to do so in any significant manner." Justice Marshall, joined by Justices Brennan and Blackmun, dissented on equal protection grounds.

***FTC v. Superior Court Trial Lawyers Ass'n*, 493 U.S. 411 (1990).** The Court, per Justice Stevens, held that an economically motivated boycott by an organization of lawyers seeking higher fees for representing indigents was not entitled to receive special First Amendment protection. A group of lawyers who were appointed by the Superior Court to represent indigents in criminal cases pursuant to the District of Columbia Criminal Justice Act (CJA) agreed to boycott taking any new CJA appointments in order to increase the fees paid to them. After the District of Columbia government acceded to their demands, the Federal Trade Commission filed a complaint against the lawyers' group alleging that they had violated the antitrust laws by entering into a conspiracy to fix prices and conduct a boycott that constituted unfair methods of competition. The FTC ruled that the boycott was illegal *per se* under the antitrust laws and entered an order prohibiting the group from initiating further boycotts. The United States Court of Appeals vacated the order.

The lawyers' association argued that even if this conduct were invalid under the antitrust laws, its action was nonetheless shielded under *NAACP v. Claiborne Hardware*, 458 U.S. 886 (1982), where First Amendment protection was accorded to a politically motivated boycott. Justice Stevens distinguished *Claiborne*, however, since the civil rights protesters who participated in the *Claiborne* boycott had not sought any "special advantage for themselves" nor had they intended "to destroy legitimate competition."

[5] Alienage and Association

***Reno v. American-Arab Anti-Discrimination Committee*, 525 U.S. 471 (1999).** This case concerned preclusion of judicial review in deportation proceedings; it also involved a claim by resident aliens that they were selectively targeted for deportation in violation of their First and Fifth Amendment rights. The Immigration and Naturalization Service (INS) instituted deportation proceedings against a number of resident aliens, all members of the Popular Front for the Liberation of Palestine, a group characterized by the government as an international terrorist organization. The plaintiff resident aliens alleged that the INS was selectively enforcing the immigration laws against them in violation of their First and Fifth Amendment rights. The federal district court issued preliminary injunctive relief against deportation proceedings. The plaintiffs were deemed likely to prove that the INS did not enforce routine status requirements against immigrants who were not members of disfavored groups. Furthermore, the possibility of deportation combined with the chill to their First Amendment rights while the proceedings were pending constituted irreparable injury.

While appeal of the federal district court's grant of injunctive relief was pending, Congress enacted the Illegal Immigration Reform and Immigrant Responsibility Act of 1996 (IIRIRA) which limited judicial review of immigration proceedings. The Ninth Circuit held that federal jurisdiction still existed and affirmed the injunctive relief granted below. The Supreme Court granted review.

Justice Scalia, for the Court, said that the issue was whether the IIRIRA deprived the federal courts of jurisdiction over this suit. The targeted resident aliens had argued that only judicial review by a federal court (as opposed to an INS hearing) would preserve the factual development necessary for an appeal. Without such review, the resident aliens contended habeas relief would also be unavailable. Indeed, even if initial federal judicial review and subsequent habeas relief thereafter were available for these resident aliens, it would come too late to prevent a "chilling effect" on their First Amendment rights. The resident aliens argued that the doctrine of constitutional doubt required the Court to interpret the IIRIRA in a manner which would allow immediate review of their claim of selective enforcement.

Justice Scalia denied that the doctrine of constitutional doubt had any application to this proceeding: "As a general matter-and assuredly in the context of claims such as those put forward in the present case-an alien unlawfully in this country has no constitutional right to assert selective enforcement as a defense against his deportation." Justice Scalia said that even in the field of criminal law a "selective prosecution claim is a rara avis." Such claims invade prosecutorial discretion, "a special province of the Executive." The standard for proving such claims is a "particularly demanding one."

Concerns that displacing the presumption that the prosecutor has acted within the law are "greatly magnified" in the deportation context: "The Executive should not have to disclose its 'real' reasons for deeming nationals of a particular country a special threat—or indeed for simply wishing to antagonize a particular foreign country's nationals—and even if it did disclose them a court would be ill equipped to determine their authenticity and utterly unable to assess their adequacy." As for the interest of the targeted alien in avoiding selective treatment in regard to deportation, Justice Scalia declared that the selective treatment factor was less compelling than it would be in the case of criminal prosecutions: "While the consequences of deportation may assuredly be grave, they are not imposed as punishment."

The Court, through an interpretation which reconciled apparently conflicting statutory provisions, held that the IIRIRA deprived the federal courts of jurisdiction over the claims of the targeted resident aliens. Justice Scalia declared that the jurisdiction limitation provision of the IIRIRA applied only to three discrete actions that the Attorney General might take-commencing proceedings, adjudicating cases or executing removal orders. The jurisdictional limitation applied only to these three actions and not to all claims that might arise in deportation proceedings. The theme behind insulating these actions from judicial review was that they were actions where executive discretion was at its height.

Justice Scalia concluded: "To resolve the present controversy, we need not rule out the possibility of a rare case in which the alleged basis of discrimination is so outrageous that the foregoing consideration can be overcome. When an alien's continuing presence in this country is in violation of the immigration laws, the Government does not offend the Constitution by deporting him for the additional reason that it believes him to be a member of an organization that supports terrorist activity." The Supreme Court vacated the judgment of the Ninth Circuit and remanded with instructions to that court to vacate the judgment of the District Court.

Justice Ginsburg, concurring in part and concurring in the judgment, said that judicial review would be available "notwithstanding a statutory bar, if the INS acts in bad faith, lawlessly or in patent violation of constitutional rights." However, because no such showing had been made and because judicial review was available for the final deportation order, immediate judicial review was not necessary. Justice Breyer concurred only in the foregoing part of Justice Ginsburg's concurrence.

In the second part of her concurrence, Justice Ginsburg observed that *certiorari* had been granted only on the jurisdictional issue and not on the selective enforcement issue. For that reason, full briefing on the selective enforcement issue was lacking: "I would therefore leave the question an open one. I note, however, that there is more to 'the other side of the ledger,' than the Court allows." Freedom of speech and press is accorded to aliens residing in the United States. *Bridges v. Wixon,* 326 U.S. 135 (1945). Under the Court's "selective prosecution doctrine, 'the decision to prosecute may not be deliberately based upon an unjustifiable standard such as race, religion, or other arbitrary classification, including the exercise of protected statutory and constitutional rights.' *Wayte v. United States,* 470 U.S. 598 (1985)." Justice Ginsburg was not persuaded that selective enforcement of the deportation laws should be exempt from that mandate. She also denied that deportation was not a grave sanction.

Justice Ginsburg concluded by saying that if the targeted resident aliens could show a "strong likelihood of ultimate success on the merits, and a chilling effect on current speech," immediate judicial review would obtain "if we were to find the agency's action flagrantly improper." The resident aliens here had not made such a demonstration: "Further, were respondents to assert a colorable First Amendment claim as a now or never matter were that claim not cognizable upon judicial review of a final order again precedent and sense would counsel immediate resort to a judicial forum."

Justice Souter, dissenting, said that the sad history of the statutory provisions in this case showed that Congress had "apparently unintentionally" passed legislation which "simultaneously grants and denies the right of judicial review to certain aliens who were in deportation proceedings before April 1, 1997." Souter reasoned that the IIRIRA either permitted judicial review of suits pending at the time of enactment (such as the instant suit) or it precluded all judicial review of such pending suits. In such a situation, he would invoke "the principle of constitutional doubt" and apply that statutory provision which afforded judicial review and thus avoid a constitutional problem: "[C]omplete preclusion of judicial review of any kind for claims brought by aliens subject to proceedings for removal would raise the serious constitutional question whether Congress may block every remedy for enforcing a constitutional right. The principle of constitutional doubt counsels against adopting the interpretation that raises this question."

Justice Souter said his "constitutional doubt" approach would avoid resolution of a troubling issue "whether selective prosecution claims have vitality in the immigration context." Yet the Court addressed this issue even though it was not briefed before the Court: "[I]n what I take as dictum, [the Court argues] that the alien's interest in avoiding selective treatment 'is less compelling than in criminal prosecutions.' The interest in avoiding selective enforcement of the criminal law, shared by the government and the accused, is that prosecutorial discretion not be exercised to violate constitutionally prescribed guarantees of equality or liberty. This interest applies to the like degree in immigration litigation, and is not attenuated because the deportation is not a penalty for a criminal act or because the violation is ongoing."

Justice Stevens, concurring, did not share Justice Souter's "constitutional doubt" about the prohibition of judicial review of collateral proceedings such as the present case. Congress could not, however, authorize the punishment of innocent people because they happen to be members of a terrorist organization. However, as stated in the last part of Justice Scalia's opinion, Justice Stevens had "no doubt" that priority could be given by the Attorney General "to the removal of deportable aliens who are members of such an organization."

[B] ASSOCIATING FOR ELECTION PURPOSES

[1] Campaign Spending

***Buckley v. Valeo,* 424 U.S. 1 (1976).** The Federal Election Campaign Act of 1971, among other things, adopted the following reforms of campaign financing in federal elections:

(1) Individual political contributions were limited to $1,000 to any single candidate per election, with an overall annual limitation of $25,000 by a contributor.

(2) Independent expenditures by individuals and groups "relative to a clearly identified candidate" were limited to $1,000 a year.

> (3) Campaign spending by candidates for various federal offices and spending for national conventions by political parties were subject to prescribed limits, depending upon the federal office sought.
>
> (4) Political committees were required to keep detailed records of contributions and expenditures, including the name and address of each individual contributing in excess of $10, and to file quarterly reports with the Federal Election Commission disclosing the source, recipient and purpose of every contribution exceeding $100.

In an extensive per curiam opinion, the Court struck down the Act's expenditure ceilings while it upheld the contribution limitations and disclosure requirements.

Expenditure limitations. In striking down the expenditure limitations, the Court emphasized that they "operate in an area of the most fundamental First Amendment activities. Discussion of public issues and debate on the qualifications of candidates are integral to the operation of the system of government established by our Constitution. In a republic where the people are sovereign, the ability of the citizenry to make informed choices among candidates for office is essential, for the identities of those who are elected will inevitably shape the course that we follow as a nation." The Court added that "[t]he First Amendment protects political association as well as political expression," citing *NAACP v. Alabama*.

The Court rejected the argument that "what the Act regulates is conduct, and that its effect on speech and association is incidental at most":

> A restriction on the amount of money a person or group can spend on political communication during a campaign necessarily reduces the quantity of expression by restricting the number of issues discussed, the depth of their exploration, and the size of the audience reached. This is because virtually every means of communicating ideas in today's mass society requires the expenditure of money.

The Court noted that "[t]he expenditure limitations contained in the Act represent substantial rather than merely theoretical restraints on the quantity and diversity of political speech."

Contribution limitations. By contrast, limits on individual campaign contributions were held valid. In support of this conclusion, the Court reasoned that

> a limit upon the amount that any one person or group may contribute to a candidate or political committee entails only a marginal restriction upon the contributor's ability to engage in free communication. A contribution serves as a general expression of support for the candidate and his views, but does not communicate the underlying basis for the support. The quantity of communication by the contributor does not increase perceptibly with the size of his contribution, since the expression rests solely on the undifferentiated, symbolic act of contributing. At most, the size of the contribution provides a very rough index of the intensity of the contributor's support for the candidate. A

> limitation on the amount of money a person may give to a candidate or campaign organization thus involves little direct restraint on his political communication, for it permits the symbolic expression of support evidenced by a contribution but does not in any way infringe the contributor's freedom to discuss candidates and issues. While contributions may result in political expression if spent by a candidate or an association to present views to the voters, the transformation of contributions into political debate involves speech by someone other than the contributor.

Although the Court acknowledged that the Act's contribution limits "impinge on protected associational freedoms," it emphasized that " '[n]either the right to associate nor the right to participate in political activities is absolute.' Even a 'significant interference' with protected rights of 'political association' may be sustained if the State demonstrates a sufficiently important interest and employs means closely drawn to avoid unnecessary abridgment of associational freedoms."

Applying this principle, the Court concluded that "[i]t is unnecessary to look beyond the Act's primary purpose — to limit the actuality and appearance of corruption resulting from large individual financial contributions — in order to find a constitutionally sufficient justification for the $1,000 contribution limitation."

Reporting and disclosure requirements. The Act's reporting and disclosure requirements were "attacked as overbroad — both in their application to minor-party and independent candidates and in their extension to contributions as small as $11 or $101." The Court found the asserted interests in the contribution, reporting and disclosure requirements to be sufficiently important to outweigh the possibility of infringement, particularly when the 'free functioning of our national institutions' is involved."

> First, disclosure provides the electorate with information "as to where political campaign money comes from and how it is spent by the candidate" in order to aid the voters in evaluating those who seek federal office.
>
> Second, disclosure requirements deter actual corruption and avoid the appearance of corruption by exposing large contributions and expenditures to the light of publicity. This exposure may discourage those who would use money for improper purposes either before or after the election.
>
> Third, and not least significant, recordkeeping, reporting, and disclosure requirements are an essential means of gathering the data necessary to detect violations of the contribution limitations.

Chief Justice Burger dissented from the portion of the Court's opinion upholding the provisions for disclosure of small contributions and for limitations on contributions.

Justice White, on the other hand, dissented from the Court's invalidation of the Act's expenditure limitations. Justice Marshall dissented from the

Court's invalidation of the provision limiting the amount a candidate may spend from his personal funds. Justice Blackmun, seeing no basis for a distinction between contribution limitations and expenditure limitations, dissented from the Court's invalidation of the expenditure limitations.

***First National Bank v. Bellotti*, 435 U.S. 765 (1978).** Massachusetts law prohibited a corporation from making either contributions or direct expenditures "for the purpose of influencing or affecting the vote on any question submitted to the voters [*e.g.* referenda on the state ballot], other than one materially affecting any of the property, business or assets of the corporation." The Supreme Court, in an opinion by Justice Powell, struck down this limitation. The state first argued that corporations should not have free speech liberties, a position which the Court rejected out of hand. The state then offered two justifications for the limitation, one having to do with protection of the electoral process and the other concerning protection of minority shareholders.

With regard to the electoral process, the Court stated:

> Referenda are held on issues, not candidates for public office. The risk of corruption perceived in cases involving candidate elections, simply is not present in a popular vote on a public issue. To be sure, corporate advertising may influence the outcome of the vote; this would be its purpose. But the fact that advocacy may persuade the electorate is hardly a reason to suppress it. We noted only recently that "the concept that government may restrict the speech of some elements of our society in order to enhance the relative voice of others is wholly foreign to the First Amendment." Moreover, the people in our democracy are entrusted with the responsibility for judging and evaluating the relative merits of conflicting arguments. They may consider, in making their judgment, the source and credibility of the advocate.

With regard to protection of shareholders, the Court pointed out that the statute was not rationally directed to that purpose. At one extreme, it did not prevent the corporation from spending money for legislative lobbying, which could be even more expensive than referendum campaigning. At the other, it would prevent a corporation from spending funds even if every shareholder desired that they be spent in that fashion. Simply put, the statute did not address the purpose of regulating internal corporate affairs.

Consider the contention of Professor Cox:

> If liberty means the opportunity of the individual man or woman to express himself or herself in a society in which ideas are judged principally by their merits, increasing the relative influence of organizations with large financial resources and shrinking the attention paid to truly individual voices means a net loss of human freedom.

Archibald Cox, *Freedom of Expression in the Burger Court*, 94 Harv. L. Rev. 1, 70 (1980). What is the Court's response to the concern that corporate power could overwhelm the electoral process? In *Bellotti*, Justice Powell cited the absence of any evidence in the record of overwhelming corporate influence on the electorate. Suppose such evidence could be introduced. Would it have to be introduced on a state-by-state basis? In *Buckley v. Valeo*, the Court stated that "the concept that government may restrict the speech of some elements of our society in order to enhance the relative voice of others is wholly foreign to the First Amendment."

***Federal Election Comm'n v. National Conservative Political Action Comm.*, 470 U.S. 480 (1985).** The Court, per Justice Rehnquist, held that § 9012(f) of the Presidential Election Campaign Fund Act (Fund Act), making it a criminal offense for independent political committees to expend more than $1,000 to further a candidate's election if the candidate received public financing, violated the First Amendment.

The Supreme Court cited *Buckley v. Valeo* for the proposition "that the expenditures in this case produce speech at the core of the First Amendment." The contributions and expenditure limitations apply to fundamental first amendment activities: the discussion of issues of public concern and debate on the qualifications of the candidates. The restriction of the amount of money expended during a political campaign reduced both the quantity and the quality of expression.

Nor did the form of organization or method of solicitation employed by PACs diminish their first amendment entitlement: "The First Amendment freedom of association is squarely implicated in this case." This was not simply a limitation on contributions constituting "speech by proxy." "The present case involves limitations on expenditures by PACs, not on the contributions they receive; and in any event these contributions are predominantly small and thus do not raise the same concerns as sizable contributions."

Justice Marshall wrote a separate dissenting opinion abandoning the position that he had supported in *Buckley*:

> I am now unpersuaded by the distinction established in *Buckley*. I have come to believe that the limitations on independent expenditures challenged in that case and here are justified by the congressional interests in promoting "the reality and appearance of equal access to the political arena," and in eliminating political corruption and the appearance of such corruption.

***Federal Election Comm'n v. Massachusetts Citizens for Life*, 479 U.S. 238 (1986).** The Federal Election Campaign Act, 2 U.S.C. § 441b, prohibits corporations from employing treasury funds for the purpose of an expenditure "in connection with any election to any public office." The section requires that such expenditures be financed by voluntary contributions to a separate segregated fund. The appellee, a nonprofit corporation designed to foster respect for human life, prepared a "Special Election Edition" of its newsletter, urging voters to vote "pro-life" in the upcoming Massachusetts primary, listing each candidate for state and federal office and indicating whether they supported or opposed the organization's positions.

The Federal Election Commission filed a complaint in federal court seeking a civil penalty, alleging that the special edition violated § 441b as an expenditure from a corporate treasury to distribute a campaign flyer on behalf of certain political candidates. The Supreme Court held that while the publication did constitute a violation of § 441b, as applied the provision violated the First Amendment.

Justice Brennan for a majority reasoned:

> Regulation of corporate political activity thus has reflected concern not about use of the corporate form per se, but about the potential for unfair deployment of wealth for political purposes. Groups such as MCFL, however, do not pose that danger of corruption. MCFL was formed to disseminate political ideas, not to amass capital. The resources it has available are not a function of its success in the economic marketplace, but its popularity in the political marketplace. In short, MCFL is not the type of "traditional corporation[s] organized for economic gain" that has been the focus of regulation of corporate political activity.

***Austin v. Michigan Chamber of Commerce*, 494 U.S. 652 (1990).** The statute in *Bellotti* prohibiting corporations from influencing referenda was held invalid. But in *Austin* the Court held constitutional a Michigan statute prohibiting corporations from using corporate treasury funds for independent expenditures in support of or in opposition to any candidate in elections for state office. Corporations were allowed, however, to make such expenditures from segregated funds used solely for political purposes. Justice Marshall, speaking for the Court, reasoned: "State law grants corporations special advantages — such as limited liability, perpetual life, and favorable treatment of the accumulation and distribution of assets — that enhance their ability to attract capital and to deploy their resources in ways that maximize the return on their shareholders' investments. The state-created advantages not only allow corporations to play a dominant role in the nation's economy, but also permit them to use 'resources amassed in the economic marketplace' to obtain 'an unfair advantage in the political marketplace.' " The Court also upheld the statute's exemption for media corporations.

The Court in *Austin* did not purport to overrule *Bellotti*. As a practical matter, however, was the Court retreating from *Bellotti*? Justice Brennan, concurring in *Austin*, responded by observing that it was a legitimate state interest "to promote the ability of investors to purchase stock in corporations without fear that their money will be used to support candidates with whom they do not agree." Justice Brennan also commented that Justice Stevens had noted in his concurrence that *Bellotti* had distinguished those federal and state laws which regulated "corporate participation in partisan *candidate* elections."

***McIntyre v. Ohio Election Comm'n*, 514 U.S. 334 (1995).** The Court held unconstitutional an Ohio statute that prohibited the distribution of any material "designed to influence the voters in any election [u]nless there appears in a conspicuous place the name and business address of the person who is responsible therefor." Justice Stevens for the majority stated:

> "Anonymous pamphlets, leaflets, brochures and even books have played an important role in the progress of mankind." *Talley v.*

> *California* (1960). Great works of literature have frequently been produced by authors writing under assumed names.
>
> The freedom to publish anonymously extends beyond the literary realm. In *Talley*, the Court held that the First Amendment protects the distribution of unsigned handbills urging readers to boycott certain Los Angeles merchants who were allegedly engaging in discriminatory employment practices. [The Court in *Talley* had referred to numerous historic incidents of anonymous protests and calls for political action.]

Ohio attempted to distinguish the current law on the ground that it had to do with regulation of elections. In response, Justice Stevens pointed out that this was not a regulation of the method of elections but speech "at the core of the protection afforded by the First Amendment. When a law burdens core political speech, we apply 'exacting scrutiny,' and we uphold the restriction only if it is narrowly tailored to serve an overriding state interest."

Ohio argued that the restriction on anonymity was justified by "its interest in preventing fraudulent and libelous statements and its interest in providing the elctorate with relevant information." The latter interest was dismissed with the comment that the name of the author would add little to the reader's ability to evaluate the message. The fraud and libel interest was held legitimate but not persuasive enough to justify a blanket prohibition.

***Nixon v. Shrink Missouri Gov't PAC,* 528 U.S. 377 (2000).** Missouri state law contains a campaign contribution law similar to the federal law, including a $1,000 (adjusted upward for inflation) per election contribution limit. Challengers asserted that Supreme Court rulings following *Buckley*; had called for actual justification in specific facts of corruption to justify a contribution limitation, but the Court held that a public perception of potential harm was enough to justify a contribution limit. Dissenters included not just Justices Thomas and Scalia, who objected to any legislative intervention into the election financing scheme, but also Justice Kennedy, who argued that Buckley had created an enormous side-effect in permitting so-called "soft money" and "issue advocacy" campaigns that escape the contribution limitation through subterfuge. *See* Richard Briffault, *Issue Advocacy: Redrawing the Elections/Politics Line*, 77 TEX. L. REV. 1751 (1999). Justice Kennedy therefore urged that *Buckley* be overruled in its entirety to allow legislatures to look at a variety of options and other constitutional tests to be considered.

***Federal Election Commission v. Colorado Republican Federal Campaign Committee,* 533 U.S. 431 (2001):** The Federal Election Campaign Act sought to provide a "functional" definition of campaign "contributions" by including within that concept "expenditures made by any person in cooperation, consultation, or concert, with, or at the request or suggestion of, a candidate, his authorized political committees, or their agents." Thus, expenditures coordinated with a candidate are deemed contributions for purposes of the Act and therefore subject to the Act's limitations on contributions. In *Colorado Republican Federal Campaign Committee v. Federal Election Commission,* 518 U.S. 604 (1996) *(Colorado I)*, the Supreme Court held that limits established by the Federal Election Campaign Act were unconstitutional as applied to the Colorado Republican Party's independent expenditures in connection with a senatorial campaign. The Court rejected the Commission's argument that all expenditures by a political party were presumptively to be deemed coordinated with the candidate. The Court found the particular expenditure to be independent.

In addition to its finding that the law was unconstitutional as applied to the facts of the case, the Court remanded for consideration of the party's assertion that all limits on expenditures by a political party in connection with congressional campaigns are facially unconstitutional, even when those expenditures have been openly coordinated with the candidate. Though the lower federal courts had agreed with that challenge, the Supreme Court rejected it. Justice Souter, writing for the majority, noted that characterizing coordinated expenditures on the part of private individuals as contributions is constitutional. The issue, therefore, was "whether a party is otherwise in a different position from other political speakers, giving it a claim to demand a generally higher standard of scrutiny before its coordinated spending can be limited."

The party argued that it was different from a private individual, because "a party and its candidate are joined at the hip" and therefore coordinated spending is essential to political parties. The Court rejected this argument: "Parties perform functions more complex than simply electing candidates; whether they like it or not, they act as agents for spending on behalf of those who seek to produce obligated officeholders." Thus, there is "good reason to view limits on coordinate spending by parties through the same lens applied to such spending by donors." The Court was unpersuaded by the argument that parties would be severely hampered by an inability to coordinate with a candidate: "Despite decades of limitation on coordinated spending, parties have not been rendered useless. In reality, parties continue to organize to elect candidates, and also function for the benefit of donors whose object is to place candidates under obligation, a fact that parties cannot escape. Indeed, parties' capacity to concentrate power to elect is the very capacity that apparently opens them to exploitation as channels for circumventing contribution and coordinated spending limits binding on other political players." The Court concluded that "contribution limits would be eroded if inducement to circumvent them were enhanced by declaring parties' coordinated spending wide open."

Justice Thomas, speaking for two other justices and in part for a third, dissented: "I continue to believe that *Buckley v. Valeo* should be overruled. We need not, however, overrule *Buckley* and apply strict scrutiny in order to hold the Party Expenditure Provision unconstitutional. Even under *Buckley* which described the requisite scrutiny as 'exacting' and 'rigorous,' the regulation cannot pass constitutional muster." He reasoned that "[t]he rationale for th[e] distinction between contributions and independent expenditures has been that, whereas ceilings on contributions by individuals and political committees, 'entai[l] only a marginal restriction' on First Amendment interests, limitations on independent expenditures 'impose significantly more severe restrictions on protected freedoms of political expression and association.' " He found coordinated expenditures, for First Amendment purposes, were indistinguishable from independent expenditures: "It is not just 'symbolic expression,' but a clear manifestation of the party's most fundamental political views. By restricting such speech, the Party Expenditure Provision undermines parties' 'freedom to discuss candidates and issues,' and cannot be reconciled with our campaign finance jurisprudence."

***FEC v. Beaumont*, 539 U.S. 146 (2003).** In what may be a preview of the Court's forthcoming consideration of a First Amendment challenge to the McCain-Finegold campaign finance reform law, the Supreme Court, per Justice Souter, held that 2 U.S.C. § 441b, which prohibits corporations from directly contributing or making expenditures to candidates for federal office can be applied to nonprofit advocacy corporations consistent with the First Amendment.

Section 441b(a) prohibits "any corporation whatever . . . to make a contribution or expenditure" in connection with a specified set of federal elections, and 2 U.S.C. § 441b(2) further defines contribution or expenditure as "anything of value." However, the statute does not preclude "the establishment, administration, and solicitation of contributions to a separate, segregated fund to be utilized for political purposes" (i.e., PACs). North Carolina Right to Life, Inc., three of its officers, and a North Carolina voter (collectively "NCRL") sued the FEC challenging the constitutionality of § 441b solely as it is applied to NCRL. North Carolina Right to Life, Inc., is a North Carolina nonprofit advocacy corporation that provides counseling to pregnant women in the form of alternatives to abortion, and is "overwhelmingly funded by private individuals," although it does receive some funding from businesses. Additionally, North Carolina Right to Life, Inc. has previously contributed to North Carolina state elections, but has not yet contributed to federal elections due to the prohibitions of § 441b. However, it has established a PAC known as "North Carolina Right to Life, Inc. PAC," which has made contributions to federal elections.

The district court granted summary judgment in favor of NCRL, finding that § 441b was unconstitutional as applied to NCRL. The Court of Appeals for the Fourth Circuit affirmed, finding that both the ban on direct contributions and independent expenditures are unconstitutional. The Supreme Court reversed.

Justice Souter began by recognizing that, for "over a century," Congress has chosen to prohibit direct corporate campaign contributions because of the corporate structure's unique potential for corruption and substantial influence of federal elections. The ban on direct contributions by corporations not only "prevents corruption or the appearance of corruption," but also protects "individuals who have paid money into a corporation or union for purposes other than the support of candidates from having that money used to support political candidates to whom they may be opposed." Still another interest for "regulating corporate electoral involvement" is that "restricting contributions by various organizations hedges against their use as conduits for 'circumvention of [valid] contribution limits.' " Specifically, "[t]o the degree that a corporation could contribute to political candidates, the individuals 'who created it, who own it, or whom it employs' could exceed the bounds imposed on their own contributions by diverting money through the corporation."

Justice Souter concluded: "In sum, our cases on campaign finance regulation represent respect for the 'legislative judgment that the special characteristics of the corporate structure require particularly careful regulation.' And we have understood that such deference to legislative choice is warranted particularly when Congress regulates campaign contributions, carrying as they do a plain threat to political integrity and a plain warrant to counter the appearance and reality of corruption and the misuse of corporate advantages."

The Court then turned to NCRL's more focused challenge to the ban on § 441b as applied to direct contributions by nonprofit advocacy corporations. Justice Souter reasoned that *FEC v. National Right to Work Comm.*, 459 U.S. 197 (1982), had all but decided that issue against NCRL. In that case, the Court had concluded "that the corporation's capacity to make contributions was legitimately limited to indirect donations within the scope allowed to PACs." Justice Souter explained: "We specifically rejected the argument made here, that deference to congressional judgments about proper limits on corporate contributions turns on details of corporate form or the affluence of particular corporations. In the same breath, we remarked on the broad applicability of § 441b to 'corporations and labor unions without great financial resources, as well as those more fortunately situated,' and made a point of refusing to 'second-guess a legislative determination as to the need for prophylactic measures where corruption is the evil feared.' " Other precedents have *National Right to Work* as "generally approving the § 441b prohibition on direct contributions, even by nonprofit corporations 'without great financial resources.' "

However, NCRL relied on *FEC v. Massachusetts Citizens for Life, Inc.* [text, p. 1233], where the "Court held the prohibition on independent expenditures under § 441(b) unconstitutional as applied to a nonprofit advocacy corporation." Justice Souter noted that the Court in MCFL had distinguished *National Right to Work* on grounds that it had involved regulation of contributions, not expenditures. Regulation of contributions requires less compelling justification. Justice Souter concluded that, given precedent, the Court could not accept NCRL's effort to invalidate the ban on direct contributions by nonprofit advocacy corporations "without recasting our understanding of the risks of harm posed by corporate political contributions, of the expressive significance of contributions, and of the consequent deference owed to legislative judgments on what to do about them." He asserted that "NCRL's efforts . . . fail to unsettle existing law on any of these points."

First, while NCRL had argued that nonprofit advocacy corporations do not pose a threat to the political system and therefore the governmental interest in combating corruption is "weak." Justice Souter contended that "concern about the corrupting potential underlying the corporate ban may indeed be implicated by advocacy corporations." He reasoned that advocacy corporations do benefit from significant state-created advantages, may amass substantial political "war chests," and often have substantial resources and political power (e.g., the NRA). Furthermore, nonprofit advocacy corporations also have potential as conduits for abuse as individuals try to bypass individual contribution limitations.

Second, the Court responded to NCRL's argument that the regulation should be subject to strict scrutiny analysis. Determining First Amendment standards for reviewing political financial restrictions, Justice Souter said, is based on the importance of the political activity at issue to effective speech or political association. Restrictions on political contributions "have been treated as merely 'marginal' speech restrictions subject to relatively complaisant review under the First Amendment, because contributions lie closer to the edges than to the core of political expression." Therefore, "instead of strict scrutiny, a contribution limit significantly interfering with associational rights" will pass muster "if it satisfies the lesser demand of being 'closely drawn' to match a 'sufficiently important interest.' " While NCRL argued that § 441b is not closely drawn, the Court determined the argument rested on the false premise that the law was a complete ban on participation. Justice Souter determined that § 441b is not a complete ban because it allows participation of unions and corporations in politics through the establishment of PACs.

The Court concluded:

> NCRL cannot prevail, then, simply by arguing that a ban on an advocacy corporation's direct contributions is bad tailoring. NCRL would have to demonstrate that the law violated the First Amendment in allowing contributions to be made only through its PAC and subject to a PAC's administrative burdens. But a unanimous Court in *National Right to Work* did not think the regulatory burdens on PACs, including restrictions on their ability to solicit funds, rendered a PAC unconstitutional as an advocacy corporation's sole avenue for making political contributions. There is no reason to think the burden on advocacy corporations is any greater today, or to reach a different conclusion here.

Justice Kennedy, concurring in the judgment, again asserted his opinion that "the Court erred in sustaining certain state and federal restrictions on political speech in the campaign finance context and misapprehended basic First Amendment basic principles in doing so." However, Justice Kennedy concluded that the Court had correctly read precedent. But Justice Kennedy indicated: "Were we presented with a case in which the distinction between contributions and expenditures under the whole scheme of campaign finance regulation were under review, I might join Justice Thomas' opinion."

Justice Thomas, joined by Justice Scalia, dissenting, said he "continues to believe that campaign finance laws are subject to strict scrutiny." Section 441b would not survive strict scrutiny review because "broad prophylactic caps on . . . giving in the political process . . . are unconstitutional 'because . . . they are not narrowly tailored to meet any relevant compelling state interest.' "

***McConnell v. FEC*, 540 U.S. 93 (2003).** The Bipartisan Campaign Reform Act of 2002 (BCRA) addressed "loopholes" in the Federal Election Campaign Act that were perceived to be emasculating the FECA limitations: the use of "soft money" and the proliferation of "issue ads." The combination of these two previously unregulated practices allowed many contributors and party organizers to evade FECA requirements.

FECA originally regulated only "contributions," which consisted of the gift or advance of anything of value "made by any person for the purpose of influencing state or local elections are therefore unaffected by FECA's requirements and prohibitions. As a result, prior to the enactment of BCRA, federal law permitted corporations and unions, as well as individuals who had already made the maximum permissible contributions to federal candidates, to contribute "nonfederal money"—also known as "soft money"—to political parties for activities intended to influence state or local elections. FEC interpretations first allowed political parties to fund mixed-purpose activities, such as get-out-the-vote drives and generic party advertising, with soft money. FEC eventually expanded the allowable uses of soft money to party advertisements that mentioned the name of a federal candidate, so long as they did not expressly advocate the candidate's election or defeat.

BCRA's key provision was that "national committees of a political party . . . may not solicit, receive, or direct to another person a contribution, donation, or transfer of funds or any other thing of value, or spend any funds, that are not subject to the limitations, prohibitions, and reporting requirements of this Act." Many plaintiffs challenged this provision as a limitation on freedom of expression and associations, claiming that it prevented contributors from supporting their preferred political parties.

Justices Stevens and O'Connor jointly authored the lead opinion among many opinions dealing with the various complicated facets of BCRA. They viewed the heart of BCRA's reforms to be a mere elimination of "soft money" and "issue ads" that were "evasion" of FECA requirements. The evasion would occur because soft money and issue ads could accomplish the same purposes as express advocacy which could lawfully be funded only with hard money. Thus, the ads enabled unions, corporations, and wealthy contributors to circumvent FECA limitations. In addition, although ostensibly independent of the candidates, the ads were often actually coordinated with, and controlled by, the campaigns.

The Stevens-O'Connor opinion stated that BCRA "does little more than regulate the ability of wealthy individuals, corporations, and unions to contribute large sums of money to influence federal elections, federal candidates, and federal officeholders."

Plaintiffs contend that we must apply strict scrutiny . . . because many of its provisions restrict not only contributions but also the spending and solicitation of funds raised outside of FECA's contribution limits. But for purposes of determining the level of scrutiny, it is irrelevant that Congress chose . . . to regulate contributions on the demand rather than the supply side. The relevant inquiry is whether the mechanism adopted to implement the contribution limit, or to prevent circumvention of that limit, burdens speech in a way that a direct restriction on the contribution itself would not. That is not the case here.

The amendments would not limit the total amount of money that political parties can spend. "Rather, they simply limit the source and individual amount of donations. That they do so by prohibiting the spending of soft money does not render them expenditure limitations."

A separate opinion for the Court by Chief Justice Rehnquist dealt with other aspects of BCRA. A challenge to amendments to the Federal Communications

Act was dismissed for lack of standing because any election campaign to which the amendments might apply was too remote to be justiciable. A provision with some complicated disclosure requirements was upheld, while a provision forbidding contributions by persons 17 or younger was struck down.

Another opinion for the Court by Justice Breyer reversed the lower court's holding of facial invalidity with respect to provisions that imposed recordkeeping and disclosure requirements on broadcasters. Challenges to these provisions must await implementation in concrete settings.

Various Justices dissented with respect to some discrete parts of the Court's holding. Justice Stevens dissented only with respect to the standing holding on the campaign broadcast provision and would have upheld it on the merits.

In essence, there were four dissents from most of the provisions regarding "soft money" and the counting of coordinated expenditures as "contributions" that could be regulated. Chief Justice Rehnquist argued that treating all that money as "contribution" that could be limited swept too broadly and that Congress should have been required to engage in more "closely drawn" regulations to get at corruption or the appearance of corruption. Justice Scalia dissented with regard to several provisions on the basis that strict regulation of the money available for campaigning ultimately will result in advantaging incumbents, thus stifling criticism of government and changes in representation. Justice Kennedy argued that the restrictions will make it more difficult for the individual citizen to express preferences for who speaks on his or her behalf. Justice Thomas dissented with a dire forecast of what could happen in the future: strict regulation of political speech and even "outright regulation of the press."

[2] Political Patronage

***Branti v. Finkel,* 445 U.S. 507 (1980).** The Court, per Justice Stevens, considered the problem of reconciling traditional political patronage practices with a more sensitive understanding of First Amendment requirements. In *Branti*, the Court held that attorneys in a county public defender's office could not be dismissed on purely political grounds. A constitutional violation could be shown if the plaintiffs could prove that they were to be dismissed solely for the reason that they were not affiliated with or sponsored by the Democratic Party. Dismissal of public employees on the basis of their party affiliation alone would violate the First and Fourteenth Amendments' freedom of political belief and association and would place an unconstitutional condition on receipt of a government benefit.

In an important distinction, the Court said that the critical issue in deciding whether public employees could be discharged because of their political affiliation was not dependent on whether a particular job could be classified as a "policy-making" job or "confidential" job. The dispositive issue was whether the government could show that party affiliation was in fact an appropriate requirement for the effective performance of the public office involved. The Court cautioned, however, that affiliation is not necessarily relevant to every "policy-making" or "confidential" position.

Three Justices, in an opinion authored by Justice Powell, dissented in part. They objected that the Court ignored the substantial interest served by patronage. It was pointed out, for example, that the President should have "the right to consider political affiliation when he selects top ranking Department of Justice officials." Justice Powell argued in essence that the First Amendment is designed to protect the political process, not to displace it.

[C] THE RIGHT OF NONASSOCIATION AND COMPELLED SPEECH

BOY SCOUTS OF AMERICA v. DALE

530 U.S. 640, 120 S. Ct. 2446, 147 L. Ed.2d 554 (2000)

Chief Justice Rehnquist delivered the opinion of the Court.

The Boy Scouts is a private, not-for-profit organization engaged in instilling its system of values in young people. The Boy Scouts asserts that homosexual conduct is inconsistent with the values it seeks to instill. Respondent is James Dale, a former Eagle Scout whose adult membership in the Boy Scouts was revoked when the Boy Scouts learned that he is an avowed homosexual and gay rights activist. The New Jersey Supreme Court held that New Jersey's public accommodations law requires that the Boy Scouts admit Dale. This case presents the question whether applying New Jersey's public accommodations law in this way violates the Boy Scouts' First Amendment right of expressive association. We hold that it does.

I

James Dale entered scouting in 1978 at the age of eight by joining Monmouth Council's Cub Scout Pack 142. Dale became a Boy Scout in 1981 and remained a Scout until he turned 18. By all accounts, Dale was an exemplary Scout. In 1988, he achieved the rank of Eagle Scout, one of Scouting's highest honors.

Dale applied for adult membership in the Boy Scouts in 1989. The Boy Scouts approved his application for the position of assistant scoutmaster of Troop 73. Around the same time, Dale left home to attend Rutgers University. After arriving at Rutgers, Dale first acknowledged to himself and others that he is gay. He quickly became involved with, and eventually became the co-president of, the Rutgers University Lesbian/Gay Alliance. In 1990, Dale attended a seminar addressing the psychological and health needs of lesbian and gay teenagers. A newspaper covering the event interviewed Dale about his advocacy of homosexual teenagers' need for gay role models. In early July 1990, the newspaper published the interview and Dale's photograph over a caption identifying him as the copresident of the Lesbian/Gay Alliance.

Later that month, Dale received a letter from Monmouth Council Executive James Kay revoking his adult membership. Dale wrote to Kay requesting the reason for Monmouth Council's decision. Kay responded by letter that the Boy Scouts "specifically forbid membership to homosexuals." In 1992, Dale filed a complaint against the Boy Scouts in the New Jersey Superior Court. The complaint alleged that the Boy Scouts had violated New Jersey's public accommodations statute and its common law by revoking Dale's membership based solely on his sexual orientation. New Jersey's public accommodations statute prohibits, among other things, discrimination on the basis of sexual orientation in places of public accommodation.

The New Jersey Superior Court's Chancery Division granted summary judgment in favor of the Boy Scouts. The court held that New Jersey's public accommodations law was inapplicable because the Boy Scouts was not a place of public accommodation, and that, alternatively, the Boy Scouts is a distinctly private group exempted from coverage under New Jersey's law.

The New Jersey Superior Court's Appellate Division reversed and remanded for further proceedings. It held that New Jersey's public accommodations law applied to the Boy Scouts and that the Boy Scouts violated it. The Appellate Division rejected the Boy Scouts' federal constitutional claims.

The New Jersey Supreme Court affirmed the judgment of the Appellate Division.

We granted the Boy Scouts' petition for certiorari to determine whether the application of New Jersey's public accommodations law violated the First Amendment.

II

In *Roberts v. United States Jaycees,* 468 U.S. 609, (1984), we observed that "implicit in the right to engage in activities protected by the First Amendment" is "a corresponding right to associate with others in pursuit of a wide variety of political, social, economic, educational, religious, and cultural ends." This right is crucial in preventing the majority from imposing its views on groups that would rather express other, perhaps unpopular, ideas. Government actions that may unconstitutionally burden this freedom may take many forms, one of which is "intrusion into the internal structure or affairs of an association" like a "regulation that forces the group to accept members it does not desire." Forcing a group to accept certain members may impair the ability of the group to express those views, and only those views, that it intends to express. Thus, "[f]reedom of association . . . plainly presupposes a freedom not to associate."

The forced inclusion of an unwanted person in a group infringes the group's freedom of expressive association if the presence of that person affects in a significant way the group's ability to advocate public or private viewpoints. But the freedom of expressive association, like many freedoms, is not absolute. We have held that the freedom could be overridden "by regulations adopted to serve compelling state interests, unrelated to the suppression of ideas, that cannot be achieved through means significantly less restrictive of associational freedoms."

To determine whether a group is protected by the First Amendment's expressive associational right, we must determine whether the group engages in "expressive association." The First Amendment's protection of expressive association is not reserved for advocacy groups. But to come within its ambit, a group must engage in some form of expression, whether it be public or private.

Because this is a First Amendment case where the ultimate conclusions of law are virtually inseparable from findings of fact, we are obligated to independently review the factual record to ensure that the state court's judgment does not unlawfully intrude on free expression. The record reveals the following. The Boy Scouts is a private, nonprofit organization. According to its mission statement:

> "It is the mission of the Boy Scouts of America to serve others by helping to instill values in young people and, in other ways, to prepare them to make ethical choices over their lifetime in achieving their full potential."

The values we strive to instill are based on those found in the Scout Oath and Law:

> Scout Oath "On my honor I will do my best To do my duty to God and my country and to obey the Scout Law; To help other people at all times; To keep myself physically strong, mentally awake, and morally straight."

Scout Law "A Scout is:

> "Trustworthy Obedient Loyal Cheerful Helpful Thrifty Friendly Brave Courteous Clean Kind Reverent."

Thus, the general mission of the Boy Scouts is clear: "To instill values in young people." The Boy Scouts seeks to instill these values by having its adult leaders spend time with the youth members, instructing and engaging them in activities like camping, archery, and fishing. During the time spent with the youth members, the scoutmasters and assistant scoutmasters inculcate them with the Boy Scouts' values — both expressly and by example. It seems indisputable that an association that seeks to transmit such a system of values engages in expressive activity.

Given that the Boy Scouts engages in expressive activity, we must determine whether the forced inclusion of Dale as an assistant scoutmaster would significantly affect the Boy Scouts' ability to advocate public or private viewpoints. This inquiry necessarily requires us first to explore, to a limited extent, the nature of the Boy Scouts' view of homosexuality.

The values the Boy Scouts seeks to instill are "based on" those listed in the Scout Oath and Law. The Boy Scouts explains that the Scout Oath and Law provide "a positive moral code for living; they are a list of 'do's' rather than 'don'ts.' " The Boy Scouts asserts that homosexual conduct is inconsistent with the values embodied in the Scout Oath and Law, particularly with the values represented by the terms "morally straight" and "clean."

Obviously, the Scout Oath and Law do not expressly mention sexuality or sexual orientation. And the terms "morally straight" and "clean" are by no means self-defining. Different people would attribute to those terms very different meanings. For example, some people may believe that engaging in homosexual conduct is not at odds with being "morally straight" and "clean."

And others may believe that engaging in homosexual conduct is contrary to being "morally straight" and "clean." The Boy Scouts says it falls within the latter category.

The New Jersey Supreme Court analyzed the Boy Scouts' beliefs and found that the "exclusion of members solely on the basis of their sexual orientation is inconsistent with Boy Scouts' commitment to a diverse and 'representative' membership . . .[and] contradicts Boy Scouts' overarching objective to reach 'all eligible youth.'" The court concluded that the exclusion of members like Dale "appears antithetical to the organization's goals and philosophy." But our cases reject this sort of inquiry; it is not the role of the courts to reject a group's expressed values because they disagree with those values or find them internally inconsistent.

The Boy Scouts asserts that it "teaches that homosexual conduct is not morally straight," and that it does "not want to promote homosexual conduct as a legitimate form of behavior," We accept the Boy Scouts' assertion. We need not inquire further to determine the nature of the Boy Scouts' expression with respect to homosexuality. But because the record before us contains written evidence of the Boy Scouts' viewpoint, we look to it as instructive, if only on the question of the sincerity of the professed beliefs.

A 1978 position statement to the Boy Scouts' Executive Committee, signed by Downing B. Jenks, the President of the Boy Scouts, and Harvey L. Price, the Chief Scout Executive, expresses the Boy Scouts' "official position" with regard to "homosexuality and Scouting":

> "Q. May an individual who openly declares himself to be a homosexual be a volunteer Scout leader?
>
> "A. No. The Boy Scouts of America is a private, membership organization and leadership therein is a privilege and not a right. We do not believe that homosexuality and leadership in Scouting are appropriate. We will continue to select only those who in our judgment meet our standards and qualifications for leadership."

Thus, at least as of 1978 — the year James Dale entered Scouting — the official position of the Boy Scouts was that avowed homosexuals were not to be Scout leaders.

A position statement promulgated by the Boy Scouts in 1991 (after Dale's membership was revoked but before this litigation was filed) also supports its current view:

> "We believe that homosexual conduct is inconsistent with the requirement in the Scout Oath that a Scout be morally straight and in the Scout Law that a Scout be clean in word and deed, and that homosexuals do not provide a desirable role model for Scouts."

The Boy Scouts publicly expressed its views with respect to homosexual conduct by its assertions in prior litigation.

We must then determine whether Dale's presence as an assistant scoutmaster would significantly burden the Boy Scouts' desire to not "promote homosexual conduct as a legitimate form of behavior." As we give deference to an association's assertions regarding the nature of its expression, we must also give deference to an association's view of what would impair its expression. That is not to say that an expressive association can erect a shield against antidiscrimination laws simply by asserting that mere acceptance of a member from a particular group would impair its message. But here Dale, by his own admission, is one of a group of gay Scouts who have "become leaders in their community and are open and honest about their sexual orientation." Dale was the copresident of a gay and lesbian organization at college and remains a gay rights activist. Dale's presence in the Boy Scouts would, at the very least, force the organization to send a message, both to the youth members and the world, that the Boy Scouts accepts homosexual conduct as a legitimate form of behavior.

Hurley v. Irish-American Gay, Lesbian and Bisexual Group of Boston, Inc., is illustrative on this point. There we considered whether the application of Massachusetts' public accommodations law to require the organizers of a private St. Patrick's Day parade to include among the marchers an Irish-American gay, lesbian, and bisexual group, GLIB, violated the parade organizers' First Amendment rights. We noted that the parade organizers did not wish to exclude the GLIB members because of their sexual orientations, but because they wanted to march behind a GLIB banner. We observed:

> [A] contingent marching behind the organization's banner would at least bear witness to the fact that some Irish are gay, lesbian, or bisexual, and the presence of the organized marchers would suggest their view that people of their sexual orientations have as much claim to unqualified social acceptance as heterosexuals . . . . The parade's organizers may not believe these facts about Irish sexuality to be so, or they may object to unqualified social acceptance of gays and lesbians or have some other reason for wishing to keep GLIB's message out of the parade. But whatever the reason, it boils down to the choice of a speaker not to propound a particular point of view, and that choice is presumed to lie beyond the government's power to control.

Here, we have found that the Boy Scouts believes that homosexual conduct is inconsistent with the values it seeks to instill in its youth members; it will not "promote homosexual conduct as a legitimate form of behavior." As the presence of GLIB in Boston's St. Patrick's Day parade would have interfered with the parade organizers' choice not to propound a particular point of view, the presence of Dale as an assistant scoutmaster would just as surely interfere with the Boy Scout's choice not to propound a point of view contrary to its beliefs.

The New Jersey Supreme Court determined that the Boy Scouts' ability to disseminate its message was not significantly affected by the forced inclusion of Dale as an assistant scoutmaster because of the following findings:

> Boy Scout members do not associate for the purpose of disseminating the belief that homosexuality is immoral; Boy Scouts discourages its leaders from disseminating any views on sexual issues; and Boy Scouts

> includes sponsors and members who subscribe to different views in respect of homosexuality.

We disagree with the New Jersey Supreme Court's conclusion drawn from these findings.

First, associations do not have to associate for the "purpose" of disseminating a certain message in order to be entitled to the protections of the First Amendment. An association must merely engage in expressive activity that could be impaired in order to be entitled to protection. For example, the purpose of the St. Patrick's Day parade in Hurley was not to espouse any views about sexual orientation, but we held that the parade organizers had a right to exclude certain participants nonetheless.

Second, even if the Boy Scouts discourages Scout leaders from disseminating views on sexual issues — a fact that the Boy Scouts disputes with contrary evidence — the First Amendment protects the Boy Scouts' method of expression. If the Boy Scouts wishes Scout leaders to avoid questions of sexuality and teach only by example, this fact does not negate the sincerity of its belief discussed above.

Third, the First Amendment simply does not require that every member of a group agree on every issue in order for the group's policy to be "expressive association." The Boy Scouts takes an official position with respect to homosexual conduct, and that is sufficient for First Amendment purposes. In this same vein, Dale makes much of the claim that the Boy Scouts does not revoke the membership of heterosexual Scout leaders that openly disagree with the Boy Scouts' policy on sexual orientation. But if this is true, it is irrelevant. The presence of an avowed homosexual and gay rights activist in an assistant scoutmaster's uniform sends a distinctly different message from the presence of a heterosexual assistant scoutmaster who is on record as disagreeing with Boy Scouts policy. The Boy Scouts has a First Amendment right to choose to send one message but not the other. The fact that the organization does not trumpet its views from the housetops, or that it tolerates dissent within its ranks, does not mean that its views receive no First Amendment protection.

Having determined that the Boy Scouts is an expressive association and that the forced inclusion of Dale would significantly affect its expression, we inquire whether the application of New Jersey's public accommodations law to require that the Boy Scouts accept Dale as an assistant scoutmaster runs afoul of the Scouts' freedom of expressive association. We conclude that it does.

We recognized in cases such as *Roberts* that States have a compelling interest in eliminating discrimination against women in public accommodations. But in each of these cases we went on to conclude that the enforcement of these statutes would not materially interfere with the ideas that the organization sought to express. In *Roberts*, we said "indeed, the Jaycees has failed to demonstrate . . . any serious burden on the male members' freedom of expressive association."

We thereupon concluded in each of these cases that the organizations' First Amendment rights were not violated by the application of the States' public accommodations laws.

In *Hurley*, we said that public accommodations laws "are well within the State's usual power to enact when a legislature has reason to believe that a given group is the target of discrimination, and they do not, as a general matter, violate the First or Fourteenth Amendments." But we went on to note that in that case "the Massachusetts [public accommodations] law has been applied in a peculiar way" because "any contingent of protected individuals with a message would have the right to participate in petitioners' speech, so that the communication produced by the private organizers would be shaped by all those protected by the law who wish to join in with some expressive demonstration of their own."

Dale contends that we should apply the intermediate standard of review enunciated in *United States v. O'Brien* to evaluate the competing interests. There the Court enunciated a four-part test for review of a governmental regulation that has only an incidental effect on protected speech — in that case the symbolic burning of a draft card. A law prohibiting the destruction of draft cards only incidentally affects the free speech rights of those who happen to use a violation of that law as a symbol of protest. But New Jersey's public accommodations law directly and immediately affects associational rights, in this case associational rights that enjoy First Amendment protection. Thus, *O'Brien* is inapplicable.

In *Hurley*, we applied traditional First Amendment analysis to hold that the application of the Massachusetts public accommodations law to a parade violated the First Amendment rights of the parade organizers. Although we did not explicitly deem the parade in Hurley an expressive association, the analysis we applied there is similar to the analysis we apply here. We have already concluded that a state requirement that the Boy Scouts retain Dale as an assistant scoutmaster would significantly burden the organization's right to oppose or disfavor homosexual conduct. The state interests embodied in New Jersey's public accommodations law do not justify such a severe intrusion on the Boy Scouts' rights to freedom of expressive association. That being the case, we hold that the First Amendment prohibits the State from imposing such a requirement through the application of its public accommodations law.

Justice Stevens' dissent makes much of its observation that the public perception of homosexuality in this country has changed. Indeed, it appears that homosexuality has gained greater societal acceptance. But this is scarcely an argument for denying First Amendment protection to those who refuse to accept these views. And the fact that an idea may be embraced and advocated by increasing numbers of people is all the more reason to protect the First Amendment rights of those who wish to voice a different view.

Justice Stevens' extolling of Justice Brandeis' comments in *New State Ice Co. v. Liebmann,* 285 U.S. 262, (1932) (dissenting opinion); confuses two entirely different principles. In *New State Ice*, the Court struck down an Oklahoma regulation prohibiting the manufacture, sale, and distribution of ice without a license. Justice Brandeis, a champion of state experimentation in the economic realm, dissented. But Justice Brandeis was never a champion of state experimentation in the suppression of free speech. To the contrary, his First Amendment commentary provides compelling support for the Court's opinion in this case.

We are not, as we must not be, guided by our views of whether the Boy Scouts' teachings with respect to homosexual conduct are right or wrong; public or judicial disapproval of a tenet of an organization's expression does not justify the State's effort to compel the organization to accept members where such acceptance would derogate from the organization's expressive message. "While the law is free to promote all sorts of conduct in place of harmful behavior, it is not free to interfere with speech for no better reason than promoting an approved message or discouraging a disfavored one, however enlightened either purpose may strike the government." *Hurley*.

JUSTICE STEVENS, with whom JUSTICE SOUTER, JUSTICE GINSBURG and JUSTICE BREYER join, dissenting.

Because every state law prohibiting discrimination is designed to replace prejudice with principle, Justice Brandeis' comment on the States' right to experiment with "things social" is directly applicable to this case.

> To stay experimentation in things social and economic is a grave responsibility. Denial of the right to experiment may be fraught with serious consequences to the Nation. It is one of the happy incidents of the federal system that a single courageous State may, if its citizens choose, serve as a laboratory; and try novel social and economic experiments without risk to the rest of the country. This Court has the power to prevent an experiment. We may strike down the statute which embodies it on the ground that, in our opinion, the measure is arbitrary, capricious or unreasonable. We have power to do this, because the due process clause has been held by the Court applicable to matters of substantive law as well as to matters of procedure. But in the exercise of this high power, we must be ever on our guard, lest we erect our prejudices into legal principles. If we would guide by the light of reason, we must let our minds be bold. *New State Ice Co. v. Liebmann,* 285 U.S. 262, 311 (1932) (dissenting opinion).

In its "exercise of this high power" today, the Court does not accord this "courageous State" the respect that is its due.

The majority holds that New Jersey's law violates BSA's right to associate and its right to free speech. But that law does not "impose any serious burdens" on BSA's "collective effort on behalf of [its] shared goals," *Roberts v. United States Jaycees* nor does it force BSA to communicate any message that it does not wish to endorse. New Jersey's law, therefore, abridges no constitutional right of the Boy Scouts.

I

The Boy Scout Handbook defines "morally straight," as such:

> To be a person of strong character, guide your life with honesty, purity, and justice. Respect and defend the rights of all people. Your relationships with others should be honest and open. Be clean in your speech and actions, and faithful in your religious beliefs. The values you follow as a Scout will help you become virtuous and self-reliant.

The Scoutmaster Handbook emphasizes these points about being "morally straight":

> In any consideration of moral fitness, a key word has to be 'courage.' A boy's courage to do what his head and his heart tell him is right. And the courage to refuse to do what his heart and his head say is wrong. Moral fitness, like emotional fitness, will clearly present opportunities for wise guidance by an alert Scoutmaster.

As for the term "clean," the Boy Scout Handbook offers the following:

> A Scout is CLEAN. A Scout keeps his body and mind fit and clean. He chooses the company of those who live by these same ideals. He helps keep his home and community clean. You never need to be ashamed of dirt that will wash off. If you play hard and work hard you can't help getting dirty. But when the game is over or the work is done, that kind of dirt disappears with soap and water.
>
> There's another kind of dirt that won't come off by washing. It is the kind that shows up in foul language and harmful thoughts. Swear words, profanity, and dirty stories are weapons that ridicule other people and hurt their feelings. The same is true of racial slurs and jokes making fun of ethnic groups or people with physical or mental limitations. A Scout knows there is no kindness or honor in such mean-spirited behavior. He avoids it in his own words and deeds. He defends those who are targets of insults.

It is plain as the light of day that neither one of these principles — "morally straight" and "clean" — says the slightest thing about homosexuality. Indeed, neither term in the Boy Scouts' Law and Oath expresses any position whatsoever on sexual matters.

The Court seeks to fill the void by pointing to a statement of "policies and procedures relating to homosexuality and Scouting" signed by BSA's President and Chief Scout Executive in 1978 and addressed to the members of the Executive Committee of the national organization. The letter says that the BSA does "not believe that homosexuality and leadership in Scouting are appropriate." But when the entire 1978 letter is read, BSA's position is far more equivocal:

> 4. Q. May an individual who openly declares himself to be a homosexual be employed by the Boy Scouts of America as a professional or non-professional?
>
> A. Boy Scouts of America does not knowingly employ homosexuals as professionals or non-professionals. We are unaware of any present laws which would prohibit this policy.
>
> 5. Q. Should a professional or non-professional individual who openly declares himself to be a homosexual be terminated?
>
> A. Yes, in the absence of any law to the contrary. At the present time we are unaware of any statute or ordinance in the United States which prohibits discrimination against individual's employment upon

> the basis of homosexuality. In the event that such a law was applicable, it would be necessary for the Boy Scouts of America to obey it, in this case as in Paragraph 4 above. It is our position, however, that homosexuality and professional or non-professional employment in Scouting are not appropriate.

Four aspects of the 1978 policy statement are relevant to the proper disposition of this case. First, at most this letter simply adopts an exclusionary membership policy. But simply adopting such a policy has never been considered sufficient, by itself, to prevail on a right to associate claim.

Second, the 1978 policy was never publicly expressed — unlike, for example, the Scout's duty to be "obedient." It was an internal memorandum, never circulated beyond the few members of BSA's Executive Committee. It remained, in effect, a secret Boy Scouts policy. Far from claiming any intent to express an idea that would be burdened by the presence of homosexuals, BSA's public posture — to the world and to the Scouts themselves — remained what it had always been: one of tolerance, welcoming all classes of boys and young men. In this respect, BSA's claim is even weaker than those we have rejected in the past.

Third, it is apparent that the draftsmen of the policy statement foresaw the possibility that laws against discrimination might one day be amended to protect homosexuals from employment discrimination. Their statement clearly provided that, in the event such a law conflicted with their policy, a Scout's duty to be obedient" and "obey the laws," even if "he thinks [the laws] are unfair" would prevail in such a contingency. *See supra*, at 4–5. In 1978, however, BSA apparently did not consider it to be a serious possibility that a State might one day characterize the Scouts as a "place of public accommodation" with a duty to open its membership to all qualified individuals. The portions of the statement dealing with membership simply assume that membership in the Scouts is a "privilege" that BSA is free to grant or to withhold. The statement does not address the question whether the publicly proclaimed duty to obey the law should prevail over the private discriminatory policy if, and when, a conflict between the two should arise — as it now has in New Jersey. At the very least, then, the statement reflects no unequivocal view on homosexuality. Indeed, the statement suggests that an appropriate way for BSA to preserve its unpublished exclusionary policy would include an open and forthright attempt to seek an amendment of New Jersey's statute. ("If he thinks these rules and laws are unfair, he tries to have them changed in an orderly manner rather than disobey them.")

Fourth, the 1978 statement simply says that homosexuality is not "appropriate." It makes no effort to connect that statement to a shared goal or expressive activity of the Boy Scouts. Whatever values BSA seeks to instill in Scouts, the idea that homosexuality is not "appropriate" appears entirely unconnected to, and is mentioned nowhere in, the myriad of publicly declared values and creeds of the BSA. That idea does not appear to be among any of the principles actually taught to Scouts. Rather, the 1978 policy appears to be no more than a private statement of a few BSA executives that the organization wishes to exclude gays — and that wish has nothing to do with any expression BSA actually engages in.

Third, BSA never took any clear and unequivocal position on homosexuality. Though the 1991 and 1992 policies state one interpretation of "morally straight" and "clean," the group's published definitions appearing in the Boy Scout and Scoutmaster Handbooks take quite another view. And BSA's broad religious tolerance combined with its declaration that sexual matters are not its "proper area" render its views on the issue equivocal at best and incoherent at worst. We have never held, however, that a group can throw together any mixture of contradictory positions and then invoke the right to associate to defend any one of those views. At a minimum, a group seeking to prevail over an antidiscrimination law must adhere to a clear and unequivocal view.

BSA's inability to make its position clear and its failure to connect its alleged policy to its expressive activities is highly significant. By the time Dale was expelled from the Boy Scouts in 1990, BSA had already been engaged in several suits under a variety of state antidiscrimination public accommodation laws challenging various aspects of its membership policy. Indeed, BSA had filed amicus briefs before this Court in two earlier right to associate cases (*Roberts v. United States Jaycees,* and *Board of Directors of Rotary Int'l v. Rotary Club of Duarte,* 481 U.S. 537 (1987)) pointing to these very cases; it was clearly on notice by 1990 that it might well be subjected to state public accommodation antidiscrimination laws, and that a court might one day reject its claimed right to associate. Yet it took no steps prior to Dale's expulsion to clarify how its exclusivity was connected to its expression. It speaks volumes about the credibility of BSA's claim to a shared goal that homosexuality is incompatible with Scouting that since at least 1984 it had been aware of this issue — indeed, concerned enough to twice file amicus briefs before this Court — yet it did nothing in the intervening six years (or even in the years after Dale's expulsion) to explain clearly and openly why the presence of homosexuals would affect its expressive activities, or to make the view of "morally straight" and "clean" taken in its 1991 and 1992 policies a part of the values actually instilled in Scouts through the Handbook, lessons, or otherwise.

III

BSA's claim finds no support in our cases. We have recognized "a right to associate for the purpose of engaging in those activities protected by the First Amendment — speech, assembly, petition for the redress of grievances, and the exercise of religion." *Roberts*. And we have acknowledged that "when the State interferes with individuals' selection of those with whom they wish to join in a common endeavor, freedom of association . . . may be implicated." But "the right to associate for expressive purposes is not . . . absolute"; rather, "the nature and degree of constitutional protection afforded freedom of association may vary depending on the extent to which . . . the constitutionally protected liberty is at stake in a given case." Indeed, the right to associate does not mean "that in every setting in which individuals exercise some discrimination in choosing associates, their selective process of inclusion and exclusion is protected by the Constitution." *New York State Club Assn., Inc. v. City of New York,* 487 U.S. 1 (1988). For example, we have routinely and easily rejected assertions of this right by expressive organizations with discriminatory membership policies, such as private schools, law firms, and labor organizations. In fact, until today, we have never once found a claimed right to associate in the selection of members to prevail in the face of a State's antidiscrimination law. To the contrary, we have squarely held that a State's antidiscrimination law does not violate a group's right to associate simply because the law conflicts with that group's exclusionary membership policy.

In *Roberts v. United States Jaycees*, we addressed just such a conflict. The Jaycees was a nonprofit membership organization " 'designed to inculcate in the individual membership . . . a spirit of genuine Americanism and civic interest, and . . . to provide . . . an avenue for intelligent participation by young men in the affairs of their community.' " The organization was divided into local chapters, described as " 'young men's organizations,' " in which regular membership was restricted to males between the ages of 18 and 35. But Minnesota's Human Rights Act, which applied to the Jaycees, made it unlawful to " 'deny any person the full and equal enjoyment of . . . a place of public accommodation because of . . . sex.' " The Jaycees, however, claimed that applying the law to it violated its right to associate — in particular its right to maintain its select

We rejected that claim. Cautioning that the right to associate is not "absolute," we held that "infringements on that right may be justified by regulations adopted to serve compelling state interests, unrelated to the suppression of ideas, that cannot be achieved through means significantly less restrictive of associational freedoms." We found the State's purpose of eliminating discrimination is a compelling state interest that is unrelated to the suppression of ideas. We also held that Minnesota's law is the least restrictive means of achieving that interest. The Jaycees had "failed to demonstrate that the Act imposes any serious burdens on the male members' freedom of expressive association." Though the Jaycees had "taken public positions on a number of diverse issues, [and] . . . regularly engage in a variety of . . .activities worthy of constitutional protection under the First Amendment," there was "no basis in the record for concluding that admission of women as full voting members will impede the organization's ability to engage in these protected activities or to disseminate its preferred views." "The Act," we held, "requires no change in the Jaycees' creed of promoting the interest of young men, and it imposes no restrictions on the organization's ability to exclude individuals with ideologies or philosophies different from those of its existing members."

We took a similar approach in *Board of Directors of Rotary Int'l v. Rotary Club of Duarte*. Rotary International, a nonprofit corporation, was founded as " 'an organization of business and professional men united worldwide who provide humanitarian service, encourage high ethical standards in all vocations, and help build goodwill and peace in the world.' " It admitted a cross section of worthy business and community leaders, but refused membership to women. "The exclusion of women," explained the group's General Secretary, "results in an 'aspect of fellowship . . . that is enjoyed by the present male membership.' " That policy also allowed the organization "to operate effectively in foreign countries with varied cultures and social mores." Though California's Civil Rights Act, which applied to Rotary International, prohibited discrimination on the basis of sex, the organization claimed a right to associate, including the right to selec

As in *Jaycees*, we rejected the claim, holding that "the evidence fails to demonstrate that admitting women to Rotary Clubs will affect in any significant way the existing members' ability to carry out their various purposes. "To be sure," we continued, "Rotary Clubs engage in a variety of commendable service activities that are protected by the First Amendment. But [California's Civil Rights Act] does not require the clubs to abandon or alter any of these activities. It does not require them to abandon their basic goals of humanitarian service, high ethical standards in all vocations, good will, and peace. Nor does it require them to abandon their classification system or admit members who do not reflect a cross section of the community." Finally, even if California's law worked a "slight infringement on Rotary members' right of expressive association, that infringement is justified because it serves the State's compelling interest in eliminating discrimination against women."

Rather, in *Jaycees*, we asked whether Minnesota's Human Rights Law requiring the admission of women "imposed any serious burdens" on the group's "collective effort on behalf of [its] shared goals." (emphases added). Notwithstanding the group's obvious publicly stated exclusionary policy, we did not view the inclusion of women as a "serious burden" on the Jaycees' ability to engage in the protected speech of its choice. Similarly, in *Rotary Club*, we asked whether California's law would "affect in any significant way the existing members' ability" to engage in their protected speech, or whether the law would require the clubs "to abandon their basic goals." The relevant question is whether the mere inclusion of the person at issue would "impose any serious burden," "affect in any significant way," or be "a substantial restraint upon" the organization's "shared goals," "basic goals," or "collective effort to foster beliefs." Accordingly, it is necessary to examine what, exactly, are BSA's shared goals and the degree to which its expressive activities would be burdened, affected, or restrained by including homosexuals.

The evidence before this Court makes it exceptionally clear that BSA has, at most, simply adopted an exclusionary membership policy and has no shared goal of disapproving of homosexuality. BSA's mission statement and federal charter say nothing on the matter; its official membership policy is silent; its Scout Oath and Law — and accompanying definitions — are devoid of any view on the topic; its guidance for Scouts and Scoutmasters on sexuality declare that such matters are "not construed to be Scouting's proper area," but are the province of a Scout's parents and pastor; and BSA's posture respecting religion tolerates a wide variety of views on the issue of homosexuality. Moreover, there is simply no evidence that BSA otherwise teaches anything in this area, or that it instructs Scouts on matters involving homosexuality in ways not conveyed in the Boy Scout or Scoutmaster Handbooks. In short, Boy Scouts of America is simply silent on homosexuality. There is no shared goal or collective effort to foster a belief about homosexuality at all — let alone one that is significantly burdened by admitting homosexuals.

As in *Jaycees*, there is "no basis in the record for concluding that admission of [homosexuals] will impede the [Boy Scouts'] ability to engage in [its] protected activities or to disseminate its preferred views" and New Jersey's law "requires no change in [BSA's] creed." And like *Rotary Club*, New Jersey's law "does not require [BSA] to abandon or alter any of" its activities. The evidence relied on by the Court is not to the contrary. The undisclosed 1978 policy certainly adds nothing to the actual views disseminated to the Scouts. It simply says that homosexuality is not "appropriate." There is no reason to give that policy statement more weight than Rotary International's assertion that all-male membership fosters the group's "fellowship" and was the only way it could "operate effectively." As for BSA's post-revocation statements, at most they simply adopt a policy of discrimination, which is no more dispositive than the openly discriminatory policies held insufficient in *Jaycees* and *Rotary Club*; there is no evidence here that BSA's policy was necessary to — or even a part of — BSA's expressive activities or was every taught to Scouts.

Equally important is BSA's failure to adopt any clear position on homosexuality. BSA's temporary, though ultimately abandoned, view that homosexuality is incompatible with being "morally straight" and "clean" is a far cry from the clear, unequivocal statement necessary to prevail on its claim. Despite the solitary sentences in the 1991 and 1992 policies, the group continued to disclaim any single religious or moral position as a general matter and actively eschewed teaching any lesson on sexuality. It also continued to define "morally straight" and "clean" in the Boy Scout and Scoutmaster Handbooks without any reference to homosexuality. As noted earlier, nothing in our cases suggests that a group can prevail on a right to expressive association if it, effectively, speaks out of both sides of its mouth. A State's antidiscrimination law does not impose a "serious burden" or a "substantial restraint" upon the group's "shared goals" if the group itself is unable to identify its own stance with any clarity.

IV

The majority pretermits this entire analysis. It finds that BSA in fact " 'teaches that homosexual conduct is not morally straight.' " This conclusion, remarkably, rests entirely on statements in BSA's briefs. Moreover, the majority insists that we must "give deference to an association's assertions regarding the nature of its expression" and "we must also give deference to an association's view of what would impair its expression." So long as the record "contains written evidence" to support a group's bare assertion, "we need not inquire further." Once the organization "asserts" that it engages in particular expression, "we cannot doubt" the truth of that asse

This is an astounding view of the law. I am unaware of any previous instance in which our analysis of the scope of a constitutional right was determined by looking at what a litigant asserts in his or her brief and inquiring no further. It is even more astonishing in the First Amendment area, because, as the majority itself acknowledges, "we are obligated to independently review the factual record." It is an odd form of independent review that consists of deferring entirely to whatever a litigant claims. But the majority insists that our inquiry must be "limited," because "it is not the role of the courts to reject a group's expressed values because they disagree with those values or find them internally inconsistent."

But nothing in our cases calls for this Court to do any such thing. An organization can adopt the message of its choice, and it is not this Court's place to disagree with it. But we must inquire whether the group is, in fact, expressing a message (whatever it may be) and whether that message (if one is expressed) is significantly affected by a State's antidiscrimination law. More critically, that inquiry requires our independent analysis, rather than deference to a group's litigating posture. Reflection on the subject dictates that such an inquiry is required.

Surely there are instances in which an organization that truly aims to foster a belief at odds with the purposes of a State's antidiscrimination laws will have a First Amendment right to association that precludes forced compliance with those laws. But that right is not a freedom to discriminate at will, nor is it a right to maintain an exclusionary membership policy simply out of fear of what the public reaction would be if the group's membership were opened up. It is an implicit right designed to protect the enumerated rights of the First Amendment, not a license to act on any discriminatory impulse. To prevail in asserting a right of expressive association as a defense to a charge of violating an antidiscrimination law, the organization must at least show it has adopted and advocated an unequivocal position inconsistent with a position advocated or epitomized by the person whom the organization seeks to exclude. If this Court were to defer to whatever position an organization is prepared to assert in its briefs, there would be no way to mark the proper boundary between genuine exercises of the right to associate, on the one hand, and sham claims that are simply attempts to insulate nonexpressive private discrimination, on the other hand. Shielding a litigant's claim from judicial scrutiny would, in turn, render civil rights legislation a nullity, and turn this important constitutional right into a farce. Accordingly, the Court's prescription of total deference will not do. In this respect, Justice Frankfurter's words seem particularly apt:

Elaborately to argue against this contention is to dignify a claim devoid of constitutional substance. Of course a State may leave abstention from such discriminations to the conscience of individuals. On the other hand, a State may choose to put its authority behind one of the cherished aims of American feeling by forbidding indulgence in racial or religious prejudice to another's hurt. To use the Fourteenth Amendment as a sword against such State power would stultify that Amendment. Certainly the insistence by individuals on their private prejudices as to race, color or creed, in relations like those now before us, ought not to have a higher constitutional sanction than the determination of a State to extend the area of nondiscrimination beyond that which the Constitution itself exacts. *Railway Mail Assn. v. Corsi,* 326 U.S. 88, 98, (1945) (concurring opinion).

There is, of course, a valid concern that a court's independent review may run the risk of paying too little heed to an organization's sincerely held views. But unless one is prepared to turn the right to associate into a free pass out of antidiscrimination laws, an independent inquiry is a necessity. Though the group must show that its expressive activities will be substantiallyburdened by the State's law, if that law truly has a significant effect on a group's speech, even the subtle speaker will be able to identify that impact. In this case, no such concern is warranted. It is entirely clear that BSA in fact expresses no clear, unequivocal message burdened by New Jersey's law.

V

Even if BSA's right to associate argument fails, it nonetheless might have a First Amendment right to refrain from including debate and dialogue about homosexuality as part of its mission to instill values in Scouts. It can, for example, advise Scouts who are entering adulthood and have questions about sex to talk "with your parents, religious leaders, teachers, or Scoutmaster," and, in turn, it can direct Scoutmasters who are asked such questions "not undertake to instruct Scouts, in any formalized manner, in the subject of sex and family life" because "it is not construed to be Scouting's proper area." Dale's right to advocate certain beliefs in a public forum or in a private debate does not include a right to advocate these ideas when he is working as a Scoutmaster. And BSA cannot be compelled to include a message about homosexuality among the values it actually chooses to teach its Scouts, if it would prefer to remain silent on that subject.

BSA has not contended, nor does the record support, that Dale had ever advocated a view on homosexuality to his troop before his membership was revoked. Accordingly, BSA's revocation could only have been based on an assumption that he would do so in the future. But the only information BSA had at the time it revoked Dale's membership was a newspaper article describing a seminar at Rutgers University on the topic of homosexual teenagers that Dale attended. The relevant passage reads:

> James Dale, 19, co-president of the Rutgers University Lesbian Gay Alliance with Sharice Richardson, also 19, said he lived a double life while in high school, pretending to be straight while attending a military academy." He remembers dating girls and even laughing at homophobic jokes while at school, only admitting his homosexuality during his second year at Rutgers. " 'I was looking for a role model, someone who was gay and accepting of me,' Dale said, adding he wasn't just seeking sexual experiences, but a community that would take him in and provide him with a support network and friends.

Nothing in that article, however, even remotely suggests that Dale would advocate any views on homosexuality to his troop. The Scoutmaster Handbook instructs Dale, like all Scoutmasters, that sexual issues are not their "proper area," and there is no evidence that Dale had any intention of violating this rule. Indeed, from all accounts Dale was a model Boy Scout and Assistant Scoutmaster up until the day his membership was revoked, and there is no reason to believe that he would suddenly disobey the directives of BSA because of anything he said in the newspaper article.

To be sure, the article did say that Dale was co-president of the Lesbian/Gay Alliance at Rutgers University, and that group presumably engages in advocacy regarding homosexual issues. But surely many members of BSA engage in expressive activities outside of their troop, and surely BSA does not want all of that expression to be carried on inside the troop. For example, a

Scoutmaster may be a member of a religious group that encourages its followers to convert others to its faith. Or a Scoutmaster may belong to a political party that encourages its members to advance its views among family and friends. Yet BSA does not think it is appropriate for Scoutmasters to proselytize a particular faith to unwilling Scouts or to attempt to convert them from one religion to another. Nor does BSA think it appropriate for Scouts or Scoutmasters to bring politics into the troop. n18. From all accounts, then, BSA does not discourage or forbid outside expressive activity, but relies on compliance with its policies and trusts Scouts and Scoutmasters alike not to bring unwanted views into the organization. Of course, a disobedient member who flouts BSA's policy may be expelled. But there is no basis for BSA to presume that a homosexual will be unable to comply with BSA's policy not to discuss sexual matters any more than it would presume that politically or religiously active members could not resist the urge to proselytize or politicize during troop meetings. As BSA itself puts it, its rights are "not implicated unless a prospective leader presents himself as a role model inconsistent with Boy Scouting's understanding of the Scout Oath and Law."

The majority, though, does not rest its conclusion on the claim that Dale will use his position as a bully pulpit. Rather, it contends that Dale's mere presence among the Boy Scouts will itself force the group to convey a message about homosexuality — even if Dale has no intention of doing so. The majority holds that "the presence of an avowed homosexual and gay rights activist in an assistant scoutmaster's uniform sends a distinct . . .message," and, accordingly, BSA is entitled to exclude that message. In particular, "Dale's presence in the Boy Scouts would, at the very least, force the organization to send a message, both to the youth members and the world, that the Boy Scouts accepts homosexual conduct as a legitimate form of behavior."

The majority's argument relies exclusively on *Hurley v. Irish-American Gay, Lesbian and Bisexual Group of Boston, Inc.* In that case, petitioners John Hurley and the South Boston Allied War Veterans Council ran a privately operated St. Patrick's Day parade. Respondent, an organization known as "GLIB," represented a contingent of gays, lesbians, and bisexuals who sought to march in the petitioners' parade "as a way to express pride in their Irish heritage as openly gay, lesbian, and bisexual individuals." When the parade organizers refused GLIB's admission, GLIB brought suit under Massachusetts' antidiscrimination law. That statute, like New Jersey's law, prohibited discrimination on account of sexual orientation in any place of public accommodation, which the state courts interpreted to include the parade. Petitioners argued that forcing them to include GLIB in their parade would violate their free speech rights.

We agreed. We first pointed out that the St. Patrick's Day parade — like most every parade — is an inherently expressive undertaking. Next, we reaffirmed that the government may not compel anyone to proclaim a belief with which he or she disagrees.We then found that GLIB's marching in the parade would be an expressive act suggesting the view "that people of their sexual orientations have as much claim to unqualified social acceptance as heterosexuals." Finally, we held that GLIB's participation in the parade "would likely be perceived" as the parade organizers' own speech — or at least as a view which they approved — because of a parade organizer's customary control over who marches in the parade. 515 U.S. at 575. Though Hurley has a superficial similarity to the present case, a close inspection reveals a wide gulf between that case and the one before us today.

First, it was critical to our analysis that GLIB was actually conveying a message by participating in the parade — otherwise, the parade organizers could hardly claim that they were being forced to include any unwanted message at all. Our conclusion that GLIB was conveying a message was inextricably tied to the fact that GLIB wanted to march in a parade, as well as the manner in which it intended to march. We noted the "inherent expressiveness of marching [in a parade] to make a point," and in particular that GLIB was formed for the purpose of making a particular point about gay pride. More specifically, GLIB "distributed a fact sheet describing the members' intentions" and, in a previous parade, had "marched behind a shamrock-strewn banner with the simple inscription 'Irish American Gay, Lesbian and Bisexual Group of Boston.' " "[A] contingent marching behind the organization's banner," we said, would clearly convey a message. Indeed, we expressly distinguished between the members of GLIB, who marched as a unit to express their views about their own sexual orientation, on the one hand, and homosexuals who might participate as individuals in the parade without intending to express anything about their sexuality by doing so.

Second, we found it relevant that GLIB's message "would likely be perceived" as the parade organizers' own speech. That was so because "parades and demonstrations . . .are not understood to be so neutrally presented or selectively viewed" as, say, a broadcast by a cable operator, who is usually considered to be "merely 'a conduit' for the speech" produced by others. Rather, parade organizers are usually understood to make the "customary determination about a unit admitted to the parade."

Dale's inclusion in the Boy Scouts is nothing like the case in *Hurley*. His participation sends no cognizable message to the Scouts or to the world. Unlike GLIB, Dale did not carry a banner or a sign; he did not distribute any fact sheet; and he expressed no intent to send any message. If there is any kind of message being sent, then, it is by the mere act of joining the Boy Scouts. Such an act does not constitute an instance of symbolic speech under the First Amendment.

It is true, of course, that some acts are so imbued with symbolic meaning that they qualify as "speech" under the First Amendment. At the same time, however, "we cannot accept the view that an apparently limitless variety of conduct can be labeled 'speech' whenever the person engaging in the conduct intends thereby to express an idea." [*United States v. O'Brien*]. Though participating in the Scouts could itself conceivably send a message on some level, it is not the kind of act that we have recognized as speech. Indeed, if merely joining a group did constitute symbolic speech; and such speech were attributable to the group being joined; and that group has the right to exclude that speech (and hence, the right to exclude that person from joining), then the right of free speech effectively becomes a limitless right to exclude for every organization, whether or not it engages in any expressive activities. That cannot be, and never has been, the law.

This is not to say that Scouts do not engage in expressive activity. It is only to say that the simple act of joining the Scouts — unlike joining a parade — is not inherently expressive.

The only apparent explanation for the majority's holding, then, is that homosexuals are simply so different from the rest of society that their presence alone — unlike any other individual's — should be singled out for special First Amendment treatment. Under the majority's reasoning, an openly gay male is irreversibly affixed with the label "homosexual." That label, even though unseen, communicates a message that permits his exclusion wherever he goes. His openness is the sole and sufficient justification for his ostracism. Though unintended, reliance on such a justification is tantamount to a constitutionally prescribed symbol of inferiority. As counsel for the Boy Scouts remarked, Dale "put a banner around his neck when he . . . got himself into the newspaper . . .. He created a reputation. . . . He can't take that banner off. He put it on himself and, indeed, he has continued to put it on himself."

Another difference between this case and Hurley lies in the fact that Hurley involved the parade organizers' claim to determine the content of the message they wish to give at a particular time and place. The standards governing such a claim are simply different from the standards that govern BSA's claim of a right of expressive association. Generally, a private person or a private organization has a right to refuse to broadcast a message with which it disagrees, and a right to refuse to contradict or garble its own specific statement at any given place or time by including the messages of others. An expressive association claim, however, normally involves the avowal and advocacy of a consistent position on some issue over time. This is why a different kind of scrutiny must be given to an expressive association claim, lest the right of expressive association simply turn into a right to discriminate whenever some group can think of an expressive object that would seem to be inconsistent with the admission of some person as a member or at odds with the appointment of a person to a leadership position in the group.

Furthermore, it is not likely that BSA would be understood to send any message, either to Scouts or to the world, simply by admitting someone as a member. Over the years, BSA has generously welcomed over 87 million young Americans into its ranks. The notion that an organization of that size and enormous prestige implicitly endorses the views that each of those adults may express in a non-Scouting context is simply mind boggling. Indeed, in this case there is no evidence that the young Scouts in Dale's troop, or members of their families, were even aware of his sexual orientation, either before or after his public statements at Rutgers University. It is equally far-fetched to assert that Dale's open declaration of his homosexuality, reported in a local newspaper, will effectively force BSA to send a message to anyone simply because it allows Dale to be an Assistant Scoutmaster. For an Olympic gold medal winner or a Wimbledon tennis champion, being "openly gay" perhaps communicates a message — for example, that openness about one's sexual orientation is more virtuous than concealment; that a homosexual person can be a capable and virtuous person who should be judged like anyone else; and that homosexuality is not immoral — but it certainly does not follow that they necessarily send a message on behalf of the organizations that sponsor the activities in which they excel. The fact that such persons participate in these organizations is not usually construed to convey a message on behalf of those organizations any more than does the inclusion of women, African-Americans, religious minorities, or any other discrete group. Surely the organizations are not forced by antidiscrimination laws to take any position on the legitimacy of any individual's private beliefs or private conduct.

VI

Unfavorable opinions about homosexuals "have ancient roots." *Bowers v. Hardwick,* 478 U.S. 186 (1986). Like equally atavistic opinions about certain racial groups, those roots have been nourished by sectarian doctrine. Over the years, however, interaction with real people, rather than mere adherence to traditional ways of thinking about members of unfamiliar classes, have modified those opinions.

That such prejudices are still prevalent and that they have caused serious and tangible harm to countless members of the class New Jersey seeks to protect are established matters of fact that neither the Boy Scouts nor the Court disputes. That harm can only be aggravated by the creation of a constitutional shield for a policy that is itself the product of a habitual way of thinking about strangers. As JUSTICE BRANDEIS so wisely advised, "we must be ever on our guard, lest we erect our prejudices into legal principles."

If we would guide by the light of reason, we must let our minds be bold. I respectfully dissent.

JUSTICE SOUTER, with whom JUSTICE GINSBURG and JUSTICE BREYER join, dissenting.

I join JUSTICE STEVENS's dissent but add this further word on the significance of Part VI of his opinion. There, JUSTICE STEVENS describes the changing attitudes toward gay people and notes a parallel with the decline of stereotypical thinking about race and gender. The legitimacy of New Jersey's interest in forbidding discrimination on all these bases by those furnishing public accommodations is, as JUSTICE STEVENS indicates, acknowledged by many to be beyond question. The fact that we are cognizant of this laudable decline in stereotypical thinking on homosexuality should not, however, be taken to control the resolution of this case.

Boy Scouts of America (BSA) is entitled, consistently with its own tenets and the open doors of American courts, to raise a federal constitutional basis for resisting the application of New Jersey's law. BSA has done that and has chosen to defend against enforcement of the state public accommodations law on the ground that the First Amendment protects expressive association: individuals have a right to join together to advocate opinions free from government interference.

The right of expressive association does not, of course, turn on the popularity of the views advanced by a group that claims protection. Whether the group appears to this Court to be in the vanguard or rearguard of social thinking is irrelevant to the group's rights. I conclude that BSA has not made out an expressive association claim, therefore, not because of what BSA may espouse, but because of its failure to make sexual orientation the subject of any unequivocal advocacy, using the channels it customarily employs to state its message. As JUSTICE STEVENS explains, no group can claim a right of expressive association without identifying a clear position to be advocated over time in an unequivocal way. To require less, and to allow exemption from a public accommodations statute based on any individual's difference from an alleged group ideal, however expressed and however inconsistently claimed, would convert the right of expressive association into an easy trump of any antidiscrimination law.

If, on the other hand, an expressive association claim has met the conditions JUSTICE STEVENS describes as necessary, there may well be circumstances in which the antidiscrimination law must yield, as he says. It is certainly possible for an individual to become so identified with a position as to epitomize it publicly. When that position is at odds with a group's advocated position, applying an antidiscrimination statute to require the group's acceptance of the individual in a position of group leadership could so modify or muddle or frustrate the group's advocacy as to violate the expressive associational right. While it is not our business here to rule on any such hypothetical, it is at least clear that our estimate of the progressive character of the group's position will be irrelevant to the First Amendment analysis if such a case comes to us for decision.

NOTES

1. *Roberts v. United States Jaycees*, 468 U.S. 609 (1984). *Roberts*, discussed extensively throughout *Dale*, was a suit by the Jaycees alleging that Minnesota's requiring the organization to admit women as regular members would infringe upon the regular male members' rights of free speech and association. Justice Brennan, speaking for the Court, held that the interference with the Jaycees' associational choices did not violate the constitutionally protected version of that right: "The undisputed facts reveal that the local chapters of the Jaycees are large and basically unselective groups. Apart from age and sex, neither the national organization nor the local chapters employs criteria for judging applicants for membership, and new members are routinely recruited and admitted with no inquiry into their backgrounds." Therefore "the Jaycees chapters lack the distinctive characteristics that might afford constitutional protection to the decision of its members to exclude women."

Nor did it violate their expressive associational rights: "In claiming that women might have a different attitude about such issues as the federal budget, school prayer, voting rights, and foreign relations, or that the organization's public positions would have a different effect if the group were not 'a purely young men's association,' the Jaycees rely solely on unsupported generalizations about the relative interests and perspectives of men and women. In the absence of a showing far more substantial than that attempted by the Jaycees, we decline to indulge in the sexual stereotyping that underlies appellee's contention that, by allowing women to vote, application of the Minnesota Act will change the content or impact of the organization's speech."

"In any event," the Court added, "even if enforcement of the Act causes some incidental abridgement of the Jaycees' protected speech, that effect is no greater than is necessary to accomplish the State's legitimate purposes."

The *Roberts* rationale was relied upon by Justice Powell in *Board of Dirs. of Rotary Int'l v. Rotary Club of Duarte,* 481 U.S. 537 (1987), but only after conducting an independent inquiry into the nature of privacy and associational claims that could be made by Rotary Clubs. The California courts had applied the state public accommodations statute to prevent the International from expelling the local club when the local took women members. The International claimed that the result violated rights of free expression and association:

> The evidence in this case indicates that the relationship among Rotary Club members is not the kind of intimate or private relation that warrants constitutional protection. The size of local Rotary Clubs ranges from fewer than 20 to more than 900. There is no upper limit on the membership of any local Rotary Club. About ten percent of the membership of a typical club moves away or drops out during a typical year. The clubs therefore are instructed to "keep a flow of prospects coming" to make up for the attrition and gradually to enlarge the membership. The purpose of Rotary "is to produce an inclusive, not exclusive, membership, making possible the recognition of all useful local occupations, and enabling the club to be a true cross-section of the business and professional life of the community." The membership undertakes a variety of service projects designed to aid the community, to raise the standards of the members' businesses and professions, and to improve international relations. Such an inclusive "fellowship for service based on diversity of interest," however beneficial to the members and to those they serve, does not suggest the kind of private or personal relationship to which we have accorded protection under the First Amendment. To be sure, membership in Rotary Clubs is not open to the general public. But each club is instructed to include in its membership "all fully qualified prospective members located within its territory," to avoid "arbitrary limits on the number of members in the club," and to "establish and maintain a membership growth pattern."
>
> Many of the Rotary Clubs' central activities are carried on in the presence of strangers. Rotary Clubs are required to admit any member of any other Rotary Club to their meetings. Members are encouraged to invite business associates and competitors to meetings. At some Rotary Clubs, the visitors number "in the tens and twenties each week" Joint meetings with the members of other organizations, and other joint activities, are permitted. The clubs are encouraged to seek coverage of their meetings and activities in local newspapers. In sum, Rotary Clubs, rather than carrying on their activities in an atmosphere of privacy, seek to keep their "windows and doors open to the whole world." We therefore conclude that application of the [statute] to local Rotary Clubs does not interfere unduly with the members' freedom of private association.

In *New York State Club Ass'n v. City of New York,* 487 U.S. 1 (1988), the Court upheld against a First Amendment overbreadth challenge New York City's Local Law 63, which prohibited discrimination in any "institution, club or place of accommodation [that] has more than four hundred members, provides regular meal service and regularly receives payment for dues, fees, use of space, facilities, services, meals or beverages directly or indirectly from or on behalf of nonmembers for the furtherance of trade or business." However, any such club "shall be deemed to be in its nature distinctly private" if it is a "benevolent" order or religious corporation. Justice White, speaking for the Court, stated:

> On its face, Local Law 63 does not affect "in any significant way" the ability of individuals to form associations that will advocate public or private viewpoints. It does not require the clubs "to abandon or alter" any activities that are protected by the First Amendment. If a club seeks to exclude individuals who do not share the views that the club's members wish to promote, the Law erects no obstacle to this end. It is conceivable, of course, that an association might be able to show that it is organized for specific expressive purposes and that it will not be able to advocate its desired viewpoints nearly as effectively if it cannot confine its membership to those who share the same sex, for example, or the same religion. In the case before us, however, it seems sensible enough to believe that many of the large clubs covered by the Law are not of this kind.

The Court noted that the "opportunities for individual associations to contest the constitutionality of the Law as it may be applied against them are adequate to assure that any overbreadth under the Law will be curable through case-by-case analysis of specific facts." Justice O'Connor, joined by Justice Kennedy, concurred separately, as did Justice Scalia.

2. *The problem of proof.* Note the sharp dispute among the Justices concerning the factual issue of the Boy Scouts' preexisting attitude towards homosexuality. According to one commentator, "[t]he question of what level of proof should be required of groups that assert a First Amendment right to an exemption from anti-discrimination laws is profoundly important. Setting the bar too low would permit such groups to circumvent democratically enacted laws on a whim, or simply because they would rather not be inconvenienced, at the expense of important legislative goals. Setting the bar too high would interfere with the ability of such groups to determine their values, how to order those values, and how to express them." Steffen N. Johnson, *Expressive Association and Organizational Autonomy,* 85 Minn. L. Rev. 1639, 1640–41 (2001). The same commentator concludes that "the *Dale* Court set the bar in approximately the right place." *Id.* at 1641.

3. *The constitutional origins of the right of nonassociation.* From what aspects of free speech theory is the right of nonassociation properly derived. In *Dale,* the Court proceeds largely on the premise that the right of nonassociation serves as a corollary to protect the affirmative right of association. Is that correct? Consider the assertion that the theoretical foundation of *Dale* is "misguidedly truncated." Martin Redish & Christopher

McFadden, *HUAC, the Hollywood Ten, and the First Amendment Right of Non-Association,* 85 MINN. L. REV. 1669, 1672 (2001). "In addition to the affirmative right of association," it is argued, "the right of non-association should be seen as an outgrowth of a completely different aspect of the First Amendment universe: the line of cases recognizing a First Amendment right not to be forced to speak. Such a recognition would extend the right of non-association to numerous instances of purely passive refusals to associate with those holding politically or ideologically offensive views." *Id.*

4. *Determining the reach of Dale.* Consider what result the majority's analysis in *Dale* would dictate in the following hypothetical assertions of a First Amendment right of non-association, and whether or not you agree with that result (in each case, assume that the act of non-association violates applicable statutes):

a. A local orchestra excludes a member, solely because it is discovered that he is the leader of a militant white supremacist organization. *See* Redish & McFadden, 85 MINN. L. REV. at 1672.

b. An organization of white supremacists excludes an individual from membership because he is African-American. (How, if at all, is this case different from *Roberts*? From the orchestra hypothetical?)

c. A restaurant owner excludes African-Americans from his restaurant because he believes in separation of the races.

5. *Hurley v. Irish-American Gay, Lesbian and Bisexual Group,* 515 U.S. 557 (1995). The Court stated the issue in this case as being "whether Massachusetts may require private citizens who organize a parade to include among the marchers a group imparting a message the organizers do not wish to convey." A group of gay, lesbian and bisexual persons of Irish descent [GLIB] sought to participate in Boston's St. Patrick's Day parade. The group in charge of the parade, the South Boston Allied War Veterans Council, chose to exclude GLIB, and that organization sued for violation of the state's public accommodations law. The state trial court found for GLIB, reasoning that because the statute merely prohibited discrimination on the basis of sexual orientation, any infringement on the Council's right to expressive association was merely "incidental" to the legitimate purpose of eradicating discrimination. The Supreme Judicial Court of Massachusetts affirmed.

The U.S. Supreme Court reversed:

> To be sure, we agree with the state courts that in spite of excluding some applicants, the Council is rather lenient in admitting participants. But a private speaker does not forfeit constitutional protection simply by combining multifarious voices, or by failing to edit their themes to isolate an exact message as the exclusive subject matter of the speech.

The Court reasoned that "[s]ince every participating unit affects the message conveyed by the private organizers, the state courts' application of the [public accommodations] statute produced an order essentially requiring [the Council] to alter the expressive content of their parade."

The Court rejected the argument that the parade presented no coherent message that was being disrupted:

> [L]ike a composer, the Council selects the expressive units of the parade from potential participants, and though the score may not produce a particularized message, each contingent's expression in the Council's eyes comports with what merits celebration on that day. Even if this view gives the Council credit for a more considered judgment then it actively made, the Council is clearly decided to exclude a message it did not like from the communication it chose to make, and that is enough to invoke its right as a private speaker to shape its expression by speaking on one subject while remaining silent on another.

Is this decision distinguishable from *Roberts*?

6. *Compulsory dues and fees.* The constitutionality under the First Amendment of compulsory service fees charged pursuant to an agency shop arrangement authorized by state law was raised in *Abood v. Detroit Bd. of Educ.,* 431 U.S. 209 (1977). Relying heavily on precedent, Justice Stewart, for the Court, initially upheld service charges when "used to finance expenditures by the union for the purposes of collective bargaining, contract administration, and grievance adjustment." Although employees may disagree with union positions, "such interference [with associational interests] as exists is constitutionally justified by the legislative assessment of the important contribution of the union shop to the system of labor relations established by Congress."

The Court held, however, that a different rule pertains when compulsory service charges are used for political or ideological purposes divorced from the union's duty as a collective bargaining representative:

> One of the principles underlying the Court's decision in *Buckley v. Valeo*, was that contributing to an organization for the purpose of spreading a political message is protected by the First Amendment. The fact that the appellants are compelled to make, rather than prohibited from making contributions for political purposes works no less an infringement of their constitutional rights. For at the heart of the First Amendment is the notion that an individual should be free to believe as he will, and that in a free society one's beliefs should be shaped by his mind and his conscience rather than coerced by the State.

These principles were held to "prohibit the appellees from requiring any of the appellants to contribute to the support of an ideological cause he may oppose as a condition of holding a job as a public school teacher." While the union can spend funds for the expression of political views or political candidates, such expenditures must be financed by charges "paid by employees who do not object to advancing those ideas and who are not coerced into doing so against their will by the threat of loss of governmental employment." Justice Stewart recognized the difficulty of drawing lines between collective bargaining activities and ideological activities but had no occasion in this instance "to define such a dividing line."

***Keller v. State Bar*, 496 U.S. 1 (1990).** Chief Justice Rehnquist, for a unanimous Court, held that an "integrated bar" like the State Bar of California could not use the dues of its members to finance political and ideological activities with which its members disagreed. An "integrated bar" conditions the right to practice law on membership and the payment of dues to the State Bar. Although lawyers admitted to practice in the state may be required to join and pay dues to an "integrated" state bar, the First Amendment restricts the dues-financed activities in which the State Bar may engage.

Members of the California State Bar challenged the use of dues for political and ideological purposes with which they disagreed. Examples of some of the activities challenged included "lobbying for or against state regulation (1) prohibiting state and local agency employers from requiring employees to take polygraph tests; (2) prohibiting possession of armor piercing handgun ammunition; (3) creating an unlimited right to action to sue anybody causing air pollution; and (4) requesting Congress to refrain from enacting a guest worker program." The petitioners also objected to the State Bar's opposition to "federal legislation limiting federal court jurisdiction over abortions, public school prayer and busing."

Was the use of dues for political or ideological purposes governed by *Abood v. Detroit Board of Education*? The United States Supreme Court answered this question in the affirmative. *Abood* had invalidated the use of "agency-shop dues" by non-union public employees for political and ideological causes unrelated to collective bargaining activities. The Supreme Court of California had distinguished *Abood* and rejected the first amendment challenge to the protested use of dues by the State Bar on the ground that the Bar's "status as a regulated state agency exempted it from any constitutional constraints on the use of its speech." Relying on the "government speech" doctrine, the State Bar contended: "The government must take substantive positions and decide disputed issues to govern. . . . So long as it bases its actions on legitimate goals, government may speak despite citizen disagreement with its message, for government is not required to be content-neutral."

Chief Justice Rehnquist was not persuaded by the effort to distinguish the "integrated state bar" from the labor union in *Abood*. The State Bar was different than most government agencies. The bar's funds came from mandatory dues not from legislative appropriations. In addition, the Bar's functions were essentially advisory since the state Supreme Court had to implement the Bar's suggestions. There was "a substantial analogy" between the State Bar and its members and the relationship of the unions to their members. Chief Justice Rehnquist declared:

> *Abood* held that a union could not expend a dissenting individual's dues for ideological activities not "germane" to the purpose for which compelled association was justified: collective bargaining. Here the compelled association and integrated bar is justified by the State's interest in regulating the legal profession and improving the quality of legal services. The State Bar may therefore constitutionally fund activities germane to these goals out of the mandatory dues of all

> members. It may not, however, in such manner fund activities of an ideological nature which fall outside those areas of activity. The difficult question, of course, is to define the latter class of activities.

What activities were in fact "germane" to the goals of the State Bar? The guiding standard should be "whether the challenged expenditures are necessarily or reasonably incurred for the purpose of regulating the legal profession or improving the quality of the legal service available to the people of the State."

7. *Compelled dues in the university setting: Bd. of Regents of Univ. of Wis. v. Southworth,* 529 U.S. 217 (2000). Student activity fees traditionally are used to fund a variety of student organizations and their expressive activities. In the Wisconsin case, the Supreme Court held first that the University was not required to limit subsidies to those activities that were "germane" to the University mission. "If it is difficult to define germane speech with ease or precision where a union or bar association is the party, the standard becomes all the more unmanageable in the public university setting, particularly where the State undertakes to stimulate the whole universe of speech and ideas." Therefore, the University was not required (although it could if it chose to do so) to have a refund or option system. Dissenting students do, however, have First Amendment interests at stake. "The proper measure, and the principal standard of protection for objecting students, we conclude, is the requirement of viewpoint neutrality in the allocation of funding support."

Rosenberger v. University of Virginia [p. 1460], although decided before *Southworth*, involved the question of how to carry out viewpoint neutrality in the difficult setting of religious speech. The University of Virginia had decided not to fund a student newspaper that carried a religious viewpoint. The Supreme Court struck this down, holding that "the school's adherence to a rule of viewpoint neutrality in administering its student fee program would prevent 'any mistaken impression that the student newspapers speak for the University.'" In the religious setting, this neutrality results in a "nonpreferential" allocation of subsidies for all religious viewpoints.

In the more typical setting, viewpoint neutrality requires some administrative judgment to ensure that there is no favoritism for certain viewpoints over others. In the Wisconsin scheme, an organization could seek funding by campus-wide referendum. The Court remanded for consideration of whether this method of obtaining funding for popular causes, and presumably not for unpopular causes, would violate viewpoint neutrality.

8. *Wooley v. Maynard,* 430 U.S. 705 (1978). The Court held, per Chief Justice Burger, that a state may not constitutionally enforce criminal sanctions against persons who cover the motto "live free or die" on passenger vehicle license plates because that motto is repugnant to their moral and religious beliefs. The freedom of thought protected by the First Amendment includes the right to speak freely and the right to be free from being compelled to speak. The state may not require an individual to participate in the dissemination of an ideological message by displaying it on his private property in a manner and for the express purpose that it be observed and read by the public. The state interests in facilitating the identification of passenger vehicles and promoting the appreciation of history, individualism and state pride are not sufficiently compelling to override the First Amendment interest at stake.

Consider the argument that the First Amendment interest asserted in *Wooley* was largely trivial. After all, no one seeing a car driven with a state slogan on the license plate would reasonably identify the driver with the view conveyed by the slogan. If you find this argument persuasive, would you find it less persuasive if the slogan were something like, "Hitler was right"?

9. *Glickman v. Wileman Brothers & Elliott*, 521 U.S. 457 (1997). The Court, per Justice Stevens, rejected a First Amendment challenge to marketing orders promulgated by the Secretary of Agriculture pursuant to the Agricultural Marketing Agreement Act of 1937, assessing fruit growers for the cost of generic advertising of their products. The growers noted their disagreement with the content of some of the generic advertising, and argued that the assessment constituted compelled speech, in violation of the First Amendment. The Supreme Court disagreed: "Three characteristics of the regulatory scheme at issue distinguish it from laws that we have found to abridge the freedom of speech. First, the marketing orders impose no restraint on the freedom of any producer to communicate any message to any audience. Second, they do not compel any person to engage in any actual or symbolic speech. Third, they do not compel the producers to endorse or to finance any political or ideological views. Indeed, since all of the respondents are engaged in the business of marketing California nectarines, plums, and peaches, it is fair to presume that they agree with the central message of the speech that is generated by the generic program."

In dissent, Justice Souter joined in whole or in part by three other justices argued: "The legitimacy of governmental regulation does not validate coerced subsidies for speech that the government cannot show to be reasonably necessary to implement the regulation, and the very reasons for recognizing that commercial speech falls within the scope of First Amendment protection likewise justifies the protection of those who object to subsidizing it against their will." Justice Souter rejected the majority's assumption that the fruit growers did not actually disagree with the generic advertising, and argued that in any event the assumption was beside the point. "[T]he requirement of disagreement," he said, "finds no legal warrant in our compelled-speech cases."

10. *United States v. United Foods, Inc.*, 533 U.S. 405 (2001): The Court distinguished *Glickman* in upholding a constitutional challenge to an assessment imposed pursuant to the Mushroom Promotion, Research, and Consumer Information Act on mushroom producers to fund re, advertisements promoting mushroom sales. United Foods wanted to convey the message to consumers that its brand of mushrooms is superior to those grown by other producers, while the messages conveyed pursuant to the assessment suggested that all mushrooms were fungible. United Foods argued that it was being compelled to subsidize expression, in violation of the First Amendment. A majority of the Court agreed, even though commercial speech was involved: "Our precedents concerning compelled contributions to speech provide the beginning point for our analysis. The fact that the speech is in aid of a commercial purpose does not deprive respondent of all First Amendment protection. [T]hose whose business and livelihood depend in some way upon the product involved no doubt deem First Amendment protection to be just as important for them as it is for other discrete, little noticed groups in a society which values the freedom resulting from speech in all its diverse parts." The Court found that "First Amendment values are at serious risk if the government can compel a particular citizen, or a discrete group of citizens, to pay special subsidies for speech on the side that it favors; and there is no apparent principle which distinguishes out of hand minor debates about whether a branded mushroom is better than just any mushroom."

The Court concluded that the case differed from *Glickman* "in a most fundamental respect. In *Glickman*, the mandated assessments for speech were ancillary to a more comprehensive program restricting marketing autonomy. Here, for all practical purposes, the advertising itself, far from being of the ancillary, is the principal object of the regulatory scheme." The Court reasoned that "[t]he features of the marketing scheme found important in *Glickman* are not present in the case now before us," because "almost all of the funds collected under the mandatory assessments are for one purpose: generic advertising." The mushroom producers "are not forced to associate as a group which makes cooperative decisions."

Justice Thomas wrote separately "to reiterate my views that 'paying money for the purposes of advertising involves speech,' and that 'compelling speech raises a First Amendment issue just as much as restricting speech.' Any regulation that compels the funding of advertising must be subjected to the most stringent First Amendment scrutiny."

Justice Breyer dissented: "The Court, in my view, disregards controlling precedent, fails properly to analyze the strength of the relevant regulatory and commercial speech interests, and introduces into First Amendment law an unreasoned legal principle that may well pose an obstacle to the development of beneficial forms of economic regulation." He found *Glickman* to be controlling: "The issue there, like here, was whether the First Amendment prohibited the Government from collecting a fee for collective product advertising from an objecting grower of those products (nectarines, peaches, and plums). We held that the collection of the fee did not 'rais[e] a First Amendment issue for us to resolve,' but rather was 'simply a question of economic policy for Congress and the Executive to resolve.' " He found *Abood* irrelevant, because "the subsidiary activities in question were political activities that might "conflict with one's 'freedom of belief.' " In the present case, by contrast, "the funded activities here, like identical activities in [*Glickman*], do not involve this kind of expression."

11. *Johanns v. Livestock Marketing Association*, 544 U.S. 550 (2005). The association brought an action against the Department of Agriculture, challenging, on First Amendment grounds, mandatory contributions collected from beef producers pursuant to the Beef Promotion and Research Act, for the purpose of funding communications by the Cattlemen's Beef and Research Board, which had been created by the Secretary of Agriculture as part of his administrative implementation of the Act. The Court, in an opinion by Justice Scalia, rejected the challenge:

> In all of the cases invalidating exactions to subsidize speech, the speech was, or was presumed to be, that of an entity other than the government itself. Our compelled-subsidy cases have consistently respected the principle that "[c]ompelled support of a private association is fundamentally different from compelled support of government"—even those programs of government one does not approve. . .is of course perfectly constitutional, as every taxpayer must attest. And some government programs involve, or entirely consist of, advocating a position.

Do you understand the distinction the Court is drawing? Does it make sense, as a matter of First Amendment theory?

In dissent, Justice Souter argued: "The [Court's] error is not that government speech can never justify compelling a subsidy, but that a compelled subsidy should not be justifiable by speech unless the government must put that speech forward as its own. Otherwise there is no check whatever on government's power to compel special speech subsidies, and the rule of *United Foods* is a dead letter. I take the view that if government relies on the government-speech doctrine to compel specific groups to fund speech with targeted taxes, it must make itself politically account able by indicating that the content actually is a government message, not just the statement of one self-interested group the government is currently willing to invest with power." On the issue, see generally Gia Lee, *Persuasion, Transparency, and Government Speech,* 56 HASTINGS L.J. 983 (2005). How different, if at all, is this case from *United Foods*?

Chapter 9

FREEDOM OF RELIGION: ESTABLISHMENT AND FREE EXERCISE

The primacy of position of freedom of religion in the Bill of Rights attests to the importance of freedom of conscience and religious belief for the Framers. Several of the colonies were established by dissident sects fleeing from the state-ordained Church of England, and other colonies experienced dissatisfaction with official religions. The search for religious tolerance played a basic part in the origins of the new nation.

Free exercise and nonestablishment are set forth in the First Amendment text as if they were complementary parts of a single guarantee of freedom of religion. In simple terms, preventing government from establishing an official religion should go hand-in-hand with assuring that each person is free to exercise his or her religious preferences.

But in fact there is often a real tension between the two religion clauses. If the Establishment Clause prohibited all forms of government support for religion, such as fire and police services, the guarantee of free exercise would be virtually worthless. But government assistance to religion or particular religions may violate the Establishment Clause. Similarly, "free exercise" may mean exemption for some persons from generally applicable laws, but it cannot mean that a person is free to claim exemption from all government regulation for her conduct merely by creating a religion and invoking the constitutional guarantee. And if government does accommodate particular religious beliefs and practices by granting exemptions from general laws, might it run afoul of the Establishment Clause? The Court has warned that the clauses "are cast in absolute terms, and either, if expanded to a logical extreme, would tend to clash with the other." The compatibility and conflict of the two aspects of religious freedom provides the central theme of this chapter.

§ 9.01 THE ESTABLISHMENT CLAUSE

[A] PRELUDE — SETTING THE MODERN ISSUES

May government prescribe activities such as moments of silence, prayers, study of religion, and observance of religious holidays in the public schoolhouse? May government provide assistance in the form of services, direct subsidies, or tax exemptions to religious schools? These illustrate the issues with which the Court has grappled in defining the meaning of a "law respecting the establishment of a religion."

A natural inclination in interpreting the constitutional language is to inquire into the historical purposes and understandings of the clauses. But the history is ambiguous. There are two metaphorical depictions of the clauses that have found support in different versions of the history.

Thomas Jefferson has been credited as the source of a metaphor that describes a "wall of separation between Church and State." As the opinion in *Everson v. Board of Education* below indicates, the First Amendment religion clauses grew out of the successful arguments of Jefferson and Madison in the Virginia legislature prior to adoption of the Constitution. The separation principle has been invoked to prohibit government aid to religion, at least in many situations in which the aid is avoidable.

But there is a competing metaphor derived from the words and actions of Jefferson and Madison as well as from other sources. That metaphor goes under the banner of "nonpreferentialism" and stems from the premise that government cannot avoid all contact with religion and religious exercises. The nonpreferentialism principle would require only that government not prefer any particular sect over another.

There was no significant Supreme Court decision interpreting the Establishment Clause prior to World War II. Professor Choper cites a study done at the end of World War II which found that "both federal and state funds 'are being allocated, in no less than 350 instances, to American parochial schools today.' " ALVIN W. JOHNSON & FRANK H. YOST, SEPARATION OF CHURCH AND STATE IN THE UNITED STATES 112 (1948). It was apparent at that time that both public and private education had a major role to play in American life. What was not apparent was how the two should interact. Most, but far from all, private schools at the time were Catholic. The issues were framed in the following 5-4 decision by the Supreme Court.

EVERSON v. BOARD OF EDUCATION

330 U.S. 1, 67 S. Ct. 504, 91 L. Ed. 711 (1947)

JUSTICE BLACK delivered the opinion of the Court.

A New Jersey statute authorizes its local school districts to make rules and contracts for the transportation of children to and from schools. The appellee, a township board of education, acting pursuant to this statute, authorized reimbursement to parents of money expended by them for the bus transportation of their children on regular buses operated by the public transportation system. Part of this money was for the payment of transportation of some children in the community to Catholic parochial schools. These church schools give their students, in addition to secular education, regular religious instruction conforming to the religious tenets and modes of worship in the Catholic faith. The superintendent of these schools is a Catholic priest.

The New Jersey statute is challenged as a "law respecting an establishment of religion." Whether this New Jersey law is one respecting the "establishment of religion" requires an understanding of the meaning of that language, particularly with respect to the imposition of taxes.

A large proportion of the early settlers of this country came here from Europe to escape the bondage of laws which compelled them to support and attend government favored churches. The imposition of taxes to pay ministers' salaries and to build and maintain churches and church property aroused indignation. It was these feelings which found expression in the First Amendment. No one locality and no one group throughout the Colonies can rightly be given entire credit for having aroused the sentiment that culminated in adoption of the Bill of Rights' provisions embracing religious liberty. But Virginia, where the established church had achieved a dominant influence in political affairs and where many excesses attracted wide public attention, provided a great stimulus and able leadership for the movement. The people there, as elsewhere, reached the conviction that individual religious liberty could be achieved best under a government which was stripped of all power to tax, to support, or otherwise to assist any or all religions, or to interfere with the beliefs of any religious individual or group.

The movement toward this end reached its dramatic climax in Virginia in 1785-86 when the Virginia legislative body was about to renew Virginia's tax levy for the support of the established church. Thomas Jefferson and James Madison led the fight against this tax. Madison wrote his great Memorial and Remonstrance against the law. In it, he eloquently argued that a true religion did not need the support of law; that no person, either believer or non-believer, should be taxed to support a religious institution of any kind; that the best interest of a society required that the minds of men always be wholly free; and that cruel persecutions were the inevitable result of government-established religions. Madison's Remonstrance received strong support throughout Virginia. And the Assembly postponed consideration of the proposed tax measure until its next session. When the proposal came up for consideration at that session, it not only died in committee, but the Assembly enacted the famous "Virginia Bill for Religious Liberty" originally written by Thomas Jefferson. This Court has previously recognized that the provisions of the First Amendment, in the drafting and adoption of which Madison and Jefferson played such leading roles, had the same objective and were intended to provide the same protection against governmental intrusion on religious liberty as the Virginia statute.

The "establishment of religion" clause of the First Amendment means at least this: Neither a state nor the Federal Government can set up a church. Neither can pass laws which aid one religion, aid all religions, or prefer one religion over another. Neither can force nor influence a person to go to or to remain away from church against his will or force him to profess a belief or disbelief in any religion. No person can be punished for entertaining or professing religious beliefs or disbeliefs, for church attendance or non-attendance. No tax in any amount, large or small, can be levied to support any religious activities or institutions, whatever they may be called, or whatever form they may adopt to teach or practice religion. Neither a state nor the Federal Government can, openly or secretly, participate in the affairs of any religious organizations or groups and vice versa. In the words of Jefferson, the clause against establishment of religion by law was intended to erect "a wall of separation between Church and State."

We must consider the New Jersey statute in accordance with the foregoing limitations imposed by the First Amendment. But we must not strike that state statute down if it is within the state's constitutional power even though it approaches the verge of that power. New Jersey cannot consistently with the "establishment of religion" clause of the First Amendment contribute tax-raised funds to the support of an institution which teaches the tenets and faith of any church. On the other hand, other language of the amendment commands that New Jersey cannot hamper its citizens in the free exercise of their own religion.

Measured by these standards we cannot say that the First Amendment prohibits New Jersey from spending tax-raised funds to pay the bus fares of parochial school pupils as a part of a general program under which it pays the fares of pupils attending public and other schools. It is undoubtedly true that children are helped to get to church schools. There is even a possibility that some of the children might not be sent to the church schools if the parents were compelled to pay their children's bus fares out of their own pockets when transportation to a public school would have been paid for by the State. Similarly, parents might be reluctant to permit their children to attend schools which the state had cut off from such general government services as ordinary police and fire protection, connections for sewage disposal, public highways and sidewalks. Of course cutting off church schools from these services, so separate and so indisputably marked off from the religious function, would make it far more difficult for the schools to operate. But such is obviously not the purpose of the First Amendment. That Amendment requires the state to be a neutral in its relations with groups of religious believers and non-believers; it does not require the state to be their adversary. State power is no more to be used so as to handicap religions, than it is to favor them.

The State contributes no money to the schools. It does not support them. Its legislation, as applied, does no more than provide a general program to help parents get their children, regardless of their religion, safely and expeditiously to and from accredited schools. The First Amendment has erected a wall between church and state. That wall must be kept high and impregnable. We could not approve the slightest breach. New Jersey has not breached it here.

JUSTICE RUTLEDGE, with whom JUSTICES FRANKFURTER, JACKSON and BURTON agree, dissenting.

The Amendment's purpose was not to strike merely at the official establishment of a single sect, creed or religion, outlawing only a formal relation such as had prevailed in England and some of the colonies. Necessarily it was to uproot all such relationships. But the object was broader than separating church and state in this narrow sense. It was to create a complete and permanent separation of the spheres of religious activity and civil authority by comprehensively forbidding every form of public aid or support for religion.

Does New Jersey's action furnish support for religion by use of the taxing power? Certainly it does, if the test remains undiluted as Jefferson and Madison made it, that money taken by taxation from one is not to be used or given to support another's religious training or belief, or indeed one's own. Today as then the furnishing of "contributions of money for the propagation of opinions which he disbelieves" is the forbidden exaction; and the prohibition is absolute for whatever measure brings that consequence and whatever amount may be sought or given to that end.

The funds used here were raised by taxation. The Court does not dispute nor could it that their use does in fact give aid and encouragement to religious instruction. It only concludes that this aid is not "support" in law. But Madison and Jefferson were concerned with aid and support in fact, not as a legal conclusion "entangled in precedents." Here parents pay money to send their children to parochial schools and funds raised by taxation are used to reimburse them. This not only helps the children to get to school and the parents to send them. It aids them in a substantial way to get the very thing they are sent to the particular school to secure, namely, religious training and teaching.

NOTES

1. *Original intent.* As *Everson* indicates, there is little consensus on the historical meaning or purpose of the Nonestablishment Clause. There is some evidence that it was only intended as a principle of federalism — that the national government would not interfere with state prerogatives in the religious sphere — or as a bar against a national church. *Everson's* incorporation of the nonestablishment principle as a part of due process liberty limiting state power essentially doomed such a narrow construction.

Jefferson and, at least at times, Madison advocated a principle of strict separation to prevent church interference with the operations of government. But there is no agreement that the First Amendment was meant simply to embody the Madison-Jefferson view of religious freedom. There is at least the competing view that nonestablishment expresses the views of Roger Williams that government not be allowed to interfere with religions — religious liberty was the prime concern. It has also been suggested that the Nonestablishment Clause was not designed to prevent aid to religion, but only to assure evenhanded treatment of churches in receiving whatever support was given.

How much emphasis should be placed on the original meaning of the religious guarantees? Justice Brennan, concurring in *Abington School District v. Schempp*, p. 1396, warned against a too literal quest for the original purpose of the founding fathers in deciding religion cases because of the ambiguity of the historical record, the changed character of education and American society since adoption of the First Amendment, the fact that "our religious composition makes us a vastly more diverse people than were our forefathers," and "the dramatic evolution of the religious diversity among the population which our public schools serve."

2. *Wall of separation.* Both Justice Black's majority opinion and the dissent in *Everson*, borrowing from Jefferson, call for an "impregnable" wall of separation between church and state. By the time of *Lemon v. Kurtzman*, p. 1374, the Court was to acknowledge that the "line of separation" is "far from a wall."

For some that acknowledgement is still too stinting. Professor Carter contends that American law and politics have trivialized religious devotion. Stephen L. Carter, The Culture of Disbelief 109 (1994). Although he agrees that separation of church and state is necessary for a vital and pluralistic democracy, he understands those who complain that separationism has led to government hostility to religion:

Proponents of the hostility thesis believe that the Supreme Court bears a heavy burden of responsibility for what they see as the disfavored position of religion in America. Justice Hugo Black in *Everson* often is said to have started the ball rolling. [T]here is nothing wrong with the metaphor of a wall of separation. The trouble is that in order to make the Framers' vision compatible with the structure and needs of modern society, the wall has to have a few doors in it.

[B] PUBLIC AID TO RELIGIOUS SCHOOLS

Everson, upholding public provision of transportation to private schools, was the starting point in 1947 for analysis of public assistance to parochial schools. In 1968 the Court upheld a state plan for providing textbooks to private schools on the propositions that the books themselves did not deal with religious matters and that the providing of this service would be no different from provision of other basic services. *Board of Educ. v. Allen,* 392 U.S. 236 (1968). In *Walz v. Tax Comm'n,* 397 U.S. 664 (1970), the Court upheld a broad tax exemption for real property used solely for religious worship. Chief Justice Burger's opinion for the Court called for a "benevolent neutrality" from government toward religion rather than asking whether the legislation had a "secular purpose." "The legislative purpose of a property tax exemption is neither the advancement nor the inhibition of religion; it is neither sponsorship nor hostility." But the opinion added: "We must be sure that the end result — the effect — is not excessive government entanglement with religion." *Excessive entanglement* then becomes a matter of separate concern in succeeding cases.

***Lemon v. Kurtzman,* 403 U.S. 602 (1971).** State legislation from Rhode Island and Pennsylvania authorized state funded teacher salary supplements and other aid to nonpublic schools provided that the funds were not used for religious subjects. Chief Justice Burger for Court held that the legislation was unconstitutional and set forth a once influential three pronged test to evaluate Establishment Clause violations. "First, the statute must have a secular purpose; second, its principal or primary effect must be one that neither advances nor inhibits religion; finally, the statute must not foster 'an excessive government entanglement with religion.' " The Court held that the legislation under review would result in "excessive entanglement between government and religion." In order to comply with the restrictions set forth in the legislation, an impermissible level of "comprehensive, discrimination and continuing state surveillance" would be required. Moreover, such legislation had the capacity to create a different kind of entanglement in the form of divisive political division along religious lines. The Court on occasion still applies the *Lemon* test but other doctrinal rivals have emerged to limit its influence. Justice Scalia in *Lamb's Chapel v. Center Moriches Union Free School District,* 508 U.S. 384 (1993), said *Lemon* was like "some ghoul in a late-night horror movie" which "stalks our Establishment Clause jurisprudence."

The entanglement test. *Lemon* adds the excessive entanglement test to the purpose-effect standard. This test stemmed from the dictum of the Chief Justice in *Walz*, which in turn stemmed from some of the Jefferson-Madison statements regarding the reasons for the nonestablishment principle. In *Lemon*, Chief Justice Burger includes excessive entanglement as a separate element of a three-part test for whether the principle has been violated. The three-part test thus has the internal potential for becoming a conundrum: government cannot grant aid that has a primary effect of advancing religion, but it cannot monitor the use of its aid without becoming entangled. Preventing entanglement may be a reason for the nonestablishment principle, but it is highly questionable as a test.

Consider the argument by Professor Choper that avoidance of administrative entanglement between government and religion and avoidance of political divisiveness, "neither should, nor can, represent a value to be judicially secured by the Establishment Clause." Jesse Choper, *The Religion Clauses of the First Amendment: Reconciling the Conflict*, 41 U. PITT. L. REV. 673 (1980). Regulation of religions and religious education is constitutionally permitted, even though this requires "administrative entanglement." Further, Choper notes that the government exempts religious practices from certain general rules, even though this involves an administrative entanglement. Does entanglement generate intra-group strife? Choper concludes: "[R]eligious antagonism in the political arena, though perhaps regrettable, is a fact of life in our pluralistic governmental system which cannot be effectively suppressed through the Establishment Clause."

***Mueller v. Allen*, 463 U.S. 388 (1983)**. Minnesota allowed a deduction on a parent's state income tax for expenses incurred for tuition, textbooks and transportation of dependents not to exceed $500 per dependent in grades K-6 and $700 in grades 7-12. Justice Rehnquist for the Court first articulated the "secular" purpose behind the deduction:

> A state's decision to defray the cost of educational expenses incurred by parents — regardless of the type of schools their children attend — evidences a purpose that is both secular and understandable. An educated populace is essential to the political and economic health of any community, and a state's efforts to assist parents in meeting the rising cost of educational expenses plainly serves this secular purpose of ensuring that the state's citizenry is well-educated. Similarly, Minnesota, like other states, could conclude that there is a strong public interest in assuring the continued financial health of private schools, both sectarian and non-sectarian. By educating a substantial number of students such schools relieve public schools of a correspondingly great burden — to the benefit of all taxpayers. All these justifications are readily available, and each is sufficient to satisfy the secular purpose inquiry of *Lemon*.
>
> We turn therefore to the more difficult but related question whether the Minnesota statute has "the primary effect of advancing the sectarian aims of the nonpublic schools." In concluding that it does not, we find several features of the Minnesota tax deduction particularly significant. First, an essential feature of Minnesota's arrangement is the fact that [this] is only one among many deductions — such as those for medical expenses and charitable contributions — available

under the Minnesota tax laws. Under our prior decisions, the Minnesota legislature's judgment that a deduction for educational expenses fairly equalizes the tax burden of its citizens and encourages desirable expenditures for educational purposes is entitled to substantial deference.

[Second,] the deduction is available for educational expenses incurred by all parents, including those whose children attend public schools and those whose children attend non-sectarian private schools or sectarian private schools. [A] program that neutrally provides state assistance to a broad spectrum of citizens is not readily subject to challenge under the Establishment Clause.

[Third,] by channeling whatever assistance it may provide to parochial schools through individual parents, Minnesota has reduced the Establishment Clause objections to which its action is subject. It is true, of course, that financial assistance provided to parents ultimately has an economic effect comparable to that of aid given directly to the schools attended by their children. It is also true, however, that under Minnesota's arrangement public funds become available only as a result of numerous, private choices of individual parents of school-age children.

***Witters v. Washington Dep't of Services for the Blind,* 474 U.S. 481 (1986)**. Witters, a student at a Christian college, applied to the Washington Commission for the Blind for vocational rehabilitation, pursuant to a state statute that authorized the Commission to provide special education or training for visually handicapped persons. The Commission denied the aid, and the state courts affirmed, on the grounds that the aid would have the effect of advancing religion and would be therefore unconstitutional. The United States Supreme Court reversed unanimously.

Justice Marshall's opinion for the Court applied the *Lemon* test, holding that the extension of aid to Witter would not have the primary effect of advancing religion. Unlike the "direct subsidy" in *Grand Rapids School Dist. v. Ball*, 473 U.S. 373 (1985) the assistance was paid directly to the student who then transferred it to an institution of his own choice. The state did not make this decision nor did it create any financial incentive for students to attend sectarian institutions. Any aid to religion resulted solely from "the genuinely independent and private choices of aid recipients. [T]he decision to support religious education is made by the individual, not by the State." In addition, there was no showing that any significant part of the aid expended under the program as a whole would end up flowing to religious education. There was not any message of "state endorsement" of religion.

AGOSTINI v. FELTON

521 U.S. 203, 117 S. Ct. 1997, 138 L.Ed. 2d 391 (1997)

JUSTICE O'CONNOR delivered the opinion of the Court.

In *Aguilar v. Felton,* 473 U.S. 402 (1985), this Court held that the Establishment Clause of the First Amendment barred the city of New York from sending public school teachers into parochial schools to provide remedial education to disadvantaged children pursuant to a congressionally mandated program. On remand, the District Court for the Eastern District of New York entered a permanent injunction reflecting our ruling. Twelve years later, petitioners — the parties bound by that injunction — seek relief from its operation. Petitioners maintain that *Aguilar* cannot be squared with our intervening Establishment Clause jurisprudence and ask that we explicitly recognize what our more recent cases already dictate: *Aguilar* is no longer good law. We agree with petitioners that *Aguilar* is not consistent with our subsequent Establishment Clause decisions and further conclude that, on the facts presented here, petitioners are entitled under Federal Rule of Civil Procedure 60(b)(5) to relief from the operation of the District Court's prospective injunction.

Title I of the Elementary and Secondary Education Act of 1965 channels federal funds, through the States, to "local educational agencies" (LEAs). The LEA's spend these funds to provide remedial education, guidance, and job counseling to eligible students. An eligible student is one (I) who resides within the attendance boundaries of a public school located in a low-income area, and (ii) who is failing, or is at risk of failing, the State's student performance standards. Title I funds must be made available to all eligible children, regardless of whether they attend public schools, and the services provided to children attending private schools must be "equitable in comparison to services and other benefits for public school children."

An LEA providing services to children enrolled in private schools is subject to a number of constraints that are not imposed when it provides aid to public schools. Title I services may be provided only to those private school students eligible for aid, and cannot be used to provide services on a "school-wide" basis. In addition, the LEA must retain complete control over Title I funds; retain title to all materials used to provide Title I services; and provide those services through public employees or other persons independent of the private school and any religious institution. The Title I services themselves must be "secular, neutral, and nonideological," and must "supplement, and in no case supplant, the level of services" already provided by the private school.

Petitioner Board of Education of the City of New York (Board), an LEA, first applied for Title I funds in 1966 and has grappled ever since with how to provide Title I services to the private school students within its jurisdiction. Approximately 10% of the total number of students eligible for Title I services are private school students. Recognizing that more than 90% of the private schools within the Board's jurisdiction are sectarian, the Board initially arranged to transport children to public schools for after-school Title I instruction. But this enterprise was largely unsuccessful. Attendance was poor, teachers and children were tired, and parents were concerned for the safety of their children. The Board then moved the after-school instruction onto private school campuses, as Congress had contemplated when it enacted Title I. After this program also yielded mixed results, the Board implemented the plan we evaluated in *Aguilar v. Felton.*

That plan called for the provision of Title I services on private school premises during school hours. Before any public employee could provide Title I instruction at a private school, she would be given a detailed set of written and oral instructions emphasizing the secular purpose of Title I and setting out the rules to be followed to ensure that this purpose was not compromised. Specifically, employees would be told that (i) they were employees of the Board and accountable only to their public school supervisors; (ii) they had exclusive responsibility for selecting students for the Title I program and could teach only those children who met the eligibility criteria for Title I; (iii) their materials and equipment would be used only in the Title I program; (iv) they could not engage in team-teaching or other cooperative instructional activities with private school teachers; and (v) they could not introduce any religious matter into their teaching or become involved in any way with the religious activities of the private schools. All religious symbols were to be removed from classrooms used for Title I services. The rules acknowledged that it might be necessary for Title I teachers to consult with a student's regular classroom teacher to assess the student's particular needs and progress, but admonished instructors to limit those consultations to mutual professional concerns regarding the student's education. To ensure compliance with these rules, a publicly employed field supervisor was to attempt to make at least one unannounced visit to each teacher's classroom every month.

In 1978, six federal taxpayers — respondents here — sued the Board in the District Court for the Eastern District of New York. Respondents sought declaratory and injunctive relief, claiming that the Board's Title I program violated the Establishment Clause. The District Court permitted the parents of a number of parochial school students who were receiving Title I services to intervene as codefendants. The District Court granted summary judgment for the Board, but the Court of Appeals for the Second Circuit reversed. In a 5-4 decision, this Court affirmed on the ground that the Board's Title I program necessitated an "excessive entanglement of church and state in the administration of [Title I] benefits." On remand, the District Court permanently enjoined the Board "from using public funds for any plan or program under [Title I] to the extent that it requires, authorizes or permits public school teachers and guidance counselors to provide teaching and counseling services on the premises of sectarian schools within New York City."

The Board, like other LEA's across the United States, modified its Title I program so it could continue serving those students who attended private religious schools. Rather than offer Title I instruction to parochial school students at their schools, the Board reverted to its prior practice of providing instruction at public school sites, at leased sites, and in mobile instructional units (essentially vans converted into classrooms) parked near the sectarian school. The Board also offered computer-aided instruction, which could be provided "on premises" because it did not require public employees to be physically present on the premises of a religious school.

It is not disputed that the additional costs of complying with *Aguilar*'s mandate are significant. Since the 1986-1987 school year, the Board has spent over $100 million providing computer-aided instruction, leasing sites and mobile instructional units, and transporting students to those sites. These "*Aguilar* costs" thus reduce the amount of Title I money an LEA has available for remedial education, and LEA's have had to cut back on the number of students who receive Title I benefits.

In October and December of 1995, petitioners — the Board and a new group of parents of parochial school students entitled to Title I services — filed motions in the District Court seeking relief under Federal Rule of Civil Procedure 60(b) from the permanent injunction entered by the District Court on remand from our decision in *Aguilar*.

In order to evaluate whether *Aguilar* has been eroded by our subsequent Establishment Clause cases, it is necessary to understand the rationale upon which *Aguilar*, as well as its companion case, *School Dist. of Grand Rapids v. Ball,* rested. Distilled to essentials, the Court's conclusion that the Shared Time program in *Ball* had the impermissible effect of advancing religion rested on three assumptions:

(i) any public employee who works on the premises of a religious school is presumed to inculcate religion in her work;

(ii) the presence of public employees on private school premises creates a symbolic union between church and state; and

(iii) any and all public aid that directly aids the educational function of religious schools impermissibly finances religious indoctrination, even if the aid reaches such schools as a consequence of private decisionmaking.

Additionally, in *Aguilar* there was a fourth assumption: that New York City's Title I program necessitated an excessive government entanglement with religion because public employees who teach on the premises of religious schools must be closely monitored to ensure that they do not inculcate religion.

Our more recent cases have undermined the assumptions upon which *Ball* and *Aguilar* relied. To be sure, the general principles we use to evaluate whether government aid violates the Establishment Clause have not changed since *Aguilar* was decided.

As we have repeatedly recognized, government inculcation of religious beliefs has the impermissible effect of advancing religion. Our cases subsequent to *Aguilar* have, however, modified in two significant respects the approach we use to assess indoctrination. First, we have abandoned the presumption that the placement of public employees on parochial school grounds inevitably results in the impermissible effect of state-sponsored indoctrination or constitutes a symbolic union between government and religion. There is no genuine basis upon which to confine *Zobrest's* underlying rationale — that public employees will not be presumed to inculcate religion — to sign-language interpreters.

Second, we have departed from the rule relied on in *Ball* that all government aid that directly aids the educational function of religious schools is invalid. In *Witters v. Washington Dept. of Servs. for Blind*, we held that the Establishment Clause did not bar a State from issuing a vocational tuition grant to a blind person who wished to use the grant to attend a Christian college and become a pastor, missionary, or youth director. Even though the grant recipient clearly would use the money to obtain religious education, we observed that the tuition grants were "made available generally without regard to the sectarian-nonsectarian, or public-nonpublic nature of the institution benefited." The grants were disbursed directly to students, who then used the money to pay for tuition at the educational institution of their choice. In our view, this transaction was no different from a State's issuing a paycheck to one of its employees, knowing that the employee would donate part or all of the check to a religious institution. In both situations, any money that ultimately went to religious institutions did so "only as a result of the genuinely independent and private choices of" individuals. The same logic applied in *Zobrest*.

Zobrest and *Witters* make clear that, under current law, the Shared Time program in Ball and New York City's Title I program in *Aguilar* will not, as a matter of law, be deemed to have the effect of advancing religion through indoctrination. First, there is no reason to presume that, simply because she enters a parochial school classroom, a full-time public employee such as a Title I teacher will depart from her assigned duties and instructions and embark on religious indoctrination, any more than there was a reason in *Zobrest* to think an interpreter would inculcate religion by altering her translation of classroom lectures.

Zobrest also repudiates *Ball's* assumption that the presence of Title I teachers in parochial school classrooms will, without more, create the impression of a "symbolic union" between church and state. We do not see any perceptible (let alone dispositive) difference in the degree of symbolic union between a student receiving remedial instruction in a classroom on his sectarian school's campus and one receiving instruction in a van parked just at the school's curbside.

Nor under current law can we conclude that a program placing full-time public employees on parochial campuses to provide Title I instruction would impermissibly finance religious indoctrination. In all relevant respects, the provision of instructional services under Title I is indistinguishable from the provision of sign-language interpreters under the IDEA. Both programs make aid available only to eligible recipients. That aid is provided to students at whatever school they choose to attend. Although Title I instruction is provided to several students at once, whereas an interpreter provides translation to a single student, this distinction is not constitutionally significant.

A number of our Establishment Clause cases have found that the criteria used for identifying beneficiaries are relevant in a second respect, apart from enabling a court to evaluate whether the program subsidizes religion. Specifically, the criteria might themselves have the effect of advancing religion by creating a financial incentive to undertake religious indoctrination. This incentive is not present, however, where the aid is allocated on the basis of neutral, secular criteria that neither favor nor disfavor religion, and is made available to both religious and secular beneficiaries on a nondiscriminatory basis. Under such circumstances, the aid is less likely to have the effect of advancing religion.

We therefore hold that a federally funded program providing supplemental, remedial instruction to disadvantaged children on a neutral basis is not invalid under the Establishment Clause when such instruction is given on the premises of sectarian schools by government employees pursuant to a program containing safeguards such as those present here. The same considerations that justify this holding require us to conclude that this carefully constrained program also cannot reasonably be viewed as an endorsement of religion. Accordingly, we must acknowledge that *Aguilar*, as well as the portion of *Ball* addressing Grand Rapids' Shared Time program, are no longer good law.

The doctrine of *stare decisis* does not preclude us from recognizing the change in our law and overruling *Aguilar* and those portions of *Ball* inconsistent with our more recent decisions. [O]ur Establishment Clause jurisprudence has changed significantly since we decided *Ball* and *Aguilar*, so our decision to overturn those cases rests on far more than "a present doctrinal disposition to come out differently from the Court of [1985]." *Casey*. We therefore overrule Ball and Aguilar to the extent those decisions are inconsistent with our current understanding of the Establishment Clause.

JUSTICE SOUTER, with whom JUSTICE STEVENS and JUSTICE GINSBURG join, and with whom JUSTICE BREYER joins as to Part II, dissenting.

In sum, nothing since *Ball* and *Aguilar* and before this case has eroded the distinction between "direct and substantial" and "indirect and incidental." That principled line is being breached only here and now. If a scheme of government aid results in support for religion in some substantial degree, or in endorsement of its value, the formal neutrality of the scheme does not render the Establishment Clause helpless or the holdings in *Aguilar* and *Ball* inapposite.

[T]he object of Title I is worthy without doubt, and the cost of compliance is high. In the short run there is much that is genuinely unfortunate about the administration of the scheme under *Aguilar*'s rule. But constitutional lines have to be drawn, and on one side of every one of them is an otherwise sympathetic case that provokes impatience with the Constitution and with the line. But constitutional lines are the price of constitutional government.

NOTES

Agostini v. Felton was criticized by one commentator as marking a break "with tradition" because it "applied the endorsement test instead of the Lemon analysis for the first time in a case involving government funding of religious schools." This critic assets that this result was accomplished by manipulating the reasoning of *Witters* and *Zobrest*, cases which involved a single religious school student who received government financial assistance: "The *Agostini* Court failed to acknowledge that [*Witters* and *Zobrest*] specifically contrasted the statute at issue with the type of massive aid program involved in *Aguilar*." Note, 71 TEMP. L. REV. 1045 (1997). *Agostini* has also been vigorously defended: "It has never made sense to deny remedial education services to disadvantaged children simply because they chose to attend religious schools instead of public schools. In *Agostini*, the Court was correct in not finding an excessive entanglement between church and state when a Title I program provides equally for both private and public school students." Note, 35 HOUS. L. REV. 1333 (1998).

MITCHELL v. HELMS

530 U.S. 793, 120 S. Ct. 2530, 147 L. Ed. 2d 660 (2000)

[Chapter 2 of the Education Consolidation and Improvement Act of 1981 channels federal funds via state educational agencies (SEAs) to local educational agencies (LEA's), which in turn lend educational materials and equipment, such as library and media materials and computer software and hardware, to public and private elementary and secondary schools to implement "secular, neutral, and nonideological" programs. The enrollment of each participating school determines the amount of Chapter 2 aid that it receives. In an average year, about 30% of Chapter 2 funds spent in Jefferson Parish, Louisiana, are allocated for private schools, most of which are Catholic or otherwise religiously affiliated. Viewing these materials to be more like teachers and other kinds of aid than like textbooks, the Fifth Circuit ruled the program to be unconstitutional. The Supreme Court reversed, upholding the program.]

JUSTICE THOMAS announced the judgment of the Court and delivered an opinion, in which THE CHIEF JUSTICE, and JUSTICES SCALIA and KENNEDY join.

[The plurality opinion by Justice Thomas declared that *Agostini* had modified the *Lemon* test by merging the "entanglement" prong into the question of "effects." As recast, the effects portion of the test states that government aid has the effect of advancing religion if it (1) results in governmental indoctrination, (2) defines its recipients by reference to religion, or (3) creates an excessive entanglement.]

[T]he question whether governmental aid to religious schools results in governmental indoctrination is ultimately a question whether any religious indoctrination that occurs in those schools could reasonably be attributed to governmental action. In distinguishing between indoctrination that is attributable to the State and indoctrination that is not, we have consistently turned to the principle of neutrality, upholding aid that is offered to a broad range of groups or persons without regard to their religion. If the religious, irreligious, and areligious are all alike eligible for governmental aid, no one would conclude that any indoctrination that any particular recipient conducts has been done at the behest of the government. As a way of assuring neutrality, we have repeatedly considered whether any governmental aid that goes to a religious institution does so "only as a result of the genuinely independent and private choices of individuals."

We have viewed as significant "whether the private choices of individual parents," as opposed to the "unmediated" will of government, determine what schools ultimately benefit from the government aid, and how much. For if numerous private choices, rather than the single choice of a government, determine the distribution of aid pursuant to neutral eligibility criteria, then a government cannot, or at least cannot easily, grant special favors that might lead to a religious establishment. To the extent that *Meek* and *Wolman* conflict with this holding, we overrule them.

JUSTICE O'CONNOR, joined by JUSTICE BREYER, concurred.

Reduced to its essentials, the plurality's rule states that government aid to religious schools does not have the effect of advancing religion so long as the aid is offered on a neutral basis and the aid is secular in content. The plurality also rejects the distinction between direct and indirect aid, and holds that the actual diversion of secular aid by a religious school to the advancement of its religious mission is permissible. Although the expansive scope of the plurality's rule is troubling, two specific aspects of the opinion compel me to write separately. First, the plurality's treatment of neutrality comes close to assigning that factor singular importance in the future adjudication of Establishment Clause challenges to government school-aid programs. Second, the plurality's approval of actual diversion of government aid to religious indoctrination is in tension with our precedents and, in any event, unnecessary to decide the instant case.

[JUSTICE O'CONNOR agreed with the plurality that *Meek* and *Wolman* should be overruled. She did not, however, go so far as the dissenters in finding that any aid that could be diverted to religious purposes was prohibited.]

[E]ven if *Meek* and *Wolman* had articulated the divertibility rationale urged by respondents and JUSTICE SOUTER, I would still reject it for a more fundamental reason. Stated simply, the theory does not provide a logical distinction between the lending of textbooks and the lending of instructional materials and equipment. An educator can use virtually any instructional tool, whether it has ascertainable content or not, to teach a religious message. I would adhere to the rule that we have applied in the context of textbook lending programs: To establish a First Amendment violation, plaintiffs must prove that the aid in question actually is or has been, used for religious purposes."

As in *Agostini*, the Chapter 2 aid is allocated on the basis of neutral, secular criteria; the aid must be supplementary and cannot supplant non-Federal funds; no Chapter 2 funds ever reach the coffers of religious schools; the aid must be secular; any evidence of actual diversion is de minimis; and the program includes adequate safeguards. Regardless of whether these factors are constitutional requirements, they are surely sufficient to find that the program at issue here does not have the impermissible effect of advancing religion.

I agree with JUSTICE SOUTER that the "plurality appears to take evenhandedness neutrality and in practical terms promote it to a single and sufficient test for the establishment constitutionality of school aid." I do not quarrel with the plurality's recognition that neutrality is an important reason for upholding government-aid programs against establishment Clause challenges. Nevertheless, we have never held that a government-aid program passes constitutional muster solely because of the neutral criteria it employs as a basis for distributing aid.

JUSTICES SOUTER, STEVENS, AND GINSBURG dissented.

[In their view, the "plurality departs from established laws" while the majority (plurality plus O'CONNOR) "misapplies" it.]

To the plurality there is nothing wrong with aiding a school's religious mission; the only question is whether religious teaching obtains its tax support under a formally evenhanded criterion of distribution. The principle of no aid to religious teaching has no independent significance. My concern with these arguments goes not so much to their details as it does to the fact that the plurality's choice to employ imputations of bigotry and irreligion as terms in the Court's debate makes one point clear: that in rejecting the principle of no aid to a school's religious mission the plurality is attacking the most fundamental assumption underlying the Establishment Clause, that government can in fact operate with neutrality in its relation to religion. I believe that it can, and so respectfully dissent.

[The dissenters thus would preserve *Meek* and *Wolman's* emphasis on whether aid was administered in a neutral fashion to promote secular interests.]

NOTE

No single opinion commanded a majority of the Court in *Mitchell v. Helms*. Yet the plurality opinion of Justice Thomas—and part of Justice O'Connor's concurrence—embarks the Court on a new direction. *Meek v. Pittenger,* 421 U.S. 349 (1973), and *Wolman v. Walter,* 433 U.S. 229 (1977), had rejected government aid to religious schools in the form of instructional materials and equipment. *Mitchell v. Helms* upheld the use of taxpayer funds by religious schools to buy computer equipment and overruled *Meek* and *Wolman* to the extent they were inconsistent with its ruling. Advocates of school vouchers took particular comfort from Justice Thomas's emphasis on neutrality and private choice. However, Justice O'Connor in her concurrence, joined by Justice Breyer, objected to making neutrality the sole criterion of the constitutionality of government to religion.

Mitchell v. Helms stimulated diverse reactions. Some hailed the Thomas plurality decision. Clint Bolick, director of litigation for the Institute of Justice which favors school vouchers funded by taxpayer dollars for use at either private or public schools, said that *Mitchell v. Helms* "make public policy much more flexible in terms of aid following students rather than aid to the public school system exclusively." But Mark D. Stern, on behalf of the American Jewish Congress, said: "Had Thomas gathered five votes for his opinion, vouchers would be constitutional. Since he didn't it leads me to think that vouchers are unconstitutional." *See* Jodi Wilgoren, "Court Ruling Fuels Debate on Vouchers for Education," WASHINGTON POST, p. A21, June 29, 2000.

ZELMAN v. SIMMONS-HARRIS

536 U.S. 639 122 S. Ct. 2460, 153 L.Ed.2d 604(2002)

CHIEF JUSTICE REHNQUIST delivered the opinion of the Court.

The State of Ohio has established a pilot program designed to provide educational choices to families with children who reside in the Cleveland City School District. The question presented is whether this program offends the Establishment Clause of the United States Constitution. We hold that it does not.

There are more than 75,000 children enrolled in the Cleveland City School District. The majority of these children are from low-income and minority families. For more than a generation, however, Cleveland's public schools have been among the worst performing public schools in the Nation. In 1995, a Federal District Court declared a "crisis of magnitude" and placed the entire Cleveland school district under state control. More than two-thirds of high school students either dropped or failed out before graduation. Of those students who managed to reach their senior year, one of every four still failed to graduate. Of those students who did graduate, few could read, write, or compute at levels comparable to their counterparts in other cities. The program provides two basic kinds of assistance to parents of children in a covered district. First, the program provides tuition aid for students in kindergarten through third grade, expanding each year through eighth grade, to attend a participating public or private school of their parent's choosing. Second, the program provides tutorial aid for students who choose to remain enrolled in public school.

The tuition aid portion of the program is designed to provide educational choices to parents who reside in a covered district. Any private school, whether religious or nonreligious, may participate in the program and accept program students so long as the school is located within the boundaries of a covered district and meets statewide educational standards.

Participating private schools must agree not to discriminate on the basis of race, religion, or ethnic background, or to "advocate or foster unlawful behavior or teach hatred of any person or group on the basis of race, ethnicity, national origin, or religion." Any public school located in a school district adjacent to the covered district may also participate in the program. Adjacent public schools are eligible to receive a $2,250 tuition grant for each program student accepted in addition to the full amount of per-pupil state funding attributable to each additional student.

Tuition aid is distributed to parents according to financial need. Families with incomes below 200% of the poverty line are given priority and are eligible to receive 90% of private school tuition up to $2,250. For these lowest-income families, participating private schools may not charge a parental co-payment greater than $250. For all other families, the program pays 75% of tuition costs, up to $1,875, with no co-payment cap. These families receive tuition aid only if the number of available scholarships exceeds the number of low-income children who choose to participate. Where tuition aid is spent depends solely upon where parents who receive tuition aid choose to enroll their child. If parents choose a private school, checks are made payable to the parents who then endorse the checks over to the chosen school.

The tutorial aid portion of the program provides tutorial assistance through grants to any student in a covered district who chooses to remain in public school. Parents arrange for registered tutors to provide assistance to their children and then submit bills for those services to the State for payment. Students from low-income families receive 90% of the amount charged for such assistance up to $360. All other students receive 75% of that amount. The number of tutorial assistance grants offered to students in a covered district must equal the number of tuition aid scholarships provided to students enrolled at participating private or adjacent public schools.

The program has been in operation within the Cleveland City School District since the 1996-1997 school year. In the 1999-2000 school year, 56 private schools participated in the program, 46 (or 82%) of which had a religious affiliation. None of the public schools in districts adjacent to Cleveland have elected to participate. More than 3,700 students participated in the scholarship program, most of whom (96%) enrolled in religiously affiliated schools. Sixty percent of these students were from families at or below the poverty line. The program is part of a broader undertaking by the State to enhance the educational options of Cleveland's schoolchildren in response to the 1995 takeover. That undertaking includes programs governing community and magnet schools.

The Establishment Clause of the First Amendment, applied to the States through the Fourteenth Amendment, prevents a State from enacting laws that have the "purpose" or "effect" of advancing or inhibiting religion. *Agostini v. Felton* [text, p. 1382]. There is no dispute that the program challenged here was enacted for the valid secular purpose of providing educational assistance to poor children in a demonstrably failing public school system. Thus, the question presented is whether the Ohio program nonetheless has the forbidden "effect" of advancing or inhibiting religion. To answer that question, our decisions have drawn a consistent distinction between government programs that provide aid directly to religious schools, and programs of true private choice, in which government aid reaches religious schools only as a result of the genuine and independent choices of private individuals. While our jurisprudence with respect to the constitutionality of direct aid programs has "changed significantly" over the past two decades, *Agostini*, our jurisprudence with respect to true private choice programs has remained consistent and unbroken. Three times we have confronted Establishment Clause challenges to neutral government programs that provide aid directly to a broad class of individuals, who, in turn, direct the aid to religious schools or institutions of their own choosing. Three times we have rejected such challenges.

In *Mueller* [text, p. 1375], we rejected an Establishment Clause challenge to a Minnesota program authorizing tax deductions for various educational expenses, including private school tuition costs, even though the great majority of the program's beneficiaries (96%) were parents of children in religious schools. In *Witters* [text, p. 1376], we used identical reasoning to reject an Establishment Clause challenge to a vocational scholarship program that provided tuition aid to a student studying at a religious institution to become a pastor. Finally, in *Zobrest v. Catalina Foothills School District*, 509 U.S. 1 (1993), we applied *Mueller* and *Witters* to reject an Establishment Clause challenge to a federal program that permitted sign-language interpreters to assist deaf children enrolled in religious schools.

Mueller, Witters, and *Zobrest* thus make clear that where a government aid program is neutral with respect to religion, and provides assistance directly to a broad class of citizens who, in turn, direct government aid to religious schools wholly as a result of their own genuine and independent private choice, the program is not readily subject to challenge under the Establishment Clause. A program that shares these features permits government aid to reach religious institutions only by way of the deliberate choices of numerous individual recipients. The incidental advancement of a religious mission, or the perceived endorsement of a religious message, is reasonably attributable to the individual recipient, not to the government, whose role ends with the disbursement of benefits.

We believe that the program challenged here is a program of true private choice, consistent with *Mueller, Witters*, and *Zobrest*, and thus constitutional.

As was true in those cases, the Ohio program is neutral in all respects toward religion. It is part of a general and multifaceted undertaking by the State of Ohio to provide educational opportunities to the children of a failed school district. It confers educational assistance directly to a broad class of individuals defined without reference to religion, *i.e.*, any parent of a school-age child who resides in the Cleveland City School District. The program permits the participation of *all* schools within the district, religious or nonreligious. Adjacent public schools also may participate and have a financial incentive to do so. Program benefits are available to participating families on neutral terms, with no reference to religion.

There are no "financial incentive[s]" that "ske[w]" the program toward religious schools. *Witters.* Such incentives "[are] not present where the aid is allocated on the basis of neutral, secular criteria that neither favor nor disfavor religion, and is made available to both religious and secular beneficiaries on a nondiscriminatory basis." *Agostini.* The program here in fact creates financial *dis*incentives for religious schools, with private schools receiving only half the government assistance given to community schools and one-third the assistance given to magnet schools. Adjacent public schools, should any choose to accept program students, are also eligible to receive two to three times the state funding of a private religious school. Families too have a financial disincentive to choose a private religious school over other schools. Parents that choose to participate in the scholarship program and then to enroll their children in a private school (religious or nonreligious) must copay a portion of the school's tuition. Families that choose a community school, magnet school, or traditional public school pay nothing. Although such features of the program are not necessary to its constitutionality, they clearly dispel the claim that the program "creates financial incentive[s] for parents to choose a sectarian school." *Zobrest.* Respondents suggest that even without a financial incentive for parents to choose a religious school, the program creates a "public perception that the State is endorsing religious practices and beliefs." But we have repeatedly recognized that no reasonable observer would think a neutral program of private choice, where state aid reaches religious schools solely as a result of the numerous independent decisions of private individuals, carries with it the *imprimatur* of government endorsement. *Mueller*; *Witters*; *Zobrest.* Any objective observer familiar with the full history and context of the Ohio program would reasonably view it as one aspect of a broader undertaking to assist poor children in failed schools, not as an endorsement of religious schooling in general.

There also is no evidence that the program fails to provide genuine opportunities for Cleveland parents to select secular educational options for their school-age children. Cleveland schoolchildren enjoy a range of educational choices: They may remain in public school as before, remain in public school with publicly funded tutoring aid, obtain a scholarship and choose a religious school, obtain a scholarship and choose a nonreligious private school, enroll in a community school, or enroll in a magnet school. That 46 of the 56 private schools now participating in the program are religious schools does not condemn it as a violation of the Establishment Clause. The Establishment Clause question is whether Ohio is coercing parents into sending their children to religious schools, and that question must be answered by evaluating *all* options Ohio provides Cleveland schoolchildren, only one of which is to obtain a program scholarship and then choose a religious school.

JUSTICE SOUTER speculates that because more private religious schools currently participate in the program, the program itself must somehow discourage the participation of private nonreligious schools. But Cleveland's preponderance of religiously affiliated private schools certainly did not arise as a result of the program; it is a phenomenon common to many American cities. Indeed, by all accounts the program has captured a remarkable cross-section of private schools, religious and nonreligious. It is true that 82% of Cleveland's participating private schools are religious schools, but it is also true that 81% of private schools in Ohio are religious schools. The constitutionality of a neutral educational aid program simply does not turn on whether and why, in a particular area, at a particular time, most private schools are run by religious organizations, or most recipients choose to use the aid at a religious school. This point is aptly illustrated here. The 96% figure upon which respondents and JUSTICE SOUTER rely discounts entirely (1) the more than 1,900 Cleveland children enrolled in alternative community schools, (2) the more than 13,000 children enrolled in alternative magnet schools, and (3) the more than 1,400 children enrolled in traditional public schools with tutorial assistance. Including some or all of these children in the denominator of children enrolled in nontraditional schools during the 1999-2000 school year drops the percentage enrolled in religious schools from 96% to under 20%. The 96% figure also represents but a snapshot of one particular school year. In the 1997-1998 school year, by contrast, only 78% of scholarship recipients attended religious schools. In sum, the Ohio program is entirely neutral with respect to religion. It provides benefits directly to a wide spectrum of individuals, defined only by financial need and residence in a particular school district. It permits such individuals to exercise genuine choice among options public and private, secular and religious. The program is therefore a program of true private choice. In keeping with an unbroken line of decisions rejecting challenges to similar programs, we hold that the program does not offend the Establishment Clause.

The judgment of the Court of Appeals is reversed.

JUSTICE O'CONNOR, concurring.

While I join the Court's opinion, I write separately for two reasons. First, although the Court takes an important step, I do not believe that today's decision, when considered in light of other longstanding government programs that impact religious organizations and our prior Establishment Clause jurisprudence, marks a dramatic break from the past. Second, given the emphasis the Court places on verifying that parents of voucher students in religious schools have exercised "true private choice," I think it is worth elaborating on the Court's conclusion that this inquiry should consider all reasonable educational alternatives to religious schools that are available to parents. To do otherwise is to ignore how the educational system in Cleveland actually functions.

These cases are different from prior indirect aid cases in part because a significant portion of the funds appropriated for the voucher program reach religious schools without restrictions on the use of these funds. The share of public resources that reach religious schools is not, however, as significant as respondents suggest. Data from the 1999-2000 school year indicate that 82 percent of schools participating in the voucher program were religious and that 96 percent of participating students enrolled in religious schools, but these data are incomplete. These statistics do not take into account all of the reasonable educational choices that may be available to students in Cleveland public schools. When one considers the option to attend community schools, the percentage of students enrolled in religious schools falls to 62.1 percent. If magnet schools are included in the mix, this percentage falls to 16.5 percent.

Even these numbers do not paint a complete picture. The Cleveland program provides voucher applicants from low-income families with up to $2,250 in tuition assistance and provides the remaining applicants with up to $1,875 in tuition assistance. In contrast, the State provides community schools $4,518 per pupil and magnet schools, on average, $7,097 per pupil. Even if one assumes that all voucher students came from low-income families and that each voucher student used up the entire $2,250 voucher, at most $8.2 million of public funds flowed to religious schools under the voucher program in 1999-2000. Although just over one-half as many students attended community schools as religious private schools on the state fisc, the State spent over $1 million more—$9.4 million—on students in community schools than on students in religious private schools because per-pupil aid to community schools is more than double the per-pupil aid to private schools under the voucher program. Moreover, the amount spent on religious private schools is minor compared to the $114.8 million the State spent on students in the Cleveland magnet schools.

A significant portion of the funds appropriated for these programs reach religiously affiliated institutions, typically without restrictions on its subsequent use. Against this background, the support that the Cleveland voucher program provides religious institutions is neither substantial nor atypical of existing government programs. While this observation is not intended to justify the Cleveland voucher program under the Establishment Clause, it places in broader perspective alarmist claims about implications of the Cleveland program and the Court's decision in these cases.

There is little question in my mind that the Cleveland voucher program is neutral as between religious schools and nonreligious schools. JUSTICE SOUTER's theory that the Cleveland voucher program's cap on the tuition encourages low-income student to attend religious schools ignores that these students receive nearly double the amount of tuition assistance under the community schools program than under the voucher program and that none of the community schools is religious. In my view the more significant finding in these cases is that Cleveland parents who use vouchers to send their children to religious private schools do so as a result of true private choice.

What appears to motivate JUSTICE SOUTER's analysis is a desire for a limiting principle to rule out certain nonreligious schools as alternatives to religious schools in the voucher program. But the goal of the Court's Establishment Clause jurisprudence is to determine whether, after the Cleveland voucher program was enacted, parents were free to direct state educational aid in either a nonreligious or religious direction. That inquiry requires an evaluation of all reasonable educational options Ohio provides the Cleveland school system, regardless of whether they are formally made available in the same section of the Ohio Code as the voucher program. Based on the reasoning in the Court's opinion, which is consistent with the realities of the Cleveland educational system, I am persuaded that the Cleveland voucher program affords parents of eligible children genuine nonreligious options and is consistent with the Establishment Clause.

JUSTICE THOMAS, concurring.

Despite this Court's observation nearly 50 years ago in *Brown v. Board of Education*, that "it is doubtful that any child may reasonably be expected to succeed in life if he is denied the opportunity of an education," urban children have been forced into a system that continually fails them. These cases present an example of such failures. Besieged by escalating financial problems and declining academic achievement, the Cleveland City School District was in the midst of an academic emergency when Ohio enacted its scholarship program.

The Establishment Clause of the First Amendment [on] its face places no limit on the States with regard to religion. The Establishment Clause originally protected States, and by extension their citizens, from the imposition of an established religion by the Federal Government. Whether and how this Clause should constrain state action under the Fourteenth Amendment is a more difficult question.

The Fourteenth Amendment fundamentally restructured the relationship between individuals and the States and ensured that States would not deprive citizens of liberty without due process of law. [I]n the context of the Establishment Clause, it may well be that state action should be evaluated on different terms than similar action by the Federal Government.

Whatever the textual and historical merits of incorporating the Establishment Clause, I can accept that the Fourteenth Amendment protects religious liberty rights. But I cannot accept its use to oppose neutral programs of school choice through the incorporation of the Establishment Clause. There would be a tragic irony in converting the Fourteenth Amendment's guarantee of individual liberty into a prohibition on the exercise of educational choice.

JUSTICE STEVENS, dissenting.

Is a law that authorizes the use of public funds to pay for the indoctrination of thousands of grammar school children in particular religious faiths a "law respecting an establishment of religion" within the meaning of the First Amendment? In answering that question, I think we should ignore three factual matters that are discussed at length by my colleagues. First, the severe educational crisis that confronted the Cleveland City School District when Ohio enacted its voucher program is not a matter that should affect our appraisal of its constitutionality.

Second, the wide range of choices that have been made available to students *within the public school system* has no bearing on the question whether the State may pay the tuition for students who wish to reject public education entirely and attend private schools that will provide them with a sectarian education. The fact that the vast majority of the voucher recipients who have entirely rejected public education receive religious indoctrination at state expense does, however, support the claim that the law is one "respecting an establishment of religion."

Third, the voluntary character of the private choice to prefer a parochial education over an education in the public school system seems to me quite irrelevant to the question whether the government's choice to pay for religious indoctrination is constitutionally permissible.

For the reasons stated by JUSTICE SOUTER and JUSTICE BREYER, I am convinced that the Court's decision is profoundly misguided. Admittedly, in reaching that conclusion I have been influenced by my understanding of the impact of religious strife on the decisions of our forbears to migrate to this continent, and on the decisions of neighbors in the Balkans, Northern Ireland, and the Middle East to mistrust one another. Whenever we remove a brick from the wall that was designed to separate religion and government, we increase the risk of religious strife and weaken the foundation of our democracy.

JUSTICE SOUTER, with whom JUSTICE STEVENS, JUSTICE GINSBURG, and JUSTICE BREYER join, dissenting.

If there were an excuse for giving short shrift to the Establishment Clause, it would probably apply here. But there is no excuse. Constitutional limitations are placed on government to preserve constitutional values in hard cases, like these.

The applicability of the Establishment Clause to public funding of benefits to religious schools was settled in *Everson v. Board of Ed. of Ewing*, which inaugurated the modern era of establishment doctrine. The Court stated the principle in words from which there was no dissent: "No tax in any amount, large or small, can be levied to support any religious activities or institutions, whatever they may be called, or whatever form they may adopt to teach or practice religion." The Court has never in so many words repudiated this statement, let alone, in so many words, overruled *Everson*.

Today, however, the majority holds that the Establishment Clause is not offended by Ohio's Pilot Project Scholarship Program, under which students may be eligible to receive as much as $2,250 in the form of tuition vouchers transferable to religious schools. In the city of Cleveland the overwhelming proportion of large appropriations for voucher money must be spent on religious schools if it is to be spent at all, and will be spent in amounts that cover almost all of tuition. The money will thus pay for eligible students' instruction not only in secular subjects but in religion as well, in schools that can fairly be characterized as founded to teach religious doctrine and to imbue teaching in all subjects with a religious dimension. Public tax money will pay at a systemic level for teaching the covenant with Israel and Mosaic law in Jewish schools, the primacy of the Apostle Peter and the Papacy in Catholic schools, the truth of reformed Christianity in Protestant schools, and the revelation to the Prophet in Muslim schools, to speak only of major religious groupings in the Republic.

How can a Court consistently leave *Everson* on the books and approve the Ohio vouchers? The answer is that it cannot. It is only by ignoring *Everson* that the majority can claim to rest on traditional law in its invocation of neutral aid provisions and private choice to sanction the Ohio law. It is, moreover, only by ignoring the meaning of neutrality and private choice themselves that the majority can even pretend to rest today's decision on those criteria.

Although it has taken half a century since *Everson* to reach the majority's twin standards of neutrality and free choice, the facts show that, in the majority's hands, even these criteria cannot convincingly legitimize the Ohio scheme.

Consider first the criterion of neutrality. "Neutrality" as the majority employs the term is, literally, verbal and nothing more. This, indeed, is the only way the majority can gloss over the very nonneutral feature of the total scheme covering "*all* schools": public tutors may receive from the State no more than $324 per child to support extra tutoring (that is, the State's 90% of a total amount of $360), whereas the tuition voucher schools (which turn out to be mostly religious) can receive up to $2,250.

The majority addresses the issue of choice the same way it addresses neutrality, by asking whether recipients or potential recipients of voucher aid have a choice of public schools among secular alternatives to religious schools. Again, however, the majority asks the wrong question and misapplies the criterion. The majority has confused choice in spending scholarships with choice from the entire menu of possible educational placements, most of them open to anyone willing to attend a public school. When the choice test is transformed from where to spend the money to where to go to school, it is cut loose from its very purpose.

If, contrary to the majority, we ask the right question about genuine choice to use the vouchers, the answer shows that something is influencing choices in a way that aims the money in a religious direction: of 56 private schools in the district participating in the voucher program (only 53 of which accepted voucher students in 1999-2000), 46 of them are religious; 96.6% of all voucher recipients go to religious schools, only 3.4% to nonreligious ones. Unfortunately for the majority position, there is no explanation for this that suggests the religious direction results simply from free choices by parents. Evidence shows, however, that almost two out of three families using vouchers to send their children to religious schools did not embrace the religion of those schools. The families made it clear they had not chosen the schools because they wished their children to be proselytized in a religion not their own, or in any religion, but because of educational opportunity.

There is, in any case, no way to interpret the 96.6% of current voucher money going to religious schools as reflecting a free and genuine choice by the families that apply for vouchers. The 96.6% reflects, instead, the fact that too few nonreligious school desks are available and few but religious schools can afford to accept more than a handful of voucher students.

Religious teaching at taxpayer expense simply cannot be cordoned from taxpayer politics, and every major religion currently espouses social positions that provoke intense opposition. My own course as a judge on the Court cannot, simply be to hope that the political branches will save us from the consequences of the majority's decision. *Everson's* statement is still the touchstone of sound law, even though the reality is that in the matter of educational aid the Establishment Clause has largely been read away. True, the majority has not approved vouchers for religious schools alone, or aid earmarked for religious instruction. But no scheme so clumsy will ever get before us, and in the cases that we may see, like these, the Establishment Clause is largely silenced. I do not have the option to leave it silent, and I hope that a future Court will reconsider today's dramatic departure from basic Establishment Clause principle.

JUSTICE BREYER, with whom JUSTICE STEVENS and JUSTICE SOUTER join, dissenting.

I join JUSTICE SOUTER's opinion, and I agree substantially with JUSTICE STEVENS. I write separately, however, to emphasize the risk that publicly financed voucher programs pose in terms of religiously based social conflict. In many places there were too many religions, too diverse a set of religious practices, too many whose spiritual beliefs denied the virtue of formal religious training. This diversity made it difficult, if not impossible, to devise meaningful forms of "equal treatment" by providing an "equal opportunity" for all to introduce their own religious practices into the public schools.

The upshot is the development of constitutional doctrine that reads the Establishment Clause as avoiding religious strife, *not* by providing every religion with an *equal opportunity* (say, to secure state funding or to pray in the public schools), but by drawing fairly clear lines of *separation* between church and state—at least where the heartland of religious belief, such as primary religious education, is at issue.

The principle underlying these cases—avoiding religiously based social conflict—remains of great concern. As religiously diverse as America had become when the Court decided its major twentieth-century Establishment Clause cases, we are exponentially more diverse today. America boasts more than 55 different religious groups and subgroups with a significant number of members. Under these modern-day circumstances, how is the "equal opportunity" principle to work—without risking the "struggle of sect against sect" against which JUSTICE RUTLEDGE warned?

Consider the voucher program here at issue. That program insists that the religious school accept students of all religions. Does that criterion treat fairly groups whose religion forbids them to do so? The program also insists that no participating school "advocate or foster unlawful behavior or teach hatred of any person or group on the basis of race, ethnicity, national origin, or religion." How will the public react to government funding for schools that take controversial religious positions on topics that are of current popular interest—say, the conflict in the Middle East or the war on terrorism? Yet any major funding program for primary religious education will require criteria. And the selection of those criteria, as well as their application, inevitably pose problems that are divisive.

In a society as religiously diverse as ours, the Court has recognized that we must rely on the Religion Clauses of the First Amendment to protect against religious strife, particularly when what is at issue is an area as central to religious belief as the shaping, through primary education, of the next generation's minds and spirits.

I do not believe that the "parental choice" aspect of the voucher program sufficiently offsets the concerns I have mentioned. Parental choice cannot help the taxpayer who does not want to finance the religious education of children. It will not always help the parent who may see little real choice between inadequate nonsectarian public education and adequate education at a school whose religious teachings are contrary to his own. It will not satisfy religious minorities unable to participate because they are too few in number to support the creation of their own private schools. It will not satisfy groups whose religious beliefs preclude them from participating in a government-sponsored program, and who may well feel ignored as government funds primarily support the education of children in the doctrines of the dominant religions. And it does little to ameliorate the entanglement problems or the related problems of social division. Consequently, the fact that the parent may choose which school can cash the government's voucher check does not alleviate the Establishment Clause concerns associated with voucher programs.

The Court, in effect, turns the clock back. It adopts, under the name of "neutrality," an interpretation of the Establishment Clause that this Court rejected more than half a century ago. In its view, the parental choice that offers each religious group a kind of equal opportunity to secure government funding overcomes the Establishment Clause concern for social concord. An earlier Court found that "equal opportunity" principle insufficient; it read the Clause as insisting upon greater seperation of church and state, at least in respect to primary education. In a society composed of many different religious creeds, I fear that this present departure from the Court's earlier understanding risks creating a form of religiously based conflict potentially harmful to the Nation's social fabric. Because I believe the Establishment Clause was written in part to avoid this kind of conflict, and for reasons set forth by JUSTICE SOUTER and JUSTICE STEVENS, I respectfully dissent.

NOTE

Professor Mark Tushnet says that now that *Zelman* has resolved the basic question of the validity of voucher programs under the Establishment Clause, the collateral issues the case raises are now front and center: "First, may a state create a voucher program and exclude religiously affiliated schools from participation? Second, are states limited in the degree of regulation they can impose on schools accepting voucher payments?. . . Third, and most expansively, given the role that choice plays in structuring *Zelman*'s doctrine, must states create voucher programs to ensure that parents have real choices with respect to their children's education?" Mark Tushnet, *Vouchers After Zelman*, 2002 SUP.CT. REV. 1, 7. As to the second question, note that Ohio law in *Zelman* had a nondiscrimination requirement. Tushnet suggests that some religiously affiliated schools may decline to participate in voucher programs that are inconsistent with their religious principles. Thus, a religiously sponsored school might limit enrollment to adherents of the religion with which the school is affiliated. Yet some religiously-sponsored schools will accept a nondiscrimination mandate. The result will be that some religious groups will benefit more than others: "In short, regulatory conditions operate to create sect preferences, and sect preferences are at the heart of the prohibitions against establishment of religion." How would you answer each of the three questions?

[C] RELIGION IN THE PUBLIC SCHOOLS

***Engel v. Vitale*, 370 U.S. 421 (1962)**. The Court, with only Justice Stewart dissenting, held unconstitutional a prescribed prayer to be said aloud in public school classes at the beginning of each school day in the presence of a teacher. The twenty-two word prayer, composed by the Board of Regents, was as follows: "Almighty God, we acknowledge our dependence upon Thee, and we beg Thy blessings upon us, our parents, our teachers, and our country." The Court, per Justice Black, held that "it is no part of the business of government to compose official prayers for any group of the American people to recite as a part of a religious program carried on by government." The most immediate purpose of the Establishment Clause, according to the Court, was "the belief that a union of government and religion tends to destroy government and to degrade religion." If the government supports a particular form of religion, it incurs "the hatred, disrespect and even contempt of those who hold contrary beliefs."

Justice Black specifically discussed the relation of the Free Exercise and Establishment Clauses:

> Although these two clauses may in certain circumstances overlap, they forbid two quite different kinds of governmental encroachment upon religious freedom. The Establishment Clause, unlike the Free Exercise Clause, does not depend upon any showing of direct governmental compulsion and is violated by the enactment of laws which establish an official religion whether those laws operate directly to coerce non-observing individuals or not. This is not to say, of course, that laws officially prescribing a particular form of religious worship do not involve coercion of such individuals. When the power, prestige and financial support of government is placed behind a particular religious belief, the indirect coercive pressure upon religious minorities to conform to the prevailing officially approved religion is plain.

Engel v. Vitale generated a wave of unpopular reaction. Critics of the decision included Billy Graham, Cardinal Spellman, and President Eisenhower. Congressional reaction was extremely critical, the harshest perhaps that of Congressman Andrews of Alabama that the Supreme Court had "put the Negroes in the schools and now they've driven God out."

Justice Douglas, somewhat mischievously, exploited this dimension of *Engel* when he suggested, in a concurring opinion, that even the announcement of the bailiff at the opening of the Supreme Court — "God Save the United States and this Honorable Court" — might be unconstitutional. In the *Schempp* case, which followed *Engel v. Vitale* by a year, the Supreme Court went out of its way to rebut Douglas' effort to put any reference to God outside of the constitutional pale. Is there any difference between forcing everyone to stand in the Supreme Court as the bailiff asks for God's blessing on the United States and the Supreme Court, and a compulsory school prayer from which school children can be excused at their request?

ABINGTON SCHOOL DISTRICT v. SCHEMPP

MURRAY v. CURLETT

374 U.S. 203, 83 S. Ct. 1560, 10 L. Ed. 2d 844 (1963)

[Two cases were decided together as "companion" cases. Pennsylvania law required that ten verses from the Bible should be read at the beginning of the day in every public school and provided that a child could be excused from the Bible reading upon the "written request of his parent on each school day." In the other case, a Baltimore school rule provided for the reading without comment of either a chapter from the Bible or the Lord's Prayer.]

JUSTICE CLARK delivered the opinion of the Court.

[I]n both cases the laws require religious exercises and such exercises are being conducted in direct violation of the rights of the appellees and petitioners. Nor are these required exercises mitigated by the fact that individual students may absent themselves upon parental request, for that fact furnishes no defense to a claim of unconstitutionality under the Establishment Clause. *See Engel v. Vitale.* Further, it is no defense to urge that the religious practices here may be relatively minor encroachments on the First Amendment. The breach of neutrality that is today a trickling stream may all too soon become a raging torrent and, in the words of Madison, "it is proper to take alarm at the first experiment on our liberties." Memorial and Remonstrance Against Religious Assessments.

[W]e cannot accept that the concept of neutrality, which does not permit a State to require a religious exercise even with the consent of the majority of those affected, collides with the majority's right to free exercise of religion. While the Free Exercise Clause clearly prohibits the use of state action to deny the rights of free exercise to anyone, it has never meant that a majority could use the machinery of the State to practice its beliefs.

MR. JUSTICE BRENNAN, concurring.

Our decision in these cases does not clearly forecast anything about the constitutionality of other types of interdependence between religious and other public institutions.

When the secular and religious institutions become involved in such a manner, there inhere in the relationship precisely those dangers — as much to church as to state — which the Framers feared would subvert religious liberty and the strength of a system of secular government. On the other hand, there may be myriad forms of involvements of government with religion which do not import such dangers and therefore should not, in my judgment, be deemed to violate the Establishment Clause.

NOTES

1. *Accommodating religion.* Not all state accommodations of the religious practices of public school children violate the nonestablishment guarantee. In

Zorach v. Clauson, 343 U.S. 306 (1952), the Court upheld a program of released time for public school children to go for religious instruction outside of the public school. Children whose parents chose not to have them participate engaged in the normal instruction program. By contrast, *McCollum v. Board of Educ.,* 333 U.S. 203 (1948), held that released time for religious instruction in the public school building violated the Establishment Clause. The Court in *Zorach* noted that no public funds or other forms of direct public support were involved. The Court also emphasized the serious negative consequences for the free exercise of religion if the Establishment Clause were read to bar all accommodation of religion. Justice Douglas, for the *Zorach* Court, stated: "When the state encourages religious instruction or cooperates with religious authorities by adjusting the schedule of public events to sectarian needs, it follows the best of our traditions. For it then respects the religious nature of our people and accommodates the public service to their spiritual needs." Should the place of the instruction control whether the practice is an impermissible establishment or a permissible accommodation? Is *Zorach* compatible with the prayer cases?

2. *Majority and minority rights.* Should religious exercises in the classroom such as were involved in *Engel* and *Schempp* be viewed as an accommodation of religious traditions and beliefs? Justice Stewart speaks of the free exercise rights of the majority in *Schempp* as being worthy of protection. Dean Griswold has suggested that for a "minority" child to participate in religious exercise desired by the majority may make the child uncomfortable but does not really involve anything more than a decent respect for the sensibilities of the majority.

> The child of a nonconforming or minority group is, to be sure, different in his beliefs. That is what it means to be a member of a minority. Is it not desirable for him to learn not so much that he is different, as that other children are different from him? He allows the majority of the group to follow their own tradition, perhaps coming to understand and to respect what they feel is significant to them.

Erwin Griswold, *Absolute Is in the Dark: A Discussion of the Approach of the Supreme Court to Constitutional Questions*, 8 Utah L. Rev. 167 (1963). But isn't the point of the Establishment Clause to forbid exactly that kind of government protection for the free exercise rights of the majority of which Griswold and Justice Stewart are speaking? Should the place of the practice, *i.e.* the classroom, be determinative? *McCullom* and *Zorach* could be read together as indicating that the Griswold view is acceptable so long as it is the majority who have to leave the room.

3. *Purpose-effects test.* To decide Establishment Clause cases, the Court in *Schempp* says it is necessary to ask "what are the purposes and the primary effect of the enactment?" Is secularism rather than sectarianism mandated by the Establishment Clause? Is the purpose-effect test consistent with the separation approach of *Everson*? Justice Clark speaks of "neutrality." Compare the following proposal offered by Professor Choper: "[T]he Establishment Clause should forbid only government action whose purpose is solely religious and that is likely to impair religious freedom by coercing, compromising, or influencing religious beliefs." Jesse Choper, *The Religion Clauses of the First Amendment: Reconciling the Conflict*, 41 U. Pitt. L. Rev. 673 (1980). Professor Choper argues that the "secular purpose" prong of the Court's test "would make virtually all accommodations for religion unconstitutional." He notes that "the primary goal of nearly all accommodations for religion is to avoid burdening religious activity," and that the purpose therefore is necessarily to aid religion.

4. *Compulsion and majoritarianism revisited*. In *Marsh v. Chambers,* 463 U.S. 783 (1983), a case dealing with state legislative prayer, Chief Justice Burger confronted objections that a single chaplain (in this case Presbyterian) had been employed by the state for a number of years and that all prayers were in the "Judeo-Christian tradition."

> We cannot, any more than Members of the Congresses of this century, perceive any suggestion that choosing a clergyman of one denomination advances the beliefs on a particular church. To the contrary, the evidence indicates that Palmer was reappointed because his performance and personal qualities were acceptable to the body appointing him.

463 U.S. at 793. The Court also pointed out that "Palmer characterizes his prayers as 'nonsectarian,' 'Judeo-Christian,' and with 'elements of the American civil religion.' " Is Chief Justice Burger's reaction to Palmer's acceptability simply a statement that if the majority is successful in having their views accepted, then the Establishment Clause does not apply to the religious practices thus established? Is the reference to nonsectarian Judeo-Christian prayers simply obtuseness about the diversity of religious beliefs and practices in this country?

EDWARDS v. AGUILLARD

482 U.S. 578, 107 S. Ct. 2573, 96 L. Ed. 2d 510 (1987)

[In *Epperson v. Arkansas,* 393 U.S. 97 (1968), the Court held that an anti-evolution law violated the Establishment Clause because it "selects from the body of knowledge a particular segment which it proscribes for the sole reason that it is deemed to conflict with a particular religious doctrine." Simply, this was a purposeful government promotion of a religious theory. It would seem that the state cannot purge the teaching of the theory of human evolution from the classroom to further religious tenets, and that the public school teaching program cannot be dictated by religious beliefs. But can a state enact a law requiring the teaching of "scientific creationism," *i.e.* the scientific support for an explanation that life resulted from a sudden moment of creation, as an alternative to evolution?

[The Louisiana legislature enacted the "Creationism Act" which required that scientific creationism be included in the public school curriculum if evolution was taught. Parents, religious leaders and teachers challenged the law on the ground that it violated the Establishment Clause. Louisiana defended the Act on the ground that it was designed to promote a legitimate secular purpose — academic freedom. The federal district court granted summary judgment in favor of the challengers. The Court of Appeals affirmed as did the Supreme Court.]

JUSTICE BRENNAN delivered the opinion of the Court.

While the Court is normally deferential to a State's articulation of a secular purpose, it is required that the statement of such purpose be sincere and not a sham. It is clear from the legislative history that the purpose of the legislative sponsor, Senator Bill Keith, was to narrow the science curriculum. During the legislative hearings, Senator Keith stated: "My preference would be that neither [creationism nor evolution] be taught." Such a ban on teaching does not promote — indeed, it undermines — the provision of a comprehensive scientific education.

It is equally clear that requiring schools to teach creation science with evolution does not advance academic freedom. The Act does not grant teachers a flexibility that they did not already possess to supplant the present science curriculum with the presentation of theories, besides evolution, about the origin of life.

Furthermore, the goal of basic "fairness" is hardly furthered by the Act's discriminatory preference for the teaching of creation science and against the teaching of evolution. While requiring that curriculum guides be developed for creation science, the Act says nothing of comparable guides for evolution. The Act forbids school boards to discriminate against anyone who "chooses to be a creation-scientist" or to teach "creationism," but fails to protect those who choose to teach evolution or any other non-creation science theory, or who refuse to teach creation science.

If the Louisiana legislature's purpose [were] solely to maximize the comprehensiveness and effectiveness of science instruction, it would have encouraged the teaching of all scientific theories about the origins of humankind. But under the Act's requirements, teachers who were once free to teach any and all facets of this subject are now unable to do so. Moreover, the Act fails even to ensure that creation science will be taught, but instead requires the teaching of this theory only when the theory of evolution is taught. Thus we agree with the Court of Appeals' conclusion that the Act does not serve to protect academic freedom, but has the distinctly different purpose of discrediting "evolution by counterbalancing its teaching at every turn with the teaching of creation science."

We do not imply that a legislature could never require that scientific critiques of prevailing scientific theories be taught. But because the primary purpose of the Creationism Act is to endorse a particular religious doctrine, the Act furthers religion in violation of the Establishment Clause.

The Louisiana Creationism Act advances a religious doctrine by requiring either the banishment of the theory of evolution from public school classrooms or the presentation of a religious viewpoint that rejects evolution in its entirety. The Act violates the Establishment Clause of the First Amendment because it seeks to employ the symbolic and financial support of government to achieve a religious purpose.

JUSTICE SCALIA, with whom THE CHIEF JUSTICE [REHNQUIST] joins, dissenting.

Even if I agreed with the questionable premise that legislation can be invalidated under the Establishment Clause on the basis of its motivation alone, without regard to its effects, I would still find no justification for today's decision. The Louisiana Legislature explicitly set forth its secular purpose ("protecting academic freedom") in the very text of the Act.

I have to this point assumed the validity of the *Lemon* "purpose" test. Our cases interpreting and applying the purpose test have made such a maze of the Establishment Clause that even the most conscientious governmental officials can only guess what motives will be held unconstitutional.

For while it is possible to discern the objective "purpose" of a statute (i.e., the public good at which its provisions appear to be directed), or even the formal motivation for a statute where that is explicitly set forth (as it was, to no avail, here), discerning the subjective motivation of those enacting the statute is, to be honest, almost always an impossible task.

In the past we have attempted to justify our embarrassing Establishment Clause jurisprudence on the ground that it "sacrifices clarity and predictability for flexibility." I think it time that we sacrifice some "flexibility" for "clarity and predictability." Abandoning [the] purpose test — a test which exacerbates the tension between the Free Exercise and Establishment Clauses, has no basis in the language or history of the amendment, and, as today's decision shows, has wonderfully flexible consequences — would be a good place to start.

NOTES

1. ***Correct but wrong?*** Professor Carter contends that *Edwards v. Aguillard* was rightly but "tragically" decided: "The decision is correct because of the difficulty of articulating the precise secular purpose for the teaching of creationism." At bottom, it is "an explanation for the origin of life that is dictated by religion." But Carter believes *Aguillard* was a "humiliating constitutional slap" to millions who do not wish to make "the separation of faith and self that secular political and legal culture demand." STEPHEN L. CARTER, THE CULTURE OF DISBELIEF 168–69 (1994).

2. ***Graduation prayer and the concept of "civil religion."*** A spate of cases in the state and lower federal courts regarding the validity of prayer at high school graduation exercises resulted in Supreme Court review of the issue in a case out of Rhode Island. *Marsh v. Chambers,* 463 U.S. 783 (1983), held that prayer at the opening of state legislative sessions served historical ceremonial purposes and did not have a prohibited effect of advancing religion. When school districts did likewise at graduation ceremonies, challengers then relied on the "purpose and effect" test of *Lemon*. There was an apparent tension between prohibiting practices with either a primary purpose or effect of advancing religion on the one hand and permitting purely ceremonial uses of prayer on the other. Would official dictation of an "American Civil Religion" be a violation of the nonestablishment principle?

LEE v. WEISMAN

505 U.S. 577, 112 S.Ct. 2649, 120 L. Ed. 2d 467 (1992)

JUSTICE KENNEDY delivered the opinion of the Court.

School principals in the public school system of the city of Providence, Rhode Island, are permitted to invite members of the clergy to offer invocation and benediction prayers as part of the formal graduation ceremonies for middle schools and for high schools. The question before us is whether including clerical members who offer prayers as part of the official school graduation ceremony is consistent with the Religion Clauses of the First Amendment, provisions the Fourteenth Amendment makes applicable with full force to the States and their school districts.

We can decide the case without reconsidering the general constitutional framework by which public schools' efforts to accommodate religion are measured. Thus we do not accept the invitation of petitioners and amicus the United States to reconsider our decision in *Lemon v. Kurtzman*. The government involvement with religious activity in this case is pervasive, to the point of creating a state-sponsored and state-directed religious exercise in a public school.

That involvement is as troubling as it is undenied. A school official, the principal, decided that an invocation and a benediction should be given; this is a choice attributable to the State, and from a constitutional perspective it is as if a state statute decreed that the prayers must occur. The principal chose the religious participant, here a rabbi, and that choice is also attributable to the State. The reason for the choice of a rabbi is not disclosed by the record, but the potential for divisiveness over the choice of a particular member of the clergy to conduct the ceremony is apparent.

We need not look beyond the circumstances of this case to see the phenomenon at work. The undeniable fact is that the school district's supervision and control of a high school graduation ceremony places public pressure, as well as peer pressure, on attending students to stand as a group or, at least, maintain respectful silence during the Invocation and Benediction. This pressure, though subtle and indirect, can be as real as any overt compulsion. Of course, in our culture standing or remaining silent can signify adherence to a view or simple respect for the views of others. And no doubt some persons who have no desire to join a prayer have little objection to standing as a sign of respect for those who do. But for the dissenter of high school age, who has a reasonable perception that she is being forced by the State to pray in a manner her conscience will not allow, the injury is no less real.

Finding no violation under these circumstances would place objectors in the dilemma of participating, with all that implies, or protesting. We do not address whether that choice is acceptable if the affected citizens are mature adults, but we think the State may not, consistent with the Establishment Clause, place primary and secondary school children in this position. Research in psychology supports the common assumption that adolescents are often susceptible to pressure from their peers towards conformity, and that the influence is strongest in matters of social convention. To recognize that the choice imposed by the State constitutes an unacceptable constraint only acknowledges that the government may no more use social pressure to enforce orthodoxy than it may use more direct means.

But the embarrassment and the intrusion of the religious exercise cannot be refuted by arguing that these prayers, and similar ones to be said in the future, are of a de minimis character. That the intrusion was in the course of promulgating religion that sought to be civic or nonsectarian rather than pertaining to one sect does not lessen the offense or isolation to the objectors. At best it narrows their number, at worst increases their sense of isolation and affront.

The essence of the Government's position is that with regard to a civic, social occasion of this importance it is the objector, not the majority, who must take unilateral and private action to avoid compromising religious scruples, here by electing to miss the graduation exercise. This turns conventional First Amendment analysis on its head. It is a tenet of the First Amendment that the State cannot require one of its citizens to forfeit his or her rights and benefits as the price of resisting conformance to state-sponsored religious practice. To say that a student must remain apart from the ceremony at the opening invocation and closing benediction is to risk compelling conformity in an environment analogous to the classroom setting, where we have said the risk of compulsion is especially high.

Inherent differences between the public school system and a session of a State Legislature distinguish this case from *Marsh v. Chambers*. The considerations we have raised in objection to the invocation and benediction are in many respects similar to the arguments we considered in *Marsh*. But there are also obvious differences. The atmosphere at the opening of a session of a state legislature where adults are free to enter and leave with little comment and for any number of reasons cannot compare with the constraining potential of the one school event most important for the student to attend. The influence and force of a formal exercise in a school graduation are far greater than the prayer exercise we condoned in *Marsh*.

We do not hold that every state action implicating religion is invalid if one or a few citizens find it offensive. People may take offense at all manner of religious as well as nonreligious messages, but offense alone does not in every case show a violation. We know too that sometimes to endure social isolation or even anger may be the price of conscience or nonconformity. But, by any reading of our cases, the conformity required of the student in this case was too high an exaction to withstand the test of the Establishment Clause. The prayer exercises in this case are especially improper because the State has in every practical sense compelled attendance and participation in an explicit religious exercise at an event of singular importance to every student, one the objecting student had no real alternative to avoid.

JUSTICE BLACKMUN, with whom JUSTICES STEVENS and O'CONNOR join, concurring.

We have believed that religious freedom cannot exist in the absence of a free democratic government, and that such a government cannot endure when there is fusion between religion and the political regime. To that end, our cases have prohibited government endorsement of religion, its sponsorship, and active involvement in religion, whether or not citizens were coerced to conform.

JUSTICE SOUTER, with whom JUSTICES STEVENS and O'CONNOR join, concurring.

I join the whole of the Court's opinion, and fully agree that prayers at public school graduation ceremonies indirectly coerce religious observance. I write separately nonetheless on two issues of Establishment Clause analysis that underlie my independent resolution of this case: whether the Clause applies to governmental practices that do not favor one religion or denomination over others, and whether state coercion of religious conformity, over and above state endorsement of religious exercise or belief, is a necessary element of an Establishment Clause violation.

Petitioners rest most of their argument on a theory that, whether or not the Establishment Clause permits extensive nonsectarian support for religion, it does not forbid the state to sponsor affirmations of religious belief that coerce neither support for religion nor participation in religious observance. I appreciate the force of some of the arguments supporting a "coercion" analysis of the Clause. But we could not adopt that reading without abandoning our settled law, a course that, in my view, the text of the Clause would not readily permit. Nor does the extratextual evidence of original meaning stand so unequivocally at odds with the textual premise inherent in existing precedent that we should fundamentally reconsider our course.

JUSTICE SCALIA, with whom THE CHIEF JUSTICE [REHNQUIST], and JUSTICES WHITE and THOMAS join, dissenting.

The deeper flaw in the Court's opinion does not lie in its wrong answer to the question whether there was state-induced "peer-pressure" coercion; it lies, rather, in the Court's making violation of the Establishment Clause hinge on such a precious question. The coercion that was a hallmark of historical establishments of religion was coercion of religious orthodoxy and of financial support by force of law and threat of penalty.

The Court relies on our "school prayer" cases. But whatever the merit of those cases, they do not support, much less compel, the Court's psycho-journey. [O]ur school-prayer cases turn in part on the fact that the classroom is inherently an instructional setting, and daily prayer there — where parents are not present to counter "the students' emulation of teachers as role models and the children's susceptibility to peer pressure," *Edwards v. Aguillard*, might be thought to raise special concerns regarding state interference with the liberty of parents to direct the religious upbringing of their children. Voluntary prayer at graduation — a one-time ceremony at which parents, friends and relatives are present — can hardly be thought to raise the same concerns.

Our religion-clause jurisprudence has become bedeviled (so to speak) by reliance on formulaic abstractions that are not derived from, but positively conflict with, our long-accepted constitutional traditions. Foremost among these has been the so-called *Lemon* test. The Court today demonstrates the irrelevance of *Lemon* by essentially ignoring it, and the interment of that case may be the one happy byproduct of the Court's otherwise lamentable decision. Unfortunately, however, the Court has replaced *Lemon* with its psycho-coercion test, which suffers the double disability of having no roots whatever in our people's historic practice, and being as infinitely expandable as the reasons for psychotherapy itself.

NOTES

1. *Lemon and coercion.* Professor Paulsen says *Weisman* shows that the *Lemon* test has been abandoned by the Court in favor of a new coercion test. Michael Paulsen, *Lemon is Dead*, 43 CASE W. RES. L. REV. 795, 797 (1993):

> The principle may be summarized as follows: Government may not, through direct legal sanction (or threat thereof) or as a condition of some other right, benefit, or privilege, require individuals to engage in acts of religious exercise, worship, expression or affirmation, nor nor may it require individuals to attend or give their direct and personal financial support to a church or religious body or ministry.

Professor Lupu argues that none of the Justices in *Weisman* accept Paulsen's "assertion that coercion is a necessary element of an Establishment Clause violation." Ira Lupu, *Which Old Witch?: A Comment on Professor Paulsen's* Lemon *Is Dead*, 43 CASE W. RES. L. REV. 883, 890 (1993). Lupu disputes Paulsen's contention that coercion is a prerequisite to finding an Establishment Clause violation:

> [P]erhaps Professor Paulsen does not believe that the Establishment Clause forbids printing "In Jesus Christ We Trust" or "Allah be Praised" on the realm's coin, but no one on the Supreme Court appears to share that view.

2. *Lemon rephrased.* Professor Conkle contends that *Lemon* has survived *Weisman*. But his conception of *Lemon* transcends literal application of the three prongs of the *Lemon* test. Daniel Conkle, *Lemon Lives*, 43 CASE W. RES. L. REV. 865, 874 (1993):

> [W]hen I refer to *Lemon*, I am referring to a pragmatic test for evaluating Establishment Clause challenges. This test considers the purpose and effect of the government's action and the resulting relationship between religion and government. Whether the Court literally recites the *Lemon* formula is less important than whether it honors the policies that *Lemon* represents.

Professor Conkle says that the endorsement test is consistent with *Lemon*. Perhaps it is because the endorsement test — unlike the coercion test — embraces the coercive as well as the noncoercive injuries which "government support for religion can inflict."

SANTA FE INDEPENDENT SCHOOL DISTRICT v. DOE

530 U.S. 290, 120 S.Ct. 2266, 147 L.Ed. 2d 205 (2000)

[The court struck down student-led, student-initiated prayers at a public high school football game. Prior to 1995, the Santa Fe, Texas High School student chaplain delivered a prayer over the public address system at each varsity home football game. The high school is part of the Santa Fe Independent School District. Two families, one Mormon and the other Roman Catholic, challenged this practice as a violation of the Establishment Clause. After suit was filed, the School District changed its policy. The new policy provided for two student elections -one to decide whether there should be invocations at football games, the other to select the student to deliver it. The students by a majority voted for an invocation and for a student to deliver it. The district court then modified the school policy by ordering that only nonsectarian, nonproselytizing prayer would be permissible. The Fifth Circuit ruled that the policy even as modified by the district court still violated the Establishment Clause. The Supreme Court, per Justice Stevens, 6-3, affirmed, ruling that the case was governed by *Lee v. Weisman*.]

JUSTICE STEVENS delivered the opinion of the Court.

[The School District sought to distinguish *Lee v. Weisman* because the messages were private student speech rather than public speech.]

[W]e are not persuaded that the pregame invocations should be regarded as "private speech." These invocations are authorized by a government policy and take place on government property at government-sponsored school-related events. Of course, not every message delivered under such circumstances is the government's own. We have held, for example, that an individual's contribution to a government-created forum was not government speech. *See Rosenberger* [text, p. 1359]. Although the [School] District relies heavily on *Rosenberger* and similar cases involving such forums, it is clear that the pregame ceremony is not the type of forum discussed in those cases.

Santa Fe's student election system ensures that only those messages deemed "appropriate" under the District's policy may be delivered. That is, the majoritarian process implemented by the District guarantees, by definition, that minority candidates will never prevail and that their views will be effectively silenced.

Like the student referendum for funding in [*Board of Regents of Univ. Of Wis. System v.*] *Southworth*, 529 U.S. 217 (2000), this student election does nothing to protect minority views but rather places students who hold such views at the emrcy of the majority. Because "fundamental rights may not be submitted to vote; they depend on the outcome of no elections," the District's elections are insufficient safeguards of diverse student speech.

[T]he only type of message that is expressly endorsed in the text [of the policy] is "invocation"—a term that primarily describes an appeal for divine assistance. In fact, as used in the past at Santa Fe High School, an "invocation" has always entailed a focused religious message. Thus, the expressed purposes of the policy encourage the selection of a religious message and that is precisely how the students understand the policy. Regardless of the listener's support for, or objection to, the message, an objective Santa Fe High School student will unquestionably perceive the inevitable pregame prayer as stamped with her school's seal of approval.

[Justice Stevens rejected the contention of the School District that it had adopted a " 'hands-off' " approach to the pregame invocation. Justice Stevens declared: "In this case, as [i]n *Lee,* the 'degree of school involvement' makes it clear that the pregame prayers bear the 'imprint of the State and thus put school-age children who objected in an untenable position." The School District argued that the invocation was intended to solemnize "sporting events, promote good sportsmanship and student safety." The Court responded that the courts had the responsibility to distinguish between sham secular purposes and sincere ones.

Most striking to us is the evolution of the current policy from the long-sanctioned office of "Student Chaplain" to the candidly titled "Prayer at Football games" regulation. School sponsorship of a religious message is impermissible because it sends the ancillary message to members of the audience who are nonadherents "that they are outsiders, not full members of the political community, and an accompanying message to adherents that they are insiders, favored members of the political community." *Lynch v. Donnelly* (O'CONNOR, J., concurring.) The delivery of such a message—over the school's public address system, by a speaker representing the student body, under the supervision of school faculty, and pursuant to a school policy that explicitly and implicitly encourages public prayer—is not properly characterized as "private" speech.

[The School District tried to distinguish the graduation prayer in *Lee v. Weisman* from its pregame message policy. There was no government coercion for two reasons: (1) The pregame messages were the result of student not government choices and (2) there was no coercion because attendance at an extracurricular event like a football game, unlike a graduation ceremony, is voluntary. Both rationales were rejected: "The [election] mechanism encourages divisiveness along religious lines in a public school setting, a result at odds with the Establishment Clause. Although it is true that the ultimate choice of student speaker is 'attributable to the students,' the District's decision to hold the constitutionally problematic election is clearly a 'choice attributable to the State.' *Lee*." As for the argument that attendance at a football game was voluntary, the Court pointed out that for cheerleaders, band members and members of the football team, attendance was really not voluntary. In fact, some of these activities were for class credit. For many students, the choice whether to attend a high school football game or "to risk facing a personally offensive religious ritual" is a difficult one.]

The Constitution, moreover, demands that the school may not force this difficult choice upon these students for "the State cannot require one of its citizens to forfeit his or her rights and benefits as the price of resisting conformance to state-sponsored religious practice." [*Lee v. Weisman*] The Religion Clauses of the First Amendment [do not] impose a prohibition on all religious activity in our public schools. Thus, nothing in the Constitution as interpreted by this Court prohibits any public school student from voluntarily praying at any time before, during, or after the schoolday. But the religious liberty protected by the Constitution is abridged when the State affirmatively sponsors the particular religious practice of prayer.

[Finally, the Court rejected the School District's argument that the facial challenge to the pregame message policy was premature because no invocation had yet been given. Serious constitutional injury is not limited to situations when students are required to participate in religious worship when they attend a school event. Others include "the mere passage by the District of a policy that has the purpose and perception of government establishment of religion. Another is the implementation of a government electoral process that subjects the issue of prayer to a majoritarian vote." [The Court's] "Establishment Clause cases involving facial challenges [h]ave not focused solely on the possible applications of the statute, but rather have considered whether the statute has an unconstitutional purpose." The constitutionality of an enactment is assessed by reference to the three factors set forth in *Lemon v. Kurtzman,* one of which is that a law is invalid if it lacks a secular religious purpose.]

Therefore, the simple enactment of this policy, with the purpose and perception of school endorsement of student prayer was a constitutional violation. We need not wait for the inevitable to confirm and magnify the constitutional injury. Government efforts to endorse religion cannot evade constitutional reproach based solely on the remote possibility that those attempts may fail. This policy likewise does not survive a facial challenge because it impermissibly imposes upon the student body a majoritarian election on the issue of prayer. Through its election scheme, the District has established a governmental electoral mechanism that turns the school into a forum for religious debate. Such a system encourages divisiveness along religious lines and threatens the imposition of coercion upon those students not desiring to participate in a religious exercise. Simply by establishing this school-related procedure, which entrusts the inherently nongovernmental subject of religion to a majoritarian vote, a constitutional violation has occurred. No further injury is required for the policy to fail a facial challenge.

CHIEF JUSTICE REHNQUIST, with whom JUSTICES SCALIA and THOMAS join, dissenting.

[T]he Court's opinion [b]ristles with hostility to all things religious in public life. We do not learn until late in the Court's opinion that respondents in this case challenged the district's student-message program at football games before it had been put into practice. [T]he fact that a policy might "operate under some conceivable set of circumstances is insufficient to render it wholly invalid." While there is an exception to this principle in the First Amendment overbreadth context because of our concern that people may refrain from speech out of fear of prosecution, there is no similar justification for overbreadth cases. No speech will be "chilled" by the existence of a government policy that might unconstitutionally endorse religion over nonreligion. Therefore, the question is not whether the district's policy may be applied in violation of the Establishment Clause, but whether it inevitably will be.

The Court, venturing into the realm of prophesy, decides that it "need not wait for the inevitable" and invalidates the district's policy on its face. To do so, it applies the most rigid version of the oft-criticized test of *Lemon v. Kurtzman.*

The Court also relies on our decision in *Lee v. Weisman.* In *Lee,* we concluded that the content of the speech at issue, a graduation prayer given by a rabbi, was "directed and controlled" by a school official. In other words at issue in *Lee* was *government* speech. Here, by contrast, the potential speech at issue, if the policy had been allowed to proceed, would be a message or invocation selected or created by a student. That is, if there were speech at issue here, it would be *private* speech.

"The 'crucial difference between *government* speech endorsing religion, which the Establishment Clause forbids, and *private* speech endorsing religion, which the Free Speech and Free Exercise Clauses protect," applies with particular force to the question of endorsement. *Mergens,* text, p. 1475] (plurality opinion) (emphasis in original)."

NOTES

1. *Virginia minute-of-silence law.* In order "that the right of every pupil to the free exercise of religion be guaranteed within the schools," Virginia in 2000 enacted a law authorizing local school boards "to establish the daily observance of one minute of silence" in each public school classrooms:

> Where such one-minute of silence period of silence is instituted, the teacher responsible for each classroom shall take care that all pupils remain seated and silent and make no distracting display to the end that each pupil may, in the exercise of his or her individual choice, meditate, pray or engage in any other silent activity which does not interfere with, distract, or impede other pupils in the like exercise of individual choice.

The ACLU filed suit in the federal district court contending that the law's purpose is to "promote organized prayer in the public schools." Kent Willis, Executive Director of the Virginia ACLU, commented: " 'A true minute-of silence law that did not mention prayer and has no religious intent would be constitutional.' " ACLU counsel argued that the use of the word "pray" and the phrase "free exercise of religion" indicate that the state intended to " 'characterize prayer as a favored practice.' " State Senator Warren Barry who introduced the bill said prayer was mentioned solely because the legislature did not want to "discriminate against prayer." *See* Patricia Davis and Liz Seymour, WASHINGTON POST, pp. B1 and B8.

The ACLU contended that *Santa Fe Independent School District* supports the ACLU challenge. Is the Virginia minute-of-silence law distinguishable from the school district's pregame message policy in Santa Fe Independent School District ? *Cf. Wallace v. Jaffree*, 472 U.S. 38 (1985), where an Alabama minute-of-silence law for purposes of "meditation or voluntary prayer" was struck down on the ground that it constituted a thinly veiled attempt to inject prayer into the official school program and was a prohibited "endorsement" of religion.

2. *Concluding thoughts on establishment in the schools*. Two metaphors have tended to dominate thought in this area, the "wall of separation" metaphor and the "nonpreference" metaphor. The student might find it useful now to review the Court opinions regarding religion in the public schools and public aid to religious schools, looking for evidences of these metaphors.

The *Lemon* test looked at purposes, effects, and entanglement. These were attempts to strike a compromise between the two metaphors but it was a compromise subject to attack from both sides. For example, a strict separationist might not be content with permitting *any* effect of a government program that favored religion and might be offended by some forms of aid to religious schools that have been permitted, such as textbooks and transportation. For this person, a rule that required a compelling state interest for any activity that benefitted religion might make sense. On the other hand, a nonpreferentialist might think that a primary effect of aiding religion would be fine so long as all religions were eligible to benefit. For the neutralist, the knotty problems are what to do with those situations in which not all religions can be aided equally (*e.g.*, posting religious texts in classrooms) and the question of whether nonreligion should also be treated neutrally with religion (*e.g.*, prayer controversies).

Santa Fe Independent School District appears to be an amalgam of the *Lemon* test, the coercion test and the endorsement test. Which of these tests predominates in Justice Stevens's opinion in the *Sante Fe* case?

[D] GOVERNMENT ACKNOWLEDGMENT OF RELIGION

During the 1980s the Supreme Court dealt with a growing number of challenges to various government practices in contexts outside the schools. Many of these practices were longstanding traditions, such as prayers to open legislative sessions and Christmas displays. As the preceding cases illustrate, when governmental action is challenged under the Establishment Clause, the tripartite test of *Lemon v. Kurtzman* usually will be applied. But adherence to *Lemon* has not been undeviating. In several instances, the Court has upheld government action under the *Lemon* tests. Sometimes the Court has invalidated governmental action under the Establishment Clause even though it has not used the tripartite test set forth in Lemon. The most recent cases indicate that there is an open rift on the Court over what should be the proper relationship between government and religion.

***Larson v. Valente,* 456 U.S. 228 (1982)**. The Court, per Justice Brennan, invalidated a Minnesota law imposing disclosure requirements only on religious organizations which solicited more than 50% of their funds from nonmembers on the ground that the law discriminated against non-traditional religions in violation of the establishment clause. (Suit had been instituted by members of the Unification Church or Moonies.) The legislation was invalidated under the strict scrutiny test rather than the *Lemon* test.

Having determined that the 50% rule granted a preference for some denominations over others, Justice Brennan invoked the principle "[t]hat the clearest command of the Establishment Clause is that one religious denomination cannot be officially preferred over another . . . unless [the rule] is justified by a compelling governmental interest and unless it is closely fitted to further that interest." While acknowledging that the state had a significant interest in protecting citizens from abusive practices involved in charitable solicitation regardless of whether the solicitation were conducted by a religious organization, the Court concluded that the 50% rule was not closely fitted to further that interest.

Three major rationales had been advanced for the 50% rule. "That members of a religious organization can and will exercise supervision and control over the organization's solicitation activities when membership contributions exceed fifty percent; that membership control, assuming its existence, is an adequate safeguard against abusive solicitations of the public by the organization; and that the need for public disclosure rises in proportion with the percentage of non-member contributions." The Court found no substantial support for any of these three propositions in the record.

***Bowen v. Kendrick*, 487 U.S. 589 (1987)**. The Court held that the Adolescent Family Life Act, which authorizes federal grants to public or nonpublic private organizations or agencies for services and research in the area of premarital adolescent sexual relations and pregnancy, does not violate the religion clauses of the First Amendment. The Act had been challenged in part on the grounds that it had been motivated by religious concerns. The Chief Justice, speaking for the Court, concluded: "As we see it, it is clear from the face of the statute that the AFLA was motivated primarily if not entirely, by a legitimate secular purpose — the elimination or reduction of social and economic problems caused by teenage sexuality, pregnancy, and parenthood." Express statutory references to the role of religious organizations were dismissed as doing nothing more than "reflect[ing] at most Congress' considered judgment that religious organizations can help solve the problems to which the AFLA is addressed. Nothing in our previous cases prevents Congress from making such a judgment or from recognizing the important part that religion or religious organizations may play in resolving certain secular problems. To the extent that this Congressional recognition has any effect of advancing religion, the effect is at most 'incidental and remote.'"

Nor did the Court express concern that the Act allows religious institutions to participate as recipients of federal funds: "[T]his Court has never held that religious institutions are disabled by the First Amendment from participating in publicly sponsored social welfare programs. . . . [T]here is no reason to assume that the religious organizations which may receive grants are 'pervasively sectarian' in the same sense as the Court has held parochial schools to be." The Court therefore expressed little concern over "the less intensive monitoring" of grants provided for in the Act.

Justice Blackmun, joined by Justices Brennan, Marshall and Stevens, dissented: "Whatever Congress had in mind, it enacted a statute that facilitated, and, indeed, encouraged the use of public funds for [religious] instruction, by giving religious groups a central pedagogical and counseling role without imposing any restraints on the sectarian quality of the participation."

[1] The Christmas Display Controversy

LYNCH v. DONNELLY

465 U.S. 668, 104 S. Ct. 1355, 79 L. Ed. 2d 604 (1984)

CHIEF JUSTICE BURGER delivered the opinion for the Court:

Each year, in cooperation with the downtown retail merchants' association, the City of Pawtucket, Rhode Island, erects a Christmas display as part of its observance of the Christmas holiday season. The display is situated in a park owned by a nonprofit organization and located in the heart of the shopping district. The display is essentially like those to be found in hundreds of towns or cities across the Nation — often on public grounds — during the Christmas season. The Pawtucket display comprises many of the figures and decorations traditionally associated with Christmas, including, among other things, a Santa Claus house, reindeer pulling Santa's sleigh, candy-striped poles, a Christmas tree, carolers, cutout figures representing such characters as a clown, an elephant, and a teddy bear, hundreds of colored lights, a large banner that reads "SEASON'S GREETINGS," and the creche at issue here. All components of this display are owned by the City.

The creche, which has been included in the display for 40 or more years, consists of the traditional figures, including the Infant Jesus, Mary and Joseph, angels, shepherds, kings, and animals, all ranging in height from 5" to 5'. In 1973, when the present creche was acquired, it cost the City $1365; it now is valued at $200. The erection and dismantling of the creche costs the City about $20 per year; nominal expenses are incurred in lighting the creche. No money has been expended on its maintenance for the past 10 years.

In every Establishment Clause case, we must reconcile the inescapable tension between the objective of preventing unnecessary intrusion of either the church or the state upon the other, and the reality that, as the Court has so often noted, total separation of the two is not possible. The Court has sometimes described the Religion Clauses as erecting a "wall" between church and state. The concept of a "wall" of separation is a useful figure of speech probably deriving from views of Thomas Jefferson. The metaphor has served as a reminder that the Establishment Clause forbids an established church or anything approaching it. But the metaphor itself is not a wholly accurate description of the practical aspects of the relationship that in fact exists between church and state. No significant segment of our society and no institution within it can exist in a vacuum or in total or absolute isolation from all the other parts, much less from government. Nor does the Constitution require complete separation of church and state; it affirmatively mandates accommodation, not merely tolerance, of all religions, and forbids hostility toward any.

Our history is replete with official references to the value and invocation of Divine guidance in deliberations and pronouncements of the Founding Fathers and contemporary leaders. Beginning in the early colonial period long before Independence, a day of Thanksgiving was celebrated as a religious holiday to give thanks for the bounties of Nature as gifts from God. President Washington and his successors proclaimed Thanksgiving, with all its religious overtones, a day of national celebration and Congress made it a National Holiday more than a century ago. That holiday has not lost its theme of expressing thanks for Divine aid any more than has Christmas lost its religious significance.

Other examples of reference to our religious heritage are found in the statutorily prescribed national motto "In God We Trust," which Congress and the President mandated for our currency, and in the language "One nation under God," as part of the Pledge of Allegiance to the American flag. That pledge is recited by thousands of public school children — and adults — every year. Art galleries supported by public revenues display religious paintings of the fifteenth and sixteenth centuries, predominantly inspired by one religious faith. The very chamber in which oral arguments on this case were heard is decorated with a notable and permanent — not seasonal — symbol of religion: Moses with the Ten Commandments. Congress has long provided chapels in the Capitol for religious worship and meditation.

This history may help explain why the Court consistently has declined to take a rigid, absolutist view of the Establishment Clause. [Instead, the] Court has scrutinized challenged legislation or official conduct to determine whether, in reality, it establishes a religion or religious faith, or tends to do so. In each case, the inquiry calls for line drawing; no fixed, per se rule can be framed. The Establishment Clause like the Due Process Clauses is not a precise, detailed provision in a legal code capable of ready application. In the line-drawing process we have often found it useful to inquire whether the challenged law or conduct has a secular purpose, whether its principal or primary effect is to advance or inhibit religion, and whether it creates an excessive entanglement of government with religion. *Lemon*. But, we have repeatedly emphasized our unwillingness to be confined to any single test or criterion in this sensitive area.

In this case, the focus of our inquiry must be on the creche in the context of the Christmas season. Focus exclusively on the religious component of any activity would inevitably lead to its invalidation under the Establishment Clause. When viewed in the proper context of the Christmas Holiday season, it is apparent that, on this record, there is insufficient evidence to establish that the inclusion of the creche is a purposeful or surreptitious effort to express some kind of subtle governmental advocacy of a particular religious message. In a pluralistic society a variety of motives and purposes are implicated. The City, like the Congresses and Presidents, however, has principally taken note of a significant historical religious event long celebrated in the Western World. The creche in the display depicts the historical origins of this traditional event long recognized as a National Holiday.

JUSTICE O'CONNOR, concurring:

I write separately to suggest a clarification of our Establishment Clause doctrine.

Our prior cases have used the three-part test articulated in *Lemon v. Kurtzman* as a guide to detecting these two forms of unconstitutional government action. It has never been entirely clear, however, how the three parts of the test relate to the principles enshrined in the Establishment Clause. Focusing on institutional entanglement and on endorsement or disapproval of religion clarifies the *Lemon* test as an analytical device.

The proper inquiry under the purpose prong of *Lemon*, I submit, is whether the government intends to convey a message of endorsement or disapproval of religion. Applying that formulation to this case, I would find that Pawtucket did not intend to convey any message of endorsement of Christianity or disapproval of nonChristian religions. The evident purpose of including the creche in the larger display was not promotion of the religious content of the creche but celebration of the public holiday through its traditional symbols. Celebration of public holidays, which have cultural significance even if they also have religious aspects, is a legitimate secular purpose.

JUSTICE BRENNAN, joined by JUSTICES MARSHALL, BLACKMUN and STEVENS, dissenting:

When government decides to recognize Christmas day as a public holiday, it does no more than accommodate the calendar of public activities to the plain fact that many Americans will expect on that day to spend time visiting with their families, attending religious services, and perhaps enjoying some respite from pre-holiday activities. [W]hen officials participate in or appear to endorse the distinctively religious elements of this otherwise secular event, they encroach upon First Amendment freedoms. For it is at that point that the government brings to the forefront the theological content of the holiday, and places the prestige, power and financial support of a civil authority in the service of a particular faith.

NOTES

1. ***Lemon revisited.*** The Court's observation in *Lynch* that its freedom of religion jurisprudence should not be limited to a single test heralded news that *Lemon*'s future was not secure. *Lynch* also demonstrated that there were problems with at least one of the doctrinal candidates available to replace *Lemon*. Justice O'Connor concurred in *Lynch* using the endorsement test. Justice Brennan, however, found that the public display of a creche by a city during the Christmas season constituted an impermissible endorsement of religion: "Clearly, the endorsement test is no panacea for the resolution of establishment clause issues." *See* JEROME BARRON & C. THOMAS DIENES, FIRST AMENDMENT IN A NUTSHELL 493–494 (3d ed. 2004).

2. ***The "Reindeer Rule.*** The *Lynch* result

> has become known as the "reindeer rule" — a tableau depicting the Nativity of Jesus doesn't amount to an establishment of religion if it is surrounded by secular symbols of Christmas. (The Pawtucket display included a "Santa Claus house," reindeer pulling Santa's sleigh, candy-striped poles, and figures representing a clown, an elephant, and a teddy bear. All that was missing were the Smurfs bearing gifts for baby Jesus.)

McGough, *Menorah Wars*, THE NEW REPUBLIC (Feb. 5, 1990), p. 12.

3. ***The Allegheny County Decision.*** In ***Allegheny County v. ACLU*, 492 U.S. 573 (1989)**, the Supreme Court considered constitutional challenges to two religious holiday displays on public property in downtown Pittsburgh, Pennsylvania. The first display was a creche which was placed on the Grand Staircase of the Allegheny County Courthouse. The second display was a Chanukah menorah which was placed immediately opposite the City-County Building, right next to a Christmas tree and a sign saluting liberty. Justice Blackmun for the Court held, 5-4, that the creche was a violation of the Establishment Clause but the menorah was not. Justice Blackmun applied

the so-called endorsement test. The critical distinction between the two displays was that the creche was displayed alone without any other secular holiday symbols. The singular display of the creche was held to be an impermissible endorsement of Christian doctrine. The menorah was but a part of an overall holiday setting. *Lynch* was distinguished because nothing detracted from the religious message of the creche. Justice Blackmum's opinion in *Allegheny County* was joined by Justices O'Connor, Stevens, Brennan and Marshall. Justice Kennedy joined by the Chief Justice and Justices White and Scalia dissented in part. They disagreed with the Court's ruling that the display of the creche on public property was a violation of the Establishment Clause. In their view, the menorah display was constitutional but so was the creche display. Justice Kennedy declared that the "endorsement test is flawed in its fundamentals and unworkable in practice. The uncritical adoption of this standard is every bit as troubling as the bizarre result it produces in the case before us."

The opinions in *Allegheny County* reflect deep division over the relevance of original intent in Establishment Clause doctrine. To what extent must government distance itself from religion? The separationist viewpoint would declare all religious displays off-limits on public property (except, perhaps, to the extent that the public forum doctrine required allowing private groups to use public property for religious purposes). The nonpreferentialist viewpoint would allow government display of many religious symbols in recognition of the cultural significance of religion.

> The prominence and longevity of the nonpreferential aid theory is remarkable in light of the weak evidence supporting it and the quite strong evidence against it.

Douglas Laycock, *The Origins of the Religion Clauses of the Constitution: "Nonpreferential" Aid to Religion: A False Claim About Original Intent*, 27 WM. & MARY L. REV. 875, 877 (1986).

In response, Professor Smith asserts that Laycock is actually advocating a nonpreferential approach as between religion and nonreligion. Smith believes it should be permissible for government to prefer religion over nonreligion so long as no person's rights of conscience are violated. Would this approach permit "noncoercive" official religious exercises. Rodney Smith, *Nonpreferentialism in Establishment Clause Analysis: A Response to Professor Laycock*, 65 ST. JOHN'S L. REV. 245 (1991).

4. *The* Allegheny County *Decision and the Endorsement Test.* *Allegheny County* has been described as a "doctrinal train wreck." Michael Paulsen, *Lemon Is Dead*, 43 CASE W. RES. L. REV. 795, 813–15 (1993). Professor Paulsen points out that there was majority support on the Court only for two points. The first was a desire to down-grade *Lemon*: "The Court did not return to *Lemon*. The test actually applied in *Allegheny* was not *Lemon*, but O'Connor's purported refinement: 'endorsement.' " The second point concerned the application of the endorsement test: "[T]his particular nativity scene, appearing in a prominent position in the public courthouse, constitutes a forbidden 'endorsement' of Christianity. The majority fractured, of course, on the application of the endorsement test to the menorah." Professor Paulsen concludes: "The basic problem with the endorsement test is that it is no test at all, but merely a label for the judge's largely subjective impressions."

Does disagreement on the Court about whether the nativity scene and a menorah both constitute an endorsement necessarily demonstrate the inadequacy of the endorsement test?

5. *Larkin v. Grendel's Den, Inc.*, 459 U.S. 116 (1982). The Court, per Chief Justice Burger, held that the following Massachusetts statute violated the Establishment Clause: "Premises located within a radius of five hundred feet of a church or school shall not be licensed for the sale of alcoholic beverages if the governing body of such church or school files written objection thereto." In 1977, appellee Grendel's Den applied to the Cambridge License Commission for a liquor license but the application was denied because of objections raised by the Holy Cross Armenian Church, located within ten feet of the proposed restaurant.

The Court applied the three-part test for determining if a law violates the Establishment Clause. First, the Court found that the "valid secular legislative purposes" of protecting "spiritual, cultural, and educational centers from the 'hurly-burly' associated with liquor outlets," could easily be accomplished by other means. The legislature might adopt an absolute ban on liquor outlets within prescribed distances from schools or churches or could provide a hearing to insure that the views of affected institutions could be expressed.

Further, giving religious institutions a veto power has a primary effect of advancing religion. The law provides no standards; it does not by its terms require that churches' power be used in a religiously neutral way. "There is, therefore, potential for a religious institution to use that statute for explicitly religious goals." The Court also noted that "the mere appearance of a joint exercise of legislative authority by church and state provides a significant symbolic benefit to religion in the minds of some by reason of the power conferred. In this way, the statute could have the primary effect of advancing religion."

Finally, the Court decided that the statute involved excessive entanglement of government with religion by enmeshing churches "in the exercise of substantial government powers contrary to our consistent interpretation of the Establishment Clause." The Framers did not intend that "important discretionary governmental powers would be delegated to or shared with religious institutions."

Justice Rehnquist, dissenting, pointed out that the current version, requiring the affected institution to object to the liquor outlet, was less restrictive than the absolute ban on liquor outlets imposed by an earlier statute. "The flat ban, which the majority concedes is valid, is more protective of churches and more restrictive of liquor sales than the present § 16C." Why, he asked, should the more flexible approach be unconstitutional?

The *Grendel's Den* decision has been ascribed to the "separationist strand" in Establishment Clause caselaw: "Although the Constitution permits participation by the clergy in the political process, governmental authority may not be delegated to religious institutions. For this reason, a flat ban that gives churches neither governmental power nor unfair influence over secular neighbors is permissible, while the potentially less restrictive selective ban is not." *The Supreme Court, 1982 Term*, 97 HARV. L. REV. 4, 145 (1983).

McCREARY COUNTY v. AMERICAN CIVIL LIBERTIES UNION OF KENTUCKY

125 S. Ct. 2722 (2005)

JUSTICE SOUTER delivered the opinion of the Court.

I

In the summer of 1999, petitioners McCreary County and Pulaski County, Kentucky (hereinafter Counties), put up in their respective courthouses large, gold-framed copies of an abridged text of the King James version of the Ten Commandments, including a citation to the Book of Exodus. In McCreary County, the placement of the Commandments responded to an order of the county legislative body requiring "the display [to] be posted in 'a very high traffic area' of the courthouse." In Pulaski County, amidst reported controversy over the propriety of the display, the Commandments were hung in a ceremony presided over by the county Judge-Executive, who called them "good rules to live by" and who recounted the story of an astronaut who became convinced "there must be a divine God" after viewing the Earth from the moon. The Judge-Executive was accompanied by the pastor of his church, who called the Commandments "a creed of ethics" and told the press after the ceremony that displaying the Commandments was "one of the greatest things the judge could have done to close out the millennium."

In each county, the hallway display was "readily visible to . . . county citizens who use the courthouse to conduct their civic business, to obtain or renew driver's licenses and permits, to register cars, to pay local taxes, and to register to vote."

In November 1999, respondents American Civil Liberties Union of Kentucky *et al.* sued the Counties in Federal District Court and sought a preliminary injunction against maintaining the displays, which the ACLU charged were violations of the prohibition of religious establishment included in the First Amendment of the Constitution. Within a month, and before the District Court had responded to the request for injunction, the legislative body of each County authorized a second, expanded display, by nearly identical resolutions reciting that the Ten Commandments are "the precedent legal code upon which the civil and criminal codes of . . .Kentucky are founded," and stating several grounds for taking that position: that "the Ten Commandments are codified in Kentucky's civil and criminal laws"; that the Kentucky House of Representatives had in 1993 "voted unanimously . . . to adjourn . . . 'in remembrance and honor of Jesus Christ, the Prince of Ethics' "; that the "County Judge and . . .magistrates agree with the arguments set out by Judge [Roy] Moore" in defense of his "display [of] the Ten Commandments in his courtroom"; and that the "Founding Father[s] [had an] explicit understanding of the duty of elected officials to publicly acknowledge God as the source of America's strength and direction."

As directed by the resolutions, the Counties expanded the displays of the Ten Commandments in their locations, presumably along with copies of the resolution, which instructed that it, too, be posted. In addition to the first display's large framed copy of the edited King James version of the Commandments, the second included eight other documents in smaller frames, each either having a religious theme or excerpted to highlight a religious element. The documents were the "endowed by their Creator" passage from the Declaration of Independence; the Preamble to the Constitution of Kentucky; the national motto, "In God We Trust"; a page from the Congressional Record of February 2, 1983, proclaiming the Year of the Bible and including a statement of the Ten Commandments; a proclamation by President Abraham Lincoln designating April 30, 1863, a National Day of Prayer and Humiliation; an excerpt from President Lincoln's "Reply to Loyal Colored People of Baltimore upon Presentation of a Bible," reading that "[t]he Bible is the best gift God has ever given to man"; a proclamation by President Reagan marking 1983 the Year of the Bible; and the Mayflower Compact.

After argument, the District Court entered a preliminary injunction ordering that the "display . . . be removed from [each] County Courthouse IMMEDIATELY" and that no county official "erect or cause to be erected similar displays." The court's analysis of the situation followed the three part formulation first stated in *Lemon v. Kurtzman*.

The Counties filed a notice of appeal from the preliminary injunction but voluntarily dismissed it after hiring new lawyers. They then installed another display in each courthouse, the third within a year. No new resolution authorized this one, nor did the Counties repeal the resolutions that preceded the second. The posting consists of nine framed documents of equal size, one of them setting out the Ten Commandments explicitly identified as the "King James Version" at Exodus 20:3-17, and quoted at greater length than before.

Assembled with the Commandments are framed copies of the Magna Carta, the Declaration of Independence, the Bill of Rights, the lyrics of the Star Spangled Banner, the Mayflower Compact, the National Motto, the Preamble to the Kentucky Constitution, and a picture of Lady Justice. The collection is entitled "The Foundations of American Law and Government Display" and each document comes with a statement about its historical and legal significance. The comment on the Ten Commandments reads:

"The Ten Commandments have profoundly influenced the formation of Western legal thought and the formation of our country. That influence is clearly seen in the Declaration of Independence, which declared that 'We hold these truths to be self-evident, that all men are created equal, that they are endowed by their Creator with certain unalienable Rights, that among these are Life, Liberty, and the pursuit of Happiness.' The Ten Commandments provide the moral background of the Declaration of Independence and the foundation of our legal tradition."

The ACLU moved to supplement the preliminary injunction to enjoin the Counties' third display, and the Counties responded with several explanations for the new version, including desires "to demonstrate that the Ten Commandments were part of the foundation of American Law and Government" and "to educate the citizens of the county regarding some of the documents that played a significant role in the foundation of our system of law and government." The court, however, took the objective of proclaiming the Commandments' foundational value as "a religious, rather than secular, purpose" and found that the assertion that the Counties' broader educational goals are secular "crumble[s] . . . upon an examination of the history of this litigation."

As requested, the trial court supplemented the injunction, and a divided panel of the Court of Appeals for the Sixth Circuit affirmed. We now affirm.

II

Twenty-five years ago in a case prompted by posting the Ten Commandments in Kentucky's public schools, this Court recognized that the Commandments "are undeniably a sacred text in the Jewish and Christian faiths" and held that their display in public classrooms violated the First Amendment's bar against establishment of religion. *Stone v. Graham* [1980]. Stone found a predominantly religious purpose in the government's posting of the Commandments, given their prominence as " 'an instrument of religion.' " The Counties ask for a different approach here by arguing that official purpose is unknowable and the search for it inherently vain. In the alternative, the Counties would avoid the District Court's conclusion by having us limit the scope of the purpose enquiry so severely that any trivial rationalization would suffice, under a standard oblivious to the history of religious government action like the progression of exhibits in this case.

Ever since *Lemon v. Kurtzman* summarized the three familiar considerations for evaluating Establishment Clause claims, looking to whether government action has "a secular legislative purpose" has been a common, albeit seldom dispositive, element of our cases. Though we have found government action motivated by an illegitimate purpose only four times since Lemon, and "the secular purpose requirement alone may rarely be determinative . . ., it nevertheless serves an important function." *Wallace v. Jaffree* (O'CONNOR. J, concurring in judgment).

The touchstone for our analysis is the principle that the "First Amendment mandates governmental neutrality between religion and religion, and between religion and nonreligion." *Epperson v. Arkansas*. When the government acts with the ostensible and predominant purpose of advancing religion, it violates that central Establishment Clause value of official religious neutrality, there being no neutrality when the government's ostensible object is to take sides. "*Lemon's* "purpose' requirement aims at preventing [government] from abandoning neutrality and acting with the intent of promoting a particular point of view in religious matters"). Manifesting a purpose to favor one faith over another, or adherence to religion generally, clashes with the "understanding, reached . . . after decades of religious war, that liberty and social stability demand a religious tolerance that respects the religious views of all citizens . . . ." *Zelman v. Simmons-Harris* (BREYER, J., dissenting). By showing a purpose to favor religion, the government "sends the . . . message to . . . nonadherents 'that they are outsiders, not full members of the political community, and an accompanying message to adherents that they are insiders, favored members. . . .' " *Santa Fe Independent School Dist. v. Doe*.

Despite the intuitive importance of official purpose to the realization of Establishment Clause values, the Counties ask us to abandon *Lemon*'s purpose test, or at least to truncate any enquiry into purpose here. Their first argument is that the very consideration of purpose is deceptive: according to them, true "purpose" is unknowable, and its search merely an excuse for courts to act selectively and unpredictably in picking out evidence of subjective intent. The assertions are as seismic as they are unconvincing.

Examination of purpose is a staple of statutory interpretation that makes up the daily fare of every appellate court in the country, and governmental purpose is a key element of a good deal of constitutional doctrine. With enquiries into purpose this common, if they were nothing but hunts for mares' nests deflecting attention from bare judicial will, the whole notion of purpose in law would have dropped into disrepute long ago.

But scrutinizing purpose does make practical sense, as in Establishment Clause analysis, where an understanding of official objective emerges from readily discoverable fact, without any judicial psychoanalysis of a drafter's heart of hearts. There is, then, nothing hinting at an unpredictable or disingenuous exercise when a court enquires into purpose after a claim is raised under the Establishment Clause.

Nor is there any indication that the enquiry is rigged in practice to finding a religious purpose dominant every time a case is filed. In the past, the test has not been fatal very often, presumably because government does not generally act unconstitutionally, with the predominant purpose of advancing religion. That said, one consequence of the corollary that Establishment Clause analysis does not look to the veiled psyche of government officers could be that in some of the cases in which establishment complaints failed, savvy officials had disguised their religious intent so cleverly that the objective observer just missed it. But that is no reason for great constitutional concern. If someone in the government hides religious motive so well that the "'objective observer, acquainted with the text, legislative history, and implementation of the statute,'" *Santa Fe Independent School Dist. v. Doe*, (O'CONNOR, J., concurring in judgment), cannot see it, then without something more the government does not make a divisive announcement that in itself amounts to taking religious sides. A secret motive stirs up no strife and does nothing to make outsiders of nonadherents, and it suffices to wait and see whether such government action turns out to have (as it may even be likely to have) the illegitimate effect of advancing religion.

III

The display rejected in Stone had two obvious similarities to the first one in the sequence here: both set out a text of the Commandments as distinct from any traditionally symbolic representation, and each stood alone, not part of an arguably secular display. Stone stressed the significance of integrating the Commandments into a secular scheme to forestall the broadcast of an otherwise clearly religious message, and for good reason, the Commandments being a central point of reference in the religious and moral history of Jews and Christians. They proclaim the existence of a monotheistic god (no other gods). They regulate details of religious obligation (no graven images, no sabbath breaking, no vain oath swearing). And they unmistakably rest even the universally accepted prohibitions (as against murder, theft, and the like) on the sanction of the divinity proclaimed at the beginning of the text. Displaying that text is thus different from a symbolic depiction, like tablets with 10 roman numerals, which could be seen as alluding to a general notion of law, not a sectarian conception of faith. Where the text is set out, the insistence of the religious message is hard to avoid in the absence of a context plausibly suggesting a message going beyond an excuse to promote the religious point of view. The display in Stone had no context that might have indicated an object beyond the religious character of the text, and the Counties' solo exhibit here did nothing more to counter the sectarian implication than the postings at issue in Stone. Actually, the posting by the Counties lacked even the Stone display's implausible disclaimer that the Commandments were set out to show their effect on the civil law. What is more, at the ceremony for posting the framed Commandments in Pulaski County, the county executive was accompanied by his pastor, who testified to the certainty of the existence of God. The reasonable observer could only think that the Counties meant to emphasize and celebrate the Commandments' religious message.

Once the Counties were sued, they modified the exhibits and invited additional insight into their purpose in a display that hung for about six months. This new one was the product of forthright and nearly identical Pulaski and McCreary County resolutions listing a series of American historical documents with theistic and Christian references, which were to be posted in order to furnish a setting for displaying the Ten Commandments and any "other Kentucky and American historical documen[t]" without raising concern about "any Christian or religious references" in them. As mentioned, the resolutions expressed support for an Alabama judge who posted the Commandments in his courtroom, and cited the fact the Kentucky Legislature once adjourned a session in honor of "Jesus Christ, Prince of Ethics."

In this second display, unlike the first, the Commandments were not hung in isolation, merely leaving the Counties' purpose to emerge from the pervasively religious text of the Commandments themselves. Instead, the second version was required to include the statement of the government's purpose expressly set out in the county resolutions, and underscored it by juxtaposing the Commandments to other documents with highlighted references to God as their sole common element. The display's unstinting focus was on religious passages, showing that the Counties were posting the Commandments precisely because of their sectarian content. That demonstration of the government's objective was enhanced by serial religious references and the accompanying resolution's claim about the embodiment of ethics in Christ. Together, the display and resolution presented an indisputable, and undisputed, showing of an impermissible purpose.

Today, the Counties make no attempt to defend their undeniable objective, but instead hopefully describe version two as "dead and buried." Their refusal to defend the second display is understandable, but the reasonable observer could not forget it.

After the Counties changed lawyers, they mounted a third display, without a new resolution or repeal of the old one. The result was the "Foundations of American Law and Government" exhibit, which placed the Commandments in the company of other documents the Counties thought especially significant in the historical foundation of American government. In trying to persuade the District Court to lift the preliminary injunction, the Counties cited several new purposes for the third version, including a desire "to educate the citizens of the county regarding some of the documents that played a significant role in the foundation of our system of law and government." The Counties' claims did not, however, persuade the court, intimately familiar with the details of this litigation, or the Court of Appeals, neither of which found a legitimizing secular purpose in this third version of the display. The conclusions of the two courts preceding us in this case are well warranted.

These new statements of purpose were presented only as a litigating position, there being no further authorizing action by the Counties' governing boards. And although repeal of the earlier county authorizations would not have erased them from the record of evidence bearing on current purpose, the extraordinary resolutions for the second display passed just months earlier were not repealed or otherwise repudiated. Indeed, the sectarian spirit of the common resolution found enhanced expression in the third display, which quoted more of the purely religious language of the Commandments than the first two displays had done. No reasonable observer could swallow the claim that the Counties had cast off the objective so unmistakable in the earlier displays.

If the observer had not thrown up his hands, he would probably suspect that the Counties were simply reaching for any way to keep a religious document on the walls of courthouses constitutionally required to embody religious neutrality.

In holding the preliminary injunction adequately supported by evidence that the Counties' purpose had not changed at the third stage, we do not decide that the Counties' past actions forever taint any effort on their part to deal with the subject matter. We hold only that purpose needs to be taken seriously under the Establishment Clause and needs to be understood in light of context; an implausible claim that governmental purpose has changed should not carry the day in a court of law any more than in a head with common sense. It is enough to say here that district courts are fully capable of adjusting preliminary relief to take account of genuine changes in constitutionally significant conditions.

Nor do we have occasion here to hold that a sacred text can never be integrated constitutionally into a governmental display on the subject of law, or American history. We do not forget, and in this litigation have frequently been reminded, that our own courtroom frieze was deliberately designed in the exercise of governmental authority so as to include the figure of Moses holding tablets exhibiting a portion of the Hebrew text of the later, secularly phrased Commandments; in the company of 17 other lawgivers, most of them secular figures, there is no risk that Moses would strike an observer as evidence that the National Government was violating neutrality in religion.

IV

The prohibition on establishment covers a variety of issues from prayer in widely varying government settings, to financial aid for religious individuals and institutions, to comment on religious questions. In these varied settings, issues of about interpreting inexact Establishment Clause language, like difficult interpretative issues generally, arise from the tension of competing values, each constitutionally respectable, but none open to realization to the logical limit.

Given the variety of interpretative problems, the principle of neutrality has provided a good sense of direction: the government may not favor one religion over another, or religion over irreligion, religious choice being the prerogative of individuals under the Free Exercise Clause. A sense of the past thus points to governmental neutrality as an objective of the Establishment Clause, and a sensible standard for applying it. To be sure, given its generality as a principle, an appeal to neutrality alone cannot possibly lay every issue to rest, or tell us what issues on the margins are substantial enough for constitutional significance, a point that has been clear from the Founding era to modern times. But invoking neutrality is a prudent way of keeping sight of something the Framers of the First Amendment thought important. The dissent, however, puts forward a limitation on the application of the neutrality principle, with citations to historical evidence said to show that the Framers understood the ban on establishment of religion as sufficiently narrow to allow the government to espouse submission to the divine will.

The dissent identifies God as the God of monotheism, all of whose three principal strains (Jewish, Christian, and Muslim) acknowledge the religious importance of the Ten Commandments. On the dissent's view, it apparently follows that even rigorous espousal of a common element of this common monotheism, is consistent with the establishment ban.

While the dissent fails to show a consistent original understanding from which to argue that the neutrality principle should be rejected, it does manage to deliver a surprise. As mentioned, the dissent says that the deity the Framers had in mind was the God of monotheism, with the consequence that government may espouse a tenet of traditional monotheism. This is truly a remarkable view. Other members of the Court have dissented on the ground that the Establishment Clause bars nothing more than governmental preference for one religion over another, but at least religion has previously been treated inclusively. Today's dissent, however, apparently means that government should be free to approve the core beliefs of a favored religion over the tenets of others, a view that should trouble anyone who prizes religious liberty.

We are centuries away from the St. Bartholomew's Day massacre and the treatment of heretics in early Massachusetts, but the divisiveness of religion in current public life is inescapable. This is no time to deny the prudence of understanding the Establishment Clause to require the Government to stay neutral on religious belief, which is reserved for the conscience of the individual.

JUSTICE O'CONNOR, concurring.

Reasonable minds can disagree about how to apply the Religion Clauses in a given case. But the goal of the Clauses is clear: to carry out the Founders' plan of preserving religious liberty to the fullest extent possible in a pluralistic society. By enforcing the Clauses, we have kept religion a matter for the individual conscience, not for the prosecutor or bureaucrat. At a time when we see around the world the violent consequences of the assumption of religious authority by government, Americans may count themselves fortunate: Our regard for constitutional boundaries has protected us from similar travails, while allowing private religious exercise to flourish. The well-known statement that "[w]e are a religious people," *Zorach v. Clauson*, has proved true. Americans attend their places of worship more often than do citizens of other developed nations, and describe religion as playing an especially important role in their lives. Those who would renegotiate the boundaries between church and state must therefore answer a difficult question: Why would we trade a system that has served us so well for one that has served others so poorly?

Our Founders conceived of a Republic receptive to voluntary religious expression, and provided for the possibility of judicial intervention when government action threatens or impedes such expression. Voluntary religious belief and expression may be as threatened when government takes the mantle of religion upon itself as when government directly interferes with private religious practices. When the government associates one set of religious beliefs with the state and identifies nonadherents as outsiders, it encroaches upon the individual's decision about whether and how to worship. In the marketplace of ideas, the government has vast resources and special status. Government religious expression therefore risks crowding out private observance and distorting the natural interplay between competing beliefs. Allowing government to be a potential mouthpiece for competing religious ideas risks the sort of division that might easily spill over into suppression of rival beliefs. Tying secular and religious authority together poses risks to both.

Given the history of this particular display of the Ten Commandments, the Court correctly finds an Establishment Clause violation. The purpose behind the counties' display is relevant because it conveys an unmistakable message of endorsement to the reasonable observer.

It is true that many Americans find the Commandments in accord with their personal beliefs. But we do not count heads before enforcing the First Amendment. Nor can we accept the theory that Americans who do not accept the Commandments' validity are outside the First Amendment's protections. There is no list of approved and disapproved beliefs appended to the First Amendment—and the Amendment's broad terms ("free exercise," "establishment," "religion") do not admit of such a cramped reading.

It is true that the Framers lived at a time when our national religious diversity was neither as robust nor as well recognized as it is now. They may not have foreseen the variety of religions for which this Nation would eventually provide a home. They surely could not have predicted new religions, some of them born in this country. But they did know that linedrawing between religions is an enterprise that, once begun, has no logical stopping point. They worried that "the same authority which can establish Christianity, in exclusion of all other Religions, may establish with the same ease any particular sect of Christians, in exclusion of all other Sects." Memorial 186. The Religion Clauses, as a result, protect adherents of all religions, as well as those who believe in no religion at all.

JUSTICE SCALIA, with whom THE CHIEF JUSTICE and JUSTICE THOMAS join, and with whom JUSTICE KENNEDY joins as to Parts II and III, dissenting.

I would uphold McCreary County and Pulaski County, Kentucky's (hereinafter Counties) displays of the Ten Commandments. I shall discuss first, why the Court's oft repeated assertion that the government cannot favor religious practice is false; second, why today's opinion extends the scope of that falsehood even beyond prior cases; and third, why even on the basis of the Court's false assumptions the judgment here is wrong.

I

George Washington added to the form of Presidential oath prescribed by Art. II, § 1, cl. 8, of the Constitution, the concluding words "so help me God." The Supreme Court under John Marshall opened its sessions with the prayer, "God save the United States and this Honorable Court." The First Congress instituted the practice of beginning its legislative sessions with a prayer. The same week that Congress submitted the Establishment Clause as part of the Bill of Rights for ratification by the States, it enacted legislation providing for paid chaplains in the House and Senate. The day after the First Amendment was proposed, the same Congress that had proposed it requested the President to proclaim "a day of public thanksgiving and prayer, to be observed, by acknowledging, with grateful hearts, the many and signal favours of Almighty God." President Washington offered the first Thanksgiving Proclamation shortly thereafter, devoting November 26, 1789 on behalf of the American people " 'to the service of that great and glorious Being who is the beneficent author of all the good that is, that was, or that will be,' " *Van Orden v. Perry* (plurality opinion) (quoting President Washington's first Thanksgiving Proclamation), thus beginning a tradition of offering gratitude to God that con

Presidents continue to conclude the Presidential oath with the words "so help me God." Our legislatures, state and national, continue to open their sessions with prayer led by official chaplains. The sessions of this Court continue to open with the prayer "God save the United States and this Honorable Court." Invocation of the Almighty by our public figures, at all levels of government, remains commonplace. Our coinage bears the motto "IN GOD WE TRUST." And our Pledge of Allegiance contains the acknowledgment that we are a Nation "under God."

With all of this reality (and much more) staring it in the face, how can the Court possibly assert that " 'the First Amendment mandates governmental neutrality between . . . religion and nonreligion,' " and that "[m]anifesting a purpose to favor . . . adherence to religion generally," is unconstitutional? Who says so? Surely not the words of the Constitution. Surely not the history and traditions that reflect our society's constant understanding of those words. Surely not even the current sense of our society, recently reflected in an Act of Congress adopted unanimously by the Senate and with only 5 nays in the House of Representatives, criticizing a Court of Appeals opinion that had held "under God" in the Pledge of Allegiance unconstitut

Besides appealing to the demonstrably false principle that the government cannot favor religion over irreligion, today's opinion suggests that the posting of the Ten Commandments violates the principle that the government cannot favor one religion over another. *See also Van Orden*, (STEVENS, J., dissenting). That is indeed a valid principle where public aid or assistance to religion is concerned, or where the free exercise of religion is at issue, but it necessarily applies in a more limited sense to public acknowledgment of the Creator. If religion in the public forum had to be entirely nondenominational, there could be no religion in the public forum at all. One cannot say the word "God," or "the Almighty," one cannot offer public supplication or thanksgiving, without contradicting the beliefs of some people that there are many gods, or that God or the gods pay no attention to human affairs. With respect to public acknowledgment of religious belief, it is entirely clear from our Nation's historical practices that the Establishment Clause permits this disregard of polytheists and believers in unconcerned deities, just as it permits the disregard of devout atheists. The Thanksgiving Proclamation issued by George Washington at the instance of the First Congress was scrupulously nondenominational—but it was monotheistic.

Historical practices thus demonstrate that there is a distance between the acknowledgment of a single Creator and the establishment of a religion. The former is, as *Marsh v. Chambers* put it, "a tolerable acknowledgment of beliefs widely held among the people of this country." The three most popular religions in the United States, Christianity, Judaism, and Islam—which combined account for 97.7% of all believers—are monotheistic. All of them, moreover (Islam included), believe that the Ten Commandments were given by God to Moses, and are divine prescriptions for a virtuous life. Publicly honoring the Ten Commandments is thus indistinguishable, insofar as discriminating against other religions is concerned, from publicly honoring God. Both practices are recognized across such a broad and diverse range of the population—from Christians to Muslims—that they cannot be reasonably understood as a government endorsement of a particular religious viewpoint.[1]

Finally, I must respond to JUSTICE STEVENS' assertion that I would "marginaliz[e] the belief systems of more than 7 million Americans" who adhere to religions that are not monotheistic. Surely that is a gross exaggeration. The beliefs of those citizens are entirely protected by the Free Exercise Clause, and by those aspects of the Establishment Clause that do not relate to government acknowledgment of the Creator. Invocation of God despite their beliefs is permitted not because nonmonotheistic religions cease to be religions recognized by the religion clauses of the First Amendment, but because governmental invocation of God is not an establishment. JUSTICE STEVENS fails to recognize that in the context of public acknowledgments of God there are legitimate competing interests: On the one hand, the interest of that minority in not feeling "excluded"; but on the other, the interest of the overwhelming majority of religious believers in being able to give God thanks

[1] This is not to say that a display of the Ten Commandments could never constitute an impermissible endorsement of a particular religious view. The Establishment Clause would prohibit, for example, governmental endorsement of a particular version of the Decalogue as authoritative. Here the display of the Ten Commandments alongside eight secular documents, and the plaque's explanation for their inclusion, make clear that they were not posted to take sides in a theological dispute.

and supplication as a people, and with respect to our national endeavors. Our national tradition has resolved that conflict in favor of the majority.

II

As bad as the *Lemon* test is, it is worse for the fact that, since its inception, its seemingly simple mandates have been manipulated to fit whatever result the Court aimed to achieve. Today's opinion is no different. In two respects it modifies *Lemon* to ratchet up the Court's hostility to religion. First, the Court justifies inquiry into legislative purpose, not as an end itself, but as a means to ascertain the appearance of the government action to an " 'objective observer.' " Because in the Court's view the true danger to be guarded against is that the objective observer would feel like an "outside[r]" or "not [a] full membe[r] of the political community," its inquiry focuses not on the actual purpose of government action, but the "purpose apparent from government action." Under this approach, even if a government could show that its actual purpose was not to advance religion, it would presumably violate the Constitution as long as the Court's objective observer would think othe

Second, the Court replaces *Lemon*'s requirement that the government have "a secular . . . purpose," with the heightened requirement that the secular purpose "predominate" over any purpose to advance religion. The Court treats this extension as a natural outgrowth of the longstanding requirement that the government's secular purpose not be a sham, but simple logic shows the two to be unrelated. If the government's proffered secular purpose is not genuine, then the government has no secular purpose at all. The new demand that secular purpose predominate contradicts *Lemon*'s more limited requirement, and finds no support in our cases.

I have urged that *Lemon*'s purpose prong be abandoned, because even an exclusive purpose to foster or assist religious practice is not necessarily invalidating. But today's extension makes things even worse. By shifting the focus of *Lemon*'s purpose prong from the search for a genuine, secular motivation to the hunt for a predominantly religious purpose, the Court converts what has in the past been a fairly limited inquiry into a rigorous review of the full record. Those responsible for the adoption of the Religion Clauses would surely regard it as a bitter irony that the religious values they designed those Clauses to protect have now become so distasteful to this Court that if they constitute anything more than a subordinate motive for government action they will invalidate it.

III

Even accepting the Court's *Lemon-based premises, the displays at issue here were constitutional.*

To any person who happened to walk down the hallway of the McCreary or Pulaski County Courthouse during the roughly nine months when the Foundations Displays were exhibited, the displays must have seemed unremarkable—if indeed they were noticed at all. The walls of both courthouses were already lined with historical documents and other assorted portraits; each Foundations Display was exhibited in the same format as these other displays and nothing in the record suggests that either County took steps to give it greater prominence.

On its face, the Foundations Displays manifested the purely secular purpose that the Counties asserted before the District Court: "to display documents that played a significant role in the foundation of our system of law and government." That the Displays included the Ten Commandments did not transform their apparent secular purpose into one of impermissible advocacy for Judeo-Christian beliefs. But when the Ten Commandments appear alongside other documents of secular significance in a display devoted to the foundations of American law and government, the context communicates that the Ten Commandments are included, not to teach their binding nature as a religious text, but to show their unique contribution to the development of the legal system. This is doubly true when the display is introduced by a document that informs passersby that it "contains documents that played a significant role in the foundation of our system of law and government."

In any event, the Court's conclusion that the Counties exhibited the Foundations Displays with the purpose of promoting religion is doubtful. In the Court's view, the impermissible motive was apparent from the initial displays of the Ten Commandments all by themselves: When that occurs, the Court says, "a religious object is unmistakable." Surely that cannot be. If, as discussed above, the Commandments have a proper place in our civic history, even placing them by themselves can be civically motivated—especially when they are placed, not in a school (as they were in the Stone case upon which the Court places such reliance), but in a courthouse.

Turning at last to the displays actually at issue in this case, the Court faults the Counties for not repealing the resolution expressing what the Court believes to be an impermissible intent. To begin with, of course, it is unlikely that a reasonable observer would even have been aware of the resolutions, so there would be nothing to "cast off." The Court implies that the Counties may have been able to remedy the "taint" from the old resolutions by enacting a new one. But that action would have been wholly unnecessary in light of the explanation that the Counties included with the displays themselves: A plaque next to the documents informed all who passed by that each display "contains documents that played a significant role in the foundation of our system of law and government." Additionally, there was no reason for the Counties to repeal or repudiate the resolutions adopted with the hanging of the second displays, since they related only to the second displays. After complying with the District Court's order to remove the second displays "immediately," and erecting new displays that in content and by express assertion reflected a different purpose from that identified in the resolutions, the Counties had no reason to believe that their previous resolutions would be deemed to be the basis for their actions.

VAN ORDEN v. PERRY
125 S. Ct. 2854 (2005)

Chief Justice Rehnquist announced the judgment of the Court and delivered an opinion, in which Justice Scalia, Justice Kennedy, and Justice Thomas join.

The question here is whether the Establishment Clause of the First Amendment allows the display of a monument inscribed with the Ten Commandments on the Texas State Capitol grounds. We hold that it does.

The 22 acres surrounding the Texas State Capitol contain 17 monuments and 21 historical markers commemorating the "people, ideals, and events that compose Texan identity." Tex. H. Con. Res. 38, 77th Leg. (2001).[2] The monolith challenged here stands 6-feet high and 3 1/2 -feet wide. It is located to the north of the Capitol building, between the Capitol and the Supreme Court building. Its primary content is the text of the Ten Commandments. An eagle grasping the American flag, an eye inside of a pyramid, and two small tablets with what appears to be an ancient script are carved above the text of the Ten Commandments. Below the text are two Stars of David and the superimposed Greek letters Chi and Rho, which represent Christ. The bottom of the monument bears the inscription "PRESENTED TO THE PEOPLE AND YOUTH OF TEXAS BY THE FRATERNAL ORDER OF EAGLES OF TEXAS 1961."

Petitioner Thomas Van Orden is a native Texan and a resident of Austin. At one time he was a licensed lawyer, having graduated from Southern Methodist Law School. Van Orden testified that, since 1995, he has encountered the Ten Commandments monument during his frequent visits to the Capitol grounds. His visits are typically for the purpose of using the law library in the Supreme Court building, which is located just northwest of the Capitol building.

Forty years after the monument's erection and six years after Van Orden began to encounter the monument frequently, he sued numerous state officials in their official capacities, seeking both a declaration that the monument's placement violates the Establishment Clause and an injunction requiring its removal. After a bench trial, the District Court held that the monument did not contravene the Establishment Clause. It found that the State had a valid secular purpose in recognizing and commending the Eagles for their efforts to reduce juvenile delinquency. The District Court also determined that a reasonable observer, mindful of the history, purpose, and context, would not conclude that this passive monument conveyed the message that the State was seeking to endorse religion. The Court of Appeals affirmed the District Court's holdings with respect to the monument's purpose and effect. We now affirm.

Our cases, Januslike, point in two directions in applying the Establishment Clause. One face looks toward the strong role played by religion and religious traditions throughout our Nation's history. The other face looks toward the principle that governmental intervention in religious matters can itself endanger religious freedom.

This case, like all Establishment Clause challenges, presents us with the difficulty of respecting both faces. Our institutions presuppose a Supreme

[2] The monuments are: Heroes of the Alamo, Hood's Brigade, Confederate Soldiers, Volunteer Fireman, Terry's Texas Rangers, Texas Cowboy, Spanish-American War, Texas National Guard, Ten Commandments, Tribute to Texas School Children, Texas Pioneer Woman, The Boy Scouts' Statue of Liberty Replica, Pearl Harbor Veterans, Korean War Veterans, Soldiers of World War I, Disabled Veterans, and Texas Peace Officers.

Being, yet these institutions must not press religious observances upon their citizens. One face looks to the past in acknowledgment of our Nation's heritage, while the other looks to the present in demanding a separation between church and state. Reconciling these two faces requires that we neither abdicate our responsibility to maintain a division between church and state nor evince a hostility to religion by disabling the government from in some ways recognizing our religious heritage.

These two faces are evident in representative cases both upholding and invalidating laws under the Establishment Clause. Over the last 25 years, we have sometimes pointed to *Lemon v. Kurtzman* as providing the governing test in Establishment Clause challenges. Yet, just two years after Lemon was decided, we noted that the factors identified in *Lemon* serve as "no more than helpful signposts." *Hunt v. McNair*. Many of our recent cases simply have not applied the *Lemon* test. Others have applied it only after concluding that the challenged practice was invalid under a different Establishment Clause test.

Whatever may be the fate of the *Lemon* test in the larger scheme of Establishment Clause jurisprudence, we think it not useful in dealing with the sort of passive monument that Texas has erected on its Capitol grounds. Instead, our analysis is driven both by the nature of the monument and by our Nation's history.

As we explained in *Lynch v. Donnelly*, "There is an unbroken history of official acknowledgment by all three branches of government of the role of religion in American life from at least 1789."

Recognition of the role of God in our Nation's heritage has also been reflected in our decisions. This recognition has led us to hold that the Establishment Clause permits a state legislature to open its daily sessions with a prayer by a chaplain paid by the State. *Marsh v. Chambers*. Such a practice, we thought, was "deeply embedded in the history and tradition of this country." With similar reasoning, we have upheld laws, which originated from one of the Ten Commandments, that prohibited the sale of merchandise on Sunday. *McGowan v. Maryland* (separate opinion of FRANKFURTER, J.).

In this case we are faced with a display of the Ten Commandments on government property outside the Texas State Capitol. Such acknowledgments of the role played by the Ten Commandments in our Nation's heritage are common throughout America. We need only look within our own Courtroom. Since 1935, Moses has stood, holding two tablets that reveal portions of the Ten Commandments written in Hebrew, among other lawgivers in the south frieze. Representations of the Ten Commandments adorn the metal gates lining the north and south sides of the Courtroom as well as the doors leading into the Courtroom. Moses also sits on the exterior east facade of the building holding the Ten Commandments tablets.

Of course, the Ten Commandments are religious—they were so viewed at their inception and so remain. The monument, therefore, has religious significance. According to Judeo-Christian belief, the Ten Commandments were given to Moses by God on Mt. Sinai. But Moses was a lawgiver as well as a religious leader. And the Ten Commandments have an undeniable historical meaning, as the foregoing examples demonstrate. Simply having religious content or promoting a message consistent with a religious doctrine does not run afoul of the Establishment Clause.

There are, of course, limits to the display of religious messages or symbols. For example, we held unconstitutional a Kentucky statute requiring the posting of the Ten Commandments in every public schoolroom. *Stone v. Graham*, 449 U.S. 39, 101 S. Ct. 192, 66 L. Ed. 2d 199 (1980) (per curiam). In the classroom context, we found that the Kentucky statute had an improper and plainly religious purpose. As evidenced by Stone's almost exclusive reliance upon two of our school prayer cases, it stands as an example of the fact that we have "been particularly vigilant in monitoring compliance with the Establishment Clause in elementary and secondary schools," *Edwards v. Aguillard*.

The placement of the Ten Commandments monument on the Texas State Capitol grounds is a far more passive use of those texts than was the case in Stone, where the text confronted elementary school students every day. Indeed, Van Orden, the petitioner here, apparently walked by the monument for a number of years before bringing this lawsuit. Texas has treated her Capitol grounds monuments as representing the several strands in the State's political and legal history. The inclusion of the Ten Commandments monument in this group has a dual significance, partaking of both religion and government. We cannot say that Texas' display of this monument violates the Establishment Clause of the First Amendment.

JUSTICE SCALIA, concurring.

I join the opinion of The Chief Justice because I think it accurately reflects our current Establishment Clause jurisprudence—or at least the Establishment Clause jurisprudence we currently apply some of the time. I would prefer to reach the same result by adopting an Establishment Clause jurisprudence that is in accord with our Nation's past and present practices, and that can be consistently applied—the central relevant feature of which is that there is nothing unconstitutional in a State's favoring religion generally, honoring God through public prayer and acknowledgment, or, in a nonproselytizing manner, venerating the Ten Commandments.

JUSTICE THOMAS, concurring.

This case would be easy if the Court were willing to abandon the inconsistent guideposts it has adopted for addressing Establishment Clause challenges, and return to the original meaning of the Clause. I have previously suggested that the Clause's text and history "resis[t] incorporation" against the States. If the Establishment Clause does not restrain the States, then it has no application here, where only state action is at issue.

Even if the Clause is incorporated, or if the Free Exercise Clause limits the power of States to establish religions, our task would be far simpler if we returned to the original meaning of the word "establishment" than it is under the various approaches this Court now uses. The Framers understood an establishment "necessarily [to] involve actual legal coercion."

There is no question that, based on the original meaning of the Establishment Clause, the Ten Commandments display at issue here is constitutional. In no sense does Texas compel petitioner Van Orden to do anything. The only injury to him is that he takes offense at seeing the monument as he passes it on his way to the Texas Supreme Court Library. He need not stop to read it or even to look at it, let alone to express support for it or adopt the Commandments as guides for his life. The mere presence of the monument along his path involves no coercion and thus does not violate the Establishment Clause. Returning to the original meaning would do more than simplify our task. It also would avoid the pitfalls present in the Court's current approach to such challenges.

Much, if not all, of this would be avoided if the Court would return to the views of the Framers and adopt coercion as the touchstone for our Establishment Clause inquiry. Every acknowledgment of religion would not give rise to an Establishment Clause claim. Courts would not act as theological commissions, judging the meaning of religious matters. Most important, our precedent would be capable of consistent and coherent application.

JUSTICE BREYER, concurring in the judgment.

If the relation between government and religion is one of separation, but not of mutual hostility and suspicion, one will inevitably find difficult borderline cases. And in such cases, I see no test-related substitute for the exercise of legal judgment. That judgment is not a personal judgment. Rather, as in all constitutional cases, it must reflect and remain faithful to the underlying purposes of the Clauses, and it must take account of context and consequences measured in light of those purposes. While the Court's prior tests provide useful guideposts—and might well lead to the same result the Court reaches today—no exact formula can dictate a resolution to such fact-intensive cases.

The case before us is a borderline case. It concerns a large granite monument bearing the text of the Ten Commandments located on the grounds of the Texas State Capitol. On the one hand, the Commandments' text undeniably has a religious message, invoking, indeed emphasizing, the Deity. On the other hand, focusing on the text of the Commandments alone cannot conclusively resolve this case. Rather, to determine the message that the text here conveys, we must examine how the text is used. And that inquiry requires us to consider the context of the display.

In certain contexts, a display of the tablets of the Ten Commandments can convey not simply a religious message but also a secular moral message (about proper standards of social conduct). And in certain contexts, a display of the tablets can also convey a historical message (about a historic relation between those standards and the law)—a fact that helps to explain the display of those tablets in dozens of courthouses throughout the Nation, including the Supreme Court of the United States.

Here the tablets have been used as part of a display that communicates not simply a religious message, but a secular message as well. The circumstances surrounding the display's placement on the capitol grounds and its physical setting suggest that the State itself intended the latter, nonreligious aspects of the tablets' message to predominate. And the monument's 40-year history on the Texas state grounds indicates that that has been its effect.

The group that donated the monument, the Fraternal Order of Eagles, a private civic (and primarily secular) organization, while interested in the religious aspect of the Ten Commandments, sought to highlight the Commandments' role in shaping civic morality as part of that organization's efforts to combat juvenile delinquency. The Eagles' consultation with a committee composed of members of several faiths in order to find a nonsectarian text underscores the group's ethics-based motives. The tablets, as displayed on the monument, prominently acknowledge that the Eagles donated the display, a factor which, though not sufficient, thereby further distances the State itself from the religious aspect of the Commandments' message.

The physical setting of the monument, moreover, suggests little or nothing of the sacred. The monument sits in a large park containing 17 monuments and 21 historical markers, all designed to illustrate the "ideals" of those who settled in Texas and of those who have lived there since that time. The setting does not readily lend itself to meditation or any other religious activity. But it does provide a context of history and moral ideals.

If these factors provide a strong, but not conclusive, indication that the Commandments' text on this monument conveys a predominantly secular message, a further factor is determinative here. As far as I can tell, 40 years passed in which the presence of this monument, legally speaking, went unchallenged (until the single legal objection raised by petitioner). And I am not aware of any evidence suggesting that this was due to a climate of intimidation. Hence, those 40 years suggest more strongly than can any set of formulaic tests that few individuals, whatever their system of beliefs, are likely to have understood the monument as amounting, in any significantly detrimental way, to a government effort to favor a particular religious sect, primarily to promote religion over nonreligion, to "engage in" any "religious practic[e]," to "compel" any "religious practic[e]," or to "work deterrence" of any "religious belief." Those 40 years suggest that the public visiting the capitol grounds has considered the religious aspect of the tablets' message as part of what is a broader moral and historical message reflective of a cultural heritage.

This case, moreover, is distinguishable from instances where the Court has found Ten Commandments displays impermissible. The display is not on the grounds of a public school, where, given the impressionability of the young, government must exercise particular care in separating church and state. This case also differs from *McCreary County*, where the short (and stormy) history of the courthouse Commandments' displays demonstrates the substantially religious objectives of those who mounted them, and the effect of this readily apparent objective upon those who view them. That history there indicates a governmental effort substantially to promote religion, not simply an effort primarily to reflect, historically, the secular impact of a religiously inspired document. And, in today's world, in a Nation of so many different religious and comparable nonreligious fundamental beliefs, a more contemporary state effort to focus attention upon a religious text is certainly likely to prove divisive in a way that this longstanding, pre-existing monument has not.

At the same time, to reach a contrary conclusion here, based primarily upon on the religious nature of the tablets' text would, I fear, lead the law to exhibit a hostility toward religion that has no place in our Establishment Clause traditions. Such a holding might well encourage disputes concerning the removal of longstanding depictions of the Ten Commandments from public buildings across the Nation. And it could thereby create the very kind of religiously based divisiveness that the Establishment Clause seeks to avoid.

JUSTICE STEVENS, with whom JUSTICE GINSBURG joins, dissenting.

The sole function of the monument on the grounds of Texas' State Capitol is to display the full text of one version of the Ten Commandments. The monument is not a work of art and does not refer to any event in the history of the State. It is significant because, and only because, it communicates the following message:

"I AM the LORD thy God.

"Thou shalt have no other gods before me.

"Thou shalt not make to thyself any graven images.

"Thou shalt not take the Name of the Lord thy God in vain.

"Remember the Sabbath day, to keep it holy.

"Honor thy father and thy mother, that thy days may be long upon the land which the Lord thy God giveth thee.

"Thou shalt not kill.

"Thou shalt not commit adultery.

"Thou shalt not steal.

"Thou shalt not bear false witness against thy neighbor.

"Thou shalt not covet thy neighbor's house.

"Thou shalt not covet thy neighbor's wife, nor his manservant, nor his maidservant, nor his cattle, nor anything that is thy neighbor's."

Viewed on its face, Texas' display has no purported connection to God's role in the formation of Texas or the founding of our Nation; nor does it provide the reasonable observer with any basis to guess that it was erected to honor any individual or organization. The message transmitted by Texas' chosen display is quite plain: This State endorses the divine code of the "Judeo-Christian" God. If any fragment of Jefferson's metaphorical "wall of separation between church and State" is to be preserved—if there remains any meaning to the "wholesome 'neutrality' of which this Court's [Establishment Clause] cases speak," *School Dist. of Abington Township v. Schemp*—a negative answer to that question is mandatory.

I

In my judgment, at the very least, the Establishment Clause has created a strong presumption against the display of religious symbols on public property. The adornment of our public spaces with displays of religious symbols and messages undoubtedly provides comfort, even inspiration, to many individuals who subscribe to particular faiths. Unfortunately, the practice also runs the risk of "offend[ing] nonmembers of the faith being advertised as well as adherents who consider the particular advertisement disrespectful."

Government's obligation to avoid divisiveness and exclusion in the religious sphere is compelled by the Establishment and Free Exercise Clauses, which together erect a wall of separation between church and state. This metaphorical wall protects principles long recognized and often recited in this Court's cases. The first and most fundamental of these principles, one that a majority of this Court today affirms, is that the Establishment Clause demands religious neutrality—government may not exercise a preference for one religious faith over another. *See, e.g., McCreary County v. American Civil Liberties Union of Ky.*

The wall that separates the church from the State does not prohibit the government from acknowledging the religious beliefs and practices of the American people, nor does it require governments to hide works of art or historic memorabilia from public view just because they also have religious significance.

This case, however, is not about historic preservation or the mere recognition of religion. The issue is obfuscated rather than clarified by simplistic commentary on the various ways in which religion has played a role in American life, and by the recitation of the many extant governmental "acknowledgments" of the role the Ten Commandments played in our Nation's heritage. Surely, the mere compilation of religious symbols, none of which includes the full text of the Commandments and all of which are exhibited in different settings, has only marginal relevance to the question presented in this case.

The monolith displayed on Texas Capitol grounds cannot be discounted as a passive acknowledgment of religion, nor can the State's refusal to remove it upon objection be explained as a simple desire to preserve a historic relic. This Nation's resolute commitment to neutrality with respect to religion is flatly inconsistent with the plurality's wholehearted validation of an official state endorsement of the message that there is one, and only one, God.

II

Though the State of Texas may genuinely wish to combat juvenile delinquency, and may rightly want to honor the Eagles for their efforts, it cannot effectuate these admirable purposes through an explicitly religious medium. The State may admonish its citizens not to lie, cheat or steal, to honor their parents and to respect their neighbors' property; and it may do so by printed words, in television commercials, or on granite monuments in front of its public buildings. Moreover, the State may provide its schoolchildren and adult citizens with educational materials that explain the important role that our forebears' faith in God played in their decisions to select America as a refuge from religious persecution, to declare their independence from the British Crown, and to conceive a new Nation. The message at issue in this case, however, is fundamentally different from either a bland admonition to observe generally accepted rules of behavior or a general history lesson.

The reason this message stands apart is that the Decalogue is a venerable religious text. As we held 25 years ago, it is beyond dispute that "[t]he Ten Commandments are undeniably a sacred text in the Jewish and Christian faiths." *Stone v. Graham.* For many followers, the Commandments represent the literal word of God as spoken to Moses and repeated to his followers after descending from Mount Sinai. The message conveyed by the Ten Commandments thus cannot be analogized to an appendage to a common article of commerce ("In God we Trust") or an incidental part of a familiar recital ("God save the United States and this honorable Court"). Thankfully, the plurality does not attempt to minimize the religious significance of the Ten Commandments. Attempts to secularize what is unquestionably a sacred text defy credibility and disserve people of faith.

Moreover, despite the Eagles' best efforts to choose a benign nondenominational text, the Ten Commandments display projects not just a religious, but an inherently sectarian message. There are many distinctive versions of the Decalogue, ascribed to by different religions and even different denominations within a particular faith; to a pious and learned observer, these differences may be of enormous religious significance. In choosing to display this version of the Commandments, Texas tells the observer that the State supports this side of the doctrinal religious debate. The reasonable observer, after all, has no way of knowing that this text was the product of a compromise, or that there is a rationale of any kind for the text's selection.

The Establishment Clause, if nothing else, forbids government from "specifying details upon which men and women who believe in a benevolent, omnipotent Creator and Ruler of the world are known to differ." *Lee v. Weisman* (SCALIA, J., dissenting). Given that the chosen text inscribed on the Ten Commandments monument invariably places the State at the center of a serious sectarian dispute, the display is unquestionably unconstitutional under our case law.

Even if, however, the message of the monument, despite the inscribed text, fairly could be said to represent the belief system of all Judeo-Christians, it would still run afoul of the Establishment Clause by prescribing a compelled code of conduct from one God, namely a Judeo-Christian God, that is rejected by prominent polytheistic sects, such as Hinduism, as well as nontheistic religions, such as Buddhism. And, at the very least, the text of the Ten Commandments impermissibly commands a preference for religion over irreligion. Any of those bases, in my judgment, would be sufficient to conclude that the message should not be proclaimed by the State of Texas on a permanent monument at the seat of its government.

Today there are many Texans who do not believe in the God whose Commandments are displayed at their seat of government. Many of them worship a different god or no god at all. Some may believe that the account of the creation in the Book of Genesis is less reliable than the views of men like Darwin and Einstein. The monument is no more an expression of the views of every true Texan than was the "Live Free or Die" motto that the State of New Hampshire placed on its license plates in 1969 an accurate expression of the views of every citizen of New Hampshire. See *Wooley v. Maynard*.

Recognizing the diversity of religious and secular beliefs held by Texans and by all Americans, it seems beyond peradventure that allowing the seat of government to serve as a stage for the propagation of an unmistakably Judeo-Christian message of piety would have the tendency to make nonmonotheists and nonbelievers "feel like [outsiders] in matters of faith, and [strangers] in the political community." Even more than the display of a religious symbol on government property, displaying this sectarian text at the state capitol should invoke a powerful presumption of invalidity.

III

The plurality relies heavily on the fact that our Republic was founded, and has been governed since its nascence, by leaders who spoke then (and speak still) in plainly religious rhetoric. Further, the plurality emphatically endorses the seemingly timeless recognition that our "institutions presuppose a Supreme Being," Many of the submissions made to this Court by the parties and amici, in accord with the plurality's opinion, have relied on the ubiquity of references to God throughout our history.

The speeches and rhetoric characteristic of the founding era, however, do not answer the question before us. I have already explained why Texas' display of the full text of the Ten Commandments, given the content of the actual display and the context in which it is situated, sets this case apart from the countless examples of benign government recognitions of religion. But there is another crucial difference. Our leaders, when delivering public addresses, often express their blessings simultaneously in the service of God and their constituents. Thus, when public officials deliver public speeches, we recognize that their words are not exclusively a transmission from the government because those oratories have embedded within them the inherently personal views of the speaker as an individual member of the polity. The permanent placement of a textual religious display on state property is different in kind; it amalgamates otherwise discordant individual views into a collective statement of government approval.

The plurality's reliance on early religious statements and proclamations made by the Founders is also problematic because those views were not espoused at the Constitutional Convention in 1787 nor enshrined in the Constitution's text.

The original understanding of the type of "religion" that qualified for constitutional protection under the Establishment Clause likely did not include those followers of Judaism and Islam who are among the preferred "monotheistic" religions JUSTICE SCALIA has embraced in his *McCreary County* opinion. The inclusion of Jews and Muslims inside the category of constitutionally favored religions surely would have shocked CHIEF JUSTICE MARSHALL and JUSTICE STORY. Indeed, JUSTICE SCALIA is unable to point to any persuasive historical evidence or entrenched traditions in support of his decision to give specially preferred constitutional status to all monotheistic religions. Perhaps this is because the history of the Establishment Clause's original meaning just as strongly supports a preference for Christianity as it does a preference for monotheism. Generic references to "God" hardly constitute evidence that those who spoke the word meant to be inclusive of all monotheistic believers; nor do such references demonstrate that those who heard the word spoken understood it broadly to include all monotheistic faiths. JUSTICE SCALIA's inclusion of Judaism and Islam is a laudable act of religious tolerance, but it is one that is unmoored from the Constitution's history and text, and moreover one that is patently arbitrary in its inclusion of some, but exclusion of other (e.g., Buddhism), widely practiced non-Christian religions.

Indeed, to constrict narrowly the reach of the Establishment Clause to the views of the Founders would lead to more than this unpalatable result; it would also leave us with an unincorporated constitutional provision—in other words, one that limits only the federal establishment of "a national religion." Under this view, not only could a State constitutionally adorn all of its public spaces with crucifixes or passages from the New Testament, it would also have full authority to prescribe the teachings of Martin Luther or Joseph Smith as the official state religion. Only the Federal Government would be prohibited from taking sides, (and only then as between Christian sects).

A reading of the First Amendment dependent on either of the purported original meanings expressed above would eviscerate the heart of the Establishment Clause. It would replace Jefferson's "wall of separation" with a perverse wall of exclusion—Christians inside, non-Christians out. It would permit States to construct walls of their own choosing—Baptists inside, Mormons out; Jewish Orthodox inside, Jewish Reform out. A Clause so understood might be faithful to the expectations of some of our Founders, but it is plainly not worthy of a society whose enviable hallmark over the course of two centuries has been the continuing expansion of religious pluralism and tolerance.

It is our duty, therefore, to interpret the First Amendment's command that "Congress shall make no law respecting an establishment of religion" not by merely asking what those words meant to observers at the time of the founding, but instead by deriving from the Clause's text and history the broad principles that remain valid today.

We serve our constitutional mandate by expounding the meaning of constitutional provisions with one eye towards our Nation's history and the other fixed on its democratic aspirations. The principle that guides my analysis is neutrality. The basis for that principle is firmly rooted in our Nation's history and our Constitution's text. I recognize that the requirement that government must remain neutral between religion and irreligion would have seemed foreign to some of the Framers; so too would a requirement of neutrality between Jews and Christians. Fortunately, we are not bound by the Framers' expectations—we are bound by the legal principles they enshrined in our Constitution. As religious pluralism has expanded, so has our acceptance of what constitutes valid belief systems. The evil of discriminating today against atheists, "polytheists[,] and believers in unconcerned deities," *McCreary County* (Scalia, J., dissenting), is in my view a direct descendent of the evil of discriminating among Christian sects. The Establishment Clause thus forbids it and, in turn, forbids Texas from displaying the Ten Commandments monument the plurality so casually affirms.

[Dissenting Opinion of Justice O'Connor is omitted.]

Justice Souter, with whom Justice Stevens and Justice Ginsburg join, dissenting.

Although the First Amendment's Religion Clauses have not been read to mandate absolute governmental neutrality toward religion, the Establishment Clause requires neutrality as a general rule, and thus expresses Madison's condemnation of "employ[ing] Religion as an engine of Civil policy," Memorial and Remonstrance Against Religious Assessments, 2 Writings of James Madison 183, 187 (G. Hunt ed. 1901). A governmental display of an obviously religious text cannot be squared with neutrality, except in a setting that plausibly indicates that the statement is not placed in view with a predominant purpose on the part of government either to adopt the religious message or to urge its acceptance by others.

[A] pedestrian happening upon the monument at issue here needs no training in religious doctrine to realize that the statement of the Commandments, quoting God himself, proclaims that the will of the divine being is the source of obligation to obey the rules, including the facially secular ones. In this case, moreover, the text is presented to give particular prominence to the Commandments' first sectarian reference, "I am the Lord thy God."

The monument's presentation of the Commandments with religious text emphasized and enhanced stands in contrast to any number of perfectly constitutional depictions of them, the frieze of our own Courtroom providing a good example, where the figure of Moses stands among history's great lawgivers. While Moses holds the tablets of the Commandments showing some Hebrew text, no one looking at the lines of figures in marble relief is likely to see a religious purpose behind the assemblage or take away a religious message from it. Only one other depiction represents a religious leader, and the historical personages are mixed with symbols of moral and intellectual abstractions like Equity and Authority. Since Moses enjoys no especial prominence on the frieze, viewers can readily take him to be there as a lawgiver in the company of other lawgivers; and the viewers may just as naturally see the tablets of the Commandments (showing the later ones, forbidding things like killing and theft, but without the divine preface) as background from which the concept of law emerged, ultimately having a secular influence in the history of the Nation.

Texas seeks to take advantage of the recognition that visual symbol and written text can manifest a secular purpose in secular company, when it argues that its monument (like Moses in the frieze) is not alone and ought to be viewed as only 1 among 17 placed on the 22 acres surrounding the state capitol.

But 17 monuments with no common appearance, history, or esthetic role scattered over 22 acres is not a museum, and anyone strolling around the lawn would surely take each memorial on its own terms without any dawning sense that some purpose held the miscellany together more coherently than fortuity and the edge of the grass. One monument expresses admiration for pioneer women. One pays respect to the fighters of World War II. And one quotes the God of Abraham whose command is the sanction for moral law. The themes are individual grit, patriotic courage, and God as the source of Jewish and Christian morality; there is no common denominator.

When the plurality finally does confront *Stone v. Graham*, it tries to avoid the case's obvious applicability by limiting its holding to the classroom setting. In fact, *Stone's* reasoning reached the classroom only in noting the lack of support for the claim that the State had brought the Commandments into schools in order to "integrat[e] [them] into the school curriculum." Accordingly, our numerous prior discussions of *Stone* have never treated its holding as restricted to the classroom.

Nor can the plurality deflect *Stone* by calling the Texas monument "a far more passive use of [the Decalogue] than was the case in *Stone*, where the text confronted elementary school students every day." Placing a monument on the ground is not more "passive" than hanging a sheet of paper on a wall when both contain the same text to be read by anyone who looks at it. The problem in *Stone* was simply that the State was putting the Commandments there to be seen, just as the monument's inscription is there for those who walk by it.

To be sure, Kentucky's compulsory-education law meant that the schoolchildren were forced to see the display every day, whereas many see the monument by choice, and those who customarily walk the Capitol grounds can presumably avoid it if they choose. But in my judgment (and under our often inexact Establishment Clause jurisprudence, such matters often boil down to judgment, this distinction should make no difference. The monument in this case sits on the grounds of the Texas State Capitol. There is something significant in the common term "statehouse" to refer to a state capitol building: it is the civic home of every one of the State's citizens. If neutrality in religion means something, any citizen should be able to visit that civic home without having to confront religious expressions clearly meant to convey an official religious position that may be at odds with his own religion, or with rejection of religion.

NOTE

Two of the editors of this book have made the following observation about the conflicting results in *McCreary* and *Van Orden*: "In sum, separationists prevailed in *McCreary* and accommodationists in *Van Orden*. Yet the critical vote in each case was that of Justice Breyer and his analysis was so fact-specific as to give neither position a decisive edge." JEROME A. BARRON & C. THOMAS DIENES, CONSTIUTIONAL LAW IN A NUTSHELL 575 (6th ed. 2005). Although it is true that Justice Breyer was the critical vote in each case, isn't it also true that on balance the two cases represented an overall victory for the accommodationists?

[2] Separate Religious Communities and the State

BOARD OF EDUCATION OF KIRYAS JOEL VILLAGE SCHOOL DISTRICT v. GRUMET

512 U.S. 687, 114 S.Ct. 2481, 129 L. Ed. 2d 546 (1994)

JUSTICE SOUTER delivered the opinion of the Court.

The Village of Kiryas Joel in Orange County, New York, is a religious enclave of Satmar Hasidim, practitioners of a strict form of Judaism. The village fell within the Monroe-Woodbury Central School District until a special state statute passed in 1989 carved out a separate district, following village lines, to serve this distinctive population. The question is whether the Act creating the separate school district violates the Establishment Clause of the First Amendment, binding on the States through the Fourteenth Amendment. Because this unusual act is tantamount to an allocation of political power on a religious criterion and neither presupposes nor requires governmental impartiality toward religion, we hold that it violates the prohibition against establishment.

Children from Kiryas Joel who needed special education (including the deaf, the mentally retarded, and others suffering from a range of physical, mental, or emotional disorders) [had been previously] forced to attend public schools outside the village, which their families found highly unsatisfactory. Parents of most of these children withdrew them from the Monroe-Woodbury secular schools, citing "the panic, fear and trauma [the children] suffered in leaving their own community and being with people whose ways were so different."

Although it enjoys plenary legal authority over the elementary and secondary education of all school-aged children in the village, the Kiryas Joel Village School District currently runs only a special education program for handicapped children.

What makes this litigation different from *Larkin* is the delegation here of civic power to the "qualified voters of the village of Kiryas Joel," as distinct from a religious leader or an institution of religious government like the formally constituted parish council in *Larkin*. [T]he difference between thus vesting state power in the members of a religious group as such instead of the officers of its sectarian organization is one of form, not substance.

[T]he second (and arguably more important) distinction between this case and *Larkin* is the identification here of the group to exercise civil authority in terms not expressly religious. [The New York law] effectively identifies these recipients of governmental authority by reference to doctrinal adherence, even though it does not do so directly.

Because the district's creation ran uniquely counter to state practice, following the lines of a religious community where the customary and neutral principles would not have dictated the same result, we have good reasons to treat this district as the reflection of a religious criterion for identifying the recipients of civil authority. We therefore find the legislature's Act to be substantially equivalent to defining a political subdivision and hence the qualification for its franchise by a religious test, resulting in a purposeful and forbidden "fusion of governmental and religious functions." *Larkin v. Grendel's Den*.

The fact that this school district was created by a special and unusual Act of the legislature also gives reason for concern whether the benefit received by the Satmar community is one that the legislature will provide equally to other religious (and nonreligious) groups. This is the second malady the *Larkin* Court identified in the law before it, the absence of an "effective means of guaranteeing" that governmental power will be and has been neutrally employed.

The fundamental source of constitutional concern here is that the legislature itself may fail to exercise governmental authority in a religiously neutral way. The anomalously case-specific nature of the legislature's exercise of state authority in creating this district for a religious community leaves the Court without any direct way to review such state action for the purpose of safeguarding a principle at the heart of the Establishment Clause, that government should not prefer one religion to another, or religion to irreligion. Because the religious community of Kiryas Joel did not receive its new governmental authority simply as one of many communities eligible for equal treatment under a general law, we have no assurance that the next similarly situated group seeking a school district of its own will receive one; unlike an administrative agency's denial of an exemption from a generally applicable law, which "would be entitled to a judicial audience," a legislature's failure to enact a special law is itself unreviewable.

In finding that Chapter 748 violates the requirement of governmental neutrality by extending the benefit of a special franchise, we do not deny that the Constitution allows the state to accommodate religious needs by alleviating special burdens. Our cases leave no doubt that in commanding neutrality the Religion Clauses do not require the government to be oblivious to impositions that legitimate exercises of state power may place on religious belief and practice.

[A]ccommodation is not a principle without limits, and what petitioners seek is an adjustment to the Satmars' religiously grounded preferences that our cases do not countenance. Prior decisions have allowed religious communities and institutions to pursue their own interests free from governmental interference, but we have never hinted that an otherwise unconstitutional delegation of political power to a religious group could be saved as a religious accommodation. Petitioners' proposed accommodation singles out a particular religious sect for special treatment, and whatever the limits of permissible legislative accommodations may be, it is clear that neutrality as among religions must be honored.

In this case we are clearly constrained to conclude that the statute before us fails the test of neutrality. It delegates a power this Court has said "ranks at the very apex of the function of a State," to an electorate defined by common religious belief and practice, in a manner that fails to foreclose religious favoritism. It therefore crosses the line from permissible accommodation to impermissible establishment.

Justice Stevens, with whom Justices Blackmun and Ginsburg join, concurring.

[The State] affirmatively supports a religious sect's interest in segregating itself and preventing its children from associating with their neighbors. The isolation of these children, while it may protect them from "panic, fear and trauma," also unquestionably increased the likelihood that they would remain within the fold, faithful adherents of their parents' religious faith. By creating a school district that is specifically intended to shield children from contact with others who have "different ways," the State provided official support to cement the attachment of young adherents to a particular faith.

Affirmative state action in aid of segregation of this character is unlike the evenhanded distribution of a public benefit or service, a "release time" program for public school students involving no public premises or funds, or a decision to grant an exemption from a burdensome general rule. It is, I believe, fairly characterized as establishing, rather than merely accommodating, religion.

JUSTICE KENNEDY, concurring in the judgment.

Whether or not the purpose is accommodation and whether or not the government provides similar gerrymanders to people of all religious faiths, the Establishment Clause forbids the government to use religion as a line-drawing criterion. In this respect, the Establishment Clause mirrors the Equal Protection Clause. Just as the government may not segregate people on account of their race, so too it may not segregate on the basis of religion. The danger of stigma and stirred animosities is no less acute for religious line-drawing than for racial.

JUSTICE SCALIA, with whom THE CHIEF JUSTICE and JUSTICE THOMAS join, dissenting.

[T]he Court's snub of *Lemon* today (it receives only two "see also" citations, in the course of the opinion's description of *Grendel's Den*) is particularly noteworthy because all three courts below (who are not free to ignore Supreme Court precedent at will) relied on it, and the parties (also bound by our case law) dedicated over 80 pages of briefing to the application and continued vitality of the *Lemon* test. To replace *Lemon* with nothing is simply to announce that we are now so bold that we no longer feel the need even to pretend that our haphazard course of Establishment Clause decisions is governed by any principle. The foremost principle I would apply is fidelity to the longstanding traditions of our people, which surely provide the diversity of treatment that JUSTICE O'CONNOR seeks, but do not leave us to our own devices.

NOTES

1. ***Homogeneous religious communities.*** Professor Carter contends that, instead of welcoming religion into the public square, American society marginalizes religion. In his view, religious communities serve as a counterpoise to the state. The variety of religions in America serves to mediate "between the citizen and the apparatus of government, providing an independent moral voice." STEPHEN L. CARTER, THE CULTURE OF DISBELIEF 36–37 (1993). These views contrast sharply with strict separationism.

Some religious communities do not wish to serve as mediators: "Consider for example, the separationist Old Order Amish who were granted an exemption in *Wisconsin v. Yoder*, or the Satmar Hasidim whose self-segregation was at issue in [*Kiryas Joel*]." Kathleen Sullivan, *Book Review, God as a Lobby*, 61 U. CHI. L. REV. 1655, 1669 (1995). Professor Sullivan fears that Carter underestimates the potential for religious strife which may follow the abandonment of separationism. Carter gives "too little consideration to the possibility that it is at least partly our separationist culture that distinguishes us from Belfast, Sarajevo, or Beirut."

For a different view, see Abner S. Greene, *Kiryas Joel and Two Mistakes About Equality*, 96 COLUM. L. REV. 1, 6 (1996):

> A true political liberalism [i]ncorporates the complete exit model ["permeable sovereignty"] by providing not only for a public arena for the advancement of a common ground, but also for an exit option for citizens according to private law. [P]ermeable sovereignty — the recognition that within one nation there exists a multiplicity of law-givers, both at the public and private level — is both normatively defensible and consonant with our constitutional structure.

2. *Pragmatic approaches.* Professor Eisgruber believes that "by inviting New York to write a general law accommodating localities that prefer segregated schools, the *Kiryas Joel* Court exacerbated the problem. A more appropriate solution would be to reverse *Aguilar v. Felton* and 'return to on-site instruction.' " Christopher Eisgruber, *Madison's Wager: Religious Liberty in the Constitutional Order*, 89 Nw. U.L. Rev. 347, 408 (1995).

The New York legislature responded to *Kiryas Joel* immediately by passing a new statute that permits any municipality meeting certain criteria to form its own school district. The *Kiryas Joel* plaintiffs have brought suit once again and contend that the new law is still unconstitutional. It is suggested that Justice O'Connor would validate the new law because it is a generally applicable one. Note, *Separatist Religious Groups and the Establishment Clause*, 30 Harv. C.R. — C.L.L. Rev. 223, 234 (1994). What about the rest of the Court?

3. *Sunday Preference Laws.* In *McGowan v. Maryland,* 366 U.S. 420 (1961), the Court rejected an establishment clause challenge to a Sunday Closing law. Chief Justice Warren, for the Court, held that while "Blue Laws" were originally motivated by religious considerations, "[t]he present purpose and effect of most of them is to provide a uniform day of rest for all citizens." To rely solely on the genesis of such laws "would give a constitutional interpretation of hostility to the public welfare rather than one of mere separation of Church and State." To the claim that the state had alternative means for achieving its secular purposes, the Court replied that the objective was to have a common day of rest and "[i]t would seem unrealistic for enforcement purposes and perhaps detrimental to the general welfare to require the State to choose a common-day-of-rest other than that which most persons would select of their own accord."

§ 9.02 FREE EXERCISE OF RELIGION

Prior to Justice Scalia's opinion for the Court in *Employment Div., Dep't of Human Resources v. Smith*, p. 1458, courts faced with this type of issue typically would balance, in some fashion, the burdens on free exercise against the state interests involved. Once the challenger demonstrated a significant burden on a sincerely held religious belief or practice, the government would be required to demonstrate that the law was narrowly tailored to serve an overriding (sometimes compelling) interest. Often, the Supreme Court also would require a showing that the government interest could not be satisfied by any less onerous alternative. But, given the burgeoning eccentric "religious" cults in our varied and pluralist society, identifying "religious" practice is increasingly difficult. Can a court inquire into the truth or falsity of the religious claim? How severe should the government's burden of justification be? In accommodating the needs and demands of the free exercise guarantee, how are the demands of the nonestablishment principle to be satisfied? One point to bear in mind is that whenever government grants exemptions from laws of general applicability to accommodate the free exercise of religious beliefs, there is potential for arguing that the exemption establishes religion.

The inherent difficulty of the foregoing questions may have been a major factor in producing the *Smith* opinion, which attempts to limit the application of the free exercise clause to one of two situations — either an overt attempt on the part of government to curtail religious practices or the combination of a free exercise claim with another constitutionally based claim such as freedom of speech. We cannot yet know what the effect of *Smith* will be.

[A] THE "DIFFERENCE" BETWEEN CONDUCT AND BELIEF

***Reynolds v. United States,* 98 U.S. 145 (1878).** Reynolds, a Mormon in the Territory of Utah, was charged with violating a federal law prohibiting polygamy in the federal territories. Reynolds defended against the charge by claiming that as a Mormon he was obliged to practice polygamy as a part of his faith. Did the federal statute prohibiting polygamy violate the free exercise of religion, at least as applied to a member of the Mormon faith? The Court held that it did not.

In *Reynolds*, Chief Justice Waite, for the Court, rhetorically asked whether government was barred from preventing human sacrifice simply because it was a fundamental part of religious worship, or whether government could not prevent a woman from burning herself on her dead husband's funeral pyre because her religion commanded it. It was necessary, he concluded, to draw a distinction between "beliefs" which are protected under the Constitution and "practices" or "actions" which are not:

> Congress was deprived of all legislative power over mere opinion, but was left free to reach actions which were in violation of social duties or subversive of good order. Laws are made for the government of actions, and while they cannot interfere with mere religious beliefs and opinions, they may with practices. Can a man excuse his practices to the contrary because of his religious belief? To permit this would be to make the professed doctrine of religious belief superior to the law of the land and in effect to permit every citizen to become a law unto himself. Government could exist only in name under such circumstances.

***United States v. Ballard,* 322 U.S. 78 (1944).** Two Ballards were convicted for using the mail to obtain funds by false representation. In soliciting funds for the "I AM" movement, they claimed that Guy Ballard (their late husband and father) had talked with Jesus, that he had been delegated by St. Germain to serve as a divine messenger, and that all three could cure both curable and incurable diseases. The jury was instructed not to consider the truth of these claims but only the question of whether the defendants had a good-faith belief in their claims. The Court of Appeals reversed on the basis that the defendants were entitled to have the truth or falsity of their claims tested by the jury under a "reasonable doubt" standard.

The Supreme Court reversed and remanded, holding that the district court properly submitted to the jury only the question of the Ballards' sincerity of religious beliefs. Justice Douglas, for the Court, stated:

> The religious views espoused by respondents might seem incredible, if not preposterous, to most people. But if those doctrines are subject to trial before a jury charged with finding their truth or falsity, then the same can be done with the religious beliefs of any sect. When the triers of fact undertake that task, they enter a forbidden domain.

Justice Jackson, dissenting, argued that

> as a matter of either practice or philosophy, I do not see how we can separate an issue as to what is believed from consideration as to what is believable. How can the Government prove these persons knew something to be false which it cannot prove to be false? If we try religious sincerity severed from religious verity, we isolate the dispute from the very considerations which in common experience provide its most reliable answer.
>
> The wrong of these things, as I see it, is not in the money the victims part with half so much as in the mental and spiritual poison they get. But that is precisely the thing the Constitution put beyond the reach of the prosecutor, for the price of freedom of religion or of speech or of the press is that we must put up with, and even pay for, a good deal of rubbish.
>
> I would dismiss the indictment and have done with this business of judicially examining other people's faiths.

Should *Reynolds* and *Ballard* be read to mean that government is free to regulate conduct, regardless of its impact on religion, so long as belief remains free of regulation? While much of the Court's language suggests such a principle, freedom to believe would be of limited value if it did not encompass the ability to express the belief through religious practices. On the other hand, the fact that regulation of conduct incidentally intrudes on what a person considers his religious worship cannot automatically render the conduct constitutionally immune from regulation.

Dictum from *Cantwell v. Connecticut,* 310 U.S. 296 (1940), follows the belief-action distinction without stripping all protection for religiously motivated conduct:

> [T]he Amendment embraces two concepts — freedom to believe and freedom to act. The first is absolute but, in the nature of things, the second cannot be. Conduct remains subject to regulation for the protection of society. The freedom to act must have appropriate definition to preserve the enforcement of that protection. In every case

> the power to regulate must be so exercised as not, in attaining a permissible end, unduly to infringe the protected freedom.

[B] SABBATH CELEBRATION AS A FREE EXERCISE PROBLEM

***Braunfeld v. Brown*, 366 U.S. 559 (1961).** Sunday closing laws were upheld against the free exercise claims of non-Sunday Sabbatarians who preferred to open their businesses on Sunday (and perhaps close on Saturday). Chief Justice Warren's plurality opinion labelled the burden imposed on the free exercise of religion as only "indirect." The law did not make the plaintiff's religious practices unlawful, but only "operate[d] so to make the practice of their religious beliefs more expensive." Further, the law was only an economic inconvenience to those orthodox Jews who believed it necessary to work on Sunday.

> Of course, to hold unassailable all legislation regulating conduct which imposes solely an indirect burden on the observance of religion would be a gross oversimplification. If the purpose or effect of a law is to impede the observance of one or all religions or is to discriminate invidiously between religions, that law is constitutionally invalid even though the burden may be characterized as being only indirect. But if the State regulates conduct by enacting a general law within its power, the purpose and effect of which is to advance the State's secular goals, the statute is valid despite its indirect burden on religious observance unless the State may accomplish its purpose by means which do not impose such a burden.

Applying this standard, the Court noted that *McGowan v. Maryland*, p. 1444, had examined alternatives to closing laws and had concluded that the "State might well find that those alternatives would not accomplish bringing about a general day of rest." *Braunfeld* rejected the argument that the state should be required to carve out an exception from the Sunday closing laws for those persons who, because of religious convictions, observed a day of rest other than Sunday. *Braunfeld* stressed the danger of perceived discrimination against Sunday observers who might claim an economic competitive disadvantage. Further, such a law "might make necessary a state-conducted inquiry into the sincerity of the individual's religious beliefs, a practice which a State might believe would itself run afoul of the spirit of constitutionally protected religious guarantees." Finally, the proposed law might well cause hiring problems since exempted employers would probably hire employees who themselves qualified for the religious exemption.

Only Justices Stewart and Brennan dissented from the Court's free exercise judgment. Justice Stewart argued that the non-Sunday Sabbatarian was being forced "to choose between his religious faith and his economic survival. This is a cruel choice. It is a choice which I think no state can constitutionally demand." Justice Brennan asked: "What overbalancing need is so weighty in the constitutional scale that it justifies this substantial, though indirect, limitation of appellants' freedom?" His answer was that "[i]t is the mere convenience of having everyone rest on the same day." He viewed this as inadequate to qualify as "grave and immediate danger to interests the State may lawfully protect."

***Sherbert v. Verner*, 374 U.S. 398 (1963)**. The Court, per Justice Brennan, held that the state could not deny unemployment compensation to an otherwise eligible person simply because she refused to accept employment on Saturday, the Sabbath Day of her faith. The state did not consider this as "good cause" justifying a refusal to accept work. While acknowledging that the burden on appellant's religion was only indirect (although more direct than those in *Braunfeld*), this was "only the beginning, not the end" of the inquiry.

> Here not only is it apparent that appellant's declared ineligibility for benefits derived solely from her practice of her religion, but the pressure upon her to forego that practice is unmistakable. The ruling forces her to choose between following the precepts of her religion and forfeiting benefits, on the one hand, and abandoning one of the precepts of her religion in order to accept work, on the other. Governmental imposition of such a choice puts the same kind of burden upon the free exercise of religion as would a fine imposed against appellant for her Saturday worship.

It does not matter, said Justice Brennan, that unemployment compensation benefits are only a privilege and not a right since "to violate a cardinal principle of her religious faith effectively penalizes the free exercise of her constitutional liberty."

In a second step, the Court considered the state justification for imposing such a significant burden. But the *Sherbert* Court did not look for simply a competing governmental interest; instead, the Court required that the government demonstrate a "compelling state interest" and "that no alternative forms of regulation" would suffice. The suggestion that fraudulent claims would be filed by unscrupulous claimants feigning religious objections to Saturday work, which would dilute the compensation fund and hinder the scheduling by employers of necessary Saturday work, was treated as speculative. Justice Brennan concluded that such concerns were not of the dimension that had motivated the Court in *Braunfeld*. In any case, the government had failed to demonstrate that there were no alternative forms of regulation that could curb abuses.

Justice Brennan then addressed the establishment issue:

> In holding as we do, plainly we are not fostering "the establishment" of the Seventh-Day Adventist religion in South Carolina, for the extension of unemployment benefits to Sabbatarians in common with Sunday worshippers reflects nothing more than the governmental obligation of neutrality in the face of religious differences, and does not represent that involvement of religious with secular institutions which it is the object of the Establishment Clause to forestall.

Justice Stewart, concurring, argued that the Court's reasoning was inconsistent with Braunfeld and the "fundamentalist rhetoric" of *Schempp*. He urged that "the court must explicitly reject the reasoning of Braunfeld."

Justice Harlan, joined by Justice White, dissented, contending that the decision "necessarily overruled *Braunfeld*." In this case, as in the prior Blue Law case, religious exemptions would require "case-by-case inquiry into religious beliefs." Further, Justice Harlan contended that the holding meant that the state "must single out for financial assistance those whose behaviour is religiously motivated, even though it denies such assistance to others whose identical behaviour (in this case, inability to work on Saturdays) is not religiously motivated." He rejected the proposition that "the state is constitutionally compelled to carve out an exception to its general rule of eligibility," noting that there are very few situations in which the Constitution requires special treatment on account of religion. The present case was deemed especially inappropriate for such an exception, "in light of the indirect, remote, and insubstantial effect of the decision on the exercise of appellant's religion and in light of the direct financial assistance to religion that [the Court's] decision requires." Justice Harlan, however, also rejected Professor Kurland's neutrality principle: "My own view, is that at least under the circumstances of this case it would be a permissible accommodation of religion for the State, if it chose to do so, to create an exception to its eligibility requirement for persons like the appellant."

THOMAS v. REVIEW BOARD OF INDIANA EMPLOYMENT SECURITY DIVISION

450 U.S. 707, 101 S. Ct. 1425, 67 L. Ed. 2d 624 (1981)

CHIEF JUSTICE BURGER delivered the opinion of the Court.

We granted certiorari to consider whether the State's denial of unemployment compensation benefits to the petitioner, a Jehovah's Witness who terminated his job because his religious beliefs forbade participation in the production of armaments, constituted a violation of his First Amendment right to free exercise of religion.

Thomas terminated his employment in the Blaw-Knox Foundry and Machinery Company when he was transferred from the roll foundry to a department that produced turrets for military tanks. He claimed his religious beliefs prevented him from participating in the production of war materials. The respondent Review Board denied him unemployment compensation benefits by applying disqualifying provisions of the Indiana Employment Security Act. The Supreme Court of Indiana, dividing 3-2, vacated the decision of the Court of Appeals, and denied Thomas benefits.

The judgment under review must be examined in light of our prior decisions, particularly *Sherbert v. Verner*.

The Indiana Supreme Court apparently took a different view of the record. It concluded that "although the claimant's reasons for quitting were described as religious, it was unclear what his belief was, and what the religious basis of his belief was." Courts should not undertake to dissect religious belief because the believer admits that he is "struggling" with his position or because his beliefs are not articulated with the clarity and precision that a more sophisticated person might employ.

The Indiana court also appears to have given significant weight to the fact that another Jehovah's Witness had no scruples about working on tank turrets; for that other Witness, at least, such work was "scripturally" acceptable. Intrafaith differences of that kind are not uncommon among followers of a particular creed, and the judicial process is singularly ill equipped to resolve such differences in relation to the Religion Clauses.

It is true that, as in *Sherbert*, the Indiana law does not compel a violation of conscience. But, "this is only the beginning, not the end of our inquiry." In a variety of ways we have said that "a regulation neutral on its face may, in its application, nonetheless offend the constitutional requirement for governmental neutrality if it unduly burdens the free exercise of religion." *Wisconsin v. Yoder*. Here, as in *Sherbert*, the employee was put to a choice between fidelity to religious belief or cessation of work; the coercive impact on *Thomas* is indistinguishable from *Sherbert*, where the Court held:

> [N]ot only is it apparent that appellant's declared ineligibility for benefits derives solely from the practices of her religion, but the pressure upon her to forego, that practice is unmistakable.

Where the state conditions receipt of an important benefit upon conduct proscribed by a religious faith, or where it denies such a benefit because of conduct mandated by religious belief, thereby putting substantial pressure on an adherent to modify his behavior and to violate his beliefs, a burden upon religion exists. While the compulsion may be indirect, the infringement upon free exercise is nonetheless substantial.

The mere fact that the petitioner's religious practice is burdened by a governmental program does not mean that an exemption accommodating his practice must be granted. The state may justify an inroad on religious liberty by showing that it is the least restrictive means of achieving some compelling state interest. The purposes urged to sustain the disqualifying provision of the Indiana unemployment compensation scheme are two-fold: (1) to avoid the widespread unemployment and the consequent burden on the fund resulting if people were permitted to leave jobs for "personal" reasons; and (2) to avoid a detailed probing by employers into job applicants' religious beliefs. When the focus of the inquiry is properly narrowed, however, we must conclude that the interests advanced by the state do not justify the burden placed on free exercise of religion.

There is no evidence in the record to indicate that the number of people who find themselves in the predicament of choosing between benefits and religious beliefs is large enough to create "widespread unemployment," or even to seriously affect unemployment — and no such claim was advanced by the Review Board. Similarly, although detailed inquiry by employers into applicants' religious beliefs is undesirable, there is no evidence in the record to indicate that such inquiries will occur in Indiana, or that they have occurred in any of the states that extend benefits to people in the petitioner's position. Nor is there any reason to believe that the number of people terminating employment for religious reasons will be so great as to motivate employers to make such inquiries.

Neither of the interests advanced is sufficiently compelling to justify the burden upon Thomas' religious liberty. Accordingly, Thomas is entitled to receive benefits unless, as the state contends and the Indiana court held, such payment would violate the Establishment Clause.

The respondent contends that to compel benefit payments to Thomas involves the state in fostering a religious faith. There is, in a sense, a "benefit" to Thomas deriving from his religious beliefs, but this manifests no more than the tension between the two Religious Clauses which the Court resolved in Sherbert. Unless we are prepared to overrule Sherbert, Thomas cannot be denied the benefits due him on the basis of the findings of the referee, the Review Board and the Indiana Court of Appeals that he terminated his employment because of his religious convictions.

Justice Rehnquist, dissenting.

Where, as here, a State has enacted a general statute, the purpose and effect of which is to advance the State's secular goals, the Free Exercise Clause does not in my view require the State to conform that statute to the dictates of religious conscience of any group. The Court's treatment of the Establishment Clause issue is equally unsatisfying. Although today's decision requires a State to provide direct financial assistance to persons solely on the basis of their religious beliefs, the Court nonetheless blandly assures us, just as it did in Sherbert, that its decision "plainly" does not foster the "establishment" of religion. I would agree that the Establishment Clause, properly interpreted, would not be violated if Indiana voluntarily chose to grant unemployment benefits to those persons who left their jobs for religious reasons. But I also believe that the decision below is inconsistent with many of our prior Establishment Clause cases.

[C] FREE EXERCISE AND ACCOMMODATION

WISCONSIN v. YODER

406 U.S. 205, 92 S. Ct. 1526, 32 L. Ed. 2d 15 (1972)

Chief Justice Burger delivered the opinion of the Court.

Respondents Jonas Yoder and Adin Yutzy are members of the Old Order Amish Religion, and respondent Wallace Miller is a member of the Conservative Amish Mennonite Church. They and their families are residents of Green County, Wisconsin. Wisconsin's compulsory school attendance law required them to cause their children to attend public or private school until reaching age 16 but the respondents declined to send their children, ages 14 and 15, to public school after completing the eighth grade. The children were not enrolled in any private school, or within any recognized exception to the compulsory attendance law, and they are conceded to be subject to the Wisconsin statute.

On complaint of the school district administrator for the public schools, respondents were charged, tried, and convicted of violating the compulsory attendance law in Green County Court and were fined the sum of $5 each. Respondents defended on the ground that the application of the compulsory attendance law violated their rights under the First and Fourteenth Amendments. The trial testimony showed that respondents believed, in accordance with the tenets of Old Order Amish communities generally, that their children's attendance at high school, public or private, was contrary to the Amish religion and way of life. They believed that by sending their children to high school, they would not only expose themselves to the danger of the censure of the church community, but, as found by the county court, endanger their own salvation and that of their children. The State stipulated that respondents' religious beliefs were sincere.

[I]n order for Wisconsin to compel school attendance beyond the eighth grade against a claim that such attendance interferes with the practice of a legitimate religious belief, it must appear either that the State does not deny the free exercise of religious belief by its requirement, or that there is a state interest of sufficient magnitude to override the interest claiming protection under the Free Exercise Clause.

In evaluating those claims we must be careful to determine whether the Amish religious faith and their mode of life are, as they claim, inseparable and interdependent. A way of life, however virtuous and admirable, may not be interposed as a barrier to reasonable state regulation of education if it is based on purely secular considerations; to have the protection of the Religion Clauses, the claims must be rooted in religious belief. Although a determination of what is a "religious" belief or practice entitled to constitutional protection may present a most delicate question, the very concept of ordered liberty precludes allowing every person to make his own standards on matters of conduct in which society as a whole has important interests. Thus, if the Amish asserted their claims because of their subjective evaluation and rejection of the contemporary secular values accepted by the majority, much as Thoreau rejected the social values of his time and isolated himself at Walden Pond, their claims would not rest on a religious basis. Thoreau's choice was philosophical and personal rather than religious, and such belief does not rise to the demands of the Religion Clauses. [T]he record in this case abundantly supports the claim that the traditional way of life of the Amish is not merely a matter of personal preference, but one of deep religious conviction, shared by an organized group, and intimately related to daily living.

The impact of the compulsory attendance law on respondents' practice of the Amish religion is not only severe, but inescapable, for the Wisconsin law affirmatively compels them, under threat of criminal sanction, to perform acts undeniably at odds with fundamental tenets of their religious beliefs.

The State advances two primary arguments in support of its system of compulsory education. It notes, as Thomas Jefferson pointed out early in our history, that some degree of education is necessary to prepare citizens to participate effectively and intelligently in our open political system if we are to preserve freedom and independence. Further, education prepares individuals to be self-reliant and self-sufficient participants in society. We accept these propositions.

Whatever their idiosyncrasies as seen by the majority, this record strongly shows that the Amish community has been a highly successful social unit within our society even if apart from the conventional "mainstream." Its members are productive and very law-abiding members of society; they reject public welfare in any of its usual modern forms. The Congress itself recognized their self-sufficiency by authorizing exemption of such groups as the Amish from the obligation to pay social security taxes.

The State, however, supports its interest in providing an additional one or two years of compulsory high school education to Amish children because of the possibility that some such children will choose to leave the Amish community, and that if this occurs they will be ill-equipped for life. The State argues that if Amish children leave their church they should not be in the position of making their way in the world without the education available in the one or two additional years the State requires. However, on this record, that argument is highly speculative. There is no specific evidence of the loss of Amish adherents by attrition, nor is there any showing that upon leaving the Amish community Amish children, with their practical agricultural training and habits of industry and self-reliance would become burdens on society because of educational shortcomings.

Contrary to the suggestion of the dissenting opinion of Mr. Justice Douglas, our holding today in no degree depends on the assertion of the religious interest of the child as contrasted with that of the parents. It is the parents who are subject to prosecution here for failing to cause their children to attend school, and it is their right of free exercise, not that of their children, that must determine Wisconsin's power to impose criminal penalties on the parent. The dissent argues that a child who expresses a desire to attend public high school in conflict with the wishes of his parents should not be prevented from doing so. There is no reason for the Court to consider that point since it is not an issue in the case. The children are not parties to this litigation. The State has at no point tried this case on the theory that respondents were preventing their children from attending school against their expressed desires, and indeed the record is to the contrary.

Our disposition of this case, however, in no way alters our recognition of the obvious fact that courts are not school boards or legislatures, and are ill-equipped to determine the "necessity" of discrete aspects of a State's program of compulsory education. This should suggest that courts must move with great circumspection in performing the sensitive and delicate task of weighing a State's legitimate social concern when faced with religious claims for exemption from generally applicable educational requirements. It cannot be over-emphasized that we are not dealing with a way of life and mode of education by a group claiming to have recently discovered some "progressive" or more enlightened process for rearing children for modern life.

JUSTICE POWELL and JUSTICE REHNQUIST took no part in the consideration or decision of this case.

JUSTICE WHITE, with whom JUSTICES BRENNAN and STEWART join, concurring.

I join the Court because the sincerity of the Amish religious policy here is uncontested, because the potentially adverse impact of the state requirement is great, and because the State's valid interest in education has already been largely satisfied by the eight years the children have already spent in school.

JUSTICE DOUGLAS, dissenting in part.

The Court's analysis assumes that the only interests at stake in the case are those of the Amish parents on the one hand, and those of the State on the other. The difficulty with this approach is that, despite the Court's claim, the parents are seeking to vindicate not only their own free exercise claims, but also those of their high-school-age children. Where the child is mature enough to express potentially conflicting desires, it would be an invasion of the child's rights to permit such an imposition without canvassing his views. As the child has no other effective forum, it is in this litigation that his rights should be considered. And if an Amish child desires to attend high school, and is mature enough to have that desire respected, the State may well be able to override the parents' religiously motivated objections.

NOTES

1. ***Exemption theory.*** It has been said that "courts have failed to develop an independent justification for religion-based exemptions." *Note*, 90 YALE L.J. 350 (1980). Do the above cases provide such justification?

Professor Galanter has written in favor of permitting exemptions for the sake of free exercise:

> [W]hatever the majority considers necessary for its religious practice is quite unlikely to be prohibited by law. And whatever the majority finds religiously objectionable is unlikely to become a legal requirement — for example, medical practices which substantial groups find abhorrent, like contraception, sterilization, euthanasia, or abortion. Exceptions then, give to minorities what majorities have by virtue of suffrage and representative government.

Marc Galanter, *Religious Freedoms in the United States: A Turning Point?*, 1966 WIS. L. REV. 215 (1966). But does this provide a basis for requiring religious exemptions? Does it matter whether the law in question imposes a duty to act which is contrary to the challenger's religious beliefs or denies benefits to those who fail to qualify because of religious beliefs?

2. ***Sunday closing laws.*** What is the status of Sunday Closing laws after *Sherbert* and *Thomas*? James Kushner, *Towards the Central Meaning of Religious Liberty: Non-Sunday Sabbatarians and the Sunday Closing Cases Revisited*, 35 SW. L.J. 557 (1981), argues that the proper issue today "is whether the state's important goal of having a quiet day when the entire family can assemble is compelling and whether an exemption for non-Sunday Sabbatarians or a 'one day in seven' type of measure would preclude the state from achieving its objectives." He concludes that the Blue Laws could not withstand such scrutiny.

An exception to a general law on behalf of free exercise is permitted in *Yoder*, *Thomas*, and *Sherbert*, but denied in *Braunfeld*. In *Braunfeld*, Chief Justice Warren did not pass on the validity of state statutes which create an exception to Sunday blue laws in order to permit Sabbatarians to work on Sunday. But he did suggest that such statutes raised difficult problems involving unwelcome governmental evaluation of the sincerity of those who invoked Sabbatarian statutes: how was one to distinguish the Sabbatarian who worked on Sunday and rested on Saturday from religious conviction from the Sabbatarian who did the same to secure a competitive advantage?

3. *The Sherbert-Yoder doctrine — areas of marginal significance?* Professor Pepper asserts that if *Yoder* had had "more generalized consequences" for mandatory public education it would not have been decided the same way. Stephen Pepper, *Conflicting Paradigms of Religious Freedom: Liberty vs. Equality*, 1993 B.Y.U. L. REV. 59–60. The Court "to an almost bizarre extent" stressed the insular and limited character of the Amish community. Pepper concludes that under *Sherbert* and *Yoder* protection for religion has been granted only in "areas of marginal concern to the state." Is this a fair criticism? Is it true of both *Sherbert* and *Thomas*?

4. *Exemption theory in Yoder.* Chief Justice Burger adopts an exemption theory in Yoder. He asserts that sometimes an exemption must be made "from a general obligation." The danger of violating the Establishment Clause is, in this view, less than the reality of violating the Free Exercise Clause. Justice Douglas states that the "law and order" record of the Amish should be irrelevant. As a constitutional matter, the no-establishment principle demands that it be irrelevant. The question of whether exemption from a general obligation can ever be anything less than an establishment certainly comes to the fore if the reason for the exemption is that the Amish have been in America for a long time, or that they are exceptionally law abiding, or industrious.

In an article in HARPER'S in 1972, significantly entitled *The Importance of Being Amish*, Professor Walter Berns described the holding in *Yoder* as stating "one's religious conviction" entitled one "to an exemption from the requirements of a valid criminal statute." In Berns' view, this holding constituted "dangerous new law." He speculated that if a citizen is entitled to disobey law which conflicts with one's religious beliefs "the proliferation of sects and of forms of worship will be wonderful to behold: drug cultists, snake worshippers, income tax haters." Is the rule of *Yoder* a rule of general application or an ad hoc example of preferential treatment?

5. *Centrality and sincerity.* In *Yoder*, the Court undertook an extended examination of the "centrality" of the Amish avoidance of formal education to the Amish religion. Is it appropriate for a court — a government agency — to scrutinize the tenets of a religion to determine the extent of the burden on the free exercise of religion? Is such an examination consistent with the *Ballard* admonition against judicial probing of the truth or falsity of religious beliefs? One commentator argues that "[t]his inquiry into centrality is beyond the practical and institutional competence of courts. Moreover, the very notion of centrality is so vague that it can obscure the use of even less defensible distinctions." *Note*, 90 YALE L.J. 350 (1980).

6. *The meaning of religion.* In *Thomas* and *Yoder*, the Court addressed the issue of when a practice or belief may be termed "religious." The framers may have had only traditional, theistic religion in mind in framing the religious guarantees, but given the degree of religious pluralism in our society, the spread of cults and nontheistic belief systems and the problems of favoring particular creeds under the establishment clause, its not surprising that the courts have generally abandoned definitions of religion limited only to traditional theistic religion. And yet, the guarantee of freedom of religion requires some determination of what will qualify as a religion under the free exercise and establishment clauses. A "way of life," the Court said in *Yoder*, would not suffice. Would a definition of religion be necessary under Professor Kurland's neutrality principle?

The Court rejected any limitation of "religion" to theistic religions in *Torcaso v. Watkins,* 367 U.S. 488 (1961), holding invalid a Maryland constitutional provision requiring appointees to public office to declare a belief in the existence of God. Justice Black, for the Court, concluded that neither the federal nor the state government can "aid all religions as against non-believers, and neither can aid those religions based on a belief in the existence of God as against those religions founded on different beliefs." In extending protection to the Secular Humanist challenging the Maryland law, Justice Black observed that a number of religions in this country are not theistic, citing "Buddhism, Taoism, Ethical Culture, Secular Humanism and others."

7. Conscientious Objection and the Draft. Section 6(j) of the Universal Military Training and Service Act of 1948 provides for exemption from combat military service for those opposed to participation in war by reason of their "religious training and belief," which was defined to require belief "in a relation to a Supreme Being." In a decision with strong constitutional overtones, the Court, in *United States v. Seeger,* 380 U.S. 163 (1965), interpreted the phrase "Supreme Being" as embracing all religions, "excluding essentially political, sociological or philosophical views." Justice Clark said the relevant test of belief

> is whether a given belief that is sincere and meaningful occupies a place in the life of its possessor parallel to that filled by the orthodox belief in God of one who clearly qualifies for the exemption. Where such beliefs have parallel positions in the lives of their respective holders we cannot say that one is "in a relation to a Supreme Being" and the other is not.

Congress later deleted the "Supreme Being" language from § 6(j).

The Court carried the "parallel beliefs" position of *Seeger* even further in *Welsh v. United States,* 398 U.S. 333 (1970). Justice Black's plurality opinion extended the provision even to those "whose conscientious objection to participation in all wars is founded to a substantial extent upon considerations of public policy." Indeed, Justice Black reasoned that the only group of sincere believers who were excluded are "those whose objection to war does not rest at all upon moral, ethical, or religious principles but instead rests solely upon considerations of policy, pragmatism, or expediency."

Of course, the determination that a religion or religious belief is implicated is only a beginning, not an end to the inquiry. The Court must still determine whether the government interests are overriding. In *Gillette v. United States,* 401 U.S. 437 (1971), the Court, per Justice Marshall, refused to extend the statutory exemption for conscientious objectors to those opposing participation in particular wars. First, no Establishment Clause violation was found: "We conclude not only that the affirmative purposes underlying § 6(j) are neutral and secular, but also that valid neutral reasons exist for limiting the exemption to objectors to all war, and that the section therefore cannot be said to reflect a religious preference." Nor was the free exercise guarantee violated:

> [T]he impact of conscription on objectors to particular wars is far from unjustified. [The conscription laws] are not designed to interfere with any religious ritual or practice, and do not work a penalty against any theological position. The incidental burdens felt by persons [objecting to a particular war] are strictly justified by substantial government interests that relate directly to the very impacts in question. And more broadly, of course, there is the Government's interest in procuring the manpower necessary for military purposes.

8. *Noncoercive impositions.* In *Lyng v. Northwest Indian Cemetery Protective Ass'n,* 485 U.S. 439 (1988), the Court held that the Free Exercise Clause did not prohibit the Federal Government from permitting timber harvesting and construction for what was known as the G-O road in an area of a national forest traditionally used for religious purposes by members of three American Indian tribes. Justice O'Connor, speaking for the Court, stated:

> It is true that this Court has repeatedly held that indirect coercion or penalties on the free exercise of religion, not just outright prohibitions, are subject to scrutiny under the First Amendment. This does not and cannot imply that incidental effects of government programs, which may make it more difficult to practice certain religions but which have no tendency to coerce individuals into acting contrary to their religious beliefs, require government to bring forward a compelling justification for its otherwise lawful actions. The crucial word in the constitutional text is "prohibit."
>
> Even if we assume that the G-O road will "virtually destroy the Indians' ability to practice their religion," the Constitution simply does not provide a principle that could justify upholding respondent's legal claims. However much we might wish that it were otherwise, government simply could not operate if it were required to satisfy every citizen's religious needs and desires. The Constitution does not, and courts cannot, offer to reconcile the various competing demands on government, many of them rooted in sincere religious belief, that inevitably arise in so diverse a society as ours. That task, to the extent that it is feasible, is for the legislatures and other institutions.
>
> Whatever rights the Indians may have to the use of the area, those rights do not divest the Government of its right to use what is, after all, *its* land.

Justice Brennan, joined by Justices Marshall and Blackmun, dissented:

> The Court does not for a moment suggest that the interests served by the G-O road are in any way compelling, or that they outweigh the destructive effect construction of the road will have on respondents'

religious practices. Instead, the Court embraces the Government's contention that its prerogative as landowner should always take precedence over a claim that a particular use of federal property infringes religious practices. Attempting to justify this rule, the Court argues that the First Amendment bars only outright prohibitions, indirect coercion, and penalties on the free exercise of religion. [W]e have never suggested that the protections of the guarantee are limited to so narrow a range of governmental burdens.

EMPLOYMENT DIV., DEP'T OF HUMAN RESOURCES v. SMITH

494 U.S. 872, 110 S. Ct. 1595, 108 L. Ed. 2d 876 (1990)

Justice Scalia delivered the opinion of the Court.

This case requires us to decide whether the Free Exercise Clause of the First Amendment permits the State of Oregon to include religiously inspired peyote use within the reach of its general criminal prohibition on use of that drug, and thus permits the State to deny unemployment benefits to persons dismissed from their jobs because of such religiously inspired use.

Oregon law prohibits the knowing or intentional possession of a "controlled substance" unless the substance has been prescribed by a medical practitioner. The law defines "controlled substance" as a drug classified in Schedules I through V of the Federal Controlled Substances Act, as modified by the State Board of Pharmacy. Persons who violate this provision by possessing a controlled substance listed on Schedule I are "guilty of a Class B felony." As compiled by the State Board of Pharmacy under its statutory authority Schedule I contains the drug peyote, a hallucinogen derived from the plant Lophophorawilliamsii Lemaire.

Respondents Alfred Smith and Galen Black were fired from their jobs with a private drug rehabilitation organization because they ingested peyote for sacramental purposes at a ceremony of the Native American Church, of which both are members. When respondents applied to petitioner Employment Division for unemployment compensation, they were determined to be ineligible for benefits because they had been discharged for work-related "misconduct". The Oregon Court of Appeals reversed that determination, holding that the denial of benefits violated respondents' free exercise rights under the First Amendment.

Respondents' claim for relief rests on our decisions in *Sherbert v. Verner, Thomas v. Review Board, Indiana Employment Security Div.,* and *Hobbie v. Unemployment Appeals Comm'n of Florida,* 480 U.S. 136 (1987), in which we held that a State could not condition the availability of unemployment insurance on an individual's willingness to forgo conduct required by his religion. As we observed in *Smith I*, however, the conduct at issue in those cases was not prohibited by law. We held that distinction to be critical, for "if Oregon does prohibit the religious use of peyote, and if that prohibition is consistent with the Federal Constitution, there is no federal right to engage in that conduct in Oregon," and "the State is free to withhold unemployment compensation from respondents for engaging in work-related misconduct, despite its religious motivation." Now that the Oregon Supreme Court has confirmed that Oregon does prohibit the religious use of peyote, we proceed to consider whether that prohibition is permissible under the Free Exercise Clause.

They contend that their religious motivation for using peyote places them beyond the reach of a criminal law that is not specifically directed at their religious practice, and that is concededly constitutional as applied to those who use the drug for other reasons. They assert, in other words, that "prohibiting the free exercise [of religion]" includes requiring any individual to observe a generally applicable law that requires (or forbids) the performance of an act that his religious belief forbids (or requires). As a textual matter, we do not think the words must be given that meaning. It is no more necessary to regard the collection of a general tax, for example, as "prohibiting the free exercise [of religion]" by those citizens who believe support of organized government to be sinful, than it is to regard the same tax as "abridging the freedom . . . of the Press" of those publishing companies that must pay the tax as a condition of staying in business. It is a permissible reading of the text, in the one case as in the other, to say that if prohibiting the exercise of religion (or burdening the activity of printing) is not the object of the tax but merely the incidental effect of a generally applicable and otherwise valid provision, the First Amendment has not been offended.

Our decisions reveal that the latter reading is the correct one. We have never held that an individual's religious beliefs excuse him from compliance with an otherwise valid law prohibiting conduct that the State is free to regulate. On the contrary, the record of more than a century of our free exercise jurisprudence contradicts that proposition. We first had occasion to assert that principle in *Reynolds v. United States*, where we rejected the claim that criminal laws against polygamy could not be constitutionally applied to those whose religion commanded the practice.

Subsequent decisions have consistently held that the right of free exercise does not relieve an individual of the obligation to comply with a "valid and neutral law of general applicability on the ground that the law proscribes (or prescribes) conduct that his religion prescribes (or proscribes)."

The present case does not present such a hybrid situation, but a free exercise claim unconnected with any communicative activity or parental right. Respondents urge us to hold, quite simply, that when otherwise prohibitable conduct is accompanied by religious convictions, not only the convictions but the conduct itself must be free from governmental regulation. We have never held that, and decline to do so now. There being no contention that Oregon's drug law represents an attempt to regulate religious beliefs, the communication of religious beliefs, or the raising of one's children in those beliefs, the rule to which we have adhered ever since *Reynolds* plainly controls.

Respondents argue that even though exemption from generally applicable criminal laws need not automatically be extended to religiously motivated actors, at least the claim for a religious exemption must be evaluated under the balancing test set forth in *Sherbert*. We have never invalidated any governmental action on the basis of the *Sherbert* test except the denial of unemployment compensation.

Even if we were inclined to breathe into *Sherbert* some life beyond the unemployment compensation field, we would not apply it to require exemptions from a generally applicable criminal law. The *Sherbert* test, it must be recalled, was developed in a context that lent itself to individualized governmental assessment of the reasons for the relevant conduct. As the plurality pointed out in *[Bowen v.] Roy*, our decisions in the unemployment cases stand for the proposition that where the State has in place a system of individual exemptions, it may not refuse to extend that system to cases of "religious hardship" without compelling reason.

Whether or not the decisions are that limited, they at least have nothing to do with an across-the-board criminal prohibition on a particular form of conduct. We conclude today that the sounder approach, and the approach in accord with the vast majority of our precedents, is to hold the test inapplicable to such challenges. The government's ability to enforce generally applicable prohibitions of socially harmful conduct, like its ability to carry out other aspects of public policy, "cannot depend on measuring the effects of a governmental action on a religious objector's spiritual development." To make an individual's obligation to obey such a law contingent upon the law's coincidence with his religious beliefs, except where the State's interest is "compelling" — permitting him, by virtue of his beliefs, "to become a law unto himself," *Reynolds v. United States,* 98 U.S. at 167 — contradicts both constitutional tradition and common sense.

The "compelling government interest" requirement seems benign, because it is familiar from other fields. But using it as the standard that must be met before the government may accord different treatment on the basis of race, or before the government may regulate the content of speech, is not remotely comparable to using it for the purpose asserted here. What it produces in those other fields — equality of treatment, and an unrestricted flow of contending speech — are constitutional norms; what it would produce here — a private right to ignore generally applicable laws — is a constitutional anomaly.

Nor is it possible to limit the impact of respondents' proposal by requiring a "compelling state interest" only when the conduct prohibited is "central" to the individual's religion. It is no more appropriate for judges to determine the "centrality" of religious beliefs before applying a "compelling interest" test in the free exercise field, than it would be for them to determine the "importance" of ideas before applying the "compelling interest" test in the free speech field. What principle of law or logic can be brought to bear to contradict a believer's assertion that a particular act is "central" to his personal faith? Judging the centrality of different religious practices is akin to the unacceptable "business of evaluating the relative merits of differing religious claims."

Values that are protected against government interference through enshrinement in the Bill of Rights are not thereby banished from the political process. Just as a society that believes in the negative protection accorded to the press by the First Amendment is likely to enact laws that affirmatively foster the dissemination of the printed word, so also a society that believes in the negative protection accorded to religious belief can be expected to be solicitous of that value in its legislation as well. It is therefore not surprising that a number of States have made an exception to their drug laws for sacramental peyote use. But to say that a nondiscriminatory religious-practice exemption is permitted, or even that it is desirable, is not to say that it is constitutionally required, and that the appropriate occasions for its creation can be discerned by the courts. It may fairly be said that leaving accommodation to the political process will place at a relative disadvantage those religious practices that are not widely engaged in; but that unavoidable consequence of democratic government must be preferred to a system in which each conscience is a law unto itself or in which judges weigh the social importance of all laws against the centrality of all religious beliefs.

Because respondents' ingestion of peyote was prohibited under Oregon law, and because that prohibition is constitutional, Oregon may, consistent with the Free Exercise Clause, deny respondents unemployment compensation when their dismissal results from use of the drug. The decision of the Oregon Supreme Court is accordingly reversed. It is so ordered.

JUSTICE O'CONNOR, with whom JUSTICE BRENNAN, JUSTICE MARSHALL, and JUSTICE BLACKMUN join as to Parts I and II, concurring in the judgment. [Part I is omitted]:

II

To say that a person's right to free exercise has been burdened, of course, does not mean that he has an absolute right to engage in the conduct. Under our established First Amendment jurisprudence, we have recognized that the freedom to act, unlike the freedom to believe, cannot be absolute. Instead, we have respected both the First Amendment's express textual mandate and the governmental interest in regulation of conduct by requiring the Government to justify any substantial burden on religiously motivated conduct by a compelling state interest and by means narrowly tailored to achieve that interest. The compelling interest test effectuates the First Amendment's command that religious liberty is an independent liberty, that it occupies a preferred position, and that the Court will not permit encroachments upon this liberty, whether direct or indirect, unless required by clear and compelling governmental interests "of the highest order."

Once it has been shown that a government regulation or criminal prohibition burdens the free exercise of religion, we have consistently asked the Government to demonstrate that unbending application of its regulation to the religious objector "is essential to accomplish an overriding governmental interest," or represents "the least restrictive means of achieving some compelling state interest." To me, the sounder approach — the approach more consistent with our role as judges to decide each case on its individual merits — is to apply this test in each case to determine whether the burden on the specific plaintiffs before us is constitutionally significant and whether the particular criminal interest asserted by the State before us is compelling. Even if, as an empirical matter, a government's criminal laws might usually serve a compelling interest in health, safety, or public order, the First Amendment at least requires a case-by-case determination of the question, sensitive to the facts of each particular claim. Given the range of conduct that a State might legitimately make criminal, we cannot assume, merely because a law carries criminal sanctions and is generally applicable, that the First Amendment never requires the State to grant a limited exemption for religiously motivated conduct.

III

The Court's holding today not only misreads settled First Amendment precedent; it appears to be unnecessary to this case. I would reach the same result applying our established free exercise jurisprudence.

[T]he critical question in this case is whether exempting respondents from the State's general criminal prohibition "will unduly interfere with fulfillment of the governmental interest." Although the question is close, I would conclude that uniform application of Oregon's criminal prohibition is "essential to accomplish" its overriding interest in preventing the physical harm caused by the use of a Schedule I controlled substance. Oregon's criminal prohibition represents that State's judgment that the possession and use of controlled substances, even by only one person, is inherently harmful and dangerous. Because the health effects caused by the use of controlled substances exist regardless of the motivation of the user, the use of such substances, even for religious purposes, violates the very purpose of the laws that prohibit them. *Cf. Jacobson v. Massachusetts,* 197 U.S. 11 (1905) (denying exemption from small pox vaccination requirement).

For these reasons, I believe that granting a selective exemption in this case would seriously impair Oregon's compelling interest in prohibiting possession of peyote by its citizens. Under such circumstances, the Free Exercise Clause does not require the State to accommodate respondents' religiously motivated conduct.

Justice Blackmun, with whom Justices Brennan and Marshall join, dissenting.

Oregon has never sought to prosecute respondents, and does not claim that it has made significant enforcement efforts against other religious users of peyote. The State's asserted interest thus amounts only to the symbolic preservation of an unenforced prohibition. But a government interest in "symbolism, even symbolism for so worthy a cause as the abolition of unlawful drugs," cannot suffice to abrogate the constitutional rights of individuals. The State proclaims an interest in protecting the health and safety of its citizens from the dangers of unlawful drugs. It offers, however, no evidence that the religious use of peyote has ever harmed anyone. The factual findings of other courts cast doubt on the State's assumption that religious use of peyote is harmful.

The State's apprehension of a flood of other religious claims is purely speculative. Almost half the States, and the Federal Government, have maintained an exemption for religious peyote use for many years, and apparently have not found themselves overwhelmed by claims to other religious exemptions. Allowing an exemption for religious peyote use would not necessarily oblige the State to grant a similar exemption to other religious groups. The unusual circumstances that make the religious use of peyote compatible with the State's interests in health and safety and in preventing drug trafficking would not apply to other religious claims. Though the State must treat all religions equally, and not favor one over another, this obligation is fulfilled by the uniform application of the "compelling interest" test to all free exercise claims, not by reaching uniform results as to all claims.

Finally, although I agree with Justice O'Connor that courts should refrain from delving into questions of whether, as a matter of religious doctrine, a particular practice is "central" to the religion, I do not think this means that the courts must turn a blind eye to the severe impact of a State's restrictions on the adherents of a minority religion.

Respondents believe, and their sincerity has never been at issue, that the peyote plant embodies their deity, and eating it is an act of worship and communion. Without peyote, they could not enact the essential ritual of their religion.

For these reasons, I conclude that Oregon's interest in enforcing its drug laws against religious use of peyote is not sufficiently compelling to outweigh respondents' right to the free exercise of their religion. Since the State could not

> constitutionally enforce its criminal prohibition against respondents, the interests underlying the State's drug laws cannot justify its denial of unemployment benefits.

NOTES

1. *Smith and the compelling state interest test.* Professor McConnell has described the impact of the *Smith* decision as follows: "The *Smith* decision is undoubtedly the most important development in the law of religious freedom in decades." Michael McConnell, *Free Exercise Revisionism and the Smith Decision*, 57 U. Chi. L. Rev. 1109, 1111 (1990). McConnell criticizes the *Smith* Court for replacing the compelling state interest test (which he contends was itself a more relaxed standard than its terms would indicate) with the deferential rationality standard that is used for legislation generally. A more searching examination is necessary, he argues, to justify legislation restricting religious exercise.

> I favor returning to the standards articulated in state constitutions at the time of the framing: repugnancy to the "peace and order of the State." Madison's formulation is also apt: that free exercise should be protected "in every case where it does not trespass on private rights or the public peace." This means that we are free to practice our religions so long as we do not injure others.

Professor McConnell says that these formulations are similar to Professor Pepper's question of "is there a real, tangible (palpable, concrete, measurable), non-speculative, non-trivial, injury to a legitimate, substantial state interest?" Stephen Pepper, *The Conundrum of the Free Exercise Clause — Some Reflections on Recent Cases*, 9 N. Ky. L. Rev. 265, 289 (1982). What characteristic differentiates these tests from the test employed by Justice Scalia in *Smith*?

2. *Smith and discrimination against minority religions.* David Williams & Susan Williams, *Volitionalism and Religious Liberty*, 76 CORNELL L. REV. 769, 848 (1991):

> In the view of the *Smith* Court, however, the primary source of protection for religious practice is plainly not the Constitution at all, but the legislature. [T]he Court rather complacently accepted the probability that minority religions will disproportionately suffer in this process of legislative "accommodation"; it knew and did not care.

How would Justice Scalia react to this criticism?

If the thrust of Justice Scalia's analysis is that neither he nor the Oregon legislature which criminalized the use of peyote had any intent to discriminate against minority religions, then consider the following rebuttal to *that* argument:

> The analysis articulated in *Smith* largely turns on a distinction between discriminatory intent and impact imported from equal protection case law. This seems curiously at odds with the plain text of the first amendment. The Constitution disallows laws that prohibit the free exercise of religion, not just those that intentionally do so.

Douglas Kmiec, *The Original Understanding of the Free Exercise Clause and Religious Diversity*, 59 U.M.K.C. L. REV. 591, 597.

Another way to explain the point Prof. Kmiec is making is that what has been significant in the law of free exercise — prior to *Smith* — is whether the right of free exercise is burdened. This has been the relevant question rather than the novel question asked by Justice Scalia: Did the legislature intend to discriminate?

For a discussion of how "burdens" should be interpreted to harmonize religion with other social concerns, see Ira Lupu, *Where Rights Begin: The Problem of Burdens on the Free Exercise of Religion*, 102 HARV. L. REV. 933 (1989). For a study of the historical background of the free exercise clause, see Michael McConnell, *The Origin and Historical Understanding of Free Exercise of Religion*, 103 HARV. L. REV. 1409 (1990).

3. *The significance of Smith.* Professor McConnell has complained that the Rehnquist Court may replace the "reflexive secularism" of the Warren and Burger Courts with an "equally inappropriate statism." Michael McConnell, *Religious Freedom At a Crossroads*, 59 U. CHI. L. REV. 115, 116 (1992). He criticizes *Smith* on four grounds. First, *Smith* subordinates the rights of religious communities to "social policy" as determined by the State. Second, *Smith* disadvantages non-majoritarian religious practices and thus favors "mainstream over non-mainstream religions." Third, *Smith* treats the claim for a free exercise exemption as the equivalent of intentional advancement of religion by government. But McConnell says the Native American Church was not asking for advancement by government. It was simply asking to be let alone. Fourth, *Smith* waters down an explicit liberty set forth in the constitutional text into a requirement of nondiscrimination: "The freedom of citizens to exercise their faith should not depend on the vagaries of democratic politics, even if expressed through laws of general applicability." *Id.* at 139-40. Professor McConnell proposes the following approach to the Religion Clauses: "The underlying principle is that governmental action should have the minimum possible effect on religion, consistent with achievement of the government's legitimate purposes." *Id.* at 169.

Critics respond that "proponents of privilege [for religion]" such as McConnell have not come up with a "satisfactory formulation" for their own accomodationist position: "Because there is no coherent normative justification for privileging religion, there is, of necessity, no principle to govern the balancing called for by the 'compelling state interest' — or any other formula." Christopher Eisgruber & Lawrence Sager, *The Vulnerability of Conscience:The Constitutional Basis for Protecting Religious Conduct*, 61 U. Chi. L. Rev. 1245, 1258 (1994). Is McConnell's approach a workable one?

Professor Sullivan says that McConnell's analysis implies that the "Court should mandate more exemptions and fewer establishments in order to maintain religious pluralism." Kathleen Sullivan, *Religion and Liberal Democracy*, 59 U. Chi. L. Rev. 195 (1992). She thinks McConnell takes too strong a position on free exercise and too weak a position on establishment. She agrees that *Smith* reinforces patterns of discrimination against minority religions: "Minority religionists, like political dissenters, rarely have the political muscle to secure exemptions for themselves on the legislative floor. *Smith* wipes out their alternative recourse." What alternative is Professor Sullivan talking about?

4. *Religious Freedom Restoration Act of 1993.* The reaction to *Smith* was highly critical. In 1993, Congress enacted the Religious Freedom Restoration Act [RFRA] of 1993. The background behind the passage of RFRA has been described as follows: "The enactment of RFRA was an extraordinary event. It represents perhaps the broadest political coalition ever assembled in support of any individual rights initiative and was passed by overwhelming margins in both houses of Congress. In effect, the President of the United States, the Congress, and most interest groups have told the Court that its doctrine is seriously flawed." Frederick Gedicks, *RFRA And the Possibility of Justice*, 56 Mont. L. Rev. 95, 117 (1995). Congress was not subtle about its purpose and proclaimed on the face of the Act that its intent was to restore the compelling interest test set forth in *Sherbert* and *Yoder*.

RFRA states that government "shall not substantially burden a person's exercise of religion" even if the burden is a consequence of generally applicable laws. But the Act provides for an exception:

> Government may substantially burden a person's exercise of religion only if it demonstrates that application of the burden to the person
>
> (1) is in furtherance of a compelling governmental interest; and
>
> (2) is the least restrictive means of furthering that compelling governmental interest.

42 U.S.C. § 2000bb-1.

The Act has been no less controversial than the decision which occasioned it. Professor Conkle argues that the Act is unconstitutional because it usurps the role of the Court as ultimate arbiter of the Constitution. He contends the Act is not authorized by Section 5 of the Fourteenth Amendment because it does not involve racial discrimination and "therefore moves beyond the core historical purpose of Section 5." *See* Daniel Conkle, *The Religious Freedom Restoration Act: The Constitutional Significance of an Unconstitutional Statute*, 56 Mont. L. Rev. 39, 78 (1995).

A more positive appraisal sees RFRA as not just as a technical undoing of *Smith*:

> Rather [RFRA] restores a fundamentally different vision of human liberty. Religious believers acting on their faith are not suspicious characters seeking unprincipled special treatment. They are exercising a fundamental human right, and the American commitment is to let them exercise it unless there is an extraordinary reason to interfere — not a rational reason, or even a substantial reason, but a compelling reason.

Douglas Laycock and Oliver Thomas, *Interpreting the Religious Freedom Restoration Act*, 73 Tex. L. Rev. 209, 244–45 (1994).

In ***City of Boerne v. Flores,* 521 U.S. 507 (1997)**, the Court held RFRA to be an unconstitutional exercise of congressional power under section 5 of the Fourteenth Amendment, because of its inconsistency with *Smith* [text, p. 1458]. In dissent, Justice O'Connor expressed the view that *Smith* had been wrongly decided: "Contrary to the [*Smith*] Court's holding, the Free Exercise Clause is not simply an antidiscrimination principle that protects only against those laws that single out religious practice for unfavorable treatment. Rather, the Clause is best understood as an affirmative guarantee of the right to participate in religious practices and conduct without impermissible governmental interference, even when such conduct conflicts with a neutral, generally applicable law. Before Smith, our free exercise cases were generally in keeping with this idea: where a law substantially burdened religiously motivated conduct — regardless whether it was specifically targeted at religion or applied generally — we required government to justify that law with a compelling state interest and to use means narrowly tailored to achieve that interest." She asserted that "[t]he Court's rejection of this principle in Smith is supported neither by precedent nor history."

In response, Justice Scalia, in a separate concurring opinion, rejected Justice O'Connor's detailed historical analysis: "The historical evidence marshalled by the dissent cannot fairly be said to demonstrate the correctness of Smith; but it is more supportive of that conclusion than destructive of it." He concluded: "The issue presented by Smith is, quite simply, whether the people, through their elected representatives, or rather this Court, shall control outcome of concrete cases."

Professor Ira Lupu has appraised RFRA and its demise: "A chasm exists between the promise of RFRA and what it managed to deliver. This gap arose from the interaction among RFRA's elastic terms, the judicial discretion those terms create, and the subject of religious exemptions generally. For some of the reasons expressed in *Smith* — risks of anarchy, unprincipled distinctions, religious favoritism, and comparing incommensurables — courts have long been deeply skeptical concerning such exemptions. RFRA's terms maximized the possibilities for judicial manipulation that a doctrine of free exercise exemptions inevitably invites." Ira Lupu, *Why the Congress Was Wrong And the Court Was Right—Reflections on City of Boerne v. Flores*, 39 WM. & MARY L. REV. 793, 805–806 (1998).

Professor Lupu asks if anything has been lost by RFRA's invalidation; he responds as follows: "Occasionally, a sympathetic religious exemption claim that might have prevailed under RFRA will be rejected when advanced under other legal theories. [But], in cases in which the equities on religion's side are strong, the state constitutional law of religious liberty may become reinvigorated." *Id.* at 807-808. Why might RFRA's demise stimulate greater recourse to state constitutional protections for religious liberty?

Professor Rodney Smolla concludes that after *City of Boerne*, free exercise cases again are largely controlled by *Employment Division v. Smith*: "[T]he Free Exercise Clause is not deemed violated by laws of general applicability that happen to place substantial burdens on religion." Rodney A. Smolla, *The Free Exercise of Religion After the Fall: The Case for Intermediate Scrutiny*, 39 WM. & MARY L. REV. 925 (1998). Professor Smolla suggests three possible scenarios for the aftermath of *City of Boerne*: (1) *Smith* should be accepted as a guide to future decisions. (2) Congress should try again and pass a new law. Relying on the Spending Power, the Commerce Power and its enforcement powers under Section Five of the Fourteenth Amendment, Congress should try to reach "most, if not all, of the activities of state and local governments." This new law would be "blostered by a more exhaustive legislative record" than that which supported RFRA. (3) Notwithstanding what Congress does, the Supreme Court should re-visit *Smith* and instead of choosing either strict scrutiny or rational basis, the Court should opt for an intermediate standard of review. Professor Smolla opts for the intermediate review standard option because it would reflect "a sensible compromise to the balance of competing interests posed by *Smith* and RFRA." Isn't the first scenario the most likely if there are no changes in Court personnel?

5. *Church of the Lukumi Babalu Aye, Inc. v. Hialeah*, 508 U.S. 520 (1993). *Smith* does not mean that every free exercise claim will be subject to deferential judicial review. In *Hialeah*, the Court distinguished *Smith* and applied strict scrutiny in unanimously invalidating Hialeah city ordinances prohibiting ritualistic animal sacrifice. The ordinances had been adopted in response to citizen concerns over the practices of the Santeria religion. The Court, per Justice Kennedy, concluded that, unlike the legislation in *Smith*, the city ordinances were not neutral because they had the impermissible objective of suppressing religion. Nor were they of general applicability "because the secular ends asserted in defense of the laws were pursued only with respect to conduct motivated by religious beliefs." Because the laws directly targeted religion, strict scrutiny applied and the laws were not narrowly tailored to advance a compelling governmental interest.

In determining the object of the Hialeah laws, Justice Kennedy first considered the text of the law — "a law lacks facial neutrality if it refers to a religious practice without a secular meaning discernable from the language or context." While the Hialeah laws referred to "sacrifice" and "ritual," today those terms also have secular meanings. Going beyond "facial neutrality," Kennedy found that suppression of Santeria religious worship was the objective of the laws; the effect of the law was limited entirely to the religious exercise of the Santeria church members. Finally, additional evidence that the laws were targeted at the Santeria religion was found "in the fact that they proscribe more religious conduct than is necessary to achieve the stated ends." It was not necessary to prohibit all Santeria sacrificial practices in order to prevent cruelty to animals.

Applying strict scrutiny, Justice Kennedy stated:

> A law that targets religious conduct for distinctive treatment or advances legitimate governmental interests only against conduct with a religious motivation will survive strict scrutiny only in rare cases. It follows from what we have already said that these ordinances cannot withstand this scrutiny. Where government restricts only conduct protected by the First Amendment and fails to enact feasible measures to restrict other conduct producing substantial harm or alleged harm of the same sort, the interest given in justification of the restriction is not compelling.

Justice Scalia, joined by Chief Justice Rehnquist, concurred in all of the Court's opinion with the exception of one part which considered "the subjective motivation of the *lawmakers*" rather than "the object of the *laws* at issue. The First Amendment refers to the *effects* of the laws enacted, not the *purposes* of the legislator."

Justice Souter, concurring, did not join that part of the Court's opinion which he read to express dicta in support of *Smith* and expressed "doubts whether the *Smith* rule merits adherence." For Justice Souter, the rule of *Smith* was at odds with other Supreme Court precedent and raised serious question about the original intent of the Free Exercise Clause.

Justice Blackmun, joined by Justice O'Connor, concurred only in the Court's judgment.

> In my view, a statute that burdens the free exercise of religion "may stand only if the law in general, and the State's refusal to allow a religious exemption in particular, are justified by a compelling interest that cannot be served by less restrictive means." The Court, however, applies a different test. It applies the test announced in *Smith*, under which "a law that is neutral and of general applicability need not be justified by a compelling governmental interest even if the law has the incidental effect of burdening a particular religious practice." I continue to believe that *Smith* was wrongly decided, because it ignored the value of religious freedom as an affirmative individual liberty and treated the Free Exercise Clause as no more than an antidiscrimination principle.

One commentator has observed that the "two-tiered approach" used by the Court in *Hialeah* was redundant: "The ordinances prohibiting animal sacrifice failed the *Smith* test for the same reasons they failed strict scrutiny." Note, *Retracting First Amendment Jurisprudence Under the Free Exercise Clause,* 27 U. Rich. L. Rev. 1127, 1148 (1993). After conceding that the coupling of strict scrutiny with the *Smith* approach assures that strict scrutiny will not be restored to the stature that standard enjoyed in free exercise cases in the pre-*Smith* era, the Note concludes: "The *Hialeah* decision was merely a small step toward the reinstatement of strict scrutiny review." Do you think *Hialeah* should be read as a step toward the restoration of strict scrutiny in free exercise cases? Consider the argument that *Smith* and *City of Boerne* do not affect the applicability of strict scrutiny in cases of direct purposeful burdens on free exercise.

LOCKE v. DAVEY

540 U.S. 712, 124 S. Ct. 1307, 158 L.Ed.2d 221 (2004)

Chief Justice Rehnquist delivered the opinion of the Court.

The State of Washington established the Promise Scholarship Program to assist academically gifted students with postsecondary education expenses. In accordance with the State Constitution, students may not use the scholarship at an institution where they are pursuing a degree in devotional theology. We hold that such an exclusion from an otherwise inclusive aid program does not violate the Free Exercise Clause of the First Amendment.

The Establishment Clause and the Free Exercise Clause, are frequently in tension. Yet we have long said that "there is room for play in the joints" between them. In other words, there are some state actions permitted by the Establishment Clause but not required by the Free Exercise Clause.

This case involves that "play in the joints" described above. Under our Establishment Clause precedent, the link between government funds and religious training is broken by the independent and private choice of recipients. *See Zelman*; *Zobrest*; *Witters*; *Mueller*. As such, there is no doubt that the State could, consistent with the Federal Constitution, permit Promise Scholars to pursue a degree in devotional theology, and the State does not contend otherwise. The question before us, however, is whether Washington, pursuant to its own constitution, which has been authoritatively interpreted as prohibiting even indirectly funding religious instruction that will prepare students for the ministry, can deny them such funding without violating the Free Exercise Clause.

Davey urges us to answer that question in the negative. He contends that under the rule we enunciated in *Church of Lukumi Babalu Aye, Inc. v. Hialeah*, the program is presumptively unconstitutional because it is not facially neutral with respect to religion.[3] We reject his claim of presumptive

[3] Davey, relying on *Rosenberger v. Rector and Visitors of Univ. of Va.,* contends that the Promise Scholarship Program is an unconstitutional viewpoint restriction on speech. But the Promise Scholarship Program is not a forum for speech. The purpose of the Promise Scholarship Program is to assist students from low-and middle-income families with the cost of postsecondary education, not to " 'encourage a diversity of views from private speakers.' " *United States v. Am. Library Ass'n.*

unconstitutionality, however; to do otherwise would extend the *Lukumi* line of cases well beyond not only their facts but their reasoning. In *Lukumi*, the city of Hialeah made it a crime to engage in certain kinds of animal slaughter. We found that the law sought to suppress ritualistic animal sacrifices of the Santeria religion. In the present case, the State's disfavor of religion (if it can be called that) is of a far milder kind. It imposes neither criminal nor civil sanctions on any type of religious service or rite. It does not deny to ministers the right to participate in the political affairs of the community. And it does not require students to choose between their religious beliefs and receiving a government benefit. The State has merely chosen not to fund a distinct category of instruction.

Because the Promise Scholarship Program funds training for all secular professions, JUSTICE SCALIA contends the State must also fund training for religious professions. *See ibid.* But training for religious professions and training for secular professions are not fungible. Training someone to lead a congregation is an essentially religious endeavor. Indeed, majoring in devotional theology is akin to a religious calling as well as an academic pursuit. And the subject of religion is one in which both the United States and state constitutions embody distinct views—in favor of free exercise, but opposed to establishment—that find no counterpart with respect to other callings or professions. That a State would deal differently with religious education for the ministry than with education for other callings is a product of these views, not evidence of hostility toward religion.

Even though the differently worded Washington Constitution draws a more stringent line than that drawn by the United States Constitution, the interest it seeks to further is scarcely novel. In fact, we can think of few areas in which a State's antiestablishment interests come more into play. Since the founding of our country, there have been popular uprisings against procuring taxpayer funds to support church leaders, which was one of the hallmarks of an "established" religion.

Without a presumption of unconstitutionality, Davey's claim must fail. The State's interest in not funding the pursuit of devotional degrees is substantial and the exclusion of such funding places a relatively minor burden on Promise Scholars. If any room exists between the two Religion Clauses, it must be here. We need not venture further into this difficult area in order to uphold the Promise Scholarship Program as currently operated by the State of Washington.

JUSTICE SCALIA, with whom JUSTICE THOMAS joins, dissenting.

When the State makes a public benefit generally available, that benefit becomes part of the baseline against which burdens on religion are measured; and when the State withholds that benefit from some individuals solely on the basis of religion, it violates the Free Exercise Clause no less than if it had imposed a special tax.

That is precisely what the State of Washington has done here. It has created a generally available public benefit, whose receipt is conditioned only on academic performance, income, and attendance at an accredited school. It has then carved out a solitary course of study for exclusion: theology. No field of study but religion is singled out for disfavor in this fashion. Davey is not asking for a special benefit to which others are not entitled. He seeks only *equal* treatment—the right to direct his scholarship to his chosen course of study, a right every other Promise Scholar enjoys.

The Court's reference to historical "popular uprisings against procuring taxpayer funds to support church leaders," is therefore quite misplaced. That history involved not the inclusion of religious ministers in public benefits programs like the one at issue here, but laws that singled them out for financial aid. One can concede the Framers' hostility to funding the clergy *specifically*, but that says nothing about whether the clergy had to be excluded from benefits the State made available to all.

The Court does not dispute that the Free Exercise Clause places some constraints on public benefits programs, but finds none here, based on a principle of " 'play in the joints.' " I use the term "principle" loosely, for that is not so much a legal principle as a refusal to apply *any* principle when faced with competing constitutional directives. There is nothing anomalous about constitutional commands that abut. A municipality hiring public contractors may not discriminate *against* blacks or *in favor of* them; it cannot discriminate a little bit each way and then plead "play in the joints" when haled into court. If the Religion Clauses demand neutrality, we must enforce them, in hard cases as well as easy ones.

Even if "play in the joints" were a valid legal principle, surely it would apply only when it was a close call whether complying with one of the Religion Clauses would violate the other. But that is not the case here. It is not just that "the State could, consistent with the Federal Constitution, permit Promise Scholars to pursue a degree in devotional theology." The establishment question *would not even be close*. Perhaps some formally neutral public benefits programs are so gerrymandered and devoid of plausible secular purpose that they might raise specters of state aid to religion, but an evenhanded Promise Scholarship Program is not among them.

What is the nature of the State's asserted interest here? It cannot be protecting the pocketbooks of its citizens. It cannot be preventing mistaken appearance of endorsement; where a State merely declines to penalize students for selecting a religious major, "no reasonable observer is likely to draw . . . an inference that the State itself is endorsing a religious practice or belief." Nor can Washington's exclusion be defended as a means of assuring that the State will neither favor nor disfavor Davey in his religious calling.

No, the interest to which the Court defers is not fear of a conceivable Establishment Clause violation, budget constraints, avoidance of endorsement, or substantive neutrality—none of these. It is a pure philosophical preference: the State's opinion that it would violate taxpayers' freedom of conscience *not* to discriminate against candidates for the ministry. This sort of protection of "freedom of conscience" has no logical limit and can justify the singling out of religion for exclusion from public programs in virtually any context. The Court never says whether it deems this interest compelling (the opinion is devoid of any mention of standard of review) but, self-evidently, it is not.

The other reason the Court thinks this particular facial discrimination less offensive is that the scholarship program was not motivated by animus toward religion. The Court does not explain why the legislature's motive matters, and I fail to see why it should.

Today's holding is limited to training the clergy, but its logic is readily extendible, and there are plenty of directions to go. What next? Will we deny priests and nuns their prescription-drug benefits on the ground that taxpayers' freedom of conscience forbids medicating the clergy at public expense? This may seem fanciful, but recall that France has proposed banning religious attire from schools, invoking interests in secularism no less benign than those the Court embraces today. When the public's freedom of conscience is invoked to justify denial of equal treatment, benevolent motives shade into indifference and ultimately into repression. Having accepted the justification in this case, the Court is less well equipped to fend it off in the future. I respectfully dissent.

JUSTICE THOMAS, dissenting.

Because the parties agree that a "degree in theology" means a degree that is "devotional in nature or designed to induce religious faith," I assume that this is so for purposes of deciding this case. With this understanding, I join JUSTICE SCALIA's dissenting opinion. I write separately to note that, in my view, the study of theology does not necessarily implicate religious devotion or faith. "Theology" is defined as "the study of the nature of God and religious truth" and the "rational inquiry into religious questions."

These definitions include the study of theology from a secular perspective as well as from a religious one. Assuming that the State denies Promise Scholarships only to students who pursue a degree in devotional theology, I believe that JUSTICE SCALIA's application of our precedents is correct.

NOTE

Professor Frank Ravitch says that the Court's recent religion cases often describe governmental action as constituting "hostility" to religion but that the term hostility is used in a rhetorical way. He argues that the term is more properly used "only when actual hostility is involved" and that in *Locke v. Davey* the Court looked for actual hostility. Since the state of Washington "allowed the scholarships to be used at religious institutions, so long as the student is not training for the clergy,. . . the denial of the scholarship in Davey's case was not evidence of hostility." In *Locke*, the Court seemed to connect "hostility with animus." *See* Frank Ravitch, *The Supreme Court's Rhetorical Hostility: What Is "Hostile" to Religion Under The Establishment Clause*, 2004 B.Y.U. L. REV. 1031, 1037–38. Ravitch concedes, however, that when the Court describes government action as hostile to religion in *Mitchell*, *Rosenberger* and *Mergens* there was "no proof of animus toward religion.''" Would it be desirable to require that a judicial conclusion of government hostility toward religion be dependent on proof of animus?

§ 9.03 GOVERNMENTAL ACCOMMODATIONS THAT TEND TOWARD ESTABLISHMENT

ESTATE OF THORNTON v. CALDOR, INC.
472 U.S. 703, 105 S. Ct. 2914, 86 L. Ed. 2d 557 (1985)

[A Connecticut statute provided employees with an absolute right not to work on their religion's designated Sabbath day. Prior to 1977, Connecticut retail stores were required to close on Sunday. In 1977, state law was amended to allow stores to open for Sunday business. Thereupon, Caldor, Inc., a chain of New England retail stores, opened its Connecticut stores for Sunday business. Until 1979, Donald Thornton, a Sabbath-observing Presbyterian, complied with his employer's requirement that he work every third or fourth Sunday. When Thornton refused to continue to do so, he was fired.

[Relying upon the statute providing that employees could not be dismissed for working on their Sabbath day, Thornton took his case to an administrative board which sustained Thornton's grievance. The state Superior Court affirmed holding that the statute did not violate the Establishment Clause. The state Supreme Court reversed and held that the state statute lacked a "clear secular purpose" and therefore, violated the Establishment Clause.]

CHIEF JUSTICE BURGER delivered the opinion of the Court.

[T]he Court has frequently relied on our holding in Lemon for guidance, and we do so here. The Connecticut statute challenged here guarantees every employee, who "states that a particular day of the week is observed as his Sabbath, [has] the right not to work on his chosen day." The State has thus decreed that those who observe a Sabbath any day of the week as a matter of religious conviction must be relieved of the duty to work on that day, no matter what burden or inconvenience this imposes on the employer or fellow workers. The statute arms Sabbath observers with an absolute and unqualified right not to work on whatever day they designate as their Sabbath.

In essence, the Connecticut statute imposes on employers and employees an absolute duty to conform their business practices to the particular religious practices of the employee by enforcing observance of the Sabbath the employee unilaterally designates. The State thus commands that Sabbath religious concerns automatically control over all secular interests at the workplace; the statute takes no account of the convenience or interests of the employer or those of other employees who do not observe a Sabbath. The employer and others must adjust their affairs to the command of the State whenever the statute is invoked by an employee.

[T]here is no exception when honoring the dictates of Sabbath observers would cause the employer substantial economic burdens or when the employer's compliance would require the imposition of significant burdens on other employees required to work in place of the Sabbath observers. Finally, the statute allows for no consideration as to whether the employer has made reasonable accommodation proposals.

This unyielding weighting in favor of Sabbath observers over all other interests contravenes a fundamental principle of the Religion Clauses, so well articulated by JUDGE LEARNED HAND:

> The First Amendment . . . gives no one the right to insist that in pursuit of their own interests others must conform their conduct to his own religious necessities.

Otten v. Baltimore & Ohio R. Co., 205 F.2d 58, 61 (CA2 1953).

[This] statute goes beyond having an incidental or remote effect of advancing religion. The statute has a primary effect that impermissibly advances a particular religious practice.

We hold that the Connecticut statute, which provides Sabbath observers with an absolute and unqualified right not to work on their Sabbath, violates the Establishment Clause of the First Amendment.

NOTES

1. *Accommodating Sabbath observation.* Professor McConnell says *Thornton* reflects an "indifference or incomprehension" to religion: "Some people like to go sailing on Saturdays; some observe the Sabbath. How could the State consider one 'choice' more worthy of respect than the other? In Stephen Carter's apt phrase, this is to 'treat religion as a hobby.' " Michael McConnell, *Religious Freedom At A Crossroads*, 59 U. Chi. L. Rev. 115, 124–25 (1992).

Professor Marshall wonders if *Thornton* presents "less of an accommodational perspective than have other cases involving government regulation and practices?" The effect of the law was found "impermissible because of its absolute requirements, its support of one particular type of belief, and the burden third-parties would have to bear in the religious observer's absence." William Marshall, *"We Know It When We See It:" The Supreme Court and Establishment,* 59 S. Cal. L. Rev. 495, 545–46 (1986).

Sherbert v. Verner left "third parties to suffer some burden caused by the rights of religious believers." What was objectionable in the accommodation provided by government in *Thornton* that was not present in *McGowan* or *Sherbert*?

2. *Cutter v. Wilkinson*, 125 S. Ct. 2113 (2005). The Court, in an opinion by Justice Ginsburg, upheld against an attack under the Establishment Clause, section 3 of the Religious Land Use and Institutionalized Persons Act of 2000 (RLUPA), 42 U.S.C. § 2000cc-1(a)(1)-(2), which provided that "[n]o government shall impose a substantial burden on the religious exercise of a person residing in or confined to an institution," unless the burden furthers "a compelling governmental interest," and does so by "the least restrictive means." Inmates of institutions operated by the Ohio Department of Rehabilitation and Correction asserted that they were adherents of "nonmainstream" religions and that Ohio prison officials had failed to accommodate their religious exercise, in violation of RLUIPA. In response, the defendant prison officials mounted a facial challenge to the relevant provision of the statute, contending that it improperly advances religion in violation of the First Amendment's Establishment Clause.

In upholding the statute, the Court recognized that there exists "some space for legislative action neither compelled by the Free Exercise Clause nor prohibited by the Establishment Clause." It found RLUIPA's institutionalized-persons provision compatible with the Exceptions Clause "because it alleviates exceptional government-created burdens on private religious exercise." It further noted that it did "not read RLUIPA to elevate accommodation of religious observances over an institution's need to maintain order and safety. Our decisions indicate that an accommodation must be measured so that it does not overrule other significant interests." The Court had "no cause to believe that RLUIPA would not be applied in an appropriately balanced way, with particular sensitivity to security concerns."

BOARD OF EDUC. OF WESTSIDE COMMUNITY SCHOOLS v. MERGENS

496 U.S. 226, 110 S. Ct. 2356, 110 L. Ed. 2d 191 (1990)

JUSTICE O'CONNOR delivered the opinion of the Court, except as to Part III:

[A majority of the Court held that a federal statute, the Equal Access Act, prohibited a public high school from denying student religious groups permission to meet on school premises after school. Through Part III of Justice O'Connor's opinion, a plurality of the Court then declared that this construction of the Equal Access Act did not violate the Establishment Clause of the First Amendment.

[Students at Westside High School in Omaha, Nebraska asked the school administration for permission to form a Christian student club for purposes of Bible reading, fellowship and prayer. The students proposed that the club would not have a faculty sponsor. The school administration responded that school policy required all student clubs to have a faculty sponsor and that the club "would not or could not" have one under the Establishment Clause. Both the school administration and the Board of Education turned down the student request to form a student Christian club.

[The students, through their parents as next friends, brought suit in federal court under the Equal Access Act which forbids public schools receiving federal financial assistance and which "maintain a 'limited open forum' from denying 'equal access' to students who wish to meet within the forum on the basis of the content of such speech at such meetings." Although the federal district court rejected the statutory and constitutional claims of the students, the Eighth Circuit reversed. The student clubs at Westside were not all curriculum related. Moreover, Westside maintained a "limited open forum" within the meaning of the Equal Access Act. The Eighth Circuit also rejected the public high school's establishment clause challenge to the Act and declared that the Equal Access Act had simply extended the ruling in *Widmar v. Vincent* to public high school students. The Equal Access Act provides that a public secondary school with a "limited open forum" may not discriminate against students who wish to meet within that forum because of the "religious, political, philosophical, or other content of the speech at such meetings." A "limited open forum" exists under the Act when a school offers an opportunity for "non-curriculum related student groups to meet on school premises during noninstructional time."

[JUSTICE O'CONNOR explained that under the Act "even if a public secondary school allows only one 'noncurriculum related student group' to meet, the Act's obligations are triggered and the school may not deny other clubs, on the basis of the content of their speech, equal access to meet on school premises during noninstructional time." The term "noncurriculum related student group" was interpreted broadly to include any student group that does not "directly relate to the body of courses offered by the school."]

III

[Part III of the O'CONNOR opinion was joined by CHIEF JUSTICE REHNQUIST, JUSTICE WHITE, and JUSTICE BLACKMUN.]

In *Widmar*, we applied the three-part *Lemon* test to hold that an "equal access" policy, at the university level, does not violate the Establishment Clause. We think the logic of *Widmar* applies with equal force to the Equal Access Act. As an initial matter, the Act's prohibition of discrimination on the basis of "political, philosophical, or other" speech as well as religious speech is a sufficient basis for meeting the secular purpose prong of the *Lemon* test. Because the Act on its face grants equal access to both secular and religious speech, we think it clear that the Act's purpose was not to " 'endorse or disapprove of religion,' " *Wallace v. Jaffree* (quoting *Lynch v. Donnelly* (O'CONNOR, J., concurring.

Petitioners' principal contention is that the Act has the primary effect of advancing religion. Specifically, petitioners urge that, because the student religious meetings are held under school aegis, and because the state's compulsory attendance laws bring the students together (and thereby provide a ready-made audience for student evangelists), an objective observer in the position of a secondary school student will perceive official school support for such religious meetings.

We disagree. First, there is a crucial difference between government speech endorsing religion, which the Establishment Clause forbids, and private speech endorsing religion, which the Free Speech and Free Exercise Clauses protect. We think that secondary school students are mature enough and are likely to understand that a school does not endorse or support student speech that it merely permits on a nondiscriminatory basis.

Second, we note that the Act expressly limits participation by school officials at meetings of student religious groups, §§ 4071(c)(2) and (3), and that any such meetings must be held during "noninstructional time," § 4071(b). The Act therefore avoids the problems of "the students' emulation of teachers as role models" and "mandatory attendance requirements."

Third, the broad spectrum of officially recognized student clubs at Westside, and the fact that Westside students are free to initiate and organize additional student clubs, counteract any possible message of official endorsement of or preference for religion or a particular religious belief. To the extent that a religious club is merely one of many different student-initiated voluntary clubs, students should perceive no message of government endorsement of religion. Thus, we conclude that the Act does not, at least on its face and as applied to Westside, have the primary effect of advancing religion.

JUSTICE KENNEDY, with whom JUSTICE SCALIA joins, concurring in part and concurring in the judgment.

It is true that when government gives impermissible assistance to a religion it can be said to have "endorsed" religion; but endorsement cannot be the test. The word endorsement has insufficient content to be dispositive.

I should think it inevitable that a public high school "endorses" a religious club, in a common-sense use of the term, if the club happens to be one of many activities that the school permits students to choose in order to further the development of their intellect and character in an extracurricular setting. But no constitutional violation occurs if the school's action is based upon a recognition of the fact that membership in a religious club is one of many permissible ways for a student to further his or her own personal enrichment. The inquiry with respect to coercion must be whether the government imposes pressure upon a student to participate in a religious activity. This inquiry, of course, must be undertaken with sensitivity to the special circumstances that exist in a secondary school where the line between voluntary and coerced participation may be difficult to draw. No such coercion, however, has been shown to exist as a necessary result of this statute, either on its face or as respondents seek to invoke it on the facts of this case.

JUSTICE STEVENS, dissenting.

Can Congress really have intended to issue an order to every public high school in the nation stating, in substance, that if you sponsor a chess club, a scuba diving club, or a French club — without having formal classes in those subjects — you must also open your doors to every religious, political, or social organization, no matter how controversial or distasteful its views may be? I think not. A fair review of the legislative history of the Equal Access Act (Act) discloses that Congress intended to recognize a much narrower forum than the Court has legislated into existence today.

Under the Court's interpretation of the Act, Congress has imposed a difficult choice on public high schools receiving federal financial assistance. The Act, as construed by the majority, comes perilously close to an outright command to allow organized prayer, and perhaps the kind of religious ceremonies involved in *Widmar*, on school premises.

NOTES

1. *The significance of* Mergens. Professor Paulsen has summarized *Mergens* as follows: "[W]hile 'school prayer' or devotional exercises of the type involved in *Engel* and *Schempp* involve government coercion, voluntary extracurricular religious student group meetings involve no such coercion. Such meetings are not rendered suspect under the Establishment Clause by virtue of peer pressure from the students or the fact that the meetings occur on school grounds." Michael Paulsen, *Lemon Is Dead*, 43 CASE W. RES. L. REV. 795, 848–49 (1993). But variations on the *Mergens* fact pattern present issues that the Supreme Court has yet to resolve. Does particpation in student religious groups on school premises by "teachers or adults from the community" change the equation? Suppose a school has "no formally recognized student club meetings"; must the school district still allow religious student groups to meet on school premises?

2. *Lamb's Chapel v. Center Moriches Sch. Dist.*, 508 U.S. 384 (1993). The Court has demonstrated that *Lemon* still has some vitality. In *Lamb's Chapel*, the Court, per Justice White, held that the denial by a school board of a church group's application to use public school facilities to show a film series on child rearing violated the Free Speech Clause of the First Amendment. A public school board rule which permitted school property — a nonpublic forum — to be used for the presentation of "all views about family issues and child-rearing except those dealing with the subject matter from a religious standpoint" impermissibly discriminated on the basis of viewpoint.

In defense of its rule excluding use of school facilities by churches, the school district contended that it had a compelling interest in preventing the use of school property in violation of the antiestablishment clause of the First Amendment. The Court pointed out that *Widmar v. Vincent*, 454 U.S. 263 (1981), had held that the use of University property for religious purposes under an open access policy was not incompatible with the Court's Establishment Clause cases:

> We have no more trouble than did the *Widmar* Court in disposing of the claimed defense on the ground that the posited fears of an Establishment Clause violation are unfounded. The showing of the film in question would not have been during school hours, would not have been sponsored by the school, and would have been open to the public, not just to church members. Under these circumstances, as in *Widmar*, there would have been no realistic danger that the community would think that the [school] district was endorsing religion or any particular creed, and any benefit to religion or to the Church would have been no more that incidental. As in *Widmar*, permitting [school] District property to be used to exhibit the film involved in this case would not have been an establishment of religion under the three-part test articulated in *Lemon*: The challenged governmental action has a secular purpose, does not have the principal or primary effect of advancing or inhibiting religion, and does not foster an excessive entanglement with religion.

In a vitriolic concurrence, Justice Scalia, joined by Justice Thomas, condemned the Court's reliance on the *Lemon* test. *Lemon* was likened to "some ghoul in a late-night horror movie" which continuously "stalks our Establishment Clause jurisprudence." Justice Scalia added:

> I cannot join [the majority opinion] for yet another reason: the Court's statement that the proposed use of the school's facilities is constitutional because (among other things) it would not signal endorsement of religion in general. What a strange notion, that a Constitution which itself gives "religion in general" preferential treatment (I refer to the Free Exercise Clause) forbids endorsement of religion in general. [I]ndifference to "religion in general" in not what our cases, both old and recent, demand.
>
> I agree that the Free Speech Clause of the First Amendment forbids what [the school district has] done here. As for the asserted Establishment Clause justification, I would hold, simply and clearly, that giving

[the church] nondiscriminatory access to school facilities cannot violate that provision because it does not signify state or local embrace of a particular religious sect.

Justice Kennedy, concurring, agreed that the Court's invocation of *Lemon* was "unsettling and unnecessary." Justice White responded to the attack on *Lemon* by observing that "*Lemon*, however frightening it might be to some, has not been overruled."

ROSENBERGER v. UNIVERSITY OF VIRGINIA

515 U.S. 819, 115 S. Ct. 2510, 132 L.Ed. 2d. 700 (1995)

[The university authorized payments from its mandatory student fees to outside contractors for printing costs associated with the publications of designated student groups. The student groups had to issue a disclaimer in all their publications that they were independent of the university and the university bore no responsibility for them. One such student group published a newspaper called *Wide Awake: A Christian Perspective at the University of Virginia*.

[The university refused to authorize payment for the printing costs of *Wide Awake*. A university guideline prohibited the use of mandatory student fees to fund those activities, among others, which primarily promoted a belief in a "deity or an ultimate reality." The student group brought a 42 U.S.C. § 1983 action contending that refusal to authorize payment violated freedom of speech. The federal district court granted summary judgment for the university. The Fourth Circuit affirmed. Although the university's action constituted viewpoint discrimination violative of freedom of speech, the Fourth Circuit concluded that it was justified by "compelling interest" in securing compliance with the Establishment Clause.]

JUSTICE KENNEDY delivered the opinion of the Court.

The SAF [Student Activities Fee] is a forum more metaphysical than in a spatial or geographic sense, but the same principles are applicable. The University's denial of [the] request for third-party payments in the present case is based upon viewpoint discrimination not unlike the discrimination the school district relied upon in *Lamb's Chapel* and that we found invalid.

The University tries to escape the consequences of *Lamb's Chapel* by urging that this case involves the provision of funds rather than access to facilities. The University urges that from a constitutional standpoint, funding of speech differs from provision of access to facilities because money is scarce and physical facilities are not. The government cannot justify viewpoint discrimination among private speakers on the economic fact of scarcity. Had the meeting rooms in *Lamb's Chapel* been scarce, had the demand been greater than the supply, our decision would have been no different.

Vital First Amendment speech principles are at stake here. The first danger to liberty lies in granting the State the power to examine publications to determine whether or not they are based on some ultimate idea and if so for the State to classify them. The second, and corollary danger, is to speech from the chilling of, individual thought and expression.

[The Court held that the university's guideline "both in its terms and in its application" violated the free speech rights of the student complainants and turned next to the Establishment Clause issue.] [W]e [have] rejected the position that the Establishment Clause even justifies, much else requires, a refusal to extend free speech rights to religious speakers who participate in broad-reaching government programs neutral in design. *See Lamb's Chapel, Mergens, Widmar.*

The governmental program here is neutral towards religion. There is no suggestion that the University created it to advance religion or adopted some ingenious device with the purpose of aiding a religious cause. The object of the Student Activities Fund is to open a forum for speech and to support various student enterprises, including the publication of newspapers in recognition of the diversity and creativity of student life.

The neutrality of the program distinguishes the student fees from a tax levied for the direct support of a church or group of churches. A tax of that sort, of course, would run contrary to Establishment Clause concerns from the earliest days of the Republic. [T]he $14 paid each semester by the students is not a general tax designed to raise revenue for the University. Our decision, then, cannot be read as addressing an expenditure from a general tax fund. Here the disbursements from the fund go to private contractors for the costs of printing that which is protected under the Speech Clause of the First Amendment. This is a far cry from a general public assessment designed and effected to provide financial support for a church.

If the expenditure of governmental funds is prohibited whenever those funds pay for a service that is pursuant to a religion-neutral program, used by a group for sectarian purposes, then *Widmar*, *Mergens*, and *Lamb's Chapel* would have to be overruled.

There is no difference in logic or principle, and no difference of constitutional significance, between a school using its funds to operate a facility to which students have access, and a school paying a third-party contractor to operate that facility on its behalf. The latter occurs here.

By paying outside printers, the University in fact attains a further degree of separation from the student publication, for it avoids the duties of supervision, escapes the costs of upkeep, repair, and replacement attributable to student use, and has a clear record of costs. It would be formalistic for us to say that the University must forfeit these advantages and provide the services itself in order to comply with the Establishment Clause. It is, of course, true that if the State pays a church's bills it is subsidizing it, and we must guard against this abuse. That is not a danger here. [T]he student publication is not a religious institution.

Were the dissent's view to become law, it would require the University, in order to avoid a constitutional violation to scrutinize the content of student speech, lest the expression in question — speech otherwise protected by the Constitution — contain too great a religious content.

To obey the Establishment Clause, it was not necessary for the University to deny eligibility to student publications because of their viewpoint. The neutrality commanded of the State by the separate Clauses of the First

Amendment was compromised by the University's course of action. The viewpoint discrimination inherent in the University's regulation required public officials to scan and interpret the student publications to discern their underlying philosophic assumptions respecting religious theory and belief. That course of action was a denial of the right of free speech and would risk fostering a pervasive bias or hostility to religion, which could undermine the very neutrality the Establishment Clause requires. There is no Establishment Clause violation in the University's honoring its duties under the Free Speech Clause.

The judgment of the Court of Appeals must be, and is, reversed.

JUSTICE O'CONNOR, concurring.

This case lies at the intersection of the principle of government neutrality and the prohibition on state funding of religious activities. [P]articular features of the University's program—such as the explicit disclaimer, the disbursement of funds directly to third-party vendors, the vigorous nature of the forum at issue, and the possibility for objecting students to opt out—convince me that providing such assistance in this case would not carry the danger of impermissible use of public funds to endorse *Wide Awake's* religious message.

JUSTICE THOMAS, concurring.

[Justice Thomas concluded that the Establishment Clause was a "prohibition on governmental preferences for some religious faiths over others" and contended, contrary to the dissent, that there was no evidence "that the Framers intended to disable religious entities from participating on neutral terms in evenhanded government programs."]

JUSTICE SOUTER, with whom JUSTICES STEVENS, GINSBURG and BREYER join, dissenting.

The Court today for the first time, approves direct funding of core religious activities by an arm of the State. Because there is no warrant for distinguishing among public funding sources for purposes of applying the First Amendment's prohibition of religious establishment, I would hold that the University's refusal to support petitioners' religious activities is compelled by the Establishment Clause. The Court [argues] that providing religion with economically valuable services is permissible on the theory that services are economically indistinguishable from religious access to governmental speech forums, which sometimes is permissible. But this reasoning would commit the Court to approving direct religious aid beyond anything justifiable for the sake of access to speaking forums.

[*Wide Awake's* content] is nothing other than the preaching of the word. Using public funds for the direct subsidization of preaching the word is categorically forbidden under the Establishment Clause, and if the Clause was meant to accomplish nothing else, it was meant to bar this use of public money.

The principle against direct funding with public money is patently violated by the contested use of today's student activity fee. Like today's taxes generally, the fee is Madison's threepence. The University exercises the power of the State to compel a student to pay it, and the use of any part of it for the direct support of religious activity thus strikes [at] the heart of the prohibition on establishment. The Court, accordingly, has never before upheld direct state funding of the sort of proselytizing published in *Wide Awake* and, in fact, has categorically condemned state programs directly aiding religious activity.

Evenhandedness as one element of a permissibly attenuated benefit is, of course, a far cry from evenhandedness as a sufficient condition of constitutionality for direct financial support of religious proselytization, and our cases have unsurprisingly repudiated any such attempt to cut the Establishment Clause down to a mere prohibition against unequal direct aid. [*Witters*, *Mueller* and *Zobrest*] explicitly distinguished the indirect aid in issue from contrasting examples in the line of case striking down direct aid, and each thereby expressly preserved the core constitutional principle that direct aid to religious is impermissible.

The Court's claim of support from [the] forum-access cases [*Widmar*, *Merge ns* and *Lamb's Chapel*] is ruled out by the very scope of these holdings. [T]hey rest on the recognition that all speakers are entitled to use the street corner (even though the State paves the roads and provides the police protection to everyone on the street) and on the analogy between the public street corner and open classroom space. The analogy breaks down entirely, however, if the cases are read more broadly than the Court wrote them, to cover more than forums for literal speaking. There is no traditional street corner printing provided by the government on equal terms to all comers, and the forum cases cannot be lifted to a higher plane of generalization without admitting that new economic benefits are being extended directly to religion is in clear violation of the principle barring direct aid.

Given the dispositive effect of the Establishment Clauses's bar to funding the magazine, there should be no need to decide whether in the absence of this bar the University would violate the Free Speech Clause by limiting funding as it has done. [But] the Court's reasoning requires a university that funds private publications about any primarily nonreligious topic also to fund publications primarily espousing adherence to or rejection of religion. [This] amounts to a significant reformulation of our viewpoint discrimination precedents and will significantly expand access to limited-access forums.

NOTES

1. *Lemon revisited again.* Does *Lamb's Chapel* breathe new life into *Lemon*? One comment states that "the *Lemon* test was resuscitated despite the Court's refusal to apply it in *Lee v. Weisman*." Note, *The Lemon Test Rears Its Ugly Head Again: Lamb's Chapel v. Center Moriches Union Free School District*, 27 U. Rich. L. Rev. 1153, 1169 (1993). This author suggests that until the Justices can agree on a doctrinal replacement for *Lemon* — whether it be the coercion test or the endorsement test — "*Lemon* is not likely to be replaced." Isn't the Court's reference to *Lemon* almost half-hearted? Doesn't it overstate things to say that *Lamb's Chapel* resuscitates *Lemon*? On the other hand, Justice White does make a point of the fact that *Lemon* has not been overruled.

2. *Capitol Square Review Board v. Pinette,* 515 U.S. 753 (1995). State officials refused to allow the Ku Klux Klan to erect a ten foot cross on a public square adjoining the state Capitol building in Columbus, Ohio. Previously, permits had been issued for a Christmas tree and a Menorah. The lower federal courts issued injunctive relief requiring issuance of a permit. In an opinion by Justice Scalia, the Supreme Court affirmed. The majority treated the display as private religious speech, which "far from being a First Amendment orphan, is as fully protected under the Free Speech Clause as secular private expression." Because the public square was a traditional public forum, content-based regulation must be evaluated under the strict scrutiny standard.

Establishment Clause compliance may sometimes constitute a compelling governmental interest. But not here: "The State did not sponsor [the Klan's] expression, the expression was made on government property that had been opened to the public for speech, and permission was requested through the same application process and on the same terms required of other private groups."

One part of Justice Scalia's opinion was joined only by Chief Justice Rehnquist, Justice Kennedy and Justice Thomas. These Justices rejected the view that the cross display could constitute an impermissible endorsement: "What distinguishes *Allegheny County* and the dictum in *Lynch* from *Widmar* and *Lamb's Chapel* is the difference between government speech and private speech."

Justice Souter, joined by Justices O'Connor and Breyer, concurring, took exception to the Scalia plurality's view of the endorsement test. They described it as a novel *per se* rule that endorsement of religious expression does not violate the establishment clause "where it (1) is private and (2) occurs in a public forum even if a reasonable observer would see the expression as indicating state endorsement." In the past, the Court had looked at specific circumstances presented by private religious speech as they appear to a reasonable observer. The plurality's new *per se* rule would make the endorsement test meaningless.

Justice O'Connor, joined by Justice Breyer and Souter, concurred. The state had not shown that it had a compelling governmental interest in rejecting the Klan's permit application. The appropriate test for evaluating whether governmental regulation dealing with speech of a religious nature was the endorsement test. But they did not believe that the cross display would be perceived as an endorsement by government. "An informed member of the community will know how the public space in question has been used in the past — and it is that fact, not that the space may meet the legal definition of a public forum, which is relevant to the endorsement inquiry."

Justice Stevens dissented. The message of the cross was "religious in character." Therefore, it was a message that the state could not transmit without violating the establishment clause: "Accordingly, I would hold that the Constitution generally forbids the placement of a symbol of a religious character, in, on, or before a seat of government."

Justice Ginsburg said that "if the Establishment Clause is genuinely to uncouple government from church," a state cannot permit and a court cannot order the display at issue.

How does the endorsement discussion in *Capitol Square* affect the *Lynch — Allegheny County* "reindeer" rule?

3. *Good News Club v. Milford Central School,* 533 U.S. 98 (2001): As authorized by New York law, a school district enacted a policy authorizing district residents to use its building after school for a variety of activities, including instruction in education or the arts and social, civic and recreational uses pertaining to the community welfare. The plaintiffs, sponsors of a Christian club for children, brought a civil rights suit against the school, alleging that the school's refusal to allow them to use the facilities under this program violated their free speech rights. The school argued that it was required to deny such use under the Establishment Clause, because the club planned to engage in religious activities on school property, not merely in discussion of secular subjects from a religious perspective.

The Court held that the school's exclusion of the Christian children's club constituted unconstitutional viewpoint discrimination and that that discrimination was not required in order to avoid a violation of the Establishment Clause. Justice Thomas, writing for the majority, found that the exclusion was indistinguishable from the situations involved in *Rosenberger* and *Lamb's Chapel*. "Like the church in *Lamb's Chapel*," he reasoned, "the Club seeks to address a subject otherwise permitted under the rule, the teaching of morals and character, from a religious standpoint." The only difference, Justice Thomas noted, was "that the Club chooses to teach moral lessons from a Christian perspective through live storytelling and prayer, whereas Lamb's Chapel taught lessons through films. This distinction is inconsequential. Both modes of speech use a religious viewpoint." Moreover, the Court could not "say that the Club's activities are any more 'religious' or deserve any less First Amendment protection than did the publication of *Wide Awake* in *Rosenberger*."

The Court rejected the lower court's conclusion that "its characterization of the Club's activities as religious in nature warranted treating the Club's activities as different in kind from the other activities permitted by the school. The 'Christian viewpoint' is unique, according to the court [of appeals], because it contains an 'additional layer' that other kinds of viewpoints do not. That is, the Club 'is focused on teaching children how to cultivate their relationship with God through Jesus Christ,' which it characterized as 'quintessentially religious.' " In response, the Court stated: "We disagree that something that is 'quintessentially religious' or 'decidedly religious in nature' cannot also be characterized properly as the teaching of morals and character development from a particular viewpoint. What matters for purposes of the Free Speech Clause is that we can see no logical difference in kind between the invocation of teamwork, loyalty, or patriotism by other associations to provide a foundation for their lessons."

While conceding that "a state interest in avoiding Establishment Clause violations 'may be characterized as compelling,' and therefore may justify content-based discrimination," the Court found that it need not "confront the issue in this case, because we conclude that the school has no valid Establishment Clause interest." The fact that elementary school children were involved and arguably might feel coercive pressure, the Court found, did not change the outcome: "[T]o the extent we consider whether the community would feel coercive pressure to engage in the Club's activities, the relevant community would be the parents, not the elementary school children. It is the parents who choose whether their children will attend the Good News Club meetings. Because the children cannot attend without their parents' permission, they cannot be coerced into engaging in the Good News Club's religious activities."

In dissent, Justice Souter, joined by Justice Ginsburg, noted: "Good News's classes open and close with a prayer. The lesson plan instructs the teacher to 'lead a child to Christ,' and, when reading a Bible verse, to '[e]mphasize that this verse is from the Bible, God's Word.'" On the basis of such evidence, he concluded: "It is beyond question that Good News intends to use the public school premises not for the mere discussion of a subject from a particular, Christian point of view, but for an evangelical service of worship calling children to commit themselves in an act of Christian conversion. The majority avoids this reality only be resorting to the bland and general characterization of Good News's activity as 'teaching of morals and character, from a religious standpoint.' If the majority's statement ignores reality, as it surely does, then today's holding may be understood only in equally generic terms. Otherwise, indeed, this case would stand for the remarkable proposition that any public school opened for civic meetings must be opened for use as a church, synagogue, or mosque."

Chapter 10

STATE ACTION

The Constitution is organic law. It deals primarily with the structure of government and limitations on the power of government. Governmental entities, acting under those structures, can then order the relations of private individuals to one another. Private acts, while they may be immoral and may be made illegal by legislation, do not generally violate constitutional guarantees. This is the underlying principle behind the doctrine of state action. It is the action of government, federal or state, that makes the constitutional engine run. The Fourteenth and Fifteenth Amendments both reflect this principle in addressing their proscription to "state action." But the Thirteenth Amendment has no comparable limitation to government action. This chapter addresses the ability of courts and Congress to deal with conduct that is nominally private but that is alleged to offend constitutional values.

§ 10.01 THE ORIGINS OF THE STATE ACTION LIMITATION

The Federal Civil Rights Act of 1875 provided criminal penalties for racial discrimination in "inns, public conveyances on land or water, theatres, and other places of public amusement." The Supreme Court in a landmark decision held that Congress had no power under the Fourteenth Amendment to enact this legislation because that Amendment dealt only with state action. In addition, the Court held that Thirteenth Amendment proscriptions did not extend to racial discrimination in places of public accommodations.

CIVIL RIGHTS CASES

109 U.S. 3, 3 S. Ct. 18, 27 L. Ed. 835 (1883)

JUSTICE BRADLEY delivered the opinion of the Court.

Has Congress constitutional power to make such a law? Of course, no one will contend that the power to pass it was contained in the Constitution before the adoption of the last three amendments. The first section of the Fourteenth Amendment (which is the one relied on), after declaring who shall be citizens of the United States, and of the several States, is prohibitory in its character, and prohibitory upon the states. It is state action of a particular character that is prohibited. Individual invasion of individual rights is not the subject-matter of the Amendment. It has a deeper and broader scope. It nullifies and makes void all state legislation, and state action of every kind, which impairs the privileges and immunities of citizens of the United States, or which injures them in life, liberty or property without due process of law, or which denies to any of them the equal protection of the laws. It not only does this, but, in order that the national will, thus declared, may not be a mere *brutum fulmen,* the last section of the Amendment invests Congress with power to enforce it by appropriate legislation. To enforce what? To enforce the prohibition. To adopt appropriate legislation for correcting the effects of such prohibited state laws and state acts, and thus to render them effectually null, void, and innocuous. This is the legislative power conferred upon Congress, and this is the whole of it. It does not invest Congress with power to legislate upon subjects which are within the domain of state legislation; but to provide modes of relief against state legislation, or state action, of the kind referred to. It does not authorize Congress to create a code of municipal law for the regulation of private rights; but to provide modes of redress against the operation of state laws, and the action of state officers executive or judicial, when these are subversive of the fundamental rights specified in the Amendment. Positive rights and privileges are undoubtedly secured by the Fourteenth Amendment; but they are secured by way of prohibition against state laws and state proceedings affecting those rights and privileges, and by power given to Congress to legislate for the purpose of carrying such prohibition into effect: and such legislation must necessarily be predicated upon such supposed state laws or state proceedings, and be directed to the correction of their operation and effect.

Of course, legislation may, and should be, provided in advance to meet the exigency when it arises; but it should be adapted to the mischief and wrong which the Amendment was intended to provide against; and that is, state laws, or state action of some kind, adverse to the rights of the citizen secured by the Amendment. Such legislation cannot properly cover the whole domain of rights appertaining to life, liberty and property, defining them and providing for their vindication. That would be to establish a code of municipal law regulative of all private rights between man and man in society. It would be to make Congress take the place of the state legislatures and to supersede them. In fine, the legislation which Congress is authorized to adopt in this behalf is not general legislation upon the rights of the citizen, but corrective legislation, that is, such as may be necessary and proper for counteracting such laws as the states may adopt or enforce, and which, by the amendment, they are prohibited from making or enforcing, or such acts and proceedings as the states may commit or take, and which, by the amendment, they are prohibited from committing or taking. It is not necessary for us to state, if we could, what legislation would be proper for Congress to adopt. It is sufficient for us to examine whether the law in question is of that character.

An inspection of the law shows that it makes no reference whatever to any supposed or apprehended violation of the Fourteenth Amendment on the part of the states. It is not predicated on any such view. It proceeds *ex directo* to declare that certain acts committed by individuals shall be deemed offenses, and shall be prosecuted and punished by proceedings in the courts of the United States. It does not profess to be corrective of any constitutional wrong committed by the states; it does not make its operation to depend upon any such wrong committed. It applies equally to cases arising in states which have the justest laws respecting the personal rights of citizens, and whose authorities are ever ready to enforce such laws, as to those which arise in states that may have violated the prohibition of the amendment. In other words, it steps into the domain of local jurisprudence, and lays down rules for the conduct of individuals in society towards each other, and imposes sanctions for the enforcement of those rules, without referring in any manner to any supposed action of the state or its authorities.

[C]ivil rights, such as are guaranteed by the Constitution against state aggression, cannot be impaired by the wrongful acts of individuals, unsupported by state authority in the shape of laws, customs, or judicial or executive proceedings. The wrongful act of an individual, unsupported by any such authority, is simply a private wrong, or a crime of that individual; an invasion of the rights of the injured party, it is true, whether they affect his person, his property, or his reputation; but if not sanctioned in some way by the state, or not done under state authority, his rights remain in full force, and may presumably be vindicated by resort to the laws of the state for redress. This abrogation and denial of rights, for which the states alone were or could be responsible, was the great seminal and fundamental wrong which was intended to be remedied. And the remedy to be provided must necessarily be predicated upon that wrong. It must assume that in the cases provided for, the evil or wrong actually committed rests upon some state law or state authority for its excuse and perpetration.

Of course, these remarks do not apply to those cases in which Congress is clothed with direct and plenary powers of legislation over the whole subject, accompanied with an express or implied denial of such power to the States, as in the regulation of commerce among the several states. In these cases Congress has power to pass laws for regulating the subjects specified in every detail, and the conduct and transactions of individuals in respect thereof. But where a subject is not submitted to the general legislative power of Congress, but is only submitted thereto for the purpose of rendering effective some prohibition against particular State legislation or State action in reference to that subject, the power given is limited by its object, and any legislation by Congress in the matter must necessarily be corrective in its character, adapted to counteract and redress the operation of such prohibited State laws or proceedings of State officers. [W]hether Congress, in the exercise of its power to regulate commerce amongst the several States, might or might not pass a law regulating rights in public conveyances passing from one State to another, is a question which is not now before us, as the sections in question are not conceived in any such view.

But the power of Congress to adopt direct and primary, as distinguished from corrective legislation, on the subject in hand, is sought, in the second place, from the Thirteenth Amendment, which abolishes slavery. This amendment, as well as the Fourteenth, is undoubtedly self-executing without any ancillary legislation. By its own unaided force and effect it abolished slavery, and established universal freedom. Still, legislation may be necessary and proper to meet all the various cases and circumstances to be affected by it, and to prescribe proper modes of redress for its violation in letter or spirit. And such legislation may be primary and direct in its character; for the amendment is not a mere prohibition of State laws establishing or upholding slavery, but an absolute declaration that slavery or involuntary servitude shall not exist in any part of the United States.

[It] is assumed, that the power vested in Congress to enforce the article by appropriate legislation, clothes Congress with power to pass all laws necessary and proper for abolishing all badges and incidents of slavery in the United States; the argument being, that the denial of equal accommodations and privileges is, in itself, a subjection to a species of servitude within the meaning of the Amendment. Conceding the major proposition to be true, that Congress has a right to enact all necessary and proper laws for the obliteration and prevention of slavery with all its badges and incidents, is the minor proposition also true, that the denial to any person of admission to the accommodations and privileges of an inn, a public conveyance, or a theatre, does subject that person to any form of servitude, or tend to fasten upon him any badge of slavery? If it does not, then power to pass the law is not found in the Thirteenth Amendment.

Can the act of a mere individual, the owner of the inn, the public conveyance or place of amusement, refusing the accommodation, be justly regarded as imposing any badge of slavery or servitude upon the applicant. [W]e are forced to the conclusion that such an act of refusal has nothing to do with slavery or involuntary servitude, and that if it is violative of any right of the party, his redress is to be sought under the laws of the State; or if those laws are adverse to his rights and do not protect him, his remedy will be found in the corrective legislation which Congress has adopted, or may adopt, for counteracting the effect of State laws, or State action, prohibited by the Fourteenth Amendment. It would be running the slavery argument into the ground to make it apply to every act of discrimination which a person may see fit to make as to the guests he will entertain, or as to the people he will take into his coach or cab or car, or admit to his concert or theatre, or deal with in other matters of intercourse or business. Innkeepers and public carriers, by the laws of all the States, so far as we are aware, are bound, to the extent of their facilities, to furnish proper accommodation to all unobjectionable persons who in good faith apply for them. If the laws themselves make any unjust discrimination, amenable to the prohibitions of the Fourteenth Amendment, Congress has full power to afford a remedy under that amendment and in accordance with it.

When a man has emerged from slavery, and by the aid of beneficent legislation has shaken off the inseparable concomitants of that state, there must be some stage in the progress of his elevation when he takes the rank of a mere citizen, and ceases to be the special favorite of the laws, and when his rights as a citizen, or a man, are to be protected in the ordinary modes by which other men's rights are protected. [The law is unconstitutional and void.]

JUSTICE HARLAN, dissenting:

[With regard to the Thirteenth Amendment, JUSTICE HARLAN contended that the Amendment gave Congress express power to enact laws to protect the emancipated slaves "against the deprivation, on account of their race, of any civil rights enjoyed by other freemen in the same state." HARLAN stated that federal civil rights legislation enacted under the Thirteenth Amendment] may be of a direct and primary character, operating upon states, their officers and agents, and also upon at least, such individuals and corporations as exercise public functions and wield power and authority under the state . . . . I am of opinion that discrimination practiced by corporations and individuals in the exercise of their public or quasi-public function is a badge of servitude, the imposition of which Congress may prevent under its power, through appropriate legislation, to enforce the Thirteenth Amendment.

It remains now to consider these cases with reference to the power Congress has possessed since the adoption of the Fourteenth Amendment.

The first clause of the first section — "all persons born or naturalized in the United States, and subject to the jurisdiction thereof, are citizens of the United States, and of the state wherein they reside" — is of a distinctly affirmative character. In its application to the colored race, previously liberated, it created and granted, as well citizenship of the United States, as citizenship of the state in which they respectively resided. Further, they were brought, by this supreme act of the nation, within the direct operation of that provision of the Constitution which declares that "the citizens of each state shall be entitled to all privileges and immunities of citizens in the several states." Article 4, § 2.

The citizenship thus acquired by that race, in virtue of an affirmative grant by the nation, may be protected, not alone by the judicial branch of the government, but by congressional legislation of a primary direct character; this, because the power of congress is not restricted to the enforcement of prohibitions upon state laws or state action. It is, in terms distinct and positive, to enforce "the *provisions* of *this article*" of amendment; not simply those of a prohibitive character, but the provisions, — *all* of the provisions, — affirmative and prohibitive, of the amendment.

But what was secured to colored citizens of the United States — as between them and their respective states — by the grant to them of state citizenship? With what rights, privileges, or immunities did this grant from the nation invest them? There is one, if there be no others — exemption from race discrimination in respect of any civil right belonging to citizens of the white race in the same state. It is fundamental in American citizenship that, in respect of such rights, there shall be no discrimination by the state, or its officers, or by individuals, of corporations exercising public functions or authority, against any citizen because of his race or previous condition of servitude. [T]o hold that the amendment remits that right to the states for their protection, primarily, and stays the hand of the nation, until it is assailed by state laws or state proceedings, is to adjudge that the amendment, so far from enlarging the powers of congress — as we have heretofore said it did — not only curtails them, but reverses the policy which the general government has pursued from its very organization. Such an interpretation of the amendment is a denial to congress of the power, by appropriate legislation to enforce one of its provisions. In view of the circumstances under which the recent amendments were incorporated into the constitution, and especially in view of the peculiar character of the new rights they created and secured, it ought not to be presumed that the general government has abdicated its authority, by national legislation, direct and primary in its character, to guard and protect privileges and immunities secured by that instrument. It was perfectly well known that the great danger to the equal enjoyment by citizens of their rights, as citizens, was to be apprehended, not altogether from unfriendly state legislation, but from the hostile action of corporations and individuals in the states. And it is to be presumed that it was intended, by [the fifth section of the Fourteenth Amendment] to clothe congress with power and authority to meet that danger.

It is said that any interpretation of the Fourteenth Amendment different from that adopted by the court, would authorize congress to enact a municipal code for all the states, covering every matter affecting the life, liberty, and property of the citizens of the several states. Not so. Prior to the adoption of that amendment the constitutions of the several states, without, perhaps, an exception, secured all *persons* against deprivation of life, liberty, or property, otherwise than by due process of law, and, in some form, recognized the right of all *persons* to the equal protection of the laws. These rights, therefore, existed before that amendment was proposed or adopted. If, by reason of that fact, it be assumed that protection in these rights of persons still rests, primarily, with the states, and that congress may not interfere except to enforce, by means of corrective legislation, the prohibitions upon state laws or state proceedings inconsistent with those rights, it does not at all follow that privileges which have been *granted by the nation* may not be protected by primary legislation upon the part of congress. That exemption of citizens from discrimination based on race or color, in respect of civil rights, is one of those privileges or immunities, can no longer be deemed an open question in this court.

But if it were conceded that the power of congress could not be brought into activity until the rights specified in the act of 1875 had been abridged or denied by some state law or state action, I maintain that the decision of the court is erroneous. In every material sense applicable to the practical enforcement of the fourteenth amendment, railroad corporations, keepers of inns, and managers of places of public amusement are agents of the state, because amenable, in respect of their public duties and functions, to public regulation. It seems to me that a denial by these instrumentalities of the state to the citizen, because of his race, of that equality of civil rights secured to him by law, is a denial by the state within the meaning of the fourteenth amendment. If it be not, then that race is left, in respect of the civil rights under discussion, practically at the mercy of corporations and individuals wielding power under the states.

I agree that if one citizen chooses not to hold social intercourse with another, he is not and cannot be made amenable to the law for his conduct in that regard; for no legal right of a citizen is violated by the refusal of others to maintain merely social relations with him. The rights which Congress, by the act of 1875, endeavored to secure and protect are legal, not social, rights. The right, for instance, of a colored citizen to use the accommodations of a public highway upon the same terms as are permitted to white citizens is no more a social right than his right, under the law, to use the public streets of a city, or a town, or a turnpike road, or a public market, or a post office, or his right to sit in a public building with others, of whatever race, for the purpose of hearing the political questions of the day discussed.

NOTES

1. *Significance of the state action requirement.* Justice Bradley's decision in the *Civil Rights Cases* was the formative element in creating an interpretation of the Fourteenth Amendment that limited its scope to state or public action rather than individual or private action. Because of the limiting function of the state action concept, state action became the critical precondition without which the promises and prohibitions of the Fourteenth Amendment were not operative.

2. *Values served by the state action requirement.* What is the purpose of the state action requirement according to Justice Bradley? What values does it serve? Could the application of the Fourteenth Amendment only to state action be thought to derive from the value our system places on individual autonomy? Consider the following argument: The Court in the *Civil Rights Cases* viewed the state action limitation more as a means of preserving federalism than fostering individual autonomy.

Some commentators have criticized the state action requirement, and urged its total abandonment.

> Limiting the Constitution's protections to government action made sense when it was believed that the common law protected people from infringements of their rights by private actors. Now, however, individuals are thought to possess many rights that have no common-law protection. Thus, the state action doctrine is based on the anachronistic premise of a common law that is coextensive with individual liberties.

Erwin Chemerinsky, *Rethinking State Action,* 80 Nw. U. L. Rev. 503, 505 (1985). He concludes that "the values embodied in constitutional rights also should be recognized as rights limiting private actions, absent sufficiently compelling justifications for the behavior." *Id.* at 507.

One commentator has suggested that acceptance of Professor Chemerinsky's thesis "will not expand individual freedom. At best, it will dilute existing liberties; at worst, it may lead to a more restrictive definition and protection of those rights." William Marshall, *Diluting Constitutional Rights: Rethinking "Rethinking State Action,"* 80 Nw. U. L. Rev. 558, 559 (1985). Another response to Professor Chemerinsky could question its impact on autonomy interests.

> If . . . human values are many, conflicting, and irreconcilable, then private persons and institutions should be presumptively free to act in accordance with manifold and differing values, lest some authentic values be submerged altogether. The state action doctrine . . . frees private persons to act in accordance with many and competing values, unless legislation—popularly enacted and popularly revocable—intervenes to require private compliance with constitutional values.

Maimon Schwarzschild, *Value Pluralism and the Constitution: In Defense of the State Action Doctrine,* 1988 Sup. Ct. Rev. 129, 137. Professor Chemerinsky answers that "autonomy can be directly protected by laws and legal principles without the state action doctrine. If the state action doctrine protects freedoms worth safeguarding, then those freedoms can be upheld by legislatures and courts." Erwin Chemerinsky, *More Is Not Less: A Rejoinder to Professor*

Marshall, 80 Nw. U. L. Rev. 571, 572 (1985). But if the Constitution forbade private discrimination, how could legislation authorize it?

3. *Congress' role under the Fourteenth Amendment.* The Court in the *Civil Rights Cases* limited congressional enforcement powers under the Civil War Amendments to a corrective or remedial role. Under this model, Congress may legislate remedies for rights only as rights are defined by the courts. And, because the Court did not construe the Thirteenth or Fourteenth Amendment to extend to private racial discrimination by owners of places of public accommodation, Congress could not legislate pursuant to those Amendments. Congress apparently could not independently define the substantive content of the guarantee and certainly could not legislate against private action. As subsequent discussion will indicate, this model of Congress' enforcement powers under the Civil War Amendments has been substantially altered. Congress today may be able to reach activities that the Court might not otherwise find offensive to the guarantees in those Amendments. Congress can, *within limits,* define the substantive content of the rights that are guaranteed. There have even been indications (although not a holding) that Congress can legislate against private action under the Fourteenth Amendment. *See United States v. Guest,* p. 1537.

4. *Commerce power.* Justice Bradley in the *Civil Rights Cases* did not pass on the question of whether Congress could enforce civil rights legislation under the federal Commerce Clause. Reservation of decision on this issue helped make possible the congressional decision reflected in the Civil Rights Act of 1964 to base that statute on the Commerce Clause rather than on the Fourteenth Amendment.

5. *Thirteenth Amendment.* The Court in the *Civil Rights Cases* rejected petitioner's argument that the federal legislation at issue could be justified under the Thirteenth Amendment, which is not limited by the state action language. Instead, the Court chose to read the proscriptions of § 1 of the Amendment (and Congress' enforcement powers under § 2) narrowly to exclude racial discrimination. Compare the modern interpretation of Congress' power to define "badges of slavery" in *Jones v. Mayer,* p. 1545, and *Runyon v. McCrary,* p. 1550. Nevertheless, in the absence of applicable congressional legislation, the Court continues to construe the guarantees of the Thirteenth Amendment, § 1, narrowly. *See City of Memphis v. Greene*, 451 U.S. 100 (1981).

If Justice Harlan's approach to the Thirteenth Amendment had been accepted, it would have made that Amendment a far more formidable and generative source of constitutional law and doctrine than in fact it has been. In addition, Harlan's view of the Thirteenth Amendment would have diminished the importance of the state action requirement of the Fourteenth Amendment as a barrier to federal civil rights legislation. Would this have been good constitutional law?

6. *The Civil Rights Cases — reviving antebellum federalism?* Professor Maltz contends, as have others, that the *Civil Rights Cases* are less conservative than they are sometimes portrayed:

> First, the opinion presupposed a state duty to protect the fundamental rights of blacks. Moreover, the decision did not completely foreclose

> the federal government from protecting the rights described in the Civil Rights Act of 1875. After noting that all states currently protected those rights, Justice Bradley relied on the enforcement provisions of the Thirteenth Amendment to suggest that Congress could constitutionally require state officials to continue that protection and punish those officials who fail to do so.

Earl Maltz, *The Civil Rights Act and the Civil Rights Cases: Congress, Court, and Constitution*, 44 FLA. L. REV. 605, 634–35 (1992).

What special problems does reliance on the Thirteenth Amendment for protection against state infringement on civil rights present? Do you agree with Professor Maltz that those who call the *Civil Rights Cases* majority reactionary and bent on resurrecting the "structure of antebellum federalism have vastly overstated their case?"

§ 10.02 MODERN THEORIES OF STATE ACTION

In the years following the *Civil Rights Cases,* both courts and commentators struggled with efforts to escape that decision's confining interpretation of the state action requirement. At the same time, those making these efforts generally recognized the need to replace that interpretation with a coherent and principled construction of state action. The following subsections describe the various theories which have, over the years, received support. As will be seen, however, exactly which of these theories today represents the current state of the law is a question not easily answered. What will become clear is that wherever the current law stands, it constitutes a much more narrow construction of the state action requirement than was available during at least the Warren Court era.

[A] THE "PUBLIC FUNCTION" THEORY

One of the earliest of the departures from a narrow construction of the state action requirement came with the Court's recognition that state action could be present for constitutional purposes, even though purely as a technical matter a private party, rather than the state itself, was acting. If those private actors could properly be deemed to have been imbued with state power in some manner, their actions could be deemed to be those of the state for purposes of the Fourteenth Amendment.

This "public function" theory manifested itself in two distinct subcategories. One, what might be called the "state-like power" theory, posited that when a private actor was exercising power equivalent in nature and scope to that of the state, the activities of that private actor should be deemed state action. The other, what could be referred to as the "state-delegation" theory, provided that when the state delegates one of its traditional functions to private actors, the activities of those private actors in the performance of those functions should be deemed state action.

In reading the following materials, consider these underlying questions: Does one of these subcategories of the "public-function" theory constitute a more defensible construction of the state-action requirement than the other? Will it always be possible to distinguish between them? What are the systemic costs and benefits of each approach?

1. *Political parties and state delegation.* In *Smith v. Allwright*, 321 U.S. 649 (1944), the Supreme Court held that rules of the Democratic Party of Texas that excluded African-Americans from voting in the party's primaries violated the Fifteenth Amendment. The Court reasoned that, while no state law expressly directed this exclusion, state action could be found because many party activities were subject to extensive statutory control. In *Terry v. Adams*, 345 U.S. 461 (1953), the Court considered "the constitutional power of a Texas county political organization called the Jaybird Democratic Association to exclude Negroes from its primaries on racial grounds." Concluding that "Jaybird activities follow a plan purposefully designed to exclude Negroes from voting and at the same time to escape the Fifteenth Amendment's command," Justice Black, announcing the judgment of the Court, held that the Jaybird primary was subject to constitutional control:

> The only election that has counted in this Texas county for more than fifty years has been that held by the Jaybirds from which Negroes were excluded. The Democratic primary and the general election have become no more than the perfunctory ratifier of the choice that has already been made in Jaybird elections from which Negroes have been excluded. It is immaterial that the state does not control that part of this elective process which it leaves for the Jaybirds to manage. The Jaybird primary has become an integral part, indeed the only effective part, of the elective process that determines who shall rule and govern in the county. The effect of the whole procedure, Jaybird primary plus Democratic primary plus general election, is to do precisely that which the Fifteenth Amendment forbids — strip Negroes of every vestige of influence in selecting the officials who control the local county matters that intimately touch the daily lives of citizens.

345 U.S. at 469–70.

2. *The shopping center cases. Marsh v. Alabama*, 326 U.S. 501 (1946). The town of Chickasaw, Alabama, was entirely owned by a private corporation. Other than that, it had all the characteristics of any American town. A Jehovah's Witness went on one of the town's sidewalks and distributed religious literature. She did this notwithstanding that she had been warned that she could not distribute the religious literature within the town without a permit and that, if she applied for a permit, she would be denied. She was arrested and charged with violating a state law making it a crime "to enter or remain on the premises of another after having been warned not to do so." The Supreme Court held that a state law which criminally punished those who attempt to distribute religious literature violated the First and Fourteenth Amendment. Justice Black declared for the Court:

> Our question narrows down to this: Can those people who live in or come to Chickasaw be denied freedom of the press and religion simply because a single Company has legal title to all the town? For

> it is the State's contention that the mere fact that all the property interests in the town are held by a single company is enough to give that company power, enforceable by a state statute, to abridge these freedoms. We do not agree that the corporation's property interests settle the question. The State urges in effect that the corporation's right to control the inhabitants of Chickasaw is coextensive with the right of a homeowner to regulate the conduct of his guests. We cannot accept that contention. Ownership does not always mean absolute dominion. The more an owner, for his advantage, opens up his property for use by the public in general, the more do his rights become circumscribed by the statutory and constitutional rights of those who use it.

In *Marsh,* "dedication to the public use" became a key constitutional inquiry, even in the context of nominally private property. *Marsh* was to become the linchpin for a tortured series of cases involving the amenability of privately owned shopping centers to constitutional obligations. While the potential of the *Marsh* holding was not exploited for a number of years, the Supreme Court, in *Amalgamated Food Employees Local 590 v. Logan Valley Plaza, Inc.*, 391 U.S. 308 (1968), invoked *Marsh* in holding that informational picketing in a private shopping center could not be totally barred. Justice Marshall, for the Court, as Justice Black in *Marsh,* began with the premise that "under some circumstances property that is privately owned may be treated as though it were publicly held." In this instance, the shopping center was deemed "the functional equivalent to the business district" involved in *Marsh.*

It is notable, however, that Justice Black, the author of *Marsh,* dissented in *Logan Valley.* He would have limited that decision to "property [that] has taken on *all* the attributes of a town, *i.e.*, 'residential buildings, streets, a system of sewers, a sewage disposal plant and a business block' on which business places are situated." The mere fact that the shopping center was a business district was not sufficient "for the Court to confiscate a part of the owner's private property and give its use to people who want to picket on it."

In *Logan Valley,* the informational picketing in controversy had a direct relationship to activities within the shopping center, because it involved a grievance against one of the stores in the center. But what if the protest activities had been more general in character? In *Lloyd Corp. v. Tanner*, 407 U.S. 551 (1972), the Court limited the *Logan Valley* principle and held that a privately owned, enclosed shopping center could, consistently with the First Amendment, prohibit the distribution of handbills on its property when the handbilling was unrelated to the shopping center's operation. Now it was the private property rights which took precedence. "There is no open-ended invitation to the public to use the Center for any and all purposes, however incompatible with the interests of both the stores and the shoppers whom they serve." *Marsh* was limited to situations "where private interests were substituting for and performing the customary functions of government."

In *Hudgens v. NLRB*, 424 U.S. 507 (1976), the Court concluded that the reasoning in *Lloyd* could not be squared with *Logan Valley. Logan Valley* was overruled. Justice Stewart, for the Court, stated that "[i]f a large self-contained shopping center *is* the functional equivalent of a municipality, as

Logan Valley held," then the Constitution would not permit distinctions between "related" and "unrelated" protests as *Lloyd* had indicated. To do so, the Court concluded, would be to discriminate on the basis of the content of expression, which is generally proscribed under the First Amendment.

Justice Marshall, the author of *Logan Valley,* joined by Justice Brennan, dissented, and argued that *Lloyd* had not undermined the rationale of *Logan Valley.* The majority's ruling in the present case, asserted Justice Marshall, arose "from an overly formalistic view of the relationship between the institution of private ownership of property and the First Amendment's guarantee of freedom of expression." While private property serves legitimate values of privacy and individual autonomy, the force of those values diminishes when private property is opened for public use. "[W]hile the owner of property opened to public view may not automatically surrender any of his autonomy interests in managing the property as he sees fit, there is nothing new about the notion that the autonomy interests must be accommodated with the interests of the public. . . . As far as these groups are concerned, the shopping center owner has assumed the traditional role of the state in its control of historical First Amendment forums."

Assuming that *Logan Valley* and *Lloyd* cannot coexist, why was *Logan Valley* overruled? As Professor Schauer has noted: "Conspicuously absent from the *Hudgens* decision is language pronouncing a preference for First Amendment rights over property rights, language explicitly used in *Marsh* and *Logan Valley."* Schauer, Hudgens v. NLRB *and the Problem of State Action in First Amendment Adjudication,* 61 MINN. L. REV. 433 (1977). In this instance at least, the right of the private owner of property took precedence over the interests of the public in carrying on communicative activity in the shopping centers.

While *Hudgens* effectively curtailed use of the United States Constitution to impose constitutional constraints on privately owned shopping centers, state constitutions can be used to achieve this end. The California Supreme Court, for example, has concluded that its state constitution protects speech and petitioning in shopping centers, even when the centers are privately owned. In upholding this decision in *Pruneyard Shopping Center v. Robins*, 447 U.S. 74 (1980), the U.S. Supreme Court, per Justice Rehnquist, noted that in the prior shopping center cases "there was no State constitutional or statutory provision that had been construed to create rights to the use of private property by strangers, comparable to those found to exist by the California Supreme Court here." In the exercise of its police power, the state could adopt reasonable restrictions on private property so long as they do not contravene constitutional guarantees.

EVANS v. NEWTON

382 U.S. 296, 86 S. Ct. 486, 15 L. Ed. 2d 373 (1966)

[The city of Macon, Georgia, became trustee under Senator Bacon's will, which provided that certain land was to be used as a park, "Baconsfield," for white people only. The park was maintained for many years by the city. The city was granted a tax exemption for the park and it was considered a part of the municipal establishment. After it became clear that management by public trustees constituted state action, the city permitted blacks to use the park. At that point, members of the all-white Board of Managers of the park brought suit in the state court, asking that the city be removed as trustee and that private trustees be appointed. Negro citizens of Macon intervened in opposition. The Georgia state court accepted the resignation of the city as trustee and appointed three individual trustees. The Georgia Supreme Court held that the testator, Senator Bacon, had the right to bequeath his property to a limited class (Whites) and that the court has the power to approve new trustees so that the purpose of the trust would not fail. The Supreme Court granted certiorari.]

Justice Douglas delivered the opinion of the Court.

There are two complementary principles to be reconciled in this case. One is the right of the individual to pick his own associates so as to express his preferences and dislikes, and to fashion his private life by joining such clubs and groups as he chooses. The other is the constitutional ban in the Equal Protection Clause of the Fourteenth Amendment against state-sponsored racial inequality, which of course bars a city from acting as trustee under a private will that serves the racial segregation cause. A private golf club, however, restricted to either Negro or white membership is one expression of freedom of association. But a municipal golf course that serves only one race is state activity indicating a preference on a matter as to which the State must be neutral.

If a testator wanted to leave a school or center for the use of one race only and in no way implicated the State in the supervision, control, or management of that facility, we assume *arguendo* that no constitutional difficulty would be encountered.

This park, however, is in a different posture. For years it was an integral part of the City of Macon's activities. From the pleadings we assume it was swept, manicured, watered, patrolled, and maintained by the city as a public facility for whites only, as well as granted tax exemption under Ga. Code Ann. § 92-201. The momentum it acquired as a public facility is certainly not dissipated *ipso facto* by the appointment of "private" trustees. So far as this record shows, there has been no change in municipal maintenance and concern over this facility. Whether these public characteristics will in time be dissipated is wholly conjectural. If the municipality remains entwined in the management or control of the park, it remains subject to the restraints of the Fourteenth Amendment. We only hold that where the tradition of municipal control had become firmly established, we cannot take judicial notice that the mere substitution of trustees instantly transferred this park from the public to the private sector.

This conclusion is buttressed by the nature of the service rendered the community by a park. The service rendered even by a private park of this character is municipal in nature. It is open to every white person, there being no selective element other than race. Golf clubs, social centers, luncheon clubs, schools such as Tuskegee was at least in origin, and other like organizations in the private sector are often racially oriented. A park on the other hand, is more like a fire department or police department that traditionally serves the community. Mass recreation through the use of parks is plainly in the public domain, and state courts that aid private parties to perform that public function on a segregated basis implicate the State in conduct proscribed by the Fourteenth Amendment. Like the streets of the company town in *Marsh v. State of Alabama* [and] the elective process of *Terry v. Adams,* the predominant character and purpose of this park is municipal.

Under the circumstances of this case, we cannot but conclude that the public character of this park requires that it be treated as a public institution subject to the command of the Fourteenth Amendment, regardless of who now has title under state law. We may fairly assume that had the Georgia courts been of the view that even in private hands the park may not be operated for the public on a segregated basis, the resignation would not have been approved and private trustees appointed. We put the matter that way because on this record we cannot say that the transfer of title per se disentangled the park from segregation under the municipal regime that long controlled it.

Since the judgment below gives effect to that purpose, it must be and is

Reversed.

JUSTICE HARLAN, whom JUSTICE STEWART joins, dissenting.

[JUSTICE HARLAN argued that the writ should have been dismissed as improvidently granted. He then considered the merits, making clear his distaste for JUSTICE DOUGLAS' "public function" theory.]

I do not think that the Fourteenth Amendment permits this Court in effect to frustrate the terms of Senator Bacon's will, now that the City of Macon is no longer connected, so far as the record shows, with the administration of Baconsfield.

More serious than the absence of any firm doctrinal support for [the Court's] theory of state action are its potentialities for the future. Its failing as a principle of decision in the realm of Fourteenth Amendment concerns can be shown by comparing — among other examples that might be drawn from the still unfolding sweep of governmental functions — the "public function" of privately established schools with that of privately owned parks. Like parks, the purpose schools serve is important to the public. Like parks, private control exists, but there is also a very strong tradition of public control in this field. Like parks, schools may be available to almost anyone of one race or religion but to no others. Like parks, there are normally alternatives for those shut out but there may also be inconveniences and disadvantages caused by the restriction. Like parks, the extent of school intimacy varies greatly depending on the size and character of the institution.

While this process of analogy might be spun out to reach privately owned orphanages, libraries, garbage collection companies, detective agencies, and a host of other functions commonly regarded as nongovernmental though paralleling fields of governmental activity, the example of schools is, I think, sufficient to indicate the pervasive potentialities of this "public function" theory of state action. It substitutes for the comparatively clear and concrete tests of state action a catch-phrase approach as vague and amorphous as it is far-reaching.

[JUSTICE BLACK also dissented.]

NOTES

1. ***Basis and impact of the* Evans *holding.*** To what extent does *Evans* illustrate the "state delegation" theory? To what extent does it illustrate the "state-like power" theory? Would the case likely have been decided the same way had either aspect been absent? After this opinion was issued, the Georgia courts held under the doctrine of *cy pres* that the land could not be used for the purpose intended in the will and therefore should revert to the heirs of Senator Bacon. This holding was upheld in *Evans v. Abney,* 396 U.S. 435 (1970), p. 1515.

2. ***Legitimacy of the delegation rationale.*** Is it possible that, as both a theoretical and practical matter, the "state delegation" theory constitutes a substantially more legitimate construction of the state action requirement than does the "state-like power" theory? In the delegation situation, it is the state itself that has created the power of the actor to invoke state authorization. In the state-like power situation, the state may have taken no steps itself to create the situation.

FLAGG BROTHERS, INC. v. BROOKS
436 U.S. 149, 98 S. Ct. 1729, 56 L. Ed. 2d 185 (1978)

Justice Rehnquist delivered the opinion of the Court.

The question presented by this case is whether a warehouseman's proposed sale of goods entrusted to him for storage, as permitted by New York Uniform Commercial Code § 7-210, is an action properly attributable to the State of New York.

According to her complaint, the allegations of which we must accept as true, respondent Shirley Brooks and her family were evicted from their apartment in Mount Vernon, N.Y., on June 13, 1973. The City Marshal arranged for Brooks' possessions to be stored by petitioner Flagg Brothers, Inc., in its warehouse. Respondent was informed of the cost of moving and storage, and she instructed the workmen to proceed, although she found the price too high. On August 25, 1973, after a series of disputes over the validity of the charges being claimed by petitioner, Brooks received a letter demanding that her account be brought up to date within 10 days "or your furniture will be sold." A series of subsequent letters from respondent and her attorneys produced no satisfaction. Brooks thereupon initiated this class action in the District Court under 42 U.S.C. § 1983, seeking damages, an injunction against the threatened sale of her belongings, and the declaration that such a sale pursuant to § 7-210 would violate the Due Process and Equal Protection Clauses of the Fourteenth Amendment. On July 7, 1975, the District Court dismissed the complaint for failure to state a claim for relief under § 1983. A divided panel of the Court of Appeals reversed.

It must be noted that respondents have named no public officials as defendants in this action. The City Marshal, who supervised their evictions, was dismissed from the case by the consent of all the parties. This total absence of overt official involvement plainly distinguishes this case from earlier decisions imposing procedural restrictions on creditors' remedies. Thus, the only issue presented by this case is whether Flagg Brothers' action may fairly be attributed to the State of New York. We conclude that it may not.

Respondents' primary contention is that New York has delegated to Flagg Brothers a power "traditionally exclusively reserved to the State." They argue that the resolution of private disputes is a traditional function of civil government, and that the State in § 7-210 has delegated this function to Flagg Brothers. Respondents, however, have read too much into the language of our previous cases. While many functions have been traditionally performed by governments, very few have been "exclusively reserved to the State."

One such area has been elections. While the Constitution protects private rights of association and advocacy with regard to the election of public officials, our cases make it clear that the conduct of the elections themselves is an exclusively public function. This principle was established by a series of cases challenging the exclusion of blacks from participation in primary elections in Texas. *Terry v. Adams.* A second line of cases under the public function doctrine originated with *Marsh v. Alabama.*

These two branches of the public function doctrine have in common the feature of exclusivity. Although the elections held by the Democratic Party and its affiliates were the only meaningful elections in Texas, and the streets owned by the Gulf Shipbuilding Corporation were the only streets in Chickasaw, the proposed sale by Flagg Brothers under § 7-210 is not the only means of resolving this purely private dispute. Respondent Brooks has never alleged that state law barred her from seeking a waiver of Flagg Brothers' right to sell her goods at the time she authorized their storage. Presumably, respondent Jones, who alleges that she never authorized the storage of her goods, could have sought to replevy her goods at any time under state law. The challenged statute itself provides a damage remedy against the warehouseman for violations of its provisions. This system of rights and remedies, recognizing the traditional place of private arrangements in ordering relationships in the commercial world, can hardly be said to have delegated to Flagg Brothers an exclusive prerogative of the sovereign.

[W]e would be remiss if we did not note that there are a number of state and municipal functions not covered by our election cases nor governed by the reasoning of *Marsh* which have been administered with a greater degree of exclusivity by States and municipalities than has the function of so-called "dispute resolution." Among these are such functions as education, fire and police protection, and tax collection. We express no view as to the extent, if any, to which a city or State might be free to delegate to private parties the performance of such functions and thereby avoid the strictures of the Fourteenth Amendment.

Respondents further urge that Flagg Brothers' proposed action is properly attributable to the State because the State has authorized and encouraged it in enacting § 7-210. Our cases state "that a State is responsible for the act of a private party when the State, by its law, has compelled the act." This Court, however, has never held that a State's mere acquiescence in a private action converts that action into that of the State.

It is quite immaterial that the State has embodied its decision not to act in statutory form. If New York had no commercial statutes at all, its courts would still be faced with the decision whether to prohibit or to permit the sort of sale threatened here the first time an aggrieved bailor came before them for relief. A judicial decision to deny relief would be no less an "authorization" or "encouragement" of that sale than the legislature's decision embodied in this statute. If the mere denial of judicial relief is considered sufficient encouragement to make the State responsible for those private acts, all private deprivations of property would be converted into public acts whenever the State, for whatever reason, denies relief sought by the putative property owner.

[T]he State of New York is in no way responsible for Flagg Brothers' decision, a decision which the State in § 7-210 permits but does not compel, to threaten to sell these respondents' belongings. Here, the State of New York has not compelled the sale of a bailor's goods, but has merely announced the circumstances under which its courts will not interfere with a private sale. Indeed, the crux of respondents' complaint is not that the State *has* acted, but that it has *refused* to act. This statutory refusal to act is no different in principle from an ordinary statute of limitations whereby the State declines to provide a remedy for private deprivations of property after the passage of a given period of time.

We conclude that the allegations of these complaints do not establish a violation of these respondents' Fourteenth Amendment rights by either respondent Flagg Brothers or by the State of New York.

JUSTICE BRENNAN took no part in the consideration or decision of this case.

JUSTICE MARSHALL, dissenting.

I cannot remain silent as the Court demonstrates, not for the first time, an attitude of callous indifference to the realities of life for the poor. It blandly asserts that "respondent Jones could have sought to replevy her goods at any time under state law." In order to obtain replevin in New York, however, respondent Jones would first have had to present to a sheriff an "undertaking" from a surety by which the latter would be bound to pay "not less than twice the value" of the goods involved and perhaps substantially more, depending in part on the size of the potential judgment against the debtor. Sureties do not provide such bonds without receiving both a substantial payment in advance and some assurance of the debtor's ability to pay any judgment awarded. [W]e cannot close our eyes to the realities that led to this litigation. Just as respondent lacked the funds to prevent eviction, it seems clear that, once her goods were seized, she had no practical choice but to leave them with the warehouseman, where they were subject to forced sale for nonpayment of storage charges.

I am also troubled by the Court's cavalier treatment of the place of historical factors in the "state action" inquiry. While we are of course not bound by what occurred centuries ago in England, the test adopted by the Court itself requires us to decide what functions have been "traditionally exclusively reserved to the State." Such an issue plainly cannot be resolved in a historical vacuum. New York's highest court has stated that "in [New York] the execution of a lien traditionally has been the function of the Sheriff." By ignoring this history, the Court approaches the question before us as if it can be decided without reference to the role that the State has always played in lien execution by forced sale. In so doing, the Court treats the State as if it were, to use the Court's words, "a monolithic, abstract concept hovering in the legal stratosphere." The state action doctrine, as developed in our past cases, requires that we come down to earth and decide the issue here with careful attention to the State's traditional role.

JUSTICE STEVENS, with whom JUSTICES WHITE and MARSHALL join, dissenting.

In determining that New York's statute cannot be scrutinized under the Due Process Clause, the Court reasons that the warehouseman's proposed sale is solely private action because the state statute "*permits* but does not compel" the sale (emphasis added), and because the warehouseman has not been delegated a power "*exclusively* reserved to the state" (emphasis added). Under this approach a State could enact laws authorizing private citizens to use self-help in countless situations without any possibility of federal challenge. [T]he distinctions between "permission" and "compulsion" on the one hand, and "exclusive" and "non-exclusive," on the other, cannot be determinative factors in state-action analysis. There is no great chasm between "permission" and "compulsion" requiring particular state action to fall within one or the other definitional camp.

While Members of this Court have suggested that statutory authorization alone may be sufficient to establish state action, it is not necessary to rely on those suggestions in this case because New York has authorized the warehouseman to perform what is clearly a state function. [T]he Court reasons that state action cannot be found because the State has not delegated to the warehouseman an *exclusive* sovereign function. This distinction, however, is not consistent with our prior decisions on state action [and] is not even adhered to by the Court in this case.

In the broadest sense, we expect government "to provide a reasonable and fair framework of rules which facilitate commercial transactions." This "framework of rules" is premised on the assumption that the State will control nonconsensual deprivations of property and that the State's control will, in turn, be subject to the restrictions of the Due Process Clause. The power to order legally binding surrenders of property and the constitutional restrictions on that power are necessary correlatives in our system. In effect, today's decision allows the State to divorce these two elements by the simple expedient of transferring the implementation of its policy to private parties. Because the Fourteenth Amendment does not countenance such a division of power and responsibility, I respectfully dissent.

NOTES

1. *The state as defendant?* Professor Alexander analyzes *Flagg Bros.* as follows:

> First, even if there *is* always state action, it does not follow that the *defendant* is a state actor subject to constitutional duties. New York may have violated Mrs. Brooks's constitutional rights through its laws permitting Flagg Brothers to sell her goods and pass good title to them.

> It doesn't follow, however, that Flagg Brothers violated any constitutional duty to her: the constitutional duty may run only from New York.

Lawrence Alexander, *The Public/Private Distinction And Constitutional Limitations on Private Power,* 10 CONST. COMM. 361, 364 (1993). Should Mrs. Brooks have sued the state of New York instead of Flagg Brothers? Is it possible, *contra* Professor Alexander, that the courts would rule there was still no state action? Why?

2. ***State authorization.*** After *Flagg Bros.,* what remains of the line of cases suggesting that state actions encouraging or authorizing private conduct might be subject to constitutional restraints? Should state creation or acknowledgement of a legal right, i.e., a permissive law, constitute state action? If the state grants a driver's license, should the driver's subsequent actions on the road be deemed state action? A positivist might argue that rights exist only by reason of state recognition. Is every exercise of a property right state action? *See* Paul Brest, *State Action and Liberal Theory: A Casenote on Flagg Brothers v. Brooks,* 130 U. PA. L. REV. 1296 (1982). Consider the following:

> The simplistic dichotomy of "compulsion" and "mere acquiescence" renders the state encouragement doctrine meaningless because the cases addressed by the doctrine are precisely those where the private act is not directly compelled by the state. In these cases, the Court should broadly consider the effect of the state's laws on the system of private relationships and the pattern of private actions, rather than make everything depend on the search for some decisive direct connection between the state and the specific private act that is at issue.

The Supreme Court, 1977 Term, 92 HARV. L. REV. at 129–30. Did the statute alter the relations of the parties?

Professor Alan Madry contends that "*Flagg Brothers* represents the Burger-Rehnquist Court's hostility to the Warren court's restriction of creditor's remedies under the Due Process Clause." Alan R. Madry, *State Action and the Due Process Clause of Self-help; Flagg Brothers Redux,* 62 U. PITT. L. REV. 1, 9 (2000). More specifically, he says it was Justice Rehnquist's challenge in *Flag Brothers* "to characterize the effect of the statute in a way so that it does not bestow the mantle of state action on the private conduct." By so doing, Madry argues, Rehnquist "can avoid addressing the legitimacy of the statute." Professor Madry concludes: "[Justice Rehnquist] characterizes the effect of the statute in such a way that the statute itself is not state action. He is thus able not only to dismiss the action against the private defendant, but also to insulate the state from scrutiny." *Id.* at 17. Assuming that Professor Madry's analysis is correct, why does Justice Rehnquist want to insulate the state from judicial scrutiny?

3. ***State Action and the privatization movement.*** Chief Justice Rehnquist had left open the question whether "a city or State might be free to delegate to private parties the performance of [its] functions and thereby avoid the strictures of the Fourteenth Amendment." Professor Barak-Erez confronts this issue in the context of privatization whereby government contracts with private entities to perform previously governmental functions. She argues that existing state action doctrine does not reach privatized services:

> [Under] the public function theory, most [privatized] services were not "traditionally and exclusively" reserved to the state. [Under] the nexus theory, privatization will usually not result in a financially symbiotic relationship between the state and the private actor. The government will probably license and regulate it and even buy its services, but not gain a pecuniary profit (as in *Burton*).

Daphne Barak-Erez, *A State Action Doctrine for an Age of Privatization,* 45 SYRACUSE L. REV. 1169 (1995).

4. *"Self-help" remedies before and after* Flagg Brothers. In *Sniadach v. Family Fin. Corp.*, 395 U.S. 337 (1969), and *Fuentes v. Shevin*, 407 U.S. 67 (1972), the Court found that the requirements of procedural due process applied to state statutory schemes permitting garnishment of an employee's wages without notice, and summary seizure of goods or chattels in a person's possession under a writ of replevin. In both cases the creditor was required to enlist the aid of a representative of the state, and in both cases the Court held that the statutory procedures provided inadequate protection to the debtors' property interest. The majority opinion in *Flagg Bros.* found these cases distinguishable because of the "total absence of overt official involvement" in *Flagg Bros.*

In *Lugar v. Edmondson Oil Co.*, 457 U.S. 922 (1982), the Court found the requisite state involvement to satisfy the state action doctrine. The case arose when Edmondson Oil Company sued in Virginia state court to collect a debt owed by Lugar, a truck stop operator. Pursuant to state law, Edmondson sought prejudgment attachment of certain of Lugar's property by alleging, in an *ex parte* petition, a belief that the property might be disposed of in order to defeat creditors. Acting on this petition, a clerk of the state court issued a writ of attachment which was executed by the county sheriff. This effectively sequestered petitioner Lugar's property, although it remained in his possession. A subsequent hearing resulted in the attachment being dismissed twenty-four days after the levy because Edmondson failed to establish the statutory grounds for attachment alleged in the petition. A suit for damages caused by the interim restraint on the property followed.

Justice White, writing for the Court, held that the defendants, "private parties, may be appropriately categorized as 'state actors.' " because of the "joint participation" between the private parties and state officials. "[W]e have consistently held that a private party's joint participation with state officials in the seizure of disputed property is sufficient to characterize that party as a 'state actor' for purposes of the Fourteenth Amendment. [T]he Court of Appeals erred in holding that in this context 'joint participation' required something more than invoking the aid of state officials to take advantage of state-created attachment procedures. [W]hatever may be true in other contexts, this is sufficient when the state has created a system whereby state officials will attach property on the *ex parte* application of one party to a private dispute."

Why is there state action in *Lugar* but not *Flagg Bros.*? Perhaps it is the involvement of a state official in *Lugar,* even though acting in a purely ministerial role, that accounts for the difference. While the state is not a partner to private acts merely because it permits or licenses them, when it takes action to assist the private action, it assumes added responsibility, analogous to liability for acts of omission versus commission.

5. *The role of law in defining rights.* In reexamining the modern viability of the state action concept, consider the argument that "since any private action acquiesced in by the state can be seen to derive its power from the state which is free to withdraw its authorization at will, positivism potentially implicates the state in every 'private' action not prohibited by law." Paul Brest, *State Action and Liberal Theory: A Casenote on Flagg Brothers v. Brooks* 130 U. Pa. L. Rev. at 1301. "The [state action] doctrine has seldom been used to shelter citizens from coercive federal or judicial power. More often, it has been employed to protect the autonomy of business enterprises against the claims of consumers, minorities, and other relatively powerless citizens." *Id.* at 1330.

6. *Peremptory challenges.* Private litigants in civil cases may not use peremptory challenges to exclude jurors because of race. Exclusion in such circumstances violates the equal protection clause. These holdings depend on first holding that race-based peremptory challenges constitute state action. In *Edmonson v. Leesville Concrete Co.*, 500 U.S. 614 (1991), Justice Kennedy held that state action was present under the standards of *Lugar v. Edmondson Oil Co.*. First, the constitutional deprivation had its source in government authority since peremptory challenges were authorized by statute. Second, the private actor must be viewed as a government actor because "peremptory challenges have no utility outside the jury system," which is established and administered by government and government officials. In addition, when government permits racial discrimination to occur in a court-house, "racial exclusion in this official forum compounds the racial insult inherent in judging a citizen by the color of his or her skin."

In *Georgia v. McCollum*, 505 U.S. 42 (1992), the Court held per Justice Blackmun that the exercise by a criminal defendant of racially discriminatory peremptory challenges constitutes state action which violates the Equal Protection Clause. Relying on *Lugar* once again, the Court noted that peremptory challenges were authorized by state law, and that they perform a traditional government function — the selection of an impartial trier of fact. When the government confers on a private actor the power to choose a "quintessential governmental body" — the jury, the private actor is bound by the constitutional requirement of racial neutrality. The criminal defendant hoped to escape this conclusion because of the adverse relationship between the government and the defendant in a criminal prosecution. But the Court rejected this contention:

> [T]he fact that a defendant exercises a peremptory challenge to further his interest in acquittal does not conflict with a finding of state action. Whenever a private actor's conduct is deemed "fairly attributable" to the government, it is likely that private motives will have animated the actor's decision.

Professor Sidney Buchanan suggests a common sense approach to the exclusivity test: "*Terry, Marsh, and Edmonson* are relatively easy [public function] cases; *Logan Valley, Jackson, Flagg Bros., Rendell-Baker, and Blum* are more difficult cases. In all these cases, however, public function analysis requires a probing, fact specific inquiry that is not hobbled by the rigid confines of the exclusivity test. Indeed, viewed factually there is a self-defeating circularity to the exclusivity test: if a particular activity is literally the exclusive function of government, observation should reveal no private actor engaging in that activity. Of course, those Justices applying the exclusivity test do not mean it in that literal sense. What they really mean is that the activity in question is so uniquely governmental in nature that even in the 'rare' instances in which the activity is delegated to a private actor, it is still, for constitutional purposes, being performed by government." Professor Buchman concludes that the "fundamental inquiry" should be whether "the challenged activity [is] of such a nature that no private person or entity should be permitted to perform it free of the constraints of the Constitution." Sidney Buchanan, *A Conceptual History of the State Action Doctrine: The Search for Government Responsibility*, 34 HOUSTON L. REV. 333, 761–762 (1997).

8. *"Amateur" athletics.* In *San Francisco Arts & Athletics, Inc. v. United States Olympic Comm.*, 483 U.S. 522 (1987), the Court found no state action in the Olympic Committee's securing of an injunction against use of the word "Olympic" in the defendant's "Gay Olympic Games." A provision of the Amateur Sports Act of 1978, 36 U.S.C. § 371-96, authorized the Olympic Committee to prohibit most commercial and promotional uses of the word "Olympic." This protection differs from normal trademark protection in that the Olympic Committee need not prove that a contested use is likely to cause confusion, and an unauthorized user of the word does not have available the normal statutory defenses. After deciding that the statute's grant of the exclusive use of the word did not violate the First Amendment, Justice Powell, speaking for the Court, rejected the argument that the Olympic Committee's enforcement of its statutory right was discriminatory in violation of the Fifth Amendment:

> The fact that Congress granted it a corporate charter does not render the USOC a government agent. This Court has also found action to be governmental action when the challenged entity performs functions that have been "traditionally the *exclusive* prerogative" of the Federal Government. Neither the conduct nor the coordination of amateur sports has been a traditional governmental function. The USOC's choice of how to enforce its exclusive right to use the word "Olympic" simply is not a governmental decision.

Justice O'Connor, joined by Justice Blackmun, dissented on the state action question, expressing the belief that "the United States Olympic Committee and the United States are joint participants in the challenged activity and as such are subject to the equal protection provisions of the Fifth Amendment." 483 U.S. at 548. Justice Brennan, joined by Justice Blackmun, also dissented, relying in part on *Evans v. Newton.* Can *San Francisco Arts & Athletics* be distinguished from *Evans*?

***National Collegiate Athletic Ass'n v. Tarkanian*, 488 U.S. 179 (1988).** The Court, per Justice Stevens, held that a state university's imposition of disciplinary sanctions against its basketball coach, Jerry Tarkanian, in compliance with NCAA rules and recommendations, did not transform the NCAA's otherwise private conduct into state action. Therefore, the NCAA could not be held liable for a violation of the coach's civil rights.

After a lengthy investigation of allegedly improper recruiting practices at the University of Nevada at Las Vegas (UNLV), a state university, the NCAA's Committee on Infractions found 38 violations, including 10 by Tarkanian, the school's basketball coach. The Committee imposed a number of sanctions upon UNLV and requested that it show cause why additional penalties should not be imposed if it failed to suspend Tarkanian from its athletic program during a probation period.

Tarkanian contended that the NCAA was a "state actor" because UNLV delegated authority to the NCAA "to adopt rules governing UNLV's athletic programs and to enforce those rules on behalf of UNLV."

Justice Stevens pointed out that this case was backwards from most.

> In the typical case raising a state action issue, a private party has taken the decisive step that caused the harm to the plaintiff, and the question is whether the State was sufficiently involved to treat the decisive conduct as state action. Thus, in the usual case we ask whether the State provided a mantle of authority that enhanced the power of the harm-causing individual actor.
>
> Here the final act challenged by Tarkanian—his suspension—was committed by UNLV. A state university without question is a state actor. Clearly, UNLV's conduct was influenced by the rules and recommendations of the NCAA, the private party. But it was UNLV, the state entity, that actually suspended Tarkanian. Thus, the question is not whether UNLV participated to a critical extent in the NCAA's activities, but whether UNLV's actions in compliance with NCAA rules and recommendations turned the NCAA's conduct into state action.
>
> In *Bates v. State Bar of Arizona* [p. 1177], we established that the State Supreme Court's enforcement of disciplinary rules transgressed by members of its own state bar was state action. Those rules had been adopted *in toto* from the American Bar Association Code of Professional Responsibility. It does not follow, however, that the ABA's formulation of those disciplinary rules was state action. The State Supreme Court retained plenary power to reexamine those standards, and if necessary, to reject them and promulgate its own. So here; . . . Neither UNLV's decision to adopt the NCAA's standards nor its minor role in their formulation is a sufficient reason for concluding that the NCAA was acting under color of Nevada law when it promulgated standards governing athlete recruitment, eligibility, and academic performance.

The Court declared, contrary to Tarkanian's contention, that "UNLV delegated no power to the NCAA to take specific action against any University employee. The commitment by UNLV to adhere to NCAA enforcement procedures was enforceable only by sanctions that the NCAA might impose on UNLV itself."

Justice White, joined by Justices Brennan, Marshall, and O'Connor, dissented: "The question here is whether the NCAA acted jointly with UNLV in suspending Tarkanian and thereby also became a state actor. I would hold that it did." Justice White pointed out that it was the NCAA's findings that Tarkanian had violated NCAA rules "made at NCAA-conducted hearings, all of which were agreed to by Tarkanian's suspension by UNLV." On these facts, Justice White concluded that "the NCAA was 'jointly engaged with [UNLV] officials in the challenged action,' and therefore was a state actor."

***Brentwood Academy v. Tennessee Secondary School Athletic Association*, 531 U.S. 288 (2001).** Does the Tennessee Secondary School Athletic Association, a non-profit statewide athletic association, which regulates interscholastic sports among Tennessee public and private high schools engage in state action when it enforces one of its rules against a member school? In an era when the Supreme Court has been reluctant to characterize the activities of private entities as governmental, the Court's surprising answer, 5-4, was, "Yes." The Association ruled that Brentwood Academy, a private parochial secondary school, violated its rules barring its member schools from using "undue influence" in recruiting athletes. In this case, the "undue influence" was writing to incoming students and their parents concerning spring football practice.

Brentwood Academy sued the association under 42 U.S.C. Sec. 1983 contending that enforcement of the rules was unconstitutional state action in violation of the First and Fourteenth Amendments. Justice Souter for the Court declared that state action may be found "if, though only if, there is such a close 'nexus between the state and the challenged action' that seemingly private behavior 'may be fairly treated as that of the state itself.' " *Tarkanian* was distinguished because Court had not viewed the NCAA as a surrogate for a single state. The NCAA's policies were shaped not by Nevada or its state university but by several hundred member institutions having no connection with Nevada. *Tarkanian* itself however, dictated a different result when all an association's members, as here, were located within the same state and when most of the members were public institutions, i.e., public high schools, established by a single state.

Justice Souter declared for the Court:

> In sum, to the extent of 84% of its membership, the Association is an organization of public schools represented by their officials acting in their official capacity to provide an integral element of secondary public schooling. There would be no recognizable association, legal or tangible, without the public school officials, who do not entirely control but overwhelmingly perform all but the purely ministerial acts by which the Association exists and functions in practical terms. Only the 16% minority of private school memberships prevents this

> entwinement of the Association and the public school system from being total and their identities totally indistinguishable.
>
> To complement the entwinement of public school officials with the Association from the bottom up, the State of Tennessee has provided for entwinement from top down. State Board members are assigned ex officio to serve as members of the board of control and legislative council [of the Association], and the Association's ministerial employees are treated as state employees to the extent of being eligible for membership in the state retirement system.
>
> The entwinement down from the State Board is therefore unmistakable, just as the entwinement up from the member public schools is overwhelming. Entwinement will support a conclusion that an ostensibly private organization ought to be charged with a public character and judged by constitutional standards; entwinement to the degree shown here requires it.

The Court denied that its ruling would "trigger an epidemic of unprecedented federal litigation" and noted that, other than the Sixth Circuit below, "every Court of Appeals to consider a statewide athletic association like the one here has found it to be a state actor." The Court found state action to exist and held that "Brentwood properly names the association as a Sec. 1983 defendant." The Court did not pass on the substantive merits of Brentwood's 1983 claim and remanded the matter to the court below.

Justice Thomas, joined by Rehnquist, Scalia and Kennedy, dissented:

> Because the majority never defines "entwinement," the scope of its holding is unclear. If we are fortunate, the majority's fact-specific analysis will have little bearing beyond this case. But if the majority's new entwinement test develops in future years, it could affect many organizations that foster activities, enforce rules, and sponsor extracurricular competition among high schools—not just in athletics but in such diverse areas as agriculture, mathematics, music, marching bands, forensics and cheerleading. Indeed, this entwinement test may extend to other organizations that are composed of, or controlled by, public officials or public entities, such as firefighters, policemen, teachers, cities, or counties. I am not prepared to say that any private organization that permits public entities and public officials to participate acts as the State in anything or everything it does, and our state-action jurisprudence has never reached that far.

Professor Erwin Chemerinsky asks whether *Brentwood* has created a new and broader exception to the Supreme Court's state action doctrine: "Justice Souter does not use the traditional term in state action cases, 'entanglement,' in his majority opinion, but uses instead the word 'entwinement.' 'Entanglement,' in prior cases like *Rendell-Baker v. Kohn*, had been found to require government encouragement of constitutional violations by private actors. But no encouragement was found in *Brentwood*. Instead, the Court found that significant government involvement with the private entity was sufficient for a finding of state action. This seems to be a much more expansive exception to the state action doctrine than that found in prior cases but the exception is not defined." Erwin Chemerinsky, *The Rhetoric of Constitutional Law*, 100 Mich. L. Rev. 2008, 2024-25 (2002). How would you define the Court's new "entwinement" exception? When does it apply?

[B] "SIGNIFICANT STATE INVOLVEMENT"

Under the "public function" theory, seemingly private action is deemed to be that of the state, either because it so closely parallels traditional state authority in nature or degree of power or because it derives ultimately from the state itself. A somewhat more viable theory of state action, under current doctrinal standards, is the so-called "state involvement" theory. Under this model, private conduct is deemed state action when that conduct is significantly facilitated, supported or encouraged by the state. As will be seen, however, this theory, too, is in a state of both practical and theoretical uncertainty.

SHELLEY v. KRAEMER
334 U.S. 1, 68 S. Ct. 836, 92 L. Ed. 1161 (1948)

Chief Justice Vinson delivered the opinion of the Court.

These cases present for our consideration questions concerning the validity of court enforcement of private agreements, generally described as restrictive covenants, which have as their purpose the exclusion of persons of designated race or color from the ownership or occupancy of real property. On August 11, 1945, pursuant to a contract of sale, petitioners Shelley, who are Negroes, for valuable consideration received from one Fitzgerald a warranty deed to the parcel in question. The trial court found that petitioners had no actual knowledge of the restrictive agreement at the time of the purchase. On October 9, 1945, respondents, as owners of other property subject to the terms of the restrictive covenant, brought suit in the Circuit Court of the city of St. Louis praying that petitioners Shelley be restrained from taking possession of the property and that judgment be entered divesting title out of petitioners Shelley and revesting title in the immediate grantor or in such other person as the court should direct. The trial court denied the requested relief on the ground that the restrictive agreement, upon which respondents based their action, had never become final and complete because it was the intention of the parties to that agreement that it was not to become effective until signed by all property owners in the district, and signatures of all the owners had never been obtained. The Supreme Court of Missouri sitting *en banc* reversed and directed the trial court to grant the relief for which respondents had prayed. That court held the agreement effective and concluded that enforcement of its provisions violated no rights guaranteed to petitioners by the Federal Constitution. At the time the court rendered its decision, petitioners were occupying the property in question.

[T]he present cases, do not involve action by state legislatures or city councils. Here the particular patterns of discrimination and the areas in which the restrictions are to operate, are determined, in the first instance, by the terms of agreements among private individuals. Participation of the State consists in the enforcement of the restrictions so defined. The crucial issue with which we are here confronted is whether this distinction removes these cases from the operation of the prohibitory provisions of the Fourteenth Amendment.

Since the decision of this Court in the *Civil Rights Cases,* the principle has become firmly embedded in our constitutional law that the action inhibited by the first section of the Fourteenth Amendment is only such action as may fairly be said to be that of the States. That Amendment erects no shield against merely private conduct, however discriminatory or wrongful. We conclude, therefore, that the restrictive agreements standing alone cannot be regarded as a violation of any rights guaranteed to petitioners by the Fourteenth Amendment. So long as the purposes of those agreements are effectuated by voluntary adherence to their terms, it would appear clear that there has been no action by the State and the provisions of the Amendment have not been violated.

But here there was more. These are cases in which the purposes of the agreements were secured only by judicial enforcement by state courts of the restrictive terms of the agreements. The respondents urge that judicial enforcement of private agreements does not amount to state action; or, in any event, the participation of the State is so attenuated in character as not to amount to state action within the meaning of the Fourteenth Amendment. We have no doubt that there has been state action in these cases in the full and complete sense of the phrase. The undisputed facts disclose that petitioners were willing purchasers of properties upon which they desired to establish homes. The owners of the properties were willing sellers; and contracts of sale were accordingly consummated. It is clear that but for the active intervention of the state courts, supported by the full panoply of state power, petitioners would have been free to occupy the properties in question without restraint.

These are not cases, as has been suggested, in which the States have merely abstained from action, leaving private individuals free to impose such discriminations as they see fit. Rather, these are cases in which the States have made available to such individuals the full coercive power of government to deny to petitioners, on the grounds of race or color, the enjoyment of property rights in premises which petitioners are willing and financially able to acquire and which the grantors are willing to sell. The difference between judicial enforcement and non-enforcement of the restrictive covenants is the difference to petitioners between being denied rights of property available to other members of the community and being accorded full enjoyment of those rights on an equal footing.

The enforcement of the restrictive agreements by the state courts in these cases was directed pursuant to the common-law policy of the States as formulated by those courts in earlier decisions. The judicial action in each case bears the clear and unmistakable imprimatur of the State. We have noted that previous decisions of this Court have established the proposition that judicial action is not immunized from the operation of the Fourteenth Amendment simply because it is taken pursuant to the state's common-law policy. Nor is the Amendment ineffective simply because the particular pattern of discrimination, which the State has enforced, was defined initially by the terms of a private agreement. State action, as that phrase is understood for the purpose of the Fourteenth Amendment, refers to exertions of state power in all forms. And when the effect of that action is to deny rights subject to the protection of the Fourteenth Amendment, it is the obligation of this Court to enforce the constitutional commands.

We hold that in granting judicial enforcement of the restrictive agreements in these cases, the States have denied petitioners the equal protection of the laws and that, therefore, the action of the state courts cannot stand. We have noted that freedom from discrimination by the States in the enjoyment of property rights was among the basic objectives sought to be effectuated by the framers of the Fourteenth Amendment. That such discrimination has occurred in these cases is clear. Because of the race or color of these petitioners they have been denied rights of ownership or occupancy enjoyed as a matter of course by other citizens of different race or color.

JUSTICE REED, JUSTICE JACKSON, and JUSTICE RUTLEDGE took no part in the consideration or decision of these cases.

NOTES

1. *Limited Scope of Shelley.* Professor John Fee has called attention to the limited scope that has been accorded to *Shelley*: "The problem with taking [the] rationale of [*Shelley*] too far is that all private rights and background principles of law depend upon the judiciary for enforcement. Although *Shelley* has never been overruled, the Supreme Court has often conspicuously ignored it, leading some to conclude that it has been limited to its facts." John Fee, *The Formal State Action Doctrine and Free Speech Analysis*, 83 N. CAR. L. REV. 569, 580 (2005). Professor Fee describes three modes of state action analysis—"the conventional approach, the formal approach, and the balancing approach." He contends that each asks a different question: "The conventional approach asks, 'is there state action?' but must take a flexible view of what counts as state action. The formal approach asks, 'what is the nature of the state action and is it constitutional?' The balancing approach disregards the state action inquiry altogether and asks instead, 'whose interests weigh more?' " *Id.* at 602. Would the result in *Shelley* be the same under all three of the foregoing approaches?

2. *Significance of Shelley*. *Shelley v. Kraemer* held at least that racially discriminatory restrictive covenants in deeds were not judicially enforceable. Because the restrictive covenants involved in *Shelley* had been entered into by private persons, *Shelley* could have sounded the death knell for any state action requirement that government officials initiate or perform the discriminatory act. After all, private persons had placed restrictive covenants in deeds under the fact pattern of the *Shelley* case. But if *Shelley* meant that state action existed whenever state law could be used to enforce private discriminatory conduct, then the state action limitation would be virtually abandoned.

Shelley presented the courts with a dramatic choice between competing constitutional ideas: liberty (the right of private persons to act even in a discriminatory fashion for whatever reason) versus equality (the right of persons to have access to the ordinary activities and opportunities of life free of discrimination).

The conflict between these warring constitutional values raised questions which would prove to be major themes in the constitutional litigation of the 1950s and 1960s. If a country club excluded members of minority groups, did *Shelley* mean that the club would not be able to use the courts to eject those whom it deemed unwelcome? If a restaurant refused to serve blacks, did *Shelley* mean that the state trespass laws could not be used to remove and prosecute blacks who demanded service against the will of the ownership? If the answers to these questions were in the affirmative, then the public accommodations provisions of the Civil Rights Act of 1964 would have been unnecessary.

Lawrence Alexander, *Cutting the Gordian Knot: State Action and Self-Help Repossession,* 2 Hastings Const. L.Q. 893, 893–94 (1975), argues that "the search for state action is a fundamentally misguided quest. State action is present in every lawsuit because the laws of the state are being applied. Indeed, as *Shelley v. Kraemer* correctly suggested, state action is present wherever a relationship has legal consequences."

3. *Discrimination and state action.* Professor Pollak contended that *Shelley* only prevented the use of judicial process to enforce private discrimination against parties who did not wish to discriminate. *Shelley,* after all, involved a willing buyer and a willing seller; it did not speak at all of the unwilling seller. Louis Pollak, *Racial Discrimination and Judicial Integrity: A Reply to Professor Wechsler,* 108 U. Pa. L. Rev. 1, 13 (1959). Does this distinction help to answer the problems raised above with respect to the scope of *Shelley*? Is Pollak's distinction one which Fourteenth Amendment analysis demands? Is it a distinction which Chief Justice Vinson's opinion in *Shelley* will support?

4. *Baconsfield revisited.* Following the Court's decision in *Evans v. Newton,* p. 1498, the Georgia courts decided that if Senator Bacon couldn't have a white-only park, he wouldn't want any park at all. The bequest of the land for a public park in Senator Bacon's will thus failed, and the trust property reverted under Georgia law to the heirs of Senator Bacon. The Supreme Court, in *Evans v. Abney*, 396 U.S. 435 (1970), per Justice Black, held that this determination by the Georgia Supreme Court did not violate the equal protection guarantee. "Any harshness" from the Georgia court's decisions "can be attributed solely to its intention to effectuate as nearly as possible the explicit terms of Senator Bacon's will." The Georgia courts had merely given effect to the relevant trust laws: "[T]he Constitution imposes no requirement upon the Georgia Court to approach Bacon's will any differently than it would approach any will creating any charitable trust of any kind." *Shelley v. Kraemer* was distinguished: "Here the effect of the Georgia decision eliminated all discrimination against Negroes in the park by eliminating the park itself, and the termination of the park was a loss shared equally by the white and Negro citizens of Macon."

Justice Brennan dissented: "When it is as starkly clear as it is in this case that a public facility would remain open but for the constitutional command that it be operated on a non-segregated basis, the closing of that facility conveys an unambiguous message of community involvement in racial discrimination." He also cited *Shelley v. Kraemer* as providing grounds for finding state action: "Nothing in the record suggests that after our decision in *Evans v. Newton* the City of Macon retracted its previous willingness to manage Baconsfield on a non-segregated basis, or that the white beneficiaries of Senator Bacon's generosity were unwilling to share it with Negroes, rather than have the park revert to his heirs." Thus, even under the more restrictive interpretation of *Shelley,* "this is a case of a state court's enforcement of a racial restriction to prevent willing parties from dealing with one another." Justice Douglas also dissented.

It might fairly be asked whether the difference between Justices Black and Brennan has to do with state action or with the question of what constitutes racial discrimination.

5. *Sit-ins and enforcement of trespass laws.* One of the foremost battlegrounds of the 1960s was the use of the "sit-in" to open up segregated lunch counters and restaurants. This occasion for wrestling with the state action problem arose within the very center of Fourteenth Amendment protection, the securement of legal equality for African-Americans. During the "sit-ins" of the 1960s, African-American protesters throughout the South took seats at "whites only" restaurants and lunch counters and remained in their seats until arrested when the owners called the police. Arrest and prosecution of the demonstrators was based on violation of state trespass laws. Fundamental constitutional questions soon arose. Could police and state courts enforce criminal trespass laws designed to protect against breach of the peace when the consequences of the state enforcement of the trespass laws led to perpetuation of a social system based on racial segregation? Arguably, the state courts were only enforcing the trespass laws rather than racial discrimination. Was prosecution under the trespass laws permitted by *Shelley*?

Discrimination in privately owned facilities, the argument ran, was the act of private persons and therefore as private action, it was beyond the reach of constitutional command. The Supreme Court skillfully sought to avoid the issue of whether a pattern of private racial discrimination was to be permitted to rely on judicial enforcement of the trespass laws for its sanction. Perhaps *Shelley* should or could have been expanded to prohibit judicial enforcement of the trespass laws in these circumstances. The Court declined to move in that direction. Instead, it struggled to find state action in the initial discrimination.

In *Peterson v. Greenville*, 373 U.S. 244 (1963), a "sit-in" conviction was reversed on the ground that a city ordinance required separation of the races in restaurants. Therefore, the requisite state involvement was present. In *Lombard v. Louisiana*, 373 U.S. 267 (1963), another "sit-in" conviction was reversed on the basis that the separation of the races in that case was instigated by the oral command of city officials. Justice Harlan dissented in *Lombard,* objecting that "announcements of the Police Superintendent and the Mayor cannot well be compared with a city ordinance commanding segregated eating facilities." What is the difference between a mayor's announcement and a city ordinance in terms of state action analysis?

In *Bell v. Maryland*, 378 U.S. 226 (1964), the decision by a restaurant owner not to serve blacks was in no sense state compelled. But intervening state legislation prohibiting discrimination in public accommodations again made it possible for the Court to dodge the question. Several opinions filed in the

Bell case, however, dealt with the constitutional issues. Certainly one of the most interesting opinions, because it revisited the debate between Justice Bradley and the first Justice Harlan concerning the purpose of the Fourteenth Amendment, was a long concurring opinion filed by Justice Goldberg in which Warren and Douglas joined.

Justice Goldberg pointed out that the congressional debates on the Fourteenth Amendment illustrated a congressional desire to grant "civil rights" to the emancipated African-Americans. He contended that civil rights "certainly included the right of access to places of public accommodation for these were most clearly places and areas of life where the relations of men were traditionally regulated by governments." Goldberg believed that it was an implied assumption of Justice Bradley's opinion in the *Civil Rights Cases* that a state could not apply its statutes or common law "to deny rather than to protect the right of access to public accommodations."

The enactment of the Civil Rights Act of 1964, 42 U.S.C. §§ 2000a–2000h (1964), mooted the controversy over the use of state trespass laws to enforce racial discrimination in public accommodations involved in interstate commerce as defined by the Act. The constitutional basis of the Civil Rights Act of 1964, however, was predicated on the federal commerce power rather than under § 5 of the Fourteenth Amendment. See Chapter 2.

6. *Reitman v. Mulkey,* 387 U.S. 369 (1967). The Supreme Court invalidated Article I, Section 26 of the California Constitution, which had been adopted as an initiative in a statewide ballot in 1964. The section provided:

> Neither the State nor any subdivision or agency thereof shall deny, limit or abridge, directly or indirectly, the right of any person, who is willing or desires to sell, lease or rent any part or all of his real property, to decline to sell, lease or rent such property to such person or persons as he, in his absolute discretion, chooses.

The real property covered by section 26 was limited to residential property and contained an exception for state-owned real estate. The state supreme court had invalidated the provision as an equal protection violation, and the Supreme Court, in an opinion by Justice White, agreed:

> This Court has never attempted the "impossible task" of formulating an infallible test for determining whether the State "in any of its manifestations" has become significantly involved in private discriminations. "Only by sifting the facts and weighing the circumstances" on a case-to-case basis can a "nonobvious involvement of the State in private conduct be attributed its true significance." Here, the California court, armed as it was with the knowledge of the facts and circumstances concerning the passage and potential impact of § 26, and familiar with the milieu in which that provision would operate, has determined that the provision would involve the State in private racial discriminations to an unconstitutional degree. We accept this holding of the California court.
>
> Here we are dealing with a provision which does not just repeal an existing law forbidding private racial discriminations. Section 26 was

intended to authorize, and does authorize, racial discrimination in the housing market. The right to discriminate is now one of the basic policies of the State.

Justice Harlan, joined by Justices Black, Clark and Stewart, dissented:

The Court attempts to fit § 26 within the coverage of the Equal Protection Clause by characterizing it as in effect an affirmative call to residents of California to discriminate. The main difficulty with this viewpoint is that it depends upon a characterization of § 26 that cannot fairly be made.

The provision is neutral on its face, and it is only by in effect asserting that this requirement of passive official neutrality is camouflage that the Court is able to reach its conclusion.

BURTON v. WILMINGTON PARKING AUTHORITY

365 U.S. 715, 81 S. Ct. 856, 6 L. Ed. 2d 45 (1961)

[A restaurant located within an off-street automobile parking building in Wilmington, Delaware, refused to serve Burton food or drink solely because he was an African-American. The building was owned and operated by the Wilmington Parking Authority, which is a Delaware state agency. The restaurant, Eagle Coffee Shoppe, Inc., was a lessee of the Parking Authority. Burton sought declaratory and injunctive relief against the Parking Authority. The Wilmington Parking Authority made long-term leases with tenants for commercial use of some of the space available. Eagle's lease with the Authority did not require that its restaurant services be made available to the general public on a nondiscriminatory basis.

[The Delaware Supreme Court held that the coffee shop was acting in a private capacity and that its action was not that of the Authority, and that, therefore, the Fourteenth Amendment had not been violated. Eagle's action did not constitute state action according to the Delaware Supreme Court.]

JUSTICE CLARK delivered the opinion of the Court.

It is clear, as it always has been since the *Civil Rights Cases,* that "individual invasion of individual rights is not the subject matter of the amendment," and that private conduct abridging individual rights does no violence to the Equal Protection Clause unless to some significant extent the State in any of its manifestations has been found to have become involved in it. Because the virtue of the right to equal protection of the laws could lie only in the breadth of its application, its constitutional assurance was reserved in terms whose imprecision was necessary if the right were to be enjoyed in the variety of individual-state relationships which the Amendment was designed to embrace. For the same reason, to fashion and apply a precise formula for recognition of state responsibility under the Equal Protection Clause is "an impossible task" which "this Court has never attempted." Only by sifting facts and weighing circumstances can the nonobvious involvement of the State in private conduct be attributed its true significance.

[T]he Delaware Supreme Court seems to have placed controlling emphasis on its conclusion, as to the accuracy of which there is doubt, that only some 15% of the total cost of the facility was "advanced" from public funds; that the cost of the entire facility was allocated three-fifths to the space for commercial leasing and two-fifths to parking space; that anticipated revenue from parking was only some 30.5% of the total income, the balance of which was expected to be earned by the leasing; that the Authority had no original intent to place a restaurant in the building, it being only a happenstance resulting from the bidding; that Eagle expended considerable moneys on furnishings; that the restaurant's main and marked public entrance is on Ninth Street without any public entrance direct from the parking area; and that "the only connection Eagle has with the public facility is the furnishing of the sum of $28,700 annually in the form of rent which is used by the Authority to defray a portion of the operating expense of an otherwise unprofitable enterprise." While these factual considerations are indeed validly accountable aspects of the enterprise upon which the State has embarked, we cannot say that they lead inescapably to the conclusion that state action is not present. Their persuasiveness is diminished when evaluated in the context of other factors which must be acknowledged.

The land and building were publicly owned. As an entity, the building was dedicated to "public uses" in performance of the Authority's "essential governmental functions." The costs of land acquisition, construction, and maintenance are defrayed entirely from donations by the City of Wilmington, from loans and revenue bonds and from the proceeds of rentals and parking services out of which the loans and bonds were payable. Assuming that the distinction would be significant, the commercially leased areas were not surplus state property, but constituted a physically and financially integral and, indeed, indispensable part of the State's plan to operate its project as a self-sustaining unit. Upkeep and maintenance of the building, including necessary repairs, were responsibilities of the Authority and were payable out of public funds. It cannot be doubted that the peculiar relationship of the restaurant to the parking facility in which it is located confers on each an incidental variety of mutual benefits. Guests of the restaurant are afforded a convenient place to park their automobiles, even if they cannot enter the restaurant directly from the parking area. Similarly, its convenience for diners may well provide additional demand for the Authority's parking facilities. Should any improvements effected in the leasehold by Eagle become part of the realty, there is no possibility of increased taxes being passed on to it since the fee is held by a tax-exempt government agency. Neither can it be ignored, especially in view of Eagle's affirmative allegation that for it to serve Negroes would injure its business, that profits earned by discrimination not only contribute to, but are indispensable elements in the financial success of a governmental agency.

Addition of all these activities, obligations and responsibilities of the Authority, the benefits mutually conferred, together with the obvious fact that the restaurant is operated as an integral part of a public building devoted to a public parking service, indicates that degree of state participation and involvement in discriminatory action which it was the design of the Fourteenth Amendment to condemn. It is irony amounting to grave injustice that in one part of a single building, erected and maintained with public funds by an agency of the State to serve a public purpose, all persons have equal rights, while in another portion, also serving the public, a Negro is a second-class citizen, offensive because of his race, without rights and unentitled to service, but at the same time fully enjoys equal access to nearby restaurants in wholly privately owned buildings. As the Chancellor pointed out, in its lease with Eagle the Authority could have affirmatively required Eagle to discharge the responsibilities under the Fourteenth Amendment imposed upon the private enterprise as a consequence of state participation. But no State may effectively abdicate its responsibilities by either ignoring them or by merely failing to discharge them whatever the motive may be. It is of no consolation to an individual denied the equal protection of the laws that it was done in good faith. Certainly the conclusions drawn in similar cases by the various Courts of Appeals do not depend upon such a distinction. By its inaction, the Authority, and through it the State, has not only made itself a party to the refusal of service, but has elected to place its power, property and prestige behind the admitted discrimination. The State has so far insinuated itself into a position of interdependence with Eagle that it must be recognized as a joint participant in the challenged activity, which, on that account, cannot be considered to have been so "purely private" as to fall without the scope of the Fourteenth Amendment.

Because readily applicable formulae may not be fashioned, the conclusions drawn from the facts and circumstances of this record are by no means declared as universal truths on the basis of which every state leasing agreement is to be tested. Owing to the very "largeness" of government, a multitude of relationships might appear to some to fall within the Amendment's embrace, but that, it must be remembered, can be determined only in the framework of the peculiar facts or circumstances present. Therefore respondents' prophecy of nigh universal application of a constitutional precept so peculiarly dependent for its invocation upon appropriate facts fails to take into account "Differences in circumstances [which] beget appropriate differences in law." Specifically defining the limits of our inquiry, what we hold today is that when a State leases public property in the manner and for the purpose shown to have been the case here, the proscriptions of the Fourteenth Amendment must be complied with by the lessee as certainly as though they were binding covenants written into the agreement itself.

JUSTICE HARLAN, whom JUSTICE WHITTAKER joins, dissenting.

The Court's opinion, by a process of first indiscriminatingly throwing together various factual bits and pieces and then undermining the resulting structure by an equally vague disclaimer, seems to me to leave completely at sea just what it is in this record that satisfies the requirement of "state action." I find it unnecessary, however, to inquire into the matter at this stage, for it seems to me apparent [that] the case should first be sent back to the state court for clarification as to the precise basis of its decision.

[JUSTICE FRANKFURTER also dissented.]

NOTES

1. *Joint participation.* The majority opinion in *Burton* indicates that the state's involvement with the restaurant made the state a "joint participant in the challenged activity." What was the nature of the "involvement" that made the state a "joint participant"? Perhaps it was the fact that the private and governmental actors derived important mutual benefits. Was it simply the multiplicity of contacts between the parties? The importance of the "symbiotic relation" between the Parking Authority and Eagle Restaurant was to become the critical aspect of *Burton* relied on in *Moose Lodge v. Irvis,* the next principal case. But, at the time, it appeared that Burton was a classic example of "summing the contacts" in order to find significant state involvement — of "focusing on the presence or absence of a substantial governmental role in the management or operation of the challenged activity." Thomas Rowe, *The Emerging Threshold Approach to State Action Determinations: Trying to Make Sense of Flagg Brothers, Inc. v. Brooks,* 69 GEO. L. REV. 745, 763–64 (1981).

2. *State failure to protect.* Justice Clark's opinion makes clear that the Wilmington Parking Authority had power to adopt rules and regulations respecting the use of the facilities. Should the failure of the Parking Authority to require that its lessees refrain from discriminating have been considered in determining state action?

> The notion that the state's *inaction* in failing to bar race discrimination at the restaurant was the crux of the case in *Burton* understandably fed the growing suspicion that, while the Court might say that state action must be shown — citing the *Civil Rights Cases* in a perfunctory manner at the outset of every opinion — in reality the Court would in the future tend always to find sufficient contacts with the state to justify the exercise of federal power.

Larry Yackle, *The Burger Court, "State Action," and Congressional Enforcement of the Civil War Amendments,* 27 ALA. L. REV. 479, 497–98 (1975).

3. *Government-created corporations.* In *Lebron v. National RR Passenger Corp.*, 513 U.S.374 (1995), an artist contracted with Amtrak to display an ad on Amtrak billboards. The ad submitted had political content and was rejected by Amtrak. The contract stated that the ad was accepted subject to approval concerning such matters as the ad's text, illustration and design. The artist sued Amtrak contending that he had been denied his Fifth and Fourteenth Amendment rights. The federal district court issued an injunction requiring that the ad be displayed. The Second Circuit reversed noting that the federal legislation creating Amtrak specifically stated that Amtrak was not a government entity. The Supreme Court, per Justice Scalia, reversed:

> But it is not for Congress to make the final determination of Amtrak's status as a government entity for purposes of determining the constitutional rights of citizens affected by its actions. We hold that where, as here, the Government creates a corporation by special law, for the furtherance of governmental objectives, and retains for itself permanent authority to appoint a majority of the members of that corporation, the corporation is part of the government for purposes of the First Amendment.

The Court remanded the issue of whether Amtrak had in fact violated the First Amendment.

MOOSE LODGE NO. 107 v. IRVIS

407 U.S. 163, 92 S. Ct. 1965, 32 L. Ed. 2d 627 (1972)

JUSTICE REHNQUIST delivered the opinion of the Court.

Appellee Irvis, a Negro, was refused service by appellant Moose Lodge, a local branch of the national fraternal organization located in Harrisburg, Pennsylvania. Appellee then brought this action under 42 U.S.C. § 1983 for injunctive relief in the United States District Court for the Middle District of Pennsylvania. He claimed that because the Pennsylvania liquor board had issued appellant Moose Lodge a private club license that authorized the sale of alcoholic beverages on its premises, the refusal of service to him was "state action" for the purposes of the Equal Protection Clause of the Fourteenth Amendment.

A three-judge district court, convened at appellee's request, upheld his contention on the merits, and entered a decree declaring invalid the liquor license issued to Moose Lodge "as long as it follows a policy of racial discrimination in its membership or operating policies or practices."

Moose Lodge is a private club in the ordinary meaning of that term. It is a local chapter of a national fraternal organization having well defined requirements for membership. It conducts all of its activities in a building that is owned by it. It is not publicly funded. Only members and guests are permitted in any lodge of the order; one may become a guest only by invitation of a member or upon invitation of the house committee.

Appellee, while conceding the right of private clubs to choose members upon a discriminatory basis, asserts that the licensing of Moose Lodge to serve liquor by the Pennsylvania Liquor Control Board amounts to such State involvement with the club's activities as to make its discriminatory practices forbidden by the Equal Protection Clause of the Fourteenth Amendment.

The Court has never held, of course, that discrimination by an otherwise private entity would be violative of the Equal Protection Clause if the private entity receives any sort of benefit or service at all from the State, or if it is subject to state regulation in any degree whatever. Since state-furnished services include such necessities of life as electricity, water, and police and fire protection, such a holding would utterly emasculate the distinction between private as distinguished from State conduct set forth in *The Civil Rights Cases,* and adhered to in subsequent decisions. Our holdings indicate that where the impetus for the discrimination is private, the State must have "significantly involved itself with invidious discriminations," in order for the discriminatory action to fall within the ambit of the constitutional prohibition.

With one exception, which is discussed *infra,* there is no suggestion in this record that the Pennsylvania statutes and regulations governing the sale of liquor are intended either overtly or covertly to encourage discrimination.

Here there is nothing approaching the symbiotic relationship between lessor and lessee that was present in *Burton.* Unlike *Burton,* the Moose Lodge building is located on land owned by it, not by any public authority. Far from apparently holding itself out as a place of public accommodation, Moose Lodge quite ostentatiously proclaims the fact that it is not open to the public at large. Nor is it located and operated in such surroundings that although private in name, it discharges a function or performs a service that would otherwise in all likelihood be performed by the State. In short, while Eagle was a public restaurant in a public building, Moose Lodge is a private social club in a private building.

With the exception hereafter noted, the Pennsylvania Liquor Control Board plays absolutely no part in establishing or enforcing the membership or guest policies of the club which it licenses to serve liquor. There is no suggestion in this record that the Pennsylvania Act, either as written or as applied, discriminates against minority groups either in their right to apply for club licenses themselves or in their right to purchase and be served liquor in places of public accommodation. The only effect that the state licensing of Moose Lodge to serve liquor can be said to have on the right of any other Pennsylvanian to buy or be served liquor on premises other than those of Moose Lodge is that for some purposes club licenses are counted in the maximum number of licenses which may be issued in a given municipality. Basically each municipality has a quota of one retail license for each 1,500 inhabitants. Licenses issued to hotels, municipal golf courses and airport restaurants are not counted in this quota, nor are club licenses until the maximum number of retail licenses is reached. Beyond that point, neither additional retail licenses nor additional club licenses may be issued so long as the number of issued and outstanding retail licenses remains above the statutory maximum.

The District Court was at pains to point out in its opinion what it considered to be the "pervasive" nature of the regulation of private clubs by the Pennsylvania Liquor Control Board. As that court noted, an applicant for a club license must make such physical alterations in its premises as the board may require, must file a list of the names and addresses of its members and employees, and must keep extensive financial records. The board is granted the right to inspect the licensed premises at any time when patrons, guests or members are present.

However detailed this type of regulation may be in some particulars, it cannot be said to in any way foster or encourage racial discrimination. Nor can it be said to make the State in any realistic sense a partner or even a joint venturer in the club's enterprise. The limited effect of the prohibition against obtaining additional club licenses when the maximum number of retail licenses allotted to a municipality has been issued, when considered together with the availability of liquor from hotel, restaurant, and retail licensees falls far short of conferring upon club licensees a monopoly in the dispensing of liquor in any given municipality or in the State as a whole. We therefore hold that, with the exception hereafter noted, the operation of the regulatory scheme enforced by the Pennsylvania Liquor Control Board does not sufficiently implicate the State in the discriminatory guest policies of Moose Lodge so as to make the latter "State action" within the ambit of the Equal Protection Clause of the Fourteenth Amendment.

The District Court found that the regulations of the Liquor Control Board adopted pursuant to statute affirmatively require that "every club licensee shall adhere to all the provisions of its constitution and by-laws." Appellant argues that the purpose of this provision "is purely and simply and plainly the prevention of subterfuge," pointing out that the *bona fides* of a private club, as opposed to a place of public accommodation masquerading as a private club, is a matter with which the State Liquor Control Board may legitimately concern itself. Appellee concedes this to be the case, and expresses disagreement with the District Court on this point. There can be no doubt that the label "private club" can and has been used to evade both regulations of State and local liquor authorities, and statutes requiring places of public accommodation to serve all persons without regard to race, color, religion, or national origin.

The effect of this particular regulation on Moose Lodge under the provisions of the constitution placed in the record in the court below would be to place State sanctions behind its discriminatory membership rules, but not behind its guest practices, which were not embodied in the constitution of the lodge. Had there been no change in the relevant circumstances since the making of the record in the District Court, our holding that appellee has standing to challenge only the guest practices of Moose Lodge would have a bearing on our disposition of this issue. Appellee stated upon oral argument, though, and Moose Lodge conceded in its Brief that the bylaws of the Supreme Lodge have been altered since the lower court decision to make applicable to guests the same sort of racial restrictions as are presently applicable to members.

Even though the Liquor Control Board regulation in question is neutral in its terms, the result of its application in a case where the constitution and bylaws of a club required racial discrimination would be to invoke the sanctions of the State to enforce a concededly discriminatory private rule. *Shelley v. Kraemer* makes it clear that the application of state sanctions to enforce such a rule would violate the Fourteenth Amendment. Although the record before us is not as clear as one would like, appellant has not persuaded us that the District Court should have denied any and all relief.

Appellee was entitled to a decree enjoining the enforcement of § 113.09 of the regulations promulgated by the Pennsylvania Liquor Control Board insofar as that regulation requires compliance by Moose Lodge with provisions of its constitution and by-laws containing racially discriminatory provisions. He was entitled to no more. The judgment of the District Court is reversed, and the cause remanded with instructions to enter a decree in conformity with this opinion.

JUSTICE DOUGLAS, with whom JUSTICE MARSHALL joins, dissenting.

[T]he fact that a private club gets some kind of permit from the State or municipality does not make it *ipso facto* a public enterprise or undertaking, any more than the grant to a householder of a permit to operate an incinerator puts the householder in the public domain. We must therefore examine whether there are special circumstances involved in the Pennsylvania scheme which differentiate the liquor license possessed by Moose Lodge from the incinerator permit.

Pennsylvania has a state store system of alcohol distribution. Resale is permitted by hotels, restaurants, and private clubs which all must obtain licenses from the Liquor Control Board. Once a license is issued the licensee must comply with many detailed requirements or risk suspension or revocation of the license. Among these requirements is Regulation No. 113.09, which says "Every club licensee shall adhere to all the provisions of its Constitution and By-laws." This regulation means, as applied to Moose Lodge, that it must adhere to the racially discriminatory provision of the Constitution of its Supreme Lodge. The result, as I see it, is the same as though Pennsylvania had put into its liquor licenses a provision that the license may not be used to dispense liquor to Blacks, Browns, Yellows — or atheists or agnostics. Regulation No. 113.09 is thus an invidious form of state action.

Were this regulation the only infirmity in Pennsylvania's licensing scheme, I would perhaps agree with the majority that the appropriate relief would be a decree enjoining its enforcement. But there is another flaw in the scheme not so easily cured. Liquor licenses in Pennsylvania, unlike driver's licenses, or marriage licenses, are not freely available to those who meet racially neutral qualifications. There is a complex quota system, which the majority accurately describes. What the majority neglects to say is that the Harrisburg quota, where Moose Lodge No. 107 is located, has been full for many years. No more club licenses may be issued in that city. This state-enforced scarcity of licenses restricts the ability of blacks to obtain liquor, for liquor is commercially available *only* at private clubs for a significant portion of each week. Access by blacks to places that serve liquor is further limited by the fact that the state quota is filled. A group desiring to form a nondiscriminatory club which would serve blacks must purchase a license held by an existing club, which can exact a monopoly price for the transfer. The availability of such a license is speculative at best, however, for, as Moose Lodge itself concedes, without a liquor license a fraternal organization would be hard-pressed to survive. Thus, the State of Pennsylvania is putting the weight of its liquor license, concededly a valued and important adjunct to a private club, behind racial discrimination.

JUSTICE BRENNAN, with whom JUSTICE MARSHALL joins, dissenting.

When Moose Lodge obtained its liquor license, the State of Pennsylvania became an active participant in the operation of the Lodge bar. Liquor licensing laws are only incidentally revenue measures; they are primarily pervasive regulatory schemes under which the State dictates and continually supervises virtually every detail of the operation of the licensee's business. Very few, if any, other licensed businesses experience such complete state involvement. Plainly, the State of Pennsylvania's liquor regulations intertwine the State with the operation of the Lodge bar in a "significant way [and] lend [the State's] authority to the sordid business of racial discrimination."

NOTES

1. *Symbiosis.* Justice Rehnquist in *Moose Lodge* indicates that "there is nothing approaching the symbiotic relationship between lessor and lessee that was present in *Burton.*" Does this reduce the "significant involvement" formulation applied in *Burton* to a requirement of a "symbiotic relationship"? Is such a reading of *Burton* warranted? And if warranted, why was the requirement not satisfied in *Moose Lodge*? Consider the following:

> [W]hile a licensee receives from the state permission to operate a lucrative business and obtains a valuable property right in the license itself, the state is provided with a distribution system for its liquor sales from which it derives substantial revenue. It is difficult to see why this is not precisely the type of "symbiotic relationship" which the Court found was lacking.

The Supreme Court, 1971 Term, 86 HARV. L. REV. 50, 73–74 (1972).

2. *Private schools.* In *Norwood v. Harrison*, 413 U.S. 455 (1973), a unanimous Court held invalid a longstanding Mississippi statutory program under which textbooks were purchased by the state and lent to students in both public and private schools, without reference to whether the participating private school had racially discriminatory practices. Chief Justice Burger, for the Court, after noting that the Court had "consistently affirmed decisions enjoining state tuition grants to students attending racially discriminatory private schools," concluded that the textbook lending program was legally indistinguishable:

> Free textbooks, like tuition grants directed to private school students, are a form of financial assistance inuring to the benefit of the private schools themselves. An inescapable educational cost is the expense of providing all necessary learning materials. When, as here, that necessary expense is borne by the State, the economic consequence is to give aid to the enterprise; if the school engages in discriminatory practices the State by tangible aid in the form of textbooks thereby gives support to such discrimination.

Chief Justice Burger distinguished state provision of generalized services from provision of textbooks which, "like tuition grants, are provided only in connection with schools." Vital services over which the state might have a practical monopoly were also distinguished.

The Court has held that a city, under an order to desegregate public recreational facilities, violates equal protection when it permits exclusive use of recreational facilities, however temporary, by segregated private schools because this enhances the attractiveness of such schools. *Gilmore v. Montgomery*, 417 U.S. 556 (1974). Justice Blackmun, for the majority, however, remanded the case on the question of nonexclusive access to such facilities by segregated schools, and by segregated nonschool groups, in common or exclusively. The question was whether such access, under *Burton,* would involve the government so directly in the actions of such users "as to warrant court intervention on constitutional grounds," *e.g.*, "direct impairment of a school desegregation order." Is *Gilmore* consistent with *Moose Lodge*?

The issue of racially discriminatory private schools has been dealt with more directly pursuant to Congress' power to legislate under the Thirteenth Amendment. *See Runyon v. McCrary,* p. 1530.

3. *Access to media.* In *Columbia Broadcasting Sys. v. Democratic Nat'l Comm.*, 412 U.S. 94 (1973), a majority of the Court held that a broadcasting policy of refusal to sell time to groups like the Democratic National Committee for purposes of editorial advertising did not offend the First Amendment. First Amendment and state action problems are closely intertwined in *CBS*. The case is reported and discussed from a First Amendment perspective on p. 1298.

Chief Justice Burger, joined by Justices Stewart and Rehnquist, found that the network ban on selling editorial advertising to citizens and groups should not be considered "governmental action" for purposes of the First Amendment. The Chief Justice considered it crucial that the Federal Communications Commission, *i.e.*, the government, "has not fostered the license policy challenged here; it has simply declined to command particular action because it fell within the area of journalistic discretion." Burger distinguished state action cases, like *Burton v. Wilmington Parking Authority,* on the ground that the government was not a partner with or engaged in a "symbiotic relationship" with the broadcasters in *CBS,* as the state was with the Parking Authority in *Burton,* because the government did not profit "from the invidious discrimination of its proxy" as it had in *Burton.*

Are different policy considerations involved when the Court considers a claim that the federal government, rather than a state government, is significantly involved in the actions of private parties? If the heart of the state action requirement is a respect for federalism, should the Court be more willing to find governmental action where acts of the federal government are challenged?

4. *Balancing interests.* Does the Court's opinion in *Moose Lodge* reflect the application of a balancing test, weighing the lodge members' property and associational interests against Irvis' interest in nondiscriminatory treatment? Compare the following views:

> The Court has always recognized an associational interest in private clubs, whether political organizations or country clubs. [T]he central issue for both majority and dissent was to balance the interests of the two private parties. The test was not a new or restrictive one; the Justices merely disagreed on the impact of the practice and on how to apply the balancing test.

Robert Glennon & John Nowak, *A Functional Analysis of the Fourteenth Amendment "State Action" Requirement,* 1976 Sup. Ct. Rev. 221.

5. *Licensing and regulation.* The relationship of licensor-licensee in *Moose Lodge* and *CBS* was not enough to establish the requisite state action whereas the lessor-lessee relationship in *Burton* was sufficient. If this were the key distinction, could licensing ever be sufficient governmental involvement to trigger state duties under the Fourteenth Amendment? Even if not determinative, should the presence of "pervasive state regulation" still play a role in determining the significance of the government's involvement? The next case explores this question.

JACKSON v. METROPOLITAN EDISON CO.
419 U.S. 345, 95 S. Ct. 449, 42 L. Ed. 2d 477 (1974)

JUSTICE REHNQUIST delivered the opinion of the Court.

Respondent Metropolitan Edison Co. is a privately owned and operated Pennsylvania corporation which holds a certificate of public convenience issued by the Pennsylvania Public Utility Commission empowering it to deliver electricity to a service area which includes the city of York, Pa. As a condition of holding its certificate, it is subject to extensive regulation by the Commission. Under a provision of its general tariff filed with the Commission, it has the right to discontinue service to any customer on reasonable notice of nonpayment of bills.

Petitioner Catherine Jackson is a resident of York, who has received electricity in the past from respondent. When her account was terminated because of asserted delinquency in payments due for service, a new account with respondent was opened in the name of one James Dodson, another occupant of the residence, and service to the residence was resumed. In August 1971, Dodson left the residence. Service continued thereafter but concededly no payments were made. Petitioner states that no bills were received during this period.

On October 6, 1971, employees of Metropolitan came to the residence and inquired as to Dodson's present address. Petitioner stated that it was unknown to her. On the following day, another employee visited the residence and informed petitioner that the meter had been tampered with so as not to register amounts used. She disclaimed knowledge of this and requested that the service account for her home be shifted from Dodson's name to that of one Robert Jackson, later identified as her 12-year-old son. Four days later on October 11, 1971, without further notice to petitioner, Metropolitan employees disconnected her service.

Petitioner then filed suit against Metropolitan in the United States District Court under 42 U.S.C. § 1983, seeking damages for the termination and an injunction requiring Metropolitan to continue providing power to her residence until she had been afforded notice, a hearing, and an opportunity to pay any amounts found due. She urged that under state law she had an entitlement to reasonably continuous electrical service to her home and that Metropolitan's termination of her service for alleged nonpayment, action allowed by a provision of its general tariff filed with the Commission, constituted "state action" depriving her of property in violation of the Fourteenth Amendment's guarantee of due process of law.

Here the action complained of was taken by a utility company which is privately owned and operated, but which in many particulars of its business is subject to extensive state regulation. The mere fact that a business is subject to state regulation does not by itself convert its action into that of the State for purposes of the Fourteenth Amendment. [*Moose Lodge*.] Nor does the fact that the regulation is extensive and detailed, as in the case of most public utilities, do so. *Public Utilities Comm'n v. Pollak*, 343 U. S. 451, 462 (1952). It may well be that acts of a heavily regulated utility with at least something of a governmentally protected monopoly will more readily be found to be "state" acts than will the acts of an entity lacking these characteristics. But the inquiry must be whether there is a sufficiently close nexus between the State and the challenged action of the regulated entity so that the action of the latter may be fairly treated as that of the State itself. *Moose Lodge No. 107.* The true nature of the State's involvement may not be immediately obvious, and detailed inquiry may be required in order to determine whether the test is met. *Burton v. Wilmington Parking Authority.*

Petitioner first argues that "state action" is present because of the monopoly status allegedly conferred upon Metropolitan by the State of Pennsylvania. As a factual matter, it may well be doubted that the State ever granted or guaranteed Metropolitan a monopoly. But assuming that it had, this fact is not determinative in considering whether Metropolitan's termination of service to petitioner was "state action" for purposes of the Fourteenth Amendment. [A]lthough certain monopoly aspects were presented in *Moose Lodge No. 107,* we found that the Lodge's action was not subject to the provisions of the Fourteenth Amendment. In each of those cases, there was insufficient relationship between the challenged actions of the entities involved and their monopoly status. There is no indication of any greater connection here.

Petitioner next urges that state action is present because respondent provides an essential public service required to be supplied on a reasonably continuous basis by [state statute], and hence performs a "public function." We have, of course, found state action present in the exercise by a private entity of powers traditionally exclusively reserved to the State. If we were dealing with the exercise by Metropolitan of some power delegated to it by the State which is traditionally associated with sovereignty, such as eminent domain, our case would be quite a different one. But while the Pennsylvania statute imposes an obligation to furnish service on regulated utilities, it imposes no such obligation on the State.

Perhaps in recognition of the fact that the supplying of utility service is not traditionally the exclusive prerogative of the State, petitioner invites the expansion of the doctrine of this limited line of cases into a broad principle that all businesses "affected with the public interest" are state actors in all their actions. We decline the invitation for reasons stated long ago in *Nebbia v. New York,* in the course of rejecting a substantive due process attack on state legislation: "It is clear that there is no closed class or category of businesses affected with a public interest." Doctors, optometrists, lawyers, Metropolitan, and Nebbia's upstate New York grocery selling a quart of milk are all in regulated businesses, providing arguably essential goods and services, "affected with a public interest." We do not believe that such a status converts their every action, absent more, into that of the State.

We also reject the notion that Metropolitan's termination is state action because the State "has specifically authorized and approved" the termination practice. In the instant case, Metropolitan filed with the Public Utility Commission a general tariff — a provision of which states Metropolitan's right to terminate service for nonpayment. This provision has appeared in Metropolitan's previously filed tariffs for many years and has never been the subject of a hearing or other scrutiny by the Commission. Although the Commission did hold hearings on portions of Metropolitan's general tariff relating to a general rate increase, it never even considered the reinsertion of this provision in the newly filed general tariff.

As a threshold matter, it is less than clear under state law that Metropolitan was even required to file this provision as part of its tariff or that the Commission would have had the power to disapprove it. The District Court observed that the sole connection of the Commission with this regulation was Metropolitan's simple notice filing with the Commission and the lack of any Commission action to prohibit it.

The nature of governmental regulation of private utilities is such that a utility may frequently be required by the state regulatory scheme to obtain approval for practices a business regulated in less detail would be free to institute without any approval from a regulatory body. Approval by a state utility commission of such a request from a regulated utility, where the commission has not put its own weight on the side of the proposed practice by ordering it, does not transmute a practice initiated by the utility and approved by the commission into "state action." At most, the Commission's failure to overturn this practice amounted to no more than a determination that a Pennsylvania utility was authorized to employ such a practice if it so desired. Respondent's exercise of the choice allowed by state law where the initiative comes from it and not from the State, does not make its action in doing so "state action" for purposes of the Fourteenth Amendment.

We also find absent in the instant case the symbiotic relationship presented in *Burton v. Wilmington Parking Authority*. Metropolitan is a privately owned corporation, and it does not lease its facilities from the State of Pennsylvania. It alone is responsible for the provision of power to its customers. In common with all corporations of the State it pays taxes to the State, and it is subject to a form of extensive regulation by the State in a way that most other business enterprises are not. But this was likewise true of the appellant club in *Moose Lodge No. 107 v. Irvis*.

All of petitioner's arguments taken together show no more than that Metropolitan was a heavily regulated, privately owned utility, enjoying at least a partial monopoly in the providing of electrical service within its territory, and that it elected to terminate service to petitioner in a manner which the Pennsylvania Public Utility Commission found permissible under state law. Under our decision this is not sufficient to connect the State of Pennsylvania with respondent's action so as to make the latter's conduct attributable to the State for purposes of the Fourteenth Amendment.

JUSTICE MARSHALL, dissenting.

Our state-action cases have repeatedly relied on several factors clearly presented by this case: a state-sanctioned monopoly; an extensive pattern of cooperation between the "private" entity and the State; and a service uniquely public in nature. Today the Court takes a major step in repudiating this line of authority and adopts a stance that is bound to lead to mischief when applied to problems beyond the narrow sphere of due process objections to utility terminations.

The fact that the Metropolitan Edison Co. supplies an essential public service that is in many communities supplied by the government weighs more heavily for me than for the majority. The Court concedes that state action might be present if the activity in question were "traditionally associated with sovereignty," but it then undercuts that point by suggesting that a particular service is not a public function if the State in question has not required that it be governmentally operated. This reads the "public function" argument too narrowly. The whole point of the "public function" cases is to look behind the State's decision to provide public services through private parties. In my view, utility service is traditionally identified with the State through universal public regulation or ownership to a degree sufficient to render it a "public function."

What is perhaps most troubling about the Court's opinion is that it would appear to apply to a broad range of claimed constitutional violations by the company. The Court has not adopted the notion, accepted elsewhere, that different standards should apply to state-action analysis when different constitutional claims are presented. Thus, the majority's analysis would seemingly apply as well to a company that refused to extend service to Negroes, welfare recipients, or any other group that the company preferred, for its own reasons, not to serve. I cannot believe that this Court would hold that the State's involvement with the utility company was not sufficient to impose upon the company an obligation to meet the constitutional mandate of nondiscrimination. Yet nothing in the analysis of the majority opinion suggests otherwise.

[Justices Brennan and Douglas also dissented.]

NOTES

1. *State encouragement, authorization and approval.* If the state had *ordered* Metropolitan to adopt its termination practice, would there have been any need for a detailed inquiry into the state action question?

> To require an order from a state agency to engage in the conduct alleged to be invalid is, of course, to eliminate from consideration any case in which the argument for state action is founded upon state involvement with private conduct. [Earlier] cases would seem to stand for the proposition that indirect state action, funneled through private hands, can also violate the Fourteenth Amendment.

Larry Yackle, *The Burger Court, "State Action," and Congressional Enforcement of the Civil War Amendments,* 27 Ala. L. Rev. 479, 520 (1975). Might a requirement that the state put its imprimatur on a particular regulation encourage the state to abdicate its responsibility to supervise utilities?

2. *The nexus test.* Justice Rehnquist states that, in determining whether state action is present, "the inquiry must be whether there is a sufficiently close nexus between the state and the challenged action of the regulated entity so that the action of the latter may be fairly treated as that of the state itself." The government must be tied to the particular conduct being challenged. Why was that nexus not satisfied in *Jackson*? Does the nexus test apply *only* to cases involving state action via regulation? It has been suggested that "the *Jackson* nexus language is a specific application in a state-action-by-regulation case of a broader principle that is equally applicable to all types of state action cases." Thomas McCoy, *Current State Action Theories, the Jackson Nexus Requirement and Employee Discharges by Semi-Public and State-Aided Institutions,* 31 VAND. L. REV. 785 (1978).

3. *Monopoly power.* Professor McCoy also observed, "One might confidently have assumed that if any state aid to a private enterprise would subject the private institution to the restrictions of the fourteenth amendment, it would be the state's use of its regulatory power to create or preserve a monopoly for the private enterprise." McCoy, 31 VAND. L. REV. at 806. Simply, state grants of a monopoly augment the private actor's power in its dealings and bargaining relations with private consumers. Metropolitan has a special advantage in dealing with its customers who lack any alternative supplier. Nevertheless, the Court in both *Moose Lodge* and *Jackson,* while suggesting that monopoly power may in some circumstances result in a finding of state action, failed to find state action. Why? After *Moose Lodge* and *Jackson,* when will a private actor's state-conferred monopoly power give rise to a finding of state action?

Does the Court in *Jackson* adequately distinguish *Public Utilities Comm'n v. Pollak*? Is *Pollak* effectively overruled by *Jackson*? If so, which of the two decisions represents a more appropriate interpretation of the state action requirement?

4. *Sum of the contacts.* Justice Rehnquist rejects each of the state action theories *seriatim.* But what of the principle articulated in *Burton* that the totality of circumstances must be weighed? Would you agree with the view that by not considering the aggregate effect of state involvement, the Court ignored the cumulative test set forth in *Burton*?

5. *Regulation, monopoly and discrimination.* Is it likely, or even conceivable, that if the utility's action in *Jackson* were alleged to be racial discrimination rather than a procedural default, the Supreme Court would have found no state action? Under the view that state action involves a balancing of interests, a regulated monopoly utility would have virtually no interest in its autonomy to engage in personal discrimination. It might, however, have a significant interest in avoiding procedural requirements.

6. *Private providers of public services.* In *Blum v. Yaretsky*, 457 U.S. 991 (1982), the Court considered a challenge by a class of Medicaid patients to decisions by nursing homes in which they resided to discharge or transfer patients without notice or an opportunity for a hearing. Justice Rehnquist, writing for the Court, framed the issue to be "whether the State may be held responsible for those decisions so as to subject them to the strictures of the Fourteenth Amendment." It was held that the discharge and transfer decisions of the nursing home did not involve "state action."

The fact that regulations imposed a range of penalties on nursing homes that failed to discharge or transfer patients whose continued stay was inappropriate did not establish state action, since "those regulations themselves do not dictate the decision to discharge or transfer in a particular case." The fact that the nursing home was required to fill out forms and that an adjustment in benefits levels might follow in response to a decision to discharge or transfer did not "constitute approval or enforcement of that decision."

Citing *Burton v. Wilmington Parking Authority,* the respondents had argued that extensive state subsidization of the operating and capital costs of the facilities, payment of the medical expenses of more than ninety percent of the patients in the facilities, and the licensing of the nursing homes, "taken together" converted the action of the homes into state action. The Court rejected this aggregation of contacts approach:

> As we have previously held, privately owned enterprises providing services that the State would not necessarily provide, even though they are extensively regulated [and licensed] do not fall within the ambit of *Burton.* That programs undertaken by the State result in substantial funding of the activities of a private entity is no more persuasive than the fact of regulation of such an entity in demonstrating that the State is responsible for decisions made by the entity in the course of its business.

Justice Brennan, joined by Justice Marshall, dissented, arguing that

> the level-of-care decisions at issue in this case have far less to do with the exercise of independent professional judgment than they do with the State's desire to save money. [T]he idea of two mutually exclusive levels of care — skilled nursing care and intermediate care — embodied in the federal regulatory scheme and implemented by the State, reflects no established medical model of health care. On the contrary, the two levels of long-term institutionalized care enshrined in the Medicaid scheme are legislative constructs, designed to serve governmental cost-containment policies.

Citing *Burton,* Justice Brennan argued that "the degree of interdependence between the State and the nursing home is far more pronounced [here] than it was between the State and the private entity [in that case]." He noted that "the State subsidizes practically all of the operating and capital costs of the facility, and pays the medical expenses of more than 90% of its residents."

7. *The Rehnquist Court: State Action Transformed?* After reviewing *Moose Lodge*, *Jackson*, *Flagg Brothers* and *Blum*, Professor David Barron has observed that Chief Justice Rehnquist "remade" the state action doctrine. State action was no longer an expansive doctrine: "There was not a single method of finding state action that he [Chief Justice Rehnquist] had not addressed and limited. With each decision, he had drawn the restrictions more tightly. Importantly, Rehnquist had not overruled a single case directly. Arguably, he had done no more than refuse to extend an already expansive doctrine." *See* David Barron, *Privatizing the Constitution: State Action and Beyond in* Rehnquist's Legacy (Craig Bradley ed. 2006). Prof. Barron contends that Rehnquist's state action decisions privatize the Constitution: "Rehnquist's state action decisions do more than decline to invalidate governmental decisions not to intervene: they bar the court from evaluating the constitutional legitimacy of such decisions. The point is not that the government has not complied with the Constitution. The point is that courts should not inquire into whether it has."

In *United States v. Morrison*, [text, p. 156], the federal government sought to validate the Violence Against Women Act on the basis of both the Commerce Clause and Sec. 5 of the Fourteenth Amendment. Consider Chief Justice Rehnquist's discussion of the state action issue in that case. Rehnquist ruled that private conduct was involved in *Morrison* and, therefore, that Congress had no authority to enact VAWA under Sec. 5. The Chief Justice "saw no need to consider the constitutional legitimacy of those state actions that permitted the private conduct to occur." Do you agree that Chief Justice Rehnquist's state action analysis sought to privatize the Constitution?

8. ***Rendell-Baker v. Kohn*, 457 U.S. 830 (1982)**. The Court held, per Chief Justice Burger, that the discharge of teachers employed by a private school for maladjusted high school students did not involve state action sufficient to implicate Fourteenth Amendment guarantees, even though most of the students were referred to the institution by public authorities or under statutory authorization and public funds accounted for at least ninety percent of the school's operating budget.

Chief Justice Burger noted that the school, in the present case, and the nursing homes in *Blum*, are not "fundamentally different from many private corporations whose business depends primarily on contracts to build roads, bridges, dams, ships, or submarines for the government. Acts of such private contractors do not become acts of the government by reason of their significant or even total engagement in performing public contracts." Nor was the pervasive regulation of the school sufficient to establish state action since "the decisions to discharge the petitioners were not compelled or influenced by any state regulation. Indeed, in contrast to the extensive regulation of the school generally, the various regulators showed relatively little interest in the school's personnel matters." Finally, the Chief Justice quickly disposed of the public function theory of state action. The legislative policy choice to provide services for maladjusted students at public expense, "in no way makes these services the exclusive province of the State." Nor was the function traditionally assumed by the state, since "until recently the State had not undertaken to provide education for students who could not be served by traditional public schools. That a private entity performs a function which serves the public does not make its acts state action." Nor did the Court find the symbiotic relationship that existed in *Burton* present in this case. "Here the school's fiscal relationship with the State is not different from that of many contractors performing services for the government."

Justice Marshall, joined by Justice Brennan, dissenting, concluded: "The State has delegated to the [school] its statutory duty to educate children with special needs. The school receives almost all of its funds from the State, and is highly regulated. This nexus between the school and the state is so substantial that the school's action must be considered State action."

9. ***American Manufacturers Mutual Insurance Co. v. Sullivan*, 526 U.S. 40 (1999)**. The Court, per Chief Justice Rehnquist, held that a private insurer's decision to withhold payment for disputed medical treatment pending a "utilization review" was not fairly attributable to the state of Pennsylvania and therefore did not constitute state action. The Pennsylvania Workers' Compensation Act provides that an employer who is determined to be liable

for an employee's injury must pay for all "reasonable" and "necessary" medical treatment within 30 days of receiving the receiving the bill. In 1993, Pennsylvania amended the Act and created a "utilization review" under which an insurer could request a review of the reasonable-treatment before paying the employee's medical bill.

Ten employees and two organizations representing employees who received benefits under the Pennsylvania's Workers' Compensation Act brought suit under 42 U.S.C. § 1983, naming as defendants several private insurance companies who provided workers' compensation coverage, various Pennsylvania officials in charge of administering the Act, the School District of Philadelphia, and the director of the state workers' insurance fund. The claimants alleged that the state and private defendants, acting "under the color of state law," violated the Due Process Clause of the Fourteenth Amendment in depriving them of property by withholding payment of their benefits without adequate notice and an opportunity to be heard.

Chief Justice Rehnquist relied on *Lugar v. Edmondson Oil Co.* [text, p. 1486]. State action requires: (1) an alleged constitutional deprivation "caused by the exercise of some right or privilege created by the State or by a rule of conduct imposed by the State or by a person for whom the State is responsible," and (2) that "the party charged with the deprivation must be a person who may fairly be said to be a state actor." While the private insurers act with knowledge of and pursuant to the state statute, the Chief Justice argued that the alleged unconstitutional conduct, i.e., withholding payment for disputed medical treatment, was not "fairly attributable to the State."

The mere fact of extensive state regulation was not sufficient to convert the private action into state action. Rather, the Court had to determine whether a "close nexus" existed between the State and the insurer so as to consider the challenged action fo the latter an action of the State itself. The Court rejected the claimants' argument that the insurers are state actors because the State has "authorized" and "encouraged" the insurers to withhold payment. While the State's decision to amend the Act to allow insurers to suspend payment of benefits during utilization review may be considered subtle encouragement, the "mere availability of a remedy for wrongful conduct, even when the private use of that remedy serves important public interests," does not significantly encourage the private activity so as to make the State responsible for it. The Amendment could just as easily be seen as a form of state inaction — a decision not to intervene in the dispute.

The Court also rejected the claimants argument that the State had delegated powers "traditionally exclusively reserved to the State." First, the Chief Justice rejected plaintiffs' reliance on precedent involving State delegation of the power to suspend public benefits to a private actor. In the present case, nothing imposed legal obligations on the State to provide benefits to injured workers; the obligation was imposed on private employers. Second, the State had not delegated to insurers "the traditionally exclusive governmental function of deciding whether to suspend payment for disputed medical treatment." Chief Justice Rehnquist asserted that before workers' compensation laws existed, an insurer could withhold payment of medical expenses without any involvement of the State. The insurer's decisions to withhold payment, the Court concluded, is not fairly attributable to the State.

Finally, the Court rejected the Court of Appeals reliance on the "joint participation" theory of state action from *Burton v. Wilmington Parking Authority* [text, p. 1518]. Later cases, such as *Blum v. Yaretsky* [text, p. 1532] and *Jackson v. Metropolitan Edison Co.* [text, p. 1527], the Chief Justice asserted had refined the theory and established that "privately owned enterprises providing services that the State would not necessarily provide, even though there are extensively regulated, do not fall within the ambit of Burton." Here the State regulatory scheme "leaves the challenged decisions to the judgment of insurers."

The Court went on to determine "whether the Due Process Clause requires workers' compensation insurers to pay disputed medical bills prior to a determination that the medical treatment was reasonable and necessary." The Court held that the employees did not have a property interest in the payment of benefits of due process purposes.

§ 10.03 LEGISLATING AGAINST PRIVATE ACTION

[A] UNDER THE FOURTEENTH AMENDMENT

Section 5 of the Fourteenth Amendment reads: "The Congress shall have power to enforce, by appropriate legislation, the provisions of this article." When Congress exercised its power to strike at private discrimination, the answer of the *Civil Rights Cases* was clear. Congress had power "to adopt appropriate legislation for correcting the effects of such prohibited *state* laws and *state* acts, and thus to render them effectively null, void, and innocuous. This is the legislative power conferred upon Congress, and this is the whole of it."

But this was before *Katzenbach v. Morgan,* p. 202. If Congress has power to implement the Civil War Amendments, could it not legislate against private action? Citing *Katzenbach* and his opinion in *Guest,* reprinted below, Justice Brennan has claimed that the rule established in the *Civil Rights Cases,* "that Congress cannot under § 5 protect the exercise of Fourteenth Amendment rights from private interference has been overruled." *Adickes v. S.H. Kress & Co.*, 398 U.S. 144 (1970). After reading the materials in this section, consider whether you agree with Justice Brennan.

In *United States v. Price*, 383 U.S. 787 (1966), the incident which provided the basis for the movie "Mississippi Burning," three Mississippi law officers were accused of having taken three civil rights workers, Schwerner, Chaney, and Goodman from their cells at night, and transporting them to a place where fifteen private persons were waiting. The indictments charged that the eighteen defendants had "punished" the three men by willfully assaulting and killing them, thus depriving them of their right "not to be summarily punished without due process of law."

The Supreme Court, per Justice Fortas, affirmed the district court holding that the three officers, even though acting contrary to state law, were acting "under color of law." *See Screws v. United States*, 325 U.S. 91 (1945) ("Misuse of power, possessed by virtue of state law and made possible only because the wrongdoer is clothed with the authority of state law, is action taken 'under color of state law' "). But the Court, reversing the district court, also held that the conduct of the fifteen private individuals constituted state action, and therefore, action under color of law. "To act 'under color' of law," said Justice Fortas, "does not require that the accused be an officer of the State. It is enough that he is a willful participant in joint activity with the State or its agents." In this case, the indictment charged

> joint activity, from start to finish. Those who took advantage of participation by state officers in accomplishment of the foul purpose alleged must suffer the consequences of the participation. In effect, if the allegations are true, they were participants in official lawlessness, acting in willful concert with state officers, and hence under color of law.

The Court then considered an indictment charging each of the eighteen defendants with a violation of 18 U.S.C. § 241, which is not limited to actions done under color of law. Treating the problem as statutory rather than constitutional, Justice Fortas concluded that the language of § 241 "includes rights or privileges protected by the Fourteenth Amendment; that whatever the ultimate coverage of the section may be, it extends to conspiracies otherwise within the scope of the section participated in by officials alone or in collaboration with private persons." But could § 241 be constitutionally employed where there was no state actor?

UNITED STATES v. GUEST

383 U.S. 745, 86 S. Ct. 1170, 16 L. Ed. 2d 239 (1966)

JUSTICE STEWART delivered the opinion of the Court.

The six defendants in this case were indicted for criminal conspiracy in violation of 18 U.S.C. § 241 (1964 ed.). In five numbered paragraphs, the indictment alleged a single conspiracy by the defendants to deprive Negro citizens of the free exercise and enjoyment of several specified rights secured by the Constitution and laws of the United States.*

The defendants moved to dismiss the indictment on the ground that it did not charge an offense under the laws of the United States. The District Court sustained the motion and dismissed the indictment as to all defendants and all numbered paragraphs of the indictment. [W]e reverse the judgment of the District Court. As in *United States v. Price,* we deal here with issues of statutory construction, not with issues of constitutional power.

The second numbered paragraph of the indictment alleged that the defendants conspired to injure, oppress, threaten, and intimidate Negro citizens of the United States in the free exercise and enjoyment of:

* [Editors' note: The Court of Appeals described the various actions of the defendants as having created a "reign of terror" in Athens, Georgia over a period of months. The defendants had fired weapons randomly at a drive-in restaurant frequented by African-Americans and at an apartment house occupied by black residents. The incidents culminated in the shooting death of Colonel Lemuel Penn, who was traveling through Athens on his way home to Maryland from Fort Benning.]

> The right to the equal utilization, without discrimination upon the basis of race, of public facilities in the vicinity of Athens, Georgia, owned, operated or managed by or on behalf of the State of Georgia or any subdivision thereof.

Correctly characterizing this paragraph as embracing rights protected by the Equal Protection Clause of the Fourteenth Amendment, the District Court held as a matter of statutory construction that 18 U.S.C. § 241 does not encompass any Fourteenth Amendment rights, and further held as a matter of constitutional law that "any broader construction of § 241 would render it void for indefiniteness." In so holding, the District Court was in error, as our opinion in *United States v. Price* makes abundantly clear.

Unlike the indictment in *Price,* however, the indictment in the present case names no person alleged to have acted in any way under the color of state law. The argument is therefore made that, since there exist no Equal Protection Clause rights against wholly private action, the judgment of the District Court on this branch of the case must be affirmed. On its face, the argument is unexceptionable. The Equal Protection Clause speaks to the State or to those acting under the color of its authority.

In this connection, we emphasize that § 241 by its clear language incorporates no more than the Equal Protection Clause itself; the statute does not purport to give substantive, as opposed to remedial, implementation to any rights secured by that Clause. Since we therefore deal here only with the bare terms of the Equal Protection Clause itself, nothing said in this opinion goes to the question of what kinds of other and broader legislation Congress might constitutionally enact under § 5 of the Fourteenth Amendment to implement that Clause or any other provision of the Amendment.

This case requires no determination of the threshold level that state action must attain in order to create rights under the Equal Protection Clause. This is so because, contrary to the argument of the litigants, the indictment in fact contains an express allegation of state involvement sufficient at least to require the denial of a motion to dismiss. One of the means of accomplishing the object of the conspiracy, according to the indictment, was "By causing the arrest of Negroes by means of false reports that such Negroes had committed criminal acts." Although it is possible that a bill of particulars, or the proof if the case goes to trial, would disclose no co-operative action by officials of the State, the allegation is enough to prevent dismissal of this branch of the indictment.

The fourth numbered paragraph of the indictment alleged that the defendants conspired to injure, oppress, threaten, and intimidate Negro citizens of the United States in the free exercise and enjoyment of:

> "The right to travel freely to and from the State of Georgia and to use highway facilities and other instrumentalities of interstate commerce within the State of Georgia."

The District Court was in error in dismissing the indictment as to this paragraph. The constitutional right to travel from one State to another, and necessarily to use the highways and other instrumentalities of interstate commerce in doing so, occupies a position fundamental to the concept of our

Federal Union. [I]f the predominant purpose of the conspiracy is to impede or prevent the exercise of the right of interstate travel, or to oppress a person because of his exercise of that right, then, whether or not motivated by racial discrimination, the conspiracy becomes a proper object of the federal law under which the indictment in this case was brought.

JUSTICE CLARK, with whom JUSTICES BLACK and FORTAS join, concurring.

Although the Court specifically rejects any such connotation, it is, I believe, both appropriate and necessary under the circumstances here to say that there now can be no doubt that the specific language of § 5 empowers the Congress to enact laws punishing all conspiracies — with or without state action — that interfere with Fourteenth Amendment rights.

JUSTICE HARLAN, concurring in part and dissenting in part.

To the extent that [the Court holds] that 18 U.S.C. § 241 (1964 ed.) reaches conspiracies, embracing only the action of private persons, to obstruct or otherwise interfere with the right of citizens freely to engage in interstate travel, I am constrained to dissent. On the other hand, I agree that § 241 does embrace state interference with such interstate travel, and I therefore consider that this aspect of the indictment is sustainable.

This right to travel must be found in the Constitution itself. My disagreement with this phase of the Court's opinion lies in this: While past cases do indeed establish that there is a constitutional "right to travel" between States free from unreasonable *governmental* interference, today's decision is the first to hold that such movement is also protected against *private* interference, and, depending on the constitutional source of the right, I think it either unwise or impermissible so to read the Constitution. I would sustain this aspect of the indictment only on the premise that it sufficiently alleges state interference with interstate travel, and on no other ground.

JUSTICE BRENNAN, with whom THE CHIEF JUSTICE [WARREN] and JUSTICE DOUGLAS join, concurring in part and dissenting in part.

I am of the opinion that a conspiracy to interfere with the right to equal utilization of state facilities described in the second numbered paragraph of the indictment is a conspiracy to interfere with a "right secured by the Constitution" within the meaning of § 241 — without regard to whether state officers participated in the alleged conspiracy. I believe that § 241 reaches such a private conspiracy, not because the Fourteenth Amendment of its own force prohibits such a conspiracy, but because § 241, as an exercise of congressional power under § 5 of that Amendment, prohibits *all* conspiracies to interfere with the exercise of a "right secured by the Constitution" and because the right to equal utilization of state facilities is a "right secured by the Constitution" within the meaning of that phrase as used in § 241.[3]

For me, the right to use state facilities without discrimination on the basis of race is, within the meaning of § 241, a right created by, arising under and

[3] Similarly, I believe that § 241 reaches a private conspiracy to interfere with the right to travel from State to State. I therefore need not reach the question whether the Constitution of its own force prohibits private interferences with that right; for I construe § 241 to prohibit such interferences, and as so construed I am of the opinion that § 241 is a valid exercise of congressional power.

dependent upon the Fourteenth Amendment and hence is a right "secured" by that Amendment. It finds its source in that Amendment. The Fourteenth Amendment commands the State to provide the members of all races with equal access to the public facilities it owns or manages, and the right of a citizen to use those facilities without discrimination on the basis of race is a basic corollary of this command. Whatever may be the status of the right to equal utilization of *privately owned facilities,* it must be emphasized that we are here concerned with the right to equal utilization of *public facilities owned or operated by or on behalf of the State.* To deny the existence of this right or its constitutional stature is to deny the history of the last decade, or to ignore the role of federal power, predicated on the Fourteenth Amendment, in obtaining nondiscriminatory access to such facilities. It is to do violence to the common understanding, an understanding that found expression in Titles III and IV of the Civil Rights Act of 1964 dealing with state facilities.

A majority of the members of the Court[6] expresses the view today that § 5 empowers Congress to enact laws punishing *all* conspiracies to interfere with the exercise of Fourteenth Amendment rights, whether or not state officers or others acting under the color of state law are implicated in the conspiracy. Although the Fourteenth Amendment itself, according to established doctrine, "speaks to the State or to those acting under the color of its authority," legislation protecting rights created by that Amendment, such as the right to equal utilization of state facilities, need not be confined to punishing conspiracies in which state officers participate. Rather, § 5 authorizes Congress to make laws that it concludes are reasonably necessary to protect a right created by and arising under that Amendment; and Congress is thus fully empowered to determine that punishment of private conspiracies interfering with the exercise of such a right is necessary to its full protection.

I acknowledge that some of the decisions of this Court, most notably an aspect of the *Civil Rights Cases,* have declared that Congress' power under § 5 is confined to the adoption of "appropriate legislation for correcting the effects of prohibited State laws and State acts, and thus to render them effectually null, void, and innocuous." I do not accept — and a majority of the Court today rejects — this interpretation of § 5. It reduces the legislative power to enforce the provisions of the Amendment to that of the judiciary;[7] and it attributes a far too limited objective to the Amendment's sponsors.[8] Moreover, the language of § 5 of the Fourteenth Amendment and § 2 of the

[6] The majority consists of the Justices joining my Brother CLARK's opinion and the Justices joining this opinion. The opinion of MR. JUSTICE STEWART construes § 241 as applied to the second numbered paragraph to require proof of active participation by state officers in the alleged conspiracy and that opinion does not purport to deal with this question.

[7] Congress, not the judiciary, was viewed as the more likely agency to implement fully the guarantees of equality, and thus it could be presumed the primary purpose of the Amendment was to augment the power of Congress, not the judiciary.

[8] As the first MR. JUSTICE HARLAN said in dissent in the *Civil Rights Cases*:

> It was perfectly well known that the great danger to the equal enjoyment by citizens of their rights, as citizens, was to be apprehended not altogether from unfriendly State legislation, but from the hostile action of corporations and individuals in the States. And it is to be presumed that it was intended, by that section [§ 5], to clothe Congress with power and authority to meet that danger.

Fifteenth Amendment are virtually the same, and we recently held in *South Carolina v. Katzenbach* that "[t]he basic test to be applied in a case involving § 2 of the Fifteenth Amendment is the same as in all cases concerning the express powers of Congress with relation to the reserved powers of the States." The classic formulation of that test by Chief Justice Marshall in *McCulloch v. Maryland,* was there adopted. It seems to me that this is also the standard that defines the scope of congressional authority under § 5 of the Fourteenth Amendment.

Viewed in its proper perspective, § 5 of the Fourteenth Amendment appears as a positive grant of legislative power, authorizing Congress to exercise its discretion in fashioning remedies to achieve civil and political equality for all citizens. No one would deny that Congress could enact legislation directing state officials to provide Negroes with equal access to state schools, parks and other facilities owned or operated by the State. Nor could it be denied that Congress has the power to punish state officers who, in excess of their authority and in violation of state law, conspire to threaten, harass and murder Negroes for attempting to use these facilities. And I can find no principle of federalism nor word of the Constitution that denies Congress power to determine that in order adequately to protect the right to equal utilization of state facilities, it is also appropriate to punish other individuals — not state officers themselves and not acting in concert with state officers — who engage in the same brutal conduct for the same misguided purpose.

NOTES

1. ***Civil actions for conspiracies.*** **42 U.S.C. § 1985(3)** provides a civil action for conspiracies to deprive a person of constitutional rights and has no "under color of law" provision. Can it be used to reach private conspiracies? What rights does it protect? In *Griffin v Breckenridge*, 403 U.S. 88 (1971), the Court recognized a § 1985(3) action brought by blacks for compensatory and punitive damages against white persons who, mistaking them for civil rights workers, stopped them on the highway, detained, assaulted, and beat them. The complaint alleged a conspiracy to prevent the plaintiffs from seeking equal protection of the laws and from enjoying the equal rights, privileges, and immunities of citizens, including but not limited to freedom of speech, movement, association, and assembly; the right to petition their government for redress of grievances; security in their homes; and their right not to be enslaved or deprived of life and liberty without due process of law.

Justice Stewart, for the Court, examining the language of § 1985(3), its companion provisions and its history, concluded that they "point unwaveringly to § 1985(3)'s coverage of private conspiracies." This did not mean that the provision was a general federal tort law since Congress intended that "there must be some racial, or perhaps otherwise class-based, invidiously discriminatory animus behind the conspirators' action. The conspiracy, in other words, must aim at a deprivation of the equal enjoyment of rights secured by the law to all." Justice Stewart noted that the Court was not deciding whether some "invidiously discriminatory intent" other than race might suffice. He claimed further that the requirement of "animus" was not equivalent to the specific intent required in *Screws*. Since the complaint set forth all of the elements of a § 1985(3) action, it was necessary to determine if Congress could constitutionally reach such action.

Justice Stewart found the requisite constitutional support for such an application of § 1985(3) in the Thirteenth Amendment: "Congress was wholly within its powers under § 2 of the Thirteenth Amendment in creating a statutory cause of action for Negro citizens who have been the victims of conspiratorial, racially discriminatory private action aimed at depriving them of the basic rights that the law secures to all free men."

Further support was found in cases, including *Guest,* which "have firmly established that the right of interstate travel is constitutionally protected, does not necessarily rest on the Fourteenth Amendment, and is assertable against private as well as governmental interference." This right of interstate travel "like other rights of national citizenship, is within the power of Congress to protect by appropriate action."

Justice Stewart concluded with the following comment:

> In identifying these two constitutional sources of congressional power, we do not imply the absence of any other. More specifically, the allegations of the complaint in this case have not required consideration of the scope of the power of Congress under § 5 of the Fourteenth Amendment. By the same token, since the allegations of the complaint bring this cause of action so close to the constitutionally authorized core of the statute, there has been no occasion here to trace out its constitutionally permissible periphery.

In a footnote, Justice Stewart cited *Guest, Katzenbach v. Morgan,* and *Oregon v. Mitchell.*

In *Bray v. Alexandria Women's Health Clinic*, 506 U.S. 263 (1993), abortion clinics and abortion rights organizations sought to enjoin Operation Rescue, an antiabortion group, from blocking access to abortion clinics. The plaintiffs unsuccessfully relied on 42 U.S.C. § 1985(3). The Court, per Justice Scalia, held that the plaintiffs had not shown that "some racial or perhaps otherwise class based, invidious discriminatory animus (lay) behind the conspirator's action and that the conspiracy aimed at interfering with rights that are protected against private as well as official encroachment" as required under *Griffin v. Breckenridge*. Operation Rescue's demonstrations had a harmful effect on women seeking abortions but did not discriminate against women as a class; some women oppose abortion. The animus requirement therefore was not satisfied.

How does "animus" differ from "specific intent"? Perhaps nonracial discriminatory animus is enough. The historical preoccupation with the needs of blacks for protection in framing the 1871 KKK Act may impose such a limitation. If the right of interstate travel is to be used as a constitutional nexus, must there be a showing that the right is somehow burdened? Can private interference with other Fourteenth Amendment rights be reached? Does the *Bray* case shed light on the latter issue?

2. *The use of other powers by Congress.* Congress can legislate under its commerce and spending powers against even private discrimination.

Further, the Thirteenth Amendment, § 2 can be used to legislate remedies for private action violating the rights therein guaranteed since the Amendment proscribes *all* slavery and involuntary servitude, not merely that imposed by government. Finally, it is established that Congress can legislate against official or private action violative of "federal rights" arising from the relation of the citizen to the national government. *See, e.g.*, *United States v. Classic*, 313 U.S. 299 (1941) (the right to vote in congressional primaries secured by Article I, § 2, as modified by Article I, § 4, and Article I, § 18, cl. 18); *In re Quarles*, 158 U.S. 532 (1895) (right of informer under federal custody to protection); *Ex parte Yarbrough*, 110 U.S. 651 (1884) (right to vote in federal elections); *United States v. Cruikshank*, 92 U.S. 542 (1876) (right to assemble and petition government). Rights secured by federal statute against private action can also be effectuated by congressional action.

Consider the statement of Justice Story in rejecting a constitutional challenge to the fugitive slave legislation in *Prigg v. Pennsylvania*, 41 U.S. (16 Peters) 539, 615 (1842): "If indeed, the Constitution guarantees the right the natural inference is, that the national government is clothed with the appropriate authority and functions to enforce it. The fundamental principle applicable to all cases of this sort, would seem to be, that where the end is required, the means are given."

Given all these vehicles available to a Congress seeking to protect civil rights against private action, consider Professor Tribe's observation that "as a grant of legislative power, the Fourteenth Amendment may be redundant." Laurence H. Tribe, American Constitutional Law 353 (2d ed. 1988).

3. *Right to interstate travel.* If Justice Stewart is adding the right of interstate movement to the catalog of federal rights, what is its source? See Chapter 7[A] on the right to travel in equal protection cases. If it is a privilege or immunity of national citizenship, a due process guarantee, or based on the equal protection guarantee, it could be argued that state action is still required. "The difficulty with the majority's analysis [in *Guest*] is that all but one of the cases cited in the opinion dealt with state interference with interstate travel. [T]he majority in *Guest* was able to cite no authority clearly supporting its holding that the right to travel is protected against private interference." Howard Feuerstein, *Civil Rights Crimes and the Federal Power to Punish Private Individuals for Interference with Federally Secured Rights,* 19 Vand. L. Rev. 641, 662–63 (1966). Consider Justice Stewart's assertion in *Griffin v. Breckenridge* that the right of interstate travel is not necessarily dependent on the Fourteenth Amendment.

4. *Original intent of the legislature.* Professor Harris identifies three primary views among the framers of the enforcement legislation. At one extreme were legislators who "embraced a construction of the amendment which sustained almost unlimited congressional power to protect constitutional rights against both official and private action, to the point of displacing state authority altogether without awaiting abridgements of constitutional rights." At the opposite extreme were those who took what has become the traditional view that "congressional power was limited to the elimination of unequal laws and the correction of official or state action alone." Finally, there was a middle ground suggesting that "Congress had the responsibility to protect constitutional rights in the event of failure of the states to do so, but only after the states had failed or refused to do their duty." ROBERT J. HARRIS, THE QUEST FOR EQUALITY 45 (1960).

5. *Access to facilities.* Assume that equal access to public facilities is a right secured by the equal protection clause. There are three possibilities for characterizing such a right: a right to a racially neutral state policy in admitting persons to public facilities; a right to be free from interference with the states' duty to provide equal protection of the laws; or a right to affirmative state action in protecting the person's nondiscriminatory access to public places. Do the rights in the Fourteenth Amendment, § 1, change depending on whether they are enforced directly by a court or through congressional legislation? Does the state owe a similar duty for access to privately-owned places of public accommodation? To public facilities generally? To private facilities generally? How do you determine the scope of the state's duty under the Fourteenth Amendment, § 1? Does it extend to state protection of all "fundamental rights"?

6. *Congressional definition of rights.* Justice Brennan in *Guest* recognizes congressional power to implement the substantive rights provided by the Fourteenth Amendment, § 1. Consider the point made by Professor Cox: "The only rights exactly correlative to the duties imposed by the Fourteenth Amendment are rights against the state, not against private individuals." He adds that if Congress may "take any action against private individuals which it judges appropriate to secure full enjoyment of the rights to life, liberty, and property," then the power of Congress is essentially unlimited. Archibald Cox, *Foreword: Constitutional Adjudication and the Promotion of Human Rights,* 80 HARV. L. REV. 91, 110, 115 (1966).

7. *Updated legislation.* In 1968, Congress provided a new criminal law remedy for denial of constitutional rights. The new statute, 18 U.S.C. § 245, punishes injury or intimidation of persons seeking to use listed federal or state facilities or most places of public accommodations. It has been suggested that compromises reflected in § 245, which were designed to mitigate potential federal-state friction resulting from civil rights prosecutions, have limited the section's effectiveness as a source of protection.

[B] UNDER THE THIRTEENTH AMENDMENT: THE HERITAGE OF SLAVERY

The Thirteenth Amendment, § 1, provides that "[n]either slavery nor involuntary servitude shall exist within the United States" and § 2 recognizes Congress' power to "enforce [the] article by appropriate legislation." In the *Civil Rights Cases,* the Court acknowledged that this would include primary legislation regulating even private action, but read the § 1 rights very narrowly. But as *Katzenbach v. Morgan* indicated, Congress may not be limited under the Civil War Amendments to providing remedies only for the violation of substantive rights recognized by the Court. Congress may have power to define the substantive right.

The principal response of the Court to this question came in the area of racial discrimination in housing. In 1968, two major blows were struck against maintenance of housing discrimination. The first was enactment of the 1968 Open Housing Act, 42 U.S.C. § 3601 et seq., prohibiting discrimination in the sale or rental of housing on the basis of race, color, religion or national origin. The Act also reaches discrimination in financing, real estate brokerage and advertising for the sale or rental of property. The second major effort against residential segregation came from the Court in *Jones v. Alfred H. Mayer Co.*

JONES v. ALFRED H. MAYER CO.

392 U.S. 409, 88 S. Ct. 2186, 20 L. Ed. 2d 1189 (1968)

JUSTICE STEWART delivered the opinion of the Court.

In this case we are called upon to determine the scope and constitutionality of an Act of Congress, 42 U.S.C. § 1982, which provides that:

> All citizens of the United States shall have the same right, in every State and Territory, as is enjoyed by white citizens thereof to inherit, purchase, lease, sell, hold, and convey real and personal property.

On September 2, 1965, the petitioners filed a complaint in the District Court alleging that the respondents had refused to sell them a home in the Paddock Woods community of St. Louis County for the sole reason that petitioner Joseph Lee Jones is a Negro. Relying in part upon § 1982, the petitioners sought injunctive and other relief. The District Court sustained the respondents' motion to dismiss the complaint, and the Court of Appeals for the Eighth Circuit affirmed, concluding that § 1982 applies only to state action and does not reach private refusals to sell. [W]e reverse the judgment of the Court of Appeals. We hold that § 1982 bars *all* racial discrimination, private as well as public, in the sale or rental of property, and that the statute, thus construed, is a valid exercise of the power of Congress to enforce the Thirteenth Amendment.[5]

At the outset, it is important to make clear precisely what this case does *not* involve. Whatever else it may be, 42 U.S.C. § 1982 is not a comprehensive open housing law. In sharp contrast to the Fair Housing Title (Title VIII) of the Civil Rights Act of 1968, the statute in this case deals only with racial discrimination and does not address itself to discrimination on grounds of religion or national origin. It does not deal specifically with discrimination in the provision of service or facilities in connection with the sale or rental of a dwelling. It does not prohibit advertising or other representations that indicate discriminatory preferences. It does not refer explicitly to discrimination in financing arrangements or in the provision of brokerage services.[10]

---

[5] Because we have concluded that the discrimination alleged in the petitioners' complaint violated a federal statute that Congress had the power to enact under the Thirteenth Amendment, we find it unnecessary to decide whether that discrimination also violated the Equal Protection Clause of the Fourteenth Amendment.

[10] In noting that 42 U.S.C. § 1982 differs from the Civil Rights Act of 1968 in not dealing explicitly and exhaustively with such matters, we intimate no view upon the question whether ancillary services, or facilities of this sort might in some situations constitute "property" as that term is employed in § 1982. Nor do we intimate any view upon the extent to which discrimination in the provision of such service might be barred by 42 U.S.C. § 1981.

It does not empower a federal administrative agency to assist aggrieved parties. It makes no provision for intervention by the Attorney General. And, although it can be enforced by injunction, it contains no provision expressly authorizing a federal court to order the payment of damages. Thus, although § 1982 contains none of the exemptions that Congress included in the Civil Rights Act of 1968, it would be a serious mistake to suppose that § 1982 in any way diminishes the significance of the law recently enacted by Congress.

On its face, § 1982 appears to prohibit *all* discrimination against Negroes in the sale or rental of property — discrimination by private owners as well as discrimination by public authorities. Stressing what they consider to be the revolutionary implication of so literal a reading of § 1982, the respondents argue that Congress cannot possibly have intended any such result. Our examination of the relevant history, however, persuades us that Congress meant exactly what it said.

[JUSTICE STEWART's lengthy review of legislative history is omitted. He concluded:]

In light of the concerns that led Congress to adopt it and the contents of the debates that preceded its passage, it is clear that the Act was designed to do just what its terms suggest: to prohibit all racial discrimination, whether or not under color of law, with respect to the rights enumerated therein — including the right to purchase or lease property. As we said in a somewhat different setting two Terms ago, "We think that history leaves no doubt that, if we are to give [the law] the scope that its origins dictate, we must accord it a sweep as broad as its language." *United States v. Price.* "We are not at liberty to seek ingenious analytical instruments," to carve from § 1982 an exception for private conduct — even though its application to such conduct in the present context is without established precedent.

The remaining question is whether Congress has power under the Constitution to do what § 1982 purports to do: to prohibit all racial discrimination, private and public, in the sale and rental of property. Our starting point is the Thirteenth Amendment, for it was pursuant to that constitutional provision that Congress originally enacted what is now § 1982.

As its text reveals, the Thirteenth Amendment "is not a mere prohibition of state laws establishing or upholding slavery, but an absolute declaration that slavery or involuntary servitude shall not exist in any part of the United States." *Civil Rights Cases.* It has never been doubted, therefore, "that the power vested in Congress to enforce the article by appropriate legislation," includes the power to enact laws "direct and primary, operating upon the acts of individuals, whether sanctioned by state legislation or not."

The constitutional question in this case, therefore, comes to this: Does the authority of Congress to enforce the Thirteenth Amendment "by appropriate legislation" include the power to eliminate all racial barriers to the acquisition of real and personal property? We think the answer to that question is plainly yes.

"By its own unaided force and effect," the Thirteenth Amendment "abolished slavery, and established universal freedom." *Civil Rights Cases.* Whether or not the Amendment *itself* did any more than that — a question not involved in this case — it is at least clear that the Enabling Clause of that Amendment empowered Congress to do much more. For that clause clothed "Congress with power to pass *all laws necessary and proper for abolishing all badges and incidents of slavery in the United States.*" *Ibid.* (Emphasis added.)

Surely Congress has the power under the Thirteenth Amendment rationally to determine what are the badges and the incidents of slavery, and the authority to translate that determination into effective legislation. Nor can we say that the determination Congress has made is an irrational one. For this Court recognized long ago that, whatever else they may have encompassed, the badges and incidents of slavery — its "burdens and disabilities" — included restraints upon "those fundamental rights which are the essence of civil freedom, namely, the same right to inherit, purchase, lease, sell and convey property, as is enjoyed by white citizens." *Civil Rights Cases.* Just as the Black Codes, enacted after the Civil War to restrict the free exercise of those rights, were substitutes for the slave system, so the exclusion of Negroes from white communities became a substitute for the Black Codes. And when racial discrimination herds men into ghettos and makes their ability to buy property turn on the color of their skin, then it too is a relic of slavery.

JUSTICE HARLAN, whom JUSTICE WHITE joins, dissenting.

I believe that the Court's construction of § 1982 as applying to purely private action is almost surely wrong, and at the least is open to serious doubt. The issues of the constitutionality of § 1982, as construed by the Court, and of liability under the Fourteenth Amendment alone, also present formidable difficulties. Moreover, the political processes of our own era have, since the date of oral argument in this case, given birth to a civil rights statute embodying "fair housing" provisions which would at the end of this year make available to others, though apparently not to the petitioners themselves, the type of relief which the petitioners now seek. It seems to me that this latter factor so diminishes the public importance of this case that by far the wisest course would be for this Court to refrain from decision and to dismiss the writ as improvidently granted.

Like the Court, I began analysis of § 1982 by examining its language. For me, there is an inherent ambiguity in the term "right," as used in § 1982. The "right" referred to may either be a right to equal status under the law, in which case the statute operates only against state-sanctioned discrimination, or it may be an "absolute" right enforceable against private individuals. To me, the words of the statute, taken alone, suggest the former interpretation, not the latter.

[JUSTICE HARLAN's counter-legislative history and comments on the ethics of the Reconstruction period are omitted. He concluded:]

In sum, the most which can be said with assurance about the intended impact of the 1866 Civil Rights Act upon purely private discrimination is that the Act probably was envisioned by most members of Congress as prohibiting official, community-sanctioned discrimination in the South, engaged in pursuant to local "customs" which in the recent time of slavery probably were embodied in laws or regulations.

I think it particularly unfortunate for the Court to persist in deciding this case on the basis of a highly questionable interpretation of a sweeping, century-old statute which, as the Court acknowledges, contains none of the exemptions which the Congress of our own time found it necessary to include in a statue regulating relationships so personal in nature. In effect, this Court, by its construction of § 1982, has extended the coverage of federal "fair housing" laws far beyond that which Congress in its wisdom chose to provide in the Civil Rights Act of 1968.

NOTES

1. *The language of § 1982: Rights and duties.* Does § 1982 have a "plain meaning"?

> Picture a situation in which a seller has placed property on the market for sale at a particular price, with the reservation that purchase is open to Whites only. Freeze the situation at that instance in time, and then ask whether black citizens in that situation have the same right to purchase real property as white citizens. Plainly they do not, if the words have any meaning at all.

Arthur Larson, *The New Law of Race Relations,* 1969 WIS. L. REV. 470, 487.

On the other hand: "The 'same rights' to purchase property could simply mean the same legal competence, that is, the same immunity from state-imposed disabilities." *The Supreme Court, 1967 Term,* 82 HARV. L. REV. 63, 96 (1968). Consider the other "rights" recognized in § 1982; do they help in clarifying the meaning of the term? Perhaps "right" could mean "liberty" or "privilege."

2. *Legislative history.* A principal point of contention among commentators has been whether the majority's or Justice Harlan's historical exegesis was correct. Professor Casper argues that the purpose of § 1982 "was to give practical effect to the repeal of discrimination laws and customs in the South." Gerhard Casper, *Jones v. Mayer: Clio, Bemused and Confused Muse,* 1968 SUP. CT. REV. 89, 99. Others argue that *Jones* did not even go as far as intended by the Reconstruction Congress. Consider again Chief Justice Warren's disparaging the value of the legislative history of the Reconstruction Congresses as a guide to decision in *Brown v. Board of Education.*

3. *Alternative constitutional rationale.* Section 1982 was reenacted in the 1870 Civil Rights Act following passage of the Fourteenth Amendment. The petitioners in *Jones* also argued a Fourteenth Amendment violation. What are the obstacles to successfully maintaining such a claim? Is it relevant that the respondent was a housing developer exercising continuing authority over a suburban housing complex having about 1,000 inhabitants? Is there any theory for overcoming the "state action" obstacle?

4. *A new Thirteenth Amendment?* Prior to *Jones,* the Thirteenth Amendment had been construed narrowly, limited primarily to federal legislation proscribing peonage and enforced labor. What is the rationale for reading "badges of slavery" into the Thirteenth Amendment, § 1? It has been observed that the framers chose neither broad natural law language nor narrow language dealing with ownership of persons:

> The language they did choose may at least be seen as lying in a middle range between "specific" and "great" concepts. Although seemingly narrow, it appears to have been designed as a full response to the evil perceived. As modern perceptions of that evil grow, the response may take on increasingly broader scope.

Note, 82 HARV. L. REV. 1294, 1302 (1969). In the absence of congressional enforcement legislation, does the Thirteenth Amendment, § 1, bar all "badges of slavery"? Has the Court adopted the first Justice Harlan's interpretation of the Thirteenth Amendment in his dissent in the *Civil Rights Cases*? Does the Thirteenth Amendment impose affirmative duties on government to eliminate "badges of slavery"? Perhaps it is a command to promote "freedom" or "liberty," the converse of slavery. Or, perhaps it is a command to eliminate, root and branch, the "relics of slavery." Or, finally, it may be a protection of all "fundamental rights."

5. *Power to deal with private discrimination.* What are the implications of *Jones* regarding congressional power? Does it open the door to broad congressional legislation against private racial discrimination? Professor Larson contends: "One certainly gets the impression from the opinion as a whole that, under the rubric of abolishing the badges and incidents of slavery, Congress would be within its constitutional rights in passing legislation striking down almost any conceivable kind of action, public or private, characterized by racial discrimination." Larson, 1969 WIS. L. REV. at 78. *See Griffin v. Breckenridge,* p. 1541, using § 1985(3) to enforce Thirteenth Amendment rights against private persons.

Can Congress reach nonracial discrimination under the *Jones* rationale?

> If *Jones* is read literally, Congress possesses a power to protect individual rights under the thirteenth amendment which is as open-ended as its power to regulate interstate commerce. Seemingly, Congress is free, within the broad limits of reason, to recognize whatever rights it wishes, define the infringement of those rights as a form of domination and thus an aspect of slavery, and proscribe such infringement as a violation of the Thirteenth Amendment.

LAURENCE H. TRIBE, AMERICAN CONSTITUTIONAL LAW 333 (2d ed. 1988). Professor Tribe cautions, however, that a literal reading of *Jones* might not come to pass since the Court's recent decisions have construed statutes that "are concerned almost entirely with racial discrimination, they raise few questions about the limits of Congress' Thirteenth Amendment power." Could Congress legislate against sex discrimination using the Thirteenth Amendment?

Beyond § 1982 Property Rights: *Runyon v. McCrary*

1. *42 U.S.C. § 1981*. This section, which was also part of the 1866 Civil Rights Act, reenacted in the 1870 legislation, seems even broader than § 1982:

> All persons shall have the same right to make and enforce contracts, to sue, be parties, give evidence, and to the full and equal benefit of

> all laws and proceedings as is enjoyed by white citizens, and shall be subject to like punishment, pains, penalties, taxes, licenses, and exactions of every kind, and to no other.

What is included in the term "contract"? Employment? Admission to public places? Education? Access to hospitals?

2. *Runyon v. McCrary,* 427 U.S. 160 (1976). Respondents claimed, and the district court found, that their children had been denied admission to two private schools because they were black. The Supreme Court held, 7-2, that 42 U.S.C. § 1981 prohibits private schools from excluding qualified children solely because they are black. Justice Stewart, writing for the Court, concluded that

> the racial exclusion practiced by [these schools] amounts to a classic violation of § 1981. The parents sought to enter into contractual relationships for educational services [under which] the schools would have received payments for services rendered, and the students would have received instruction for those payments. The educational services of [the schools] were advertised and offered to members of the general public. But neither school offered services on an equal basis to white and nonwhite students.

The Court also found that § 1981, as applied, did not violate "constitutionally protected rights of free association and privacy, or a parent's right to direct the education of his children."

Justice White, joined by Justice Rehnquist, dissenting, argued that "[t]he legislative history of 42 U.S.C. § 1981 confirms that the statute means what it says and no more, i.e., that it outlaws any legal rule disabling any person from making or enforcing a contract, but does not prohibit private racially motivated refusals to contract." The dissent also cautioned that the majority's holding

> threatens to embark the judiciary on a treacherous course. As the associational or contractual relationships become more private, the pressures to hold § 1981 inapplicable to them will increase. Imaginative judicial construction of the word "contract" is foreseeable; Thirteenth Amendment limitations on Congress' power to bar "badges and incidents of slavery" may be discovered; the doctrine of the right to association may be bent to cover a given situation.

Courts would be forced "to balance sensitive policy considerations," and all this would occur "under the guise of 'construing' a statute." Finally, Justice White concluded that the majority's construction of § 1981 was not compelled by *Jones*. "[§ 1982] is a Thirteenth Amendment statute under which the Congress may and did reach private conduct, at least with respect to sales of real estate. [§ 1981] is a Fourteenth Amendment statute under which Congress may and did reach only state action."

3. *Scope of the Thirteenth Amendment.* As he had done in *Jones,* Justice Stewart began his analysis in *Runyon* by noting the questions not presented in the case. It did not present questions involving "the right of a private social organization to limit its membership on racial or other grounds," "the right of a private school to limit its student body to boys, to girls, or to adherents of a particular religious faith, since 42 U.S.C. § 1981 is in no way addressed to such categories of selectivity"; or "the application of § 1981 to private sectarian schools that practice *racial* exclusion on religious grounds." Do Justice Stewart's qualifications suggest that § 1981 might not reach such activities? If so, would the limitations be statutory or constitutional in nature?

In the wake of *Runyon,* attempts have been made to identify the boundaries of § 1981. These efforts stem from a concern that § 1981 could be used to justify extensive federal court oversight of private activities. *See* Note, 29 STAN. L. REV. 747 (1977), which concludes that the rights of privacy and association have been so narrowly defined as to provide no real barrier to a broad application of § 1981 to discriminatory practices (e.g., segregated social clubs).

Are there any viable limits on the potential of the *Jones* rationale? Instead of looking at the values furthered by the Thirteenth Amendment's expansion, the question can be approached by looking at the competing values such as the rights of privacy, freedom of expression, and freedom of association. A balancing of values may be required. *See* Note, 82 HARV. L. REV. at 1312–15.

For example, social relationships may be partly contractual, as in a marriage, but privacy interests might still predominate:

> The same should be true where a person is seeking to establish a contractual relationship with a genuinely private club. Here, as in marriage, the dominant motive on both sides for entering into the relationship is personal and associational rather than economic. In such relationships, the legal system can justly place a higher premium on preserving an unfettered right of personal choice.

Sidney Buchanan, *Federal Regulation of Private Racial Prejudice: A Study of Law in Search of Morality,* 56 IOWA L. REV. 473, 507 (1971); *see Roberts v. United States Jaycees,* p. 1359.

4. ***The "private" sphere.*** It has been suggested that, with *Runyon,* the Court has completed the formulation of a "public/private sphere doctrine" which will not only replace the state action requirement of the Fourteenth Amendment but will also be used as a means of defining the breadth of the Thirteenth Amendment. This unitary response to Thirteenth and Fourteenth Amendment issues, it is argued, was dictated by the underlying question common to both Amendments: to what extent should civil rights efforts be allowed to interfere with private life?

> The developments in the civil rights cases of the last five years are fully compatible with two lines of doctrinal development extending over the past fifteen years that have more clearly distinguished the public sphere from the private. Racial discrimination was prohibited by Congress in the public spheres of service by private hotels and restaurants involved in interstate commerce, of employment practices by certain private commercial establishments, and of the private sale and rental of real estate under many circumstances. Meanwhile, the

> Supreme Court was discovering a constitutionally protected sphere of privacy in which individual liberty is the preferred value. These two developments would be wholly consonant with an explicit announcement by the Court that the Thirteenth or Fourteenth Amendment prohibits racial discrimination in the public but not in the truly private sphere.

Leslie Goldstein, "*Death and Transfiguration of the State Action Doctrine — Moose Lodge v. Irvis to Runyon v. McCrary,*" 4 HASTINGS CONST. L.Q. 1, 31–32 (1977).

5. *Reconsideration of Jones.* In its October, 1987 term, the Court shocked civil rights advocates when it set *Patterson v. McLean Credit Union*, 485 U.S. 617 (1988), for reargument on the question: "Whether or not the interpretation of 42 U.S.C. § 1981 adopted by this Court in *Runyon v. McCrary*, 427 U.S. 160 (1976), should be reconsidered." But in *Patterson v. McLean Credit Union*, 491 U.S. 164 (1989), the Court, per Justice Kennedy, unanimously concluded that "*Runyon* should not be overruled and we now reaffirm that § 1981 prohibits racial discrimination in the making and enforcement of private contracts."

The Court, however, held that "racial harassment relating to the conditions of employment is not actionable under § 1981 because the provision does not apply to conduct which occurs after the formation of a contract and which does not interfere with the right to enforce established contract obligations." The question under § 1981 is "whether the employer, *at the time of the formation of the contract,* in fact intentionally refused to enter a contract with the employee on racially neutral terms."

In the Civil Rights Act of 1991, Congress expanded the scope of § 1981 by redefining "make and enforce" to read "making, performance, modification, and termination of contracts, and the enjoyment of all benefits, privileges, terms and conditions of the contractual relationship."

Chapter 11

LIMITATIONS ON JUDICIAL REVIEW

The appropriate exercise of judicial review has formed the dominant theme of constitutional law for almost two centuries. Ever since *Marbury v. Madison* established the judicial review power over federal legislation and *Martin v. Hunter's Lessee* established judicial review over state legislation along with Supreme Court review over state courts, every constitutional law case has included at least two questions: whether a law is constitutional and whether the Court should say so. The Court's power has rarely been questioned, but whether the power should be used in given instances occasionally has surfaced as a burning issue. In some rare instances, the Court's exercise of the judicial review power has resulted in suggestions that the power should be curtailed or taken away. This Chapter explores these themes in detail.

The first topic is that of congressional control over the jurisdiction of the Supreme Court's appellate jurisdiction. Although Article III sets the outer boundaries of the judicial power, common doctrine is that Congress need not vest all of that power in the federal courts. Indeed, on its face it would seem that Congress' power to make exceptions to jurisdictional grants would allow it to carve out specific subjects on which the federal courts cannot act at all. There have been numerous proposals by politicians upset over a particular course of court decisions to divest the courts of power on that subject. Recent examples involve busing, school prayer, and abortion. There are a variety of theories that have been offered as restrictions on Congress' power to curtail federal court jurisdiction.

Beyond the possibility of congressional control over court jurisdiction, there exist a number of limitations on the review power both within the constitutional structure itself and within the Court's own sense of discretion. For example, the case-or-controversy requirement of Article III limits the variety of disputes that the federal courts can hear, and the courts have on occasion claimed the power to refuse to adjudicate a case for "prudential" reasons.

The doctrines that arise out of the case-or-controversy requirement and the claimed prudential considerations include standing, ripeness, and mootness. We have already seen one variation on the theme known as the political question doctrine. The others are similar in that they formally deny review over the issues presented by some party for decision. As you will see, when the Court decides that an issue is not justiciable in a case presenting a constitutional question, the result is that the defending party (often a federal or state official) is not constrained by the Constitution in the circumstances of that particular lawsuit.

As you study these materials, do not become excessively concerned with the variety of terms used to identify similar concepts. "Case or controversy," "justiciability," and the names of the specific doctrines within them, are used by different persons for different reasons. In some cases, they are all part of the same concept, while in others they identify strikingly different concepts. What is important is that you understand the processes at work and that you can use the tools available for analyzing a problem.

§ 11.01 CONGRESSIONAL CONTROL OF THE SUPREME COURT'S APPELLATE JURISDICTION: THE "EXCEPTIONS" CLAUSE

Article III, section 2 of the Constitution extends the Supreme Court's original jurisdiction (i.e., its jurisdiction to adjudicate cases in the first instance, without any other court having initially adjudicated them) to an extremely limited category of cases. "In all the other cases before mentioned," the provision then states, "the supreme court shall have appellate jurisdiction, both as to law and fact, with such exceptions, and under such regulations as the Congress shall make." If one were to take these words literally, they would seem to vest in Congress a vast power to exclude cases from the purview of the Supreme Court.

The potential extent of this congressional power has given rise to significant concern among scholars. *See, e.g.*, Henry Hart, *The Power of Congress to Limit the Jurisdiction of Federal Courts: An Exercise in Dialectic,* 66 HARV. L. REV. 1362 (1953); Leonard Ratner, *Congressional Power Over the Appellate Jurisdiction of the Supreme Court,* 109 U. PA. L. REV. 157 (1960). What do you think are the concerns?

It has never been definitively determined in the courts whether the language of the Exceptions Clause should, in fact, be read literally and unqualifiedly. The most important case considering the question is *Ex parte McCardle*, to which we now turn.

The Background of Ex Parte McCardle

McCardle, a sympathizer with the Southern cause, had published some editorials criticizing the federal military occupation of Mississippi in the Vicksburg, Mississippi TIMES between October 2 and November 6, 1867. The substance of these editorials resulted in McCardle's arrest and detention by the commanding general of the the federal military government in Mississippi. A military commission was convened to try McCardle on charges, among others, of disturbing the peace, inciting insurrection, and impeding reconstruction. McCardle sought a writ of habeas corpus from the federal court and invoked the Act of February 5, 1867 which gave the federal courts jurisdiction to grant writs of habeas corpus in cases where persons were detained in violation of law; the statute also provided for appeal to the United States Supreme Court. The federal court denied the writ, and McCardle appealed to the Supreme Court. McCardle filed his appeal on December 23, 1867. After oral argument was heard in the McCardle case, Congress, by a bill enacted over veto on March 27, 1868, repealed that part of the Habeas Corpus Act of February 5, 1867 which gave appellate jurisdiction to the Supreme Court. For a detailed historical account of *Ex parte McCardle*, see IV CHARLES FAIRMAN, HISTORY OF THE SUPREME COURT OF THE UNITED STATES: RECONSTRUCTION AND REUNION 1864–88, at 433–514 (1971).

In *Ex parte McCardle*, the Supreme Court upheld the right of Congress to withdraw appellate jurisdiction from the Supreme Court over a pending case. Congress had repealed the statute which gave the Court appellate jurisdiction in *McCardle* and the Court acquiesced in the repeal. Professor Pritchett describes the political background behind the repeal of the Act of 1867 by Congress as follows:

> That Court had just declared Lincoln's wartime use of military commissions unconstitutional in *Ex parte Milligan* [7 U.S. (4 Wall.) 2 (1866)], and Congress feared that it would use the McCardle appeal to invalidate the Reconstruction legislation. Consequently in March, 1868, the Radical Republicans rushed through Congress, and repassed over the President's veto, a statute repealing the Act of 1867 so far as it granted appeals to the Supreme Court, and withdrawing "any such jurisdiction by said Supreme Court, on appeals which have been, or may hereafter be taken."

Charles Pritchett, American Constitutional System 130 (2d. ed. 1968).

Professor Fairman, in his account of *Ex parte McCardle* in History of the Supreme Court of the United States, at 486, says that the question Chief Justice Chase wanted to have argued was whether Congress could "oust an appeal already perfected." The Supreme Court ultimately held unanimously, per Chief Justice Chase, that the Supreme Court's jurisdiction had been constitutionally ousted. As you read the *McCardle* case, consider the following question: should federal legislation which deprives the Supreme Court of its undoubted jurisdiction over an appeal in the middle of its consideration of that appeal be regarded as a violation of separation of powers? *See generally* William Van Alstyne, *A Critical Guide to Ex Parte McCardle,* 15 Ariz. L. Rev. 229 (1973).

Ex Parte McCARDLE

74 U.S. (7 Wall.) 506, 19 L. Ed. 264 (1869)

[Chief Justice Chase] delivered the opinion of the Court.

The first question necessarily is that of jurisdiction; for, if the act of March 1868, takes away the jurisdiction defined by the act of February, 1867, it is useless, if not improper, to enter into any discussion of other questions. It is quite true, as was argued by the counsel for the petitioner, that the appellate jurisdiction of this Court is not derived from acts of Congress. It is, strictly speaking, conferred by the Constitution. But it is conferred "with such exceptions and under such regulations as Congress shall make."

It is unnecessary to consider whether, if Congress had made no exceptions and no regulations, this Court might not have exercised general appellate jurisdiction under rules prescribed by itself. For among the earliest acts of the first Congress, at its first session, was the act of September 24th, 1789, to establish the judicial courts of the United States. That act provided for the organization of this Court, and prescribed regulations for the exercise of its jurisdiction.

The source of that jurisdiction, and the limitations of it by the Constitution and by statute, have been on several occasions subjects of consideration here. In the case of *Durousseau v. United States*, 6 Cranch 312, particularly, the whole matter was carefully examined, and the Court held, that while "the appellate powers of this Court are not given by the judicial act, but are given by the Constitution," they are, nevertheless, "limited and regulated by that act, and by such other acts as have been passed on the subject." The Court said, further, that the judicial act was an exercise of the power given by the Constitution to Congress "of making exceptions to the appellate jurisdiction of the Supreme Court." "They have described affirmatively," said the Court, "its jurisdiction, and this affirmative description has been understood to imply a negation of the exercise of such appellate power as is not comprehended within it." The principle that the affirmation of appellate jurisdiction implies the negation of all such jurisdiction not affirmed having been thus established, it was an almost necessary consequence that acts of Congress, providing for the exercise of jurisdiction, should come to be spoken of as acts granting jurisdiction, and not as acts making exceptions to the constitutional grant of it.

The exception to appellate jurisdiction in the case before us, however, is not an inference from the affirmation of other appellate jurisdiction. It is made in terms. The provision of the act of 1867, affirming the appellate jurisdiction of this Court in cases of habeas corpus is expressly repealed. It is hardly possible to imagine a plainer instance of positive exception.

We are not at liberty to inquire into the motives of the legislature. We can only examine into its power under the Constitution: and the power to make exceptions to the appellate jurisdiction of this Court is given by express words. What, then, is the effect of the repealing act upon the case before us? We cannot doubt as to this. Without jurisdiction the Court cannot proceed at all in any cause. Jurisdiction is power to declare the law, and when it ceases to exist, the only function remaining to the Court is that of announcing the fact and dismissing the cause. And this is not less clear upon authority than upon principle.

It is quite clear, therefore, that this Court cannot proceed to pronounce judgment in this case, for it has no longer jurisdiction of the appeal; and judicial duty is not less fitly performed by declining ungranted jurisdiction than in exercising firmly that which the Constitution and the laws confer.

Counsel seem to have supposed, if effect be given to the repealing act in question, that the whole appellate power of the Court, in cases of habeas corpus, is denied. But this is an error. The act of 1868 does not except from that jurisdiction any cases but appeals from Circuit Court under the act of 1867. It does not affect the jurisdiction which was previously exercised.

NOTES

1. *Ex parte Yerger*, 75 U.S. (8 Wall.) 75 (1869). This case suggested limits on *McCardle* both on the specifics of habeas corpus jurisdiction and on the general authority of Congress. Yerger was being held for trial by a military court just as McCardle had been. His petition for a writ of habeas corpus was denied by the lower courts and the Supreme Court asked for briefing and argument solely on the question of the Court's appellate jurisdiction.

The Court pointed out that Congress had granted habeas corpus jurisdiction in several statutory provisions, including acts of 1789 (prisoners pending trial by United States authorities, committed for trial by United States courts, or to be brought into court to testify), 1833 (prisoners confined under any authority, state or federal, for acts done under color of federal authority), 1842 (foreign citizens acting under color of foreign authority), and 1867 (any person confined in violation of federal constitution, treaty, or statute). Although the 1867 habeas corpus provision had been repealed, the courts and the Supreme Court still possessed other means, in view of the earlier legislation, to free a prisoner from unlawful confinement.

2. *United States v. Klein*, 80 U.S. (13 Wall.) 128 (1872). *Klein* placed a gloss on *McCardle*. Under a series of Reconstruction statutes, Congress provided that rebels would forfeit their property to the United States and created the Court of Claims to adjudicate title to property confiscated by the government. President Johnson offered pardons to rebels who would take an oath of loyalty; in return, they could have their property back. When the Supreme Court held that the Court of Claims was to enforce the President's promise, Congress passed additional legislation declaring that a pardon should have the effect of establishing guilt, directing the Court of Claims to deny claims from pardoned rebels, and withdrawing appellate jurisdiction by the Supreme Court over the Court of Claims.

> Undoubtedly the legislature has complete control over the organization and existence of that court and may confer or withhold the right of appeal from its decisions. And if this act did nothing more, it would be our duty to give it effect. If it simply denied the right of appeal in a particular class of cases, there could be no doubt that it must be regarded as an exercise of the power of Congress to make "such exceptions from the appellate jurisdiction" as should seem to it expedient.
>
> But the language of this proviso shows plainly that it does not intend to withhold appellate jurisdiction except as a means to an end. Its great and controlling purpose is to deny to pardons granted by the President the effect which this court had adjudged them to have. The proviso declares that pardons shall not be considered by this court on appeal. We had already decided that it was our duty to consider them and give them effect, in cases like the present as equivalent to proof of loyalty.
>
> The court is required to ascertain the existence of certain facts and thereupon to declare that its jurisdiction on appeal has ceased, by dismissing the bill. What is this but to prescribe a rule for the decision of the cause in a particular way? In the case before us, the Court of Claims has rendered judgment for the claimant and an appeal has been taken to this court. We are directed to dismiss the appeal, if we find that the judgment must be affirmed, because of a pardon granted to the intestate of the claimants. Can we do so without allowing one party to the controversy to decide it in its own favor? Can we do so

without allowing that the legislature may prescribe rules of decision to the Judicial Department of the government in cases pending before it? We must think that Congress has inadvertently passed the limit which separates the legislative from the judicial power.

The rule prescribed is also liable to just exception as impairing the effect of a pardon, and thus infringing the constitutional power of the Executive. To the executive alone is intrusted the power of pardon; and it is granted without limit. Pardon includes amnesty. It blots out the offence pardoned and removes all its penal consequences. It may be granted on conditions. In these particular pardons, that no doubt might exist as to their character, restoration of property was expressly pledged, and the pardon was granted on condition that the person who availed himself of it should take and keep a prescribed oath. Now it is clear that the legislature cannot change the effect of such a pardon any more than the executive can change a law. Yet this is attempted by the provision under consideration. This certainly impairs the executive authority and directs the court to be instrumental to that end.

3. *Felker v. Turpin*, 518 U.S. 651 (1996). Congress has considered a variety of measures over the years by which to curtail prisoner access to the federal courts, particularly with regard to repeated petitions for habeas corpus by state prisoners. Those petitions typically allege constitutional defects in the prisoner's trial or incarceration. In 1996, Congress declared that a prisoner could have only one habeas petition considered on its merits unless a new claim arose as a matter of change in constitutional law or the petitioner could demonstrate factual innocence of the crime along with reasons why the facts were not fully developed at trial. The Supreme Court granted expedited review of a claim by a petitioner who was on death row and who had previously been denied habeas relief by the federal courts. The arguments that the statute unconstitutionally stripped the federal courts of judicial review authority and that it interfered with the prohibition on suspension of the writ of habeas corpus were met by the government's contention that the statute did not preclude original jurisdiction in the Supreme Court of extraordinary habeas petitions. The Court accepted the government's view:

> We hold that the Act does not preclude this Court from entertaining an application for habeas corpus relief, although it does affect the standards governing the granting of such relief. We also conclude that the availability of such relief in this Court obviates any claim by petitioner under the Exceptions Clause of Article III, § 2, of the Constitution, and that the operative provisions of the Act do not violate the Suspension Clause of the Constitution, Art. I, § 9.

Felker did not resolve the issue raised in *McCardle*: Can Congress abolish all Supreme Court review of a constitutional issue? Professor Cole argues that the question cannot be answered satisfactorily.

> If the Court were to hold that Congress may make whatever "exceptions" it pleases, judicial independence would be seriously

> impaired. If, on the other hand, the Court were to impose precise limits on how Congress can limit its jurisdiction, the checking function of the "exceptions" clause would be substantially diminished. Thus, the clause best serves its function as long as its scope remains ambiguous.

David Cole, *The Question That Cannot Be Answered*, LEGAL TIMES, June 3, 1996, p. 21, 25. What is the downside of leaving this issue unresolved?

4. *The breadth of* McCardle. Viewing *Ex parte Yerger* and *McCardle* together, it has been argued by some commentators that the Court in *McCardle* had approved only a limited contraction of the Court's appellate jurisdiction in habeas cases. Professor Bernard Schwartz makes clear, for example, that the key point in *McCardle* is that the Court did not hold "that Congress could validly oust it of all appellate jurisdiction in habeas corpus cases." *See* BERNARD SCHWARTZ, CONSTITUTIONAL LAW, A TEXTBOOK 19 (1972). The implication of Professor Schwartz' analysis is that a modest contraction of appellate jurisdiction is permissible, but a severe contraction of that jurisdiction is impermissible because it would be a violation of separation of powers.

Can Congress eliminate the only effective remedy for vindicating a constitutional right? Does the due process guarantee limit Congress' power under Article III, § 2? If so, does that in any way limit Congress' power under the exceptions clause? That power extends only to the Supreme Court's appellate jurisdiction. If Congress were to leave unaffected the authority of the federal district and appellate courts to review the constitutionality of federal or state statutes, and remove only the Supreme Court's jurisdiction, would due process be violated? *See* Martin H. Redish, *Congressional Power to Regulate Supreme Court Appellate Jurisdiction Under the Exceptions Clause: An Internal and External Examination*, 27 VILL. L. REV. 900, 915—16 (1982): "Since the Supreme Court itself has unequivocally held that due process does not require the provision of any level of appellate review, there can be no doubt that mere removal of the Supreme Court's appellate jurisdiction would fail to present any due process problems."

5. *The arguments from original intent.* ROBERT BORK, CONSTITUTIONALITY OF THE PRESIDENT'S BUSING PROPOSALS 7 (1972): "Would the framers have couched a general power to control the Court, to nullify its function as a final interpreter of the law, in the language of 'exceptions' and 'regulations'? Or does that language more probably imply authority over relatively minor problems, matters of detail and convenience?" Judge Bork makes the following comment about *McCardle*:

> *McCardle* is a rather enigmatic precedent. If it stands for the proposition that Congress may take away any category of the Supreme Court's jurisdiction, it obviously is capable of destroying the entire institution of judicial review since *Marbury v. Madison*. So read, there is good reason to doubt *McCardle's* vitality as a precedent today.

Justice Douglas made an even broader disclaimer in dissent in *Glidden v. Zdanok*, 370 U.S. 530, 605 n.11 (1962): "There is a serious question whether the *McCardle* case could command a majority view today."

A very different view is found in Justice Frankfurter's dissent in *National Mut. Ins. Co. v. Tidewater Transfer Co.*, 337 U.S. 582, 655 (1948): "Congress need not give this Court any appellate power; it may withdraw appellate jurisdiction once conferred and it may do so even while a case is *sub judice.*" Professor Wechsler states the point bluntly:

> Federal courts, including the Supreme Court, do not pass on constitutional questions because there is a special function vested in them to enforce the Constitution or police the other agencies of the government. They do so rather for the reason that they must decide a litigated issue that is otherwise within their jurisdiction and in doing so must give effect to the supreme law of the land.

Herbert Wechsler, *The Courts and the Constitution*, 65 COLUM. L. REV. 1001, 1005—06 (1965). Professor Wechsler also points out that citizens may rely on "state courts, bound as they are by the Constitution as 'the supreme Law of the Land any Thing in the Constitution or Laws of any State to the Contrary notwithstanding.'" Is the power of the state judiciary over federal enactments persuasive as an alternative?

6. *Jurisdiction-stripping proposals.* The existence of *Ex parte McCardle* as a precedent has served to stimulate repeated congressional efforts to deprive the lower federal courts of original jurisdiction and the Supreme Court of appellate jurisdiction in one or another controversial area where court decisions met with legislative displeasure. These proposals have proceeded on the implicit assumption that by exercising its power to limit jurisdiction under the Exceptions Clause, Congress is—either legally or practically—overturning a preexisting line of Supreme Court doctrine or particular Supreme Court decisions. Illustrative examples are busing of students to effect school integration, school prayer, and abortion.

a. School prayer. A typical example of a jurisdiction-stripping bill is one introduced by Senator Jesse Helms of North Carolina, introduced in January, 1985 (S.47, 99th Cong., 1st Sess.):

> The Supreme Court shall not have jurisdiction to review, by appeal, writ of certiorari, or otherwise, any case arising out of any State statute, ordinance, rule, regulation, practice, or any part thereof, which relates to voluntary prayer, Bible reading, or religious meetings in public schools or public buildings.
>
> Notwithstanding any other provision of law, the district courts shall not have jurisdiction of any case or question which the Supreme Court does not have jurisdiction to review under [the previous section].

Earlier, the Reagan administration had backed a proposal for a constitutional amendment to allow prayer in the public schools. When that proposal was defeated in the Senate, Senator Helms warned that "there is more than one way to skin a cat, and there is more than one way for Congress to provide a check on arrogant Supreme Court Justices who routinely distort the Constitution to suit their own notions of public policy." 130 CONG. REC. S2901 (March 20, 1984 daily ed.).

b. Abortion. Another Helms initiative was contained in the so-called "Human Life Statute," H.R. 900 & S. 158, 97th Cong., 1st Sess. (1981). After declaring the view of Congress that life begins at conception, the proposal would go on to provide:

> Notwithstanding any other provision of law, no inferior Federal court ordained and established by Congress under article III of the Constitution of the United States shall have jurisdiction to issue any restraining order, temporary or permanent injunction, or declaratory judgment in any case involving or arising from any State law or municipal ordinance that (1) protects the rights of human persons between conception and birth, or (2) prohibits, limits, or regulates (a) the performance of abortions or (b) the provision at public expense of funds, facilities, personnel, or other assistance for the performance of abortions.

Notice that this proposal would not limit the Supreme Court's jurisdiction to hear cases coming out of the state courts dealing with abortions. It would only prevent the district courts from issuing injunctions. By contrast, H.R. 867, introduced in the same session of Congress, would have stripped both the Supreme Court and the lower federal courts of jurisdiction in abortion cases. With *Casey* on the books as the latest Supreme Court precedent, if Congress stripped the Court of jurisdiction, what would be the law of the land with respect to constitutional protection for abortion? Would such legislative action have the effect of overruling *Casey* and *Roe*? Consider the following argument: A congressional exception to the Supreme Court's appellate jurisdiction to review the constitutionality of anti-abortion legislation would-at least as a theoretical matter-have the ironic effect of locking in those decisions. *See* Martin H. Redish, *Congressional Power to Limit Supreme Court Appellate Jurisdiction: An Internal and External Examination,* 27 VILL. L. REV. 900 (1982).

7. The internal and external theories of limits on Congress. The various proposals to limit federal jurisdiction have spawned extensive hearings in the Senate and commentaries in the press. As might be expected, the professional academics are at the heart of attempting to elaborate the bases for validity or invalidity of these proposals.

Professor Ratner finds limits within the structure of the Constitution and separation of powers. He argues that Congress cannot destroy the "essential constitutional functions of the Court to maintain the supremacy and uniformity of federal law." Leonard Ratner, *Congressional Power Over the Appellate Jurisdiction of the Supreme Court,* 109 U. PA. L. REV. 157 (1960); *Majoritarian Constraints on Judicial Review: Congressional Control of Supreme Court Jurisdiction,* 27 VILL. L. REV. 929 (1982). This position stems from the position of Professor Henry Hart that Congress ultimately cannot "destroy the essential role of the Supreme Court in the constitutional plan." Henry Hart, *The Power of Congress to Limit the Jurisdiction of Federal Courts: An Exercise in Dialectic,* 66 HARV. L. REV. 1362, 1365 (1953). Examine the text of the Exceptions Clause in Art. III, § 2. Does it provide a basis to support such a limited construction? A variation on the theme is that, although Congress may have the sheer power to limit federal court jurisdiction, abusive exercise of the power would violate the spirit of the Constitution. Paul Bator, *Congressional Power Over the Jurisdiction of the Federal Courts*, 27 VILL. L. REV. 1030, 1039 (1982).

Most critics discount this notion of "internal" checks based on the "essential functions" theory. Professor Gunther, for example, points out that it is difficult to imply internal checks from the very document that contains the clauses allowing Congress to make exceptions to federal court jurisdiction. Gerald Gunther, *Congressional Power to Curtail Federal Court Jurisdiction: An Opinionated Guide to the Ongoing Debate*, 36 STAN. L. REV. 895, 907 (1984).

Another "internal" view is that, although Congress can make some exceptions to either the appellate or the original power of the federal courts, it cannot leave a litigant without some federal forum for assertion of constitutional rights. Lawrence Sager, *Foreword: Constitutional Limitations on Congress' Authority to Regulate the Jurisdiction of the Federal Courts*, 95 HARV. L. REV. 17 (1981).

The leading advocate of "external" restraints is probably Professor Tribe, who argues that forcing certain disfavored federal constitutional claims to proceed through the state courts would constitute a denial of equal protection. Laurence Tribe, *Jurisdictional Gerrymandering: Zoning Disfavored Rights Out of the Federal Courts*, 16 HARV. C.R. -C.L.L. REV. 129 (1981). To this argument, Professor Gunther replies that Congress' "disaffection" with the results of certain Supreme Court cases can be expressed in this fashion unless there is something in the Constitution itself to restrain it. In other words, the Tribe position does not address the initial question of Congress' explicit authority to make exceptions to federal court jurisdiction. Gunther, 36 STAN. L. REV. at 920.

Finally, it must be noted that even those accepting broad congressional discretion strongly urge Congress not to abuse its power with regard to the federal courts. Congress has rejected jurisdiction-stripping proposals on every occasion since the days of Reconstruction. (Although some limited deferrals of federal jurisdiction have given the state courts first crack at certain kinds of cases.) Gunther goes so far as to suggest that there is enough support in the literature to warrant a defensive Court in invalidating a harsh measure from Congress despite the theoretical problems. 36 STAN. L. REV. at 922.

8. *Demore v. Hyung Joon Kim*, 538 U.S. 510 (2003). Chief Justice Rehnquist, writing for the Court, began by evaluating the petitioner's claim that 8 U.S.C. § 1226(e) prohibited judicial review of the Attorney General's decision to detain the respondent. This claim was based on a provision within the statute that such decisions by the Attorney General are not reviewable by any court. First, the Court distinguished between judicial review of an operational decision to detain an individual, which is barred by the language of the provision, and judicial review of the constitutional validity "of the statutory framework that permits his detention without bail." When Congress intends to bar review of constitutional claims, its intent must be clear. The "clear text" of this statute does not bar such a claim. Furthermore, "where a provision precluding review is claimed to bar habeas review, the Court has required a particularly clear statement that such is Congress' intent." The Court concluded that the statute did not contain such a clear statement of congressional intent to bar habeas review.

Justice O'Connor, joined by Justices Scalia and Thomas, concurred in part and concurred in the judgment. She asserted that the only "plausible reading" of Sec. 1226(e) was that Congress intended to bar the federal courts from setting aside the Attorney General's decision to detain criminal aliens during deportability proceedings. She contended that Congress should not be deemed to repeal habeas jurisdiction without a "specific and unambiguous directive to that effect." She considered the argument that the statute violated the Suspension Clause, which provides: "The Privilege of the Writ of Habeas Corpus shall not be suspended, unless when in Cases of Rebellion or Invasion the public Safety may require it." Art. I, Sec. 9, cl.2, "is likely unavailing," since the Clause protects the Writ as it existed in 1789. She pointed out that in 1789 "and thereafter until very recently" habeas corpus was not "generally available" to aliens to challenge detention during deportation proceedings. However, since the majority have determined that judicial review exists here, "I need not conclusively determine the thorny question whether 8 U.S.C. § 1226 (e) violates the Suspension Clause."

§ 11.02 CONSTITUTIONAL AND POLICY LIMITATIONS

[A] THE CASE OR CONTROVERSY REQUIREMENT

The case-or-controversy requirement has been understood to prohibit the federal courts from giving advisory opinions on constitutional matters. The courts may decide only "flesh and blood" controversies. They cannot reach out to resolve an issue until it comes to the court bearing the hallmarks of actual controversy between two litigants who are adversaries in fact.

Professor Lea Brilmayer suggests three policies underlying the Article III requirement: "the smooth allocation of power among courts over time [avoiding premature decisions]; the unfairness of holding later litigants to an adverse judgment in which they have not been properly represented [representational interests]; and the importance of placing control over the political processes in the hands of the people most closely involved [self-determination interests]." Lea Brilmayer, *The Jurisprudence of Article III: Perspectives on the "Case or Controversy" Requirement*, 93 Harv. L. Rev. 297, 306 (1979). In her view, these interests reflect the significance of ensuring that the court is adequately informed on the consequences of an action before rendering decision. The major debate in the materials that follow is whether the courts have any discretion to "reject" a "case" because it does not serve these or similar interests. *See* Mark Tushnet, *The Sociology of Article III: A Response To Professor Brilmayer*, 93 Harv. L. Rev. 1698 (1980); Lea Brilmayer, *A Reply*, 93 Harv. L. Rev. 1727 (1980).

The requirement that the federal courts adjudicate only cases or controversies implements the principles of separation of powers among the branches. *See* Martin H. Redish, The Federal Courts in the Political Order 89–90 (1991): "The 'case-or-controversy' prerequisite was presumably designed to ensure that the unrepresentative branch would not function in a manner identical to that of the representative branches. By confining the judiciary's operation to the adjudication of live, adversary disputes capable of being resolved and whose resolution may be enforced, Article III ensures that the judicial branch will neither be able to initiate or enact wholly generalized legislative edicts, nor carry out the day-to-day executive or administrative tasks of government. Article III, then, requires that the judiciary perform its essential political role in a manner unique among the branches."

The fact that a case-or-controversy requirement exists, however, does not automatically explain how one is to be able to determine whether such a case or controversy is actually present in an individual situation. In the next case, consider whether the Court (a) adequately defined the indicia of case or controversy, and (b) properly applied those criteria to the facts.

MUSKRAT v. UNITED STATES

219 U.S. 346, 31 S. Ct. 250, 55 L. Ed. 246 (1911)

[Under federal legislation enacted in 1902, certain property was set aside for some Cherokee Indians, although it was to be administered by the federal government. Federal laws, enacted in 1904 and 1906, attempted to enlarge the number of Indians who would share in the property. Also, the duration of the period prohibiting restraints on alienation of the property was lengthened by the 1904 and 1906 federal legislation.

[Indians whose claims derived from the 1902 Act were adversely affected because their property rights would be diminished to the extent that they had to share the land with a larger class. Some persons whose claims derived from the 1902 Act, among them Muskrat, were authorized by Congress in 1907 to bring suit in the United States Court of Claims in order to obtain a determination of the constitutionality of the 1904 and 1906 Acts. The Court of Claims sustained the validity of the Acts and dismissed the petitions. In a decision that has since been often cited, the Supreme Court held that the 1907 statute was itself unconstitutional on the ground that it violated the case or controversy requirement of Article III.]

JUSTICE DAY delivered the opinion of the Court.

The first question in these cases, as in others, involves the jurisdiction of this court to entertain the proceeding, and that depends upon whether the jurisdiction conferred is within the power of Congress, having in view the limitations of the judicial power as established by the Constitution of the United States. [The Court quotes Article III.] It will serve to elucidate the nature and extent of the judicial power thus conferred by the Constitution to note certain instances in which this court has had occasion to examine and define the same.

In 1793, by direction of the President, Secretary of State Jefferson addressed to the Justices of the Supreme Court a communication soliciting their views upon the question whether their advice to the executive would be available in the solution of important questions of the construction of treaties, laws of nations and laws of the land, which the Secretary said were often presented under circumstances which "do not give a cognizance of them to the tribunals of the country." The answer to the question was postponed until the subsequent sitting of the Supreme Court, when CHIEF JUSTICE JAY and his associates answered to President Washington that in consideration of the lines of separation drawn by the Constitution between the three departments of government, and being judges of a court of last resort, afforded strong arguments against the propriety of extra-judicially deciding the question alluded to, and expressing the view that the power given by the Constitution to the President of calling on heads of departments for opinions "seems to have been purposely, as well as expressly, united to the executive departments."

It therefore becomes necessary to inquire what is meant by the judicial power thus conferred by the Constitution upon this Court, and with the aid of appropriate legislation upon the inferior courts of the United States. "Judicial power," says MR. JUSTICE MILLER in his work on the Constitution, "is the power of a court to decide and pronounce a judgment and carry it into effect between persons and parties who bring a case before it for decision. As we have already seen by the express terms of the Constitution, the exercise of the judicial power is limited to "cases" and "controversies." Beyond this it does not extend, and unless it is asserted in a case or controversy within the meaning of the Constitution, the power to exercise it is nowhere conferred.

What, then, does the Constitution mean in conferring this judicial power with the right to determine "cases" and "controversies"? A "case" was defined by MR. CHIEF JUSTICE MARSHALL as early as the leading case of *Marbury v. Madison*, to be a suit instituted according to the regular course of judicial procedure. [I]n the case of *In re Pacific Railway Commission* [the Court stated:]

> By cases and controversies are intended the claims of litigants brought before the courts for determination by such regular proceedings as are established by law or custom for the protection or enforcements of rights, or the prevention, redress, or punishment of wrongs. Whenever the claim of a party under the Constitution, laws, or treaties of the United States takes such a form that the judicial power is capable of acting upon it, then it has become a case. The term implies the existence of present or possible adverse parties whose contentions are submitted to the court for adjudication.

Applying the principles thus long settled by the decisions of this court to the act of Congress undertaking to confer jurisdiction in this case, [it is] evident that there is neither more nor less in this procedure than an attempt to provide for a judicial determination, final in this court, of the constitutional validity of an act of Congress. Is such a determination within the judicial power conferred by the Constitution? We think it is not. That judicial power, as we have seen, is the right to determine actual controversies arising between adverse litigants, duly instituted in courts of proper jurisdiction. The right to declare a law unconstitutional arises because an act of Congress relied upon by one or the other of such parties in determining their rights is in conflict with the fundamental law. The exercise of this, the most important and delicate duty of this court, is not given to it as a body with revisory power over the action of Congress, but because the rights of the litigants in justiciable controversies require the court to choose between the fundamental law and a law purporting to be enacted within constitutional authority, but in fact beyond the power delegated to the legislative branch of the Government. This attempt to obtain a judicial declaration of the validity of the act of Congress is not presented in a "case" or "controversy," to which, under the Constitution of the United States, the judicial power alone extends. It is true the United States is made a defendant to this action, but it has no interest adverse to the claimants. The object is not to assert a property right as against the Government, or to demand compensation for alleged wrongs because of action upon its part. The whole purpose of the law is to determine the constitutional validity of this class of legislation, in a suit not arising between parties concerning a property right necessarily involved in the decision in question, but in a proceeding against the Government in its sovereign capacity, and concerning which the only judgment required is to settle the doubtful character of the legislation in question. Such judgment will not conclude private parties, when actual litigation brings to the court the question of the constitutionality of such legislation. In a legal sense the judgment could not be executed, and amounts in fact to no more than an expression of opinion upon the validity of the acts in question.

Nor can it make any difference that the petitioners had brought suits in the Supreme Court of the District of Columbia to enjoin the Secretary of the Interior from carrying into effect the legislation subsequent to the act of July 1, 1902, which suits were pending when the jurisdictional act here involved was passed. The latter act must depend upon its own terms and be judged by the authority which it undertakes to confer. If such actions as are here attempted, to determine the validity of legislation, are sustained, the result will be that this court, instead of keeping within the limits of judicial power and deciding cases or controversies arising between opposing parties, as the Constitution intended it should, will be required to give opinions in the nature of advice concerning legislative action, a function never conferred upon it by the Constitution, and against the exercise of which this court has steadily set its face from the beginning.

The questions involved in this proceeding as to the validity of the legislation may arise in suits between individuals, and when they do and are properly brought before this court for consideration they, of course, must be determined in the exercise of its judicial functions. For the reasons we have stated, we are constrained to hold that these actions present no justiciable controversy within the authority of the court, acting within the limitations of the Constitution under which it was created. The judgments will be reversed and the cases remanded to the Court of Claims, with directions to dismiss the petitions for want of jurisdiction.

NOTES

1. *Advisory opinions.* Do you think our constitutional tradition would be richer if the Supreme Court had acceded to Secretary of State Jefferson's request to answer the many questions of law with which the Department of State was faced but which were not of the type which were likely to develop into litigation? As the *Muskrat* decision makes clear, Chief Justice Jay reacted negatively to this request on the ground that the Supreme Court must not give advisory opinions. This position has been followed in theory by Article III federal courts to this day. Yet in some states whose own constitutions erect no barriers against the rendition of advisory opinions, state supreme courts give advisory opinions on proposed state legislation with regard to questions of validity under both state and federal constitutions. For example, in 1973, the Supreme Judicial Court of Massachusetts declared that a proposed bill requiring newspapers within the state to publish political ads for all candidates running for an office, if the paper published the political ad of one such candidate, was violative of the First Amendment. *See Opinion of the Justices*, 298 N.E.2d 829 (Mass. 1973). Is the Supreme Court necessarily without jurisdiction to review an advisory opinion from a state supreme court?

2. *The remedial posture of* Muskrat. Should not a less rigorous definition of the case or controversy requirement have been arrived at by the Court in *Muskrat*? Surely, from the point of view of a reasonable and serviceable definition of the case or controversy requirement, there is more apparent adversity described in Muskrat's claim that the 1904 and 1906 acts invalidly infringed on his property rights, than there is in the Secretary of State's desire to have the Supreme Court do some authoritative legal research for him. The *Muskrat* fact situation could easily have produced a case or controversy. When someone whose claims derived under the 1904 and 1906 acts went upon Muskrat's land to take possession, Muskrat could sue for ejectment. The issue of the validity of the title would be a case or controversy. Does this possibility of suit make the Court's decision in *Muskrat* more or less reasonable?

Is the reason the *Muskrat* suit was not a case or controversy primarily due to the fact that Muskrat had no quarrel with the federal government, the nominal defendant under the Act of 1907, but with the new class of Indians who had been given rights to his property under the Acts of 1904 and 1906? This new class of Indians should have been the appropriate parties defendant. Yet even if the Act of 1907 had made this new class of Indians the parties defendant, there might still not have been an Article III case or controversy under the theory of the *Muskrat* decision. Two things would have had to occur to make the situation an actual case or controversy. The new class of Indians would have had to have taken possession of property claimed by Muskrat, and the first class of Indians and Muskrat would have had to manifest their objection to that possession by filing a law suit on their own motion.

[B] DISCRETIONARY AVOIDANCE OF CONSTITUTIONAL ISSUES

While some limitations on the exercise of judicial review flow from the jurisdictional provisions of Article III, others are a result of the Court's own sense of self-restraint, an attempt to define its proper place within the legal-political system. These policy parameters on the judicial review power are indicated in the following case.

RESCUE ARMY v. MUNICIPAL COURT

331 U.S. 549, 67 S. Ct. 1409, 91 L. Ed. 1666 (1947)

JUSTICE RUTLEDGE delivered the opinion of the Court.

[T]his Court has followed a policy of strict necessity in disposing of constitutional issues. The policy, however, has not been limited to jurisdictional determinations. For, in addition, "the Court [has] developed, for its own governance in the cases confessedly within its jurisdiction, a series of rules under which it has avoided passing upon a large part of all the constitutional questions pressed upon it for decision." Thus, as those rules were listed in support of the statement quoted, constitutional issues affecting legislation will not be determined in friendly, nonadversary proceedings; in advance of the necessity of deciding them; in broader terms than are required by the precise facts to which the ruling is to be applied; if the record presents some other ground upon which the case may be disposed of; at the instance of one who fails to show that he is injured by the statute's operation, or who has availed himself of its benefits; or if a construction of the statute is fairly possible by which the question may be avoided. [*See Ashwander v. TVA*, 297 U.S. 288 (1936).]

Like the case and controversy limitation itself and the policy against entertaining political questions, [the policy] is one of the rules basic to the federal system and this Court's appropriate place within that structure. Indeed in origin and in practical effects, though not in technical function, it is a corollary offshoot of the case and controversy rule. And often the line between applying the policy or the rule is very thin. They work, within their respective and technically distinct areas, to achieve the same practical purposes for the process of constitutional adjudication, and upon closely related considerations.

The policy's ultimate foundations, some if not all of which also sustain the jurisdictional limitation, lie in all that goes to make up the unique place and character, in our scheme, of judicial review of governmental action for constitutionality. They are found in the delicacy of that function, particularly in view of possible consequences for others stemming also from constitutional roots; the comparative finality of those consequences; the consideration due to the judgment of other repositories of constitutional power concerning the scope of their authority; the necessity, if government is to function constitutionally, for each to keep within its power, including the courts; the inherent limitations of the judicial process, arising especially from its largely negative character and limited resources of enforcement; withal in the paramount importance of constitutional adjudication in our system.

All these considerations and perhaps others, transcending specific procedures, have united to form and sustain the policy. Its execution has involved a continuous choice between the obvious advantages it produces for the functioning of government in all its coordinate parts and the very real disadvantages, for the assurance of rights, which deferring decision very often entails. On the other hand it is not altogether speculative that a contrary policy, of accelerated decision, might do equal or greater harm for the security of private rights, without attaining any of the benefits of tolerance and harmony for the functioning of the various authorities in our scheme. For premature and relatively abstract decisions, which such a policy would be most likely to promote, have their part too in rendering rights uncertain and insecure.

NOTES

1. *The "policy of strict necessity" and "prudential considerations."* The first step in understanding *Rescue Army* is to identify the "policy" that Justice Rutledge was describing. First, he says that it is a policy "not limited to jurisdictional determinations" and that it can apply to "cases confessedly within [the Court's] jurisdiction." Defining the policy consists of listing a number of "considerations" that would seem to make the Court wary of exercising its judicial review function. Between these two steps, the opinion presents a list of "rules" that the Court follows in deciding cases. That list is drawn from Justice Brandeis' opinion for the Court in *Ashwander v. TVA.*

The rules provided in *Ashwander* have to do with the hierarchy of decisions that a Court would consider in deciding a case. They are used in *Rescue Army* as if they justified a policy of not deciding a case.

It still remains to determine what the policy is that is described in *Rescue Army*. It appears to be an open-ended discretion on the part of the Court to refuse to decide an issue. In justifying such a policy, some writers have described it as an exercise of "prudence" on the part of the Court. Thus has arisen a practice of referring to factors such as those listed in *Rescue Army* as the "prudential considerations" governing the Court's willingness or unwillingness to exercise its jurisdiction. There is clearly a fine line separating the *Rescue Army* principles of judicial self-restraint and the policies underlying the case or controversy requirement. As the cases set forth in the remainder of the chapter indicate, the vagueness of the dividing line often makes it difficult to determine whether the obstacle to constitutional decision is a jurisdictional bar, or whether it reflects judicial self-restraint expressed through a policy of avoidance of judicial review.

2. *Judicial duty to decide.* Not everyone would agree that a federal court should ever decline to exercise the judicial power. Consider the statement of John Marshall in *Cohens v. Virginia*, p. 30:

> It is most true that this Court will not take jurisdiction if it should not: but it is equally true, that it must take jurisdiction if it should. The judiciary cannot, as the legislature may, avoid a measure because it approaches the confines of the constitution. We cannot pass it by because it is doubtful. With whatever doubts, with whatever difficulties, a case may be attended, we must decide it, if it be brought before us. We have no more right to decline the exercise of jurisdiction which is given, than to usurp that which is not given. The one or the other would be treason to the constitution. Questions may occur which we would gladly avoid; but we cannot avoid them. All we can do is, to exercise our best judgment, and conscientiously to perform our duty.

Is this statement consistent with *Ashwander*? with *Rescue Army*?

3. *Adequate and independent state grounds for decision.* One of the principles set out in *Ashwander* is that the Supreme Court will not decide a federal question on appeal from a state court, even if wrongly decided, if there is an adequate and independent state ground also given for the decision that would produce the same result. In *Michigan v. Long*, 463 U.S. 1032 (1984), the Court elaborated that

> when, as in this case, a state court decision fairly appears to rest primarily on federal law, or to be interwoven with the federal law, and when the adequacy and independence of any possible state law ground is not clear from the face of the opinion, we will accept as the most reasonable explanation that the state court decided the case the way it did because it believed that federal law required it to do so. If a state court chooses merely to rely on federal precedents as it would on the precedents of all other jurisdictions, then it need only make clear by a plain statement in its judgment or opinion that the federal cases are being used only for the purpose of guidance, and do not themselves compel the result that the court has reached. If the state court decision indicates clearly and expressly that it is alternatively based on bona fide separate, adequate, and independent grounds, we, of course, will not undertake to review the decision.

This principle has become increasingly important as lawyers bring suit in "favorable" state courts claiming both federal and state constitutional violations. State courts can decide such cases using both grounds for decision. It can then be argued that the Supreme Court should not review the decision because there is an adequate independent state basis for the decision.

§ 11.03 JUSTICIABILITY LIMITATIONS

[A] THE STANDING LIMITATION: WHO CAN LITIGATE?

The Supreme Court requires that every federal litigant have "standing" to make the claims in her action or defense. In part this standing requirement is deemed to derive directly from Article III's case-or-controversy requirement: If constitutionally dictated standing is absent, no case or controversy exists. In addition to the requirements of Article III, however, the Supreme Court has imposed what have been referred to as "prudential" limits on standing. These are limits that the Court has recognized, not because they derive from Article III, but rather because the Court deems them wise as a matter of judicial administration. As a consequential matter, the key difference between the two forms of standing limitations is that Congress may explicitly revoke the prudential limits, while Congress may not extend litigant standing to exceed the limits imposed by the Constitution.

As you will see from the cases that follow, the Court has construed the Constitution to require that three factors be present: injury in fact, traceability, and redressability. In other words, the plaintiff must (1) have suffered a concrete injury, (2) that injury must be traceable to the challenged acts of the defendant, and (3) the court must be in a position to redress the plaintiff's injury by providing some form of relief. How do you think each one of these requirements is thought to foster the policies underlying the case-or-controversy requirement?

Prudential limits come into play only once it has been determined that the three prerequisites of constitutionally dictated standing have been satisfied. These limits, then, are relevant only to plaintiffs who satisfy the constitutional requirements. An example is the prohibition on so-called "third-party standing," where a litigant seeks to benefit in his own litigation by asserting the rights of third parties. Consider the following argument: Perhaps paradoxically, the Supreme Court's imposition of prudential limits, authorized by neither the Constitution nor congressional statute, constitutes improper judicial activism in the name of judicial restraint.

[1] TAXPAYER AND CITIZEN STANDING: THE IDEOLOGICAL PLAINTIFF AND THE REQUIREMENT OF INJURY IN FACT

This section deals with what are referred to as "taxpayer suits." The plaintiff claims to be a taxpayer who has been injured because the government to which he pays his taxes has expended funds in a manner that violates law. In the following cases, ask yourself how well the three requirements of constitutional standing are satisfied in taxpayer suits, and whether it is possible to distinguish among different categories of taxpayer suits for these purposes. Also consider whether those who bring taxpayer suits are usually more appropriately characterized as "ideological" plaintiffs, and what the consequences of such a concept are for the case-or-controversy requirement.

MASSACHUSETTS v. MELLON
FROTHINGHAM v. MELLON

262 U.S. 447, 43 S. Ct. 597, 67 L. Ed. 1078 (1923)

Justice Sutherland delivered the opinion of the Court.

Both cases challenge the constitutionality of the Act of November 23, 1921, c. 135, 42 Stat. 224, commonly called the Maternity Act. Briefly, it provides for an initial appropriation and thereafter annual appropriations for a period of five years, to be apportioned among such of the several states as shall accept and comply with its provisions, for the purpose of cooperating with them to reduce maternal and infant mortality and protect the health of mothers and infants.

In the Massachusetts case it is alleged that the plaintiff's rights and powers as a sovereign state and the rights of its citizens have been invaded and usurped by these expenditures and acts; and that, although the state has not accepted the act, its constitutional rights are infringed by the passage thereof and the imposition upon the state of an illegal and unconstitutional option either to yield to the federal government a part of its reserved rights or lose the share which it would otherwise be entitled to receive of the moneys appropriated. In the *Frothingham* case plaintiff alleges that the effect of the statute will be to take her property, under the guise of taxation, without due process of law. We have reached the conclusion that the cases must be disposed of for want of jurisdiction without considering the merits of the constitutional questions.

In the first case, the State of Massachusetts presents no justiciable controversy either in its own behalf or as the representative of its citizens. The appellant in the second suit has no such interest in the subject-matter, nor is any such injury inflicted or threatened, as will enable her to sue.

First. The State of Massachusetts in its own behalf, in effect, complains that the act in question invades the local concerns of the state, and is a usurpation of power, viz: the power of local self-government reserved to the states. In the last analysis, the complaint of the plaintiff state is brought to the naked contention that Congress has usurped the reserved powers of the several states by the mere enactment of the statute, though nothing has been done and nothing is to be done without their consent; and it is plain that that question, as it is thus presented, is political and not judicial in character, and therefore is not a matter which admits of the exercise of the judicial power.

It follows that in so far as the case depends upon the assertion of a right on the part of the state to sue in its own behalf we are without jurisdiction. In that aspect of the case we are called upon to adjudicate, not rights of persons or property, not rights of dominion over physical domain, not quasi-sovereign rights actually invaded or threatened, but abstract questions of political power, of sovereignty, of government. No rights of the state falling within the scope of the judicial power have been brought within the actual or threatened operation of the statute.

We come next to consider whether the suit may be maintained by the state as the representative of its citizens. To this the answer is not doubtful. We need not go so far as to say that a state may never intervene by suit to protect its citizens against any form of enforcement of unconstitutional acts of Congress; but we are clear that the right to do so does not arise here. Ordinarily, at least, the only way in which a state may afford protection to its citizens in such cases is through the enforcement of its own criminal statutes, where that is appropriate, or by opening its courts to the injured persons for the maintenance of civil suits or actions. But the citizens of Massachusetts are also citizens of the United States. It cannot be conceded that a state, as parens patriae, may institute judicial proceedings to protect citizens of the United States from the operation of the statutes thereof. While the state, under some circumstances, may sue in that capacity for the protection of its citizens, it is no part of its duty or power to enforce their rights in respect of their relations with the federal government. In that field it is the United States, and not the state, which represents them as parens patriae, when such representation becomes appropriate; and to the former, and not to the latter, they must look for such protective measures as flow from that status.

Second. The attack upon the statute in the *Frothingham* case is, generally, the same, but this plaintiff alleges in addition that she is a taxpayer of the United States; and her contention, though not clear, seems to be that the effect of the appropriation complained of will be to increase the burden of future taxation and thereby take her property without due process of law. The right of a taxpayer to enjoin the execution of a federal appropriation act, on the ground that is invalid and will result in taxation for illegal purposes, has never been passed upon by this Court. The interest of a taxpayer of a municipality in the application of its moneys is direct and immediate and the remedy by injunction to prevent their misuse is not inappropriate. But the relation of a taxpayer of the United States to the federal government is very different. His interest in the moneys of the Treasury — partly realized from taxation and partly from other sources — is shared with millions of others; is comparatively minute and indeterminable; and the effect upon future taxation, of any payment out of the funds, so remote, fluctuating and uncertain, that no basis is afforded for an appeal to the preventive powers of a court of equity.

The administration of any statute, likely to produce additional taxation to be imposed upon a vast number of taxpayers, the extent of whose several liability is indefinite and constantly changing, is essentially a matter of public and not of individual concern. If one taxpayer may champion and litigate such a cause, then every other taxpayer may do the same, not only in respect of the statute here under review but also in respect of every other appropriation act and statute whose administration requires the outlay of public money, and whose validity may be questioned. The bare suggestion of such a result, with its attendant inconveniences, goes far to sustain the conclusion which we have reached, that a suit of this character cannot be maintained. It is of much significance that no precedent sustaining the right to maintain suits like this has been called to our attention, although, since the formation of the government, as an examination of the acts of Congress will disclose, a large number of statutes appropriating or involving the expenditure of moneys for non-federal purposes have been enacted and carried into effect.

The functions of government under our systems are apportioned. To the legislative department has been committed the duty of making laws; to the executive the duty of executing them; and to the judiciary the duty of interpreting and applying them in cases properly brought before the courts. The general rule is that neither department may invade the province of the other and neither may control, direct or restrain the action of the other. We are not now speaking of the merely ministerial duties of officials. We have no power per se to review and annul acts of Congress on the ground that they are unconstitutional. That question may be considered only when the justification for some direct injury suffered or threatened, presenting a justiciable issue, is made to rest upon such an act. Then the power exercised is that of ascertaining and declaring the law applicable to the controversy. It amounts to little more than the negative power to disregard an unconstitutional enactment, which otherwise would stand in the was of the enforcement of a legal right. The party who invokes the power must be able to show not only that the statute is invalid but that he has sustained or is immediately in danger of sustaining some direct injury as the result of its enforcement, and not merely that he suffers in some indefinite way in common with people generally. If a case for preventive relief be presented the court enjoins, in effect, not the execution of the statute, but the acts of the official, the statute notwithstanding. Here the parties plaintiff have no such case. Looking through forms of words to the substance of their complaint, it is merely that officials of the executive department of the government are executing and will execute an act of Congress asserted to be unconstitutional; and this we are asked to prevent. To do so would be not to decide a judicial controversy, but to assume a position of authority over the governmental acts of another and co-equal department, an authority which plainly we do not possess.

NOTES

1. *Unenforceable limitations?* With respect to the state of Massachusetts, did the Court hold that the state cannot complain of congressional breaches of constitutional limitations on the apportionment of tax revenues among the states or that there indeed were no such limitations? Is it possible that there are limitations but that they are not judicially enforceable? The Court states that the question of whether "Congress has usurped the reserved powers of the several states" is "political and not judicial in character." Is this a holding "on the merits" that Congress is not subject to any legal restraints in its relationship to the states? Is it an expression of the political question doctrine? The broad question behind each of these questions is whether there is a consistent theme with respect to the proper role of the Court in assessing the findings and policies of the other branches of government.

With respect to Mrs. Frothingham, did the Court hold that Congress is not limited in the purposes for which it may spend or that the taxpayer has no basis to complain of breaches of any such limitations? Is it possible that there are limitations but that they are not judicially enforceable?

2. *State taxpayer suits — Doremus v. Board of Educ.*, 342 U.S. 429 (1952). The *Frothingham* case established a general rule barring federal taxpayer standing to challenge federal action. This rule differs from the rules of standing established by many states for state taxpayers challenging state action as violative of the United States Constitution. In *Doremus*, two plaintiffs, state and municipal taxpayers, challenged a New Jersey statute requiring certain portions of the Old Testament to be read without comment at the opening of each public school day. The taxpayers were unable to show that their taxes were affected by the state statute. Nevertheless, the state court took the position that there was standing but then ruled against the plaintiffs on the merits.

The Supreme Court dismissed the appeal on the ground that the basis on which standing was conferred by New Jersey was inadequate to evidence a case or controversy which is required for the litigation of a case in a federal court. Justice Jackson said in *Doremus*:

> The taxpayer's action can meet this [case or controversy] test, but only when it is a good-faith pocketbook action. It is apparent that the grievance which it is sought to litigate here is not a direct dollars-and-cents injury but is a religious difference. If appellants established the requisite special injury necessary to a taxpayer's case or controversy, it would not matter that their dominant inducement to action was more religious than mercenary. It is not a question of motivation but of possession of the requisite financial interest that is, or is threatened to be, injured by the unconstitutional conduct.

The Court's quarrel with the fact situation in *Doremus* was that a good-faith taxpayer's suit was not present. The Bible reading did not affect the taxes of the plaintiffs. In dissent, Justice Douglas, joined by Justices Reed and Burton, said that the Bible reading statute deflected the public schools "from the education program for which the taxes were raised."

The conventional rationale for allowing state and municipal taxpayer suits while refusing federal taxpayer suits is that an individual taxpayer's "pocket-book" injury is a more significant part of total revenues on the state or municipal level than is the case on the federal level. Obviously, when we are dealing with corporate taxpayers at the federal level compared to individual taxpayers in populous and wealthy states like New York and California, the taxpayer's over-all stake in any given expenditure may be greater at the federal level.

Some states' willingness to see taxpayer status as sufficient to satisfy a standing requirement is obviously based on the view that it is desirable to provide judicial oversight for state and local government. Is there any reason that such accountability should not be desirable at the federal level as well? Or does the case and controversy requirement of Article III present a barrier which is not present on the state or local level?

3. *Defendant standing — Asarco Inc. v. Kadish,* 490 U.S. 605 (1989). The Supreme Court, per Justice Kennedy, held that "when a state court has issued a judgment in a case where plaintiffs in the original action had no standing to sue under the principles governing the federal courts, we may exercise our jurisdiction on certiorari if the judgment of the state court causes direct, specific, and concrete injury to the parties who petition for our review, where the requisites of a case or controversy are also met." The plaintiffs in the state court could not have met the *Doremus* "good-faith pocketbook" requirement, but the judgment of the state court invalidated oil and gas leases held by the defendants. Thus the defendants, petitioners in the Supreme Court, had suffered actual injury by the action of the state court.

FLAST v. COHEN

392 U.S. 83, 88 S. Ct. 1942, 20 L. Ed. 2d 947 (1968)

Chief Justice Warren delivered the opinion of the Court.

The gravamen of the appellants' complaint was that federal funds appropriated under the [federal] Act were being used to finance instruction in reading, arithmetic, and other subjects in religious schools, and to purchase textbooks and other instructional materials for use in such schools. Such expenditures were alleged to be in contravention of the Establishment and Free Exercise Clauses of the First Amendment.

[O]ur point of reference in this case is the standing of individuals who assert only the status of federal taxpayers and who challenge the constitutionality of the federal spending program. Whether such individuals have standing to maintain that form of action turns on whether they can demonstrate the necessary stake as taxpayers in the outcome of the litigation to satisfy Article III requirements.

The nexus demanded of federal taxpayers has two aspects to it. First, the taxpayer must establish a logical link between that status and the type of legislative enactment attacked. Thus, a taxpayer will be a proper party to allege the unconstitutionality only of exercises of congressional power under the taxing and spending clause of Art. I, § 8, of the Constitution. It will not be sufficient to allege an incidental expenditure of tax funds in the administration of an essentially regulatory statute. This requirement is consistent with the limitation imposed upon state taxpayer standing in federal courts in *Doremus v. Board of Education*. Secondly, the taxpayer must establish a nexus between that status and the precise nature of the constitutional infringement alleged. Under this requirement, the taxpayer must show that the challenged enactment exceeds specific constitutional limitations imposed upon the exercise of the congressional taxing and spending power and not simply that the enactment is generally beyond the powers delegated to Congress by Art. I, § 8. When both nexuses are established, the litigant will have shown a taxpayer's stake in the outcome of the controversy and will be a proper and appropriate party to invoke a federal court's jurisdiction.

The taxpayer-appellants in this case have satisfied both nexuses to support their claim of standing under the test we announce today. Their constitutional challenge is made to an exercise by Congress of its power under Art. I, § 8, to spend for the general welfare, and the challenged program involves a substantial expenditure of federal tax funds. In addition, appellants have alleged that the challenged expenditures violate the Establishment and Free Exercise Clauses of the First Amendment. Our history vividly illustrates that one of the specific evils feared by those who drafted the Establishment Clause and fought for its adoption was that the taxing and spending power would be used to favor one religion over another or to support religion in general. The Establishment Clause was designed as a specific bulwark against such potential abuses of governmental power, and that clause of the First Amendment operates as a specific constitutional limitation upon the exercise by Congress of the taxing and spending power conferred by Art. I, § 8.

We have noted that the Establishment Clause of the First Amendment does specifically limit the taxing and spending power conferred by Art. I, § 8. Whether the Constitution contains other specific limitations can be determined only in the context of future cases. However, whenever such specific limitations are found, we believe a taxpayer will have a clear stake as a taxpayer in assuring that they are not breached by Congress. Under such circumstances, we feel confident that the questions will be framed with the necessary specificity, that the issues will be contested with the necessary adverseness and that the litigation will be pursued with the necessary vigor to assure that the constitutional challenge will be made in a form traditionally thought to be capable of judicial resolution. We lack that confidence in cases such as *Frothingham* where a taxpayer seeks to employ a federal court as a forum in which to air his generalized grievances about the conduct of government or the allocation of power in the Federal System.

JUSTICE DOUGLAS, concurring.

While I have joined the opinion of the Court, I do not think that the test it lays down is a durable one for the reasons stated by my Brother Harlan.

I think, therefore, that it will suffer erosion and in time result in the demise of *Frothingham v. Mellon*. It would therefore be the part of wisdom, as I see the problem, to be rid of *Frothingham* here and now.

JUSTICE STEWART, concurring.

I join the judgment and opinion of the Court, which I understand to hold only that a federal taxpayer has standing to assert that a specific expenditure of federal funds violates the Establishment Clause of the First Amendment. Because that clause plainly prohibits taxing and spending in aid of religion, every taxpayer can claim a personal constitutional right not to be taxed for the support of a religious institution. The present case is thus readily distinguishable from *Frothingham v. Mellon* where the taxpayer did not rely on an explicit constitutional prohibition but instead questioned the scope of the powers delegated to the national legislature by Article I of the Constitution.

JUSTICE HARLAN, dissenting.

The complaint in this case, unlike that in *Frothingham*, contains no allegation that the contested expenditures will in any fashion affect the amount of these taxpayers' own existing or forseeable tax obligations. Even in cases in which such an allegation is made, the suit cannot result in an adjudication either of the plaintiff's tax liabilities or of the propriety of any particular level of taxation. The relief available to such a plaintiff consists entirely of the vindication of rights held in common by all citizens.

Surely it is plain that the rights and interests of taxpayers who contest the constitutionality of public expenditures are markedly different from those of "Hohfeldian" plaintiffs,[5] including those taxpayer-plaintiffs who challenge the validity of their own tax liabilities. We must recognize that these non-Hohfeldian plaintiffs complain, just as the petitioner in *Frothingham* sought to complain, not as taxpayers, but as "private attorneys-general." The interests they represent, and the rights they espouse, are bereft of any personal or proprietary coloration. They are, as litigants, indistinguishable from any group selected at random from among the general population, taxpayers and nontaxpayers alike. These are and must be, to adopt Professor Jaffe's useful phrase, "public actions" brought to vindicate public rights.

It seems to me clear that public actions, whatever the constitutional provisions on which they are premised, may involve important hazards for the continued effectiveness of the federal judiciary. Although I believe such actions to be within the jurisdiction conferred upon the federal courts by Article III of the Constitution, there surely can be little doubt that they strain the judicial function and press to the limit judicial authority. There is every reason to fear that unrestricted public actions might well alter the allocation of authority among the three branches of the Federal Government. [S]uch

[5] The phrase is Professor Jaffe's, adopted, of course, from W. HOHFELD, FUNDAMENTAL LEGAL CONCEPTIONS (1923). I have here employed the phrases "Hohfeldian" and "non-Hohfeldian" plaintiffs to mark the distinction between the personal and proprietary interests of the traditional plaintiff, and the representative and public interests of the plaintiff in a public action. I am aware that we are confronted here by a spectrum of interests of varying intensities, but the distinction is sufficiently accurate, and convenient, to warrant its use at least for purposes of discussion.

actions would, even without conscious abuse, go far toward the final transformation of this Court into the Council of Revision which despite Madison's support, was rejected by the Constitutional Convention. The powers of the federal judiciary will be adequate for the great burdens placed upon them only if they are employed prudently, with recognition of the strengths as well as the hazards that go with our kind of representative government.

This Court has previously held that individual litigants have standing to represent the public interest, despite their lack of economic or other personal interests, if Congress has appropriately authorized such suits. I would adhere to that principle. Any hazards to the proper allocation of authority among the three branches of the Government would be substantially diminished if public actions had been pertinently authorized by Congress and the President. I appreciate that this Court does not ordinarily await the mandate of other branches of the Government, but it seems to me that the extraordinary character of public actions, and of the mischievous, if not dangerous, consequences they involve for the proper functioning of our constitutional system, and in particular of the federal courts, makes such judicial forbearance the better part of wisdom.

NOTES

1. *The nexus holding.* The Court in *Flast* stated that a taxpayer would have standing when "the challenged enactment exceeds specific constitutional limitations imposed upon the exercise of the congressional taxing and spending power and not [when] the enactment is generally beyond the powers delegated to Congress by Art. I, § 8." To reach the conclusion on standing, therefore, it was necessary to decide that there was a specific limitation on the spending power. The "double nexus" required by *Flast* purports to be between (1) taxpayer status and challenged enactment, and (2) taxpayer status and the constitutional provision. There necessarily then is a link between the enactment and the constitutional provision. In other words, standing exists because there is a specific constitutional provision limiting the spending power.

2. *Distinguishing* Frothingham. After *Flast*, is *Frothingham* still good law? If the distinction between the two cases is only the nature of the constitutional provision invoked, what would be wrong with saying forthrightly that Art. I, § 8 imposes no limits on Congress' spending power? If that statement had been a bad idea in 1923, would it have been an equally bad idea in 1968? If *Frothingham* had been reversed in its entirety, as Justice Douglas urged, what would the result be — complete judicial review of all federal legislation under which expenditures are made?

3. *Injury in fact: citizens' suits.* Professor Davis has long advocated standing for any party who is aggrieved or injured by administrative action and challenges that action in the courts. The critical point, argues Professor Davis, is that the would-be litigant has suffered "injury in fact," no matter how slight. This requirement could be satisfied, in Davis' view, even by a taxpayer's investment in a federal spending program. Does *Flast* adopt this approach? Professor Davis believes that Justice Harlan misinterpreted the concept of "private attorney-general" by reading it as a basis for standing where the plaintiff has no personal stake in the suit. Kenneth Davis, *Standing: Taxpayers and Others*, 35 U. Chi. L. Rev. 601, 611–17, 628–36 (1968). Professor Davis' analysis of *Flast* prompted a reply by another commentator, who argued that *Flast* would eventually be seen as the first step in the abandonment of all standing requirements. *See* Boris Bittker, *The Fictitious Taxpayer: The Federal Taxpayer's Suit Twenty Years After Flast v. Cohen,* 36 U. Chi. L. Rev. 364 (1968).

Why should a plaintiff have to demonstrate injury in fact—i.e., a personal stake in the outcome of the controversy—in order to satisfy Article III case or controversy? For example, in *Frothingham* why could the plaintiff not assert, simply, that she possessed a strong interest in this particular legal issue? Would the policies underlying the case-or-controversy requirement have been undermined if such a suit were allowed to proceed? To what extent is the injury-in-fact requirement designed to foster principles of judicial restraint? Consider the following argument: Absent the injury-in-fact requirement, the courts would constantly be placed in the position of reviewing the constitutionality of the actions of the other two branches, thereby giving rise to significant interbranch tensions and undermining the democratically based value of having primary policy making flowing out of the representative and accountable branches of the federal government. Judge, now Justice, Antonin Scalia wrote "that the judicial doctrine of standing is a crucial and inseparable element of [the separation of powers] principle, whose disregard will inevitably produce — as it has in the past few decades — an overjudicialization of the processes of self-governance." Antonin Scalia, *The Doctrine of Standing as an Essential Element of the Separation of Powers*, 17 Suffolk L. Rev. 881 (1983). Scalia goes on to point out that wrapping the question of whether a plaintiff has suffered injury to a "legal right" in "prudential" standing language makes it seem as if the Court itself is deciding not to adjudicate rather than making it clear that the legislature has decided that the claimed right does not exist. Comparing the legislature to the Framers of the Constitution, has not the Court in cases like *Valley Forge* decided that the claimed establishment clause limitation on property transfers does not exist while purporting to exercise its own discretion not to decide the issue?

Dean Nichol is highly critical of what he sees to be a further movement "away from clarity" in the standing doctrine. Gene Nichol, *Abusing Standing: A Comment on Allen v. Wright,* 133 U. Pa. L. Rev. 635 (1985). "If a case threatens the appropriate separation of powers, it should be dismissed; but it should be dismissed under a doctrine that considers such intrusion as its decisive factor—that is, the political question doctrine." He goes on to observe that the lack of clarity in the doctrine means that "standing can apparently be either rolled out or ignored in order to serve unstated and unexamined values."

See also Martin H. Redish, The Federal Courts in the Political Order 94–95 (1991), asserting that "[i]njury-in-fact is neither a necessary nor sufficient feature of judicial restraint, as that concept is properly understood. [It is accurate to believe] that use of an injury-in-fact requirement reduces the sum total of constitutional challenges to majoritarian action, and in that sense the requirement could be thought to foster judicial restraint. But that fact alone should not serve as a sufficient justification for adoption of a jurisdictional rule. For example, a rule randomly excluding from federal court jurisdiction every fourth constitutional case that has been filed would reduce the number of constitutional challenges by 25 percent, yet surely no one would suggest that therefore such a practice represents a wise instrument of judicial restraint. [T]here is no reason to believe that the injury-in-fact requirement is any more rational a means of ensuring judicial restraint than a process of random selection."

To what extent may the injury-in-fact requirement be explained on the basis that litigants who have a concrete interest in the case can be presumed to take the case more seriously in the role of an advocate than would someone who lacked such a concrete interest? Is this necessarily true? For example, compare the zealousness of an anti-abortion activist group (which presumably cannot satisfy the injury-in fact-requirement) in challenging the existence of a constitutional right to an abortion to an individual litigant who is suing to recover $50. Which of those two litigants is more likely to take the case seriously?

The injury-in-fact requirement has been subjected to scathing attacks in the scholarly literature. For discussions of the requirement that are largely critical, see REDISH at 87-103; Henry Monaghan, *Constitutional Adjudication: The Who and When,* 82 YALE L.J. 1363 (1979); Gene Nichol, *Rethinking Standing,* 72 CAL. L. REV. 68 (1984); Mark Tushnet, *The Sociology of Article III: A Response to Professor Brilmayer,* 93 HARV. L. REV. 1698 (1980). Does a plaintiff in a taxpayer suit fail to satisfy the injury-in-fact requirement?

4. *Associational standing — Sierra Club v. Morton,* 405 U.S. 727 (1972). For a few years, it appeared as if these predictions of the demise of standing might bear fruit, at least in reduction of the doctrine's significance. A major standing suit arose out of a Walt Disney proposal for a multi-million-dollar ski and recreation resort to be built in the Mineral King Valley. The Sierra Club brought suit to block the development. As a basis for standing, the Sierra Club cited its special interest in conservation and wildlife preservation which, it argued, made it, under the Administrative Procedure Act, § 10, "[a] person suffering legal wrong because of agency action or adversely affected or aggrieved by agency action within the meaning of a relevant statute." 5 U.S.C. § 702. Sierra Club's "relevant statute" was the Forest Service's enabling legislation which charged the Service with preserving and protecting the nation's forests. The Sierra Club could have sued on behalf of its individual members but deliberately chose not to do so. Instead, Sierra sought to make this a test case of public interest litigation. The Supreme Court, 4-3, rejected the Sierra Club's theory of standing.

The Court, per Justice Stewart, decided the case in terms of the Administrative Procedure Act. While recognizing that aesthetic, conservational and recreational values would suffice as injury, Justice Stewart contended that "a mere 'interest in a problem,' no matter how long-standing the interest and no matter how qualified the organization is in evaluating the problem, is not sufficient by itself to render the organization 'adversely affected' or 'aggrieved' within the meaning of the APA."

Justice Douglas, dissenting, noted that "[t]he issue of statutory standing aside, no doubt exists that 'injury in fact' to 'aesthetic' and 'conservational' interests is here sufficiently threatened to satisfy the case or controversy clause." He concluded:

> The critical question of "standing" would be simplified and also put neatly in focus if we fashioned a federal rule that allowed environmental issues to be litigated in the name of the inanimate object about to be despoiled, defaced, or invaded by roads and bulldozers and where injury is the subject of public outrage.

Justice Blackmun, joined by Justice Brennan argued that the Court ought to have remanded with directions that Sierra Club be permitted to amend its complaint to allege "injury in fact." Blackmun supported creating an exception in the law of standing to permit "sincere, dedicated, established" organizations to bring actions even where they cannot allege a direct personal interest in the outcome of the suits. Environmental issues, he noted, often touch upon matters of public interest without necessarily affecting any single individual directly.

On remand, the Sierra Club included allegations of personal interest in its members' use of the area and was able to litigate the substantive issue.

5. *United States v. SCRAP*, 412 U.S. 669 (1973). The Court, per Justice Stewart, held that various environmental groups, including SCRAP, an unincorporated association of five law students, had standing as "persons adversely affected or aggrieved" under the APA to challenge an ICC failure to suspend a railroad freight surcharge. The plaintiffs alleged that they "suffered economic, recreational and aesthetic harm" since the rate hike would encourage increased use of nonrecyclable goods, further depleting national resources and resulting in more refuse, thus polluting the environment.

While the Court stated that "a plaintiff must allege that he has been or will in fact be perceptibly harmed by the challenged agency action," it stressed that

> the fact that many persons shared the same injury [is not] sufficient reason to disqualify from seeking review of an agency's action any person who had in fact suffered injury. To deny standing to persons who are in fact injured simply because many others are also injured, would mean that the most injurious and widespread Government actions could be questioned by nobody. We cannot accept that conclusion.

Justice White, joined by Chief Justice Burger and Justice Rehnquist, dissenting, argued that "[t]he allegations here do not satisfy the threshold requirement of injury in fact for constituting a justiciable case or controversy" because they were remote, speculative and insubstantial. The dissenters warned that "we are well on our way to permitting citizens at large to litigate any decisions of the Government which fall in an area of interest to them and with which they disagree."

Professor Davis suggests that *SCRAP* "represents an all-time high in Supreme Court liberality on the subject of standing" and establishes that "a trifle may be enough for standing." KENNETH C. DAVIS, ADMINISTRATIVE LAW OF THE SEVENTIES 489 (1976).

6. *United States v. Richardson,* 418 U.S. 166 (1974). A return to more rigorous justiciability requirements began almost immediately after *SCRAP*. In *Richardson*, the Court held, 5-4, per Chief Justice Burger, that a federal taxpayer lacks standing to challenge the constitutionality, under Article I, § 9, cl. 7, requiring a regular accounting of public funds, of a statute which permits the CIA to account for its expenditures "solely on the certificate of the Director."

The Court said taxpayer standing did not exist for two reasons. First, the suit was not brought to challenge the exercise of the federal taxing or spending power but rather to challenge statutes regulating the CIA. Second, there was no allegation that appropriated funds were being spent in violation of any specific constitutional limitation upon taxing and spending powers. Therefore, the Court reasoned there was no logical nexus between the taxpayer's status as a taxpayer and his claim.

Chief Justice Burger, for the Court, stated:

> [Respondent is seeking] to employ a federal court as a forum in which to air his generalized grievances about the conduct of government. As our society has become more complex, our numbers more vast, our lives more varied, and our resources more strained, citizens increasingly request the intervention of the courts on a greater variety of issues than at any period of our national development. The acceptance of new categories of judicially cognizable injury has not eliminated the basic principle that to invoke judicial power the claimant must have a "personal stake in the outcome," *Baker v. Carr*, or a "particular concrete injury," *Sierra Club*, "or a direct injury," *Ex parte Levitt*; in short, something more than "generalized grievances," *Flast*.

What would be wrong with "judicial supervision of the coordinate branches" if the Constitution sets judicially enforceable limitations on those branches? To ask the same question in another form, does not the majority make a judicial decision on the proper interpretation of the Accounts Clause when it holds that that clause does not authorize judicial intervention to limit the spending power?

VALLEY FORGE CHRISTIAN COLLEGE v. AMERICANS UNITED FOR SEPARATION OF CHURCH & STATE, INC.

454 U.S. 464, 102 S. Ct. 752, 70 L. Ed. 2d 700 (1982)

[Pursuant to its authority under the property clause, Congress enacted the Federal Property and Administrative Services Act of 1949, designed to provide "an economical and efficient system for the disposal of surplus property." The Act gives the Secretary of Health, Education and Welfare the power to dispose of surplus property by transferring it to private or public institutions. The Secretary may sell the property to non-profit, tax-exempt educational institutions, and may discount the transfer price on the basis of "any benefit which has accrued or may accrue to the United States from the use of such property for educational purposes." In 1976, HEW conveyed a 77-acre tract of surplus property, formerly used as a military hospital, to petitioner Valley Forge, a college devoted to training men and women for Christian service. The appraised value of the property at the time was $577,500 but this value was discounted by the Secretary's computation of a 100% public benefit allowance, enabling petitioner to acquire the property with no financial consideration.

[Respondent (Americans United) and four of its employees brought suit in federal district court challenging the conveyance on the ground that it violated the establishment clause of the First Amendment. Their complaint alleged that each of the organization's 90,000 members "would be deprived of the fair and constitutional use of his (her) tax dollars." The district court granted summary judgment and dismissed the case on the ground that respondents lacked standing to sue as taxpayers under *Flast v. Cohen*, and that they "failed to allege any actual injury beyond a generalized grievance common to all taxpayers." The court of appeals reversed, holding that although respondents lacked standing as taxpayers, they did have standing to sue as "citizens," claiming " 'injury in fact' to their shared individuated right to a government that "shall make no law respecting the [sic] establishment of religion." The respondents had thus satisfied the "case or controversy" requirement of Article III. The Supreme Court reversed.]

Justice Rehnquist delivered the opinion of the Court.

The term "standing" subsumes a blend of constitutional requirements and prudential considerations, and it has not always been clear in the opinions of this Court whether particular features of the "standing" requirement have been required by Art. III *ex proprio vigore*, or whether they are requirements that the Court itself has erected and which were not compelled by the language of the Constitution. A recent line of decisions, however, has resolved that ambiguity, at least to the following extent: at an irreducible minimum, Art. III requires the party who invokes the court's authority to "show that he personally has suffered some actual or threatened injury as a result of the putatively illegal conduct of the defendant," and that the injury "fairly can be traced to the challenged action" and "is likely to be redressed by a favorable decision." In this manner does Art. III limit the federal judicial power "to those disputes which confine federal courts to a role consistent with a system of separated powers and which are traditionally thought to be capable of resolution through the judicial process."

The requirement of "actual injury redressable by the court" serves several of the "implicit policies embodied in Article III." It tends to assure that the legal questions presented to the court will be resolved, not in the rarified atmosphere of a debating society, but in a concrete factual context conducive to a realistic appreciation of the consequences of judicial action. The "standing" requirement serves other purposes. Because it assures an actual factual setting in which the litigant asserts a claim of injury in fact, a court may decide the case with some confidence that its decision will not pave the way for lawsuits which have some, but not all, of the facts of the case actually decided by the court.

The Art. III aspect of standing also reflects a due regard for the autonomy of those persons likely to be most directly affected by a judicial order. The federal courts have abjured appeals to their authority which would convert the judicial process into "no more than a vehicle for the vindication of the value interests of concerned bystanders."

The exercise of the judicial power also affects relationships between the coequal arms of the National Government. The effect is, of course, most vivid when a federal court declares unconstitutional an act of the Legislative or Executive Branch. While the exercise of that "ultimate and supreme function" is a formidable means of vindicating individual rights, when employed unwisely or unnecessarily it is also the ultimate threat to the continued effectiveness of the federal courts in performing that role. Proper regard for the complex nature of our constitutional structure requires neither that the Judicial Branch shrink from a confrontation with the other two coequal branches of the Federal Government, nor that it hospitably accept for adjudication claims of constitutional violation by other branches of government where the claimant has not suffered cognizable injury.

Beyond the constitutional requirements, the federal judiciary has also adhered to a set of prudential principles that bear on the question of standing. Thus, this Court has held that "the plaintiff generally must assert his own legal rights and interests, and cannot rest his claim to relief on the legal rights or interests of third parties." In addition, even when the plaintiff has alleged redressable injury sufficient to meet the requirements of Art. III, the Court has refrained from adjudicating "abstract questions of wide public significance" which amount to "generalized grievances," pervasively shared and most appropriately addressed in the representative branches. Finally, the Court has required that the plaintiff's complaint fall within "the zone of interests to be protected or regulated by the statute or constitutional guarantee in question."

Merely to articulate these principles is to demonstrate their close relationship to the policies reflected in the Art. III requirement of actual or threatened injury amenable to judicial remedy. But neither the counsels of prudence nor the policies implicit in the "case or controversy" requirement should be mistaken for the rigorous Art. III requirements themselves. Satisfaction of the former cannot substitute for a demonstration of " 'distinct and palpable injury'. . .that is likely to be redressed if the requested relief is granted." That requirement states a limitation on judicial power, not merely a factor to be balanced in the weighing of so-called "prudential" considerations.

The injury alleged by respondents in their amended complaint is the "depriv[ation] of the fair and constitutional use of [their] tax dollar." Unlike the plaintiffs in *Flast*, respondents fail the first prong of the test for taxpayer standing. Their claim is deficient in two respects. First, the source of their complaint is not a congressional action, but a decision by HEW to transfer a parcel of federal property. *Flast* limited taxpayer standing to challenges directed "only [at] exercises of congressional power." Second, and perhaps redundantly, the property transfer about which respondents complain was not an exercise of authority conferred by the Taxing and Spending Clause of Art.

I, § 8. The authorizing legislation, the Federal Property and Administrative Services Act of 1949, was an evident exercise of Congress' power under the Property Clause, Art. IV, § 3, cl. 2.

Although the Court of Appeals properly doubted respondents' ability to establish standing solely on the basis of their taxpayer status, it considered their allegations of taxpayer injury to be "essentially an assumed role." In the court's view, respondents had established standing by virtue of an " 'injury in fact' to their shared individuated right to a government that "shall make no law respecting the [sic] establishment of religion." The court distinguished this "injury" from "the question of 'citizen standing' as such." Although citizens generally could not establish standing simply by claiming an interest in governmental observance of the Constitution, respondents had "set forth instead a particular and concrete injury" to a "personal constitutional right."

In finding that respondents had alleged something more than "the generalized interest of all citizens in constitutional governance," the Court of Appeals relied on factual differences which we do not think amount to legal distinctions. The court decided that respondents' claim differed from those in *Schlesinger* and *Richardson*, which were predicated, respectively, on the Incompatibility and Accounts Clauses, because "it is at the very least arguable that the Establishment Clause creates in each citizen a 'personal constitutional right' to a government that does not establish religion." The court found it unnecessary to determine whether this "arguable" proposition was correct, since it judged the mere allegation of a legal right sufficient to confer standing.

This reasoning process merely disguises, we think with a rather thin veil, the inconsistency of the court's results with our decisions in *Schlesinger* and *Richardson*. The plaintiffs in those cases plainly asserted a "personal right" to have the government act in accordance with their views of the Constitution; indeed, we see no barrier to the assertion of such claims with respect to any constitutional provision. But assertion of a right to a particular kind of Government conduct, which the Government has violated by acting differently, cannot alone satisfy the requirements of Art. III without draining those requirements of meaning.

Nor can *Schlesinger* and *Richardson* be distinguished on the ground that the Incompatibility and Accounts Clauses are in some way less "fundamental" than the Establishment Clause. Each establishes a norm of conduct which the Federal Government is bound to honor — to no greater or lesser extent than any other inscribed in the Constitution. To the extent the Court of Appeals relied on a view of standing under which the Art. III burdens diminish as the "importance" of the claim on the merits increases, we reject that notion. The requirement of standing "focuses on the party seeking to get his complaint before a federal court and not on the issues he wishes to have adjudicated." Moreover, we know of no principled basis on which to create a hierarchy of constitutional values or a complementary "sliding scale" of standing which might permit respondents to invoke the judicial power of the United States.

The complaint in this case shares a common deficiency with those in *Schlesinger* and *Richardson*. Although they claim that the Constitution has been violated, they claim nothing else. They fail to identify any personal injury suffered by the plaintiffs as a consequence of the alleged constitutional error, other than the psychological consequence presumably produced by observation of conduct with which one disagrees. That is not an injury sufficient to confer standing under Art. III, even though the disagreement is phrased in constitutional terms. It is evident that respondents are firmly committed to the constitutional principle of separation of church and State, but standing is not measured by the intensity of the litigant's interest or the fervor of his advocacy. "[T]hat concrete adverseness which sharpens the presentation of issues" is the anticipated consequence of proceedings commenced by one who has been injured in fact; it is not a permissible substitute for the showing of injury itself.

In reaching this conclusion, we do not retreat from our earlier holdings that standing may be predicated on noneconomic injury. We simply cannot see that respondents have alleged an injury of any kind, economic or otherwise, sufficient to confer standing. Respondents complain of a transfer of property located in Chester County, Pennsylvania. The named plaintiffs reside in Maryland and Virginia; their organizational headquarters are located in Washington, D.C. They learned of the transfer through a news release. Their claim that the Government has violated the Establishment Clause does not provide a special license to roam the country in search of governmental wrongdoing and to reveal their discoveries in federal court. The federal courts were simply not constituted as ombudsmen of the general welfare.

JUSTICE BRENNAN, with whom JUSTICES MARSHALL and BLACKMUN join, dissenting.

It is clear in the light of history, that one of the primary purposes of the Establishment Clause was to prevent the use of tax monies for religious purposes. The taxpayer was the direct and intended beneficiary of the prohibition on financial aid to religion.

It may be that Congress can tax for almost any reason, or for no reason at all. There is, so far as I have been able to discern, but one constitutionally imposed limit on that authority. Congress cannot use tax money to support a church, or to encourage religion. Each, and indeed every, federal taxpayer suffers precisely the injury that the Establishment Clause guards against when the Federal Government directs that funds be taken from the pocketbooks of the citizenry and placed into the coffers of the ministry.

[JUSTICE STEVENS also dissented]

NOTES

1. *Distinguishing* Flast. After *Valley Forge*, is *Flast* still good law? The Court says that there are two distinctions between the cases.

First, what difference does it make that the school received land and buildings worth $577,500 rather than receiving $577,500 in cash to purchase land and buildings? Does the taxpayer-citizen have less interest in land than in cash? Or does the Constitution prohibit transfers of cash without prohibiting transfers of land? The Court says that the transfer was accomplished under the Property Clause rather than the spending clause and that *Flast* held the Establishment Clause to be a limitation only on Congress' spending power.

Second, what difference does it make that the transfer was accomplished without implicating the validity of a congressional enactment? Would *Flast* have been decided differently if the statute left HEW free to decide which schools received subsidies and the administrator had decided to give money to a religious school? A statute dictating that money or land is to be given to religious schools leaves less doubt about the overall impact of a subsidy program than does a statute giving discretion to the executive branch, but the amount of money and amount of impact on religious values may be just as great under either. Moreover, if the Establishment Clause prohibits support of religion, then it should be triggered as easily by a transfer of $100 as by a transfer of $500,000. On the other hand, allowing judicial challenge of every decision by an administrative agency creates a "floodgate" issue that might not be present with challenges to statutes. Should the Court have spelled out its reasons for making this distinction by dealing with these arguments?

2. *Ideological plaintiffs.* A substantial clue to the Court's actual holding, or at least its attitude toward the plaintiffs in *Valley Forge*, might lie in its characterization of the plaintiffs themselves. Might the case have been decided differently if the plaintiffs had been residents of Chester County, Pennsylvania? What if one of the plaintiffs had been an unsuccessful applicant for the surplus property who wanted to use the buildings for a charitable clinic or as offices for the Americans United for Separation of Church and State?

The Court has frequently disparaged citizen-litigants who present no "particularized claim of injury not suffered by the citizenry at large." With regard to the *Valley Forge* plaintiffs, the Court said: "Although they claim that the Constitution has been violated, they claim nothing else. They fail to identify any personal injury suffered by the plaintiffs as a consequence of the alleged constitutional error, other than the psychological consequence presumably produced by the observation of conduct with which one disagrees." In other words, the alleged constitutional violation is not a "legal injury." Why not? Because the Establishment Clause does not create a private right of action to sue the government official who violates it? Does that holding avoid adjudication of the merits of the claim?

Professor Doernberg argues that many constitutional provisions, particularly the Establishment Clause, were specifically designed to create "collective interests" that the Court is refusing to recognize. "The effect is that certain constitutional provisions effectively exist only at the whim and during the good will of the government, because the collective interest in enforcement of such provisions will not be protected by the courts." Donald Doernberg, *"We the People": John Locke, Collective Constitutional Rights, and Standing to Challenge Government Action*, 73 CAL. L. REV. 52, 56 (1985).

[2] DETERMINING THE EXISTENCE OF INJURY AND CAUSATION

ALLEN v. WRIGHT

468 U.S. 737, 104 S. Ct. 3315, 82 L. Ed. 2d 556 (1984)

JUSTICE O'CONNOR delivered the opinion of the Court.

Parents of black public school children allege in this nationwide class action that the Internal Revenue Service (IRS) has not adopted sufficient standards and procedures to fulfill its obligation to deny tax-exempt status to racially discriminatory private schools. They assert that the IRS thereby harms them directly and interferes with the ability of their children to receive an education in desegregated public schools. The issue before us is whether plaintiffs have standing to bring this suit. We hold that they do not.

The Internal Revenue Service denies tax-exempt status under §§ 501(a) and (c)(3) of the Internal Revenue Code—and hence eligibility to receive charitable contributions deductible from income taxes under §§ 170(a)(1) and (c)(2) of the Code — to racially discriminatory private schools. The IRS policy requires that a school applying for tax-exempt status show that it "admits the students of any race to all the rights, privileges, programs, and activities generally accorded or made available to students at that school and that the school does not discriminate on the basis of race in administration of its educational policies, admissions policies, scholarship and loan programs, and athletic and other school-administered programs." To carry out this policy, the IRS has established guidelines and procedures for determining whether a particular school is in fact racially nondiscriminatory. Failure to comply with the guidelines "will ordinarily result in the proposed revocation of" tax-exempt status.

In 1976 respondents challenged [the IRS] guidelines and procedures in a suit filed in Federal District Court against the Secretary of the Treasury and the Commissioner of Internal Revenue. The plaintiffs named in the complaint are parents of black children who, at the time the complaint was filed, were attending schools in seven States in school districts undergoing desegregation. They brought this nationwide class action "on behalf of themselves and their children, and. . .on behalf of all other parents of black children attending public school systems undergoing, or which may in the future undergo, desegregation pursuant to court order [or] HEW regulations and guidelines, under state law, or voluntarily." They estimated that the class they seek to represent includes several million persons.

Respondents allege in their complaint that many racially segregated private schools were created or expanded in their communities at the time the public schools were undergoing desegregation. According to the complaint, many such private schools, including 17 schools or school systems identified by name in the complaint (perhaps some 30 schools in all), receive tax exemptions either directly or through the tax-exempt status of "umbrella" organizations that operate or support the schools. Respondents allege that, despite the IRS policy of denying tax-exempt status to racially discriminatory private schools and despite the IRS guidelines and procedures for implementing that policy, some of the tax-exempt racially segregated private schools created or expanded in desegregating districts in fact have racially discriminatory policies. Respondents allege that the IRS grant of tax exemptions to such racially discriminatory schools is unlawful.

Respondents allege that the challenged Government conduct harms them in two ways. The challenged conduct

> (a) constitutes tangible federal financial aid and other support for racially segregated educational institutions, and
>
> (b) fosters and encourages the organization, operation and expansion of institutions providing racially segregated educational opportunities for white children avoiding attendance in desegregating public school districts and thereby interferes with the efforts of federal courts, HEW and local school authorities to desegregate public school districts which have been operating racially dual school systems.

Thus, respondents do not allege that their children have been the victims of discriminatory exclusion from the schools whose tax exemptions they challenge as unlawful. Indeed, they have not alleged at any stage of this litigation that their children have ever applied or would ever apply to any private school. Rather, respondents claim a direct injury from the mere fact of the challenged Government conduct and, as indicated by the restriction of the plaintiff class to parents of children in desegregating school districts, injury to their children's opportunity to receive a desegregated education. The latter injury is traceable to the IRS grant of tax exemptions to racially discriminatory schools, respondents allege, chiefly because contributions to such schools are deductible from income taxes under §§ 170(a)(1) and (c)(2) of the Internal Revenue Code and the "deductions facilitate the raising of funds to organize new schools and expand existing schools in order to accommodate white students avoiding attendance in desegregating public school districts."

Respondents request only prospective relief. They ask for a declaratory judgment that the challenged IRS tax-exemption practices are unlawful. They also ask for an injunction requiring the IRS to deny tax exemptions to a considerably broader class of private schools than the class of racially discriminatory private schools. Under the requested injunction, the IRS would have to deny tax-exempt status to all private schools

> which have insubstantial or nonexistent minority enrollments, which are located in or serve desegregating public school districts, and which either
>
> (1) were established or expanded at or about the time the public school districts in which they are located or which they serve were desegregating;
>
> (2) have been determined in adversary judicial or administrative proceedings to be racially segregated; or
>
> (3) cannot demonstrate that they do not provide racially segregated educational opportunities for white children avoiding attendance in desegregating public school systems . . . .

Finally, respondents ask for an order directing the IRS to replace its 1975 guidelines with standards consistent with the requested injunction.

The District Court considered and granted the defendants' motion to dismiss the complaint. The United States Court of Appeals for the District of Columbia reversed. We now reverse.

[T]he law of Art. III standing is built on a single basic idea — the idea of separation of powers. It is this fact which makes possible the gradual clarification of the law through judicial application. Determining standing in a particular case may be facilitated by clarifying principles or even clean rules developed in prior cases. Typically, however, the standing inquiry requires careful judicial examination of a complaint's allegations to ascertain whether the particular plaintiff is entitled to an adjudication of the particular claims asserted. Is the injury too abstract, or otherwise not appropriate, to be considered judicially cognizable? Is the line of causation between the illegal conduct and injury too attenuated? Is the prospect of obtaining relief from the injury as a result of a favorable ruling too speculative?

Respondents allege two injuries in their complaint to support their standing to bring this lawsuit. First, they say that they are harmed directly by the mere fact of Government financial aid to discriminatory private schools. Second, they say that the federal tax exemptions to racially discriminatory private schools in their communities impair their ability to have their public schools desegregated. We conclude that neither suffices to support respondents' standing. The first fails under clear precedents of this Court because it does not constitute judicially cognizable injury. The second fails because the alleged injury is not fairly traceable to the assertedly unlawful conduct of the IRS.[19]

Respondents' first claim of injury can be interpreted in two ways. It might be a claim simply to have the Government avoid the violation of law alleged in respondents' complaint. Alternatively, it might be a claim of stigmatic injury, or denigration, suffered by all members of a racial group when the Government discriminates on the basis of race. Under neither interpretation is this claim of injury judicially cognizable.

This Court has repeatedly held that an asserted right to have the Government act in accordance with law is not sufficient, standing alone, to confer jurisdiction on a federal court. Neither do they have standing to litigate their claims based on the stigmatizing injury often caused by racial discrimination. There can be no doubt that this sort of noneconomic injury is one of the most serious consequences of discriminatory government action and is sufficient in some circumstances to support standing. *See Heckler v. Mathews*. Our cases

[19] The "fairly traceable" and "redressability" components of the constitutional standing inquiry were initially articulated by this Court as "two facets of a single causation requirement." To the extent there is a difference, it is that the former examines the causal connection between the assertedly unlawful conduct and the alleged injury, whereas the latter examines the causal connection between the alleged injury and the judicial relief requested. Cases such as this, in which the relief requested goes well beyond the violation of law alleged, illustrate why it is important to keep the inquiries separate if the "redressability" component is to focus on the requested relief. Even if the relief respondents request might have a substantial effect on the desegregation of public schools, whatever deficiencies exist in the opportunities for desegregated education for respondents' children might not be traceable to IRS violations of law — grants of tax exemptions to racially discriminatory schools in respondents' communities.

make clear, however, that such injury accords a basis for standing only to "those persons who are personally denied equal treatment" by the challenged discriminatory conduct. [Respondents] do not allege a stigmatic injury suffered as a direct result of having personally been denied equal treatment.

The consequences of recognizing respondents' standing on the basis of their first claim of injury illustrate why our cases plainly hold that such injury is not judicially cognizable. If the abstract stigmatic injury were cognizable, standing would extend nationwide to all members of the particular racial groups against which the Government was alleged to be discriminating by its grant of a tax exemption to a racially discriminatory school, regardless of the location of that school. All such persons could claim the same sort of abstract stigmatic injury respondents assert in their first claim of injury. A black person in Hawaii could challenge the grant of a tax exemption to a racially discriminatory school in Maine. Recognition of standing in such circumstances would transform the federal courts into "no more than a vehicle for the vindication of the value interests of concerned bystanders." *United States v. SCRAP*. Constitutional limits on the role of the federal courts preclude such a transformation.

It is in their complaint's second claim of injury that respondents allege harm to a concrete, personal interest that can support standing in some circumstances. The injury they identify — their children's diminished ability to receive an education in a racially integrated school — is, beyond any doubt, not only judicially cognizable but, as shown by cases from *Brown v. Board of Education* to *Bob Jones University v. United States*, one of the most serious injuries recognized in our legal system. Despite the constitutional importance of curing the injury alleged by respondents, however, the federal judiciary may not redress it unless standing requirements are met. In this case, respondents' second claim of injury cannot support standing because the injury alleged is not fairly traceable to the Government conduct respondents challenge as unlawful.[22]

The illegal conduct challenged by respondents is the IRS's grant of tax exemptions to some racially discriminatory schools. The line of causation between that conduct and desegregation of respondents' schools is attenuated at best. From the perspective of the IRS, the injury to respondents is highly indirect and "results from the independent action of some third party not before the court," *Simon v. Eastern Kentucky Welfare Rights Org.*

The diminished ability of respondents' children to receive a desegregated education would be fairly traceable to unlawful IRS grants of tax exemptions only if there were enough racially discriminatory private schools receiving tax exemptions in respondents' communities for withdrawal of those exemptions to make an appreciable difference in public-school integration. Respondents have made no such allegation. It is, first, uncertain how many racially

[22] Respondents' stigmatic injury, though not sufficient for standing in the abstract form in which their complaint asserts it, is judicially cognizable to the extent that respondents are personally subject to discriminatory treatment. The stigmatic injury thus requires identification of some concrete interest with respect to which respondents are personally subject to discriminatory treatment. That interest must independently satisfy the causation requirement of standing doctrine.

discriminatory private schools are in fact receiving tax exemptions. Moreover, it is entirely speculative, as respondents themselves conceded in the Court of Appeals, whether withdrawal of a tax exemption from any particular school would lead the school to change its policies. It is just as speculative whether any given parent of a child attending such a private school would decide to transfer the child to public school as a result of any changes in educational or financial policy made by the private school once it was threatened with loss of tax-exempt status. It is also pure speculation whether, in a particular community, a large enough number of the numerous relevant school officials and parents would reach decisions that collectively would have a significant impact on the racial composition of the public schools.

The links in the chain of causation between the challenged Government conduct and the asserted injury are far too weak for the chain as a whole to sustain respondents' standing. It involves numerous third parties (officials of racially discriminatory schools receiving tax exemptions and the parents of children attending such schools) who may not even exist in respondents' communities and whose independent decisions may not collectively have a significant effect on the ability of public-school students to receive a desegregated education.

The idea of separation of powers that underlies standing doctrine explains why our cases preclude the conclusion that respondents' alleged injury "fairly can be traced to the challenged action" of the IRS. *Simon v. Eastern Kentucky Welfare Rights Org.* That conclusion would pave the way generally for suits challenging, not specifically identifiable Government violations of law, but the particular programs agencies establish to carry out their legal obligations. Such suits, even when premised on allegations of several instances of violations of law, are rarely if ever appropriate for federal-court adjudication.

The same concern for the proper role of the federal courts is reflected in cases like *O'Shea v. Littleton, Rizzo v. Goode,* and *City of Los Angeles v. Lyons.* In all three cases plaintiffs sought injunctive relief directed at certain systemwide law enforcement practices. [Each case involved allegations of police abuse or discriminatory judicial treatment aimed at racial minorities. — Ed.] The Court held in each case that, absent an allegation of a specific threat of being subject to the challenged practices, plaintiffs had no standing to ask for an injunction. Animating this Court's holdings was the principle that "[a] federal court. . .is not the proper forum to press" general complaints about the way in which government goes about its business.

Most relevant to this case is the principle articulated in *Rizzo v. Goode.*

> When a plaintiff seeks to enjoin the activity of a government agency, even within a unitary court system, his case must contend with the well-established rule that the Government has traditionally been granted the widest latitude in the "dispatch of its own internal affairs."

When transported into the Art. III context, that principle, grounded as it is in the idea of separation of powers, counsels against recognizing standing in a case brought, not to enforce specific legal obligations whose violation works a direct harm, but to seek a restructuring of the apparatus established by the Executive Branch to fulfill its legal duties. The Constitution, after all, assigns to the Executive Branch, and not to the Judicial Branch, the duty to "take Care that the Laws be faithfully executed." We could not recognize respondents' standing in this case without running afoul of that structural principle.[26]

"The necessity that the plaintiff who seeks to invoke judicial power stand to profit in some personal interest remains an Art. III requirement." *Simon v. Eastern Kentucky Welfare Rights Org.* Respondents have not met this fundamental requirement. The judgment of the Court of Appeals is accordingly reversed, and the injunction issued by that court is vacated.

Justice Marshall took no part in the decision of the case.

Justice Brennan, dissenting.

One could hardly dispute the proposition that Article III of the Constitution, by limiting the judicial power to "cases" or "controversies," embodies the notion that each branch of our National Government must confine its actions to those that are consistent with our scheme of separated powers.

The Court's attempt to obscure the standing question must be seen, therefore, as no more than a cover for its failure to recognize the nature of the specific claims raised by the respondents in these cases. By relying on generalities concerning our tripartite system of government, the Court is able to conclude that the respondents lack standing to maintain this action without acknowledging the precise nature of the injuries they have alleged. In so doing, the Court displays a startling insensitivity to the historical role played by the federal courts in eradicating race discrimination from our nation's schools. Because I cannot join in such misguided decisionmaking, I dissent.

Viewed in light of the injuries they claim, the respondents have alleged a direct causal relationship between the government action they challenge and the injury they suffer: their inability to receive an education in a racially integrated school is directly and adversely affected by the tax-exempt status granted by the IRS to racially discriminatory schools in their respective school districts. Common sense alone would recognize that the elimination of tax-exempt status for racially discriminatory private schools would serve to lessen the impact that those institutions have in defeating efforts to desegregate the public schools.

The Court admits that "[t]he diminished ability of respondents' children to receive a desegregated education would be fairly traceable to unlawful IRS grants to tax exemptions . . . if there were enough racially discriminatory private schools receiving tax exemptions in respondents' communities for withdrawal of those exemptions to make an appreciable difference in public-school integration," but concludes that "[r]espondents have made no such allegation." With all due respect, the Court has either misread the complaint

[26] We disagree with Justice Stevens' suggestions that separation of powers merely underlie standing requirements, have no role to play in giving meaning to those requirements, and should be considered only under a distinct justiciability analysis. Moreover, our analysis of this case does not rest on the more general proposition that no consequence of the allocation of administrative enforcement resources is judicially cognizable. Rather, we rely on separation of powers principles to interpret the "fairly traceable" component of the standing requirement.

or is improperly requiring the respondents to prove their case on the merits in order to defeat a motion to dismiss. For example, the respondents specifically refer by name to at least 32 private schools that discriminate on the basis of race and yet continue to benefit illegally from tax-exempt status. Eighteen of those schools — including at least 14 elementary schools, two junior high schools, and one high school — are located in the city of Memphis, Tennessee, which has been the subject of several court orders to desegregate. Similarly, the respondents cite two private schools in Orangeburg, South Carolina that continue to benefit from federal tax exemptions even though they practice race discrimination in school districts that are desegregating pursuant to judicial and administrative orders. At least with respect to these school districts, as well as the others specifically mentioned in the complaint, there can be little doubt that the respondents have identified communities containing "enough racially discriminatory private schools receiving tax exemptions . . . to make an appreciable difference in public-school integration."

More than one commentator has noted that the causation component of the Court's standing inquiry is no more than a poor disguise for the Court's view of the merits of the underlying claims. The Court today does nothing to avoid that criticism. What is most disturbing about today's decision, therefore, is not the standing analysis applied, but the indifference evidenced by the Court to the detrimental effects that racially segregated schools, supported by tax-exempt status from the federal government, have on the respondents' attempt to obtain an education in a racially integrated school system. I cannot join such indifference, and would give the respondents a chance to prove their case on the merits.

JUSTICE STEVENS, with whom JUSTICE BLACKMUN joins, dissenting.

Three propositions are clear to me: (1) respondents have adequately alleged "injury in fact"; (2) their injury is fairly traceable to the conduct that they claim to be unlawful; and (3) the "separation of powers" principle does not create a jurisdictional obstacle to the consideration of the merits of their claim.

Respondents, the parents of black school children, have alleged that their children are unable to attend fully desegregated schools because large numbers of white children in the areas in which respondents reside attend private schools which do not admit minority children. The Court, Justice Brennan, and I all agree that this is an adequate allegation of "injury in fact." This kind of injury may be actionable whether it is caused by the exclusion of black children from public schools or by an official policy of encouraging white children to attend nonpublic schools. A subsidy for the withdrawal of a white child can have the same effect as a penalty for admitting a black child. In final analysis, the wrong the respondents allege that the Government has committed is to subsidize the exodus of white children from schools that would otherwise be racially integrated. The critical question in this case, therefore, is whether respondents have alleged that the Government has created that kind of subsidy.

The purpose of [the IRS] subsidy is to promote the activity subsidized; the statutes "seek to achieve the same basic goal of encouraging the development of certain organizations through the grant of tax benefits." *Bob Jones University v. United States.* If the granting of preferential tax treatment would "encourage" private segregated schools to conduct their "charitable" activities, it must follow that the withdrawal of the treatment would "discourage" them, and hence promote the process of desegregation.

This causation analysis is nothing more than a restatement of elementary economics: when something becomes more expensive, less of it will be purchased. Sections 170 and 501(c)(3) are premised on that recognition. If racially discriminatory private schools lose the "cash grants" that flow from the operation of the statutes, the education they provide will become more expensive and hence less of their services will be purchased. Conversely, maintenance of these tax benefits makes an education in segregated private schools relatively more attractive, by decreasing its cost. Accordingly, without tax exempt status, private schools will either not be competitive in terms of cost, or have to change their admissions policies, hence reducing their competitiveness for parents seeking "a racially segregated alternative" to public schools, which is what respondents have alleged many white parents in desegregating school districts seek.[6]

Considerations of tax policy, economics, and pure logic all confirm the conclusion that respondents' injury in fact is fairly traceable to the Government's allegedly wrongful conduct. The Court therefore is forced to introduce the concept of "separation of powers" into its analysis.

The Court could mean one of three things by its invocation of the separation of powers. First, it could simply be expressing the idea that if the plaintiff lacks Article III standing to bring a lawsuit, then there is no "case or controversy" within the meaning of Article III and hence the matter is not within the area of responsibility assigned to the Judiciary by the Constitution. While there can be no quarrel with this proposition, in itself it provides no guidance for determining if the injury respondents have alleged is fairly traceable to the conduct they have challenged.

Second, the Court could be saying that it will require a more direct causal connection when it is troubled by the separation of powers implications of the case before it. That approach confuses the standing doctrine with the justiciability of the issues that respondents seek to raise. The purpose of the standing inquiry is to measure the plaintiff's stake in the outcome, not whether a court has the authority to provide it with the outcome it seeks.

The strength of the plaintiff's interest in the outcome has nothing to do with whether the relief it seeks would intrude upon the prerogatives of other branches of government; the possibility that the relief might be inappropriate does not lessen the plaintiff's stake in obtaining that relief. If a plaintiff

[6] This causation analysis explains the holding in the case on which the Court chiefly relies, *Simon v. Eastern Kentucky Welfare Rights Organization*. However, while here the source of the causal nexus is the price that white parents must pay to obtain a segregated education, which is inextricably intertwined with the school's tax status, in *Simon* the plaintiffs were seeking free care, which hospitals could decide not to provide for any number of reasons unrelated to their tax status. Moreover, in *Simon*, the hospitals had to spend money in order to obtain charitable status. Therefore, they had an economic incentive to forgo preferential treatment.

[T]he tax benefits private schools receive here involve no "financial drain" since the schools need not provide "uncompensated services" in order to obtain preferential tax treatment. Thus, the economic effect of the challenged tax treatment in this case is not "speculative," as the Court concluded it was in *Simon*. Here the financial incentives run in only one direction.

presents a nonjusticiable issue, or seeks relief that a court may not award, then its complaint should be dismissed for those reasons, and not because the plaintiff lacks a stake in obtaining that relief and hence has no standing.

Third, the Court could be saying that it will not treat as legally cognizable injuries that stem from an administrative decision concerning how enforcement resources will be allocated. This surely is an important point. Respondents do seek to restructure the IRS' mechanisms for enforcing the legal requirement that discriminatory institutions not receive tax-exempt status. Such restructuring would dramatically affect the way in which the IRS exercises its prosecutorial discretion. The Executive requires latitude to decide how best to enforce the law, and in general the Court may well be correct that the exercise of that discretion, especially in the tax context, is unchallengeable.

Here, respondents contend that the IRS is violating a specific constitutional limitation on its enforcement discretion. There is a solid basis for that contention. Surely the question whether the Constitution or the Code limits enforcement discretion is one within the Judiciary's competence, and I do not believe that the question whether the law imposes such an obligation upon the IRS is so insubstantial that respondents' attempt to raise it should be defeated for lack of subject-matter jurisdiction on the ground that it infringes the Executive's prerogatives.

In short, I would deal with the question of the legal limitations on the IRS' enforcement discretion on its merits, rather than by making the untenable assumption that the granting of preferential tax treatment to segregated schools does not make those schools more attractive to white students and hence does not inhibit the process of desegregation. I respectfully dissent.

NOTES

1. *Simon v. Eastern Kentucky Welfare Rights Org.*, 426 U.S. 26 (1976). The Court, per Justice Powell, held that indigents and organizations composed of indigents do not have standing to bring a federal suit against the Secretary of the Treasury and the IRS to challenge a revenue ruling allowing favorable tax treatment to a nonprofit hospital that offered only emergency room service to indigents. The petitioner had argued that by extending tax benefits to such hospitals despite their refusals fully to serve the indigents, the defendants were "encouraging" the hospitals to deny services to the individual plaintiff and to the members and clients of the plaintiff organizations.

Justice Powell reasoned that even where injury at the hands of a hospital by denial of services is alleged, this is insufficient in itself to establish a case or controversy where no hospital is a defendant. "A federal court may act only to redress injury that fairly can be traced to the challenged action of the defendant and not injury that results from the independent action of some third party not before the court." It was deemed pure speculation whether the denial of services to indigents resulted from government "encouragement" or was an independent hospital decision made without regard to tax implications. "Moreover, the complaint suggests no substantial likelihood that victory in this suit would result in respondents' receiving the hospital treatment they desire."

Justice Brennan, concurring in the judgment, characterized the plaintiffs' claim as follows:

> Respondents' claim is not, and by its very nature could not be, that they have been and will be illegally denied the provision of indigent medical services by the hospitals. Rather, if respondents have a claim cognizable under the law, it is that the Internal Revenue Code requires the government to offer economic inducements to the relevant hospitals only under conditions which are likely to benefit respondents. The relevant injury in light of this claim is, then, injury to this beneficial interest — as respondents alleged, injury to their "opportunity and ability" to receive medical services.

2. *Separation of powers revisited.* What is meant by the statement in the footnote that "we rely on separation of powers principles to interpret the 'fairly traceable' component of the standing requirement?" Is the Court trying to say that it is solely an executive function to determine whether the executive has caused harm to a citizen? The Court says that it is an executive, not a judicial function, to "take care that the Laws be faithfully executed." Why is the requirement of faithful execution itself not a vehicle for judicial review under the notion that it "is emphatically the province and duty of the judicial department to say what the law is?"

When the Court says that standing is built on the single idea of separation of powers, does it mean that judicial review is an appropriate judicial function only when the Court is forced to exercise it because government itself has initiated the judicial process? This limited view of judicial review actually could be squared with the opinion in *Marbury* by focusing on Marshall's reading of the necessity of a court's choosing the law to apply in a given case. Under this view, the law of justiciability is essentially a part of the law of remedies; the Constitution could be read in some instances not to create an affirmative right to relief but only a shield against government action. *See* Walter Dellinger, *Of Rights and Remedies: The Constitution as a Sword*, 83 Harv. L. Rev. 1532 (1972).

3. *Causation as an issue decided on the pleadings.* In *Simon* and *Allen*, it was possible that plaintiff's requested relief would not have brought complete satisfaction because the third parties (schools and hospitals) still could behave as they did before the lawsuit even without their tax exemption. But wasn't a more favorable situation likely? What is lost by not giving the plaintiff the opportunity for discovery and some form of fact-finding on the causation issue? Referring to the *Allen* issue of whether government subsidies had contributed to "white flight," Dean Nichol makes this argument.

> Under the majority's application of the traceability requirement, the connection between government action and the enrollment of white students in discriminatory private schools must be alleged in such a specific manner that there could be no speculation as to its truth. As a result, the plaintiffs were required to prove their case in the complaint without benefit of discovery or trial.

Gene Nichol, *Abusing Standing: A Comment on Allen v. Wright,* 133 U. PA. L. REV. 635, 640 n.27 (1985).

Notice that in *Gladstone Realtors v. Village of Bellwood*, 441 U.S. 91 (1979), Justice Powell for the Court emphasized that the plaintiffs were entitled to a trial on the issue of whether they had been caused harm by the realtors' steering practices. In *Warth, Simon* and *Allen* the complaints were dismissed in advance of trial because the plaintiffs could not persuade the Court that their harm was the result of government action. Justice Brennan accuses the majority of "improperly requiring plaintiffs to prove their case on the merits in order to defeat a motion to dismiss."

4. *Enforcing the government's obligation to enforce the law.* The "redressability" portion of the majority opinion in *Allen* implies that a court will not issue an injunction requiring the executive to enforce the law. In *Linda R.S. v. Richard D.*, 410 U.S. 614 (1973), an unwed mother brought suit seeking an injunction to require state officials to enforce a child support law against the father of her child. The Court said that "appellant has made no showing that her failure to secure support payments results from the nonenforcement, as to her child's father," of the child support law. The Court also stated that "in American jurisprudence at least, a private citizen lacks a judicially cognizable interest in the prosecution or nonprosecution of another." Is this case based on a lack of causation or a lack of a right? Obviously, the government officials did not cause the father to refuse to pay child support, but on the other hand their prosecution of him might cause him to make the payments. Therefore, the question to be decided was whether the officials owed a duty to the mother to bring a prosecution. Arguably, the Court resolved this issue by dismissing for lack of standing.

Most state courts take the view that prosecutorial discretion is unreviewable. Prosecutors do not have sufficient personnel or funds to prosecute every case and must make some selective choices and there are usually no standards by which to judge whether the discretion was properly exercised in a given case. The result is to say that the citizen has no litigable interest in whether a given case should be prosecuted, much like the second rationale in *Linda R.S.*

The citizen's law enforcement issue arose in an unusual way in *Diamond v. Charles*, 476 U.S. 54 (1986). Dr. Diamond intervened as a party-defendant at the district court in a suit brought by physicians against a new Illinois statute regulating abortions, asserting his interest in preventing abortions. When the statute was declared unconstitutional in part, the state appealed to the Court of Appeals for the Seventh Circuit, which affirmed. Dr. Diamond then appealed to the Supreme Court but the state did not. The Court held that Dr. Diamond had no standing to pursue the appeal. Citing *Linda R.S.*, the Court said that "a private citizen lacks a judicially cognizable interest in the prosecution or nonprosecution of another." The Court also dismissed as too speculative Dr. Diamond's claims that if the abortion law were upheld, there would be more babies born and thus his practice as a pediatrician would improve.

The following two Supreme Court decisions should be read together. In reading them, ask yourself whether the two can be adequately distinguished, or whether the second decision in reality constitutes a significant departure from the first decision.

LUJAN v. DEFENDERS OF WILDLIFE

504 U.S. 555, 112 S. Ct. 2130, 119 L.Ed. 2d 351 (1992)

JUSTICE SCALIA delivered the opinion of the Court with respect to Parts I, II, III-A, and IV, and an opinion with respect to Part III-B in which THE CHIEF JUSTICE, JUSTICE WHITE, and JUSTICE THOMAS join.

This case involves a challenge to a rule promulgated by the Secretary of the Interior interpreting § 7 of the Endangered Species Act of 1973 (ESA), in such fashion as to render it applicable only to actions within the United States or on the high seas. The preliminary issue, and the only one we reach, is whether the respondents here, plaintiffs below, have standing to seek judicial review of the rule.

I

The ESA seeks to protect species of animals against threats to their continuing existence caused by man. The ESA instructs the Secretary of the Interior to promulgate by regulation a list of those species which are either endangered or threatened under enumerated criteria, and to define the critical habitat of these species. Section 7(a)(2) of the Act then provides, in pertinent part: "Each Federal agency shall, in consultation with and with the assistance of the Secretary [of the Interior], insure that any action authorized, funded, or carried out by such agency . . . is not likely to jeopardize the continued existence of any endangered species or threatened species or result in the destruction or adverse modification of habitat of such species which is determined by the Secretary, after consultation as appropriate with affected States, to be critical."

In 1978, the Fish and Wildlife Service (FWS) and the National Marine Fisheries Service (NMFS), on behalf of the Secretary of the Interior and the Secretary of Commerce respectively, promulgated a joint regulation stating that the obligations imposed by § 7(a)(2) extend to actions taken in foreign nations. The next year, however, the Interior Department began to reexamine its position. A revised joint regulation, reinterpreting § 7(a)(2) to require consultation only for actions taken in the United States or on the high seas, was proposed in 1983 and promulgated in 1986.

Shortly thereafter, respondents, organizations dedicated to wildlife conservation and other environmental causes, filed this action against the Secretary of the Interior, seeking a declaratory judgment that the new regulation is in error as to the geographic scope of § 7(a)(2), and an injunction requiring the Secretary to promulgate a new regulation restoring the initial interpretation.

II

Over the years, our cases have established that the irreducible constitutional minimum of standing contains three elements: First, the plaintiff must have suffered an "injury in fact" — an invasion of a legally-protected interest which is (a) concrete and particularized and (b) "actual or imminent, not conjectural or hypothetical." Second, there must be a causal connection between the injury and the conduct complained of — the injury has to be "fairly. . .trace[able] to the challenged action of the defendant, and not. . .th[e] result [of] the independent action of some third party not before the court." *Simon v. Eastern Kentucky Welfare Rights Org.* Third, it must be "likely," as opposed to merely "speculative," that the injury will be "redressed by a favorable decision."

The party invoking federal jurisdiction bears the burden of establishing these elements. Since they are not mere pleading requirements but rather an indispensable part of the plaintiff's case, each element must be supported in the same way as any other matter on which the plaintiff bears the burden of proof, i.e., with the manner and degree of evidence required at the successive stages of the litigation.

When the suit is one challenging the legality of government action or inaction, the nature and extent of facts that must be averred (at the summary judgment stage) or proved (at the trial stage) in order to establish standing depends considerably upon whether the plaintiff is himself an object of the action (or forgone action) at issue. If he is, there is ordinarily little question that the action or inaction has caused him injury, and that a judgment preventing or requiring the action will redress it. When, however, as in this case, a plaintiff's asserted injury arises from the government's allegedly unlawful regulation (or lack of regulation) of someone else, much more is needed. In that circumstance, causation and redressability ordinarily hinge on the response of the regulated (or regulable) third party to the government action or inaction — and perhaps on the response of others as well. The existence of one or more of the essential elements of standing "depends on the unfettered choices made by independent actors not before the courts and whose exercise of broad and legitimate discretion the courts cannot presume either to control or to predict," and it becomes the burden of the plaintiff to adduce facts showing that those choices have been or will be made in such manner as to produce causation and permit redressability of injury. Thus, when the plaintiff is not himself the object of the government action or inaction he challenges, standing is not precluded, but it is ordinarily "substantially more difficult" to establish.

III

Respondents had not made the requisite demonstration of (at least) injury and redressability.

A

Respondents' claim to injury is that the lack of consultation with respect to certain funded activities abroad "increas[es] the rate of extinction of endangered and threatened species." Of course, the desire to use or observe an animal species, even for purely aesthetic purposes, is undeniably a cognizable interest for purpose of standing. "But the 'injury in fact' test requires more than an injury to a cognizable interest. It requires that the party seeking review be himself among the injured." To survive the Secretary's summary judgment motion, respondents had to submit affidavits or other evidence showing, through specific facts, not only that listed species were in fact being threatened by funded activities abroad, but also that one or more of respondents' members would thereby be "directly" affected apart from their "special interest in th[e] subject."

With respect to this aspect of the case, the Court of Appeals focused on the affidavits of two of Defenders' members — Joyce Kelly and Amy Skilbred. Ms. Kelly stated that she traveled to Egypt in 1986 and "observed the traditional habitat of the endangered nile crocodile there and intend[s] to do so again, and hope[s] to observe the crocodile directly," and that she "will suffer harm in fact as a result of [the] American . . . role . . . in overseeing the rehabilitation of the Aswan High Dam on the Nile . . . and [in] develop [ing] . . . Egypt's . . . Master Water Plan." Ms. Skilbred averred that she traveled to Sri Lanka in 1981 and "observed th[e] habitat" of "endangered species such as the Asian elephant and the leopard" at what is now the site of the Mahaweli Project funded by the Agency for International Development (AID), although she "was unable to see any of the endangered species"; "this development project," she continued, "will seriously reduce endangered, threatened, and endemic species habitat including areas that I visited . . . [, which] may severely shorten the future of these species"; that threat, she concluded, harmed her because she "intend[s] to return to Sri Lanka in the future and hope[s] to be more fortunate in spotting at least the endangered elephant and leopard." When Ms. Skilbred was asked at a subsequent deposition if and when she had any plans to return to Sri Lanka, she reiterated that "I intend to go back to Sri Lanka," but confessed that she had no current plans: "I don't know [when]. There is a civil war going on right now. I don't know. Not next year, I will say. In the future."

We shall assume for the sake of argument that these affidavits contain facts showing that certain agency-funded projects threaten listed species — though that is questionable. They plainly contain no facts, however, showing how damage to the species will produce "imminent" injury to Mss. Kelly and Skilbred. Such "some day" intentions — without any description of concrete plans, or indeed even any specification of when the some day will be — do not support a finding of the "actual or imminent" injury that our cases require.

Besides relying upon the Kelly and Skilbred affidavits, respondents propose a series of novel standing theories. The first, inelegantly styled "ecosystem nexus," proposes that any person who uses any part of a "contiguous ecosystem" adversely affected by a funded activity has standing even if the activity is located a great distance away. This approach, as the Court of Appeals correctly observed, is inconsistent with our opinion in *National Wildlife Federation*, which held that a plaintiff claiming injury from environmental damage must use the area affected by the challenged activity and not an area roughly "in the vicinity" of it. It makes no difference that the general-purpose section of the ESA states that the Act was intended in part "to provide a means whereby the ecosystems upon which endangered species and threatened species depend may be conserved." To say that the Act protects ecosystems is not to say that the Act creates (if it were possible) rights of action in persons who have not been injured in fact, that is, persons who use portions of an ecosystem not perceptibly affected by the unlawful action in question.

Respondents' other theories are called, alas, the "animal nexus" approach, whereby anyone who has an interest in studying or seeing the endangered animals anywhere on the globe has standing; and the "vocational nexus" approach, under which anyone with a professional interest in such animals can sue. Under these theories, anyone who goes to see Asian elephants in the Bronx Zoo, and anyone who is a keeper of Asian elephants in the Bronx Zoo, has standing to sue because the Director of AID did not consult with the Secretary regarding the AID-funded project in Sri Lanka. This is beyond all reason. Standing is not "an ingenious academic exercise in the conceivable," but as we have said requires, at the summary judgment stage, a factual showing of perceptible harm. It is clear that the person who observes or works with a particular animal threatened by a federal decision is facing perceptible harm, since the very subject of his interest will no longer exist. It is even plausible — though it goes to the outermost limit of plausibility — to think that a person who observes or works with animals of a particular species in the very area of the world where that species is threatened by a federal decision is facing such harm, since some animals that might have been the subject of his interest will no longer exist. It goes beyond the limit, however, and into pure speculation and fantasy, to say that anyone who observes or works with an endangered species, anywhere in the world, is appreciably harmed by a single project affecting some portion of that species with which he has no more specific connection.

B

Besides failing to show injury, respondents failed to demonstrate redressability. Instead of attacking the separate decisions to fund particular projects allegedly causing them harm, the respondents chose to challenge a more generalized level of government action (rules regarding consultation), the invalidation of which would affect all overseas projects. This programmatic approach has obvious practical advantages, but also obvious difficulties insofar as proof of causation or redressability is concerned.

The most obvious problem in the present case is redressability. Since the agencies funding the projects were not parties to the case, the District Court could accord relief only against the Secretary: He could be ordered to revise his regulation to require consultation for foreign projects. But this would not remedy respondents' alleged injury unless the funding agencies were bound by the Secretary's regulation, which is very much an open question. Whereas in other contexts the ESA is quite explicit as to the Secretary's controlling authority, with respect to consultation the initiative, and hence arguably the initial responsibility for determining statutory necessity, lies with the agencies. When the Secretary promulgated the regulation at issue here, he thought it was binding on the agencies. The Solicitor General, however, has repudiated that position here, and the agencies themselves apparently deny the Secretary's authority. (During the period when the Secretary took the view that § 7(a)(2) did apply abroad, AID and FWS engaged in a running controversy over whether consultation was required with respect to the Mahaweli project, AID insisting that consultation applied only to domestic actions.)

Respondents assert that this legal uncertainty did not affect redressability (and hence standing) because the District Court itself could resolve the issue of the Secretary's authority as a necessary part of its standing inquiry. Assuming that it is appropriate to resolve an issue of law such as this in connection with a threshold standing inquiry, resolution by the District Court would not have remedied respondents' alleged injury anyway, because it would not have been binding upon the agencies. They were not parties to the suit, and there is no reason they should be obliged to honor an incidental legal determination the suit produced. The Court of Appeals tried to finesse this problem by simply proclaiming that "[w]e are satisfied that an injunction requiring the Secretary to publish [respondents' desired] regulatio-[n]. . .would result in consultation." We do not know what would justify that confidence, particularly when the Justice Department (presumably after consultation with the agencies) has taken the position that the regulation is not binding. The short of the matter is that redress of the only injury-in-fact respondents complain of requires action (termination of funding until consultation) by the individual funding agencies; and any relief the District Court could have provided in this suit against the Secretary was not likely to produce that action.

A further impediment to redressability is the fact that the agencies generally supply only a fraction of the funding for a foreign project. AID, for example, has provided less than 10% of the funding for the Mahaweli Project. Respondents have produced nothing to indicate that the projects they have named will either be suspended, or do less harm to listed species, if that fraction is eliminated. As in *Simon*, it is entirely conjectural whether the nonagency activity that affects respondents will be altered or affected by the agency activity they seek to achieve. [6] There is no standing.

IV

The Court of Appeals found that respondents had standing for an additional reason: because they had suffered a "procedural injury." The so-called "citizen-suit" provision of the ESA provides, in pertinent part, that "any person may commence a civil suit on his own behalf (A) to enjoin any person, including the United States and any other governmental instrumentality or agency. . .who is alleged to be in violation of any provision of this chapter." 16 U.S.C. § 1540(g). The court held that, because § 7(a)(2) requires interagency consultation, the citizen-suit provision creates a "procedural righ[t]" to consultation in all "persons" — so that anyone can file suit in federal court to challenge the Secretary's (or presumably any other official's) failure to follow the assertedly correct consultative procedure, notwithstanding their inability to allege any discrete injury flowing from that failure. To understand

[6] The dissent criticizes us for "overlook[ing]" memoranda indicating that the Sri Lankan government solicited and required AID's assistance to mitigate the effects of the Mahaweli Project on endangered species, and that the Bureau of Reclamation was advising the Aswan Project. The memoranda, however, contain no indication whatever that the projects will cease or be less harmful to listed species in the absence of AID funding. In fact, the Sri Lanka memorandum suggests just the opposite: it states that AID's role will be to mitigate the "negative impacts to the wildlife," which means that the termination of AID funding would exacerbate respondent's claimed injury.

the remarkable nature of this holding one must be clear about what it does not rest upon: This is not a case where plaintiffs are seeking to enforce a procedural requirement the disregard of which could impair a separate concrete interest of theirs (*e.g.*, the procedural requirement for a hearing prior to denial of their license application, or the procedural requirement for an environmental impact statement before a federal facility is constructed next door to them). Nor is it simply a case where concrete injury has been suffered by many persons, as in mass fraud or mass tort situations. Nor, finally, is it the unusual case in which Congress has created a concrete private interest in the outcome of a suit against a private party for the government's benefit, by providing a cash bounty for the victorious plaintiff. Rather, the court held that the injury-in-fact requirement had been satisfied by congressional conferral upon all persons of an abstract, self-contained, noninstrumental "right" to have the Executive observe the procedures required by law. We reject this view.

Vindicating the public interest (including the public interest in government observance of the Constitution and laws) is the function of Congress and the Chief Executive. The question presented here is whether the public interest in proper administration of the laws (specifically, in agencies' observance of a particular, statutorily prescribed procedure) can be converted into an individual right by a statute that denominates it as such, and that permits all citizens (or, for that matter, a subclass of citizens who suffer no distinctive concrete harm) to sue. If the concrete injury requirement has the separation-of-powers significance we have always said, the answer must be obvious: To permit Congress to convert the undifferentiated public interest in executive officers' compliance with the law into an "individual right" vindicable in the courts is to permit Congress to transfer from the President to the courts the Chief Executive's most important constitutional duty, to "take Care that the Laws be faithfully executed," Art. II, § 3. It would enable the courts, with the permission of Congress, "to assume a position of authority over the governmental acts of another and co-equal department," and to become "virtually continuing monitors of the wisdom and soundness of Executive action." "Individual rights" do not mean public rights that have been legislatively pronounced to belong to each individual who forms part of the public.

Nothing in this contradicts the principle that "[t]he. . .injury required by Art. III may exist solely by virtue of statutes creating legal rights, the invasion of which creates standing." [T]he cases used as an illustration of that principle involved Congress's elevating to the status of legally cognizable injuries concrete, de facto injuries that were previously inadequate in law (namely, injury to an individual's personal interest in living in a racially integrated community, *see Trafficante v. Metropolitan Life Ins. Co.*, and injury to a company's interest in marketing its product free from competition, *see Hardin v. Kentucky Utilities Co*). As we said in *Sierra Club*, "[Statutory] broadening [of] the categories of injury that may be alleged in support of standing is a different matter from abandoning the requirement that the party seeking review must himself have suffered an injury."

We hold that respondents lack standing to bring this action and that the Court of Appeals erred in denying the summary judgment motion filed by the

United States. The opinion of the Court of Appeals is hereby reversed, and the cause remanded for proceedings consistent with this opinion.

Justice Kennedy, with whom Justice Souter joins, concurring in part and concurring in the judgment.

Although I agree with the essential parts of the Court's analysis, I write separately to make several observations.

While it may seem trivial to require that Mss. Kelly and Skilbred acquire airline tickets to the project sites or announce a date certain upon which they will return, this is not a case where it is reasonable to assume that the affiants will be using the sites on a regular basis, nor do the affiants claim to have visited the sites since the projects commenced. With respect to the Court's discussion of respondents' "ecosystem nexus," "animal nexus," and "vocational nexus" theories, I agree that on this record respondents' showing is insufficient to establish standing on any of these bases. I am not willing to foreclose the possibility, however, that in different circumstances a nexus theory similar to those proffered here might support a claim to standing.

I also join Part IV of the Court's opinion with the following observations. As government programs and policies become more complex and far-reaching, we must be sensitive to the articulation of new rights of action that do not have clear analogs in our common-law tradition. Modern litigation has progressed far from the paradigm of Marbury suing Madison to get his commission, or Ogden seeking an injunction to halt Gibbons' steamboat operations. In my view, Congress has the power to define injuries and articulate chains of causation that will give rise to a case or controversy where none existed before, and I do not read the Court's opinion to suggest a contrary view. In exercising this power, however, Congress must at the very least identify the injury it seeks to vindicate and relate the injury to the class of persons entitled to bring suit. The citizen-suit provision of the Endangered Species Act does not meet these minimal requirements, because while the statute purports to confer a right on "any person. . .to enjoin. . .the United States and any other governmental instrumentality or agency. . .who is alleged to be in violation of any provision of this chapter," it does not of its own force establish that there is an injury in "any person" by virtue of any "violation."

Justice Stevens, concurring in the judgment.

Because I am not persuaded that Congress intended the consultation requirement in § 7(a)(2) of the Endangered Species Act of 1973 (ESA), to apply to activities in foreign countries, I concur in the judgment of reversal. I do not, however, agree with the Court's conclusion that respondents lack standing because the threatened injury to their interest in protecting the environment and studying endangered species is not "imminent." Nor do I agree with the plurality's additional conclusion that respondents' injury is not "redressable" in this litigation.

In my opinion a person who has visited the critical habitat of an endangered species, has a professional interest in preserving the species and its habitat, and intends to revisit them in the future has standing to challenge agency action that threatens their destruction. Congress has found that a wide variety of endangered species of fish, wildlife, and plants are of "aesthetic, ecological, educational, historical, recreational, and scientific value to the Nation and its people." Given that finding, we have no license to demean the importance of the interest that particular individuals may have in observing any species or its habitat, whether those individuals are motivated by aesthetic enjoyment, an interest in professional research, or an economic interest in preservation of the species. Indeed, this Court has often held that injuries to such interests are sufficient to confer standing, and the Court reiterates that holding today.

The Court nevertheless concludes that respondents have not suffered "injury in fact" because they have not shown that the harm to the endangered species will produce "imminent" injury to them. I disagree. An injury to an individual's interest in studying or enjoying a species and its natural habitat occurs when someone (whether it be the government or a private party) takes action that harms that species and habitat. In my judgment, therefore, the "imminence" of such an injury should be measured by the timing and likelihood of the threatened environmental harm, rather than — as the Court seems to suggest — by the time that might elapse between the present and the time when the individuals would visit the area if no such injury should occur.

We must presume that if this Court holds that § 7(a)(2) requires consultation, all affected agencies would abide by that interpretation and engage in the requisite consultations. Certainly the Executive Branch cannot be heard to argue that an authoritative construction of the governing statute by this Court may simply be ignored by any agency head. Moreover, if Congress has required consultation between agencies, we must presume that such consultation will have a serious purpose that is likely to produce tangible results. As Justice Blackmun explains, it is not mere speculation to think that foreign governments, when faced with the threatened withdrawal of United States assistance, will modify their projects to mitigate the harm to endangered species.

Although I believe that respondents have standing, I nevertheless concur in the judgment of reversal because I am persuaded that the Government is correct in its submission that § 7(a)(2) does not apply to activities in foreign countries.

JUSTICE BLACKMUN, with whom JUSTICE O'CONNOR joins, dissenting.

Were the Court to apply the proper standard for summary judgment, I believe it would conclude that the sworn affidavits and deposition testimony of Joyce Kelly and Amy Skilbred advance sufficient facts to create a genuine issue for trial concerning whether one or both would be imminently harmed by the Aswan and Mahaweli projects. In the first instance, as the Court itself concedes, the affidavits contained facts making it at least "questionable" (and therefore within the province of the factfinder) that certain agency-funded projects threaten listed species. The only remaining issue, then, is whether Kelly and Skilbred have shown that they personally would suffer imminent harm.[7]

[7] The record is replete with genuine issues of fact about the harm to endangered species from the Aswan and Mahaweli projects. For example, according to an internal memorandum of the Fish and Wildlife Service, no fewer than eight listed species are found in the Mahaweli project area (Indian elephant, leopard, purple-faced languar, toque macaque, red face malkoha, Bengal

I think a reasonable finder of fact could conclude from the information in the affidavits and deposition testimony that either Kelly or Skilbred will soon return to the project sites, thereby satisfying the "actual or imminent" injury standard.

The Court also concludes that injury is lacking, because respondents' allegations of "ecosystem nexus" failed to demonstrate sufficient proximity to the site of the environmental harm. Many environmental injuries, however, cause harm distant from the area immediately affected by the challenged action. Environmental destruction may affect animals traveling over vast geographical ranges or rivers running long geographical courses. It cannot seriously be contended that a litigant's failure to use the precise or exact site where animals are slaughtered or where toxic waste is dumped into a river means he or she cannot show injury.

The Court also rejects respondents' claim of vocational or professional injury. The Court says that it is "beyond all reason" that a zoo "keeper" of Asian elephants would have standing to contest his government's participation in the eradication of all the Asian elephants in another part of the world. I am unable to see how the distant location of the destruction necessarily (for purposes of ruling at summary judgment) mitigates the harm to the elephant keeper. If there is no more access to a future supply of the animal that sustains a keeper's livelihood, surely there is harm.

The plurality overlooks an Interior Department memorandum listing eight endangered or threatened species in the Mahaweli project area and recounting that "[t]he Sri Lankan government has requested the assistance of AID in mitigating the negative impacts to the wildlife involved." Further, a letter from the Director of the Fish and Wildlife Service to AID states: "The Sri Lanka government lacks the necessary finances to undertake any long-term management programs to avoid the negative impacts to the wildlife. The donor nations and agencies that are financing the [Mahaweli project] will be the key as to how successfully the wildlife is preserved. If wildlife problems receive the same level of attention as the engineering project, then the negative impacts to the environment can be alleviated. This means that there has to be long-term funding in sufficient amounts to stem the negative impacts of this project." I do not share the plurality's astonishing confidence that, on the record here, a factfinder could only conclude that AID was powerless to ensure the protection of listed species at the Mahaweli project.

As for the Aswan project, the record again rebuts the plurality's assumption that donor agencies are without any authority to protect listed species. Kelly

---

monitor, mugger crocodile, and python). The memorandum recounts that the Sri Lankan government has specifically requested assistance from the Agency for International Development in "mitigating the negative impacts to the wildlife involved." In addition, a letter from the Director of the Fish and Wildlife Service to AID warns: "The magnitude of the Accelerated Mahaweli Development Program could have massive environmental impacts on such an insular ecosystem as the Mahaweli River system." It adds: "The Sri Lankan government lacks the necessary finances to undertake any long-term management programs to avoid the negative impacts to the wildlife." Finally, in an affidavit submitted by petitioner for purposes of this litigation, an AID official states that an AID environmental assessment "showed that the [Mahaweli project] could affect several endangered species."

asserted in her affidavit — and it has not been disputed — that the Bureau of Reclamation was "overseeing" the rehabilitation of the Aswan project.

II

The Court concludes that any "procedural injury" suffered by respondents is insufficient to confer standing. It rejects the view that the "injury-in-fact requirement. . .[is] satisfied by congressional conferral upon all persons of an abstract, self-contained, noninstrumental 'right' to have the Executive observe the procedures required by law." Whatever the Court might mean with that very broad language, it cannot be saying that "procedural injuries" as a class are necessarily insufficient for purposes of Article III standing.

The Court expresses concern that allowing judicial enforcement of "agencies' observance of a particular, statutorily prescribed procedure" would "transfer from the President to the courts the Chief Executive's most important constitutional duty, to 'take Care that the Laws be faithfully executed,' Art. II, sec. 3." In fact, the principal effect of foreclosing judicial enforcement of such procedures is to transfer power into the hands of the Executive at the expense — not of the courts — but of Congress, from which that power originates and emanates.

It is to be hoped that over time the Court will acknowledge that some classes of procedural duties are so enmeshed with the prevention of a substantive, concrete harm that an individual plaintiff may be able to demonstrate a sufficient likelihood of injury just through the breach of that procedural duty.

III

In conclusion, I cannot join the Court on what amounts to a slash-and-burn expedition through the law of environmental standing. In my view, "[t]he very essence of civil liberty certainly consists in the right of every individual to claim the protection of the laws, whenever he receives an injury." *Marbury v. Madison.*

NOTES

1. *The state of standing law after* Lujan. In *Lujan,* does Justice Scalia do more than apply the injury-in-fact test to the facts of the case? Does he effectively increase the burdens on plaintiffs to demonstrate injury? Note that the injury-in-fact issue here differs from most of the cases we have seen presenting that issue, in that determination of injury turns on assessment of plaintiff's future behavior, while the majority of standing cases inquire whether the defendant's behavior has already caused damage of some kind to the plaintiff. Does that difference adequately explain this decision? According to one commentator, the lower federal courts, "following the lead" of *Lujan,* "have made it more difficult to show individual members' standing by imposing even stricter requirements for establishing the Article III requirement of 'injury in fact.' " Karl S. Coplan, *Direct Environmental Standing for Chartered Conservation Corporations,* 12 DUKE ENVTL. L. & POLICY F. 183, 185 (2001).

2. *Standing and executive power.* To what extent should *Lujan* be viewed as a case about unconstitutional legislative interferences with the executive branch, rather than a standing case? Do you see how the two issues intersect in this context? *See* William K. Kelley, *Avoiding Constitutional Questions as a Three-Branch Problem,* 86 Cornell L. Rev. 831 (2001).

3. *Standing and "procedural" injury.* What is the impact of *Lujan* on Congress's power to create an injury in fact? Should Congress be permitted to enable plaintiffs to satisfy the injury-in-fact requirement by legislatively establishing an injury, where, absent such legislative creation, no injury could be demonstrated? If it could, what role would be played by Article III's case-or-controversy requirement?

4. *Raines v. Byrd,* 521 U.S. 811 (1997). In a suit challenging the constitutionality of the Line Item Veto Act, brought by members of Congress who had voted against the Act, the Court held that the members of Congress lacked standing under Article III to bring the suit. The plaintiffs, said the Court, "do not claim that they have been deprived of something to which they personally are entitled—such as their seats as Members of Congress after their constituents had elected them." Indeed, their "claim of standing is based on a loss of political power, not loss of any private right, which would make the injury more concrete."

In denying standing, the Court distinguished its decision in *Coleman v. Miller*, 307 U.S. 433 (1939), where it had held that state legislators had standing to challenge the validity of the process used to resolve a tie legislative vote: "It is obvious that our holding in *Coleman* stands (at most) for the proposition that legislators who voted to defeat (or enact) a specific legislative act have standing to sue if that legislative action goes into effect (or does not go into effect), on the ground that their votes have been completely nullified." Plaintiffs, in contrast, "have not alleged that they voted for a specific bill, that there were sufficient votes to pass the bill, and that the bill was nonetheless deemed defeated. In the vote on the Line Item Veto Act, their votes were given full effect. They simply lost that vote."

The Court emphasized that its conclusion "neither deprives members of Congress of an adequate remedy (given they may repeal the Act or exempt appropriations bills from its reach), nor forecloses the Act from constitutional challenge (by someone who suffers judicially cognizable injury as a result of the Act). Whether the case would be different if any of these circumstances were different we need not now decide."

Justice Stevens, dissenting, argued that the plaintiffs "convincingly explain how the immediate, constant threat of the partial veto power has a palpable effect on their current legislative choices." Justice Breyer, in dissent, found the decision inconsistent with *Coleman*.

The Court held that the plaintiffs in *Clinton v. New York*, p. 328, *supra*, had standing to challenge the Line Item Veto Act. President Clinton cancelled provisions of the Balanced Budget Act of 1997 resulting in a multimillion dollar liability for New York State. The City of New York, which was subject to paying a portion of the liability, was held to suffer an economic injury in fact. The President also cancelled provisions of a tax relief act resulting in a loss of tax benefits to food refiner and processor sellers. Farmers' cooperatives that purchased from these sellers were held to be intended beneficiaries under the tax act. They lost a "bargaining chip" sufficient to constitute concrete economic injury sufficient to satisfy Article III. Unlike the plaintiffs in *Raines v. Byrd*, the plaintiffs in *Clinton* had a concrete personal stake, not simply an abstract general or an institutional interest in challenging the constitutionality of the Line Item Veto Act. The Act was held unconstitutional.

5. *Bennett v. Spear,* 520 U.S. 154 (1997). Ranch operators and irrigation districts filed an action against the regional director of the Fish and Wildlife Service and the Secretary of the Interior under the citizen-suit provision of the Endangered Species Act, alleging violations of the Act concerning the proposed restrictions of the use of reservoir water to protect lost river and shortnose species of sucker fish. The complaint alleged that the plaintiffs currently receive irrigation water from Clear Lake, and that the Bureau of Reclamation (not named as a defendant) would abide by the restrictions imposed by the "Biological Opinion" issued by the Service. The "Opinion" was required by the Act. It explained how the proposed action would "jeopardize the continued existence of any [listed] species or result in the destruction or adverse modification of [critical habitat]." The Court held that the plaintiffs had alleged sufficient injury in fact to establish standing under Article III.

Justice Scalia, speaking for the Court, reasoned: "Given [plaintiffs'] allegation that the amount of available water will be reduced and that they will be adversely affected thereby, it is easy to presume specific facts under which [plaintiffs] will be injured—for example, the Bureau's distribution of the reduction pro rata among its customers." Since the citizen-suit provision of the ESA authorizes suit by "any person," Congress expanded the zone of interests to the full extent permitted by Article III, thereby removing any prudential obstacle to plaintiffs' standing.

6. *Steel Co. v. Citizens for a Better Environment,* 523 U.S. 83 (1998). The Court held, per Justice Scalia, that Citizens for a Better Environment ("CBE") did not have standing to sue Steel Co. under the Emergency Planning and Community Right-To-Know Act of 1986 ("EPCRA"), 42 U.S.C. § 11046(a)(1) (1994), for failing in the past to file annual emergency and hazardous chemical inventory forms and toxic chemical release forms. These forms contain information about the name and location of facilities using hazardous and toxic chemicals, the name and quantity of the chemicals, as well as the method the facility uses to dispose of toxic chemicals and the annual quantity released into the environment. The EPCRA has several enforcement mechanisms. CBE sued under the citizen-suit provision, which authorizes civil penalties and injunctive relief. The EPCRA, however, required CBE to give Steel Co. sixty days notice before CBE could file a suit. During the sixty-day period, Steel Co. submitted the overdue forms. After the Administrator of the EPA decided not to bring an action against Steel Co., and when the sixty-day period expired, CBE filed suit in federal district court.

Steel Co. moved to dismiss for lack of subject matter jurisdiction and failure to state a claim upon which relief could be granted. Steel Co. argued that because its filings were up to date when the complaint was filed, the court had no jurisdiction to entertain a suit for a present violation. It further argued that, because EPCRA does not allow a suit for past violations, CBE's suit was "not a claim upon which relief could be granted." The district court agreed but the Seventh Circuit reversed and held that the EPCRA does allow private suits for past violations.

Justice Scalia, writing for the majority, addressed two issues: (1) whether a court should decide if CBE had Article III standing before deciding whether the EPCRA granted the court jurisdiction to hear the case; and (2) whether CBE had standing to sue for past violations of the EPCRA. On the first issue, the Court split as to whether a court *must decide* standing issues, whether under certain circumstances a court *should decide* standing issues first, or whether the court *should avoid* addressing the standing issue if it can resolve the case on statutory jurisdictional grounds. A majority, however, agreed that in this case it was appropriate to decide the standing issue first.

Justice Scalia repudiated the notion of "hypothetical jurisdiction": "The Ninth Circuit has denominated this practice—which it characterizes as 'assuming jurisdiction for the purpose of deciding the merits—the "doctrine of hypothetical jurisdiction.' " We decline to endorse such an approach because it carries the [federal] courts beyond the bounds of authorized judicial action and thus offends fundamental principles of separation of powers."

On the standing issue, the Court held that even assuming that CBE suffers a concrete injury in fact by being denied the information required by the EPCRA, CBE does not have standing to sue because "the complaint fails the third test of standing, redressability." CBE had requested a declaratory judgment that Steel Co. violated the EPCRA. Justice Scalia noted that there was no controversy over whether Steel Co. violated the EPCRA and that "the declaratory judgment is not only worthless to [CBE], it is seemingly worthless to all the world."

CBE also requested an order requiring Steel Co. to pay civil penalties of $25,000 per day for each violation. Justice Scalia denied that this request constituted a redressable claim since the penalties were payable to the U.S. Treasury and not to CBE: "In requesting [these damages], therefore, respondent seeks not remediation of its own injury . . . but vindication of the rule of law—the 'undifferentiated public interest' in faithful execution of EPCRA. [A]lthough a suitor may derive great comfort and joy from the fact that the United States Treasury is not cheated, that a wrongdoer gets his just deserts, or that the nation's laws are faithfully enforced, that psychic satisfaction is not an acceptable Article III remedy because it does not redress a cognizable Article III injury. Relief that does not remedy the injury suffered cannot bootstrap a plaintiff into federal court; that is the very essence of the redressibility requirement."

CBE further requested the investigation and prosecution costs of filing the suit against Steel Co. Justice Scalia bluntly refuted this claim stating that "a plaintiff cannot achieve standing to litigate a substantive issue by bringing suit for the cost of bringing suit."

Finally CBE requested prospective injunctive relief — authorization to inspect Steel Co.'s facility and records and an order requiring Steel Co. to provide CBE copies of all compliance reports submitted to the EPA. This relief,

Justice Scalia declared, "cannot conceivably remedy any past wrong but is aimed at deterring petitioner from violating EPCRA in the future." Justice Scalia noted that had CBE alleged a continuing violation or the imminence of a future violation, the relief requested would remedy the harm. Justice Scalia, however, doubted whether CBE could even allege such a harm based on the facts of the case.

Justice Breyer, concurring in part and concurring in the judgment, agreed with the Court that CBE lacked Article III standing and that federal courts "often and typically should decide standing questions at the outset of a case." Such a sequence — "first jurisdiction then the merits" — serves to restrict the federal courts to disputes that are adversarial: "But my qualifying words 'often' and 'typically' are important. The Constitution, in my view, does not always require us to replace those words with the word 'always.' The Constitution does not impose a rigid judicial 'order of operations' when doing so would cause serious practical problems. I would not make the ordinary sequence an absolute requirement."

Justice Stevens, with whom Justices Souter and Ginsburg joined in part, concurring in the judgement, rejected the majority's decision to address the standing issue first. Justice Stevens contended the majority needlessly created constitutional law about the redressability requirement of standing since the Court could simply have held that the EPCRA does not grant the federal courts jurisdiction to hear claims for past violations. Justice Stevens criticized the redressability requirement as a "judicial creation of the past 25 years." Justice Stevens distinguished previous redressability cases: "In every previous case in which the Court has denied standing because of a lack of redressability, the plaintiff was challenging some governmental action or inaction. None of these cases involved an attempt by one private party to impose a statutory sanction on another private party." In addition, Justice Stevens declared that imposing civil punishment on Steel Co. would redress CBE's injuries regardless of to whom the penalties are paid. "[CBE] clearly believes that the punishment of the Steel Company, along with future deterrence of the Steel Company and others, redresses its injury, and there is no basis in our previous standing holdings to suggest otherwise."

7. *Federal Election Commission v. Akins*, 514 U.S. 11 (1998). The Court held that an ordinary voter has standing to challenge the refusal of the Federal Election Commission (FEC) to designate the American Israel Public Affairs Committee (AIPAC) as a "political committee." Such a designation places limits on a group's contributions to campaigns, limits the amount that can be spent on candidates and imposes extensive recordkeeping and disclosure requirements. Akins and other voters politically opposed to AIPAC sought to force the FEC to designate AIPAC as a political committee subject to the statutory recordkeeping and disclosure requirements. The Court granted review to determine if ordinary voters have standing to challenge FEC's decision not to bring an enforcement action against AIPAC.

Justice Breyer, for the Court, addressed the Solicitor General's claim that the voters failed to satisfy prudential standing requirements. The Federal Election Campaign Act (FECA) broadly grants standing, stating "[a]ny person who believes a violation of this Act . . . has occurred, may file a complaint with the Commission." The injury suffered by voters such as Akins is their failure to obtain relevant information. This is an "injury of a kind that FECA seeks to address," and is within the zone of interests Congress sought to protect. The Court held: "Given the language of the statute and the nature of the injury, we conclude that Congress, intending to protect voters such as respondents from suffering the kind of injury here at issue, intended to authorize this kind of suit. Consequently, respondents satisfy 'prudential' standing requirements."

Justice Breyer then turned to the FEC claim that Congress lacks constitutional power under Article III to authorize federal courts to adjudicate this lawsuit. The voters' "injury in fact" consists of their inability to obtain information they believe they are entitled to under the statute. This is a "concrete and particular" injury since it would help them evaluate candidates for office and the role played by AIPAC's financial assistance. Justice Breyer acknowledged that "[w]hether styled as a constitutional or prudential limit on standing, the Court has sometimes determined that where large numbers of Americans suffer alike, the political process, rather than the judicial process, may provide the more appropriate remedy for the widely shared grievance." But rejection of a claim as a "generalized grievance" usually occurs where the harm is also abstract and indefinite, not where it is concrete though widely shared. While the fact that the injury is widely shared may counsel against interpreting a statute as conferring standing, it does not "automatically disqualify an interest for Article III purposes." The Court held: "We conclude that similarly, the informational injury at issue here, directly related to voting, the most basic of political rights, is sufficiently concrete and specific such that the fact that it is widely shared does not deprive Congress of constitutional power to authorize its vindication in federal courts."

The other elements of Article III standing were also satisfied. While the FEC might have accepted Akin's view of the law and still have exercised its enforcement discretion not to require disclosure, "[y]et those adversely affected by a discretionary agency decision generally have standing to complain that the agency based its decision upon an improper legal ground." The Court held: "Thus respondents' 'injury in fact' is 'fairly traceable' to the FEC's decision not to issue its complaint, even though the FEC might reach the same result exercising its discretionary powers lawfully. For similar reasons, the courts in this case can 'redress' respondents' 'injury in fact.' "

Justice Scalia, joined by Justices Thomas and O'Connor dissenting, argued that the majority read the statutory provision granting standing to "any party aggrieved" too broadly. A voter is not injured by the refusal of information but "the refusal (for an allegedly improper reason) to commence an agency enforcement action against a third person." That, in and of itself, does not constitute an injury in fact for voters. Justice Scalia notes that a narrow reading of the statute "is supported by the doctrine of constitutional doubt, which counsels us to interpret statutes, if possible, in such fashion as to avoid grave constitutional questions" as well as the holding in *Richardson*.

Justice Scalia also notes that a voter does not suffer a particularized injury which "must affect the plaintiff in a personal and individual way." The injury claimed by the voters who brought this action is common to all other voters in America and therefore is a generalized, abstract grievance. "A system in which the citizenry at large could sue to compel Executive compliance with the law would be a system in which the courts, rather than of the President, are given the primary responsibility to 'take Care that the Laws be faithfully executed.' "

FRIENDS OF THE EARTH, INC. v. LAIDLAW ENVIRONMENTAL SERVICES

528 U.S. 167, 120 S. Ct. 693, 145 L. Ed.2d 610 (2000)

JUSTICE GINSBURG delivered the opinion of the Court.

This case presents an important question concerning the operation of the citizen-suit provisions of the Clean Water Act. Congress authorized the federal district courts to entertain Clean Water Act suits initiated by "a person or persons having an interest which is or may be adversely affected." 33 U.S.C. §§ 1365(a), (g). To impel future compliance with the Act, a district court may prescribe injunctive relief in such a suit; additionally or alternatively, the court may impose civil penalties payable to the United States Treasury. § 1365(a). In the Clean Water Act citizen suit now before us, the District Court determined that injunctive relief was inappropriate because the defendant, after the institution of the litigation, achieved substantial compliance with the terms of its discharge permit. The court did, however, assess a civil penalty of $405,800. The "total deterrent effect" of the penalty would be adequate to forestall future violations, the court reasoned, taking into account that the defendant "will be required to reimburse plaintiffs for a significant amount of legal fees and has, itself, incurred significant legal expenses."

The Court of Appeals vacated the District Court's order. The case became moot, the appellate court declared, once the defendant fully complied with the terms of its permit and the plaintiff failed to appeal the denial of equitable relief.

We reverse the judgment of the Court of Appeals. The appellate court erred in concluding that a citizen suitor's claim for civil penalties must be dismissed as moot when the defendant, albeit after commencement of the litigation, has come into compliance. In directing dismissal of the suit on grounds of mootness, the Court of Appeals incorrectly conflated our case law on initial standing to bring suit, with our case law on post-commencement mootness. A defendant's voluntary cessation of allegedly unlawful conduct ordinarily does not suffice to moot a case. The Court of Appeals also misperceived the remedial potential of civil penalties. Such penalties may serve, as an alternative to an injunction, to deter future violations and thereby redress the injuries that prompted a citizen suitor to commence litigation.

I

A

In 1972, Congress enacted the Clean Water Act (Act), also known as the Federal Water Pollution Control Act, 33 U.S.C. § 1251 et seq. Section 402 of the Act, 33 U.S.C. § 1342, provides for the issuance, by the Administrator of the Environmental Protection Agency (EPA) or by authorized States, of National Pollutant Discharge Elimination System (NPDES) permits. NPDES permits impose limitations on the discharge of pollutants, and establish related monitoring and reporting requirements, in order to improve the cleanliness and safety of the Nation's waters. Noncompliance with a permit constitutes a violation of the Act. Under § 505(a) of the Act, a suit to enforce any limitation in an NPDES permit may be brought by any "citizen," defined as "a person or persons having an interest which is or may be adversely affected." Sixty days before initiating a citizen suit, however, the would-be plaintiff must give notice of the alleged violation to the EPA, the State in which the alleged violation occurred, and the alleged violator."[T]he purpose of notice to the alleged violator is to give it an opportunity to bring itself into complete compliance with the Act and thus. . .render unnecessary a citizen suit." *Gwaltney of Smithfield, Ltd. v. Chesapeake Bay Foundation, Inc.* Accordingly, we have held that citizens lack statutory standing under § 505(a) to sue for violations that have ceased by the time the complaint is filed. The Act also bars a citizen from suing if the EPA or the State has already commenced, and is "diligently prosecuting," an enforcement action.

The Act authorizes district courts in citizen-suit proceedings to enter injunctions and to assess civil penalties, which are payable to the United States Treasury. § 1365(a). In determining the amount of any civil penalty, the district court must take into account "the seriousness of the violation or violations, the economic benefit (if any) resulting from the violation, any history of such violations, any good-faith efforts to comply with the applicable requirements, the economic impact of the penalty on the violator, and such other matters as justice may require." § 1319(d). In addition, the court "may award costs of litigation (including reasonable attorney and expert witness fees) to any prevailing or substantially prevailing party, whenever the court determines such award is appropriate." § 1365(d).

B

In 1986, defendant-respondent Laidlaw Environmental Services (TOC), Inc., bought a hazardous waste incinerator facility in Roebuck, South Carolina, that included a wastewater treatment plant. Shortly after Laidlaw acquired the facility, the South Carolina Department of Health and Environmental Control (DHEC), granted Laidlaw an NPDES permit authorizing the company to discharge treated water into the North Tyger River. The permit, which became effective on January 1, 1987, placed limits on Laidlaw's discharge of several pollutants into the river, including — of particular relevance to this case — mercury, an extremely toxic pollutant. The permit also regulated the flow, temperature, toxicity, and pH of the effluent from the facility, and imposed monitoring and reporting obligations.

Once it received its permit, Laidlaw began to discharge various pollutants into the waterway; repeatedly, Laidlaw's discharges exceeded the limits set by the permit. In particular, despite experimenting with several technological fixes, Laidlaw consistently failed to meet the permit's stringent 1.3 ppb (parts per billion) daily average limit on mercury discharges. The District Court later found that Laidlaw had violated the mercury limits on 489 occasions between 1987 and 1995.

On April 10, 1992, plaintiff-petitioners Friends of the Earth (FOE) and Citizens Local Environmental Action Network, Inc. (CLEAN) (referred to collectively in this opinion, together with later joined plaintiff-petitioner Sierra Club, as "FOE") took the preliminary step necessary to the institution of litigation. They sent a letter to Laidlaw notifying the company of their intention to file a citizen suit against it under § 505(a) of the Act after the expiration of the requisite 60-day notice period, i.e., on or after June 10, 1992. Laidlaw's lawyer then contacted DHEC to ask whether DHEC would consider filing a lawsuit against Laidlaw. The District Court later found that Laidlaw's reason for requesting that DHEC file a lawsuit against it was to bar FOE's proposed citizen suit through the operation of 33 U.S.C. § 1365(b)(1)(B). DHEC agreed to file a lawsuit against Laidlaw; the company's lawyer then drafted the complaint for DHEC and paid the filing fee. On June 9, 1992, the last day before FOE's 60-day notice period expired, DHEC and Laidlaw reached a settlement requiring Laidlaw to pay $100,000 in civil penalties and to make " 'every effort' " to comply with its permit obligations.

On June 12, 1992, FOE filed this citizen suit against Laidlaw under §505(a) of the Act, alleging noncompliance with the NPDES permit and seeking declaratory and injunctive relief and an award of civil penalties. Laidlaw moved for summary judgment on the ground that FOE had failed to present evidence demonstrating injury in fact, and therefore lacked Article III standing to bring the lawsuit. In opposition to this motion, FOE submitted affidavits and deposition testimony from members of the plaintiff organizations. The record before the District Court also included affidavits from the organizations' members submitted by FOE in support of an earlier motion for preliminary injunctive relief. After examining this evidence, the District Court denied Laidlaw's summary judgment motion, finding — albeit "by the very slimmest of margins"—that FOE had standing to bring the suit.

On January 22, 1997, the District Court issued its judgment. It found that Laidlaw had gained a total economic benefit of $1,092,581 as a result of its extended period of noncompliance with the mercury discharge limit in its permit. The court concluded, however, that a civil penalty of $405,800 was adequate in light of the guiding factors listed in 33 U.S.C. § 1319(d). In particular, the District Court stated that the lesser penalty was appropriate taking into account the judgment's "total deterrent effect." In reaching this determination, the court "considered that Laidlaw will be required to reimburse plaintiffs for a significant amount of legal fees." The court declined to grant FOE's request for injunctive relief, stating that an injunction was inappropriate because "Laidlaw has been in substantial compliance with all parameters in its NPDES permit since at least August 1992."

On July 16, 1998, the Court of Appeals for the Fourth Circuit issued its judgment. The Court of Appeals assumed without deciding that FOE initially had standing to bring the action, but went on to hold that the case had become moot. The appellate court stated, first, that the elements of Article III standing — injury, causation, and redressability — must persist at every stage of review, or else the action becomes moot. [T]he Court of Appeals reasoned that the case had become moot because "the only remedy currently available to [FOE]—civil penalties payable to the government — would not redress any injury [FOE has] suffered." The court therefore vacated the District Court's order and remanded with instructions to dismiss the action.

According to Laidlaw, after the Court of Appeals issued its decision but before this Court granted certiorari, the entire incinerator facility in Roebuck was permanently closed, dismantled, and put up for sale, and all discharges from the facility permanently ceased.

II

A

The Constitution's case-or-controversy limitation on federal judicial authority, Art. III, §2, underpins both our standing and our mootness jurisprudence, but the two inquiries differ in respects critical to the proper resolution of this case, so we address them separately. Because the Court of Appeals was persuaded that the case had become moot and so held, it simply assumed without deciding that FOE had initial standing. But because we hold that the Court of Appeals erred in declaring the case moot, we have an obligation to assure ourselves that FOE had Article III standing at the outset of the litigation. We therefore address the question of standing before turning to mootness.

In *Lujan v. Defenders of Wildlife*, we held that, to satisfy Article III's standing requirements, a plaintiff must show (1) it has suffered an "injury in fact" that is (a) concrete and particularized and (b) actual or imminent, not conjectural or hypothetical; (2) the injury is fairly traceable to the challenged action of the defendant; and (3) it is likely, as opposed to merely speculative, that the injury will be redressed by a favorable decision. An association has standing to bring suit on behalf of its members when its members would otherwise have standing to sue in their own right, the interests at stake are germane to the organization's purpose, and neither the claim asserted nor the relief requested requires the participation of individual members in the lawsuit.

Laidlaw contends first that FOE lacked standing from the outset even to seek injunctive relief, because the plaintiff organizations failed to show that any of their members had sustained or faced the threat of any "injury in fact" from Laidlaw's activities. In support of this contention Laidlaw points to the District Court's finding, made in the course of setting the penalty amount, that there had been "no demonstrated proof of harm to the environment" from Laidlaw's mercury discharge violations.

The relevant showing for purposes of Article III standing, however, is not injury to the environment but injury to the plaintiff. To insist upon the former rather than the latter as part of the standing inquiry (as the dissent in essence does, is to raise the standing hurdle higher than the necessary showing for success on the merits in an action alleging noncompliance with an NPDES permit. Focusing properly on injury to the plaintiff, the District Court found that FOE had demonstrated sufficient injury to establish standing. For example, FOE member Kenneth Lee Curtis averred in affidavits that he lived a half-mile from Laidlaw's facility; that he occasionally drove over the North Tyger River, and that it looked and smelled polluted; and that he would like to fish, camp, swim, and picnic in and near the river between 3 and 15 miles downstream from the facility, as he did when he was a teenager, but would not do so because he was concerned that the water was polluted by Laidlaw's discharges. Curtis reaffirmed these statements in extensive deposition testimony. For example, he testified that he would like to fish in the river at a specific spot he used as a boy, but that he would not do so now because of his concerns about Laidlaw's discharges.

Other members presented evidence to similar effect. CLEAN member Angela Patterson attested that she lived two miles from the facility; that before Laidlaw operated the facility, she picnicked, walked, birdwatched, and waded in and along the North Tyger River because of the natural beauty of the area; that she no longer engaged in these activities in or near the river because she was concerned about harmful effects from discharged pollutants; and that she and her husband would like to purchase a home near the river but did not intend to do so, in part because of Laidlaw's discharges. CLEAN member Judy Pruitt averred that she lived one-quarter mile from Laidlaw's facility and would like to fish, hike, and picnic along the North Tyger River, but has refrained from those activities because of the discharges. FOE member Linda Moore attested that she lived 20 miles from Roebuck, and would use the North Tyger River south of Roebuck and the land surrounding it for recreational purposes were she not concerned that the water contained harmful pollutants. In her deposition, Moore testified at length that she would hike, picnic, camp, swim, boat, and drive near or in the river were it not for her concerns about illegal discharges. CLEAN member Gail Lee attested that her home, which is near Laidlaw's facility, had a lower value than similar homes located further from the facility, and that she believed the pollutant discharges accounted for some of the discrepancy. Sierra Club member Norman Sharp averred that he had canoed approximately 40 miles downstream of the Laidlaw facility and would like to canoe in the North Tyger River closer to Laidlaw's discharge point, but did not do so because he was concerned that the water contained harmful pollutants.

These sworn statements, as the District Court determined, adequately documented injury in fact. We have held that environmental plaintiffs adequately allege injury in fact when they aver that they use the affected area and are persons "for whom the aesthetic and recreational values of the area will be lessened" by the challenged activity. *Sierra Club v. Morton. See also Defenders of Wildlife.* ("Of course, the desire to use or observe an animal species, even for purely esthetic purposes, is undeniably a cognizable interest for purposes of standing.")

Our decision in *Lujan v. National Wildlife Federation*, is not to the contrary. In that case an environmental organization assailed the Bureau of Land Management's "land withdrawal review program," a program covering millions of acres, alleging that the program illegally opened up public lands to mining activities. The defendants moved for summary judgment, challenging the plaintiff organization's standing to initiate the action under the Administrative Procedure Act, 5 U.S.C. § 702. We held that the plaintiff could not survive the summary judgment motion merely by offering "averments which state only that one of [the organization's] members uses unspecified portions of an immense tract of territory, on some portions of which mining activity has occurred or probably will occur by virtue of the governmental action."

In contrast, the affidavits and testimony presented by FOE in this case assert that Laidlaw's discharges, and the affiant members' reasonable concerns about the effects of those discharges, directly affected those affiants' recreational, aesthetic, and economic interests. These submissions present dispositively more than the mere "general averments" and "conclusory allegations" found inadequate in *National Wildlife Federation*. Nor can the affiants' conditional statements — that they would use the nearby North Tyger River for recreation if Laidlaw were not discharging pollutants into it — be equated with the speculative " 'some day' intentions" to visit endangered species halfway around the world that we held insufficient to show injury in fact in *Defenders of Wildlife*.

Los Angeles v. Lyons, relied on by the dissent, does not weigh against standing in this case. In *Lyons*, we held that a plaintiff lacked standing to seek an injunction against the enforcement of a police chokehold policy because he could not credibly allege that he faced a realistic threat from the policy. In the footnote from *Lyons* cited by the dissent, we noted that "[t]he reasonableness of Lyons' fear is dependent upon the likelihood of a recurrence of the allegedly unlawful conduct," and that his "subjective apprehensions" that such a recurrence would even take place were not enough to support standing. Here, in contrast, it is undisputed that Laidlaw's unlawful conduct—discharging pollutants in excess of permit limits—was occurring at the time the complaint was filed. Under *Lyons*, then, the only "subjective" issue here is "[t]he reasonableness of [the] fear" that led the affiants to respond to that concededly ongoing conduct by refraining from use of the North Tyger River and surrounding areas. Unlike the dissent, we see nothing "improbable" about the proposition that a company's continuous and pervasive illegal discharges of pollutants into a river would cause nearby residents to curtail their recreational use of that waterway and would subject them to other economic and aesthetic harms. The proposition is entirely reasonable, the District Court found it was true in this case, and that is enough for injury in fact.

Laidlaw argues next that even if FOE had standing to seek injunctive relief, it lacked standing to seek civil penalties. Here the asserted defect is not injury but redressability. Civil penalties offer no redress to private plaintiffs, Laidlaw argues, because they are paid to the government, and therefore a citizen plaintiff can never have standing to seek them.

Laidlaw is right to insist that a plaintiff must demonstrate standing separately for each form of relief sought. But it is wrong to maintain that citizen plaintiffs facing ongoing violations never have standing to seek civil penalties.

We have recognized on numerous occasions that "all civil penalties have some deterrent effect." *Hudson v. United States*. More specifically, Congress has found that civil penalties in Clean Water Act cases do more than promote immediate compliance by limiting the defendant's economic incentive to delay its attainment of permit limits; they also deter future violations. This congressional determination warrants judicial attention and respect.

It can scarcely be doubted that, for a plaintiff who is injured or faces the threat of future injury due to illegal conduct ongoing at the time of suit, a sanction that effectively abates that conduct and prevents its recurrence provides a form of redress. Civil penalties can fit that description. To the extent that they encourage defendants to discontinue current violations and deter them from committing future ones, they afford redress to citizen plaintiffs who are injured or threatened with injury as a consequence of ongoing unlawful conduct.

The dissent argues that it is the availability rather than the imposition of civil penalties that deters any particular polluter from continuing to pollute. This argument misses the mark in two ways. First, it overlooks the interdependence of the availability and the imposition; a threat has no deterrent value unless it is credible that it will be carried out. Second, it is reasonable for Congress to conclude that an actual award of civil penalties does in fact bring with it a significant quantum of deterrence over and above what is achieved by the mere prospect of such penalties. A would-be polluter may or may not be dissuaded by the existence of a remedy on the books, but a defendant once hit in its pocketbook will surely think twice before polluting again.

We recognize that there may be a point at which the deterrent effect of a claim for civil penalties becomes so insubstantial or so remote that it cannot support citizen standing. The fact that this vanishing point is not easy to ascertain does not detract from the deterrent power of such penalties in the ordinary case.

In this case we need not explore the outer limits of the principle that civil penalties provide sufficient deterrence to support redressability. Here, the civil penalties sought by FOE carried with them a deterrent effect that made it likely, as opposed to merely speculative, that the penalties would redress FOE's injuries by abating current violations and preventing future ones — as the District Court reasonably found when it assessed a penalty of $405,800.

Laidlaw contends that the reasoning of our decision in *Steel Co. v. Citizens for a Better Environment* directs the conclusion that citizen plaintiffs have no standing to seek civil penalties under the Act. We disagree. *Steel Co.* established that citizen suitors lack standing to seek civil penalties for violations that have abated by the time of suit. We specifically noted in that case that there was no allegation in the complaint of any continuing or imminent violation, and that no basis for such an allegation appeared to exist. In short, *Steel Co.* held that private plaintiffs, unlike the Federal Government, may not sue to assess penalties for wholly past violations, but our decision in that case did not reach the issue of standing to seek penalties for violations that are ongoing at the time of the complaint and that could continue into the future if undeterred.[4]

[4] In insisting that the redressability requirement is not met, the dissent relies heavily on *Linda R.S. v. Richard D.* That reliance is sorely misplaced. In *Linda R.S.*, the mother of an out-of-wedlock child filed suit to force a district attorney to bring a criminal prosecution against the absentee father for failure to pay child support. In finding that the mother lacked standing to seek this

[The Court's consideration of mootness is discussed at p. 1620.]

For the reasons stated, the judgment of the United States Court of Appeals for the Fourth Circuit is reversed, and the case is remanded for further proceedings consistent with this opinion.

[The concurring opinion of JUSTICE STEVENS is omitted.]

JUSTICE KENNEDY, concurring.

Difficult and fundamental questions are raised when we ask whether exactions of public fines by private litigants, and the delegation of Executive power which might be inferable from the authorization, are permissible in view of the responsibilities committed to the Executive by Article II of the Constitution of the United States. The questions presented in the petition for certiorari did not identify these issues with particularity; and neither the Court of Appeals in deciding the case nor the parties in their briefing before this Court devoted specific attention to the subject. In my view these matters are best reserved for a later case. With this observation, I join the opinion of the Court.

JUSTICE SCALIA, with whom JUSTICE THOMAS joins, dissenting.

The Court begins its analysis by finding injury in fact on the basis of vague affidavits that are undermined by the District Court's express finding that Laidlaw's discharges caused no demonstrable harm to the environment. It then proceeds to marry private wrong with public remedy in a union that violates traditional principles of federal standing — thereby permitting law enforcement to be placed in the hands of private individuals. Finally, the Court suggests that to avoid mootness one needs even less of a stake in the outcome than the Court's watered-down requirements for initial standing. I dissent from all of this.

I

Plaintiffs, as the parties invoking federal jurisdiction, have the burden of proof and persuasion as to the existence of standing. The plaintiffs in this case fell far short of carrying their burden of demonstrating injury in fact. The

extraordinary remedy, the Court drew attention to "the special status of criminal prosecutions in our system," and carefully limited its holding to the "unique context of a challenge to [the non-enforcement of] a criminal statute." Furthermore, as to redressability, the relief sought in *Linda R.S.*—a prosecution which, if successful, would automatically land the delinquent father in jail for a fixed term, with predictably negative effects on his earning power — would scarcely remedy the plaintiff's lack of child support payments. In this regard, the Court contrasted "the civil contempt model whereby the defendant 'keeps the keys to the jail in his own pocket' and may be released whenever he complies with his legal obligations." The dissent's contention, that "precisely the same situation exists here" as in *Linda R.S.* is, to say the least, extravagant. Putting aside its mistaken reliance on *Linda R.S.*, the dissent's broader charge that citizen suits for civil penalties under the Act carry "grave implications for democratic governance," seems to us overdrawn. Certainly the federal Executive Branch does not share the dissent's view that such suits dissipate its authority to enforce the law. In fact, the Department of Justice has endorsed this citizen suit from the outset, submitting amicus briefs in support of FOE in the District Court, the Court of Appeals, and this Court. [T]he Federal Government retains the power to foreclose a citizen suit by undertaking its own action. And if the Executive Branch opposes a particular citizen suit, the statute allows the Administrator of the EPA to "intervene as a matter of right" and bring the Government's views to the attention of the court.

Court cites affiants' testimony asserting that their enjoyment of the North Tyger River has been diminished due to "concern" that the water was polluted, and that they "believed" that Laidlaw's mercury exceedances had reduced the value of their homes. These averments alone cannot carry the plaintiffs' burden of demonstrating that they have suffered a "concrete and particularized" injury, *Lujan*. General allegations of injury may suffice at the pleading stage, but at summary judgment plaintiffs must set forth "specific facts" to support their claims. And where, as here, the case has proceeded to judgment, those specific facts must be " 'supported adequately by the evidence adduced at trial.' " In this case, the affidavits themselves are woefully short on "specific facts," and the vague allegations of injury they do make are undermined by the evidence adduced at trial.

Typically, an environmental plaintiff claiming injury due to discharges in violation of the Clean Water Act argues that the discharges harm the environment, and that the harm to the environment injures him. This route to injury is barred in the present case, however, since the District Court concluded after considering all the evidence that there had been "no demonstrated proof of harm to the environment," that the "permit violations at issue in this citizen suit did not result in any health risk or environmental harm," that "[a]ll available data . . . fail to show that Laidlaw's actual discharges have resulted in harm to the North Tyger River," and that "the overall quality of the river exceeds levels necessary to support . . . recreation in and on the water."

The Court finds these conclusions unproblematic for standing, because "[t]he relevant showing for purposes of Article III standing. . .is not injury to the environment but injury to the plaintiff." This statement is correct, as far as it goes. We have certainly held that a demonstration of harm to the environment is not enough to satisfy the injury-in-fact requirement unless the plaintiff can demonstrate how he personally was harmed. In the normal course, however, a lack of demonstrable harm to the environment will translate, as it plainly does here, into a lack of demonstrable harm to citizen plaintiffs. While it is perhaps possible that a plaintiff could be harmed even though the environment was not, such a plaintiff would have the burden of articulating and demonstrating the nature of that injury. Ongoing "concerns" about the environment are not enough, for "[i]t is the reality of the threat of repeated injury that is relevant to the standing inquiry, not the plaintiff's subjective apprehensions," *Los Angeles v. Lyons*. At the very least, in the present case, one would expect to see evidence supporting the affidavits' bald assertions regarding decreasing recreational usage and declining home values, as well as evidence for the improbable proposition that Laidlaw's violations, even though harmless to the environment, are somehow responsible for these effects. Plaintiffs here have made no attempt at such a showing, but rely entirely upon unsupported and unexplained affidavit allegations of "concern."

Indeed, every one of the affiants deposed by Laidlaw cast into doubt the (in any event inadequate) proposition that subjective "concerns" actually affected their conduct. Linda Moore, for example, said in her affidavit that she would use the affected waterways for recreation if it were not for her concern about pollution. Yet she testified in her deposition that she had been to the river only twice, once in 1980 (when she visited someone who lived by the river) and once after this suit was filed. Similarly, Kenneth Lee Curtis, who claimed he was injured by being deprived of recreational activity at the river, admitted that he had not been to the river since he was "a kid," and when asked whether the reason he stopped visiting the river was because of pollution, answered "no." As to Curtis's claim that the river "looke[d] and smell[ed] polluted," this condition, if present, was surely not caused by Laidlaw's discharges, which according to the District Court "did not result in any health risk or environmental harm." The other affiants cited by the Court were not deposed, but their affidavits state either that they would use the river if it were not polluted or harmful (as the court subsequently found it is not), or said that the river looks polluted (which is also incompatible with the court's findings). These affiants have established nothing but "subjective apprehensions."

Although we have previously refused to find standing based on the "conclusory allegations of an affidavit," *Lujan v. National Wildlife Federation*, the Court is content to do just that today. By accepting plaintiffs' vague, contradictory, and unsubstantiated allegations of "concern" about the environment as adequate to prove injury in fact, and accepting them even in the face of a finding that the environment was not demonstrably harmed, the Court makes the injury-in-fact requirement a sham. If there are permit violations, and a member of a plaintiff environmental organization lives near the offending plant, it would be difficult not to satisfy today's lenient standard.

II

The Court's treatment of the redressability requirement — which would have been unnecessary if it resolved the injury-in-fact question correctly — is equally cavalier. As discussed above, petitioners allege ongoing injury consisting of diminished enjoyment of the affected waterways and decreased property values. They allege that these injuries are caused by Laidlaw's continuing permit violations. But the remedy petitioners seek is neither recompense for their injuries nor an injunction against future violations. Instead, the remedy is a statutorily specified "penalty" for past violations, payable entirely to the United States Treasury. Only last Term, we held that such penalties do not redress any injury a citizen plaintiff has suffered from past violations. *Steel Co. v. Citizens for a Better Environment*. The Court nonetheless finds the redressability requirement satisfied here, distinguishing *Steel Co.* on the ground that in this case the petitioners allege ongoing violations; payment of the penalties, it says, will remedy petitioners' injury by deterring future violations by Laidlaw. It holds that a penalty payable to the public "remedies" a threatened private harm, and suffices to sustain a private suit.

That holding has no precedent in our jurisprudence, and takes this Court beyond the "cases and controversies" that Article III of the Constitution has entrusted to its resolution. Even if it were appropriate, moreover, to allow Article III's remediation requirement to be satisfied by the indirect private consequences of a public penalty, those consequences are entirely too speculative in the present case. The new standing law that the Court makes — like all expansions of standing beyond the traditional constitutional limits — has grave implications for democratic governance. I shall discuss these three points in turn.

A

In *Linda R.S. v. Richard D.*, the plaintiff, mother of an illegitimate child, sought, on behalf of herself, her child, and all others similarly situated, an injunction against discriminatory application of Art. 602 of the Texas Penal Code. Although that provision made it a misdemeanor for "any parent" to refuse to support his or her minor children under 18 years of age, it was enforced only against married parents. That refusal, the plaintiff contended, deprived her and her child of the equal protection of the law by denying them the deterrent effect of the statute upon the father's failure to fulfill his support obligation. The Court held that there was no Article III standing. There was no " 'direct' relationship," it said, "between the alleged injury and the claim sought to be adjudicated," since "[t]he prospect that prosecution will, at least in the future, result in payment of support can, at best, be termed only speculative." [Our cases] demonstrate that, in American jurisprudence at least, a private citizen lacks a judicially cognizable interest in the prosecution or nonprosecution of another."

There was no "logical nexus" between nonenforcement of the statute and Linda R.S.'s failure to receive support payments because "[t]he prospect that prosecution will. . .result in payment of support" was "speculative," *Linda R.S.*,—that is to say, it was uncertain whether the relief would prevent the injury.[1] Of course precisely the same situation exists here. The principle that "in American jurisprudence. . .a private citizen lacks a judicially cognizable interest in the prosecution or nonprosecution of another" applies no less to prosecution for civil penalties payable to the State than to prosecution for criminal penalties owing to the State.

The Court's opinion reads as though the only purpose and effect of the redressability requirement is to assure that the plaintiff receive some of the benefit of the relief that a court orders. That is not so. If it were, a federal tort plaintiff fearing repetition of the injury could ask for tort damages to be paid, not only to himself but to other victims as well, on the theory that those damages would have at least some deterrent effect beneficial to him. Such a suit is preposterous because the "remediation" that is the traditional business of Anglo-American courts is relief specifically tailored to the plaintiff's injury, and not any sort of relief that has some incidental benefit to the plaintiff. Just as a "generalized grievance" that affects the entire citizenry cannot satisfy the injury-in-fact requirement even though it aggrieves the plaintiff along with everyone else, see *Lujan*, so also a generalized remedy that deters all future unlawful activity against all persons cannot satisfy the

[1] The decision in *Linda R.S.* did not turn, as today's opinion imaginatively suggests, on the father's short-term inability to pay support if imprisoned. The Court's only comment upon the imprisonment was that, unlike imprisonment for civil contempt, it would not condition the father's release upon payment. The Court then continued: "The prospect that prosecution will, at least in the future,"—i.e., upon completion of the imprisonment—"result in payment of support can, at best, be termed only speculative."

remediation requirement, even though it deters (among other things) repetition of this particular unlawful activity against these particular plaintiffs.

Thus, relief against prospective harm is traditionally afforded by way of an injunction, the scope of which is limited by the scope of the threatened injury. In seeking to overturn that tradition by giving an individual plaintiff the power to invoke a public remedy, Congress has done precisely what we have said it cannot do: convert an "undifferentiated public interest" into an "individual right" vindicable in the courts. A claim of particularized future injury has today been made the vehicle for pursuing generalized penalties for past violations, and a threshold showing of injury in fact has become a lever that will move the world.

B

As I have just discussed, it is my view that a plaintiff's desire to benefit from the deterrent effect of a public penalty for past conduct can never suffice to establish a case or controversy of the sort known to our law. Such deterrent effect is, so to speak, "speculative as a matter of law." Even if that were not so, however, the deterrent effect in the present case would surely be speculative as a matter of fact.

The Court recognizes, of course, that to satisfy Article III, it must be "likely," as opposed to "merely speculative," that a favorable decision will redress plaintiffs' injury, *Lujan*. Further, the Court recognizes that not all deterrent effects of all civil penalties will meet this standard — though it declines to "explore the outer limits" of adequate deterrence. It concludes, however, that in the present case "the civil penalties sought by FOE carried with them a deterrent effect" that satisfied the "likely [rather than] speculative" standard. There is little in the Court's opinion to explain why it believes this is so.

The Court cites the District Court's conclusion that the penalties imposed, along with anticipated fee awards, provided "adequate deterrence." There is absolutely no reason to believe, however, that this meant "deterrence adequate to prevent an injury to these plaintiffs that would otherwise occur." The statute does not even mention deterrence in general (much less deterrence of future harm to the particular plaintiff) as one of the elements that the court should consider in fixing the amount of the penalty. (That element can come in, if at all, under the last, residual category of "such other matters as justice may require." 33 U.S.C. § 1319(d).) The statute does require the court to consider "the seriousness of the violation or violations, the economic benefit (if any) resulting from the violation, any history of such violations, any good-faith efforts to comply with the applicable requirements, [and] the economic impact of the penalty on the violatorY." The District Court meticulously discussed, in subsections (a) through (e) of the portion of its opinion entitled "Civil Penalty," each one of those specified factors, and then — under subsection (f) entitled "Other Matters As Justice May Require," it discussed "1. Laidlaw's Failure to Avail Itself of the Reopener Clause," "2. Recent Compliance History," and "3. The Ever-Changing Mercury Limit." There is no mention whatever — in this portion of the opinion or anywhere else — of the degree of deterrence necessary to prevent future harm to these particular plaintiffs.

The Court points out that we have previously said " 'all civil penalties have some deterrent effect,' " That is unquestionably true: As a general matter, polluters as a class are deterred from violating discharge limits by the availability of civil penalties. However, none of the cases the Court cites focused on the deterrent effect of a single imposition of penalties on a particular lawbreaker. Even less did they focus on the question whether that particularized deterrent effect (if any) was enough to redress the injury of a citizen plaintiff in the sense required by Article III. They all involved penalties pursued by the government, not by citizens. If the Court had undertaken the necessary inquiry into whether significant deterrence of the plaintiffs' feared injury was "likely," it would have had to reason something like this: Strictly speaking, no polluter is deterred by a penalty for past pollution; he is deterred by the fear of a penalty for future pollution. That fear will be virtually nonexistent if the prospective polluter knows that all emissions violators are given a free pass; it will be substantial under an emissions program such as the federal scheme here, which is regularly and notoriously enforced; it will be even higher when a prospective polluter subject to such a regularly enforced program has, as here, been the object of public charges of pollution and a suit for injunction; and it will surely be near the top of the graph when, as here, the prospective polluter has already been subjected to state penalties for the past pollution. The deterrence on which the plaintiffs must rely for standing in the present case is the marginal increase in Laidlaw's fear of future penalties that will be achieved by adding federal penalties for Laidlaw's past conduct.

I cannot say for certain that this marginal increase is zero; but I can say for certain that it is entirely speculative whether it will make the difference between these plaintiffs' suffering injury in the future and these plaintiffs' going unharmed. In fact, the assertion that it will "likely" do so is entirely farfetched. It is much greater than the speculativeness we found excessive in *Linda R.S. v. Richard D.*, where we said that "the prospect that prosecution [for nonsupport] will . . . result in payment of support can, at best, be termed only speculative."

In sum, if this case is, as the Court suggests, within the central core of "deterrence" standing, it is impossible to imagine what the "outer limits" could possibly be. The Court's expressed reluctance to define those "outer limits" serves only to disguise the fact that it has promulgated a revolutionary new doctrine of standing that will permit the entire body of public civil penalties to be handed over to enforcement by private interests.

C

By permitting citizens to pursue civil penalties payable to the Federal Treasury, the Act does not provide a mechanism for individual relief in any traditional sense, but turns over to private citizens the function of enforcing the law. A Clean Water Act plaintiff pursuing civil penalties acts as a self-appointed mini-EPA. Where, as is often the case, the plaintiff is a national association, it has significant discretion in choosing enforcement targets. Once the association is aware of a reported violation, it need not look long for an injured member, at least under the theory of injury the Court applies today.

And once the target is chosen, the suit goes forward without meaningful public control. The availability of civil penalties vastly disproportionate to the individual injury gives citizen plaintiffs massive bargaining power — which is often used to achieve settlements requiring the defendant to support environmental projects of the plaintiffs' choosing. Thus is a public fine diverted to a private interest.

To be sure, the EPA may foreclose the citizen suit by itself bringing suit. This allows public authorities to avoid private enforcement only by accepting private direction as to when enforcement should be undertaken — which is no less constitutionally bizarre. Elected officials are entirely deprived of their discretion to decide that a given violation should not be the object of suit at all, or that the enforcement decision should be postponed. This is the predictable and inevitable consequence of the Court's allowing the use of public remedies for private wrongs.

By uncritically accepting vague claims of injury, the Court has turned the Article III requirement of injury in fact into a "mere pleading requirement," *Lujan*, and by approving the novel theory that public penalties can redress anticipated private wrongs, it has come close to "mak[ing] the redressability requirement vanish," *Steel Co.* The undesirable and unconstitutional consequence of today's decision is to place the immense power of suing to enforce the public laws in private hands. I respectfully dissent.

NOTES

1. *Contrasting* Laidlaw *and* Lujan. Does *Laidlaw* represent an effective overruling of *Lujan*, or is it possible to reconcile the two decisions? A number of commentators have viewed the two decisions as inconsistent. *See, e.g.*, Maxwell Stearns, *From Lujan to Laidlaw: A Preliminary Model of Environmental Standing,* 11 Duke Envtl. L. & Pol'y F. 321, 327 (2001), suggesting that "[i]n a short span of just eight years, the Court appears to have issued a major retrenchment upon *Lujan*'s logic, if not its holding." Do you agree? If the two decisions are, in fact, deemed inconsistent, which puts forth the wiser approach to standing? Professor Stearns suggests that "*Laidlaw* appears poised to be commended as a restoration of sound principles of standing." *Id.* at 327. See also Kristen M. Shults, Comment, *Friends of the Earth v. Laidlaw Environmental Services: A Resounding Victory for Environmentalists, Its Implications on Future Justiciability Decisions, and Resolution of Issues on Remand,* 89 Geo. L.J. 1001, 1008 (2001), suggesting that "[t]he *Laidlaw* Court may be signaling a change in direction for the standing doctrine."

Does the answer to this question change if one considers solely the impact of these decisions on standing *in environmental cases*? *See* Robert V. Percival & Joanna B. Goger, *Escaping the Common Law's Shadow: Standing in the Light of Laidlaw,* 12 Duke Envtl. L. & Pol'y F. 119, 121 (2001), asserting that "[a]s a result of *Laidlaw,* citizens who live near sources of pollution or who recreate in areas affected by violations of environmental law may sue to enforce the laws without having to demonstrate observable impacts of the illegal acts." Is that necessarily a good result? In any event, is it legitimate to distinguish between environmental standing and other applications of the doctrine?

2. *The nature of the requisite injury.* Do you understand the Court's distinction between injuries to the environment and injuries to the plaintiff? Is the dissent correct in asserting that there can be no injury to the plaintiff absent a showing of injury to the environment? Or could one reason that even if the environment has not itself been harmed, an individual plaintiff could nevertheless suffer "harm" because of the *fear* of environmental harm induced by defendant's conduct?

Consider the relevance to this question of *City of Los Angeles v. Lyons*, 461 U.S. 95 (1983), which was discussed in *Laidlaw*. The complaint alleged that Lyons had been stopped by police officers for a traffic violation and that although he had offered no resistance the officers applied a "chokehold" to him, rendering him unconscious and causing damage to his larynx. The complaint sought both damages and injunctive relief against the police force's continued use of the chokehold in routine traffic stops. The Court found that Lyons lacked standing to seek injunctive relief, reasoning that "it is surely no more than speculation to assert either the Lyons himself will again be involved in one of those unfortunate instances, or that he will be arrested in the future and provoke the use of a chokehold." The fact that Lyons may personally have *feared* the possibility of such future action against him, as a result of his experience, presumably would have still been insufficient to provide standing. Can *Lyons* be distinguished from *Laidlaw*'s dichotomy between injury to the plaintiff and injury to the environment?

The Court in the University of Michigan Affirmative action case, *Gratz v. Bollinger* [p. 756, *supra*], rejected the dissent's argument that the named class representative lacked Article III standing to seek prospective relief and that the case should be dismissed. Because the challenger claimed he was denied equal treatment by the University's admissions policy and was ready to apply for a transfer to the University, he had standing to seek prospective relief. His future injury claim for declaratory and injunctive relief was not conjectural and hypothetical. The University's use of race in the transfer policies was sufficiently similar to its use of race in initial freshman admissions that the named representative had standing to represent unnamed class members in challenging the freshman admissions policy.

3. *Standing and regulatory policy.* Is there a basis on which to distinguish standing issues when private citizens are viewed as vehicles to enforce federal regulatory policy? See Percival and Goger, 12 DUKE ENVTL. L. & POL'Y F. at 120–21, suggesting that "*Laidlaw* is best understood not as having worked a fundamental change in standing doctrine, but rather as a rejection of the extreme consequences of employing a private law model in assessing litigants' standing. *Laidlaw* returns standing jurisprudence to a model more consistent with the realities of the modern regulatory state." Is there a principled basis for shifting the controlling model of standing from one grounded in private rights to a regulatory state model when private plaintiffs bring suit? What are the implications of such a standing model for Article II's vesting of executive power in the President, an issue raised by the dissent?

4. *Utah v. Evans,* 122 S.Ct. 2191 (2002). The Court, per Justice Breyer, held that Utah had Art. III standing to challenge the Census Bureau's use of "hot-deck imputation," which affected the 2000 census results in a way that led to Utah's loss of a seat in the House of Representatives. "Hot deck imputation" involves imputing to the unit or address for which a gap in census information exists, the same characteristics as the closest, similar neighbor that also did not mail a questionnaire response. This practice in the year 2000 census increased the Census Bureau's calculation of North Carolina's population and decreased its calculation of Utah's population, resulting in the loss of one congressional seat by Utah and the gain of a seat by North Carolina. Utah claimed that the use of hot-deck imputation violated a federal statute prohibiting "sampling" and the Census Clause, Art. I, § 2, cl. 3, which it argued required that an "actual Enumeration" be made. Utah sought an injunction compelling the Census Bureau to change the census results and North Carolina intervened. Following a district court finding in favor of the Census Bureau, Utah appealed. The Supreme Court held that Utah had standing to challenge this practice because its grievance was sufficiently concrete and because the court had the power to redress this grievance by ordering revision of the Census report.

North Carolina argued that Utah lacked Art. III standing to challenge the census methodology because the courts had no power to redress Utah's injury. North Carolina asserted that a court could do no more than order a new, proper census report, which would have no effect on Utah's congressional representation. The statute governing the census process requires that the census be taken on the first day of April, its results reported to the President by the first of January, 2001 and transmitted to Congress by January 12th, and each state's congressional representation be certified by January 16th. The statute provides that upon completion of this process, each state is "entitled" to the number of Representatives specified in the certificate. In North Carolina's view, because this reporting and certification process had been completed, the state was legally entitled to the congressional representation apportioned to it following the final count, notwithstanding any court-ordered revision in the census report.

Justice Breyer rejected the argument that, under the relevant certification statute, North Carolina was legally entitled to its already-apportioned representation. Noting that the census statute in question contained no express provision for handling erroneous census reports, Justice Breyer contended that the statute's certification process did not legally bar correction of mistakes in the count. Justice Breyer declared: "we read the statute as permitting certificate revision in such cases of court-determined error, and we include among them cases of court determined legal error leading to a court-required revision of the underlying Secretarial report."

Justice Scalia, dissenting from the Court's ruling on Art. III standing, argued that Utah lacked standing because its relief would depend upon action on a revised Census report by third parties—the President and Congress—not before the Court. Justice Scalia argued that the revision of the Census report by the Secretary of Commerce would have no impact on Utah's congressional apportionment unless the President chose to follow the policy recommendations reflected in the revised report. This element of presidential discretion "is fatal to appellants' standing because appellants have not sued the President to force him to take these steps—and could not do so even if they tried, since 'no court has authority to direct the President to take an official act.' " Justice Scalia concluded: "Thus, because appellant's 'standing depends on the unfettered choices made by independent actors not before the courts and whose exercise of broad and legitimate discretion the courts cannot presume either to control or to predict,' standing in this case does not exist."

§ 11.04 THIRD-PARTY STANDING: RAISING THE RIGHTS OF OTHERS

***Tileston v. Ullman,* 318 U.S. 44 (1943).** Tileston, a Connecticut physician, sought a declaratory judgment in state court that the Connecticut law prohibiting the use of contraceptive devices, or the giving of advice on their use, was unconstitutional. His complaint alleged that three of his patients had health problems which made pregnancy a threat to their lives, and that the anti-birth control statute deprived them of life without due process of law. The Connecticut law, Tileston alleged, precluded him from offering his patients the medical advice on contraception which their precarious health situations demanded. The Connecticut court reached the merits of the complaint but upheld the validity of the statute. The appeal to the Supreme Court was dismissed without regard to the merits of the complaint. Tileston was held to lack standing because his suit did not allege any injury to himself. Rather his suit was directed to the constitutional rights of his patients, nonparties to the litigation.

In *Griswold v. Connecticut,* p. 496, a doctor and the nonphysician director of a birth control clinic were convicted of aiding and abetting married persons in violating the criminal provisions of the Connecticut birth control statute. The Court held that these defendants had standing to raise the rights of privacy of their patients and reversed the convictions. The Court emphasized that the defendants had a "professional relationship" with the persons whose rights were at stake. In *Eisenstadt v. Baird,* p. 512, a pharmacist was allowed to raise the rights of unmarried persons to receive contraceptives. After *Griswold* and *Eisenstadt*, would it be accurate to say that a health care provider has a right to distribute contraceptives or must it still be said that the provider must rely on the rights of the recipients?

It is possible that the Court gained two advantages by delaying a "substantive" ruling between *Tileston* and *Griswold*. One is that the Court itself could profit from further debate and reflection on the issues. Another is that signaling its interest in the issue while not ruling directly on it could force the issue back into the political arena for another round of debate and possible resolution in those fora. Weighed against these advantages, how significant are the costs of "lost" constitutional "rights" to the women of Connecticut during the intervening 20 years?

***Singleton v. Wulff,* 428 U.S. 106 (1976).** The Court held that two physicians who would benefit financially if they succeeded in challenging the constitutionality of a state statute excluding abortions that are not "medically indicated" from Medicaid benefits, had standing to challenge such a statute; the physicians had a financial stake in the outcome, and thus had standing in the classic sense. The Court also held that the physicians had standing to assert the rights of their women patients to be free of governmental interference with the abortion decision. The closeness of the relationship between the doctor and the patient in this context justified permitting the assertion of the woman patient's constitutional rights by the doctor. A woman cannot safely get an abortion without the aid of a doctor and an impecunious woman cannot secure a doctor unless the doctor receives compensation from the state. Finally, the constitutionally protected abortion decision is one in which the doctor is himself intimately involved.

***Elk Grove Unified School Dist. v. Newdow*, 124 S. Ct. 2301 (2004).** The Ninth Circuit had declared the phrase "under God" in the Pledge of Allegiance to be an unconstitutional establishment of religion in the context of daily recitation of the Pledge in public school. In an opinion by Justice Stevens, the Supreme Court reversed on the ground that the father who brought the action lacked standing. The father and mother were engaged in a "protracted custody dispute" but the mother had legal custody and had intervened in the federal action to object to the father's representing their daughter's interests. Indeed, she had obtained a state court order directing him not to undertake representation of the daughter or to bring suit as the daughter's "next friend." The federal court nevertheless had held that this did not deprive Newdow "as a noncustodial parent, of Article III standing to object to unconstitutional government action affecting his child."

Justice Stevens began by invoking the "prudential limits to the powers of an unelected, unrepresentative judiciary in our kind of government," quoting from *Allen v. Wright*.

> The command to guard jealously and exercise rarely our power to make constitutional pronouncements requires strictest adherence when matters of great national significance are at stake. Even in cases concededly within our jurisdiction under Article III, we abide by "a series of rules under which [we have] avoided passing upon a large part of all the constitutional questions pressed upon [us] for decision. Always we must balance "the heavy obligation to exercise jurisdiction," against the "deeply rooted" commitment "not to pass on questions of constitutionality" unless adjudication of the constitutional issue is necessary.
>
> Without such limitations—closely related to Art. III concerns but essentially matters of judicial self-governance—the courts would be called upon to decide abstract questions of wide public significance even though other governmental institutions may be more competent to address the questions and even though judicial intervention may be unnecessary to protect individual rights.

Justice Stevens then focused on "prudential standing, which embodies judicially self-imposed limits on the exercise of federal jurisdiction." In the present case, the state courts had recognized that the mother had authority to make final decisions for the child if the two parents disagreed. Newdow contended that, despite the mother's final authority, he retained an "unrestricted right to inculcate in his daughter—free from governmental interference—the atheistic beliefs he finds persuasive." Justice Stevens responded that Newdow's rights could not be viewed in isolation from the rights of the child's mother as a parent and as legal custodian and, most importantly, the interests of the child. "What makes this case different is that Newdow's standing derives entirely from his relationship with his daughter, but he lacks the right to litigate as her next friend. In marked contrast to our case law on *jus tertii, see, e.g., Singleton v. Wulff,* the interests of this parent and this child are not parallel and, indeed, are potentially in conflict."

Justice Stevens concluded:

> In our view, it is improper for the federal courts to entertain a claim by a plaintiff whose standing to sue is founded on family law rights that are in dispute when prosecution of the lawsuit may have an adverse effect on the person who is the source of the plaintiff's standing. When hard questions of domestic relations are sure to affect the outcome, the prudent courses is for the federal court to stay its hand rather than reach out to resolve a weighty question of federal constitutional law. . . . There is a vast difference between Newdow's right to communicate with his child—which both California law and the First Amendment recognize—and his claimed right to shield his daughter from influences to which she is exposed in school despite the terms of the custody order. We conclude that, having been deprived under California law of the right to sue as next friend, Newdow lacks prudential standing to bring this suit in federal court.

Chief Justice Rehnquist, joined by Justices O'Connor and Thomas, dissented from the standing holding:

> The Court concludes that the California cases "do not stand for the proposition that Newdow has a right to dictate to others what they may or may not say to his child respecting religion." Surely, under California case law and the current custody order, respondent may not tell Banning what she may say to their child respecting religion, and respondent does not seek to. Just as surely, respondent cannot name his daughter as a party to a lawsuit against Banning's wishes. But his claim is different: Respondent does not seek to tell just anyone what he or she may say to his daughter, and he does not seek to vindicate solely her rights.
>
> Respondent asserts that the School District's pledge ceremony infringes his right under California law to expose his daughter to his religious views. While she is intimately associated with the source of respondent's standing (the father-daughter relationship and respondent's rights thereunder), the daughter *is not the source* of respondent's standing; instead it is their relationship that provides respondent his standing, which is clear once respondent's interest is properly described.

Reaching the "merits" of the Establishment claim, Chief Justice Rehnquist and Justice O'Connor both held that the phrase "under God" was neither an endorsement of religion nor itself a religious exercise so as to warrant condemnation as an establishment of religion. To the Chief Justice, the phrase is simply a recognition of the role of religion in the country's history: "Reciting the Pledge, or listening to others recite it, is a patriotic exercise, not a religious one; participants promise fidelity to our flag and our Nation, not to any particular God, faith, or church." To Justice O'Connor, the Establishment Clause allows a form of "ceremonial deism" that prefers no particular religion and endorses no particular religious belief.

Justice Thomas took the opportunity to express his view that the Establishment Clause is not capable of incorporation against the states, and that at most only the Free Exercise Clause would restrain state behavior.

***Kowalski v. Tesmer*, 125 S. Ct. 564 (2004)**: The Court held that attorneys lacked third-party standing to bring an action on behalf of hypothetical future clients. The attorneys had brought an action in federal court to challenge the constitutionality of Michigan's practice of denying appointed appellate counsel to indigents who had pleaded guilty. The attorneys claimed standing based on a future attorney-client relationship with as yet unascertained Michigan criminal defendants who will request, but be denied, appellate counsel. In rejecting third-party standing, the Court distinguished its earlier decisions allowing attorneys to assert third-party standing on behalf of litigants. In its earlier decisions, the attorneys were asserting the rights of *existing* clients, a relationship that is "quite distinct from the *hypothetical* attorney-client relationship posited here." The suit failed to satisfy the Court's two prerequisites for asserting third-party standing: (1) that the party have a "close relationship" with the party whose rights are being asserted, and (2) that there exists a "hindrance" to the possessor's ability to protect his own interests. Neither criterion was satisfied. An attorney could not possess a close relationship with a hypothetical litigant, and there was no reason that these attorneys could not volunteer to assist those future litigants when they wished to appeal. While the Court acknowledged that it had been "quite forgiving" with these criteria in the past under limited circumstances, it emphasized that as a general matter it had "not looked favorably upon third-party standing."

§ 11.05 THE TIMING LIMITATION: WHEN CAN CONSTITUTIONAL LITIGATION BE BROUGHT?

[A] MOOTNESS AND THE TIMING OF JUDICIAL REVIEW

When an issue that has provoked litigation has been resolved by events, the court may refuse to decide the case on the basis of mootness. Mootness is one of the many doctrines which concern the timing of judicial review. As the Court emphasizes in its per curiam opinion in *DeFunis v. Odegaard*, it is closely intertwined with the case or controversy requirement of Article III. If an issue that brought parties to court has in fact been resolved, then there is not that adversity between them which the case and controversy clause requires.

Some of the affirmative action issues raised in *DeFunis* were answered in the famous *Bakke* case, p. 708. *Bakke* was decided only four years after *DeFunis* and purported to resolve the merits. Had the Court gained any insights in the four-year delay?

DeFUNIS v. ODEGAARD

416 U.S. 312, 94 S. Ct. 1704, 40 L. Ed. 2d 164 (1974)

PER CURIAM.

In 1971 the petitioner, Marco DeFunis, applied for admission as a first-year student at the University of Washington Law School, a state-operated institution. The size of the incoming first-year class was to be limited to 150 persons, and the Law School received some 1,600 applications for these 150 places. DeFunis was eventually notified that he had been denied admission. He thereupon commenced this suit in a Washington trial court, contending that the procedures and criteria employed by the Law School Admissions Committee invidiously discriminated against him on account of his race in violation of the Equal Protection Clause of the Fourteenth Amendment to the United States Constitution.

DeFunis brought the suit on behalf of himself alone, and not as the representative of any class, against the various respondents, who are officers, faculty members, and members of the Board of Regents of the University of Washington. He asked the trial court to issue a mandatory injunction commanding the respondents to admit him as a member of the first-year class entering in September of 1971, on the ground that the Law School admissions policy had resulted in the unconstitutional denial of his application for admission. The trial court agreed with his claim and granted the requested relief. DeFunis was, accordingly, admitted to the Law School and began his legal studies there in the fall of 1971. On appeal, the Washington Supreme Court reversed the judgment of the trial court and held that the Law School admissions policy did not violate the Constitution. By this time DeFunis was in his second year at the Law School.

He then petitioned this Court for a writ of certiorari, and MR. JUSTICE DOUGLAS, as CIRCUIT JUSTICE, stayed the judgment of the Washington Supreme Court pending the "final disposition of the case by this Court." By virtue of this stay, DeFunis has remained in law school, and was in the first term of his third and final year when this Court first considered his certiorari petition in the fall of 1973. Because of our concern that DeFunis' third-year standing in the Law School might have rendered this case moot, we requested the parties to brief the question of mootness before we acted on the petition. In response, both sides contended that the case was not moot. The respondents indicated that, if the decision of the Washington Supreme Court were permitted to stand, the petitioner could complete the term for which he was then enrolled but would have to apply to the faculty for permission to continue in the school before he could register for another term.[2]

[2] By contrast, in their response to the petition for certiorari, the respondents had stated that DeFunis "will complete his third year [of law school] and be awarded his J.D. degree at the end of the 1973-1974 academic year regardless of the outcome of this appeal."

In response to questions raised from the bench during the oral argument, counsel for the petitioner has informed the Court that DeFunis has now registered "for his final quarter in law school." Counsel for the respondents have made clear that the Law School will not in any way seek to abrogate this registration.[3] In light of DeFunis' recent registration for the last quarter of his final law school year, and the Law School's assurance that his registration is fully effective, the insistent question again arises whether this case is not moot, and to that question we now turn.

The starting point for analysis is the familiar proposition that "federal courts are without power to decide questions that cannot affect the rights of the litigants before them." The inability of the federal judiciary "to review moot cases derives from the requirement of Art. III of the Constitution under which the exercise of judicial power depends upon the existence of a case or controversy." Although as a matter of Washington state law it appears that this case would be saved from mootness by "the great public interest in the continuing issues raised by this appeal," the fact remains that under Art. III "[e]ven in cases arising in the state courts, the question of mootness is a federal one which a federal court must resolve before it assumes jurisdiction."

The respondents have represented that, without regard to the ultimate resolution of the issues in this case, DeFunis will remain a student in the law school for the duration of any term in which he has already enrolled. Since he has now registered for his final term, it is evident that he will be given an opportunity to complete all academic and other requirements for graduation, and, if he does so, will receive his diploma regardless of any decision this Court might reach on the merits of this case. In short, all parties agree that DeFunis is now entitled to complete his legal studies at the University of Washington and to receive his degree from that institution. "determination by this Court of the legal issues tendered by the parties is no longer necessary to compel that result, and could not serve to prevent it. DeFunis did not cast his suit as a class action, and the only remedy he requested was an injunction commanding his admission to the Law School. He was not only accorded that remedy, but he now has also been irrevocably admitted to the final term of the final year of the law school course. The controversy between the parties has thus clearly ceased to be "definite and concrete" and no longer "touch[es] the legal relations of parties having adverse legal interests."

It matters not that these circumstances partially stem from a policy decision on the part of the respondent Law School authorities. The respondents, through their counsel, the Attorney General of the State, have professionally represented that in no event will the status of DeFunis now be affected by any view this Court might express on the merits of this controversy. And it has been the settled practice of the Court, in contexts no less significant, fully to accept representations such as these as parameters for decision.

There is a line of decisions in this Court standing for the proposition that the "voluntary cessation of allegedly illegal conduct does not deprive the

[3] In their memorandum on the question of mootness, counsel for the respondents unequivocally stated: "If Mr. DeFunis registers for the spring quarter under the existing order of this Court during the registration period from February 20, 1974, to March 1, 1974, that registration would not be canceled unilaterally by the university regardless of the outcome of this litigation."

tribunal of power to hear and determine the case, *i.e.*, does not make the case moot." These decisions and the doctrine they reflect would be quite relevant if the question of mootness here had arisen by reason of a unilateral change in the admissions procedures of the Law School. For it was the admissions procedures that were the target of this litigation, and a voluntary cessation of the admissions practices complained of could make this case moot only if it could be said with assurance "that there is no reasonable expectation that the wrong will be repeated." Otherwise, "[t]he defendant is free to return to his old ways," and this fact would be enough to prevent mootness because of the "public interest in having the legality of the practices settled." But mootness in the present case depends not at all upon a "voluntary cessation" of the admissions practices that were the subject of this litigation. It depends, instead, upon the simple fact that DeFunis is now in the final quarter of the final year of his course of study, and the settled and unchallenged policy of the Law School to permit him to complete the term for which he is now enrolled.

It might also be suggested that this case presents a question that is "capable of repetition, yet evading review," *Roe v. Wade*, and is thus amenable to federal adjudication even though it might otherwise be considered moot. But DeFunis will never again be required to run the gauntlet of the Law School's admission process, and so the question is certainly not "capable of repetition" so far as he is concerned. Moreover, just because this particular case did not reach the Court until the eve of the petitioner's graduation from law school, it hardly follows that the issue he raises will in the future evade review. If the admissions procedures of the Law School remain unchanged,[4] there is no reason to suppose that a subsequent case attacking those procedures will not come with relative speed to this Court, now that the Supreme Court of Washington has spoken. This case, therefore, in no way presents the exceptional situation in which [this] doctrine might permit a departure from "[t]he usual rule in federal cases that an actual controversy must exist at stages of appellate or certiorari review, and not simply at the date the action is initiated." *Roe v. Wade*.

Because the petitioner will complete his law school studies at the end of the term for which he has now registered regardless of any decision this Court might reach on the merits of this litigation, we conclude that the Court cannot, consistently with the limitations of Art. III of the Constitution, consider the substantive constitutional issues tendered by the parties. Accordingly, the judgment of the Supreme Court of Washington is vacated, and the cause is remanded for such proceedings as by that Court may be deemed appropriate.

JUSTICE BRENNAN, with whom JUSTICES DOUGLAS, WHITE, and MARSHALL concur, dissenting.

I respectfully dissent. Many weeks of the school term remain, and petitioner may not receive his degree despite respondents' assurances that petitioner will

[4] In response to an inquiry from the Court, counsel for the respondents has advised that some changes have been made in the admissions procedures "for the applicants seeking admission to the University of Washington law schoolfor the academic year commencing September, 1974." The respondents' counsel states, however, that "[these] changes do not affect the policy challenged by the petitioners in that special consideration still is given to applicants from 'certain ethnic groups.' "

be allowed to complete this term's schooling regardless of our decision. Any number of unexpected events — illness, economic necessity, even academic failure — might prevent his graduation at the end of the term. Were that misfortune to befall, and were petitioner required to register for yet another term, the prospect that he would again face the hurdle of the admissions policy is real, not fanciful; for respondents warn that "Mr. DeFunis would have to take some appropriate action to request admission for the remainder of his law school education, and some discretionary action by the University on such request would have to be taken." Thus, respondents' assurances have not dissipated the possibility that petitioner might once again have to run the gauntlet of the University's allegedly unlawful admissions policy. The Court therefore proceeds on an erroneous premise in resting its mootness holding on a supposed inability to render any judgment that may affect one way or the other petitioner's completion of his law studies. For surely if we were to reverse the Washington Supreme Court, we could insure that, if for some reason petitioner did not graduate this Spring, he would be entitled to re-enrollment at a later time on the same basis as others who have not faced the hurdle of the University's allegedly unlawful admissions policy.

In these circumstances, and because the University's position implies no concession that its admissions policy is unlawful, this controversy falls squarely within the Court's long line of decisions holding that the "[m]ere voluntary cessation of allegedly illegal conduct does not moot a case." Since respondents' voluntary representation to this Court is only that they will permit petitioner to complete this term's studies, respondents have not borne the "heavy burden," of demonstrating that there was not even a "mere possibility" that petitioner would once again be subject to the challenged admissions policy. On the contrary, respondents have positioned themselves so as to be "free to return to [their] old ways."

I can thus find no justification for the Court's straining to rid itself of this dispute. While we must be vigilant to require that litigants maintain a personal stake in the outcome of a controversy to assure that "the questions will be framed with the necessary specificity, that the issues will be contested with the necessary adverseness and that the litigation will be pursued with the necessary vigor to assure that the constitutional challenge will be made in a form traditionally thought to be capable of judicial resolution," there is no want of an adversary contest in this case. Indeed, the Court concedes that, if petitioner has lost his stake in this controversy, he did so only when he registered for the Spring term. But appellant took that action only after the case had been fully litigated in the state courts, briefs had been filed in this Court and oral argument had been heard. The case is thus ripe for decision on a fully developed factual record with sharply defined and fully canvassed legal issues.

Moreover, in endeavoring to dispose of this case as moot, the Court clearly disserves the public interest. The constitutional issues which are avoided today concern vast numbers of people, organizations, and colleges and universities, as evidenced by the filing of twenty-six *amici curiae* briefs. Few constitutional questions in recent history have stirred as much debate, and they will not disappear. They must inevitably return to the federal courts and ultimately again to this Court. Because avoidance of repetitious litigation serves the public interest, that inevitability counsels against mootness determinations, as here, not compelled by the record. Although the Court should, of course, avoid unnecessary decisions of constitutional questions, we should not transform principles of avoidance of constitutional decisions into devices for sidestepping resolution of difficult cases.

ROE v. WADE

410 U.S. 113, 93 S. Ct. 705, 35 L. Ed. 2d 147 (1973)

JUSTICE BLACKMUN delivered the opinion of the Court.

The appellee notes that the record does not disclose that Roe was pregnant at the time of the District Court hearing on May 22, 1970, or on the following June 17 when the court's opinion and judgment were filed. And he suggests that Roe's case must now be moot because she and all other members of her class are no longer subject to any 1970 pregnancy. The usual rule in federal cases is that an actual controversy must exist at stages of appellate or certiorari review, and not simply at the date the action is initiated. But when, as here, pregnancy is a significant fact in the litigation, the normal 266-day human gestation period is so short that the pregnancy will come to term before the usual appellate process is complete. If that termination makes a case moot, pregnancy litigation seldom will survive much beyond the trial stage, and appellate review will be effectively denied. Our law should not be that rigid. Pregnancy often comes more than once to the same woman, and in the general population, if man is to survive, it will always be with us. Pregnancy provides a classic justification for a conclusion of nonmootness. It truly could be "capable of repetition, yet evading review."

We, therefore, agree with the District Court that the termination of [Jane Roe's] 1970 pregnancy has not rendered her case moot.

NOTES

1. *Mootness and merits.* Was *DeFunis* moot because mootness promised a refuge from the intractable constitutional issues raised by the merits of the case? But *Roe v. Wade* was a case raising issues of difficulty equal to those presented by DeFunis and yet the mootness problem was given short shrift. Is the difference that in *Roe* a clear majority for a particular result was present while such a clear majority might have been lacking in *DeFunis*? As a doctrinal matter, does it make any sense to say that the litigant in *Roe* might become pregnant again while it was unlikely DeFunis would need to go to law school again? On this point it should be noted that the University of Washington School of Law did not concede that DeFunis would be allowed to matriculate to the point of graduation if, for example, he failed a course or became ill in his "last" semester.

2. *The Mootness-standing intersection: The impact of* Laidlaw. Though much of the Supreme Court's decision in *Friends of the Earth, Inc. v. Laidlaw Environmental Services, Inc.,* concerned standing, the decision also included an important discussion of mootness. In reversing the Court of

Appeals' decision that the case was moot, Justice Ginsburg's opinion for the Court stated:

> The Court of Appeals justified its mootness disposition by reference to *Steel Co.*, which held that citizen plaintiffs lack standing to seek civil penalties for wholly past violations. In relying on *Steel Co.*, the Court of Appeals confused mootness with standing. The confusion is understandable, given this Court's repeated statements that the doctrine of mootness can be described as "the doctrine of standing set in a time frame: The requisite personal interest that must exist at the commencement of the litigation (standing) must continue throughout its existence (mootness)." *Arizonans for Official English*, 520 U.S., at 68, n. 22, (*quoting United States Parole Comm'n v. Geraghty*, 445 U.S. 388, 397 (1980), in turn quoting Monaghan, *Constitutional Adjudication: The Who and When*, 82 Yale L.J. 1363, 1384 (1973)).
>
> Careful reflection on the long-recognized exceptions to mootness, however, reveals that the description of mootness as "standing set in a time frame" is not comprehensive. As just noted, a defendant claiming that its voluntary compliance moots a case bears the formidable burden of showing that it is absolutely clear the allegedly wrongful behavior could not reasonably be expected to recur. By contrast, in a lawsuit brought to force compliance, it is the plaintiff's burden to establish standing by demonstrating that, if unchecked by the litigation, the defendant's allegedly wrongful behavior will likely occur or continue, and that the "threatened injury [is] certainly impending." *Whitmore v. Arkansas*. The plain lesson of these cases is that there are circumstances in which the prospect that a defendant will engage in (or resume) harmful conduct may be too speculative to support standing, but not too speculative to overcome mootness. Furthermore, if mootness were simply "standing set in a time frame," the exception to mootness that arises when the defendant's allegedly unlawful activity is "capable of repetition, yet evading review" could not exist.
>
> Standing doctrine functions to ensure, among other things, that the scarce resources of the federal courts are devoted to those disputes in which the parties have a concrete stake. In contrast, by the time mootness is an issue, the case has been brought and litigated, often (as here) for years. To abandon the case at an advanced stage may prove more wasteful than frugal. This argument from sunk costs does not license courts to retain jurisdiction over cases in which one or both of the parties plainly lacks a continuing interest, as when the parties have settled or a plaintiff pursuing a nonsurviving claim has died. *See, e.g., DeFunis v. Odegaard* (non-class-action challenge to constitutionality of law school admissions process mooted when plaintiff, admitted pursuant to preliminary injunction, neared graduation and defendant law school conceded that, as a matter of ordinary school policy, plaintiff would be allowed to finish his final term). But the argument surely highlights an important difference between the two doctrines.

Do you understand the distinction the Court seeks to draw between mootness and standing? Do you understand why the speculativeness of injury is sufficient to preclude standing, but the speculativeness concerning the likelihood that challenged behavior will reoccur?

3. *Class actions and repetition.* The *DeFunis* majority indicates that the mootness doctrine is a mandate of Article III and that a federal court lacks jurisdiction to review a moot case. If this is true, then how does the *Roe* Court obtain jurisdiction? Through the "capable of repetition, yet evading review" exception? Moreover, the Court also notes that DeFunis "brought suit on behalf of himself alone, and not as the representative of any class" as if that made a difference. Should it? The truth may be that both the class action and the repetition exception are elaborations of the case or controversy requirement.

Rule 23 of the Federal Rules of Civil Procedure allows a named party to represent a class of persons similarly situated in certain defined categories of cases. Once a case is properly certified as a class action, the named party can continue to represent the class even if the case becomes moot as to that party or it is determined that the named party is not entitled to individual relief.

In *Sosna v. Iowa*, 419 U.S. 393 (1975), the named plaintiff challenged a state one-year durational residency requirement on the ability to seek a divorce within that state's courts. The case was certified as a class action on behalf of all persons who might in the future seek a divorce less than one year after establishing residency in the state. Obviously, the named party would pass the one-year period before the case could be finally determined on appeal. Although the case could have been decided through the repetition rubric if repetition to other persons were sufficient, the Supreme Court instead held that class status was sufficient to satisfy Article III. "When the district court certified the propriety of the class action, the class of unnamed persons described in the certification acquired a legal status separate from the interest asserted by [the named representative]."

A similar result was reached in *Franks v. Bowman Transp. Co.*, 424 U.S. 747 (1976), a case in which the possibility of repetition did not seem to exist. In Franks the named representative [a person named Lee] of a class of job applicants attacked racially discriminatory hiring practices under Title VII of the Civil Rights Act of 1964, but Lee was found not to be entitled to relief after the class had been certified. The Court relied on the "tenacity and competence of their counsel" in finding that the unnamed members of the class were adequately represented and thus that there was a live controversy with respect to them.

Has the Court implicitly held that Sosna and Lee have standing to assert the rights of third parties? Or are the absent members of the class actually before the court through their representatives? Can something so important as Article III justiciability requirements actually turn on something so amorphous and conceptual as "presence" through a surrogate? If "tenacity and competence of counsel" is the deciding factor, why is that not adequate in cases like *Valley Forge* and *Allen*?

4. *The same party issue.* Is the repetition exception dependent on the possibility of repetition with respect to the same parties? In *First National Bank v. Bellotti*, 438 U.S. 907 (1978), the plaintiff challenged a state law that prohibited corporations from spending money on campaigns affecting state referendums. The particular election in which the issue arose had already been held when the case reached the Supreme Court. The Court noted that *Sosna* would resolve the issue if a class action were certified and stated that, in the absence of class certification, the repetition doctrine requires two elements to coalesce: "(1) The challenged action was in its duration too short to be fully litigated prior to its cessation or expiration, and (2) there [is] a reasonable expectation that the same complaining party [will] be subjected to the same action again."

Applying this standard to the present case, the Court found both elements to be satisfied. There were "no reasonably foreseeable circumstances" through which the corporate litigant could obtain review by the Supreme Court prior to a referendum on a similar constitutional amendment. Further, there was every reason to believe that the corporate litigant would again be faced with the threat of criminal prosecution for resisting the constitutional amendment. The challenged statutory provision would continue to restrain influence by corporate expenditures on vaild questions thereby restraining arguably protected speech.

5. *Honig v. Doe,* 484 U.S. 305 (1988). The Court, in an opinion by Justice Brennan, dealt with suits seeking injunctive relief against school district officials who had suspended emotionally disturbed students for violent and disruptive conduct related to their disability, allegedly in violation of the Education of the Handicapped Act [EHA]. The Court held moot the claim of a student who had turned 21 and thus was outside the protection of the Act, but held that a 20-year-old student presented a live controversy.

> Although at present he is not faced with any proposed expulsion or suspension proceedings, and indeed no longer even resides within the [same school district], he remains a resident of California and is entitled to a "free appropriate public education" within that State. His claims under the EHA, therefore, are not moot if the conduct he originally complained of is "capable of repetition, yet evading review." Given Smith's continued eligibility for educational services under the EHA, the nature of his disability and petitioner's insistence that all local school districts retain residual authority to exclude disabled children for dangerous conduct, we have little difficulty concluding that there is a "reasonable expectation" that Smith would once again be subjected to a unilateral "change in placement" for conduct growing out of his disabilities were it not for the state-wide injunctive relief issued below.
>
> Our cases reveal that, for purposes of assessing the likelihood that state authorities will re-inflict a given injury, we generally have been unwilling to assume that the party seeking relief will repeat the type of misconduct that would once again place him or her at risk of that injury. No such reluctance, however, is warranted here. It is respondent Smith's very inability to conform his conduct to socially accepted

norms that renders him "handicapped" within the meaning of the EHA. In the absence of any suggestion that respondent has overcome his earlier difficulties, it is certainly reasonable to expect, based on his prior history of behavioral problems, that he will again engage in classroom misconduct.

[B] RIPENESS, PREMATURITY AND ABSTRACTNESS

UNITED PUBLIC WORKERS v. MITCHELL

330 U.S. 75, 67 S. Ct. 556, 91 L. Ed. 754 (1947)

[In *United Public Workers*, the Supreme Court, 4-3, dealt with an attack on the Hatch Act, which imposes a ban on the political activities of federal employees. None of the appellants in United Public Workers, except one, had violated the provisions of the Act but they wished to engage in political activities forbidden to federal employees by the Act. Therefore, the appellants sought a declaratory judgment on the constitutional limits to regulation of the political activities of government employees. The Court, per Mr. Justice Reed, denied the request for declaratory relief of the appellants who had not yet violated the Hatch Act. With regard to the appellant who had violated the Act and who was being threatened with removal from his job with the Civil Service Commission, the Court held that declaratory relief should obtain.]

Justice Reed delivered the opinion of the Court.

As is well known the federal courts established pursuant to Article III of the Constitution do not render advisory opinions. For adjudication of constitutional issues, "concrete legal issues, presented in actual cases, not abstractions," are requisite. This is as true of declaratory judgments as any other field. These appellants seem clearly to seek advisory opinions. As these appellants are classified employees, they have a right superior to the generality of citizens, but the facts of their personal interest in their civil rights, of the general threat of possible interference with those rights by the Civil Service Commission under its rules, if specified things are done by appellants, does not make a justiciable case or controversy. Appellants want to engage in "political management and political campaigns," to persuade others to follow appellants' views by discussion, speeches, articles and other acts reasonably designed to secure the selection of appellants' political choices. Such generality of objection is really an attack on the political expediency of the Hatch Act, not the presentation of legal issues. It is beyond the competence of courts to render such a decision.

The power of courts, and ultimately of this court, to pass upon the constitutionality of acts of Congress arises only when the interests of litigants require the use of this judicial authority for their protection against actual interference. A hypothetical threat is not enough. We can only speculate as to the kinds of political activity the appellants desire to engage in or as to the contents of their proposed public statements or the circumstances of their publication. It would not accord with judicial responsibility to adjudge, in a matter involving constitutionality, between the freedom of the individual and the requirements of public order except when definite rights appear upon the one side and definite prejudicial interferences upon the other.

Should the courts seek to expand their power so as to bring under their jurisdiction ill-defined controversies over constitutional issues, they would become the organ of political theories. Such abuse of judicial power would properly meet rebuke and restriction from other branches. By these mutual checks and balances by and between the branches of government, democracy undertakes to preserve the liberties of the people from excessive concentrations of authority No threat of interference by the Commission with rights of these appellants appears beyond that implied by the existence of the law and the regulations. [T]he determination of the trial court, that the individual appellants, other than Poole, could maintain this action, was erroneous.

NOTE

The Connecticut statute involved in *Tileston* and *Griswold*, prohibiting the use of birth control devices and advice on their use, came under constitutional attack from contraception users in *Poe v. Ullman*, 367 U.S. 497 (1961). In a 5-4 decision, the Court dismissed the appeals and declined to adjudicate the question of the constitutionality of the Connecticut statute. A plurality opinion was delivered by Justice Frankfurter, joined by Chief Justice Warren, and Justices Clark and Whittaker.

The appellants, said Frankfurter, had not alleged any immediate threat of prosecution should they proceed to disobey the Connecticut statute in question. Furthermore, even if the complaints contained an allegation of immediate threat of prosecution, "we are not bound to accept as true all that is alleged." The Connecticut law, though on the statute books since 1879, had almost never been enforced through criminal prosecutions. Given this history of non-enforcement, Justice Frankfurter declared the appellants' allegation of fear of prosecution "collide[d] with plausibility." The law, he noted, was widely flouted in Connecticut, where birth control devices "are commonly and notoriously sold in Connecticut drug stores." In his view, Connecticut had nullified the proscriptive force of the statute by deliberately not enforcing the law. It posed no threat and no immediate controversy, and the constitutional challenge to its validity was more hypothetical than real. For these reasons, Justice Frankfurter stated that he thought the case was nonjusticiable:

> Justiciability is of course not a legal concept with a fixed content or susceptible of scientific verification. Its utilization is the result of many subtle pressures, including the appropriateness of the issues and the actual hardship to the litigants of denying them the relief sought. Both these factors justify withholding adjudication of the constitutional issues raised under the circumstances and in the manner in which they are now before the Court.

Is ripeness an Article III limitation or a matter of policy? Are the same doctrines involved in *Mitchell* and *Poe*? What would the litigants in *Mitchell* and *Poe* have to do to make their case appropriate for review?

SOCIALIST LABOR PARTY v. GILLIGAN

406 U.S. 583, 92 S. Ct. 1716, 32 L. Ed. 2d 317 (1972)

[The Socialist Labor Party sought a declaratory judgment from a three-judge federal panel that certain sections of the Ohio election law were unconstitutional. The party had brought a similar action in 1968. In that case, *Socialist Labor Party v. Rhodes*, 393 U.S. 23 (1968), the Court held that the challenged election code provisions violated the Fourteenth Amendment guarantee of equal protection. Following the 1968 Supreme Court decision, Ohio revised much of its election law. The Socialist Labor Party was not satisfied with the changes and brought a second suit in 1970. A three-judge panel was convened to hear the new challenge. The panel struck down as unconstitutional all the pertinent election law provisions except a loyalty oath requirement, which it sustained as valid.

[Both sides to the litigation appealed to the Supreme Court. Meanwhile, the Ohio legislature again revamped the state's election law, modifying those provisions which the three-judge panel had held invalid. All issues in the case were thus mooted, except for the Socialist Labor Party's claim that the Ohio loyalty oath requirement was unconstitutional. Under this provision, an elaborate loyalty oath and disclaimer of subversive activities was established for all political parties seeking access to the ballot except "any political party or group which has had a place on the ballot in each national and gubernatorial election since the year 1900." In other words, the two major national parties, the Democrats and Republicans, were exempt. The Socialist Labor Party argued that the law was an unconstitutional denial of equal protection.]

JUSTICE REHNQUIST delivered the opinion of the Court.

Appellants did not in their action that came here in 1968 challenge the loyalty oath. Their 1970 complaint respecting the loyalty oath is singularly sparse in its factual allegations. There is no suggestion in it that the Socialist Labor Party has ever refused in the past, or will now refuse, to sign the required oath. There is no allegation of injury that the party has suffered or will suffer because of the existence of the oath requirement. It is fairly inferable that the absence of such allegations is not merely an oversight in the drafting of a pleading. The requirement of the affidavit under oath was enacted in 1941, and has remained continuously in force since that date. The Socialist Labor Party has appeared on the state ballot since the law's passage, and, unless the state officials have ignored what appear to be mandatory oath provisions, it is reasonable to conclude that the party has in the past executed the required affidavit.

It is axiomatic that the federal courts do not decide abstract questions posed by parties who lack "a personal stake in the outcome of the controversy." Appellants argue that the affidavit requirement violates the First and Fourteenth Amendments, but their pleadings fail to allege that the requirement has in any way affected their speech or conduct, or that executing the oath would impair the exercise of any right that they have as a political party or as members of a political party. They contend that to require it of them but not of the two major political parties denies them equal protection, but they do not allege any particulars that make the requirement other than a hypothetical burden. Finally, they claim that the required affidavit is impermissibly vague and that its enforcement procedures do not comport with due process. But the record before the three-judge District Court, and now before this Court, is extraordinarily skimpy in the sort of proved or admitted facts that would enable us to adjudicate this claim. Since appellants have previously secured a position on the ballot with no untoward consequences, the gravamen of their claim that it injures them remains quite unclear. In the usual case in which this Court has passed on the validity of similar oath provisions, the party challenging constitutionality was either unable or unwilling to execute the required oath, and in the circumstances of the particular case sustained, or faced the immediate prospect of sustaining, some direct injury as a result of the penalty provisions associated with the oath.

The long and the short of the matter is that we know very little about the operation of the Ohio affidavit procedure as a result of this lawsuit than we would if a prospective plaintiff who had never set foot in Ohio had simply picked this section of the Ohio election laws out of the statute books and filed a complaint in the District Court setting forth the allegedly offending provisions and requesting an injunction against their enforcement. These plaintiffs may well meet the technical requirement of standing, and they may be parties to a case or controversy, but their case has not given any particularity to the effect on them of Ohio's affidavit requirement.

This Court has recognized in the past that even when jurisdiction exists it should not be exercised unless the case "tenders the underlying constitutional issues in clean-cut and concrete form." *Rescue Army v. Municipal Court.* Problems of prematurity and abstractness may well present "insuperable obstacles" to the exercise of the Court's jurisdiction, even though that jurisdiction is technically present.

Notwithstanding the indications that appellants have in the past executed the required affidavit without injury, it is, of course, possible that at some future time they may be able to demonstrate some injury as a result of the application of the provision challenged here. Our adjudication of the merits of such a challenge will await that time. This appeal must be dismissed.

[Justice Douglas, joined by Justices Brennan and Marshall, dissented.]

NOTES

1. *Abstractness.* The Court dismissed the appeal because of the abstract and speculative posture of the case despite the presence of jurisdiction. If the plaintiffs had standing, and the case met the case or controversy requirement of Article III, what made the case abstract and speculative? Was it the Court's concern that there was no certainty either of injury to the plaintiffs or of controversy between the parties?

Justice Rehnquist said that the older loyalty oath cases were distinguishable from the instant case because they presented an immediate or threatened injury to the party challenging the oath. The Socialist Labor Party had failed to allege such injury in its complaint. Justice Douglas, dissenting, argued that in the next election in Ohio, the Socialist Labor Party would be faced with the choice of taking the oath or being kept off the ballot. Justice Douglas, unlike the Court, was willing to assume for the purposes of deciding the instant case that the Socialist Labor Party would seek a place on the Ohio ballot in the next election, and that the loyalty oath would present a cruel choice at least for the party's officers and individual members.

Suppose the Socialist Labor Party had alleged the following in its complaint: (1) inability in good conscience to comply with the Ohio law; (2) an intention to apply for a place on the ballot in the forthcoming Ohio election; and (3) a fear that Ohio election officials would refuse to give the party access to the ballot if the Ohio law were not complied with. Would the Supreme Court still have declined to decide the appeal?

2. *Requiring violations of the law.* The Court decided in *Mitchell* that the "threat of interference by the Commission with rights of these appellants . . . implied by the existence of the law and the regulations" was not a current constitutional violation. What is the point of using language of ripeness when at least that issue has been decided? The Court in *Gilligan* decided that the Socialist Labor Party was not unconstitutionally injured by being forced to file an affidavit and oath. What is the point of pretending not to decide the "substantive merits" of the dispute?

Mitchell, Gilligan, and *Poe* all suggest that a person who wants to challenge a criminal statute alleged to be restricting his or her First Amendment freedoms must first violate the statute and be prosecuted before the Court will listen to the complaint. The social utility of forcing people to violate an existing law is certainly open to question, particularly when their First Amendment interests in speech and privacy are at stake.

The Supreme Court has recognized at least one rather interesting exception to the doctrine. In *Ex parte Young*, 209 U.S. 123 (1908), the shareholders of a railroad sought to enjoin the state attorney general from enforcing a rate regulation scheme on the railroad's operations. Violation of the regulations would have occasioned a heavy fine. The Court held that the railroad need not violate the statute and face the risk of having to pay the fine if its constitutional attack failed; the risk was deemed to be excessive in light of the benefits to be gained from violation. In dozens, if not hundreds, of cases businesses have been able to challenge state and local government regulation or licensing schemes without having to violate the provisions of state law prior to the challenge. Is it fair to say that the Court values corporate dollars more than individual interests in free speech and privacy, or is there some other explanation?

In *Steffel v. Thompson*, 415 U.S. 452 (1974), the plaintiff sought declaratory relief that a state trespass law could not be applied to his distribution of leaflets at a private shopping center. He and a companion had gone to the shopping center to hand out leaflets protesting the Vietnam War. The police were called by the shopping center management and threatened to arrest them if they did not leave. Steffel left but his companion defied the order and continued handing out leaflets. She was arrested, prosecuted, and convicted of criminal trespass. He then sought federal court relief. The Supreme Court held that the specific threat in light of specific conduct was sufficient to provide a live controversy for a declaratory judgment that the statute was unconstitutional as applied to that conduct. A similar result was reached in

Dombrowski v. Pfister, 380 U.S. 479 (1965), when the Court decided that threatened enforcement of a state anti-subversive statute had a "chilling effect" on rights of free expression.

But what is protected by the judgment in *Steffel*? What if Steffel goes back to the shopping center at a more crowded time of day? with leaflets on a different subject? with several rough-looking companions? The difficulty with deciding a case in advance of enforcement, unless the decision is addressed to the validity of the statute in its entirety (on its face), lies in knowing what has been decided. *Dombrowski* presented no similar problem because the statute was found to be void on its face rather than as applied.

3. *National Park Hospitality Association v. Department of the Interior*, 538 U.S. 803 (2003). The Court held 7-2 that a challenge by concessionaires to an administrative regulation by the National Park Service (NPS) rendering the Contract Disputes Act of 1978 (CDA) inapplicable to concession contracts was not ripe for federal judicial resolution. NPS issued regulations in 2000 stating that concession contracts were not subject to the procedures of the CDA, which included recourse to the Department of Interior Board of Contract Appeals. An association representing oncessionaires wanting access to that procedure brought suit to challenge the new regulations.

Justice Thomas, writing for the Court, relied primarily on the nature of the regulation. Rather than an administrative regulation with the "force of law," Justice Thomas characterized the regulation as a statement of policy, "designed to inform the public of NPS' views on the proper application of the CDA." The regulation could not have the force of law, Justice Thomas reasoned, because NPS was not delegated rulemaking authority under the CDA nor any power to administer it. NPS therefore lacks the power to determine which contracts the provision should or should not apply to. The regulation "does not create adverse effects of a strictly legal kind" normally required to show hardship; it does not create affirmative legal rights or obligations, it does not "grant, withhold, or modify any formal legal license, power, or authority," nor does it "subject anyone to any civil or criminal liability."

Moreover, the regulation "does not affect a concessioner's primary conduct." Rather, it "leaves a concessioner free to conduct its business as it sees fit." Since "[c]oncessioners suffer no practical harm as a result of Section 51.3," and in fact, the regulation does not even prevent them from "following the procedures set forth in the CDA once a dispute over a concession contract actually arises," there is not a sufficient showing of hardship if the Court refuses to decide the case.

Justice Stevens, concurring in the judgment, argued that ripeness was not the appropriate doctrine to apply to the case. "Petitioner seeks this Court's resolution of the straightforward legal question whether the [CDA] applies to concession contracts with the [NPS]. Though this question is one that would otherwise be appropriate for this Court to decide, in my view petitioner has not satisfied the threshold requirement of alleging sufficient injury to invoke federal-court jurisdiction."

According to Justice Stevens, the petitioner had failed to allege sufficient injury in fact to satisfy Art. III standing requirements. "In the complaint filed in the District Court, petitioner . . . failed to allege that the existence of the regulation had caused any injury to it or to its members." Rather, petitioner had simply alleged that resolution of the question was important as a practical matter because of the length of concession contracts and the size of the investments involved. Because petitioner had failed to identify a single instance "in which the Park Service's regulation caused a concessionaire to refuse to bid on a contract, to modify its bid, or to suffer any other specific injury," there was no indication that "any specific injury . . . would be redressed by a favorable decision on the merits of the case."

Justice Breyer, joined by Justice O'Connor, dissenting, agreed with the Court that the petitioner had satisfied standing requirements. The Park Service's denial to petitioner's members, many of whom "are parties to, as well as potential bidders for, park concession contracts," of the "significant protections" provided by the CDA in potential contract disputes "is concrete and likely to occur." According to the dissent, the threat of immediate concrete harm in the form of increased bidding costs also made the case ripe for judicial review. Like Justice Stevens, the dissent concluded: "The Park Service's interpretation is definite and conclusive, not tentative or likely to change." Justice Breyer acknowledged the majority's concerns, such as the fact that "concessioners can raise the legal question at a later time, after a specific contractual dispute arises," and that the case might encourage "premature challenges in other cases where agency interpretations may be less formal, less final, or less well suited to immediate judicial determination." But he concluded that the "fact of immediate and particularized (and not totally reparable) injury during the bidding process" was sufficient evidence of hardship to overcome concerns about ripeness.

TABLE OF CASES

[References are to page numbers and footnotes]

A

B

[References are to page numbers and footnotes]

C

[References are to page numbers and footnotes]

[References are to page numbers and footnotes]

D

E

F

[References are to page numbers and footnotes]

G

[References are to page numbers and footnotes]

[References are to page numbers and footnotes]

K

L

[References are to page numbers and footnotes]

[References are to page numbers and footnotes]

N

[References are to page numbers and footnotes]

O

P

[References are to page numbers and footnotes]

[References are to page numbers and footnotes]

[References are to page numbers and footnotes]

T

U

V

W

[References are to page numbers and footnotes]

X

Y

Z

INDEX

[References are to page numbers.]

A

B

C

[References are to page numbers.]

[References are to page numbers.]

[References are to page numbers.]

[References are to page numbers.]

[References are to page numbers.]

G

[References are to page numbers.]

[References are to page numbers.]

[References are to page numbers.]

S

[References are to page numbers.]